BEST RECIPES from AMERICA'S KITCHENS

BEST RECIPES from AMERICA'S KITCHENS

WEATHERVANE BOOKS
New York

Originally published as *The American-International Encyclopedic Cookbook*

This 1988 edition is published by Weathervane Books, distributed by Crown Publishers, Inc.,
225 Park Avenue South, New York, New York 10003, by arrangement with Harper & Row,
Publishers, Inc.

Printed and Bound in the United States of America

Library of Congress Cataloging-in-Publication Data

American-international encyclopedic cookbook.
Best recipes from America's Kitchens.

Reprint. Originally published: The American-international encyclopedic cookbook. New
York: Crowell, 1972.
Compiled by the Homemakers Research Institute.
Includes index.
1. Cookery, American.   2. Cookery, International.
I. London, Anne.   II. Homemakers Research Institute.   III. Title.
TX715.A518   1988   641.5   88-10792
ISBN 0-517-66554-9

h g f e d c b

CONTENTS

BEST
RECIPES
from
AMERICA'S
KITCHENS

APPETIZERS

An appetizer, by its very name, should tempt the appetite, not destroy it. As a starter for a meal it should be complement and contrast for the dishes which follow it, and may run the gamut of hot or cold appetite-provoking foods including fruit cups, seafood cocktails, small salads, canapés, and hors d'oeuvres. The latter is a French term which literally means "outside of work," hence served before a meal. In French, hors d'oeuvre means any appetizer. Americans tend to limit it to a bit of food small enough to be eaten with the fingers—or, if it is too greasy or hot, speared with a cocktail pick. Canapé is culinary French for an individual appetizer on a bread or other edible base in a one-bite finger form. Canapés may be the same tasty concoctions as hors d'oeuvres but they are not usually served at the table.

Parties, whether in the afternoon or evening, also call for canapés and hors d'oeuvres. How many they will be and in what variety depends upon the type of party. If your party is to be an open-end affair that is likely to last for several hours, your guests will be craving substantial fare, especially if it's a cocktail party that often spans the dinner hour.

In such cases the "menu" should be hearty enough to substitute for a meal. It should include four to six cold appetizers, and two or three hot ones. Include some meat, cheese, relishes, a dip, a spread, a finger food—things that can be made in advance and refrigerated or popped into the oven just a few minutes before your guests arrive. Make choices from among appetizers

that can be kept warm for several hours in a chafing dish or in a casserole over a candle warmer.

The recipes in this book are extremely varied and give specific methods and seasonings. Nevertheless these recipes should in the last analysis serve only as a guide. They are offered with the suggestion that each be sampled and seasoned to taste as they are made. We believe they will stimulate your imagination and that you will want to elaborate on them and create your own favorites. With these recipes as a base, you can evolve many hundreds of variations with contrasts in colors, textures, designs, and seasonings. They include so many favorite flavors and foods that when the impromptu occasion arises anyone can find enough ingredients on the pantry shelf to make up a delectable array of dainties.

Dips

Give your guests a bit of something crisp, and a bowl of something spicy to dip it in and serving is simplified. Arrange a choice of dips on platters or trays large enough to hold an assortment of hors d'oeuvres and crackers as well as the containers holding the dips.

Nothing is better to dunk than raw vegetables. Surround dips with a variety including celery, raw carrot cut in thin strips or very long slices curled in iced water, kohlrabi or turnips cut paper-thin, cauliflower broken and sliced in flowerets, asparagus tips, slices of cucumber and zucchini, as well as green onions, crisp radishes, and tiny cherry or plum tomatoes.

Many savory mixtures are adaptable as dips. Before making your choices, see not only the recipes that follow for dips but check also canapé spreads in this section and the sandwich fillings in the sandwich section. Some of these make excellent dips if thinned with mayonnaise or sour cream. Prepared spreads are a convenience, however they may need more seasoning.

ROQUEFORT COTTAGE CHEESE DIP

2½ ounces Roquefort cheese
1 8-ounce package creamed cottage cheese
½ teaspoon onion juice
About 6 tablespoons sour cream

Crumble Roquefort cheese and add to cottage cheese, mixing well. Stir in onion juice. Add enough sour cream to give good dipping consistency.

Serve with potato chips, dip crackers, or crisp raw vegetables.

CHEESE AND CLAM DIP

1 clove garlic, cut in half
1 8-ounce package cream cheese
2 teaspoons lemon juice
1½ teaspoons Worcestershire sauce
½ teaspoon salt
Dash of freshly ground pepper
1 7-ounce can minced clams, drained
4 tablespoons clam broth

Rub a small mixing bowl with cut clove of garlic. Place remaining ingredients in bowl. Blend well.

For a thinner dip, add more clam broth.

For an appealing hors d'oeuvre idea that is easy to prepare and very interesting to serve, try fresh vegetable relishes accompanied by a cold dip or a hot one such as cheese fondue.

SPICY DIP FOR SEAFOOD

1 cup mayonnaise
1 tablespoon anchovy paste
1/2 teaspoon dry mustard
1/2 teaspoon Tabasco sauce
1/4 teaspoon garlic salt
2 tablespoons tarragon vinegar
3 hard-cooked eggs, finely chopped
3 tablespoons finely chopped, stuffed olives
3 tablespoons finely chopped gherkins
1 tablespoon chopped parsley
1 teaspoon finely chopped onion

Combine ingredients in order given and mix well.
Serve with chunks of lobster meat, shrimp, or other seafood on picks.

PINK DIP FOR SHRIMP

1 cup mayonnaise
1/4 cup chili sauce
1/4 cup ketchup
2 tablespoons horseradish
2 tablespoons vinegar or lemon juice
Few grains of cayenne pepper or dash of Tabasco

Combine ingredients and chill thoroughly.

SARDINE AND CHEESE DIP

2 3 1/4-ounce cans sardines
2 3-ounce packages cream cheese
1 clove garlic, finely minced
3 tablespoons minced onion
1/4 teaspoon salt
2 tablespoons Worcestershire sauce
1 tablespoon lemon juice
Strips of pimiento

Mash drained sardines with cheese and blend with other seasonings. Chill several hours before serving to blend flavors.
Serve garnished with pimiento strips. Use as a dip for crackers, potato, or corn chips.

AVOCADO-CHEESE DIP

1 cup mashed avocado pulp
1 8-ounce package cream cheese
3 tablespoons lemon juice
Dash of Worcestershire sauce
1/3 cup finely chopped green onions
1 teaspoon salt
Crackers

Gradually add the avocado to the cream cheese, blending until smooth. Add the lemon juice, Worcestershire sauce, onions, and salt and mix until thoroughly blended.
Place in a bowl on a tray or round chop plate, and surround with crackers.

SOUR CREAM-CAVIAR DIP

1 3-ounce package cream cheese
Dash of Tabasco sauce
1 1/2 cups sour cream
1/2 teaspoon grated onion
1/4 cup red salmon caviar or whitefish roe

Soften cream cheese with fork. Add Tabasco, sour cream, and onion. Mix well. Put in serving dish. Sprinkle caviar or roe over top.
Serve as dip for potato chips, crackers, or Melba toast.

ANCHOVY-CELERY COCKTAIL DIP

1 8-ounce package cream cheese
Dash of paprika
1/2 teaspoon whole celery seed
2 teaspoons minced onion
1 tablespoon lemon juice
2 teaspoons anchovy paste
2 tablespoons cream

Cream the cheese until smooth. Add the remaining ingredients and blend until fluffy.
Serve with potato chips or crackers.

WINE AND CHEESE DIP

2 cups shredded Cheddar cheese
2 tablespoons butter
1/3 cup Port or sherry

Combine cheese, butter, and wine; beat with spoon until blended. Pack in small container and chill well.
Serve as dip for crackers or Melba toast. Makes about 1 cup.

GUACAMOLE

This avocado dish is of Mexican origin; it may be used as a cocktail dip, canapé spread, or as a salad. If this must be made long ahead of serving time, it's a good idea to put a thin layer of mayonnaise over it to be sure it will not darken. Stir in the mayonnaise before you serve the guacamole.

1 large clove garlic, crushed
1 small onion, grated
1 teaspoon salt
1/4 teaspoon pepper
1 avocado
1 tomato, skinned
1 teaspoon olive oil

Combine garlic, onion, salt, and pepper. Cut avocado in half and remove seed. Scoop out pulp; mash. Add to first mixture along with mashed tomato and oil.
Serve in the scooped-out skins with salty-crisp crackers.

ZESTY EGG DIP

4 hard-cooked eggs, minced
3 slices crisp bacon, crumbled
1 teaspoon minced onion
1 teaspoon Worcestershire sauce
1 teaspoon horseradish
Mayonnaise, enough to give nice spreading consistency

Mix ingredients thoroughly; heap into bowl and chill before serving.

VEGETABLE-COTTAGE CHEESE DIP

2 cups cottage cheese
1/4 cup heavy cream
1/4 cup grated raw carrot
1/2 cup finely cut green onions
1/4 cup chopped green pepper
6 radishes, sliced very thin

Mix ingredients thoroughly; heap into bowl and chill before serving.

Nowadays dips and dunks and nibblers on picks are favorites for most parties. Guests love making their own "sticks and picks" while the hostess takes care of last-minute doings, or greets her guests, then joins in the fun.

Bases for Canapés

PREPARED BASES FOR CANAPÉS

A variety of ready-to-use bread, cracker, pastry, and many novelty bases may be purchased. Thin crackers or wafers of all types, corn and potato chips, flaked or shredded cereals of dainty sizes make simple, attractive bases.

All bases other than untoasted bread should be crisp. If it is necessary to crisp or freshen them, spread over the bottom of a pan and heat in a moderate oven (350°F.) about 10 minutes.

TOASTED BREAD CANAPÉ BASES

Slice bread 1/4-inch thick and cut into dainty shapes (rounds, stars, crescents, triangles, strips, etc.) with cooky or sandwich cutters.

Place on broiler rack in preheated broiler oven. Place rack about 3 inches from flame. Toast bread on one side.

Brush toasted side with melted butter, if desired. Spread canapé mixture on untoasted side.

CANAPÉ TOAST ROUNDS

To quickly prepare toast rounds, use small pan rolls, and slice each into several thin slices. Toast the slices.

This is quicker and less wasteful than cutting rounds from slices of bread.

FRIED (SAUTÉED) BREAD BASES

Method #1: Cut bread into desired shapes. Sauté on one side in a little butter or margarine in a heavy skillet over very low heat. Drain on absorbent paper. Spread plain side with desired canapé spreads.

Method #2: Cut bread into desired shapes. Toast on one side. Sauté untoasted side as in Method #1 above. Drain. Spread untoasted side.

Hints: Most people find that sautéed canapé bases are more desirable than ordinary toasted bread bases; they have far more flavor.

All canapé bases should be spread as close to serving time as possible. Allowing them to stand too long will ruin them. If possible, don't spread them more than 1/2 hour before serving time.

PUFF PASTRY BASES

Use recipe for puff pastry. Roll very thin (about 1/8 inch). Cut into small rounds and put 2 together to form patty cases and bake. Fill with any canapé filling, such as cheese, fish, or fruit.

Or roll puff pastry slightly thicker and cut into small, fancy shapes. Bake, and use with any canapé spreads, such as cheese, fish, meat, poultry, or seasoned caviar.

PASTRY CANAPÉ BASES

Use plain pastry recipe or any of its variations. Roll very thin (about 1/8 inch). Cut into fancy shapes and bake in very hot oven (450°F.) until lightly browned.

For variety, sprinkle, before baking, with allspice, cardamom, caraway seed, coriander, cayenne, curry powder, mace mustard, paprika, or grated cheese. Use with desired canapé spreads.

COCKTAIL TURNOVERS

Roll out piecrust dough on a floured board to 1/8-inch thickness. Cut in 3-inch squares or circles for each turnover.

Fill with desired filling. Lift one corner of a square and fold over the filling to the opposite corner, making a triangle tart. Moisten edges to seal. Press edges together with the prongs of a fork. Cut vent in each to permit escape of steam.

Bake on baking sheet in very hot oven (450°F.) for about 12 to 15 minutes.

JIFFY COCKTAIL BISCUITS

Use a prepared ready-mix and follow directions on package. Cut biscuits 1 inch in diameter. Bake as directed and fill with desired spread or filling.

PASTRY COCKTAIL SLICES

Roll out plain pastry. Spread lightly with anchovy paste or a ham spread mixed with melted butter, or very finely chopped ham.

Cover with sheet of waxed paper. Roll lightly to press spread into pastry. Remove paper. Roll jelly roll fashion and slice. Or leave flat and cut in sticks or fancy shapes.

Bake in very hot oven (450°F.) until lightly browned.

CANAPÉ CRÊPES

1/2 cup sifted enriched flour
1/2 teaspoon salt
2 egg yolks, beaten
1 cup water

Mix and sift flour and salt. Mix egg yolks and water. Gradually combine the two mixtures, beating until smooth.

Bake on a greased griddle or skillet. Cool and spread with desired canapé filling and roll. Makes about 20 very thin crêpes.

SAVORY CRACKER CANAPÉ BASES

Any of the large variety of crisp savory crackers may be used. Brush them lightly with melted butter and toast in a moderate oven (350°F.) until delicately browned.

For variations, sprinkle before toasting with caraway seeds, celery salt, garlic salt, grated cheese, paprika, or onion salt.

Fill tiny cream puffs or èclair shells with chopped cooked shrimp mixed with mayonnaise, or with chicken, lobster, shrimp, or crabmeat salad, or with cream cheese blended with Roquefort and beaten with a little heavy cream.

MACARONI SHELL CANAPÉ BASES

Cook macaroni shells as directed on package until tender but not soft. Drain on paper towels.

Fill the shells with desired filling when quite dry. If giant macaroni shells are used, they may be cut in half. Different manufacturers use different Italian names for giant macaroni shapes.

CREAM CHEESE PASTRY BASES

3/4 cup sifted enriched flour
1/8 teaspoon salt
1/2 cup butter
2 3-ounce packages cream cheese
1 tablespoon cold water

Mix and sift flour and salt. Cut in butter and cheese with 2 knives or pastry blender. Stir in water and chill thoroughly.

Roll very thin and cut into rounds or sticks. Bake in very hot oven (450°F.) until lightly browned, about 6 minutes. Spread with any desired canapé fillings. Makes about 60 to 70 canapé bases.

You can give variety to your hors d'oeuvre tray by using different fillings and garnishes with one cheese pastry recipe.

Butters for Canapés

To prepare any of the following butters, combine softened butter and other ingredients as directed below. Blend thoroughly and store in a covered container in the refrigerator until ready to use.

If hard, leave at room temperature about 1 hour, or cream the mixture until of desired spreading consistency.

Savory butters add flavor to canapés; if desired, some may be used alone without additional spreads. Just spread on canapé bases and garnish as desired.

Anchovy Butter: To ¼ cup butter add 1 tablespoon anchovy paste, or mashed anchovy fillets, and ½ teaspoon lemon juice.

Caper Butter: To ¼ cup butter add 1 tablespoon finely minced capers.

Caviar Butter: To ¼ cup butter add 2 teaspoons caviar, ¼ teaspoon grated onion, and a few drops lemon juice.

Cheese Butter: To ¼ cup butter add ¼ cup soft snappy cheese.

Chili Butter: To ¼ cup butter add 2 tablespoons chili sauce.

Chives Butter: To ¼ cup butter add 1 tablespoon finely minced chives and 1 teaspoon lemon or lime juice.

Crabmeat Butter: To ¼ cup butter add 3 tablespoons finely shredded crabmeat and ½ teaspoon lemon juice.

Curry Butter: To ¼ cup butter add ¼ teaspoon curry powder.

Egg Butter: To ¼ cup butter add 2 mashed hard-cooked egg yolks, ½ teaspoon lemon juice, a dash of Tabasco sauce, salt and cayenne to taste.

Garlic Butter: To ¼ cup butter add 1 small clove of garlic, minced fine.

Green Savory Butter: To ¼ cup butter add 3 tablespoons spinach purée, 1 tablespoon anchovy paste, a dash of paprika, 1 teaspoon capers, and salt to taste. Put through a sieve.

Green Pepper Butter: To ¼ cup butter add 2 tablespoons grated green pepper, well-drained, and a few drops lemon juice.

A happy trend is the serving of only two or three kinds of nibblers, with plenty of each. Preparation is certainly easier, and the results more appealing than an overwhelming array.

Herring Butter: To ¼ cup butter add 2 teaspoons ground smoked herring or herring paste, and a few drops lemon juice.

Honey Butter: To ¼ cup butter add ¼ cup honey. Use on hot biscuits, griddlecakes, and waffles.

Horseradish Butter: To ¼ cup butter add 2 tablespoons drained horseradish.

Ketchup Butter: To ¼ cup butter add 2 to 3 tablespoons ketchup.

Lemon Butter: To ¼ cup butter add ½ teaspoon grated lemon rind and 1 tablespoon lemon juice. (Lime and orange rind and juice may be substituted.)

Liverwurst Butter: To ¼ cup butter add 2 tablespoons mashed liverwurst sausage and ½ teaspoon finely grated onion.

Lobster Butter: To ¼ cup butter add 2 tablespoons lobster paste, ½ teaspoon lemon juice, and a dash each of dry mustard and paprika.

Mint Butter: To ¼ cup butter add 2 tablespoons minced mint leaves and 1 teaspoon lemon juice. Color lightly green with food coloring.

Mustard Butter: To ¼ cup butter add 1 tablespoon prepared mustard.

Nut Butter: To ¼ cup butter add 2 tablespoons finely ground salted nuts.

Olive Butter: To ¼ cup butter add ⅛ cup finely minced green or stuffed olives and a few drops onion juice.

Olive-Pimiento Butter: To ¼ cup butter add 1 pimiento rubbed through a sieve, and ⅛ cup finely minced stuffed olives.

Onion Butter: To ¼ cup butter add 1 teaspoon onion juice.

Parmesan Butter: To ¼ cup butter add 2 tablespoons grated Parmesan cheese.

Parsley Butter: To ¼ cup butter add 2 tablespoons minced parsley and 1 teaspoon lemon juice.

Peanut Butter: To ¼ cup butter add ¼ cup peanut butter, 1 teaspoon honey, and salt to taste.

Pimiento Butter: To ¼ cup butter add 2 tablespoons mashed pimiento and 1 teaspoon finely minced pickles.

Roquefort Butter: To ¼ cup butter add 1 tablespoon Roquefort cheese.

Salmon Butter: To ¼ cup butter add 1 tablespoon salmon paste, or mashed smoked salmon (1 ounce), and 1 teaspoon lemon juice.

Sardine Butter: To ¼ cup butter add 1 tablespoon sardine paste, or mashed sardines, and ½ teaspoon each of lemon and onion juice.

Shrimp Butter: To ¼ cup butter add 2 tablespoons ground cooked or canned shrimp and ¼ teaspoon each lemon juice and onion juice.

Arrange hors d'oeuvres in contrasting shapes and colors.

Tarragon Butter: To ¼ cup butter add 2 or 3 tarragon leaves, finely chopped, and a few drops tarragon vinegar.

Watercress Butter: To ¼ cup butter add 2 tablespoons finely chopped watercress, 1 teaspoon lemon juice, and a few drops Worcestershire sauce.

Worcestershire Butter: To ¼ cup butter add ¼ teaspoon Worcestershire sauce.

HERB BUTTERS—HINTS

Herb butters are excellent to use on piping hot steaks, chops, hamburger, pot roasts, and broiled fish. Or the mixture is used as a savory cracker or sandwich spread.

Try one herb at a time, then try blending two herbs to give distinction to your cookery.

HERB BUTTERS WITH FRESH HERBS

Combine minced tender leaves of such fresh herbs as chives, chervil, fennel, marjoram, and tarragon and a few crumbs of dry bread in a mortar.

Add a drop or two of brandy or an aromatic liqueur and grind with a pestle.

Then blend with butter or margarine and force through a fine sieve. The crumbs and liqueur help distribute and hold the flavor of the herbs in the butter.

Place in covered jar and chill the mixture.

HERB BUTTERS WITH DRIED OR POWDERED HERBS

To ¼ pound (½ cup) butter or margarine add 1 teaspoon dried herb or ½ teaspoon powdered herb. A half teaspoon of lemon juice may be added, too.

Combine with a fork and keep in a covered jar at room temperature for about 2 hours to get the full bouquet of flavor.

Then keep in a covered jar in the refrigerator for use within two or three days.

Canapé "Pies" and "Cakes"

Canapé pies are deservedly very popular because they can be prepared well in advance of a party; they encourage the use of your imagination; they can often be made from ingredients in your refrigerator and cupboard; they are fun to make. The base for it is a large round loaf of rye bread, which you can slice crosswise into big circles. You spread each slice with softened butter or margarine or a thin layer of mayonnaise or cream cheese, and then let your fancy dictate how you finish it.

It should consist of circles of various appetizing mixtures that blend well in flavors and contrast in colors. Each spread may be separated by rings of seasoned cream cheese rippled from a decorating tube. The cream cheese, too, may be divided up and tinted in various contrasting shades with food coloring.

CANAPÉ PIE

1 round loaf of rye bread
1/3 cup softened butter or margarine
1/4 cup mayonnaise
Caviar
Sieved egg yolk
Cream cheese
Sardine paste
Shrimp paste
Salmon paste
Pickled onions

Cut a slice horizontally (1/2 inch thick) from the widest part of the loaf of bread. Trim off the crusts.

Mix the butter or margarine and mayonnaise and spread generously on the slice of bread. Mark the slice in concentric circles, using cutters and bowls of various sizes.

Fill the center ring with caviar, marking the center point with a sieved egg yolk. Fill the next ring with cream cheese pressed through a pastry tube. Fill the next rings with sardine paste, shrimp paste, and salmon paste, separated by cream cheese.

Pipe an edge of cream cheese around the outer edge. Line the rim of the plate with tiny pickled onions.

Cut the canapé in wedges like pie. Serve cold.

APPETIZER PIE

Cut a large round loaf of rye bread in circular slices 1/4 inch thick. Spread with soft butter.

Place a teaspoon of caviar in center. Surround with a ring of cream cheese, then with a ring of rolled anchovies, a ring of chopped ripe olives, and another ring of cream cheese.

Garnish outer edge with small pickled onions, whole stuffed green olives, and halves of cooked or canned shrimp, alternating the foods.

Chill and serve in pie-shaped wedges.

SANDWICH "CAKE"

Crust
Use 1 package yeast roll mix

Filling No. 1
1 12-ounce can luncheon meat, mashed or ground
1 tablespoon pickle relish
2 tablespoons mayonnaise

Filling No. 2
4 hard-cooked eggs
1/2 teaspoon salt
1/8 teaspoon pepper
1/4 teaspoon celery seed
1 tablespoon chopped parsley

Filling No. 3
1 12-ounce can luncheon meat, mashed or ground
2 tablespoons chili sauce

Topping
2 cans deviled ham
1 8-ounce package cream cheese
Milk
Sliced stuffed olives
Pitted ripe olives

Prepare roll mix according to directions on package. Bake in two 8-inch cake pans. Cool. Trim side crusts and split each layer.

Spread each layer with softened butter, margarine or mayonnaise.

Combine ingredients for each filling, as given above, and put layers together with filling No. 1 on the bottom layer, No. 2 on the second layer, and No. 3 on the third layer. Spread top of loaf with deviled ham.

Frost sides with cream cheese which has been softened to spreading consistency with milk.

Decorate with cream cheese forced through a pastry tube and garnish with slices of stuffed and ripe olives.

To make umbrella, cut pimiento in half and use a strip of green pepper for the handle; make scallops with halves of sliced stuffed olive and tube "seams" on umbrella using cream cheese.

APPETIZER "CAKE"

The appetizer "cake" may be made from a commercial bakery loaf if you use one of the small round loaves of white, rye, or pumpernickel made by Swedish, Jewish, German, French, or Italian bakeries. You may prefer, however, to bake your own loaf in a deep round pan using a prepared mix or half of a roll recipe. After baking, cool and remove crusts with sharp knife.

Cut the loaf into 4 slices to form 4-inch "layers" of the appetizer "cake."

Spread the individual layers with sticky sandwich fillings. For example,

Canapé Pie

chicken salad, alternating with vegetable salad, egg salad alternating with fish salad. Put the spread slices together to form original shape of loaf.

Frost the loaf with softened cream cheese. Garnish as desired with sliced olives, pickles, radishes, etc.

Chill thoroughly in refrigerator. To serve, cut into individual wedges as you would a cake.

HALLOWEEN CANAPÉ PIE

Cheese Spread: Cream together 6 ounces cream cheese and 1 1/2 ounces blue cheese. Season to taste with Worcestershire sauce and chopped parsley. Mix in enough milk or cream to make it spreading consistency. Spread in an even layer in bottom of 8-inch pie plate.

Ham Layer: Spread 4 1/2 ounces (2 small cans) deviled ham over cheese layer.

Egg Layer: Chop 4 hard-cooked eggs. Season to taste with salt, pepper, pimiento, and mayonnaise. Spread on top of ham layer. Cover with waxed paper. Chill in refrigerator several hours or overnight.

To Decorate and Serve: Make Jack O'Lantern face with pimiento strips. Cut pie in thin wedges for serving and accompany with crisp crackers.

Sandwich "Cake"

Cheese Canapés and Spreads

Pecan Cheese Ball

PECAN CHEESE BALL

2   8-ounce packages cream cheese
1   8½-ounce can crushed pineapple, drained
2   cups chopped pecans
¼   cup chopped green pepper
2   tablespoons chopped onion
1   tablespoon seasoned salt
Pineapple slices
Maraschino cherries
Parsley

Soften cream cheese; gradually stir in crushed pineapple, 1 cup pecans, green pepper, onion, and salt. Chill well.

Form into a ball and roll in 1 cup pecans. Chill until serving.

Garnish with twists of pineapple slices, maraschino cherries, and parsley. Serve with assorted crackers.

GORGONZOLA OR ROQUEFORT SPREAD

Soften Gorgonzola cheese and butter (about half and half) and mix it together into a soft paste.

If Roquefort is used, sweet butter is advisable if the cheese is very salty. Season with sweet Italian vermouth and spread on rounds of toast or bread.

GREEN PEPPER-CHEESE SPREAD

Blend 1 3-ounce package cream cheese with 4 tablespoons minced green pepper, 2 tablespoons minced onion, 1 teaspoon French dressing, and a few grains cayenne.

COTTAGE CHEESE SLICES

1   cup cottage cheese
¼   cup crumbled blue cheese
4   stuffed olives, chopped
1   tablespoon chopped parsley
1   pimiento, chopped
1   tablespoon minced green pepper
3   tablespoons creamed butter
¼   teaspoon paprika

Mix cheeses together until well blended. Add remaining ingredients and form into a roll 2 inches in diameter.

Chill thoroughly. Slice and serve on crackers.

LIPTAUER CHEESE

This is sometimes referred to as Liptauer Käse or Hungarian cheese; it is a classic European appetizer and like any classic dish it usually appears in many versions. In Europe, goat's milk pot cheese is often used. Other versions may include part cottage cheese and part cream cheese. Some specialty stores sell a ready-to-serve packaged mixture. A popular version is given below:

1   cup (8-ounce carton) cottage cheese
1   cup (½ pound) butter
1   tablespoon crushed or whole caraway seeds
1   tablespoon finely chopped chives or onion
1   tablespoon finely chopped capers
1   tablespoon mild prepared or dry mustard
1   anchovy, chopped, or ½ teaspoon anchovy paste
1   tablespoon Hungarian paprika

Put the cheese through a fine sieve. Cream the butter with caraway seeds, chives or onion, capers, mustard, anchovy, and half the paprika, then gradually stir in the cheese.

Shape mixture into a mound; sprinkle with remaining paprika and garnish with salad greens. Serve as an appetizer with rye and pumpernickel bread. Serves 8 to 10.

Note: If chives are used, serve within 6 hours as the taste of the chives may grow strong.

STUFFED EDAM

1   Edam cheese
2   teaspoons onion juice
½   teaspoon Worcestershire sauce
¾   teaspoon prepared mustard
¼   to ⅓ cup cream

Cut a small section off the top of the cheese. Hollow out inside.

Combine cheese with other ingredients. Beat together until smooth. Refill cheese shell with mixture. Refrigerate 3 hours to blend seasonings. Serve at room temperature.

ROQUEFORT-COTTAGE CHEESE SPREAD

1   pound cottage cheese
2   3-ounce packages cream cheese
1   glass Roquefort cheese spread
2   tablespoons Worcestershire sauce
¼   cup melted butter
2   tablespoons cream
½   cup finely minced onion

Mix all ingredients together and beat well. Cover and chill overnight to permit flavors to blend.

Serve in lettuce-lined bowl with crackers or Melba toast.

COCKTAIL CHEESE LOG

1   3-ounce package cream cheese
3   ounces butter
1   teaspoon capers
1   teaspoon paprika
½   teaspoon caraway seed
½   teaspoon anchovy paste
1   tablespoon finely chopped onion

Blend cheese and butter. Add remaining ingredients. Shape into roll. Wrap in waxed paper. Chill thoroughly.

Let your guests cut and spread it on crackers, Melba toast, or thinly sliced bread.

TOMATO AND CREAM CHEESE SPREAD

1   cut clove garlic
2   very ripe tomatoes
1   8-ounce package cream cheese
1   teaspoon Worcestershire sauce
1   teaspoon grated onion
½   teaspoon salt

Rub a chopping bowl with garlic. Chop tomatoes in same bowl until completely mashed.

Add remaining ingredients. Beat until smooth. Serve with crackers and potato chips.

CHEESE-ANCHOVY SPREAD

2   3-ounce packages cream cheese
½   tube anchovy paste
1   tablespoon lemon juice
1   teaspoon Worcestershire sauce
1   teaspoon minced onion

Mix all ingredients together and chill to blend flavors.

Use as spread for crackers, potato or corn chips, or as canapé topping.

A large tray of assorted crackers and cheese, as well as crisp, cold vegetable sticks and spicy bite-size fruits are the main ingredients for a "choose your partners" snack assortment.

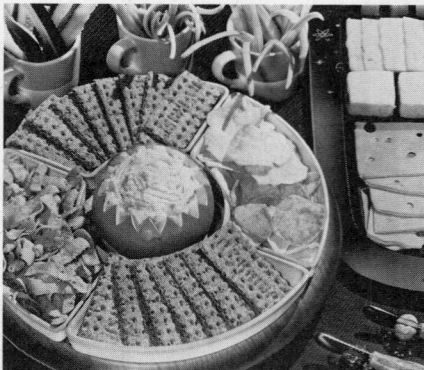

PROVOLONE AND SALAMI SPREAD

1/4 pound Provolone cheese
1/4 pound salami
2 small sweet pickles
1/2 cup mayonnaise

Put cheese, salami, and pickles through food chopper, using medium blade. Add mayonnaise, and mix well. Store mixture in covered jar in refrigerator.

Flavor improves after spread has stood a day or two. Especially good on rye bread. Makes about 1 1/2 cups.

Variations: Muenster, Cheddar, or Swiss cheese may be substituted for Provolone.

CREAM CHEESE COCKTAIL MOLD

2 3-ounce packages cream cheese
1/4 cup soft butter
1/2 teaspoon caraway seed
1 tablespoon anchovy paste
1 teaspoon paprika
1 tablespoon chopped chives
1/2 teaspoon salt
1 teaspoon capers

Cream the cheese and butter together until fluffy. Add remaining ingredients and mix well.

Pack into small mold. Chill several hours. Unmold on tray or plate. Serve with potato chips and crackers.

SAGE-CHEESE SPREAD

Blend thoroughly 1/2 pound cream cheese, 1/4 teaspoon salt, and 3/4 teaspoon ground sage.

Chill overnight in refrigerator. Spread on crackers, thin toast, or Melba toast.

WINE-CHEESE SPREAD

Combine aged American or Cheddar cheese with enough sherry to make a smooth spread. Add half as much chopped stuffed olives. Mix well.

PICKLE-CREAM CHEESE SPREAD

Mix finely chopped sweet pickles with cream cheese. Spread on canapé bases and garnish with slices of stuffed olives.

PISTACHIO-CHEESE SPREAD

Combine 1 3-ounce package of Roquefort cheese and 1 3-ounce package cream cheese with 1 tablespoon heavy cream, 1 teaspoon minced onion, 2 tablespoons chopped ripe olives, and 1/2 cup blanched pistachio nuts. Mix well and chill.

SOUR CREAM-CHEESE SPREAD

Blend cream cheese with sour cream. Season with salt and pepper.

WATERCRESS-CHEESE SPREAD

Cream 1 3-ounce package cream cheese. Dry and chop 1 cup watercress. Blend together with 1 teaspoon Worcestershire sauce and 1/4 teaspoon salt.

CHUTNEY-CHEESE SPREAD

Blend 1 3-ounce package cream cheese with 1/3 cup chutney.

BERMUDA SWISS SPREAD

Grind and mix together equal parts of Swiss cheese and Bermuda onions. Spread on rounds of buttered white or cocktail rye bread.

CHEESE-STUFFED ROLL SLICES

Cut off ends of frankfurter rolls. Scoop out centers with fork, and stuff rolls with any cheese spread. Wrap in waxed paper; chill. To serve, cut in 1/2-inch slices.

NUT AND CHEESE SPREAD

Blend cream cheese with chopped nuts. Sweeten to taste with confectioners' sugar.

OLIVE-CHEESE SPREAD

Put 2 parts American cheese and 1 part stuffed or pitted olives through the food chopper using a fine knife. Mix together well.

DEVILED HAM-CREAM CHEESE SPREAD

4 3-ounce packages cream cheese
1/2 cup light cream
2 tablespoons deviled ham
1 teaspoon finely chopped chives

Soften cream cheese with cream. Blend with remaining ingredients. Pile into a bowl.

HORSERADISH-CHEESE SPREAD

Combine 1 3-ounce package of cream cheese with 1 1/2 teaspoons drained horseradish, 1/2 teaspoon scraped onion, and 1/8 teaspoon salt.

Blend thoroughly and spread on toast bases. Top with bits of crisp bacon.

GARLIC-CREAM CHEESE SPREAD

Rub a salad bowl with a cut clove of garlic. Moisten cream cheese with a bit of cream and work in the bowl until cheese is softened and has absorbed some of the garlic aroma.

Garnish the spread canapés with a piping of finely minced parsley.

LIEDERKRANZ OR CAMEMBERT SPREAD

Blend Liederkranz or Camembert cheese with half as much cream cheese.

TOMATO-PARMESAN CANAPÉS

Place thin slices of tomato on toasted canapé bases. Sprinkle with grated Parmesan cheese and then with chopped parsley.

OLIVE AND SHARP CHEESE SPREAD

Combine 1/4 cup grated soft sharp cheese with 1/4 cup butter. Add 1/4 cup finely chopped green or stuffed olives. Season to taste with salt and pepper.

COMMODORE'S CHEESE

1/2 pound sharp Cheddar cheese
1/4 pound Roquefort or blue cheese
1 3-ounce package cream cheese
Minced chives
Heavy cream
Paprika

Put Cheddar and blue cheese through food chopper, or grate fine and blend with cream cheese, chives, and heavy cream. Beat until fluffy. Mound on a serving plate and sprinkle with paprika to serve.

(Try this as dessert sometime with preserved fruit and toasted crackers!)

One savory cheese spread may be used in different variations of hors d'oeuvres: ham pinwheels, triangular bologna stacks; salami cornucopias, and tiny filled patty shells. A versatile spread is made by blending 1 8-ounce package cream cheese with 1/4 cup cream and 1 tablespoon Worcestershire sauce.

Egg Appetizers

HINTS ABOUT STUFFED EGGS

Although hard-cooked eggs are frequently referred to incorrectly as "hard-boiled," it should be noted that eggs are not "boiled" if cooked properly. They should be hard-cooked in water just below the boiling point for 12 to 15 minutes.

If the eggs are taken directly from the refrigerator start them in cold or lukewarm water. Hot water may crack the shells. When done, chill in cold water to prevent darkening of the yolks and to make shelling easier.

Cut the eggs in half lengthwise, or if you want to cut them crosswise, trim the bottoms so they won't roll over.

Remove the yolks and put through a sieve or mash with a fork. Combine with seasonings and refill the whites of eggs. To get a more decorative effect, use a pastry tube.

Garnish the filled eggs with slices of stuffed olives, tiny pearl onions, chopped chives, chopped parsley, bits of pimiento, or paprika.

How To Center Egg Yolks for Stuffed Eggs

If eggs are allowed to remain in one position while being hard-cooked there is a tendency for the yolks to sink to the bottom. For stuffed eggs it is desirable to have egg yolks in the center of hard-cooked eggs.

To obtain such a result gently stir the eggs, keeping them in motion for the first 6 or 7 minutes of cooking.

Deviled Eggs With Scalloped Edge

DEVILED EGGS

6   hard-cooked eggs, shelled
1   tablespoon cream or mayonnaise
1½ teaspoons vinegar
Dash of pepper
¾   teaspoon prepared mustard
½   teaspoon Worcestershire sauce (optional)
¼   teaspoon salt

Cut eggs in halves lengthwise. Remove yolks; force through sieve. Add seasonings and beat until smooth and fluffy.

Fill egg whites with mixture. Garnish tops with dash of paprika, chopped parsley, or chopped chives.

Hot Deviled Eggs: If desired, substitute cream or evaporated milk for mayonnaise. To serve, heat eggs in top of double boiler and serve with hot cheese or tomato sauce.

Serve on buttered hot toast or arrange around boiled rice ring.

STUFFED EGG VARIATIONS

Follow method for Deviled Eggs. The ingredients given are used with 6 hard-cooked eggs unless otherwise indicated.

Anchovy Stuffed Eggs: For 6 eggs use 2 tablespoons anchovy paste, 1 tablespoon minced chives, and 1 teaspoon lemon juice.

Bacon Stuffed Eggs: Cook bacon until crisp. Chop and mix with mashed egg yolk and minced parsley. Moisten with mayonnaise.

Caviar Stuffed Eggs: For 6 eggs use 2 ounces caviar, 3 tablespoons mayonnaise, ¼ teaspoon salt, and a pinch of pepper. Garnish tops with caviar.

Celery Stuffed Eggs: Chop celery very fine. Mix with mashed egg yolk and moisten with mayonnaise or salad dressing.

Cheese Stuffed Eggs: For 6 eggs use 2 tablespoons creamed butter, ⅓ cup grated Swiss cheese, and salt and pepper to taste.

Chicken or Veal Stuffed Eggs: Chop cooked chicken or veal very fine. Mix with equal amounts mashed egg yolk. Season to taste.

Chicken Livers Stuffed Eggs: Sauté chicken livers. Chop fine and mix with mashed egg yolk.

Crabmeat Stuffed Eggs: For 6 eggs use ½ cup flaked crabmeat, ½ cup finely chopped celery, 1 tablespoon chopped green pepper, ½ teaspoon dry mustard, and ⅓ cup mayonnaise.

Deviled Ham or Liver Sausage Stuffed Eggs: Blend deviled ham or liver sausage with the mashed yolks. Smooth to a paste with mayonnaise.

Dried Beef Stuffed Eggs: For 6 eggs frizzle ⅓ cup dried beef in butter in heavy skillet before combining with juice of ½ lemon, ¼ teaspoon Worcestershire sauce, and mashed egg yolks.

Ham Stuffed Eggs: For 6 eggs use ¼ cup ground ham, 1 teaspoon dry mustard, about ½ teaspoon salt, and enough mayonnaise to form a smooth paste with the mashed egg yolks.

Mushroom and Onion Stuffed Eggs: Sauté chopped mushrooms and onions in butter. Mix with mashed egg yolk.

Pickle Stuffed Eggs: Mix finely mashed egg yolks with finely chopped pickle. Moisten with mayonnaise.

Sardine Stuffed Eggs: Mash sardines. Season with salt and lemon juice. Mix with mashed egg yolk. Moisten with mayonnaise.

Shrimp Stuffed Eggs: Marinate small whole cooked or canned cleaned shrimp in French dressing for ½ hour. Place a whole shrimp in the cavity of each egg half.

Cover with mashed egg yolk mixed with mayonnaise and a little lemon juice.

Stuffed Eggs En Casserole: Place stuffed eggs in a casserole. Cover with cheese, tomato, mushroom, or other desired sauce. Sprinkle with buttered crumbs or grated cheese.

Bake in moderate oven (350°F.) until browned on top and heated through.

Deviled Egg Faces: To make, first stuff the egg whites. Fasten a gherkin with a toothpick at the rounded end of the egg. Cut two tiny pimiento squares and a 1 x ¼-inch strip for the eyes and mouth. Place these on the filling. Spread the top of the pointed end of the egg with mayonnaise. Dust mayonnaise with chopped parsley. Chill.

TOMATO-EGG CANAPÉS

Toast rounds of bread on one side. Spread untoasted sides with mayonnaise. Add thin slices of tomato, then slices of hard-cooked egg.

Sprinkle lightly with salt. Garnish with a slice or two of olive.

EGG AND SALMON CANAPÉS

Blend hard-cooked egg yolks, flaked salmon, and mayonnaise or salad dressing to a smooth paste.

Toast sliced bread on one side. Spread salmon mixture on untoasted side.

Garnish with finely chopped parsley and hard-cooked egg white.

BACON AND EGG SPREAD

Mash 2 hard-cooked eggs; combine with 4 slices finely crumbled cooked bacon. Moisten with 1 tablespoon mayonnaise.

Season with 1 tablespoon desired dried herb and 1 tablespoon wine or herb vinegar. Mix to a smooth spread.

ZESTY EGG SPREAD

Mash 4 hard-cooked egg yolks; season with 1 teaspoon ketchup, 1 teaspoon onion juice, 1 teaspoon prepared mustard, 1/4 teaspoon salt, 1/8 teaspoon pepper, and 3 drops Worcestershire sauce.

EGG AND CHEESE SPREAD

3 3-ounce packages cream cheese
1 ounce blue cheese
2 hard-cooked eggs, chopped
1 teaspoon onion juice
1 tablespoon Worcestershire sauce
Cream to moisten
Salt and pepper to taste

Combine all ingredients. Mash with fork, adding enough cream to moisten.

Form into ball. Chill until firm. Serve with crackers or Melba toast.

WATERCRESS-EGG SPREAD

Mash hard-cooked eggs; combine with finely chopped watercress. Moisten with mayonnaise.

Fish and Shellfish Canapés and Spreads

FLAKED FISH SPREADS

Cook, cool, and flake fillets or use canned flaked fish. Serve in any of the three following ways:

1. Mix equal quantities of flaked fish and chopped pearl onions. Mix with mayonnaise and chili sauce. Serve on whole-wheat crackers.

2. Mix equal quantities of flaked fish and chopped mustard pickle. Serve on crackers or toast strips.

3. Moisten flaked fish with cream and horseradish. Serve on crackers or toast strips, garnished with green pepper.

SARDINE AND EGG SPREAD

Combine mashed sardines with mashed hard-cooked egg yolk. Season to taste with lemon juice. Add enough butter to form a smooth paste.

Spread on toasted canapé bases. Garnish with riced egg white. Sprinkle with chopped parsley.

CHOPPED HERRING SPREAD

Wash, clean, bone and chop salted herring which has been soaked in cold water for several hours.

For each herring use 1 onion, 1 tart apple, 1 slice of toast soaked in vinegar or lemon juice. Chop all together very fine.

Add 1 teaspoon salad oil, and a dash each of cinnamon and pepper.

Serve garnished with finely chopped hard-cooked egg.

ANCHOVY-EGG SPREAD

Mash and blend 4 hard-cooked egg yolks and 4 anchovies. Moisten to spreading consistency with mayonnaise. Season with grated onion and freshly ground black pepper.

Spread and garnish with chopped egg white.

CRABMEAT OR LOBSTER SPREAD

Make a paste of canned or cooked seafood. Moisten with mayonnaise. Season with lemon juice and grated onion.

KIPPERED HERRING SPREAD

1 cup mashed, kippered herring
1 chopped hard-cooked egg
1/4 cup minced cucumber
Mayonnaise to moisten
2 drops lemon juice

Blend ingredients to a smooth spread.

DEVILED LOBSTER SPREAD

1 cup cooked or canned flaked lobster
1/2 teaspoon grated onion
2 tablespoons mayonnaise
1 tablespoon Worcestershire sauce
1/2 teaspoon prepared mustard
Salt and pepper to taste

Blend ingredients to a smooth spread.

STURGEON-CHEESE SPREAD

1 cup flaked kippered sturgeon or herring
1 1/2 cups grated Cheddar cheese
1/2 medium-sized Bermuda onion, grated

Blend to a smooth spreading consistency. Spread and garnish with slices of stuffed olives.

CLAM-CHEESE SPREAD

1 7-ounce can minced clams, drained
1 3-ounce package cream cheese
1 tablespoon Worcestershire sauce
About 1 tablespoon onion juice
Pinch of dry mustard
Salt to taste

Mix thoroughly and use as spread for canapé bases.

SMOKED SALMON FINGERS

Spread pumpernickel or dark rye bread with sweet butter. Cut into fingers. Cover with thin slices of smoked salmon. Sprinkle with minced parsley.

Serve with lemon wedges. If desired, season with olive oil and freshly ground black pepper.

OYSTER CANAPÉS

Use round canapé bases toasted on one side. Spread untoasted side with mustard butter. Dip chilled raw oysters in mayonnaise and press one into each round.

Garnish with sieved hard-cooked egg yolk mixed with minced chives.

PICKLED HERRING CANAPÉS

Place small slices of Bermuda or Spanish onion on squares of rye or pumpernickel bread.

Top each with small squares of pickled herring. Sprinkle with chopped parsley or watercress.

CHEESE AND SMOKED SALMON CANAPÉS

Split small hard rolls. Spread with cream cheese. Top with thinly sliced smoked salmon.

Cut into bite-size wedges.

JIFFY SHRIMP CANAPÉS

Spread untoasted side of canapé bases with mayonnaise. Place a whole cooked shrimp on each.

Garnish with finely chopped parsley.

You'll get compliments when you serve a colorful, attractive array of canapés and hors d'oeuvres.

CAVIAR SERVING HINTS

Caviar sounds extravagant but a little of it goes a long way, and to many people it represents absolute perfection as an appetizer. If you can't afford imported caviar, settle for some nice domestic red or black caviar. Many of the most prominent hostesses do. The red is usually less expensive than the black.

To serve caviar by itself, bed the jars in a bowl of cracked ice and serve with accompaniments of dark rye bread, Melba toast, sour cream, minced onion, and lemon wedges.

It is wise not to make caviar canapés too far ahead of time because caviar has a tendency to soak through ordinary bread or toast.

It is usually preferable to use the packaged kind of canapé base inasmuch as these ready-made bases do not become as soaked as the usual homemade bases. However, if a layer of cream cheese is spread over toasted bread bases, the soaking can be prevented.

The simple traditional caviar canapé is made as follows: Spread toast squares or rounds with caviar; sprinkle lightly with grated onion and lemon juice. Decorate with finely chopped whites and yolks of hard-cooked eggs.

RED CAVIAR CANAPÉS

2   3-ounce packages cream cheese
1   tablespoon chopped onion
1   tablespoon chopped parsley
Few leaves sage, shredded
1   medium-sized jar red caviar
Mayonnaise
Toasted canapé bases

Mix cream cheese with onion, parsley, and sage. Cover half of each toast round with cream cheese mixture. Cover other half with caviar.

With a pastry tube place a garnish of mayonnaise between the caviar and cheese and around the edges.

Always a favorite—an attractive tray of cooked shrimp with a spicy cocktail sauce dip.

RED AND BLACK CAVIAR CANAPÉS

Use black and red caviar. Spread diamond or round canapé bases with cream cheese seasoned with onion juice.

Divide the canapé down the middle with a ridge of cream cheese, minced parsley, or minced chives.

Put red caviar on 1 side and black caviar on other side.

If desired, border canapés with grated hard-cooked egg yolk or white, or with minced parsley.

WAGON-WHEEL CANAPÉS

Remove seed sections from small slices of tomatoes. Place on buttered toast rounds.

Fill alternate sections with chopped hard-cooked egg and black caviar.

CAVIAR-CHEESE SPREAD

Soften cream cheese with cream. Spread on small crackers. Dot with caviar.

CAVIAR-EGG SPREAD

Combine 2 finely chopped hard-cooked eggs with 2 tablespoons caviar; moisten with mayonnaise.

SALMON-AVOCADO CANAPÉS

½   cup flaked cooked or canned salmon
2   tablespoons mayonnaise
1½ tablespoons lemon juice
¼   teaspoon salt
Dash of pepper
8   large toast rounds
3   tablespoons softened butter
½   cup mashed avocado
8   strips pimiento

Mix salmon, mayonnaise, ½ tablespoon lemon juice, salt, and pepper.

Spread toast rounds with softened butter. Spread half of each round with salmon mixture, the other half with avocado mixed with remaining lemon juice.

Mark the division with a pimiento strip.

EGG AND LOBSTER CANAPÉS

3   tablespoons lobster paste
3   tablespoons butter
6   small rounds of toast
2   hard-cooked eggs
3   stuffed olives

Cream together the lobster paste and butter. Spread evenly on toast rounds. Arrange thick slices of hard-cooked egg in center.

Cut olives in halves and press a half into the center of egg slices, cut side up.

SARDINE SPREAD

Mash and blend together 3 sardines and 1 3-ounce package cream cheese. Season with lemon juice to taste.

SARDINE-CUCUMBER CANAPÉS

Soak thin slices of cucumber in salted ice water to crisp. Cut canapé bases to size of cucumber and spread with cream cheese. Top each with a cucumber slice.

Top cucumber with chopped sardines mixed with mayonnaise and lemon juice. Garnish with a bit of pimiento.

CRABMEAT OR LOBSTER AND DEVILED EGG SPREAD

1   6- or 7-ounce can crabmeat or lobster
2   hard-cooked eggs
½   teaspoon mustard
2   tablespoons mayonnaise
1   tablespoon lemon juice
About 1 teaspoon curry powder

Drain, bone and wash the seafood. Mash and blend with remaining ingredients to a smooth spread.

CRABMEAT SPREAD

1   cup finely flaked crabmeat
2   tablespoons chopped parsley
1   tablespoon minced onion
3   tablespoons mayonnaise
¼   teaspoon curry powder
1   teaspoon lemon juice

Blend ingredients to a smooth spread.

SHRIMP-AVOCADO CANAPÉS

Peel and mash a small avocado. Season with 1 teaspoon lemon juice, 1 teaspoon minced onion, and a dash of salt.

Spread on crackers and top each with a whole shrimp.

EGG-SARDINE CANAPÉS

Mix equal parts of yolks of hard-cooked eggs and sardines and a little lemon juice. Spread on toast bases.

Sprinkle with chopped egg whites mixed with finely chopped parsley.

HERRING AND SALMON CANAPÉS

Spread canapé bases with lemon butter. Arrange thin strips of smoked salmon and smoked herring on the bases.

Decorate with chopped hard-cooked egg yolk. Sprinkle with finely chopped parsley.

SHRIMP AND TOMATO CANAPÉS

Marinate cleaned, cooked shrimp in French dressing for 1 hour. Cover each toast round with a slice of tomato.

Place a marinated shrimp in center. Top with a bit of mayonnaise.

ANCHOVY CANAPÉS

Spread rounds of Melba toast with cream cheese. Cover with slice of hard-cooked egg. Top each with rolled anchovy fillet.

Meat And Poultry Canapés And Spreads

PÂTÉ DE FOIE GRAS

Genuine pâté de foie gras (literally, a pâté of fat livers) is imported. It is made from the oversized marbled livers of geese that have been fattened by being confined to pens and stuffed with food; they are cooked with madeira, seasonings, and usually truffles. The forced feeding of geese to obtain the necessary fat livers is not legal in the United States. However, pâtés of chicken livers properly prepared make a more than acceptable substitute.

MOCK PÂTÉ DE FOIE GRAS
(Pâté of Chicken Livers)

1/2 pound chicken livers
1 teaspoon salt
Pinch of cayenne
1/2 cup rendered chicken fat, goose fat, or softened butter
1/4 teaspoon nutmeg
1 teaspoon dry mustard
1/8 teaspoon ground cloves
2 tablespoons finely minced onion

Cover chicken livers with water; bring to a boil, reduce heat and simmer in covered saucepan 15 to 20 minutes. Drain and put the hot livers through the food chopper using finest blade.

Mix with remaining ingredients until thoroughly blended. Pack in a crock or jar and chill in refrigerator. Makes about 1 1/4 cups.

Note: A few canned truffles may be added to above.

Blender Pâté: Cook and chop the livers as above, then whip in electric blender until very smooth. Mix with 1/2 cup rendered chicken or goose fat or with 1/2 cup softened butter. Season very lightly with salt and 1 tablespoon port or sherry. If desired, a few truffles may be added.

CHICKEN OR TURKEY SPREAD

Chop or grind cooked chicken or turkey. Moisten with mayonnaise. Add finely chopped celery or almonds. Season to taste. Garnish with watercress.

CURRIED CHICKEN SPREAD

1 cup finely chopped cooked chicken and giblets
1/2 cup chopped toasted almonds
1 teaspoon grated onion
1/2 teaspoon curry powder
About 1/2 cup mayonnaise

Mix ingredients thoroughly; using just enough mayonnaise to moisten spread.

HAM-CHEESE-PINEAPPLE SPREAD

Combine equal parts of finely ground cooked ham, cream cheese, and drained crushed pineapple.

BRAUNSCHWEIGER PINEAPPLE

This is a popular centerpiece for a buffet spread. Use 1 1/2 to 2 pounds cold, firm braunschweiger (liver) sausage. Remove covering and mold it into shape like a fresh pineapple.

Spread surface with a little soft butter or brush with lemon juice. Cover surface with slices of stuffed olive to resemble "eyes" of pineapple.

If desired, top with 3 or 4 green onions or leaves from fresh pineapple. Serve surrounded with crackers and potato chips.

Note: The Braunschweiger Pineapple may be wrapped in waxed paper or aluminum foil and stored in the refrigerator 2 to 3 days before serving.

HAM SPREAD

Moisten finely chopped cooked ham with mayonnaise. Add a little chopped dill or sweet pickle relish and pimiento. Season to taste with salt and pepper.

Spread on bases and garnish with stuffed olive slices.

CRUNCHY HAM SPREAD

1 cup finely chopped cooked ham
1/4 cup chopped walnuts or almonds
2 tablespoons finely chopped celery
1/4 cup chopped pineapple
Mayonnaise to moisten

Mix ingredients thoroughly.

DEVILED HAM AND EGG SPREAD

1/4 cup deviled ham
1 tablespoon finely chopped celery
1 hard-cooked egg, chopped
1/4 teaspoon curry powder
1/2 teaspoon olive oil
Mayonnaise to moisten
Salt to taste

Mix ham, celery, and egg. Combine curry powder and olive oil. Add to ham mixture and moisten with mayonnaise. Add salt to taste.

HAM-CHICKEN-OLIVE SPREAD

1/2 cup chopped cooked ham
1/2 cup chopped cooked chicken
1/4 cup chopped green olives
Mayonnaise to moisten

Mix ingredients thoroughly.

CHICKEN LIVER AND EGG SPREAD

Mix 1/2 cup chopped, cooked chicken livers and 2 hard-cooked eggs, chopped. Season with 1 teaspoon finely chopped onion and salt and pepper to taste. Moisten with cream.

DEVILED HAM AND CHEESE SPREAD

Combine 6 ounces deviled ham with 1/4 cup pimiento cheese spread and 2 tablespoons chopped sweet pickle. Moisten with mayonnaise.

DEVILED HAM AND EGG SPREAD

Mix deviled ham and chopped hard-cooked egg; season with horseradish.

Spread on canapé base and garnish with bit of watercress.

ROAST BEEF OR VEAL SPREAD

Moisten finely ground cooked meat with mixture of horseradish and mayonnaise. Season to taste.

CHOPPED CHICKEN OR CALVE'S LIVER

1/2 pound chicken or calve's liver
1 or 2 hard-cooked eggs
1/2 small onion
1/2 cup finely chopped celery, optional
Salt and pepper

Lightly fry the chicken livers in a little chicken fat or butter.

Chop together with the other ingredients until fine. Season to taste with salt and pepper.

Moisten with melted chicken fat or butter.

A tray of "self-service" spreads with a variety of breads, crackers, and vegetable hors d'oeuvres simplifies service.

BEEF OR STEAK TARTARE

2 pounds raw finely ground, fresh lean steak
2 raw egg yolks
½ cup finely chopped onion
4 anchovies, mashed
Finely chopped watercress, parsley, or other desired herbs
Salt and pepper, to taste
Worcestershire sauce, to taste
Capers, to taste

Combine steak, egg yolks, onion, and anchovies. Add watercress or parsley, salt, pepper, Worcestershire sauce, and capers to taste.

Serve in a mound as an hors d'oeuvre with squares of pumpernickel or rye bread. Or shape the mixture into small balls and roll in chopped parsley.
Note: The same beef mixture may be served as a main dish.

LIVERWURST AND BACON SPREAD

Chop cold crisp bacon very fine. Combine 1 part bacon and with 3 parts liverwurst.

Season with salt, pepper, Worcestershire sauce, and Tabasco sauce to taste.

SPICY SNACKING TREE

3 hard-cooked eggs
2 4½-ounce cans deviled ham
1 tablespoon grated onion
¼ teaspoon Tabasco
1 teaspoon Worcestershire
1 3-ounce package cream cheese, softened
Chopped chives
Pimiento

Chop hard-cooked eggs. Combine with deviled ham, grated onion, Tabasco, and Worcestershire. Chill.

Shape into tree form. Decorate around the edge of the tree with softened cream cheese, then top edging with chopped chives. Cover "tree trunk" with pimiento. Serve with assorted crackers and toast rounds. Serves 20 to 30.

Spicy Snacking Tree

HAM HOURGLASS

1 pound cooked ground ham
½ cup dark raisins
1 medium onion, shredded
½ teaspoon curry powder
¾ cup mayonnaise
2 3-ounce packages cream cheese, softened
2 tablespoons milk
2 tablespoons pimiento, chopped
2 tablespoons ripe olives, chopped

In a bowl thoroughly blend ham, raisins, onion, curry powder, and mayonnaise. Shape mixture into an hourglass, approximately 10 inches long on a tray. Chill.

Blend softened cream cheese and milk. Frost ham mixture with the cream cheese mixture. Make sand effect with chopped pimiento and ripe olives. Make frame of hourglass using assorted crackers. Makes about 4½ cups.

HAM AND ONION CANAPÉS

1 cup ground cooked ham
1 sweet red onion
1 tablespoon sour cream
1 tablespoon mayonnaise
Freshly ground pepper
Toasted canapé bases

Grind the ham with medium-sized onion and make a light smooth spread with the other ingredients. Spread on small pieces of buttered toast.

SALAMI AND EGG CANAPÉS

½ pound hard salami
3 hard-cooked eggs
½ cup salad dressing
Bread, sliced thin

Put salami and hard-cooked eggs through food chopper 2 or 3 times. Blend with salad dressing.

Trim crust from bread and cut into small squares. Toast on one side. Spread untoasted side with salami mixture.

Sprinkle with chopped parsley and garnish with pimiento strips.

CHOPPED LIVER AND MUSHROOMS

½ pound chicken or calve's liver
½ cup sliced fresh mushrooms
3 tablespoons chicken fat or butter
Salt and pepper
Onion juice

Lightly fry the liver in a little fat, then remove and fry the mushrooms in the same fat for about 5 minutes.

Chop liver and mushrooms fine and add the fat in which they were fried. Season to taste with salt, pepper, and onion juice.

Moisten, if necessary, with a little additional melted chicken fat or butter.

Ham Hourglass: A zesty spread for a New Year's party is this flavorful combination of ham, raisins, and curry powder shaped into an hourglass and frosted with cream cheese.

BAKED BEAN AND FRANK CANAPÉS

Mash baked beans and spread on toasted canapé bases. Garnish with slices of frankfurters and stuffed olives.

PARSLEY ROUNDS

Spread edges of toast rounds with softened butter; roll in chopped parsley.

Combine chopped cooked chicken or grated-style tuna fish with butter, onion juice, salt, and pepper. Spread on toast.

BACON AND TOMATO CANAPÉS

Toast rounds of bread the size of tomato slices. Spread with crisp, chopped bacon blended with mayonnaise.

Top with very thin tomato slice, cucumber slice, and stuffed-olive slice.

HAM AND EGG CANAPÉS

Combine yolks of 2 hard-cooked eggs, ½ teaspoon dry mustard, 1 teaspoon mayonnaise, and 1½ tablespoons deviled ham. Mix until smooth.

Spread on rounds of rye bread. Top with ring slices of hard-cooked egg white. Sprinkle with paprika.

HAM AND CHEESE SPREAD

1 cup finely chopped cooked ham
¼ cup grated American cheese
½ teaspoon finely chopped onion
1 teaspoon chili sauce or ketchup

Mix ingredients thoroughly.

LIVERWURST AND ONION CANAPÉS

Spread very thin slices of mild onion with liverwurst which has been mashed and moistened with mayonnaise.

Place on toast rounds. Garnish edges with sieved hard-cooked egg.

HAM AND RELISH SPREAD

Combine 1 cup ground cooked ham and ½ cup pepper relish.

Fruit and Vegetable Hors D'Oeuvres

Many raw fresh vegetables are delicious appetizers. Some of the best are carrots, cauliflower, celery, cucumber, green onions, tiny whole tomatoes, and turnips. They must be of top quality. Cut the vegetables in small, attractive pieces or slices and have them crisp and well-chilled. Provide salt for those who prefer to eat them without sauce. Some cooked vegetables are also excellent, especially cooked or canned artichoke hearts and asparagus tips. Drain these and marinate in French dressing.

STUFFED BRUSSELS SPROUTS

Drain canned or cooked Brussels sprouts. Cut out centers and stuff with favorite canapé spread to which may be added the chopped centers of sprouts.

BEETS

Use tiny canned beets, plain or pickled. Provide a bowl of sour cream for dunking.

CARROT STICKS

Carrot sticks, if they are crisp, make an excellent appetizer by themselves, or accompanied by a dunking sauce.

CAULIFLOWERETS

Break cauliflower into small flowerets. Crisp in ice water. Drain and sprinkle with paprika.

Or, pre-cook flowerets for just a few minutes, then marinate in sharp French dressing until serving time.

MARINATED CELERIAC

Chill cooked celery root or celeriac and cut into oblongs. Marinate in French dressing for several hours.

STUFFED MUSHROOM CAPS

Wash and drain small fresh mushroom caps. Fry gently in a little butter until tender. Remove while still firm, drain on paper towels, chill and fill with desired filling.

SHERRIED MUSHROOMS

Use small mushrooms. Remove skin and stems. Cover with sherry and soak several hours.

Drain and fill with Roquefort cheese or caviar. Serve each on a cocktail pick.

STUFFED TOMATO SLICES

Cut medium-sized tomatoes in eighths and cut out centers, leaving 1/2-inch thick piece.

Chop 2 hard-cooked eggs fine; add 1/2 teaspoon salt, a little finely chopped celery, 1 tablespoon mayonnaise, and 1 teaspoon mustard-with-horseradish.

Fill the tomato boats and garnish with a bit of parsley.

PICKLED COCKTAIL MUSHROOMS

2 4-ounce cans button mushrooms
1 cup white wine or cider vinegar
1 tablespoon sugar
1 teaspoon salt
1 shredded bay leaf
3 cloves
3 whole black peppers
1 clove garlic, sliced
1 slice lemon

Combine vinegar, seasonings, and mushroom liquid. Boil 3 to 4 minutes. Add mushrooms. Turn into a jar and let stand overnight.

Letting them stand from 1 to 2 weeks will improve the flavor. Serve whole on picks or chop and use as a canapé spread.

STUFFED RAW CARROTS

Make raw carrots into cylinders by hollowing out centers with an apple corer.

Or raw carrots may be shaped into troughs or cones hollowed for fillings.

STUFFED PLUM TOMATOES

Select firm cherry or plum tomatoes. Cut out centers and stuff with a favorite fish, seafood, or meat mixture.

TURNIPS

Turnip sticks or thin slices of turnip which have been crisped in ice water make an excellent appetizer.

GARLIC OLIVES

Drain green or ripe olives; place in a bowl. Add 6 to 12 peeled cloves of garlic. Cover with salad oil. Cover and store in refrigerator for 24 hours.

Drain and use the oil for salad dressing. Sprinkle the olives with chopped parsley.

STUFFED RADISHES

Hollow out good-sized radishes with a small sharp-pointed knife. Crisp in ice water.

Stuff with a mixture of caviar, minced parsley, mayonnaise, lemon juice, and onion juice, seasoned to taste. Or fill with softened cheese.

STUFFED CUCUMBER

Remove center of pared cucumber with vegetable corer.

Stuff with a mixture of 1 cup flaked tuna or salmon, 2 tablespoons mayonnaise, 1/2 teaspoon each of onion and lemon juice, a dash of Worcestershire sauce, and salt and pepper to taste.

Chill and cut into 1/2-inch slices.

GHERKIN FANS

Slice gherkins to within 1/2 inch of top. Spread the finger-like slices fan shape. This can also be done with half a gherkin cut lengthwise.

Vegetable Hors d'Oeuvres with Dipping Sauce

CUCUMBER SLICES

Peel cucumber. Score it by running a 4-tined fork down the lengthwise surface of the cucumber. Cut into very thin slices. Chill in a tray of ice. Drain and sprinkle lightly with chopped parsley.

When skin is tender, score without peeling and slice, thus adding a touch of color.

CUCUMBER STICKS

Peel cucumber. Cut in half. Remove seeds. Cut solid part into narrow strips about 3 inches long.

Cover with damp cloth. Chill well before serving. Sprinkle with paprika.

MARINATED ONIONS

Skin and slice Bermuda onions. Soak in a brine made of 2/3 cup water to 1 tablespoon salt. Drain and soak in vinegar for 20 to 30 minutes. Drain again. Chill thoroughly.

CUCUMBER CUPS

Scoop out centers of 2-inch lengths of cucumbers. Fill with a mixture of 1 cup flaked tuna, 1/4 cup minced sweet pickle, 1 tablespoon lemon juice, 1/2 teaspoon onion juice, and salt and pepper to taste. Chill.

Serve garnished with slices of stuffed olives.

ITALIAN OLIVE MIXTURE

1/2 pound green olives
1/2 pound black olives
3 stalks celery, chopped
1 green pepper, chopped
1 red pepper, chopped
1 clove garlic, crushed
1/4 cup olive oil
1/4 cup vinegar
Black pepper, to taste
Oregano, to taste

Crack the olives with a hammer until the pits show. Combine with remaining ingredients. Let stand at room temperature 2 days. Store in refrigerator in sealed, sterilized jars. Serves 8 to 10.

STUFFED CELERY

Use only the tender white stalks showing no discoloration. The inside stalks are preferable.

Wash and leave tips of leaves on stalks or remove leaves from coarser stalks. Crisp in ice water. Dry on paper towels before stuffing.

Use a pastry tube or a knife and fill grooves with one of the following fillings.

Garnish with chopped parsley, green pepper, chives, pimiento, or a dash of paprika. Chill before serving.

STUFFED CELERY FILLINGS

Almond-Cream Cheese Filling: Combine 1/4 cup finely chopped almonds, 1 3-ounce package cream cheese, 1 tablespoon chili sauce, 3/4 teaspoon curry powder, and a dash of salt.

Avocado Filling: Mash ripe avocado pulp. Sprinkle with lemon juice. Season to taste with salt and pepper. If desired, mix with finely chopped olives. Moisten slightly with mayonnaise.

Stuff and garnish with bits of pimiento.

Avocado-Roquefort Filling: Mash avocado pulp. Combine with Roquefort or other blue cheese and make a smooth paste, adding lemon juice and onion juice to taste.

Stuff and garnish with bits of pimiento.

Chicken-Cream Cheese Filling: Blend 1 cup ground cooked white chicken meat, 1 3-ounce package cream cheese, 2 tablespoons lemon juice, 1/2 teaspoon salt, and a few grains cayenne pepper.

Clam-Cream Cheese Filling: Drain 1 small can minced clams (about 7-ounce size) and combine with 1 3-ounce package cream cheese, 1 tablespoon lemon juice, and 3 tablespoons butter. Chill slightly before filling celery stalks.

Cottage Cheese Filling: Season cheese with salt, and spread into grooves. Garnish with thin slices of radish with red edge showing.

Cottage Cheese Filling #2: Mix creamy cottage cheese with chopped sweet pickles, minced pimiento, or chopped chives.

Snappy Cheese Filling: Combine 1/2 cup grated cheese, 11/2 teaspoons mustard-with-horseradish, 11/2 teaspoons mayonnaise, and 1/8 teaspoon paprika. Press firmly into celery stalks. Sprinkle with paprika.

Crabmeat-Cream Cheese Filling: Remove cartilage from 1 6 1/2-ounce can crabmeat. Mash and combine with 1 3-ounce package cream cheese, adding just enough sherry to bind mixture. Season to taste.

Cream Cheese Filling: Mix cream cheese with finely chopped nuts. Spread in celery grooves.

Or mix cheese with finely chopped, stuffed olives.

Cream Cheese Filling #2: Season cream cheese with prepared horseradish.

Egg Filling: Chop hard-cooked eggs fine. Moisten with mayonnaise. Season with salt and pepper. Stuff, and sprinkle with paprika or minced parsley.

Deviled Ham Filling: Combine deviled ham, cream cheese, and mayonnaise to taste. Season with prepared mustard and horseradish.

Pimiento Cheese Filling: Blend pimiento cheese with chopped crisp bacon and chopped sweet pickle.

Roquefort Filling: Combine Roquefort or other blue cheese with a little butter or cream cheese. Season with grated onion.

Seafood Filling: Combine crabmeat, tuna fish, or other flaked, cooked, or canned seafood with a little lemon juice to flavor and mayonnaise to moisten.

Stuffed Celery with Sardines: Stuff lengths of celery cut to sardine size with cream cheese blended with a little onion juice and parsley.

Lay a whole sardine (small one, of course) on each stuffed celery stalk and garnish with a strip of pimiento.

Stuffed celery and deviled eggs are always a treat. Put your imagination to work on fillings; their variety is infinite.

Celery Pinwheels

CELERY PINWHEELS

Blend cream cheese with Roquefort-type cheese. Add mayonnaise or cream until firm spreading consistency. Season with Worcestershire sauce.

Separate stalks of pascal celery. Wash and dry. Fill stalks with cheese mixture and press stalks back into original form of the bunch.

Roll in waxed paper and hold overnight in refrigerator. Just before serving slice celery crosswise forming pinwheels. Arrange on chilled iceberg lettuce cups. Two or 3 slices make 1 serving.

STUFFED PEPPER SLICES

Select long thin peppers in a variety of shades of green and red. Stuff so that all corners are filled with a seasoned cream cheese mixture. Chill 2 to 3 hours.

To serve, cut with a very sharp knife into 1/4-inch slices.

STUFFED ARTICHOKE HEARTS

Remove centers from drained canned artichoke hearts leaving 1/8 inch wall.

Chop centers and add equal amount of chopped pimiento and 1/2 quantity chopped browned almonds or peanuts. Fill centers.

AVOCADO SPREAD

Pare avocados and mash pulp with a fork. Season with lemon or lime juice and salt. Spread on canapé bases.

Garnish with minced parsley and strips of green pepper or pimiento.

GREEN PEPPER AND EGG SPREAD

Mix finely chopped green pepper and finely chopped hard-cooked egg. Moisten with mayonnaise.

Season to taste with salt, pepper, and a tiny bit of dry mustard.

SPICED PINEAPPLE

Sauté pineapple chunks in a little butter or margarine.

Sprinkle with brown sugar, spices, and a dash of vinegar. Stir gently until glazed.

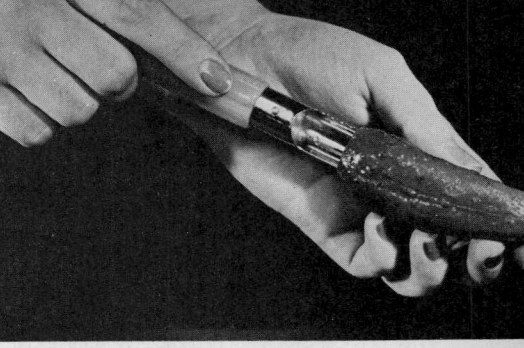

EGGPLANT "CAVIAR"

1 medium-sized eggplant
2 small onions, minced
2 cloves, minced
1 clove garlic, minced
1 ripe tomato, peeled and minced
Salt and pepper
Vinegar
Olive oil

Broil the whole eggplant over direct flame, or in a broiler for 15 to 20 minutes, turning to cook evenly on all sides. Test with a cake tester to see if it is soft all through.

Remove the skin and mash the pulp; mix with the onions, cloves, and garlic. Add the tomato, and season to taste with salt, pepper, vinegar, and oil.

Serve on greens, garnished with quartered tomatoes and black olives or use as a canapé spread.

STUFFED PRUNES

Stuff steamed or soaked plump prunes with a mixture of highly seasoned cream cheese or other suggested fillings.

1. Cottage cheese seasoned with chili sauce.
2. Very crisp chopped celery.
3. Anchovy, shrimp, salmon, tuna, smoked whitefish, or sardine canapé fillings.
4. Roquefort cheese softened with cream.
5. Roquefort moistened with mayonnaise.
6. Aged Cheddar cheese softened with cream.
7. Cream cheese and chopped chives.
8. Finely chopped ham, seasoned with prepared mustard, finely chopped pickle, moistened with mayonnaise.
9. Cream cheese and chopped nuts, moistened with pineapple juice.

MILWAUKEE CANAPÉS

1 cup well-drained sauerkraut
¾ cup mayonnaise
Rounds of rye bread
Stuffed olives

Chop sauerkraut very fine and mix with ¼ cup mayonnaise.

Spread on rye bread rounds which have already been spread with remaining mayonnaise. Garnish with sliced olives.

TOMATO-EGG CANAPÉS

3 slices peeled tomato, chopped
1 hard-cooked egg, chopped
2 tablespoons minced pickle
2 tablespoons minced onion
⅛ teaspoon salt
Dash of pepper
2 tablespoons softened butter

Combine ingredients and use as spread for toasted bread canapés or crackers.

STUFFED DILL PICKLE SLICES

Remove centers from dill pickles with a vegetable corer.

Stuff pickles with a snappy cheese spread, well-seasoned ground cooked meat, mock pâté de foie gras, deviled ham, or liver sausage.

Chill thoroughly and cut them crosswise into ⅓-inch slices.

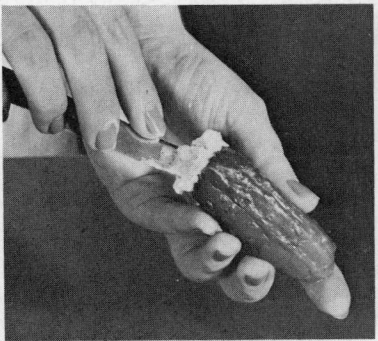

ONION AND EGG SPREAD

Combine 1 finely chopped medium-sized mild onion and 1 finely chopped hard-cooked egg. Moisten with about 4 tablespoons melted chicken fat. Season with salt and pepper to taste.

Serve on crackers or squares of dark rye or pumpernickel bread.

GREEN ONION AND BUTTER SPREAD

Cream ½ cup butter or margarine until soft. Add ¼ cup minced green onion tops and beat with a rotary beater until light and fluffy.

Store in covered jar in refrigerator.

WATERCRESS SPREAD

Combine 1 cup chopped dry watercress, 3 tablespoons cream cheese, ½ teaspoon Worcestershire sauce, 1 tablespoon French dressing, and salt and pepper to taste.

Spread on crackers or potato chips.

STRAWBERRIES

Serve whole, perfect strawberries with the stems on, arranging them around a bowl of sour cream.

AVOCADO-CREAM CHEESE SPREAD

3 3-ounce packages cream cheese
½ cup light cream
1 large avocado, peeled, pitted, and mashed
1½ teaspoons lemon juice
1½ teaspoons onion juice
1 teaspoon salt

Avocado pulp and cream cheese should be about equal in amount. Soften cream cheese with cream. Blend with remaining ingredients. Chill thoroughly.

PIMIENTO ROLLS

Drain pimientos on paper towels and use as a base for fillings. Roll and fasten with picks.

Chill, then slice into bite-size portions.

WHOLE RADISHES

Select firm red or white radishes. Wash and scrub thoroughly. Leave enough stem on to serve as a handle.

Wrap in damp cloth. Chill thoroughly in refrigerator.

ASPARAGUS ROLL CANAPÉS

Roll tiny canned asparagus tips in thinly sliced boiled ham.

Serve on toasted canapé bases which have been spread with mustard butter.

MUSHROOM SPREAD

Wash and chop or grind mushrooms fine. Fry lightly in butter for 5 minutes. Cool and season to taste with lemon juice, salt, and pepper.

SURPRISE RADISHES

Cut small radishes in half lengthwise. Put together with cheese spread. Chill.

It's nice to let a bit of the stem and leaves remain on each radish.

MUSHROOMS WITH PÂTÉ

Sauté mushrooms in butter. Cool and fill caps with pâté de foie gras. Chill and serve on crisp crackers.

OLIVES IN FRENCH DRESSING

Place green or ripe olives in a bowl. Cover with a well-seasoned French dressing to which a cut clove of garlic has been added.

Let stand several hours or overnight in a cold place. Drain and serve.

Cold Skewered Tidbits

Sometimes the hostess does the sticking, sometimes the guest. The toothpick, plain or colorful, is universally accepted.

If the guests are doing the picking, provide a small container of picks. The thoughtful hostess also provides a receptacle for disposing of used picks.

Sometimes edible picks like raw carrot sticks or celery sticks may be used, in which case the hostess will make holes in the food cubes with a skewer, before stringing them.

PORCUPINE SERVERS FOR SNACKS ON PICKS

An attractive way to serve snacks on picks that not only saves space but also creates colorful centerpieces for platters and trays is to use the wooden or metal figures made especially for this purpose and frequently referred to as "porcupine servers."

If you don't have any use a large grapefruit, a big red apple, a large orange, an eggplant, a cantaloupe or other melons. These may be left whole and studded with the snacks on picks porcupine fashion.

Some fruits such as melons, apples, grapefruit, and pineapples may be cut in halves, placed flat side down on the platters or trays and studded with the snacks on picks. Seeds should, of course, be removed from melons. Or melons such as honeydew or cantaloupe may be placed cut side up, the centers filled with fruit balls or such snacks as ripe or stuffed olives, cheese balls, and radish roses, and the edges used for the hors d'oeuvres' base.

Any sort of toothpicks may be used but an assortment of colored wooden or plastic picks is most attractive. Surround the porcupine servers with assorted canapés.

Colorful cocktail picks make for convenience in service and are appreciated by your guests.

BOLOGNA-CHEESE STACKS

4   tablespoons cream cheese
1/4 teaspoon minced onion
1/8 teaspoon salt
1   teaspoon horseradish
3   1/16-inch thick slices large bologna
2   1/8-inch thick slices Cheddar cheese

Blend together first 4 ingredients. Alternate slices of bologna with Cheddar cheese, putting cream cheese mixture between slices; chill.

When cheese is firm, cut into strips, wedges, or cubes. Stick each with a wooden pick.

HAM AND SWISS CHEESE STACKS

Have ham and Swiss cheese cut into very thin slices. Cream butter with horseradish-mustard and curry powder to taste.

Spread a slice of ham with seasoned butter. Cover with slice of cheese. Spread with butter and continue in this way until stack is 1/2 inch thick.

Wrap tightly in waxed paper. Chill thoroughly. To serve, cut into cubes or small wedges. Place one cube and a tiny pickled onion on each pick.

STUFFED FRANKS

Cut franks in half lengthwise. Spread cut surface of half the franks generously with a cheese spread.

Top each spread half with an unspread half, pressing back into original shape. Scrape off excess cheese.

Wrap in waxed paper. Chill. Cut into 1/2-inch pieces and serve on cocktail picks.

APPLES AND CHEESE

Cut firm red eating apples into 1/2 inch slices, after coring. Do not pare. Dip in orange juice to prevent darkening.

Spread with softened Roquefort or blue or other sharp cheese and cut into wedges. Spear each wedge with a pick.

ARTICHOKE HEARTS

Marinate tiny canned artichoke hearts in highly seasoned French dressing to which a clove of garlic has been added. Drain well.

HAM AND CHEESE

Alternate cubes of boiled ham and Swiss or American cheese on picks.

HAM AND MELON

Cut fresh cantaloupe or other melon into cubes. Dip in lemon juice. Spear each cube with a cube of ham or canned spiced meat.

SAUSAGE AND CHEESE

Spear short pieces of Vienna or other sausage and cubes of Cheddar or Swiss cheese.

A grapefruit makes a handy porcupine server for nibblers on picks.

SWISS AND DILL PICKLE

Cut Swiss cheese into 1/2-inch cubes. Put between 2 thin slices of dill pickle, and skewer with pick.

SAUSAGE AND PICKLED BEETS

Spear cubes of bologna or other sausage and cubes of pickled beets.

CHEESE AND PINEAPPLE

Spear a cube of fresh pineapple, then a cube of sharp Cheddar cheese and top with a cherry.

CHEESE STUFFED OLIVES

Fill large pitted olives with cream cheese spread. Serve on picks.

ROAST BEEF AND CHUTNEY BALLS

Mix 1 cup ground leftover roast beef with 4 tablespoons chutney chopped fine with syrup, 1/4 cup ground almonds, 1/4 teaspoon curry powder, and 1 to 2 tablespoons mayonnaise to bind. Shape into balls and chill.

COTTAGE CHEESE BALLS

Mix dry cottage cheese with just enough milk or cream to form a smooth paste. Season with salt, pepper, and minced onion.

Chill, then form into balls. Roll in chopped parsley.

HAM AND PEANUT BUTTER BALLS

Add enough peanut butter to 1 cup ground cooked ham to give a good shaping consistency.

Form into small balls and roll in chopped fresh parsley. Chill thoroughly.

BRAUNSCHWEIGER BALLS

Mash braunschweiger with a fork. Form into small balls. Roll in finely chopped dried beef or parsley.

Or scoop about a heaping tablespoon of the mashed sausage onto palm of left hand. Pat to flatten, then place a stuffed olive or a piece of dill pickle in the center. Roll into a ball to cover the olive or pickle. Roll in chopped parsley.

BACON-CELERY-CHEESE BALLS

Combine 1 cup crisp bacon broken into bits, with ½ cup finely chopped celery, ½ medium-sized apple diced fine, and 1 3-ounce package cream cheese. Add just enough mayonnaise to bind.

Shape into balls and roll in chopped walnuts.

HAM AND CREAM CHEESE BALLS

Combine 1 cup ground cooked ham, 1 3-ounce package cream cheese, 1 teaspoon prepared horseradish, ½ teaspoon prepared mustard, and just enough mayonnaise to bind if needed.

Form into small balls and roll in chopped fresh parsley. Chill thoroughly.

GREEN BALLS

½ cup grated Swiss cheese
½ cup minced cooked ham
½ teaspoon prepared mustard
1 egg yolk
¼ teaspoon salt
Dash of pepper
Minced chives or parsley

Blend first 6 ingredients together and chill thoroughly. Form into balls and roll in minced chives or parsley.

CHEESE-ONION BALLS

Blend 1 cup grated American cheese with 2 tablespoons grated onion. Add enough thick sour cream to bind.

Shape into small balls. Roll in chopped chipped beef and chill thoroughly.

CHICKEN-CHEESE BALLS

Mash a small can (about 6-ounce size) chicken with 1½ cups Gruyère cheese and blend well. There is usually enough gelatin in canned chicken to act as a binder.

Shape into small balls, then roll in chopped almonds. Chill thoroughly.

An attractive and easy cheese tidbit tray is made with colored picks, skewered stuffed olives and little white pearl onions, topping Cheddar cheese cubes.

LOBSTER TAIL PICK 'N' DIP

1 cup mayonnaise
1 tablespoon anchovy paste
½ teaspoon dry mustard
½ teaspoon Tabasco sauce
¼ teaspoon garlic salt
2 tablespoons tarragon vinegar
3 hard-cooked eggs, finely chopped
3 tablespoons finely chopped, stuffed olives
3 tablespoons finely chopped gherkins
1 tablespoon chopped parsley
1 teaspoon finely chopped onion
2 12-ounce lobster tails

Blend mayonnaise, anchovy paste, mustard, Tabasco sauce, and garlic salt. Stir in vinegar. Add hard-cooked eggs, stuffed olives, gherkins, parsley, and onion. Mix well. Makes 2 cups sauce.

Boil lobster tails; remove meat, chill and cube, saving 1 shell to serve sauce in. Place a wooden pick in each cube and arrange around sauce-filled shell.

Decorate platter with watercress or parsley. Makes about 24 appetizers.

ROQUEFORT CHEESE BALLS

2 3-ounce packages cream cheese
⅛ pound Roquefort cheese
2 tablespoons finely chopped celery
1 tablespoon finely chopped onion
Dash of cayenne
Salad dressing
1½ cups finely chopped walnuts

Blend cream and Roquefort cheeses. Add celery, onion, cayenne, and salad dressing. Chill, then form into small balls. Roll in nuts.

APPLE AND CHEESE BALLS

Peel large eating apples and with a vegetable ball scoop make as many small apple balls as possible. Soak the balls in lemon juice to keep from discoloring. Drain on paper towels.

Spread with a seasoned softened cheese moistened with mayonnaise to get a spreading consistency. Roll each cheese-spread ball in chopped nuts.

CREAM CHEESE-CARROT BALLS

Blend 1 3-ounce package cream cheese with ½ cup grated raw carrot, and a few grains cayenne pepper.

Shape into small balls. Roll in chopped parsley and chill thoroughly.

BURNING BUSH

Season 1 3-ounce package of cream cheese with ½ teaspoon minced onion. Chill, then form into balls. Roll in minced dried beef.

CREAM CHEESE "STRAWBERRIES"

Form seasoned cream cheese to resemble strawberries in shape. Chill.

Dust with paprika. Stick pieces of parsley in the ends.

Lobster Tail Pick 'n' Dip: As appealing to your guests as a dish of candy to a child is this offering of chilled lobster tail with its spicy sauce.

LIVER SAUSAGE BALLS

½ pound liver sausage
1 tablespoon minced parsley
2 teaspoons grated onion
2 teaspoons celery seeds
½ teaspoon Worcestershire sauce
Finely grated raw carrot or minced dried beef
36 to 40 pretzel sticks

Mash liver sausage; add parsley, onion, celery seeds, and Worcestershire sauce; mix well.

Form into 36 to 40 small balls. Roll in grated carrot or dried beef. Insert pretzel sticks for handles.

TONGUE AND CHEESE STACKS

Spread 2 slices of smoked boiled tongue with cream cheese softened with cream. Stack together and top with an unspread slice of tongue.

Trim edges (use trimmings in spreads) and cut into cubes. Stick each with a pick.

THURINGER WITH PICKLED ONION

Spear cubes of thuringer and top with pickled onion.

PICKLES IN BLANKETS

Roll thin slices of roast beef, tongue, smoked salmon, strips of anchovy, or strips of pickled herring around tiny sour-sweet or other gherkins. Secure the rolls with picks.

WATERMELON PICKLE

Spear cubes of watermelon pickle on picks with pieces of ham.

SALAMI AND OLIVES

Alternate bite-size cubes of salami or other sausage and olives on picks.

CHEESE AND ONION

Place a ½-inch square of American cheese, a tiny slice of pickle, and a tiny pickled onion on each pick.

Miscellaneous Cold Hors D'Oeuvres

SHRIMP REMOULADE

1   large clove garlic
3   tablespoons olive oil
1   tablespoon vinegar
5   tablespoons chili sauce
¾   teaspoon salt
Few grains of pepper
⅛   teaspoon paprika
½   teaspoon dry mustard
1½   teaspoons prepared horseradish
2   cans jumbo shrimp

Mince garlic very fine; add olive oil, vinegar, chili sauce and seasoning; mix well.

Remove black vein from shrimp. Add shrimp to sauce. Let stand in refrigerator several hours.

Pierce shrimp with toothpicks; remove from sauce and arrange on serving platter. Pour remaining sauce over shrimp. Serves 8.

DRIED BEEF-COTTAGE CHEESE ROLLS

1   cup cottage cheese
2   teaspoons minced parsley
2   teaspoons prepared horseradish
⅛   teaspoon paprika
Mayonnaise
12   small dried beef slices

Combine cottage cheese, parsley, horseradish, paprika, and mayonnaise.

Spread on dried beef slices and roll. Fasten with picks. Chill thoroughly.

PARSLEY ROLLS

White bread, fresh
Olive-pimiento cheese spread
Parsley

Cut the bread in thin slices; trim the crusts and spread each slice with the cheese spread softened at room temperature.

Roll up each slice and garnish the ends with small sprigs of parsley.

Parsley Rolls

PICKLE-FILLED HAM ROLLS

1   4½-ounce can liver paté
2   tablespoons mayonnaise
2   teaspoons prepared mustard
¼   teaspoon salt
6   slices boiled ham, cut ⅛-inch thick
2   large dill pickles

Combine liver paté, mayonnaise, mustard, and salt; blend well. Spread each ham slice with part of liver mixture.

Cut pickles in thirds, lengthwise, and place a pickle strip crosswise on the end of each ham slice.

Roll up each slice crosswise starting from the pickle end. Fasten with picks. Chill thoroughly. Cut in halves and serve as finger food. Makes 12.

GLAZED COCKTAIL SHRIMP

1   cup canned tomatoes
6   tablespoons water
2   tablespoons chopped celery
1   carrot, sliced
1   tablespoon chopped green pepper
1   whole clove
¼   teaspoon salt
⅛   teaspoon pepper
¾   tablespoon unflavored gelatin
1½   teaspoons lemon juice
1   pound fresh cooked, cleaned shrimp, chilled

Put tomatoes and 4 tablespoons water in saucepan. Add vegetables and seasoning and bring to boiling point on high heat. Reduce heat and cook 15 minutes; strain.

Soften gelatin in 2 tablespoons cold water 5 minutes. Add to hot tomato juice and stir until gelatin is dissolved. Stir in lemon juice. Chill in refrigerator until of syrupy consistency.

Dip cold shrimp in gelatin mixture. Drain on cake rack and chill. Repeat several times to build up heavy coating of aspic on shrimp.

SALAMI CORNUCOPIAS

Spread thinly sliced salami with mustard. Roll into cornucopias and fasten with picks.

Serve plain or place a small pickle, a stuffed olive, or a small ball of cream cheese mixed with chopped chives in the center as a filling, or roll each around a few stalks of watercress.

HAM AND ASPARAGUS ROLLS

Spread small strips of thinly sliced boiled or baked ham with mayonnaise seasoned with mustard.

Roll each prepared ham slice around a cooked or canned asparagus tip. Fasten with a pick.

Or marinate asparagus tips in French dressing before rolling in the ham slices.

Pickle-filled Ham Rolls

CHEESE "CARROTS"

1   3-ounce package cream cheese
⅓   cup grated carrot
¼   teaspoon salt
Dash of cayenne
4   drops Worcestershire sauce
1   tablespoon chopped chives or onion
Sprigs of parsley

Mix cream cheese and carrot; season with salt, cayenne, Worcestershire sauce, and chives. Roll into miniature carrot shapes. Chill until firm.

Stick a tiny sprig of parsley into each "carrot" to resemble tops.

CHEESE "CARROTS" #2

1   teaspoon unflavored gelatin
2   tablespoons cold water
½   cup smoked cheese spread
¼   teaspoon Worcestershire sauce
2   medium-sized carrots, grated
Parsley

Soften gelatin in cold water 5 minutes. Melt over hot water. Cool slightly. Blend with cheese and Worcestershire sauce.

Place in refrigerator until of pliable consistency. Divide into 1 teaspoon portions. Shape into cones.

Roll in grated carrots, and stick sprig of parsley in large end to represent carrot top.

SMITHFIELD HAM ROLLS

Spread thin slices of Smithfield ham with cottage cheese mixed with piccalilli; roll up tightly and spear with picks.

ROQUEFORT LETTUCE ROLLS

Mix and cream well 3 parts Roquefort cheese with 1 part cream cheese. Chill.

Wrap small portions in small, crisp lettuce leaves. Fasten with picks.

CHICKEN ROLLS

Soften cream cheese with brandy and season with salt. Spread on thin slices of chicken meat and roll. Fasten with picks and chill.

SMOKED SALMON-CAVIAR CORNUCOPIAS

Roll thin slices of smoked salmon into cone shape. Fasten with picks.

Fill each with caviar seasoned with lemon juice, or caviar mixed with riced hard-cooked eggs seasoned with lemon juice and paprika.

CHEESE AND PRETZELS

Form small balls from tasty cheese. Place a cheese ball at each end of a small pretzel stick.

HAM PINWHEELS

3 slices boiled ham
2 tablespoons olive-pimiento cheese spread
About 12 small stuffed olives

Spread each slice of ham with 2 teaspoons cheese spread. Cut into ¾-inch strips. Place an olive at end of each strip and roll. Secure with pick and chill.

When cheese is firm, remove picks and cut each roll in half to form 2 pinwheels. Serve with cut side up.

MELON AND HAM ROLLS

Wrap small chilled wedges of honeydew melon with very thin slices of Italian prosciutto ham. Fasten with picks.

CHEESE-BOLOGNA ROLLS

2 ounces Cheddar cheese
2 teaspoons softened butter
1 large stuffed olive, chopped fine
6 slices large bologna
4 large stuffed olives, cut into lengthwise strips

Cream the cheese and butter together. Stir in chopped olive. Spread each round of bologna with 2½ teaspoons of cheese mixture.

Cut rounds crosswise into 4 triangular parts. Beginning at point of triangle, roll and secure with pick. Garnish ends of roll with slice of olive. Chill.

HAM STICKS

Spread ham with prepared mustard. Wrap around bread sticks allowing 1 inch of bread stick to be free as a handle.

JIFFY SNACK TRAY ➤

To make gay pinwheels, just spread slices of boiled ham with pasteurized process cheese spread; roll up jell-roll fashion and chill well. Slice and serve on crackers.

For ribbon loaf, spread 12 slices of processed American cheese with canned deviled ham and stack them up. Cut through the center of the stack to make two "loaves." Chill well and slice off as needed. Serve with crackers.

LOBSTER TAIL, PAN AMERICAN STYLE

4 to 6 (6-ounce) lobster tails
1 can tomato sauce
¼ cup olive oil
2 tablespoons vinegar
2 tablespoons minced onion
¼ cup minced celery
¼ cup minced stuffed olives
1 teaspoon salt
1 teaspoon aromatic bitters

Cook lobster tails as directed on package, or see index. Drench with cold water, drain. Cut down both sides of undershell with kitchen scissors, peel off undershell. Insert thumb between shell and meat, gently pull meat from shell, in one piece. Reserve shells. Chill meat and cut in large cubes.

Mix tomato sauce with remaining ingredients. Add lobster meat and allow to marinate several hours. Serve in shells with toothpicks, as appetizer. **Note:** The lobster meat may be heated after marinating, and served as a main course with boiled rice. Serves 4 to 6.

ROAST BEEF PINWHEELS

Spread thin slices of roast beef with garlic butter. Roll each prepared slice, then wrap individual rolls in waxed paper.

Chill thoroughly and when ready to serve slice with a sharp knife into bite-size pinwheels. Spear each with a pick.

Variations: Use liver paste or Roquefort cheese thinned with butter instead of the garlic butter.

SMOKED SALMON ROLLS

Spread thin slices of smoked salmon with cream cheese seasoned with horseradish, salt, and black pepper. Roll carefully, skewering with picks.

TONGUE-ASPARAGUS ROLLS

Season mayonnaise with dry mustard to taste. Spread on small slices of tongue or dried beef.

Roll each slice around an asparagus tip. Secure with a pick.

Lobster Tail, Pan American Style

SMOKED SALMON CORNUCOPIAS

12 thin slices smoked salmon
½ cup cottage cheese
½ teaspoon onion juice
¼ teaspoon salt
Dash of pepper
Paprika
Watercress or parsley

Shape very thinly sliced smoked salmon into cornucopias; fasten with picks.

Combine cheese, onion juice, salt, and pepper. Fill each cornucopia with some of the mixture.

Garnish with a dash of paprika, a sprig of parsley or watercress. Chill.

Variations: Salami or other sausage may be used instead of smoked salmon. Roquefort cream cheese, cream cheese seasoned with chopped chives, or well-seasoned chicken salad may be used as the filling.

CHEESE-FILLED HAM ROLLS

1 3-ounce package cream cheese
6 chopped stuffed olives
1 teaspoon prepared horseradish
2 tablespoons cream
Salt and pepper
Boiled ham slices

Combine cheese, olives, horseradish, and cream; season to taste. Spread on slices of boiled ham. Roll and fasten with picks.

First Course Fish and Shellfish Appetizers

HINTS ABOUT SEAFOOD COCKTAILS

Chilled crabmeat, lobster, shrimp, tuna fish, etc. with a sharp cocktail sauce are always a perfect at-table beginning for a dinner. They are traditionally served in sherbet (cocktail) glasses, lined with lettuce. Other nice ways to serve them include the following:

1. Arrange seafood on small plates with romaine leaf or lettuce cup filled with cocktail sauce in center of each plate.

2. Pile seafood in green pepper rings placed on small plates; cover with sauce.

3. Hollow out small tomatoes; place on beds of watercress or other greens on small plates. Fill tomatoes with seafood which has been dipped into sauce.

OYSTER OR CLAM COCKTAIL

Drain small oysters or clams and chill thoroughly. Place 5 or 6 oysters in each lettuce-lined cocktail glass.

Cover with cocktail sauce. Serve with wedge of lemon.

LOBSTER COCKTAIL

Cut cooked or canned lobster in pieces. Serve in lettuce-lined cup with cocktail sauce or with very highly seasoned mayonnaise.

SHRIMP IN MUSTARD SAUCE
(Shrimp New Orleans)

1½ pounds fresh shrimp, cooked, or
      two 5¾-ounce cans shrimp
2   tablespoons vinegar
⅓   cup salad oil
Salt and pepper
2   tablespoons prepared mustard
1   teaspoon paprika
2   green onions with tops, minced
1   celery heart, minced

Clean shrimp. Combine remaining ingredients and pour over shrimp. Toss lightly. Chill 2 hours.

Serve on shredded lettuce or in scallop shells. Serves 6.

LOBSTER TAIL COCKTAILS

4   small rock lobster tails, boiled
¼   cup ketchup
2   tablespoons lemon juice
1   tablespoon vinegar
2   tablespoons mayonnaise
1   teaspoon prepared mustard
⅛   teaspoon celery salt
3   drops Tabasco sauce

Remove meat from cooked lobster tails. Chill, dice and refill individual shells.

Top with sauce made by combining remaining ingredients. Serve icy cold with lemon wedges. Serves 4.

SHRIMP COCKTAIL

Clean canned or fresh-cooked shrimp, removing black line from back. Chill.

Serve in lettuce-lined cocktail cups with cocktail sauce or with very highly seasoned mayonnaise. Finely chopped celery may be added.

CANNED CRABMEAT COCKTAIL

Flake canned crabmeat, remove bony tissue and combine with chopped celery. Chill. Serve in lettuce-lined cocktail glasses with cocktail sauce.

FRESH CRABMEAT COCKTAIL

Combine equal quantities cooked fresh crabmeat and Russian dressing. Toss well. Serve from salad bowl or in individual lettuce-lined cups.

SCALLOP COCKTAIL

Clean scallops and cook in boiling water until they begin to shrivel, about 5 minutes. Drain and chill.

Serve in lettuce-lined cocktail cups with desired sauce.

SEAFOOD AND AVOCADO COCKTAIL

Use half and half avocado cubes and pieces of tuna, lobster meat, crabmeat, or shrimp.

Serve in lettuce-lined cocktail cups with cocktail sauce.

SEAFOOD AND GRAPEFRUIT COCKTAIL

Arrange cooked, cleaned shrimp, pieces of lobster meat, or chilled tiny oysters in alternate layers with grapefruit segments in lettuce-lined cocktail cups.

Top with mayonnaise seasoned with lemon juice and Tabasco sauce.

Seafood Cocktails: If you like, combine two or more kinds of seafood such as canned or cooked crabmeat, lobster, or shrimp in each seafood cocktail. Use about ⅓ cup of seafood for each serving. Mix with cocktail sauce or serve the sauce separately. Put the seafood on lettuce or watercress in chilled dessert glasses.

Lobster Tail Cocktails

STANDARD COCKTAIL SAUCE

¾   cup chili sauce or ketchup
1½   tablespoons lemon juice
1   tablespoon Worcestershire sauce
1   tablespoon prepared horseradish
Few drops of Tabasco sauce
¼   teaspoon salt
1   teaspoon grated onion

Mix ingredients and chill thoroughly. Yield: about 1 cup.

CREAM COCKTAIL SAUCE

2   tablespoons tarragon vinegar
1   teaspoon dry mustard
Juice of ½ lemon
1   teaspoon prepared horseradish
1   cup chili sauce
1   cup whipped cream
1   tablespoon mayonnaise
½   teaspoon Worcestershire sauce

Mix the mustard in the vinegar. Add other ingredients and mix well. Yield: about 2 cups.

CELERY COCKTAIL SAUCE

¾   cup ketchup or chili sauce
1½   tablespoons lemon juice
1   teaspoon Worcestershire sauce
¼   cup chopped celery
Dash each of salt and cayenne

Mix ingredients and chill thoroughly. Yield: about 1 cup.

COCKTAIL DRESSING

½   cup mayonnaise
1   tablespoon lemon juice
1   tablespoon ketchup
1   tablespoon horseradish
3   drops Worcestershire sauce
2   drops Tabasco sauce
Salt and paprika to taste

Mix ingredients and chill thoroughly. Yield: about ¾ cup.

CURRY COCKTAIL DRESSING

1   cup mayonnaise
½   teaspoon curry powder
1   tablespoon minced onion
2   tablespoons chutney
1   tablespoon lemon juice

Mix ingredients and chill thoroughly. Yield: about 1¼ cups.

First Course Fruit Appetizers

HINTS ABOUT FRUIT CUPS

Simple combinations of fruit make excellent first courses for they stimulate the appetite. Mixtures of almost any fruits may be used, canned, fresh or frozen. Choose combinations that contrast in color, texture, and taste; dice them in attractive sizes, not too small. Prepare them in advance and chill in the refrigerator so the flavors will mingle. If canned ready-mixed fruit cocktail is used, it is frequently advisable to add some fresh, tart fruit to vary the texture and flavor.

Allow ½ cup of fruit mixture per serving.

Sweetening: Canned fruits are usually sweet enough without additional sweetening. If fresh, tart fruits are used a little thin sugar syrup may be added; however, appetizer fruit cups must never be too sweet. The addition of a little lemon or lime juice will usually improve a fruit cup, whether fresh or canned fruits are used.

A simple lemon sauce may be made by mixing lemon juice with confectioners' sugar to the consistency of a sauce.

Sugar Syrup: Boil 1 cup sugar and ½ cup water gently for 5 minutes. Cool and dilute with juices from canned or fresh fruits or berries. Lemon or orange juice may be added.

Coloring: For variety, the syrup may be delicately colored with a little red or green food coloring. Or, add color by using the syrup of maraschino or mint cherries or a little crème de menthe or grenadine syrup.

Garnishing: Fruit cups may be garnished with a sprig of mint, a red or green cherry, a whole strawberry, or a small scoop of fruit ice or sherbet.

Crushed Mints: Crushed after-dinner mints are an interesting addition to some fruit cups, especially those made of citrus fruits and other tart combinations.

Preserved Ginger: With tart fruits try syrup from preserved ginger and chopped ginger. Use 1 tablespoon syrup and 1 tablespoon chopped ginger with 3 cups fruit mixture.

Wine Cocktail Sauce: Mix ½ cup sugar, ⅓ cup sherry wine, and 2 tablespoons lemon juice or Madeira wine. Chill and serve with any fruit cocktail.

Serving Cups: Serve fruits in cocktail glasses, sherbet glasses, glass bowls, or in shells from grapefruit, oranges, melons, or pineapples. When shells are used, part of the fruit removed from the shells should be one of the ingredients in the fruit cup mixture.

Ginger Ale Fruit Cup: Pour small amount of chilled ginger ale over any combination of canned fruits.

MELON BALL COCKTAILS

Cut balls from cantaloupe, honeydew, watermelon, or other melons, using melon-ball cutter or half-teaspoon measure.

Serve very cold, alone or in combination with other fruits. Sweeten to taste with thin sugar syrup.

HONEYDEW MELON COCKTAIL

Cook ½ cup sugar and ⅓ cup water 5 minutes; cool and add 2 tablespoons each of lemon, lime and orange juice. Pour over chilled melon balls.

PEACH COCKTAIL

2½ cups diced, fresh peaches
1 tablespoon lemon juice
2 tablespoons sugar
Chilled ginger ale
Fresh mint

Combine peaches, lemon juice, and sugar. Fill fruit cocktail glasses. Add 1 to 2 tablespoons ginger ale to each glass. Garnish with sprig of mint. Serves 4.

GRAPE-MELON COCKTAIL

Mix equal amounts seedless grapes, diced honeydew melon, and diced orange sections. Flavor with lemon juice. Sweeten with sugar.

CANTALOUPE SALAD COCKTAIL

1 cantaloupe
1 cup honeydew melon cubes
2 fresh peaches, sliced
1 cup Tokay grapes, pitted and cut in halves
¼ cup fruit French dressing

Have all ingredients thoroughly chilled. Pare cantaloupe and cut into 8 wedges. Combine remaining ingredients.

Arrange 2 cantaloupe wedges on each salad dish to form circle or oval. Fill centers with salad mixture. Serves 4.

FRUIT SHERBET CUP

Fill sherbet cup half full with combined diced orange and grapefruit sections. Top with scoop of lemon or other fruit sherbet. Arrange fruit sections around sherbet. Garnish with mint leaves.

PINEAPPLE BOATS

Trim ⅔ from leafy top of large pineapple and chill. Cut into 8 lengthwise wedges. Cut out cores. Pare skin in one piece, leaving it in place.

Cut pulp downward into 5 or 6 slices, retaining shape. Serve each portion garnished with whole berries and confectioners' sugar.

Normandy Fruit Cocktail

NORMANDY FRUIT COCKTAIL

½ cup granulated sugar
¼ teaspoon ground cloves
½ cup water
¾ cup port wine
1 cup melon balls
1 cup sliced, seeded Tokay grapes
1 cup sliced bananas

Combine sugar, cloves, and water and bring to a boil. Boil 5 minutes.

Cool; add wine and pour over melon and grapes and place in refrigerator for several hours. Add bananas just before serving. Serves 4 to 5.

BANANA-ORANGE COCKTAIL

Cut ripe bananas into thin slices. Place in cocktail glasses and cover with chilled orange juice.

Decorate tops with orange sections. Sprinkle lightly with confectioners' sugar. Garnish with a sprig of mint, a cherry, or a strawberry.

SEMI-TROPIC COCKTAIL

3 oranges, diced
1 cup diced pineapple
3 bananas, diced
3 tablespoons confectioners' sugar
1 cup grated coconut
1 pint grape juice

Mix together the fruit, sugar, and coconut. Fill cocktail glasses about ⅔ full. Chill thoroughly.

When ready to serve, pour the chilled grape juice over each cocktail and garnish with pieces of candied orange peel or the grated rind of oranges. Serves 6.

FRESH PINEAPPLE COCKTAIL

1 fresh pineapple
1 cup sugar
⅓ cup water
½ cup chilled orange juice
3 tablespoons lime juice

Peel, core, and dice the pineapple. Chill thoroughly. Combine sugar and water; boil 1 minute.

Chill syrup and add orange and lime juices. Place pineapple in cocktail glasses and pour syrup mixture over it. Serves 6.

21

GRAPEFRUIT IN COCKTAIL GLASSES

Allow one-half grapefruit per person. To remove whole segments, a very sharp knife is essential. Peel off the yellow skin, then peel off the white skin so that none shows on whole fruit.

Remove segments by cutting the first few from the outside toward the center. The remainder are usually easy to remove by cutting from the core toward the edge.

Place grapefruit segments and juice in glasses and fill the glasses with a dessert wine, orange juice, or ginger ale.

STRAWBERRY COCKTAIL

Cover chilled hulled strawberries with chilled pineapple juice. Add, if desired, confectioners' sugar.

Variation: Sprinkle strawberries with lemon juice and confectioners' sugar. Garnish with mint leaves.

PINEAPPLE-MINT COCKTAIL

2 cups canned pineapple cubes
1 cup halved and seeded Tokay grapes
1 cup ginger ale
1/2 cup mild, white candy mints

Drain pineapple and add grapes, ginger ale, and mints. Chill thoroughly.

GRAPE-SHERRY COCKTAIL

Wash small white seedless grapes; remove stems and cut in halves. Place shaved ice in bottom of each sherbet glass and fill with grapes.

Pour 3 tablespoons sherry on each serving. Serve at once.

Fruit in Orange or Grapefruit Shells: Orange or grapefruit shells filled with grapes, berries, or other assorted fruits make a colorful and refreshing first course appetizer, or arranged on a silver platter, a beautiful addition to your punch party table.

For the fluted shells, choose clean-skinned oranges and grapefruit. Halve the orange or grapefruit by making zigzag cuts to center as shown in illustration. Separate the halves and remove meat from shells.

GRAPE-FILLED AVOCADOS

3 cups seeded and halved red grapes (1 1/2 pounds)
3 ripe avocados
Lemon juice
Madeira wine

Cut avocados in halves and remove pits. Rub avocados with lemon juice to prevent darkening. Chill thoroughly.

Fill avocado halves with grapes. Pour wine over. Serves 6.

AVOCADO COCKTAIL

3 cups avocado cubes or balls
1/2 cup ketchup
1 teaspoon prepared horseradish
1 teaspoon Worcestershire sauce
2 tablespoons lemon or lime juice
1 tablespoon mayonnaise
1/4 teaspoon salt
Dash of Tabasco sauce

Apportion 1/2 cup avocado cubes or balls to each cocktail. Combine ketchup, horseradish, Worcestershire sauce, lemon or lime juice, mayonnaise, salt, and Tabasco sauce; blend and pour over fruit. Serve chilled. Serves 6.

Variations: Add half as much of any of the following as the amount of avocado used: asparagus tips; balls or cubes of cooked celery root; diced tomato and cucumber; diced celery; seafoods as lobster, shrimp, tuna, salmon, and crab. Oysters require a very nippy sauce.

These citrus fruit cups are made by combining fresh, frozen, or chilled grapefruit sections with sliced bananas and diced apple (leave red peel on for color contrast); with finely cut dates and shredded coconut; with diced avocado and chopped pimiento (omit sugar); with sliced strawberries; with orange or lime sherbet.

PINEAPPLE GRAPE FREEZE

1/4 cup powdered sugar
1 No. 2 can (2 1/2 cups) pineapple juice
1 egg white
1 1/2 cups halved, seeded red grapes

Dissolve sugar in pineapple juice. Beat egg white until stiff and fold in. Pour into refrigerator freezing tray.

Freeze to mush-like consistency and fold in grapes. Serve immediately. Serves 6.

WATERMELON COCKTAIL

This is a good way to use the ends of watermelon. Make balls with melon-ball scoop, or cut in 1-inch cubes, removing seeds.

Sprinkle melon with lemon juice and powdered sugar, using 1/2 tablespoon lemon juice and 1 tablespoon powdered sugar for each portion. Cover and chill. Serve in cocktail glasses. Garnish with fresh mint.

BRAZILIAN GRAPEFRUIT COCKTAIL

Cut grapefruit into halves. Remove seeds and pulpy center. With a sharp knife remove membrane between segments. Sprinkle tops with ground Brazil nuts and finely cut fresh mint. Add light cover of powdered sugar. Chill.

Just before serving, pour a teaspoonful of sherry in the center of each half.

If the fresh mint cannot be obtained, take a little of the grapefruit juice which will form in the hollow of the fruit and flavor with a few drops of oil, or essence, of peppermint.

Pour this over the fruit before adding the powdered sugar. Sherry may be omitted.

French – Fried Hot Appetizers

If you can solve the service problem and get this type of hors d'oeuvre to your guests while hot and just out of the fryer, nothing is more delicious. Consider the suggestions given in this chapter plus other dishes such as deep-fat fried shrimp and other shellfish, bite-size croquettes, etc.

BATTER DIPPED HORS D'OEUVRES

Easy Batter Dip:

1 cup pancake mix
1/4 teaspoon salt
3/4 cup water

Combine and beat with a rotary egg beater or an electric mixer about 2 minutes.

Use as suggested below and for other simple batter dipped French fried appetizers.

Cocktail Frankfurters: Dip cocktail frankfurters in batter; drain and fry in hot deep fat (375°F.) 2 to 3 minutes.

Corned Beef Fingers: Cut corned beef into finger length strips. Dip in batter; drain and fry in hot deep fat (375°F.) 2 to 3 minutes.

Chicken Livers: Prick chicken livers well with a fork. Dip in batter; drain and fry in hot deep fat (375°F.) 2 to 3 minutes.

Surprise Cheese Balls: Cut processed cheese into small cubes or roll small spoonfuls of ready-spread cheese into balls.

Spear each ball or cube with a wooden pick. Dip in batter. Fry in hot deep fat (375°F.) 2 to 3 minutes.

Pineapple Frank Kebobs: Alternate drained pineapple cubes and cocktail frankfurters on skewers.

Dip in batter; drain and fry in hot deep fat (375°F.) 2 to 3 minutes.

CHEESE BOURAG (Armenian)

2 cups sifted enriched flour
1/4 teaspoon salt
3 teaspoons baking powder
3 tablespoons sweet butter
About 1/2 cup milk
1/2 pound sharp cheese, grated
3 tablespoons finely chopped parsley
1/4 teaspoon salt

Sift flour, salt, and baking powder together. Cut in butter with a pastry blender or 2 knives and mix to a dough with milk, handling as little as possible.

Roll out very thin on a floured board; cut into 2-inch squares.

Mix remaining ingredients together. Put squares together by pairs with tablespoon of cheese mixture between. Seal edges well by pressing with tines of a fork.

Fry until brown in deep hot fat (365° to 375°F.). Drain and serve.

TURKISH CHEESE APPETIZERS (Beureks)

Cut 1/2 pound Gruyère cheese into small pieces. Put into a saucepan with 1/4 cup thick white sauce. Stir until cheese is melted and mixture is thick.

Spread on a platter to cool. Chill in refrigerator if necessary. Shape into small sausage-like shapes.

Wrap each in a thin piece of plain pastry and fry in deep hot fat (385°F.) until golden brown. Drain. Serve hot or cold.

FRENCH FRIED PARSLEY

1 egg yolk
1/2 cup milk
1/2 cup enriched flour
1/2 teaspoon salt
Sprigs of parsley

Beat egg yolk; add milk, then add flour and salt.

Dip sprigs of parsley in the batter and fry in hot deep fat (365°–375°F.) until crisp. Serve with dipping sauce.

CHEESE AND NUT BALLS

2 teaspoons flour
1/8 teaspoon cayenne
1/2 teaspoon salt
1 cup grated American cheese
1 egg white, stiffly beaten
1/4 cup finely chopped nuts

Mix flour, cayenne, salt, and grated cheese. Fold egg white lightly into cheese mixture until well blended. Form into small balls and roll in chopped nuts.

Fry in hot deep fat (375°F.) until golden brown. Drain on paper towels. Serve hot on picks. Makes about 15 balls.

JIFFY CODFISH BALLS

Shape canned codfish cakes into small balls the size of marbles. Fry in hot deep fat (375°F.) until brown.

Insert cocktail pick and serve hot on hors d'oeuvres tray with a dipping sauce or ketchup.

MEAT AND SAUERKRAUT BALLS (German)

1/2 pound lean ham
1/2 pound lean pork
1/2 pound corned beef
1 medium-sized onion
1 teaspoon minced parsley
3 tablespoons shortening
2 cups enriched flour
1 teaspoon salt
1 teaspoon dry mustard
2 cups milk
2 pounds sauerkraut, cooked and drained
Flour
2 slightly beaten eggs
Dry breadcrumbs

Put ham, pork, corned beef, and onion through food chopper, using medium blade. Add parsley and blend well.

Sauté in shortening until browned. Add flour, salt, mustard, and milk. Blend thoroughly. Cook, stirring constantly, until thick.

Add sauerkraut and put entire mixture through food chopper. Mix thoroughly.

Cook in skillet, stirring constantly, until thick. Cool then form into balls the size of a walnut.

Roll balls in flour. Dip in beaten egg. Roll in crumbs. Fry in deep fat (370°F.) until browned. Serve hot on picks.

BEEF BURGUNDY BALLS

1/2 pound round steak, ground
1 egg
2 tablespoons flour
2 teaspoons finely chopped onion
1/4 teaspoon Worcestershire
1 tablespoon burgundy wine
Salt and pepper to taste

Combine all ingredients; mix well; form in small balls. Roll balls in fine cracker crumbs.

Fry in hot deep fat (375°F.) until brown. Drain. Serve hot on picks.

A tray of hot hors d'oeuvres will add luster to your entertaining—try it and hear the cheers.

FRIED RICE BALLS

Form 1 cup of snappy cheese into small balls not over a 1/2-inch in diameter. Spread lightly with a tangy prepared mustard.

Then roll each ball in salted, cooked rice. The rice should not be blanched or fluffed; kernels should stick together. Roll balls in hands to make them firm and compact.

Drop into hot deep fat (375°F.) and fry until golden brown. These may be reheated in the oven. Serve hot on picks.

Variations:

1. Substitute cooked shrimp for cheese.

2. Substitute ball of anchovy paste for cheese.

3. Substitute stuffed olive for cheese.

CODFISH-POTATO BALLS

1   cup salt codfish
2 1/2 cups potatoes
1/2   tablespoon butter
1   egg, well beaten
1/8   teaspoon pepper

Wash fish in cold water. Pick in very small pieces or cut, using scissors.

Wash, pare and soak potatoes, cutting in pieces of uniform size before measuring.

Cook fish and potatoes in boiling water to cover until potatoes are nearly soft.

Drain thoroughly through strainer and return to kettle in which they were cooked. Shake over heat until thoroughly dry.

Mash thoroughly and add butter, egg, and pepper. Beat with fork 2 minutes. Add salt if necessary.

Take up by spoonfuls and sauté in butter or fry 1 minute in hot deep fat (385°F.) until brown. Drain on paper. Serve hot on picks.

CAVIAR RISSOLES

Roll puff paste 1/4-inch thick and cut in small rounds. Place 1 teaspoon caviar, seasoned with lemon juice in the center of each.

Moisten edges and cover with a second round. Press edges together with the tines of a fork.

Fry in hot deep fat (370°F.) 3 to 4 minutes, or until golden brown. Drain on paper towels.

SAUSAGE-POTATO BALLS

Form seasoned sausage meat in 3/4-inch balls. Coat with mashed potatoes. Roll in beaten egg diluted with 1 tablespoon cold water, then in fine dry breadcrumbs.

Let stand for an hour to dry. Fry in hot deep fat (370°F.) until golden. Serve hot on picks.

TUNA BALLS

2   6 1/2-ounce cans tuna
1   tablespoon flour
1/3   cup milk
1   teaspoon minced onion
1/2   teaspoon salt
1/8   teaspoon pepper
Few grains of cayenne
1   beaten egg

Drain and shred tuna, saving the oil. Heat 1 tablespoon of the tuna oil in a saucepan. Blend in flour until smooth.

Remove from heat and slowly add milk, stirring until well blended. Add onion, salt, pepper, and cayenne.

Return to heat and, stirring constantly, cook until smooth and thick. Remove from heat; add beaten egg and tuna.

Chill until firm then form into 3/4-inch balls. Roll in flour.

Fry in hot deep fat (375°F.) until golden brown. Serve on picks with a dipping sauce. Makes 30 to 36 balls.

CLAM CAKE HORS D'OEUVRES

2   cups sifted enriched flour
1   teaspoon baking powder
1/2   teaspoon salt
2   eggs, well beaten
1   cup milk
1/2   cup clam liquid
1   pint fresh clams
Deep fat for frying

Sift flour with baking powder and salt. Add well beaten eggs, milk, and clam liquid slowly; stir well and add clams which have been ground quite fine in a food chopper.

Drop by spoonfuls into hot deep fat (375°F.). When nicely browned, remove from kettle and drain. Serve hot. Provide a dipping sauce.

CORNED BEEF BALLS

2   cups finely chopped corned beef
1   egg, slightly beaten
2   tablespoons ketchup or chili sauce
About 1 tablespoon Worcestershire sauce

Mix ingredients and form into 3/4-inch balls. Roll in fine dry bread or cracker crumbs, then in a beaten egg diluted with 1 tablespoon cold water, and again in crumbs.

Fry in hot deep fat (375°F.) until golden brown. Serve hot on picks with a dipping sauce. Makes about 36 to 40 balls.

Ham Balls: Use finely chopped cooked ham instead of corned beef.

SOYED CHICKEN LIVERS

Cut chicken livers into small strips. Dip in soy sauce then in a very light batter made of egg and flour. Fry in hot deep fat (375°F.).

OYSTER BALLS—FRENCH FRIED

1   pint oysters
1   teaspoon grated onion
1   teaspoon minced parsley
1/4   teaspoon salt
1/4   teaspoon pepper
Dash of Tabasco or cayenne
Pinch of mace
1   cup soft breadcrumbs
2   eggs
2   tablespoons butter
Corn meal or fine dry breadcrumbs

Pour 1 quart of boiling water over drained oysters then drain well and chop fine.

Season with onion, parsley, salt, pepper, cayenne, and mace.

Add soft breadcrumbs and mix to stiff paste with 1 beaten egg and the butter. Form into small balls.

Roll in beaten egg, then in corn meal or dry crumbs. Fry in hot deep fat (350°F.) until browned. Drain on absorbent paper. Serve hot on picks.

CHEESE BISCUIT BALLS

Knead 1 cup grated Cheddar cheese and 1/3 teaspoon cayenne pepper into 1 cup prepared baking powder biscuit dough.

Shape into tiny balls and fry in hot deep fat (365°F.) until lightly browned. Serve hot on picks. Makes about 24.

CHEESE BALLS

Blend 1 1/2 cups grated American cheese with 1/2 green pepper chopped very fine, and 1 beaten egg. Season with 1/4 teaspoon salt.

Shape into small balls. Roll in cracker crumbs or dry breadcrumbs. Fry in hot deep fat (365°F.).

CHEESE AND RICE BALLS

Mix 1 1/2 cups grated American cheese, 1/4 cup dry cooked cold rice, 2 egg whites, 1/4 teaspoon cayenne pepper, and a pinch of salt.

Shape into 1-inch balls. Fry in hot deep fat (375°F.). Drain on absorbent paper.

The chafing dish should be your "steady" for serving almost any hot hors d'oeuvre at any time.

Hot Cheese Appetizers

HAM-CHEESE CANAPÉS

1 cup freshly grated American cheese
½ cup finely chopped ham
2 tablespoons light cream
1 teaspoon prepared mustard
Dash of cayenne
¼ teaspoon Worcestershire sauce
Toasted bread bases
Grated American cheese

Combine cheese, ham, cream, and seasoning. Heat in top of double boiler until cheese melts.

Spread warm mixture on bases. Sprinkle with grated cheese. Broil lightly. Serve hot.

TOMATO-CHEESE CANAPÉS

Cut white bread into small rounds with cooky cutter. Toast on 1 side and butter untoasted side.

Cut slices of small firm tomatoes ¼-inch thick. Place tomato slices on buttered side. Season with salt and a speck of grated onion.

Pile grated Cheddar cheese on tomato and broil until cheese is melted. Serve hot.

AMERICAN CHEESE CANAPÉS

Spread toast fingers or squares with mustard butter. Spread with a mixture of equal parts of minced parsley and finely chopped olives. Top each with a thin slice of American cheese.

Broil under moderate heat until cheese melts. Sprinkle with paprika and serve hot.

PARMESAN-ONION CANAPÉ

Make circles of crustless bread with a round cooky cutter. Blend grated Parmesan cheese and mayonnaise until the mixture is very thick. Place a paper-thin slice of onion on the bread circle.

Heap with the cheese-mayonnaise mixture. Dust with paprika. Place under the broiler until the bread is toasted and the top is bubbly.

CREAM CHEESE PUFF CANAPÉS

1 3-ounce package cream cheese
2 tablespoons mayonnaise
1 tablespoon minced onion or other seasoning
2 tablespoons chopped nuts, optional

Soften cream cheese with mayonnaise and add seasoning and nuts. Spread ¼-inch thick on salted crackers.

Brown quickly under broiler and serve hot.

OLIVE-CHEESE-BACON ROLLS

Cut large stuffed olives into halves and put together with Cheddar cheese spread. Wrap in bacon. Broil until crisp.

OLIVE SURPRISE PUFFS

1 cup grated process Cheddar cheese
2 tablespoons melted butter or margarine
½ cup enriched flour
1 teaspoon dry mustard
Dash of cayenne
3 tablespoons sherry
1 3-ounce jar stuffed green olives

Combine ingredients except olives. Pat mixture around each drained olive to cover completely.

Arrange on greased cooky sheet and bake in hot oven (400°F.) 10 minutes. Serve hot. Makes 16 to 18.

ROQUEFORT-CREAM CHEESE PUFFS

1 3-ounce package cream cheese
3 tablespoons or more Roquefort cheese
¼ cup chopped pecans or walnuts
Thin bread slices

Mix the two cheeses and the nuts; season to taste. Cut crusts from bread slices.

Spread the cheese mixture between slices and cut into squares or triangles.

Toast under broiler and serve very hot.

CHEESE-OLIVE FINGERS

Cut bread into thin strips, lengthwise. Spread with butter. Sprinkle with grated cheese and season with salt and cayenne.

Bake until delicately browned in moderate oven (350°F.).

Sprinkle with finely minced ripe olives and serve.

CHEESE PASTRY TWIRLS

1 package piecrust mix
1 5-ounce jar Cheddar cheese spread
2 tablespoons sherry
¼ teaspoon Worcestershire sauce
Dash of cayenne

Prepare pie pastry according to package directions and roll into a rectangle about 10 by 15 inches. Cut crosswise in halves to make two smaller rectangles.

Blend cheese spread, wine, and seasonings; spread evenly over pastry. Roll jelly-roll fashion, from one wide side to the other. Wrap in waxed paper; chill 1 hour or longer.

With a sharp knife, cut in slices about ⅜ inch thick. Place on greased baking sheet. Bake in hot oven (425°F.) about 15 minutes or until golden brown. Serve hot. Makes about 36.

SWISS-ONION CANAPÉS

Cover toast rounds with a thin slice of onion, then with mayonnaise and top with a circle of Swiss cheese.

Melt cheese under broiler.

HOT CANAPÉ PUFFS

Soften 1 8-ounce package of cream cheese at room temperature and cream it until it is soft. Add 1 teaspoon grated onion, ½ teaspoon baking powder, 1 egg yolk, and salt and pepper to taste. Blend all ingredients thoroughly.

Toast 18 small bread rounds. Spread 2 2½-ounce cans of deviled meat on the bread rounds.

Place a heaping spoonful of the cream cheese mixture on top of the deviled meat.

Place in a moderate oven (375°F.) until heated through, lightly browned, and puffy, about 8 to 10 minutes.

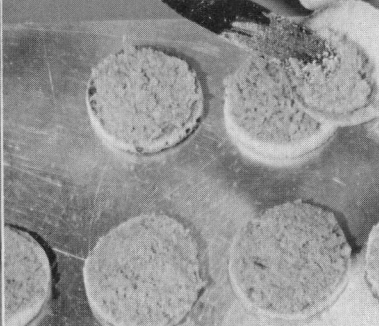

Hot Canapé Puffs

Appetizer Filling on French Rolls

APPETIZER FILLING ON FRENCH ROLLS

Put 1 small onion, half of a medium-sized green pepper, and 6 slices of broiled bacon through a food chopper.

Cut ½ pound of process cheese food into quarters lengthwise. Put the process cheese food through the food chopper and add it to the chopped onion, pepper, and bacon. Add ½ cup condensed tomato soup, ½ teaspoon salt, a dash of cayenne, and a dash of Worcestershire sauce.

Split 2½-inch finger rolls and spread half of each with 1 tablespoon of the filling; cover with the other halves. Bake in moderate oven (350°F.) until rolls are hot and filling is melted.

Serve hot as an appetizer. This filling also may be used in frankfurter buns and cut in inch pieces before baking.

HOT CHEESE BALLS

2 cups sharp Cheddar cheese, grated
½ cup butter
1 cup enriched flour
⅛ teaspoon salt
¼ teaspoon dry mustard
¼ teaspoon paprika

Blend cheese and butter; add flour, salt, mustard, and paprika. Roll into balls the size of marbles.

Place on greased baking sheet and bake in moderate oven (350°F.) for 10 minutes.

PIMIENTO CHEESE AND DRIED BEEF ROLLS

Use ½ cup pimiento cheese for filling. Spread 12 thin bread slices (crusts removed) with mayonnaise, using 3 tablespoons. Cover with cheese and top with dried beef.

Roll and cut each in half. Fasten with picks.

Toast under broiler and serve hot. Makes 2 dozen rolls.

BACON, BREAD AND CHEESE ROLLS

Place thin slices of cheese on thin slices of bread. Roll up and wrap in bacon slices. Broil slowly until bacon is done.

PUFFY CHEESE AND BACON CANAPÉS

1 egg yolk, well beaten
½ cup grated nippy cheese
1 tablespoon cream
Salt and pepper
1-inch strips of bacon
Bread squares

Combine egg yolk, cheese, and cream. Season to taste.

Toast bread squares or rounds on one side and spread mixture on untoasted side. Top each with a bacon strip.

Bake in moderate oven (350°F.) until bacon is crisp.

TOASTED SNAPPY CHEESE ROLLS

4 ounces snappy spreading cheese
2 tablespoons butter
½ loaf unsliced fresh bread

Cream the cheese and butter together until very soft. Slice bread very thin and remove crusts.

Place slices on a damp cloth and spread each slice with some of the cheese mixture. Roll jelly-roll fashion tightly and fasten with picks.

Cover with waxed paper and chill in refrigerator.

Brush each roll with melted butter and toast in very hot oven (450°F.) or under broiler and serve hot. Makes 12 to 15 canapés.

Toasted Anchovy-Cheese Rolls: Substitute 1 3-ounce package cream cheese, 1 tablespoon anchovy paste, and 1½ tablespoons heavy cream for the snappy cheese and butter.

Toasted Pimiento-Cheese Rolls: Substitute pimiento cream cheese for the snappy cheese spread and cream it with the butter.

CHEESE PUFFS

½ cup butter
2 cups shredded American cheese
1 cup sifted enriched flour
⅛ teaspoon salt
¼ teaspoon paprika

Cream butter; add cheese and cream well. Sift flour with seasonings and add to creamed mixture. Shape in 1-inch balls.

Freeze on baking sheet and when frozen, store cheese balls in freezer bag.

If you do not want to freeze them, chill for several hours before baking.

Place on baking sheet in moderate oven (350°F.) for about 15 minutes or until puffed and brown. Makes 30 puffs.

CHEESE CRACKER PUFFS

24 rich round crackers
⅓ cup grated sharp American process cheese
¼ teaspoon Worcestershire sauce
Dash of dry mustard
Dash of paprika
1 stiffly beaten egg white

Sprinkle top of each cracker with cheese, then stack 3 together. Fold Worcestershire sauce, mustard, and paprika into egg white.

Place a small mound of egg-white mixture on top of each stack of crackers.

Bake on ungreased cooky sheet in very hot oven (450°F.) about 4 minutes or until cheese melts and meringue browns. Makes 8.

ST. REGIS CHEESE CANAPÉS

¼ pound sharp process Cheddar cheese
¼ cup butter
½ cup enriched flour
¼ teaspoon salt
Paprika

Cream the cheese and butter together. Blend in flour and salt. Form into small balls the size of marbles.

Place on an ungreased cooky sheet and flatten with tines of a fork to make a waffle design. Dust lightly with paprika. Chill in refrigerator for 2 to 3 hours.

Bake in very hot oven (450°F.) until browned, 8 to 10 minutes. Makes about 24 to 30 canapés.

PARMESAN SQUARES

Moisten grated Parmesan cheese with cream. Spread on toast squares or crackers.

Toast in moderate oven until cheese melts.

Toasted Cheese Dreams: Rolled hot canapés to delight your family as well as your friends.

TOASTED CHEESE DREAMS

1/2 pound sharp cheese, grated
1 3-ounce package cream cheese
2 tablespoons butter, melted
1 egg, beaten
1 tablespoon cream
1 whole loaf white bread (unsliced)

Combine grated cheese with softened cream cheese, melted butter, and beaten egg, adding cream to moisten.

Slice bread lengthwise or crosswise of loaf, as preferred.

Spread lengthwise slices with the cheese mixture. Roll up like jelly roll and slice 3/8 inch thick.

Spread thin crosswise slices with the mixture and roll from corner to corner, fastening with toothpick.

Sliced bread may be cut in rounds or other shapes and spread with cheese mixture, if desired.

Toast under broiler until golden brown. Serve hot. Makes about 2 1/2 to 3 dozen.

CHEESE DREAMS AMERICAN

2 egg whites
1/8 teaspoon salt
1 cup grated American cheese
1 teaspoon Worcestershire sauce
Bread squares or rounds, toasted on one side
Tiny pieces of bacon

Beat egg whites with salt until very stiff. Fold in grated cheese seasoned with Worcestershire sauce.

Spread untoasted sides of bread bases with cheese-egg mixture. Top each with a tiny piece of bacon.

Broil under moderate flame until cheese is lightly browned and puffed.

AMERICAN CHEESE CANAPÉS

Cut a package of 8 slices of pasteurized process American cheese in half and then in quarters.

Place the 32 squares of cheese on assorted crackers arranged on a baking sheet. Place in moderate oven or under low broiler heat until cheese is melted.

Garnish each cheese square with an olive slice, an anchovy curl, or a cocktail onion.

Arrange the canapés on a round tray or chop plate and garnish the center with olives.

CHEESE PUFFS AMERICAN

1/4 pound natural American cheese, grated
1/4 cup butter or margarine
1/2 cup sifted enriched flour
1/8 teaspoon salt

Place all ingredients in bowl. With fingers, blend all ingredients together until smooth; chill 1/2 hour.

Form into 1/2-inch balls. Place on cooky sheet. Chill. Bake in moderate oven (350°F.) 10 to 15 minutes. Makes 2 1/2 dozen.

WAFFLED TEASERS

Place a very thin slice of Swiss cheese or ham or both between thinly sliced buttered bread. Spread lightly with horseradish mustard.

Make sandwiches very small. Toast in waffle iron.

ROQUEFORT PUFF CANAPÉS

Beat 1 egg white until stiff. Cream 2 ounces Roquefort cheese spread and fold into egg white. Heap on crackers or bread rounds.

Bake in slow oven (300°F.) until browned (about 15 minutes). Garnish with paprika. Makes 8 2-inch puffs.

CHEESE-NUT CANAPÉS

Mix grated American cheese, paprika, and onion juice. Spread on toast rounds. Place under broiler to melt cheese.

Sprinkle with chopped Brazil nuts.

TOASTED CREAM CHEESE ROLLS

Trim crusts from unsliced loaf of bread with a very sharp knife. Cut into extremely thin slices. If necessary, flatten slices with rolling pin.

Spread with softened butter, then with cream cheese. Roll up and place on baking sheet with open end at bottom.

Toast under moderate broiler heat until delicately browned. Serve hot.

Variations: Snappy cheese spreads or other fillings may be substituted for cream cheese.

TOASTED AMERICAN CHEESE ROLLS

3/4 cup grated American cheese
1 beaten egg yolk
2 teaspoons Worcestershire sauce
2 tablespoons ketchup

Mix ingredients thoroughly into a paste and spread evenly on slices of fresh bread, cut thin the long way of the loaf.

Roll bread like jelly roll and wrap tightly in waxed paper. Store in refrigerator about 3 hours.

Remove paper with hot, sharp knife. Cut off thin slices. Place on pan and toast under broiler on one side, then on the other.

PIMIENTO CHEESE PUFFS

1 8-ounce package pimiento cheese
1 well-beaten egg
Salt and pepper
Bread bases

Blend cheese and egg; season to taste. Make bread cutouts in various shapes with a cooky cutter. Toast on one side; brush other side with melted butter.

Spread with cheese mixture. Just before serving, broil until brown and puffed. Makes about 35.

CHEESE AND CHUTNEY CANAPÉS

Spread round crackers or toast with chutney. Top with a thin slice of American cheese. Broil to melt cheese. Serve hot.

ONION-CHEESE PASTRY ROLLS

1 recipe plain pastry
1/2 cup grated cheese
1/2 cup chopped onion
Salt and pepper

Roll pastry into thin sheet and cut strips 4 inches long and 1/2 inch wide.

Sprinkle with cheese, onion, salt, and pepper. Roll jelly-roll fashion and fasten with picks.

Place on baking sheet, cut side down. Bake in very hot oven (450°F.) until done, 12 to 15 minutes. Makes about 4 dozen.

American Cheese Canapés

Hot Fish and Shellfish Appetizers

ANGELS ON HORSEBACK

For each angel, lay a medium-sized oyster on a thin slice of bacon. Salt and pepper the oyster; sprinkle with paprika and minced parsley. Roll the bacon around the oyster, securing it with a pick.

Place in a shallow pan and brown slowly in moderate oven (375°F.) until bacon is crisp. Serve very hot.

Note: It's a good idea to precook the bacon slightly to shorten the baking time, as oysters should not be overcooked. Cook bacon only long enough to remove some of the fat. It should be very limp.

OYSTER-ROQUEFORT CANAPÉS

Toast rounds of bread on one side. Spread untoasted side with anchovy butter.

Cook oysters in white wine until edges curl, about 1 minute.

Place an oyster on each round. Cover with Roquefort cheese which has been creamed with sweet butter and seasoned with pepper.

Sprinkle with paprika. Broil until bubbly and lightly browned.

OYSTER TURNOVERS

Marinate small oysters for about 3 hours in French dressing to which a piece of garlic clove has been added. Drain oysters well and dry on paper towels.

Roll out plain pastry very thin; cut into 2½ inch rounds. Place an oyster in each round; fold over and seal the edges with the tines of a fork. Prick each with fork to make vents.

Bake in very hot oven (450°F.) about 15 minutes. Serve very hot.

EASY OYSTER CANAPÉS

Place small oysters on small toast rounds. Sprinkle with salt, pepper, and lemon juice, then with grated cheese.

If desired, add a tiny piece of bacon. Broil just until cheese melts. Serve immediately.

LOBSTER-BACON ROLLS

Use canned or freshly cooked lobster meat. Season with salt and paprika. Brown in melted butter in which a little minced onion is cooked.

Roll when brown in slices of uncooked bacon. Fasten with toothpicks. Broil until bacon is crisp.

Serve on toast squares or rounds with coating of tartar sauce. Garnish with pimiento strips.

SHAD ROE WITH BACON

Wrap small pieces of canned shad roe in small pieces of bacon. Fry until crisp. Spear each with a pick.

LOBSTER RUMAKI

Remove the shells from raw lobster tails and cut the meat into pieces about ½ inch thick. Marinate (soak) in equal parts of soy sauce and sherry.

Drain and combine each piece with a slice of water chestnut. Wrap each in bacon and secure with a toothpick. Bake in hot oven (400°F.) until bacon is crisp.

FINNAN HADDIE CANAPÉS

½ tablespoon finely chopped onion
2 tablespoons finely chopped mushrooms
3 tablespoons butter
2 tablespoons flour
⅔ cup light cream
2 tablespoons grated cheese
2 egg yolks, slightly beaten
1 cup finnan haddie, soaked and flaked
Salt and cayenne
Bread rounds, toasted on 1 side
Grated cheese
Buttered breadcrumbs

Fry onion and mushrooms in butter for 5 minutes. Blend in flour. Add cream gradually and heat to boiling, stirring constantly.

Remove from heat and stir in 2 tablespoons cheese, egg yolks, and finnan haddie. Season with salt and cayenne.

Heap mixture on untoasted side of bread rounds. Sprinkle with cheese and buttered crumbs. Brown lightly in hot oven (400°F.).

PUFFY SHRIMP CANAPÉS

12 canned or cooked shrimp
1 egg white
¼ cup grated cheese
⅛ teaspoon salt
⅛ teaspoon paprika
Dash of pepper
½ cup mayonnaise

Cut the cleaned shrimp in half lengthwise. Beat egg white until stiff; fold in remaining ingredients.

Pile this mixture on toast rounds or crackers. Top each canapé with a shrimp half.

Broil under moderate heat until puffy and delicately browned. Serve hot.

DEVILED SHAD ROE CANAPÉS

1 tablespoon melted butter
⅓ teaspoon mustard
1¼ teaspoons Worcestershire sauce
¼ teaspoon salt, about
4 pieces canned shad roe

Mix first 4 ingredients. Drain the roe and roll in this mixture. Mash the roe and spread on toast squares.

Place in hot oven (425°F.) for 5 minutes. Serve with lemon wedges.

Hot Seafood Hors d'Oeuvres: To make these hot bites of seafood, melt ½ cup butter or margarine; add ½ teaspoon garlic salt, 1 teaspoon tarragon, and ¼ cup sherry. Cook bite-size pieces of seafood in the wine-butter mixture. Use lobster tails, fish sticks, bacon-wrapped shrimp, or bacon-wrapped white fish, cut in bite-sized pieces. Keep hot and serve with assorted wafers or crackers.

ANCHOVY STICKS

1 cup sifted enriched flour
⅓ cup butter
2 tablespoons anchovy paste
Cold water

Cut the butter into the flour with a pastry blender or two knives. Rub in the anchovy paste and add enough water to make a dough that will roll.

Cut into sticks and bake in a very hot oven (450°F.) about 5 minutes.

To form rings, fasten the ends of the sticks together or cut with a ring cutter, then bake.

ANCHOVY-TOMATO ROUNDS

2 tablespoons butter
2 tablespoons anchovy paste
8 toast rounds
8 tomato slices
3 tablespoons grated American cheese

Mix butter and anchovy paste. Spread on toast rounds. Place a thin slice of tomato on top of each. Sprinkle with grated cheese.

Place under moderate broiler until cheese is melted. Serve at once very hot, garnished with chopped parsley.

ANCHOVY-CHEESE PUFFS

1 3-ounce package cream cheese
½ cup butter or margarine
1 cup sifted enriched flour
Anchovy paste

Blend cheese and butter. Mix with flour. Chill.

Roll very thin and cut with 2-inch cooky cutter. Spread with anchovy paste.

Fold over and bake in hot oven (400°F.) 10 minutes. Serve hot. Makes about 48.

MINCED CLAM CRISPETS

    2 3-ounce packages cream cheese, at
        room temperature
    ½ cup drained minced clams
    1 teaspoon Worcestershire sauce
    Dash or two of Tabasco sauce
    ¼ teaspoon salt

Mix together above ingredients. Remove crusts from bread slices and cut in squares or rounds. Brown in butter on moderately hot griddle, on 1 side only.

Spread other side heavily with clam mixture. Place on cooky sheet.

Just before ready to serve, place low under broiler or in hot oven (400°F.) until topping is puffed and browned. Serve at once.

How many appetizers it will make depends upon how large bread is cut and how generously spread is used.

Variations: 1. Serve cold as spread for crisp crackers or on shredded wheat wafers.

2. Add 2 or 3 tablespoons of liquid drained from minced clams to make consistency for dipping. Serve with large potato chips or very thin slices of rye or pumpernickel bread toasted in slow oven.

3. This mixture is good used as an open-face sandwich, following the Crispet directions, or as topping for stuffed baked potatoes; bake in moderately hot oven to heat through and brown top. Serve as an entrée.

SARDINE TURNOVERS

Roll plain pastry thin. Cut into squares the length of sardines. Cut each square diagonally to form triangles.

Have small sardines drained on absorbent paper. Lay a sardine on each piece of pastry. Sprinkle with lemon juice.

Fold point of triangle opposite diagonal over sardine. Press tightly to opposite side. Prick with fork to form vent. Place on ungreased baking sheet. Store in refrigerator until ready to use. Bake in very hot oven (450°F.) 15 to 20 minutes.

CRABMEAT-CHEESE CANAPÉS

Moisten flaked canned crabmeat with mayonnaise. Toast bread bases on one side.

Spread untoasted side with crabmeat. Cover thickly with grated mild cheese. Sprinkle with a little paprika.

Toast under moderate heat until cheese melts and is lightly browned.

SHRIMP-VEGETABLE KEBOB

Alternate on a skewer whole cleaned shrimp, tomato wedges, okra, and bacon. Broil until done.

Fried shrimp are always a favorite appetizer. Your only problem is to keep the tray replenished. ➤

TUNA OR CRABMEAT-CUCUMBER CANAPÉS

    1 7-ounce can tuna, drained and
        flaked
    ¼ cup mayonnaise
    1 tablespoon ketchup
    1 tablespoon vinegar
    Few grains of cayenne
    ¼ teaspoon salt
    ¼ teaspoon Worcestershire sauce
    1 cucumber
    Paprika
    Bread rounds, toasted on 1 side

Combine the drained and flaked tuna with mayonnaise, ketchup, vinegar, cayenne, salt, and Worcestershire.

Peel the cucumber and flute it by scraping the sides lengthwise with the tines of a fork. Slice very thin and dip edges in paprika.

Place a slice of cucumber on untoasted side of each bread round. Heap a little of the tuna mixture in center of each. Brown lightly in the broiler. Serve hot.

CRABMEAT-MUSHROOM CANAPÉS

    1 cup canned flaked crabmeat
    ⅔ cup (½ can) condensed cream of
        mushroom soup
    1 tablespoon finely chopped green
        pepper
    1 tablespoon finely chopped pimien-
        to
    ¼ teaspoon salt
    Few grains of cayenne
    1 tablespoon sherry, optional
    Bread rounds, toasted on 1 side
    Buttered bread crumbs

Combine crabmeat, soup, pepper, pimiento, salt, and cayenne; heat through. Remove from heat and add sherry.

Spread untoasted side of canapé bases with crabmeat mixture. Sprinkle with breadcrumbs. Brown lightly under broiler and serve hot.

Lobster or Shrimp-Mushroom Canapés: Substitute flaked cooked or canned lobster or shrimp for the crabmeat in the above recipe.

TUNA OR CRABMEAT CANAPÉS

Combine drained, mashed tuna or crabmeat with enough mayonnaise or French dressing to make a creamy paste.

Spread on toast rounds. Sprinkle with grated cheese. Brown lightly in broiler.

SHRIMP-PINEAPPLE KEBOB

Marinate cooked, cleaned shrimp in soy sauce. Spear a small whole shrimp and a cube of canned pineapple on each pick. Bake or broil until hot.

HOT SHRIMP WITH DIPPING SAUCE

    ¼ cup butter
    6 tablespoons lemon juice
    3 pounds cooked shrimp

Melt butter in heavy skillet; add lemon juice. When mixture bubbles add shrimp. Keep heat very low.

This can be done in a chafing dish at buffet table. Serve with shrimp dipping sauce (below).

Shrimp Dipping Sauce:

    1½ cups ketchup
    ¼ cup lemon juice
    ½ teaspoon salt
    1 tablespoon Worcestershire sauce
    1 tablespoon prepared horseradish
    1 teaspoon finely minced celery
    Few drops onion juice
    Few drops Tabasco sauce

Combine and chill ingredients.

FRIED BABY SCALLOPS

    1 pound scallops
    ¼ cup flour
    ¼ teaspoon salt
    ⅛ teaspoon pepper
    ¼ cup butter or margarine

Wipe scallops with a damp paper towel. Roll in flour seasoned with salt and pepper.

Melt butter in skillet. Add scallops and cook only 5 minutes over high heat, turning constantly to brown evenly. Serve at once on picks. Serve with a dipping sauce.

If large sea scallops are used, cut in small pieces.

Fried Baby Scallops

TUNA-CHEESE CANAPÉS

Mix flaked canned tuna fish with chopped stuffed olives and mayonnaise or salad dressing. Season with Worcestershire sauce.

Spread on small squares, strips, or rounds of toast. Sprinkle with grated American cheese.

Place under moderate broiler until cheese is melted. Serve hot.

SMOKED SALMON FINGERS

Spread toast fingers with lemon butter. Place 1/4-inch slice smoked salmon on toast.

Cover with buttered crumbs and brown under broiler.

SARDINE CANAPÉS WITH CHEESE

Drain and bone skinless sardines. Mash and season with finely minced celery, ketchup, minced onion, and pepper.

Add enough mayonnaise to make a paste of spreading consistency. Spread lightly on thin slices of ice-box rye bread.

Sprinkle with Parmesan cheese. Broil until well heated throughout.

WHOLE SARDINE CANAPÉS

Mix 2 tablespoons soft butter with 1 teaspoon dry mustard and a few drops Worcestershire sauce.

Drain large sardines and brush with mixture. Dip in cracker crumbs. Broil quickly.

Serve on toast strips and sprinkle with lemon juice. Garnish with minced parsley.

SARDINE ROLLS

Drain oil from sardines; mash sardines and mix with horseradish and lemon juice to taste.

Spread on thin squares of very fresh bread (crusts removed). Roll up and secure with pick.

Brush with melted butter and toast in a hot oven (400°F.) until lightly browned. Serve at once.

Scallop Soufflé Snacks

DEVILED CRABMEAT CANAPÉS

1 cup flaked canned crabmeat
1 tablespoon butter
1 tablespoon onion juice
1 teaspoon Worcestershire sauce
1/4 teaspoon mustard
1/4 cup thick white sauce

Combine ingredients and heat thoroughly. Season with salt and pepper.

Serve hot on crackers or toasted bread rounds.

CLAM CANAPÉS

Combine finely chopped, drained fresh or canned clams with enough mayonnaise to hold together. Season to taste with drained chili sauce and salt and pepper.

Toast bread rounds on one side and spread clam mixture on untoasted side. Sprinkle with grated mild cheese. Top with a dash of paprika.

Toast under broiler until cheese is melted and canapés are lightly browned.

BROILED SHRIMP-BACON ROLLS

Wrap cleaned, cooked or canned shrimp in small slices of bacon. Fasten with picks.

Brown slowly in frying pan, or grill in the broiler, or bake in hot oven until bacon is done.

Replace burnt picks with fresh ones.

ANCHOVY-BACON ROLLS

Place one or two anchovy fillets on each slice of bacon. Roll tightly jelly roll fashion. Secure with a pick. Broil until bacon is crisp. Replace burnt picks with fresh ones and serve hot.

SCALLOP SOUFFLÉ SNACKS

1 pound sea scallops (about 12), fresh or frozen
1/4 cup mayonnaise
2 tablespoons drained pickle relish
1 tablespoon minced parsley
1 1/2 teaspoons lemon juice
1/8 teaspoon salt
1/4 teaspoon Worcestershire sauce
Few grains pepper
1 egg white

Defrost scallops, if frozen. Cook scallops in about 1 cup water in covered saucepan, keeping water below boiling point, until just tender (about 10 minutes). Drain, cool, cut in halves.

Combine all remaining ingredients except egg white; mix well. Beat egg white stiff; fold into mayonnaise mixture.

Place scallop halves on baking sheet or in shallow pan; top each with mayonnaise mixture. When ready to serve, run under broiler with surface of food 3 inches below broiler heat. Broil about 3 minutes or until golden brown. Serve at once, as hot hors d'oeuvres. Makes 24.

SHAD ROE AND BACON CANAPÉS

Shad roe
Butter
2 or 3 slices of bacon
Salt and pepper
Few drops of lemon juice
Toast rounds

Fry the shad roe a few minutes in a little butter, then mash it. Mince the bacon and fry until crisp; drain and add to the roe.

Season to taste with the lemon juice, salt and pepper. Spread on toast rounds and broil a few seconds before serving hot.

BROILED BREADED OYSTERS

Roll fresh oysters in mixture of half bread and half cracker crumbs. Press flat with hands.

Broil 2 minutes on each side. Salt lightly and brush with melted butter. Serve on buttered hot toast rounds.

LOBSTER, SHRIMP, OR CRABMEAT CANAPÉS

Season finely chopped cooked or canned lobster, shrimp, or crabmeat with salt, cayenne, and a few drops of lemon juice.

Moisten with thick white sauce. Spread on toasted bread rounds. Sprinkle with cheese. Brown in the oven.

CLAM-CREAM CHEESE ROUNDS

1 large can minced clams
1 8-ounce package cream cheese
2 tablespoons lemon juice
Garlic to taste

Drain clams and combine with other ingredients. Spread on rounds of toast. Sprinkle with paprika.

Toast under broiler until thoroughly heated and slightly browned.

OYSTER AND MUSHROOM CANAPÉS

Peel large mushrooms and remove stems. Dip in melted butter or olive oil.

Put a fresh oyster in each. Season to taste with salt, pepper, paprika, and celery salt, if desired.

Broil under moderate heat. Serve on hot toasted canapé bases or in the oyster shells.

SCALLOP-BACON ROLLS

Parboil scallops in their own liquid for 3 minutes. Drain and dry with paper towels.

Cut scallops into bite-size pieces. Wrap each in a piece of bacon. Fasten with a pick.

Broil or bake in a hot oven until bacon is crisp. Serve hot with a bowl of cocktail sauce.

Hot Meat And Poultry Appetizers

SWEDISH MEAT BALLS WITH RED WINE SAUCE

- 1 pound twice-ground beef
- 1 cup fine dry breadcrumbs
- 1 teaspoon cornstarch
- 1 teaspoon salt
- 1/4 teaspoon pepper
- Dash of allspice or mace
- 1 beaten egg
- 1 cup rich milk or light cream
- 1 small onion, minced
- Fat or oil
- 3 tablespoons flour
- 2 cups water
- 2/3 cup claret, cabernet, burgundy or any red wine
- Salt and pepper

Add breadcrumbs, cornstarch, salt, pepper, allspice or mace, beaten egg and milk to the ground meat. Sauté onion lightly in fat or oil. Mix with ground meat mixture. Blend ingredients thoroughly.

Shape into tiny balls 40 to 42 in all. Brown lightly in a little oil or fat. Remove balls from pan.

Make gravy by slowly blending the flour into the fat in pan and then slowly adding the water and the wine. Add salt and pepper to gravy to taste. Return meat balls to pan; simmer 20 minutes.

ROQUEFORT-BEEF BALLS

- 1/4 pound ground beef
- 1/4 teaspoon salt
- 1/8 teaspoon pepper
- 1 teaspoon Worcestershire sauce
- 1 ounce Roquefort cheese
- 2 tablespoons butter

Mix meat and seasonings. Divide into 12 portions. Press flat into patties about 1 1/2 inches in diameter.

Place a piece of cheese in center of each patty; form into balls in palms of hands.

Brown on all sides in butter. Serve hot on picks.

Use a chafing dish, a candle warmer, or electric skillet to keep Swedish Meat Balls warm in their wine sauce.

BEEF FONDUE OR FONDUE A LA BOURGUIGNONNE

Your guests cook their own bite-sized morsels of tender beef in hot vegetable oil, then dip in a choice of tasty sauces from among a variety set out. A deep metal chafing dish pot which narrows at the top is preferred to keep the fat from sputtering. Since everything is pre-assembled this sumptuous dish makes entertaining easy. And it's a good choice to help people get acquainted; they just have to be friendly sharing the same central cooking dish and then personally dipping the meat into succulent sauces.

Allow for each person about 1/3 to 1/2 pound beef tenderloin, trimmed and cut in 3/4 inch cubes. Less tender cuts of beef may be used if prepared with instant meat tenderizer following directions on label.

Use smaller tid-bits of meat to serve as an hors d'oeuvre, larger ones when it is to be the main course. Have beef cubes at room temperature.

Have ready 2 to 4 sauces: such as Tomato Dipping Sauce, Horseradish Cream Sauce, Garlic Butter. Make other selections such as a curry sauce or a sweet-sour sauce from sauce section.

Heat 1 1/2 inches cooking oil in saucepan. (You may use deep fryer or electric skillet; bring to 425°F.) Each guest holds beef cube in hot oil with fork until cooked to desired doneness. Special forks, though nice, are not required; improvise with your kitchen utensils. It even adds to the fun to use skewers.

The cooked meat is dipped into one of the sauces. Or each guest may arrange servings of sauces on individual plates. Compartmented plates are desirable for main course use but not necessary. Serve with crusty French bread or rolls and a tossed salad.

Tomato Dipping Sauce: Combine 1 8-ounce can tomato sauce, 1/4 cup bottled steak sauce, 2 tablespoons brown sugar, and 2 tablespoons vegetable cooking oil. Bring to a boil. Serve hot.

Horseradish Cream Sauce: Combine 1 cup sour cream, 2 tablespoons prepared horseradish, and 1/4 teaspoon salt. Serve chilled.

Garlic Butter: Whip 1/2 cup softened butter and 1 minced clove of garlic until light and fluffy.

HAM ON PICKS

This one's easy. Cube cooked ham, spear on toothpicks, heat, and serve in a bath of hot kirsch, red wine, pineapple juice with mustard in it, or sweet-sour sauce, in the chafing dish.

Beef Fondue: Your guests cook their own bite-sized morsels of tender meat, then dip them in a choice of tasty sauces.

HOT PORK CUBE HORS D'OEUVRES

Cut fresh pork shoulder into small, even cubes and sprinkle with salt and pepper. Cook on a baking sheet in a preheated very slow oven (200°F.) until the cubes are crisp, 1 1/2 to 2 hours. Serve on picks.

COCKTAIL SAUSAGES OR FRANKFURTERS

Broil or sauté cocktail-size sausages or larger ones cut into 1-inch lengths. Serve hot on picks.

Provide a small bowl of heated barbecue sauce in which to dunk them.

CHICKEN BALLS

- 2 1/2 cups finely chopped cooked chicken
- 1/2 teaspoon minced onion
- 1/4 teaspoon salt
- 2 tablespoons mayonnaise

Combine ingredients and form into small balls. Roll balls in flour; dip in melted butter or margarine.

Brown quickly in hot oven (400°F.). Serve hot.

HAM AND CREAM CHEESE PUFFS

- 1 cup ground cooked ham
- 3 tablespoons minced green pepper
- 1 tablespoon prepared mustard
- 1/4 teaspoon Worcestershire sauce
- 1/2 cup thick white sauce
- 1 3-ounce package cream cheese
- 1 beaten egg yolk
- 1 teaspoon grated onion
- 1/4 teaspoon baking powder
- 18 2-inch toast rounds

Combine ham, green pepper, mustard, and Worcestershire sauce. Stir in white sauce and mix well. Combine cheese, egg yolk, onion, and baking powder.

Spread toast rounds with ham mixture. Top with cheese mixture. Broil under moderate heat until topping puffs and browns. Serve hot. Makes 18.

PASTRY WRAPS

Roll broiled or pan cooked cocktail sausages or short lengths of any cooked spicy sausage in chili sauce, prepared mustard, or barbecue sauce and wrap with pie pastry.

Bake in a hot oven at (425° F.) 8 minutes, or enough to brown the pastry lightly.

Transfer to chafing dish and keep hot. Provide guests with cocktail picks. These can be prepared early in the day and heated in the chafing dish.

HAMBURGER CANAPÉS

½ pound lean ground beef
1 teaspoon minced onion
½ teaspoon salt
⅛ teaspoon pepper
Dash of Worcestershire sauce

Mix ingredients thoroughly and spread in thin layer on toasted canapé bases.

Broil until done. Makes about 24 2-inch canapés.

BEEF AND PINEAPPLE KABOBS

1 pound ground beef
¼ cup sour cream
1 teaspoon seasoned salt
1 No. 2 can pineapple chunks, drained
Teriyaki sauce (below)

Have meatman grind beef twice. Mix beef, sour cream, and seasoned salt. Form into 56 small balls (about 1 teaspoon of mixture for each).

Place 2 meat balls and 1 pineapple chunk on wooden cocktail pick, with pineapple in center. Marinate kabobs 1 hour or more in Teriyaki sauce or other desired sauce. Broil 3 minutes on each side under broiler. Makes 28 kabobs.

Teriyaki Sauce: Combine ½ cup soy sauce, ¼ cup sugar, ½ teaspoon monosodium glutamate, ⅛ cup salad or olive oil, 1 teaspoon grated fresh ginger or ½ chopped clove of garlic (optional), and ¼ cup sherry (optional). Stir until blended.

BEEF BITS EN BROCHETTE

2 pounds boneless beef round or pork loin
1 cup soy sauce
1 tablespoon Worcestershire sauce
1 clove garlic, mashed
¼ cup sherry
1 teaspoon sugar

Cut meat into thin ¼-inch slices. Cut slices into small 1½-inch squares. Combine remaining ingredients. Blend well. Pour mixture over meat, stirring well to coat. Marinate for several hours, or overnight.

Spear 5 to 6 pieces of meat on a bamboo skewer. Broil over an indoor hibachi, alcohol burner, or in an electric broiler until brown, about 5 minutes. Turn occasionally. Serve with hot mustard and sweet-sour sauce. Serves 6.

BEEF BALLS IN BACON BLANKETS

Season freshly ground beef with salt, pepper, and grated onion. Shape into balls.

Rub half slices of bacon with a piece of cut garlic. Roll a bacon slice around each meat ball and secure with a pick. Broil until the meats are cooked.

COCKTAIL SAUSAGE RISSOULES

Make puff paste and roll out ⅛-inch thick. Cut into rounds.

Place a tiny cooked sausage in center. Fold pastry over. Press edges together with tines of fork or a pastry marker. Prick top.

Brush tops lightly with a mixture of 1 egg yolk beaten with 1 teaspoon cold water.

Bake in very hot oven (450°F.) 10 minutes. To vary, substitute small sardines or rolled anchovy fillets for sausage. Serve hot.

CHEESE AND HAM COCKTAIL BISCUITS

⅔ cup sifted enriched flour
½ teaspoon salt
6 tablespoons grated American cheese
2 tablespoons butter
2 to 3 tablespoons milk
Deviled ham

Mix and sift flour with salt. Cut or rub in the cheese and butter. Add milk to form dough. Roll out ⅛ inch thick. Cut into tiny rounds.

Spread deviled ham on alternate rounds. Cover with unspread rounds. Pinch edges together. Bake in very hot oven (450°F.) 12 to 15 minutes.

For variety, you may want to try other favorite fillings in place of deviled ham.

Beef Bits en Brochette: Get everyone cooking his own snack and you have a perfect party icebreaker.

HOT HAMBURGER APPETIZERS

¼ pound bologna
1 small onion
½ pound ground beef
½ teaspoon salt
¼ teaspoon pepper
⅓ cup fine, dry breadcrumbs
½ cup milk
1 egg

Put bologna and onion through medium blade of food chopper. Combine with remaining ingredients. Pack into 9-inch pie pan.

Bake in moderate oven (350°F.) about 45 minutes. Then cut in ¾-inch squares. Insert a toothpick in each.

Serve with sour cream mixed with horseradish or with mustard relish. Good, too, with chili sauce, or ketchup. Serves 6 to 8.

HAM AND CHEESE ROUNDS

1 package refrigerated biscuits
1 2¼-ounce can deviled ham
1 tablespoon mayonnaise
1 teaspoon salt
5 slices sharp process American cheese
Stuffed olives, sliced

Bake the biscuits as directed on package. Split.

Combine deviled ham, mayonnaise, and salt. Spread on biscuit halves. Cut cheese in quarters and place a square atop each biscuit. Decorate with a slice of olive.

Broil at low heat until cheese melts, about 4 minutes. Serve hot. Makes 20.

PINEAPPLE WITH BACON

Wrap pineapple sticks in narrow slices of bacon. Fasten with picks.

Broil or bake in moderate oven (375°F.) until bacon is done, turning to brown on all sides. Serve hot.

BOLOGNA CURLS

Spread thin slices of bologna, with the casings on, with any cheese spread.

Broil until bologna curls. Serve on picks.

Piping hot beef and pineapple kabobs may be broiled in the oven or have your guests cook their own on a hibachi.

CHUTNEY-HAM ROUNDS

Spread toasted or sautéed rounds of bread with a mixture of equal parts of chutney sauce and boiled ham put through the food chopper, or deviled ham.

Sprinkle with grated Parmesan cheese or other well-flavored cheese. Brown in a hot oven (400°F.). Serve hot or cold garnished with parsley.

BRAUNSCHWEIGER CANAPÉS

Toast bread canapé bases on one side. Spread untoasted side with mustard butter. Cover thickly with mashed Braunschweiger which has been seasoned with a little grated onion.

Broil under moderate heat until hot and puffy, 8 to 10 minutes. Garnish with stuffed olive slices before serving. Serve hot.

PORK SAUSAGE TEMPTERS

1   pound pork sausage meat
1/4   cup minced onion
1/3   cup water
1/4   cup lemon juice
2   tablespoons vinegar
2   teaspoons Worcestershire sauce
2   tablespoons sugar
1/2   teaspoon salt
1   teaspoon prepared mustard
      Dash of cayenne or Tabasco sauce

Form sausage meat into 3/4-inch balls. Brown slowly on all sides. Remove balls and drain off all but 1 tablespoon fat.

Brown onion lightly, stirring frequently. Add remaining ingredients. Simmer until thickened, about 20 minutes. Pour sauce into a chafing dish or top of double boiler.

Stick each ball with a pick and stand up in sauce. Makes about 4 dozen balls.

SAVORY BOLOGNA ROLLS

Cut thin slices of bologna. Spread with mixture of cream cheese, chopped pickles, chopped chives, and chopped olives.

Roll slices and fasten each with picks. Dip in salad dressing seasoned with ketchup and Worcestershire sauce. Broil a few minutes. Serve hot.

CHICKEN GIBLET CANAPÉS

Cover squares or rounds of toast with chopped cooked chicken giblets seasoned to taste.

Sprinkle generously with grated Parmesan cheese. Broil under moderate heat until cheese melts.

HAM AND BRAZIL NUT FINGERS

Cut slices of rye bread into finger-length sandwiches.

Spread with prepared mustard, then with a mixture of 1/2 cup ground ham mixed with 1 tablespoon chili sauce and 1/4 cup thinly sliced Brazil nuts.

Toast and serve hot.

CHICKEN LIVERS WITH MUSH-ROOMS AND BACON

Cut livers in bite-size pieces. Cut sliced bacon in 1-inch pieces.

Fill skewers with alternate pieces of chicken liver, bacon, and small button mushrooms.

Dip in melted butter and roll in breadcrumbs.

Broil under moderate heat until browned on all sides. Season with salt and pepper.

DEVILED FRANKS

Broil cocktail franks then slit half-way down on one side. Spread with mixture of prepared mustard and horseradish.

Use in proportion of 1 tablespoon prepared mustard to 1/2 teaspoon horseradish. Fasten with picks.

LIVER SAUSAGE SURPRISES

Mash liver sausage and roll it around stuffed olives, pickled onions, or cubes of sharp cheese.

Roll in chopped parsley, finely chopped nuts, or toasted fine breadcrumbs. Bake or French fry until hot, then keep that way in a chafing dish.

RUMAKI

12   ounces (20) chicken livers
      Salt and pepper
1/2   teaspoon Ac'cent
2   tablespoons butter or margarine
2   tablespoons minced onion
10   slices bacon, cut in half
20   walnut halves (3/4 cup) or 20
      slices water chestnut
      Wooden picks

Cut livers in half; sprinkle with salt, pepper, and Ac'cent.

Melt butter; add onion; cook until soft but now brown. Add chicken livers; cook until just tender.

Fry bacon half done but not crisp; drain. Place a liver in center of bacon slice with a walnut half. Wrap bacon around both; secure with wooden pick.

Broil with moderate heat until bacon is crisp. Makes 20.

DEVILED HAM PASTRY SNAILS

3/4   cup sifted enriched flour
1/8   teaspoon salt
1/4   cup shortening
      About 2 tablespoons cold water
1   3 1/4-ounce can deviled ham

Sift flour and salt, cut in shortening, then add water to make a stiff dough.

Roll very thin into oblong shape. Spread with deviled ham. Roll up jelly roll fashion.

Wrap in waxed paper and chill thoroughly. Slice thin and bake in hot oven (400°F.) 15 minutes. Serve hot or cold. Makes 36.

Pastry Snail Variations: You may want to experiment with many of the fillings suggested for canapé spreads such as the cheese, fish, and seafood fillings, or try the suggestions given below.

Anchovy-Cheese: Soften cream cheese and blend with equal amount of anchovy paste or anchovy fillets mashed to a paste.

American Cheese: Spread with grated American cheese seasoned to taste.

Cottage Cheese: Season cottage cheese with salt and pepper to taste and a little paprika, if desired.

Cream Cheese: Soften cream cheese with just a little cream. Season with salt and paprika.

Deviled Ham and Cheese: Spread with deviled ham. Season with mustard and salt. Sprinkle with grated cheese, then with a little paprika.

Roquefort Cheese: Crumble Roquefort or blue cheese and blend with equal amount cream cheese which has been softened with just a bit of cream.

HAM AND PINEAPPLE ON PICKS

Place chunks of pineapple and cubes of ham on picks. Brush with corn syrup. Broil until golden brown.

Chicken livers, water chestnuts, and bacon, blend flavors in the Japanese appetizer, Rumaki.

SAUSAGE TEMPTERS

A chafing dish can do the heating of these little tempters while the guests arrive.

Cut cooked pure pork sausage links in half-inch pieces. If canned or fully cooked brown and serve sausage is used, no pre-cooking is needed.

Pour pineapple juice into the chafing dish pan. Add the sausage pieces. Stab a pineapple chunk on a pick and then stick the point into a piece of sausage. Just heat and let the guests help themselves.

FRANK AND CHEESE CANAPÉS

Simmer frankfurters until thoroughly heated. Drain and remove casings. Put through food chopper, using medium blade. Season to taste with prepared mustard. Add a little piccalilli and enough mayonnaise to give spreading consistency.

Spread on toasted bread bases. Sprinkle with grated Cheddar cheese. Just before serving, heat under moderate broiler until cheese melts. Serve hot.

If desired, the frankfurter mixture may be used as a cold spread.

DEVILED HAM WITH MUSHROOMS

Spread canapé base with a mixture of deviled ham, chopped pickle, and tart mayonnaise.

Top with fresh or canned button mushroom and place under broiler flame to brown mushroom. Sprinkle with paprika. Serve hot.

CHILI-HAMBURGER CANAPÉS

1 pound ground beef
1 tablespoon chili powder
1 teaspoon salt
Dash of Tabasco sauce
¼ cup ketchup
12 slices toast, buttered and crusts cut off
Chili sauce

Stir and heat meat, chili powder, salt, Tabasco, and ketchup in skillet until red color disappears and mixture becomes spreadable. Spread on hot buttered toast.

At serving time, cut toast into 8 triangles or 9 squares. Bake in very hot oven (450°F.) 10 minutes. To serve, garnish with a dash of chili sauce.

CHICKEN-CHEESE CANAPÉS

Whip a small jar of nippy cheese spread until creamy. Add an equal amount of boned canned chicken or turkey. Season with Worcestershire sauce. Mix lightly but do not mash.

Spread on cocktail crackers. Place on baking sheet. Bake in very hot oven (450°F.) or broil until cheese melts, about 5 minutes. Serve hot.

FRANK TOP-NOTCHERS

Slit franks lengthwise down the middle without cutting all the way through. Insert a stick of cheese.

Cut into 1-inch pieces and wrap each piece in bacon. A pick holds all in place.

Broil to heat and crisp the bacon. Keep hot on a grill or in pan set over hot water.

HAM AND CHEESE TARTLETS

2 cups enriched flour
2 teaspoons baking powder
½ teaspoon salt
5 tablespoons butter and lard mixed
1 cup grated cheese
About 1 cup milk
2 cups ground cooked ham
1 beaten egg
Sour or sweet cream

Mix and sift flour, baking powder, and salt. Cut in shortening with a pastry blender or 2 knives, then add the cheese. Add just enough milk so the dough can be rolled out, handling it as little as possible. Roll very thin and cut into small rounds.

Moisten the ham with the egg and a little cream so that it is stiff but smooth. Put a rounded teaspoonful on one round and cover with another. Press down the edges with a fork.

Bake in a moderate oven (375°F.) about 15 minutes. Serve hot.

Variations: Other fillings may be used such as creamed finely chopped mushrooms, shrimp, or crabmeat.

FRANKS AND MUSHROOMS ON PICKS

Place small canned mushrooms and 1-inch pieces of frankfurter on picks. Brush with melted butter. Broil.

WAFFLED WAFERS

2 cups sifted enriched flour
3 teaspoons baking powder
1 teaspoon salt
2 to 4 tablespoons shortening
⅔ to ¾ cup milk
¾ cup deviled ham or minced olive spread or other finely minced sandwich filling

Sift together flour, baking powder, and salt. Cut or rub in shortening. Add milk to make a soft dough.

Turn out on lightly floured board and knead gently ½ minute. Roll out biscuit dough ¼-inch thick. Cut with biscuit cutter.

Spread half the biscuits with sandwich spread. Cover with another biscuit.

Place a "sandwich" in each section of a hot waffle iron and bake until well browned, about 3½ minutes. Serve hot. Makes 9 sandwich wafers.

Frank Top-Notchers

BACON AND CHEESE CANAPÉS

2 cups grated cheese
¼ cup crisp minced bacon
1 tablespoon Worcestershire sauce
Few grains of cayenne
Toasted canapé bases

Mix cheese with bacon, Worcestershire sauce, and cayenne. Spread untoasted side of canapé bases.

Broil under moderate heat until cheese melts.

BACONWICHES

Have Canadian bacon cut into slices ⅛ inch thick. Cut the slices into quarters.

Place ½ teaspoon softened American cheese in the center of each small cracker. Cover with a quarter slice of Canadian bacon.

Broil until bacon is hot and crisp at edges. Serve on toast bread bases.

BACON-PEANUT BUTTER CANAPÉS

Method #1: Mix peanut butter with diced, crisp bacon. Toast rounds or squares of bread on one side. Spread untoasted side with mixture.

Place under broiler just long enough to heat slightly. Serve warm.

Method #2: Spread untoasted side of canapé bases with peanut butter. Cover with small thin slices of bacon.

Toast in broiler until bacon is crisp. Serve warm.

Waffled Wafers

Miscellaneous Hot Appetizers

MUSHROOM CANAPÉS
(Italian Style)

Olive oil
3 cloves garlic
1 pound small mushrooms
Salt and pepper
1 tablespoon onion juice
1 tablespoon lemon juice
Chopped parsley

Mash the garlic in the olive oil in an iron skillet. Add washed mushrooms and fry over low heat until tender, adding salt and pepper to taste. Add onion and lemon juice.

Serve hot or cold on toasted bread bases. Garnish with parsley.

MUSHROOM-HAM CANAPÉS

1 cup chopped mushrooms
2 tablespoons butter
1/2 cup ground cooked ham
1 tablespoon pepper relish
1 tablespoon salad dressing
Bread rounds, toasted
Stuffed olives
Pimiento

Fry mushrooms in butter over low heat 5 minutes. Add ham and cook 3 minutes.

Stir in pepper relish and salad dressing. Spread on toast rounds.

Bake in very hot oven (450°F.) 3 to 5 minutes.

Garnish with sliced olives and pimiento strips. Makes about 30 canapés.

STUFFED MUSHROOM CANAPÉS

Spread toast rounds with pimiento butter. Top with sautéed mushroom cap filled with cooked ground meat or fish mixed with relish and salad dressing.

Bake in very hot oven (450°F.) about 5 minutes.

CHILI-OLIVE-CHEESE SNACKS

2/3 cup chopped ripe olives
2/3 cup grated American cheese
3/4 teaspoon chili powder
1 package piecrust mix or pastry (basis 1 1/2 cups flour)

Combine olives with cheese and chili powder. Roll pastry thin and cut with 2-inch biscuit cutter.

Place a teaspoon filling on one-half of each round. Moisten edges and fold other half over filling in half-moon shape. Pinch edges to seal.

Place on cooky sheet and bake in very hot oven (450°F.) about 10 to 12 minutes. Serve hot. Makes about 36 snacks.

TAMALE CURLS

For an unusual hot hors d'oeuvre, cut hot canned tamales into bite-sized segments and spear with toothpicks for serving.

SCRAMBLED EGG ROLLS

Scramble eggs until thick but not dry; season with salt, pepper, and Worcestershire sauce.

Pile on thin bread slices (crusts removed). Roll and fasten with picks. Toast under broiler.

ASPARAGUS-CHEESE FINGERS

Heat tiny canned asparagus tips in melted butter until hot throughout. Place on toast fingers.

Sprinkle heavily with grated American cheese. Broil under moderate heat until cheese melts.

ASPARAGUS IN BREAD ROLLS

Slice fresh bread in 1/4-inch slices. Spread with creamed butter or with anchovy paste. Remove crusts. Roll 1 canned asparagus tip in bread.

Wrap in waxed paper and chill several hours. Remove paper and toast in hot oven. Serve hot.

BACON-TOMATO ROUNDS

Cover rounds of buttered toast with thick slices of tomato. Season tomato slices with salt, paprika, and brown sugar.

Cover with small thin bacon slices. Broil until bacon is crisp.

FRUIT BITS AND BACON

Roll in small bacon slices, 1-inch squares of watermelon, peach, pear, or any spiced fruit.

Fasten with a pick and broil, turning to brown all sides. Serve hot.

BAKED BEAN ROLLS

Season 1/2 cup baked beans with 1 tablespoon chili sauce. Pile on thin slices of bread. Roll and fasten with picks.

Wrap in slice of bacon and toast under broiler until bacon is crisp, turning to brown on all sides. Serve hot.

BACON-AVOCADO FINGERS

Mash avocado pulp with fork. Season with salt, paprika, and lemon juice to taste.

Spread on toast strips. Sprinkle with chopped bacon. Broil until bacon is crisp.

ASPARAGUS-HAM ROLLS

Trim crusts from thin slices of fresh bread. Trim ham slices to fit bread slices and spread with mustard.

Dip cooked or canned asparagus tips in mayonnaise and place one tip at end of prepared slice of bread and ham.

Roll jelly roll fashion. Fasten with picks. Toast in broiler, turning to brown evenly. Serve hot.

Hot and Bubbly Appetizers: No one will deny the glamour of a hot appetizer—a little more work perhaps, but worth it. Many of the hot appetizers presented in this book may be assembled in advance, ready to pop into the oven or broiler when guests assemble.

And of course an electric tray, chafing dish, or electric skillet really becomes a valuable asset for keeping hot appetizers hot until the last bite.

ANCHOVY AND EGG ON FRENCH TOAST

4 anchovies, chopped
2 hard-cooked eggs, finely chopped
6 small squares French toast
3 stuffed olives
Melted butter

Mix anchovies and eggs. Spread on French toast. Press a half of stuffed olive into center. Brush with melted butter and place under broiler 3 minutes.

SCRAMBLED EGG AND MEAT CANAPÉS

2 eggs, slightly beaten
3 tablespoons chopped ham, cervelat, salami, or other sausage
1 teaspoon minced parsley
Salt and pepper
Butter or margarine
Bread bases, toasted on 1 side
Grated cheese

Combine eggs with ham or sausage and parsley. Season to taste and cook in butter or margarine over low heat until thick but not dry. Mix with fork while cooking.

Spread on untoasted side of bread bases. Sprinkle with cheese. Just before serving, broil under moderate heat until cheese melts. Serve hot.

EGG AND SALAMI CANAPÉS

1 cup ground hard salami
4 to 6 eggs
1 onion, minced
Salt and pepper

Beat all ingredients together until frothy. Drop by spoonfuls into a well-greased hot skillet. Serve on canapé bases spread with mustard.

EGG AND MUSHROOM CANAPÉS

1 cup sliced fresh mushrooms or ½ cup sliced canned mushrooms
2 tablespoons minced onion
½ cup butter or margarine
4 hard-cooked eggs, finely chopped
2 tablespoons minced parsley
Salt and pepper
1 slightly beaten egg
Canapé bases toasted on 1 side
Grated cheese

Sauté mushrooms and onion in melted butter or margarine. Add hard-cooked eggs, parsley, and salt and pepper to taste. Add beaten egg and cook only until thick.

Spread on untoasted sides of canapé bases. Sprinkle with grated cheese. Place under broiler until cheese melts. Serve hot.

OLIVES IN PASTRY BLANKETS

Prepare plain pastry. Roll out ⅛ inch thick on a slightly floured board. Cut into 2-inch squares.

Place a medium-sized stuffed olive in each square and fold pastry around it. Roll lightly between the palms of hands to form balls.

Bake on ungreased cooky sheet in very hot oven (450°F.) until crisp and delicately browned, about 15 minutes.

These snacks may be prepared in advance and kept in refrigerator until ready to be baked.

AVOCADO AND BACON SNACKS

Cut a peeled ripe but firm avocado into cubes. Dip in chili sauce, then roll each cube in ⅓ to ½ inch slice of bacon.

Fasten with a pick and broil not too close to heat. Serve hot when bacon is crisp.

PEARL ONION AND BACON

Wrap pearl onions in small slices of bacon. Fasten with picks. Broil until bacon is crisp. Serve hot.

Serve Chili Corn Quaso from a chafing dish with crackers or tortillas.

SHASHLIK TYPE HORS D'OEUVRES

2 12-ounce cans luncheon meat
¼ cup olive oil
2 medium-sized onions
Juice of 1 lemon or 3 tablespoons wine vinegar
Dash of salt
¼ teaspoon coarsely ground pepper
½ teaspoon Worcestershire sauce
2 8-ounce cans cocktail sausage
Small whole onions

Cut meat in 1-inch cubes and oblongs. Put olive oil in bowl; add coarsely grated onions, lemon juice, and seasonings. Mix thoroughly.

Add meat, sausage, and small whole onions. Rub sauce mixture into meat and place covered in refrigerator for 4 to 5 hours or overnight.

When nearly ready to serve remove meats to shallow pan and place under broiler to brown lightly.

Keep hot in chafing dish. Have cocktail picks conveniently at hand for serving.

WATERMELON PICKLES AND BACON

Cut watermelon pickles into cubes and wrap each piece in a slice of bacon which has been precooked just enough to shrink it some and remove excess fat.

Skewer with picks and bake until hot in moderate oven (350°F.). Serve hot.

FAT RASCALS

Pit and stuff small steamed or partially cooked prunes with a piece of Cheddar or process cheese. Wrap in slice of uncooked bacon, fastened with a wooden pick.

Broil on all sides until bacon is crisp. Serve hot.

PINEAPPLE-CHEESE CANAPÉS

Place a thick slice of pineapple on a toasted bread base. Sprinkle with grated cheese.

Top with small slices of bacon. Broil until bacon is crisp. Serve hot.

CHILI CORN QUASO

¼ cup finely-chopped onion
1 clove garlic, minced
1 tablespoon butter or margarine, melted
1 pound Cheddar cheese, shredded
1 6-ounce can tomato paste
1 12-ounce can yellow whole kernel corn with sweet peppers, drained
½ teaspoon Worcestershire sauce
1 teaspoon chili powder

Sauté onion and garlic in melted butter or margarine in large heavy saucepan. Add cheese; melt over low heat, stirring frequently. Stir in remaining ingredients. Serve from chafing dish with crackers or tortillas. Makes about 2½ cups dip.

Shashlik Type Hors d'Oeuvres

PICKLE AND CHEESE ROUNDS

Top untoasted sides of canapé rounds with slices of pickle. Sprinkle liberally with grated cheese.

Bake in moderate oven (350°F.) until cheese melts.

OLIVES AND BACON

Wrap ½-inch slices of bacon around large stuffed olives. Fasten with a pick. Place on rack in shallow pan.

Bake in hot oven (400°F.) until bacon is crisp, 12 to 15 minutes. Serve hot.

OLIVE-STUFFED PRUNES

Steam prunes until tender. Remove pits. Fill each prune with a stuffed olive.

Wrap in a thin slice of bacon and fasten with a pick.

Bake in a very hot oven (450°F.) until bacon is crisp, turning to crisp all sides. Remove picks and insert fresh ones. Serve hot.

FRIED BRUSSELS SPROUTS

Cook Brussels sprouts until just tender.

Drain well and dip in egg which has been beaten with a dash of salt and a few grains of cayenne pepper. Then dip in breadcrumbs and fry in bacon or sausage fat until golden brown.

Serve hot on picks with a dip of thinned mayonnaise.

ARTICHOKE HEARTS

Drain canned artichoke hearts well and slowly fry in butter until lightly browned.

Sprinkle with salt, pepper, chopped parsley, and lemon juice. Serve hot on picks.

HOT MEXICAN ROLLS

Combine 1 can tomato sauce, ½ teaspoon oregano, 1 teaspoon Worcestershire, ¼ teaspoon chili powder, ¾ teaspoon garlic salt, ½ teaspoon sugar, dash of Tabasco, and 1 can Vienna sausages, drained.

Heat to serving temperature. Serve on tiny cocktail rolls.

BARBECUE COOKING

More and more homemakers are discovering that it is more fun to cook over an outdoor grill with a husband than over an indoor stove alone.

The jointed chicken, the two-inch steak, and the rack of pork spareribs are natural and favorite candidates for roasting over a bed of coals. Experts enlarge the scope of barbecuing beyond broiling and roasting over open coals. Many of your favorite recipes may be "moved out of the kitchen" into the patio or plain backyard.

Here you'll find a large variety of recipes to keep grill, spit, and skewers busy for many months, plus numerous side dishes, hints, and sauces to give outdoor meals variety and flavor.

TOOLS AND EQUIPMENT

Have a work table near the grill, so tools, pots, pans, skillets, and ingredients can be handy. Here is a check-list of articles you will want to have handy before you plan your first outdoor meal:

Paper and kindling
Charcoal or dry wood
Poker to tame fire
Matches in small jar with
    screw top
Paper towels and napkins
Bib-type apron
Canvas or asbestos gloves
    and pot holders
Grill
Long-handled fork and spoon
Skewers of various lengths
Tongs for turning food
Hinged, long-handled
    wire broiler
Dutch oven
Platter or pan for cooked meat

Small saucepan for barbecue
    sauce
Swab or brush for barbecue
    sauce
Large coffee pot
Condiment kit of salt, pepper,
    ketchup, Worcestershire
    sauce, and mustard
Bottle opener
Can opener
Big carving board and a very
    sharp sturdy carving knife

FUEL AND FIREMAKING HINTS

If you have some dry hardwood stacked away, even if it's only fallen limbs, you're in luck. This is good fuel, especially if it's hickory, oak, maple, pecan, or walnut; these burn slowly and make a long-lasting bed of coals. If you picnic in the woods, you'll probably find plenty of wood with a little hunting. But for most barbecues, including those in public parks, on the beach, or at lakeside, it is best to carry your own fuel. Most convenient and satisfactory all-around are charcoal or the more condensed "briquettes." The latter costs more but burns longer and more evenly. Both provide an unmistakable outdoorsy aroma. For hickory fragrance, buy packaged hickory discs. Plenty of dry paper and kindling are needed to ignite this fuel.

Place crumpled newspapers and kindling in the fire pit first, then arrange the fuel on top loosely so that air can circulate freely throughout. Gasoline and kerosene are almost as dangerous as dynamite, so never use them. For a quick starting of charcoal or briquettes, use charcoal lighting fuel or several stubs of candles. Fan the fire gently.

The main points are:

1. Build your fire early enough so that it will have burned down to glowing coals by the time you are ready to cook the meal. If you use charcoal or briquettes, start the fire an hour ahead. Allow 1½ hours for wood.

2. Build a big enough fire to provide heat for cooking food for all your guests at one time. A shallow bed of coals will do for chops, hamburgers, or hot dogs. Roasts and thick meats need a deeper bed.

3. Replenish fuel occasionally but avoid flames.

4. Low, even heat from a flameless fire is the secret of outdoor cooking. Once the coals have burned down to a gray color, lit by a ruddy glow, you will have the steady even heat necessary for barbecuing.

5. Keep a poker and a bulb syringe (or child's water pistol) on hand, and if the fire blazes up from meat drippings, extinguish flames with a few drops of water.

6. Keep the fire near the front of the grill for cooking meat. There will be enough heat at the back of the grill for making coffee and warming foods.

7. If your grill is movable, the temperature can be controlled by changing the distance between grill and coals. If your grill is stationary, you can increase the temperature by adding fuel; and reduce it by removing a few coals or pushing them away from the cooking area of the grate.

8. Put the fire out when through. Always keep a bucket of water by the fireplace ready to use in case the fire threatens to get out of control completely.

OUTDOOR MENU HINTS

Choose a menu to suit grill space. Keep it simple, tasty, and portable. Plan the meal so that first grilling feeds all guests. Try out your barbecue menu on the family before inviting anyone else.

Serve some help-yourself appetizers to keep appetites from getting out of hand, so that the chef can carry on unmolested.

Don't overload the menu with fancy frills. The center of attraction should be the grill-cooked meat or poultry. Another hot dish such as baked beans in a casserole can be prepared on the grill, or other casserole dishes such as creamed potatoes, scalloped potatoes, or vegetables in a cheese sauce may be prepared in advance in the kitchen and kept hot by the barbecue fire or a candle warmer.

A tossed salad, some deviled eggs, potato chips or sizzling French fried potatoes, toasted split rolls or hot garlic bread or cheese bread chunks, mixed pickles, and olives round out a good barbecue menu.

Salads and Relishes: Green salads, which must be kept crispy-cool, are better prepared just before eating. Relishes such as carrot sticks, celery sticks, olives, and tiny green onions should be kept crisp and chilled in crushed ice or a vacuum container until serving time. Potato salad is a universal favorite, but, of course, it requires at-home preparation and must be kept cold. A simple cole slaw may be prepared at home and served at the barbecue site.

Beverages: Individual cold drinks should be set out in serve-yourself form in a tub of ice. Include a variety of carbonated beverages in individual bottles as well as individual servings of milk drinks and lemonade poured in advance into saved-up small jars. Instant coffee is a time-saver at a picnic for both iced and hot coffee.

Picnic Coffee: Heat 2 quarts freshly drawn cold water to boiling. Combine 1 cup regular grind coffee, 1 egg, and 3 tablespoons cold water. Pour the boiling water over coffee in coffee pot. Heat just to boiling. Cover and let stand 12 minutes over very low heat. Strain to serve.

Desserts: Individual pies and cookies are easy to serve. If whole cakes or pies are taken on a picnic, they should be carried in a basket with separate shelves to keep them intact. Apple or cherry pie can be warmed at the side of the grill in heavy foil plates. Marshmallows can be toasted. Ice cream, especially in individual cups, is a universal favorite, but keeping it can be a problem. Arrange for packing it in natural or dry ice so that it will keep firm.

After the Meal: Roast nuts (pecans, walnuts, etc.) in the shell over the fire. Place the nuts in a wire basket and shake over the heat to roast evenly.

Finally, be sure to have food that appeals to all tastes and pack it so it may be brought forth, set out, and served without too much fuss or bother. After all, a barbecue or any outdoor meal should be a "picnic"—one of America's finest outdoor occasions.

SETTING THE OUTDOOR TABLE

Take fire, smoke, sun, and wind into consideration when setting the outdoor table. The appointments of an outdoor meal should be in harmony with the setting.

Fine linens, silver, and glassware should be left in the home. You'll like sturdy plastic dinnerware or paper plates (or plastic-surface) and cups.

Inexpensive knives, forks, and spoons may be purchased and kept for this purpose.

Heavy paper spoons are a good choice because they can be destroyed, but the use of paper forks is inadvisable since they are difficult to use for cutting purposes, as for a meat loaf.

Paper napkins and a paper table cloth are very satisfactory. Don't use white, for it dazzles in the sun.

Candle warmers to keep coffee and casseroles hot are convenient and attractive. Use extra-large salt and pepper shakers.

Beef Steaks for the Barbecue

Think of charcoal broiling and almost everyone thinks first of steaks. This is not for lack of imagination but rather that they are such good eating. Though a plain and perfectly broiled steak is beef perfection, even that delight may pall if served too often. Therefore we include variations—classic recipes that taste even better outdoors.

Steak chefs are a divided clan, starting with stubborn preferences as to the cut and the method of cooking. Some char the steak, then grill it slowly; some do it the other way around. And among steak purists the charcoal grill vs. the wood fire can start an argument comparable to a major breach of the peace.

HOW TO BUY AND CHARCOAL-BROIL A STEAK

When Buying Beefsteak: Two things on which chefs do agree are that steak must be thick (1½ to 2 inches) for open fire cooking and of top quality.

Prime quality is the best you can buy but very often a porterhouse or sirloin from choice or good-quality beef is a good buy.

If you broil rump steaks, however, they should be prime quality. You can, of course, use a meat tenderizer with some cuts.

Amount to Buy: Consider the number of people to be served, the cooking area of your grill and the amount of money you intend to spend. For the average appetite ½ to 1 pound of steak is not too much to allow. You'll find, however, that ½ pound each will rarely seem enough for hearty outdoor appetites.

If your grill is small and your party

large, cook one large thick steak so it can be sliced to make the rounds. If grill is large, individual steaks are in order.

The Fire: A wood fire for steak broiling should be built just big enough to burn down to a 4-inch-deep bed of coals, which, when spread out evenly, is only slightly larger than the steak. The fire is ready when the coals are glowing but have a light film of white ash.

Broiling with charcoal takes much less time than broiling over wood fire. Although many like to use hickory or fruit woods to give flavor to the steak, small uniform charcoal briquettes of top quality give the best performance. A good charcoal fire takes fewer briquettes than most amateur chefs use.

Preliminaries: Take steak out of refrigerator before grilling—but not more than 1 hour ahead.

Trim, leaving minimum of fat so drippings won't blaze up too much. Gash edges.

Spear steak trimmings on fork and rub hot grill or folding wire broiler to keep steak from sticking.

Optional Before Broiling: If desired, rub the steak with garlic or spread with prepared mustard, or rub with a mixture of 1 tablespoon flour, 1 tablespoon mustard, 1/4 teaspoon salt, and 1/8 teaspoon pepper.

Broiling: The time it takes to cook a steak over an open fire depends not only on how thick the steak is but also on four highly variable conditions: the temperature of the steak, how hot the fire is, the temperature of the air, the drafts or breezes.

As a rule of thumb, if a 1½-inch sirloin steak is at room temperature and placed about 6 inches from a good bed of coals, it should be rare after 6 minutes on each side, medium rare at 7 minutes, medium at 9 minutes, and well done at 12 minutes per side.

A 2-inch steak may require as much as 16 minutes each side for rare, 18 minutes for medium, and 20 for well done.

Broil on one side, then turn carefully without sticking fork into meat so as not to lose juices.

If drippings flare up, put out the blaze with a sprinkle of water. Salt and pepper the browned meat.

To Test: Surest method is to test the steak before the alloted time is up by making a small cut near the center and judging by the color.

Since meat continues to cook for 5 to 10 minutes after it is removed from the fire, the stickler for an exact degree of rareness should stop when the color is still a bit too red.

STEAK SPREADS

Mustard Spread: Cream 1/4 cup (1/2 stick) butter with 2 tablespoons prepared mustard. Spread over cooked steak.

Horseradish-Tabasco Spread: Cream 1/4 cup (1/2 stick) butter with 1½ teaspoons horseradish and 1/8 teaspoon Tabasco sauce. Spread over cooked steak.

Roquefort Spread: Cream 2 tablespoons butter with 3 ounces Roquefort cheese. Spread over cooked steak.

MUSHROOM TOPPER FOR STEAKS

1/2 **pound fresh mushrooms**
Flour
3 **tablespoons butter or margarine**
1/2 **teaspoon soy sauce**
Salt and pepper

Wash mushrooms gently in a little cold water (don't soak). Drain thoroughly.

Cut off tip of stem and leave mushrooms whole or slice. Sprinkle lightly with flour.

Melt butter in skillet; add mushrooms, cover and cook over low heat until tender, 7 to 10 minutes, turning occasionally.

Add soy sauce and season to taste with salt and pepper. Serve over steak or hamburgers. Serves 4.

PEPPER TOPPER FOR STEAKS

1 **clove garlic, chopped fine**
1/4 **cup salad oil**
5 **green peppers, very thinly sliced**
2 **tablespoons wine vinegar**
1/2 **teaspoon salt**

Cook garlic in oil until golden; add peppers and cook gently until tender, stirring frequently.

Season with vinegar and salt. Serve over steak or hamburgers. Makes 1 cup.

INDIVIDUAL STEAK SANDWICHES

Count on at least 1/2 pound steak per person. Let the steaks stand at room temperature for at least 1/2 hour.

Rub both sides with salt and pepper; spread with a thin layer of prepared mustard. Grill or broil until brown on one side.

Turn and brown on second side until desired doneness. Remove from heat; top with a dollop of butter.

Butter a split loaf of French bread, split hamburger buns or slices of white bread.

Place steaks on half the buttered bread or buns. Top other half with onion and tomato slices. Put together to form sandwiches.

Slice the French bread diagonally to make individual servings.

Trim steaks, leaving minimum of fat so drippings won't blaze up too much. Gash edges at intervals to prevent curling.

SALT-BROILED STEAK

Sirloin steak, 2 inches thick
Box coarse salt
Water
Barbecue sauce

Remove the steak from the refrigerator long enough before cooking to completely remove chill.

When fire is very hot, moisten salt until it is like a thick paste. Spread over both sides of steak.

Broil 7 to 12 minutes for each side. Knock off salt; slice browned steak and serve on French bread with hot barbecue sauce.

MARINATED RIB STEAKS

Pound finely crushed or minced garlic into the steaks. Cover with wine vinegar and let stand several hours at room temperature. Drain and cook over hot coals.

BLUE CHEESE BROILED STEAK

Crush a clove of garlic; add 1/2 pound blue cheese and mash well.

Grill a thick steak on one side until browned, turn and spread with cheese. When steak is done on the bottom, cheese should have melted to a savory sauce.

STEAK ROSEMARY

Cover both sides of steak with rosemary pressed in with your hand.

Grill as usual and season just before serving. Top each serving with a pat of butter.

Individual Steak Sandwiches

WINE-BARBECUED STEAK

1/2 cup salad oil
1/2 cup red wine
2 tablespoons grated onion
1 garlic clove, slashed
1 1/2 teaspoons salt
1 teaspoon Ac'cent
Few drops Tabasco sauce
1 sirloin steak, cut 1 to 1 1/2-inches thick

Combine all ingredients except steak. Cover; chill several hours or overnight.

At the cook-out, heat the sauce. Use to brush steak as it broils, turning steak and brushing frequently.

To serve, cut steak in slices 1/2 inch thick, from bone to edge. Serve in toasted frankfurter buns. Serves 8.

STUFFED ROLLED FLANK STEAK

1/4 cup butter or margarine
1 clove garlic, crushed
1/2 cup chopped celery
1 4-ounce can drained mushrooms, pieces and stems
1/4 teaspoon ground black pepper
2 cups finely rolled cracker crumbs, beef flavored
1/4 cup crumbled Bleu cheese
1/4 cup water
2 flank steaks

Melt butter or margarine; add garlic, celery, mushrooms, and pepper. Cook until celery is tender. Stir in crumbs, cheese, and water.

Pound flank steaks lightly to flatten. Spread 1/2 of the stuffing on each steak. Roll up and tie with twine.

Broil over low fire turning frequently until cooked, about 1/2 hour. Makes 8 to 10 servings.

Stuffed Rolled Flank Steak: Make the stuffing in the morning, roll the steak and chill until cooking time. Serve with cold, crisp finger vegetables and bacon-wrapped corn on the cob roasted in foil.

STEAK WITH GARLIC OIL

Soak 2 cut cloves of garlic in 1 cup olive oil the night before the barbecue.

Prepare 1-inch-thick steak by gashing around the edges to prevent curling during grilling.

Pour the oil in a shallow pan; remove the garlic. Dip the steak in the oil, coating both sides. Grill as usual and season with salt and pepper when it is about done.

STUFFED ROUND STEAK

1 1/2 pounds round steak, cut 1/4-inch thick
1 1/2 cups breadcrumbs
1/4 cup minced onion
3 tablespoons minced parsley
3 tablespoons melted butter or margarine
Salt and pepper
8 strips bacon
8 hamburger rolls

Cut steak into 8 (2 x 4-inch) strips. Spread with dressing made by combining breadcrumbs, onion, parsley, melted butter, and seasonings. Roll up and wrap in bacon. Fasten with wooden picks.

Broil over hot coals until bacon is crisp, turning frequently.

Serve sizzling on buttered rolls. If desired, make hollows in centers of hamburger rolls (using the crumbs in the dressing) so that finished sandwiches won't be too "fat" to bite. Makes 8.

SOYED STEAK

Chop 1 clove garlic very fine and combine with 1/2 to 1 cup soy sauce in a shallow pan.

Marinate steak in this sauce for about 15 minutes, turning frequently to thoroughly impregnate the steak with the sauce. Then grill as usual.

Note: Do not use a metal utensil for the marinade as it may affect the taste. The same marinade may be used for other meats.

LONDON BROIL

This requires aged top-quality flank steak, quick broiling, and thin serving slices. Do not attempt this method of cooking unless you are sure of the quality of the steak. When in doubt, braise it.

Have a 2- to 3-pound top-quality flank steak trimmed of excess fat and membrane and, if desired, scored on both sides.

Brush well with salad oil or bottled sauce for gravy.

Broil over hot coals until brown but still rare, about 5 minutes on each side.

Season with butter, salt, and pepper. Cut into very thin slices diagonally across the grain.

Blue Cheese-Topped: Cover the flank steak with a mixture of 1 cup salad oil, 2 tablespoons vinegar, and 1 mashed, peeled clove of garlic; let stand in refrigerator 8 to 24 hours, turning 2 or 3 times.

Remove from marinade and broil on 1 side; turn, cover with mashed blue cheese for the last few minutes of broiling.

MARINATED GIANT SIRLOIN STEAK

Select a sirloin steak at least 2 1/2 inches thick.

Marinate (soak) 1 hour in 1/3 cup salad oil to which has been added 3 minced cloves garlic.

Place in folding wire broiler. Season with salt and pepper.

Grill over hot coals 6 to 10 minutes, 1 minute at a time on each side.

Remove from wire broiler and place right on hot coals until charred, at least 6 minutes per side. Slice 3/4 inch thick (the meat will look raw).

Meanwhile, heat 1 or 2 cups water with 1 cup butter or margarine in a roasting pan. Place steak slices in pan. Simmer 1/2 minute per side—no longer—or 15 seconds for rare. Lift out and serve as is or in buns.

MARINATED CUBE STEAKS

Use top-quality sirloin, round, or chuck steak, 1/3 inch thick. Have it scored.

Marinate (soak) 15 minutes in barbecue sauce or in 1/2 cup soy sauce with 1 clove garlic, minced.

Let guests cook their own on long sharp-pointed green sticks or long-handled forks, or cook several on a wire broiler or grill.

RIB ROAST OR STEAK

1 3-rib roast, separated into steaks or 1 4-pound steak
4 cloves garlic, crushed in salt
3/4 cup olive oil

Rub both sides of meat well with garlic salt. Brush generously with olive oil. Broil 10 to 15 minutes on each side.

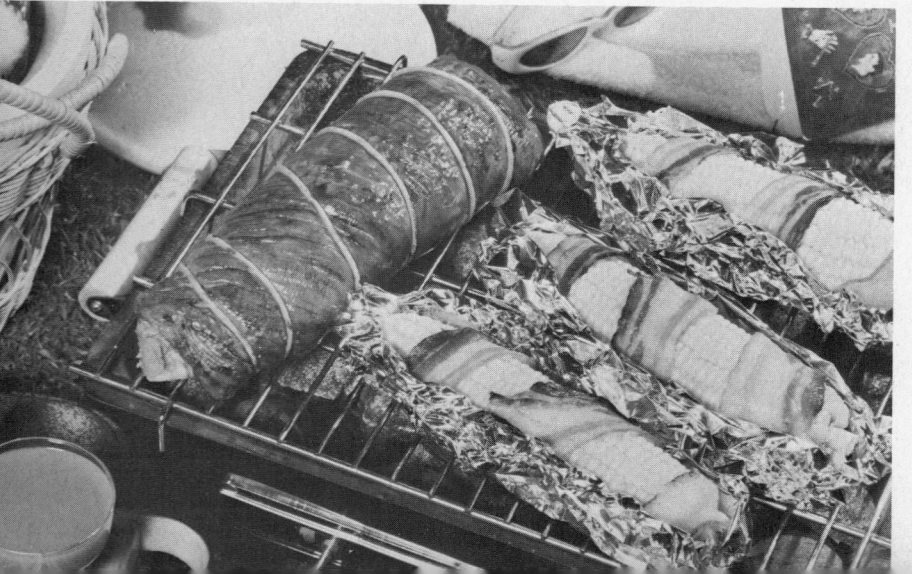

Aluminum Foil Cooking

Many foods take an exciting new flavor when slowly roasted in foil over or in the coals. All the flavor and food value are wrapped right in and seasonings can be added at the beginning. An additional advantage of foil-packet cooking is that the food stays hot and moist longer if there is a delay in serving.

It is best to use 18-inch heavy-duty aluminum foil. If the regular 12-inch-wide household foil is used, cut off twice the length required to wrap food and wrap double. Always be sure to wrap securely and seal edges tightly.

The following timing directions will serve as a general guide for your own recipes cooked directly on hot coals; turn each packet at half time:

Thick Steak: 20 minutes per pound.
'Burgers, Medium Thin: 10 to 12 minutes.
Frankfurters: 5 to 8 minutes.
Chicken: Whole, 1 to 1½ hours; very small pieces, in individual packets, 30 to 35 minutes.

MASTER METHOD FOR CHICKEN-IN-FOIL DINNERS

Many combinations of chicken with vegetables and other ingredients may be cooked in foil. The pattern for preparing these easy eat-from-the-foil dinners is as follows:

Have chicken cut in half or in quarters; rinse. Small protruding and easily removed bones are pulled out.

Sufficient chicken for one serving is placed skin side down in the center of a double thickness of regular household foil or one thickness of heavy-duty foil measuring about 12 x 14 inches. Vegetables, butter or margarine, seasonings, and a little liquid are added.

Bring the foil up over the food and seal the edges together with a double fold. Seal the ends the same way turning them up to hold in the juice.

Place the bundles on the grate over an outdoor fire and cook, chicken side down, for about 40 to 50 minutes. Have a good fire when the chicken starts cooking, so that the chicken will brown through the foil. Eat right from the foil. Delicious gravy is formed from the juice of the chicken mingled with the butter and other ingredients.

CHICKEN, SWEET POTATO AND APPLE IN A FOIL PACKAGE

Prepare chicken according to master method. Place on pieces of foil and season with salt and pepper.

Peel and slice thinly sweet potatoes or yams and place around chicken, allowing about ½ potato to each serving. Add 4 ½-inch slices of apple to each serving.

In a small bowl, combine 2 tablespoons lemon juice, a little grated lemon rind, 4 tablespoons light brown sugar, and 1 tablespoon softened butter or margarine. Spread over apples and potatoes.

Seal in a package and cook on a grate over an open fire as described above.

CHICKEN, SEASONED RICE AND TOMATO IN A FOIL PACKAGE

Prepare chicken according to master method, placing each quarter chicken in center of a piece of aluminum foil.

In a frying pan, fry 2 strips of bacon until crisp. Drain bacon and lightly brown the chicken liver in fat. Dice liver and bacon.

Pour off all but 1 tablespoon bacon fat from pan and add 1 cup of quick-cooking rice (uncooked) to pan.

Add 1 cup canned tomatoes, half juice and half pulp, cut up so that tomato is equally mixed through. Stir in bacon and liver, 1 teaspoon finely minced onion, ½ teaspoon salt, a dash of pepper and garlic salt.

Spoon one-quarter of this mixture over each chicken piece. Seal packages and cook on grill as described.

CHICKEN, ZUCCHINI AND SAVORY TOMATO SAUCE IN A FOIL PACKAGE

Prepare chicken according to master method. Place each piece skin-side-down on foil. Season with salt, pepper, a little fresh tarragon and chives minced fine or a prepared ground herb mixture for seasoning chicken.

Have ready sliced tender young zucchini and sliced onion and add a

generous serving to each portion of chicken.

Season vegetable with salt and pepper, then add 1 tablespoon canned tomato sauce to each serving and top with a generous piece of butter or margarine. Seal packages and cook on grill as described.

CHICKEN DINNER IN FOIL

For each serving:

2 or 3 pieces frying chicken
1 pared potato
1 tomato
1 peeled onion
2 mushroom caps
2 green pepper rings
2 tablespoons raw rice
1 tablespoon Worcestershire sauce
¾ teaspoon salt
Dash of pepper
Sprinkling of paprika
Small pat of butter or margarine

Use a large piece of heavy-duty aluminum foil or a double thickness of regular household foil.

Arrange chicken, potato, tomato, onion, mushrooms, and green pepper neatly on the foil.

Sprinkle with rice and seasonings. Dot with butter.

Fold the foil to make a neat package, securing the ends well.

Cook over glowing coals until all is tender, about 1¼ hours, turning package every 20 or 30 minutes. Serve in the foil. Serves 1.

For very easy and delicious outdoor cooked meals, try chicken-in-foil dinners. Make them up the night before, wrap securely in aluminum foil and store in the refrigerator. Corn, too, can be prepared ahead and wrapped in foil. Cook over an outdoor fire, then eat right from the foil.

Frank and Bean Buns: Partially fill split buns with canned baked beans or chili con carne. Wrap each filled bun in a double thickness of foil and seal securely. Heat buns for 10 minutes, turning frequently, on the cooler side of the grill. Grill frankfurters over hot coals until heated through. To serve, open bun packages and place a grilled frankfurter in each.

CHICKEN BREASTS IN FOIL

6   chicken breasts
1½ teaspoons salt
⅛ teaspoon pepper
1   can condensed cream of mushroom soup
1   clove garlic, finely chopped
1   tablespoon finely chopped green onion
2   tablespoons finely chopped parsley
Dash of thyme
½ teaspoon crushed tarragon

Season chicken with salt and pepper.

Combine remaining ingredients and mix well. Spread equal portions on the surface and in the cavities of the 6 chicken breasts.

Put each breast on a square of aluminum foil; bring edges together and seal with drugstore wrap, folding corners under.

Cook over hot coals until tender, turning once. Total time about 40 to 45 minutes. Serves 6.

Note: Use heavy-duty aluminum foil or a double thickness of regular household foil.

PORK CHOP DINNER IN FOIL

Pork chops
Sweet potatoes, pared
Tart apples, pared
Onion slices
Seasonings

Use heavy-duty foil or a double thickness of ordinary household foil. In the center of each large square of foil place a pork chop which has been lightly browned in a skillet.

Add two or more thick slices of ap-

ple, sweet potato, and onion. Season each dinner well with salt, pepper, and a little thyme.

Bring foil up over food and seal into tight packages by double folding edges together. Place on grill over medium heat and cook about 1 hour.

STEAK DINNER IN FOIL

Chili sauce
Flour
Celery, cut into 3-inch lengths
Carrots, scraped and quartered
Small onions, peeled
Baking potatoes, pared and quartered
1-inch cubes of beef sirloin tip
Ac'cent, salt, pepper

Use heavy-duty foil or double thickness of regular household foil.

For each serving, combine 2 tablespoons chili sauce and 2 teaspoons flour; spread in center of large square of foil.

On sauce arrange several pieces of celery, 1 scraped and quartered carrot, 3 peeled onions, and 2 pieces pared and quartered potato.

Top with about ⅓ pound beef sirloin cubes; sprinkle with ⅓ teaspoon salt, dash of pepper, and ½ teaspoon Ac'cent.

Fold the foil into a secure package, using drugstore wrap, and fasten ends underneath securely.

Cook over glowing coals until all is tender, about 1 hour.

INDIVIDUAL HAM DINNERS IN FOIL PACKAGES

1-inch thick ham slices (ready-to-eat type)
Brown sugar
Prepared mustard
Whole cloves
Pineapple slices
Butter or margarine
Sweet potatoes, pared and quartered

Use heavy duty foil or a double thickness of ordinary household foil. In each large square of foil place a serving portion of ham; spread each serving with 2 tablespoons brown sugar and 1 teaspoon prepared mustard.

Stick a clove or two into drained pineapple slice and place on ham. Dot with butter.

Place 2 pieces of pared and quartered sweet potato at side of ham.

Fold the foil into a secure package using drug store wrap and fasten the ends underneath securely.

Cook over glowing coals until potato is tender, about 1 hour. Serve in the package.

FRANKFURTERS IN FOIL

Wrap individual frankfurters with 2 tablespoons any barbecue sauce in foil. Heat on hot coals 10 minutes.

FISH DINNER IN FOIL

Use a square of heavy-duty aluminum foil (or a double thickness of regular foil) for each serving.

In the center, place a slice of halibut, salmon, or other desired fish (fresh or thawed frozen). Season to taste with salt and pepper.

Cover with thin slice of pared small eggplant, bay leaf, 1 thin slice each of tomato, onion, and lemon.

Wrap, double folding the edges. Place on hot grayish coals. Cook about 8 minutes, turning once.

FISH DINNER IN FOIL #2

Place on a piece of heavy-duty foil, 1 to 2 pounds of fish with 2 medium onions, thinly sliced; 2 tomatoes, cut in quarters; ¼ pound mushrooms, sliced, and 1 green pepper, finely chopped.

Add 3 tablespoons butter, salt and pepper to taste.

Wrap tightly in foil and secure the edges well. Cook 10 to 15 minutes near the coals, turning halfway through cooking.

FOIL-PACKAGED KEBABS

Let your guests skewer their own assortment of cubes of round steak, onion slices, tomato halves, small frankfurters, mushroom caps, and squares of bacon.

Place the filled skewers on squares of heavy duty foil, brush with a peppy barbecue sauce and sprinkle with salt and pepper. Close the foil by twisting it at the ends to hold it secure.

Place the kebabs on the grate over a good charcoal briquet fire and cook, turning once or twice. It takes up to 40 minutes depending on size of pieces.

To serve, place the skewers on paper plates and with a pot holder, push the foil wrapped food off the skewer. Open the foil and savor the well cooked food with delicious juices intact.

Individual packaged dinners to cook on the grill can be prepared ahead of time, ready to be carried outdoors. French bread, sliced and buttered and wrapped in foil, can heat during the last 15 minutes.

Skewer Cookery

Skewer cookery is spectacular and never fails to intrigue guests, but actually it's not at all new and may be the earliest form of cookery. Centuries ago Armenian shepherds placed their food on sticks and cooked it over open fires. The dish Armenians made famous, shish kebab, consists of marinated lamb alternated on a skewer with pieces of green pepper and onion and broiled until done and crispy brown.

Specialty restaurants have popularized a flaming version by serving it on long swords tipped with cotton which can be ignited for an impressive parade to the table of the diner.

Your skewers may be green twigs, wires, metal spikes. Your food may be almost anything: meat, game, fish, poultry, fruit, vegetables, alone or in combination. Sometimes they are marinated, sometimes merely brushed with oil or sauce—always succulent, delicious.

BEEF OR LAMB KEBABS (Master Recipe)

2 pounds boneless lean meat (lamb shoulder or leg, beef chuck or sirloin)
¾ pound fresh mushrooms
2 medium-sized onions
3 medium-sized firm tomatoes
2 green peppers

Marinade and Basting Sauce:

2 bay leaves, crumbled
6 whole black peppers, crushed
¾ cup vinegar
⅓ cup water
1½ teaspoons sugar
3 tablespoons olive or salad oil
½ cup chopped onions
1 clove garlic, minced

Marinade: Combine bay leaves, black peppers, vinegar, water, and sugar in small pan. Bring to boil; boil slowly 3 to 4 minutes.

Cool and pour into pint jar with the oil. Shake well before using.

Meat: Cut meat into 1½-inch cubes and put in 2-quart bowl. Sprinkle with chopped onions and minced garlic. Pour on marinade and stir well.

Cover and let stand in refrigerator 3 to 4 hours or longer, stirring occasionally.

Vegetables: Wash mushrooms quickly in cold water. Dry with towel; remove stems. Peel onions, quarter, ready to separate into layers. Wash tomatoes and peppers. Cut tomatoes into 6 wedges each. Cut pepper shells into 1½-inch squares.

Fill Skewers: Drain marinade from meat; keep for basting. Slide a piece of meat on skewer, then pieces of green pepper, a whole mushroom, a layer of onion. Continue to alternate meat and vegetables, ending with meat.

Press filled skewers at ends so all will fit together tightly. Brush with marinade.

Broil: Broil until meat is desired doneness, turning several times to brown evenly on all sides. Baste often with marinade. Sprinkle with salt and pepper and push from skewers with fork onto serving plates.

About Tomatoes: Since tomatoes cook more quickly than the meat and other ingredients, be sure to broil them separately.

Cut the tomatoes into 4 to 6 wedges, depending upon their size, then thread the pieces on a skewer and broil only until heated through and lightly browned.

Variations: Squares of luncheon meat or quarters of frankfurters may be used instead of beef or lamb. Keep in marinade only an hour or two, or just brush with salad oil.

Oven Broiling: To prepare in the broiler, just lay the filled skewers across a shallow roasting pan and broil slowly, turning and basting as they cook.

SHISH KEBAB

1 leg of lamb (5 or 6 pounds), boned
½ pound onions, sliced
1 tablespoon salt
½ teaspoon pepper
⅓ cup sherry
2 tablespoons oil
1 teaspoon oregano

Remove all fat and gristle from the leg of lamb. Bone it and cut meat into 1-inch squares.

Mix meat with sliced onions, seasonings, and other ingredients. Let meat marinate in sauce at least 1 hour, and preferably overnight.

Put on skewers and broil over charcoal fire or in gas broiler until crisply brown on all sides. Serves 8.

STEAK KEBABS WITH RED WINE

1 pound sirloin steak, cut in cubes
12 large fresh mushrooms
½ cup claret, Burgundy, or cabernet
1 teaspoon Worcestershire sauce
½ cup salad oil
2 tablespoons ketchup
1 tablespoon sugar
1 tablespoon vinegar
½ teaspoon powdered marjoram
½ teaspoon powdered rosemary

Marinate steak cubes and mushrooms 2 hours in marinade made by blending wine, salad oil, Worcestershire, ketchup, sugar, vinegar, and herbs.

Arrange 4 beef cubes and 3 mushrooms alternately on skewers.

Broil, turning to brown well on all sides. Baste frequently with remaining marinade. Serves 4.

SKEWERED LAMB INTERNATIONAL

½ cup pineapple juice
¼ cup soy sauce
2 teaspoons brown sugar
½ teaspoon Worcestershire sauce
½ small garlic clove, minced
¼ teaspoon ground ginger
½ teaspoon Ac'cent
⅛ teaspoon thyme
1 pound boned lamb shoulder
6 bacon slices
8 mushroom caps
8 pineapple chunks

Combine first 8 ingredients; mix well.

Cut lamb into 12 cubes. Cut bacon slices in halves, fold each piece in two.

On each of 4 long skewers, alternately string 3 pieces of lamb, 3 bacon folds, 2 mushroom caps, and 2 pineapple chunks, beginning and ending with lamb.

Place in shallow pan; pour pineapple juice mixture over. Chill several hours.

Drain, saving sauce. Broil 10 minutes, with surface of meat 3 inches from heat; brush twice with sauce.

Turn, broil 10 minutes longer, brushing twice with sauce. Serve on rice. Heat any remaining sauce; pour over all. Serves 4.

Lamb on skewers appears under many names and with many flavors. It is the shish kebab of the Near East, the shashlik of Russia, the brochette d'agneau of France, the souvlakia of Greece. And each nationality adds a distinctive flair by way of flavor in the sauce in which meaty squares of lamb are soaked before stringing on skewers.

The rules for kebab cookery are simple. Select foods that cook in the same length of time and are complementary in flavor. Of course, the meats must be the broiling type and, therefore, tender and cut for relatively quick cooking.

TERIYAKIS

1   can (20 ounces) pineapple chunks
1   pound top round or sirloin of beef, cut ¾-inch thick
¼   cup soy sauce
1   clove garlic, minced
¾   teaspoon ginger
1   small jar stuffed olives (about 22)
22   short skewers (about 4 inches long)
    Ac'cent

Drain pineapple; reserve ½ cup of the syrup.

Cut beef into cubes about the size of pineapple chunks.

Combine reserved pineapple syrup, soy sauce, garlic, and ginger. Add meat cubes and pineapple chunks; marinate at least 1 hour.

Alternate meat cubes and pineapple on skewers, ending with an olive. Broil to desired doneness. Sprinkle with Ac'cent. Serve hot.

LAMB AND PINEAPPLE KEBABS

1½   pounds lamb, ½ inch thick
6   slices canned pineapple
Salt and pepper
⅓   cup butter or margarine, melted
¾   cup fine cracker crumbs

Choose steak from shoulder or leg; cut meat and pineapple in 1-inch squares.

Alternate pieces on skewers and sprinkle with salt and pepper; dip in melted butter and roll in crumbs.

Broil with moderate heat, turning often; serve on toast. Serves 6.

HAM AND PINEAPPLE KEBABS

Spear 1½-inch cubes of ready-to-eat ham and canned pineapple chunks, allowing 3 cubes of ham and 2 of pineapple to each skewer.

Broil for 8 minutes, turning frequently, basting with pineapple juice.

LIVER AND BACON KEBABS

Cut calf, lamb, or veal liver into 1-inch cubes.

Alternate liver and strips of bacon which have been folded into quarters on metal skewers. Brush liver with melted fat.

Brown about 5 inches from heat, turning to brown evenly. Broil until bacon is crisp and liver is browned, 10 to 15 minutes. Season with salt and pepper.

Variations: Alternate mushroom caps or small whole boiled onions with the liver and bacon. Chicken livers cut in half may be used. Sliced canned water chestnuts are a good combination with the chicken livers.

SPICED HAM AND POTATO KEBABS

Cut 1 12-ounce can of ham into 9 cubes. Score each cube on sides. Insert on skewer, alternating with small cooked or canned potatoes.

Baste with your favorite barbecue sauce and broil 8 to 10 minutes, turning and basting with additional sauce throughout the broiling period.

Variations: Proceed as above, substituting canned spiced crabapples, canned sweet potatoes, and pineapple chunks for potatoes.

Baste with glaze of equal parts of brown sugar and pineapple syrup.

QUICK BEEF TENDERLOIN KEBABS

Buy beef tenderloin in one piece. Cut into 1½ x 2-inch cubes.

Place on skewers alternately with fresh mushroom caps and chunks of onion.

Brush with melted beef fat (your meat man will supply the suet to melt).

Broil quickly over coals until meat is browned but still rare and juicy inside, about 4 to 7 minutes.

Teriyakis have come to us from Japan via Hawaii. The cast iron broiler (hibachi) is much used in the Islands. Heat from the charcoal fire is controlled by draft door at bottom of broiler. The hibachi can be used in the indoor fireplace during the winter months.

CAUCASIAN SHASHLIK

1   leg of lamb (about 6 pounds), boned
2   cups Burgundy wine
2   cups olive oil
Juice of 2 lemons
Salt and pepper
½   Bermuda onion, finely chopped
Vegetables, as desired

Cut lamb in 2-inch squares.

Combine Burgundy, oil, lemon juice, seasonings, and onion. Place mixture in earthenware crock or in deep china or glass dish; do not use metal. Marinate 3 days in the refrigerator.

When ready to cook, use 12-inch skewers. On each skewer alternate pieces of lamb with ⅓ tomato, ⅓-inch slice of onion (1 inch in diameter) and a ring of green pepper, if desired.

Each 12-inch skewer will take about 5 cubes of lamb, 2 tomatoes and 2 onion slices.

To cook: Broil on both sides gently, about 8 minutes on each side, depending on thickness of meat. If possible, finish off in a moderate oven 10 minutes.

For indoor service, make this quick, appetizing sauce:

Blend ¼ cup Burgundy wine or tarragon vinegar with 2 to 3 tablespoons melted warm butter; pour over each serving as a sauce.

Serve with hot steamed rice and a green vegetable or tossed salad. Serves 8.

STEAK AND MUSHROOM KEBABS

1½   pounds round steak, cut in 1½ inch cubes
½   pound mushroom caps, washed and drained
Sauce:
1   teaspoon Worcestershire sauce
½   teaspoon Ac'cent
1   clove garlic
⅛   teaspoon rosemary
½   cup red wine
½   cup oil
1   tablespoon horseradish

Remove mushroom stems and save for another dish. Marinate steak and mushrooms in combined sauce ingredients for several hours.

Arrange steak cubes and mushrooms alternately on skewers. Allow 3 cubes of steak and 2 mushrooms per skewer.

Broil over hot coals, basting frequently with sauce. Serve with remaining sauce. Serves 4.

Hamburgers for the Cook-Out

TIPS FOR BETTER HAMBURGERS

● Freshly ground beef is bright red in color and should have a little fat for flavor.

● When meat is ground to order, check the leanness of the meat and if it is very lean have 2 to 3 ounces suet ground with each pound of meat.

● Medium or coarsely ground meat (ground only once) gives extra juicy, light-textured hamburgers.

● For improved flavor, add ½ teaspoon Ac'cent (pure monosodium glutamate) to each pound of ground beef.

● When shaping patties, handle the meat lightly; the less handling ground beef gets, the more juicy and tender it will be.

● To avoid sticking, spread patties with soft butter or margarine before broiling.

● While cooking, turn hamburgers only once. Don't flip back and forth.

● Don't pack patties down with the spatula.

● If the grids on the grill are too widely spaced to hold hamburgers and if there is no skillet or wire broiler available, use a piece of aluminum foil on the grill.

● For extra juicy hamburgers, serve them with a zippy sauce. While the 'burgers cook over the grill, melt 3 or 4 tablespoons butter or margarine in a skillet for each 4 hamburgers. Season with Worcestershire sauce. When the 'burgers are cooked, put into skillet and turn once so both sides are coated; serve piping hot with the sauce.

● Always have hot toasted buns or bread ready for immediate service when the hamburgers are done.

DOUBLE HAMBURGERS

1   pound hamburger
1   teaspoon salt
1   egg
¼   cup milk
2   tablespoons prepared mustard
6   thin slices onion
2   tablespoons pickle relish or chili
     sauce

Combine hamburger, salt, egg, and milk. Mix well. Make 12 small flat patties. Spread mustard on 6 patties. Top each with onion slice and a teaspoon of relish.

Place remaining patties on top of relish. Press patties together, sealing well around the edges.

Broil 3 inches from heat source about 5 minutes on each side or pan-fry in 1 tablespoon fat in a heavy skillet. Makes 6 patties.

HAMBURGERS WITH EVERYTHING

2   pounds lean hamburger
2   teaspoons salt
½   teaspoon pepper
Relishes

Combine hamburger, salt, and pepper. Shape into 12 patties. Broil to desired doneness, turning once. Serve with choice of relishes.

Hot and Sharp Sauce: Mix ¾ cup mayonnaise, ½ cup prepared mustard, and 2 tablespoons horseradish. Top with sliced dill pickle.

Green and Red Relish: Mix 1 cup chili sauce and a dash of Tabasco. Put in serving dish and top with ¼ cup pickle relish.

Sweet and Sour Sauce: Fry 2 slices bacon. Remove from pan. Stir 2 tablespoons flour into fat. Add ½ cup water, ½ cup vinegar, 2 tablespoons sugar, ½ teaspoon salt, and ½ chopped red pepper. Cook until thickened. Add crumbled bacon.

Minted Cucumber: Peel and dice 1 medium-sized cucumber. Sprinkle with ½ teaspoon salt and 1 tablespoon sugar. Add 2 tablespoons each of wine vinegar and chopped fresh mint.

Green Onion with Caraway: Mix 1 cup sliced green onions with a few caraway seeds and 2 tablespoons vinegar. Add salt and pepper to taste.

Herbed Sour Cream: Mix 1 cup sour cream, 2 tablespoons chopped green onion tops, and 1 tablespoon chopped fresh herbs or 1 teaspoon dried herbs.

HAMBURGER PICNIC "PIZZA"

Fry 1 pound lean hamburger until brown. Add ⅔ cup tomato sauce, ¾ teaspoon salt, ¼ teaspoon garlic salt, ¼ cup sliced stuffed olives, and 1 cup diced Mozzarella or Muenster cheese.

Cut deep slits into top of 8 oblong hard rolls. Fill rolls and sprinkle with oregano.

Wrap in aluminum foil. Cook on rack over hot coals about 15 minutes, turning frequently. Serves 4.

CAMPFIRE HAMBURGER-BACON SPECIALS

For each serving, shape around the end of a green stick ¼ pound lean hamburger seasoned with minced onion, salt, and pepper.

Wrap diagonally with a slice of bacon; fasten with toothpick.

Cook slowly over hot coals, turning often, until bacon is crisp.

Remove picks. Slip meat from stick into a split toasted frankfurter bun. Serve with mustard and pickle relish.

For Cheeseburger Stacks: Season hamburger with salt and pepper. Shape into thin patties, using ¼ cup meat per patty and flatten into 4 inch circles. Between each two patties, place a thin slice of process cheese; press edges together to seal cheese inside. Grill over the coals on both sides. Serve in heated buns.

JUICY PICNIC PATTIES

Season each pound of ground beef with 1 teaspoon salt and ⅛ teaspoon pepper. Add ¼ cup cold water per pound of meat.

Shape into patties and wrap in waxed paper before taking to the picnic spot.

JUICY PICNIC PATTIES #2

Season each pound of beef with 1 teaspoon salt and ⅛ teaspoon pepper.

Pat out into thin patties. Dot a patty with 4 or 5 bits of chipped ice in center. Top with a second patty and press gently to seal edges.

As the hamburgers cook, the ice melts and steam forms.

BARBECUE-STYLE HAMBURGER

Shape a pound of lean hamburger into 4 patties and cook to desired doneness.

Meanwhile heat quick barbecue sauce prepared at home by combining ¾ cup chili sauce, ¼ cup picalilli, and a dash each of Tabasco and garlic salt.

Put each patty in a split heated roll and cover generously with sauce.

Serves 4.

GROUND BEEF-OLIVE 'BURGERS

1   pound ground beef
12 stuffed olives, sliced
1   small onion, finely chopped
½   teaspoon salt
⅛   teaspoon pepper

Combine ground beef, olives, onion, salt, and pepper. Shape into patties.

Broil patties with surface of meat 2 inches from heat. When one side is browned, turn and finish cooking on second side.

Serve each patty topped with an onion and tomato slice. Serves 4 to 6.

STUFFED HAMBURGER OBLONGS

1½ pounds ground beef
Salt and pepper
Prepared mustard
¼ pound processed American cheese
1   dill pickle
8   frankfurter rolls

Season ground beef with salt and pepper and divide into 8 equal portions. Pat each portion into thin oblong patty and spread with prepared mustard.

Cut cheese into 8 sticks; cut pickle into 8 strips.

Place one cheese stick and one pickle strip on each patty.

Roll up and grill over hot charcoal until cheese melts and meat is cooked.

Serve in toasted frankfurter rolls. Serves 8.

NUTBURGERS

1½ pounds ground beef chuck
1   teaspoon salt
⅛   teaspoon pepper
1   small onion, to be chopped
⅓   cup walnuts, to be chopped
8   sprigs parsley, to be chopped
4   hamburger buns

Season meat with salt and pepper; blend, then form into 8 thin patties.

Chop and combine onion, walnuts, and parsley; spread mixture on 4 patties. Cover with remaining patties; press edges of meat together so filling is sealed in.

Grill until brown; serve on split buns. Makes 4 sandwiches.

CHEESEBURGERS

1   pound ground beef
1   teaspoon salt
Pepper
1   tablespoon Worcestershire sauce
Slices of sharp cheese
Hot buttered toasted buns

Combine beef and seasonings; mix thoroughly. Shape into 4 to 6 patties, depending upon how thick they are desired.

Broil or pan fry in skillet. Lay a slice of cheese over the top of each patty for the last few minutes to melt cheese.

Serve in buttered toasted buns.

HAMBURGER-PEPPER STEAK

Cut 3 large sweet peppers (1 red and 2 green) into chunks. Fry in a little oil until tender.

Shape a pound of lean hamburger into a steak 1½ inches thick and 3 inches wide. Broil on rack over coals to desired doneness. Cut into 8 slices.

Cut loaf of French bread into 4-inch pieces. Split and butter each and fill with 2 slices of steak and ¼ of the peppers. Season to taste. Serves 4.

BARBECUED HAMBURGERS IN FOIL

1½ pounds hamburger
1½ teaspoons salt
Chili sauce
Prepared mustard
Ketchup
Thick steak sauce

Mix hamburger and salt; shape into 8 large thin patties. Spread with prepared condiments.

Wrap each patty in aluminum foil, and freeze in freezer or freezing compartment of refrigerator.

To cook, put wrapped hamburgers directly on hot coals; cover with more coals and cook for 8 to 10 minutes. Serves 4.

MUSHROOM-HAMBURGERS

Mix 1 pound lean hamburger with 1 teaspoon salt, ¼ teaspoon pepper, ½ cup minced fresh mushrooms (or minced drained canned mushrooms), and ½ cup grated Cheddar cheese.

Shape into 4 to 6 patties. Broil or fry to desired doneness. Serve in toasted hamburger buns. Serves 4.

SURPRISE CHEESEBURGERS

1   pound chopped beef
½   teaspoon salt
About 1 cup cheese cracker crumbs
2   tablespoons ketchup

Blend all ingredients together well. Divide mixture into 8 equal parts; form into patties.

Broil until well browned on both sides. Serve on toasted bun. Makes 8 cheeseburgers.

CARNATZLACH
(Rumanian Hamburger Rolls)

1½ pounds lean ground beef
1   onion, grated
1   garlic clove, minced
1   carrot, grated
Dash of cayenne (optional)
1   teaspoon salt
About 1½ teaspoons poultry seasoning
2   slightly beaten eggs
3   tablespoons flour
⅛   teaspoon paprika

Combine ground beef, onion, garlic, carrot, cayenne, salt, poultry seasoning, and eggs; mix well.

Form into 1-inch thick rolls, 3 to 4 inches long, tapering at the ends. Or form into smaller rolls, if desired. The former are called carnatzei; the latter are called by the diminutive, carnatzlach.

Roll the hamburgers in flour seasoned with paprika and broil under or over moderate heat. These are traditionally cooked over charcoal. Serves 6.

HOT STUFFED PICNIC ROLLS

2   tablespoons fat
1   chopped onion
¼   cup chopped green pepper
½   cup chopped celery
1   pound hamburger
½   cup ketchup
1   teaspoon salt
¼   teaspoon pepper
1   tablespoon Worcestershire sauce
1   cup shredded aged Cheddar cheese
6   frankfurt buns
Butter or margarine
Prepared mustard

Melt fat in heavy skillet. Add onion, green pepper, and celery. Cook and stir 5 minutes. Add hamburger and cook until redness is gone.

Add ketchup, salt, pepper, Worcestershire sauce, and cheese. Cook slowly 10 minutes. Chill.

Split buns and hollow out inside. Spread inside surface with butter and mustard. Fill each bun with hamburger mixture. (These are easier to fill if mixture is chilled).

Wrap individually in aluminum foil.

At serving time, heat wrapped rolls on outdoor picnic grate or in moderate oven (350°F.) 30 minutes.

Serve with pickles, cole slaw, and potato chips. Makes 6 rolls.

JUMBO CHEESE-ONION BURGERS

2   pounds hamburger
2   tablespoons prepared horseradish or ½ teaspoon Worcestershire sauce
½   teaspoon savory or poultry seasoning
Salt and pepper
1   medium onion, cut in 4 slices
4   slices process cheese
1   tablespoon olive or salad oil

Combine hamburger, horseradish or Worcestershire sauce, savory or poultry seasoning, and salt and pepper. Mix lightly and shape into 4 thick patties.

Cover each onion slice with a slice of cheese; press slightly so they hold together.

Broil the meat patties on 1 side about 5 minutes. Turn and broil on other side about 4 minutes.

Cover each with a cheese-onion slice; brush with oil and broil again, just long enough to melt the cheese. Serve with fresh hamburger rolls and sliced tomatoes. Serves 4.

HAMBURGER-PICKLE DOGS

Divide 1 pound hamburger into 4 parts. Shape each part over a long dill pickle strip.

Cook over slow fire to desired doneness. Serve in toasted split frankfurter rolls with mustard and chili sauce, or ketchup. Serves 4.

Ham Steaks and Pork Chops

BROILED HAM SLICE

Cut rind off slice of smoked ham and cut edges of fat in several places to prevent curling. Brush with melted butter or margarine.

Place in hinged wire broiler and broil over moderate heat 10 to 30 minutes according to thickness of slice, turning frequently. Allow 10 minutes for slice 1/4 inch thick; 15 to 20 minutes for slice 1/2 to 3/4 inch thick, and 20 to 30 minutes for slice 1 inch thick. Tenderized ham slices require from 1/3 to 1/2 less time.

Serve with broiled pineapple and sweet potato slices, or with sautéed apples if desired. Allow 1/4 to 1/3 pound per portion.

Fruited Ham Steak: Prepare as above and while broiling over moderate heat, baste with pineapple juice, white wine, or vermouth from time to time. To serve, slice in thin strips.

HAM STEAK WITH SOY-SHERRY SAUCE

Prepare broiled ham steak and, while broiling, brush both sides frequently with a mixture of 1/2 cup each soy sauce and sherry.

Serve with pineapple slices which have been brushed with the same sauce and broiled.

BARBECUED PORK CHOPS

Combine 1 cup soy sauce and 1 crushed clove of garlic. Marinate 6 1-inch thick pork chops in mixture for 1 hour, turning frequently.

Broil chops for 45 minutes, turning and basting often with Barbecue Chili Sauce (see sauces). Serves 6.

HERB PORK CHOPS

Cover loin or rib chops with tomato juice which has been seasoned with salt, pepper, and a generous amount of crushed basil. Marinate for several hours.

Remove chops carefully so basil clings. Broil over low heat until well done. A 1-inch chop will take 15 to 20 minutes on each side.

Serve with a sauce made out of tomato juice, using 1 clove garlic, 1 tablespoon olive oil, and 1 tablespoon flour to each cup of tomato juice.

BROILED HAM WITH PINEAPPLE SAUCE

1 cup brown sugar
1/2 cup vinegar
2 tablespoons dry mustard
1 cup pineapple juice
Thin ham slices

Combine sugar, vinegar, and mustard; simmer gently for 3 minutes. Remove from heat and add pineapple juice.

Broil the thin ham slices on the grill. When slightly browned, baste with the sauce, then baste occasionally while it cooks until tender and well seasoned.

BARBECUED HAM STEAKS

1/4 cup melted butter or margarine
2 cups sherry wine
2 teaspoons powdered cloves
1/4 cup brown sugar
1/4 cup dry mustard
2 teaspoons paprika
3 to 4 cloves garlic, minced
3 ham slices, 1-inch thick

Combine sauce ingredients and marinate ham slices in it for 2 hours, turning once.

Drain ham slices and broil about 20 minutes, turning often and basting with the sauce. Serves 6.

HAM STEAKS WITH MUSHROOM SAUCE

2 ham steaks, 1/2-inch thick
3 tablespoons vinegar
1 1/2 teaspoons dry mustard
1/2 teaspoon sugar
2 tablespoons currant jelly
1/2 pound fresh mushrooms, peeled and sliced
Butter or margarine as needed
Salt, pepper, paprika

Score fat edges of ham steaks to prevent curling. Put ham in skillet; add a little water, cover and let steam 10 minutes.

Mix vinegar, mustard, sugar, and jelly in saucepan and heat, but do not boil.

Broil ham in hinged wire broiler. Lightly brown the mushrooms in butter and combine with sauce.

Place broiled ham on a heated platter; pour mushroom sauce over. Salt, pepper, and paprika may be added to sauce if desired. Serves 4.

GLAZED-BROILED THICK HAM SLICE

1 1 1/2- to 2-inch slice ready-to-eat ham
2 tablespoons orange or peach marmalade, honey, or brown sugar mixed with a tablespoon of mustard

Slash fat edges to prevent curling. Broil ham slice 3 inches from heat source for 10 minutes. Turn with tongs and broil until brown.

Spread with orange or peach marmalade or other sweet topping. Serve hot. Serves 6.

Note: Slices of ready-to-eat picnic or cooked boneless shoulder butt or Canadian style bacon may be broiled in this way.

QUICK AND EASY HAM BARBECUE

Use fully cooked boneless ham roll. It may be left whole and skewered from end to end or cut into 1-inch serving portions to speed heating.

A tasty daub sauce is made by combining 3/4 cup brown sugar, 3 tablespoons vinegar, 1/4 cup pineapple juice, 1/2 cup apricot nectar, 1/4 teaspoon powdered cloves, and 1/4 teaspoon powdered garlic.

Brush ham liberally with sauce, using a long-handled brush or cloth on a stick. Continue to daub on sauce as the ham heats. Constant turning over hot coals should heat the ham in 20 to 30 minutes. Because fully-cooked ham is used, there's no worry about under-cooking. When the slices are lightly browned, they are ready to serve.

Quick and Easy Ham Barbecue

Barbecued Spareribs

SPEEDY BARBECUED SPARERIBS

Barbecued spareribs are an outdoor favorite, but because of the necessity for thorough cooking of pork, many persons prefer this method.

Cut 4 pounds spareribs into 3 to 4 rib sections. Simmer in 2 cups water until almost tender (about 1 hour) or pressure cook in 1 cup water at 15 pounds pressure 20 minutes according to manufacturer's directions.

Dip each piece in Texas barbecue sauce (see sauces) and grill over hot coals, turning often to brown well. Brush with more Texas barbecue sauce frequently during grilling. Serves 3 to 4.

"SMOKY" BARBECUED SPARERIBS

3 pounds spareribs, cut in pieces
1 to 2 tablespoons liquid smoke
1 clove garlic, chopped
1 medium onion, chopped
Few sprigs parsley, chopped
Pinch each of black pepper, ginger, and rosemary
½ cup dry sherry
2 tablespoons sugar
2 tablespoons tomato paste

Brush the ribs with liquid smoke and place in shallow roasting pan. Sprinkle with a mixture of garlic, onion, parsley, pepper, ginger, and rosemary.

Cover pan with foil or waxed paper and let stand overnight.

To cook, remove ribs from pan and cook over coals until tender, basting occasionally with a mixture of sherry, sugar, and tomato paste. Serves 3 to 4.

SWEET AND SOUR SPARERIBS

3½ to 4 pounds spareribs
Salt
2 cups master barbecue sauce (see sauces)
1 cup crushed pineapple
4 tablespoons orange marmalade

Cut ribs into serving-size pieces. Season with salt. Brown over hot coals. When golden, place in frying pan.

Combine barbecue sauce, pineapple, and marmalade. Pour over spareribs. Brown, basting often, until tender, 1 to 1½ hours. Serves 4.

Just-right ribs are crispy-brown outside, tender and juicy inside. Lean shows no pink when cut. Long slow cooking and frequent turning are required.

BARBECUED SPARERIBS

1 cup ketchup
4 tablespoons vinegar
2 to 4 tablespoons dark brown sugar
Few drops Tabasco or other hot sauce
4 tablespoons prepared mustard
3 to 4 pounds spareribs

Mix sauce ingredients well and use to baste spareribs often during cooking. If a thinner sauce is desired, add a little tomato juice.

Have the spareribs cracked down the middle and cut into 6-inch serving pieces. Sprinkle with salt and pepper. Broil over low heat until tender, 1 to 1½ hours, turning and basting often with this sauce or with barbecue chili sauce, or special hot barbecue sauce. Serves 4.

SPICY BARBECUED SPARERIBS

¼ cup brown sugar
1 tablespoon salt
1 tablespoon celery seed
1 tablespoon chili powder
1 teaspoon paprika
2½ to 3 pounds spareribs
¼ cup vinegar
1 cup (8-ounce can) tomato sauce

Mix dry ingredients and rub about ⅓ into the ribs.

Combine remaining mixture with vinegar and tomato sauce.

Let the ribs stand an hour, if possible, before cooking. Then cook over moderate heat until tender, basting occasionally with the sauce. Serves 3 to 4.

GOURMET BARBECUED SPARERIBS

5 pounds spareribs
1 cups soy sauce
1 cup Cointreau
1 cup honey
2 cups canned crushed pineapple
2 lemons, sliced
4 teaspoons powdered ginger
1 cup white wine vinegar
8 cloves garlic, finely chopped

Combine sauce ingredients. Marinate ribs in mixture for ½ hour, turning once.

Broil until done, 1 to 1½ hours, basting with this same sauce or with special hot barbecue sauce or with barbecue chili sauce. Serves 5 to 6.

GARLIC SPARERIBS

4 to 5 pounds spareribs
4 cloves garlic
1 cup stock or consommé
1 cup orange marmalade
¼ cup vinegar
¼ cup ketchup
1 tablespoon salt

Marinate (soak) the whole racks of ribs in a mixture of crushed or finely chopped garlic and all remaining ingredients for 12 hours or more in refrigerator.

Then lift ribs from the liquid and weave the bony strips onto a spit.

Broil 1 to 1½ hours or until meat is tender and glazed. Baste with the marinade during the cooking period. Serves 4 to 5.

Lamb and Veal for the Barbecue

LAMB CHOPS WITH LEMON

4 thick (1½ inches) loin lamb chops
Grated rind of 1 lemon
Juice of 1 lemon

Cut little pockets in the fat of each chop. Stuff pockets well with grated lemon rind.

Arrange chops on broiling rack or in hinged wire broiler and broil on one side for about 10 minutes, then turn and broil second side for the same length of time.

For well done lamb, broil a little longer on both sides. Season with salt and pepper. Serve on heated dishes, with a little lemon juice poured over each chop. Serves 4.

MINTED SHOULDER LAMB CHOPS

½ cup orange juice
¼ cup lemon juice
1 tablespoon sugar
½ teaspoon marjoram
½ teaspoon rosemary
½ teaspoon Ac'cent
¼ teaspoon salt
Few grains nutmeg
Bouquet of fresh mint
4 double shoulder lamb chops, boned and rolled

Combine all ingredients except mint and chops. Let stand 1 hour.

Tie mint bouquet in cheesecloth.

Dip chops in sauce; place on grill. Turn frequently, brushing each time with sauce, using mint "switch" as a brush.

Broil 15 to 25 minutes, depending on degree of "doneness" desired. Serves 4.

Lamb Shanks: Always a good buy and highly favored by men. Although they are usually braised, they can be barbecued on the grill—with delicious results.

BROILED VEAL CHOPS AND STEAKS

Veal needs long, slow cooking over moderate heat.

For steaks, use cuts from the leg, 1 to 1½ inches thick. Have kidney chops cut 1 to 1½ inches thick.

Season to taste as they cook. Inasmuch as veal is improved with extra seasoning, serve with well heated barbecue sauce.

BROILED LAMB STEAKS

Lamb steaks about 1 inch thick, cut from the leg, may be cooked in much the same way as beef steaks. Broil slowly, turning often, and season to taste just before serving.

Many people like them seasoned with tarragon or rosemary. The rosemary should be rubbed into the steak before cooking. If tarragon flavor is preferred, sprinkle a little on the steak as it cooks.

BARBECUED LAMB SHANKS

½ cup olive oil
1 tablespoon lemon juice
1 teaspoon salt
½ teaspoon thyme
1 tablespoon tomato paste
1 teaspoon dry mustard
1 small onion, grated
4 garlic cloves
4 lamb shanks
4 whole chili peppers

Combine first seven ingredients for marinade. Insert split garlic clove in each lamb shank. Arrange shanks on long skewers, alternately with whole chili peppers. Prick meat all over with fork, then pour marinade over it. Let meat stand in marinade about 2 hours, then remove.

Roast directly over coals 4 to 5 inches from heat for about 1 hour or until meat is tender. Serves 4.

BARBECUED LEG OF LAMB

Leg of lamb, boned, flattened (about 6 pounds)
2 tablespoons vinegar
½ cup olive oil
1 clove garlic, crushed
1 teaspoon salt
½ teaspoon pepper

Combine vinegar, oil, garlic, salt, and pepper. Marinate lamb in this sauce for 2 hours or more, turning often.

When ready to cook, lift lamb from marinade and place on a basket-broiler. Flatten and shape, then lock the racks firmly in place. Broil over coals 1½ to 2 hours, turning often and brushing every 5 minutes with special hot barbecue sauce. Serves 6 to 8.

STUFFED BREAST OF LAMB CHOPLETS

Have the meatman remove the breast bone, cut off the first 2 or 3 ribs from point end of breast, and remove the boneless flank end. Have a pocket cut in the breast.

Cut meat and some fat from the trimmings; add an extra pound of lamb shoulder and put through the food chopper. Season the ground meat with salt, pepper, and ½ teaspoon mace.

Stuff the lamb breast tightly with ground meat. Chill, if possible, then cut between ribs to make choplets. Grill over hot coals.

LAMB RIBLETS WITH SPICY SAUCE

1 strip of lamb breast or riblets
Garlic salt
¼ cup chili sauce
⅛ teaspoon celery salt
Dash of Tabasco sauce
Juice of 1 lemon

Cut breast into one-rib pieces. Sprinkle ribs with garlic salt. Combine remaining ingredients.

Broil until ribs are browned. Brush with sauce and broil until ribs are tender. Serves 3.

LAMB CHOPS AND KIDNEY GRILL

4 lamb loin or shoulder chops
2 lamb kidneys, split
Butter or oil
Salt and pepper
2 tomatoes, cut in halves crosswise
4 whole cooked carrots

Place chops and kidneys on broiler rack or in hinged wire broiler. Brush kidneys with oil or butter. Broil about 7 minutes or until chops are well browned.

Season with salt and pepper. Turn and arrange tomatoes and carrots on grill, first seasoning with salt and pepper and brushing with oil or butter. Broil about another 7 minutes and serve hot. Serves 4.

MARINATED BREAST OF LAMB

1   large lamb breast (3 pounds)
1   cup orange juice
1/2   cup lemon juice
2   tablespoons sugar
1/2   cup chopped mint leaves

Cut up the breast into riblets or leave whole. Cover with mixture of the juices and sugar. Place in refrigerator overnight.

The next day add the chopped mint to the marinade 2 hours before cooking time.

Remove the meat from the marinade; rub with oil and cook over a slow fire for 1 to 1¼ hours, or until tender on the inside and rather crisp outside. While cooking, baste with a sauce made of 1/2 cup of the marinade mixed with 1/4 cup salad oil.

Heat remaining marinade and serve as a sauce. Serves 4 to 6.

Marinated Lamb Shanks: Place 4 to 6 pounds lamb shanks in a heavy kettle. Add a little water; cover and simmer gently until partially tenderized.

Drain, cool, and cover with above marinade and proceed as directed in recipe for marinated lamb breast.

MARINATED BREAST OF LAMB #2

1   cup lemon juice
1/3   cup olive or salad oil
1   medium onion, thinly sliced
Breast of lamb (about 3 pounds)
1/2   teaspoon Ac'cent
1/2   teaspoon salt
Dash of pepper

Mix lemon juice, oil, and onion. Pour over lamb and let stand for 1 hour at least, longer if possible.

Lift meat from marinade and thread on spit. Sprinkle with Ac'cent, salt, and pepper.

Broil over a slow fire for 1 to 1¼ hours or until tender on the inside, rather crisp outside. Serves 4 to 6.

MARINATED LAMB STEAKS

Use steaks about 1 inch thick from leg or shoulder. Rub with garlic and salt.

Marinate in both white wine and tarragon leaves (to 1 cup wine, add 1½ teaspoons dry tarragon). Let steak absorb this for about 2 hours, turning frequently.

Remove to piece of absorbent paper.

Melt 6 tablespoons butter in saucepan; add the wine and tarragon; heat and save.

Put steak over medium-hot coals, brushing from time to time with the wine-tarragon mixture. A 1-inch steak will take 4 to 6 minutes per side to cook to medium rare.

BROILED LAMB CHOPS

Have English lamb chops or shoulder chops cut about two inches thick. Place the chops in a hinged wire broiler over a good bed of coals.

Brown on one side, turn and brown on second side. Should require about 30 to 40 minutes to cook these chops. Serve on heated plates.

LAMB BARBECUE—HUNGARIAN

Before barbecuing a roast of lamb or chops, rub with salt in which garlic has been crushed.

Then place a layer of sliced onion in the bottom of a pan or crock. Put in the meat and pile sliced lemon and sliced onion on top and around sides.

Cover and let stand in a cool place overnight, or longer if possible.

Before cooking, sprinkle lots of paprika over the meat. The meat is then ready for roasting or broiling.

BARBECUED VEAL CHOPS

4   veal chops, 1 inch thick
1/4   cup oil
2   tablespoons lemon juice
1/2   teaspoon salt
1/4   teaspoon pepper
1   clove garlic, mashed
Pinch of marjoram
2   tablespoons Worcestershire sauce
2   tablespoons ketchup

Combine ingredients for barbecue sauce. Place chops in a wire folding broiler and sear chops near the coals.

Remove to a higher position. Turn and baste with sauce frequently until tender. This should take about 35 minutes. Serve on hot plates with remaining warm barbecue sauce. Serves 4.

HERB VEAL CHOPS OR STEAKS

Roll veal chops or steaks in oil or butter, then in a mixture of chopped chives, parsley, and tarragon. Let stand for an hour.

Broil over low heat until cooked through. A 1-inch steak will take about 15 minutes on each side.

LAMB WHIRLS

1/2   pound sliced bacon
1½   pounds ground lamb
1   teaspoon salt
1/8   teaspoon pepper
1/4   teaspoon marjoram
1   tablespoon Worcestershire sauce
1   cup corn flakes
2   tablespoons water

Arrange bacon in overlapping slices on a sheet of paper about 10 inches wide.

Combine remaining ingredients, pat out on bacon.

Roll as for jelly roll, wrap tightly in waxed paper and chill thoroughly.

Before slicing, place wooden picks through roll at inch intervals to hold bacon in place. Cut 1-inch slices.

Broil over hot coals 6 to 7 minutes on each side, turning when brown. Serves 6.

CURRIED LAMB STEAKS

Combine 3/4 cup soy sauce with 1 tablespoon curry powder, 1 mashed clove of garlic, and a bit of ginger.

Soak lamb steaks in this mixture for 1 hour before broiling.

Economy-wise homemakers choose lamb breast for the cook-out. It makes a delicious dish when marinated and prepared in much the same way as barbecued pork spareribs. Prepare the breast whole, cut between the ribs for lamb riblets, or cut in 2- or 3-rib portions.

Spit Barbecued Meats

SELECTING THE ROAST

Make a friend of a good meatman. He will advise about best cuts for "over the coals." These are popular cuts for roasting on a spit: standing ribs of beef, rolled ribs, top-quality rump, sirloin or tenderloin of beef; leg, rolled shoulder, or saddle of lamb; fresh or smoked ham, loin of pork or double loin of pork (2 loins boned and tied together so fat is all on the outside), and Canadian bacon.

Meat for spit barbecuing should be at room temperature; remove from refrigerator 1 to 2 hours before you start the fire.

HOW TO SPIT A ROAST

The object is to have the meat secured to the spit so that, as nearly as possible, it is in balance and it is compact and well fastened. If one side of the roast is much heavier than the other, which it usually is in standing ribs, run the spit through diagonally. A rolled roast or leg of lamb is spitted directly through center.

USE A MEAT THERMOMETER

Use a meat thermometer when roasting and you won't have to guess when your roast is done. After the meat has been spitted, insert the thermometer at an angle into the heaviest end to center of the roast so it won't strike coals or heating element as the roast turns. The tip must not touch bone, fat, or the metal spit.

The thermometer probably won't register a change for the first hour, or until the heat penetrates center of the roast.

ROASTING HINTS

A fairly slow fire should be used. If the roast has a good covering of fat it will acquire a beautiful glaze as it evenly bastes itself with its own juices.

Lean cuts of meat are best basted with butter or oil while they cook. Or you can baste the roast with an herb-seasoned or barbecue sauce.

In either type, lean or fat, basting will add to the flavor and improve the glaze.

A drip pan made of aluminum foil can be set in place before or after you build the fire. Put it in front of the coals directly under meat on spit. The juices caught that way make a far better gravy, just as they are, than the usual flour and water variety.

Timing of cooking periods will vary with the size of firebox, degree of heat, amount and direction of wind, and type of grill used.

WHOLE BEEF TENDERLOIN ON A SPIT

Have the meatman roll the whole tenderloin in a thin sheet of rounded suet and tie securely.

Spit it through the center and season with salt and pepper. Other seasonings such as garlic or a little rosemary may be used, if desired.

Roast until it is crisp on the outside but still rare in the center, about 35 to 45 minutes. Slice and serve with a wine or mushroom sauce.

STUFFED ROUND STEAK

2 pounds round steak cut about ½-inch thick
½ pound ground beef
2 to 3 slices liverwurst, mashed
4 mushrooms, chopped
4 tablespoons cream, tomato juice, or meat stock
2 teaspoons salt
Dash of pepper
6 bacon slices

Have the meatman pound the steak, or pound it yourself with a meat mallet.

Mix ground beef with liverwurst, mushrooms, cream, salt, and pepper to make the stuffing.

Spoon mixture onto steak, shaping it down the center in a narrow strip.

Roll sides of steak over stuffing and tie tightly with string.

Wrap bacon slices around the roll at even intervals and fasten bacon ends securely with wooden picks.

Insert spit in center of the meat and broil over hot coals or in electric unit 30 to 45 minutes. Serves 4 to 6.

BARBECUED BOLOGNA ROLL

Remove casing from a large piece of round bologna. Score surface crosswise at 1-inch intervals to depth of ¼ inch.

Insert spit through the center and broil over coals or in rotisserie about 30 minutes, basting frequently with barbecue sauce.

A few minutes before bologna is done, split and toast sandwich rolls. Slice bologna, and serve between rolls with additional sauce, if desired.

RUMP ROAST ON A SPIT

Rump roast
2½ cups vinegar
2½ cups water
3 onions, sliced
1 lemon, sliced
12 whole cloves
2 or 3 bay leaves
6 whole black peppers
1½ tablespoons salt

Because beef rump roast is a less-tender cut it is best to marinate 2 or 3 days in the refrigerator before roasting.

Combine the marinade ingredients in a bowl and let stand at room temperature for several hours before adding meat.

Then add the meat and, for a mild flavor, let stand in the refrigerator for only 24 hours.

Remove the meat from the refrigerator about 4 hours before roasting on a spit over coals or in rotisserie, until tender, 1½ to 2 hours.

Baste roast with barbecue sauce several times during cooking.

Note: You can keep the chilled marinade for the next roast.

STUFFED LEG OR SHOULDER OF LAMB

Leg or shoulder of lamb, boned and rolled, but not tied

Stuffing:

2 medium onions, finely chopped
2 cloves garlic, finely chopped
¼ cup butter or margarine
¼ pound pork sausage meat
1½ cups breadcrumbs
1 teaspoon tarragon

Cook onions and garlic in butter until onions look limp.

Cook sausage in a little hot water about 5 minutes; drain thoroughly.

Combine all stuffing ingredients; mix well. Spread on lamb; roll up and tie securely.

Insert spit and roast over coals or in rotisserie, basting occasionally with pan juices mixed if desired with a little white wine. Season the roast with salt just before removing from spit.

ROTISSERIE ROASTING GUIDE		
Kind of roast	Approximate cooking time*	Thermometer reading
Beef		
Rare	2 to 2½ hours	140°F.
Medium	2½ to 3 hours	160°F.
Well-done	3 to 4 hours	170°F.
Pork, fresh	2 to 3½ hours	185°F.
Lamb		
Medium	1½ to 2 hours	175°F.
Well-done	2 to 2½ hours	180°F.

*For a 4- to 6-pound roast at room temperature.

ROAST SUCKLING PIG

Suckling pigs range in size from 10 to 30 pounds and it takes a rather large spit to roast one.

Choose the largest pig your equipment will hold. The smallest pigs will be nothing but skin and bones when cooked. Sprinkle the inside with salt, pepper, and a little oregano or sweet basil. Rub the skin well with oil, salt, and a little of the same herb.

Head and feet can be cut off before or after cooking; however, it won't look much like a pig if they are removed before cooking. Insert a piece of wood in the mouth to simplify adding an apple later.

Tie the legs in a kneeling position and arrange the pig on the spit so that it is perfectly balanced.

Place over a deep bed of hot coals arranged in such a way to allow for a pan to be placed in the center to catch the drippings from the roasting meat. These should be used for basting. The pig may be basted with oil; however, the pig will lose much of its flavor.

Like all pork, the pig must be roasted until thoroughly done. The skin should be very crisp. The time will be about 2½ hours for a very small pig, up to 6 to 10 hours for a large stuffed suckling pig, depending on the fire.

If the pig is stuffed with a sage or fruit dressing, stuff loosely to allow for expansion, and sew or lace up closely and tightly.

When done, remove from the spit, place a red apple in the mouth and cranberries in the eyes. Hang a necklace of cranberries around the neck, if desired, for additional garnish.

MARINATED ROUND OF BEEF

1 4-pound eye round of beef
1 tablespoon meat tenderizer
3 cups dry white wine
¾ cup salad oil
1 teaspoon rosemary
Pinch of sage
Pinch of thyme
1 tablespoon black pepper
2 onions, thinly sliced
2 tablespoons butter or margarine, melted
1 teaspoon celery seeds

Pierce surface of the meat in many places with a fork or skewer and sprinkle with meat tenderizer.

Put beef in a deep bowl and pour in marinade mixture of wine, oil, rosemary, sage, thyme, pepper, and onions.

Cover and let stand for 24 hours at room temperature, turning the meat occasionally to season and tenderize all over.

Drain meat, saving the marinade, and insert spit through center.

Roast over coals or in rotisserie, about 1½ hours, basting frequently with a mixture of 2 cups of the reserved marinade combined with melted butter or margarine and celery seeds.

BARBECUED LOIN OF PORK

Have the backbone removed from pork loin. Tie securely. Insert spit through center and cook over moderate heat, basting frequently with a barbecue sauce.

If the cooking is done over coals instead of in rotisserie, place a drip pan made of aluminum foil under it to catch drippings. It should take about 2 to 2½ hours over moderate coals.

ROLLED RIB OF BEEF

Make several incisions in the surface of the roast and insert small pieces of peeled onion and fresh thyme.

Rub lightly with smoked salt.

Place on spit and roast, basting frequently with barbecue sauce. When done, slice in rounds and serve on buttered rolls.

BARBECUED LEG OF LAMB #2

Leg of lamb, 5 to 6 pounds
4 cloves garlic
Salt and pepper
⅓ cup dry vermouth
⅓ cup olive or salad oil

Cut little slashes in lamb and tuck in slivers of garlic.

Rub surface with salt and pepper and insert spit in center of meat.

Roast over coals or in rotisserie until heated through, then start basting with the mixture of vermouth and oil.

Roasting time is about 1½ to 2 hours for medium-well-done meat.

Variations: If desired, the leg of lamb may be boned, rolled, and tied. Instead of the vermouth-oil basting sauce, it may be basted with pan juices mixed with a little white wine.

BARBECUED SHOULDER OF LAMB

Shoulder of lamb, boned and rolled, can be prepared in ways suggested for leg of lamb.

Here is a popular spicy basting sauce:

½ cup salad oil
Juice of 1 lime
1 small onion, minced
1 clove garlic, minced
1 teaspoon salt
¼ teaspoon pepper
1 teaspoon ginger
¼ teaspoon rosemary

Combine ingredients to make sauce.

Insert spit through center of tied 3- to 4-pound lamb shoulder. Roast over coals or in rotisserie, basting frequently with the sauce.

BARBECUED LEG OF LAMB, HAWAIIAN

Have the leg of lamb boned but not rolled and tied. Sprinkle the inside with curry powder and salt. Add a light sprinkling of small strips of pineapple.

Roll up and tie securely. Insert spit and roast over coals or in rotisserie, basting occasionally with pineapple juice mixed with salad oil, and seasoned with a little curry powder.

A roast is a top choice for entertaining out-of-doors if you have a grill with a revolving spit. The sight of it turning over the fire fascinates everyone and stimulates the appetite. But most important, a roast actually tastes better cooked this way.

Poultry

BARBECUED CHICKEN, DUCK, GOOSE, TURKEYS
(Master Recipe)

The birds should be halved beforehand, washed, drained, and kept chilled.

Brush them with all-purpose barbecue sauce and lay on grill with skin side up.

Use two forks or fork and spoon to turn halves occasionally. Avoid piercing the meat as this lets the juices drain away.

Baste with brush, spoon, or, best of all, a green stick or long fork wrapped on one end with clean cloth to make a "daubing" stick.

Keep fire or coals very low so the birds won't scorch or cook too quickly.

Place sauce near fire to keep warm and for convenience.

Serve the birds, cut according to size, on paper plates, or on warmed serving plates, if desired, at small barbecues. Half of an average-size chicken suits most persons. A quarter is enough for children.

Birds that weigh more than $3\frac{1}{2}$ pounds may be quartered, if desired, for serving to a group. Ducks may be served in halves or quarters. Small turkeys may be quartered. A goose halved for barbecuing may be disjointed, then sliced for serving.

The remaining sauce may be simmered down and poured over the warm birds just before serving, or it may be passed around.

Test for doneness by cutting into thick part of drumstick. If it cuts easily and no pink shows, the bird is done.

LEMON-BARBECUED TURKEY

1 4- to 6-pound turkey
2 lemons
3 tablespoons melted fat
1 teaspoon salt
$\frac{1}{8}$ teaspoon pepper
$\frac{1}{4}$ teaspoon paprika
1 teaspoon sugar

Have turkey split in half lengthwise. Break the joints of the drumsticks, hip and wing. Skewer the legs and wings into position.

Rub both sides of turkey pieces with cut lemon, squeezing lemon to obtain plenty of juice. Brush with melted fat. Sprinkle with a mixture of salt, pepper, paprika, and sugar.

Place turkey halves in a large folding wire broiler and broil slowly for about an hour. Turn every 15 minutes, brushing with melted fat each time.

The turkey is done when the meat on the thickest part of the drumstick cuts easily and there is no pink color visible. Serves 8.

HOW TO ROAST CHICKEN OR TURKEY ON A SPIT

You can't beat a fine plump chicken, capon, or turkey cooked over coals.

Select chicken or capon weighing 4 to 8 pounds. The spit should enter through the backbone about 1 inch above the tail and come out through extreme front end of breast bone.

Any size turkey may be roasted on a spit provided it is young and tender. Large birds require a longer cooking time, of course, and frequent basting. The new small turkeys (4- to 8-pound ready-to-cook) are popular for spit roasting; however, the 15- to 18-pound turkeys are also ideal.

They should first be trussed, having legs and wings tied close to body and neck skin fastened to back with a skewer.

Insert spit as for chicken (a hammer may have to be used to drive the spit); fasten holding forks securely and balance.

It is important that the bird be spitted so that it is balanced well.

Stuffing: Either chicken or turkey may be stuffed before roasting. In this case the spit must emerge a little farther forward to compensate for the added off-center weight. Also the cooking time is longer.

Roasting: Roast over a moderate fire, basting or not as you wish with a barbecue or basting sauce. Chicken is good basted with a mixture of melted butter and white wine.

You may test for doneness by pulling the leg; if it moves easily at the joint, it is done. A turkey of 14 to 16 pounds will take about 3 hours to cook; a 5-pound chicken may take as long as 1 hour and 40 minutes.

The insertion of a meat thermometer in the thickest part of the thigh of a very large chicken or a turkey will eliminate any guessing about when the bird is done.

Spit roasting may be done with charcoal, electricity, or gas supplying the heat. All methods roast meats equally well under properly controlled conditions. The choice may depend upon the convenience, the location, and the cost.

SPIT ROASTED DUCK WITH ORANGE GLAZE

Brush duck inside and out with undiluted frozen orange juice concentrate.

Follow directions for chicken in putting on spit and roasting; baste with orange juice. A 4- to 6-pound duck takes about 1 to $1\frac{1}{2}$ hours.

TURKEY STEAKS

Have meatman cut whole frozen turkey on electric meat saw in crosswise slices 1 inch thick. When turkey is completely sliced, cut each slice in half at the center. Reserve end pieces and small organ pieces for soups, salads, etc.

Place frozen steaks on grill over medium fire. Salt and baste steaks well with all-purpose barbecue sauce.

Broil slowly about 20 minutes on each side, turning once.

SPIT ROASTED ORANGE STUFFED DUCK

1 duck, about 6 pounds
3 unpeeled oranges, quartered
$\frac{1}{4}$ cup olive oil
$\frac{1}{2}$ cup orange juice
1 tablespoon grated orange rind
$\frac{1}{2}$ cup melted butter or margarine
1 tablespoon chopped watercress

Stuff duck with quartered oranges. Place on spit. Brush with oil. Broil $1\frac{1}{2}$ to 2 hours, turning often.

Serve with sauce made by combining remaining ingredients and heating until just below boiling point. Do not boil. Serves 6.

For Eating Pleasure: Spit barbecued poultry (duckling, chicken, Cornish hens, turkey)—a delight to the most discerning gourmet when rotisserie roasted over charcoal. To simplify the task line grill with aluminum foil. It reflects heat upward, increases cooking efficiency, and keeps grill clean. Form drip pan from foil to catch and hold juices.

To Make Foil Drip Pan for Rotisserie Roasting: Prepare this from 18 inch wide heavy duty aluminum foil. Tear off a sheet about 5 inches longer than the food on the spit. Fold this in half lengthwise, then turn up edges all around $1\frac{1}{2}$ inches and miter corners to seal them and make the sides firm. Place this pan in front of the hot briquets and under the meat; juices will fall into it.

Barbecued Baby Turkey Halves: When showing off your mastery of grilling, don't overlook this delicacy.

WINE BARBECUED STUFFED TURKEY

4- to 5-pound turkey
⅘ quart red wine
½ pound chestnuts, canned or fresh
1   medium potato
1   pound ground pork
1   teaspoon salt
¼ teaspoon pepper
½ pound sliced salt pork

Put turkey in a large bowl. Pour over the wine and marinate (soak) for 24 hours in refrigerator. Turn bird occasionally.

To make stuffing: Cook fresh chestnuts in boiling water for about 20 minutes or until tender, then remove shells and inner brown coating. Just drain liquid from canned chestnuts.

Cook potato until tender.

Fry ground pork until lightly browned.

Chop chestnuts and potato very fine; mix with ground pork, salt, and pepper.

Lift turkey from marinade; fill the cavity with stuffing.

Sew or skewer opening in turkey and truss tightly.

Arrange strips of salt pork over breast and back of bird and fasten the ends with wooden picks.

Insert spit in center of turkey; fasten holding forks securely.

Roast over hot coals or in rotisserie 2 to 2½ hours, or until tender. During the last 15 minutes of roasting, baste with the wine marinade.

Remove salt pork, wooden picks, and string before serving. Serves 8.

WINE BARBECUED CHICKEN

Combine 2 parts olive oil to 1 part dry white wine.

Add 1 chopped onion, crushed or finely minced clove of garlic, tarragon, and salt and pepper to taste.

Marinate (soak) the cut-up prepared broilers in this mixture for 2 to 3 hours, turning several times.

Remove from marinade and broil,

basting with the sauce while the chickens cook.

MARINATED BARBECUED CHICKEN

Cut ready-to-cook broilers into serving pieces. Let stand in any of the barbecue sauces 8 to 24 hours, or as long as possible.

Grill over hot coals slowly, about 25 minutes or until tender, turning often. Baste frequently with additional barbecue sauce.

Marinated Barbecued Turkey Broilers: Prepare and broil as for chicken (above), using 3- to 6-pound ready-to-cook turkey broilers.

SAVORY CHICKEN ON A SPIT

2   broilers-fryers (2½ to 3 pounds)
½ cup white wine
½ cup salad oil, melted butter, or margarine
1   teaspoon dried tarragon or rosemary
1   teaspoon salt
Dash of pepper

Fasten chickens on the spit. Mix wine, salad oil or melted butter or margarine, tarragon or rosemary, salt, and pepper together.

Brush or baste chickens every 15 minutes with sauce.

Cook until tender, 45 to 60 minutes. Serve with remaining sauce poured over. Serves 4.

SPIT ROASTED STUFFED DUCK

1   5-pound duck
3   teaspoons anise seeds
4   teaspoons ground coriander
1   medium onion, chopped
¾ pound ground beef
1   tablespoon butter or margarine
1   cup raisins
1   teaspoon salt
Dash of pepper

Put the clean singed duck in a deep bowl. Sprinkle with 3 teaspoons each of anise seeds and coriander. Cover with water. Let stand for 2 hours at least, then remove from water and drain.

To make the stuffing: Cook chopped onion and ground beef in butter or margarine until slightly browned.

Stir in raisins, 1 teaspoon coriander, salt, and pepper.

Spoon the stuffing into duck cavity and sew or skewer the opening. Insert spit through center of birds and fasten holding forks securely.

Roast over hot coals or in rotisserie for 2 to 2¼ hours or until tender. Serves 4.

CHICKEN CANTONESE ON A SPIT

2   whole broiler-fryers (about 2½ pounds each ready-to-cook)
4   stalks celery, coarsely chopped
¼ cup soy sauce
¼ cup sherry wine
1   clove garlic, crushed or minced
1   teaspoon dry mustard
¼ teaspoon pepper
½ teaspoon ginger
2   teaspoons Worcestershire sauce
3   tablespoons salad oil

Spoon celery into chicken cavities; close openings securely with skewers. Place on spit.

Combine remaining ingredients and use as basting sauce.

Brush chickens with sauce; cook over coals, basting frequently with sauce, about 45 to 50 minutes. Serves 4.

GRILL-BROILED CHICKEN OR DUCKLING

2   broiler-fryer chickens (not over 2½ pounds each, ready-to-cook weight)
½ cup salad oil
2   teaspoons salt
½ teaspoon pepper
½ teaspoon Ac'cent

Cut chickens in halves lengthwise. Break the drumstick, wing joints, and hip so birds stay flat during broiling.

Brush with oil. Season with salt, pepper, and Ac'cent. Lay on grill with skin side up or inside nearest the hot coals.

When inside is well browned, turn without piercing the meat as this lets the juices drain away. Brown skin side, brushing with fat.

Test for doneness by cutting into thick part of drumstick. If it cuts easily and no pink shows, chicken is done. Serves 4.

Barbecue a turkey for a bountiful July 4 buffet supper. A hearty macaroni casserole and crusty French bread are ideal additions to the meal.

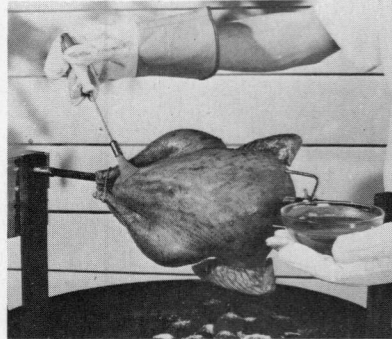

Frankfurters

RELISHES FOR FRANKFURTERS

1. Sliced mild, raw onion, separated into rings and then marinated in French dressing.

2. Hot seasoned sauerkraut plus caraway seeds or grated cheese.

3. Hot canned baked beans.

4. Strips of red and green pepper, fried lightly in oil for a few minutes.

5. Chutney or pickle relish.

6. Chopped onions and cucumbers, vinegar-dressed.

7. Chili sauce and chopped pickles.

8. Cheese spread or sauce.

9. Mayonnaise mixed with India relish and spiked with a generous amount of cayenne or Tabasco sauce.

10. Cole slaw or potato salad.

11. Bottled meat sauce.

12. Prepared mustard, sparked up with a teaspoon of horseradish and a few celery seeds.

13. Hot applesauce.

14. Hot crushed pineapple.

15. Chive cream cheese.

16. A sweet-sour bacon relish, made by heating equal parts of vinegar and brown sugar to the boiling point, then adding chopped, dry, crisp bacon. Serve hot.

GLAZED FRANKFURTERS

Slash 1 pound frankfurters. Combine 1/3 cup brown sugar and 1/3 cup prepared mustard. Spread into slashes and on franks. Broil 3 to 5 minutes or until golden. Serves 4 to 6.

WIENER CANOES

Slit frankfurters lengthwise, not quite through. Stuff with fillings like those suggested below.

Wrap filled frankfurters in double thickness of foil, sealing edges together with a tight double fold. Heat on grill over medium fire 6 to 8 minutes. Do not turn. Remove foil and serve in warm buns.

1. Sliced green onions, sautéed in butter and dotted with pimiento.

2. Cooked macaroni and cheese.

3. Horseradish, chopped stuffed olives, and cheese cubes.

4. Chopped celery, chopped onions, and pickle relish.

Wiener Canoes

Everybody's Favorite: Flavored franks wrapped in bacon. Slash franks lengthwise without cutting all the way through. Fill with mustard (or ketchup or pickle relish, or strips of cheese). Wrap bacon around filled franks, fastening bacon ends with toothpicks. Arrange, cut side up, on broiler rack or grill. Broil or grill until bacon is light brown. ➤

FRANKFURTER TOASTIES

1 pound frankfurters (about 8 frankfurters)
8 slices thinly sliced sandwich bread
Melted butter or margarine
Prepared mustard
Wooden picks

Pour boiling water over frankfurters and let stand 8 minutes. Drain.

Spread bread with softened butter and mustard. Place frankfurter cornerwise on bread and fasten the opposite corners together with wooden picks.

Brush each toastie with melted butter and broil until toast is golden brown. Serve with barbecue sauce. Serves 8.

FRANKS WITH BLUE CHEESE TOPPING

1/4 cup crumbled blue cheese (2 1/2 ounces)
2 tablespoons prepared mustard
1 pound frankfurters

Mash cheese with fork. Add mustard and combine thoroughly. Slice franks lengthwise.

Spread cut surface with cheese and mustard mixture. Broil until cheese is bubbly and brown. Serves 6 to 8.

FRANK KEBABS WITH QUICK BARBECUE SAUCE

1/2 pound frankfurters
1/2 pound processed cheese
1 4-ounce can whole mushrooms

Cut frankfurters into quarters. Cube processed cheese. Alternate frankfurter quarters, cheese cubes, and mushrooms on skewers and broil 3 to 4 minutes on each side.

Serve with quick barbecue sauce. Serves 8.

Quick Barbecue Sauce:

1 cup ketchup
2 tablespoons prepared mustard
2 tablespoons Worcestershire sauce
1/2 teaspoon onion powder

Combine ingredients and simmer 5 minutes.

FRANKFURTERS AND BEANS

Heat canned green, lima beans, or baked beans. Stir in sliced frankfurters.

If desired, season with mustard, ketchup, or a little shredded cheese.

CONEY ISLAND HOT DOGS

1 No. 2 can chili con carne
1 6-ounce can tomato paste
1 teaspoon prepared mustard
1/2 teaspoon salt
8 frankfurters
8 frankfurter rolls
Butter or margarine

Mix the chili con carne, tomato paste, mustard, and salt in a pan. Heat thoroughly.

Slit frankfurters diagonally in 4 or 5 places; grill until brown.

Split rolls, spread with butter, and then toast.

Place a frankfurter in each roll and cover generously with chili con carne. Makes 8 sandwiches.

FRANKS IN BLANKETS

1 1/4 cups prepared biscuit mix
1/3 cup milk
8 frankfurters
8 gherkins
Prepared mustard

Make rolled biscuit dough in accordance with package directions, reducing milk to 1/3 cup. Roll dough to 1/8-inch thickness on floured board. Cut into four 3 1/2-inch squares.

Split the frankfurters and gherkins lengthwise. Spread center of each frankfurter with mustard and insert 2 pickle halves.

Place 1 filled frankfurter on each dough square and roll it so that the center portion of frankfurter is encased. Cook slowly over coals until dough is browned on all sides. Makes 8.

STUFFED FRANKFURTERS

Split 1 pound frankfurters lengthwise and stuff with a mixture of 2 cups hot seasoned mashed potatoes mixed with 1/4 cup grated cheese and 1/4 cup finely minced onion. Broil 10 to 15 minutes. Serves 4 to 6.

FRANK KEBABS

Thread small salted tomatoes, onions, and frankfurters alternately on skewers. Rotate over coals until savory brown.

Put pieces between split buns or slices of bread.

Fish and Shellfish for the Barbecue

BARBECUED WHOLE FISH

Any fish can be broiled over the fire whether it's a small smelt or the largest salmon your grill can accommodate. For large fish, have more moderate fire than for smaller ones.

Sprinkle the inside of the cleaned fish with salt, pepper, and lemon juice before broiling. Large fish may be split.

Put in a greased hinged wire broiler and brown carefully on both sides.

If desired, baste the fish as it cooks with equal parts of melted butter and white wine or with melted butter flavored with lemon juice and thyme or tarragon. Fish with substantial skin and rich in fat need not be basted.

A fish weighing about 5 or 6 pounds will take anywhere from 20 to 45 minutes, or until the fish flakes easily with a fork. Small whole fish will cook in 15 minutes.

BARBECUED FISH FILLETS AND STEAKS

Have both fish and hinged wire broiler well oiled to prevent sticking. If fish is thick it will take a more moderate fire for a longer time than if it is thin.

A fish steak 2 inches thick takes about 15 minutes, one 1½ inches thick takes about 12 minutes, and one an inch thick about 7 minutes.

Fillets cook in 5 to 7 minutes, depending on size.

Brush fish well with softened butter or oil; heat the hinged wire broiler and grease it.

Brush fish while cooking with melted butter to which lemon juice or herbs have been added. Season with salt and pepper.

Barbecued Fish Steaks

FISH KEBABS

2 pounds quick-frozen ocean perch fillets
¾ cup ketchup
1 teaspoon Worcestershire sauce
Few drops Tabasco sauce
¾ teaspoon salt
¾ teaspoon Ac'cent
Few grains pepper
4 strips bacon
Dill pickle slices

Cut fish, while frozen, into 1½-inch cubes.

Combine ketchup, Worcestershire sauce, Tabasco, salt, Ac'cent, and pepper. Pour over fish cubes; let stand 1½ hours at room temperature, stirring occasionally with fork. Drain, saving sauce.

Cut each strip of bacon in fourths. Cut dill pickle crosswise into 16 slices.

On each of 8 skewers string a fish cube, a square of bacon, and a pickle slice; repeat, ending with a third fish cube.

Place in folding wire broiler and broil with medium heat 8 to 10 minutes, turning once and brushing several times with ketchup mixture.

Garnish with lemon wedges dipped in parsley. Makes 8 fish kebabs.

FISH KEBABS #2

2 pounds swordfish, cut in 1-inch cubes
2 cucumbers, cut in 1-inch slices
1 large jar stuffed olives

Sauce:

¾ cup olive oil
⅓ cup lemon juice
1 bay leaf, broken
4 drops Tabasco sauce

Combine sauce ingredients. Marinate fish for ½ hour.

On a skewer, alternate kebab ingredients. Broil 10 minutes, basting with marinade. Serves 6.

FISH FRY

Small fish may be cleaned and fried whole. Larger fish are boned and cut into steaks or fillets before frying.

Dip cleaned fish in water, then in a mixture of ½ cup flour, ½ cup yellow corn meal, and 1 tablespoon salt.

Fry in ¼ inch hot fat until brown on 1 side; turn and brown other side. Cook until fish flakes easily when tested with a fork. Do not overcook.

For Sandwiches: Heat sliced buttered buns in a foil picnic plate over grill. Insert a fried fish fillet and a serving of cole slaw in each bun. Serve immediately.

Racks and skewers for fish kebabs can usually be purchased at any outdoor supply or housewares stores. Or you can make your own from green wooden sticks.

SOYED BROILED FISH FILLETS

1 pound fish fillets
Salt and pepper
2 teaspoons soy sauce
2 tablespoons salad oil
2 tablespoons lemon juice
2 tablespoons minced parsley

Cut fillets into serving pieces; sprinkle with salt and pepper. Combine soy sauce and oil.

Place fish in oiled hinged wire broiler and broil until golden brown, about 5 to 8 minutes on each side. Baste frequently with soy-oil mixture.

Place on warm platter. Heat remaining soy-oil mixture; add lemon juice and parsley; pour over fish. Serves 4.

TROUT BROILED IN BACON

Wrap cleaned trout in bacon. Cook in folding wire broiler over coals, turning to cook both sides. Serve when bacon is done.

There are all kinds of tempting epicurean methods for preparing the harvest from the sea and fresh water sources, but none surpasses the outdoor fish fry. Shredded cabbage and tomato wedges combined with a tartar sauce can be added to the fried fillets served in buttered buns for a big bite sandwich.

SHELLFISH IDEAS TO COOK ON SKEWERS

1. Scallops with partially cooked strips of bacon woven on skewers around the scallops. Secure at ends with wedges of lemon.

2. Scallops alternated with mushroom caps. Brush with butter while broiling.

3. Scallops dipped in melted butter to which lemon juice, chopped parsley, and crushed garlic have been added. Broil quickly.

4. Raw oysters, dipped in melted butter, then rolled in mixture of half crumbs and half grated Parmesan cheese.

5. Small raw oysters dipped 'in butter, each put in a mushroom cap and strung on skewers.

6. Raw oysters, each rolled in bacon which has first been sprinkled with chopped green onion.

7. Raw shrimp, shelled, cleaned, then marinated in melted butter, olive oil, chopped garlic, and curry powder, alternated with squares of green pepper.

8. Raw shrimp, shelled and cleaned, with pineapple chunks, and brown-and-serve sausage.

9. Use fresh or frozen shrimp; do not shell. Dip in barbecue sauce. Spear on long fork or skewer.

Hold over fire until shells are brown-tinged. Pull shell off shrimp and eat.

Scallops en Brochette: Skewer whole scallops, medium size mushrooms, and squares of bacon. Grill over charcoal or in broiler about 10 minutes, turning often and brushing with highly seasoned French dressing throughout the cooking.

BROILED LOBSTER TAILS

Split thawed lobster tails along the top. Place on grill or in hinged wire broiler.

Broil with the meat side up at the start; finish cooking with shell side up. Total broiling time about 12 minutes for medium-sized tails, 13 to 15 minutes for large tails.

While broiling, brush frequently with melted butter. Serve with additional melted butter and lemon wedges.

BROILED LOBSTERS

Split live lobsters with a heavy knife or cleaver. Remove intestinal vein and stomach. Crack the claws with a hammer.

Brush meat well with melted butter and cook for a few minutes, flesh side up, then turn.

Baste lavishly with melted butter and finish broiling with shell to the fire. This will take about 15 minutes, depending on size of the lobsters.

After cooking, the empty part of the shell may be filled with hot toasted buttered crumbs. Serve with melted butter and lemon wedges.

BROILED CRABS

1/4 cup melted butter or margarine
1 tablespoon lemon juice
Dash of salt
Few grains pepper
6 soft-shelled crabs, cleaned
Flour

Combine butter, lemon juice, salt, and pepper. Roll crabs in mixture, then in flour.

Place in hinged wire broiler and cook over hot coals 5 minutes on each side, brushing often with butter mixture. Serve in toasted hamburger buns with tartar sauce.

Broiled Lobster Tails

Skewers threaded through the thawed lobster tails will keep tails flat during cooking.

SHRIMP AND PINEAPPLE KEBABS

3 pounds shrimp, fresh or frozen
1 cup soy sauce
1/2 cup lemon juice
1 No. 2 can pineapple chunks
1 pound bacon, cut in half slices

Shell shrimp, cut down back and remove sand vein.

Marinate shrimp in mixture of soy sauce and lemon juice for 1/2 hour.

On skewers, alternate shrimp, pineapple, and bacon (1/2 slice folded). Broil until bacon is crisp. Serves 6.

BACON AND SCALLOPS

8 slices bacon
1/2 pound scallops (Cape scallops preferably)
3 slices white bread, cut into 1-inch cubes

Using one slice of bacon for each skewer, thread alternately with scallops, bread cubes, and bacon (beginning and ending with bacon).

Broil 5 inches from heat source for 3 minutes on each side. Serve immediately. Serves 4.

ROAST CLAMS OR OYSTERS

Scrub 1 dozen unshelled cherrystone clams or oysters per person, changing water several times.

Place on grill or wire screening put across hot coals. Or wrap in aluminum foil and place on coals.

Turn occasionally and serve when shells open with melted butter or barbecue sauce for dipping.

Barbecue Sauces and Marinades

HINTS ON CHOOSING A SAUCE

Fish, meat, or poultry grilled out-of-doors over charcoal or wood should be basted frequently or they may dry out. There are sauces of an infinite variety of flavors, colors, and consistencies. One that is cool to a Texan's tongue may scorch that of a Maine Down Easter. But most Americans agree that barbecue sauce should have some sort of spice, sparkle, zing, zest, and kick, with more than a hint of wild, woodsy, outdoor flavor. It need not be fiery or fierce, but it should have a barbecue flavor.

A sauce recipe should be selected that will best suit the fish, meat, or poultry with which it will be served.

Fish and chicken call for a sauce that is delicately seasoned—mostly oil and herbs.

Barbecue sauce for pork chops and spareribs should have little oil or other fat, lots of chili sauce or ketchup.

Lamb calls for a sauce with a liberal amount of oil and garlic.

Thick steaks and other thick beef cuts such as thick cubes on skewers require a well seasoned sauce fairly rich in oil.

The all-purpose barbecue sauce which follows teams up well with all kinds of poultry cooked on outdoor pits or in ovens. It has been tested and retested for years at small and large barbecues in home kitchens, hotel kitchens, restaurants, church kitchens, Grange halls, and elsewhere over a large part of the United States. Spooned or brushed over cooking meat, it browns to a tasty, reddish brown crust full of flavor. In roasting pans it cooks down with the drippings into a rich, thick gravy to be served over the meat or separately.

The recipes for sauces given here should be only a beginning for the outdoor chef. The range and variety of vinegars (wine, cider, distilled, herb-flavored), fats, oils, spices, herbs, juices, and vegetables you may put into your sauce are limitless. So, use your imagination and experiment until you find the "Perfect Sauce," if there be one. There is certainly no set rule. If you don't have one ingredient, try another similar one. But taste frequently while mixing the ingredients. If your sauce is underflavored, you can quickly correct that lack. Make plenty of it. Leftover sauce keeps well in the refrigerator.

ALL-PURPOSE BARBECUE SAUCE

To Serve 6 with 3 Chickens:

¾ teaspoon salt
½ teaspoon pepper
¾ teaspoon paprika
2 teaspoons sugar
¼ teaspoon garlic salt
⅓ cup ketchup
⅓ cup tomato juice
1 small onion, chopped fine
⅔ cup water
¼ cup vinegar or lemon juice
½ teaspoon Worcestershire sauce
2 tablespoons butter, margarine, or salad oil

To Serve 24 with 12 Chickens:

1 tablespoon salt
1¾ teaspoons pepper
1 tablespoon paprika
3 tablespoons sugar
1 teaspoon garlic salt
1⅓ cups ketchup
1⅓ cups tomato juice
3 medium onions, chopped fine
2⅔ cups water
1 cup vinegar or lemon juice
2 teaspoons Worcestershire sauce
¼ pound or ½ cup butter, margarine, or salad oil

To Serve 50 with 25 Chickens:

2 tablespoons salt
2½ teaspoons pepper
2 tablespoons paprika
⅓ cup sugar
2 teaspoons garlic salt
2⅔ cups ketchup
2⅔ cups tomato juice
1¼ pounds onion, chopped fine
5½ cups water
1¾ cups vinegar or lemon juice
1½ tablespoons Worcestershire sauce
½ pound or 1 cup butter, margarine, or salad oil

Method: Measure all ingredients in pan or kettle. Heat to boiling. Keep hot for basting on grill.

Oven Barbecuing: Pour sauce over halved birds in roasting pan to about 1 inch deep. If sauce becomes too thick, add a little hot water.

The success secret of tasty barbecued ribs is the barbecue sauce. Choose your favorite from the recipes given here.

BARBECUE CHILI SAUCE

¾ cup finely chopped onion
¾ cup finely chopped green pepper
4 cloves garlic, finely chopped
6 tablespoons butter or margarine
4 cups canned tomatoes
¾ cup red wine
¾ cup bouillon
1½ tablespoons salt
¼ teaspoon pepper
1½ tablespoons chili powder
1½ tablespoons cornstarch
1½ teaspoons sugar

Cook onion, green pepper, and garlic in butter until soft.

Add remaining ingredients and bring to a boil. Reduce heat and cook until thickened, stirring constantly.

Cover and simmer gently 10 minutes longer. Serve with frankfurters, ham, pork, and spareribs.

TEXAS BARBECUE SAUCE

2 cups water
½ teaspoon black pepper
4 tablespoons brown sugar
1 teaspoon garlic salt or 2 cloves garlic, chopped fine
2 teaspoons salt
1 cup cider vinegar
1 5-ounce bottle Worcestershire sauce
Juice of 4 lemons
4 tablespoons butter (see note below)

Bring water to boil in a large 2-quart kettle; add pepper and simmer 5 minutes.

Add brown sugar; stir until dissolved, then add garlic salt or chopped garlic, salt, and vinegar, and stir.

Add ½ the bottle of Worcestershire; simmer for a few minutes, then add lemon juice and stir. Then add balance of the Worcestershire and stir while heating.

Add butter as sauce heats during use. Makes 1 quart.

Note: In making up this sauce it is easier to make it in a larger quantity than you need for a single barbecue. By omitting the butter, it will keep for weeks in the refrigerator. When ready to use, heat slowly with the butter. Omit butter when barbecuing pork.

CHINESE BASTING SAUCE FOR PORK, SPARERIBS, HAM STEAKS

½ cup chicken stock or consommé
¼ cup honey
¼ cup soy sauce
½ clove garlic, crushed
⅛ teaspoon ginger
2 tablespoons ketchup

Combine ingredients and cook over low heat for 8 to 10 minutes. Makes 1 cup.

SPECIAL HOT BARBECUE SAUCE

2 cups finely chopped onion
2 cloves garlic, finely chopped
1 bay leaf
1 teaspoon crushed chili pepper
1 teaspoon dry mustard
1 teaspoon salt
1 tablespoon brown sugar
2½ cups chili sauce
¾ cup olive oil
⅓ cup lemon juice
2 tablespoons tarragon vinegar
2 teaspoons Tabasco sauce
⅓ cup water

Combine all ingredients in pan or kettle; bring to boil. Reduce heat and simmer 15 minutes. Serve with chicken, lamb, or spareribs.

BARBECUED STEAK SAUCE

⅔ cup water
½ teaspoon dry mustard
1 cup tomato juice
⅔ cup vinegar
1½ tablespoons butter or margarine
1 tablespoon Worcestershire sauce
¼ cup pepper flakes
1 teaspoon paprika
1 teaspoon salt
¼ teaspoon black pepper

Combine in saucepan and simmer 10 minutes. Makes 2 cups.

Grill steak over coals. Brush with barbecue sauce as steak cooks. Serve with remaining sauce.

WINE MARINADE AND BASTING SAUCE

¼ cup salad oil
½ cup red or white wine
1 clove garlic, grated
1 teaspoon onion, grated
½ teaspoon salt
1 tablespoon Worcestershire sauce
½ teaspoon black pepper

Mix oil and wine; add rest of ingredients and chill several hours.

Pour over poultry or meat; let chill 3 hours. Baste again with sauce during cooking. Makes ¾ cup.

Note: Use red wine for steaks or lamb; white wine for chicken or veal.

MASTER BASTING SAUCE

½ cup salad oil
½ cup wine vinegar
½ cup lemon juice
¼ cup soy sauce
½ teaspoon Ac'cent
Salt, pepper, herbs to taste

Mix ingredients and store in covered jar in refrigerator.

This master sauce is used by many barbecue experts for basting all types of meat and poultry while cooking over hot coals or in rotisserie.

TARRAGON MARINADE FOR STEAK

1 large yellow onion, sliced
1 lemon
5 cloves garlic
1 whole bay leaf
½ teaspoon dry mustard
Salt
Freshly ground black pepper
1 cup oil
3 tablespoons tarragon vinegar
½ cup dry red wine

Line a shallow glass baking dish with whole onion slices. Squeeze lemon juice over onion, toss in lemon rinds.

Add 4 split garlic cloves, spices, ½ teaspoon salt, and ½ teaspoon pepper. Pour in oil, vinegar, and wine.

Lay the steak in the marinade and spread the rest of the onion slices on the steak.

Squeeze the juice of another clove of garlic over all, and sprinkle with additional salt and pepper. Baste and marinate for 3 hours.

This amount is enough for 2 pounds of 2-inch sirloin. Serve the marinated onions raw with the cooked steak.

HERB BARBECUE SAUCE FOR CHICKEN

½ cup salad oil
¼ cup olive oil
¼ cup lemon juice
½ teaspoon salt (part garlic salt if desired)
⅛ teaspoon marjoram
⅛ teaspoon thyme
⅛ teaspoon black pepper
⅛ teaspoon Ac'cent
Pinch of oregano

Mix ingredients well and let stand several hours to blend flavors.

Use a sprig of fresh rosemary or marjoram for a "basting brush" if you have some growing in your garden. This will be enough sauce for basting chickens to serve 6.

MINT MARINADE FOR LAMB KEBABS

6 sprigs fresh mint
2 tablespoons vinegar
⅓ cup salad oil
1 teaspoon salt
¼ teaspoon pepper
2 tablespoons minced onion
¼ teaspoon paprika

Wash the mint and finely chop the leaves. Add chopped mint to remaining ingredients.

Mix well, pour sauce over lamb cubes and place in refrigerator for 2 to 4 hours.

Thread on skewers and broil.

Use the sauce for basting during the broiling process. Makes about ½ cup sauce.

JIFFY NO-COOK SAUCE FOR CHICKEN

½ teaspoon pepper
1 teaspoon salt
1 teaspoon onion powder, or 1 medium onion, grated
1 teaspoon prepared mustard
2 teaspoons sugar
1 can (10½ ounces) condensed tomato soup
1 cup vinegar
1 cup water
1 tablespoon Worcestershire sauce
¼ cup cooking oil

Blend dry ingredients in mixing bowl or quart jar. Add remaining ingredients in order given. Mix thoroughly. Makes about 1 quart.

Barbecues 4 chickens outdoors and 3 indoors.

For oven barbecuing, add ½ cup water to sauce and pour over chicken halves in baking pan.

After marinating the meat, pour the marinade in a handy pitcher for easy basting as the meat cooks.

Outdoor Ways with Vegetables

FROZEN VEGETABLES IN FOIL

Thaw vegetables until they can be broken into chunks.

Make individual packets of chunks, or place on large sheet of heavy foil or 2 sheets light foil.

Add salt, pepper, a little Ac'cent, and plenty of butter or margarine.

Shape into long, flat package with edges tucked under.

Cook on grill over hot coals about 5 minutes longer than package label directs. If fire is too hot, move packages over to side of grill. Serve from foil with edges folded back.

MUSHROOMS IN FOIL

Put 5 or 6 mushrooms on a square of foil; add a pat of butter and salt and pepper.

Wrap in tight secure packet and broil about 8 minutes, turning once.

SAVORY VEGETABLE COMBO IN FOIL

Slice eggplant, onion, tomato, and mushroom. Place a portion of each on square of foil.

Brush with oil; season with salt, pepper, and oregano.

Fold and seal edges securely. Cook on hot coals about 12 minutes.

CORN ROASTED IN FOIL

Remove husks and silk from fresh corn or use frozen corn. Brush with butter or margarine; season with salt pepper and maybe chili or oregano.

Wrap in foil. Bake in coals, turning 2 or 3 times. Takes about 15 to 20 minutes.

Or cream together softened butter or margarine, minced parsley, paprika, and a bit of salt, and freshly ground pepper. Spread this mixture liberally over each ear of corn before wrapping in foil.

Serve either with plenty of butter or margarine to brush over corn as it is being eaten.

CORN ROASTED ON THE COB

Pull back husks from corn; remove silk. Replace husks and tie in place.

Soak corn in salted water 5 minutes; drain.

Roast on grill over hot fire for about 10 to 12 minutes, turning frequently.

Remove husks, and serve corn with butter or margarine and salt.

To Roast in Coals: After draining corn, bury it in hot coals for 10 to 12 minutes.

To preserve the natural flavor and color of vegetables, prepare them in aluminum foil packages.

TOMATOES AND BACON

Cut a thick slice of tomato, sprinkle with salt and and pepper, and wrap with a thin strip of bacon. Place in a wire toaster and cook over the hot coals.

PEANUT BUTTER GRILLED CORN

Remove husks and spread ears lightly with peanut butter. Wrap each corn in a bacon slice; fasten with a wooden pick.

Place on grill over hot coals and cook 10 minutes, turning often. Or grill on long skewers.

WESTERN-STYLE ONIONS

Cut peeled sweet onions in 1/3-inch slices. Fry slowly in butter or margarine until yellow, turning often. Season and serve with hamburgers.

TOMATO-CORN-ONION BARBECUE

Simmer small whole onions and fresh corn on the cob until just underdone. Break ears of corn into halves or thirds.

String onions, corn, and small whole fresh tomatoes on heavy skewers. Brush with garlic butter.

Lay on grill of hot coals to finish cooking and brown lightly. Turn and baste with additional garlic butter during the barbecuing.

BROILED EGGPLANT SLICES

This vegetable is especially good with barbecued meats. Peel eggplant and cut in 3/4-inch slices.

Sprinkle lightly with flour; dot with butter or brush with oil.

Place in hinged wire broiler and broil, turning once during the cooking.

Brush again with oil after turning and season with salt and pepper.

With Cheese: Sprinkle lightly with grated cheese before broiling.

VEGETABLE IDEAS TO COOK ON SKEWERS

1. Alternate green pepper squares, small onions, tomatoes, mushroom caps, and squash wedges. Brush with barbecue sauce before broiling.

2. Eggplant cubes, wrapped in bacon, alternated with pieces of green peppers and onions.

3. Eggplant cubes, small onions, and cherry tomatoes or tomato wedges. Marinate in olive oil seasoned with crushed garlic and oregano before broiling.

4. Small tomatoes and mushroom caps. Brush with melted butter or olive oil while broiling.

5. Chunks of carrots, parboiled onions, and slices of zucchini or other summer squash. Marinate in garlic-flavored olive oil before broiling.

ONIONS ROASTED IN FOIL

Method #1: Wrap onions, peeled or not, in foil and bake until fork-tender, about 30 minutes. Serve with butter, salt, and pepper.

Method #2: Stuff onions before wrapping with chopped apples, chicken livers, ripe olives, or nuts.

BROILED ONION SLICES

Put large slices of sweet (Bermuda) onion in a hinged wire broiler. Brush with butter and broil until golden brown. Leave them a little underdone in the center and still crunchy.

TOMATOES AND ONION IN FOIL

Choose medium, firm tomatoes (one per serving). Cut each in half crosswise. Sprinkle cut surfaces with salt and pepper.

Put together with a thin slice of onion between halves. Fasten with a wooden pick.

Wrap each tomato in a square of foil and bake at edge of grill 15 to 20 minutes.

Skewered Vegetable Barbecue

SKEWERED VEGETABLE BARBECUE

1 pound squash (banana, hubbard, or other winter-type squash), cut in 1-inch squares
1 bunch carrots, pared and cut into 1½-inch lengths
6 small potatoes (¾ pound), pared
2 green peppers, washed and seeded, cut into 1½-inch squares
¾ pound plum tomatoes (20)
¼ cup cooking oil
½ teaspoon salt
¼ teaspoon pepper
½ teaspoon Ac'cent

Simmer squash, carrots, and potatoes separately ahead of time (each in ½ cup water, ½ teaspoon salt, and ¼ teaspoon Ac'cent) until vegetables are just underdone. Drain and cool.

Combine vegetables, including whole tomatoes, in large bowl with oil, salt, pepper, and Ac'cent. Toss lightly to coat. Let stand 1 hour to marinate.

Thread vegetables alternately on long skewers.

Broil over hot coals 4 to 5 minutes, turning 4 times and basting with warm butter mixture. Remove from skewer. Serve as accompaniment to main dish. Serves 6.

Individual cups of aluminum foil add new interest to traditional baked beans. Two thicknesses of aluminum foil are formed over coffee cups. Canned beans are heated and served right in the attractive foil containers. Or home-baked beans can be prepared in these containers in the oven.

POTATOES BAKED IN CANS

Scrub baking potatoes; place in coffee or shortening cans. Put on lids loosely. Bake on grill when heat is low until tender, rolling cans occasionally. They take about 1 hour and 15 minutes.

When potatoes are done, cut slit in each, season with salt, pepper, and butter or margarine.

JIFFY FRENCH FRIES

Place thawed frozen French-fried potatoes in corn popper. Shake over hot coals until piping hot. Season with salt.

Or heat a bit of shortening or salad oil in heavy skillet. Add potatoes and toss until hot.

Note: Canned shoestring potatoes may be prepared in the same way.

JIFFY FRENCH FRIES #2

Punch a hole in the top of can of French-fried potatoes with a beverage can opener.

Place can on grill and roll occasionally as it heats. Open and serve.

Jiffy French-Fried Onions: Prepare in the same way as Method #2 above.

POTATOES ROASTED IN FOIL

Method #1: Potatoes may be baked pared or not. Scrub unpared baking potatoes well.

Brush with oil, melted butter or margarine; sprinkle with salt and pepper.

Wrap each securely in a square of foil. Bake on the grill or right on top of coals, or in hot ashes. It will take about an hour for good-sized potatoes. Give them pinch test to tell when ready to eat.

To serve, cut crisscross with fork in top; add a pat of butter.

Method #2: Scrub baking potatoes but do not pare. Cut each potato into 3 or 4 lengthwise slices. Brush with butter; season with salt and pepper.

Reassemble potato and wrap in foil. Bake in coals or at edge of grill about 45 to 60 minutes.

Method #3: Pare and slice potatoes. Season with salt, pepper, and butter or margarine. Wrap individual portions securely in foil and bake as in Method #1 above.

Method #4: Scrub baking potatoes well. Remove a lengthwise piece from each potato with an apple corer but do not cut clear to the other end.

Put a spoonful or two of evaporated milk into the hole. Seal the hole with outer ½-inch piece of the potato removed with the corer.

Wrap each potato securely in foil and bake on grill until tender.

RODEO POTATOES

Scrub new potatoes well. Cook in jackets in heavily salted water (3 tablespoons salt to 1 quart water).

Drain and peel potatoes. Season with salt and pepper.

Brown well in hot bacon fat over medium heat. Keep turning potatoes carefully so they become crusty brown all over.

SKILLET-FRIED POTATOES

Pare and cut potatoes into ¼-inch strips. Cover with cold salted water (1 tablespoon salt to 1 cup water). Let stand about 25 minutes.

Drain and dry with paper toweling. Cook, covered, in small amount hot fat in heavy skillet. Uncover and cook until brown, turning often.

SWEET POTATOES

Pan-Fried (Sautéed): Fry canned or cooked sweets in a little hot salad oil in skillet until golden brown on all sides.

Baked in Foil: Follow method for potatoes baked in foil.

Grilled: Cut peeled, cooked sweets in halves lengthwise. Spread with butter or margarine. Grill in hinged wire broiler over hot coals, turning often, until bubbly. Top with butter, salt, and pepper.

POTATO BAKE—OUTDOORS OR INDOORS

8 Idaho baking potatoes
1 cup melted butter
⅓ cup Worcestershire sauce
¼ cup chopped parsley, dill, or chives

Bake potatoes until half baked (about 40 minutes). Cool.

Cut potato into ½-inch slices leaving slices joined at the bottom. Combine butter, Worcestershire sauce, and chopped herbs.

Place each sliced potato on a square of foil. Spoon about 3 tablespoons of the butter mixture over each potato. Wrap tightly in foil sealing all edges.

Bake over gray coals, turning occasionally, for 30 to 40 minutes or until potatoes, when pierced, are tender. Serves 8. Indoors: Bake in moderate oven (375°F.) 30 to 40 minutes.

Potato Bake—Outdoors or Indoors

Outdoor Ways with Fruit

FRUIT MIXED GRILL

Brush tomato or pineapple slices, or peeled banana or peach halves, with melted butter, margarine, or salad oil.

Sprinkle with salt, pepper, and, if desired, lemon juice, nutmeg, etc.

Grill in hinged wire broiler over hot coals, turning to brown.

FRUIT KEBABS

1 No. 2½ can peach halves, halved
3 bananas, thickly sliced
2 apples, cut in wedges
1 fresh pineapple, cubed
3 grapefruit, sectioned

Sauce:

1 cup grapefruit juice
2 tablespoons Cointreau
½ cup honey
½ teaspoon chopped mint

Combine sauce ingredients and marinate the fruit for ½ hour.

Alternate fruit on skewer and broil 5 to 8 minutes, basting with marinade.

FLAMED BANANAS

Peel firm, ripe bananas and rub with sugar. Arrange in folding wire broiler and sprinkle with lemon juice.

Broil until just delicately browned but not mushy.

Place on a flameproof platter. Sprinkle with a little more sugar. Pour ¼ cup rum over them; ignite the rum and serve while flaming.

BACON, BANANA AND ORANGE GRILL

½ cup firmly packed brown sugar
½ teaspoon cinnamon
4 bananas
Lemon juice
4 slices bacon
3 oranges

Mix sugar and cinnamon. Peel bananas; roll in lemon juice, then in sugar mixture.

Wrap bacon slice around each banana; fasten with wooden picks.

Peel oranges; slice and sprinkle with remaining sugar mixture.

Place fruit in hinged wire broiler and broil over moderate heat 8 minutes, turning bananas once. Serves 4.

BANANA-HAM ROLLUPS

Cut peeled bananas in lengthwise halves, then crosswise.

Roll each in very thin cooked ham slice. Grill in folding wire broiler, turning to cook both sides.

Let your family and guests help themselves to cool eating from a deep salad bowl filled with chilled fruits served with wedges of lime or lemon.

SKEWER-COOKED FRUITS

1. Apple quarters, dipped in melted butter and sprinkled with sugar.
2. Halves of orange slices alternated with pieces of banana. Brush with honey, then broil and serve sprinkled with toasted coconut.
3. Dip pineapple chunks in butter, then roll in macaroon crumbs before serving.

FRESH PINEAPPLE IN FOIL

Cut off top and the bottom slice. Set aside. Cut around inside of shell.

Push out fruit in one piece; cut into sticks, discarding core. Return to shell. Replace top and bottom.

Wrap in foil. Bake on medium coals, turning once, about 30 minutes.

ROASTED BANANAS

Wash firm bananas (yellow with green tips), allowing at least one for each person.

Roast them right on the grill. It will take 10 to 15 minutes for them to cook through and don't be alarmed when they darken as they cook.

Serve hot as a vegetable, same as a baked potato. Let each person split his own banana lengthwise and eat the rich fruit out of skin with a fork. No need to add butter, but some like a bit of lemon juice.

BANANAS ROASTED IN FOIL

Method #1: Wrap unpeeled bananas in foil. Put them around the edge of coals, turning once or twice during cooking. They take 10 to 15 minutes.

Method #2: Slit banana skins lengthwise. Insert brown sugar and wrap in foil. Bake 8 minutes over hot coals, turning once.

Method #3: Remove peels from bananas and place each in a section of foil cut large enough to wrap bananas securely.

Sprinkle 1 tablespoon granulated sugar and 1 teaspoon cinnamon on each banana.

Wrap securely and nestle them into hot but not flaming coals; cook 10 to 15 minutes, depending on heat of coals. Serve with spoons and eat directly from foil cases.

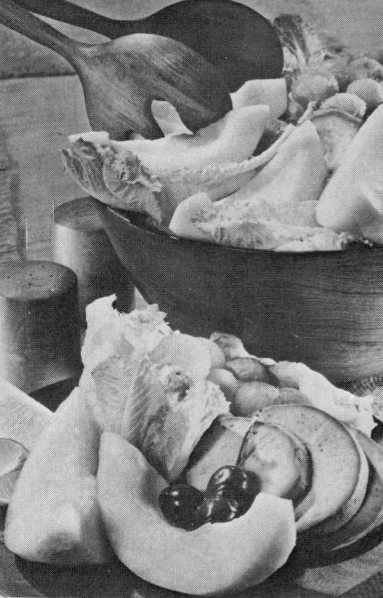

APPLES ROASTED IN FOIL

Method #1: Wrap whole apples each in a piece of foil and put them around the edge of coals, turning them once or twice during the cooking. Test with a fork through the foil and serve in the foil. They take about 30 minutes.

Method #2: Core the apples and fill the centers with sugar, cinnamon, and butter before roasting. Or fill the centers with peppermint candies before roasting.

CAMPFIRE APPLES

Stick an apple through the stem end on the end of a stick (one for each person).

Roast over coals until the skin can be easily peeled off. Tear off the peel and roll the hot apple in a pan of brown sugar.

Turn the sugared apple slowly over the coals until the sugar melts into the apple.

CARAMEL APPLES

½ pound caramels
2 tablespoons water
Apples, cut in quarters

Fold up sides of a double square of aluminum foil to serve as a disposable pan.

Place caramels and water in this; put on grill to melt. Stir smooth.

Remove cores from quartered apples. Hold over fire on sticks or long-handled forks to heat slightly. Then dip in melted caramel; twirl to coat with caramel. Cool and eat from stick.

BEVERAGES

Beverages take the spotlight at the beginning and at the end of a well-planned meal. An icy juice, tart and refreshing, makes a good start for any meal. From this liquid first course to after-dinner coffee, you'll find a broad selection of beverage ideas to complement your dinner or party menus.

The recipes given here, except for some variations of coffee, are non-alcoholic. Alcoholic drinks of all types are in a separate section, **Drinks.**

Juice Cocktails

Juice cocktails, except the hot varieties, should always be served thoroughly chilled. Fruit juices to be served as an appetizer should never be too sweet. Many of the canned juices may be improved by the addition of a little lemon or lime juice to give zest and to offset the natural sweetness of the fruit.

Innumerable interesting flavors may be created by combining two or more juices before chilling. Some suggestions are given below.

Many of the fruit and vegetable cocktails may be enriched in texture and food value if they are prepared in the electric blender.

FROSTED GLASSES FOR COCKTAILS
Method 1: Just before filling cocktail glasses, dip rims in lemon or orange juice to depth of half an inch, then dip immediately into granulated sugar. If time permits, place the glasses in the refrigerator to frost for about 20 minutes.
Method 2: Dip rims into unbeaten egg white, then in granulated sugar. Let glasses dry before serving.

CHILLED FRUIT JUICE SUGGESTIONS
1. Mix pineapple juice, fresh or canned, with orange or lemon juice.
2. Mix equal parts unsweetened grapefruit juice and apricot nectar.
3. Mix equal parts unsweetened pineapple or orange juice and prune juice.
4. Mix one part grape juice and two parts unsweetened pineapple juice.
5. Mix equal parts pineapple juice and orange juice and flavor with a dash of fresh lime juice.
6. Mix equal parts grape juice and unsweetened grapefruit juice.
7. Mix 2 cups sweet cider, ½ cup pineapple juice, and ½ cup orange juice.
8. Flavor cranberry juice with a dash of lemon juice, and sweeten to taste.
9. Mix equal parts of grapefruit and cranberry juices.
10. Mix equal parts of loganberry juice and pineapple juice.
11. Add chopped mint or 1 or 2 drops of oil of peppermint to canned or fresh grapefruit juice.
12. Mix 2 parts grape juice and 1 part ginger ale, and add lemon juice to taste.

SPARKLING FRUIT COCKTAILS

Method 1: Combine equal parts canned fruit juices (apple, cranberry juice cocktail, orange, whole fruit nectar) with chilled ginger ale.

Method 2: Reconstitute frozen juice concentrates (grape, grapefruit, lemonade, limeade, orange) with chilled ginger ale instead of water. Serve at once.

GRAPE JUICE COCKTAIL

2 cups grape juice
3 tablespoons lemon juice
1 pint chilled ginger ale

Combine grape and lemon juices and chill thoroughly. Just before serving add the ginger ale. Serve in frosted glasses. Serves 6.

PINEAPPLE-GRAPEFRUIT COCKTAIL

½ cup sugar
½ cup water
1¾ cups pineapple juice
1 cup grapefruit juice

Boil sugar and water together 5 minutes, stirring until sugar is dissolved. Add fruit juices to the cooled syrup. Chill. Serves 6.

SPICED CIDER COCKTAIL

2 cups cider
⅛ teaspoon salt
3 whole cloves
3 whole allspice
2 cinnamon sticks
¼ cup lemon juice
¾ cup orange juice
1 cup chilled ginger ale

Combine cider, salt, and spices; bring to a boil, then simmer about 5 minutes. Cool and strain.

Add lemon and orange juices. Sweeten slightly if desired. Chill thoroughly. Just before serving add ginger ale. Serves 8.

SAUERKRAUT COCKTAIL

3 cups canned sauerkraut juice
½ teaspoon Worcestershire sauce
¼ teaspoon prepared mustard
Dash of pepper

Combine and chill thoroughly. Shake well before serving. Serves 6.

TOMATO JUICE COCKTAIL

3 cups tomato juice
⅛ teaspoon pepper
¾ teaspoon salt
¼ teaspoon sugar
5 teaspoons lemon juice
5 drops Tabasco sauce

Shake ingredients together and chill thoroughly before serving. Serve with tiny wedges of lemon. Serves 6.

CLAM JUICE COCKTAIL

3 cups clam juice
3 tablespoons lemon juice
2 tablespoons ketchup
1 or 2 drops Tabasco sauce

Combine and chill thoroughly. Shake well before serving. Serves 6.

Variations: Other seasonings such as horseradish, Worcestershire sauce, grated onion, celery seed, etc. may be used as desired.

BLENDER APPETIZER COCKTAILS

In each of the following recipes, combine all ingredients in the blender container. Cover and turn on blender. Run until all ingredients are blended and smooth. Serve immediately. Each recipe makes about 3 cups.

EMERALD JUICE COCKTAIL

1 cup grapefruit juice
1 cup pineapple juice
1 tablespoon lemon juice
¼ package frozen spinach, unthawed, cut up
½ cup cracked ice

FRUIT AND VEGETABLE COCKTAIL

1 cup orange juice
1 cup grapefruit juice
1 cup shredded green cabbage
¼ green pepper
1 tablespoon lemon juice
1 cup cracked ice

GOLDEN JUICE COCKTAIL

1 cup canned apricot nectar
1 cup grapefruit juice
½ cup frozen pineapple, unthawed
½ carrot, cut up
1 tablespoon lemon juice
½ cup cracked ice

MINTED PINEAPPLE CUCUMBER COCKTAIL

1 cup pineapple juice
1 tablespoon lemon juice
1 cup unpeeled diced cucumber
Few sprigs mint
1 cup cracked ice

TOMATO JUICE CHEESE COCKTAIL

1½ cups canned tomato juice
½ cup cottage cheese
1 cup cracked ice
½ teaspoon Worcestershire sauce
Chives
Few celery leaves

VEGETABLE COCKTAIL

2 cups canned tomato juice
½ carrot, cut up
¼ small onion
Few celery leaves
Few sprigs parsley
1 cup cracked ice

CRANBERRY JUICE COCKTAIL

2 cups cranberries
3 cups water
½ cup sugar

Cook cranberries in water until skins pop; strain through cheesecloth.

Cook juice and sugar until sugar is dissolved, about 2 minutes.

Chill and add lemon juice, orange juice, unsweetened pineapple juice, or pale ginger ale to suit taste. Serves 6.

CLAM AND TOMATO JUICE COCKTAIL

Combine equal amounts of clam juice and tomato juice or use two-thirds clam juice and one-third tomato juice.

Season to taste with lemon juice, a dash of Tabasco sauce, and salt and pepper. Chill thoroughly before serving with a wedge of lemon.

FROZEN FRUIT COCKTAIL

Freeze ginger ale to a mush in freezing trays. Spoon into sherbet glasses and top with well-chilled and drained canned fruit cocktail.

FROZEN GRAPE JUICE

2 cups grape juice
1 tablespoon lemon juice

Combine and turn into freezing tray. Freeze to a mush, stirring once. Turn into a chilled bowl and beat with a fork. Serve at once. Serves 4.

FROSTED JUICE COCKTAILS

Add a tiny ball of any fruit ice to each cocktail glass of fruit juice just before serving. Add a sprig of mint for garnish.

Two popular combinations are: (1) lime ice on pineapple juice; (2) cranberry sherbet on pineapple juice.

FROZEN TOMATO JUICE

Season tomato juice as desired. Turn into freezing tray. Freeze to mush, stirring once.

Turn into a chilled bowl and beat with a fork. Serve at once.

TOMATO JUICE FRAPPÉ

1 pint-2-ounce can tomato juice
1 small onion, sliced
Few celery leaves
Dash of Tabasco sauce
½ teaspoon salt
1 teaspoon unflavored gelatin
1 tablespoon cold water

Combine tomato juice, onion, celery leaves, Tabasco, and salt in saucepan. Bring to boil and simmer about 5 minutes. Strain.

Sprinkle gelatin over cold water and let stand 5 minutes. Add to hot tomato mixture and stir until dissolved. Cool.

Pour into refrigerator tray and freeze to a mush, stirring occasionally. Serve in sherbet glasses. Serves 6.

BEET JUICE COCKTAIL

1 cup liquid drained from canned beets
1½ cups water
⅓ cup lemon juice
½ teaspoon salt
Dash of cayenne

Combine and chill thoroughly. Shake well before serving. Serves 6.

Tomato Juice—Winter Style: Serve in hot cups or in soup bowls. Some favorite garnishes for hot juice are: a slice of clove-spiked lemon; a generous spoonful of whipped cream; a slice of stuffed olive; a sprinkling of chopped chives; a few pieces of popcorn.

SPICED TOMATO COCKTAIL

2 cups canned tomato juice
½ cup sugar
2 lemons, sliced
¼ teaspoon cinnamon
⅛ teaspoon nutmeg
6 whole cloves
½ cup lemon juice
2 cups iced water

Combine tomato juice, sugar, sliced lemons, cinnamon, nutmeg, and cloves; heat to boiling point.

Strain, chill thoroughly and add lemon juice and iced water. Serve in cocktail glasses, garnished with bits of candied ginger. Serves 6.

SAUERKRAUT-TOMATO JUICE COCKTAIL

No. 1: Combine equal parts of sauerkraut juice and tomato juice. Season to taste with Worcestershire sauce. Chill thoroughly before serving with lemon wedges.

No. 2: Combine 1 part sauerkraut and 3 parts tomato juice. Season to taste with lemon juice and salt and pepper. Chill thoroughly before serving.

FRESH MINT COCKTAIL

1 cup fresh mint leaves
1 cup sugar
½ cup water
Green food coloring
Cracked ice cubes
1 cup ginger ale
4 sprigs fresh mint

Crush mint in saucepan with sugar. Add water. Mix thoroughly and boil 10 minutes. Strain. Add food coloring to make syrup a delicate mint green.

Half fill cocktail glasses with cracked ice. Add 2 tablespoons mint syrup and fill to top with ginger ale. Garnish with sprig of mint. Serves 4.

Coffee

COFFEE

The coffee bean grows on an evergreen tropical shrub or small tree believed to be native to Ethiopia. Popular in Arabia probably since the 15th century, coffee was not introduced into Europe until late in the 17th century. It quickly became a craze, and coffeehouses—the forerunners of modern clubs—were the meeting places of social, literary, and political leaders.

The flavor and aroma of the coffee bean are not released until it is roasted. Instant coffee is made by dehydrating brewed coffee. Despite its stimulating properties, coffee by itself has no food value.

The French word for coffee (and also for coffeehouse or restaurant serving light refreshments) is café.

Café Au Lait: Equal parts of strong hot coffee and scalded milk, usually poured simultaneously from separate pots into the cup.

Café Brûlot, Café Diable, Café Diabolique: Black coffee prepared with spices and orange peel, served in a demitasse (small cup) with flaming brandy.

Café Creole Bourbon: A carefully filtered, strong, fragrant coffee, which takes over an hour to prepare.

Café Glacé: A mixture of coffee, water, sugar, and boiled milk, frozen and served in cups.

Café Liégeois: Café Glacé to which whipped cream has been added.

Café Noir: Black coffee.

The Italian word for coffee and coffeehouse is caffè. Italian coffee is roasted very dark, almost charred, which gives it a pungent flavor.

Caffè Espresso: Coffee made in a special machine that forces steam through finely ground (pulverized) coffee identified as "espresso" on the container. To make at home, use the recipe which comes with your equipment. Serve espresso after dinner in a small coffee cup (demitasse) or in an espresso glass with or without a twist of lemon peel. Some fanciers add a dash of brandy.

Caffè Latte: Coffee with milk, usually half and half.

Cappucino: Either black coffee topped with whipped cream and cinnamon or coffee served in a tall, narrow glass or cup with frothy boiled milk.

Caffè Borgia: Equal parts of hot espresso and hot chocolate, topped with whipped cream and sprinkled with grated orange rind.

In the Near East, finely powdered (pulverized) coffee is used and the beverage is drunk unfiltered and heavily sweetened. This is commonly known in Western countries as Turkish coffee.

RULES FOR MAKING GOOD COFFEE

1. Measure coffee and water accurately. Use 2 level standard measuring tablespoons to each 8-ounce standard measuring cup of water.

2. Use fresh water for making coffee. For best results, start with freshly drawn cold water. Water that has been pre-heated or drawn from the hot water faucet may impart an undesirable taste to the brew.

3. Serve as soon as possible after brewing. If necessary to let brewed coffee stand any length of time, hold at serving temperature by placing pot in pan of hot water or over very low heat on asbestos pad. Keep coffee hot but do not boil. Coffee that has cooled cannot be reheated without loss of flavor.

4. For best results always brew coffee at full capacity of the coffee maker.

5. Consistent timing is important. After you find the exact timing to secure the results desired with your method of coffee-making, stick to it in order to get uniform results.

6. Never boil coffee.

7. Never re-use coffee grounds.

8. Never allow cloth filters to become dry. Keep immersed in cold water. Never use soap in washing cloth filters.

9. Keep coffee maker immaculately clean. Wash thoroughly after each use and rinse with clear hot water.

10. Always scald coffee maker before using.

PERCOLATOR COFFEE METHOD

1. Measure required amount of fresh cold water into percolator and place on heat.

2. When water boils, remove from heat.

3. Measure required amount of ground coffee into basket and insert basket into percolator.

4. Cover, return to heat and allow to percolate slowly for 6 to 8 minutes.

5. Remove coffee basket and serve.

STEEPED COFFEE METHOD

1. Preheat pot by scalding with hot water.

2. Measure required amount of ground coffee into pot.

3. Pour on measured amount of fresh boiling water.

4. Stir coffee and water for at least half a minute. Let stand 5 to 10 minutes, depending on grind of coffee used and strength of brew desired.

5. Pour coffee off grounds, through a strainer if desired, and serve.

STORING COFFEE

Coffee in bean form retains its flavor longer than in ground form.

Roasted coffee, whether in whole bean or ground, should be kept in a container as nearly air tight as possible. If market containers are not air tight, the coffee should be transferred to a tight sealing fruit jar.

Refrigerate for best flavor retention. Approximate time limit for storage of opened ground coffee is 14 days at room temperature, considerably longer in the refrigerator.

If it becomes weak, use more. If it becomes bitter, it's usable if the bitterness is not objectionable.

VACUUM-MADE COFFEE

1. Measure required amount of fresh cold water into lower bowl; place on heat.

2. Place filter into upper bowl, and add measured quantity of ground coffee, but *do not* insert in lower bowl. If you have a vacuum maker with a vented stem (a small hole in the side of the tube above the hot water line) the pot may be completely assembled before placing on heat. In this type of vacuum maker the water in the lower bowl will not start to rise until the water boils. When water starts to rise, reduce heat and follow the regular procedure.

3. When water in lower bowl boils actively, reduce heat. (If electricity is used, turn it off.)

4. Insert upper bowl with a slight twist to insure a tight seal.

5. When the water has risen into upper bowl (some water will always remain in the lower bowl) stir water and coffee thoroughly.

6. In 1 to 3 minutes (depending on grind—finer grinds require the shorter time) turn off heat. (If electricity is used remove coffee maker from unit.)

7. When all coffee has been drawn into lower bowl, remove upper bowl and serve.

8. Cloth filters should be washed in cold water immediately after being used and kept immersed in cold water until used again. Never use soap in washing cloth filters.

DRIP COFFEE METHOD

1. Preheat pot by scalding with hot water.

2. Measure required amount of ground coffee into filter section.

3. Measure required amount of fresh boiling water into upper container, then cover.

4. When dripping is completed remove upper section immediately.

5. Stir brew and serve.

6. Cloth filters should be washed in cold water immediately after using and *kept immersed in cold water* until next used. Never use soap in washing filters.

PICNIC COFFEE

Use 1 pound coarsely ground coffee to 2 gallons water. Tie coffee rather loosely in a sugar sack or muslin bag. There must be room for swelling of grounds, and for the water to circulate.

Bring water to a boil, and when boiling rapidly, push the kettle away from highest heat, so that water is held just under boiling point. Add sack of coffee and use a stick or paddle to agitate it. Slosh it up and down frequently for a 12 to 15 minute brewing period.

Lift sack out, let it drain, then discard it. Do not allow coffee to boil.

URN COFFEE

Use 1 pound coffee for 2 gallons water. Fill water jacket of urn with water until glass gauge registers ¾ full and heat just to boiling point. Put coffee in basket or filter, and pour briskly boiling water over it. Cover.

When water has dripped through, remove coffee container immediately. One pound of coffee will make 32 standard measuring cups (8-ounces each).

TURKISH COFFEE

6 rounded tablespoons pulverized coffee
6 tablespoons sugar
3 cups cold water
Rosewater (optional)

Place coffee, sugar, and water in a lidless coffee pot or pan. Heat until mixture comes to a brisk boil, stirring constantly.

Remove from heat and let the froth subside. Replace pot on very hot heat and repeat process 3 more times.

Add a little cold water to pot just before serving to settle brew. Add a few drops of rosewater, if desired, to each cup. Serve in demitasses.

IRISH COFFEE

Put in a pre-warmed 7-ounce goblet or coffee cup 1 jigger Irish whiskey and 1 teaspoon sugar. Fill the glass with freshly made strong, hot coffee. Stir until sugar is dissolved. Top with a spoonful of whipped cream.

CAFÉ BRÛLOT OR DIABLE
(French Flaming Coffee)

Peel of 1 orange
4 sticks cinnamon
12 whole cloves
6 lumps sugar
½ cup brandy or Cognac
4 cups freshly made coffee

Slice orange peel thinly and place in a silver bowl or chafing dish with cinnamon, cloves, and sugar.

Pour brandy over sugar mixture and ignite; ladle it until the sugar is dissolved. Add freshly made coffee. Serve in demitasse cups. Serves 6 to 8.

ICED COFFEE

Method 1 (With Cracked Ice): Prepare double-strength coffee by any method. Pour hot freshly made coffee over cracked ice in tall glasses.

The double-strength will make up for dilution by the ice without loss of flavor.

Serve iced coffee with sugar and plain or whipped cream.

Method 2 (Precooled): Prepare regular strength coffee by any method. Pour into earthenware, enamel, or glass container. Cool and place, securely covered, in refrigerator.

Freshly made coffee can be kept in the refrigerator many hours without seriously impairing the flavor quality.

Method 3 (With Coffee Cubes): Prepare regular strength coffee by any method. Cool and pour into refrigerator trays. Freeze.

To serve, pour freshly made regular strength hot coffee over coffee ice cubes in tall glasses.

CINNAMON CHOCOLATE COFFEE

2 ounces (2 squares) unsweetened chocolate
1 cup double-strength freshly made coffee
3 tablespoons sugar
⅛ teaspoon salt
3 cups milk
Cracked ice
Powdered cinnamon

Melt chocolate in coffee in top of double boiler. Add sugar and salt. Keep over hot water; add milk gradually and stir to blend.

Chill and pour over cracked ice in tall glasses. Sprinkle generously with powdered cinnamon. Serves 4.

ICED CHOCOLATE-CAFÉ

Combine and beat thoroughly 1 cup double-strength coffee, 1 tablespoon chocolate syrup, 2 tablespoons whipped cream, and 3 tablespoons crushed ice. Serve immediately.

Spiced Iced Coffee

SPICED ICED COFFEE CONCENTRATE

1 quart warm water
1 cup instant coffee (as it comes from jar)
¼ teaspoon ground cloves
1 teaspoon cinnamon

To make concentrate: Empty instant coffee as it comes from the jar into suitable container or jar. Add cloves and cinnamon. Slowly add water. Stir or shake to dissolve coffee and spices. Cover and stir or shake before using. Makes 1 quart or about 20 servings.

To use concentrate: For each serving pour 3 tablespoons concentrate over ice cubes into an 8-ounce glass. Add cold water. Sweeten to taste. If desired, serve with plain or whipped cream. Garnish with nutmeg.

VIENNESE ICED COFFEE

Half fill tall glass with cracked ice. Sprinkle with confectioners' sugar to taste. Add 1 tablespoon whipped cream. Fill with hot double-strength coffee.

MEXICAN ICED COFFEE

Chill 4 cups double-strength coffee. To serve add 6 tablespoons sugar and 2 teaspoons vanilla. Stir well to dissolve sugar.

Pour into glasses about ¼ full of cracked ice. Add cream as desired. Serves 6.

SPANISH CREAM COFFEE

Caramelize 1 cup sugar by melting in heavy skillet, stirring constantly. Add 1 cup boiling water and stir until sugar is dissolved. Boil 2 minutes and add 1 quart double-strength fresh coffee.

Add 1 cup thin cream and serve in tall glasses with cracked ice. Garnish with small spoonful of ice cream.

MOCHA ICED COFFEE

Combine freshly made double-strength coffee with an equal amount of cooled cocoa.

Pour into tall glass filled with ice. Add powdered sugar and cream to taste.

RUM ICED COFFEE

Pour precooled regular-strength coffee over ice in glass. Serve with whipped cream topping to which rum flavoring has been added.

Tea and Tea Base Beverages

RULES FOR BREWING TEA

Use spotlessly clean teapot made of glass, china, or earthenware. Scald teapot with boiling water and drain.

Measure tea into teapot, using one teaspoon tea leaves, or one teabag, for each measuring cup of water, plus one extra teaspoon or bag "for the pot."

Bring measured cold water to a galloping boil and pour over tea leaves. Let steep 4 to 5 minutes to develop full flavor. Dilute to the desired strength with clear, boiling water.

Variations: Serve tea with sugar, honey, fruit preserves, cream, lemon or orange slices, crystallized ginger, or cloves.

RUSSIAN TEA

Scald an earthenware teapot with boiling water and drain. Put in 2 teaspoons of tea leaves for each cup of water. Pour boiling water over the tea leaves.

Cover tightly and keep warm for 5 minutes. Strain into another scalded pot.

To serve, pour ¼ cup of tea infusion into each cup. Fill with boiling water and serve with lemon and sugar.

BOHEMIAN TEA

    3   quarts boiling water
    1   cup sugar
    1   teaspoon whole cloves
    1   stick cinnamon
    2   tablespoons black tea
    ¾   cup orange juice
    Juice of 2 lemons

Tie spices loosely in cheesecloth bag and add with sugar to hot water. Boil 10 minutes. Turn off heat and add tea tied in another bag.

Cover and let stand 5 minutes. Remove spices and tea bag. Add fruit juices and serve hot. Serves 20.

ICED TEA

Method 1: Make double-strength hot tea, allowing 2 teaspoons of tea for each cup of boiling water. Pour hot over crushed ice in tall glasses.

Method 2: Make regular-strength tea. Freeze in refrigerator trays. To serve, pour freshly made regular-strength hot tea over tea cubes in tall glasses.

Method 3: Cool regular-strength tea to room temperature and place in refrigerator to chill. Serve over crushed ice in tall glasses.

ICED TEA CONCENTRATE

Pour 1½ quarts boiling water over ¼ pound tea leaves. Let steep 6 minutes. Strain concentrate into glass or earthenware container (**Note:** one pint of water will be absorbed by the tea leaves.) and dissolve 1 cup sugar in it.

To serve, dilute concentrate with 7 parts cold water and add ice and lemon. The concentrate is best when made fresh.

HOT FRUIT PUNCH

    3   tablespoons tea leaves
    2   quarts boiling water
    1½ cups sugar or syrup
    1   cup lemon juice
    5   cups fresh or canned orange
        juice, or orange and pineap-
        ple juice or apricot nectar

Steep tea in boiling water. Add sugar and bring to boiling point. Add fruit juices and heat until just hot, but do not boil.

Garnish punch in bowl with sliver-thin slices of lemon and orange. Serves 30.

HOT MINTED TEA

    4   sprigs fresh mint
    4   teaspoons tea
    1   quart boiling water
    Lemon or lime slices

Add fresh mint to dry tea. Pour boiling water over tea. Cover and allow to steep 3 to 5 minutes.

Strain and serve hot with slice of lemon or lime.

One tablespoon mint jelly may be substituted for fresh mint. Serves 4 to 6.

HAWAIIAN TEA—HOT OR COLD

    ½   cup water
    1   cup sugar
    1⅓ cups lemon juice
    1   No. 2 can (2½ cups) pineapple
        juice
    2   quarts freshly brewed black tea
        (3 tablespoons tea for 2
        quarts boiling water)
    1   8-ounce bottle maraschino cher-
        ries and syrup

Boil sugar and water together 5 minutes. Combine with remaining ingredients and serve hot. Or pour over crushed ice and serve cold. Serves about 18.

ICED SPICED TEA

    3   tablespoons tea leaves
    4   cups boiling water
    12 whole cloves
    12 allspice berries
    1   2-inch cinnamon stick
    Lemon wedges

Put tea leaves in a heated pot and add boiling water. Add spices and let stand 5 minutes.

Pour through a strainer into tall glasses filled with ice. Serves 4.

SPICED TEA FROST

    ⅔   cup granulated sugar
    2   cups cold water
    Grated rind of 1 lemon
    8   whole cloves
    2   1-inch cinnamon sticks
    ¼   teaspoon ginger
    5   cups freshly made hot tea
    Lemon sections

Combine all ingredients but the tea and lemon sections, and boil 15 minutes. Strain and cool.

Add tea, mix well, and pour over ice in tall glasses. Serve with lemon sections. Serves 6.

MOCK CLARET PUNCH

    3   lemons
    5   oranges
    1   cup currant juice
    Small stick cinnamon
    2   cups water
    1   cup tea infusion
    Sugar or corn syrup
    ¼   cup stemmed fresh currants

Squeeze juice from lemons and oranges and add to currant juice. Chill.

Grate rind of 1 lemon and 1 orange, and add with cinnamon stick to water. Boil together 10 minutes, then strain and cool.

Add fruit juices and tea infusion to water. Sweeten to taste with syrup. Garnish with currants. Serves 6 to 8.

STORING TEA

Whether bulk or package, tea should be kept in moderately cool, dry place, away from foods of distinctive flavors.

Dampness will spoil tea by starting secondary fermentation.

Exposure to air will cause tea to lose flavor, strength, and aroma.

Do not keep tea more than nine months to a year.

A parfait pie and iced tea strike a cool note for summer patio gatherings.

Milk Drinks

COCOA

1/4 to 1/3 cup sugar to taste
6 tablespoons cocoa
Dash of salt
1 cup water
5 cups milk

Combine sugar, cocoa, and salt in a pan. Add water slowly and boil 2 minutes, stirring until thickened. Add milk and heat slowly to just below boiling point.

Before serving, beat with rotary beater until frothy. Serve topped with whipped cream or marshmallow.

Serves 6.

HOT CHOCOLATE

2 ounces (2 squares) unsweetened chocolate
1 cup cold water
1/8 teaspoon salt
3 tablespoons sugar
3 cups milk

Heat chocolate and water together, stirring until chocolate is melted and blended. Add salt and sugar and boil 4 minutes, stirring constantly.

Place over hot water and gradually stir in milk. Heat thoroughly. To serve, beat with rotary beater until light and frothy. Serves 6.

ICED BRAZILIAN CHOCOLATE

2 ounces (2 squares) unsweetened chocolate
1 cup strong coffee
3 tablespoons sugar
1/8 teaspoon salt
3 cups milk

Add chocolate to coffee in top of double boiler. Place over low heat and stir until chocolate is melted and blended. Add sugar and salt and boil 3 minutes, stirring constantly.

Place over boiling water. Add milk gradually, stirring constantly, then heat. Beat with rotary beater until light and frothy. Pour over ice in tall glasses. Serves 4.

ICED MINTED COCOA

6 tablespoons cocoa
2 sprigs fresh mint, crushed
1 cup boiling water
1/2 cup sugar
1 quart scalded milk
1/2 teaspoon vanilla

Add cocoa to well crushed mint and pour boiling water over all. Let stand until cold.

Add sugar to scalded milk, stirring until dissolved. Add to cocoa mixture and strain. Cool and add vanilla.

Serve well chilled in tall glasses with whipped cream topping. Serves 4 to 6.

EGGNOG
(Master Recipe)

1 egg
Few grains salt
1 tablespoon sugar
1/4 teaspoon vanilla
1 cup cold milk
Dash of nutmeg

Beat egg, salt, and sugar. Add vanilla and milk. Beat thoroughly. Pour into glass and sprinkle lightly with nutmeg. Serves 1.

Almond Eggnog: Omit vanilla and flavor eggnog with 6 drops almond extract.

Chocolate Eggnog: Omit sugar. Add 1 1/2 tablespoons chocolate syrup and 1 tablespoon malted milk (optional). Beat well. Top with whipped cream.

Fruit Juice Eggnog: Flavor eggnog with 2 tablespoons fresh or canned fruit juice.

Honey Eggnog: Substitute 2 tablespoons honey for sugar.

Malted Milk Eggnog: Add 1 to 2 tablespoons malted milk to eggnog.

Sherry Eggnog: Flavor eggnog with 2 tablespoons sherry or other favorite wine.

MEXICAN COCOA

3 egg whites
3/4 cup cocoa
1 teaspoon cinnamon
1/4 cup sugar or more
1 cup cold milk
2 3/4 quarts scalded milk

Make thin paste of egg whites, cocoa, cinnamon, sugar, using 1 cup cold milk.

Slowly add scalded milk to paste over low heat, beating constantly with rotary beater. Serve when thoroughly hot and foamy. Serves 10 to 12.

FRENCH CHOCOLATE MIX

2 1/2 ounces (2 1/2 squares) unsweetened chocolate
1/2 cup water
3/4 cup sugar
1/4 teaspoon salt
1/2 cup heavy cream, whipped

Place chocolate and water in saucepan and cook over low heat until thick, stirring frequently. Add sugar and salt and bring to boil. Let cool, then fold in whipped cream. Store in covered jar in refrigerator. Makes 1 pint. To serve as hot chocolate, pour hot milk over 1 or 2 tablespoons of mixture in cup.

To serve as cold chocolate milk, stir 1 or 2 tablespoons of mix into glass of milk with fork or use rotary beater.

The idea of a "home soda fountain" offers fun for the whole family—children love "make-your-own" drinks and milk drinks are real energy builders.

FRUIT MILK SHAKES

Use thoroughly chilled milk, fruit juice, or fruit pulp. Shake or beat with fruit or syrup until well blended. Sweeten to taste. Garnish with whipped cream if desired.

Evaporated milk diluted with an equal amount of water may be used instead of fresh milk.

Each of the following makes 4 generous servings.

Banana Shake: Combine 3 mashed ripe bananas with 3 cups milk.

Fruit Juice Shake: Combine 4 cups milk with 1/2 cup fruit syrup from cooked or canned fruit. Use apricot, peach, plum, pineapple, prune, or fruit nectar.

Grape Juice Shake: Combine 2 1/2 cups milk, 1 1/2 cups grape juice, and 1 teaspoon lemon juice.

Orange Shake: Combine 2 cups milk, 2 cups orange juice, and 1/4 teaspoon almond extract.

Prune Shake: Combine 2 cups milk, 2 cups prune juice, and 1 teaspoon lemon juice.

Strawberry Shake: Combine 4 cups of milk and 1 cup crushed sweetened strawberries.

BLENDER MILK DRINKS

In recipes given below, pour 1 cup milk into container. Add fruit, 1 cup finely cracked ice, and if a richer drink is desired, 2 or 3 marshmallows or 1 scoop ice cream. Blend until smooth.

Banana: Use 1 ripe medium-sized banana.

Chocolate-Mint: Use chocolate syrup to taste, 4 drops peppermint extract, and 4 marshmallows.

Peach: Use 1 cup fresh or canned sliced peaches or 1/2 cup frozen peaches and 2 tablespoons sherry.

Pineapple: Use 1 cup fresh or canned, diced or crushed pineapple.

Prune: Use 1/2 cup soaked pitted prunes and 1 tablespoon molasses.

Strawberry: Use 2 cups fresh strawberries and 4 tablespoons sugar or 1 cup frozen berries.

CHOCOLATE MILK SHAKE

Add 2 tablespoons or more chocolate syrup to 1 cup milk. Beat with egg beater. Top with ice cream—vanilla or chocolate.

Frosted Chocolate: Beat into the chocolate and milk mixture a scoop of ice cream. Malted milk may be added.

Maple Milk Shake: Use 2 to 3 tablespoons of maple syrup instead of chocolate.

Minted Chocolate Shake: Flavor each chocolate milk shake with 3 drops of peppermint extract. Garnish with whipped cream and sprig of fresh mint.

CHOCOLATE MALTED MILK

½ cup cold chocolate syrup
¼ cup malted milk powder
2 cups chilled milk
1 large scoop vanilla or chocolate ice cream
Dash of salt

Put all ingredients into mixer and shake or beat until well mixed and frothy. Serve at once. Serves 2.

COFFEE MALTED

6 tablespoons malted milk powder
2 cups fresh, hot double strength coffee
⅔ cup sugar
1½ cups milk
½ cup cream

Combine coffee with malted milk powder and beat until smooth. Add sugar to mixture and stir until dissolved. Add milk and cream.

Chill thoroughly and serve with plenty of crushed ice. Serves 6.

CHOCOLATE-MOCHA SHAKE

Mix ¼ cup hot, double-strength coffee, 1 cup milk, and 2 tablespoons chocolate syrup.

Cool, and pour over cracked ice in glasses. Top with whipped cream. Serves 2.

Flavored Milk Drinks

There's practically no end to the variety that can be made. The nice part of such a versatile concoction is that, provided with makings, each one likes to create his own.

Mint Delight

MINT DELIGHT

6 cups milk
4 tablespoons sugar
1½ teaspoons peppermint extract
5 to 6 drops green food coloring
Few grains salt
1 pint vanilla ice cream
Maraschino cherries and pineapple chunks

Add sugar, peppermint, food coloring, and salt to cold milk, stirring to blend. Pour into cold glasses. Top with vanilla ice cream.

Garnish with maraschino cherries and pineapple chunks on sippers. Serves 6.

MOLASSES SHAKE

2 tablespoons light molasses
2 tablespoons lemon juice
1 teaspoon sugar
¼ teaspoon grated lemon rind
1 cup milk
1 large scoop vanilla ice cream

Combine ingredients in shaker. Shake or beat until frothy. Makes 1½ cups.

BLACK BOTTOM COMBO

½ cup chocolate flavored syrup
⅔ cup milk
2 large scoops vanilla ice cream
Dash of cinnamon
1 egg white
¼ teaspoon vanilla
2 tablespoons sugar

Pour ¼ cup chocolate flavored syrup into each of 2 10-ounce glasses. Put milk, ice cream, and cinnamon in deep 1-quart bowl. Beat with rotary beater until ice cream is well blended and mixture is thick.

Pour slowly over syrup. Beat egg white until foamy. Add vanilla. Gradually beat in sugar, beating until mixture forms stiff peaks. Fill glasses with beaten egg white and garnish with maraschino cherries. Makes 2 10-ounce servings.

BLUEBERRY MILK SHAKE

1 cup crushed blueberries
½ cup sugar
Few grains salt
3 tablespoons grated lemon rind
6 tablespoons lemon juice
6 cups cold milk
1 pint vanilla ice cream

Mash fresh blueberries and add sugar, salt, lemon rind, and juice. Blend thoroughly and add cold milk. Pour into cold glasses and top with vanilla ice cream.

Garnish with fresh blueberries or thin lemon slices. Serves 6.

REDUCER'S COFFEE MILK SHAKE

Combine 1 cup skim milk, 1 teaspoon instant coffee, and saccharin to taste. Add an ice cube and blend until creamy.

BANANA MILK SHAKE #2

1 fully ripe banana
1 cup (8 ounces) milk

Peel banana. Slice into a bowl and beat with a rotary egg beater or electric mixer until smooth and creamy. Add milk; mix well. Serve immediately. Makes 1 large or 2 medium-sized drinks.

Variations:

Banana Chocolate Milk Shake: Add 1 tablespoon chocolate syrup before mixing milk shake.

Banana Chocolate Malted Milk Shake: Add 4 teaspoons chocolate malted milk and ¼ teaspoon vanilla before mixing milk shake.

Banana Orange Milk Shake: Use ½ cup orange juice in place of half of the milk. Add ½ teaspoon sugar before mixing milk shake.

Banana Pineapple Milk Shake: Use ¼ cup canned, unsweetened pineapple juice in place of a fourth of the milk before mixing milk shake.

Banana Spiced Milk Shake: Sprinkle ground nutmeg or cinnamon on top of milk shake just before serving.

Banana Vanilla Milk Shake: Add ½ teaspoon vanilla before mixing milk shake.

Banana Frosted Milk Shake: Add 3 tablespoons vanilla ice cream before mixing milk shake.

Important: For a colder drink, add about 2 tablespoons of crushed ice, and ice cream if desired, before mixing milk shake.

For a sweeter drink, add ice cream or plain sugar syrup.

Fruit Drinks

LEMONADE

1 cup sugar syrup (or to taste)
Juice of 6 lemons
1 quart water

Combine sugar syrup, juice, and water. Chill. Pour over cracked ice in tall glasses.

Variations: Substitute carbonated water, ginger ale, grape juice (reduce sugar syrup to taste), or orange juice. To serve, garnish with lemon or orange slices, mint leaves, fresh berries, crushed fruit, etc.

LIMEADE

Use 1 cup lime juice, 1 cup sugar syrup, and 1 quart water.

ORANGEADE

Use juice of 5 oranges, juice of 1 lemon, 1 cup sugar syrup, and 1 quart water.

LEMONADE READY-MIX

2 cups lemon juice
4 teaspoons grated lemon rind
1 cup sugar, honey, maple or corn syrup

Combine and stir until sugar dissolves. Store in covered glass (not metal) jar in refrigerator or cool place until ready to use.

For each serving of lemonade, combine 1/4 cup lemonade mix with ice water. Makes 8 to 10 large glasses.

GRAPEFRUIT JUICE FRAPPÉ

1 1/2 teaspoons (1/2 envelope) unflavored gelatin
2 tablespoons cold water
1/2 cup boiling water
1/3 cup sugar
2 cups grapefruit juice
1/4 cup lemon juice
Ginger ale

Soften gelatin in cold water. Dissolve in boiling water. Add sugar and cool. Add fruit juices and freeze to mush in refrigerator tray.

To serve, fill tall glasses half full and fill with ginger ale. Garnish with cherries and orange slices. Serves 4.

Lemonade-Mint Punch

ORANGE FROSTED

1 cup orange juice, fresh, frozen, or canned
2 scoops vanilla ice cream

Blend orange juice and ice cream with egg beater, electric beater, malted milk machine, or blender until ice cream is dissolved. Serves 1.

SPICED LEMONADE

Combine 1 cup sugar syrup with 12 whole cloves and 1 3-inch cinnamon stick. Cook 5 minutes. Strain.

Add juice of 6 lemons and 1 quart water. Chill. Serve over crushed ice.

MOCK MINT JULEP

3/4 cup sugar
1 cup water
Juice of 3 lemons
4 sprigs of mint, bruised
1 pint ginger ale

Boil sugar and water. Cool. Add lemon juice, mint, and ginger ale. Serve in glasses half filled with crushed ice. Garnish each with 2 sprigs of mint. Serves 4.

ORANGE PEACH FREEZE

For each serving, put 2 tablespoons frozen orange juice concentrate in tall glass. Add 3 or 4 ice cubes. Fill glass 3/4 full with ginger ale. Add a scoop of orange sherbet.

Garnish with fresh peach slices dipped in orange juice to prevent discoloration.

FRUIT VELVET

1 6-ounce can frozen fruit juice concentrate
1/2 pint vanilla ice cream
2 6-ounce cans cold water
2 6-ounce cans ginger ale

Empty can of frozen orange, grape, or pineapple juice concentrate and 1/2 pint vanilla ice cream into small mixer bowl and beat at a medium speed until well blended.

Using the frozen juice can as a measure, add 2 cans of cold water and 2 cans of ginger ale and beat at slow-to-medium speed until well blended and frothy. Serve immediately. Makes 4 to 6 servings.

LEMONADE-MINT PUNCH

1 6-ounce can frozen concentrate for lemonade
4 tablespoons green mint jelly
1 large bottle ginger ale
Ice cubes

Combine concentrate for lemonade (undiluted) and mint jelly; mix well until jelly has softened in the concentrate for lemonade.

Add ginger ale and ice cubes and stir well. Serve immediately. Makes 1 quart.

GRAPE RICKEY

1 quart grape juice
1 quart water
1/4 cup lemon or lime juice
1 cup orange juice
Sugar syrup to sweeten

Combine ingredients and pour over cracked ice in tall glasses. Serves 8 to 10.

Syrups

An endless variety of drinks may be made by using as a foundation fruit syrup and juices which can easily be made in the home, bottled, and kept for future use. Syrups left over from canned or pickled fruit may be used.

SUGAR SYRUP

Boil 2 cups sugar and 2 cups water 5 minutes. Cool and keep well chilled.

To substitute syrup for sugar, use 1 1/4 tablespoons syrup for each tablespoon sugar called for in recipe.

Fruit Syrups: (Strawberry, pineapple, raspberry, grape, apricot, etc.) Combine 1 cup fruit juice, 1 quart sugar syrup, and juice of 1 lemon.

COCOA SYRUP

1/2 cup hot water
6 tablespoons cocoa
1 1/2 cups corn syrup or 8 tablespoons sugar
1/8 teaspoon salt
1 teaspoon vanilla

Pour hot water over cocoa and stir until smooth. Add corn syrup or sugar, and salt. Simmer 10 minutes, stirring constantly. Add vanilla.

Serve hot or cold over ice cream or other dessert. Syrup may be covered and stored 4 to 6 weeks in refrigerator.

Chocolate Syrup: Substitute 2 ounces (2 squares) unsweetened chocolate for cocoa.

To make cocoa or chocolate: Add 1 1/2 to 2 tablespoons of cocoa syrup or chocolate syrup to each cup hot or cold milk. Serve iced drinks over chipped ice in tall glass. Top with whipped cream.

Variations: Flavor with cinnamon, ginger, a drop of peppermint extract, or crushed mint leaves.

COFFEE SYRUP

1 cup strong coffee
1 cup sugar
1 teaspoon vanilla
Few grains salt

Cook coffee and sugar together 5 minutes; add vanilla and salt. Cool.

Keep in covered jar to use as needed. Makes about 1 cup.

Party Punches

TEA PUNCH
(Master Recipe)

- 2 cups hot tea infusion (pour 1 pint boiling water over 1 teaspoon tea leaves)
- 6 cups fruit juice
- 4 cups ginger ale or carbonated water
- Sugar

Just before serving, combine, sweeten to taste, and pour over ice block in punch bowl. Makes 24 4-ounce servings.

California Punch: Use 3 cups loganberry juice, 2½ cups orange juice, and ½ cup lemon juice as the fruit juice.

Golden Punch: Use 1 cup lime juice, 2 cups orange juice, and 3 cups pineapple juice as the fruit juice.

Royal Punch: Use 4 cups grape juice and 2 cups grapefruit juice as the fruit juice.

COFFEE PUNCH

- 1 2-ounce jar instant coffee
- 1 quart warm water
- 1 cup sugar
- 3 quarts cold water
- 2 quarts vanilla, chocolate, or coffee ice cream

Combine coffee, warm water, and sugar; stir until sugar is dissolved. Chill.

Pour mixture into punch bowl. Stir in cold water. Beat 1 quart ice cream into coffee mixture. Spoon remaining ice cream over top. Makes 44 4-ounce servings.

LEMONADE-CIDER PUNCH BOWL

- 4 6-ounce cans lemonade concentrate
- 4 quarts cider

Combine concentrate for lemonade with chilled cider (instead of water) and place in punch bowl, over a chunk of ice or with ice cubes.

Purple Cow Punch

STRAWBERRY PUNCH

- 1 quart water
- 1 cup sugar
- 2 cups corn syrup
- 1 quart grapefruit juice
- 2 cups lemon juice
- 1 quart strawberries
- 1 bunch mint
- 1 quart ginger ale

Cook water, sugar, and corn syrup together to make a syrup. Chill and add to fruit juices.

Wash strawberries and mint. Reserve half of berries to garnish each punch cup. Mash remaining berries and add to fruit juice mixture. Add ginger ale just before serving. Makes 1 gallon.

FRUIT PUNCH

- 4 cups sugar
- 2 cups water
- 1 quart lemon juice
- 3 cups orange juice
- 1 quart grape juice
- 3½ quarts water

Make syrup of sugar and 2 cups water. Cool. Add strained fruit juices and water. Pour over block of ice in punch bowl. Makes about 50 small servings.

Variations: Ginger ale may be used instead of part of water. Pineapple juice may be used in place of part or all of grape juice. Garnish with thin wedges of orange and lemon.

ROSY LEMONADE PUNCH

- 3 12-ounce packages frozen strawberries or raspberries
- 4 6-ounce cans frozen concentrate for lemonade
- 2 tall bottles ginger ale
- 2 tall bottles sparkling water
- Sliced bananas for garnish

Let berries unfreeze and put through sieve if you wish.

Combine concentrate for lemonade with berries and berry juice and add ginger ale and sparkling water just before serving. Pour over ice in punch bowl.

Sliced bananas make an interesting garnish for this rosy lemonade punch. Makes about 36 4-ounce servings.

PURPLE COW PUNCH

- 2 quarts chocolate milk
- 1 28-ounce bottle black raspberry soda
- 4 teaspoons aromatic bitters
- Chocolate sprinkles

Have chocolate milk and soda well chilled. At serving time, combine all ingredients in a punch bowl. Sprinkle chocolate sprinkles on top, if desired. Makes 17 servings.

Frosty Sherbet Punch

FROSTY SHERBET PUNCH

- 3 cans (1 quart, 14 ounces each) orange-grapefruit juice
- 3 cans (1 quart, 14 ounces each) pineapple juice
- 3 cans (12 ounces each) apricot nectar
- 3 quarts ginger ale
- 3 quarts lemon sherbet

Have juices and ginger ale thoroughly chilled. Empty one can of each juice and one quart of ginger ale into punch bowl. Add a quart of sherbet. Spoon the liquid over the sherbet until partly melted. Serve.

When supply runs low, repeat the process adding another unit of each ingredient. Makes about 3 gallons.

GRAPE PUNCH

- 3 cups boiling water
- ¼ cup tea leaves
- ½ cup sugar
- Ice cubes
- ¾ cup lemon juice
- 1 6-ounce can frozen concentrated grape juice, plus 2¼ cups water or 1 pint bottled grape juice
- 1 12-ounce bottle carbonated water

Pour boiling water over tea leaves. Cover and steep 5 minutes. Strain. Add sugar.

Pour hot over ice cubes in large punch bowl or pitcher. Add juices and carbonated water. Mix thoroughly. Makes 2 quarts.

CREAMY SPICED MILK PUNCH BOWL

- 1 quart milk
- 2 teaspoons cinnamon
- 1 teaspoon nutmeg
- ⅛ teaspoon salt
- 1 quart vanilla ice cream
- ½ pint whipping cream
- 1 teaspoon vanilla
- 4 tablespoons grated orange rind

Pour milk into cold punch bowl; mix in seasonings. Add ½ of the ice cream, stirring until partially melted.

Whip cream until stiff and fold in vanilla. Place remaining ice cream and whipped cream on top of spiced milk. Sprinkle with grated orange rind. Serve in mugs with stick cinnamon stirrers. Serves 10 to 12.

Easy Party Punch

EASY PARTY PUNCH

1 can (46 ounces) grapefruit juice, chilled
1 can (46 ounces) orange juice, chilled
1 can (18 ounces) tangerine juice, chilled
1 quart ginger ale, chilled

Combine chilled citrus juices in punch bowl with ice cubes. Add ginger ale.

If desired, garnish with grapefruit sections, lime slices, mint, and cherries. Makes about 4½ quarts or 36 ½-cup servings.

ORANGE SHERBET FLOAT

4 quarts orange sherbet
8 quarts chilled ginger ale
1 quart chilled fresh orange juice (8 to 10 oranges)

Turn orange sherbet into large punch bowl. If sherbet is very hard, let stand in cartons at room temperature to soften somewhat.

Add orange juice and ginger ale. Stir to blend. No ice is required. Makes about 75 servings.

GOLDEN FRUIT PUNCH

2 No. 2 cans apricots
1 cup lemon juice
2 cups orange juice
4 28-ounce bottles ginger ale
Fresh mint

Put apricots through strainer. Add fruit juices.

Mix with ginger ale before serving and pour over ice cubes in tall glasses. Garnish with slices of lemon and mint. Serves 25.

HOLIDAY PARTY PUNCH

1½ quarts apple juice
1 quart gingerale
Lemon and lime slices
Green and red maraschino cherries

Chill apple juice and ginger ale. Combine just before serving. Pour into punch bowl over ice cubes.

Garnish with lemon and lime slices topped with quarters of green and red cherries. Allow about ½ cup per serving. Makes 10 to 12 servings.

FRUIT AND MINT PUNCH BOWL

Freeze water with sprigs of fresh mint in 1½-quart ring mold or loaf pan. Mix 1 46-ounce can each chilled orange drink and pineapple juice and 1 can frozen lemonade concentrate in punch bowl.

Shortly before serving, add 1 29-ounce bottle ginger ale and ice ring. Garnish with orange and lemon slices. Makes 15 large or 30 small glasses.

Hot Holiday Punches

HOT MULLED CIDER

1 gallon sweet cider
6 cinnamon sticks, broken in 1-inch pieces
1 tablespoon whole cloves
1 tablespoon whole allspice
2 pieces whole mace
3 cups brown sugar
2½ cups canned, spice crab apples

Put cider in kettle. Add cinnamon. Tie other spices in cheesecloth bag, and drop into cider. Stir in sugar. Heat slowly and simmer 20 minutes. Add apples 5 minutes before serving.

Remove spice bag before serving. Serve hot in earthen mugs with an apple in each mug. Makes 3½ quarts.

HOT BUTTERED PUNCH

¾ cup brown sugar
¼ teaspoon salt
¼ teaspoon nutmeg
½ teaspoon cinnamon
½ teaspoon allspice
¾ teaspoon cloves
4 cups water
2 1-pound cans jellied cranberry sauce
1 quart unsweetened pineapple juice
¼ cup butter

Mix brown sugar, salt, spices, and 3 cups water in saucepan and bring to a boil.

Add 1 cup water to cranberry sauce; beat with rotary beater until smooth.

Add pineapple juice and cranberry mixture to hot syrup; heat to just below boiling.

Serve hot with ½ teaspoon butter in each cup. Makes about 24 4-ounce servings.

HOT CRANBERRY PUNCH

1 cup apple juice
3 cups cranberry juice
½ cup strained orange juice (1 large orange)
Juice of 1 lemon, strained (2½ to 3 tablespoons)
3 whole cloves
1 small piece stick cinnamon (about 1½-inch stick)
2 to 4 tablespoons sugar
1 orange, sliced
1 lime, sliced
Cloves to stud orange and lime slices

Combine apple juice, cranberry juice, orange juice, lemon juice, cloves, cinnamon, and sugar in a 2-quart saucepan; stir to dissolve sugar and blend ingredients.

Cover and heat on a low heat until punch comes to boil. Carefully strain punch into punch bowl. Serve while hot.

Slice orange and lime and stud with cloves. Float for a garnish on top of punch. Makes about 1 quart or about 16 one-half cup servings.

Note: This recipe can be multiplied successfully. Heat punch in 6-8 quart container on medium heat until punch comes to boil.

LEMONADE-CRANBERRY PUNCH

4 pints cranberry cocktail
4 6-ounce cans frozen concentrate for lemonade
½ teaspoon salt
½ teaspoon cinnamon
1 teaspoon allspice
4 cups water

Combine ingredients in large kettle; heat and simmer gently 10 to 15 minutes. Do not boil.

Pour into punch bowl and serve in mugs. Makes about 1 gallon punch.

HOT SPICED GRAPE JUICE

1 quart grape juice
½ cup sugar
2 short pieces stick cinnamon
12 whole cloves
⅛ teaspoon salt

Mix all the ingredients and bring to boiling point. Cool, and let stand several hours.

When ready to serve, reheat, remove spices, and add lemon juice if desired. Serve hot. Serves 6.

HOT CALYPSO CIDER

2 quarts apple cider or juice
¼ cup brown or maple sugar
3 slices orange
3 slices lemon
2 tablespoons aromatic bitters

Heat cider with sugar. Stir until sugar is dissolved. Add orange slices and lemon slices. Let simmer 10 minutes. Add bitters, stir, and serve. Makes about 2 quarts.

Hot Calypso Cider

BREADS AND ROLLS MADE WITH YEAST

WHAT TO KNOW BEFORE YOU START

Baking with yeast is one of the most rewarding forms of the culinary art. Mixing yeast doughs and batters is fascinating, and not at all difficult when you understand the hows and whys. Shaping the dough is more play than work. Baking produces the fragrant, delicious treats that bring you compliments by the baker's dozen.

If you are just starting your yeast-baking "career," or if you want to know how to improve your yeast breads, the following instructions cover everything you need to know.

INGREDIENTS

Really good bread begins with good ingredients. The amounts and flavorings in different breads vary, but the basic ways of mixing them are the same.

Yeast

Active yeast in compressed or dry form is a living plant especially suited to breadmaking. It is responsible for the fermentation action which produces the light, porous grain and unusual texture of baked yeast products. One of the most important functions of yeast is that during the fermentation process carbon dioxide gas is formed which causes yeast doughs and yeast batters to rise. This process results in light porous baked products and is partly responsible for their delicious flavor and aroma.

There is also another type of yeast which is dry but inactive, sometimes called primary grown or brewers' yeast. It is used as a source of protein and vitamin B complex factors in pharmaceuticals, animal and special dietary foods. But it will not raise bread.

Dry Yeast: For those who bake at home, active dry yeast is fast replacing compressed yeast, long sold in foil-wrapped cakes. Active dry yeast in airtight, moisture-proof packages stays fresh for many months on any cool shelf and gives uniformly fine results until the expiration date on package.

Active dry yeast can be used in place of compressed yeast in any recipe when dissolving directions are followed. One package or 1 scant tablespoon of dry yeast is equivalent to 1 cake (3/5 ounce) of compressed yeast.

No-Dissolve Dry Yeast

No-dissolve and instant blend yeasts can be used according to manufacturers' general directions (blending undissolved yeast with flour) or can be used in the traditional way (dissolving yeast in warm water). We have provided recipes following the traditional and the more recently developed no-dissolve methods.

Compressed Yeast: Perishable compressed yeast cakes must be kept in the refrigerator—and for not longer than a week or two. Compressed yeast can be frozen but must be defrosted at room temperature and used immediately. To determine whether compressed yeast is usable, crumble it between the fingers. If it crumbles easily, even though there is slight browning at the edges due to drying, it is still good.

Compressed yeast comes in 3/5-ounce, 1-ounce, and 2-ounce cakes.

Research shows that in dissolving yeast, the best results are obtained when the water temperature is 95°F. to 105°F. with the ideal temperature near 95°F. for compressed yeast and near 105°F. for active dry yeast. In using active dry or compressed yeast, too much heat can kill the action of the yeast. Not enough heat, however, can retard its action.

For best results, dissolve active dry yeast in warm, not hot, water (105°F. to 115°F.), compressed yeast in lukewarm water (85°F. to 95°F.).

Flour

Wheat flour is used for breadmaking because it contains a particular protein called gluten which has unique physical properties. The gluten stretches to form an elastic framework capable of holding the bubbles of gas produced by the yeast. Without gluten, you cannot make satisfactory yeast-raised breads. The amount and quality of gluten vary with different flours. The variety of wheat, where grown, and the milling process all influence the character of the flour and the amount and kind of gluten which in turn influence the volume and texture of the yeast-raised products. Yeast recipes usually specify approximate instead of exact amounts of flour and do not indicate an exact number of minutes for kneading the dough or beating the batter. The amount of flour required and the time and manipulation necessary are determined by the character of the flour, particularly its absorptive property, amount and quality of gluten. For best results, follow recipe directions. But also learn to recognize good consistency in a mixture and proper kneading in a dough.

The flour used for breadmaking in the home is enriched all-purpose flour—sometimes called family flour. Other types of flour such as cake flour and self-rising flour are sometimes used but do not produce the same results. Rolled oats, bran, corn meal, and rye flour are sometimes used in combination with all-purpose wheat flour to make special breads and rolls.

Liquid

Milk and water are the liquids ordinarily used in making yeast breads. Occasionally other liquids such as fruit juices are added for special flavor. The milk may be whole, evaporated, or dry. When using whole milk to make yeast breads and rolls, it should be scalded to obtain best grain and texture. Whatever the liquid, it should be lukewarm when mixed with the dissolved yeast because too much heat can make the yeast inactive.

Water is the best and fastest liquid medium for yeast rehydration. So for best results, use only water when dissolving active dry yeast. In a recipe using liquid other than water for dissolving the yeast, substitute 1/4 cup warm, not hot, water for 1/4 cup of the liquid in the recipe. Dissolve dry yeast in the water and then proceed with the recipe.

Bread and rolls made with all water have a wheaty flavor and crisp crust, while those made with milk have a more velvety grain and a creamy white crumb. Milk breads also keep better and make better toast.

Sugar and Salt

Yeast and sugar work together to form the carbon dioxide gas which causes the dough—or batter—to rise. Salt helps control this rate of rise. The right proportion of sugar and salt contributes to flavor of the product, and, in addition, sugar helps give a golden brown color to the crust.

The usual sugar is white granulated, but brown sugar, molasses, honey, and corn syrup are sometimes used depending upon the type of product being made. Salt may be plain or iodized .

Shortening

Some type of fat or oil is included in nearly all yeast-raised products. It conditions the gluten, making a dough or batter that stretches easily as the bubbles of gas expand. Shortening also adds flavor, contributes to a tender crust and an attractive sheen. Hydrogenated shortenings, lard, vegetable oils, fortified margarine, and butter are all suitable shortenings when used in tested recipes specifying these shortenings.

Eggs

Eggs give extra flavor and richness and make the product more nutritious. They also help produce a fine and delicate texture and, like sugar, encourage a golden brown crust. Sometimes, before baking, a beaten-egg mixture is brushed on the surface of the rolls or bread to give them a shiny golden sheen.

Other Ingredients

Spices and herbs, fruits, nuts, and other tasty ingredients are added for flavor, variety, and extra food value.

Utensils for Yeast Breads

Standard household measuring cups and measuring spoons are essential.

Select a bowl big enough to allow room for easy mixing and fermentation, and a wooden mixing spoon that is comfortable to handle.

Ordinarily, a clean towel is used to cover the dough or batter—or the shaped bread or rolls—when they are set to rise. But you can cover them just as efficiently with waxed paper, paper toweling, or even a plate for the bowl rise.

The utensils shown in the photographs throughout this book are good examples to follow. Do try to use pans of the same size called for in the recipes. The sizes given are inside measurements.

BASIC MIXING METHODS

When you combine a yeast mixture, you automatically follow a basic pattern or method. It may be one of several such as the time-saving batter method, the straight-dough method, or the sponge method. The yeast used may be either compressed or active dry. Understanding the various basic ways of combining yeast mixtures makes any yeast recipe easier to follow.

The Batter Method

The Batter Method is a relatively new way to bake with yeast. Because yeast batter breads and rolls are so quick to make, the batter recipes in this book are sure to become favorites. As the name implies, this type of yeast mixture is a batter rather than the usual yeast dough. And not only is it lighter and easier to handle but also requires no kneading or shaping. These quick and easy yeast batters may be quite thin or fairly thick, depending on what you are making; for example, a casserole bread or yeast-raised waffles. But in any case, the yeast batter is merely mixed and then allowed to rise in a bowl or in the baking pan.

The Straight-Dough Method

The Straight-Dough Method is the one with which you may be most familiar. The mixing is done in continuous operation. The time it takes a dough to rise by the Straight-Dough Method is affected by the amount of yeast. More yeast (as specified in recipes) produces an Action-Quick Dough and speeds up the rising time.

The Sponge Method

The Sponge Method is one of the very oldest ways of combining yeast mixtures. The mixing is done in two operations. First a sponge is made by combining the dissolved yeast, some sugar, and part of the flour and liquid, and allowing it to ferment until it is raised, bubbly, and spongelike. The other ingredients are added with the remaining flour to make a dough that can be kneaded.

During the three rising periods, characteristic flavor and special lightness develop.

What About Refrigerator Dough?

If you have wondered about keeping doughs in the refrigerator, the answer is not to refrigerate any dough unless the recipe has been designed for refrigeration.

A refrigerator dough should have sugar and salt in the proportions that will extend the action of the yeast over several days.

A satisfactory refrigerator dough recipe specifies amounts that are carefully worked out according to a tested formula.

Temperature Is Important

Temperature plays an important role in the preparation of any yeast product. Because yeast is a living plant, too much heat can kill the action of the yeast, and not enough heat can slow down the action of the yeast.

For best results, dissolve active dry yeast in warm, not hot water (105°F.) and compressed yeast in lukewarm water (95°F.). To test the temperature of the water, drop a little water on the inside of your wrist. Warm, not hot, water feels comfortably warm. Lukewarm water feels neither warm nor cool.

Before combining any mixture—such as scalded milk mixed with sugar, salt, and shortening—with dissolved yeast, the mixture must be cooled to lukewarm.

STEPS IN MIXING STRAIGHT-DOUGH METHOD

Mixing a yeast dough is a simple step-by-step process that goes along quickly. Few special techniques are involved. Here are the steps for mixing by the Straight-Dough Method. To make bread and rolls by other methods, follow the recipes.

Step 1: Pour milk into saucepan and heat to the scalding point (this is just below boiling or at about 180°F.). Turn off heat. Stir in sugar, salt, and shortening. Let mixture cool to lukewarm to protect the action of the yeast.

Step 2: Measure water into a large mixing bowl. Test for warm, not hot, for active dry yeast; lukewarm for compressed yeast (see above). Sprinkle active dry yeast or crumble compressed yeast into the water. Stir until dissolved.

Step 3: Test the milk mixture to make sure it is lukewarm. When lukewarm, add to dissolved yeast. If the recipe calls for eggs, stir them in.

Step 4: Stir in half of the flour (previously sifted and carefully measured) or the amount called for in the recipe. Beat or mix until smooth.

Step 5: Add the remaining half of the sifted flour. You may need a little less or a little more flour, depending on the characteristics of the flour, to make a yeast dough that has a rough dull appearance and will be a bit sticky to handle.

Step 6: Continue to stir until an irregular ball forms and comes away from the bowl, leaving only a small amount sticking to the sides. The mixed dough is now ready to be turned out on a lightly floured breadboard or cloth.

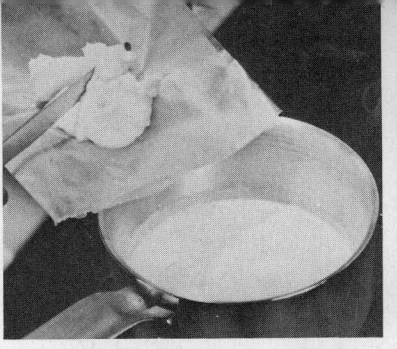

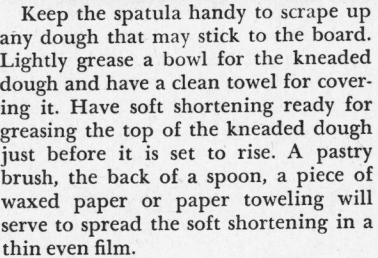

HOW TO KNEAD

Kneading is part of the process of mixing yeast dough during which the rough uneven texture of the dough changes to a smooth elastic ball. You can actually feel this fascinating change take place as you work the responsive dough with your hands.

Kneading helps blend ingredients. It improves flavor. And it develops the gluten which, in turn, develops good grain and texture in the bread and rolls. As you knead, the manipulation of the dough makes the gluten flexible and pliable so that it will stretch when the leavening gas expands, and trap the bubbles of gas produced by the yeast.

Getting Ready to Knead: Before you turn the dough out on the floured board, get out the things you'll need, such as extra flour, shortening, spatula, pastry brush, and a clean towel. You'll get better results and kneading will go along smoothly.

You can knead on a large board, a cloth, or a table top, whichever is most convenient. Measure out a half to a cup of flour to be used on the board as you knead the dough. How much of this flour you will use is determined by the amount the dough requires.

Keep the spatula handy to scrape up any dough that may stick to the board. Lightly grease a bowl for the kneaded dough and have a clean towel for covering it. Have soft shortening ready for greasing the top of the kneaded dough just before it is set to rise. A pastry brush, the back of a spoon, a piece of waxed paper or paper toweling will serve to spread the soft shortening in a thin even film.

Now that you're all set, flour the board very lightly and turn the dough out on the board. With floured hands, flatten the dough very slightly by pressing it firmly, and shape it into a round, rather flat ball. Now you are ready to knead the dough.

As you knead, sprinkle the extra flour little by little onto the board and knead it into the dough. Enough has been added when the dough no longer sticks to your hands or the board. Work the dough firmly. This will make a smooth, springy ball and produce better results than too gentle handling. In fact, some like to give the dough an occasional slap against the board while kneading. Vigorous handling will give you a livelier dough and one that is easier to shape.

Kneading

Fold, push, and turn the dough working in a rocking motion. At first kneading may be a little awkward, but once you get used to the 1-2-3 steps kneading becomes easy and you will develop a rhythm. The rough and slightly sticky dough changes to a smooth ball. The ball of dough becomes more elastic and as you knead you can feel the springiness develop. Generally, a dough is kneaded enough in about 8 to 10 minutes. The time may vary depending on the type of flour used, and the speed and energy with which you knead. The characteristics of the dough—the look and feel—tell you when the dough is kneaded enough.

The Kneaded Dough

Pick the dough up in your hands. Look at it and feel it. The dough itself tells you when it is well kneaded and is a better guide than any set time for kneading. A well kneaded dough looks full and rounded, smooth, satiny, and tightly stretched. By looking at it closely, you can see tiny gas bubbles under the surface. They have many sizes and shapes due to the stretching of the dough during kneading. The surface of the dough appears slightly irregular although it has a satiny sheen.

In your hands, the dough feels springy and elastic. Press it firmly with your fingers and you will feel the springiness gently pushing back. When the dough has been kneaded enough, place it in the greased bowl and spread the top with soft shortening.

THE YEAST AT WORK

The yeast batter or dough rises as a result of the changes produced by the fermentation of the yeast. While the carbon dioxide gas bubbles are forming, the gluten is becoming more pliable allowing the batter or dough to expand. These changes within the batter or dough contribute to the characteristic flavor and texture of yeast products.

Temperature Is Important In Rising

For proper fermentation, yeast batters and doughs should be placed to rise at a temperature of about 85°F. In summer, this means you have to be careful about too much heat, and in winter, find a way to keep the batter or dough warm and cozy. Yeast is a living plant that likes an atmosphere neither too hot nor too cold. Maintain steady warmth during this rising period.

(1) Rising: Always grease the surface of the dough and cover the bowl with a clean towel or cloth—or with waxed paper. Set the bowl in a warm place, free from draft. In hot weather, keep it out of the direct sunlight and away from the extra heat of the kitchen. In cold weather, warm the bowl before putting in the dough. Place it in a warm place—near a range or radiator, but never on top of either. If the room is cold, you can place the dough in an unheated oven with a large pan of hot water on the shelf beneath it, or on the broiler rack with hot water in the broiler pan. Or set the bowl of dough in a deep pan of water just warm enough so your hands feel comfortable in it.

(2) Doubled in Bulk: When the dough looks double its original size, called "doubled in bulk," the proper fermentation changes have taken place. The time varies with temperature, the amount of yeast, kind of flour, and the other ingredients in the recipe. The time given in recipes for double in bulk is approximate, a useful guide to tell you when to test the dough. To test for

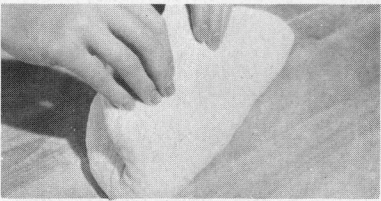
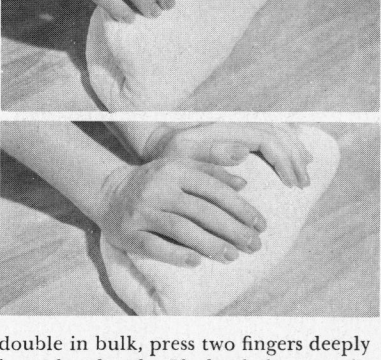

double in bulk, press two fingers deeply into the dough. If the holes remain when the fingers are withdrawn, the dough has probably doubled in bulk. Doughs that are bubbly and that collapse are overfermented. At high altitudes, test for double in bulk well before the time indicated in the recipe has elapsed.

(3) Punch Down: When the dough has doubled in bulk, it is ready for punching down. Punching the dough down after the first rising releases some of the gas in the dough, thus speeding up the rate of fermentation by accelerating yeast activity. It also breaks up the big air pockets into smaller ones, producing a fine-textured product. After you punch it down with your fist, pull the sides into center and turn dough out onto a lightly floured board, pastry cloth, or table top. A resting period makes dough easier to handle.

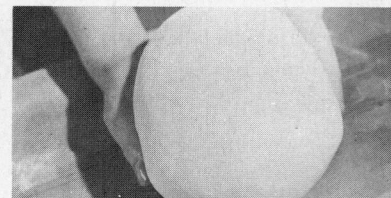

Step 1: With floured hands, flatten the dough very slightly by pressing it into a round, rather flat ball.
Step 2: Fold the dough toward you with a rolling motion, using the fingers of both hands.
Step 3: Push the ball of dough away from you, using the heels of your hands.
Step 4: Turn the dough one-quarter way around on the board. Repeat steps 2, 3, and 4.
Step 5: The dough should look full and rounded, smooth, satiny, and tightly stretched.

(4) Shaping: The dough, ready for shaping, feels warm and is easy to handle. If any flour is needed on the board for shaping, use it in small amounts. Shape the dough as desired, following the recipe-shaping directions. After the dough is shaped, it is ready for a second and final rising in a warm, cozy spot.

(5) Ready to Bake: When the shaped dough is puffy and light, press very gently with your finger tip. If the slight indentation remains, it is ready to bake. Dough shaped for bread is ready to bake when the center of the loaf is slightly higher than the edge of the pan.

Yeast Bread in Loaves

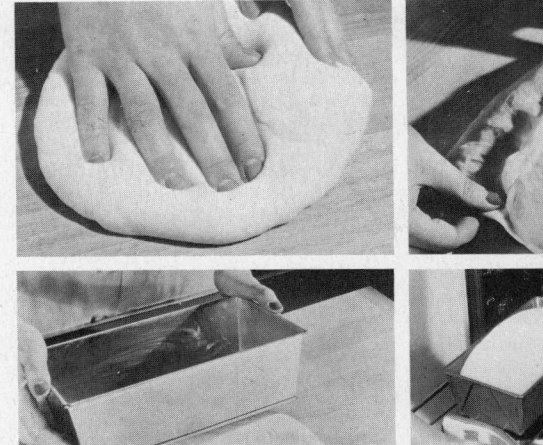

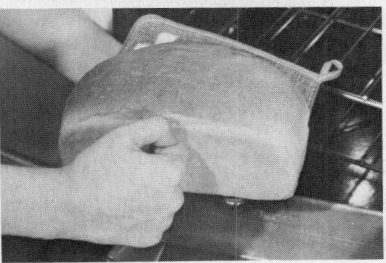
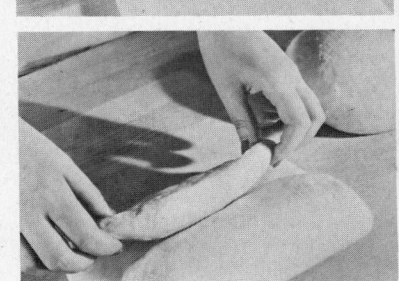

SHAPING AND BAKING THE LOAF

1. Form the dough into a smooth round ball on the pastry cloth or breadboard. Cut it in half with a sharp knife. With the fingers flatten one half of the dough.

2. Press the flattened dough into an oblong about 9 x 7 x 1-inches. The width will be about the same as the length of your bread pan.

3. Fold each end of the oblong to the center overlapping slightly. Press each side down firmly. Working with both hands helps to shape it evenly.

4. To seal the dough into shape, pinch the center fold and ends. Place the loaf, sealed edge down, in a greased pan, 9 x 5 x 3-inches.

5. When baking two loaves, place pans on the center shelf with 2 inches between them to allow heat to circulate. For four loaves use two shelves. Place at right front, left back, left front and right back.

6. Using pot holders, remove a pan from the oven and tip the loaf out of the pan.

Tap the bottom or sides of the loaf for a hollow sound.

If not done, return it to the oven for a few minutes for more baking.

WHITE BREAD
(Straight-Dough Method)

1	cup milk
3	tablespoons sugar
2½	teaspoons salt
6	tablespoons shortening
1	cup warm (not hot) water
1	package or cake yeast, active dry or compressed
3	cups sifted enriched flour

Additional 3 cups sifted enriched flour (about)

Scald milk. Stir in sugar, salt, and shortening. Cool to lukewarm.

Measure warm water into bowl (cool to lukewarm for compressed yeast). Sprinkle or crumble in yeast and stir until dissolved. Stir in lukewarm milk mixture.

Add 3 cups flour and beat until smooth. Stir in additional flour. Turn out on lightly floured board. Knead until smooth and elastic. Place in greased bowl; brush with shortening.

Cover. Let rise in warm place, free from draft, until doubled in bulk, about 1 hour. Punch down, turn out on board.

Divide in half, let rest 15 to 20 minutes. Shape into loaves. Place in greased bread pans 9 x 5 x 3 inches.

Cover. Let rise in warm place, free from draft, until center is slightly higher than edge of pan, about 1 hour.

Bake in hot oven (400°F.) about 50 minutes. Makes 2 loaves.

For Faster Bread (Action-Quick Dough): Use 2 packages or cakes yeast; bowl rise about 30 minutes, pan rise about 45 minutes.

Note: For 1 loaf use 1 package or cake yeast and ½ of all other ingredients; bowl rise about 30 minutes, pan rise about 45 minutes.

For 4 loaves use double the amount of each ingredient; bowl rise about 1 hour, pan rise about 1 hour.

WHITE BREAD
(Sponge Method)

1½	cups warm (not hot) water
2	tablespoons sugar
1	package or cake yeast, active dry or compressed
2	cups sifted enriched flour
1	cup milk
2	tablespoons sugar
1	tablespoon salt
3	tablespoons shortening

Additional 5 cups sifted enriched flour (about)

To Make Sponge: Measure warm water and 2 tablespoons sugar into bowl. (Cool to lukewarm for compressed yeast.) Sprinkle or crumble in yeast and stir until dissolved. Add flour and beat until smooth.

Cover. Let rise in warm place, free from draft, until light and spongy, about 1 hour.

To Make Bread: Scald milk. Stir in 2 tablespoons sugar, salt, and shortening. Cool to lukewarm.

Stir sponge down. Stir in lukewarm milk mixture. Stir in additional 5 cups flour.

Turn dough out on lightly floured board. Knead until smooth and elastic. Place in greased bowl; brush with shortening.

Cover. Let rise in warm place, free from draft, until doubled in bulk, about 45 minutes.

Punch down and turn out on lightly floured board.

Divide in half, let rest 15 to 20 minutes.

Shape into loaves. Place in greased bread pans 9 x 5 x 3 inches.

Cover. Let rise in warm place, free from draft, until center is slightly higher than edge of pan, about 1 hour.

Bake in hot oven (400°F.) about 50 minutes. Makes 2 loaves.

WHOLE WHEAT BREAD
(Straight-Dough Method)

- ¾ cup milk
- 3 tablespoons sugar
- 4 teaspoons salt
- ⅓ cup shortening
- ⅓ cup molasses
- 1½ cups warm (not hot) water
- 2 packages or cakes yeast, active dry or compressed
- 4½ cups whole wheat flour
- 2 cups sifted enriched flour

Scald milk. Stir in sugar, salt, shortening, and molasses. Cool to lukewarm.

Measure into bowl 1½ cups warm water (cool to lukewarm for compressed yeast). Sprinkle or crumble in yeast and stir until dissolved. Stir in lukewarm milk mixture.

Add ½ mixture of whole wheat flour and enriched flour. Beat until smooth. Stir in remaining flour mixture. Turn dough out on lightly floured board. Knead until smooth and elastic. Place in greased bowl; brush top with soft shortening.

Cover. Let rise in warm place, free from draft, until doubled in bulk, about 1 hour and 15 minutes.

Punch down and turn out on lightly floured board. Divide in half; shape into loaves. Place in greased bread pans 9 x 5 x 3 inches.

Cover. Let rise in warm place, free from draft, until center is slightly higher than edge of pan, about 1 hour.

Bake in hot oven (400°F.) about 50 minutes. Makes 2 loaves.

100% WHOLE WHEAT BREAD
(No-Dissolve Method)

- 8¾ to 9¾ cups unsifted whole wheat flour
- 4 teaspoons salt
- 2 packages active dry yeast
- 1½ cups milk
- 1½ cups water
- ½ cup honey
- 6 tablespoons (¾ stick) margarine

In a large bowl thoroughly mix 3 cups flour, salt, and undissolved active dry yeast.

Combine milk, water, honey, and margarine in a saucepan. Heat over low heat until liquids are warm. (Margarine does not need to melt.) Gradually add to dry ingredients and beat 2 minutes at medium speed of electric mixer, scraping bowl occasionally. Add 1 cup flour, or enough flour to make a thick batter. Beat at high speed 2 minutes, scraping bowl occasionally. Stir in enough additional flour to make a soft dough. Turn out onto lightly floured board; cover dough with bowl and let rest for 10 minutes. Then knead until smooth and elastic, about 8 to 10 minutes.

Place in greased bowl, turning to grease top. Cover; let rise in warm place, free from draft, until doubled in bulk, about 50 minutes.

Punch dough down; turn out onto lightly floured board. Divide dough in half; shape each half into a loaf. Place in 2 greased 8½ x 4½ x 2½-inch loaf pans. Cover; let rise in warm place, free from draft, until doubled in bulk, about 50 minutes.

Bake in moderate oven (375°F.) about 35 to 40 minutes, or until done. Remove from pans and cool on wire racks. Makes 2 loaves.

NO-KNEAD WHITE BREAD
(Master Recipe)

- 1½ cups scalded milk
- ½ cup shortening
- ¼ cup sugar
- 2 tablespoons salt
- 1½ cups water
- 3 cakes compressed yeast
- 3 eggs
- 9 cups sifted enriched flour

Combine milk, shortening, sugar, and salt. Cool to lukewarm by adding 1½ cups water.

Add yeast and mix well. Blend in eggs.

Add flour slowly. Mix until dough is well blended.

Place in large, greased bowl and cover if the dough is to be chilled.

Shape into 3 loaves on well-floured board. Place in greased pans, 9 x 4 x 3-inches, and cover.

Let rise in warm place until doubled in bulk, about 2 hours for chilled dough and 1 hour for unchilled dough.

Bake in moderate oven (375°F.) 1 hour. Makes 3 loaves.

Variations:

Cheese Bread: Blend in 2 cups grated cheese when flour is added.

Cinnamon Loaves: Roll ⅓ the dough into 16 x 8 inch rectangle. Sprinkle with ¼ cup sugar and 1 teaspoon cinnamon. Roll as for jelly roll, starting with 8-inch edge and sealing edges. Place in greased pan.

Use remaining dough plain or make 2 more cinnamon loaves from it.

Nut Bread: Blend in 1 cup chopped nuts before flour is added.

WHITE BREAD
(No-Dissolve Method)

- 5½ to 6½ cups unsifted all-purpose flour
- 3 tablespoons sugar
- 2 teaspoons salt
- 1 package active dry yeast
- 1½ cups water
- ½ cup milk
- 3 tablespoons margarine

In a large bowl thoroughly mix 2 cups flour, sugar, salt, and undissolved active dry yeast.

Combine water, milk, and margarine in a saucepan. Heat over low heat until liquids are warm. (Margarine does not need to melt.) Gradually add to dry ingredients and beat 2 minutes at medium speed of electric mixer, scraping bowl occasionally. Add ¾ cup flour, or enough flour to make a thick batter. Beat at high speed 2 minutes, scraping bowl occasionally. Stir in enough additional flour to make a soft dough. Turn out onto lightly floured board; knead until smooth and elastic, about 8 to 10 minutes. Place in greased bowl, turning to grease top. Cover; let rise in warm place, free from draft, until doubled in bulk, about 1 hour.

Punch dough down; turn out onto lightly floured board. Cover; let rest 15 minutes. Divide dough in half and shape into loaves. Place in 2 greased 8½ x 4½ x 2½-inch loaf pans. Cover; let rise in warm place, free from draft, until doubled in bulk, about 1 hour.

Bake in hot oven (400°F.) about 25 to 30 minutes, or until done. Remove from pans and cool on wire racks. Makes 2 loaves.

ONE BOWL ANADAMA BREAD
(No-Dissolve Method)

- 5½ to 6½ cups unsifted all-purpose flour
- 2½ teaspoons salt
- 1 cup yellow corn meal
- 2 packages active dry yeast
- ¼ cup (½ stick) softened margarine
- 2 cups very hot tap water
- ½ cup molasses (at room temperature)

In a large bowl thoroughly mix 2½ cups flour, salt, corn meal, and undissolved active dry yeast. Add softened margarine.

Gradually add very hot tap water and molasses to dry ingredients and beat 2 minutes at medium speed of electric mixer, scraping bowl occasionally. Add ½ cup flour, or enough flour to make a thick batter. Beat at high speed 2 minutes, scraping bowl occasionally. Stir in enough additional flour to make a soft dough. Turn out onto lightly floured board; knead until smooth and elastic, about 8 to 10 minutes. Place in greased bowl, turning to grease top. Cover; let rise in warm place, free from draft, until doubled in bulk, about 1 hour.

Punch dough down; turn out onto lightly floured board. Divide dough in half and shape into loaves. Place in 2 greased 8½ x 4½ x 2½-inch loaf pans. Cover; let rise in warm place, free from draft, until doubled in bulk, about 45 minutes. Bake in a moderate oven (375°F) about 35 minutes, or until done. Remove from pans and cool on wire racks. Makes 2 loaves.

SALT-RISING BREAD

A type of bread leavened by micro-organisms which have a yeast-like effect and produce a distinctive flavor.

1   cup whole milk
2   tablespoons sugar
1½ teaspoons salt
⅓   cup white corn meal
1   cup lukewarm water
4¼ cups sifted enriched flour
2   tablespoons melted shortening

Scald the milk, remove from the heat, and stir in 1 tablespoon of the sugar, the salt, and the corn meal. Mix thoroughly and place the mixture in a large fruit jar or pitcher.

Cover the container and place it in a pan of water which is hot to the hand (120°F.).

Allow it to stand in a warm place for 7 or 8 hours, or overnight, or until it has fermented.

Make a soft sponge by adding to the fermented mixture the water, 2 cups of the flour and the remaining sugar.

Beat thoroughly, using an electric mixer if available.

Place the sponge in the hot-water bath (120°F.) and allow it to rise until it is very light and full of bubbles.

Turn the sponge into a large, warm mixing bowl and gradually stir in the remaining flour, or enough to make a fairly stiff dough which does not stick to the hands and can be kneaded. Knead for 10 minutes.

Divide the dough in half, shape into loaves, and place in generously greased bread pans.

Brush the loaves with melted shortening; cover the loaves with a light, clean towel, and allow them to rise in a warm place until the dough is twice its original size.

Bake in hot oven (400°F.) for 10 minutes; reduce oven temperature to (350°F.) and bake for another 30 minutes. Makes 2 loaves.

Note: Salt rising bread has a disagreeable odor while it is rising and baking. This odor is diffused in the baking. It is never as light as other breads, but is close-grained and has a distinctive flavor. It dries out quickly, but it makes excellent toast.

SWEDISH LIMPE

Sometimes spelled limpa, this is a famous cake-like bread.

2   cups water
½   cup brown sugar
2   teaspoons caraway seed
1   tablespoon shortening
1   teaspoon chopped orange peel or
      1 scant teaspoon anise seed

½   cake compressed yeast
3   cups sifted enriched flour (about)
1   teaspoon salt
About 2 cups rye flour

Boil together water, sugar, caraway seed, shortening, and orange peel (or anise seed) for 3 minutes. Let mixture become lukewarm.

Add yeast. Stir thoroughly, gradually adding sufficient white flour to make a soft dough.

Place dough in a warm place and let rise for 1½ hours. Then add salt and enough rye flour to make a stiff dough. Let rise again for 2 hours.

Knead slightly and shape into loaf. Put into greased loaf pan, 9 x 5 x 3-inches. Let rise again for half an hour.

Bake in moderate oven (350°F.) for 1 hour. Makes 1 loaf.

RYE BREAD
(No-Dissolve Method)

2½ cups unsifted rye flour
2½ cups unsifted white flour
      (about)
1   tablespoon sugar
1   tablespoon salt
1   tablespoon caraway seeds
      (optional)
1   package active dry yeast
1   cup milk
¾   cup water
2   tablespoons honey
1   tablespoon margarine
¼   cup corn meal
1   egg white
2   tablespoons water

Combine flours; in a large bowl thoroughly mix 1⅔ cups flour mixture, sugar, salt, caraway seeds, and undissolved active dry yeast.

Combine milk, ¾ cup water, honey, and margarine in a saucepan. Heat over low heat until liquids are warm. (Margarine does not need to melt.) Gradually add to dry ingredients and beat 2 minutes at medium speed of electric mixer, scraping bowl occasionally. Add 1 cup flour mixture, or enough flour mixture to make a thick batter. Beat at high speed 2 minutes, scraping bowl occasionally. Stir in enough flour mixture to make a soft dough. (If necessary, add additional white flour to obtain desired dough.)

Turn dough out onto lightly floured board; knead until smooth and elastic, about 8 to 10 minutes. Place in greased bowl, turning to grease top. Cover; let rise in warm place, free from draft, until doubled in bulk, about 1 hour.

Punch dough down; turn out onto lightly floured board. Divide in half; form each piece into a smooth ball. Cover; let rest 10 minutes. Flatten each piece slightly. Roll lightly on board to form tapered ends. Sprinkle 2 greased

baking sheets with corn meal. Place breads on baking sheets. Combine egg white and 2 tablespoons water; brush breads. Let rise, uncovered, in warm place, free from draft, 35 minutes.

Bake in hot oven (400°F.) about 25 minutes, or until done. Remove from baking sheets and cool on wire racks. Makes 2 loaves.

CHEESE POTATO BREAD
(Italian)

1   cake compressed or 1 package dry
      yeast
½   cup scalded milk or ¼ cup luke-
      warm water and ¼ cup
      scalded milk
3   cups sifted enriched flour
1   teaspoon sugar
1   teaspoon salt
⅔   cup riced or mashed potatoes
⅓   cup melted butter or margarine
3   ounces (about 1 cup) shredded
      Gruyère cheese or other firm
      cheese
2   unbeaten eggs

Soften compressed yeast in ½ cup scalded milk, cooled to lukewarm. If dry yeast is used, dissolve in ¼ cup lukewarm water as directed on package; decrease amount of scalded milk to ¼ cup. Let stand 5 minutes.

Sift together flour, sugar, and salt. Combine potatoes, melted butter or margarine, cheese, and eggs in large bowl. Beat until well combined. Blend in yeast-milk mixture and dry ingredients; mix thoroughly.

Knead on well floured board until smooth and satiny, 5 to 8 minutes. Place in greased bowl and cover. Let rise in warm place (85° to 90°F.) until doubled in bulk, about 1 hour.

Punch down dough by plunging fist in center. Knead gently on floured board about 2 minutes. Shape into long roll and fit into well-greased 9-inch ring mold. Pinch ends together to seal. Let rise in warm place until light, about 30 minutes.

Bake in moderate oven (375°F.) 25 to 35 minutes. Serve warm. Makes 1 9-inch bread ring.

Cheese Potato Bread

ONE BOWL WHEAT GERM CASSEROLE BREAD
(No-Dissolve Method)

2¾ to 3¼ cups unsifted
    all-purpose flour
2 teaspoons salt
½ cup wheat germ
2 packages active dry yeast
2 tablespoons softened margarine
1⅓ cups very hot tap water
2 tablespoons molasses (at room
    temperature)

In a large bowl thoroughly mix 1 cup flour, salt, wheat germ, and undissolved active dry yeast. Add softened margarine.

Gradually add very hot tap water and molasses to dry ingredients and beat 2 minutes at medium speed of electric mixer, scraping bowl occasionally. Add ½ cup flour, or enough flour to make a thick batter. Beat at high speed 2 minutes, scraping bowl occasionally. Stir in enough additional flour to make a stiff batter. Cover; let rise in warm place, free from draft, until doubled in bulk, about 45 minutes.

Stir batter down. Beat vigorously, about ½ minute. Turn into a greased 1½-quart casserole. Bake in moderate oven (375°F.) about 45 minutes, or until done. Remove from casserole and cool on wire rack. Makes 1 loaf.

IRISH FRECKLE BREAD
(No-Dissolve Method)

4¾ to 5¾ cups unsifted
    all-purpose flour
½ cup sugar
1 teaspoon salt
2 packages active dry yeast
1 cup potato water or water
½ cup (1 stick) margarine
2 eggs (at room temperature)
¼ cup mashed potatoes (at room
    temperature)
1 cup seedless raisins

In a large bowl thoroughly mix 1½ cups flour, sugar, salt, and undissolved active dry yeast.

Combine potato water or water and margarine in a saucepan. Heat over low heat until liquid is warm. (Margarine does not need to melt.) Gradually add to dry ingredients and beat 2 minutes at medium speed of electric mixer, scraping bowl occasionally.

Add eggs, potatoes, and ½ cup flour, or enough flour to make a thick batter. Beat at high speed for 2 minutes, scraping bowl occasionally.

Stir in raisins and enough additional flour to make a soft dough. Turn out onto lightly floured board; knead until smooth and elastic, about 8 to 10 minutes.

Place in greased bowl, turning to grease top. Cover; let rise in warm place, free from draft, until doubled in bulk, about 1 hour and 15 minutes.*

Punch dough down; turn out onto lightly floured board. Divide dough

into 4 equal pieces. Shape each piece into a slender loaf, about 8½ inches long.

Put 2 loaves, side by side, in each of 2 greased 8½ x 4½ x 2½-inch loaf pans. Cover; let rise in warm place, free from draft, until doubled in bulk, about 1 hour.

Bake in moderate oven (350°F.) about 35 minutes, or until done. Remove from pans and cool on wire racks. Makes 2 loaves.

*Note: If plain water is used, rising time will be about 1 hour 45 minutes.

ONE BOWL LOW CHOLESTEROL BREAD
(No-Dissolve Method)

7 to 8 cups unsifted
    all-purpose flour
2 tablespoons sugar
2 teaspoons salt
1 package active dry yeast
1 tablespoon softened margarine
2½ cups very hot tap water

In a large bowl thoroughly mix 2½ cups flour, sugar, salt, and undissolved active dry yeast. Add softened margarine.

Gradually add very hot tap water to dry ingredients and beat 2 minutes at medium speed of electric mixer, scraping bowl occasionally. Add ¾ cup flour, or enough flour to make a thick batter. Beat at high speed 2 minutes, scraping bowl occasionally. Stir in enough additional flour to make a soft dough. Turn out onto lightly floured board; knead until smooth and elastic, about 8 to 10 minutes. Place in greased bowl, turning to grease top. Cover; let rise in warm place, free from draft, until doubled in bulk, about 1 hour.

Punch dough down; turn out onto lightly floured board. Divide dough in half; shape each half into a loaf. Place in 2 greased 9 x 5 x 3-inch loaf pans. Cover; let rise in warm place, free from draft, until doubled in bulk, about 1 hour.

Bake in hot oven (400°F.) about 40 to 45 minutes, or until done. Remove from pans and cool on wire racks. Makes 2 loaves.

GLUTEN BREAD

Gluten is a nutritious substance found in wheat flour; the component that gives dough its elasticity. When isolated it is gray and sticky. Gluten flour is low in starch and high in gluten.

1 cup milk
1 tablespoon sugar
1 teaspoon salt
1 cake compressed yeast
1 cup lukewarm water
4 cups gluten flour
1 tablespoon melted shortening

Scald milk. Add sugar and salt. Cool to lukewarm. Dissolve yeast in luke-

warm water and add to lukewarm milk.

Add half the flour and beat until smooth. Add melted shortening and remaining flour, or enough to make easily handled dough.

Knead dough quickly and lightly until smooth and elastic. Place dough in greased bowl. Cover and set in warm place, free from draft. Let rise until doubled in bulk, about 1¾ hours.

When light, divide into 2 equal portions and shape into loaves. Place in greased bread pans. Cover and let rise until doubled in bulk, about 1 hour.

Bake in hot oven (400°F.) 45 minutes. Makes 2 loaves.

PUMPERNICKEL BREAD (SWEET)

German name for a coarse-textured, black or dark-brown bread, also called schwarzbrod, or black bread.

1½ cups cold water
¾ cup corn meal
1½ cups boiling water
1½ tablespoons salt
1 tablespoon sugar
2 tablespoons shortening
1 tablespoon caraway seed
2 cups cooled mashed potato
1 cake compressed yeast
¼ cup lukewarm water
6 cups rye meal or rye flour
About 2 cups whole wheat flour

Stir cold water into corn meal. Add to boiling water and cook, stirring constantly until thick. Add salt, sugar, shortening, and caraway seed. Let stand until lukewarm.

Add potato and the yeast which has been softened in the lukewarm water. Add rye meal or rye flour and enough whole wheat flour to form a soft dough. Stir in at first with a spoon and then with the hand.

Turn out on a lightly floured board. Knead until it is smooth and elastic and does not stick to board. Place in greased bowl. Grease surface and let stand in a warm place (85°F.) until double in bulk.

Divide dough into 3 portions; form into balls. Let rest a few minutes. Roll 1 ball at a time, about twice the length and twice the breadth of loaf pans.

Fold in both ends so they overlap at center. Press sides to seal and then fold in the pressed sides so they overlap at center. Roll the loaf under the hands until it fits the pan.

Place in greased pan with seam-side of loaf underneath. Grease surface; let rise until double in bulk. Bake in moderate oven (375°F.) about 1 hour. Makes 3 loaves.

Sour Dough Pumpernickel: Before shaping loaves, take out 1 cup of dough and place it in a jar. Cover and set aside to ferment. When baking fresh batch of bread, stir down sour dough and substitute it for yeast in above recipe.

BUTTERMILK BREAD
(No-Dissolve Method)

5½ to 6½ cups unsifted
    all-purpose flour
3 tablespoons sugar
2½ teaspoons salt
¼ teaspoon baking soda
1 package active dry yeast
1 cup buttermilk
1 cup water
⅓ cup margarine

In a large bowl thoroughly mix 2 cups flour, sugar, salt, baking soda, and undissolved active dry yeast.

Combine buttermilk, water, and margarine in a saucepan. Heat over low heat until liquids are warm. (Margarine does not need to melt.) Mixture will appear curdled. Gradually add to dry ingredients and beat 2 minutes at medium speed of electric mixer, scraping bowl occasionally. Add 1 cup flour, or enough flour to make a thick batter. Beat at high speed 2 minutes, scraping bowl occasionally. Stir in enough flour to make a soft dough.

Turn out onto lightly floured board; knead until smooth and elastic, about 8 to 10 minutes. Place in greased bowl, turning to grease top. Cover; let rise in warm place, free from draft, until doubled in bulk, about 1 hour.

Punch dough down; turn out onto lightly floured board. Divide dough in half. Shape each half into a loaf. Place in 2 greased 8½ x 4½ x 2½-inch loaf pans. Cover; let rise in warm place, free from draft, until doubled in bulk, about 1 hour.

Bake in a moderate oven (375°F.) about 35 minutes, or until done. Remove from pans and cool on wire rack. Makes 2 loaves.

ONE BOWL WHITE SALT-FREE BREAD
(No-Dissolve Method)

2¾ to 3¼ cups unsifted
    all-purpose flour
1 tablespoon sugar
1 package active dry yeast
1 cup very hot tap water
2 tablespoons peanut oil

In a large bowl thoroughly mix 1 cup flour, sugar, and undissolved active dry yeast.

Gradually add very hot tap water and peanut oil to dry ingredients and beat 2 minutes at medium speed of electric mixer, scraping bowl occasionally. Add ¼ cup flour, or enough flour to make a thick batter. Beat at high speed 2 minutes, scraping bowl occasionally. Stir in enough additional flour to make a soft dough.

Turn out onto lightly floured board; knead until smooth and elastic, about 8 to 10 minutes. Place in greased bowl,

turning to grease top. Cover; let rise in warm place, free from draft, until doubled in bulk, about 45 minutes.

Punch down dough; turn out onto lightly floured board. Shape into a loaf and place in greased 9 x 5 x 3-inch loaf pan. Cover; let rise in warm place, free from draft, until doubled in bulk, about 45 minutes.

Bake in hot oven (400°F.) about 30 minutes, or until done. Remove from pan and cool on wire rack. Makes 1 loaf.

CASSEROLE WHITE BREAD
(Batter Method)

1 cup milk
3 tablespoons sugar
1 tablespoon salt
1½ tablespoons shortening
1 cup warm (not hot) water
2 packages or cakes yeast, active
    dry or compressed
4½ cups sifted enriched flour

Scald 1 cup milk. Stir in sugar, salt, and shortening. Cool to lukewarm.

Measure into bowl 1 cup warm water (cool to lukewarm for compressed yeast). Sprinkle or crumble in yeast. Stir until dissolved. Stir in lukewarm milk mixture.

Add flour and stir until well blended, about 2 minutes. Cover. Let rise in warm place, free from draft, about 40 minutes or until more than doubled in bulk.

Stir batter down. Beat vigorously, about ½ minute. Turn into greased 1½ quart casserole. A square pan 8 x 8 x 2 inches or an 8 inch tube pan may also be used.

Bake uncovered in moderate oven (375°F.) about 1 hour. Makes 1 loaf.

SOUR DOUGH BREAD
(No-Dissolve Method)

Starter:
1¾ cups unsifted all-purpose flour
1 tablespoon sugar
1 tablespoon salt
1 package active dry yeast
2½ cups warm water

Dough:
5 to 6 cups unsifted all-purpose
    flour
3 tablespoons sugar
1 teaspoon salt
1 package active dry yeast
1 cup milk
2 tablespoons margarine
1½ cups starter

To make starter, combine the flour, sugar, salt, and undissolved active dry yeast in a large bowl. Gradually add warm water to dry ingredients and beat 2 minutes at medium speed of electric mixer, scraping the bowl occasionally. Cover; let stand at room temperature (78°-80°F.) 4 days. Stir down daily.

To make dough, combine 1 cup flour,

sugar, salt, and undissolved active dry yeast in a large bowl.

Combine milk and margarine in a saucepan. Heat over low heat until liquid is warm. (Margarine does not need to melt.) Gradually add to dry ingredients and beat 2 minutes at medium speed of electric mixer, scraping bowl occasionally.

Add 1½ cups starter and 1 cup flour, or enough flour to make a thick batter. Beat at high speed 2 minutes, scraping bowl occasionally. Stir in enough additional flour to make a soft dough. Turn out onto lightly floured board; knead until smooth and elastic, about 8 to 10 minutes. Place in greased bowl, turning to grease top. Cover; let rise in warm place, free from draft, until doubled in bulk, about 1 hour.

Punch dough down; turn out onto lightly floured board. Let rest 15 minutes. Divide dough in half. Shape each half into a loaf and place in greased 9 x 5 x 3-inch loaf pan. Cover; let rise in warm place, free from draft, until doubled in bulk, about 1 hour.

Bake in hot oven (400°F.) about 30 minutes, or until done. Remove from pans and cool on wire racks. Makes 2 loaves.

To Reuse Starter: Add 1½ cups lukewarm water, ¾ cup unsifted all-purpose flour, and 1½ teaspoons sugar to unused starter. Beat for 1 minute at medium speed of electric mixer. Cover and let stand until ready to make bread again. Stir down daily.

RAISIN CASSEROLE BREAD
(Batter Method)

⅔ cup hot water
½ cup sugar
1½ teaspoons salt
¼ cup shortening
½ cup warm (not hot) water
2 packages or cakes yeast, active
    dry or compressed
1 egg, beaten
3¼ cups sifted enriched flour
1 cup seedless raisins

Mix together water, sugar, salt and shortening. Cool to lukewarm.

Measure into bowl ½ cup warm water (cool to lukewarm for compressed yeast). Sprinkle or crumble in yeast. Stir until dissolved. Stir in lukewarm water mixture.

Add beaten egg, flour, and raisins. Stir until well blended, about 2 minutes.

Let rise in warm place, free from draft, about 50 minutes or until more than doubled in bulk. Stir down. Beat vigorously about ½ minute. Turn into greased 1½ quart casserole.

Bake uncovered in hot oven (400°F.) about 45 minutes. Makes 1 loaf.

HIGH PROTEIN BREAD
(Rich Flour Formula Health Bread)

1   package dry or 1 cake compressed yeast
1/4 cup warm water (lukewarm for compressed yeast)
5   cups sifted enriched flour
1   tablespoon salt
1/4 cup sugar
1/3 cup full-fat soy flour
1/2 cup nonfat dry milk solids
1/4 cup wheat germ
1   tablespoon melted shortening
1¾ cups water

Dissolve yeast in 1/4 cup water. Combine dry ingredients in mixing bowl. Add dissolved yeast, melted shortening, and water, mixing to blend well.

Knead dough until smooth and satiny, then place in well greased bowl. Cover and allow to rise in warm place for about 1½ hours.

Punch down by plunging fist in center of dough, then fold over edges of dough and turn whole mass upside down. Cover and allow to rise again for 15 to 20 minutes.

Shape into 2 loaves and place in greased pans. Cover and allow to stand about 55 to 60 minutes in warm place or until dough rises and fills pans.

Bake in hot oven (400°F.) 45 minutes. Makes 2 loaves.

SALLY LUNN
(No-Dissolve Method)

3½ to 4 cups unsifted flour
1/3 cup sugar
1   teaspoon salt
1   package active dry yeast
1/2 cup milk
1/2 cup water
1/2 cup (1 stick) margarine
3   eggs (at room temperature)

In a large bowl thoroughly mix 1¼ cups flour, sugar, salt, and undissolved active dry yeast.

Combine milk, water, and margarine in a saucepan. Heat over low heat until liquids are warm. (Margarine does not need to melt.) Gradually add to dry ingredients and beat 2 minutes at medium speed of electric mixer, scraping bowl occasionally. Add eggs and 1 cup flour, or enough flour to make a thick batter. Beat at high speed 2 minutes, scraping bowl occasionally. Stir in enough additional flour to make a stiff batter. Cover; let rise in warm place, free from draft, until doubled in bulk, about 1 hour.

Stir batter down and beat well, about ½ minute. Turn into a well-greased and floured 9-inch tube pan. Cover; let rise in warm place, free from draft, until doubled in bulk, about 1 hour.

Bake in slow oven (325°F.) about 45 to 50 minutes, or until done. Remove from pan and cool on wire rack. Best when served warm. Makes 1 bread.

CHALLAH OR HALLAH

A Yiddish term for twisted loaves of yeast-raised white bread prepared originally for the Jewish Sabbath. The dough is usually braided, but a variety of forms are made for the various holidays of the year.

2   cups hot water
1   tablespoon salt
1   tablespoon sugar
2   tablespoons vegetable oil
1   cake compressed or 1 package dry granular yeast
1/4 cup lukewarm water (warm for dry yeast)
2   beaten eggs
8   cups sifted enriched flour

Pour 2 cups hot water over salt, sugar, and oil in mixing bowl. When lukewarm, add the yeast which has been dissolved in the 1/4 cup lukewarm water.

Add eggs and flour gradually. Mix and stir, then knead until smooth and elastic. Cover and let rise in a warm place until double in bulk.

Turn half of the dough onto a board and cut into 4 equal parts. Roll each part 1½ inches thick and form 3 into a braid. Fasten the ends well and place in a floured bread pan.

Cut remaining 1/4 into 3 parts and roll each part 1/2 inch thick. Form into a braid and place on top of braid in pan.

Let rise until doubled in bulk. Brush with beaten egg yolk; sprinkle with poppy seed, if desired.

Bake in hot oven (400°F.) 1 hour, then reduce heat to moderate (350°F.) and bake 15 minutes longer. To form a hard crust, let cool in a draft. Makes 2 loaves.

ITALIAN CHRISTMAS BREAD
(Panettone)

2   packages or cakes yeast, active dry or compressed
1   cup warm (not hot) water
1/2 cup butter, melted
2   teaspoons salt
1/2 cup sugar
2   beaten eggs
3   beaten egg yolks
About 5½ cups sifted enriched flour
1   cup thinly sliced citron
1   cup seedless raisins

Soften dry yeast in warm water (cool to lukewarm for compressed yeast).

Mix butter, salt, sugar, eggs, and egg yolks. Add yeast and butter mixtures to 5 cups flour and stir until blended.

Knead on floured board until smooth and no longer sticky, adding more flour as needed. The dough should be soft. Knead in citron and raisins.

Place dough in greased bowl. Grease surface and cover with cloth towel. Let

rise in warm place (80°F.) until doubled in bulk, about 2 hours.

Knead dough again until smooth. Place in greased 3-quart round baking pan. Brush top with melted butter. Cover and let rise until doubled in bulk, about 40 minutes.

With a sharp knife, cut deep cross in top of loaf. Bake in hot oven (425°F.) until surface begins to brown, about 9 minutes. Lower oven temperature to slow (325°F.) and bake until done, about 1 hour longer. Makes 1 large loaf.

BARM BRACK
(No-Dissolve Method)

The Irish are famous for many types of breads—Irish soda bread, gingerbread, and their own special crusty whole wheat bread. One of their most popular loaves is Barm Brack. This bread is filled with candied fruits and acquired its name from "barm" the Gaelic word for yeast.

4½ to 5½ cups unsifted all-purpose flour
1/2 cup sugar
1½ teaspoons salt
1   teaspoon grated lemon peel
3   packages active dry yeast
3/4 cup water
1/2 cup milk
1/4 cup (1/2 stick) margarine
2   eggs (at room temperature)
1¼ cups golden seedless raisins
1/3 cup chopped mixed candied fruits

In a large bowl thoroughly mix 1½ cups flour, sugar, salt, lemon peel, and undissolved active dry yeast.

Combine water, milk, and margarine in saucepan. Heat over low heat until liquids are warm. (Margarine does not need to melt.) Gradually add to dry ingredients and beat 2 minutes at medium speed of electric mixer, scraping bowl occasionally. Add eggs and 3/4 cup flour, or enough flour to make a thick batter. Beat at high speed 2 minutes, scraping the bowl occasionally. Stir in enough additional flour to make a soft dough. Turn out onto lightly floured board; knead until smooth and elastic, about 8 to 10 minutes. Place in greased bowl, turning to grease top. Cover; let rise in warm place, free from draft, until doubled in bulk, about 40 minutes.

Punch dough down; turn out onto lightly floured board. Knead in raisins and candied fruits. Divide in half. Shape into loaves. Place in 2 greased 8½ x 4½ x 2½-inch loaf pans. Cover; let rise in warm place, free from draft, until doubled in bulk, about 50 minutes.

Bake in a moderate oven (375°F.) about 30 to 35 minutes, or until done. Remove from pans and cool on wire racks. Makes 2 loaves.

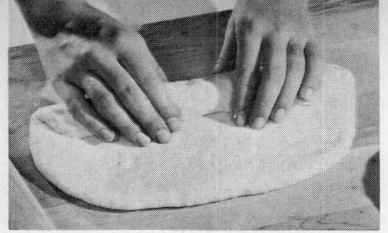

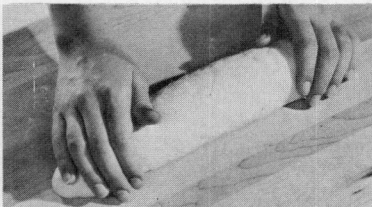

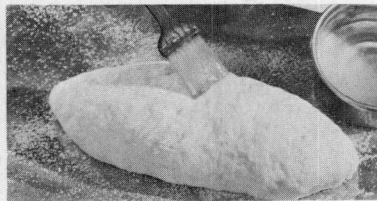

French Bread

FRENCH BREAD

1¼ cups warm, not hot, water (luke-
     warm for compressed yeast)
1   package or cake yeast, active dry
     or compressed
1½ teaspoons salt
1   tablespoon soft shortening
1   tablespoon sugar
3½ cups sifted enriched flour

Measure water into a large mixing
bowl (warm, not hot, water for active
dry yeast; lukewarm water for compressed yeast). Sprinkle or crumble in
yeast. Stir until dissolved.

Add salt, shortening, and sugar. Stir
in flour.

Turn dough out on lightly floured
board. Knead 8 to 10 minutes or until
dough is springy and elastic and does
not stick to the board.

Place in greased bowl and brush top
lightly with melted shortening. Cover
with a cloth. Let rise in a warm place,
free from draft, until doubled in bulk,
about 40 minutes.

Punch dough down. Let rise again
until almost doubled in bulk, about 30
minutes.

Punch down, turn out on floured
board and cut dough into two equal
portions.

Roll each half into an oblong about
8 x 10 inches. Beginning with the wide
side, roll up tightly. Seal edges by
pinching together.

With hands on each end of roll, roll
gently back and forth to lengthen loaf
and taper ends.

Place loaves on a greased baking
sheet sprinkled lightly with yellow corn
meal. Brush loaves with cornstarch
glaze. Let rise, uncovered about 1½
hours.

Brush again with cornstarch glaze.
With a sharp knife, make ¼ inch
slashes in dough at 2-inch intervals.
Bake in hot oven (400°F.) 10 minutes.

Remove from oven, brush again with
cornstarch glaze. Return and bake
about 30 minutes or until golden
brown. Makes 2 loaves.

Cornstarch Glaze: Mix 1 teaspoon
cornstarch with 1 teaspoon cold water.
Combine with ½ cup boiling water.
Cook until smooth. Let cool slightly.

WHITE BATTER BREAD
(No-Dissolve Method)

4 to 4½ cups unsifted all-purpose
        flour
3   tablespoons sugar
1   tablespoon salt
2   packages active dry yeast
1   cup milk
1   cup water
2   tablespoons margarine

In a large bowl thoroughly mix 1½
cups flour, sugar, salt, and undissolved
active dry yeast.

Combine milk, water, and margarine
in a saucepan. Heat over low heat until
liquids are warm. (Margarine does not
need to melt.) Gradually add to dry
ingredients and beat 2 minutes at medium speed of electric mixer, scraping
bowl occasionally. Add 1 cup flour, or
enough flour to make a thick batter.
Beat at high speed 2 minutes, scraping
bowl occasionally. Stir in enough additional flour to make a stiff batter. Beat
until well blended. Cover; let rise in
warm place, free from draft, until doubled in bulk, about 40 minutes.

Stir batter down. Beat vigorously,
about ½ minute. Turn into a greased
9 x 5 x 3-inch loaf pan.

Bake in a moderate oven (375°F.)
about 40 to 50 minutes, or until done.
Remove from pan and cool on wire
racks. Makes 1 large loaf.

Herb Batter Bread: Combine ¼ teaspoon basil leaves, ¼ teaspoon oregano
leaves, and ¼ teaspoon thyme leaves
with the 1½ cups flour, sugar, salt,

and yeast. Then proceed with recipe as
directed. Makes 1 large loaf.

RUSSIAN BLACK BREAD
(No-Dissolve Method)

4   cups unsifted rye flour
3   cups unsifted white flour
1   teaspoon sugar
2   teaspoons salt
2   cups whole bran cereal
2   tablespoons caraway seed,
        crushed
2   teaspoons instant coffee
2   teaspoons onion powder
½   teaspoon fennel seed, crushed
2   packages active dry yeast
2½ cups water
¼   cup vinegar
¼   cup dark molasses
1   square (1 ounce) unsweetened
        chocolate
¼   cup (½ stick) margarine
1   teaspoon cornstarch
½   cup cold water

Combine rye and white flours. In a
large bowl thoroughly mix 2⅓ cups
flour mixture, sugar, salt, cereal, caraway seed, instant coffee, onion powder,
fennel seed, and undissolved active dry
yeast.

Combine 2½ cups cold water, vinegar, molasses, chocolate, and margarine in a saucepan. Heat over low heat
until liquids are warm. (Margarine and
chocolate do not need to melt.) Gradually add to dry ingredients and beat
2 minutes at medium speed of electric
mixer, scraping bowl occasionally. Add
½ cup flour mixture, or enough flour
mixture to make a thick batter. Beat
at high speed 2 minutes, scraping bowl
occasionally. Stir in enough additional
flour mixture to make a soft dough.
Turn out onto lightly floured board.
Cover dough with bowl and let rest 15
minutes. Then knead until smooth and
elastic, about 10 to 15 minutes (dough
may be sticky). Place in greased bowl,
turning to grease top. Cover; let rise in
warm place, free from draft, until doubled in bulk, about 1 hour.

Punch dough down; turn out onto
lightly floured board. Divide dough in
half. Shape each half into a ball, about
5 inches in diameter. Place each ball in
the center of greased 8-inch round cake
pan. Cover; let rise in warm place, free
from draft, until doubled in bulk,
about 1 hour.

Bake in a moderate oven (350°F.)
about 45 to 50 minutes, or until done.

Meanwhile, combine cornstarch and
½ cup cold water. Cook over medium
heat, stirring constantly, until mixture
boils; continue to cook, stirring constantly, 1 minute. As soon as bread is
baked, brush cornstarch mixture over
tops of loaves. Return bread to oven
and bake 2 to 3 minutes, or until glaze
is set. Remove from pans and cool on
wire racks. Makes 2 loaves.

Yeast Rolls

ROLL DOUGH
(Straight-Dough Method)

- 3/4 cup milk
- 1/4 cup sugar
- 2 1/4 teaspoons salt
- 4 1/2 tablespoons shortening
- 3/4 cup warm (not hot) water
- 1 package or cake yeast, active dry or compressed
- 2 1/4 cups sifted enriched flour
- Additional 2 1/4 cups sifted enriched flour (about)

Scald milk. Stir in sugar, salt, and shortening. Cool to lukewarm.

Measure 3/4 cup warm water into bowl (cool to lukewarm for compressed yeast). Sprinkle or crumble in yeast. Stir until dissolved. Stir in lukewarm milk mixture.

Add 2 1/4 cups flour. Beat until smooth. Stir in additional flour.

Turn out on lightly floured board. Knead until smooth and elastic. Place in greased bowl; brush with shortening.

Cover. Let rise in warm place, free from draft, until doubled in bulk, about 1 hour.

Punch down and turn out on lightly floured board.

Proceed according to directions for shapes.

For Faster Roll Dough (Action-Quick Dough): Use 2 packages or cakes yeast; bowl rise about 40 minutes.

WHOLE WHEAT ROLLS
(Batter Method)

- 1 1/4 cups milk
- 1/4 cup sugar
- 2 1/2 teaspoons salt
- 1/4 cup shortening
- 1/4 cup honey*
- 1/4 cup warm (not hot) water
- 2 packages or cakes yeast, active dry or compressed
- 3 1/2 cups whole wheat flour

Scald milk. Stir in sugar, salt, shortening, and honey. Cool to lukewarm.

Measure into bowl 1/4 cup warm water (cool to lukewarm for compressed yeast). Sprinkle or crumble in yeast. Stir until dissolved. Stir in lukewarm milk mixture.

Add flour. Stir until well blended, about 1/2 minute. Cover. Let rise in warm place, free from draft, until doubled in bulk, about 45 minutes.

Stir batter down. Beat vigorously about 1/2 minute. Fill greased muffin pans 2 3/4 x 1 1/4 inches about 3/4 full.

Bake in hot oven (400°F.) about 25 minutes. Makes 12 rolls.

* Corn syrup or molasses may be substituted, if necessary.

REFRIGERATOR ROLL DOUGH
(Straight-Dough Method)

- 3/4 cup milk
- 6 tablespoons sugar
- 1 tablespoon salt
- 5 tablespoons shortening
- 1/2 cup warm (not hot) water
- 2 packages or cakes yeast, active dry or compressed
- 1 egg, beaten
- 2 cups sifted enriched flour
- Additional 2 1/2 cups sifted enriched flour

Scald milk. Stir in sugar, salt, and shortening. Cool to lukewarm.

Measure into bowl 1/2 cup warm water (cool to lukewarm for compressed yeast). Sprinkle or crumble in yeast and stir until dissolved. Stir in lukewarm milk mixture.

Add beaten egg and 2 cups flour. Beat until smooth. Stir in additional 2 1/2 cups flour.

Place dough in greased bowl; brush top with soft shortening. Cover tightly with waxed paper or aluminum foil. Store in refrigerator at least 2 hours or until needed.

To use, punch down and cut off dough needed.

Proceed according to directions for shapes selected.

May be kept 2 to 3 days in refrigerator.

WHOLE WHEAT ROLL DOUGH
(Straight-Dough Method)

- 1 cup milk
- 3 tablespoons molasses
- 2 tablespoons sugar
- 2 1/2 teaspoons salt
- 1/4 cup shortening
- 1/2 cup warm (not hot) water
- 1 package or cake yeast, active dry or compressed
- 2 1/4 cups whole wheat flour
- 2 1/4 cups sifted enriched flour

Scald milk. Stir in molasses, sugar, salt, and shortening. Cool to lukewarm.

Measure warm water into bowl (cool to lukewarm for compressed yeast). Sprinkle or crumble in yeast and stir until dissolved. Stir in lukewarm milk mixture.

Add 1/2 mixture of whole wheat flour and enriched flour. Beat until smooth. Stir in remaining flour mixture.

Turn dough out on lightly floured board. Knead until smooth and elastic. Place in greased bowl; brush top with soft shortening.

Cover. Let rise in warm place, free from draft, until doubled in bulk, about 1 hour and 20 minutes. Punch down and turn out on lightly floured board.

Proceed according to directions for shapes desired.

ONE BOWL DINNER ROLLS
(No-Dissolve Method)

- 2 3/4 to 3 1/4 cups unsifted all-purpose flour
- 1/4 cup sugar
- 1/2 teaspoon salt
- 1 package active dry yeast
- 5 tablespoons softened margarine
- 2/3 cup very hot tap water
- 1 egg (at room temperature)
- Melted margarine

In a large bowl thoroughly mix 3/4 cup flour, sugar, salt, and undissolved active dry yeast. Add softened margarine. Gradually add very hot tap water to dry ingredients and beat 2 minutes at medium speed of electric mixer, scraping bowl occasionally. Add egg and 1/2 cup flour, or enough flour to make a thick batter. Beat at high speed 2 minutes, scraping bowl occasionally. Stir in enough additional flour to make a soft dough.

Turn out onto lightly floured board; knead until smooth and elastic, about 8 to 10 minutes. Place in greased bowl, turning to grease top. Cover; let rise in warm place, free from draft, until doubled in bulk, about 1 hour.

Punch dough down; turn out onto lightly floured board. Proceed according to directions for desired shape. Cover; let rise in warm place, free from draft, until doubled in bulk, about 1 hour.

Carefully brush rolls with melted margarine. Bake in a hot oven (400°F.) about 10 to 15 minutes, or until done. Remove from baking sheets and cool on wire racks. Makes 2 or 3 dozen rolls.

Curlicues: Divide dough into 2 or 3 equal pieces.* Roll out each piece into a 9 x 12-inch oblong. Brush generously with melted margarine. Cut into 12 strips (about 1 inch wide). Hold one end of each strip firmly and wind dough loosely to form coil; tuck end firmly underneath. Place on greased baking sheets, about 2 inches apart.

Pretzels: Divide dough into 2 or 3 equal pieces.* Then divide each piece into 12 pieces. Roll each into a pencil-shaped 16-inch roll. Shape into pretzels and place on greased baking sheets, about 2 inches apart.

*Divide dough into 2 pieces to make family-size rolls or divide into 3 pieces to make smaller dinner rolls.

Parkerhouse Rolls: Divide dough in half. Roll each half into a 1/4-inch thick circle. Cut into rounds with a 2 1/2-inch biscuit cutter. Crease each round with dull edge of knife to one side of center. Brush each round to within 1/4-inch of the edges with melted margarine. Fold larger side over smaller so edges just meet. Pinch well with fingers to seal. Place on greased baking sheets so rolls are almost touching.

CLOVER LEAF ROLLS

Divide Roll Dough in half. Form each half into 9-inch roll. Cut into 9 equal pieces. Form each piece into 3 small balls. Brush sides with melted margarine or butter.

Place 3 balls in each section of greased muffin pans 2¾ x 1¼ inches.

Cover. Let rise in warm place, free from draft, until doubled in bulk. (Whole Wheat, White, Refrigerator Doughs about 1 hour; Action-Quick Dough about 30 minutes.) Brush lightly with melted margarine or butter.

Bake in hot oven at 400°F. (Whole Wheat Rolls about 20 minutes; White Rolls about 15 minutes.) Makes 18 rolls.

Clover Leaf Rolls

HONEY PECAN ROLLS

½ cup pecan halves

While Roll Dough is rising prepare Honey Syrup.

Spread one-half syrup in each of two pans 8 x 8 x 2 inches. Arrange pecan halves in each pan. Divide Roll Dough in half. Form each half into 12-inch roll. Cut into 12 equal pieces. Form into balls. Place in prepared pan about ¼ inch apart. Cover. Let rise in warm place, free from draft, until doubled in bulk, about 1 hour. Bake in hot oven (400°F.) about 25 minutes. Turn out of pans immediately. Makes 24.

Honey Syrup:

⅓ cup dark brown sugar
⅔ cup honey
3 tablespoons margarine or butter, melted

Combine ingredients.

Honey Pecan Rolls

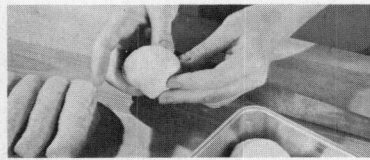

BOWKNOTS

When Roll Dough is ready for shaping, roll dough under hand to ½-inch thickness. Cut in pieces about 6 inches long. Tie in knots. Place on greased baking sheet.

Bowknots

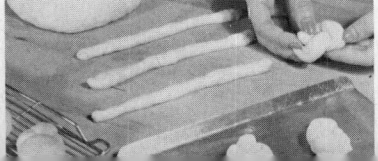

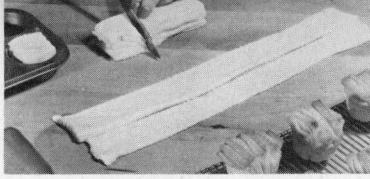

Fan Tans

FAN TANS

Divide Roll Dough into 3 equal pieces. Roll out each piece into an oblong about 11 x 9 inches. Brush lightly with melted margarine or butter.

Cut into 7 equal strips (about 1½ inches wide). Pile strips one on top of other. Cut into 6 equal pieces (about 1½ inches long). Place cut side up in greased muffin pans 2¾ x 1¼ inches.

Cover. Let rise in warm place, free from draft, until doubled in bulk. (Straight-Dough Method about 1 hour; Action-Quick Dough about 30 minutes; Refrigerator Dough about 1 hour.) Brush lightly with melted margarine or butter.

Bake in hot oven (400°F.) about 20 minutes. Makes 18.

Bubble Loaf

BUBBLE LOAF

Divide Roll Dough in half. Form each half into a roll about 12 inches long. Cut each roll into 24 equal pieces. Form into balls.

Place a layer of balls about ½ inch apart in greased bread pan 9 x 5 x 3 inches or 9 inch tube pan. Brush lightly with melted butter or margarine.

Arrange a second layer of balls on top of first.

Cover. Let rise in warm place, free from draft, until top of loaf is slightly higher than edge of pan. (Straight-Dough Method about 1 hour; Action-Quick Dough about 30 minutes; Refrigerator Dough about 1 hour.)

Brush lightly with melted margarine or butter.

Bake in moderate oven (375°F.) about 30 minutes. Makes 2 loaves.

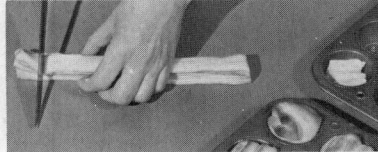

Butterflakes

BUTTERFLAKES

When Roll Dough is ready for shaping, roll out to thin rectangular sheet ⅛ inch thick. Brush dough with melted butter or margarine. Fold dough into layers about 1 inch wide and 6 or 7 layers deep. Cut pieces 1½ inches long. A pastry wheel gives the edges a crinkly effect. Set on end in greased muffin pans.

CURLICUES

Divide Roll Dough in half. Roll out each half into an oblong about 12 x 9 inches. Brush generously with melted margarine or butter.

Cut into 12 equal strips (about 1 inch wide). Hold one end of strip firmly and wind closely to form coil. Tuck end firmly underneath. Place on greased baking sheets about 2 inches apart. Cover. Let rise in warm place, free from draft, until doubled in bulk. (Straight-Dough Method about 1 hour; Action-Quick Dough about 30 minutes; Refrigerator Dough about 1 hour.) Brush lightly with melted margarine or butter. Bake in hot oven at 400°F. about 15 minutes. Makes 24.

Curlicues

CRESCENTS

Divide Roll Dough into 3 equal pieces. Roll out each piece into a circle about 9 inches in diameter. Brush lightly with melted margarine or butter.

Cut into 8 pie-shaped pieces. Roll up tightly beginning at wide end. Seal points firmly.

Place on greased baking sheets, with points underneath, about 2 inches apart. Curve to form crescents.

Cover. Let rise in warm place, free from draft, until doubled in bulk. (Straight-Dough Method about 1 hour; Action-Quick Dough about 30 minutes; Refrigerator Dough about 1 hour.)

Brush lightly with melted margarine or butter.

Bake in hot oven (400°F.) about 15 minutes. Makes 24.

Crescents

BUTTERFLIES

When Roll Dough is ready for shaping, roll dough into rectangular sheet ¼ inch thick and 6 inches wide. Brush with melted margarine or butter. Roll up like jelly-roll. Cut into pieces 2 inches long. Press across center of each piece with knife handle or small rolling pin.

Butterflies

LUCKY CLOVERS

Divide Roll Dough in half. Form each half into 9-inch roll. Cut into 9 equal pieces. Form into balls.

Place in greased muffin pans 2¾ x 1¼ inches. With scissors cut each ball in half, then into quarters, cutting through almost to bottom of rolls. Brush lightly with melted margarine or butter.

Cover. Let rise in warm place, free from draft, until doubled in bulk. (Whole Wheat, White, Refrigerator Doughs about 1 hour; Action-Quick Dough about 30 minutes.)

Bake in hot oven at 400°F. (Whole Wheat Rolls about 20 minutes; White Rolls about 15 minutes.) Makes 18.

Lucky Clovers

PARKER HOUSE ROLLS

Divide Roll Dough in half. Roll out each half into 9-inch circle. Cut into rounds with 2½-inch cooky cutter.

Crease with dull edge of knife to one side of center. Brush lightly with melted margarine or butter. Fold larger side over smaller so edges just meet. Seal.

Place on greased baking sheet about 1 inch apart.

Cover. Let rise in warm place, free from draft, until doubled in bulk. (Straight-Dough Method about 1 hour; Action-Quick Dough about 30 minutes; Refrigerator Dough about 1 hour.)

Brush lightly with melted margarine or butter.

Bake in hot oven at 400°F. about 15 minutes. Makes 24 rolls.

Parker House Rolls

PAN ROLLS

Divide Roll Dough in half. Form each half into a roll about 12 inches long. Cut into 12 equal pieces. Form into smooth balls.

Place in greased shallow pans about ¼ inch apart.

Cover. Let rise in warm place, free from draft, until doubled in bulk. (Straight-Dough Method about 1 hour; Action-Quick Dough about 30 minutes; Refrigerator Dough about 1 hour.)

Brush lightly with melted margarine or butter.

Bake in moderate oven at 375°F. about 20 minutes. Makes 24 rolls.

Pan Rolls

ROSETTES

When Roll Dough is ready for shaping, roll dough under hand to ½-inch thickness. Cut in pieces about 6 inches long. Tie in knots, and bring one end through center and the other over the side. Place on greased baking sheet.

Rosettes

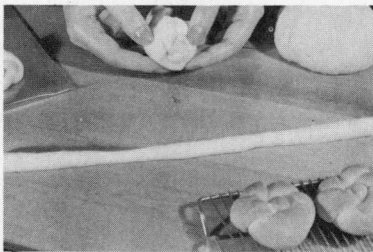

SNAILS

When Roll Dough is ready for shaping, roll dough under hand to form long pieces ½ inch in diameter. Cut into 8-inch lengths. Twist each piece by rolling ends in opposite directions. Coil to form snail. Tuck end under edge of roll to hold it in place. Place on greased baking sheet.

Snails

BUTTERMILK ROLLS

1   cake compressed or 1 package dry granular yeast
¼   cup lukewarm water
1½   cups buttermilk
2   tablespoons shortening
½   teaspoon baking soda
2   tablespoons sugar
1½   teaspoons salt
4   cups sifted enriched flour

Soften the yeast in the lukewarm (warm for dry yeast) water. Scald the buttermilk and add to it the shortening, soda, sugar, salt, and 2 cups of the flour.

Beat for several minutes, then add enough additional flour to make a light but not sticky dough. Turn out on lightly floured board and knead for 8 minutes.

Place in a greased bowl, grease the surface of the dough, cover, and allow it to rise in warm place until doubled in bulk (about 1½ hours).

Punch down and roll out on a lightly floured board. Cut into rounds and place in a high-sided, greased pan, close together but not touching. Allow to rise until doubled in bulk, 45 minutes. Bake in moderate oven (350°F.) for 20 to 25 minutes.

ENGLISH MUFFINS

These are small, flat, yeast-raised cakes baked on a griddle. They may be cut from rolled-out dough or shaped by allowing balls of dough to rise in muffin rings. English muffins are broken apart (not cut) and toasted before serving. Always store them in the refrigerator.

1   cup scalded milk
3   tablespoons butter or margarine
1¼   teaspoons salt
2   tablespoons sugar
1   cake compressed yeast
¼   cup lukewarm water
1   beaten egg
About 3½ cups sifted enriched flour
White corn meal

Pour scalded milk over butter, salt, and sugar. Soften yeast in water.

Cool milk mixture to lukewarm, then add yeast, egg, and 2 cups flour.

Stir to blend well, then knead in remaining flour until dough is thick and elastic.

Turn batter into greased bowl. Cover and allow to rise in warm place until doubled in bulk, about 1 hour.

Sprinkle about ¼ cup white corn meal on lightly floured pastry board or cloth. Roll dough out ¼ inch thick. Cut with medium English muffin rings or 3½-inch cooky cutter.

Let cut dough rise, covered, until doubled in size. Bake on lightly greased griddle over moderate heat, about 15 minutes on first side and 7 minutes on other side. Makes about 1 dozen.

REFRIGERATOR POTATO ROLLS
(Master Recipe)

    1   cup milk, scalded
    1   cup hot mashed potato
    ½   cup shortening
    ¼   cup sugar
    2   teaspoons salt
    1   cake compressed yeast
    ½   cup lukewarm water
    2   eggs, beaten
    5   to 6 cups sifted enriched flour

Combine milk, potato, shortening, sugar, and salt in a large bowl. Let stand until lukewarm.

Soften yeast in lukewarm water and add with eggs.

Add 1½ cups flour and beat well. Cover and let stand in warm place (85°F.) until full of bubbles, about 1 hour.

Stir in enough flour (3½ to 4½ cups) to make a fairly stiff dough. Knead on a lightly floured board until smooth. Return to lightly greased bowl, and grease top of dough. Cover, and chill in refrigerator.

About 1½ hours before serving time, shape desired number of rolls. Place on greased pans. Let rise until doubled in bulk, about 1 hour. Bake in hot oven (425°F.) 15 to 20 minutes. Makes about 3 dozen rolls.

Note: Remaining dough may be kept in refrigerator several days. Punch down before placing in refrigerator.

Variations:

Butterscotch Rolls: Butter muffin pans. Add 1 teaspoon butter, 1 teaspoon brown sugar, and 1 tablespoon chopped nuts.

Form dough into medium-sized balls. Place 1 ball in each tin. Allow to rise until double in bulk.

Bake in hot oven (425°F.) 25 minutes. Turn out while hot.

Date and Walnut Rolls: Prepare recipe for refrigerator potato rolls using half white flour and half whole wheat flour.

Substitute brown sugar for white. Add 1 cup chopped, pitted dates and ½ cup chopped nuts.

Shape into rolls. Allow to rise until double in bulk.

Bake in hot oven (425°F.) 20 minutes. Frost with confectioners' sugar icing.

Nut and Prune Rolls: To the recipe for refrigerator potato rolls add ½ cup chopped nuts, 1 cup prunes, diced, and 1 teaspoon baking powder.

Shape into rolls. Allow to rise until doubled in bulk. Sprinkle with cinnamon-sugar mixture.

Bake in hot oven (425°F.) 20 minutes.

BRIOCHE

Brioche is a yeast-raised bread rich in eggs and shortening, popular in France as a breakfast roll. It may be made in many shapes and sizes, but the most familiar form is the roll made by topping one ball of dough with a smaller ball before baking to form a bun with a little hat on it.

    ½   cup milk
    ½   cup margarine or butter
    ⅓   cup sugar
    ½   teaspoon salt
    ¼   cup warm (not hot) water
    1   package or cake yeast, active dry
          or compressed
    1   egg yolk, beaten
    3   whole eggs, beaten
    3¼ cups sifted enriched flour
    1   egg white
    1   tablespoon sugar

Scald milk. Cool to lukewarm.

Cream margarine or butter thoroughly. Add gradually and cream together ⅓ cup sugar and salt.

Measure warm water into bowl (cool to lukewarm for compressed yeast). Sprinkle or crumble in yeast and stir until dissolved. Stir in lukewarm milk and creamed mixture.

Add beaten egg yolk, beaten whole eggs, and flour. Beat 10 minutes.

Cover. Let rise in warm place, free from draft, about 2 hours or until more than doubled in bulk.

Stir down. Beat thoroughly. Cover tightly with waxed paper or aluminum foil. Store in refrigerator overnight.

Stir down and turn out soft dough on floured board.

Divide into 2 pieces, one about ¾ weight of dough and the other about ¼ weight of dough.

Cut larger piece into 16 equal pieces. Form into smooth balls. Place in well greased muffin pans 2¾ x 1¼ inches.

Cut smaller piece into 16 equal pieces. Form into smooth balls.

Make a deep indentation in center of each large ball; dampen slightly with cold water. Press a small ball into each indentation.

Cover. Let rise in warm place, free from draft, about 1 hour or until more than doubled in bulk. Brush with mixture of 1 egg white and 1 tablespoon sugar.

Bake in moderate oven (375°F.) about 20 minutes. Makes 16.

ENGLISH BATH BUNS

Shape Brioche Dough into large round buns. Place about 2 inches apart on greased baking sheet. Cover and set in warm place, free from draft. Let rise until light, about 1½ hours.

Before baking, press into the tops sliced blanched almonds, chopped cit-

Brioche

ron, and chopped candied orange peel.

Brush with 1 tablespoon water mixed with one egg white beaten. Bake in moderate oven (350°F.) about 40 to 45 minutes.

CRUMPETS

These are English breakfast or tea cakes very similar to English muffins except that buttered muffin rings are always used in preparing them.

    2   cups scalded milk
    ½   cup butter
    ¾   teaspoon salt
    1   package dry or 1 cake compressed
          yeast
    About 3 cups sifted flour

Combine scalded milk, butter, and salt in a large mixing bowl; let cool to lukewarm.

Soften yeast in a little lukewarm water and add to the milk. Stir in 3 or more cups flour to make a stiff dough which can be beaten with a spoon. Beat well.

Cover the dough with a towel and set in a warm place to rise until light.

Put buttered muffin rings on a hot buttered griddle. Fill the rings half-full with the dough. Bake slowly until the crumpets are well risen and lightly browned on the under-side.

Turn, ring and all, and brown on the other side. The crumpets must be watched carefully. If they brown too quickly, lower the heat. To serve, split and toast the crumpets and butter generously. Makes about 1 dozen.

BAGEL

Bagel is a Yiddish term for an old-time Jewish yeast-dough roll shaped (traditionally by hand) like a doughnut with a hole in the center. It is cooked in simmering water before being baked. Its hard crust is notorious. It is often served with lox (smoked salmon) and cream cheese.

1/4 cup butter
1 1/2 tablespoons sugar
1/2 teaspoon salt
1 cup scalded milk
1 ounce compressed yeast
1 egg white
3 3/4 cups sifted enriched flour

Add butter, sugar, and salt to scalded milk. When lukewarm, add yeast, well beaten egg white, and the flour.

Combine well, knead, and let rise until doubled in bulk. Cut off small pieces and roll the width of a finger and twice the length, tapering at the ends.

Shape into rings, pinching the ends together well. Let stand on a floured board only until they begin to rise.

Fill a large shallow pan half full of water. Place over heat and when very hot, but not boiling, drop the dough rings in carefully one at a time.

Cook under the boiling point until they hold their shape, then turn with a skimmer and continue to cook. They must be light and keep their shape when handled.

Place on thin ungreased baking sheet and bake in a hot oven (400°F.) until crisp and golden brown, first on one side, then on the other.

Note: If desired, the bagel can be sprinkled with salt and caraway seed before baking.

ONE BOWL CHEESY ONION BURGER BUNS
(No-Dissolve Method)

5 3/4 to 6 3/4 cups unsifted flour
3 tablespoons sugar
1 1/2 teaspoons salt
2 packages active dry yeast
2 tablespoons softened margarine
2 cups very hot tap water
1 1/2 cups grated sharp Cheddar cheese
1/4 cup finely chopped onion

In a large bowl thoroughly mix 2 cups flour, sugar, salt, and undissolved active dry yeast. Add softened margarine.

Gradually add very hot tap water to dry ingredients and beat 2 minutes at medium speed of electric mixer, scraping bowl occasionally. Add 1 cup flour, or enough flour to make a thick batter. Beat at high speed 2 minutes, scraping bowl occasionally. Stir in cheese, onion, and enough additional flour to make a soft dough. Turn out onto lightly floured board; knead until smooth and elastic, about 8 to 10 minutes. Place in greased bowl, turning to grease top. Cover; let rise in warm place, free from draft, until doubled in bulk, about 1 hour.

Punch dough down; turn out onto lightly floured board. Divide dough into 20 equal pieces. Form each piece into a smooth ball; place balls 2 inches apart on greased baking sheets. Cover; let rise in warm place, free from draft, until doubled in bulk, about 45 minutes.

Bake in hot oven (400°F.) about 15 to 20 minutes, or until done. Remove from baking sheets and cool on wire racks. Makes 20 buns.

CROISSANTS

Croissant is the French term for crescent and refers to a particularly flaky roll of that shape.

1 package dry yeast
3/4 cup milk
2 cups sifted enriched flour
1/2 teaspoon salt
1/2 cup sweet butter
1 egg yolk

Dissolve yeast in warm milk (110°F.). Sift together flour and salt, and add dissolved yeast. Knead until smooth and elastic.

Place in greased bowl and grease top of dough. Let rise in warm place (85°F.) until double in bulk.

Roll it out in a long strip. Dot with bits of butter and fold in thirds. Turn so an open edge is toward you. Pat and roll into another long strip. Fold in thirds. Wrap in waxed paper and chill well.

Roll out and fold ends to center. Fold again, wrap and refrigerate.

Remove and repeat the process a fourth time. The last time, roll the dough out a little thinner but do not fold. Cut into triangles.

Brush one tip of each with beaten egg yolk mixed with a little water and roll from wide end to tip, pressing to seal.

Shape into half moons. Place on well buttered cooky sheets. Cover with waxed paper and let rise until double in bulk.

Brush tops with beaten egg yolk. Bake in hot oven (425°F.) 20 to 25 minutes. Serve hot. Makes 18 rolls.

BRAN REFRIGERATOR ROLLS

1 cup shortening
3/4 cup sugar
1 cup whole bran
2 teaspoons salt
1 cup boiling water
2 cakes compressed or 2 packages dry yeast
1 cup water (lukewarm for compressed yeast or warm for dry yeast)
2 well beaten eggs
6 1/2 cups sifted enriched flour

Measure shortening, sugar, bran, and salt into large mixing bowl. Add boiling water, stirring until shortening is melted. Let stand until lukewarm.

Soften yeast in lukewarm water; stir into bran mixture together with eggs. Add half of the flour and beat until smooth; add remaining flour and beat well. Cover bowl tightly and place in refrigerator overnight or until ready to use.

Shape balls of dough to fill greased muffin pans about half full. Let rise in warm place about 2 hours or until double in bulk. Bake in hot oven (425°F.) about 15 minutes. Makes 3 1/3 dozen rolls, about 2 1/2 inches in diameter.

ONE BOWL HARD ROLLS
(No-Dissolve Method)

4 1/2 to 5 1/2 cups unsifted all-purpose flour
2 tablespoons sugar
2 teaspoons salt
1 package active dry yeast
3 tablespoons softened margarine
1 1/2 cups very hot tap water
1 egg white (at room temperature)
Corn meal
1/2 cup water
1 teaspoon cornstarch

In a large bowl thoroughly mix 1 1/3 cups flour, sugar, salt, and undissolved active dry yeast. Add softened margarine. Gradually add very hot tap water to dry ingredients and beat 2 minutes at medium speed of electric mixer, scraping bowl occasionally. Add egg white and 1 cup flour, or enough flour to make a thick batter. Beat at high speed 2 minutes, scraping bowl occasionally. Stir in enough additional flour to make a soft dough. Turn out onto lightly floured board; knead until smooth and elastic, about 8 to 10 minutes. Place in greased bowl, turning to grease top. Cover; let rise in warm place, free from draft, until doubled in bulk, about 45 minutes.

Punch dough down; turn out onto lightly floured board. Cover; let rest 10 minutes. Divide in half. Form each half into a 9-inch roll. Cut into nine 1-inch pieces. Form into smooth balls. Place about 3 inches apart on greased baking sheets sprinkled with corn meal. Cover; let rise in warm place, free from draft, until doubled in bulk, about 45 minutes.

Slowly blend remaining 1/2 cup water into cornstarch. Bring mixture to a boil. Cool slightly. When read to bake, brush each roll with cornstarch glaze. Slit tops with a sharp knife criss-cross fashion. If desired, sprinkle with sesame or poppy seeds.

Bake in a very hot oven (450°F.) about 15 minutes, or until done. Remove from baking sheets and cool on wire racks. Makes 1 1/2 dozen rolls.

SPEEDY PAN ROLLS

1 cup lukewarm water
1/3 cup melted shortening
1 tablespoon sugar
2 teaspoons salt
2 cakes compressed yeast or 2 packages dry granular yeast
1 egg
3½ cups sifted enriched flour

Combine water, shortening, sugar, and salt. Add yeast and mix well.

Blend in egg and add flour. Mix until dough is well blended and soft.

Roll out on well floured board and fit into greased pan (12 x 8 inches). Cut dough into rectangles (1 x 4 inches) with knife that has been dipped in melted butter.

Let rise in warm place (80 to 85°F.) until double in bulk, about 30 minutes.

Bake in hot oven (400°F.) 20 minutes. Makes 2 dozen rolls.

BAPS
(From Scotland)

1 package dry granular yeast
½ cup warm water
4 cups sifted enriched flour
1 teaspoon sugar
1½ teaspoons salt
¼ cup lard
½ cup undiluted evaporated milk

Soften yeast in warm water. Mix and sift dry ingredients; add lard, mixing well with pastry blender.

Add yeast mixture and evaporated milk. Mix well and knead 2 minutes; put in greased bowl. Cover, let rise until double in bulk.

Knead lightly; shape into ovals about 3 x 2 inches.

Brush with a little additional milk, let rise until double in bulk.

Bake in hot oven (400°F.) 15 to 20 minutes. Makes 1 dozen.

FIG-BRAN MUFFIN BUNS

1 cup milk, scalded
½ cup coarsely chopped dried figs
½ cup whole bran
1 teaspoon salt
3 tablespoons brown sugar
1 tablespoon shortening
2 cakes compressed yeast
2 cups sifted enriched flour

Pour hot milk over figs, bran, salt, sugar, and shortening in mixing bowl. Cool to lukewarm, then crumble in the yeast and beat in the flour.

Drop at once by spoonfuls into greased muffin pans, filling them half full.

Let rise in warm place until the muffins fill the pans.

Bake in hot oven (400°F.) about 20 minutes. Makes 12 good sized muffins or 16 to 18 small ones.

BUTTERFLAKE ROLLS
(Master Recipe)

2 cakes compressed yeast
¼ cup sugar
1½ cups milk (room temperature)
2½ tablespoons cider or distilled white vinegar
¼ cup butter
¼ cup lard
5½ cups sifted enriched flour
½ teaspoon baking soda
1 teaspoon salt

Crumble yeast in bowl and add sugar. To the milk, slowly add vinegar stirring rapidly. Pour over yeast and sugar, then let stand 10 minutes.

Melt butter and lard; then cool. Sift together flour, baking soda, and salt.

Add the melted shortening to yeast mixture. Mix well, then add sifted dry ingredients, beating until a smooth dough is formed.

Transfer dough to a well greased bowl and brush top with butter. Place bowl in warm place until dough is about tripled in bulk.

Turn out of bowl, without stirring, onto well floured board. Sprinkle top of dough lightly with flour, then roll out to desired thickness. Make into fancy shapes as desired.

Set rolls in warm place 10 to 15 minutes or until light. Bake in a hot oven (400°F.) 15 to 20 minutes, depending upon shape and size of rolls. Remove from pan at once to cake rack, unless to be served hot.

Crisscross Rolls: Roll Butterflake Roll dough ¼ inch thick. Brush with melted butter. Cut into long strips 1½ inches wide.

Cut strips into 2 inch lengths, then place 3 into each well greased muffin pan in crisscross fashion, having 3rd strip in position of first. Brush tops with butter, then let rise. Bake according to directions.

Nut Rolls: Roll Butterflake Roll dough ⅛ inch thick. Brush with melted butter. Sprinkle with brown sugar and chopped nuts. Cut strips ¾ inch wide and 4 long. Roll, then place end up in greased muffin pan. Let rise and bake according to directions.

Poppy Seed Twists: Roll Butterflake Roll dough about ⅛ inch thick. Cut into strips ¾ inch wide and 3 inches long. Place one on top of another in braid fashion. Brush tops with melted butter, then sprinkle with poppy seeds. Let rise and bake according to directions.

Butterflake Rolls

Crisscross Rolls

Poppy Seed Twists

Nut Rolls

TWISTED PLAIN OR SWEET ROLLS

Roll plain Roll Dough or Sweet Dough into long oblong shape a little less than ¼ inch thick. Spread with very soft or melted butter.

Fold ½ of dough over the other half. Trim edges to square corners.

Cut into strips ½ inch wide and 6 inches long. Use strips to make any of the following rolls:

Clothespin Cruller Rolls: Wrap strip around greased wooden clothespin so edges barely touch. After baking, twist clothespin and pull out.

Crooked Mile Rolls: Twist and tie knot in one end of strip. Then pull longer end through center of knot; bring it around and up through center opening again.

Toad-In-The-Hole Or Turk's Cap: Twist and tie knot in one end of strip. Then pull longer end through center of knot.

Figure 8's: Hold one end of strip firmly in one hand. Twist the other end, stretching it slightly until the 2 ends when brought together will naturally form a figure 8. Seal ends well.

Twists: Make the same way as Figure 8's, but give each roll an additional twist just before placing it on baking sheet.

Sweet Dough Recipes

SWEET DOUGHS

A sweet dough is a basic yeast-flour-liquid mixture containing more sugar, shortening, and eggs than the dough for non-sweet (plain) breads and rolls. It may be a kneaded dough such as Basic Sweet Dough (Straight-Dough Method); or a stiff batter such as Rich Sweet Dough. Some breads that are considered sweet breads, such as Danish Pastry, are made from a plain dough; the sweetness comes from the filling they contain.

Many of the recipes that follow for sweet breads and rolls, coffee cakes, and tea rings call for all or part of a basic sweet dough; either the basic sweet dough or the rich sweet dough may be used.

BASIC SWEET DOUGH
(Straight-Dough Method)

An easy-to-handle kneaded dough for sweet rolls and coffee cake.

½ cup milk
½ cup sugar
1½ teaspoons salt
¼ cup shortening
½ cup warm (not hot) water
2 packages or cakes yeast, active dry or compressed
2 eggs, beaten
3 cups sifted enriched flour
2 cups sifted enriched flour (about)

Scald milk. Stir in sugar, salt, and shortening. Cool to lukewarm.

Measure into bowl ½ cup warm water (cool to lukewarm for compressed yeast). Sprinkle or crumble in yeast. Stir until dissolved. Stir in lukewarm milk mixture.

Add beaten eggs and 3 cups flour. Beat until smooth. Stir in additional 2 cups flour.

Turn dough out on lightly floured board. Knead until smooth and elastic. Place in greased bowl; brush top with soft shortening. Cover. Let rise in warm place, free from draft, until doubled in bulk, about 1 hour.

Punch down and turn out on lightly floured board. Proceed according to directions for shapes selected.

For Faster Sweet Dough (Action-Quick Dough): Use 3 packages or cakes yeast; bowl rise about 45 minutes.

Note: For ½ recipe use ½ of each ingredient.

For double the recipe use double the amount of each ingredient; bowl rise about 1 hour.

RICH SWEET DOUGH

A no-knead refrigerator dough that makes a rich, tender product.

¾ cup milk
½ cup sugar
2 teaspoons salt
½ cup (1 stick) butter or margarine
½ cup warm water (105°-115°F.)
2 packages or cakes yeast, active dry or compressed
1 egg
4 cups unsifted enriched flour

Scald milk; stir in sugar, salt, and butter or margarine. Cool to lukewarm.

Measure warm water into large warm bowl. Sprinkle or crumble in yeast; stir until dissolved. Stir in lukewarm milk mixture, egg, and half the flour; beat until smooth. Stir in remaining flour to make a stiff batter.

Cover tightly with waxed paper or aluminum foil. Refrigerate dough at least 2 hours. Dough may be kept in refrigerator 3 days. To use, cut off amount needed and shape as desired.

FROSTED SNAILS

1 recipe Sweet Dough
Confectioners' sugar frosting
Chopped nuts

When Sweet Dough is light, punch down. Let rest 10 minutes.

Roll into long rolls a scant ½ inch thick. Cut into pieces 9 inches long.

Coil each piece loosely to form snail, tucking end of strip under roll. Let rise until doubled, about 45 minutes.

Bake in moderate oven (350°F.) 20 minutes.

When slightly cool, frost with confectioners' sugar frosting and sprinkle with chopped nuts. Makes about 3 dozen snails.

JACK HORNER ROLLS

Use 1 recipe for Sweet Dough and when it is light punch down and divide into portions for individual rolls.

Round up each portion to a smooth ball. Cover and let rest 10 minutes.

Flatten each ball to ¼ inch. Mix together ½ cup sugar and ½ teaspoon cinnamon. Sprinkle each with ½ teaspoon of sugar and cinnamon mixture.

Place a pitted cooked prune in center of each portion. Bring edges together, seal, and place rolls smooth side up on greased baking sheet.

Cover and let rise until doubled in bulk. Bake in moderate oven (375°F.) 20 to 25 minutes.

When cooled, brush with confectioners' sugar frosting. Makes about 3½ dozen rolls.

SWEDISH TEA RING

Use ½ recipe for Sweet Dough and when it is light roll into a rectangular sheet about ½ inch thick.

Brush with melted butter and cinnamon. Nuts or raisins may be added.

Roll jelly-roll fashion and shape into a ring on a greased baking sheet. Cut with scissors at 1-inch intervals, almost through the ring. Turn each slice slightly on its side.

Cover and let rise until doubled.

Bake in moderate oven (375°F.) 25 to 30 minutes.

Frost while warm with confectioners' sugar frosting. Sprinkle thickly with chopped nuts. Makes 1 tea ring.

Swedish Tea Ring

CINNAMON BUN LOAF

Prepare as for Cinnamon Buns, cutting each long roll into 18 equal pieces (about ½-inch wide).

Place pieces ½-inch side down in greased bread pan 9 x 5 x 3 inches. Brush top generously with melted margarine or butter. If desired, top with additional sugar and cinnamon mixture.

Let rise as directed for Cinnamon Buns.

Bake in moderate oven (350°F.) about 40 minutes. Makes 2 loaves.

Cinnamon Bun Loaf

Jack Horner Rolls

ROSEBUDS

1 recipe Sweet Dough
½ cup raspberry, strawberry, or apricot jam
1 egg yolk
2 tablespoons milk

Divide Sweet Dough in half. Roll out each half into a square about 12 x 12 inches.

Spread ¼ cup jam evenly on each square. Roll up as for jelly roll. Cut into 12 equal pieces (about 1 inch wide).

Place, cut side up, in greased muffin pans 2¾ x 1¼ inches. With sharp knife or scissors cut crosses, about ½ inch deep, across tops of buns.

Cover. Let rise in warm place, free from draft, until doubled in bulk. (Straight-Dough Method about 1 hour; Action-Quick Dough about 30 minutes.)

Beat egg yolk and milk together. Brush tops of buns with egg mixture.

Bake in moderate oven (350°F.) about 30 minutes.

Ice tops with plain icing. Makes 24.

Rosebuds

RUM ROLLS

Add ½ cup currants to ½ recipe for Sweet Dough. When dough is light, punch down and divide into small portions for individual rolls.

Shape each portion into a smooth round ball. Place on greased baking sheet. Cover and let rise until doubled in bulk.

Bake in moderate oven (375°F.) 15 to 20 minutes. Ice at once with confectioners' sugar frosting to which has been added a few drops of rum flavoring. Makes about 2 dozen small rolls.

Rum Rolls

HOT CROSS BUNS

1 recipe Sweet Dough
1 teaspoon cinnamon
¼ teaspoon allspice
1 cup currants

To recipe for Sweet Dough add remaining ingredients. When dough is light, punch down. Let rest 10 minutes.

Divide into pieces the size of a walnut. Shape each piece into ball.

Place ½ inch apart in greased pans or 1½ inches apart on greased baking sheets. Let rise until doubled (about 45 minutes).

Bake in moderate oven (350°F.) 20 to 25 minutes.

Remove at once from pans and make cross of white frosting on each roll. Makes about 3½ dozen rolls.

Hot Cross Buns

STOLLEN

Stollen is a German name for a rich yeast coffee cake, usually with raisins and almonds.

Use ½ recipe for Sweet Dough and when it is light add ½ cup raisins and ½ cup blanched chopped almonds and knead them in.

Divide dough in 2 equal portions and round them up. Cover and let rest 10 to 15 minutes.

Flatten out each ball of dough into an oval sheet. Brush ½ of each sheet with melted butter. Fold unbuttered half over buttered half, like Parker House rolls.

Place on greased baking sheets. Let rise until doubled in bulk.

Bake in moderate oven (350° to 375°F.) 25 to 30 minutes. Brush with confectioners' sugar frosting and sprinkle with chopped nuts. Makes 2 stollen.

Stollen

CINNAMON BUNS

1 recipe Sweet Dough
1½ cups sugar
2 teaspoons cinnamon
⅔ cup raisins

Divide Sweet Dough in half. Roll out each half into an oblong about 14 x 9 inches. Brush lightly with melted margarine or butter.

Sprinkle each oblong with one-half mixture of sugar, cinnamon, and raisins. Roll up as for jelly roll to make roll 9 inches long. Seal edges firmly.

Cut into 9 equal pieces. Place cut side up about 1 inch apart in greased 9-inch layer cake pan or square pan 8 x 8 x 2 inches. Cover. Let rise in warm place, free from draft, until double in bulk. (Straight-Dough Method about 1 hour; Action-Quick Dough about 30 minutes.) Bake in moderate oven (350°F.) about 35 minutes. Ice top with plain icing. Makes 18.

Cinnamon Buns

KOLACKY

Kolacky (also spelled kolachy and kolachen) were originally Bohemian dessert breads but are now popular in other European countries and in the United States. They may be round buns topped with a fruit, cheese, or poppy-seed filling or filled square buns.

1 recipe Sweet Dough
2 tablespoons melted butter
Fruit filling
Confectioners' sugar

When sweet dough is light, punch down. Let rest 10 minutes.

Divide into pieces the size of walnuts. Shape each piece into ball. Place 2 inches apart on greased baking sheets. Let rise 15 minutes.

With fingertip press down center of each roll to make hollow. Brush with butter or margarine. Fill hollows with fruit filling. Let rise until doubled, about 30 minutes.

Bake in moderate oven (350°F.) 20 minutes. Sprinkle with confectioners' sugar. Makes about 4 dozen kolacky.

Fruit Filling For Kolacky:

1½ cups chopped, cooked prunes or 1½ cups chopped, cooked apricots
¼ cup prune juice or ¼ cup apricot juice
½ cup sugar
1 tablespoon lemon juice
½ teaspoon cinnamon
¼ teaspoon cloves

Combine all ingredients and mix well.

PALM LEAF ROLLS

1 recipe Sweet Dough
1½ cups sugar
2 teaspoons cinnamon
⅔ cup raisins

Divide Sweet Dough in half. Roll out each half into a square about 12 x 12 inches. Brush lightly with melted margarine or butter.

Sprinkle each square with one-half mixture of sugar, cinnamon, and raisins. Roll up as for jelly roll. Seal edges firmly.

Cut into 8 equal pieces (about 1¼ inches wide). Make two cuts through each piece, parallel to cut sides and extending to within ½ inch of other side. Turn each loaf on its side and spread the three leaves apart into fan shape. Place on greased baking sheets about 2 inches apart.

Cover. Let rise in warm place, free from draft, until doubled in bulk. (Straight-Dough Method about 1 hour; Action-Quick Dough about 30 minutes.)

Bake in moderate oven (350°F.) about 35 minutes.

Ice tops with plain icing. Makes 16.

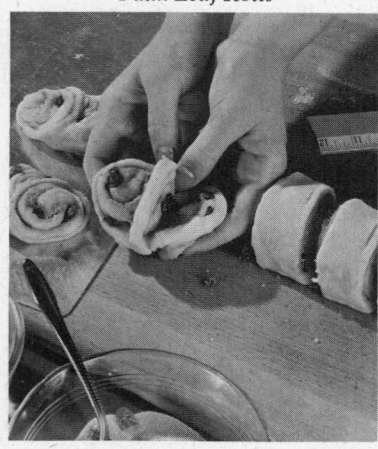

Palm Leaf Rolls

BOHEMIAN BRAID

Use ½ recipe for Sweet Dough and when it is light, divide into 9 portions.

Roll each portion into a long roll. Braid 4 rolls loosely and place on greased baking sheet. Then braid 3 portions and place on top of first braid. Twist last 2 portions together and place on top, tucking ends under.

Cover and let rise until doubled in bulk.

Bake in moderate oven (350° to 375°F.) 40 to 45 minutes. Brush with confectioners' sugar frosting and sprinkle with chopped nuts. Makes 1 large braided loaf.

Bohemian Braid

BUTTERSCOTCH PECAN ROLLS

Into each muffin cup put ½ teaspoon butter and 1 teaspoon brown sugar. Sprinkle with ½ teaspoon water. Arrange 3 or 4 pecan halves in each muffin cup.

Use 1 recipe for Sweet Dough and when it is light punch down and let rest 10 minutes.

Roll dough out to rectangular sheet ½ inch thick and 9 inches wide. Brush lightly with melted butter and sprinkle generously with brown sugar.

Roll jelly-roll fashion, sealing edges. Cut into 1-inch slices.

Place slices, cut side down, into prepared muffin pans.

Cover and let rise until doubled in bulk.

Bake in moderate oven (375°F.) 20 to 25 minutes.

Let rolls stand in pans 1 minute before turning them out. Makes about 3½ dozen rolls.

Butterscotch Pecan Rolls

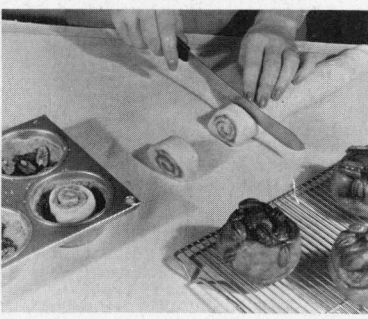

HONEY ALMOND CAKE

1 recipe Sweet Dough
6 tablespoons flour
½ cup sugar
½ teaspoon salt
2 cups milk
2 eggs, beaten
1 teaspoon vanilla
¼ cup sugar
½ cup honey
2 tablespoons margarine or butter
2 tablespoons slivered, blanched almonds

While Sweet Dough is rising prepare Cream Filling:

Mix together in top of double boiler flour, sugar, and salt. Gradually stir in milk. Cook over hot water, stirring constantly until thickened, about 15 minutes.

Stir slowly into beaten eggs. Return to top of double boiler and cook over hot water for 3 minutes longer. Remove from heat. Stir in vanilla. Cool until thick enough to spread.

Divide Sweet Dough in half; form each half into smooth ball. Place in greased 8-inch layer cake pan. Cover. Let rise in warm place, free from draft, until doubled in bulk. (Straight-Dough Method about 1 hour; Action-Quick Dough about 30 minutes.)

Bring to boil in saucepan sugar, honey, and margarine or butter. Brush tops of cakes with half of honey syrup.

Sprinkle on each cake the almonds.

Bake in moderate oven (350°F.) about 35 minutes.

Brush cakes while still hot with remaining syrup. Cool.

Slice each into 2 layers; fill with Cream Filling. Makes 2 cakes.

Honey Almond Cake

CINNAMON LOAF

Use ½ recipe for Sweet Dough and, when it is light, roll it into a rectangular sheet ½ inch thick and about 8 inches wide.

Brush with butter and spread with a mixture of 3 teaspoons cinnamon and 1 cup sugar.

Roll jelly-roll fashion and cut to make 2 loaves.

Place in greased bread pans, and let them rise.

Before baking, brush with milk, and sprinkle with sugar. Bake in hot oven (400°F.) 30 to 35 minutes. Makes 2 loaves.

BABA AU RHUM

Baba is the French term for a yeast-raised cake often containing fruit or flavored with fruit juices. It may be soaked with rum or a rum substitute before being served, and is then called baba au rhum.

1   cake compressed yeast
1/2 cup scalded milk
2   cups sifted enriched flour
1/2 cup sugar
1/2 cup butter
1/2 teaspoon salt
1   tablespoon grated lemon rind
3   eggs, well beaten

Dissolve yeast in milk, which has been cooled to lukewarm. Add 1/2 cup flour and 1 tablespoon sugar. Beat until smooth.

Cover and let rise in warm place (80° to 85°F.) until doubled in bulk, about 1 hour.

Cream butter. Add remaining sugar gradually. Cream until light and fluffy. Add salt, lemon rind, and eggs and beat until smooth.

Stir in the remaining flour. Add the yeast mixture. Beat 15 minutes by hand or 5 minutes by electric mixer.

Pour in greased casserole dish or mold of 1 1/2 to 2 quart capacity. Cover and let rise until doubled in bulk, about 1 hour.

Bake in moderate oven (350°F.) 40 to 50 minutes.

Remove from oven. Prick top with tines of sharp fork. Turn out of pan and place cake (inverted) in pie plate. Pour baba sauce over top and sides, then brush with apricot glaze.

Allow cake to stand until most of baba sauce is absorbed before serving. Makes one 9-inch cake.

Baba Sauce: Boil 1 cup sugar and 1 cup strong clear tea 5 minutes. Cool. Add 2 teaspoons rum.

Apricot Glaze: Soak 1/4 pound apricots overnight in just enough water to cover. Press through sieve. Measure equal parts pulp and sugar. Boil together 5 minutes, stirring constantly.

NO-KNEAD SWEET ROLLS

1/2 cup milk
3   tablespoons shortening
3   tablespoons sugar
2   teaspoons salt
1/2 cup water
1   cake compressed yeast
1   egg
3   cups sifted enriched flour
Mixture of:
    2   tablespoons melted butter
    1/4 cup sugar
    1   teaspoon cinnamon

Scald milk, and combine with shortening, sugar, and salt. Cool to lukewarm with 1/2 cup water. Add yeast and mix well.

Blend in egg. Add flour gradually. Mix until dough is well blended and soft. Roll out dough on well floured board to form rectangle (18 x 12 inches).

Spread with mixture listed above. Prepared prune, apricot, or date-nut fillings may be used.

Roll as for jelly roll and cut into 1-inch slices. Place slices, cut side down, in greased pan (12 x 8 x 2 inches) or greased muffin pans. Let rise until light, about 1 hour. Bake in moderate oven (375°F.) 25 to 30 minutes. Makes 18 medium-sized rolls.

ELECTION CAKE

This rich yeast cake, often called Hartford Election Cake after Hartford, Conn., where it originated in the 19th century, is sometimes made with various other candied fruits added to it.

1   cake compressed yeast
1/2 cup lukewarm water
2   cups scalded milk
1   teaspoon salt
6   cups sifted enriched flour
2   cups raisins, chopped
1/2 cup sliced citron
2/3 cup butter (at room temperature)
2   cups firmly packed brown sugar
1   teaspoon cinnamon
1/2 teaspoon nutmeg
3   large eggs or 4 medium eggs
Molasses

Soften yeast in lukewarm water. Cool milk to lukewarm and add salt and softened yeast.

Add 1/3 cup flour to chopped raisins and sliced citron. Mix well.

Add yeast mixture to remaining flour and beat with wooden spoon until well blended and "stringy." Set in warm place (80° to 90°F.) to rise until double in bulk.

Setting the pan of dough in water of 90° to 100°F. in temperature helps to give rapid rising, 45 to 60 minutes.

While dough is rising, cream butter, add sugar gradually and cream until fluffy. Add cinnamon and nutmeg.

Add eggs 1 at a time and mix thoroughly.

Add creamed mixture to dough and beat until no spots of white dough show. Add raisins and citron and mix. Let dough rise until double in bulk, 30 to 40 minutes.

Cut down dough and stir until smooth.

Turn into 3 1-quart pans or casseroles, well greased, and let rise until dough reaches tops of pans, 45 to 60 minutes.

Bake on lower shelf of moderate oven (350°F.) 30 minutes; lower temperature to slow (325°F.) and continue baking 30

to 35 minutes longer.

If tops brown too fast, cover after first 30 minutes with aluminum foil.

Glaze when done with molasses and return to oven for 5 minutes to set glaze. Serves 24.

BUTTER SCHNECKEN

Schnecken is the German word for snails; hence snail-shaped buns.

1   cake compressed yeast
1/2 cup sugar
3/4 cup butter
1/2 cup milk, scalded
2   eggs
1   cup sour cream
4 1/2 cups sifted enriched flour
1 1/2 teaspoons salt

Crumble yeast into mixing bowl; add sugar and stir together until yeast liquifies. Let stand about 20 minutes. Meanwhile, melt butter in scalded milk. Beat eggs, add sour cream; blend well with yeast and sugar mixture. Add lukewarm milk, butter, flour, and salt all at once. Beat 8 to 10 minutes. Long beating improves the dough, which should be soft. Store in refrigerator.

The next day, let dough rise in warm place to double its original bulk, or more. Knead in 1 1/2 cups more flour. Roll out into 2 sheets about 1/4 inch thick.

Spread with mixture of 1 part pecans to 2 parts raisins and sprinkle with mixture of 1/4 teaspoon cinnamon to 1/4 cup sugar. Roll lengthwise; cut like a jelly roll into slices 1 1/2 inches thick.

Place in buttered muffin pans lined with mixture of 1 cup brown sugar, 1/4 cup melted butter, 2 tablespoons water, and whole pecans, using 1 tablespoon of this mixture in the bottom of each pan. Set schnecken in warm place to rise to double in bulk. Bake in hot oven (400°F.) about 25 minutes; reduce temperature to 350°F., and bake 10 minutes longer.

Butter Schnecken

SOUR CREAM KOLACKY

1 cake compressed yeast
3 tablespoons sugar
2 tablespoons lukewarm milk
⅓ cup shortening
5 egg yolks, well beaten
Grated rind of 1 lemon
1 cup thick sour cream
3 cups sifted enriched flour
½ teaspoon salt
1 teaspoon baking soda
Raisins or cherries
1 egg white, well beaten

Soften yeast and 1 tablespoon sugar in lukewarm milk. Cream shortening and 2 tablespoons sugar. Add egg yolks, lemon rind, sour cream, and yeast mixture. Mix well.

Add flour sifted with salt and soda and beat thoroughly. Drop from teaspoon on well-greased pans or fill greased muffin cups half full.

Place a raisin or cherry on top of each cake. Brush with beaten egg white. Sprinkle with sugar and let rise in a warm place until light, about 2 hours.

Bake in moderate oven (375°F.) 25 minutes. Makes about 36.

SAVARIN

A yeast-raised cake baked in a ring mold and then saturated with a syrup flavored with rum or kirsch. The hollow center is filled with cut-up fruit, custard, or whipped cream, or a combination of these. It is named after Jean Anthelme Brillat-Savarin, a French gastronome (1755-1826), the author of *The Physiology of Taste*, a classic work on cookery. His name has been given to several dishes.

1 package or cake yeast, active dry or compressed
¼ cup warm water (105°-115°F.)
1½ cups sifted enriched flour
1 tablespoon sugar
½ teaspoon salt
2 large or 3 small eggs
¼ cup milk
⅔ cup butter, at room temperature
1 teaspoon grated lemon rind
Rum syrup (below)

Sprinkle or crumble yeast into warm water; stir until dissolved.

Combine flour, sugar, and salt in a large bowl. Stir in yeast and eggs which have been beaten slightly with the milk. Beat until the batter is smooth, about 100 strokes.

Add butter and lemon rind; beat until butter is blended into batter, about 50 strokes.

Spoon the batter into a 9-inch ring mold, filling it only half full. Cover with a cloth and let rise until the batter just fills the mold, about 1 hour.

Bake in hot oven (400°F.) 30 to 35 minutes, or until browned.

Turn the cake out of the mold onto a serving plate. Spoon hot rum syrup over it until cake is saturated. If desired, keep warm and fill with whipped cream or a light custard just before serving. Makes 8 to 10 servings.

Rum Syrup: Combine 1 cup water, 1 cup sugar, 2 slices lemon, 1 slice orange, 1-inch piece vanilla bean, a 2-inch stick cinnamon, and 1 clove; bring to boil, stirring until sugar is dissolved. Simmer 5 minutes; strain and add ½ cup light rum.

HOSKA

Hoska is a spectacular braided yeast bread from old Czechoslovakia. It's light and delicately sweet. Fruit and chopped almonds throughout the tender bread provide delightful texture contrast. It is not frosted, but is glazed and decorated before baking with whole almonds that toast to a beautiful brown.

1 cup milk
½ cup shortening
¾ cup sugar
½ teaspoon salt
¼ cup warm (not hot) water
2 packages or cakes yeast, active dry or compressed
2 eggs, beaten
3 cups sifted enriched flour
¼ cup chopped citron
¼ cup raisins
¼ cup chopped almonds
Additional 2½ cups sifted enriched flour (about)
1 egg
1 tablespoon water
¼ cup whole blanched almonds

Scald milk. Stir in shortening, sugar, and salt. Cool to lukewarm.

Measure warm water into bowl (cool to lukewarm for compressed yeast). Sprinkle or crumble in yeast and stir until dissolved. Stir in lukewarm milk mixture.

Add 2 beaten eggs and 3 cups flour. Beat until smooth.

Stir in citron, raisins, and almonds. Stir in an additional 2½ cups flour.

Turn out on lightly floured board. Knead until smooth and elastic. Place in greased bowl; brush with shortening.

Cover. Let rise in warm place, free from draft, until doubled in bulk, about 1 hour and 15 minutes.

Punch down and turn out on lightly floured board. Divide in half. Divide one half into 3 equal pieces; roll each piece into a strip about 18 inches long. Place 3 strips on greased baking sheets. Form into braid. Brush top lightly with melted margarine or butter.

Divide ⅔ of remaining dough into 3

equal pieces. Form into a second braid about 18 inches long. Place on top of first braid. Brush top lightly with melted margarine or butter.

Form remaining dough into a third braid about 18 inches long. Place on top of second braid. If necessary, use tooth picks to hold braids in place.

Let rise in warm place, free from draft, until doubled in bulk, about 1 hour.

Brush with mixture of egg and water. Decorate with blanched almonds.

Bake in moderate oven (375°F.) about 45 minutes. Makes 1 cake.

Hoska

DANISH PASTRY

The flaky, flavorful pastry known to us as "Danish" actually originated in Vienna. From there it traveled to Denmark, and became so popular that we now associate it with its adopted country rather than with the country of origin. In Denmark it is still called "Vienna bread," but it's "Danish Pastry" to us.

1 ounce compressed yeast
2 tablespoons lukewarm water
¾ cup milk
¾ teaspoon salt
3 tablespoons sugar
2 tablespoons butter
2 eggs
¼ teaspoon nutmeg
¼ teaspoon lemon extract
¼ teaspoon almond extract
About 3½ cups enriched flour
½ cup cold sweet butter for rolling

Dissolve yeast in lukewarm water and set aside. Scald milk with salt, sugar, and butter. Cool to lukewarm and add to yeast mixture.

Beat eggs; add nutmeg and flavorings and stir mixture into the milk-yeast combination. Work in 1 cup flour. Beat until smooth, then add enough more flour to make a very soft dough.

Turn out onto floured board and knead until smooth. Round up, place in greased bowl, and let rise until light, about 1 hour.

Punch down, then roll out to a rectangle about 7 by 10 inches. Place ⅓ of sweet butter, cut into tiny pieces, over ⅔ of the rectangle. Fold unbuttered third of dough towards you over the buttered part and fold last third over the first 2 to give 3 thicknesses. Press edges together and chill in refrigerator for ½ hour.

Repeat rolling, buttering, and chilling process 2 times, making 3 rollings in all.

Now divide dough into 5 pieces and while working with 1 piece, keep remainder in refrigerator.

Dough may seem hard to roll when removed from refrigerator, but the chilling produces flakiness in the finished product. Shape as indicated below.

After shaping rolls, place on ungreased baking sheets, preferably those with lips to prevent drippings of melted butter spilling on oven surface.

Cover with cloth and allow to rise until double in bulk.

Bake in moderate oven (375°F.) 15 to 20 minutes. When rolls are cool, brush lightly with light corn syrup. Makes about 2 dozen.

SHAPING DANISH PASTRY

Cinnamon Fans: Combine 2 tablespoons sugar, 1 teaspoon cinnamon, and ¼ cup finely chopped nuts.

Roll pastry into a rectangle 9 by 12 inches and sprinkle mixture over it.

Roll as for jelly roll. Cut into 1½ inch slices. Make 2 deep gashes in each slice and separate the gashed sections and open like a fan.

Snails: Make almond filling by grinding ¼ pound unblanched almonds, and mixing with 1 cup sugar. Gradually add 1 egg blended with 2 teaspoons cream. Mix well and spread half of it over the 9-inch half of pastry (again rolled to rectangle 9 by 12 inches).

Cut into 9 1-inch strips. Roll filled halves toward center, turn over and spread on remaining filling. Roll this filled strip to center. Press 2 rolls together. Turn on flat side and press down firmly with palm of hand. (Use jam as a filling if you prefer.)

Raspberry Stars: Roll dough into square, 12 by 12 inches. Cut into 3 inch squares. Moisten center of each square with a drop of milk.

Cut each corner 1 inch toward center. Turn every other point toward center, pressing down firmly.

Place teaspoon of thick raspberry jam in center of each star.

Almond Butterflies: Prepare same amount of almond filling as used for snails.

Roll well chilled dough into 10 by 12 inch rectangle. Brush with melted butter, then spread on almond filling.

Roll like jelly roll. Cut into 1½ inch slices. Make a deep crease with handle of knife through center of each piece parallel with cut side.

KUGELHUPF OR GUGELHUPF

Kugelhupf is a rich cake-like bread made from a batter instead of a dough. In Vienna, where this cake-like bread was perhaps most famous, it is frequently served for dessert or as a special-occasion refreshment.

½ cup milk
½ cup sugar
½ teaspoon salt
¼ cup margarine or butter
¼ cup warm (not hot) water
1 package or cake yeast, active dry or compressed
2 eggs, beaten
2½ cups sifted enriched flour
14 to 16 whole blanched almonds
½ cup seedless raisins
½ teaspoon grated lemon rind

Scald milk. Stir in sugar, salt, and margarine or butter. Cool to lukewarm.

Measure warm water into bowl (cool to lukewarm for compressed yeast). Sprinkle or crumble in yeast and stir until dissolved. Stir in lukewarm milk mixture.

Add beaten eggs and flour. Beat vigorously, about 5 minutes.

Cover. Let rise in warm place, free from draft, until doubled in bulk, about 1 hour and 30 minutes.

Sprinkle fine breadcrumbs over sides and bottom of well greased 1½ quart casserole or fancy mold. Arrange almonds on bottom.

Stir batter down. Beat thoroughly. Stir in raisins and grated lemon rind. Turn into prepared casserole or mold.

Let rise in warm place, free from draft, until doubled in bulk, about 1 hour.

Bake in moderate oven (350°F.) about 50 minutes. Makes 1 cake.

VIENNESE COFFEE RING

2 packages compressed or dry yeast
¼ cup lukewarm water for compressed or warm for dry yeast
1 cup milk
½ cup sugar
1 teaspoon salt
¼ cup shortening
About 3¼ cups sifted enriched flour
1 egg, beaten

Topping:

⅓ cup sugar
¼ teaspoon cinnamon
¼ cup chopped nuts

Soften yeast in lukewarm water. Scald milk. Add sugar, salt, and shortening. Cool to lukewarm.

Add 1 cup flour and beat well. Add softened yeast and egg. Beat thoroughly.

Add remaining flour to make a stiff batter. Beat 3 minutes.

Pour into greased spring form pan. Mix sugar, cinnamon, and nuts for topping and sprinkle over batter. Let rise until doubled.

Bake in moderate oven (375°F.) 35 to 40 minutes. Makes 1 coffee ring.

Viennese Coffee Ring

DATE BRAIDED CAKE

1 recipe Sweet Dough
1 cup chopped, pitted dates
1/4 cup brown sugar
2/3 cup water
1/2 cup chopped nuts
1 tablespoon lemon juice
1 egg yolk
2 tablespoons milk
2 tablespoons margarine or butter
2 tablespoons sugar
1/3 cup sifted enriched flour
1/2 teaspoon cinnamon

While Sweet Dough is rising prepare Date Filling:

Combine in saucepan 1 cup dates, brown sugar, water, chopped nuts, and lemon juice. Bring to a boil over medium heat, stirring constantly, and continue boiling until mixture is thick enough to spread.

Divide Sweet Dough in half. Roll out each half into an oblong about 16 x 8 inches.

Spread half the Date Filling down center third of each oblong. Cut 15 slits in dough along each side of filling, making strips about 1 inch wide.

Fold strips at an angle across filling, alternating from side to side. Place on greased baking sheet. If desired, form into a ring. Place one end in the other and seal together firmly.

Cover. Let rise in warm place, free from draft, until doubled in bulk. (Straight-Dough Method about 1 hour; Action-Quick Dough about 30 minutes.)

Combine and brush cakes with egg yolk and milk.

Sprinkle with mixture of margarine or butter, sugar, flour, and cinnamon.

Bake in moderate oven (350°F.) about 35 minutes. Makes 2 cakes.

Date Braided Cake

BEATEN BATTER
(Master Recipe)

1 cake compressed yeast
1/4 cup lukewarm water
1 cup milk
1/4 cup sugar
1 teaspoon salt
1/2 cup shortening
About 3 1/4 cups sifted enriched flour
2 eggs
1/2 teaspoon vanilla, optional

Soften yeast in lukewarm water. Scald milk and add sugar, salt, and shortening. Cool to lukewarm. Add 1 cup flour and beat well.

Add softened yeast, eggs, and vanilla. Beat well.

Add remaining flour to make a thick batter. Beat thoroughly until smooth. Cover and let rise until doubled, about 1 hour.

Use with different toppings to make coffee cakes and puff rolls. Makes 2 coffee cakes 8 x 8 inches or 2 9-inch cakes, or about 2 1/2 dozen 2-inch puffs.

CRUMBLE COFFEE CAKE

1/2 recipe Beaten Batter
3 tablespoons milk
Crumble Topping

When beaten batter is light, stir down. Spread evenly in greased pan (8 x 8 inches) or 9-inch layer pan.

Brush with milk and sprinkle with crumble topping.

Let rise until doubled, about 45 minutes.

Bake in moderate oven (375°F.) 30 minutes. Makes 1 coffee cake.

Crumble Topping:

1/2 cup sifted enriched flour
1/4 cup dry breadcrumbs
2 tablespoons sugar
1/2 teaspoon cinnamon
2 tablespoons butter

Mix flour, breadcrumbs, sugar, and cinnamon. Cut in or rub in butter until crumbly.

CRANBERRY SWIRL COFFEE CAKE

1/2 recipe Beaten Batter
1/2 cup sweetened cranberry sauce
1/4 cup sugar
1/4 teaspoon cinnamon

When beaten batter is light, stir down. Spread evenly in greased 9-inch layer pan.

With a floured spoon make grooves in swirl design on top of batter. Fill grooves wtih cranberry sauce.

Mix sugar and cinnamon. Sprinkle evenly over top. Let rise until doubled, about 45 minutes.

Bake in moderate oven (375°F.) 30 minutes. Makes 1 coffee cake.

TEA PUFFS

1/2 recipe Beaten Batter
1/2 cup sliced almonds
1/4 cup sugar
1/2 teaspoon cinnamon

When beaten batter is light, stir down. Drop by spoonfuls into greased muffin pans.

Mix almonds, sugar, and cinnamon. Sprinkle over muffins.

Let rise until doubled, about 45 minutes.

Bake in moderate oven (375°F.) 25 minutes. Makes about 16 2-inch puffs.

APPLE COFFEE CAKE

1/2 recipe Beaten Batter
3 to 4 medium apples
2 tablespoons melted butter
1/4 cup sugar
1 teaspoon cinnamon

When beaten batter is light, stir down. Spread evenly in greased 9-inch layer pan.

Peel and slice apples. Arrange apple slices on top of batter, overlapping them in 2 circles.

Brush with melted butter. Mix sugar and cinnamon and sprinkle over apples.

Let rise until doubled, about 45 minutes.

Bake in moderate oven (375°F.) 30 minutes. Makes 1 coffee cake.

SUGARPLUM LOAF

3/4 cup scalded milk
1/2 cup shortening
1/2 cup sugar
2 eggs
1 cake compressed yeast
2 tablespoons lukewarm water
5 cups sifted enriched flour
1 teaspoon salt
1/2 cup seedless raisins
1/2 cup chopped walnuts
1/2 cup chopped citron
1/2 cup chopped candied cherries

Cool scalded milk to lukewarm. Cream together shortening and sugar. Beat eggs and add.

Dissolve yeast in lukewarm water. Add with milk to creamed mixture. Add 1 cup flour and mix well.

Cover and let rise in warm place until doubled in bulk.

Add salt, raisins, chopped nuts, citron, and cherries. Gradually add remaining flour and knead on lightly floured board until thoroughly mixed.

Place in greased round pan 8 inches in diameter and 3 inches high. Cover and let rise in warm place until doubled in bulk.

Bake in moderate oven (350°F.) 1 hour and 15 minutes.

Remove from pan and cool on wire rack. If desired, spread with confectioners' sugar icing. Makes 1 loaf.

Cinnamon Rolls

CINNAMON ROLLS

Use ½ recipe for Sweet Dough and when it is light roll out to long narrow sheet ¼ inch thick. Brush with ¼ cup melted butter.

Mix 1 cup sugar and 1½ teaspoons cinnamon, and sprinkle over dough. If desired, ½ cup raisins may be added.

Roll up jelly-roll fashion and seal edge. Cut into 1-inch slices and place cut side down into well greased muffin pans, ring mold, or deep cake pan.

Brush tops with milk, and sprinkle with cinnamon and sugar mixture.

Let rise until doubled in bulk. Bake in moderate oven (375°F.) 25 minutes. Makes 3½ dozen rolls.

JULE KAGA

Jule Kaga is a Norwegian fruited sweet bread flavored with cardamom, a favorite spice in Scandinavian countries.

1   cup milk
½   cup sugar
1   teaspoon salt
½   cup shortening
¼   cup warm (not hot) water
2   packages or cakes yeast, active dry or compressed
2   cups sifted enriched flour
1½ teaspoons ground cardamom
½   cup raisins
¼   cup chopped citron
¼   cup chopped candied cherries
¼   cup chopped almonds
Additional 2½ cups sifted enriched flour (about)

Scald milk. Stir in sugar, salt, and shortening. Cool to lukewarm.

Measure warm water into bowl (cool to lukewarm for compressed yeast). Sprinkle or crumble in yeast and stir until dissolved. Stir in lukewarm milk mixture.

Add 2 cups flour. Beat thoroughly. Cover. Let rise in warm place, free from draft, until doubled in bulk, about 30 minutes. Stir down.

Stir in cardamom, raisins, citron, cherries, and almonds. Stir in an additional 2½ cups flour.

Turn out on lightly floured board. Knead until smooth and elastic. Place in greased bowl; brush with shortening. Cover. Let rise in warm place, free from draft, until doubled in bulk, about 55 minutes.

Punch down. Form into round ball

and place on large greased baking sheet.

Cover. Let rise in warm place, free from draft, until doubled in bulk, about 1 hour.

Bake in hot oven (400°F.) for 10 minutes; reduce to moderate heat (350°F.) and continue baking for 40 minutes.

Cool. Frost with plain icing, decorate with nuts and candied fruit. Makes 1 round loaf.

BUTTER HORNS

1   package dry or 1 cake compressed yeast
¼   cup warm water for dry yeast or lukewarm for compressed yeast
½   cup scalded milk
¼   cup sugar
½   teaspoon salt
1   beaten egg
¼   cup soft butter
About 2¾ cups sifted enriched flour

Soften yeast in warm water about 5 minutes. Pour scalded milk over sugar and salt. Cool to lukewarm.

Add softened yeast, beaten egg, and soft butter. Blend well, then stir in 1 cup flour, or enough to make soft batter.

Beat well, then add enough more flour to make soft, but kneadable dough. Knead until smooth and elastic on lightly floured board.

Place in greased bowl. Grease surface lightly. Cover and set in warm place until doubled in bulk, about 1 hour.

Divide dough in half. Roll each half on lightly floured board into a circular sheet about ¼ inch thick. Cut into pie-shaped wedges, 12 to a circle for tiny rolls, or 8 to a circle for larger ones.

Spread with a little melted butter. Roll each wedge from wide end, pressing tip of dough against roll to keep it from unrolling.

Place on greased baking sheets 1 inch apart. Cover with cloth and let rise again until light, about ½ hour.

Bake in hot oven (425°F.) 12 to 15 minutes. Makes 2 dozen.

HOLLAND CAKE

½   cup butter
1   cup sugar
1   cup strong black coffee
2   eggs, well beaten
4   tablespoons cream
1   cake compressed yeast
2   tablespoons lukewarm water
About 4½ cups sifted enriched flour
1   cup seeded raisins
2   tablespoons whole anise seed

Cream butter and sugar together until light and fluffy. Add cold coffee and the eggs and cream.

Soften yeast in lukewarm water and add to first mixture. Add flour to make soft dough. Mix well, cover and let rise

until doubled in bulk, about 1½ hours.

Punch down and knead in raisins and anise seeds, continuing kneading until dough is smooth and satiny. Cover and let rise until doubled in bulk, about 1 hour.

Bake in moderate oven (350°F.) until done, about 50 minutes. When cold, ice with confectioners' sugar frosting. Makes one 9 x 15-inch loaf.

CHERRY-GO-ROUND
(No-Dissolve Method)

3½ to 4½ cups unsifted all-purpose flour
½   cup sugar
1   teaspoon salt
1   package active dry yeast
1   cup milk
¼   cup water
½   cup (1 stick) margarine
1   egg (at room temperature)
½   cup unsifted all-purpose flour
½   cup chopped pecans
½   cup firmly packed light brown sugar
1   can (1-pound) pitted red sour cherries, well drained
Confectioners' sugar frosting

In a large bowl thoroughly mix 1¼ cups flour, sugar, salt, and undissolved active dry yeast.

Combine milk, water, and margarine in a saucepan. Heat over low heat until liquids are warm. (Margarine does not need to melt.) Gradually add to dry ingredients and beat 2 minutes at medium speed of electric mixer, scraping bowl occasionally. Add egg and ¾ cup flour, or enough flour to make a thick batter. Beat at high speed 2 minutes, scraping the bowl occasionally. Stir in enough additional flour to make a stiff batter. Cover bowl tightly with aluminum foil. Refrigerate dough at least 2 hours. (Dough may be kept in refrigerator 3 days.)

When ready to shape dough, combine ½ cup flour, pecans, and brown sugar.

Turn dough out onto lightly floured board and divide in half. Roll ½ of the dough to a 14 x 7-inch rectangle. Spread with ¾ cup cherries. Sprinkle with ½ the brown sugar mixture. Roll up from long side as for jelly roll. Seal edges. Place sealed edge down in circle on greased baking sheet. Seal ends together firmly. Cut slits ⅔ through ring at 1-inch intervals; turn each section on its side. Repeat with remaining dough, cherries, and brown sugar mixture. Cover; let rise in warm place, free from draft, until doubled in bulk, about 1 hour.

Bake in a moderate oven (375°F.) about 20 to 25 minutes, or until done. Remove from baking sheets and cool on wire racks. Frost while warm with confectioners' sugar frosting. Makes 2 coffeecakes.

HAMANTASCHEN

Hamantaschen is a Yiddish term for triangular yeast-raised cakes filled with a poppyseed and honey filling or other fillings and eaten at Purim, a Jewish holiday. The word is derived from the Bible character Haman, and possibly, from German taschen (pockets), probably with reference to the manner in which the cakes are filled. Their shape recalls the triangular hat Haman is supposed to have worn.

Hamantaschen may be made from the basic recipes for sweet dough. Roll small balls of dough to ¼-inch thickness into rounds 4 to 6 inches in diameter. On each round place a mound of filling (below) and bring the edges together to form a triangle, pinching the edges together from the top down to corners.

Let the filled rolls rise in warm place until double in bulk. Brush tops with diluted egg yolk, evaporated milk, or melted shortening.

Bake in moderate oven (375°F.) until lightly browned, 20 to 25 minutes for medium-sized rolls.

Note: Similar shaped cookies may be made from a rolled sugar cooky dough using the traditional poppyseed and honey filling.

POPPYSEED AND HONEY FILLING FOR HAMANTASCHEN

2 cups poppyseed
1 cup milk or water
½ cup honey
¼ cup sugar
⅛ teaspoon salt
2 eggs, if desired

If the poppyseed are large they should be scalded, drained well, and put through the finest blade of the food chopper or pounded.

Combine the poppyseed with milk or water, honey, sugar, and salt in a saucepan. Cook over moderate heat until thick, stirring to prevent scorching.

Let cool, then beat in the eggs. If the addition of eggs thins out the filling too much, place the mixture over moderate heat and cook 1 or 2 minutes, stirring constantly.

Variations: Chopped almonds or other nuts (¼ cup) and ¼ cup seedless raisins or currants may be added. The filling may be flavored with 1 tablespoon lemon juice and ½ teaspoon grated lemon rind.

SOUR CREAM FAN TAN ROLLS

1 package dry yeast
¼ cup warm water
¾ cup scalded, cooled sour cream
⅛ teaspoon baking soda
1 teaspoon salt
2 tablespoons sugar
About 2 cups sifted enriched flour

Soften yeast in warm water about 5 minutes. Add cooled sour cream. Stir in soda, salt, and sugar. Then gradually work in flour to make soft dough.

Round dough up and place in greased bowl. Brush top with melted fat. Cover and let rise in warm place until doubled in bulk, 1 to 1½ hours.

Turn out on lightly floured board and knead lightly 1 minute. Roll dough into rectangular sheet about ⅛ inch thick. Brush with melted butter or margarine.

Cut into strips 1½ inches wide. Pile in stacks of 6 strips. Cut in pieces 1½ inches long and place in greased muffin pans, cut edges up.

Let rise again in warm place until doubled in size.

Bake in hot oven (425°F.) 15 minutes or until nicely browned. Makes 1 dozen.

ORANGE ROLLS

1 cake compressed or 1 package dry yeast
¼ cup water (lukewarm for compressed yeast, warm for dry yeast)
½ cup scalded milk
¼ cup shortening
¼ cup sugar
1¼ teaspoons salt
½ cup orange juice
1 teaspoon grated orange rind
1 beaten egg
About 4 cups sifted enriched flour

Soften yeast in water. Pour milk over shortening, sugar, and salt.

When lukewarm add orange juice, grated rind, egg, yeast, and 2 cups flour. Beat until smooth.

Add enough flour to make dough which can be handled on board. Knead until light and elastic, about 3 minutes.

Form into ball and place in warm bowl. Grease top lightly. Cover and keep in warm place (80° to 85°F.) until doubled in bulk.

Punch down, form into rolls, and place on well greased pan. Let rise until very light and doubled in bulk.

Bake in hot oven (400°F.) 15 to 25 minutes, depending on size. Makes about 30 rolls.

Orange Refrigerator Rolls: Follow above recipe. After placing dough in bowl, grease top. Cover and place in refrigerator.

Two hours before baking, put required amount of dough in a warm, greased bowl. Let rise in warm place about 1½ hours.

Knead and shape into rolls. Bake as directed.

CORNISH SPLITS

1 cake compressed yeast
¼ cup sugar
4 cups sifted enriched flour

¼ teaspoon salt
⅓ cup shortening
¾ cup lukewarm milk
2 eggs, well beaten
Melted butter
½ cup whipped cream
¼ cup apricot jam

Combine yeast and 2 tablespoons sugar. Let stand until yeast is liquefied.

Sift flour and salt with remaining sugar. Add yeast. Cut in the shortening.

Add milk to beaten eggs, and combine with the yeast mixture. Mix quickly to a soft dough. Spread with melted butter. Cover and let rise until doubled in size.

Knead and form into flat, small cakes. Place on baking sheet, brush with butter and let rise again until doubled.

Bake in hot oven (400°F.) about 20 to 25 minutes. Cool. Split side of each and fill with the whipped cream mixed with apricot jam.

ENGLISH TEA CAKE

1 cake compressed or 1 package dry granular yeast
½ cup scalded milk
¼ cup shortening
¼ cup sugar
1 egg or 2 egg yolks, beaten
½ teaspoon salt
½ cup currants
About 1½ cups sifted enriched flour

Topping:

2 tablespoons sugar
¼ teaspoon cinnamon
¼ cup chopped nuts

Soften yeast in milk which has been cooled to lukewarm. Add shortening, sugar, egg, salt, currants, and enough flour to make a rather stiff drop batter. Beat until smooth. Let rise until doubled.

Stir down and pour into greased 8 x 8 x 2-inch pan, filling pan about ½ full. Mix sugar, cinnamon, and nuts for topping and sprinkle over the batter. Let rise until puffy and doubled. Bake in hot oven (400°F.) 25 to 30 minutes. Makes 1 tea cake, 8 x 8 x 2 inches.

English Tea Cake

NORWEGIAN TEA BREAD

2   cups milk
1   cup butter
1   cup sugar
¼   teaspoon salt
1   cake compressed yeast
9   cups sifted enriched flour
2   teaspoons ground cardamom
½   cup finely sliced citron, packed in cup
½   cup raisins

Scald milk; add butter, sugar, and salt; cool. When lukewarm, crumble yeast into milk mixture in mixing bowl. Add 4 cups sifted flour and beat until smooth.

Pour into large clean buttered bowl, cover closely, and set in warm place out of draughts until doubled in bulk, about 2½ hours.

Then stir in remaining flour, turn out on floured board, and knead thoroughly until smooth and elastic.

Knead in cardamom, citron, and raisins a little at a time. Total time given to kneading should be at least 15 minutes.

Replace in buttered bowl, cover, and again let rise to double in bulk.

Turn out onto floured board and again knead down. Divide into 3 equal portions. Shape in loaves and place in buttered loaf pans.

Cover and set in warm place until slightly more than doubled in bulk; then slash each loaf 3 times across the top and brush with melted butter.

Bake in moderate oven (375°F.) 10 minutes; then reduce to 300°F. and bake 40 to 50 minutes longer.

Remove to cake racks and cool. Makes 3 loaves.

COCONUT PINEAPPLE COFFEE CAKE
(Batter Method)

3   tablespoons margarine or butter
2   tablespoons dark brown sugar
½   cup shredded coconut
⅓   cup pineapple tidbits
⅓   cup milk
⅓   cup sugar
¾   teaspoon salt
¼   cup shortening
¼   cup warm (not hot) water
1   package or cake yeast, active dry or compressed
1   egg, beaten
½   teaspoon vanilla
2   cups sifted enriched flour

Melt margarine or butter in pan 8 x 8 x 2 inches. Spread evenly brown sugar and coconut. Arrange pineapple tidbits.

Scald in saucepan ⅓ cup milk. Stir in sugar, salt, and shortening. Cool to lukewarm.

Measure into bowl ¼ cup warm water (cool to lukewarm for compressed yeast). Sprinkle or crumble in yeast. Stir until dissolved. Stir in lukewarm milk mixture.

Add beaten egg, vanilla, and flour. Stir until well blended, about 1 minute. Turn batter into prepared pan. Let rise in warm place, free from draft, until doubled in bulk, about 1 hour and 15 minutes.

Bake in moderate oven (375°F.) about 35 minutes. Turn out of pan immediately. Serve warm. Makes 1 cake.

Orange Coffee Cake:
3   tablespoons margarine or butter
¼   cup dark brown sugar
2   oranges, peeled and sectioned

Melt margarine or butter in pan 8 x 8 x 2 inches. Spread evenly brown sugar. Arrange orange sections.

Proceed as for Coconut Pineapple Coffee Cake. Makes 1 cake.

HUNGARIAN FILLED BUNS

1   cake compressed or 1 package dry granular yeast
2   tablespoons lukewarm water for compressed yeast or warm for dry yeast
½   cup butter
3   cups sifted enriched flour
6   tablespoons sour cream
3   egg yolks, beaten
2   tablespoons sugar
½   teaspoon salt
Lukewarm milk

Soften the yeast in the lukewarm water. Cut the butter into the flour with 2 knives or a pastry blender.

Add the sour cream and egg yolks and mix well. Add the sugar, salt, and the softened yeast, and enough milk to make a dough that is soft but not sticky. Allow to rise in a warm place until doubled in bulk.

Punch down and allow to rest for 10 minutes. Roll out thinly; spread lightly with softened butter; fold the sides over the center and the ends to the center, envelope fashion. Roll thinly and fold again. Repeat this procedure twice more.

The dough is now ready to be cut into rolls; rolled and cut into pinwheels or made into filled squares; or triangles of dough may be filled and rolled to form horns and crescents.

Brush the rolls with beaten egg white and sprinkle with anise or poppy seed.

Allow to rise again until doubled in bulk and bake in moderate oven (350°F.) for 20 minutes. Makes 2 dozen rolls.

Cheese Filling: Press 2 cups cottage cheese through a sieve and mix to a paste with 3 beaten eggs, 1 tablespoon

sugar, the grated rind of 1 lemon, ½ cup raisins, and ¼ teaspoon nutmeg.

Prune Filling: Mix together into a stiff paste 2 cups chopped, cooked prunes, the grated rind of 1 lemon, 2 tablespoons sugar, and ½ teaspoon cinnamon.

Raisin Filling: Boil together 1 cup sugar and 1 cup water. Add 1 cup chopped raisins, 1 cup chopped nuts, 1 teaspoon cinnamon, and the grated rind of 1 lemon. Cook for about 8 minutes, stirring until thick.

BABKA
(No-Dissolve Method)

This Polish Easter bread derives its name from the word meaning old woman, because the cake, which is tall and wide, looks like an old woman with wide skirts. It is also served in Czechoslovakia where young girls put love messages on Easter eggs and present them with Babka to their boyfriends.

2   cups unsifted all-purpose flour
¼   cup sugar
1   package active dry yeast
½   cup milk
¼   cup (½ stick) margarine
3   eggs (at room temperature)
¼   cup mixed candied fruits
¼   cup seedless raisins

In a large bowl thoroughly mix ¾ cup flour, sugar, and undissolved active dry yeast.

Combine milk and margarine in a saucepan. Heat over low heat until liquid is warm. (Margarine does not need to melt.) Gradually add to dry ingredients and beat 2 minutes at medium speed of electric mixer, scraping bowl occasionally. Add eggs and ½ cup flour, or enough flour to make a thick batter. Beat at high speed 2 minutes, scraping bowl occasionally. Add remaining flour and beat 2 minutes at high speed. Cover; let rise in warm place, free from draft, until bubbly, about 1 hour.

Stir in candied fruits and raisins. Turn into greased and floured 2-quart Turk's Head pan or tube pan. Let rise, uncovered, in warm place, free from draft, for 30 minutes.

Bake in moderate oven (350°F.) about 40 minutes, or until done.

Before removing from pan, immediately prick surface with fork. Pour Rum Syrup (below) over cake. After syrup is absorbed, remove from pan and cool on wire rack. When cool, if desired, frost with confectioners' sugar frosting. Makes 1 cake.

Rum Syrup: Combine ½ cup sugar, ⅓ cup water, and 2 teaspoons rum extract in a saucepan; bring to a boil.

CINNAMON ORANGE CRESCENTS
(No-Dissolve Method)

        4 to 5 cups unsifted all-purpose
             flour
    ½ cup sugar
    2 teaspoons salt
    1 tablespoon grated orange peel
    2 packages active dry yeast
    ¾ cup milk
    ½ cup water
    ½ cup (1 stick) margarine
    1 egg (at room temperature)
    Melted margarine
    ¾ cup sugar
    1 tablespoon ground cinnamon
    Confectioners' sugar frosting

In a large bowl thoroughly mix 1½ cups flour, ½ cup sugar, salt, orange peel, and undissolved active dry yeast.

Combine milk, water, and ½ cup margarine in a saucepan. Heat over low heat until liquids are warm. (Margarine does not need to melt.) Gradually add to dry ingredients and beat 2 minutes at medium speed of electric mixer, scraping bowl occasionally. Add egg and ½ cup flour, or enough flour to make a thick batter. Beat at high speed 2 minutes, scraping bowl occasionally. Stir in enough additional flour to make a soft dough. Turn out onto lightly floured board; knead until smooth and elastic, about 8 to 10 minutes. Place in greased bowl, turning to grease top. Cover; let rise in warm place, free from draft, until doubled in bulk, about 1 hour.

Punch dough down; turn out onto lightly floured board. Divide dough into 8 equal pieces. Roll 1 piece of dough into an 8-inch circle. Brush with melted margarine. Combine ¾ cup sugar and cinnamon. Sprinkle circle with about 1½ tablespoons cinnamon-sugar mixture. Cut into 8 pie-shaped pieces. Roll up tightly, beginning at wide end; seal points firmly. Place on greased baking sheet with points underneath. Curve to form crescents. Repeat with remaining pieces of dough and cinnamon-sugar mixture. Cover; let rise in warm place, free from draft, until doubled in bulk, about 1 hour.

Bake in moderate oven (350°F.) about 12 minutes, or until done. Remove from baking sheets and cool on wire racks. Frost with confectioners' sugar frosting. Makes 64 small rolls.

LEMON DROP BALLS

    1 recipe Sweet Dough
    ¼ cup melted butter
    Lemon sugar

When sweet dough is light, punch down. Divide into 4 equal parts and let rest 10 minutes.

Roll each part into long roll about ¾ inch thick. Cut into pieces ¾ inch long.

Shape each piece into ball. Dip into melted butter, then into lemon sugar.

Place 5 balls in each cup of greased muffin pans. Let rise until doubled, about 45 minutes.

Bake in moderate oven (350°F.) 25 minutes. Makes about 3 dozen rolls.

Lemon Sugar: Combine ½ cup sugar and 2 tablespoons grated lemon rind. Mix well.

SUGAR CRISP ROLLS
(No-Dissolve Method)

    2 to 2½ cups unsifted
             all-purpose flour
    1¼ cups sugar
    ½ teaspoon salt
    1 package active dry yeast
    ¼ cup milk
    ¼ cup water
    ¼ cup (½ stick) margarine
    1 egg (at room temperature)
    1 cup chopped pecans
    Melted margarine

In a large bowl thoroughly mix ¾ cup flour, ¼ cup sugar, salt, and undissolved active dry yeast.

Combine milk, water, and ¼ cup margarine in a saucepan. Heat over low heat until liquids are warm. (Margarine does not need to melt.) Gradually add to dry ingredients and beat 2 minutes at medium speed of electric mixer, scraping bowl occasionally.

Add egg and ¼ cup flour, or enough flour to make a thick batter. Beat at high speed 2 minutes, scraping bowl occasionally. Stir in enough additional flour to make a soft dough.

Turn out onto lightly floured board; knead until smooth and elastic, about 8 to 10 minutes. Cover; let rise in warm place, free from draft, until doubled in bulk, about 1 hour. Punch down and let rise an additional 30 minutes.

Combine remaining 1 cup sugar and pecans.

Punch dough down; turn out onto lightly floured board. Roll dough to a 9 x 18-inch rectangle. Brush with melted margarine. Sprinkle dough with half the sugar mixture. Roll up from long side as for jelly roll; seal edges. Cut into 1-inch slices. Roll each slice of dough into a 4-inch circle using remaining sugar mixture in place of flour on board, coating both top and bottom of each circle. Place on greased baking sheets. Cover; let rise in warm place, free from draft, until doubled in bulk, about 30 minutes.

Bake in a moderate oven (375°F.) about 10 to 15 minutes, or until done. Remove from baking sheets and cool on wire racks. Makes 1½ dozen rolls.

DOUBLE-QUICK COFFEE BREADS
(Master Recipe)

    1 package active dry yeast
    ¾ cup warm water (not hot—110°
            to 115°F.)
    ¼ cup sugar
    1 teaspoon salt
    2¼ cups sifted enriched flour
    1 egg
    ¼ cup soft shortening or butter

In mixing bowl dissolve yeast in water. Add sugar and salt, and about half the flour.

Beat thoroughly 2 minutes. Add egg and shortening. Then gradually beat in remaining flour until smooth.

Drop small spoonfuls over entire bottom of greased pan. (Use 8 inch oven-glass pan, or 9 inch square aluminum pan, or 10 inch iron skillet or 9 inch ring mold.) Cover. Let rise in warm place (85°) until double in bulk, 50 to 60 minutes.

Bake in moderate oven (375°F.) until brown, 30 to 35 minutes. Immediately turn out to avoid sticking. Serve warm.

Variations of Double-Quick Coffee Breads:

Jam Puffs: Fill half full 16 to 20 medium-sized greased muffin cups. Let rise. Bake 15 to 20 minutes. When baked, spread with ½ cup thick red jam. Garnish with coconut or chopped nuts.

Cinnamon Streusel: Mix thoroughly 2 tablespoons butter, ⅓ cup white or brown sugar, 2 tablespoons enriched flour, 2 teaspoons cinnamon, ½ cup chopped nuts. Spoon dough into pan. Sprinkle with Streusel mixture.

Tutti-Frutti: Mix into finished dough ½ cup candied fruit and ¼ cup chopped nuts. Spoon into pan. When baked, ice with a mixture of ¾ cup sifted confectioners' sugar and 1 to 2 tablespoons cream. Decorate top with candied fruit and nuts.

Browned Butter Almond: Melt in pan ⅓ cup butter. Add ½ cup slivered blanched almonds. Heat until butter foams up in pan and browns and almonds are light golden brown. (Almonds brown a little more while cooling.) Cool to warm. Mix in 2 tablespoons white corn syrup, ½ cup sugar, ½ teaspoon almond extract. Spoon over dough.

Spicy Sugar Puffs: Fill half full 16 to 20 medium-sized greased, muffin cups. Let rise. Bake 15 to 20 minutes. Immediately after baking, roll in ½ cup melted butter, then in a mixture of ¾ cup sugar and 2 teaspoons cinnamon. Serve hot.

Dress-Ups with Hot Roll Mix

EASY CINNAMON ROLLS

1 package hot roll mix
2 tablespoons melted butter or margarine
1/4 cup brown sugar
1 teaspoon cinnamon
1 cup brown sugar
2 tablespoons light corn syrup
1 tablespoon butter or margarine

Prepare dough as directed on package. On lightly floured surface, roll
dough into oblong shape 1/4 inch thick.
Brush with melted butter; sprinkle with
1/4 cup brown sugar and the cinnamon.
Roll as for jelly roll; pinch edges to
seal; cut in 1-inch slices.

Combine 1 cup brown sugar, the syrup, and butter; heat. Spread in greased
9 x 9 x 2-inch pan. Place rolls cut side
down in mixture. Cover; let double in
bulk, about 30 minutes.

Bake in moderate oven (375°F.)
about 30 minutes. Invert to remove
from pan; cool. Makes 16.

QUICK LEMON ROLLS

1 package hot roll mix
3/4 cup warm water or milk
1 egg, beaten
1/2 cup sugar
2 tablespoons grated lemon rind
2 teaspoons lemon juice

Place yeast from package of mix (in
small envelope) in bowl. Add warm water (98° to 115°F.) and stir until dissolved. Add beaten egg and roll mix
from package. Blend thoroughly.

Grease top, cover with waxed paper,
and let stand in a warm place (85° to
90°F.) until light and double in bulk,
45 to 60 minutes.

Drop by spoonfuls into 2-inch muffin cups, filling them 1/2 full. Blend
sugar, lemon rind, and juice and sprinkle over rolls. Let rise until double in
bulk.

Bake in moderate oven (375°F.)
about 20 minutes. Makes 24 small rolls.

Hot Deviled Ham Braids

NUT TWISTS

1 package hot roll mix
2 tablespoons melted shortening or
salad oil
3/4 cup chopped walnuts
1/2 cup sugar
1 teaspoon cinnamon

Prepare dough as hot roll mix package directs, adding shortening to yeast-
water liquid. Cover. Let rise in warm
place (85° to 90°F.) about 30 minutes.

Combine nuts, sugar, and cinnamon.
Divide dough into small pieces. Stretch
each until about 8-inches long; roll in
nut mixture; twist into S or other shape.

Place on greased baking sheet. Sprinkle with nut mixture. Let rise in warm
place until light, 30 to 60 minutes. Bake
in hot oven (400°F.) 12 to 15 minutes.
Makes 11/2 dozen rolls.

ORANGE PINWHEELS

1 package hot roll mix
1/2 cup sugar
1 tablespoon grated orange rind
2 tablespoons melted butter or margarine
2 tablespoons orange juice
1/4 cup sugar
1 tablespoon grated orange rind

Prepare dough as hot roll mix package directs. Cover. Let rise in warm
place (85° to 90°F.) until double in
bulk, 30 to 60 minutes.

Combine 1/2 cup sugar and next 3 ingredients. Spread evenly in bottoms of
greased 21/2 inch muffin pan cups. On
lightly floured board, roll dough into
20 x 12 inch rectangle.

Combine 1/4 cup sugar and 1 tablespoon grated orange rind. Sprinkle over
dough. Roll up jelly roll fashion, starting at 20-inch edge. Cut into 1-inch
slices. Place, cut sides down, in muffin
cups.

Let rise in warm place until light, 30
to 60 minutes. Bake in moderate oven
(375°F.) 20 to 25 minutes. Makes 11/2
dozen rolls.

HOT DEVILED HAM BRAIDS

1 package hot roll mix
2 41/2-oz. cans deviled ham
1/4 cup chili sauce
1/4 cup chopped nuts

Prepare dough according to package
recipe. Roll into rectangle about 16 x
10 inches.

Combine deviled ham, chili sauce,
and nuts. Spread in 3-inch strip down
center of dough.

On either side, perpendicular to ham
strip, cut 1-inch strips of dough just
to mixture. Make braid by crossing
opposite strips.

Cover braid and allow to rise for an
hour. Bake in hot oven (425°F.) 20
minutes or until golden brown. Makes
about 14 servings.

HERB BREAD STICKS

1/2 teaspoon nutmeg
1 teaspoon leaf sage
2 teaspoons caraway seeds
1 package hot roll mix

Combine first 3 ingredients with hot
roll mix. Then prepare dough as package directs. Cover. Let rise in warm
place (85° to 90°F.) until double in
bulk, 30 to 60 minutes.

Shape into 2 dozen bread sticks. Place
on greased baking sheet, 1 inch apart.

Let rise in warm place until light, 30
to 60 minutes. Bake in hot oven
(400°F) about 15 minutes. Makes 2
dozen sticks.

EASY PLUM KUCHEN

1 package hot roll mix
1 quart halved plums
1/2 cup or more sugar
1 teaspoon cinnamon
2 egg yolks
1/2 cup cream

Prepare dough from hot roll mix as
directed on package and let rise until
double in bulk.

Roll to fit a greased deep 7 x 12-inch
pan. Place in pan, grease surface and let
rise until almost double in thickness.

Arrange plums in parallel rows on
dough. Mix sugar and cinnamon and
sprinkle over dough.

Mix egg yolks with cream and drip
over plums.

Bake in a hot oven (400°F.) about 20
minutes. Makes 8 servings.

Apple or Peach Kuchen: Substitute
apples or peaches for plums in the
above recipe.

RED AND GREEN TWIST

1 package hot roll mix
1 No. 2 can crushed pineapple
1/4 cup sugar
1/2 cup raspberry or strawberry jam
2 tablespoons butter or margarine
1 tablespoon dark corn syrup

Prepare hot roll mix as package directs. Cook pineapple with sugar until
thick; cool.

Divide dough into 3 parts. On floured
board, roll 1 part into rectangle about
10 x 6-inches. Spread with half of pineapple mixture; roll up from long side,
jelly-roll fashion.

Repeat with second part of dough,
using rest of pineapple tinted green.

Repeat with third part, using raspberry jam. On greased cooky sheet,
braid the 3 rolls (2 with pineapple filling, 1 with raspberry). Pinch ends to
seal. Let rise until double in bulk.

Bake in hot oven (400°F.) 20 minutes
or until done. Melt butter; mix with
corn syrup; heat; brush on braid.

Cranberry Twist

CRANBERRY TWIST

½ package of hot roll mix (14½ ounce package)
1 cup cranberry sauce (½ can)
½ cup chopped nuts
2 tablespoons grated orange rind

Prepare roll mix according to directions on package. Roll out dough to an oblong about 10 by 14 inches.

Spread cranberry sauce evenly over surface of dough; sprinkle with nuts and grated orange rind.

Lift long edge of dough, and roll, jelly-roll fashion, into an even and plump roll. Seal seam by pinching along edge.

Join ends to form ring and place in well greased 11-inch pie plate, with seam side of roll down.

Mark ring in 12 equal sections. With kitchen shears cut through roll on these marks to about ½ inch from center edge of ring. Take each cut piece and twist over on its side so that each piece rests partly on pie plate and partly on next piece with all pieces twisted in same direction.

Cover and let rise until doubled in bulk.

Bake in moderate oven (375°F.) 20 minutes or until nicely browned and top springs back when depressed. Makes 12 servings.

Mincemeat Twist: Substitute prepared moist mincemeat for cranberry sauce.

STREUSEL RAISIN BREAD

1 package hot roll mix
¼ cup sugar
1 cup seedless raisins, rinsed and drained
1 egg, slightly beaten
2 tablespoons melted butter or margarine
Few drops almond extract
1 tablespoon sugar
2 tablespoons flour
1 tablespoon soft butter or margarine

Combine hot roll mix, sugar, and raisins. Dissolve yeast as package directs, using ¼ cup less water; combine with egg, melted butter, almond extract. Stir into dry mixture, blending thor-

oughly. Cover; let rise in warm place until double in bulk.

Turn out onto lightly floured surface; knead lightly. Shape into loaf; place in pan. Sprinkle top with combined 1 tablespoon sugar, 2 tablespoons flour, 1 tablespoon butter; cover with clean towel. Let rise until double in bulk.

Bake in moderate oven (350°F.) 45 minutes or until done. Turn out onto wire rack. Mix confectioners' sugar with water to make thin frosting; drizzle over bread. Serve as is, or warm up in 325°F. oven.

JACK HORNER COFFEE RING

1 package hot roll mix
1 egg, lightly beaten
2 tablespoons melted butter or margarine (for mix)
12 small pitted cooked prunes
1 tablespoon melted butter
3 tablespoons sugar
1 teaspoon cinnamon
⅓ cup chopped almonds

Make dough with hot roll mix as directed on package, using ½ cup less liquid than specified. Beat in 1 lightly beaten egg and 2 tablespoons melted butter. Cover dough and let rise in warm place until doubled in bulk, about 1 to 1½ hours.

Turn out on floured board and roll into rectangle about 9 x 12 inches. Cut into 3-inch squares.

Place a well-drained prune in center of each square and wrap dough, around it. Dip each in melted butter, then in sugar blended with spice. Then dip in almonds.

Arrange balls in greased 8-inch ring mold. Let rise about ½ hour. Bake in moderate oven (375°F.) about 30 minutes. Remove from pan. Sprinkle with any remaining almonds. Serve at once. Makes 8-inch ring.

BOHEMIAN FRUIT BUNS

1 package hot roll mix
1 cup warm water
12 pitted prunes or 12 cooked dried apricots
⅓ cup chopped nuts

Place yeast from package of mix (in small envelope) in bowl and add warm water (98° to 115°F.). Stir until completely dissolved. Add mix from package and blend thoroughly.

Grease top and cover with waxed paper. Let stand in warm place (85° to 90°F.) until light and double in bulk (45 to 60 minutes).

Turn out and knead about 30 strokes on a floured board. Roll to ½ inch thickness and cut into rounds with 2½-inch biscuit cutter.

Place on greased baking sheet. Let

rise as before until double in bulk (about 45 minutes).

Press an indentation in center of each bun. Roll a prune or apricot in nuts and place in depression of each roll.

Bake in moderate oven (350°F.) 20 minutes.

Drip confectioners' frosting over warm buns. To make frosting, mix 1 cup sifted confectioners' sugar with 4 teaspoons water and ½ teaspoon vanilla. Makes 12 buns.

DATE MUMS

1 package hot roll mix
1 cup warm water
1 tablespoon sugar
1 slightly beaten egg
¼ cup melted butter or margarine

Date Filling:

2 cups fresh California dates
½ cup honey
½ teaspoon nutmeg
½ teaspoon cinnamon
2 tablespoons butter or margarine
Powdered sugar icing

Remove packet of yeast and dissolve in warm water. Stir in sugar and beaten egg. Gradually add flour mixture, beating well between each addition until smooth dough forms.

Grease top; cover with damp cloth and let rise in warm place (85°F.) until doubled in bulk.

Add melted butter; kneading gently. Let rest 30 minutes on lightly floured surface.

Divide dough into six equal parts and roll out to 4 by 14-inch rectangles, about ¼ inch thick. Spread with date filling.

Roll dough lengthwise as for jelly roll to make 14-inch rolls; cut each in half and form wreaths on greased cooky sheet, pinching ends together.

Clip with kitchen shears about ¼ inch apart. Separate clips by pulling every other one to center of wreath.

Let rise until almost doubled in bulk (about 20 minutes) in warm place.

Bake in moderate oven (375°F.) 12 to 15 minutes. Drizzle with powdered sugar icing. Makes 12 individual coffee cakes.

Date Filling: Pit and slice dates. Combine with honey, spices, and butter mixing well. Warm gently.

Date Mums

QUICK BREADS

Quick bread is a term used to describe any bread leavened with baking powder, baking soda, air, or steam rather than with yeast. They include biscuits, muffins, coffee cakes, shallow loaves such as corn breads, deep loaves such as nut breads, spoon breads, griddlecakes, waffles, and steamed breads such as popovers. They are quick to make because they require no rising period.

Quick Breads in Loaves

Most quick breads in loaves are hard to buy so you'll have to make them if you want to serve them. Most of them taste better and slice easier if stored at least a day. Wrap the thoroughly cooled whole loaves in plastic wrap or aluminum foil or place in an airtight container. These breads may be stored in the refrigerator for short periods or in the freezer.

PINEAPPLE BRAN BREAD

2/3 cup pineapple syrup
2/3 cup whole bran
2 cups sifted enriched flour
1/2 cup sugar
2 teaspoons baking powder
1/4 teaspoon baking soda
1 teaspoon salt
1/2 cup chopped walnuts
1/2 cup drained, canned, crushed pineapple
1 well beaten egg
2 tablespoons melted shortening

Measure pineapple syrup and add water if necessary to make 2/3 cup. Pour over bran and let stand 15 minutes.

Mix and sift flour, sugar, baking powder, baking soda, and salt.

Add walnuts, crushed pineapple, egg, and melted shortening to bran mixture and add to sifted dry ingredients. Mix until just blended.

Turn into greased loaf pan, 9 x 5 x 3 inches. Bake in slow oven (325°F.) 1 hour and 15 minutes. Makes 1 loaf.

WHITE NUT BREAD (Master Recipe)

2 cups sifted enriched flour
3 teaspoons baking powder
1/4 cup sugar
1/2 teaspoon salt
1 cup chopped nuts
1 egg, well beaten
1 cup milk

Sift dry ingredients together. Stir in nuts.

Combine egg and milk. Pour milk mixture into dry ingredients and stir quickly to mix.

Turn into greased loaf pan, 8 1/2 x 4 1/2 inches. Bake in moderate oven (350°F.) 45 minutes. Makes 1 loaf.

Variations:

Candied Orange Peel Bread: In master recipe substitute 1 cup chopped candied orange peel for nuts.

Date Nut Bread: In master recipe substitute brown sugar for white, and 1/2 cup chopped dates for 1/2 cup nuts.

Fruit Nut Bread: In master recipe substitute 1 cup chopped dried apricots, raisins, or currants for 1/2 cup nuts.

Orange Nut Bread: In master recipe substitute 1/2 cup orange marmalade for sugar. Use only 1/2 cup milk. Add 1 tablespoon grated orange rind.

Whole Wheat Bread: In master recipe substitute 1 cup whole wheat (graham) flour for 1 cup white flour and 1/4 cup firmly packed brown sugar for granulated sugar.

BANANA TEA BREAD

1 3/4 cups sifted enriched flour
2 3/4 teaspoons baking powder
1/2 teaspoon salt
1/3 cup shortening
2/3 cup sugar
2 eggs, well beaten
1 cup mashed, ripe bananas (2 to 3 bananas)

Sift together flour, baking powder, and salt. Beat shortening until creamy in mixing bowl. Add sugar gradually to shortening and continue beating until light and fluffy. Add eggs and beat well.

Add flour mixture alternately with bananas, a small amount at a time, mixing after each addition only enough to moisten dry ingredients.

Turn into a greased loaf pan (8 1/2 x 4 1/2 x 2 1/2-inches) and bake in a moderate oven (350°F.) about 1 hour and 10 minutes or until bread is done. Makes 1 loaf.

Variations:

Banana Apricot Tea Bread: Add 1 cup finely cut dried apricots to egg mixture.

Banana Nut Tea Bread: Add 1/2 cup coarsely chopped nuts to egg mixture.

Banana Prune Tea Bread: Add 1 cup finely cut dried prunes to egg mixture.

Banana Raisin Tea Bread: Add 1 cup seedless raisins to egg mixture.

Holiday Banana Tea Bread: Add 1 cup mixed, candied fruit, 1/4 cup raisins, and 1/2 cup coarsely chopped nuts to egg mixture.

Important: If apricots or prunes are very dry, soak them in warm water until soft. Drain and dry well before using them in the bread.

A crack down the center of a nut loaf is no mistake—it's typical.

WHOLE WHEAT NUT BREAD #2 (Master Recipe)

1½ cups sifted enriched flour
5 teaspoons baking powder
1 teaspoon salt
¾ cup sugar
1½ cups whole wheat flour
1 cup chopped nuts
1 egg
1¼ cups milk
6 tablespoons melted shortening

Sift white flour, baking powder, salt, and sugar together. Add whole wheat flour and nuts and mix well.

Beat egg slightly. Add milk and melted shortening. Combine with dry ingredients, stirring only enough to blend.

Place in a well greased loaf pan. Bake until golden brown in moderate oven (350°F.) for 50 to 60 minutes. Remove from pan. Cool before slicing. Makes 1 large or 2 small loaves.

Variations:

Fruit Bread: In master recipe substitute 1 cup chopped dates, raisins, prunes, or figs for nuts.

Honey Nut Bread: In master recipe use honey instead of sugar.

Orange Nut Bread: In master recipe substitute ½ cup chopped candied orange peel for ½ cup chopped nuts.

SALLY LUNN

2 cups sifted enriched flour
3 teaspoons baking powder
½ teaspoon salt
3 tablespoons sugar
2 eggs, separated
½ cup milk
½ cup melted shortening

Mix and sift flour, baking powder, salt, and sugar.

Combine beaten egg yolks and milk. Add to flour mixture, stirring only enough to moisten the dry ingredients. Add the shortening. Fold in stiffly beaten egg whites.

Turn into a greased square pan 8 x 8 x 2 inches. Bake in moderate oven (350°F.) about 30 minutes. Cut into squares. Serve hot.

BRAN BREAD

3 cups sifted enriched flour
1 teaspoon salt
¼ cup sugar
4 teaspoons baking powder
1 cup whole bran
2 eggs
1 cup milk
¼ cup melted shortening

Sift flour, salt, sugar, and baking powder together and add bran.

Beat eggs. Stir in milk and melted shortening.

Pour liquid into dry ingredients all at once and stir only until dry ingredients are mixed. If desired, add ½ cup chopped raisins.

Pour into a well greased bread pan. Bake in moderate oven (375°F.) 50 to 60 minutes. Will keep well if wrapped in waxed paper when cool. Makes 1 loaf.

BRAN RAISIN BREAD

1 egg
1 cup sugar
¼ cup molasses
1 cup sour milk
2 tablespoons melted shortening
1 cup whole bran
2 cups sifted enriched flour
½ teaspoon baking soda
3 teaspoons baking powder
1 teaspoon salt
½ cup raisins

Beat egg slightly. Add sugar, molasses, milk, shortening, and bran.

Sift flour, baking soda, salt, and baking powder. Mix raisins with flour, and add to the first mixture. Beat well.

Bake in a well greased loaf pan in moderate oven (350°F.) for 1¼ hours. Cool before slicing. Makes 1 large loaf.

BUTTERSCOTCH BREAD

2 eggs
2 cups firmly packed brown sugar
3 tablespoons melted butter or margarine
4 cups sifted enriched flour
1 teaspoon baking soda
1½ teaspoons baking powder
1 teaspoon salt
2 cups sour milk or buttermilk
1 cup chopped nuts

Beat eggs. Add sugar gradually, beating it in. Add shortening.

Sift together flour, soda, baking powder, and salt. Add to egg mixture alternately with milk. Add nuts.

Pour into greased loaf pans. Bake in moderate oven (350°F.) 45 minutes. Makes 2 1-pound loaves.

Irish Soda Bread: For a sugary topping, brush top surface of loaf with melted butter and sprinkle with sugar before baking.

APPLE BREAD

½ cup shortening
⅔ cup sugar
2 eggs
1 cup ground unpeeled apples
2 cups sifted enriched flour
1 teaspoon baking powder
1 teaspoon baking soda
½ teaspoon salt
¼ cup chopped nuts

Cream shortening and sugar together. Blend in beaten eggs and fruit. Include juice with the apple. Stir in mixed and sifted dry ingredients. Blend in nuts.

Pour batter into greased loaf pan (8 x 4 inches). Bake in moderate oven (350°F.) 55 to 60 minutes. Makes 1 loaf.

IRISH SODA BREAD

4 cups sifted enriched flour
¼ cup granulated sugar
1 teaspoon salt
1 teaspoon baking powder
¼ cup butter or margarine
2 cups seedless raisins
1⅓ cups buttermilk
1 egg
1 teaspoon baking soda

Mix and sift flour, sugar, salt, and baking powder. Cut in butter or margarine with pastry blender or two knives until it resembles coarse corn meal. Stir in raisins.

Combine buttermilk, egg, and baking soda. Stir buttermilk mixture into flour mixture until just moistened.

Bake in greased 1-quart pudding pan or casserole in moderate oven (375°F.) 45 to 50 minutes, until golden brown.

Note: This recipe has been slightly modified for today's American taste. This new version adds a little butter or margarine and one egg. In it's original form, Irish soda bread is known as "bannock" if baked, or "soda farls" if cooked on a griddle and cut into triangles.

Variations: The above recipe can be varied as is done in Ireland: add caraway seeds to taste; substitute ½ cup molasses for ½ cup buttermilk (omitting sugar); use half whole wheat flour, half white.

BOSTON BAKED BREAD

1½ cups sifted enriched flour
2½ teaspoons baking soda
1½ teaspoons salt
¼ cup sugar
2 cups whole wheat flour
⅓ cup shortening
1 cup raisins
1 well-beaten egg
2 cups sour milk or buttermilk
¾ cup molasses

Mix and sift flour, soda, salt, and sugar. Add whole wheat flour and mix well. Cut in shortening until mixture resembles coarse meal. Add raisins.

Combine egg, milk, and molasses; add to dry ingredients. Mix only until flour is dampened.

Turn into 2 greased and floured loaf pans. Bake in moderate oven (350°F.) 45 to 50 minutes. Makes 2 loaves.

STEAMED BROWN BREAD

1 cup sifted enriched flour
1 teaspoon baking powder
1½ teaspoons baking soda
1 teaspoon salt
1 cup whole wheat flour
1 cup yellow corn meal
1½ cups seedless raisins
2 cups buttermilk or sour milk
¾ cup molasses

Sift white flour with baking powder, baking soda, and salt. Add whole wheat flour, corn meal, and raisins.

Combine buttermilk or sour milk and molasses. Add dry ingredients and mix thoroughly.

Fill 3 No. 2 cans ⅔ full. The cans should be well greased. Cover with waxed paper and tie firmly with string.

Steam in deep-well cooker or large kettle containing 2 cups hot water. Turn to high until boiling, then down to low. Total steaming time: 3½ hours.

Fruit Brown Bread: Add 1½ cups chopped uncooked prunes or dates to batter in place of raisins.

CHOCOLATE TEA BREAD

3 cups sifted cake flour
1½ teaspoons baking soda
1 teaspoon salt
1 cup sugar
½ cup cocoa
1 egg
6 tablespoons vinegar plus milk to make 1¼ cups liquid
⅓ cup melted shortening

Sift flour, soda, salt, sugar, and cocoa together. Beat egg, add liquid and shortening, and stir all at once into flour mixture until batter is smooth.

Turn into greased 8¾ x 4½ x 2½-inch loaf pan.

Bake in moderate oven (350°F.) 1 hour or until done. Remove from pan

and cool several hours or overnight before slicing. Makes 1 loaf.

PRUNE-OATEN BREAD

2 cups sifted enriched flour
½ cup sugar
2½ teaspoons baking powder
½ teaspoon baking soda
1 teaspoon salt
1 cup rolled oats, uncooked
1¼ cups buttermilk or sour milk
2 tablespoons melted fat
1 cup diced, drained, cooked prunes
½ cup chopped nuts

Sift together flour, sugar, baking powder, soda, and salt. Add rolled oats and mix thoroughly.

Combine buttermilk with slightly cooled fat. (To make sweet milk sour, add 1 tablespoon of vinegar to 1¼ cups of sweet milk.) Add to flour mixture with prunes and nuts, stirring just enough to moisten the dry ingredients. (Batter should be lumpy.)

Put into well greased loaf pan, 9 x-5 x 3 inches. Place extra halves of prunes and whole nutmeats on top.

Bake in moderate oven (350°-375°F.) about 1 hour or until done. Turn out on rack to cool. Makes 1 loaf.

CHEESE NUT BREAD

2 cups sifted enriched flour
1 tablespoon baking powder
¾ teaspoon salt
½ tablespoon sugar
1 cup grated American cheese
¼ cup chopped pecans
1 egg
¾ cup milk
2 tablespoons butter, melted

Mix and sift flour twice with baking powder, salt, and sugar. Add cheese and nuts and mix thoroughly.

Beat egg, add milk and melted butter and pour into dry ingredients. Stir quickly until dry ingredients are just dampened; batter should not be smooth.

Pour into buttered bread pan (8 x-4 x 3 inches) and let stand 15 minutes at room temperature.

Bake in moderate oven (350°F.) 1 hour or until toothpick inserted in center comes out clean. Turn loaf out onto cake cooler and cool before slicing. Makes 1 loaf.

BRAZIL NUT BREAD

3 cups whole wheat flour
1½ cups sifted enriched flour
5 teaspoons baking powder
2 teaspoons baking soda
1½ teaspoons salt
1½ cups brown sugar
1½ cups sliced Brazil nuts
3 cups sour milk or 3 cups buttermilk

Prune-Oaten Bread

Mix dry ingredients together. Add Brazil nuts and mix well. Add milk and stir well. Pour into 2 greased loaf pans.

Bake about 1 hour in slow oven (325°F.). Makes 2 loaves.

LEMON NUT BREAD

4 tablespoons butter or margarine
1¼ cups sugar
2 eggs
1½ teaspoons finely grated lemon rind
3¼ cups sifted enriched flour
3 teaspoons baking powder
½ teaspoon salt
½ teaspoon baking soda
⅔ cup milk
4 tablespoons lemon juice
¾ cup coarsely chopped pecans or walnuts

Cream butter or margarine and sugar together in mixing bowl. Blend in the eggs one at a time and the lemon rind.

Stir in sifted dry ingredients alternately with liquids (milk and lemon juice). Fold in nuts.

Spoon batter into lightly greased loaf pan (9 x 5 x 2½ inches), being sure thick batter is well into corners of pan.

Bake in moderate oven (350°F.) 1 hour or until knife inserted in center comes out clean. Remove from pan. Cool.

Nut bread cuts more easily and flavors are more mellowed if it is cooled and wrapped for 24 hours before serving.

Note: If you prefer a nut bread without a cracked top crust, allow the batter to stand in the pan at room temperature for about 20 minutes before baking.

Make quick loaf breads the day before they are to be used, to make neat slices. Very fresh bread crumbles easily.

Nut bread sandwiches call for simple fillings: soft butter or margarine, softened cream cheese, jelly, or jam.

SCOTCH OATMEAL BREAD

2 eggs
1 cup sugar
2 cups sour milk or buttermilk
2/3 cup molasses
3 cups sifted enriched flour
1 teaspoon salt
1 teaspoon baking powder
2 teaspoons baking soda
1 1/2 cups quick or regular uncooked oats
1/2 cup chopped nuts
1 1/2 cups raisins

Beat eggs until light; add sugar gradually, beating until fluffy. Add sour milk and molasses, mixing well.

Sift together flour, salt, baking powder, and soda and add to creamed mixture.

Add rolled oats, nuts and raisins, stirring only enough to combine.

Bake in 2 greased paperlined bread pans (4 1/2 x 8 1/2 inches) in moderate oven (350°F.) 1 hour.

Store in bread box one day before slicing.

ARKANSAS DATE BREAD

1 cup sifted enriched flour
1/2 teaspoon salt
1 teaspoon baking soda
1 cup whole wheat flour
1 cup whole bran
1 cup dates
1/2 cup molasses
1 1/4 cups sour milk
1 1/2 tablespoons melted fat
1 egg, slightly beaten

Sift white flour once. Measure and sift again with salt and baking soda. Add whole wheat flour and bran.

Cut dates in small pieces and mix through dry ingredients, with the finger tips. Add the molasses, sour milk, and fat to the egg, and stir this mixture into dry ingredients.

Pour into a well greased loaf pan. Bake in moderate oven (350°F.) for 1 1/2 hours. Cool before slicing. Makes 1 loaf.

PECAN BREAD

2 cups sifted enriched flour
3 teaspoons baking powder
1/2 teaspoon salt
1/2 cup firmly packed brown sugar
1 cup milk
1 beaten egg
2 tablespoons melted butter
1 cup broken pecans

Sift flour, baking powder, and salt together. Stir in brown sugar.

Combine milk and egg and add to dry ingredients mixing until just moistened. Then add melted butter and nuts.

Spread batter into well greased loaf

pan, about 9 1/4 x 5 1/4 x 2 3/4 inches.

Bake in moderate oven (350°F.) 1 hour or until lightly browned. Makes 1 loaf.

APPLE SPICE BREAD

2 cups sifted enriched flour
1 teaspoon baking soda
1 teaspoon salt
1 teaspoon cinnamon
1/2 teaspoon nutmeg
1/4 teaspoon cloves
1/2 cup shortening
3/4 cup firmly packed light brown sugar
2 eggs
1 teaspoon vanilla
1 cup grated raw apples
2 tablespoons vinegar plus water to make 1/2 cup
1/2 cup chopped nuts

Sift flour, soda, salt, and spices together. Cream shortening; blend in sugar and add eggs one at a time and beat until smooth.

Add vanilla. Add flour mixture alternately with grated apple and liquid. Stir in nuts. Turn into greased 8 3/4 x 4 1/2 x 2 1/2-inch loaf pan.

Bake in moderate oven (350°F.) 1 hour or until done. Remove from pan and cool several hours or overnight before slicing. Makes 1 loaf.

CRANBERRY RELISH BREAD

2 cups sifted enriched flour
1 teaspoon baking soda
1 teaspoon salt
3/4 cup sugar
1 egg
1/3 cup orange juice
3 tablespoons white (distilled) vinegar plus water to make 2/3 cup
1 teaspoon grated orange rind
1/4 cup melted shortening
1 cup halves or coarsely chopped raw cranberries
1 cup chopped nuts

Sift together flour, soda, salt, and sugar into mixing bowl.

Beat egg; add liquid, orange rind, and melted shortening. Add all at once to flour mixture and stir until flour is just dampened.

Add cranberries and nuts; stir just enough to blend well.

Turn into greased 8 3/4 x 4 1/2 x 2 1/2-inch loaf pan. Bake in moderate oven (350°F.) 60 to 70 minutes or until done.

Remove from pan and cool several hours or overnight before slicing. Makes 1 loaf.

CEREAL FLAKE ORANGE NUT BREAD

2 cups sifted enriched flour
3 teaspoons baking powder

1 teaspoon salt
1/2 cup sugar
1 tablespoon grated orange rind
1/2 cup chopped nuts
1 egg, well beaten
3/4 cup orange juice
3 tablespoons melted fat or salad oil
1 cup whole wheat flakes

Sift together flour, baking powder, salt, and sugar; stir in orange rind and nuts.

Combine egg, orange juice, and fat, and add to flour mixture, stirring only until well mixed. Stir in whole wheat flakes.

Turn into greased loaf pan, 8 1/2 x 4 1/2 x 2 1/2-inches, and bake in moderate oven (350°F.) about 1 hour. Cool on rack. Makes 1 loaf.

PRUNE NUT BREAD

1 cup prunes
3 cups sifted enriched flour
4 teaspoons baking powder
1/2 teaspoon baking soda
1 1/2 teaspoons salt
2 tablespoons sugar
1/4 cup shortening
2 eggs
1/2 cup evaporated milk diluted with 1/2 cup water
1/2 cup chopped nuts

Rinse prunes; drain and dry on towel. If prunes are very dry, boil them 5 minutes. Remove pits, and put prunes through food chopper.

Sift flour with baking powder, soda, salt, and sugar. Cut shortening into flour mixture.

Beat eggs; add diluted evaporated milk and stir into flour mixture. Add prunes and nuts.

Pour into well greased loaf pan about 9 x 5 x 3 inches. Place extra halves of prunes and whole nuts on top.

Bake in moderate oven (350° to 375°F.) 1 hour or until brown. Turn out on rack to cool. Makes 1 loaf.

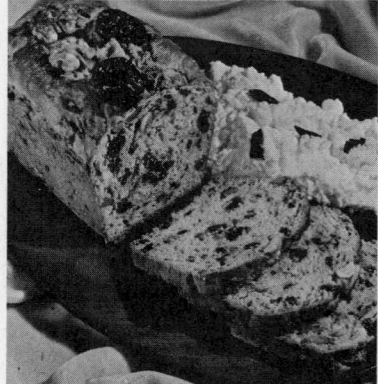

Prune Nut Bread

MOLASSES WHOLE WHEAT NUT BREAD

2	tablespoons brown sugar
2	cups whole wheat flour
1	cup sifted enriched flour
3/4	teaspoon baking soda
2 1/2	teaspoons baking powder
1 1/4	teaspoons salt
3/4	cup milk
3/4	cup water
3/4	cup molasses
1	cup chopped walnuts

Mix together sugar, whole wheat flour, white flour, baking soda, baking powder, and salt.

Combine milk, water, and molasses; add to dry ingredients. Mix smooth. Add nuts.

Pour into 9 1/4 x 5 1/4 x 2 1/2-inch greased loaf pan. Let stand 20 minutes.

Bake in moderate oven (350°F.) 1 1/2 hours.

Cool 5 minutes. Remove from pan. Cool. Bread will slice in uniformly thin slices if stored overnight.

BANANA BREAD

2	cups sifted enriched flour
1	teaspoon baking soda
1	teaspoon salt
1/2	cup shortening
1	cup sugar
2	eggs
1	cup mashed ripe banana (2 to 3 bananas)
1	tablespoon vinegar plus milk to make 1/2 cup liquid

Sift together flour, soda, and salt. Cream shortening, blend in sugar, add eggs one at a time, and beat until fluffy.

Add flour mixture alternately with bananas and liquid, beating well after each addition.

Turn into greased 9 1/2 x 5 1/2 x 2 3/4-inch loaf pan. Bake in moderate oven (350°F.) 60 to 70 minutes or until done. Remove from pan and cool several hours or overnight before slicing. Makes 1 loaf.

ORANGE NUT BREAD #2

2 1/2	cups sifted enriched flour
2/3	cup sugar
1	teaspoon salt
2 1/2	teaspoons baking powder
1/2	cup chopped walnuts
1	egg
1	cup milk
1	tablespoon grated orange rind
1/4	cup orange juice
2	tablespoons melted shortening

Sift together flour, sugar, salt, and baking powder. Stir in chopped walnuts.

Beat egg and mix with milk, grated orange rind, orange juice, and melted shortening. Add orange mixture to flour mixture and stir only until dry ingredients are moistened.

Pour batter into a well greased 8 x 6 x 2-inch baking dish. Bake in a moderate oven (350°F.) for 1 hour and 15 minutes.

Slice and serve with butter, orange marmalade, and cream cheese.

BUTTERMILK NUT BREAD

3	cups sifted enriched flour
1/2	teaspoon salt
3/4	teaspoon baking soda
2	teaspoons baking powder
1	cup firmly packed brown sugar
1	cup coarsely chopped walnuts
1	egg
2	tablespoons molasses
1 1/2	cups buttermilk
3	tablespoons melted butter

Sift together flour, salt, baking soda, and baking powder. Add sugar and walnuts.

Beat egg until thick and lemon-colored. Add molasses and buttermilk. Combine with first mixture along with melted butter. Stir only to blend ingredients. Do not beat. (This will be very thick.)

Spoon mixture into well buttered loaf bread pan (9 x 5 x 3-inches) making a slight hollow in center. Let stand 20 minutes before baking.

Bake in moderate oven (350°F.) about 60 minutes or until a wooden pick thrust into center comes out clean.

Turn out of pan onto wire rack to cool. (Breads of this type frequently crack across top during baking.) Makes 1 loaf.

Buttermilk-Fruit Bread: One-half to 3/4 cup chopped figs, dates, or raisins may be added along with nuts.

CINNAMON RAISIN COFFEE BREAD

1/4	cup butter or margarine, melted
1/2	cup sugar
2	teaspoons cinnamon
2 1/2	cups sifted enriched flour
1	teaspoon salt
1 1/4	teaspoons baking soda
1/2	cup sugar
2	eggs
5	tablespoons white (distilled) vinegar plus milk to make 1 cup liquid
1/4	cup melted shortening
1/2	cup raisins
1/4	cup chopped nuts

Combine butter or margarine, 1/2 cup sugar, and cinnamon. Set aside. Sift flour, salt, soda, and other 1/2 cup sugar into mixing bowl.

Beat eggs, add liquid, blend well; then add shortening and raisins. Pour all at once into flour mixture and stir until flour is just dampened.

Spread 1/2 of batter in greased 8 x 8 x 2-inch baking pan; sprinkle with 1/2 the cinnamon mixture. Cover with remaining batter and draw knife through batter several times to distribute filling slightly. Sprinkle top with rest of cinnamon mixture and nuts.

Bake in moderate oven (350°F.) 45 minutes. Serve warm, cutting in squares. Makes 1 loaf.

APPLE BREAD #2

2 1/4	cups enriched flour
1	teaspoon baking powder
1/2	teaspoon salt
1/2	teaspoon nutmeg
1	teaspoon baking soda
1/2	cup sugar
2	eggs
1/2	cup light corn syrup
1	teaspoon grated lemon rind
1	tablespoon lemon juice
1	cup unpeeled raw red apple, chopped fine
1/4	cup chopped nuts
1/2	cup melted butter or margarine
	Apple wedges

Sift, measure flour, and resift with baking powder, salt, nutmeg, soda, and sugar into mixing bowl.

Break in eggs and add corn syrup mixed with rest of ingredients. Mix as little as possible to form dough and leave ingredients evenly distributed.

Turn into well greased loaf pan. Top with thin apple wedges dipped in butter or margarine, then in sugar.

Bake in moderate oven (350°F.) about 1 hour. Cover pan for first 20 minutes. Makes 1 loaf, 4 1/2 x 9 inches.

DATE NUT BREAD

2 1/2	cups sifted enriched flour
1 1/4	teaspoons baking soda
1	teaspoon salt
1/2	cup chopped dates
2	eggs
5	tablespoons white (distilled) vinegar
3/4	cup milk
1/4	cup firmly packed brown sugar
1/4	cup melted shortening
3/4	cup chopped nuts

Sift flour, soda, and salt together into mixing bowl. Stir in chopped dates until all are separated.

Beat eggs, combine with vinegar and milk, and stir in brown sugar. Add melted shortening and pour all at once into flour mixture. Stir only until all flour is dampened; then add nuts and mix lightly.

Turn into greased 8 3/4 x 4 1/2 x 2 1/2-inch loaf pan. Bake in moderate oven (350°F.) 60 to 70 minutes or until done.

Remove from pan and cool several hours or overnight before slicing. Makes 1 loaf.

Corn Breads

Corn breads can justly be called a truly American dish. The best corn bread is made from the traditional "water-ground" corn meal which retains its germ and has a much-prized flavor. It is still extensively used in the South; however, it has poor keeping qualities. New process or granulated corn meal is highly refined, consisting only of the endosperm, and consequently has better keeping quality but a less desirable flavor.

When making corn breads use heavy metal utensils. A thin pan permits the bread to overcook on the outside before the inside is done. Grease the pans heavily and heat them well for 5 minutes before adding the batter.

CORN BREAD

1 cup sifted enriched flour
3 teaspoons baking powder
½ teaspoon salt
½ cup sugar
½ cup yellow corn meal
1 cup milk
1 egg, well beaten
1 tablespoon melted shortening

Mix and sift flour, baking powder, salt, and sugar. Stir in corn meal.

Add milk to beaten egg and stir into first mixture. Add shortening and blend.

Turn into shallow, greased 8-inch pan. Bake in hot oven (400°F.) about 20 minutes. Cut into 6 squares. Serve hot.

Variations:

Bacon Corn Bread: Add ½ cup diced crisp cooked bacon to sifted flour mixture.

Corn Bread Sticks: Combine ingredients as directed. Turn into hot well-greased corn-stick pans.

Bake in hot oven (400°F.) 15 to 20 minutes. Makes about 12 sticks.

OLD SOUTH CORN BREAD

1 teaspoon salt
1 cup white corn meal
1 cup boiling water
¼ cup vinegar
1¾ cups sweet milk
2 well beaten eggs
2 tablespoons melted shortening
1 teaspoon baking soda

Combine salt and corn meal. Add slowly to boiling water while stirring constantly to prevent lumping.

Combine vinegar and milk. Add 1½ cups of the vinegar and milk to corn meal mixture, and mix well. Add eggs and melted shortening. Stir until well blended.

Dissolve soda in remaining ½ cup of vinegar and milk. Add to corn meal mixture and stir until completely blended. Turn into greased 1½-quart casserole.

Bake in hot oven (400°F.) 1 hour. Serve immediately with a spoon. Serves 5 to 6.

CRACKLING CORN BREAD

2 ounces salt pork, chopped
2 cups white corn meal, preferably stone ground
1½ teaspoons baking powder
½ teaspoon baking soda
1 teaspoon salt
2 beaten eggs
About 1 cup buttermilk
Shortening

Cook salt pork slowly, stirring often until lightly browned. Mix and sift corn meal, baking powder, baking soda, and salt.

Mix eggs, buttermilk, and 2 tablespoons fat from cracklings. Drain off remaining fat and reserve. Add liquid ingredients to corn meal. Add cracklings and stir until corn meal is dampened.

Batter should be stiff enough almost to hold its shape when dropped from spoon.

In a skillet heat reserved fat (without sediment) or use shortening. Drop cornbread mixture from a spoon into fat to form cakes. Brown slowly on both sides. Makes about 12 corn cakes.

SOUTHERN SPOON BREAD

2½ cups scalded milk
1 cup sifted white corn meal
1 teaspoon salt
1½ tablespoons melted butter
4 eggs, separated
1 teaspoon baking powder

Add scalded milk to corn meal, stirring until smooth. Add salt.

Cook over hot water, stirring constantly, until thick. Stir in melted butter.

Cool slightly. Beat egg yolks and add to cooled corn meal mixture. Add baking powder and mix well.

Fold in stiffly beaten egg whites. Turn into hot, buttered casserole.

Bake in moderate oven (375°F.) until firm and brown on top. Serve from casserole. Serves 8 to 10.

Bacon Spoon Bread: Add ½ cup diced, crisp bacon to corn meal mixture with the butter. Bacon fat may be used instead of butter.

Cheese Spoon Bread: Add ¾ cup grated cheese to batter after fat has been added.

NEW ORLEANS CORN PONE

3 cups yellow corn meal
1 teaspoon salt
2 tablespoons melted shortening
1½ cups boiling water
1 cup milk

Certain meals seem to demand corn bread. Serve it piping hot with plenty of butter.

1 well beaten egg
2 teaspoons baking powder

Combine corn meal, salt, and shortening. Add boiling water gradually, stirring until well mixed. Stir in milk and set aside for 1 hour to cool. Beat well and stir in egg and baking powder.

Pour into corn stick pans or into shallow greased pans. Bake in hot oven (400°F.) 40 minutes or until done. Makes 2 dozen corn sticks.

SKILLET CORN BREAD

1 cup yellow corn meal
¾ cup boiling water
1 tablespoon fat
¾ teaspoon salt
2 tablespoons corn syrup
1 tablespoon flour
1 teaspoon baking powder
2 tablespoons milk
1 egg

Pour corn meal into boiling water. Add fat and salt; mix well. Stir in syrup, flour, baking powder, and milk. Add egg and beat well.

Spread in well greased, heavy 8-inch skillet. Cover, and cook over low heat 10 minutes. Turn, cover, and cook about 8 minutes longer. Makes 1 8-inch round.

CORN DODGER

1 cup yellow corn meal
½ cup sifted enriched flour
1 teaspoon salt
1½ teaspoons baking powder
2 teaspoons sugar
1 cup milk
1 egg, beaten
2½ tablespoons hot bacon drippings

Sift the dry ingredients into a mixing bowl. Combine the milk and egg and stir into the dry ingredients. Beat well and then stir in the hot drippings.

Pour into a hot casserole. Bake in a hot oven (425°F.) for 30 minutes, or until golden brown. Serve hot in pie-shaped pieces.

Spoon bread, also called batter bread, is a moist bread, soft enough to be eaten with a spoon.

CHEESE SPOON BREAD

3/4 cup corn meal
1 teaspoon salt
Dash of pepper
1 tablespoon sugar
1 cup water
2 tablespoons fat
2 cups milk
1/2 pound process cheese, sliced
3 eggs, beaten

In saucepan, mix corn meal, salt, pepper, sugar, water, fat, and 1 cup milk. Cook over medium heat until thick and boiling, stirring constantly.

Remove from heat; add sliced cheese, reserving a few slices to put on top of mixture before baking. Stir until cheese melts.

Add remaining milk and beaten eggs. Pour into greased 1 1/2-quart shallow baking dish. Put reserved slices of cheese on top.

Bake in slow oven (325°F.) until almost set, about 50 minutes. Serve at once from dish. Serves 4.

RICE SPOON BREAD

3 cups milk
2/3 cup corn meal
2 tablespoons butter, margarine, or
    salad oil
1 teaspoon salt
1 cup cooked rice
3 well beaten eggs

Scald 2 cups milk in saucepan. Mix remaining milk with corn meal, then stir into hot milk.

Over low heat, stir mixture until it thickens, about 5 minutes.

Remove from heat. Add butter, salt, and rice. Stir into eggs gradually.

Pour into greased 1 1/2-quart baking dish. Bake in hot oven (425°F.) until silver knife inserted in center comes out clean, about 45 to 50 minutes. Serve with butter or margarine. Serves 5 to 6.

SHORT'NEN BREAD

1 1/2 cups corn meal
3/4 cup sifted enriched flour
1/2 teaspoon baking soda
1/4 teaspoon salt
1 cup sour milk
1 cup cracklings (see below)

Sift the dry ingredients together; add milk and stir in cracklings.

Pour into a greased baking pan. Bake in hot oven (425°F.) 30 minutes, or until brown. Makes 1 loaf.

Note: Cracklings are the crisp brown bits left when lard is made. A modern version of cracklings can be made by heating fat salt pork or bacon in a frying pan. Pour off the fat until only crisp, lean bits remain. Chop fine and use in recipe.

OLD TIME MAINE TOGUS LOAF (STEAMED)

1/2 cup sifted enriched flour
1/2 teaspoon baking soda
1 teaspoon salt
1 1/2 cups yellow corn meal
1 1/2 cups sweet milk
1/2 cup sour milk
1/4 cup molasses

Mix and sift flour, baking soda, and salt. Add corn meal. Mix together sweet milk, sour milk, and molasses. Add to dry ingredients. Mix all ingredients together.

Pour into greased mold. Cover with waxed paper tied securely and steam 3 hours.

The batter will be very thin, but corn meal absorbs the moisture while steaming.

Serve hot with butter, or use as a base for creamed chicken. Makes 1 medium-sized loaf.

CUSTARD CORN BREAD

3/4 cup yellow corn meal
1/2 cup sifted enriched flour
2 tablespoons sugar
1/2 teaspoon salt
1 teaspoon baking powder
1 beaten egg
1 cup milk
2 tablespoons melted butter
1/2 cup milk

Mix and sift corn meal, flour, sugar, salt, and baking powder.

Combine egg, 1 cup milk, and butter; add to dry ingredients and mix well. (The batter is very thin.)

Pour batter in greased pan, 8 x 8 x 2-inches. Pour 1/2 cup milk carefully over top of batter.

Bake in hot oven (400°F.) 20 minutes. Then cut in squares and serve hot with chicken, turkey, or pork.

CORN STICKS #2

1 1/4 cups corn meal
1/4 cup sifted enriched flour
2 tablespoons sugar
3 teaspoons baking powder
1 teaspoon salt
1 1/8 cups milk
1 egg, beaten
4 tablespoons melted butter

Place corn stick pans in the oven to heat.

Sift all the dry ingredients into a mixing bowl.

Combine the milk and egg and stir into the dry ingredients. Stir in the melted butter.

Brush the hot corn stick pans with butter and fill them almost full with the mixture.

Bake in a very hot oven (450°F.) for 10 to 12 minutes. Makes 12 sticks.

JOHNNY CAKE

2 cups yellow corn meal
1/2 cup sifted enriched flour
1/2 teaspoon salt
2 teaspoons baking powder
2 tablespoons sugar
1 egg, well beaten
1 cup milk
2 tablespoons melted shortening

Mix and sift dry ingredients. Add well beaten egg, milk, and melted shortening. Pour into greased pan, 8 inches square.

Bake in hot oven (425°F.) until golden brown (about 25 minutes). Makes 1 loaf.

YANKEE APPLE CORN BREAD

2 cups yellow corn meal
1/4 cup sugar
1 1/2 teaspoons salt
2 cups sour milk or buttermilk
2 tablespoons melted shortening
2 well beaten eggs
1 teaspoon baking soda
1 tablespoon cold water
1 cup chopped raw apple

Mix corn meal, sugar, salt, milk, and shortening in top part of double boiler. Cook over hot water 10 minutes, stirring frequently. Cool.

Add eggs, soda, which has been dissolved in cold water, and apples. Bake in greased pan in hot oven (400°F.) 20 to 25 minutes. Serves 8.

SOUR MILK CORN BREAD

3 cups corn meal
2 teaspoons baking powder
1 teaspoon salt
1 tablespoon sugar
1/2 teaspoon baking soda
2 cups sour milk or buttermilk
2 eggs, beaten
1 cup thick sour cream

Sift together the corn meal, baking powder, salt, and sugar.

Stir the soda into the buttermilk and combine with the eggs and the cream. Mix all the ingredients together and bake in a very hot oven (450°F.) for 20 minutes.

Corn Sticks

Quick Coffee Cakes

QUICK COFFEE CAKE
(Master Recipe)

    2 cups sifted enriched flour
    2 teaspoons baking powder
    ½ teaspoon salt
    ½ cup sugar
    6 tablespoons butter or margarine
    1 egg, beaten
    ½ cup milk

Mix and sift the flour, baking powder, salt, and sugar into a mixing bowl. Cut in the shortening.

Combine the egg and milk and stir into the dry ingredients until the mixture is blended.

Spread the dough evenly in a buttered 9-inch layer pan. Bake in a hot oven (400°F.) for 25 to 30 minutes.

Quick Coffee Cake Variations:

Crumb Topping For Quick Coffee Cake: Spread the dough evenly in a buttered 9-inch layer pan.

Brush the top with 1½ tablespoons melted butter or margarine.

Mix together 4 tablespoons sugar, 1 tablespoon flour, and 1 teaspoon cinnamon and sift this mixture evenly over the top of the dough.

Bake in hot oven (400°F.) for 30 minutes.

Cut into pie-shaped wedges while still in the pan and remove each piece to a serving dish.

Dutch Apple Coffee Cake: Spread dough in a shallow pan. Brush with melted butter.

Cover with thinly sliced tart apples in parallel rows. Sprinkle generously with sugar and cinnamon.

Bake in hot oven (400°F.) about 30 minutes.

Iced Coffee Cake: After baking, ice cake with confectioners' sugar icing, then sprinkle with minced candied fruit, chopped nuts, or combination of fruits and nuts.

Nut Coffee Cake: Glaze the top of the cake before baking with a mixture of slightly beaten egg white and water, or with a mixture of 3 tablespoons sugar and 1 tablespoon water.

Sprinkle thickly with chopped nuts. Almonds are particularly good.

Currant Coffee Cake: Currants may be used in the same way as nuts, in nut coffee cake, or may be combined with them.

Prune or Plum Coffee Cake: Arrange pitted canned plums or prunes over batter.

Pour over a little of the juice. Sprinkle with cinnamon and sugar.

Bake in hot oven (400°F.) about 30 minutes.

Upside-Down Cherry Coffee Cake: In a deep cake pan melt 2 tablespoons butter.

Sprinkle 4 tablespoons sugar over bottom of pan.

Cover with sour canned cherries (or other fruit) that have been well drained. Cover with coffee cake dough.

Bake in hot oven (400°F.) about 20 minutes.

APPLE COFFEE CAKE

    1 recipe Quick Coffee cake
    3 medium apples, peeled and sliced
    2 tablespoons melted butter or margarine
    ¼ cup sugar
    ½ teaspoon cinnamon

Spread the coffee cake batter in a buttered 9-inch layer pan.

Arrange the apple slices on top in circles until the entire top of the dough is covered.

Brush with the butter and sprinkle with the sugar and cinnamon. Bake in hot oven (400°F.) for 25 minutes.

APRICOT UPSIDE-DOWN COFFEE CAKE

    1 recipe Quick Coffee cake
    ¼ cup butter or margarine
    ¼ cup brown sugar
    16 cooked dried apricot halves

Melt the butter in an 8-inch square pan. Sprinkle with the brown sugar and arrange the apricot halves evenly over the butter-sugar mixture.

Cover with coffee cake batter. Bake in hot oven (400°F.) for 25 minutes.

QUICK KUGELHUPF

    1 cup butter
    1 cup sugar
    5 eggs
    4 cups sifted enriched flour
    ½ teaspoon salt
    4 teaspoons baking powder
    1 cup milk
    1 cup seedless raisins
    1 teaspoon grated lemon rind
    1 teaspoon vanilla
    ½ cup chopped nuts (optional)
    Confectioners' sugar

Cream butter until soft and fluffy. Sift in sugar gradually and beat until creamy and light. Add 1 egg at a time, beating well after each addition.

Sift flour with salt and baking powder. Add sifted mixture in 3 parts to butter mixture alternating with milk in thirds. Beat smooth after each addition.

Add raisins, lemon rind, vanilla, and nuts (if desired).

Mix well and pour into greased 7-inch tube pan. Bake in moderate oven (350°F.) about 1 hour.

When cooled, dust with confectioners' sugar.

Orange Blossom Coffee Ring

ORANGE BLOSSOM COFFEE RING

    1 cup whole bran dry cereal
    ¾ cup orange juice
    1 egg
    ¼ cup soft shortening
    1 teaspoon grated orange rind
    1 cup sifted all-purpose flour
    1½ teaspoons baking powder
    ¼ teaspoon baking soda
    ½ teaspoon salt
    ¼ cup sugar
    ½ cup seedless raisins

Combine whole bran cereal and orange juice; let stand until most of moisture is taken up. Add egg, shortening, and orange rind; beat well.

Sift together flour, baking powder, soda, salt, and sugar. Add to first mixture together with raisins, stirring only until combined.

Fill greased 8-inch ring mold about ⅔ full. Bake in hot oven (400°F.) about 25 minutes. Remove from ring mold; let cool. Frost with thin confectioners' icing and decorate with pecan halves and candied fruit. Makes 8 to 10 servings.

FRENCH COFFEE CAKE

    ½ cup firmly packed brown sugar
    1 tablespoon cornstarch
    1 tablespoon butter
    Grated rind 1 orange
    ¼ cup water
    ⅓ cup orange juice
    1 tablespoon lemon juice
    1 cup sifted enriched flour
    2 teaspoons baking powder
    1 teaspoon salt
    3 tablespoons shortening
    ⅓ cup milk

Blend sugar, cornstarch, butter, and orange rind. Reserve 2 tablespoons mixture for topping.

To remainder, add water and juices. Simmer 5 minutes. Cool.

Mix and sift flour, baking powder, and salt. Cut in shortening and then add milk.

Divide dough in 3 portions. Roll to fit 8-inch square pan.

Spread layer of orange mixture in greased pan. Add layer of dough. Repeat, ending with orange mixture. Sprinkle with sugar mixture.

Bake in hot oven (425°F.) 20 minutes. Serves 6.

Quick Coffee Ring

QUICK COFFEE RING

1 cup light or dark raisins
2 cups sifted all-purpose flour
4 teaspoons baking powder
1 teaspoon salt
1/3 cup shortening
2/3 cup milk
3 tablespoons melted butter or margarine
1/3 cup brown sugar (packed)
1/4 teaspoon cinnamon

Rinse and drain raisins. Sift together flour, baking powder, and salt. Cut in shortening. Add milk and mix well. Turn out onto lightly floured board and roll to rectangle about 10 x 14 inches.

Combine 2 tablespoons of the butter with brown sugar, cinnamon, and raisins. Spread over dough. Roll up as for jelly roll.

Place sealed edge down on lightly greased baking sheet. Join ends to form ring, seal. With scissors make cuts 2/3 of way through ring at 1-inch intervals. Turn each section on its side. Brush with remaining butter.

Bake in hot oven (400°F.) about 25 minutes, until well browned. Serve hot. Makes 1 ring.

SOUR CREAM BISCUIT CAKE

2 cups sifted enriched flour
2 teaspoons baking powder
1/2 teaspoon baking soda
Dash of salt
1/2 cup sugar
1/4 cup butter or margarine
1 cup sour cream
1 slightly beaten egg

Mix and sift flour, baking powder, soda, salt, and sugar. Cut in butter.

Add sour cream to beaten egg and stir lightly into dry ingredients. Turn

into 8-inch square pan or loaf pan.

Bake in hot oven (400°F.) 25 minutes for 8-inch square pan or 45 minutes in loaf pan.

If desired, sprinkle top of cake with sugar and cinnamon before baking. Makes 1 cake square or loaf.

OPEN-FACED APPLE CAKE

2 cups sifted enriched flour
2 1/2 teaspoons baking powder
1 teaspoon salt
6 tablespoons shortening
About 3/4 cup milk
3 medium-sized apples
3 tablespoons sugar
1/4 teaspoon cinnamon

Mix and sift flour, baking powder, and salt. Cut in 4 tablespoons shortening thoroughly. Add just enough milk to hold dry ingredients together.

Turn into 2 lightly greased 8-inch layer-cake pans.

Peel and slice apples thinly and arrange over dough. Dot with remaining fat. Sprinkle with sugar and cinnamon.

Bake in moderate oven (375°F.) about 20 minutes. Serve with cream.

RAISIN COCONUT COFFEE CAKE

3/4 cup seedless raisins
1 1/3 cups sifted enriched flour
2/3 cup brown sugar (packed)
1/3 cup shortening (part butter or margarine)
1/2 teaspoon baking powder
1/4 teaspoon salt
1/4 teaspoon cinnamon
1/4 teaspoon baking soda
1 egg
1/3 cup buttermilk or sour milk
2/3 cup shredded coconut

Rinse raisins and drain thoroughly. Combine flour, sugar, and shortening and blend until crumbly. Set aside 1/2 cup of this mixture.

To remainder, add baking powder, salt, cinnamon, and soda. Stir in raisins. Beat egg lightly; add buttermilk. Stir into dry mixture and blend well.

Turn into greased 8-inch cake pan. Sprinkle reserved crumbly mixture evenly over batter and top with coconut. Bake in moderate oven (350°F.) 30 to 40 minutes. Cut in wedges; serve warm. Serves 6.

DUTCH PEACH CAKE

Part 1:

2 cups sifted enriched flour
1/2 teaspoon salt
4 teaspoons baking powder
1/2 cup sugar
1/4 teaspoon mace
1 egg
1 cup milk
1/4 cup melted butter (1/2 stick butter)

Sift together the dry ingredients. Beat the egg until thick and lemon-colored.

Add the milk and stir into the dry mixture along with the melted butter. Do not beat. Spread into a well buttered 9-inch square glass baking dish or pan.

Part 2:

2 tablespoons butter
1/4 cup sugar
2 tablespoons flour
1 teaspoon cinnamon
Peach slices, quantity depends on design

Crumble the butter into the dry ingredients, using a coarse-tined fork. (Double the quantity if the family likes lots of topping.)

Arrange peach slices in rows or in any desired design on top of batter. Sprinkle the crumbly butter mixture over the top. Bake in a moderate oven (375°F.) for 25 to 30 minutes. Serve hot.

Note: This is good as dessert for dinner, cut in squares and topped with whipped cream or hard sauce, or served with a pitcher of cream

BLUEBERRY BUCKLE

Crumb Topping:

1/2 cup sugar
1/3 cup sifted enriched flour
1/2 teaspoon cinnamon
3 tablespoons soft butter or margarine

Measure sugar, flour, and cinnamon into small bowl. Mix well.

Add butter or margarine and cut in with fork or pastry blender until mixture is consistency of crumbs.

Batter:

1/4 cup soft butter or margarine
3/4 cup sugar
1 egg
1/2 cup milk
1 1/2 cups sifted enriched flour
2 teaspoons baking powder
1/2 teaspoon salt
1 14-ounce can blueberries, drained

Stir butter or margarine until creamy. Add sugar, gradually, mixing until creamy. Beat in egg. Add milk.

Sift together flour, baking powder, and salt. Stir into butter or margarine mixture, stirring until smooth. Gently fold in about 1 cup well drained blueberries.

Spread batter into well buttered pan, 8 x 8 inches.

Sprinkle with crumb topping. Bake in moderate oven (375°F.) 45 to 50 minutes.

BAVARIAN MOCK STRUDEL

    2   cups sifted enriched flour
    ½   cup sugar
    4   teaspoons baking powder
    ¼   cup non-fat dry milk solids
    ½   teaspoon salt
    ½   cup shortening
    ⅓   cup water

Topping:

    1   cup light canned sweet cherries
    2   tablespoons melted butter
    ¼   cup brown sugar
    ⅓   cup whole almonds

Sift dry ingredients together. Cut in shortening. Add water and mix. Spread in greased 6 x 12-inch pan.

Arrange cherries in rows over dough. Mix other topping ingredients together and sprinkle over cherries.

Bake in hot oven (400°F.) for 35 minutes.

Make icing with ½ cup powdered sugar, 2 teaspoons water, and ⅛ teaspoon almond extract. Drizzle over hot bread. Serve warm.

ORANGE COFFEE CAKE

Orange Crumb Topping:

    1   cup sifted enriched flour
    ¾   cup brown sugar
    2.   tablespoons melted shortening
    2   tablespoons orange juice
    1½   teaspoons grated orange rind
    ½   teaspoon cinnamon

Mix above ingredients together with a fork before mixing coffee cake.

Coffee Cake:

    2   cups sifted enriched flour
    ¼   teaspoon salt
    ½   cup sugar
    4   teaspoons baking powder
    1½   teaspoons grated orange rind
    4   tablespoons shortening
    1   egg
    ½   cup orange juice
    ½   cup milk

Mix and sift dry ingredients. Add orange rind and cut in shortening. Blend in well beaten egg mixed with orange juice and milk.

Spread in greased and floured 8-inch square pan. Drop bits of Orange Crumb Topping over top.

Bake in moderate oven (375°F.) 30 to 35 minutes.

HONEY COFFEE CAKE

    ¾   cup sifted enriched flour
    2½   teaspoons baking powder
    ¼   teaspoon salt
    ½   cup milk
    ¼   cup honey
    1   egg, well beaten
    3   tablespoons melted shortening
    1½   cups wheat flakes or 1½ cups
         bran flakes

Sift flour with baking powder and salt. Combine milk, honey, and egg, and add to flour mixture.

Add shortening, mixing only enough to combine. Fold in flakes. Pour into greased pan. Sprinkle topping (see below) over batter.

Bake in hot oven (400°F.) until done (25 minutes). Makes 1 square cake (8" x 8" x 2").

Honey Coffee Cake Topping: Mix together ¼ cup brown sugar, ½ teaspoon cinnamon, ¼ teaspoon nutmeg, 2 tablespoons melted butter, and ½ cup wheat or bran flakes. Sprinkle over batter in pan.

POPPY SEED KUCHEN

    1½   cups sifted enriched flour
    4   tablespoons sugar
    ½   teaspoon baking powder
    ⅛   teaspoon salt
    1   cup milk
    1   egg yolk, beaten
    ½   pound poppy seeds
    ¼   cup butter
    ½   cup cream
    1   tablespoon grated lemon rind or
         1 tablespoon grated orange
         rind

Mix and sift flour, 1 tablespoon sugar, baking powder, and salt. Blend milk with egg yolk. Add to flour mixture. Blend well and let stand ½ hour.

Grind poppy seeds well. Add remaining ingredients and mix well.

Roll dough out ½-inch thick on a floured board. Place in a cake pan. Cover with poppy seed mixture.

Bake in moderate oven (350°F.) about 30 minutes.

DUTCH BANANA COFFEE CAKE

    1   cup sifted enriched flour
    1¼   teaspoons baking powder
    ½   teaspoon salt
    2   tablespoons sugar
    ¼   cup shortening
    1   egg, well beaten
    3   tablespoons milk
    3   firm bananas
    2   tablespoons melted butter
    2   tablespoons sugar
    ¼   teaspoon cinnamon
    1   teaspoon grated orange rind

Mix and sift flour, baking powder, salt, and sugar. Cut in shortening.

Combine egg and milk. Add to flour mixture and stir until mixture is blended.

Turn the stiff dough into a greased baking pan (8 x 10 x 2 inches), and spread evenly over bottom of pan.

Peel bananas and cut into ½-inch diagonal pieces. Cover surface of dough with overlapping pieces of bananas. Brush bananas with butter.

Mix together sugar, cinnamon, and orange rind and sprinkle over top of bananas.

Bake in moderate oven (350°F.) about 35 minutes. Serves 6 to 8.

STAR COFFEE CAKE

    1   No. 2 can (2½ cups) crushed pine-
         apple, drained
    ¾   cup syrup drained from pineapple
    1   recipe biscuit dough using 2 cups
         flour or biscuit mix
    ¼   cup butter or margarine, melted
    ½   cup firmly packed brown sugar
    ¼   teaspoon cinnamon
    ½   cup pecans or other nuts, chopped
    Small red and green gumdrops,
         halved

Drain pineapple thoroughly. Make biscuit dough, using pineapple syrup instead of milk. Roll out about ½ inch thick on lightly floured board, making a circle 10½ inches in diameter.

Melt butter; stir in brown sugar, cinnamon, nuts, drained pineapple.

Transfer circle of dough to greased cooky sheet. Make 5 slashes from outside edge to center. (These should be about 3 inches long and 6 inches apart at edge.)

Put 2 tablespoons pineapple mixture in each of the 5 sections.

Then, taking the corner of one section, fold it over toward center, then overlap the other corner on top of this, making a point.

Pinch together at the tip and along double thickness to keep pineapple from oozing out.

Repeat with other 4 sections to make a 5-point star.

Spread remainder of pineapple mixture in center area.

Brush surface of dough with melted shortening. Decorate with gumdrops.

Bake in very hot oven (450°F.) 20 to 25 minutes. Serve hot.

Star Coffee Cake

Fig Loaf Roll

FIG LOAF ROLL

Fig Filling:

- ¾ cup dried figs
- ¼ cup water
- ¼ cup sugar
- 1 tablespoon flour
- Dash of salt
- 2 tablespoons lemon juice

Cover figs with boiling water and let stand about 10 minutes; drain, clip off stems, and snip figs fine with scissors.

Add water and heat. Add sugar mixed with flour and salt, and cook gently, stirring, about 10 minutes, or until thickened.

Add lemon juice, and cool before using.

Dough For Fig Roll Loaf:

- 3 cups sifted enriched flour
- 4½ teaspoons baking powder
- ¾ teaspoon salt
- ¼ cup sugar
- 6 tablespoons shortening
- 1 egg, beaten
- 1 cup milk

Mix and sift flour with baking powder, salt, and sugar into mixing bowl. Cut or rub in shortening until like corn meal.

Add milk to beaten egg; add all at once to flour mixture and stir just until dough will hold together.

Turn out on lightly floured board or canvas, and roll or pat out about ½ inch thick.

The sheet of dough should be as wide as your bread pan is long, or about 8 inches.

Spread the fig filling evenly over the dough, roll up, and cut into slices about ¾ inch thick.

Stand the slices up in their original position in a well greased 8 x 4 x 4-inch bread loaf pan, placing each slice tightly against the other until the pan is full.

Bake in hot oven (400°F.) 30 to 35 minutes, until done and nicely browned. Cool slightly before cutting. Serves 6.

TOPSY-TURVEY DUTCH APPLE CAKE

- ¼ cup margarine
- ¾ cup firmly packed brown sugar
- 1 teaspoon cinnamon
- 1 tablespoon milk
- 2 baking apples, peeled and sliced thin
- 2 cups sifted enriched flour
- 3 teaspoons baking powder
- 2 tablespoons sugar
- ½ teaspoon salt
- ⅓ cup margarine
- 1 egg
- ¾ cup milk

Melt margarine and add brown sugar, cinnamon, and milk. Pour into 9-inch layer pan or 9-inch square pan.

Arrange sliced apples in brown sugar mixture.

Sift together flour, baking powder, sugar, and salt. Cut in margarine.

Combine egg with milk and add to flour mixture. Stir only until flour disappears. Spread dough carefully over apples.

Bake in moderate oven (350°F.) 45 to 50 minutes. Serve upside-down, garnished with whipped cream, if desired.

SWEDISH CHERRY RING

- 1 recipe biscuit dough
- Melted butter
- ¼ cup sugar
- 1 teaspoon cinnamon
- ¼ cup chopped nuts
- Cherry preserves

Roll dough into rectangle ¼ inch thick. Spread with melted butter and sprinkle with sugar, cinnamon, and nuts.

Roll dough jelly-roll fashion. Shape into ring on greased cooky sheet. Press ends together.

From outer edge, snip almost to center at 1-inch intervals with scissors. Pull slices apart and twist so cut surface is turned upward.

Place one teaspoon of cherry pre-

serves in crevice of each cut. Bake in very hot oven (450°F.) about 15 minutes, or until nicely browned.

STRAWBERRY COFFEE CAKE

- 2 cups sifted enriched flour
- 2 teaspoons baking powder
- 6 tablespoons sugar
- ¾ teaspoon salt
- ⅓ cup butter or shortening
- 1 well beaten egg
- ⅓ cup milk
- 1½ cups strawberries, cleaned and hulled

Topping:

- 3 tablespoons butter
- 3 tablespoons flour
- ¼ cup sugar

Mix and sift flour, baking powder, sugar, and salt. Cut in shortening.

Combine egg and milk and add to dry ingredients, stirring with fork only to blend well.

Spread dough in well greased 8-inch square pan. Cover with strawberries, whole or cut in halves. Sprinkle with topping.

Bake in hot oven (400°F.) 25 to 30 minutes.

Prepare topping by blending ingredients together until crumbly. Makes 1 8-inch square cake.

BLUEBERRY COFFEE CAKE

- ½ cup shortening
- ½ cup sugar
- 2 eggs
- 1¾ cups sifted enriched flour
- 3 teaspoons baking powder
- ½ teaspoon salt
- 1 cup milk
- ⅔ cup blueberries
- ¼ cup brown sugar, firmly packed
- ½ teaspoon cinnamon

Cream shortening. Add sugar and cream thoroughly. Beat eggs, and add.

Mix and sift flour, baking powder, and salt. Add alternately with milk to creamed mixture. Fold in blueberries.

Turn into a greased 8-inch square pan. Sprinkle with mixture of brown sugar and cinnamon.

Bake in moderate oven (350°F.) 50 minutes. Serve hot.

Swedish Cherry Ring

SPICE NUT COFFEE CAKE

1½ cups sifted enriched flour
⅔ cup sugar
2 teaspoons baking powder
½ teaspoon salt
½ teaspoon cloves
½ teaspoon nutmeg
1 teaspoon cinnamon
⅓ cup shortening
1 egg, beaten
2 tablespoons molasses
⅔ cup milk
½ cup chopped walnuts

Sift together into a bowl the flour, sugar, baking powder, salt, and spices.

Cut in shortening with fork or pastry blender until mixture is like coarse crumbs. Reserve ½ cup of this mixture for top of coffee cake.

To rest of crumb mixture add beaten egg, molasses, and milk. Mix lightly.

Pour into large well greased baking dish. Sprinkle top with remaining ½ cup of crumb mixture and the chopped walnuts.

Bake in moderate oven (350°F.) about 45 minutes. Serves 8.

FILLED CINNAMON COFFEE CAKE

¼ cup shortening
¾ cup sugar
1 well beaten egg
2 cups sifted enriched flour
2 teaspoons baking powder
½ teaspoon salt
¾ cup milk

Filling:

½ cup sugar
3 teaspoons cinnamon
2 tablespoons flour
3 tablespoons melted butter

Cream shortening and sugar together. Add egg and mix well.

Mix and sift flour, baking powder, and salt. Add sifted dry ingredients and milk alternately to creamed mixture.

Spread ½ the batter in greased pan about 7 by 11 inches.

Mix all ingredients for filling together until crumbly. Sprinkle ½ the filling over batter. Cover with remaining batter and sprinkle with remaining topping.

Bake in moderate oven (375°F.) 30 minutes. Serves 8.

MOCK APPLE STRUDEL

2 cups sifted enriched flour
3 teaspoons baking powder
½ teaspoon salt
2 tablespoons sugar
4 tablespoons shortening
⅔ to ¾ cup milk
3 cups chopped apple
½ cup sugar
1 teaspoon cinnamon
Confectioners' sugar
Vanilla

Chopped nuts

Mix and sift flour, baking powder, salt, and sugar. Cut in shortening. Add milk to make a soft dough.

Turn out on floured board and knead gently. Roll out ¼-inch thick. Brush with melted butter or margarine. Cover with chopped apple. Sprinkle sugar and cinnamon over apple.

Roll jelly-roll fashion and form into a semicircle on a greased baking sheet.

Bake in hot oven (425°F.) 20 to 25 minutes.

While warm, frost with white frosting made by beating confectioners' sugar with a little hot water until smooth, and flavor with vanilla. Sprinkle chopped nuts over frosting. Makes 12 1-inch slices.

CRANBERRY TWISTS
Cranberry Filling:

1 cup cranberries
2 tablespoons cornstarch
½ cup sugar
2 tablespoons water
2 tablespoons margarine
Dash of nutmeg

Wash and pick over cranberries, removing stems. Mix cornstarch and sugar. Add to cranberries in saucepan. Mix well. Add water.

Cook over gentle heat, stirring constantly until thickened. Sauce will be quite thick.

Remove from heat. Stir in margarine and nutmeg. Let cook while making the dough.

Dough:

2 cups sifted enriched flour
3 teaspoons baking powder
¾ teaspoon salt
2 tablespoons sugar
6 tablespoons margarine
About ¾ cup milk

Sift together flour, baking powder, salt, and sugar into mixing bowl.

Cut or rub in margarine until mixture is like coarse corn meal.

Add milk and stir until dough clings together in ball.

Turn out on floured board or pastry cloth.

Roll out to long narrow sheet a scant ½ inch thick.

Spread cranberry filling on dough, leaving a strip about ⅓ of the width of dough uncovered. Fold this strip over center ⅓ of dough; then fold over third strip. This makes 3 layers of dough and 2 layers of filling.

Cut crosswise into 1-inch slices. Twist each slice once, twisting ends in opposite directions.

Place an inch apart on greased baking sheet.

Bake in hot oven (425°F.) 15 minutes. Serve hot.

Mock Apple Strudel

PINEAPPLE PINWHEELS

2 cups sifted enriched flour
3 teaspoons baking powder
2 tablespoons granulated sugar
1 teaspoon salt
⅓ cup shortening
⅔ cup syrup drained from crushed pineapple
1 cup drained crushed pineapple
½ cup firmly packed brown sugar
¼ teaspoon cinnamon
2 tablespoons melted butter or margarine

Sift flour, baking powder, granulated sugar, and salt together into mixing bowl. Using pastry blender or 2 knives cut in shortening until finely divided. Add pineapple syrup and mix until dough holds together.

Turn out on lightly floured board and knead gently several strokes to smooth dough. Roll out to an oblong shape, about 8 x 16 inches.

Spread with following mixture: 1 cup drained crushed pineapple, ½ cup brown sugar, ¼ teaspoon cinnamon, and 2 tablespoons melted butter or margarine.

Starting from long side roll up as for jelly roll; seal long edge, using fingers.

With sharp knife cut into 16 slices, 1-inch thick. Place slices, cut side down, in well greased square baking pan, 9 x 9 x 1¾ inches.

Bake in hot oven (425°F.) 25 minutes. Makes 16 pineapple pinwheels.

Pineapple Pinwheels

Biscuits and Quick Rolls

BAKING POWDER BISCUIT HINTS

For high, light, and tender—piping hot, crusty biscuits

1. Turn on the oven first as correct baking temperature is important for perfect results. After assembling the ingredients and utensils, measuring dry ingredients and sifting them together into mixing bowl, measure shortening into mixing bowl and cut into flour mixture with pastry blender (or 2 knives used scissors fashion) until finely blended. Mixture should look like coarse crumbs.

2. Measure the maximum amount of milk specified. Do not add all of it at first. Add almost all of it, mix it in and see if the dough seems easy to handle. Then add the rest if necessary. Too much milk makes the dough sticky and difficult to handle. Not enough milk makes the dough stiff and the finished biscuits tough and dry.

3. Round up on a lightly floured board. Knead very gently and fast just to thoroughly mix ingredients and to even up texture. This means turning the dough 2 or 3 times—not more than 15 or 20 punches with flour-dusted hands. Too much handling at this point makes the biscuits tough.

4. Roll dough or pat it out (with floured hand) until dough is ½-inch thick.

5. Cut with biscuit cutter (dipped in flour first to prevent sticking. Cut as close together as possible. (Leftover bits of dough should be fitted and pushed together, patted out and cut—not re-rolled.) Place biscuits close together on baking sheet for biscuits with soft sides —or far apart for biscuits with crusty sides.

BAKING POWDER BISCUITS

(Master Recipe)

    2 cups sifted enriched flour
    3 teaspoons baking powder
    1 teaspoon salt
    4 tablespoons shortening
    ⅔ to ¾ cup milk or ⅔ to ¾ cup
       water

Sift together dry ingredients. Cut shortening into flour with 2 knives or pastry blender until consistency of coarse meal.

Add liquid, mixing lightly with a fork until a ball forms that separates from the sides of bowl.

Turn out on lightly floured board. Knead gently ½ minute. Roll or pat out dough ½ inch thick. Cut with floured biscuit cutter.

Bake on ungreased baking sheet in very hot oven (450°F.) 12 to 15 minutes. Serve immediately. Makes 1½ dozen biscuits.

Biscuit Variations:

Biscuit Teasers: Place preserves or seasoned chopped meat between 2 thin biscuits. Press edges together. Brush with shortening or milk and bake.

Bran Biscuits: In master recipe substitute 1 cup whole bran for 1 cup white flour.

Cheese Biscuits: In master recipe add ¼ cup grated cheese to dry ingredients.

Chive Biscuits: In master recipe add ¼ cup freshly chopped chives to mixture of flour and shortening.

Cream Biscuits: In master recipe use 1 scant cup medium cream instead of shortening and milk or water.

Drop Biscuits: Increase liquid in master recipe to 1 cup. Drop from teaspoon on lightly greased baking sheet or muffin pans.

Fried Biscuits: Prepare master recipe; drop spoonfuls of dough into hot greased pan. Turn when brown.

Fruit Biscuits: In master recipe add ½ cup chopped dates, figs, prunes, or raisins to mixture of flour and shortening.

Mint Biscuits: In master recipe add ¼ cup freshly chopped mint to mixture of flour and shortening.

Nut Biscuits: In master recipe add ½ cup chopped nuts to mixture of flour and shortening.

Orange Biscuits: In master recipe add 1 tablespoon grated orange rind to mixture of flour and shortening.

Orange Tea Biscuits: In master recipe add 1 teaspoon grated orange rind to dry ingredients. When biscuits have been cut, press into the top of each a small cube of sugar which has been dipped in orange juice or other fruit juice.

Peanut Biscuits: Substitute ½ cup peanut butter for shortening in master recipe.

Rich Shortcake Biscuits: To master recipe, add 1 egg and 2 tablespoons sugar. Increase shortening to 6 tablespoons.

Savory Biscuits: Add 1 teaspoon poultry seasoning to dry ingredients of master recipe.

Sour Milk or Buttermilk Biscuits: Follow master recipe. Add ½ teaspoon baking soda, sifting it with flour. Use sour milk or buttermilk for liquid.

Whole Wheat Biscuits: In master recipe substitute 1 cup whole wheat flour for 1 cup white flour. Use ¾ teaspoon salt instead of 1 teaspoon salt.

OLD-FASHIONED SODA BISCUITS

    2 cups sifted enriched flour
    ¾ teaspoon baking soda
    ½ teaspoon salt
    ¼ cup shortening
    ¼ cup distilled vinegar
    ½ cup sweet milk

Mix and sift flour, soda, and salt. Cut in shortening. Add vinegar and milk and stir lightly.

Turn onto floured board and knead lightly.

For Northern-style, roll about ½ inch thick; **Southern-style,** roll about ¼ inch thick.

Cut biscuits and prick with fork for Southern-style. Place on greased baking sheet.

Bake in very hot oven (450°F.) 12 to 15 minutes. Makes 16 to 18 2-inch Northern-style biscuits or 32 to 34 2-inch Southern-style biscuits.

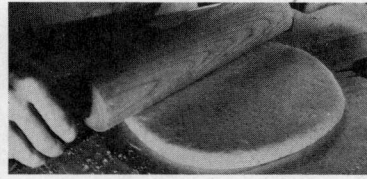
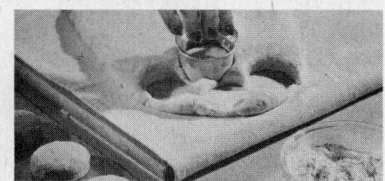

VARIETY BISCUITS FROM MASTER BISCUIT RECIPE

Banana Curls: Roll dough for baking powder biscuits into rectangular shape about 1/4 inch thick. Brush with 2 tablespoons melted butter or margarine.

Slice 2 medium-sized ripe bananas evenly over the dough.

Mix 3 tablespoons brown sugar and 1/2 teaspoon cinnamon together and sprinkle over bananas.

Roll as for jelly roll and cut in 1-inch slices.

Place cut side up in well greased muffin pans and brush top with melted butter. Bake in hot oven (400°F.) 15 minutes. Makes 18 curls.

Biscuit Sticks: Roll or pat out dough for baking powder biscuits and cut into sticks 1/2 inch wide and 3 inches long. Brush with melted butter.

Bake in hot oven (425°F.) and serve them stacked log-cabin fashion.

Blueberry Biscuits: Prepare baking powder biscuit dough. Roll out 1/4 inch thick. Fill as in method #1 or #2.

Bake in very hot oven (450°F.) 12 to 15 minutes.

Method #1: Form shells by lining muffin pans halfway up with dough. Fill the middle with sugared berries. Cover with a round of dough. Moisten edges of shells and rounds and press lightly together.

Method #2: Cut the dough into small squares or rounds. Place sugared berries between two pieces and pinch edges together.

Cheese Rosettes: To recipe for baking powder biscuits add 1/2 cup grated American cheese before adding liquid. Substitute water for milk.

Chill slightly before using. Roll out on floured surface to 1/4-inch thickness.

Cut into 1/2-inch strips about 6 inches long. Tie in bowknot. After tying bring one end through center and other end over the side and turn under.

Place on greased baking sheet, dust with paprika, and bake in hot oven (400°F.) 10 to 15 minutes.

Cheese Squares: Roll or pat dough for baking powder biscuits 1/4-inch thick. Sprinkle lightly with grated cheese.

With a sharp knife, cut dough into squares. Bake in hot oven (425°F.).

Cherry Delights: Cut dough for baking powder biscuits into small rounds.

With a smaller cutter, remove centers from half the rounds. Brush with rich milk. Place the rings on top of the whole rounds.

Place 1/2 teaspoon cherry preserves in the center of each and bake in hot oven (425°F.) 12 to 15 minutes.

Marmalade Crescents: Prepare dough for baking powder biscuits. Roll out 1/2 inch thick.

Brush with 2 tablespoons melted butter or other melted shortening. Spread with marmalade or jam.

Cut into 3-inch squares, then cut each square diagonally in half to make triangles.

Roll each triangle jelly-roll fashion, starting with the long edge of the triangle. Shape into a crescent.

Place on greased baking sheet and bake in a very hot oven (450°F.) 12 to 15 minutes. Makes about 16 crescents.

Pineapple Squares: Add 2 tablespoons sugar to recipe for baking powder biscuits and roll out into rectangular sheet.

Cut into strips 3 inches wide and 6 inches long. Brush with melted butter.

Place 1 teaspoon crushed pineapple on 1/2 of each strip and fold the other end of the strip over the fruit. Press edges together with a fork. Prick tops with fork.

Bake in hot oven (425°F.) 25 minutes. Serve hot or cold with cream or with fruit sauce.

GRIDDLE SODA SCONES (No Fat)

4	cups sifted enriched flour
1	teaspoon baking soda
1	teaspoon cream of tartar
1 1/2	teaspoons salt
1	cup buttermilk

Mix all ingredients thoroughly. Pat out on floured board to 1/2-inch thickness; cut with 2 1/2-inch cutter.

Put on hot greased griddle; cook until well-risen and light brown underneath. Turn, cook on other side until brown.

When the edges are dry, the scones are done. Makes about 15 scones.

CHEESE FAN TANS

Prepare baking powder biscuit dough. Shape into a smooth ball after a quick light kneading. Roll into a rectangle about 1/3-inch thick and 8-inches wide.

Cut in 4 strips 2 inches wide. Spread with softened (not melted) butter. Sprinkle 3 strips with a generous cup of shredded American natural or process Cheddar cheese ranging from mild to nippy as family taste suggests.

Pile the 3 strips on top of each other, covering with the fourth strip (no cheese on this). Cut across into 6 pieces. Carefully place in buttered deep muffin pans or custard cups, having the cut side up. Brush with melted butter.

Bake in a very hot oven (450°F.) for 10 to 12 minutes or until cooked through with a light browning. Serve at once.

Scotch Scones

SCOTCH SCONES

A scone was originally a Scottish griddlecake made usually of oats, sometimes of barley or wheat; nowadays, it refers to a small cake resembling a baking powder biscuit, cut in various shapes, baked in a hot oven or on a griddle, and usually served with butter.

2	cups sifted enriched flour
3	teaspoons baking powder
1	teaspoon salt
1	tablespoon sugar
4	tablespoons shortening
1/4	cup currants (optional)
2	eggs
1/2	cup milk

Sift together flour, baking powder, salt, and sugar. Cut in shortening. Add currants, if desired.

Beat together 1 whole egg and 1 egg yolk, reserving 1 white for the tops. Add milk to beaten eggs, and add all to dry ingredients. Stir only enough to make dough hold together.

Turn out on lightly floured board and knead 1/2 minute. Roll out in circular shape to 1/2 inch thickness.

Cut into pie-shaped wedges. Brush tops with white of egg, and sprinkle with sugar. Bake in hot oven (425°F.) 12 to 15 minutes. Makes 10 to 12 scones.

SWEET POTATO BISCUITS

1 1/2	cups sifted enriched flour
2	tablespoons baking powder
3/4	teaspoon salt
1/2	cup chilled shortening
1	cup milk
1 1/2	cups mashed sweet potatoes

Mix and sift flour, baking powder, and salt. Cut in shortening with a pastry blender or 2 knives.

Combine milk and sweet potatoes. Add to flour-shortening mixture and stir quickly.

Knead lightly on board using as little flour as possible on board. Roll 1/2 inch thick. Cut with floured biscuit cutter.

Place on greased baking sheet. Bake in hot oven (425°F.) 12 to 15 minutes. Makes about 2 dozen.

Cheese Fan Tans

HOMEMADE BISCUIT MIX

8 cups sifted enriched flour
1 tablespoon salt
4 tablespoons baking powder
1 cup shortening

Mix and sift flour, salt, and baking powder into a large bowl.

Have shortening at room temperature. Cut it into flour mixture with pastry blender or fork until mixture is like coarse corn meal.

Store in a closely covered container. Biscuit mix will keep 3 to 4 weeks in a cool cupboard and much longer in the refrigerator.

Rich Homemade Biscuit Mix: Sift in with the flour 1 cup dried skim milk solids.

To Make 6 Biscuits: Measure 1 cup biscuit mix into a bowl. Stir in 1/4 to 1/3 cup milk.

To cut out and bake follow method in master recipe for Biscuits.

To Make 6 Muffins: Measure 1 cup biscuit mix into a bowl. Add 1 tablespoon sugar, 1 well beaten egg, and about 1/2 cup milk.

To mix and bake follow method in master recipe for Plain Muffins.

To Make 6 Pancakes: Measure 1 cup biscuit mix. Beat 1 egg well; combine with 1/2 cup milk and 2 tablespoons flour. Add to mix and stir only to dampen flour.

Then add more milk to make batter just thin enough to pour. To bake follow method in master recipe for Griddle Cakes.

To Make 6 Waffles: Measure 2 cups mix; add 1 teaspoon sugar and 1/8 teaspoon salt.

Combine 2 tablespoons melted butter, 1 well beaten egg, and 1 1/2 cups sweet or sour milk. Beat liquid ingredients into biscuit mix.

To bake, follow method in master recipe for Waffles.

QUICK ORANGE ROLLS

1 can frozen orange juice concentrate
1/4 cup water
1 cup sugar
2 cups sifted enriched flour
4 teaspoons baking powder
1 teaspoon salt
1/4 cup shortening
2/3 to 3/4 cup milk
1 cup chopped dates

Combine orange juice concentrate, water, and sugar and cook to thick syrup, about 10 minutes. Cool.

Mix and sift flour, baking powder, and salt. Cut in shortening wtih pastry blender until mixture resembles coarse meal. Add milk to make a soft dough, while stirring quickly.

Roll out to rectangle about 8 by 16 inches. Sprinkle on the chopped dates. Roll up long way as for jelly roll. Cut into 16 slices.

Place cut side down in deep 9-inch pie pan, placing rolls close together. Pour cooled syrup over biscuits.

Bake in very hot oven (450°F.) 15 to 20 minutes. Makes about 16.

BISCUIT PINWHEELS

Prepare dough for standard baking powder biscuits. Roll into an oblong about 12 inches long and 1/4 inch thick.

Spread with desired filling as directed in the following variations.

Roll lengthwise as tightly as possible, jelly-roll fashion. Pinch edge to the roll.

Cut into 1-inch slices and place cut side down in greased muffin pans.

Bake in hot oven (400°F.) 18 to 20 minutes. Makes about 12 pinwheels.

Butterscotch Pinwheels: Spread dough with 2 tablespoons melted shortening and 1/2 cup brown sugar. Roll and cut as directed above.

Cream together 1/3 cup butter and 1/2 cup brown sugar.

Spread thickly in each muffin pan and place 2 or 3 pecan halves in bottom of each pan before adding pinwheels. Bake.

Cinnamon Currant Pinwheels: Spread dough with 2 tablespoons melted shortening and mixture of 1/2 cup sugar and 1 1/4 teaspoons cinnamon.

Sprinkle with 1/2 cup currants. Roll, cut, and bake.

Honey or Maple Pinwheels: Brush rolled dough with melted fat. Sprinkle with brown sugar. If desired, add chopped nuts, dates, or raisins. Roll and cut as directed.

Place 1 tablespoon honey or maple syrup in bottom of each greased muffin pan. Press cut biscuit into each section.

Jam Pinwheels: Spread dough with 2 tablespoons melted shortening and 1/2 cup jam or marmalade; roll, cut, and bake.

Peanut Butter Pinwheels: Spread dough with 2 tablespoons melted shortening and 1/2 cup peanut butter; roll, cut, and bake.

CORN MEAL DROP BISCUITS

3/4 cup sifted enriched flour
2 1/2 teaspoons baking powder
1/2 teaspoon salt
3/4 cup corn meal
1/4 cup shortening
3/4 cup milk

Mix and sift flour, baking powder, and salt. Blend in corn meal.

Cut in shortening until mixture resembles coarse meal. Add milk all at once and stir only until all flour is dampened.

Drop by spoonfuls onto meat and vegetable mixture in casserole. Bake in hot oven (400°F.) 35 to 40 minutes.

BEATEN BISCUITS

These are unleavened Southern biscuits that depend for tenderness on long beating or the use of a special biscuit machine.

3 cups sifted enriched flour
1/2 teaspoon salt
1/2 cup chilled lard
2/3 cup milk

Mix flour and salt. Cut in shortening as for pastry. Add milk and mix until dough holds together.

Turn out onto a board and beat dough vigorously with a small bat shaped ice crusher, a rolling pin, an old-fashioned wooden potato masher, or a miniature baseball bat, unless you have a biscuit machine.

Beat until dough becomes smooth and velvety in texture. Cut tiny biscuits and prick each clear through twice with the tines of a fork.

Bake on cooky sheet in moderate oven (350°F.) 30 minutes. Split and butter while hot. Makes 3 dozen.

PECAN ROLLS

2 cups sifted enriched flour
3 teaspoons baking powder
1/2 teaspoon salt
4 tablespoons shortening
2/3 to 3/4 cup milk
2 tablespoons melted butter or margarine
1/2 cup firmly packed brown sugar
Pecan halves

Prepare muffin pans by spreading thickly with a creamy mixture made by creaming together 3 tablespoons butter and 6 tablespoons brown sugar. Put 2 or 3 pecan halves into each muffin cup.

Sift together flour, baking powder, and salt. Cut in shortening. Add milk, stirring only until dough holds together.

Turn out on slightly floured board and knead lightly for 1/2 minute. Roll out to 1/4-inch thickness. Brush with melted butter or margarine and sprinkle with brown sugar.

Roll jelly-roll fashion and cut into 1-inch slices. Place slices cut side down into muffin pans.

Bake in hot oven (425°F.) 20 to 25 minutes. Let stand in pan for a minute before turning out. Serve hot or cold. Makes 16 to 18 small rolls.

Pecan Rolls

STIR AND ROLL BISCUITS
(Master Recipe)

2 cups sifted enriched flour
3 teaspoons baking powder
1 teaspoon salt
1/3 cup salad oil
2/3 cup milk

Sift flour once, measure and add baking powder and salt. Sift together into a bowl.

Pour oil and milk in 1 measuring cup but do not stir together. Then pour all at once into flour.

Stir with a fork until mixture cleans side of bowl and rounds up into a ball.

For Dropped Biscuits: Drop dough onto ungreased cooky sheet.

For Rolled Or Patted Biscuits: Smooth by kneading dough about 10 times without additional flour.

With the dough on waxed paper, press out 1/4-inch thick with hands, or roll out between waxed paper.

For higher biscuits, roll dough 1/2-inch thick. Cut with unfloured biscuit cutter.

Bake on ungreased cooky sheet in very hot oven (475°F.) 10 to 12 minutes. Makes about 16.

UPSIDE-DOWN ORANGE BISCUITS

1/4 cup melted butter or margarine
1/2 cup orange juice
3/4 cup sugar
2 teaspoons grated orange rind
2 2/3 cups sifted enriched flour
3 teaspoons baking powder
3/4 teaspoon salt
6 tablespoons butter or margarine
1 1/8 cups milk
1/2 teaspoon cinnamon

Combine melted margarine, orange juice, 1/2 cup sugar, and orange rind; boil 2 minutes. Pour into greased round 9-inch baking pan.

Sift together flour, baking powder, and salt. With pastry blender cut 6 tablespoons butter or margarine into flour until coarse crumbs are formed. Add milk and stir with fork until soft dough is formed.

Knead 1/2 minute on lightly floured board. Roll out to 1/4 inch thickness. Brush with a little melted butter or

Cheese Corn Meal Biscuit Ring

margarine and sprinkle with 1/4 cup sugar and 1/2 teaspoon cinnamon.

Roll as for a jelly roll. Cut in 1-inch slices; place, cut side down, over orange mixture. Bake in very hot oven (450°F.) 20 to 25 minutes. Serves 6.

CORN FLAKE HONEY ROLLS

2 cups sifted enriched flour
3 teaspoons baking powder
1/2 teaspoon salt
1/4 cup fat
2/3 cup milk
3 tablespoons melted butter or margarine
3 cups corn flakes
2/3 cup seedless raisins
1/2 cup honey

Sift together flour, baking powder, and salt. Cut in fat until a coarse even texture is obtained. Add milk, stirring enough to make a soft dough.

Turn onto a lightly floured board and knead about 20 seconds. Roll dough to 1/2-inch thickness. Brush with melted butter.

Combine slightly crushed corn flakes, raisins, honey, and sliced maraschino cherries if you like. Spread over biscuit dough, roll as for a jelly roll.

Using a knife dipped in flour, cut into 1-inch slices. Place slices on greased baking sheet.

Bake in hot oven (400°F.) about 15 to 20 minutes. Serve at once. Makes 10 to 12 rolls.

CHEESE CORN MEAL BISCUIT RING

2 cups sifted enriched flour
3/4 cup corn meal
5 teaspoons baking powder
2 teaspoons salt
1/3 cup shortening
3 tablespoons chopped pimiento
1 cup milk
1/2 cup grated sharp cheese

Sift together flour, corn meal, baking powder, and salt. Cut in shortening until mixture resembles coarse crumbs. Add pimiento.

Add milk, mixing lightly only until mixture is dampened. Turn out on lightly floured board and knead gently a few seconds.

Roll out to 3/8-inch thickness; brush with melted butter. Cut with floured biscuit cutter, small size.

Dip the buttered side of each biscuit in grated cheese.

In well greased 8-inch ring mold, stand biscuits on end with flat sides of biscuits together. Sprinkle remaining cheese over top.

Bake in hot oven (400°F.) 20 to 25 minutes.

Let stand in ring mold 2 or 3 minutes. Invert and turn right side up. Brush with melted butter. Makes 1 8-inch ring.

Cinnamon Flake Kuchen

CINNAMON FLAKE KUCHEN

1/4 cup shortening
1/3 cup granulated sugar
1 egg
1 1/2 cups sifted enriched flour
2 teaspoons baking powder
3/4 teaspoon salt
1/2 teaspoon nutmeg
2/3 cup milk
1/2 cup brown sugar
1/2 teaspoon cinnamon
1/2 teaspoon nutmeg
2 tablespoon butter or margarine, melted
1 cup whole wheat flakes

Blend shortening and granulated sugar; add egg and beat well.

Sift together flour, baking powder, salt, and 1/2 teaspoon nutmeg. Add to shortening mixture alternately with milk, being careful not to overmix. Spread in greased shallow 9 x 9-inch baking pan.

Mix together brown sugar, spices, butter, and whole wheat flakes; sprinkle over batter.

Bake in hot oven (400°F.) about 25 minutes. Serve hot. Serves 12.

TRICKS WITH CHEESE AND BISCUITS

Cheese Pocketbooks: Roll biscuit dough 1/4-inch thick. Cut in 2-inch rounds. Spread each with softened butter. Place a piece of Cheddar cheese on each. Fold it over. Press edges together. Brush tops with melted butter. Bake.

Cheese-Tomato Biscuit: Add 1/2 cup shredded dry American Cheddar cheese to flour mixture; use tomato juice for the liquid.

Coral Reefs: Make up regular biscuit mix except use tomato juice in place of milk. Roll dough 1/3-inch thick. Cut in small rounds. Put together in pairs with a round slice of Cheddar cheese between. Brush tops with melted butter. Bake as usual.

Cheese Frosted Biscuit: Melt over hot water and mix together soft spreading Cheddar cheese (with pimiento if desired), a 6 to 8 ounce glass with 3 tablespoons butter. Place biscuits close together in pan. Top each with a spoonful of the cheese mixture. The cheese runs down, over and through the biscuits, as they bake.

IRISH SCONES

3 cups sifted enriched flour
1 teaspoon salt
1 teaspoon cream of tartar
1 teaspoon baking powder
About 1 cup buttermilk

Mix and sift together dry ingredients. Make a hollow in the center and add enough buttermilk to make a soft dough.

Turn onto a floured board and knead quickly and lightly until the dough is free from cracks. Roll out the required thickness and cut in scones.

Place on a greased and floured baking sheet and bake in hot oven (400°F.) until thoroughly baked, about 15 minutes for medium-sized scones.

BUTTERFLY CINNAMON ROLLS

2 cups sifted enriched flour
3 teaspoons baking powder
1 teaspoon salt
½ cup shortening
1 slightly beaten egg
½ cup milk
2 tablespoons melted butter or margarine
⅓ cup sugar
1 teaspoon cinnamon

Sift dry ingredients. Cut in shortening until mixture resembles texture of coarse corn meal.

Combine egg and milk and stir in dry ingredients until just blended.

Turn out on floured board or cloth. Pat out dough. Fold in half. Repeat 6 times. The last time roll to ¼-inch thickness.

Spread with melted butter, sugar, and cinnamon. Roll up and cut into 1-inch slices.

Cut slit through center parallel to cut edges of slice down to but not through bottom layer of dough. Spread halves from center out on baking sheet.

Bake in hot oven (425°F.) until browned, 15 to 20 minutes. Makes 12 rolls.

GOLDEN WHEAT STICKS

¾ cup Wheatena or other whole wheat cereal, uncooked
1¼ cups sifted enriched flour
¼ cup sugar
½ teaspoon salt
3 teaspoons baking powder
1 egg, beaten
¾ cup milk
¼ cup melted butter or margarine

Combine cereal, flour, sugar, salt, and baking powder. Add beaten egg and milk; mix. Stir in butter.

Place in greased corn stick pans. Bake in hot oven (425°–450° F.) about 25 to 30 minutes. Makes 12 sticks.

DATE SURPRISES

2 cups sifted enriched flour
3 teaspoons baking powder
1 teaspoon salt
2 teaspoons sugar
2 tablespoons melted shortening
2 egg yolks
¾ cup milk
1½ tablespoons butter
6 dates

Sift flour with baking powder, salt, and sugar.

Stir melted shortening, beaten egg yolks, and milk into flour mixture. Turn out on slightly floured board; roll to ½ inch thickness and cut with biscuit cutter into circles 2½ inches in diameter.

Spread each biscuit with butter and put half a date on each. Fold biscuit over and press edges together. Place in greased layer cake pan.

Bake in moderate oven, (350°F.) 20 to 25 minutes or until browned. Makes 12 rolls.

QUICK SALT STICKS

2 cups sifted enriched flour
1 teaspoon baking soda
½ teaspoon salt
⅓ cup shortening
¼ cup vinegar
½ cup milk
1 cup oven-popped rice cereal
1 teaspoon salt
1½ teaspoons caraway or poppy seeds

Sift together flour, soda, and salt; cut in shortening until mixture resembles coarse corn meal. Add vinegar and milk, stirring only until combined.

Turn out on lightly floured board and knead gently a few times.

Divide into 16 equal parts. Roll each ball on board with palms of hands until it becomes a cylinder about 6 inches long. Brush with milk.

Crush rice cereal; mix in salt and caraway seeds. Roll each stick in rice cereal mixture. Place on greased baking sheets. Bake in very hot oven (450°F.) about 15 minutes. Makes 16 sticks, 6 inches long.

SOUTHERN BUTTERMILK BISCUITS

2 cups sifted enriched flour
2 teaspoons baking powder
¾ teaspoon baking soda
½ teaspoon salt
¼ cup shortening
1¼ cups buttermilk

Sift flour, measure, resift 3 times with remaining dry ingredients, the last time into a bowl.

Cut in shortening with pastry blender or fork to consistency of rice grains.

Add buttermilk and mix lightly, only enough to blend ingredients.

Turn onto lightly floured board and knead lightly 5 or 6 times. Roll out ½-inch thick. Cut with 2-inch biscuit cutter. Place on ungreased cooky sheet.

Bake in very hot oven (450°F.) 15 to 18 minutes until light golden brown. Makes 1 dozen.

POTATO BISCUITS

1 cup sifted enriched flour
3 teaspoons baking powder
1 teaspoon salt
2 tablespoons shortening
1 cup mashed potato
About ½ cup water or milk

Mix and sift flour, baking powder, and salt. Blend in shortening.

Add potato and mix thoroughly. Then add enough liquid to make a soft dough.

Roll dough lightly to about ½ inch in thickness. Cut into biscuits. Bake in hot oven (400°F.) 12 to 15 minutes.

CHEESE-FROSTED BISCUITS #2

2 cups sifted enriched flour
½ teaspoon salt
4 teaspoons baking powder
½ teaspoon cream of tartar
2 teaspoons sugar, if desired
½ cup (1 stick) butter
⅔ cup milk

Sift together dry ingredients. Cut butter in using pastry blender, 2 knives, or coarse tined fork, until mixture resembles coarse crumbs. Add milk all at once and stir just until dough follows fork around the bowl.

Turn out on floured cloth. Knead lightly for a few seconds until smooth. Pat or roll out to ½-inch thickness. Cut with 2-inch biscuit cutter.

Place close together in shallow biscuit or cake pan. Just before sending to the oven, spread with cheese frosting.

Cheese Frosting: Melt over hot water about ½ pound (2 generous cups) of shredded or thinly sliced natural or process American Cheddar cheese and 4 tablespoons butter. Whip up well before topping each biscuit with spoonful of mixture.

Bake at once in very hot oven (450°F.) 10 to 12 minutes. Makes 16 medium biscuits.

Cheese-Frosted Biscuits #2

Muffins

MUFFIN HINTS

Perfect muffins should be light, tender, and fine in texture. Many variations can be made from a single master recipe or from a packaged mix. Here are a few steps in making perfect muffins.

1. After lighting the oven and assembling the ingredients and utensils, measure the shortening and put on stove to melt. Let cool while mixing batter. Grease muffin pans with any sweet unsalted shortening.

2. Sift and measure flour into the sifter. Measure other dry ingredients (baking powder, salt, etc.) and put into sifter with the flour.

3. Sift the dry ingredients together into a mixing bowl. This sifting of the flour and other dry ingredients together distributes them evenly through the flour—an aid to good texture.

4. Combine the milk, well beaten egg, and melted shortening.

5. Stir the liquid into the dry ingredients just until mixed. Mix just enough to blend the ingredients, because too much mixing or beating makes tough, coarse-textured muffins.

6. Fill the greased muffin cups 2/3 full. Use a rubber scraper to push batter off the mixing spoon. Muffin cups vary in size. The surface area varies from very small to large. The depth varies from shallow to deep. This accounts for the differences in baking times.

Standards for Good Muffins

Well-proportioned shape and size . . . no peaks . . . evenly browned . . . tender crust . . . even tender grain . . . no tunnels . . . good flavor.

Causes of Poor Muffins

Incorrect proportions . . . inaccurate measurements . . . overmixed batter . . . pans too full . . . incorrect baking procedure.

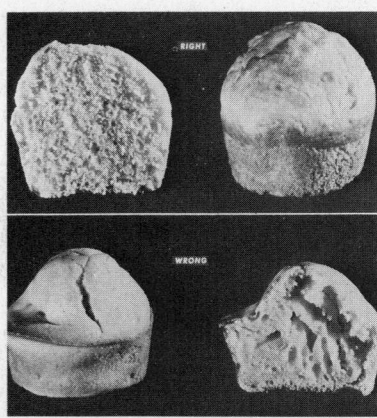

MUFFINS
(Master Recipe)

    2   cups sifted enriched flour
    3   teaspoons baking powder
    1/2 teaspoon salt
    2   tablespoons sugar
    1   egg, well beaten
    1   cup milk
    3   tablespoons melted shortening

Sift together dry ingredients. Combine egg, milk, and shortening. Add quickly to flour mixture, stirring only until just moistened. Do not beat.

Drop batter gently by spoonfuls into greased muffin pans, filling 2/3 full.

Bake in hot oven (425°F.) 20 to 25 minutes, or until golden brown. Makes 1 dozen 2-inch muffins.

Muffin Variations:

Apple Muffins: In master recipe add 1/4 teaspoon cinnamon and 2 tablespoons shortening. Fold 1 cup finely chopped apples into batter.

Bacon Muffins: In master recipe use bacon fat for shortening. Add 1/4 cup chopped, cooked bacon to sifted dry ingredients.

Berry Muffins: In master recipe add 1 cup berries (blueberries, sweetened blackberries, sweetened strawberries) to dry ingredients.

Bran Muffins: In master recipe substitute 1 cup whole bran for 1 cup white flour. Soak bran in milk 5 minutes before mixing.

Cheese Muffins: In master recipe add 1/2 cup grated mild cheese to dry ingredients.

Cherry Muffins: In master recipe add to muffin batter, 3/4 cup drained, chopped cherries, fresh or canned.

Corn Meal Muffins: In master recipe substitute 1 cup corn meal for 1 cup white flour.

Cranberry Muffins: Follow master recipe; to sifted dry ingredients add 3/4 cup chopped cranberries mixed with 3 tablespoons sugar.

Dried Fruit Muffins: In master recipe add 1/2 cup chopped pitted dates, figs, or raisins to dry ingredients.

Ham Muffins: In master recipe add 1/2 cup diced ham to sifted dry ingredients.

Marmalade Muffins: Follow master recipe; put 1/2 teaspoon butter or margarine and 1 teaspoon marmalade into each muffin cup. Drop batter for plain muffins on top.

Nut Muffins: Add 1/2 cup chopped nuts to dry ingredients.

Oatmeal Muffins: In master recipe substitute 1 cup quick-cooking oats (uncooked) for 1 cup white flour.

Orange Muffins: In master recipe add 1 tablespoon grated orange rind to dry ingredients. Substitute orange juice for milk.

Parsley Muffins: In master recipe omit sugar. Add 2 tablespoons minced parsley, stirring it into sifted dry ingredients.

Rice Muffins: Follow master recipe; to flour mixture add 1 cup cold cooked rice and 2 well beaten eggs.

Muffin Variations:

Sour Cream Muffins: Follow master recipe. Use only 1 teaspoon baking powder. Add 1/2 teaspoon baking soda. Increase salt to 3/4 teaspoon. Substitute 1 1/4 cups thick sour cream for milk and shortening.

Sour Milk or Buttermilk Muffins: In master recipe reduce baking powder to 1 teaspoon. Add 1/2 teaspoon baking soda, sifting it with flour. Use sour milk or buttermilk instead of sweet milk.

Soy Muffins: In master recipe substitute 1/2 cup soy flour for 1/2 cup white flour.

Sweet Cream Muffins: In master recipe increase salt to 3/4 teaspoon. Substitute 1 1/4 cups heavy cream for milk and shortening.

Whole Wheat Muffins: In master recipe substitute 1 cup whole wheat flour for 1 cup white flour.

WHEAT GERM MUFFINS

1 1/4 cups sifted enriched flour
3/4 teaspoon salt
3 teaspoons baking powder
1/2 cup dehydrated natural wheat germ
2 tablespoons melted shortening
1 beaten egg
3/4 cup milk
1/4 cup unsulphured molasses

Mix and sift flour, salt, and baking powder and mix with wheat germ.

Combine remaining ingredients and add to flour mixture. Stir only until blended. Fill greased muffin pans 2/3 full. Bake in hot oven (425°F.) 20 minutes.

Variations:

Raisin, Date or Fig Wheat Germ Muffins: To above batter add 1/2 cup raisins, diced dates, or diced figs.

Wheat Germ Muffins with Dry Milk: Sift 3 tablespoons dried skim milk powder with dry ingredients, and continue as directed.

Muffins keep well, so wrap leftovers in plastic wrap or aluminum foil and refrigerate or freeze to serve at another meal. Be sure to heat them before serving. Enclose muffins loosely in foil and heat about 5 minutes in preheated very hot oven (450°F.).

BUTTER CRUST MUFFINS

1 cup sifted enriched flour
1/2 teaspoon salt
3 teaspoons baking powder
1 tablespoon sugar
1/2 cup corn meal
1 cup milk
1 beaten egg
1/4 cup peanut butter
1 tablespoon melted shortening

Mix and sift flour, salt, baking powder, and sugar. Stir in corn meal.

Combine milk, egg, peanut butter, and melted shortening. Add to dry ingredients and mix only until flour is moistened. Fill greased muffin pans 2/3 full. Bake in hot oven (400° F.) about 20 minutes. Makes 12.

BLUEBERRY BUTTERMILK MUFFINS

2 cups sifted enriched flour
1/2 cup sugar
1 teaspoon salt
1/4 teaspoon baking soda
2 1/4 teaspoons baking powder
1/4 cup melted butter
1 slightly beaten egg
1 cup buttermilk
1 cup blueberries

Mix and sift flour, sugar, salt, baking soda, and baking powder.

Mix butter, egg, and buttermilk together. Stir into dry ingredients mixing just enough to moisten. Fold in blueberries.

Fill greased muffin pans about 2/3 full. Bake in hot oven (425°F.) 25 minutes. Makes 12 medium muffins.

CEREAL FLAKE MUFFINS

1 cup sifted enriched flour
2 1/2 teaspoons baking powder
1/2 teaspoon salt
1/4 cup sugar
1 egg, beaten
1/2 cup milk
4 tablespoons melted fat
1 1/2 cups bran flakes, whole wheat flakes, or 3 cups corn flakes, slightly crushed

Sift together flour, baking powder, salt, and sugar. Combine egg, milk, and slightly cooled fat. Add to flour mixture, stirring only enough to dampen flour. Fold in cereal flakes, being careful not to overmix.

Fill well greased muffin pans, 2 1/2 inches in diameter, 2/3 full. Bake in hot oven (400°F.) 15 to 18 minutes. Makes 12 muffins.

Blueberry Flake Muffins: Add 3/4 cup fresh blueberries or drained defrosted frozen blueberries to mixture.

Nut Muffins: Add 1/2 cup chopped walnuts, Brazil nuts, or pecans to sifted ingredients.

Banana Nut Muffins: Add 1/2 cup mashed bananas and 1/2 cup chopped nutmeats to egg mixture.

ORANGE PECAN MUFFINS

1/3 cup shortening
3/4 cup sugar
3 eggs
1 3/4 cups sifted enriched flour
3 teaspoons baking powder
1/4 teaspoon salt
1/4 cup orange juice
1/4 cup milk
1 teaspoon grated orange rind
3/4 cup chopped pecans

Cream shortening and sugar until light and fluffy. Add eggs and mix well.

Mix and sift dry ingredients and add alternately with orange juice, and then milk. Fold in rind and nuts.

Turn into well greased muffin pans filling 2/3 full. Bake in moderate oven (375°F.) 20 minutes. Makes 18 medium muffins.

PEACH MUFFINS

2 cups sifted enriched flour
1/2 teaspoon salt
2 1/2 teaspoons baking powder
1/4 cup sugar
1 cup milk
1 slightly beaten egg
1/4 cup shortening, melted
3/4 cup sliced canned peaches, well drained
2 tablespoons sugar
1 teaspoon cinnamon
1/2 teaspoon nutmeg

Mix and sift flour, salt, baking powder, and 1/4 cup sugar.

Combine milk, egg, and shortening; stir into dry ingredients quickly. Fold in peaches. Turn into well greased muffin pans, filling 2/3 full.

Mix and sift 2 tablespoons sugar, cinnamon, and nutmeg and sprinkle over muffins.

Bake in hot oven (400°F.) 25 minutes. Makes 12 medium muffins.

BANANA TEA MUFFINS

1 3/4 cups sifted cake flour
2 teaspoons baking powder
3/4 teaspoon salt
1/4 teaspoon baking soda
1/4 cup shortening
1/3 cup sugar
1 egg
1 cup mashed bananas (2 to 3 bananas)

Mix and sift flour, baking powder, salt, and baking soda.

Beat shortening until creamy. Add sugar gradually and continue beating until light and fluffy.

Add egg and beat well. Add flour mixture alternately with bananas, mixing until batter is smooth.

Fill well greased muffin pans 2/3 full. Bake in hot oven (400°F.) until done, about 20 minutes. Serve hot or cold. Makes 16 small muffins.

MOLASSES MUFFINS
(Master Recipe)

2   cups sifted enriched flour
1/8 teaspoon baking soda
2   teaspoons baking powder
1/2 teaspoon salt
1/2 cup raisins, optional
1   unbeaten egg
1/4 cup unsulfured molasses
1   cup milk
3   tablespoons melted shortening

Sift together flour, soda, baking powder, and salt. Add raisins and mix well.

Combine egg, molasses, milk and melted shortening. Stir into dry ingredients, mixing only enough to blend.

Spoon mixture into well greased muffin pans about 2/3 full.

Bake in hot oven (400°F.) 15 to 20 minutes. Makes about 10 to 12 large or 18 small muffins.

Variations:

Bran Molasses Muffins: Reduce flour to 1 cup and add 3/4 cup whole bran with raisins to sifted flour, soda, baking powder, and salt. Reduce milk to 3/4 cup and proceed as directed in master recipe.

Corn-Meal Molasses Muffins: Reduce flour to 1 cup and add 1 cup corn meal with raisins to sifted flour, soda, baking powder, and salt.

Oatmeal Molasses Muffins: Reduce flour to 1 cup and add 1 cup uncooked rolled oats with raisins to sifted flour, soda, baking powder, and salt. Reduce milk to 3/4 cup and proceed as directed in master recipe.

PINEAPPLE MUFFINS

2   cups sifted enriched flour
4   teaspoons baking powder
1/2 teaspoon salt
1/2 cup sugar
1   slightly beaten egg
1   cup undrained, crushed pineapple
1/4 cup shortening, melted

Mix and sift flour, baking powder, salt, and sugar. Add egg and pineapple and mix lightly. Blend in shortening.

Turn into greased muffin pans, filling 2/3 full. Bake in moderate oven (375°F.) 20 minutes. Makes 18 medium muffins.

STRAWBERRY MUFFINS

1/4 cup shortening
1/2 cup sugar
2   eggs
2   cups sifted enriched flour
4   teaspoons baking powder
1   teaspoon salt
2/3 cup milk
1 1/2 cups strawberries

Cream shortening and add sugar gradually. Beat eggs and add to mixture.

Mix and sift flour, baking powder, and salt. Add alternately with milk to

first mixture.

Wash berries, hull, and cut in halves. Stir gently into batter.

Turn into greased muffin pans, filling 2/3 full. Bake in hot oven (400°F.) 25 minutes. Makes 12 muffins.

LOUISIANA CORN MUFFINS

1 1/2 cups sifted enriched flour
3   teaspoons baking powder
1   teaspoon salt
3   tablespoons sugar
3/4 cup corn meal
1   well beaten egg
1   cup milk
1/2 cup melted shortening
1   tablespoon chopped green pepper
1   teaspoon minced onion
1/2 cup grated cheese

Mix and sift flour, baking powder, salt, and sugar. Add corn meal and mix.

Combine egg, milk, and shortening. Turn liquid mixture into dry ingredients and stir vigorously until all flour is dampened. Add green pepper, onion, and cheese.

Turn batter into greased muffin pans. Bake in hot oven (400°F.) 25 to 30 minutes. Serve hot. Makes 18 muffins.

MAPLE BRAN MUFFINS

1   cup sour cream
1   cup maple syrup
2   well beaten eggs
1   cup sifted enriched flour
1   teaspoon baking soda
1   cup whole bran
1/4 cup chopped raisins
1/4 cup chopped nuts

Combine cream, syrup, and eggs. Mix and sift flour and baking soda and mix with bran, raisins, and nuts.

Add liquid to dry ingredients and mix quickly.

Turn into greased muffin pans. Bake in hot oven (400°F.) 25 minutes. Makes 24 medium muffins.

BANANA BRAN MUFFINS

1   cup sifted enriched flour
3/4 teaspoon baking soda
1/2 teaspoon salt
1/4 cup sugar
1   cup whole bran
1   well beaten egg
2   tablespoons sour milk or buttermilk
2   tablespoons melted shortening or oil
2   cups thinly sliced ripe bananas

Mix and sift together flour, soda, salt, and sugar. Add bran and mix well.

Combine egg, milk, shortening, and bananas. Add to dry ingredients, mixing only enough to dampen all flour.

Turn into well greased muffin pans. Bake in moderate oven (375°F.) 35 minutes. Makes 6 large muffins.

OATMEAL-APPLE MUFFINS

1 1/4 cups milk
2   tablespoons butter or margarine
3/4 cup quick cooking oats, uncooked
1   egg
1 1/2 cups sifted enriched flour
1/4 cup plus 3 tablespoons sugar
1/2 teaspoon salt
4   teaspoons baking powder
1/2 teaspoon cinnamon
1   apple

Scald milk. Add butter or margarine and pour over oats. Beat egg and add. Sift flour, 3 tablespoons sugar, salt, and baking powder. Add to oat mixture, stirring only enough to moisten. Fill 12 greased muffin pans 2/3 full.

Combine 1/4 cup sugar and cinnamon. Peel, core, and quarter apple. Cut into thirds and dip each slice in sugar mixture, and press, curved side up, into each muffin.

Bake in hot oven (400°F.) 20 to 25 minutes. Makes 12 muffins.

ORANGE RAISIN GEMS

2   cups sifted enriched flour
3/4 teaspoon baking soda
1/2 teaspoon salt
1/3 cup sugar
1/2 cup raisins
1   well beaten egg
1/3 cup orange juice
1/2 teaspoon grated orange rind
1 1/3 tablespoons vinegar and sweet
     milk to make 2/3 cup
1/3 cup shortening, melted

Sift flour, soda, salt, and sugar together in mixing bowl. Add raisins.

Combine egg, orange juice and rind, vinegar and milk, and melted shortening. Add to dry ingredients and stir only until dry ingredients are dampened.

Fill greased muffin pans 2/3 full. Bake in hot oven (425°F.) 20 minutes. Remove from oven and let stand several minutes before removing from pans.

Variation: If desired, add 1/2 cup nuts with raisins.

CORN KERNEL MUFFINS

1   well beaten egg
1 1/4 cups milk
3   tablespoons shortening
1   cup whole kernel corn, drained
1 1/2 cups sifted enriched flour
3 1/2 teaspoons baking powder
1   teaspoon salt
3   tablespoons sugar
1   cup yellow corn meal

Combine egg, milk, shortening, and corn. Mix thoroughly. Mix and sift dry ingredients, add and mix quickly.

Turn into oiled muffin pans. Bake in hot oven (425°F.) about 25 minutes. Makes 12 large muffins.

POTATO FLOUR MUFFINS

1/2 cup potato flour
1 teaspoon baking powder
1/2 teaspoon salt
2 teaspoons cold water
4 eggs, separated
1 tablespoon sugar

Mix and sift potato flour and baking powder. Add salt and water to egg whites and beat to a coarse foam. Sprinkle sugar over surface and beat until stiff but moist and glossy.

Beat egg yolks until thick and lemon colored. Fold into egg whites. Fold in flour. Turn into ungreased muffin pans.

Bake in moderate oven (350°F.) until delicately browned on top, 15 to 20 minutes. Remove by loosening from sides. Serve immediately. Makes 12 medium muffins.

OATMEAL MUFFINS #2

1 cup buttermilk or sour milk
1 cup quick or old fashioned uncooked oats
1 cup sifted enriched flour
1/4 cup sugar
1/2 teaspoon baking soda
2 teaspoons baking powder
1/2 teaspoon salt
3/4 cup seedless raisins (optional)
1 beaten egg
3 tablespoons melted shortening

Pour buttermilk over rolled oats and let stand a few minutes.

Sift together dry ingredients; add to rolled oats mixture with raisins.

Add beaten egg stirring lightly; fold in melted shortening.

Fill greased muffin pans 2/3 full and bake in a hot oven (425°F.) 15 to 25 minutes, depending on size of muffins. Makes 8 large or 16 small muffins.

Variations: One cup sweet milk may be substituted for buttermilk. Omit soda and increase baking powder to 3 teaspoons.

BRAN MUFFINS #2

1 cup whole bran
3/4 cup milk
1 egg
1/4 cup soft shortening
1 cup sifted enriched flour
2 1/2 teaspoons baking powder
1/2 teaspoon salt
1/4 cup sugar

Combine bran and milk; let stand until most of moisture is taken up. Add egg and shortening and beat well.

Sift together flour, baking powder, salt, and sugar. Add to first mixture, stirring only until combined.

Fill greased muffin pans 2/3 full. Bake in hot oven (400°F.) about 30 minutes. Makes 9 muffins, 2 1/2 inches in diameter.

CRUMB MUFFINS

1/4 cup shortening
1/4 cup sugar
1 egg, beaten
1 cup sifted enriched flour
3 teaspoons baking powder
1/2 teaspoon salt
1 cup fine, dry crumbs
1 cup milk

Cream the shortening. Stir in sugar, and add egg.

Sift flour, baking powder, and salt together. Add crumbs. Add to first mixture alternately with milk.

Fill greased muffin pans 2/3 full. Bake in moderate oven (375°F.) 25 minutes. Makes 1 dozen muffins.

Berry Crumb Muffins: Add 1 cup huckleberries.

Date Crumb Muffins: Add 3/4 cup chopped, pitted dates.

HONEY BRAN MUFFINS

2 cups sifted enriched flour
4 teaspoons baking powder
3/4 teaspoon salt
2 cups bran flakes
1/2 cup raisins
1/2 cup chopped walnuts or pecans
1/2 cup honey
1 1/4 cups milk
2 tablespoons melted butter or margarine
1 well beaten egg

Mix and sift flour, baking powder, and salt. Combine bran, raisins, and nuts. Add to flour mixture.

Add honey, milk, and melted butter to beaten egg and blend well.

Pour liquids into dry mixture, stirring only until dry ingredients are dampened. Fill medium-sized greased muffin pans 2/3 full.

Bake in hot oven (400°F.) 20 to 25 minutes. Serve warm. Makes 18 medium muffins.

GINGER GEMS

1/4 cup shortening
1/2 cup sugar
1 egg
1 3/4 cups sifted enriched flour
1 teaspoon baking soda
1/4 teaspoon salt
1/4 teaspoon nutmeg
1/4 teaspoon ginger
1/4 teaspoon cinnamon
1/2 cup molasses
1/2 cup cold strong coffee

Cream shortening and sugar until light and fluffy. Add egg and beat well.

Add sifted dry ingredients alternately with molasses and coffee in thirds, beating until smooth after each addition.

Fill greased small muffin pans about 2/3 full. Bake in moderate oven (375°F.) 20 minutes. Makes 24 small muffins.

CORN MEAL MUFFINS #2

1 egg, unbeaten
1 cup milk
1/4 cup melted shortening
1 cup sifted enriched flour
1 cup yellow corn meal
2 tablespoons sugar
3 teaspoons baking powder
1/2 teaspoon salt

Place egg, milk, and melted shortening in medium-sized mixing bowl. Beat with a kitchen fork until thoroughly blended (about 100 strokes).

Sift flour, corn meal, sugar, baking powder, and salt together over surface of liquid ingredients. Using gentle strokes, carefully mix until ingredients are just blended (about 25 strokes).

Bake in greased 2 1/2 x 1 1/4-inch muffin pans in hot oven (425°F.) for 20 to 25 minutes. Makes 12 muffins.

CHEESE MUFFINS #2

2 1/4 cups sifted enriched flour
3 teaspoons baking powder
3/4 teaspoon salt
2/3 cup grated American Cheese
1 egg
1 cup milk
1/4 cup melted butter

Mix and sift flour, baking powder, and salt.

Add grated cheese and mix thoroughly. Beat egg, add milk and melted butter, and pour into center of dry ingredients.

Stir quickly until dry ingredients are just dampened. Batter should not be smooth. Fill greased muffin pans about 2/3 full.

Bake in hot oven (425°F.) 15 to 20 minutes or until golden brown. Makes 12 medium muffins.

DATE CHEESE MUFFINS

1 egg, unbeaten
1 cup milk
1/4 cup melted shortening
2 cups sifted enriched flour
3 teaspoons baking powder
2 tablespoons sugar
1/2 teaspoon salt
1/4 cup grated American cheese
1/4 cup chopped dates

Place egg, milk, and melted shortening into medium-sized mixing bowl. Beat with a kitchen fork until thoroughly blended (about 100 strokes).

Sift flour, baking powder, sugar, and salt evenly over surface of liquid ingredients. Add cheese and dates. Using gentle strokes, carefully mix until ingredients are just blended (about 25 strokes).

Bake in greased 2 1/2 x 1 1/4-inch muffin pans in hot oven (425°F.) for 20 to 25 minutes. Makes 12 muffins.

Popovers

POPOVER HINTS

Successful popovers may be baked not only in old-fashioned cast-iron popover pans but also in earthenware and oven glass custard cups and in modern heavy aluminum muffin pans. The cups should be deeper than they are wide.

If custard cups of oven glass or earthenware are used, preheat them while mixing the batter.

Grease the preheated cups just before filling.

If the cups are made of aluminum or other metal that heats quickly, they do not have to be preheated.

The batter for popovers should be thin—about as thick as whipping cream. Do not overbeat the batter.

Good popovers really have the appearance of having tried to "pop over." They should be crisp and glazed in appearance with a thin, golden-brown crust, hollow and slightly moist inside without being wet or soggy.

When popovers won't "pop" often the difficulty lies not with the recipe or the mixing, but with the baking. Steam supplies the leavening action and since they tend to rise quickly in the oven, the mistake of removing them from the oven before they are fully baked is fairly common. They should be left in the oven for the full baking time, at the correct temperature to make sure they stay "popped."

When the popovers are punctured with a sharp fork 5 minutes before the baking is finished, the steam is allowed to escape and the insides dry a little.

CHEESE POPOVERS

    1   egg
    3/8 teaspoon salt
    1   cup milk
    1   cup sifted enriched flour
    1/4 pound Cheddar cheese, grated

Beat egg slightly; add salt and milk and gradually stir into flour to make a smooth batter.

Beat with rotary beater until full of air bubbles.

Have popover pans, muffin pans, or glass custard cups thoroughly heated and well greased.

Drop a rounded teaspoon of batter into each. Spread with a teaspoon of cheese and cover with a second teaspoon of batter.

Bake in very hot oven (450°F.) until brown and well popped, about 20 minutes. Makes 8 or more popovers, depending on pan size.

POPOVERS
(Master Recipe)

    1   cup sifted enriched flour
    1/2 teaspoon salt
    2   eggs
    1   cup milk
    1   tablespoon melted shortening

Mix and sift flour and salt. Beat eggs with a rotary beater until light and thick.

Add flour and 1/3 cup of the milk and continue to beat slowly until all the flour is moistened, about half a minute.

Gradually add remaining milk and melted shortening, beating only until the mixture is free from lumps, 1 to 2 minutes.

Fill greased custard cups or iron muffin pans a little less than half full. Bake in a hot oven (425°F.) 35 to 40 minutes or until the popovers are firm. Serve at once. Makes 6 to 8 large popovers.

Variations: To vary, add a few grains of paprika, dried sage, crushed mint, or other herbs or spices.

Stuffed Popovers: Split popovers. Fill with scrambled eggs, creamed fish, or creamed vegetables, etc.

CORN MEAL POPOVERS

    1 1/2 cups milk
    1/3 cup yellow corn meal
    3   eggs
    1   cup sifted enriched flour
    1   teaspoon salt

Scald 1 cup milk and pour over corn meal; stir well.

Combine remaining milk with eggs and beat well with a rotary beater.

Combine all ingredients and beat with rotary beater until batter is smooth and thick, about 2 minutes.

Fill well greased popover pans or tall custard cups 1/3 to 1/2 full.

Bake in hot oven (425°F.) 30 minutes; reduce heat to slow (325°F.) and bake 15 to 20 minutes longer. Makes 6 to 8. Serve at once.

ORANGE POPOVERS

    2   eggs
    1   cup milk
    1   cup orange juice
    Grated rind of 1 orange
    1/2 teaspoon salt
    2   cups sifted enriched flour

Beat eggs. Add milk, orange juice, rind, and salt. Add to flour, beating with rotary beater until smooth.

Fill preheated popover or custard cups 1/2 full.

Bake in very hot oven (450°F.) 25 minutes. Reduce heat to moderate (350°F.) and bake until popovers dry out inside, 25 minutes longer. Serve hot. Makes 12 large or 18 small popovers.

Serve popovers piping hot and puffy right out of the oven.

OATMEAL POPOVERS

    3   eggs
    1 1/2 cups milk
    1/2   cup quick rolled oats, uncooked
    1   cup sifted enriched flour
    1   teaspoon salt

Combine eggs and milk; beat well. Add remaining ingredients and beat with a rotary beater until batter is smooth and thick, about 2 minutes.

Fill well greased popover pans or tall custard cups 1/3 to 1/2 full.

Bake in hot oven (425°F.) 30 minutes. Reduce heat to slow (325°F.) and bake 30 minutes longer. Makes 6 to 8. Serve at once.

RYE POPOVERS

    3/4 cup sifted rye flour
    1/4 cup sifted enriched flour
    1/4 teaspoon salt
    1   teaspoon sugar
    2   eggs
    1   cup milk

Mix and sift dry ingredients. Beat eggs and add milk; stir gradually into flour mixture to make a smooth batter. Beat with rotary beater until full of air bubbles.

Fill hot greased custard cups 2/3 full.

Bake in very hot oven (450°F.) 20 minutes. Reduce heat to moderate (350°F.) and bake 20 minutes or until crisp.

CHEESE COCKTAIL POPOVERS

    1   cup boiling water
    1/2 cup butter
    1/2 cup enriched flour
    1/2 cup Parmesan cheese
    Pinch of salt
    2   eggs

Put the boiling water in a saucepan and melt the butter in it. Then stir in the flour, cheese, and salt. Stir hard over low heat until mixture is smooth. Let it cool.

Half hour before ready to serve, stir in the eggs one at a time and beat well. Drop by small teaspoonfuls on a greased, floured cooky sheet.

Bake in moderate oven (350°F.) 30 minutes. Serve immediately. Makes about 30 small popovers.

Dress-Ups with Biscuit Mix

NUT BREAD
(Master Recipe)

½ cup sugar
1 egg
1¼ cups milk
1½ cups chopped nuts
3 cups biscuit mix

Mix sugar, egg, milk, and chopped nuts. Stir in biscuit mix and beat hard for 30 seconds.

Pour into a well greased loaf pan 9½ x 5¼ x 2¾-inches.

Bake in moderate oven (350°F.) 45 to 50 minutes, until wooden pick thrust into center comes out clean.

A slight crack in top is characteristic. Cool slightly before cutting with a bread knife.

Variations:

Fruit Nut Bread: Follow directions for Nut Bread (above) except use ¾ cup sugar and instead of milk use orange juice. Use only ¾ cup chopped nuts and add 1 cup raisins or other chopped dried fruit. Bake 55 to 60 minutes.

Banana Nut Bread: Follow directions for Nut Bread (above) except use ¾ cup sugar and only ½ cup milk. Use only ¾ cup chopped nuts and add 1 cup mashed bananas (2 to 3 bananas).

Orange Nut Bread: Follow directions for Nut Bread (above) except use ¾ cup sugar and instead of milk use orange juice plus 1 tablespoon grated orange rind. Use only ¾ cup chopped nuts. Bake 50 to 55 minutes.

CHERRY NUT BREAD

½ cup sugar
1 egg
1¼ cups milk
1 cup chopped nuts
¾ cup cut-up candied cherries
3 cups biscuit mix

In large mixing bowl, stir together sugar, egg, milk, nuts, and cherries. Then add biscuit mix and beat briskly

Cheese Tea Ring

30 seconds. (Just count to 30.)

Turn into greased loaf pan, 10 x 5 x 3-inches. Bake in moderate oven (350°F.) 45 to 50 minutes or until done. Cool. This bread cuts best next day. Makes 1 loaf.

HEARTY SHRIMP-AND-CHEESE BISCUITS

1½ cups biscuit mix
½ cup milk
1 tablespoon instant minced onion
2 tablespoons finely chopped green pepper
2 tablespoons chopped pimiento
1 can (4½ ounces) deveined shrimp
½ cup grated American cheese
1 tablespoon mayonnaise
1 teaspoon prepared mustard

Combine biscuit mix, milk, onion, green pepper, and pimiento. Shape into dough and knead 10 times.

Shred shrimp and add cheese, mayonnaise, and mustard.

Roll dough into a rectangle 18 x 9 inches; cut into 3-inch squares.

Place a spoonful of shrimp mixture in the middle of each square. Shape into long rolls, crescents, and square shells.

Bake in very hot oven (450°F.) 10 to 12 minutes, or until done. Serve hot. Makes 18 biscuits.

CHEESE TEA RING

¾ cup milk or light cream
3 cups biscuit mix
1½ cups shredded American Cheddar cheese
Softened butter

Add milk to the biscuit mix, stirring lightly, until it can be shaped up into a ball. Turn out on floured cloth. Knead slightly until smooth.

Roll into a ½ inch thick rectangle.

Spread with softened butter. Sprinkle liberally with the shredded cheese.

Carefully roll up like a jelly roll. Bring the two ends together, sealing with a bit of milk, to form a ring.

Place on a buttered cooky sheet. Using sharp scissors, make slanting cuts through the ring almost to the center, making slices 2 inches thick.

Turn each section cut side down on the sheet, so that the cut sides lie almost flat.

Brush lightly with melted butter.

Bake in a hot oven (400°F.) about 25 minutes or until done and lightly browned.

Brush top again with melted butter before serving.

Serve piping hot with plenty of butter and crab apple, currant, or quince jelly.

Makes 6 to 8 servings.

Hearty Shrimp and Cheese Biscuits: A filling featuring shrimp and cheese and an easy-to-make biscuit dough seasoned with instant minced onion turn "Hearty Shrimp-and-Cheese Biscuits" into flavorsome delights.

RING-O-GOLD COFFEE CAKE
Butter Crunch Mixture:

½ cup melted butter
½ cup sugar
½ cup finely chopped pecans
½ cup fine dry breadcrumbs
Grated rind of 1 orange

Coffee Cake Batter:

⅓ cup sugar
1 egg, beaten
⅓ cup milk
1 cup biscuit mix
3 tablespoons melted shortening

For the butter crunch, combine all ingredients thoroughly. Press on bottom and sides of one-quart ring mold.

For the coffee cake, add sugar to beaten egg, beating until fluffy. Add milk and biscuit mix, stirring lightly until combined. Lightly stir in melted shortening. Pour into butter crunch-lined mold.

Bake in a moderate oven (375°F.) 25 to 30 minutes. Let cool 5 minutes; turn out, crunch side up on a platter. Serve warm. Makes 1 coffee cake.

APRICOT WALNUT BREAD

2 cups biscuit mix
1 cup quick-rolled oats, uncooked
¾ cup sugar
1 teaspoon baking powder
¼ teaspoon salt
½ cup dried apricots, cut up
1 cup broken walnuts
1 well beaten egg
1¼ cups milk or diluted evaporated milk

Stir biscuit mix with oats, sugar, baking powder, and salt. Add apricots and nuts. Combine egg and milk and add to dry ingredients. Beat hard 30 seconds.

Turn into greased loaf pan, 9 x 5 x 3-inches. Bake in moderate oven (350°F.) until done, about 1 hour.

Cool in pan 10 minutes and remove. Cuts best when day old. Makes 1 loaf.

ORANGE GLAZE BREAKFAST BUNS

Quick Buns:

2 cups biscuit mix
1/4 cup sugar
1 teaspoon grated orange rind
1/4 cup shortening
1 egg, beaten
1 cup milk
1/2 cup chopped dates

Glaze:

1/2 cup confectioners' sugar
1 tablespoon orange juice
Few grains salt
Chopped nuts, optional

Mix together biscuit mix, sugar, and grated orange rind. Cut in shortening until mixture resembles coarse crumbs.

Combine beaten egg and milk; add all at once to dry ingredients, stirring only until combined. Fold in chopped dates.

Drop batter by tablespoons onto greased baking sheet. Bake in hot oven (425°F.) about 15 minutes. Remove from baking sheet and drizzle glaze (made by combining sugar, orange juice, and salt) over hot buns. Sprinkle with nuts. Serve immediately. Makes 12 quick buns.

HIDDEN BERRY COFFEE CAKE

Batter:

1 egg, beaten
1/3 cup sugar
1/3 cup milk
Grated rind of 1/2 lemon
1 cup biscuit mix
1/4 cup melted butter or margarine
1/2 cup fresh or frozen blueberries, drained

Topping:

2 tablespoons brown sugar
Grated rind of 1/2 lemon
1 tablespoon biscuit mix
1/4 cup finely chopped nuts
2 tablespoons butter or margarine

For coffee cake batter, place all ingredients in bowl except blueberries; beat with rotary egg beater until fairly smooth. Do not overbeat. Stir in blueberries. Spread batter in a greased 8-inch round layer pan.

Combine topping ingredients; sprinkle over batter. Bake in a hot oven (400°F.) 15 to 20 minutes. Makes 8 servings.

FIVE-MINUTE PRUNE COFFEE CAKE

2 cups biscuit mix
1/3 cup sugar
1 egg
1/2 cup milk

1 cup cooked prunes, pitted, halved

Combine biscuit mix and sugar. Beat egg, add milk and stir into dry mixture, mixing well.

Turn into greased 8-inch square pan and top with prune halves. Sprinkle on topping. Bake in moderate oven (375°F.) about 35 minutes.

Topping: Mix 1/3 cup brown sugar, 3 tablespoons biscuit mix, and 1/4 teaspoon cinnamon.

CHERRY COFFEE CAKE

3 cups biscuit mix
1/3 cup granulated sugar
3/4 cup milk
2 beaten eggs
1/2 cup firmly packed brown sugar
2 tablespoons enriched flour
2 teaspoons cinnamon
3 tablespoons melted butter or margarine
1/2 cup chopped walnuts
2/3 cup cherry jam

Combine biscuit mix and granulated sugar. Combine milk and eggs; add to biscuit mix, stirring just until moistened.

Spread 1/2 of mixture in bottom of greased 9 x 11 1/2-inch round pan.

Mix brown sugar, flour, cinnamon, butter, and nuts. Sprinkle over mixture in pan.

Drop remaining dough by spoonfuls around outer edge of pan.

Bake in moderate oven (350°F.) 30 to 35 minutes. Spread with cherry jam when removed from oven. Serve warm.

Toppings and Fillings for Coffee Cakes

CINNAMON TOPPING

6 tablespoons butter
3/4 cup sugar
6 tablespoons sifted enriched flour
1 1/2 teaspoons cinnamon
1/8 teaspoon salt

Cream butter. Add sugar gradually, mixing well. Add remaining ingredients and stir until well mixed and crumbly.

STREUSEL TOPPING

1/3 cup butter
1/3 cup sugar
1/2 cup sifted enriched flour
1 cup dry cake or 1 cup breadcrumbs, ground
1 teaspoon cinnamon

Cream butter. Add sugar gradually, mixing well. Add remaining ingredients and stir until well mixed and crumbly.

HONEY NUT TOPPING

4 tablespoons butter
4 tablespoons sugar
4 tablespoons sifted enriched flour
4 tablespoons honey
1/2 cup chopped nuts

Cream butter. Add sugar, mixing well. Add flour and honey and beat until well mixed. Add nuts.

RUM AND HONEY TOPPING

3/4 cup confectioners' sugar
2 tablespoons honey
1 tablespoon rum
Hot water

Blend sugar, honey, and rum. Add just enough hot water to make an icing of spreading consistency. Makes 1 cup.

PINEAPPLE TOPPING

1/2 cup drained crushed pineapple
1/2 cup raisins or currants
1/2 cup brown sugar
1/4 cup soft butter or margarine

Combine ingredients and spread over dough. Bake as directed. Makes 1 1/2 cups.

CHEESE FILLING

1 egg yolk
1/4 cup sugar
1 cup cottage cheese, sieved
1 1/2 tablespoons flour
Grated rind of 1/2 lemon
1/2 teaspoon vanilla

Beat egg yolk, add sugar, then the rest of ingredients. Mix well. Makes 1 1/2 cups.

POPPY SEED FILLING

1 cup black poppy seed
1 cup milk
2 tablespoons butter
2 tablespoons honey
1/2 cup chopped almonds
Grated rind of 1/2 lemon
1 tablespoon chopped citron
1/4 cup sugar
1 tart apple, grated

Grind poppy seed and boil seed with milk, butter, honey, almonds, lemon rind, citron, and sugar until thick.

When cool, add apple. You may substitute raspberry jam for apple, if you wish. Makes 2 cups.

NUT FILLING

1 egg yolk, beaten slightly
1/4 cup sugar
2 tablespoons butter, salted
1/2 cup finely chopped walnuts or pecans
1/2 teaspoon almond extract

Mix ingredients thoroughly and use to fill any yeast or quick coffee cake. Bake as directed. Makes 1 cup.

CAKES

Explore the wonderful world of cakes. You can make selections from a vast variety of forms and flavors in simple or rich layers with moist creamy fillings and luscious frostings, some large and elaborate, others small and dainty, the famous torten of European cooks, the golden sponge cakes, high angel food cakes, and the traditional holiday cakes, rich in nuts and fruits.

Cakes may be divided into three basic types: (1) those made with shortening (the conventional or one-bowl "quick-method" cakes), still commonly called "butter" cakes because originally butter was the shortening most frequently used and now largely replaced by hydrogenated vegetable shortening; (2) those made without shortening (the angel and sponge cakes); and (3) a combination angel and shortening-type cake (the chiffon cake). Although they are different in ingredients, in the way they are mixed, and in their final appearance and texture, nevertheless many rules for cakemaking apply to all three.

TIPS FOR SUCCESSFUL CAKE-MAKING

1. Read the complete recipe carefully; be sure you understand it before proceeding.

2. Assemble all ingredients you will need. Have them at room temperature. This is especially important for eggs, which will not whip to full volume when cold, and for fats that are to be creamed.

3. Assemble all utensils and other tools needed.

4. Choose the size and shape of pan to fit the cake to be baked and prepare the pans for baking before mixing the batter.

5. Set the oven at the correct temperature early enough to be sure that it will be preheated to indicated temperature by the time your cake is ready to bake. (The oven thermostat should be checked frequently by utility service department or check it yourself with a portable oven thermometer.)

6. Measure ingredients accurately with standard measuring cups and spoons and use level measurements. Cake recipes are carefully balanced and careless measuring can cause inferior results.

Flour should be sifted before measuring. Then lightly fill the measuring cup to the desired level with a spoon. Do not shake or tap cup; level off with a knife or spatula. Sift the flour again with the dry ingredients as the recipe directs. Waxed paper is helpful in the sifting process. Use only the amount of flour called for.

For additional hints on how to measure, see **Facts About Food and Cooking.**

7. Mix ingredients according to the directions of the specific recipe. If a recipe says stir, beat, cream, whip, or fold in, do exactly that.

Definitions of terms used in recipes will be found in **Facts About Food and Cooking.**

8. Because the cake will rise in baking, the pans should usually not be filled more than two-thirds full. Spread the batter evenly in the pan. For layers and cupcakes be sure the batter is divided evenly among the pans.

The following guide will be helpful in determining the size of pans for any recipes: A cake with shortening containing 2 cups flour may be baked in (a) 2 layer-cake pans 9 inches in diameter or 8 inches square, (b) 1 loaf pan 4 x 8 inches, (c) 12 average muffin cups, (d) 1 sheet pan 8 x 9 inches square and 2 inches deep.

The pans should usually not be filled more than two-thirds full. Spread the batter evenly in the pan. For layers and cupcakes be sure the batter is divided evenly among the pans.

9. Place pans in carefully controlled preheated oven, as near the center of the oven as possible and away from the sides. Don't let pans touch each other or the sides of the oven. And don't place pans directly under each other. If necessary, stagger the pans on two shelves. There should be plenty of space around each pan for complete circulation of heat. Check to see that the oven temperature is accurate and correctly set.

Place pans in carefully controlled preheated oven, as near the center as possible and away from the sides. Allow space around each pan for circulation of heat.

10. Regardless of the time given in a recipe, always test the cake for doneness. Test the cake near the end of the baking time given in the recipe to see if it is done, opening the oven door just enough for a quick test.

There are several tests you can apply to decide when your cake is done: (a) the surface will spring back when pressed lightly with a finger; if the impression of the finger remains, bake longer and test again, (b) a cake tester or a wooden toothpick inserted in center will come out clean, (c) a cake will shrink slightly from the sides of the pan. Considerable shrinkage from the sides of the pan usually means the cake is overbaked.

Your cake is done when the center surface will spring back when pressed lightly with a finger.

A cake is done when a cake tester or a wooden toothpick inserted in center will come out clean.

11. Specific directions are given in certain recipes for removing cakes and torten from the oven, how to cool, etc. Follow these directions carefully.

The following applies to cakes with shortening ("butter" cakes): Upon removing the cake from the oven, place the pan on a wire cake rack. Let it stand and cool in the pan for 5 to 10 minutes. Then carefully loosen cake from edges of pan. Place cake rack over top of cake and invert quickly. Leave cake on rack to cool. If warm cake is placed on a board or plate, the bottom becomes soggy. If paper was used in the bottom of the pan, remove it from cake immediately.

12. Cool cake before frosting. If cakes are frosted while still warm, they absorb too much frosting and become soggy. To frost, brush off loose crumbs and place bottom sides together with filling and frosting. Cover sides first, then the top, spreading frosting to edges with a light swirling motion.

Leave cake on rack to cool. If warm cake is placed on a board or plate, the bottom becomes soggy.

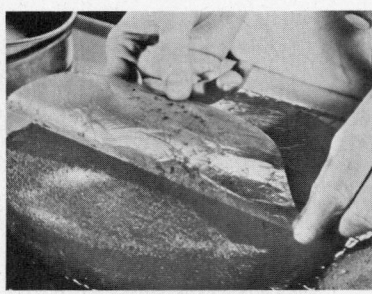

If paper was used in the bottom of the pan, remove it from the cake immediately.

Brush off loose crumbs from the cooled cake. Place bottom sides together with filling, then cover sides with frosting.

Cover the top last, spreading frosting to edges with a light swirling motion.

FACTS ABOUT CAKE INGREDIENTS

The finished cake can be only as good as the ingredients that go into it; therefore use only high quality ingredients.

Flour: Cake flour, made from soft wheat, has a tender gluten and should be used when called for in the recipe for fine-textured results. Cake flour is usually best for cakes with shortening and for angel and sponge cakes.

The recipes that follow specify the kind of flour to be used. When cake flour is not specified in a recipe, enriched (all purpose) flour is used. Although we do not recommend the substitution of flours, enriched flour may be used instead of cake flour in some recipes with some loss in the fineness of the cake's texture. If enriched flour is substituted for cake flour, use two tablespoons less per cup of enriched flour.

Self-Rising Cake Flour: Some special cake flours on the market already contain baking powder and salt. When this type of flour is used follow directions on package.

Baking Powder: Recipes in this book call for double-acting baking powder. For an explanation of the different actions of the three different types of baking powders and how to make substitutions, see baking powder entry in index.

Sugar: Fine granulated sugar is used in all the recipes unless otherwise indicated—but cane or beet sugar may be used. Coarse sugar makes a coarse-textured cake. Fine grain sugar is especially important for sponge and angel cakes because there is no preliminary creaming with shortening. If sugar is lumpy sift before measuring.

Brown sugar and maple sugar add flavor in addition to sweetening cake. Follow directions for using brown sugar, packing firmly in cup.

Shortening: Hydrogenated shortenings will insure consistently good baking results and are easy to use. Softened hydrogenated vegetable shortening must be used in recipes for one-bowl "quick-method" cakes. In other recipes for cakes with shortening, you may use vegetable fats, lard, butter, or margarine as shortening. Butter may be substituted for part of the shortening for the real butter flavor prized by many cake bakers.

The water displacement method is the easiest way to measure fats. See **Facts About Food and Cooking.**

When a pound of butter or margarine is divided into four sticks, each stick equals ½ cup or 4 ounces.

Eggs: Use good quality fresh eggs because if they are stale the flavor of cake is affected. Fresh eggs should have thick whites and yolks that don't spread when eggs are broken. They beat to their best volume after they are three days old. Eggs should be kept refrigerated; however they beat easier if they are at room temperature at time of beating. Therefore remove eggs at least an hour before using in cakemaking.

You will note in some of our recipes that we call for measured eggs because this is the most accurate way of using eggs. When cup-measure is not specified, use medium-sized eggs.

In separating eggs it is important that none of the yolk gets into the white. If this occurs the white will not whip to a stiff foam.

Liquid: Milk (sweet or sour, buttermilk, evaporated, and reconstituted dry milk powder) is most commonly used, but water, coffee, or fruit juices may be used.

For hints about safe substitutions in recipes, see **Facts About Food and Cooking.**

Preparing Pans: Choose the size and shape of pan to fit the type of cake to be baked. Prepare pans before mixing the batter. For cakes with shortening the bottom and sides of the pan should be greased lightly. A piece of waxed paper cut to fit the bottom may be placed in the greased pan if desired. As an extra precaution, some like to grease the waxed paper too. Another method is to grease the pan lightly and then dust lightly with flour or rub with pancoat made by creaming until smooth two parts shortening with one part flour.

Do not grease the pans for cakes made without shortening (angel and sponge cakes) as the batter needs to cling to the sides of pan in order to reach top volume. Do not fill pans more than two-thirds full.

CAUSES OF FAULTS IN CAKES

Although you think you have followed directions very carefully for mixing and baking your cake, the cake may not turn out as expected. This is not a matter of chance but is caused by something you did or failed to do during mixing or baking. Study the following chart, note the sections that name any faults of your cake, and try to determine where you have slipped.

Cake is burned:
1. Oven heats unevenly.
2. Oven too full for good circulation of heat.
3. Oven too hot.
4. Cake placed too near side of oven.
5. Oven too hot for kind of baking pan used.

Cake is heavy:
1. Too much mixing.
2. Too much fat or liquid.
3. Not enough sugar, baking powder, or baking soda.
4. Baking temperature not right.

Cake is not sufficiently risen:
1. Not enough baking powder or baking soda.
2. Pan too large for amount of batter.
3. Baking temperature wrong.

Cake is tough:
1. Too little fat or sugar.
2. Too much flour.
3. Batter overmixed (in a plain cake).
4. Oven too hot.
5. Cake baked too long.

Cake ran over pan:
1. Too much batter for size of pan.
2. Oven not hot enough.
3. Too much baking powder or baking soda.
4. Too much sugar.

Color of crust is uneven:
1. Ingredients not well blended.
2. Oven temperature uneven.
3. Oven too crowded.
4. Cake placed too close to edge of oven.

Cake has a sticky crust:
1. Too much sugar.
2. Not baked long enough.
3. Not cooled properly.

Cake is higher on one side than other:
1. Oven grate not level.
2. Oven temperature uneven (crust forms sooner in the hotter part of the oven, so the side of the cake on the hot side of the oven will not rise as much as on the other).
3. Batter spread unevenly in pan.
4. Dented pan used.

Cake is coarse-grained:
1. Insufficient creaming of fat and sugar.
2. Oil used instead of a hard fat (in conventional or quick-mix cakes).
3. Enriched (all-purpose) flour used.
4. Too much baking powder or baking soda.
5. Oven not hot enough.

Cake falls apart while being taken from pan:
1. Too much fat, sugar, baking powder, or baking soda.
2. Insufficient baking time.
3. Baked in too slow an oven.
4. Carelessly removed from pan.
5. Removed from pan before cooled.

Crust is soggy or doughy:
1. Cake allowed to steam while cooling.
2. Insufficient baking period.
3. Cake baked too slowly.

Cake sticks to pan, or crust comes off in balls:
1. Pan not properly greased.
2. Too much sugar.
3. Cake left in pan too long.

Cake falls:
1. Too much sugar, fat, liquid, baking powder, or baking soda.
2. Too little flour.
3. Too short a baking period.
4. Oven not hot enough.
5. Cake pans jarred during baking before cake was firm enough to hold shape.

Crust is too light in color:
1. Oven not hot enough, especially at last period.
2. Not enough sugar, fat, baking powder, or baking soda.
3. Not enough batter to fill pan properly.
4. Baking temperature too low for type of baking pan used.

Top of cake is cracked or rounded too much:
(*Top of a standard loaf cake should be slightly cracked.*)
1. Too much flour.
2. Not enough liquid.
3. Batter overmixed after addition of flour.
4. Oven too hot at beginning of baking.

Cake has soggy layer at bottom:
1. Ingredients not thoroughly mixed.
2. Fat too soft.
3. Too little baking powder or baking soda.
4. Too much liquid.
5. Lower part of oven not hot enough.
6. Egg whites not beaten sufficiently (in chiffon cakes).

Cake is dry and crumbly:
1. Too much flour, baking powder, or baking soda.
2. Too little fat, sugar, or liquid.
3. Cornstarch used with an enriched (all-purpose) flour.
4. Cocoa substituted for chocolate without adding more fat.
5. Egg whites overbeaten (in conventional cakes).
6. Cake overbaked or baked too long in too slow an oven.

Cake has a tough crust:
1. Not enough fat or sugar.
2. Too much flour.
3. Baked in floured pan.
4. Baked too long.
5. Oven too hot.

Conventional Method Cakes with Shortening

CONVENTIONAL MIXING METHOD

Complete mixing directions are given in each recipe; however some homemakers frequently find a step-by-step chart such as the following useful.

1. Remove butter or shortening, eggs, and milk from refrigerator about an hour before making cake so ingredients will be at room temperature.

2. Sift flour once; measure by piling in measuring cup and leveling off with knife or spatula. Sift together with dry ingredients.

3. Measure extracts into specified liquid or measure and add to creamed mixture later.

4. Melt chocolate if called for in recipe.

5. Cream shortening and sugar until smooth and fluffy. (With electric mixer use medium speed.)

6. Beat in whole eggs or yolks. Add chocolate if called for in recipe. Beat mixture until well blended. (With mixer use medium speed.)

7. Add and stir in dry ingredients alternately with liquid in recipe. Stir flour and liquid around bowl in same direction after each addition for a cake with more even grain. (With mixer, use low speed, adding flour and liquid at the same time.) Avoid over-stirring when using mixer because this will cause reduced cake volume. Stir enough to make batter smooth.

8. Add and blend in fruits, nuts, etc., if called for in recipe.

9. If stiffly beaten egg whites are specified in a recipe, fold them into cake batter lightly but quickly with a down-up-and-over motion, gradually turning bowl.

10. Turn cake batter into prepared pans.

CLASSIC BUTTER CAKE

2 cups sifted cake flour
3 teaspoons baking powder
1/2 teaspoon salt
2/3 cup butter or other shortening
1 cup sugar
3 eggs, separated
2/3 cup milk
1 teaspoon flavoring

Sift together three times flour, baking powder, and salt.

Cream butter until soft and gradually add sugar, creaming until light and fluffy. Mix in well beaten egg yolks.

Add dry ingredients alternately with milk, stirring vigorously after each addition. Continue stirring for 2 minutes or about 300 strokes.

Fold in the stiffly beaten egg whites and flavoring. Turn into lightly greased baking pans and place in center of preheated oven.

Bake in 2 9-inch layer pans in moderate oven (375° F.) 25 to 30 minutes, or in loaf pan (8 x 8 x 2 inches) in moderate oven (350° F.) 40 to 60 minutes.

Remove from oven, loosen edges with knife, and turn out, inverted, on cake rack. Cool and ice. If cake fails to come out immediately spread a cold damp cloth over bottom of pan for a moment or two.

Variations of Classic Butter Cake

White Classic Cake: Omit egg yolks. Add 1/2 cup shortening.

Banana Nut Cake: Bake in 2 layers. Cool and fill with banana nut filling.

Coconut Cake: With stiffly beaten egg whites and flavoring fold in 1/2 cup shredded coconut and 2 additional tablespoons milk.

Ice with boiled frosting. Cover with coconut or with chocolate sprinkles.

Gold Cake: Omit egg whites. Substitute 1/2 cup butter and 3/4 cup milk for butter and milk stated. Use 1/2 teaspoon orange extract flavoring.

Lady Baltimore Cake: Bake White Cake above in 2 9-inch layers. Fill with Lady Baltimore filling. Ice with boiled frosting.

Marble Cake: Divide batter in two parts. To one part, add 1 1/2 ounces (1 1/2 squares) of melted, unsweetened chocolate, stirring it in well.

Put the 2 batters into a greased loaf baking pan by alternate tablespoonfuls. Pass a spatula through the batter to blend slightly.

Spice Cake: Sift 3/4 teaspoon each of cloves, cinnamon, and nutmeg with the flour. Substitute brown sugar, packed firmly, for white sugar. Ice with caramel frosting.

Raisin Cake: At the last add 2/3 cup seedless raisins dredged with a little of the flour. Ice with caramel frosting.

SPICE CAKE #2

2 1/3 cups sifted cake flour
3 teaspoons baking powder
1 teaspoon salt
1 teaspoon cinnamon
1/4 teaspoon nutmeg
1/4 teaspoon mace
1/4 teaspoon cloves
1 tablespoon boiling water
1/2 cup shortening
1 1/2 cups sugar
3 eggs, unbeaten
2/3 cup milk

Sift flour, measure, resift 3 times with baking powder and salt.

Measure spices into cup; add boiling water and stir to smooth paste.

Cream shortening and sugar. Add eggs, one at a time, beating thoroughly. Stir in spice paste.

Add flour mixture alternately with milk in 4 or 5 portions, beginning and ending with flour and beat until smooth after each addition.

Turn batter into 2 ungreased 9-inch cake pans lined with thin plain paper on bottoms.

Bake in moderate oven (375°F.) about 30 minutes. Remove from oven and cool on cake racks 5 minutes.

Turn out of pans, invert and cool. Remove paper and spread layers with molasses butter frosting or rum nut filling and frosting.

Variation: For variety, make 1 recipe creamy vanilla frosting. Divide in half, add rum and nuts to 1/2 the frosting and chocolate to the other.

Spread one layer of cake (top and sides) with one frosting and the other layer with the second frosting.

APPLESAUCE FIG CAKE

1/2 cup shortening
1 cup sugar
2 eggs
1 3/4 cups sifted all-purpose flour
1 teaspoon salt
1 teaspoon baking powder
1/2 teaspoon baking soda
1/2 teaspoon cinnamon
1/2 teaspoon nutmeg
1 cup sweetened applesauce
1/3 cup chopped walnuts
1 cup chopped dried figs

Cream shortening; gradually add sugar, creaming until light. Add eggs; beat until fluffy.

Sift dry ingredients; add to creamed mixture alternately with applesauce, beating after each addition. Stir in nuts and figs. Pour into greased angel food cake pan.

Bake in moderate oven (350°F.) about 45 minutes. Cool in pan 10 minutes; remove. While still warm, spread top with thin frosting, if desired.

Applesauce Fig Cake

BURNT SUGAR CAKE

3 cups sifted cake flour
3 teaspoons baking powder
¾ teaspoon salt
¾ cup butter or margarine
1¼ cups sugar
3 eggs, separated
3 tablespoons burnt sugar syrup (below)
1 cup milk
1 teaspoon vanilla

Sift flour, baking powder, and salt together.

Cream butter thoroughly; add sugar gradually, creaming until light and fluffy. Add egg yolks, one at a time, beating well after each. Blend in burnt sugar syrup.

Add flour mixture alternately with milk, beating after each addition. Add vanilla.

Beat egg whites until stiff but not dry. Fold carefully into batter.

Pour into 2 well greased 8 x 8 x 2-inch square pans. Bake in moderate oven (375°F.) 25 to 30 minutes.

Cool thoroughly on cake rack. Fill and frost layers with burnt sugar frosting. Arrange salted pecans around sides of cake.

Burnt Sugar Syrup: Melt ½ cup granulated sugar in a heavy skillet, stirring constantly. When dark in color, remove from heat and slowly add ⅓ cup hot water, blending thoroughly.

Burnt Sugar Frosting:

2 egg whites
1½ cups sugar
5 tablespoons water
1½ teaspoons light corn syrup
2 tablespoons burnt sugar syrup

Combine egg whites, sugar, water, and corn syrup in top of double boiler. Beat until thoroughly blended.

Place over rapidly boiling water; beat constantly while cooking about 7 minutes, or until frosting stands in peaks.

Remove from water; add burnt sugar syrup and beat until thick enough to spread on cake.

APPLESAUCE CAKE

½ cup shortening
1 cup brown sugar
2 well beaten eggs or 4 well beaten egg yolks
2 cups sifted cake flour
½ teaspoon salt
1 teaspoon cinnamon
½ teaspoon cloves
½ teaspoon nutmeg
1 teaspoon baking soda
¾ cup chopped dates
1 cup chopped nuts
1 cup cold applesauce

Cream shortening. Add sugar gradually, and cream together until smooth and fluffy. Mix in eggs or egg yolks.

Sift flour with salt, spices, and baking soda. Add dates and nuts, blend with flour. Add flour mixture alternately with applesauce to shortening sugar-egg mixture and mix until smooth. Pour into greased pans.

Bake in moderate oven (350°F.) 30 to 35 minutes for layer pans, and 45 to 50 minutes for loaf pan.

Cool in pans 5 to 10 minutes, then remove and cool on wire rack. Ice with brown sugar frosting; decorate with walnut halves.

SOUR CREAM SPICE CAKE

¼ cup shortening
1 cup brown sugar
1 egg
¾ cup thick sour cream
1¾ cups sifted cake flour
¼ teaspoon baking soda
2 teaspoons baking powder
⅛ teaspoon salt
¼ teaspoon cloves
2 teaspoons cinnamon

Cream shortening. Add sugar gradually. Add egg and beat well. Add sour cream.

Sift flour with baking soda, baking powder, salt, cloves, and cinnamon.

Add 2 tablespoons of the dry ingredients to the creamed mixture. Beat thoroughly. Add dry ingredients to the first mixture, beating well.

Pour into a well greased and floured pan (8 x 12 x 2 inches). Bake in moderate oven (350°F.) 30 minutes.

Spread confectioners' sugar icing on top and sides.

FRENCH ORANGE FIG CAKE

1½ cups sifted cake flour
2 teaspoons baking powder
½ teaspoon salt
⅓ cup butter
1 cup sugar
1 egg plus 1 egg yolk
1 teaspoon orange juice
½ cup milk

Mix and sift flour, baking powder, and salt.

Cream butter. Add sugar gradually, beating until very fluffy. Add beaten eggs combined with orange juice.

Add dry ingredients alternately with milk. Start and end with flour. Beat until well blended.

Pour into 2 greased and floured cake pans. Bake in moderate oven (350°F.) 25 minutes.

Remove and cool. Put together with fig filling. Frost with orange frosting.

DAISY PARTY CAKE

½ cup soft shortening
1½ cups sugar
4 egg whites
2½ cups sifted cake flour
2½ teaspoons baking powder
½ teaspoon salt
1 cup milk
½ teaspoon lemon extract
½ teaspoon almond extract

Cream shortening and sugar until fluffy; blend in each egg white.

Sift in dry ingredients alternately with milk; add flavorings.

Pour into well greased, floured oblong pan (14 x 9 x 2-inches).

Bake in moderate oven (375°F.) 20 to 25 minutes or until top springs back when lightly touched.

Make up your favorite boiled or 7-minute frosting using 2 egg whites and 1½ cups sugar.

To one-half the icing stir in 8 drops yellow food coloring and ¼ teaspoon lemon extract.

Swirl on sides and top half of the cake crosswise; to other half of icing mix in 8 drops green food coloring and ¼ teaspoon mint extract. Swirl on the rest of the cake.

Mark "yellow" cake into 16 squares; place a small daisy atop each square. Mark "green" cake first into 6 diagonal strips; then divide cake crosswise into 3 strips. This marking gives 6 triangles and 6 diamonds. Place a nut dipped in yellow frosting in center of each piece —walnut halves for diamonds and almonds for triangles. Serves 12 to 14.

Daisy Party Cake

PRUNE SPICE CAKE

    3   cups sifted enriched flour
    1¼ teaspoons baking soda
    1   teaspoon salt
    1½ teaspoons nutmeg
    1   teaspoon allspice
    1½ teaspoons cinnamon
    ¾   teaspoon cloves
    ¾   cup shortening
    1½ cups sugar
    3   eggs
    1½ cups sour milk or 1½ cups but-
          termilk
    1½ cups cut up, cooked, pitted prunes

Sift together dry ingredients three times.

Cream shortening and sugar until light and fluffy. Beat in eggs, one at a time.

Add dry ingredients alternately with sour milk or buttermilk, beating until smooth after each addition. Add prunes and blend well. Turn into large, greased tube pan.

Bake in moderate oven (350°F.) 1½ hours, or until done.

Cool. Spread with 7-minute frosting. Decorate with grated orange rind.

MASTER BUTTER CAKE
(With 4 Eggs)

    3   cups sifted cake flour
    4   teaspoons baking powder
    ¼ to ½ teaspoon salt
    1   cup butter or other shortening
    2   cups sugar
    4   eggs
    1   cup milk
    ½ to 1 teaspoon vanilla

Sift together, flour, baking powder, and salt.

Cream shortening until soft and smooth. Gradually add sugar, creaming until light and fluffy. Add eggs, one at a time, beating after each addition.

Add dry ingredients alternately with milk. Add vanilla. Turn into lightly greased pans.

For layer cake, bake in moderate oven (375°F.) 25 minutes. For a loaf cake, bake in slow oven (325°F.) 40 to 45 minutes.

Cool in pans 5 to 10 minutes. Remove from pans and cool on wire rack.

Variations of 4-Egg Master Butter Cake

Chocolate Cake: Use ⅞ cup shortening instead of 1 cup, and 2⅞ cups flour instead of 3 cups, and 2 ounces (2 squares) melted unsweetened chocolate added with the vanilla.

Cupcakes: Pour into lightly greased cupcake pans, ⅔ full. Bake in moderate oven (375°F.) 20 to 25 minutes.

Remove from pans and cool on wire rack. Makes 24 cupcakes.

LORD BALTIMORE CAKE

    2½ cups sifted cake flour
    2½ teaspoons baking powder
    ¼   teaspoon salt
    ¾   cup butter
    1¼ cups sugar
    8   egg yolks
    ¾   cup milk
    1   teaspoon lemon extract
    1   teaspoon orange extract

Sift flour 3 times with baking powder and salt.

Cream butter thoroughly; add sugar gradually, and cream together until light and fluffy. Add egg yolks which have been beaten until very thick and lemon colored. Beat well.

Add dry ingredients alternately with milk and flavorings, beating after each addition. Turn into 2 9-inch greased, waxed paper lined, again greased layer pans.

Bake in moderate oven (375°F.) 25 minutes.

Cool. Put layers together with Lord Baltimore filling and frosting. Garnish top and sides of cake with pecan halves.

HONEY CAKE

    Scant 3 cups sifted cake flour
    2   teaspoons baking powder
    ½   teaspoon salt
    1   cup butter
    1   cup strained honey
    4   well beaten eggs
    1   tablespoon lemon juice
    1   teaspoon grated lemon rind
    1   cup cut citron
    ¾   cup chopped nuts

Mix and sift flour, baking powder, and salt.

Cream butter with honey. Blend in eggs, lemon juice, and lemon rind. Add dry ingredients. Blend smoothly. Mix in citron and nuts. Pour into large loaf pan lined with greased paper. Bake in moderate oven (350°F.) 1 hour.

BANANA LAYER CAKE

    1¾ cups sifted cake flour
    1   teaspoon baking powder
    ¼   teaspoon salt
    ⅓   cup shortening
    ⅓   cup granulated sugar
    ½   cup brown sugar
    2   well beaten eggs
    1   teaspoon vanilla
    1   teaspoon baking soda
    4   tablespoons milk
    1   cup mashed bananas

Sift flour with baking powder and salt.

Cream shortening until soft and smooth. Gradually add granulated sugar and brown sugar, beating until fluffy. Beat in eggs and vanilla.

Dissolve baking soda in milk. Add with bananas to creamed mixture. Add dry ingredients, beating until smooth.

Turn into 2 greased 8-inch layer pans. Bake in moderate oven (350°F.) 30 to 35 minutes. Cool 5 to 10 minutes in pans.

Remove from pans and cool on wire rack. Spread lemon filling between layers. Cover top and sides with whipped cream.

Decorate with border of fluted sliced bananas on top. To flute, draw lines with fork down sides of bananas, then slice.

MOLASSES ZIG-ZAG CAKE

    2   cups sifted enriched flour
    2   teaspoons baking powder
    ¼   teaspoon salt
    ½   cup shortening
    1   cup sugar
    2   unbeaten eggs
    ⅔   cup milk
    1   teaspoon black walnut flavoring
    2   tablespoons dark molasses
    1   teaspoon allspice
    ¼   cup chopped nuts

Sift together flour, baking powder, and salt.

Blend together shortening and sugar, creaming well. Add eggs. Beat 1 minute.

Combine milk and flavoring. Add alternately with dry ingredients to creamed mixture, beginning and ending with dry ingredients. Blend thoroughly after each addition. (With electric mixer use low speed.)

Place ⅓ of batter in a second bowl. Add molasses and allspice.

Spoon light and dark batters alternately into well greased and lightly floured 9 x 5 x 3-inch pan. Run fork through batter several times in both directions.

Bake in moderate oven (350°F.) 70 to 75 minutes. Let cool in pan 15 minutes before turning out. Cool thoroughly; frost with cinnamon glaze. Sprinkle with chopped nuts.

Cinnamon Glaze: Combine 1 cup sifted confectioners' sugar, 3 tablespoons cream, 1 teaspoon vanilla, ¼ teaspoon cinnamon, and ¼ teaspoon salt. Mix thoroughly.

Molasses Zig-Zag Cake

Regal Gold Cake

REGAL GOLD CAKE

3   cups sifted enriched flour
1½ tablespoons baking powder
¼   teaspoon salt
⅔   cup butter
1   teaspoon vanilla
1⅓ cups sugar
5   egg yolks
½   cup evaporated milk mixed with
         ½ cup water

Sift flour; measure and resift with baking powder and salt.

Cream butter with vanilla; add sugar gradually and continue creaming until light and fluffy. Add egg yolks and beat well.

Add dry ingredients alternately with milk, beginning and ending with dry ingredients.

Pour into 3 9-inch layer cake pans. Bake in moderate oven (375°F.) about 25 minutes. Frost with caramel frosting. Chopped pecans may be sprinkled over top of frosted cake while frosting is still soft or beaten into the frosting.

LADY BALTIMORE CAKE

2   cups sifted cake flour
2½ teaspoons baking powder
1   teaspoon salt
½   cup shortening
1   cup sugar
1   teaspoon vanilla
¾   cup milk
3   egg whites

Sift flour, measure, resift 3 times with baking powder and salt.

Cream shortening and ¾ cup sugar. Stir in vanilla.

Add flour mixture alternately with milk in 4 or 5 portions, beginning and ending with flour; beat until smooth after each addition.

Beat egg whites with rotary beater until foamy, gradually beat in remaining ¼ cup sugar; beat until mixture stands in soft peaks. Fold in batter lightly but thoroughly.

Turn batter into 2 ungreased 8-inch cake pans lined with thin plain paper on bottoms.

Bake in moderate oven (350°F.) 20 to 25 minutes. Remove from oven and cool on cake racks 5 minutes. Turn out of pan. Invert and cool. Remove paper and spread Lady Baltimore frosting between layers, on top and sides.

OLD-FASHIONED POUND CAKE

1   cup butter
1   cup sugar
5   well beaten eggs
2   cups sifted cake flour
¼   teaspoon mace
1   tablespoon brandy or 1 teaspoon
         lemon extract

Cream butter thoroughly; add sugar gradually and continue beating until light and fluffy. Add well beaten eggs, then beat about 10 minutes on electric mixer at moderate speed.

Blend in flour, mace, and brandy, using low speed.

Pour into greased 9½ x 5½ x 2¾-inch loaf pan. Bake in slow oven (325° F.) 1 hour and 15 minutes.

Note: If desired, substitute rose water for brandy or lemon extract.

FLUFFY WHITE BUTTER CAKE

½   cup butter
1½ cups sugar
1   teaspoon vanilla
3   cups sifted cake flour
3   teaspoons baking powder
1   cup milk
4   egg whites

Let butter stand at room temperature until softened. Cream softened butter thoroughly, adding sugar gradually and continuing to cream until fluffy. Add vanilla and blend well.

Sift flour and baking powder together. Add flour mixture and milk alternately to butter-sugar mixture, beating after each addition until smooth.

Beat egg whites stiff but not dry and fold gently into cake batter.

Pour into 3 8-inch greased cake pans. Bake in moderate oven (375° F.) 25 minutes.

Makes 3 layer cake.

SILVER CAKE

2⅔ cups sifted cake flour
3   teaspoons baking powder
1   teaspoon salt
5   egg whites
½   cup sugar
⅔   cup shortening (at room tempera-
         ture)
1¼ cups sugar
1   cup milk
1   teaspoon vanilla or grated lemon
         rind

Measure sifted flour, add baking powder and salt, and sift together three times.

Beat egg whites until foamy; add ½ cup sugar gradually, and continue beating only until meringue will hold up in soft peaks.

Cream shortening; add 1¼ cups sugar gradually, and cream together until light and fluffy. Add flour, alternately with milk, in small amounts, beating after each addition until smooth.

Add flavoring and blend. Then beat meringue into batter.

Use two round 9-inch layer pans, 1½ inches deep and line bottoms with paper. Pour batter into pans.

Bake in moderate oven (375°F.) about 30 minutes.

This cake may be baked in two 9 x 9 x 2-inch square pans or in 16 x 10 x 2-inch pan at (375°F.) 25 to 30 minutes.

Spread with fluffy lime frosting and lime fruit filling, seven minute frosting or strawberry fluff.

PARTY BUTTER CAKE

3   cups sifted cake flour
3   teaspoons baking powder
½   teaspoon salt
¾   cup butter
1½ cups sugar
3   eggs, separated
1½ teaspoons vanilla
1   cup milk

Sift flour, measure; sift 3 times with baking powder and salt.

Cream butter thoroughly, until soft and smooth; then gradually blend in all but ¼ cup of the sugar.

Add beaten egg yolks and vanilla, and beat until fluffy. Add flour mixture and milk alternately in several portions, beginning and ending with flour and beating well after each addition.

Beat egg whites until stiff, and gradually beat in the remaining ¼ cup sugar. Fold into cake batter, lightly but thoroughly.

Turn batter into 3 8-inch cake pans, which have been lined with waxed paper in the bottom and buttered on the sides.

Bake in moderate oven (350°F.) about 20 to 25 minutes, or until a toothpick inserted in the center comes out clean. Remove to cake racks to cool.

Put together with the chocolate butter icing between layers, and spread top and sides with vanilla butter icing. Garnish top with shaved semi-sweet chocolate. Serves 12.

Party Butter Cake

Caramel Syrup Cake

MASTER BUTTER CAKE
(With 2 Eggs)

1/2 cup butter or other shortening
1 1/2 cups sugar
2 large eggs or 3 medium eggs
3 cups sifted cake flour
4 teaspoons baking powder
1/4 to 1/2 teaspoon salt
1 cup milk
1/4 to 1 teaspoon vanilla

Cream together shortening and sugar. Add eggs, 1 at a time, beating after each.

Sift together flour, baking powder, and salt.

Add alternately with milk to creamed mixture.

Add vanilla. Pour into lightly greased pans.

For a 2-layer cake, bake in moderate oven (375°F.) 25 minutes.

For a loaf cake, bake in slow oven (325°F.) 40 to 45 minutes.

Cool in pans for 5 to 10 minutes. Remove from pans and cool on wire racks.

Variations of Master 2-Egg Butter Cake

Banana Cake: Add crushed bananas to cake filling. Ice with banana frosting.

Chocolate Cake: Use 3/8 cup shortening instead of 1/2 cup, and 2 7/8 cups flour instead of 3 cups.

Melt 2 ounces (2 squares) unsweetened chocolate, over warm (not boiling) water, and add with vanilla.

Cocoa Cake: Reduce flour to 2 1/2 cups. Add 5 tablespoons cocoa. Sift cocoa with dry ingredients.

Coconut Cake: Add 1/2 cup shredded coconut to batter. Ice with coconut frosting.

Marble Layer Cake: Divide batter into 2 parts and add 1 ounce (1 square) melted chocolate to one part. Put by spoonfuls into 2 greased layer pans, alternating light and dark mixtures. Decorate with chocolate frosting.

Mocha Cake: Use 1/2 cup strong coffee and 1/2 cup water, instead of milk.

Nut Cake: Add 1/2 cup nutmeats broken in pieces to batter.

Orange Coconut Cake: Flavor with 1 tablespoon orange rind instead of vanilla. Substitute orange juice for milk. Mix in 1/2 cup grated coconut with the liquid. Cover cake with orange frosting and shredded coconut.

Spice Cake: Reduce cake flour to 2 3/4 cups and add 1 teaspoon cinnamon, 1/2 teaspoon cloves, and 1/2 teaspoon allspice or nutmeg.

White Cake: Use 4 to 6 egg whites, instead of 2 to 3 whole eggs.

Yellow Cake: Use 4 to 6 egg yolks, instead of 2 to 3 whole eggs, and add extra teaspoon of baking powder.

(1 1/2 teaspoons grated orange rind may be used instead of vanilla.)

CARAMEL SYRUP CAKE
Syrup:

1 1/4 cups sugar
3/4 cup boiling water

Place 1 1/2-quart saucepan, containing sugar, on medium-high heat. Stir constantly with wooden spoon until sugar changes to greyish lumps (sugar masses) and then to dark brown liquid.

Slowly pour boiling water down side of pan, stirring liquid sugar as you do (it will steam and bubble). Boil 5 minutes. Keep warm. Makes 1 cup.

Cake:

1/2 cup butter or margarine
1 cup sugar
1 teaspoon vanilla
2 eggs
2 cups sifted enriched flour
2 1/2 teaspoons baking powder
1/2 teaspoon salt
2/3 cup burnt sugar syrup (above)
1/4 cup milk

Cream butter or margarine and sugar together until fluffy. Stir in vanilla and each egg well.

Alternately fold in sifted dry ingredients with syrup and milk. Stir-beat vigorously for several minutes.

Pour into well greased and floured 9-inch square pan. Bake in moderate oven (350°F.) about 35 minutes or until center springs back when touched lightly.

Remove from pan; cool on cake rack. Ice with burnt sugar frosting.

Burnt Sugar Frosting:

1/2 cup sugar
1/3 cup burnt sugar syrup
1 egg white

In top of double boiler combine sugar, burnt sugar syrup, and egg white.

Place over boiling water, beating until frosting stands in peaks when beater is drawn out (takes about 4 minutes). Makes enough for top and sides of 9-inch square cake.

LEMON PECAN CRUNCH CAKE

3/4 cup butter or margarine
1 1/2 cups sugar
3 well beaten eggs
3 cups sifted enriched flour
3 teaspoons baking powder
1/2 teaspoon salt
1 cup milk
Juice and grated rind of 1 lemon
1 cup chopped pecans

Cream butter until light and gradually beat in sugar, beating until light and fluffy.

Add eggs and blend well.

Sift dry ingredients together and add alternately with milk to creamed mixture, mixing until blended.

Stir in lemon juice and rind.

Generously grease 10-inch tube pan with butter or margarine and cover bottom with chopped nuts. Pour in batter.

Bake in moderate oven (375°F.) 1 hour. Turn out on rack to cool.

WASHINGTON CREAM PIE #2

1/3 cup butter
1 cup sugar
2 eggs, unbeaten
1 3/4 cups sifted cake flour
2 teaspoons baking powder
1/4 teaspoon salt
1/2 cup milk
1 teaspoon vanilla

Cream butter thoroughly. Add sugar gradually. Add eggs, 1 at a time, beating after each addition.

Mix and sift dry ingredients and add alternately with milk and vanilla, beginning and ending with flour mixture.

Bake in 2 greased 9-inch layer pans in moderate oven (375°F.) 20 to 25 minutes. When cool, put together with cream filling between layers and dust confectioners' sugar over top. Makes two 9-inch layers.

MAPLE CREAM CAKE

1/3 cup butter
1 cup sugar
2 eggs
1 3/4 cups sifted cake flour
1 teaspoon baking powder
1 teaspoon baking soda
2 1/2 tablespoons cocoa
1 cup sour milk
1 teaspoon vanilla

Cream butter and sugar until light and fluffy. Add eggs and mix well.

Mix and sift dry ingredients and add alternately with milk and vanilla, beating smooth after each addition.

Pour into 3 greased and floured 8-inch layer pans. Bake in moderate oven (375°F.) 25 minutes.

Turn out on cake racks to cool. Fill with maple cream filling. Frost with chocolate frosting.

MASTER BUTTER CAKE
(With 1 Egg)

2   cups sifted cake flour
1/4 teaspoon salt
2 1/2 teaspoons baking powder
1/3 cup butter or other shortening
1   cup sugar
1   egg
1   teaspoon vanilla
2/3 cup milk

Sift together flour, salt, and baking powder.

Cream shortening until soft and smooth, and gradually add sugar, beating until light and fluffy. Beat in egg and vanilla. Add dry ingredients alternately with milk.

Turn into greased pan and bake. In single square pan: moderate oven (350°F.) 50 minutes. In 2 layer pans: moderate oven (375°F.) 25 minutes. In cupcake pans: moderate oven (375°F.) 25 minutes.

Cool layers 5 to 10 minutes in pan before removing and cooling on wire rack. Remove cupcakes from pans at once and cool on wire rack.

Makes 2 8-inch layers, 1 8-inch square cake, or 1 1/2 dozen cupcakes.

Variations of One-Egg Butter Cake

Boston Cream Pie: Bake in 2 layers. Spread cream filling between layers. Sift powdered sugar over top.

Caramel Cake: Add 4 tablespoons caramel flavoring with the liquid.

Chocolate Cake: Add 1 ounce (1 square) melted chocolate to creamed shortening.

Raisin Cake: Prepare batter. At the last, add 1/2 cup raisins which have been dredged with 2 tablespoons cake flour.

Short Cake: Bake in shallow pan. Cut in rounds. Split each round in 2 parts. Spread fruit between each part and on top. Serve with whipped cream. Garnish with fruit.

Spice Cake: Reduce cake flour to 1 7/8 cups and add 1 teaspoon cinnamon, 1/4 teaspoon cloves, and 1/4 teaspoon allspice or nutmeg.

Washington Pie: Bake in 2 layers. Spread jam or jelly between layers. Sift powdered sugar over top.

White Cake: Use 2 egg whites in place of whole egg. Fold in stiffly beaten whites last.

Yellow Cake: Use 2 egg yolks in place of whole egg, and 1 teaspoon grated orange rind for the flavoring.

BUTTERMILK CAKE

2   cups sifted cake flour
3/4 teaspoon baking soda
1/2 teaspoon salt
2/3 cup shortening
1   cup sugar
3   eggs, separated
1   teaspoon vanilla
1/2 teaspoon lemon extract
1/2 cup buttermilk
2   tablespoons distilled vinegar

Sift flour, soda, and salt together.

Cream shortening; add sugar gradually, creaming until light and fluffy. Add egg yolks and beat until very light. Add vanilla and lemon extract; blend well.

Add dry ingredients alternately with combined buttermilk and vinegar. Beat until batter is smooth.

Fold in stiffly beaten egg whites. Pour into greased 7 x 10 x 2-inch loaf pan or two 8-inch layer cake pans, 1 1/2-inches deep.

Bake loaf in moderate oven (350°F.) 40 to 45 minutes; layers at (375°F.) 25 to 30 minutes.

SILHOUETTE CAKE

1 1/4 cups butter or margarine
2 1/2 cups sugar
1/4 teaspoon salt
1   teaspoon vanilla
4   eggs
3   cups sifted cake flour
4   teaspoons baking powder
1   cup milk
3   1-ounce squares baking chocolate, melted

Cream butter or margarine, sugar, salt, and vanilla until light and fluffy. Beat in eggs well.

Sift together flour and baking powder and add alternately with milk, adding flour first and last.

Pour 1/3 of batter into one 8-inch cake pan lined with greased wax paper.

Add melted chocolate to remaining 2/3 batter and pour equal portions into two 8-inch layer pans.

Bake in moderate oven (375°F.) about 30 minutes.

Cool and frost with boiled frosting. Melt 2 1-ounce squares baking chocolate and spread lightly over top.

POUND CAKE

1 1/4 cups butter
1/2 teaspoon mace
Grated rind of 1/2 lemon
1 1/2 cups sugar
6   eggs, separated
3   cups sifted cake flour
1/4 to 1/2 teaspoon salt

Cream butter until soft. Add mace and lemon rind, then gradually add sugar, beating until mixture is light and fluffy.

Slowly add well beaten egg yolks. Fold in stiffly beaten egg whites. Add flour and salt, beating until batter is smooth.

Turn into a tube pan which has been lined with waxed paper. Bake in slow oven (300° to 325°F.) 1 to 1 1/4 hours.

Praline Cake

PRALINE CAKE

Cake:
1/4 cup shortening
3/4 cup granulated sugar
1   egg
1 1/2 cups sifted cake flour
1/4 teaspoon salt
1 1/2 teaspoons baking powder
2/3 cup milk
1   teaspoon vanilla

Topping:
1/4 cup brown sugar
2   teaspoons flour
1   tablespoon water
2   tablespoons melted butter or margarine
1/2 cup chopped pecans

Cream shortening; add granulated sugar gradually, creaming until fluffy. Beat in egg thoroughly.

Sift together 1 1/2 cups flour, salt, and baking powder; add to shortening mixture alternately with milk, beating until smooth after each addition. Stir in vanilla.

Pour into well greased round cake dish. Bake in slow oven (325°F.) about 40 minutes or until done. Cool slightly.

Topping: Mix together brown sugar, 2 teaspoons flour, water, melted butter, and chopped nuts; carefully spread on top of slightly cooled cake. Return to slow oven (325°F.) and bake 10 minutes.

RICH WHITE BUTTER CAKE

1 cup butter
2 cups sugar
1 teaspoon vanilla
3 cups sifted cake flour
1 cup milk
2 teaspoons baking powder
7 egg whites

Cream butter and sugar. Add vanilla. Sift flour with baking powder; add alternately with milk, beating well after each addition of flour.

Beat egg whites until stiff but not dry and fold into cake batter.

Bake in 3 greased 9-inch cake pans in slow oven (325°F.) 35 minutes. Turn out on cake racks. When cool, frost with 7-minute frosting.

Makes 3-layer 9-inch cake.

MARASCHINO CHERRY-NUT CAKE

3/4 cup butter or margarine
1 1/2 cups sugar
3 eggs, separated
3 cups sifted cake flour
3 teaspoons baking powder
1/2 teaspoon salt
1 cup milk
1/3 cup chopped, drained red maraschino cherries (about 16 cherries)
1/2 cup chopped pecans
1/4 teaspoon almond flavoring

Cream butter or margarine, add sugar gradually and cream well together. Add egg yolks and beat thoroughly.

Sift flour, baking powder, and salt together and add to creamed mixture alternately with milk, beginning and ending with dry ingredients.

Add well drained maraschino cherries, nuts, and almond flavoring.

Beat egg whites until stiff but not dry. With a rubber spatula or a spoon fold in the egg whites with an up and over motion.

Divide batter evenly into 2 9-inch cake pans that have been oiled on the bottom.

Bake in moderate oven (375°F.) 20 minutes or until inserted toothpick comes out clean.

Cool on racks until pans are cool enough to handle. Turn out on racks and cool before frosting. Frost with 7-minute or butter frosting. Decorate with red maraschino cherries and green spearmint leaf gumdrops.

WHOLE WHEAT NUT CAKE

1 cup sifted enriched flour
2 teaspoons baking powder
1/4 teaspoon salt
1/2 teaspoon cinnamon
1/2 teaspoon nutmeg
1/4 teaspoon allspice
1/2 cup whole wheat flour
3/4 cup chopped nuts
1/4 cup butter
3/4 cup sugar
2 beaten eggs
1/2 teaspoon vanilla
2/3 cup milk

Sift together enriched flour, baking powder, salt, cinnamon, nutmeg, and all-spice. Blend in whole wheat flour and chopped nuts.

Cream butter. Add sugar gradually. Add eggs and vanilla and blend well. Add sifted dry ingredients alternately with milk, beating until smooth after each addition.

Turn into well greased loaf pan. Bake in moderate oven (350°F.) 40 to 50 minutes. Remove from pan and cool on cake rack. Cover with orange cream cheese icing.

HONEY ORANGE CAKE

1/2 cup shortening
1/2 cup sugar
1/2 cup honey
1 egg
2 cups sifted enriched flour
2 teaspoons baking powder
1/4 teaspoon baking soda
1/4 teaspoon salt
1/2 cup fine-shredded orange peel
1/4 cup orange juice
1 teaspoon grated lemon rind or 1 teaspoon lemon flavoring

Cream shortening. Add sugar gradually, creaming until light and fluffy. Add honey, beating until smooth. Beat in egg.

Sift together dry ingredients three times. Add orange peel.

Combine orange juice and lemon rind or flavoring. Add dry ingredients alternately with orange juice to creamed mixture beginning and ending with flour mixture.

Spread in well greased square cake pan. The mixture is quite thick.

Bake in moderate oven (350°F.) about 45 to 60 minutes.

Let stand 7 or 8 minutes before removing cake from pan. Serve plain, iced, or with hot fruit sauce, warm or cold. Makes 16 2-inch squares.

Honey Orange Sauce: Blend 1/2 cup orange juice with 1/3 cup honey. Pour over the warm or cold cake or serve separately.

GOLDEN LOAF CAKE

3 1/2 cups sifted enriched flour
3 teaspoons baking powder
1 teaspoon baking soda
1 1/4 teaspoons salt
1 1/2 teaspoons cinnamon
3/4 teaspoon ground cloves
3/8 teaspoon nutmeg
1/4 teaspoon mace
1/2 cup shortening
1 1/2 cups firmly packed brown sugar
2 cups seedless raisins
2 cups water
1 cup chopped nuts

Sift flour, measure, resift 3 times with baking powder, soda, salt, and spices.

Combine shortening, sugar, raisins, and water in saucepan. Boil vigorously 3 minutes. Cool. Add chopped nuts, then flour mixture in 3 or 4 portions and mix thoroughly.

Pour into ungreased loaf pan (5 x 9 x 2 1/2 inches), lined with thin plain paper. Bake in moderate oven (350°F.) 1 to 1 1/4 hours.

Remove from oven. Cool on cake rack 5 minutes. Turn out of pan, invert and cool thoroughly. Remove paper and spread with creamy vanilla or mocha frosting.

Lemon Filled Layer Cake

LEMON FILLED LAYER CAKE

2 cups sifted cake flour
2 teaspoons baking powder
1/2 teaspoon salt
1/2 cup butter
1 cup sugar
4 egg yolks
3/4 cup milk
1 teaspoon vanilla

Sift flour, baking powder, and salt together three times.

Cream butter thoroughly; add sugar gradually, and cream until light and fluffy.

Beat egg yolks until thick and lemon colored; add to creamed mixture and blend well.

Add flour mixture alternately with milk and vanilla, beating after each addition until smooth.

Pour in two 8-inch, greased, waxed paper lined, and again greased layer pans. Bake in moderate oven (375°F.) 25 to 30 minutes.

Put layers together with lemon filling. Make design on top by laying fancy paper doily on top layer and sifting confectioners' sugar over it. Gently remove doily. Keep cake chilled in refrigerator, especially in warm weather.

CRANBERRY SPICE CAKE

1/2 cup shortening
1 cup sugar
1 beaten egg
1 cup raisins
1/2 cup chopped nuts
1 3/4 cups sifted enriched flour
1/4 teaspoon salt
1 teaspoon baking soda
1 teaspoon baking powder
1 teaspoon cinnamon
1/2 teaspoon cloves
1 cup cranberry sauce, jellied or whole

Cream shortening and sugar. Add egg. Stir in raisins and nuts.

Combine dry ingredients and sift; add to first mixture. Stir in cranberry sauce.

Bake in moderate oven (350°F.) about 1 hour in greased tube pan, or for 30 to 40 minutes in greased 8-inch layer cake pans.

Frost with cranberry cream cheese frosting.

SPICY MARBLE CAKE

⅔ cup butter or margarine
2 cups sugar
3 well beaten eggs
3 cups sifted cake flour
1 teaspoon baking powder
1 teaspoon baking soda
½ teaspoon salt
1 cup sour milk
1 tablespoon molasses
1 square (1 ounce) unsweetened chocolate, melted, cooled
1 teaspoon cinnamon
1 teaspoon nutmeg
½ teaspoon cloves

Cream butter until light; gradually add sugar, creaming until very light and fluffy. Beat in eggs.

Mix and sift flour, baking powder, soda, and salt. Add to creamed mixture alternately with sour milk, blending quickly but thoroughly.

Divide batter in half. To one-half add molasses, melted chocolate, and spices sifted together. Blend well.

Place alternate spoonfuls of white and dark batter in well greased 10-inch tube pan. Bake in moderate oven (350°F.) 1 hour and 10 minutes.

Turn out on cake rack and cool thoroughly. Cover top and sides with chocolate frosting. Decorate outer edge of cake with walnut halves.

ALMOND MERINGUE CAKE

½ cup butter
½ cup sugar
4 beaten egg yolks
1 cup sifted cake flour
½ cup milk
1 teaspoon baking powder
¼ teaspoon salt
2 tablespoons cake flour

Cream butter and sugar. Add beaten egg yolks. Add alternately the 1 cup of cake flour and the milk.

Sift on top of mixture and fold in baking powder, salt, and 2 tablespoons cake flour.

Pour into 2 8-inch greased layer cake pans. Set in cool place while preparing meringue topping.

Meringue Topping:

4 egg whites
¾ cup sugar
1 teaspoon vanilla
¾ cup blanched almonds, chopped

Beat egg whites to a froth; add sugar gradually and continue beating until all sugar is added. Meringue stands in peaks when beaters are pulled out.

Add vanilla and spread on unbaked layers. Sprinkle with chopped almonds.

Bake in moderate oven (350° F.) 35 minutes.

Cool and remove from pans. Meringue will shrink a little on cooling. Place 1 layer upside down on serving plate.

Cover with lemon filling and top with second layer, meringue side up.

Note: Ice cream, cream pudding, or whipped cream and orange marmalade blended together may be used for filling.

HUNGARIAN PLUM CAKE

½ cup butter
1 cup sugar
2 eggs
1 cup sifted enriched flour
1 teaspoon baking powder
½ teaspoon salt
2 teaspoons cinnamon
½ teaspoon lemon extract
10 fresh or canned plum halves

Cream butter, add ½ cup sugar, and cream until light and fluffy. Add eggs one at a time and beat well.

Add flour which has been sifted with baking powder, salt, and 1 teaspoon cinnamon. Add lemon extract.

Pour into a well greased pan (11 x 6 x 2 inches). Press the plum halves into batter. Sprinkle mixture of ½ cup sugar and 1 teaspoon cinnamon over top.

Bake in hot oven (400°F.) 30 minutes. Serves 5 to 6.

Variations:

Hungarian Apple Cake: Substitute 3 sliced tart apples for plums.

Hungarian Peach Cake: Substitute 10 halves of fresh or canned peaches for plums.

PINK MARBLE CAKE

2 cups sifted cake flour
2½ teaspoons baking powder
¾ teaspoon salt
3 egg whites
¼ cup sugar
½ cup shortening (at room temperature)
1 cup sugar
1 cup minus 2 tablespoons milk
1 teaspoon vanilla
Red food coloring

Measure sifted flour, add baking powder and salt, and sift together three times.

Beat egg whites until foamy; add ¼ cup sugar gradually and continue beating until meringue will hold up in soft peaks.

Cream shortening, add 1 cup sugar gradually, and cream together until light and fluffy. Add flour, alternately with milk, in small amounts, beating after each addition until smooth. Add vanilla and blend. Add meringue and beat thoroughly into batter.

Tint one-third of the batter pink. Use two round 8-inch layer pans, 1¼ inches deep; line bottoms with paper.

Put large spoonfuls of batters into pans, alternating pink and white mixtures. With a knife, cut through batter in a wide zigzag course to marble.

Bake in moderate oven (375°F.) about 25 minutes. Spread with Hungarian chocolate frosting.

LEMONADE BOSTON CREAM CAKE

¾ cup sugar
⅓ cup butter
2 eggs
1 teaspoon frozen concentrate for lemonade
1½ cups sifted cake flour
2 teaspoons baking powder
⅓ teaspoon salt
½ cup milk

Sift sugar. Cream butter and sugar together and beat until they are very light. Beat in eggs one at a time. Add concentrate for lemonade.

Resift flour with baking powder and salt. Add sifted dry ingredients to the batter alternately with the milk.

Line two 8-inch layer cake pans with waxed paper; pour batter in them and bake in moderate oven (375°F.) about 25 minutes. Cool the layers.

Lemonade Filling:

2 tablespoons butter or margarine
¼ cup sugar
3 tablespoons flour
¼ teaspoon salt
¾ cup milk or water
2 egg yolks
3 tablespoons frozen concentrate for lemonade

Melt butter and add sugar, flour, and salt. Stir in milk gradually, and cook over boiling water until thickened.

Add slightly beaten egg yolks, mixed with the concentrate for lemonade, and cook 1 minute longer.

Cool before putting between cake layers. Put cake together and sift powdered sugar over the top.

Lemonade Boston Cream Cake

APPLESAUCE LOAF CAKE

2½ cups sifted enriched flour
¾ teaspoon baking powder
1 teaspoon baking soda
1 teaspoon salt
½ teaspoon cinnamon
¼ teaspoon cloves
½ cup shortening
1 cup sugar
1 teaspoon vanilla
1 egg
1½ cups unsweetened, thick, applesauce
1 cup raisins
1 cup chopped nuts

Sift flour, measure, resift 3 times with baking powder, soda, salt, and spices.

Cream shortening and sugar. Stir in vanilla, then egg; beat well. Stir in applesauce, raisins, and nuts. Fold in flour mixture thoroughly in 4 or 5 portions.

Turn into loaf pan (5¼ x 9¼ inches) lined with thin plain paper. Bake in moderate oven (350°F.) about 1½ hours.

Remove from oven, cool on cake rack 5 minutes, turn out of pan. Invert on rack and cool. Remove paper and spread with creamy vanilla frosting.

WESTERN POUND CAKE

6 tablespoons butter
1 cup sugar
3 eggs, unbeaten
1 cup sour milk
½ teaspoon baking soda
2 cups sifted cake flour
1 teaspoon baking powder
2 teaspoons vanilla
⅓ cup each of nuts, raisins, and candied fruit

Cream butter and sugar thoroughly. Add unbeaten eggs, 1 at a time, beating after each addition.

Sift dry ingredients together. Add milk and dry ingredients alternately to creamed mixture, mixing only until well blended. Add vanilla, fruit, and nuts and mix.

Pour into a greased 5½ x 9½ x 3-inch loaf pan, or in a tube pan 8 or 9 inches in diameter.

Regal Banana Cake

Bake in moderate oven (350°F.) 1 hour. If the loaf should be well browned after 30 minutes of baking cover with brown paper to prevent scorching.

ORANGE GOLD CAKE

2 cups sifted cake flour
2¼ teaspoons baking powder
1 teaspoon salt
½ cup shortening
1 cup sugar
5 egg yolks
1 whole egg
Orange juice
½ cup milk

Sift flour, measure, resift 3 times with baking powder and salt.

Cream shortening and sugar. Stir in lightly beaten egg yolks and whole egg.

Add enough orange juice to milk to make ⅔ cup.

Add flour mixture alternately with liquid to the creamed mixture in 4 or 5 portions, beginning and ending with flour. Beat until smooth after each addition.

Turn into an ungreased cake pan (9 x 9 x 2 inches) lined with thin plain paper on bottom.

Bake in slow oven (325°F.) 50 to 60 minutes. Remove from oven, invert and cool slightly. Remove paper and spread with orange glaze while cake is still warm.

REGAL BANANA CAKE

½ cup shortening
1 cup sugar
3 eggs, separated
1½ cups sifted enriched flour
2 teaspoons baking powder
½ teaspoon baking soda
¾ teaspoon salt
14 graham crackers, finely rolled
1 cup mashed bananas
⅓ cup sour milk
½ cup chopped nuts
1½ cups heavy cream, whipped
Banana slices

Cream shortening and ½ cup sugar; beat in egg yolks.

Sift together flour, baking powder, soda, and salt. Combine with graham cracker crumbs. Stir into creamed mixture alternately with mashed banana and milk.

Beat egg whites until almost stiff. Beat in remaining ½ cup sugar until whites are very stiff and glossy. Fold into cake mixture along with ½ cup chopped nuts. Pour into 3 8-inch greased and lined cake pans.

Bake in moderate oven (350°F.) 35 minutes or until done. Cool 10 minutes; remove from pans.

When thoroughly cooled put layers together with whipped cream and banana slices. Garnish top with chopped nuts if desired.

SPECIAL NUT CAKE

3 cups sifted cake flour
2 teaspoons baking powder
¾ teaspoon salt
1 cup butter (at room temperature)
1¾ cups sugar
3 eggs, unbeaten
1 egg yolk, unbeaten
¾ cup milk
1 teaspoon orange extract
1 teaspoon almond extract
¾ to 1 cup very finely chopped nuts

Measure sifted flour, add baking powder and salt, and sift together three times.

Cream butter, add sugar gradually, and cream together until light and fluffy. Add eggs and yolk; beat well. Then add flour, alternately with milk, in small amounts, beating after each addition until smooth. Add flavorings and nuts; mix well.

Grease and lightly flour a 9-inch tube pan. Pour batter into tube pan.

Bake in moderate oven (375°F.) 1 hour, or until wire cake tester comes out clean and dry.

Cool slightly before removing from pan.

This cake may be baked in two 8 x 4 x 3-inch pans, lined on bottoms with paper, in slow oven (325°F.) about 1 hour.

Serve unfrosted to accompany fruit desserts or ice cream. Or spread with fruit frosting.

BLITZKUCHEN

1⅛ cups sifted cake flour
1 teaspoon baking powder
½ cup butter
1 cup sugar
4 eggs, separated
1 teaspoon grated lemon rind
3 tablespoons milk
1 egg white diluted with 1 tablespoon water
¼ teaspoon salt
¾ cup sugar
2 tablespoons cinnamon
½ cup chopped nuts

Mix and sift flour and baking powder.

Cream butter until soft and smooth. Gradually add sugar, beating until light and fluffy. Add well beaten egg yolks and lemon rind. Gradually add flour, beating well. Add milk and beat again.

Beat egg whites with salt until stiff, but not dry. Gently fold into batter.

Pour into 2 greased pans (8 x 12 inches) and spread with diluted egg white. Sprinkle liberally with combination of sugar, cinnamon, and nuts.

Bake in moderate oven (375°F.) 20 minutes. Serve either hot or cold.

WINE CAKE

1/2 cup butter
1 cup sugar
1 teaspoon baking powder
1 3/4 cups sifted cake flour
6 tablespoons port, muscatel, or to-kay
Juice of 1/2 lemon
4 egg whites
Grated rind of 1 lemon

Cream butter thoroughly, add half the sugar gradually, and beat until light and fluffy.

Sift flour and baking powder together several times and add to creamed mixture alternately with wine and lemon juice. Beat batter until light.

Beat egg whites until light and fold in the remaining half cup of sugar. Beat until sugar is dissolved and meringue will stand in peaks. Fold lightly but thoroughly into batter.

Fill greased loaf pan two-thirds full. Bake in slow oven (325°F.) for 1 hour.

TOMATO SOUP CAKE

2 cups sifted cake flour
1 tablespoon baking powder
1/2 teaspoon baking soda
1/2 teaspoon powdered cloves
1/2 teaspoon cinnamon or mace
1/2 teaspoon nutmeg
1 cup seedless raisins
1/2 cup shortening
1 cup sugar
2 well beaten eggs
1 can (1 1/4 cups) condensed tomato soup

Sift together flour, baking powder, soda, and spices.

Wash and cut raisins. (Roll in a small amount of the flour mixture.)

Cream shortening; add sugar gradually; then eggs, mixing thoroughly. Add flour mixture alternately with soup; stir until smooth. Fold in raisins.

Pour into 2 greased and floured 8-inch layer pans.

Bake in moderate oven (375°F.) about 35 minutes, or until done. Frost as desired.

Tomato Soup Cake

MOLASSES MARBLE CAKE

1/2 cup shortening
1 cup sugar
2 beaten eggs
2 cups sifted cake flour
2 teaspoons baking powder
1/4 teaspoon salt
2/3 cup milk
2 teaspoons allspice
3 tablespoons molasses

Cream shortening. Add sugar gradually and beat until light and fluffy. Add eggs, and cream thoroughly.

Mix and sift flour, baking powder, and salt. Add alternately with the milk to the creamed mixture. Beat after each addition.

Remove 2/3 of batter from bowl. Add allspice and molasses to the remaining batter and beat well.

Drop by tablespoons into greased loaf pan, alternating light and dark mixtures.

Bake in moderate oven (350°F.) 1 hour. Serve plain or frost as desired.

EGGLESS APPLESAUCE CAKE

1/4 teaspoon cloves
1/2 teaspoon nutmeg
1/2 teaspoon cinnamon
1/4 teaspoon salt
2 cups sifted cake flour
1 teaspoon baking soda
1/3 cup shortening
3/4 cup strained honey
1 cup cold applesauce, slightly sweetened
1 cup seedless raisins
1/4 cup broken nutmeats

Sift together dry ingredients.

Cream shortening. Add honey and cream thoroughly. Add applesauce, then sifted dry ingredients. Add raisins and nuts, mixing well.

Pour batter into a greased and floured 8-inch square cake pan. Bake in moderate oven (350°F.) 1 hour.

HUNGARIAN APPLESAUCE CAKE

2 cups sifted cake flour
1 teaspoon baking powder
1/2 teaspoon salt
1/2 cup butter
1 cup sugar
1 teaspoon cinnamon
Grated rind of 1 lemon
1 well beaten egg
1 1/2 cups thick applesauce
1 teaspoon baking soda
1/2 cup seedless raisins
1/2 cup chopped nuts

Mix and sift flour, baking powder, and salt.

Cream together butter, sugar, cinnamon, and lemon rind until soft and smooth. Add egg and beat until fluffy.

Add applesauce, baking soda, raisins, and nuts. Add dry ingredients and mix

well.

Turn into well greased and floured cake pan. Bake in moderate oven (350° F.) 1 1/2 hours.

PUMPKIN CAKE

2 1/4 cups sifted cake flour
3 teaspoons baking powder
1/2 teaspoon salt
1/4 teaspoon baking soda
1 1/2 teaspoons cinnamon
1/2 teaspoon ginger
1/2 teaspoon allspice
1/2 cup butter or other shortening
1 cup firmly packed brown sugar
1/2 cup granulated sugar
1 egg and 2 egg yolks, unbeaten
3/4 cup buttermilk or sour milk
3/4 cup canned pumpkin
1/2 cup finely chopped walnut meats

Measure sifted flour, add baking powder, salt, soda, and spices. Sift together 3 times.

Cream butter, add sugars gradually and cream well. Add egg and egg yolks, one at a time, beating until light. Add flour alternately with buttermilk, in small amounts, beating after each addition until smooth. Add pumpkin and nuts; mix well.

Bake in 2 round 8-inch layer pans, lined on bottoms with paper, in moderate oven (350°F.) 30 to 35 minutes, or until done.

Cool and frost with fluffy frosting, tinted orange. Garnish with small flowers.

GOLD BUTTER CAKE

2 cups sifted cake flour
3 teaspoons baking powder
1/2 teaspoon salt
1/2 cup butter
1 cup sugar
5 egg yolks
1 whole egg, beaten
2/3 cup milk
1 teaspoon vanilla

Sift together flour, baking powder, and salt 3 times.

Cream butter and sugar until light and fluffy. Mix in egg yolks and whole egg. Add dry ingredients alternately with milk and vanilla, beating only until smooth after each addition.

Turn into greased 9-inch square pan. Bake in moderate oven (350°F.) about 45 minutes.

Spread top with chocolate frosting and frost sides with butterscotch nut frosting.

Apricot Gold Butter Cake: Prepare half the recipe for Gold Butter Cake. Line well greased shallow pan with 1 cup drained, cooked, sweetened dried apricots. Pour batter over apricots.

Bake in moderate oven (350°F.) about 35 minutes. Serve hot with apricot sauce.

Conventional Method Chocolate Cakes

STEPS IN MAKING A DELICATE CHOCOLATE CAKE

This picture story for a delicate chocolate cake gives hints that apply to other cakes with shortening.

1. Assemble all ingredients and utensils needed. Have ingredients at room temperature. Measure with standard measuring spoons and cups. Prepare pans before mixing cake.

2. Cream shortening and sugar until smooth and fluffy. (With electric mixer use medium speed.)

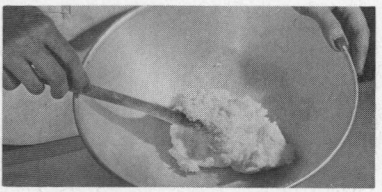

3. Add the beaten eggs, then the melted chocolate. Beat mixture until well blended. (With mixer use medium speed.)

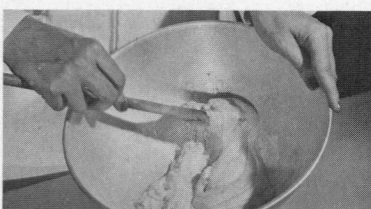

4. Stir in the dry ingredients alternately with liquid in recipe. (With mixer use low speed, adding flour and liquid at the same time.)

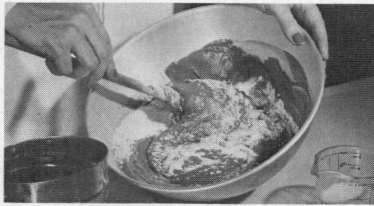

5. Spread the batter evenly over the prepared pans.

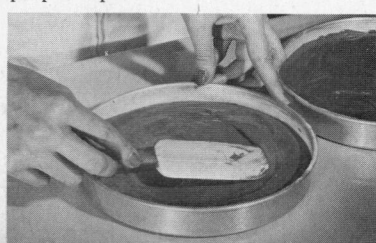

OLD-FASHIONED CHOCOLATE CAKE

½ cup shortening
1 cup granulated sugar
½ cup firmly packed light brown sugar
2 well beaten eggs
1 teaspoon vanilla
3 1-ounce squares chocolate
½ cup hot water
2 cups sifted cake flour
¼ teaspoon salt
1 teaspoon baking soda
⅔ cup buttermilk

Cream shortening; add sugars gradually and cream thoroughly.

Beat eggs well; add vanilla and add to first mixture, beating well.

Melt chocolate in hot water; blend thoroughly and cool slightly. Add to creamed mixture, blending well.

Sift flour with salt and soda; add alternately with buttermilk to creamed mixture. Mix well until smooth.

Turn into 2 9-inch greased layer cake pans Bake in moderate oven (375° F.) 25 to 30 minutes, or until cake springs back to touch of finger.

Cool cake in pans 5 minutes. Remove and cool thoroughly on cake racks. Frost with mocha frosting.

MASTER DEVIL'S FOOD CAKE

¾ cup cocoa
¾ cup brown sugar
1¼ cups milk
½ cup shortening
1 cup granulated sugar
3 eggs
1¼ teaspoons vanilla
2 cups sifted cake flour
1 teaspoon baking powder
1 teaspoon salt
¾ teaspoon baking soda

Mix cocoa with brown sugar. Scald milk over medium heat, add gradually to brown sugar mixture. Beat until smooth. Cool.

Cream shortening. Add granulated sugar gradually, creaming together until light and fluffy. Add eggs 1 at a time, beating after each addition. Add vanilla.

Sift together flour, baking powder, salt, and soda. Add alternately with cocoa mixture to fat-sugar-egg mixture, mixing until smooth.

Pour into greased layer pans. Bake in moderate oven (350° F.) 25 to 30 minutes.

Cool in pans 5 to 10 minutes. Remove from pans and cool on wire rack. Frost with caramel frosting. Sprinkle with chopped nuts.

Old-Fashioned Chocolate Cake

SOUR CREAM DEVIL'S FOOD CAKE

2 cups sifted cake flour
1½ teaspoons baking soda
½ teaspoon salt
⅓ cup butter or other shortening (at room temperature)
1¼ cups sugar
1 egg, unbeaten
3 1-ounce squares unsweetened chocolate, melted
1 teaspoon vanilla
½ cup thick sour cream
1 cup sweet milk

Measure sifted flour, add soda and salt, and sift together three times.

Cream shortening; add sugar gradually, and cream together until light and fluffy. Add egg and beat well. Stir in chocolate and vanilla.

Add ¼ of the flour and blend. Then add sour cream and beat well. Add rest of flour, alternately with milk, beating after each addition until smooth.

Use 2 round 9-inch layer pans, 1½ inches deep; line the bottoms with paper. Pour quickly into pans.

Bake in moderate oven (350° F.) 30 to 35 minutes. Frost with peppermint frosting or easy fudge frosting.

RED DEVIL'S FOOD CAKE

½ cup shortening
1½ cups sugar
½ cup cocoa
2 eggs
2 cups sifted cake flour
½ cup milk
2 teaspoons baking soda
1 cup boiling water
1 teaspoon vanilla

Cream shortening and add sugar and cocoa. Cream thoroughly and then add eggs and beat well.

Add flour alternately with milk in which soda has been dissolved. Add boiling water and vanilla.

Line bottoms of 2 8-inch cake pans with waxed paper. Turn into cake pans.

Bake in moderate oven (350° F.) 30 minutes. Frost as desired.

Feather Devil's Food Cake

FEATHER DEVIL'S FOOD CAKE

1/2 cup shortening
1 cup granulated sugar
1 cup light brown sugar
2 beaten eggs
3 squares (3 ounces) chocolate
1/2 cup hot water
2 1/2 cups sifted cake flour
1/2 teaspoon baking soda
2 teaspoons baking powder
1 teaspoon salt
2/3 cup milk
1 teaspoon vanilla

Cream shortening until soft and smooth. Gradually add sugars, beating until light and fluffy. Beat in eggs.

Melt chocolate in the hot water in top of double boiler, stirring until thick and smooth. Cool slightly. Add to fat-sugar-egg mixture and mix well.

Sift together flour, soda, baking powder, and salt 3 times. Add alternately with milk and vanilla, beating well after each addition.

Turn into 2 greased 9-inch layer pans. Bake in moderate oven (350° F.) 30 to 35 minutes.

Put layers together and cover cake with 7-minute frosting. Garnish with chopped nuts or chocolate shot.

FUDGE NUT CAKE

1/4 cup shortening
1/2 cup sugar
1 egg
1/2 teaspoon vanilla
1 square (1 ounce) bitter chocolate
1 cup sifted cake flour
1 teaspoon baking powder
1/2 teaspoon salt
1/3 cup milk

Cream shortening until light; add sugar gradually and continue creaming until fluffy. Beat in egg and add vanilla.

Melt chocolate over hot water and blend with creamed mixture.

Mix and sift flour, baking powder, and salt; add alternately with milk to creamed mixture.

Pour into well greased glass layer cake dish. Bake in moderate oven (350°F.) about 35 minutes or until

toothpick comes out clean.

Frost with easy fudge frosting and serve directly from baking dish. Serves 10 to 12.

CHOCOLATE HONEY CAKE

3 squares (3 ounces) unsweetened chocolate, melted
2/3 cup honey
1 3/4 cups sifted cake flour
1 teaspoon baking soda
3/4 teaspoon salt
1/2 cup butter or other shortening
1/2 cup sugar
1 teaspoon vanilla
2 eggs, unbeaten
2/3 cup water

Blend melted chocolate and honey.

Sift flour once, measure, add soda and salt, and sift together 3 times.

Cream butter until soft. Add sugar gradually, creaming until light and fluffy. Add chocolate-honey mixture and vanilla. Mix well.

Add eggs, one at a time, beating thoroughly after each addition.

Add flour, alternately with water, a small amount at a time, beating after each addition until smooth.

Bake in 2 greased 8-inch layer pans in moderate oven (350° F.) 30 to 35 minutes. Spread with chocolate honey frosting.

POTATO CHOCOLATE CAKE

1 cup hot unseasoned mashed potatoes
2 cups sugar
2/3 cup shortening
4 eggs, unbeaten
1 teaspoon vanilla
2 cups sifted all-purpose flour
1/2 cup cocoa
3 teaspoons baking powder
1 teaspoon each cinnamon and nutmeg
1/2 teaspoon salt
1/2 cup milk
1 cup chopped walnuts

Line bottoms of 2 9-inch layer pans or a 13 x 9 x 2-inch oblong pan with waxed paper cut to fit.

Prepare mashed potatoes. (Easy way: follow directions for 2 servings on packaged mashed potatoes.) Measure; set aside.

Gradually beat sugar into shortening until fluffy. Add eggs 1 at a time, beating well. Add vanilla and potatoes. Add sifted dry ingredients and milk alternately, about 1/4 of each at a time, beating smooth. Stir in walnuts.

Bake in moderate oven (350°F.), layers 40 to 45 minutes, loaf about 50 minutes, or until done when tested.

Let stand 5 minutes. Turn out on racks, peel off paper. When cool, frost with butter cream or other frosting and sprinkle thickly with walnuts.

CHOCOLATE CAKE
(Master Recipe)

2 cups sifted cake flour
3 teaspoons baking powder
1/4 teaspoon salt
1/2 teaspoon baking soda
1/2 cup butter or other shortening
1 cup sugar
2 eggs, separated
3 ounces (3 squares) melted chocolate
1 1/4 cups milk
1 teaspoon vanilla

Sift flour once before measuring, then sift 3 times with baking powder, salt, and soda.

Cream butter until soft and smooth. Gradually add sugar, creaming until light and fluffy. Add beaten egg yolks. Then add melted chocolate.

Add milk alternately with dry ingredients, beating until smooth after each addition.

Continue beating for two minutes (about 300 strokes). Fold in flavoring and stiffly beaten egg whites. Turn into lightly greased pans.

Bake layers in 2 9-inch pans, in moderate oven (375°F.) 30 minutes or bake in loaf pan (8 x 8 x 2 inches) in moderate oven (350°F.) 50 to 60 minutes.

Turn out on cake rack to cool. Ice with chocolate frosting.

Variations of Master Chocolate Cake

Chocolate Almond Cake: Prepare chocolate layers. Prepare chocolate seven-minute frosting. Add chopped almonds to 1/3 of frosting. Spread between layers. Decorate top with almonds.

Chocolate Cream Cake: Prepare chocolate layers. Spread cream filling between layers. Spread boiled frosting on top and sides of cake.

Chocolate Maple Cake: Prepare chocolate layers. Spread maple walnut frosting between layers and on top of cake. Decorate with walnut halves.

Chocolate Marshmallow Cake: Bake cake in a loaf pan (8 x 8 x 2 inches). While still warm, place over the top, marshmallows cut in half and rinsed in cold water. Let cool. Cover with chocolate butter frosting.

Potato Chocolate Cake

OLD-TIME FUDGE CAKE

3 1-ounce squares unsweetened chocolate, melted
½ cup milk
1 well beaten egg
⅔ cup sugar
½ cup shortening
1 cup sugar
1 teaspoon vanilla
2 eggs
2 cups sifted cake flour
1 teaspoon baking soda
¼ teaspoon salt
⅔ cup milk

Combine chocolate, ½ cup milk, well beaten egg, and ⅔ cup sugar in saucepan; cook over low heat until thickened, stirring constantly. Cool.

Stir shortening to soften. Gradually add 1 cup sugar, and cream together until light and fluffy. Add vanilla.

Add remaining eggs, 1 at a time, beating well after each.

Sift flour, soda, and salt together 3 times.

Add flour mixture to creamed mixture alternately with ⅔ cup milk, a small amount at a time.

Beat after each addition until smooth. Blend in chocolate mixture.

Bake in 2 paper-lined 9 x 1½-inch round pans in moderate oven (350° F.) 25 to 30 minutes.

Frost with chocolate frosting. Garnish with walnut halves.

CHOCOLATE MARASCHINO CAKE

½ cup shortening
1 cup sugar
1 square (1 ounce) chocolate, melted
1 beaten egg
1¾ cups sifted cake flour
1 teaspoon baking soda
½ teaspoon salt
1 cup liquid (use juice from 3-ounce bottle of maraschino cherries plus buttermilk or sour milk to make 1 cup)
Maraschino cherries from 3-ounce bottle, cut in small pieces
½ cup chopped nuts

Cream shortening. Gradually add sugar, and cream until light and fluffy. Add melted chocolate and egg. Blend well.

Mix and sift flour, soda, and salt, and add alternately with liquid. Stir in cherries and nuts.

Turn into a greased loaf pan (8 x 8 x 2 inches). Bake in moderate oven (350° F) 30 to 35 minutes. Frost with 7-minute frosting.

STARLIGHT DOUBLE-DELIGHT CAKE

Chocolate Frosting:

2 3-ounce packages cream cheese
½ cup shortening
½ teaspoon vanilla
½ teaspoon mint flavoring
6 cups (about 1½ pounds) sifted confectioners' sugar
¼ cup hot water
4 squares (4 ounces) unsweetened chocolate, melted

Cream the cream cheese, shortening, vanilla, and mint flavoring or 2 to 3 drops oil of peppermint. Blend well. (If desired, mint flavoring may be omitted and vanilla increased to 1 teaspoon).

Measure and blend half of sugar into creamed cheese mixture. Add water alternately with balance of sugar.

Blend in chocolate. Mix until smooth.

Cake:

¼ cup shortening
3 eggs, unbeaten
2¼ cups sifted enriched flour
1½ teaspoons baking soda
1 teaspoon salt
¾ cup milk

Combine shortening and 2 cups of the chocolate frosting mixture; mix thoroughly.

Blend in the eggs, one at a time. Beat for 1 minute.

Sift together flour, soda, and salt. Add milk alternately with the dry ingredients to creamed mixture, beginning and ending with dry ingredients. Blend thoroughly after each addition. (With electric mixer use a low speed).

Pour mixture into two 9-inch round layer pans, well greased and lightly floured on the bottoms only.

Bake in moderate oven (350°F.) 30 to 40 minutes. Cool; frost with remaining chocolate frosting.

FUDGE NUT LOAF CAKE

½ cup shortening
2 cups sugar
1¼ teaspoons salt
2 teaspoons vanilla
2 eggs
4 squares (4 ounces) chocolate
2 cups sifted cake flour
2 teaspoons baking powder
1½ cups milk
1 cup chopped nuts

Cream shortening. Add sugar, salt, and vanilla. Cream until fluffy. Add eggs, one at a time, beating well after each addition.

Melt chocolate and add to creamed mixture. Beat until well combined.

Mix and sift flour and baking pow-

Starlight Double-Delight Cake

der. Add alternately with milk, adding flour first and last. Add nuts, and mix until thoroughly blended.

Grease bottom of cake pan (13 x 9 x 1½ inches). Dust lightly with flour. Turn batter into pan.

Bake in moderate oven (350° F.) 40 minutes. Cool and frost with chocolate nut frosting.

Fudge Nut Layer Cake: Bake in 2 8-inch layer pans in moderate oven (375° F.) 25 to 30 minutes. Cool and spread a custard filling between layers. Frost as above.

CHOCOLATE PEPPERMINT CAKE

⅔ cup shortening
1¼ cups sugar
2 eggs
1 teaspoon vanilla
2 cups sifted cake flour
2½ teaspoons baking powder
¼ teaspoon baking soda
1 teaspoon salt
½ cup cocoa
½ cup evaporated milk diluted with ½ cup water
2 drops oil of peppermint

Cream shortening and sugar. Beat eggs slightly with vanilla and add.

Sift dry ingredients together. Add alternately with diluted evaporated milk to first mixture. Beat well. Add oil of peppermint.

Bake in 2 greased 8-inch cake pans in moderate oven (350° to 375°F.) about 30 to 40 minutes.

Frost with pink icing; decorate with crushed peppermint. Serves 8 to 10.

Chocolate Peppermint Cake

Gingerbreads

GINGERBREAD
(Master Recipe)

2 cups sifted enriched flour
1 teaspoon ground ginger
¾ teaspoon baking soda
¾ teaspoon cinnamon
¼ teaspoon ground cloves
1 teaspoon salt
¼ cup shortening
¼ cup sugar
1 egg
¾ cup molasses
¾ cup milk

Sift together dry ingredients. Cream shortening. Gradually add sugar, beating until light and fluffy. Add egg and beat well. Stir molasses into the milk.

Add dry ingredients alternately with molasses mixture, beating thoroughly.

Turn into greased layer or loaf pans or in muffin pans.

Bake in moderate oven (350°F.) 30 to 40 minutes for layers, 35 to 45 minutes for loaf, and 20 to 25 minutes for cupcakes. Makes 2 8-inch layers or 1 large loaf or 1½ dozen cupcakes.

Ginger Nut or Raisin Cake: In master recipe stir in one cup of nuts or raisins.

Ginger Orange Cake: In master recipe replace milk with orange juice and add 1 tablespoon grated orange rind to creamed shortening and sugar.

Gingerbread Washington Pie: Prepare the recipe for Gingerbread and bake in well greased pie plate. When cool, split in two. Make half the recipe of Cornstarch Pudding (see index). Cool. Spread between layers. Sprinkle top layer with powdered sugar.

Gingerbread Upside-Down Cake: Melt 2 tablespoons butter in 9-inch-square cake pan. Add ¼ cup molasses. Arrange 1 cup sliced fruit in decorative pattern in the pan. Pour 1 recipe of Gingerbread over fruit.

Bake in moderate oven (350°F.) 45 minutes to 1 hour. Turn out upside-down.

WHITE HOUSE GINGERBREAD

2½ cups sifted enriched flour
1 teaspoon salt
1 teaspoon ginger
2 teaspoons cinnamon
½ teaspoon nutmeg (optional)
½ teaspoon cloves
½ cup lard
½ cup sugar
1½ teaspoons baking soda
1 cup unsulphured molasses
2 eggs, unbeaten
1 cup sour milk

Mix and sift flour, salt, and spices. Cream together the lard, sugar, and soda until fluffy. Add molasses to lard-sugar mixture, then stir ½ cup of the dry ingredients into this mixture.

Add eggs, one at a time, beating well after each addition. Then add sour milk and remaining dry ingredients alternately, beating after each addition.

Pour batter into a well buttered and lightly floured pan (9 x 9 x 2 inches or 8 x 12 x 2 inches). Bake in moderate oven (350°F.) until done, 45 minutes. **Note:** Gingerbread—the moist, rich kind, made with sour milk, has been a White House favorite.

ORANGE GINGERBREAD

½ cup butter
1 cup orange marmalade
½ cup molasses
½ teaspoon salt
2 cups sifted enriched flour
1 teaspoon ginger
1 teaspoon cinnamon
½ teaspoon nutmeg
¼ teaspoon cloves
2 eggs
1 teaspoon baking soda
1 tablespoon hot water

Cream butter; add orange marmalade and molasses. Mix well.

Sift salt, flour, and spices together and fold into first mixture. Add unbeaten eggs, one at a time.

Dissolve soda in hot water and add to all. Mix thoroughly.

Turn into well greased 8-inch square pan. Bake in moderate oven (350°F.) 30 minutes. Serve warm.

HOT WATER GINGERBREAD

2½ cups sifted enriched flour
1 teaspoon salt
1 teaspoon baking powder
1 teaspoon ginger
2 teaspoons cinnamon
½ teaspoon cloves
½ cup shortening
½ cup sugar
¾ teaspoon baking soda
1 cup unsulphured molasses
2 eggs
1 cup hot water

Sift together flour, salt, baking powder, ginger, cinnamon, and cloves.

Cream shortening, sugar, and soda. Add unsulphured molasses. Stir in ½ cup flour mixture. Beat in eggs. Add hot water alternately with remaining flour mixture. Beat ½ minute.

Turn into 12 well greased 2¾-inch muffin pans and 12 2¼-inch muffin pans.

Bake in a moderate oven (350°F.) 20 minutes.

For gingerbread layer, turn batter into a well greased, lightly floured 9 x 9 x 2-inch pan.

Bake in a moderate oven (350°F.) 45 minutes.

Gingerbread is an adaptable type of cake which can be presented in many ways.

FLUFFY BRAN GINGERBREAD

⅓ cup shortening
⅓ cup sugar
⅓ cup molasses
1 egg
⅔ cup whole bran
1¼ cups sifted enriched flour
1 teaspoon baking powder
½ teaspoon baking soda
½ teaspoon salt
¾ teaspoon ginger
½ teaspoon cinnamon
¾ cup boiling water

Beat shortening until creamy; add sugar slowly and beat until light and fluffy.

Stir in molasses and add unbeaten egg; beat mixture thoroughly. Add bran and let stand 5 minutes.

Sift together all dry ingredients; add to bran mixture and blend thoroughly. Add boiling water and beat until smooth.

Pour out into well greased 9-inch pie plate and bake in moderate oven (350°F.) about 30 minutes. Serve warm. Serves 6 to 8.

MAPLE SYRUP GINGERBREAD

1 egg, beaten
1 cup maple syrup
1 cup sour cream
2⅓ cups sifted enriched flour
1 teaspoon baking soda
2 teaspoons ginger
½ teaspoon salt
4 tablespoons melted butter

Combine egg, maple syrup, and sour cream. Sift together twice the flour, baking soda, ginger, and salt.

Stir the liquid ingredients into the sifted dry ingredients, beating well until smooth.

Add the melted butter and beat thoroughly. Pour into a buttered oblong pan.

Bake in moderate oven (350°F.) for 30 minutes. Cool on cake rack and frost with maple frosting.

One-Bowl Cakes

ONE-BOWL MIXING METHOD

Complete mixing directions are given in each recipe; however some homemakers frequently find a step-by-step chart such as the following useful.

Use special recipes (called "easy-mix," "pastry-blend," or "quick-method") for one-bowl cakes. Attempts to adapt conventional cake recipes to the one-bowl method may bring you poor results.

1. Sift flour once, measure by piling lightly in measuring cup and leveling off with knife or spatula. Sift together with dry ingredients into mixing bowl.

2. Softened hydrogenated vegetable shortening must be used with this method. Stir the shortening to soften, then add with two-thirds of the liquid in the recipe (if enriched flour is used, add all the liquid).

3. Beat at medium speed in electric mixer for 2 minutes, scraping down the batter in the bowl constantly or beat with a spoon for 2 minutes (150 strokes are equal to 1 minute of beating by mixer).

4. Add remaining liquid and unbeaten eggs (yolks or whites). Beat 2 minutes more (scraping bowl frequently in electric mixer).

5. Turn into prepared pans.

SPICE CAKE

2 cups sifted enriched flour
3 teaspoons baking powder
1 teaspoon salt
1 teaspoon cinnamon
1 teaspoon allspice
1 teaspoon cloves
1/2 teaspoon nutmeg
1 cup granulated sugar
1/3 cup firmly packed brown sugar
1/2 cup vegetable shortening
3/4 cup plus 2 tablespoons milk
2 eggs, unbeaten
1 teaspoon vanilla

Mix and sift flour, baking powder, salt, cinnamon, allspice, cloves, nutmeg, and granulated sugar.

Add sieved brown sugar, shortening, and 3/4 cup milk. Beat for 2 minutes, 300 strokes, until batter is well blended. (With electric mixer blend at low speed, then beat at medium speed for 2 minutes.)

Add remaining 2 tablespoons milk, eggs, and vanilla. Beat for 2 minutes.

Pour batter into 2 well greased and floured 8-inch layer cake pans, at least 1 1/4 inches deep.

Bake in moderate oven (350° F.) 30 to 35 minutes. Cool and frost with banana frosting.

BANANA LAYER CAKE

2 1/4 cups sifted cake flour
1 1/4 cups sugar
2 1/2 teaspoons baking powder
1/2 teaspoon baking soda
1/2 teaspoon salt
1/2 cup vegetable shortening
1 1/2 cups mashed ripe bananas
2 eggs, unbeaten
1 teaspoon vanilla

Sift together flour, sugar, baking powder, soda, and salt into large mixing bowl.

Add shortening, 1/2 cup of bananas, and eggs. Beat 2 minutes at slow to medium speed with electric mixer or 2 minutes by hand. Scrape down bowl and beater or spoon frequently during mixing.

Add remaining 1 cup bananas and vanilla. Beat 1 minute longer scraping down bowl and beater or spoon frequently during mixing.

Turn into 2 well greased, 8-inch layer cake pans. Bake in moderate oven (375° F.) about 25 minutes, or until layers are done.

Frost with your favorite frosting; any flavor blends well with banana cake.

Variations:

Banana Spice Layer Cake: Sift together with the dry ingredients 1/8 teaspoon ground cloves, 1 1/4 teaspoons cinnamon, and 1/2 teaspoon nutmeg.

Banana Cupcakes: Turn batter into well greased cupcake pans. Bake in moderate oven (375° F.) about 25 minutes or until cupcakes are done. Makes 18 to 20 cupcakes.

DEVIL'S FOOD CAKE

2 cups sifted cake flour
1 teaspoon baking soda
3/4 teaspoon salt
1 1/3 cups sugar
1/2 cup vegetable shortening
1 cup milk
1 teaspoon vanilla
2 eggs, unbeaten
3 1-ounce squares chocolate, melted

Mix and sift flour, soda, salt, and sugar.

Cream shortening until soft. Add sifted dry ingredients and 3/4 cup milk. Mix until all flour is dampened, then beat 2 minutes with medium speed of mixer.

Add vanilla, eggs, melted chocolate, and remaining milk. Beat 1 minute longer. If mixed by hand beat the same length of time, allowing 150 strokes per minute.

Bake in moderate oven (350° F.) 30 minutes in 2 9-inch layer pans or 40 minutes in 13 x 9 x 2-inch pan.

Banana Layer Cake

GOLDEN CAKE

1/2 cup vegetable shortening
2 1/2 cups sifted cake flour
1 1/2 cups sugar
4 teaspoons baking powder
1 teaspoon salt
1 cup milk
1 teaspoon vanilla
4 egg whites, unbeaten, or 2 whole eggs

Place shortening in bowl. Mix and sift flour, sugar, baking powder, and salt. Add to shortening.

Add 2/3 cup milk and the vanilla. Beat all together for 2 minutes with medium speed of electric mixer or 300 strokes by hand (150 strokes per minute).

With rubber scraper keep batter scraped from sides and bottom of mixing bowl throughout the mixing. Scrape bowl and beaters thoroughly.

Add whole eggs or egg whites and 1/3 cup milk. Beat again for 2 minutes. Scrape bowl and beaters.

Turn into 2 9-inch round pans each of which has been fitted with two circles of heavy waxed paper.

Bake in moderate oven (375° F.) about 25 minutes.

Cool on rack 5 minutes. Use end of knife to loosen sides of cake from pan. Turn out on rack to cool. Frost with golden cream frosting. Top with pecans.

BLUEBERRY CAKE

1/3 cup vegetable shortening
2 cups sifted enriched flour
2 teaspoons baking powder
1/4 teaspoon salt
1 cup sugar
3/4 cup milk
1 egg, unbeaten
1 cup blueberries

Stir shortening to soften. Sift dry ingredients together and add. Stir in milk. Beat vigorously 2 minutes.

Add egg. Beat 1 minute. Stir in blueberries.

Turn into greased 8 x 8 x 2-inch pan. Bake in moderate oven (350° F.) about 50 minutes. Serve warm with whipped cream.

LEMON CLOUD CAKE

2 cups sifted all-purpose flour
1½ cups sugar
⅓ cup instant nonfat dry milk
2½ teaspoons baking powder
½ teaspoon salt
½ cup soft butter or margarine
1 cup water
1 tablespoon grated lemon rind
3 egg whites, unbeaten
Lemon Cream Filling (below)

Sift flour, sugar, nonfat dry milk, baking powder, and salt into a 3-quart bowl. Add butter or margarine, water, and lemon rind. Beat 2 minutes at medium speed. Add egg whites and beat 2 minutes more.

Pour batter into 2 greased and floured 8-inch round pans.

Bake near center of moderate oven (350°F.) 30 to 40 minutes or until cake springs back when touched lightly with finger.

Cool thoroughly. Spread lemon cream filling between layers and on top to within ½-inch of edge of cake. Frost sides and top edge with seven minute frosting mix, prepared according to package directions. Sprinkle 1 cup finely-cut coconut over seven minute frosting.

Lemon Cream Filling:

⅔ cup instant nonfat dry milk
2 tablespoons cornstarch
½ cup sugar
1¼ cups water
3 egg yolks, slightly beaten
1 tablespoon grated lemon rind
¼ cup lemon juice
2 tablespoons soft butter or margarine

Mix nonfat dry milk, cornstarch, and sugar in a 2-quart saucepan. Stir in gradually until smooth a mixture of water and egg yolks.

Cook and stir constantly over medium heat until mixture is thick and just begins to bubble. Lower heat and cook and stir 2 minutes more.

Remove from heat and stir in lemon rind, lemon juice, and butter or margarine until smooth. Cool thoroughly before spreading on Lemon Cloud Cake.

Lemon Cloud Cake

ORANGE LOAF CAKE

2 cups sifted cake flour
1¼ cups sugar
1½ teaspoons baking powder
1 teaspoon salt
½ cup vegetable shortening
½ cup orange juice
1 tablespoon grated orange rind
½ to ⅔ cup eggs, unbeaten

Mix and sift flour, sugar, baking powder, and salt into mixing bowl. Add shortening, orange juice, and orange rind. Beat 2 minutes at slow speed, or 300 strokes by hand.

Add eggs and again beat 2 minutes at low speed, or 300 strokes by hand.

Turn into greased loaf baking pan (5 x 9¼ x 2¾ inches). Bake in slow oven (325° F.) 1½ hours.

WHITE LAYER CAKE
(Master Recipe)

2 cups sifted cake flour
1⅓ cups sugar
1 teaspoon salt
½ cup vegetable shortening
1 cup milk
1 teaspoon vanilla
3½ teaspoons baking powder
4 egg whites, unbeaten

Sift flour, sugar, and salt into mixing bowl or bowl of electric mixer.

Add shortening, which is at room temperature, ⅔ of milk to which vanilla has been added.

Beat 150 strokes, scraping bowl and spoon frequently. (Or beat 2 minutes on No. 2 speed of electric mixer.) Add baking powder and beat a few seconds.

Add egg whites and remaining milk. Beat 300 strokes. (Or 2 minutes on No. 2 speed of electric mixer.)

Scrape sides of bowl and spoon frequently during beating process.

Bake in 2 well greased, floured 9-inch layer pans in moderate oven (350° F.) 30 minutes.

Variations:

Cupcakes: Fill pans ½ full. Bake in moderate oven (350° F.) 15 to 18 minutes.

Chocolate Cake: Omit ¼ cup of flour. Add ½ cup cocoa to dry ingredients before sifting.

Orange Cake: Spread orange confectioners' frosting between layers and on top.

Spice Cake: Omit vanilla. Add and sift with flour 1 teaspoon nutmeg, ½ teaspoon cinnamon, and ¼ teaspoon cloves.

Coconut Berry Cake: Spread a tart berry jelly between layers and on top. Sprinkle with shredded coconut.

Coconut Fluff Cake

COCONUT FLUFF CAKE

2¼ cups sifted cake flour
4½ teaspoons baking powder
1½ teaspoons salt
1¾ cups sugar
¾ cup vegetable shortening
1⅛ cups milk
1 teaspoon vanilla
1 teaspoon almond extract
⅔ cup egg whites, unbeaten

Mix and sift flour, baking powder, salt, and sugar. Add shortening and milk. Beat for 2 minutes until batter is well blended and glossy.

If electric mixer is used, beat at low to medium speed for same period of time. Add vanilla, almond extract, and egg whites. Beat 2 minutes.

Pour into 2 slightly greased, floured, 8-inch square layer cake pans or 9-inch round layer cake pans. Bake in moderate oven (350° F.) 35 to 40 minutes.

Frost with fluffy white frosting. Cover with coconut.

Loaf Cake: Turn batter into lightly greased, floured loaf pan. Bake in moderate oven (350° F.) 40 to 45 minutes.

CHOCOLATE ICICLE CAKE

1¾ cups sifted cake flour
3 teaspoons baking powder
1 teaspoon salt
1¼ cups sugar
½ cup cocoa
⅔ cup vegetable shortening
1 cup milk
2 eggs, unbeaten
1 teaspoon vanilla

Sift together flour, baking powder, salt, sugar, and cocoa. Add shortening and ⅔ cup milk. Beat for 2 minutes until batter is well blended and glossy.

If electric mixer is used, beat at low to medium speed for same period of time.

Add ⅓ cup milk, eggs, and vanilla. Beat 2 minutes.

Pour into 2 lightly greased, floured, 8-inch layer cake pans. Bake in moderate oven (350° F.) 30 to 35 minutes.

Frost cooled layers with fluffy cooked frosting. Decorate edges with melted chocolate, letting the chocolate run down the sides to form "icicles."

ORANGE KISS-ME CAKE

1   large orange
1   cup seedless raisins
1/3   cup walnuts
2   cups sifted enriched flour
1   teaspoon baking soda
1   teaspoon salt
1   cup sugar
1/2   cup vegetable shortening
3/4   cup milk
2   eggs, unbeaten
1/4   cup milk

Grind together pulp and rind of orange (reserve juice for topping), raisins, and walnuts, using coarse blade of food chopper.

Sift together flour, soda, salt, and sugar. Add shortening and 3/4 cup milk. Beat for 1 1/2 minutes, 150 strokes per minute, until batter is well blended. (With electric mixer blend at low speed, then beat at medium speed for 1 1/2 minutes.)

Add eggs and 1/4 cup milk. Beat for 1 1/2 minutes. Fold orange-raisin mixture into batter.

Pour into 12 x 8 x 2 or 13 x 9 x 2-inch pan, well greased and lightly floured on the bottom only.

Bake in moderate oven (350° F.) 40 to 50 minutes.

Note: Cake may be baked in two 8- or 9-inch round layer pans at 350° F. for 35 to 40 minutes.

Orange-Nut Topping:

1/3   cup orange juice
1/3   cup sugar
1   teaspoon cinnamon
1/4   cup chopped walnuts

Drip orange juice over warm cake.

Combine sugar, cinnamon, and walnuts; sprinkle over cake. Decorate with orange slices, if desired.

LADY BALTIMORE CAKE

1 3/4   cups sifted enriched flour
3   teaspoons baking powder
1   teaspoon salt
1 1/4   cups sugar
1/2   cup vegetable shortening
3/4   cup milk
3   egg whites, unbeaten
1   teaspoon vanilla

Mix and sift flour, baking powder, salt, and sugar.

Add shortening and 1/2 cup milk. Beat for 2 minutes, 300 strokes, until batter is well blended. (With electric mixer blend at low speed, then beat at medium speed for 2 minutes.)

Add remaining milk, egg whites, and vanilla. Beat for 2 minutes.

Turn batter into 2 well greased and floured 8-inch layer pans, at least 1 1/4 inches deep.

Bake in moderate oven (350° F.) 25 to 30 minutes. Cool and frost with Lady Baltimore frosting.

Orange Kiss-Me Cake

PINEAPPLE LAYER CAKE

2   cups sifted cake flour
1 1/2   cups sugar
3 1/2   teaspoons baking powder
1   teaspoon salt
1   teaspoon grated lemon rind
1/2   cup vegetable shortening
1   cup less 2 tablespoons canned
        pineapple juice
1   teaspoon vanilla
3   egg whites, unbeaten
Pineapple filling
1   cup whipping cream, whipped

Mix and sift flour, 1 1/4 cups sugar, baking powder, and salt. Add lemon rind, shortening, pineapple juice, and vanilla.

Beat all together 200 strokes (2 minutes by hand or with mixer at low speed). Scrape bowl and spoon or beater.

Add egg whites and beat 200 strokes (2 minutes by hand or with mixer at low speed).

Turn into 2 square greased pans (8 x 8 x 2 inches). Bake in moderate oven (350° F.) 25 to 30 minutes.

Chill layers and split in half. Sweeten whipped cream with 1/4 cup sugar. Spread pineapple filling and sweetened whipped cream between layers. Cover top with whipped cream.

Garnish corners with bits of pineapple. Chill cake several hours in refrigerator before serving, and keep in refrigerator until used up.

SMALL LEMON CAKE

1 1/4   cups sifted cake flour
3/4   cup sugar
2   teaspoons baking powder
1/2   teaspoon salt
1   teaspoon grated lemon rind
1/3   cup vegetable shortening
1/2   cup milk
1   teaspoon vanilla
1   egg, unbeaten

Mix and sift flour, sugar, baking powder, and salt into mixing bowl. Add lemon rind. Drop in shortening.

Add milk and vanilla and beat 150 strokes (1 1/2 minutes by hand or on mixer at low speed). Scrape bowl and spoon or beater. Add egg and again beat 150 strokes.

Bake in 8 x 8 x 2-inch greased pan in moderate oven (375° F.) 25 to 35 minutes. Cool. Spread with lemon frosting.

ORANGE CAKE

1/4   teaspoon grated orange rind
1/2   cup strained orange juice
2 1/4   cups sifted cake flour
3   teaspoons baking powder
1   teaspoon salt
1 1/4   cups sugar
1/2   cup vegetable shortening
1/2   cup milk
2   eggs, unbeaten

Steep orange rind in orange juice for 5 minutes and strain. Discard rind.

Sift flour, measure, resift 3 times with baking powder, salt, and sugar, the last time into bowl.

Add shortening and stir with spoon enough to distribute evenly. Combine orange juice and milk; add 2/3 cup to flour mixture.

Beat 2 minutes in electric mixer at low speed or by hand. (While beating by hand, if necessary to rest, count beating time only.) When using electric mixer, scrape bowl frequently and scrape beaters at the end of the 2 minutes.

Add remaining milk and eggs; beat 1 minute.

Pour into 2 ungreased 8-inch layer cake pans lined with thin plain paper on bottoms. Bake in moderate oven (375° F.) about 25 minutes.

Remove from oven and cool 5 minutes. Turn out of pans and cool. Remove paper and spread with 7-minute or creamy vanilla frosting and sprinkle with coconut.

FUDGE CAKE

3 squares (3 ounces) chocolate
1/4 cup boiling water
2 cups sifted cake flour
1 teaspoon baking soda
1 teaspoon salt
1 1/4 cups sugar
1/3 cup melted vegetable shortening
1 cup sour cream
2 eggs, unbeaten
1 teaspoon vanilla

Melt chocolate in water, stirring until well blended and thick.

Sift together flour, soda, salt, and sugar. Add shortening and sour cream. Beat for 2 minutes, or until batter is well blended and glossy.

If electric mixer is used, beat at low to medium speed for same period of time.

Add cooled chocolate mixture, eggs, and vanilla. Beat for 2 minutes.

Pour into 2 lightly greased, floured, 8-inch layer cake pans. Bake in moderate oven (350° F.) for 35 to 40 minutes. When cool, frost with creamy chocolate frosting.

Note: Sweet cream may be substituted for sour cream but add 1 tablespoon lemon juice.

EASY CHOCOLATE CAKE

2 1-ounce squares chocolate
1 1/3 cups sifted enriched flour
1 cup sugar
1 teaspoon baking soda
1/2 teaspoon salt
1/4 cup vegetable shortening
1 cup buttermilk or sour milk
1 egg, unbeaten
1 teaspoon vanilla

Melt chocolate and cool.

Mix and sift flour and sugar. Add soda, salt, shortening, buttermilk, egg, vanilla, and cooled chocolate in large bowl.

Beat with rotary beater for 3 minutes. (With electric mixer blend at low speed, then beat at medium speed for 3 minutes.)

Turn batter into greased and floured 9 x 9 x 2-inch pan. Bake in moderate oven (350° F.) 40 to 45 minutes.

Serve warm topped with whipped cream or frost as desired.

HURRY-UP LOAF CAKE

2 1/4 cups sifted cake flour
2 1/4 teaspoons baking powder
1/2 teaspoon salt
1 cup sugar
1/3 cup softened shortening
1 cup milk
1 teaspoon vanilla

Sift flour once. Measure. Add baking powder, salt, and sugar and sift together 3 times.

Add shortening, milk, and vanilla. Mix only enough to dampen all flour, then beat vigorously about 1 minute.

Turn into greased, lined loaf pan (8 x 8 x 2 inches.) Bake in moderate oven (375° F.) until done, about 40 minutes.

PENUCHE LAYER CAKE

2 1/4 cups sifted cake flour
1 1/2 cups sugar
2 1/2 teaspoons baking powder
1 teaspoon salt
3/4 cup vegetable shortening
3/4 cup milk
1 teaspoon orange extract
1/2 teaspoon almond extract
3 eggs, unbeaten

Mix and sift flour, sugar, baking powder, and salt into mixing bowl. Drop in shortening.

Add 1/2 cup milk, flavoring extracts, and 1 egg and beat 200 strokes (2 minutes by hand or on mixer at low speed). Scrape bowl and spoon or beater.

Add remaining milk and 2 eggs and beat 200 strokes.

Turn into 2 deep 9-inch greased layer pans. Bake in moderate oven (375° F.) 25 to 30 minutes.

Spread penuche pecan frosting between layers and on top and sides.

GINGER CAKE

2 cups sifted cake flour
1 3/4 teaspoons baking powder
1/4 teaspoon baking soda
1 teaspoon salt
1 cup sugar
1 1/2 teaspoons ginger
1 teaspoon cinnamon
1/2 cup vegetable shortening
1/4 cup molasses
3/4 cup plus 1 tablespoon milk
2 eggs, unbeaten

Sift flour, measure, resift 3 times with baking powder, soda, salt, sugar, ginger, and cinnamon, the last time into bowl. Add shortening, molasses, and 1/2 cup milk. Stir with spoon until all flour is dampened.

Beat 2 minutes in electric mixer at low speed or by hand. (While beating by hand, if necessary to rest, count beating time only.) When using electric mixer, scrape bowl frequently, and scrape beaters at end of 2 minutes.

Add eggs and remaining milk; beat 1 minute longer.

Pour batter into 2 greased 8-inch layer pans lined with thin plain paper on bottoms. Bake in moderate oven (350° F.) about 25 to 30 minutes.

Remove from oven and cool on cake racks 5 minutes. Turn out of pans, invert and cool. Remove paper. Spread with lemon frosting.

PRUNE WHIP SPICE CAKE

2 1/4 cups sifted enriched flour
1 1/3 cups sugar
2 teaspoons baking powder
1/4 teaspoon baking soda
1 teaspoon salt
1/2 teaspoon cinnamon
1/4 teaspoon nutmeg
1/4 teaspoon allspice
1/2 cup shortening
1/2 cup prune juice
1/2 cup milk
2 eggs, unbeaten
1 teaspoon vanilla

Sift together flour, sugar, baking powder, soda, salt, cinnamon, nutmeg, and allspice into large bowl.

Add shortening, prune juice, and milk. Beat for 1 1/2 minutes. (With electric mixer, blend at a low speed, then beat at medium speed. By hand, beat with a spoon 150 strokes per minute).

Add eggs and vanilla. Beat for 1 1/2 minutes.

Turn batter into pans (see sizes below), well greased and lightly floured on the bottoms only.

Bake in moderate oven (375° F.). For two 8-inch round pans, 25 to 30 minutes; two 9-inch round pans, 20 to 25 minutes; 13 x 9 x 2-inch pan, 30 to 35 minutes; 12 x 8 x 2-inch pan, 35 to 40 minutes.

Cool and frost. (Use 1/2 recipe of frosting for loaf cake.)

Fluffy Prune Frosting: Combine 1 cup firmly packed brown sugar*, 1/4 cup light corn syrup, 1/4 cup prune juice*, 2 egg whites, 2 teaspoons lemon juice, and 1/4 teaspoon salt in top of double boiler.

Cook over boiling water, beating constantly with electric mixer or rotary beater, until mixture stands in peaks.

Remove from heat. Continue beating about 2 minutes. Fold in 1/2 cup well drained cooked prunes, cut fine, and 2 tablespoons chopped nuts.

* Or substitute 3/4 cup granulated sugar and reduce prune juice to 2 tablespoons.

Prune Whip Spice Cake

Chiffon Cakes

HINTS ABOUT CHIFFON CAKES

These airy, delicate, high and luscious cakes are prepared by a method that combines some of the steps in making an angel cake and a shortening-type cake. Because the method is different be sure to read the recipe very carefully before starting to mix the cake.

The mixing directions in each of the recipes are complete. As with other recipes, assemble all the ingredients and utensils, preheat the oven, and measure ingredients accurately. Use the type and size pans specified in recipe and note particularly that you do *not* grease pans unless the recipe specifically calls for it.

MOCHA MARBLE CHIFFON CAKE

- 2¼ cups sifted cake flour
- 1½ cups sugar
- 3 teaspoons baking powder
- 1 teaspoon salt
- ½ cup salad oil
- 6 egg yolks, unbeaten
- ¾ cup cold water
- 2 teaspoons vanilla
- 7 egg whites
- ½ teaspoon cream of tartar
- 1 1-ounce square unsweetened chocolate, melted

Mix and sift flour, sugar, baking powder, and salt into large bowl. Make well in the center and add oil, egg yolks, water, and vanilla. Beat with rotary beater until smooth.

Beat egg whites until foamy; add cream of tartar and beat until stiff.

Remove 1 cup batter and to it add melted chocolate, then fold in a little beaten egg white.

Fold remaining egg white into white batter.

Alternately spoon batters into ungreased 10-inch tube pan. Bake in slow oven (325° F.) 55 minutes.

Remove from oven. Turn upside down on cake rack. Cool for 1 minute. Loosen sides of cake and around tube. Remove from pan.

Frost with mocha frosting. Decorate with toasted almonds.

LEMON CHIFFON CAKE
(Master Recipe)

- 2¼ cups sifted cake flour
- 1½ cups sugar
- 3 teaspoons baking powder
- 1 teaspoon salt
- ½ cup salad oil
- 5 egg yolks, unbeaten
- ¾ cup cold water
- 2 teaspoons vanilla
- Grated rind of 1 lemon (optional)
- 1 cup egg whites (7 or 8)
- ½ teaspoon cream of tartar

Mix and sift flour, sugar, baking powder, and salt. Make a well and add oil, egg yolks, water, vanilla, and (if desired) lemon rind. Beat with a spoon until smooth.

Use a very large mixing bowl in which to whip egg whites with cream of tartar until very stiff peaks are formed. Gently fold cake mixture into egg whites until well blended. Do not stir.

Pour into ungreased 10-inch tube pan (4 inches deep) immediately.

Bake in slow oven (325°F.) 55 minutes, then at 350°F. 10 to 15 minutes, or until top springs back when lightly touched.

Invert pan on rack until cold. To remove from pan, loosen from sides and tube with spatula.

Lemon Chiffon Cake Variations

Banana Chiffon Cake: Reduce water to ⅓ cup. Use only 1 teaspoon vanilla or lemon rind. Add 1 cup sieved very ripe bananas (2 to 3 bananas) to egg yolk mixture. Bake in slow oven (325° F.) 65 to 70 minutes.

Orange Chiffon Cake: Omit vanilla and lemon rind. Add grated rind of 2 oranges (about 3 tablespoons) to egg yolk mixture. Baking time same as for lemon chiffon cake.

Walnut Chiffon Cake: Omit lemon rind. After egg mixture has been folded into egg whites, sprinkle over top of batter, gently folding in with a few strokes 1 cup very finely chopped walnuts. Baking time same as for lemon chiffon cake.

PECAN CHIFFON CAKE

- 1 cup sifted cake flour
- ½ cup firmly packed brown sugar
- ¾ teaspoon salt
- 1½ teaspoons baking powder
- ¼ cup salad oil
- 3 egg yolks
- 6 tablespoons water
- ½ teaspoon vanilla
- ½ teaspoon almond flavoring
- ½ cup egg whites
- ¼ teaspoon cream of tartar
- ¼ cup granulated sugar
- ½ cup finely chopped pecans

Mix and sift into a mixing bowl the flour, brown sugar, salt, and baking powder. Make a hollow in center and add salad oil. Add in order: egg yolks, water, vanilla, and almond flavoring. Beat with a spoon until smooth.

Put egg whites into a large mixing bowl. Add cream of tartar. Beat with rotary or electric beater until whites form soft peaks. Add granulated sugar gradually, beating after each addition.

Beat until meringue is just stiff enough not to slide when bowl is inverted.

Pour egg yolk mixture over meringue. Gently fold yolks and pecans into meringue until well blended.

Turn into ungreased loaf pan (5 x 10 x 3 inches). Bake in a slow oven (325° F.) 50 minutes. Frost with butter frosting.

WALNUT CHIFFON CAKE #2

- 2¼ cups sifted cake flour
- 1½ cups sugar
- 3 teaspoons baking powder
- 1 teaspoon salt
- ½ cup salad oil
- 5 egg yolks, unbeaten
- ¾ cup cold water
- 2 teaspoons vanilla
- 1 cup egg whites (7 or 8)
- ½ teaspoon cream of tartar
- 1 cup very finely chopped walnuts

Sift dry ingredients into bowl. Make a well and add oil, egg yolks, water, and vanilla. Beat with spoon until smooth or with electric mixer on medium speed 1 minute.

Measure egg whites and cream of tartar into large mixing bowl. Beat by hand until whites form very stiff peaks or with electric mixer on high speed 3 to 5 minutes. Do not underbeat. Pour egg yolk mixture gradually over beaten whites folding just until blended. Fold in chopped nuts. Pour into ungreased 10 x 4-inch tube pan.

Bake 55 minutes in slow oven (325° F.), then increase to 350° F. and bake 10 to 15 minutes longer, or until top springs back when lightly touched.

Turn pan upside down with tube over neck of funnel or bottle. Let hang until cold.

Loosen from sides and tube with spatula; turn pan over, hit edge sharply on table. Frost with browned butter icing (below). Then make it truly gift-gorgeous by wreathing the top with walnut halves.

Browned Butter Icing: Melt, then keep over low heat until golden brown, ¼ cup butter. Remove from heat.

Blend in 2 cups sifted confectioners' sugar, 2 tablespoons cream, and 1½ teaspoons vanilla.

Stir vigorously until cool and of a consistency to spread. (If it becomes too thick to spread, stir in a little hot water.)

In High Altitudes: Adjust baking powder amounts and oven temperature as follows:

Altitudes	Baking Powder
3000–4000 ft.	2¼ tsp.
4000–6500 ft.	1½ tsp.
over 6500 ft.	¾ tsp.

Over 3500 feet, increase each oven temperature 25°.

YELLOW 2-EGG CHIFFON CAKE

    2   eggs, separated
    1½ cups sugar
    2¼ cups sifted cake flour
    3   teaspoons baking powder
    1   teaspoon salt
    ⅓   cup salad oil
    1   cup milk
    1½ teaspoons flavoring

Heat oven to 350° F. (moderate). Grease generously and dust with flour 2 round layer pans, 8 inches by at least 1½ inches deep or 9 x 11½ inches.

Beat egg whites until frothy. Gradually beat in ½ cup of the sugar. Continue beating until very stiff and glossy.

Sift remaining sugar, flour, baking powder, and salt into another bowl. Pour in salad oil, half of milk, and flavoring. Beat 1 minute, medium speed on mixer or 150 vigorous strokes by hand. Scrape sides and bottom of bowl constantly. Add remaining milk, egg yolks. Beat 1 minute more, scraping bowl constantly.

Fold meringue into batter by cutting down gently through batter, across the bottom up and over, turning bowl often. Pour into prepared pans. Bake layers 30 to 35 minutes. Cool.

Variations of 2-Egg Chiffon Cake

Orange-Filled Cake: Spread clear orange filling between layers. Ice with white mountain icing. Sprinkle generously with coconut.

Clear Orange Filling: Mix in saucepan 1 cup sugar, 4 tablespoons cornstarch, ½ teaspoon salt, 1 cup orange juice, 1½ tablespoons lemon juice, and 2 tablespoons butter.

Boil 1 minute, stirring constantly. Stir in 2 tablespoons grated orange rind. Chill.

White Mountain Icing: Stir until well blended in small saucepan ⅔ cup sugar, 2⅔ tablespoons water, and ⅓ cup white corn syrup. Boil rapidly to 242° F. (mixture spins a 6- to 8-inch thread or a few drops form a firm ball when dropped into cold water).

When mixture begins to boil, start beating ⅓ cup egg whites (2 large). Beat until stiff enough to hold a peak.

Pour hot syrup slowly in a thin steady stream into beaten egg whites, beating constantly with electric or rotary beater until mixture stands in very stiff peaks. Blend in 1½ teaspoons vanilla.

French Cream Cake: Split each layer into two layers. Spread cream filling, made with packaged vanilla pudding mix, between layers and on top.

Ice sides of cake with brown beauty icing. Sprinkle top edge of cake with toasted slivered almonds.

Brown Beauty Icing: Place bowl in ice water. Mix thoroughly 1 cup sifted confectioners' sugar, ¼ teaspoon salt, 3 tablespoons milk, 3 tablespoons soft shortening, 2 squares (2 ounces) unsweetened chocolate, melted, and ¾ teaspoon vanilla.

Add 2 or 3 egg yolks (or 1 small egg). Beat until thick enough to spread (3 to 5 minutes).

Peppermint Chocolate Chip Cake: After folding in meringue, fold in 2 squares (2 ounces) unsweetened chocolate, grated. Pour into prepared pans. Bake layers 30 to 35 minutes. Cool. Ice with pink peppermint icing. Trim swirls of icing with grated chocolate.

Pink Peppermint Icing: Stir until well blended in small saucepan ⅔ cup sugar, 2⅔ tablespoons water, and ⅓ cup white corn syrup.

Boil rapidly to 242° F. (mixture spins a 6- to 8-inch thread or a few drops form a firm ball when dropped into cold water).

When mixture begins to boil, start beating ⅓ cup egg whites (2 large). Beat until stiff enough to hold a peak.

Pour hot syrup slowly in a thin steady stream into beaten egg whites, beating constantly with electric or rotary beater until mixture stands in very stiff peaks.

Blend in ¼ teaspoon peppermint extract. Tint a delicate pink with red food coloring.

PINEAPPLE COCONUT CHIFFON CAKE

    2¼ cups sifted cake flour
    1   cup sugar
    3   teaspoons baking powder
    1   teaspoon salt
    ½   cup salad oil
    5   egg yolks, unbeaten
    ¾   cup canned pineapple juice
    1   cup egg whites (8 or 9 medium
        eggs)
    ½   teaspoon cream of tartar
    ½   cup sugar
    1   cup shredded coconut

Mix and sift together flour, 1 cup sugar, baking powder, and salt. Make a well in the center and add in order: oil, egg yolks, and juice. With spoon, beat until very smooth.

With electric mixer at high speed or with egg beater, beat whites with cream of tartar until soft peaks are formed. Gradually add ½ cup sugar, beating until very stiff peaks are formed.

Gently fold yolk mixture into whites until blended. During last few strokes fold in coconut.

Turn into ungreased 10-inch tube pan. Bake in slow oven (325°F.) about 1 hour or until done.

Invert pan and cool. Loosen cake with spatula and invert pan. Strike edge sharply on table so cake will drop out.

Serve with whipped cream into which drained canned crushed pineapple has been folded.

CHOCOLATE CHIFFON CAKE

    2¼ cups sifted cake flour
    1⅔ cups sugar
    3   teaspoons baking powder
    2   teaspoons instant coffee
    1   teaspoon salt
    ¼   teaspoon cinnamon
    ½   cup salad oil
    6   egg yolks
    ¾   cup water
    2   teaspoons vanilla
    2   to 3 1-ounce squares unsweet-
        ened chocolate, melted
    ½   teaspoon cream of tartar
    6   egg whites

Mix and sift first 6 ingredients. Make a well in the center and add in order: oil, egg yolks, water, and vanilla. Beat with spoon until smooth. Add melted chocolate and blend well.

Add cream of tartar to egg whites. Beat until egg whites form very stiff peaks.

Gently fold first mixture into egg whites until well blended. Fold, do not stir.

Turn batter into ungreased 10-inch tube pan. Bake in slow oven (325° F.) 70 to 75 minutes or until cake springs back when touched lightly with finger.

Immediately invert pan over funnel or bottle to cool. When cold, loosen side of cake with spatula.

Chocolate Chiffon Cake

Upside-Down Cakes

These are cakes served with the bottom side up. Fruit, sugar, butter, or whatever else is specified in the recipe as a topping is placed in the cake pan before the batter is added.

PEACH UPSIDE-DOWN CAKE

4   tablespoons melted butter
¾   cup firmly packed brown sugar
6   canned peach halves
¼   cup shortening
¾   cup sugar
1   egg, unbeaten
1   teaspoon lemon juice
2   teaspoons grated lemon rind
1½ cups sifted cake flour
2   teaspoons baking powder
½   teaspoon salt
½   cup milk

Mix butter and brown sugar together and pat into bottom of square 8-inch cake pan. Arrange peach halves over this, cut side down.

Cream shortening and sugar together. Add egg, lemon juice, and rind. Beat until fluffy.

Mix and sift flour, baking powder, and salt. Add to creamed mixture alternately with milk.

Pour batter over peaches carefully. Bake in moderate oven (375°F.) 45 minutes.

Turn out upside down. Serve plain or with whipped cream.

BANANA UPSIDE-DOWN CAKE

2   tablespoons butter
½   cup firmly packed brown sugar
3   medium bananas, cut in quarters
½   cup raisins
Walnut halves
¼   cup shortening
⅔   cup sugar
2   beaten eggs
1   teaspoon vanilla
1½ cups sifted cake flour
2   teaspoons baking powder
½   teaspoon salt
⅓   cup milk

Melt butter. Add brown sugar, and stir until well blended. Pat into the bottom of a square 8-inch baking pan. Arrange bananas, raisins, and nuts over this and pat down gently.

Cream shortening. Add sugar gradually and cream thoroughly. Add eggs and beat well. Add vanilla.

Mix and sift flour, baking powder, and salt.

Add flour mixture alternately with milk to creamed mixture, stirring and blending after each addition.

Beat slightly to make smooth. Pour batter carefully over bananas.

Bake in moderate oven (350°F.) until done, about 55 minutes. Turn out upside down.

BLUEBERRY UPSIDE-DOWN CAKE

1   quart fresh blueberries
1   tablespoon lemon juice
¾   cup sugar
1   teaspoon aromatic bitters
4   tablespoons shortening
½   cup sugar
1   egg
1½ cups all-purpose flour
Dash of salt
1½ teaspoons baking powder
¾   cup milk

Wash and drain blueberries. Squeeze lemon juice over top and sprinkle with ¾ cup sugar and bitters. Place in bowl and set aside.

Cream shortening and ½ cup sugar together. Add egg. Sift together flour, salt, and baking powder. Add to shortening. Then add milk and beat for 2 minutes until smooth.

Place sweetened blueberries in 8-inch square cake pan which has been well greased on sides. Arrange berries in even layer and smooth cake dough over berries.

Bake in moderate oven (350°F.) 30 minutes. When cake is done, invert on platter. Cut in squares and serve warm with plain or whipped cream. Makes 8 to 10 servings.

PINEAPPLE UPSIDE-DOWN CAKE

(Master Recipe)

¼   cup butter
½   cup firmly packed brown sugar
4   slices pineapple, cut in wedges
1⅓ cups sifted cake flour
2   teaspoons baking powder
¼   teaspoon salt
¾   cup granulated sugar
¼   cup butter or other shortening
1   egg, unbeaten
½   cup milk
1   teaspoon vanilla

Melt butter in 8 x 8 x 2-inch square pan or 8-inch skillet. Add brown sugar and blend well. Remove from heat.

Arrange pineapple wedges on sugar mixture and set aside.

Measure sifted flour, add baking powder, salt, and granulated sugar, and sift together 3 times.

Cream shortening. Add dry ingredients, egg, milk, and vanilla. Stir until all flour is dampened, then beat vigorously 1 minute. Pour batter over fruit mixture in pan.

Bake in moderate oven (350°F.) about 50 minutes.

Cool cake in pan 5 minutes. Then invert on plate and let stand a minute before removing pan.

Upside-down cake is best when served warm. It may be garnished with whipped cream or a variation. It is also delicious with ice cream.

Blueberry Upside-Down Cake

Variations:

Apricot or Peach Upside-Down Cake: Use batter for plain or spiced pineapple upside-down cake.

For the topping, substitute 20 cooked dried apricot halves or 12 canned apricot halves, or 1¼ cups of well drained sliced peaches for the pineapple slices in recipe.

Arrange on sugar mixture. Cover with batter and bake as directed. Serve plain or with ice cream.

Coconut Butterscotch Upside-Down Cake: Prepare as for pineapple upside-down cake.

For the topping gently cook 1 cup finely cut coconut in 1 tablespoon melted butter in 8 x 8 x 2-inch square pan until golden brown.

Then add 3 tablespoons more butter, ½ cup firmly packed brown sugar, and ¼ cup water; heat until blended, stirring constantly. Serve plain or with whipped cream.

Pineapple-Spice Upside-Down Cake: Follow recipe for pineapple upside-down cake, adding 1 teaspoon cinnamon, ½ teaspoon nutmeg, and ⅛ teaspoon cloves to flour mixture.

Cranberry Upside-Down Cake: Use pineapple upside-down cake batter.

For topping, melt 3 tablespoons butter in 8 x 8 x 2-inch square pan. Add 6 tablespoons sugar and 1 tablespoon grated orange rind; mix well.

Sprinkle 1½ cups fresh cranberries, coarsely cut, over sugar mixture. Cover with batter and bake as directed.

Fresh Blueberry Upside-Down Cake: Prepare as for pineapple upside-down cake.

For the topping, melt 3 tablespoons butter in 8 x 8 x 2-inch square pan.

Add ⅓ cup firmly packed brown sugar and mix well.

Pour 1¾ cups fresh blueberries over sugar mixture; sprinkle with ½ teaspoon grated lemon rind and 2 teaspoons lemon juice. Serve with plain whipped cream.

MINCEMEAT UPSIDE-DOWN CAKE

3 tablespoons butter or margarine
2 tablespoons brown sugar
1½ cups canned or packaged mince-
    meat*
1 cup sifted cake flour
1 teaspoon baking powder
¼ teaspoon salt
½ teaspoon cinnamon
⅛ teaspoon nutmeg
¼ teaspoon ground cloves
¼ teaspoon allspice
¼ cup sugar
⅓ cup milk
½ cup light or dark corn syrup
1 teaspoon vanilla
¼ cup shortening
1 egg, unbeaten

Melt butter in an 8-inch square pan. Sprinkle with brown sugar and spread mincemeat lightly over the mixture.

Sift flour with the baking powder, salt, spices, and sugar.

Combine milk, corn syrup, and vanilla. Add shortening with half of the liquid and the egg to the dry ingredients. Mix until all flour is dampened, then beat 1 minute longer (100 full strokes per minute).

Add the remaining liquid and beat 2 minutes. Pour over mincemeat and bake in a moderate oven (350°F.) 35 minutes. Turn out immediately. Serves 6.

*Note: If packaged mincemeat is used prepare according to the directions given.

PEAR UPSIDE-DOWN GINGERBREAD

1 cup sifted enriched flour
½ teaspoon baking soda
¼ teaspoon salt
1 teaspoon cinnamon
¾ teaspoon ginger
¼ teaspoon nutmeg
1 egg, slightly beaten
5 tablespoons brown sugar
¼ cup dark molasses
½ cup sour milk or buttermilk
¼ cup shortening, melted
3 ripe pears, peeled and halved
6 walnuts
2 tablespoons chopped walnuts

Sift together all dry ingredients. Combine egg, sugar, molasses, milk, and shortening; gradually add flour mixture, stirring until mixed. Beat vigorously about 1 minute until batter is smooth.

Place pear halves, cut side down into well greased 9-inch pie plate. Place a walnut in center of each pear.

Pour gingerbread mixture over pears. Sprinkle with chopped walnuts.

Bake in moderate oven (350°F.) about 30 minutes. Serves 6.

FRESH PEAR UPSIDE-DOWN CAKE

2 tablespoons butter or margarine
⅓ cup brown sugar
1 large fresh pear
⅛ teaspoon nutmeg
2 eggs, separated
1 cup warm light corn syrup
1 teaspoon vanilla
1 tablespoon melted shortening
1 cup sifted enriched flour
1½ teaspoons baking powder
¼ teaspoon salt
½ cup bran

Combine butter and sugar in 9-inch cake pan; cook over low heat until butter melts. Spread evenly over bottom of cake pan. Pare fruit and cut into slices lengthwise. Remove core. Arrange slices in circle in bottom of pan; sprinkle with nutmeg.

Beat egg yolks well; add corn syrup and continue beating. Add flavoring and melted shortening. Stir in sifted dry ingredients and bran.

Beat egg whites until stiff but not dry; fold into batter. Spread over pears. Bake in moderate oven (350°F.) about 45 minutes. Turn upside down on plate while hot. Serve with whipped cream or lemon sauce if desired.

CRANBERRY-ORANGE UPSIDE-DOWN CAKE

Topping:

2 tablespoons butter
1 cup firmly packed brown sugar
2 cups cranberries
2 oranges, sectioned and broken

Melt butter in shallow baking pan (8 x 10 inches). Stir in sugar and spread evenly over bottom of pan.

Wash and pick over cranberries. Cut them in halves. Spread berries over sugar. Scatter orange pieces over cranberries.

Cake Batter:

1½ cups sifted cake flour
2 teaspoons baking powder
¼ teaspoon salt
¼ cup shortening
Grated rind of 1 orange
¾ cup sugar
1 egg, unbeaten
¼ cup evaporated milk mixed with
    ¼ cup orange juice

Sift flour with baking powder and salt.

Cream shortening with orange rind. Add sugar gradually and continue creaming until light and fluffy. Add egg and beat until well blended.

Add flour mixture alternately with milk and orange juice, beginning and ending with flour.

Turn batter over cranberry mixture. Bake in moderate oven (375°F.) 30 to 40 minutes. Serve warm.

Marbapple Ginger Cake

MARBAPPLE GINGER CAKE

4 cups (4 to 5 medium) cooking
    apples, pared and sliced
1 cup sugar
1 tablespoon flour
1 teaspoon cinnamon
2 tablespoons butter or margarine
2 tablespoons water
1 tablespoon lemon juice

Batter:

2¼ cups sifted enriched flour
2 teaspoons baking powder
1 teaspoon ginger
½ teaspoon salt
½ cup shortening
1 cup sugar
2 eggs, unbeaten
⅔ cup mik
¼ cup molasses
1 teaspoon cinnamon
¼ teaspoon cloves
¼ teaspoon nutmeg
¼ teaspoon baking soda

Combine apples, 1 cup sugar, 1 tablespoon flour, 1 teaspoon cinnamon, butter, water, and lemon juice in saucepan.

Cook over medium heat, occasionally stirring gently, until apples are tender. Pour into well greased 13 x 9 x 2-inch pan.

Sift together 2¼ cups flour, baking powder, ginger, and salt.

Blend together shortening and 1 cup sugar, creaming well. Add eggs; beat for 1 minute.

Add milk alternately with the dry ingredients to creamed mixture, beginning and ending with dry ingredients. Blend thoroughly after each addition. (With electric mixer use low speed.)

Place half of batter in second bowl. Blend in molasses, 1 teaspoon cinnamon, cloves, nutmeg, and soda.

Spoon light and dark batters alternately over apples in pan.

Bake in moderate oven (350°F.) 50 to 60 minutes.

Cool in pan 15 to 20 minutes, then invert on serving plate or on wire rack covered with waxed paper. Serve warm or cold, plain or with whipped cream.

Cheese Cakes and Pies

MASTER CHEESE CAKE

1 package (6 ounces) zwieback
1/2 cup melted butter
3 tablespoons powdered sugar
3 eggs, separated
1 cup granulated sugar
Grated rind and juice of 1 lemon
1/2 teaspoon salt
1/2 teaspoon grated nutmeg
1 cup heavy cream, whipped stiff
1 teaspoon vanilla (optional)
1/2 cup enriched flour, sifted twice
1 pound cottage cheese, sieved

Crush zwieback with a rolling pin. Combine crumbs with butter and powdered sugar. Press half of mixture in bottom and around sides of a well greased, deep, round baking pan or spring form.

Beat egg yolks until light. Gradually add granulated sugar, beating thoroughly. Add grated rind and juice of lemon, salt, nutmeg, vanilla-flavored whipped cream, and flour.

Mix thoroughly with the cheese and rub through a sieve to insure absolute smoothness.

Fold in stiffly beaten egg whites. Pour carefully on top of zwieback mixture. Spread remaining crumb mixture over the top.

Bake in very slow oven (275°F.) until firm, 1 hour, or until set. Turn off heat. Let stand in oven 1 hour, or until cooled.

Remove rim of spring form, and place with tin bottom on serving plate.

Master Cheese Cake Variations

Apricot Cheese Cake: Arrange layer of strained, cooked dried apricots on zwieback crust. Cover with cheese mixture.

Pineapple Cheese Cake: Arrange a layer of well drained crushed pineapple on zwieback crust. Cover with cheese mixture.

Strawberry Cheese Cake: Place a layer of well drained, mashed strawberries, which have been cooked for 5 minutes in a little sugar syrup, on zwieback crust. Cover with cheese mixture.

Prune Cheese Cake: Place a layer of strained, cooked prunes on zwieback

Petal Cheese Cake

crust. Cover with cheese mixture.

CHEESE REFRIGERATOR CAKE

2 eggs
1/4 cup milk
3/4 pound cottage cheese
6 tablespoons sugar
2 tablespoons flour
1/4 teaspoon salt
1/2 teaspoon grated lemon rind
3/4 teaspoon lemon juice
2/3 cup cream, whipped
1/2 package zwieback, rolled fine
1/4 cup sugar
1/4 teaspoon cinnamon
1/8 teaspoon salt
2 tablespoons butter or margarine, melted

Beat eggs. Add milk and cottage cheese.

Combine 6 tablespoons sugar, flour, 1/4 teaspoon salt, and lemon rind. Add to cheese mixture and cook in top of double boiler until thick, about 10 minutes, stirring occasionally.

Remove from heat. Add lemon juice. Cool and fold in whipped cream.

Combine zwieback crumbs, 1/4 cup sugar, cinnamon, 1/8 teaspoon salt, and butter.

Line a loaf pan with waxed paper. Arrange cheese and crumb mixtures in alternate layers. Chill in refrigerator about 5 hours, or overnight.

Serves 6 to 8.

PETAL CHEESE CAKE

1 6-ounce package zwieback, finely rolled
1/2 cup butter or margarine, softened
2 tablespoons sugar
3 8-ounce packages cream cheese
3 eggs
3/4 cup sugar
1 teaspoon vanilla
1 3-ounce package strawberry flavored gelatin
1 1/2 cups boiling water
1 package frozen sliced peaches, thawed and drained
3 or 4 large fresh strawberries, cut in halves

Blend zwieback crumbs, softened butter or margarine, and 2 tablespoons sugar. Press firmly against bottom and sides of a 9-inch spring form pan.

Blend softened cream cheese, eggs, 3/4 cup sugar, and vanilla. Pour into crust. Bake in moderate oven (375°F.) 40 minutes. Cool.

Dissolve strawberry flavored gelatin in boiling water and cool until sirupy.

Arrange peach slices in a ring around edge of cake and place strawberry halves petal fashion in the center. Spoon gelatin over fruit. Chill thoroughly. Makes 10 to 12 servings.

Fresh Date Cheese Cake

FRESH DATE CHEESE CAKE

1 3/4 cups buttered graham cracker crumbs
1 1/2 cups fresh dates
4 large eggs (7/8 cup)
1 cup sugar
3 8-ounce packages cream cheese, softened
1 tablespoon vanilla
1/4 teaspoon salt
1/2 pint sour cream
1 tablespoon sugar
1 teaspoon finely grated orange rind
Halved fresh dates

Line bottom and sides of greased 9-inch spring form pan with crumbs; press firmly into place. Cut dates into small pieces and arrange on bottom crust.

Beat eggs; gradually add 1 cup sugar, beating until thickened. Add cream cheese gradually, beating after each addition until smooth. Stir in vanilla and salt.

Spoon mixture over dates. Bake in moderate oven (350°F.) about 45 minutes. Cool several hours or overnight, first on wire rack and then in refrigerator.

Blend sour cream, 1 tablespoon sugar, and orange rind. Spread over cake. Garnish with halved dates.

Bake 5 minutes in very hot (475°F.) oven. Cool before cutting. Makes 12 servings.

FLUFFY CHEESE CAKE

1 package (6 ounces) zwieback
1 1/4 cups sugar
1/2 teaspoon cinnamon
1/2 cup melted butter
3 eggs, separated
1/4 cup sifted enriched flour
1 1/2 pounds dry cottage cheese
1 teaspoon vanilla
1 tablespoon grated lemon rind
1 cup whipping cream

Crush zwieback. Add 1/4 cup sugar, cinnamon, and melted butter. Mix thoroughly and line bottom and sides of an 8-inch spring form pan. Chill while making filling.

Beat egg yolks until thick and lemon-colored. Blend 1 cup sugar and the flour together. Add to beaten yolks, mixing thoroughly.

Fluffy Cheese Cake, Continued

Rub cottage cheese through a sieve and add to yolk mixture, beating well. Stir in vanilla and lemon rind.

Whip cream until stiff. Lightly fold cream into cheese mixture, and fold in stiffly beaten egg whites. Turn cheese mixture into crumb-lined spring form pan.

Bake in a slow oven (300°F.) for 1¼ hours.

Cool thoroughly on cake rack before removing sides of pan. Serves 8.

CHEESE TORTE

2   cups breadcrumbs
1½   cups sugar
1   teaspoon cinnamon
½   cup melted butter
4   eggs
⅛   teaspoon salt
1½   teaspoons lemon juice
1½   teaspoons grated lemon rind
1   cup cream
3   cups dry cottage cheese
4   tablespoons flour
¼   cup chopped nuts

Combine crumbs with ½ cup sugar, cinnamon, and butter.

Set aside ¾ cup crumb mixture for topping.

Press remaining mixture into 9-inch pan, lining bottom and sides.

Beat eggs with remaining sugar until light.

Add salt, lemon juice, lemon rind, cream, cheese, and flour.

Beat thoroughly until well blended. Turn into lined pan, sprinkle with remaining crumbs and nuts.

Bake in moderate oven (350°F.) about 1 hour, or until center is set.

Turn off or reduce heat. Open oven door and let stand in oven 1 hour, or until cooled. Serves 10 to 12.

CHERRY CREAM CHEESE PIE

1   baked 9-inch pie shell
1⅓   cups (15-ounce can) sweetened condensed milk
¼   cup lemon juice
1   3-ounce package cream cheese
2   eggs, separated
1½   cups (No. 2 can) red, sour, pitted cherries, well drained
¼   teaspoon cream of tartar
4   tablespoons sugar

Blend together condensed milk and lemon juice.

Cherry Cream Cheese Pie

Beat cream cheese, softened at room temperature, until smooth. Add one egg yolk at a time, beating well after each addition. Add cherries and mix thoroughly.

Fold cheese and cherry mixture into the condensed milk mixture. Put into cooled, baked pie shell.

Add cream of tartar to egg whites; beat until almost stiff enough to hold a peak. Add sugar gradually, beating until egg whites are stiff and dry.

Pile egg white mixture lightly on pie filling. Bake in slow oven (325°F.) 15 minutes or until lightly browned. Cool.

HOLLYWOOD CHEESE CAKE

18   rolled zwieback or 1½ cups zwieback crumbs
3   tablespoons butter
2   tablespoons sugar
1   pound cream cheese
½   cup sugar
⅛   teaspoon cinnamon
½   teaspoon vanilla
1   teaspoon grated lemon rind
1   tablespoon lemon juice
2   eggs, separated
1   cup thick sour cream
1   tablespoon sugar
1   teaspoon vanilla

Blend zwieback crumbs with butter and 2 tablespoons sugar. Press onto the bottom of a 9-inch spring pan. Bake in a slow oven (300°F.) for 5 minutes. Cool.

Blend cream cheese, softened at room temperature, with ½ cup sugar, cinnamon, ½ teaspoon vanilla, lemon rind, and lemon juice. Add egg yolks, one at a time, mixing well after each yolk is added.

Fold in stiffly beaten egg whites and pour the mixture on top of the crumbs.

Bake in a slow oven (300°F.) 45 minutes.

Blend the sour cream with 1 tablespoon sugar and 1 teaspoon vanilla. Spread this mixture over the top of cake.

Return to oven for an additional 10 minutes. Cool before removing from pan. Do not invert.

ITALIAN RICOTTA CHEESE PIE

Flaky pastry for 9-inch pie shell and lattice strips for the top
3   cups (1½ pounds) ricotta cheese
¼   cup flour
2   tablespoons grated orange rind
2   tablespoons grated lemon rind
1   tablespoon vanilla
⅛   teaspoon salt
4   eggs
1   cup sugar

Combine ricotta cheese, flour, grated orange and lemon rinds, vanilla, and salt.

Beat eggs until foamy. Add sugar

Hollywood Cheese Cake

gradually, beating until eggs are thick and piled softly.

Stir beaten eggs into ricotta mixture until well blended and smooth. Pour ricotta filling into pastry lined pan. Cover with lattice strips.

Bake in moderate oven (350°F.) about 50 to 60 minutes, until filling is firm and pastry is golden brown.

Remove from oven and place on cooling rack. Before serving, sprinkle with 2 tablespoons sifted confectioners' sugar.

JIFFY CHEESE CAKE— BLENDER METHOD

1   tablespoon (1 envelope) unflavored gelatin
1   tablespoon lemon juice
Yellow peel of 1 lemon
½   cup hot water or milk
⅓   cup sugar
2   egg yolks
1   8-ounce package cream cheese
1   heaping cup crushed ice
1   cup sour cream
Graham cracker crust (below)

Combine gelatin, lemon juice, lemon peel, and hot liquid in electric blender. Cover and blend at high speed 40 seconds.

Add sugar, egg yolks, and cheese; cover and blend 10 seconds. Add ice and sour cream; cover and blend 15 seconds.

Pour mixture into a 4-cup spring form pan lined with half a recipe for crumb crust. Sprinkle top with remaining crumb crust mixture. Chill until set. Serves 6.

Crumb Crust—Blender Method:

15   graham crackers
1   tablespoon sugar
½   teaspoon cinnamon
¼   cup butter, melted

Break 5 crackers into quarters; place in electric blender. Blend to crumbs by flicking the motor on and off at high speed 4 times. Empty crumbs into a bowl and continue until all crackers are crumbed.

Stir in sugar and cinnamon. Add melted butter and mix until all crumbs are moistened.

Press crumbs against sides and bottom of buttered spring-form pan or 9-inch pie pan. Chill before adding the filling.

Pineapple Cheese Refrigerator Cake

PINEAPPLE CHEESE REFRIGERATOR CAKE

Butter-Crumb Crust:

2 cups fine graham cracker crumbs (24 graham crackers)
1/4 cup granulated sugar
1/2 cup melted butter or margarine

Mix all ingredients together until mixture is crumbly. Save out about 1/3 cup. Using back of spoon, press mixture against bottom and sides of 10-inch spring-form pan.

Allow crust to chill while preparing the filling.

Filling:

2 tablespoons (2 envelopes) unflavored gelatin
1/2 cup cold water
2 egg yolks
1/4 cup granulated sugar
1 teaspoon salt
1/2 cup milk
2 cups cottage cheese (sieved)
1 cup canned crushed pineapple with syrup
1 tablespoon grated lemon rind
2 to 3 tablespoons lemon juice
2 egg whites
1/4 cup sugar
1 cup whipping cream

Soften gelatin in cold water.

Beat egg yolks, add 1/4 cup sugar, salt, and milk, and cook over hot water about 5 minutes or until beginning to thicken.

Remove from heat. Add softened gelatin. When cool, fold in sieved cottage cheese, pineapple, lemon juice, and rind.

Beat egg whites until stiff, but not dry, and gradually fold in the second 1/4 cup sugar.

Fold egg whites and whipped cream into cheese mixture. Turn into buttercrumb crust. Sprinkle remaining 1/4 cup crumb mixture around edge. Place in refrigerator to chill.

To serve, remove sides of spring pan, but do not try to remove bottom. Garnish with strawberries and pineapple. Cut in wedges and top with sugared sliced strawberries and pineapple. Serves 10 to 12.

GERMAN CHEESE CAKE

Muerbe Teig (Cookie Dough Piecrust):

1 cup sifted enriched flour
1/2 teaspoon baking powder
1/4 cup sugar
1 tablespoon butter
1 well beaten egg

Mix and sift flour, baking powder, and sugar. Work in butter with fingertips. Mix in egg.

Roll out 1/4-inch thick on a slightly floured board and line a spring form pan or a large pie plate with it.

Cheese Cake Filling:

3/4 cup creamed butter
1 cup sugar
3 eggs, unbeaten
2 cups cottage cheese, sieved
1 tablespoon cornstarch
Grated rind of 1 large lemon

Cream together the butter and sugar. Add unbeaten eggs one at a time, beating well.

Mix cottage cheese, cornstarch, and lemon rind; beat into creamed mixture until well blended.

Spread mixture in the spring form pan or pie plate.

Bake in a very hot oven (450°F.) 10 minutes.

Reduce to moderate (350°F.) and bake 20 to 30 minutes or until lightly browned and done. Serve cold.

STRAWBERRY CHEESE PIE

1 3-ounce package cream cheese
2 tablespoons milk
1 baked 9-inch pie shell
1 quart fresh strawberries
1 1/2 cups water
Few drops red food coloring
1 cup sugar
3 tablespoons cornstarch
1/2 pint whipping cream, whipped

Soften cheese with milk and spread over bottom of baked pie shell. Fill shell with the choicest berries, using about 1 pint.

Cook remaining berries in water until soft. Put through a sieve or mash well and add red food coloring.

Combine sugar and cornstarch. Add to sieved fruit. Cook until thickened, stirring often. Pour over berries in pie shell. Chill and top with whipped cream.

PINEAPPLE COTTAGE CHEESE PIE

1/2 recipe plain pastry
1 1/2 cups creamed cottage cheese
2 eggs, separated
1/4 cup melted butter or margarine
1/2 cup sugar
1/4 teaspoon salt
1 tablespoon flour

Grated rind of 1 lemon
1/2 cup chopped nuts
1/4 cup milk

Press cheese through a sieve twice. Combine all ingredients except egg whites, blending well.

Beat egg whites until stiff and fold into mixture.

Pour into pastry lined 9-inch pie pan.

Bake in very hot oven (450°F.) 10 minutes. Reduce heat to moderate (350°F.) and bake until filling is firm and pie is nicely browned, 40 minutes longer.

Spread with pineapple glaze (below) and return to oven until glaze is set, 5 minutes.

Pineapple Glaze: Drain 1 No. 2 can crushed pineapple thoroughly. Combine with 1/2 cup sugar and 2 tablespoons cornstarch.

Add 3/4 cup pineapple juice and cook slowly, stirring constantly, until thick and clear. Add pineapple and cool. Spread by spoonfuls over cheese filling.

LEMON CHEESE PIE

1 baked 8-inch pie shell
1 8-ounce package cream cheese
2 eggs
1/2 cup sugar
1 teaspoon vanilla
1 teaspoon grated lemon rind
1 tablespoon lemon juice
1/2 cup whipping cream
2 tablespoons confectioners' sugar
1 teaspoon vanilla

Soften cream cheese; whip until fluffy. Add eggs, one at a time, beating well after each.

Blend in sugar, vanilla, lemon rind, and lemon juice. Mix well. Turn into baked pie shell.

Bake in moderate oven (350°F.) 15 to 20 minutes, until slightly firm.

Cool. Chill at least 1 hour before serving.

Whip cream until stiff. Fold in confectioners' sugar and vanilla. Spread over pie before serving. Garnish with grated lemon rind, if desired.

Lemon Cheese Pie

Angel Food and Sponge Cakes

HINTS ABOUT SPONGE AND ANGEL FOOD CAKES

The sponge cake family includes yellow sponge cakes made with whole eggs, and white angel cakes made with egg whites. A true sponge or angel cake contains no shortening and no leavening except the air beaten into it in the mixing. Various other cakes such as thrifty sponge cake and butter sponge cake are included in this group of recipes although they are really mock sponge cakes.

Since true sponge cakes are leavened just with the air which is beaten into the eggs, particularly the egg whites, during the mixing process, the secret of getting a light, tender cake will depend on proper beating of egg whites, the lightness with which you fold in the flour and sugar mixtures to prevent the escape of the incorporated air, and the temperature at which you bake the cake.

You'll find that methods vary from recipe to recipe. As for other cakes, read recipe carefully. Assemble all ingredients; use standard measuring utensils and measure accurately. Prepare pans according to directions in recipe. Do not grease pans. Some sponge cake recipes specify that pans be lined with plain paper. Spread mixed batter to sides of pan and fill all corners.

Angel and sponge cakes are done when the top springs back to the touch of the finger. Cool cakes in inverted pans. If the cake falls away from the pan, it may be because pan was greased or because of insufficient baking.

If you want a brown crust, remove the cake from pan just as soon as it is cool. The longer you keep cool sponge cakes in the pan, the more crust will adhere to pan. The flavor of most sponge cakes is improved by standing overnight before cutting. Store the cooled cake in a tightly covered container.

STEPS IN MAKING ANGEL FOOD CAKE

1. Assemble all utensils and ingredients. Use standard measuring utensils and measure exactly. Prepare pans according to directions in recipe. Do not grease.

2. Beat egg whites until foamy.

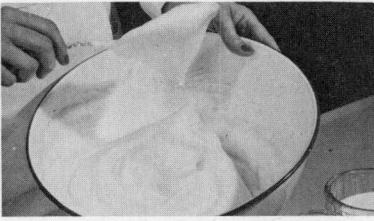

3. Add cream of tartar, continue beating until stiff but not dry. Whites should be glossy and moist, and should cling to bottom and sides of bowl.

4. Using a whisk-type beater, blend in flavoring and fold in dry ingredients. Do not stir.

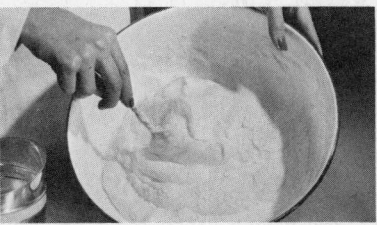

5. Turn into a dry tube pan. Cut through the batter in the pan to break any large air bubbles.

ANGEL FOOD CAKE

(Master Recipe)

1¼ cups sifted cake flour
1¾ cups sugar
½ teaspoon salt
1½ cups egg whites
     (11 to 13 eggs)
1¼ teaspoons cream of tartar
1 teaspoon vanilla
1 teaspoon almond extract

Sift and measure flour. Sift together 5 times the flour, sugar, and salt.

Beat egg whites with a rotary beater until foamy; add cream of tartar, and continue beating until stiff but not dry. Whites should be glossy and moist, and should cling to bottom and sides of bowl.

Using a whisk type beater, blend in flavoring and fold in dry ingredients. Do not stir.

Turn into 10-inch ungreased tube pan. Bake in slow oven (325° F.) 1 to 1¼ hours.

Invert pan on rack until cake is cold or about 1 hour. Loosen from sides and center with knife and remove from pan.

Angel Food Cake Variations:

Smaller Angel Food Cake: Use 1 cup flour, 1¼ cups sugar, ¼ teaspoon salt, 1 teaspoon cream of tartar, 1 cup egg whites, 1 teaspoon vanilla, ½ teaspoon almond extract. Bake in 9-inch tube pan.

Chocolate Angel Food: In master recipe substitute ¼ cup cocoa for ¼ cup flour. Sift cocoa with 1 cup of sugar. Omit almond extract.

Maraschino Angel Food: Follow master recipe. Drain and cut up ½ cup maraschino cherries. Pour ¼ of batter into pan. Sprinkle cherries over batter. Add another ¼ of batter. Continue alternating batter and fruit until all used.

Marble Angel Food: In master recipe add 2 tablespoons chocolate syrup to half the batter. Omit almond extract. Alternate layers of white and chocolate batters in pan.

Orange Angel Food: Follow master recipe. Fold in 1 tablespoon grated orange rind. Substitute 1 teaspoon orange extract for almond extract. Cover with Orange Frosting.

Peppermint Angel Food: In master recipe use 1 teaspoon peppermint extract or a few drops peppermint oil as flavoring. Add a few drops red or green coloring.

Pineapple Angel Food: Dice ½ cup pineapple. Follow method for maraschino angel food above.

Spice Angel Food: In master recipe sift 1 teaspoon cinnamon, ¼ teaspoon nutmeg, ¼ teaspoon allspice with flour.

Angel Food Cake Variations:

Tutti-Frutti Angel Food: Follow master recipe and tint batter to a pink color with food coloring. Fold in 1 cup finely chopped candied fruits.

Yellow and White Angel Food: Prepare master recipe, omitting flavoring. Divide batter into 2 parts.

Into one part fold in 4 well beaten egg yolks, 2 tablespoons flour, and 1 teaspoon lemon extract.

Into the second part fold in 1 teaspoon vanilla.

Drop by spoonfuls into pan, alternating white and yellow batter.

Layered Angel Cake: Cut angel food cake crosswise in 2 layers. Fold toasted almonds into flavored whipped cream for filling. Frost with whipped cream; sprinkle generously with toasted shredded almonds. Serve at once.

WHIPPED CREAM ANGEL FOOD CAKE

- 2 cups sifted cake flour
- 3 teaspoons baking powder
- 1/2 teaspoon salt
- 1 1/2 cups sugar
- 1 cup whipping cream
- 3 egg whites
- 1/2 cup water
- 1 teaspoon vanilla

Sift together the flour, baking powder, salt, and sugar 3 times.

Whip cream stiff. Beat egg whites until stiff. Combine carefully. Add water and vanilla. Gradually fold in dry ingredients.

Bake in layers in moderate oven (350°F.) until done, about 30 minutes. Spread lemon filling between layers.

ANGEL PEPPERMINT LOAF CAKE

- 1/2 cup sifted cake flour
- 3/4 cup sifted sugar
- 2/3 cup egg whites
- 1/8 teaspoon salt
- 1/2 teaspoon cream of tartar
- 1/2 teaspoon vanilla
- 1/4 teaspoon almond extract
- 2 tablespoons finely crushed peppermint stick candy

Measure sifted flour; add 1/4 cup sugar and sift 4 times.

Combine egg whites, salt, cream of tartar, and flavorings in large bowl. Beat with flat wire whip, egg beater, or at high speed of electric mixer until soft peaks are formed.

Blend in remaining sugar, 2 tablespoons at a time. Fold in flour mixture, 1/2 at a time. Then fold in crushed candy.

Turn batter into ungreased 10 x 5 x 3-inch loaf pan. Bake in moderate oven (375°F.) about 25 minutes.

Cool upside down 1 hour. Serve plain or with chocolate ice cream.

MASTER SPONGE CAKE

- 1 cup sifted cake flour
- 5 eggs, separated
- 1 cup sugar
- 2 tablespoons lemon juice
- 1 teaspoon grated lemon rind
- 1/2 teaspoon salt

Sift flour three times.

Using a rotary beater, beat egg yolks until thick and lemon-colored. Gradually add half the sugar, beating thoroughly, and then the lemon juice and grated lemon rind. Beat until thick.

Beat egg whites with salt until stiff enough to form peaks but not dry. Fold in remaining sugar, then the yolk mixture. Fold in flour gently. Turn at once into ungreased tube pan.

Powdered sugar sifted over top makes a delicate crust.

Bake in preheated slow oven (325°F.) 50 to 60 minutes or until done.

Remove from oven and invert pan 1 hour, or until cake is cool.

Master Sponge Cake Variations:

Sponge Layer Cake: Bake master sponge cake in layer pans in moderate oven (350°F.) about 30 minutes. Spread jam or jelly between layers. Sprinkle powdered sugar on top.

Cocoa Sponge Cake: In master sponge cake replace 1/4 cup flour with 1/4 cup cocoa. Replace 1 tablespoon lemon juice with 1 tablespoon water. Sift cocoa with flour.

Orange Sponge Cake: In master sponge cake add grated rind and juice of 1/2 orange. Grate rind before cutting orange. Omit 1 tablespoon lemon juice.

Pineapple Meringue Sponge: Bake master sponge cake in layers. Spread crushed pineapple between layers and on top. Top with meringue. Place in slow oven with door ajar, until meringue is delicate brown in color.

Jelly Roll: Omit 2 eggs from recipe for master sponge cake. Add 1/4 cup water and 1 teaspoon baking powder.

Line bottom of flat rectangular pan with greased paper. Spread cake evenly in thin layer. Bake in moderate oven (350°F.) about 15 minutes.

While hot turn onto cloth sprinkled with powdered sugar and remove greased paper. Trim edges. Spread with soft jelly and roll up.

MATZO SPONGE CAKE

- 8 eggs, separated
- 1 1/2 cups sugar
- Pinch of salt
- Grated rind and juice of 1/2 lemon
- 1 cup sifted matzo cake meal

Beat egg yolks until light; add sugar and beat again. Add salt, lemon juice

and rind, then add cake meal and finally fold in the egg whites beaten until stiff but not dry.

Turn into a 10-inch spring form pan. Bake in moderate oven (350°F.) 45 minutes. Cool, then cut into layers.

Serve with sweetened strawberries between the layers. Spread top and side with flavored and sweetened whipped cream.

ZUPPA INGLESE

Zuppa Inglese is an Italian term which means literally, English soup; it is the name of a superb Italian cake with a custard filling and a topping of whipped cream.

- 1/2 cup sugar
- 1/4 cup enriched flour
- 1/4 teaspoon salt
- 2 cups milk, scalded
- 4 egg yolks
- 1/2 teaspoon vanilla
- 1/2 cup light rum
- 2 tablespoons crème de cacao
- 2 sponge cake layers, homemade or purchased
- 1 cup heavy cream, whipped
- 2 tablespoons candied fruits, chopped fine

Mix sugar, flour, and salt in top of a double boiler. Gradually stir in scalded milk. Place over boiling water and cook, stirring until thickened.

Beat egg yolks until blended. Gradually add part of milk mixture to egg yolks while stirring. Slowly pour into hot mixture; cook over simmering water, stirring occasionally, until thickened. Let cool, then chill.

Divide mixture into 3 parts. Add vanilla to 1 part, 1 tablespoon rum to second, and crème de cacao to third.

Split cake layers to make 4 layers. Place 1 layer on a serving dish. Sprinkle with 1/4 of remaining rum and spread with one of the three custard mixtures. Repeat with second and third layers. Cover with the fourth layer of cake and sprinkle it with remaining rum. Chill overnight in refrigerator.

At serving time, spread whipped cream over top and sides of cake; sprinkle top with candied fruits. Serves 8.

Sponge cakes are usually served plain or with only a light sprinkling of confectioners' sugar.

Almond Candy Cake

ALMOND CANDY CAKE

1   large sponge or chiffon cake
Filling (below)
Maple Crisp Topping (below)
1   cup toasted blanched almond
     halves

Split cake into 4 equal layers. Spread about half of filling between cake layers. Spread remainder over top and sides of cake. Cover cake very thickly with Maple Crisp Topping, and stick almond halves porcupine fashion over top and sides of cake. Makes 16 to 20 servings.

Filling:

2   cups whipping cream
2   tablespoons sugar
1/8 teaspoon maple flavoring

Whip cream with sugar and flavoring.

Maple Crisp Topping:

1½ cups sugar
1/3 cup water
1/4 cup light corn syrup
1   tablespoon sifted baking soda
2   teaspoons maple flavoring

Combine sugar, water, and corn syrup in top of double boiler, stirring until well blended. Boil over moderate heat to hard crack stage (310°F.), until a small amount of syrup dropped into cold water will break with a brittle snap.

Remove from heat, and stir in soda and maple flavoring. Stir vigorously until well blended, but not enough to destroy foam made by soda.

Turn at once into ungreased shallow pan, about 9 inches square. Let stand without moving until completely cold. Knock out of pan and crush between sheets of waxed paper to make coarse crumbs.

SUNSHINE CAKE

5   egg yolks
½ cup sugar
1   cup sifted cake flour
2   tablespoons cold water
½ teaspoon vanilla
½ teaspoon almond extract
½ teaspoon lemon extract
8   egg whites
½ teaspoon cream of tartar
½ teaspoon salt
1   cup sugar

Beat egg yolks until thick (at least 5 minutes). Gradually beat ½ cup sugar into egg yolks. Beat in flour alternately with cold water mixed with vanilla, almond, and lemon extracts.

In another large bowl beat egg whites with cream of tartar and salt until stiff. Gradually beat remaining 1 cup sugar into stiffly beaten egg whites.

Gradually and gently cut and fold egg yolk mixture into beaten egg whites.

Pour into ungreased 10-inch tube pan (4 inches deep). Bake in slow oven (325° F.) 60 to 65 minutes.

Note: A 13 x 9-inch oblong pan may be used. Grease bottom of pan and bake only 35 to 40 minutes.

GENOISE

The genoise is a superb French cake. It does not contain a leavening agent other than the air that is beaten into the eggs. The name means "pertaining to Genoa" and since similar cakes are popular in Italy, it probably originated in that country.

1   cup (about 5) eggs
1   cup sugar
½ teaspoon salt
1   teaspoon vanilla
1¼ cups sifted enriched flour
Toasted slivered almonds or grated
    chocolate

Beat eggs until light and fluffy. Gradually add sugar, salt, and vanilla. Beat until thick and lemon-colored.

Fold in flour, 8 tablespoons at a time. Fold gently but thoroughly.

Pour into 2 8-inch round layer pans, well greased and lined with waxed paper on bottoms. Bake in moderate oven (350° F.) 25 to 30 minutes.

Cool in pan. Remove layers from pans and split to form 4 layers. Spread cool crème au beurre (below) between layers and on sides of cake.

Decorate sides with toasted slivered almonds or grated chocolate. Frost top with chocolate icing (below).

Crème au Beurre: Combine ¾ cup sugar and 2 tablespoons cornstarch in saucepan. Mix well. Add 3 eggs (or 6 egg yolks). Beat until light and fluffy.

Stir in 1½ cups milk; cook over medium heat until thick, stirring constantly.

Remove from heat; add 1 teaspoon vanilla. Cool. Blend in ½ cup creamed butter or margarine.

Chocolate Icing: Cream 2 tablespoons butter or margarine. Blend in 1 cup sifted confectioners' sugar. Add 1 small egg; beat well.

Blend in 1 square (1 ounce) melted chocolate and ½ teaspoon vanilla. Beat until smooth.

BUTTER SPONGE CAKE

2¼ cups sifted enriched flour
2   teaspoons baking powder
1   teaspoon salt
11 egg yolks
2   cups sugar
1   cup scalded milk
1   teaspoon vanilla
½ teaspoon lemon extract
½ cup melted butter

Have all ingredients at room temperature. Mix and sift flour, baking powder, and salt.

Beat egg yolks until thick, light colored, and fluffy. Add sugar gradually, beating thoroughly.

Combine scalded milk, vanilla, and lemon extract. Add gradually to beaten egg yolks, beating well after each addition. Gradually fold in sifted dry ingredients.

Add melted butter, blending well. Turn batter into ungreased 10-inch tube pan. Cut through batter with spatula to break large air pockets.

Bake in moderate oven (350°F.) 50 to 60 minutes. Cool in inverted pan about 1 hour.

SUPREME SPONGE CAKE

1⅔ cups sifted cake flour
½ teaspoon baking powder
½ teaspoon salt
½ cup hot water
10 slightly beaten egg yolks
1   cup sugar
1   teaspoon lemon extract

Sift flour once. Measure and add baking powder and salt. Sift together 3 times.

Add hot water gradually to egg yolks, beating constantly. Continue beating for about 10 minutes, or until mixture is very light and has almost doubled in bulk.

Add sugar gradually, beating constantly. Add lemon extract.

Sift in dry ingredients gradually, folding gently but thoroughly.

Turn into ungreased 10-inch tube pan at once. Bake in moderate oven (350° F.) about 1 hour.

When done, invert pan and let cool before removing.

Genoise

NORWEGIAN CROWN CAKE

1½ cups sifted enriched flour
1 teaspoon baking powder
6 egg yolks
½ cup water
1 cup sugar
4 egg whites (½ cup)
½ teaspoon salt
Sliced almonds
1 No. 303 can apricot halves
Peach slices, pineapple cubes, maraschino cherries, fresh berries or grapes

Sift together flour and baking powder. Beat egg yolks with water and ½ cup sugar until thick and ivory-colored. (With electric mixer beat at high speed about 10 minutes.)

Fold in dry ingredients, ⅓ at a time, with wire whisk or large slotted spoon.

Beat 4 egg whites with salt until slight mounds form when beater is raised. Add gradually ½ cup sugar, beating well after each addition. Continue beating until mixture stands in stiff, glossy peaks when beater is raised. Fold carefully but thoroughly into batter.

Turn into 2 well greased and lightly floured 9-inch round layer pans. Bake in moderate oven (350° F.) 25 to 30 minutes.

Remove from pans immediately; cool thoroughly on wire racks.

Split cooled layers to form 4 layers. Place on oven-proof plate, spreading cream filling (below) between layers. Spread only sides with meringue (below); decorate with sliced almonds. Brown in moderate oven (375°F.) 10 to 12 minutes.

Drain apricot halves well. Just before serving, arrange fruit on top of cake to resemble jewels in a crown. Place 4 halves in center and remaining halves around edge.

For additional color, between apricots place drained, canned peach slices, pineapple cubes, maraschino cherries, fresh berries or grapes.

Cream Filling: Blend together ½ cup sugar, ¼ cup flour, 2 tablespoons cornstarch, and ¼ teaspoon salt in top of double boiler. Blend in 1 slightly beaten egg yolk and ½ cup milk. Gradually add 2 cups scalded milk.

Cook over boiling water, stirring constantly, until thick. Remove from heat.

Blend in 1 tablespoon butter and 2 teaspoons vanilla. Cover. Cool thoroughly.

Meringue: Beat 3 egg whites until slight mounds form when beater is raised. Add 6 tablespoons sugar gradually, beating well after each addition. Continue beating until meringue stands in stiff, glossy peaks when beater is raised.

Norwegian Crown Cake

FEATHERY-LIGHT SPONGE CAKE

3 eggs
1¼ cups sugar
½ teaspoon vanilla
½ teaspoon almond extract
1¼ cups sifted cake flour
1½ teaspoons baking powder
¼ teaspoon salt
½ cup hot milk

In mixing bowl beat eggs until thick and lemon-colored (about 5 minutes). Gradually add sugar and flavorings.

Fold in dry ingredients, sifted together 3 times. Then, quickly stir in hot milk.

Pour thin batter into an ungreased loaf pan (9 x 5 x 2½ inches). Bake in moderate oven (350° F.) about 40 minutes or until top springs back when touched lightly.

Remove from oven. Invert 1 hour on cake rack to cool. Turn out on serving plate. Frost with orange-flavored icing; sprinkle top with coarsely chopped walnut meats (⅓ cup). Serves 6 to 8.

DAFFODIL CAKE

¾ cup plus 2 tablespoons sifted cake flour
1 cup plus 2 tablespoons sifted sugar
¾ cup egg whites
¼ teaspoon salt
¾ teaspoon cream of tartar
¼ teaspoon orange extract
3 egg yolks
¼ teaspoon vanilla

Sift ¾ cup flour and ½ cup sugar together twice.

Beat egg whites with salt until foamy. Sprinkle cream of tartar over egg whites and continue beating until stiff, but not dry.

Fold in ½ cup additional sugar, a small amount at a time. Sift in dry ingredients gradually, folding in carefully.

Divide batter in half. Combine 2 tablespoons sugar, 2 tablespoons cake flour, orange extract, and egg yolks, beaten until thick and lemon-colored. Fold into ½ of batter.

Blend ¼ teaspoon vanilla into remaining ½ of batter.

Place by spoonfuls yellow and white batters alternately into ungreased 9-inch tube pan.

Bake in slow oven (325° F.) 60 minutes. Invert pan until cake is cold, or about 1 hour.

SPONGE LAYER CAKE

3 eggs
1 cup sugar
Grated rind of 1 lemon
1 tablespoon melted butter
⅓ cup hot water
1 cup sifted cake flour
1½ teaspoons baking powder
¼ teaspoon salt

Beat eggs until light and lemon-colored. Add sugar gradually, beating well. Add grated rind with butter and hot water.

Mix and sift flour, baking powder, and salt and fold into first mixture.

Pour into 2 greased and floured 8-inch layer cake pans. Bake in moderate oven (375°F.) 20 to 25 minutes.

Remove cakes from pans when cool, and frost.

Sponge Cake Roll: Bake sponge layer cake in greased jelly roll pan (10 x 15 inches) in moderate oven (375° F.) 15 to 20 minutes.

Invert pan on cloth sprinkled with confectioners' sugar. Roll up in cloth. Place cake seam down and cool.

Unroll gently and spread with ice cream. Roll up and serve at once. Serves 8 to 10.

Sponge Drop Cakes: Prepare batter for sponge layer cake. Fill well greased muffin pans ⅔ full.

Bake in moderate oven (375°F.) about 20 minutes. Remove from pans. Cool and frost if desired.

THRIFTY SPONGE CAKE

1½ cups sifted cake flour
1 teaspoon baking powder
⅛ teaspoon salt
3 eggs
1 cup sugar
⅓ cup water
1 teaspoon vanilla or lemon extract

Sift flour with baking powder and salt.

Beat eggs with rotary beater until very light and frothy. Gradually add sugar, beating until thick and light colored. Then add water and vanilla or lemon extract.

Fold in dry ingredients, blending well. Turn into ungreased tube pan or two 8-inch layer pans.

Bake in moderate oven (350°F.) 25 to 35 minutes.

Invert pan 1 hour, or until cold, before removing cake.

Orange Sponge Cake: In thrifty sponge cake recipe substitute orange juice for water and 1 tablespoon grated orange rind for other flavoring.

Sponge Cupcakes: Fill cupcake pans ⅔ full. Bake in moderate oven (350°F.) about 15 minutes. Top with lemon frosting, orange frosting, or pineapple frosting.

MOSAIC CAKE—ITALIAN

Sponge Cake:

1 cup sifted cake flour
5 large or 6 medium eggs, separated
1/8 teaspoon salt
1 cup sugar
1 teaspoon grated lemon rind
4 1/2 teaspoons lemon juice

Sift flour, measure; sift twice again.

In large bowl, beat egg whites until frothy; sprinkle salt over top and continue beating until stiff but still moist. Beat in sugar, sprinkling in about 2 tablespoons at a time and beating after each addition until glossy.

In a small bowl beat egg yolks until thick and lemon-colored; add lemon rind and juice, continue beating until very thick.

Gently fold egg yolk mixture into egg whites. Fold in flour, sifting in about 1/4 cup at a time.

Turn into ungreased 9-inch tube pan. Bake in slow oven (325° F.) about 1 hour or until top springs back when touched gently. Invert pan until cool, about 1 hour; remove from pan.

To Frost and Decorate: Slice cake into 3 layers; spread chocolate cheese filling between the layers. Cover top and sides with almond frosting.

Decorate sides with 2 cups (1 pound) mixed candied fruits. Make circle of candied fruits on top around hole in center.

Chocolate Cheese Filling: Melt 1 package (6 ounces) semi-sweet chocolate pieces and 2 tablespoons butter over hot (not boiling) water. Add 3 tablespoons hot water and blend well. Sieve 1 cup cottage cheese and combine with chocolate mixture. Add 1/2 teaspoon almond extract and mix until well blended and creamy.

Almond Frosting: Beat 1 egg white until frothy; add 1 cup sifted confectioners' sugar and beat until smooth. Add another 1/2 cup sifted confectioners' sugar and blend well.

Stir in 1 teaspoon almond extract and 1/2 teaspoon lemon juice; blend until smooth.

MATZO HONEY CAKE

6 eggs, separated
1/2 cup sugar
1/2 cup honey
1/2 cup matzo cake meal
2 tablespoons potato starch

Beat egg whites until they hold a peak. Gradually beat in the sugar.

Beat egg yolks until light, and beat in the honey thoroughly.

Fold the egg white mixture into the yolk mixture. Fold in the sifted dry ingredients. Bake in slow oven (325°F.) 50 minutes in an ungreased angel cake

pan. When done leave in pan, turned upside down, until cool.

CINDERELLA SPONGE CAKE

1 cup sifted cake flour
1/2 teaspoon salt
2 tablespoons lemon juice
1 1/2 teaspoons grated lemon rind
1 tablespoon water
1/3 cup egg yolks
1 cup sugar
3/4 cup egg whites

Sift together flour and salt twice.

Combine lemon juice, lemon rind, water, and egg yolks and beat with rotary beater until very thick. Gradually add sugar, a tablespoon at a time, beating thoroughly after each addition.

Sift dry ingredients into egg mixture gradually, folding in carefully.

Beat egg whites stiff, but not dry, and fold into batter, handling gently.

Turn into ungreased 9-inch tube pan. Bake in slow oven (325°F.) 60 to 70 minutes.

Cool in inverted pan about 1 hour. Serve unfrosted, or cut across into 2 layers and fill with lemon filling and frost with meringue.

HOT MILK SPONGE CAKE

1 1/4 cups sifted cake flour
2 teaspoons baking powder
1/4 teaspoon salt
2 eggs
1 cup sugar
1 tablespoon lemon juice or 1 teaspoon vanilla
1/2 cup hot milk

Sift together 3 times the flour, baking powder, and salt.

Beat eggs until very thick and light, about 10 minutes. Gradually add sugar, beating constantly. Add flavoring.

Fold in dry ingredients, a small amount at a time. Add milk, mixing quickly until batter is smooth.

Turn into an ungreased 9-inch tube pan. Bake in moderate oven (350° F.) 35 to 45 minutes.

Remove from oven. Invert pan on rack until cold before removing cake.

GOLD CAKE

3 cups sifted cake flour
2 teaspoons baking powder
10 egg yolks
1 teaspoon vanilla or lemon extract
1/4 teaspoon salt
2 cups sugar
1 cup cold water

Sift flour with baking powder.

Beat egg yolks until thick and very light. Add flavoring and salt. Gradually beat in sugar.

Add flour alternately with water, beating after each addition until smooth.

Turn batter into ungreased 10-inch tube pan. Bake until golden brown in moderate oven (350° F.) 50 to 60 minutes.

Invert pan on cake rack 1 hour, or until cold, before removing from pan.

ANGEL FOOD SWIRL CAKE

3/4 cup sifted cake flour
1/2 cup sifted sugar
1 1/4 cups egg whites
1/4 teaspoon salt
1 1/4 teaspoons cream of tartar
Additional 3/4 cup sugar
1 teaspoon vanilla
1/4 teaspoon almond extract
2 tablespoons cake flour
4 tablespoons sugar
3 tablespoons cocoa

Sift together 2 times the 3/4 cup flour and 1/2 cup sugar.

Beat egg whites with salt until foamy. Sprinkle 1 1/4 teaspoons cream of tartar over egg whites and continue beating until stiff, but not dry. Fold in 3/4 cup additional sugar, a small amount at a time.

Add vanilla and almond extract. Sift in dry ingredients gradually, folding in carefully.

Divide batter in half. Sift together 2 tablespoons cake flour and 2 tablespoons sugar. Add to one half of batter.

Sift together 2 tablespoons sugar and 3 tablespoons cocoa and fold into remaining half of batter. Into an ungreased 9-inch tube pan, place alternate spoonfuls of light and dark batters.

Bake in slow oven (325° F.) 60 minutes. Invert pan until cake is cold, or about 1 hour.

LEMON-ORANGE SUNSHINE CAKE

8 eggs, separated
1/4 cup lemon juice
1/4 cup orange juice
1 1/2 cups sugar
1 1/2 cups sifted cake flour
1 1/2 teaspoons baking powder
1/2 teaspoon salt
1 teaspoon grated lemon rind
1 teaspoon grated orange rind

Beat egg yolks until thick, light-colored, and fluffy. Add fruit juices. Gradually add half the sugar, beating well until sugar is dissolved. Fold in mixed and sifted flour, baking powder, and salt.

Beat egg whites until stiff but not dry; add remaining sugar and beat until well blended.

Fold egg yolk mixture into egg whites with grated lemon and orange rind.

Turn into ungreased 10-inch tube pan. Bake in moderate oven (350° F.) 1 hour and 15 minutes.

Invert pan, but do not remove cake until thoroughly cooled. Frost with orange butter frosting.

Roll Cakes

JELLY ROLL

1 cup sifted cake flour
2 teaspoons baking powder
1/4 teaspoon salt
3 eggs
1/4 cup cold water
1 cup sugar
1 teaspoon vanilla
Confectioners' sugar
1 glass jelly
Cherries and nuts for garnish

Sift flour, baking powder, and salt.

Beat eggs until thick and lemon-colored. Add cold water and sugar, beating well. Gradually fold in sifted ingredients. Add vanilla.

Turn into well greased cake pan (10 x 15 inches) lined with greased brown or waxed paper.

Bake in hot oven (425° F.) 12 to 15 minutes.

Place tea towel on table, cover with waxed paper, sprinkle with confectioners' sugar. Turn hot cake onto waxed paper. Spread with jelly. Hold paper and towel firmly with thumb and first finger. Lift and roll. Cool.

Unwrap. Garnish with cherries and nuts. Serves 6.

Chocolate Roll: In jelly roll recipe, replace 1/4 cup of the flour with 1/4 cup cocoa before sifting. Fill with cream filling, or with whipped cream if cooled before rolling.

BRAZIL NUT CHOCOLATE ROLL

4 eggs
3/4 cup sugar
3/4 cup sifted cake flour
1 teaspoon baking powder
1/4 teaspoon salt
1 teaspoon vanilla
1/2 cup confectioners' sugar
1/2 cup ground Brazil nuts

Beat eggs with rotary beater. Add sugar gradually until mixture becomes thick and light-colored.

Strawberry Whip Roll

Sift flour with baking powder and salt, and fold into egg mixture. Add vanilla.

Pour into pan (15 x 10 inches) lined with heavy greased paper. Bake in hot oven (400° F.) 13 minutes.

Turn from pan at once onto waxed paper, covered with confectioners' sugar and ground Brazil nuts. Remove paper on which cake has been baked.

Spread with chocolate Brazil nut filling and roll up. Wrap in paper and cool on rack.

YULE ROLL

4 eggs, separated
3/4 cup sugar
1 teaspoon vanilla
12 graham crackers, finely rolled (1 cup crumbs)
1 teaspoon baking powder
1/4 teaspoon salt

Beat egg whites until stiff; gradually beat in 1/4 cup sugar.

In separate bowl, beat egg yolks until thick and lemon-colored; mix in vanilla. Fold egg yolks into egg whites.

Combine graham cracker crumbs, remaining sugar, baking powder, and salt. Gently fold crumb mixture into egg mixture.

Pour batter into jelly roll pan (15 1/2 x 10 1/2 inches) lined with greased brown paper; spread evenly. Bake in hot oven (400° F.) 15 minutes or until done.

Loosen sides and turn out onto towel sprinkled with confectioners' sugar. Carefully remove brown paper.

Fold cake over about one inch to start roll. With left hand raise towel and roll cake, guiding it with right hand. Leave in towel to cool on rack.

When thoroughly cooled, unroll and spread with chocolate cream. Roll up again.

Serve as is, or freeze for an ice cream roll.

Chocolate Cream: Pour 1 1/2 cups heavy cream into well chilled bowl; add 1/2 cup instant sweet cocoa mix. Beat with rotary egg beater until cream stands in peaks.

GINGER ROLL

1 1/4 cups sifted enriched flour
1/3 cup sugar
1 1/4 teaspoons baking soda
1 teaspoon each ginger, cinnamon, nutmeg, and allspice
1/3 cup melted butter
1/3 cup molasses
1 well beaten egg
1/2 cup warm water
Confectioners' sugar
1 cup heavy cream, whipped

Grease a 10 1/2 x 15 1/2-inch jelly roll pan; line with paper and grease paper.

Brazil Nut Chocolate Roll

Sift together twice flour, sugar, soda, and spices. Add butter, molasses, egg, and water. Stir until smooth. Spread in pan.

Bake in moderate oven (350° F.) until cake rebounds when pressed with finger, about 15 minutes.

Cool cake briefly in pan. Cover with thin cloth, wrung out of cold water. Finish cooling in refrigerator.

Remove cloth, sprinkle cake with sugar, turn out on waxed paper. Remove paper adhering to under side of cake.

Spread with whipped cream, roll. Wrap in waxed paper.

STRAWBERRY WHIP ROLL

1/2 cup enriched flour
3/4 teaspoon baking powder
1/4 teaspoon salt
1/4 cup sugar
3 beaten eggs
1 1/4 teaspoons vanilla
3 tablespoons melted butter or margarine
1 egg white
1/4 cup sugar
1 cup sliced fresh strawberries
Whole berries
Confectioners' sugar

Sift, measure flour, and resift with baking powder and salt.

Add 1/4 cup sugar to eggs gradually and beat until thick and light-colored. Add vanilla; fold in flour mixture and add melted butter or margarine.

Pour into well greased pan (7 x 11 x 1 1/4 inches) lined with waxed paper and brushed with melted butter or margarine. Bake in hot oven (400° F.) 10 minutes.

Turn out on damp cheese cloth; roll cake up and cool.

Beat egg white until stiff but not dry. Gradually beat in 1/4 cup sugar.

Unroll cake and spread with meringue. Top meringue with sliced strawberries.

Reroll and sprinkle top with confectioners' sugar. Garnish with mounds of meringue topped with whole strawberries. Serves 6.

Fruit Cakes

LIGHT FRUIT CAKE

1   cup chopped candied orange peel
1/2 cup chopped candied lemon peel
2   cups sliced citron
1 1/2 cups raisins, candied cherries, or other dried or candied fruit, or a mixture of several fruits, sliced or chopped
1   teaspoon mace
1/2 teaspoon each cloves and allspice
1 1/4 cups orange or pineapple juice
1   cup honey
1   cup shortening
1   cup sugar
4   beaten eggs
1   teaspoon vanilla
1/4 cup brandy or rum
1   cup nutmeats—preferably blanched, shredded, and slightly toasted almonds
5   cups sifted enriched flour
1 1/2 teaspoons salt
1/2 teaspoon baking soda
3   teaspoons baking powder

Mix peels and fruits with spices, fruit juice, and honey and let stand overnight.

Cream shortening with sugar; add eggs, vanilla, and brandy or rum. Blend thoroughly and mix with fruit combination and nuts.

Sift together remaining ingredients and stir into fruit mixture. Mix well.

Pour into a tube pan or 2 loaf pans that have been greased, lined with paper and greased again.

Cover with several thicknesses of waxed paper and tie it on securely.

Place on rack in kettle, surround with boiling water that extends halfway up around cake, cover pot and steam 1 large cake 3 hours or 2 small cakes 2 hours.

Remove paper covering and, if desired, glaze surface by coating it with honey and decorate with nuts and candied fruits.

Bake in very slow oven (250°F.) about 2 hours. Makes about 5 pounds.

TO DECORATE FRUIT CAKES

A week or two before serving cake, make a glaze by combining 1 1/2 cups sugar and 1 cup sieved cooked, dried apricot pulp and juice. Boil to 240° F. or until sticky. Apply immediately to cake while glaze is still sticky.

Decorate top with bits of candied fruits and blanched almonds. When first coat of glaze is dry, add another coat of hot glaze syrup.

Let dry, then wrap cake lightly so that some air reaches cake to keep glaze dry.

DARK FRUIT CAKE

1   pound raisins
1/2 pound candied cherries, halved
1/2 pound citron, thinly sliced
1/4 pound figs, dates, or candied pineapple, sliced
3   ounces candied orange peel, sliced
3   ounces candied lemon peel, sliced
1 2/3 cups sifted enriched flour
1/4 teaspoon baking soda
1/2 teaspoon each of allspice, cinnamon, nutmeg, and salt
2/3 cup shortening
2/3 cup brown sugar, sifted
4   eggs, separated
1/3 cup molasses
6   tablespoons grape, apple, or pineapple juice, or rum, brandy, or sherry

If fruits are dry and hard place in a sieve and steam until soft over boiling water. Cool and prepare as indicated.

Dredge well with 1/3 cup of the flour, using the hand to do this.

Sift together twice the remaining flour, soda, spices, and salt.

Cream shortening, add sugar and cream until fluffy. Add well beaten egg yolks and mix thoroughly. Stir in molasses.

Add sifted dry ingredients and fruit juice or liquor alternately to creamed mixture, mixing well after each addition.

Beat egg whites until stiff and fold into batter.

Add dredged fruits and mix evenly through batter.

Line 1 large or 2 medium loaf pans with 3 thicknesses of waxed paper.

Press batter into pans, filling them 3/4 full. If desired decorate top with candied cherries and citron. Cover with three thicknesses of paper and tie it on securely.

Set on a rack in a kettle or pan that has a tight-fitting cover. Add boiling water to half the depth of the cakes. Cover kettle; steam cakes 3 hours, adding more water to kettle if necessary.

Remove top paper coverings and bake in very slow oven (250°F.) 2 hours. Remove from pans and cool.

To store, wrap in waxed paper or a cloth saturated with brandy. Store in an airtight container in a cool place. Dampen cloth with more brandy about every 3 weeks. Makes about 5 pounds of cake.

ELEGANT WHITE FRUIT CAKE

A cake for an anniversary of great importance. May be used as an alternate with dark fruit cake as a wedding cake. Cut the candied (glacé) fruits into large uniform pieces, then when the cake is sliced for serving, the beautiful rich

Elegant White Fruit Cake

colors will shine against the white background.

Makes a 5 1/2 pound cake in a spring form pan with a tube center, or a 10-inch angel food cake pan.

1 1/2 cups (6 slices) pineapple chunks
1   cup cubed citron
1   cup halved, candied (glacé) cherries
1   cup each cut candied (glacé) lemon and orange rinds
1   cup golden seedless raisins
1 1/2 cups slivered blanched almonds
4   cups sifted enriched flour
2   teaspoons baking powder
2   teaspoons salt
3/4 cup shortening
1/4 cup butter or margarine
2   cups sugar
3/4 cup milk
8   egg whites

Prepare baking pan.

Combine fruits and almonds with sifted dry ingredients.

Cream together shortening, butter or margarine, and sugar until light and fluffy.

Stir in combined fruits, nutmeats, and sifted dry ingredients alternately with milk to make a stiff batter.

Fold in egg whites, beaten until stiff; spoon batter into prepared pan.

Bake in slow oven (300°F.) about 2 1/2 hours or until top is firm to light touch. (If top seems to be browning too fast, cover with heavy paper during last 45 minutes of baking.)

FRUIT CAKE WITH WHOLE NUTS

4   eggs, separated
1   cup sugar
1/4 cup wine
1   cup sifted enriched flour
1   teaspoon baking powder
1/8 teaspoon salt
1   cup chopped candied pineapple
1   pound whole pitted dates
1/2 pound whole candied cherries
1/2 pound walnut halves
1/2 pound pecan halves
1/2 pound whole Brazil nuts

Beat egg yolks. Add sugar, and cream together thoroughly. Add wine and mix well.

Add flour sifted with baking powder and salt. Fold in stiffly beaten egg

*Fruit Cake with Whole Nuts,
Continued*

whites. Add chopped pineapple, dates, cherries, and nuts to batter. Mix well.

Grease 2 pans (4½ x 9 x 5 inches). Line with waxed paper and grease again. Carefully add cake mixture with a spoon.

Bake in a slow oven (325°F.) about 1½ hours.

Cool thoroughly. Remove paper and store in an airtight container.

HOLIDAY STAR CAKE

½ cup butter or margarine
½ cup sugar
¼ cup honey
2 eggs
2 cups sifted enriched flour
1 teaspoon baking powder
½ teaspoon salt
1 cup mincemeat
1 cup diced apples
½ cup raisins
1 cup mixed diced fruit (orange and lemon peel, citron, cherries)
½ cup chopped nuts
1 tablespoon brandy flavoring

Cream butter or margarine, sugar, and honey together; beat in eggs one at a time.

Sift dry ingredients together and combine with egg mixture. Stir in fruit, nuts, and flavoring.

Line the bottom of a well greased mold with waxed paper. Fill mold to within 1 to 1½ inches from the top. Bake in slow oven (325°F.) 1½ to 2 hours. Make 6 cups unbaked batter or amount suitable for a 1 pound bread loaf pan, or 1½ quart mold.

DUNDEE CAKE

A Scotch cake often made with currants and candied peel, usually covered with almonds before baking; named for a city in Scotland.

2¼ cups sifted enriched flour
1 teaspoon baking powder
½ teaspoon salt
¾ cup butter
¾ cup sugar
3 eggs
½ cup milk
1 cup raisins, chopped
½ cup currants, washed and dried
¼ cup candied orange peel or citron, chopped
¼ cup chopped blanched almonds
12 blanched almonds, split

Mix and sift flour, baking powder, and salt.

Cream butter well; add sugar and cream until fluffy. Add eggs 1 at a time and beat after each addition until very fluffy.

Add flour mixture alternately with milk to butter mixture, stirring after each addition only until mixed. Do not beat.

Fold in raisins, currants, orange peel, and chopped almonds.

Turn into 9 x 3½ inch pan which has been lined on the bottom with greased waxed paper. Arrange split almonds on top.

Bake in slow oven (325°F.) until cake begins to shrink from sides of pan, about 75 minutes. Cool about 15 minutes before removing from pan. Makes 1 loaf.

NO-BAKE FESTIVE FRUIT CAKE

For 2¼ pound cake:

½ cup evaporated milk
16 finely cut marshmallows
3 tablespoons orange juice*
4 dozen 2½-inch graham crackers
¼ teaspoon cinnamon
¼ teaspoon nutmeg
⅛ teaspoon cloves
1 cup dark or light seedless raisins
½ cup finely cut dates
¾ cup broken English walnuts
¾ cup candied fruit**

For 4½ pound cake:

1 cup evaporated milk
32 finely cut marshmallows
6 tablespoons orange juice*
8 dozen 2½-inch graham crackers
½ teaspoon cinnamon
½ teaspoon nutmeg
¼ teaspoon cloves
2 cups dark or light seedless raisins
1 cup finely cut dates
1½ cups broken English walnuts
1½ cups candied fruit**

Line with waxed paper bottom and sides of one or two 5-cup loaf or tube pan or pans (depending upon size of cake).

Place milk, marshmallows, and orange juice into a bowl and let stand until needed.

Roll graham crackers into fine crumbs. Put crumbs into a large bowl; add cinnamon, nutmeg, cloves, raisins, dates, and walnuts.

Add bulk or canned ready-mixed, cut-up candied fruit.

Add milk mixture. Mix with spoon, then with hands until crumbs are moistened. Press firmly into pan.

Top with fruit and nuts. Cover tightly.

Chill 2 days before slicing. Keep in cool place.

* Alcoholic flavoring can replace the orange juice if desired.

** For 2¼-pound cake you can replace the ¾ cup of ready-mixed candied fruit with: ⅓ cup finely cut candied pineapple, ⅓ cup finely cut candied cherries, 2 tablespoons finely cut candied orange peel.

For 4½-pound cake you can replace the 1½ cups of ready-mixed candied fruit with: ⅔ cup finely cut candied pineapple, ⅔ cup finely cut candied cherries, and ¼ cup finely cut candied orange peel.

Butter Fruit Cake

BUTTER FRUIT CAKE

2 pounds raisins
2 pounds currants
1 pound almonds
1 pound pecans
1 pound citron
4 cups sifted enriched flour
1 teaspoon nutmeg
1 teaspoon mace
1 teaspoon cinnamon
2 cups sweet butter
1 pound brown sugar
12 eggs
6 ounce glass jelly (blackberry, currant, or grape)
¼ cup lemon juice
¼ cup canned peach juice
½ cup cream

Wash and dry raisins and currants. Blanch almonds, drain and cut with pecans into quarters. Cut citron into thin slices. Place fruit in large mixing bowl.

Sift flour, measure and sift with spices and mix with fruit until well coated.

Cream butter and add sugar gradually. Add beaten eggs and jelly.

Next stir in flour, nut and fruit mixture alternately with fruit juice first, then cream.

Line pans with heavy waxed paper and butter lightly. Fill pans almost to top.

Bake small loaf cakes in very slow oven (275°F.) 3 to 3½ hours. Bake large loaf cakes in very slow oven (250°F.) 4 to 4½ hours. The cakes will shrink from edges when done.

Cool cakes on wire rack, without removing waxed paper. When cool, wrap in heavy waxed paper and store in tightly covered container until ready to use.

No-Bake Groom's Fruit Cake   *Groom's Dark Fruit Cake*

NO-BAKE GROOM'S FRUIT CAKE

3   cups mixed nuts (almonds, walnuts, Brazil nuts, etc.)
1   pound seedless raisins
1   cup (8 ounces) diced, mixed, glazed fruit
1   8-ounce jar maraschino cherries, drained
1   pound graham crackers
1   tablespoon (1 envelope) unflavored gelatin
1/3 cup orange juice
1/2 cup sugar
2/3 cup unsulphured molasses
1   tablespoon grated orange rind
1/4 teaspoon each: cinnamon, nutmeg, cloves
1/8 teaspoon each: allspice, ginger

Line a 9¼ x 5¼ x 2¾-inch loaf pan, or 2 loaf pans, 7¼ x 3½ x 2 inches, with two strips waxed paper, extending paper 3 inches above rim. Set aside.

Put nuts in a large mixing bowl, with raisins, glazed fruit, and maraschino cherries; mix well.

Finely crush graham crackers with a rolling pin; add to nut-fruit mixture.

Soften gelatin in orange juice; place over boiling water and stir until gelatin is dissolved. Add sugar; stir until dissolved.

Pour molasses into large bowl of electric mixer; add gelatin mixture, orange rind, and spices. Beat on highest speed of electric mixer 15 minutes.

Add to nut-fruit mixture; blend thoroughly with spoon or hands. Turn into prepared pan, pressing down firmly. If desired, garnish with additional maraschino cherries and sliced Brazil nuts.

Fold waxed paper over cake. Chill in refrigerator 6 to 8 hours. To store, wrap in aluminum foil and keep in refrigerator. Makes 4½ pounds fruit cake.

GROOM'S DARK FRUIT CAKE

3/4 cup raisins
3/4 cup chopped nuts
1/3 cup diced citron
2   cups sifted enriched flour
1/2 teaspoon baking soda
1/2 teaspoon salt
1   teaspoon cinnamon
1/2 teaspoon allspice
1/2 teaspoon mace
1/4 teaspoon cloves
1/2 cup shortening
1/2 cup sugar
2   eggs
3/4 cup unsulphured molasses
1/2 cup milk

Combine raisins, nuts, and citron in mixing bowl.

Sift together flour, soda, salt, cinnamon, allspice, mace, and cloves; mix ½ cup with the fruit-nut mixture.

Cream shortening; add sugar and cream well. Beat in eggs one at a time.

Combine molasses and milk; add alternately with remaining flour mixture to shortening mixture. Mix in prepared fruit and nuts.

Turn into a greased and waxed-paper-lined 9¼ x 5¼ x 2¾ -inch pan.

Bake in slow oven (325°F.) 1 hour and 25 minutes.

Cool 15 minutes; remove from pan. Makes 2½ pounds fruit cake.

CALIFORNIA FRUIT CAKE

1   cup prunes
1   cup dried white figs
3   cups seedless raisins
2   cups candied cherries
1   cup cut preserved lemon peel
1   cup cut preserved orange peel
2   cups cut preserved citron
1   teaspoon cloves
2   teaspoons cinnamon
2   teaspoons nutmeg
2   teaspoons mace
1/4 teaspoon black pepper
1   cup thick orange marmalade
1/3 cup fruit juice or white wine
1½ cups butter or margarine
2   cups granulated sugar
1   tablespoon rum flavoring
7   eggs
5   cups sifted enriched flour
1   teaspoon salt
1   teaspoon baking soda
1   cup coarsely chopped blanched almonds

1   cup broken walnuts
Blanched almonds for top
Thin strips of candied citron for top

Rinse dried fruits. Drain figs and raisins and dry thoroughly.

Cover prunes with water and boil 15 minutes. Drain and dry. Cut from pits into small pieces.

Clip stems from figs and cut figs into thin strips. Slice cherries.

•Combine fruits, peels, spices, marmalade, and fruit juice and blend well. Cover and let stand overnight.

Cream butter and sugar together thoroughly. Add flavoring and well beaten eggs and beat. Add a portion of flour sifted with salt and soda and mix well. Add fruit mixture and nuts, and stir to blend. Add remainder of flour and stir until fruit is well distributed.

Pour into 10-inch tube pan which has been lined with 2 thicknesses of greased brown paper and 1 of greased waxed paper. (Allow paper to extend about ¾ inch above rim for safety.)

Bake in slow oven (250°F.) about 3 hours, raise temperature to 300°F. and continue baking about 1½ hours.

Decorate top with whole blanched almonds and thin strips of candied citron. Baked weight about 7½ pound cake.

ORANGE FRUIT CAKE

2½ cups sifted cake flour
1½ teaspoons baking soda
1/2 teaspoon salt
1   teaspoon cinnamon
1/2 teaspoon cloves
1/4 teaspoon allspice
1/2 cup finely cut citron
1/2 cup finely cut candied pineapple
1/2 cup quartered candied cherries
1/2 cup broken nutmeats
1/2 cup shortening
2   cups sugar
2   well beaten eggs
1   tablespoon grated orange rind
3½ tablespoons vinegar and enough sour cream to make 1 cup
3/4 cup orange juice

Sift flour, soda, salt, cinnamon, cloves, and allspice together. Add cut fruits and nuts and mix well.

Cream shortening. Add 1 cup sugar gradually and cream until fluffy.

Add eggs and grated orange rind. Beat well. Add vinegar and sour cream alternately with the flour mixture to the creamed ingredients. Mix until thoroughly blended.

Pour into well greased 9-inch tube pan. Bake in moderate oven (350° F.) 1 hour.

After cake is removed from oven, and while it is still hot, pour over it 1 cup sugar mixed with orange juice. Let cake cool before removing from pan.

Tortes and Miscellaneous Cakes

HINTS ABOUT TORTES

The German word for tart or cake is torte (plural—torten) and the term refers to the cakes of European cooks in which ground nuts or crumbs (cake, cracker, or bread) are usually used instead of flour. Torten are made light with eggs and generally contain no shortening. In this country there is a tendency also to apply the term to cakelike desserts, frequently differing very little from conventional cakes. The famous European torten may vary from one to twelve layers.

Many of the following recipes are baked in 9-inch spring form pans. The spring form pan should be greased and sprinkled lightly with flour.

The making of torten is not difficult although they sometimes require long beating. Some traditional recipes are at their best if beaten for as much as thirty minutes.

To remove torte from pan, be sure to run a spatula around the edge of torte, then release the side spring of pan. Do not remove torte from bottom of pan until thoroughly cooled unless specifically directed to do so in the recipe.

Fruit pulp or chilled jellies whipped are favorite torte fillings. Nut torten are frequently spread with whipped jelly, particularly currant jelly, and then sprinkled with blanched, browned, slivered almonds.

Whipped cream flavored with brandy, rum, extracts, or coffee is the outstanding favorite for frostings.

ALMOND MOCHA TORTE

4 egg yolks
1 cup sugar
1 tablespoon melted butter or margarine
½ teaspoon vanilla
½ cup sifted all-purpose flour
½ teaspoon salt
1 teaspoon baking powder
4 egg whites
1 cup ground almonds
Toasted almonds
Candied cherry slices

Beat egg yolks with sugar until thick

Almond Mocha Torte

and ivory-colored. Beat in butter and vanilla.

Sift flour with salt and baking powder; blend into egg yolk mixture.

Beat egg whites until soft peaks form; fold in ground almonds. Combine with yolk mixture, and spread into two greased and floured 9-inch layer cake pans.

Bake in moderate oven (350°F.) 25 minutes. Turn out on racks at once; layers get crisp as they cool.

Spread with filling (below). Decorate with almond slices and candied cherries. Let stand 12 hours in cool place before serving. Makes 1 9-inch torte.

Filling:
1 cup whipping cream
1 tablespoon powdered instant coffee
1 tablespoon powdered sugar

Whip cream; blend in coffee and sugar.

APPLE TORTE

4 eggs, separated
¾ cup sugar
3 apples, grated
1 cup lady finger or sponge cake crumbs
Juice and grated rind of ½ lemon
¼ cup chopped almonds

Beat egg yolks and sugar until light; blend in apples, crumbs, lemon juice and rind, and then fold in the stiffly beaten whites.

Pour into a greased and floured 8-inch spring form pan. Sprinkle with almonds, pressing them into mixture with the back of spoon.

Bake in moderate oven (350°F.) 20 to 25 minutes. Leave torte on bottom of spring form. Serve with cream.

NUT ZWIEBACK TORTE

5 eggs, separated
1 cup sugar
1 cup chopped nuts
1 cup zwieback crumbs
1 teaspoon baking powder

Beat egg yolks until light; add sugar gradually and beat until thick and lemon-colored.

Blend in nuts and crumbs, then fold in the stiffly beaten egg whites and baking powder.

Turn into 2 round 8-inch layer cake pans. Bake in moderate oven (350°F.) 20 minutes.

Fill the cooled layers and cover the top and sides with sweetened whipped cream flavored with sherry. Decorate the top with pecan halves.

Imperial Waltz Torte

IMPERIAL WALTZ TORTE

2 6-ounce packages butterscotch pieces
½ cup sugar
½ cup water
2 teaspoons vanilla
1 package pie crust mix or pastry mix for 2-crust, 9-inch pie
1 cup whipping cream, whipped
1 cup toasted chopped pecans
Whole pecans
Cream

In a saucepan combine butterscotch pieces, sugar, and water. Cook over low heat, stirring constantly, until smooth. Add vanilla; cool.

Blend ½ cup butterscotch sauce into pie crust mix. Divide pastry into 6 equal parts (should be slightly less than ¼ cup each).

On foil-covered cooky sheets draw 7-inch circles. Place a pastry portion in center of a circle; pat and press out dough to cover circle.

Bake in hot oven (425°F.) 5 minutes or until done; cool. Run tip of knife under edges of layers to loosen; lift off carefully. Repeat until six layers are made.

Fold all but ½ cup remaining butterscotch sauce into whipped cream. Spread each layer with butterscotch cream and sprinkle with about 3 tablespoons pecans.

Stack layers; garnish top with whole pecans. Chill until serving. Thin remaining ½ cup butterscotch sauce with a little cream and serve with torte.

MATZO ALMOND TORTE

5 eggs, separated
1 cup sugar
1 cup almonds, ground without blanching
½ cup matzo meal
1 teaspoon baking powder
1 teaspoon cinnamon
¼ teaspoon cloves
1 tablespoon lemon juice or brandy

Beat egg yolks and sugar until light; add remaining ingredients in order given, adding the stiffly beaten whites last.

Pour into greased and floured 8-inch spring form pan. Bake in moderate oven (350°F.) 1 hour.

SCHAUM TORTE

Schaum Torte is the German name for a meringue baked in layers or in a spring-form pan and served with fruit and whipped cream.

6   egg whites
1¾ cups powdered sugar
1   teaspoon vinegar
1   teaspoon almond extract
Strawberries or raspberries, crushed
Extra powdered sugar
Whipped cream
Whole strawberries or raspberries

Beat egg whites until stiff. Gradually add sifted powdered sugar, vinegar, and almond extract.

Bake in 2 loose-bottomed, buttered, 8-inch cake pans in slow oven (275°F.) 40 minutes.

Turn off oven and leave oven door open to allow meringue to cool 30 minutes.

When cool, fill layers with strawberries or raspberries crushed with powdered sugar. Also put fruit on top layer and cover with whipped cream. Decorate with whole berries. Serve immediately.

DOBOS TORTE

The Dobos Torte, created by a famous Hungarian pastry chef named Dobos, consists of a sponge type cake made in several layers with a rich chocolate filling between layers and a caramel glaze spread over the top.

Batter:

¾ cup sifted cake flour
¼ teaspoon salt
6   eggs, separated
1   cup sugar
1   teaspoon vanilla

Filling:

½   cup sugar
4   large eggs
4   squares (4 ounces) bittersweet
      chocolate
2   tablespoons boiling water
⅞   cup butter
1   teaspoon vanilla

Mix and sift flour and salt 4 times.

Beat egg yolks until light and lemon-colored. Gradually beat in sugar, and with last addition add vanilla. Gradually add flour. Beat well.

Beat egg whites until stiff, but not dry, and fold in lightly.

Grease 4 8-inch cake pans and pour in a thin layer of batter, spreading evenly. Reserve half the batter for remaining 4 layers.

Bake in moderate oven (375°F.) 5 to 8 minutes.

Remove cake at once from pans. Grease and refill pans with remaining batter. Set layers aside to cool.

Filling: Combine in top of double boiler sugar and eggs. Cook over boiling water, beating constantly until mixture begins to thicken. Cool slightly.

Cut chocolate into small pieces. Dissolve in boiling water and keep warm until needed.

Cream butter until light. Add melted chocolate and vanilla. Combine with egg mixture.

Spread filling between layers. Place toothpicks through top layers to hold layers in place until filling sets. Spread with caramel glaze (below).

Caramel Glaze: Melt and brown in a skillet 3 tablespoons powdered sugar and pour over the cake. Spread with a hot knife. Let cake stand in cool place 24 hours before serving.

BREAD TORTE

The bread torte or brottorte is an old-time German cake.

5   eggs, separated
1   cup sugar
1   cup grated breadcrumbs
Juice and grated rind of ½ lemon or
      2 tablespoons wine
1   cup almonds, blanched and grated
1½ teaspoons baking powder

Beat egg yolks and sugar until very light.

Soak breadcrumbs in lemon juice or wine. Mix all ingredients folding in the stiffly beaten egg whites last.

Turn into 2 greased and floured 9-inch layer pans. Bake in moderate oven (350°F.) 45 minutes. Fill with walnut filling.

GRAHAM CRACKER DATE-NUT TORTE

2   cups graham cracker crumbs (about
      20 crackers)
1   teaspoon salt
1   teaspoon baking powder
1   tablespoon sugar
3   well beaten eggs
3   cups chopped pitted dates
3   tablespoons flour
½   cup chopped walnuts or pecans
1   teaspoon vanilla
⅓   cup milk
Whipped cream

Combine crumbs, salt, baking powder, and sugar. Add eggs.

Toss dates in flour to keep them from sticking. Add floured dates, nuts, vanilla, and milk.

Pour mixture into a greased 8-inch square pan. Bake in slow oven (325°F.) 45 minutes.

Cut into squares. Top each with whipped cream.

LINZER TORTE

A rich German cake that resembles an open-face jam pie.

1½ cups sifted enriched flour
¼   cup sugar
½   teaspoon baking powder
½   teaspoon salt
½   teaspoon cinnamon
½   cup firmly packed brown sugar
½   cup butter or margarine
1   egg, unbeaten
½   cup ground unblanched almonds

Sift together flour, sugar, baking powder, salt, and cinnamon. Cut in brown sugar and butter or margarine. Add egg and almonds. Blend with pastry blender or fork.

Reserve a generous ½ cup of dough for topping and chill. Press remaining dough evenly into bottom and sides of 8-inch pie pan. (Do not cover rim of pie pan.)

Fill with cream filling (below). Top with raspberry sauce (below).

Roll out chilled ½ cup of dough on floured pastry cloth or board to ⅛-inch thickness. Cut into ½-inch strips with pastry wheel or knife. Arrange over filling, crisscross fashion.

Cover ends of lattice strips with another strip, circling pie but not covering rim of pie pan. Press to seal.

Bake in moderate oven (375°F.) 30 to 35 minutes. Serve warm or cool.

Cream Filling: Beat 1 egg until fluffy, about 2 minutes. Add gradually ⅓ cup sugar; beat until thick and lemon-colored. Blend in ¼ cup sifted enriched flour and ¼ teaspoon salt.

Gradually add 1½ cups milk, which has been scalded in top of double boiler.

Return mixture to top of double boiler. Cook over boiling water, stirring constantly, until thick. Cover and continue cooking 4 to 5 minutes, stirring occasionally. Add 1 teaspoon vanilla. Cool.

Raspberry Sauce: Combine 1 package thawed, frozen raspberries, undrained, 2 tablespoons sugar, and 2 tablespoons cornstarch in saucepan. (If desired, 1½ cups fresh raspberries and ¼ cup sugar may be substituted. Omit cornstarch.)

Add 1 tablespoon lemon juice. Bring to boil and cook 5 to 10 minutes until mixture begins to thicken. Cool.

Linzer Torte

POPPY SEED TORTE

¾ cup poppy seed
¾ cup milk
¾ cup butter
1½ cups sugar
2 cups sifted cake flour
2 teaspoons baking powder
¼ teaspoon salt
4 stiffly-beaten egg whites
Filling (see below)

Soak poppy seed in milk overnight.

Cream butter to soften; add sugar gradually and cream together. Mix in milk and poppy seed.

Sift dry ingredients together; add to creamed mixture. Fold in egg whites.

Bake in 3 paper-lined 8 x 1¼-inch round pans in moderate oven (350°F.) 25 to 30 minutes.

Cool 10 minutes; remove from pans.

Filling: Mix ½ cup sugar and 1 tablespoon cornstarch in double boiler. Combine 1½ cups milk and 4 well beaten egg yolks; gradually stir into sugar mixture and cook, stirring constantly, until thick.

Cool slightly; add 1 teaspoon vanilla and ¼ cup chopped walnuts. Cool.

Spread between cooled cake layers. For design on top, cut a daisy stencil from cardboard or heavy paper; lay it on torte. Sift confectioners' sugar over top; lift off stencil. Center daisy with grated orange rind.

SWEDISH APPLE CAKE

4 tablespoons butter
2 cups zwieback crumbs
Few drops lemon juice
1 tablespoon Angostura bitters
2 cups applesauce

Melt butter in skillet, add sifted zwieback crumbs and stir until nicely brown. Add lemon juice and bitters.

Butter baking dish well and arrange crumbs and applesauce in alternating layers finishing with crumbs.

Bake in moderate oven (375°F.) 25 to 35 minutes. Cool before unmolding and serve with whipped cream.

Swedish Apple Cake

YAEGERTORTE
(Hunter's Cake)

½ pound whole unpeeled almonds
8 small eggs
1 cup sugar
Grated rind of 1 lemon
1 tablespoon lemon juice
Fine breadcrumbs

Grind unpeeled almonds in food chopper.

Beat 2 whole eggs and 6 yolks thoroughly for about 5 minutes. Stir in ground almonds, sugar, lemon rind, and juice. Last, fold in stiffly beaten egg whites thoroughly.

Sprinkle some fine breadcrumbs on bottom of a greased 9-inch spring form pan. Pour in the batter.

Bake in moderate oven (375°F.) about 1 hour. Let cool before gently removing from pan.

Frost top and sides of cake with chocolate confectioners' sugar frosting, and decorate with whole peeled almonds. This cake improves in flavor if held a day or two.

Chocolate Frosting: Melt 2 1-ounce squares unsweetened chocolate with 3½ tablespoons milk and 1 tablespoon butter.

Cool, then add ¼ teaspoon vanilla, and work in about 2½ cups sifted confectioners' sugar, or enough to make soft spreadable frosting.

CHOCOLATE WALNUT TORTE

6 eggs, separated
1 cup sugar
1 cup chopped or ground walnuts or pecans
2 tablespoons graham cracker crumbs
1 teaspoon vanilla
1 cup sweet butter
1 cup confectioners' sugar
4 ounces (4 squares) chocolate
2 teaspoons sherry

Beat egg yolks, gradually adding the sugar. Add nuts and cracker crumbs, then vanilla. Fold in stiffly beaten egg whites.

Bake in 2 greased, floured 9-inch pans in moderate oven (350°F.) about 30 minutes. Cool.

Cream butter; add sugar and beat until fluffy.

Melt chocolate in top of double boiler; add to sugar-butter mixture, blending well.

Spread one layer of the torte with marmalade or strawberry jam to a thickness of ¼ inch. Sprinkle with sherry.

Place on top layer and cover top and sides of cake with butter frosting.

Place in refrigerator and it will keep at least two weeks, or without refrigeration for 2 to 3 days. Serves 6.

ALMOND TORTE

1 pound almonds
8 eggs, separated
1 cup sugar
Pinch of salt
1 teaspoon baking powder
½ teaspoon almond extract
1 teaspoon vanilla

Blanch almonds, dry and grind to a fine meal.

Beat egg whites until stiff and beat into them half the sugar.

Beat egg yolks with remaining sugar until light and lemon-colored.

Fold the yolks into whites, then carefully fold in almond meal, salt, and baking powder. Add almond extract and vanilla.

Pour into 9-inch spring form pan. Bake in slow oven (300°F.) 1¼ hours.

Cool and cover with whipped cream to which sugar has been added to taste.

Garnish with blanched almonds, slivered and sautéed in butter until lightly browned.

Hazelnut Torte: Substitute hazelnuts for almonds.

LEKACH
(Traditional Jewish Honey Cake)

6 eggs
1 cup sugar
1 cup honey
2 tablespoons salad oil or melted shortening
3½ cups sifted enriched flour
1½ teaspoons baking powder
1 teaspoon baking soda
¼ teaspoon ground cloves
½ teaspoon cinnamon
½ teaspoon allspice
½ cup chopped nuts
½ cup raisins
¼ cup finely cut citron or mixed candied fruit
2 tablespoons brandy

Beat eggs well, then gradually add sugar and beat until light and creamy. Stir in honey and shortening.

Mix and sift flour, baking powder, soda, and spices; stir in the nuts and fruit, then combine with first mixture. Add brandy last.

Pour into a paper-lined and oiled rectangular pan. Sprinkle a few blanched, halved almonds on top, if desired.

Bake in a slow oven (325°F.) about 1 hour.

Invert pan and allow cake to cool before removing. When ready to serve, cut into squares or diamond shapes.

Variation: Instead of the 6 eggs, use 4 eggs plus ½ cup coffee or tea. Dilute the honey with the hot coffee or tea before combining. The 6-egg recipe makes a cake of finer texture.

CHOCOLATE TORTE

- 8 eggs, separated
- 1 cup sugar
- 2 squares (2 ounces) unsweetened chocolate, grated
- ½ cup breadcrumbs

Beat egg yolks and sugar together until thick and lemon-colored. Add grated chocolate and stir until mixture is well combined.

Add crumbs and then fold in stiffly beaten egg whites.

Turn into 2 buttered 8-inch layer cake pans. Bake in moderate oven (350°F.) 40 minutes.

Remove from pans and cool on cake rack. When cool, split each layer in half, making 4 layers.

Fill between the layers and cover top and sides with following frosting:

Mix together 1 cup sugar, 1 cup milk, and 2 ounces (2 squares) unsweetened chocolate, grated. Cook until a soft ball is formed when dropped into cold water.

Remove from heat; then add 1 teaspoon vanilla and 1 tablespoon butter, which has been creamed thoroughly with 2 egg yolks. Beat until cool enough to spread.

Whip 1 pint heavy cream and fold the chocolate mixture into the cream. Add sugar to taste.

BLITZ TORTE

- 1⅓ cups sifted cake flour
- 1⅓ teaspoons baking powder
- ⅛ teaspoon salt
- ½ cup shortening
- 1½ cups sugar
- 4 eggs, separated
- 5 tablespoons milk or cream
- 1 teaspoon vanilla
- ½ teaspoon cinnamon
- ½ cup shredded blanched almonds

Mix and sift flour, baking powder, and salt 3 times.

Cream shortening. Gradually beat in ½ cup sugar. Add egg yolks, one at a time, beating after each addition until the mixture is light and fluffy.

Alternately add dry ingredients with milk, starting and ending with flour and beating after each addition until smooth.

Add vanilla. Spread batter in two 9-inch greased pans.

Beat egg whites until stiff. Gradually beat in 1 cup sugar and cinnamon. Spread in equal amounts on top of each layer. Sprinkle thickly with almonds.

Bake in slow oven (325°F.) 25 minutes. Increase heat to (350°F.) and bake 30 minutes longer.

Remove cake from pans. Cool. Put layers together with crushed sweetened fruit and whipped cream.

SACHER TORTE

A rich chocolate cake named for a famous Viennese restaurant.

- ½ cup sweet butter
- ½ cup plus 2 tablespoons confectioners' sugar
- 4 ounces (4 squares) sweet chocolate, melted
- 6 eggs, separated
- 1 tablespoon grated lemon rind
- 1 teaspoon cinnamon
- ½ teaspoon cloves
- 1 cup plus 2 tablespoons very fine toasted white breadcrumbs
- ⅛ teaspoon salt

Apricot jam

Cream butter until soft and creamy. Gradually add sugar and continue beating until well blended.

Beat in chocolate and egg yolks, one at a time, beating well after each addition. Stir in lemon rind, cinnamon, cloves, and breadcrumbs. Mix well.

Beat egg whites with salt until stiff, but not dry. Fold lightly into batter.

Bake in 2 greased 8-inch cake pans in slow oven (325°F.) 25 minutes.

Remove from pans and cool. Spread apricot jam between layers. Frost with chocolate frosting.

MERINGUE MOLASSES TORTE

Cake:

- 2 cups sifted enriched flour
- ½ teaspoon salt
- ¾ teaspoon baking powder
- ½ teaspoon baking soda
- ⅓ cup granulated sugar
- 1 egg
- ¾ cup dark molasses
- ¾ cup boiling water
- ½ cup shortening

Sift flour, salt, baking powder, baking soda, and granulated sugar together. Add egg and molasses, mix well.

Pour boiling water over shortening in a pint measure. Add to flour mixture and beat.

Bake in square cake dish in slow oven (325°F.) for 40 minutes.

Meringue:

- 2 egg whites
- ½ cup brown sugar
- ½ teaspoon vanilla
- ¼ cup chopped nuts

Beat egg whites until stiff. Beat in brown sugar gradually. Add vanilla; fold in chopped nuts.

Remove cake from oven after 40 minutes of baking; spread meringue evenly over top.

Return to slow oven (325°F.) for 12 to 15 minutes or until meringue is browned.

FRUIT-FILLED CROWN CAKE
(French)

- ½ cup butter or margarine
- 1 cup sifted enriched flour
- ½ teaspoon baking powder
- 4 egg yolks
- ¾ cup sugar
- 2 tablespoons water
- 1 tablespoon rum extract or 1 teaspoon vanilla
- 4 egg whites
- ½ teaspoon salt
- 1 cup apricot jam

Melt butter or margarine; cool. Sift together flour and baking powder.

Beat egg yolks in small mixing bowl until blended. Gradually add sugar, beating well after each addition. Continue beating thoroughly until very thick and ivory colored. (With electric mixer beat at high speed at least 5 minutes.)

Blend in water and rum extract or vanilla. Fold in dry ingredients, ⅓ at a time. Fold carefully but thoroughly until dry ingredients disappear.

Beat egg whites with salt until stiff but not dry. Fold in egg yolk and flour mixture gently. Add cooled, melted butter; fold just until blended.

Turn into well greased and lightly floured 9-inch ring mold pan. Fill no more than ½ full.

Bake in moderate oven (350°F.) 25 to 30 minutes. Cool. Spread with apricot jam. Fill center with fruit salad just before serving.

Fruit Salad: Combine 4 oranges, sectioned (reserve 6 sections for garnish), 2 bananas, sliced, 1 apple, diced, and ½ cup well drained pineapple.

Whip 1 cup whipping cream; fold in 2 tablespoons confectioners' sugar and 1 teaspoon vanilla. Fold ¾ of cream into fruit.

Spoon lightly into center of cake. Decorate with remaining whipped cream and orange sections.

Fruit-Filled Crown Cake

Meringue Molasses Torte

CHESTNUT TORTE

1 pound chestnuts
3 egg yolks
6 whole eggs
6 tablespoons sugar
2 teaspoons vanilla
3 egg whites
Pinch of salt
1/2 pint whipping cream
3 tablespoons crushed pineapple

Make a gash in each chestnut. Place chestnuts in boiling water and cook 20 minutes. Drain and remove both outer and inner shell; press through sieve.

Beat egg yolks and whole eggs; add sugar and beat together thoroughly about 5 minutes with electric mixer or 10 minutes with rotary beater.

Add chestnuts gradually and beat 15 minutes longer. Add vanilla.

Beat the 3 egg whites with salt until stiff, and fold in gently.

Bake in unbuttered torte pan in moderate oven (350°F.) 50 minutes.

Frost with 1/2 pint whipping cream, whipped with vanilla sugar (see index) to taste; then fold in 3 tablespoons well drained crushed pineapple.

ORANGE TORTE

1 orange
1 cup raisins
1 cup sifted enriched flour
1/2 teaspoon baking soda
1 teaspoon baking powder
1/4 teaspoon salt
1 cup firmly packed brown sugar
1/2 cup shortening
1 egg
1 cup buttermilk
1 cup uncooked rolled oats

Squeeze orange and set juice aside. Grind orange rind and raisins through medium blade of food chopper.

Mix and sift flour, soda, baking powder, and salt into a bowl. Add brown sugar, shortening, egg, and orange juice. Beat until smooth.

Fold in orange rind and raisin mixture, buttermilk, and rolled oats. Turn into a greased square cake pan.

Bake in a moderate oven (350°F.) 45 to 50 minutes. Serve warm with whipped cream or hard sauce.

Fruit Cocktail Torte

HUNGARIAN TORTE

1 whole egg
6 eggs, separated
3/4 cup sugar
1 2/3 cups ground walnuts
1 square (1 ounce) unsweetened chocolate, grated
1/2 cup dried cake crumbs
1/2 teaspoon almond extract
Currant jelly
1/2 pint heavy cream, whipped

Beat egg yolks and whole egg until light and lemon-colored.

Add sugar, nuts, chocolate, and cake crumbs, beating after each addition.

Add almond extract. Fold in stiffly beaten egg whites.

Bake in 2 well buttered and floured 9-inch cake pans in moderate oven (350°F.) 15 or 20 minutes.

When cold, cut layers in half and fill with currant jelly. Cover with chocolate frosting and top with whipped cream.

FRUIT COCKTAIL TORTE

1/2 cup shortening
1 1/4 cups sugar
4 eggs, separated
1 cup sifted cake flour
1 teaspoon baking powder
1/8 teaspoon salt
3 tablespoons milk
1 teaspoon vanilla
Cream filling (below)
1/2 of No. 2 1/2 can (1 3/4 cups) fruit cocktail

Cream shortening; add 1/2 cup sugar gradually. Cream until light and fluffy. Add well beaten egg yolks and blend.

Mix and sift flour, baking powder, and salt. Add dry ingredients to creamed mixture alternately with milk, beginning and ending with dry ingredients. Mix well. Add vanilla.

Spread batter in 2 greased 9-inch layer cake pans that have been lined with waxed paper.

Beat egg whites stiff, then gradually add remaining 3/4 cup sugar while continuing to beat. Cover batter with this meringue.

Bake in moderate oven (350°F.) about 35 minutes.

Remove from pan and cool, meringue side up on cake racks. When cake is cool, put the 2 layers together with cream filling (below). Top with drained fruit cocktail.

Cream Filling: Scald 1 cup milk. Combine 1/4 cup sugar and 1 tablespoon cornstarch; add to 1 beaten egg and blend well.

Add scalded milk gradually, stirring constantly. Cool. Add 1/2 teaspoon almond extract.

Strawberry Cream Torte

STRAWBERRY CREAM TORTE

1/4 cup shortening
1/4 cup sugar
1/2 teaspoon vanilla
2 egg yolks
3/4 cup sifted cake flour
1/4 teaspoon salt
1 teaspoon baking powder
1/4 cup milk

Cream shortening until fluffy. Gradually beat in 1/4 cup sugar. Beat in vanilla and egg yolks.

Sift flour, salt, and baking powder together and add alternately with milk to egg mixture.

Pour batter into a well greased 8-inch square cake pan. Top with a meringue made of:

3 egg whites
1/8 teaspoon cream of tartar
1/2 cup sugar

Beat egg whites until stiff. Add cream of tartar. Beat in sugar gradually. Spread on cake batter.

Bake in very slow oven (250°F.) 25 minutes. Increase heat to moderate (350°F.) and bake 20 minutes longer.

Remove from oven and cool. Top with 1 cup of heavy cream, whipped until stiff, then mixed with 1 cup sliced strawberries. Garnish with whole berries.

CHOCOLATE WHIPPED CREAM TORTE

7 eggs, separated
2 cups powdered sugar
6 squares (6 ounces) chocolate, grated
1 teaspoon vanilla
2 1/3 cups almonds, ground
Whipped cream, almond-flavored

Beat egg yolks with 1 1/2 cups powdered sugar until lemon-colored.

Add grated chocolate, vanilla, and ground almonds. Beat thoroughly.

Beat egg whites until stiff, and fold in 1/2 cup powdered sugar. Fold into first mixture.

Bake in 3 well buttered and floured 8-inch cake pans in a slow oven (325°F.) about 30 minutes.

When cold, fill and cover with sweetened, almond-flavored whipped cream.

SICILIAN STRUFOLI

About 2 cups sifted enriched flour
1/4 teaspoon salt
3 eggs
2 cups shortening or salad oil
1/2 cup mild-flavored honey
1/2 cup sugar
Pine nuts
Colored candy sprinkles

Place 1½ cups flour and the salt on a board. Make a depression in the center and add eggs. Use a spatula and mix, adding enough more of the flour to make a fairly stiff dough. Knead until smooth.

Using half the dough at a time, roll on a floured board to 1/4-inch thickness. Cut into 1/4-inch strips. Roll each strip of dough under the hands to form a rope.

Arrange several of these ropes, side by side, and cut into 1/4-inch squares. Place these separately on a floured board or tray.

Heat shortening or oil to 350°F. in a deep saucepan. Carefully lower the dough by spoonfuls into fat and fry, stirring constantly, until light brown. Remove with a perforated spoon and drain on absorbent paper. Keep warm.

Mix sugar and honey in a large skillet. Cook over low heat, stirring constantly, to consistency of a heavy syrup, about 5 minutes.

Add fried dough and toss to coat each piece with syrup.

Shape into a mound (or other desired shape) on a platter and sprinkle with pine nuts and colored candies. Serves 8.

VIENNA TORTE

7 eggs, separated
1¼ cups sugar
1 cup sifted enriched flour
1/4 cup cornstarch
2 teaspoons baking powder
Pinch of salt

Beat egg whites until frothy. Add 1/2 cup sugar gradually and beat until stiff.

Beat egg yolks until thick; then gradually beat in remaining sugar. Combine with first mixture.

Mix and sift flour with cornstarch, baking powder, and salt and fold in carefully.

Turn into 4 greased 8-inch layer cake pans. Bake in moderate oven (350° F.) about 20 minutes.

Vienna Torte Filling: Heat 1¼ cups milk in double boiler. Mix 1/3 cup flour, 1/3 cup sugar, and 1/4 cup cold milk. Add to heated milk and stir until thick, then cover and cook 15 minutes. Cool.

When cool, add 1 cup melted butter; mix well, then add 1 teaspoon vanilla and 1 cup confectioners' sugar. Spread between the layers and on top and sides. Cover well with chopped nuts.

ALMOND TORTE #2

7 egg whites
1 cup sugar
2 cups ground blanched almonds
1/2 teaspoon almond extract

Beat egg whites until stiff. Fold in sugar gradually. Fold in ground almonds. Add almond extract last.

Turn into 2 buttered and floured 9-inch cake pans. Bake in slow oven (325°F.) about 40 minutes.

Fill and cover cooled layers with almond torte filling and frosting (below).

Almond Torte Filling And Frosting:

7 egg yolks
8 tablespoons sugar
Pinch of salt
1/2 cup sweet butter
1/2 teaspoon vanilla
1 teaspoon grated orange rind
Shaved almonds

Place egg yolks in top of double boiler over hot water.

Beat yolks until creamy, gradually adding sugar and salt. Remove and cool.

Cream butter until lemon-colored and add to first mixture. Add vanilla and orange rind.

Fill and cover layers. Sprinkle with shaved almonds.

ORANGE TORTE #2

2½ cups sifted cake flour
1¼ teaspoons baking soda
1/2 teaspoon salt
1 teaspoon cinnamon
1/2 teaspoon cloves
1/4 teaspoon allspice
1/2 cup finely cut citron
1/2 cup finely cut candied pineapple
1/2 cup quartered candied cherries
1/2 cup broken nuts
1/2 cup shortening
1 cup sugar
2 well beaten eggs
1 tablespoon grated orange rind
3½ teaspoons vinegar and sour cream to make 1 cup
1 cup sugar
3/4 cup orange juice

Sift flour, soda, salt, cinnamon, cloves, and allspice together. Add fruit and nuts; mix well.

Cream shortening. Add sugar gradually and cream until fluffy. Add eggs and grated orange rind. Beat well.

Mix vinegar and sour cream together. Add alternately with flour mixture to creamed ingredients. Mix until thoroughly blended.

Pour into well greased 9-inch tube pan. Bake in moderate oven (350°F.) 1 hour.

After cake is removed from oven and while it is still hot, pour over it the 1 cup sugar mixed with orange juice. Let cake cool before removing from pan.

MERINGUE CRADLE CAKE

4 egg whites
1 cup sugar
1 cup finely chopped pecans (filberts, almonds, or other nuts may also be used)
1 square (1 ounce) grated unsweetened chocolate
2 cups sifted enriched flour
3 teaspoons baking powder
1 teaspoon salt
1/2 cup butter or margarine
1 cup sugar
4 egg yolks
3/4 cup milk
1 teaspoon vanilla

Beat egg whites until soft mounds form. Gradually add 1 cup sugar, beating constantly until straight, glossy peaks are formed when beater is raised. Fold in pecans and chocolate.

Spread evenly over bottom and three-fourths up sides of 10-inch tube pan, well greased and lined with waxed paper on the bottom only.

Sift together flour, baking powder, and salt.

Cream butter. Gradually add 1 cup sugar, creaming well. Add egg yolks; beat well.

Combine milk and vanilla. Add alternately with the dry ingredients to creamed mixture, beginning and ending with dry ingredients. Blend thoroughly after each addition. (With electric mixer use a low speed.) Pour into meringue-lined pan.

Bake in slow oven (325°F.) 75 to 85 minutes until cake springs back completely, leaving no imprint when touched lightly in center.

Let cool in pan 20 minutes; loosen from sides and center tube with spatula and let cool 30 minutes longer before removing from pan.

Note: Cake may also be baked in two 9 x 5 x 3 inch bread pans for 50 to 60 minutes.

Meringue Cradle Cake

ROCOCO TORTE

5 eggs, separated
5 tablespoons sugar
2 tablespoons fine breadcrumbs
2 tablespoons flour
2 squares (2 ounces) sweet chocolate, grated

Beat egg yolks until light and lemon-colored. Add sugar gradually and beat well.

Blend in breadcrumbs, flour, and grated chocolate, then fold in stiffly beaten egg whites.

Turn into two 8-inch well buttered layer cake pans. Bake in a moderate oven (350°F.) 30 minutes.

Remove from pans and cool on cake rack. When cool, fill layers and cover the top with creamy walnut frosting (below).

Creamy Walnut Frosting: Cream together 6 tablespoons butter and 2 tablespoons sugar. Combine 1 cup ground walnuts and ½ cup light cream and stir into the butter-sugar mixture. Add 1 teaspoon vanilla and beat until the mixture is thick and foamy.

ALMOND ANGEL TORTE

2 cups almonds
½ pound dates
5 eggs, separated
¾ cup confectioners' sugar
2 teaspoons baking powder

Blanch almonds, reserving a few to decorate the top. Grind the nuts. Pit the dates; pour boiling water over them, drain and rub to a smooth paste.

Beat egg yolks and gradually add sugar and date pulp; then lightly stir in almonds.

Fold baking powder into stiffly beaten egg whites and fold whites into the above mixture.

Turn into a well greased and floured 9-inch spring form pan. Bake in moderate oven (350°F.) about 45 minutes.

When cool, cut in 2 layers and spread layers and top with whipped cream. Sprinkle with remaining almonds, sliced.

DATE TORTE

½ cup sifted enriched flour
⅛ teaspoon salt
1 teaspoon baking powder
2 beaten eggs
½ cup sugar
½ teaspoon vanilla
½ teaspoon almond extract
1 cup chopped pecans
2 cups chopped dates
¼ cup chopped candied cherries

Mix and sift flour, salt, and baking powder; add eggs beaten with sugar. Add vanilla and almond extract, nuts, and fruits.

Bake in greased 8-inch square pan in slow oven (300°F.) 1 hour. Serve topped with whipped cream or with custard sauce. Serves 8.

LEMON ANGEL TORTE

1 teaspoon vanilla
1 teaspoon vinegar
1 teaspoon water
3 egg whites
½ teaspoon baking powder
⅛ teaspoon salt
1 cup sifted granulated sugar
1 beaten whole egg
4 beaten egg yolks
½ cup sugar
1½ tablespoons flour
¾ cup water
Grated rind and juice of 1½ lemons
1 cup heavy cream
½ teaspoon vanilla

Combine 1 teaspoon vanilla, vinegar, and water.

Beat egg whites, baking powder, and salt until stiff. Add 1 cup sugar in tablespoon portions, alternating with a few drops of combined liquids. Beat until stiff and glossy.

Heap lightly into greased pie pan. Press into shape of pie shell with a spoon.

Bake in very slow oven (275°F.) 1 hour.

Combine remaining ingredients except cream and vanilla. Cook in top of double boiler until thick, stirring constantly. Cool.

Whip cream and flavor with ½ teaspoon vanilla.

When meringue shell is cool, spread part of whipped cream in a layer on the bottom. Pour in the cooled lemon mixture.

Decorate top of pie with remaining whipped cream. Chill several hours before serving.

CHERRY ZWIEBACK TORTE

1 cup drained pitted cherries
¾ cup zwieback crumbs
4 eggs, separated
2 cups sugar
¼ cup hot cherry juice
¼ cup chopped nuts
1 teaspoon cinnamon

Mix cherries with ¼ cup crumbs. Set aside.

Beat egg yolks and sugar until lemon-colored. Blend in cherry juice, then add ½ cup crumbs and beat until smooth.

Add nuts and cinnamon, then the crumbed cherries and then fold in the stiffly beaten egg whites.

Turn into a greased 9-inch spring form pan sprinkled with crumbs.

Bake in moderate oven (350°F.) 40 to 50 minutes. Serve with whipped cream.

Square Dance Nut Cake

SQUARE DANCE NUT CAKE

1⅔ cups sifted enriched flour
2 teaspoons baking powder
½ teaspoon salt
1 cup sugar
½ cup soft butter (half shortening may be used)
⅔ cup milk
3 egg whites, unbeaten
½ teaspoon vanilla
¼ teaspoon lemon extract
½ cup chopped walnuts

Sift together flour, baking powder, salt, and sugar. Add butter and milk.

Beat for 1½ minutes, 150 strokes per minute, until batter is well blended. (With electric mixer blend at low speed, then beat at medium speed for 1½ minutes.)

Add egg whites, vanilla, and lemon extract. Beat for 1½ minutes.

Blend in walnuts. Pour into 8 x 8 x 2-inch pan, well greased and lightly floured on the bottom only.

Bake in moderate oven (350° F.) 40 to 50 minutes.

Cool. Cut cake into four squares; frost with checkerboard frosting.

Checkerboard Frosting: Combine 1 tablespoon warm milk, 2 tablespoons melted butter, 2¼ cups sifted confectioners' sugar, 1 egg yolk, and ½ teaspoon vanilla. Beat until smooth and creamy.

Add 1 square (1 ounce) melted unsweetened chocolate and 1 tablespoon milk to one third of the frosting.

Frost two cake squares with white frosting, two with chocolate.

Arrange squares checkerboard fashion. Decorate with chopped nuts.

BREADCRUMB CAKE

3 eggs
1 cup sugar
2 cups crumbs, from very dry oven-toasted bread
¼ teaspoon cinnamon
¼ teaspoon almond extract
¼ teaspoon salt
1 teaspoon vanilla

Beat eggs, add sugar, and stir in other ingredients. Spread mixture evenly into shallow greased pan.

Bake in slow oven (300°F.) about 30 minutes. Cake has a texture and flavor similar to macaroons.

GRAHAM CRACKER TORTE

22   graham crackers
1¼   teaspoons baking powder
½   cup chopped pecans
¼   cup shortening
¾   cup sugar
1   egg
¾   cup milk
1   teaspoon vanilla

Crush graham crackers through food mill or with rolling pin and mix with baking powder and chopped pecans.

Cream shortening and sugar together; add egg, milk, and vanilla. Add to first mixture, mix well, and pour into 11 x 7-inch pan.

Bake in moderate oven (375°F.) 20 minutes. Cut in squares and top with whipped cream, or put two layers together with a custard filling and frost with a butter icing. Serves 6.

DUTCH PLUM CAKE

2   cups sifted enriched flour
4   teaspoons baking powder
½   teaspoon salt
1   tablespoon sugar
⅓   cup butter
1   beaten egg
About ⅔ cup milk
Plums, pitted and quartered
Sugar, cinnamon, butter

Mix and sift flour, baking powder, salt, and sugar. Cut butter into this; add egg and enough milk to make a soft dough.

Spread dough in greased baking pan; cover with a layer of plums. Sprinkle plums with sugar and a little cinnamon; dot with bits of butter.

Bake in hot oven (400°F.) about 30 minutes. Serve with cream.

RUSSIAN STRAWBERRY TORTE

2   cups sifted enriched flour
½   teaspoon salt
1   cup sweet butter
1   cup strawberry jam
2   cups whipped cream
⅛   teaspoon almond extract

Sift together flour and salt. Cut in butter with 2 knives or pastry blender until mixture looks like fine barley.

Add enough cold water to hold dough together. Roll out on lightly floured board. Fold 4 times and roll out again. Separate dough into 3 parts and roll out into 3 rounds.

Prick each with a fork several times. Bake in hot oven (400°F.) until brown, about 30 to 45 minutes.

Spread 1 round with jam and cover with whipped cream flavored with almond extract.

Cover with another baked round, spread with jam and whipped cream, and top with third round. Spread with jam and a thick layer of whipped cream.

FRUIT TORTE

8   egg whites
1   teaspoon cream of tartar
Pinch of salt
2   cups sugar
2   teaspoons mint or almond extract
2   cups sweetened fresh or frozen peaches, crushed pineapple or any fresh berries
½   cup heavy cream, whipped

Beat egg whites until frothy and add cream of tartar and salt. Gradually beat in sugar, sprinkling 1 tablespoon at a time over top of egg whites.

Add flavoring and beat until stiff and peaked. Pour into an ungreased 9-inch spring form pan.

Bake in very slow oven (275°F.) 55 to 60 minutes.

Allow to cool. With a spatula or knife, loosen torte by running knife around edge of pan.

When thoroughly cool, remove sides of spring form pan. Fill slight hollow that forms with fruit and top with flavored whipped cream. Serves 8 to 12.

DATE AND NUT TORTE

1   cup sifted enriched flour
1½   teaspoons baking powder
½   teaspoon salt
½   cup shortening
1   teaspoon vanilla
1   cup sugar
2   whole eggs
2   egg yolks (reserve whites for meringue)
2   tablespoons water
½   cup chopped dates
1   cup chopped walnuts
⅛   teaspoon salt
⅛   teaspoon cream of tartar

Mix and sift flour, baking powder, and ½ teaspoon salt.

Cream shortening with vanilla and gradually add ½ cup sugar, creaming well.

Beat thoroughly 2 whole eggs plus 2 egg yolks, and 2 tablespoons water.

Add eggs and dry ingredients alternately to creamed mixture, beginning and ending with dry ingredients. Blend thoroughly after each addition. (With electric mixer use low speed.) Blend in dates and walnuts.

Turn into greased and floured 9-inch round spring form pan (2¾ inches deep) or 8 x 8 x 2- inch pan lined with waxed paper.

Beat 2 egg whites until foamy. Add ⅛ teaspoon salt and cream of tartar; beat until egg whites form slight mounds when beater is raised. Gradually add remaining sugar and beat until meringue forms peaks.

Spread meringue over batter. Bake in slow oven (325°F.) 1 hour.

BRAZIL NUT TORTE

½   cup sifted enriched flour
2   teaspoons baking powder
2   cups fine graham cracker crumbs
½   cup soft shortening
1   cup sugar
3   egg yolks
¾   cup chopped Brazil nuts
1   teaspoon vanilla
Milk*
3   stiffly beaten egg whites
1   package vanilla pudding pie filling
1½ cups milk
½   cup heavy cream, whipped

Line bottoms of 2 11¼-inch deep 8-inch layer pans with waxed paper.

Sift together flour and baking powder; add cracker crumbs.

With electric mixer at medium speed, or "cream" (or with spoon), thoroughly mix shortening with sugar, then with egg yolks, until very light and fluffy, about 4 minutes altogether. Add nuts and vanilla.

Then, at low speed, or "blend," beat in flour mixture alternately with indicated amount of milk, beating after each addition.

Quickly fold in egg whites. Turn into pans.

Bake in moderate oven (375°F.) 30 minutes or until done. Cool in pans on wire rack.

Meanwhile, combine vanilla pudding with 1½ cups milk. Cook, stirring, over medium heat until mixture comes to boil.

Remove from heat; pour into bowl; place waxed paper directly on surface of pudding. Refrigerate several hours.

Beat pudding until smooth; fold in whipped cream.

Split each cake layer; spread filling between layers and on top of cake. Refrigerate at least 1 hour.

*Note: With butter, margarine, or lard, use 1 cup milk. With vegetable or any other shortening, use 1 cup plus 2 tablespoons milk.

SAND TORTE

1   cup butter
1   cup sugar
6   eggs, separated
1   cup sifted enriched flour
1   cup cornstarch
2   teaspoons baking powder
Juice and grated rind of ½ lemon
1½ tablespoons rum or brandy

Cream butter and sugar very well; add beaten yolks.

Mix and sift flour, cornstarch, and baking powder; add to creamed mixture with lemon juice and rum or brandy.

Fold in stiffly beaten whites. Turn into greased tube pan. Bake in moderate oven (350°F.) 45 minutes.

APPLE TORTE #2

¾ cup sugar
1 well beaten egg
½ cup sifted enriched flour
½ teaspoon salt
1 teaspoon baking powder
1½ cups pared and grated tart apples
1 teaspoon almond flavoring
½ cup chopped pecans
¼ cup chopped dates
1 cup cream, whipped

Beat sugar into egg gradually, using electric mixer. Add sifted dry ingredients and mix thoroughly. Stir in remaining ingredients except cream.

Turn into greased 8 x 8 x 2 inch cake pan. Bake in moderate oven (350°F.) 30 minutes.

Cut into squares and serve warm topped with whipped cream. Serves 8.

APPLE TORTE #3

1 package zwieback
¾ cup sugar
1½ teaspoons cinnamon
½ cup butter, melted
3 large apples
¼ cup water
4 eggs, separated
1 can (1⅓ cups) sweetened condensed milk
Juice of 1 lemon
1 teaspoon vanilla
⅛ teaspoon salt

Roll zwieback fine; add sugar, cinnamon, and butter. Press ¾ of this mixture into the bottom and around the sides of a spring form pan.

Cut the cored apples into pieces; add water and cook slowly until tender, then press through a seive.

Beat egg yolks until light; add milk, lemon juice, vanilla, salt, and cooked apples. Fold in stiffly beaten whites.

Pour into pan and sprinkle remaining crumbs on top. Bake in moderate oven (375°F.) 30 minutes.

CHOCOLATE NUT LOAF

2½ cups sifted cake flour
1 teaspoon baking soda
¾ teaspoon salt
1 cup shortening
2 cups sugar
5 eggs
1 cup finely cut nutmeats
3 1-ounce squares unsweetened chocolate, melted
1 cup sour milk or buttermilk
2 teaspoons vanilla

Sift flour once, measure, add soda and salt, and sift together 3 times.

Cream shortening, add sugar gradually, and cream together until light and fluffy.

Beat eggs until very thick and light; add to creamed mixture and beat well. Add nuts and chocolate and blend.

Add flour, alternately with sour milk, a small amount at a time, beating after each addition until smooth. Add vanilla.

Bake in greased pan, 13 x 9 x 2 inches, in slow oven (325°F.) 1 hour, or until done. Spread with mocha frosting.

DARK MYSTERY CAKE

1¼ cups California figs, steamed and chopped fine
1¾ cups sifted cake flour
1 teaspoon salt
1 teaspoon baking soda
2 teaspoons baking powder
¾ cup shortening
1 cup sugar
3 eggs, separated
3 1-ounce squares chocolate, melted
1¼ cups milk
⅓ cup sugar for egg whites

Prepare figs, snipping off stems with scissors, then chopping fine.

Measure, mix and sift dry ingredients. Reserve ½ cup flour mixture for dredging chopped figs.

Cream shortening; add sugar and cream thoroughly. Add egg yolks and beat until light, then add melted chocolate. Mix thoroughly.

Add sifted flour mixture alternately with milk, adding in thirds and beating until smooth after each addition. Add fig-flour mixture last.

Beat egg whites until light and gradually beat in ⅓ cup sugar. Fold into cake mixture.

Pour into greased 9-inch cake pans. Bake in moderate oven (350°F.) 40 minutes or bake in loaf pan at 325° F., 1 hour. Frost with fluffy 7-minute frosting or with butter cream frosting.

VANILLA TORTE

4 eggs, separated
1½ cups sugar
5 unsalted soda crackers, rolled fine
1 teaspoon baking powder
1 teaspoon vanilla
1 cup heavy cream, whipped
½ cup finely chopped nuts

Beat egg yolks with sugar until thick and lemon-colored.

Blend in cracker crumbs, baking powder, and vanilla, then fold in stiffly beaten egg whites.

Turn into 2 buttered 9-inch layer cake pans. Bake in moderate oven (350° F.) 25 minutes.

Cool on cake rack, then put layers together with half the whipped cream. Sprinkle top with chopped nuts. Dust with confectioners' sugar and decorate with remaining whipped cream.

Easter Cake

EASTER CAKE

Cake:
1½ cups sifted cake flour
1½ teaspoons baking powder
¼ teaspoon salt
⅜ cup shortening
¾ cup sugar
1 egg
1 teaspoon vanilla
½ cup milk

Fluffy Icing:
¼ cup cold water
¾ cup sugar
1/16 teaspoon salt
⅛ teaspoon cream of tartar
2 teaspoons light corn syrup
1 egg white
½ teaspoon vanilla
Few drops of yellow food coloring

Sift together flour, baking powder, and ¼ teaspoon salt.

Cream shortening with ¾ cup sugar until fluffy; add egg and 1 teaspoon vanilla and beat until very light.

Add sifted dry ingredients alternately with milk to creamed mixture, combining thoroughly.

Pour batter into 8-inch square glass cake dish. Bake in moderate oven (350°F.) 30 to 35 minutes or until cake is done. Remove from oven and cool on rack.

Fluffy Icing: Place all icing ingredients except vanilla and coloring in top of double boiler. Beat with rotary beater until ingredients are combined.

Place over boiling water; continue beating and cook until frosting will stand in peaks. Remove from heat; add ½ teaspoon vanilla and yellow coloring and beat until thick enough to spread. Spread on cooled cake.

Decorations: Measure ⅔ cup moist shredded coconut in 2-cup measure; add 2 drops green food coloring, mixing with fork until coconut is uniformly green.

Make a nest of coconut on each corner of cake and fill with jelly bean eggs.

To make a bunny, elongate a marshmallow to an oval shape with fingers. With scissors, snip long triangular cuts to make ears; push ears up and forward. Shape nose, front feet, and tail by pinching with fingers.

Using red food coloring, paint on eyes, nose, and mouth with wooden pick. Place a bunny on or near each nest.

Cupcakes and Other Finger Cakes

Petits Fours

PETITS FOURS

The French term petits fours may be applied to a wide variety of small cakes, pastries, fancy cookies, and even some candied fruits; however in the United States it usually refers to very small cakes made in various shapes (squares, diamonds, rectangles, triangles, rounds, hearts, etc.) with a frosting on the top and sides and delicately decorated.

2	cups sifted cake flour
2½	teaspoons baking powder
½	teaspoon salt
1¼	cups sugar
1	cup heavy cream
½	cup egg whites, unbeaten
1	teaspoon vanilla

Sift together flour, baking powder, salt, and sugar.

Whip heavy cream until stiff and add sifted dry ingredients, egg whites, and vanilla. Beat for 2 minutes, or until batter is well blended and glossy.

If electric mixer is used, beat at low to medium speed for same period of time.

Pour into lightly greased shallow pan lined with waxed paper. Bake in moderate oven (350° F.) 20 to 25 minutes.

Turn out on cake rack while warm and remove waxed paper. Cool.

Cut with fancy cutters or sharp knife into small squares, diamonds, triangles or any desired shape.

Frost with petits fours frosting and ornamental frosting. Decorate with colored sugar, candied fruits and nuts. Makes 1 sheet cake, 15 x 10 inches.

GRAHAM CRACKER PETITS FOURS

Bake delicate graham cracker cake (below) in 12½-inch rectangular baking dish. Cool thoroughly, overnight if possible.

Cut into small squares, triangles, and diamonds as desired. Place on 2 wire racks over waxed paper.

Delicate Graham Cracker Cake:

⅔	cup sifted enriched flour
¾	cup sugar
2½	teaspoons baking powder
½	teaspoon salt
20	graham crackers, finely rolled (about 1⅔ cups crumbs)
½	cup shortening
¾	cup milk
1	teaspoon vanilla
2	eggs

Mix and sift flour, sugar, baking powder, and salt; combine with graham cracker crumbs.

Place shortening in a bowl. Add dry ingredients, milk, and vanilla; mix until dry ingredients are dampened.

Beat 2 minutes in electric mixer or 300 strokes by hand.

Add eggs and beat 1 minute in mixer or 150 strokes by hand.

Pour into 2 greased paper-lined 8-inch layer cake pans. Bake in moderate oven (375° F.) about 25 minutes. Cool. Fill and frost.

Petits Fours Frosting:

1	cup granulated sugar
¼	cup butter or margarine
¼	cup shortening
½	cup milk
½	teaspoon salt
3	cups confectioners' sugar
½	teaspoon vanilla

Combine granulated sugar, butter or margarine, shortening, milk, and salt in saucepan. Bring to a boil over moderate heat; stir constantly. Boil vigorously 1 minute.

Remove from heat; stir in confectioners' sugar and vanilla. Tint with food coloring as desired.

Cool 2 to 3 minutes or until frosting is a good consistency for pouring. Pour over petit fours, covering sides with aid of spatula. Re-use drippings until all cakes are covered.

Unsweetened chocolate added to the drippings makes a delicious chocolate frosting.

Note: Garnish using pastry tube and decorators frosting, a can of pressurized whipped cream, or fruit and nuts in any pretty design. Makes about 2½ dozen.

PETITS FOURS FROSTING HINTS

In France Fondant Frosting is traditional and the small cakes are often dipped first in Apricot Glaze before the frosting is applied.

To apply the glaze, insert a fork into each piece of cake and dip into glaze just to cover the top and sides. Place the pieces with uncoated side down about 1 inch apart on wire racks placed on waxed paper or cooky sheets. Let stand until glaze sets, about 1 hour. Then cover with warm Fondant Frosting. The waxed paper or cooky sheets will catch excess frosting which can be reheated and used again.

LADYFINGERS

3	eggs, separated
½	cup sifted confectioners' sugar
½	cup sifted cake flour
⅛	teaspoon salt
½	teaspoon vanilla

Beat egg whites until stiff but not dry. Gradually beat in sugar.

Beat egg yolks until thick. Fold into egg whites. Fold in sifted flour and salt.

Add vanilla.

With a pastry bag and plain hole tube, shape into fingers (1x4½ inches) on baking sheet covered with ungreased heavy paper. Sprinkle with additional confectioners' sugar.

Bake in moderate oven (350°F.) 10 to 12 minutes.

Remove from paper with a long sharp knife. Press together in pairs. Makes about 12.

Sponge Drops: Arrange by spoonfuls on cooky sheet. Bake as above. Put together in pairs with whipped cream.

MADELEINES

These small French cakes are baked in special molds shaped like scallop shells—or if not available, muffin pans may be used.

2	eggs
1	cup sugar
1	cup sifted cake flour
¾	cup butter, melted and cooled
1	tablespoon light rum
1	teaspoon vanilla or 1 teaspoon grated lemon rind

Combine eggs and sugar in double boiler; heat until lukewarm, stirring constantly. Remove from heat and beat until thick, but light and creamy.

When cool, gradually add cake flour. Add cool, melted butter with rum and vanilla.

Pour into molds and bake in very hot oven (450°F.) about 15 minutes. Makes about 15 cakes.

PEANUT BUTTER CUPCAKES

⅓	cup shortening
1½	cups brown sugar, firmly packed
½	cup peanut butter
2	beaten eggs
2	cups sifted enriched flour
½	teaspoon salt
2½	teaspoon baking powder
¾	cup milk
1	teaspoon vanilla

Cream shortening and 1 cup sugar well. Add peanut butter and mix well. Add eggs with remaining ½ cup sugar.

Mix and sift dry ingredients and add alternately with milk and vanilla.

Fill greased muffin pans ½ full. Bake in moderate oven (350°F.) 25 minutes. Makes about 24 cupcakes.

FINGER CAKES

2¼ cups sifted cake flour
3¼ teaspoons baking powder
1 teaspoon salt
1½ cups sugar
½ cup vegetable shortening
1 cup milk
4 egg whites, unbeaten
1½ teaspoons vanilla
¼ teaspoon almond extract

(Mix by hand or in electric mixer. Count only the actual beating time or strokes. Scrape bowl and spoon or beater often.)

Measure sifted flour into sifter and add baking powder, salt, and sugar.

Stir shortening just to soften. Sift in dry ingredients. Add ¾ cup of the milk. Mix until all flour is dampened. Then beat 2 minutes at a low speed of electric mixer or 300 strokes by hand.

Add egg whites, remaining milk, and flavorings. Beat 1 minute longer at a low speed of electric mixer or 150 strokes by hand.

Use a 13 x 9 x 2-inch pan or two 9 x 9 x 2-inch square pans. Line bottom with paper. Pour batter into pan.

Bake in moderate oven (350°F.) 25 to 30 minutes.

For a white layer cake, bake in two 9-inch square or round layer pans 25 to 30 minutes. Frost as desired.

When cooled, cut oblong cake in thirds or quarters, or cut square cakes in halves. Spread each section with frosting of different tint.

Mark off "fingers" about 3 x 1 inch, scoring through frosting. Decorate with tiny candies, cut citron, etc., to give an assortment. Before serving, cut through cake as marked.

LOW CALORIE CUPCAKES

1 cup sifted enriched flour
1 teaspoon baking soda
½ teaspoon salt
½ teaspoon nutmeg
1 teaspoon cinnamon
⅓ cup firmly packed brown sugar
3 tablespoons soft shortening
2 eggs, unbeaten
¾ cup buttermilk
1 cup rolled oats, uncooked
¼ cup raisins

Mix and sift flour, soda, salt, and spices into bowl.

Add sugar, shortening, eggs, and about half the buttermilk. Beat until smooth, about 2 minutes.

Fold in remaining buttermilk, rolled oats, and raisins. Fill small paper baking cups or greased small muffin cups ½ full.

Bake in moderate oven (375°F.) 12 to 15 minutes. Makes 20 cupcakes, about 82 calories each.

THREE-IN-ONE CUPCAKES

2 cups sifted enriched flour
3 teaspoons baking powder
¼ teaspoon salt
½ cup butter
1 cup sugar
2 eggs, unbeaten
¾ cup milk
1 teaspoon vanilla

Sift together flour, baking powder, and salt.

Cream butter and sugar until soft and creamy. Add eggs. Beat until light and fluffy. Add dry ingredients alternately with milk, mixing thoroughly. Add vanilla.

Divide batter into 3 parts. Leave ⅓ of batter plain. Fill muffin pans ⅔ full and bake in moderate oven (375° F.) 20 to 30 minutes.

Frost plain batter cupcakes with chocolate frosting and chocolate shots when cool.

Prepare fruit cupcakes and spice nut cakes from remainder of batter.

Fruit Cupcakes: To ⅓ of batter add ⅓ cup raisins, ⅓ cup citron, and ⅓ cup coconut. Bake. Frost with butter frosting. Garnish with fruits.

Spice Nut Cakes: To ⅓ of batter add ⅓ cup grated nuts and ¼ teaspoon each of cinnamon and cloves. Serve plain or frosted.

CHOCOLATE CHIP CUPCAKES

⅓ cup vegetable shortening
¾ cup sugar
2 eggs, unbeaten
1 teaspoon vanilla
2¼ cups sifted cake flour
3 teaspoons baking powder
1 teaspoon salt
⅔ cup milk
1 package chocolate chips

Cream shortening. Add sugar gradually, creaming continually. Beat in 1 egg at a time and add vanilla.

Mix and sift flour, baking powder, and salt. Add to first mixture alternately with milk.

Place half of batter in greased muffin pans. Sprinkle with half of chocolate chips.

Add remaining batter and sprinkle with remaining chocolate chips.

Bake in moderate oven (375°F.) 20 to 25 minutes. Makes 18 cupcakes.

ORANGE CUPCAKES

1⅓ cups sifted cake flour
2 teaspoons baking powder
¼ teaspoon salt
¼ cup shortening
1 teaspoon grated orange rind
¾ cup sugar
1 egg, unbeaten
¼ cup orange juice
¼ cup evaporated milk

Mix and sift flour, baking powder, and salt.

Cream shortening with orange rind. Add sugar gradually and cream until fluffy. Add egg and beat until well blended.

Mix the orange juice and evaporated milk. Add flour mixture alternately with juice-milk mixture, beginning and ending with flour.

Fill well greased muffin pans ⅔ full. Bake in moderate oven (375°F.) until golden brown, about 20 minutes. Makes about 15 medium-sized cupcakes.

COCONUT PINEAPPLE CUPCAKES

1¾ cups sifted cake flour
1½ teaspoons baking powder
¼ teaspoon salt
½ cup shortening
1 cup sugar
2 eggs, unbeaten
Water*
½ cup canned crushed pineapple
1 teaspoon vanilla
1 cup shredded coconut

Measure sifted flour, add baking powder and salt, and sift together 3 times.

Cream shortening, add sugar gradually, and cream together until light and fluffy. Add eggs, one at a time, beating well.

Combine water, crushed pineapple, and vanilla; add to egg mixture, alternately with flour, beating after each addition until smooth. Add ¼ of the coconut.

Spoon batter into paper baking cups (set in muffin pans), filling each only half-full. Sprinkle batter with remaining coconut. Bake in moderate oven (375°F.) 20 to 25 minutes. Makes 24.

*Note: With vegetable shortening, use 3 tablespoons water. With butter or margarine, use 1 tablespoon water.

LEMON MOLASSES CUPCAKES

½ cup shortening
½ cup sugar
1 well beaten egg
½ cup molasses
2 cups sifted cake flour
2 teaspoons baking powder
½ teaspoon baking soda
1½ teaspoons cinnamon
¼ teaspoon salt
½ cup milk
1 tablespoon grated lemon rind

Cream shortening until soft and smooth. Gradually add sugar, beating until fluffy. Beat in egg, then molasses. Beat vigorously.

Mix and sift flour with baking powder, soda, cinnamon, and salt. Add alternately with milk, beating briskly after each addition. Add lemon rind.

Fill greased, floured muffin pans ½ full. Bake in moderate oven (350°F.) 30 minutes. Makes 15 to 20 cupcakes.

Dress-Ups with Cake Mixes

THREE-COLOR LAYER CAKE

Prepare white cake mix as directed on package.

Divide into 3 parts. Use 1/3 for white layer. Color 1/3 pink with a few drops of red food coloring. Color 1/3 yellow or other desired color.

Pour batter into 3 prepared 8-inch layer pans.

Bake in moderate oven (350° F.) about 18 minutes. Spread orange marmalade between layers. Frost top and sides with orange butter frosting.

SURPRISE COFFEE CAKE

To dry white cake mix, add 4 teaspoons instant coffee, then proceed as directed on package.

SHADOW CAKE

Prepare white cake mix batter and just before turning into pan, fold in 1/2 cup ground semi-sweet chocolate pieces and 1/2 teaspoon mint extract.

STRAWBERRY WHIP CAKE

1   package white cake mix
2   10-ounce cans frozen sliced straw-
      berries
1   envelope unflavored gelatin
1   tablespoon lemon juice
1   cup whipping cream, whipped

Make cake according to package directions, baking in two 8-inch layers. Cool; split layers in half to make 4 layers.

Meanwhile, defrost strawberries according to directions on can; drain, reserving syrup. Cover strawberries and place in refrigerator.

Soften gelatin in strawberry syrup; heat to a full boil; remove from heat. Cool.

Add strawberries and lemon juice and chill until mixture is slightly thickened. Fold whipped cream into gelatin mixture. Spread strawberry mixture between layers and frost sides and top of cake. Chill thoroughly before slicing. Makes 10 to 12 servings.
Variation: Use Strawberry Whip as a topping for slices of angel food cake, sponge cake, or pound cake.

Strawberry Whip Cake

WEDDING CAKE

Four tiered cake requires 13 1-pound 1-ounce packages pound cake mix. Prepare according to package directions. Line all pans with paper.

Bake two 13 x 2½-inch round layers, using 3 packages of cake mix for each pan; two 10 x 2½-inch round layers, using 2 packages of cake mix for each layer; three 8-inch round layers, using 2 packages of cake mix divided evenly into the three 8-inch round pans; and one 5 x 4-inch round spring form pan, using 1 package of cake mix.

Bake all layers in a slow oven (325°F.). Bake the 13-inch layers 2¼ hours or until toothpick inserted in center comes out clean, 10-inch layers 2 hours, 8-inch layers 35 minutes, 5-inch layer 1 hour.

Cool all cakes before removing from pans. Cakes may be baked ahead and frozen until needed.

Wedding Cake Icing:

1   cup white shortening
1   teaspoon salt
24 cups sifted confectioners' sugar
      (about 8 pounds)
10 egg whites, unbeaten
1   cup milk
1   tablespoon rum extract (or de-
      sired flavoring)

Cream shortening; add salt. Gradually add about 1 cup confectioners' sugar. Blend well. Add remaining sugar alternately with egg whites and milk; beat until thick enough to spread. Add rum extract.

Keep frosting bowl covered with a damp cloth while frosting cake.

Cut a circle of cardboard to fit under each tier and put cake layers together with frosting. (Cardboard will keep tiers level.)

Frost entire cake with a very thin layer of icing. Allow to dry thoroughly. Frost cake. Smooth with a spatula dipped in boiling water. Use remaining frosting for decorations.

To make scallop design, as shown, mark design outline by pressing a teacup into icing around top edge of bottom tier. Use round cooky cutters in graduated sizes to mark design on remaining tiers. Cake makes about 130 slices.

SEAFOAM CAKE SQUARES

Prepare batter from 1 package plain cake mix. Pour into greased 13 x 9½ x-2-inch pan. Top with mixture made by beating ¾ cup brown sugar into 2 stiffly-beaten egg whites. Sprinkle with ½ cup chopped nuts.

Bake in moderate oven (375° F.) until cake is done.

For the Bride: Pound cake mix baked in four graceful tiers and iced in pure white makes the wedding cake of her dreams. The layers may be baked ahead and frozen until you are ready to decorate the cake.

CRANBERRY UPSIDE-DOWN CAKE

Use 1 package white cake mix. Substitute ½ cup pineapple juice for part of liquid.

Melt ¼ cup butter or margarine in an ungreased 12 x 8 x 2-inch pan. Add ½ cup brown sugar, firmly packed, and stir until sugar is dissolved. Add 2 cups fresh cranberries and 1 cup drained, crushed pineapple.

Cover with cake batter. Bake in moderate oven (375° F.) 30 to 40 minutes.

For variations add any of the following fruits, well drained, cut side up. Use liquid specified in directions on label in preparing batter:

Apricot or Peach Upside-Down Cake: 12 apricot halves or 6 peach halves.

Pineapple Upside-Down Cake: 6 slices pineapple; fill centers with whole maraschino cherries.

PINEAPPLE CAKE

Use 1 package white cake mix. Fold in ½ cup drained, crushed pineapple and 1 tablespoon grated lemon rind, just before turning into pan.

Fill and frost the baked cake with pineapple butter frosting.

CHERRY PASTEL CAKE

Prepare white cake mix batter and just before turning batter into pan, fold in ⅓ cup minced, well drained maraschino cherries and ½ cup finely chopped toasted almonds.

LEMON PUDDING CAKE

Prepare 1 package lemon pie filling following package directions.

Spread filling in oblong pan (13 x 9-1/2 x 2 inches). Let stand while making cake batter.

Make white cake mix batter according to directions on package. Pour over lemon filling.

Bake in moderate oven (350° F.) 35 to 40 minutes. Sift confectioners' sugar over the top.

Serve warm or cold. If served cold, lemon filling will be stiffer.

BRAZIL NUT CAKE

Use 1 package white cake mix. Fold in 1/2 cup chopped, toasted Brazil nuts, just before turning batter into pans. (Toast nuts by spreading 1/2 cup nuts in shallow pan; dot with 1 tablespoon butter or margarine and bake in moderate oven (350°F.) 10 minutes.)

OLD WOMAN IN A SHOE CAKE

Prepare two 17-ounce packages pound cake mix according to directions on package for loaf cakes.

When cakes are cool, cut 1/3 from end of one loaf. Cut other end of this loaf in a rounded shape for toe of shoe.

Cut a small amount from one end of second loaf. Stand on end at the straight end of the first loaf, with bottom of cake against the other loaf and rounded side facing out.

Cut the top of the vertical loaf to make it level. Spread with a little frosting and place the 1/3 cut from first cake on top.

Frost entire cake with your favorite fluffy icing made from a recipe or a mix.

Make shoe laces and windows from pieces of licorice ropes with shutters of sugar wafers. The door is made of graham crackers and the chimney is pieces of waffle cremes. The children are small lollipops with pipe cleaner arms and faces piped in frosting.

FRUIT COCKTAIL UPSIDE-DOWN CAKE

Coat bottom of buttered 2-quart fruit mold with 3 tablespoons brown sugar and arrange drained fruit from 1/2 No. 2 1/2 can fruit cocktail in bottom.

Cover with cake batter made from a package of white cake mix and bake according to directions on package for loaf cake.

Serve warm with rum-flavored whipped cream to which remaining half of fruit cocktail is added. Serves 8.

MOCHA DATE CAKE

Use 1 package white cake mix. Reduce the liquid specified on package by 1/2 cup.

Combine 1/2 cup finely chopped dates with 1/2 cup hot strong instant coffee and allow to cool. Add coffee-date mixture with last addition of liquid.

Fill with date and nut filling; frost with coffee frosting.

ALMOND PISTACHIO ANGEL FOOD CAKE

Use 1 package angel cake food mix. Add 1/4 teaspoon almond extract to batter and color with a few drops green food coloring.

Fold in 3/4 cup finely sliced blanched almonds just before turning into pan.

PINK PEPPERMINT ANGEL FOOD CAKE

Use 1 package angel food cake mix. Add 1 teaspoon mint flavoring to liquid and tint batter a delicate pink with red food coloring. Bake as directed on package.

COFFEE ANGEL FOOD CAKE

Use 1 package angel food cake mix. Stir 1 tablespoon instant coffee into liquid called for on package.

COCONUT ANGEL FOOD CAKE

Use 1 package angel food cake mix. Fold 1/2 to 3/4 cup finely cut shredded coconut into batter just before turning into pan.

PINK ANGEL CAKE

Prepare and bake angel food cake mix according to package directions.

Split the cool cake into 2 layers. Put together and frost with fluffy frosting (made from a mix) tinted pale pink with red food coloring.

Note: For a party touch, garnish with sliced strawberries.

Old Woman in a Shoe Cake: "There was an old woman who lived in a shoe" —you remember the Old Mother Goose nursery rhyme! Well, here is the storybook shoe in edible form—made of pound cake mix and cookies—an ideal centerpiece and theme for a children's party.

BANANA SPICE CAKE

1   package spice cake mix
1   pint heavy cream, whipped and sweetened
3   to 4 bananas

Use your favorite spice cake mix. Prepare according to package directions. Bake in 2 9-inch square greased pans 25 to 30 minutes, or until cake tester comes out clean and dry.

Cool, remove from pan and cover one square with some of the whipped cream.

Place 3 or 4 whole bananas on top; cover with whipped cream. Top with other cake layer; frost top and sides with remaining whipped cream.

Banana Spice Cake

ANGEL FOOD SPICE CAKE

Use 1 package angel food cake mix. Add 1 teaspoon cinnamon, 1/4 teaspoon nutmeg, and 1/2 teaspoon allspice to dry ingredients. Bake as directed on package.

FRUIT COCONUT CAKE

1   18 1/2- to 20-ounce package yellow cake mix
1   can (1 lb. 14 oz.) fruit cocktail
1   cup orange marmalade
1   cup flaked coconut
Whipped cream (optional)

Mix cake and bake according to package directions, baking in 9 x 13 x 2-inch pan.

While cake is warm, drain fruit cocktail thoroughly and arrange over top of cake.

Warm marmalade gently, stir in coconut, and spread over fruit. Place under broiler until lightly browned. Serve warm, plain or topped with whipped cream. Makes 12 to 15 servings.

Fruit Coconut Cake

COCONUT BUTTERSCOTCH CAKE

1 package white cake mix
1/4 cup butter or margarine
1 cup firmly packed brown sugar
2 tablespoons light cream or top milk
1 cup shredded coconut

Prepare cake according to directions on package. Pour into greased 11 x 7- x 1½-inch pan. Bake in moderate oven (375° F.) 25 to 30 minutes.

Cream butter and sugar. Add cream or milk, mix well and add coconut.

Remove cake from oven while warm; spread with coconut mixture. Broil until golden brown, about 5 minutes. Cool. Cut in squares.

MARSHMALLOW CUPCAKES

Make cupcakes from a package of cake mix. Top each baked cupcake with a marshmallow. Put back in oven until marshmallows melt and toast.

WINE JELLY CREAM CAKE

Prepare 2 (8-inch) "butter" cake layers, using a packaged mix. Let cool thoroughly, then split each layer crosswise with a sharp knife to make two thinner layers.

For filling, beat 1¼ cups wine jelly (made with port or red table wine) with a rotary or electric beater for a few seconds to make it easy to spread.

Put the four layers together with the jelly between.

Frost top and sides of cake with jelly cream frosting (below).

Store cake in refrigerator until time to serve.

Wine Jelly Cream Frosting:

1 cup heavy cream
½ cup wine jelly (use same flavor jelly as for cake filling)

Whip cream until stiff. Using the same beater, whip jelly for a few seconds. Gently fold jelly into cream. Spread on cake.

Birthday Girl Cake

CHRISTMAS WREATH CAKE

Use 1 package white cake mix. Divide white cake batter into two bowls.

To one half add ¼ teaspoon almond extract and add red food coloring to make batter a delicate pink.

To other half add ½ teaspoon vanilla and tint delicate green with food coloring.

Pour pink batter into prepared 9-inch ring mold; cover with green batter. Streak lightly with spatula.

Fill prepared mold half full; bake remaining batter in cupcake pans. Frost with a fluffy frosting. Decorate with candied cherries and angelica.

SUNNY LEMON CAKE

Prepare yellow cake mix batter as directed on package. Add 2 teaspoons grated lemon rind just before turning into pan.

BIRTHDAY GIRL CAKE

Bake two layers of delicate white cake, using one of the ready-prepared packaged mixes.

Cool the layers, then put them together and cover with this soft and fluffy frosting.

Blushing Pink Frosting:

1½ cups sugar
⅓ cup warm water
2 egg whites (at room temperature)
1 teaspoon lemon juice
3 drops oil of peppermint
Red food coloring

Place sugar, water, egg whites, and lemon juice in the top section of double boiler; beat with an electric or rotary beater for about 1 minute, stirring around sides and bottom with a rubber scraper. (This pre-cook beating helps to dissolve the sugar and prevent graininess in the completed frosting.)

Set top section of double boiler over boiling water and continue beating until frosting stiffens and holds its shape. (Be sure to use the rubber scraper occasionally during this cooking.) The beating will take about 7 minutes, a little more or less depending upon the size of the double boiler and the vigor of beating.

Turn frosting out into a wide-topped bowl and add flavoring, and red coloring, a few drops at a time to get desired shade. Beat for about 2 minutes (this helps to get the frosting to perfect smoothness) until frosting is slightly cooled.

Frost cake between layers, around sides and top swirling it generously. Group fat deep pink candies on top, with pink and blue satin ribbon bows, clusters of baby roses and forget-me-nots. Place small bouquets at intervals around cake.

CRANBERRY LOAF CAKE

1 17-ounce package pound cake mix
¾ cup milk
2 eggs

Prepare pound cake mix according to package directions using milk and eggs. Bake in a slow oven (325°F.) 1¼ hours. Cool.

Slice cake lengthwise into three layers. Spread Cranberry Filling (below) on two layers. Stack and top with third layer. Frost with Cranberry Butter Frosting (below).

Cranberry Filling:

¼ cup sugar
2 tablespoons cornstarch
1 1-pound can whole cranberry sauce
1 tablespoon lemon juice
½ cup chopped walnuts

Combine sugar and cornstarch. Add cranberry sauce, lemon juice, and walnuts. Cook until mixture thickens and clears. Cool.

Cranberry Butter Frosting:

½ cup softened butter or margarine
3½ cups sifted confectioners' sugar
⅓ cup cranberry juice cocktail

Cream butter with 1 cup confectioners' sugar. Add remaining sugar alternately with cranberry juice cocktail. Beat until smooth and of spreading consistency. Frost top and sides of cake. Makes 8 to 10 servings.

Cranberry Loaf Cake

POLKA DOT CAKE

Use 1 package white cake mix. Fold in ½ cup finely ground semi-sweet chocolate pieces and ½ teaspoon mint flavoring.

Frost the baked cake with a white frosting to which mint flavoring has been added. Decorate with semi-sweet chocolate pieces.

MAPLE NUT CAKE

Flavor white cake mix batter with a few drops maple flavoring. After turning batter into pan, sprinkle with ½ cup finely chopped nuts.

DATE CAKE

Prepare white cake mix batter and just before turning into pan, add ½ cup finely chopped pitted dates and 1 teaspoon grated lemon rind.

EASTER LAMB CAKE

Prepare 1 package white cake mix as directed on package.

Pour batter into the face half of well greased lamb mold. (Be sure some batter is placed in each ear.) Cover with back of mold and wire or tie mold together.

Place mold face down on baking sheet and bake in very hot oven (450° F.) 10 minutes. Reduce heat to 350° F. and bake 35 minutes longer.

Remove mold from oven and open, removing back of mold first. Allow lamb to cool in face of mold about 5 minutes. Loosen cake from sides of mold and remove carefully. Stand lamb cake upright on cake rack until cool.

Frost with fluffy frosting (below). Cover with 1 can moist coconut. Use raisins for eyes and nose and slice of maraschino cherry for mouth.

Fluffy Frosting: Combine 1 unbeaten egg white, ¾ cup sugar, dash of salt, 3 tablespoons water, and 1 teaspoon light corn syrup in top of small double boiler. Beat with rotary egg beater about 1 minute, or until thoroughly mixed.

Cook over rapidly boiling water, beating constantly with rotary egg beater 4 minutes or until frosting will stand in stiff peaks.

Remove from boiling water. Add ½ teaspoon vanilla and beat 1 minute or until thick enough to spread.

CHOCOLATE FLECK CAKE

Prepare yellow cake mix batter as directed on package. Grate 1 or 2 1-ounce squares unsweetened chocolate and fold into batter just before turning into pan.

CHOCOLATE-MINT CAKE SQUARES

Prepare and bake a loaf cake as directed on package of white cake mix.

Place chocolate-covered peppermints on top of hot loaf cake. Return to oven for a few minutes. As chocolates melt, spread evenly over cake.

RAINBOW PARTY CAKE

Prepare cake batter, using any recipe desired.

Divide into 4 portions. Tint 1 portion yellow, 1 green, and 1 red. Leave 4th portion uncolored. Place alternate spoonfuls of each color in buttered layer cake pans. Bake.

Put layers together with fluffy boiled frosting. Serve with ice cream.

For special occasions, use a cake plate large enough so that a few flowers may be placed around the border of the dish for decoration. Green leafy sprays, such as philodendron are also nice to use.

BANANA SPICE CAKE

Use 1 package white cake mix. Mix 2 teaspoons cinnamon, ¼ teaspoon cloves, ½ teaspoon nutmeg, and 1 teaspoon allspice with mix.

Substitute ⅔ cup mashed bananas for ⅓ cup liquid specified in directions on label. Fold in ½ cup chopped walnuts.

Frost the baked cake with a fluffy white frosting.

CHRISTMAS TREE UPSIDE-DOWN CAKE

Use 1 package white cake mix. Fold in ½ cup finely chopped glacé fruits, just before turning batter into pan.

Fill prepared Christmas tree mold half full. Bake remaining batter in cupcake pans.

ANGEL PEACH COCONUT CAKE

1 package angel cake mix
1 3-ounce package orange-flavored gelatin
1 No. 303 can (2 cups) sliced peaches, drained
1 cup heavy cream, whipped
1 4-ounce can or package (1⅓ cups) shredded coconut, toasted

Prepare and bake angel cake mix in tube pan as directed on package. Cool.

Remove from pan. Cut center from cake to make hole 4-inches across. Place cake on flat plate.

Prepare gelatin as directed on package. Chill until partially set and fold in peaches. Fill center of cake with this mixture. Chill until set.

Frost top and sides with whipped cream and sprinkle with toasted coconut.

ENCORE CAKE

8 unsweetened dried figs, stewed
1 package spice cake mix
½ cup plus 2 tablespoons juice from stewed figs
2 whole eggs
2 tablespoons water
1 can moist coconut

With scissors snip the stems off the stewed figs. Then place the figs in a mixing bowl and beat hard with electric or hand beater. The figs will be whirled into small bits.

Add the contents from the spice cake mix, plus the juice from the stewed figs. Beat for 2 minutes.

Add the eggs and beat 1 minute. Then add the 2 tablespoons water and beat at low speed for 1 more minute.

Place in two well-buttered 9-inch layer pans. Bake in moderate oven (350°F.) about 25 minutes. Cool slightly.

Frost with your favorite vanilla flavored seven minute frosting with lots of coconut sprinkled on frosting, between layers and on top.

PARTY TORTE

1 package angel food mix
1 rounded tablespoon instant coffee
½ cup brown sugar, packed down
20 fig cookies, crumbled
1 cup milk
2 tablespoons butter
2 lightly beaten egg yolks
1 teaspoon vanilla
2 cups heavy cream
2 teaspoons instant coffee
½ cup confectioners' sugar
1 teaspoon vanilla
½ cup English Toffee crumbs

Follow directions on the angel food mix package, placing water in the mixing bowl. Then spoon out 3 tablespoons water, add the instant coffee, stir to dissolve, return to bowl.

Proceed as usual in making the cake. Bake it in two 9-inch ungreased layer pans. Bake in a moderate oven (375° F.) for about 20 minutes or until just done.

Cool upside down on cake racks. When cold remove from the pans.

Meanwhile, in a saucepan combine the brown sugar, crumbled fig cookies, milk, and butter.

Stir over slow heat until the fig cookies almost blend with the milk. Pour onto the egg yolks and cook for a minute more. Cool and add vanilla.

Meanwhile, stir the second measure of instant coffee into a little of the cream. Add to the cream, sugar, and vanilla and whip until very stiff.

Spread both cake layers with the fig mixture, then with the cream. Sprinkle top generously with the candy crumbs. Place in refrigerator at once. Serve very cold. Serves 8 to 10.

Party Torte

YELLOW NUT CAKE

Prepare yellow cake mix batter as directed on package. Add ½ cup finely chopped nuts just before turning into pan.

Encore Cake

MYSTERY MOCHA CAKE

1 package cake mix (white, yellow, spice, or chocolate)
½ cup brown sugar
½ cup granulated sugar
4 tablespoons cocoa
1 cup cold strong coffee

Prepare cake mix as directed on package. Pour into greased 9-inch square cake pan.

Combine sugars and cocoa. Sprinkle evenly over batter. Pour coffee over top.

Bake in moderate oven (350° F.) 40 minutes. Serve warm.

SPICY PUMPKIN CAKE

1 package honey spice cake mix (see note below)
½ teaspoon baking soda
½ cup chopped walnuts
1 cup cooked or canned pumpkin
½ cup finely-cut pitted dates

Combine cake mix and baking soda, then proceed according to package directions, substituting the pumpkin for the last addition of liquid. Fold in nuts and dates.

Pour batter into 2 greased and floured 9-inch layer cake pans; bake as directed on package.

Fill and frost with honey whipped cream (below). Garnish top with mixed diced candied fruits and peels.

Honey-Whipped Cream: Whip 1 cup heavy cream until fluffy; whip in 3 tablespoons honey and ¼ teaspoon cinnamon.

Note: Or use white or yellow cake mix with spices added as suggested on package, adding baking soda at the same time. Add 1 cup pumpkin instead of last addition of liquid. You can use either the type of cake mix which calls for fresh eggs or the type which calls for the addition of liquid only.

JIFFY MARBLE CAKE

Prepare marble-cake batter, using 1 package marble-cake mix. Bake in paper-lined 13 x 9 x 2-inch pan.

Remove from pan; cool on rack. Cut in half lengthwise to give two layers. Frost between layers, on sides and top with fudgy cream-cheese frosting (below).

Fudgy Cream-Cheese Frosting: Have two 3-ounce packages cream cheese at room temperature. Blend with 2 tablespoons milk. Gradually beat in 5 cups sifted confectioners' sugar.

Melt and slightly cool two 1-ounce squares unsweetened chocolate; blend into sugar mixture. Stir in 1 teaspoon vanilla and dash of salt.

COCOA MERINGUE TORTE

1 package yellow cake mix
4 egg whites
⅛ teaspoon cream of tartar
Dash of salt
¾ cup sugar
¾ cup finely chopped walnuts
Cocoa whipped cream (below)

Prepare cake mix according to package directions and pour into 2 paper-lined 9 x 1½-inch round pans.

Beat egg whites until foamy. Add cream of tartar and salt; continue beating until soft peaks form. Add sugar gradually, beating until glossy and sugar is dissolved.

Fold in nuts. Spread mixture carefully over cake batter in both pans.

Bake in moderate oven (375° F.) 25 to 30 minutes.

Cool cake in pans 10 minutes; then remove from pans to finish cooling. Frost tops and sides with cocoa whipped cream.

Cocoa Whipped Cream: Combine 1-½ cups heavy cream, ½ cup sugar, and ⅓ cup cocoa; chill 1 hour. Beat until stiff. Trim frosted torte with walnut halves.

CHOCOLATE POLKA-DOT CAKE WITH WHITE FROSTING

1 package chocolate or devil's food cake mix
2 egg whites
1½ cups sugar
1½ teaspoons light corn syrup or ¼ teaspoon cream of tartar
⅓ cup cold water
Dash of salt
1 teaspoon vanilla
Semi-sweet chocolate pieces

Prepare chocolate cake mix and bake in round layer pans as directed on package. Cool.

Combine egg whites, sugar, corn syrup, water, and salt in double boiler. Beat 1 minute with electric mixer or rotary beater. Then cook over boiling water, beating constantly until frosting forms peaks, about 7 minutes.

Remove from boiling water; add vanilla; beat until of spreading consistency, about 2 minutes.

Frost tops and sides of cake layers. Polka dot with semi-sweet chocolate pieces.

FLAMING PEACH CAKE

Prepare a honey spice cake from a package of prepared mix. Let cake cool, then fill and top with sweetened whipped cream.

Arrange well drained cling peach halves on top, pit side up.

In the center of each peach, place a sugar lump soaked in lemon extract. Then light up the sugar lumps and serve while flaming.

JELLY FLUFF FROSTED LAYER CAKE

Prepare 2 (8- or 9-inch) "butter" cake layers, using a packaged mix or your favorite recipe. Let cool thoroughly, then spread jelly fluff frosting (below) between layers and over top and sides of cake.

Jelly Fluff Frosting:
¾ cup wine jelly (preferably made with port or red table wine for color)
2 egg whites
Dash of salt

Place jelly in a small saucepan; stir over medium heat until melted and bubbling. Beat egg whites until stiff but not dry.

Add salt, then gradually beat in the hot jelly. Continue to beat until frosting holds its shape when the beater is drawn through it. Spread on cake.

Wine Jelly:

Measure 3 cups sugar into top of double boiler. Add 2 cups wine (sherry, sauterne, burgundy, port, muscatel, or tokay); mix well.

Place over rapidly boiling water and heat 2 minutes, stirring constantly.

Remove from water and at once stir in ½ bottle liquid fruit pectin. Pour quickly into glasses. Paraffin at once. Makes about 5 6-ounce glasses.

Jelly Fluff Frosted Layer Cake

MAPLE-NUT DEVIL'S FOOD CAKE

Use 1 package devil's food cake mix. Add a few drops maple flavoring to batter. After turning into pan, sprinkle with ½ cup finely chopped nuts.

DEVIL'S FOOD NUT CAKE

Prepare devil's food cake mix batter and fold in ½ cup finely chopped nuts before turning into pan.

COCONUT DEVIL'S FOOD CAKE

Prepare devil's food cake mix batter and fold in ½ to ¾ cup finely cut shredded coconut before turning into pan.

APRICOT STAR CAKE

Use 1 package chocolate cake mix. Substitute ½ cup apricot nectar for part of liquid. Fold in 1 cup chopped dried apricots. Fill prepared star mold half full.

Bake remaining batter in cupcake pans. Frost with ornamental frosting. Decorate with dragées, candied cherries, angelica.

CHERRY-NUT ANGEL FOOD CAKE

Use 1 package angel food cake mix. Fold in ½ cup chopped, drained maraschino cherries and ½ cup chopped walnuts. Bake as directed on package.

CHOCOLATE ANGEL FOOD CAKE

Use 1 package angel food cake mix. Sift 2 tablespoons cocoa with ¼ of dry ingredients.

Fold into beaten egg white mixture. Bake as directed on package.

GINGERBREAD WASHINGTON PIE

Bake gingerbread mix in a greased pie pan. When cool split in two. Prepare molasses cornstarch pudding (below) or use desired packaged pudding. Cool; spread between layers. Sprinkle top layer with powdered sugar.

Molasses Cornstarch Pudding:

2½ tablespoons cornstarch
1¼ cups cold milk
1 beaten egg
⅛ teaspoon salt
¼ cup molasses
1 tablespoon butter or margarine
1 teaspoon vanilla

Mix cornstarch with ¼ cup of the cold milk. Scald remaining milk and stir into cornstarch mixture. Cook over hot water until thick and smooth.

Combine well beaten egg, salt, and molasses. Add gradually to milk, stirring all the while. Continue cooking until thick and smooth.

Remove from heat. Stir in butter or margarine. Cool slightly, then add vanilla.

Gingerbread Washington Pie

TUTTI-FRUTTI GINGERBREAD

Use 1 package gingerbread or ginger cake mix. Fold in 1 cup ground fresh cranberries and ½ cup chopped raisins. Bake as directed on package.

CHEESE-FROSTED GINGERBREAD

Prepare 1 package gingerbread or ginger cake mix and bake as directed on package.

Add ¼ cup light cream to 1 3-ounce package cream cheese; beat until fluffy, adding additional cream if necessary. Spread over gingerbread after it has been removed from pan.

CRUNCHY-TOP GINGERBREAD

Prepare 1 package gingerbread mix. Bake in greased 10 x 6 x 11½-inch pan in moderate oven (350°F.) 30 minutes. Sprinkle with crunchy topping (below). Bake 10 minutes.

Crunchy Topping: Combine ¼ cup brown sugar, 2 tablespoons enriched flour, 2 tablespoons butter or margarine, dash of salt, 1 teaspoon cinnamon, and ½ cup broken walnuts; mix thoroughly.

SPICY APPLESAUCE GINGERBREAD

Use 1 package gingerbread or ginger cake mix; add 1 teaspoon cinnamon and 1 teaspoon nutmeg to dry mix.

Substitute 1 cup canned applesauce for ¾ cup of liquid. Bake as directed on package.

SUGAR AND SPICE GINGER CAKE

Use 1 package gingerbread or ginger cake mix. Pour batter into prepared pan.

Before baking, sprinkle lightly with this topping: Mix together ½ cup firmly packed brown sugar, 2 tablespoons enriched flour, and 2 teaspoons cinnamon; blend in 2 tablespoons melted butter or margarine; stir in ½ cup chopped walnuts.

CAFÉ GINGERBREAD

Use 1 package gingerbread or ginger cake mix; add 1½ tablespoons powdered instant coffee mix. Fold in ½ cup finely ground semi-sweet chocolate pieces. Bake as directed on package.

COCONUT GINGERBREAD

Use 1 package gingerbread or ginger cake mix; fold in 1 cup chopped shredded coconut. Bake as directed on package.

CHOCOLATE SPICE CAKE

Use 1 package chocolate cake mix. Add ½ teaspoon cloves, 1 teaspoon cinnamon, and ¾ teaspoon allspice to dry mix.

Fold into batter ¼ cup each chopped candied orange and grapefruit peel just before turning into pan. Bake as directed on package.

PEPPERMINT DEVIL'S FOOD CAKE

Prepare devil's food cake mix batter and flavor with a few drops peppermint extract before turning into pan.

Devil's Food Cake—Fluffy White Frosting

COFFEE-SPICE DEVIL'S FOOD CAKE

Use 1 package devil's food cake mix. To dry mix add 4 teaspoons instant coffee, ¼ teaspoon nutmeg, ¼ teaspoon allspice, and ½ teaspoon cinnamon.

CHOCOLATE BANANA CREAM CAKE

Prepare devil's food cake mix as directed on package. Bake as directed.

Split one of the warm layers in half crosswise to make 2 thin layers. Put layers together with sweetened whipped cream and sliced bananas in the middle. Place more whipped cream and sliced bananas on top.

Frost remaining layer as desired and save for another meal.

CHOCOLATE CRUNCH CAKE

Use 1 package chocolate cake mix. Add ¼ cup peanut butter with liquid. Fold in ½ cup chopped peanuts into batter. Bake as directed on package.

COCONUT CHOCOLATE CAKE

Prepare 1 package chocolate cake mix. Add 1 cup chopped shredded coconut to batter. Bake as directed on package.

WALNUT MOCHA CAKE

Prepare 1 package chocolate cake mix. Add 1½ tablespoons powdered instant coffee to dry mix.

Fold into batter ½ cup chopped black walnuts, just before turning into pan. Bake as directed on package.

BLACK AND WHITE SWIRL CAKE

Use 1 package chocolate cake mix. Prepare chocolate cake mix, substituting ½ cup orange juice for part of liquid; fold in 1 tablespoon grated orange rind.

Use 1 package white cake mix. Pour white cake batter into 2 prepared 10-inch round layer pans. Cover with chocolate batter. Swirl lightly with spatula.

Fill and frost with a chocolate frosting to which 1 tablespoon grated orange rind has been added.

High-Altitude Cake Recipes

BAKING CAKES AT HIGH ALTITUDES

In a high altitude region (3,000 feet above sea level) you may find that cakes made from sea level recipes may tend to fall and give unpredictable results. For a general guide to changes in sea level recipes, see **Cooking at High Altitudes.** In addition, specific recipes for various altitudes are given in this section.

QUICK-METHOD CAKE

Preparations: Have the shortening at room temperature. Line bottoms of pans with paper; grease. Use two round 8-inch layer pans, 1¼ inches deep. Start oven for moderate heat (375°F.). Sift flour once before measuring.

(For 5000 feet altitude)

Measure into sifter:

2   cups sifted cake flour
1¾ teaspoons double acting baking
      powder
¾   teaspoon salt
1¼ cups sugar*

Measure into mixing bowl:

½   cup vegetable shortening (see be-
      low*)

Measure into cup:

1   cup minus 2 tablespoons milk*
1   teaspoon vanilla

Have ready:

2   eggs, unbeaten

* If the shortening used is butter, margarine, or lard, decrease sugar and milk.... Use 1 cup plus 2 tablespoons sugar and ¼ cup milk.

Mixing Method: Stir shortening just to soften. Sift in dry ingredients. Add ¾ of the milk and mix until all flour is dampened. Then beat 2 minutes.

Add remaining milk and the eggs and beat 1 minute longer.

(Mix cake by hand or at low speed of electric mixer. Count only actual beating time. Or count beating strokes. Allow about 150 full strokes per minute. Scrape bowl and spoon often.)

Baking: Turn batter into pans. Bake in moderate oven (375°F.) 25 minutes, or until done.

Or bake in a 9 x 9 x 2-inch pan or 10 x 10 x 2-inch pan in moderate oven (350°F.) 25 to 35 minutes, or until done.

(For 3000 feet altitude)

Measure into sifter:

2   cups sifted cake flour
1¾ teaspoons double acting baking
      powder
¾   teaspoon salt
1¼ cups sugar

Measure into mixing bowl:

½   cup vegetable shortening (see be-
      low*)

Measure into cup:

¾   cup plus 1 tablespoon milk*
1   teaspoon vanilla

Have ready:

2   eggs, unbeaten

* If the shortening used is butter, margarine, or lard, decrease milk to ¾ cup.
Follow the mixing method above.

(For 7000 feet altitude)

Measure into sifter:

2   cups sifted cake flour
1½ teaspoons double acting baking
      powder
¾   teaspoon salt
1   cup plus 2 tablespoons sugar*

Measure into mixing bowl:

½   cup vegetable shortening (see be-
      low*)

Measure into cup:

1   cup minus 1 tablespoon milk*
1   teaspoon vanilla

Have ready:

2   eggs, unbeaten

* If the shortening used is butter, margarine, or lard, decrease sugar and milk.... Use 1 cup sugar and ¾ cup plus 1 tablespoon milk.
Follow the mixing method above.

SILVER MOON WHITE CAKE

Preparations: Have the shortening at room temperature. Line bottoms of pans with paper; grease. Use two round or square 9-inch pans, 1½ inches deep. Start oven for moderate heat (375°F.). Sift flour once before measuring.
Prepare meringue by beating 5 egg whites with rotary egg beater (or at a high speed of electric mixer) until foamy. Add ½ cup sugar gradually, beating only until meringue will hold up in soft peaks.

(For 5000 feet altitude)

Measure into sifter:

2½ cups sifted cake flour
2¼ teaspoons double acting baking
      powder
1   teaspoon salt
1¼ cups sugar*

Measure into mixing bowl:

⅔   cups vegetable shortening (see be-
      low*)

Measure into small bowl:

1¼ cups milk*
1½ teaspoons vanilla

Have ready: meringue of

5   egg whites and ½ cup sugar

* If butter, margarine, or lard is used, decrease sugar and milk.... Use 1 cup plus 2 tablespoons of each.

Mixing Method: Stir shortening just to soften. Sift in dry ingredients. Add ¾ of the milk and mix until all flour is dampened. Then beat 2 minutes.

Add remaining milk, blend; then add meringue mixture and beat 1 minute longer.

(Mix cake by hand or at low speed of electric mixer. Count only actual beating time. Or count beating strokes. Allow about 150 full strokes per minute. Scrape bowl and spoon often.)

Baking: Turn batter into pans. Bake in moderate oven (375°F.) 25 minutes, or until done.

This cake may also be baked in a 13 x 9 x 2-inch pan 35 minutes, or until done. Spread with fluffy pineapple frosting.

(For 3000 feet altitude)

Measure into sifter:

2½ cups sifted cake flour
2½ teaspoons double acting baking
      powder
1   teaspoon salt
1¼ cups sugar

Measure into mixing bowl:

⅔   cups vegetable shortening (see be-
      low*)

Measure into small bowl:

1   cup plus 2 tablespoons milk*
1½ teaspoons vanilla

Have ready: meringue of

5   egg whites and ½ cup sugar

* If the shortening used is butter, margarine, or lard, decrease milk to 1 cup.
Follow the mixing method above.

Silver Moon White Cake, Continued
(For 7000 feet altitude)
Measure into sifter:

2½ cups sifted cake flour
2 teaspoons double acting baking powder
1 teaspoon salt
1 cup plus 2 tablespoons sugar*

Measure into mixing bowl:

⅔ cup vegetable shortening (see below*)

Measure into small bowl:

1¼ cups milk*
1½ teaspoons vanilla

Have ready: meringue of

5 egg whites and ½ cup sugar

* If the shortening used is butter, margarine, or lard, decrease sugar and milk. . . . Use 1 cup sugar and 1 cup plus 2 tablespoons milk.
Follow the mixing method above.

MIX-EASY DEVIL'S FOOD

Preparations: Have the shortening at room temperature. Line bottoms of pans with paper; grease. Use two round 9-inch layers, 1½ inches deep. Start oven for moderate heat (350°F.). Sift flour once.

(For 5000 feet altitude)
Measure into sifter:

2 cups sifted cake flour
½ teaspoon double acting baking powder
¾ teaspoon baking soda
¾ teaspoon salt
1⅓ cups sugar*
½ cup cocoa

Measure into mixing bowl:

⅔ cup vegetable shortening (see below*)

Measure into small bowl:

1¼ cups milk*
1 teaspoon vanilla

Have ready:

2 eggs, unbeaten

* With butter, margarine, or lard, decrease sugar and milk to 1¼ cups sugar and 1 cup plus 2 tablespoons milk.
Mixing Method: Sift dry ingredients together twice. Stir shortening just to soften. Sift in dry ingredients. Add ¾ of the milk and mix until all flour is dampened. Then beat 2 minutes.
Add remaining milk and the eggs, and beat 1 minute longer.
(Mix cake by hand or at low speed of electric mixer. Count only actual beating time. Or count beating strokes. Allow about 150 full strokes per minute. Scrape bowl and spoon often.)

Baking: Turn batter into pans. Bake in moderate oven (350°F.) 25 minutes, or until done. Spread with seven-minute frosting.
This cake may also be baked in a 13 x 9 x 2-inch pan in moderate oven (350°F.) 30 to 35 minutes.

(For 3000 feet altitude)

Measure into sifter:

2 cups sifted cake flour
½ teaspoon double acting baking powder
1 teaspoon baking soda
¾ teaspoon salt
1⅓ cups sugar
½ cup cocoa

Measure into mixing bowl:

⅔ cup vegetable shortening (see below*)

Measure into small bowl:

1 cup plus 2 tablespoons milk*
1 teaspoon vanilla

Have ready:

2 eggs, unbeaten

* If the shortening used is butter, margarine, or lard, decrease milk to 1 cup.
Follow the mixing method above.

(For 7000 feet altitude)

Measure into sifter:

2 cups sifted cake flour
½ teaspoon double acting baking powder
¾ teaspoon baking soda
¾ teaspoon salt
1¼ cups sugar*
⅓ cup cocoa

Measure into mixing bowl:

½ cup vegetable shortening (see below*)

Measure into small bowl:

1¼ cups milk*
1 teaspoon vanilla

Have ready:

2 eggs, unbeaten

* If butter, margarine, or lard is used, decrease sugar and milk. . . . Use 1 cup plus 2 tablespoons of each.
Follow the mixing method above.

SPONGE CAKE

Preparations: Have eggs at room temperature. Start oven for moderate heat (375°F.). Sift flour once before measuring. Use 9-inch tube pan.

(For 5000 feet altitude)
Ingredients:

1 cup sifted cake flour
1 cup minus 1 tablespoon sifted granulated sugar
5 egg yolks
1½ teaspoon grated lemon rind
1½ tablespoons lemon juice
2 tablespoons water
5 egg whites
¼ teaspoon salt
¼ teaspoon cream of tartar

Mixing Method: Measure sifted flour, add ¼ cup sugar, and sift together four times.
Place egg yolks in small bowl. Add lemon rind and beat with rotary egg beater until thick and lemon-colored. Add lemon juice and water gradually, beating until thick and light.
Beat egg whites and salt with flat wire whisk or rotary egg beater until foamy.
Sprinkle in cream of tartar and continue beating until egg whites are stiff enough to hold up in soft peaks but are still moist and glossy.
Add remaining sugar in three additions, beating 50 strokes after each. Then fold in egg yolk mixture with flat wire whisk or spoon until well blended.
Sift about ¼ of flour over mixture and fold in lightly with whisk or spoon (15 fold-over strokes), turning bowl gradually. Continue folding in flour by fourths in this way, folding well after last addition (25 strokes).

Baking: Turn into ungreased round 9-inch tube pan. Bake in moderate oven (375°F.) 30 minutes, or until done. Remove from oven, invert pan, and let stand 1 hour, or until cake is cool.

(For 3000 feet altitude)
Ingredients:

1 cup sifted cake flour
1 cup sifted granulated sugar
5 egg yolks
1½ teaspoons grated lemon rind
1½ tablespoons lemon juice
2 tablespoons water
5 egg whites
¼ teaspoon salt
¼ teaspoon cream of tartar

Follow the mixing method given above.

(For 7000 feet altitude)
Ingredients:

1 cup sifted cake flour
1 cup minus 2 tablespoons sifted granulated sugar
5 egg yolks
1½ teaspoons grated lemon rind
1½ tablespoons lemon juice
2 tablespoons water
5 egg whites
¼ teaspoon salt
½ teaspoon cream of tartar

Follow the mixing method given above.

FAMILY SIZE ANGEL FOOD

Preparations: Have eggs at room temperature. Start oven for moderate heat (375°F.). Sift flour once before measuring. Use 9-inch tube pan.

(For 5000 feet altitude)

Ingredients:

1 cup sifted cake flour
1 cup plus 2 tablespoons sifted granulated sugar
1 cup egg whites plus 1 white
1/4 teaspoon salt
1 teaspoon cream of tartar
1 teaspoon vanilla
1/4 teaspoon almond extract

Mixing Method: Measure sifted flour, add 1/4 cup sugar, and sift together four times.

Beat egg whites and salt with flat wire whisk or rotary egg beater until foamy.

Sprinkle in cream of tartar and continue beating until egg whites are stiff enough to hold up in soft peaks, but are still moist and glossy.

Sprinkle remaining sugar over egg whites, about 4 tablespoons at a time, and beat after each addition to blend (25 strokes). Beat in flavoring (10 strokes).

Sift about 1/4 of flour over mixture and fold in lightly with whisk or spoon (15 fold-over strokes), turning bowl gradually. Continue folding in flour by fourths in this way, folding well after last addition (25 strokes).

Baking: Turn into ungreased round 9-inch tube pan. Bake in moderate oven (375°F.) 30 minutes, or until done.

Remove from oven, invert pan, and let stand 1 hour, or until cake is cool. Spread with icing.

(For 3000 feet altitude)

Ingredients:

1 cup sifted cake flour
1 1/4 cups sifted granulated sugar
1 cup egg whites
1/4 teaspoon salt
1 teaspoon cream of tartar
1 teaspoon vanilla
1/4 teaspoon almond extract

Follow the mixing method given above.

(For 7000 feet altitude)

Ingredients:

1 cup sifted cake flour
1 cup sifted granulated sugar
1 cup egg whites plus 1 white
1/4 teaspoon salt
1 1/4 teaspoons cream of tartar
1 teaspoon vanilla
1/4 teaspoon almond extract

Follow the mixing method given above.

GOLD CAKE

Preparations: Have the shortening at room temperature. Line bottom of 10 x 5 x 3-inch loaf pan with paper; grease. Start oven for moderate heat (350°F.). Sift flour once before measuring.

(For 5000 feet altitude)

Measure into sifter:

2 cups sifted cake flour
1 1/2 teaspoons double acting baking powder
3/4 teaspoon salt
1 cup sugar

Measure into mixing bowl:

1/2 cup vegetable shortening (see below*)

Measure into cup:

1 cup minus 2 tablespoons milk*
1 teaspoon vanilla

Have ready:

5 egg yolks, unbeaten

* If the shortening used is butter, margarine, or lard, decrease milk to 3/4 cup.

Mixing Method: Stir shortening just to soften. Sift in dry ingredients. Add egg yolks and 1/2 cup of the milk and mix until all flour is dampened. Then beat 2 minutes.

Add remaining milk and beat 1 minute longer.

(Mix cake by hand or at low speed of electric mixer. Count only actual beating time. Or count beating strokes. Allow about 150 full strokes per minute. Scrape bowl and spoon often.)

Baking: Turn batter into pan. Bake in moderate oven (350°F.) 1 hour, or until done. Spread with butter frosting.

(For 3000 feet altitude)

Measure into sifter:

2 cups sifted cake flour
1 3/4 teaspoons double acting baking powder
3/4 teaspoon salt
1 cup sugar

Measure into mixing bowl:

1/2 cup vegetable shortening (see below*)

Measure into cup:

3/4 cup milk*
1 teaspoon vanilla

Have ready:

5 egg yolks, unbeaten

* If the shortening used is butter, margarine, or lard, decrease milk to 2/3 cup.

Follow the mixing method above.

(For 7000 feet altitude)

Measure into sifter:

2 cups sifted cake flour
1 1/2 teaspoons double acting baking powder
3/4 teaspoon salt
1 cup minus 1 tablespoon sugar*

Measure into mixing bowl:

1/2 cup vegetable shortening (see below*)

Measure into cup:

1 cup minus 2 tablespoons milk*
1 teaspoon vanilla

Have ready:

5 egg yolks, unbeaten

* If the shortening used is butter, margarine, or lard, decrease sugar and milk. . . . Use 1 cup minus 2 tablespoons sugar and 3/4 cup milk.

Follow the mixing method above.

Gold Cake Variations:

Sunshine Party Loaf: Omit vanilla and add 2 teaspoons grated orange rind to shortening. Mix and bake as directed. Spread cake with lemon icing.

Old-Fashioned Loaf Cake: Omit vanilla in Gold Cake. Add 1 1/2 teaspoons grated lemon rind to shortening, and sift 1/4 teaspoon nutmeg with dry ingredients.

MIX-EASY ONE-EGG CAKE

Preparations: Have the shortening at room temperature. Line bottom of pan with paper; grease. Use 9 x 9 x 2-inch pan. Start oven for moderate heat (375°F.).

(For 5000 feet altitude)

Measure into sifter:

2 cups sifted cake flour
1 1/2 teaspoons double acting baking powder
3/4 teaspoon salt
1 cup sugar

Measure into mixing bowl:

1/3 cup butter or other shortening

Measure into cup:

1 cup minus 2 tablespoons milk
1 teaspoon vanilla

Have ready:

1 egg, unbeaten

Mixing Method: Stir shortening just to soften. Sift in dry ingredients. Add 3/4 of the milk and mix until all

Mix-Easy One-Egg Cake, Continued
flour is dampened. Then beat 2 minutes.

Add remaining milk and the egg and beat 1 minute longer.

(Mix cake by hand or at low speed of electric mixer. Count only actual beating time. Or count beating strokes. Allow about 150 full strokes per minute. Scrape bowl and spoon often.)

Baking: Turn batter into pan. Bake in moderate oven (375°F.) 30 minutes, or until done.

This cake may also be baked in two round 8-inch layer pans 25 minutes, or until done.

(For 3000 feet altitude)

Measure into sifter:

2   cups sifted cake flour
1¾ teaspoons double acting baking powder
¾   teaspoon salt
1   cup sugar

Measure into mixing bowl:

⅓   cup butter or other shortening

Measure into cup:

¾   cup milk
1   teaspoon vanilla

Have ready:

1   egg, unbeaten

Follow the mixing method above.

(For 7000 feet altitude)

Measure into sifter:

2   cups sifted cake flour
1¼ teaspoons double acting baking powder
¾   teaspoon salt
1   cup minus 1 tablespoon sugar

Measure into mixing bowl:

⅓   cup butter or other shortening

Measure into cup:

1   cup minus 1 tablespoon milk
1   teaspoon vanilla

Have ready:

1   egg, unbeaten

Follow the mixing method above.

LUCKY DAY NUT LOAF

Preparations: Have the shortening at room temperature. Line bottom of 10 x 5 x 3-inch loaf pan with paper; grease. Start oven for moderate heat (350°F.). Sift flour once before measuring.

(For 5000 feet altitude)

Measure into sifter:

2   cups sifted cake flour
1½ teaspoons double acting baking powder
¾   teaspoon salt
1   cup plus 2 tablespoons sugar*

Measure into mixing bowl:

½   cup vegetable shortening (see below*)

Measure into cup:

¾   cup plus 1 tablespoon milk*
1   teaspoon vanilla

Have ready:

2   eggs, unbeaten
¾   cup nutmeats, finely chopped

* If the shortening used is butter, margarine, or lard, decrease sugar and milk. . . . Use 1 cup sugar and ⅔ cup milk.

Mixing Method: Stir shortening just to soften. Sift in dry ingredients. Add ¾ of the milk and mix until all flour is dampened. Then beat 2 minutes.

Add remaining milk and the eggs and beat 1 minute longer. Add nuts.
(Mix cake by hand or at low speed of electric mixer. Count only actual beating time. Or count beating strokes. Allow about 150 full strokes per minute. Scrape bowl and spoon often.)

Baking: Turn batter into pan. Bake in moderate oven (350°F.) 1 hour and 10 minutes, or until cake is done.

(For 3000 feet altitude)

Measure into sifter:

2   cups sifted cake flour
1¾ teaspoons double acting baking powder
¾   teaspoon salt
1¼ cups sugar

Measure into mixing bowl:

½   cup vegetable shortening (see below*)

Measure into cup:

¾   cup milk*
1   teaspoon vanilla

Have ready:

2   eggs, unbeaten
¾   cup nutmeats, finely chopped

If the shortening used is butter, margarine, or lard, decrease milk to ⅔ cup.
Follow the mixing method above.

(For 7000 feet altitude)

Measure into sifter:

2   cups sifted cake flour
1½ teaspoons double acting baking powder
¾   teaspoon salt
1   cup sugar*

Measure into mixing bowl:

½   cup vegetable shortening (see below*)

Measure into cup:

1   cup minus 2 tablespoons milk*
1   teaspoon vanilla

Have ready:

2   eggs, unbeaten
¾   cup nutmeats, finely chopped

* With butter, margarine, or lard, decrease sugar and milk to 1 cup minus 2 tablespoons sugar and ¾ cup milk.
Follow the mixing method above.

Quick Cupcakes: Mix batter for Lucky Day Nut Loaf (above), omitting nutmeats.

Turn into muffin pans that have been greased lightly on bottoms only, filling each only half full.

Bake in moderate oven (375°F.) 20 minutes, or until done. Makes 18 medium or 36 small cupcakes.

Standards for a Good Layer Cake

Well-proportioned shape and size, slightly rounded top, straight sides, evenly browned, tender crust, velvety even-grained crumb, good flavor.

This Should Happen

This Should Not Happen

CAKE FROSTINGS, FILLINGS, AND GLAZES

The term frosting originally meant an uncooked cake covering, while icing referred to a cooked sugar mixture used to coat a cake; the two are now used interchangeably. The same frosting that covers a cake may be used for filling between the layers, but often a different filling is preferable.

CHOOSING A FROSTING

A frosting should complement or flatter the flavor or color of your cake. A rich frosting should be chosen for a simple economy cake, a fluffy frosting for a light moist cake, and so on. A sponge cake, angel food, or a pound cake may be served unfrosted or finished off with a simple icing or glaze or with a topping. For good looks, frostings must be soft and manageable, yet not the least "runny."

Uncooked butter frostings call for confectioners' sugar (XXXX). Coarser sugar will make them grainy. If too soft these frostings can be thickened by the addition of a little more sugar. If too stiff, thin with a few drops of cream or other liquid.

Fluffy frostings such as the 7-minute, boiled, and uncooked meringue types are luscious and lavish looking. Make these the day the cake is to be served. Overcooking gives these frostings sugary texture. Undercooking leaves them too soft.

Creamy cooked frostings are fudge-like in consistency, creamy, and delicious. They harden more quickly than uncooked frostings, so need to be spread more quickly. The bowl of frosting may be placed over warm water to keep the frosting soft and workable.

CAKE DECORATING WITH FROSTING

A plain cake is a pleasant dessert—but a decorated cake is a party. The difference is simply a skillful hand with frosting. Special decorating may consist of the simple decorative touches described below, arranged in an appropriate design, or it may include more elaborate borders, rosettes, and festoons made with frosting and a cake decorator. Even the elaborately decorated cakes which are seen in caterers' windows are not so difficult to do as might be supposed. A few simple rules and practice with cake decorating equipment will soon give you artistically decorated cakes. The equipment may consist merely of homemade paper cornucopias with a few inexpensive basic metal tubes or it may include a special cloth, rubber, or metal holder and a large variety of tubes. These may be purchased at most house furnishing stores.

Preparing the Cake

First, frost cake as directed, but spread frosting smoothly over the top and sides unless a rough surface or swirl pattern is part of the desired decorative effect.

Not all frostings can be used for decorating. The frosting must be stiff enough to hold its shape and yet be soft enough to pass through the small opening of a decorating tube. Butter frostings are usually preferred as they keep well; a frosting must be one that will not harden or dry too quickly because the decorating process often takes some time.

The frosting may be tinted delicately as desired. Pastel tints are usually best but brighter colors may be used for color accents.

HINTS AND STEPS IN FROSTING A CAKE

1. Have the cake thoroughly cool. Brush or rub off all loose crumbs. Trim off ragged edges with a scissors.
2. Choose a flat plate or tray that will "frame" the cake. A 9-inch cake looks best on a plate or tray 12 to 13 inches in diameter. This allows a border of about 2 inches all around the cake. If the plate is too large or too deep, it dwarfs the cake. If too small, it make the cake appear clumsy and overbalanced.
3. To keep the plate clean while frosting, cover the outer area of the plate with pieces of waxed paper extending beyond the edge of plate.
4. If your cake is quite moist, a little powdered sugar sprinkled on the plate will keep it from sticking.

5. Place cake in position (on the papers) on the cake plate. If there is any difference in cake layers, choose the thicker layer for the bottom layer, and keep a smooth-crusted layer for the top.
6. Use a flexible spatula to spread frosting.
7. For a layer cake, place some frosting on the bottom layer. Spread it smoothly, almost to the edge. With a soft filling, spread to 1 inch from the edge. Then adjust the second layer so that edges are even and cake uniform in height. If top layer slides, insert a wire cake tester or slender knitting needle through both layers to anchor. This can be removed before frosting the top.

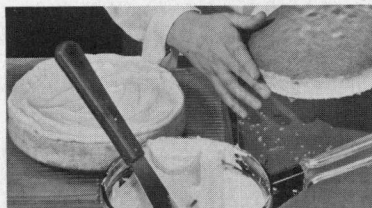

Spread frosting carefully on lower layer, then fit top.

Start frosting at the sides, then fill in the top.

8. To frost outside of cake, spread frosting over edge and sides. Then pile remaining frosting on top and spread lightly to the edges. Swirl the frosting attractively as you frost.
9. Work quickly so that the frosting will not crust over before you finish. Let frosting set slightly, then draw out the pieces of waxed paper carefully from under cake.
10. For very special cakes, it pays to frost smoothly first with a thin layer of frosting to hold down any crumbs and

to give an even base coat. When set or firm, the final frosting may be spread more easily.

Light strokes with a spatula will vary the decorative effect.

11. For cupcakes, hold each cake, turning as you spread frosting on the top. To frost the sides as well, hold cake, top and bottom, while frosting sides, then place on cake rack or hold on a fork while frosting the top (or the bottom).

To Frost Cupcakes Quickly: Dip the top of each cupcake into soft frosting. Twirl slightly and quickly turn right side up.

SIMPLE DECORATIVE TOUCHES

Confectioners' Sugar: (1) Sprinkle the sugar through a small sieve onto unfrosted cake. (2) For special designs, place a fancy paper doily or a cut-out pattern, or letters on top of the cake. Then sprinkle with confectioners' sugar. Carefully lift the pattern up and away. The design will be embossed on the cake.

Candies: Use colored or silver candies for forming letters, festoons, or simple borders. With a toothpick, draw or space out the design lightly on frosted cake. Then place candies carefully on design. If necessary, use a tweezers to place each candy in position.

Chocolate: Melt chocolate over boiling water with 1 teaspoon butter for each square (ounce) of chocolate. Use to dribble over fluffy frosting from a teaspoon. Or paint the chocolate onto a smooth frosting to form a design, greeting, or name.

Frosting Sculpture: Frost cake with 7-minute frosting. Then tint more frosting with food coloring and use to form swirls or "ferns" at intervals on top and sides of cake.

Fruit and Nuts: For flower and leaf designs, colored candies may be used with citron cut in leaf shapes. Other fruits such as raisins, candied cherries, citron, etc. may be arranged on cakes in designs. Try cluster raisins with toasted almonds, cherry bits with strips of citron.

Pecan or walnut halves may be centered on cupcakes or cake squares. Chopped pecans, walnuts, or pistachios are attractive pressed against sides of frosted cakes or around top edge in a border or scattered freely on the top.

To Toast Nuts: Place nuts in a shallow pan with a little butter (1 teaspoon butter for each cup of nuts). Heat in moderate oven (350°F.) until lightly browned, 15 to 20 minutes. Or heat and stir in a heavy skillet.

To Sliver Almonds: Blanch shelled almonds by covering with boiling water and letting stand until skins wrinkle, about 3 minutes. Drain and rub off brown skins. Split nuts and cut in slivers.

Coconut, Plain, Toasted, or Tinted: Sprinkle it over fluffy frostings or press it against sides of cake while frosting is still soft.

To Tint Coconut: Sprinkle shredded coconut on white paper. Dilute a tiny bit of food coloring in a small amount of water; sprinkle over coconut and rub evenly through it until the coconut is evenly tinted. Or put the coconut in a glass jar, filling no more than half full. Sprinkle with a few drops of diluted coloring. Cover jar and shake until all coconut is tinted.

To Toast Coconut: Spread shredded coconut in a thin layer on a baking sheet. Toast in moderate oven (350°F.) until golden brown, stirring it frequently to toast evenly.

Jelly: Use beaten or melted jelly for designs; for example, a red jelly heart or a green shamrock. Use a toothpick to mark the design on the cake, then spread the jelly inside the design.

Flowers: Dainty fresh flowers or a spray of green leaves are an especially inviting garnish on a simply frosted cake. Place small flowers and feathery greens in a small glass and insert in center of a frosted tube cake. Place matching flowers around the cake. Use tiny rosebuds or nosegays tied with ribbon for small cakes. Flowers around cakes should be grouped low enough so that the base of the cake can be seen.

Candles: Select candles and holders in the right color and size for the cake. A single large candle or candle-flower may be used in the center or a few medium-sized candles near the center instead of many small candles for older birthdays.

HOW TO CUT CAKES

Use a long, sharp knife for cutting cakes and cut with a gently sawing motion. Do not press down. For best results with frosted cakes, rinse the knife frequently in hot water. (This cannot be done at the table but it is an excellent aid when cutting cakes in kitchen for a party.)

Round layer cakes may be cut in wedges so that each piece has equal frosting. To serve sponge cake and angel food, cut lightly with a very sharp or serrated knife, or "tear" off each piece, using two forks or a cake breaker.

Here are diagrams for cutting round cakes when serving a crowd. Use the largest one for deep, single-layered cakes or try the other two for 9- or 10-inch layer cakes.

To cut a square cake 8 x 8 x 2 inches or larger.

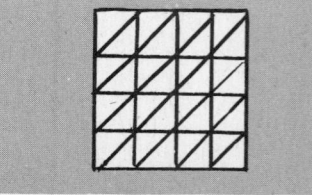

HOMEMADE CAKE DECORATOR

If you have no cake decorating set, you can make your own decorator bag for special borders and writing. For the bags, cut squares or 10x8- or 12x9-inch rectangles of sturdy waxed or thin parchment paper into two triangles (step 1).

Roll each triangle into a cone shape, making sure it is tightly rolled so as not to give under pressure (steps 2, 3, and 4). Fold down the top point of the cone to keep it from unfolding (step 5).

Washable bags may be shaped similarly from muslin or light canvas, then stitched.

For writing, snip off the tip of the paper cone to give a small opening. Designs can be made by cutting this tip. An inverted "v" cut will shape leaf designs or flutings; a series of tiny "y's" will form shell designs and ridged borders.

If preferred, metal tips may be inserted at the bottom of the canvas bag or paper cone. Cut the tip off on the dotted line and drop the metal tube in as shown in steps 6 and 7.

For best results, fill cake decorator tube, bag, or cone only half-full of frosting at a time. Use one hand to guide the tip, the other to force out frosting gently.

Practice on paper or an inverted pan before attempting to decorate a cake in order to make sure that the frosting is of the right consistency.

If it is too soft it will not spread and the design will not be clear cut, and it will be difficult to break off the flow of frosting at the right point. If it is too stiff it will be difficult to push through the tube and will tend to break or crack.

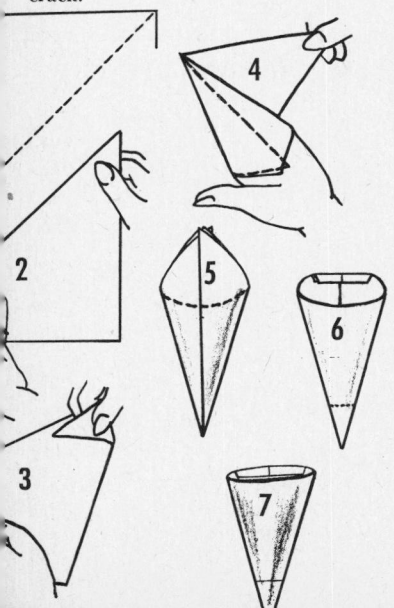

1. Begin the cutting at the lowest tier. To make the cuts even in depth, run a knife all the way around where it abuts the second lowest layer.

2. Continue this process with the next lowest tier, then with the third tier.

HOW TO CUT A WEDDING CAKE

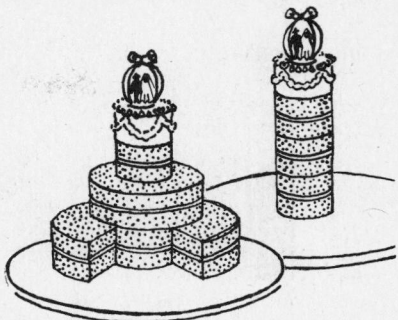

3. Then cut the lowest tier again, cutting successive slices until a single cylindrical central core remains with the ornate top in place.

4. Save the ornate top for the bride to be frozen, if desired, for the first anniversary party.
5. Then finish slicing the central core beginning at the top.

Uncooked and Quick Frostings

PLAIN CONFECTIONERS' FROSTING

(Master Recipe)

2 cups sifted confectioners' sugar
2 tablespoons soft butter or margarine
1 teaspoon vanilla or almond extract
About 2 tablespoons boiling water, hot milk, hot cream, or fruit juice

Combine sugar, butter, and vanilla in a bowl. Add liquid, a little at a time, beating well with fork or spoon between additions.

Add only enough liquid to give the mixture easy spreading consistency.

Variations of Confectioners' Frosting

Glossy Chocolate Frosting: Add 1½ ounces (1½ squares) unsweetened chocolate melted over hot water, or ⅓ cup cocoa, sifted in with the sugar.

Coconut Confectioners' Frosting: Just before spreading plain confectioners' frosting or glossy chocolate frosting, add ½ cup moist shredded coconut. Garnish top of cake with more coconut.

Coffee Confectioners' Frosting: Use strong hot coffee for the liquid.

Maple Confectioners' Frosting: Use maple syrup for the liquid.

Nut Confectioners' Frosting: Add about ½ cup chopped nuts just before spreading. Garnish cake with nut halves or finely chopped nuts.

Raspberry Confectioners' Frosting: Omit flavoring in plain confectioners' frosting and use crushed raspberries and their juice as the liquid.

Raisin Confectioners' Frosting: Add about ½ cup chopped raisins to plain confectioners' frosting just before spreading.

Rum Confectioners' Frosting: Substitute rum or rum flavoring for other flavoring.

Strawberry Confectioners' Frosting: Omit flavoring in plain confectioners' frosting and use crushed strawberries and their juice as the liquid.

Simple Lemon Confectioners' Frosting: Substitute lemon juice for 1 tablespoon of the water. Add ½ teaspoon grated lemon rind.

Simple Orange Confectioners' Frosting: Omit flavoring. Use orange juice for the liquid. Add 1 teaspoon grated orange rind.

BUTTER FROSTING
(Master Recipe)

¼ cup butter or margarine
2 cups sifted confectioners' sugar
⅛ teaspoon salt
3 tablespoons cream
1 teaspoon vanilla

Cream butter until soft. Slowly stir in 1 cup sugar and the salt. Add additional sugar alternately with cream, beating thoroughly after each addition until creamy and smooth. Beat in vanilla.

Additional cream may be added to give frosting spreading consistency.

Makes frosting to cover top and sides of two 8-inch layer cakes or 2 dozen cupcakes.

Butter Frosting Variations

Almond Butter Frosting: Omit vanilla in master recipe. Add 1 teaspoon almond flavoring.

Apricot Butter Frosting: Omit cream in master recipe. Add ¼ cup cooked apricot pulp and 1 teaspoon lemon juice.

Chocolate Butter Frosting: Melt 2 ounces (2 squares) unsweetened chocolate over hot water. Blend with 2 tablespoons boiling water. Add vanilla reduced to ½ teaspoon and salt. Substitute 2 tablespoons milk for cream.

Cinnamon Butter Frosting: Substitute cinnamon for vanilla in master recipe.

Coffee Butter Frosting: Substitute strong coffee for cream in master recipe.

Lemon Butter Frosting: Substitute lemon juice and 1 egg yolk for the cream and vanilla in master recipe. Add 1½ teaspoons grated lemon rind.

Maple Walnut Butter Frosting: In master recipe, substitute maple flavoring for vanilla. Add ½ cup chopped walnuts with the last of the sugar.

Mint Butter Frosting: Prepare master recipe. Color frosting green. Substitute mint flavoring for vanilla.

Or melt peppermint candy and add to frosting for flavor and color.

Mocha Butter Frosting: In master recipe, substitute coffee for cream. Add 1½ tablespoons cocoa with the creamed butter.

Orange Butter Frosting: In master recipe, substitute 1 egg yolk and 2 tablespoons orange juice for the cream. Substitute grated orange rind for vanilla.

Pineapple Butter Frosting: In master recipe, omit cream. Add about ¼ cup drained crushed pineapple. Use lemon juice for flavoring.

Pistachio Butter Frosting: Prepare master recipe. Color frosting pale green. Add a few drops of almond extract.

Strawberry Butter Frosting: Omit liquid in master recipe. Add about ¼ cup crushed strawberries.

Use lemon juice for flavoring. Decorate with whole strawberries.

CREAM CHEESE ICING
(Master Recipe)

1 package (3 ounces) cream cheese
1 tablespoon milk
1½ cups sifted confectioners' sugar
1 teaspoon vanilla

Soften cheese with milk. Gradually add confectioners' sugar and vanilla. Beat until creamy.

Variations:

Cream Cheese Chocolate Icing: Increase milk to 3 tablespoons, and confectioners' sugar to 2½ cups. Add 2 ounces (2 squares) melted unsweetened chocolate and ⅛ teaspoon salt. Omit vanilla.

Orange Cream Cheese Icing: Substitute 2 tablespoons orange juice and 1 teaspoon grated orange rind for milk and vanilla.

FLUFFY LIME FROSTING

6 tablespoons butter or margarine
¼ teaspoon salt
1 teaspoon vanilla
1 egg white, unbeaten
3½ cups sifted confectioners' sugar
2½ tablespoons lime juice
2½ teaspoons grated lime rind

Cream together butter, salt, and vanilla. Add egg white. Then add sugar, alternately with lime juice, beating well after each addition. Add lime rind and beat well.

Makes frosting for tops and sides of two 8-inch layers, or top and sides of a 9- or 10-inch angel food cake.

Fluffy Orange Frosting: Use above recipe, substituting orange rind and juice for lime rind and juice.

GOLDEN CREAM FROSTING

¼ cup shortening
¼ cup butter or margarine
½ teaspoon salt
1 teaspoon vanilla
1 egg yolk
1¾ to 2 cups sifted confectioners' sugar
1 tablespoon milk

Cream shortening and butter until soft and fluffy. Beat in salt, vanilla, and

Strawberry Meringue

egg yolk. Add sugar alternately with milk, beating constantly.

Makes frosting for top and sides of two 9-inch layers.

STRAWBERRY MERINGUE FOR SPONGE CAKE

2 egg whites
⅛ teaspoon salt
½ cup sugar
1 teaspoon lemon juice
1½ cups sliced strawberries

Beat egg whites until stiff, but not dry. Blend in salt, sugar, and lemon juice. Continue beating until meringue stands in peaks and is well blended. Fold in strawberries.

Serve over sponge or angel food cake. Makes strawberry meringue for one 13½-ounce sponge cake.

MOLASSES BUTTER FROSTING

2 tablespoons shortening
2 tablespoons butter or margarine
¼ teaspoon salt
¼ cup light molasses
¼ cup cream
4 cups firmly packed sifted confectioners' sugar

Cream shortening and butter. Add salt, molasses, and cream; mix well. Add confectioners' sugar gradually and stir until smooth.

Spread between, on top and sides of two 9-inch layers. Use with spice cake.

CREAMY VANILLA FROSTING

2 tablespoons shortening
2 tablespoons soft butter or margarine
⅛ teaspoon salt
1 teaspoon vanilla
2 cups firmly packed confectioners' sugar
2 tablespoons warm cream

Cream shortening and butter together. Add salt, vanilla, and 1 cup sugar. Stir in warm cream.

Add remaining sugar and beat until thoroughly blended.

Spread on top and sides of cake. Makes frosting for two 8-inch layers.

Creamy Lemon Frosting: In above, substitute 1 tablespoon lemon juice and ¼ teaspoon grated lemon rind for vanilla.

ORNAMENTAL FROSTING

Cream 2 tablespoons butter. Blend in 2 cups sifted confectioners' sugar, mixing well.

Add 1/2 teaspoon vanilla and 2 to 4 tablespoons hot cream, a little at a time, until frosting is of right consistency to press through a cone made from heavy brown paper.

Divide into 3 or more parts and tint each a different pastel color by adding food coloring, a drop at a time.

Decorate cakes by pressing frosting through paper cones.

LEMON CONFECTIONERS' FROSTING
(Master Recipe)

1   egg yolk
1 1/2   tablespoons lemon juice
1   tablespoon grated orange rind
1/8   teaspoon salt
2   cups confectioners' sugar

Combine egg yolk, lemon juice, orange rind, and salt. Beat until smooth.

Gradually mix in sugar and beat until of spreading consistency.

Makes frosting for 2 layers or 20 cupcakes.

Variations:

Lime Confectioners' Frosting: Substitute lime for lemon juice and 1/4 teaspoon grated lemon rind for orange rind. Tint lightly with green food coloring.

Orange Confectioners' Frosting: Substitute 2 tablespoons orange juice for lemon juice and omit grated orange rind.

BANANA BUTTER FROSTING

1/2   cup mashed ripe banana
1/2   teaspoon lemon juice
1/4   cup butter or margarine
3 1/2   cups sifted confectioners' sugar

Mix together banana and lemon juice.

Beat butter until creamy. Add sugar and banana alternately, a small amount at a time, beating until frosting is light and fluffy.

Makes enough frosting for top and sides of two 9-inch layers.

BROILED FROSTING

1/2   cup butter or margarine
1   cup firmly packed brown sugar
6   tablespoons cream
1   cup shredded coconut
1   cup chopped nuts

Heat butter and brown sugar together until melted and well blended. Add cream, coconut, and nuts, and spread on warm cake immediately.

Place under broiler until delicately brown, about 3 minutes.

"NO-COOK" MARSHMALLOW FROSTING

1/4   teaspoon salt
2   egg whites
1/4   cup sugar
3/4   cup corn syrup, light or dark
1 1/4   teaspoons vanilla

Add salt to egg whites and beat with electric or rotary beater until mixture forms soft peaks.

Gradually add sugar, about 1 tablespoon at a time, beating until smooth and glossy. Continue beating and add corn syrup, a little at a time, beating thoroughly after each addition, until frosting peaks. Fold in vanilla.

Makes enough to frost top and sides of two 9-inch layers.

Variations:

Coffee Frosting: Omit vanilla; add 1 tablespoon instant coffee with corn syrup.

Lemon or Orange Frosting: Omit vanilla; fold in 2 teaspoons grated lemon or orange rind.

Spice Frosting: Omit vanilla; add 1/2 teaspoon ginger, 1/4 teaspoon cinnamon, and a few grains of cloves with dark corn syrup.

Coconut Frosting: Sprinkle 1 cup shredded coconut over top and sides of frosted cake, or fold in 1 cup shredded coconut with vanilla.

SUPREME CHOCOLATE NUT FROSTING

1/2   cup butter or margarine
1   egg
2   ounces (2 squares) chocolate
1 1/3   cups confectioners' sugar
1/8   teaspoon salt
1   teaspoon vanilla
1   cup chopped nuts

Cream butter until soft and creamy. Beat in egg.

Melt chocolate and add to butter-egg mixture. Add confectioners' sugar, salt, and vanilla. Beat until smooth and creamy. Stir in chopped nuts.

Makes frosting for 1 large loaf cake or 24 cupcakes.

FLUFFY UNCOOKED FROSTING

2   egg whites
1   tablespoon vinegar
1   teaspoon lemon juice
Few grains salt
2   teaspoons cornstarch
About 2 1/2   cups sifted confectioners' sugar

Beat egg whites until stiff. Add vinegar, lemon juice, salt, and cornstarch. Continue beating.

Gradually add sugar until of consistency to spread.

QUICK FUDGE FROSTING

6   to 8 ounces semisweet chocolate
1/4   cup butter or margarine
1 1/2   cups sifted confectioners' sugar
1/2   teaspoon cinnamon
1/8   teaspoon salt
1/2   cup warm milk
1   teaspoon vanilla

Melt chocolate over hot water. Blend in butter.

Combine sugar, cinnamon, and salt. Add alternately with milk to chocolate-butter mixture, beating after each addition. Add vanilla and cool.

Makes frosting for 24 cupcakes or tops and sides of two 9-inch layers.

CHOCOLATE MOCHA FROSTING

1/4   cup butter or margarine
1/4   cup strong coffee
2   cups confectioners' sugar
1/4   cup cocoa
1/2   teaspoon salt
1   teaspoon vanilla

Have butter and coffee at room temperature. Sift together sugar, cocoa, and salt.

Combine all ingredients and beat until smooth and fluffy. Spread on cake.

Makes enough frosting for two 9-inch layers.

FLUFFY HONEY FROSTING

1   egg white
Dash of salt
1/2   cup honey

Beat egg white with salt until stiff enough to hold up in peaks, but not dry.

Pour honey in fine stream over egg white, beating constantly until frosting holds its shape. (Beat about 2 1/2 minutes with electric mixer, or about 4 minutes by hand.)

Makes frosting to cover tops of two 8-inch layers.

For a quick decoration, confectioners' sugar is sprinkled through a paper doily.

MOLASSES MOCHA FROSTING
(Master Recipe)

2 cups sifted confectioners' sugar
1/4 cup butter or margarine
1 egg white, unbeaten
1 tablespoon cold coffee
1 tablespoon molasses
1 teaspoon vanilla

Add 1 cup sugar gradually to butter and egg white. Mix well.

Add remaining sugar alternately with coffee, molasses, and vanilla. Beat well.

Makes enough for tops and sides of two 8-inch layers or tops of two 9-inch layers.

Variations:

Molasses Chocolate Frosting: Add 3 tablespoons cocoa or 1 square (1 ounce) melted chocolate.

Molasses Orange Frosting: Omit coffee and vanilla. Add 2 tablespoons orange juice, 1 teaspoon grated orange rind, and 1/2 teaspoon grated lemon rind.

SPICY RAISIN FROSTING

1 3/4 cups confectioners' sugar
1 tablespoon cocoa
1/2 teaspoon cinnamon
1/2 teaspoon cloves
1/2 teaspoon nutmeg
1/2 cup sweetened condensed milk
1/2 teaspoon vanilla
1/2 cup raisins

Combine ingredients in order given. Use to frost spice cakes.

EASY CHOCOLATE FROSTING

3 tablespoons butter or margarine
2 squares (2 ounces) chocolate
2 3/4 cups sifted confectioners' sugar
1 teaspoon vanilla
1/3 cup hot milk

Combine butter and chocolate in top of double boiler. Cook over boiling water until chocolate is melted.

Combine sifted confectioners' sugar with vanilla and hot milk and blend well.

Add melted chocolate and beat until smooth and thick.

To get our famous date on a cake prepare paper cutouts and put in place, then sprinkle with powdered sugar.

BUTTERFLY FROSTING

2 tablespoons butter or margarine
2 1/2 cups sifted confectioners' sugar
1 egg white, unbeaten
About 1 tablespoon cream
3/4 teaspoon vanilla
1/8 teaspoon salt
Coloring

Cream butter; add part of sugar gradually, blending after each addition. Add remaining sugar, alternately with egg white, then with cream, until of right consistency to spread. Beat after each addition until smooth.

Add vanilla and salt. Tint delicately with coloring.

For assorted frostings, divide untinted frosting into four small bowls. Use one plain or flavor with 1/2 square (1/2 ounce) melted unsweetened chocolate. Tint the remaining frostings to give delicate, yet decided shades of yellow, green, and pink.

While using assorted frostings, keep bowls covered to avoid crusting. If necessary, one or two drops of cream or milk may be added to keep frostings of right consistency to spread. Use for decorating, if desired.

QUICK FRUIT FROSTING

3 cups sifted confectioners' sugar
3 teaspoons grated orange rind
About 1/4 cup lemon juice
Dash of salt
1/4 cup butter or other shortening, melted

Combine sugar, rind, juice, and salt in small bowl. Add melted butter and beat.

Makes frosting for tops and sides of two 8-inch layers (thinly). Use half recipe for top of 8 x 8 x 2-inch square cake.

ALMOND PASTE FROSTING

Blanch or skin 1 pound of almonds and put through food chopper, using medium blade.

Mix in 1 pound confectioners' sugar, sifted very well.

Beat 3 egg whites slightly, then mix them in. Finally, add 1 teaspoon almond extract.

Because this makes a heavy and stiff paste, you have to place it on the cake and work it into a smooth, even layer with your hands.

ALMOND FROSTING

Cream 1/2 cup butter. Add dash of salt. Blend in 1 3/4 cups sifted confectioners' sugar gradually.

Add 1 unbeaten egg yolk, 1/2 teaspoon almond extract, and 4 teaspoons milk. Beat until of spreading consistency.

Add few drops of yellow food coloring, if desired.

HEART'S DELIGHT CAKE

1. Soften one 8-ounce package cream cheese at room temperature.

2. Blend 4 cups sifted confectioners' sugar into cream cheese. Add 2 tablespoons maraschino cherry juice and blend again.

3. Add 2 tablespoons chopped maraschino cherries, mixing them in lightly.

4. Spread frosting on bottom layer of your favorite cake baked in 2 heart-shaped pans.

5. Cover with second layer of cake and spread remaining frosting on sides and top of cake.

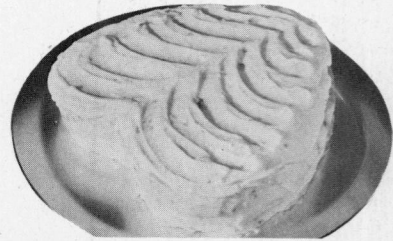

Cooked Frostings

BOILED FROSTING
(Master Recipe)

1½ cups sugar
Dash of salt
½ cup water
3 tablespoons corn syrup
2 egg whites
½ teaspoon vanilla

Cook sugar, salt, water, and corn syrup to the soft ball stage (238°F.). Remove mixture from heat.

Beat egg whites quickly with a rotary beater. Pour hot syrup slowly in a fine stream over egg whites, beating constantly.

Add vanilla and continue beating until frosting stands up in peaks. Quickly spread on cake.

On a rainy or humid day, boil syrup to higher temperature. If frosting hardens before spreading, beat in a few drops of hot water.

Makes frosting for top and sides of 2 9-inch layer cakes or 24 cupcakes.

Boiled Frosting Variations

Apricot Frosting: Fold ½ cup cooked apricot pulp into beaten frosting.

Brown Sugar Frosting: In master recipe, substitute brown sugar for granulated. Omit corn syrup and cook to 250°F. instead of 238°F.

Chocolate Frosting: In master recipe, add ¼ cup cocoa or 2 squares (2 ounces) melted chocolate to sugar, and cook with sugar and water.

Coconut Frosting: Sprinkle plain, tinted, or toasted shredded coconut over frosting.

Coffee Walnut Frosting: In master recipe, substitute coffee for water. Omit vanilla. Add ½ cup chopped walnuts to beaten frosting.

Colored Frosting: Tint frosting with food coloring as desired. Flavor as desired.

Fruit Frosting: Prepare master recipe. Fold chopped candied cherries, chopped candied pineapple, or other chopped candied fruit into beaten frosting.

Ginger Frosting: In master recipe, use ¼ cup brown sugar and 1 cup granulated sugar. Fold in ½ cup finely chopped, drained preserved ginger just before spreading.

Lady Baltimore Frosting or Filling: Prepare master recipe. Chop and fold ¼ cup each of dried figs, pitted dates, seedless raisins, walnuts, and blanched almonds into beaten frosting. If desired, substitute almond extract for vanilla.

Lemon Frosting: Prepare master recipe. Fold into frosting 2 tablespoons lemon juice and 1 teaspoon lemon rind just before spreading.

Lord Baltimore Frosting or Filling: Prepare master recipe. Fold ½ cup toasted coconut, ¼ cup chopped candied cherries or chopped maraschino cherries, ¼ cup chopped, toasted, blanched almonds or chopped pecans into beaten frosting.

Marshmallow Frosting: Prepare master recipe. Cut marshmallows into quarters. Arrange on top of cake. Spread frosting over them, or fold in half-melted marshmallows just before spreading.

Molasses Frosting: In master recipe, substitute 3 tablespoons molasses for corn syrup.

Nut Frosting: Sprinkle whole or chopped nuts over frosting.

Peppermint Frosting: Flavor master recipe with a few drops of peppermint instead of vanilla.

Strawberry Frosting: Prepare master recipe and fold ½ cup crushed strawberries into beaten frosting.

SEVEN MINUTE FROSTING
(Master Recipe)

2 egg whites, unbeaten
1½ cups sugar
⅛ teaspoon salt
⅓ cup cold water
1 tablespoon light corn syrup
1 teaspoon vanilla

Place egg whites, sugar, salt, water, and corn syrup in top of double boiler.

Place over boiling water and beat constantly with a large double rotary beater or electric mixer at high speed until frosting will stand in peaks, about 7 minutes.

Remove from heat; beat in vanilla. Quickly spread on cake.

Makes enough frosting for top and sides of 2 9-inch layer cakes or 2 dozen cupcakes.

Seven-Minute Frosting Variations

Chocolate Frosting: Stir into beaten frosting 2 ounces (2 squares) melted chocolate.

Coconut Frosting: Sprinkle plain, tinted, or toasted coconut over frosting while still soft.

Coffee Frosting: In master recipe, omit vanilla. Substitute coffee for water.

Colored Frosting: Tint frosting as desired with food coloring. Flavor as desired.

Fruit Frosting: Prepare master recipe. Fold ½ cup chopped candied cherries, chopped candied pineapple, or other candied fruit into beaten frosting.

Lemon Frosting: In master recipe, substitute 2 tablespoons lemon juice and grated rind of 1 lemon for 2 tablespoons water, the corn syrup, and vanilla.

Orange Frosting: In master recipe, substitute 3 tablespoons orange juice and grated rind of 1 orange for 3 tablespoons water, the corn syrup, and vanilla.

Marshmallow Frosting: Follow master recipe and fold in 1 dozen quartered marshmallows with flavoring.

Peppermint Candy Frosting: Prepare master recipe. Fold ¼ cup crushed hard peppermint candy into beaten frosting. Garnish sides of cake with additional ¼ cup of crushed hard peppermint candy.

Sea Foam Frosting: Omit corn syrup in master recipe. Substitute 1½ cups brown sugar for granulated sugar.

PENUCHE (PANOCHA) PECAN FROSTING

1½ cups firmly packed light brown sugar
1½ cups granulated sugar
2 tablespoons light corn syrup
¾ cup milk
¼ cup shortening
¼ cup butter or margarine
¼ teaspoon salt
1 teaspoon orange extract
1 cup chopped pecans

Place both sugars, corn syrup, milk, shortening, butter, and salt in saucepan. Bring slowly to full rolling boil, stirring constantly, and boil briskly 2 minutes. Cool to lukewarm.

Add orange extract and beat until thick enough to spread. Add pecans and mix.

Makes frosting to cover tops and sides of two 9-inch layers.

Homemade frosting gives a simple "bought" cake an appetizing look.

CARAMEL FROSTING

1½ cups firmly packed brown sugar
1 cup top milk or light cream
2 tablespoons butter or margarine
½ teaspoon vanilla
⅛ teaspoon salt

Combine sugar and milk and bring to boil, stirring constantly.

Stirring occasionally, boil to soft ball stage (236°F.).

Remove from heat and add butter, vanilla, and salt. Cool to lukewarm and beat until of spreading consistency.

Makes frosting for top and sides of two 8-inch layers or 24 cupcakes.

BUTTERSCOTCH FROSTING

1 cup firmly packed light brown sugar
⅓ cup granulated sugar
⅓ cup hot water
1 beaten egg white
½ teaspoon vanilla
Few grains salt

Mix together brown sugar, granulated sugar, and water over low heat until thoroughly dissolved. Bring to a boil and cook until syrup spins a long thread.

Pour syrup slowly over egg white, beating constantly. Add vanilla and salt.

If desired, ⅓ cup chopped nuts may be added.

HONEY ALMOND FROSTING

2 egg whites, unbeaten
¼ cup honey
1 cup toasted, chopped almonds

Combine egg whites and honey in top of double boiler, beating with rotary egg beater until thoroughly mixed.

Place over rapidly boiling water, beating constantly with rotary egg beater, and cook 7 minutes, or until frosting will stand up in peaks.

Remove from boiling water. Add ½ of nuts. Spread on cake, sprinkling remaining nuts over top of cake while frosting is still soft.

Makes frosting to cover tops and sides of two 8- or 9-inch layers.

MAPLE FROSTING

¾ cup firmly packed brown sugar
2½ tablespoons water
1 egg white
¼ teaspoon maple flavoring

Cook sugar, water, and egg white in top of double boiler, beating constantly until mixture stands up in peaks (about 7 minutes).

Remove from heat and add maple flavoring. Beat until of spreading consistency.

FONDANT FROSTING

2 cups sugar
1 cup water
½ teaspoon cream of tartar or 2 tablespoons light corn syrup

Combine the ingredients in a saucepan and stir over low heat until sugar is dissolved. Cover and bring to a rapid boil.

Uncover and continue to boil, without stirring, until a small amount of syrup forms a soft ball when dropped into cold water, or to 238°F. on a candy thermometer. Remove from heat and allow to cool to lukewarm.

Then beat with wooden spoon until syrup becomes white and creamy. Spread quickly over cake.

If it becomes too dry for smooth spreading, add a little hot water and beat until smooth. The fondant may be delicately tinted with food coloring and flavored as desired.

Dipping with Fondant: Make fondant frosting and keep it soft over boiling water, stirring in a few drops of boiling water if mixture becomes too stiff.

Add flavoring or food coloring desired, but stir as little as possible to avoid crystallization.

Lower small cakes or cookies into the liquid fondant on a dipping fork. Raise cake and draw the dipping fork lightly across the edge of the pan to remove any excess fondant, then invert the dipped cake onto a platter or waxed paper.

Work quickly so that the fondant will not become too thick. If it should thicken, however, add a few more drops of boiling water to bring it back to the right consistency.

Decorate the little cakes with a bit of candied fruit or rind, nuts, or tiny sugar flowers.

CREAMY CHOCOLATE FROSTING

1 cup firmly packed brown sugar
3 squares (3 ounces) chocolate
¼ teaspoon salt
⅓ cup evaporated milk or ⅓ cup cream
3 tablespoons butter or margarine
1 teaspoon vanilla
Confectioners' sugar

Combine brown sugar, chocolate, salt, and milk or cream in a saucepan. Bring to boiling point. Cook on medium heat until slightly thickened, about 5 minutes. Remove from heat.

Add butter and vanilla. Cool slightly. Add enough sifted confectioners' sugar for proper consistency to spread. Beat until smooth.

Spread between layers and on top and sides of cake.

WHITE MOUNTAIN FROSTING

2 egg whites
1½ cups sugar
½ cup cold water
1 tablespoon light corn syrup or ¼ teaspoon cream of tartar
1 teaspoon vanilla

Put the egg whites in a mixing bowl.

Combine sugar, water, and corn syrup or cream of tartar in a small saucepan. Stir over low heat until the sugar has dissolved. Boil rapidly until a small amount of syrup forms a soft ball when dropped into cold water (238°F.). Remove from heat.

Beat the egg whites quickly until stiff. Continue beating while pouring the hot syrup in a fine stream over the egg whites. Add the flavoring and continue beating until the mixture is stiff enough to spread.

STRAWBERRY FLUFF

2 egg whites, unbeaten
1 cup sugar
Dash of salt
1⅓ cups sliced fresh strawberries or 1 package frozen sliced strawberries, thawed and drained

Combine egg whites, sugar, salt, and ⅔ cup strawberries in top of double boiler. Beat about 1 minute to blend.

Place over rapidly boiling water and beat constantly with rotary egg beater or at high speed with electric mixer 7 minutes, or until frosting will stand up in stiff peaks.

Remove from boiling water and beat until cool. Fold in remaining drained berries and spread at once.

Frosts tops and sides of two 9-inch layers; top and sides of 13 x 9 x 2-inch cake. Or fills 16 x 10 x 2-inch cake roll.

Flower Garden Cake Decoration: Frost top and sides of a rectangular cake with a white frosting. Spread frosting evenly. Mark cake into serving-size pieces, then sprinkle with colored sugar. Decorate with fresh garden flowers. Wrap stems with aluminum foil; place one blossom on each serving. Insert colored picks to form "Xs" on the top of outer edge of cake.

MOCHA FROSTING

About 1/3 cup strong coffee
4 cups firmly packed sifted confectioners' sugar
1/2 cup shortening
1/8 teaspoon salt
1 teaspoon vanilla

To make strong coffee, add 1/2 cup medium-ground coffee to 1 cup cold water. Heat to boiling. Remove from heat and let stand 2 minutes. Strain and cool slightly.

Combine sugar gradually with shortening and add coffee as needed to make a creamy-smooth mixture. Add salt and vanilla. Spread on cooled cake.

Makes frosting for tops and sides of two 9-inch layers.

Mocha Chocolate Frosting: To above recipe, add 1 square (1 ounce) melted unsweetened chocolate. A little more coffee may be needed for good spreading consistency.

HUNGARIAN CHOCOLATE FROSTING

3 1-ounce squares unsweetened chocolate
1 1/2 cups sifted confectioners' sugar
2 1/2 tablespoons hot water
3 egg yolks
1/4 cup softened butter or other shortening

One whole egg may be substituted for the 3 egg yolks; use only 2 tablespoons water.

Melt chocolate. Remove from heat; add sugar and water, and blend. Add egg yolks, one at a time, beating well after each. Add butter gradually, beating well after each addition.

Makes frosting for tops and sides of two 8- or 9-inch layers, or top and sides of 8-, 9-, or 10-inch square cake, 10 x 5 x 3-inch loaf, a 9-inch 3-layer cake, or 24 cupcakes.

FLUFFY COOKED FROSTING

1 1/4 cups sugar
1/4 teaspoon cream of tartar
1/2 cup water
3 egg whites
1/2 cup confectioners' sugar
1/2 teaspoon vanilla

Combine 1 cup sugar, cream of tartar, and water; stir over low heat until thoroughly dissolved. Bring to a boil and cook to the medium-hard ball stage (250°F.).

Beat egg whites until stiff but not dry. Fold in remaining 1/4 cup sugar, a tablespoon at a time, beating after each addition.

Slowly pour syrup into egg whites, beating constantly. Beat in sifted confectioners' sugar and vanilla.

Makes frosting to cover top and sides of two 9-inch layers.

EASY FUDGE FROSTING

3 1-ounce squares unsweetened chocolate
2 tablespoons butter or margarine
2 3/4 cups sifted confectioners' sugar
7 tablespoons light cream or top milk
Dash of salt
1 teaspoon vanilla

Melt chocolate and butter over boiling water and blend.

Add 1 1/2 cups confectioners' sugar, cream, and salt, all at once and beat until smooth. Cook and stir over low heat until mixture bubbles up well around edges.

Remove from heat; add vanilla and remaining sugar in thirds, beating after each addition until smooth.

Place over bowl of ice water until thick enough to spread on cake.

Frosts tops and sides of two 8-inch layers or two 8-inch square cakes.

PETITS FOURS FROSTING

2 cups granulated sugar
1 cup water
1/8 teaspoon cream of tartar
1 to 2 cups sifted confectioners' sugar

Combine granulated sugar, water, and cream of tartar. Cook over direct heat to 226°F., or a thin syrup. Stir only until sugar is dissolved. Remove from heat.

Pour into top of double boiler and cool to somewhat above lukewarm (110°F.). Gradually add 1 to 2 cups sifted confectioners' sugar until frosting is of proper consistency to pour.

Place a few cakes in rows on a wire rack over a cooky sheet, allowing considerable space between cakes. Pour frosting over cakes, covering tops and sides and allowing frosting to drip onto cooky sheet. Keep over hot water when not pouring.

If it becomes too thick, add a few drops of hot water. If too thin, add a little more sifted confectioners' sugar. Scrape frosting from cooky sheet, reheat, and use for other cakes. Repeat the process until cakes are completely coated.

Decorate with ornamental frosting, colored sugar, candied fruit, or nuts.

SHADOW FROSTING

Spread cake with white mountain frosting.

When the frosting has set, melt 2 squares (2 ounces) chocolate in double boiler over hot water, heating only until the chocolate is melted. Pour the chocolate over top of cake slowly and let it trickle down the sides.

For use on small tea cakes, frost the top only with the white mountain frosting. Smooth the frosting in the center and make a rim around the outside edge.

Pour the chocolate in the center to be held in place by the rim until it sets.

BOILED MARSHMALLOW FROSTING

2 1/2 cups granulated sugar
1/2 cup light corn syrup
1/4 teaspoon salt
1/2 cup water
2 egg whites
1 teaspoon vanilla
8 marshmallows, cut in quarters

Place sugar, corn syrup, salt, and water together in a saucepan and cook to the firm ball stage (250°F.).

Pour the hot syrup slowly into the well beaten egg whites, beating constantly.

Add vanilla and continue beating until the frosting will hold its shape when tossed over the back of a spoon. Add marshmallows.

This frosting recipe will stand in swirls an inch or more high.

FOUR MINUTE FROSTING

1 egg white, unbeaten
3/4 cup sugar
Dash of salt
3 tablespoons water
1 teaspoon light corn syrup
1/2 teaspoon vanilla

Prepare as for the seven-minute frosting, beating only 4 minutes.

Frosts tops and sides of two 8-inch layers (thinly) or two 8 x 4 x 3-inch loaves, or top and sides of 9 or 10-inch tube cake.

A pumpkin of orange frosting tops this cake; face is painted on with chocolate.

Cake Fillings

CRÈME PÂTISSIÈRE OR PASTRY CREAM

4 beaten egg yolks
⅔ cup sugar
6 tablespoons flour
1 teaspoon cornstarch
2 cups milk, scalded
1 vanilla bean or ½ teaspoon vanilla

Cream egg yolks and sugar together until light and creamy. Blend in flour and cornstarch.

Gradually add milk in which vanilla bean has been scalded. (If vanilla extract is used, add at the end.) Cook, stirring constantly, over low heat until thick and boiling.

Set pan immediately in cold water to cool it quickly or empty into a cold bowl. Stir occasionally to keep a skin from forming on top. Chill before using. Use for filling éclairs, napoleons, and other cakes.

Variations: For chocolate cream, flavor with melted chocolate; for mocha cream, flavor with coffee extract.

FRANGIPANE CREAM

A custard cream used as a pastry filling or topping. Also spelled frangipani; it is said to be named after a Marquis Frangipani, major general under Louis XIV.

To Make: Prepare Crème Pâtissière (Pastry Cream), but after removing from the heat, beat in 2 tablespoons butter and ¼ cup dried and rolled macaroon crumbs. If desired, flavor with lemon extract, sherry, brandy, or rum.

LORD BALTIMORE FILLING AND FROSTING

1½ cups sugar
½ teaspoon cream of tartar
Dash of salt
½ cup hot water
3 egg whites
½ teaspoon vanilla
2 teaspoons lemon juice
½ cup macaroon crumbs
12 candied cherries, chopped
½ cup chopped blanched almonds
¼ cup chopped pecans

Blend sugar, cream of tartar, salt, and hot water. Cook, without stirring, to soft ball stage or 240°F. on candy thermometer.

Beat egg whites until stiff. Pour syrup in a fine stream over beaten whites, beating constantly. Add vanilla.

Add lemon juice to crumbs. Fold crumbs, cherries, and nuts into 1½ cups of frosting and use this for cake filling.

CREAM FILLING
(Master Recipe)

¾ cup sugar
5 tablespoons flour
¼ teaspoon salt
2 cups scalded milk
2 slightly beaten eggs
1 teaspoon vanilla

Combine sugar, flour, and salt. Slowly stir in scalded milk. Cook in double boiler over boiling water for 15 minutes, or until thick.

Add a little of the hot mixture to eggs. Stir in remaining hot mixture. Cook over simmering water for 3 minutes. Cool and add vanilla.

For a richer filling, add 2 tablespoons butter to hot cooked custard.

Makes filling for 4 large layers or 24 large cream puffs or 24 éclairs.

Cream Filling Variations:

Banana Cream Filling: In master recipe, substitute 1 teaspoon lemon juice for vanilla. Add medium-sized mashed banana to filling.

Butterscotch Cream Filling: In master recipe, substitute ¾ cup brown sugar for granulated sugar. Add 2 tablespoons butter to cooked filling.

Chocolate Cream Filling: In master recipe, increase sugar to 1 cup. Add 2 ounces (2 squares) unsweetened chocolate to milk before cooking. Beat until smooth.

Coconut Cream Filling: In master recipe, add 1 cup shredded coconut to filling.

Coffee Cream Filling: In master recipe, substitute ½ cup strong fresh coffee for ½ cup milk. Proceed as directed.

Creamy Custard Filling: Prepare master recipe. Fold ½ cup whipped heavy cream into chilled filling.

Pineapple Cream Filling: In master recipe, substitute lemon juice for vanilla. Add ½ cup crushed, drained pineapple to filling.

DATE FILLING

1 pound chopped, pitted dates
1 tablespoon lemon juice
½ cup water
⅓ cup sugar
⅛ teaspoon salt
1 cup finely chopped nuts

Combine all ingredients except nuts and bring to boiling point, stirring constantly until thick.

Add nuts and cool. Spread between layers.

Almond Luxor Cake

ALMOND LUXOR CAKE

Make 2 (or 3) 8-inch layers (cake mix or your recipe), put together with Luxor Custard Filling (below), frost with white icing or whipped cream, sprinkle with roasted almonds, diced.

Luxor Custard Filling:
2 cups milk
⅔ cup sugar
Few grains salt
3 tablespoons cornstarch
3 egg yolks, beaten
1 teaspoon vanilla
½ cup roasted almonds, diced

Combine 1½ cups milk, sugar, and salt in top of double boiler. Scald.

Blend remaining ½ cup milk, cornstarch, and beaten egg yolks; stir into hot milk, cook and stir until thick. Blend in vanilla and almonds. Cool and spread on cake.

CHOCOLATE BRAZIL NUT FILLING

2 squares (2 ounces) chocolate
¾ cup milk
4 tablespoons flour
½ cup sugar
1 tablespoon butter or margarine
½ teaspoon vanilla
½ cup ground Brazil nuts

Add chocolate to milk in double boiler. Beat over low heat until chocolate is melted and well blended.

Add a small amount of the chocolate mixture to the flour, which has been sifted with the sugar.

Return to double boiler. Stir until smooth and cook until thickened. Add butter and vanilla.

When cool, add Brazil nuts and spread on cake.

WALNUT TORTE FILLING

2 beaten egg yolks
½ cup sugar
¾ cup milk
½ teaspoon vanilla or rum flavoring
1 pound chopped walnuts

Mix egg yolks and sugar; add milk and cook in top of double boiler until thick.

Cool; add vanilla or rum and nuts. Spread between layer of walnut torte.

LEMON FILLING
(Master Recipe)

3/4 cup sugar
5 tablespoons flour
1/8 teaspoon salt
2/3 cup water
1 slightly beaten egg
1 tablespoon butter or margarine
1 teaspoon grated lemon rind
1/3 cup lemon juice

Combine sugar, flour, and salt in top of double boiler. Add water and blend thoroughly. Cook over boiling water until thickened, stirring constantly.

Cover and cook additional 10 minutes, stirring occasionally.

Stir in a little of the hot mixture into slightly beaten egg. Slowly stir into the remaining hot mixture. Cook over simmering water for 2 minutes, stirring constantly.

Cool slightly. Add butter and lemon rind. Chill and add lemon juice. Makes filling for two 9-inch layers.

Lemon Filling Variations

Lemon Cream Filling: Fold 1/2 cup whipped, heavy cream into chilled lemon filling.

Orange Filling: Proceed as for lemon filling. Decrease sugar to 1/2 cup, water to 1/2 cup, lemon juice to 1 tablespoon, lemon rind to 1/2 teaspoon.

Add 1 tablespoon orange rind. When chilled, add 1/2 cup orange juice.

Orange Date Filling: Add 1/2 cup chopped dates to orange filling.

Orange Coconut Filling: Add 1/2 cup shredded coconut to orange filling.

Orange Cream Filling: When orange filling is chilled, fold in 1/2 cup whipped heavy cream and 1/2 cup plain or toasted shredded coconut.

WHIPPED CREAM FILLING
(Master Recipe)

1/2 teaspoon unflavored gelatin
1 tablespoon cold water
3 tablespoons confectioners' sugar
1/4 teaspoon vanilla
1/2 cup heavy cream

Soften gelatin in cold water. Place over boiling water. Stir until dissolved. Let cool.

Mix with sugar, vanilla, and cream. Whip until stiff. Chill thoroughly before spreading. Makes filling for two 9-inch layers.

Variations of Whipped Cream Filling

Applesauce Filling: Omit vanilla in master recipe. Decrease cream to 1/3 cup. Before chilling, fold in 1/2 cup chilled, thick applesauce and 1/2 teaspoon cinnamon.

Chocolate Filling: In master recipe, increase sugar to 4 tablespoons. Mix with 2 tablespoons cocoa before adding cream.

Coffee Filling: Substitute coffee for water in master recipe.

Pineapple Filling: Omit vanilla in master recipe. Decrease cream to 1/3 cup. Before chilling, fold in 1/2 cup drained, crushed pineapple.

BANANA FILLING

1 cup sugar
1/4 cup water
3 large bananas, mashed
2 lightly beaten egg yolks

Heat sugar and water until syrup spins a thread when dropped from fork or spoon (234°F.).

Combine mashed bananas with beaten egg yolk. Add syrup gradually, beating thoroughly.

Place over hot water. Heat through, beating thoroughly. Cool before spreading.

Banana Nut Filling: Add about 1/2 cup chopped nuts just before spreading.

PINEAPPLE FILLING

3/4 cup sugar
2 1/2 tablespoons cornstarch
1/8 teaspoon salt
Grated rind of 1 lemon
1/4 cup lemon juice
3 slightly beaten egg yolks
1/2 cup canned pineapple juice
2 tablespoons butter or margarine

Mix sugar, cornstarch, and salt in top of double boiler. Add lemon rind and lemon juice and mix well. Add egg yolks, pineapple juice, and butter and blend.

Place over boiling water. Cook until thick and smooth, stirring constantly, about 15 minutes.

Makes filling for two 8-inch layers.

RUM NUT FILLING AND FROSTING

1/4 cup enriched flour
3/4 cup milk
1/4 cup butter or margarine
1/2 cup shortening
3/4 cup granulated sugar
1/2 teaspoon salt
1/2 teaspoon vanilla
3/4 cup chopped nuts
3 tablespoons rum flavoring
4 cups tightly packed sifted confectioners' sugar

Measure flour into saucepan. Add milk gradually, stirring until smooth. Cook to thick paste over slow heat, stirring constantly. Cool to lukewarm.

Cream butter, shortening, granulated sugar, and salt thoroughly. Add lukewarm paste and beat with rotary beater until fluffy. Fold in vanilla and nuts.

Spread 1/3 of mixture between layers of 9-inch layer cake.

Add rum flavoring and confectioners' sugar to remaining mixture and stir until well blended.

Spread over top and sides of cake. Makes filling and frosting for two 9-inch layers.

LIME FRUIT FILLING

To 1/2 cup of fluffy lime frosting (see Index), add 2 tablespoons each of chopped raisins, nuts, candied cherries, and citron.

Spread between layers of cake. Use remaining frosting to cover top and sides of cake. For a gay effect, sprinkle silver dragées or tiny colored candies on top of cake.

MAPLE CREAM FILLING

4 egg yolks
3/4 cup confectioners' sugar
3/4 cup milk
1/2 cup butter or margarine
2 teaspoons maple flavoring

Beat egg yolks until thick and lemon colored. Add sugar and milk and cook in double boiler, stirring constantly, until thick, about 10 minutes. Cool.

Cream butter until fluffy. Add thoroughly cold custard and maple flavoring. Beat with rotary beater until smooth.

Makes filling for 3-layer 8-inch cake.

CARAMEL FILLING

1/2 cup firmly packed brown sugar
2 cups granulated sugar
1 cup buttermilk
1/2 teaspoon baking soda
1/2 cup butter or margarine
1 tablespoon vanilla

Combine sugars, buttermilk, baking soda, and butter. Cook until syrup forms a soft ball when a small amount is dropped into cold water (238°F.).

Cool. Add vanilla. Beat until creamy. Spread over cake.

SOUR CREAM FILLING

2 eggs
2/3 cup sugar
1 cup sour cream
Pinch of salt
1/2 teaspoon vanilla

Beat eggs until thick. Gradually add sugar, beating constantly. Add sour cream and salt.

Cook over boiling water until thickened, stirring constantly, about 15 minutes.

Cool. Add vanilla. Makes filling for two 9-inch layers.

GOLDEN CREAM FILLING

1½ tablespoons (1½ envelopes) un-
    flavored gelatin
4   tablespoons cold water
8   egg yolks
⅛   teaspoon salt
1   cup confectioners' sugar
4   tablespoons strong fresh coffee
1   pint cream, whipped

Soften gelatin in cold water.

Beat egg yolks with salt until thick. Beat sugar in gradually.

Dissolve softened gelatin in hot coffee. Add to egg-sugar mixture.

Let stand until partially set. Fold in whipped cream.

Makes filling and topping for two 9-inch layers.

APPLE FILLING

¾   cup sugar
1   tablespoon flour
3   tablespoons lemon juice
1   tablespoon water
1   beaten egg
1   cup grated apple

Combine all ingredients. Cook over very low heat until thick, 8 to 10 minutes. Cool.

Spread between layers. Frost cake with seven-minute frosting.

Pineapple Coconut Filling: In above recipe, substitute 1 cup drained crushed pineapple for the grated apple, and add ½ cup freshly grated coconut.

Glazes

When used on cakes, glazes are jiffy substitutes for frostings. The thin coating helps to keep a cake moist but requires no particular ability to apply.

Glazes are most frequently used on angel food and chiffon cakes; however they may be used on sweet breads, fruitcakes, cookies, and small cakes such as petits fours.

A cake such as fruitcake, sweet breads, or Christmas cookies may be decorated with bits of fruit and nuts just after applying a glaze and when it dries the decorations will be held in place.

CHOCOLATE GLAZE

1   tablespoon butter or margarine
1   1-ounce square unsweetened chocolate
1½ tablespoons hot milk
½   cup sifted confectioners' sugar
Dash of salt

Melt butter and chocolate together. Combine milk, sugar, and dash of salt in bowl. Blend in chocolate mixture gradually.

Pour over cake and spread with spatula. Makes enough glaze to cover cake roll or 8- or 9-inch layer.

APRICOT GLAZE

Wash and drain 1 cup dried apricots. Put in saucepan with 2½ cups water and boil uncovered 10 minutes.

Put through sieve or food mill. There should be 2 cups apricot purée; if not, add water to make that amount.

Combine purée with 2½ cups sugar. Bring to a boil and boil gently 5 to 8 minutes, stirring constantly until purée is as thick as marmalade.

Cool and use for tarts, pastries, and under frostings of decorated cakes to give a smooth surface over which to spread the outer frosting.

To Store: Keep unused glaze in covered container in refrigerator. When ready to use again, warm slightly to facilitate spreading.

APRICOT JAM GLAZE

1   cup sugar
1   cup boiling water
¾   cup apricot jam

Stir and cook combined sugar and water in saucepan over medium heat until sugar is dissolved. Bring to boiling point, uncovered, and boil 10 minutes.

Heat apricot jam in another pan until it bubbles around the edge of pan. Remove from heat and put through a sieve into the syrup. Mix well and keep hot until ready to use, or reheat just before using to make thin enough to pour. Use for glazing petits fours, fruit pies, tarts, and coffee cakes.

LEMON GLAZE

1½ tablespoons milk
1   tablespoon butter or margarine
1   cup sifted confectioners' sugar
1½ tablespoons lemon juice
½   teaspoon grated lemon rind

Heat milk and butter together. Measure sugar into bowl. Add liquid and stir until smooth. Then add juice and rind.

Pour over cake, letting it run down sides. Makes enough glaze to cover a 9-inch or 10-inch tube cake.

ORANGE GLAZE

1   teaspoon grated orange rind
1   tablespoon orange juice
1   cup firmly packed sifted confectioners' sugar
About 1 tablespoon water

Combine orange rind and juice; let stand 5 minutes. Strain and discard rind.

Stir juice into sugar and add enough water to make a good spreading consistency.

Spread on slightly warm cake. Makes enough glaze for top of one 9-inch square cake.

Glazed Fruit Cake

GLAZE FOR FRUITCAKES

1¼ cups sifted confectioners' sugar
2   tablespoons soft butter or margarine
¼   teaspoon vanilla
1½ to 2 tablespoons milk

Combine sugar, butter, vanilla and 1½ tablespoons milk in a bowl. Beat with a spoon until smooth. If thinner glaze is desired, add remaining milk.

JIFFY BLENDER GLAZE

1¼ cups confectioners' sugar
¼   cup fruit juice (lemon, lime, or orange)
1   teaspoon vanilla

Combine ingredients in blender and mix until smooth. No heating is necessary. Just spread on warm cakes or holiday cookies. Glaze has just the right consistency for embedding decorative fruits and nuts. Makes enough glaze for 4 square 8-inch cakes.

VANILLA GLAZE

2   cups sifted confectioners' sugar
⅛   teaspoon salt
3   to 4 tablespoons hot cream

Combine sugar and salt in bowl. Blend in cream until mixture has consistency of a glaze. Spread on top of cake, letting it drip down sides. Makes glaze for 9-inch tube cake.

Note: In above 2 tablespoons soft butter and 2 to 3 tablespoons milk may be substituted for cream.

Cinnamon Glaze: Combine ½ teaspoon cinnamon and ¼ teaspoon nutmeg with the sugar and salt.

COFFEE GLAZE

2½ tablespoons water
1   tablespoon butter or margarine
1⅓ cups sifted confectioners' sugar
Dash of salt
2   teaspoons instant coffee

Heat water and butter together. Measure sugar, salt, and instant coffee into bowl. Add hot liquid and stir until smooth.

Pour over cake, letting it run down sides. Makes glaze to cover tube cake.

CANDY AND CONFECTIONS

HINTS FOR MAKING CANDY

Before you begin candymaking read the basic hints given here and follow the recipes exactly. Don't try to substitute ingredients or double the recipes.

Candies are usually classified into two general types, cream candies and hard candies. Each type has many variations. The two types are determined by the thickness of the syrup or the extent to which the sugar is carmelized in the candymaking process. The syrup becomes thick as it boils. The creamy candies, such as fondant and fudge, form crystals, which must be very small in order to avoid a coarse, grainy texture. Note that these candies are stirred only until the sugar is dissolved. The hard candies, such as butterscotch and caramels, are non-crystalline. It's important to pour and cool hard candies quickly.

EQUIPMENT FOR CANDY-MAKING

The saucepans should be sufficiently heavy to minimize scorching. Use heavy aluminum or enamel pans large enough to allow the candy to boil vigorously without danger of boiling over.

Use a wooden spoon for stirring or beating. A medium-sized spatula is best for removing candy from the pans. Bowls should be smooth. For cooling fondant and brittle candies a marble slab is ideal but an inverted baking sheet for brittle or a large platter for fondant make acceptable substitutes. For fudge and similar candies use shallow pans with straight sides.

Before starting to make candy, assemble all ingredients and utensils so that they will be handy.

USE OF CANDY THERMOMETER

A candy thermometer is necessary to insure uniformity and consistency in results.

The bulb should be entirely immersed in mixture without touching pan. Have your eye on level with part of scale being tested.

The accuracy of your candy thermometer should be checked each time you use it. Let the thermometer stand in boiling water for 10 minutes. The thermometer should register 212° F. If there is any variation, subtract or add to make the same degree of allowance in testing candy.

COLD WATER TESTS

With practice the cold water tests given below will give satisfactory results.

To make cold water test, remove pan from heat. Pour small amount of syrup from spoon into cup of cold water, not ice water. The hardness of ball formed indicates temperature of candy.

COOKING TEMPERATURES FOR CANDY

Soft Ball: (236°–238° F.) When dropped into cold water, syrup will form soft ball which quickly loses its shape on removal.

When using brown sugar, or on rainy or damp days, boil to higher temperature.

Firm Ball: (244°–250° F.) Syrup will form a firm but plastic ball in cold water which can be easily handled in the water and becomes soft on removal. Use for caramels.

Hard Ball: (250°–258° F.) Syrup forms firm ball in cold water but is plastic and can easily be handled in cold water.

Use higher temperature on rainy or damp days. Use for divinity, nougat, popcorn balls.

Very Hard Ball: (258°–266° F.) Syrup loses most of plastic quality in cold water. Ball will roll on buttered plate. Use for taffy.

Light Crack: (290°–300° F.) Syrup will form brittle threads in cold water. Spiral softens when removed from water. Use for butterscotch.

Hard Crack: (300°–310° F.) Syrup forms brittle threads in cold water which remain brittle on removal. Use for brittle candy.

HIGH ALTITUDE ADJUSTMENTS

For general information about effect of high altitudes on cooking temperatures, see **Cooking at High Altitudes.** When using a thermometer, adjust for temperatures as follows: If soft ball is called for at sea level at 236°F., test for soft ball at 226°F. at 3,000 feet; 223°F. at 5,000 feet; and 220°F. at 7,000 feet.

Use a candy thermometer to insure results.

Quick and Uncooked Candies

Bourbon or Rum Balls

UNCOOKED FONDANT
(Master Recipe)

1   egg white
1/2 tablespoon water
3/4 teaspoon vanilla
2¾ cups confectioners' sugar

Combine egg white, water, and vanilla in a bowl. Beat until well blended.

Add sugar gradually until mixture is very stiff. Knead with hands until smooth.

Wrap in waxed paper. Store in refrigerator to use as desired.

Uncooked Fondant Variations

Cherry Fondant Balls: Color fondant pink. Form into balls. Press a maraschino cherry into each.

Chocolate Fondant: Add 2 squares (2 ounces) melted, unsweetened chocolate to fondant. Blend thoroughly.

Chocolate Nut Cubes: Combine fondant and chopped pecans. Cut into tiny cubes and dip in melted chocolate.

Fondant Chocolate Peppermints: Add a few drops of essence of peppermint to fondant. Mix it thoroughly.

Melt 2 squares (2 ounces) unsweetened chocolate in top of double boiler.

Form small balls of fondant. Press into round, flat patties. Dip in melted chocolate. Place on waxed paper to dry.

Coconut or Chocolate Fondant Balls: Form fondant balls. Roll in shredded coconut or chocolate.

Fondant Nougats: Add chopped dates, nuts, figs, and maraschino cherries to fondant.

Spread on waxed paper. Cut into squares. Dip each square in powdered sugar.

Fondant Nut Brown Patties: Make small balls of fondant. Roll in dry cocoa. Press flat with half a nut on each.

Pistachio Fondant Balls: Color fondant green. Form into small balls. Press flat with a pistachio nut.

Strawberry Fondant: Coat ripe, unhulled strawberries with fondant, leaving stems uncoated. Roll in powdered sugar.

Store in refrigerator until ready to serve.

UNCOOKED BUTTER FONDANT

Add 2 teaspoons butter to 3 tablespoons boiling water.

Add sifted confectioners' sugar a little at a time until the mixture is pliable and may be molded by hand. Use as other fondants.

MARZIPAN (ALMOND PASTE CANDY)

Marzipan, also called marchpane or almond paste candy, is a confection made of sweetened almond paste, usually colored and formed into tiny fruit and vegetable shapes.

2 egg whites
1 cup almond paste
1/2 teaspoon vanilla or lemon extract
1 cup confectioners' sugar

Beat egg whites. Mix with almond paste. Add flavoring and enough sugar to make mixture stiff enough to handle. Allow to stand overnight.

Divide, color, and flavor to imitate fruits or vegetables, such as pears, apples, etc. Mold into shapes.

It may also be cut into small pieces and dipped into chocolate or other coating, or used as the center of candied cherries, dates, or prunes.

Note: Commercial almond paste may be used. To prepare 1 cup almond paste blanch and pound 2⅔ cups shelled almonds into fine consistency.

CHOCOLATE CREAM CHEESE FUDGE

1 3-ounce package cream cheese
2 cups sifted confectioners' sugar
2 1-ounce squares unsweetened chocolate, melted
1/4 teaspoon vanilla
Dash of salt
1/2 cup chopped pecans

Place cream cheese in bowl and cream until soft and smooth. Slowly blend sugar into it. Add melted chocolate. Mix well.

Add vanilla, salt, and chopped pecans and mix until well blended.

Press into well greased shallow pan. Place in refrigerator until firm, about 15 minutes. Cut into squares.

Note: For slightly softer fudge blend in 1 teaspoon of cream.

MOCHA CREAMS

1/2 cup strong coffee
2 tablespoons butter
5 tablespoons cocoa
3/4 cup finely chopped walnuts
1/2 teaspoon vanilla
4 cups confectioners' sugar

Heat coffee to boiling point. Remove from heat and add butter and cocoa. Blend well. Add nuts and mix thoroughly.

Add vanilla and sugar, a little at a time, working in well until candy is stiff enough to form into balls about size of large marbles.

Flatten balls slightly. Place on buttered plate to harden. Makes 3/4 pound.

BOURBON OR RUM BALLS

3 cups finely crushed vanilla wafers
1 cup finely chopped walnuts
1⅓ cups (15-ounce can) sweetened condensed milk
1/3 cup bourbon or rum
Confectioners' sugar or sprinkles

Combine wafer crumbs and nuts. Add sweetened condensed milk and bourbon (or rum); blend well. Chill about 1 hour.

Dip palms of hands into confectioners' sugar. Shape, by teaspoonfuls into small balls. Roll in confectioners' sugar or colored sprinkles. Store in covered container in refrigerator. Candies can be kept moist and fresh for several weeks.

FUDGE BALLS

Melt 2 squares (2 ounces) chocolate in double boiler. Add 1⅓ cups (15-ounce can) sweetened condensed milk.

Stir mixture over boiling water until it thickens, about 5 minutes.

Drop halves of marshmallows into mixture and lift out covered with chocolate. Roll in finely chopped nuts until well covered.

FUDGE WEDGES

1 4-ounce can flaked coconut
1 6-ounce package semi-sweet chocolate pieces
3 tablespoons light corn syrup
2½ cups sifted confectioners' sugar
1 cup chopped walnuts
1/3 cup orange juice
About 1⅔ cups finely rolled graham cracker crumbs

Sprinkle 2/3 of the flaked coconut over bottom of a 9-inch pie plate.

Melt chocolate over hot water. Add remaining ingredients, except flaked coconut, and mix well.

Turn into coconut-lined pie plate. Sprinkle remaining coconut over top and press down gently. Chill. Cut into thin wedges. Makes 14 to 16 wedges.

Fudge Wedges

Fruit Candies

GLAZED APRICOTS

2 cups dried apricots
2 cups granulated sugar
1 teaspoon cream of tartar
1 cup water

Rinse apricots. Cover with boiling water and let stand 10 minutes. Drain thoroughly.

Combine sugar, cream of tartar, and water; bring to a boil, stirring until sugar is dissolved.

Add apricots and boil slowly for 30 minutes or until fruit is transparent and syrup sheets from spoon.

Remove fruit to wire rack and drain overnight. Roll in granulated sugar.

APRICOT COCONUT BALLS

¾ cup dried apricots
½ cup nuts
¾ cup coconut
1 teaspoon grated orange rind
1 teaspoon grated lemon rind
1 tablespoon lemon juice

Put apricots, nuts, and coconut through food chopper or chop fine.

Combine with remaining ingredients, mixing well. Shape into small balls. Roll in ground nuts if desired.

CRYSTALLIZED MINT LEAVES

Remove fresh mint leaves from stems. Wipe each leaf and brush with stiffly beaten egg white.

Dip in granulated sugar flavored with oil of peppermint. Place on waxed paper to dry or place on cake rack.

Cover with waxed paper. Let stand in very slow oven (250°F.) until dry. Repeat if leaves are not thoroughly coated.

DRIED FRUIT SNACK TRAY

Steam fruits over boiling water 10 minutes or until soft. Remove pits from prunes and stuff with a piece of marshmallow, an almond, or a pecan or walnut half.

To coat prunes with chocolate, melt semi-sweet or milk chocolate over warm, not boiling, water, stirring frequently. Dip pitted prunes, one at a time, using two forks. Drain off excess chocolate. Set on waxed paper to harden.

Dried Fruit Snack Tray

CARAMEL APPLES

15 to 20 apples
2 pounds granulated sugar (4 cups)
Scant cup light corn syrup
2⅔ cups evaporated milk
1½ cups chopped pecans

Select small apples, free from blemishes. Wash and dry thoroughly and stick on wooden skewers.

Put sugar, syrup, and ⅔ cup of the evaporated milk in a large heavy kettle. Stir to blend well. Heat slowly until sugar is dissolved, stirring constantly. Then cook briskly to a thick syrup, stirring all the while.

Add remainder of milk slowly, keeping mixture boiling briskly, and cook to firm ball stage (242°F.), stirring constantly to prevent scorching. Remove from heat and let stand until caramel stops bubbling.

Working quickly, dip apples, one at a time, in caramel and twirl to get rid of surplus coating and make smooth.

Dip bottoms in chopped nuts. Place on aluminum foil or a well buttered baking sheet to set.

If coating becomes too hard for dipping, add a little evaporated milk and reheat, stirring to keep smooth.

The caramel should be kept quite hot so that coating will not be too heavy. Makes 15 to 20 caramel apples.

STUFFED DATES

Remove pits and stuff as suggested below. Roll in powdered or granulated sugar or shake a few at a time in paper bag containing a little sugar.

If desired, mix 1 teaspoon cinnamon with each ¼ cup sugar.

Suggested stuffings include: marshmallows, cut in quarters; candied ginger, cut in bits; candied pineapple, cut in bits; peanut butter moistened with orange juice; salted almonds; broken nutmeats such as Brazil nuts, pecans, and walnuts; fondant.

Stuffed Prunes: Follow suggestions for stuffed dates. If prunes are very dry, steam until tender. Cool before stuffing.

SPANISH SWEETS (DULCES)

2 cups walnuts
¾ cup almonds
1 7- to 8-ounce package pitted dates
2 cups pecans
¾ cup candied cherries
¾ cup seeded raisins
Confectioners' sugar

Put all ingredients except confectioners' sugar through food chopper, using medium blade.

On board covered with confectioners' sugar, knead ground mixture until

Caramel Apples

thick and smooth.

Shape into 1-inch balls. Wrap in waxed paper. Refrigerate. Makes about 5 dozen.

PEANUT BUTTER FRUIT CONFECTIONS

1 cup pitted dates
½ cup seedless raisins
½ cup currants
1 cup peanut butter
¼ cup sweetened condensed milk

Put fruits through food chopper. Add peanut butter and sweetened condensed milk. Mix well.

Press into bottom of 8 x 8 x 2-inch buttered pan which has been sprinkled with confectioners' sugar. Smooth surface of candy and sprinkle with confectioners' sugar if desired.

Chill until firm. Cut in squares. Makes about 1⅛ pound.

CANDIED GRAPEFRUIT PEEL

Peel fruit, keeping peel in large pieces. Wash and trim out most of white from inside. Cut into strips or triangles.

Cover with cold water. Boil 5 minutes. Drain. Cover again with cold water. Boil 5 minutes. Drain. Repeat twice, or until peel is tender.

Weigh drained peel. Weigh an equal amount of honey and sugar, using half of each.

Add ⅓ cup water for each cup honey and sugar. Add peel.

Simmer until peel is glazed, about 20 minutes. Drain. Roll in granulated sugar.

Candied Orange or Lemon Peel: Simmer peel until tender without changing water, 20 to 30 minutes. Proceed as above.

Chocolate Citrus Peel: Dip candied peel in melted sweet chocolate.

Candied Fruit Peel

Dipped Stuffed Figs

DIPPED STUFFED FIGS

Fillings: Nutmeats as walnut, almond, Brazil, pecan, hickory, or peanuts. Preserved or candied fruits as orange or lemon peel, citron, cherries, pineapple, ginger, or marshmallows. Dipping chocolate or fondant for coating.

Rinse California dried figs, drain, wrap in towel and steam over hot water about 15 minutes, or until tender.

Remove and dry with cloth. Slit down 1 side and stuff with preferred fruit or nut filling, or fruit-nut combinations. Chill well before dipping.

Chocolate Coating: Dip stuffed figs, blossom end down, in dipping chocolate melted over warm (not hot) water. Place on waxed paper to harden.

Fondant Coating: Dip in fondant melted over hot water and place on waxed paper to harden. Melted fondant may be tinted as desired with food coloring.

Double Coating: Dip in fondant as directed, then in dipping chocolate.

APRICOT CANDY ROLL

3 cups sugar
1 cup evaporated milk
1 cup finely chopped dried apricots
¼ cup butter
½ teaspoon salt
2 teaspoons vanilla
½ cup finely chopped nuts

Combine sugar, evaporated milk, apricots, butter, and salt in saucepan. Stirring constantly, bring to a boil.

Boil, stirring occasionally, to the soft ball stage, 236° F. Cool to lukewarm (120° F.).

Add vanilla and nuts and beat until stiff enough to knead.

Place on bread board and knead until smooth.

Shape into four small rolls about an inch in diameter.

Place in the refrigerator to chill for several hours. Cut into small slices. Makes 80 small pieces.

Chocolate Nut Candy Roll: Omit apricots and add 2 squares (2 ounces)

unsweetened chocolate to the evaporated milk and sugar mixture.

FRUIT NUGGETS

3 cups light brown sugar
1 cup sour cream
½ teaspoon salt
½ square (½ ounce) chocolate
2 tablespoons butter
½ cup dates, cut fine
½ cup chopped walnuts, pecans, or coconut

Cook sugar, cream, and salt to the soft ball stage, 234° F. stirring occasionally, wiping crystals down from side of pan.

Pour immediately into a well buttered clean pan.

Drop in chocolate and butter, and allow to stand without stirring until pan can be held comfortably on palm of hand.

Beat until mass begins to thicken and color becomes lighter; stir in dates and nuts.

Drop by teaspoonfuls into chopped nuts or coconut; roll until balls are coated, and place on waxed paper to cool.

Makes 2 pounds, or 3 dozen nuggets 1¼ inches in diameter.

FRUIT SLICES

1 cup pitted, plumped prunes
1 cup figs
1 cup raisins
½ cup nuts

Grind fruit and nuts. Mix thoroughly and shape into long, slender rolls. Roll in coconut or finely chopped nuts.

Wrap in waxed paper and chill. Slice off pieces as desired. Or slice off pieces and wrap in waxed paper.

PARISIAN SWEETS

½ pound figs
½ pound dried apricots or seedless raisins
½ pound nutmeats
Confectioners' sugar

Wash and pick over fruits. Combine with nutmeats. Grind through a food

chopper, using medium blade.

Roll out about ½-inch thick on a board sprinkled with confectioners' sugar.

Cut into small pieces or make balls and roll them in confectioners' sugar. Store in a tin box or a tight jar.

FRUIT BALLS

6 cups puffed rice or puffed wheat
¼ cup chopped candied cherries
½ cup chopped dates
½ cup chopped nuts
¾ cup light corn syrup
¼ cup light molasses
½ teaspoon salt
1 teaspoon vinegar
2 tablespoons shortening
1 teaspoon vanilla

Crisp puffed rice in a moderate oven (350°F.) 10 minutes; place in large greased bowl and mix with chopped fruits and nuts.

Combine syrup, molasses, salt, and vinegar in saucepan; cook until a few drops in cold water form a hard ball (255°F.).

Remove from heat; add shortening and vanilla, stirring only enough to mix. Slowly pour cooked syrup over puffed rice, mixing quickly. Form into balls immediately. Makes 8 large balls.

Candied Fruit Bars: Prepare as above and pack at once into greased 7 x 11-inch pan. Cool and cut into bars. Makes about 30 bars.

YULE FIG BALLS

1 cup chopped dried figs
2 cups sugar-coated rice cereal
⅓ cup chopped dried apricots
⅔ cup light corn syrup
3 tablespoons honey
½ teaspoon vinegar
¼ teaspoon salt
2 tablespoons butter or margarine
½ teaspoon grated lemon rind

Combine figs, cereal, and apricots in greased mixing bowl; set aside.

Combine syrup, honey, vinegar, and salt in small saucepan. Place over low heat and bring to boil. Cook, stirring constantly, until mixture forms a hard ball in cold water (250°F.).

Remove from heat; add butter and lemon rind. Pour over cereal mixture and mix quickly. Butter hands and shape into balls.

Yule Fig Balls

Nut Treats

SUGARED ALMONDS

1 cup sugar
1/2 cup water
1/2 pound blanched almonds
1 teaspoon vanilla
1/2 teaspoon cinnamon

Cook sugar and water in heavy iron skillet 5 minutes. Add nuts and cook until syrup begins to appear white and slightly sugared.

Add flavorings and remove pan from heat for 10 minutes.

Replace over low heat. Stir constantly until sugar starts to melt.

Pour the whole mixture onto a cake rack which has been placed over waxed paper. Separate the nuts as they dry.

PEANUT CLUSTERS

Melt 1/2 pound semi-sweet chocolate in bowl over hot water. Remove from heat; add 1/2 pound roasted Spanish peanuts and stir well.

Drop from teaspoon onto waxed paper. Chill overnight in refrigerator. Keep in cool place. Makes about 36 clusters.

ALMOND PASTE

1 pound blanched almonds
2 cups sugar
1 cup water
1/2 cup orange juice
Few drops rose water
Confectioners' sugar

Put almonds through food chopper at least 4 times, using finest blade.

Cook sugar and water just past soft ball stage (240° F.). Mix with ground almonds. Add orange juice and rose water. Stir until thoroughly blended and creamy.

Turn out on a hard surface dusted with confectioners' sugar. Let stand until cool.

Pack in closely covered container. Store in cool, dry place and let ripen at least 1 week.

In various European countries this traditional almond paste is shaped into flat cakes or a variety of forms, decorated and served during the Christmas season. Makes 2 pounds.

CHEESE STUFFED PECANS

Choose the biggest pecan (or walnut) halves you can find; toast them lightly in a moderate oven and cool.

Put two together with highly seasoned cream cheese, Roquefort type cheese, or smoked cheese.

CURRIED NUTS

Toast nuts in the oven, and while toasting sprinkle generously with curry powder and a little butter or oil.

BRAZIL NUT CHIPS

Shell Brazil nuts. Cover with cold water and bring slowly to a boil. Simmer 2 to 3 minutes. Drain and cut while damp into thin lengthwise slices, about 1/8 inch thick.

Spread out in a shallow pan. Dot with butter, allowing 2 tablespoons of butter for each 1 1/2 cups of the shelled nuts. Sprinkle with salt.

Bake in moderate oven (350° F.) 15 to 20 minutes, stirring occasionally.

Variations: Chips also may be curried or spiced. Follow above directions, and for 1 1/2 cups shelled Brazil nuts combine 1 teaspoon curry powder with the salt. Or omit salt and substitute 1 tablespoon sugar mixed with 1/4 teaspoon cinnamon.

ALMONDS IN OLIVE OIL

Shell almonds and remove the brown inner skins by blanching.

To blanch, pour boiling water over the nuts, hold at simmering temperature 3 minutes, then drain and slip off the loosened skins by pressing the kernels between thumb and forefinger. Dry.

Place blanched almonds in a shallow pan; add 1 teaspoon olive oil for each cup of nuts and heat in slow oven (300° F.) until pale brown, 25 to 30 minutes. Stir occasionally.

Salt while hot and let cool before serving.

TOASTED PUMPKIN OR SQUASH SEEDS

Remove the fiber from unwashed seeds. To 2 cups of seeds add 1 1/2 tablespoons melted butter or salad oil and 1 1/4 teaspoons salt.

Spread the seeds in a shallow pan. Toast in a very slow oven (250° F.) until brown and crisp, stirring occasionally.

DEVILED ALMONDS

Sauté 2 cups blanched almonds in 2 tablespoons salad oil until crunchy, about 5 minutes. Drain on absorbent paper.

Add 1/8 teaspoon chili powder, 1 teaspoon salt, and 1/8 teaspoon cayenne. Toss well.

SALTED NUTS

Shell and blanch nuts, if necessary. Wash and dry thoroughly. Melt 1/2 teaspoon butter in a shallow pan. Add a layer of shelled nuts.

Place in moderate oven (350° F.) about 10 minutes. Stir and turn nuts frequently.

Pour onto absorbent paper to drain off any excess butter.

Sprinkle with salt, to taste. About 1 1/2 to 2 teaspoons salt per pound nuts is the usual amount.

SALTED SOYBEANS

Use varieties which are good for cooked dried beans. Wash and soak dried soybeans overnight. Drain and spread in a single layer and let dry at room temperature, or dry with a towel.

Fry a small handful at a time in hot deep fat (360° F.) for 8 to 10 minutes. Drain on paper towels and sprinkle with salt while still warm.

FRENCH FRIED NUTS

Fry shelled dry nuts in deep hot fat (370° F.) until lightly browned, 4 to 5 minutes.

Drain on absorbent paper. Sprinkle with salt.

GARLIC NUTS

Sprinkle nuts with garlic salt and melted butter and toast in oven until crisp.

Or, mash a garlic clove and let stand in butter 1/2 hour. Strain butter and use to season nuts while toasting them.

LITTLE SNOWTOPS

1/2 cup granulated sugar
Pinch of cream of tartar
1/4 cup hot water
1/4 teaspoon vanilla
Drop or two of mint extract
1 1/4 cups sifted confectioners' sugar
2 cups roasted unblanched almonds

Combine granulated sugar, cream of tartar, and hot water in small saucepan. Cook over low heat until sugar dissolves. Continue cooking to 226° F. or to a thin syrup.

Cool to lukewarm. Stir in flavorings and confectioners' sugar.

Hold almonds 1 at a time by pointed end and dip rounded end into sugar mixture. Place on waxed paper to dry. Makes about 1 1/4 pounds.

Little Snowtops

GLACÉ NUTS

1   cup sugar
1/8   teaspoon cream of tartar
1/2   cup water
Nutmeats

Combine ingredients and heat to boiling. Stir until sugar is dissolved. Wipe all grains of sugar from sides of saucepan with a damp cloth. Boil without stirring to the light crack stage (290° F.).

Remove sugar crystals around edge of pan with wet cloth. Remove saucepan from heat. Set in pan of cold water to stop boiling immediately.

Remove from cold water and set in pan of hot water. Using a fork, dip each nut into syrup, drain, and place on waxed paper. If syrup becomes too thick, reheat over hot water.

BRANDIED ALMONDS OR PECANS

1/4   cup butter
2 1/4   cups confectioners' sugar
1/4   cup brandy or sherry
2   cups blanched almonds or pecan halves

Cream butter and work in sugar and brandy or sherry.

Toast almonds in moderate oven (350° F.) until golden, stirring frequently in a shallow pan.

Stir nuts into sugar mixture while hot. When nuts are well coated, spread them out on paper to cool.

ORANGE SUGARED NUTS

1 1/2   cups sugar
1/4   cup water
3   tablespoons orange juice
1/2   teaspoon grated orange rind
1/2   pound pecans or other nuts

Cook sugar, water, and orange juice to soft ball stage (238° F.).

Remove from heat; add rind and nuts. Stir constantly until syrup looks cloudy.

Drop onto waxed paper or greased surface. Separate nuts into small clusters. Makes about 3/4 pound.

SPICED NUTS

1/4   cup sugar
2   teaspoons cinnamon
1/8   teaspoon nutmeg
1/8   teaspoon cloves
1   cup nuts (almonds, pecans, English walnuts, Brazil nuts, etc.)
1   slightly beaten egg white

Mix sugar and spices in a small bowl. Add nuts to egg white, a few at a time, in order to coat them well.

Drop into the bowl of sugar and spices. When well coated, place on buttered baking sheet and brown in slow oven (300° F.) for 30 minutes.

CARAMEL ALMONDS

2   cups granulated sugar
1/4   cup butter
Unblanched almonds

Combine sugar and butter in skillet. Stir over low heat until sugar is melted and browned.

When mixture looks golden and slightly lumpy stir in almonds.

Coat them quickly and separate while hot on waxed paper.

RAISIN-WALNUT LOAF

2   cups raisins
1   cup walnuts
1/4   cup sweetened condensed milk

Put raisins and nuts through food chopper. Blend thoroughly with sweetened condensed milk.

Scrape mixture into buttered pan which has been sprinkled with confectioners' sugar.

Smooth the top and sprinkle with more confectioners' sugar. Cut into squares.

CHOCOLATE PEPPERMINT NUT CLUSTERS

4   ounces (4 squares) semi-sweet chocolate
1/4   cup crushed peppermint stick candy
1   cup walnuts

Melt chocolate over warm, not hot, water. Stir in peppermint stick candy and walnuts, mixing until nuts are coated.

Drop by teaspoonful onto waxed paper to harden.

RAISIN PEANUT CLUSTERS— UNCOOKED

Wash 2 1/2 cups seedless raisins and dry thoroughly on a towel.

Melt 1/2 pound sweet or dripping chocolate over warm water and cool to lukewarm. Add raisins, 1 cup shelled, roasted peanuts, and 1/4 teaspoon salt. Mix well. Drop from teaspoon onto waxed paper or shape in paper candy cups. Chill overnight in refrigerator. Makes about 50 small clusters.

Pulled Candies

PEPPERMINT CANDY CANES

2   cups sugar
1/2   cup light corn syrup
1/2   cup water
1/4   teaspoon cream of tartar
3/4   teaspoon peppermint extract
3/4   to 1 teaspoon red food coloring

Combine sugar, corn syrup, water, and cream of tartar; stir until sugar dissolves.

Cook without stirring to hard-ball stage (265° F.). Remove from heat and add peppermint extract.

Divide in 2 portions and add coloring to 1 part.

Pour out on greased platters. When candy is cool enough to handle, pull each part separately.

Form in ropes and twist red part around white. Cut in 8-inch lengths and form in the shape of candy canes. Makes about 10.

WHITE TAFFY

2   cups sugar
2/3   cup water
1/2   cup light corn syrup
2   tablespoons white (distilled) vinegar
1   tablespoon butter or margarine
1/8   teaspoon salt
1/2   teaspoon baking soda
Few drops of mint extract

Combine sugar, water, corn syrup, and vinegar in heavy 2-quart saucepan. Stir over low heat until sugar is dissolved. Cover and boil 3 minutes.

Uncover and boil over moderate heat without stirring until candy thermometer registers 280° F. (soft crack stage).

Remove from heat. Blend in butter or margarine, salt, and baking soda. Pour onto an oiled marble slab or enameled pan.

As candy cools, turn edges with spatula toward center. Sprinkle extract over candy.

When cool enough to handle, gather candy into a ball and pull until white and porous. Use soft butter or margarine on fingers to prevent candy from sticking to hands.

Pull and twist into a rope about 1/2 inch in diameter. Cut into 1/2-inch serving pieces with scissors. Wrap each piece in waxed or cellophane paper for storing. Makes 1 pound.

CRACK TAFFY

1 1/4   cups molasses
1   tablespoon vinegar
3/4   cup sugar
1/8   teaspoon salt
1/8   teaspoon baking soda
1   tablespoon butter

Blend molasses, vinegar, and sugar. Boil carefully to very hard ball stage (270° F.). Remove from the heat.

Add remaining ingredients, stirring until well mixed.

Pour into greased pans. Let stand until cool. Crack with a mallet or hammer.

SALT WATER TAFFY

Mix 1 cup sugar, 3 tablespoons cornstarch, and few grains salt. Add 1/2 cup water and 2/3 cup honey. Cook to very hard ball stage (266° F.).

Pour into greased pan. Cool. Pull until porous. Cut in 1-inch pieces.

Hard Candies and Brittles

LOLLYPOPS
(Master Recipe)

2   cups sugar
2/3 cup light corn syrup
1   cup water
1/2 teaspoon oil of lemon
Few drops yellow food coloring

Place sugar, corn syrup, and water in saucepan. Cook over low heat, stirring until sugar dissolves. Continue cooking, without stirring, to hard crack stage (310° F.).

Wrap wet cloth around a fork. While cooking, wipe crystals from sides of pan with wet cloth.

Grease lollypop molds or flat surface.

When temperature of 310°F. is reached, add oil of lemon and coloring, stirring both in quickly.

Pour immediately into greased molds, or drop from end of spoon onto flat greased surface.

Press end of stick into each pop as soon as each is dropped from spoon. Loosen lollypops as soon as they are firm and before they are cold.

Lollypop Variations: Vary flavoring and coloring by using oil of lime and green food coloring, oil of peppermint and pink food coloring, and oil of cinnamon and red food coloring.

To form faces, use Life Savers or raisins for eyes, pieces of prune for mouth, and coconut for hair. Have all decorations ready to add while lollypops are hot.

ENGLISH TOFFEE

1   cup sugar
1   cup butter or margarine
1   tablespoon corn syrup
3   tablespoons water
3/4 cup chopped almonds or peanuts
1 small chocolate bar, cut fine

Cook sugar, butter or margarine, corn syrup, and water until a few drops tested in cold water crack (290°F. on candy thermometer).

While syrup cooks, chop nuts fine and sprinkle almost all of them over bottom of pie-pan.

Pour hot syrup over nuts, sprinkle with finely chopped chocolate bar and top it off with remaining almonds or peanuts. When cool, break into chunks.

NUT CRUNCH

2/3 cup butter or margarine
1   cup sugar
1/2 teaspoon vanilla
3/4 cup chopped nuts
3   ounces (3 squares) semi-sweet chocolate

Melt butter, add sugar and, with constant stirring, cook slowly to 300°F.

(very brittle in ice water).

Add vanilla and half the nuts. Pour out on a smooth, greased surface (not a pan). Spread thin and cool.

Loosen candy from greased surface and mark into squares before it becomes crisp.

Melt chocolate over hot water, spread over cooled candy and sprinkle with remaining nuts.

When chocolate is cool, break crunch into squares. Makes 1¾ pounds.

BUTTERSCOTCH
(Master Recipe)

2   cups brown sugar
1/4 cup light corn syrup
1   cup water
1/4 teaspoon salt
1/3 cup butter
1/4 teaspoon vanilla

Place sugar, corn syrup, water, and salt in saucepan. Cook over low heat, stirring until sugar dissolves.

Continue cooking without stirring until mixture reaches temperature of 290°F. Add butter, remove from heat, and add vanilla.

Pour into a buttered shallow pan. Cool slightly. Mark into squares. When cold, break into pieces. Makes about 1⅛ pounds.

Lemon Butterscotch: In master recipe substitute a few drops oil of lemon for vanilla.

Butterscotch Lollypops: In master butterscotch recipe cook sugar mixture to 290°F. Stir in butter and vanilla quickly.

Pour into greased lollypop molds, or drop from end of teaspoon onto greased flat pan. Place stick in each pop.

PEANUT BRITTLE

1½ cups shelled peanuts
1/4 teaspoon salt
1   cup sugar
1/2 cup light corn syrup
1/2 cup water
1½ tablespoons butter
1/2 teaspoon lemon extract

Sprinkle nuts with salt and warm in oven.

Put sugar, corn syrup, and water in pan. Stir until it boils. Wash down sides with wet pastry brush and cook to 295°F., or until mixture is very brittle when tried in cold water.

Add butter, lemon extract, and nuts; pour into a shallow greased pan.

As soon as it can be handled, turn the mass over and pull and stretch it out as thin as possible. Break into irregular pieces.

Popcorn Balls

POPCORN BALLS
(Master Recipe)

1   tablespoon butter
1   cup sugar
1   cup molasses
1/2 teaspoon salt
4   quarts popped corn

Melt butter. Add sugar, molasses, and salt. Boil on medium heat until very hard ball stage (260°F.).

Pour over corn. Stir corn thoroughly while pouring syrup over it.

Butter hands lightly. Shape into balls. Makes 12 to 14.

Popcorn Ball Variations

Cereal Popcorn Balls: Substitute 3 cups puffed cereal for similar amount of popcorn and mix before adding syrup.

Colored Popcorn Balls: Omit molasses. Use 1½ cups light corn syrup and add any desired food coloring and 1 teaspoon vanilla.

Nut Caramel Corn: Add 1/2 cup nuts to popcorn before adding syrup. Cool slightly. Shape into balls.

Popcorn Chop Suey: Substitute 1 cup shelled roasted peanuts and 1 cup shredded coconut for similar amount of popcorn. Mix before adding syrup.

Raisin Popcorn Balls: Add 1/2 cup raisins to popcorn before adding syrup.

MOLASSES PEANUT CRUNCH

1   cup molasses
1   cup sugar
2   tablespoons shortening
1/8 teaspoon baking soda
2½ cups chopped peanut meats

Combine molasses, sugar, and shortening; cook slowly, stirring constantly to 252°F. (or when a small quantity dropped in cold water forms firm ball).

Remove from heat; add baking soda; stir until bubbling stops. Add nuts.

Pour into greased shallow pan. Cool slightly; cut in small squares or bars. Wrap in waxed paper. Makes about 1¾ pounds.

Beaten Candies

FONDANT
(Master Recipe)

  2 cups sugar
  ¾ cup boiling water
  ⅛ teaspoon cream of tartar
  ⅛ teaspoon salt
  ½ teaspoon vanilla

Place sugar, water, cream of tartar, and salt in saucepan over hot fire. Stir constantly until, but not after, sugar has dissolved. Do not splash syrup. Remove spoon. Do not use it again after syrup boils.

Remove sugar crystals around edge of pan with wet cloth.

Let syrup boil until it reaches 238°F., or until it forms soft ball in cold water. Be sure bulb of thermometer is down in syrup yet does not touch bottom of pan.

Add vanilla without stirring. Pour syrup in a thin sheet onto chilled platter to cool quickly. Do not scrape out saucepan.

When syrup is cool, work it with flat wooden spoon until it creams. When it forms a soft creamy mass, work it with palms of hands in the same way as bread dough until it is smooth.

Place fondant in an earthenware or glass dish. Cover with damp cloth. After 24 hours fondant is ready to mold. It will keep for months in a cold place if covered with moist cloth or stored in tightly covered jar.

Fondant Variations

Brown Sugar Fondant: Substitute 1 cup firmly packed brown sugar for 1 cup granulated sugar.

Cherry or Nut Fondant Balls: Form ripened fondant into tiny balls. Press each between two halves of cherries or nutmeats, or roll each in chopped coconut, chopped nuts, cocoa, or chopped semi-sweet chocolate.

Chocolate Fondant: Knead 2 squares (2 ounces) melted unsweetened chocolate and ½ teaspoon vanilla into 1 cup ripened fondant.

Coffee Fondant: Substitute strong fresh coffee for water.

Fondant Loaves: Add fruit and nuts to fondant. Pack into loaf pan. Let stand until firm. Cut into slices.

Fondant Mints: Melt ripened fondant slowly over hot water. Color and flavor. Drop from teaspoon onto waxed paper.

Fondant Nut Creams: Knead fondant, and flavor with almond extract or coffee extract.

Knead into it a mixture of chopped nuts or moist coconut.

Shape into balls, squares, or patties which may be dipped in melted dipping chocolate.

Fruits Stuffed With Fondant: Prepare dates, figs, or prunes. Stuff with fondant.

Tutti-Frutti Fondant: Knead fondant. Add cherry extract or almond extract.

Knead chopped mixture of raisins, dates, figs, candied cherries, citron, orange peel, or other candied fruit into ripened fondant.

Shape into a flat cake. Cut after it stands 1 hour.

Fondant Wintergreen Creams: Melt portion of fondant in top part of double boiler until soft enough to drop from a spoon.

Add a tiny bit of red food coloring to tint delicate pink and 1 to 2 drops oil of wintergreen flavoring, stirring enough to blend.

If fondant is too thick add few drops of hot water. If too thin, let stand 5 to 10 minutes to thicken.

Drop from a teaspoon onto waxed paper or lightly buttered flat surface.

Dipped Almonds: Melt fondant over warm water; tint with food coloring. Dip almonds or other nuts. Cool on racks.

PANOCHA #2
(Also spelled penuchi and penuche)

  2 tablespoons butter or margarine
  ¾ cup half cream and half milk, or rich top milk
  1 cup firmly packed brown sugar
  1½ cups granulated sugar
  1 teaspoon vanilla
  ½ to ¾ cup broken nuts

Melt butter or margarine in 2-quart saucepan, using rubber spatula to bring it up around sides of pan, greasing well. Pour cream and milk into pan. Place over heat and bring to boiling point.

Add sugars and stir well to dissolve. Cover pan and bring mixture to boil slowly. Cook about 1 minute or until sugar crystals are melted down from sides of pan.

Remove cover and continue cooking gently with stirring to soft ball stage (238°F.), about 20 minutes. Remove from heat.

Let stand without moving, until candy is lukewarm (110°F.) and bottom of saucepan is barely warm to the hand. This will take about 1 hour.

Add vanilla and nuts; beat with a heavy spoon. Continue beating until candy becomes creamy and starts to lose its gloss.

Pour into a buttered 8-inch square pan. Cut into pieces while still warm. Makes about 24 pieces.

MEXICAN ORANGE CANDY

  1 cup sugar
  1½ cups rich sweet milk
  2 cups sugar
  Grated rind of 2 oranges
  Pinch of salt
  ½ cup butter
  1 cup nutmeats (walnuts or pecans)

Melt 1 cup sugar in a large kettle while the milk is scalding in a double boiler. When the sugar is melted to a rich yellow, add hot milk all at once, stirring. It will boil up quickly, so be sure to use a good-sized kettle.

Add 2 cups sugar to this mixture, stirring until dissolved; cook until it forms an almost hard ball in water (238°F.). Just before it is done add grated orange rind, salt, butter, and nutmeats. Beat until creamy and pour on a buttered platter to cool.

PRALINES

  1 cup granulated sugar
  1 cup firmly packed brown sugar
  ½ teaspoon baking soda
  1 cup buttermilk
  ⅛ teaspoon salt
  2 tablespoons butter or margarine
  1¼ cups pecan halves
  1 teaspoon vanilla

In heavy 4-quart saucepan combine sugars, baking soda, buttermilk, and salt. Stir over low heat until sugar is dissolved. Boil over moderate heat until candy thermometer registers 230°F. (thread stage).

Remove from heat. Add butter or margarine, nuts, and vanilla.

Beat candy until it starts to become thick and slightly sugary. Then place saucepan over low heat to prevent candy from becoming too hard before it is dropped into patties.

Dip by tablespoonful onto waxed paper, forming patties about 3 inches in diameter.

Cool. Remove from paper and wrap individually in waxed or cellophane paper. Makes 15.

Pralines

Chocolate and Vanilla Fudge

CHOCOLATE FUDGE
(Master Recipe)

2 squares (2 ounces) **unsweetened chocolate**
⅔ cup milk
2 cups sugar
⅛ teaspoon salt
2 tablespoons butter
1 teaspoon vanilla

Break chocolate into small pieces. Add to milk in saucepan. Cook over low heat, stirring constantly until mixture is smooth.

Add sugar and salt and stir until sugar is dissolved and mixture boils.

Cook slowly, without stirring, until a small quantity dropped into cold water forms a soft ball (236°F.). Remove from heat.

Add butter and vanilla without stirring. Cool to lukewarm (110°F.). Beat until fairly thick.

Pour at once into greased pan. Cool. Cut into squares. Makes about 1¼ pounds.

Chocolate Fudge Variations

Brown Sugar Fudge: In master recipe substitute 1 cup firmly packed brown sugar for 1 cup granulated sugar.

Coconut Fudge: Add ½ cup chopped, shredded coconut just before pouring into greased pan.

Creamy Chocolate Fudge: In master recipe add 2 tablespoons light corn syrup with sugar.

Fruit Fudge: Stir ½ cup chopped dates, figs, candied fruit, dried fruit, or raisins into fudge just before pouring into pan.

Fudge Nut and Fruit Balls: Add chopped nuts and chopped cherries, dates, or figs to beaten fudge and mix until just blended.

Mold into even-sized balls with hands. Roll each in finely ground nuts.

Marshmallow Fudge: Follow master recipe. Cut 12 marshmallows into small pieces. Add to fudge just before pouring into pan.

Mocha Fudge: In master recipe decrease milk to ⅓ cup. Add ⅔ cup fresh strong coffee.

Nut Fudge: Add ½ cup broken nutmeats just before pouring into pan.

Peanut Butter Fudge: In master recipe substitute ¼ cup peanut butter for butter and add when beating fudge after it has cooled to lukewarm (110°F.).

Panocha: In master recipe substitute brown sugar for white and water for milk.

Sour Cream Fudge: In master recipe substitute sour cream for milk. Omit butter and cook to slightly higher temperature (238°F.).

Vanilla Fudge: Omit chocolate from recipe for chocolate fudge and increase vanilla to 1½ teaspoons.

DIVINITY
(Master Recipe)

2 cups sugar
1 cup water
¼ cup corn syrup
⅛ teaspoon salt
2 egg whites
1½ cups chopped walnuts
1 teaspoon vanilla

Heat sugar, water, corn syrup, and salt, stirring constantly until sugar has dissolved. Continue to cook without stirring until syrup when dropped in cold water forms a hard ball (250°F.).

Beat egg whites. Pour syrup slowly into them and continue to beat until candy is stiff enough to hold its shape. Add nuts and vanilla.

Drop by spoonful onto waxed paper, or turn into buttered pan and cut in 1-inch squares when firm.

Pack in a tin box. Keep covered because it dries out quickly.

Divinity Variations

Brazil Nut Divinity: Use Brazil nuts instead of walnuts.

Brown Sugar Divinity or Sea Foam: In master recipe substitute 1 cup firmly packed brown sugar for 1 cup granulated sugar.

Cherry Divinity: Prepare master recipe. Color delicate pink with food coloring. Add ½ cup chopped candied cherries.

Chocolate Divinity: Follow master recipe. After syrup and egg whites have been combined, add 2 squares (2 ounces) melted unsweetened chocolate.

Coconut Divinity: Add ½ cup toasted shredded coconut.

Fruit Divinity: Chopped dates, figs, or other dried or candied fruit may be added.

Maple Divinity: In master recipe decrease water to ¼ cup. Add ¾ cup maple syrup.

Neapolitan Divinity: Prepare master recipe. Divide candy into 3 parts. Color 1 part with strawberry or cherry coloring.

Add 1 square (1 ounce) melted unsweetened chocolate to second part.

Spread white, or third, part in bottom of buttered pan. Add pink part, then chocolate part. Press together. Let harden before cutting into squares.

Orange Divinity: In master recipe add 3 tablespoons coarsely grated orange rind with vanilla and nuts.

NOUGAT

½ cup honey
2 cups sugar
¼ cup water
2 stiffly beaten egg whites
⅛ teaspoon salt
¾ cup chopped nuts

Combine honey, sugar, and water. Cook to hard ball stage (258°F.).

Beat egg whites with salt until stiff. Add syrup gradually, beating constantly until it stands up in peaks.

Spread in greased shallow square pan. Top with nuts. Cool and cut in rectangular pieces. Makes about 24 pieces.

MAPLE PECAN PRALINES

1 cup firmly packed maple sugar
1 cup firmly packed brown sugar
1 cup milk
1 tablespoon butter
1½ cups pecans

Combine all ingredients except nuts in saucepan. Cook to soft ball stage or 240°F. on candy thermometer. Cool to lukewarm. Beat until creamy and thick.

Place pan over hot water until candy is soft enough to drop in flat cakes from spoon.

Arrange nuts in groups on a buttered pan. Drop candy over them. Cool and remove pralines with spatula. Wrap in waxed paper.

SEA FOAM

1 cup firmly packed dark brown sugar
1 cup granulated sugar
¾ cup water
3 tablespoons corn syrup
2 stiffly beaten egg whites
1 teaspoon vanilla
1 cup chopped nuts

Put sugars and water into saucepan. Stir until well dissolved. Add syrup and cook to 252°F. or hard ball stage.

Pour slowly over well beaten egg whites.

Beat until mixture is light and fluffy, and piles up without spreading.

Add vanilla and nuts. Drop by spoonful onto waxed paper. Makes 3 dozen pieces.

Poured Candies

VANILLA CARAMELS
(Master Recipe)

2 cups sugar
1/16 teaspoon salt
2 cups corn syrup
1/2 cup butter
1 tall can evaporated milk
1 teaspoon vanilla

Combine sugar, salt, and syrup in saucepan. Cook over low heat until sugar is completely dissolved. Bring to boil. Cook until a little syrup dropped from teaspoon into cold water forms firm ball (244° F.).

Add butter and milk a little at a time so that mixture does not stop boiling. Continue cooking to 242° F.

Remove from heat. Add vanilla, stirring only to blend.

Pour into buttered pan. Mark into squares. Cut when cold. Makes about 72 pieces.

Vanilla Caramel Variations

Chocolate Caramels: In master recipe cook 4 squares (4 ounces) unsweetened chocolate with sugar, salt, and syrup.

Coconut Caramels: Add 1 cup toasted shredded coconut after removing from heat.

Coffee Caramels: In master recipe substitute 1 teaspoon coffee extract for vanilla.

Fruit Caramels: Add 1 cup diced figs, dates, or raisins before pouring into buttered pan.

Honey Caramels: In master recipe substitute 2 cups honey for corn syrup. Decrease butter to 1/4 cup. Cook to firm ball stage (244° F.).

Nut Caramels: Add 1 to 1 1/2 cups chopped nuts before pouring into pan.

BUTTERSCOTCH CARAMELS

1 pint cream
1 3/4 cups light corn syrup
2 cups granulated sugar
3/4 cup butter
1 cup chopped pecans
1/2 teaspoon vanilla

Place 1/2 pint cream, syrup, and sugar in pan over low heat, stirring constantly. When mixture is boiling hard, add remaining cream and butter slowly, so that candy does not stop boiling.

Cook slowly until candy makes a firm ball when dropped in cold water, 246° to 248° F.

Sprinkle chopped nuts on well buttered baking pan. Add vanilla to mixture and pour over nuts. Let stand several hours.

Cut in inch pieces and wrap separately in waxed paper. This quantity fills a 10-inch square baking pan and makes 2 1/2 pounds of caramels.

FIVE-MINUTE FUDGE

2/3 cup undiluted evaporated milk (small can)
1 2/3 cups sugar
1 1/2 cups (about 16) medium diced marshmallows
1/2 cup chopped nuts
1 1/2 cups semi-sweet chocolate pieces
1 teaspoon vanilla

Place evaporated milk and sugar in large saucepan. Heat to boiling, then cook 5 minutes. Begin timing after mixture begins bubbling around edges of pan.

Remove from heat; add marshmallows, nuts, chocolate, and vanilla. Stir until marshmallows and chocolate are melted. Pour into buttered 8-inch square pan. Cool; cut in squares. Makes about 2 pounds.

Caramel Fudge: Prepare fudge as directed above, using caramel chips in place of semi-sweet chocolate.

Five-Minute Fudge Rolls: Make Five-Minute Fudge as directed above. Spread about 1 cup chopped nuts on heavy waxed paper. Pour fudge mixture over nuts. As fudge cools, form into roll. Slice.

CREAM CARAMELS

1 cup sugar
1/8 teaspoon salt
1 cup corn syrup
1/4 cup butter
3/4 cup evaporated milk, undiluted
1 teaspoon vanilla

Stirring occasionally, boil sugar, salt, and corn syrup rapidly to 245° F. Add butter and evaporated milk gradually so that the mixture does not stop boiling at any time.

Cook rapidly to firm ball stage (242° F.). Stir constantly because the mixture sticks easily at the last. Add flavoring and pour into a buttered pan. Cool thoroughly before cutting.

Cut with a heavy sharp knife with a sawlike motion.

About 25 minutes are required for cooking. Makes 1 pound or 22 caramels (3/4 x 1/2 inch).

NEVER-FAIL FUDGE

1/2 pound sweet chocolate
1/4 cup butter
1/4 cup cream
1/2 pound (32) marshmallows
1/2 pound (1 3/4 cups) confectioners' sugar
1 teaspoon vanilla
1/8 teaspoon salt

Five-Minute Fudge

1 cup chopped nuts

Place chocolate, butter, cream, and marshmallows in top of double boiler and cook over boiling water until melted.

Stir until well blended, then add confectioners' sugar, vanilla, and salt and stir until smooth.

Add nuts and pour into buttered pan. Cut when cool.

Allow to cool thoroughly before eating. The fudge will be somewhat soft when first cut but becomes firm overnight.

HOLIDAY CANDY SLICES

1 cup brown sugar (packed)
1 cup sugar
3/4 cup water
1/4 teaspoon cream of tartar
1 teaspoon vanilla
3/4 cup chopped or ready-diced almonds

Combine sugars, water, and cream of tartar; stir over low heat until sugar is dissolved. Heat to boiling, cover and boil slowly 3 or 4 minutes, to dissolve any crystals on sides of pan. Uncover, and boil without stirring to medium hard ball (242° F.).

Pour out at once onto platter which has been rinsed in cold water. Allow to cool until barely warm. Add vanilla and stir until creamy.

Shape with hands into two rolls, 1-inch in diameter. Roll each in almonds, wrap in waxed paper and allow to set until firm. Cut into slices with sharp knife. Makes about 1 1/2 pounds.

Holiday Candy Slices

Miscellaneous Cooked Candies

COCONUT KISSES

1/2 cup evaporated milk, undiluted
1/2 cup sugar
2 cups shredded coconut
1/4 teaspoon almond extract

Combine ingredients. Drop from a teaspoon onto a well oiled (not buttered) baking sheet.

Bake in a slow oven (325° F.) 15 minutes. Remove from pan while hot.

CHOCOLATE SLICES

8 cups corn flakes or 2 cups packaged corn flake crumbs
1/2 cup soft butter or margarine
1/3 cup sugar
1/3 cup cocoa
1 egg, slightly beaten
1 teaspoon vanilla
1 cup shredded or flaked coconut
1/2 cup chopped nutmeats
1/4 cup soft butter or margarine
1 teaspoon vanilla
2 cups sifted confectioners' sugar
2 tablespoons milk

If using corn flakes, crush into fine crumbs. Combine 1/2 cup butter, sugar, cocoa, and egg, in top of double boiler. Cook over hot but not boiling water, stirring constantly until mixture is well-blended and slightly thickened. Remove from heat. Add 1 teaspoon vanilla.

Add coconut, nutmeats, and corn flake crumbs; mix well. Press into ungreased 8 x 8-inch pan. Chill.

Beat 1/4 cup butter until soft; add 1 teaspoon vanilla and confectioners' sugar gradually, stirring until well-blended. Stir in just enough milk so that mixture will spread easily. Spread over chocolate mixture. Chill.

Cover with Chocolate Glaze. Cut into squares to serve. Makes 25 1 1/2-inch squares.

Chocolate Glaze: Melt 2 squares (2 ounces) unsweetened chocolate with 1 tablespoon butter or margarine over hot but not boiling water; mix well. Spread over vanilla mixture.

Chocolate Slices

COFFEE FUDGE

1 cup water
2 teaspoons instant coffee
1/2 cup milk
1 1/2 cups granulated sugar
1 1/2 cups firmly packed brown sugar
1/8 teaspoon salt
1/4 cup margarine
1 teaspoon vanilla
3 1-ounce squares semi-sweet chocolate

Heat water in 2-quart saucepan. Add instant coffee and stir to dissolve.

Add milk, sugars, and salt. Mix well. Bring to boil and cook to 230°F. on candy thermometer. At this stage syrup begins to spin a thread.

Add margarine. Continue cooking over moderate heat to 235°F., or until a scant teaspoon of syrup dropped into a cup of cold water forms a soft ball.

Remove from heat and pour into large bowl. Do not scrape sides of pan. Let cool without stirring to 110–115°F. Then stir until creamy.

Add vanilla and continue stirring until candy becomes thick and cheese-like.

Rub palms of hands lightly with margarine and knead candy in bowl until soft and creamy.

Break off bits and roll in hand to form date-shaped pieces. Or roll into long roll and cut into 1 1/2-inch lengths.

Put pieces on margarined baking sheet or shallow pan. Cover with waxed paper and let stand 10 to 15 minutes.

Melt semi-sweet chocolate in small pitcher set into hot water. Stir smooth. Pour in thin stream over pieces of candy. If preferred, dip ends of pieces into chocolate and then into chopped coconut or nuts.

Store in tightly closed container, or pack in waxed paper-lined boxes and store in freezer. Makes about 1 3/4 pounds or 65 pieces.

CHOCOLATE BONBONS
(Chocolate Dipping)

Melt very slowly in top part of double boiler a good quality of specially prepared dipping chocolate, sweetened or unsweetened. Do not heat water under chocolate above 120°F. (slightly more than lukewarm), since overheating spoils chocolate for dipping. Stir constantly while melting to keep constant temperature.

When melted, beat thoroughly. Keep heat very low while dipping.

To dip centers, use a fork or confectioners' dipper. Drop a center into chocolate. Cover completely with chocolate. Remove with dipping fork. Drop onto waxed paper.

The room in which dipping is done should be cool, so that chocolate may harden quickly.

Fruit, nuts, mints, plain fondant, and other candies may be dipped in chocolate. One pound dipping chocolate will cover 70 to 80 assorted centers.

TURKISH PASTE

3 tablespoons (3 envelopes) unflavored gelatin
1/2 cup cold water
1/2 cup hot water
1 pound (2 1/4 cups) sugar
1/4 teaspoon salt
3 tablespoons lemon juice
Green food coloring
Mint flavoring
1 cup finely chopped nuts

Soften gelatin in cold water for 5 minutes. Bring hot water and sugar to boiling point. Add salt and gelatin. Stir until gelatin has dissolved. Simmer 20 minutes.

Remove from heat and when cool add lemon juice, coloring, and mint flavoring. Stir in nuts.

Let mixture stand until it begins to thicken. Stir again before pouring into a pan that has been rinsed with cold water. Have the layer of paste about 1-inch thick.

Let stand overnight in cool place. Moisten sharp knife in boiling water. Cut candy in cubes. Roll in powdered sugar.

FROSTED PEANUT SQUARES

1 cup brown sugar, firmly packed
1 cup peanut butter
1 cup corn syrup
2 cups salted peanuts
10 cups corn flakes

Combine sugar, peanut butter, and corn syrup in large saucepan. Cook and stir until mixture begins to bubble (185°F.).

Remove from heat; stir in peanuts and corn flakes. Press warm mixture evenly and firmly into buttered 15 x 10-inch pan. Cool; frost with fudge icing or melted chocolate and butterscotch pieces, if desired. Cut into squares when firm. Makes 60 1 1/2-inch squares.

Frosted Peanut Squares

ORANGE CREAM BON BONS

3 cups sugar
½ cup evaporated milk
⅔ cup orange juice
½ cup (1 stick) butter
1 tablespoon grated orange rind
½ cup chopped nuts
6 ounces (6 squares) semi-sweet chocolate

Combine sugar, evaporated milk, orange juice, and butter in a saucepan. Stir constantly until the mixture boils. Boil, stirring occasionally, to a soft ball stage, 236°F.

Remove from heat and cool to lukewarm. Beat until thick enough to knead, then turn out onto a wooden board.

This candy may get quite hard in the pan, but it will soften up when kneaded.

Divide it in two equal parts, and into one half knead the grated orange rind and into the other the chopped nuts.

Wrap in waxed paper and refrigerate for several days to mellow. When ready to use, shape the candy into balls.

Melt the chocolate over low heat. Dip the balls into the chocolate until well coated, remove with a spoon, place on waxed paper until the chocolate hardens. Makes 4 dozen pieces.

FRENCH CHOCOLATES

2 1-ounce squares unsweetened chocolate
1⅓ cups (15-ounce can) sweetened condensed milk

Melt chocolate in double boiler. Add milk and stir over boiling water 5 minutes until mixture thickens.

Finish in one of the following ways and chill 2 hours before serving. Makes about 1 pound.

Chocolate Nut Balls: Drop by teaspoonful into finely chopped nuts and roll until well covered with nuts.

Chocolate Fruit Balls: Add chopped dates, raisins, nuts, or quartered marshmallows to chocolate mixture. Form in balls and roll in cocoa or cocoa and confectioners' sugar, which have been mixed.

SOUR CREAM PANOCHA

3 cups light brown sugar
½ cup granulated sugar
1½ cups thick sour cream
1 tablespoon butter
½ cup broken nutmeats

Combine sugars, sour cream, and butter and cook to soft ball stage (236° F.). Cool to lukewarm and beat until mixture loses its gloss.

Add nuts just before end of beating period. Pour into buttered pan. Cut when hardened.

ALMOND BRITTLE

3 cups corn flakes
½ cup seedless raisins
½ cup coarsely chopped blanched almonds
1 cup sugar
½ teaspoon butter
⅛ cup vinegar
¼ cup water
¼ teaspoon salt

Combine corn flakes, raisins, and almonds in large pan and warm in oven.

Boil remaining ingredients to hard crack stage (300°F.).

Pour slowly over corn flake-almond mixture, blending lightly but thoroughly.

Spread in pan lined with waxed paper. When cool, break or cut in pieces. Makes 1 pound.

COFFEE COCOA FUDGE

2 tablespoons shortening
5 tablespoons hot coffee
¼ teaspoon salt
1 pound (3½ cups) sifted confectioners' sugar
¼ cup cocoa

Place shortening and the hot coffee in top of double boiler and heat over boiling water until shortening is melted.

Mix salt, sugar, and cocoa and sift together. Stir in confectioners' sugar in 3 installments, beating thoroughly after each addition. If necessary, add a little more hot coffee.

When mixture is well blended and smooth, remove at once from hot water, pour in greased 7 x 7-inch pan and cut in squares.

QUICK BRAZIL NUT FUDGE

4 squares (4 ounces) chocolate
2 tablespoons butter
¼ teaspoon salt
1 teaspoon vanilla
1 pound sifted confectioners' sugar
⅓ cup milk
1 cup chopped Brazil nuts
Whole Brazil nuts

Melt chocolate and butter over low heat. Stir in salt and vanilla. Stir in sugar alternately with the milk, keeping pan over hot water.

Remove from heat and stir in chopped Brazil nuts.

Pour fudge into a 7-inch square pan. Garnish with Brazil nuts, cut in halves. Let stand several hours. Cut in squares.

WALNUT CLUSTERS

Break up ½ pound sweet cooking chocolate and melt over hot water, stirring constantly. Stir in 1½ cups broken walnut meats.

Drop by tablespoons onto waxed paper. Chill. Makes 24 clusters.

CANTONESE FUDGE

1 pound brown sugar
Few grains salt
1 tablespoon light corn syrup
1 tablespoon butter
¾ cup evaporated milk
1 teaspoon vanilla
¼ cup finely cut candied ginger

Mix sugar, salt, syrup, butter, and milk thoroughly in heavy saucepan.

Cook over medium heat to soft ball stage (237°F.), stirring constantly. Cool.

Stir in vanilla and candied ginger. Beat until crystalline.

Turn into buttered pan. Mark in squares. Makes 1⅛ pounds.

MOLASSES NUT CRUNCH

1 cup unsulphured molasses
1 cup sugar
1 tablespoon butter or margarine
¼ teaspoon baking soda
2½ cups chopped peanuts or other nuts

Combine unsulphured molasses, sugar, and butter or margarine in a 2-quart saucepan. Place over low heat and stir until sugar is dissolved.

Cook over medium heat until syrup, when dropped in very cold water, separates into threads which are hard but not brittle, or until candy thermometer reaches 270°F.

Remove from heat; stir in baking soda. Add nuts. Turn into a greased 8-inch square pan; spread quickly.

When candy is slightly cool, cut into squares. Wrap in waxed paper. Makes about 1¾ pounds.

CHRISTMAS DIVINITY FUDGE

2 cups sugar
½ cup water
¼ cup light corn syrup
⅛ teaspoon salt
2 egg whites
1 teaspoon vanilla
¼ teaspoon almond extract
Few drops pink food coloring
½ cup glacé cherries, halved
¼ cup citron, sliced

Heat sugar, water, syrup, and salt, stirring until sugar is dissolved. Boil to 255°F. (firm ball in cold water).

In a large bowl beat egg whites until stiff but not dry; pour the syrup mixture slowly into them, beating with a wire whisk until mixture holds up in peaks.

Add vanilla and almond extract, pink coloring, and fruits. Pour into a greased 8-inch square pan or drop from the tip of a spoon onto waxed paper.

Remove candy from pan before cutting. Store in airtight container. Makes about 1½ pounds.

Note: If candy is over-beaten and becomes dry, add a small amount of water to soften it and to restore the glaze.

CANNING

Canning is a method of food preservation by the use of heat and airtight containers with retention of the maximum amount of flavor, texture, and food value.

Tiny organisms—molds, yeasts, and bacteria—are normally present in fruits, vegetables, and meats, and will eventually cause fresh foods to spoil. The aim in canning is to destroy or inactivate by heat the action of the microorganisms. Molds, yeasts, and bacteria are present at all times in the air, water, and soil.

In the canning process fruits and vegetables are heated sufficiently to stop the action of these tiny organisms with the exception of some types of bacteria. There are certain heat-resistant bacteria that go through a spore phase in their life cycle, a form in which they are very difficult to kill.

In canning foods high in acid, like fruits, tomatoes, and pickled beets, the spores are readily destroyed at the boiling temperature in a reasonable length of time. In all vegetables other than tomatoes it may take 12 to 15 hours or more to destroy or inactivate the spores at the boiling temperature.

If cooked at 10 pounds pressure in a steam pressure cooker, these same spores are destroyed in less than 1 hour.

On the other hand the enzymes are useful to a degree in that they are responsible for the normal ripening process of fruits and vegetables. They will, however, cause decay after the normal ripening point has been reached if their action is not stopped. Extreme heat or extreme cold will inhibit and delay the action of enzymes.

DIRECTIONS FOR USING BOILING WATER BATH

This method is used for fruits and acid vegetables (tomatoes).

Any big, clean vessel will do for a boiling-water canner, if it's deep enough to let water boil well over tops of the jars at least 2 inches, has a tight-fitting lid, and a rack to keep the jars at least ½ inch from the bottom of the vessel.

Place rack in canner. Fill with boiling water. Jars must be hot when placed in the canner. If necessary, heat in hot water.

Bring water to a rolling boil. If necessary, add water to keep jars covered 2 inches.

When processing time is completed open cover by tilting toward you so that steam will not come in contact with face and hands.

Remove jars one at a time. Complete seal. (See directions.)

DIRECTIONS FOR USING PRESSURE CANNER

Use only this method for processing all non-acid vegetables and meats.

Follow manufacturer's directions carefully for use and care of cooker.

Each time cooker is used, be sure it contains enough water to come just below the level of rack (1 to 2 inches of water).

Place jars on rack, leaving ample space between jars for free circulation of steam.

Adjust cover and fasten on securely.

Air must be exhausted by leaving petcock open until a steady stream of steam escapes for 5 to 10 minutes.

Close petcock. Allow pressure to rise to specified point, counting pressure time when gauge reaches desired pressure.

Maintain constant pressure by regulation of heat.

When processing time is completed remove cooker from heat.

Do not open cooker until pressure gauge registers zero. Cool slowly until zero point is registered.

Slowly open petcock until all steam has escaped.

To open cover, tilt toward you, so escaping steam will not burn face or hands.

Let jars stand a few minutes before removing one at a time.

Complete seal (see directions).

HIGH ALTITUDE ADJUSTMENTS

Adjust cooking time or pressure to match the altitude. For water bath, add 1 minute to the processing time, if time specified is 20 minutes or less, for each 1,000 feet above sea level. Add 2 minutes for every 1,000 feet if the time called for is more than 20 minutes. For a pressure cooker, increase pressure 1 pound for each 2,000 feet.

CANNING TOOLS

Gather together tools needed for canning before beginning to work.

Use good cooking utensils with tight-fitting lids, measuring cups, a wire basket, or plenty of cheesecloth, bowls, a colander, large spoons, a ladle, a sharp knife or two, plenty of clean towels, dishcloths, and pot holders.

A wide-mouthed funnel, wire clamps, or tongs for removing hot jar from pressure canner or water bath are helpful aids.

CHECKING JARS AND COVERS

Inspect jars carefully for possible defects, cracks, chips, or dents.

Have ample supply of jar tops, new rubbers, or self-sealing lids. Make sure they fit. Do not reuse rubber rings or self-sealing lids. Check to see that zinc screw lids have no loose linings. Clamp lids must be tight. If necessary, remove top clamp, bend down in center, and bend in sides to tighten.

PREPARING JARS AND COVERS

Wash jars, caps, and rubber rings in soapy water. Rinse with clear hot water.

Sterilize by placing jars, caps, and rings in pan of hot water with a rack or cloth on the bottom of it.

Bring to a boil just before ready to fill jars.

Do not boil metal caps with self-sealing compound. Just dip in boiling water before using.

PACKING JARS

Remove 1 jar at a time from water. Pack hot jars as quickly as possible and seal immediately.

Keep jars in hot water or on cloth or several layers of paper while packing.

Don't pack food too solidly or heat will not penetrate thoroughly.

Using knife blade, work out any air bubbles formed in jar.

When packed always wipe food particles with clean damp cloth from rim of jar and from rubber ring.

COOLING JARS

Never invert jars of any type after processing—even for a moment.

Place jars on several thicknesses of cloth or newspaper.

Avoid drafts. Leave air space between jars.

Never cover jars while cooling.

LABELING JARS

After jars have cooled for 24 hours, wipe clean, label with name, date, and with lot number, if more than one lot is prepared.

STORING JARS

Store jars upright in cool, dry, dark place. Handle jars a minimum amount.

CHECKING JARS

Examine jars after week or ten days for signs of spoilage.

Remove and dispose of spoiled jars of food immediately.

OPENING JARS

To open glass-top or zinc screw lids, pull out jar rubber with a pair of pliers.

To open self-sealing metal lids puncture top and lift up.

On opening canned foods, odor should be characteristic of product with no outrush of air or liquid.

Never taste to test for spoilage.

Before every serving, all home-canned meats and vegetables (except tomatoes) should be cooked at boiling temperature for at least 10 minutes (spinach and other leafy vegetables for 15 minutes) in a covered container even when they are to be served cold.

HOW TO CLOSE LIDS

Metal self-sealing lids: Use only on jars with smooth, even top edges.

Put lid in place with sealing compound touching rim of jar, attach screw band, then hold your index finger on lid so it won't slip while you screw band down firmly without exerting unusual force.

Don't invert, move, or handle jars for at least 24 hours after processing.

Screw bands may be removed and re-used.

Test seal by tapping lids gently with a spoon. If properly sealed, they will sound a clear, ringing note, and the lid will have a slight dip caused by the vacuum inside.

If lids bulge upward and give off a dull sound when tapped, the seal is imperfect. If seal is imperfect, open and use the food at once or immediately replace the lid with a new one and reprocess the jar for half the original time.

Glass top self-sealing lids: Use on jars with smooth, even rims free of nicks, cracks, or sharp edges.

Leave 1 inch of space in top of jar regardless of type of food being canned.

Fit wet rubber ring around projection on under side of glass lid.

Place lid so rubber lies between lid and top edge of jar.

Turn bands tight, then loosen slightly (about 1/4 turn). Bands must fit loosely during processing.

Immediately after processing, screw bands tightly to complete seal.

Remove bands 24 hours after canning, and test seal by pulling on lid gently with the finger tips.

If screw bands are not replaced on jars, handle jars gently to prevent breaking the seal.

Do not turn filled jars upside down.

Clamp lids: Place rubber on ridge. Fasten top clamp only.

Process. Then snap down side clamp. Do not invert jars.

Zinc screw lids: Place rubber ring on sealing shoulder of jar. Screw lid down until lid and rubber ring just touch.

After processing, tighten lids the moment jars are removed.

Do not invert jars after processing.

SYRUPS FOR CANNING FRUITS

Thin syrup: Use 1 part sugar and 3 parts juice or water. Bring to a boil, keep hot.

Use on apples, blueberries, huckleberries, pears, pineapple, sweet cherries.

Medium syrup: Use 1 part sugar and 2 parts juice or water. Bring to a boil. Keep hot.

Use on apricots, blackberries, peaches, plums, raspberries, strawberries, gooseberries, sour cherries, rhubarb.

Thick or heavy syrup: Use 1 part sugar and 1 part juice or water. Bring to a boil. Keep hot.

Use on larger sour fruits.

Variations:

Honey may be used to replace as much as half the sugar required.

Corn syrup may be used to replace as much as 1/3 of the sugar required.

Do not use sweeteners that have a strong flavor, such as brown sugar or sorghum.

CANNING POINTERS

Use only the very best fresh foods for canning. The finished product will not be any better than what went into it.

Fruits and vegetables should be canned while they are fresh and at their best. The fresher the fruits and vegetables the higher their vitamin content and the lower the bacteria count.

Most vegetables are best before they are fully matured, so choose young, fresh vegetables.

Select fresh, firm, ripe fruits.

Remove any spots and bruises which may cause spoilage.

Sort and wash carefully, removing all traces of sand and dirt.

To keep apples, peaches, and pears from turning dark after peeling, place in a solution of 2 tablespoons each of salt and vinegar to gallon of water.

Scald peaches and tomatoes in boiling water for 1 minute to loosen skin, then dip into cold water 1/2 minute and remove skin.

Canning Vegetables in Pressure Cooker

ASPARAGUS

Select fresh, tender asparagus. Sort. Wash thoroughly, and trim off scales.

Long Pieces: Cut stalks into lengths to fit upright in container. Tie in bundles.

Place upright in kettle, with boiling water to cover lower part of stalks. Cover tightly. Boil 3 minutes.

Pack hot, removing string as asparagus slips into containers.

Add 1/2 teaspoon salt to each pint. Cover with fresh boiling water.

Process at 10-pound pressure: pint jars, 25 minutes; quart jars, 55 minutes, and No. 2 and No. 2 1/2 cans, 20 minutes.

Short Pieces: Cut stalks into 1-inch lengths. Cover with boiling water and boil 3 minutes.

Pack hot into containers. Add 1/2 teaspoon salt to each pint and cover with boiling water.

Process same as above.

Allow 2 to 3 pounds for each quart.

BEANS (Lima)

Select young, tender beans. Shell and wash. Cover with boiling water and bring to a boil.

Pack hot. Add 1/2 teaspoon salt to each pint and cover with boiling water.

Process at 10-pound pressure: pint jars, 35 minutes; quart jars, 60 minutes,

Beans (Lima), Continued

and No. 2 and No. 2½ cans, 40 minutes.

Allow 4 to 5 pounds beans (in pods) for each quart jar.

BEANS (fresh green soybeans)

Cover shelled beans with boiling water and boil 3 or 4 minutes.

Pack hot, and add ½ teaspoon salt to each pint. Cover with fresh boiling water.

Process at 10-pound pressure: pint jars or No. 2 cans, 60 minutes, and quart jars, 70 minutes.

Allow 4 to 5 pounds beans (in pods) for each quart jar.

BEANS (snap)

Wash thoroughly, trim off ends, and remove strings if stringy. Cut into pieces (½ to 1 inch) or cut lengthwise or leave whole.

Cover with boiling water and boil 5 minutes.

Pack hot. Add ½ teaspoon salt to each pint and cover with fresh boiling water.

Process at 10-pound pressure: pint jars, 20 minutes; quart jars and No. 2 cans, 25 minutes, and No. 2½ cans, 30 minutes.

Allow 1½ to 2 pounds for each quart.

THIS IS THE WAY TO CAN GREEN BEANS

1. Check jars for nicks, cracks, and sharp edges. Wash jars and caps in hot soapy water; rinse. Leave jars in hot water until ready to use. Use new lids and good bands.

2. Thoroughly wash freshly gathered beans, which are young, tender, and crisp in several changes of water. Lift beans out of water and drain.

3. Trim ends; remove any strings; cut or break into pieces. Prepare only enough for one canner load.

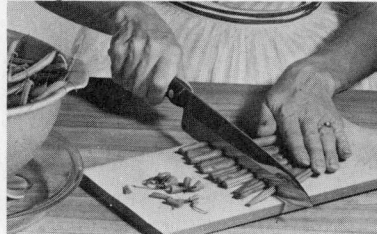

4. Cover beans with boiling water and boil for 5 minutes, or pack raw.

5. Stand hot jar on wood or cloth. Add 1 teaspoon salt per quart; cover beans with boiling water, leaving 1-inch head space.

6. Wipe top and threads of jar with clean, damp cloth. Put lid on, red rubber sealing compound next to jar. Screw band down evenly and tight.

7. Put jars into steam-pressure canner containing 2 to 3 inches of hot water, or the amount recommended by the manufacturer.

8. Place canner over heat. Lock cover according to the manufacturer's instructions.

9. Leave vent open until steam escapes steadily for 10 minutes. Close vent. At altitudes less than 2,000 feet above sea level bring pressure to 10 pounds. Keep pressure steady for 20 minutes for pints, 25 minutes for quarts.

10. Remove canner from heat. Let pressure fall to zero. Wait 2 minutes. Slowly open vent. Open canner. Remove jars. Do not tighten bands.

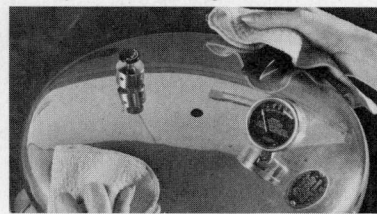

11. Stand jars several inches apart, out of drafts, to cool for about 12 hours. Remove bands.

12. Test the seal by pressing center of lid. If dome is down, or stays down when pressed, jar is sealed. Store without bands in dry, dark, reasonably cool place.

BEETS

Select tender baby beets. Trim off tops, leaving 1 inch of stems. Wash thoroughly.

Cook in boiling water about 15 minutes or steam until skins slip off easily. Skin and trim. Or peel beets before boiling them.

Leave small beets whole. Cut large beets in sections.

Pack quickly into containers before beets cool. Add ½ teaspoon salt to each pint. Cover with fresh boiling water (1 teaspoon vinegar added to each pint will help to retain the red color).

Process at 10-pound pressure: pint jars, 25 minutes; quart jars, 55 minutes, and No. 2 and No. 2½ cans, 30 minutes.

Allow 2½ to 3 pounds fresh beets (without tops) for each quart jar.

Note: Pickled beets may be processed in boiling-water bath.

CARROTS

Select tender carrots. Wash thoroughly. If desired, remove skins by scraping.

Leave small carrots whole. Cut large carrots into lengthwise quarters or cubes.

Cover with boiling water. Boil 5 minutes.

Pack hot into containers. Add ½ teaspoon salt to each pint. Cover with boiling water—the same water in which the carrots were cooked.

Process at 10-pound pressure: pint jars and No. 2 cans, 20 minutes, and quart jars and No. 2½ cans, 25 minutes.

Allow about 2½ pounds fresh carrots (without tops) for each quart jar.

CORN

Use freshly picked corn in the milk stage. Work with small quantities at a time and complete the whole canning process as quickly as possible. Husk and silk the corn, using a stiff brush, if necessary, to remove the silk.

Cut corn from cob so that kernels are whole. Do *not* scrape the cob.

Add ½ as much boiling water as corn. Heat to boiling point.

Pack into pint glass jars, or No. 2 C-enameled tin cans. Add ½ teaspoon salt and ½ to 1 teaspoon sugar, if desired, to each pint.

Process at 10-pound pressure: pint jars, 55 minutes; quart jars, 85 minutes, and No. 2 and No. 2½ cans, 60 minutes.

Allow 8 to 12 ears for each quart jar.

PEAS

Select young, tender peas. Wash pods and shell only enough to fill containers to be processed at one time. Wash shelled peas. Cover with boiling water and bring to boiling point.

Pack hot into pint jars or No. 2 cans. Add ½ teaspoon salt and ½ teaspoon sugar, if desired, to each pint. Cover with boiling water.

Process at 10-pound pressure: pint and quart jars, 40 minutes, and No. 2 and 2½ cans, 30 minutes.

Allow 2 to 2½ pounds unshelled peas for each pint jar.

PUMPKIN AND SQUASH

Wash and peel pumpkin and winter squash; do not peel summer squash. Cut into 1-inch cubes. Boil or steam until tender and press through colander. Heat to simmering (190°F.).

Pack hot. Add ½ teaspoon salt to each pint if desired.

Process at 10-pound pressure: pint jars, 60 minutes; quart jars, 80 minutes; No. 2 cans, 75 minutes, and No. 2½ cans, 90 minutes.

Allow 2 to 2½ pounds fresh pumpkin or squash for each quart jar.

SPINACH OR OTHER GREENS

Pick over and wash greens carefully. Discard imperfect leaves and tough stems.

Heat greens in covered kettle containing small amount of water until completely wilted.

Pack into pint jars or No. 2 cans, being careful not to pack too solidly. Add ½ teaspoon salt to each pint and cover greens with boiling water.

Process at 10-pound pressure: pint jars, 45 minutes; quart jars, 70 minutes; No. 2 cans, 60 minutes, and No. 2½ cans, 75 minutes.

Allow 2 to 3 pounds for each quart jar.

Canning Fruits and Vegetables in Boiling Water Bath

APPLES

Wash, pare, and cut apples into pieces of desired size.

Prepare only as many as can be processed at one time.

Boil in thin syrup 5 minutes. Pack hot into jars. Cover with boiling syrup.

There is less shrinkage by this method and the jars are better filled. Process, in boiling water bath, pint or quart jars or No. 2½ cans 15 minutes. No. 2 cans, 10 minutes.

Allow 2 to 3 pounds of apples for each quart jar.

APRICOTS

Wash, cut into halves, and remove pits. (If they are to be peeled, scald in boiling water to loosen skins before cutting.)

Cold Pack: Pack apricots in glass jars. Cover with boiling syrup.

Process, in boiling water bath, pint or quart jars 30 minutes.

Hot Pack: Simmer 3 to 5 minutes in thin or medium syrup.

Pack apricots hot into containers. Cover with boiling syrup.

Process, in boiling water bath, pint or quart jars or No. 2½ cans 20 minutes; No. 2 cans, 15 minutes.

BEETS, PICKLED

Select tender beets. Wash thoroughly.

Cook in boiling water, or steam 10 minutes or until skins slip easily. Remove skins.

Leave small beets whole. Cut large beets into sections.

Pack quickly into containers before beets cool.

Add ½ teaspoon salt, 1 teaspoon or more of sugar, and 3 to 6 whole cloves, if desired, to each pint.

Cover with boiling vinegar (unless vinegar is very strong, use it full strength).

Process, in boiling water bath, pint or quart jars 30 minutes.

CHERRIES

Wash and pit cherries.

Cold Pack: Pack into jars. Cover with boiling syrup.

Process pint jars in boiling water bath 20 minutes, quart jars 25 minutes.

Hot Pack: Add ½ to 1 cup sugar to each quart of cherries.

Bring slowly to boiling point. Boil 2 minutes.

Pack hot into glass jars or sanitary R-enamel cans. Cover with boiling syrup.

Process, in boiling water bath, pint or quart jars or No. 2 or 2½ cans 15 minutes.

Allow 1½ to 2 quarts cherries for each quart jar.

GOOSEBERRIES

Wash berries and remove stems.

Cold Pack: Pack into containers. Cover with boiling syrup.

Process, in boiling water bath, pint or quart jars 20 minutes.

Hot Pack: Cover with boiling medium syrup. Boil 1 or 2 minutes. Pack into jars or cans.

Process, in boiling water bath, pint or quart jars or No. 2½ cans 15 minutes; No. 2 cans, 10 minutes.

Allow 1½ to 2 quarts fresh berries for each quart jar.

THIS IS THE WAY TO CAN PEACHES

1. Check jars. Be sure there are no nicks, cracks, or sharp edges. Use new lids.

2. Wash and rinse jars and caps. Leave jars in hot water until ready to use.

3. Sort, wash, and drain only enough firm-ripe peaches for one canner load. Fill water-bath canner half full with hot water. Put canner on to heat. Prepare sugar syrup.

4. Put peaches in wire basket or cheesecloth. Dip peaches into boiling water ½ to 1 minute to loosen skins. Dip into cold water. Drain.

5. Cut peaches into halves, pit and peel. Drop halves into salt-vinegar water (2 tablespoons each to 1 gallon cold water). Rinse before packing.

6. Stand hot jar on rubber tray, wood or cloth. Pack peaches, cavity-side down, layers overlapping. Leave ½-inch head space.

7. Cover peaches with boiling hot syrup, leaving ½-inch head space. It will take 1 to 1½ cups syrup for each quart jar.

8. Run rubber bottle scraper or similar non-metal utensil between fruit and jar to release air bubbles. Add more syrup, if needed.

9. Wipe top and threads of jar with clean, damp cloth. Put lid on; screw band tight . . . it must screw down evenly to hold red rubber sealing compound against top of jar.

10. As each jar is filled, stand it on rack in canner. Water should be hot, but not boiling. If needed, add more water to cover jars 1 to 2 inches. Put cover on canner.

11. Bring water to a boil. At altitudes less than 1,000 feet above sea level process pints 25 minutes, quarts 30 minutes, at gentle but steady boil.

12. Remove jars from canner. Let cool for about 12 hours. Remove bands. Test for seal by pressing center of lid. If dome is down, or stays down when pressed, jar is sealed. Store without bands in dry, dark, reasonably cool place.

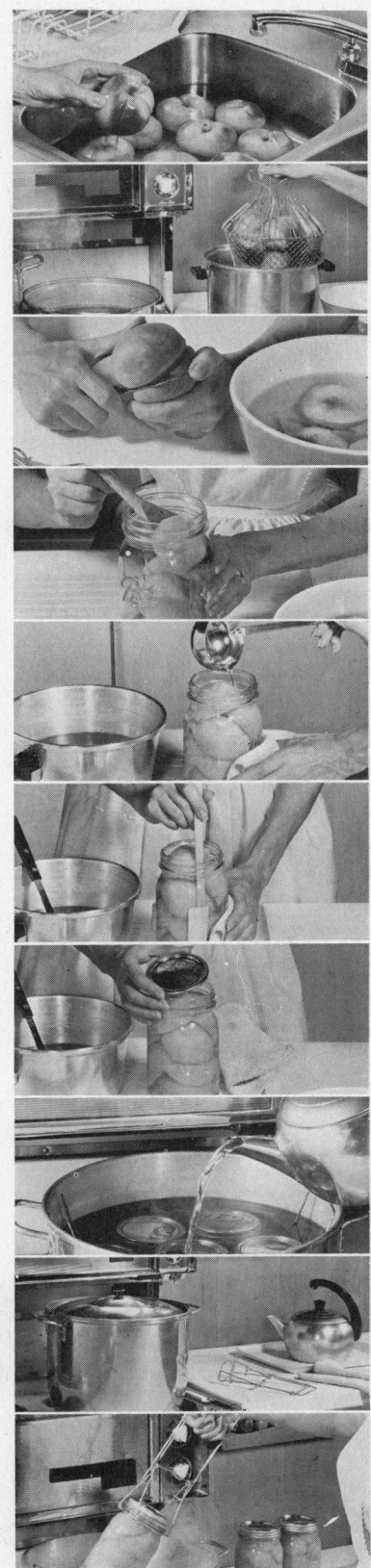

PEACHES

Select ripe, firm peaches. Plunge into boiling water to loosen skins. Remove and plunge into cold water. Peel.

Prepare only as many as can be processed at one time.

Cold Pack: Pack peaches into glass jars. Cover with boiling syrup.

Process, in boiling water bath, pint or quart jars 30 minutes.

Hot Pack: Simmer 3 to 5 minutes in syrup.

Pack peaches into containers. Cover with boiling syrup.

Process, in boiling water bath, pint or quart jars or No. 2 or 2½ cans 20 minutes.

Allow 2 to 2½ pounds fresh fruit for each quart jar.

PEARS

Wash, peel, cut in half, and remove core. Prepare only as many as can be processed at one time. Drain.

Boil in thin or medium syrup 4 to 8 minutes, according to size and softness.

Pack pears into containers. Cover with boiling syrup.

Process, in boiling water bath, pint or quart jars or No. 2 or 2½ cans 20 minutes.

Allow 2 to 2½ pounds fresh pears for each quart.

PINEAPPLE

Peel, core, and remove "eyes." Slice or cut in pieces.

Boil pineapple in thin syrup 5 minutes.

Pack into containers. Cover with boiling syrup.

Process, in boiling water bath, pint or quart jars or No. 2½ cans 30 minutes; No. 2 cans, 25 minutes.

Allow 1 large pineapple for each quart jar.

PLUMS

Wash. Prick each plum to prevent bursting of skin.

Cold Pack: Pack plums into glass jars. Cover with boiling syrup (medium or thick).

Process pint jars 20 minutes, quart jars 25 minutes, in boiling water bath.

Hot Pack: Simmer in medium syrup 5 minutes.

Pack plums into containers. Cover with boiling syrup.

Process, in boiling water bath, pint or quart jars or No. 2 to 2½ cans 15 minutes.

Allow 2 to 2½ pounds for each quart jar.

RHUBARB

Select young, tender rhubarb. Wash, cut into ½-inch lengths, but do not skin.

Boil rhubarb in water or syrup until soft. Pack boiling hot into glass jars.

Process, in boiling water bath, pint or quart jars 10 minutes.

Allow 1½ to 2 pounds for each quart jar.

RASPBERRIES (BLACK)

Wash carefully, remove caps, and drain.

Cold Pack: Fill glass jars, shaking or jarring against hand to make a more solid pack. Cover with boiling syrup (medium or thick).

Process, in boiling water bath, pint or quart jars 20 minutes.

Hot Pack: Boil berries in medium syrup 2 minutes.

Pack into containers. Cover with boiling syrup.

Process, in boiling water bath, pint or quart jars or No. 2½ cans 15 minutes; No. 2 cans, 10 minutes.

Allow 1½ to 2 quarts fresh berries for each quart jar.

RASPBERRIES (RED)

Wash berries, being careful not to crush them. Drain.

Pack into glass jars or sanitary R-enamel cans, alternating berries and boiling red syrup until containers are filled.

Process the same as black raspberries.

To prepare red syrup, use overripe or soft berries not firm enough for canning. Heat slowly to boiling point using ½ cup water to 1 cup berries.

Extract juice by straining through fine sieve or cheese cloth. To each cup of juice add ½ cup sugar. Bring slowly to boiling point.

Allow 1½ to 2 quarts fresh berries for each quart jar.

STRAWBERRIES

Wash, cap, and drain fresh, firm berries.

Heat Immediately: Add ½ to 1 cup sugar to each quart berries. Heat slowly to boiling point and let stand several hours or overnight.

Reheat slowly to boiling point. Pack berries hot into containers.

Process, in boiling water bath, pint or quart jars or No. 2½ cans 15 minutes; No. 2 cans, 10 minutes.

Heat Later: Add ½ to 1 cup sugar to each quart of berries, alternating layers of berries and sugar. Let stand several hours or overnight.

Heat slowly to boiling point. Pack

berries hot into containers. Process same as above.

Allow 1½ to 2 quarts fresh berries for each quart jar.

TOMATOES

Select firm, well-ripened tomatoes. Wash.

Scald, plunge in cold water to peel, and remove cores. Quarter.

Cold Pack: Pack tomatoes solidly into containers. Add ½ teaspoon salt to each pint. When packing tomatoes in glass jars, leave ½ inch head space. When using tin cans, leave ¼-inch head space.

Set in boiling water and keep there until contents in center of container are at least 160°F.

Partially seal glass jars. Seal tin cans.

Process, in boiling water bath, pint jars 35 minutes, quart jars 45 minutes, No. 2 or No. 2½ cans 45 minutes.

Hot Pack: Heat slowly to boiling point. Boil 2 minutes. Pack into containers.

Process, in boiling water bath, pint or quart jars or No. 2 or 2½ cans 10 minutes.

Allow 2½ to 3 pounds for each quart jar.

Canning Meats

Can only fresh meat from government-inspected-and-approved healthy animals, slaughtered and handled under strictly sanitary conditions. Beef, veal, lamb, mutton, and pork may be successfully canned at home.

Refrigerate the meat at a freezing temperature until ready for canning. If frozen, can it as soon as it thaws.

Meats may be processed by either the hot pack or the raw pack method.

Raw Pack: Cut up meat as for Hot Pack (see below); add salt if desired.

Pack raw, lean strips in clean, hot jars, leaving 1-inch head space.

Place open jars in large container of warm water filled up to about 2 inches from top of containers.

Cover vessel and boil slowly until meat is medium done, about 75 minutes in glass jars, 50 minutes in tin cans. Meat thermometer should register 170°F. in center of jar or can.

Add boiling stock or water to fill container.

Adjust covers; partially seal and process quart jars in pressure canner 70 minutes at 15-pound pressure.

Hot Pack: Use cuts suitable for chops, steaks, and roasts for canning large pieces; use less-tender cuts and smaller pieces for stew meat.

Cut meat away from bone, remove

all excess fat; use bones for soup. Cut meat across grain ½ to 1 inch thick or cut into cubes for stews.

Precook meat slowly in covered pan until about half done with just enough water or stock added to keep meat from sticking; stir or turn occasionally.

Do not coat meat with flour or cracker crumbs.

Do not fry meats for canning; they become hard and dry and develop an "off" flavor in processing.

Pack strips of hot meat at once in sterilized jars kept hot in boiling water. If salt is desired, add ½ teaspoon to each pint jar and 1 teaspoon to each quart.

Cover with hot broth (fat removed) or water, leaving 1-inch head space in jars. Work out air bubbles with knife.

Wipe jar rims; partially seal and process quarts in pressure canner 60 minutes at 15-pound pressure.

CANNING POULTRY

Select plump stewing hens for best flavor. Disjoint and cut into convenient pieces; sort meaty and bony pieces; set giblets aside.

Cover bony pieces with cold water; cook for stock. Drain broth into bowl; skim off fat.

Poultry should be bled well and hung in a cool place for 6 to 12 hours before canning.

Raw Pack: Wash thoroughly. Cut up poultry into convenient pieces; sort meaty and bony pieces; add salt if desired; pack into hot jars as directed for hot pack.

Place filled open jars in large container filled with warm water to about 2 inches from top of jars.

Cover vessel and boil slowly until meat is steaming hot and medium done, about 75 minutes for glass jars and 50 minutes for tin cans. Meat thermometer should register 170°F. for center of jar.

Process at once at 15-pound pressure for 60 minutes.

Hot Pack: Remove excess fat from meaty pieces. Pour hot broth or water over meat to cover; cover and simmer until about half done. When cut in center, pieces will show little or no pink color. Stir occasionally.

Add salt, if desired, ½ teaspoon to each pint and 1 teaspoon to each quart jar.

Pack second joints and drumsticks into hot jars with skin sides next to glass; place breast pieces in center; fit small pieces into spaces. Leave 1-inch head space in glass containers.

Cover meat with hot broth and work out air bubbles.

Partially seal and process at once for 60 minutes at 15-pound pressure.

CASSEROLES AND ONE-DISH MEALS

When you find it a problem to think of something to serve, prepare a casserole. A main dish casserole reduces the job of good menu planning to simplicity. It's the hostess' best friend and the busy homemaker's helper because it is often the solution to time-saving beforehand meal preparation. Usually casseroles can be prepared hours in advance, stored in the refrigerator ready for baking later, or can be three-fourths baked and finished just before serving.

Modern homemakers think of a casserole as a combination of protein (meat, fish, cheese, or eggs), an extender like a pasta (macaroni, spaghetti, noodles, etc.) or rice, all bound together with a sauce. A wisely chosen recipe will mean that you have used ingredients with flavors that blend well together, offer well-balanced nutrition, and are convenient to use. Since casseroles are generally range-to-table utensils, there's less trouble serving, less washing up to do afterward.

Beef Casseroles

SWISS STEAK EN CASSEROLE

2 pounds round steak
1/2 clove garlic
1 teaspoon salt
1/8 teaspoon pepper
About 1/2 cup flour
1/4 cup fat
1/2 cup chopped onions
1 cup grated carrots, green pepper, and chopped celery, combined
1 cup chopped tomatoes
1 cup boiling water
6 to 12 small potatoes, pared

Rub steak with garlic. Pound combined salt, pepper, and flour into it.

Cook onion until tender in hot fat in heavy skillet. Add steak and sear both sides. Transfer to casserole.

Combine vegetables and boiling water and add to seared steak.

Cover closely and cook in very slow oven (275°F.) until tender; about 2 hours.

About 40 minutes before meat is done, brown potatoes in a little fat; add to casserole. Serves 6.

ROUND OR CHUCK STEAK CASSEROLE

1 to 1 1/2 pounds round or chuck steak, cut 1/4-inch thick
2 teaspoons salt
1 teaspoon paprika
About 2 tablespoons flour
2 tablespoons fat
1 medium onion, sliced
4 small potatoes, sliced
1 cup canned tomatoes
1 tablespoon ketchup

Cut steak into 4 pieces. Season with 1 teaspoon salt and paprika. Coat with flour. Brown in hot fat in a heavy skillet. Transfer to casserole.

Place onion and potatoes over top. Mix tomatoes, ketchup, and remaining teaspoon salt; pour over potatoes.

Cover and bake in moderate oven (350°F.) until tender, about 1 1/4 hours. If necessary, add a little water. Serves 4.

Variations: Substitute breast of lamb or lamb riblets for beef.

SHORT RIBS—NEW ENGLAND STYLE

1 pound dried navy beans
1 No. 2 1/2 can tomatoes
2 tablespoons prepared mustard
1/2 cup molasses
3 tablespoons chopped onion
3 teaspoons salt
1/2 teaspoon pepper
3 pounds short ribs of beef

Soak navy beans if necessary. Add tomatoes and seasonings. Cover and cook slowly for 1 1/2 hours.

Brown short ribs on all sides. Add short ribs to beans.

Cover closely and cook slowly on top of range or in a slow oven (300°F.) for 2 hours. Serves 6.

HUNGARIAN GOULASH EN CASSEROLE

2 pounds beef chuck, cut in 2-inch cubes
1 cup chopped onions
6 tablespoons hot fat
1 tablespoon flour
1 1/2 teaspoons salt
1 tablespoon paprika
2 bouillon cubes in 2 cups boiling water or 2 cups stock
1 cup (8-ounce can) tomato sauce
2 cups peeled, diced tomatoes
1 clove garlic, chopped fine
1 Bouquet Garni, (see below)

Pan fry beef and onions in hot fat until onions are soft and yellow.

Stir in lightly the flour, salt, and paprika; cook 5 minutes. Add remaining ingredients and heat to boiling. Turn into heated casserole.

Bake in moderate oven (350°F.) until meat is tender, about 1 1/2 hours. Remove Bouquet Garni. Serve with hot macaroni. Serves 6.

Bouquet Garni: Tie in a small piece of cheesecloth, 1 bay leaf, 2 tablespoons chopped parsley, a blade of thyme, and a stalk of celery and leaves.

ROUND STEAK WITH TOMATOES AND CORN

1 1/2 pounds round steak, cut into 1 1/2-inch cubes
2 tablespoons fat
1 No. 2 can tomatoes, drained
1 cup whole kernel corn
1/2 teaspoon basil
Few grains nutmeg
Salt and pepper

Brown meat lightly in hot fat; transfer to casserole. Add tomatoes, corn, and seasoning.

Bake in moderate oven (350°F.) 25 to 30 minutes. Serves 4.

Prepare your casseroles in range-to-table dishes that either harmonize with or present pleasant color contrasts to the table dishes.

Beef Pot Pie

BEEF POT PIE

1½ pounds boneless beef (chuck, bottom round, neck)
2   tablespoons flour
2   tablespoons fat
1   cup chopped onion
2   cups hot water
2   teaspoons salt
4   whole cloves
1   bay leaf
4   carrots, sliced
4   potatoes, quartered
1   cup sliced celery
Pastry for 1-crust pie

Cut meat into 1-inch cubes, dust with the flour and brown slowly and thoroughly in the fat. To the browned meat add onion, water, salt, cloves, and bay leaf. Cover and simmer over low heat for 1½ hours.

Add vegetables. Cook for 30 minutes more or until vegetables are tender.

To make gravy, stir in 2 tablespoons flour mixed with ½ cup water. When thickened, place mixture in 1½-quart casserole.

Roll pastry to a circle the same size as casserole. Cut into 6 pie-shaped pieces and place on top of pie.

Bake in hot oven (425°F.) 25 to 30 minutes or until crust is browned. Serves 6.

BEEF STROGANOFF EN CASSEROLE

2   large mild onions, chopped fine
About 3 tablespoons butter
1¼ pounds round steak
Flour
½   pound fresh mushrooms, sliced
1   can condensed tomato soup
¼   cup sherry
1   cup beef bouillon or stock
Salt and pepper
Sour cream
Cooked noodles

Pan fry onions in butter until soft, then transfer to casserole.

Cut steak into narrow strips, 2 inches long. Roll meat in flour. Then brown in hot melted butter. Transfer meat to casserole.

Brown mushrooms in remaining butter, adding more butter if necessary.

Transfer mushrooms to casserole.

Combine soup, sherry, and bouillon and pour over contents of casserole. Season to taste with salt and pepper.

Bake in moderate oven (350°F.) until meat is tender, about 40 minutes.

Serve over hot cooked noodles, topping each portion with sour cream. Serves 4 to 5.

BEEF AND VEGETABLE PIE

1½ pounds beef (chuck, round, or shoulder arm, cut in 1-inch cubes)
2   tablespoons fat or bacon drippings
1½ teaspoons salt
4   medium carrots, sliced
4   medium potatoes, diced
1   medium onion, sliced
Salt and pepper
½   recipe plain pastry or biscuit dough

Brown meat slowly in hot fat. Add boiling water to just cover meat. Add salt. Cover and simmer until almost done, 30 to 60 minutes depending upon meat used.

Add vegetables and more boiling water if necessary to just cover. Simmer until all are tender, about 20 minutes longer.

Thicken gravy by making a paste of 2 tablespoons of flour and ¼ cup cold water, then stirring into hot gravy and cooking 2 or 3 minutes longer. Add salt and pepper to taste. Bring to boil and pour into buttered 2-quart casserole.

Cover with pastry rolled thin with several slashes cut in to allow escape of steam or cover with baking powder biscuits.

Bake in hot oven (425°F.) until golden brown, about 15 minutes. Serves 5.

Variation: Ground beef may be substituted for beef cubes. Add salt and cover with water as above but cook only 15 to 20 minutes.

OVEN BEEF STEW

2   pounds chuck
4   tablespoons flour
3   tablespoons hot fat
1   teaspoon salt
3   tablespoons prepared mustard
1   teaspoon Ac'cent
2½ cups tomato juice or water
6   medium potatoes, cut in halves
12 small carrots, scraped and cut in lengthwise quarters
12 small white onions
1   package frozen peas or corn kernels, thawed just enough to separate

Cut meat into 2-inch cubes. Sprinkle meat with flour. Brown in hot fat and transfer to 3-quart casserole.

Stir remaining flour and seasonings into fat in pan. Gradually add tomato juice or water, stirring constantly. Pour over meat.

Cover and cook in moderate oven (350°F.) 1 hour.

Add potatoes, carrots, and onions; cover and cook 45 minutes longer. Add peas, cover and cook until vegetables are tender, about 15 minutes longer.

Before serving, stir stew to bring meat to top.

Note: If corn is used, potatoes may be omitted.

Oven Lamb Stew: Substitute 2 pounds boned lamb shoulder for beef. Have fat trimmed off. Increase flour to 5 tablespoons.

Before serving stew, spoon off excess surface fat.

Oven Veal Stew: Substitute 2 pounds boned veal shoulder for beef.

Use 1 to 1½ cups white wine instead of tomato juice or water. Increase flour to 5 tablespoons.

If desired substitute ½ pound fresh mushrooms for peas.

OLD FASHIONED BEEF AND KIDNEY POT PIE

1½ pounds veal kidneys
1½ pounds top sirloin of beef
½   cup butter or margarine
2   tablespoons flour
3   cloves garlic, crushed
1   tablespoon tomato purée
⅔   cup red Burgandy wine
1   quart beef stock or water
1   sprig parsley
1   small stalk celery
½   bay leaf
¼   teaspoon thyme
½   pound salt pork
½   pound very small onions, boiled
10 fresh mushrooms
Pastry for 1-crust pie

Trim kidneys and mince. Mince beef. Pan fry slowly together in ⅓ cup butter or margarine until golden brown. Blend in flour. Add garlic, purée, wine, and stock.

Tie in a small piece of cheesecloth the parsley, celery, bay leaf, and thyme. Add with garlic to meat mixture. Add salt and pepper to taste.

Bake in moderate oven (350°F.) about 40 minutes.

Remove garlic and herb bag.

Boil salt pork in water to cover until tender. Cut into cubes and fry until crisp. Pan fry mushrooms in remaining fat. Combine ingredients and bake 15 minutes.

Spread in deep pie pan and cool. Cover with thin pastry crust. Cut gashes to allow steam to escape.

Bake in hot oven (425°F.) until crust is golden brown, about 30 minutes. Serves 6 to 8.

ROUND STEAK WITH WINE

3 slices bacon
1 clove garlic, crushed
1½ pounds round steak, cut in 1-inch cubes
Flour
½ cup consommé
½ cup dry red wine
½ teaspoon salt
6 small onions, peeled
3 medium carrots, diced
5 whole black peppers
2 whole cloves
2 bay leaves

Cook bacon in heavy skillet until brown but not crisp. Remove bacon and add garlic to fat in pan.

Coat steak cubes with flour and brown meat on all sides. Add consommé, wine, and salt. Heat to boiling and turn into large casserole. Add bacon, cut into 1-inch pieces, and remaining ingredients.

Cover and bake in slow oven (300°F.) about 2 hours. Serves 6.

BEEF CASSEROLE— HUNGARIAN STYLE

2 pounds round steak, cut in ½-inch cubes
3 tablespoons fat
1 large onion, chopped
1 clove garlic, chopped fine
2 tablespoons flour
¾ cup canned browned mushrooms and broth
½ cup chopped celery
1 cup thick sour cream
1 cup tomato sauce (8-ounce can)
1 teaspoon salt
⅛ teaspoon pepper
1 tablespoon Worcestershire sauce

Brown meat in hot fat. Add onion and garlic and cook until golden. Stir in flour slowly. Add remaining ingredients and mix well.

Turn into greased 3-quart casserole. Bake, uncovered, in slow oven (325° F.) until meat is tender, about 1½ hours. Serves 6.

SHORT RIBS OF BEEF CASSEROLE

2 pounds short ribs of beef
1½ teaspoons salt
⅛ teaspoon pepper
2 tablespoons flour
1 tablespoon fat
½ cup water
1 tablespoon Worcestershire sauce
4 medium potatoes, pared
4 small onions, peeled
3 medium carrots, pared and sliced
1½ cups canned or cooked peas (optional)

Have ribs cut into serving size pieces. Season with salt and pepper. Roll in flour. Brown in hot fat in heavy skillet.

Turn into a heated casserole with the fat. Add water, cover, and bake in moderate oven (350°F.) 1 hour.

Add Worcestershire sauce, potatoes cut in halves, onions, carrots, and peas. Add up to ¼ cup additional water if required.

Cover and bake until meat begins to separate from bones. Baste with sauce from casserole just before serving. Serves 4.

MEAT PIE—SOUTHERN STYLE

2 pounds cubed raw beef
2 tablespoons fat
1 cup chopped onions
2 cups chopped celery
½ cup chopped green pepper
3 cups canned tomatoes, juice and pulp
3 tablespoons flour
2 teaspoons salt
¼ teaspoon pepper
¼ teaspoon paprika
½ cup kernel corn, drained
Corn Meal Biscuit Topping

Sear meat in hot fat until nicely browned, about 10 to 15 minutes. Remove meat from fat.

Cook onions, celery, and green pepper in the fat until tender and lightly browned. Add tomatoes gradually to flour and seasonings; add meat and vegetables. Turn into 2½-quart casserole.

Cover and cook in moderate oven (350°F.) about 30 minutes. Top with corn meal biscuit topping and bake as directed. Serves 8 to 10.

BEEF-PORK SAUSAGE-BEAN CASSEROLE

1 pound dried red kidney beans
½ pound link pork sausages
1 pound boneless chuck beef, cut in small cubes
2 onions, chopped
2 cloves garlic, minced
½ teaspoon dried rosemary
¾ cup dry red wine
2 teaspoons salt
¼ teaspoon pepper
Dash of cayenne
1½ cups bean liquid

Wash beans and bring to boil in 6 cups water; boil 2 minutes.

Turn off heat and let stand 1 hour. Then simmer until almost tender.

Cut sausages in half and fry until brown. Remove sausage from pan.

Brown beef in fat with onions and garlic.

Add rosemary, wine, salt, pepper, and cayenne. Cover and simmer 1 hour.

Combine with beans, 1½ cups bean liquid, and sausages. Put in 3-quart casserole.

Cover and bake in moderate oven (350°F.) until beans and meat are tender, about 1½ hours. Serves 4 to 6.

CUBE STEAK AND MUSHROOM CASSEROLE

4 cube steaks
4 tablespoons bacon drippings
2 medium onions, sliced
1 pound mushrooms, sliced
1 can condensed cream of mushroom soup
⅔ cup buttermilk
2 tablespoons minced parsley
1 teaspoon salt
¼ teaspoon pepper
¼ teaspoon dry mustard
4 medium potatoes, sliced

Brown steaks in drippings. Remove steaks from pan and sauté onion and mushroom slices until tender.

Drain steak, onions, and mushrooms on absorbent paper.

Combine soup, buttermilk, parsley, and seasonings. Place alternate layers of potatoes, onion, mushroom slices, and steaks in a 2½-quart greased casserole. Pour a little soup mixture on each layer.

Bake uncovered in moderate oven (350°F.) for 1 hour. Serves 4.

STEAK AND ONION PIE

1 pound round steak, cubed
¼ cup flour
2 teaspoons salt
⅛ teaspoon pepper
½ teaspoon paprika
Dash of ginger
Dash of allspice
¼ cup fat
1 cup sliced onions
2½ cups hot water
2 cups diced potatoes
½ recipe plain pastry

Roll meat in mixture of flour, salt, pepper, paprika, ginger, and allspice. Brown in hot fat.

Add onions and cook until light yellow. Add water. Cover and simmer until meat is tender.

Add potatoes; turn into greased shallow casserole.

Cover with plain pastry. Brush with slightly beaten egg.

Bake in very hot oven (450°F.) until pastry is nicely browned, about 25 minutes. Serves 6.

For variety season biscuits for topping with your favorite herb and sprinkle with caraway seeds.

Ground Meat Casseroles

Hamburger and Potato Puffs

GROUND BEEF LAYERED CASSEROLE

2 pounds ground beef
2 tablespoons shortening
1 clove garlic
1 tablespoon oil
4 cups sliced potatoes
1 12-ounce package frozen green beans, thawed
1 12-ounce can small white onions
1½ teaspoons salt
¼ teaspoon pepper
¼ teaspoon thyme
1 tablespoon cornstarch
1 8-ounce can tomato sauce
⅔ cup bouillon
¼ cup grated Cheddar cheese
¼ cup breadcrumbs
3 tablespoons melted butter

Sauté beef in shortening until browned and crumbling. Rub a 3-quart casserole with cut garlic clove and oil.

Arrange in it a layer each of half the potatoes, meat, beans, and all the onions. Finish with layers of remaining beans, meat, and finally potatoes, sprinkling salt, pepper, and thyme on each layer.

Mix cornstarch to a thin paste with a little tomato sauce. Mix with remaining tomato sauce and bouillon. Pour over potatoes.

Top with a mixture of grated cheese and breadcrumbs. Drizzle butter over all.

Bake uncovered in moderate oven (350°F.) for 1¼ hours. Serves 6 to 8.

CHILI CON CARNE CASSEROLE

1 pound chuck
1 large onion, chopped
2 cloves garlic, minced
3 tablespoons bacon drippings
1½ teaspoons salt
2 tablespoons chili powder
1 teaspoon oregano
¼ teaspoon cummin
1 bay leaf, crushed
1 No. 2 can (2½ cups) tomatoes
1 No. 2 can (2½ cups) red kidney beans

Have beef coarsely ground or chop it fine. Brown meat, onion, and garlic in drippings. Sprinkle with seasonings.

Combine with tomatoes and turn into a 2-quart greased casserole. Cover and bake in slow oven (325°F.) for 1½ hours.

Remove from oven. Stir in heated beans. Replace cover and continue baking for 20 minutes. Serves 6.

Note: The cooking may be done on the top of the range. Place casserole on an asbestos pad to protect it from direct heat. Cook over low heat for 2 hours. Add beans and heat through.

HAMBURGER AND POTATO PUFFS

1 pound ground beef
1 onion, chopped
½ green pepper, chopped
1 clove garlic, minced
¼ teaspoon basil
½ teaspoon seasoned salt
1 can (3-ounce) sliced mushrooms
1 can (8-ounce) tomato sauce
1 package (5⅝-ounce) instant mashed potatoes
⅓ cup grated Parmesan cheese
1 tablespoon chopped parsley

Brown beef, onion, green pepper, and garlic in skillet. Add seasonings, mushrooms, and tomato sauce. Simmer 5 minutes.

Prepare mashed potatoes for 4 according to package directions. Add Parmesan cheese and parsley to potatoes; place spoonfuls around edge of skillet on beef mixture. Bake in hot oven (400°F.) 10 minutes or until potato puffs are lightly browned. Serves 4.

SPANISH MEAT PIE

3 tablespoons fat
1 clove garlic
1 pound hamburger
4 tablespoons flour
2 cups cooked tomatoes
2 cups whole kernel corn
1 teaspoon salt
¼ teaspoon paprika
¼ teaspoon chili powder
Dash of cayenne
3 slices buttered bread

Melt fat in heavy skillet. Brown garlic in hot fat. Remove garlic, and add meat. Brown well.

Blend in flour and, when well mixed, add tomatoes, corn, and seasonings. Pour into buttered 1-quart casserole.

Cut slices of bread in half and place on top of casserole. Bake in hot oven (400°F.) 15 minutes, or until top is browned. Serves 6.

BEEF AND NOODLE CASSEROLE

2 tablespoons finely chopped onion
2 tablespoons fat
1 pound hamburger
1½ teaspoons salt
⅛ teaspoon pepper
8 ounces wide noodles, cooked
1 10½-ounce can condensed cream of tomato soup
½ cup shredded cheese

Pan-fry onion in hot fat in a heavy skillet. Add hamburger and brown thoroughly.

Combine meat, seasonings, noodles, and soup in a 3-quart casserole. Top with shredded cheese.

Bake in a moderate oven (350°F.) for 30 minutes. Serves 8.

ORLEANS MEAT PIE

Filling:

¼ cup fat
½ cup chopped onion
1 pound hamburger
1 teaspoon salt
3 tablespoons ketchup or chili sauce

Biscuit:

2 cups biscuit mix
About ⅔ cup milk

Topping:

1 cup drained, cooked tomatoes

Heat fat. Cook onion slowly to a golden brown. Add meat and brown well. Add salt and ketchup.

Put biscuit mix into mixing bowl. Pour milk quickly into dry ingredients. Stir until well blended. Turn onto lightly floured board. Knead 6 times. Roll into circular shape. Put into a 9-inch pie pan. Do not flute edges.

Fill with cooked meat. Cover with drained tomatoes. Bake in very hot oven (450°F.) 30 minutes. Serve hot. Serves 6.

COMPANY CASSEROLE

1 pound hamburger
1 tablespoon butter or margarine
2 8-ounce cans tomato sauce
8 ounces noodles
1 cup cottage cheese
8 ounces cream cheese
¼ cup thick sour cream
⅓ cup chopped green onions
1 tablespoon chopped green pepper
2 tablespoons butter or margarine, melted

Brown hamburger in butter in a heavy skillet. Stir in tomato sauce. Remove from heat.

Boil noodles in salted water 10 minutes. Drain.

Combine cottage cheese, cream cheese, sour cream, onions, and green pepper.

In a buttered 2-quart casserole, spread half the noodles. Cover with cheese mixture, then cover this with remaining noodles. Pour melted butter over noodles. Pat hamburger sauce mixture on top.

Bake in moderate oven (350°F.) 20 to 30 minutes. Serve hot. Makes 6 generous servings.

MOUSAKA

This is a Greek casserole, which bakes in 4 distinct layers of eggplant and sauce with cheese topping.

1 pound hamburger
2 cups chopped onion
1/2 cup water
1/4 cup ketchup
1 tablespoon chopped parsley
1 teaspoon salt
1/8 teaspoon pepper
1 cup fine breadcrumbs
2 slightly beaten egg whites
1/4 cup butter or margarine
1/2 cup flour
3 cups milk
1/2 teaspoon salt
1/8 teaspoon nutmeg
2 egg yolks
1 large eggplant (about 2 pounds)
1/4 cup fat
1/4 cup shredded cheese

Brown hamburger in a heavy skillet. Add onion, water, ketchup, parsley, 1 teaspoon salt, and pepper; simmer 10 minutes.

Combine breadcrumbs with egg whites and add half of the meat mixture.

Make a white sauce from the butter, flour, milk, 1/2 teaspoon salt, and nutmeg. Add a little of the white sauce to egg yolks; return to saucepan. Cook until thick.

Pare eggplant and cut into 1/2-inch slices. Brown slices in hot fat.

Place half of the slices in the bottom of a buttered baking dish (12 x 8 x 2 inches). Spread half the meat mixture over the eggplant. Add 1 cup of white sauce. Add second layer of eggplant, meat, and remaining white sauce.

Mix cheese with remaining breadcrumbs and egg white mixture. Sprinkle over top of mixture. Bake in a moderate oven (350°F.) for 30 minutes. Serves 10.

HAMBURGER HARVEST CASSEROLE

1 pound hamburger
1 cup chopped onions
2 cups cooked tomatoes
1 teaspoon curry powder or chili powder or 1 tablespoon Worcestershire sauce
2 tablespoons salt
2 potatoes, sliced thin
1/3 cup flour
2 cups whole kernel corn, drained
2 cups cooked lima beans, drained
1/2 cup sliced green pepper
1 1/2 cups shredded cheese or buttered crumbs

Combine hamburger, onions, tomatoes, one of the seasonings, and salt. Pat into a 1-inch layer in a 3-quart casserole.

Over this place, in layers, the pota-toes, flour, corn, lima beans, and green pepper. Top with cheese or crumbs.

Bake in a moderate oven (350°F.) for 1 hour. Serve hot. Serves 8 to 10.

HAMBURGER "PIZZA"

1 pound ground beef
1 1/2 teaspoons salt
1/2 teaspoon pepper
1 cup well drained canned tomatoes
1/2 cup shredded soft cheese
2 tablespoons chopped parsley
1/4 teaspoon dried basil
2 tablespoons finely chopped onion

Mix ground beef with salt and pepper. Pat out in a 9-inch pie pan.

Spread tomatoes over hamburger and sprinkle with the remaining ingredients.

Bake in a moderate oven (375°F.) 15 to 20 minutes. Cut in wedges to serve. Serves 4.

Variation: To make Sunshine Meat Pie, fill hamburger "crust" with a mixture of 1 1/2 cups well drained whole kernel corn (12-ounce can), 1 cup well drained canned tomatoes, 1/2 teaspoon salt, and 1/4 teaspoon basil. Bake as above.

HAMBURGER CORN PONE PIE

1 pound ground beef
1/3 cup chopped onion
1 tablespoon shortening
2 teaspoons chili powder
3/4 teaspoon salt
1 teaspoon Worcestershire sauce
1 cup canned tomatoes
1 cup drained canned kidney beans
1 cup corn bread batter (1/2 standard recipe) or 1/2 package corn muffin mix

Brown meat and onion in melted shortening. Add seasonings and toma-toes. Cover and simmer over low heat for 15 minutes. Add kidney beans.

Pour into a greased casserole. Top with corn bread batter and bake in a hot oven (425°F.) for 20 minutes. (When using package muffin mix, if recipe calls for 1 egg, use the whole egg in the half recipe.) Serves 4.

HAMBURGER CURRY BAKE

1 pound hamburger
1/2 cup chopped onion
1 tablespoon flour
1 teaspoon salt
1 teaspoon curry powder
1 cup milk
3 cups corn flakes, crushed
2 tablespoons butter or margarine

Stir and cook hamburger and onion in a heavy skillet to brown meat. Stir in flour, salt, curry powder, and milk. Mix thoroughly.

Spoon half of this mixture over bottom of a 1 1/2-quart casserole. Sprinkle half of the corn flakes over surface. Spread remaining meat mixture on top of corn flakes. Top with layer of corn flakes.

Dot with butter and bake in a moderate oven (350°F.) for 1 hour. Serves 4 to 6.

SWEDISH CABBAGE ROLLS

1 pound ground beef
1/2 pound ground pork
3 cups cooked rice
1 teaspoon sugar
1 onion, chopped
1 teaspoon salt
1/4 teaspoon pepper
1 head cabbage
1 tablespoon butter or margarine
1 cup hot water
1 can (10 1/2 ounce) cream of tomato soup

Combine the beef, pork, rice, sugar, onion, salt, and pepper.

Wilt the cabbage leaves by placing in boiling water for a few minutes.

Place about 1/2 cup of the mixture in each cabbage leaf and roll up securely. Place rolls in a baking pan. Dot each with butter.

Combine water and soup and pour over the rolls. Bake in a moderate oven (350°F.) 1 hour. Serves 6.

SHEPHERD'S PIE

Shepherd's pie is a meat pie often made with leftovers moistened with a sauce or a gravy and baked in a cas-serole, with a topping or border of mashed potatoes. This popular version contains ground beef.

1 pound ground beef
2 tablespoons chopped onion
2 tablespoons fat
1 teaspoon salt
2 cups cooked diced carrots
2 1/2 cups mashed potatoes
Parsley for garnish, if desired

Brown beef and onion lightly in melted fat in a skillet. Add salt.

Arrange carrots in bottom of a well greased 1 1/2-quart heat-resistant glass bowl. Pour browned beef mixture over carrots. Top with mashed potato, pip-ing some on with a cake decorator, if desired.

Bake in hot oven (400°F.) 15 to 20 minutes or until potatoes are lightly browned and food is piping hot. Garnish with parsley and serve.

Serves 5 to 6.

Shepherd's Pie

Pork and Ham Casseroles

PORK CHOP-NOODLE CASSEROLE

6 pork chops
1 tablespoon fat
2 teaspoons salt
2 tablespoons grated onion
1 tablespoon Worcestershire sauce
1 can condensed tomato soup
½ cup water
4 cups cooked noodles

Brown chops in fat until golden brown. Season with 1 teaspoon salt.

Combine remaining salt, onion, Worcestershire sauce, tomato soup, and water.

Place noodles in a casserole; add tomato soup mixture. Arrange chops overlapping around inner edge.

Cover and bake in moderate oven (350°F.) 1½ hours. Serves 4 to 6.

PORK CHOP VEGETABLE CASSEROLE WITH RICE

6 or 8 pork chops
½ cup chopped onion
½ cup chopped green pepper
1 can cream of mushroom soup
1 cup water
3 cups cooked rice
2 cups cooked peas
1 teaspoon salt
⅛ teaspoon pepper

Place pork chops in a skillet and brown on both sides. Enough fat should cook out of the pork shops so that it is not necessary to add any to the skillet. Lift pork chops out of skillet.

Place onion and green pepper in skillet and cook until tender. It may be necessary to add a small amount of fat to prevent onions and peppers from sticking.

Add mushroom soup, water, rice, peas, salt, and pepper. Mix well.

Pour half the rice and pea mixture into a greased baking dish. Arrange half the chops over the rice and peas. Add the rest of the rice and peas.

Top with remaining chops and bake in a moderate oven (350°F.) about 30 minutes.

Serves 6 or 8 depending upon the number of pork chops used.

Pork Chop Vegetable Casserole with Rice

PORK CHOPS WITH POTATOES AND CABBAGE

4 pork chops, about ½-inch thick
1½ teaspoons salt
⅛ teaspoon pepper
¼ cup chopped onion
1 can condensed cream of celery soup
½ cup milk
3 medium potatoes, pared and sliced
1 pound shredded cabbage
¼ cup flour

Cut excess fat from pork chops. Season with salt and pepper. Grease skillet very lightly with a piece of the fat. Brown chops on both sides over moderate heat, about 15 minutes. Remove chops. Pour off fat.

Measure 2 tablespoons fat into skillet. Add onion, celery soup, and milk. Stir to blend well.

Put 2 alternating layers of potatoes and cabbage in 2½-quart casserole. Sprinkle each layer with flour and pour about ¼ of celery-milk mixture over each layer. Top with chops.

Cover and bake in moderate oven (350° F.) 1 hour and 15 minutes. Serves 4.

SPARERIBS AND BEANS

1 No. 2 can (2½ cups) kidney or lima beans
2 large onions, chopped
3 pounds spareribs
Salt and pepper
1 cup apple juice

Place a layer of beans in a greased baking dish. Season with some of the onion. Repeat layers.

Cut spareribs into serving pieces. Place on beans. Season with salt and pepper. Pour apple juice over all.

Cook, uncovered, in moderate oven (350° F.) until spareribs are done, about 1 hour. Serves 4.

SPARERIBS AND SAUERKRAUT

3 pounds spareribs
1 teaspoon salt
¼ teaspoon pepper
1 quart sauerkraut
1 tart apple, chopped
1 cup water
1 raw potato, grated
1 teaspoon caraway seed

Season ribs with salt and pepper. Brown in open roasting pan in extremely hot over. (500°F.) 30 minutes. Place sauerkraut and apple on top of meat; add water and cover pan.

Reduce heat to moderate (350° F.) and roast 1 hour longer. Stir in potato and caraway seed. Bake 30 minutes longer. Serves 6.

Pork and Vegetable Pie

PORK AND VEGETABLE PIE

1½ pounds diced pork shoulder
½ cup sliced onions
2 cups water or bouillon
1 teaspoon salt
¼ teaspoon pepper
1 cup sliced carrots
1 cup sliced celery
1 cup cooked green beans or peas
2 teaspoons Worcestershire sauce
Baking powder biscuit dough

Have meat man cut pork into 1-inch cubes. Trim off fat and fry out in a heavy saucepan. Remove solid pieces and brown pork and onions in the fat.

Add water or bouillon and salt and pepper. Cook for 45 minutes, then add carrots and celery and cook 15 minutes. Thicken liquid with 2 tablespoons flour mixed to a smooth paste with a little water.

Add green beans or peas with Worcestershire sauce. Pour while hot into a 1½-quart casserole. Top with baking powder biscuit dough cut into circles or fancy shapes.

Bake in very hot oven (450° F.) for 20 minutes or until biscuits are well browned. Serves 6 to 8.

HAM AND MUSHROOM RISOTTO

1 medium onion, minced
1½ cups slivered boiled or baked ham
⅓ cup olive oil
1½ cups uncooked rice
Pinch of saffron
2½ cups chicken stock or canned broth
½ cup sauterne or other white wine
Salt and pepper
1 4-ounce can mushroom stems and pieces, drained
¼ cup chopped parsley
Grated Parmesan cheese

Sauté onion and ham gently in oil 5 minutes. Add rice and cook, stirring, for about 1 or 2 minutes.

Steep saffron in a little chicken stock, and add to rice mixture. Add remaining stock, wine, salt, and pepper to taste. Bring to boil, then pour into 2-quart casserole.

Cover and bake in moderate oven (375°F.) 30 minutes.

Stir in mushrooms and parsley. Cover and bake 10 minutes longer. Serve with grated Parmesan cheese. Serves 6.

Ham and Rice Casserole

HAM AND RICE CASSEROLE

1   egg
2   tablespoons milk
1   teaspoon dry mustard
1/8   teaspoon pepper
1/3   cup fine cereal crumbs
1/4   cup grated Parmesan cheese
6   large slices ham, 1/8-inch thick
1/4   cup shortening
3   cups hot cooked rice
1/2   pound sliced American cheese
1   can condensed cream of tomato soup

Beat egg with a fork. Stir in milk, mustard, and pepper. Combine cereal crumbs with Parmesan cheese. Dip ham slices in egg mixture then in crumbs.

Melt shortening in large skillet. Sauté prepared ham slices in shortening until lightly browned on both sides.

Spoon rice into greased baking pan. Arrange ham slices on rice. Top ham with cheese slices; cover with tomato soup. Cover and bake in moderate oven (375°F.) 20 minutes. Serves 6.

HAM WITH NOODLES AND PINEAPPLE

4   ounces medium noodles
3   tablespoons butter or margarine
3   tablespoons flour
1   cup milk
1/4   cup pineapple juice
1   cup pineapple chunks
1 1/2   cups cubed ham (1/2-pound)
1/4   cup buttered breadcrumbs

Cook noodles in boiling, salted water until tender. Drain and rinse.

Melt butter in saucepan. Stir in flour. Gradually add milk and pineapple juice, stirring constantly until thickened. Add noodles, pineapple chunks, and cubed ham. Blend well. Pour into greased 1 1/2-quart casserole. Sprinkle with crumbs.

Bake in moderate oven (350° F.) 30 minutes. Serve hot. Serves 4.

HAM WITH NOODLES

1 1/2   cups cooked noodles
2   cups ground cooked ham
2   cups thin white sauce
Crumbs mixed with melted fat

Place half the noodles in a greased baking dish and top with half the ham. Add another layer of noodles and ham.

Pour white sauce over mixture. Top with crumbs. Bake in moderate oven (350°F.) 20 minutes. Serves 4.

HAM, POTATOES, AND CHEESE SCALLOP

3/4   pound cooked ham, sliced thin or 1 can (12 ounces) luncheon meat
1   small onion, finely chopped
4   to 6 potatoes, pared and sliced thin
3   tablespoons flour
1/2   teaspoon salt
1/4   teaspoon pepper
1   cup grated sharp process Cheddar cheese
1   cup milk
2   tablespoons butter or margarine
1/4   cup ketchup

Arrange ham in greased 1 1/2-quart casserole. Sprinkle onion over ham. Add layer of potatoes. Sprinkle with half of flour, salt, pepper, and cheese. Repeat layers.

Heat milk with butter and pour over casserole.

Cover and bake in moderate oven (350°F.) 40 minutes. Then sprinkle with ketchup and bake uncovered until potatoes are tender, about 30 minutes longer. Serves 4 to 6.

LAYERED HAM AND VEGETABLES

1   large potato, thinly sliced
1   cup coarsely chopped celery
1   large onion, sliced
1   green pepper, coarsely chopped
4   slices boiled ham, cut in small pieces
1   can condensed cream of tomato soup
1   teaspoon salt
Dash of pepper
1/4   cup fine breadcrumbs
2   teaspoons melted butter or margarine

Place a layer each of potato, celery, onion, green pepper, and ham in a greased 1-quart casserole.

Season tomato soup with salt and pepper. Pour over vegetables and ham. Toss crumbs with butter and sprinkle over top.

Bake in moderate oven (350°F.) until vegetables are tender, about 1 hour. Serves 4.

PORK CHOP-CORN CASSEROLE

5   thick pork chops
1 1/2   tablespoons fat
1 1/2   teaspoons salt
Dash of pepper
1   No. 2 can (2 1/2 cups) cream style corn
1/2   cup diced green pepper
2   tablespoons hot water

Brown chops slowly in hot fat in heavy skillet. Sprinkle with salt and pepper.

Mix corn and green pepper; arrange in layers with chops in greased casserole. Add hot water.

Cover and bake in moderate oven (350° F.) 45 minutes. Remove cover and bake 15 minutes longer. Serves 5.

CRUSTY HAM AND CORN PIE

1   cup cubed ham or luncheon meat
2   tablespoons butter or margarine
1/2   cup finely diced onion
1   cup finely diced celery
1/4   cup finely diced green pepper
2   tablespoons flour
1 1/2   teaspoons salt
1/4   teaspoon pepper
2   cups canned tomatoes
1/2   cup drained whole kernel corn
Corn meal biscuit topping (below)

Brown ham in melted butter in skillet.

Add onion, celery, and green pepper; cook until partially tender.

Blend in flour, salt, and pepper. Add tomatoes and corn. Cook until thickened.

Turn into shallow 10-inch casserole (or leave in skillet).

Top with corn meal biscuit topping.

Bake in hot oven (400°F.) about 40 minutes. Serves 6.

CORN MEAL BISCUIT TOPPING

1 1/4   cups milk, scalded
1/4   cup yellow or white corn meal
2   cups sifted enriched flour
2 1/4   teaspoons baking powder
1   teaspoon salt
1/4   cup shortening

Pour hot milk over corn meal and let cool completely.

Sift flour once, measure; add baking powder and salt and sift together twice. Cut in shortening until mixture resembles coarse meal.

Add corn meal mixture all at once, stirring only until all flour is dampened. Drop by spoonfuls over meat-vegetable mixture.

Bake in hot oven (400°F.) 40 to 45 minutes. Serve at once.

Pastry Toppings: These lend themselves to imaginative variations in design. Use cooky cutters to shape pastry toppings into attractive patterns.

Lamb Casseroles

LAMB CHOPS CREOLE CASSEROLE

- 4 lamb shoulder chops, cut ½ to ¾-inch thick
- 1 tablespoon fat
- 1 No. 2 can (2½ cups) tomatoes
- ½ cup uncooked rice
- 1 medium onion, cut in 4 slices
- 1 green pepper, cut in 4 rings
- 1 teaspoon salt
- ½ teaspoon pepper
- 1 tablespoon flour

Brown chops on all sides in hot fat. Place in casserole.

Drain tomatoes and save juice. On each chop arrange in this order, the following: 2 tablespoons rice, 1 slice onion, ½ tomato, and 1 green pepper ring. Season. Heat ½ cup tomato juice to boiling and pour around chops.

Cover closely. Bake in slow oven (300°F.) 1½ hours.

Thicken cooking liquid with flour. Serve over chops. Serves 4.

LAMB WITH EGGPLANT AND RICE

- 1 medium eggplant, cut in large cubes
- 1½ pounds lamb shoulder, cut in 1-inch squares
- 3 tablespoons butter
- 1 medium onion, diced
- 1 teaspoon marjoram
- Pinch of thyme
- Salt and pepper
- 1 cup consommé
- 1 cup raw rice
- 1 No. 2 can (2½ cups) tomatoes

Soak cubes of eggplant in salted water for 15 minutes; rinse and drain well.

Brown lamb on all sides in hot fat. Transfer to casserole.

Pan fry onion until golden. Add onion, eggplant, seasonings, and consommé to casserole.

Brown rice in a dry skillet; add tomatoes with juice to rice. Pour over casserole.

Bake in moderate oven (350°F.) until lamb is tender, about 1½ hours. Serves 6.

Bake-Alongs: For efficient baking along with the casserole, select vegetables, fruits, desserts, and hot breads that call for the same temperature. The same timing is desirable, but not always possible. To insure top crispness in the main dish, vegetables, fruits, and desserts which fill the oven with steam should be covered.

Plan contrast in color. Use bright-colored foods to perk up the paler casseroles.

LAMB WITH RICE

- 1½ pounds lean boneless lamb, cut in 1-inch cubes
- ¼ cup wine vinegar
- ½ cup sweet cider or apple juice
- 2 medium onions, sliced
- ½ teaspoon pickle spice
- 2 tablespoons flour
- 1 teaspoon salt
- ⅛ teaspoon pepper
- ½ teaspoon Ac'cent
- 2 tablespoons butter or margarine
- ¾ cup uncooked rice
- 3 cups boiling water
- 3 beef bouillon cubes

Cover lamb with mixture of vinegar, cider or apple juice, onions, and pickle spice. Let marinate in refrigerator overnight. Then, drain meat, reserving spiced liquid. Sprinkle meat with flour mixed with seasonings. Brown slightly on all sides in hot fat.

Place meat in alternating layers with rice in a casserole. Add boiling water in which bouillon cubes have been dissolved and the spiced liquid. Cover and bake in moderate oven (350°F.) 2 hours. Serves 4.

LAMB STEW CASSEROLE

- 1 pound lamb, cut in small chunks
- Salt and pepper
- ⅓ cup salad oil
- 8 small whole onions, peeled
- 1 can condensed tomato soup
- ⅓ cup water
- ½ cup slivered almonds

Season lamb with salt and pepper. Brown in hot oil. Put in casserole.

Add onions. Mix soup and water in meat skillet until it bubbles; pour over meat. Sprinkle with almonds.

Bake in moderate oven (350°F.) until meat is tender, about 1 hour. Serves 4.

BAKED LAMB CHOPS

- 6 shoulder lamb chops
- 1 clove garlic
- Salt and pepper
- 2 tablespoons fat
- 2 medium onions, chopped
- 2 cups cooked diced carrots
- 4 tablespoons flour
- 4 tablespoons chili sauce
- ½ cup Rhine or sauterne wine

Rub chops with cut clove of garlic. Season with salt and pepper. Brown on both sides in hot fat in skillet. Transfer to casserole.

Sauté onions and carrots in skillet until onions are soft and yellow. Stir in flour, chili sauce, and wine. Cook, stirring, until thickened. Place mound of this mixture on each chop.

Bake in moderate oven (350°F.) 45 minutes. Serves 6.

Lamb Shank Casserole

LAMB SHANK CASSEROLE

- 6 lamb shanks (about 1 pound each)
- Seasoned flour
- 3 tablespoons salad oil
- ¼ cup lemon juice
- ¼ cup water
- 1 tablespoon sugar
- 6 bay leaves
- 6 medium-sized sweet potatoes, cooked, pared and quartered, or two 1-pound cans sweet potatoes, drained
- 3 cups cooked cut green beans

Dredge lamb shanks with flour. Heat salad oil; add lamb shanks and brown well on all sides. Place lamb shanks in 6 individual casseroles; reserve lamb drippings.

Combine lamb drippings, lemon juice, water, sugar, and bay leaves; pour over lamb shanks. Cover and bake in slow oven (325°F.) about 1½ hours, or until lamb is tender.

Add sweet potatoes and beans. Cover and bake 10 minutes, or until vegetables are thoroughly heated. Serves 6.

LAMB RIBLET CASSEROLE

- 3 pounds lamb riblets
- 1½ teaspoons salt
- 1 teaspoon paprika
- 2 tablespoons flour
- 2 tablespoons fat
- 1 small onion, sliced
- 4 medium potatoes, pared and sliced
- 1 cup canned or cooked tomatoes
- 1 teaspoon salt
- 1 tablespoon ketchup

Season riblets and roll in flour to cover evenly. Brown on all sides in hot fat in heavy skillet or flameproof casserole. Cover meat with onion and potatoes.

Mix tomatoes, 1 teaspoon salt, and ketchup. Pour over potatoes.

Cover and bake in moderate oven until meat is tender, about 1¼ hours. If necessary, add a little water. Serves 4.

Lamb Breast Casserole: Use breast of lamb, cut into serving pieces, instead of lamb riblets.

Veal Casseroles

VEAL CUTLETS BAKED IN MUSHROOM SAUCE

6   slices bacon
1/2 cup finely chopped onion
2   pounds veal cutlets, 1/2-inch thick, cut into serving pieces
1   slightly beaten egg
2   tablespoons water
1/2 cup sifted dry breadcrumbs
1   tablespoon bottled meat sauce
2   cans condensed cream of mushroom soup

Fry bacon in skillet until crisp; remove. Cook onion in bacon fat until tender; remove.

Dip meat in egg-water mixture, then into breadcrumbs. Brown on both sides in bacon fat.

Place in flat casserole (12 x 8 x 2-inches). Sprinkle with onions and meat sauce. Top with bacon. Pour on condensed soup.

Bake in moderate oven (350°F.) until tender, about 30 minutes. Serves 8.

VEAL SCALLOPINI CASSEROLE

2 1/2 pounds boneless shoulder of veal
1/2 cup flour
2   teaspoons salt
1/4 teaspoon pepper
1/2 cup finely chopped onion
1/2 cup fat or salad oil
1   No. 2 can tomatoes, strained
3/4 cup sliced canned or fresh mushrooms
1   teaspoon sugar

Cut veal into 1 1/4-inch cubes. Roll in flour seasoned with 1/2 teaspoon salt and a dash of pepper.

Cook onions in hot fat until tender and yellow. Transfer onions to 2-quart casserole.

Brown veal in the fat on all sides and transfer to casserole. Add tomatoes, mushrooms, sugar, and remaining salt and pepper.

Cover and cook in moderate oven (350°F.) until tender, about 1 1/2 hours. Serve with boiled white rice or cooked spaghetti and tomato sauce. Serves 5 to 6.

VEAL CUTLETS PARMIGIANA

1 1/2 pounds veal cutlets, cut 1/2-inch thick
1   teaspoon salt
1/8 teaspoon pepper
2   slightly beaten eggs
1/4 cup grated Parmesan cheese
1/2 cup sifted breadcrumbs
Oil for browning
1   cup tomato sauce
1/2 pound mozzarella or mild American cheese

Have cutlets divided into serving pieces and flattened with mallet to 1/8-inch thickness. Season with salt and pepper.

Dip meat in eggs and then coat evenly with a mixture of Parmesan cheese and crumbs.

Brown cutlets evenly on both sides in hot oil, allowing about 3 minutes for each side.

Place in shallow casserole or individual casseroles. Put a spoonful of tomato sauce on each, then a slice of mozzarella cheese.

Bake in moderate oven (350°F.) until cheese browns lightly, about 15 minutes. Serves 4 to 6.

VEAL CHOPS HUNGARIAN #1

6   veal chops
Salt, pepper, Ac'cent
Flour, for coating
1/4 cup fat or oil
1   medium onion, diced
Paprika
1/2 cup stock or water
1   cup sour cream
1/2 teaspoon Ac'cent
Salt and pepper
Cooked noodles
Melted butter

Sprinkle chops on both sides with salt, pepper, and Ac'cent; coat lightly with flour.

Brown chops, in the heated fat, on both sides, over moderate heat. Toward end of browning add onion and sprinkle chops generously with paprika. Add stock or water to skillet; cover tightly. Simmer over low heat until tender, about 30 minutes.

Remove chops to hot platter. Stir sour cream, the 1/2 teaspoon Ac'cent, salt and pepper into pan gravy. Heat; correct seasoning.

Place hot cooked noodles around chops; drizzle melted butter over noodles; shake on Ac'cent lightly. Pour gravy over chops. Serves 6.

VEAL PAPRIKASH CASSEROLE

1/4 pound lean salt pork, cut into small pieces
3   pounds boneless stewing veal, cut in 1 1/2-in. pieces
Flour
1   pound sliced fresh mushrooms
1   cup sliced onions
3   beef bouillon cubes, dissolved in 1 1/2 cups water
1 1/2 teaspoons salt
1/2 teaspoon pepper
2   tablespoons paprika
1   cup sour cream
Chopped parsley

Fry salt pork until crisp in heavy kettle; remove pork.

Roll veal in flour and lightly brown in pork fat. Add mushrooms and onions. Cook 15 minutes, stirring often.

Add beef bouillon cubes and water, salt, pepper, and paprika. Turn into 2 1/2-quart casserole.

Cover and bake in moderate oven (350°F.) until veal is tender, 1 1/2 to 2 hours. Just before serving, put 1 cup sour cream on top. Sprinkle with chopped parsley. Serves 6.

Note: Topping with sour cream rather than stirring it in, prevents curdling and preserves bright red color.

SOUR CREAM VEAL AND NOODLES

1   pound veal steak
Salt and pepper
1   small onion, finely chopped
1   cup sliced celery
1   can (6 ounces) mushrooms or 1 cup sautéed fresh mushrooms
1/2 cup water
1   package (8 ounces) egg noodles
1   cup sour cream
Bread or cracker crumbs
Butter for cooking

Cut meat into 1/2-inch cubes. Brown in butter. Add seasonings, onion, celery, mushrooms, and water.

Add noodles which have been cooked in boiling salted water until tender and drained.

Add sour cream. Turn into buttered casserole. Sprinkle top with crumbs. Dot with butter. Place uncovered in moderate oven (350°F.) until butter melts and forms a brown crust. Cover and bake 1 hour. Serves 8 to 10.

VEAL STEW CASSEROLE

2   pounds veal for stew
1/4 cup flour
2   teaspoons salt
1/4 teaspoon pepper
3   tablespoons fat
3   medium onions
1   pound or 1 No. 2 can green beans
3   stalks celery, cut in 4-inch pieces
1   green pepper, cut in rings
1   No. 2 can (2 1/2 cups) tomatoes

Roll veal in seasoned flour. Brown slowly in hot fat. Add whole onions, green beans, celery, green pepper rings, and tomatoes.

Cover and cook in slow oven (300°F.) about 1 1/2 hours or until meat is tender and vegetables are done. Serves 6 to 8.

Plan contrast in size and shape. Many casseroles contain foods in small pieces. As a contrast to avoid monotony in size and shape, serve firm whole fruits or vegetables or sections with definite form.

Franks, Pork Sausage, Canned Meat Casseroles

PORK SAUSAGE WITH SWEET POTATOES AND APPLES

3 medium cooked sweet potatoes
3 medium apples
1/3 cup brown sugar
1/2 teaspoon salt
1/2 pound pork sausage links

Pare and slice sweet potatoes and apples. Place in alternate layers in greased 1-quart casserole. Sprinkle with brown sugar and salt.

Cover and bake in hot oven (400°F.) 15 minutes. At the same time bake pork sausage in an open pan.

Remove cover from casserole. Top with sausages. Bake uncovered 15 minutes longer. Serves 3 to 4.

CORNED BEEF-RICE CASSEROLE

4 cups cooked rice
2 cups cubed cooked or canned corned beef
1 No. 2 can (2 1/2 cups) tomatoes
1/4 cup finely chopped onion
1 teaspoon salt
Few grains of pepper
1 teaspoon Worcestershire sauce

Put alternate layers of rice and beef in greased casserole.

Mix tomatoes and seasonings; pour over rice-beef mixture.

Cover and bake in moderate oven (350°F.) 30 minutes. Serves 4.

CORNED BEEF HASH CASSEROLE

1 1-pound can corned beef hash
1/4 cup finely chopped parsley
1/4 cup chopped pimiento
1 small clove garlic, minced
1 tablespoon lemon juice
1/2 cup cream
1/4 teaspoon celery seed
Dash of sage
1/4 teaspoon Worcestershire sauce
Dash of Tabasco sauce
1/4 teaspoon salt
1/2 cup crushed potato chips

Combine corned beef hash, parsley, pimiento, garlic, and lemon juice. Turn into 1 1/2-quart buttered casserole.

Mix cream, celery seed, sage, Worcestershire, Tabasco, and salt. Pour over hash mixture. Sprinkle with potato chips.

Bake in moderate oven (350°F.) 20 minutes. Serves 4.

CHILI CON CARNE WITH CORN BREAD TOPPING

Fill individual casseroles about 3/4 full with canned chili con carne. Top with prepared corn bread mix batter in rows. Put ripe olives between rows.

Bake in moderate oven (375°F.) 20 to 25 minutes.

FRANKFURTER AND TOMATO CASSEROLE

3 medium tomatoes, cut in 1-inch thick slices
Flour
6 frankfurters, cut into 1/2-inch pieces
1 large onion, sliced thin
1 medium green pepper, sliced
1 cup grated sharp Cheddar cheese
1 clove garlic, minced
1/2 teaspoon salt

Sprinkle tomato slices with flour and arrange in greased 1 1/2-quart casserole in alternate layers with frankfurter pieces, onion, green pepper, and cheese. Season each layer with garlic and salt.

Cover and bake in moderate oven (350°F.) until cheese is bubbly. Serves 4 to 5.

Variation: Substitute 1 can whole kernel corn for cheese.

DRIED BEEF AND MACARONI

2 cups (2 3 1/2-ounce glasses) dried beef
1/4 cup butter or margarine
2 tablespoons diced green pepper
1/4 cup grated sharp Cheddar cheese
2 cups thin white sauce
1 8-ounce package macaroni

Cut dried beef into pieces. Fry until crisp in melted butter. Add green pepper and cook 3 minutes longer. Melt cheese in white sauce.

Break macaroni into small pieces. Cook until tender in boiling salted water. Drain.

Combine all ingredients. Turn into 2-quart buttered casserole Set casserole in shallow pan of hot water and bake in moderate oven (350°F.) about 30 minutes. Serves 6.

Stuffed Green Peppers: Fill parboiled green pepper shells with above mixture. Cover with buttered crumbs. Bake in moderate oven to heat and brown.

FRANKFURTERS WITH HOT POTATO SALAD

4 cups cooked potatoes, sliced thin
1/3 cup salad oil
3 tablespoons vinegar
1 1/2 teaspoons salt
Dash of pepper
1 1/2 cups canned or cooked green beans, drained
1/4 cup onions, sliced thin
4 large frankfurters, sliced

Gently mix potatoes with oil, vinegar, salt, and pepper.

Place green beans in layer in greased 1 1/2-quart casserole. Add alternate layers of potato salad, onion, and frankfurters.

Cover and bake in hot oven (400°F.) 30 minutes. Serves 4.

RICE AND FRANKFURTER CASSEROLE

3/4 cup uncooked rice
1 1/2 cups sliced onions
3 tablespoons fat or salad oil
3 1/2 cups canned tomatoes
1 tablespoon sugar
1 1/2 teaspoons salt
1/4 cup chopped green pepper
3 whole cloves
1 bay leaf
9 frankfurters

Cook and drain rice. Cook onions in hot fat until transparent. Add remaining ingredients except frankfurters and simmer 15 minutes. Remove bay leaf and cloves. Add rice.

Arrange in alternate layers in greased casserole, using 1/3 of rice mixture first, then 3 frankfurters, whole or sliced. Reserve 3 frankfurters for top layer.

Cover and bake in moderate oven (350°F.) 50 to 60 minutes. Uncover for last 15 minutes of baking. Serves 6.

CORNED BEEF CASSEROLE

1 can cream of mushroom soup
1/2 cup evaporated milk
1 can (12-ounce) corned beef, cut up
1 cup grated process American cheese
1/4 cup finely cut onion
1 1/2 cups broken noodles (cooked in unsalted water)
1/2 cup crumbled potato chips

Combine soup, evaporated milk, corned beef, cheese, onion, and noodles in a 3-quart bowl. Pour into a greased 1 1/2-quart casserole.

Top with potato chips. Bake in hot oven (425°F.) 15 minutes or until bubbly hot. Serves 4.

Tuna Casserole: Use 1 can (7-ounce) tuna (drained) in place of corned beef.

Corned Beef Casserole

BOLOGNA OR CERVELAT CASSEROLE

¾ cup grated cheese
1 cup medium white sauce
1 tablespoon minced onion
1 teaspoon Worcestershire sauce
¼ teaspoon celery salt
¼ teaspoon garlic salt
1½ cups cooked vegetables (whole kernel corn, beans, peas, or cabbage)
½ pound cold cuts (bologna or cervelat) cubed
¾ cup buttered breadcrumbs or cubes

Add ½ cup cheese to white sauce and stir until melted. Add onion and seasonings.

Arrange vegetables, meat, and sauce in layers. Mix remaining ¼ cup cheese with crumbs and sprinkle over top.

Bake in moderate oven (350°F.) until top has browned, about 20 minutes. Serves 4.

PANTRY-SHELF COMPANY CASSEROLE

2 No. 303 cans (4 cups) whole kernel corn, mixed vegetables, or hominy
1 can chopped ham, pork loaf, ground meat, franks, or sausage
½ cup water
1 can condensed cream of celery, tomato, chicken, or mushroom soup
1 teaspoon Worcestershire sauce
¼ teaspoon prepared mustard
½ cup shredded cheese (optional)

Spread vegetables in 2-quart shallow casserole. Cover with canned meat cut into serving portions.

Combine soup, water, and seasonings. Pour over meat. Sprinkle with cheese.

Bake in moderate oven (375°F.) 30 to 40 minutes. Serve hot. Serves 6.

LIMA BEAN-PORK SAUSAGE CASSEROLE

1 pound pork sausage meat
1 tablespoon fat
3 cups cooked or canned lima beans
2 cups cooked or canned tomatoes
1 teaspoon salt
¼ teaspoon pepper
1 onion, sliced
1 green pepper, sliced
3 tablespoons breadcrumbs

Form sausage meat into small patties, brown slightly in hot fat in skillet.

Combine beans, tomatoes, salt, and pepper. Put layer of bean mixture in greased casserole. Add layers of onion and pepper slices, and meat patties.

Repeat layers until all ingredients are used. Top with breadcrumbs.

Bake in moderate oven (350°F.) 1 hour. Serves 6 to 8.

BARBECUED SAUERKRAUT AND FRANKFURTER BAKE

1 No. 2½ can (3½ cups) sauerkraut
6 frankfurters
2 tablespoons butter or margarine
½ cup chopped onions
2 teaspoons sugar
1 teaspoon dry mustard
¼ teaspoon salt
⅛ teaspoon freshly ground pepper
1 teaspoon paprika
⅓ cup chili sauce
2 teaspoons Worcestershire sauce
½ cup water

Open sauerkraut; drain off 3 tablespoons juice and reserve.

Cut frankfurters in halves lengthwise; cut each lengthwise half into quarters.

In a saucepan, melt butter or margarine over low heat. Add onions and sauté until golden brown.

Remove from heat; add sugar, dry mustard, salt, pepper, paprika, chili sauce, Worcestershire sauce, water, 3 tablespoons sauerkraut juice, and frankfurter pieces. Cook over low heat 10 minutes.

Turn sauerkraut into a shallow baking dish, leaving a section free in the center. Arrange cooked frankfurter pieces in center of space and pour barbecue sauce over them. Bake in moderate oven (350°F.) 15 minutes. Serves 6.

SURPRISE COMPANY CASSEROLE

½ cup chopped onion
⅓ cup chopped green pepper
2 tablespoons fat
1 12-ounce can pork-ham luncheon meat, diced
¾ cup fine breadcrumbs
½ cup shredded American cheese
1 can condensed cream of mushroom soup
½ cup milk
3 slightly beaten eggs

Cook onion and green pepper in hot fat until onion is yellow. Add remaining ingredients and mix well. Pour into greased 2-quart casserole.

Bake in moderate oven (350°F.) about 1 hour. Garnish top with green pepper rings. Serves 6 to 8.

VIENNA SAUSAGE WITH RICE

2 small cans Vienna sausage
1 cup coarse breadcrumbs or corn flakes
2 cups fluffy cooked rice
1 cup canned tomatoes, sieved
1 small green pepper, chopped
1 small onion, chopped
6 ripe olives, chopped
Salt and pepper to taste
Butter

Leave Vienna sausage whole or cut in half as desired. Combine remaining

Barbecued Sauerkraut and Frankfurter Bake

ingredients and mix lightly.

Turn half of rice mixture into greased casserole. Spread half of sausages on rice. Add rice to fill casserole. Top with remaining sausages and dot with butter.

Bake in moderate oven (350°F.) 25 minutes. Serves 4 to 6.

HAWAIIAN PARTY CASSEROLE

2 cans (12 ounces each) luncheon meat, coarsely grated
1 No. 2 can pineapple slices, drained
5 teaspoons cornstarch
Juice drained from pineapple
½ cup sliced celery
½ cup finely chopped green pepper
2 pounds potatoes, pared and cooked

Reserve 3 slices pineapple and arrange layers of meat and remaining pineapple in 3-quart casserole.

Blend cornstarch with a little pineapple juice and add to remaining juice; cook until thickened, stirring constantly.

Add celery and green pepper to pineapple mixture and cook until crisply tender. Pour over contents of casserole.

Season and mash potatoes; place in 5 mounds around edge of casserole. Make a depression in each.

Arrange reserved pineapple slices in center of casserole.

Bake in hot oven (400°F.) 35 to 40 minutes. Before serving, dot potatoes with butter. Serves 6 to 8.

SAUSAGE AND RICE CASSEROLE

1 pound pork sausage meat
3 cups cooked rice
1 can condensed tomato soup

Brown sausage meat, stirring constantly to keep separated. When lightly brown, drain off fat and add cooked rice. Put rice and sausage into casserole.

Add soup. Bake, covered, in moderate oven (350°F.) 40 minutes. Serves 4 to 5.

Topping Tip: It's good planning to keep a package of piecrust, muffin, corn bread, or biscuit mix on hand for days when time's short and you want to turn out a meat pie fast. Other equally speedy and versatile helpers are plain or seasoned instant mashed potatoes, and the wonderful variety of refrigerated biscuits.

Variety Meat Casseroles

SPANISH LIVER

1 pound sliced beef, lamb, or pork
  liver
1½ tablespoons flour
2 tablespoons fat
¼ cup chopped onion
¼ cup chopped green pepper
½ clove garlic, chopped
½ cup sliced mushrooms, if desired
2½ cups fresh or canned tomatoes
1½ teaspoons salt
Pepper to taste
2 cups cooked noodles or spaghetti
1 cup soft breadcrumbs

Dip liver slices in flour and cut in cubes. Brown liver in fat; add onion, green pepper, garlic, mushrooms, to-matoes, salt, and pepper. Cover and simmer 10 minutes.

Place noodles or spaghetti and liver mixture in alternate layers in greased baking dish. Top with breadcrumbs.

Bake in moderate oven (375°F.) un-til mixture is heated through and crumbs are browned, 15 to 20 minutes. Serves 6.

TONGUE AND RICE CASSEROLE

2 tablespoons melted butter
⅓ cup breadcrumbs
1 teaspoon minced parsley
1 teaspoon minced onion
1 egg yolk
1 pound cooked or canned tongue
1 cup cooked seasoned rice
⅛ teaspoon paprika
¼ cup grated cheese
1 tablespoon butter

Mix 2 tablespoons butter, crumbs, parsley, onion, and egg yolk. Spread in bottom of casserole.

Cover with layer of sliced tongue. Top with layer of cooked rice.

Sprinkle with paprika and grated cheese. Dot with 1 tablespoon butter.

Bake in moderate oven (375°F.) 30 minutes. Serves 6.

SWISS-STYLE LIVER

1½ pounds beef or pork liver
Flour
2 teaspoons salt
½ teaspoon pepper
2 tablespoons fat
2 onions, sliced
2½ cups cooked tomatoes

Buy liver in one piece. Dredge with flour mixed with salt and pepper. Brown in hot fat.

Transfer to casserole. Add onions and tomatoes.

Cover closely and cook in moderate oven (350°F.) 1½ hours.

Add water, if needed. Serves 6 to 8.

TRIPE EN CASSEROLE

1½ pounds honeycomb tripe
3 cups chopped celery
2 cups chopped onion
⅓ cup chopped parsley
¼ cup butter or olive oil
1 No. 2 can (2½ cups) tomato juice
1 teaspoon salt
Pepper
¼ cup grated Parmesan cheese
¼ cup fine dry breadcrumbs

Wash tripe well and cut into 2½-inch squares.

Sauté celery, onion, and parsley in hot oil until lightly browned. Turn into heated casserole. Cover with tripe.

Add tomato juice, salt, and pepper to taste.

Cover tightly and bake in slow oven (325°F.) until tender, about 3 hours.

Remove cover. Sprinkle with cheese mixed with breadcrumbs. Raise oven temperature to hot (400°F.) and bake until nicely browned on top, about 30 minutes. Serves 6.

LIVER-RICE CASSEROLE

¾ pound beef, lamb, or pork liver
¼ cup fat
¼ cup diced onion
¼ cup diced green pepper
½ cup diced celery
2 cups cooked rice
1 cup canned tomatoes or tomato
  juice
1 teaspoon salt
Dash of pepper

Cover liver with boiling water and simmer 10 minutes. Drain and grind or chop coarsely.

Brown liver, onion, green pepper, and celery in hot fat. Combine with rice and tomatoes in a casserole. Season to taste.

Cover and bake in moderate oven (350°F.) ½ hour. Remove cover and bake 10 minutes longer. Serves 5 to 6.

LIVER AND POTATO BAKE

1 pound sliced liver
Flour, salt, pepper
3 tablespoons fat
3½ cups thinly sliced potatoes
1 cup thinly sliced onions
1½ cups medium white sauce

Roll liver in flour seasoned with salt and pepper; brown in hot fat. Cut liver in 1½-inch cubes.

Pan fry potatoes and onion in re-maining fat until brown and tender.

Place alternate layers of liver, pota-toes, and onion in baking dish. Add white sauce.

Bake in moderate oven (350°F.) 20 minutes. Serves 4.

OXTAILS EN CASSEROLE

2 large oxtails
3 tablespoons fat
6 small onions, peeled and quartered
6 small carrots, scraped and quartered
1 cup diced celery
1 teaspoon salt
¼ teaspoon pepper
½ teaspoon Ac'cent
¼ teaspoon thyme
1 garlic clove, crushed
4 cups boiling water
2 beef bouillon cubes
3 tablespoons flour
2 tablespoons cold water

Have oxtails cut into pieces at joints. Rinse and dry.

Pan fry oxtails in hot fat until lightly browned. Place half of oxtail pieces in 2½-quart casserole. Cover with vege-tables. Add seasonings. Cover with re-maining oxtail pieces

Combine water and bouillon cubes in a saucepan. Bring to boil and stir in flour which has been blended with 2 tablespoons cold water to a smooth paste. Bring to boil and pour into casse-role.

Cover and cook in moderate oven (350°F.) until tender. Serves 4.

Variation: When nearly done, add ½ cup dry red wine to casserole

KIDNEY STEW

8 lamb kidneys
½ pound sliced fresh mushrooms
6 or 8 green onions, chopped
¼ cup butter or margarine
3 tablespoons flour
½ cup stock or bouillon
½ cup red wine (or use additional
  stock)
Salt and pepper
1½ cups potato balls, cooked or
  canned

Wash kidneys and remove outer skin. Split in half lengthwise and remove any membranes. Slice about ¼-inch thick.

Cook sliced kidneys, mushrooms, and green onions in butter about 10 min-utes, then put them in greased casserole.

Add flour to butter still in skillet; mix well.

Add stock and wine gradually to make a gravy; stir and cook until thickened.

Season to taste. Add to kidneys.

Brown potatoes in a little more but-ter or margarine; place in casserole.

Cover and simmer in moderate oven (350°F.) about 25 minutes. Serves 4.

Plan contrast in texture. Most cas-seroles are moist or soft in texture. As a contrast to softness use crispness, and serve raw or firm cooked vegetables and fresh crisp salad greens.

Poultry Casseroles

WITH COOKED OR CANNED POULTRY

CHICKEN NOODLE CASSEROLE

2 cups noodles
½ pound mushrooms, sliced
2 cups diced, cooked chicken
1 cup dry breadcrumbs
¼ cup minced onion
2 sprigs parsley, chopped
1 teaspoon salt
⅛ teaspoon pepper
2 cups hot chicken stock
3 tablespoons chicken fat

Cook noodles in 2 quarts boiling salted water. Drain.

Alternate noodles, mushrooms, and chicken in a well greased casserole.

Sprinkle each layer with breadcrumbs, minced onion, parsley, and salt, and pepper. Pour hot stock over all. Top with crumbs. Dot with fat.

Bake uncovered in moderate oven (350°F.) until top layer of crumbs is golden brown, about 30 minutes.

Serves 6.

CHICKEN AND ASPARAGUS AU GRATIN

4 cups soft bread, cut in small cubes
1 cup grated Cheddar cheese
½ cup melted butter
2 cups cooked asparagus tips
½ cup enriched flour
2 teaspoons salt
¼ teaspoon pepper
3 cups milk
2 cups diced cooked chicken

Mix bread cubes with cheese and ¼ cup melted butter. Line 2-quart baking dish with half the cubes. Arrange asparagus tips on cubes.

Blend flour, salt, and pepper in remaining ¼ cup butter, then add milk and cook, stirring until thick and smooth. Add chicken and pour over asparagus. Sprinkle top with remaining bread cubes.

Bake in moderate oven (350°F.) 30 minutes. Bread cubes should be golden brown before removing from oven. Serves 6.

Chicken and Asparagus Au Gratin

HOT CHICKEN SALAD
(Mrs. Richard M. Nixon's Recipe)

4 cups cooked cold cut-up chicken chunks
2 tablespoons lemon juice
¾ cup mayonnaise
1 teaspoon salt
½ teaspoon monosodium glutamate
2 cups chopped celery
4 hard-cooked eggs, sliced
¾ cup cream of chicken soup
1 teaspoon onion, finely minced
2 pimientos, cut fine
1 cup grated cheese
1½ cups crushed potato chips
⅔ cup finely chopped toasted almonds

Combine all except cheese, potato chips, and almonds. Place in a large rectangular dish. Top with cheese, potato chips, and almonds. Let stand overnight in refrigerator.

Bake in hot oven (400°F.) 20 to 25 minutes. Serves 8.

CHICKEN JAMBALAYA CASSEROLE

1½ cups diced cooked chicken
1 cup cooked rice
1½ cups canned tomatoes
1 large onion, chopped fine
1 small green pepper, chopped fine
½ cup chopped celery
1 teaspoon salt
⅛ teaspoon pepper
½ cup fine dry breadcrumbs
2 tablespoons melted butter

Combine chicken, rice, and tomatoes. Cook 10 minutes.

Add onion, green pepper, celery, and seasonings. Turn into casserole.

Combine crumbs and melted butter. Sprinkle over casserole.

Bake in moderate oven (350°F.) 1 hour. Serve very hot. Serves 4.

TURKEY CASHEW CASSEROLE

1 cup chopped cooked turkey
1 can condensed cream of mushroom soup
1½ cups coarsely cut celery
¼ pound cashew nuts, coarsely chopped
1 tablespoon minced onion
Dash of pepper
Salt, if nuts are unsalted
About 2 cups cracker crumbs, coarsely crumbled

Mix together first 6 ingredients. Taste; add salt if necessary.

In 1½-quart casserole layer turkey mixture and cracker crumbs ending with crumbs.

Bake in slow oven (325°F.) 40 minutes. Serves 4.

Variations in toppings add glamour and individuality to your favorite casseroles. Consider these as topping materials: crisp cereals, crackers, corn or potato chips, in designs or as crumbs; tiny sausages, bologna as is or in overlapping slices, grated cheese, bacon strips, mashed potatoes, breadcrumbs, biscuits, and pastry.

CHICKEN-VEGETABLE-RICE CASSEROLE

1 cup diced cooked chicken
1 cup chopped stuffed olives
1 cup cooked peas
½ cup diced cooked celery
1½ teaspoons salt
¼ teaspoon pepper
1 tablespoon lemon juice
2 tablespoons fat
2 tablespoons flour
2 cups milk
1½ cups cooked rice
2 tablespoons melted butter
½ cup breadcrumbs

Combine chicken, olives, peas, celery, salt, pepper, and lemon juice.

Melt fat and blend in flour; add milk gradually, stirring constantly to prevent lumping. Cook until consistency of thin white sauce. Add chicken mixture to sauce.

Spread rice in buttered 1½-quart casserole. Pour sauce mixture over rice. Toss crumbs with melted butter and sprinkle over casserole.

Bake in moderate oven (350°F.) 25 minutes. Serves 5 to 6.

CURRIED CHICKEN CASSEROLE

1 cup finely chopped celery
2 tablespoons butter or margarine
1 cup cooked rice
2 cups cooked or canned chicken, cut in chunks
1 small can (about 3 ounces) whole mushrooms
¼ cup mayonnaise
2 teaspoons minced onion
About 1 teaspoon curry powder
¼ teaspoon salt
1 tablespoon lemon juice

Pan fry celery in butter until tender. Add remaining ingredients and combine well.

Turn into greased casserole.

Bake in moderate oven (350°F.) until bubbly, about 20 minutes. Serves 4.

Hot Chicken Salad Tarts

CHICKEN NEAPOLITAN #1

1/3 cup butter or margarine
3/4 pound fresh mushrooms, sliced
5 tablespoons flour
1/2 teaspoon celery salt
1/8 teaspoon white pepper
2 cups chicken broth or bouillon
1 cup evaporated milk, undiluted
1/3 cup ketchup
2 teaspoons Worcestershire sauce
Dash of Tabasco sauce
8-ounce package spaghetti
2 1/2 cups coarsely diced cooked chicken
1/2 cup fine breadcrumbs
3 tablespoons melted butter or margarine
Grated Parmesan cheese

Pan fry mushrooms in melted butter in saucepan over low heat until tender; remove mushrooms.

Add flour and seasonings; blend until smooth. Gradually add chicken broth and milk. Cook, stirring constantly, until mixture thickens and comes to a boil. Cook a few minutes longer, adding ketchup, Worcestershire sauce, and Tabasco sauce.

Cook spaghetti in boiling salted water until tender; drain. Combine with half the sauce.

Fill baking dish or casserole with spaghetti, heaping it around sides of dish. Fill center with remaining sauce, diced chicken, and mushrooms. Sprinkle with breadcrumbs, which have been moistened with melted butter, and Parmesan cheese.

Bake in moderate oven (350° F.) until breadcrumbs are browned, about 10 minutes. Serves 6.

HOT CHICKEN SALAD TARTS

2 packages pie crust mix
1 green pepper, finely diced
1 1/2 cups diced celery
3 cups diced chicken, cooked or canned
1 1/2 cups mayonnaise
3/4 teaspoon salt
Few drops Tabasco sauce
1 teaspoon Ac'cent
1 1/2 teaspoons Worcestershire sauce

Prepare pie crust mix as directed on package. Chill.

Meanwhile combine remaining ingredients.

Roll half of pastry 1/8 inch thick on lightly floured board. Cut in 4 circles 7 inches in diameter. Fit loosely into 4 6-inch pie pans. Trim edges.

Fill pans with chicken salad mixture.

Roll out remaining pastry 1/8 inch thick. Cut in 4 circles 6 inches in diameter. Cut out center of these circles with a 3-inch cooky cutter. Scallop by hand, if desired.

Place pastry rings on pies; press edges together with floured fork. Bake in hot oven (425°F.) 20 to 25 minutes, or until pastry is golden brown. Serve hot. Makes 4 tarts.

RICE AND CHICKEN AMANDINE

1 tablespoon minced onion
4 tablespoons butter or chicken fat
1/3 cup flour
2 cups chicken bouillon
1 cup heavy cream
3 cups cooked rice
2 1/2 cups diced cooked chicken
1/2 cup blanched, slivered, toasted almonds
2 tablespoons diced pimiento
1 tablespoon minced parsley
1/4 teaspoon nutmeg
1/4 teaspoon thyme
1/4 teaspoon sweet marjoram
1 teaspoon salt

Sauté onion in butter. Blend in flour. Gradually add bouillon, stirring constantly until sauce thickens.

Simmer 10 minutes; add cream and heat thoroughly but do not boil.

Add rest of ingredients, mixing well.
Pour into buttered 2-quart casserole. Bake in moderate oven (375°F.) 20 to 30 minutes. Serves 6.

CHICKEN SLICES IN CHEESE SAUCE

1 pound asparagus, cooked (fresh, frozen or 1 No. 2 can)
6 slices cooked chicken
1 can (1 1/4 cups) condensed cream of chicken soup
1/2 cup shredded American cheese

Place asparagus in flat baking dish or pan; top with sliced chicken.

Stir soup and cheese together; pour over chicken.

Place under broiler, or in very hot oven (450°F.) until lightly browned. Serves 6.

CHICKEN-WINE CASSEROLE

1 can condensed mushroom soup
1/3 cup dry white wine
1 cup cooked or canned chicken or turkey, diced
3-ounce package potato chips, crushed
2 hard-cooked eggs, diced
Celery salt and pepper to taste

Put soup and wine in a mixing bowl; stir until well blended. Add remaining ingredients (reserving a few potato chip crumbs for topping) and mix well.

Turn into a greased casserole. Sprinkle with remaining potato chip crumbs.

Bake in moderate oven (375° F.) about 25 minutes. Serves 4.

CHICKEN-RICE GOURMET

1 5 1/2-ounce package quick-cooking rice
4 tablespoons butter or margarine
4 tablespoons flour
1 cup chicken broth (canned or bouillon-cube broth may be used)
1 cup cream or undiluted evaporated milk
1/3 cup sherry
1/2 teaspoon Worcestershire sauce
Salt and pepper to taste
1 1/2 to 2 cups diced, cooked chicken
1 4-ounce can sliced mushrooms
2 pimientos, finely chopped
2 tablespoons chopped parsley
Buttered fine breadcrumbs

Cook rice according to directions on package.

Melt butter and stir in flour; add broth and cream and cook, stirring constantly, until mixture is thickened and smooth. Add sherry, Worcestershire sauce, salt, and pepper.

Combine this sauce with rice, chicken, mushrooms, pimientos, and parsley, mixing gently but thoroughly.

Turn into greased casserole, top with buttered breadcrumbs and bake in moderate oven (350°F.) about 45 minutes. Serves 4.

Chicken-Rice Gourmet

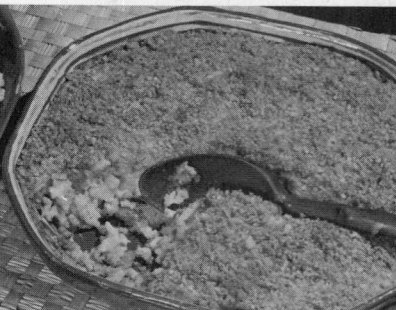

Chicken Broccoli Casserole

CHICKEN TAMALE PIE

3 cups chicken stock or water and bouillon cubes
1½ teaspoons salt
1 cup yellow corn meal
1 large onion, minced
1 clove garlic, minced
2 ounces diced salt pork
¼ cup salad oil
1 No. 2 can (2½ cups) whole kernel corn, drained
1 cup canned tomatoes
2 teaspoons chili powder
¼ teaspoon pepper
½ teaspoon paprika
2 cups diced cooked chicken
2 beaten eggs
½ cup grated American cheese

Heat stock or water to boiling. Add salt. Stir in corn meal slowly and cook to a thick mush.

Pan fry onion, garlic, and pork in hot fat until onion is light golden color. Add corn, tomatoes, and seasonings. Heat and stir until well blended.

Combine with corn meal mixture. Add chicken. Fold in beaten eggs. Pour into buttered 2-quart casserole.

Bake in moderate oven (350° F.) 50 to 60 minutes. Fifteen minutes before tamale is removed from oven sprinkle with grated cheese. Serve at once. Serves 6 to 8.

MUSHROOM CHICKEN PIE

4 small white onions, thinly sliced
1 tablespoon chopped green pepper
2 tablespoons shortening
1 can (1¼ cups) condensed cream of mushroom soup
½ cup milk or light cream
1 cup cubed, cooked chicken
½ cup diced cooked carrots (or cooked peas)
1 cup biscuit mix

Cook onion and green pepper until soft in shortening in skillet.

Combine with soup, ¼ cup milk, chicken, and carrots; pour into 8-inch pie plate.

Add remaining ¼ cup milk to biscuit mix; roll dough into a circle about 9-inches in diameter. Place on top of chicken mixture; flute edge.

Bake in very hot oven (450°F.) 15 minutes. Serves 4.

CHICKEN BROCCOLI CASSEROLE

1 cup firmly packed white sauce mix (below)
2 cups warm water
1 cup finely cubed cheese
4 chicken breasts, cooked
1 package frozen broccoli, cooked until just tender
Parmesan cheese

Place water in top of double boiler or heavy saucepan. Add white sauce mix and stir until smooth and thickened. Add cheese and cook until cheese has all melted, stirring occasionally.

Cook broccoli until just tender. Place broccoli in flat casserole or individual dishes. Place chicken breasts on top of broccoli. Pour cheese sauce over this.

Sprinkle with Parmesan cheese and place under broiler until nicely browned. Serves 4.

White Sauce Mix: Sift ½ cup nonfat dry milk solids, ¼ cup enriched flour, and slightly more than ½ teaspoon salt into a bowl.

Add ¼ cup firm butter with a pastry blender until the mixture is about the consistency of coarse corn meal.

CHICKEN SUPPER CASSEROLE

1 tablespoon minced onion
1 tablespoon butter or margarine
2 cups canned tomatoes
1 teaspoon salt
¼ teaspoon thyme
2 cups cooked or canned chicken, in small chunks
1 cup cooked rice
¼ cup chopped stuffed green olives
1 cup grated American cheese
Buttered crumbs (optional)

Pan fry onion in butter until golden. Add ½ cup tomatoes, salt, and thyme. Cook 5 minutes.

Add chicken, rice, olives, and cheese.

Put remaining 1½ cups tomatoes in greased casserole. Then turn chicken mixture over tomatoes.

If desired, top with buttered crumbs. Bake in moderate oven (350° F.) 30 to 40 minutes. Serves 4.

CHICKEN BISCUIT PIE

1 can condensed cream of chicken soup
¼ cup water or juice from peas
1 cup cooked chicken, cubed
½ cup cooked peas
2 tablespoons chopped pimiento
Biscuit dough for 12 biscuits

Stir soup; add water slowly. Blend in chicken, peas, and pimiento. Put in greased 13 x 9 x 2-inch baking dish; top with biscuits.

Bake in very hot oven (425°F.) 15 to 20 minutes. Serves 6.

CHICKEN PUFF

¼ cup butter or margarine
¼ cup enriched flour
1 cup milk
¼ teaspoon basil
¾ teaspoon salt
Dash of pepper
Dash of red pepper
3 well beaten egg yolks
½ teaspoon finely chopped parsley
1 tablespoon chopped pimiento
1½ cups chopped cooked chicken
3 stiffly beaten egg whites

Melt butter; blend in flour. Stir milk in gradually. Add seasonings and cook until thick, stirring constantly. Remove from heat.

Stir in yolks, parsley, pimiento, and chicken. Cool to lukewarm. Fold in egg whites.

Pour into 1½-quart casserole. Bake in moderate oven (350°F.) 35 to 40 minutes, or until knife inserted comes out clean. Serves 6.

CHICKEN VEGETABLE PIE

¼ cup margarine
¼ cup enriched flour
2 cups milk
½ teaspoon salt
⅛ teaspoon pepper
1 cup cubed cooked chicken, or 1 6-ounce can boned chicken
1 2-ounce can mushrooms
1 cup cooked peas
1 cup cooked diced carrots
1 hard-cooked egg, diced
1 tablespoon Worcestershire sauce, if desired
1 tablespoon diced pimiento
Biscuit dough

Melt margarine in saucepan. Add flour, stirring smooth. Add milk gradually, stirring constantly until sauce comes to boil and is thickened.

Add liquid from mushrooms. Season with salt and pepper. Fold in chicken, vegetables, egg, Worcestershire sauce, and pimiento. Turn into 6 individual bakers, or into one 2-quart baking dish.

Top with biscuit rings and bake in hot oven (400° F.) 25 minutes, or until biscuits are delicately browned. Serves 6.

Chicken Vegetable Pie

Baked Mexican Chicken

BAKED MEXICAN CHICKEN

2 cups canned corn
1 teaspoon salt
½ teaspoon pepper
2 cups cooked chicken, cut in large pieces
2 onions, thinly sliced
2 peppers, thinly sliced
1 small clove garlic, chopped
2 tablespoons chicken fat
1 tablespoon flour
2 cups canned tomatoes or 5 fresh tomatoes, peeled and quartered

Place corn in bottom of well greased 2-quart casserole. Sprinkle with half of salt and pepper; cover with chicken.

Cook sliced onions, peppers, and garlic in chicken fat until brown. Add remaining salt and pepper and flour; stir until well blended, add tomatoes and cook about 5 minutes or until thickened. Pour this sauce over corn and chicken.

Bake in moderate oven (350°F.) about 30 minutes or until brown. Serves 6.

CHICKEN AND RICE, BLACKSTONE

4 tablespoons butter or margarine
5 tablespoons flour
1 cup rich milk or evaporated milk
½ cup chicken stock (canned or bouillon cube broth may be used)
½ cup sauterne or other white wine
1 teaspoon celery salt
Salt and pepper to taste
2 cups diced cooked or canned chicken
3 cups cooked rice (1 cup uncooked)
¼ cup minced pimiento
1 4-ounce can mushroom stems and pieces, drained
½ cup slivered blanched almonds
Buttered fine breadcrumbs
Paprika

Melt butter and stir in flour; add milk, chicken stock, and wine. Cook, stirring constantly, until the mixture boils and thickens. Add seasoning.

Combine chicken, rice, pimiento, mushrooms, almonds, and sauce, and mix lightly. Turn into a buttered casserole; sprinkle with breadcrumbs and paprika.

Bake in moderate oven (375°F.)

about 25 minutes or until bubbly and delicately browned. Serves 8.

SPICY CHICKEN "SOUFFLE"

5 slices bread
2 cups cooked or canned chicken, cut in pieces
2 cups grated American cheese
3 eggs
2 cups milk
½ teaspoon salt
½ teaspoon dry mustard
¼ teaspoon thyme
Dash of pepper
Dash of paprika

Butter bread slices; trim off crusts and cut into ½-inch cubes.

Arrange in layers in greased 1½-quart casserole as follows: bread cubes, chicken, 1½ cups grated cheese, bread cubes, chicken, bread cubes.

Beat eggs with milk and seasonings. Pour over contents of casserole.

Place casserole in shallow pan and pour hot water into pan until 1-inch deep.

Bake in slow oven (325° F.) 45 minutes.

Sprinkle with remaining ½ cup cheese and bake 40 minutes longer. Serves 6 to 8.

CURRIED TURKEY AND RICE CASSEROLE

1 cup raw rice
1 medium onion, chopped
⅓ cup butter or margarine
2 tablespoons curry powder
3 cups diced, cooked turkey meat
2½ cups turkey broth
Salt

Slowly fry rice and onion in butter, stirring often until rice turns pale yellow. Blend in curry powder and cook 2 minutes.

Combine with turkey, broth, and salt to taste depending on seasoning in broth.

Turn into a 2-quart greased casserole. Bake uncovered in moderate oven (350°F.) 25 minutes or until liquid is absorbed and rice is fluffy. Serves 4.

CHICKEN-OKRA CASSEROLE

1 can condensed mushroom soup
¼ cup milk
1 teaspoon Worcestershire sauce
1 cup chopped cooked or canned chicken
1 cup cooked or canned sliced okra
Potato chips

Combine soup, milk, and Worcestershire sauce. Add chicken and okra. Turn into casserole.

Bake in moderate oven (350° F.) 20 minutes.

Cover with potato chips and bake 5 minutes longer. Serves 4.

CHICKEN HINT

Here's a guide to amount to buy when you plan to make a casserole with cooked chicken.

1 3½-pound ready-to-cook chicken will give you about 3 cups diced cooked chicken.

2 whole chicken breasts (10 ounces each) will give you 1½ to 2 cups diced cooked chicken or 12 thin slices cooked chicken.

Note: Cook chicken breasts as for stewed chicken but cook only until tender, about 30 minutes.

CHICKEN AND BROWN RICE CASSEROLE

1 cup celery, cut in 1-inch lengths plus a few minced leaves
1 small onion, chopped
2 cups cooked chicken, cut in 1-inch chunks
2½ cups chicken stock
1 cup uncooked brown rice
1½ teaspoons salt
1 bay leaf
Dash of Tabasco sauce
3 tablespoons butter or chicken fat
3 medium carrots, cut in ½-inch rounds
1 medium green pepper, cut in 1-inch strips

Arrange celery, onion, and chicken evenly in greased 2-quart casserole.

Add chicken stock, rice, salt, bay leaf (tuck to one side for easy removal), Tabasco, and butter.

Cover and bake in moderate oven (350°F.) 45 minutes.

With a fork lightly mix in carrots and green pepper.

Cover and bake 45 minutes longer. Serves 6.

CHICKEN-LIMA CASSEROLE

1 package frozen limas, cooked
1 cup cooked or canned chicken, in large chunks
1 can condensed cream of mushroom soup
½ cup milk
1¼ cups crushed potato chips
Salt and pepper

Combine limas, chicken, soup, milk, and 1 cup crushed potato chips in 1½-quart casserole.

Season to taste. Sprinkle with remaining chips.

Bake in moderate oven (350° F.) until bubbling, about 30 minutes. Serves 4.

Garnish Your Casseroles: When the dish is ready to come to the table add a final bit of colorful contrasting garnish such as fresh green parsley, pepper rings, watercress, pimiento strips, sliced olives, sliced carrots, slices of fruit.

Chicken pie may be topped with individual biscuits or a biscuit crust.

For a glazed biscuit crust, brush the topping with beaten egg yolk, mixed with equal amount of milk.

CHICKEN PIE

1 can (3 to 4 ounces) broiled mushrooms, sliced
1½ cups cooked or 2 6-ounce cans chicken, cut in pieces
2 tablespoons sliced stuffed green olives
2 tablespoons chopped pimiento
2 chicken bouillon cubes
1 cup hot water
6 tablespoons flour
½ teaspoon salt
Dash of pepper
2 cups biscuit mix

Drain mushrooms, reserving liquid. Combine mushrooms, chicken, olives, and pimiento. Place in shallow casserole or baking dish (8 x 8 x 1¾-inches).

Dissolve bouillon cubes in hot water. Add enough cold water to mushroom liquid to make 1 cup. Make a paste of the flour and a little of this cold liquid. Blend in remaining cold liquid and bouillon.

Cook until thick and smooth, stirring constantly. Add seasonings. Pour over mixture in casserole.

Prepare biscuit dough. Roll to fit casserole and place on top.

Bake in very hot oven (450° F.) 15 minutes. Serves 5 to 6.

TURKEY CORN PUDDING

1 tablespoon grated onion
2 tablespoons melted butter or margarine
1 teaspoon salt
¼ teaspoon pepper
¼ teaspoon paprika
3 eggs, well beaten
1 tall can undiluted evaporated milk
1½ cups diced cooked or canned turkey
1 cup whole kernel corn

Combine onion, butter, and seasonings with well beaten eggs; blend thoroughly. Mix in remaining ingredients. Pour into greased 1½-quart casserole. Set it in pan of warm water and bake in moderate oven (375°F.) 40 minutes, or until knife inserted in center comes out clean. Serves 6.

BAKED CHICKEN AND CORN #2

1½ tablespoons butter
1 small onion, chopped
1 tablespoon chopped green pepper
1 cup cooked or 6-ounce can chicken, cut in small pieces
1 cup whole kernel corn
½ teaspoon salt
⅛ teaspoon pepper
¼ cup milk
1 egg
1 tablespoon finely crushed breadcrumbs

Pan fry onion and green pepper in 1 tablespoon butter until onion is slightly brown. Add chicken, corn, salt, and pepper.

Beat milk and egg together; add to chicken and corn mixture.

Pour into small casserole.

Sprinkle with breadcrumbs. Dot with remaining ½ tablespoon butter.

Bake in moderate oven (375° F.) about 40 minutes. Serves 3 to 4.

OKLAHOMA CHICKEN LOAF

4 cups diced cooked chicken, or meat of 5-pound stewing chicken
1 cup cooked rice
¼ cup diced pimientos
1 tablespoon grated onion
1 cup milk
2 cups soft breadcrumbs (2 or 3-day-old bread) firmly packed
2 cups rich chicken broth
4 beaten eggs
1 teaspoon salt
1 teaspoon pepper

Combine all ingredients. Taste and add more seasonings if desired.

Place in shallow 2-quart baking dish, about 2 x 6 x 12 inches.

Bake in slow oven (325°F.) until firm, about 1 hour. Knife inserted near center should come out clean.

Cut in squares or thick oblong slices. Loaf is nice served with chicken giblet gravy to which has been added 1 can mushroom soup. Serves 12 to 15.

Chicken Saucer Pies

CHICKEN BARLEY CASSEROLE

1 medium onion
4 leeks or green onions
2 tablespoons shortening
1 cup barley
4 cups water
1 8-ounce can tomato sauce
2 bouillon cubes
1 tablespoon salt
2 cans (5-ounce size) boned chicken

Chop onion and leeks or green onions coarsely and cook in melted shortening until slightly golden.

Mix in the barley and cook a few minutes longer.

Add remaining ingredients; transfer to greased casserole or baking dish. Bake in moderate oven (350°F.) 2 hours or until barley is tender. Serves 6.

CHICKEN SAUCER PIES

1 package pie crust mix
1 egg white, slightly beaten
4 tablespoons butter or margarine
4 tablespoons flour
½ teaspoon salt
Few grains pepper
½ teaspoon Ac'cent
2 cups chicken bouillon or stock
2 tablespoons chopped chives
½ teaspoon Worcestershire sauce
Few drops Tabasco sauce
3 cups finely diced, cooked or canned chicken

Line individual pie pans with pastry; brush with egg white.

Melt butter or margarine; blend in flour, salt, pepper, and Ac'cent. Add bouillon; stir over low heat until smooth and thickened. Add remaining ingredients.

Fill pie pans. Brush inside of top crusts with egg white; cover pies; press edges together; prick with tines of fork.

Bake in very hot oven (450°F.) 30 minutes. Makes 4 6-inch or 6 4-inch pies.

Chicken Saucer Pies make perfect lunch box fare, because they are good served cold as well as hot. Half a six-inch pie is enough for a dainty eater, but the man of the house can put away a whole one with no trouble at all.

We recommend these pies especially to homemakers who pack more than one lunch every day.

Chicken and Broccoli Casserole

CHICKEN AND BROCCOLI CASSEROLE

2 cups corn flakes or 1/2 cup packaged corn flake crumbs
1 tablespoon butter or margarine, melted
1/2 cup flour
1 cup milk
2 cups chicken broth
1 cup mayonnaise
1 teaspoon lemon juice
1/2 teaspoon curry powder
2 10-ounce packages frozen broccoli
2 1/2 cups cubed, cooked chicken

If using corn flakes, crush into fine crumbs. Combine corn flake crumbs with melted butter. Reserve for topping.

Blend flour and milk to make a smooth paste; stir in chicken broth. Cook until thickened, stirring constantly. Remove from heat. Stir in mayonnaise, lemon juice, and curry powder.

Cook broccoli according to package directions only until tender. Drain well. Cut broccoli stalks in half; arrange in 2-quart casserole. Cover broccoli with chicken; pour on sauce. Top with buttered corn flake crumbs.

Bake in moderate oven (350°F.) about 30 minutes or until thoroughly heated and crumbs are browned. Serve immediately. Serves 6 (1 cup each).

HAM AND TURKEY BRUNCH PIE

1 2/3 cups cheese cracker crumbs, finely rolled
1/4 cup softened butter or margarine
1/2 pound ham, cut in strips
1/2 pound turkey, cut in strips
1 10 1/2-ounce can condensed cream of chicken soup
1/4 cup milk
1/2 cup grated Cheddar cheese
3 eggs, beaten
2 teaspoons prepared mustard
1 teaspoon Worcestershire sauce

Ham and Turkey Brunch Pie

Thoroughly blend cheese cracker crumbs and butter or margarine. Press firmly against bottom and sides of a 9-inch pie plate.

Layer ham and turkey strips in pie shell, reserving a few strips for garnish.

Combine soup, milk, and grated cheese. Heat, stirring, until cheese melts. Add beaten eggs, prepared mustard, and Worcestershire sauce. Pour over ham and turkey. Top with reserved strips. Bake in slow oven (300°F.) 45 minutes or until knife inserted in center comes out clean. Serves 4 to 6.

CHICKEN DIVAN

This dish is a simplified version of a recipe said to have originated many years ago in a French-American restaurant in New York. Turkey may be substituted for the chicken. Broccoli is sometimes used instead of asparagus.

8 stalks asparagus
1 tablespoon melted butter or margarine
3 tablespoons grated Parmesan cheese
1/2 cup sherry
4 thick slices cooked breast of chicken
2 egg yolks
1 cup white sauce

Cook asparagus; drain well and arrange on heat-proof platter or in shallow casserole.

Sprinkle with butter, 1 tablespoon cheese, and 2 tablespoons sherry. Top with chicken meat.

Sprinkle with another tablespoon of cheese and 2 tablespoons sherry.

Beat egg yolks and add to white sauce; season and add remaining sherry. Pour over chicken. Top with remaining cheese.

Bake in hot oven (400°F.) until delicately browned, about 12 minutes. Serves 2 or 3.

BAKED CHICKEN À LA KING

1/2 cup butter or margarine
1/2 cup flour
3/4 teaspoon salt
Few grains pepper
1 1/2 teaspoons Ac'cent
1 1/2 teaspoons paprika
1 6-ounce can broiled mushrooms
About 4 cups milk
3 to 4 cups diced cooked chicken
1/3 cup diced pimiento
2 cups cooked or canned peas
4 cups cooked rice

Melt butter or margarine; blend in flour, salt, pepper, Ac'cent, and paprika. Drain liquid from mushrooms into measuring cup; add milk to make 4 cups; add to first mixture. Cook over low heat, stirring constantly, until smooth and thickened.

Add mushrooms, chicken, pimiento, and peas.

Line oblong baking dish 12 x 7 1/2 x 2-inches with rice. Fill with chicken mixture. Dot rice with butter or margarine.

Bake in slow oven (325°F.) 15 to 20 minutes. Serves 8.

CHICKEN FONDUE

1 cup chicken broth
1 cup milk
2 cups cooked, diced chicken
2 cups stale bread cubes
2 tablespoons chopped pimiento
1 1/2 teaspoons salt
Dash of freshly ground black pepper
4 slightly beaten egg yolks
4 stiffly beaten egg whites

Heat chicken broth and milk to boiling point.

Add chicken, bread cubes, pimiento, salt, pepper, and egg yolks.

When mixture has cooled to lukewarm, fold in egg whites beaten stiff but not dry.

Turn into greased casserole and bake in moderate oven (350°F.) 45 to 50 minutes. Serves 6.

SUPPER PARTY TURKEY

1/4 cup butter or margarine
1/3 cup all-purpose flour
1 1/4 teaspoons salt
2 cups milk
1 tablespoon instant minced onion
2 tablespoons white wine, or 1/2 teaspoon Worcestershire sauce
2 cups diced cooked turkey
1 cup cooked or canned green peas
1/3 cup toasted slivered almonds
Cooked brown rice

Melt butter; blend in flour and salt. Add milk; cook and stir until mixture boils and is thickened. Stir in onion and wine. Add turkey and peas; heat thoroughly.

Just before serving, stir in part of almonds. Sprinkle remaining almonds on top. If desired, add a few whole blanched almonds. Serve on brown rice. Serves 3 to 4.

Supper Party Turkey

Casseroles with Fresh or Frozen Chicken

CHICKEN ALMOND CASSEROLE

1 4-pound stewing chicken
1 7-ounce package egg noodles
1 small can mushrooms or ¼ pound
   fresh cooked mushrooms
½ pound blanched almonds, browned
   in oil
1 cup medium white sauce
Salt and pepper
½ cup cracker crumbs

Cook chicken until tender in salted water to cover. Remove meat from bones and measure out 3 cups skimmed broth. Cook noodles in broth until tender.

Arrange half the noodles in bottom of greased casserole. Cover with half the chicken, then add a layer of mushrooms and one of almonds. Season to taste. Repeat layers of noodles, chicken, and mushrooms.

Mix broth left from cooking noodles with white sauce and pour over all. Sprinkle with cracker crumbs and top with remaining almonds.

Bake in moderate oven (350°F.) 1 hour. Serves 6 to 8.

CHICKEN Ā LA WARWICK

¼ cup uncooked rice
4 tablespoons fat or salad oil
¼ cup chopped blanched almonds
¼ cup chopped onion
1 3-pound chicken, cut into serving
   pieces
¼ cup flour
1½ cups milk
1 teaspoon salt
1 teaspoon sugar
3 tablespoons chopped pimiento
⅛ teaspoon pepper
⅛ teaspoon cayenne
¼ teaspoon thyme

Brown rice in 2 tablespoons hot fat or oil, stirring constantly. Add almonds and onion; cook until onion is soft. Turn into 2-quart casserole.

Roll chicken in flour. Brown in remaining 2 tablespoons hot oil. Put chicken in casserole.

Combine milk and seasonings. Pour over chicken. Bake in slow oven (325°F.) 1 hour. Serves 6 to 8.

Baked Chicken Supreme

CHICKEN GRUCCI

4 leg and thigh sections of frying
   chickens
1 large clove garlic, minced
Juice of 1 lime or lemon
5 tablespoons olive oil
1 tablespoon sugar
4 medium onions, cut in eighths
   and lightly browned in oil
1 green pepper, cut in strips
4 large potatoes, cut into balls and
   lightly browned in oil
2 tablespoons flour
½ teaspoon paprika
½ cup sherry
1½ cups water
Salt and pepper
1 can mushrooms
1 small can tiny green peas, heated
4 pimientos, cut in strips

Put chicken in bowl; sprinkle with garlic and lime or lemon juice. Chill at least 3 hours or overnight. Remove from marinade; dry.

Heat oil in heavy skillet; sprinkle sugar in and quickly brown chicken. Place chicken in large casserole or individual ones; add vegetables.

Stir flour into oil left in skillet; add paprika, and slowly stir in wine and water. Cook, stirring, until slightly thickened. Season with salt and pepper. Add mushrooms and pour over chicken.

Cover and bake in moderate oven (350°F.) 30 to 50 minutes. Sprinkle on heated peas. Garnish each serving with pinwheel made of pimento strips. Serves 4.

BAKED CHICKEN SUPREME

1 young chicken, 2 to 2½ pounds
   ready-to-cook weight, cut up
½ cup fat for frying
½ to 1 clove garlic
1 teaspoon salt
½ cup sliced onion
2 tablespoons flour
2 cups strained cooked tomatoes
1 cup (½ pint) sour cream
¼ cup grated Parmesan cheese

Brown chicken in hot fat. Place chicken in casserole.

Prepare sauce: Slice garlic and mash with salt. Cook garlic-salt mixture and onion until onion is transparent in 1 tablespoon of drippings left in frying pan.

Blend in flour. Add tomatoes and heat to boiling. Remove from heat.

Add sour cream gradually, stirring vigorously. Add Parmesan cheese. Mix thoroughly and pour over browned chicken.

Cover and bake in slow oven (325°F.) until chicken is fork-tender, about 45 minutes. Serves 4 to 5.

Old-Fashioned Chicken Pie

OLD-FASHIONED CHICKEN PIE

1 chicken (4 to 5 pounds), disjointed
1 bay leaf
2 teaspoons salt
Few grains pepper
Dash celery salt
1½ teaspoons Ac'cent
Boiling water
1 pound small white onions
1 bunch carrots, sliced
6 tablespoons flour
6 tablespoons cold water
1 tablespoon prepared horseradish
2½ cups biscuit mix

Place chicken in deep kettle; add bay leaf, salt, pepper, celery salt, and 1 teaspoon Ac'cent. Add enough boiling water to cover. Simmer 2 hours, or until chicken is tender.

Meanwhile, cook onions and carrots separately, adding ¼ teaspoon Ac'cent to each vegetable.

Remove chicken and drained vegetables to large, shallow baking dish.

Strain broth in kettle; measure 3 cups. Add vegetable waters to broth, to make 4 cups in all, adding water if necessary.

Add flour, mixed smooth with cold water; cook over low heat, stirring, until thickened; add remaining Ac'cent and horseradish; pour over chicken and vegetables.

Make biscuit dough as directed on package of mix. Roll ½ inch thick; cut with chicken-shaped cooky cutter. Arrange on baking dish. Add bits of raisins for eyes, if desired.

Bake in hot oven (425°F.) 25 to 30 minutes, or until biscuits are golden brown. Serves 6 to 8.

CHICKEN GIZZARDS WITH RICE

2 pounds gizzards
2 green onions, chopped
½ clove garlic, minced
⅓ cup chopped celery
¼ teaspoon paprika
Salt and pepper
2 tablespoons butter or margarine
¾ cup water
3 cups cooked rice

Wash fresh gizzards and cut into small pieces. Place in casserole.

Add onions, garlic, celery, and paprika. Season to taste with salt and pepper. Dot with butter. Add water.

Cover and bake in slow oven (325°F.) 2 hours. Serve with hot cooked rice. Serves 6 or more.

CHICKEN BATTER PUDDING

1 stewing chicken
Salt and pepper
1 whole onion
1 bay leaf (optional)
Minced onion
Chopped parsley

Batter:

3 cups sifted enriched flour
2 teaspoons baking powder
½ teaspoon salt
4 eggs, separated
1 quart milk
2 teaspoons melted butter or margarine

Simmer chicken until tender in water to cover. While cooking season broth with salt, pepper, onion, and a bay leaf, if desired.

Remove chicken from broth; strain broth and cool. Remove chicken meat from bones and cut into pieces.

Make batter by mixing dry ingredients, then stirring in beaten egg yolks and milk. Add butter or margarine and fold in stiffly beaten egg whites.

Place layer of chicken in greased casserole or baking dish. Season with salt, pepper, minced onion, and parsley, then cover with 1 cup of the batter. Alternate layers of chicken and batter, having the last layer of batter.

Bake in moderate oven (350°–375° F.) 1 hour.

Serve at table from casserole with gravy made by boiling down the broth and thickening it with a flour paste. Serves 6 to 8.

CHICKEN CREOLE CASSEROLE

1 frying chicken, 3 to 3½ pounds
Flour
5 tablespons fat
2 medium onions, thinly sliced
1 cup tomatoes
2 raw carrots, diced
½ teaspoon paprika
¼ teaspoon pepper
1½ teaspoons salt
2 whole cloves
3 cups boiling water
1 cup uncooked rice
Sliced stuffed olives

Cut chicken into frying pieces and sprinkle lightly with flour.

Pan fry onions in hot fat until golden; remove from fat.

Pan fry chicken in same fat until well browned on all sides. Place chicken in center of 2-quart casserole with tightly fitting cover.

Combine tomatoes, carrots, and seasonings with boiling water. Pour around chicken. Sprinkle rice and fried onion slices evenly around chicken. Cover tightly.

Cook in moderate oven (350° F.) until chicken is tender, rice fluffy, and water has evaporated, 1 to 1½ hours.

Remove cover for last 5 to 10 minutes. To serve, garnish with sliced stuffed olives. Serves 4 to 6.

CHICKEN WITH VEGETABLES

1 stewing chicken (4 to 5 pounds)
Salt and pepper
Flour
2 tablespoons butter or other fat
3 carrots, chopped
1 bunch celery, chopped
1 onion, chopped
1 green pepper, chopped
1 cup hot water
1 cup milk

Cut up chicken and season with salt and pepper. Sprinkle with flour. Brown in hot fat in frying pan. Transfer the browned pieces to a casserole.

Place vegetables in frying pan to let them absorb remaining fat. Transfer to casserole. Add hot water.

Cover and cook in very slow oven (275° F.) until chicken is tender, 3 to 4 hours. Add more water as necessary.

Just before serving, remove the pieces of chicken and skim off excess fat from the mixture of broth and vegetables.

Mix 2 tablespoons of this fat with 2 tablespoons flour; add with milk to contents of casserole. Cook 10 minutes longer, stirring a few times. Season to taste. Return chicken to casserole and serve. Serves 4 to 5.

CHICKEN PIE WITH BUTTER-CRISP CRUST

1 5-pound chicken, cut in serving pieces
2 quarts cold water
1 large onion, sliced
4 coarse stalks of celery with tops
8 sprigs parsley
1½ tablespoons salt
1 cup undiluted evaporated milk
¾ cup sliced American cheese
Thin flour paste
Cooked vegetables, if desired
Butter-crisp crust (below)

Simmer first 6 ingredients until tender. Let chicken cool in stock.

Then remove chicken and place in casserole. If desired, (a good idea because it stretches the dish as well as making a whole meal of it) add cooked vegetables—carrots (cut in pieces), small white onions, peas, mushrooms, cubed potatoes, hard-cooked eggs—any or all. A few thin slices or cubes of cooked ham may be arranged in with the chicken.

For the gravy, to 4 cups of the strained stock, add the undiluted evaporated milk with salt and pepper to suit the taste. Bring to a boil and stir in a

Chicken Pie with Butter-Crisp Crust

thin flour paste (½ cup flour and 1 cup water mixed smooth). Add the sliced cheese. Simmer 5 minutes while stirring until thickened. Pour over chicken.

Top with a round of butter-crisp pastry cut a bit larger than the top of the casserole. Crimp edges and slash top here and there.

Bake in a very hot oven (450° F.) about 30 minutes until golden brown. Makes 8 to 10 servings depending upon whether or not vegetables and so on have been added.

Butter-Crisp Crust:

3 3-ounce packages cream cheese
½ cup (1 stick) butter
1½ cups sifted enriched flour

Have cheese and butter at room temperature. Mix together thoroughly. Then, using a fork or pastry blender, cut this mixture into the flour and shape to form a ball. Wrap in waxed paper and chill in the refrigerator several hours.

When ready to use, roll the pastry to about ⅛-inch thickness. Cut slightly larger than top of casserole, following its shape. Any leftover pastry dough may be made into tart shells or used for jelly turnovers.

Baked Chicken-Dumpling Casserole: Use dumplings instead of the crust and bake them atop the chicken combination. Be sure to use a casserole or Dutch oven with a tightly-fitting cover.

Dumplings: For the eggless dumplings, sift together 2 cups sifted enriched flour, 1 teaspoon salt, and 4 teaspoons baking powder. Add 1 tablespoon minced parsley or finely cut chives. Stir in a mixture of ½ cup evaporated milk, ½ cup cold water, adding 2 tablespoons melted butter. Mix only until the dough holds together.

Drop by tablespoons on top of hot chicken, vegetables and gravy. Cover tightly. Bake in a hot oven (400° F.) for 25 minutes. Do not lift the lid, no matter how curious you get!

CHICKEN WITH YELLOW RICE

2 ready-to-cook fryers, cut up
1/3 cup olive oil
1 2/3 cups uncooked rice
1 large onion, minced
1 green pepper, minced
2 or 3 cloves garlic, minced
2 tablespoons salt
1/4 teaspoon pepper
Large pinch of saffron
8 tomatoes, cut in quarters
1 package frozen peas, thawed
2 cups water

Fry chicken in oil in large heavy skillet or Dutch oven until browned. Transfer to 3-quart casserole.

In same skillet, fry rice until golden; add onion, green pepper, and garlic; cook a few minutes. Stir in remaining ingredients. Pour mixture over chicken.

Cover and bake in hot oven (400°F.) 30 minutes. Remove cover and bake until chicken is tender, about 40 minutes longer. Serves 8.

PINEAPPLE CHICKEN CASSEROLE

1 roasting chicken, about 4 pounds
1/2 cup flour
1 teaspoon salt
1/4 teaspoon pepper
1/3 cup margarine
1 can (No. 1 flat) sliced pineapple
1 medium-sized onion, chopped
Chicken bouillon

Cut chicken into serving-size pieces and coat with a mixture of flour, salt, and pepper.

Drain pineapple slices, saving juice, and brown in melted margarine. Remove from skillet and set aside.

Sauté chopped onion in the same margarine until lightly browned and remove from pan.

Brown pieces of chicken on all sides in remaining fat.

Arrange chicken and sautéed onion in a baking dish or casserole with a cover.

Measure pineapple juice and add enough bouillon to make 2 cups. Pour over chicken. Arrange pineapple slices (or you may use chunks) on top. Cover.

Bake in moderate oven (350°F.) for 1 hour and 15 minutes or until chicken is easily pierced with a fork.
Serves 4 to 6.

Pineapple Chicken Casserole

CHICKEN AND RICE VALENCIA

1/4 cup salad oil
3 1/2-pound frying chicken, cut up
3/4 pound raw ham, cubed or 2 cups cubed cooked ham
1 large onion, chopped
2 cloves garlic, finely chopped
2 4-ounce cans pimiento, cut in strips
2 tablespoons paprika
1/2 cup concentrated tomato paste
4 1/2 cups water
2 cups uncooked rice
2 cups cooked peas
1/2 cup coarsely chopped toasted almonds or peanuts

Brown chicken well in hot oil in skillet; set aside.

Cook ham cubes, onion, and garlic in large kettle, Dutch oven, or flame resistant casserole until onion is limp and lightly browned. Add pimiento, paprika, tomato paste, and water; simmer 1 hour. Add rice and bring to boiling. Then add browned chicken.

Cover and bake in moderate oven (350° F.) until rice is done and has absorbed liquid, about 45 minutes to 1 hour. About 5 minutes before serving, stir in peas and toasted nuts. Serves 6.

CHICKEN BAKED IN SOUR CREAM

1 2- to 2 1/2-pound chicken, ready-to-cook weight
1/2 cup flour
1 teaspoon salt
1/8 teaspoon pepper
1/4 cup butter or margarine
1/2 cup sliced mushrooms, canned or fresh
1 cup sour cream
1 cup water
1/4 teaspoon thyme

Dredge chicken pieces in mixture of the flour, salt, and pepper and brown in butter or margarine. Transfer to a casserole.

Add mushrooms and sour cream diluted with water. Sprinkle with thyme and cover closely.

Bake in slow oven (325°F.) for 1 hour. Serve in the cream with fluffy rice or boiled potatoes. Serves 4.

LATTICE-TOPPED CHICKEN PIES
Chicken Pie Filling:

1/3 cup chicken fat or shortening
1/2 cup sifted enriched flour
3 cups chicken stock (or part milk)
3 cups cooked chicken, cut in pieces
1 1/2 cups cooked celery, diced
2 cups cooked peas
1 1/2 cups cooked potatoes, diced

Melt chicken fat or shortening. Blend in flour. Add chicken stock, stirring constantly until thickened. Season to taste.

Lattice-Topped Chicken Pies

Divide chicken and vegetables into 6 individual casseroles allowing 1/2 cup chicken and 1/4 cup of each vegetable per casserole. Cover with hot chicken gravy. Top with lattice strips.

Lattice Topping:

1 1/2 cups sifted enriched flour
1/2 teaspoon salt
1/2 teaspoon curry powder
1/2 cup lard
4 tablespoons cold water

Sift flour, salt, and curry powder together. Cut in lard with pastry blender or 2 knives until mixture resembles coarse meal. Add water; mix only until flour is dampened. Chill dough in refrigerator for a short time.

Roll dough on floured board to 1/8- to 1/4-inch thickness; cut into strips 1/2 inch wide. Arrange strips of dough lattice fashion over filling.

Bake in hot oven (425° F.) 12 to 15 minutes. Serve with a cranberry relish. Serves 6.

CHICKEN SAUTERNE

1 to 2 young chickens, disjointed (set aside neck, wings, and backs for chicken soup)
1/4 cup olive oil
1/4 cup butter or margarine
1/4 pound dried mushrooms (soaked for a few hours—save liquid)
1 to 2 stalks celery, cut fine
1 small onion, minced
1/2 cup tomato juice
1/2 teaspoon salt
1/4 teaspoon pepper
1 bay leaf
1/2 cup sour cream
1 package mixed quick frozen vegetables, cooked, or 1 No. 2 can vegetables
1 cup sauterne wine

Brown chicken on all sides in hot oil in a deep pan. Cook, uncovered, over low heat 30 minutes.

Meanwhile, melt butter and add soaked and drained mushrooms, celery, onion, tomato juice, and seasonings. Cover and simmer gently 30 minutes.

Stir in sour cream 5 minutes before cooking is finished.

Pour sauce into casserole. Add chicken and any chicken liquid left in pan. Cover with hot vegetables. Add wine.

Cover casserole. Bake in moderate oven (350°F.) 15 to 20 minutes. Serves 4.

Chicken Andalusia

CHICKEN ANDALUSIA

1 broiler-fryer chicken, 2½ to 3 pounds, quartered
2 tablespoons olive or salad oil
1 pound new potatoes
2 teaspoons salt
¼ teaspoon pepper
2 tablespoons tomato paste or ketchup
½ cup dry sherry
¼ cup water
1 tablespoon flour
½ cup sliced, pimiento-stuffed olives
1 package (10 ounces) frozen artichoke hearts, cooked according to package directions

Brown chicken on all sides in hot oil in Dutch oven; remove chicken, then brown potatoes.

Mix together salt, pepper, tomato paste, sherry, and water; slowly stir into flour. Stir flour mixture into drippings in pan.

Add chicken and olives; cover and cook over low heat 30 minutes, or until chicken and potatoes are tender. Serve with artichoke hearts. Serves 4.

CHICKEN LEGS WITH BROCCOLI CASSEROLE

1 pint sour cream
1 envelope dehydrated onion soup mix
About 2 cups saltine cracker crumbs, finely rolled
6 chicken legs
2 packages frozen broccoli spears

Mix sour cream, onion soup mix, and cracker crumbs. Spread this mixture in bottom of a 7½ x 11¾-inch baking pan.

Place chicken legs on sour cream mixture. Cover and bake in moderate oven (350°F.) 1 hour or until chicken legs are almost done.

Add broccoli spears and cook uncovered until broccoli is tender. Serves 4 to 6.

Chicken Legs with Broccoli Casserole

BARBECUED CHICKEN CASSEROLE

1 frying chicken, cut up
2 tablespoons butter or margarine
½ cup chopped onion
½ cup chopped celery
¼ cup chopped green pepper
1 cup ketchup
1 cup water
2 tablespoons Worcestershire sauce
2 tablespoons brown sugar
⅛ teaspoon pepper

Coat chicken with ¾ cup flour mixed with 2 teaspoons salt and brown in ½ cup hot lard or shortening. As pieces are browned, arrange in casserole.

Sauté onion in melted butter or margarine until clear. Add all other ingredients and bring to a boil. Pour over chicken in casserole.

Cover and bake in moderate oven (350°F.) about 1 hour, until tender. Serves 4 to 5.

CHICKEN BIARRITZ

1 stewing chicken, cut into serving pieces
Butter or other fat
2 carrots, sliced
2 small onions, diced
2 bay leaves
Salt and pepper
2 cups water
1 dozen potato balls
1 dozen button mushrooms
2 cups water
2 tablespoons sherry
1 tablespoon minced parsley

Brown chicken thoroughly in hot fat. Place in deep casserole. Add carrots, onions, bay leaves, seasonings, and water.

Cover tightly and bake in slow oven (325°F.) 1½ to 2 hours.

Add the potato balls and mushrooms for the last half hour. Add sherry and parsley and bake 10 minutes longer. Serves 6.

FLORENTINE CHICKEN

1 2½-pound ready-to-cook fryer, cut up
¼ cup butter
3 cloves garlic
¼ cup minced onion
1 cup ketchup
¼ cup vinegar
2 tablespoons sugar
1 teaspoon salt
¼ cup Worcestershire sauce

½ cup water

Brown chicken on all sides in butter. Place in greased 3-quart baking dish. Combine remaining ingredients and pour over chicken.

Bake, covered, in moderate oven (350°F.) for 1 to 1½ hours. Serves 4.

TURKEY WITH WINE SAUCE

2 medium onions, sliced
1 large green pepper, sliced
1 stalk celery, diced
¼ cup butter or margarine
½ small turkey (about 3 pounds), cut in pieces
Salt and pepper
3 tablespoons brandy
¾ cup white wine

Gently fry onions, green peppers, and celery in a heavy skillet in hot butter for 5 minutes. Remove from pan.

Sprinkle turkey with salt and pepper and brown on all sides.

Heat brandy in a small saucepan; set ablaze and pour over turkey pieces. When flames die out add white wine, onions, and peppers.

Cover tightly and simmer for 1¾ hours, or until fork-tender in thickest parts. Serves 4.

SMOTHERED CHICKEN EN CASSEROLE

1 broiler-fryer chicken, cut in serving pieces
1 tablespoon flour
½ teaspoon salt
1/16 teaspoon pepper
½ teaspoon paprika
½ stalk finely chopped celery with leaves
1 small onion, sliced
2 tablespoons butter or margarine
½ cup hot water
½ cup light cream

Place chicken in a casserole pan; do not overlap pieces. Combine flour, salt, pepper, and paprika; sprinkle over chicken pieces. Add celery and onion. Dot with butter.

Bake uncovered in moderate oven (375°F.) 20 minutes. Add water, bake 20 minutes longer. Add cream, cover and bake 10 minutes. Serve with hot cooked rice. Serves 4.

Smothered Chicken En Casserole

Chicken Catalan

CHICKEN CATALAN

1   broiler-fryer chicken, 3 pound quartered
1   clove garlic
2   tablespoons olive or salad oil
8   small white onions
2   teaspoons salt
½   teaspoon pepper
½   cup chicken stock or bouillon
4   medium tomatoes, peeled and diced, or 1 can (1 pound) tomatoes, drained
½   pound fresh mushrooms, sliced
1   cup sliced, pimiento-stuffed olives
½   cup dry sauterne wine
⅓   cup flour
Hot cooked rice

Brown chicken with garlic in hot oil in Dutch oven; discard garlic. Add onions, salt, pepper, chicken stock, and tomatoes. Cover and bake in moderate oven (375°F.) 1 hour.

Add mushrooms and olives to chicken; bake 15 minutes longer.

Remove chicken and onions. Blend sauterne and flour; stir into tomato-olive sauce. Cook, stirring constantly, until thickened. Add chicken and onions. Serve with hot rice. Serves 4.

CHICKEN ALMOND PIE

1   frying chicken (2½ pounds), cut up
2   cups water
½   cup chopped celery (and a few minced leaves)
1   tablespoon instant minced onion
1½ teaspoons salt
1   can (4 ounces) sliced mushrooms
¼   cup butter or margarine
¼   cup all-purpose flour
1   cup light cream or milk
⅛   teaspoon pepper
¼   teaspoon dill weed
½   cup toasted blanched slivered almonds
Unbaked pastry as for 9-inch pie shell

Chicken Almond Pie

In a pot slowly cook chicken, water, celery, onion, salt, and liquid from mushrooms about 30 minutes, or until tender. Cool chicken and remove skin and bones, leaving meat in large pieces (about 2 cups).

Melt butter and stir in flour, then cream, 1 cup stock from chicken, pepper, and dill weed. Cook and stir until mixture boils and is thickened. Stir in chicken, mushrooms, and almonds.

Turn into shallow 1-quart baking dish. Top with pastry; flute and prick. Bake in hot oven (400°F.) 25 to 30 minutes, until golden brown. Serves 5 to 6.

CHICKEN WITH RICE ORLEANS

1   large fryer, cut up
½   cup olive oil
1½ teaspoons salt
⅓   cup minced onion
⅛   teaspoon powdered ginger
1   cup raw rice
1   clove garlic
Tip of bay leaf
1   No. 2½ can (3½ cups) tomatoes

Pan-fry chicken in oil until golden brown. Place in bottom of casserole with the oil.

Sprinkle over it salt, onion, ginger, and rice, the latter washed and drained.

Bury the clove of garlic and tip of bay leaf in the ingredients. Pour tomatoes over all.

Bake, covered, in moderate oven (350°F.) until rice is tender and fluffy and tomato juice has been absorbed, about 1 hour or slightly longer. Remove clove of garlic and bay leaf before serving.

To serve, arrange rice in a mound with chicken around it. Garnish with stuffed olives and parsley. Serves 6.

Note: If preferred, cook, covered, on top of range, keeping heat very low.

CHICKEN-NOODLE PARTY CASSEROLE

1   4-pound ready-to-cook stewing chicken, cut up
4   cups water
1   tablespoon salt
2   sliced onions
6   whole black peppers
1   clove garlic, minced
1   carrot, cut in half
Few celery leaves
1   cup sliced celery
1   cup chopped green pepper
⅓   cup flour
Broth plus water to make 3½ cups
3   chopped pimientos
½   teaspoon pepper
1   pound broad noodles
2   cups (½ pound) shredded sharp cheese
Paprika

Combine chicken with water, salt, onions, whole black peppers, garlic, carrot, and celery leaves. Cover and cook slowly 3 hours.

Remove meat from chicken; cut in chunks. Strain broth; cool and skim off fat.

Fry sliced celery and green pepper in chicken fat 5 minutes. Stir in flour, then add broth and water. Cook until thickened, stirring constantly. Add pimientos, pepper, and chicken.

Cook noodles in boiling salted water until tender; drain. Put in 4-quart shallow casserole or two smaller casseroles.

Pour chicken mixture over noodles. Mix lightly with fork. Add more salt, if desired. Sprinkle with cheese and paprika.

Bake in moderate oven (375°F.) until bubbly hot, about 40 minutes. Serves 12.

"CHICKEN IN THE CORN" PIES

1   stewing chicken, 3½ pounds
1   quart hot water
4   teaspoons salt
1   stalk celery
1   small onion
2   cups cooked peas
3   cups broth
6   tablespoons flour
½   cup cold water
1   recipe corn meal pastry (see below)

Cover chicken with hot water. Add salt, celery, and onion. Cover and let simmer 2 to 2½ hours or until tender.

Remove meat from bones. Cube meat and place in 6 small casseroles. Add ⅓ cup peas to each.

Thicken broth with flour that has been mixed to a paste with the cold water. Fill casseroles with the gravy to ½-inch from top.

Roll out pastry to ⅛-inch thickness and cut circles 1 inch larger than casseroles. Place rounds on the pies and crimp edges. Prick tops to allow steam to escape. Bake in hot oven (425°F.) 25 to 30 minutes or until pastry is nicely browned. Serves 6.

Corn Meal Pastry for Meat or Chicken Pies: For corn meal pastry, stir ⅓ cup yellow corn meal into sifted flour and salt of 9-inch 2-crust pie pastry recipe. Cut in shortening and use same amount of liquid as in recipe.

"Chicken in the Corn" Pies

Chicken Casserole Fredona

CHICKEN CASSEROLE FREDONA

1 chicken, 3 to 4 pounds
Salt and pepper
Flour
4 tablespoons butter
4 carrots, diced
2 small turnips, diced
2 onions, diced
3 medium potatoes, diced
6 medium tomatoes, sliced
½ teaspoon salt
¼ teaspoon pepper
1 teaspoon sugar
2 chicken bouillon cubes
2 cups boiling water
2 tablespoons flour
1 tablespoon aromatic bitters

Cut chicken into serving pieces. Sprinkle both sides with salt and pepper. Put a little flour in paper bag, add chicken pieces and shake.

In heavy skillet, fry pieces in butter until golden brown. Remove chicken and in same butter brown carrots, turnips, onions, and potatoes. Add tomatoes, salt, pepper, and sugar. Remove vegetables.

Dissolve bouillon cubes in boiling water. Blend flour with fat in skillet, gradually add hot bouillon and aromatic bitters. Cook gravy, stirring constantly, until slightly thickened.

Place vegetables in bottom of deep casserole, pour half the gravy over them, arrange chicken pieces on top and pour on remaining gravy. Cook, covered, in moderate oven (350°F.) 45 minutes. Serves 6.

CHICKEN NEAPOLITAN #2

1 4-pound chicken, cut in pieces
Salt and pepper
1 teaspoon Ac'cent
Flour
½ cup olive or other salad oil
1 medium onion, chopped
1 clove garlic, crushed
1 small green pepper, seeded and slivered
1 cup sliced mushrooms
1 tablespoon chopped parsley
2 tablespoons tomato paste
1½ cups water
¾ cup dry sherry
Cooked spaghetti or spaghettini
Grated Parmesan cheese

Wipe chicken pieces with damp cloth; sprinkle flesh sides with salt, pepper, and Ac'cent. Coat lightly with flour. Brown pieces well in heated oil.

Arrange browned chicken in casserole or Dutch oven, or leave in the skillet if it is large enough and can be covered. Add vegetables, tomato paste, and water.

Cover; simmer until chicken is almost tender. Stir occasionally and add very little more water. Sauce should be quite thick.

About 15 to 20 minutes before serving, add sherry.

Serve with cooked spaghetti or spaghettini. Pass cheese. Serves 6.

CHICKEN WITH ALMOND SAUCE

3½-pound frying chicken, cut up
2 tablespoons butter
2 tablespoons olive oil
4 medium tomatoes, cut in small wedges
¼ cup sherry or other white wine
¾ cup salted shredded almonds
1½ cups chicken stock
⅛ teaspoon rosemary
Salt and pepper to taste
1 cup sour cream
Cooked rice

Brown chicken on all sides in butter and olive oil in heavy skillet. Transfer to casserole. Add tomatoes, sherry, almonds, chicken stock, and seasonings.

Cover and cook in moderate oven (350°F.) 40 minutes. Stir in cream and heat in oven about 5 minutes.

Serve with hot cooked rice. Serves 4.

POT-LUCK CHICKEN CASSEROLE

1 4- to 5-pound drawn stewing chicken, cut in pieces
⅓ cup flour
Salt and pepper
¼ cup rendered chicken or cooking fat
12 small carrots, scraped
18 small white onions, peeled
3 stalks celery, cut in 1-inch lengths
Dash of allspice
1 bay leaf
¼ teaspoon powdered marjoram
1 teaspoon Ac'cent
½ cup red wine

Roll chicken pieces in flour seasoned with salt and pepper. Brown in hot fat, turning frequently to brown evenly.

Place in a large casserole. Add carrots, onions, and celery.

Pour 1 cup water into pan in which chicken was browned; add 1 teaspoon salt, a few grains pepper, allspice, bay leaf, marjoram, and Ac'cent. Simmer until pan juices are loosened. Strain into casserole.

Cover and bake in slow oven (300°F.) 1½ hours.

Add wine. Increase heat to hot oven (400°F.) and bake, covered, for 1 hour. Serves 6.

SAUCY CHICKEN WITH HERB PEACHES

2 cut-up frying chickens, 3½ pounds each
Flour, salt, pepper, shortening
1 can (1 pound) cream-style corn
1 can (10½ ounces) condensed cream of chicken soup, undiluted
1 cup undiluted evaporated milk
½ cup water
¼ cup instant minced onion
¼ cup finely chopped green pepper
¾ teaspoon salt
1 can (1 pound, 13 ounces) cling peach halves
¼ cup melted butter
2 tablespoons lemon juice
Powdered thyme

Dip chicken into flour seasoned with salt and pepper. Brown in shortening in heavy skillet. Transfer to large baking dish with a cover.

In a saucepan, combine corn, soup, evaporated milk, water, onion, green pepper, and ¾ teaspoon salt. Heat until bubbly, stirring occasionally; pour over chicken.

Cover and bake in moderate oven (350°F.) 40 to 45 minutes.

Drain peaches; place cup-sides up in shallow baking dish. Combine butter and lemon juice; drizzle over peaches. Sprinkle with thyme. Place in oven during last 10 to 15 minutes that chicken is baking. Serves 6 to 8.

Saucy Chicken with Herb Peaches

Fish and Shellfish Casseroles

WITH CANNED OR COOKED FISH

THRIFTY TUNA CASSEROLE

1 can condensed cream of mushroom soup
1/2 cup milk
1 7-ounce can drained flaked tuna
1 1/4 cups crushed potato chips
1 cup unsalted cooked green peas,
   drained

Empty soup into a small casserole.
Add milk and mix thoroughly.

Add tuna, 1 cup potato chips, and
peas. Stir well. Sprinkle top with remaining potato chips.

Bake in moderate oven (375°F.) 25
minutes. Serves 4.

TUNA-SPAGHETTI CASSEROLE

6 tablespoons butter or margarine*
6 tablespoons flour
1 teaspoon salt
Few grains pepper
1 tall can (1 2/3 cups) evaporated milk
1 8-ounce can tomato sauce
2/3 cup water
1/4 teaspoon thyme
3/4 teaspoon Ac'cent
1 13-ounce can tuna
1 8-ounce package thin spaghetti,
   cooked
2 cups cooked or canned green peas
2 cups well seasoned mashed potatoes
Melted butter or margarine

Melt butter or margarine in top of
double boiler; blend in flour, salt, and
pepper.

Combine evaporated milk, tomato
sauce, and water; add all at once. Stir
over low heat until smooth and thickened. Add thyme and Ac'cent; cover;
set over hot water; cook 10 minutes.

Meanwhile break tuna into fairly
large pieces; combine with spaghetti
and peas. Add sauce; mix well; pour
into casserole. Top with ring of mashed
potatoes; brush with melted butter or
margarine.

Bake in hot oven (425°F.) about 15
minutes or until potatoes are golden
brown. Serves 6.

*Note: Or, measure oil from tuna and
add enough butter or margarine to
make 6 tablespoons.

Tuna-Spaghetti Casserole

CHOPSTICK TUNA

1 10 1/2-ounce can cream of mushroom soup
2 7-ounce cans tuna, well drained
   and broken into chunks
1 cup celery, cut in 1/4-inch diagonal
   pieces
1 cup cashew nuts
1/4 cup evaporated milk
1 tablespoon instant minced onion
2 cups chow mein noodles
1 11-ounce can mandarin orange
   sections, well drained
Few sprigs of parsley

Mix soup, tuna, celery, nuts, evaporated milk, onion, and 1 cup chow mein
noodles in a 2-quart bowl. Put into a
greased 1 1/2-quart deep baking dish.
Top with remaining 1 cup chow mein
noodles.

Bake near center of moderate oven
(375°F.) about 20 minutes, or until
bubbly hot. Take from oven. Top with
mandarin orange sections and parsley.
Serve immediately. Serves 4 to 6.

MUSHROOM-TUNA-NOODLE CASSEROLE

8 ounces noodles
1 7-ounce can tuna
2 hard-cooked eggs, sliced
1 cup drained, cooked or canned
   peas
1 can condensed cream of mushroom soup
Liquid from cooked or canned peas
1/4 cup grated cheese

Cook noodles in boiling salted water
until tender. Drain well and rinse with
hot water. Drain and discard oil from
tuna.

Arrange layers of cooked noodles,
sliced egg, flaked tuna, and peas in
greased 1 1/2-quart casserole starting and
ending with noodles.

Dilute mushroom soup with equal
amount of liquid from peas or milk.
Heat to boiling point, stirring to keep
smooth.

Pour over tuna-noodle mixture in casserole, pushing mixture aside gently to
allow soup to run down to bottom.
Sprinkle with grated cheese.

Bake in moderate oven (375°F.) until cheese is nicely browned and mixture is heated through, 15 to 20 minutes. Serve at once. Serves 5.
Variation: Substitute 1 cup crumbled
potato chips for grated cheese.

TUNA COMPANY CASSEROLE

1 6-ounce package egg noodles
1 can condensed cream of mushroom
   soup
1 cup milk

Chopstick Tuna

1/4 pound pimiento cheese, sliced
2 hard-cooked eggs, chopped
1 7-ounce can tuna*
6 tablespoons flaked cereal crumbs,
   buttered

Cook noodles in boiling salted water
until tender.

Empty soup into a pan and stir well,
then add milk and heat. Add pimiento
cheese and stir until cheese melts.

Combine drained noodles, eggs, and
tuna with sauce. Turn into buttered
casserole. Sprinkle buttered flaked
cereal crumbs over top.

Bake in moderate oven (350°F.) 25
to 30 minutes. Serves 8.

*Note: Pour a cup of hot water over
the tuna fish just as it comes from the
can to take off the excess oil.

TUNA AND RICE CASSEROLE

1 7-ounce can tuna
2 tablespoons chopped green pepper
1 can condensed cream of mushroom
   soup
1 cup milk
3 cups cooked rice
Buttered breadcrumbs (optional)

Pour oil from tuna into a saucepan;
add green pepper and cook over low
heat 5 minutes, stirring occasionally.

Blend in soup, stirring constantly until smooth. Add milk; heat.

Place hot rice in greased 1 1/2-quart
casserole. Arrange tuna chunks on rice.
Pour sauce over top. If desired, sprinkle
with buttered breadcrumbs.

Bake in moderate oven (350°F.) 20
to 30 minutes. Serves 4 to 5.

JIFFY TUNA-RICE CASSEROLE

1 12-ounce can cooked converted rice
1 6 1/2-ounce can grated tuna
1 cup grated American cheese
1/4 to 1/2 cup minced parsley
2 tablespoons minced onion
1 cup milk
2 beaten eggs
Salt and pepper
1/2 teaspoon Ac'cent

Combine all ingredients, seasoning
to taste. Turn into greased casserole.

Bake in moderate oven (350°F.)
about 1 hour. Serves 4 to 5.

TUNA-CORN BREAD CASSEROLE

    1   7-ounce can tuna, flaked
    1/3 cup canned mushrooms
    2   cups frozen mixed vegetables, cooked
    2   cups medium white sauce
    1/4 cup sifted enriched flour
    3/4 cup yellow corn meal
    1   teaspoon baking powder
    1   tablespoon sugar
    1/2 teaspoon salt
    1/4 teaspoon baking soda
    3/4 cup sour milk
    1 1/2 tablespoons shortening, melted

Combine tuna, mushrooms, and vegetables. Season well and turn into buttered 1 1/2-quart casserole. Pour white sauce over mixture.

Mix flour, corn meal, baking powder, sugar, salt, and soda. Add sour milk to dry ingredients. Stir in melted shortening and mix until smooth. Spread lightly on top of casserole.

Bake in moderate oven (350°F.) until corn bread is done, about 25 minutes. Remove from oven and invert on a hot serving plate or if desired, serve from the casserole. Serves 4 to 6.

TUNA-LIMA BEAN CASSEROLE

    1   7-ounce can tuna, coarsely flaked
    1   package frozen lima beans, thawed
    1   can condensed cream of celery soup
    1/4 cup water
    3   or 4 slices toast
    3   or 4 slices process American cheese

Combine tuna, lima beans, soup, and water. Turn into shallow casserole.

Cover each slice of toast with a slice of cheese. Cut into triangles or other decorative pattern and arrange on top of casserole.

Bake in moderate oven (375°F.) 45 minutes. Serves 3 or 4.

SALMON, NOODLES, AND MUSHROOMS

    2   tablespoons chopped onion
    4   tablespoons melted butter
    3   tablespoons flour
    1 1/2 teaspoons salt
    1/4 teaspoon pepper
    2   cups milk
    2   tablespoons horseradish
    1/4 teaspoon Worcestershire sauce
    1   cup (8-ounce can) salmon, flaked
    1/2 cup (4-ounce can) mushrooms
    2   tablespoons chopped pimiento
    1   cup cooked peas
    1   cup cooked noodles (3/4 cup uncooked)
    1/2 cup breadcrumbs

Pan fry onion in 2 tablespoons butter until golden. Blend in flour, salt, and pepper.

Gradually add milk and cook, stirring constantly, until thickened.

Remove from heat. Add horseradish and Worcestershire sauce.

Gently combine salmon, mushrooms, pimiento, peas, and noodles with white sauce.

Turn into buttered 1 1/2-quart casserole. Toss breadcrumbs with remaining 2 tablespoons butter and sprinkle over casserole.

Bake in moderate oven (350°F.) 20 minutes. Serves 4 to 6.

TOMATO-SALMON PIE

Biscuit Crust:

    2   cups enriched flour
    3   teaspoons baking powder
    1/2 teaspoon salt
    1/4 cup margarine or butter
    2/3 cup milk

Sift, measure flour. Resift with baking powder and salt. Cut in margarine or butter.

Add milk and toss lightly with fork. Knead lightly on floured pastry cloth until smooth on one side. Roll out 1/4 inch thick. Fit into baking dish.

Filling:

    3   tablespoons chopped onion
    1/4 cup chopped green pepper
    1/4 cup margarine or butter
    3   tablespoons enriched flour
    2 1/2 cups canned tomatoes
    1/4 teaspoon salt
    1/8 teaspoon pepper
    2   teaspoons sugar
    1   1-pound can salmon
    Grated cheese

Sauté onion and green pepper in margarine or butter. Blend in flour. Add tomatoes, seasonings, and sugar and cook 15 minutes.

Spread salmon on top of biscuit dough. Cover with tomato sauce.

Bake in hot oven (400°F.) 20 to 25 minutes. Sprinkle with cheese. Serves 6.

THRIFTY FISH CASSEROLE

    1   onion, sliced
    1/4 cup diced celery and leaves
    1   cup cubed potatoes
    1   cup diced carrots
    1   cup boiling water
    1/2 teaspoon salt
    1/4 teaspoon pepper
    1/2 bay leaf
    1   7-ounce can fish flakes
    1   tablespoon flour
    1   cup evaporated milk
    2   tablespoons breadcrumbs
    1   tablespoon butter or margarine

Cook vegetables with water and seasonings until tender.

Add fish, flour, and milk, mixed together. Heat to boiling. Pour into 1 1/2-quart casserole. Cover with crumbs. Dot with butter or margarine. Brown in moderate oven (350°F.). Serves 4.

Tomato-Salmon Pie

SALMON CHEESE PIE

    2 1/4 cups sifted enriched flour
    3   teaspoons baking powder
    1/2 teaspoon salt
    1/3 cup shortening
    2   eggs
    1/2 cup milk
    1   1-pound can salmon
    1   tablespoon grated onion
    2   tablespoons salmon juice
    1/3 pound cheese, thinly sliced

Sift together flour, baking powder, and salt. Cut in shortening until mixture resembles coarse meal.

Combine eggs and milk; beat well. Add liquid to dry ingredients and mix only until all flour is dampened.

Roll out 2/3 of dough on well floured pastry cloth or board to 11-inch circle. Fit into 9-inch piepan or layer cake pan.

Drain salmon. Flake into bowl, removing skin and bones. Add onion and salmon juice.

Turn into biscuit-lined pan. Cover with cheese.

Roll out remaining 1/3 of dough to 7-inch circle. Place on top of cheese.

Bake in moderate oven (375°F.) 25 to 30 minutes. Serve hot with vegetable sauce. Serves 6.

Vegetable Sauce: Melt 1/4 cup butter in saucepan. Blend in 1/4 cup flour and 1 teaspoon prepared mustard; mix well.

Gradually add 2 cups milk. Cook over low heat, stirring constantly, until thick. Add 1/2 teaspoon salt and 2 cups any desired cooked green vegetable. Or garnish with 1/4 cup chopped parsley.

Salmon Cheese Pie

FISH AND NOODLES

3 tablespoons chopped onion
⅓ cup diced celery
1 tablespoon butter or margarine
½ teaspoon salt
Pepper to taste
1⅔ cups cooked or canned tomatoes
1⅔ cups cooked noodles
2 cups flaked cooked fish
Crumbs mixed with melted butter or margarine

Cook onion and celery in butter a few minutes. Add salt, pepper, and tomatoes; heat to boiling. (2 cups raw tomatoes, cut in pieces, may be used instead of 1⅔ cups cooked.)

Put alternate layers of noodles, fish, and hot tomato mixture into greased baking dish. Top with crumbs.

Bake in moderate oven (350°F.) 20 minutes or until the mixture is heated through and breadcrumbs are browned.

Variations: Use cooked spaghetti or macaroni instead of noodles. Instead of tomatoes, use cheese sauce—a thin white sauce to which ½ cup grated sharp cheese has been added for each cup of sauce. Sprinkle with grated cheese the last 10 minutes of baking.

TUNA FISH-AVOCADO CASSEROLE

2 7-ounce cans tuna
4 tablespoons butter or margarine
4 tablespoons flour
2 teaspoons dry mustard
1½ cups milk
½ cup light cream or top milk
Salt and pepper
1 avocado, peeled and diced
Cracker crumbs

Drain tuna; shred fine. Melt butter or margarine in double boiler and blend with flour and mustard.

Add milk and cream. Cook over hot water, stirring constantly, until smooth and thickened.

Add tuna. Season to taste with salt and pepper. Remove from heat. Fold in avocado.

Fill casserole with alternate layers of cracker crumbs and tuna mixture, ending with crumbs. Dot with butter or margarine.

Bake in hot oven (400°F.) until mixture begins to bubble. Serve at once. Serves 6.

Baked Tuna in Sea Shells

TUNA HOLIDAY PIE

3 6½-ounce cans chunks-style tuna
1 chicken bouillon cube
¾ cup boiling water
2 tablespoons butter or margarine
⅓ cup enriched flour
¾ cup heavy cream
3 medium-sized onion slices
¼ cup grated Parmesan cheese
¾ cup shredded Swiss cheese
1 tablespoon lemon juice
⅔ cup chili sauce
½ teaspoon salt
2 tablespoons chopped parsley
1 unbaked 10-inch pastry shell, well chilled

Drain tuna, reserving 3 tablespoons oil for use in cheese sauce.

Dissolve chicken bouillon cube in boiling water.

In a saucepan, melt butter or margarine over low heat; add tuna oil and flour and blend. Add chicken bouillon, cream, and onion slices. Cook over low heat until thickened, stirring constantly.

Remove onion slices; add cheese and stir until melted. Add lemon juice, chili sauce, salt, parsley, and tuna; mix well.

Pour into unbaked pie shell. Bake in hot oven (400°F.) 30 to 35 minutes, or until pastry is done and cheese is browned and bubbly. Serves 6 to 8.

RICE AND FISH CASSEROLE

1 tablespoon shortening
1 tablespoon flour
Salt, pepper, paprika to taste
1 cup milk
1 cup flaked cooked or canned fish
1½ cups cooked rice

Melt shortening in saucepan. Add flour, salt, pepper, and paprika, stirring until blended and smooth. Add milk slowly, stirring constantly to avoid lumps. Cook until smooth, add fish and heat thoroughly.

Pour creamed fish over cooked rice in attractive casserole dish. Garnish with parsley, grated cheese or chopped olives. Serves 4.

BAKED TUNA IN SEA SHELLS

1 7-ounce can tuna
¼ cup chopped green pepper
¼ cup chopped onion
½ cup chopped celery
¼ teaspoon salt
Dash of pepper
½ teaspoon Worcestershire sauce
½ cup mayonnaise
½ cup buttered breadcrumbs

Break tuna into chunks and combine ingredients except breadcrumbs.

Place in individual sea shells or baking dishes. Sprinkle with buttered crumbs.

Bake in a moderate oven (350°F.) about 30 minutes. Serves 4.

Tuna Holiday Pie

SCALLOPED SALMON AND LIMA BEANS

1 8-ounce can salmon
1 No. 2 can or 1 12-ounce package frozen lima beans
Milk
4 tablespoons butter or margarine
¼ cup flour
1 teaspoon salt
Few grains pepper
½ teaspoon Ac'cent
1 cup milk
1 cup buttered soft breadcrumbs

Drain salmon liquid into measuring cup.

Cook lima beans according to directions on package; drain; pour cooking water into cup of salmon liquid. Fill cup with milk.

Melt butter or margarine; blend in flour, salt, pepper, and Ac'cent.

Add contents of measuring cup plus the milk; stir over low heat until smooth and thickened.

Flake salmon, removing bones. Combine with lima beans in 1-quart casserole.

Pour sauce over all; top with buttered crumbs.

Bake in moderate oven (375°F.) until crumbs are brown, 15 to 20 minutes. Serves 4.

TUNA-GREEN BEAN CASSEROLE

3 to 4 slices bread
2 tablespoons butter or margarine, melted
1 1-pound can green beans
1 can condensed cream of mushroom soup
1 7-ounce can tuna, flaked

Cut bread slices into cubes or cut into fish shapes with a cooky cutter. Toss in melted butter.

Drain beans; add liquid to pan in which butter was melted. Cook until liquid is reduced to ½ cup.

Add soup, beans, and undrained tuna; heat. Turn into shallow casserole. Arrange cubes or "fish" on top. Bake in hot oven (400°F.) 15 minutes. Serves 4.

Scalloped Salmon and Lima Beans

Salmon Casserole

SALMON DINNER CASSEROLE

1 1-pound can salmon
1½ tablespoons butter or other fat
2 tablespoons flour
½ teaspoon salt
Dash of pepper
1¾ cups liquid (liquid from canned salmon plus milk to make volume)
¼ pound Cheddar cheese, grated
2 cups fluffy cooked rice
1 cup cooked peas
2 tablespoons butter or other fat, melted
½ cup dry breadcrumbs

Drain and flake salmon, saving liquid.

Melt butter, and blend in flour and seasonings. Add liquid gradually, and cook until thick and smooth, stirring constantly. Stir in cheese, and heat until melted.

Combine salmon with rice, peas, and cheese sauce. Place mixture in well greased casserole. Combine butter and crumbs; sprinkle over casserole.

Bake in moderate oven (375°F.) until brown, 30 minutes. Serves 6.

SHERRIED TUNA-CRAB CASSEROLE

3 tablespoons butter or margarine
3 tablespoons flour
3 cups milk
1 cup grated American cheese
⅓ cup sherry
3 slightly beaten eggs
1 6½-ounce can crabmeat, or 1 cup fresh crabmeat
1 7-ounce can tuna, drained and flaked
Salt, celery salt, onion salt, and pepper to taste
½ cup buttered fine breadcrumbs

Melt butter and stir in flour; add milk and cook, stirring constantly, until mixture is thickened and smooth. Add cheese and stir over low heat until melted.

Remove from heat. Stir in sherry, then eggs; add crabmeat and tuna; season to taste.

Pour mixture into a greased baking dish (10x6x2 inches); sprinkle with buttered breadcrumbs.

Bake in a slow oven (325°F.) for 1 hour, or until a knife inserted comes out clean. Serves 6.

Quick Salmon Macaroni Bake

MACARONI AND SALMON SURPRISE

1 1-pound can salmon, drained
2 15¼-ounce cans macaroni with cheese sauce
¾ cup sliced peeled cucumber
2 medium tomatoes, thinly sliced
⅓ cup soft breadcrumbs
2 tablespoons melted butter or margarine
¼ cup grated process American cheese

Remove skin and bones from salmon; flake. Arrange macaroni, salmon, cucumber, and tomatoes in alternate layers in greased 2-quart casserole.

Mix breadcrumbs, butter, and cheese; sprinkle over top.

Bake in moderate oven (375°F.) for 45 minutes. Serves 4 to 6.

MEXICAN SALMON

1 1-pound can salmon (pink), undrained
1 egg
1 green pepper, minced
1 small onion, minced
1 cup canned tomatoes
⅛ teaspoon pepper
2 teaspoons chili powder
1 teaspoon salt
⅓ cup breadcrumbs
3 sprigs parsley, minced

Bone salmon and blend with egg in skillet. Add next 7 ingredients, reserving 2 tablespoons of the crumbs. Simmer 10 minutes; add parsley.

Turn into buttered baking dish or individual casseroles. Top with balance of breadcrumbs.

Bake in hot oven (400°F.) until crumbs are brown. Serves 6.

QUICK SALMON MACARONI BAKE

1 can (7¾ ounces) salmon
2 cans (about 1 pound each) macaroni and cheese
½ cup finely chopped celery
1 teaspoon grated onion
½ teaspoon dry mustard
2 tablespoons milk
Garlic bread cubes (below)

Drain and flake salmon. Combine with macaroni and cheese, celery, onion, and mustard.

Spoon into 1½-quart baking dish; pour milk over top; sprinkle with garlic bread cubes.

Bake in moderate oven (350°F.) 25 to 30 minutes, or until bubbling and browned.

To make garlic bread cubes: Melt 1½ tablespoons butter or margarine with ½ clove garlic; sauté 5 minutes; remove garlic. Toss ⅓ cup small bread cubes in butter or margarine. Serves 4.

SALMON CASSEROLE

⅓ cup chopped onion
¼ cup chopped green pepper
¼ cup diced celery
½ cup sliced mushrooms
¼ cup butter or margarine
3 tablespoons flour
1½ teaspoons salt
¼ teaspoon pepper
1 tall can (1⅔ cups) evaporated milk
1 cup water
1 1-pound can salmon, boned and flaked
2 cups fresh, frozen, or canned peas
2 cups crushed potato chips

Sauté onion, green pepper, celery, and mushrooms in melted butter until lightly browned. Add flour, salt, and pepper and mix well.

Gradually stir in evaporated milk, then water and cook until smooth and thickened, stirring constantly.

Arrange layers of salmon, peas, white sauce, and potato chips in buttered 2-quart casserole. Top with layer of potato chips and dot with butter.

Cover and bake in moderate oven (375°F.) 25 minutes. Uncover and bake 10 minutes longer or until top is brown.

When using individual casseroles, cut cooking time in half. Serves 6.

THRIFTY FISH PIE— POTATO TOPPING

3 tablespoons butter or margarine
¼ cup flour
1 teaspoon salt
¼ teaspoon pepper
2 cups milk
1 7-ounce can fish flakes
1 small onion, grated
1 cup cooked or canned carrots
1 cup canned peas
2 cups mashed potatoes

Melt butter or margarine in heavy kettle. Add flour, salt, and pepper; mix well.

Add milk, stirring constantly, and cook over low heat until sauce is thick and smooth.

Add fish flakes, onion, carrots, and peas. Pour into 2-quart casserole. Cover with mashed potatoes.

Bake in hot oven (425°F.) 20 minutes. Serves 4.

CASSEROLES

WITH FRESH OR FROZEN FISH

FISH AND VEGETABLE CASSEROLE

1 pound frozen fish fillets, thawed
Salt and pepper
Salad oil
1 No. 2 can small white potatoes
¼ cup finely chopped onion
3 medium tomatoes, peeled and thinly sliced
1 cup sour cream
1 tablespoon lemon juice
½ teaspoon dry mustard
¼ teaspoon salt
Dash of pepper
Paprika

Cut fish into serving pieces and season with salt and pepper. Cook fish gently in hot oil in skillet until golden.

Cook potatoes and onion in hot oil until golden.

Arrange fish, potatoes, and onion in a wide shallow casserole. Cover with tomato slices. Season with salt.

Combine sour cream, lemon juice, mustard, salt, and pepper. Pour over tomato slices. Sprinkle with paprika.

Bake in moderate oven (350°F.) 15 to 20 minutes. Serves 4.

Variations: Substitute 1½ pounds halibut or swordfish steaks for 1 pound frozen fish fillets. Substitute (do not brown) 1 cup cooked or canned green beans for potatoes.

FISH FILLETS FLORENTINE

4 tablespoons butter or margarine
4 tablespoons flour
1¼ cups rich milk
1 can (4 ounces) mushroom stems and pieces
½ cup sauterne, Rhine, chablis, or other white wine
¼ cup grated Parmesan cheese
½ teaspoon Worcestershire sauce
Salt and pepper to taste
3 to 3½ cups chopped, well drained cooked spinach
1½ pounds fish fillets (sole, halibut, salmon, or other favorite fish)

Melt butter or margarine and stir in flour. Add milk and liquid from mushrooms. Cook, stirring constantly, until mixture is thickened and smooth.

Add mushrooms, wine, cheese, and seasonings.

Spread spinach evenly over bottom of greased shallow baking dish (large enough so that layer of spinach is not more than 1-inch deep, about 8 x 12 x 2-inches). Lay fillets on top of spinach. Cover with wine-cream sauce.

Bake in moderate oven (375°F.) until fish flakes when tested with fork, about 25 minutes. Serves 4 to 5.

FISH FILLETS DIVAN

2 pounds fish fillets
2 tablespoons melted butter
Salt and pepper
2 packages frozen broccoli
4 tablespoons butter
3 tablespoons flour
1½ cups milk
¼ pound process cheese, cubed
¼ teaspoon salt
½ teaspoon dry mustard
⅛ teaspoon garlic salt
½ teaspoon Worcestershire sauce

Brush fillets with melted butter; sprinkle with salt and pepper. Pre-heat broiler. Broil 3 inches from source of heat for 10 to 15 minutes, or until fish flakes easily when tested with a fork.

Cook broccoli according to directions on package.

Prepare cheese sauce as follows: melt butter in a saucepan; remove from heat, stir in flour, then milk. Return to heat and cook, stirring constantly, until thickened. Add remaining ingredients and continue cooking until cheese is melted and sauce smooth.

Arrange broccoli in baking dish. Pour half of sauce over it; arrange fish fillets on top. Top with remaining sauce. Place in moderate oven (350°F.) for about 10 minutes to heat thoroughly. Serves 6.

FISH DINNER CASSEROLE

½ cup butter or margarine
1 small onion, thinly sliced
1½ tablespoons flour
1½ cups milk
1 package frozen fish fillets (cod, haddock, or ocean perch), cut in pieces
1 small can shrimp, drained, or 1 12-ounce package frozen shrimp (cleaned)
1 teaspoon chopped parsley
1 small can sliced mushrooms, drained
3 raw potatoes, sliced

Melt butter in saucepan. Add onion and cook until soft. Remove pan from heat; stir in flour and then milk.

Return to heat. Cook, stirring constantly, until smooth and thickened.

Arrange fish and shrimp in a buttered casserole. Sprinkle with parsley and mushrooms. Pour half of the sauce over fish. Top with layer of sliced potatoes and pour remaining sauce over all.

Bake in moderate oven (375°F.) 40 minutes or until potatoes are done. Serves 6.

Fish Fillets Divan

SWEDISH HALIBUT

2 large sweet onions
3 tablespoons melted butter or margarine
4 tablespoons flour
1 teaspoon salt
3 cups cooked tomatoes
2 bay leaves
2 pounds halibut steak

Cut onions in ¼-inch slices, and place all but 2 slices in well greased baking dish.

Slip the 2 slices into rings; dip into melted butter or margarine and then into seasoned flour and set aside.

Blend 3 tablespoons flour and 2 tablespoons butter with tomatoes and add to baking dish. Place fish on it. Brush with rest of butter. Sprinkle with flour and salt. Top with onion rings.

Bake in very hot oven (450°F.) 30 minutes. Serves 6.

FISH FILLET AND CHEESE CASSEROLE

1 pound frozen fish fillets, thawed (flounder, haddock, halibut, or sole)
½ cup milk
½ pound (2 cups) finely cut sharp Cheddar cheese
¼ teaspoon paprika
¼ teaspoon dry mustard
¼ teaspoon Worcestershire sauce
2 cups soft breadcrumbs

Cut fish into serving pieces and put in shallow 1½-quart casserole.

Combine milk, cheese, and seasonings in top of double boiler. Cook over boiling water, stirring constantly, until cheese melts. Add breadcrumbs and pour over fish.

Bake in moderate oven (375°F.) until puffy and lightly browned on top, about 25 minutes. Serves 4.

Fish Dinner Casserole

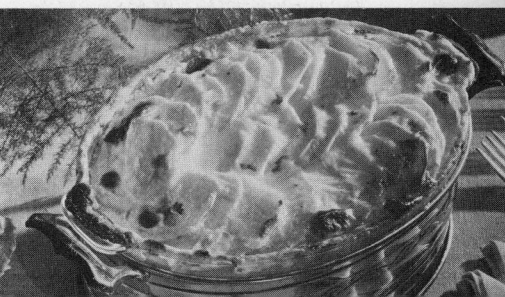

FISH NEWBURG CASSEROLE

2½ pounds haddock
½ pound fresh mushrooms, sliced
4 tablespoons butter or margarine
2 tablespoons flour
1¼ cups milk
½ pound process American cheese, shredded
Salt and pepper
2 teaspoons Worcestershire sauce
¼ cup sherry
½ cup buttered crumbs

Simmer fish in small amount of water until tender. Remove skin and flake fish into large pieces. There should be 4 cups, loosely packed.

Cook mushrooms gently in 2 tablespoons butter about 4 minutes over low heat.

Melt 2 tablespoons butter in a saucepan; blend in flour.

Slowly add milk and cook, stirring constantly, until sauce thickens.

Add cheese and cook, stirring constantly, until cheese is melted and blended in, about 3 minutes.

Add seasonings, sherry, fish, and mushrooms.

Turn into buttered casserole. Sprinkle with buttered crumbs.

Bake in slow oven (300° F.) 20 minutes. Serves 6.

HADDOCK CASSEROLE

1 small onion, minced
½ pound fresh mushrooms, sliced
2 tablespoons salad oil
2 cups medium white sauce
1 cup sour cream
1 cup grated sharp cheese
1 package frozen peas, cooked and drained
2 pounds haddock fillets, cooked and flaked

Gently cook onions and mushrooms in salad oil for 5 minutes. Add to hot white sauce with remaining ingredients. Turn into a casserole.

Place under broiler until bubbly and delicately browned. Serves 8.

SALMON ORIENTALE

2 pounds salmon steaks, cut 1-inch thick
2 teaspoons salt
Dash of pepper
½ cup of flour
¼ cup melted butter or margarine
2 cups chopped celery
1 cup onion rings
3 tablespoons chopped green pepper
2 cups whole kernel corn
2 tablespoons soy sauce

Sprinkle salmon on both sides with 1 teaspoon salt and dash of pepper. Roll in flour.

Brown steaks quickly in fat. Place browned steaks in large, well greased casserole.

Cook celery, onion, and green pepper in remaining fat until almost tender. Add corn and soy sauce; pour over the salmon. Sprinkle with remaining salt.

Cover and bake in moderate oven (350°F.) 25 to 30 minutes. Serves 6.

HALIBUT AND SAUERKRAUT CASSEROLE

3 tablespoons butter or margarine
1½ tablespoons flour
⅔ cup finely chopped onion
¼ teaspoon salt
⅛ teaspoon pepper
¼ teaspoon marjoram
½ teaspoon dill seed
2 cups sauerkraut
1 pound halibut
⅛ teaspoon salt
Dash of paprika

Melt butter. Blend in flour gradually, stirring constantly, until lightly browned. Add onion, salt, pepper, marjoram, dill seed, and sauerkraut. Mix thoroughly and turn into casserole. Put fish on top. Cover.

Bake in moderate oven (350°F.) 40 to 45 minutes. Sprinkle with remaining salt and paprika. Brown under broiler. Serves 4.

FISH DINNER CASSEROLE #2

4 to 6 medium potatoes
1 pound frozen fish fillets, thawed (cod, ocean perch, or sole)
¼ cup melted butter or margarine
Salt and pepper
½ cup minced parsley
1 package frozen or 1 No. 2 can peas

Boil and cool the potatoes.

If fish fillets are large cut them lengthwise to make 8 pieces. Lay fish skin-side up and brush with melted butter or margarine. Sprinkle with salt, pepper, and parsley.

Roll each and fasten with wooden picks. Place in center of large shallow casserole. Cut potatoes in thin slices and stand them around inside edge of casserole so slices overlap. Leave a space between fish and potatoes for peas to be added later.

Brush potatoes and fish with remaining butter. Sprinkle fish with paprika.

Bake in hot oven (400°F.) 30 minutes. Cook or heat peas. Drain. Season to taste. Place in space left in casserole. Remove picks before serving. Serves 4.

SUNSET SCALLOP

1 cup tomatoes
½ cup water
4 whole cloves
1 tablespoon sugar

1 teaspoon salt
2 tablespoons butter or margarine
2 tablespoons flour
2 tablespoons fat
¼ cup minced onion
2 pounds fish fillets

Cook tomatoes, water, cloves, sugar, and salt for 5 minutes. Strain.

Melt butter in top of double boiler; add flour and stir until well blended. Cook 1 minute.

Slowly add the hot strained tomato mixture and stir until thickened. Cook 2 minutes longer.

Melt fat and cook onions until clear. Place cooked onions in a greased casserole.

Wipe fillets with a damp cloth and place on onions. Pour hot sauce over fish.

Bake in very hot oven (450°F.), allowing 10 minutes per inch thickness of fish.

If frozen fillets are used, increase time to 20 minutes for each inch thickness of fish. Serves 6.

STUFFED FILLETS IN CHEESE SAUCE

2 pounds fish fillets
2 tablespoons lemon juice
Salt and pepper
¼ cup melted butter or margarine
Bread stuffing (below)
Cheese sauce (below)

Dip the fillets in melted butter. Stuff them with bread stuffing, roll up, and fasten with toothpicks.

Place in a 12 inch rectangular baking dish. Pour the lemon juice over them and sprinkle with salt and pepper.

Pour the cheese sauce into the dish, and bake in slow oven (325°F.) for 30 minutes. Serves 6.

Bread Stuffing:

1 cup fine, dry breadcrumbs
½ cup melted butter or margarine
¼ teaspoon salt
⅛ teaspoon pepper
2 tablespoons chopped parsley

Combine ingredients in the order given and mix well.

Cheese Sauce:

2 tablespoons butter or margarine
2 tablespoons flour
1½ cups milk
2 cups grated sharp Cheddar cheese
½ teaspoon salt
⅛ teaspoon paprika
½ teaspoon dry mustard

Melt butter, add flour and mix well. Slowly add milk, grated cheese, and seasonings and stir until thickened.

CASSEROLES
WITH SHELLFISH, FRESH, FROZEN, AND CANNED

HOT SEAFOOD SALAD

¾ cup chopped green pepper
¾ cup chopped onion
1 cup diced celery
1 cup canned or cooked crabmeat, flaked
1 cup canned or cooked shrimp, cut in pieces
½ to ¾ teaspoon salt
Dash of pepper
1 teaspoon Worcestershire sauce
1 cup mayonnaise
1 cup soft breadcrumbs
2 tablespoons melted butter

Combine vegetables, crabmeat, salt, pepper, shrimp, Worcestershire sauce, and mayonnaise.

Put mixture in greased 1-quart casserole or 8 individual shells. Toss crumbs in butter; sprinkle over top.

Bake in moderate oven (350°F.) until hot and crumbs are golden brown, 30 minutes. Serves 6 to 8.

SEAFOOD DINNER CASSEROLE

1 cup cooked or canned shrimp, cleaned and chopped
1 cup clams, chopped
1 cup flaked canned crabmeat
Salt and pepper
1 tablespoon minced celery leaves
¾ cup medium white sauce
2 cups canned corn
6 buttered toast triangles

Place the shrimp, clams, and crabmeat in bottom of buttered casserole. Season with salt and pepper. Sprinkle with celery leaves. Pour over white sauce.

Season corn and add to casserole. Arrange toast to cover most of the top. If the corn is dry, moisten with a little milk.

Bake in moderate oven (350°F.) about 25 minutes. Serves 6.

SHRIMP CREOLE CASSEROLE

1 No. 1 picnic can shrimp
2 cans condensed tomato soup
⅓ cup chopped onion
1 can (12 ounces) whole kernel corn
¼ cup pimiento, cut in strips
3 tablespoons chopped green pepper
1 teaspoon chili powder
⅔ cup buttered crumbs

Clean black veins from shrimp and combine all ingredients except crumbs.

Place in baking dish. Top with buttered crumbs.

Bake in moderate oven (375°F.) about 30 minutes. Serves 6.

PARTY SHRIMP PIE

½ cup butter or margarine
¼ cup flour
½ teaspoon salt
⅛ teaspoon pepper
¼ teaspoon mace
2 cups milk
1 tablespoon sherry (optional)
2 cups cooked cleaned shrimp
1 tablespoon lemon juice
3 cups (½ pound) sliced fresh mushrooms
1 cup oven-popped rice cereal
1 tablespoon melted butter or margarine

Melt ¼ cup butter and stir in flour and seasonings. Add milk slowly, stirring constantly, and cook until thickened, stirring occasionally. Stir in sherry.

Sprinkle shrimp with lemon juice. Cook mushrooms in remaining butter until golden brown. Reserve a few shrimp and mushrooms for garnish, if desired.

Fold remaining shrimp and mushrooms into sauce. Pour into buttered 1½-quart casserole.

Mix oven-popped rice cereal with melted butter and sprinkle over mixture. Garnish with shrimp and mushrooms.

Bake in hot oven (400° F.) about 20 minutes or until browned. Garnish with parsley, if desired. Serves 6.

SHRIMP—CORN MEAL—TOMATO CASSEROLE

3 cups boiling water
1 teaspoon salt
¾ cup corn meal
2 slices bacon, chopped
1 cup canned tomatoes
3 tablespoons finely chopped onion
3 tablespoons finely chopped green pepper
1 teaspoon salt
⅛ teaspoon pepper
½ teaspoon Worcestershire sauce
1 cup ripe olives
1 10½-ounce can shrimp, cleaned
⅔ cup grated American cheese

Add 1 teaspoon salt to boiling water; gradually stir in corn meal and cook until thickened.

Fry bacon until crisp; add tomatoes, onion, green pepper, 1 teaspoon salt, pepper, and Worcestershire sauce to bacon and drippings. Cook 10 minutes.

Cut olives from pits in large pieces. Add with shrimp to vegetable mixture.

Place half of corn meal in 1½-quart casserole. Cover with half of shrimp-vegetable mixture and half of cheese. Repeat layers.

Bake in moderate oven (350°F.) 30 minutes. Serves 6.

Party Shrimp Pie

CLAM AND CORN CASSEROLE

2 eggs
1 cup milk
1¼ cups coarsely crumbled soda crackers
1 7-ounce can minced clams, undrained
1 cup frozen corn, thawed just enough to separate
3 tablespoons melted butter or margarine
1 tablespoon minced green pepper
2 tablespoons finely chopped onion
½ teaspoon Worcestershire sauce
About ¼ teaspoon salt
½ cup grated process American cheese

Beat eggs; add milk and crumbled crackers. Let stand a few minutes to soften.

Add remaining ingredients except cheese and gently mix together. Add more salt to taste if crackers are unsalted. Turn into 1½-quart casserole.

Bake in moderate oven (350°F.) until firm, about 50 minutes. Sprinkle with cheese. Bake until cheese melts, about 5 minutes longer. Serves 4 to 6.

SCALLOPS NEWBURG CASSEROLE

1 pint scallops
3 tablespoons butter
1 teaspoon lemon juice
2 teaspoons flour
¼ teaspoon salt
Dash of cayenne pepper
½ cup plus 2 tablespoons cream
2 well beaten egg yolks
½ cup buttered breadcrumbs

If scallops are very large cut into pieces. Cook scallops in salted water 3 to 5 minutes. Drain and dry.

Put 2 tablespoons butter in a fry pan and add scallops. Heat 3 minutes and add lemon juice.

Melt remaining 1 tablespoon butter in saucepan. Add flour and stir until well blended.

Add salt and cayenne. Add cream gradually, stirring constantly, until mixture thickens.

Remove from heat and very slowly add to beaten egg yolks. Add scallops. Pour into 1½-quart casserole. Sprinkle with crumbs.

Brown in hot oven (425°F.) 10 minutes. Serves 4.

CRABMEAT AND CHEESE BAKE

3 tablespoons mayonnaise or salad dressing
1 tablespoon prepared mustard
¼ teaspoon salt
1 6½-ounce can crabmeat
1 cup diced celery
8 thin bread slices
¾ pound sliced American cheese
2 eggs
1 cup milk
1 teaspoon Worcestershire sauce

Combine mayonnaise, mustard, and salt. Mix with combined crabmeat and celery. Spread between bread slices. Cut sandwiches in halves.

Alternate layers of sandwiches and cheese in greased casserole. Beat eggs; add milk and Worcestershire sauce. Pour into casserole. Cover and bake in slow oven (325°F.) 45 minutes. Serves 4.

SHRIMP IN BARBECUE SAUCE

1 cup cleaned shrimp, home cooked or canned
2 cups cooked rice
Mexican barbecue sauce (below)
½ cup grated cheese
Ripe olives (optional)

Make alternate layers of shrimp and rice in a casserole. Pour sauce over rice and shrimp layers.

Top with grated cheese and bake in moderate oven (350°F.) for 20 minutes. Garnish with olives. Serves 4 to 5.

Mexican Barbecue Sauce:

½ cup butter or margarine
1 small onion, minced
1 clove garlic, minced
1½ teaspoons mustard
2 tablespoons chili powder
1 cup tomato ketchup
½ cup vinegar or lemon juice
½ cup water
1 tablespoon sugar
1 tablespoon Worcestershire sauce

Sauté onion and garlic in butter; add other ingredients and boil 5 minutes or until thick.

Note: This is a delicious sauce for broiling or roasting meat or for adding new flavor to leftover meats.

Shrimp in Barbecue Sauce

OYSTER AND MACARONI SCALLOP

3 tablespoons butter or margarine
½ cup finely chopped celery
¼ cup finely chopped green pepper
3 tablespoons flour
⅛ teaspoon pepper
½ teaspoon salt
2 cups milk
1 pint shucked oysters
½ pound macaroni shells, cooked
½ cup breadcrumbs
Additional 2 tablespoons butter or margarine
1 tablespoon minced parsley

Pan fry celery and green pepper in 3 tablespoons melted butter until tender. Blend in flour and seasonings. Gradually add milk, stirring over low heat until smooth and thick.

Add oysters, which have been cut in halves if very large.

In a greased 2-quart casserole place a layer of one-third of the cooked macaroni. Cover with half the oyster mixture.

Add a second layer of macaroni, then a layer of oyster mixture, and top with final layer of macaroni. Press down slightly with a large spoon.

Brown the breadcrumbs slightly in remaining butter or margarine. Combine with parsley and sprinkle over top of casserole.

Bake in moderate oven (350°F.) 30 minutes. Serves 6 to 8.

Variations:

Clam and Macaroni Scallop: Substitute 1 pint shucked clams for oysters.

Ham and Macaroni Scallop: Substitute 2 cups diced cooked or canned ham for oysters.

Crabmeat, Bonito, Salmon, or Tuna-Macaroni Scallop: Substitute 2 cans (6½ or 7 ounces each) of other seafood for oysters. Break into bite-size pieces before using.

LOBSTER AND MUSHROOM CASSEROLE

4 tablespoons butter
1½ tablespoons flour
2 tablespoons grated Parmesan or Romano cheese
½ cup dry white wine
¼ pound fresh mushrooms, sliced
Salt and pepper
1 slightly beaten egg
1 package frozen lobster, thawed

Melt butter in saucepan. Blend in flour and cheese. Gradually stir in wine.

Heat mushrooms in sauce. Add salt and pepper to taste. Remove from heat. Let cool, then stir in egg. Add lobster. Turn into buttered casserole.

Bake in moderate oven (350°F.) 30 minutes. Serves 4.

Oyster and Macaroni Scallop

CRABMEAT WITH CORN AND EGGS

1 cup fresh-cooked or 1 6½-ounce can crabmeat, flaked
1½ cups drained canned whole kernel corn
3 hard-cooked eggs, chopped fine
1 tablespoon chopped parsley
2 teaspoons lemon juice
1 tablespoon finely chopped onion
4 tablespoons butter or margarine
2 tablespoons flour
1 teaspoon dry mustard
1 cup milk
½ teaspoon salt
½ teaspoon Worcestershire sauce
½ cup soft breadcrumbs
¼ cup grated Parmesan cheese

Combine crabmeat, corn, eggs, parsley, and lemon juice; turn into 1½-quart casserole.

Cook onion in 3 tablespoons melted butter in saucepan until tender, about 3 minutes. Stir in flour and mustard. Gradually add milk and cook, stirring constantly, until thickened. Add salt and Worcestershire. Turn into casserole and combine with crabmeat mixture.

Combine crumbs and cheese with 1 tablespoon melted butter; sprinkle over casserole.

Bake in moderate oven (375°F.) until hot and browned on top, 20 to 25 minutes. Serves 6.

CLAM AND VEGETABLE PIE

4 carrots, sliced
4 onions, sliced
4 potatoes, sliced
½ cup chopped celery tops
1 bay leaf
Dash of garlic salt
½ teaspoon thyme
1 teaspoon salt
⅛ teaspoon pepper
1 cup water
1 10½-ounce can minced clams
1 tablespoon butter or margarine
Pastry for top

Cook vegetables with seasoning in water for 8 minutes covered. Add undrained clams.

Turn into 2-quart casserole. Dot with butter or margarine.

Top with pastry. Bake in very hot oven (450°F.) 25 minutes. Serves 4.

LOBSTER NEWBURG CASSEROLE

2   cups canned, frozen, or fresh
      cooked lobster
½   teaspoon dry mustard
6   tablespoons butter
1½ cups sliced fresh mushrooms
3   egg yolks
1½ cups heavy cream
1   teaspoon salt
Dash of cayenne
¼   cup sherry

Separate cooked lobster meat into
small pieces.

Blend mustard into melted butter
in skillet. Add lobster and mushrooms
and sauté lightly about 5 minutes.

Mix egg yolks, cream, and seasonings
together and cook in double boiler,
stirring constantly, until mixture coats
a spoon.

Combine with lobster and mushrooms. Heat through, then stir in
sherry. Fill individual casseroles or
shells and bake in hot oven (400° F.)
until mixture is heated through, about
10 minutes. Serve at once. Serves 4.

SHRIMP, RICE, AND CHEESE DELIGHT

¼   pound fresh mushrooms, sliced
2   tablespoons butter or margarine
1   pound fresh cooked shrimp or 2
      cans (5¾ ounces each)
1½ cups cooked rice
1½ cups shredded process American
      cheese
½   cup cream or undiluted evapor-
      ated milk
3   tablespoons ketchup
½   teaspoon Worcestershire sauce
Salt and pepper

Sauté mushrooms in butter or margarine until tender, about 5 minutes.
Mix lightly with shrimp, rice, and
cheese.

Combine cream or evaporated milk,
ketchup, Worcestershire sauce, and salt
and pepper to taste. Add to shrimp mixture. Pour into individual casseroles.

Bake in moderate oven (350°F.) 25
minutes. Serves 5 to 6.

Variations: Two cups cooked cubed
chicken may be used instead of shrimp.
Cooked noodles or macaroni may be
used instead of rice.

Crabmeat Cobbler

SHRIMP WITH RICE AND MUSHROOMS

1   pound fresh mushrooms, sliced
¼   cup butter or margarine
1   pound fresh cooked shrimp,
      cleaned or 2 cans (5¾ ounces
      each)
2   cups cooked rice
½   pound Cheddar cheese, shredded
1   cup evaporated milk or cream
⅓   cup ketchup
1   teaspoon Worcestershire sauce
Salt and pepper

Sauté mushrooms in butter until tender, about 5 minutes. Add shrimp, rice,
and cheese.

Combine milk or cream, ketchup,
Worcestershire sauce, and salt and pepper to taste. Add to first mixture. Turn
into casserole.

Bake in moderate oven (350°F.) 45
minutes. Serves 6 to 8.

CRABMEAT COBBLER

½   cup butter or margarine
½   cup chopped green pepper
½   cup chopped onion
½   cup sifted enriched flour
1   teaspoon dry mustard
½   teaspoon Ac'cent
1   cup milk
1   cup shredded American cheese
1   cup (6½-ounce can) crabmeat,
      boned
1½ cups drained tomatoes (No. 2
      can)
2   teaspoons Worcestershire sauce
½   teaspoon salt

Melt butter or margarine in top of
double boiler.

Add green pepper and onion. Cook
over boiling water until tender, about
10 minutes.

Blend in flour, mustard, Ac'cent,
milk, and cheese. Cook, stirring constantly, until cheese is melted and mixture is very thick.

Add crabmeat, tomatoes, Worcestershire sauce, and salt. Blend thoroughly.
Pour into 2-quart casserole.

Cheese Biscuit Topping:

1   cup sifted enriched flour
2   teaspoons baking powder
½   teaspoon salt
¼   cup shredded American cheese
2   tablespoons shortening
½   cup milk

Sift together flour, baking powder,
and salt into mixing bowl. Add cheese.

Cut in shortening thoroughly until
particles are fine.

Add milk; mix only until all flour is
moistened. Drop by rounded teaspoonfuls on top of hot crabmeat mixture.

Bake in very hot oven (450°F.) 20 to
25 minutes. Serves 6 to 8.

*Lobster Tails Thermidor
en Casserole*

LOBSTER TAILS THERMIDOR EN CASSEROLE

2   packages frozen rock lobster tails
      (4 tails)
1   tablespoon butter or margarine
1   tablespoon flour
1   cup milk
1   beaten egg
1   teaspoon dry mustard
¼   teaspoon salt
Dash of cayenne pepper
About ¾ cup cracker crumbs, coarsely
      crumbled

Cook lobster tails according to directions on package. Remove meat from
shell; cut into small pieces.

Melt butter or margarine; blend in
flour. Gradually stir in milk; cook and
stir constantly until mixture thickens
and boils 2 minutes. Remove from heat.

Stir a little hot mixture into egg;
combine with remaining mixture; stir
in mustard, salt, cayenne, and lobster
meat (and a dash of sherry if you wish).
Pour into 1½-quart casserole. Sprinkle
top with cracker crumbs.

Bake in moderate oven (350° F.) 15
minutes. Before bringing to table, arrange shells on top. To serve, put shells
on plates and spoon lobster into shells.
Serves 4.

CRABMEAT-SPAGHETTI PARTY CASSEROLE

2½ cups thin spaghetti, broken in
      pieces
1   can condensed tomato soup
1   tall can evaporated milk
1   6½-ounce can crabmeat, flaked
1   cup grated process American
      cheese
1   tablespoon finely chopped onion
¼   cup finely chopped green pepper
½   teaspoon salt
Dash of thyme
1   tablespoon melted butter
½   cup soft breadcrumbs

Cook spaghetti in boiling salted
water; drain.

Combine in 2-quart casserole the
spaghetti, soup, milk, crabmeat, cheese,
onion, green pepper, salt, and thyme.

Combine melted butter and breadcrumbs; sprinkle over top.

Bake in moderate oven (350°F.) 45
minutes. Serves 8.

CRABMEAT WITH EGGS AND MUSHROOMS

1   6½-ounce can crabmeat, flaked
1½ cups (3 to 4) chopped hard-cooked eggs
½   cup (4-ounce can) mushrooms
2   tablespoons chopped onion
3   tablespoons melted butter
1   cup cooked peas
¼   pound American cheese, grated
2   teaspoons lemon juice
Dash of curry powder
½   teaspoon salt
2   cups thin white sauce
½   cup breadcrumbs

Combine crabmeat, eggs, and mushrooms.

Pan fry onion in 1 tablespoon melted butter until golden; add to crabmeat mixture.

Lightly mix in peas, grated cheese, lemon juice, curry powder, and salt.

Turn into buttered 1½-quart casserole. Pour white sauce over top. Toss breadcrumbs with remaining 2 tablespoons melted butter and sprinkle over top of casserole.

Bake in moderate oven (350°F.) 25 minutes. Serves 4 to 6.

TOMATO CRAB CASSEROLE

2½ cups thin spaghetti, broken
1   cup evaporated milk
1   can cream of tomato soup
1   6½-ounce can crabmeat, flaked
1½ cups shredded sharp Cheddar cheese
¼   cup chopped green pepper
2   tablespoons minced onion
¼   teaspoon marjoram
½   teaspoon salt
⅛   teaspoon pepper
Buttered breadcrumbs

Cook spaghetti in boiling salted water until tender, about 10 minutes. Drain.

Mix evaporated milk, tomato soup, flaked crabmeat, 1 cup shredded cheese, green pepper, onion, and seasonings. Mix in the spaghetti.

Pour into a buttered 1½-quart casserole. Top with the remaining ½ cup shredded cheese and the buttered crumbs. Bake in a moderate oven (350°F.) 45 minutes. Serves 4 to 6.

Tomato Crab Casserole

SHRIMP WITH SPAGHETTI AND CHEESE

½   cup chopped onion
3   tablespoons butter or margarine
¼   cup chopped green pepper
1   No. 2 can (2½ cups) tomatoes
1½ teaspoons salt
¼   teaspoon paprika
1   teaspoon Worcestershire sauce
4   ounces spaghetti, cooked and drained
½   pound fresh cooked shrimp or 1 7-ounce can
1   cup grated Parmesan cheese

Sauté onion in butter until soft and yellow. Add green pepper, tomatoes, and seasonings. Simmer 10 minutes.

Add spaghetti, cleaned shrimp, and ½ cup grated cheese. Turn into casserole. Sprinkle with remaining cheese.

Bake in moderate oven (350°F.) until cheese is melted, about 20 minutes. Serves 4.

SHRIMP WITH ARTICHOKES AND MUSHROOMS

8   to 12 cooked artichoke hearts or 1 No. 2 can artichoke hearts
1   7-ounce can shrimp, cleaned
½   pound fresh mushrooms or 1 cup drained canned mushrooms
2   tablespoons butter or margarine
1½ cups medium white sauce
1   tablespoon Worcestershire sauce
¼   cup sherry
Salt and pepper
¼   cup grated Parmesan cheese

Arrange artichoke hearts in buttered shallow casserole. Spread cleaned shrimp around them.

Cook mushrooms in butter 5 minutes and add to casserole. Season white sauce with Worcestershire, sherry, and salt and pepper to taste and pour over all. Sprinkle top with cheese and paprika.

Bake in moderate oven (375°F.) 20 minutes. Serves 4 or more.

Variation: If desired, substitute canned or fresh flaked, cooked crabmeat for shrimp. Fresh cooked and cleaned shrimp may also be used.

CURRIED SHRIMP IN ZUCCHINI

2   pounds zucchini
3   tablespoons fat
1   tablespoon minced onion
1   teaspoon curry powder
½   teaspoon salt
Dash of cayenne
2   tablespoons flour
¼   cup undiluted evaporated milk or top milk
2   8-ounce cans shrimp, cleaned,
½   cup dry breadcrumbs

Split zucchini lengthwise and cook in boiling salted water 5 minutes. Hollow

out the centers; chop it and drain shells.

Melt fat; add onion, curry, salt, cayenne, flour, and milk. Stir well.

When thickened add shrimp cut in small bits. Season to taste. Add chopped zucchini. Stuff shells and sprinkle with crumbs.

Brown in moderate oven (350°F.) 15 minutes. Serves 6.

SPAGHETTI CLAM BAKE

¼   cup finely chopped onion
¼   cup finely chopped green pepper
2   tablespoons melted butter or margarine
1   cup (7-ounce can) minced clams, drained
¼   cup clam liquid
½   teaspoon salt
2   cans spaghetti with tomato sauce and cheese
⅓   cup grated sharp process cheese

Sauté onion and green pepper in butter until tender. Combine with clams and next 3 ingredients; pour into 1½-quart casserole. Top spaghetti mixture with cheese.

Bake in moderate oven (375°F.) 30 minutes or until cheese is melted and casserole is hot. Serves 4 to 6.

SHRIMP THERMIDOR EN CASSEROLE

½   pound fresh mushrooms, sliced
¼   cup butter
Additional ⅓ cup butter
½   cup sifted flour
3   cups warm light cream
¼   cup grated Parmesan cheese
2   tablespoons dry white wine
¼   teaspoon dry mustard
Pinch of cayenne
3   cups cooked shrimp, cut in 1-inch pieces
1½ teaspoons salt
Additional grated Parmesan cheese
Additional melted butter

Cook mushrooms in ¼ cup butter until lightly browned.

Melt additional ⅓ cup butter in saucepan. Stir in flour until smooth. Gradually add cream, and cook over low heat, stirring constantly, until thickened. Simmer 3 minutes.

Add ¼ cup grated cheese, wine, mustard, cayenne, cooked mushrooms, shrimp, and salt. Mix well. Turn into casserole.

Sprinkle top generously with additional grated Parmesan cheese, then sprinkle with additional melted butter.

Bake in hot oven (400°F.) 15 minutes, then place under broiler to brown top. Serves 6.

Variations: Cooked lobster, crabmeat, and other shellfish may be substituted for shrimp.

Miscellaneous Casseroles and One-Dish Meals

CHOP SUEY AND CHOW MEIN

Chop Suey is an American-Chinese dish that originated in the United States and is unknown in China. It is made of a great variety of ingredients, which may include chicken, other meats, seafood, bamboo shoots, bean sprouts, water chestnuts, mushrooms, and stock. It is served with rice. Chow Mein is a dish similar to Chop Suey but served with fried noodles instead of rice.

CHICKEN CHOP SUEY
(Master Recipe)

4 tablespoons butter, margarine, shortening, or salad oil
2 medium onions, chopped
4 outside stalks celery, sliced fine
1/2 pound fresh mushrooms, sliced through stems
1/2 cup boiling chicken stock or 1/2 cup boiling bean sprout liquid
1/2 teaspoon salt
1/4 teaspoon pepper
2 cups cooked chicken
1 can bean sprouts, drained
2 tablespoons cornstarch
1 teaspoon sugar
1/2 cup cold bean sprout liquid
2 tablespoons soy sauce
Hot boiled rice

Heat fat or oil over low heat in large heavy saucepan or Dutch oven. Add onions, celery, and mushrooms. Cover and cook over low heat until celery is almost tender, about 10 minutes.

Add 1/2 cup boiling stock, salt, and pepper; simmer 5 minutes.

Add chicken, cut into matchlike slivers, and drained sprouts.

Mix cornstarch and sugar with 1/2 cup cold liquid and add soy sauce.

Add 1/2 cup of hot chicken mixture and mix well, then pour back into remaining chicken mixture.

Cook, stirring constantly, until mixture thickens. Serve with additional soy sauce and hot boiled rice. Serves 6.

Chow Mein

Chicken Chop Suey Variations

Lobster Chop Suey: Substitute cooked or canned lobster, cut into thin strips, for cooked chicken. Add lobster meat just before serving and heat through. Overcooking toughens lobster meat.

Crabmeat Chop Suey: Substitute flaked cooked or canned crabmeat for chicken.

Pork Chop Suey: Substitute cooked pork for chicken.

Other Variations of Chop Suey: Veal may be substituted for chicken to make Mock Chicken Chop Suey. Raw seafood or meat may be substituted for cooked or canned seafood or meat; however, it must be cut up into matchlike strips and fried in fat until delicately browned, about 5 to 10 minutes, before continuing as directed with vegetables and other ingredients in Chicken Chop Suey.

Chow Mein: Prepare Chicken Chop Suey or any variation and serve over fried noodles or canned chow mein noodles instead of boiled rice. If desired, garnish with slivered, blanched almonds.

SHRIMP CHOW MEIN

1/2 pound fresh or frozen shrimp
1 1/2 tablespoons butter or peanut oil
1/4 cup chopped onion
1/2 green pepper, cut in 2-inch strips
1 cup hot water
1 cup celery, cut in 2-inch strips
3/4 teaspoon salt
Dash of pepper
1 No. 2 can bean sprouts, drained
2 tablespoons cold water
2 tablespoons cornstarch
2 teaspoons soy sauce
1 teaspoon sugar
Chow mein noodles
Hot boiled rice

Remove shells and black veins from shrimp. Rinse in cold water and cut in half, then again in half lengthwise.

Melt butter in large heavy skillet over medium heat. Add onion and green pepper and cook 5 minutes.

Add hot water, celery, salt, pepper, bean sprouts, and shrimp. Cover and simmer 5 minutes or until celery is tender but still slightly crisp.

Combine cold water, cornstarch, soy sauce, and sugar; stir lightly into hot mixture and cook uncovered 4 minutes longer.

Serve on chow mein noodles with rice. Serves 4 to 5.

Note: You can use 1 5-ounce can shrimp or 1 package frozen cooked shrimp (first thawed). Add these with cornstarch mixture at the end.

CHICKEN SUBGUM CHOW MEIN OR CHOP SUEY

1/3 cup peanut oil
1 clove garlic, minced
1 cup diced canned water chestnuts
1 cup diced canned bamboo shoots
1/2 cup thinly sliced green beans
6 green onions, chopped
2 cups finely diced celery
1 1/2 cups sliced Chinese cabbage
1/2 cup diced fresh mushrooms
1 medium green pepper, diced
1 tablespoon salt
1/2 teaspoon pepper
1 1/2 teaspoons sugar
2 cups chicken stock or 2 bouillon cubes and 2 cups water
3 tablespoons soy sauce
2 tablespoons cornstarch
2 cups finely shredded cooked chicken
1/2 cup toasted almonds
Chow mein noodles

Heat oil in large heavy saucepan or Dutch oven.

Add garlic, vegetables, salt, pepper, and sugar. Add stock and mix well. Cover and bring to boil. Stir well. Cover again and boil 10 minutes.

Combine soy sauce, 4 tablespoons cold water, and cornstarch. Blend thoroughly and add to hot vegetable mixture. Cook, stirring, until thickened. Add chicken and cook 5 minutes longer.

Serve with chow mein noodles. Sprinkle almonds over each serving. Serves 6.

Variations: Beef, pork, veal, lamb, shrimp, or lobster may be substituted for chicken.

To serve as Subgum Chop Suey, serve with hot boiled rice instead of chow mein noodles.

PORK AND APPLE CHOP SUEY

1 pound boneless pork
1/4 cup fat
3 medium-sized onions
1 1/2 cups water
1 No. 2 can bean sprouts
1/2 teaspoon Ac'cent
2 cups slivered celery
2 tart apples, thinly sliced
Soy sauce to taste
3 tablespoons cornstarch

Cut pork in narrow strips about 2 inches long. Brown in hot fat; remove. Add onions; brown lightly.

Return pork to frying pan; add water, liquid from bean sprouts, and Ac'cent. Cover; simmer 30 minutes.

Add celery and apples; cook 10 minutes longer. Add soy sauce if desired.

Dissolve cornstarch in little cold water; add stirring constantly until thickened.

Add bean sprouts; bring to boiling point. Serve with hot cooked rice. Serves 6.

Vegetables are at their best when cooked just to "crispy-doneness" the Chinese way. Whether you cook authentically in a Chinese Wok or in a frying pan, this vegetable flavor of Cha'O Yuk will long be remembered.

VEGETABLE CHA'O YUK

2 tablespoons cooking oil
½ pound boneless pork, cut in thin strips
¼ cup soy sauce
1 teaspoon sugar
4 stalks celery, sliced diagonally
1 bell pepper, cut in bite-size squares
1 cup sliced cauliflowerets
1 5-ounce can bamboo shoots, sliced
1 onion, cut in large slices
1 cup mushroom slices
1 cup bean sprouts (fresh or canned)
2 tablespoons broth
1 tablespoon cornstarch
¼ cup broth

Heat oil in frying pan or Chinese wok on high flame for about 2 minutes. Brown pork strips quickly. When no longer pink, add soy sauce, sugar, celery, bell pepper, cauliflowerets, bamboo shoots, and onion. Cook 1 minute.

Add mushrooms, bean sprouts, and 2 tablespoons of broth. Cook 1 minute.

Mix cornstarch with ¼ cup broth. Stir into vegetables. Cook 1 to 2 minutes longer or until slightly thickened. Serve over rice. Serves 4 to 6.

PINEAPPLE CHICKEN CHOW MEIN

¼ cup salad oil
1 cup thinly sliced onions
3 cups thinly sliced celery
1 No. 2 can bean sprouts, undrained
1 14-ounce can pineapple tidbits, drained
2 chicken bouillon cubes, dissolved in ½ cup hot water
3 teaspoons salt
¼ teaspoon pepper
2 tablespoons brown sugar
2 tablespoons cornstarch
¼ cup soy sauce
2 cups slivered, cooked or canned chicken
Chow mein noodles

Heat oil in Dutch oven or large heavy saucepan.

Add onions, celery, bean sprouts with liquid, drained pineapple, bouillon dissolved in water, salt, pepper, and brown sugar. Cover and bring to boil.

Blend cornstarch with soy sauce and stir into vegetable mixture. Add chicken.

Cook, stirring, 3 to 5 minutes, until thickened. Serve over crisp chow mein noodles. Serves 4 to 5.

SUKIYAKI

Sukiyaki is a Japanese term which means, literally, roasted on a plow; it is a traditional Japanese dish with innumerable variations. Basically it consists of thin strips of meat (usually tender beef, sometimes chicken) with vegetables such as green pepper, celery, bamboo shoots, bean sprouts, mushrooms, green onion, leeks, water chestnuts, and tender young spinach. Tofu (bean curd) and shirataki (gelatinous noodles) are often included. The latter resembles vermicelli or thin spaghetti and is sometimes called cellophane noodles. Tofu and shirataki are available in many Oriental grocery stores. The recipe given below is an Americanized version without the "hard-to-find" Japanese ingredients.

Sukiyaki is prepared at the table over a hot plate or in a chafing dish, and care is taken not to overcook the vegetables, which must remain crisp. It is served with rice.

2 tablespoons salad oil
1½ pounds sirloin steak, cut in thin diagonal slices about 2 inches long and ½ inch wide
¼ cup sugar
¾ cup soy sauce
¼ cup water or mushroom stock
2 medium onions, sliced thin
1 green pepper, sliced in thin strips
1 cup sliced celery, cut into diagonal 1½-inch strips
1 can (12-ounce size) bamboo shoots, sliced thin
1 can (8 ounces) mushrooms, sliced thin
1 bunch green onions, cut in 1-inch lengths with tops

Heat oil in skillet. Add meat and brown lightly.

Mix sugar, soy, and water or mushroom stock. Add half of this to meat.

Push meat to one side of pan and add onion, green pepper, and celery. Cook a few minutes.

Add remaining soy sauce liquid, bamboo shoots, and mushrooms. Cook 3 to 5 minutes.

Add green onions and tops. Cook 1 minute longer. Stir well.

Serve at once with steamed rice and hot tea. Serves 8.

WAR MEIN

⅓ cup butter, margarine, or shortening
½ pound lean pork, cut in thin strips
½ pound lean veal, cut in thin strips
½ cup onions, cut fine
2 teaspoons salt
⅛ teaspoon pepper
2 cups celery, cut fine
1 cup hot water or stock
1 cup bamboo shoots, drained and sliced thin
1 cup water chestnuts, drained and sliced thin
1 can bean sprouts, drained well
Flavoring and Thickening:
3 tablespoons cold water
3 tablespoons cornstarch
1 teaspoon Chinese brown gravy sauce
2 teaspoons soy sauce
2 teaspoons sugar

Heat fat in large skillet; add meat and sear quickly, without browning. Add onions; stir and cook for 2 minutes.

Add salt, pepper, celery, and hot water. Cover and cook for 5 minutes at a quick boil, stirring once.

Add well drained bamboo shoots, water chestnuts, and bean sprouts. Mix thoroughly and let come to boil.

Add thickening and flavoring mixture. Stir lightly and cook 2 or 3 minutes.

Serve over hot, boiled egg noodles or vermicelli noodles.

Garnish with slices of hard-cooked eggs and thin strips of green onions. Serves 6.

Sukiyaki

Bean Bakes

BOSTON BAKED BEANS

    2   cups navy beans
    1½ quarts cold water
    ¼   to ½ pound salt pork
    4   tablespoons molasses
    1   to 2 teaspoons salt
    ½   teaspoon mustard
        Hot water

Wash beans. Add water, boil 2 minutes, then remove from heat, and let soak 1 hour. Or, add water and let soak overnight in cool place.

Boil soaked beans gently in the same water for 45 minutes or until they begin to soften.

Make cuts through rind of the pork about ½ inch apart. Put half the pork in a bean pot or deep baking dish. Add beans and bury rest of the pork in them, exposing only the scored rind.

Mix molasses, salt, and mustard with a little hot water. Pour over the beans, and add enough hot water to cover beans.

Cover bean pot. Bake in very slow oven (250°F.) 6 or 7 hours; add a little hot water from time to time.

During last hour of baking remove lid to let beans brown on top. Serves 6 to 8.

Baked Lima Beans: Substitute dried lima beans for navy beans.

Baked Kidney Beans: Substitute dried kidney beans for navy beans.

Baked Beans and Spareribs: Substitute 6 pork spareribs for salt pork in Boston Baked Beans.

SCALLOPED LIMA BEANS AND PIMIENTOS

    1   cup medium white sauce
    2   teaspoons grated onion
    ¼   teaspoon celery salt
    1   teaspoon salt
    ⅛   teaspoon pepper
    3   pimientos, chopped
    1   can dried lima beans
    ¾   cup buttered soft breadcrumbs

To the medium white sauce add the onion, celery salt, salt, pepper, and chopped pimientos. Add sauce mixture to the canned lima beans and blend together.

Place in a greased casserole and cover the top with the buttered soft bread crumbs.

Bake in moderate oven (350°F.) until crumbs are lightly browned, about 30 minutes. Serves 5.

Variations: To make a more hearty dish add to the sauce when mixing with the beans, 1 cup canned shrimp or 1 cup cooked or canned meat that is cubed.

ALL-AMERICAN BAKED BEANS
(Jiffy Recipe)

    2   slices bacon
    3   tablespoons finely minced onion
    1   tablespoon molasses
    1½ tablespoons ketchup
    ¼   teaspoon salt
    ¼   teaspoon dry mustard
    ½   teaspoon Worcestershire sauce,
        optional
    2 to 3 cups canned or cooked dry beans

Fry bacon, remove from pan, and cook onion for a few minutes in bacon fat. Add molasses, ketchup, salt, mustard, and Worcestershire sauce. Add beans and mix lightly.

Pour into baking dish. Break bacon into bits and sprinkle over top. Bake in moderate oven (350°F.) 20 minutes. Or heat in a saucepan on top of stove, crumbling bacon over top before serving.

Baked Lima Beans: Use soaked lima beans and omit molasses. Place in baking dish and add other ingredients, and water to cover. Bake in moderate oven (350°F.) until tender.

BAKED BEANS WITH MEAT
(Jiffy Recipe)

    2   1-pound cans baked beans
    1   can canned pork loaf, chopped
        ham, sausage, or franks
    ¼   cup ketchup
    1   teaspoon prepared mustard

Pour baked beans into 2-quart shallow wide casserole. Cover with canned meat cut into serving pieces.

Combine ketchup and mustard; spread over meat. Bake in moderate oven (375°F.) 30 minutes. Serves 6.

COWBOY BEAN CASSEROLE

    1   cup diced ham
    2   tablespoons butter or margarine
    1   clove garlic, minced
    1   large can baked beans
    1   large can red kidney beans,
        drained
    1   large can green lima beans,
        drained
    1   tablespoon brown sugar
    1   tablespoon mustard-with-horserad-
        ish
    ½   cup ketchup
    3   tablespoons vinegar
        Salt and pepper
    1   medium onion, sliced

Brown ham in butter or margarine. Combine garlic, beans, ham, mustard, and seasonings.

Pour into greased casserole. Top with onion slices.

Bake in moderate oven (350°F.) 45 to 60 minutes. Serves 6.

The Indians gave us the idea of baking beans—and beans still rank as one of America's favorite foods.

CHILI KIDNEY BEANS
WITH TOMATOES

    2   cups dry kidney beans
    1   large onion, sliced
    1   large clove garlic, sliced
    1   green pepper, minced
    ¼   cup bacon drippings
    1   No. 2½ can or 3½ cups fresh to-
        matoes
    2   teaspoons salt
    2   teaspoons chili powder

Boil beans 2 minutes in water to cover, and soak 1 hour in the hot water. Or, boil as above and soak overnight.

Add onion, garlic, green pepper, bacon drippings, tomatoes, and salt; and simmer 2 hours in the soaking water. Add more water if needed during cooking.

Add chili powder, stirring as little as possible to avoid mashing the beans.

Place in baking dish or bean pot. Cover and bake in moderate oven (350°F.) about 2 hours.

Uncover during last part of cooking if brown beans are desired. Serves 6.

Variations: If preferred, use lima or navy beans in place of kidney beans.

TEXAS BEAN BAKE
(Jiffy Recipe)

    5   slices bacon
    1   minced onion
    ¼   cup chopped green pepper
    2   1-pound cans red kidney beans
    2   cups drained canned tomatoes
    1   4-ounce can deviled ham
    ¾   teaspoon dry mustard
    1   teaspoon curry powder dissolved
        in 1 tablespoon hot water
    3   tablespoons molasses
        Salt

Dice 1 bacon slice; fry with onion and green pepper. Mix kidney beans, tomatoes, ham, mustard, curry powder, molasses, and salt to taste. Add onion-pepper mixture.

Turn into casserole. Top with bacon slices.

Bake in hot oven (400°F.) until bacon is crisp, about 25 minutes. Serves 6.

LIMA BEAN-PORK SAUSAGE CASEROLE
(Dutch Style)

1½ cups large dry limas
3½ cups cold water
2½ teaspoons salt
1 pound link sausages
1 onion, thinly sliced
2 red apples, cored and sliced
¼ cup firmly packed brown sugar
1 tablespoon vinegar
½ cup ketchup

Rinse lima beans and cover with the cold water. Soak 6 to 8 hours or overnight. Add 1½ teaspoons salt. Bring to boil in saucepan and simmer until limas are tender, ½ to 1 hour.

Fry sausages until half done. Remove half of them from pan. Pour off all but 2 tablespoons fat.

Cut sausages in pan in bite-size pieces with fork. Add onion and apples; cover and cook 5 minutes. Sprinkle with sugar, vinegar, and remaining salt.

Drain limas and reserve ¾ cup liquid. Stir ketchup and reserved liquid into sausage mixture.

Turn beans into baking dish. Pour sausage mixture over beans. Put whole sausages on top.

Bake in moderate oven (350°F.) 1 hour. Serves 4.

LAST MINUTE LIMA SUPPER

1 small onion
¼ cup minced sweet green pepper
¼ cup butter or margarine
⅓ cup sifted enriched flour
1 teaspoon salt
2 cups milk
1 cup cooked ham, chicken, or tuna pieces
½ cup grated American cheese
3 quartered hard-cooked eggs
3 cups cooked California large dry limas (about 1½ cups before cooking)
¼ cup minced pimiento

Chop onion fine and cook with green pepper in butter until soft. Blend in flour and salt. Add milk slowly, stirring constantly.

Continue cooking until smooth and thick, about 5 minutes. Add all remaining ingredients.

Last Minute Lima Supper

Keep hot on top of stove until ready to serve. Or, turn into casserole, top with buttered crumbs, if desired, and heat in moderate oven (350°F.) until bubbly and hot. Serves 6.

LIMA SCALLOP

2 cups chopped tomatoes
2 tablespoons chopped onion
6 tablespoons butter or margarine
2 cups thinly sliced zucchini
2 cups cooked California large dry limas, about 1 scant cup before cooking
3 tablespoons flour
1 teaspoon salt
1 cup milk
3 slices bread
¼ cup soft cheese spread

Cook tomatoes and onion in 4 tablespoons butter until softened. Add zucchini and simmer until just barely tender.

Arrange tomato mixture and limas in a 10 x 6 x 2-inch casserole.

Then measure into saucepan the remaining 2 tablespoons butter, flour, and salt. Blend until butter melts. Stir in milk and cook until smooth and thickened, about 5 minutes. Pour over vegetables.

Spread bread with cheese and cut into cubes. Arrange over top of casserole. Bake in moderate oven (350°F.) 20 minutes. Serves 6.

BAKED CHILI BEANS AND GROUND BEEF

1⅓ cups dry chili or kidney beans
Water
½ pound ground beef
3 tablespoons drippings or other fat
1 medium onion, sliced
1 clove garlic, sliced
1 green pepper, minced
2 cups cooked or canned tomatoes
1 teaspoon salt
Chili powder to taste

Soak beans overnight in cold water or 4 to 5 hours in lukewarm water to cover. Cook in the same water until almost tender.

Brown meat in fat. Add onion, garlic, green pepper, tomatoes, and salt, and cook a few minutes. (2½ cups raw tomatoes, cut in pieces, may be used instead of 2 cups cooked.) Add meat mixture and chili powder to beans.

Place in baking dish or bean pot. Cover and bake in moderate oven (350°F.) about 2 hours. Uncover during the last half hour to brown the beans if desired.

Or cook the mixture slowly for about 1 hour in a covered kettle on top of the range. Stir occasionally. Serves 6.

Lima Scallop

LENTIL-SAUSAGE CASSEROLE

1 cup lentils
4 cups cold water
⅔ cup minced green onions
1 tablespoon minced parsley
½ clove garlic, minced
3 tablespoons minced celery
2 teaspoons salt
⅛ teaspoon pepper
1 tablespoon fat
1 tablespoon flour
Sliced sausage
1 tablespoon tomato purée or 2 medium tomatoes, sliced

Wash lentils and soak overnight in cold water. Drain, reserving liquid. Heat 2 cups liquid; add lentils, onions, parsley, garlic, celery, salt, and pepper. Cook, covered, until nearly tender.

Drain; measure liquid; add enough of reserved liquid or water to make 1¼ cups liquid. Place lentil mixture in greased baking dish.

Melt fat in saucepan; blend in flour. Slowly add reserved 1¼ cups liquid and cook, stirring until thickened. Pour over lentils. Pan fry sausage slices lightly, draining off fat. Place sausage and tomatoes (or diluted tomato purée) sprinkled with salt on top of lentils.

Bake in moderate oven (375°F.) 20 minutes. Serve hot. Serves 4.

BEAN AND CHEESE CASSEROLE

1 cup dry beans (pea beans, limas, red kidney beans, etc.)
3 cups water
1 teaspoon salt
2 tablespoons butter or margarine
1 cup medium white sauce
1 cup grated sharp cheese
1 cup soft bread cubes or crumbs

Boil beans in water 2 minutes and soak 1 hour or longer. Add salt and 1 tablespoon fat and boil until tender, about 2 hours. Add sauce and cheese and turn into a casserole.

Toss crumbs with remaining 1 tablespoon fat and sprinkle over beans.

Bake in moderate oven (350°F.) until crumbs are brown, about 20 minutes. Serves 4.

Beans with Frizzled Beef: Substitute 2 ounces dried beef for cheese in above recipe.

Cook the beef until the edges curl in the butter or margarine before making the white sauce.

LIMA SUNSHINE CASSEROLE

1 cup California large dry limas
Salt
¼ cup chopped onion
¼ cup diced green sweet pepper
2 tablespoons butter or margarine
1½ cups canned tomatoes
1 cup cream-style canned corn
1 cup cubed cooked ham
Buttered crumbs, optional

Stir rinsed limas into 1 quart rapidly boiling water. Boil gently over low heat until tender, about 1½ to 2 hours. Season with 1 teaspoon salt last ½ hour.

Sauté onion and green pepper lightly in heated butter. Stir in tomatoes, corn, limas, and ham. Mix thoroughly and turn into greased casserole.

Top with buttered crumbs or some of ham pieces if desired.

Bake in moderate oven (350°F.) until heated through and flavors are blended, 45 minutes to 1 hour. Serves 4 to 5.

BARBECUED LIMAS

1½ cups California large dry limas
3½ cups water
1½ teaspoons salt
4 strips bacon
1 medium-sized onion
1 clove garlic
1 10½-ounce can tomato soup
1 tablespoon vinegar
1 tablespoon prepared mustard
1 teaspoon chili powder
1 teaspoon Worcestershire sauce

Rinse limas, add water and soak overnight or several hours. Add salt and simmer 1 to 1½ hours, or until barely tender.

Drain, reserving ½ cup liquid. Cook bacon partially and set aside. Drain off all but 1 tablespoon fat. Chop onion and mince garlic. Cook onion and garlic until transparent in remaining bacon fat.

Add remaining ingredients and ½ cup cooking liquid from limas. Heat to boiling, add drained limas and turn into 1-quart baking dish.

Top with partially cooked bacon. Bake in moderate oven (350°F.) about 1 hour. Serves 6.

Barbecued Limas

HAWAIIAN BAKED BEANS
(Jiffy Recipe)

1 16-ounce can baked beans
2 slices canned pineapple, cut into pieces
1 tablespoon pineapple syrup
2 tablespoons light brown sugar
Dash of ground cloves

Combine all ingredients in 1-quart casserole.

Bake in moderate oven (375°F.) for 30 minutes or until hot. Serves 3 to 4.

Note: This recipe may be doubled by using ⅛ teaspoon ground cloves and doubling other ingredients.

Alternate Method: Combine all ingredients in saucepan. Heat thoroughly.

BAKED BEANS WITH RED WINE

6 to 8 slices bacon
1 onion, sliced
½ cup claret, burgundy, cabernet, or any red wine
1 large can baked beans

Fry bacon until partly done, not crisp. Remove bacon. Pour off all but about 2 tablespoons fat. Add sliced onion and fry gently 5 minutes in hot fat. Then add wine and beans; mix thoroughly.

Pour into shallow casserole or individual casseroles. Bake in hot oven (400°F.) until bubbly, about 20 minutes.

Top with partly cooked bacon slices and put back in oven until bacon is crisp. Serves 4.

SAVORY BAKED BEANS
(Jiffy Recipe)

¼ cup unsulphured molasses
1 tablespoon vinegar
1 tablespoon prepared mustard
¼ teaspoon Tabasco sauce
2 1-pound cans baked beans
1 onion, sliced

Combine unsulphured molasses, vinegar, mustard, and Tabasco sauce; mix well.

Empty beans into skillet or casserole and stir in molasses mixture.

Arrange onion slices on top of beans or layer with beans.

Simmer in skillet on top of range 10 to 15 minutes, or bake in casserole in a hot oven (425°F.) 30 minutes. Serves 4 to 5.

BAKED BEANS—WISCONSIN STYLE
(Jiffy Recipe)

1 16-ounce can baked beans in tomato sauce
2 tablespoons thick sour cream
¾ cup grated process sharp cheese

Combine ingredients in casserole. Bake in moderate oven (350°F.) 20 minutes. Serves 3.

Hawaiian Baked Beans

Thrifty baked bean dishes are not only budget balancers but close-to-the-top choices for buffet meals, picnics, and many special occasions.

SURPRISE COMPANY SPECIAL

1 1-pound can baked beans
1 No. 2 can kidney beans
¼ cup unsulphured molasses
1 tablespoon vinegar
1 tablespoon prepared mustard
1 12-ounce can luncheon meat, diced
Onion and tomato slices

Combine beans in casserole; stir in molasses, vinegar, mustard, and meat. Top with onion and tomato slices. Bake in moderate oven (375°F.) 45 minutes. Serves 6.

HAM SHANK AND BEANS

1 ham shank
Water
2 cups navy beans
1 onion, sliced
2 teaspoons dry mustard
¼ cup molasses

Cover ham shank with water. Bring to a boil, then reduce heat and simmer until ham drops from bone, about 2½ hours.

Cover beans with warm water. Soak 2½ hours.

Drain. Cover with ham broth and boil 10 minutes. Add diced ham and sliced onion. Mix mustard and molasses with ham broth. Add to beans. Add ham broth to cover beans.

Simmer slowly or bake in slow oven (325°F.) 1 hour. Serves 6 to 8.

Variations: If desired, pour ¼ cup chili sauce or ketchup over beans before baking. Black-eyed peas or red kidney beans may be substituted for navy beans.

BACHELORS' BEEF AND BEANS

2 tablespoons butter or margarine
1 small jar dried beef
1 can condensed tomato soup
½ cup milk
2 cups cooked or canned large limas
¼ cup grated American cheese

Melt butter and shred dried beef into it. Heat through. Add soup and blend in milk. Heat to simmering.

Place drained beans in baking dish. Pour sauce over them. Top with grated cheese.

Bake in moderate oven (350°F.) about 20 minutes. Serves 4.

KIDNEY BEANS À LA CREOLE

1/4 pound bacon ends, chopped
1 large onion, minced
1/4 cup diced green pepper
1 tablespoon sugar
1/2 teaspoon salt
1/2 teaspoon pepper
1 cup canned tomatoes
2 1-pound cans red kidney beans

Cook bacon in skillet until crisp. Drain off all but 2 tablespoons fat. Add onion and green pepper. Cook until onion is tender.

Add remaining ingredients, except beans, and simmer 10 minutes.

Put beans in 1-quart casserole; add sauce. Cover and bake in moderate oven (350°F.) 30 minutes. Serves 4.

PINEAPPLE BAKED BEANS

2 No. 2 cans baked beans
1 No. 2 can pineapple chunks

Place the contents of one of the cans of beans in a 1½-quart casserole.

Drain pineapple and reserve 5 or 6 of the chunks to use to decorate the top.

Place remaining chunks in an even layer over beans and cover with second can of beans. Arrange the 5 or 6 pineapple chunks on top and bake covered in a moderate open (350° F.) for 20 to 30 minutes. Serves 6.

LIMA BEANS IN CREAMY CHEESE SAUCE

4 tablespoons butter or margarine
4 tablespoons flour
2½ cups milk
1 teaspoon salt
1/8 teaspoon pepper
1 cup grated American cheese
4 cups dried lima beans, cooked
1½ cups diced celery, cooked

Melt butter in top of double boiler, blend in flour; add milk and cook until sauce is thick. Add seasonings and cook 10 minutes.

Add cheese and cook until cheese is melted.

Add drained, cooked lima beans, and celery that has been diced or sliced in julienne strips and cooked until tender.

Pour into individual or one large casserole. Bake in moderate oven (350°F.) 15 to 20 minutes. Serves 6.

Lima Beans in Creamy Cheese Sauce

BOSTON BEAN CASSEROLE
(Jiffy Recipe)

4 slices bacon
1 to 2 tablespoons finely chopped onion
2 to 4 tablespoons chopped green pepper
1/2 cup chopped celery
2 cans (18 ounces each) oven-baked beans, Boston style

Cut 3 slices bacon into squares and fry with onion and green pepper until bacon is crisp. Pour off excess fat and combine with celery and baked beans in a casserole. Sprinkle with 1 slice raw bacon, finely diced. Bake in moderate oven (375°F.) until top is browned, 40 minutes. Serves 6.

BAKED BEAN SPECIAL

1/4-pound bacon square or 6 slices bacon
1/3 cup finely chopped celery
1/4 cup chopped onion
1/4 cup finely chopped green pepper
2 1-pound-5-ounce cans pork and beans
1/4 cup ketchup
2 tablespoons brown sugar
2 tablespoons molasses
5 drops Tabasco sauce

Score bacon square and brown. Cook celery, onion, and green pepper in 2 tablespoons bacon drippings until soft but not brown.

Combine all ingredients except bacon and pour into square (8 x 8 x 2-inch) baking dish.

Put bacon square, scored side up, in center. Bake in moderate oven (375°F.) 45 to 60 minutes. Serves 8 to 10.

LIMA BEAN-GROUND BEEF-CHILI BAKE

2 cups dried lima beans
1 teaspoon salt
1/2 pound ground beef
1/2 cup onion rings
1 clove garlic, mashed
1 tablespoon chopped hot red peppers
2 tablespoons fat
1 No. 2 can (2½ cups) tomatoes, drained
1 teaspoon chili powder
1/2 cup grated sharp American cheese

Cover lima beans with water; soak overnight. Add water if necessary and bring slowly to boiling point. Simmer uncovered 1 hour. Add salt for last hour of cooking. Drain and reserve 1 cup bean liquid.

Brown meat, onion rings, garlic, and red pepper in hot fat. Add tomatoes, chili powder, lima beans, 1 cup bean liquid, and cheese.

Turn into wide shallow casserole.

Bake in moderate oven (350°F.) 1 hour. Serve topped with extra grated cheese, if desired. Serves 6 to 8.

BRAZILIAN LIMA BEANS

2 cups dried lima beans
2 teaspoons salt
1 quart water
1 cup ground ham
1 cup diced onions
1 clove garlic, minced
1/4 cup bacon fat
1 cup tomato juice
1 cup tomato purée
2 teaspoons chili powder
2 teaspoons salt
1/2 cup grated cheese

Soak lima beans overnight. Add beans and 2 teaspoons salt to 1 quart water and cook beans until tender. Drain.

Brown ground ham, onions, and garlic in bacon fat. Add tomato juice, tomato purée, chili powder, and 2 teaspoons salt to ham mixture; cook together for 5 minutes.

Pour cooked tomato sauce over cooked lima beans in 2-quart casserole. Sprinkle top with grated cheese.

Bake in moderate oven (350°F.) about 25 minutes or until cheese is melted. Serves 6 to 8.

BAKED BEANS DELUXE

2 cups dried pea beans
6 cups cold water
1 medium onion, chopped
2 cups tomato pulp or 2 8-ounce cans tomato sauce
1/2 cup salad oil
2 small sweet pickles, chopped
1/2 cup stuffed olives, chopped
1 small stalk celery, chopped
1/2 cup grated sharp cheese

Combine washed beans with cold water. Bring to boiling point and cook 1 hour, adding water if necessary; drain.

Combine onion, tomato pulp (or tomato sauce), and oil. Simmer until thick.

Add pickles, olives, and celery to beans; turn into casserole. Pour tomato mixture over bean mixture.

Cover and bake in moderate oven (350°F.) until beans are tender, about 1½ hours.

Sprinkle with cheese and bake uncovered until cheese melts and browns. Serves 8.

BAKED BEAN RAREBIT
(Jiffy Recipe)

Combine 1 18-ounce can Boston style baked beans with 1 cup (1/4 pound) grated American cheese, and 1/2 green pepper, sliced.

Pour into casserole. Bake in moderate oven (350°F.) 45 minutes. Serves 4.

CEREALS, RICE, AND OTHER GRAINS

Cereal Cookery

BASIC CEREAL COOKING RULES

Quick-Cooking Oats: To 3 cups rapidly boiling salted water, gradually add 1½ cups quick-cooking oats.

Stirring constantly, cook 2½ minutes or longer if desired.

Quick-Cooking Wheat Cereal: To 2½ cups rapidly boiling salted water, gradually add ½ cup quick-cooking wheat cereal. Stir constantly until thickened. Cook slowly 5 minutes.

Rolled Oats: To 3 cups rapidly boiling salted water, gradually add 1½ cups rolled oats.

Stirring constantly, cook 5 minutes or longer, if desired.

Wheat Cereal: To 3 cups rapidly boiling salted water, gradually add ½ cup wheat cereal. Stir constantly until thickened. Cook slowly 15 minutes.

Cereal Cooked in Milk: Substitute scalded milk for water in the recipe. Add cereal to scalded milk. Cook, covered, over hot water until thickened and done.

Cereal Cooked with Fruit: Follow recipes given above, adding ¼ cup chopped dried apricots, pitted dates, figs, pitted prunes, raisins, or nutmeats a few minutes before cooking is completed.

FRIED MUSH

Turn cooked cereal into a greased mold. Cover to prevent crust from forming. Chill until firm.

Cut into ½-inch-thick slices. Dip in flour or corn meal.

Sauté in butter or salad oil, browning on both sides. Cook slowly, if desired dry and crisp. Serve with maple or corn syrup or molasses.

TEMPTING WAYS TO SERVE COOKED CEREALS

● Add dried fruits such as raisins, dates, and prunes.
● Cook cereal with milk or use part milk instead of water.
● Combine 2 or more cereals and cook together.
● Serve cereals with honey, molasses, brown sugar, or maple syrup instead of white sugar.
● Slice cold leftover cereal and fry. Serve with butter and syrup.
● Mix leftover cereal with ground cooked meat, fish, or vegetables. Chill. Slice and fry.
● Use leftover cereal as part of stuffing for fish, meats, and poultry.
● Use leftover cereal as a stuffing for baked apples. Fill cored centers. Top with brown sugar and bake.
● Add sweetening and desired flavorings to leftover cereal. Turn into custard cups. Chill and serve with dessert sauces.

WHITE CORN MEAL MUSH

Using top of double boiler over direct heat, add 1 teaspoon salt to 3 cups briskly boiling water.

Gradually add ½ cup white corn meal. Cook, stirring constantly, until thick, about 10 minutes. Place over boiling water.

Cover and cook ½ hour longer, stirring occasionally. Serves 4 to 6.

YELLOW CORN MEAL MUSH

Using top of double boiler over direct heat, add 1 teaspoon salt to 2½ cups briskly boiling water.

Combine ½ cup yellow corn meal and ½ cup water. Slowly add to boiling water. Cook, stirring constantly, until thick, about 5 minutes.

Place over boiling water. Cover and cook ½ hour longer, stirring occasionally. Serves 4 to 6.

HOMINY

Hominy is hulled corn (maize) coarsely broken or ground into small pieces of about the same size. When it is very coarse, hominy is sometimes called samp. Pearl hominy: whole-grain hominy with the hulls removed by machinery; lye hominy: whole grains with the hulls removed by soaking in lye water; granulated hominy: a ground form; grits: broken grains.

BOILED HOMINY GRITS

5 cups water
1½ teaspoons salt
1 cup hominy grits

Bring water with salt to a rapid boil in the upper part of a double boiler. Add grits slowly, while stirring, and cook until thickened over direct heat.

Cover, place over lower part of double boiler and cook over boiling water, stirring occasionally, for 2 hours. Serves 6

FRIED HOMINY GRITS

3 cups water
¾ teaspoon salt
1 cup hominy grits
3 tablespoons corn meal
3 tablespoons fat

Boil 3 cups water; add salt. Gradually stir hominy grits into rapidly boiling water. Cook about 1 hour over hot water, stirring occasionally.

Pour hominy into greased 1-quart loaf pan. Place in refrigerator until cold.

Cut into slices about ½ inch thick and dip into corn meal.

Heat fat in skillet. Cook hominy slices in hot fat until brown on each side. Serve piping hot with syrup or honey. Makes 8 slices.

Polenta

HOMINY CAKES

Drain 1 No. 2 can hominy. Mix with 1 slightly beaten egg, 2 tablespoons flour, and salt and pepper to taste.

Form into small flat cakes. Brown on both sides in butter or margarine. Serve with syrup or honey.

BUTTERED CANNED HOMINY

Heat canned hominy in its own liquid or drain and heat in top of double boiler.

Add butter and season to taste with salt and pepper. Serve in place of potato with desired sauce.

HOMINY AND CHEESE TIMBALES

2   cups drained, canned hominy
2/3 cup grated cheese
2   beaten eggs
3/4 teaspoon salt
Dash of pepper
2   teaspoons chopped green pepper
2   teaspoons chopped pimiento
2   tablespoons minced parsley
1   cup scalded milk

Combine all ingredients well. Turn into individual baking dishes.

Place in pan of hot water and bake in moderate oven (350°F.) 1/2 hour.

Unmold and serve with cheese, tomato, or Spanish sauce. Serves 6.

HOMINY WITH DRIED BEEF

2   tablespoons butter
2   2½-ounce jars sliced dried beef
1   15-ounce can hominy, drained
½   cup sour cream
Dash of black pepper

Melt butter in frying pan. Chop dried beef and cook in butter until slightly crisp and frizzled. Add drained hominy and cook until hominy is hot.

Add sour cream and pepper. Heat briefly to serving temperature, stirring constantly. Serves 4.

Hominy with Dried Beef

POLENTA

Polenta is an Italian dish; a porridge or mush made usually of corn meal but also of chestnut meal, barley, or semolina. It is spread thinly on a large platter and covered with tomato or meat sauce, Parmesan cheese, and sometimes sausages. Polenta al forno: cold polenta baked in the oven with sauce and cheese; originally a way of using up leftovers.

ITALIAN POLENTA

1   cup white corn meal
4   cups water
1   teaspoon salt
1   onion, chopped
1   clove garlic, minced
½   pound Italian sausage, chicken livers, or other meat, shredded
2   tablespoons olive oil
1   No. 2 can plum tomatoes
¼   teaspoon oregano or thyme
1   bay leaf
Pepper
½   cup or more grated Parmesan or Romano cheese

Mix corn meal with 1 cup water. Heat remaining 3 cups water to boiling with salt in top of a double boiler. Add corn meal and cook, stirring, until thickened.

Place over hot water in lower part of double boiler and cook, covered, stirring occasionally, 1 hour.

Brown onion, garlic, sausage, or other meat in olive oil. Add tomatoes, oregano or thyme, bay leaf, pepper, and additional salt to taste. Simmer, stirring often, until thickened.

To serve, spread half the mush on a platter. Cover with half the sauce and half the cheese. Repeat the layers. Serves 5 to 6.

Polenta Variations

Prepare corn meal mush as directed for polenta and serve as follows:

Baked Cheese Squares: Pour hot polenta into a pan, making it about ¾ inch thick. Cool and chill.

Cut into squares and dip in lightly beaten egg that has been mixed with 2 tablespoons water. Roll in grated cheese, place in a baking pan and dot with bits of butter.

Bake in moderate oven (350°F.) until cheese has browned lightly. Serve with tomato sauce or sour cream.

Romanian Mamaliga: Fry 4 bacon slices until crisp. Grease a casserole with bacon fat.

Arrange corn meal mush, bacon fat and bacon, and grated Swiss or pot cheese in layers, using plenty of cheese and fat.

Bake in moderate oven (350°F.) about 25 minutes. Serve with sauerkraut.

Grits Au Gratin with Creole Shrimp

GRITS

Grain, especially hominy, hulled and coarsely ground. It is used as a breakfast cereal; in the South, it is served with gravy in place of potatoes.

GRITS AU GRATIN

¾   cup grits
3   cups boiling water
1   teaspoon salt
½   pound sharp cheese, grated
1   cup milk
½   cup buttered breadcrumbs
¼   teaspoon paprika

Slowly stir grits into boiling, salted water in top of double boiler over direct heat. Cover, place over boiling water and continue cooking 45 minutes, stirring occasionally.

Alternate layers of cooked grits and grated cheese in greased baking dish.

Add milk and sprinkle with breadcrumbs and paprika. Bake in slow oven (325°F.) 30 minutes. Serves 6.

Note: Grits au gratin may be baked in a greased ring mold and served with Creole shrimp or creamed meat or vegetables.

TORTILLAS

Tortillas are thin, flat unleavened cakes made of pounded corn (a kind of coarse corn meal) baked on a hot iron plate or flat stone. They are used throughout Mexico in place of bread and are used as a base for many dishes. The recipe given here is designed to be used with corn meal generally available in American groceries.

3   cups yellow corn meal
2   cups sifted enriched flour
3   teaspoons salt
4   tablespoons shortening
1   to 1¼ cups lukewarm water

Mix corn meal, flour, and salt together in bowl.

Cut in shortening until mixture is finely divided. Make a well in mixture and add 1 cup water and stir.

If necessary, add more water until all ingredients form a ball and bowl is clean.

Turn onto cloth and knead well. Form dough into small balls about 1½ inches in diameter. Let balls stand 15 minutes. Then flatten each ball by rolling with rolling pin until 6 inches in diameter.

Place on ungreased skillet or griddle and cook about 2 minutes. Turn and cook about 1 minute longer. Makes 18 tortillas.

ENCHILADAS

An enchilada is a tortilla rolled around a meat, chicken, or cheese mixture, served with a sauce usually containing chili; a Mexican dish. Enchiladas may also be made by stacking the tortillas and filling like griddlecakes.

ENCHILADAS WITH LETTUCE

12 corn meal tortillas
2 cups enchilada sauce
1 small onion, cut fine
1 pound aged Cheddar cheese, shredded
1 medium head lettuce, shredded
4 fried eggs (optional)

Heat sauce in skillet. Combine onion, cheese, and lettuce.

For each enchilada, dip a tortilla into the hot enchilada sauce and place it on a plate. Sprinkle with lettuce mixture.

Cover with another tortilla dipped into the hot sauce. Sprinkle with lettuce mixture. Repeat with a third tortilla.

Pour about 2 tablespoons of the hot sauce over the top and serve at once. If desired, place a fried egg on top of each enchilada. Serves 4.

Note: Tortillas and enchilada sauce may be bought at a Mexican store.

ENCHILADA SAUCE

1/4 cup salad oil
1 medium-sized onion, peeled and cut fine
1 clove garlic, peeled and mashed
1 sprig parsley, chopped fine
1 6-ounce can tomato paste
1 1/2 cups water
1 teaspoon vinegar
1/2 teaspoon oregano
1/2 teaspoon salt
1 teaspoon sugar
1/8 teaspoon cayenne
2 teaspoons chili powder

Heat oil in heavy skillet. Add onion, garlic, parsley, and tomato paste. Simmer 3 minutes.

Add water, vinegar, oregano, salt, sugar, cayenne, and chili powder. Bring to boil. Simmer 15 minutes to blend flavors. Makes about 2 cups.

TACOS

Tacos are Mexican sandwiches made of tortillas rolled or folded to enclose fillings of meat, fish, refried beans, or other food, then fried or baked, sometimes toasted.

TOSTADAS

Tostadas are tortillas fried golden and crisp and often served with appetizers and soups. They are sometimes served covered with spoonfuls of various mixtures including refried beans, cheese, Mexican sausage, shredded lettuce, and sauce.

TAMALE

A Mexican and Central American dish basically of minced meat and corn meal wrapped in corn husks or banana leaves, tied up, dipped in oil, and steamed. There are a number of variations, and the Mexican ones always include chili peppers. U.S. versions in casserole form, usually less highly seasoned, are called tamale pies.

TAMALE PIE

1 No. 1 tall can ripe olives
1 pound ground lean beef
2 tablespoons salad oil
1 cup chopped onion
1/2 cup chopped green pepper
2 cups sliced celery
1 No. 2 1/2 can (3 1/2 cups) tomatoes
2 teaspoons salt
2 teaspoons chili powder
1 1/2 cups corn meal
1 1/2 teaspoons salt
4 1/2 cups boiling water
2 cups grated American cheese

Cut olives from pits into large pieces, reserving a few whole ones.

Brown beef in oil. Add onion and pepper and cook until clear. Stir in celery, tomatoes, 2 teaspoons salt, and chili powder and simmer 10 minutes.

Stir corn meal and 1 1/2 teaspoons salt slowly into boiling water. Turn heat low and cook 10 minutes, stirring occasionally.

Stir olives into meat mixture.

In greased 3-quart casserole arrange alternate layers of corn meal, meat mixture, and cheese, topping with a few spoonfuls of corn meal and a layer of cheese over all.

Bake in moderate oven (350°F.) 45 minutes to 1 hour. Place a whole ripe olive in each corn meal puff.

Serves 6 to 8.

KASHA OR BUCKWHEAT GROATS

Kasha is a Russian and Yiddish term for buckwheat groats. The recipe given here is an old-time Jewish dish.

1 1/4 cups fine buckwheat groats
1/2 teaspoon salt
1/2 teaspoon paprika
1 slightly beaten egg
1 cup boiling water
1 tablespoon chicken fat, butter, or shortening

Combine buckwheat groats, salt, paprika, and egg; blend thoroughly.

Place in a greased 1-quart casserole. Bake in moderate oven (350°F.) for 20 minutes.

Stir in the boiling water and fat. Cover and bake 20 minutes longer.

Serve with meat and gravy, with buttered noodles and sautéed mushrooms, as a cereal, or use as a filling for blintzes and knishes, or as a stuffing for meat or poultry. Makes about 3 cups.

SCRAPPLE

Scrapple is a firm mush made by boiling cooked, shredded pork in its own spicy broth with corn meal. When cold, it is sliced and fried. A Pennsylvania-Dutch dish, it was originally made only from pig's head. Buckwheat or other cereals are sometimes used in place of corn meal.

PORK SCRAPPLE

Select 3 pounds of bony pieces of pork. Simmer in 3 quarts water until meat drops from bone.

Strain off broth and carefully remove all pieces of bone. Chop meat fine.

There should be about 2 quarts of broth. If necessary, add water to make this quantity. Bring broth to boiling point; slowly add 2 cups corn meal and cook mixture until thick, stirring almost constantly.

Add chopped meat, salt, and any other seasoning desired, such as onion juice, sage, and thyme.

Pour hot scrapple into oblong enamelware pans which have been rinsed with cold water. Chill until firm.

Slice and brown in hot skillet. If scrapple is rich in fat, additional fat is not necessary for frying.

VEGETABLE SCRAPPLE

1 medium-sized onion
1 medium-sized carrot
1/2 green pepper
1 cup yellow corn meal
1 tablespoon salt
3 1/2 cups boiling water
1 teaspoon Ac'cent
1 cup chopped peanuts
Fat or salad oil

Mince onion, carrot, and green pepper.

Add corn meal and salt to boiling water slowly, stirring constantly until thickened.

Add minced vegetables and Ac'cent. Cook over hot water 1 hour.

Add peanuts. Pour into well greased loaf pan. Chill.

When cold, slice and sauté until golden brown in small amount fat or salad oil. Serves 4 to 6.

Vegetable Scrapple

BULGUR WHEAT

Bulgur wheat is a special kind of cracked wheat that since Biblical times has been a basic food of the Middle East. It is now processed in the United States. Because it is so delicious and so rich nutritionally, it is worth searching for. If it is not available in your local market, you can buy it in health-food stores or in Armenian and Syrian neighborhood groceries. Bulgur is a traditional accompaniment to shish kebab. It is cooked like rice. Also spelled bulghour, boulghour, bulgor, and burghul.

BULGUR PILAF

½ cup butter or margarine
3 cups bulgur
1 small onion, chopped fine
6 cups broth (chicken, lamb, or beef)
Salt and pepper

Melt butter in heavy skillet; add dry bulgur. Cook over low heat until butter begins to bubble.

Fry onion in separate pan until golden brown. Mix with bulgur; add broth, and salt and pepper to taste.

Stir well and place in moderate oven (375°F.) for 30 minutes. Then remove from oven, stir well, and bake 30 minutes longer. Serves 8 or more.
Armenian Rice Pilaf: Omit onions, substitute rice for bulgur and proceed as directed above.

PARTY TAMALE PIE

1 cup yellow corn meal
4 cups boiling water
1 large onion, chopped
2 tablespoons salad oil
½ pound hamburger
1 small can tomato paste
½ cup sliced stuffed olives
1 cup sliced ripe olives
½ cup chopped green pepper
2 teaspoons chili powder
1 cup beef bouillon or consommé
1 No. 2 can whole kernel corn
Dash of cayenne pepper
2 teaspoons salt
1 cup shredded cheese

Stir corn meal into rapidly boiling water. Cook and stir until thick with a long-handled spoon. Remove from heat.

Brown onion in oil in a heavy skillet. Add hamburger. Cook and stir until redness of meat disappears. Add tomato paste, stuffed olives, ripe olives, green pepper, chili powder, bouillon, corn, cayenne, and salt. Stir well. Taste to be sure there is enough salt.

Pour into a shallow baking pan (12 x 8 x 2 inches). Sprinkle shredded cheese over top. Dash paprika liberally over surface. Bake in a moderate oven (350°F.) 1 hour. Serves 16.

Rice Cookery

While rice has never been to us the all-important food it is in many parts of the world, nevertheless it should be remembered that it is one of the most versatile of all our foods. It can be a breakfast cereal, an alternate for potatoes, or a dessert. It makes fine casseroles with other ingredients to give flavor and color. It is the base for many favorite foreign recipes such as sukiyaki, chop suey, the Spanish and Mexican rice dishes, Indian curries, pilafs, and other Oriental dishes.

TYPES OF RICE

Rice is marketed in a variety of ways —each kind labeled to tell you what it is and each has its special advantage.

Precooked Rice: This quick type is completely cooked and requires only to be steamed in boiling water. Follow directions on the package.

This rice will more than double in volume as it steams.

Converted Rice: The grains of this rice are parboiled before milling by means of a special steam-pressure method which aids in the retention of much of the natural vitamins and minerals.

Specific directions for cooking are given on the package. After cooking, the grains will be separate, plump, and fluffy. Each cup of uncooked converted rice will give about 4 cups cooked rice.

Regular Rice: This rice is cleaned, washed, and graded in the milling process.

It is not necessary to wash before cooking if it comes clean from the package. You just measure, add water and salt as suggested on the package. Or follow directions for fluffy boiled rice given below.

Short- and Long-Grain Rice: Regular rice may be either short grain or long grain. Short-grain rice cooks tender and moist and the particles tend to cling together. It is usually the favored choice for croquettes, pudding, or rice rings, where you desire a tender rice which will mold more readily.

Long-grain rice will be fluffy and the grains will be separate after cooking. For this reason it is often preferred for serving with stews and curries and the like.

Brown Rice: This is often preferred to white rice because it is a whole-grain rice, retaining the essential food values. It has a pleasing nutty flavor. It is, however, more perishable than white rice and requires greater care in packing and storing.

Wild Rice: This is not a real rice but is actually the seed of a marsh grass. The grains are long, dark, and greenish, chewier when cooked than other rice.

It has a distinctive flavor but it is quite expensive because wild rice has to be gathered by hand. It is considered a delicacy when served with game as accompaniment or stuffing.

HOW TO COOK FLUFFY, WHITE RICE

Put 1 cup uncooked rice, 2 cups cold water, and 1 teaspoon salt into a 2-quart saucepan and bring to vigorous boil.

Turn the heat as low as possible. Cover the saucepan with a lid. Do not remove lid or stir rice while it is cooking. Leave saucepan over this low heat for 14 minutes.

Turn heat off. The rice is now ready to use. However, leave the cover on the saucepan to keep the rice warm if you are not ready to use it immediately. Makes 3 heaping cups.
For Extra-Fluffy, Tender, Separate Grains: Allow the rice to steam for an additional 10 minutes—with heat off, but without removing lid.

HOW TO COOK BROWN RICE

Wash ¾ cup brown rice. Gradually add to 4½ cups boiling water to which 1 teaspoon salt has been added. Cover and cook over low heat until all liquid is absorbed, 40 to 60 minutes.

Uncover and let stand over low heat to let rice dry out and fluff. Makes about 3⅔ cups cooked rice.
Note: Meat or chicken stock may be substituted for water and salt.

HOW TO COOK WILD RICE

Combine 1 cup washed wild rice; add 3 cups water or consommé (and 1 teaspoon salt if you use water).

Place in saucepan, cover, and bring to boil rapidly. Reduce heat and cook about 25 minutes, or until rice swells and absorbs water.

Uncover and let steam dry. Add a little butter and serve with game, or add onion and chopped giblets, and use as stuffing for a bird. Serves 4 to 6.

STEEPED WILD RICE

Wash rice thoroughly in cold water. Drain. Cover 1 cup rice with 1 quart boiling water. Let stand about 40 minutes.

Drain and cover again with boiling water. Let stand 20 minutes. Repeat this twice again, using fresh boiling water each time.

Last time, add 2 teaspoons salt and then drain thoroughly. Serve with 1 tablespoon melted butter and season to taste.

Top O' Range Rice Dishes

RISOTTO

Risotto is an Italian term for various rice dishes, often for rice sautéed in oil, butter, or margarine, then cooked in stock, sometimes with chicken, meat, seafood, cheese, and other ingredients.

RISOTTO ALLA MILANAISE

- ¼ pound butter or margarine
- 2 onions, chopped
- 2 cups rice
- ½ cup white wine
- 3 cups stock (chicken or beef, canned or cubes)
- Pinch of saffron
- Salt and pepper
- 2 cups grated Parmesan cheese

Melt half the butter or margarine in deep skillet, add onions and brown lightly. Add rice, stir well and cook 15 minutes.

Add wine, stock, saffron, salt and pepper to taste. Cover and simmer gently about 20 minutes, until rice is fluffy and tender. Stir occasionally while cooking.

Just before serving, melt remaining butter or margarine, sprinkle over rice with grated cheese. Serves 4.

RICE AND CHEESE

Serve cooked rice with cheese sauce or add ¾ to 1 cup grated cheese to hot cooked rice.

PINEAPPLE RICE

Blend 3 to 4 cups cooked rice with the contents of 1 No. 2 can chunks or crushed pineapple, drained.

RICE MEDLEY

- 2 tablespoons butter or margarine
- ½ cup diced celery
- 2 cups cooked rice
- 1 4½-ounce can deviled ham
- 1 egg, beaten
- ¼ teaspoon salt
- Dash of pepper
- ½ cup Cheddar cheese, grated
- Crumbled cooked bacon

Melt butter in skillet; sauté celery until tender but not brown. Add rice, ham, egg, salt, and pepper. Heat thoroughly, stirring constantly.

Pour into buttered casserole. Top with cheese and bacon. Place under broiler only until cheese is melted. Serves 4.

Rice Medley

SPANISH RICE

- ½ cup uncooked rice
- 3 slices finely diced bacon
- 2 tablespoons chopped onion
- 2 tablespoons chopped green pepper
- 1 cup tomato juice
- 1 teaspoon salt
- ⅛ teaspoon pepper

Cook rice uncovered in boiling salted water until tender. Drain and blanch with boiling water.

Cook bacon until crisp; remove from frying pan. Cook onion and pepper in bacon fat until golden brown and tender.

Add rice, tomato juice, salt, pepper, and bacon. Simmer 10 minutes, or until most of tomato juice has been absorbed by rice. Stir occasionally to prevent sticking. Serves 4.

CURRIED RICE

- 2 tablespoons fat or salad oil
- 1 cup uncooked rice
- 1 tablespoon chopped onion
- 3 cups boiling water or meat stock
- 1 to 2 tablespoons curry powder
- 2 teaspoons salt

Heat fat in a saucepan. Add rice and onion and stir until rice is golden brown.

Add boiling water or stock and seasonings. Cover and cook slowly until tender, about 30 minutes. Serves 4.

PILAF

Pilaf, also spelled pilau, pilaff, and pilaw, is a term applied to any of a number of Near Eastern rice dishes, usually highly seasoned. The rice is often cooked with butter or oil before the liquid is added; nuts, bits of meat, poultry, or fish are sometimes mixed in or served on top. The same term is often applied to other grain dishes, for example Bulgur Pilaf (which see).

RICE PILAF

- 1 cup uncooked rice
- 3 chicken bouillon cubes
- 1½ cups boiling water
- ½ cup slivered blanched almonds
- ¼ cup butter or margarine

Brown rice lightly in uncovered heavy pan, kettle, or skillet with tight-fitting lid. Stir occasionally to distribute heat evenly.

Dissolve bouillon cubes in water and add to rice. Cover and let come to boil over medium heat. Reduce heat to low and cook until rice is fluffy and done, 25 to 30 minutes.

Cook almonds in half the butter until lightly browned, stirring constantly.

Melt remaining butter with nuts, then mix with rice, tossing lightly with a fork. Serves 4 to 5.

Rice Indienne may be molded before serving.

RICE INDIENNE

- 1 cup uncooked rice
- 2 cups bouillon
- 2 tablespoons butter or margarine
- ½ cup white raisins
- ½ teaspoon salt
- ¼ cup toasted slivered almonds

Combine rice, bouillon, butter, raisins, and salt in saucepan. Bring to a boil and stir. Cover and simmer 14 minutes. Add almonds and mix lightly with a fork. Serves 4 to 6.

MEXICAN RICE

- 1 cup rice
- ½ clove garlic, minced
- 1 small onion, chopped
- 2 tablespoons fat
- 2 teaspoons salt
- ½ medium-sized green pepper, chopped
- 2 teaspoons chili powder
- 1 cup canned tomatoes
- 2 cups beef stock

Wash rice; sauté with garlic and onion in hot fat until browned.

Add salt, green pepper, chili powder, tomatoes, and stock; cover and simmer 20 to 30 minutes, or until rice is soft. Remove cover during last 5 minutes to finish evaporation and let mixture dry out.

One-half pound ground beef may be cooked with rice, if desired. Serves 6.

TEXAS RICE AND RED BEANS

- 2 cups kidney beans
- ¼ pound salt pork
- 2 quarts water
- 1 small clove garlic, minced
- 1 tablespoon chili powder
- 1 teaspoon salt
- 3 cups cooked rice

Cook beans with salt pork in boiling water until tender.

Add garlic, chili powder, and salt to taste. Simmer until gravy is heavy. Add rice; serve. Serves 6.

Texas Rice and Red Beans

Paella Valenciana

PAELLA

Paella is a classic Spanish rice dish with many variations. The most famous is the Valencia-style, which is made of several kinds of seafood, chicken, sausage, pimiento, peas, and tomatoes, flavored with garlic and saffron.

PAELLA VALENCIANA

2   ready-to-cook frying chickens (about 2 pounds each)
1/3 cup olive oil
3½ teaspoons salt
1½ cups uncooked rice
2   cloves garlic, minced
1   bay leaf, crumbled
Large pinch of saffron
¼   teaspoon pepper
3   quartered tomatoes or 1 cup canned tomatoes
1   green pepper, sliced
1   pimiento or sweet red pepper, sliced
Dash of cayenne
1   pound fresh hot Spanish or Italian sausage or link pork sausage, cut in 1-inch pieces
1   dozen shucked littleneck clams
1   pound cooked shrimp
½   pound cooked lobster, cut up
1   cup cooked peas

Cut chicken into 20 pieces; fry until browned in hot oil in skillet. Transfer to large casserole; season with 1 teaspoon salt.

Put rice and garlic in skillet and cook slowly until rice browns a little. Add bay leaf, saffron, 2½ teaspoons salt, pepper, tomatoes, green pepper, pimiento, and cayenne. Bring to boil, stirring gently with fork. Pour over chicken.

Cover and bake in hot oven (425°F.) 25 minutes. Reduce heat to moderate (375°F.) and add sausage which has been fried until brown. Add clams, shrimp, lobster, and peas. Stir lightly with fork.

Cover and bake until rice is dry and fluffy, about 15 minutes longer. Serves 8 to 10.

QUICK MEXICAN RICE

Toss cooked rice lightly with butter and chili powder.

PIMIENTO RICE

To 2 cups hot cooked rice, add ¾ to 1 cup grated cheese and 2 chopped pimientos.

JIFFY SAFFRON RICE

2   tablespoons butter or margarine
½   medium onion, minced
½   teaspoon dried saffron
2   cups canned chicken broth or 2 chicken bouillon cubes dissolved in 2 cups boiling water
1⅓ cups packaged precooked rice*

Sauté onion until golden in 2 tablespoons butter in skillet.

Mix saffron with 1 tablespoon chicken broth; set aside.

Bring remaining broth to boil in saucepan. Add rice and onion; mix until all rice is moistened. Cover and remove from heat; let stand 13 minutes.

Lightly mix in saffron and 2 tablespoons butter with fork. Serve with broiled chicken or chicken or seafood curry. Serves 4.

*Note: Or use 1 cup raw regular or processed white rice; combine with 2⅔ cups chicken broth in saucepan; bring to boil; simmer, covered, 20 minutes; add sautéed onion, saffron, and butter.

JAMBALAYA

Jambalaya is a Creole dish of highly seasoned rice, ham, shrimp or other shellfish, and tomatoes. The name is believed to come in part from the French word for ham, jambon.

1   tablespoon fat
1   tablespoon flour
1   cup cleaned cooked or raw shrimp
1   pound chopped cooked ham
1½ cups canned or fresh tomatoes
1   onion, sliced
1   red pepper, chopped
1   green pepper, chopped
1   clove garlic, crushed
Sprig of thyme (optional)
1   tablespoon minced parsley
1   teaspoon Worcestershire sauce
1   teaspoon salt
Dash of pepper
Paprika
4   cups water
1   cup raw rice

Melt fat; blend in flour, stirring constantly, until smooth and slightly brown.

Add shrimp, ham, and tomatoes; cook 3 minutes. Add onion, red and green pepper, garlic, thyme, parsley, Worcestershire sauce, about 1 teaspoon salt, dash of pepper, a sprinkling of paprika, and water. Bring to boiling-point and simmer about 12 minutes.

Add rice, cover and cook until tender, about 30 minutes.

Do not stir the mixture but lift occasionally with a fork from bottom of pot to keep rice from burning. Serves 6 or more.

RISOTTO WITH SHRIMP

1   cup chopped onion
⅔   cup chopped celery
½   cup sliced mushrooms (fresh or canned)
¼   cup cooking oil
2   cups uncooked rice, washed
1   6-ounce can tomato paste
1¾ cups hot water
2   teaspoons salt
1   teaspoon Worcestershire sauce
¼   teaspoon thyme
¼   teaspoon pepper
1   clove garlic, mashed
2   cups shrimp, cooked and cleaned
1   cup cooked green peas

Cook onion, celery, and mushrooms in oil until lightly browned.

Remove vegetables from pan; add rice and brown over low heat, stirring constantly.

Add remaining ingredients except shrimp and peas. Cover and simmer 1 hour, or until rice is tender.

Stir in shrimp and peas. Heat through, about 10 minutes longer. Serves 4 to 5.

CREOLE RICE PILAF WITH MUSHROOMS

1   pound mushrooms, sliced
1   medium sized onion, chopped
1   green pepper, chopped
Few sprigs of parsley, chopped
1   cup canned tomatoes
1   tablespoon tomato paste
¼   cup salad oil
1   tablespoon butter or margarine
Salt and pepper to taste
1   cup uncooked rice
1   cup water

Slice mushrooms into a skillet. Add onion, green pepper, parsley, tomatoes, tomato paste, oil, butter or margarine, salt and pepper. Place on low heat; in about 10 minutes add the rice and the water. Cook 20 minutes in all.

Add hot water, a little at a time as needed, if the mixture becomes too dry; but when the rice is tender, the liquid should be completely absorbed. (Watch carefully to keep from burning. If a lid is put on the skillet during part of the cooking time, the rice cooks more quickly and is less likely to stick.) Serves 4.

Jambalaya

Rice Oven Dishes

DOLMAS

Dolmas are combinations of meat, rice, vegetables, and spices wrapped in lettuce, fig, or especially grape leaves and stewed. Variations of such dishes with or without meat are popular throughout the Near East. Originally Turkish, the word is sometimes applied to anything similarly stuffed—green peppers, tomatoes, cucumbers, zucchini, etc.

GRAPE LEAF ROLLS (DOLMAS)

2 medium-sized onions, chopped fine
1/4 cup olive oil
1 cup uncooked rice
1/3 cup pine nuts
1 tablespoon chopped parsley
Juice of 1/2 lemon
1/2 teaspoon allspice
Salt and pepper
1 can grape leaves, well drained, or 12 fresh leaves (see note below)

Brown onions in oil. Add rice, pine nuts, parsley, lemon juice, allspice, salt, and pepper.

Add 1 cup warm water and cook until liquid is absorbed.

Put a spoonful of mixture on each leaf. Roll up and fasten with a wooden pick.

Put the plump rolls in casserole with 1 cup water.

Cover and bake in moderate oven (350°F.) 45 minutes, until liquid is absorbed. Serves 4.

Note: Canned grape leaves can be bought in Greek or Syrian stores, or fresh ones (12 or more large leaves for this amount of rice) may be dropped into boiling water for 1 or 2 minutes to make them pliable. Drain and use as directed.

WILD RICE AND MUSHROOMS

1 cup canned mushrooms
1/2 cup butter or margarine
2 tablespoons flour
1 cup milk and mushroom liquid
3 cups cooked wild rice
1/2 teaspoon salt
Dash of pepper
Buttered crumbs

Brown mushrooms in melted butter. Blend in flour, then milk to make a sauce. Add rice and seasonings.

Mix and turn into greased casserole. Top with buttered crumbs. Bake in moderate oven (375°F.) until browned. Serves 6.

BAKED RICE WITH CHEESE

Combine 3 cups cooked rice with 2 cups cheese sauce.

Turn into baking dish or individual baking cups. Bake in hot oven (400°F.) about 15 minutes.

TURKISH RICE

3 tablespoons butter or margarine
1 onion, chopped
1 green pepper, chopped
1 clove garlic, finely minced (optional)
1/2 pound fresh mushrooms, sliced
2/3 cup diced celery
1 pound uncooked rice (2 1/8 cups)
1 1/2 teaspoons salt
2 cups canned tomatoes
2 cups water
Buttered crumbs
Grated cheese (optional)
2 tablespoons chopped parsley

Melt butter in saucepan; add onion, green pepper, garlic, mushrooms, and celery. Brown over low heat, then add rice, salt, tomatoes, and water. Stir to blend.

Pour mixture into large buttered casserole. Cover and bake until rice has absorbed liquid and is tender.

Uncover, stir to blend ingredients, then top with crumbs. Dot with grated cheese if desired.

Brown uncovered in moderate oven (375°F.). Garnish with chopped parsley. Serves 6 to 8.

ORANGE RICE

1/4 cup margarine
2 cups hot water
1 cup uncooked rice
1 tablespoon chopped onion
2/3 cup diced celery
2 tablespoons grated orange rind
3/4 cup orange juice
1 1/2 teaspoons salt

Add 1/4 cup margarine to hot water. Mix together rice, chopped onion, diced celery, orange rind, orange juice, and salt. Add hot water to rice mixture.

Place in a 3-quart casserole dish. Cover and bake in moderate oven (350°F.) 3/4 hour. Serves 6.

BAKED RICE À LA GRUCCI

3 cups cooked rice
1/2 cup grated American cheese
1/4 cup chopped pimiento
1 1/2 cups tomato juice
1 1/2 teaspoons salt
Dash of pepper
2 cups corn flakes
2 tablespoons melted butter or margarine

Combine rice, cheese, pimiento, tomato juice, and seasonings. Pour into greased 1 1/2-quart casserole.

Crush corn flakes slightly and mix with melted butter. Sprinkle over rice mixture.

Bake in moderate oven (350°F.) about 30 minutes, until well heated. Serve at once. Serves 6.

GREEN RICE CASSEROLE

2 cups cooked rice
1/2 cup grated sharp cheese
1 cup milk
1 beaten egg
2 tablespoons minced onion
1/2 cup minced parsley

Combine and mix all ingredients. Add salt to taste.

Turn into greased casserole. Bake in slow oven (325°F.) 30 minutes. Serve with creamed seafoods. Serves 6.

BROWN RICE AND MUSHROOMS

1 cup fresh mushrooms, sliced
2 tablespoons shortening
1/4 cup chopped onion
1/4 cup chopped green pepper
1 teaspoon minced pimiento
1/2 teaspoon salt
2 cups cooked brown rice
3 tablespoons grated yellow cheese
1 cup hot water

Sauté mushrooms in shortening. Add onion and green pepper and cook gently 5 minutes.

Add pimiento, salt, rice, cheese, and hot water. Turn into greased casserole.

Bake in moderate oven (350°F.) until heated through, about 30 minutes. Serves 4 to 5.

PILAF WITH SALAMI

3/4 cup uncooked rice
2 tablespoons butter or margarine
2 cups hot bouillon or broth
1 tablespoon chopped onion
2 teaspoons Worcestershire sauce
1 1/2 cups cubed salami

Add rice to melted butter in heavy skillet and heat until golden brown.

Add bouillon, onion, and Worcestershire sauce. Heat to boiling point. Add salami and turn into casserole.

Bake in moderate oven (375°F.) about 40 minutes. Add more water if necessary. Serves 4.

BAKED RICE FREDONA

Fill a greased casserole with 3 to 4 cups cooked rice.

Beat 2 eggs lightly with 1 1/2 to 2 cups milk and pour over rice. Season with salt and pepper. Dot with butter and sprinkle with paprika.

Bake in moderate oven (350°F.) until browned.

Baked Rice À La Grucci

Fried Rice and Croquettes

FRIED RICE CROQUETTES
(Master Recipe)

       3 tablespoons butter or margarine
       3 tablespoons flour
     1/2 teaspoon salt
       1 cup milk
   1 1/2 cups cooked rice
         Fine dry breadcrumbs
       1 slightly beaten egg

Melt butter in a saucepan; blend in flour and salt. Add milk and cook until thickened, stirring constantly.

Add rice; mix and spread on shallow plate to cool.

Shape into 6 croquettes. Roll in crumbs, then in beaten egg and again in crumbs.

Fry in deep, hot fat (375°F.) until brown. Drain on absorbent paper.

Rice Croquette Variations

Cheese-Rice Croquettes: Prepare and chill rice as directed in master recipe.

Mix grated cheese with a few drops onion juice. If necessary, moisten with a little milk.

Shape into small balls. Coat with thick layer of rice mixture. Proceed as in master recipe.

Cranberry-Rice Croquettes: Cut chilled cranberry sauce into cubes. Coat with chilled rice mixture. Proceed as in master recipe.

Pimiento-Rice Croquettes: Add 2 tablespoons chopped pimiento to rice mixture of master recipe.

Rice Croquettes with Jelly: Make a depression in the top of each croquette when shaping them, or form into balls, then into nests. Proceed as in master recipe.

To serve, place a spoonful of tart red jelly in each.

Savory Rice Croquettes: Prepare master recipe and add 1/4 teaspoon paprika and 1 tablespoon ketchup to rice mixture.

Sweet Rice Croquettes: Prepare master recipe; add 2 tablespoons powdered sugar and grated rind of 1/2 lemon before cooling mixture.

Tomato-Rice Croquettes: In master recipe, substitute tomato juice for milk. Cook 1 tablespoon grated onion with the flour.

CREOLE RICE CAKES

       4 slices bacon, chopped
       3 tablespoons minced onions
       3 tablespoons minced green pepper
       1 teaspoon salt
     1/2 teaspoon black pepper
       3 cups cooked rice
       1 cup sifted enriched flour

       1 teaspoon baking powder
       1 to 1 1/2 cups tomato pulp

Sauté bacon until crisp. Reserve fat.

To the bacon, add rest of ingredients and mix well. Form into small, round, flat cakes.

Brown cakes in reserved bacon fat. Serve as a vegetable. Serves 6.

BAKED CHEESE AND RICE CROQUETTES

     1/3 cup mayonnaise
       2 tablespoons flour
     2/3 cup flour
   1 1/2 teaspoons salt
     1/8 teaspoon pepper
     1/4 teaspoon paprika
       1 teaspoon onion juice
     3/4 cup grated cheese
   2 1/2 cups cooked rice
         Dry breadcrumbs

In a saucepan, combine mayonnaise and flour. Stir in milk. Cook until thickened.

Add seasonings, onion juice, and grated cheese and cook until cheese is melted.

Cool. Add cooked rice to cheese sauce and mix thoroughly.

Shape into 12 croquettes. Roll in dry breadcrumbs. Let stand in refrigerator for several hours.

Place on baking sheet and bake in hot oven (400°F.) 20 minutes, or until well browned. Serve with a tomato sauce. Serves 6.

Note: These croquettes may be made and held in the refrigerator for 24 hours, if desired. Bake just before serving.

MUSHROOM FRIED RICE
(CHINESE)

     1/4 cup dried mushrooms
       2 tablespoons oil
       1 onion, chopped
       1 cup sliced fresh mushrooms
       2 tablespoons chopped green onions
       4 cups boiled rice, cold
       2 tablespoons soy sauce
     1/2 teaspoon sugar
       2 tablespoons chopped parsley

Wash and soak dried mushrooms in hot water for 1/2 hour.

Heat oil and stir-fry onion, fresh mushrooms, and green onions.

Shred soaked mushrooms which have been drained and add. Add rice and stir until heated.

Add soy sauce and sugar and, when all is heated, serve topped with chopped parsley. Serves 5 to 6.

Fried Rice

FRIED RICE

Fried Rice is a Chinese dish of previously boiled rice sautéed in oil or bacon fat with eggs, onions, soy sauce, and bits of cooked beef, pork, chicken, ham, or shellfish.

     1/2 pound roasted or fried ham or
           bacon (a can of lobster or
           shrimp may be substituted for
           meat)
       2 eggs, slightly beaten
       3 cups cooked rice
       1 tablespoon chopped onion
         Dash of pepper
     1/2 teaspoon salt
       2 tablespoons soy sauce

Cut ham or bacon in small pieces and fry. It is not necessary to heat or fry cold roasted meat, canned lobster or shrimp. Simply cut small.

Fresh shrimp or lobster should be sautéed in butter 3 minutes.

Fry eggs slightly on both sides in hot, well greased skillet. Add rice, onion, pepper, salt, meat or seafood, and mix thoroughly while cooking about 3 minutes.

Remove from heat; add soy sauce and stir. Serve while hot. Serves 4.

SHRIMP SUBGUM FRIED RICE

       4 tablespoons salad oil
       1 cup diced fresh mushrooms
     1/2 cup diced, cooked green pepper
       2 cups diced onions
     1/2 cup diced water chestnuts, optional
   1 1/2 teaspoons Ac'cent, optional
         Salt and pepper to taste
       3 slightly beaten eggs
       6 cups cooked rice
       1 cup diced, cooked cleaned shrimp
       2 finely chopped green onions
       4 tablespoons soy sauce

Heat oil in skillet. Add mushrooms, green pepper, onions, chestnuts, Ac'cent, and salt and pepper. Mix well and stir 4 minutes over moderate heat.

Add eggs and let fry about 1 minute, or until firm. Add rice and shrimp; mix well and stir constantly for 4 minutes.

Add green onions and soy sauce; mix thoroughly. Serves 4 to 6.

Variations: Substitute for the shrimp an equal amount of cooked lobster, chicken, roast pork, or boiled ham.

Rice Rings, Loaves, and Timbales

RICE RING
(Master Recipe)

For a 4- to 5-cup ring mold, use 1 cup uncooked rice and 1/4 cup melted butter or margarine.

For a 7-cup ring mold, use 1 1/2 cups uncooked rice and 6 tablespoons melted butter or margarine.

Cook rice and add melted butter to hot rice. Pack into well buttered ring mold. Let stand a minute; invert on warmed platter.

Fill center with creamed dried beef, fish, vegetables, or chicken.

Rice-Cheese Ring: Omit butter in above. Blend 1 cup grated cheese through cooked rice.

Mold and serve with creamed celery, eggs, or fish.

Rice-Pea Ring: Arrange layer of buttered peas in bottom of mold before adding rice.

Serve with creamed chicken, salmon, or tuna fish.

Rice-Chili Ring: Add 1 to 2 teaspoons chili powder to hot rice. Mold.

Serve with meat balls or meat sauce in center.

RICE TIMBALES

Pack cooked rice in buttered molds. Let stand in hot water about 10 minutes.

Unmold, garnish with a mushroom cap and serve with cheese sauce.

TO KEEP RICE RING HOT OR TO REHEAT

If a rice ring has been made the day before or prior to serving time, it must be reheated or kept hot until the meal is to be served.

To do this, cover the mold with foil or waxed paper to prevent the rice from becoming dry. Place a string just under the edge of the mold to hold the paper secure.

Put the ring in a pan of hot water and leave in a slow oven or over a low heat on top of the range until time to serve. No special timing is necessary. However, the ring must be left long enough for the rice to be hot when served.

To keep ring mold hot or to reheat.

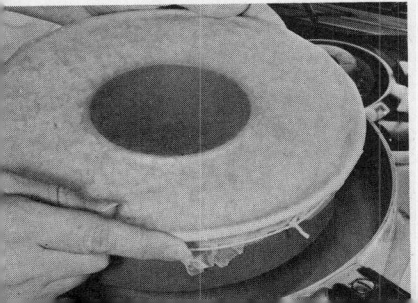

NUT LOAF

1/4 cup butter or margarine
1 cup chopped celery
1/4 cup chopped onion
1/4 cup chopped green pepper
1/4 cup flour
1 1/2 teaspoons salt
1/4 teaspoon pepper
1 1/2 cups milk
2 cups chopped pecans
2 cups cooked rice
2 tablespoons minced parsley
2 tablespoons pimiento
4 eggs, beaten
1/2 cup fine dry breadcrumbs

Melt butter or margarine. Add celery, onion, and green pepper; cook slowly until soft but not brown. Blend in flour, salt, pepper, then milk; cook until thickened stirring constantly. Add remaining ingredients; mix well.

Press into greased 9 x 5 x 3-inch loaf pan. Bake in moderate oven (375°F.) until set, 35 to 40 minutes. Cool in pan 5 minutes, then remove from pan and let stand 10 minutes before slicing. Serve with Carrot Sauce (below). Serves 6.

Carrot Sauce:

1/3 cup butter or margarine
2 cups shredded raw carrots (about 8 medium)
2 tablespoons chopped onion
1/4 cup flour
1/4 teaspoon salt
2 cups water
2 vegetable or beef bouillon cubes

Melt butter or margarine. Add carrots and onion; cook, stirring constantly, until carrots are almost tender. Blend in flour and salt. Add water and bouillon cubes. Cook, stirring constantly until thickened. Serve with Nut Loaf. Makes 2 1/2 cups sauce.

MUSHROOM RICE RING

1 cup uncooked rice
1/2 pound mushrooms, chopped
2 tablespoons butter or margarine
1/4 cup hot stock or water
Salt and paprika

Cook rice until tender. Drain.

Sauté mushrooms in butter 3 minutes and stir in stock or water.

Combine mushroom mixture with cooked rice. Season to taste. Turn into greased 7-inch ring mold.

Set in pan of hot water. Bake in moderate oven (350°F.) about 30 minutes.

To serve, unmold on platter. Fill center with creamed fish, meat, or buttered vegetables Serves 6.

Nut Loaf

BAKED RICE RING

Combine 2 cups cooked rice with 2 tablespoons melted fat and 1 teaspoon salt. Turn into greased ring mold.

Place mold in pan of hot water. Bake in moderate oven (350°F.) 25 minutes.

Unmold on platter and fill center with creamed fish, meat, vegetable, as desired. Sprinkle with paprika. Garnish outside of ring with border of cooked peas.

Baked Brown Rice Ring: Substitute steamed brown rice in above recipe.

CHEESE RICE RING (BAKED)

1/2 cup uncooked rice
1 beaten egg
2 tablespoons melted butter or margarine
1/4 cup milk
1/3 cup grated cheese
1/2 teaspoon grated onion
1/4 teaspoon salt
2 tablespoons chopped parsley
1 teaspoon Worcestershire sauce

Cook rice until tender and drain. Combine with remaining ingredients and turn into greased 7-inch ring mold.

Set in pan of hot water and bake in moderate oven (350°F.) about 40 minutes. To serve, unmold on platter. Serves 4.

ALMOND RICE RING WITH BEEF STEW

3 cups cooked rice
1/2 cup coarsely chopped toasted almonds
1/4 cup melted butter or margarine
2 cans (1-lb. each) beef stew

Combine rice, almonds, and butter. Put into a well greased ring mold. Set the mold in a pan of hot water and bake in moderate oven (350°F.) about 20 minutes.

Loosen the edges with a knife and invert on a platter. Fill the center with heated stew. Serves 4 to 6.

Almond Rice Ring with Beef Stew

CHEESE AND CHEESE DISHES

Foods come alive with flavor when cheese is a principal ingredient. Take your choice of main dish casseroles, tangy sauces and salad dressings, cool salads enriched with cheese, crusty cheese breads, tempting cheese desserts, etc. Throughout this book you'll find hundreds of recipes with new ideas in cheese uses and cheese cookery. To find everything we have published on this subject, consult the index.

CHOOSING CHEESE

Selecting and buying the right cheese is largely a matter of personal preference. Some persons prefer mild cheese; others favor sharp or strong-flavored cheeses. Children generally like mild cheeses and their elders the more pungent varieties.

Information follows on the various forms of cheese available in retail markets. These facts may enlarge your acquaintance with the cheese family and help you use cheese more interestingly and appetizingly.

CHEESE COOKERY HINTS

● Successful cheese cookery depends on brief heating at a low temperature. High temperatures and too-long cooking make cheese tough and stringy, and cause the fat to separate out. Some of the flavor is lost, too.

● Cheese blends more readily with other ingredients if you shred or dice it first. One-half pound of cheese yields about 2 cups of shredded cheese.

● Soft, well-aged Cheddar melts and blends with other ingredients more readily than less ripened cheese, and less of it is needed because it has a more pronounced flavor. Process cheese also melts and blends readily, but has a much milder flavor.

● Melt cheese in the top of a double boiler over simmering water, or add it to a hot mixture. When making cheese sauce, stir in the shredded cheese after the white sauce is completely cooked, and heat only enough to melt the cheese. When making a cheese omelet, add the shredded cheese after the omelet is cooked—just before folding.

● Cheese can be melted under the broiler, too. Open-face cheese sandwiches can be made this way. Place the sandwich so the cheese is 4 to 5 inches from the heat. Broil just until the cheese begins to melt.

● Casserole dishes containing cheese should be baked at low to moderate temperatures. To prevent cheese toppings from toughening or hardening during baking, cover them with crumbs or add the cheese just before removing the food from the oven.

STORING CHEESE

Cheese keeps best in the refrigerator. How long it will keep depends on the kind of cheese and the wrapping. Soft cheeses—such as cottage, cream, and Neufchatel—are highly perishable. Hard cheeses—Cheddar and Swiss, for example—keep much longer than soft cheeses if protected from drying out. Approximate storage times are given below.

Leave cheese in its original wrapper, if possible. Cover cut surfaces tightly with waxed paper, foil, or plastic to protect the surface from drying out, or store the cheese in a tightly covered container. If you want to store a large piece of cheese for an extended time, dip the cut surface in melted paraffin. Store cheese that has a strong odor, such as Limburger, in a tightly covered container.

Any surface mold that develops on hard natural cheese should be trimmed off completely before the cheese is used. In mold-ripened cheeses such as Blue or Roquefort, mold is an important part of the cheese and can be eaten. If mold penetrates the interior of cheeses, such as Cheddar and Swiss, that are not ripened by molds, cut away the moldy portions or discard the cheeses.

Cheese that has dried out and become hard may be grated and stored in a tightly covered jar.

Home Storage Guide for Cheese

Cottage, fresh Ricotta: Refrigerate, covered; use within 3 to 5 days.

Cream, Neufchatel, other soft varieties: Refrigerate, covered or tightly wrapped; use within 2 weeks.

Cheddar, Swiss, other hard varieties: Refrigerate, tightly wrapped; will keep for several months unless mold develops.

Cheese spreads and cheese foods: Store unopened jars at room temperature; after opening, refrigerate, tightly covered; will keep for several weeks.

TO ENHANCE CHEESE FLAVOR

Except for soft, unripened cheeses such as cottage or cream cheese, all cheeses taste better when served unchilled. This usually requires from 20 minutes to 1 hour at room temperature to bring out the distinctive flavor and texture.

TO SLICE CHEESE

You may prefer to buy a cheese cutter in order to have slices of uniform thickness. A heavy thread or fine wire can also be used to slice cheese; this works especially well with Blue cheese.

GRATED CHEESE

If cheese is to be grated or shredded, the job is easier if you work with cold cheese taken directly from the refrigerator. Use ends of cheese or dry hard cheese such as Cheddar, Gruyère, Parmesan, or Romano. Grate small quantities as needed just before using.

Guide to Natural Cheeses

AMERICAN CHEESE

American Cheddar cheese. The term usually is taken to mean mild Cheddar, either natural or pasteurized process Cheddar. See **Cheddar; Process Cheeses.**

APPETITOST

A Danish cheese made from sour buttermilk. Some is imported, and a small quantity is made in the United States.

ASIAGO

A cheese of Italian origin with a dark surface, cream-colored interior, piquant flavor, and granular texture.

Use it for general table use when fresh, for grating when old and drier.

BEL PAESE

Light yellow. Mellow flavor. Soft to solid consistency.

Delicious with plain crackers or with fruit for dessert.

BLUE

Blue, blue-mold, or blue-veined cheese is the name for cheese of the Roquefort type that is made in the United States and Canada. It is made from cow's or goat's milk, rather than ewe's milk. The French word for this type of cheese is bleu.

As a general term, blue is sometimes used to refer to many Roquefort-type cheeses marbled with a blue-green mold, including the English Stilton, French Roquefort, Danish Danablu, Italian Gorgonzola, etc. All have a mild-to-sharp sort of pungent salty flavor.

Use crumbled in crunchy salads, in salad dressings, for canapé spreads, and' snacks. Particularly delicious with fresh pears or toasted unsalted crackers and sherry. Makes an excellent topping for broiled steaks.

BONDOST

A Swedish cow's milk cheese now made in the United States. It is sometimes flavored with cumin or caraway seeds. The flavor is mild to pronounced, depending upon age. Use it for general table use.

BRICK

Creamy white to light yellow in color. Has small eyes and an elastic texture. Mild-to-sharp flavor.

Use on cheese trays, with crackers, and in sandwiches.

BRIE

Soft, creamy interior with light russet-brown crust. It has a pronounced odor and sharp flavor.

Spread it, crust and all, on crackers, dark, whole grain breads, on French bread, or on slices of unpeeled apple.

CACIOCAVALLO

This cheese, originally from Italy, is made in a number of unusual shapes, often tied in pairs. The surface is light brown. The cured cheese has a smooth, firm body, and preferably the interior of the cheese is white. It has a somewhat salty, smoky flavor.

Use it as a table cheese when it's fresh, that is, cured not more than 2 to 4 months. When fully cured, 6 to 12 months, it is suitable for grating.

CAMEMBERT

Soft, creamy, yellowish interior with a thin, whitish crust. Rich, mild flavor.

To serve, soften it at room temperature. At its peak, interior will be like thick cream. World-wide favorite dessert cheese. Spread it, crust and all, on slices of unpeeled apple, on crackers, plain or toasted, and on French bread.

CHANTELLE

A trade name of a semi-soft ripened cheese made from cow's milk. It has a pale yellow interior with a mild-to-pronounced flavor, depending on age.

Use it for dessert, sandwiches, snacks, and on cheese trays. Serve wedges with apple, pears, or pineapple.

CHEDDAR

Cheddar cheese is named for the village of Cheddar in Somersetshire, England, where it was first made probably in the latter part of the 16th century.

About 75 percent of all the cheese made in the United States is a Cheddar or Cheddar-type cheese. In fact, it is made and used so widely that it often is called American cheese, or American Cheddar cheese, and cheeses similar to Cheddar but made by a slightly modified process are called American-type cheeses.

The color may be light cream to orange; the flavor mild when fresh, pronounced and pleasing when cured or aged.

It is the national favorite for sandwiches, with pies, cobblers, etc. Use in cooking, as in casseroles, soufflés, etc. Adds heartiness to tossed salads.

COLBY

Mild to mellow flavor, similar to Cheddar; softer body and more open texture than Cheddar; light cream to orange in color.

Use it for sandwiches and snacks.

COTTAGE CHEESE

Sometimes called pot cheese and also Dutch cheese or Schmierkäse, it is a soft, uncured cheese made from skim milk or from reconstituted skim milk or nonfat dry milk solids.

Usually some cream is mixed with the cheese curd before it is marketed or consumed. If the cheese contains 4 percent or more of fat, it is called creamed cottage cheese. Flavoring materials, such as peppers, olives, pimientos, may be added also.

Use it in salads or spreads, plain or flavored with chives, nuts, pickle relish, diced fruit, etc.

CREAM CHEESE

Delicately flavored, white, mild, and fresh as cream. Soft texture. Made from a mixture of cream and milk with minimum fat content of 35 percent (usually 35 to 38 per cent).

Thin with cream to top fruit salads and desserts. Use as a sandwich filling particularly with date and nut breads. Cube it for fruit salads. Season and form into balls for hors d'oeuvres.

EDAM OR GOUDA

Round cheeses with flattened ends and red coatings. Mild flavor which is sometimes salty and nut-like. Edam weighs 2 to 4 pounds. "Baby" Gouda weighs less than a pound.

They are pretty to look at and the mild flavor blends well with tart apples, grapes and tangerines. Use as a bright hub for a dessert or snack tray.

EMMENTALER

The native name for Swiss cheese which was first made, probably about the middle of the 15th century, in the Canton of Bern, in the Emmental Valley in Switzerland. See **Swiss.**

GAMMELOST

A brown-colored, strong-flavored Norwegian cheese made of skimmed sour milk. Use for snacks and general table use.

GJETOST

A hard, dark brown, smooth-textured cheese with a full sweet flavor. It is made in Norway from goat's milk. Slice it thin and serve on crackers or dark breads.

GOMOST

A whole milk Norwegian cheese, made usually from cow's milk but also from goat's milk. A nice snack cheese.

GORGONZOLA

A blue mold cheese made from cow's milk with a delicate, piquant flavor.

Crumble it into salads and salad dressings. Use it on cheese snack tray and as a dessert cheese with crackers or fruit.

GRUYÈRE

A Swiss cheese with smaller holes and a taste similar to Swiss. In the United States, Gruyère means a light yellow semi-hard process cheese that is foil-wrapped in small wedges. The flavor is mild.

KOSHER CHEESE

Kosher cheese is made especially for Jewish consumers, to conform with Jewish dietary custom. Typically, it is made without animal rennet. Sometimes the milk is curdled by natural souring; sometimes a starter is added to the milk.

Among the kosher cheeses are soft cheeses like cream and cottage cheese, kosher gouda, and a cheese that is made by the limburger process but, unlike limburger, is eaten fresh. Kosher cheese bears a label by which it can be identified.

LIEDERKRANZ

A trade name of a creamy yellow cheese with a hearty, robust flavor. Odor somewhat resembles Limburger. Soft, creamy spreading consistency. Spreads easily.

Serve with toast, crackers, rye and pumpernickel breads. The thin crust should be eaten for fullest flavor enjoyment.

LIMBURGER

Soft textured cheese. Very characteristic odor and flavor. Despite the fact that there is so much jesting about it, Limburger is considered by many cheese fanciers as among the most delicious of cheese flavors. Actually, once you have got past the pungent smell of Limburger, you will find its taste rather mild. Serve the same way as Liederkranz.

MONTEREY

Monterey (or Monterey Jack) is a California cheese with a semi-soft, white interior. It hardens with age.

It is delicate and fragrant, good for general table use and as a dessert cheese.

MOZZARELLA

A semi-soft, light, cream-colored cheese made from cow's milk with a mild flavor.

It is used for the most part in cooking, especially in such dishes as eggplant or veal parmigiana and pizza. It's a "must" for real pizza.

MUENSTER

Orange-colored rind with light-yellow interior full of tiny holes. Often flavored with anise or caraway seed. It has a semi-hard texture.

Serve with vegetable relish tray. Good with green onions (scallions), cucumbers, carrot sticks, radishes, etc. Excellent with pumpernickel bread or date-nut bread.

MYSOST

A light brown cheese with a sweetish flavor made in the Scandinavian countries from goat's milk, in the United States from cow's milk. Nice to slice thin and serve on crackers or dark breads.

NEUFCHÂTEL

A cream cheese-type product of French origin with a smooth soft texture, mild flavor, white color. In the United States it is made from pasteurized milk or a milk-and-cream mixture in much the same way as cream cheese, but it contains less fat (20 percent minimum). Excellent for sandwiches, on crackers, in salads.

OKA

A type of Port du Salut cheese made in the Trappist monastery at Oka, Canada. It has a russet surface, creamy yellow interior with a semi-soft texture that slices well.

It is an excellent dessert cheese. The flavor teams up especially good with port wine.

PARMESAN

Delicate yellow color. Mild to full flavor. Texture is firm to hard—usually the latter.

Grate to serve on spaghetti, soups like minestrone and onion, on some salads and casseroles.

PINEAPPLE

A Cheddar type, named for its shape. Yellow to orange color.

Use as centerpiece in a tray. Hollow out cone-shaped piece in center; cut in cubes and return to shell. Serve with cocktail picks.

PORT DU SALUT

Delicate in flavor. It has a moderately soft interior but it slices well.

Serve with plain bland crackers or all by itself. Good either way.

PROVOLONE

A smoky tasting cheese that comes in several shapes. It's commonly seen hanging in ball shapes or long cylindrical forms in stores in Italian neighborhoods.

Excellent with rye or whole wheat crackers.

RICOTTA

This soft-textured cheese is often called "Italian cottage cheese." It is made from whey with whole or skim milk added. Fresh, moist ricotta is the type usually found in our markets and it is popularly used in ravioli, lasagna, etc. Cured dry ricotta is suitable for grating.

ROMANO

An Italian cheese with a somewhat granular texture and practically no holes or eyes.

Excellent with rye bread or whole wheat crackers if it hasn't been aged more than about 8 months. More frequently it is cured for a year or more and then it is hard, very sharply piquant, and suitable for grating.

ROQUEFORT

A blue-veined and semi-soft-to-hard cheese, named for the village of Roquefort in southeastern France, where its manufacture has been an important industry for more than two centuries. A French regulation limits use of the word Roquefort to cheese made in the Roquefort area from ewe's milk.

Other French cheese of the Roquefort type is called bleu cheese, and Roquefort-type cheese made in the United States and other countries is known as blue cheese. In addition, there are the distinctive blue-veined cheeses of England (Stilton) and Italy (Gorgonzola).

Only genuine Roquefort is allowed to have the name Roquefort. Imports are marked Roquefort-France. For uses, see **Blue.**

SAP SAGO

This cheese has been made in the Canton of Glarus, Switzerland, for at least 500 years and perhaps more; it is made also in Germany. It has a sharp, pungent, cloverlike flavor; very hard texture suitable for grating; light green or sage green in color. Grate it for seasoning.

SCAMORZE

A soft mild cheese of Italian origin, much like mozzarella and used in the same way. It is excellent in many Italian dishes, especially pizza. It is very tasty when toasted with bread or fried with an egg.

STILTON

Famous English cheese with a ridged or wrinkled rind, creamy color with blue or green mold interior. It has a semi-hard texture and sharp flavor.

Use it as a table cheese and for other purposes suggested for blue cheese. See **Blue.**

SWISS (EMMENTALER)

Originally from Switzerland, this cheese has a grayish brown surface, a white or slightly glossy cream interior color. The texture is semi-hard with round, rather large holes throughout. It has a mild nutlike sweetish flavor.

Slice thin to serve on platters with cold meats and other foods. Use with rye breads or serve in small sticks with salad plates. Adds heartiness to fruit and vegetable salads. Use it in such dishes as Swiss cheese pies, fondues, etc.

TRAPPIST

Trappist cheese made in various monasteries in Europe is much the same as the Port du Salut cheese made in France and the Oka cheese made in Canada (often called Canadian Port du Salut), but there are variations in the manufacturing process. See **Port du Salut.**

NATURAL CHEESE

Natural cheese is a product made by coagulating milk and then separating the curd, or solid part, from the whey, or watery part. Some natural cheeses are ripened (aged) to develop their characteristic flavor and texture; others are used unripened. Ripened cheeses sometimes are labeled as to the degree of ripening or aging. Cheddar cheese may be labeled "mild," "medium," or "mellow," "aged," or "sharp."

Many persons prefer natural cheeses to other forms of cheese because each natural cheese has its own characteristic flavor and texture. Flavors range from bland cottage cheese to tangy Blue or pungent Limburger. Textures vary too—from the smooth creaminess of cream cheese to the firm elasticity of Swiss cheese.

The guide to natural cheeses lists cheeses likely to be found in grocery and specialty stores. Characteristics and suggested uses are given for each cheese.

PROCESS CHEESES

Process (or pasteurized process) cheese is made by grinding fine, and mixing together by heating and stirring, one or more cheeses of the same or two or more varieties, together with an added emulsifying agent, into a homogeneous, plastic mass. Other ingredients may be used such as small amounts of cream, water, salt, color, and spices or flavoring materials. The cheese may be smoked, or it may be made from smoked cheese, or so-called liquid smoke or smoke "flavor" may be added.

During the manufacturing process it must be heated to pasteurizing temperature; therefore, it keeps well and does not ripen further.

Because it melts easily, it's excellent for all cheese cookery. It must be labeled "process cheese."

PROCESS CHEESE FOOD

Process cheese food (or pasteurized process cheese food) is made in the same ways as process cheese, except that certain dairy products (cream, milk, cheese whey, or whey albumin) or concentrates or mixtures of any of these may be added, but at least 51 percent of the weight of the finished cheese food must be cheese.

PROCESS CHEESE SPREADS

Process cheese spreads (or pasteurized process cheese spreads) are made in the same way as process cheese foods, except that they contain more moisture (44 to 60 percent) and less fat (but not less than 20 percent) and must be spreadable at a temperature of 70°F. Fruits, vegetables, or meats may be added.

COLDPACK CHEESE OR CLUB CHEESE

This a combination of fresh and aged natural cheese blended into a uniform product without heating. No emulsifier is used. Spices or smoke flavoring and food acids may be added.

The flavor of coldpack cheese is usually sharp and characteristic of the natural cheese or cheeses used. Coldpack cheese is softer than natural cheese and spreads more easily.

COLDPACK CHEESE FOOD

This is prepared like coldpack cheese, but contains added milk or whey solids. It may include fruits, vegetables, pimientos, meats, spices, or smoke flavoring. Sugar or corn syrup may also be added. Coldpack cheese food is milder, softer, and more spreadable than coldpack cheese.

TO FREEZE CHEESE

Freezing is not recommended for most cheeses because they become crumbly and mealy when frozen. Small pieces (1 pound or less, not more than 1 inch thick) of the following varieties can be frozen satisfactorily: Brick, Cheddar, Edam, Gouda, Muenster, Port du Salut, Swiss, Provolone, Mozzarella, and Camembert. You can also freeze small quantities of Blue, Roquefort, and Gorgonzola for salads or salad dressings, or other uses where a crumbly texture is acceptable. Wrap cheeses tightly, freeze quickly at 0°F. or below, and store no more than 6 months. When removed from the freezer, cheese should be thawed in the refrigerator and used as soon as possible after thawing.

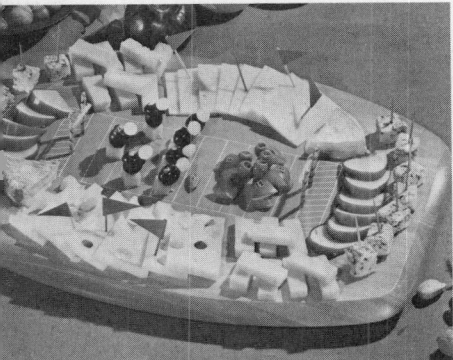

Appealing Ways with Cheese

THE CHEESE TRAY—FOR SNACKS OR DESSERT

The cheese tray is a simple-to-do and easy-to-serve dessert or snack. Cheese and crackers are a favorite finish to dinner with many people and particularly with men. A perfect accompaniment to cheese are luscious bits of fresh fruit; apples, pears, and grapes are the most popular.

Cheese arrangements may be made on any type of tray or Lazy Susan. Vary the decorative effects by cutting cheeses into attractive shapes: cubes, balls, finger sticks, wedges, etc. Ground-aged Cheddar may be molded to look like pumpkins, pears, etc.

Recipes Featuring Cheese

WELSH RABBIT
(Master Recipe)

This dish is often, and mistakenly, called Welsh rarebit. Actually, the name is humorous and slightly derogatory in origin; other examples of the same kind of joke are Cape Cod turkey (codfish) and Scotch woodcock (eggs with anchovy paste).

Welsh rabbit is a thick sauce traditionally of melted Cheddar cheese and ale or beer, seasoned with Worcestershire sauce, mustard, salt, sometimes pepper, and paprika. There are many variations. Milk is often substituted for the ale or beer and egg or egg yolk is sometimes added for a smoother mixture. Ideally, rabbits are made at the table in a chafing dish and accompanied by a dry white wine or beer. Good Welsh rabbit can be bought canned, ready to be heated and served.

2   tablespoons butter or margarine
2   tablespoons flour
1/2 teaspoon salt
Few grains cayenne
1   cup milk or cream
1/2 teaspoon dry mustard
1   cup grated cheese
4   slices of toast

Prepare white sauce by melting butter, blending in flour, salt, and cayenne, and gradually adding milk. Cook over hot water, stirring constantly until thick.

Add mustard and cheese, stirring until cheese is melted and mixture smooth. Serve hot on toast or salted crackers. Serves 4.

Welsh Rabbit Variations

Bacon Rabbit: Dice 2 or 3 strips of crisp, drained bacon and add to sauce with the cheese.

Baked Rabbit: Pour rabbit over toast. Bake in slow oven (325°F.) until golden brown, about 15 minutes.

Dried Beef Rabbit: Add 1/2 cup dried beef after soaking slightly in hot water and draining.

English Monkey: Substitute 1/2 cup stale breadcrumbs for flour in sauce. Add 1 slightly beaten egg to sauce.

Olive Rabbit: Add 1/2 cup sliced stuffed olives to sauce.

Welsh Rabbit

Onion Rabbit: Sprinkle grated or minced onion over rabbit.

Oyster Rabbit: Add 1 cup parboiled oysters to sauce.

Rum Tum Tiddy: Add 1 teaspoon Worcestershire sauce and 1 slightly beaten egg to tomato rabbit (below).

Sardine Rabbit: Arrange 3 or 4 sardines on each slice of buttered toast. Place under hot broiler 2 to 3 minutes. Pour over rabbit sauce. Serve at once.

Tomato Rabbit: Substitute 1 cup condensed tomato soup for milk. If desired, add 1 tablespoon each minced onion and green pepper.

Tuna Rabbit: Add 1/2 cup flaked tuna fish to sauce.

WELSH RABBIT WITH ALE OR BEER

1   tablespoon butter or margarine
1/2 cup ale or beer
1   pound grated Cheddar or aged
        American cheese
2   egg yolks
2   teaspoons Worcestershire sauce
1   teaspoon prepared mustard
Salt
1/4 cup milk
Paprika

Place butter and ale or beer in chafing dish or double boiler. When hot, add cheese and melt slowly, stirring continually.

When smooth, add egg yolks mixed with seasonings and milk and stir for a few minutes until thickened.

Serve on the soft side of bread toasted on one side with crusts removed. Garnish with dash of paprika. Serves 6.

EGG RABBIT WITH ASPARAGUS SPEARS

2/3 cup diced celery
1/4 cup chopped onion
2   tablespoons butter
1   can (10 1/2 ounces) condensed
        cream of tomato soup
1/2 teaspoon prepared mustard
Dash of Tabasco, optional
1/2 cup milk
1   cup shredded sharp or mild proc-
        essed American cheese (1/4
        pound)
6   hard-cooked eggs, coarsely chopped
2   packages frozen asparagus spears,
        cooked, or 2 No. 2 cans aspar-
        agus spears, drained

Cook celery and onions, slowly, in butter until tender but not brown. Stir in soup, seasonings, and milk; heat.

Fold in cheese and eggs and allow cheese to melt and eggs to heat, stirring frequently. Pour over hot cooked drained asparagus spears. Serve plain or on toast points. Serves 6.

Swiss Fondue

SWISS FONDUE

This is a hot mixture of melted cheese and wine, sometimes thickened with cornstarch. Traditionally Swiss cheese (Emmentaler or Gruyère) is used. The cheese or combination of cheeses used must be natural cheese, not pasteurized types. The wine may be any light dry white wine of the Rhine, Riesling, or Chablis types. For an authentic Swiss touch kirsch is added; however you may substitute a non-sweetened fruit brandy such as applejack, slivovitz, cognac, etc., or light rum. Swiss fondue is usually made and served in a chafing dish. It is accompanied by thick cubes of crusty French bread to dip (on forks) into the fondue. The bread cubes are speared with the fork going through the soft part first.

1   clove garlic
1 1/2 to 2 cups dry white wine
1   pound natural Swiss cheese,
        grated
2   teaspoons cornstarch
3   tablespoons kirsch
Freshly-ground black pepper
1   loaf French or Italian bread

Rub the bottom and sides of an earthenware casserole or chafing dish with garlic. Add wine and heat to boiling point but do not boil.

Add cheese, stirring constantly with wooden spoon. When cheese is creamy and barely simmering, add cornstarch blended with kirsch. Stir until mixture bubbles. Add pepper to taste.

Place casserole over an alcohol burner or transfer to a chafing dish or electric skillet adjusted to low heat. Keep the fondue hot but not simmering. If it becomes too thick, add a little more wine. To serve, accompany with 1-inch cubes of bread for dipping into the warm fondue. Makes about 3 cups or about 4 servings.

Egg Rabbit with Asparagus Spears

Cheese Custard Luncheon Pie

CHEESE CUSTARD LUNCHEON PIE

Pastry for 9-inch pie crust
4   slices bacon, cut in small pieces
1/3   cup finely chopped onion
2   tablespoons finely chopped green
     pepper
1½   cups milk
3   eggs
1   tablespoon minced pimiento
1/4   teaspoon pepper
1/2   pound American cheese, grated
Sliced stuffed olives for garnish

Prepare pastry and place in pie pan. Chill.

Fry bacon until crisp. Remove from pan. Pour off all but 2 tablespoons fat. Cook onions and green pepper until soft but not brown.

Heat milk to scalding, then add slowly to slightly beaten eggs. Add bacon, onion-green pepper mixture, pimiento, and pepper. Add cheese.

Pour into chilled pastry crust and bake in slow oven (325°F.) 45 minutes to 50 minutes or until set. Garnish if desired with stuffed olive slices. Serve immediately. Serves 6.

TOMATO SUPER SUPPER DISH

1/4   cup soft butter or margarine
6   slices bread, toasted
2½   cups shredded American cheese
3   eggs, slightly beaten
2   cans (2½ cups) condensed tomato
     soup
1/4   teaspoon salt
1/4   teaspoon dry mustard

Spread butter on toasted bread; cut each slice into 6 squares.

Grease a 2-quart baking dish; place in it alternate layers of toast squares and cheese, ending with a top layer of cheese.

Combine eggs, soup, salt, and mustard; pour over bread-cheese layers.

Bake in slow oven (325°F.) about 1 hour.

Garnish with border of finely chopped green pepper and sprigs of parsley. Serve piping hot as a hearty luncheon or supper dish. Serves 6.

Variation: This dish may be made with condensed cream of mushroom soup instead of tomato for Mushroom Super Supper Dish.

BLENDER WELSH RABBIT

1½   cups milk
1   egg
1   teaspoon Worcestershire sauce
1   teaspoon salt
1/4   teaspoon dry mustard
1/2   teaspoon paprika
1   tablespoon cornstarch
1/2   pound diced sharp Cheddar
     cheese

Heat milk. Put all ingredients except milk in container in order given. Add hot milk gradually and blend thoroughly, about 1 minute.

Heat in double boiler over hot water until thick, about 5 minutes. Serve over hot toast. Serves 4.

GOLDEN LUNCHEON

2   tablespoons butter or margarine
2   teaspoons cornstarch
3/4   cup light cream
1/2   teaspoon salt
1/2   teaspoon dry mustard
1/2   teaspoon Worcestershire sauce
3/4   pound Cheddar cheese, cut in small
     pieces
1   beaten egg
Toast
6   poached eggs

Melt butter over low heat or in top of double boiler. Blend in cornstarch; add cream.

Add salt, mustard, and Worcestershire sauce and cook until slightly thickened, about 2 or 3 minutes.

Add cheese and cook, stirring constantly, until cheese is melted.

Add beaten egg and stir while cooking, until very smooth.

Serve at once on toast on preheated plates. Top each serving with a poached egg. Serves 6.

CHEESE AND VEGETABLE CASSEROLE

1½   cups scalded milk
1   cup soft breadcrumbs
1/4   cup melted butter or margarine
2   pimientos, chopped
1   tablespoon chopped parsley
1½   tablespoons chopped onion
1½   cups grated, American cheese
3/8   teaspoon salt
Pepper and paprika
3   eggs, well beaten
1   cup cooked or canned vegetables,
     drained

Pour scalded milk over breadcrumbs. Add butter, pimientoes, parsley, onion, grated cheese, and seasoning. Add well beaten eggs.

Put vegetables in well greased casserole and pour milk-cheese mixture over them.

Bake in slow oven (325°F.) 1¼ hours. Serves 4 to 5.

CHEESE AND CORN MEAL CASSEROLE

2   cups boiling water
1   teaspoon salt
2/3   cup corn meal
1   tablespoon butter or margarine
1   pound Cheddar cheese, shredded

Bring water with salt to rolling boil. Gradually add corn meal, stirring constantly to prevent lumping. Cook over low heat 8 minutes, stirring occasionally.

Remove from heat and stir in butter until melted.

Cover bottom of greased shallow 9-inch casserole with cheese. Add alternate layers of corn meal and cheese until full.

Bake in moderate oven (350°F.) 30 minutes. Serve with hot tomato sauce. Serves 4.

OLIVE CHEESE PIE

2/3   cup ripe olives
6   slices bacon
2   tablespoons chopped onion
3   eggs
1¼   teaspoons salt
1/2   teaspoon prepared mustard
1/2   teaspoon Worcestershire sauce
Dash of Tabasco sauce
Dash of black pepper
2   cups grated packed American
     cheese
2   cups milk
Pastry for 1 9-inch crust

Cut olives into large pieces. Cut bacon into 1/4-inch pieces and fry until crisp. Remove bacon from pan and drain off all but 1 tablespoon fat.

Cook onion slowly in bacon fat until clear and yellow.

Beat eggs lightly and add seasonings. Blend in cheese, milk, olives, bacon, and onion. Turn into pastry-lined pan.

Bake in very hot oven (450°F.) 15 minutes. Reduce heat to slow (300°F.) and bake 30 to 40 minutes longer, or until set in center.

Allow to stand 5 to 10 minutes before serving. Garnish with bacon curls and ripe olives. Serves 6 to 8.

Olive Cheese Pie

CHEESE PUDDING

1½ cups milk
2½ cups cubed stale bread
1½ cups coarsely grated cheese
1½ tablespoons butter or margarine
¾ teaspoon salt
½ teaspoon pepper
Pinch of nutmeg
3 eggs, separated

Combine milk, bread, cheese, butter, and seasonings; cook over low heat until cheese is melted. Remove from heat.

Blend in egg yolks which have been beaten until lemon-colored. Then fold in egg whites which have been beaten until stiff but not dry.

Pour into 2-quart buttered baking dish. Bake in moderate oven (350°F.) 30 to 35 minutes. Serves 6.

CHEESE SURPRISE DUMPLINGS

1 recipe pastry or 1 package (8 to 9 ounces) prepared pie crust mix
½ cup chopped onion
3 tablespoons butter or margarine
¼ cup finely chopped green pepper
1 cup chopped celery stalks
½ pound process Cheddar cheese, shredded
¾ cup (5 ounce can) cooked, shelled and cleaned shrimp, cut in small pieces

Roll pastry ⅛-inch thick; cut into 8 5-inch squares.

Cook onion in butter until light golden brown. Add green pepper and celery. Cover tightly and allow to cook slowly until celery is tender, about 10 minutes, stirring occasionally.

Remove cover. Add cheese and keep over very low heat until cheese is melted, stirring constantly. Add shrimp and mix well.

Place ¼ cup cheese mixture in center of square, moisten edges with cold water. Fold so that corners of square meet in center over mixture and press edges firmly together to prevent leakage of filling. Prick top several places with tines of fork.

Bake in hot oven (400°F.) until light golden brown, about 20 to 25 minutes.

Serve hot with horseradish mustard sauce. Makes 8.

Cheese Surprise Dumplings

AMERICAN CHEESE FONDUE

20 saltine crackers
¼ pound (1 cup) grated sharp cheese
1 tablespoon butter or margarine
½ teaspoon salt
1¼ cups milk, scalded
2 eggs, separated

Crumble saltine crackers. Add cracker crumbs, cheese, butter or margarine, and salt to scalded milk.

Beat egg yolks; gradually stir in cracker mixture.

Beat egg whites stiff enough to stand in peaks, but not dry. Fold into cracker mixture.

Pour into 1-quart buttered baking dish. Bake in moderate oven (375°F.) 40 minutes or until knife inserted in center comes out clean. Serves 4.

NUT AND CHEESE LOAF

1 tablespoon chopped onion
1 tablespoon butter or margarine
1 cup grated cheese
1 cup chopped walnuts
1 cup dry breadcrumbs
¾ cup boiling water
1 egg, beaten
Salt and pepper, to taste

Cook onion in butter for a few minutes. Mix cheese, nuts, breadcrumbs, and water. Add melted butter, onion, egg, and salt and pepper.

Bake in a small pan in moderate oven (350°F.) about 30 minutes. Serve with tomato sauce. Serves 4 to 6.

CHEESE-MACARONI CUSTARD

½ cup elbow macaroni
½ cup sharp cheese
1 cup milk, scalded
4 eggs, beaten
2 tablespoons melted butter or margarine
¾ teaspoon salt
Dash of pepper
⅛ teaspoon fresh onion juice
2 medium tomatoes, sliced

Cook macaroni in boiling, salted water until tender. Drain, but do not rinse. Divide macaroni into 5 buttered custard cups (¾-cup size).

Soften cheese in mixing bowl and add milk gradually, mixing until smooth.

Stir in beaten eggs, butter, ¾ teaspoon salt, pepper, and onion juice. Pour mixture over macaroni.

Set cups in pan of hot water which reaches almost to top rim of custard cups. Bake in slow oven (325°F.) 30 minutes.

Brush tomato slices with butter and place one on top of each custard. Continue baking 20 minutes, then test for doneness (a sharp knife inserted in center should come out clean). Serve at once. Serves 5.

American Cheese Fondue

BREAD AND CHEESE PUFF

8 slices buttered enriched bread
½ pound package sliced American Cheddar cheese (8 slices)
Salt and pepper
1 teaspoon Ac'cent
4 eggs, beaten
1 quart milk
½ teaspoon Worcestershire sauce
Dash of Tabasco sauce

Place 4 slices bread on bottom of shallow baking dish, cutting to fit bottom.

Cover bread with half the cheese; sprinkle with salt, pepper, and ½ teaspoon Ac'cent. Repeat.

Combine remaining ingredients; pour over bread and cheese. Bake in moderate oven (350°F.) 40 minutes or until top is golden brown, puffed and shiny. Serve at once. Serves 6.

CHEESE-RICE TIMBALES

¼ cup finely chopped green pepper
1 tablespoon finely chopped onion
2 tablespoons melted fat
1 tablespoon flour
¾ cup milk
½ teaspoon salt
½ teaspoon dry mustard
¼ pound grated cheese, (about 1 cup)
2 eggs, beaten
1 cup cooked rice

Cook green pepper and onion in fat until tender. Blend in flour; add milk and cook, stirring constantly, until thickened. Add salt and mustard.

Remove from heat. Add cheese and stir until it is melted. If necessary, place pan over very low heat to melt cheese. Stir sauce into eggs and add rice.

Turn into greased custard cups. Bake in moderate oven (350°F.) until firm, about 35 minutes.

Unmold and serve plain or with tomato sauce. Serves 4.

Bread and Cheese Puff

Tomato Cheeserole Dinner

TOMATO CHEESEROLE DINNER

1 tablespoon green pepper, chopped
2 tablespoons onion, chopped
2 tablespoons shortening
2 tablespoons flour
1 No. 2½ can tomatoes (about 3¼ cups)
1 tablespoon chopped celery tops
1 teaspoon sugar
½ teaspoon salt
⅛ teaspoon pepper

Sauté green pepper and onion in shortening in deep saucepan until tender. Blend in flour; stir until smooth.

Add tomatoes, celery tops, sugar, salt, and pepper. Continue cooking until mixture comes to a boil, stirring constantly. Simmer over low heat 5 minutes, stirring occasionally.

Cheese Dumplings:

1 cup sifted enriched flour
2 teaspoons baking powder
½ teaspoon salt
2 tablespoons shortening
½ cup American or Cheddar cheese, grated
1 tablespoon chopped parsley
½ cup milk

Sift together flour, baking powder, and salt. Cut in shortening until mixture resembles coarse meal.

Blend in grated cheese and parsley. Add milk all at once and mix only until all flour is dampened.

Dip tablespoon into cold water. Then drop batter from spoon onto above hot tomato sauce. Cover tightly.

Steam 20 to 25 minutes. Do not remove the cover during steaming process. Serve immediately. Serves 4 to 6.

CHEESE AND RICE PATTIES

3 tablespoons butter or margarine
1 tablespoon chopped green pepper
1 tablespoon chopped onion
3 cups cooked rice
1½ cups grated American cheese
1 tablespoon chopped pimiento
1 egg, beaten
¾ teaspoon salt
Dash of black pepper
Fine dry breadcrumbs

Melt butter in top part of double boiler. Add green pepper and onion.

Simmer over direct heat for 5 minutes.

Blend in rice, add cheese and pimiento, and heat over hot water until cheese is melted, stirring constantly. Fold in beaten egg, salt, and pepper. Cool.

Shape into 12 patties of uniform size. Dip in breadcrumbs.

Pan fry patties in butter until golden brown. Serve with creamed vegetable. Serves 6.

WINE CHEESE PUFF

4 slices white bread
Butter or margarine
⅓ pound American or Cheddar cheese, grated
4 eggs
2 cups milk
½ cup sherry
¾ teaspoon dry mustard
Salt to taste

Remove crusts from bread and spread both sides with butter or margarine.

Place 2 slices in bottom of a greased baking dish. Cover with half of the cheese. Place remaining slices of bread over this and cover with rest of cheese.

Beat eggs lightly; add milk, sherry, mustard, and salt. Pour over bread and cheese and set in refrigerator for several hours or overnight.

Allow to come to room temperature before baking. Bake in a slow oven (325°F.) for 1 hour. Serves 6.

Variations: Add 1 7-ounce can tuna, drained and flaked, 1 cup crabmeat or shrimp, or 1 cup finely chopped, cooked ham along with the cheese.

CHEESE AND EGGPLANT CASSEROLE

1 medium eggplant, washed and peeled
1 beaten egg
¼ cup milk
1 teaspoon salt
Fine bread or cracker crumbs
½ cup butter
1½ cups shredded sharp Cheddar cheese

Cut peeled eggplant into slices about ½ inch thick.

Mix egg, milk, and salt. Dip slices of eggplant into egg mixture, then into fine bread or cracker crumbs. Sauté in butter until golden brown.

Arrange alternate layers of eggplant, cheese, and tomato sauce (see below) in 1½-quart casserole. Top with cheese.

Bake in moderate oven (350°F.) 20 to 30 minutes. Serves 4.

Tomato Sauce: Sauté 2 tablespoons chopped onion in 2 tablespoons butter until transparent. Add 1 6-ounce can tomato paste, 1½ cups water, 1 teaspoon salt, and ¼ teaspoon pepper. Simmer 5 minutes. Remove from heat.

Creole Cheese Puff

CREOLE CHEESE PUFF

Sauce:

2 tablespoons butter or margarine
½ cup sliced onion
½ cup diced green pepper
1 No. 2 can (2¼ cups) tomatoes
1 cup diced celery
1½ teaspoons salt
Dash of cayenne
⅛ teaspoon powdered cloves
1 teaspoon sugar
4 tablespoons flour
¼ cup cold water

Make sauce by cooking onion and green pepper in butter over low heat until tender; do not brown. Add tomatoes, celery, seasonings, and sugar.

Cover and simmer gently 15 minutes, stirring occasionally.

Blend flour and water and add to sauce, cooking until smooth and thick and stirring constantly. Pour into greased baking pan.

Sandwiches:

6 slices white bread
Butter or margarine
1½ cups freshly grated American cheese
1 egg, beaten slightly
½ cup milk
1 teaspoon minced onion

Butter bread slices; add grated cheese to make sandwiches. Cut into triangles.

Blend together egg, milk, and minced onion.

Dip sandwiches in mixture and arrange on top of sauce.

Bake in slow oven (325°F.) 30 minutes or until lightly browned. Serve with sauce. Serves 6.

Cheese and Eggplant Casserole

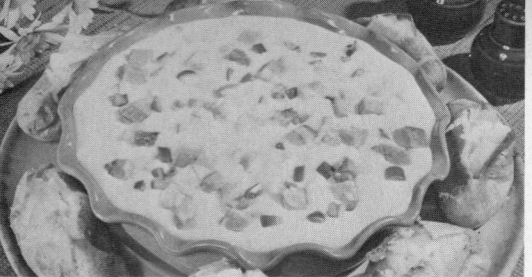

Ham and Cheese Rabbit

HAM AND CHEESE RABBIT

1/4 pound ham
4 tablespoons chopped green pepper
2 tablespoons chopped onion
3 tablespoons butter or margarine
4 tablespoons flour
1 cup milk
1/2 teaspoon salt
Dash of pepper
Dash of cayenne pepper
1 teaspoon prepared mustard
2 cups grated American cheese

Cut ham into cubes and brown in frying pan. Remove ham and set aside.

Cook green pepper and onion in butter until tender, about 5 minutes. Add flour and blend.

Stir in milk gradually, and cook over low heat until thickened, stirring constantly.

Add salt, pepper, cayenne pepper, mustard, and grated cheese; stir until cheese is melted. Add ham cubes and heat.

Serve on baked potatoes, toasted English muffins, or toast points. Serves 6.

QUICHE AU DIABLE

3/4 pound Swiss cheese, grated
3 eggs, beaten
1 3/4 cups light cream
1/4 cup minced onion
1 teaspoon Worcestershire sauce
1 teaspoon salt
Dash of black pepper
2 cans (4 1/2 ounces each) deviled ham
1 9-inch unbaked pie shell
1/4 cup grated Parmesan cheese

Combine Swiss cheese, eggs, cream, onion, Worcestershire sauce, salt, pepper, and deviled ham. Mix well. Pour into pie shell and sprinkle with grated Parmesan cheese.

Bake in very hot oven (450°F.) 15 minutes. Reduce heat to 300°F. and continue baking about 25 minutes or until set. Cool slightly before serving in narrow wedges. Serves 8 to 10.

Quiche Au Diable

FLUFFY TOMATO RABBIT

1 can (1 1/4 cups) condensed tomato soup
2 cups shredded American cheese
1/2 teaspoon dry mustard
1/2 teaspoon Worcestershire sauce
2 eggs, separated
Toast or crackers

Heat soup slowly; add cheese and heat until melted, stirring constantly.

Add mustard and Worcestershire sauce to beaten egg yolks; stir into hot mixture.

Gently fold in beaten egg whites and heat thoroughly. Serve on hot toast or crackers. Serves 4.

WOODCHUCK

2 cups tomatoes
1/4 pound diced American cheese (1 cup)
1 beaten egg
Salt and pepper to taste
Brown sugar to taste
Few grains cayenne
Hot toast or hot toasted crackers

Cook until very soft 2 cups tomatoes (1 1/2 cups tomato purée heated may be substituted). Beat them with a wire whisk into a purée.

Stir in cheese over low heat. Cook and stir these ingredients until the cheese is melted.

Add egg; cook and stir the mixture until the egg is slightly thickened. Add salt, pepper, brown sugar, and cayenne.

Serve at once over hot toast or hot toasted crackers. Serves 4.

ONION CHEESE PIE

1 1/2 cups fine soda cracker crumbs (about 33 crackers 2 x 2 inches)
1/2 cup butter or margarine, melted
2 1/2 cups onions, sliced thin
2 tablespoons butter or margarine
1 1/2 cups milk, scalded
3 eggs, slightly beaten
1 teaspoon salt
1/4 teaspoon pepper
1/2 pound process American cheese, finely shredded

Combine cracker crumbs and melted butter. Blend thoroughly and press evenly in buttered, deep 9-inch pie plate.

Fry onions in butter until lightly browned. Place in bottom of cracker-crumb crust.

Scald milk and slowly add to eggs, stirring constantly. Add salt, pepper, and cheese. Pour over onions.

Bake in slow oven (325°F.) 40 to 45 minutes or until silver knife inserted in center comes out clean. Serves 4 to 6.

Quiche Lorraine

QUICHE LORRAINE

Quiche Lorraine is a rich open-faced pie, traditional in France, made of custard with cheese and bacon. It may be served as a luncheon dish or as an hors d'oeuvre.

Pastry:

1 cup sifted enriched flour
1/2 teaspoon salt
1/3 cup shortening
3 to 4 tablespoons cold water

Sift together flour and salt. Cut in shortening until particles are size of small peas. Sprinkle cold water over mixture, tossing lightly with fork until dough is moist enough to hold together. Form into a ball.

Roll out on floured pastry cloth or board to a circle 1 1/2 inches larger than inverted 8-inch piepan. Fit pastry loosely into pan. Fold edge to form a standing rim. Flute the edges.

Filling:

1/2 pound bacon (about 12 slices)
1/4 pound Swiss or American cheese, grated
3 eggs
2 cups milk or light cream
1 teaspoon salt
1/16 teaspoon pepper
1/16 teaspoon cayenne pepper

Fry bacon until crisp (1/4-pound cooked ham, diced, may also be used). Crumble into pastry-lined pan. Arrange grated cheese over bacon (3 ounces Gruyère cheese may also be used).

Beat eggs slightly with rotary beater; add milk or cream and seasonings. Blend and pour over bacon and cheese in pan.

Bake in hot oven (400°F.) 35 to 45 minutes. Do not overbake. Remove from oven while center still appears soft. Cool 5 to 10 minutes before serving. Serves 6.

Onion Cheese Pie

Cheese Timbales with Tomato Sauce

CHEESE TIMBALES

3 tablespoons butter or margarine
3 tablespoons flour
1 teaspoon salt
2 teaspoons mustard-with-horseradish
Dash of cayenne
1 onion, finely minced
3 cups milk
2 cups grated Cheddar cheese
5 eggs

Melt butter or margarine in top of double boiler; blend in flour and seasonings. Add onion and milk. Cook about 5 minutes, until sauce thickens.

Add grated cheese; stir constantly until cheese melts and sauce is smooth. Beat eggs slightly; gradually stir cheese mixture into eggs. Blend well.

Pour mixture into greased 6-ounce custard cups. Place cups in pan of hot water. Bake in moderate oven (350°F.) about 30 minutes or until a knife inserted in center comes out clean.

Loosen, turn out on platter. Serve hot with a spicy tomato sauce to which ½ cup sliced mushrooms has been added. Garnish top of each timbale with a sprig of parsley. Serves 6.

CHEESE AND CORN PUDDING

⅓ cup butter or margarine
⅓ cup flour
1½ cups milk
1 teaspoon dry mustard
½ teaspoon salt
½ teaspoon pepper
1½ cups cheese, coarsely grated
1 cup cooked fresh corn, cut off the cob or drained canned whole kernel corn
1 cup breadcrumbs
5 large or 6 small eggs, separated

Melt butter, add flour, and blend; gradually add milk and cook over low heat, stirring constantly until thickened.

Add mustard, salt, pepper, and cheese. Remove from heat; add corn and breadcrumbs, and mix.

Add egg yolks, one at a time, blending each in. Fold in egg whites which have been beaten until stiff but not

Rice and Cheese Stuffed Cabbage Rolls

dry.

Pour into greased 2-quart baking dish and set in a pan filled with hot water.

Bake in moderate oven (350°F.) 1 hour. Serves 6.

OLIVE-CHEESE CUSTARD

5 slices bread
2 tablespoons butter or margarine
Salt and pepper
½ cup sliced stuffed olives
1 cup shredded process American cheese
3 eggs
¼ teaspoon dry mustard
2⅓ cups milk

Spread both sides of bread slices with butter or margarine. Cut into cubes.

Put a layer of bread cubes in a shallow casserole. Sprinkle lightly with salt and pepper. Cover with a layer of olives, then with a layer of cheese. Repeat until all ingredients have been used.

Beat the eggs. Add mustard and milk and beat again. Pour over mixture in casserole.

Bake in slow oven (300°F.) until set, about 40 minutes. Serves 4.

Mushroom-Cheese Custard: Substitute ½ cup sautéed sliced mushrooms for olives. If desired, mushroom stems may be used, and the whole caps kept for other dishes.

RICE AND CHEESE STUFFED CABBAGE ROLLS

8 large cabbage leaves
2 cups cooked rice (⅔ cup raw rice)
2 tablespoons butter or margarine
½ teaspoon salt
Dash of pepper
½ pound process Cheddar cheese, shredded
½ cup sliced celery
1 cup tomato sauce

Cook cabbage leaves in boiling water until slightly tender and transparent, about 5 minutes. Drain and cool.

Add butter, salt, pepper, cheese, and celery to rice and mix well.

Place ½ cup firmly packed rice-cheese mixture into each cabbage leaf. Wrap securely into a bundle and place side by side in shallow 8x12-inch baking dish. Pour tomato sauce over bundles.

Bake, basting occasionally, in moderate oven (350°F.) until cabbage is tender, about 40 minutes. Serve garnished with parsley. Serves 4.

Variations: Substitute ½ cup diced raw carrots, ¼ cup chopped stuffed olives, or ½ cup chopped green pepper for ½ cup sliced celery.

CHEESE CUSTARD

2 cups milk, scalded
1 cup grated process American cheese
4 eggs, separated
½ teaspoon salt

Add grated cheese to scalded milk and stir carefully until cheese melts. Let cool.

Beat egg yolks until light; add to cooled cheese-milk mixture.

Beat egg whites with salt until stiff but not dry. Fold into cheese-milk-egg mixture.

Turn into buttered 1½-quart casserole. Place in pan of hot water and bake uncovered in moderate oven (350°F.) until firm to the touch, 40 to 60 minutes. Serves 6.

SPANISH CHEESE FONDUE

½ cup semi-cooked minced onion
¼ cup semi-cooked minced green pepper
1 cup semi-cooked mushroom caps
1 cup whole kernel corn
1 cup canned tomatoes
3 tablespoons butter or margarine
1½ cups milk
2 cups soft breadcrumbs
1½ cups grated American Cheese
1 teaspoon salt
⅛ teaspoon paprika
Dash of pepper
1 tablespoon butter, melted
3 eggs, separated

Combine vegetables and 3 tablespoons butter. Heat thoroughly and divide mixture into 6 individual baking dishes or place all in large buttered casserole. Keep in warm place until cheese fondue mixture is ready for baking.

Pour milk over breadcrumbs and let stand until milk is absorbed. Add cheese, seasonings, melted butter, and well beaten egg yolks, mixing lightly.

Fold in stiffly beaten egg whites. Turn into individual baking dishes or large casserole on top of vegetable mixture.

Bake in moderate oven (350°F.) until delicately browned and firm to the touch 30 to 45 minutes.

Serve at once. If prepared in individual baking dishes, turn out on serving plates upside down. Serves 6.

Spanish Cheese Fondue

LUNCHEON FONDUE

- 3 tablespoons butter or margarine
- 3 tablespoons flour
- 3½ cups milk
- 1½ pounds Muenster or Cheddar cheese, grated
- 1 teaspoon salt
- ½ teaspoon pepper
- ¼ teaspoon nutmeg
- ¾ teaspoon caraway seed
- French bread, cut in large cubes

Melt butter in top of double boiler. Add flour, blend well and add milk. Bring to boiling point, stirring constantly to avoid lumps.

Place over hot water; add cheese and seasonings. Cook until cheese is melted.

Serve over cubed French bread in preheated soup bowls or plates. Serves 6.

Variation: Cook in an earthenware casserole over low heat, using an asbestos pad. Then serve in the casserole, letting each person spear a cube of bread and dunk into the fondue. If possible, keep the casserole hot over an alcohol flame.

CHEESE LAYERED CASSEROLE

- 6 to 8 thin slices bread
- ¼ to ⅓ pound American cheese, shredded or sliced
- ¾ teaspoon salt
- ¼ teaspoon prepared mustard
- ¼ teaspoon paprika
- 4 beaten eggs
- 2 cups milk

Arrange bread and cheese in layers in greased casserole. Have 2 or 3 layers of bread, with bread on bottom and top layers. Sprinkle seasoning between layers.

Mix beaten eggs and milk; pour over bread and cheese. Let stand 50 minutes.

Bake in moderate oven (350°F.) until puffy and firm, 45 to 60 minutes. Knife inserted in center should come out clean. Serves 6 to 8.

Bacon-Cheese Layered Casserole: Dice 4 slices bacon; cook until done but not crisp. Sprinkle between layers of bread and cheese. Or, cut bacon in 2-inch pieces and use as top layer.

Cheese Onion Bake

CHEESE AND EGG CASSEROLE

- 2 cups cracker crumbs (use about 3 to 4 dozen saltines and roll)
- 1 pound cheese, coarsely grated
- 6 hard-cooked eggs, coarsely chopped
- 3 tablespoons chopped parsley
- 3 cups milk
- ¾ teaspoon Worcestershire sauce
- ½ teaspoon dry mustard
- Juice of 1 lemon
- Salt and pepper to taste
- 2 eggs, well beaten

In a baking dish or casserole, arrange a layer of cracker crumbs, a layer of grated cheese, a layer of chopped eggs, and sprinkle with some of the parsley; continue until all is used up.

Heat milk to lukewarm; add Worcestershire sauce, mustard, and lemon juice and season to taste with salt and pepper.

Add the eggs, beat, and pour the liquid over the layers in the casserole. Shake gently to distribute the liquid evenly.

Bake in moderate oven (350°F.) 40 to 45 minutes. Serve in the casserole. Serves 6.

CHEESE AND TOMATO CASSEROLE

- 4 medium tomatoes, cut in ½-inch slices
- 1 cup shredded Cheddar cheese
- ⅓ cup thinly sliced onion
- ½ teaspoon salt
- ⅛ teaspoon pepper
- 1 cup crushed potato chips

Place layer of tomato slices in greased 1½-quart casserole, using half the tomatoes.

Add alternate layers of cheese and onion, using half of each for each layer, until all are used. Season layers with salt and pepper. Sprinkle top with potato chips.

Bake in moderate oven (350°F.) until cheese is melted and bubbly, about 30 minutes. Serves 4.

CHEESE ONION BAKE

- 1 cup shredded Cheddar cheese
- 1 cup cheese-flavored cracker crumbs
- 1 can (10½ ounces) condensed cream of mushroom soup
- ¼ teaspoon pepper
- 2 pounds small white onions
- Paprika

Combine ½ cup of shredded cheese, ½ cup cracker crumbs, soup, and pepper.

Peel and cook onions in boiling water until tender. Drain well. Pour into a 1½-quart casserole.

Pour sauce over onions. Sprinkle with remaining cheese and crumbs. Sprinkle with paprika. Bake in moderate oven (350°F.) 30 minutes. Serves 8 to 10.

Chili-Cheese Bake

CHILI-CHEESE BAKE

- 2 15½-ounce cans chili
- 30 or 32 crisp round cheese crackers
- ⅓ pound (1½ cups) sharp Cheddar cheese, grated
- 1½ teaspoons onion flakes
- 3 or 4 slices bacon

Spoon ⅓ of the chili over the bottom of a 10 x 6 x 1½-inch baking dish. Arrange a layer of crackers over chili; sprinkle with cheese and onion. Repeat layers.

Cook bacon until lightly browned. Arrange over casserole. Bake in hot oven (400°F.) 15 to 20 minutes or until hot. Serves 6.

CHEESE-VEGETABLE PIE

- Pastry for 1 crust pie
- 1 cup freshly grated American cheese
- 1 cup milk, scalded
- 2 eggs
- 1½ teaspoons salt
- ⅛ teaspoon pepper or paprika
- 1 teaspoon Worcestershire sauce
- 2½ cups mixed, cooked vegetables
- 2 fresh tomatoes

Blend ½ cup grated cheese with dry ingredients when making pastry. Roll out on floured board to ⅛-inch thickness. Line pie pan and bake in very hot oven (450°F.) 10 minutes.

Meanwhile, add milk to slightly beaten eggs; add seasonings and vegetables except tomatoes.

Pour into partially baked pie shell. Cut tomatoes into eighths and arrange on top. Sprinkle top with remaining ½ cup cheese.

Bake in moderate oven (350°F.) about 30 minutes or until clean knife inserted in center comes out clean. Serves 6.

Cheese-Vegetable Pie

COOKIES, BARS, AND SMALL CAKES

One of the first projects for a beginner in baking should be cookies because modern cooky recipes cut time and effort to a minimum and produce the maximum in goodness. Here we present a broad selection of favorite American drop cookies, cooky-cutter treats to fill or frost, cooky bars, and favorite recipes from around the world.

HINTS FOR COOKY BAKERS

As in all other baking, flour for cookies is always sifted once before measuring.

Preheat oven to temperature given in the recipe about 15 minutes before you want to bake the cookies.

Prepare the baking sheets and pans in advance by greasing them, unless otherwise specified, with any mild-flavored unsalted shortening. Use a pastry brush or soft paper. Only doughs containing a high proportion of shortening are baked on ungreased sheets or pans.

If cooky sheet is not available, a pan with sides may be turned upside down and the cookies baked on the bottom of the pan.

INGREDIENTS FOR COOKIES

Individual preferences may be followed in choosing some of the ingredients.

Any mild-flavored fat is acceptable for cookies; however, part butter or margarine, preferably half, will improve flavor unless the recipe specifically calls for another shortening.

The flour may be cake flour, whole wheat, or enriched. Many recipes name a specific flour to be used. Where just "flour" is called for, that means enriched (all-purpose) flour.

When substituting cake flour for enriched flour, add 2 more tablespoons of cake flour for each cup called for in the recipe.

Flavoring may be vanilla, or a combination of flavors.

Nuts may be peanuts, pecans, walnuts, Brazil nuts, hickory nuts, black walnuts, or whatever kind is available.

All recipes in this book call for double-acting baking powder.

SHAPING COOKIES

For easy handling it is often advisable or necessary to chill the dough.

For rolled cookies, shape the dough into medium-sized balls, roll out, and cut with cutters dipped in flour. Shake off excess flour each time. Save the scraps from each rolling, re-chill, and roll out again.

A pastry wheel may be used for cutting rectangular-, diamond-, or triangle-shaped cookies. It saves time and makes re-rolling of dough unnecessary.

The recipes in this section give directions for dropped, molded, sliced, pressed and rolled cookies, and bar cookies. Whichever method is followed, remember that all cookies should be uniform in size and thickness so that they will bake evenly.

To obtain a glaze over the cookies, brush with egg white or beaten egg yolk before baking.

When making drop cookies, chilling the dough keeps it from spreading and flattening. Allow ample space (usually at least 2 inches) between cookies.

DECORATING COOKIES

For decorating cookies the following materials may be used: nuts, chocolate bits or shavings, shredded coconut, candied bits of fruit such as pineapple, cherries, citron, colored candies and sugars, dots of marmalade and jellies.

For putting cookies together fruit fillings, softened marshmallows, and frosting may be used.

HOW TO TELL WHEN COOKIES ARE DONE

Crisp cookies; when delicately browned. Drop cookies; when touched lightly with finger, spring back in shape. Bar cookies; still moist when done, follow time given in recipe.

Overbaking makes cookies hard and dry. Watch timing carefully and test when minimum time is reached. Better yet, bake and test 1 cooky before placing panful in oven.

HINTS ABOUT BAKING SHEETS

● Baking sheets with little or no sides will let your cookies bake evenly and quickly. The sheets should be shiny for best results.

● Do not grease a cooky sheet unless the recipe calls for it because it may cause the cookies to spread too much.

● Baking sheets should clear the sides of the oven by at least two inches for best circulation of heat and even baking.

● When re-using baking sheets, cool them before placing unbaked cookies on them or the heat will melt the shortening in the dough and cause the cookies to spread too much during baking.

● When you bake two sheets of cookies at one time, place one on each rack. Reverse the sheets once during baking for better browning.

TO FREEZE COOKY DOUGH

Most cooky doughs freeze satisfactorily. Pack drop or rolled cooky dough in freezer containers; label and freeze. To use, thaw in refrigerator until dough is easy to handle. Prepare and bake as directed in recipes.

Form refrigerator cooky dough into rolls or use special molds. Wrap in aluminum foil or plastic wrap; seal and label. To use, cut frozen or slightly thawed dough into slices. Bake as directed in recipes.

TO FREEZE COOKIES

Wrap cooled cookies in aluminum foil, plastic wrap, or place in plastic bags. Label and freeze. Fragile cookies should be packed in freezer containers with plastic wrap or waxed paper between layers.

To serve, thaw frozen baked cookies

unwrapped, 15 to 30 minutes, then just before serving heat them for a moment on a cooky sheet in a very slow oven (300°F.) to restore crispness.

STORING COOKIES

Cool cookies thoroughly before storing. Remove from baking sheet with a spatula and place in a single layer on a wire cake rack. When cool, store different types of cookies in separate containers. If the cookies are very fragile, put sheets of waxed paper between layers.

Crisp Cookies: To keep cookies crisp, use a container with loose-fitting cover. The cookies will remain dry and crisp except in very humid weather, and may then be dried out by placing them in a slow oven (300°F.) for 3 to 5 minutes.

Soft Cookies: To keep cookies soft and chewy, use a tightly covered container. A slice of apple, orange, or bread helps keep cookies moist. Change the fruit and bread frequently to insure freshness.

Bar Cookies: If the bar cookies are to be used soon after baking, store in the pan in which they were baked. Cover tightly with foil or plastic wrap. To prolong freshness, they may be wrapped individually after cooling and cutting. Then they are ready for serving, freezing, or for packing in lunch boxes.

TO MAIL COOKIES

Cooky bars and drop cookies will usually hold up well in shipment if packed correctly. Wrap each cooky individually or put them into a strong plastic bag. Line a heavy cardboard box with waxed paper or aluminum foil. Bed the cookies in popcorn. Fill the box completely, stuffing all corners, with popcorn until it just touches the top cover. Wrap and tie securely. Attach a "fragile" sticker.

If Christmas cookies are to be used as tree decorations, you can bake the strings for hanging right into the cookies.

Cookie Bars

Bar cookies are made by spreading batter evenly and using the size pan recommended in the recipe. Cut bars and squares when they have cooled unless otherwise directed in the recipe.

MASTER BAR COOKIES

1½	cups sifted enriched flour
1	teaspoon baking powder
¼	teaspoon salt
¾	cup shortening
½	cup sugar
2	eggs, unbeaten
6	tablespoons milk
1	teaspoon vanilla

Sift flour once. Measure and add baking powder and salt. Sift together twice.

Cream shortening and add sugar gradually, creaming until light. Add eggs, one at a time, and beat thoroughly after each addition.

Add dry ingredients alternately with combined milk and flavoring, mixing well after each addition. Beat well after last addition only.

Spread evenly in well greased pan (12x9x2 inches). Bake in moderate oven (350°F.) until done, 20 to 25 minutes.

When cold, spread with strawberry jam and pour a lemon confectioners' sugar icing in thin streams over top, or frost with chocolate frosting. Cut into bars to serve.

Master Bar Cooky Variations

Date-Nut Bars: In master recipe, add 1 cup chopped dates and 1 cup chopped nuts after adding dry ingredients. Cut into squares after baking; roll in confectioners' sugar before serving.

Tangy Spice Bars: In master recipe, add 1 teaspoon cinnamon, ½ teaspoon nutmeg, ½ teaspoon allspice, and ¼ teaspoon cloves; sift with the dry ingredients.

Add ¼ cup molasses, ½ cup chopped nuts, and 1 cup chopped raisins; blend into batter before spreading in baking pan.

Frost with Lemon Butter Frosting when cold.

Chocolate Frosted Bars: In master recipe, add 2 squares (2 ounces) chocolate, melted, then blend in ½ cup chopped nuts just before pouring into baking pan.

When cold, frost with Bittersweet Chocolate Frosting.

Bar cookies are usually best when eaten within a day or so after baking, as the cut surfaces dry out with longer storage.

Master Bar Cookies

MOLASSES BROWNIES

⅔	cup butter or margarine
⅔	cup confectioners' sugar
⅔	cup molasses
1	teaspoon vanilla
1	egg
1¾	cups sifted enriched flour
⅛	teaspoon baking soda
1	cup chopped nuts

Cream butter and sugar until fluffy. Stir in molasses and vanilla. Beat in egg.

Add flour which has been sifted with soda. Mix well and stir in nuts.

Spread batter in 2 well greased and slightly floured 9-inch square pans. If desired, sprinkle top with chopped nuts or place a pecan half in the center of each brownie.

Bake in moderate oven (350°F.) 25 minutes. Makes about 3 dozen.

ORANGE AND NUT SQUARES

1	cup sifted enriched flour
1½	teaspoons baking powder
1	teaspoon salt
3	tablespoons soft butter or margarine
½	cup sugar
2	eggs
½	cup orange marmalade
1	cup whole bran cereal
½	cup chopped salted almonds

Sift together flour, baking powder, and salt. Blend butter and sugar; add eggs and beat well. Stir in marmalade and whole bran cereal. Add sifted dry ingredients and almonds; mix well.

Spread in greased 9 x 9-inch pan. Bake in moderate oven (375°F.) about 25 minutes. While warm, cut into squares. Roll in or sift with confectioners' sugar when cool, if desired. Makes 25 1¾-inch squares.

Orange and Nut Squares

Golden Crunchies

GOLDEN CRUNCHIES

1/4 cup butter or margarine
3/4 cup sugar
2 eggs
1 1/2 teaspoons vanilla
1/2 cup dry milk powder
1/2 teaspoon baking powder
1/4 teaspoon salt
1 cup sugared honey wheat germ
1 cup chopped walnuts

Cream butter or margarine with sugar. Add 2 eggs and beat well. Add vanilla.

Combine dry milk powder, baking powder, salt, and wheat germ. Add dry ingredients to butter-sugar-egg mixture and blend thoroughly. Fold in nuts.

Bake in greased 8-inch square pan in moderate oven (350°F.) 35 to 40 minutes. Cut into squares.

BUTTERSCOTCH BROWNIES

1/4 cup butter or margarine
1 cup dark brown sugar
1 egg, unbeaten
1 teaspoon vanilla
1/2 cup sifted enriched flour
1 teaspoon baking powder
1/2 teaspoon salt
1/2 cup broken nuts

Melt butter. Stir in brown sugar until dissolved. Cool slightly, then beat in egg and vanilla.

Mix and sift flour, baking powder, and salt. Stir in with nuts. Turn into greased 8x8-inch pan.

Bake in moderate oven (350°F.) 25 to 30 minutes.

Cut immediately into bars. Makes 16 or more bars.

APPLE SLICES

4 cups sifted enriched flour
1/2 teaspoon salt
2 cups sugar
1 cup butter or margarine
5 cups peeled and sliced tart apples
1 teaspoon cinnamon

Combine flour, salt, and sugar; cut in butter until crumbly.

Reserve 1/2 cup and lightly press half of the remainder into bottom of greased pan (about 9x12 inches).

Bake in moderate oven (375°F.) 10 minutes.

Remove from oven and spread with apple slices which have been mixed with the reserved 1/2 cup crumbs and cinnamon. Top with remaining crumbs and return to oven.

Continue baking at 375°F. until lightly browned, about 30 minutes. Makes about 24.

LEMON-GLAZED RAISIN BARS

2 cups sifted cake flour
1 1/4 teaspoons baking powder
1/2 teaspoon salt
2 eggs
1 cup sugar
1 tablespoon soft butter
1 No. 2 can (2 1/2 cups) raisin pie filling
1 cup finely chopped pecans

Topping:
3 tablespoons milk
2 tablespoons butter
2 cups sifted confectioners' sugar
1 teaspoon grated lemon rind
3 tablespoons lemon juice

Sift flour with baking powder and salt. Beat eggs well, gradually adding sugar. Beat in butter. Stir in pie filling, nuts, and flour mixture.

Spread mixture in 2 greased 9 x 9 x 2-inch baking pans. Bake in slow oven (325°F.) 30 to 35 minutes. Cool.

Topping: Combine milk, butter, and 1 cup confectioners' sugar; add remaining sugar, lemon rind, and juice. Blend well. Spread over cooled cookies and cut into bars. Makes about 4 dozen.

BROWNIES
(Master Recipe)

3/4 cup sifted enriched flour
1/2 teaspoon baking powder
1/2 teaspoon salt
2 squares (2 ounces) unsweetened chocolate
1/3 cup shortening
1 cup sugar
2 eggs
1/2 cup broken nuts

Sift together flour, baking powder, and salt.

Melt chocolate with shortening over hot water and beat in sugar and eggs. Add dry ingredients and mix thoroughly. Stir in nuts.

Spread in well greased square pan (8x8x2 inches). Bake in moderate oven (350°F.) until top has dull crust, about 30 to 35 minutes. When done a slight imprint will be left when top is touched lightly with finger.

Cool and cut into squares before removing from pan. Makes 16 2-inch squares.

Chocolate Frosted Brownies: Prepare Brownies and frost with Chocolate Frosting before cutting into squares.
Tea Brownies: Follow master recipe, chopping nuts finely. Spread batter in 2 well greased oblong pans (9x13x2 inches). Sprinkle with 3/4 cup blanched and finely sliced green pistachio nuts. Bake 7 to 8 minutes. Cut immediately into squares or diamonds. Remove

from pan while warm.

PECAN TOAST

2 cups sifted enriched flour
1/4 teaspoon baking soda
1/2 teaspoon salt
1/3 cup shortening
3/4 cup sugar
3/4 teaspoon anise extract
2 eggs
1 tablespoon milk
1 tablespoon vinegar
3/4 cup chopped pecans

Sift flour, baking soda, and salt together.

Cream shortening, sugar, and anise extract together thoroughly. Beat in eggs. Stir in milk and vinegar. Blend in dry ingredients and nuts.

Spread in greased 8-inch square cake pan. Bake in moderate oven (375°F.) about 25 minutes or until lightly browned.

Cool on cake rack. Turn out of pan. Cut into 2 1/2x1/2-inch bars. Lay bars on cooky sheet.

Bake in moderate oven (375°F.) 15 to 20 minutes or until lightly toasted.

Cool on cake rack. Makes 46 2 1/2x1/2-inch bars.

PRUNE RICHES

1 cup pitted cooked prunes
1/4 cup granulated sugar
1 teaspoon grated lemon rind
1 tablespoon lemon juice
1 1/2 cups rolled oats, uncooked
1/2 cup firmly packed brown sugar
3/4 cup sifted enriched flour
1/4 teaspoon salt
2/3 cup shortening (part butter or margarine)

Chop prunes; combine with granulated sugar, lemon rind and juice, and cook and stir over low heat until thick. Cool.

Blend rolled oats, brown sugar, flour, salt, and shortening until crumbly. Put 1/2 of mixture in bottom of greased 8-inch square pan and pack firmly.

Spread with prune mixture and top with remaining crumb mixture. Pat lightly into filling.

Bake in moderate oven (350°F.) 35 to 40 minutes, until lightly browned. Makes 18 bars.

Prune Riches

FLORENTINES

2 cups sifted enriched flour
1 teaspoon baking powder
1 teaspoon salt
½ cup shortening
1 cup granulated sugar
2 eggs, unbeaten
1 teaspoon vanilla
⅓ cup raspberry or strawberry jam
⅔ cup chopped nuts
2 egg whites
1 cup firmly packed brown sugar
1 teaspoon vanilla

Sift flour with baking powder and salt.

Cream shortening; add granulated sugar and continue creaming. Add unbeaten eggs and vanilla and beat until fluffy. Add sifted dry ingredients. Mix thoroughly.

Spread in greased 8 x 12-inch pan. Spread with jam and sprinkle with nuts.

Beat egg whites until stiff. Add brown sugar and vanilla slowly. Continue beating until smooth. Spread meringue over first mixture.

Bake in moderate oven (350°F.) 35 to 40 minutes.

When cool, cut into 2-inch squares. Makes 24 squares.

PECAN SPICE BARS

3 egg yolks
1 cup firmly packed dark brown sugar
⅔ cup sifted enriched flour
1 teaspoon baking powder
⅛ teaspoon salt
1 teaspoon cinnamon
½ teaspoon cloves
1 teaspoon vanilla
3 egg whites, beaten stiff
½ cup broken pecans

Beat egg yolks until thick and lemon-colored. Add sugar and beat well.

Sift flour with baking powder, salt, and spices, and add to above. Stir well. Fold in vanilla, stiffly beaten egg whites, and nuts.

Pour into greased, waxed paper-lined square pan. Bake in moderate oven (350°F.) 25 minutes.

Cool for 5 minutes; cut into thin bars, and roll in spicy sugar (⅓ cup confectioners' sugar mixed with ¼ teaspoon cloves). Makes 16 bars.

Chocolate Indians

PIRATE BLOCKS

2 eggs
1 cup firmly packed brown sugar
14 graham crackers
1½ teaspoons baking powder
½ teaspoon salt
½ cup chopped pitted dates or raisins
½ cup chopped nuts

Beat eggs and sugar together until light and fluffy.

Roll graham crackers into fine crumbs. Mix with baking powder and salt and add to egg mixture. Add dates and nuts.

Spread in greased 8-inch square pan. Bake in slow oven (300°F.) 25 minutes.

Cut in squares while warm. Sprinkle with confectioners' sugar, if desired. Makes about 16.

SCOTCH TEAS

½ cup butter or margarine
1 cup firmly packed brown sugar
2 cups rolled oats, uncooked
½ teaspoon salt
1 teaspoon baking powder

Melt butter and stir in sugar. When well blended add rolled oats, salt, and baking powder, mixed together. Spread in greased 8-inch square pan.

Bake in moderate oven (350°F.) 30 minutes.

Cool about 5 minutes and cut into squares. Remove from pan as soon as cookies are cool enough to hold together, and before entirely cooled. Makes 12 squares.

CHOCOLATE INDIANS

¾ cup sifted enriched flour
½ teaspoon baking powder
½ teaspoon salt
2 squares (2 ounces) unsweetened chocolate
⅓ cup shortening
1 cup sugar
2 eggs, well beaten
1 teaspoon vanilla
¾ cup chopped walnuts or pecans

Sift together flour, baking powder, and salt twice.

Melt chocolate and shortening in top of double boiler over boiling water.

Gradually add sugar to beaten eggs, beating well between additions. Add melted chocolate and blend well. Gradually stir in flour, mixing thoroughly. Add vanilla and nuts.

Bake in greased baking pan (about 8x8 inches) in moderate oven (350°F.) about 25 minutes, or until brown and slightly shrunk from side of pan.

Remove from oven. Cut into squares in the pan while still warm. Makes 18 to 24 bars.

Norwegian Almond Bars

NORWEGIAN ALMOND BARS

2 cups sifted enriched flour
1 teaspoon baking powder
1 teaspoon salt
¾ cup sugar
¾ cup butter or margarine
½ cup cold mashed potatoes
1¼ cups sifted confectioners' sugar
1½ cups almonds, ground
1 teaspoon cinnamon
½ teaspoon cardamom
1 tablespoon water
1 egg white
1 egg yolk

Sift together flour, baking powder, salt, and sugar. Cut in butter until particles are the size of small peas.

Press ¾ of mixture into ungreased 13x9x2-inch pan. Reserve remainder for topping.

Bake in moderate oven (375°F.) 10 minutes.

Blend together potatoes, confectioners' sugar, almonds, cinnamon, cardamom, water, and egg white. Mix thoroughly. Spread over partially baked dough.

Combine remaining crumb mixture with egg yolk. Press together. Roll out on floured pastry cloth or board to a 10x6-inch rectangle. Cut into strips ½ inch wide. Place across filling, crisscross fashion.

Bake in moderate oven (375°F.) 20 to 25 minutes.

Cut into bars or squares while still warm. Makes about 2 dozen bars.

TOFFEE SQUARES

1 cup butter or margarine
1 cup firmly packed brown sugar
1 egg yolk
1 teaspoon vanilla
2 cups sifted enriched flour
1 8-ounce bar milk chocolate
1 cup chopped nuts

Cream butter. Add brown sugar and cream until light and fluffy. Add beaten egg yolk, vanilla, and sifted flour. Spread thinly on cooky sheet.

Bake in moderate oven (350°F.) 15 to 20 minutes.

Melt chocolate and spread over top while warm. Sprinkle with nuts. Cut into squares while warm. Makes 24 bars.

Bran Blondies

BRAN BLONDIES

¾ cup sifted enriched flour
½ teaspoon baking powder
¼ teaspoon baking soda
½ teaspoon salt
½ cup ready-to-eat bran
½ cup chopped nuts
½ cup butter or margarine
1 cup firmly packed brown sugar
1 egg, slightly beaten
1 teaspoon vanilla
½ cup (3 ounces) semi-sweet chocolate, chopped or bits

Sift together flour, baking powder, soda, and salt; mix in bran and nuts.

Melt butter in saucepan. Remove from heat and stir in sugar; cool. Stir in egg and vanilla.

Add sifted dry ingredients a small amount at a time, beating well after each addition. Spread in greased 9x9-inch pan. Sprinkle with chocolate.

Bake in moderate oven (350°F.) about 15 minutes. Makes 24 bars 2x1½ inches.

Note: Blondies are done when still soft in center but pulled away from sides of pan.

NUT CAKE BARS

1 cup sifted enriched flour
1 teaspoon baking powder
½ teaspoon salt
¾ cup shortening
1 cup sugar
4 eggs
1 teaspoon vanilla
2 teaspoons cinnamon
½ cup chopped nuts

Sift together flour, baking powder, and salt.

Cream together shortening and sugar until light and fluffy. Add eggs, one at a time, beating well after each addition. Add vanilla. Add dry ingredients and beat thoroughly.

Spread in shallow greased pan (11x16 inches). Sprinkle cinnamon and nuts over top of batter.

Bake in moderate oven (375°F.) 25 minutes.

Cut into bars or squares. Makes 55 bars 1x3¼ inches.

BANANA BARS

2 cups sifted enriched flour
2 teaspoons baking powder
½ teaspoon salt
¼ cup shortening
1 cup sugar
2 eggs
1 cup mashed bananas (3 medium)
½ teaspoon lemon extract
½ teaspoon vanilla
½ cup chopped nuts
Confectioners' sugar frosting

Sift together flour, baking powder, and salt.

Cream together shortening and sugar; add eggs, beating well. Add dry ingredients alternately with mashed bananas. Add flavoring extracts and nuts and beat thoroughly.

Spread batter in greased pan (8x13 inches). Bake in moderate oven (350°F.) 30 minutes.

While still warm, frost with thin confectioners' sugar frosting. When cool, cut into bars or squares.

Banana Drop Cookies: Drop dough by teaspoonfuls on greased baking sheets and bake in moderate oven (350°F.) 12 to 15 minutes. Makes 32 bars 1x4 inches, or about 4 dozen cookies.

SOUTHERN PECAN BARS

1⅓ cups sifted enriched flour
½ teaspoon baking powder
⅓ cup butter or margarine
½ cup firmly packed brown sugar
¼ cup pecans, chopped fine

Sift together flour and baking powder.

Blend butter or margarine and brown sugar together, creaming well. Add dry ingredients; mix with an electric mixer or spoon until mixture resembles coarse meal.

Stir in pecans; mix well. Pat firmly into bottom of well greased 12x8x2- or 13x9x2-inch pan.

Bake in moderate oven (350°F.) 10 minutes only.

Pecan Topping: Beat 2 eggs until foamy. Add ¾ cup dark corn syrup, ¼ cup firmly packed brown sugar, 3 tablespoons flour, ½ teaspoon salt, and 1 teaspoon vanilla. Mix well. Pour over partially baked crust.

Sprinkle with ¾ cup pecans, coarsely chopped. If desired, fold the chopped pecans into filling before pouring over crust and arrange 30 pecan halves evenly over top, one for each bar. Bake in moderate oven (350°F.) 25 to 30 minutes. Let cool in pan; cut into bars. Store in tightly covered container. Makes about 2½ dozen bars.

COCONUT PINEAPPLE SQUARES

1 tablespoon butter or margarine
1 tablespoon sugar
1 cup sifted enriched flour
3 teaspoons baking powder
1 teaspoon salt
3 eggs, well beaten
1 cup drained, crushed pineapple
1 cup sugar
1 tablespoon melted butter or margarine
2 cups shredded coconut

Cream 1 tablespoon butter and 1 tablespoon sugar.

Sift flour, baking powder, and salt together. Add to creamed mixture and mix until crumbly. Add half the eggs and mix thoroughly.

Spread in 8-inch square pan. Cover with pineapple.

Mix 1 cup sugar, melted butter, and coconut; add remaining eggs and blend well. Spread over top of pineapple.

Bake in moderate oven (350°F.) 30 to 35 minutes. Cut into squares. Makes 24 bars.

DATE SQUARES

1 7-ounce package pitted dates
1 cup boiling water
1 teaspoon baking soda
¼ teaspoon salt
½ cup margarine
1 cup sugar
1 egg
2 cups sifted enriched flour
1 teaspoon vanilla
½ pint heavy cream
24 walnut-stuffed dates

Cut up dates. Pour boiling water over dates in bowl. Add soda and salt. Cool.

Cream margarine. Add sugar gradually, creaming until light and smooth. Add egg and beat well. Add flour and cooled date mixture alternately, mixing smooth after addition. Spread batter in greased 7x11-inch pan. Bake in moderate oven (350°F.) 1 hour.

Cut in squares. To serve, garnish each square with whipped cream topped with nut-stuffed dates. Makes about 24 squares.

Southern Pecan Bars

GUMDROP SQUARES

4 eggs
2 cups firmly packed brown sugar
1 tablespoon water
2 cups sifted cake flour
1/8 teaspoon salt
1 teaspoon baking powder
1 teaspoon cinnamon
1 cup tiny mixed gumdrops (fresh and soft)
1/2 cup nutmeats

Beat eggs until light. Add brown sugar gradually and water. Continue beating until blended.

Add flour, which has been sifted with salt, baking powder, and cinnamon. Stir smooth. Add gumdrops and nuts.

Spread batter 1/2 inch thick in greased, floured pan. Bake in moderate oven (350°F.) 30 minutes.

Cut into squares. Makes about 18 to 24 bars.

OLD-FASHIONED RAISIN BARS

2 cups sifted enriched flour
1/4 teaspoon baking soda
1/2 teaspoon salt
1 teaspoon ground cinnamon
1/2 teaspoon ground nutmeg
1/2 teaspoon ground allspice
1/2 teaspoon ground ginger
1/4 teaspoon ground cloves
2/3 cup shortening
1/3 cup sugar
1/4 cup light molasses
1 egg
2 tablespoons water
1 tablespoon vinegar
1 1/2 cups seedless raisins
3/4 cup chopped nuts

Sift together flour, soda, salt, and spices.

Cream together shortening and sugar thoroughly. Beat in molasses and egg. Stir in water and vinegar. Blend in dry ingredients, raisins, and nuts.

Spread in greased 15 1/2 x 10 1/2 x 1-inch baking pan. Bake in moderate oven (375°F.) about 20 minutes or until lightly browned.

Cool slightly. Mark into 3 x 2-inch bars. While still warm, spread bars with thin confectioners' sugar frosting. Cool. Cut into bars. Makes 20 3x2-inch bars.

Old-Fashioned Raisin Bars

WINE FRUIT COOKY BARS

2 cups sifted enriched flour
1/2 teaspoon baking soda
1/2 teaspoon salt
1/2 teaspoon nutmeg
1 cup raisins, chopped prunes, currants, or any dried chopped fruit
1/2 cup butter or margarine
2/3 cup firmly packed brown sugar
1 egg
1/4 cup port or muscatel

Mix and sift dry ingredients. Mix fruit with dry ingredients.

Cream the butter; add sugar and cream well.

Beat egg into butter-sugar mixture.

Add dry ingredients to mixture alternately with wine.

Pour onto an oiled cooky sheet; spread evenly.

Bake in moderate oven (375°F.) about 12 minutes. Cut into bars while still warm. Cool and frost with wine icing (below).

Wine Icing:

1 tablespoon butter or margarine
1 1/2 cups confectioners' sugar
1/2 teaspoon nutmeg
Port or muscatel

Blend butter into sugar. Add nutmeg and enough wine to give mixture a smooth spreading consistency.

FRUIT FILLED BARS

1 pound pitted dates, prunes, apricots, or figs
1/2 cup granulated sugar
3/4 cup light corn syrup
1/4 cup orange juice
2 teaspoons grated orange rind
1/4 teaspoon salt
1 teaspoon baking soda
2 1/2 cups sifted enriched flour
1 teaspoon salt
1 cup shortening
1 cup firmly packed brown sugar
1/2 cup water
2 1/2 cups rolled oats, uncooked

Combine fruit, granulated sugar, syrup, orange juice, orange rind, and 1/4 teaspoon salt; cook until thick. Cool.

Sift together flour, soda, and 1 teaspoon salt into bowl. Add shortening, brown sugar, and water. Beat until smooth, about 2 minutes. Fold in oats.

Spread half of dough over greased 12x15-inch baking sheet. Cover with fruit filling. Roll remaining dough between 2 sheets of waxed paper. Chill, then remove paper and place dough over filling.

Bake in moderate oven (350°F.) 30 to 35 minutes.

Cool and cut into bars. Makes 5 dozen bars.

Butterscotch Squares

BUTTERSCOTCH SQUARES

1/2 cup butter or margarine
2 cups firmly packed brown sugar
2 eggs
1 teaspoon vanilla
1 1/2 cups sifted enriched flour
2 teaspoons baking powder
1 cup chopped nuts

Melt butter in heavy saucepan. Add sugar and bring to boil over low heat, stirring constantly. Cool.

Add eggs one at a time, beating thoroughly. Stir in vanilla and flour which has been sifted with baking powder. Mix in chopped nuts.

Turn into greased and floured 7x9-inch pan. Bake in moderate oven (350°F.) 30 to 35 minutes. When cool, cut into squares. Makes 3 dozen 1 1/2-inch squares.

COCONUT BEAUTIES

1 1/2 cups sifted cake flour
1 teaspoon baking powder
1 teaspoon salt
1/3 cup shortening
1 cup granulated sugar
2 eggs, (reserve 1 egg white)
2 tablespoons milk
1/2 teaspoon vanilla
1/2 teaspoon lemon juice
1 egg white
1 cup firmly packed brown sugar
1/2 teaspoon vanilla
2/3 cup shredded coconut

Mix and sift flour, baking powder, and salt.

Cream shortening and granulated sugar; add eggs (reserving 1 egg white for meringue) and mix well. Add dry ingredients alternately with milk. Mix well. Add 1/2 teaspoon vanilla and lemon juice.

Spread 1/4-inch thick in 8x12-inch greased pan.

Beat egg white until stiff. Beat in brown sugar, adding 1/3 cup at a time. Add 1/2 teaspoon vanilla. Fold in coconut. Spread meringue over first mixture.

Bake in slow oven (325°F.) about 30 minutes.

Cut into squares and cool. Makes 24 small bars.

ALMOND JAM BARS

1½ cups sifted enriched flour
½ cup sugar
½ teaspoon baking powder
½ teaspoon salt
½ teaspoon cinnamon
¼ teaspoon cloves
½ cup shortening
½ teaspoon almond extract
¼ teaspoon vanilla
1 egg, beaten
¼ cup milk
¾ cup jam

Sift together flour, sugar, baking powder, salt, cinnamon, and cloves.

Cream together shortening and flavoring. Cut or rub shortening into flour mixture.

Combine egg and milk and add to flour mixture. Mix until well blended. Spread about ⅓ of the mixture into greased pan (7x11 inches). Cover evenly with jam.

Spread remaining mixture over jam. Bake in hot oven (400°F.) 25 to 30 minutes.

When cool, cut into bars. Makes 28 bars 1x2½ inches.

PEANUT BUTTER DATE BARS

½ cup sifted cake flour
1¼ teaspoons baking powder
¼ teaspoon salt
½ teaspoon nutmeg
½ teaspoon cinnamon
¼ teaspoon allspice
¼ cup butter or margarine
½ cup peanut butter
1 cup sugar
2 eggs, well beaten
⅔ cup finely cut dates
½ teaspoon vanilla

Sift flour with baking powder, salt, and spices.

Cream butter and peanut butter thoroughly. Add sugar gradually to beaten eggs and beat until light and deep yellow. Stir into creamed mixture.

Add flour mixture and beat until blended. Add dates and vanilla. Turn into shallow greased, waxed paper-lined pan.

Bake in moderate oven (350°F.) 45 minutes. Turn out on rack. Remove paper.

Cool and cut into bars or squares. Makes about 24 bars.

Quick Fudge Squares

BUTTER CHEWS

¾ cup butter or margarine
3 tablespoons granulated sugar
1½ cups sifted enriched flour
2¼ cups firmly packed brown sugar
3 egg yolks, beaten
1 cup chopped nuts
¾ cup shredded coconut
3 egg whites, stiffly beaten
Confectioners' sugar

Cream butter; add granulated sugar, and blend with flour. Pat in bottom of 8x12-inch greased pan.

Bake in moderate oven (375°F.) 15 minutes.

Add brown sugar to beaten egg yolks. Add nuts and coconut. Stir in stiffly beaten egg whites and spread over first mixture. Return to oven for 25 to 30 minutes.

Dust with confectioners' sugar. Cut any desired size. Makes 2 dozen 2-inch squares.

PEANUT BUTTER BROWNIES

¼ cup butter or margarine
¼ cup peanut butter
1 cup sugar
2 eggs, beaten
2 squares (2 ounces) unsweetened chocolate, melted
½ cup sifted enriched flour
½ teaspoon baking powder
⅛ teaspoon salt

Cream butter and peanut butter with sugar.

Add beaten eggs, melted chocolate, and flour which has been sifted with baking powder and salt. Spread in shallow waxed paper-lined and greased pan.

Bake in moderate oven (350°F.) about 20 minutes.

Cut in squares while still warm. Makes 16 bars.

QUICK FUDGE SQUARES

2 squares (2 ounces) unsweetened chocolate
⅓ cup butter or margarine
¼ cup light corn syrup
⅔ cup sugar
½ teaspoon salt
1½ teaspoons vanilla
2 cups uncooked oats
¼ cup chopped nuts

Melt chocolate and butter in top of double boiler over boiling water. Add remaining ingredients, blending thoroughly.

Pack firmly into greased 8-inch square pan. Sprinkle a few chopped nuts on top if desired.

Bake in hot oven (425°F.) 12 minutes. When thoroughly cool, turn out of pan and cut in squares or bars. Store in refrigerator. Makes 36 squares or 18 bars.

Date Orange Bars

DATE ORANGE BARS

2 eggs
½ cup orange juice
¼ cup melted butter or margarine
1 cup sifted enriched flour
1 teaspoon baking powder
½ teaspoon salt
1 cup sugar
¾ cup coarsely chopped walnuts
½ cup pitted, coarsely cut dates

In small mixing bowl, beat eggs until light and fluffy. Slowly add orange juice; stir in melted butter or margarine.

Sift dry ingredients into second mixing bowl; add nuts and dates; toss lightly with fork to completely coat with flour. Stir in liquid mixture thoroughly.

Pour into well greased 8-inch square pan. Bake in moderate oven (350°F.) about 30 minutes or until center springs back when lightly touched. Cut into bars while still warm. Makes 16 bars.

CRANBERRY SQUARES

½ cup shortening
½ cup sugar
1 teaspoon grated lemon rind
2 egg yolks
1 cup sifted enriched flour
½ teaspoon salt
¼ teaspoon baking soda
1- pound can whole cranberry sauce, drained
2 egg whites
¼ cup sugar
½ cup finely chopped walnuts

Cream shortening, sugar, and lemon rind. Add egg yolks 1 at a time, beating after each addition.

Sift together flour, salt, and soda. Add to creamed mixture. Mix well.

Spread or press dough evenly into greased 12x8x2-inch pan (or one with approximate measurements). Spread cranberry sauce evenly over dough.

Beat egg whites until stiff but not dry. Gradually add sugar and continue beating until mixed. Fold in finely chopped walnuts. Spread meringue over cranberry sauce.

Bake in moderate oven (350°F.) 45 minutes. Cool. Cut into strips or squares. Sprinkle with confectioners' sugar.

APPLE SLICES #2

2 cups sifted enriched flour
½ teaspoon salt
½ cup shortening
2 egg yolks
1 tablespoon lemon juice
½ cup cold water
8 apples, peeled and sliced
½ cup sugar
¼ teaspoon salt
1 tablespoon flour
½ teaspoon cinnamon
½ teaspoon nutmeg
½ cup raisins

Mix and sift flour and salt; cut in shortening as for pastry.

Beat together thoroughly egg yolks, lemon juice, and cold water. Add gradually to dry ingredients and stir until all flour is moistened.

Divide dough in 2 parts. Roll 1 portion as thin as pie crust and line 7x12-inch pan. Fill with apple mixture made by combining remaining ingredients.

Roll second portion of dough to fit top of pan and place over apples. Press edges of dough firmly together.

Bake in moderate oven (350°F.) until crust is nicely browned and apples are tender, about 45 minutes.

When cool, drizzle a thin Confectioners' Sugar Frosting over top and cut into slices. Serves 6.

CHOCOLATE DIAMONDS

1 square (1 ounce) unsweetened chocolate
¼ cup butter or margarine
½ cup sugar
1 unbeaten egg
¼ cup sifted enriched flour
⅛ teaspoon salt
¼ teaspoon vanilla
⅓ cup finely chopped nuts

Melt chocolate and butter over hot water. Remove from heat and add remaining ingredients except nuts.

Spread in 2 8x8x2-inch greased pans. Sprinkle with nuts. Bake in hot oven (400°F.) about 12 minutes.

Cool slightly and cut in 1½-inch diamonds in pans. When cold, remove to wire racks. Makes about 30.

EASY MOLASSES BROWNIES

1⅓ cups (1 can) sweetened condensed milk
¼ cup molasses
1 egg
2 cups graham cracker crumbs
¼ teaspoon cinnamon
¼ teaspoon salt
1 cup chopped nuts

Combine condensed milk and molasses; cook over low heat, stirring constantly, until mixture thickens, about 5 minutes. Cool.

Beat egg; add molasses mixture.

Combine graham cracker crumbs, cinnamon, salt, and nuts; add to molasses mixture.

Line 8x8x2-inch pan with greased waxed paper; pour in batter.

Bake in moderate oven (350°F.) 40 minutes.

Remove from pan immediately, remove paper; cut in squares. If desired, sprinkle top with confectioners' sugar.

COCONUT PEANUT BUTTER BARS

1 cup sifted enriched flour
1 teaspoon baking powder
¼ teaspoon salt
¼ cup shortening
½ cup peanut butter
1 cup sugar
2 eggs, well beaten
1 cup shredded coconut
½ teaspoon vanilla

Sift flour, baking powder, and salt several times.

Cream shortening; beat in peanut butter. Gradually beat in sugar until the texture is spongy. Add eggs. Stir in dry ingredients, coconut, and vanilla.

Spread in paper-lined, greased 8x12-inch pan. Bake in moderate oven (350°F.) until done, about 25 minutes.

Cut into strips while still warm and roll in confectioners' sugar. Makes about 36.

FROSTED COFFEE BARS

1½ cups sifted enriched flour
½ teaspoon baking powder
½ teaspoon baking soda
½ teaspoon salt
½ teaspoon cinnamon
¼ cup shortening
1 cup firmly packed brown sugar
1 egg
½ cup hot coffee
½ cup raisins
¼ cup chopped nuts
Coffee Frosting

Sift together flour, baking powder, soda, salt, and cinnamon.

Cream together shortening and sugar. Add egg and beat well. Add coffee and gradually stir in dry ingredients. Add raisins and nuts and beat thoroughly.

Spread in greased pan (11x16 inches). Bake in moderate oven (350°F.) 15 to 20 minutes.

While still warm, frost with Coffee Frosting. Cool and cut into bars. Makes 28 bars.

FIG BARS

1 cup dried figs
1½ cups sifted enriched flour
½ teaspoon baking powder
½ teaspoon baking soda
½ teaspoon salt
2 eggs, separated

1 cup sugar
1 teaspoon vanilla
½ cup buttermilk or sour milk
½ cup chopped nuts

Pour boiling water over figs and let stand 10 minutes. Drain. Cut off stems. Cut figs in small pieces.

Sift together flour, baking powder, soda, and salt.

Beat egg yolks. Add sugar gradually, beating until light. Add vanilla. Add dry ingredients alternately with buttermilk or sour milk. Fold in figs and nuts. Fold in stiffly beaten egg whites.

Spread in greased pan (8x13 inches). Bake in moderate oven (375°F.) 25 minutes.

Cut into bars. Makes 48 bars 1x2 inches.

HAZELNUT SLICES

2 large egg whites
1 cup sugar
1 tablespoon enriched flour
1 teaspoon vanilla
1½ cups coarsely ground unblanched hazelnuts (filberts)

Beat egg whites until stiff in top of double boiler. Beat in sugar gradually. Fold in flour.

Cook over boiling water, stirring constantly, 3 minutes. Remove from over hot water. Blend in vanilla and nuts.

Spread smoothly ¼ inch thick in ungreased paper-lined 13x9-inch pan. Dip fingers in warm water and moisten top by patting gently.

Bake in moderate oven (350°F.) until top looks dull, 15 to 20 minutes.

While warm, cut into slices 2x1½ inches. Cool slightly, then turn paper over, slices and all. Dampen entire surface with cold water. Slices are easily removed when water penetrates paper. Makes 32 slices.

QUICK COCONUT BARS

¼ cup butter or margarine
1 cup light brown sugar, sifted
1 egg
1 teaspoon vanilla or grated rind of 1 orange
½ cup sifted enriched flour
1 teaspoon baking powder
½ teaspoon salt
1 cup finely chopped coconut

Melt butter in a quart saucepan. Add sugar and stir until very well blended. Cool slightly. Beat in egg and vanilla.

Sift together onto waxed paper the flour, baking powder, and salt. Add to butter mixture and stir until blended. Fold in ¾ cup of the coconut.

Turn into greased 8x8-inch pan. Sprinkle with remaining ¼ cup coconut. Bake in moderate oven (350°F.) about 30 minutes.

When almost cool cut into bars. Makes 32 1x2-inch bars.

Refrigerator Cookies

Refrigerator cookies are made from a very stiff dough which can be prepared and shaped into rolls or in special molds and stored in the refrigerator usually up to three weeks. The advantage of refrigerator cookies is that cookies can be sliced and baked as you need them.

RIBBON COOKIES

1½ cups sifted enriched flour
1 teaspoon baking powder
¼ teaspoon salt
½ cup shortening
½ cup sugar
½ teaspoon vanilla
1 egg, beaten
1 square (1 ounce) chocolate, melted

Mix and sift flour, baking powder, and salt.

Cream together shortening and sugar until light and fluffy. Add vanilla and egg. Add flour mixture to creamed mixture.

Divide dough into two parts, and add melted chocolate to one part. Wrap each portion in waxed paper and chill until firm.

Pat dough in alternate layers (chocolate, then vanilla, then chocolate) in small rectangular pan. Chill until firm. Cut into ⅛-inch slices.

Bake on ungreased cooky sheet in hot oven (400°F.) 6 to 8 minutes. Makes about 42.

PEANUT BUTTER REFRIGERATOR COOKIES

½ cup peanut butter
½ cup shortening
2 cups firmly packed brown sugar
1 teaspoon vanilla
2 eggs
2¼ cups sifted enriched flour
2 teaspoons baking soda
1 teaspoon salt
1 cup raisins, cut fine
2 cups rolled oats, uncooked
½ cup chopped nuts

Cream peanut butter and shortening until well combined. Add sugar and vanilla and continue creaming until fluffy. Add eggs and beat well.

Sift together flour, soda, and salt. Add raisins, dry ingredients, rolled oats, and nuts to peanut butter mixture, blending well.

Shape into rolls, wrapping each roll in waxed paper. Chill. Slice into ⅛-inch slices.

Bake on cooky sheet in moderate oven (350°F.) about 15 minutes. Store in loosely covered container to keep cookies crisp. Makes about 90.

BUTTERSCOTCH REFRIGERATOR COOKIES
(Master Recipe)

4 cups sifted enriched flour
1 teaspoon baking soda
1 teaspoon cream of tartar
½ teaspoon salt
1 cup butter, margarine, or shortening
2 cups brown sugar, firmly packed
2 eggs
1 teaspoon vanilla
1 cup chopped nuts

Sift together flour, soda, cream of tartar, and salt.

Cream butter or shortening and sugar until light and fluffy. Add eggs and vanilla, beating well. Add dry ingredients and nuts and mix thoroughly.

Shape into rolls. Wrap each in waxed paper, or press into cooky molds. Chill until very firm.

Slice thin and bake on ungreased baking sheet in hot oven (400°F.) 8 to 10 minutes. Makes about 6 dozen 2-inch cookies.

Butterscotch Cookie Variations

Butterscotch Coconut Cookies: Omit chopped nuts and add 2 cups shredded coconut to fat-sugar-egg mixture.

Butterscotch Date Cookies: Omit nuts and add 2 cups of finely chopped dates to sifted dry ingredients.

Chocolate Nut Cookies: Add 3 squares (3 ounces) melted, unsweetened chocolate to fat-sugar-egg mixture.

Coconut Orange Cookies: Substitute 1 cup granulated sugar for 1 cup brown sugar. Add 3 cups shredded coconut to sifted dry ingredients. Omit vanilla and flavor with 2 tablespoons grated orange rind and ¾ teaspoon lemon extract.

Filled Butterscotch Cookies: Prepare dough and shape into rolls. Chill and cut into thin slices.

Put raisin filling (below) between two, pressing together with fork. Bake in moderate oven (375°F.) 10 to 12 minutes.

Raisin Cooky Filling: Mix together 2 cups ground raisins, ½ cup brown sugar, ⅛ teaspoon salt, and 2 tablespoons cornstarch. Add 1 cup water gradually, mixing well. Cook until thickened, stirring constantly. Cool before using.

DANISH DANDIES

8 hard-cooked egg yolks
1 cup shortening (use at least ½ butter or margarine)
¾ cup sugar
½ teaspoon salt
½ teaspoon vanilla
½ teaspoon lemon extract
1¾ to 2 cups sifted enriched flour

Press hard-cooked egg yolks through

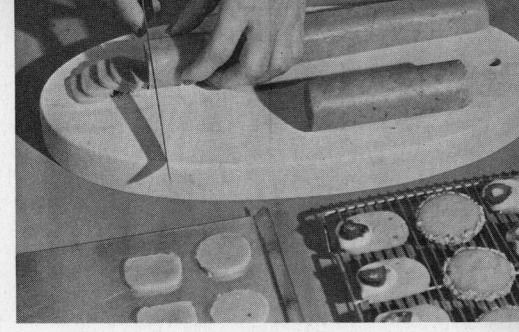

Butterscotch Refrigerator Cookies

a sieve.

Cream shortening and sugar until light and fluffy. Add salt, flavoring extracts, and egg yolks. Mix well. Add flour to make moderately stiff dough.

Shape into rolls and wrap in waxed paper or press into cooky molds. Chill. Slice ⅛-inch thick.

Bake on ungreased baking sheets in hot oven (400°F.) 8 to 10 minutes.

Note: Dough may be formed into balls an inch in diameter. Press with fork, or with bottom of tumbler. Makes about 8½ dozen.

Spritz Cookies: Force dough through cooky press into various shapes.

CARROT COOKIES

1 cup shortening
2 cups sifted enriched flour
½ cup sugar
½ teaspoon salt
½ teaspoon cinnamon
¼ teaspoon nutmeg
1 teaspoon vanilla
1 egg
1 cup finely-grated raw carrots
½ cup chopped nuts
Powdered sugar

Cream shortening until fluffy. Sift flour, sugar, salt, and spices together. Add to shortening and mix well. Add vanilla, egg, carrots, and nuts.

Form into 2 rolls 1-inch in diameter. Wrap in waxed paper and chill at least 2 hours.

Slice ½-inch thick and bake on ungreased cooky sheet in moderate oven (375°F.) 10 to 12 minutes. Roll in powdered sugar while warm. Makes 6 dozen cookies.

Carrot Cookies

MASTER REFRIGERATOR COOKIES

½ cup shortening
½ cup firmly packed brown sugar
¾ cup granulated sugar
1 egg
1 teaspoon vanilla
½ cup chopped nuts
2 cups sifted enriched flour
2 teaspoons baking powder
½ teaspoon salt

Cream shortening; add sugars and cream thoroughly. Add egg and beat well. And vanilla and nuts.

Mix and sift flour, baking powder, and salt. Add to creamed mixture and mix well.

Shape into rolls about 1½ inches in diameter. Wrap each in waxed paper. Chill in refrigerator several hours or overnight. Cut chilled rolls in ⅛-inch slices.

Place on greased cooky sheet. Bake in hot oven (425°F.) 8 to 10 minutes. Makes 4 dozen.

Master Refrigerator Cooky Variations

Almond Refrigerator Cookies: Substitute ½ cup finely ground blanched almonds for chopped nuts.

Checkerboard Cookies: Divide dough into 2 equal parts. Add 1 square (1 ounce) cooled, melted chocolate to 1 part. Leave other part plain.

Line a freezing tray with waxed paper.

Pack half the chocolate dough into bottom and cover with uniform layer of plain dough. Add another layer of chocolate and top with final layer of plain dough.

Cover with waxed paper and chill several hours.

Turn the layered loaf out onto waxed paper. Slice with thin sharp knife into ¼-inch slices.

Place 4 slices together so that, when viewed from the end, each chocolate strip lies above a plain strip.

Slice thinly across checkerboard pattern. Bake as directed in master recipe.

Chocolate Refrigerator Cookies: In master recipe, add 2 ounces (2 squares) melted chocolate or 4 tablespoons cocoa to fat-sugar-egg mixture.

Master Refrigerator Cookies

Coconut Refrigerator Cookies: In master recipe, substitute ½ cup coconut for nuts.

Coconut Orange Refrigerator Cookies: Omit vanilla and add 2 tablespoons grated orange rind to coconut cookies.

Fruit Refrigerator Cookies: In master recipe, substitute ½ cup currants, raisins, or any mixture of dried fruits, cut into small pieces, for nuts.

Ginger Refrigerator Cookies: In master recipe, substitute 2 tablespoons molasses for 2 tablespoons sugar and add ¼ cup finely chopped candied ginger or 1 tablespoon ginger.

Pinwheel Cookies: Divide dough of master recipe into 2 equal parts.

Add 1 square (1 ounce) cooled melted chocolate to 1 part. Leave other part plain.

Roll each part ⅛-inch thick and place one sheet on top of the other.

Roll up as for jelly roll. Wrap firmly in waxed paper and chill. Slice and bake.

Spice Refrigerator Cookies: In master recipe, add and sift with dry ingredients 1 to 2 teaspoons mixed spices (cinnamon, ginger, and nutmeg).

RAISIN-ORANGE FILLED COOKIES

1 teaspoon vinegar
½ cup milk
1 cup sifted enriched flour
1 teaspoon baking powder
¼ teaspoon salt
½ cup soft butter
½ cup soft shortening
¾ cup sugar
5 cups quick-cooking rolled oats
1 No. 2 can (2½ cups) raisin pie filling
1 cup chopped candied orange peel

Stir vinegar into milk and set aside.

Sift flour with baking powder and salt. Cream butter, shortening, and sugar until light and fluffy. Blend in ½ flour mixture. Add milk and mix well. Blend in remaining flour. Stir in rolled oats. Chill at least 4 hours.

Cut off ⅓ of chilled dough, leaving remainder in refrigerator. Roll on a floured surface to ⅛ inch thickness; cut ½ with a floured 3-inch round cutter and ½ with a floured 3-inch doughnut cutter.

Combine pie filling and orange peel. Place ½ tablespoon of filling on each round and top with doughnut-shaped dough. Seal edges with a fork.

Place on ungreased cooky sheet and bake in moderate oven (350°F.) 10 to 12 minutes. Cool. Repeat with remaining dough and filling. Makes about 2 dozen.

Chocolate Nut Slices

CHOCOLATE NUT SLICES

2 cups sifted enriched flour
¼ teaspoon baking soda
½ teaspoon salt
¾ cup shortening
1¾ cups sugar
2 teaspoons vanilla
1 egg
4 squares (4 ounces) baking chocolate, melted
1 tablespoon vinegar
¾ cup chopped pecans

Sift together flour, baking soda, and salt.

Cream together shortening, sugar, and vanilla. Beat in egg and chocolate. Stir in vinegar. Blend in dry ingredients and nuts.

Shape into 2 rolls, 2 inches in diameter. Chill several hours. Slice dough into ¼-inch slices.

Bake on cooky sheet in moderate oven (375°F.) about 10 minutes.

Cool on cake rack. Makes 7 dozen.

OATMEAL CRISPIES

¾ cup sifted enriched flour
½ teaspoon salt
½ teaspoon baking soda
½ cup shortening
½ cup firmly packed brown sugar
½ cup granulated sugar
1 egg
½ teaspoon vanilla
1½ cups rolled oats, uncooked
¼ cup chopped nuts

Mix and sift flour, salt, and soda into bowl. Add shortening, sugars, egg, and vanilla. Beat until smooth, about 2 minutes. Fold in oats and nuts.

Shape dough in 2 rolls. Wrap in waxed paper and chill.

Slice ¼-inch thick and place on ungreased baking sheet.

Bake in moderate oven (350°F.) 10 to 12 minutes. Makes 3½ dozen.

Raisin-Orange Filled Cookies
Lemon-Glazed Raisin Bars

Oatmeal Cookies with Fig Filling

OATMEAL COOKIES WITH FIG FILLING

1/2 cup shortening
1/2 cup butter
1 1/2 cups dark brown sugar
2 eggs
1 teaspoon vanilla
2 cups sifted enriched flour
1 teaspoon baking powder
1 teaspoon salt
1/2 teaspoon baking soda
2 1/2 cups quick-cooking rolled oats

Cream shortening, butter, and sugar until fluffy. Add eggs and vanilla; beat well.

Sift together flour, baking powder, salt, and soda; add to creamed mixture and beat well. Stir in rolled oats. Chill at least 1 hour.

Roll half the dough at a time on well floured pastry cloth to a little less than 1/4 inch. Cut with round cutter. Place about 1 tablespoon filling on half the rounds. Cut small circle out of centers of remaining rounds. Place on filling; press edges to seal.

Bake on ungreased cooky sheet in moderate oven (350°F.) 12 minutes. Makes about 30 cookies.

Fig Filling:

10 dried figs, chopped
1/2 cup water
3 tablespoons lemon juice
1 teaspoon grated lemon peel
1/3 cup sugar

Combine ingredients; simmer 10 to 15 minutes.

THREE-IN-ONE COOKIES

2 cups sifted enriched flour
1 teaspoon baking powder
1/2 teaspoon salt
1/2 cup shortening
1 cup sugar
1 egg
1 tablespoon milk
1/2 teaspoon vanilla
1 square (1 ounce) chocolate, melted
1 tablespoon orange juice
1 tablespoon grated orange rind

Sift together flour, baking powder,

Fig Star Cookies

and salt.

Cream shortening and sugar until light and fluffy. Add egg, milk, and vanilla; stir in dry ingredients. Mix thoroughly. Divide dough into thirds.

To one-third add melted chocolate, mixing it in thoroughly.

To another third add orange juice and rind, mixing well.

Leave remaining third plain.

Shape each third into a roll. Wrap in waxed paper. Chill until very firm. Slice thin and bake on greased cooky sheets in hot oven (400°F.) 10 minutes. Makes about 5 dozen small cookies.

CHRISTMAS REFRIGERATOR COOKIES

2 1/2 cups sifted enriched flour
1 1/2 teaspoons baking powder
1/2 teaspoon salt
1 cup butter or margarine
1 1/2 cups sugar
1 egg, beaten
1 teaspoon vanilla
1/4 cup chopped candied cherries
1/4 cup chopped or broken pecans
1 ounce (1 square) sweet milk chocolate, melted

Sift flour, measure; sift twice with baking powder and salt.

Cream butter until soft and gradually blend in sugar. Add egg and vanilla, and beat vigorously until smooth and fluffy. Add flour mixture and mix thoroughly.

Divide dough into 3 portions. Add chopped cherries to one portion, and nuts and chocolate to the second. Roll part of each dough in waxed paper and chill several hours in the refrigerator.

When ready to bake, slice very thin. Place on buttered cooky sheets and bake in hot oven (400°F.) about 10 minutes or until delicately browned.

The remaining dough may be placed in a cooky press and pressed out into fancy shapes on buttered cooky sheets. Bake at the same time and same temperature as those that are sliced. Makes about 8 dozen thin cookies.

FIG STAR COOKIES

1 cup shortening (part butter or margarine for flavor)
1/2 cup sugar
3/4 cup corn syrup
1/4 teaspoon maple flavoring
2 eggs, beaten
4 1/2 cups sifted enriched flour
1 teaspoon baking powder
1/2 teaspoon salt

Cream shortening and sugar; beat in syrup, flavoring, and eggs. (Maple-flavored syrup may be used in this recipe, in which case omit maple flavoring.)

Stir in flour sifted with baking powder and salt.

Shape into two rolls about 2 1/2 inches in diameter, wrap in waxed paper, and chill in refrigerator several hours.

Slice thin. For filled cookies, put together in pairs, sandwich fashion, with a dot of Fig Filling #2 between; press edges together, and prick top with fork or mark with knife.

To Make Star Cookies: Put a small spoonful of fig filling in the center of a cooky slice, then with the fingers fold up edges and pinch in place to make a reasonable facsimile of a star.

Bake filled or star cookies in hot oven (400°F.) 8 to 10 minutes, or until delicately browned around edges. Cool on racks.

Makes about 3 dozen filled cookies, or six dozen stars. To freshen cookies, reheat them in the oven for a few minutes before serving, and serve warm.

DATE PINWHEEL COOKIES

3/4 cup pitted, diced dates (5 ounces)
6 tablespoons granulated sugar
6 tablespoons water
2 teaspoons lemon juice
1/2 teaspoon grated lemon rind
1/4 cup finely chopped nuts
2 cups sifted enriched flour
1/4 teaspoon baking soda
1/4 teaspoon salt
2/3 cup butter or margarine
1 1/4 cups firmly packed brown sugar
1 1/2 teaspoons grated orange rind
1 egg
1 tablespoon vinegar

Combine dates, granulated sugar, and water in heavy saucepan. Cook until thickened, about 5 minutes, stirring constantly. Remove from heat. Blend in lemon juice, 1/2 teaspoon lemon rind, and nuts. Cool.

Sift together flour, soda, and salt.

Cream together butter or margarine, brown sugar, and 1 1/2 teaspoons orange rind. Beat in egg and vinegar. Blend in dry ingredients. Chill dough several hours or overnight.

Roll dough into 15x10-inch rectangle. Spread with date mixture. Starting from a long side, roll as for jelly roll. Chill 1 hour.

Slice into 1/4-inch slices. Place slices on cooky sheet.

Bake in moderate oven (375°F.) 12 to 15 minutes or until lightly browned. Cool on cake rack. Makes 5 dozen.

Date Pinwheel Cookies

Drop Cookies

Drop cookies are made from a soft dough and dropped from a spoon onto a cooky sheet. Actually the term "drop" is a little misleading since the mixture must be stiff enough to be pushed from the spoon. Keep the cookies about two inches apart unless the recipe states otherwise. Keep them uniform in size; however the shape may be irregular since they spread on the baking sheet.

SUGAR JUMBLES
(Master Recipe)

1⅛ cups sifted enriched flour
¼ teaspoon baking soda
½ teaspoon salt
½ cup soft shortening (part butter or margarine)
½ cup sugar
1 egg
1 teaspoon vanilla

Sift together flour, soda, and salt. Mix shortening, sugar, egg, and vanilla together thoroughly. Stir in dry ingredients.

Drop rounded teaspoonfuls about 2 inches apart onto lightly greased baking sheet.

Bake in moderate oven (375°F.) until delicately browned (cookies should still be soft), about 8 to 10 minutes. Cool slightly, then remove from baking sheet. Makes about 3 dozen 2-inch cookies.

Variations of Sugar Jumbles

Chocolate Chip Jumbles: Substitute ¾ cup (half granulated and half brown) sugar for ½ cup granulated sugar. Add ½ cup chopped nuts and 1 package (7 ounces) chocolate chips.

Orange Chocolate Chip Jumbles: Add 1 teaspoon grated orange rind to the shortening mixture of above.

Coconut Jumbles: Add 1 cup moist shredded coconut to batter of master recipe.

Glazed Orange Jumbles: Add 1½ teaspoons grated orange rind and 1 cup chopped nuts to batter of master recipe. Bake.

While hot, dip tops of cookies in an

Sugar Jumbles

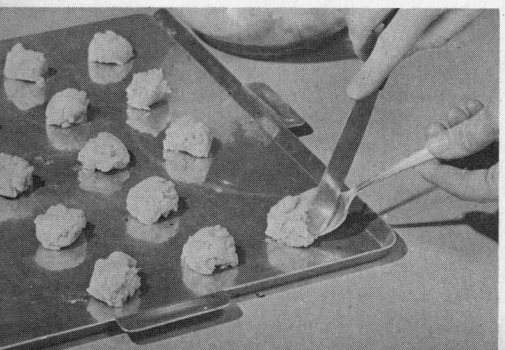

orange glaze made as follows: Heat together ⅓ cup sugar, 3 tablespoons orange juice, and 1 teaspoon grated orange rind.

Nut Jumbles: Add 2 cups nutmeats to batter of master recipe.

3-in-1 Jumbles: Divide dough of master recipe into 3 parts. Add ½ square melted unsweetened chocolate to 1 part. Drop ½ cup whole nutmeats into batter, coating each nut well.

Add ½ cup moist shredded coconut to second part.

Leave third part plain and drop 14 nut-stuffed dates into batter. Coat each date well. Each coated date and nut makes a cooky.

COCONUT MACAROONS
(Master Recipe)

2 tablespoons sifted cake flour
½ cup sugar
¼ teaspoon salt
2 egg whites
½ teaspoon vanilla
2 cups shredded coconut

Mix and sift flour, salt, and sugar.

Beat egg whites until stiff and peaky but not dry. Fold whites into dry ingredients.

Add vanilla and fold in coconut.

Drop by teaspoonfuls onto lightly greased paper-covered baking sheet. Allow space for spreading and rising.

Bake in moderate oven (350°F.) about 20 minutes, or until golden brown and dry on surface. Makes about 20 2-inch macaroons.

Coconut Macaroon Variations

Cake Crumb Macaroons: Substitute ¾ cup cake crumbs for 1 cup coconut.

Caramel Nut Macaroons: Substitute ½ cup brown sugar and 1 cup chopped nuts for granulated sugar and coconut.

Cherry Coconut Macaroons: Add ½ cup chopped candied cherries.

Chocolate Chip Macaroons: Substitute ½ cup chocolate chips for 1 cup coconut.

Condensed Milk Macaroons: Omit sugar and egg whites. Mix coconut, flour, salt, and vanilla with sweetened condensed milk.

Corn Flake Macaroons: Substitute 2 cups corn flakes for coconut.

Orange Macaroons: Add 1 tablespoon grated orange rind with egg whites. Sprinkle grated orange rind over macaroons when done.

Popcorn Macaroons: Substitute 2 cups popcorn for coconut.

Rice Macaroons: Substitute puffed rice for coconut and add ¼ cup chopped nuts.

Blueberry Drop Cookies

BLUEBERRY DROP COOKIES

1 cup fresh blueberries
2 cups sifted enriched flour
2 teaspoons baking powder
¼ teaspoon salt
¾ cup vegetable shortening
1 cup sugar
2 eggs
1½ teaspoons grated lemon rind
½ cup milk

Wash blueberries and spread on paper towel to dry thoroughly.

Sift together flour, baking powder, and salt. Cream shortening until soft and gradually beat in sugar. Add eggs and lemon rind and beat until well mixed. Add flour mixture alternately with milk, beating until smooth after each addition. Lightly fold in blueberries.

Drop by teaspoonfuls on greased baking sheet and bake in moderate oven (375°F.) 10 to 12 minutes. Makes about 2½ dozen cookies.

ALMOND MACAROONS

1 cup blanched almonds
1 egg
½ cup sugar
¼ teaspoon salt
1 tablespoon enriched flour
1 tablespoon melted butter or margarine
½ teaspoon vanilla
Additional almonds for decoration

Grind almonds, using fine blade of food chopper. Beat egg and gradually beat in sugar, salt, and flour. Stir in butter, vanilla, and ground almonds.

Drop by teaspoonful onto greased baking sheet. Top each cooky with an almond half or a few chopped almonds. Bake in moderate oven (350°F.) 10 to 15 minutes, until lightly browned. Remove from pan at once. Makes about 20 cookies.

Almond Macaroons

Banana Oatmeal Cookies

BANANA OATMEAL COOKIES

1½ cups sifted enriched flour
1 cup sugar
½ teaspoon baking soda
1 teaspoon salt
¼ teaspoon nutmeg
¾ teaspoon cinnamon
¾ cup shortening
1 egg, well beaten
1 cup mashed ripe bananas
1¾ cups rolled oats, uncooked
½ cup chopped nuts

Sift into mixing bowl: flour, sugar, soda, salt, nutmeg, and cinnamon. Cut in shortening. Add egg, bananas, rolled oats, and nuts. Beat until thoroughly blended.

Drop by teaspoonfuls, about 1½ inches apart, onto ungreased cooky sheet. Bake in hot oven (400°F.) about 15 minutes, or until edges are browned. Remove from pan immediately and cool on rack. Makes about 3½ dozen cookies.

ALMOND PASTE MACAROONS

1 pound almond paste (see below)
2 cups sugar
¼ teaspoon salt
4 tablespoons sifted cake flour
⅔ cup sifted confectioners' sugar
⅔ cup egg whites, unbeaten

Soften almond paste with hands and work in sugar, salt, flour, confectioners' sugar, and egg whites.

Drop by teaspoonfuls 2 inches apart on ungreased wrapping paper placed on baking sheet. Pat tops lightly with fingers dipped in cold water.

Bake in slow oven (325°F.) until set and delicately browned, about 18 to 20 minutes.

Remove from paper. Makes about 5 dozen 2-inch macaroons.

Almond Paste for Macaroons:

Grind 2 cups blanched almonds, thoroughly dried (not toasted), through finest knife of food chopper. Then grind twice again. Mix in 1½ cups sifted confectioners' sugar. Blend in ¼ cup egg whites, unbeaten, and 2 teaspoons almond extract. Mold into ball. Place in tightly covered container in refrigerator for at least 4 days to age. Makes 1 pound.

COFFEE AND SPICE DROPS
(Master Recipe)

1 cup soft shortening
2 cups firmly packed brown sugar
2 eggs
½ cup cold coffee
3½ cups sifted enriched flour
1 teaspoon baking soda
1 teaspoon salt
1 teaspoon nutmeg
1 teaspoon cinnamon

Cream shortening; gradually beat in sugar and eggs and beat thoroughly. Stir in cold coffee.

Sift together flour, soda, salt, nutmeg, and cinnamon and stir in. Chill at least 1 hour.

Drop rounded teaspoonfuls about 2 inches apart onto lightly greased baking sheet.

Bake in hot oven (400°F.) until set (when touched lightly with finger, almost no imprint remains), about 8 to 10 minutes. Makes about 6 dozen 2½-inch cookies.

Variations of Coffee and Spice Drops

Applesauce Drop Cookies: Include 1 teaspoon cloves with other spices. Add 2 cups well drained thick applesauce, 1 cup cut-up raisins, and ½ cup coarsely chopped nuts to batter. Bake 9 to 12 minutes.

Hermits: Add 2½ cups halved seedless raisins and 1¼ cups broken nuts to batter. Be careful not to overbake.

Mincemeat Drop Cookies: Add 2 cups well drained mincemeat to batter.

Spiced Prune Drops: Include ¼ teaspoon cloves with other spices. Add 2 cups cut-up cooked prunes (pitted and well drained), and 1 cup broken nuts to batter.

PECAN DROP COOKIES

1¼ cups sifted enriched flour
¼ teaspoon baking soda
¼ teaspoon salt
⅓ cup shortening
1¼ cups firmly packed brown sugar
1 egg
1 cup coarsely broken pecans

Resift flour 3 times with soda and salt.

Cream shortening and sugar. Add egg and mix thoroughly.

Stir in flour mixture in 2 or 3 portions, mixing each portion until smooth. Stir in nuts.

Drop by tablespoonfuls 2 inches apart onto lightly greased cooky sheet.

Bake in moderate oven (375°F.) 10 to 12 minutes. Cool about 5 minutes on cooky sheet, then remove cookies to cake rack. Makes about 3½ dozen 2½-inch cookies.

NO-BAKE RUM DROPS

2 cups vanilla wafer crumbs or graham cracker crumbs
1 cup sifted confectioners' sugar
2 tablespoons cocoa
⅛ teaspoon salt
1 cup finely chopped nuts or chopped coconut
2 tablespoons white corn syrup or honey
¼ to ⅓ cup brandy, rum, or Cointreau

Roll crumbs fine. Add sugar, cocoa, salt, and nuts.

Combine liquid ingredients and slowly add to first mixture. Use just enough liquid to hold ingredients together nicely.

Shape by teaspoonfuls into firm 1-inch balls. Roll balls in confectioners' sugar or dry cocoa.

Store in tightly covered box at least 24 hours before using. Makes 45 to 50 1-inch balls.

CRANBERRY DROP COOKIES

½ cup butter or margarine
1 cup granulated sugar
¾ cup brown sugar (packed)
¼ cup milk
2 tablespoons orange juice
1 egg
3 cups sifted enriched flour
1 teaspoon baking powder
¼ teaspoon baking soda
½ teaspoon salt
1 cup chopped nuts
2½ cups coarsely chopped cranberries

Cream butter and sugars together. Beat in milk, orange juice, and egg.

Sift together flour, baking powder, soda, and salt. Combine with creamed mixture and blend well. Stir in chopped nuts and cranberries.

Drop by teaspoonfuls onto greased cooky sheet. Bake in moderate oven (375°F.) 10 to 15 minutes. Makes about 12 dozen tea-size cookies.

Cranberry Bar Cookies: To bake as bar cookies, spread batter on a well-greased 11 x 15 x 1-inch pan and bake in moderate oven (350°F.) 45 minutes or until golden brown. For a sugary crust, sprinkle with granulated sugar. Makes 4 dozen 1 x 2 inch bars.

Cranberry Drop Cookies
Cranberry Bar Cookies

OATMEAL DROP COOKIES
(Master Recipe)

1 cup sifted enriched flour
1 teaspoon baking powder
½ teaspoon salt
¾ cup shortening
1 cup firmly packed brown sugar
2 eggs
1 teaspoon vanilla
⅓ cup milk
3 cups rolled oats, uncooked

Sift together flour, baking powder, and salt into bowl. Cut in shortening; add sugar, eggs, vanilla, and about half the milk. Beat until smooth, about 2 minutes.

Fold in remaining milk and the rolled oats. Drop from a teaspoon onto greased baking sheet.

Bake in moderate oven (375°F.) 12 to 15 minutes. Makes 4 dozen.

Variations of Oatmeal Cookies

Chocolate Chip Oatmeal Cookies: Add 1 7-ounce package chocolate chips to batter.

Coconut Oatmeal Cookies: Add 1 cup coconut to batter.

Date Oatmeal Cookies: Add 1 cup chopped dates to batter.

Nut Oatmeal Cookies: Add 1 cup chopped nuts to batter.

Raisin Spice Oatmeal Cookies: Sift 1 teaspoon cinnamon and ¼ teaspoon nutmeg with dry ingredients. Omit vanilla. Add 1 cup raisins to batter.

CRISP CHOCOLATE CHIP COOKIES

½ cup butter or margarine
¼ cup granulated sugar
½ cup firmly packed brown sugar
1 egg
½ teaspoon vanilla
1½ cups sifted enriched flour
½ teaspoon baking soda
½ teaspoon salt
1½ cups oven-popped rice cereal
1 cup (6-ounces) semi-sweet chocolate pieces

Blend butter and sugars thoroughly; add egg and vanilla and beat well.

Crisp Chocolate Chip Cookies

Sift together flour, soda, and salt. Add to first mixture and stir until combined. Stir in rice cereal and chocolate.

Drop by teaspoonfuls onto greased baking sheets. Bake in moderate oven (375°F.) about 12 minutes. Makes 4 dozen 1½-inch cookies.

KICHLACH

Kichlach is a Yiddish term for various old-time cookies. The recipe given here has been popular for many years.

1¼ cups sifted enriched flour
2 tablespoons sugar
¼ teaspoon salt
3 eggs, slightly beaten

Mix and sift flour, sugar, and salt. Make a "well" in the center and add the eggs. Beat with a fork until formed into a smooth dough.

Drop from a teaspoon onto a slightly greased cooky sheet at least an inch apart.

Bake in slow oven (325°F.) until lightly browned at the edges and puffed, about 20 minutes. Makes about 36.

Variation: Combine as above, adding ½ cup salad oil or melted shortening; beat until well blended. If desired, add 3 tablespoons fine poppy seed to this variation.

CORNUCOPIAS

½ cup sifted cake flour
1 egg
⅓ cup sugar
2 tablespoons water

Measure sifted flour and sift again. Beat egg slightly in small deep bowl; add sugar, and continue beating until very thick. Then add water gradually, beating constantly until very thick and light.

Add flour all at once and fold in with a spoon until just blended.

Grease baking sheet and dust lightly with flour, tapping sheet to remove any excess flour.

Drop cooky dough from tablespoon onto sheet, spreading each cooky with a spoon into a very thin 5-inch circle. (It is best to bake only 3 cookies at a time so they may be rolled quickly when baked). Bake in moderate oven (350°F.) until golden brown, 10 minutes.

Remove each cooky from baking sheet with a spatula and roll at once into a cone. If necessary, place baking sheet over low heat or return to oven for a moment or two in order to remove cookies easily. Set aside to cool.

When cornucopias are cold, fill with strawberry whipped cream. Serve at once. Makes 12.

Strawberry Whipped Cream: Mix ½ cup sugar and 1½ cups sliced strawberries. Let stand 10 minutes. Drain. Fold into 1 cup cream whipped.

Raisin Peek-a-Boo Drops

RAISIN PEEK-A-BOO DROPS

1 cup shortening (half butter or margarine)
2 cups light brown sugar (packed)
3 eggs, beaten
3 cups sifted enriched flour
1 teaspoon baking soda
1 teaspoon salt
1 teaspoon vanilla
Rich raisin filling (below)

Cream shortening and sugar together until light and fluffy; beat in eggs. Sift flour, soda, and salt together twice. Add to creamed mixture along with vanilla.

Drop dough in small mounds on ungreased baking sheet. Press a small amount of rich raisin filling in center of each mound. Top filling with a small bit of dough.

Bake in moderate oven (350°F.) about 10 to 15 minutes. Use a wide spatula to carefully remove cookies to wire rack to cool. Makes about 3½ dozen cookies.

Rich Raisin Filling: Measure 1½ cups dark or golden raisins, ½ cup sugar blended with 1 tablespoon cornstarch, and ½ cup water into a saucepan.

Cook and stir until thick, about 10 to 15 minutes; remove from heat and cool slightly.

Add 1 tablespoon each lemon juice and soft butter and ¼ cup each chopped filberts and halved candied cherries. Stir to blend, let stand until cold.

Cornucopias

Chocolate Peek-A-Boos

CHOCOLATE PEEK-A-BOOS

1   cup sifted enriched flour
1/4   teaspoon salt
1/4   cup sugar
1   cup milk
1/2   cup butter or margarine
4   eggs
1 1/2   teaspoons vanilla
About 1/2 of 6-ounce package semi-sweet chocolate bits

Sift together flour, salt, and sugar.
Measure milk into saucepan. Add butter; heat just to boiling point.
Add dry ingredients, all at once, to hot liquid, stirring constantly. Cook, stirring vigorously, until mixture leaves sides of pan in smooth compact ball. Remove from heat.
Add eggs, one at a time, beating vigorously after each addition until mixture is smooth again. Blend in vanilla; mix well.
Drop dough by half teaspoonfuls, 2 inches apart, onto ungreased baking sheet. Place 1 chocolate bit on each cooky. Then cover with a teaspoon of dough.
Bake in moderate oven (375°F.) 15 to 20 minutes. Sprinkle with confectioners' sugar, if desired. Cool. Makes about 4 1/2 dozen.

SOFT GINGER COOKIES

3/4   cup evaporated milk
1   tablespoon vinegar
1   cup shortening
1/2   cup sugar
1   egg, unbeaten
1/2   cup molasses
3   cups sifted enriched flour
2   teaspoons baking soda
1   teaspoon salt
1   teaspoon ginger
1   teaspoon cinnamon

Combine milk and vinegar. Cream shortening and sugar thoroughly. Add unbeaten egg and molasses and beat well. Add the soured milk and blend well.
Sift flour with other dry ingredients into mixture and mix well. Drop from teaspoon onto greased baking sheet.
Bake in moderate oven (375°F.) about 15 minutes. Makes 5 dozen.

BROWN SUGAR DROPS
(Master Recipe)

3 1/2   cups sifted enriched flour
1   teaspoon baking soda
1   teaspoon salt
1   cup soft shortening
2   cups firmly packed brown sugar
2   eggs
1/2   cup sour milk or buttermilk

Sift together flour, soda, and salt.
Cream shortening, gradually beat in sugar and eggs. Stir in sour milk or buttermilk. Gradually stir in flour mixture and beat thoroughly. Chill at least 1 hour.
Drop rounded teaspoonfuls about 2 inches apart onto lightly greased baking sheet.
Bake in hot oven (400°F.) until set (when touched lightly with finger almost no imprint remains), about 8 to 10 minutes. Makes about 6 dozen 2 1/2-inch cookies.

Brown Sugar Drop Variations

Coconut Drops: Add 1 cup moist shredded coconut to batter.

Fruit Drop Cookies: Add 1 1/2 cups broken pecans, 2 cups candied cherries, cut in halves, and 2 cups cut-up dates to batter. Decorate each cooky with a pecan half. Make cookies slightly smaller.

Nut Drops: Add 1 cup cut-up nutmeats to batter.

Salted Peanut Drop Cookies: Follow recipe for Brown Sugar Drops, using 2 instead of 3 1/2 cups flour and adding 2 cups uncooked rolled oats and 1 cup wheat flakes cereal. Add 1 cup coarsely chopped salted peanuts (without husks). Bake until brown, 12 to 14 minutes.

NUT CRUNCHES

1 1/2   cups sifted enriched flour
1/2   teaspoon baking soda
1   teaspoon salt
1/2   cup shortening
1/2   cup brown sugar
1/4   cup granulated sugar
1   egg, beaten
1/2   teaspoon vanilla
1/2   cup chopped nuts
1/2   cup chopped raisins

Sift together flour, soda, and salt.
Cream shortening and sugars together until light and fluffy. Add egg and vanilla. Beat well.
Add flour mixture to creamed mixture. Mix well. Fold in nuts and raisins.
Drop by teaspoonful onto ungreased baking sheets. Bake in moderate oven (375°F.) 10 minutes. Makes about 5 dozen.

MARMALADE COOKIES

2   cups sifted enriched flour
1   teaspoon baking powder
1/2   teaspoon salt
1/2   cup butter or margarine
2/3   cup sugar
1   egg, unbeaten
1   tablespoon cream or milk
1/4   cup marmalade
1/2   teaspoon vanilla

Mix and sift flour, baking powder, and salt.
Cream butter or margarine until soft and gradually blend in sugar. Add egg and beat thoroughly, then beat in milk, marmalade, and vanilla. Add dry ingredients and mix well.
Drop from teaspoon, about 1 inch apart, onto lightly greased cooky sheet.
Cover bottom of water glass with a piece of clean cloth (can be fastened on with a rubber band or string), dip in flour and press cookies flat about 1/8 inch thick.
Bake in moderate oven (375°F.) until delicately browned, 10 to 12 minutes.
Remove to cake rack to cool. Makes about 3 dozen.

Variations: If desired, substitute other preserves such as apricot, orange, pineapple, etc., for marmalade.

LACE COOKIES

1   cup dark molasses
1   cup sugar
1   cup butter or margarine
1/8   teaspoon salt
2   cups sifted enriched flour
1   teaspoon baking powder
1/2   teaspoon baking soda

Combine molasses, sugar, and butter in saucepan. Bring mixture to boil and cook 1 minute. Remove from heat.
Add dry ingredients, sifted together, and mix well.
Place in pan of hot water to keep batter from hardening. Drop from 1/4 teaspoon measure, 3 inches apart, on greased cooky sheets.
Bake in moderate oven (350°F.) 10 minutes or until brown.
Cool slightly and quickly remove from sheet with spatula. Makes 3 dozen.

Nut Crunches

RAISIN CHERRYETTES

4 cups corn flakes or 1 cup corn flake crumbs
1 cup sifted enriched flour
1/2 teaspoon salt
3/4 cup soft butter or margarine
3/4 cup sugar
1 egg
1 teaspoon grated lemon rind
1 cup flaked coconut
3/4 cup golden or dark raisins
1/4 cup coarsely chopped candied cherries

If using corn flakes, crush into fine crumbs. Sift together flour and salt; mix with corn flake crumbs.

Blend butter and sugar until light and fluffy. Stir in egg and lemon rind. Add dry ingredients; mix well. Stir in coconut, raisins, and cherries.

Drop by teaspoonfuls onto greased baking sheets. Bake in moderate oven (350°F.) about 15 minutes. Makes about 4 dozen cookies, 2 inches in diameter.

Raisin Cherryettes

CHOCOLATE WHEAT GERM GEMS

1 1/2 cups sifted enriched flour
1/2 teaspoon baking powder
1/2 teaspoon salt
1/2 cup butter or margarine
1 cup brown sugar, firmly packed
1/2 cup milk
2/3 cup wheat germ
2 squares (2 ounces) bitter chocolate, melted
1/2 cup coarsely chopped nuts
1 1/2 teaspoons vanilla

Sift together flour, baking powder, and salt. Cream butter or margarine and brown sugar together. Add dry ingredients and milk; mix well. Blend in remaining ingredients.

Drop teaspoonfuls of batter on greased baking sheet. Bake in moderate oven (375°F.) until done, 12 to 15 minutes. Makes about 2 1/2 dozen cookies.

Chocolate Wheat Germ Cookies

SOUR CREAM DROP COOKIES
(Master Recipe)

2 3/4 cups sifted enriched flour
1/2 teaspoon baking soda
1/2 teaspoon baking powder
1/2 teaspoon salt
1/2 cup soft shortening
1 1/2 cups sugar
2 eggs
1 cup thick sour cream
1 teaspoon vanilla

Sift together flour, soda, baking powder, and salt.

Cream shortening. Gradually beat in sugar and eggs. Stir in sour cream and vanilla. Gradually stir in dry ingredients. Chill at least 1 hour.

Drop rounded teaspoonfuls about 2 inches apart onto lightly greased baking sheet.

Bake in hot oven (425°F.) until delicately brown (when touched lightly with finger, almost no imprint remains), about 8 to 10 minutes. Makes about 5 dozen 2 1/2-inch cookies.

Sour Cream Drop Variations

Chocolate Cream Drops: Add 2 squares (2 ounces) melted unsweetened chocolate to fat-sugar-egg mixture. Add 1 cup cut-up nuts to batter. Frost cooled cookies with chocolate icing.

Coconut Cream Drops: Add 1 cup moist shredded coconut to batter of master recipe.

Fruit and Nut Drops: In master recipe, add and sift with dry ingredients 1 teaspoon cinnamon, 1/2 teaspoon cloves, and 1/4 teaspoon nutmeg.

Add 1 cup cut-up dates or raisins and 1 cup cut-up nuts to batter. The spices may be omitted if desired.

CHOCOLATE CHIP COOKIES

1 cup shortening
3/4 cup firmly packed brown sugar
3/4 cup granulated sugar
2 eggs, well beaten
1 cup chopped nuts
1/2 pound sweet or semi-sweet chocolate, cut in small pieces
1 teaspoon vanilla
2 1/2 cups sifted enriched flour
2 teaspoons baking powder
1/4 teaspoon salt

Cream shortening and sugars together until light. Add eggs and blend. Add nuts, chocolate, and vanilla.

Sift flour, baking powder, and salt together and add. Mix thoroughly. Drop onto cooky sheets.

Bake in slow oven (325°F.) about 20 minutes. Makes about 4 dozen.

Display your creative talents in shaping and decorating cookies, but for best results follow the recipe for the dough.

Lemon Drops

LEMON DROPS

2 cups sifted enriched flour
1/2 teaspoon baking soda
1/2 teaspoon salt
1/2 cup shortening
1 cup sugar
2 eggs
1 teaspoon vanilla
1/4 cup lemon juice
1 tablespoon grated lemon rind
1/4 cup lemon sugar (below)

Sift together flour, soda, and salt.

Cream together shortening and sugar until light and fluffy. Add eggs and vanilla, beating well.

Add dry ingredients alternately with lemon juice and rind, mixing well after each addition. Drop by teaspoonfuls onto greased baking sheet. Sprinkle with lemon sugar.

Bake in moderate oven (375°F.) 15 minutes. Makes about 5 dozen.

Lemon Sugar: Mix 1 teaspoon grated lemon rind with 1/4 cup sugar.

OATMEAL ORANGE LACE COOKIES

1/2 cup sifted enriched flour
1/2 teaspoon salt
2/3 cup sugar
1 cup fat (at room temperature)
2 eggs
1/2 teaspoon vanilla
1 teaspoon grated orange rind
1 cup rolled oats, uncooked
1/2 cup grated or shredded moist or fresh coconut

Sift dry ingredients together into mixing bowl. Add fat, eggs, vanilla, and grated orange rind; blend thoroughly. Fold in rolled oats and coconut.

Drop from teaspoon 2 inches apart onto cooky sheet. Flatten with knife which has been dipped in cold water.

Bake in moderate oven (350°-375°F.) 10 to 12 minutes. Remove from cooky sheet immediately. Makes 4 dozen.

Oatmeal Orange Lace Cookies

St. Patrick's Day Cookies

MOLASSES DROP COOKIES

(Master Recipe)

2   cups sifted enriched flour
1½ teaspoons baking powder
½   teaspoon salt
¼   teaspoon baking soda
1   teaspoon ground ginger
1   teaspoon cinnamon
½   cup shortening
¼   cup sugar
1   egg
¼   cup milk
¾   cup molasses

Mix and sift together flour, baking powder, salt, soda, ginger, and cinnamon.

Cream shortening and gradually add sugar, creaming well; add egg.

Mix milk and molasses. Add dry ingredients alternately with liquid, beating until smooth after each addition.

Drop from teaspoon onto lightly greased baking sheet.

Bake in moderate oven (350°F.) about 12 minutes. Makes 4 dozen.

Variations of Molasses Cookies

Coconut Gems: Add 1 cup shredded coconut and 1 tablespoon milk.

Oatmeal Molasses Cookies: Use only 1 cup flour and add 1½ cups uncooked rolled oats.

Raisin Molasses Cookies: Add ½ cup nuts and raisins to any of the variations.

Whole Wheat Molasses Cookies: Replace ½ the enriched flour with whole wheat flour.

Coconut Orange Jumbos

ST. PATRICK'S DAY COOKIES

2   cups sifted enriched flour
2   teaspoons baking powder
1   teaspoon cinnamon or allspice
¼   teaspoon cloves
½   teaspoon nutmeg
½   teaspoon salt
½   cup small raisins
¼   to ½ cup coarsely chopped nuts
½   cup sugar
¾   cup corn syrup
1   cup butter or margarine
1¼ cups hot mashed potatoes
1   egg

Sift flour with baking powder, spices, and salt. Stir in raisins and nuts.

Cream sugar, syrup, and butter or margarine and beat into mashed potatoes. Combine mixtures.

Use teaspoon-size measuring spoon and drop 3 mounds close together on lightly greased cooky sheet. Arrange a bit of dough for stem. Brush with slightly beaten egg and sprinkle with sugar.

Bake in moderate oven (375°F.) 20 minutes. Makes 2½ dozen.

COCONUT ORANGE JUMBOS

2½ cups sifted enriched flour
¼   teaspoon salt
½   teaspoon baking soda
¾   cup shortening
½   cup sugar
½   cup light corn syrup
2   eggs
2   cups chopped, shredded coconut
3   tablespoons grated orange rind
½   cup orange juice

Sift together flour, salt, and soda.

Cream shortening. Add sugar gradually and cream until light and fluffy.

Add syrup, blend thoroughly. Add eggs, one at a time, beating well after each addition. Stir in coconut and orange rind.

Add sifted dry ingredients, alternately with orange juice. Drop by teaspoonfuls onto lightly greased baking sheet.

Bake in moderate oven (350°F.) 15 minutes.

Cool and frost with a butter cream frosting. Makes 5 dozen.

MAPLE NUT DROPS

⅔   cup maple syrup
1   can (1⅓ cups) sweetened condensed milk
2   cups crushed graham cracker crumbs
1   teaspoon vanilla
1   cup chopped nuts

Cook maple syrup and condensed milk in heavy pan until thickened, about 3 minutes. Be careful not to scorch. Cool slightly and add remaining ingredients.

Drop from teaspoon onto greased baking sheet.

Bake in moderate oven (350°F.) 15 minutes.

Remove from pan at once. Cookies will be hard if overbaked. Store in jar to soften. Makes about 36 small cookies.

Note: Be sure to use sweetened condensed milk. Same results will not be obtained with evaporated milk.

SHERRIED BUTTER-NUT DROPS

1½ cups softened butter or margarine
1¾ cups sifted confectioners' sugar
¼   teaspoon salt
3⅓ cups sifted enriched flour
½   cup sherry
1   cup finely chopped walnuts or pecans

Cream butter and sugar thoroughly and add salt.

Add flour alternately with wine, mixing well after each addition. Stir in nuts.

Drop by teaspoonfuls onto greased, floured cooky sheets.

Bake in moderate oven (350°F.) 20 to 25 minutes. Makes about 100.

CEREAL JUMBLES

⅓   cup shortening
½   cup sugar
1   well beaten egg
1½ tablespoons milk
1   cup sifted enriched flour
½   teaspoon baking powder
¼   teaspoon baking soda
½   teaspoon salt
½   teaspoon vanilla
½   cup finely cut dates
½   cup chopped nuts
1½ cups whole wheat flakes

Cream shortening; add sugar gradually, and blend. Add egg and milk.

Sift together flour, baking powder, soda, and salt. Stir into the creamed mixture. Add vanilla, dates, and nuts.

Crush cereal flakes slightly. Drop cooky dough from teaspoon into crushed cereal flakes and roll so that balls of dough are entirely coated. Top with nut meat halves, if desired.

Place about 3 inches apart on greased heavy baking sheet.

Bake in hot oven (400°F.) about 12 minutes. Makes 2 to 3 dozen.

Cereal Jumbles

MOLASSES PECAN COOKIES

1/2 cup shortening
1/2 cup sugar
2 eggs
1/2 cup molasses
1 1/2 cups sifted enriched flour
1/4 teaspoon baking soda
1/4 teaspoon mace
1/4 teaspoon salt
1 cup finely chopped pecans

Cream together shortening and sugar; add eggs one at a time, beating after each. Add molasses; mix well.

Sift together flour, soda, mace, and salt; add 1/2 cup nuts; mix well.

Drop by teaspoons onto greased baking sheet 2 inches apart. Sprinkle tops with remaining nuts.

Bake in moderate oven (350°F.) 12 minutes. Remove from pan immediately. Makes 4 dozen.

CHRISTMAS FRUIT COOKIES

1 1/2 cups raisins
1 1/2 cups currants
1 1/2 cups candied pineapple
1 1/2 cups candied cherries
1/2 cup thinly sliced citron
1 1/2 cups broken nuts
1/2 cup butter or margarine
1 1/2 cups firmly packed brown sugar
3 eggs, separated
1/2 cup evaporated milk
1 1/2 teaspoons vinegar
2 cups sifted enriched flour
1/2 teaspoon baking soda
1/2 teaspoon salt
1 teaspoon cinnamon
1 teaspoon cloves
1 teaspoon allspice
Dash of nutmeg

Wash raisins and currants and drain well. Cut other fruit into small pieces.

Cream butter until smooth and plastic. Add sugar gradually and continue creaming until free from sugar granules. Beat in egg yolks.

Stir vinegar into milk and add to butter mixture.

Mix and sift flour, soda, salt, and spices. Stir into butter mixture with the fruit and nuts.

Beat egg whites until stiff but not dry. Fold into batter. Drop by teaspoonsful onto greased cooky sheet.

Bake in slow oven (325°F.) 20 to 25 minutes. Makes 8 to 10 dozen.

Christmas Fruit Cookies

ORANGE HONEY DROPS

3 cups sifted enriched flour
3 teaspoons baking powder
1/2 teaspoon salt
1/2 cup shortening
1/2 cup sugar
1 egg
1 teaspoon vanilla
1 cup honey
1/4 cup chopped nuts
1/4 cup chopped candied orange peel
1/4 cup chopped candied lemon peel

Sift together flour, baking powder, and salt.

Cream together shortening and sugar until light and fluffy. Add egg and vanilla, beating well. Blend in honey.

Add dry ingredients, nuts, orange and lemon peels, mixing thoroughly. Drop by teaspoonfuls onto greased baking sheet.

Bake in moderate oven (375°F.) 10 minutes. Makes about 7 1/2 dozen.

PENNSYLVANIA-DUTCH RAISIN CAKES

1/4 cup butter or margarine
3/4 cup sugar
1 egg
1/2 teaspoon baking soda
1 tablespoon hot water
1 1/2 cups sifted enriched flour
1/4 teaspoon salt
1/4 teaspoon cinnamon
1/4 teaspoon nutmeg
1 cup ground raisins

Cream the butter and sugar thoroughly. Add the beaten egg and mix well.

Dissolve soda in hot water and add alternately with a sifted mixture of the flour, salt, cinnamon, and nutmeg. Stir in the raisins.

Drop by teaspoonsful onto a greased cooky sheet and bake in a moderate oven (375°F.) 8 minutes. Makes 4 dozen small cookies.

BRANDY WAFERS

1/2 cup molasses
1/2 cup butter or margarine
1 1/4 cups sifted cake flour
1/4 teaspoon salt
2/3 cup sugar
1 tablespoon ginger
3 tablespoons brandy

Heat molasses to boiling. Add butter. Add sifted dry ingredients gradually, stirring constantly. Stir in brandy.

Drop by 1/2 measuring teaspoonfuls 3 inches apart on greased cooky sheets.

Bake 6 cookies at a time in slow oven (300°F.) 8 to 10 minutes. Cool 1 minute.

Remove with spatula and roll at once around handle of wooden spoon. If removed too soon, wafers will break. If not soon enough, they will not roll. Makes about 60.

Tropical Treats

TROPICAL TREATS

4 dozen pitted dates
4 dozen quartered walnut meats
1/2 cup margarine
1/4 cup brown sugar
1/2 cup granulated sugar
1/2 teaspoon vanilla
1 egg
1 3/4 cups sifted enriched flour
1/2 teaspoon salt
1 1/2 teaspoons baking powder
1/2 cup milk
Creamy vanilla frosting
Cashew nuts or walnuts

Stuff dates with walnut quarters. Cream margarine and sugars together until light and fluffy. Beat in vanilla and egg.

Sift together flour, salt, and baking powder. Add flour mixture alternately with milk to margarine mixture, mixing smooth after each addition.

Drop batter by teaspoonfuls onto greased baking sheet. Press a stuffed date into each mound of batter. Cover dates with another teaspoonful of batter, spreading it to cover dates completely.

Bake in moderate oven (375°F.) 10 to 12 minutes. When cool, frost with creamy vanilla frosting and garnish with cashew nut or walnut half. Makes about 48.

BUTTERSCOTCH COFFEE WAFERS

2 cups sifted enriched flour
2 teaspoons baking powder
1/2 teaspoon salt
1 1/2 cups chopped nuts
1/2 cup shortening
2 cups firmly packed brown sugar
2 well beaten eggs
1/2 cup strong coffee

Mix and sift flour, baking powder, and salt; add nuts.

Melt shortening; add sugar gradually and mix thoroughly over low heat.

Remove from heat and add well beaten eggs. Stir in flour and nut mixture alternately with coffee.

Drop by teaspoonfuls onto greased baking sheet. Spread with wet knife and bake in moderate oven (350°F.) 12 to 15 minutes. Remove at once with thin knife or spatula. Makes 6 to 9 dozen, depending on size.

Fig Oatmeal Cookies

FIG OATMEAL COOKIES

1   cup dried figs, coarsely chopped
2   cups sifted enriched flour
2   teaspoons baking powder
1/2 teaspoon salt
1   teaspoon cinnamon
2   cups quick-cooking oats, uncooked
1/2 cup chopped nuts
3/4 cup shortening
1   cup firmly packed brown sugar
2   eggs
8   tablespoons water

Cover figs with hot water and allow to stand 10 minutes. Pour off water and reserve for liquid. Snip off stems from figs, then chop coarsely.

Sift flour with baking powder, salt, and cinnamon. Add oats, chopped figs, and nuts.

Cream shortening; add sugar, cream together thoroughly. Add well beaten eggs, then add sifted dry ingredients alternately with water to form dough.

Drop by teaspoonfuls onto greased cooky sheet. Bake in hot oven (400°F.) 10 minutes. Makes 48 cookies.

SPICED FIG BALLS

1/2 cup dried figs (packed in cup)
1/2 cup shortening
1/2 cup molasses
1/4 cup sugar
1/4 teaspoon ginger
1   egg, beaten
1   teaspoon vanilla
1/2 teaspoon lemon extract
1   teaspoon baking soda
1/2 teaspoon cinnamon
1/4 teaspoon nutmeg
1/4 teaspoon salt
2 7/8 cups sifted enriched flour (3 cups, less 2 tablespoons)

Cover figs with boiling water and let stand 10 minutes. Drain, clip off stems, and cut fine with scissors (if moist figs are used softening may be eliminated).

Combine shortening, molasses, and sugar. Heat to boiling. Cool to lukewarm and add ginger, beaten egg, vanilla, and lemon extract.

Add sifted soda, spices, salt, and flour. Stir in chopped figs.

Drop by teaspoonfuls onto greased baking sheet.

Bake in moderate oven (375°F.) 12 minutes. Makes 3 dozen.

NEW ORLEANS DROP COOKIES

3/4 cup shortening
3/4 cup molasses
2   eggs
2 1/4 cups sifted enriched flour
4   teaspoons baking powder
1/2 teaspoon salt
1 1/2 teaspoons cinnamon
1/2 teaspoon baking soda
1/2 cup milk
1/2 cup seedless raisins
1/2 cup chopped walnuts

Slowly melt shortening; cool. Add molasses and eggs; beat well.

Sift together flour, baking powder, salt, cinnamon, and soda; add alternately with milk to first mixture. Add raisins and nuts.

Drop by teaspoonfuls onto greased baking sheet. Bake in hot oven (425°F.) 8 to 10 minutes. Makes 4 to 5 dozen.

PEANUT DROP COOKIES

2   cups sifted enriched flour
2   teaspoons baking powder
1/2 teaspoon salt
1/2 cup shortening
1   cup sugar
2   eggs
1/2 teaspoon vanilla
1/4 cup milk
1 1/2 cups chopped peanuts

Sift together flour, baking powder, and salt.

Cream together shortening and sugar until light and fluffy. Add eggs and vanilla. Mix well.

Add dry ingredients alternately with milk, beating after each addition. Stir in peanuts.

Drop by teaspoonfuls on ungreased baking sheets. Bake in hot oven (400°F.) 10 minutes. Makes about 4 dozen.

CHOCOLATE MOUNDS

2   cups sifted enriched flour
2   teaspoons baking powder
1/2 teaspoon baking soda
1   teaspoon salt
1/2 cup cocoa
1/2 cup shortening
1   cup sugar
2   eggs
1/2 teaspoon vanilla
1   cup buttermilk or sour milk

Sift together flour, baking powder, soda, salt, and cocoa.

Cream together shortening and sugar until light and fluffy. Add eggs and vanilla, beating well.

Add dry ingredients alternately with buttermilk or sour milk. Drop by teaspoonfuls onto ungreased baking sheet.

Bake in moderate oven (350°F.) 12 to 15 minutes. While still warm, brush with confectioners' sugar icing. Makes 4 dozen.

POPPY SEED COOKIES

1   cup poppy seed
1/2 cup scalded milk
1/2 cup butter or margarine
1/2 cup sugar
2   ounces (2 squares) chocolate, melted
1/4 cup currants (optional)
1 1/2 cups sifted enriched flour
1   teaspoon baking powder
1/8 teaspoon salt
1/2 teaspoon cinnamon
1/4 teaspoon ground cloves
1/4 cup raisins (optional)

Soak poppy seed in hot milk for 1/2 hour.

Cream butter and sugar. Add remaining ingredients and mix thoroughly. Drop by teaspoonfuls onto greased baking sheets.

Bake in moderate oven (350°F.) 20 minutes. Makes about 30.

BRAN FLAKE CHIP COOKIES

1 1/4 cups sifted enriched flour
1   teaspoon baking powder
1/4 teaspoon salt
3/4 cup butter or margarine
1/2 cup firmly packed brown sugar
1/2 cup granulated sugar
2   eggs
1   teaspoon vanilla
1/4 cup milk
1/2 cup chopped nuts
3   cups bran flakes
1   (7-ounce) bar semi-sweet or bitter-sweet chocolate, cut in tiny pieces

Sift flour with baking powder and salt.

Cream butter; add sugars gradually, beating thoroughly after each addition. Beat in eggs, one at a time; stir in vanilla.

Add flour mixture alternately with milk, beating until smooth after each addition.

Stir in nuts, bran flakes, and finally chocolate pieces.

Drop from teaspoon onto buttered cooky sheet. Bake in moderate oven (375°F.) 12 minutes or until done. Makes about 3 dozen.

Bran Flake Chip Cookies

COCONUT ISLANDS

2 cups sifted enriched flour
1/2 teaspoon salt
1/2 teaspoon baking soda
3 squares (3 ounces) unsweetened chocolate
1/4 cup hot strong coffee
1/2 cup butter or shortening
1 cup firmly packed brown sugar
1 egg, unbeaten
2/3 cup thick sour cream
1/3 cup finely cut coconut (canned, packaged, or grated fresh)
Additional 2/3 cup coconut

Sift together flour, salt, and soda.

Melt chocolate in hot coffee in small saucepan over low heat. (If desired, 1/4 teaspoon instant coffee and 1/4 cup boiling water may be substituted.) Cool.

Cream butter or other shortening; gradually add brown sugar, creaming well. Add unbeaten egg and the cool chocolate mixture. Beat well.

Add sour cream alternately with the dry ingredients to cream mixture. Mix until well blended. Stir in 1/3 cup coconut.

Drop by heaping teaspoonfuls onto greased baking sheets.

Bake in moderate oven (375°F.) 12 to 15 minutes.

Frost while warm with chocolate frosting (see below.) Sprinkle tops with additional 2/3 cup coconut. Store in tightly covered container. Makes 3 1/2 dozen.

Chocolate Frosting: Heat 1 1/2 squares (1 1/2 ounces) unsweetened chocolate, 1/4 cup sour cream, and 1 tablespoon butter in top of double boiler over hot water, stirring until chocolate melts. Immediately remove from heat.

Gradually blend in 1 1/2 to 2 cups sifted confectioners' sugar, until consistency to spread. Thin with water or cream, a few drops at a time, if necessary.

NORWEGIAN AND DANISH KRINGLE (COOKIES)

1 cup rich sour cream
1 cup sugar
3 cups sifted cake flour
1 teaspoon salt
1 teaspoon cinnamon
3/4 teaspoon baking soda
1 ounce (1 square) melted bitter chocolate, optional

Combine sugar and sour cream and stir until dissolved.

Sift the flour, salt, cinnamon, and soda; add to sour cream mixture. Add the melted chocolate (this may be left out if desired).

Mix well and drop by 1/2 teaspoons onto greased cooky sheet. Bake 20 minutes in a moderate oven (350°F.). Makes 72 cookies.

MONKEY FACES

2 1/2 cups sifted enriched flour
1 teaspoon baking soda
1/2 teaspoon salt
1/2 teaspoon ginger
1/2 teaspoon cinnamon
1/2 cup shortening
1 cup firmly packed brown sugar
1 teaspoon vinegar
1/2 cup buttermilk or 1/2 cup sour milk
1/2 cup molasses
Raisins or currants for faces

Sift together flour, soda, salt, ginger, and cinnamon.

Cream together shortening and sugar until light and fluffy. Add vinegar and blend well.

Combine buttermilk or sour milk with molasses. Add dry ingredients alternately with milk. Drop by teaspoonfuls onto ungreased baking sheet. Make faces with currants or raisins.

Bake in moderate oven (350°F.) 10 to 15 minutes. Makes about 6 dozen.

TUTTI FRUTTI COOKIES

1 cup shortening
1 cup molasses
1 egg
2 cups sifted enriched flour
1 1/2 teaspoons baking soda
1 teaspoon salt
1 teaspoon cinnamon
1 teaspoon nutmeg
1 cup seedless raisins
1 cup chopped nuts
3/4 cup chopped citron, candied orange, and lemon peels

Slowly melt shortening; cool. Add molasses and egg; beat well.

Sift together flour, soda, salt, cinnamon, and nutmeg; add to first mixture.

Put raisins, nuts, and fruit peels through fine-blade food chopper. Add to batter.

Drop by teaspoonfuls 2 inches apart onto greased baking sheet.

Bake in hot oven (425°F.) 8 to 10 minutes, until brown. Makes about 60.

COCONUT CHIP DROPS

2 cups sifted enriched flour
1/4 teaspoon baking soda
1/4 teaspoon salt
3 eggs
1 1/2 cups firmly packed brown sugar
1 teaspoon vanilla
1 tablespoon vinegar
1 tablespoon melted butter or margarine
1 1/2 squares (1 1/2 ounces) baking chocolate, chopped
1 cup chopped pecans
1 cup chopped coconut

Sift together flour, soda, and salt.
Beat eggs, brown sugar, and vanilla

together until thick. Stir in vinegar and melted butter or margarine. Blend in dry ingredients, chocolate, nuts, and coconut. Drop by teaspoonfuls onto greased cooky sheet. Bake in moderate oven (375°F.) about 10 minutes or until lightly browned. Cool on cake rack. Makes 4 1/2 dozen.

HOLIDAY OATMEAL DROPS

2/3 cup butter or margarine
3/4 cup firmly packed brown sugar
1 egg
1 teaspoon vanilla
2 cups sifted enriched flour
2 teaspoons baking powder
1/2 teaspoon salt
1 cup quick oats, uncooked
1/2 cup chopped candied fruit
1/2 cup shredded coconut
1/4 cup milk
Pecan halves

Cream butter or margarine and sugar until fluffy; add egg and vanilla and beat well.

Sift flour, baking powder, and salt; stir in oats, candied fruit, and coconut. Add oat mixture and milk to creamed mixture. Stir well.

Drop by teaspoonfuls onto lightly greased cooky sheets. Press a pecan half into each cooky.

Bake in moderate oven (375°F.) 10 to 12 minutes. Makes 4 dozen.

COFFEE MINCEMEAT COOKIES

1 9-ounce package dehydrated mincemeat
1 cup strong coffee
1/2 cup melted shortening or drippings
1/2 cup molasses
1 beaten egg
1 1/2 cups sifted enriched flour
3/4 teaspoon baking soda
1/2 teaspoon salt
1/2 teaspoon mace

Combine mincemeat and coffee; simmer 10 minutes, or until mixture has consistency of mincemeat pie filling. Cool.

Add shortening and molasses. Add egg and beat well.

Mix and sift remaining ingredients and stir in. Drop by tablespoons onto greased cooky sheet about 2 inches apart.

Bake in hot oven (400°F.) 15 minutes or until cookies are brown. Makes about 2 1/2 dozen.

Cooky snitchers are not always the youngsters of the family. The aroma of freshly baked cookies is likely to bring everyone into the kitchen for a sample.

Rolled and Filled Cookies

Rolled cookies are made from a dough stiff enough to roll thin and cut with a cooky cutter, sharp knife, or a pastry wheel.

The dough should be chilled if it is too soft to be rolled out easily. If the dough is not chilled, it may be too soft to roll without adding more flour; therefore making the cookies less tender.

Dip cooky cutters in flour each time before cutting dough to prevent sticking.

A lightly floured pastry cloth and stockinette cover for the rolling pin will help in rolling the dough and keep it from sticking.

MASTER ROLLED SUGAR COOKIES

2 cups sifted enriched flour
1½ teaspoons baking powder
½ teaspoon salt
½ cup butter, margarine, or shortening
1 cup sugar
1 egg, well beaten
1 teaspoon vanilla
1 tablespoon milk or cream

Sift together 1½ cups flour, baking powder, and salt.

Cream butter; add sugar gradually and cream until light and fluffy. Add egg, vanilla, and milk.

Add sifted dry ingredients, then gradually add remaining flour until dough is stiff enough to handle. Chill at least 1 hour.

Roll ⅛-inch thick on lightly floured board and shape with floured cooky cutters. Place on ungreased cooky sheets. Sprinkle with plain or tinted sugar.

Bake in moderate oven (375°F.) 8 to 10 minutes. Makes 50 to 60 small cookies.

Variations of Master Rolled Sugar Cookies

Dropped Sugar Cookies: Use only 1½ cups flour and 1 teaspoon baking powder. Drop by teaspoonfuls 2 to 3 inches apart onto greased cooky sheets. For flat cookies, press with knife or fork dipped in cold water or flatten with floured bottom of glass.

If mixture is too firm, shape into small balls and flatten as above.

Bake in moderate oven (375°F.) 8 to 10 minutes.

Almond Rolled Cookies: In master recipe, add ⅓ cup chopped, blanched almonds and grated rind of ½ lemon, to flour mixture. Sift with dry ingredients ½ teaspoon each of cinnamon, clove, and nutmeg.

Butterscotch Rolled Cookies: In master recipe, substitute 1 cup firmly packed brown sugar for granulated sugar.

Candied Fruit Rolled Cookies: In master recipe, add ¼ cup chopped cherries, pineapple, orange, lemon, or grapefruit peel to flour mixture. Cookies may also be garnished with bits of fruit before baking.

Caraway Seed Rolled Cookies: In master recipe, add 2 tablespoons caraway seed.

Chocolate Rolled Cookies: In master recipe, add 2 squares (2 ounces) melted unsweetened chocolate with beaten egg. One cup finely chopped nuts may be added to sifted dry ingredients.

Coconut Orange Rolled Cookies: In master recipe, omit vanilla and add 1¼ teaspoons grated orange rind. Add 1 cup shredded coconut to flour mixture.

Coconut Rolled Cookies: In master recipe, add ½ cup shredded coconut to flour mixture, or sprinkle coconut over cookies before baking.

Crisp Rolled Sugar Cookies: Follow master recipe and roll dough ¼-inch thick. Cover with sugar before baking.

Date Nut Rolled Cookies: In master recipe, add ¼ cup each chopped dates and nuts to flour mixture.

Fruit Rolled Cookies: In master recipe, add ½ cup of chopped apricots, prunes, dates, figs, or raisins to flour mixture.

Ginger Rolled Cookies: In master recipe, add ¼ cup candied ginger, cut fine.

Lemon Rolled Cookies: In master recipe, substitute 1 teaspoon lemon extract and 2 teaspoons grated lemon rind for vanilla.

Maple Sugar Rolled Cookies: In master recipe, substitute finely crushed maple sugar for granulated sugar.

Molasses Rolled Cookies: In master recipe, substitute ¼ cup brown sugar and ¼ cup molasses for granulated sugar. Omit milk. Add 1 teaspoon ginger and ½ teaspoon baking soda.

Nut Rolled Cookies: In master recipe, add ½ cup chopped nuts to flour mixture.

Orange Rolled Cookies: In master recipe, substitute orange juice for milk. Add grated rind of ½ orange. Use 2 egg yolks instead of whole egg.

Peanut Butter Rolled Cookies: In master recipe, use ½ cup peanut butter and ½ cup brown sugar instead of butter and granulated sugar. Add 1 tablespoon milk or cream.

Pinwheel Cookies: Divide dough of master recipe into 2 equal parts. Blend 1 square (1 ounce) melted chocolate into one part.

Roll each part to ⅛-inch thickness on separate pieces of floured waxed paper. Then place white dough on top of chocolate dough, removing waxed paper.

Roll up as for a jelly roll. Wrap firmly in waxed paper. Chill.

Slice and bake in hot oven (400°F.) about 8 minutes.

Raisin Rolled Cookies: In master recipe, add ½ cup raisins to butter and sugar-egg mixture.

Sand Tarts: Roll chilled dough of master recipe ¼ inch thick and cut in desired shapes.

Brush with egg white and sprinkle with mixture of 4 tablespoons sugar and 1 teaspoon cinnamon.

Decorate with blanched almond halves and candied fruits.

Sour Cream Rolled Cookies: In master recipe, reduce baking powder to ½ teaspoon. Add ¼ teaspoon nutmeg and ¼ teaspoon baking soda. Sift with flour.

Substitute ½ teaspoon lemon extract for vanilla. Use ⅓ cup sour cream instead of 1 tablespoon milk.

Spice Rolled Cookies: In master recipe, omit vanilla. Sift with dry ingredients ¼ teaspoon each allspice, cinnamon, and cloves.

FILLED SUGAR COOKIES

Method No. 1: Prepare recipes for Master Rolled Sugar Cookies and desired filling. Bake the sugar cookies.

When cool, spread filling on half the cookies and cover with remaining cookies to make "sandwiches."

Method No. 2: Prepare recipes for Master Rolled Sugar Cookies and desired filling.

Roll out dough ⅛-inch thick. Cut into desired shapes with cooky cutters.

Place 1 teaspoon filling on half the cookies. Cover with remaining rounds, pressing edges together with fork.

Bake on ungreased baking sheet in moderate oven (375°F.) 10 to 15 minutes. Makes about 2 dozen (2½-inch) filled cookies.

Method No. 3: Prepare recipe for Master Rolled Sugar Cookies. Roll out and cut into squares.

Fill and fold over diagonally to make triangles with filling in pocket thus formed.

Bake in moderate oven (375°F.) 8 to 10 minutes.

Method No. 4: Proceed as in No. 3 and fold squares or roll into cornucopias, with filling peeking out at wide end of horn.

Twist pointed end of horn to give curled effect. Bake in moderate oven (375°F.) 8 to 10 minutes.

Orange Mincemeat Squares

ORANGE MINCEMEAT SQUARES

2 cups sifted enriched flour
2 teaspoons baking powder
1 teaspoon salt
¾ cup sugar
½ cup melted shortening
2 eggs
½ teaspoon orange extract
1 tablespoon shredded orange rind
¾ cup mincemeat or orange marmalade

Sift together flour, baking powder, and salt.

Add sugar to melted shortening and mix well. Add eggs, beating until mixture is smooth and well blended.

Stir in orange extract and orange rind. Gradually add flour mixture, stirring until mixture is smooth.

Cover and place in refrigerator for several hours or until dough can be easily handled.

Divide dough in half, returning one half to refrigerator. Place other half on floured board or pastry cloth.

Roll out to 12-inch square. Cut into 16 3-inch squares. Place about 1 teaspoon mincemeat or orange marmalade in center of each square. Bring corners of each square together in center of square, sealing edges.

Place on baking sheet and bake in moderate oven (375°F.) 12 to 15 minutes.

Roll out remaining half of dough and bake in same way. Makes 32 squares.

HUNGARIAN BUTTER COOKIES

1½ cups butter or margarine
1 cup sugar
2 eggs, separated
1 tablespoon rum
4 cups sifted enriched flour
½ cup chopped nuts

Cream butter, gradually add sugar, creaming until fluffy.

Beat in egg yolks and rum. Work in flour to a smooth dough.

Roll out to ⅛-inch thickness. Cut into desired shapes with cooky cutters.

Beat 2 egg whites very stiff. Drop ½ teaspoon egg white on each cooky. Sprinkle a few chopped nuts on top.

Bake in moderate oven (350°F.) about 10 minutes or until golden brown.

PRUNE COOKY FILLING

1 cup chopped cooked prunes
¼ cup sugar
2 teaspoons grated orange rind
½ cup nuts, optional
¼ teaspoon salt
¼ teaspoon vanilla

Mix all ingredients, stirring until sugar is dissolved.

DATE RAISIN COOKY FILLING

½ cup chopped raisins
1 cup chopped dates
½ cup sugar
2 teaspoons grated lemon rind
3 teaspoons cornstarch
¼ cup cold water
3 teaspoons lemon juice
½ cup chopped nuts

Combine raisins, dates, sugar, and lemon rind in a saucepan.

Dissolve cornstarch in cold water and add to fruit mixture. Cook over low heat, stirring constantly until thickened. Blend in lemon juice and nuts.

Use in Method No. 2, Filled Cookies.

FIG COOKY FILLING

1 cup ground figs
¼ cup orange juice
2 teaspoons grated orange rind
¼ cup water
⅛ teaspoon salt
¼ cup sugar
¼ cup chopped nuts

Mix together all ingredients except nuts.

Cook until mixture thickens, about 5 minutes, stirring constantly.

Cool and add nuts.

FIG COOKY FILLING #2

1½ cups dried figs
1 cup cold water
½ cup corn syrup
1 teaspoon grated lemon rind
6 tablespoons sugar
2 tablespoons flour
Few grains salt
1 tablespoon lemon juice
½ cup chopped nuts

Cover dried figs with boiling water and let stand 10 minutes; drain, clip off stems, and cut fairly fine, using scissors.

Add cold water and cook until tender, about 10 minutes. Add corn syrup and grated lemon rind, and cook a few minutes longer.

Mix sugar, flour, and salt; add all at once, and cook, stirring until thickened and clear.

Remove from heat; add lemon juice and nuts, and cool before using. Makes about 2 cups of filling.

FILLED SUGAR COOKIE HINTS

Prepare Master Rolled Sugar Cooky Dough. Roll dough to ⅛ inch in thickness and cut with a medium sized plain cooky cutter and a cutter with a scalloped edge.

Place cookies on lightly greased cooky sheet, then place in center of cookies a heaping teaspoon of desired filling.

Cover plain cookies with cookies of equal size and the scalloped cookies with ones from which centers have been removed.

Press edges of plain cookies together with tines of a fork which has been dipped in flour.

Bake as directed and remove from pans at once onto cake rack.

Rainbow Cookies

SPRINGERLE

Springerle are anise-flavored German Christmas cookies. Designs are embossed into the rolled out dough with special rolling pins or boards.

    2   eggs
    1¼ cups granulated sugar
        Grated rind of 1 lemon
    1   teaspoon anise seed
    2½ cups sifted enriched flour
    ½   teaspoon baking powder
    ½   teaspoon salt

Beat eggs until thick and lemon colored.

Add sugar gradually, then beat with electric mixer 10 minutes or with rotary beater 20 minutes. Add flavorings and sifted dry ingredients.

Roll to ¼-inch thickness. Let stand until dry on top.

To emboss designs, press floured springerle rolling pin or board very hard on dough. Cut around designs and let dry on board overnight.

Remove to greased cooky sheets. Bake in slow oven (300°F.) 25 to 30 minutes.

Store in airtight container at least 1 week before using. Makes about 36.

BERLINER KRANZ COOKIES

    ¾   cup butter or margarine
        Granulated sugar
    1   teaspoon grated orange rind
    1   egg
    2   cups sifted enriched flour
    ¼   teaspoon salt
    1   egg white
        Green sugar
        Red cinnamon candies

Cream butter. Add ½ cup sugar, orange rind, and egg, and beat until light. Add flour and salt. Chill several hours or until firm enough to roll.

Roll to ⅛-inch thickness. Cut with floured 2-inch doughnut cutter. Put on cooky sheets. Beat egg white until foamy; add 2 tablespoons sugar gradually and beat until stiff. Brush cookies with mixture.

Decorate cookies with green sugar and cinnamon candies.

Bake in hot oven (400°F.) 10 to 12 minutes.

Remove to wire racks while hot. Makes about 48.

RAINBOW COOKIES

    1   cup butter or margarine
    1   teaspoon vanilla
    1   cup sifted confectioners' sugar
    2½ cups sifted enriched flour

Blend together butter or margarine, vanilla, and confectioners' sugar, creaming well. Blend in flour gradually.

Divide dough into four parts. Color one part red, one yellow, and one green by adding 4 drops food coloring to each. Blend color in dough thoroughly with spoon or knead in with hands. Leave fourth portion uncolored. You will have four portions of dough, each a different color.

Shape one-fourth of each color dough into a long strip ½-inch thick. Place the four strips side by side on floured pastry cloth or board.

Roll out lengthwise into a long strip 2½ to 3 inches wide and ⅛ inch thick. Cut into rounds with 2½-inch cutter so that each cooky has 4 colored stripes.

Repeat this process three more times, using remaining dough. Reroll all extra pieces of dough together to ⅛-inch thickness and cut into rounds. Cookies made from this dough will be marbled. Place on greased baking sheets.

Bake in moderate oven (350°F.) 8 to 10 minutes. Do not brown. Cool.

Place cookies together with peanut butter filling (see below), sandwich style, if desired. Or serve cookies plain. Store in tightly covered container. Makes 2 dozen filled or 4 dozen unfilled cookies.

Peanut Butter Filling: Combine ⅓ cup firmly packed brown sugar and 1 tablespoon flour in saucepan. Add ½ cup water. Cook over medium heat, stirring constantly, until thickened.

Remove from heat; add ¼ cup creamy-style peanut butter. Use 1 teaspoon between each pair of cookies.

MARMALADE RINGS

    2   cups sifted enriched flour
    3   teaspoons baking powder
    1   teaspoon salt
    6   tablespoons shortening
    ¾   cup milk
        Marmalade

Mix and sift dry ingredients. Cut in shortening thoroughly. Blend in milk to make a soft dough.

Roll out on lightly floured board to ¼-inch in thickness. Cut in 2-inch rounds. Cut centers from half the rounds.

Arrange rounds on baking sheet. Cover with those from which centers have been cut. Reroll scraps.

Bake in very hot oven (450°F.) about 12 to 15 minutes.

Remove from oven. Fill centers with marmalade. Makes about 1½ dozen.

RAGALACH

    1   cup soft sweet butter
    ½   pound soft cream cheese
    ¼   teaspoon salt
    2   cups sifted enriched flour
    1   cup chopped walnuts
    ½   cup sugar
    1   tablespoon cinnamon

Mix together the butter, cheese, and salt until creamy. Mix in flour. Form into 14 balls. Chill overnight.

Roll each ball to 6-inch circle, on lightly floured cloth. Cut each into quarters.

Mix nuts, sugar, and cinnamon. Drop rounded teaspoonful onto each quarter. Pinch together edges of dough and form into crescents. Place on ungreased cooky sheet.

Bake in moderate oven (350°F.) until light brown, about 12 minutes. Makes about 60.

OATMEAL SUGAR STARS

    ⅔   cup soft shortening
    ¾   cup sugar
    1   egg
    1   tablespoon milk
    1   teaspoon vanilla
    1¾ cups sifted enriched flour
    1   teaspoon baking powder
    ½   teaspoon salt
    ¾   cup quick or old fashioned uncooked oats
    ¼   cup chopped candied fruit

Beat shortening and sugar together until creamy. Add egg, milk, and vanilla; beat until mixture is light and fluffy.

Sift flour, baking powder, and salt together; stir into shortening mixture. Stir in oats. Chill dough about 30 minutes.

Roll out on lightly floured board or canvas to ⅛-inch thickness. Cut out cookies with well-floured star-shaped cooky cutter. Place a few pieces of candied fruit in center of each star. Sprinkle with granulated sugar. Bake on greased cooky sheets in moderate oven (375°F.) 10 to 12 minutes. Cool. Makes 3 dozen cookies.

Oatmeal Sugar Stars

OLD-FASHIONED BUTTER COOKIES

1 cup butter
2 cups sugar
1 teaspoon vanilla
3 eggs, well beaten
4 cups sifted enriched flour
1/2 teaspoon salt

Cream butter; add sugar and vanilla and continue creaming until light. Beat eggs and add to butter mixture. Blend well.

Sift flour, measure; sift with salt and add to dough, using more flour if necessary to make stiff dough. Chill 20 to 30 minutes.

Roll out to 1/4-inch thickness. Cut with cooky cutter and bake on lightly greased cooky sheet in hot oven (400°F.) about 10 minutes. (Cookies may be sprinkled with sugar before baking.)

Remove from pans to cake racks to cool. Makes 5 to 6 dozen.

Filled Butter Cookies: Roll dough to 1/8-inch thickness and cut with scalloped cooky cutter.

Place cookies on cooky sheet; place in center of each a heaping teaspoon of date and raisin filling. Cover with cookies of equal size with scalloped edge. Centers may be removed with small scalloped cutter.

Bake in hot oven (400° to 425°F.) 15 minutes. Remove from pans to cake rack.

SWEDISH TEA CAKES

1 cup butter or margarine
3 tablespoons cream
2 cups sifted enriched flour
1 egg white, slightly beaten
2 tablespoons finely chopped pecans
2 tablespoons sugar
1/3 cup raspberry jam

Cream butter until light and fluffy. Add cream and beat well. Add flour, mixing thoroughly.

Roll dough in waxed paper and chill several hours.

Divide into 2 parts. Roll 1 part about 1/4-inch thick on well floured pastry cloth. Cut with 2 1/2-inch doughnut cutter with center cutter removed to make whole rounds. Place on ungreased cooky sheets.

Roll and cut remaining dough in rings as for doughnuts with 2 1/2-inch cutter. Brush rings with egg white and place egg side down on rounds of dough.

Brush tops of cookies with egg white and sprinkle with nuts and sugar. Fill centers with jam.

Bake in hot oven (400°F.) until delicately browned, about 12 to 15 minutes. Makes about 24.

SCOTCH SHORTBREAD
(Master Recipe)

1 cup soft butter or margarine
3/4 cup sugar
2 1/2 cups sifted enriched flour

Cream butter and add sugar gradually, blending thoroughly. Add flour slowly and mix thoroughly to a smooth dough. Chill.

Roll out about 1/2-inch thick. Cut into desired shapes with cooky cutters (small leaves, ovals, squares, etc.). Flute edges if desired by pinching between fingers as for pie crust.

Place on ungreased baking sheet. Bake in slow oven (300°F.) about 20 to 25 minutes or until golden brown. Makes about 2 dozen 1x1 1/2-inch cookies.

Scotch Shortbread Variations

Basic Shortbread Cookies: Roll dough to 1/4-inch thickness. Cut into desired shapes. Prick all over with fork. Bake about 20 minutes.

Butterscotch Shortbread: Substitute 1 cup firmly packed brown sugar for granulated sugar.

Whole Wheat Shortbread: Substitute 1 cup whole wheat flour for 1 cup enriched flour.

Honey Shortbread: Use only 1/2 cup sugar and add 4 tablespoons honey.

GINGERSNAPS

2 cups sifted enriched flour
1/4 cup sugar
1 teaspoon baking soda
1/2 teaspoon salt
3 teaspoons ginger
1/2 teaspoon cinnamon
1/2 cup dry breadcrumbs
1/2 cup molasses
1/2 cup melted shortening
2 tablespoons ice water

Sift together flour, sugar, soda, salt, ginger, and cinnamon. Add crumbs, molasses, shortening, and water. Mix thoroughly.

Roll 1/8-inch thick on lightly floured board or canvas. Shape with cooky cutter.

Bake on ungreased baking sheet in moderate oven (375°F.) about 10 minutes. Makes about 7 dozen 2-inch cookies.

Refrigerator Gingersnaps: Dough may be shaped in roll, wrapped in waxed paper and stored in refrigerator. Cut chilled roll in 1/8-inch slices and bake as above.

NORWEGIAN ALMOND STICKS

3 1/2 cups sifted enriched flour
1/2 teaspoon baking powder
3 eggs, well beaten
1 cup sugar
1 cup butter or margarine, melted

1 egg white, unbeaten
1/4 cup chopped almonds

Sift together flour and baking powder.

Beat together eggs and sugar and blend in melted butter. Gradually stir in flour and mix well.

Roll out thin on lightly floured board and cut into narrow finger-length strips.

Place on greased and lightly floured cooky sheet. Brush with unbeaten egg white and dot with chopped almonds.

Bake in moderate oven (350°F.) 8 to 10 minutes. Makes 50 to 70.

DATE-FILLED ORANGE COOKIES

1 1/2 cups chopped dates
1/2 cup sugar
1 tablespoon grated orange rind
1/4 cup orange juice
1 cup butter, margarine, or shortening
1 cup light brown sugar
3 1/2 cups sifted enriched flour
2 teaspoons baking powder
1/4 teaspoon salt
1/2 cup water
1/2 teaspoon vanilla
2 cups corn flakes, slightly crushed

Combine dates, sugar, orange rind, and juice; cook over low heat until a soft paste is formed. Let cool.

Cream fat and brown sugar well. Sift flour, baking powder, and salt together; add alternately with water and vanilla to first mixture. Stir in corn flakes. Chill.

Roll dough to 1/8-inch thickness. Cut with floured 2 1/2- to 3-inch cutter.

Put a teaspoonful of filling on one round and place a second round on top, pressing edges together.

Bake on greased cooky sheet in moderate oven (375°F.) about 15 minutes. Makes 3 1/2 dozen.

Date-Filled Orange Cookies

California Fig Holiday Wreaths

CALIFORNIA FIG HOLIDAY WREATHS

1/2 cup butter or margarine
1 cup sugar
3 tablespoons cream
1 teaspoon vanilla
1 egg
2¾ cups sifted cake flour
1/2 teaspoon salt
1½ teaspoons baking powder

Cream butter; add sugar gradually and cream thoroughly. Add milk, vanilla, and beaten egg.

Sift flour with salt and baking powder; combine with other ingredients. Chill thoroughly.

Roll out 1/4-inch thick. Cut half the dough in full rounds, the remainder in doughnut shapes the same size.

Spread lower layer with Fig Filling #2; top with doughnut ring, pinch together and place on baking sheet.

Bake in moderate oven (375°F.) 12 to 15 minutes.

LECKERLIS

1 cup sugar
1/2 cup honey
1/2 cup chopped candied orange and
     lemon peel
1½ teaspoons cloves
1½ teaspoons nutmeg
1 tablespoon cinnamon
1 teaspoon baking soda
Grated rind of 1/2 lemon
1 cup unblanched almonds, sliced
   thin
2¾ cups sifted enriched flour

Heat 1/2 cup sugar and honey to boiling. Remove from heat and add peel, spices, and soda dissolved in 2 tablespoons cold water. Add remaining ingredients.

Knead until well blended. Roll dough to 1/2-inch thickness. Put on greased waxed paper on cooky sheet.

Bake in slow oven (325°F.) about 25 minutes.

Turn out on wire rack and remove paper at once. Turn right side up.

Cook remaining 1/2 cup sugar and 1/4 cup water until mixture spins a thread. Spread on Leckerlis. Cut in diamonds. Store in airtight container at least 1 week before using. Makes about 60.

GINGERBREAD BOYS

1/3 cup soft shortening
1 cup firmly packed brown sugar
1½ cups dark molasses
1/2 cup cold water
7 cups sifted enriched flour
1 teaspoon salt
1 teaspoon allspice
1 teaspoon ginger
1 teaspoon cloves
1 teaspoon cinnamon
2 teaspoons baking soda
3 tablespoons cold water

Mix shortening thoroughly with sugar and molasses. Stir in 1/2 cup cold water.

Mix and sift flour, salt, allspice, ginger, cloves, and cinnamon. Stir into first mixture.

Dissolve soda in 3 tablespoons cold water and stir in. Chill dough.

Roll out 1/2-inch thick. Cut with gingerbread boy cutter or cut around a greased cardboard cutout with a sharp knife.

Place on greased baking sheet carefully, using a wide pancake turner.

Press raisins into cookies to form eyes, nose, mouth, and shoe and cuff buttons.

Use strips of citron for tie and pieces of candied cherries or small red gumdrops for coat buttons.

Bake in moderate oven (350°F.) 15 to 18 minutes. Cool slightly.

Use white frosting to make outlines of collar, cuffs, belt, and shoes. Makes 1 dozen.

SWISS CINNAMON STARS

2 cups blanched almonds
4 egg whites
Grated rind and juice of 1/2 lemon
About 1½ pounds confectioners'
   sugar
2 tablespoons cinnamon

Grate almonds in rotary grater.

Beat egg whites until stiff. Add rind, juice, and 2 cups sugar. Continue beating until very stiff. Measure 1 cup and reserve.

To remaining mixture, add almonds and cinnamon. Put on board generously sprinkled with confectioners' sugar.

Sprinkle top with sugar. Roll very thin with sugar-dusted rolling pin. Cut with star-shaped cutter.

Put on brown paper on cooky sheets. Spread with egg white mixture.

Bake in very slow oven (250°F.) about 30 minutes.

Slip paper onto wet table or board. Let stand 1 minute. Loosen stars and lift to wire rack.

Store in airtight container 1 week before using. Makes about 60.

NORWEGIAN CHRISTMAS WREATHS

2 hard-cooked egg yolks
1/2 cup butter or margarine
1/4 cup sugar
1 cup sifted enriched flour
1/2 teaspoon vanilla

Put egg yolks through sieve and cream them with butter. Add sugar gradually and continue creaming. Then add flour and vanilla.

Roll thin and cut into doughnut-shaped cookies. Decorate with bits of candied cherry, citron, and angelica to resemble Christmas wreaths, or use red and green colored sugar.

Bake on ungreased cooky sheet in moderate oven (350°F.) 8 to 10 minutes. Makes about 24.

VALENTINE COOKIES

6 tablespoons butter or margarine
2/3 cup sugar
1 egg, well beaten
1/2 teaspoon vanilla
2 cups sifted enriched flour
2 teaspoons baking powder
1/4 teaspoon salt
1/4 cup milk

Cream butter or margarine and sugar. Add egg and vanilla and beat well.

Sift flour, baking powder, and salt; add to creamed mixture with milk to form a dough. Chill.

Roll out to 1/8-inch thickness; cut with heart-shaped cooky cutter.

Place half of the cookies on a lightly greased baking sheet; brush each with water.

Cut smaller heart-shaped centers from remaining cookies and place the heart frames on top of cookies on baking sheet. Reroll scraps.

Bake in moderate oven (375°F.) 10 to 12 minutes. Cool. Fill center heart space with cherry filling. Makes 2 dozen.

Cherry Filling: Mix 1/4 cup sugar, 1½ tablespoons cornstarch, and 1/4 teaspoon salt. Add 1/2 cup water and 1/2 cup maraschino cherry juice. Cook over low heat until thickened, stirring constantly.

Remove from heat and add 18 chopped cherries and 1 tablespoon butter or margarine. Cool.

Valentine Cookies

CITRON COOKIES

2 cups sifted cake flour
1 teaspoon cream of tartar
1/2 teaspoon baking soda
1/2 teaspoon salt
1/2 cup butter or margarine
1 cup sugar
2 eggs, separated
1/4 teaspoon each vanilla and almond extract
Candied citron
Candied cherries

Sift together flour, cream of tartar, soda, and salt.

Cream butter and sugar until light and fluffy and beat in egg yolks 1 at a time, beating well after each addition. Gradually stir in dry ingredients and mix well.

Fold in stiffly beaten egg whites flavored with vanilla and almond. Add enough flour to make dough soft enough to roll out easily.

Roll out on floured board to 1/8-inch thickness. Cut with floured cooky cutters. Arrange cherries and candied citron (cut into small pieces and strips) in flower designs on cookies. Place on greased cooky sheet.

Bake in hot oven (400°F.) 8 to 10 minutes.

Store between layers of waxed paper in airtight container.

COFFEE JUMBLES

3 cups sifted enriched flour
2 teaspoons baking powder
1/2 teaspoon salt
2/3 cup shortening
1 cup sugar
2 eggs
1/2 teaspoon almond flavor
1/4 cup strong hot coffee
Sugar
Cinnamon
Raisins
Almonds, halved

Mix and sift flour, baking powder, and salt.

Cream shortening, stir in sugar and beat until fluffy. Stir in eggs, 1 at a time, and beat well after each addition. Stir in almond flavoring.

Add sifted flour ingredients alternately with coffee. Chill in refrigerator.

Roll part of mixture 1/4-inch thick. Cut into rounds. Press edges with fork or use fancy cutter. To make bowknots, break off small pieces of dough, roll thin with fingers and knot.

Glaze cookies with egg white diluted with a little water. Sprinkle around cookies with sugar and cinnamon, and garnish with plumped raisins or halved blanched almonds.

Bake on ungreased sheet in hot oven (400°F.) 10 to 12 minutes. Makes 3 to 5 dozen cookies, depending upon size.

PINEAPPLE LEI COOKIES

1 1/4 cups drained, crushed pineapple
1/3 cup sugar
1 tablespoon cornstarch
1 teaspoon grated lemon rind
1 tablespoon lemon juice
2 cups sifted enriched flour
1/4 teaspoon baking soda
1/2 teaspoon salt
1/2 cup butter or margarine
3/4 cup sugar
1 teaspoon lemon extract
1 egg
2 tablespoons pineapple juice
1 tablespoon white (distilled) vinegar
1/4 cup shredded coconut, optional

Combine pineapple, 1/3 cup sugar, cornstarch, and lemon rind in heavy saucepan. Cook until thickened, about 5 minutes, stirring constantly. Remove from heat. Blend in lemon juice. Cool.

Sift flour, soda, and salt together.

Cream together butter or margarine, 3/4 cup sugar, and lemon extract. Beat in egg, pineapple juice, and vinegar. Blend in dry ingredients. Chill several hours.

Roll out dough 1/8-inch thick. Cut cookies with a 2 1/2-inch cutter. Cut a 1-inch hole in center of half the cookies. Place cooky circles on cooky sheet.

Drop a teaspoon of filling in center of each circle. Top with cooky rings. Press edges together firmly. If desired, sprinkle filling with coconut.

Bake in moderate oven (375°F.) 15 minutes or until lightly browned.

Cool on cake rack. Makes 2 1/2 dozen.

Pineapple Lei Cookies

CHOCOLATE HEARTS

1 cup butter or margarine
1 cup sugar
1/2 teaspoon vanilla
2/3 cup sour cream
2 ounces (2 squares) chocolate, melted
2 1/4 cups sifted enriched flour
1/4 teaspoon salt
Red food coloring

Put butter or margarine into a large bowl. Add sugar gradually and cream thoroughly. Add vanilla, sour cream, and chocolate; mix well.

Sift together flour and salt; fold into creamed mixture until thoroughly

Chocolate Hearts

blended. Chill dough in refrigerator overnight, or for several hours.

Spoon off small amount at a time; roll each to 1/4-inch thickness on a lightly floured board. Cut with heart-shaped cooky cutter.

Place 1 inch apart on lightly greased cooky sheet. Bake in moderate oven (350°F.) about 10 minutes.

Put a smaller heart-shaped cutter over each cooky. Frost inside with confectioners' sugar frosting tinted pink with a few drops of red food coloring, or frost whole cooky. Makes 3 dozen.

FANCY HOLIDAY COOKIES

1 cup butter or margarine
1 cup sugar
2 eggs
1 1/2 teaspoons vanilla
3 1/2 cups sifted enriched flour
1/2 teaspoon baking powder
1/2 teaspoon salt
1 ounce (1 square) chocolate, melted
1/2 teaspoon cinnamon
1/8 teaspoon cloves
1/8 teaspoon nutmeg
1 egg white

Cream butter or margarine and sugar; beat in eggs and vanilla.

Sift together flour, baking powder, and salt and combine with creamed mixture.

To half the mixture, add the melted chocolate and blended seasonings. Chill the doughs until firm.

Roll to 1/4-inch thickness and cut into desired shapes. Bake in the upper part of moderate oven (350°F.) 15 minutes.

Brush with egg white, decorate, and return to oven for 5 minutes. Makes 6 dozen.

Fancy Holiday Cookies

Witch Hat Cookies

WITCH HAT COOKIES

2 cups sifted enriched flour
1/3 cup nonfat dry milk powder
1 teaspoon baking powder
3/4 teaspoon salt
1/2 cup shortening
1 cup sugar
1 egg, unbeaten
1 teaspoon vanilla
2 tablespoons water
2 ounces (2 squares) unsweetened chocolate, melted

Sift together flour, nonfat milk powder, baking powder, and salt.

Cream shortening. Add sugar gradually, beating until light and fluffy. Beat in egg. Stir in vanilla and water.

Add dry ingredients gradually, beating until smooth. Stir in cooled, melted chocolate.

Divide dough into 3 portions. Wrap in waxed paper and chill several hours.

Roll out 1/8-inch thick on lightly floured board. Cut into witch hat shape. (Make hat shape out of cardboard.)

Place on well greased cooky sheet. Bake in hot oven (400°F.) 5 minutes. Decorate cooled cookies with children's names, using a confectioners' sugar frosting. Makes 38 4-inch cookies.

POLISH HONEY CAKES

1/2 cup honey
1/2 cup sugar
1 whole egg and 2 egg yolks
4 cups sifted enriched flour
1 teaspoon baking soda
1/2 teaspoon cinnamon
1/2 teaspoon nutmeg
1/4 teaspoon cloves
1/4 teaspoon ginger
Blanched almonds, halved

Warm honey slightly and combine with sugar. Add eggs, reserving a small amount of egg white, and beat well.

Sift flour with soda and spices and stir thoroughly into honey mixture. Let the dough rest overnight.

Next day roll dough to a 1/4-inch thickness; cut out with a cooky cutter. Brush with the reserved egg white, which has been beaten slightly.

Press half a blanched almond into each cooky and bake in moderate oven (375°F.) for about 15 minutes.

DATE CREAM CHEESE ROLL-UPS

1 cup butter or margarine
1/2 pound cream cheese
2 cups sifted enriched flour
1/4 teaspoon salt
Confectioners' sugar
Pitted dates

Cream butter and cheese together. Blend in flour and salt. Chill several hours or until firm enough to roll.

Roll to 1/8-inch thickness on board sprinkled with confectioners' sugar. Cut in 1x3-inch strips with pastry wheel. Put a date in center of each strip and roll up. Place folded side down, on cooky sheets.

Bake in moderate oven (375°F.) about 15 minutes.

If desired, sprinkle with confectioners' sugar. Makes about 8 dozen.

Variations: For variety, substitute nuts or candied cherries for dates.

ALMOND TEA COOKIES

1 cup butter or margarine
2/3 cup sugar
3 egg yolks
2 1/2 cups sifted enriched flour
1/2 teaspoon salt
1/2 cup ground almonds
1/2 teaspoon vanilla
Whole almonds

Cream butter and sugar together thoroughly. Blend in unbeaten egg yolks. Stir in flour, salt, ground almonds, and flavoring. Work mixture with hands until smooth.

Roll dough 1/8 to 1/4-inch thick and cut into desired shapes. (Dough may be shaped into 1-inch balls and flattened with fork.) Top with half or whole almond, using the natural (unroasted) kernel, blanched or unblanched. Bake on ungreased cooky sheet in hot oven (400°F.) about 8 to 10 minutes or until a very light brown. Makes about 5 dozen.

SWEDISH GINGERSNAPS
(Pepperkakor)

1/2 cup dark corn syrup or light molasses
1/2 cup firmly packed brown sugar
1/2 cup granulated sugar
1/2 cup butter or margarine
1 egg and 1 egg yolk, beaten
2 tablespoons sour cream
2 teaspoons cinnamon
1/2 teaspoon cloves
1 teaspoon ginger
1/2 teaspoon baking soda
1 teaspoon baking powder
2 1/2 cups sifted enriched flour

Heat syrup to boiling and add sugars and butter. Stir until dissolved. Add beaten egg and yolk and sour cream, beating well.

Sift dry ingredients together and add.

Chill several hours or until firm enough to roll thin.

Cut with floured cooky cutter and decorate, if desired, with split almonds.

Bake in hot oven (400°F.) until lightly browned, about 10 minutes. Makes about 50.

LEMON FILLED COOKIES

3/4 cup butter or margarine
1 cup sugar
1 egg, well beaten
1 1/2 teaspoons vanilla
2 1/2 cups sifted enriched flour
3/4 teaspoon baking powder
1/4 teaspoon salt
Lemon Filling (below)

Cream butter or margarine; add sugar gradually and blend ingredients until light. Add egg and vanilla and blend thoroughly.

Sift dry ingredients together and stir into creamed mixture. Mix thoroughly and chill dough.

Roll out as thin as possible on a lightly floured board and cut with a fluted cooky cutter. Place a spoonful of Lemon Filling on one round; cut two gashes in another round and cover filling. Gently lift points so filling will show. Press edges together and seal with a fork.

Place on greased baking sheet and bake in moderate oven (375°F.) 8 to 10 minutes. Makes 40 filled cookies.

Note: If cookies lose crispness because of damp weather, return them to oven for 2 to 3 minutes to crisp.

Variations: These cookies may be filled with mincemeat, preserves, or a mixture of marmalade, dates, and nuts, if desired. Or, for a single cooky, brush the unbaked cookies with beaten egg white, sprinkle with grated almonds and sugar, and bake as directed.

Lemon Filling for Cookies:

1/2 cup sugar
2 tablespoons cornstarch
1/4 teaspoon salt
1/2 cup orange juice
1 tablespoon grated lemon rind
1/4 cup lemon juice
1 tablespoon butter or margarine

Mix ingredients together in a saucepan. Bring to a rolling boil and boil 1 minute, stirring constantly. Chill before using.

Lemon Filled Cookies

Miscellaneous Small Cakes and Cookies

HINTS ABOUT MOLDED AND SHAPED COOKIES

Molded and shaped cookies are more easily made if the dough is chilled first. The dough is formed into balls or sticks, sometimes with the palms of the hands. Flouring the hands will help in handling sticky doughs.

Balls are sometimes flattened with the palms of the hands or the bottom of a glass which has been greased and dipped into flour. Redip the glass for each cooky.

ALMOND PRETZELS

- 1 cup butter or margarine
- 1 cup sugar
- 2 eggs and 2 egg yolks
- 2 cups sifted enriched flour
- 1/2 pound almonds, unblanched and ground (about 2 cups)

Cream butter; add sugar and cream thoroughly.

Add eggs and egg yolks, and beat well. Add flour and ground almonds and mix.

Knead into a large roll and place in refrigerator to harden. When thoroughly cold, cut into pieces the size of a walnut. Roll out 1/4- to 1/2-inch thick and twist into pretzel shapes.

Bake in slow oven (325°F.) until browned, about 25 minutes.

GERMAN ALMOND CRESCENTS

- 1 1/4 cups sifted enriched flour
- 1 cup blanched almonds, grated
- 1/4 cup confectioners' sugar
- 1/2 cup butter or margarine, creamed

Mix flour with almonds and confectioners' sugar. Cut in butter with the fingers as for making pastry. Knead until well blended and smooth.

Form into rolls 2 inches thick. Cut crosswise into 1/2-inch slices and shape into crescents.

A little beaten egg yolk may be added if dough is too crumbly to handle.

Place on greased baking sheet. Bake in slow oven (325°F.) until crisp. They must remain almost white. Dip in Vanilla Sugar (see Index) while still hot.

Jelly-Filled Dainties

CHINESE ALMOND COOKIES

- 2 cups sifted enriched flour
- 1/4 teaspoon baking soda
- 1/4 teaspoon salt
- 1/2 cup butter or margarine
- 2/3 cup granulated sugar
- 2/3 cup firmly packed brown sugar
- 1/2 teaspoon almond extract
- 1 egg, separated
- 2 tablespoons milk
- 1 tablespoon vinegar
- 1/2 cup finely chopped blanched almonds, toasted
- 1/3 cup blanched almonds, split in half

Sift together flour, soda, and salt.

Cream together butter or margarine, sugars, and almond extract.

Beat in egg yolk, milk, and vinegar. Blend in dry ingredients and chopped almonds.

Shape dough into 1-inch balls. Place on cooky sheet 2 1/2 inches apart. Flatten with bottom of floured water glass.

Beat egg white slightly. Brush cookies with egg white.

Press a half almond in center of each cooky.

Bake in moderate oven (375°F.) 10 to 12 minutes or until lightly browned. Cool on cake rack. Makes 4 dozen cookies

JELLY-FILLED DAINTIES

- 2 cups sifted enriched flour
- 1/2 teaspoon salt
- 1 cup soft butter or margarine
- 1/2 cup brown sugar, firmly packed
- 1 egg
- 1/2 teaspoon vanilla
- 2 cups corn flakes or 1/2 cup corn flake crumbs
- Currant, raspberry, or strawberry jelly

Sift together flour and salt. Blend butter and sugar. Add egg and vanilla; beat well. Stir in sifted dry ingredients.

Shape dough into balls about 1 inch in diameter. If using corn flakes, crush into fine crumbs. Roll cookies in corn flake crumbs. Place about 2 inches apart on ungreased baking sheets. Make dent in center of each cooky.

Bake in slow oven (300°F.) 10 minutes. Remove from oven; press down dent in top of each cooky. Return to oven and bake about 10 minutes longer. Fill centers of cookies with jelly when ready to serve. Makes about 4 dozen cookies, 1 1/2 inches in diameter.

FATTIGMANDS

Fattigmands are fried cookies of Norwegian and Swedish origin.

- 3 beaten eggs
- 3 tablespoons cream
- 3 tablespoons sugar

Chinese Almond Cookies

- 1 1/2 tablespoons melted butter or margarine
- 1 tablespoon lemon juice
- 1/2 teaspoon ground cardamom seed
- 1/4 teaspoon salt
- 4 1/2 to 5 cups sifted enriched flour

Mix together eggs, cream, and sugar. Stir in butter, lemon juice, cardamom, salt, and 2 cups flour. Mix well. Stir in enough more flour to make a stiff dough.

Wrap in waxed paper and chill at least 1 hour. Remove 1/4 of the dough at a time, and roll out on a lightly floured board or pastry cloth until paper thin.

Cut into 2-inch diamonds. Cut a slit in the center of each and pull one corner through.

Fry in hot deep fat (350°F.) until delicately browned.

Dust with confectioners' sugar before serving. Makes 10 dozen.

CINNAMON BALLS

- 1 cup soft butter or margarine
- 1/3 cup sugar
- 2 teaspoons vanilla
- 2 cups sifted cake flour
- 1 teaspoon cinnamon
- 1/2 cup corn flake crumbs
- 1 cup finely chopped pecan meats
- 1 1/2 cups sifted confectioners' sugar

Blend butter, sugar, and vanilla. Sift together flour and cinnamon; add with corn flake crumbs and pecan meats to butter mixture; mix well.

Shape into small balls; place on greased baking sheets. Bake in moderate oven (350°F.) about 25 minutes. Roll at once in confectioners' sugar. Makes about 4 dozen cookies, 1 1/2 inches in diameter.

Cinnamon Balls

ROLLED SWEDISH WAFERS

½ cup butter or margarine
½ cup sugar
2 slightly beaten eggs
1⅓ cups sifted enriched flour
¼ teaspoon lemon extract
Shredded almonds or coconut

Cream butter. Gradually add sugar and beat until smooth. Beat in eggs, flour, and lemon extract.

Drop by teaspoonfuls onto an inverted baking pan. Spread to make very thin round cookies, about 3 inches in diameter. Sprinkle with almonds or coconut.

Bake in slow oven (325°F.) 8 to 10 minutes.

Remove from pan and roll up at once, nut side up, over handle of wooden spoon. Makes 6 dozen.

PEANUT CRUNCHIES (UNBAKED)

½ cup (1 stick) butter
½ cup chunk-style peanut butter
½ pound marshmallows
2 squares (2 ounces) unsweetened chocolate
3 cups sugar-coated corn flakes

In a saucepan place butter, peanut butter, marshmallows, and chocolate; cook over low heat, stirring constantly, until ingredients are melted and well blended. Add corn flakes and mix well.

Pack into buttered 8-inch square pan and let stand until set. When cool, cut into bars. Makes 28 bars.

MARSHMALLOW-CORN FLAKE DROPS (UNBAKED)

¼ cup (½ stick) butter
½ pound marshmallows,
3 cups corn flakes

In a saucepan over low heat, cook butter and marshmallows, stirring constantly, until melted. Remove from heat and add corn flakes; mix well.

Moisten 2 spoons with cold water and form mixture into small balls; place on waxed paper-lined cooky sheets. Let stand until firm. Makes 2 dozen drops.

Peanut Crunchies
Marshmallow-Corn Flake Drops

PEANUT BUTTER FIG CRUNCHIES

¾ cup butter or margarine
¾ cup sugar
½ cup brown sugar
⅔ cup peanut butter
1 egg, slightly beaten
1 teaspoon vanilla
1¾ cups enriched flour
½ teaspoon baking soda
½ teaspoon salt
1 cup chopped dried figs
Additional sugar

Cream butter and sugars. Blend in peanut butter, egg, and vanilla. Add sifted flour, soda, salt, and figs; mix well.

Form into small balls; roll in sugar. Bake on ungreased cooky sheets in moderate oven (375°F.) 10 to 12 minutes. Makes about 5 dozen cookies.

MANDELBRODT

A German and Yiddish term meaning literally, almond bread. Mandelbrodt is an old-time almond-flavored Jewish cooky. The cooky dough is baked in a long roll, then cut into thin diagonal slices which are browned in the oven.

3 eggs
1 cup sugar
6 tablespoons salad oil
1 teaspoon lemon juice
Grated rind of 1 lemon
¼ teaspoon almond extract
2¾ cups sifted enriched flour
4 teaspoons baking powder
¼ teaspoon salt
½ cup coarsely cut blanched almonds

Beat eggs with sugar until light, then stir in oil, juice and grated rind of lemon, and almond extract.

Mix and sift flour, baking powder, and salt. Combine the 2 mixtures, adding nuts as dough is formed.

Knead on lightly floured surface and form into long rolls about 3 inches wide and 1 inch thick.

Bake in moderate oven (350°F.) until light brown, 40 to 45 minutes. Transfer to a bread board while warm and cut into ½-inch slices.

Place slices cut side up on a cooky sheet and place on top shelf of oven or under moderate broiler heat until lightly browned. Makes 36 to 40 cookies.

Chocolate Mandelbrodt: Before shaping into rolls, remove ¼ of the dough and work into it 2 tablespoons cocoa mixed with 1 tablespoon sugar and a dash of cinnamon.

Wrap remaining rolled and flattened white dough around the chocolate roll. Shape into 2 rolls and bake as directed above.

Peanut Butter Fig Crunchies

LEMON ANGEL HALOS

2 cups sifted enriched flour
1 teaspoon salt
1 teaspoon baking soda
⅔ cup shortening
1 cup firmly packed brown sugar
1 teaspoon vanilla
1 unbeaten egg
Lemon Filling (below)
Meringue (below)

Sift together flour, salt, and soda.

Blend together shortening and brown sugar, creaming well. Add vanilla and unbeaten egg; beat well. Blend in the dry ingredients gradually; mix thoroughly. Chill.

Prepare lemon filling and then meringue while dough is chilling.

Shape chilled dough into balls, using a level teaspoonful of dough for each. Place on ungreased baking sheets. Flatten to ⅛-inch thickness.

Place a rounded teaspoonful of meringue on each cooky. Then form a hollow in the center of each, using the back of a teaspoon dipped in cold water.

Bake in slow oven (300°F. 10 to 12 minutes until cream-colored. When cool, fill hollow in top of each cooky with ½ teaspoon lemon filling. Makes about 7 dozen.

Lemon Filling: Combine 1 cup sugar, ¼ cup lemon juice, 1 teaspoon grated lemon rind, and 3 slightly beaten egg yolks in saucepan. Heat to boiling, stirring constantly.

Remove from heat. Add 3 tablespoons butter; cover and cool.

Meringue: Beat 3 egg whites until slight mounds form when beater is raised. Gradually add ¾ cup sugar, beating well after each addition. Continue beating until mixture stands in stiff, glossy peaks when beater is raised.

Blend in 2 teaspoons lemon juice; beat until mixture again forms stiff peaks.

Lemon Angel Halos

MERINGUES (KISSES)
(Master Recipe)

4 egg whites
1/4 teaspoon salt
1 cup fine granulated sugar
1 teaspoon vanilla

Beat egg whites with salt until stiff and dry. Beat in sugar gradually, sprinkling in 2 tablespoonfuls at a time. Add vanilla and continue beating until mixture holds its shape.

Shape in mounds with a spoon, pastry bag, or tube on greased cooky sheets covered with lightly greased heavy paper.

Bake in very slow oven (250°F.) 50 to 60 minutes.

Remove from paper while still warm. If desired, shape in pairs. Makes about 30 large or 60 small meringues.

Meringue Variations

Coconut Kisses: In master recipe, fold in 1 cup shredded coconut before shaping.

Creole Kisses: In master recipe, fold in 1 cup finely pounded nut brittle before shaping.

Date and Walnut Meringues: In master recipe, fold 1 cup each chopped dates and nuts into meringue mixture.

Maple Nut Kisses: In master recipe, substitute 1 cup finely grated maple sugar for granulated sugar. Fold 1 cup ground nuts into meringue mixture.

Marguerites: Follow master recipe and, at the last, fold in 1 cup finely chopped nuts. Drop from a teaspoon on small chocolate or vanilla wafers. Sprinkle with granulated sugar. Bake in slow oven (300°F.) 30 minutes. Makes about 48 marguerites.

Meringue Shells: Prepare master recipe and shape in 3-inch mounds. Bake 1 to 1¼ hours. Remove from oven. Scoop out soft center with a spoon and place in oven to dry.

To serve, fill center with ice cream or sweetened fruit, and top with whipped cream or dessert sauce.

Meringue Shells with Pie Filling

Mushroom Meringues: Prepare master recipe. Shape with pastry bag or tube into rounds the size of mushroom caps. Sprinkle with cocoa or chocolate. Shape stems like mushroom stems. Bake, remove from paper, and place caps on stems.

Nut Meringue Shells: In master recipe, fold in 1 cup chopped nuts (almonds, cashews, English walnuts, pecans, or pistachio nuts) before shaping into 3-inch mounds.

Pecan Kisses: In master recipe, substitute 1 cup firmly packed brown sugar for granulated. Fold 1 cup chopped nuts into meringue mixture.

LANGUES DE CHAT OR CAT TONGUES

1/4 cup butter
1/4 cup sugar
1/2 teaspoon vanilla
2 egg whites
1/4 cup sifted enriched flour

Cream the butter; add sugar and vanilla and cream together until light and fluffy. Add egg whites, one at a time, mixing well after each addition. Sift flour a little at a time over the surface and fold in carefully.

On a buttered and floured baking sheet make small strips about 2 inches long and as thick as a pencil by putting the batter through a pastry bag fitted with a small plain tube.

Bake in very hot oven (450°F.) until edges become golden brown, about 4 minutes. Remove from baking sheet and cool on absorbent paper. Makes about 20.

Variations: These may be frosted or put a filling between two of the cakes using 3 parts chocolate frosting and 1 part crushed nut brittle.

CHERRY COOKIES

1/2 cup shortening
1/2 cup sugar
1 teaspoon salt
1 teaspoon vanilla
1/4 teaspoon almond extract
2 egg yolks
1 1/3 cups sifted enriched flour
Glacéed or well drained maraschino cherries, cut in quarters

Cream shortening, sugar, and salt. Add flavorings and egg yolks and blend well. Stir in flour until well mixed.

Quickly roll dough into long cylinder, 1 inch in diameter and cut into 1/2-inch lengths. Form balls from cut pieces and place on ungreased cooky sheet. Press a quarter cherry gently into center of each.

Bake in moderate oven (375°F.) until golden brown, 10 to 12 minutes.

Remove from pan to cake rack. Makes 3½ to 4 dozen.

Snappy Turtle Cookies

SNAPPY TURTLE COOKIES

1½ cups sifted enriched flour
1/4 teaspoon baking soda
1/4 teaspoon salt
1/2 cup butter or margarine
1/2 cup firmly packed brown sugar
1 egg
1 egg yolk (reserve white)
1/4 teaspoon vanilla
1/8 teaspoon maple flavoring, if desired
Pecan halves

Sift together flour, soda, and salt.
Cream butter or margarine; gradually add brown sugar, creaming well. Add egg and egg yolk; beat well. Blend in vanilla and maple flavoring, if desired. Add dry ingredients gradually; mix thoroughly. Dough will be soft. Chill, if desired.

Arrange split pecan halves in groups of three or five on greased baking sheets to resemble head and legs of a turtle.

Mold dough into balls; dip bottom into unbeaten egg white and press lightly onto nuts. Use a rounded teaspoonful of dough for each, so tips of nuts will show when cooky is baked.

Bake in moderate oven (350°F.) 10 to 12 minutes. Do not overbake.

Cool and frost tops generously with chocolate frosting (see below).

Chocolate Frosting: Combine 2 squares (2 ounces) chocolate or 1/3 cup semi-sweet chocolate pieces, 1/4 cup milk, and 1 tablespoon butter in top of double boiler. Heat over boiling water until chocolate melts; blend until smooth.

Remove from heat; add 1 cup sifted confectioners' sugar. Beat until smooth and glossy. If too thin, add additional confectioners' sugar until of desired consistency.

Press cookies are made by forcing the dough through a cooky press to form a variety of shapes. They are usually made from a very rich dough, and it is not necessary to grease the baking sheet unless directed otherwise in the recipe.

Spritz Cookies

SPRITZ COOKIES

Spritz cookies are Scandinavian cookies made in various shapes by means of a cooky press or pastry bag.

4½ cups sifted enriched flour
¼ teaspoon baking soda
1 teaspoon salt
2 cups shortening
1½ cups sugar
3 eggs, beaten

Sift together flour, soda, and salt.

Cream together shortening and sugar until light and fluffy. Add eggs. Add flour mixture, mixing well.

Force dough through cooky press onto cooky sheets. Bake in moderate oven (375°F.) 15 minutes. Makes 70 2-inch cookies.

VIENNESE VANILLA CRESCENTS

4 cups sifted enriched flour
1½ cups butter or margarine
Pinch of salt
4 tablespoons powdered sugar
1 cup unblanched almonds or hazelnuts, ground fine

On a pastry board, work into a soft dough the flour, butter, salt, and sugar. When blended, work in the ground nuts. Chill the dough at least 2 hours.

Then on a lightly floured board shape the dough into little-finger-thick rolls. Cut off pieces 2 inches long.

Bend them into crescents and bake on a lightly floured cooky sheet in a moderate oven (350°F.) for 10 to 15 minutes without allowing them to color. While still hot remove with a broad knife and roll them carefully in Vanilla Sugar (see Index).

TEXAS STARS

Chocolate Dough:

2 tablespoons butter or margarine
1 package (6 ounces) semi-sweet chocolate pieces
1 can (15 ounces) minus 2 tablespoons sweetened condensed milk (reserve remaining milk)
1 cup sifted enriched flour
½ cup walnuts, chopped
1 teaspoon vanilla

Melt butter or margarine with chocolate pieces over boiling water. Remove from heat.

Blend in condensed milk; add flour and mix thoroughly. Stir in walnuts and vanilla. Mix well. Chill at least 1 hour.

White Dough:

¾ cup soft butter or margarine
½ cup sugar
1½ cups sifted enriched flour
2 tablespoons sweetened condensed milk (reserved from chocolate dough recipe
¾ cup crisp ready-to-eat cereal (shredded type or crumbled flakes)
1 cup chopped coconut
Additional ½ cup crushed ready-to-eat cereal
¼ cup sifted confectioners' sugar

Cream the butter or margarine. Gradually add sugar, creaming well.

Blend in flour and 2 tablespoons condensed milk. Mix thoroughly. Add cereal; mix well. Chill 15 to 30 minutes, if desired.

Combine coconut and the additional ½ cup cereal.

Roll out chilled white dough to ⅛-inch thickness on pastry cloth or board which has been sprinkled with confectioners' sugar. Cut into rounds with 2-inch cutter; place ½ inch apart on ungreased baking sheet.

Drop chilled chocolate dough by teaspoonfuls into coconut-cereal mixture and roll to coat thoroughly. Mold into balls and flatten into 2-inch circles.

Place chocolate circles on top of white circles and press down to seal.

Shape into five-pointed stars by pinching white and chocolate doughs together with left thumb and index finger to form each point.

Bake in moderate oven (350°F.) 12 to 15 minutes.

Cool and store in tightly covered container. Makes 4 dozen.

Peanut Butter Cookies

PEANUT BUTTER COOKIES

1⅔ cups sifted enriched flour
1½ teaspoons baking powder
Few grains salt
½ cup butter or margarine
½ cup firmly packed brown sugar
½ cup dark corn syrup
½ cup peanut butter
1 well beaten egg
½ teaspoon vanilla
Additional ½ cup peanut butter, optional*

Mix and sift together flour, baking powder, and salt.

Cream butter or margarine; gradually add sugar, and cream until light and fluffy.

Add syrup and ½ cup peanut butter, beating until smooth and well blended. Add beaten egg and vanilla.

Add sifted dry ingredients, a little at a time, mixing well after each addition.

Shape dough into balls, about 1 inch in diameter. Place on ungreased baking sheet; flatten cookies with a fork. Place about ½ teaspoon of peanut butter on top of each cooky.

Bake in moderate oven (350°F.) 12 to 15 minutes. Makes about 3½ dozen.

*Note: If desired, chopped peanuts may be substituted for peanut butter.

Texas Stars

PFEFFERNÜSSE

Literally, German for peppernuts; these are hard, spicy cookies the size of a large nut, sometimes containing black pepper. They are traditionally made at Christmas time.

4   cups sifted enriched flour
1   teaspoon baking soda
1/2 teaspoon salt
1   tablespoon cinnamon
1   teaspoon cloves
1   teaspoon nutmeg
1/4 teaspoon black pepper
1   tablespoon crushed cardamom seed
1   teaspoon anise seed
1/4 pound candied orange peel
1/2 pound citron
2   tablespoons butter or margarine
2 1/2 cups powdered sugar
5   eggs, separated
1 1/2 teaspoons grated lemon rind
About 1/4 cup milk or water
1   cup confectioners' sugar

Mix and sift flour, soda, salt and spices. Stir in seeds, then ground orange peel and citron.

Mix together butter and sugar; add well beaten egg yolks and lemon rind and beat thoroughly. Gradually stir in flour-fruit mixture and fold in stiffly beaten egg whites. Chill 1 hour.

Shape in small balls the size of walnuts. Place on cloth and let stand, uncovered, overnight at room temperature.

In the morning brush balls with thin confectioners' icing made by gradually stirring milk into confectioners' sugar.

Place on ungreased baking sheet and bake in moderate oven (350°F.) 15 to 20 minutes. Makes about 7 1/2 dozen.

TEIGLACH (HONEY BALLS)

Teiglach is a Yiddish term for a Jewish holiday confection made of small pieces of rich dough, sometimes with nuts added, cooked in a syrup of honey, sugar, and often spices. They may be stored and served in the syrup. There is also a dry version.

Dough:
3   eggs
2   cups sifted enriched flour
1/4 teaspoon salt
1/2 teaspoon cinnamon or nutmeg
Chopped almonds, optional

Honey Syrup:
1   cup honey (1 pound)
1   cup sugar
1   teaspoon ginger

Beat eggs slightly in a large mixing bowl. Mix and sift flour, salt, and cinnamon or nutmeg; stir into eggs to form a stiff dough.

Turn out onto a lightly floured surface and knead 1 or 2 minutes. Pat a small ball of this dough into 1/2-inch

thickness and cut into 1/4-inch squares. Remove the cut squares to a large platter and continue with the remaining dough until all has been cut.

Or roll small pieces of dough to form long 1/4-inch rolls, and then cut into 1/4-inch pieces.

Combine honey, sugar, and ginger in a large kettle and bring to a rolling boil.

Drop in the bits of dough a few at a time to prevent lowering of temperature of syrup.

After all have been dropped in, reduce heat and cook about 20 minutes, using a wooden spoon to prevent boiling over. Do not stir while cooking.

Turn out on a wet wooden board and pat with wet wooden spoon to an even thickness, about 1/2 inch.

If almonds are used, spread them evenly over the wet board before turning out the teiglach carefully over them without spreading the chopped nuts too far apart.

Let cool, then cut into small diamond or square shapes 1 to 1 1/2 inches in diameter.

Teiglach may be prepared well in advance of the day on which they are to be served. Store in jars or a crock after they are thoroughly cold.

Variation: If desired, individual cuts of the dough may be dropped into the boiling syrup and cooked a few at a time, skimming out as they rise to the top, about 7 or 8 minutes, then placed on a platter. When cold, store in jars.

COOKY DESSERT SHELLS

1/3 cup butter or margarine
1/2 cup sugar
1   egg
1   tablespoon orange juice
1 1/2 cups sifted enriched flour
1   teaspoon baking powder
1/4 teaspoon salt

Add sugar gradually to butter or margarine and cream thoroughly. Add egg and orange juice and mix well.

Sift flour, baking powder, and salt into creamed mixture. Blend well. Chill dough a few hours.

Roll dough to 1/8-inch thickness on lightly floured board; cut into large rounds. Invert muffin cups and grease outside of cups. Place rounds over cups; press down and pinch edges of dough at intervals to fit cups. Prick with a fork.

Bake in moderate oven (375°F.) 6 to 8 minutes.

Cool 1 minute before removing shells. Fill with fresh strawberries, chocolate pudding, or vanilla ice cream topped with apricot marmalade or any other favorite sauce. Makes 10 to 12 shells.

Chocolate Twin Dots

CHOCOLATE TWIN DOTS

1/2 cup dates
1/4 cup water
1   package (6 ounces) semi-sweet chocolate pieces
1 1/2 cups sifted enriched flour
1   teaspoon salt
1/2 teaspoon baking soda
3/4 cup shortening
1 1/2 cups firmly packed brown sugar
1   egg, unbeaten
1   teaspoon vanilla
1/2 cup quick-cooking oats, uncooked
1   cup currants or raisins
1/2 cup sifted confectioners' sugar
1/2 cup finely chopped nuts

Place dates, cut fine, in 1/4 cup water in saucepan and simmer until soft, 2 to 3 minutes. Cool.

Melt 2/3 cup chocolate pieces over hot water. (Reserve remaining 1/3 package.)

Sift together flour, salt, and soda.

Blend together shortening and brown sugar, creaming well. Add egg and vanilla and the melted chocolate. Beat well.

Blend in the dry ingredients gradually. Stir in the oats and currants or raisins and the cool dates. Chill if necessary for easy handling.

Drop by rounded teaspoonfuls into sifted confectioners' sugar. Coat thoroughly and form into balls. Dip tops into chopped nuts.

Place on greased baking sheets. Press two of the reserved semi-sweet chocolate pieces close together into the top of each cooky.

Bake in moderate oven (375°F.) 10 to 12 minutes.

Cool 1 minute before removing from baking sheets. Cool thoroughly and store in tightly covered container. Makes about 5 dozen.

Cooky Dessert Shells

Sparkling Almond Rounds

SPARKLING ALMOND ROUNDS

¼ cup butter or margarine
½ cup shortening
1 cup sugar
¼ teaspoon almond extract
1 egg
1⅓ cups sifted enriched flour
1¼ teaspoons baking powder
¼ teaspoon each mace, cinnamon, salt
⅓ cup finely chopped unblanched almonds

Brown butter or margarine in 1½-quart saucepan; remove from heat and add shortening, stirring to melt. Then blend in sugar and almond extract.

Beat in egg with spoon. (Mixture will thicken and become smooth). Mix in sifted dry ingredients and almonds.

Use teaspoon measure to take out pieces of dough; form small balls and drop into a dish of sugar; roll to coat well.

Place sugared balls about 2 inches apart on greased cooky sheet. Bake in moderate oven (375°F.) about 10 minutes or until light golden brown. Makes about 4½ dozen 2-inch cookies.

Keep crisp by storing in a canister or jar with a loose-fitting cover.

HUNGARIAN CREAM CHEESE KIPFEL

1 cup butter or margarine
1 cup (½ pound) cream cheese
2 cups sifted enriched flour
½ teaspoon salt
½ pound chopped nuts
4 tablespoons sugar
Grated rind of 1 lemon
Dash of cinnamon

Combine quickly with hands the butter, cheese, flour, and salt. Place in refrigerator overnight.

Roll out ⅛-inch thick on floured board. Cut into 2-inch squares.

Mix together nuts, sugar, lemon rind, and cinnamon. Place a small amount on each square, fold over, and seal edges.

Bake in moderate oven (375°F.) 10 to 15 minutes.

Sprinkle with powdered sugar. Makes about 80.

Variations: Kipfel may also be filled with jam or stewed dried fruit.

PRALINE COOKIES

½ cup butter or margarine
1½ cups firmly packed brown sugar
1 egg, unbeaten
1½ cups sifted enriched flour
1 teaspoon vanilla
1 cup coarsely chopped pecans

Cream butter. Add sugar and egg and blend. Add flour, vanilla, and nuts. Mix well.

Shape into balls the size of a walnut. Place on greased cooky sheet and flatten out to about ⅛-inch thick.

Bake in moderate oven (375°F.) 12 minutes or until browned. Makes 3 dozen.

SWEDISH FRIED COOKIES

3 beaten eggs
3 tablespoons cream
3 tablespoons sugar
½ teaspoon salt
Flour

Combine eggs, cream, sugar, salt, and flour. Use enough flour to make very firm dough. Roll out dough very thin. Cut in diamond shapes.

Cut a slit in center of each diamond; draw one point of cooky through it.

Fry in hot deep fat (350°F.) ½ to 1 minute or until golden brown.

Drain on absorbent paper. Sprinkle with granulated sugar. Makes about 36.

MAPLE RICE CRISP COOKIES

1¾ cups sifted enriched flour
¾ teaspoon baking soda
1 teaspoon salt
1 teaspoon cinnamon
¼ cup milk
1 egg, beaten
1 teaspoon maple flavoring
½ cup shortening
1 cup sugar
1 cup pre-sweetened rice cereal
½ cup chopped nuts
1½ cups pre-sweetened rice cereal for rolling cookies

Combine and sift flour, soda, salt, and cinnamon. Combine milk, egg, and flavoring.

Cream shortening and sugar until light and fluffy. Add dry ingredients and liquids alternately one-half at a time. Stir only until dry ingredients are moistened. Fold in cereal and nuts carefully.

Roll rounded teaspoonfuls of cooky dough in additional pre-sweetened rice cereal.

Place on greased cooky sheet and bake in moderate oven (350°F.) until done, about 15 minutes. Remove from cooky sheet; cool. Makes 40 to 42 cookies.

Three-Way Banana Oatmeal Cookies

THREE-WAY BANANA OATMEAL COOKIES

2 cups sifted enriched flour
1 teaspoon cinnamon
¼ teaspoon nutmeg
1½ teaspoons salt
1 teaspoon baking powder
¼ teaspoon baking soda
1 cup sugar
1 cup soft shortening
1 cup mashed bananas (2 to 3)
2 eggs
2 cups uncooked oats

Sift together flour, spices, salt, baking powder, soda, and sugar; add shortening, mashed bananas, and eggs.

Beat until smooth, about 2 minutes; fold in rolled oats. Divide cooky dough in three parts.

Bar Cookies: Spread one-third of dough in a well greased 8-inch square pan. Bake in moderate oven (375°F.) 15 to 20 minutes. Let stand 10 minutes.

Turn out of pan; cut in bars or squares; roll in confectioners' sugar while still warm.

Drop Cookies: Drop second portion of cooky dough by teaspoons onto well greased cooky sheet. Decorate with chocolate chips, nuts, or raisins, if desired.

Bake in moderate oven (375°F.) 10 to 12 minutes.

Rolled Cookies: Refrigerate third portion of dough overnight.

Sprinkle a board or canvas generously with confectioners' sugar. Roll out cooky dough to ¼-inch thickness, sprinkling with additional sugar while rolling if necessary to prevent sticking. Cut in 2-inch circles or fancy shapes.

Bake on greased cooky sheet in moderate oven (350°F.) 8 to 10 minutes, or until brown.

Maple Rice Crisp Cookies

ROCKS

1   cup butter or margarine
1   cup sugar
4   eggs, separated
2¼ cups sifted enriched flour
1   teaspoon cinnamon
1   teaspoon cloves
1   cup black walnut meats
1½ cups raisins
1   teaspoon baking soda
1½ tablespoons boiling water

Cream butter; add sugar and beat until smooth. Beat in egg yolks one at a time.

Sift flour, cinnamon, and cloves together. Add walnuts and raisins to flour. Stir into creamed mixture, mixing well.

Dissolve soda in boiling water; add to batter.

Beat egg whites until stiff; fold into batter.

Drop from teaspoon onto baking sheet. Bake in moderate oven (350°F.) 15 to 20 minutes or until done. Makes about 4 dozen.

PEANUT BRITTLE COOKIES

1   cup sifted enriched flour
¼   teaspoon baking soda
½   teaspoon cinnamon
½   cup butter or other shortening
½   cup firmly packed brown sugar
2   tablespoons beaten egg (reserve remainder)
1   teaspoon vanilla
½   cup salted peanuts, finely chopped
1   tablespoon egg
Additional ½ cup salted peanuts or other nuts

Sift together flour, soda, and cinnamon.

Cream butter or other shortening; gradually add sugar, creaming well. Add 2 tablespoons beaten egg and vanilla; beat well.

Blend in dry ingredients and ½ cup chopped peanuts. Mix thoroughly.

Spread or pat dough on greased baking sheet to a 14x10-inch rectangle. Brush with remaining 1 tablespoon egg. Sprinkle with ½ cup salted peanuts or other nuts.

Bake in slow oven (325°F.) 20 to 25 minutes. Do not overbake.

Cut or break into pieces while warm. Makes about 2 dozen.

Peanut Brittle Cookies

LEBKUCHEN
(German Honey Cakes)

A frosted spicy rectangular German cooky, frequently served during the Christmas season.

4   cups sifted cake flour
¼   teaspoon baking soda
¾   teaspoon cinnamon
⅛   teaspoon nutmeg
⅛   teaspoon cloves
⅔   cup honey
½   cup firmly packed brown sugar
2   tablespoons water
1   egg, slightly beaten
¾   cup shredded candied orange peel
¾   cup shredded candied citron
1   cup almonds, blanched and shredded

Sift flour once and measure. Add soda and spices, and sift together 3 times.

Combine honey, sugar, and water and boil 5 minutes. Cool. Add flour, egg, orange peel, citron, and nuts.

Press dough into a cake and wrap in waxed paper. Store in refrigerator 2 or 3 days to ripen.

Roll ¼ inch thick on lightly floured board. Cut in 1x3-inch strips.

Bake on greased baking sheet in moderate oven (350°F.) 15 minutes.

When cool, spread with Transparent Glaze (see below). Store at least 1 day before serving. Makes about 5 dozen strips.

Transparent Glaze: Combine 2 cups sifted confectioners' sugar and 3 tablespoons boiling water. Add 1 teaspoon vanilla. Beat thoroughly. Spread on cookies while glaze is still warm.

Note: These cookies are characteristically hard and chewy. They develop a better flavor upon storage. Store 2 weeks or longer for best flavor.

SNICKERDOODLES

2¾ cups sifted enriched flour
2   teaspoons cream of tartar
1   teaspoon baking soda
½   teaspoon salt
1   cup soft shortening
1½ cups sugar
2   eggs

Sift together flour, cream of tartar, soda, and salt.

Cream shortening; gradually beat in sugar and eggs; stir in dry ingredients. Chill dough.

Form into balls the size of small walnuts. Roll in mixture of 2 tablespoons sugar and 2 teaspoons cinnamon. Place about 2 inches apart on ungreased baking sheet.

Bake in hot oven (400°F.) until lightly browned, but still soft, about 8 to 10 minutes.

These cookies puff up at first, then flatten out with crinkled tops. Makes about 5 dozen 2-inch cookies.

Slice 'N Serve Cookies

SLICE 'N SERVE COOKIES

¾   cup (5 ounces) dates
1   tablespoon flour
⅔   cup sifted enriched flour
½   teaspoon baking powder
½   teaspoon salt
3   eggs
¾   cup granulated sugar
½   teaspoon vanilla
½   cup pecans, finely chopped
20 maraschino cherries
1   tablespoon confectioners' sugar
1   cup pecans, finely chopped

Prepare dates by placing in a sieve and pouring boiling water over them. Cut fine with scissors or knife which has been dipped in hot water. Coat with 1 tablespoon flour.

Sift together ⅔ cup flour, baking powder, and salt.

Beat eggs until foamy. Gradually add ¾ cup sugar, beating constantly until thick and ivory colored. Blend in vanilla.

Fold in the dry ingredients carefully but thoroughly. Then fold in ½ cup pecans, finely chopped, and the cut-up dates.

Spread in 15x11-inch jelly roll pan which has been lined with waxed paper, then greased generously and floured lightly.

Drain maraschino cherries. Arrange 10 cherries across each end of batter about ½ inch in from edge of pan.

Bake in slow oven (325°F.) 30 to 35 minutes.

Turn hot cake out onto waxed paper which has been sprinkled with 1 tablespoon confectioners' sugar. Remove paper, trim the edges and cut crosswise into two 11x7½-inch rectangles.

Roll each rectangle tightly, beginning with the cherry end. Wrap in waxed paper and chill.

Spread chilled rolls thinly with butter frosting (below) and roll in 1 cup chopped pecans. Chill. To serve, cut in ¼- to ½-inch slices.

Butter Frosting: Cream 2 tablespoons butter or margarine. Blend in 1¼ cups sifted confectioners' sugar alternately with 3 to 4 teaspoons cream. Add ¼ teaspoon vanilla. Beat until creamy and smooth.

FRIED BOHEMIAN TWISTS

2 cups sifted enriched flour
1 tablespoon sugar
1 teaspoon butter or margarine
1/2 teaspoon salt
2 egg yolks
1 whole egg
2 tablespoons cream

Mix the flour, sugar, butter and salt together until smooth. Add the egg yolks one at a time, mixing well. Now add the whole egg and mix well. Add the cream gradually.

Turn onto a board and knead until dough does not cling to hands or board. Roll to paper thinness.

Cut dough into oblongs 4x6 inches, using pastry-wheel. Gash pieces with 5 or 6 cuts through center lengthwise and parallel. Do not cut to edges of rectangle.

Lift with fork; poke a corner or two through the gashes, twist and drop into deep hot fat (370°F.). Fry until golden brown, turning once. Sprinkle with confectioners' sugar. Makes 12 oblongs.

PECAN CANDY COOKIES

1/4 cup sugar
1/4 cup pecans
1/3 cup butter or margarine
1/3 cup shortening
1/4 cup firmly packed brown sugar
1 1/2 cups sifted enriched flour
1/2 teaspoon salt
1 teaspoon vanilla
Confectioners' sugar

Place 1/4 cup sugar and pecans in heavy skillet. Place over low heat and cook, stirring constantly, until sugar is melted and golden brown. Turn out onto buttered waxed paper and cool. When hard, chop fine.

Cream butter and shortening until light and fluffy. Blend in brown sugar, flour, and salt. Add vanilla and pecan candy.

Form into balls in palms of hands. Place on ungreased cooky sheets. Bake in slow oven (300°F.) 30 minutes.

Roll in confectioners' sugar while warm. Makes about 36.

SUGAR AND SPICE BALLS

2 cups corn flakes
1 cup butter or margarine
1/3 cup sugar
2 teaspoons vanilla
2 cups sifted cake flour
1 teaspoon cinnamon
1 cup finely chopped nuts
1 1/2 cups sifted confectioners' sugar

Crush corn flakes into fine crumbs. Blend butter, sugar, and vanilla.

Sift together flour and cinnamon; add with corn flake crumbs and nuts to butter mixture; mix well.

Shape into small balls and place on greased baking sheets. Bake in moderate oven (350°F.) about 30 minutes.

Roll at once in confectioners' sugar. Makes about 4 dozen balls 1 1/2 inches in diameter.

CRISP SWEDISH NUT CRESCENTS

1/4 cup butter or margarine
3/4 cup sugar
1 well beaten egg
2 tablespoons milk
1 teaspoon vanilla
1 1/3 cups sifted enriched flour
2 teaspoons salt
1 teaspoon baking powder
1 cup chopped pecans
1/2 cup sugar

Cream butter and sugar together. Add egg, milk, and vanilla.

Mix and sift flour, salt, and baking powder; stir into butter mixture.

Spread dough very thin and evenly on bottom of buttered, inverted 8x8-inch pans.

Sprinkle with pecans and sugar. Mark in strips 3/4x4 inches.

Bake 1 pan at a time in slow oven (325°F.) 10 to 12 minutes.

While hot, cut into strips and shape over a rolling pin. If strips become too brittle to shape, return to oven to reheat and soften. Makes 9 dozen.

NORWEGIAN ANISE COOKIES

2 3/4 cups sifted enriched flour
2 1/2 teaspoons baking powder
1/2 teaspoon salt
1/2 cup sugar
1/2 cup shortening
1 teaspoon anise seed
1 egg, beaten
1/3 cup milk
Sesame or poppy seed

Mix and sift flour, baking powder, salt, and sugar. Cut in shortening with pastry blender or 2 knives until mixture resembles coarse corn meal. Add anise seed.

Add beaten egg to milk. Make a "well" in the dry ingredients and add egg mixture. Stir until a smooth stiff dough is formed.

Pinch off balls of dough about 3 inches in diameter. Roll into strip about 1/4 inch in diameter. Cut in lengths about 6 inches long.

Twist into various shapes, such as S, U, rosettes, figure 8, etc. Press gently into sesame seed. Place seed side up, on ungreased cooky sheet.

Bake in moderate oven (375°F.) about 15 minutes.

These cookies should be short and rich. Makes about 3 dozen.

GINGER COOKIES

5 cups sifted enriched flour
3 teaspoons baking soda
1/2 teaspoon salt
3 teaspoons ginger
1 cup shortening
2 cups firmly packed brown sugar
2 eggs, beaten
1 teaspoon vinegar
1/2 cup dark molasses

Mix and sift flour, soda, salt, and ginger.

Cream shortening; add sugar and cream until fluffy. Add beaten eggs, vinegar, and molasses. Mix in dry ingredients.

Form into balls, using about 1 tablespoon dough for each. Place on cooky sheet.

Bake in hot oven (400°F.) 12 to 15 minutes.

The cookies are very soft when done, but harden when cool. Makes 5 dozen.

SWEETHEARTS

1/4 cup butter or margarine
3/4 cup sugar
1 egg
1/2 teaspoon vanilla
1 1/4 cups sifted enriched flour
1 1/2 teaspoons baking powder
1/4 teaspoon salt
1/3 cup milk

Cream butter or margarine with sugar until light; add egg and vanilla and beat until fluffy.

Sift flour, baking powder, and salt. Add to creamed mixture with milk and stir smooth.

Brush a flat baking pan with butter or margarine; line with waxed paper and brush with butter or margarine again. Spread batter into pan.

Bake in moderate oven (375°F.) 15 to 20 minutes.

Remove from pan; cool and, with cooky cutter, cut out in heart shapes. Spread pink icing between hearts, sandwich fashion, and on top and sides. Decorate each with a candy heart if desired.

Pink Icing: Combine 2 1/2 cups sifted confectioners' sugar, 4 tablespoons cream, 1/4 teaspoon salt, and 1 teaspoon vanilla. Tint a delicate pink with red food coloring. Makes 11 double hearts or 22 single hearts.

Sweethearts

PECAN BUTTER BALLS

2 cups sifted enriched flour
1/4 cup sugar
1/2 teaspoon salt
1 cup butter or margarine
2 teaspoons vanilla
3 cups finely chopped pecans

Mix and sift flour, sugar, and salt. Work in butter and vanilla. Add 2 cups nuts and mix well.

Shape in 1-inch balls. Roll balls in remaining 1 cup nuts. Bake on cooky sheets in slow oven (325°F.) about 25 minutes. Makes about 4 1/2 dozen.

Variations: Almonds, filberts, or walnuts can also be used. If desired, omit 1 cup nuts and roll cookies while warm in fine granulated sugar.

HEDGEHOGS

2 cups walnuts
1 cup dates, pitted
1 cup firmly packed brown sugar
2 cups shredded coconut
2 unbeaten eggs

Grind walnuts and dates in food chopper. Add sugar, 1 cup coconut, and eggs, and mix thoroughly.

Shape into rolls about 1 inch long and 1/2 inch in diameter. Roll each cooky in remaining coconut.

Place on greased cooky sheets and bake in moderate oven (350°F.) 15 minutes. Makes about 60.

CHILEAN LOVE KNOTS

1 egg
2 tablespoons heavy cream
2 tablespoons sugar
Pinch of salt
1 teaspoon cinnamon
Sifted flour

Beat the egg until very light. Beat in the cream, sugar, salt, and cinnamon. Beat hard, then add enough sifted flour to make a stiff paste. Roll out thin and cut into long narrow strips. Tie each into two or three knots. Fry until golden brown in deep hot fat.

Drain and dust with powdered sugar while hot. Serve with fruit sauce of any kind.

Heart-Shaped Tea Cakes

SWEDISH SPRITZBAAKEN COOKIES

(Mrs. Dwight D. Eisenhower's favorite cooky recipe.)

1 pound butter
1 cup sugar
2 whole eggs
2 extra egg yolks
4 1/2 cups sifted enriched flour
Vanilla

Cream sugar and butter. Add beaten eggs, then flour gradually, then vanilla to taste. Use cooky press and form your own design.

Bake in a moderate oven (350° to 375°F.) 20 minutes or until done.

Should be light in color. These bake very quickly and need to be watched constantly. Makes 100 cookies.

SWEDISH AMMONIA COOKIES (DROMMAR)

(These are the famous Swedish Dreams)

1/2 pound butter (1 cup)
1/2 pound sugar (1 1/8 cups)
1/2 pound sifted enriched flour (2 cups)
1 scant teaspoon ammonia salt
1 teaspoon vanilla

Cream the butter; add sugar and cream thoroughly, using an electric beater if possible.

Beat in the sifted flour, ammonia salt, and vanilla.

Put in refrigerator for a few hours, then shape into small balls and bake in a slow oven (300°F.).

HEART-SHAPED TEA CAKES

1/2 cup butter or margarine
1/4 cup sugar
1 egg plus 1 egg yolk
3/4 cup mild old-fashioned molasses
3/4 cup milk
1 teaspoon vanilla
2 cups sifted enriched flour
3 teaspoons baking powder
1/4 teaspoon salt

Cream butter; gradually add sugar and beat until fluffy. Add whole egg and egg yolk one at a time and beat until mixture is puffy light.

Measure molasses into milk. Add vanilla. Sift together the dry ingredients. Add dry ingredients and liquid, alternately to first mixture, mixing until smooth.

Bake in well greased heart-shaped tea cake pans in moderate oven (350°F.) 20 to 25 minutes.

Frost with confectioners' icing. Decorate cakes while frosting is moist with vari-colored candy bits, chopped nuts, or halves of nuts.

Pecan Roll Cookies

PECAN ROLL COOKIES

1/2 cup butter or margarine
1/3 cup confectioners' sugar, unsifted
1/4 teaspoon vanilla
1/2 teaspoon almond extract
1 1/2 cups sifted cake flour
1/2 cup chopped pecans
Whole pecan halves

Cream butter thoroughly; add sugar, and beat until creamy. Stir in flavorings.

Add flour in several portions, beating after each addition. Add chopped nuts.

Shape small portions of dough into rolls about 2 inches long and 1/2 inch in diameter. Press a pecan half on top of each cooky.

Bake on buttered cooky sheet in moderate oven (350°F.) 10 to 15 minutes.

While hot, sprinkle lightly with confectioners' sugar. Cool on cake racks. Makes 2 1/2 to 3 dozen cookies, depending upon size.

MELTING MOMENTS

1/2 cup butter or margarine
5 tablespoons confectioners' sugar
1 teaspoon almond extract
1/4 teaspoon salt
1 cup sifted enriched flour
1 teaspoon baking powder

Cream butter, sugar, almond extract, and salt until light and fluffy. Add flour and baking powder and blend. Chill.

Form into balls, using a teaspoonful of cooky dough for each ball. Place on ungreased cooky sheet. Flatten with fork dipped in flour.

Bake in moderate oven (350°F.) until edges are browned, 8 to 10 minutes.

Cool before removing from pan. Makes 4 dozen.

Variations: If desired, decorate with candy decorations or colored sugar before baking.

Melting Moments
For a crisscross effect, flatten each cooky with the floured tines of a fork.

DESSERTS

Desserts, plain or fancy, are the crowning touch to a meal. Whether you choose a traditional recipe or one that takes advantage of today's easy-on-the-cook ingredients, you can turn out wonderful desserts that will please your family or dazzle company.

The desserts presented here run the gamut from homelike simplicity to high sophistication. Included are the desserts every family depends on from day to day as well as the famous desserts of many lands. Choosing the right dessert is as much of an art as preparing it. Well cooked and attractively served, the plain ones, too, can be exciting.

Always choose a dessert that suits your menu. If the meal has been light choose a rich dessert, or select a light one for a heavy meal. Plan to make your choice of desserts an essential part of your food planning pattern. They can go a long way in rounding out the needs for essential nutrients—especially for the children.

Custards and Other Puddings

BAKED CUSTARD

(Master Recipe)

⅓ cup sugar
¼ teaspoon salt
4　eggs, slightly beaten
3　cups milk, scalded
½ teaspoon vanilla
Few grains nutmeg

Add sugar and salt to eggs. Beat until thoroughly mixed. Add milk to egg mixture, stirring constantly. Add vanilla.

Strain into buttered custard cups and sprinkle lightly with nutmeg. Set molds in baking pan. Pour enough hot water into pan to reach level of custard.

Bake in slow oven (325°F.) until firm, 25 to 35 minutes, or until silver knife put into center comes out clean. Chill. Serves 6 to 8.

Baked Custard Variations

Large Mold: Use 6 eggs; bake 1 to 1½ hours. Use silver knife test.

Bread Custard Pudding: In master recipe, substitute 1 cup breadcrumbs for 2 of the eggs. Add raisins, candied peel, or other chopped fruit. Mix and bake.

Caramel Custard: In master recipe, add ½ cup caramelized sugar syrup to milk. Or pour 1 to 1½ tablespoons caramel syrup into each cup before pouring in custard mixture. Bake. Unmold to serve.

Chocolate Custard: In master recipe, add 2 squares (2 ounces) unsweetened chocolate to milk before scalding. Beat with rotary beater until blended.

Coconut Custard: Add ¾ cup shredded coconut to custard mixture of master recipe.

Date or Nut Custard: Follow master recipe; mix 1 cup either chopped dates or nuts with custard before baking.

Fruit Custard: Place pieces of soft or soaked dried apricots or other fruit in bottom of molds before pouring in custard.

Gingerbread Custard: Prepare master recipe. Use 1½ cups crumbled gingerbread. Place 3 tablespoons in each buttered cup before pouring in custard.

Golden Custard: In master recipe, use 8 egg yolks. Omit whites.

Honey Custard: In master recipe, substitute ½ cup honey for sugar. Omit vanilla and nutmeg. Add dash of cinnamon.

Maple Custard: Prepare master recipe. Pour 1 to 1½ tablespoons maple syrup into each cup. Pour in custard mixture carefully so that syrup is not disturbed. Bake. Unmold to serve.

Or substitute 4 tablespoons maple syrup or sugar for granulated sugar in master recipe.

Marshmallow Custard: Put 2 cut-up marshmallows into bottom of each cup. Sprinkle with shredded coconut before pouring in custard.

Rice Custard: Prepare master recipe. Add 1 cup cooked rice to strained custard and grated rind of ½ lemon.

Silver Custard: In master recipe, substitute 2 egg whites for each whole egg.

MEXICAN FLAN

½ cup sugar
1　14-ounce can sweetened condensed milk
¾ cup milk
½ teaspoon vanilla
⅛ teaspoon salt
4　eggs, lightly beaten
2　ripe bananas, mashed
2　tablespoons lemon juice

Caramelize sugar by heating in a heavy skillet. Pour into a shallow 1-quart mold, coating the bottom and sides well.

In a saucepan combine sweetened condensed milk, milk, vanilla, salt, eggs, bananas, and lemon juice. Heat, stirring, until well blended. Pour into mold.

Set mold in pan of hot water. Bake in moderate oven (350°F.) 65 to 70 minutes or until set. Cool. Unmold and chill until ready to serve. Garnish with mandarin orange sections and serve with shortbread cookies. Serves 6 to 8.

SOFT CUSTARD
(Master Recipe)

3 to 4 eggs, slightly beaten, or 4 to 6
      egg yolks
3 tablespoons sugar
1/8 teaspoon salt
2 cups milk, scalded
1 teaspoon vanilla

Combine beaten eggs, sugar, and salt. Slowly stir in scalded milk, stirring constantly.

Strain, then cook over simmering water 5 minutes or until mixture thickens and coats back of spoon.

Add flavoring, strain at once, and chill. Serve as sauce or dessert. Serves 4 to 6.

Soft Custard Variations

Almond Custard: Top each portion with chopped toasted almonds before serving.

Chocolate Custard: Follow master recipe. Melt 2 squares (2 ounces) unsweetened chocolate. Blend with scalded milk before adding to eggs. Add 1 tablespoon sugar.

Coconut Custard: Pour soft custard into baking dish. Beat 3 egg whites until stiff; fold in 1/3 cup sugar and 1/2 cup coconut.

Spread over custard. Brown delicately in slow oven (300°F.). Chill.

Coffee Custard: In master recipe, substitute 1 cup strong coffee for 1 cup milk.

Cornstarch Pudding: In master recipe, substitute 3 tablespoons cornstarch for eggs.

Custard Whip: Prepare master recipe. Fold 1/2 cup whipped cream into cool custard.

Floating Island: Prepare soft custard with 4 egg yolks. Pour into sherbet glasses and chill.

Beat 2 egg whites, sweeten, and drop by spoonfuls on top of each serving. Garnish with a bit of jelly or cherry on top of egg white.

Fruit Custard: Prepare master recipe. Add any desired fresh or dried fruit to cup before pouring in custard.

Fruit Delight: Prepare soft custard. Slice fruit (peaches, oranges, strawberries, or bananas) into a bowl. Pour over the custard, or alternate layers of fruit and stale sponge cake.

Chill and serve with whipped cream.

Macaroon Pudding: Pour soft custard over macaroon or cooky crumbs. Chill.

Orange Custard: In master recipe, substitute 1 tablespoon grated orange rind for vanilla. Put orange sections in bottom of each cup before pouring in custard.

Or add 1/4 cup chopped candied orange peel to cool custard.

Spanish Custard Cream: Substitute 1 tablespoon (1 envelope) unflavored gelatin for 2 eggs. Soften gelatin in 1/4 cup cold milk. While gelatin is softening prepare soft custard with balance of milk.

When soft custard is done, pour it slowly over soaked gelatin. Stir until dissolved. Chill.

Tapioca Custard: In master recipe, substitute 3 tablespoons tapioca for 2 of the eggs. Cook tapioca in milk until transparent, 5 to 10 minutes. Then add to egg yolk mixture. Proceed as for soft custard.

Tipsy Custard Pudding: In master recipe, substitute sherry for vanilla. Pour over pieces of stale sponge cake. Chill.

Yellow Custard: In master recipe, substitute 4 egg yolks for whole eggs. Serve plain or with fruit, or use for Floating Island.

CRÈME BRULÉE

Brulé is a French term meaning burnt; it is usually applied to caramelized sugar. Crème brulée is a rich custard with a caramelized sugar coating.

3 cups heavy cream
1- inch piece vanilla bean
6 egg yolks
6 tablespoons granulated sugar
1/2 cup or more brown sugar

Heat cream with vanilla bean in upper part of double boiler.

Beat egg yolks with granulated sugar until light and creamy. Stir warm cream into egg yolks very carefully, discarding vanilla bean. Return to double boiler.

Place over boiling water and cook, stirring constantly, until custard coats spoon. Pour into shallow glass baking dish. Place in refrigerator to set and chill thoroughly.

When ready to serve, cover top with layer of brown sugar thick enough so none of cream shows through. Set dish on layer of crushed ice or surround with ice cubes in a pan.

Place under broiler flame until the sugar forms a bubbly brown crust. Watch it very carefully or the sugar will burn.

Serve at once or chill thoroughly and serve as is or over peaches. Serves 6.

Note: Two teaspoons vanilla may be substituted for vanilla bean. Combine with the sugar and egg yolks. Maple sugar may be substituted for brown sugar.

SABAYON OR ZABAGLIONE

This is a delicate soft custard served hot or cold alone as a dessert or as a dessert sauce. The French name is sabayon, a corruption of the Italian word zabaglione. In Italian it is also spelled zabaione. It is composed basically of beaten egg yolks, sugar, and heavy wine; however it is often varied by using various wines and combinations of favorite liqueurs. Marsala is the traditional wine in Italy. For a fluffier dessert or sauce, egg whites are sometimes beaten until stiff and folded into the custard just before serving.

4 egg yolks
3 tablespoons sugar
1/2 cup Sherry, Marsala, or Madeira

Beat yolks until light and thick. Add sugar. Continue beating until thoroughly blended. Slowly beat in wine.

Cook in top of double boiler over hot, not boiling, water. Beat constantly until mixture leaves sides of pan.

Remove from heat and beat 1 minute more. Serve hot or cold in sherbet glasses as a dessert, or over chilled fruits as a sauce. Serves 4.

BAKED BLUEBERRY CUSTARD

1 cup fresh blueberries
1 quart milk
5 eggs
5 tablespoons sugar
1/2 teaspoon salt
1/4 teaspoon nutmeg
1 1/2 teaspoons vanilla

Wash and drain blueberries, being careful not to crush or break berries. Dry on paper towel.

Scald milk. Break eggs into a bowl and beat well. Add sugar, salt, nutmeg, and vanilla. Pour in scalded milk and stir well with spoon.

Pour into custard cups. Carefully arrange blueberries on top of custard (some will sink). If desired sprinkle additional nutmeg on top.

Place cups in pan of hot water and bake in moderate oven (350°F.) about 15 to 20 minutes. Test with silver knife. When knife comes out clean, custard is done. Do not overcook, as custard will then turn watery. Remove custard cups from water and cool, then chill in refrigerator. Serve icy cold. Serves 8.

Baked Blueberry Custard

Chocolat Pots De Crème

CHOCOLAT POTS DE CRÈME

2½ 1-ounce squares unsweetened
      chocolate
3   cups milk
½   to ⅔ cup sugar
¼   teaspoon salt
5   egg yolks
½   teaspoon vanilla

Melt chocolate in a little milk in top of double boiler, over hot water; add sugar, salt, and remaining milk; cook until chocolate is completely melted.

Remove from heat; slowly stir into beaten egg yolks. Return to double boiler; cover and cook at simmering temperature 20 to 30 minutes or until medium thick, stirring occasionally. Remove from heat and stir in vanilla.

Pour into custard cups or serving dishes that have been rinsed in cold water. Chill. Serve cold with cream. Serves 6.

BLUEBERRY GRUNT

A grunt is an old-fashioned New England pudding, usually made of blueberries although other fruits are sometimes used.

1⅓ cups blueberries
1½ cups water
⅔   cup sugar
¼   teaspoon salt
1¾ teaspoons baking powder
1⅓ cups sifted enriched flour
1   tablespoon shortening
⅓   cup milk or more

Pick over and wash blueberries. Put in a well greased 2-quart casserole. Add water and sugar and put into hot oven (400°F.).

Mix and sift salt, baking powder, and

Blueberry Grunt

flour. Cut shortening into flour mixture with a knife.

Gradually add milk to make a soft dough, handling the mixture as little as possible.

When the blueberries have been in the oven about 5 minutes, drop in spoonfuls of the dough. Cover and continue baking about 25 minutes. Serves 5 to 6.

ENGLISH APPLE TRIFLE

5   cups sponge cake cubes
¾   cup sherry
1   3½-ounce package vanilla pudding mix
3   cups milk
⅔   cup black raspberry jam
2½ cups (1 can) apple slices
1   teaspoon grated lemon rind
1   tablespoon lemon juice
½   cup sugar
1   cup heavy cream, whipped

Place cake cubes in dish 8 x 12½ x 2 inches. Sprinkle sherry over cake cubes.

Combine pudding mix with milk; cook slowly until thickened, stirring constantly. Pour over cake cubes; spoon raspberry jam over all.

Chop apples; combine with lemon rind, lemon juice, and sugar. Heat. Spoon over cake mixture.

Chill several hours. Just before serving spoon whipped cream over apple mixture. Serves 8 to 10.

English Apple Trifle

OLD-FASHIONED APPLE CRISP

6   medium cooking apples
1½ cups moist breadcrumbs
¾   cup sugar
1½ teaspoons cinnamon
1½ tablespoons butter or margarine
2   tablespoons grated orange rind
⅓   cup water

Pare, core, and slice apples and place ½ in casserole.

Combine breadcrumbs, sugar, and cinnamon and sprinkle ½ over apples. Dot with ½ the butter.

Repeat with remaining apples, crumbs, and butter. Sprinkle with orange rind and add water.

Cover and bake in moderate oven (375°F.) 45 minutes. Serves 6.

APPLE CUSTARD

1½ cups milk
3   eggs, beaten
⅓   cup sugar
1   tablespoon grated orange rind
2   tablespoons orange juice
¼   teaspoon salt
1   cup strained, sweetened applesauce
⅛   teaspoon nutmeg

Add milk to beaten eggs. Mix together the sugar, grated orange rind, orange juice, salt, applesauce, and nutmeg. Add to milk and eggs and stir until all the ingredients are well blended.

Pour into 6 well greased custard cups. Place the cups in a pan filled with hot water to a depth of about 1 inch.

Bake in a moderate oven (350°F.) about 30 minutes or until the custards are firm. Serves 6.

APPLE PAN DOWDY

Apple Pan Dowdy is an old-fashioned New England dessert of sliced apples, molasses or brown sugar, nutmeg, and cinnamon, topped with a soft biscuit dough and baked.

2   cups sliced apples
¼   cup molasses or brown sugar
¼   teaspoon nutmeg
¼   teaspoon cinnamon
¼   teaspoon salt
¼   cup butter or margarine
½   cup sugar
1   well beaten egg
1½ cups sifted enriched flour
2   teaspoons baking powder
½   teaspoon salt
½   cup milk

Place apples in greased baking dish. Sprinkle with molasses or brown sugar, spices, and salt.

Bake in moderate oven (350°F.) until apples are soft.

Meanwhile prepare batter: Cream butter. Add sugar gradually, and add egg.

Mix and sift flour, baking powder, and salt. Add alternately with milk to first mixture. Pour over apples and continue baking. Total baking time about 35 minutes.

Serve from baking dish or turn out with apples on top. Serve with hard sauce or cream. Serves 6.

Apple Pan Dowdy

BLANC MANGE OR CORNSTARCH PUDDING
(Master Recipe)

Old-fashioned cornstarch pudding which in its many variations continues to be a favorite in many homes. The name, blancmange, is derived from the French words blanc (white) and manger (to eat).

3 to 4 tablespoons cornstarch
1/4 cup sugar
1/8 teaspoon salt
1/4 cup cold milk
1 3/4 cups scalded milk
1 teaspoon vanilla

Mix cornstarch, sugar, and salt with cold milk. Add scalded milk slowly to cornstarch mixture. Cook in top of double boiler over simmering water until smooth and thickened throughout, about 10 minutes.

Cover and cook 10 to 15 minutes, stirring 2 or 3 times. Cool slightly. Add vanilla. Mix thoroughly.

Pour into molds and chill. Serve plain or with fruit, nuts, and whipped cream, or sauce. Serves 6.

Blanc Mange Variations

Butterscotch Blanc Mange: In master recipe, substitute 1/2 cup firmly packed brown sugar for granulated. Add 2 tablespoons butter to mixture before cooling.

Caramel Blanc Mange: In master recipe, add 1/4 cup caramelized sugar syrup to milk after scalding.

Chocolate Blanc Mange: In master recipe, add 2 ounces (2 squares) bitter chocolate to scalded milk. Beat until chocolate and milk are smooth. Add 2 extra tablespoons sugar to cold milk mixture.

Or add 3 to 4 tablespoons cocoa and 2 extra tablespoons cornstarch. Mix with cold milk mixture.

Chocolate Cream Blanc Mange: Fold 1/2 cup whipped cream or 2 beaten egg whites into chocolate pudding.

Coconut Blanc Mange: In master recipe, add 1/2 cup shredded coconut before molding.

Coffee Blanc Mange: In master recipe, substitute 1 cup strong coffee for 1 cup milk.

Creamy Blanc Mange: To master recipe add 2 egg whites, beaten stiff with vanilla.

Fluffy Blanc Mange: Follow master recipe. When pudding is cooked, stir a small amount of hot mixture into 2 slightly beaten egg yolks. Stir into remaining hot mixture and cook 2 minutes, stirring constantly.

Cool slightly. Fold in 2 egg whites, beaten stiff, but not dry. Cool.

Fruit Blanc Mange: Add 1/2 cup crushed pineapple or other chopped or crushed fruits or berries before molding, or fill bottom of mold with fruits and pour pudding over fruit.

Layered Blanc Mange: Use food coloring; add to part of pudding before molding. Mold in layers, alternating colors.

Molded Blanc Mange: Increase cornstarch to 4 tablespoons. Flour may be substituted for cornstarch (5 to 7 tablespoons).

Nut Blanc Mange: Add 1/2 cup broken nutmeats to pudding.

PERSIMMON PUDDING

1 cup persimmon pulp (about 3 large persimmons)
2 well beaten eggs
About 1 cup milk
1 1/2 tablespoons melted butter or margarine
1 cup sifted enriched flour
1/2 teaspoon baking soda
3/4 cup sugar
1/2 teaspoon salt
1/4 teaspoon cinnamon
1/4 teaspoon nutmeg
1/2 cup raisins or chopped nuts, optional

Mix persimmon pulp with eggs; add milk and butter.

Mix and sift flour, soda, sugar, salt, and spices. Combine with first mixture and mix to a soft batter, adding more milk if necessary. Add raisins or nuts if used.

Pour into buttered 8 x 8 x 2-inch pan. Bake in moderate oven (350°F.) 30 to 45 minutes.

Serve with hard sauce or with plain or whipped cream. Serves 6.

CHEESE APPLE CRISP

5 cups (2 cans) apple slices
3/4 teaspoon cinnamon
1 cup sugar
1/4 cup water
2 teaspoons lemon juice
2/3 cup sifted all-purpose flour
1/8 teaspoon salt
1/3 cup butter or margarine
1 cup grated American cheese

Arrange apple slices in a greased 9 x 9 x 2 inch pan. Combine cinnamon with 1/4 cup of the sugar; sprinkle over apples. Add water and lemon juice.

Combine remaining 3/4 cup sugar, flour, and salt; work in butter or margarine to form a crumbly mixture; lightly stir in grated cheese. Sprinkle flour-cheese mixture over apples.

Bake in moderate oven (350°F.) 55 minutes, or until apples are tender, and topping is crisp and delicately browned. If desired, serve with whipped cream, ice cream, or lemon sauce. Serves 8 to 10.

Applesauce Rum Pudding

APPLESAUCE RUM PUDDING

2 cups canned applesauce
1 cup light brown sugar
1 cup broken pecans
1 cup seedless raisins
1/4 cup rum or 1 1/2 teaspoons rum extract
2 teaspoons cinnamon
1 teaspoon nutmeg
1/2 teaspoon allspice
4 egg whites
1 teaspoon lemon extract
1/2 cup sugar

Combine applesauce, brown sugar, pecans, raisins, rum (or rum extract), cinnamon, nutmeg, and allspice; heat. Pour into 1 1/2 quart casserole.

Beat egg whites stiff with rotary egg beater; add lemon extract and gradually beat in sugar until mixture stands in peaks. Mound meringue in center in a ring or spread over top of applesauce mixture. Bake in slow oven (325°F.) 15 to 20 minutes, or until meringue is delicately brown. Serve immediately. Serves 6.

Note: The applesauce mixture can be made up the day before it is to be served, and stored in the refrigerator. The flavor is enhanced by allowing it to stand 24 hours.

Cheese Apple Crisp

Cottage Pudding

COTTAGE PUDDING
(Master Recipe)

The name Cottage Pudding is misleading because it is not a pudding but a simple cake served usually while still warm with a sauce.

1/4 cup shortening
3/4 cup sugar
1 egg
2 cups sifted enriched flour
1/4 teaspoon salt
2 teaspoons baking powder
Dash of nutmeg
1 cup milk

Cream shortening and sugar. Add egg and beat until light and frothy.

Sift together flour, salt, baking powder, and nutmeg. Add alternately with milk to creamed mixture, beating after each addition.

Bake in greased baking pan in moderate oven (350°F.) about 35 minutes.

Serve warm with butterscotch, chocolate, or lemon sauce, or with sweetened fresh or canned fruits. Serves 6.

Cottage Pudding Variations

Individual Cottage Puddings: Bake in muffin pans in hot oven (400°F.) 20 to 25 minutes.

Berry Cottage Pudding: Add 1 cup blueberries to batter. Serve with hard sauce.

Other drained, canned, or fresh fruits may be used the same way.

Chocolate Chip Cottage Pudding: Add 1 cup chocolate bits to pudding.

Fruit-Topped Cottage Pudding: Place any desired fruits in bottom of baking pan before adding batter. Invert to serve.

Sweet Potato Pudding with Fluffy Lemon Sauce

SWEET POTATO PUDDING

1 1/4 cups mashed sweet potato
1/4 teaspoon nutmeg
1/4 teaspoon allspice
1/2 teaspoon salt
1/2 cup boiling water
1/2 cup sugar
2 eggs, beaten
1 cup evaporated milk

Boil 2 large sweet potatoes in jackets until tender, skin and mash.

Mix spices and salt; add water slowly. Add spice mixture with sugar and beaten eggs to sweet potatoes. Blend well, then add milk.

Pour into custard cups or baking dish. Bake in slow oven (325°F.) until set, about 1 hour. If a deep baking dish is used, set in a pan of hot water to bake.

Serve hot or cold with Fluffy Lemon Sauce #2. Serves 6.

GRATED SWEET POTATO PUDDING

2 eggs
1 cup granulated or brown sugar
1 cup rich milk
1/4 cup melted butter or margarine
1 tablespoon lemon juice
1/2 teaspoon grated lemon rind
1/2 teaspoon salt
1/4 teaspoon cloves
1/4 teaspoon ginger
2 cups grated raw sweet potatoes

Beat eggs until light; gradually beat in sugar. Stir in milk, butter, lemon juice, lemon rind, salt, and spices.

Combine with sweet potatoes, mixing well.

Turn into greased baking dish. Bake in moderate oven (350°F.) about 30 minutes. Stir the pudding with a spoon and bake 15 minutes longer. Serve with cream and a tart jam. Serves 6.

Variations: This Southern pudding has many variations. Nuts, currants, raisins, minced citron are often added. Molasses is sometimes substituted for part of the sugar. A half teaspoon cinnamon may be substituted for the lemon juice and rind.

Jiffy Fruit Trifles: Prepare instant pudding mix according to package directions. When pudding has set, spoon into individual sherbet or fruit dishes, making alternate layers with vanilla wafers and fruit.

Many variations may be made by combining different flavors of pudding with any one or combinations of fresh or frozen fruit. Try instant vanilla pudding with blueberries, peaches, strawberries, or raspberries; instant coconut pudding with cherries, oranges, or pineapple; or instant chocolate pudding with bananas or oranges.

INDIAN PUDDING
(Master Recipe)

Indian Pudding is an old-fashioned New England baked dessert made with corn meal and molasses. Other ingredients vary widely.

1/3 cup yellow corn meal
1/2 teaspoon salt
4 1/2 cups milk
1/2 cup molasses
1/2 teaspoon ginger
1/2 teaspoon cinnamon

Combine corn meal, salt, and 1/2 cup milk.

Scald 4 cups milk in top of double boiler. Add moistened corn meal, stirring constantly. Cook 20 minutes, or until thickened. Add molasses, ginger, and cinnamon.

Pour into a greased baking dish. Bake in slow oven (300°F.) for 2 hours.

Serve warm with vanilla ice cream, or chill and serve with cream. Serves 6.

Apple Indian Pudding: Pare and slice 2 apples. Add to thickened mixture. Add sugar to taste.

Date or Fig Indian Pudding: Add 1/2 cup pitted, chopped dates or chopped figs to thickened mixture.

INDIAN PUDDING WITH EGGS

1 quart milk
5 tablespoons corn meal
2 tablespoons butter
1 cup dark molasses
1 teaspoon salt
1 teaspoon cinnamon
2 well beaten eggs
1 cup cold milk

Scald 1 quart milk in a double boiler. Slowly stir in corn meal and cook over hot water 20 minutes. Add butter, molasses, salt, cinnamon, and beaten eggs.

Mix and spoon into a buttered baking dish. Pour 1 cup cold milk over top. Bake in moderate oven (350°F.) 1 hour. Serves 6 to 8.

Variations: Vary seasoning by using only 3/4 teaspoon cinnamon and adding 1/4 teaspoon nutmeg or ginger.

With Apples: Use 1 cup sliced apples. Arrange in layer in baking dish before spooning in the pudding.

Danish Apple Cake

BROWN BETTY
(Master Recipe)

Brown Betty is traditionally an apple pudding made with breadcrumbs, spices, and sweetening. The term Betty has been extended to similar puddings made of other fruits.

1/3 cup melted butter or margarine
2 cups soft breadcrumbs
3 cups sliced apples
1/2 cup sugar
Cinnamon or nutmeg, to taste
1/3 cup chopped nuts, optional
Grated rind of 1 lemon
2 tablespoons lemon juice
1/2 cup water

Mix butter with breadcrumbs. Arrange in a buttered baking dish, first a layer of crumbs, then a layer of apples. Sprinkle apples with some of the sugar, spice, and chopped nuts. Repeat until fruit and crumbs are used, topping dish with crumbs.

Combine lemon rind, juice, and water. Pour over top of dish.

Bake in moderate oven (350°F.) 45 minutes. If crumbs get too brown before time is up, cover dish.

Serve with cream, lemon sauce, or hard sauce. Serves 6.

Brown Betty Variations

Apricot or Prune Betty: Substitute 2½ cups stewed apricots or prunes for apples. Use fruit juice in place of lemon juice and water.

Banana Betty: Substitute sliced bananas for apples.

Blueberry Betty: Substitute 2½ cups blueberries or other berries for apples. Sugar may be reduced to ¼ cup.

Cherry Betty: Substitute 3 cups pitted cherries for apples.

Corn Flake Betty: Substitute corn flakes for breadcrumbs. Bake in shallow dish.

Peach Betty: Substitute sliced peaches for apples.

Pineapple Betty: Substitute 3 cups diced, canned pineapple for apples. Reduce sugar to ¼ cup.

Rhubarb Betty: Substitute 2½ cups stewed rhubarb for apples. Omit water.

DANISH APPLE CAKE

2 large or 3 medium tart apples (1½ pounds), peeled, cored, and diced
¼ cup Cherry Heering (liqueur)
⅓ cup sugar
2 cups dry breadcrumbs
¼ cup sugar
½ teaspoon cinnamon or nutmeg
3 ounces (¾ stick) butter

In a saucepan combine apples, Cherry Heering, and the ⅓ cup sugar. Cover and simmer for 30 minutes, or until apples are tender.

Mix breadcrumbs, the ¼ cup sugar, and cinnamon or nutmeg. Melt butter in a frying pan, add crumb mixture, and stir over moderate heat until crumbs are brown. Let cool and crisp in pan.

Serve in glasses as described above, or butter a 6-inch x 2 inch deep round cake pan. Put in a layer of crumbs, then a layer of apples. Alternate crumbs and apples until all ingredients are used. Bake in moderate oven (350°F.) 30 minutes. Let cool, then invert on serving plate. Serve with Custard Sauce (below). Serves 6.

Custard Sauce with Liqueur

3 egg yolks
2 tablespoons sugar
½ cup Cherry Heering
½ cup cream

In top of double boiler combine egg yolks and sugar. Heat Cherry Heering and cream until very hot, stir into egg yolk mixture and cook, stirring constantly over simmering water until sauce coats the spoon (from 10 to 15 minutes). Serve lukewarm over warm Danish Apple Cake.

NORWEGIAN PRUNE PUDDING

½ pound prunes
2 cups cold water
1 cup sugar
Dash of salt
1 stick cinnamon (1 inch)
1⅓ cups boiling water
⅓ cup cornstarch
1 tablespoon lemon juice

Wash and soak prunes in cold water 1 hour. Boil until soft in same water. Drain and reserve juice.

Pit the prunes. Crack pits, remove meats, and add to prunes. Combine prunes and juice.

Add sugar, salt, cinnamon stick, and boiling water. Simmer 10 minutes.

Mix cornstarch with enough cold water to give pouring consistency. Add to prune mixture and cook 5 minutes, stirring constantly. Remove stick of cinnamon. Add lemon juice.

Turn into a mold. Chill thoroughly. Serve with cream. Serves 6.

Layer Puddings are easy to make with instant pudding mixes prepared according to package directions. Use brandy snifters or any large deep stemmed glasses. Make one flavor at a time, allowing it to set about 10 minutes before adding the next flavor.

CABINET PUDDING

2 cups milk
2 tablespoons butter or margarine
2 tablespoons sugar
2 cups bread or cake crumbs
2 slightly beaten eggs
¼ teaspoon salt
½ teaspoon vanilla

Combine milk, butter, and sugar in saucepan. Cook over low heat until milk reaches scalding point. Cool slightly. Add crumbs.

Combine eggs, salt, and vanilla; slowly stir into milk mixture.

Turn into greased 1-quart casserole. Place in pan of hot water and bake in moderate oven (375°F.) about 1 hour. Serves 6.

LEMON FIG PUDDING

2 packages lemon pudding and pie filling mix
15 fig cakes
4 egg whites
½ cup sugar

Prepare both packages of mix according to directions for pie filling. Cut fig cakes into quarters, fold into slightly cooled lemon filling. Pile into 8 individual ovenproof dishes.

Beat egg whites until foamy. Add sugar gradually, beating until mixture forms peaks. Pile on top of pudding.

Bake in hot oven (425°F.) 5 minutes or until lightly browned. Cool. For festive occasions place dishes in sherbet glasses and serve with additional fig cakes. Serves 8.

Lemon Fig Pudding

TAPIOCA CREAM PUDDING

(Master Recipe)

⅓ cup quick-cooking tapioca
⅓ cup sugar
⅛ teaspoon salt
2 eggs, separated
4 cups milk, scalded
1 teaspoon vanilla

Combine tapioca, sugar, salt, and egg yolks in top of double boiler. Add milk slowly and mix thoroughly.

Cook until tapioca is transparent, stirring often. Remove from heat.

Fold into stiffly beaten egg whites. Add vanilla.

Serve warm or cold with cream. Serves 6.

Tapioca Cream Variations

Butterscotch Tapioca: In master recipe, substitute light brown sugar for granulated. Add 2 tablespoons butter to cooked mixture before folding in egg whites. When done, fold in ½ cup chopped nuts.

Chocolate Tapioca: Add 2 squares (2 ounces) unsweetened chocolate to milk. Heat and beat with rotary beater until blended. Increase sugar to ⅔ cup. Proceed as in master recipe.

Coconut Tapioca: Add ½ cup shredded coconut to milk. Instead of folding in egg whites, pour mixture into buttered baking dish. Fold ½ cup sugar into stiffly beaten egg whites. Pile on top. Bake in slow oven (300°F.) 15 minutes.

Date, Apricot or Prune Tapioca: Add ½ cup chopped dates, prunes, or steamed apricots to mixture before folding in egg whites.

Fresh Berry Tapioca: Fold 2 cups crushed blueberries, raspberries, or strawberries into partially cooked tapioca. Chill.

Fruit Tapioca: Arrange slices of fruit, canned or fresh, in sherbet glasses before pouring in mixture. Chill.

Honey Tapioca: In master recipe, substitute ⅓ cup honey for sugar.

Jelly Tapioca Parfait: Arrange tapioca cream pudding in alternate layers with a berry jelly in parfait glasses. Use just enough jelly to cover cream. Serve with whipped cream.

Nut Tapioca: Add ½ cup chopped nuts to mixture before pouring into molds.

Tapioca Gelatin Parfait: Prepare colored gelatin. Fill half of each parfait glass with gelatin. Fill rest of glass with tapioca cream pudding. Garnish with cubes of gelatin.

PEARL TAPIOCA PUDDING

1 cup pearl tapioca
4 cups milk
5 eggs, separated
¾ cup sugar
Grated rind of 1 lemon
Juice of ½ lemon

Soak tapioca in 1 cup milk overnight in refrigerator. The next day add 3 cups milk and cook 3 hours in a double boiler over, not in, hot water. Let cool.

Beat egg yolks with sugar, lemon rind, and lemon juice; add to cooled tapioca mixture.

Beat egg whites until stiff but not dry.

Line a baking dish with a layer of tapioca mixture; add a layer of beaten egg whites, another layer of tapioca, and top with a layer of egg whites.

Bake in slow oven (325°F.) about 15 minutes. Serve hot or cold with a sauce, if desired. Serves 6 to 8.

CHERRY TAPIOCA

1½ cups canned sour cherries
2½ cups cherry juice and water
2 teaspoons lemon juice
1½ tablespoons melted butter or margarine
¾ cup firmly packed brown sugar
¾ teaspoon salt
Dash of nutmeg
⅓ cup quick-cooking tapioca

Combine ingredients in buttered casserole, mixing well.

Bake in moderate oven (375°F.) 30 minutes, stirring every 10 minutes and again when removing from oven.

If desired, top with halved marshmallows and leave in oven just long enough to lightly brown. Serves 6.

DATE AND NUT PUDDING

(Master Recipe)

¾ cup sifted enriched flour
1½ teaspoons baking powder
½ teaspoon salt
1½ cups chopped, pitted dates
¾ cup chopped almonds, walnuts, or pecans
3 eggs
¾ cup sugar

Mix and sift flour, baking powder, and salt. Add dates and nuts.

Beat eggs until light. Add sugar and mix well. Add to dry ingredients.

Turn into greased, deep 9-inch pie pan. Bake in slow oven (325°F.) 35 to 40 minutes. Cut into wedges while warm.

Tear into pieces and serve in dessert glasses topped with whipped cream or desired sauce. Serves 6.

Apricot and Nut Pudding: Substitute well drained, soaked, dried apricots for the dates. Cut apricots in strips.

Prune and Nut Pudding: Substitute well drained, soaked, dried prunes for dates. Pit prunes and cut in strips.

FRENCH WINE CUSTARD

6 eggs, separated
⅔ cup sugar
¾ cup sweet sherry
¼ teaspoon salt
Cherries or strawberries

Mix egg yolks and sugar in top of 1½-quart double boiler. Set over simmering water and beat with rotary beater until fluffy. Do not let water boil.

Add sherry gradually and continue beating until mixture resembles whipped cream. Cool quickly and chill.

Before serving, beat egg whites stiffly with salt. Fold into chilled custard. Turn into glass serving dish. Serve plain or garnish with cherries or strawberries. Serves 8.

Variations: This wine custard is especially delightful served as a sauce over canned peaches, frozen strawberries or raspberries, or most fresh fruit in season.

For jellied wine custard soften ½ tablespoon (½ envelope) unflavored gelatin in 2 tablespoons water. Add to hot mixture while beating. Chill until syrupy. Fold in egg whites, beaten with salt.

DANISH APPLE BAKE

1 quart applesauce
2 cups toasted breadcrumbs
3 egg yolks, beaten
⅓ cup melted butter or margarine
½ teaspoon cinnamon
¼ cup sugar
3 egg whites
6 tablespoons sugar
½ teaspoon vanilla

Combine applesauce, breadcrumbs, egg yolks, butter, cinnamon, and ¼ cup sugar.

Bake in greased 2-quart casserole in slow oven (325°F.) 45 minutes. Remove from oven.

Beat egg whites until stiff. Add 6 tablespoons sugar gradually, continuing to beat until mixture stands in peaks. Add vanilla.

Top apple bake with meringue and return to oven for 15 minutes, or until brown. Serves 8.

Danish Apple Bake

BREAD PUDDING
(Master Recipe)

    2 beaten eggs
    About ¼ cup sugar
    ½ teaspoon salt
    1 teaspoon vanilla
    ¼ teaspoon nutmeg
    4 cups milk, scalded
    ¼ cup soft butter or margarine
    2 cups bread cubes

Combine eggs, sugar, salt, vanilla, and nutmeg. Add scalded milk and butter; mix well. Add bread and pour into buttered baking dish. Set baking dish in pan of hot water.

Bake in moderate oven (350°F.) 45 to 50 minutes, or until a knife inserted in center comes out clean.

Serve warm or cold with cream, plain or whipped, hard sauce or lemon sauce.

Cake, gingerbread, or breadcrumbs may be substituted for bread cubes. Serves 6.

Bread Pudding Variations

Individual Bread Puddings: Pour mixture into 6 buttered individual baking cups.

Bake as directed 35 to 45 minutes, or until knife inserted in center comes out clean.

Banana Bread Pudding: Slice 1 or 2 bananas over top before baking.

Butterscotch Bread Pudding: In master recipe, substitute ½ cup firmly packed brown sugar for granulated.

Melt butter with sugar in a skillet, stirring until evenly brown. Slowly add to milk. Cook until blended. Proceed as directed.

Caramel Bread Pudding: In master recipe, use ½ cup sugar. Caramelize sugar and dissolve in milk before pouring over crumbs.

Chocolate Bread Pudding: Follow master recipe and melt 2 squares (2 ounces) unsweetened chocolate in milk. Beat until blended.

Coconut Bread Pudding: Follow master recipe and add ½ cup moist shredded coconut just before pouring into baking pan. Sprinkle top with extra coconut if desired.

Fruit Bread Pudding: Follow master recipe; add ½ cup chopped raisins, dates, or figs just before pouring mixture into baking pan.

Honey Bread Pudding: In master recipe, substitute ¾ cup strained honey for sugar and ¾ teaspoon lemon extract for vanilla.

Marmalade Bread Pudding: Add ½ cup orange marmalade to mixture of master recipe.

Marshmallow Bread Pudding: Cover top of baked pudding with marshmallows. Return to oven until melted and slightly browned.

Mocha Bread Pudding: In master recipe, substitute 2 cups light cream and 2 cups fresh coffee for milk.

Nut Bread Pudding: Add ½ cup chopped nuts to chocolate or butterscotch bread pudding.

RENNET PUDDING
(Master Recipe)

    1 rennet tablet
    1 tablespoon cold water
    2 cups milk
    3 tablespoons sugar
    Few grains salt
    ½ teaspoon vanilla

Crush rennet tablet and dissolve thoroughly in cold water.

Heat milk until barely lukewarm (110°F.). (Do not use evaporated, condensed, or scalded milk.) Add sugar, salt, and vanilla. Stir until sugar is completely dissolved.

Add dissolved rennet and stir quickly for a few seconds. Pour at once into dessert glasses. Let stand undisturbed until set, about 10 minutes. Chill in refrigerator. Serves 4 to 5.

Rennet Pudding Variations

To Color: Add a few drops of food coloring with the milk.

Chocolate Rennet: Add chocolate syrup to the milk.

Maple Rennet: Substitute maple sugar for granulated.

Brown Sugar Rennet: Substitute brown sugar for granulated.

Package Rennet: Follow directions on package of flavored rennet.

Floating Island Bread Pudding: The "floating island" is a meringue made by beating egg whites to soft peaks, then slowly beating in sugar to make a stiff meringue. Spoon the meringue onto top of each pudding. Return to oven and bake about 10 minutes or until meringue is set and nicely browned.

Fluffy Lemon Bread Pudding

FLUFFY LEMON BREAD PUDDING

    2 cups milk, scalded
    3 cups soft ½-inch bread cubes
    3 egg yolks, beaten
    ⅔ cup sugar
    ¼ teaspoon nutmeg
    1½ teaspoons grated lemon rind
    ¼ teaspoon lemon extract

Meringue:

    3 egg whites
    ⅓ cup sugar
    ½ teaspoon lemon extract

Pour scalded milk over bread cubes. Let stand until bread is soaked.

Add beaten egg yolks, sugar, nutmeg, lemon rind, and lemon extract and beat well with a rotary beater.

Pour into a well greased 1½-quart casserole; set in a shallow pan of hot water.

Bake in a moderate oven (350°F.) until an inserted knife comes out clean, about 1 hour. Remove from oven, leaving casserole in pan of hot water.

Beat egg whites until stiff. Add sugar gradually, continuing to beat until mixture stands in peaks. Add lemon extract.

Top pudding with meringue and return to oven for 15 minutes, or until brown. Serves 8.

OZARK PUDDING
(MRS. HARRY S. TRUMAN'S)

    1 egg
    ¾ cup sugar
    2 tablespoons flour
    1¼ teaspoons baking powder
    ⅛ teaspoon salt
    ½ cup chopped nuts
    ½ cup chopped raw apple
    1 teaspoon vanilla

Beat egg. If an electric mixture is used, set at lowest speed and beat 1 minute. Gradually add sugar, continuing to beat until very smooth.

Mix and sift flour, baking powder, and salt. Add to sugar-egg mixture, stirring with a spoon. Add nuts, apple, and vanilla. Turn into generously buttered 9-inch shallow pie pan.

Bake in moderate oven (350°F.) 35 minutes. Serve with whipped cream or ice cream. Serves 4.

Apple Rice Pudding with Butterscotch Meringue

APPLE RICE PUDDING WITH BUTTERSCOTCH MERINGUE

1   cup uncooked white rice
6   medium apples, thinly sliced
1   teaspoon salt
1   cup sugar
1   teaspoon cinnamon
3   cups milk
2   egg yolks
2   egg whites
4   tablespoons brown sugar
1   teaspoon vanilla

Cook rice in saucepan with 1 quart boiling water and 1 teaspoon salt for 10 minutes; drain.

Place half the apple slices in a buttered 2-quart casserole. Blend together salt, sugar, and cinnamon and sprinkle 1/3 of mixture over apples.

Add 1/2 of the rice and remainder of apples and sprinkle with second 1/3 of sugar mixture. Top with remaining rice and sugar mixture.

Pour in milk which has been blended with beaten egg yolks.

Cover and bake in slow oven (300°F.) about 2 hours, stirring occasionally, adding extra milk, as needed. Uncover and cook 30 minutes longer to brown.

To Make Meringue: Beat egg whites until they peak; add brown sugar, 1 tablespoon at a time, beating between each addition and continue beating until very stiff. Fold in vanilla.

Spread on pudding and return to oven for 20 minutes, or until lightly browned. Cool. Serve with ice cream or plain cream. Serves 6 to 8.

CREAMY RAISIN RICE PUDDING

1   quart milk
1/2 cup uncooked rice
1/2 teaspoon salt
1/2 cup light or dark raisins
1/2 cup sugar
1   teaspoon vanilla

Combine milk, rice, and salt; heat slowly to boiling. Turn into greased 1 1/2-quart baking dish.

Bake in slow oven (300°F.) 45 minutes, stirring 3 or 4 times.

Rinse and drain raisins. Stir raisins, sugar, and vanilla into rice, and bake 15 minutes longer. Serves 6.

Note: For extra-creamy pudding, reduce rice to 1/3 cup.

OLD-TIME RICE PUDDNG
(Master Recipe)

3/4 cup uncooked rice
1 1/2 quarts milk
3/4 cup sugar
1/4 teaspoon nutmeg
1/2 teaspoon salt
3/4 cup seedless raisins

Wash rice. Add milk, sugar, nutmeg, and salt. Place in a buttered 2 1/2-quart baking dish.

Bake in slow oven (325°F.) 2 1/2 hours, stirring twice during first hour. Stir brown crust into pudding several times during the remainder of baking.

Add raisins 1/2 hour before pudding is done. Then allow crust to form again on pudding. Serve warm or cold with cream, if desired.

To reduce baking time, cook rice 10 to 15 minutes in the milk in double boiler before baking. Serves 6 to 8.

Variations of
Old-Time Rice Pudding

Apricot Rice Pudding: Substitute well drained, soaked apricots for raisins. Cut apricots in strips.

Brown Rice Pudding: Substitute 3/4 cup brown rice for white. Bake same way.

Brown Sugar Rice Pudding: Substitute 3/4 cup firmly packed brown sugar for granulated. Omit raisins. Serve cold.

Chocolate Rice Pudding: Mix 1/4 cup cocoa with rice and sugar mixture. Serve with sweetened whipped cream.

Date Rice Pudding: Substitute 3/4 cup chopped, pitted dates for raisins.

Honey Rice Pudding: Substitute 1/2 cup honey for sugar.

Molasses Rice Pudding: Substitute 1/2 cup molasses for sugar and 1/2 teaspoon cinnamon for nutmeg. Add 1 1/2 tablespoons butter at last stirring.

Prune Rice Pudding: Substitute 3/4 cup well drained, pitted, soaked prunes for raisins. Cut prunes in strips.

FRUIT FILLED RICE DESSERT RING

2   cups fluffy cooked rice
2   cups milk
1/4 cup sugar
2   tablespoons butter or margarine
1/2 teaspoon salt
4   tablespoons cornstarch
1/2 cup cold milk
2   teaspoons vanilla
3   egg whites, beaten stiff

Place the cooked rice, the 2 cups of milk, sugar, butter, and salt in a double boiler.

Add the 1/2 cup of milk to the cornstarch. Mix well. Pour into the double boiler. Cook 15 minutes, or until the

Fruit Filled Rice Dessert Ring

milk has cooked into the rice, stirring occasionally. Cool.

Add vanilla. Fold in stiffly beaten egg whites.

Turn into a well buttered ring mold. Chill at least 4 hours. Unmold on a large platter and fill with fresh fruit in season or canned or frozen fruit. Surround the ring with extra fruit if desired.

To unmold the ring, dip the mold quickly in hot water or cover it with a hot towel for several seconds. Place a plate over the mold, invert the plate and mold together. Shake and tap the mold until the ring is released. Serves 6.

STRAWBERRY RICE PARFAIT

4   cups sweetened cooked rice
4   tablespoons sugar
1/2 pint whipping cream
1 to 2 drops red food color
1/2 teaspoon almond flavoring
1   package frozen strawberries, defrosted
Additional tinted whipping cream, if desired

To sweeten rice, add 2 tablespoons sugar to water in which rice is cooked. Chill.

Just before serving, whip the cream, fold in food color, flavoring, and remaining 2 tablespoons sugar. Then fold into the rice. Fill serving dishes with alternate layers of rice and strawberries. (Reserve a strawberry for the top of each serving.) Top with whipped cream and the reserved berries. Serves 6.

Strawberry Rice Parfait

BANANA MERINGUE PUDDING
(Master Recipe)

⅓ cup cornstarch
1 cup sugar
¾ teaspoon salt
3 cups scalded milk
3 eggs, separated
1½ teaspoons vanilla
24 small or 16 large vanilla wafers
3 large ripe bananas, sliced

Mix cornstarch with ⅔ cup sugar and ½ teaspoon salt in double boiler. Pour scalded milk over this mixture. Cook over boiling water until mixture thickens, stirring almost constantly. Cover and cook 15 minutes, stirring occasionally.

Add hot mixture very slowly to beaten egg yolks, stirring constantly. Return to double boiler and cook 2 minutes. Let cool and add vanilla.

Put alternate layers of vanilla wafers, banana slices, and pudding mixture in 1½-quart casserole, having top layer pudding.

To Make Meringue: Beat egg whites with ¼ teaspoon salt until foamy. Gradually add ⅓ cup sugar, beating until it will stand up in soft peaks. Pile lightly on pudding.

Bake in moderate oven (350°F.) until delicately browned, about 15 minutes. Let cool, then chill in refrigerator before serving. Serves 6.

Variations of
Banana Meringue Pudding

Apple Meringue Pudding: Substitute 2 cups drained canned pie apples for bananas. Substitute grated lemon or orange rind for vanilla.

Coconut Meringue Pudding: Substitute 1 cup shredded coconut for bananas. Sprinkle ¼ cup coconut over meringue before baking. If fresh coconut is used, substitute coconut milk for an equal amount of milk.

Grapefruit Meringue Pudding: Substitute 1½ cups drained sweetened grapefruit segments for bananas. Substitute 1 tablespoon grated grapefruit rind for vanilla.

Orange Meringue Pudding: Substitute 1½ cups drained orange segments for bananas. Substitute 1 tablespoon grated orange rind for vanilla.

Chocolate Meringue Pudding: Add 2 1-ounce squares unsweetened chocolate to milk before scalding. Use 1 egg less and decrease sugar in meringue to ¼ cup.

Peach Meringue Pudding: Substitute 2 cups fresh or drained canned sliced peaches for bananas. Substitute 1 tablespoon grated orange rind for vanilla.

Pineapple Meringue Pudding: Substitute 2 cups drained canned pineapple chunks for bananas. Substitute grated lemon or orange rind for vanilla.

PORT WINE-APPLE PUDDING

4 tart apples, sliced
2 tablespoons lemon juice
⅔ cup port, angelica, muscatel, tokay, or any dessert wine
⅓ cup butter or margarine
⅓ cup sugar
2 beaten eggs
¼ teaspoon salt
¼ teaspoon nutmeg
½ teaspoon cinnamon
2 cups dry bread cubes

Pour lemon juice and wine over sliced apples and let stand.

Cream together butter and sugar. Add beaten eggs, salt, and spices. Combine with apples and wine and bread cubes.

Turn into a baking dish; cover and bake in moderate oven (350°F.) 35 or 40 minutes. Serve while still warm with Fluffy Wine Sauce. Serves 6.

Fluffy Wine Sauce:

Cream 2 tablespoons butter or margarine until light and fluffy. Blend in ¾ cup confectioners' sugar.

Add 3 tablespoons any dessert wine and beat until mixture is smooth. Add 2 teaspoons grated lemon rind.

BLUEBERRY CRISP PUDDING

4 cups fresh blueberries
⅓ cup granulated sugar
2 teaspoons lemon juice
4 tablespoons butter or margarine
⅓ cup firmly packed brown sugar
⅓ cup sifted enriched flour
¾ cup quick-cooking oats, uncooked

Put blueberries in 1½-quart baking dish. Sprinkle with granulated sugar and lemon juice.

Cream butter or margarine; gradually add brown sugar and cream well. Blend in flour and oats with a fork. Spread topping over blueberries.

Bake in moderate oven (375°F.) 35 to 40 minutes. Serve with plain or whipped cream. Serves 6.

Note: Canned berries may be substituted for fresh. Use two 15-ounce cans, drained, syrup-packed blueberries and ⅓ cup syrup. Omit granulated sugar. Bake in 1-quart baking dish.

SWEDISH APPLE PUDDING

¼ cup butter or margarine, melted
2 cups zwieback crumbs
1 No. 2 can (2½ cups) sweetened applesauce

Mix butter and crumbs. Butter baking dishes thoroughly and arrange crumbs and applesauce in alternating layers, finishing with crumbs.

Bake in moderate oven (375°F.) 15 minutes. Serve warm or cold with Vanilla Whipped Cream Sauce (see Index). Serves 8

Port Wine-Apple Pudding

MAGNOLIA MANOR DESSERT

1 cup sifted enriched flour
⅔ cup sugar
¼ teaspoon cinnamon
⅛ teaspoon ginger
Dash of cloves
3 tablespoons butter
⅓ cup pecans, chopped
½ cup boiling water
1 teaspoon baking soda
¼ cup molasses

Sift together flour, sugar, cinnamon, ginger, and cloves. Cut in butter until mixture resembles coarse meal. Add chopped pecans.

Press ⅔ of crumb mixture in well greased 8x8x2-inch pan.

Combine water and soda. Add molasses. Mix thoroughly. Pour over crumb mixture in pan. Sprinkle with remaining ⅓ crumb mixture.

Bake in moderate oven (350°F.) 30 to 35 minutes. Serve warm topped with whipped cheese topping and warm orange sauce. Serves 6 to 8.

Whipped Cheese Topping: Soften 1 package (3 ounces) cream cheese with 1 tablespoon cream and ½ teaspoon vanilla. Blend in 3 tablespoons sifted confectioners' sugar; cream well.

Orange Sauce: Combine ½ cup sugar, 1 tablespoon flour, 1 tablespoon cornstarch, and ⅛ teaspoon salt in saucepan. Add ¾ cup boiling water and 2 tablespoons butter. Cook over medium heat, stirring constantly, until thick and clear.

Remove from heat; add grated rind and juice of 1 orange and juice of 1 lemon.

Magnolia Manor Dessert

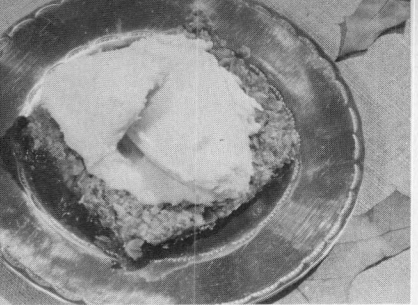

Cranberry Crunch

CRANBERRY CRUNCH

1   cup uncooked rolled oats
1/2 cup sifted enriched flour
1   cup firmly packed brown sugar
1/2 cup butter or margarine
1- pound can cranberry sauce (jellied or whole)
1   quart vanilla ice cream

Mix oats, flour, and brown sugar. Cut in butter until crumbly.

Place half of this mixture in an 8 x 8-inch greased cake pan. Cover with cranberry sauce. Top with balance of mixture. Bake in moderate oven (350°F.) 45 minutes.

Serve hot in squares topped with scoops of vanilla ice cream. Serves 6 to 8.

TIPSY PUDDING
(Master Recipe)

2   stale sponge layers
1/2 cup sherry
3   cups milk
1/3 cup sugar
1/4 teaspoon salt
2   eggs
1   teaspoon vanilla
2   tablespoons chopped candied cherries
2   tablespoons slivered, toasted almonds

Break cake into about 12 pieces and arrange in serving bowl. Pour sherry over cake and chill several hours or overnight.

Scald milk in top of double boiler. Mix together sugar, salt, and eggs. Add scalded milk very slowly, stirring constantly. Return to double boiler.

Cook over boiling water until mixture thickens slightly and will coat back of spoon, about 5 minutes. Cool. Add vanilla. Chill.

Pour 3/4 of custard over cake. Chill several hours before serving. Pour remaining custard over pudding when ready to serve. Garnish with cherries and almonds. Serves 6.

Tipsy Pudding Variations

Layered Tipsy Pudding: Instead of breaking cake into pieces, split cake layers. Spread with jam. Put together and place in large bowl. Pour sherry over cake and proceed as directed.

Individual Tipsy Puddings: Use 6 small squares of cake. Place in individual dishes. Pour an equal amount of sherry over each. Proceed as directed.

Ladyfinger Tipsy Pudding: Use 24 ladyfingers instead of sponge cake. Split ladyfingers. Spread 12 with jelly.

Sandwich together and put 2 in bottom of each dessert cup. Stand 4 halves up around inside edge. Pour sherry and custard over each.

CHOCOLATE FUDGE BATTER PUDDING
(Master Recipe)

2   tablespoons melted butter or margarine
1   cup sugar
1   teaspoon vanilla
1   cup sifted enriched flour
8   tablespoons cocoa
1   teaspoon baking powder
3/4 teaspoon salt
1/2 cup milk
1/2 cup chopped nuts, if desired
1 2/3 cups boiling water

Mix butter, 1/2 cup sugar, and vanilla.

Sift flour with 3 tablespoons cocoa, baking powder, and 1/2 teaspoon salt. Add alternately with milk to first mixture. Mix well and stir in nuts.

Mix together 1/2 cup sugar, 5 tablespoons cocoa, 1/4 teaspoon salt, and boiling water. Turn into casserole (10 x 5 x 2 inches). Drop batter by tablespoons on top.

Bake in moderate oven (350°F.) 40 to 45 minutes. Serve warm.

This pudding when baked has a chocolate sauce on bottom and cake on top. Spoon out a portion of cake and cover with sauce. If served cold, serve plain or whipped cream over the thickened sauce. Serves 6.

Variations of Chocolate Fudge Batter Pudding

Black and White Fudge Batter Pudding: Mix 1/2 package white cake mix as directed on package and substitute for chocolate batter in master recipe. Use same sauce.

Butterscotch Batter Pudding: Follow master recipe, omitting cocoa altogether. Substitute 1 1/2 cups firmly packed brown sugar for granulated sugar. (Use 1/2 cup in batter.)

To make sauce: Mix 1 cup brown sugar, 1 tablespoon flour, 1/4 teaspoon salt, 2 tablespoons butter, and 2 cups boiling water. Chopped pecans go well with this variation.

Chocolate-Ginger Batter Pudding: Mix 1/2 package gingerbread mix as directed on package and substitute for chocolate batter in master recipe. Use same sauce.

Spice Batter Pudding: Follow recipe for Butterscotch Batter Pudding, adding 1 teaspoon cinnamon, 1/2 teaspoon cloves, and 1/2 teaspoon nutmeg to batter. Add 1/2 cup raisins to sauce.

SYLLABUB

2   cups heavy cream
1/2 cup confectioners' sugar
1   teaspoon vanilla
1/4 cup Crème de Cacao, apricot brandy, or sauterne
12 ladyfingers, split
    Chopped almonds

Whip cream until it begins to hold shape. Then gradually beat in sugar, beating until stiff. Stir in vanilla and Crème de Cacao gradually so that mixture does not curdle. Spoon into small dessert glasses.

Split ladyfingers and place 4 halves in each glass. Sprinkle wtih almonds. Serve at once. Serves 6.

SKILLET FRUIT BETTY

1 1/2 cups stale bread cubes
2   tablespoons butter or margarine
1/2 cup honey
2   cups thinly sliced fruit (peaches, apples, whole berries)
    Heavy cream

Brown bread cubes in butter. Add honey and fruit. Cover and cook until fruit is tender, about 8 minutes.

Serve hot or cold with cream. Serves 4.

APPLE BATTER PUDDING

1   quart thinly sliced apples
1   cup sugar
1/8 teaspoon allspice
1/4 teaspoon nutmeg
2   tablespoons shortening
1   egg, beaten
1/2 teaspoon vanilla
1   cup sifted enriched flour
2   teaspoons baking powder
1/4 teaspoon salt
1/2 cup milk

Mix sliced apples with half the sugar, the allspice, and nutmeg. Place in a well greased 9-inch round baking dish.

Beat the shortening and remaining sugar until creamy; add egg and vanilla and beat thoroughly.

Sift together flour, baking powder, and salt; add alternately with milk to shortening mixture, beating well between each addition. Pour over apples and bake in moderate oven (350°F.) about 60 minutes. Serve hot with top milk. Serves 6 to 8.

Apple Batter Pudding

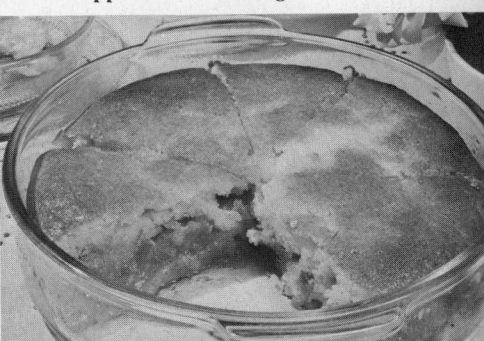

PEACH CRISP

1 quart tightly packed sliced peaches
½ teaspoon cinnamon
½ cup water
1 teaspoon grated lemon rind
1 cup sugar
½ cup butter or margarine
¼ teaspoon salt
¾ cup enriched flour

Arrange peaches in shallow, greased casserole (8x9 inches). Sprinkle with cinnamon. Add water and lemon rind.

Work together sugar, butter, salt, and flour until crumbly. Spread over peaches.

Bake uncovered in moderate oven (350°F.) until peaches are tender and top is nicely browned, 30 to 45 minutes.

Serve warm, plain or with cream. Serves 6.

Apple, Pear, Prune, Apricot Crisp:
Sliced apples or pears or soaked dried fruit may be subsituted for peaches.

Peach Crisp with Brown Sugar: Substitute firmly packed brown sugar for granulated sugar.

Peach Crisp with Corn Flakes: Substitute crushed corn flakes for flour.

BAKED CRANBERRY DESSERT

½ cup sugar
1½ cups graham cracker crumbs
1 teaspoon cinnamon
½ cup chopped walnuts
⅓ cup melted butter or margarine
1 tablespoon grated orange rind
3 cups cranberry sauce
½ cup cream, whipped

Mix together sugar, crumbs, cinnamon, walnuts, and melted butter or margarine. Pat ⅔ of mixture into well greased large baking dish.

Add grated orange rind to cranberry sauce and pour on top of crumb mixture in dish. Place remaining crumb mixture on top of cranberry sauce.

Bake in moderate oven (350°F.) 30 minutes. Cool and decorate top with whipped cream. Serves 8.

Baked Cranberry Dessert

PEACH CRUMB PUDDING
(Master Recipe)

2 cups milk
2 cups soft breadcrumbs
¼ teaspoon salt
⅔ cup sugar
2 eggs, beaten
2 tablespoons soft butter or margarine
¼ teaspoon nutmeg
2 cups sliced peaches, fresh or canned

Scald milk and pour over breadcrumbs. Cool.

Add salt, sugar, eggs, butter, and nutmeg. Mix. Fold in peaches.

Turn into buttered casserole. Bake in moderate oven (350°F.) 1¼ hours.

Cover with meringue or serve with cream. Serves 6.

Peach Crumb Pudding Variations

Apple Crumb Pudding: Use 2 cups peeled sliced apples in place of peaches.

Blueberry Crumb Pudding: Use 2 cups blueberries or other berries to replace peaches.

Cherry Crumb Pudding: Use 2 cups pitted, halved cherries to replace peaches.

Plum Crumb Pudding: Use 2 cups sliced pitted plums to replace peaches.

MATZO KUGEL

3 matzos
3 eggs, separated
½ cup sugar
¼ teaspoon salt
¼ teaspoon cinnamon
¼ cup raisins (optional)
3 tablespoons shortening or other fat
3 tart apples, thinly sliced
¼ cup chopped nuts
Grated rind of 1 lemon or orange

Soak matzos in cold water to cover. Drain well but do not press out the water.

Beat egg yolks until light; add sugar, salt, and cinnamon. Stir in the drained matzos.

Fold in stiffly beaten egg whites and raisins.

Turn half the mixture into a well greased and heated baking dish. Cover evenly with the sliced apples; sprinkle with nuts and grated rind.

Cover with remaining matzo mixture. Dot with remaining fat; sprinkle with additional cinnamon and sugar.

Bake in moderate oven (350°F.) until nicely browned, about 45 to 50 minutes.

Serve with a wine or fruit sauce or with stewed berries or other fruit. Serves 6.

Sunshine Pudding with Peaches

SUNSHINE PUDDING WITH PEACHES

2 cups milk
¼ cup cornstarch
½ cup sugar
⅛ teaspoon salt
2 eggs, separated
⅓ cup lemon juice
1 teaspoon grated lemon rind
2 tablespoons butter

Heat milk in double boiler to scalding point.

Blend cornstarch, ¼ cup sugar, and salt. Pour a little hot milk on dry ingredients while stirring; add remaining hot milk, stirring to blend. Return to double boiler and cook 20 minutes over hot water, stirring occasionally.

Beat egg yolks, pour a little hot mixture onto yolks; return to double boiler and cook 2 minutes longer. Remove from heat; add lemon juice, lemon rind, and butter, beating until smooth. Cool.

Beat egg whites until frothy, add remaining ¼ cup sugar, a tablespoon at a time, beating between each addition. Beat until stiff and fold into pudding.

Pour into custard cups or pudding molds that have been rinsed in cold water. Chill. Serve in pudding dishes with sliced peaches. Serves 6.

CANADIAN BERRY BATTER PUDDING

2 cups sifted enriched flour
1 teaspoon baking soda
½ teaspoon salt
⅓ cup shortening
¾ cup sugar
2 eggs
¼ cup white vinegar
½ cup milk
1¾ cups blueberries

Mix and sift flour, soda, and salt.

Cream shortening and sugar; add eggs one at a time, beating well after each addition.

Combine vinegar and milk; add to creamed mixture alternately with sifted dry ingredients, stirring until flour is just dampened. Fold in berries.

Spread in greased 8 x 8-inch pan. Bake in moderate oven (375°) about 45 minutes.

Serve warm with sauce or whipped cream. Serves 8.

Spiced Cottage Custard

BROWNIE PUDDING

½ cup sifted enriched flour
1 teaspoon baking powder
½ teaspoon salt
⅓ cup granulated sugar
1 tablespoon cocoa
¼ cup milk
1 tablespoon melted shortening
½ teaspoon vanilla
¼ cup chopped nuts
½ cup firmly packed brown sugar
2 tablespoons cocoa
¾ cup boiling water

Sift flour with baking powder, salt, granulated sugar, and 1 tablespoon cocoa into bowl. Add milk, shortening, and vanilla; mix only until smooth. Then add chopped nuts.

Turn into greased casserole or small baking dish.

Mix brown sugar and 2 tablespoons cocoa together and sprinkle over batter. Then pour boiling water over top of batter. This forms sauce in bottom of pan after pudding is baked.

Bake in moderate oven (350°F.) 30 to 40 minutes. Serves 6 to 8.

DATE CRUNCH

1 cup chopped dates
1 cup water
½ cup granulated sugar
½ cup chopped pecans
½ cup butter or margarine
1 cup firmly packed brown sugar
1 cup sifted enriched flour
1 teaspoon baking powder
1 cup uncooked quick rolled oats

Combine dates, water, and granulated sugar; cook over medium heat to consistency of soft jam. Cool and add pecans.

Cream butter and brown sugar; add flour which has been sifted with baking powder. Add rolled oats and mix until crumbly.

Pat ½ of crumb mixture into an 8x8-inch pan. Spread filling over crumbs. Top with remainder of crumb mixture.

Bake in slow oven (325°F.) 45 minutes. Serve with whipped cream flavored with vanilla and cinnamon. Serves 6 to 9.

SPICED COTTAGE CUSTARD

2 cups milk
3 eggs
6 tablespoons sugar
1 cup sieved cottage cheese
¼ teaspoon salt
1 teaspoon grated lemon rind
1 teaspoon vanilla
½ teaspoon cinnamon
Cooked, drained apricot halves

Heat milk in top of double boiler.

Beat 2 whole eggs and 1 yolk, reserving extra white for meringue. Add 4 tablespoons sugar, cottage cheese, salt, lemon rind, vanilla, and cinnamon, stirring to blend. Slowly add hot milk, while stirring.

Place 2 or 3 apricot halves in each of 6 buttered custard cups and pour cheese custard over them.

Place in pan of warm water and bake in slow oven (300°F.) 35 to 40 minutes, until custards are almost completely set and lightly browned.

Beat egg white until stiff. Add remaining 2 tablespoons sugar, 1 at a time, beating between each addition.

Top each custard with meringue and place in broiler about 3 minutes or until meringues are lightly browned. Serves 6.

CHERRY PUDDING

1¼ cups sifted enriched flour
1½ teaspoons baking powder
½ teaspoon salt
½ cup sugar
½ cup milk
2 tablespoons melted shortening
1¾ cups drained pitted red sour cherries, fresh or canned
2 cups hot water or cherry juice and water
½ to ¾ cup sugar
2 tablespoons butter or margarine

Sift flour with baking powder, salt, and ½ cup sugar into bowl. Add milk and melted shortening; stir only until smooth.

Spread dough evenly in greased shallow pan, about 12x8x2 inches. Arrange cherries over top.

Combine hot water or cherry juice, sugar, and butter; bring to a boil. Pour over cherries.

Bake immediately in moderate oven (375°F.) 45 to 50 minutes. Serve warm. Serves 8.

Fig Nut Pudding: Use recipe for Cherry Pudding, omitting cherries. Add ½ cup chopped figs to batter and spread evenly in greased pan, about 10x6x2 inches. Sprinkle with ¼ to ½ cup chopped nuts.

Use brown sugar in the sauce mixture. Pour hot sauce over batter and bake immediately in moderate oven (350°F.) 45 to 50 minutes. Serve warm. Serves 8.

CHOCOLATE RUM PUDDING

1 ounce (1 square) unsweetened chocolate
½ cup sugar
2 cups milk
⅛ teaspoon salt
5 tablespoons cornstarch
1 slightly beaten egg
1 tablespoon butter or margarine
2 teaspoons rum flavoring
Whipped cream

Place chocolate, sugar, 1¾ cups scalded milk, and salt in top of double boiler. Heat to boiling point, stirring until chocolate is melted.

Stir cornstarch into remaining ¼ cup milk, blending well, then slowly stir into hot milk mixture. Cook over boiling water about 20 minutes, or until thickened. Add a little of hot mixture to slightly beaten egg.

Return to custard mixture and cook 5 minutes longer. Add butter and rum flavoring.

Chill in individual serving dishes. Top with whipped cream before serving. Serves 4.

APPLESAUCE PUDDING

3 cups applesauce
1 cup sugar
1 teaspoon grated lemon rind
1 teaspoon lemon juice
2 teaspoons vanilla
3 egg yolks
3 egg whites
⅛ teaspoon salt
9 maraschino cherries

Mix together applesauce, ⅔ cup sugar, lemon rind, lemon juice, and 1 teaspoon vanilla.

Beat egg yolks into applesauce mixture. Pour into 8-inch square baking pan.

Beat egg whites until fluffy. Add salt and beat until stiff but not dry. Gradually beat in ⅓ cup sugar until egg whites stand in peaks. Beat in 1 teaspoon vanilla.

Arrange meringue in 9 mounds on top of applesauce mixture. Bake in slow oven (300°F.) about 15 minutes or until meringue is slightly browned.

Garnish with maraschino cherries. Serve either hot or cold. Serves 9.

Applesauce Pudding

LEMON TRIFLE

1 cup hot scalded milk
3 eggs, separated
1 tablespoon sugar
Dash of salt
2 tablespoons butter or margarine
Grated rind of 2 lemons
4 cups cake crumbs
Juice of 2 lemons
6 tablespoons sugar

Gradually stir scalded milk into slightly beaten egg yolks. Beat in 1 tablespoon sugar and dash of salt.

Cook over boiling water 5 minutes or until mixture coats a spoon, stirring constantly. Add butter; cool slightly, stirring occasionally; add lemon rind.

Put cake crumbs into baking dish. Pour custard over; sprinkle with lemon juice.

Spread over a meringue made by beating egg whites until stiff and gradually beating in 6 tablespoons sugar.

Bake in moderate oven (350°F.) 15 minutes or until browned.

Cool. Serves 6.

BLACKBERRY FLUMMERY

2 cups blackberry juice, from canned or cooked fresh blackberries
½ cup sugar (if juice is unsweetened)
3 tablespoons cornstarch
¼ teaspoon salt
2 tablespoons lemon juice

Heat blackberry juice in a double boiler. Mix and sift sugar, cornstarch, and salt. Add to juice and stir until mixture thickens.

Cover and cook 15 to 20 minutes. Remove from heat and add lemon juice. Beat well.

Pour into serving dish. Chill. Serve with plain or whipped cream. Serves 6.

QUEEN OF PUDDINGS

1 cup fine breadcrumbs
2 cups milk
2 tablespoons butter or margarine
¾ cup sugar
3 eggs, separated
1 pint strawberries or raspberries

Soak crumbs in milk until thickened, about 5 minutes.

Cream butter; stir in ½ cup sugar, then add well beaten egg yolks. Stir into soaked breadcrumbs.

Pour into buttered casserole, place in pan of hot water, and bake in moderate oven (350°F.) until firm, about 1 hour.

Place berries on top. Make a meringue of egg whites and remaining ¼ cup sugar; pile on top of berries and bake until golden brown, about 10 minutes. Serve either warm or thoroughly cooled. Serves 6.

Variation: A layer of strawberry or raspberry jam may be substituted for fresh berries.

MOLASSES APPLE COTTAGE PUDDING

2 tablespoons butter or margarine
2 tart apples
6 tablespoons molasses
⅓ cup shortening
⅔ cup sugar
1 egg
1 cup sifted enriched flour
1½ teaspoons baking powder
¼ teaspoon salt
½ cup milk
½ teaspoon vanilla

Melt butter; place in 6 greased custard cups, dividing butter equally.

Pare apples; core; chop fine. Divide evenly in the cups; add 1 tablespoon molasses to each.

Cream together shortening and sugar; add egg; beat well.

Sift together flour, baking powder, and salt; add alternately with milk to creamed mixture. Add vanilla; mix well. Pour over apple mixture, filling cups ¾ full.

Bake in moderate oven (350°F.) 45 to 50 minutes. Turn upside down on serving dish. Serve immediately with any preferred sauce, or whipped cream. Serves 6.

BROWN NUTTY PUDDING

¼ cup butter or margarine
1 cup sugar
¼ teaspoon salt
½ teaspoon cloves
½ teaspoon nutmeg
1 teaspoon cinnamon
1 egg, unbeaten
1⅔ cups milk
2 cups dry bread cubes
½ cup seedless raisins
½ cup chopped nuts
1 teaspoon baking soda
2 tablespoons water

Cream butter with sugar, salt, and spices. Add egg. Beat until smooth.

Pour milk over bread cubes, raisins, and nuts. Combine with creamed mixture.

Dissolve soda in water and add to pudding. Pour into a deep 1½-quart greased casserole.

Bake in slow oven (300°F.) 1 to 1¼ hours or until deep dark brown. Stir pudding after 30 minutes of baking. Serve warm with Lemon Sauce. Serves 8.

PINK MARBLE PUDDING

About 2 cups fresh, frozen, or canned stewed and sweetened rhubarb
About 2 cups fresh, frozen, or canned and sweetened raspberries
1 cup sugar (or to taste)
14 fig cookies, crumbled
1 cup heavy cream

Molasses Apple Cottage Pudding

1 teaspoon vanilla
3 tablespoons confectioners' sugar

Combine sweetened rhubarb and raspberries. Purée them through the food mill or a sieve. Place in a saucepan with the sugar and the fig cookies crumbled into small bits. Heat slowly, stirring constantly until the fig cookies are almost blended into the mixture.

When cool, place in the refrigerator to chill.

Just before serving, whip the cream with the vanilla and the sugar.

Place the fig mixture in dessert glasses alternately with spoonfuls of the whipped cream.

Top with cream and serve very cold. Serves 6 to 8.

APPLESAUCE FLOATING ISLAND

2 cups milk
2 tablespoons cornstarch
6 tablespoons sugar
2 eggs
⅛ teaspoon salt
1 teaspoon vanilla
1½ cups chilled applesauce

Scald milk in double boiler. Add cornstarch to 4 tablespoons of sugar and mix.

Separate eggs, saving whites for meringue. Beat yolks; add to sugar mixture and blend gradually; add the scalded milk, stirring to mix thoroughly. Return mixture to double boiler and cook 5 minutes, or until thickened.

Remove from heat; add salt and vanilla. Chill.

Beat egg whites until stiff; add 2 tablespoons sugar gradually, beating thoroughly.

Fold chilled applesauce into the chilled pudding mixture before serving. Top with spoonfuls of meringue; sprinkle with cinnamon or nutmeg. Serves 6.

Applesauce Floating Island

Steamed Puddings

General Directions for Steaming Puddings

Pudding mixtures may be prepared in special pudding molds, or small cylindrical cans with tight covers such as baking powder cans.

Molds should be tightly covered with parchment paper, aluminum foil, or several layers of heavy waxed paper, letting it extend at least an inch over the edge and tied in place. The mold and cover should be thoroughly greased. Mold should be only ⅔ full.

If a steamer is not available, place a trivet or wire rack in a large covered kettle or roasting pan. Place the covered molds on the trivet or rack. Add water to just below the top of trivet. Cover, let water boil slowly to form steam. Water should be boiling in kettle or steamer when food is ready for cooking.

Keep water boiling, constantly refilling with boiling water as needed.

When done, remove molds and let stand a few minutes, or set in cold water for a few seconds before unmolding.

If desired, the batter may be poured directly into the upper part of a double boiler and cooked over boiling water. The water should not touch the upper part. The sides and cover of double boiler insert should be well greased.

Individual Date-Nut Puddings

PLUM PUDDING—STEAMED

Plum pudding is a spicy suet pudding of English origin, traditionally served at Thanksgiving and Christmas dinners, often flaming. It contains mixed dried and candied fruits but no plums.

1	pound seedless raisins
1	pound currants
¼	cup chopped nuts
2½	cups sifted enriched flour
2	teaspoons baking soda
1	teaspoon cloves
1	teaspoon allspice
1	teaspoon nutmeg
1	teaspoon cinnamon
2	teaspoons salt
4	eggs
1	cup sugar
2	cups molasses
2	cups buttermilk
1½	cups finely chopped suet
½	cup grape juice
2½	cups fine dry breadcrumbs
	Hard sauce

Clean raisins and currants; combine with nuts. Dredge with 1 cup flour.

Sift remaining flour, soda, cloves, allspice, nutmeg, cinnamon, and salt.

Beat eggs; add sugar, molasses, buttermilk, suet, grape juice, and crumbs. Add raisin mixture; mix well. Add flour mixture; mix well.

Pour into 2 greased 3-pound molds. Cover; steam 3 hours.

Cool puddings, wrap in heavy waxed paper; store. The puddings keep for weeks in a cool place. Resteam to heat.

Serve hot with sauce. Each pudding serves 12.

INDIVIDUAL DATE-NUT PUDDINGS

¼	cup soft butter or margarine
½	cup sugar
1	teaspoon vanilla
½	teaspoon salt
2	eggs, beaten
¼	cup milk
1½	quarts soft bread cubes
2	teaspoons baking powder
1	cup chopped, pitted dates
½	cup chopped walnuts

Combine butter, sugar, vanilla, and salt; add beaten eggs and milk.

Combine bread cubes and baking powder; add to first mixture. Add dates and walnuts.

Grease 7 individual (6-ounce) fruit juice cans on inside and put ¾ cup pudding mixture into each can. Cover top of can with aluminum foil and press it down over sides of can.

Put 1 pint water in pressure cooker; place cans on rack in cooker. Place cover on cooker and steam pudding for 15 minutes. Close steam valve and pressure cook pudding for 30 minutes.

Let pudding cool 5 minutes before loosening with spatula and turning it out. Serve with foamy sauce. Makes 7 individual puddings.

NEW ENGLAND PLUM PUDDING

½	cup butter or margarine
1	cup sugar
1	egg, unbeaten
1	cup sifted enriched flour
1	teaspoon baking soda
¾	teaspoon cloves
1½	teaspoons cinnamon
1	teaspoon nutmeg
1	cup dry sifted breadcrumbs
1	cup broken walnuts
1½	cups raisins
¾	cup hot water

Cream butter or margarine; add sugar gradually, creaming continually. Beat in egg.

Sift dry ingredients over breadcrumbs, walnuts, and raisins; mix well. Add to first mixture alternately with hot water.

Turn into greased 2-quart pudding mold and cover tightly.

Place on rack in very slow oven (250°F.) and oven steam 2½ to 3 hours. Serve with foamy sauce. Serves 8.

APPLE PUDDING—STEAMED

6	apples
¼	cup sugar
¼	teaspoon cinnamon
¼	cup water
1	cup sifted enriched flour
2½	teaspoons baking powder
½	teaspoon salt
1	tablespoon shortening
	About ⅓ cup milk

Wash, pare, and quarter apples. Cut into slices about ¼ inch thick. Add sugar, cinnamon, and water. Cover and cook over low heat until tender. Stir carefully if necessary.

Mix and sift flour, baking powder, and salt. Cut in shortening. Add milk, mixing quickly to make a soft dough. Pat out to fit the size of pan in which the apples are cooking. Place dough over apples. Cover pan and put in steamer.

Steam pudding about 1 hour. Turn out onto a large plate, apple side up. Serve warm with lemon sauce. Serves 6.

Plum Pudding

VANILLA PUDDING—STEAMED
(Master Recipe)

1/3 cup shortening
1 cup sugar
1 teaspoon vanilla
1 1/2 cups sifted cake flour
1 1/2 teaspoons baking powder
1/8 teaspoon salt
1/2 cup milk
3 egg whites

Cream shortening; add 2/3 cup sugar and vanilla. Cream until light and fluffy.

Mix and sift dry ingredients. Add in thirds to creamed mixture, alternating with milk, mixing well after each addition.

Beat egg whites until stiff but not dry. Gradually add remaining 1/3 cup sugar, beating continuously. Carefully fold into batter.

Fill individual greased molds 3/4 full. Steam until done, about 1/2 hour. Serve with fruit sauce. Serves 6 to 8.

Vanilla Pudding Variations

Almond Pudding: Substitute almond extract for vanilla.

Chocolate Pudding: Melt and cool 2 squares (2 ounces) unsweetened chocolate. Add with sugar-egg mixture.

Raisin Nut Pudding: Add 1/2 cup each seedless raisins and nuts with sugar-egg mixture.

Raisin Pudding: Add 1 cup seedless raisins with sugar-egg mixture.

MOLASSES PUDDING—STEAMED

1 egg
3/4 cup molasses
2 tablespoons melted shortening
1 teaspoon vanilla
1 3/4 cups sifted enriched flour
1 cup raisins or 1/2 cup raisins and 1/2 cup nutmeats
1/4 teaspoon salt
1 teaspoon baking powder
1 teaspoon cinnamon
1/2 teaspoon baking soda
1/2 cup cold water

Beat egg; stir in molasses, shortening, and vanilla.

Sift flour and dust part of it over raisins and nutmeats.

Resift the rest of flour with salt, baking powder, and cinnamon.

Dissolve soda in cold water. Add sifted dry ingredients in 3 parts to molasses mixture alternately with thirds of water and soda. Beat batter well after each addition.

Pour batter into greased pudding mold. Cover closely and steam 1 1/2 hours. Serve hot with hard sauce or whipped cream. Serves 6.

Coconut Pudding: Add 1 cup shredded coconut to batter.

SUET PUDDING—STEAMED

1/2 pound suet, finely chopped
2 cups packaged breadcrumbs
1 cup seedless raisins
1/2 cup mixed candied fruits, citron, or nuts, chopped
1 1/4 cups firmly packed brown sugar
2 tablespoons molasses
1/2 cup milk, cider, or grape juice (liquid may be 1/4 brandy)
1 beaten egg
1/2 teaspoon each of baking soda, salt, cloves, and allspice
1 teaspoon cinnamon

Mix all ingredients except soda, salt, and spices, using the hand.

Mix soda, salt, and spices; sprinkle over batter. Blend in well.

Fill individual greased custard cups about 2/3 full and cover each with aluminum foil.

Set on rack in large pot or covered roaster. Add boiling water to depth of about 1 inch.

Cover and steam 1 hour, adding more water, if needed. Remove covers and cool thoroughly. Replace covers before storing.

To reheat: steam, covered, during service of first courses of meal. Serve with hard sauce or whipped cream. Serves 8.

HUNGARIAN PLUM PUDDING

2 cups stale breadcrumbs
1 cup scalded milk
1/2 cup sugar
2 eggs, separated
1 1/4 cups seedless raisins
1 1/4 cups currants
1/4 cup finely cut citron
1/2 cup butter or margarine, melted
1/4 cup grape juice
1/2 teaspoon nutmeg
1 teaspoon cinnamon
1/4 teaspoon each cloves and mace
1 1/2 teaspoons salt

Soak breadcrumbs in milk and let cool.

Combine sugar, beaten egg yolks, raisins, currants, and citron. Add milk mixture and butter. Mix well.

Add remaining ingredients; then fold in stiffly beaten egg whites.

Pour into buttered mold. Cover and steam 5 hours. Serve hot with hard sauce. Serves 6.

GINGER-FIG PUDDING—STEAMED

1 cup dried figs (1/2 pound)
1 egg
1 cup molasses
1/2 cup melted shortening
2 teaspoons ginger
1 teaspoon baking soda
1 teaspoon salt
2 1/2 cups sifted enriched flour
3/4 cup warm water

Ginger-Fig Pudding

Cover figs with boiling water for 10 minutes; drain, reserving warm water to use in pudding; clip off stems with scissors and cut fine.

Beat egg; add molasses and shortening. Sift dry ingredients together and add alternately with water.

Lastly add figs; mix well and turn into a greased pudding mold.

Set in a pan of boiling water. Put a cover over the pan and steam for 2 1/2 hours in slow oven (325°F.) or in conventional steamer. This will make 2 puddings and each pudding will serve 6. Keeps nicely and may be reheated. Serve with hard sauce.

ST. PATRICK'S DAY PUDDING

2 (7 3/4-ounce) packages fig newtons cakes
1/2 cup milk
1/4 cup butter or margarine
1 egg, well beaten
1 teaspoon cinnamon
1/4 teaspon ground cloves
1/4 teaspoon nutmeg
1 teaspoon lemon juice
1/4 teaspoon grated lemon rind
1 tablespoon baking powder

Break fig newtons cakes into milk. Let stand 15 minutes; stir to blend.

Cream butter; add egg, cinnamon, cloves, nutmeg, lemon juice, lemon rind, and baking powder. Stir into fig mixture.

Divide into 12 small greased molds; cover tightly with aluminum foil.

Steam 30 minutes. Cool a few minutes before unmolding.

Garnish with hard sauce or whipped cream.

Note: If desired, steam half the recipe in individual molds and the remainder in a quart mold to reheat for another day.

St. Patrick's Day Pudding

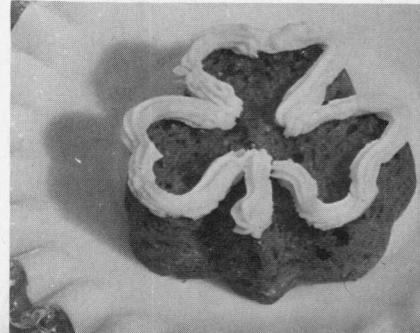

Dumplings, Cobblers, Shortcakes

CHERRY DUMPLINGS

Cherry Sauce:

2   tablespoons butter or margarine
1/2 cup sugar
Dash of salt
1/2 cup cherry juice
1 1/2 cups sour pitted cherries
1 1/2 cups boiling water

Combine all ingredients in order given in heavy skillet or large saucepan.

Bring mixture to boil, reduce heat and simmer gently about 5 minutes.

Dumplings:

1   cup sifted enriched flour
1 1/2 teaspoons baking powder
Dash of salt
1/4 cup sugar
2   tablespoons butter or margarine
1/2 teaspoon vanilla
1/3 to 1/2 cup milk

Sift together flour, baking powder, salt, and sugar. Cut or rub in butter or margarine until mixture is crumbly.

Add vanilla to milk. Add milk to flour mixture and stir only enough to moisten flour. Drop by spoonfuls into boiling sauce.

Cook uncovered 5 minutes. Cover and steam gently 15 minutes longer.

Serve dumplings warm with cherry sauce. Serves 4.

Cherry Dumplings

WESTERN APPLE DUMPLINGS

1   cup sifted enriched flour
1/4 teaspoon salt
2   teaspoons baking powder
2   teaspoons sugar
1/4 cup butter or margarine
1   slightly beaten egg
3   tablespoons milk
2   tablespoons melted butter or margarine
1 1/2 cups finely diced, pared, cored apples
1/4 cup seedless raisins
1   tablespoon sugar
1   teaspoon cinnamon

Sauce:

1/2 cup brown sugar
1/2 cup granulated sugar
1   tablespoon cornstarch
3/4 cup water
1   tablespoon butter or margarine

Mix and sift flour, salt, baking powder, and 2 teaspoons sugar. Cut in butter with pastry blender or blending fork until pieces are size of small peas.

Combine beaten egg with milk and stir into first mixture, forming smooth dough. Knead dough about 1 minute, then roll out in rectangle 1/4 inch thick on well floured pastry cloth. Brush with 2 tablespoons melted butter.

Mix apples and raisins and spread over dough. Combine 1 tablespoon sugar and 1 teaspoon cinnamon and sprinkle over apples and raisins.

Roll up as for jelly roll and cut into 6 slices with sharp knife. Place rolls in individual custard cups or tart pans.

Cover with sauce made by mixing sugars and cornstarch; add water and butter and bring mixture to boiling point.

Bake in moderate oven (375°F.) 25 minutes. Serve warm with plain cream, if desired. Serves 6.

BAKED FRUIT DUMPLINGS
(Master Recipe)

Roll biscuit dough 1/4-inch thick. Cut into 4-inch squares.

Use 6 small apples, apricots, or peaches. Place whole fruit, pared and cored or pitted, in center of each square. Sprinkle 1 tablespoon sugar and cinnamon or nutmeg mixture over fruit in each dumpling. Dot with butter.

Bring corners up over fruit. Pinch edges together. Prick with fork.

Bake in moderate oven (350°F.) 30 minutes. Serve with dessert sauce.

One recipe for biscuit dough makes 6 dumplings. The amount of sugar and cinnamon or nutmeg mixture may be varied, depending upon individual taste or sweetness of fruit.

HUNGARIAN PLUM DUMPLINGS

1 1/2 pounds boiled potatoes
2   eggs, slightly beaten
1   teaspoon salt
About 2 cups sifted enriched flour
12   to 15 ripe plums
1   teaspoon cinnamon
1/2 cup sugar
1   cup breadcrumbs
About 1/4 cup butter or margarine

Cook potatoes in jackets. Peel and mash. Add eggs and salt. Mix well. Sift in enough flour to make a smooth dough.

Roll out to 1/2-inch thickness on a floured board and cut into 3-inch squares.

Pit the plums; fill cavities with cinnamon and sugar. Place a plum on each square. Fold dough around plums to form balls. Cook 10 minutes, covered in boiling salted water. Drain well.

Roll dumplings in breadcrumbs which have been browned in butter. Serve hot. Serves 6 to 8.

Variations: Apricots filled with cinnamon and sugar, or sliced and sugared apples, may be substituted for plums.

OLD-FASHIONED APPLE DUMPLINGS

1   recipe plain pastry
6   medium (tart) cooking apples
6   teaspoons butter
1/4 cup brown sugar
1   teaspoon cinnamon
1/8 teaspoon salt

Prepare pastry and roll 1/8-inch thick on floured board. Cut into 6-inch squares.

Wash, thinly peel and core apples. Make 2 crosswise cuts through top of each apple, about 1/2 inch deep.

Place 1 apple on each pastry square. Put 1 teaspoon butter into each cavity. Sprinkle apple with brown sugar, cinnamon, and salt. Moisten edges of pastry squares with water. Fold corners to center and press edges together.

Place in ungreased pan (7 x 11 x 1 1/4 inches). Bake in very hot oven (450°F.) 10 minutes. Reduce to moderate heat (350°F.) and bake 25 to 30 minutes longer or until apples are tender and crust delicately browned.

Serve hot with butterscotch or hard sauce, or with cream. Serves 6.

Old-Fashioned Apple Dumplings

Saucy Apple Dumplings

SAUCY APPLE DUMPLINGS

2 cups sifted enriched flour
3 teaspoons baking powder
1 teaspoon salt
6 tablespoons shortening
½ to ¾ cup milk
4 medium-sized apples
½ cup brown sugar

Mix and sift flour, baking powder, and salt. Cut or rub in shortening. Add milk to make a soft dough.

Turn out on lightly floured board and knead gently ½ minute. Roll into rectangular sheet about 8 inches wide and ⅛ inch thick.

Pare and core apples and chop coarsely. Spread evenly over dough.

Sprinkle with brown sugar. Roll up like a jelly roll and seal edge. Cut into 2-inch slices. Place in greased baking pan.

Pour 1 cup Cinnamon Candy Sauce (below) over slices in pan.

Bake in moderate oven (375°F.) 40 minutes. Makes 8 dumplings.

Cinnamon Candy Sauce: Mix ¼ cup cornstarch and ½ cup brown sugar together. Add ½ cup red cinnamon candies and 2½ cups water.

Cook until clear and thickened, stirring constantly. Serve warm or cold over dumplings.

STEAMED BERRY DUMPLINGS

Stew enough blueberries, loganberries, or blackberries to make 1 quart. Sweeten to taste with sugar.

If desired, use canned berries, heated to boiling point.

Roll biscuit dough to ½-inch thickness. Cut into small biscuits. Drop into boiling berries.

Cover and cook 12 to 15 minutes. Serve hot with berry sauce poured over dumplings.

Steamed Apple Dumplings: Use thin applesauce instead of berries. Proceed as directed for Steamed Berry Dumplings.

BLUSHING BEAUTY DUMPLINGS

6 tart medium-sized baking apples
Apple peelings
1½ cups water
½ cup sugar
¼ teaspoon red food coloring
1½ cups sifted enriched flour
¼ teaspoon salt
½ cup shortening
1 teaspoon grated orange rind
5 to 6 tablespoons cold orange juice
2 tablespoons sugar
1 teaspoon nutmeg
3 tablespoons butter

Peel and core apples. Combine apple peelings and water in saucepan. Cover; cook until tender, 5 to 10 minutes. Drain juice and to it add ½ cup sugar. Cover and cook 10 minutes. Remove from heat; add red food coloring. Set aside.

Sift together flour and salt. Cut in shortening and orange rind until particles are the size of small peas. Sprinkle cold orange juice over mixture, tossing lightly with fork until dough is moist enough to hold together. Form into a ball.

Roll out on floured pastry cloth or board to 18 x 9-inch rectangle. Cut into 9 x 3-inch strips.

Wrap strip around each apple, sealing tightly at bottom only.

Combine 2 tablespoons sugar and the nutmeg. Place 1 teaspoonful in center of each apple. Top with butter (½ tablespoon on each dumpling).

Place in 12 x 8-inch baking pan so dumplings do not touch one another. Pour reserved syrup around dumplings.

Bake in moderate oven (350°F.) 50 to 60 minutes. Baste with syrup after baking 40 minutes. Serve warm, plain or with cream. Serves 6.

CARAMEL NUT DUMPLINGS

1½ cups sugar
2½ cups water
¼ teaspoon salt
1 teaspoon vanilla

Melt ¾ cup sugar over high heat, stirring constantly until amber in color. Remove from heat and stir until liquid thickens and cools slightly.

Slowly stir in water and return to heat. Add remaining sugar, salt, and vanilla and mix well. Remove from heat.

Prepare Dumplings: Mix and sift 1 cup sifted enriched flour, 2 tablespoons sugar, 1¾ teaspoons baking powder, and dash of salt. Stir in ⅓ cup chopped walnuts. Add ½ cup milk and stir quickly until flour is just moistened.

Drop by teaspoons into simmering caramel sauce. Cover tightly and steam 20 minutes over low heat. Serves 6 to 8.

Blushing Beauty Dumplings

ROLLED FIG DUMPLINGS

Filling:

2 cups figs, chopped fine
1 tablespoon lemon juice
3 tablespoons cold water

Add lemon juice and water to figs. Heat to boiling, stir, and cool.

Syrup:

1 cup sugar
1½ cups water
Grated rind and juice of 1 lemon

Mix sugar, water, lemon juice, and rind and bring to boil.

Dough:

2 cups sifted enriched flour
3 teaspoons baking powder
½ teaspoon salt
4 tablespoons shortening
1 well beaten egg
½ cup rich milk

Sift flour, baking powder, and salt together into bowl. Add shortening and cut in finely.

Beat egg well, add to milk, and blend with dry ingredients.

Knead dough lightly about ½ minute, then roll out into rectangle about ¼ inch thick. Spread with fig filling, then roll up.

Cut into 9 even slices and arrange in 8-inch baking dish, cut side down. Pour boiling syrup over top.

Bake immediately in hot oven (400°F.) 25 minutes. Serve hot or cold either in sauce or with cream. Makes 9.

Rolled Fig Dumplings

Master Fruit Cobbler

BLUEBERRY COBBLER

Filling:

2 cups blueberries
Few grains salt
Sugar
1 egg, well beaten
  or 1 tablespoon quick tapioca
  or 1 tablespoon flour
Butter or margarine

Batter:

1/4 cup butter or margarine
1/2 cup sugar
1 egg, well beaten
1 1/2 cups sifted enriched flour
2 teaspoons baking powder
1/2 teaspoon salt
1/2 cup milk

Filling: Add salt and sugar to taste to berries. Add egg or other thickening. Spread in buttered baking dish and dot with butter.

Batter: Cream butter. Add sugar gradually, and add egg.

Mix and sift flour, baking powder, and salt. Add alternately with milk to creamed mixture.

Cover berries with batter and bake in hot oven (425°F.) about 30 minutes.

Serve warm with whipped cream, vanilla sauce or other desired sauce. Serves 6.

Variations of Blueberry Cobbler

Blackberry or Loganberry Cobbler: Use blackberries or loganberries instead of blueberries.

Apple Cobbler: Use 2 cups sliced fresh or canned apples instead of berries.

Peach Cobbler: Use 2 cups fresh or canned sliced peaches instead of berries. If fresh peaches are used, put in a pit or two for especially good flavor.

Sour Cherry Cobbler: Pit cherries; cook 5 minutes in just enough water to keep from burning. Sweeten to taste and pour into baking dish.

MASTER FRUIT COBBLER

Filling:

1/2 cup sugar, or to taste
1/8 teaspoon salt
2 tablespoons cornstarch
3 cups sliced peaches, or other fruit

Crust:

1 cup sifted enriched flour
1/2 teaspoon salt
1/3 cup butter or margarine
3 to 4 tablespoons cold water

Filling: Mix sugar, salt, cornstarch, and fruit and pour into buttered, shallow casserole or deep oven glass cake pan, 2 1/2 inches deep preferably.

Crust: Sift flour with salt. Cut in butter until size of wheat grains. Add water a little at a time until mixture holds together. Chill dough 15 to 20 minutes.

Roll pastry out 1/8- to 1/4-inch thickness and cut into decorative pieces with cooky cutters. Place pieces of pastry at regular intervals over fruit mixture.

Bake in very hot oven (450°F.) 20 to 25 minutes or until crust is browned. Serve hot with hard sauce. Serves 6.

APPLE-CHEESE COBBLER

4 cups peeled and sliced apples
1 cup sugar
1 teaspoon cinnamon
6 to 8 slices cheese
1/3 cup shortening
2 cups sifted enriched flour
3 teaspoons baking powder
1/2 teaspoon salt
1 cup milk

Combine apples, sugar, and cinnamon and arrange evenly over bottom of 8 x 8 x 2-inch baking dish. Cover with slices of cheese.

Top with a drop biscuit dough made by cutting shortening into flour which has been combined with baking powder and salt. When mixture is of a coarse corn meal-like texture, add all of milk and stir until moisture is evenly distributed.

Bake in hot oven (400°F.) 35 to 45 minutes, or until crust is brown and biscuit topping is baked. Serve warm with cream. Serves 6 to 8.

The Patriotic Cobbler topping is easily made from pastry for a 1-crust pie. Roll pastry on a lightly floured surface to a 10 x 4-inch rectangle. Cut into three 10-inch strips, two 6-inch strips, and one 4 x 2 1/2-inch rectangle. Cut small stars out of the rectangle and place star-studded rectangle in one corner of pie. Arrange 6-inch strips beside rectangle and 10-inch strips over remainder of pie.

RHUBARB COBBLER

4 cups diced rhubarb
1 1/2 cups sugar
1 tablespoon margarine
1 cup sifted enriched flour
1 1/2 teaspoons baking powder
1/2 teaspoon salt
3 tablespoons sugar
1/8 teaspoon nutmeg
1/4 cup margarine
1 egg, beaten
1/4 cup milk

Combine rhubarb and 1 1/2 cups sugar, mixing well. Spread into well-margarined 8 x 8-inch or 7 x 9-inch pan. Dot with 1 tablespoon margarine.

Mix and sift flour, baking powder, salt, 1 tablespoon sugar, and nutmeg into mixing bowl. Cut 1/4 cup margarine into flour mixture until mixture is like fine corn meal.

Combine beaten egg and milk. Add all at one time to flour mixture and stir until well blended.

With spoon, arrange batter in lattice-effect over rhubarb in pan, or drop by spoonfuls or spread thinly over rhubarb. Sprinkle batter with 2 tablespoons sugar.

Bake in moderate oven (350°F.) 40 to 45 minutes. Serve warm with cream or ice cream. Serves 6.

BUTTER-FRUIT COBBLER

1 quart strawberries
1 medium-sized fresh pineapple
2 tablespoons lemon juice
1 1/2 cups sifted cake flour
1/4 teaspoon salt
1/2 cup butter or margarine
3 to 4 tablespoons cold water
2 tablespoons flour
1/2 cup sugar

Wash berries thoroughly with cold water before hulling them.

Slice pineapple, peel, and cut in wedges.

Combine fruits, add lemon juice, and mix together lightly. Place in refrigerator while mixing crust.

Sift flour, measure 1 1/2 cups and re-sift with the salt. Add butter and cut in with pastry blender or 2 knives until mixture has texture of rice grains. Add cold water a few drops at a time, tossing with fork until dry ingredients are just dampened.

Form into round patty and roll out on lightly floured board.

Cut with floured cooky cutter into fancy shapes.

Butter the casserole, turn the fruit into it, and sprinkle with the 2 tablespoons flour mixed with the sugar.

Arrange the rolled pastry on top in any desired arrangement, and bake in a very hot oven (450°F.) for 15 to 20 minutes, until crust is golden brown. Serve warm or cold. Serves 6.

EASY-DO SHORTCAKES

All you have to do to make these strawberry shortcakes with their old-fashioned ways is—for 6 man-sized servings—to measure into bowl 4 cups packaged biscuit mix and ¼ cup sugar.

Add about 1½ cups cream, mixing with fork. Keep dough soft but, if it is sticky, add a bit more biscuit mix. Don't overmix.

Turn out on floured board or pastry cloth. Knead 10 times to shape in ball. Pat or roll out in rectangle to ½ inch thickness. Spread with softened butter.

Fold over, keeping in rectangular shape with a bit of patting and shaping at corners.

Note: This shortcake dough can be made with milk—about 1½ cups—and 6 to 8 tablespoons melted butter instead of cream.

Using knife dipped in flour, cut dough in 6 or 8 squares depending upon size desired.

For round shortcakes, cut with large floured cutter but knife method is easier and saves fussing with the "scraps."

Place a little apart on cooky sheet. Spread tops with softened butter and sprinkle with sugar if desired.

Bake in very hot oven (450°F.) about 10 minutes. These shortcakes should be baked just before serving so they'll be piping hot.

To serve, split shortcakes. Arrange on serving plate or plates. While hot, spread with butter.

Cover lower half with sweetened strawberries, both sliced and whole, depending on size. Use ¾ to 1 cup sugar for quart of berries, allowing them to stand at room temperature for a while.

Put on top crust. Cover with strawberries and juice. Serve at once, topped with plenty of slightly sweetened whipped cream.

Plantation Peach Shortcake

PLANTATION PEACH SHORTCAKE

2 cups sifted enriched flour
3 teaspoons baking powder
½ teaspoon salt
¼ cup firmly packed brown sugar
½ cup shortening
½ cup chopped pecans
1 well beaten egg
⅔ cup light cream
Sweetened, sliced peaches (fresh, frozen, or canned)
Whipped cream

Sift together flour, baking powder, and salt into large bowl. Cut in brown sugar and shortening until mixture resembles coarse meal. Add pecans.

Combine well beaten egg and cream; add to flour-shortening mixture, mixing only until all flour is dampened.

Spread in two well greased 8-inch round layer cake pans. (For individual shortcakes, turn out dough on well floured board or pastry cloth; knead a few strokes. Roll to ½-inch thickness. Cut into rounds with floured 3-inch cutter. Place on ungreased baking sheet.)

Bake in very hot oven (450°F.) 10 to 12 minutes.

Place peaches between layers or split individual shortcakes. Top with sweetened whipped cream and peaches.

PARTY "SHORT" CAKE

Prepare white, yellow, or spice cake mix as directed on package. Bake as directed. Allow cake to cool.

Split layer crosswise to make 2 thin layers. Spoon between layers about 1½ cups sweetened prepared fruit—fresh, frozen, or drained canned fruit such as berries, peaches, bananas, etc.

Spread over top ½ cup heavy cream, whipped. Serve at once, or keep in refrigerator until serving time.

Ice remaining layer as desired, and save for another meal.

Party "Short" Cake

RICH SHORTCAKE

    2   cups sifted enriched flour
    3   teaspoons baking powder
    ¾   teaspoon salt
    2   tablespoons sugar, if desired
    ½   cup shortening
    About ¾ cup milk

Sift flour 3 times with remaining dry ingredients, the last time into bowl. (Omit sugar for chicken, fish, or meat shortcake.)

Cut in shortening with pastry blender or blending fork until mixture is consistency of rice grains. Add milk all at once and mix lightly with fork. Do not stir vigorously.

Spread to uniform thickness in lightly greased 8-inch cake pan.

Bake in very hot oven (450°F.) 20 to 25 minutes until golden brown. Split through center crosswise and spoon desired sweetened fruit and juice such as berries, peaches, or grapefruit between and over hot layers just before serving.

Creamed chicken or fish may be used with unsweetened shortcake.

GRAPE COBBLER

    Plain pastry or 2 cups packaged mix
    4   cups stemmed washed Concord
        grapes (about 2 pounds)
    1   cup sugar
    2   tablespoons butter or margarine
    1   tablespoon lemon juice
    ½   teaspoon cinnamon
    2   tablespoons flour

Line bottom and sides of 9-inch square pan with pastry.

Slip grape skins away from pulp. Put pulp in saucepan. Put skins in bowl.

Cook pulp about 5 minutes, or until seeds loosen. Then put fruit through sieve to remove seeds.

Mix grape skins, grape pulp, and remaining ingredients together and turn into pastry lined pan.

Cover with top crust, which has been slashed in several places to allow escape of steam.

Bake in very hot oven (450°F.) 15 minutes. Reduce heat to moderate (375°F.) and bake 30 minutes longer, or until crust is lightly browned.

Serve cooled to room temperature, plain or with cream or vanilla ice cream. Serves 6.

Peach Skillet Shortcake

CRANBERRY NUT COBBLER

    2   cups sugar
    1   cup water
    4   cups cranberries
    ½   cup chopped walnuts
    Grated rind 1 orange
    2   tablespoons butter or margarine
    1   cup sifted enriched flour
    2   tablespoons sugar
    2   teaspoons baking powder
    ¼   teaspoon salt
    2   tablespoons shortening
    6   tablespoons milk

Heat sugar and water to boiling point; add cranberries, walnuts, orange rind, and butter and let stand while mixing biscuit dough.

Sift dry ingredients together; blend in shortening and add milk.

Roll out dough to ¼-inch thickness. Fill individual baking dishes (shallow custard cups, ramekins, or deep-dish pie dishes) with cranberry mixture.

Cover each with round of biscuit dough. Prick holes in top of each to allow steam to escape.

Bake in very hot oven (450°F.) about 15 minutes.

Serve with hard sauce flavored with ¼ cup chopped fresh cranberries and 1 tablespoon cranberry syrup from filling. Serves 6.

PEACH SKILLET SHORTCAKE
(With Prepared Mix)

    2   cups biscuit mix
    2   tablespoons sugar, optional
    ½   cup milk
    ¼   cup butter or margarine, melted
    3   cups sliced peaches, sweetened and
        chilled
    1   cup heavy cream, whipped, or 1
        pint vanilla ice cream

Place a heavy skillet on asbestos or other heat pad. Cover and heat slowly while mixing dough.

Combine biscuit mix and sugar. Add milk and melted butter or margarine and mix well with fork. Knead about 10 times. Pat or roll on board dusted with additional mix into 9-inch round.

Grease skillet well with shortening. Place round of dough in pan and cover. Be sure heat is low to prevent burning. Let bake until brown on bottom and sides and firm to touch in center, about 20 minutes.

Turn shortcake out onto serving plate and split in half, using a plate to lift off top half. If desired, spread lower half with soft butter. Cover bottom half with ½ the peaches. Cover with top of cake, add peaches and garnish with whipped cream or ice cream. Serves 8.

Strawberry Skillet Shortcake: Substitute strawberries for peaches. Other desired fruits may be used.

BLUEBERRY SKILLET COBBLER

    3   cups fresh blueberries, or 2½ cups
        canned berries and juice
    Sugar
    Dash of salt
    1   tablespoon cornstarch
    2   tablespoons butter or margarine
    1   cup biscuit mix
    ⅓   cup cream
    1   tablespoon sugar

Heat fresh berries and ¾ cup water or canned berries and juice in skillet. Sweeten to taste. Add salt and cornstarch blended in 2 tablespoons cold water.

Bring to boil, stirring frequently. Cook 1 minute. Dot with butter.

Mix biscuit mix with cream and 1 tablespoon sugar, according to directions on package for drop-shortcake dough. Drop dough from tablespoon over berries in skillet. Cover, and cook over very low heat 20 minutes.

Serve hot with cream, if desired. Serves 4 to 6.

STRAWBERRY PINWHEEL SHORTCAKE

    1½ cups sifted enriched flour
    1   teaspoon salt
    2   teaspoons baking powder
    2   tablespoons sugar
    2   tablespoons shortening
    1   egg, beaten
    ⅓   cup milk
    2   tablespoons melted butter or mar-
        garine
    ½   cup sugar
    1   tablespoon grated orange rind
    1   quart strawberries

Sift together flour, salt, baking powder, and 2 tablespoons sugar. Cut shortening into flour until mixture is like coarse corn meal. Add beaten egg and milk all at once and mix lightly.

Pat out dough on a floured board into a 9-inch square. Spread dough with melted butter or margarine. Mix together ½ cup sugar and the grated orange rind; sprinkle on dough.

Roll as for jelly roll; cut into 6 slices. Arrange biscuits, cut side up, around edge of lightly greased 10-inch pie pan. Bake in moderate oven (375°F.) for about 25 minutes.

Wash and hull strawberries. When biscuits are cool heap fresh strawberries in center of pie plate for serving. Serves 6.

Strawberry Pinwheel Shortcake

Miscellaneous Desserts

COEUR À LA CRÈME (CHEESE AND CREAM HEART)

Coeur is French for heart; coeur à la crème is a French cheese dessert molded in individual heart-shaped molds with perforated bottoms or in one large traditional heart-shaped wicker basket lined with moistened cheesecloth. It is served with crushed or whole strawberries, raspberries, or other fruit. The heart molds are usually available in specialty shops.

1 pound cottage cheese
1 pound cream cheese, softened
Pinch of salt
2 cups heavy cream
Crushed fresh strawberries or defrosted frozen strawberries

Combine cottage cheese, cream cheese, and salt thoroughly. Gradually add cream, beating until mixture is smooth.

Turn into individual molds or one large mold. Place on deep plate and refrigerate to drain overnight.

At serving time unmold onto chilled plates. Serve with crushed sweetened strawberries. If desired, garnish with whole strawberries and mint or parsley. Serve with French bread. Serves 6.

STRAWBERRY TRIFLES

2 cups sifted enriched flour
3 teaspoons baking powder
1 teaspoon salt
½ cup shortening
1 cup sugar
2 eggs, beaten
1 teaspoon vanilla
¾ cup milk

Sift together flour, baking powder, and salt.

Cream together shortening and sugar until light and fluffy. Add eggs, beating well. Add vanilla. Add flour mixture to creamed mixture alternately with milk.

Fill greased 3-inch muffin pans ½ full

Bake in moderate oven (375°F.) about 25 minutes.

Cut off tops of cupcakes, and spread with whipped cream and halves of strawberries. Replace tops of cupcakes, garnish with more strawberry halves,

Cherry Meringue Dessert

and top with whipped cream and one whole strawberry. Makes about 14 3-inch cakes.

CHERRY MERINGUE DESSERT

1¼ cups sifted enriched flour
½ teaspoon baking powder
¼ teaspoon salt
⅓ cup shortening
⅓ cup sugar
2 egg yolks, unbeaten
1 tablespoon milk
½ cup chopped pecans
1 No. 2 can pie cherries, drained (reserve juice)
2 tablespoons cornstarch
½ cup sugar
¾ cup cherry juice (reserved)
¼ teaspoon almond extract
2 egg whites
¼ cup sugar

Sift together flour, baking powder, and salt.

Blend shortening and sugar, creaming well. Add egg yolks and milk; beat well.

Add flour mixture all at once; stir until mixture is well blended and forms a ball. Press into bottom of well greased and lightly floured 9-inch round layer cake pan.*

Reserve 2 tablespoons pecans for meringue. Sprinkle remainder over dough in pan.

Bake in moderate oven (375°F.) 12 to 15 minutes until golden brown. Cool.

Transfer cooled, baked cooky circle to baking sheet. Drop meringue (see below) by tablespoonfuls in a ring around edge on top of cooky circle. Sprinkle meringue with the 2 tablespoons reserved pecans.

Bake in moderate oven (350°F.) 12 to 15 minutes, until meringue is lightly browned. Fill center with the cooled cherry filling (see below). Serves 8 to 10.

Cherry Filling: Blend together cornstarch and ½ cup sugar in saucepan. Stir in cherry juice until sugar dissolves. Cook over medium heat, stirring constantly, until thick and clear. Remove from heat. Add almond extract and cherries. Cool.

Meringue: Beat egg whites until slight mounds form when beater is raised. Add ¼ cup sugar gradually, beating well after each addition. Continue beating until meringue stands in stiff, glossy peaks when beater is raised.

*Note: Dough may be rolled out to a 9-inch circle on greased baking sheet. Bake, cool and top with meringue and cherry filling as directed.

Blueberry Dream Dessert

BLUEBERRY DREAM DESSERT

2 cups quick rolled oats, uncooked
1 cup sifted enriched flour
1 cup firmly packed brown sugar
¾ cup butter, melted
2 cups blueberries
1 tablespoon flour
½ cup sugar
2 tablespoons lemon juice
⅛ teaspoon salt
¾ cup water or juice from canned blueberries

Mix rolled oats, 1 cup flour, and brown sugar. Add melted butter and mix well. Line bottom of 8-inch square pan with oatmeal mixture, reserving about ½ cup for topping.

Combine blueberries, 1 tablespoon flour, sugar, lemon juice, salt, and liquid in saucepan. Simmer about 5 minutes.

Remove from heat and pour into oatmeal crust. Sprinkle with remaining crumbs and bake in moderate oven (350°F.) 45 minutes. Serve topped with whipped cream or ice cream. Serves 6 to 8.

Note: One No. 2 can of prepared blueberry pie filling may be substituted for the blueberry filling mixture.

RASPBERRY MERINGUE CUPCAKES

For a quickly prepared dessert, serve bakery cupcakes with a meringue into which fresh, canned, or well drained frozen fruit has been folded.

Slice the cupcakes into wedges, cutting only half way through; open gently, fill the cavity with the meringue and fruit.

Raspberry Meringue Cupcakes

Swedish Chocolate Dessert

SWEDISH CHOCOLATE DESSERT

2¼ cups sifted enriched flour
½ cup sugar
⅓ cup cocoa
½ teaspoon baking powder
½ teaspoon salt
¾ cup shortening
1 unbeaten egg
2 tablespoons milk

Sift together flour, sugar, cocoa, baking powder, and salt into mixing bowl. Cut in shortening until particles are the size of small peas. Add egg and milk. Blend with fork or pastry blender until well combined.

Place dough on large ungreased baking sheet, at least 15x12 inches.* Roll out on baking sheet with floured rolling pin to 15x11-inch rectangle.

Trim edges with sharp knife or pastry wheel; divide into three 11x5-inch rectangles. Bake in moderate oven (375°F.) for 12 to 15 minutes. Avoid overbaking. Cool on baking sheets. When cold, loosen carefully with spatula.

Place a piece of cardboard (about 12x6 inches) on a sheet of aluminum foil or waxed paper (which is large enough to wrap dessert for chilling).

Stack layers on top of cardboard, spreading filling (see below) between layers but not quite to edge. Frost top (see below). If desired, decorate top with toasted slivered almonds.

Chill until frosting has set. Then wrap loosely in the aluminum foil (or waxed paper); chill overnight. Cut into 6 or 8 rectangular-shaped pieces to serve.

*Note: If a large baking sheet is not available, roll dough to fit the bottom of an inverted 15x10-inch shallow pan, then divide into 3 equal rectangles. Or, divide the dough into 3 portions, roll each to an 11x5-inch rectangle. Then use smaller baking sheets or pans.

Vanilla Filling:

1 egg
¼ cup sugar
¼ cup enriched flour
1 cup milk, scalded in top of double boiler
1 teaspoon vanilla
½ cup whipping cream

Beat egg until light and fluffy. Gradually add sugar, beating constantly until thick and light. Blend in flour. Gradually add scalded milk; return mixture to top of double boiler.

Cook over boiling water, stirring constantly, until thick and smooth. Add vanilla; cool.

Beat whipping cream until thick and fold into cooled filling.

Chocolate Filling: Follow recipe above but combine the whipping cream with 3 tablespoons cocoa and 3 tablespoons sugar.

Chill for 30 minutes. Then beat until thick and fold into filling.

Chocolate Icing:

2 tablespoons butter or margarine
2 tablespoons cocoa
½ cup sifted confectioners' sugar
1 egg yolk
¼ teaspoon vanilla

Melt butter in saucepan. Remove from heat; blend in cocoa. Add confectioners' sugar, egg yolk, and vanilla. Beat until smooth.

FROMAGE À LA CRÈME (FRENCH CHEESE AND CREAM)

Fromage is French for cheese; fromage à la crème is a French molded cream cheese dessert served with fresh unhulled strawberries, or other fresh fruit or berries.

2 8-ounce packages cream cheese
2 tablespoons cream
⅛ teaspoon salt
1 cup whipped cream or 1 cup sour cream

Beat cream cheese with 2 tablespoons cream and the salt until soft; fold into whipped cream or sour cream. Turn into rinsed individual molds or one large mold.

Chill thoroughly, then unmold onto chilled plates. Serve with fresh unhulled strawberries or other fresh fruit or berries. Serves 6.

CRUMBLED TORTE

2 eggs, separated
1 cup sugar
1 cup coarsely cut dates
1 cup finely cut nutmeats
1 tablespoon enriched flour
1 teaspoon baking powder

Beat egg yolks until frothy. Add sugar gradually, continuing to beat until well mixed.

Add dates, nutmeats, flour, and baking powder. Stir until all ingredients are moistened.

Fold in stiffly beaten egg whites until mixture is blended.

Spread batter into greased 9-inch square pan. Bake in a hot oven (425°F.) 15 minutes. Let stand until cold.

Crumble torte into stemmed glasses. Crown with sweetened whipped cream and cherries. Serves 4 to 6.

NORWEGIAN APPLE CAKE

2 cups toasted crumbs
½ teaspoon nutmeg
2 cups applesauce
Butter or margarine
Whipped cream
Jelly

Combine crumbs and nutmeg. Arrange alternate layers of crumbs and applesauce in a buttered pudding dish, dotting each with butter. Top with crumbs; press down well.

Bake in slow oven (325°F.) 45 minutes. Cool, then turn out of dish. Spread with whipped cream. Dot with jelly. Serves 6.

CRANBERRY GRUNT

2 cups cranberries
1 cup chopped apples
½ cup water
⅓ cup plus 2 tablespoons sugar
¼ cup plus 2 tablespoons butter or margarine
¼ teaspoon powdered cloves
½ teaspoon nutmeg
1½ cups sifted enriched flour
3 teaspoons baking powder
¼ teaspoon salt
⅓ cup milk

Simmer cranberries and apples in water about 10 minutes.

Blend ⅓ cup sugar, 2 tablespoons butter, and spices with cranberries and apple. Pour 1¾ cups of mixture into a baking dish which has been brushed with butter.

To make dough for pinwheels, sift together the flour, 2 tablespoons sugar, baking powder, and salt. Cut in ¼ cup butter with pastry blender or 2 knives. Add milk, stirring until flour is just moistened.

Place on floured board, roll ½ inch thick. Brush with melted butter. Spread with remaining cranberry-apple mixture, drained. Roll as for jelly roll. Cut into 1-inch slices. Arrange slices, cut side down, over cranberry mixture.

Bake in a hot oven (425°F.) about 20 minutes, or until crust is nicely browned. Serve warm, or chilled with whipped cream. Serves 6.

Cranberry Grunt

CHERRY ROLY POLY

2 cups sifted enriched flour
3 teaspoons baking powder
1/4 cup sugar
3/4 teaspoon salt
4 to 6 tablespoons shortening
1/3 to 1/2 cup milk
1 No. 2 can (2 cups) pitted sour cherries
1/2 cup sugar
2 tablespoons cornstarch
1 cup liquid

Mix and sift flour, baking powder, 1/4 cup sugar, and salt.

Cut in shortening until mixture has fine even crumb. Add enough milk to make a soft dough.

Turn onto lightly floured surface and knead gently 1/2 minute. Roll into rectangle 1/4 inch thick.

Drain cherries and save juice. Place cherries on dough and roll as for jelly roll. Cut into 1-inch slices. Place cut surface down in greased 9-inch square baking dish.

Mix sugar and cornstarch. Add enough water to cherry juice to make 1 cup liquid and add to sugar-cornstarch mixture. Cook until thick and clear.

Bake rolls in hot oven (425°F.) 15 minutes.

Pour juice over rolls and bake 10 minutes longer. Makes 8 to 10 rolls.

RHUBARB ROSETTES

1 cup sifted enriched flour
1 1/2 teaspoons baking powder
1 tablespoon sugar
1/4 teaspoon salt
1/4 cup margarine
1/3 cup milk
3/4 cup sugar
2 cups rhubarb, cut 1/2-inch pieces

Sift together into mixing bowl flour, baking powder, 1 tablespoon sugar, and salt. Cut or blend in margarine with fork or pastry blender until mixture is like corn meal.

Add milk. Stir until flour is well moistened and dough holds together in a ball.

Turn out on lightly floured board or pastry cloth and knead lightly 4 or 5 times. Roll out to long sheet, a scant 1/2 inch thick and about 12 inches long.

Mix 3/4 cup sugar with rhubarb. Spread evenly over dough. Dot with margarine. Roll up like a jelly roll. Seal edge.

With sharp knife, cut across roll to make 9 slices about 1 1/2 inches thick. Set rolls cut side down into prepared pan.

Bake in hot oven (400°F.) 30 minutes. Serve warm. Put each rosette in dessert dish and spoon sauce from bottom of pan. Makes 9.

DEEP DISH PLUM DESSERT

3 cups unsweetened chopped plums
3/4 cup light corn syrup
1/4 teaspoon cinnamon
1/4 teaspoon nutmeg
2 tablespoons butter or margarine

Wash, pit, and chop plums. Add corn syrup and spices. Pour into a shallow greased baking dish. Dot plums with 2 tablespoons butter. Cover with crust.

To Make Crust: Use 1 1/2 cups sifted enriched flour, 2 teaspoons baking powder, 2 tablespoons sugar, 1/2 teaspoon salt, 6 tablespoons shortening, and about 1/2 cup milk.

Sift flour with baking powder, sugar, and salt. Cut in shortening. Add milk to make a soft dough. Roll out 1/2 inch thick.

Make several slashes in dough for steam to escape. Place over fruit to fit dish. Sprinkle with 2 tablespoons sugar. Bake in hot oven (400°F.) 45 minutes. Serve warm. Serves 8.

Variations: Apples, blackberries, cranberries, huckleberries, cherries, or peaches may be substituted for plums. Amount of syrup will vary according to fruit used. Sugar and fruit juice may be used instead of corn syrup.

SPICY APPLESAUCE CRUNCH

16 zwieback, finely rolled (1 1/3 cups crumbs)
1/2 cup butter or margarine
1/2 cup brown sugar
1 teaspoon cinnamon
2 cups thick tart applesauce

Sauté zwieback crumbs in butter or margarine until browned; mix in sugar and cinnamon.

Pour applesauce into 8-inch round baking dish or 9-inch pie plate. Top with crumbs.

Bake in slow oven (325°F.) 30 minutes. Serve hot garnished with whipped cream and jelly. Serves 6.

APPLE ROLY POLY

Biscuit or shortcake dough
4 tablespoons butter or margarine
3 tablespoons sugar
1/2 teaspoon cinnamon
3 or 4 tart apples, chopped
1/2 cup brown sugar
1 tablespoon lemon juice
1/2 cup water

Prepare recipe for biscuit or shortcake dough and pat dough into a rectangle about 1/2 inch thick. Brush with soft butter, sprinkle with sugar and cinnamon mixture.

Spread chopped apples over this. Roll like jelly roll. Cut into 1 1/2-inch crosswise slices.

Place slices cut side up in a buttered

baking dish about 2 inches deep, leaving space between.

Make a syrup of brown sugar, lemon juice, and water. Pour over biscuits.

Bake in hot oven (400°F.) 30 to 40 minutes. Serve warm, with whipped or plain cream. Serves 6.

Fruit Dumplings: Follow Roly Poly recipe, patting dough to 1/4-inch thickness. Cut into individual servings (squares or triangles). Fill with fruit, moisten edges with milk, pinch together. Bake in the syrup.

ANGEL FOOD SURPRISE CAKE

1 1/2 ounces (1/2 package) cherry-flavored gelatin
1 cup hot water
1/4 cup pitted red cherries
1 bakers' 13 1/2-ounce angel food cake
1/4 teaspoon vanilla
3/4 cup heavy cream, whipped

Dissolve cherry gelatin in water and stir until dissolved. Chill until slightly thick; fold in cherries.

Slice 1/2 inch of cake away from inner rim of angel food cake and cut it into 1/2-inch cubes; add to cherry gelatin.

Refill cake center with cherry gelatin and cake mixture.

Add vanilla to whipped cream. Cover top and sides of cake with whipped cream.

Place in refrigerator until ready to serve. Serves 8.

Angel Food Surprise Cake

Gelatin Desserts

Many wonderful desserts are made from a gelatin base. These are usually called creams, whips, or snows, according to the fruit combination, such as Bavarian Cream, Lemon Snow, or Prune Whip. Other desserts may be combinations of fruit, gelatin, or cream fillings plus cake or cooky foundation. These are often an ideal way of using the last of the angel food, sponge, or plain cake or extending a small amount of a food to fit your dessert needs.

Snow puddings attain a characteristic light airy texture through the addition of egg whites which have been folded in when the gelatin mixture begins to set. The same holds true of Bavarian creams except that whipped cream takes the place of the egg whites.

FRUIT WHIP

1   tablespoon (1 envelope) unflavored gelatin
1/4   cup fresh lime juice
1   teaspoon grated lime rind
3/4   cup syrup from canned fruit cocktail
1/2   cup sugar
1/4   teaspoon salt
Few drops almond extract
1   cup chilled evaporated milk
1 1/2   cups drained canned fruit cocktail
Ladyfingers (optional)

Soften gelatin in lime juice. Combine lime rind, syrup from fruit cocktail, sugar, and salt; heat, and dissolve softened gelatin in it. Blend in almond extract. Cool until slightly thickened.

Whip chilled evaporated milk in chilled bowl until light and fluffy. Fold in gelatin mixture. Chill a few minutes, until mixture mounds on a spoon.

Line serving dish with ladyfingers, if desired, and spoon pudding into dish Chill several hours, or overnight. Garnish with additional fruit cocktail, if desired. Serves 6 to 8.

Fruit Whip

FRUIT COCKTAIL MOLD

1   16-ounce can (2 cups) fruit cocktail
1   package strawberry-flavored gelatin
1   tablespoon (1 envelope) unflavored gelatin
2   tablespoons cold water
2   cups milk
2   eggs, separated
1/4   cup sugar
1/4   teaspoon salt
2   tablespoons sugar
1   teaspoon vanilla

Drain fruit cocktail thoroughly. Dissolve fruit flavored gelatin according to directions on package, replacing part of water with syrup drained from fruit cocktail. Chill until slightly thickened.

Fold in fruit cocktail. Pour into bottom half of ring mold or other fancy mold. Chill until firm.

Soften unflavored gelatin in 2 tablespoons water.

Heat milk to scalding in top of double boiler. Beat egg yolks, sugar, and salt together until light. Slowly stir in hot milk.

Return to double boiler. Cook, stirring constantly, until mixture coats spoon.

Remove from heat; add gelatin and stir until dissolved.

When cool and slightly thickened, fold in egg whites beaten stiff with remaining sugar and vanilla.

Pour into top half of mold. Chill until firm. Serves 6.

APPLESAUCE BAVARIAN PIE

1   tablespoon (1 envelope) unflavored gelatin
1/4   cup cold water
2   cups canned applesauce
1   (15-ounce) can sweetened condensed milk
1/3   cup lemon juice
1/4   cup orange juice
1   tablespoon grated orange rind
2   egg yolks
1   package chocolate wafers (2 1/4-inch diameter)
1/2   cup heavy cream

Soften gelatin in water. Heat applesauce; add gelatin. Stir until dissolved. Cool.

Combine condensed milk, lemon juice, orange juice, orange rind, and egg yolks; stir until mixture thickens. Add applesauce; mix well.

Line bottom and sides of 9-inch pie plate with chocolate wafers, standing wafers around edge. Cover with 1/2 applesauce mixture. Add layer of cookies, cover with remaining applesauce mixture. Place an overlapping circle of cookies on top. Chill. Just before serving; whip cream stiff, use as garnish. Serves 8.

Saucy Raspberry Dessert

SAUCY RASPBERRY DESSERT

1   package raspberry-flavored gelatin
1   cup hot water
1   cup canned applesauce
2   tablespoons sugar
1   teaspoon grated lemon rind
1   tablespoon lemon juice
2/3   cup chopped walnuts
3/4   cup tiny marshmallows
1/2   cup heavy cream, whipped

Dissolve raspberry gelatin in hot water; add applesauce, sugar, lemon rind and juice. Chill over ice water until slightly thickened. Fold in walnuts and marshmallows.

Pour into 1 quart mold. Chill until firm. Unmold and serve with whipped cream. Serves 6.

SNOW PUDDING

1   tablespoon (1 envelope) unflavored gelatin
1/2   cup cold water
3/4   cup boiling water
3/4   cup sugar
1/4   teaspoon salt
1/4   cup lemon juice
1   teaspoon grated lemon rind
2   egg whites, stiffly beaten

Soften gelatin in cold water. Add boiling water, sugar, and salt. Stir until dissolved. Add lemon juice and rind.

Chill until mixture is slightly thicker than consistency of unbeaten egg whites. Whip until light. Add stiffly beaten egg whites.

Place bowl in ice water. Continue beating until mixture begins to hold its shape. Pour into large or individual molds. Chill until firm.

Unmold and serve with soft custard, chocolate sauce, or fresh crushed berries or fruit. Serves 6.

Applesauce Bavarian Pie

ABOUT CHARLOTTES

A true charlotte is a fruit pudding, traditionally of apples only, cooked in a mold lined with bread that has been dipped in melted butter. Nowadays a vast variety of dishes are referred to as charlottes. They include many types of cold molded dishes; cream fillings, gelatin fillings, mixtures of nuts and fruits in various fillings, ices, etc., prepared in molds lined with ladyfingers, sponge cake, cookies, etc. The Charlotte Russe usually specifically refers to a cold dessert of Bavarian cream stiffened in a mold lined with ladyfingers or sometimes with cake or graham crackers.

COFFEE CHARLOTTE RUSSE

    1   tablespoon (1 envelope) unfla-
            vored gelatin
    1/2   cup sugar
    1/8   teaspoon salt
    2   tablespoons instant coffee
    1 1/4   cups milk
    2   eggs, separated
    1/2   teaspoon vanilla
    1   cup heavy cream, whipped
    Lady fingers or sponge cake

In top of double boiler, mix gelatin, 1/4 cup sugar, salt, and coffee. Stir in cold milk. Place over boiling water and scald, stirring constantly.

Beat egg yolks slightly. Slowly pour small amount of hot mixture over egg yolks. Return to double boiler and cook, stirring constantly, until mixture coats spoon, about 3 minutes.

Remove from heat and add vanilla. Chill until mixture is slightly thicker than consistency of unbeaten egg white.

Beat egg whites until stiff and gradually beat in remaining 1/4 cup sugar. Fold in gelatin mixture and whipped cream.

Spoon into individual serving dishes which have been lined with lady fingers or sponge cake, or turn into paper baking cups in muffin pan.

Chill until firm. Garnish with additional whipped cream, pecans, or chocolate cooky crumbs. Serves 10.

Coffee Charlotte Russe

LEMON GELATIN
(Master Recipe)

    2   tablespoons (2 envelopes) unfla-
            vored gelatin
    1/2   cup cold water
    2 1/2   cups boiling water
    3/4   cup sugar
    1/8   teaspoon salt
    3/4   cup lemon juice
    1   teaspoon grated lemon rind

Soften gelatin in cold water 5 minutes. Add hot water, sugar, and salt; stir until dissolved.

Add fruit juice and grated rind. Pour into molds and chill until firm.

Serve with plain or whipped cream, custard sauce, or fruits. Serves 6 to 8.

Lemon Gelatin Variations

Fruit Bavarian Cream: When gelatin begins to set, beat until foamy. Fold in 1 cup heavy cream which has been whipped and sweetened.

Add desired fruit pulp. Mold and chill.

Fruit Gelatin: Substitute canned fruit juices for water. If juices are sweet, they may replace sugar as well as the liquid and flavoring.

Add fruit when gelatin starts to set.

Gelatin Squares: Cut firm gelatin into cubes. Pile one or more colors in each cup or serve with cubed fruit.

Grape Gelatin: In master recipe substitute 1 teaspoon orange rind for lemon rind. Reduce sugar to 1/2 cup and reduce lemon juice to 1 tablespoon.

Substitute 1 1/2 cups grape juice for 1 1/2 cups water.

Lemon Snow or Sponge Pudding: When gelatin begins to set, beat with rotary beater until foamy.

Beat 2 to 3 egg whites until stiff and beat into gelatin foam. Mold and chill.

Molded Fruit Salads: Use lemon gelatin to mold fruits, vegetables, fish, or meat.

Tomato juice, chicken, or meat stock may be substituted for liquid; seasonings may be varied.

For specific recipes see salads.

Orange Gelatin: In master recipe substitute 1 1/2 cups orange juice for 1 cup water. Reduce lemon juice to 1/4 cup. Substitute orange rind for lemon rind.

Prune Jelly: In master recipe, substitute 1 1/2 cups prune juice for 1 1/2 cups liquid.

Add 1/2 cup each of raisins, cooked chopped prunes, and chopped nuts. Mold and chill.

Riced Gelatin: Chill gelatin until very firm. Force through potato ricer. Pile into serving dishes. Combine several colors per serving.

Whipped Gelatin: When gelatin is soft and quivery, beat with a rotary beater until light and fluffy. Mold or pile into serving dishes.

Please read about gelatin
in **Ingredients—**
How to Use Them.

LALLA ROOKH CREAM

    3   eggs, separated
    1/2   cup sugar
    1/2   cup cream
    1   tablespoon (1 envelope) unfla-
            vored gelatin
    2   tablespoons cold milk
    1   tablespoon rum
    1   cup heavy cream, whipped

Beat yolks and add sugar and cream. Cook over hot water, stirring constantly, until mixture coats spoon.

Soften gelatin in 2 tablespoons cold milk; add to mixture and stir until dissolved.

Remove from heat. Cool, add rum, stiffly beaten egg whites, and whipped cream.

Turn into mold. Chill until mixture holds its shape. Serve garnished with maraschino cherries and cherry juice. Serves 4.

APPLE STRAWBERRY SNOW

    1   tablespoon (1 envelope) unfla-
            vored gelatin
    1/4   cup cold water
    2   cups canned applesauce
    1/4   teaspoon nutmeg
    Dash of salt
    1   cup sliced, fresh strawberries
    1   teaspoon vanilla
    2   egg whites
    1/3   cup sugar

Soften gelatin in cold water 5 minutes. Combine applesauce, nutmeg, and salt; heat. Add gelatin, stirring until dissolved. Cool until slightly thickened. Add strawberries and vanilla.

Beat egg whites stiff, gradually add sugar, beating constantly. Fold into applesauce mixture. Pour into 1 quart mold; chill until firm. Unmold on serving plate. If desired, garnish with whipped cream and whole strawberries. Serves 6 to 8.

Apple Strawberry Snow

Apricot Charlotte Russe

APRICOT CHARLOTTE RUSSE

1½ tablespoons (1½ envelopes) un-
    flavored gelatin
1   can apricot nectar (1½ cups)
2   eggs, separated
½ cup sugar
⅛ teaspoon salt
⅔ cup evaporated milk
3   tablespoons lemon juice
1   cup evaporated milk, chilled icy
    cold

Soften gelatin in ½ cup of the apricot nectar.

Beat egg yolks, sugar, and salt in the
top of a double boiler. Gradually add
the remaining cup of apricot nectar,
then the ⅔ cup evaporated milk.

Cook over boiling water until thickened, about 7 to 10 minutes, stirring
constantly.

Add softened gelatin to the custard
and stir until gelatin is dissolved. Remove from heat and cool.

When the mixture is slightly thicker
than unbeaten egg white, add lemon
juice. Then whip the chilled milk very
stiff and fold into the apricot mixture.

Spoon into a spring form pan that
has been lined with vanilla wafers or
lady fingers.

Chill until set, about 2 to 3 hours.
Makes 8 generous servings.

SHERRY GELATIN

2   tablespoons (2 envelopes) unfla-
    vored gelatin
¼ cup cold water
1¼ cups boiling water
¾ cup sugar
¼ teaspoon salt
¼ cup orange juice
2   tablespoons lemon juice
1   cup sherry

Soften gelatin in cold water 5 minutes. Add boiling water, sugar, and salt.
Stir until dissolved.

Add orange and lemon juices and

sherry. Mix well. Turn into molds and
chill. Serves 6.

BAVARIAN CREAM
(Master Recipe)

1   tablespoon (1 envelope) unfla-
    vored gelatin
¼ cup cold water
2   egg yolks
½ cup sugar
¼ teaspoon salt
1   cup milk
1   cup heavy cream, whipped
½ teaspoon vanilla

Soften gelatin in cold water 5 minutes.

Beat egg yolks with sugar and salt.
Add to milk and cook in double boiler
until thick. Add softened gelatin. Stir
until dissolved.

Cool and, when mixture begins to
thicken, fold in whipped cream and
vanilla.

Turn into dampened mold and chill.
Unmold and serve with fruit sauce.
Serves 6.

Butterscotch Bavarian Cream: In
master recipe, omit granulated sugar.
Cook ¾ cup brown sugar with 2 tablespoons butter a few seconds, then add
to hot mixture.

Maple Bavarian Cream: In master
recipe, substitute shaved maple sugar
for granulated sugar. Add ½ cup
chopped pecans or walnuts.

STRAWBERRY BAVARIAN CREAM
(Master Recipe)

1   tablespoon (1 envelope) unfla-
    vored gelatin
2   tablespoons cold water
1½ cups crushed strawberries
About ½ cup sugar
⅛ teaspoon salt
1   tablespoon lemon juice
1   cup heavy cream, whipped

Soften gelatin in cold water 5 minutes. Place over hot water; stir until
dissolved.

Remove from heat. Add berries, sugar,
salt, and lemon juice. Mix well.

Cool until slightly thickened. Fold in
whipped cream. Turn into mold and
chill. Bottom of mold may be garnished with whole berries.

Unmold and serve plain, or with additional whole berries and whipped
cream. Serves 6.

Variations of
Strawberry Bavarian Cream

Apricot Bavarian Cream: In master
recipe, substitute diced apricots for
strawberries.

Berry-Banana Bavarian Cream: In
master recipe, substitute ¾ cup of
mashed ripe banana for ¾ cup crushed
berries.

Macaroon Bavarian Cream: In master recipe, add ¾ cup crushed macaroons with whipped cream.

Nut Bavarian Cream: In master
recipe, add ¾ cup chopped nuts with
whipped cream.

Peach Bavarian Cream: In master
recipe, substitute diced peaches for
strawberries.

Raspberry Bavarian Cream: In master recipe, substitute crushed raspberries for strawberries.

CHARLOTTE RUSSE

Line parfait glasses with lady fingers,
thin strips of angel food or sponge cake,
or macaroons.

Fill with any Bavarian cream mixture; garnish with pieces of fruit. Chill.

CHOCOLATE SPONGE
(Master Recipe)

1½ tablespoons (1½ envelopes) un-
    flavored gelatin
¼ cup cold water
1½ ounces (1½ squares) chocolate
⅓ cup sugar
¼ teaspoon salt
¼ cup boiling water
3   eggs, separated
1   teaspoon vanilla

Soften gelatin in cold water 5 minutes.

Melt chocolate in top of double
boiler; add sugar, salt, and boiling water. Bring to boil.

Remove from heat; add softened gelatin and stir until dissolved. Slowly add
to slightly beaten egg yolks.

Chill until mixture begins to thicken,
then fold in stiffly beaten egg whites
and vanilla.

Turn into dampened mold and chill.
Serve with whipped cream. Serves 6.

Variations of Chocolate Sponge

Chocolate Charlotte: Prepare chocolate sponge recipe. Line mold with lady
fingers or sponge cake before pouring
in gelatin mixture.

Macaroon Chocolate Sponge: To
master recipe, add ¾ cup crushed macaroons.

Nut Chocolate Sponge: To master
recipe, add ¾ cup chopped nuts.

Fruit Bavarian Cream

Double-Ring Dessert

SPANISH CREAM
(Master Recipe)

1 tablespoon (1 envelope) unflavored gelatin
¼ cup cold water
2 cups milk, scalded
3 eggs, separated
½ cup sugar
⅛ teaspoon salt
1 teaspoon vanilla

Soften gelatin in cold water 5 minutes; add scalded milk, stirring to dissolve gelatin.

Combine egg yolks, sugar, salt, and
gelatin mixture in top of double boiler.
Cook over hot water 5 minutes, stirring
constantly until sugar is dissolved.

Cool until slightly thickened. Add
vanilla. Fold in stiffly beaten egg whites.
Turn into molds. Chill until firm.

Unmold and serve with chocolate
sauce, whipped cream, or fruit. Serves 6.

Variations of Spanish Cream

Chocolate Spanish Cream: Follow
master recipe. Melt 2 1-ounce squares
unsweetened chocolate in milk. Beat
with rotary beater until blended.

Coffee Spanish Cream: In master
recipe, increase sugar to ⅔ cup. Substitute 1½ cups fresh hot coffee for
1½ cups milk.

Macaroon Spanish Cream: Follow
master recipe. Fold ¾ cup crushed
macaroons into egg whites.

Mocha Spanish Cream: In master
recipe, increase sugar to ⅔ cup. Decrease milk to ½ cup. Add 1½ cups
fresh hot coffee with 2 1-ounce squares
unsweetened chocolate dissolved in it.

Orange Spanish Cream: In master
recipe, omit vanilla and water. Add ½
teaspoon each grated lemon and orange
rind and 1 tablespoon lemon juice. Reduce scalded milk to 1½ cups. Soften
gelatin in ½ cup orange juice.

Angel Cream Loaf

DOUBLE-RING DESSERT

2 packages lemon-flavored gelatin
2½ cups hot water
1 quart vanilla ice cream
½ cup toasted slivered almonds
½ cup chopped maraschino cherries

Dissolve gelatin in hot water in 3-
quart saucepan. Spoon in ice cream;
stir until melted.

Chill until thickened but not set
(about 15 to 25 minutes); fold in almonds and cherries. Turn into 2 1-
quart ring molds. Chill until firm.

(If only one ring mold is available,
make up half the recipe, turn out of
mold when set, then make other half.)

To serve, cut a section (about ⅓
from one ring, place inside second ring
and line up remaining ⅔ of cut ring
alongside to give entwined circles effect. Serves 12.

ANGEL CREAM LOAF

20 thin chocolate wafers
2 tablespoons sugar
¼ teaspoon salt
1 tablespoon (1 envelope) unflavored gelatin
2 cups canned applesauce
3 egg yolks, beaten
½ teaspoon ground mace
1 tablespoon lemon juice
3 egg whites
2 tablespoons sugar
1 cup heavy cream

Line an 8½ x 4½ x 2¾-inch pan
with waxed paper. Place 3 chocolate
wafers in bottom of pan.

In top of double boiler mix 2 tablespoons sugar, salt, and gelatin. Add
applesauce and egg yolks. Stir well.
Cook over boiling water, stirring constantly, until gelatin is dissolved, about
7 minutes.

Remove from heat; stir in mace and
lemon juice. Chill until mixture is the
consistency of unbeaten egg white.

Beat egg whites until they hold a
stiff peak. Add 2 tablespoons sugar,
beating constantly. Fold into applesauce mixture until well blended. Whip
cream; fold into mixture.

Spoon ¼ of mixture on top of wafers
in prepared pan. Add a layer of wafers.
Repeat 3 times, ending with applesauce
mixture. Chill in refrigerator several
hours or overnight. Unmold on serving platter. Peel off paper. If desired,
serve with additional whipped cream.
Serves 8.

RUM PUDDING

1 tablespoon (1 envelope) unflavored gelatin
¾ cup milk
3 egg yolks
6 tablespoons sugar
¼ teaspoon salt
2 tablespoons rum

1 cup heavy cream, whipped

Soften gelatin in ¼ cup milk 5 minutes. Heat remaining ½ cup milk and
dissolve softened gelatin in it.

Beat egg yolks and sugar until light
and fluffy; add salt, rum, and dissolved
gelatin. Chill.

When partially thickened, fold in
whipped cream. Turn into individual
molds. Chill.

Unmold and serve with a fruit sauce.
Serves 4 to 6.

FRUIT MOUSSE

1½ cups sugar
2 tablespoons grated orange rind
½ cup boiling water
2 tablespoons (2 envelopes) unflavored gelatin
⅓ cup cold water
1½ cups orange juice
⅓ cup pineapple juice
¾ cup nonfat dry milk solids
¾ cup ice water
⅓ cup lemon juice
½ cup chopped, drained maraschino
  cherries
½ cup drained, crushed canned
  pineapple
1½ cups chopped blanched almonds

Chill a small bowl and beater for
whipping nonfat dry milk.

Put sugar, grated orange rind, and
boiling water into saucepan. Stir and
boil 1 minute.

Soften gelatin in cold water. Dissolve
it in hot syrup. Add orange juice and
pineapple juice.

Cool until mixture is partially set
and of a jelly-like consistency. When
gelatin mixture has thickened, fold in
whipped nonfat dry milk solids.

To whip nonfat dry milk, put ice
water in chilled bowl, sprinkle nonfat
dry milk on top. When mixture is partially whipped, add lemon juice and
beat until stiff (about 10 minutes).

After folding in whipped nonfat dry
milk, fold in cherries, nuts, and pineapple.

Pour into 1½-quart mold or 2 refrigerator trays and put in refrigerator
until set. Serve garnished with fresh or
canned fruit. Serves 10 to 12.

Fruit Mousse

Chilled Lemon Fluff

CHILLED LEMON FLUFF

18 to 20 large chocolate wafers, rolled fine (1½ cups)
⅓ cup melted butter or margarine
1 tablespoon (1 envelope) unflavored gelatin
¼ cup cold water
3 eggs, separated
½ cup sugar
¼ teaspoon salt
⅔ cup evaporated milk
⅓ cup water
1 teaspoon vanilla
1 cup evaporated milk, whipped
Grated rind and juice of 1 lemon

Chill bowl and beater to whip evaporated milk.

Mix chocolate crumbs and butter thoroughly. Press thin layer over sides and bottom of lightly buttered 8-inch square cake pan. Set in refrigerator to chill.

Soften gelatin in ¼ cup cold water.

Mix egg yolks, sugar, salt, evaporated milk, and the ⅓ cup water in top of double boiler. Cook until mixture thickens.

Add softened gelatin and stir until dissolved. Add vanilla and fold in stiffly beaten egg whites.

Chill until slightly congealed. Fold in whipped evaporated milk.

To whip evaporated milk, first chill milk in ice cube tray until crystals form around edge. Pour in chilled bowl. Add lemon juice after it is partially whipped and continue beating until it stands in peaks.

Fold in grated lemon rind. Pour into crust and chill until firm. Garnish with shaved milk chocolate or semi-sweet chocolate. Serves 9.

Prune Chiffon Melva

CRANBERRY WHIP

1½ cups cranberry juice cocktail
1 package lemon gelatin
½ cup evaporated milk, icy cold

Heat 1 cup cocktail. Pour over lemon gelatin. Stir until gelatin is dissolved. Add remaining ½ cup cocktail. Set in cool place to jell.

When mixture begins to jell, beat with egg beater until light and fluffy.

Beat cold evaporated milk in chilled bowl until very stiff. Fold into gelatin mixture. Spoon into individual molds or 1 large mold and chill until firm. Serves 4 to 6.

STRAWBERRY GELATIN WHIP

1 teaspoon grated lemon rind
1 cup sugar
1 tablespoon (1 envelope) unflavored gelatin
¼ cup cold water
¼ cup boiling water
3 tablespoons lemon juice
2 cups crushed fresh strawberries
4 egg whites
⅛ teaspoon salt
Whipped cream

Mix lemon rind and ½ cup sugar.

Soften gelatin in cold water and dissolve in boiling water. Add sugar mixture and stir until dissolved. Add lemon juice and berries. Chill over bowl of ice cubes.

When thickened and completely chilled, whip mixture until frothy.

Beat egg whites with salt until stiff. Gradually beat in remaining ½ cup sugar, blending well. Fold into gelatin mixture.

Spoon into serving dishes and chill. Serve with whipped cream. Serves 8.

PRUNE CHIFFON MELVA

1 tablespoon (1 envelope) unflavored gelatin
½ cup cold water
¼ cup sugar
¼ teaspoon salt
2 5-ounce cans strained cooked prunes or 1½ cups chopped, cooked prunes
3 tablespoons lemon juice
1 teaspoon Angostura bitters
1 cup heavy cream, whipped or ⅔ cup icy-cold evaporated milk, whipped

Sprinkle gelatin in cold water, place over boiling water (or in double boiler) and stir until dissolved. Add sugar and salt, stir until dissolved; remove from heat. Add prunes, lemon juice, and bitters.

Chill mixture until it is slightly thickened. Fold into whipped cream or whipped evaporated milk; pile gelatin mixture into sherbet or parfait glasses and chill until firm. Serves 4 to 6.

Cranberry Whip

PARTY DESSERT TO SERVE 25

1 1-pound 4½-ounce can pineapple chunks
2 12-ounce packages frozen sliced peaches, thawed
2 10-ounce packages frozen sliced strawberries, thawed
2 packages strawberry-flavored gelatin
2 quarts heavy cream
⅔ cup confectioners' sugar
¼ teaspoon salt
1 teaspoon ginger
1 7¼-ounce package coconut covered marshmallow cakes, cut in pieces

Drain fruit; combine peach and strawberry syrups and add enough water to make 4 cups. Heat to boiling. Add strawberry gelatin, stirring until gelatin is dissolved. Cool.

Combine heavy cream, sugar, salt, and ginger. Whip until cream holds peaks. Fold in drained fruits (cut peaches, if very large) and coconut covered marshmallow cake pieces. When gelatin is firm enough to mound when dropped from a spoon, fold into cream.

Turn into 3 greased molds in graduated sizes, 6-inch, 7-inch, and 8-inch. Freeze until firm. Unmold and stack together. Garnish with sliced fresh strawberries, whipped cream, and coconut covered marshmallow cakes. Serves 25.

Party Dessert to Serve 25

Pastel Snow Squares

PASTEL SNOW SQUARES

1   3-ounce package strawberry-fla-
    vored gelatin
1½ cups hot water
3   egg whites
¼   teaspoon salt
1   cup graham cracker crumbs, finely
    rolled, (about 12)

Sauce:
3   egg yolks
⅓   cup sugar
½   cup melted butter or margarine
1   tablespoon grated lemon rind
1   tablespoon lemon juice
½   cup heavy cream, whipped

Dissolve gelatin in hot water. Chill
until thick and syrupy. Beat egg whites
with salt until stiff but not dry. Fold
into gelatin. Turn into a 9-inch square
pan.

Cut gelatin into squares. Roll each
square in graham cracker crumbs. Pile
in sherbet glasses and top with sauce.
Sauce: Beat egg yolks until thick and
lemon-colored, gradually adding sugar.
Blend in melted butter, grated lemon
rind, and lemon juice. Fold in whipped
cream. Chill about 1 hour. Serves 6.
Variations: For variety make recipe
using different flavors of gelatin and
mix the colors in each serving.

Two-In-One Strawberry Charlotte

CHRISTMAS STAR MOLDS

1   tablespoon (1 envelope) unfla-
    vored gelatin
½   cup cold milk
¼   cup sugar
¼   teaspoon salt
1   cup sliced, pitted dates
1½ cups milk
⅓   cup sliced, candied cherries
⅓   cup slivered, blanched almonds
½   teaspoon vanilla
¼   teaspoon almond flavoring
½   cup heavy cream, whipped

Soften gelatin in cold milk about 5
minutes.

Combine sugar, salt, dates, and milk
and heat together to scalding. Remove
from heat; add gelatin and stir to dissolve.

Chill mixture until it begins to set.
Stir in fruits and flavorings. Whip
cream and fold in.

Turn into individual star molds or
1-quart mold that has been rinsed in
cold water. Chill until set. Serve with
whipped cream if desired. Serves 6.

BANANA BAVARIAN CREAM

1   package lemon-flavored gelatin
2   cups hot water
¼   teaspoon salt
⅔   cup sugar
½   cup heavy cream
5   bananas

Dissolve gelatin in hot water. Add
salt and sugar. Chill until cold and
syrupy.

Fold in cream, whipped only until
thick and shiny, but not stiff.

Crush bananas to pulp with silver
fork and fold at once into mixture.

Chill until slightly thickened. Turn
into mold.

Chill until firm. Unmold. Serve with
tart fruit sauce. Serves 8.

TWO-IN-ONE STRAWBERRY
CHARLOTTE

1   tablespoon (1 envelope) unfla-
    vored gelatin
2   tablespoons cold water
1½ cups finely crushed strawberries
1   tablespoon lemon juice
¾   cup sugar
⅛   teaspoon salt
1   cup heavy cream, whipped
Sugar wafers

Soften gelatin in cold water 5 minutes. Place over boiling water; stir until dissolved. Blend in strawberries,
lemon juice, sugar, and salt. When almost set, fold in whipped cream.

Line 1-quart mold or casserole with
sugar wafers. Spoon in strawberry mixture. Chill several hours until firm.
Serves 6.

Christmas Star Molds

GINGER-ORANGE REFRIGERATOR
PUDDING

1   tablespoon (1 envelope) unfla-
    vored gelatin
2   tablespoons cold water
2   cups milk
2   tablespoons cornstarch
½   cup sugar
2   egg yolks, beaten
1   cup orange juice
2   tablespoons grated orange rind
2   egg whites, stiffly beaten
2   cups (½ pound) crumbled ginger-
    snaps

Soften gelatin in cold water. Scald
milk in top of double boiler.

Sift together cornstarch and sugar.
Add milk. Cook 10 minutes, stirring
constantly.

Gradually add small amounts of hot
pudding to beaten egg yolks until both
are combined.

Return to double boiler and cook
an additional 2 minutes, stirring constantly.

Remove from heat and add softened
gelatin, orange juice, and rind. Let chill
1½ hours.

Fold stiffly beaten egg whites into
pudding.

Line serving dishes with gingersnaps.
Fill with alternate layers of orange pudding and gingersnaps, ending with layer
of gingersnaps.

Chill in refrigerator several hours or
overnight. Garnish edge of serving
dishes with gingersnap halves. Serves 8.

Ginger-Orange Refrigerator Pudding

RUSSIAN CREAM WITH STRAWBERRIES

    4   teaspoons (1⅓ envelopes) unfla-
          vored gelatin
    ¼   cup cold water
    2   cups cream
    ¼   cup sugar
    2   cups sour cream
    1   pint fresh or frozen strawberries
    Heavy cream, whipped

Soften gelatin in cold water.

Combine cream and sugar; heat to scalding but do not boil.

Dissolve softened gelatin in hot cream and sugar mixture. Chill until it begins to thicken, stirring occasionally.

Fold in sour cream, blending until smooth. Turn mixture into an oiled quart mold. Chill until firm.

Unmold on serving dish. Top with strawberries and garnish with whipped cream. Serves 8.

APRICOT ORANGE REFRIGERATOR DESSERT

    1   tablespoon (1 envelope) unfla-
          vored gelatin
    ¼   cup cold water
    ½   cup hot water
    ½   cup canned apricot juice
    ½   cup orange juice
    1   tablespoon lemon juice
    ¼   cup sugar
    Few grains of salt
    2   egg whites
    1½ cups crushed macaroons
    Whole macaroons

Soften gelatin in cold water. Add hot water and stir until dissolved. Add fruit juices, sugar, and salt. Chill.

When thickened, beat with rotary beater until frothy. Fold in stiffly beaten egg whites and crushed macaroons.

Line mold with additional macaroons. Fill with whipped mixture. Chill 6 hours.

Unmold and garnish top with small drained apricot halves, alternating with orange sections. Serves 6.

ANGEL FOOD GELATIN DESSERT

    1   package strawberry- or raspberry-
          flavored gelatin
    2   cups boiling water
    1   cup heavy cream, whipped
    4   cups crumbled angel food cake
    1   package frozen strawberries or
          raspberries

Dissolve gelatin in boiling water and let stand until partially thickened.

Whip thickened gelatin until light and fluffy. Fold in whipped cream and angel food cake pieces. Chill in 7-cup mold until firm.

Unmold and garnish with thawed berries and additional whipped cream. Serves 8.

ORANGE BAVARIAN CREAM

    2   tablespoons (2 envelopes) unfla-
          vored gelatin
    ½   cup cold water
    ½   cup boiling water
    1   cup sugar
    4   to 5 tablespoons lemon juice
    1½ cups orange juice and pulp
    ¼   teaspoon salt
    3   egg whites
    2   cups heavy cream, whipped

Soften gelatin in cold water 5 minutes. Add boiling water and sugar; stir until dissolved. Add lemon and orange juice and pulp.

Chill until partially set, then beat until foamy.

Add salt to egg whites and beat until stiff; fold into gelatin. Fold in whipped cream and turn into a dampened mold.

Chill until firm. Unmold on platter and garnish with orange sections. Serves 8 to 10.

Variations: Substitute other fresh fruits or cooked dried fruits for orange juice and pulp. Use drained juice instead of orange juice. Reduce sugar in accordance with sweetness of cooked fruit.

ORANGE CHARLOTTE RUSSE

Line mold with split lady fingers. Fill with orange Bavarian cream mixture.

SHERRY CREAM

    1   teaspoon grated lemon rind
    1¼ cups milk
    2   tablespoons sugar
    Few grains salt
    2   slightly beaten egg yolks
    1   tablespoon (1 envelope) unfla-
          vored gelatin
    ¼   cup cold water
    ¼   teaspoon vanilla
    2   tablespoons sherry
    2   egg whites
    1   cup heavy cream
    2½ tablespoons confectioners' sugar

Add lemon rind to milk and scald in top of double boiler over simmering water.

Add sugar and salt to egg yolks and blend. Pour hot milk gradually over egg yolks, stirring constantly.

Return to top of double boiler and cook over simmering water, stirring constantly, until mixture thickens. Remove from heat.

Meanwhile soften gelatin in cold water 5 minutes. Add to hot custard and stir to dissolve completely. Add vanilla and sherry and blend well.

Beat egg whites until stiff but not dry, then fold carefully into mixture. Chill until mixture begins to thicken.

Beat cream until stiff, adding confec-

tioners' sugar gradually. Fold into custard mixture. Turn into mold.

Cover with waxed paper. Place in refrigerator to chill until firm.

Unmold on serving plate and cover with thawed but icy-cold frozen strawberries. Serves 6.

PEAR MINT DELIGHT

    1   12-ounce jar mint jelly
    2   teaspoons (⅔ envelope) unfla-
          vored gelatin
    ¼   cup cold water
    Juice of 2 lemons
    1   cup heavy cream, whipped
    1   No. 2½ can large pear halves
    ¼   cup crème de menthe
    6   maraschino cherries

Beat jelly with fork until broken into small pieces. Soften gelatin in cold water, then dissolve over hot water.

Add lemon juice and gelatin to jelly.

Fold in whipped cream. Spoon into serving dishes.

Place a pear half cut-side-up in each dish.

Pour 2 teaspoons crème de menthe over each pear. Garnish centers with maraschino cherries. Chill thoroughly. Serves 6.

BANANA GELATIN DESSERT

    1   package fruit-flavored gelatin or 1
          tablespoon (1 envelope) unfla-
          vored gelatin
    2   ripe firm bananas
    Dessert topping

Mix gelatin according to package directions. Chill only until slightly thickened.

Partly fill 1 pint-sized mold with gelatin. (4 to 6 individual molds may be used in place of 1 large mold.)

Peel bananas, slice and arrange on top of the gelatin. Fill mold with remaining gelatin. Chill until firm.

Unmold. Garnish with additional slices of ripe banana or other fruit, if desired.

Serve plain or topped with cream, custard sauce or fruit sauce.

Serves 4 to 6.

Banana Gelatin Salad: Serve with sour cream, mayonnaise, or a tart French-style salad dressing. Garnish with crisp salad greens.

Banana Gelatin Dessert

LIME AND GRAPEFRUIT BAVARIAN

1   No. 2 can grapefruit segments
1   package lime-flavored gelatin
1/4 cup sugar
1 2/3 cups (1 tall can) evaporated milk, chilled icy cold
1/4 cup coarsely chopped pecans toasted

Drain juice from grapefruit segments. There should be 1 1/4 cups. If not, add water to make that amount. Heat to boiling point.

Combine gelatin with the sugar. Pour hot grapefruit juice over gelatin-sugar mixture and stir until dissolved.

Chill mixture to the consistency of unbeaten egg white. Then whip chilled milk very stiff, and fold lightly but thoroughly into the gelatin mixture.

Put a grapefruit segment into the bottom of each of 8 sherbet glasses. Pile Bavarian on top and garnish each serving with grapefruit segments. Chill at least 2 hours.

Just before serving, toast pecans in a moderate oven (375°F.) until crisp, about 5 minutes, and sprinkle over the top of each serving. Makes 8 generous servings.

MASTER CLEAR ORANGE GELATIN—FIVE WAYS

1   tablespoon (1 envelope) unflavored gelatin
1/2 cup cold orange juice
1 1/4 cups hot orange juice
1/3 cup sugar
1/8 teaspoon salt

Soften gelatin in cold orange juice. Add hot orange juice, sugar, and salt; stir until dissolved.

Pour into molds and chill until firm. Serves 4.

ORANGE SPANISH CREAM

Use recipe for orange gelatin with the following changes.

Soften gelatin in 1 cup cold milk in top of double boiler.

Place over boiling water. Add sugar and salt and stir until gelatin and sugar are dissolved.

Beat 2 egg yolks slightly. Pour small amount of hot mixture slowly over egg yolks. Return to double boiler and cook over hot, not boiling water, stirring constantly until mixture coats spoon.

Remove from heat; cool. Stir in 3/4 cup cold orange juice; chill until mixture is slightly thicker than unbeaten egg white consistency.

Beat 2 egg whites until stiff; fold in gelatin mixture. Turn into molds and chill until firm.

ORANGE CHARLOTTE

Use recipe for orange gelatin with the following changes.

Reduce hot orange juice to 1 cup.

Chill mixture until slightly thicker than unbeaten egg white consistency.

Whip 1 cup heavy cream and fold into gelatin mixture. Turn into molds and chill until firm. If desired, serve with chocolate sauce.

ORANGE SNOW

Use recipe for orange gelatin with the following changes.

Reduce hot orange juice to 1 cup; increase sugar to 1/2 cup.

Chill until mixture is slightly thicker than unbeaten egg white consistency; beat with rotary beater until light and fluffy.

Beat 2 egg whites until stiff; add gelatin mixture. Place bowl in ice water; continue to beat until mixture begins to hold its shape. Turn into molds and chill until firm.

ORANGE WHIP

Use recipe for orange gelatin with the following change.

Chill gelatin mixture until slightly thicker than unbeaten egg white consistency; beat with rotary beater until light and fluffy. Turn into molds and chill until firm.

RICE TIGER PARFAIT

White Layer:

1   tablespoon (1 envelope) unflavored gelatin
3/4 cup milk
1   cup hot rice
1/2 cup sugar
1/2 teaspoon salt
1/2 cup heavy cream, whipped

Dark Layer:

1   cup milk
1   cup cooked rice
2   tablespoons cocoa
1/4 cup sugar
1/4 teaspoon salt
1/4 teaspoon vanilla

White Layer: Soften gelatin in 3/4 cup cold milk until dissolved. Then add 1 cup hot cooked rice. Add 1/2 cup sugar and 1/2 teaspoon salt and let cool.

When cold, fold in cream which has been whipped stiff. Chill until firm.

Dark Layer: Heat 1 cup milk in double boiler. Add 1 cup cooked rice. Add cocoa which has been mixed with 1/4 cup sugar and 1/4 teaspoon salt. Cook about 35 minutes until thick, stirring occasionally. Add vanilla. Chill.

To Assemble Parfait: When both mixtures are cool, layer light and dark rice mixtures in parfait glasses. Chill until ready to serve.

Serve plain or topped with sweetened whipped cream and maraschino cherries. Serves 4.

RICE STRAWBERRY BAVARIAN

1/2 cup cold water
1   tablespoon (1 envelope) unflavored gelatin
1   cup hot cooked rice
1/4 cup sugar
1/4 teaspoon salt
1   teaspoon vanilla
1   cup heavy cream, whipped
1/2 cup mashed strawberries

Pour cold water into saucepan and sprinkle gelatin on top of water. Let stand 5 minutes.

Place saucepan over low heat and stir until gelatin has dissolved. Add hot cooked rice, sugar, salt, and vanilla. Mix well and cool.

When mixture begins to thicken, fold in cream which has been whipped. Add mashed strawberries and mix well. (Some strawberries are sweeter than others, so taste to see that sugar used is enough.)

Turn into greased mold or individual molds or pile into individual dessert dishes.

If rice strawberry bavarian has been molded, chill until firm. Then unmold and serve with sliced sweetened strawberries. Serves 5.

Orange Gelatin Desserts

Refrigerator Cakes

The term refrigerator cakes covers a wide variety of chilled desserts usually of some kind of small cakes, pieces of cake, or wafers combined with a filling of whipped cream, gelatin mixtures, fruits, nuts, etc. They are made at least several hours before serving and are kept cold in the refrigerator.

MARSHMALLOW REFRIGERATOR CAKE

2   cups marshmallows, quartered
3/4 cup heavy cream
2   cups stale cake crumbs
3   tablespoons chopped nuts
3   tablespoons chopped maraschino cherries
1/4 cup chopped dates

Soak marshmallows in cream 1/2 hour. Add remaining ingredients.

Press mixture into a mold. Let stand in refrigerator overnight. Serves 6.

CHOCOLATE REFRIGERATOR TORTE

2   1-ounce squares bitter chocolate
1/2 cup sugar
1/4 cup milk
4   beaten egg yolks
1   cup butter or margarine
1   cup confectioners' sugar
4   stiffly beaten egg whites
1/4 teaspoon salt
Lady fingers or sponge cake

Melt chocolate over hot water in top of double boiler.

Combine 1/2 cup sugar, milk, and beaten egg yolks. Add to chocolate and cook until thick and smooth. Cool.

Cream butter until very soft. Add confectioners' sugar and cream thoroughly. Add chocolate mixture and mix well.

Fold in stiffly beaten egg whites to which salt has been added.

Pour into straight-sided cake or torte pan that has been lined with lady fingers.

Chill in refrigerator several hours. Serve with whipped cream to which crushed peppermint candy has been added. Serves 6.

Chocolate Refrigerator Torte

ORANGE REFRIGERATOR CAKE

5   tablespoons lemon juice
1/2 cup orange juice
1   teaspoon grated orange rind
1/3 teaspoon grated lemon rind
1/4 teaspoon vanilla
3   tablespoons chopped, blanched almonds
1 1/3 cups (15-ounce can) sweetened condensed milk
Lady fingers or sponge cake

Combine fruit juices, grated rind, vanilla, almonds, and condensed milk.

Line mold with waxed paper. Put layer of lady fingers in bottom. Cover with fruit mixture and another layer of lady fingers, repeating until mixture is used, and topping with lady fingers. Chill overnight. Slice to serve. Serves 6.

ANGEL FOOD CHOCOLATE TORTE

1   large angel food cake
1   cup sweet butter or margarine
2 1/2 cups confectioners' sugar
1 1/2 teaspoons vanilla
2   1-ounce squares chocolate, melted
6   tablespoons cocoa
1/8 teaspoon salt
2   cups heavy cream
1/2 cup salted pistachio nuts, chopped

Slice cake into 3 layers.

Cream butter well. Beat 2 cups confectioners' sugar into the butter and cream well. Add 1 teaspoon vanilla and melted chocolate. Mix well and spread between layers.

Mix and sift 1/2 cup confectioners' sugar, cocoa, and salt. Add to the cream and chill 2 hours or more.

Add 1/2 teaspoon vanilla to cream and whip until stiff. Spread on tops and sides of cake. Sprinkle chopped nuts around sides of cake.

Chill thoroughly (2 hours or more) before serving. Serves 12 to 16.

MOCHA LOG

1   cup heavy cream
1/4 cup confectioners' sugar
1   tablespoon instant coffee powder
20 chocolate wafers
Chocolate curls (below)

Whip cream with confectioners' sugar and instant coffee until stiff. Spread chocolate wafers with cream and put together in stacks of 4 or 5. Freeze until cream is set.

Lay stacks on edge on a platter to make one long roll. Spread remaining cream on outside of roll. Freeze.

Remove from freezer about one hour before serving and store in refrigerator. Garnish with chocolate curls. (To make chocolate curls, slightly soften, but do not melt, a large bar of sweet chocolate. Use potato peeler to shave curls from back of candy bar.) To serve, slice diagonally. Serves 6 to 8.

Strawberry Angel Cake

STRAWBERRY ANGEL CAKE

1   large angel food cake
Powdered sugar
1   10-ounce package frozen strawberries
Juice from strawberries plus water to make 1 cup
1   3-ounce package strawberry-flavored gelatin
1/2 cup marshmallow whip
1   cup undiluted evaporated milk
2   tablespoons lemon juice

Prepare cake by cutting around cake 3/4-inch in from the outer edge and 1/2-inch in from center edge. Cut to within 1 inch of bottom. Scoop out cake between cuts with a fork. Dust powdered sugar on sides of cake.

Defrost strawberries. Drain juice. Add water to make 1 cup liquid. Heat to boiling.

Place gelatin in large bowl. Add hot liquid. Stir until dissolved. Add marshmallow whip to hot gelatin. Stir until blended. Chill until consistency of unbeaten egg white.

Chill evaporated milk in refrigerator tray until soft crystals form around edges (about 10 to 15 minutes). Whip until stiff (about 1 minute). Add lemon juice and whip until very stiff (about 2 minutes longer).

Fold strawberries and whipped evaporated milk into marshmallow mixture until well blended. Fill cake cavity and frost top with mixture. Chill until firm (about 3 hours). Slice and serve. Garnish with strawberries if desired. Serves 8 to 10.

Mocha Log

Chocolate Crumb Cake

CHOCOLATE CRUMB CAKE

18   large chocolate wafers
1/4   cup butter or margarine, melted
Dash of salt
2   cups milk
3   tablespoons cornstarch
1/2   cup sugar
1/4   teaspoon salt
3   eggs, separated
1   tablespoon (1 envelope) unfla-
    vored gelatin
3   tablespoons cold water
1 1/2   teaspoons vanilla
1/2   cup finely chopped nuts
Grated chocolate

Crush wafers with rolling pin (there should be about 1 1/2 cups); combine thoroughly with butter and dash of salt.

Press firmly onto sides and bottom of buttered 7 1/2-inch spring-form or straight-sided pan; set in refrigerator to chill.

Add milk to cornstarch which has been combined with 1/4 sugar and the salt. Add this mixture to slightly beaten egg yolks in top of double boiler. Cook over hot water until mixture is smooth and thickened; stir constantly.

Soften gelatin in cold water and set in pan of boiling water to melt. Add to custard.

Remove from heat and fold in egg whites, beaten stiff with remaining sugar.

Cool; add vanilla and nuts and pour into crumb-lined pan.

Grate chocolate over top and set in refrigerator 3 to 4 hours, or until firm. Serves 8.

Note: Serve cake on large plate garnished with small bunches of white or tokay grapes and mint leaves. And when grapes are no longer in season, maraschino cherries with stems make a pleasant color contrast.

Date and Nut Cream Roll

PEACH REFRIGERATOR TORTE

1   cup finely crushed graham
    crackers
1/4   cup and 1 tablespoon granulated
    sugar
4   tablespoons melted butter or mar-
    garine
3/4   cup syrup from canned cling
    peaches
1/8   teaspoon salt
2   teaspoons (2/3 envelope) unfla-
    vored gelatin
2   tablespoons lemon juice
1/4   teaspoon grated lemon rind
1/2   cup heavy cream, whipped
1 1/2   cups canned cling peach slices

Blend crumbs, 1 tablespoon sugar, and butter. Pat into bottom and halfway up sides of loaf pan (about 7 1/2 x 3 1/2 x 3 inches). Chill.

Heat syrup, 1/4 cup sugar, and salt together. Soften gelatin in lemon juice and dissolve in hot syrup. Blend in rind.

Cool until mixture reaches consistency of unbeaten egg white. Fold in whipped cream and well drained peach slices. Pour into crumb-lined pan.

Chill thoroughly. Cut into slices to serve. Serves 6.

VANILLA WAFER CAKE

Arrange a layer of vanilla wafers in bottom of a loaf pan.

Spread slightly sweetened whipped cream over wafers to a depth of about 1/4 inch. Then place another layer of wafers and whipped cream, repeating until pan is 3/4 full and ending with wafers.

Chill in refrigerator overnight. Serve with chocolate syrup.

DATE AND NUT CREAM ROLL

2   3-ounce packages cream cheese
1   8-ounce can date and nut bread
1   tablespoon light cream or orange
    juice
1   tablespoon finely chopped crystal-
    lized ginger, if desired

Allow cream cheese to soften at room temperature. Meanwhile, remove bread from can. Cut into slices about 3/8 inch thick.

Cream the cheese until fluffy. Stir in cream or orange juice. Add ginger, if desired.

Spread each slice evenly with cream cheese mixture. Place one slice on top of another. Frost entire roll with remaining cream cheese mixture.

Cover carefully so that cover does not touch roll and place in refrigerator until well chilled and cheese is firm, about 2 hours.

Just before serving, cut in diagonal slices to give striped appearance. Serves 6.

Chocolate Chiffon Cake

CHOCOLATE CHIFFON CAKE

12   lady fingers
1   tablespoon (1 envelope) unfla-
    vored gelatin
1/2   cup sugar, divided
1/4   teaspoon salt
3   eggs, separated
3/4   cup milk
1   cup semi-sweet chocolate pieces
1   teaspoon vanilla
2/3   cup icy cold evaporated milk,
    whipped

Split lady fingers; cut off one end to stand upright and fit sides of 8-inch spring-form pan.

Mix gelatin, 1/4 cup sugar, and salt in top of double boiler.

Combine egg yolks and milk; add to gelatin mixture. Add semi-sweet chocolate pieces.

Cook over boiling water, stirring occasionally, until gelatin is dissolved and chocolate is melted. Beat with rotary beater until blended.

Remove from heat; add vanilla. Chill until mixture mounds slightly when dropped from spoon.

Beat egg whites until stiff, but not dry. Gradually add remaining 1/4 cup sugar and beat until very stiff. Fold in chocolate mixture and whipped evaporated milk.

Turn into prepared pan; chill until firm. If desired, top with additional whipped cream and shaved chocolate. Serves 8 to 10.

PINEAPPLE-NUT REFRIGERATOR CAKE

1/2   cup butter or margarine
1   cup sugar
3   egg yolks
1   cup crushed canned pineapple
1/2   cup chopped nuts
14   graham crackers, crumbed
1/4   cup pineapple juice
1/2   cup heavy cream, whipped

Cream together butter and sugar. Add egg yolks and continue creaming until well blended. Add pineapple and nuts.

Arrange alternate layers of crumbs and pineapple mixture in a loaf pan, having crumbs as bottom and top layer.

Moisten with juice. Refrigerate for 12 hours. Serve in slices with whipped cream. Serves 6 to 8.

MOCHA REFRIGERATOR CAKE

2 teaspoons (2/3 envelope) unflavored gelatin
2 tablespoons cold water
1 cup hot water
1 tablespoon instant coffee
1/4 cup sugar
1/8 teaspoon salt
1 cup heavy cream, whipped
2/3 cup chocolate cooky crumbs

Soften gelatin in cold water 5 minutes.

Combine hot water and instant coffee. Add softened gelatin to hot coffee, stirring until dissolved. Add sugar and salt. Mix well.

Chill, stirring occasionally, until mixture becomes syrupy. Fold into whipped cream.

Turn half into a loaf or spring-form pan which has been lined with waxed paper. Sprinkle with 1/2 the cooky crumbs. Repeat, alternating layers of mixture and cooky crumbs.

Chill in refrigerator until firm, about 6 hours.

Unmold and cut loaf cake into slices or round cake into wedges. Garnish with whipped cream if desired. Serves 6.

PEPPERMINT CANDY CAKE

1/4 pound peppermint candy
1/2 cup milk
1 tablespoon (1 envelope) unflavored gelatin
2 tablespoons cold water
1 1/2 cups heavy cream, whipped
12 lady fingers, split

Put candy in cloth bag and pound with hammer to crush it. Add to milk and heat in double boiler until melted.

Soften gelatin in cold water 5 minutes. Dissolve in hot peppermint mixture.

Chill until it thickens, then whip until light. Fold in whipped cream.

Line loaf pan with waxed paper and cover bottom with layer of split lady fingers. Add 1/2 of peppermint mixture, then add another layer of lady fingers, the remaining filling, and finally, the remaining lady fingers. Chill until firm.

Garnish servings with shaved sweet chocolate, if desired. Serves 6.

Molded Jelly Roll

STRAWBERRY CREAM CAKE

1 tablespoon (1 envelope) unflavored gelatin
1/4 cup cold water
1 cup crushed strawberries
1 tablespoon lemon juice
1/2 cup sugar
1/4 teaspoon salt
1 1/2 cups heavy cream, whipped
24 lady fingers

Soften gelatin in cold water and dissolve over boiling water. Add to strawberries which have been combined with lemon juice, sugar, and salt.

Cool and, when mixture begins to congeal, fold in whipped cream.

Line sides and bottom of large square pan with split lady fingers. Cover with strawberry mixture. Top with layer of lady fingers, repeating until pan is full. Chill. Unmold on large platter. Serves 6.

ALMOND REFRIGERATOR CAKE

2/3 cup butter or margarine
2 cups powdered sugar
4 eggs, separated
1 teaspoon orange extract
1/4 teaspoon almond extract
1/2 cup shredded almonds
Lady fingers
18 macaroons

Cream butter and sugar. Add egg yolks, beating well. Add flavorings and almonds.

Fold in stiffly beaten egg whites.

Line mold with lady fingers. Add layer of filling, then a layer of macaroon crumbs. Repeat until 3 layers of filling are used.

Cover with macaroons and chill at least 24 hours before serving. Serves 6.

MOLDED JELLY ROLL

1 package raspberry-flavored gelatin
1 cup boiling water
1 cup raspberry juice
2 1/2 cups canned drained raspberries
1 1/2 cups heavy cream, whipped
1 jelly roll with red jelly
Additional 1 cup heavy cream, whipped
Fresh raspberries

Dissolve gelatin in boiling water. Add berry juice. Set aside to thicken.

Fold canned berries into whipped cream and add to gelatin mixture.

Line a spring-form pan with 1/2-inch-thick slices of jelly roll. Pour in gelatin mixture and chill 5 hours in refrigerator.

Turn out on platter; garnish with whipped cream and fresh raspberries. Serves 10 to 12.

Variations: Use strawberries, blackberries, etc., instead of raspberries.

Chocolate Nut Cake

CHOCOLATE NUT CAKE

2 8-ounce cans ready-to-serve chocolate nut roll
1 cup peanut butter
1 cup heavy cream
1/4 cup instant sweet milk cocoa
1/4 cup slivered blanched almonds

Slice each chocolate nut roll into 10 slices. Spread each slice, except one, with peanut butter. Stack slices and press together gently.

Whip heavy cream with cocoa. Lay log on side; cover with whipped cream. Garnish with slivered blanched almonds. Chill.

To serve, slice on a diagonal. Serves 12 to 14.

PEACH BLOSSOM CAKE

1 No. 2 1/2 can cling peach slices
1 envelope (1 tablespoon) unflavored gelatin
1/4 cup cold water
1 tablespoon lemon juice
1 1/2 cups whipping cream
1 1/2 cups crushed peanut brittle
1 8- or 9-inch bought round sponge cake
Mint sprigs

Drain peach slices, saving syrup. Chop 1 1/2 cups peach slices; reserve remainder for decorating. Heat 1/2 cup of the syrup to boiling.

Soften gelatin in cold water; dissolve in hot syrup. Cool slightly and add chopped peaches and lemon juice. Chill until partially set.

Whip 1/2 cup of the cream. Fold into peach mixture along with peanut brittle.

Slice cake in three layers. Fill with peach mixture; let stand in refrigerator at least 3 hours before serving.

Whip remaining cream; frost cake. Decorate with peach slices and mint sprigs. Serves 8 to 10.

Peach Blossom Cake

Yule Log

YULE LOG

21 graham crackers
2¼ cups canned applesauce
1 teaspoon nutmeg
½ cup finely chopped walnuts
½ cup heavy cream
Citron
Red cinnamon candies

Arrange 3 graham crackers in row in loaf pan lined with waxed paper.

Combine applesauce, nutmeg, and nuts. Add layer of applesauce mixture; repeat, using 7 layers of crackers and 6 layers of applesauce, ending with layer of crackers.

Chill in refrigerator several hours.

Just before serving, cover with whipped cream. Garnish with citron, cut in shape of holly leaves and red cinnamon candies. Slice and serve. Serves 6.

Variation: Instead of whipped cream cover, a white confectioners' sugar frosting may be used, if desired.

ALMOND COFFEE REFRIGERATOR CAKE

1 cup butter or margarine
1½ cups confectioners' sugar
2 egg yolks, well beaten
½ cup cold extra strong coffee
⅛ teaspoon salt
1 teaspoon vanilla
½ cup chopped toasted almonds
18 to 20 lady fingers
Whipped cream

Cream butter or margarine and cream in sugar gradually. Add egg yolks. Beat mixture until smooth and fluffy.

Add coffee, a little at a time, mixing enough to blend well after each addition. Add salt, vanilla, and chopped nuts.

Line loaf pan with waxed paper. Cover bottom of pan with split lady fingers flat-side-down.

Spread layer of coffee mixture over lady fingers. Cover with another layer of split lady fingers. Add more coffee mixture, then another layer of lady fingers.

Chill in refrigerator at least 4 hours. Turn out on small platter. Garnish with whipped cream. Serves 8.

VANILLA REFRIGERATOR CAKE PUDDING
(Master Recipe)

¾ cup sweet butter or margarine
1½ cups powdered sugar
6 eggs, separated
About 1 teaspoon vanilla
Sponge cake or lady fingers

Cream butter until light and fluffy. Add sugar. Cream well.

Beat in egg yolks, one at a time. Add vanilla or other flavoring. Fold in stiffly beaten egg whites.

Line mold with ladyfingers or strips of cake. Cover with mixture. Chill in refrigerator 24 hours. Serves 6.

Variations of
Vanilla Refrigerator Cake Pudding

Chocolate: Melt 1½ ounces (1½ squares) chocolate. Add slowly to first mixture.

Fruit: Add ¼ cup each well drained crushed pineapple and chopped maraschino cherries to mixture before folding in egg whites.

Lemon: Omit vanilla. Add juice and rind of 1 lemon to first mixture.

Macaroon: Add ¾ cup finely crushed, sifted macaroon crumbs to mixture before folding in egg whites.

LEMON REFRIGERATOR CAKE

1 cup sweet butter or margarine
1 cup sugar
3 egg yolks, unbeaten
Grated rind and juice of 1 lemon
3 egg whites
3½ dozen lady fingers

Cream butter and sugar together until very creamy. Add egg yolks and beat until very light. Add grated lemon rind and juice and beat.

Beat egg whites until stiff but not dry and fold into butter mixture.

Line bottom and sides of spring-form pan with lady fingers. Add filling and remaining lady fingers in layers, the top layer being lady fingers.

Refrigerate for 24 hours. Serve with whipped cream. Serves 8 to 10.

GRAHAM CRACKER PASTRIES

½ cup heavy cream
2 tablespoons jelly, whipped smooth
12 graham crackers

Whip cream stiff; blend in whipped jelly.

Spread cream on each graham cracker and put together in stacks of 4. Frost outside of stacks with remaining cream.

Chill in refrigerator about 3 hours.

To serve, cut stacks in half diagonally. Makes 6 pastries.

BANANA-BERRY REFRIGERATOR CAKE

1 pint raspberries or strawberries
10 tablespoons sugar
1 tablespoon (1 envelope) unflavored gelatin
¼ cup cold water
1 pint heavy cream
2½ dozen lady fingers
3 large ripe bananas, sliced

Pick over berries. Wash and drain. Add 4 tablespoons sugar and chill until ready to use.

Soften gelatin in cold water. Place over boiling water to dissolve.

Whip cream, beating in 4 tablespoons sugar gradually. Add gelatin and beat to smooth consistency.

Spread layer of whipped cream mixture over mold lined with lady fingers. Over this spread half the sugared berries.

Add another layer of lady fingers, then a layer of bananas, sprinkled with 2 tablespoons sugar. Add another layer of cream and finally a layer of lady fingers. Chill overnight. Serves 8.

CHOCOLATE REFRIGERATOR CAKE

4 1-ounce squares unsweetened chocolate
½ cup sugar
Dash of salt
¼ cup hot water
4 eggs, separated
1 teaspoon vanilla
1 cup heavy cream, whipped
2 dozen lady fingers

Melt chocolate over hot water. Add sugar, salt, and water, stirring until sugar is dissolved and mixture is blended. Remove from boiling water.

Add egg yolks, 1 at a time, beating thoroughly after each addition.

Place over boiling water and cook 2 minutes, stirring constantly.

Remove from heat. Add vanilla and fold in beaten egg whites. Chill. Fold in whipped cream.

Line bottom and sides of a waxed paper-lined mold with lady fingers. Turn chocolate mixture into mold. Place remaining lady fingers on top. Chill overnight in refrigerator. Serves 8.

Graham Cracker Pastries

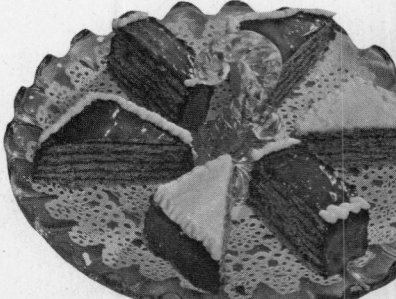

APRICOT REFRIGERATOR CAKE

    ¾ cup vanilla wafer crumbs
    1 teaspoon (⅓ envelope) unfla-
        vored gelatin
    2 tablespoons cold water
    ¼ cup butter or margarine
    1 cup confectioners' sugar
    1 egg yolk
    ¼ teaspoon almond extract
    12 cooked apricots, puréed
    1 cup heavy cream

Line bottom of 8-inch-square cake pan with ½ cup wafer crumbs.

Soften gelatin in cold water. Dissolve by placing in pan of hot water.

Cream butter or margarine and sugar until light and fluffy. Add egg yolk and almond extract and blend well. Blend in puréed apricots.

Whip cream and slowly whip in dissolved gelatin. Fold whipped cream into first mixture and spread over crumbs.

Top with remaining wafer crumbs. Chill in refrigerator overnight. Serves 8.

FRENCH REFRIGERATOR CAKE

    2 cups vanilla wafer crumbs (about
        ½ pound)
    ½ cup butter
    1 cup confectioners' sugar
    2 beaten eggs
    1 cup heavy cream, whipped
    ½ cup chopped nuts
    1 cup drained, crushed pineapple

Place 1 cup crumbs in ungreased, 8-inch square pan. Thoroughly cream butter and sugar; add eggs and beat well. Spread carefully over crumbs.

Combine cream, nuts, and pineapple. Spread over creamed mixture, then sprinkle with remaining crumbs. Let stand 18 to 24 hours. Cut in squares and serve on lace-paper doilies. Serves 8.

PINEAPPLE-CHERRY REFRIGERATOR TORTE

    ½ pound vanilla wafers (1½ cups
        crumbs)
    ½ cup butter
    1 cup confectioners' sugar
    2 beaten egg yolks
    2 stiffly-beaten egg whites
    1 8-ounce can crushed pineapple
    1 3-ounce bottle maraschino cher-
        ries, chopped
    1½ cups heavy cream, whipped

Roll wafers to crumbs; place half in 8-inch square pan. Thoroughly cream butter and sugar; add egg yolks and beat well. Fold in egg whites.

Spread over crumbs. Arrange pineapple, pineapple syrup, and cherries over creamed mixture.

Add cherry syrup to whipped cream; spread over fruit. Top with remaining crumbs. Chill in refrigerator overnight. Serves 8.

REFRIGERATOR FRUIT CAKE

    ½ cup butter or margarine, melted
    1½ cups quick oats
    1 pound chopped pecans or walnuts
    1 tablespoon (1 envelope) unfla-
        vored gelatin
    2 tablespoons water
    1 cup marshmallow creme
    ½ pound chopped dates
    ½ pound chopped figs
    ½ pound chopped candied mixed
        fruits
    ½ teaspoon salt
    2 teaspoons orange extract
    1 cup heavy cream, whipped
    Cherries
    Candied fruit peel

Combine butter or margarine, quick oats, and nuts. Toast until brown in shallow pan in hot oven (400°F.). Turn frequently.

Soak gelatin in water 5 minutes. Dissolve over hot water. Add to marshmallow creme.

Mix ¾ of the toasted oats and nuts, marshmallow creme, dates, figs, mixed fruits, salt, and flavoring. Fold in whipped cream.

Sprinkle remaining toasted oats and nuts in bottom of waxed paper-lined 8-inch-deep layer or spring-form pan. Pack cake mixture into pan firmly. Cover and chill overnight.

Unmold and garnish with cherries and candied fruit peel in any desired design. Serves 8 to 10.

PEACH REFRIGERATOR CAKE

    1⅓ cups (15-ounce can) sweetened
        condensed milk
    ¼ cup lemon juice
    1 cup sliced peaches
    2 stiffly beaten egg whites
    2 dozen chocolate wafers

Blend milk and lemon juice thoroughly. Add sliced peaches. Fold in egg whites.

Line pan with waxed paper. Cover with fruit mixture, topping with layer of chocolate wafers. Repeat until fruit mixture is all used, topping with layer of wafers.

Chill in refrigerator 6 to 8 hours. Unmold. Remove waxed paper. Serves 6.

FROZEN TRIFLE

    1 slice butter cake, 1 inch thick
    ½ cup sherry
    ½ cup toasted almonds, chopped
    ½ cup strawberry or raspberry jam
    2 egg yolks
    6 tablespoons sugar
    Pinch of salt
    1 cup scalded milk
    1 cup heavy cream, whipped

Cut cake to fit refrigerator tray. Pour sherry over it slowly so that it will absorb the wine. Add half the nuts and cover with jam.

Beat together egg yolks, sugar, and salt. Pour scalded milk slowly over this. Cook over boiling water, stirring constantly, until the mixture coats a spoon.

Chill and add stiffly whipped cream. Pour over cake, cover with the remaining nuts, and place in freezing tray until frozen just enough to slice. Serves 6.

LEMON ANGEL REFRIGERATOR CAKE

    1 tablespoon (1 envelope) unfla-
        vored gelatin
    ¼ cup cold water
    6 egg yolks, slightly beaten
    ¾ cup sugar
    ¾ cup lemon juice
    1½ teaspoons grated lemon rind
    6 egg whites
    ¾ cup sugar
    1 large angel food cake
    1 cup cream, whipped

Soften gelatin in cold water. Combine egg yolks, ¾ cup sugar, and lemon juice and rind, and cook over hot water (not boiling) until mixture coats a spoon.

Remove from heat, add gelatin. Stir until dissolved; cool. Stir in a drop or two of yellow food coloring if you wish to deepen the color.

Beat egg whites until stiff, and gradually add remaining sugar while beating constantly. Fold into custard.

Cut large angel food cake into 3 layers. When filling is slightly congealed, spread between layers and very thinly over top and sides of cake.

Chill until nearly ready to serve, then frost with thin coating of whipped cream. Make about 5 flower decorations on top of cake, using pastel-colored Jordan almonds for petals.

CHOCOLATE RIBBON LOAF

    1 package chocolate pudding
    2 cups milk
    24 graham crackers
    ½ cup heavy cream, whipped stiff

Prepare chocolate pudding according to directions on package, using 2 cups milk; cool.

Spread pudding on 23 graham crackers and put together in stacks of 4 or 5. Then lay stacks on edge on a long platter to make one long roll, with crackers and pudding alternating. (Leave last cracker plain.)

Spread remaining pudding on top of loaf; frost sides and ends with whipped cream.

Chill in refrigerator about 3 hours. To serve, slice diagonally, at a 45° angle. Serves 6.

RUSSIAN TORTE

Angel food cake
2 tablespoons (2 envelopes) unfla-
    vored gelatin
1/4 cup water
1 cup confectioners' sugar
1/8 teaspoon salt
2 tablespoons strong liquid coffee
8 egg yolks
1 pint heavy cream
1 teaspoon vanilla
1/2 cup chopped almonds, roasted

Cut angel food cake in two, the bottom layer a little thicker than the top.
Soften gelatin in cold water about 5
minutes. Put over boiling water to dissolve.
Add confectioners' sugar, salt, coffee,
and set aside until it begins to jell.
In the meantime, have egg yolks well
beaten, add the cream, beaten stiff, and
vanilla.
Combine the two mixtures before
the gelatin sets. Then beat thoroughly.
Spread between layers and over top.
Sprinkle with almonds. Chill thoroughly.

CRANBERRY REFRIGERATOR CAKE

1 egg white
2 cups cranberry sauce
1/2 cup chopped nuts
Sponge cake
1/2 cup heavy cream, whipped and
    sweetened

Beat egg white until stiff. Combine
with cranberry sauce and fold in
chopped nuts.
Slice layers of sponge cake to fit a
loaf pan. Alternate layers of cake and
sauce until pan is full, finishing with
a layer of cake.
Place weight on top. Let stand in
refrigerator 8 hours.
Unmold. Garnish with whipped
cream. Cut in slices to serve. Serves 6.

APPLESAUCE REFRIGERATOR CAKE

2 teaspoons cornstarch
1/2 cup sugar
1 cup applesauce
1 tablespoon melted butter or mar-
    garine
4 eggs, separated
Juice of 1 lemon
24 lady fingers

Combine cornstarch, sugar, applesauce, butter, and beaten egg yolks.
Cook in top of double boiler, stirring
constantly, until thick.
Remove from heat. Add lemon juice
and, when partially cold, fold in stiffly
beaten egg whites.
Spread layer of filling over small
mold lined with split lady fingers. Cover
with layer of lady fingers. Repeat until
mold is filled. Chill 24 hours. Serves 6.

WALNUT PRINCESS CAKE

1 tablespoon (1 envelope) unfla-
    vored gelatin
3 tablespoons cold water
1 cup maple syrup
Dash of salt
1 cup heavy cream, whipped
1/2 cup chopped walnuts
Walnut halves
1 10-inch angel cake

Soften gelatin in cold water. Heat
syrup and dissolve gelatin and salt in
it. Cool until slightly thickened.
Fold in whipped cream and chopped
walnuts. Chill a few minutes until mixture is almost set.
Spread on sides and top of large
angel cake or sponge cake. Decorate
with walnut halves. Chill.

TOFFEE REFRIGERATOR CAKE

1 package baker's sponge cake
    (2 layers)
1 package butterscotch pudding mix
2 cups milk
1 cup heavy cream, whipped, or 1
    can pressure-whipped cream

Cut sponge layers in half, crosswise,
to make 4 layers.
Prepare pudding mix as directed on
package, using the 2 cups milk.
Press one of the cake layers into a
medium-sized mixing bowl. Add 1/3 of
the cooked pudding, another cake layer,
and so on, ending with the 4th cake
layer. Chill several hours or overnight.
Unmold on serving plate. Swirl
whipped cream on top and sides. Decorate with chocolate-tipped salted almonds (melt 1 square unsweetened
chocolate over hot water, dip wide ends
of almonds in chocolate). Serves 8.

FIG BAR REFRIGERATOR CAKE

1 package lemon-flavored gelatin
1 cup hot water
2 packages fig bars or newtons
1 small can evaporated milk
Grated rind of 1/2 lemon

Dissolve gelatin in hot water. Chill
until slightly thickened. Line baking
pan or deep refrigerator tray with
waxed paper; then line with fig bars
or newtons, standing them on end
around sides of pan. Reserve half of
the fig bars for the top.
When gelatin is partially thick, beat
it until light.
Chill evaporated milk and whip. Fold
into gelatin, together with the lemon
rind.
Pour half of mixture over fig bars.
Add a layer of crumbled figs bars, then
the rest of the gelatin mixture. Cover
top with the rest of the whole fig bars.
Chill until firm, then unmold, decorate with fig flowers, and serve with
whipped cream. Serves 6 to 8.

Walnut Princess Cake

GINGERSNAP REFRIGERATOR CAKE

1/2 cup soft butter or margarine
1 cup confectioners' sugar
2 eggs
1 teaspoon vanilla
1 cup pineapple, cut fine
3 bananas, cut fine
1/2 cup chopped almonds
3/4 cup heavy cream, whipped
1/2 pound gingersnaps, crushed fine

Cream butter and sugar. Beat in
eggs and vanilla. Whip mixture until
creamy.
Combine fruit, nuts, and whipped
cream. Fold in 1 tablespoon confectioners' sugar.
Cover bottom of a deep pan with
crumbs. Pour creamed mixture over
this, and sprinkle with crumb mixture.
Add layer of whipped cream mixture. Sprinkle remaining crumbs on
top.
Chill in refrigerator overnight.
Serves 6 to 8.

MAPLE REFRIGERATOR CAKE

2/3 cup maple syrup
1 1/3 cups (15-ounce can) sweetened
    condensed milk
1/2 cup heavy cream, whipped
24 vanilla wafers

Blend syrup and milk and bring
slowly to boil in heavy saucepan. Cook
gently until thickened, about 4 minutes. Cool and fold in whipped cream.
Pour into a waxed paper-lined pan
in a thin layer. Cover with layer of
wafers. Repeat until all of maple mixture is used. Finish with layer of wafers.
Chill in refrigerator 6 hours. Turn
out on small platter. Remove waxed
paper. Serves 6.

Fig Bar Refrigerator Cake

Miscellaneous Chilled Desserts

FRENCH CREAM PUDDING

½ pound vanilla wafers
½ cup butter or margarine
1 cup confectioners' sugar
2 eggs
1 cup heavy cream, whipped
¾ cup black walnut meats, finely chopped
¾ cup maraschino cherries, finely chopped

Crush vanilla wafers fine. Place ½ the crumbs in bottom of buttered loaf pan.

Cream together butter or margarine and sugar until light and fluffy.

Beat eggs until well blended and add to first mixture and blend well.

Fold in whipped cream, nuts, and cherries. Spread over crumbs. Top with remaining crumbs.

Chill in refrigerator 24 hours before serving. Cut in squares to serve.

Serves 6 to 8.

FRUIT FLUFFS

2 cups (1 pint) heavy cream, whipped
2 cups drained mandarin orange sections
1 cup drained canned pineapple tidbits
1 cup seedless grapes
1 cup sliced bananas
1 cup maraschino cherries, cut in halves
1 10¼-ounce package shortbread cookies, crushed
½ teaspoon mace

Whip 1 cup heavy cream until stiff. Fold in 1½ cups mandarin orange sections and next four ingredients.

Line a 9-inch square pan with wax paper, allowing edges to extend above pan. Spread half of the crushed shortbread cookies mixed with mace evenly over bottom of pan; fill with fruit mixture, top with remaining crumbs. Chill overnight.

Remove from pan, cut into 10 rectangular pieces. Garnish individual pieces with reserved whipped cream and orange sections. Serves 10.

Fruit Fluffs

ALMOND STRAWBERRY TRIFLE

1 package (regular) vanilla pudding and pie filling mix (not instant)
1½ cups milk
Dash of salt
⅓ cup orange juice or white dinner wine
20 ladyfingers
½ cup toasted blanched slivered almonds
¼ cup strawberry jelly
1 cup whipping cream
Additional almonds for garnish
Fresh strawberries or strawberry jelly

Prepare pudding mix as package directs using only 1½ cups milk and salt. Remove from heat and add ¼ cup orange juice. Chill.

To make trifle; arrange ladyfingers over bottom and around sides of 8-inch spring-form pan or serving dish. Sprinkle with remaining orange juice and the almonds. Spoon on jelly. Pour chilled pudding over jelly; refrigerate several hours.

Whip cream and spread over top of pudding. Garnish with additional almonds and fresh strawberries, or dollops of strawberry jelly, if desired. Serves 6 to 8.

TOFFEE REFRIGERATOR DESSERT

1 cup vanilla wafer crumbs
½ cup butter or margarine
1 cup confectioners' sugar
3 eggs, separated
1 1-ounce square unsweetened chocolate, melted
½ teaspoon vanilla
½ cup finely chopped nuts

Line bottom of 8-inch square cake pan or large freezing tray with ½ the vanilla wafer crumbs.

Cream butter or margarine and sugar together until light and fluffy. Beat in slightly beaten egg yolks and melted chocolate.

Cool slightly and fold in stiffly beaten egg whites and vanilla. Spread over crumbs. Top with remaining crumbs and nuts.

Place in freezing compartment of refrigerator to chill 24 hours. It will become firm but not frozen. Cut in squares and serve plain or top each serving with small scoop of ice cream.

Serves 6 to 8.

FRUIT COCKTAIL MARLOW

Cut ½ pound marshmallows into quarters and dissolve in 1 cup strong, hot coffee in the top of a double boiler.

Cool until mixture begins to thicken. Fold in 1 cup whipped cream and 2 cups drained canned fruit cocktail. Pour into sherbet glasses and chill. Serves 6.

Almond Strawberry Trifle

PINEAPPLE REFRIGERATOR DESSERT

6 ounces vanilla sugar wafers
½ cup butter or margarine
1 cup confectioners' sugar
2 well beaten eggs
4 large slices canned pineapple, cut up
½ pint heavy cream, whipped

Crush wafers. Line buttered 11 x 7 x 1½-inch cake pan with ¾ of the crumbs.

Cream butter and sugar together until light and fluffy; add eggs and blend thoroughly. Spread over crumbs.

Arrange pineapple pieces over egg mixture.

Whip cream and spread over pineapple. Sprinkle remaining crumbs over cream.

Cover with waxed paper. Refrigerate for 24 hours. Serves 8 to 10.

FRUITED SYLLABUB

2 cups heavy cream
4 egg whites
½ cup confectioners' sugar
¼ teaspoon salt
½ cup chopped blanched almonds
½ cup glacé cherries, chopped fine
½ cup orange juice
1 teaspoon lemon juice
¼ teaspoon almond extract

Whip cream. Beat egg whites to soft-peak stage. Combine with the whipped cream. Fold in sugar and salt.

Add the almonds and cherries.

Combine juices and almond extract and fold into mixture.

Chill until very cold. Serve in parfait or sherbet glasses. Serves 10 to 12.

Fruit Cocktail Marlow

FROSTY SECRET

1 egg
¾ cup sugar
¾ cup cocoa
⅓ cup margarine
1 cup chopped toasted pecans
1 cup vanilla wafer crumbs

Beat egg and sugar together until lemon colored and fluffy. Add cocoa and continue beating until well blended.

Add margarine to cocoa mixture and beat thoroughly. Add pecans and cooky crumbs.

Turn mixture into 8-inch pie pan and place in refrigerator several hours. Garnish with whipped cream.

Serves 8 to 12.

SCOTCH REFRIGERATOR DESSERT

3 tablespoons butter or margarine
1 cup firmly packed brown sugar
¼ cup sifted flour
1½ cups milk
2 eggs, separated
½ teaspoon vanilla
1 cup coarsely chopped pecans
1 box vanilla or gingersnap wafers, crushed

Melt butter or margarine in top of a double boiler over direct heat.

Mix sugar and flour; add to melted butter or margarine. Blend well.

Add milk; cook over hot water, stirring constantly, until thick and smooth. Cook 15 minutes longer.

Pour slowly over slightly beaten egg yolks, stirring constantly. Cook 2 minutes longer. Cool. Add vanilla.

Gently fold in stiffly beaten egg whites.

Cover bottom of refrigerator tray with ⅓ cooky crumbs. Cover with ½ cooked filling; top with another layer of crumbs and chopped pecans. Continue until all are used.

Place in freezing compartment and chill several hours. To serve, cut into squares or oblong pieces. Top with whipped cream. Serves 6.

DOUBLE CHOCOLATE ROLL

1 cup heavy cream
½ cup instant sweet cocoa mix
Dash of salt
23 large chocolate wafers

Pour cream into well chilled bowl; add cocoa mix and salt. Beat with rotary egg beater until cream stands in peaks.

Spread cream on chocolate wafers and put together in stacks of 4 or 5. Then lay stacks on edge on a platter to make one long roll, with cookies and cream alternating.

Spread remaining cream on outside of roll. Chill in refrigerator for 3 hours.

To serve, slice diagonally at a 45° angle about 1 inch thick. Serves 6.

CHEESE FREEZE

2 cups chocolate cooky crumbs
½ cup soft butter or margarine
½ cup confectioners' sugar
4 eggs, separated
¾ cup granulated sugar (¼ cup in custard mixture, ½ cup in egg whites)
⅓ cup flour
½ cup milk
2 tablespoons (2 envelopes) unflavored gelatin
½ cup cold water
1½ pounds cottage cheese, sieved
Grated rind of 2 lemons
2 tablespoons lemon juice
2 teaspoons lemon extract
1 teaspoon vanilla
½ pint heavy cream, whipped

Line a spring-form pan with a mixture of chocolate cooky crumbs, butter, and confectioners' sugar.

Make a custard by combining egg yolks, ¼ cup sugar, and flour in top of double boiler; gradually stir in warm milk and cook over boiling water for a few minutes.

Soften gelatin in cold water for 5 minutes; stir into custard. Let cool and add cheese, lemon rind, lemon juice, lemon extract, vanilla, and whipped cream.

Finally fold in stiffly beaten egg whites to which ½ cup sugar has been added. Turn into crumb-lined pan. Chill until firm. When ready to serve, garnish top with some chocolate crumbs and strawberry halves. Serves 10 to 12.

CHOCOLATE REFRIGERATOR DESSERT

½ cup milk
⅔ cup sugar
5 beaten egg yolks
1 cup butter or margarine
1 cup confectioners' sugar
2½ 1-ounce squares chocolate, melted and cooled
5 egg whites
1 cup fine vanilla wafer or graham cracker crumbs

Combine milk, sugar, and beaten egg yolks. Cook over low heat or over boiling water, stirring constantly, until thickened. Cool.

Cream together butter, confectioners' sugar, and cooled chocolate; blend into cold custard mixture.

Beat egg whites stiff. Fold chocolate mixture into egg whites. Blend well.

Sprinkle half of crumbs over bottom of 8 x 8 x 2-inch pan. Pour above mixture into pan. Cover top with remaining crumbs.

Chill in refrigerator at least 12 hours. Cut into squares. Serve with whipped cream. Serves 12 to 16.

Cheese Freeze

MACAROON MALLOW CRÈME

16 marshmallows, cut up
1 cup milk
10 almond macaroons
1 cup heavy cream, whipped
Few grains salt
Vanilla or almond flavoring

Dissolve marshmallows in milk over hot water. Cool.

Macaroons should not be too fresh. Break apart into coarse crumbs. (If macaroons are fresh, toast them in slow oven to dry out; then break up or crush coarsely.) Fold macaroon crumbs into whipped cream.

Fold in cooled marshmallow-milk mixture and salt. Add flavoring to taste.

Freeze, stirring several times during freezing period, until firm. Serves 4.

CROWN ROYALE

1¼ cups boiling water
1 package cherry-flavored gelatin
1 pint vanilla ice cream
Vanilla wafers
Maraschino cherries
Whipped cream

Dissolve gelatin in boiling water. Stir in ice cream until well blended.

Chill until thickened, then place a small amount in bottom of 1-quart casserole.

Carefully arrange vanilla wafers around edge of casserole; pour in remaining filling. Chill until set.

Unmold onto serving plate. Garnish with maraschino cherries, whipped cream, and a cooky in the center, topped with a cherry. Serves 6.

Crown Royale

Frozen Desserts

CLASSES OF FROZEN DESSERTS

The family of frozen desserts includes many kinds of delicacies which are divided into several classes.

1. Ice Cream

a. Plain or Philadelphia ice cream: Milk or cream is sweetened, flavored and frozen. It may or may not contain either gelatin or eggs.

b. French, New York or cooked ice cream: Cream is folded into a custard foundation containing many egg yolks and the mixture is frozen.

c. American ice cream: Similar to French ice cream except that flour or cornstarch is substituted for part or all of the egg yolks.

d. Parfait: Whipped cream and flavoring are folded into a foundation of beaten egg whites or yolks cooked with hot syrup, and the mixture is frozen.

e. Frozen pudding: Actually French ice cream which has the egg whites added separately. Contains generous amounts of fruit or nuts.

2. Frozen Custard

Similar to New York ice cream except that the egg whites are added separately. Usually has a lower fat content than is legal for ice creams.

3. Ice

Fruit juice, sweetened with sugar, diluted with water and frozen. May or may not contain gelatin or eggs. Frappés are ices frozen to a slushy consistency.

4. Sherbet

Frozen mixture of fruit juice, sugar and milk, cream or ice cream. Usually contains a stabilizer such as gelatin. A sorbet is a sherbet made with a combination of fruit juices; a lacto is a sherbet made with sour milk; soufflés are sherbets made with whole eggs.

5. Mousse

Still-frozen dessert of sweetened, flavored whipped cream. May or may not contain fruits.

General Directions for Preparing Frozen Desserts in Refrigerator

1. Rapid freezing is important to make refrigerator ice creams that are smooth. Speed up freezing by turning temperature control to coldest point 1/2 hour before preparing dessert. Allow control to remain at this point until dessert is frozen.

2. The dessert is apt to freeze more rapidly if ice cubes are not being frozen at the same time.

3. Measure sugar or any other sweetening agent carefully; excess sugar retards freezing.

4. Remove ice cubes from tray to be used and replace empty tray in refrigerator to chill while preparing dessert.

5. Pour mixture into cold tray and place tray in fastest freezing position in the unit. Usually this is the bottom of freezing unit.

6. For more rapid freezing, moisten inside bottom of freezing unit with a little water before replacing tray. This way the tray will contact the freezing unit immediately.

7. Most frozen desserts are smoother when beaten once during the freezing process. Freeze mix to consistency of mush (don't let it get too hard if you want a smooth product); empty into a chilled bowl and beat until fluffy but not melted. Return quickly to chilled tray moistened on bottom and continue to freeze.

8. When mix is frozen sufficiently, turn thermostat halfway between the coldest setting and normal.

9. When beating cream or egg whites for folding into half-frozen mixtures, beat them only until they hold a soft peak, not until stiff.

10. When beating egg whites, reserve 2 tablespoons sugar for each egg white to add gradually to the egg whites after the foamy stage is reached. This meringue-like mixture holds up better during the folding-in process than plain egg white does.

General Directions for Hand-Turned or Motor-Driven Freezers

1. A 1-quart freezer requires about 6 pounds of ice to freeze the dessert and pack it for 2 hours. A 2-quart freezer requires about 10 pounds. Allow a few extra pounds for the ice that melts while the dessert is being frozen.

2. Be sure ice is chipped from the top of the block in an ice refrigerator. Modern ice boxes are regulated so that ice must cover the bottom of the ice chamber to insure correct food compartment temperature.

3. Ice cubes from an automatic refrigerator can be used as an ice supply. Two cups of water yield about 1 pound of ice.

4. Put pieces (or cubes) of ice into a canvas bag and crush with a mallet.

5. Finely crushed ice melts faster and hastens the freezing of ice cream.

6. Scald and cool the can, the cover and dasher of the freezer.

7. The ice cream mixture should be cold when it is put into the freezer. A warm mixture may result in a coarser-textured dessert.

8. Fill the can only two-thirds full. As the dasher turns, air is whipped into the dessert, causing it to "swell."

9. Ice cream freezes as heat from it is absorbed by the ice and salt. Ice alone is not cold enough to freeze foods; therefore, salt is added which lowers the temperature of the ice.

10. Use 8 parts ice to 1 part ice cream salt. This allows for a moderate rate of freezing so that a rather large amount of air may be incorporated. This helps to produce a smooth ice cream. In addition, this proportion of ice to salt prevents waste of ice due to too rapid melting.

11. Crank the freezer a few times before adding the ice to be sure the freezer turns freely. Then, turn the crank while adding the ice and salt.

12. Turn the crank slowly for the first 3 minutes to chill the mixture thoroughly. Then crank rapidly to make desserts creamier.

13. When the crank becomes too difficult to turn, the dessert is frozen.

14. To improve flavor, let frozen desserts "ripen" 1 to 2 hours before serving. To do this, remove dasher, press down mixture in can with a spoon, place a cork in the hole of the lid and put the lid in place. Repack the freezer with a mixture of 3 parts crushed ice to 1 part ice cream salt, and cover the freezer with newspapers or a heavy cloth.

15. The dessert can be ripened, also, in the tray of an automatic refrigerator. Pack the dessert firmly in tray, cover with a double layer of waxed paper and turn the control of the refrigerator to the coldest point. The dessert will remain smooth for several hours.

General Directions for Molded Frozen Desserts

1. Use a regular ice cream mold, or an ordinary tin can, such as a baking powder or coffee can with a tightly fitting cover.

2. Chill mold thoroughly before filling with cold ice cream mixture.

3. Fill mold to overflowing. Cover with waxed paper and put on lid.

4. Seal lid edge with a piece of adhesive tape or a strip of cloth dipped in melted fat or paraffin, covering the crack completely. When fat or paraffin cools it hardens, making a seal to keep out the salty water.

5. Bury the mold in a mixture of 3 parts crushed ice to 1 part ice cream salt. Cover ice mixture with newspaper or heavy cloth. Allow about 3 hours to freeze a quart-sized mold. Drain off water and add more ice and salt in same proportions, if necessary.

6. When frozen, remove mold, dip in warm water for a few seconds, or wrap in a cloth wrung out of hot water. Remove the strip around lid, the cover and waxed paper. Invert on a serving dish.

Homemade Ice Creams

MASTER REFRIGERATOR ICE CREAM
(Uncooked Base)

2   teaspoons (2/3 envelope) unflavored gelatin
1/2 cup cold water
1 3/4 cups evaporated milk
1/2 cup sugar
2   teaspoons vanilla
1 1/2 cups heavy cream, whipped

Soften gelatin in cold water. Dissolve in hot milk. Add sugar and vanilla. Cool.

Turn into freezing tray and chill until slightly thickened. Fold in whipped cream.

Return to tray and freeze to mush-like consistency. Turn into chilled bowl and beat until smooth, but not melted.

Return to cold tray and freeze. Makes 1 quart.

MASTER REFRIGERATOR ICE CREAM
(Cooked Base)

2/3 cup sugar
1 1/2 tablespoons cornstarch
1 1/2 cups top milk
2   eggs, separated
2 1/2 teaspoons vanilla
1/4 teaspoon salt
1   cup cream, whipped

Combine sugar and cornstarch in top of double boiler. Gradually stir in milk. Cook over boiling water, stirring constantly, until mixture thickens. Cover and cook 10 minutes.

Stir a little of hot mixture into beaten egg yolks. Add yolks to remaining hot mixture. Cook over hot, not boiling, water, stirring constantly for 3 minutes.

Cool. Add vanilla and salt. Fold beaten egg whites into cooled custard. Pour into refrigerator tray and freeze until firm throughout.

Remove to chilled bowl. Quickly beat with rotary beater until smooth. Fold in whipped cream. Return to cold tray. Freeze. Makes 6 to 8 servings.

Variations of Refrigerator Ice Cream

Banana: Add 1 cup ripe mashed bananas and 1 teaspoon lemon juice with whipped cream.

Chocolate: Melt 2 squares (2 ounces) chocolate in milk; beat with rotary beater until blended. Increase sugar to 3/4 cup. Use only 1 teaspoon vanilla.

Cherry: Add 1 1/4 cups chopped pitted cherries to chilled mixture just before folding in whipped cream.

Coffee: Substitute 1/2 cup strong coffee for 1/2 cup milk.

Frozen Pudding: Combine and add with the whipped cream, 1/2 teaspoon grated orange rind, 1/2 cup mixed chopped candied fruit, 1/4 cup chopped maraschino cherries, and 3 tablespoons maraschino cherry juice.

Ginger: Add 2 tablespoons ginger syrup with vanilla. Add 3 tablespoons chopped preserved ginger with whipped cream.

Mint: Reduce vanilla to 1 teaspoon. Add oil of peppermint to taste (few drops) and green coloring.

Nut Brittle: Grind or crush 1/4 pound nut brittle and fold in before final freezing.

Peach: Add 1 1/4 cups mashed peaches to chilled mixture just before folding in whipped cream.

Pistachio: Use only 1 teaspoon vanilla. Add 1/2 teaspoon almond extract. Add green food coloring. Add 1/2 cup chopped pistachio nuts with whipped cream.

Raspberry or Strawberry: Add 1 1/4 cups crushed berries to chilled mixture just before folding in whipped cream.

BUTTER PECAN ICE CREAM

1 1/3 cups sweetened condensed milk (15 ounce can)
1/4 cup melted butter or margarine
1   cup cold water
1   teaspoon vanilla
1   pint heavy cream
1   cup pecans, chopped

Combine condensed milk and melted butter thoroughly. Add water and vanilla. Mix well and chill.

Whip cream until fluffy but not stiff. Fold into chilled mixture.

Pour into freezer tray and freeze to consistency of mush. Do not allow to freeze too much or ice cream will be coarse.

Remove half-frozen mixture from refrigerator. Scrape into a chilled bowl and beat until smooth but not melted.

Add nuts and blend in well. Return to freezing tray and freeze until firm. Serves 10 to 12.

PEPPERMINT CANDY ICE CREAM

2   tablespoons cornstarch
1   cup sugar
1/8 teaspoon salt
2   cups light cream
3   well beaten egg yolks
3   egg whites, stiffly beaten
2   cups heavy cream, whipped
1   cup finely crushed peppermint sticks

Mix cornstarch, sugar, and salt in top of double boiler. Add cream and cook over boiling water 10 minutes, stirring constantly.

Add small amount of hot mixture to egg yolks and blend thoroughly. Return to double boiler and cook 5 minutes longer, stirring constantly.

Cool. Fold in stiffly beaten egg whites and pour into large refrigerator tray. Freeze until mushy.

Turn into large chilled bowl and beat with electric or rotary beater until smooth. Fold in whipped cream and crushed candy. Blend thoroughly.

Return to cold refrigerator tray and freeze firm. Stir well once during first hour of freezing. Makes 1 quart.

BUTTERSCOTCH ICE CREAM

3   tablespoons butter or margarine
1/2 cup brown sugar
1   cup milk
1 1/2 tablespoons cornstarch
2   tablespoons cold milk
Pinch of salt
1/4 teaspoon vanilla
1   cup heavy cream, whipped

Heat butter and sugar in top of double boiler until butter is melted and well blended with sugar. Add 1 cup milk and heat to boiling.

Mix cornstarch with 2 tablespoons cold milk; stir into butter and sugar mixture.

Add salt and cook, stirring constantly, until thickened.

Cool and add vanilla. Fold in whipped cream.

Turn into refrigerator tray. Freeze to a mush.

Remove to chilled bowl and beat quickly but thoroughly with rotary beater until smooth and fluffy. Return to tray and freeze. Serves 6.

CARAMEL ICE CREAM

3   tablespoons granulated sugar
1   cup milk
1/2 cup confectioners' sugar
1/8 teaspoon salt
1 1/2 tablespoons flour
2   eggs, separated
1   pint coffee cream
1   teaspoon vanilla

Stir granulated sugar in heavy skillet over low heat until sugar is melted and becomes light brown in color. Remove from heat. Gently stir in milk. Cook until sugar is dissolved.

Mix confectioners' sugar, salt, and flour in top of double boiler.

Add sugar-milk mixture. Cook over hot water until thickened, stirring constantly, about 15 minutes.

Combine with beaten egg yolks and cook 5 minutes longer, stirring constantly. Add cream and blend well.

Freeze in refrigerator tray until firm. Remove to chilled bowl.

Add vanilla and beat until mixture is light and creamy. Fold in stiffly beaten egg whites. Return to freezing tray. Freeze firm. Serves 8.

BLACK WALNUT ICE CREAM

2 cups milk
3/4 cup sugar
1 tablespoon flour
1/4 teaspoon salt
2 eggs, separated
2 teaspoons vanilla
2 cups light cream
3/4 cup chopped black walnuts

Scald milk in top of double boiler. Mix sugar, flour, and salt. Gradually stir into scalded milk. Cook 5 minutes over simmering water, stirring constantly.

Beat egg yolks slightly. Add about 1/2 cup of hot milk mixture to egg yolks, blending well. Add to remaining milk and cook 2 minutes over simmering water, stirring constantly.

Chill. Add vanilla, cream, and nuts and blend well.

Beat egg whites until stiff but not dry and gently fold into mixture. Pour into 2 refrigerator trays. Freeze until nearly solid.

Turn into chilled bowl and beat until creamy. Return to trays and freeze firm. Makes 1 1/2 quarts.

FRENCH ICE CREAM
(Freezer)

1/2 cup sugar
1/8 teaspoon salt
5 slightly beaten egg yolks
2 cups scalded milk
2 cups heavy cream
2 to 3 vanilla beans, crushed or 2 teaspoons vanilla

Mix sugar, salt, and egg yolks. Add scalded milk slowly, mixing well. Cook over hot water until mixture coats spoon, 5 to 8 minutes. Cool.

Strain and add cream and vanilla. Freeze. Makes 1 1/2 quarts.

GELATIN ICE CREAM
(Freezer)

1 tablespoon (1 envelope) unflavored gelatin
2 tablespoons cold water
2 cups milk
3/4 cup sugar
1/8 teaspoon salt
2 cups light cream
2 teaspoons vanilla

Soften gelatin in cold water.

Scald milk; add gelatin, sugar, and salt. Stir until dissolved. Cool.

Add cream and vanilla. Freeze. Makes 1 1/2 quarts.

PHILADELPHIA ICE CREAM
(Freezer)

1 quart light cream
1 cup sugar
Dash of salt

2 teaspoons vanilla

Scald cream. Add sugar and stir until dissolved.

Add salt and vanilla. Cool and freeze. Makes 1 1/2 quarts.

CUSTARD ICE CREAM
(Freezer)

2 cups milk
1 tablespoon flour
3/4 cup sugar
1/4 teaspoon salt
2 slightly beaten egg yolks
2 cups heavy cream
1 tablespoon vanilla

Scald 1 1/2 cups milk. Mix flour, sugar, and salt. Add remaining cold milk. Add scalded milk slowly.

Cook over hot water 7 minutes, stirring constantly.

Stir hot mixture slowly into egg yolks. Cook and stir 2 minutes longer. Cool.

Add cream and vanilla. Freeze. Makes 1 1/2 quarts.

RENNET ICE CREAM
(Freezer)

1 rennet tablet
1 tablespoon cold water
3 cups lukewarm milk
3/4 cup sugar
1/8 teaspoon salt
1 cup heavy cream
2 teaspoons vanilla

Dissolve rennet tablet in cold water.

Mix remaining ingredients and heat until lukewarm. Add rennet and mix well.

Let stand until slightly thickened. Freeze. Makes 1 1/2 quarts.

FREEZER ICE CREAM VARIATIONS

(Use French, Gelatin, Custard, Philadelphia, or Rennet Recipes)

Bisque: In master recipe, substitute 2 tablespoons sherry for vanilla. Add 3/4 cup chopped nuts just before freezing.

Butter Crunch: In master recipe, add 3/4 pound finely crushed butter crunch to mixture just before freezing.

Caramel: In master recipe, add 1/4 cup caramel flavoring with cream and vanilla.

Burnt Almond: Add 1 cup finely chopped, blanched, and toasted almonds to caramel ice cream mixture.

Chocolate: Melt 2 squares (2 ounces) unsweetened chocolate. Add 1/4 cup hot water and blend thoroughly. Add to hot mixture in master recipe.

Coffee: Scald 1/3 cup ground coffee with milk or cream. Strain before adding other ingredients. Omit vanilla in master recipe.

Macaroon: In master recipe, add 1 cup crushed macaroons just before freezing. Reduce sugar to 1/2 cup.

Maple: In master recipe, substitute maple syrup or maple sugar for granulated sugar. If desired, stir in 1 cup chopped nuts when partially frozen.

Mint: In master recipe, substitute mint flavoring for vanilla; add green food coloring.

Peach: In master recipe, use only 1 teaspoon vanilla; add 1/2 teaspoon almond extract. Just before freezing, add 2 cups crushed peaches, sweetened with 1/2 cup sugar.

Peanut Brittle: In master recipe, add 3/4 cup finely crushed peanut brittle to mixture just before freezing.

Peppermint: In master recipe, add 3/4 cup finely crushed peppermint stick candy to mixture just before freezing.

Pineapple: In master recipe, substitute 1 tablespoon lemon juice for vanilla. Add 2 cups well drained, crushed pineapple just before freezing.

Pistachio: To master recipe, add 1 teaspoon almond extract and green food coloring. Add 3/4 cup chopped pistachio nuts.

Strawberry or Raspberry: Combine 2 cups mashed berries with 1/2 cup sugar; add to master recipe just before freezing.

Tutti-Frutti: In master recipe, use only 1/2 teaspoon vanilla. Combine and add 4 teaspoons maraschino cherry juice, 1/2 cup chopped maraschino cherries, 1/2 cup drained crushed pineapple, and 1/2 cup chopped nuts just before freezing.

AVOCADO ICE CREAM
(Freezer)

2 cups milk
1/2 cup granulated sugar
1/4 teaspoon salt
2 well beaten eggs
1 cup heavy cream
1 teaspoon lemon extract
1 cup sieved avocado

Combine milk, sugar, and salt; scald. Pour over eggs, stirring constantly. Add cream and lemon extract and cool.

Add fruit and mix thoroughly. Freeze in ice cream freezer. Makes about 1 quart.

Since the smooth texture of this ice cream is due to the emulsified avocado oil, it is best done in a freezer.

Homemade Sherbets

REFRIGERATOR SHERBET
(Master Recipe)

2 teaspoons (⅔ envelope) unfla-
    vored gelatin
2¼ cups cold water
1 cup sugar
Pinch of salt
Fruit and juice as desired (see below)
2 egg whites

Soften gelatin in ¼ cup cold water.
Cook sugar and 2 cups water together
2 to 3 minutes. Add softened gelatin
and dissolve thoroughly. Add salt and
fruit juice.

Freeze in refrigerator tray to mush-
like consistency.

Remove mixture to a chilled bowl
and break into small pieces. Add unbeaten egg whites and beat until fluffy
(1 minute).

Turn into chilled trays and freeze
until firm. Serves 6.

Refrigerator Sherbet Variations

Apricot Sherbet: Use 2 cups apricot
pulp and 2 tablespoons lemon juice.

Lemon or Lime Sherbet: Use ½ cup
lemon or lime juice and grated rind
of ½ lemon.

Orange Sherbet: Omit 1 cup of water. Use 1½ cups orange juice, grated
rind of ½ orange, and ¼ cup lemon
juice.

Peach and Cherry Sherbet: Use 1½
cups peach pulp, 2 tablespoons orange
juice, and ¼ cup maraschino cherries,
diced fine.

Pineapple Sherbet: Use 1 cup crushed
pineapple and 1 tablespoon lemon
juice.

Raspberry Sherbet: Use 1½ cups
crushed fresh or canned raspberries
and 2 tablespoons lemon juice.

CRANBERRY ORANGE SHERBET

1 pound (4 cups) cranberries
2 cups water
2 cups sugar
2 teaspoons (⅔ envelope) unflavored
    gelatin
1 cup orange juice
2 teaspoons grated orange rind
⅓ cup lemon juice

Cook cranberries with water until
skins pop open.

Strain and add sugar and gelatin
which has been softened in orange
juice. Add grated rind and lemon juice.

Turn into refrigerator tray. Freeze
until firm, stirring once or twice during freezing. Serves 6 to 8.

ORANGE FREEZER SHERBET
(Master Recipe)

2 cups milk and 1 cup cream or 3
    cups rich milk
1¼ cups sugar
1½ cups orange juice
2 tablespoons lemon juice
¼ teaspoon salt

Heat 1 cup milk. Add sugar and stir
until dissolved. Add other ingredients.

Use freezing mixture of 1 part salt
to 4 to 6 parts ice. Turn crank freezer
slowly.

After freezing, remove dasher. Pack
freezer with more ice and salt. Let
sherbet stand an hour or more to ripen.
Makes about 3 pints.

Variations:

Lemon Sherbet: In master recipe,
omit orange juice. Use 1 cup lemon
juice and ½ cup water.

Pineapple Sherbet: In master recipe,
substitute 1 cup drained crushed pineapple for ½ cup orange juice.

MINT SHERBET

1 cup sugar
2 cups boiling water
¼ cup chopped fresh mint
1 tablespoon (1 envelope) unflavored
    gelatin
½ cup cold water
1 cup lemon juice
Few drops green food coloring
2 egg whites

Add sugar to boiling water. Bring to
boil again, stirring to dissolve sugar.

Add mint. Remove from heat. Cover
pan and let steep 1 hour.

Soften gelatin in cold water 5 minutes and dissolve over boiling water.
Stir into steeped mixture, mixing well.

Add lemon juice. Tint a pale green
with food coloring.

Pour into refrigerator tray. Freeze to
mush.

Beat egg whites stiff. Turn sherbet
into chilled bowl. Beat quickly and
fold in egg whites. Return to tray.
Freeze firm.

To serve, garnish scoops of sherbet
with sprigs of fresh mint. Serves 6.

LEMON CREAM SHERBET

1⅓ cups sugar
1⅔ cups milk
Juice and grated rind of 2 lemons
1 cup heavy cream

Combine sugar and milk and mix
well. Add lemon juice and rind.

Whip cream until stiff and fold into
lemon mixture.

Pour into freezer tray. Freeze until
firm. Stir once or twice while freezing.
Serves 6.

ORANGE CREAM SHERBET

¾ cup sugar
¾ cup water
Grated rind of 1 orange
1½ cups orange juice
1 tablespoon lemon juice
½ cup light cream
2 egg whites
Few grains salt

Cook sugar and water together slowly
10 minutes. Add grated rind, cooking
2 minutes longer. Strain. Add syrup to
fruit juices. Cool.

Pour into freezing tray. Freeze until
firm.

Remove to a chilled bowl; beat
quickly until light. Add cream. Fold
in stiffly beaten egg whites to which
the salt has been added.

Turn into tray and freeze. If mixture separates, stir occasionally. Serves
6 to 8.

WATERMELON SHERBET

About 2 cups diced watermelon
24 marshmallows
¼ cup lemon juice
2 stiffly beaten egg whites

Press diced watermelon through sieve
to extract 1 cup juice.

Heat marshmallows and watermelon
juice over hot water, stirring until
marshmallows are melted and smooth.

Cool. Add lemon juice.

Combine marshmallow mixture with
stiffly beaten egg whites. Fold gently
until blended.

Pour into small refrigerator tray and
freeze. When partially frozen, turn into
chilled bowl. Beat quickly with rotary
beater. Return to tray and freeze.
Serves 5.

CANTALOUPE SHERBET

1½ cups water
½ cup sugar
3 cups cantaloupe, pulp and juice
    (2 medium cantaloupes)
⅓ cup lemon juice

Boil water and sugar together for 5
minutes. Cool. Add cantaloupe and
lemon juice. Pour into shallow pan and
freeze until firm around the edges of
the pan.

Turn into a bowl and beat until
smooth. Return to tray and freeze until
firm. Serves 6.

Cantaloupe Sherbet

Homemade Ices

REFRIGERATOR ICE
(Master Recipe)

⅔ cup sugar
Pinch of salt
1½ cups water
1½ teaspoons (½ envelope) unfla-
    vored gelatin
3 tablespoons cold water
Fruit juice, as desired (see below)

Boil sugar, salt, and water 5 minutes.
Soften gelatin in 3 tablespoons cold
water. Dissolve in hot syrup. Cool and
add fruit juices.

Freeze in refrigerator tray to a mush-
like consistency.

Remove to a chilled bowl; break into
small pieces. Beat with rotary beater
until fluffy (1 to 2 minutes). Return to
freezing tray and freeze until firm.
Serves 6.

Variations of Refrigerator Ice

Berry Ice: Follow master recipe. Use
2 cups red raspberries or strawberries
crushed and sieved and 1 tablespoon
lemon juice.

Cherry Ice: Follow master recipe. Use
2 cups ground cherries and juice, 1 tablespoon lemon juice, and few grains
nutmeg. Omit ½ cup water.

Cranberry Ice: Follow master recipe.
Use 2 cups cooked strained cranberries.

Lemon or Lime Ice: Follow master
recipe. Use ⅓ cup of lemon or lime
juice.

Mint Ice: To lemon ice, add ¼ teaspoon peppermint flavoring and 2 tablespoons finely minced mint leaves.

Orange Ice: Follow master recipe.
Add 1 tablespoon grated orange rind
to hot syrup and cool. Use 1½ cups
orange juice and 2 tablespoons lemon
juice.

PINEAPPLE MINT ICE

1 teaspoon (⅓ envelope) unfla-
    vored gelatin
2 tablespoons cold water
1½ cups pineapple juice
½ cup sugar
⅛ teaspoon salt
1 tablespoon chopped fresh mint
1 cup crushed pineapple
2 tablespoons lemon juice
Grated rind of 1 lemon
2 egg whites

Soften gelatin in cold water 5 minutes.

Heat pineapple juice to boiling
point and add softened gelatin, sugar,
and salt. Stir until dissolved.

Cool. Add mint, crushed pineapple,
lemon juice, and rind. Freeze to mush.

Turn into large chilled bowl. Add
unbeaten egg whites and beat until
light and fluffy. Return to tray and
freeze, stirring several times. Serves 8.

FREEZER LEMON ICE
(Master Recipe)

1 quart water
1¼ to 1½ cups sugar
1 cup strained lemon juice
¼ teaspoon salt
1 egg white

Boil water and sugar together 2 minutes, then put aside.

When cold, add lemon juice, salt, and
unbeaten egg white. Freeze with a mixture of 1 part salt to 4 to 6 parts ice.

Turn crank slowly until ice is firm.
Remove dasher and pack freezer with
more ice and salt. Let ice stand 1 hour
or more to ripen.

Lemon Ice Variations

Lime Ice: In master recipe, substitute
lime juice for lemon juice. Add green
food coloring.

Mint Ice: To lemon ice, add ¼ teaspoon mint flavoring and 2 tablespoons
finely minced mint leaves.

Berry Ice: Make syrup of 1 cup sugar
and 2 cups water. Mash 1 quart berries
and press through sieve. Add to syrup.
Cool and freeze. Raspberries, blackberries, or strawberries may be used.

Cherry Ice: Make syrup of 1 cup sugar
and 2 cups water. Grind 1 quart pitted
cherries and press through sieve. Add
to syrup. Cool and freeze.

Grape Ice: Make syrup of 1 cup sugar
and 2 cups water. Add 2 cups grape
juice, ¼ cup orange juice, and ¼ cup
lemon juice. Cool, strain, and freeze.

Orange Ice: Make syrup of 1 cup
sugar and 2 cups water. Add 2 cups
orange juice and 4 tablespoons lemon
juice. Cool, strain, and freeze.

AVOCADO GRAPEFRUIT ICE

⅔ cup sieved avocado
2 cups grapefruit juice
½ cup sugar
¼ teaspoon salt

Cut a large avocado in halves lengthwise. Remove seed and skin, and force
pulp through sieve.

Blend in grapefruit juice, sugar, and
salt. Pour into refrigerator tray. Freeze
firm.

Turn into chilled bowl. Beat with
rotary beater until smooth and fluffy.

Return to tray and freeze to desired
consistency. Makes 1½ pints.

Cranberry Mint Ice

CRANBERRY MINT ICE

1 1-pound can jellied cranberry
    sauce
1 cup pineapple juice
¼ teaspoon peppermint extract

Crush cranberry sauce with a fork.
Add pineapple juice and peppermint
extract.

Pour into freezing tray of refrigerator. Freeze.

Serve immediately. Use to top fresh
fruit cup.

CRÈME DE MENTHE ICE

1⅔ cups sugar
3 cups water
½ cup lemon juice
¼ cup crème de menthe

Cook sugar and water together 5
minutes.

Cool and add lemon juice and crème
de menthe. Pour into small refrigerator tray.

Freeze, stirring several times during
freezing. Serves 6 to 8.

GRAPEFRUIT MINT ICE

2 teaspoons (⅔ envelope) unfla-
    vored gelatin
2½ cups grapefruit juice, fresh or
    canned unsweetened
¾ cup sugar
½ cup water
Few drops peppermint extract
Green food coloring
2 egg whites, stiffly beaten

Soften gelatin in ¼ cup cold grapefruit juice.

Boil sugar and water together 5 minutes and dissolve softened gelatin in it
while hot.

Cool. Combine with remaining fruit
juice. Add peppermint flavoring and a
few drops of food coloring to tint pale
green.

Turn into refrigerator tray. Freeze to
mush.

Turn partially frozen ice into chilled
bowl. Beat until smooth. Fold in stiffly
beaten egg whites. Freeze firm, stirring
several times. Serves 6.

Variation: Mint flavoring and coloring may be omitted if plain grapefruit
sherbet is desired.

Mousses

VANILLA MOUSSE
(Master Recipe)

1   teaspoon (1/3 envelope) unflavored gelatin
1   cup light cream or rich milk
6   tablespoons sugar
1/16   teaspoon salt
1/2   teaspoon vanilla
1   cup heavy cream, whipped
2   egg whites

Soften gelatin in a little light cream
or milk.

Heat remainder of light cream or
milk and pour over gelatin. Add sugar
and salt; stir until dissolved. Chill.

When gelatin mixture has thickened
slightly, beat to incorporate air. Add
vanilla. Fold in whipped cream and
well beaten egg whites.

Mold, pack into ice and salt and
freeze or turn into freezing trays and
freeze until firm. Makes about 1 quart.

Vanilla Mousse Variations

Applesauce Mousse: In master recipe,
omit vanilla. Add 2 cups cinnamon-
flavored applesauce and 2 tablespoons
lemon juice with the cream.

Banana Mousse: In master recipe,
add 1 cup mashed ripe banana and 2
teaspoons lemon juice with whipped
cream.

Burnt Almond Mousse: Melt 8 teaspoons sugar carefully and stir in 1/2
cup ground almonds. Heat until almonds are browned. Add to milk or
light cream in master recipe. Add 1/4
teaspoon almond extract. Omit vanilla.

Chocolate Mousse: Add 2 squares (2
ounces) unsweetened chocolate to milk
or light cream in master recipe. Add
1/2 cup sugar. Heat in top of double
boiler, beating with rotary beater until blended.

Coffee Mousse: In master recipe, substitute 1/2 cup strong coffee for 1/2 cup
light cream.

Maple Mousse: In master recipe, substitute 1/3 cup maple syrup for sugar.

Peach Mousse: Omit vanilla in master recipe. Add 1/4 teaspoon almond
extract. Add 2 cups peach pulp and
1/4 cup sugar.

Peanut Brittle Mousse: In master
recipe, substitute 1/4 pound finely
ground peanut brittle candy for sugar.

Peppermint Mousse: In master recipe, substitute 1/4 crushed peppermint
stick candy for sugar. Add green food
coloring.

Strawberry or Raspberry Mousse:
Omit vanilla in master recipe. Add 1
to 2 cups crushed berries and 1 to 2
tablespoons lemon juice with whipped
cream.

PERSIMMON MOUSSE

1 1/2   cups ripe persimmon pulp
1/4   cup diced orange
1/2   cup diced canned pineapple
About 1/4 cup sugar
Dash of salt
1   tablespoon lemon juice
1   cup evaporated milk, whipped

Select 4 to 6 very ripe persimmons.
Wash, dry, cut away from stem. Carefully strip off thin skin, quarter, discarding pit and any black specks. Put
pulp through a sieve and measure.

Combine persimmon pulp, orange,
pineapple, sugar, salt, and lemon juice;
gently blend, not to destroy the delicate
persimmon flavor. Fold in whipped
milk.

Pour into a refrigerator tray and
freeze. Serves 6.

SPUMONE

1/2   cup sugar
1/2   cup maraschino cherries, drained
and cut into quarters
3   tablespoons candied orange peel,
cut into thin strips
1   teaspoon lemon juice
1 1/2   cups heavy cream, whipped
1/2   cup chopped blanched almonds
1 1/2   quarts vanilla ice cream
1/4   teaspoon almond extract

Fold sugar, cherries, orange peel, and
lemon juice into whipped cream. Put
into refrigerator tray to harden.

Add chopped nuts to ice cream, then
flavor with almond extract. If ice cream
becomes soft, put in freezer to harden.

To Pack Mold: Line a chilled 1-quart
melon mold with ice cream to depth of
1 inch. Leave hollow in center but bring
ice cream well up on sides of mold.

Fill mold with whipped cream mixture. Cover with waxed paper; fit lid on
tightly. Put in freezing compartment
for 24 hours.

Unmold onto chilled plate. To serve,
cut into 1-inch slices. Serves 10 to 12.

Note: If desired, use a mixture of
chopped candied angelica, citron, apricot, and lemon and orange peel instead
of 3 tablespoons candied orange peel.

MAPLE NUT MOUSSE

4   beaten egg yolks
1   cup maple syrup
1/8   teaspoon salt
1   teaspoon vanilla
1/2   cup chopped black walnuts
1   pint heavy cream, whipped

Combine beaten egg yolks, maple
syrup, and salt in top of double boiler.
Cook over hot water, stirring constantly, until mixture coats spoon.

Remove immediately from heat and
stir over ice cubes until cool. Add vanilla and walnuts.

Gently fold whipped cream into custard. Pour into 2 refrigerator trays.
Freeze without stirring.

To serve, pile into parfait glasses.
Top with additional whipped cream.
Garnish with chopped walnuts. Makes
about 1 quart.

GOLDEN MOUSSE

1   cup mashed ripe bananas
2   tablespoons orange juice
1/4   cup shredded coconut
3   tablespoons brown sugar
Few grains salt
1/8   teaspoon grated orange rind
1   cup heavy cream, whipped

Combine and mix first 6 ingredients.
Fold in stiffly whipped cream.

Turn into freezing tray. Freeze rapidly, without stirring, until firm. Serves
6 to 8.

BISQUE MOUSSE

3   well beaten egg yolks
1   cup sugar
3   egg whites, stiffly beaten
2   cups heavy cream, whipped
1/2   pound dry macaroons, crumbled
2   teaspoons vanilla or brandy flavoring

Beat egg yolks and sugar until thick
and lemon colored. Fold in remaining
ingredients.

Pour into large refrigerator tray.
Freeze firm. Serves 12.

MOLASSES MOUSSE

4   eggs
1/2   cup molasses
2   tablespoons orange juice
1/2   teaspoon cinnamon
Few grains salt
2   cups heavy cream

Beat eggs; add molasses. Cook over
hot water, stirring constantly until
slightly thickened.

Cool quickly by setting pan in ice
water, stirring occasionally. Add orange
juice, cinnamon, and salt.

Beat cream until slightly stiff, fold in
molasses mixture.

Pour into refrigerator tray and freeze
firm.

Or pour into 1 1/2-quart mold with
cover. Seal tight. Pack in equal parts
crushed ice and ice cream salt. Freeze
4 hours. Makes about 1 1/2 quarts.

Molasses Mousse

Parfaits

VANILLA PARFAIT
(Master Recipe)

1 cup sugar
¾ cup water
2 egg whites
¼ teaspoon salt
3 teaspoons vanilla
1½ cups whipping cream, whipped

Boil sugar and water to 230°F. or until it forms a thread.

Beat egg whites until frothy. Add salt and beat until stiff but not dry.

Slowly pour hot syrup over egg whites, beating constantly. Continue beating until mixture is cool and holds shape. Add vanilla and fold in whipped cream.

Turn into chilled trays and freeze until firm. Serve with additional whipped cream, fruits, and nuts. Serves 8.

Vanilla Parfait Variations

Banana Parfait: Omit vanilla in master recipe. Add 1 teaspoon lemon juice. Fold in 1 cup mashed ripe banana with whipped cream.

Chocolate Parfait: In master recipe, add 2 squares (2 ounces) unsweetened shaved chocolate to hot syrup. Beat with rotary beater until blended before adding other ingredients.

Coffee Parfait: In master recipe, substitute ¾ cup strong coffee for water.

Maple Parfait: In master recipe, substitute 1 cup hot maple syrup for sugar syrup.

Maraschino Cherry Parfait: In master recipe, substitute ¼ cup maraschino cherry juice for equal amount of water in making syrup. Add ⅓ cup or more diced maraschino cherries with whipped cream.

Pineapple Parfait: Omit vanilla in master recipe. Add 1 cup crushed well drained pineapple and 1½ tablespoons lemon juice with whipped cream.

Strawberry or Raspberry Parfait: Omit vanilla in master recipe. Add 2 cups crushed berries and 1¼ tablespoons lemon juice with whipped cream.

Toasted Coconut Parfait: In master recipe, add ½ cup toasted shredded coconut with whipped cream.

BLUEBERRY AND PEACH PARFAIT

2 cups blueberries
1 cup heavy cream, whipped
2 fresh peaches, pared
⅓ cup sugar

Fold washed blueberries into whipped cream.

Mash peaches; add sugar and fold into blueberry mixture.

Chill, but do not freeze, in refrigerator tray. Serve in parfait glasses. Serves 6.

GOLDEN PARFAIT

½ cup sugar
¼ cup water
4 egg yolks
Few grains salt
1½ teaspoons vanilla
1½ cups heavy cream, whipped

Boil sugar and water together. Pour slowly over well beaten egg yolks. Cook until mixture coats spoon.

Cool. Add salt and vanilla. Fold in whipped cream.

Turn into chilled tray. Freeze until firm. Serve with additional whipped cream, if desired. Serves 6.

Golden Parfait Variations

Butterscotch Parfait: In golden parfait, substitute ⅔ cup brown sugar for the granulated sugar and add 2 tablespoons butter.

Maple Nut Parfait: In golden parfait, substitute ½ cup maple syrup for sugar and water. Heat syrup over low heat and proceed as directed. Add ½ cup chopped nuts.

APPLE-LIME PARFAIT

1½ teaspoons (½ envelope) unflavored gelatin
2 tablespoons cold water
1½ cups cold water
¾ cup sugar
¼ cup lime juice
⅓ cup orange juice
2 tablespoons lemon juice
Few grains salt
Green food coloring
2 egg whites
Cinnamon apple sauce (below)

Soften gelatin in 2 tablespoons cold water for 5 minutes.

Combine remaining water and sugar; boil for 2 minutes. Add gelatin; stir until dissolved. Add lime, orange, lemon juices and salt; cool. Tint light green.

Pour into freezing tray and freeze to mush.

Place in chilled bowl. Beat with rotary beater until smooth. Beat egg whites stiff and fold in. Return to tray and freeze firm. Stir several times.

Just before serving, spoon alternate layers of applesauce and lime sherbet into parfait glasses. If desired, garnish with green maraschino cherry and sprig of mint. Serves 4 to 6.

Cinnamon Applesauce:

2 cups canned applesauce
¼ cup light brown sugar
¼ teaspoon cinnamon
½ teaspoon grated lemon rind

Combine applesauce, sugar, cinnamon, and lemon rind. Chill.

PEPPERMINT STICK PARFAIT

½ cup sugar
½ cup water
Few grains salt
2 egg whites
1 tall can evaporated milk (1⅔ cups), chilled icy cold
½ cup finely crushed peppermint stick candy

Combine sugar and water and bring slowly to a boil. Boil rapidly until syrup spins a thread (230°F.).

Add salt to egg whites and beat until stiff but not dry.

Pour syrup slowly into egg whites, beating constantly.

Chill. Beat milk until very stiff. Fold in egg white mixture and candy. Pour at once into freezing trays. Freeze. Makes 1½ quarts.

PISTACHIO PARFAIT

1 cup sugar
¼ cup water
2 egg whites
Green food coloring
½ cup chopped pistachio nuts
1 teaspoon almond extract
Few grains salt
2 cups heavy cream

Combine sugar and water; boil to 238°F. (or when small amount dropped from tip of spoon spins long thread).

Beat egg whites stiff; gradually add syrup, beating constantly. Tint light green. Cool. Add nuts, almond extract, and salt.

Whip cream; fold in. Pour into freezing tray and freeze firm. Serves 4 to 6.

For jiffy parfaits layer ice cream and fruit or other sauce, then freeze until ready to serve. Create your own imaginative combinations of ice cream and sauce. Usually parfaits are served in their special glasses, but stemmed water glasses work just as well. These have been topped, just before serving, with crunchy star-shaped sugar-coated cereal instead of the usual whipped cream.

Tricks with Ice Cream

GOOD LUCK HORSESHOE

2 pints ice cream
About 20 shortbread cookies
1 cup heavy cream
2 tablespoons confectioners' sugar
1 teaspoon vanilla
1/4 cup chopped maraschino cherries

Slice ice cream about 3/4-inch thick to size of shortbread cookies. Alternate ice cream with cookies in shape of a horseshoe, cutting the ice cream in wedges where the horseshoe curves. Freeze.

Whip cream with confectioners' sugar and vanilla. Frost horseshoe with cream and freeze until serving time. Sprinkle with chopped maraschino cherries. Slice diagonally. Serves 6.

Good Luck Horseshoe

ICE CREAM CHERRY TARTS

6 individual pastry shells
1 quart vanilla ice cream
1 pint fresh or frozen cherries or
2 cups canned sweet red cherries

Fill cooled individual pastry shells generously with vanilla ice cream. Top with red cherries and cherry sauce (below). Serves 6.

Cherry Sauce:

1 cup cherry juice (sweetened juice from fresh, frozen, or canned sweet red cherries)
1/4 cup sugar
1 1/2 teaspoons cornstarch
1 teaspoon lemon juice

Blend sugar, cornstarch, and lemon juice. Add to cherry juice and cook, stirring until slightly thickened. Cool and serve over the ice cream. If canned cherries are used, add more sugar to suit taste.

Frozen Trifle

RIBBON CAKE

Cut baker's pound cake into 4 rectangular slices. Cut 1 pint strawberry ice cream into slices. Alternate cake and ice cream layers. Freeze until firm. Serve with thawed frozen strawberries or raspberries.

Ribbon Cake

REFRIGERATOR TRAY PIE

1/4 cup butter or margarine
1/4 cup sugar
1 1/2 cups chocolate wafer crumbs
1 1/2 pints vanilla or coffee ice cream, softened

Cream butter and add crumbs and sugar. Blend together. Pack half the crumb mixture into a refrigerator tray. Chill.

Spoon ice cream over crumb mixture and pack down well. Press remaining crumbs on top of the ice cream. Spread with whipped cream, if desired. Return to refrigerator to freeze. Serves 6.

HONEYDEW-RASPBERRY DELIGHT

1 medium honeydew melon
1 quart vanilla ice cream
2 cups sweetened raspberries

Cut honeydew melon into 8 crosswise slices 1/4- to 1/2-inch thick. Remove seeds and rind.

With a sharp knife, make diagonal slashes around edge of melon slices.

Place slices of melon on dessert plates and top each with a large scoop of ice cream. Circle scoop of ice cream with sweetened raspberries. Serves 8.

FROZEN TRIFLE

1 quart vanilla ice cream
Vanilla wafers
1 cup strawberry preserves
1 pint strawberry ice cream

Pack 1 pint vanilla ice cream into bottom of 1 1/2-quart ring mold. Add a layer of vanilla wafers; spread with 1/2 cup strawberry preserves.

Stand vanilla wafers around sides of mold. Continue layering strawberry ice cream, vanilla wafers, strawberry preserves, and vanilla ice cream. Freeze until firm. Unmold on serving plate. Garnish with sliced strawberries. Serves 6 to 8.

Cut off the tops of éclair shells (homemade or baker's). Fill with ice cream and put tops back on. Serve with chocolate sauce and lots of whipped cream.

STRAWBERRY ICE CREAM PIE

3 egg whites
1/4 teaspoon salt
1/4 teaspoon cream of tartar
3/4 cup sugar
3/4 teaspoon vanilla
1 quart vanilla ice cream
1 quart strawberries
4 tablespoons confectioners' sugar
1/2 cup heavy cream, whipped
1/2 teaspoon vanilla

Beat egg whites with salt and cream of tartar until stiff but not dry. Gradually add 3/4 cup sugar and 3/4 teaspoon vanilla and beat until it holds up in peaks.

Cut a circle of brown paper to fit bottom of 9-inch pie pan. Spread meringue on paper in pie pan and build up edges.

Bake in very slow oven (250°F.) 1 hour.

Turn off heat and allow to remain in oven 1 hour longer or until dry.

Fill cooled shell with ice cream. Top with sliced strawberries to which have been added 2 tablespoons confectioners' sugar. Top with whipped cream sweetened with 2 tablespoons confectioners' sugar and flavored with 1/2 teaspoon vanilla. Decorate with a few whole berries. Serves 8.

Three-Ring Circus: Mold one quart each of vanilla, chocolate, and strawberry ice cream in 6-inch round cake pans or cut 2-inch slices from a round half gallon. Decorate with animal crackers and arrange on a tiered dish. Use a clown centerpiece and circus decorations. Dessert makes about 15 servings.

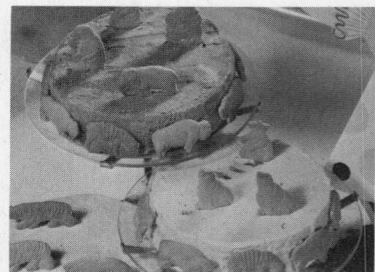

ICE CREAM SHADOW CAKE

1 bought large angel food cake ring
2 pints chocolate ice cream
1 pint heavy cream, whipped and
  sweetened
Chocolate sauce

Cut angel cake in 3 layers. Spread 1 pint ice cream (softened) between each layer. Spread whipped cream on top and sides of cake; freeze.

When ready to serve, remove from freezer, and dribble cooled chocolate sauce over top and sides of cake. Cut in wedges to serve. Serves 12.

Note: If freezer isn't available, chill cake and have cream whipped before filling cake. Fill with ice cream; spread with cream. Dribble sauce over top and sides, and serve at once.

CRUNCHY CHOCOLATE SUNDAE

8 chocolate chip cookies
1 pint vanilla ice cream

Break chocolate chip cookies into coarse crumbs.

Scoop out ice cream in 4 balls; roll in crumbs.

Serve immediately, or store in freezer until needed. Top with chocolate sauce and serve with additional chocolate chip cookies.

Variations: Use other crumbled cookies such as coconut macaroons, vanilla wafers or use chocolate cake or baked meringue crumbs. Ice cream balls or squares may be prepared in advance by rolling in crumbs and stored in freezing compartment of refrigerator or freezer until time to serve

Flaming Sundae: Pile ice cream high in sherbet glasses, spoon on your favorite sauce or sliced canned fruits. Then add a sugar cube dipped in lemon extract at the very top of the sundae. Light the cubes and carry your special dessert to the table in its flaming glory.

PARTY CLOWNS

Place a scoop of ice cream in center of each cooky or cake round for clown's head. Then make his face, using raisins for eyes, nose, and mouth.

Place an ice cream cone on each scoop of ice cream for the hat. (If desired, cones may be decorated ahead of time with candy. Use a little confectioners' sugar mixed with water to hold candy decoration on cones.)

Party Clown

JIFFY ICE CREAM SUNDAE SAUCES

Marshmallow Sauce: In saucepan, combine 1/4 pound (16) marshmallows with 1/3 cup honey, 1/3 cup heavy cream and pinch of salt.

Cook until marshmallows are almost melted, stirring occasionally. Remove from heat; stir until completely melted.

Chocolate Marshmallow Sauce: Add 1 1/2 squares unsweetened chocolate to marshmallows. Cook as in marshmallow sauce (above).

Maple Walnut Syrup: Heat some maple syrup and chopped walnuts over boiling water about 5 minutes. Good hot or cold.

Honey Almond Syrup: Heat honey and chopped toasted almonds over boiling water about 5 minutes. Good hot or cold.

Coffee Coconut Syrup: Heat 1 cup of light corn syrup with 1 tablespoon instant coffee and 1/2 cup coconut over boiling water about 5 minutes. Good hot or cold.

Pineapple or Grape Sauces: Slightly thaw frozen pineapple or grape juice concentrate.

Honey Sauce: Stir together 1/4 cup honey and 2 tablespoons melted butter or margarine.

Coffee Sauce: Mix 1 to 2 tablespoons instant coffee with 1 cup canned sweetened condensed milk.

Ice Cream Snowballs

ICE CREAM SNOWBALLS

Make large snowballs of vanilla ice cream, using ice cream scoop or large spoon.

Quickly roll each ball in chopped pecans or walnuts. Serve plain or with a butterscotch sauce.

ICE CREAM BUTTERFLIES

Buy or prepare 6 cupcakes from instant cake mix, or use own recipe; cool. Cut off tops of cupcakes; cut tops in half.

Using 1 quart ice cream, place a large scoop of it on each cupcake; insert halves of top of cupcake in ice cream to resemble butterfly wings. Serve plain or with sauce and whipped cream. Serves 6.

SPONGE CAKE SUNDAE

2 1-ounce squares unsweetened chocolate
1 cup light or dark corn syrup
1/4 teaspoon vanilla
4 sponge cake dessert shells
1 pint peppermint ice cream
Hot chocolate sauce

Melt chocolate in top of double boiler. Add syrup, stir only until blended, then add vanilla.

Place dessert shells on dessert plates. Top with pink peppermint ice cream. Pass hot chocolate sauce.

Easter Sundaes: Surround a scoop of ice cream with whipped cream. Sprinkle with flaked coconut and jelly beans. Serve with Easter Bunnies made from coconut covered marshmallow cakes, joined with toothpicks. Use sugar wafers for ears and a marshmallow for a tail.

Circus Party: Make round ice cream balls using a large scoop. Roll in flaked coconut. Store in freezer. Just before serving top each with an animal cracker and use a circus wagon from the dime store as a server for more animal crackers.

APRICOT ICE CREAM PIE

1/4 pound marshmallows
Apricot preserves
2 egg whites
1/8 teaspoon salt
1/4 cup sugar
2 pints vanilla ice cream
1 9-inch baked pastry shell, chilled

Heat marshmallows and 2 tablespoons preserves in top part of double boiler over boiling water, until marshmallows are half melted. Remove from heat, and beat until smooth.

Beat egg whites with salt until foamy; gradually add sugar, and beat until stiff. Fold in marshmallow mixture.

Press ice cream quickly into chilled shell. Spread with 1/2 cup preserves. Cover with marshmallow meringue, spreading to cover ice cream completely.

Put under preheated broiler 1 or 2 minutes, or until lightly browned. (This meringue browns very quickly.) Cut in wedges, and garnish with spoonful of preserves.

Banana Split: Peel a banana and cut in half lengthwise. Place the two halves on a shallow dish and top with 3 scoops of ice cream. Then spoon over chocolate sauce and fruit syrups and garnish with whipped cream, fruits, and nuts.

CRANBERRY ICE CREAM PIE

1 1/2 cups gingersnap crumbs
1/4 cups sugar
1/4 cup melted butter or margarine
1 quart vanilla ice cream
1 cup canned whole cranberry sauce

Combine gingersnap crumbs, sugar, and melted butter in bowl. Mix until thoroughly blended.

Cover bottom and sides of a buttered 8-inch pie pan with crumb mixture. Pack down firmly. Chill in refrigerator.

When crust is thoroughly chilled, fill with vanilla ice cream. Top with whole cranberry sauce. Place in freezing unit and freeze until serving time.

Ice Cream Tarts

ICE CREAM TARTS

Fill baked tart shells with fresh, sliced, sweetened peaches or strawberries. Top with a scoop of vanilla ice cream.

Serve with additional fruit, if desired.

Strawberry Pineapple Sundae

STRAWBERRY PINEAPPLE SUNDAE

Cut 1 large pineapple in half lengthwise, through green tops. Remove meat with sharp knife, cutting to within 1/4 inch of edges. Remove core and cut in cubes.

Wash 1 pint strawberries and remove hulls. Slice and sweeten with 1/4 cup sugar. Combine with pineapple and chill until serving time.

Place pineapple shells on large serving tray. Fill each half with ice cream (use 1 quart in all). Serve with pineapple strawberry sauce. Serves 6.

Cherry Cantaloupe Sundae

CHERRY CANTALOUPE SUNDAE

3 small cantaloupes
2 cups pitted Bing cherries
1 cup cherry juice or water
1 1/2 cups sugar
Few grains of salt
2 tablespoons lemon juice
2 drops almond extract
1 quart vanilla ice cream

Wash cantaloupes and cut in halves crosswise. Remove seeds and cut out inside of each to within 1/4 inch of edge; dice. Chill halves. Wash and pit cherries.

Combine remaining ingredients except ice cream. Heat to boiling and cook until syrup is thick. Add diced cantaloupe and cherries and chill.

Add a little sauce to each cantaloupe half. Top with ice cream and garnish with Bing cherries and diced cantaloupe. Serve with extra sauce. Serves 6.

RED AND WHITE SWIRL

Soften 1 quart vanilla ice cream. Swirl 1/2 cup strawberry sundae topping through ice cream. Turn into refrigerator tray and freeze until firm.

ORANGE CHOCOLATE SWIRL

Soften 1 quart chocolate ice cream. Swirl one 3-ounce can frozen orange juice concentrate through ice cream. Turn into refrigerator tray and freeze until firm.

JIFFY CHOCOLATE PARFAIT

Alternate chocolate ice cream, whipped cream, and canned crushed pineapple.

CHOCOLATE MERINGUES

Fill cooled meringue shells (see Index) with scoops of chocolate ice cream. Top with chocolate sauce.

Ice cream and meringue shells are a traditional combination in some European countries.

Baked Alaskas

BAKED ALASKA
(Master Recipe)

Baked Alaska is an impressive dessert and not at all difficult to make. It needs last minute preparation but if everything is prepared in advance, the Alaska may be put together and finished in the oven in minutes.

- 1- to 1½-inch layer sponge or layer cake
- ⅛ teaspoon salt
- 5 egg whites
- ⅔ cup sugar
- 1 quart or 2 pints firm, brick ice cream

Cover a wooden cutting board with a strip of heavy wrapping paper. If a thick wooden board is not available, a heavy baking sheet may be used. The wood is preferred because it is an extremely slow heat conductor, an advantage when "cooking" ice cream.

Arrange cake on the paper. (The paper will help slide dessert onto plate.)

Add salt to egg whites and beat until soft peaks form. Add sugar gradually and continue to beat until meringue holds stiff peaks.

After making meringue, center ice cream on cake. The layer of cake should be large enough to extend ½ to 1 inch beyond edge of ice cream.

Spread meringue over entire surface of ice cream and cake edge, carefully sealing to edges of cake. Sprinkle top with granulated sugar for a snowy effect.

Bake in very hot oven (450°F.) until golden brown, about 5 minutes.

To serve, slide from board to plate. Slice at the table in front of guests. Garnish servings with whole berries. Serves 6.

Baked Alaska in Pie Shells: Fill baked pie shell or individual tart shells with firm ice cream. Cover with meringue and finish as directed in Baked Alaska.

Individual Baked Alaska: Cut individual rounds or squares of sponge cake. Cover and bake as above.

Fruit Alaska: Cover cake with a layer of fresh or stewed fruit. Arrange ice cream on top. Cover with meringue. Bake as above.

Rum Alaska: Place 2 half egg shells open side up in top of meringue before baking. Bake. Fill shells with rum. Set aflame and serve.

Alaska with Nuts: Sprinkle chopped nuts over meringue.

Strawberry Alaska: Use 2 pint bricks of vanilla or strawberry ice cream.

Place 1 pint brick on the cake. Cover with a 1-inch layer of sliced and chilled strawberries; place the other pint brick on top.

Proceed as in master recipe.

Orange Alaska: The procedure is the same as in the master recipe but the ice cream is replaced by orange ice.

Remove the Alaska from the oven and surround by orange sections which have been cooked in a thin syrup until glazed.

SURPRISE ALASKA

- 1 cooled 9-inch sponge cake
- 6 egg whites
- ½ teaspoon cream of tartar
- 1 cup sugar
- 1 quart vanilla or strawberry ice-cream

Place cooled cake on several thicknesses of waxed paper (trimmed to size of cake) on a wooden board.

Using a small plate as a guide, cut a 3½-inch circle from center of cake, hollowing out a depression for the ice cream. Leave about a 1-inch layer of cake in the bottom of the depression.

Beat egg whites with cream of tartar until stiff. Beat in sugar a little at a time until meringue forms stiff, glossy peaks but is not dry.

Firmly pack the hollow with 1 quart ice cream; level off with top of cake.

Quickly spread meringue on sides and top of cake, covering completely.

Brown in very hot oven (450°F.) for 4 to 5 minutes, or until meringue is lightly browned. Slip the cake from board onto a serving platter and garnish with fresh flowers or fruit. Cut into wedge-shaped pieces and serve at once with extra ice cream, if desired. Serves 8.

RASPBERRY ALASKA PIE

About 1⅔ cups graham cracker crumbs, finely rolled
- ¼ cup softened butter or margarine
- ¼ cup sugar
- ¼ cup flaked coconut
- 2 10-ounce packages frozen raspberries
- 1 tablespoon cornstarch
- ¼ cup lemon juice
- 1 tablespoon grated lemon rind
- 1 quart vanilla ice cream
- 4 egg whites
- ½ cup sugar
- ¼ cup flaked coconut

Mix graham cracker crumbs, butter or margarine, sugar, and coconut. Blend thoroughly. Pour into a 9-inch pie plate and press firmly against bottom and sides of pie plate. The easy way is to press crumbs into place using an 8-inch pie plate. Bake in moderate oven (375°F.) 7 minutes. Cool and

Surprise Alaska

freeze.

Heat frozen raspberries with cornstarch, lemon juice, and rind. Simmer until juice is clear and slightly thickened. Cool.

Make very thin layers of sauce and ice cream in pie crust using about ½ of sauce (serve remaining sauce with pie.) Freeze.

Beat egg whites until foamy. Continue beating, gradually adding sugar until stiff peaks form when beaters are lifted. Spread over ice cream sealing to edges of crust. Sprinkle with coconut. Freeze until serving time.

Just before serving, pre-heat oven to 500°F. Place pie in oven for 2 to 4 minutes or only until meringue is lightly browned. Serve immediately. Spoon remaining sauce over individual servings. Serves 8 to 10.

Raspberry Alaska Pie

PINK LADY ALASKA

Crumb Crust:

20 graham crackers, finely rolled (about 1⅔ cups crumbs)
¼ cup softened butter or margarine
¼ cup sugar

Blend together graham cracker crumbs, butter or margarine, and sugar. Press firmly against bottom and sides of 9-inch pie plate.

If desired, bake in moderate oven (375°F.) 8 minutes. Chill.

(Make the crumb crust early in the day—ready to fill at serving time.)

Filling:

16 marshmallows
2 tablespoons crushed strawberries
2 stiffly beaten egg whites
¼ cup sugar
¼ teaspoon salt
1 pint vanilla ice cream, very firm
1 cup fresh sliced strawberries

Stir and melt marshmallows and crushed strawberries over low heat until smooth. Beat sugar gradually into stiffly beaten egg whites until they hold a peak.

Add salt. Gradually beat in cooled marshmallow mixture.

Fill crumb crust with ice cream, cover with sliced strawberries. Top with gay swirls of marshmallow meringue (be sure meringue completely covers ice cream). Brown quickly in broiler and serve at once. Serves 6 to 8.

Pink Lady Alaska

PEPPERMINT ALASKA PIE

1⅔ cups graham cracker crumbs, finely rolled
¼ cup sugar
¼ cup softened butter or margarine
1 4-ounce jar chocolate sprinkles
1 quart vanilla ice cream
½ cup crushed peppermint candy
3 egg whites
¾ cup sugar

Thoroughly blend graham cracker crumbs, sugar, softened butter or margarine, and chocolate sprinkles. Press firmly against bottom and sides of 9-inch pie plate. (The easy way is to press crumbs into place using an 8-inch pie plate.) Bake in moderate oven (375°F.) 8 minutes. Cool and freeze.

Soften ice cream slightly and stir in crushed peppermint candy. Pile into crust and freeze until firm.

Just before serving beat egg whites with sugar until stiff. Spread meringue over pie, sealing edges to crust. Bake in hot oven (500°F.) 3 to 4 minutes. Serve immediately. Serves 6 to 8.

Marlows

FROZEN HAWAIIAN MARLOW

1½ cups milk
¼ pound marshmallows, cut in halves (about 16)
½ cup heavy cream, whipped with 1 teaspoon vanilla
1½ cups (No. 2 can) drained crushed pineapple
¼ cup maraschino cherry halves
¼ cup chopped pecans or other nuts

Measure milk and marshmallows into top part of a double boiler. Heat over boiling water until marshmallows melt. Remove from heat and cool.

Fold vanilla flavored whipped cream, fruit, and nuts into cooled mixture and pour into 1-quart refrigerator tray. Freeze. Makes about 1 quart or 6 to 8 servings.

STRAWBERRY MARLOW

1 cup crushed sweetened strawberries
1 tablespoon orange juice
¼ pound marshmallows (16)
¼ cup water
1 cup whipping cream
½ teaspoon vanilla
Few grains salt

Combine strawberries and orange juice.

Combine marshmallows and water; cook over hot water, stirring occasionally, until melted. Fold into strawberry mixture. Cool.

Whip cream slightly stiff; add vanilla and salt. Fold into strawberry mixture.

Pour into freezing tray and freeze firm. Serves 4.

Peppermint Alaska Pie

VANILLA MARLOW
(Master Recipe)

30 marshmallows
¾ cup hot milk or water
2 teaspoons vanilla
1½ cups heavy cream, whipped

Melt marshmallows in hot milk or water.

Cool. Add flavoring. Chill.

When mixture begins to thicken, combine with whipped cream. Pour into tray and freeze without stirring. Serves 4 to 6.

Vanilla Marlow Variations

Banana Marlow: Omit vanilla in master recipe. Add 1 cup mashed ripe banana and 1 tablespoon lemon juice to hot milk.

Chocolate Marlow: Add 2 squares (2 ounces) melted chocolate to hot milk in master recipe.

Peach Marlow: Add 2 cups peach pulp and 1 tablespoon lemon juice to hot milk in master recipe. Substitute 1 teaspoon almond extract for vanilla.

BANANA GRAPE MARLOW

10 marshmallows
⅓ cup grape juice
2 tablespoons lemon juice
1 cup mashed ripe bananas (2 to 3 bananas)
½ cup heavy cream

Combine marshmallows and 2 tablespoons grape juice. Heat slowly, folding over and over, until marshmallows are half melted.

Remove from heat and continue folding until mixture is smooth and fluffy. Fold in remaining grape juice, then fold in lemon juice and bananas.

Turn into freezing tray and chill until mixture begins to freeze. Turn into a bowl and beat well.

Whip cream until thickened. Fold into marshmallow-banana mixture. Return to tray and freeze firm.

Serves 4 to 6.

Miscellaneous Frozen Desserts

BISCUIT TORTONI

Also called Tortoni or Bisque Tortoni on menus, this Italian dessert is sometimes flavored with sherry or rum.

2 teaspoons (2/3 envelope) unflavored gelatin
1/4 cup cold water
1/3 cup light corn syrup
1/4 cup sugar
2 egg yolks
1/4 teaspoon salt
1 teaspoon vanilla
1/2 teaspoon almond extract
1 cup heavy cream or evaporated milk, whipped
1/4 cup chopped pistachio nuts (optional)
1/2 cup vanilla wafer or macaroon crumbs

Soften gelatin in cold water. Heat corn syrup and sugar to boiling, stir until sugar is dissolved and stir into gelatin.

Beat egg yolks until very light and add syrup mixture gradually, beating constantly.

Cool thoroughly; add salt and flavorings, and fold in whipped cream or milk.

Add pistachio nuts and pour into small fluted paper cups (the kind in which biscuit tortoni is served generally) or into a tray of refrigerator. Dust top thickly with crumbs.

Freeze without stirring until firm. Makes enough for about 14 small cups or 6 to 8 servings.

CHOCOLATE ORANGE VELVET

2 8-ounce packages cream cheese, softened
1 cup heavy cream
1 6-ounce package semi-sweet chocolate pieces, melted
1/2 cup sugar
2 tablespoons grated orange rind

Whip cream cheese and heavy cream together. Add remaining ingredients and beat at high speed until light and fluffy. Pour into ice cube tray and freeze until firm.

Cut into pie shaped pieces. Serve with chocolate sandwich cookies. Serves 6 to 8.

Chocolate Orange Velvet

GRAHAM CRACKER FREEZE
(Master Recipe)

2 cups graham cracker crumbs
10 marshmallows, quartered
1 cup walnuts, chopped
1/2 cup confectioners' sugar
1 teaspoon vanilla
1 cup shredded coconut
1/2 cup cream
1/2 cup heavy cream, whipped

Mix crumbs, marshmallows, walnuts, sugar, vanilla, coconut, and cream.

Pack into refrigerator tray lined with waxed paper. Freeze until firm.

To serve, slice with knife dipped in hot water. Top with whipped cream. Serves 8 to 10.

Graham Cracker Freeze Variations

Macaroon Crumb Freeze: Substitute 2 cups macaroon crumbs for graham crackers.

Pineapple Crumb Freeze: In master recipe, substitute 1/2 cup crushed pineapple for coconut and 1/2 cup pineapple juice for 1/2 cup cream.

Prune Crumb Freeze: In master recipe, substitute 1 cup cooked prune pulp for 1/2 cup cream.

Vanilla or Chocolate Crumb Freeze: In master recipe, substitute 2 cups vanilla or chocolate crumbs for graham crackers.

FROZEN LEMON CHIFFON PIE

10 vanilla wafers, 2 inches in diameter
2 eggs, separated
1/3 cup light corn syrup
Dash of salt
1/2 teaspoon grated lemon rind
1/4 cup lemon juice
1/4 cup sugar
3/4 cup cream or evaporated milk, whipped

Roll wafers into fine crumbs. Grease a refrigerator tray with butter or margarine and coat well with crumbs. Place in freezing compartment.

Mix well in the top of a double boiler the egg yolks, syrup, salt, lemon rind and juice. Cook over boiling water, stirring constantly until mixture is slightly thickened, and cool.

Beat egg whites until stiff, add sugar and whip until mixture stiffens again.

Whip lemon juice–egg yolk mixture into whipped cream or milk, then fold in the blend of egg whites and sweetening.

Pour into the prepared tray and freeze quickly. To serve, cut into slices or pie-shaped wedges. To make the latter, cut across the tray diagonally from corner to corner, and then crosswise through center. Serves 6.

Lemon Berry Frost

LEMON BERRY FROST

3/4 cup (6-ounce can) softened frozen lemonade concentrate
1 1/2 cups (8-ounce jar) marshmallow whip
1 2/3 cups (large can) undiluted evaporated milk
1 10- or 12-ounce package frozen strawberries or raspberries

Beat lemonade concentrate and marshmallow whip together until smooth.

Chill evaporated milk in refrigerator tray until soft crystals form through milk (about 20 to 25 minutes). Whip until stiff (2 to 3 minutes). Slowly add marshmallow mixture. Whip very stiff (2 to 3 minutes longer).

Freeze in 1 1/2 quart mold until firm (2 to 3 hours). Serve with fresh or defrosted berries. Makes about 1 1/2 quarts.

FROZEN CHOCOLATE DESSERT

1 cup sugar
1/2 cup butter or margarine
4 eggs
1 square (1-ounce) unsweetened chocolate, melted
1 cup finely chopped walnuts
1 cup vanilla wafer crumbs, finely rolled
1/2 pint heavy cream, whipped

Cream sugar and butter together thoroughly. Add eggs one at a time, beating well after each egg. Stir in chocolate and walnuts.

Line an 8 1/2-inch loaf pan with wax paper. Pour in 1/3 of the filling, add a layer of crumbs. Repeat both layers twice, freeze.

Unmold onto serving plate, frost with whipped cream. Return to freezer or serve at once. Serves 6 to 8.

Frozen Chocolate Dessert

Frozen Cranberry Loaf

FROZEN CRANBERRY LOAF

3/4 cup finely ground toast crumbs
1/2 cup brown sugar
1 teaspoon cinnamon
1/2 teaspoon nutmeg
1/4 teaspoon allspice
1/4 teaspoon cloves
1/4 teaspoon ginger
3 tablespoons melted butter
1 pound can jellied cranberry sauce
1/2 cup whipping cream
1 3-ounce package cream cheese

Mix first seven ingredients together. Work in melted butter. Press mixture evenly against sides and bottom of an ice cube tray. Chill in freezing compartment for at least 1 hour.

Crush jellied cranberry sauce with a fork and spread over crumb crust. Whip cream. Soften cream cheese and whip with cream. Spread whipped cream-cheese mixture over cranberry sauce.

Place in freezing compartment and freeze until firm. Slice to serve. Serves 8.

Variation: Thick sour cream can be spread over cranberry sauce in place of cream cheese and whipped cream for excellent flavor.

APRICOT VELVET CREAM

1 No. 2 1/2 can apricot halves
1/4 cup confectioners' sugar
1/8 teaspoon salt
1 cup evaporated milk, chilled for whipping

Mash apricots, reserving a few for garnish, and add sugar and salt.

Whip chilled milk until thick. Fold in apricot mixture.

Freeze in freezing tray for 2 hours. Serves 6.

Apricot Velvet Cream

FROZEN VANILLA CUSTARD

1 egg, separated
1/4 cup sugar
1/2 teaspoon vanilla
1 small can (2/3 cup) evaporated milk, chilled

Beat egg yolk. Add sugar and vanilla. Beat until sugar is dissolved.

Beat egg white stiff. Fold into yolk mixture.

Whip milk very stiff. Fold in egg mixture lightly. Pour at once into cold freezing tray. Freeze until firm. Makes 1 pint.

Variations of Vanilla Custard

Frozen Chocolate Chip Custard: In frozen vanilla custard, fold in 2 ounces (2 squares) semi-sweet chocolate, shaved or grated, after combining egg and sugar mixture with whipped milk.

Frozen Cocoa Custard: In frozen vanilla custard, omit sugar. Use in its place a syrup made by blending 1/4 cup sugar, 1/4 cup cocoa, and 1/2 cup water and boiling until thick. Chill syrup, then add to the beaten egg yolk.

Frozen Lemon Custard: Follow recipe for frozen vanilla custard and omit vanilla. Fold 3 tablespoons lemon juice and 1/2 teaspoon grated lemon rind into whipped milk before adding egg and sugar mixture.

Frozen Peanut Brittle Custard: In frozen vanilla custard, fold 2/3 cup crushed peanut brittle into egg and sugar mixture, then add to whipped milk.

FROZEN ORANGE BALLS IN ORANGE CUPS

2 teaspoons (2/3 envelope) unflavored gelatin
1/4 cup cold water
1 cup water
3/4 cup sugar
1 teaspoon grated lemon rind
1 teaspoon grated orange rind
1 can frozen orange juice concentrate, thawed, or 1 cup fresh orange juice
1/3 cup lemon juice
2 egg whites
1/8 teaspoon salt
8 orange shell halves

Soften gelatin in 1/4 cup cold water 5 minutes.

Boil 1 cup water with sugar 10 minutes. Dissolve gelatin in hot syrup. Cool.

Add lemon and orange rind and juices. Chill until it begins to thicken. Turn into chilled bowl and beat with rotary beater until fluffy.

Beat egg whites with salt until stiff. Fold gently into fruit mixture. Turn mixture into freezer tray and freeze firm.

Form balls with an ice cream scoop. Place balls in scalloped orange shells. Cut a thin slice off bottom side of shells to make them stand secure.

Serve on galax leaves in chilled serving dishes. Serves 8.

FROZEN STRAWBERRY SHORTCAKE

1 pint strawberries
1/2 cup sugar
1 teaspoon (1/3 envelope) unflavored gelatin
2 tablespoons cold water
Sponge cake
1 cup heavy cream, whipped

Crush strawberries and mix with sugar.

Soften gelatin in cold water and dissolve over boiling water. Add gelatin to strawberries and mix thoroughly.

Cover bottom of refrigerator tray with 3/4-inch layer of sponge cake. Pour strawberry mixture over cake.

Chill and, when set, cover with whipped cream. Return to refrigerator and freeze. Serves 6.

LEMON VELVET

2 cups sugar
2 cups rich milk
Grated rind of 2 lemons
1/2 cup lemon juice
2 cups heavy cream

Combine sugar and milk and let stand 1 hour. Add lemon rind and juice, stirring well. Mixture will thicken slightly.

Whip cream until fairly stiff. Fold into milk mixture.

Pour into 2 refrigerator trays and freeze rapidly, 3 or 4 hours. Stir twice during freezing process to avoid separation. Serves 6 to 8.

Variation: One tall can undiluted evaporated milk (1 2/3 cups) may be used in place of heavy cream. To prepare for whipping, pour into refrigerator tray and freeze until fine ice crystals form around edges. Scrape milk into chilled bowl and beat until stiff.

Frozen Orange Balls in Orange Cups

CHERRY MACAROON FREEZE

1 No. 2 can black cherries, drained or 1 16-ounce package frozen cherries
1 cup dry macaroon crumbs
2 cups heavy cream, whipped

Pit cherries if necessary; cut in quarters. (Reserve cherry juice for cold beverage, sauce, gelatin dessert, or some other purpose.) Save out enough whole cherries to use one on each serving for garnish.

Fold macaroon crumbs into whipped cream, then the cherries. Pour at once into freezing tray; freeze quickly without stirring. Serves 6 to 8.

FROZEN FIG SHORTCAKE

1 cup dried figs, chopped
1 cup water
¼ cup sugar
1 teaspoon lemon juice
1 tablespoon (1 envelope) unflavored gelatin
1 tablespoon water
1 egg
4 tablespoons sugar
1 teaspoon vanilla
½ cup heavy cream, whipped
Sponge, angel cake, or jelly roll, 1 inch thick, or fig newtons

Simmer chopped figs and water with ¼ cup sugar 15 minutes; add lemon juice. Dissolve gelatin in cold water, then dissolve in the fig mixture. Cool.

Beat egg with 4 tablespoons sugar until light; add vanilla and fold in whipped cream.

Line deep refrigerator tray with waxed paper; place inch-thick slice or layer of cake on bottom. Spread cooled fig mixture over cake, then top off with the cream.

Freeze several hours or overnight. Garnish with fig flowers and whipped cream. Serves 6 to 8.

Frozen Fig Shortcake

STRAWBERRY BOMBE
Graham Cracker Crust:

¼ cup (½ stick) butter or margarine
¼ cup sugar
20 graham crackers, finely rolled

Let butter or margarine stand at room temperature until softened. Blend all ingredients well with pastry blender or hands.

Pour crumb mixture into 1¼-quart mixing bowl. Set a smaller bowl on top of crumbs, and press them firmly into an even layer against bottom and sides of bowl.

Strawberry Bombe Filling:

2 eggs, separated
1 15-ounce can sweetened condensed milk
¼ cup lemon juice
1 pint strawberries, sliced
Few drops red food coloring

Beat egg yolks until thick and lemon colored; mix in condensed milk. Add lemon juice; mix until thick. Beat in half the berries.

Beat egg whites stiff; fold in egg yolk mixture and remaining berries. Tint pink with a few drops of red coloring.

Pour into graham cracker crumb crust in bowl. Freeze for at least 6 hours.

To unmold, run a spatula around sides of bowl. Put serving plate upside down on bowl and invert. Serve garnished with whipped cream and strawberry halves. Serves 8.

FROZEN LIME CREAM CUPS

2 eggs
½ cup sugar
½ cup light corn syrup
1 cup cream
1 cup milk
⅓ cup lime juice
1 teaspoon grated lime rind
Green food coloring
Whipped cream

Beat eggs until lemon colored. Slowly add sugar to eggs, beating until mixture is thick and custard-like.

Add corn syrup, cream, milk, lime juice, and grated lime rind, blending well. Tint a delicate green with food coloring.

Turn into refrigerator tray and freeze. When frozen, remove to chilled bowl and beat with rotary beater until light and creamy.

Line muffin pans with pastel colored fluted paper cups or use standard ice cream cups. Spoon mixture into them, filling almost to top. Freeze firm.

To serve, pipe whipped cream over tops with pastry tube. Decorate with thin slivers of lime. Serves 12.

Strawberry Bombe

FROZEN LEMON CREAM

Grated rind of 2 large lemons
Strained juice of 4 large lemons
1 cup sugar
4 tablespoons water
4 eggs, separated
2 cups heavy cream, whipped

Put lemon rind, lemon juice, ¾ cup of the sugar, and water together in top of double boiler, over direct heat. Stir to dissolve sugar.

Beat egg yolks until thick and foamy; stir in hot mixture gradually; return mixture to double boiler over hot water. Stir and cook until mixture is thickened and smooth. Remove from hot water; cool completely; then chill.

Beat egg whites until foamy; gradually beat in remaining sugar, as for meringue. Fold mixture into cooled lemon custard. Fold in whipped cream.

Freeze in one large or 2 small trays, stirring gently once or twice during freezing period. Freeze until firm.
Serves 6 to 8.

FROZEN PEACH MALLOW

20 marshmallows, cut small
1 cup milk
1 cup sugar
2 cups fresh peaches or 1 package (16-ounce) frozen peaches
Few drops almond flavoring
2 cups whipped cream

Put marshmallows and milk in top of double boiler over hot water. Stir occasionally until marshmallows are dissolved. Stir in sugar. Set aside to cool completely.

Crush peaches to pulp, but do not strain; stir in flavoring. Combine cooled marshmallow mixture and peaches; fold in whipped cream.

Freeze until crystals begin to form around edge of tray.

Turn into chilled bowl and whip until smooth and light; return to freezing tray or, if mixture is not whipped, stir several times during freezing. (Stir from outer edges toward center.) Freeze until firm. Serves 4 to 5.

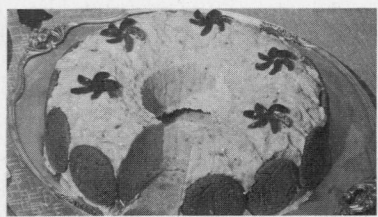

Holiday Mousse

HOLIDAY MOUSSE

1 No. 2 can crushed pineapple
3 bananas
1/2 cup sugar
1 1/2 cups finely rolled gingersnap crumbs
1 cup evaporated milk, chilled icy cold
1 tablespoon lemon juice
1 cup heavy cream
Whole gingersnaps

Combine fruit with sugar and gingersnap crumbs. Add lemon juice to evaporated milk; whip until stiff.

Whip cream stiff. Combine whipped mixtures; fold in fruit mixture.

Line a 2-quart mold with whole gingersnaps; pour in mousse. Freeze overnight. To serve, unmold onto a platter. Serves 12.

FROZEN MINT PUDDING

1 1/2 teaspoons (1/2 envelope) unflavored gelatin
2 tablespoons water
1/2 cup crushed white peppermint candy (2 ounces)
1/4 cup milk
2 eggs, separated
6 drops green food coloring
1/4 teaspoon salt
6 tablespoons sugar
1 cup heavy cream
12 plain chocolate cookies, crushed (3/4 cup)

Sprinkle gelatin on the water and soak a few minutes.

Dissolve candy in milk over boiling water.

Beat egg yolks well. Pour a little of the hot liquid into them. Add to the rest of the hot mixture, and cook until thick, stirring constantly. Stir in the coloring.

Add gelatin to the cooked mixture and stir until dissolved. Cool until thick but not set.

Add salt to egg whites, beat until stiff but not dry. Gradually add sugar, beating constantly. Combine the beaten egg whites and gelatin mixture.

Whip the cream and fold it in.

Put half the crumbs into two freezing trays. Pour in prepared mixture, and cover with rest of crumbs.

Freeze without stirring, at the coldest refrigerator temperature, 3 to 4 hours. Serves 8.

SHERRY PEACH DELIGHT

1 cup light cream or 1 cup evaporated milk, chilled
4 peaches, sliced fine
1/2 cup sherry
1 teaspoon unflavored gelatin
2 tablespoons cold water
2 eggs
1/3 cup sugar
1/2 teaspoon salt
2 cups milk
1 teaspoon almond extract

Pour light cream into freezing tray, allowing about 1 hour for the cream to begin to freeze. When crystals have formed throughout, it is ready to whip.

Slice peaches and marinate in sherry. Soften gelatin in cold water.

Beat eggs with sugar and salt; stir in milk. Cook over boiling water, stirring constantly, until mixture coats the spoon. Do not overcook. Remove from heat. Stir in softened gelatin. Cool.

Add peaches and sherry. Add almond extract.

Whip the frozen cream (or evaporated milk) and fold into peach-custard. Turn into tray and freeze partially. Whip with rotary beater. Freeze until firm. Makes 1 quart.

FROZEN PLUM PUDDING

1/2 cup sugar
2 ounces (2 squares) chocolate
1/2 cup milk
2 cups heavy cream
1 teaspoon vanilla
1/2 cup chopped nuts
1/4 cup chopped maraschino cherries
1 cup chopped raisins
1/4 cup chopped dates

Add sugar and grated chocolate to milk in a saucepan and cook until chocolate is melted and mixture is slightly thick. Chill.

Whip the cream until thick but not stiff; add chocolate mixture, vanilla, nuts, cherries, and the raisins and dates which have been "plumped" by cooking in a small amount of water which is allowed to evaporate.

Freeze at coldest temperature for 1 1/2 hours, then reduce cold for remainder of freezing period. Serves 8.

EASY STRAWBERRY FROZEN CREAM

1 cup strawberry preserves
3 tablespoons lemon juice
2 drops almond flavoring
1 cup heavy cream, whipped

Stir preserves, lemon juice, and flavoring together; fold into whipped cream.

Pour into freezing tray and freeze until firm, stirring several times during freezing period. Serves 4.

FRUIT SHERBET TARTS

20 graham crackers, finely crushed
1/4 cup softened butter or margarine
1/4 cup sugar
1 large banana
1/4 cup orange juice
2 tablespoons lime juice
3/4 cup sugar
1 1/4 cups milk
1 egg white

Thoroughly blend together graham cracker crumbs, butter, and sugar.

Divide mixture into 8 fluted paper cups set in muffin pans. Press crumbs firmly against bottom and sides of paper cups with a spoon or a straight-sided glass. Place in freezing compartment of refrigerator.

Mash banana with a fork; add orange juice, lime juice, and sugar. Stir in milk. Freeze 1 hour.

Beat mixture with a rotary beater. Beat egg white until stiff but not dry and fold into sherbet mixture.

Spoon sherbet into tart shells. Place in freezing compartment of refrigerator and freeze 3 to 4 hours. Remove fluted paper cups before serving. Makes 8 tarts.

COCONUT MOUSSE

1 cup filberts
2/3 cup sugar
1/4 cup water
6 egg yolks, stiffly beaten
2 teaspoons vanilla
1/2 teaspoon salt
2 cups heavy cream
Coconut bars, snack size

Cook filberts in water to cover 15 minutes; drain and chop.

Combine sugar and water; bring to boiling, stirring constantly; boil 5 minutes without stirring. Pour in a fine stream over egg yolks, beating constantly. Mix in vanilla and salt; beat until cool.

Whip cream stiff; fold cream and filberts into egg yolk mixture. Stand coconut bars (snack size) around sides of 8-inch square cake pan. Set a glass in center of pan. Pour filbert mixture around glass. Freeze until firm.

To serve, remove glass, unmold mousse on serving plate. Replace glass in center and fill with flowers. Decorate mousse with whipped cream and nut slices. Serves 9.

Coconut Mousse

DESSERT SAUCES

Almost everybody loves desserts, but everyone, without exception, loves desserts dressed up with a delicious sauce. The right sauce makes your dessert even better. Choose your sauce with flavor and eye appeal in mind.

LEMON SAUCE
(Master Recipe)

$\frac{1}{2}$ cup sugar
1 tablespoon cornstarch
$\frac{1}{8}$ teaspoon salt
1 cup boiling water
Juice of $\frac{1}{2}$ lemon
Grated rind of $\frac{1}{2}$ lemon
$\frac{1}{8}$ teaspoon nutmeg, optional
1 tablespoon butter or margarine

Mix together sugar, cornstarch, and salt. Gradually add boiling water; bring to boil. Cook over low heat until thickened and clear, about 15 minutes.

Stir in lemon juice and rind. Add nutmeg and butter. Serve hot over puddings and other desserts. Makes about $1\frac{1}{4}$ cups.

Lemon Sauce Variations

Fluffy Lemon Sauce: Just before removing from heat, quickly stir in 1 slightly beaten egg yolk and cook 1 minute, stirring constantly.

Remove from heat and fold in 1 stiffly beaten egg white.

Orange Lemon Sauce: Substitute fresh or canned orange juice for water.

Pineapple Lemon Sauce: Substitute pineapple juice for water.

Lime Sauce: Omit nutmeg; substitute juice and rind of 1 lime for lemon.

Whipped Cream Lemon Sauce: Fold together equal parts of lemon sauce and whipped cream.

Corn Syrup Lemon Sauce: Substitute $\frac{3}{4}$ cup corn syrup for sugar. Use only $\frac{1}{2}$ cup water.

CHOCOLATE SAUCE
(Master Recipe)

$\frac{1}{2}$ cup light corn syrup
1 cup sugar
1 cup water
3 1-ounce squares unsweetened chocolate
1 teaspoon vanilla
1 cup evaporated milk

Cook syrup, sugar, and water to soft ball stage (236°F.). Remove from heat.

Add chocolate and stir until melted. Add vanilla. Slowly add evaporated milk, stirring constantly. Cool.

Serve hot or cold. Store in covered jar in refrigerator. Makes about 3 cups.

Chocolate Sauce Variations

Hot Fudge: Reheat chocolate sauce in top part of double boiler.

Chocolate Whipped Cream Sauce: Fold an equal part of whipped cream into chocolate sauce.

Mint Chocolate Sauce: Substitute 2 drops oil of peppermint for vanilla.

Mocha Sauce: Substitute strong, fresh coffee for all or part of water.

Orange Chocolate Sauce: Substitute orange juice for half or all of water; add grated rind of 1 orange.

Rum or Brandy Chocolate Sauce: Add 1 tablespoon rum or brandy.

HOT FUDGE SAUCE

1 1-ounce square unsweetened chocolate
1 cup sugar
2 tablespoons light corn syrup
$\frac{1}{8}$ teaspoon salt
$\frac{1}{3}$ cup water
1 tablespoon butter or margarine
$\frac{1}{2}$ teaspoon vanilla

Combine chocolate, sugar, corn syrup, salt, and water in saucepan. Heat slowly until chocolate is melted and sugar is dissolved.

Boil, stirring constantly, until a small amount forms a soft ball in cold water (230°F.). Add butter and vanilla.

Serve hot over ice cream, puddings, or plain cake. Makes about $1\frac{1}{2}$ cups.

CHERRY SAUCE

2 cups sweet cherries, fresh or canned, drained
1 tablespoon sugar
$\frac{1}{4}$ cup orange juice
$\frac{1}{4}$ cup water or cherry juice

If fresh cherries are used, cook in water until tender. Press through a sieve.

Add sugar and juices to puréed or whole fruit mixture and serve cold.

More sugar may be added for tart fruit. Makes $2\frac{1}{2}$ cups.

Variations: Pineapple, strawberries, raspberries, peaches, apricots, etc., may be treated in a similar fashion.

BUTTERSCOTCH SAUCE

$1\frac{1}{2}$ cups firmly packed brown sugar
$\frac{2}{3}$ cup white corn syrup
$\frac{1}{2}$ cup water
$\frac{1}{2}$ cup evaporated milk

Boil sugar, syrup, and water to soft ball stage (235°F.).

Cool. Stir in milk. Makes 2 cups.

QUICK BUTTERSCOTCH SAUCE

Melt 30 small vanilla caramels in 1 cup water over hot water.

JELLY SAUCE

Stir a glass of jelly into $\frac{1}{4}$ cup hot water. Add 1 tablespoon butter and cook in a double boiler for a few minutes.

Thicken slightly with cornstarch smoothly blended with a little water, then add to mixture in double boiler.

HARD SAUCE
(Master Recipe)

A cold, firm sauce of butter, sugar, and flavoring. It is usually served over hot desserts such as plum pudding.

1/3 cup sweet butter or margarine
1 cup confectioners' sugar
1/2 teaspoon vanilla
1 tablespoon boiling water

Cream butter until soft. Gradually add sugar, creaming well.

Mix in vanilla and water a few drops at a time, beating until fluffy.

Pile lightly in serving dish. Chill until cold, but not hard.

Makes about 3/4 cup (4 to 6 servings).

Hard Sauce Variations

Apricot Hard Sauce: Omit vanilla. Beat in 1/2 cup strained apricot pulp with the sugar. Add 1 teaspoon apricot brandy.

Banana Hard Sauce: Omit vanilla. Beat in 1/3 to 1/2 cup mashed bananas.

Berry Hard Sauce: Omit vanilla. Beat in 1/2 cup crushed berries.

Brandy or Rum Hard Sauce: Substitute 2 tablespoons brandy or rum for vanilla.

Brown Sugar Hard Sauce: Substitute 2/3 cup brown sugar for confectioners' sugar. Flavor as desired.

Butterscotch Hard Sauce: Substitute 1/2 cup firmly packed brown sugar for confectioners' sugar. Add 1 teaspoon vanilla and 1 tablespoon light cream.

Cherry Hard Sauce: Substitute 2 tablespoons cherry syrup for vanilla. Add 1/2 cup drained chopped cherries.

Cocoa Hard Sauce: Add 2 tablespoons cocoa with the confectioners' sugar. Rum, brandy, or orange juice and rind may be used for the flavoring instead of vanilla.

Cream Hard Sauce: Add 1/4 cup heavy cream. Beat in thoroughly.

Date and Ginger Hard Sauce: Omit vanilla. Add 1/3 cup chopped dates and 1/3 teaspoon ginger.

Fluffy Hard Sauce: Fold in 1 stiffly beaten egg white. Add vanilla to taste.

Ginger Hard Sauce: Omit vanilla. Add 4 tablespoons chopped preserved ginger.

Lemon Hard Sauce: Substitute 1 teaspoon grated lemon rind and 1 teaspoon lemon juice for vanilla.

Liqueur Hard Sauce: Omit vanilla. Add 2 tablespoons desired liqueur or fruit-flavored cordial.

Orange Hard Sauce: Substitute 2 teaspoons grated orange rind and 1 tablespoon orange juice for vanilla.

Orange Marmalade Hard Sauce: While beating, work in 2 tablespoons orange marmalade.

Peach Hard Sauce: Omit vanilla and hot water. Beat into sauce 1/2 cup mashed peaches.

Spicy Hard Sauce: Add 1/8 teaspoon each of powdered cinnamon and ginger and a slight grating of nutmeg to hard sauce.

Walnut Hard Sauce: Add 2 tablespoons chopped walnuts or other nuts.

Whipped Cream Hard Sauce: Fold in 1/4 cup heavy cream, whipped.

Wine Hard Sauce: Add 1 to 3 tablespoons sherry, madeira, or port to hard sauce.

Yellow Hard Sauce: Add 1 beaten egg yolk. Use any desired flavoring.

LOW CALORIE WHIPPED TOPPING
(Use Instead of Whipped Cream)

1/2 cup ice water
1 tablespoon lemon juice
1 teaspoon vanilla
1/2 cup nonfat dry milk solids
3 tablespoons sugar

Put water, lemon juice, and vanilla in a bowl. Sprinkle dry milk on top. Beat until stiff with electric mixer or rotary beater, about 10 minutes.

Beat in sugar; continue beating until stiff enough to hold soft peaks, about 5 minutes longer. Makes about 2 1/2 cups.

Coffee Topping: Add 1 teaspoon instant coffee with vanilla.

WHIPPED JELLY SAUCE

Add 1/2 cup tart jelly to 1 unbeaten egg white. Beat with rotary beater until fluffy and light.

Serve on angel food cake, sponge cake, or pudding.

VANILLA WHIPPED CREAM SAUCE

1 slightly beaten egg
2 tablespoons sugar
1/2 cup cream, heated
1 teaspoon vanilla
1/2 cup heavy cream, whipped

Mix egg and sugar in top of double boiler. Add heated cream and cook until thick, stirring constantly.

Remove from heat. Add vanilla and cool, beating occasionally.

When cold, fold in whipped cream carefully.

Bread pudding in its many variations becomes a party dessert when garnished with a whipped topping.

VANILLA SAUCE
(Master Recipe)

1/2 cup sugar
1 tablespoon cornstarch
1/8 teaspoon salt
1 cup boiling water
1 egg yolk
2 teaspoons vanilla
2 tablespoons butter or margarine
1 egg white

Mix sugar, cornstarch, and salt. Gradually add hot water. Cook over moderate heat in saucepan until thick, stirring constantly, 6 to 7 minutes.

Add egg yolk. Cook 1 to 2 minutes, then add flavoring and butter.

Cool slightly. Fold in beaten egg white. Makes about 1 1/2 cups sauce.

Vanilla Sauce Variations

Chocolate Sauce: Add 1 square (1 ounce) grated chocolate with hot water.

Lemon Sauce: Add 2 tablespoons lemon juice and 1 teaspoon grated lemon rind to sauce. Omit vanilla.

Marshmallow Sauce: Cut up 6 marshmallows. Fold in last, leaving sauce somewhat lumpy.

Nutmeg Sauce: Add 1/2 to 3/4 teaspoon nutmeg to sauce.

Raisin Nut Sauce: Add 1/2 cup raisins and nuts, diced, and 1 teaspoon grated orange rind to sauce.

FRUIT JUICE SAUCE

1 tablespoon cornstarch
1 cup sugar
1/2 cup boiling water
2 tablespoons lemon juice
1 cup fruit juice, fresh or canned

Mix cornstarch and sugar. Add boiling water and boil 5 minutes. Cool and add fruit juice.

If sweetened juices are used, the sugar may be reduced as desired. Makes about 2 1/2 cups.

Variations: Any type of juice (strawberry, raspberry, pineapple, grape, peach, rhubarb, etc.) may be used.

Everybody loves desserts with strawberries. Plain cake makes a delicious dessert when topped with whipped cream and served with Rhubarb Strawberry Sauce.

RHUBARB STRAWBERRY SAUCE

3 cups diced fresh rhubarb
2 tablespoons water
3/4 cup sugar
1 tablespoon margarine
1 cup sliced strawberries

Cook rhubarb in the water in a covered saucepan over low heat. Add sugar and margarine. Cool.

Fold in strawberries. Serve over squares of whipped cream-topped cottage pudding. Garnish with whole strawberries. This makes enough sauce for 9 servings.

ALL-PURPOSE FRUIT DESSERT SAUCE

This recipe is called "all-purpose" because it has so many uses. It may be used by itself or combined with whipped cream and served over waffles, ice cream, puddings, custards, etc., and its ingredients are available at any season of the year.

2 cups dried apricots
1 1/4 cups water
1 1/2 cups sugar
5 cups canned crushed pineapple

Cook apricots in water in a wide-bottomed pan until the fruit is pulpy and disintegrates readily when stirred with a wire whisk.

Add sugar and stir until dissolved, then add crushed pineapple. Bring to a boil. Pour into jars and cover. Store in refrigerator. Makes about 8 cups.

FLUFFY LEMON SAUCE #2

1/2 tablespoon butter or margarine
1/2 cup confectioners' sugar
1/2 cup evaporated milk, chilled
1 tablespoon lemon juice
Grated rind of 1 lemon

Cream butter. Add sugar, a little at a time, mixing well.

Whip milk until stiff. Add lemon juice and whip to blend.

Fold sugar mixture and lemon rind into whipped milk. Serves 6.

BRANDY CREAM SAUCE

1/3 cup butter
1 cup confectioners' sugar
3 tablespoons brandy
2 egg yolks
1/2 cup cream

Place the butter in top of double boiler over (not in) hot water; beat until soft. Gradually add sugar and beat until creamy. Slowly beat in brandy, then beat in egg yolks, 1 at a time. Add cream and cook until slightly thickened. Serve over cottage pudding or gingerbread. Makes about 1 1/2 cups.

With Liqueurs: Substitute any favorite liqueur for the brandy.

ALMOND HONEY SAUCE

1 cup almonds
1 tablespoon butter or margarine
1 1/4 cups strained honey
Few grains salt

Blanch almonds by covering with boiling water and letting stand a few minutes until skins are wrinkled. Drain and rub between fingers to remove skins; dry on paper toweling.

Melt butter in pie pan in moderate oven (350°F.). Spread blanched almonds over melted butter. Bake until nuts are lightly browned, stirring occasionally, about 15 minutes.

Cool and slice or cut nuts in halves. Stir nuts into honey. Add salt.

Serve with ice cream or other desserts. Serves 6.

HOT SPICED CHERRY SAUCE

1 No. 2 can (2 1/2 cups) pitted sour red cherries
1/2 cup sugar
2 2-inch sticks cinnamon
16 whole cloves
2 teaspoons cornstarch

Drain cherries and reserve syrup.

Measure syrup and add enough water to make 1 cup. Add sugar and spices and bring to boiling point. Cook 10 minutes. Strain out spices.

Blend a little hot syrup with cornstarch. Add to hot mixture. Cook until slightly thickened, about 10 minutes. Add cherries and heat.

Serve hot. Serves 4.

LINGONBERRY SAUCE

1 quart lingonberries
1/2 cup water
1 1/2 cups sugar

Pick over berries and rinse well. Drain. Add water and sugar. Bring slowly to boiling point.

Reduce heat and cook slowly uncovered for 10 minutes.

Serve with meat or as sauce for pudding. Makes about 3 cups.

SPECIAL FUDGE SAUCE

1 1/4 cups cocoa
3/4 cup sugar
1/2 teaspoon salt
1 tablespoon cornstarch
1/2 cup light corn syrup
1/2 cup milk
2 tablespoons butter or margarine
2 tablespoons vanilla

Mix dry ingredients; add corn syrup and milk and mix thoroughly. Cook 15 minutes over hot water, stirring until thickened. Add butter.

Cool and add vanilla. Makes about 3 cups.

FLUFFY MAPLE SAUCE

3/4 cup dark corn syrup
1/4 cup brown sugar or corn syrup
2 tablespoons water
1/8 teaspoon salt
1 egg white
1/4 teaspoon maple flavoring

Mix corn syrup, sugar, and water in saucepan. Cook until it forms very soft ball when dropped into cold water (236°F.).

Pour syrup slowly over egg white beaten stiff with salt added. Add flavoring and beat until mixture holds peaks. Serve with hot pudding. Makes about 2 cups.

MELBA SAUCE

1/2 cup currant jelly
1/2 cup sugar
1 cup pulp and juice of raspberries
1/2 tablespoon cornstarch
1 tablespoon cold water

Add jelly and sugar to raspberries. Bring to boiling point. Add cornstarch mixed with cold water.

Cook, stirring constantly until mixture becomes thick and clear. Cool and strain. Makes about 2 cups.

Note: A package of thawed frozen raspberries may be used.

Peach Melba: Place a canned peach half, cut side up, in each of 6 individual dessert dishes. Top each with a scoop of ice cream and pour the cooled sauce over the top.

Peach Melba

SWEETENED WHIPPED CREAM OR CREME CHANTILLY

Whip 1 cup heavy cream until stiff. Then fold in 1 to 3 tablespoons sifted confectioners' sugar and 1/2 teaspoon vanilla. Serve with cold puddings or frozen desserts, or use as a filling for cakes.

Variations: The sweetened whipped cream may be varied in innumerable ways. Here are a few examples: (1) To the whipped cream above add 1/2 cup jam or orange marmalade; (2) add 1/2 cup blanched, toasted, slivered almonds or other nuts; (3) add 1/2 cup crushed peppermint stick candy; (4) add 1/2 cup lightly toasted coconut and 1 tablespoon light rum.

BANANA SAUCE

1 tablespoon butter or margarine
1 tablespoon flour
1/4 cup sugar
1/2 cup milk, scalded
1 egg yolk
1 banana, well mashed
1/2 cup heavy cream, whipped with a few grains salt

Cream the butter and add flour. Blend thoroughly, then add sugar gradually.

Combine with scalded milk. Cook until thickened, stirring constantly. Add egg yolk, slightly beaten. Cook 3 minutes.

Remove from heat. Add bananas. Chill. Fold in whipped cream. Makes about 1 1/2 cups.

Variations: Substitute berries and other fresh or canned fruits for banana.

LIQUEUR SAUCES

Allow for each serving about 1 1/2 tablespoons of your favorite liqueur. Crème de menthe is especially popular as a sauce. Pour over ice cream, ices, or lightly sugared fruits. Garnish with maraschino cherries.

MAPLE NUT SAUCE

1/3 cup broken pecans
1/4 cup butter or margarine
1/4 cup brown sugar or corn syrup
3/4 cup corn syrup
1 tablespoon cold water
2 tablespoons flour
1/2 cup boiling water
1/2 teaspoon maple flavoring or vanilla

Sauté pecans in butter or margarine to delicate brown and combine with sugar and syrup.

Mix cold water with flour in saucepan. Add boiling water and cook thick. Add sugar mixture and bring to a boil. Add flavoring. Serve hot. Makes about 1 1/2 cups.

CARAMEL SAUCE

1/4 cup butter or margarine, melted
1 cup brown sugar
1 tablespoon cornstarch
1 cup cold water
2 teaspoons vanilla

Combine butter, sugar, and cornstarch dissolved in water in top part of double boiler. Bring slowly to boiling point, stirring to blend.

Remove from heat. Add vanilla. Cover until ready to serve.

Should mixture congeal, place over low flame, heat slowly, then thin to desired consistency with hot water, beat with spoon until smooth. Makes about 2 cups.

Brandy, Rum or Lemon Caramel Sauce: Vary caramel sauce by substituting 2 tablespoons of any of these flavorings for vanilla.

CARAMEL SAUCE #2

Melt 1 cup sugar in heavy frying pan over low heat until light brown in color.

Remove from heat and slowly add 1 cup boiling water. Boil 10 minutes or until caramel is dissolved. Makes about 1 cup.

WHIPPED FRUIT SAUCE

1 cup fresh berries
1/2 to 1 cup sugar
Few grains salt
1 teaspoon lemon juice

Amount of sugar depends upon the sweetness of berries.

Combine ingredients in a deep bowl and beat until fluffy. Serve on cake or pudding.

COFFEE SAUCE

1/3 cup ground coffee
3/4 cup boiling water
1/3 cup sugar
1 tablespoon cornstarch
1/8 teaspoon salt
1 egg yolk
1 tablespoon shortening
1/2 teaspoon vanilla
1/3 cup thin cream

Place coffee in saucepan, add boiling water, heat to boiling. Cover, turn off heat, steep 5 minutes; strain through double thickness of cheesecloth.

Combine sugar, cornstarch, and salt in top of double boiler. Add egg yolk; mix thoroughly. Stir in coffee gradually.

Place mixture over hot water; cook 8 to 10 minutes until thickened, stirring frequently. Remove from hot water, stir in shortening and vanilla.

Set in cold water to cool, stirring frequently. Stir in cream gradually. Chill; serve over ice cream. Makes 3/4 cup sauce.

SOUR CREAM SAUCE

1/3 cup butter or margarine
1 cup confectioners' sugar
1/4 teaspoon lemon juice
1/4 teaspoon vanilla
1/4 to 1/2 cup sour cream, plain or whipped

Cream butter. Add sugar slowly and beat well. Add lemon juice and vanilla.

Beat in enough sour cream to make sauce light and fluffy.

Serve on fruit brown betty, hot baked apples or dumplings, steamed or baked puddings. Makes about 1 cup.

RUM SAUCE

4 tablespoons butter or margarine
1 cup firmly packed brown sugar
2 egg yolks, well beaten
1/2 cup cream
1/8 teaspoon salt
3 tablespoons rum

Cream together butter and sugar. Add egg yolks, cream, and salt.

Cook over boiling water until creamy and thickened.

Remove from heat. Cool, add rum. Makes 1 cup.

HOT BROWN SUGAR SAUCE

1/2 cup dark corn syrup
1/2 cup firmly packed brown sugar
4 teaspoons flour
1/4 teaspoon salt
1 cup water
2 teaspoons butter or margarine
1 teaspoon vanilla

Combine corn syrup, brown sugar, flour, salt, water, and butter in small saucepan.

Boil 10 minutes, stirring occasionally. Add vanilla. Serve hot. Makes 1 cup.

STRAWBERRY SAUCE

1/3 cup butter or margarine
1 cup powdered sugar
1 egg white
2/3 cup strawberries

Cream butter; add sugar gradually, then egg white with berries.

Beat until fruit is mashed. Makes about 1 1/2 cups.

Variations: Almost any variety of fresh fruit may be substituted for strawberries.

RUM TOFFEE SAUCE

1 cup light brown sugar
1/8 cup thin cream
2 tablespoons butter or margarine
4 teaspoons rum

Combine sugar, cream, and butter. Bring to a boil and simmer 5 minutes. Cool to lukewarm and add rum.

Serve warm on vanilla ice cream or cottage pudding. Makes about 1 1/4 cups.

PINEAPPLE SAUCE

    2   cups crushed pineapple
    1/4 cup sugar
    1   tablespoon cornstarch
    1   tablespoon butter or margarine
    1/4 teaspoon salt

Drain juice from crushed pineapple. Mix cornstarch and sugar. Add to juice. Cook over direct heat until sauce thickens, stirring constantly.

Add drained fruit, butter, and salt. Cook a few minutes longer.

Serve hot or cold over cottage pudding or plain cake. Makes about 2 cups.

MARSHMALLOW MINT SAUCE

    1   cup sugar
    1/2 cup water
    16 marshmallows, cut fine
    Few grains salt
    1   egg white
    1   or 2 drops oil of peppermint
    Green food coloring

Combine sugar and water in saucepan.

Simmer 5 minutes, stirring occasionally. Add marshmallows, stirring to blend.

Add salt to egg white and beat until stiff.

Gradually fold marshmallow mixture into egg white.

Add oil of peppermint and green coloring to tint delicately. Serve hot or cold on ice cream. Serves 6.

Marshmallow Sauce: For plain marshmallow sauce, omit oil of peppermint and green food coloring. The egg white may also be omitted.

FOAMY EGG SAUCE

    1/3 to 1/2 cup butter or margarine
    1   cup confectioners' sugar
    1   well beaten egg
    2   tablespoons hot water
    1   teaspoon vanilla

Cream butter and add sugar gradually. Beat in egg and hot water.

Heat over hot water, beating constantly, until mixture thickens. Add vanilla.

Serve hot or cold. Makes about 1 cup.

HOT BRANDY SAUCE

    1/3 cup sugar
    1/2 tablespoon cornstarch
    1/8 teaspoon salt
    1   cup hot water
    1   tablespoon butter or margarine
    2   tablespoons brandy

Combine sugar, cornstarch, and salt in a saucepan. Add hot water slowly. Cook until clear, stirring constantly. Add butter and flavoring.

Serve hot over mincemeat pie or steamed pudding. Makes 1 cup.

PEPPERMINT SAUCE

    4   teaspoons butter or margarine
    1 1/4 cups sugar
    2/3 cup light corn syrup
    3/4 cup undiluted evaporated milk
    Green food coloring
    Few drops of peppermint oil

Combine butter, sugar, and syrup; bring to boil. Cook to soft ball stage (235°F.). Cool slightly; add milk and stir until mixed.

Add green food coloring to produce desired light green color. Add peppermint oil to taste. Serve over vanilla ice cream. Makes 2 cups.

MADEIRA SAUCE

    1   cup sugar
    2 1/2 tablespoons flour
    1/8 teaspoon salt
    2   cups boiling water
    1 1/2 tablespoons lime juice
    1/2 cup madeira wine
    2   tablespoons melted butter or margarine

Mix sugar, flour, and salt. Stir gradually into boiling water. Cook until thickened, 5 to 10 minutes, stirring constantly.

Add lime juice, madeira wine, and butter. Stir well. Do not boil. Remove from heat. Makes 2 cups.

MOLASSES SAUCE

    1   cup molasses
    1   tablespoon lemon juice
    2   tablespoons butter or margarine
    1/8 teaspoon salt
    1   egg, well beaten

Simmer molasses 15 minutes or until quite thick. Add lemon juice, butter, and salt; pour mixture over well beaten egg, beating while pouring.

Then cook 3 minutes in top part of double boiler, stirring constantly. Makes about 1 1/2 cups.

HONEY-WINE FRUIT SAUCE

    1/2 cup honey
    1/2 cup water
    3   cardamom seeds, peeled and crushed fine
    1/2 teaspoon salt
    6   or 8 mint leaves, crushed or cut fine
    1   tablespoon lemon juice
    1/2 cup sherry, madeira, or port wine
    Chilled fruit as desired

Mix honey, water, and crushed cardamom seeds; simmer 5 minutes. Add salt and mint leaves. Cool and strain. Add lemon juice and wine.

Pour over chilled fruit and serve. Makes 1 1/4 cups.

Note: Cantaloupe balls, honeydew melon balls, and blueberries make a delicious combination. The sauce is excellent, too, on grapefruit segments.

SHERRY SAUCE

    2   eggs, separated
    1   cup powdered sugar
    3   tablespoons sherry

Beat yolks until thick. Gradually beat in 1/2 cup sugar.

Beat egg whites until stiff; add 1/2 cup powdered sugar gradually, beating until sugar disappears. Fold into yolk mixture. Flavor with sherry. Makes about 1 1/2 cups.

FOAMY ORANGE SAUCE

    1/3 cup butter or margarine
    1   cup confectioners' sugar
    1   egg, separated
    1/4 cup orange juice

Cream butter until soft, beat in sugar gradually, then egg yolk and orange juice.

Just before serving, fold in stiffly beaten egg white.

Variations: Flavor with 1 tablespoon brandy, or substitute sherry for orange juice. Whipped cream may also be folded into the mixture. Makes about 1 1/2 cups.

HONEY SAUCE

    2   teaspoons cornstarch
    2   tablespoons melted butter or margarine
    1/2 cup honey

Add cornstarch to melted butter and stir until smooth.

Add honey and cook 6 minutes. Makes 3/4 cup.

LEMONADE HARD SAUCE

    1/4 cup soft butter or margarine
    1   cup powdered sugar, sifted
    1   tablespoon plus 1 teaspoon frozen concentrate for lemonade (undiluted)

Cream butter; add powdered sugar, creaming and beating until light and fluffy. Add concentrate for lemonade and beat well again.

Chill slightly and mold in small balls or drop from a teaspoon onto waxed paper. Top with a clove, slices of maraschino and a clove, or a nut half.

Chill and serve with hot steamed pudding.

Lemonade Hard Sauce

DATE PECAN SAUCE

½ cup sliced, pitted dates
¼ cup water
¼ cup firmly packed brown sugar
½ cup corn syrup
⅛ teaspoon salt
½ teaspoon vanilla
½ cup chopped pecans

Combine dates, water, sugar, syrup, and salt. Bring to boil; cook 1 minute, stirring constantly.

Remove from heat. Add vanilla and nuts. Let cool. Serve over vanilla ice cream. Serves 6.

HONEY AND ORANGE SAUCE

1 cup honey
¼ cup chopped orange peel
½ cup orange juice
Pinch of salt

Combine all ingredients. Let stand over hot, not boiling, water about 30 minutes to blend flavors.

Serve on gingerbread, steamed puddings, or ice cream. Makes 1½ cups.

HOT BUTTER SAUCE

½ cup butter or margarine
1 cup sugar
½ cup cream
1 teaspoon vanilla

Melt butter or margarine. Blend in sugar and cream. Heat. Add vanilla.

Serve hot over puddings. Serves 6.

PLUM PUDDING SAUCE

¼ cup butter or margarine
1 cup confectioners' sugar
2 tablespoons cider
2 eggs, separated
½ cup evaporated milk, undiluted

Cream butter and confectioners' sugar. Add cider.

Beat egg yolks until lemon colored and add. When well mixed, stir in evaporated milk.

Cook in double boiler until sauce is thick as custard. Remove from heat.

Beat egg whites until stiff. Gradually add hot mixture, beating constantly until blended. Makes 1 cup.

PEANUT BUTTER-FRUIT SAUCE

½ cup sugar
½ cup dark corn syrup
⅓ cup water
½ teaspoon salt
¼ cup peanut butter
¼ cup raisins or chopped candied fruit

Mix sugar, corn syrup, water, and salt. Simmer 10 minutes; cool.

Stir syrup slowly into the peanut butter and raisins or candied fruit.

Serve on baked custard, ice cream, or steamed puddings. Makes about 1 cup.

LEMON SAUCE #2

½ cup butter or margarine
1 cup sugar
1 egg, beaten
3 tablespoons boiling water
1 lemon, grated rind and juice

Cream butter. Add sugar and continue creaming. Stir in egg and mix well. Add water gradually.

Cook over low heat or in top of double boiler, stirring constantly, until mixture thickens. Add lemon juice and rind. Blend well. Serves 6.

HOT BURNT SUGAR SAUCE

1¾ cups sugar
1 cup hot water
1¼ tablespoons cornstarch
¼ teaspoon salt
1½ tablespoons butter or margarine

Melt ¼ cup sugar in heavy skillet, stirring occasionally. When lightly browned, stir in hot water.

Let simmer until caramel is melted.

Mix remaining 1½ cups sugar with cornstarch and salt and add to hot mixture. Cook, stirring constantly, until thickened and clear. Add butter and serve hot. Serves 8 to 12.

FOAMY LEMON SAUCE

⅓ cup butter or margarine
¼ teaspoon salt
2 cups sifted confectioners' sugar
1 egg yolk
1 teaspoon grated lemon rind
¼ cup lemon juice

Cream butter with salt. Add 1¾ cups sugar gradually. Beat in egg yolk. Blend in lemon rind and juice.

Add remaining sugar and blend. Makes 1¼ cups.

HOT SPICY SAUCE

1 tablespoon cornstarch
2 cups sugar
¼ teaspoon cinnamon
¼ teaspoon nutmeg
2 cups water
¼ cup butter or margarine

Combine cornstarch, sugar, cinnamon, and nutmeg. Add water gradually, stirring to mix well. Add butter.

Heat to boiling, stirring constantly, and cook 5 minutes. Serve hot with puddings. Serves 6.

FOAMY BRANDY SAUCE

2 egg yolks
1 cup confectioners' sugar
Few grains salt
2 tablespoons brandy or 1 teaspoon vanilla
1 cup cream, whipped

Beat egg yolks very light, gradually adding sugar and salt. Add brandy or vanilla. Fold in whipped cream. Makes 2 cups.

FOAMY SAUCE

⅛ teaspoon salt
1 egg white
¼ cup brown sugar
¼ teaspoon vanilla
1 egg yolk
¼ cup heavy cream, whipped

Add salt to egg white and beat until foamy.

Sift brown sugar and gradually add 2 tablespoons sugar to the egg white, beating until well blended and egg white is stiff.

Add remaining sugar and vanilla to egg yolk and beat until fluffy. Combine both mixtures and fold in whipped cream. Makes 1½ cups.

Note: Sauce should not stand more than 2 hours before serving.

HOT WALNUT SAUCE

½ cup margarine
2 tablespoons cornstarch
½ cup firmly packed brown sugar
1⅓ cups boiling water
⅔ cup chopped walnuts
1 tablespoon lemon juice

Melt margarine in top of a double boiler.

Combine cornstarch and brown sugar; blend with margarine. Add water and cook until thick, stirring constantly. Add walnuts and lemon juice. Serve hot. Serves 12.

BUTTERSCOTCH SAUCE #2

½ cup butter or margarine
2⅔ cups firmly packed brown sugar
1 tablespoon lemon juice
½ cup heavy cream

Combine all ingredients. Cook in double boiler 1 hour, stirring occasionally.

Add toasted almonds to sauce if desired. Makes 3 cups.

HONEY HARD SAUCE

Cream ⅓ cup butter and gradually beat in ¾ cup honey. Add 1 teaspoon lemon juice. Chill until cold, but not hard.

Set out several sauces and balls of ice cream for a "make-your-own" ice cream sundae dessert.

DOUGHNUTS

A doughnut is defined as a small cake of sweetened leavened dough, usually ring-shaped, fried in deep, hot fat. The names friedcakes and crullers are often applied to the same product; however usage differs as to the names. The name doughnut may be derived from the fact that early doughnuts were balls or "nuts" of dough. Crullers derived their name from the Dutch word krullen, meaning curled, and they differed from doughnuts mainly in shape, being twisted, curled, or gashed across. Bismarcks are variations of the doughnut in which the dough is filled with jam, jelly, or marmalade before or, more often, after being fried in deep fat. In some places a distinction is made between a doughnut and a fried cake. The former being made with yeast and the latter a baking powder dough.

DOUGHNUT MAKING HINTS

Mixing and Cutting: The dough for quick doughnuts (made with baking powder or baking soda) should be as soft as can be handled. Chill the dough for at least an hour for ease in rolling.

Roll and cut a little of the dough at a time, keeping the balance in the refrigerator. Use a floured cutter to cut doughnuts. For variety, cut dough into strips 1 inch wide and 3 inches long to make "Long Johns." Quick doughnuts should be allowed to stand about 15 minutes before frying.

Yeast-raised doughnuts should be handled in much the same way as other yeast breads. The doughnuts should rise in a warm place until almost double in bulk before frying.

Frying: Fry in deep hot fat (375°F.). The kettle should be about half full or have at least 3 inches of fat. The temperature of the fat is very important be-cause if the fat is too cold, the doughnuts will be fat-soaked; if too hot, the doughnuts will brown before they are cooked through.

Fry only a few doughnuts at a time or the fat will cool too rapidly. Turn the doughnuts when they are brown on the underside—usually when they rise to the top of the fat. Drain on absorbent paper.

To Sugar Doughnuts: When cool, place a few at a time in a paper bag with confectioners' or granulated sugar and shake well.

To Glaze Doughnuts: Gradually add ⅓ cup boiling water to 1 cup confectioners' sugar and mix well. Dip warm doughnuts into glaze.

PLAIN DOUGHNUTS

3 tablespoons butter
1 cup sugar
2 beaten eggs
3¾ cups sifted enriched flour
4 teaspoons baking powder
½ teaspoon salt
¾ cup milk
1 teaspoon vanilla

Cream the butter; add sugar gradually and cream until light. Stir in beaten eggs.

Mix and sift flour, baking powder, and salt; add to creamed mixture alternately with the milk. Stir in vanilla. Chill thoroughly.

Roll out ⅓ inch thick on lightly floured surface. Cut with floured cutter. Fry in deep hot fat (375°F.) until brown, turning once. Drain. Makes about 3 dozen.

Variations of Plain Doughnuts:

Plain Crullers: Increase shortening in Plain Doughnuts to ¼ cup. Roll out ½ inch thick and cut into strips. Twist or form in knots. Fry in deep hot fat (375°F.). Drain on absorbent paper.

Bismarcks: Make Plain Doughnut dough and roll out ¼ inch thick. Let the rolled dough stand for 5 minutes and then cut into rounds with a lightly floured cooky cutter. Again let the dough stand for 5 minutes.

Put 1 teaspoon jam or marmalade in the center of half the rounds. Cover with a second round of dough, sandwich fashion and seal the entire edge by pressing between the fingers. Fry in deep hot fat (375°F.) and drain.

Chocolate Doughnuts: Increase the sugar in Plain Doughnuts to 1¼ cups and add 1½ squares unsweetened chocolate, melted, to the egg-sugar mixture. If desired, chopped nuts may also be added.

Drop Doughnuts: Drop dough from a spoon into the hot fat. For drop doughnuts the dough may be slightly softer than for rolled doughnuts.

Fruit Doughnuts: To the dry ingredients add ½ cup fruit such as raisins or chopped peel.

Sour Milk or Buttermilk Doughnuts: Reduce baking powder to 2 teaspoons and add ½ teaspoon baking soda. Use sour milk or buttermilk instead of sweet milk. Flavor with ¾ teaspoon nutmeg if desired.

Spice Doughnuts: Add ½ teaspoon nutmeg and ¼ teaspoon mace to the dry ingredients.

Nut Doughnuts: Add ½ cup chopped pecans or walnuts to the dough.

Orange Doughnuts: Add 1 teaspoon mace to dry ingredients and stir in 1 teaspoon grated orange rind.

RAISED DOUGHNUTS
(Master Recipe)

1¼ cups scalded milk
1 cake compressed yeast
¾ cup sugar
4½ cups sifted enriched flour
3 tablespoons butter
1 egg, well beaten
1½ teaspoons nutmeg
1 teaspoon salt

Cool milk to lukewarm. Add crumbled yeast and 1 tablespoon sugar. Stir until dissolved. Add 1½ cups of flour and beat well. Cover and let rise in a warm place about 1 hour.

Cream butter until fluffy. Add sugar, and cream together until light. Add egg, nutmeg, and salt, and stir into yeast mixture. Add remaining 3 cups flour, knead lightly, and place in a greased bowl.

Brush with salad oil, cover with towel, and let rise until double in bulk, about 1½ hours.

Roll on a floured board to ½-inch thickness. Cut with floured doughnut cutter. Let rise until double in bulk, about 1 hour.

Fry in deep hot fat (370°F.) until brown, turning once. Drain on absorbent paper. Makes about 2½ dozen.

Raised Doughnut Variations:
Bismarcks: Roll dough ½ inch thick. Cut rounds with a 3-inch cooky cutter. Fry as for raised doughnuts.

When cool, cut a short slit in side of each to the center. Put a teaspoon of jelly in center. Close tightly. Roll in sugar.

Crullers: 1. Roll dough ½ inch thick. Cut into strips ¾ inches long. Shape into twists or figure 8's. Fry as for raised doughnuts.

2. Roll dough ¼ inch thick. Cut into 2-inch squares. Make four slits in each. Then lift by picking up alternate strips between fingers and thumb. Fry same way.

RICH CRULLERS

4¼ cups sifted enriched flour
1¼ teaspoons baking soda
2½ teaspoons cream of tartar
½ teaspoon salt
1 teaspoon nutmeg
3 eggs
1 cup sugar
1 cup heavy cream

Mix and sift the dry ingredients. Beat the eggs until thick and lemon-colored; gradually beat in the sugar, then stir in the cream.

Gradually stir in the flour mixture, blending until almost smooth.

Turn out on floured board and roll out ¼ inch thick. Cut with floured doughnut cutter and fry in deep hot fat (370°F.) until golden brown.

POTATO DOUGHNUTS

4½ cups sifted enriched flour
4 teaspoons baking powder
1 teaspoon salt
1 teaspoon baking soda
1 teaspoon nutmeg
2 eggs, well beaten
1 cup sugar
2 tablespoons salad oil
1 cup mashed potato
1 cup sour milk

Mix and sift flour, baking powder, salt, baking soda, and nutmeg.

Beat eggs and sugar until light. Add oil, potato, and milk, beating until smooth. Stir in flour mixture. Chill thoroughly.

Roll on a floured board to ½-inch thickness. Cut with doughnut cutter. Fry in deep hot fat (370°F.). Drain on absorbent paper. Makes about 3 dozen.

FRENCH CRULLERS

¼ cup sugar
½ teaspoon salt
¼ cup shortening
1 cup water
1 cup sifted enriched flour
3 eggs
1 teaspoon vanilla

Combine sugar, salt, shortening, and water in heavy saucepan and heat. When briskly boiling, add flour all at once, stirring vigorously with a wooden spoon.

Beat until mixture forms a smooth ball which leaves sides of pan clean.

Place in a bowl. Beat in thoroughly one egg at a time then continue beating until mixture is smooth and shiny and breaks off when spoon is raised. Add vanilla. Chill.

Force through a pastry tube in the shape of rings onto strips of oiled waxed paper.

Carefully turn the paper upside-down so that the crullers will drop into deep hot fat.

Fry at 380°F. until golden brown on all sides. Drain. Cool. Brush with confectioners' sugar icing. Makes 10 crullers.

JIFFY DOUGHNUT PUFFS

1 tube refrigerated pan-ready biscuits
Cinnamon sugar
Confectioners' sugar

Fry pan-ready biscuits in hot deep fat (375°F.). Fry only a few at a time, and as soon as doughnuts rise to surface, turn with a long-handled fork (don't pierce). Turn often thereafter until golden and done.

Drain on absorbent paper. Serve warm, letting guests dip doughnut puffs in cinnamon or confectioners' sugar. Makes 10.

RICE CRULLERS OR FRITTERS
(Calas)

2 cups cooked rice
3 beaten eggs
¼ teaspoon vanilla
½ teaspoon nutmeg or grated lemon rind
6 tablespoons flour
½ cup sugar
½ teaspoon salt
3 teaspoons baking powder

Combine rice, eggs, vanilla, and nutmeg. Mix and sift flour, sugar, salt, and baking powder. Mix thoroughly with rice-egg mixture.

Drop by spoonfuls into deep fat (365°F.) and fry until golden brown. Drain on absorbent paper.

Sprinkle with confectioners' sugar. Serve very hot with tart jelly. Makes about 1½ dozen.

CALAS—YEAST-RAISED
These rice fritters are a famous New Orleans dish.

1½ cups cooked rice, very soft
½ package yeast, active dry or compressed
½ cup warm, not hot, water
3 eggs, beaten
1¼ cups sifted flour
¼ cup sugar
½ teaspoon salt
¼ teaspoon nutmeg

Mash rice grains and cool to lukewarm. Soften yeast in warm water and stir in lukewarm rice. Mix well. Cover and let rise overnight.

The next morning, add eggs, flour, sugar, salt, and nutmeg. Beat until smooth. Let stand in a warm place for 30 minutes.

Drop by tablespoons into deep hot fat (360°F.) and fry until golden brown, about 3 minutes. Serve sprinkled with powdered sugar or sugar mixed with cinnamon. These are excellent served with fruit or maple syrup. Makes 2 dozen.

Yeast-Raised Calas

BANANA DOUGHNUTS

5 cups sifted enriched flour
4 teaspoons baking powder
1 teaspoon baking soda
2 teaspoons salt
1 teaspoon nutmeg
1/4 cup shortening
1 cup sugar
3 eggs, well beaten
3/4 cup mashed bananas
1/2 cup sour milk or buttermilk
1 1/2 teaspoons vanilla
1/2 cup flour for rolling
Melted fat or oil

Sift together flour, baking powder, soda, salt, and nutmeg.

Beat shortening until creamy. Add sugar gradually and continue beating until light and fluffy. Add eggs and beat well.

Add combined bananas, milk, and vanilla to creamed mixture and blend. Add flour mixture and mix until smooth.

Turn a small amount of dough onto a floured board. Knead very lightly. Roll out to 3/8-inch thickness. Cut with floured 2 1/2-inch doughnut cutter.

Heat fat to 375°F. or until a 1-inch cube of bread will turn golden brown in about 40 seconds. Slip doughnuts into fat with spatula. Fry about 3 minutes, or until golden brown, turning them frequently.

Drain on absorbent paper. Makes 3 1/2 dozen. Sugar the doughnuts, if desired.

MOLASSES DOUGHNUTS

1/2 cup molasses
1/2 cup granulated sugar
2 eggs
1 1/2 tablespoons melted butter
5 cups sifted enriched flour
1 teaspoon baking soda
1 teaspoon salt
1/2 teaspoon ginger or 1 teaspoon nutmeg
1 cup thick sour milk

Beat molasses, sugar, and eggs until smooth. Add butter.

Mix and sift 2 cups flour with the soda, salt, and ginger or nutmeg. Add alternately with the sour milk to the first mixture.

Add sifted flour to make dough that can be handled easily. Chill in refrigerator.

Roll dough a little at a time. Shape with small doughnut cutter. Fry in deep hot fat (370°F.). Drain on absorbent paper. Makes about 4 dozen.

RUM OR BRANDY CRULLERS

5 egg yolks
2 whole eggs
3/4 cup sugar
2 tablespoons sour cream
2 tablespoons rum or brandy
2 teaspoons vanilla
About 3 1/2 cups sifted enriched flour

Beat egg yolks and whole eggs until thick and lemon colored. Add sugar gradually, beating well. Blend in sour cream, rum, and vanilla.

Add flour gradually until dough becomes too hard to handle in the bowl.

Toss on floured pastry cloth and knead until smooth and elastic.

Roll out portion of dough on floured cloth until paper-thin; cut into 1-inch by 3-inch strips. Slit center of each strip and take one end and pull it through slit on other side.

Fry in deep fat (375°F.) first on one, then on the other side, until pale, golden brown, about 2 minutes on the first and 1 minute on other side. Drain on absorbent paper; sprinkle with confectioners' sugar. Makes 3 to 4 dozen.

BROWN SUGAR DOUGHNUTS

2 eggs
1 1/2 cups brown sugar
4 tablespoons melted butter
1 cup milk
4 cups sifted enriched flour
4 teaspoons baking powder
1/2 teaspoon cinnamon
1/2 teaspoon salt

Beat eggs until they are light and stir into sugar. Stir butter and milk into above.

Add baking powder, cinnamon, and salt to flour and sift again. Add to above, stirring only enough to get ingredients thoroughly blended.

Chill in refrigerator at least 24 hours if possible. This prevents the doughnuts from soaking up the fat when fried.

Roll out a little of the dough at a time on floured board; cut with floured doughnut cutter.

Fry in hot deep fat (365°F.) until brown on one side. Turn and brown the other side. Drain and roll in powdered sugar.

This dough may be kept at least a week in a covered container in the refrigerator. Break off and cook only enough of the dough at a time to fill your requirements, as freshly cooked doughnuts are better than those left standing overnight. Makes about 35.

QUICK DOUGHNUTS
(With Prepared Mix)

1 package muffin mix
1 tablespoon sugar
1 1/2 teaspoons cinnamon
1 teaspoon nutmeg
About 3/4 cup water

Combine muffin mix, sugar, and spices. Add water and knead 30 seconds on lightly floured board. Roll out to 1/2-inch thickness. Cut with doughnut cutter.

Fry in deep hot fat (375°F.) 3 minutes, turning once. Drain on absorbent paper. Makes 1 dozen.

RAISED ORANGE CRULLERS

1 package dry granular yeast or 1 ounce compressed yeast
1/4 cup warm water (lukewarm for compressed)
1 cup sifted enriched flour
1 cup milk, scalded and cooled
1/4 cup butter or margarine
1/4 cup sugar
1 egg
1 teaspoon salt
About 3 cups sifted enriched flour
3/4 cup sugar
1 tablespoon grated orange rind

Dissolve yeast in water and let stand for 5 minutes.

Add 1 cup flour to milk and beat until smooth, using electric mixer. Add yeast and let stand for 30 minutes.

Cream butter and sugar until light and fluffy. Add egg and salt and beat well. Add to first mixture. Add remaining flour gradually. Knead until smooth and elastic.

Place in a greased bowl, cover, and let rise until doubled in bulk.

Turn out on floured pastry cloth and cut into 24 uniform pieces. Roll each piece until smooth and about 3/4 inch in diameter and 12 inches long.

Fold in halves and pinch end together; twist lightly. Cover and let rise until light, about 45 minutes.

Fry in deep fat (350°F.) until crullers are golden brown. Drain on absorbent paper. Roll in mixture of granulated sugar and orange rind. Makes 2 dozen.

BAKING POWDER CRULLERS

4 cups sifted enriched flour
3 1/2 teaspoons baking powder
1/2 teaspoon salt
1/2 teaspoon nutmeg
1 cup sugar
2 tablespoons shortening
2 well beaten eggs
1 cup cream

Mix and sift flour, baking powder, salt, and nutmeg.

Cream sugar and shortening together thoroughly; add eggs and beat well. Add sifted flour mixture alternately with cream to creamed mixture and mix thoroughly.

Roll out on floured board to 1/2-inch thickness. Cut into strips 6 x 1 inches. Twist strips, pressing ends together.

Fry in deep fat (370°F.) until brown, about 3 minutes. Drain on absorbent paper. When slightly cooled, sprinkle with confectioners' sugar. Makes about 24.

PIED PIPER DOUGHNUTS

2 eggs
1¼ cups sugar
1 cup mashed potatoes
5 tablespoons shortening, melted
5 cups sifted enriched flour
5 teaspoons baking powder
1 teaspoon baking soda
1 tablespoon cinnamon
½ teaspoon nutmeg
½ teaspoon cloves
1 can (1¼ cups) condensed tomato
soup
Fat for frying

Beat eggs and sugar until fluffy; add potatoes and melted shortening.

Sift flour with baking powder, soda and spices; add to egg-sugar mixture alternately with soup; mix well after each addition.

Roll dough on floured board until about ½ inch thick. Cut with doughnut cutter. Fry in 3 to 4-inch deep fat (380°F.) until brown, about 2 minutes.

Drain on absorbent paper. Dust while hot with a mixture of 1 teaspoon cinnamon and ½ cup of sugar. Makes about 40 doughnuts.

OLD-TIME DOUGHNUTS

2 cups sifted enriched flour
½ teaspoon baking soda
⅛ teaspoon nutmeg
¼ teaspoon salt
2 tablespoons shortening
½ cup sugar
1 egg
½ teaspoon vanilla
2 tablespoons vinegar and sweet milk
to make ½ cup

Mix and sift flour, soda, nutmeg, and salt.

Cream shortening; add sugar gradually and continue creaming. Add egg and beat well. Add vanilla. Add combined vinegar and milk alternately with dry ingredients and stir only until well blended.

Roll small quantities of dough at a time, about ⅓-inch thick. Cut doughnuts (2½-inch cutter) and let stand about 10 minutes. Fry in deep hot fat (365°F.) to delicate brown. Turn once. (Fry only 4 or 5 doughnuts at a time so fat will not cool unduly). Drain on absorbent paper. Makes 1½ dozen.

ONE BOWL FAST NIGHT CAKES (FASTNACHTSKUCHEN)
(No-Dissolve Method)

In Germany, and here in America, persons of German ancestry serve Fastnachts on Shrove Tuesday. The delicious little holeless doughnuts are part of a lavish feast the night before the Lenten fasting begins, just as pancakes are eaten in Ireland and England, and Shrovetide buns in Scandinavia.

3¾ to 4¼ cups unsifted
all-purpose flour
⅓ cup sugar
½ teaspoon salt
1 package active dry yeast
¼ cup (½ stick) softened margarine
1 cup very hot tap water
1 egg (at room temperature)
Peanut oil

In a large bowl thoroughly mix 1¼ cups flour, sugar, salt, and undissolved active dry yeast. Add softened margarine.

Gradually add very hot tap water to dry ingredients and beat 2 minutes at medium speed of electric mixer, scraping bowl occasionally. Add egg and ½ cup flour, or enough flour to make a thick batter. Beat at high speed 2 minutes, scraping bowl occasionally. Stir in enough additional flour to make a soft dough. Cover; let rise in warm place, free from draft, until doubled in bulk, about 1 hour.

Turn dough out onto lightly floured board; knead until smooth and elastic, about 8 to 10 minutes. Roll out into an 8 x 16-inch rectangle. Cut into 2-inch squares. Cut a slit about ¼-inch deep in the top of each square. Place on ungreased baking sheets. Cover; let rise in a warm place, free from draft, until doubled in bulk, about 45 minutes.

Fry in deep hot (375°F.) peanut oil until golden brown on both sides. Drain on paper towels. If desired, dip warm doughnuts in cinnamon-sugar mixture. Makes 32 doughnuts.

ORANGE TEA DOUGHNUTS

1 pound shortening
1 egg, beaten
½ cup milk
1 teaspoon vanilla
2 teaspoons grated orange rind
⅓ cup sugar
1⅓ cups sifted enriched flour
2 teaspoons baking powder
¼ teaspoon salt
1 tablespoon cooled melted shortening

Place shortening in a small, deep kettle or saucepan. Depth of melted fat should be at least 2 inches. Heat slowly to 350°F. when dough is ready for frying.

Combine egg, milk, vanilla, and orange rind. Sift together sugar, flour, baking powder, and salt. Mix dry with liquid ingredients. Do not beat. Stir in 1 tablespoon cooled, melted shortening.

Dip teaspoon into hot shortening, then dip up a spoonful of batter. Quickly immerse spoon into hot shortening and drop off the batter. Turn doughnut balls when they come to surface. Do not crowd kettle; fry only 4 or 5 doughnuts at a time. Fry for 3 to 5 minutes or until delicately browned.

Drain doughnuts over kettle, then

place on absorbent paper. When cool, roll in confectioners' sugar or frost with Orange Butter Frosting. Makes 14 medium or 18 small doughnuts.

CORN MEAL DOUGHNUT DROPS

½ cup corn meal
1 cup boiling water
¼ cup margarine
1 teaspoon salt
½ cup sugar
1 package (1 tablespoon) dry yeast
¼ cup warm water
About 3 cups sifted enriched flour
3 tablespoons dry milk solids
2 eggs
1 teaspoon grated lemon rind, if desired
Fat for frying
Sugar

Measure corn meal into a large mixing bowl. Pour boiling water over the meal, stirring smooth. Add margarine, salt, and sugar. Stir to melt margarine. Let stand 15 minutes.

Meanwhile, sprinkle yeast over warm water in cup. Let stand 5 minutes.

To corn meal mixture, add 1 cup of flour and dry milk solids. Mix well.

Stir yeast and mix into batter. Add eggs and beat hard. Add lemon rind, if desired, and enough flour to make a thick batter. Beat smooth.

Batter should drop from spoon and hold its shape. Scrape down sides of the bowl. Cover and set in a warm place to rise until doubled (about 1 hour).

Heat deep fat for frying to 365°F. Dip a tablespoon into hot fat; then take up batter by tablespoonfuls and drop into hot fat. Fry until golden brown on under side and turn doughnuts to brown top side. Turn doughnuts several times until done, 6 to 8 minutes altogether.

Remove from fat and drain on paper towels or brown paper.

Fry only as many doughnuts at one time as can float easily and without crowding on top of the fat in the pan.

When all doughnuts are fried, roll in granulated sugar or dust with confectioners' sugar. Makes about 3 dozen.

Corn Meal Doughnut Drops

DRINKS

Cocktails and other alcoholic drinks are countless in the variations of mixtures and the names by which they are designated in various parts of the country. Research, however, indicates that fewer than fifty drinks are served with any regularity and about one hundred more are served from time to time.

The wide selection in this section include the most popular drinks as well as the correct names by which they should be designated. Some standard drink recipes may not be mixed precisely the way you like your particular drink, but they are the recipes most generally followed by professional bartenders, mixed to please most tastes. In addition to the standard cocktails and long drinks, we have included a variety of quantity party punches for special occasions as well as guidance about serving wines with meals.

HINTS FOR MIXING COCKTAILS AND OTHER DRINKS

Most of the cocktails in this book are proportioned for one. Amounts may be increased proportionately. The drinks are based on the table of measurements given below. By using these measurements, it's easy to compute the requirements for greater quantities.

To compute the number of drops required where they are called for in a recipe, use the following figures based on three drops per dash:

For 6 cocktails .... ⅕ teaspoon
For 10 cocktails ... ⅓ teaspoon
For 25 cocktails ... ¾ teaspoon
For 100 cocktails . 3⅓ teaspoons

The term "part" is equivalent to a measure which may mean more or less than a jigger, depending upon individual taste.

A silver or glass cocktail shaker or a large tumbler is ideal for shaking or mixing drinks. There is no inflexible rule about mixing drinks; some are shaken, some stirred. If shaking is called for, add the ice and shake vigorously. Strain and serve promptly.

Usually cocktails containing wine as a principal ingredient are stirred, but there are exceptions to the rule.

Never stir or shake a carbonated water vigorously because this releases the gas and leaves the drink flat in a very short time.

SHOPPING GUIDE FOR THE HOME BAR

Watch a professional mixer in a large bar, and you'll see that he uses only a few gadgets; his basic tools are functional. Fancy pouring devices and trick shakers are all very well but they take up space. The basic utensils and tools are listed below. Most of them may be bought in hardware or hotel supply stores; for long service, buy the best.

2 mixing glasses and 1 metal top which may be combined with a glass for a shaker.
Glass cocktail shaker for special events.
Long-handled bar spoon for stirring.
Measuring spoon.
Cocktail strainer (rounded and perforated, or flat with flexible spring around the edge).
2 squeezers (regular one for lemons and oranges; pincer-type for limes and lemon sections).
Sharp small-bladed knife (stainless steel).
Corkscrew (lever type or double-action French corkscrew).
Ice pick or crusher.
Canvas bag and mallet for pounding ice.
Bar towels and wash cloths.
1 vacuum ice bucket—to eliminate frequent trips to the kitchen.
1 hard-wood muddler—a round-base wooden stick used for mashing various ingredients.
1-ounce measuring glass with lip (the type used by chemists).
1 bottle opener.

STANDARD BAR MEASUREMENTS

1	dash	3 drops
1	teaspoon	⅛ oz. (approx.)
3	teaspoons	1 tablespoon (½ oz.)
1	pony	1 ounce
1	jigger	1½ ounces
1	large jigger	2 ounces
1	wine glass (aver.)	4 ounces
1	cup	8 ounces
1	pint	16 ounces
1	quart	32 ounces
⅘	quart (fifth)	25.6 ounces
1	imperial quart	40 ounces (5 cups)
	(Canadian and British)	
½	bottle wine	12 ounces
1	bottle wine (aver.)	24 ounces
1	split of Champagne	6½ ounces
	Quart of Champagne	26 ounces
	Magnum (2 bottles)	52 ounces
	Jeroboam (4 bottles)	104 ounces
	Rehoboam (6 bottles)	156 ounces
		(1 gallon, 1 pint, 12 ounces)
A twist or curl of lemon		A thin slice of outer rind cut with curved knife

Note: The generally accepted size of a jigger is 1½ ounces. However, there has been an attempt to standardize the size at 2 ounces instead of 1½ ounces. If you use a jigger, test it and find out how much it really holds.

CHAMPAGNE

HIGHBALL

JIGGER

BRANDY INHALER

COCKTAIL

OLD-FASHIONED

BRANDY

WINE

CORDIAL

TO FROST RIMS OF GLASSES

Put lemon juice into shallow dish. Sift some granulated or powdered sugar onto plate about 1/4 inch deep.

Invert each glass in lemon juice. Lift out of juice into sugar for a minute.

Lift carefully out of sugar so as not to jar the sugar coating which has formed on rim. Place in refrigerator until "set."

Fill glasses with beverage, being careful not to disturb frost.

GLASSES—SELECTION AND USE

Most cocktails are served in 2½-, 4-, or 5-ounce glasses. Get the large ones—not measuring less than 3 ounces. The average bar cocktail measures about 2 to 2½ ounces, but the glass should never be filled to the brim. Cocktail glasses should preferably have stems because a drink is warmed by the hand, and a cocktail should remain cold.

Old-Fashioneds are traditionally served in broad, almost straight tumblers measuring 6 ounces.

Highballs are served in tumblers measuring 8 to 10 ounces.

Collins and rickeys are served in 10-, 12,- or 14-ounce glasses.

Goblets can be used for wines, flips, and sours. Get the larger sizes of the highball glasses if you want to keep the number to a minimum and make them do for highballs, collins, and juleps.

Liqueurs are traditionally served in tiny liqueur glasses, primarily because fine liqueur is expensive. If you want to dispense with the necessity of acquiring this extra set of glasses, you need only remember that a little in a larger glass will taste just as good and, in addition, you will get the pleasure of the aroma which is a goodly measure of the pleasure obtained from sipping a fine liqueur from a large glass. That's why fine old brandies are traditionally served in 18-ounce inhalers or "Napoleons."

Selections of glasses may always be made so that various glasses may serve several purposes—but, above all, let your cocktail glasses be made of *glass*. They may be either expensive crystal or the five- or ten-cent variety, but be sure they are *glass*. Metal, even gold-lined, sterling may be beautiful to look at but a cocktail drunk from them may taste like rusty tin.

For most cocktails and wines, we recommend the all-purpose tulip-shaped wine glass which may be obtained in any well-stocked store.

SIMPLE BAR SYRUP

Sugar and water boiled together to use when sugar alone might be hard to dissolve, as in cold drinks.

    4 cups sugar
    1 cup water

Combine sugar and water and place over heat. Stir until sugar is dissolved; reduce heat so mixture is simmering. Simmer until the liquid is clear.

The mixture may be bottled and kept either in the refrigerator or in an air-tight container.

Note: If you wish to clarify syrup further, add 1 well beaten egg white. Skim until perfectly clear.

Brandy Cocktails

ABOUT BRANDY

When no specific qualification is added, the term brandy means an alcoholic spirit distilled from grape wine or from marc, the residue of the grape press. Since the fermented juice of apples, apricots, cherries, peaches, pears, and other fruits can also be distilled, U.S. law requires that brandies made from fruits other than grapes be referred to by the name of the fruit —for example, apple brandy, apricot brandy, cherry brandy.

The difference between a brandy and a liqueur or cordial is in the distillation. Brandy is made by distilling the fermented juice of the fruit itself, whereas liqueurs or cordials are the result of infusing fruits or other flavoring material in grain alcohol or other liquors (chiefly brandy).

One of the most famous brandies is Cognac, which is distilled from grapes grown in a prescribed region around the French city of Cognac. Cognac labels often carry various initials and symbols supposed to denote quality, but these have no recognized authority.

Armagnac is another famous French brandy, less well known than Cognac but scarcely less fine. A little darker and heavier-flavored than Cognac, it is produced in a legally delimited area in southwest France.

Good brandies are produced also in Italy, Spain, Portugal, Germany, the Balkan countries, North Africa, and the United States (chiefly California).

Brandies should not be bottled at less than 80 proof (40 per cent alcohol). They are frequently allowed to age for many years. If a brandy is less than 2 years old, a statement showing the age must appear on the bottle. In extremely rare cases brandies have been allowed to age up to 60 years, but fine brandies are at their best after aging 25 to 40 years. It should be noted that most of the good Cognacs on the market are between 5 and 10 years old.

Brandy is aged in oak barrels, which give it a little color. For additional color caramel is added when the brandy is bottled.

APPLEJACK OLD-FASHIONED

    1½ ounces applejack
    1   lump sugar
    2   dashes Angostura bitters
    Dash of soda

Use an Old-Fashioned glass. Muddle sugar in a little soda until dissolved. Add 2 dashes Angostura bitters and a good-sized ice cube. Pour in applejack. Stir.

Decorate with fruit or twist of lemon peel. Serve with stirring rod.

APPLE CAR COCKTAIL

⅔ applejack
⅓ Cointreau
Juice of ½ lemon

Shake with ice. Serve in cocktail glass.

BETWEEN-THE-SHEETS

⅓ brandy
⅓ rum
⅓ Cointreau
Juice of ½ lemon

Shake with ice. Serve in 4-ounce cocktail glass.

BRANDY ALEXANDER
(Panama Cocktail)

1½ ounces brandy
¾ ounce crème de cacao
½ ounce heavy cream

Shake vigorously with ice. Serve in 4-ounce wine glass.

BRANDY COCKTAIL

1½ ounces brandy
½ ounce curaçao
1 teaspoon simple syrup

Stir with ice. Strain into cocktail glass. Add twist of lemon peel. Serve.

BRANDY EGG SOUR

1 ounce brandy
1 ounce curaçao
1 egg
1 teaspoon powdered sugar
2 dashes lemon juice

Shake with ice. Strain into Delmonico glass.

COFFEE COCKTAIL

1 ounce brandy
1 ounce port wine
1 teaspoon sugar
Yolk of egg

Pour brandy and port wine into mixing glass. Add ice. Then drop egg and sugar on top of ice. Shake well and serve in wine glass.

CUBAN COCKTAIL

1½ ounces brandy
½ ounce apricot brandy
Juice of ½ lime

Shake well with ice. Serve in cocktail glass.

STINGER COCKTAIL

⅔ brandy
⅓ white crème de menthe

Shake with ice. Serve in cocktail glass.

STAR COCKTAIL

½ applejack
½ Italian vermouth

Stir with ice. Strain into cocktail glass. Decorate with maraschino cherry.

SIDECAR COCKTAIL

⅓ brandy
⅓ Cointreau
⅓ lemon juice

Shake with ice. Serve in cocktail glass.

JACK ROSE COCKTAIL

1½ ounces applejack
Juice of ½ lemon
2 dashes grenadine

Shake with ice. Serve in cocktail glass.

Gin Cocktails

ABOUT GIN

Gin may be regarded as the simplest of alcoholic liquors, consisting as it does merely of neutral spirits (a pure grade of alcohol), water, and flavoring. The name is derived from genièvre, the French word for juniper, which was corrupted in English to geneva and then to gin.

Most American and British gins are of the type known as London Dry. They are neutral spirits redistilled over juniper berries and other aromatics such as angelica root, coriander, cardamom, and cassia bark, so as to absorb the flavors. Gins are never aged.

Holland was the first country to produce gin, and present-day Holland gin is a distinctive type, more aromatic and heavier in body than others. It is usually drunk straight with bitters and has too much flavor to be used in cocktails.

Old Tom gin is somewhat similar to London Dry but is sweetened. When using Old Tom, decrease the amount of sugar or syrup called for in the recipe.

Sloe gin, made from sweetened dry gin flavored with sloes (small, acid blue-black plums), is drunk as a cordial.

ADMIRAL COCKTAIL

1½ ounces dry gin
1 ounce cherry cordial
Juice of ½ lime

Shake with ice. Strain into cocktail glass.

ALEXANDER COCKTAIL

1½ ounces gin
¾ ounce crème de cacao
½ ounce heavy cream

Shake vigorously with ice. Serve in 4-ounce wine glass.

ARMY COCKTAIL

⅔ dry gin
⅓ Italian vermouth
2 dashes grenadine
Slice of orange

Shake with ice. Strain into cocktail glass. Add slice of orange.

AVIATION COCKTAIL

2 ounces dry gin
Juice of ½ lemon
4 dashes maraschino

Shake with ice. Strain into cocktail glass.

BERMUDA COCKTAIL

1¾ ounces dry gin
¾ ounce peach brandy
2 dashes grenadine
2 dashes orange juice

Shake with ice. Strain into cocktail glass.

BLACKOUT COCKTAIL

1¾ ounces dry gin
¾ ounce blackberry brandy
Juice of ½ lime

Shake with ice. Strain into cocktail glass.

BRONX COCKTAIL

½ dry gin
¼ Italian vermouth
2 half slices of orange

Add orange to ingredients and ice in mixing glass and shake vigorously. Strain into cocktail glass.

CAFE DE PARIS COCKTAIL

1½ ounces dry gin
½ ounce anisette
½ ounce heavy cream
1 egg white

Shake well with ice. Serve in 4-ounce wine glass.

CLOVER CLUB COCKTAIL

1½ ounces dry gin
4 dashes grenadine
Juice of ½ lemon
1 egg white

Shake well with ice. Serve in 4-ounce wine glass.

CLOVER LEAF COCKTAIL

1½ ounces dry gin
Juice of ½ lemon
4 dashes grenadine
1 egg white
4 or 5 mint leaves

Shake well with ice. Serve in 4-ounce wine glass. Decorate with one mint leaf on top.

COOPERSTOWN COCKTAIL

½ dry gin
¼ French vermouth
¼ Italian vermouth
2 sprigs mint

Shake well with ice. Strain into cocktail glass.

LONE TREE COCKTAIL

¾ dry gin
¼ Italian vermouth

Stir with ice. Strain into cocktail glass. Twist orange peel on top.

FOURTH ESTATE COCKTAIL

⅓ dry gin
⅓ French vermouth
⅓ Italian vermouth
3 dashes absinthe

Shake with ice. Strain into cocktail glass.

GIBSON COCKTAIL

1 ounce gin
¼ ounce Italian vermouth
¼ ounce French vermouth

Stir with cracked ice. Strain into cocktail glass. Serve with pickled onion. Twist lemon peel over drink.

GIMLET

1 teaspoon fine grain sugar
Juice of ½ lime
1½ ounces dry gin

Dissolve sugar in the lime juice in a 6-ounce glass. Add gin, and ice if desired. Fill with chilled soda. Stir slightly.
Note: Vodka has become a popular substitute for gin in this drink.

HAWAII COCKTAIL

1½ ounces dry gin
1 ounce pineapple juice
1 dash orange bitters
1 egg white

Shake well with ice. Serve in 4-ounce wine glass.

MARTINI COCKTAIL

⅔ dry gin
⅓ French vermouth

Stir with ice. Strain into cocktail glass. Decorate with olive. (Do not wash the brine off the olive.)

DRY MARTINI COCKTAIL

¾ dry gin
¼ French vermouth

Stir with ice. Strain into cocktail glass. Decorate with olive.

SWEET MARTINI COCKTAIL

⅔ dry gin
⅓ Italian vermouth

Stir with ice. Strain into cocktail glass. Decorate with maraschino cherry.

NAPOLEON COCKTAIL

1½ ounces dry gin
½ ounce Dubonnet
2 dashes Fernet Branca
2 dashes curaçao

Stir with ice. Add twist of lemon peel.

ORANGE BLOSSOM COCKTAIL

½ dry gin
½ orange juice

Shake with ice. Strain into cocktail glass.

PARADISE COCKTAIL

½ dry gin
¼ apricot brandy
¼ orange juice

Shake with ice. Strain into cocktail glass.

PERFECT COCKTAIL

⅓ dry gin
⅓ French vermouth
⅓ Italian vermouth

Stir with ice. Strain into cocktail glass. Add twist of lemon peel.

PARISIAN COCKTAIL

⅔ dry gin
⅓ French vermouth
3 dashes crème de cassis

Shake with ice. Strain into cocktail glass.

PINK LADY COCKTAIL

1½ ounces dry gin
½ ounce applejack
4 dashes grenadine
1 egg white

Shake well with ice. Serve in 4-ounce wine glass.

RED LION COCKTAIL

1½ ounces dry gin
¾ ounce Grand Marnier
¼ ounce lemon juice
3 dashes grenadine

Shake with ice. Strain into cocktail glass.

ROYAL SMILE COCKTAIL

⅔ dry gin
⅓ applejack
4 dashes grenadine
Juice of ½ lime

Stir with ice. Serve in cocktail glass.

SOCIETY COCKTAIL

¾ dry gin
¼ French vermouth
4 dashes grenadine

Shake with ice. Strain into cocktail glass.

GIN TODDY

1½ ounces dry gin
1 lump of sugar
Dash of Angostura bitters

Muddle sugar and bitters in an Old-Fashioned glass. Add gin, cube of ice, and a little water. Serve with stirring rod.

TURF COCKTAIL

½ dry gin
¼ French vermouth
¼ Italian vermouth
Dash of Angostura bitters
Dash of absinthe

Stir with ice. Strain into cocktail glass.

TORPEDO COCKTAIL

⅔ dry gin
⅓ French vermouth
Dash of Pernod

Stir with ice. Strain into cocktail glass.

WHITE LADY COCKTAIL

⅔ dry gin
⅓ Cointreau
Juice of ½ lemon
1 egg white

Shake well with ice. Serve in 4-ounce wine glass.

Rum Cocktails

ABOUT RUM

Rum is an alcoholic beverage distilled from fermented sugar-cane juice, fermented molasses, or mixtures of these. It may range in flavor from almost characterless to extremely full-bodied, in color from white to very dark. As a rule of thumb, the lighter the color the lighter the flavor. Actually, however, color has nothing to do with either the flavor or the alcoholic content, since it comes chiefly from added caramel. The real differences are due to variations in ingredients, in methods of fermentation and distillation, and in subsequent aging.

Rum is made in most of the islands of the West Indies and on the eastern seaboard of the United States (primarily New England and Philadelphia). Most of the light rums on the U.S. market come from Puerto Rico; the heavy ones from Jamaica, Barbados, Demerara, and Martinique. A good illustration of the range is that, whereas a tablespoonful of Jamaica rum will give a cup of strong coffee a marked rum flavor, a tablespoonful of strong coffee will give a cup of white rum a predominantly coffee flavor. It is therefore important to know which kind to use. While there are no hard-and-fast rules, the following classifications should be kept in mind.

White Label: A light-bodied, light-colored rum with a delicate flavor and aroma. It is usually 86 proof. Use it in delicate cocktails such as Bacardis and Daiquiris.

Gold Label: A darker-colored rum with a stronger flavor and aroma but about the same alcoholic content. Use it in cooking and in such drinks as Cuba Libres, Collinses, and rum Manhattans.

Heavy Rum: A very dark rum with a pungent flavor and aroma, ranging from 90 to 151 proof. Use it in cooking and in punches and swizzles.

BACARDI COCKTAIL

1½ ounces Bacardi rum
Juice of ½ lime
1 teaspoon sugar or 2 dashes grenadine

Shake well with ice. Strain into cocktail glass.

DAIQUIRI (Standard)

1½ ounces white rum
Juice of ½ lime
1 teaspoon sugar

Shake well with ice. Strain into cocktail glass.

DAIQUIRI (Frozen)

2 ounces white rum
Juice of ½ lime
1 teaspoon sugar
Dash of maraschino

Pre-chill glass of electric mixer. Put in ingredients. Then add a heaping champagne glass of shaved ice. Serve unstrained in chilled champagne glass with short straws.

JAMAICA RUM COCKTAIL

1½ ounces Jamaica rum
Juice of ½ lime
1 teaspoon sugar

Shake with ice and strain into cocktail glass.

LATIN MANHATTAN COCKTAIL

½ rum
½ Italian vermouth

Stir with ice. Serve in cocktail glass. Decorate with maraschino cherry.

PRESIDENTE COCKTAIL

1½ ounces Puerto Rican rum
¾ ounce French vermouth
1 dash grenadine
Twist of orange peel

Stir with ice. Serve in cocktail glass.

Vodka Cocktails and Other Drinks

ABOUT VODKA

Vodka is the national drink of Russia, now made in the United States, also. The best vodka is distilled from rye and barley malt; however the cheaper maize and potatoes are commonly used. In Russia it is drunk straight, with food. In the United States, however, it is usually mixed. It can be used in almost any drink calling for gin and it is often substituted for whiskey in some mixed drinks. Since vodka is colorless, nearly tasteless going down, and almost odorless afterwards it can be a deceptively strong drink when mixed. It may not be legally sold at less than 80 proof (40 per cent alcohol) and ranges up to 120 proof.

BLOODY MARY

3 ounces vodka
6 ounces tomato juice
2 dashes Angostura bitters
Juice of ½ lemon

Shake well with ice. Strain into 12-ounce glass.

MOSCOW MULE

2 ounces vodka
Juice of 1 lime
Ginger beer

Fill a Moscow Mule brass mug with shaved ice. Squeeze in lime juice. Add vodka. Fill with ginger beer. Stir and serve.

SCREWDRIVER

1½ ounces vodka
Orange juice

Pour the vodka over cracked ice in a highball glass. Add fresh orange juice to fill glass and stir briskly.

TWISTER

Pour 1 jigger of vodka into a rather small highball glass. Add ice and fill with 7-Up. Garnish with a slice of lemon.

VODKA DAIQUIRI

1 jigger vodka
1 teaspoon sugar
Juice of ½ lemon

Shake in cracked ice. Strain into a cocktail glass.

VODKA COLLINS

1 jigger vodka
1½ teaspoons powdered sugar
1 ounce lemon juice

Shake well with cracked ice. Pour into 12-ounce serving glass.
Fill with soda; garnish with a cherry and a slice of lemon.

VODKA FIZZ

2 ounces vodka
1 teaspoon powdered sugar
3 ounces pineapple juice

Shake well with cracked ice and pour into an 8-ounce glass. Fill with soda.

VODKA MARTINI

4 parts vodka
1 part dry vermouth

Pour into stirring glass filled with cracked ice. Add a couple of strips of lemon peel. Stir until frosty.
Strain into cocktail glass and serve with a garnish of lemon peel.

VODKA COOLERS

Pour 1 jigger of vodka into a rather small highball glass. Add ice and fill with the specified mixer requested: cola, ginger ale, grape juice, ginger beer, grapefruit juice. No garnish is used.

Whiskey Cocktails

ABOUT WHISKEY

All whiskey, whether rye, bourbon, Scotch, Irish, or Canadian, is a spirit distilled from a fermented grain mash. The grain may be corn, rye, oats, barley, or any other. Good whiskey is aged for a number of years before it is bottled—American whiskey in charred oak barrels, Scotch and Irish in sherry casks. Once it is bottled, the aging stops.

Bourbon, which is made from at least 51 per cent corn, is usually bottled straight; Scotch, Irish, and Canadian are usually blends of straight whiskies. American blends are usually a combination of whiskey and neutral spirits and are therefore mild in flavor. Most of the whiskeys called rye are actually this sort of blend.

Purely as a matter of custom, the U.S. and Irish products are called whiskey, with an e; the Scotch and Canadian, whisky.

ABOUT PROOF

Proof is an arbitrary measurement of alcoholic strength. In the United States, 200 is taken as pure ethyl alcohol and 100 as 50 per cent alcohol by volume. Each degree of proof, therefore, equals half of 1 per cent. A spirit of 86 proof, for example, contains 43 per cent alcohol by volume. Bonded whiskies, which are always straight (unblended), must by law be of 100 proof. The term is applied only to distilled liquors.

MANHATTAN COCKTAIL

⅔ rye
⅓ Italian vermouth
Dash of Angostura bitters

Stir with ice. Decorate with maraschino cherry.

DRY MANHATTAN COCKTAIL

⅔ rye
⅓ French vermouth
Dash of Angostura bitters

Stir with ice. Add twist of lemon peel.

ROB ROY COCKTAIL

⅔ Scotch whisky
⅓ Italian vermouth
Dash of Angostura bitters

Stir with ice. Serve in cocktail glass. Add twist of lemon peel.

WARD EIGHT

1½ ounces rye
Juice of ½ lemon
3 dashes grenadine

Shake with ice and serve in goblet with finely cracked ice.
Decorate with fruit. Serve with straws.

OLD-FASHIONED COCKTAIL

1½ ounces rye
1   lump sugar
Dash of soda
2   dashes Angostura bitters

Use an Old-Fashioned glass. Muddle sugar in a little soda until dissolved. Add two dashes Angostura bitters and a good-sized ice cube. Pour in whiskey. Stir. Decorate with fruit or twist of lemon peel. Serve with stirring rod.

ZAZERAC COCKTAIL

1½ ounces bourbon
1   dash Pernod
1   lump sugar
1   teaspoon water
2   dashes Peychaud bitters

Use two Old-Fashioned glasses. Muddle the sugar and water and bitters in one glass and add bourbon. Stir thoroughly.

Rinse other glass with 2 or 3 drops of Pernod and rub edge of glass with wet cork from anisette bottle. Add lump of ice.

Pour contents of first glass into this one and serve with twist of lemon peel.

BLARNEY COCKTAIL

1½ ounces Irish whiskey
1   ounce Italian vermouth
2   dashes green crème de menthe

Shake well with ice. Strain into cocktail glass. Serve with green cherry.

SHAMROCK COCKTAIL

1   ounce Irish whiskey
1   ounce French vermouth
3   dashes green crème de menthe
3   dashes green chartreuse

Stir with ice. Serve in cocktail glass.

BOURBON SOCIETY COCKTAIL

Serve 1 ounce bourbon in Old-Fashioned glass over tiny ice cubes. Add twist of lemon peel.

SCOTCH MIST

Fill Old-Fashioned glass ¾ full of shaved ice. Pour in 1½ ounces Scotch whisky. Add twist of lemon peel. Serve with straws.

SANTA ANITA

Shake 1½ ounces Scotch whisky with cracked ice and serve unstrained in Old-Fashioned glass. Add twist of lemon peel.

BLACKTHORN COCKTAIL

1½ ounces Irish whiskey
1   ounce French vermouth
Dash of anisette

Stir with ice. Serve in cocktail glass.

Wine and Liqueur Cocktails

ABOUT LIQUEURS AND CORDIALS

A liqueur is any combination of potable spirit with sugar syrup and flavoring. The terms liqueur and cordial are interchangeable, but cordial tends to be restricted to fruit-flavored liqueurs.

Unlike whiskey and brandy, which are made by fermentation and subsequent distillation, liqueurs are made by adding the flavoring (herbs, spices, fruits, flowers) to already distilled grain alcohol or other liquor, chiefly brandy. Some are then redistilled.

The alcoholic content of liqueurs varies a great deal. Most are sweet, but even some of these have a dry aftertaste. Certain liqueurs are fairly standard, with very similar ones produced by a number of manufacturers. Examples are fruit liqueurs such as apricot, blackberry, and peach, or non-fruit liqueurs such as menthe (white or green), triple sec or curaçao (orange), kümmel (caraway), anisette (anise), and cacao (cocoa). Others are proprietary, with distinctive flavors achieved by formulas that are closely guarded by the makers. Examples are Bénédictine, Forbidden Fruit, Drambuie, Chartreuse, Cordon Rouge, Cordial Médoc, and Grand Marnier.

Serve liqueurs at the end of the meal. Many drinkers, particularly men, express a decided aversion to the sweeter ones and prefer those that have a dry aftertaste, such as Drambuie, Bénédictine, or B and B. Non-drinkers usually like the sweet fruit liqueurs.

CHAMPAGNE COCKTAIL

Pre-chilled champagne
1   lump sugar
Dash Angostura bitters

Chill saucer champagne glass. Put in sugar. Dash sugar with bitters. Add small ice cube.

Fill with champagne and top with twist of lemon peel.

ARMOUR COCKTAIL

1½ ounces dry sherry
1   ounce Italian vermouth

Stir with ice and strain into cocktail glass. Serve with twist of lemon peel.

SCARLETT O'HARA

1½ ounces Southern Comfort
3   dashes grenadine
Juice of ½ lime

Shake with ice and strain into cocktail glass.

RHETT BUTLER

1½ ounces Southern Comfort
Juice of ¼ lemon
Juice of ¼ lime
2   dashes curaçao

Shake well with ice and strain into cocktail glass.

DUBONNET COCKTAIL

½ dry gin
½ Dubonnet

Stir with ice. Add twist of lemon peel.

CORONATION COCKTAIL

1½ ounces dry sherry
1   ounce Italian vermouth
2   dashes maraschino
2   dashes orange bitters

Stir with ice and strain into cocktail glass.

DOCTOR COCKTAIL

⅔ aquavit
⅓ Swedish punch
Juice of 1 lime

Shake with ice and strain into cocktail glass.

MERRY WIDOW COCKTAIL

½ French vermouth
½ Dubonnet

Stir with ice. Add twist of lemon peel.

SUISSESS COCKTAIL

1½ ounces absinthe
½ ounce anisette
White of egg

Shake well with ice and strain into Delmonico glass.

ANISETTE COCKTAIL

1   ounce anisette
½ teaspoon Benedictine
2   drops Angostura bitters

Shake with fine ice. Strain into frosted cocktail glass; drip water through ice to fill glass.

VERMOUTH COCKTAIL

1½ ounces Italian vermouth
1   dash Angostura bitters

Stir with cracked ice. Strain into chilled cocktail glass. Serve with pickled onion.

VERMOUTH COCKTAIL #2

1½ ounces French vermouth
1   dash Pernod

Shake with cracked ice. Strain into chilled cocktail glass.

Long Drinks, Coolers, and Juleps

BAHAMAS HIGHBALL

1½ ounces dry gin
1 ounce French vermouth
1 slice lemon
Quinine water

Serve with ice in 10-ounce highball glass. Stir.

BLACK VELVET

½ Guinness stout
½ champagne

Pre-chill wine and stout and pour into tall glass.

CLARET PUNCH

3 ounces claret
2 dashes curaçao
Juice of ½ lemon
1 teaspoon powdered sugar

Fill goblet with fine ice. Add all ingredients. Stir. Garnish with fruit.

JOHN COLLINS

2 ounces Holland gin
Juice of medium-sized lemon
1 teaspoon sugar

Shake well. Strain into Collins glass in which ice cubes have been placed. Add soda to fill.

ORANGE BLOSSOM COLLINS

2 ounces dry gin
Juice of small orange
1 teaspoon sugar

Shake well. Strain into Collins glass in which ice cubes have been placed. Add soda to fill.

RUM COLLINS

1½ ounces rum
Juice of small lemon
1 teaspoon sugar

Shake well and strain into Collins glass with 2 ice cubes. Fill glass with soda.

SALTY DOG COLLINS

1½ ounces dry gin
Pinch of salt
Juice of 1 lime

Shake well. Strain into Collins glass in which ice cubes have been placed. Add soda to fill.

RAMOS FIZZ

2 ounces Old Tom gin
Juice of ½ lemon
Juice of ½ lime
2 dashes orange flower water
1 ounce heavy cream
1 egg white
1 teaspoon sugar

Shake vigorously with ice. Strain into 10-ounce highball glass. Add soda to fill.

TOM COLLINS

2 ounces dry gin
Juice of medium-sized lemon
1 teaspoon sugar

Shake well. Strain into Collins glass in which ice cubes have been placed. Add soda to fill.

WHISKEY COLLINS

2 ounces rye
Juice of medium-sized lemon
1 teaspoon sugar

Shake well. Strain into Collins glass in which ice cubes have been placed. Add soda to fill.

COBBLERS

Cobblers are tall drinks made with finely cracked ice, fruit, and liquor. The berries and fresh fruits used for garnish make them particularly attractive.

Fill goblet with finely shaved ice. Add 1 teaspoon sugar. Add 3 ounces of burgundy, claret, sauterne, sherry, port, or Rhine wine, brandy, or whisky.

Stir well and garnish with slices of orange or slivers of pineapple, and a sprig of mint.

RUM COBBLER

1½ ounces rum
½ ounce curaçao
Juice of ½ lemon

Stir and strain into goblet of fine ice. Decorate with fruit and sprig of mint.

GIN FIZZ

1½ ounces dry gin
Juice of small lemon
1 teaspoon sugar

Shake with ice. Strain into 10-ounce highball glass. Add soda.

Golden Fizz: Add 1 egg yolk to Gin Fizz.

Royal Fizz: Add 1 whole egg to Gin Fizz.

Silver Fizz: Add 1 egg white to Gin Fizz.

Southside Fizz: Garnish Gin Fizz with mint leaves.

SLOE GIN FIZZ

1½ ounces sloe gin
Juice of ½ lemon
1 teaspoon sugar

Shake well with ice. Strain into highball glass and add soda.

STRAWBERRY FIZZ

1½ ounces dry gin
Dash of sweet cream
1 teaspoon sugar
4 ripe strawberries
Juice of ½ lemon

Shake well with ice. Strain into 10-ounce highball glass. Add soda to fill.

MINT JULEP

2 ounces bourbon
1 teaspoon powdered sugar
4 sprigs mint

Strip leaves from stem and drop into a 12-ounce glass or metal mug. Add sugar and dash of water.

Mash these ingredients with a muddler until sugar is dissolved.

Add whiskey and fill with shaved ice.

Stir until outside of glass or mug is frosted.

Decorate with a bouquet of mint. Sprinkle with powdered sugar.

PLANTER'S PUNCH

2 ounces Jamaica rum
Juice of 1 lime
1 teaspoon fine grain sugar

Shake well and strain into tall glass filled with shaved ice. Decorate with thin slice of lime and long stick of fresh pineapple.

HIGHBALLS

All highballs should be served in 8- or 10-ounce highball glasses. To prepare any highball, place an ice cube in the glass, add 1½ ounces of the liquor desired, and fill up the glass with carbonated water or ginger ale.

Serve with a small bar spoon in glass and a twist of lemon peel, if desired.

The following liquors may be used in preparing highballs: Applejack, bitters, bourbon, Cognac, gin, rye, rum, Scotch whisky, and cordials.

REMSEN COOLER

2 ounces dry gin
Lemon rind

Insert spiral of lemon rind in tall glass. Add ice cubes, gin, and soda to fill. Stir and serve.

WINE COOLER

Pour half a glass (or more) of your favorite wine over ice cubes in a tall glass. Appetizer wine, red or white table wine or dessert wine may be used.

Add sparkling water to fill, stir slightly and serve. Most people like the fruit-flavored soda best for this, such as the lemon-lime mixes.

Wine Coolers

ALABAMA FIZZ

1½ ounces dry gin
1 teaspoon brown sugar
Juice of ½ lemon

Stir with ice. Add soda. Garnish with mint sprigs. Serve in 10-ounce highball glass.

CUBA LIBRE

1½ ounces rum
Coca-Cola
Juice and rind of ½ lime

Squeeze lime juice into 12-ounce glass. Drop in rind. Add ice cubes and Coca-Cola and stir.

GIN AND TONIC

1½ ounces gin
Slice of lemon
Quinine water

Serve in tall glass containing ice cubes.

GIN BUCK

1½ ounces dry gin
Juice of ½ lemon
Ginger ale

Serve in highball glass with ice cubes. Fill with ginger ale. Stir.

GIN RICKEY

1½ ounces dry gin
Juice of ½ lime

Squeeze juice of lime into highball glass. Drop in rind and cube of ice. Add gin. Top with soda. Stir.

GIN SLING

1½ ounces dry gin
1 teaspoon sugar

Place ice cubes in 10-ounce highball glass. Add twist of lemon peel. Add soda. Stir.

RUM SLING

1½ ounces Jamaica rum
2 dashes Angostura bitters

Serve in highball glass with cracked ice. Fill with soda. Add twist of lemon peel. Stir.

SINGAPORE GIN SLING

2 ounces dry gin
⅔ ounce cherry brandy
Juice of 1 lemon
Dash of Benedictine

Shake. Strain into tall glass containing ice cubes. Garnish with slice of orange and sprig of mint. Add soda. Top with dash of Benedictine.

VERMOUTH CASSIS

3 ounces French vermouth
1 ounce crème de cassis

Pour into tall glass with ice cubes. Fill with soda. Stir. Add twist of lemon peel.

NEW ORLEANS FIZZ

2 ounces dry gin
Juice of ½ lemon
1 ounce heavy cream
2 dashes of orange flower water
1 egg white
1 teaspoon sugar

Shake vigorously with ice. Strain into 10-ounce highball glass. Add soda to fill.

ZOMBIE

1 ounce amber rum
1 ounce silver rum
1 ounce Jamaica rum
½ ounce cherry brandy
½ ounce apricot brandy
Juice of half lime
1 dash papaya juice
½ ounce 150-proof Jamaica rum

Fill a 14-ounce Zombie glass half full of finely cracked ice. Put in ingredients and stir. Top with the 150-proof Jamaica rum. Decorate with a sprig of mint. Serve with straws.

SPRITZER

3 ounces Rhine wine, chablis, or dry
 sauterne
Soda

Put one cube of ice in highball glass. Add wine. Fill with soda and stir.

RUM PUNCH

1½ ounces rum
Juice of ½ lemon
Orange juice equal to amount of lemon juice
Pineapple juice equal to amount of lemon juice
1 teaspoon fine grain sugar
Dash of brandy

Shake well and strain into goblet half full of shaved ice. Top with dash of brandy. Decorate with fruit.

MAMIE TAYLOR

2 ounces Scotch whisky
Slice of lemon
Split of ginger ale

Serve with two cubes of ice in a tall glass.

BRANDY COBBLER

½ teaspoon sugar
1 teaspoon curaçao
2 ounces brandy

Add to goblet ¾ filled with cracked ice; stir and decorate with fruit. Serve with straws and a spoon.

GIN FIX

¾ ounce dry gin
¾ ounce cherry brandy
1 teaspoon sugar
Juice of 1 lemon

Dissolve sugar in a little water. Add lemon juice, gin, and brandy. Fill highball glass with fine ice. Stir slowly.

Eggnogs and Milk Punches

BRANDY EGGNOG

1 egg
1 tablespoon sugar
2 ounces brandy
¾ glass milk

Shake well with cracked ice. Strain. Serve with nutmeg on top.

Variations: Substitute port, rum, sherry, or whiskey for brandy.

MILK PUNCH

1½ ounces rye whiskey
½ pint milk
1 teaspoon sugar

Shake, strain, and serve in 12-ounce glass. Sprinkle a little nutmeg on top.

BALTIMORE EGGNOG

1 ounce brandy
1½ ounces Madeira wine
2 teaspoons sugar syrup
½ ounce rum
1 whole egg
4 ounces fresh milk

Shake vigorously with cracked ice. Strain into 12-ounce glass, adding cold milk to fill glass. Stir gently and sprinkle with nutmeg.

HOLIDAY EGGNOG

6 eggs, separated
¾ cup sugar
2 cups milk, chilled
1 to 1½ cups Cognac or brandy
¼ cup rum
2 cups heavy cream, chilled
Nutmeg

Beat egg whites until almost stiff enough to hold a peak. Add sugar gradually, beating until stiff but not dry.

Beat egg yolks until thick; stir in milk, Cognac, and rum, blending well.

Whip cream until stiff and fold into egg-milk mixture. Fold in beaten egg whites.

Keep cold until ready to serve. Pour into punch bowl. Sprinkle each serving with nutmeg, if desired. Makes about 3 quarts.

Holiday Eggnog

After Dinner Drinks

ABSINTHE FRAPPÉ

1½ ounces absinthe*
¾ ounce water
1 teaspoon sugar

Shake well with ice and strain into Delmonico glass.

*Note: Genuine absinthe contains a toxic drug (Artemisia or wormwood) hence its manufacture and sale are now illegal in many countries and its importation into the United States is prohibited. Absinthe substitutes include Pernod, Oxygénée, Herbsaint, and others. These do not include the harmful wormwood content, are sweeter and less strong, though very similar in taste. To serve plain, add about ⅔ plain water just before serving.

BRANDY AND BENEDICTINE (B AND B)

½ ounce Benedictine
½ ounce brandy

Pour Benedictine into a cordial glass, then float brandy on top, so that the liqueurs are separate.

CAFÉ AU KIRSCH

1½ ounces kirsch
1½ ounces black coffee
1 teaspoon sugar
White of egg

Shake with ice and strain into wine glass.

CRÈME DE MENTHE FRAPPE

Fill frappé glass with shaved ice. Pour in crème de menthe until glass is almost full. Serve with short straws. (This is sometimes served with brandy on top; it may then be called—incorrectly—a Brandy Float.)

GRASSHOPPER

⅓ white crème de cacao
⅓ green crème de menthe
⅓ heavy cream

Shake vigorously with ice and serve in a 4-ounce wine glass.

POUSSE CAFE

⅙ ounce grenadine (red)
⅙ ounce crème de cacao (brown)
⅙ ounce maraschino (white)
⅙ ounce green crème de menthe (green)
⅙ ounce crème Yvette (violet)
⅙ ounce brandy (amber)

Pour, in the order named, very carefully and slowly into a cordial glass. This may be best accomplished by pouring the different liqueurs from a thin sherry glass.

FRAPPÉS

Pack a frappé glass with shaved ice and fill with preferred cordial or liqueur. Serve with cut straws.

Hot Drinks

BLUE BLAZER

1 wine glass Scotch whisky
1 wine glass boiling water
1 teaspoon powdered sugar

Use two silver-plated mugs with long handles. Put the whisky into one mug and the boiling water in the other.

Set the whisky afire, and while it blazes mix the ingredients by pouring them four or five times from one mug to the other. If this is properly done it will have the appearance of a continued stream of liquid fire.

Pour into an 8-ounce highball glass in which a silver teaspoon has been placed. Add powdered sugar. Stir. Serve with twist of lemon peel.

HOT BUTTERED RUM

1½ ounces Jamaica rum
4 cloves
1 lump sugar or 1 tablespoon honey
1 small pat butter

Scald an Old-Fashioned glass or mug. Put in rum, cloves, and sugar or honey. Fill glass with boiling water. Top with butter. Stir. Serve with a small silver spoon.

HOT RUM TODDY

1½ ounces Jamaica rum
Slice of lemon
1 teaspoon sugar
3 cloves
Stick of cinnamon

Scald an Old-Fashioned glass. Put ingredients in and fill with boiling water. Sprinkle powdered cinnamon on top. Stir. Serve with a small silver spoon.

HOT WHISKEY TODDY

1½ ounces rye
Juice of ½ lemon
1 teaspoon sugar

Scald an Old-Fashioned glass. When glass has been thoroughly heated, pour water out.

Muddle sugar and lemon juice until sugar is dissolved. Add whiskey and fill with boiling water. Stir. Serve with a small silver spoon.

TOM AND JERRY (Single Serving)

1½ ounces Jamaica rum
1 teaspoon sugar
1 egg
Dash of brandy
Pinch of allspice

Separate yolk and white of egg and beat yolk.

Beat egg white until fairly stiff, then add sugar, and beat to a stiff froth.

Combine yolk and white and add allspice. Put the mixture into a scalded Tom and Jerry mug. Add rum, then fill with boiling water. Stir well. Top with the brandy.

SWEDISH GLOGG

¾ cup granulated sugar
2 ounces Angostura bitters
1 pint claret
1 pint sherry
½ pint brandy

Combine ingredients and heat in saucepan until piping hot, but do not boil.

Preheat Old-Fashioned glass with boiling water and place in bottom of it 1 large raisin and 1 unsalted almond.

Place spoon in glass to prevent breaking and fill ⅔ full with hot wine mixture.

MULLED WINE (Gluehwein)

½ cup water
1 lemon, sliced
1 stick cinnamon
1 tablespoon cloves
⅓ cup sugar
1 bottle claret
2 cups pineapple juice
1 cup orange juice

Boil water with lemon slices, cinnamon, cloves, and sugar for 5 minutes.

Strain and mix with wine and fruit juices. Serve hot. Serves 8.

JERSEY LIGHTHOUSE

2 lumps sugar
2 dashes Angostura bitters
4 whole cloves
1 spiral lemon peel
3 ounces applejack

Mix in preheated mug. Fill with boiling water. Add float of applejack; set afire and serve blazing.

TOM AND JERRY (To Serve 6)

6 eggs, separated
½ cup sugar
1 cup rum
1 cup brandy
½ teaspoon cinnamon
½ teaspoon nutmeg
3 cups boiling water

Beat egg whites until stiff. Beat yolks until thick with the sugar.

Blend whites and yolks together lightly and add rum and brandy.

Add spices and gradually add the boiling water, stirring the mixture until well mixed. Serve in earthenware mugs with a dash of nutmeg.

Miscellaneous Cocktails and Other Drinks

GROG

Grog originally referred to rum diluted with water, and was named for Old Grog, nickname of Admiral Vernon (1684-1757), a British naval officer who introduced the drink about 1745. He was so called because he wore a *grogram* cloak. The following is a popular version of the drink.

1 teaspoon bar syrup
1 tablespoon strained lemon juice
1 jigger dark rum

Stir together in an 8-ounce mug and fill with very hot water or tea. Garnish with twist of lemon peel.
Variation: Substitute molasses for bar syrup. Sprinkle with ground nutmeg or cinnamon.

HORSE'S NECK

Rind of lemon peeled in a spiral
Ginger ale

Arrange spiral of lemon rind so that one end curls over edge of glass. Add ice cubes. Fill with ginger ale.

With a Spike: Add 1½ ounces rye whiskey. Serve with stirring rod.

PRAIRIE OYSTER

Yolk of egg
1 dash Lea & Perrin's sauce
Red pepper and salt to taste
1½ ounces brandy or Madeira wine

Mix well and serve in Old-Fashioned glass. Add dash of vinegar on top.

WHISKEY SOUR

1½ ounces rye or Scotch
Juice of ½ lemon
1 teaspoon sugar

Shake with ice and strain into a Delmonico glass.
Decorate with half slice of orange and maraschino cherry.

GIN SMASH

1 lump sugar
Mint leaves
1½ ounces dry gin

Muddle sugar and mint leaves that have been dashed with soda in an Old-Fashioned glass. Add gin and 1 ice cube. Stir. Top with soda. **Decorate** with small sprig of mint.

PORT OR SHERRY FLIP

2 ounces port or sherry
1 teaspoon sugar
1 whole egg

Shake well with ice in mixing glass. Strain into wine glass; then pour back and forth until smooth. Sprinkle with nutmeg.

BRANDY FLOAT

Place Old-Fashioned glass upside down tightly over pony filled with brandy. Holding pony in place, reverse Old-Fashioned glass and pour half full of soda. Lift pony along edge of larger glass to leave brandy floating on top of soda.

DAISIES

1½ ounces dry gin
3 dashes grenadine
Juice of ½ lemon

Stir into a goblet half filled with finely shaved ice. Add a squirt of plain soda water. Garnish with fruit and a sprig of mint.

Variations: Brandy, applejack, rum, or whiskey may be used instead of gin.

MAJOR BAILEY

Mint leaves
Juice of ½ lemon
1 teaspoon sugar
2 ounces dry gin

Bruise mint leaves in the lemon juice and sugar with muddler. Fill tall glass with shaved ice. Add gin.
Stir until all ingredients are thoroughly combined and outside of glass is frosted. Do not touch glass with hands in performing this rite.
Decorate with sprigs of mint. Serve with straws.

RUM SCOUNDREL

1½ ounces rum
Juice of half lime
1 teaspoon sugar
Dash of Angostura bitters

Serve in Old-Fashioned glass with ice, slices of lemon and orange. Rub the rim of the glass with a cut lemon and dip it in sugar to coat it.

RUM CRUSTAS

1½ ounces rum
½ ounce maraschino
Juice of 1 lime
2 dashes of Angostura bitters
½ teaspoon sugar
Round of orange peel

Frost the rim of a Tom Collins glass and fill with cracked ice. Cut a large circle of orange peel from circumference of large orange; fit in glass so that it is even with edge. Shake ingredients and strain into glass. Add soda.

WINE LEMONADE

Prepare lemonade in the usual manner with ice. For each glass, add 2 to 4 ounces any red or white table wine. Sweeten to taste.

FRENCH SEVENTY-FIVE

2 ounces dry gin
1 teaspoon sugar
Juice of ½ lemon
Champagne

Shake well with ice. Strain into tall glass in which ice cubes have been placed. Top with champagne.

ABOUT BEER AND ALE

Beer is an alcoholic beverage—one of the oldest—made by brewing and fermenting cereals, particularly malted barley, to which hops are usually added as a flavoring agent and stabilizer. Modern beers usually contain from 3 to 6 per cent alcohol. Although the beers of the United States, Britain, and continental Europe differ notably in flavor and content, the brewing processes are similar.

In the United States, brewing has followed the German rather than the British tradition; hence the typical beer of the U.S. breweries is lager. This is characterized by bottom fermentation—that is, the yeast sinks to the bottom after its work is over instead of floating to the top—and by the fact that it is stored at a low temperature for several weeks or months before it is marketed. (The name comes from the German word for storage place.)

Ale used to be a kind of beer made without hops. Nowadays, the term is applied in England to any light-colored beer except lager. In the United States, ale is a pale, strongly hopped beverage generally brewed by top fermentation.

Bock Beer, first made in Einbeck, Prussia, is a heavy, dark beer commonly brewed in the winter and consumed in the spring.

Porter is a strong, dark, top-fermented beer with roasted malt added for flavor and color.

Canadian Ale is heavier in body and higher in alcoholic content than U.S. ales.

Stout, darker and maltier than porter, has a more pronounced hop aroma and may attain an alcoholic content of 6 to 7 per cent.

East India Ale is a term used in Canada and Britain to describe a type of soft, full-bodied ale formerly shipped to the East.

Export is another term for a full-bodied brew that, because of its higher alcoholic content, was supposed to be better able to withstand a sea voyage.

Continental beers are generally named after the towns in which they are brewed, each town producing its special type. In this, the beer-producing localities may be compared to the vineyard districts of France, which produce their characteristic local wines.

Punch Bowl and Cup Mixes

Punch bowl and cup mixes are very similar. The former are usually mixed in a bowl to be served buffet style, while the latter are served in garnished pitchers at the table.

CLARET CUP

½ ounce maraschino liqueur
1 ounce orange curaçao
3 tablespoons fine grain sugar
1 quart claret

Mix liquor with sugar in large pitcher. Add cracked ice and stir thoroughly. Stir in chilled claret and garnish with fruits and berries. Serve in wine glasses.

RHINE WINE CUP

1 ounce maraschino liqueur
½ ounce curaçao
½ ounce simple syrup
1 quart Rhine wine

Mix liqueurs and syrup in large pitcher. Add cracked ice and pour in Rhine wine. Stir and serve in wine glasses.

FISHERMAN'S PUNCH

1 quart rye whiskey
1 pint sweet vermouth
1 pint sherry
½ pint Jamaica rum
½ cup lemon juice
4 teaspoons orange bitters
4 teaspoons grenadine
1 pint sparkling water

Mix all ingredients except sparkling water and place in refrigerator for at least 2 hours, preferably overnight, to ripen.

Add sparkling water and ice just before serving. Makes about 30 servings.

WINE PUNCH

1 bottle port or claret wine
2 cups lemon juice
1 cup grenadine, grape juice, or pineapple juice
2 cups orange juice
1 bottle carbonated water
1 pint ginger ale
Sugar syrup (1 cup or more)

Combine ingredients, adding enough sugar syrup to sweeten, and pour into punch bowl in which a block of ice has been placed. Garnish with sliced oranges. Serves 30.

CHAMPAGNE PUNCH

2 bottles champagne
2 bottles sparkling water
½ bottle or 8 jiggers each curaçao, brandy, maraschino
4 jiggers grenadine or sugar to taste
2 bottles sauterne
Fruit to garnish, if desired

Chill champagne and sparkling water thoroughly. Place large block of ice in punch bowl. Slice fruit over it, if used.

Add liqueurs and sauterne. Pour in champagne slowly and add sparkling water last. Stir gently, not vigorously. Serves 75.

WEDDING BELL LEMONADE PUNCH

4 6-ounce cans frozen concentrate for lemonade
4 cansful water (fill each lemonade can once)
4 6-ounce cans frozen pineapple juice
4 cansful water (fill each pineapple juice can once)
2 quarts ginger ale
1 quart sparkling water
1 quart dry champagne
Ice cubes (or block of ice)

Combine the juices and water to keep chilled.

When ready to use, add ginger ale and sparkling water and pour over ice cubes (or block of ice) in a large punch bowl.

Then pour the well chilled champagne as evenly as possible over the punch and stir it gently through the punch. Makes approximately 50 4-ounce servings.

WASSAIL

The term wassail was formerly used in England as a salutation given in drinking the health of a person on festive occasions. By association it came to mean any liquor in which healths are drunk, especially old English punches of spiced beer, ale, or wine. Such punches are served hot from a big bowl (Wassail Bowl) at holiday time. The Wine Wassail given below is a modern version of such a punch.

WINE WASSAIL

1 quart apple juice
1 quart orange juice
⅔ cup sugar
⅔ cup slivered blanched almonds
⅔ cup raisins
2 sticks cinnamon
24 whole cloves
2 quarts Burgundy

Combine apple juice with next 4 ingredients. Tie cinnamon sticks and cloves in a cheesecloth bag. Add to apple juice mixture. Boil 5 minutes.

Remove bag. Add Burgundy. Heat very slowly. Do not boil. Strain if desired. Serve hot. For garnish, float notched orange slices in punch bowl. Makes 4 quarts.

MAY WINE

2 quarts sauterne, Rhine, or chablis wine
¼ cup sugar
1 cup orange juice
1 cup strawberries, sliced
2 oranges, sliced

Chill wine. Dissolve sugar in orange juice in chilled punch bowl. Add wine, sliced strawberries, and orange slices.

Float a few flowers (violet blossoms are good) on surface of punch just before serving. Serves 12 to 15.

FROSTY NEW YEAR'S PUNCH

2 quarts orange ice or sherbet
3 (⅘ quart) bottles sauterne or other white wine, chilled
2 6-ounce cans frozen orange juice
Sugar to taste
1 large bottle California champagne, well chilled

Place sherbet in punch bowl. Pour in sauterne and frozen juice, diluted with water according to directions on can. Stir until no lumps of sherbet remain.

Add sugar, if desired, and stir until dissolved. Add champagne. Makes about 75 (⅓ cup) servings.

ANNIVERSARY PUNCH

1 12-ounce package frozen strawberries
2 teaspoons grated lime rind
Juice of 1 lime
1 bottle (⅘) sparkling burgundy
1 bottle (⅘) dry champagne
1 bottle (⅘) sauterne
Block of ice for punch bowl

Combine strawberries, lime rind, and lime juice in saucepan. Simmer together 10 minutes; put through food mill or sieve. Cool.

Pour fruit mixture over ice in punch bowl. Add wines just before serving.

Garnish with whole strawberries and lime slices, if desired. Makes about 25 servings.

Variation: Instead of the frozen berries, use 2 cups fresh, sliced strawberries, 1 tablespoon water, and ¼ cup sugar.

Anniversary Punch

Wines and Wine Service

Wine may be simply defined as the fermented juice of sound, ripe grapes which have been crushed after harvesting. If we crush a handful of grapes and leave it in a cup, it will turn into wine. The alcohol in wine is simply Nature's way of preserving the juice of the grape.

Wine production, however, cannot be so simply presented inasmuch as there are actually hundreds of varieties of wines. Many of them may be made according to special formulas and processes which will give them the qualities particular wineries are attempting to achieve.

The quality of really fine wines is contingent upon a number of factors, each of which can very greatly influence the finished product. When one of these factors changes, the wine will also change.

The extremely wide variations among wines arise primarily from the differences in the soil and climate in which the grapes were grown. As a matter of fact, the influence of these two factors is so great that if a vine is transplanted a very short distance from its original site a very different wine may be obtained from the grapes grown on the transplanted vine. For example, there are areas in France where certain exceptional wines come from grapes grown on the hillsides of one side of a valley and a quite entirely different wine of ordinary quality will result from similar vines growing on hillsides on the opposite side of that same valley. Then again, a variety of grapes grown in a volcanic soil will produce a different wine than the same variety of grapes grown in a gravel or clay soil.

A good wine is one which is satisfactory in taste, odor, and in appearance. It must be made naturally, without the aid of chemicals, or excess sugar, and there must be no secondary fermentation of the alcohol into vinegar.

WINE NAMES

There are hundreds of different names for wines. This need not be confusing as long as we remember that virtually all wines fit into one of these five groups:

(1) appetizer wines, (2) white table wines, (3) red table wines, (4) sweet dessert wines, and (5) sparkling wines.

THE TWELVE PRINCIPAL WINE TYPES

In the above-named five groups and among the hundreds of wine names, there are 12 distinct internationally known wine types or wine "families." If you can recognize by sight, taste, and smell these 12 well-known wine types,

you may consider yourself as well informed about wines as the average wine merchant.

These 12 distinct wine types are:

Sherry and Vermouth (appetizer wines).

Claret and Burgundy (red table wines).

Sauterne and Rhine Wine (white table wine).

Port, Muscatel, Tokay, and White Port (dessert wines).

Champagne and Sparkling Burgundy (sparkling wines).

Practically all other wines fall into these "families" but, because of various minor differences in the grapes used, in the blending methods, or even in trade names applied by vintners, they may be known by other names to indicate varying shades of color, flavor, and richness.

Don't expect to be able to recognize all the minor differences of the wines bearing other names than these 12. Not even a professional wine taster knows them all.

For those who want to delve more deeply into wine lore, the information that follows will be helpful.

RED AND WHITE WINES

All wines are classified as either red or white wines, although the variation in hues from true red to true white is endless. If a wine, however, has any tinge of red in it, that wine is a red wine and if a wine has no trace of red in it, that wine is a white wine. Hence, white wines vary in shade from a very pale straw color to an almost deep dark brown.

"DRY" AND SWEET WINES

Wines may also be classified by taste or by alcoholic content. The term "dry" is applied to wines having a low sugar content (usually less than 1%). The term therefore means the the opposite of sweet—and at no time does it mean sour. Sour wines taste of vinegar and are spoiled through secondary fermentation.

Most red wines are dry. The exceptions are port and port-style wines.

White wines vary in sweetness from the very dry manzanilla sherry to the extremely sweet tokay.

The dry wines are generally used for table wines i.e., drunk with meals. Dry wines are usually produced in sections where the summers are relatively short, and the grapes when they are ripe are not too sweet.

Sweet wines are made from extremely sweet, sometimes overripe, grapes. Their sugar content may go as high as 10%.

NATURAL AND FORTIFIED WINES

Wines may be additionally classified as either "natural" or "fortified," depending upon their alcoholic content. A natural wine contains 12% to 14% alcohol, which is the maximum normally obtainable through natural fermentation.

The alcoholic content of fortified wines ranges from 17% to 21%. This high alcoholic content is obtainable by the addition of brandy to the wine at some stage in the fermentation. If the brandy is added early in the fermentation process, the fortified wine will be sweet since little of the natural grape sugar will have been transformed into alcohol. If the brandy is added at the end, the wine may be quite dry.

In any case, after the addition of the brandy the high alcoholic concentration prevents the further natural fermentation which in time causes wine to spoil when exposed to air.

The two fortified wines of outstanding importance are sherry, originally imported from Spain, and port, originally from Portugal. Other fortified wines that are popular are madeira, muscatel, malaga, and tokay.

As a general rule, most fortified wines are too heavy and too sweet for consumption during meals, are known as dessert wines and are usually served at the end of the meal as are other desserts. The most usual exceptions are some sherries which are served slightly chilled before the meal.

The popular dry wines (red and white burgundy, red bordeaux, moselle, and rhine) are all natural wines and are used as table wines.

Some semi-sweet wines such as the sauternes are also used, especially in this country, for the same purpose.

OTHER PLANT AND FRUIT WINES

The term "wine" is also applied to alcoholic beverages made from plants and fruit other than grape. Examples of these are blackberry, elderberry, and dandelion wine.

VERMOUTHS AND OTHER APPETIZER WINES

Appetizer wines are so-called because they are favored for cocktail use and before-meal drinking. They include dry sherry, vermouth, Dubonnet, Byrrh (red), St. Raphael (white), and other brand name appetizer wines served chilled.

In this country the use of appetizer or "apéritif" wines as such is rather limited. Cocktails have displaced them almost entirely. A great deal of vermouth is used in various cocktails, and other apéritif wines are becoming increasingly popular in a large variety of cocktails.

Apéritif wines (with the exception of

sherry) are not true wines but have been modified by the addition of herbs, roots, seed, flowers, or other flavoring materials which were steeped in the wine for periods ranging from a few weeks to several years. Many of them are made from sweet wines but the various flavoring ingredients used in blending them give them a dry after-taste.

There are two types of vermouth—French and Italian. The French type is made of a relatively dry white wine and it is used in cocktail recipes in this book which call for "dry" vermouth. The alcoholic content is 19%. Italian-type vermouth has as its base a much sweeter wine as well as a different assortment of flavoring constituents. The alcoholic content is 17%. Recipes in this book calling for "sweet" vermouth refer to the Italian type.

In France and Italy both vermouths are drunk "straight." In this country their use is confined for the most part to the preparation of cocktails, although an increasing number of Americans are gradually learning to drink the vermouths in the "continental" manner.

American Wines
Types of Grapes Used in U. S. A.

In general, there are two distinct types of grapes grown in the United States.

One type is a broad group of grapes grown on all types of vines of European origin. With certain qualifications given below, it may then be said that almost every type of wine is made right here in the United States.

The second broad group of grapes are grown on vines of native American origin. As a matter of fact, early settlers found the land dotted with grape vines. Examples of these native American grapes are the Delaware, Concord, Elvira, Scuppernong, and the Catawba.

The better American producers make a variety of wines from native American grapes that should be considered on their own merits. The best of them have a distinctly wild, tangy, pleasant flavor.

Grapes are grown in 44 of the nation's 50 states and wine is produced commercially in 27 states; California, New York, and Ohio are the leaders. California, with its variations in weather from north to south and its many valleys suitable for varied types of grape vines, is the largest producer with the largest variety. From 85% to 90% of the domestic wines consumed are from this state. Most of the California grapes are grown on vines of European stock which, through transplanting, have acquired distinct charac-

teristics. While these vines came from famous wine-producing regions of Europe, nevertheless it must be remembered that very often the similarity between these vines and their European prototypes ends with the names.

As we explained in the beginning of our discussion of wines, the characteristics of a wine are as much dependent upon the soil and climate in which the grapes are grown, the treatment it is given, and the methods used in the making of the wine as upon the variety of the grapes used.

Any of these variable factors when changed result also in a change in the wine that is produced. European grape vines when transplanted to other soils and climates soon develop quite different characteristics. Many of the American wines bear the names of European wines; others bear the names of grape types.

Many American Wines Are Distinctive Types

Some of the more forward-looking and important producers have, in recent years, been coining their own descriptive names for their wines and a number of these have become well established as distinctive wines in their own rights. That is true both of wines made from grapes of native American origin and of wines made of grapes grown on vines of transplanted stock. Their distinctive qualities should be considered on their own merits.

It must be remembered that many years of intensive research by state and business-financed organizations have been devoted to the methods of American grape growing and wine making. The superior and, in many instances, really "fine" wines which have been developed in recent years in several of the wine-producing states attest to the excellent results attained from this intensive research and experimentation in the growing, production, and aging methods.

We have now reached the point where some wine lovers will argue about the differences in quality between good wines of a similar nature produced in different states as those same wine lovers once argued about the gradations of difference between two very similar French, Spanish, or German wines.

There should be no hesitation, therefore, in serving a good honest American wine in preference to an imported one of doubtful quality.

California Wines

Both sweet and dry wines are produced not only in California but also in the other principal wine-producing states.

From the southern part of California come natural sweet wines because the climate there is dry and hot enough to produce grapes with the sugar content that is required for dessert wines.

The grapes for drier wines come from the northern sections which are colder and damper.

Judging by the progress that has been made, there is no doubt that, in time, names such as Sacramento Valley, San Joaquin, Fresno, and Southern California when appearing on labels of sweet wines, and names such as Santa Clara, Napa, and Sonoma on dry wines, will mean in their own distinctive ways as much as the names Bordeaux, Burgundy, Médoc, Graves, etc. mean on French wine labels.

When purchasing California wines, keep in mind the fact that the larger producers, while maintaining only one production plant either in the northern or the southern part of the state, may be producing both sweet and dry wines by "importing" from the other section the necessary grapes. Some producers, of course, maintain plants in both sections of the state.

Somewhat the same methods are employed by major producers in other states. Some eastern and middle-western producers "round out" their varieties of wines through contractual arrangements with California vineyards who will produce quantities of wines for them in accordance with specified standards.

American Sparkling Wines

The most popular American sparkling wines are made in the East—particularly from grapes grown in the famous Finger Lakes district of New York. Many experts agree that they have a nice dry quality that compares favorably to the famous French wines—and certainly makes them a better buy than many doubtful French importations. In fact, they are preferred by many people over the sweet champagnes because the sweetening used in some instances may disguise a poor wine.

How to Compare Domestic and Imported Wines

We believe firmly that it will be interesting experience for wine lovers to explore the many varieties of American wines—particularly if they enter into that exploration with the thought in mind that many of them are new wine types that should be judged on their own merits. At the same time, a number of other factors should be remembered that are all too frequently overlooked by self-styled experts.

While the bulk of American wines (like the bulk of the wines of any wine-producing land) is ordinary wine, nevertheless a lot of really "fine" wines are produced here.

For example, France normally produces over a billion gallons of wine. Only a very small percentage of these wines are in the "fine" wine classifications which are described under French wines, and which are generally thought of when French wines are being discussed.

France consumes so much *"vin ordinaire"* that they even import large quantities of wines from areas in North Africa.

Really "fine" wines are in a class by themselves, and here in America we have our own distinctive "breeds" as do other wine-producing countries.

Why "Vintage Years" Are Not Important

Another factor against the American product was the belief that only wines of certain years were good because such a belief held true in Europe. That is one great fallacy insofar as American wines are concerned which has been exploded.

There is no such question of vintage years, that is, "good" and "bad" years, because of the immense size of our country. Our climate and soil conditions are so varied that if climate conditions for a particular year in one producing area are relatively bad, at the same time conditions in another producing area may be ideal.

That's why American wine producers can, for the most part, ignore the question of "good" and "bad" years which has become so all-important in European wine-producing areas.

In contrast, in one of the small area countries of Europe if a bad climate results in a poor wine-producing year that is almost invariably general throughout the wine-producing area.

It's obvious then why experts, who have been able to attain enough objectivity to overcome the influence of the long traditions of some of the old wine-producing areas of Europe, agree nowadays that very much of the American wines are quite as good as those produced abroad.

Serving Wines

The amount of misinformation regarding wines is so tremendous and the number of "do's" and "don'ts" about wine service that have been enumerated by so-called connoisseurs are so great in number that the average host or hostess has frequently hestitated to serve wines.

Yet for hundreds and even thousands of years before this long list of rules was elaborated wine added much pleasure to dining and entertaining.

It certainly is not necessary then to memorize these numerous and complex rules before serving wine.

In fact wine service need be no more complex than serving good coffee or tea. Many of us enjoy our "cup of tea" without making a study of the almost infinite variations of tea grown in the tea-raising areas of the world. There is no doubt, of course, that this study as well as the pastime of testing and knowing wines may be entertaining.

The few simple suggestions that follow are based on the assumption that one drinks and serves wines for enjoyment. They are based on the preferences of the vast majority of wine drinkers who do abide by certain preferences in order to get the maximum enjoyment from drinking wine.

In addition a chart is offered for the benefit of those people who would like to know the rules laid down for "formal" dinners where a variety of wines may be served, and specific types of wines chosen for each course.

Basic Hints for Serving Wines

● **Remember that really "fine" wines are rare treats for special occasions. The important consideration when choosing a table wine for ordinary occasions is that the wine should be sound—and that does not mean high-priced.**

● **Choose good domestic products rather than dubious imported wines.**

● **Your guests will be more impressed, if they know anything about wines, with a sound wine rather than one that has a fancy foreign label.**

● **If they are uninformed you may enjoy the pleasure of starting their education.**

● **Unless you have the necessary cool wine cellar, buy only enough wine to fill immediate needs. They may deteriorate rapidly in a warm closet.**

● **Buy from a well-informed, reputable dealer who may be a storehouse of reliable information in guiding you and helping you avoid impressive names that would just cause you to waste money.**

● **It is quite proper to serve only one wine with a meal. For this purpose select a plain sound wine such as a medium dry sherry or claret.**

● **One good wine is far simpler and more palatable than half a dozen of doubtful quality.**

● **For formal occasions champagne or another sparkling wine is often served throughout a meal.**

● **Red or white light wines may be served with almost any dishes.**

● **Avoid however serving dry wines with sweet dishes or foods that have sweet sauces and avoid serving red**

wines with shellfish.

● **This last is one of the few basic rules that have come down to us that seems to make sense. For some inexplicable reason shellfish seem to have a property that makes red wine taste unpleasantly metallic to some people. If it doesn't have that effect on you then there is no reason why you shouldn't forget about it insofar as your own preferences are concerned but remember that may not be the case with your guests.**

● **Your own experience will tell you that a dry wine would not necessarily go well with sweet dishes nor would a very sweet wine go well with the usual foods in a meal for the same reason that you wouldn't serve candy with roast beef.**

● **Experience indicates that most Americans like their wines, whether red or white, slightly chilled. This is quite contrary to the rule that red still wines should always be served at room temperature.**

● **Most people like white wines slightly colder than red wines but this, too, is a matter of personal preference.**

● **The ideal temperature for white wines is 45° to 50° F.**

● **Sparkling wines should always be well-chilled. Champagne, for example, is at its best when served at a temperature of 40° F. or slightly less.**

● **To chill wine thoroughly place the bottle in a refrigerator for an hour or two and then in a wine cooler (a bucket of ice) for 20 to 30 minutes.**

● **If you plan to serve a wine at room temperature allow it to stand in the room where it is to be served for several hours.**

● **Never warm wine artificially or it will spoil.**

● **A few customs have entrenched themselves so well that they have become almost traditional. They include the service of white wines with hors d'oeuvres, fish, and white meats, and the service of red wines with cheeses, salads, and dark meats—the serving of white wines before red wines, and dry wines before sweet wines. The reasons for some of these are obvious as explained above.**

● **Others have grown out of the fact that white wines are not generally as full flavored as the reds and as a result may be happier choice with the more delicately flavored dishes, and red wines which are usually more fully flavored may make a better accompaniment for the more highly flavored and seasoned dishes.**

GUIDE TO FORMAL WINE SERVICE		
Food	*Kind of Wine*	*How to Serve*
Apéritif When wine is served alone as an appetizer	Champagne or American sparkling wines Dubonnet or Byrrh Sherry (dry), or Vermouth	Chilled 35°–40° F. Chilled 40°–50° F.
Appetizers (canapés, hors d'oeuvres, etc.)	Dry white wines such as: dry Sherry Chablis (white Burgundy) Graves (white Bordeaux) Rhine or Moselle Champagne or sparkling American wines	All chilled 40°–50° F. Chilled 35°–40° F.
Soups	Dry Sherry (with clear soups) Other dry white wines such as: dry Sauternes, dry Madeira, Moselle, Rhine, Chablis Champagne or sparkling American wines	Chilled 50°–60° F. or room temperature (70° F.) All chilled 45°–50° F. Chilled 35°–40° F.
Fish or Seafood	Any white tables wines such as: Rhine, Moselle, Chablis, Graves, or dry Sauternes Dry Champagne or sparkling American wines	All chilled 50° F. Chilled 35°–40° F.
Poultry or other white meats	Any dry white table wine as suggested for fish or seafood Dry Champagne or sparkling American wines	All chilled 45°–50° F. Chilled 35°–40° F.
Wild fowl, game, and dark turkey meat	Red table wines such as: red Burgundy, Claret, Chianti, Barbera, Côte Rôtie, Zinfandel, etc.	All at cellar 55°–60° F. or room temperature 70° F.
Red Meats	Red table wines such as suggested for wild fowl, Zinfandel, and dry native American red wines Sparkling Burgundy	All at cellar 55°–60° F. or room temperature 70° F. Chilled 35°–40° F.
Cheese	Red tables wines such as: Claret, Burgundy, moderately dry Sherry, Madeira, or Port	All at room temperature 70° F.
Dessert	Sweet wines such as: Marsala, Madeira, Sherry, Tokay and Port Sweet Sauternes Sweet Champagne or sweet sparkling American wines	All at room temperature 70° F. Chilled 50° F. Chilled 35°–40° F.
Coffee	Fine old Port, Madeira, or Sherry Recommended instead of wines, however, are brandy and liqueurs	All at room temperature 70° F.

How to Keep Wines

QUANTITY WINE STORAGE FOR LONG PERIODS

To keep all wines in quantity the ideal storage place is a dark, dry cellar which maintains a uniform temperature of about 55° F. It should be well-aired but free of draft. It must also be free of vibrations and that includes slight ones caused by street traffic.

Shelves should be away from furnaces or electric wiring or heating pipes of any kind.

Such really ideal conditions for the storage of wines in quantity are found only in deep underground cellars.

The chief problem for most of us in keeping a small stock of wines is the change in temperature in the average cellar or closet in an apartment. If it is gradual and doesn't go above 70° or 75° or below 40°F. no serious damage will be done. Freezing temperatures or temperatures above 75°F. will be very harmful.

In addition proper racks should be installed in a closet so that one bottle may be removed at a time without disturbing the others.

NATURAL AND FORTIFIED WINES

In caring for wines, you must distinguish between natural wines and fortified wines.

Natural (unfortified) wines continue to change after being bottled. They have to be kept tightly sealed to keep out all air. If these wines are allowed to stand up for any length of time the corks will dry up enough to allow air to come in and permit additional fermentation which, in time, will cause the wine to turn sour.

For this reason, it is necessary to store all wines which have an alcoholic content of 14% or less on its side with the cork slightly down so that it will be kept moist by the wine.

Fortified wines have had sufficient alcohol added to them to prevent further fermentation.

They should be kept standing in such a way that you may remove one bottle at a time without disturbing the others.

When bottles of corked table wines and sparkling wines must be kept upright for display or sales purposes, old stocks should be moved to the front of shelves every time new stocks are added.

WHEN WINE IS LEFT OVER

Natural Wines (Table Wines): Because of their low alcoholic content, these are perishable after opening of their containers brings them into contact with air. If table wines are left in a partly empty container they will "go off" (spoil) even though corked.

Actual spoilage begins within a few days or a few weeks, depending upon the individual wine and the weather.

Storage in the refrigerator slows but does not prevent spoilage.

What to Do: If it's a fifth bottle of wine, cork it tightly, place in refrigerator, and use in a day or two.

If it must be held longer, pour into clean smaller bottles, close with a conical cork from drugstore, and place in refrigerator. Plan to use it within a week.

If it's a gallon jug of wine, pour what is left into clean smaller bottles. Cork tightly, store in refrigerator, and plan to use within a week.

If you plan to use leftover wine for cooking, it need not be refrigerated if you add enough olive oil to form a thin film on the wine. Such wines should be used in fish and meat cookery, not in desserts or with fruit.

Fortified Wines (Appetizer and Dessert Wines): On opening, there is no danger from further fermentation; they will keep well for many weeks unless they are exposed to air for long periods.

DUMPLINGS

There is something very middle- or Eastern-European about dumplings and in some European countries the way of a woman with dumplings is as important as her charm and beauty. A good old-fashioned dumpling gives a hearty and tasty touch to soups and stews.

SOME HINTS ABOUT MAKING DUMPLINGS FOR SOUPS AND STEWS

● Use a wide-topped cooking vessel and never crowd it.
● Use ample liquid and give each dumpling room to expand.
● Cook in *gently* boiling liquid, close to a simmer.
● Cover the vessel as soon as instructed in the recipe so the steam can begin functioning.
● Resist temptation and do not lift the cover until the dumplings are done. You can see the dumplings swell without lifting the lid if you use a tight-fitting, heat-resistant glass cover or pie pan.
● Test for doneness when the dumplings look fluffy by inserting a toothpick. If it comes out clean, the dumplings are done.

BAKING POWDER DUMPLINGS
(Master Recipe)

2 cups sifted enriched flour
1 teaspoon salt
4 teaspoons baking powder
2 tablespoons shortening
¾ to 1 cup milk or ¾ to 1 cup water

Sift together the flour, the salt, and baking powder. Cut in shortening with pastry blender or 2 knives.

Add liquid until a thick drop batter is obtained.

Drop by tablespoonfuls into boiling soup or stew; cover tightly. Cook 12 minutes. Serves 5.

Dumpling Variations

Parsley Dumplings: In master recipe add ½ cup finely chopped parsley to flour mixture.

Meat Dumplings: Add leftover cooked meat or cracklings to master recipe just before dropping dumplings into boiling soup or stew.

Puffy Cheese Dumplings: In master recipe reduce shortening to 1 tablespoon and add ½ cup grated sharp American cheese to flour mixture.

CORN MEAL DUMPLINGS

1 cup corn meal
1 teaspoon salt
1⅓ cups boiling water
1 teaspoon chopped parsley
2 slightly beaten eggs
½ teaspoon minced onion
¼ to ½ cup enriched flour

Combine corn meal and salt and gradually add to boiling water, stirring constantly.

Remove from heat and stir until smooth. Cool.

Add remaining ingredients except flour. Mix thoroughly.

Drop by spoonfuls onto waxed paper heavily sprinkled with flour. Roll around on flour to form balls.

Drop into boiling meat or chicken stew. Cover tightly. Cook 10 minutes. Serves 6.

GERMAN LIVER DUMPLINGS OR LEBERKLOESSE

1 cup chopped, cooked liver
1 cup water
1 cup breadcrumbs
1 teaspoon salt
⅛ teaspoon pepper
½ teaspoon grated onion
1 slightly beaten egg
Grated lemon rind (optional)

Chicken, goose, beef, or calves liver may be used.

Cook water and breadcrumbs to a paste, stirring to prevent burning.

Cool. Add remaining ingredients. Mix well.

Form into balls the size of walnuts. Drop into rapidly boiling salted water or boiling soup. Cook 5 to 10 minutes. Serves 6.

Liver Dumpling Variations

Fried Liver Dumplings: Roll cooked liver dumplings in fine breadcrumbs and fry in hot fat.

Chicken Gizzard Dumplings: In liver dumplings use cooked heart and tender part of gizzards with or without chopped liver.

Marrow Dumplings: In liver dumplings substitute cooked or uncooked beef marrow for chopped liver and proceed as directed.

NOCKERLN

Nockerln is a German term for light dumplings made in several different ways. The recipe that follows is one of the most popular types. Egg Foam Dumplings are another type of nockerln.

4 tablespoons butter or margarine
1 egg
1 cup enriched flour
Pinch of salt
6 tablespoons milk

Cream together the butter and egg.

Stir in flour and a pinch of salt. Moisten to form a stiff batter by adding milk gradually.

Cut out the batter with a teaspoon to form small balls or Nockerln.

Drop them into boiling soup stock; cover the pan, and cook for 10 minutes.

MATZO MEAL DUMPLINGS
(Knaidlach)

Knaidlach or knaidel are Yiddish terms for dumplings. These light matzo meal dumplings are traditionally served at Passover.

2   eggs, separated
1/2 cup matzo meal
1/2 teaspoon salt

Beat egg yolks and whites in separate bowls, then combine and add matzo meal and salt gradually while stirring until smooth.

Chill in refrigerator for 30 minutes or longer before shaping into small balls with a teaspoon or by rolling in the palms of hands.

Drop one at a time into boiling clear soup; cover and simmer for 20 minutes. Serves 4.

Variations of Matzo Meal Dumplings

1. Add 1 tablespoon cooked or uncooked beef marrow to the mixture with or without 2 tablespoons chopped parsley.

2. Add 2 tablespoons chopped liver to the mixture just before shaping into balls.

3. Add 1 tablespoon finely chopped nuts to the mixture; season with a dash of cinnamon or ginger.

4. Season mixture with a dash of ginger; if desired, add 2 tablespoons chopped parsley.

GRATED RAW POTATO DUMPLINGS

2   cups grated raw potatoes
Scant 2/3 cup enriched flour
1   egg
1/2 teaspoon salt
1/2 teaspoon grated onion
2   tablespoons breadcrumbs

Drain grated potatoes well. Combine all ingredients to form a batter thick enough to shape into balls the size of a walnut.

Drop into rapidly boiling soup or salted water; cook 20 minutes.

When done, the dumplings will rise to top. If cooked in salted water, remove with a skimmer when done. Drain. Serve with gravy or soup. Serves 6.

LITTLE DROP DUMPLINGS

3   eggs, separated
Milk
1   tablespoon butter or margarine
1   cup sifted enriched flour
1/4 teaspoon salt
Dash of pepper

Combine egg whites with enough milk to make 1 cup liquid. Pour into hot buttered pan.

Add flour and stir constantly until mixture leaves side of pan. Cool.

Add egg yolks 1 at a time, stirring well. Season. Drop by teaspoonful into boiling soup. Cook 10 minutes.

GNOCCHI

Gnocchi is Italian food, a dish that cannot be described in a word. Perhaps the closest approximation is dumpling. Gnocchi may be made of flour, mashed potatoes, or farina.

GNOCCHI WITH POTATOES

2   medium-sized potatoes
1/2 cup milk
5   tablespoons butter
1   cup flour
2   eggs
1   teaspoon salt
1/4 teaspoon paprika
3   tablespoons grated Parmesan cheese, optional

For gnocchi, use a dry mealy type of potato. Boil the potatoes in their jackets, peel and mash.

Heat combined milk and butter to boiling point. Stir in flour until dough forms a ball. Remove from heat, then beat in eggs, salt, paprika, and the mashed potatoes.

Sprinkle the dough with a little flour to prevent sticking. Cut into 5 pieces and shape each into a long roll about 1/2 inch thick. Cut into pieces about 1 inch long.

Drop about a third of the gnocchi at a time in large pan of boiling salted water and cook gently uncovered for 3 to 5 minutes. Remove to a heated bowl and keep warm. Repeat until all the gnocchi have been cooked. Serve with melted butter and grated Parmesan cheese. Serves 6.

Variation: The gnocchi may be served with 1 1/2 cups canned or homemade Italian-style tomato sauce and 1 cup grated Parmesan cheese. Toss the cooked gnocchi with 1 cup sauce and 1/2 cup cheese. Turn onto serving platter and pour 1/2 cup sauce over it. Then sprinkle with remaining 1/2 cup grated cheese.

GNOCCHI WITH FLOUR

2   tablespoons butter
2   tablespoons flour
2   tablespoons cornstarch
1/2 teaspoon salt
1   cup milk, scalded
1   egg yolk
1/2 cup grated cheese, optional

Melt butter in a skillet. Mix the flour, cornstarch, and salt; blend into melted butter and stir until smooth.

Stir in scalded milk; lower heat, add egg yolk and, if desired, the grated cheese. Beat the batter until egg has thickened and cheese has melted.

Pour into shallow greased pan. Let cool, then cut into narrow pieces about 2 inches long. Drop the pieces into gently boiling water and cook about 2 minutes. Drain and serve with melted butter. Serves 4.

Variation: If desired, do not boil the gnocchi. Place the pieces in a pan; pour additional melted butter over them, and sprinkle with additional grated cheese. Heat through in moderate oven, then serve.

GNOCCHI WITH FARINA

1/2 cup farina
1   tablespoon butter or margarine
1/2 teaspoon salt
2   cups hot milk
1   beaten egg
1/2 pound sharp cheese, grated
1/4 cup chopped onions
1/4 cup chopped green pepper
2   tablespoons fat
2   cups canned tomatoes
1   teaspoon salt
1/8 teaspoon pepper
Pinch of cayenne

Stir farina, butter, and salt into hot milk and cook in top of double boiler 15 minutes.

Add egg and cheese. Reserve 1/2 cup grated cheese.

Pour into shallow, greased pan. Chill, then cut into 12 squares and place in large, flat baking dish.

Brown chopped onion and green pepper in hot fat. Add other ingredients and cook 10 minutes. Pour sauce over farina squares. Sprinkle with remaining cheese.

Bake in slow oven (325° F.) until cheese is melted, about 15 minutes. Serves 4.

MARROW BALLS FOR SOUP

1/4 cup fresh marrow
2   tablespoons butter or margarine
3   eggs
1/4 teaspoon salt
1/8 teaspoon paprika
2   tablespoons chopped parsley
Cracker crumbs

Combine marrow and butter and beat until creamy.

Add eggs, salt, paprika, parsley, and just enough cracker crumbs to make the right consistency to shape into balls.

Cook in simmering soup 15 minutes.

Gnocchi with Farina

SPATZEN OR SPAETZEL

A German term for tiny dumplings, sometimes called German egg dumplings.

2½ cups flour
½ teaspoon salt
¼ teaspoon baking powder
Small grating of nutmeg, optional
2 eggs, lightly beaten
½ cup milk
½ cup water
½ cup melted butter

Combine flour, salt, baking powder, and nutmeg in a bowl. Mix together the eggs, milk, and water; gradually stir into the flour mixture.

The consistency of the dough depends upon the method of shaping to be used. The dough may be made softer by the addition of a small amount of water or stiffer by adding more flour. The softer the dough, the lighter the dumplings; however, it must be firm enough to retain its shape. Spatzen should be light and delicate; try out a sample and if it is too heavy, add a little water to the dough.

Cut or break off small bits of the dough with a spoon (about ¼ x 1 inch) and drop into 3 to 4 quarts rapidly boiling salted water. Cook 1 or 2 minutes. Or place the dough on a plate and cut shreds with a knife from the side of the plate into the water. Or the dough may be forced through a metal colander into the boiling water.

When done, remove them with a slotted ladle to absorbent paper to remove excess water. Toss with melted butter. Serves 6.

Variations: (1) Cook spatzen in clear soup just before serving; serve with the soup; (2) Place drained spatzen in a dish and cover with ¼ cup breadcrumbs which have been sautéed in ½ cup butter; (3) Toss spatzen with ¾ cup warm sour cream and a little butter; (4) Toss with butter and ½ cup crumbled crisp bacon bits; (5) Toss with ½ cup grated sharp Cheddar cheese and butter.

There's plenty of flavor and nourishment in an old-time stew with dumplings.

MASHED POTATO DUMPLINGS
(Kartoffel Kloesse)

1 cup ¼-inch bread cubes
Fat
2 cups mashed potatoes
1 tablespoon minced onion
1 slightly beaten egg
¾ cup sifted enriched flour
1½ teaspoons salt
½ teaspoon pepper

Fry bread cubes in hot fat. Add 1 tablespoon fat to hot mashed potatoes. Cool.

Add onion and egg; mix well with fork. Sift in flour, salt, and pepper. Mix well.

Shape into 12 balls, forming each around 4 to 5 fried bread cubes. Cook, covered, in boiling salted water 10 to 12 minutes.

If desired, brown in melted fat before serving. Serves 6.

Variations of
Mashed Potato Dumplings

Savory Potato Dumplings: Add 1 teaspoon nutmeg and marjoram to dry ingredients.

Potato Meat Dumplings: Add leftover cooked meat to potato dumplings just before shaping in balls.

Potato Dumplings with Farina: Omit bread cubes; add ½ cup farina to flour and proceed as for potato dumplings.

Potato Dumplings with Matzo Meal: Omit bread cubes; use ¾ cup matzo meal in place of flour in dumplings.

EGG FOAM DUMPLINGS

3 eggs, separated
Dash of salt
3 tablespoons flour

Beat egg whites with salt until stiff. Add egg yolks one at a time; beating slightly after each addition.

Fold in flour and pour into clear, boiling soup. Cook 5 minutes.

Lift out of soup; cut into ovals with the side of a tablespoon. Serve with hot soup.

LIVER SAUSAGE DUMPLINGS

¼ pound Braunschweiger sausage
½ egg or 1 egg white or yolk
½ cup cracker crumbs, or more if the egg is large
1 tablespoon chopped parsley or chives
1 tablespoon ketchup

Combine sausage, egg, cracker crumbs, parsley or chives, and ketchup. Shape the mixture into 1 inch balls. Cook gently for about 2 minutes in soup stock. Makes about 20 1-inch balls.

KNISHES

Knishes is a Yiddish term for any of several types of patties or dumplings, baked or fried and frequently served with soup. A popular type is made of thinly rolled or stretched dough, filled with seasoned chopped meat, cottage cheese, mashed potatoes, or kasha (cooked buckwheat groats). It is an old-time Jewish dish.

2 cups sifted enriched flour
1 teaspoon baking powder
½ teaspoon salt
2 eggs, well beaten
½ cup salad oil
Cheese or meat filling (see below)

Mix and sift flour, baking powder, and salt. Mix beaten eggs and oil and combine with flour mixture; mix to a smooth dough.

Roll out on a floured board to ⅛-inch thickness. Fold in three and roll out again to ⅛-inch thickness. Repeat the folding and rolling.

Cut into 2½-inch squares. Place a spoonful of filling in the center of each square. Bring the dough up over the filling and press dough firmly together.

Place on a baking sheet and bake in moderate oven (375°F.) until golden brown, about 25 minutes. Serve hot. Makes about 30.

Note: These may be made in advance, wrapped in aluminum foil and stored in the refrigerator. To serve, heat in slow oven (325°F.) for 15 minutes.

MEAT FILLING FOR KNISHES

2 cups ground cooked meat, chicken, or turkey
2 tablespoons finely chopped celery
2 tablespoons finely chopped onion
1 tablespoon chicken fat
1½ teaspoons salt, about
¼ teaspoon pepper, about
1 egg, well beaten
Gravy or soup stock to moisten

Remove all fat and gristle from meat before grinding. Lightly brown the celery and onion in fat, about 5 minutes.

Mix all ingredients until well blended, using just enough gravy or soup stock to make a stiff paste. Makes about 2 cups.

CHEESE FILLING FOR KNISHES

1 pound dry cottage cheese
1 egg, slightly beaten
1 tablespoon sugar
¼ teaspoon cinnamon
¼ teaspoon salt
¼ cup seedless raisins, optional

Mix all ingredients until well blended. Makes about 2 cups.

KISHKE

Kishke, often called stuffed derma, is a Yiddish term for the intestine of beef stuffed with any of various savory fillings, then roasted; an old-time Jewish dish. The most common filling is made of flour and fat seasoned with onions, salt, and pepper. Nowadays it is sold already prepared and quick frozen, ready for cooking. It is usually served with meat or poultry.

Beef casings for stuffing may be purchased from your meat man, usually requiring additional cleaning at home. Wash the casings in cold water and scrape free of any fat. As a final cleansing, use lukewarm water and turn the casings inside out. (They should be cut into short lengths—about 12 inches—to make it easy to do this.)

Sew up one end of each piece and stuff with kishke filling.

Kishke Filling for Each 12-Inch Piece:

1 cup sifted enriched flour
½ cup chopped beef suet (fat from casings may be used)
1 small onion, grated
2 tablespoons fine bread or cracker crumbs
⅛ teaspoon salt
Dash of pepper

Combine in the order given and mix well in a shallow bowl.

Place the sewed end of the casing in the center of the mixture and begin stuffing by turning in the end with the mixture as you fill the entire length of the casing.

Do not stuff too tightly because the filling expands and the casing shrinks during cooking.

Sew or tie the open end and rinse the outer surface free of any filling mixture.

Drop into boiling water for 1 minute to shrink the casing. To cook, place in roasting pan with poultry. Or it may be roasted separately on a bed of sliced onions to which rendered poultry fat has been added. Cook until lightly browned in moderate oven (350°F.), about 1½ to 2 hours.

CHEESE DUMPLINGS

1 cup enriched flour
1½ teaspoons baking powder
½ teaspoon salt
1 tablespoon shortening
1 cup grated American cheese
½ cup water

Mix and sift flour, baking powder, and salt. Cut in shortening with pastry blender or 2 knives. Add cheese. Gradually add water and mix smooth.

Drop by tablespoonfuls into boiling soup. Cover closely. Cook 12 minutes without removing cover. Serves 5.

PIROSHKI

Piroshki is the Russian and Yiddish name for little cases of raised dough (baking powder or yeast) or pastry with various fillings, which are baked or fried. They are served with soup, as canapés, or—filled with fruit—as desserts. In Poland, similar little pies are called pirogi or pirogen; they are sometimes simmered or steamed like dumplings.

Filling:

¾ pound cooked beef
2 broiled chicken livers
1 onion, sliced and fried
1 egg
Salt, pepper, cinnamon

Dough:

1½ cups sifted enriched flour
1½ teaspoons baking powder
1 slightly beaten egg
¼ cup chicken fat or shortening
Pinch of salt
About ¼ cup water

Put the cooked beef, chicken livers, and onion through the food chopper. Add the egg; season to taste and mix well.

Combine the dough ingredients, adding just enough water to make a soft dough.

Roll out about ⅛-inch thick and cut in 3½-inch rounds.

Fill each round with 1 tablespoon meat mixture. Shape in half moons by folding the edges together over the filling. Pinch the edges together securely.

Bake on a greased baking sheet in hot oven (400°F.) until nicely browned, 25 to 30 minutes. Serve with clear soups.

Variations: These old-time European baked dumplings or turnovers may also be made with a yeast dough or pie crust (homemade or packaged mix).

If a yeast dough is used, allow the filled pirogen to rise 1 to 1½ hours on the greased baking sheet, then brush with chicken fat, melted shortening, or egg yolk diluted with equal amount of water.

Bake in moderate oven (375°F.) until nicely browned, 20 to 25 minutes.

Other well seasoned fillings such as cooked liver, or poultry, or kasha (cooked buckwheat groats) may be used.

SPONGE DUMPLINGS

6 tablespoons milk
2 eggs, separated
4 tablespoons soft butter or margarine
⅔ cup sifted enriched flour
¼ teaspoon salt

Combine milk, egg whites, butter, flour, and salt in a small pan. Cook over low heat, stirring constantly.

When thick, remove pan from heat. Beat in egg yolks.

When cool, drop by spoon into simmering soup. Simmer 5 minutes and serve. Serves 6.

FLUFFY CHEESE DUMPLINGS

1 pound dry cottage cheese
2 eggs
1 cup sifted enriched flour
1 teaspoon salt
3 quarts boiling water
3 tablespoons butter or margarine
½ pint sour cream

Mash cheese; add eggs and mix well. Stir in sifted dry ingredients.

Drop by tablespoonfuls into rapidly boiling salted water. Cover and boil 15 minutes.

Drain and pour melted butter or margarine over dumplings. Serve with sour cream. Serves 4.

MATZO BALLS FOR SOUP

3 tablespoons melted chicken fat
2 eggs, separated
¾ to ⅞ cup matzo meal
½ cup hot water
Salt
⅛ teaspoon ginger (optional)

Place chicken fat and egg yolks in a large bowl; beat until well blended.

Add ¾ cup matzo meal alternately with hot water (3 additions of each).

Taste and add up to 1 teaspoon salt; stir in ginger.

Form a trial ball, about 1 inch in diameter. Drop into a pan of simmering water. Cover and cook 5 minutes. It should hold its shape. If it crumbles, add a little more matzo meal (1 to 3 tablespoonfuls) and make another trial ball.

When consistency is satisfactory, chill mixture from 1 to 3 hours.

Then form into small balls and simmer 15 to 20 minutes in hot water or hot soup. For larger balls, use a longer period of time, up to 25 minutes. Serves 6.

Matzo Balls for Soup

EGGS

In most homes in this country, eggs are a staple food that homemakers find indispensable in planning and preparing family meals. Eggs can be served in so many ways and are an ingredient in so many types of recipes that they are likely to appear in some form at any meal.

And, in addition to their versatility as a food, eggs make a worthwhile contribution to the nutrient content of diets. They are highly valued as a source of protein, iron, vitamin A, and riboflavin, and are one of the few foods that contain vitamin D. Because of the amount and quality of their proteins, eggs make a good alternate for meat.

Nutritionists usually suggest that a person eat from four to seven eggs a week, including those used in cooking. If you are counting calories, you can figure that a large egg has 80 calories, 60 of which come from the yolk.

BUYING EGGS

When you shop for shell eggs, you may find several grades, two or more sizes within one grade, and considerable range in price per dozen.

To be sure of getting quality eggs, buy graded eggs at a market that keeps them in refrigerated cases. The grade mark gives assurance that the eggs were of a specific quality at the time of testing. If they have been properly handled since testing, there will be little loss of quality.

GRADES AND SIZES OF EGGS

The U.S. Department of Agriculture has developed standards widely used throughout the country that classify eggs into three consumer grades: U.S. grade AA or fresh fancy quality, U.S. grade A, and U.S. grade B.

Cartons of Government-graded eggs are marked to show quality and size. The mark, in the form of a shield, printed on the carton or on a paper tape used to seal it, certifies that each egg has been graded for quality and sorted for size.

Grade AA or grade A eggs are a good choice for poaching, frying, or cooking in the shell because of their superior appearance and delicate flavor. Lower quality eggs are generally satisfactory for scrambling, for making omelets, and for combining with other ingredients in cooked dishes.

The grade of the egg does not affect its food value; lower grades are as high in nutrients as top grades. Shell color is determined by breed of hen and does not affect the nutritive value or quality of an egg.

The size classifications of eggs are based on weight per dozen. Size is independent of quality; eggs of any size may be included in each quality grade.

Common market sizes and minimum weight per dozen are:

Extra large—27 ounces
Large—24 ounces
Medium—21 ounces
Small—18 ounces

Two other sizes—Jumbo at 30 ounces per dozen and Peewee (pullet eggs) at 15 ounces per dozen—are sometimes available.

COMPARE PRICES

When small and medium eggs are plentiful in the late summer or fall, they are often more economical as a source of protein than larger sizes. To find which size is the most economical, compare prices within a quality grade.

Medium eggs are as good a buy as large eggs when they cost one-eighth less. Small eggs are as good a buy when they cost one-sixth less than medium or one-fourth less than large eggs.

STORING EGGS

To store eggs properly, keep them clean, cold, and covered.

Most graded eggs sold in retail stores are clean. Eggs should not be washed before storing because washing removes the thin protective film or "bloom" that seals the pores, retains moisture, and keeps out bacteria, mold, and odors.

Covering eggs retards moisture loss and helps prevent absorption of odors. The paper carton in which eggs are sold makes an excellent storage container. See that eggs are large end up in the carton to help keep the yolk centered.

Put eggs in the refrigerator promptly after purchase—they cannot be expected to maintain their quality if held in a hot car or kitchen.

For best flavor and cooking quality, use eggs within a week. They may still be usable after a few weeks' storage in a home refrigerator. With prolonged storage, however, eggs are likely to develop off-flavors and lose some thickening and leavening power.

Cover leftover yolks with cold water and store in the refrigerator in a tightly closed container. Extra egg whites should also be refrigerated in a tightly covered container. Use leftover yolks and whites within a day or two.

HINTS ABOUT USING EGGS

Everyone can cook eggs so that they retain their flavor, tenderness, and attractiveness if a few simple rules are followed.

Moderate to low temperature cookery is important. Cook eggs at low to moderate temperature to assure uniformly tender attractive eggs and egg dishes. High temperature and overcooking toughen eggs—egg-rich cakes, soufflés, and other dishes leavened with eggs will fall, the crust will be thick and tough, and inside heavy and soggy.

In dishes thickened with eggs such as custards and sauces, high temperature and overcooking cause curdling or watering.

Eggs, Separated: It is easier to separate eggs when they are still chilled, just after being taken from the refrigerator.

Crack each egg by striking it at middle against edge of bowl or with cutting edge of knife. Then, holding egg over bowl, insert thumb in crack and pull shell apart. (Yolk settles to bottom half and most of white flows out.) Carefully turn yolk into other half of shell, letting remaining white drop into bowl (repeat if necessary); drop yolk into second bowl.

Eggs, Beaten: Whole eggs whipped until whites and yolks are well blended. They're used principally to give light texture to batters and dough, and also as a binder in these products and in salad dressings.

Eggs, Slightly Beaten: Whole eggs beaten just enough to blend yolks and whites. This is enough beating when you are using them to thicken foods like custard. If you're using eggs with crumbs to coat foods before deep-fat frying, beat them only slightly.

Eggs, Well Beaten: Whole eggs beaten until whites and yolks are well blended and look light and frothy. They are beaten to this stage for use in many baked products.

Egg Yolks, Well Beaten: Egg yolks beaten until thick and lemon-colored. This is important in producing fine texture in sponge cakes.

Egg Whites, Beaten Stiff: Egg whites beaten until they stand in peaks when beater is lifted from surface, with points of peaks drooping over a bit and surface still moist and glossy. In this stage, they hold air which expands when heated.

If you don't beat the egg whites enough, they won't hold enough air; if you beat them too stiff, the foam will break down when the other ingredients are added.

When you add sugar to beaten egg whites in small amounts, the air-holding property of the egg whites is increased.

Angel cake is leavened by the expansion of air held in the egg whites and by steam during baking.

Egg Whites, Beaten Very Stiff: Egg whites beaten until points of peaks stand upright, without drooping, when beater is lifted from surface. Surface should look dry.

SOFT-COOKED EGGS
Cold Water Method: Cover eggs in pan with water to come at least 1 inch above the eggs. Bring rapidly to boiling. Turn off heat and, if necessary, set pan off burner to prevent further boiling. Cover and let stand 2 to 4 minutes, depending on individual taste.

Cool eggs promptly in cold water for several seconds to prevent further cooking and to make them easy to handle.

Boiling Water Method: Bring water in pan to rapid boiling, using enough to cover eggs as above. Meanwhile warm very cold eggs slightly in warm water to avoid cracked shells. Transfer eggs to water with spoon, turn off heat, and if necessary set pan off burner to prevent further boiling. Cover and let stand 6 to 8 minutes. Cool as above.

Cooking More Than 4 Eggs: Use either method. Do not turn off but reduce heat to keep water below simmering. Hold 4 to 6 minutes. Cool as above.

Coddled Eggs: See Boiling Water Method above.

HARD-COOKED EGGS
Cold Water Method: Follow directions for Soft-Cooked Eggs—Cold Water Method. Let stand 15 minutes. Cool promptly and thoroughly in cold water—this makes the shells easier to remove and helps prevent dark surface on yolks.

Boiling Water Method: Follow directions for Soft-Cooked Eggs—Boiling Water Method, but reduce heat to keep water below simmering and hold 20 minutes. Cool as above.

To Remove the Shell: Crackle the shell. Roll egg between hands to loosen shell, then start the peeling at the large end of the egg. Dipping in a bowl of water helps to ease the shell off.

FRIED EGGS
Method #1: Heat 1 to 2 tablespoons fat in a skillet just hot enough to sizzle a drop of water. Break and slip eggs into skillet—from a sauce dish if preferred. Reduce heat immediately. Cook slowly to desired doneness, 3 to 4 minutes.

Baste with fat during cooking. Instead of basting, skillet may be covered, or eggs may be turned over.

Method #2: Use just enough fat to grease skillet. Proceed as above. Cook

> ← *Egg whites won't beat up if there is any moisture, egg yolk, or other food on the egg beater.*

over low heat until edges turn white, about 1 minute. Add ½ teaspoon water for one egg, decreasing proportion slightly for each additional egg. Cover skillet tightly to hold in steam which bastes the egg. Cook to desired doneness.

FRIED EGGS AU BEURRE NOIR
(With Black Butter)
Fry eggs and transfer to hot platter. Sprinkle with grated onion or chopped chives if desired. Add 1 tablespoon butter to frying pan. Cook until brown. Add 1 tablespoon lemon juice or vinegar. Heat and pour over eggs.

FRENCH OMELET
(Master Recipe)
    6 eggs
    ⅓ cup milk
    ¾ teaspoon salt
    ⅛ teaspoon pepper
    2 tablespoons butter or margarine

Beat eggs until whites and yolks are well mixed. Add milk, salt, and pepper.

Melt butter in skillet. Pour in mixture and place over moderate heat.

While cooking, lift edges and tip skillet so uncooked mixture flows under cooked portion. When bottom is browned, fold over. Serves 3 to 4.

French Omelet Variations
Bacon or Ham Omelet: Add ½ cup diced crisp bacon or chopped cooked ham to egg mixture.

Cheese Omelet: Sprinkle omelet with ¼ cup grated American cheese before folding.

Mushroom Omelet: Sauté ½ to 1 cup chopped mushrooms in butter for 3 or 4 minutes. Add egg mixture and cook as directed.

Crouton Omelet: Sauté 1 cup small bread cubes in butter. Add to mixture.

Rum Omelet: Omit milk and decrease salt to ⅛ teaspoon. Add 2 tablespoons water, 2 teaspoons powdered sugar and 2 tablespoons rum to beaten eggs. Cook as directed.

After turning omelet onto hot platter pour 3 to 4 tablespoons rum around it. Ignite rum and serve at once. Sprinkle omelet with additional sugar if desired.

Vegetable Omelet: Sauté 2 tablespoons minced onion in butter. Add ½ to 1 cup canned or cooked peas, lima beans, or mixture of vegetables.

Season to taste and heat. Pour over omelet before folding or add to white sauce and pour over folded omelet.

Sweet Omelet: Omit pepper. Add 1½ tablespoons confectioners' sugar and ½ teaspoon vanilla. Serve sprinkled with confectioners' sugar.

PUFFY ("SOUFFLÉ") OMELET (Master Recipe)

4   eggs, separated
½ teaspoon salt
Pinch of pepper
4   tablespoons milk
1   tablespoon butter or margarine

Beat egg yolks until thick. Add salt, pepper, and milk.

Beat egg whites until they form peaks. Fold whites into yolks.

Pour into well buttered hot skillet, spreading mixture evenly and cooking slowly until omelet puffs up and is firm on the bottom.

Bake in moderate oven (350°F.) until top is slightly dry, about 5 minutes, and springs back when pressed lightly with fingertip.

Cut about halfway through omelet at the center, fold over with a spatula.

Serve immediately on hot platter. Serves 2 or 3.

Puffy ("Soufflé") Omelet Variations

Puffy Bacon or Ham Omelet: Add ½ cup minced cooked ham or diced crisp bacon to egg yolk mixture, or sprinkle over omelet before folding.

Puffy Cheese Omelet: Add 2 tablespoons grated cheese to egg yolk mixture.

Puffy Omelet with Chicken: Sprinkle 1 cup diced cooked chicken over omelet just before folding.

Puffy Omelet with Chicken Livers: Dice chicken livers and sauté in butter. Season with salt and pepper and Worcestershire sauce. Pour over omelet just before serving.

Puffy Omelet with Seafood: Sauté canned or cooked whole shrimp, chunks of canned or cooked crabmeat or lobster in butter and serve around omelet. Garnish with lemon wedges.

Or, pour creamed seafood over omelet before folding.

Jelly Omelet: Spread jelly on omelet before folding.

Puffy Omelet with Kidney: Sprinkle cooked and minced kidney (see index) over omelet before folding.

Puffy Onion Omelet: Sauté minced onion in butter. Fold in before cooking omelet.

Puffy Parsley Omelet: Add 2 tablespoons minced parsley when folding in egg whites.

Puffy Potato Omelet: Add ½ cup seasoned mashed potatoes to egg yolk mixture.

Puffy Omelet with Sauce: Pour cheese, tomato, or mushroom sauce over omelet after folding.

Puffy Rice Omelet: Add ⅓ cup cooked rice and ½ teaspoon tomato ketchup to egg yolk mixture.

Puffy Spanish Omelet #1: Serve Spanish Sauce (see index) in fold and around omelet.

PUFFY ("SOUFFLÉ") OMELET HINTS

Cook on top of range slowly until omelet puffs up and is firm on the bottom.

Bake in moderate oven until top is slightly dry, then cut halfway through the omelet at center.

Fold omelet over with a spatula.

Serve immediately on a hot platter, attractively garnished.

Puffy Spanish Omelet #2: Sauté 1 tablespoon each finely chopped onion and green pepper in 2 tablespoons butter until tender.

Add 1¼ cups canned tomatoes and cook until moisture is almost evaporated.

Add 1 to 2 tablespoons sliced mushrooms, about ¼ teaspoon salt, a few grains cayenne pepper, and 2 teaspoons capers. Serve in fold and around omelet.

Puffy Tomato Omelet: Cover half of omelet with slices of broiled or grilled tomato before folding, or serve omelet with hot tomato sauce.

NOODLE OMELET

4   ounces (1½ cups) noodles
3   tablespoons butter or margarine
2   tablespoons chopped onion
3   eggs
2   tablespoons milk or water
½ teaspoon salt
⅛ teaspoon pepper

Cook noodles according to package directions. Drain well. Cook onion in the butter until softened but not browned. Add noodles and blend.

Meanwhile, blend eggs, milk, salt and pepper with a fork. Mix well but do not beat frothy, and pour over noodles.

Cook rapidly, lifting mixture with fork, at the same time tipping skillet to let uncooked egg mixture flow to bottom of skillet. Keep mixture as level as possible. Shake skillet while cooking to be sure mixture is not sticking at any point.

When mixture no longer flows, reduce heat for a minute or two to completely "set" the omelet and brown the bottom. Loosen edges if necessary and slide spatula underneath to be sure omelet is free. Fold in half. Serve promptly. Serves 4.

MATZO BRIE OR FRIED MATZO

2   eggs
½ cup milk or water
¼ teaspoon salt
Dash of cinnamon
2   matzos
3   tablespoons butter or shortening

Beat eggs; add milk or water, salt, and cinnamon. Break matzos into this mixture.

Melt butter in skillet; pour in matzo mixture. Cover and cook over moderate heat about 10 minutes or until browned on under side. Turn and cook, uncovered, until browned, about 3 minutes.

Serve hot, plain or with a sprinkling of sugar and cinnamon, honey, or applesauce. Serves 2.

KAISER SCHMARREN

Kaiser Schmarren is a German name for dessert omelets sometimes referred to on American menus as Emperor's Omelets. It is an Austrian dish that is made in various ways in other Central European countries.

4 eggs, separated
2½ tablespoons sugar
⅞ cup milk
1 cup sifted enriched flour
⅛ teaspoon salt
3 tablespoons butter or margarine
Vanilla sugar
Additional 1 tablespoon butter or margarine
3 tablespoons seedless raisins
Powdered sugar

Combine egg yolks with 2½ tablespoons sugar, milk, flour, and salt to make a smooth paste.

Beat egg whites until stiff and carefully fold into first mixture.

In a large pan or skillet, melt ¼ of the 3 tablespoons butter. Pour in ¼ of mixture. It should be thinner than ¼ inch.

Cook gently and allow to puff. Turn and brown lightly on other side. Do not cook too long or it will become dry.

With 2 forks, tear bits of the schmarrn off, about the size of a quarter, until all is torn to pieces.

Cook 3 more omelets. Put each torn schmarrn onto a plate sprinkled with powdered sugar in which a bit of vanilla bean has been kept, and leave until others have been cooked.

Then put 1 tablespoon butter into skillet; add all torn schmarrn with 3 tablespoons seedless raisins washed and dried; sprinkle with powdered sugar, and stir in the skillet until heated, or about 5 minutes.

Serve on warmed plates with a fine tart fruit compote (sour cherries, cranberries, or stewed plums). Serves 4.

Spanish Rice Omelet

PENNSYLVANIA-DUTCH SMOKEHOUSE EGGS

¼ cup cooked ham and bacon (4 parts ham to 1 of bacon)
Handful of watercress
6 eggs
¼ cup thick buttermilk (or heavy cream)

Dice the cooked ham and bacon. While this is browning lightly over medium heat, take scissors and snip up the watercress.

Beat eggs and add the thick buttermilk or cream. Pour into well buttered pan on low heat. When bottom has just set, toss in the browned minced ham-bacon and cress. With fork, gently fold in these and stir egg only enough to work into inch-long flakes—not whipped and frazzled into fine, overcooked crumbs. Cook only until set throughout. Serves 4 to 6.

SPANISH RICE OMELET

6 eggs, beaten
½ cup milk
½ teaspoon salt
Dash of pepper
1 tablespoon butter or margarine
Rice Filling (below)
3 slices Mozzarella cheese

Combine eggs, milk, salt, and pepper. Mix well. Melt butter in a 10-inch skillet. Add egg mixture and cook over medium heat. As the eggs begin to set, draw the edges toward center with a spatula, tilting skillet to hasten flow of uncooked eggs on bottom.

When eggs have set, spoon half of the Spanish rice filling over the eggs and arrange Mozzarella cheese slices on top. Place under broiler until cheese is melted. Cut in wedges and serve. Serves 6.

Rice Filling:

3 tablespoons butter or margarine
½ cup green onions, chopped fine
½ cup green pepper, chopped
½ teaspoon garlic powder
2 cups canned tomatoes (1 No. 2 can)
½ bay leaf
½ teaspoon sugar
1 teaspoon salt
⅛ teaspoon pepper
⅛ teaspoon cinnamon
½ cup sliced ripe olives
3 cups cooked rice

Melt butter in saucepan. Add onions, green pepper, and garlic powder; sauté until tender.

Stir in tomatoes, seasonings, and ripe olives. Simmer about 15 minutes. Stir in cooked rice.

Note: Use leftover rice filling as a vegetable for a future lunch or dinner or freeze for later use.

CREAMED EGGS
(Master Recipe)

Blend ¼ cup flour thoroughly with ¼ cup melted butter or margarine. Gradually add 2 cups milk.

Cook over hot water, stirring constantly, until thick.

Quarter 6 hard-cooked eggs and add to sauce. Season with salt and pepper, and heat. Serve on hot toast. Serves 4.

Optional: About 2 teaspoons Worcestershire sauce or grated onion may be added.

Creamed Egg Variations

Creamed Eggs with Fish, Meat, or Poultry: Make a thin white sauce by reducing fat and flour to 2 tablespoons each.

Use fewer eggs, if desired, and add 1 to 2 cups flaked cooked fish, shrimp, or diced meat or poultry.

Creamed Eggs with Bacon: Add diced crisp bacon to creamed mixture or place slices of crisp bacon over hot buttered toast. Pour over creamed mixture.

Creamed Eggs with Peas or Asparagus Tips: Cut eggs into slices or chop fine. Add 1 cup cooked or canned peas or asparagus tips.

Creamed Eggs with Tomatoes: Sauté or broil 1-inch-thick slices of tomatoes. Arrange tomato slices on toast. Cover with creamed eggs.

Curried Creamed Eggs: Season sauce with curry powder.

Eggs A La King: Add ½ to 1 cup sliced cooked mushrooms, ½ cup cooked peas, and 1 pimiento (canned) sliced in thin strips to creamed mixture. Heat thoroughly.

Broil thick slices of tomato for 5 minutes. Place one slice on each serving of buttered hot toast, and pour over creamed mixture.

Eggs Goldenrod: Separate whites and yolks. Chop or slice whites and add to sauce.

Press yolks through sieve and sprinkle over each serving. Sprinkle with paprika.

Creamed Eggs with Asparagus

EGG FOO YONG
(Master Recipe)

Egg foo yong is a Chinese omelet made with additions of vegetables and almost any cooked meat or seafood. It is served with a sauce of thickened chicken stock seasoned with soy sauce. The name is spelled in various ways.

1   cup chopped cooked ham or roast pork
1/2 cup chopped onion
1   cup drained canned bean sprouts
3   tablespoons chopped green onion tops
1   tablespoon soy sauce
1   teaspoon salt
3   eggs
Oil for deep frying

Put meat, onion, sprouts, green onion tops, soy sauce, and salt in a bowl; mix well.

Stir the eggs lightly into the mixture.

Use a deep-bowl ladle to spoon out the mixture and lower into the hot oil. Tip the ladle at once to release the omelets.

Let them fry until they rise to the top. Turn each to brown the other side.

Lift out with a large slotted spoon. Serve on a hot dish covered with a little sauce (below). Serve additional soy sauce separately. Serves 4.

Egg Foo Yong Variations

Chicken Foo Yong: Use cooked chicken or turkey instead of ham or pork.

Crabmeat Foo Yong: Use canned or cooked crabmeat instead of ham or pork.

Lobster Foo Yong: Use canned or cooked lobster meat instead of ham or pork.

Shrimp Foo Yong: Use canned or cooked shrimp instead of ham or pork.

Vegetable Foo Yong: Omit meat; use 2 cups chopped green pepper, celery, onion, and canned bean sprouts combined. Season with an additional 1 teaspoon salt.

Subgum Foo Yong: To the master

Egg Foo Yong

recipe or any variation, add 1 cup diced mushrooms, 1/2 cup diced green beans, and 1/2 cup diced canned bamboo shoots. Mix and cook as directed.

Sauce for Egg Foo Yong:

1 1/2 cups chicken stock
1   teaspoon molasses
1   teaspoon soy sauce
1   teaspoon cornstarch
2   tablespoons cold water

Heat stock with molasses and soy sauce. Combine cornstarch with cold water; stir in until smooth. Let come to boiling point and cook until thickened.

ARTICHOKE OMELET

1   package frozen artichoke hearts
1/4 cup olive oil
1   clove garlic, minced
2   to 4 tablespoons parsley
1   onion, thinly sliced
4   eggs
Salt and pepper

Cut artichoke hearts into 1/4 to 1/2 inch lengthwise slices. Heat oil; add artichokes, garlic, and parsley; cook, stirring frequently, until lightly browned. Add onion and cook a little longer.

Slightly beat eggs seasoned with salt and pepper; pour over artichoke mixture. Cook very slowly until browned on bottom; turn out on large frying pan lid, then slide back into pan and brown on the other side. Cut into wedges. Serves 6.

Artichoke Omelet

SWEDISH OMELETS

10 eggs
2/3 cup milk
1   teaspoon salt
1/4 cup butter or margarine
6   servings sautéed ham
Parsley

Beat eggs; add milk and salt. Pour a portion of the mixture into a small frying pan in which butter or margarine has been melted. Cook over low heat until set; lift occasionally from the bottom of pan with spatula while cooking.

Place a piece of sautéed ham on each omelet and roll omelet around ham.

Prepare omelets individually, or two large ones. Serves 6.

ITALIAN ZUCCHINI OMELET
(Frittata di Zucchini)

6   tablespoons olive oil
2   tablespoons butter or margarine
2   cups sliced or chopped zucchini
4   eggs
3   tablespoons chopped parsley
1/4 teaspoon salt
Dash of pepper
1   tablespoon grated Parmesan cheese

Heat 2 tablespoons oil and 1 tablespoon butter in a frying pan. Add zucchini and cook slowly, stirring often, until vegetable is limp and lightly browned, or about 5 minutes. Cool thoroughly.

Beat eggs until fluffy. Add parsley, salt, pepper, cheese, and cooled zucchini.

Heat remaining oil and butter in a clean pan. Add egg-zucchini mixture and cook over a moderately high heat, lifting mixture around edge, until only center remains uncooked.

Place under a very low broiler heat and cook until center is firm. Turn out on a platter and cut into pie-shaped wedges to serve. Serves 2.

SWISS OMELET

2   eggs
2   tablespoons milk or water
1/2 teaspoon salt
Few grains pepper
1/3 cup creamed chicken, meat, or fish
2   strips Swiss cheese

Prepare each omelet separately as follows: Mix eggs, milk, salt, and pepper thoroughly. Avoid foaminess.

Heat fat in skillet (6- to 7-inch) just hot enough to sizzle a drop of water. Pour in egg mixture. Reduce heat.

As the mixture at the edge begins to thicken, draw the cooked portions with the fork toward the center so that the uncooked portions flow to the bottom. Tilt skillet as it is necessary to hasten flow of uncooked eggs.

Do not stir and keep mixture as level as possible. Shake skillet occasionally to be sure omelet is not sticking. When eggs no longer flow and surface is still moist, increase heat to brown bottom quickly. Loosen edge.

Place creamed chicken, meat or fish in center of omelet. Fold in half or roll.

Set omelet on heatproof platter or baking sheet until required number of omelets are cooked. Then top with the cheese strips.

Broil or place in hot oven several minutes until cheese begins to melt. Serve promptly.

For pleasing texture, flavor and color contrast, serve with cranberry sauce. Makes 1 omelet.

SHIRRED (BAKED) EGGS
(Master Recipe)

Place 1 tablespoon cream in each buttered ramekin or custard cup.

Break an egg into each; season with salt and pepper.

Place cups on a baking sheet and bake in slow oven (325°F.) until eggs are firm, 8 to 10 minutes.

Note: Watch the timing carefully but do not try to hurry shirred eggs by increasing the heat. They must be cooked by gentle oven heat. Care must be taken not to overcook the eggs as the whites can become quite hard and rubbery. The centers should be soft and the whites just set. Note that baking dishes will retain heat and continue cooking the eggs after they are removed from the oven. Many cooks prefer to set the baking dishes in a pan of hot water deep enough to reach within ½ inch of the top of the baking dishes.

Shirred Egg Variations

Shirred Eggs in Bacon Rings: Cook bacon slightly and line each cup with a slice of bacon while still soft.

Break egg into each cup. Bake in slow oven (325°F.) until eggs are set.

Shirred Eggs in Ham Cups: Line each cup with slice of boiled ham large enough to form cup.

Break an egg into each and bake in slow oven (325°F.) until eggs are set.

Shirred Eggs in Noodle Cups: Make nest of seasoned cooked noodles in each cup.

Break an egg in each and bake until set.

Shirred Eggs in Potato Cups: Make nest of seasoned mashed potatoes. Break egg in each and bake.

For additional flavoring, add finely chopped chives.

Shirred Eggs in Rice Cups: Line cups with cooked rice. Break an egg into each.

Bake in slow oven (325°F.) until eggs

Eggs Florentine may be prepared in single servings as given in variations of Shirred (Baked) Eggs or it may be prepared as a family size casserole dish.

are set, 15 to 20 minutes. Serve with hot cheese sauce.

Shirred Eggs in Toast Cups: Cut crust from slices of bread and gently press bread into greased cups. The four corners will extend up to the tops of the custard cups, forming a cup.

Break an egg into each cup. Season with salt and pepper. Dot with butter or add 1 tablespoon cream for each egg.

Bake for 15 minutes in moderate oven (350°F).

Shirred Eggs in Tomatoes: Cut a slice from stem end of each tomato. Remove enough pulp so that an egg may be placed in each. Season with salt and pepper. Cover with buttered breadcrumbs.

Arrange in pan or cups. Bake in slow oven (325°F.) until crumbs are brown and eggs are set, about 25 minutes.

Shirred Eggs with Cheese: Sprinkle grated cheese over each egg or mix grated cheese with breadcrumbs and sprinkle over eggs.

Shirred Eggs with Crumbs: Dot eggs with butter. Sprinkle with seasoned fine, dry breadcrumbs.

Bake until eggs are set and crumbs lightly browned.

Eggs Florentine: Place 3 or 4 tablespoons chopped, cooked spinach in each cup. Season with salt and pepper. Dot with butter. Drop an egg in each and sprinkle with fine breadcrumbs.

Bake 10 minutes in slow oven (325°F.), then sprinkle with grated cheese and bake additional 10 minutes.

SCOTCH WOODCOCK

Scotch Woodcock may be scrambled eggs or creamed chopped eggs served on toast spread with anchovy butter or paste, then garnished with capers and anchovy fillets. Or it may be the special version given below.

2 slices toast
6 anchovy fillets
4 egg yolks
½ cup heavy cream
3 tablespoons butter or margarine
Pepper
Parsley, chopped

Butter toast generously and cut into finger lengths. Keep hot.

Wash anchovy fillets and pound to a paste. Spread on the toast.

Beat together lightly the egg yolks and the cream. Put this mixture into a saucepan over boiling water with the butter and a little freshly ground pepper. Stir with a wooden spoon until the eggs yolks and cream are like a creamy sauce.

Strain over the prepared toast and garnish with parsley. Serves 2.

BAKED SPANISH EGGS

4 tablespoons onion, chopped
4 tablespoons green pepper, chopped
4 tablespoons butter or margarine
8 to 10 eggs
½ cup day-old breadcrumbs
¾ cup grated process American cheese
1 cup beer
Paprika

Sauté onion and green pepper in butter until tender. Pour into shallow baking dish. Carefully break eggs into dish without breaking yolks. Mix breadcrumbs with cheese and sprinkle over eggs. Spoon beer over eggs; sprinkle with paprika.

Bake in moderate oven (350°F.) until eggs are set as you like them, about 12 to 15 minutes. Serves 4 to 5.

Baked Spanish Eggs make a hearty winter supper dish that is sophisticated enough for guests. Serve with a hearty vegetable such as lima beans and beer or ale.

EGGS MORNAY

½ teaspoon paprika
⅓ cup grated cheese
2 cups thin white sauce
2 egg yolks
4 to 6 whole eggs

Add paprika and cheese (reserve about 2 tablespoons cheese for top) to hot well seasoned sauce. Beat in the 2 egg yolks.

Pour layer of sauce into well greased casserole or individual casseroles. Slip eggs into sauce, one at a time.

Pour remaining sauce around edge, leaving yolks partially exposed.

Sprinkle with remaining cheese.

Bake in moderate oven (375°F.) 15 to 20 minutes, depending upon doneness of eggs desired. Serves 2 to 3.

Eggs Mornay

SCRAMBLED EGGS
(Master Recipe)

> 5 eggs
> 1/2 cup milk or cream
> 1/2 teaspoon salt
> 1/8 teaspoon pepper
> 2 tablespoons butter or margarine

Beat eggs, milk, and seasoning slightly.

Melt butter in skillet or top of double boiler. Pour in eggs and cook until soft and creamy, stirring and scraping mixture from bottom and sides of pan occasionally.

Serve at once on warm dish. Garnish with parsley and dash of paprika. Serves 3 to 4.

Scrambled Egg Variations

Scrambled Eggs with Bacon: Use 2 slices of diced cooked bacon. Omit butter, using bacon grease for cooking eggs.

Scrambled Eggs with Cheese: Place scrambled eggs on toast. Cover with grated cheese and brown in oven.

Cream Cheese Rabbit: Use 2/3 cup milk. When almost done, crumble and stir in 1 small package (3 ounces) cream cheese. Serve on toast.

Scrambled Eggs with Fish: Add 1/2 cup cooked, flaked fish.

Scrambled Eggs with Green Peppers: Remove seeds and membranes from 2 medium green peppers. Parboil 5 minutes. Chop fine. Add when eggs begin to thicken.

Scrambled Eggs with Meat or Poultry: Add 1/2 cup chopped dried beef, cooked ham, sausage, chicken, or leftover meat.

Scrambled Eggs with Mushrooms: Drain and chop canned mushrooms. Add to egg mixture before cooking. If fresh mushrooms are used, chop and sauté in fat before adding egg mixture.

Savory Scrambled Eggs: Add 1 tablespoon chopped parsley, 1/2 teaspoon grated onion, and 1/2 tablespoon chopped chives.

Scrambled eggs and their many variations are good chafing dish "starters" for the newcomer in this form of cookery.

Scrambled Eggs with Brains: Add 1 cup chopped parboiled brains.

Scrambled Eggs with Cottage Cheese: Reduce milk to 1/4 cup. Add 1/2 to 3/4 cup cottage cheese and 1 tablespoon chopped chives or parsley when eggs are almost done.

Scrambled Eggs with Sour Cream: Substitute sour cream for milk. Add chopped young onions, if desired.

Scrambled Eggs with Toast Cubes: Sauté 1 cup toast cubes until golden brown before adding egg mixture.

Scrambled Eggs with Spinach: Add 1/2 cup well drained, finely chopped cooked spinach.

Scrambled Eggs with Sweetbreads: Add 1 cup diced parboiled sweetbreads.

Scrambled Eggs with Tomatoes: Add 1/2 cup cooked tomatoes.

Scrambled Eggs with Leftover Vegetables: Add 1/2 cup chopped cooked vegetables.

POACHED EGGS
(Master Recipe)

Fill heavy shallow pan 2/3 full of water to which 1/8 teaspoon salt has been added. Bring to boiling point.

Break eggs into a saucer and slip into gently boiling, salted water. Bring to simmering, remove from heat and cover. Let stand about 5 minutes, or until eggs are as firm as you want them.

Remove eggs carefully with a skimmer or perforated spoon and serve on toast. Add salt and pepper to taste.

Egg poachers may be used to help keep the shape of the egg.

One tablespoon of vinegar may be added to each quart of water to help set the white of egg.

Poached Egg Variations

Poached Eggs and Corned Beef Hash: Serve poached eggs on cakes of corned beef hash. Garnish with parsley.

Poached Eggs Au Gratin: Arrange poached eggs in shallow, buttered baking dish. Pour over medium white sauce. Sprinkle with grated cheese. Brown in slow oven (325°F.).

Poached Eggs in Cheese Sauce: Pour 2 cups cheese sauce into shallow pan. Poach eggs in sauce. Serve on buttered toast.

Poached Eggs in Milk: Substitute milk for water in poaching eggs. Pour milk over toast.

Poached Eggs on Creamed Toast: Pour hot white sauce over toast. Place poached egg on each slice. Sprinkle with chopped parsley.

Poached Eggs on Tomatoes: Sauté thick tomato slices in olive oil. Season to taste with salt and pepper and, if desired, a pinch of basil. Place on hot plates. Top with poached eggs.

Poached Egg Oriental: Mix cooked rice with white sauce. Season with grated onion and minced celery. Top each serving with poached egg.

POACHED EGG HINTS

1. Slide the egg into the bubbling water very gently. Poach as many eggs at a time as will fit into the pan without running together.

2. Test for doneness by gently pressing back of fork tines against yolk.

3. Remove with slotted spoon and drain well by holding spoon on a piece of toweling for a few seconds.

4. Serve immediately on hot buttered toast, rusks, or toasted English muffins.

EGGS GOLDILOCKS

Cut 4 hard-cooked eggs in half lengthwise. Remove the yolks, mash and combine with 4 tablespoons mayonnaise. Season to taste with salt and pepper. Fill the whites.

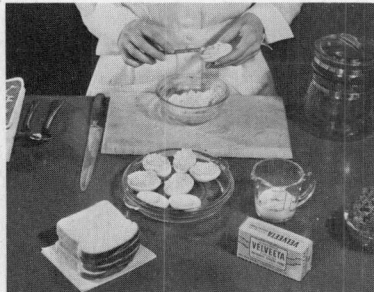

Remove the crusts from 4 slices of bread. Cut in half diagonally and toast. Arrange the toast points on a chop plate and top each with a stuffed egg half.

Melt ½ pound of pasteurized process cheese food in the top of a double boiler.

Gradually add ⅓ cup milk, stirring constantly until the sauce is smooth.

Pour the cheese sauce over the eggs.

Garnish with parsley and serve at once.

MUSHROOMS AND EGGS IN TOMATO-CHEESE SAUCE

⅔ cup margarine
1 cup milk
3 cups grated sharp cheese
1 cup sliced, cooked mushrooms, fresh or canned
2 cans (about 2⅔ cups) condensed tomato soup
1 teaspoon Worcestershire sauce
¼ teaspoon pepper
8 hard-cooked eggs, cut in quarters

Combine all ingredients except eggs in saucepan. Cook over medium heat, stirring constantly, until mixture comes to a boil.

Add and stir in hard-cooked eggs. Serves 8.

CURRIED EGGS

2 tablespoons butter or margarine
¼ teaspoon curry powder
1½ teaspoons salt
½ teaspoon sugar
½ teaspoon prepared mustard
Dash of cayenne pepper
½ cup chopped onion
¼ cup chopped green pepper
1 clove garlic, finely minced
1 No. 2 can (2½ cups) tomatoes
½ cup water
4 hard-cooked eggs, cut in quarters

Melt butter in a saucepan; add curry, salt, sugar, mustard, and pepper; blend well. Add onion, green pepper, and garlic; cook until green pepper and onion are soft, about 5 minutes.

Add tomatoes and water; cook until thickened, about 15 minutes.

Arrange eggs in a buttered 1½-quart casserole. Pour sauce over eggs.

Heat in moderate oven (350°F.) 10 minutes. Serves 4.

SCALLOPED EGGS AND CHEESE

1½ tablespoons butter or margarine
1½ tablespoons flour
¼ teaspoon salt
⅛ teaspoon pepper
⅛ teaspoon paprika
1 teaspoon Worcestershire sauce
1 cup milk
1 cup breadcrumbs
6 hard-cooked eggs, sliced
½ cup grated sharp cheese
3 tablespoons butter or margarine

Melt 1½ tablespoons butter in saucepan; blend in flour and seasonings. Slowly add milk and cook over low heat, stirring constantly, until thick.

Arrange in greased casserole in layers: half the crumbs, eggs, cheese, and sauce. Top with remaining crumbs mixed with 3 tablespoons butter.

Bake in moderate oven (375°F.) until sauce is bubbly and top nicely browned, about 40 minutes. Serve plain, or with tomato sauce. Serves 4.

Egg Cutlets

EGG CROQUETTES OR CUTLETS

4 tablespoons butter or margarine
4 tablespoons flour
1 cup milk, scalded
8 hard-cooked eggs, chopped
¾ teaspoon salt
½ teaspoon pepper
¼ teaspoon paprika
1 tablespoon finely chopped parsley
Pinch of cayenne pepper
2 raw eggs beaten with 2 tablespoons water
Fine breadcrumbs

Melt butter in the top of a double boiler. Blend in flour and gradually add milk. Stir and cook until thickened; then add chopped eggs, salt, pepper, paprika, parsley, and cayenne. Mix well and chill thoroughly.

Shape into croquettes or patties, as desired. Roll in egg beaten with water, then in breadcrumbs, coating completely and evenly.

Fry in hot deep fat (390°F.) for 1 minute. Drain on absorbent paper. Serve with tomato sauce. Serves 6.

EGG AND CHEESE CAKES

4 eggs, beaten
1 tablespoon grated onion
⅓ cup enriched flour
½ teaspoon salt
⅛ teaspoon pepper
1 teaspoon baking powder
⅓ pound sharp cheese
⅓ cup fat for frying

Combine eggs with onion, flour, salt, pepper, and baking powder. Add cheese, cut in ¼-inch cubes.

Heat fat in frying pan until a drop of water sizzles. Dip large spoon of mixture and drop into hot fat.

Brown well on both sides, turning once. Serve promptly with marmalade or jelly. Makes 12 cakes.

Scalloped Eggs and Cheese

TOAD-IN-THE-HOLE

1 slice bread
1 tablespoon butter or margarine
1 egg
Salt and pepper

Remove center from bread with biscuit cutter.

Brown in butter on one side, then turn. Slip egg into "hole." Cook egg to desired firmness. Season to taste. Serves 1.

Toad-in-the-Hole

EGGS BENEDICT

Split and toast English muffins, allowing two halves for each serving or cut slices of bread into 3-inch rounds and toast.

Cover each muffin half or toast round with a slice of broiled or sautéed ham or Canadian bacon and top with a poached egg.

Pour over 1 tablespoon Hollandaise sauce and serve hot.

Eggs Benedict

MUSHROOM EGGS BENEDICT

4 thin slices ham, fried
4 slices toast, buttered
4 eggs, poached
1 can (1¼ cups) condensed cream of
  mushroom soup
⅓ cup milk
1 tablespoon minced parsley

Place fried ham on buttered toast; top each with a poached egg.

Blend soup and milk; heat and pour over ham and eggs. Sprinkle with minced parsley. Serves 4.

MOCK EGGS BENEDICT

Fry thin slices of luncheon meat or ham in butter or margarine until lightly browned on both sides.

Meanwhile, poach number of eggs desired.

Arrange luncheon meat or ham on toast. Top with eggs and spoonful of slightly heated mayonnaise or white sauce.

EGGS CARLTON

Cook bacon slices until crisp.

Season tomato slices with salt and pepper. Roll in flour and sauté in bacon fat. Sprinkle each tomato slice with minced bacon. Serve topped with a poached egg.

Pour Hollandaise sauce over the eggs.

SMOKED SALMON AND EGGS ON TOAST

Thin slices of smoked salmon
Buttered toast
Poached or fried eggs

Dip salmon into boiling water. Drain and place on toast.

Cover with poached or fried eggs.

BROILED EGGS

Heat just enough fat to grease a shallow skillet or flame-proof baking dish. When fat is just hot enough to sizzle a drop of water, break eggs and slip into skillet—from a sauce dish if preferred. Cook on top the range just until edges turn white, about 1 minute.

Place skillet in heated broiler and broil eggs at moderate temperature to desired doneness, 2 to 4 minutes.

Variations: (1) Pour 1 tablespoon of cream per egg into skillet when edges are white and before placing in broiler. (2) Sprinkle over eggs 1 teaspoon grated cheese or buttered crumbs before placing in broiler.

Broiled Eggs

American Fondue

AMERICAN FONDUE
(Master Recipe)

1 cup milk
1 cup soft bread, broken or cubed
1 tablespoon fat
½ teaspoon salt
⅛ teaspoon pepper
3 eggs, separated

Scald milk in double boiler. Add pieces of bread, fat, and seasonings. Cool, then add well beaten egg yolks. Fold in stiffly beaten egg whites.

Place in greased baking dish or in individual molds which have been greased on bottom only. Set in pan of hot water and bake in moderate oven (350°F.) until firm to gentle touch, 50 to 60 minutes.

A knife inserted in center should come out clean. Serves 4 to 6.

American Fondue Variations

Cheese Fondue: Add 1 cup grated cheese to milk mixture. Stir until cheese is melted. Cool and follow master recipe.

Fish Fondue: Follow master recipe, adding 1 to 1½ cups shredded cooked codfish, salmon, lobster, or fresh fish just before folding in egg whites. Serve with any fish sauce. Reduce salt if seafood is salty.

Ham Fondue: Follow master recipe, adding 1 to 1½ cups ground ham just before folding in egg whites. Reduce salt if ham is salty.

Vegetable Fondue: Follow master recipe, adding 1 to 1½ cups corn, chopped spinach, or other vegetable just before folding in egg whites. Reduce salt if necessary. Serve with vegetable or Hollandaise sauce.

PICKLED EGGS—CANADIAN STYLE

2 cups white vinegar
1 teaspoon mixed pickling spice
1 medium-sized lemon, peeled and
  sliced
2 tablespoons sugar
1 teaspoon salt
12 hard-cooked eggs, shelled

Combine first 5 ingredients and simmer 8 minutes. Place the shelled eggs in a wide-mouthed 1½-quart jar. Strain in the hot vinegar.

Cover and chill in refrigerator for several hours before using. The eggs will keep in the pickling solution for several days.

Deviled Eggs En Casserole

DEVILED EGGS EN CASSEROLE

Deviled Eggs:

8 hard-cooked eggs, shelled
1 tablespoon butter or margarine
1/4 teaspoon salt
Few grains pepper
1 teaspoon prepared mustard
1 tablespoon mayonnaise

Cut eggs in half lengthwise; remove yolks and mash until smooth with remaining ingredients.

Refill whites with deviled mixture. Level off filling; put together in pairs, reserving a few halves for garnish.

Cheese Sauce:

3 tablespoons butter or margarine
2 tablespoons minced onion
3 tablespoons flour
1/2 teaspoon salt
1/8 teaspoon pepper
2 cups milk
1 1/4 cups grated American cheese
Fluffy mashed potatoes

Melt butter over low heat, add onion and simmer until tender. Add flour and seasonings; blend.

Gradually add milk and cook until mixture boils and thickens, stirring constantly. Stir in cheese until smooth.

Arrange whole deviled eggs in buttered casserole; pour cheese sauce over them.

Mash 5 or 6 medium-cooked potatoes, season with butter, salt, and pepper. Beat in about 3/4 cup of milk until potatoes are fluffy. Make a border of mashed potatoes on casserole.

Lightly brown potatoes under broiler about 4 inches from source of heat. Serves 6.

POACHED EGGS NEW ORLEANS

3 tablespoons butter or margarine
2 tablespoons flour
1 cup milk
1/2 cup minced cooked shrimp
1/2 teaspoon salt
1/8 teaspoon pepper
1 tablespoon spicy pickle relish
4 poached eggs
4 slices buttered toast

Melt butter or margarine in a saucepan over low heat. Blend in flour. Add milk and cook over low heat until the mixture boils and thickens, stirring constantly.

Add cooked shrimp, salt, pepper, and relish. Cook for 2 minutes, stirring occasionally.

Place poached eggs over buttered toast; cover with hot sauce. Serves 4.

EGGS CREOLE

4 tablespoons oil
1/2 cup chopped onion
1/4 clove garlic, minced (optional)
1/2 cup chopped green pepper
1 cup canned or fresh tomatoes, skinned and quartered
1 cup rice, cooked
Salt and pepper to taste
Tomato juice, if needed
6 eggs
1/2 cup grated cheese
1/4 cup melted butter or margarine

Heat oil; add onion and garlic, and cook over low heat for 10 minutes. Add green pepper and cook 5 minutes longer. Add tomatoes and cooked rice and season to taste. The mixture should be well moistened, so, if fresh tomatoes were not very ripe and juicy, add some tomato juice.

Divide the mixture between 6 individual baking dishes. Make a depression in the middle and break an egg into each. Sprinkle with grated cheese and melted butter.

Bake in a moderate oven (350°F.) 15 to 25 minutes, depending on whether the eggs are to be baked soft or well done. Serve in the dishes. Serves 6.

CREAMED EGG BAKE

4 tablespoons butter or margarine
4 tablespoons flour
1 teaspoon salt
1/8 teaspoon pepper
2 cups milk
2 tablespoons minced onion
1 cup grated American cheese
6 shelled, hard-cooked eggs
1 cup cooked diced celery
1/4 cup slivered olives (green or stuffed)
1/3 cup buttered breadcrumbs

Melt butter; add flour and seasonings and blend. Gradually add milk and cook over low heat until smooth and thickened, stirring constantly.

Add minced onion and grated cheese and stir until cheese is melted.

Cut hard-cooked eggs in quarters lengthwise. Place half the egg slices, half of celery and olive slivers in bottom of buttered 1 1/2-quart casserole. Top with half the sauce. Repeat, sprinkling buttered crumbs on top.

Bake in slow oven (325°F.) for 20 minutes, until lightly browned. Serves 6.

Ham and Egg Surprise

HAM AND EGG SURPRISE

1/2 cup breadcrumbs
1/2 cup milk
1 cup ground baked ham or luncheon meat
1/2 teaspoon prepared mustard
1/4 teaspoon pepper
1 beaten egg
6 hard-cooked eggs, shelled

Mix crumbs and milk in saucepan. Heat slowly. Stir into a paste. Add meat, mustard, pepper, and beaten egg. Mix well.

Cover each hard-cooked egg completely with mixture.

Fry in hot deep fat (375°F.) until lightly browned, 3 to 4 minutes. Drain on absorbent paper.

Serve hot with medium tomato sauce. Serves 6.

EGG-CHEESE-TOMATO CASSEROLE

1 can condensed tomato soup
6 tablespoons mayonnaise
1/4 cup sour cream
1/2 cup milk
2 tablespoons chopped parsley
1/4 teaspoon salt
6 hard-cooked eggs, sliced
1/4 pound American cheese

Combine all ingredients but eggs and cheese. Heat thoroughly. Cut cheese in small thin slices.

In a greased shallow casserole, place an egg slice, overlap with a slice of cheese, then another egg slice and continue until bottom of casserole is covered and all slices have been used. Pour tomato sauce over egg and cheese.

Bake in moderate oven (375°F.) 15 minutes. Serves 4.

Creamed Egg Bake

HOW TO CONVERT DRIED EGGS

Dried Whole Egg: Use 2 tablespoons powdered whole egg plus 2½ tablespoons lukewarm water to equal each fresh whole egg. Add a little water to dried egg. Stir to blend into a medium thick paste with no lumps of egg powder. Gradually add remainder of water and stir or beat until smooth.

Dried Egg Yolk: Use 1½ tablespoons powdered egg yolk plus 1 tablespoon lukewarm water to equal each fresh egg yolk. Follow directions for Dried Whole Egg.

Dried Egg Whites: Use 1 tablespoon powdered egg white plus 2 tablespoons lukewarm water to equal each fresh egg white. Sprinkle egg powder onto water. Let stand 15 minutes or longer to dissolve, stirring occasionally.

MEXICAN EGGS

2   green peppers chopped
1   large sweet onion chopped
1   clove garlic, minced fine, optional
¾ pound luncheon meat or salami sausage, diced
2   tablespoons butter or margarine
1   teaspoon salt
3   large tomatoes, peeled and diced
1   teaspoon chili powder, optional
9   eggs
Melted butter or margarine
Watercress

Cut 6 slices from small end of peppers and chop the rest. after removing seeds.

Peel, slice onion and reserve 6 small slices of small size and chop the rest.

Add chopped vegetables, garlic, and luncheon meat or sausage to butter melted in skillet. Sauté until light brown and add salt and tomatoes. Cook 5 minutes. Add chili powder.

Beat eggs frothy and add tomato mixture to them.

Grease generously the bottom of deep 9-inch layer cake or pudding pan. Pour in egg mixture.

Bake in moderate oven (350°F.) 25 to 30 minutes or until set. Cut in wedges and serve at once garnished with watercress. Serves 6.

Mexican Eggs

EGG AND CHEESE TIMBALES

1½ tablespoons butter or margarine
1   tablespoon flour
1½ cups milk
⅓ pound sharp cheese, chopped
½ teaspoon salt
⅛ teaspoon pepper
1½ teaspoons Worcestershire sauce
½ teaspoon mustard, scant
1½ teaspoons chopped pimiento
3   eggs, beaten

Melt butter. Add flour and blend well. Add milk and cook over low heat, stirring constantly until thickened. Add cheese and stir until blended.

Remove from heat and add seasonings and pimiento. Pour slowly into beaten eggs, stirring constantly. Pour into well greased custard cups.

Set cups in pan of hot water and bake in slow oven (325°F.) until firm, about 45 minutes, or until knife inserted in center comes out clean.

Unmold to serve. Chopped pickle relish, chili sauce, or whole cranberry sauce are good accompaniments. Serves 4.

EGGS BARCELONA

2   tablespoons olive oil
½ cup minced onions
2   cups canned tomatoes
½ teaspoon salt
1   teaspoon chili powder (or less to taste)
1   cup mushrooms, chopped fine
4   tablespoons minced cooked ham
6   eggs
Buttered toast

Heat olive oil in skillet; add onions and cook until light brown.

Add tomatoes, salt, chili powder, mushrooms, and ham. Stir and cook 3 minutes.

Add whole raw eggs, keeping them unbroken. Let cook until eggs are set.

Remove with skimmer and place on slices of buttered toast on a hot platter. Pour sauce around; serve hot. Serves 6.

SWISS PUFF

6   slices buttered toast, cubed
2   cups grated Swiss cheese (½ pound)
3   eggs, slightly beaten
2   cups milk
1   teaspoon salt
¼ teaspoon pepper
½ teaspoon dry mustard
1   teaspoon Worcestershire sauce

Butter a 2-quart casserole and fill with alternate layers of toast cubes and cheese.

Combine eggs, milk, and seasonings; pour over toast-cheese mixture.

Bake in moderate oven (350°F.) 35 minutes, or until a knife inserted in center comes out clean. Serves 4.

Egg Potato Pie

EGG POTATO PIE

2   tablespoons fat
1   tablespoon flour
¼ cup milk
¼ cup grated sharp cheese
½ teaspoon salt
Dash of pepper
6   medium potatoes, cooked and mashed
5   hard-cooked eggs, sliced
2   tablespoons chopped parsley

Melt fat, add flour, blend well and cook over low heat until bubbly.

Add cold milk all at once and cook, stirring constantly, until thickened. Stir in grated cheese. Add salt and pepper.

Line bottom and sides of a greased 8- or 9-inch pie plate or shallow casserole with half of the well seasoned mashed potatoes. Arrange the sliced eggs in potato shell. Top with parsley, cheese sauce, salt and pepper. Cover with remaining mashed potatoes. Brush top with milk.

Bake in moderate oven (350°F.) until nicely browned and thoroughly heated, about 30 minutes. If desired, garnish top with slices of hard-cooked egg. Serves 5.

EGGS TETRAZZINI

½ cup sliced fresh mushrooms
½ cup diced celery
1   tablespoon minced onion
2   tablespoons chopped green pepper
½ cup butter or margarine
¼ cup flour
2   cups milk
1   teaspoon Worcestershire sauce
½ teaspoon salt
Dash of pepper
4   hard-cooked eggs
4   ounces spaghetti, cooked

Cook mushrooms, celery, onion, and green pepper in ¼ cup butter until lightly browned.

Prepare sauce: Blend flour into remaining ¼ cup butter, then gradually add milk. Cook over low heat, stirring constantly, until smooth and thickened. Blend in seasonings and sautéed vegetables.

Chop 3 of the eggs coarsely and blend into mixture. Pile hot cooked spaghetti in center of warm platter. Pour sauce over it. Garnish with slices of remaining hard-cooked egg. Serves 4.

OMELET MAISON

3 ounces (¾ cup chopped) aged American cheese
¼ cup milk
½ cup heavy cream, whipped
2 large mushrooms
4 tablespoons butter or margarine
⅛ teaspoon minced chives
⅛ teaspoon minced parsley
¼ teaspoon salt
⅛ teaspoon pepper
2 eggs, separated
8 stalks or tips of canned or cooked asparagus

Heat together over hot water the cheese and milk. Stir until smooth. Chill and add ½ cup whipped cream. Reserve.

Peel mushrooms, wash, and slice. Sauté in 2 tablespoons butter and add chives, parsley, salt, pepper, and remaining whipped cream.

Beat egg whites stiff and fold in beaten egg yolks. Add mushroom mixture and fold in.

Melt remaining 2 tablespoons butter in small frying pan. Add egg mixture, cover and cook over very low heat until top is dry and bottom a golden brown.

Fold, turn out on serving platter and surround with asparagus. Pour reserved cheese sauce over all and broil quickly until surface is golden brown. Serves 2.

ZESTY BAKED EGGS

⅓ cup salad dressing or mayonnaise
¼ teaspoon salt
⅛ teaspoon pepper
½ teaspoon paprika
½ teaspoon Worcestershire sauce
½ cup milk
1 cup grated sharp cheese
8 eggs

Combine salad dressing and seasoning. Gradually add milk, stirring after each addition until smooth. Add cheese and cook over low heat until cheese is melted, about 5 minutes.

Pour 2 tablespoons of the sauce into each of 4 individual greased baking dishes. Break 2 eggs into each dish and top with remaining sauce. Place in pan of hot water.

Bake in moderate oven (350°F.) until eggs are desired consistency, 12 to 15 minutes. Serves 4.

TOMATO-DEVILED EGGS

4 hard-cooked eggs
¼ cup mayonnaise
1 tablespoon minced parsley
1 teaspoon minced onion
1 can (1¼ cups) condensed tomato soup
2 teaspoons prepared mustard
1 teaspoon lemon juice or vinegar

Split eggs lengthwise; scoop out yolks and combine with mayonnaise, parsley, and onion. Fill egg whites with this mixture.

Place eggs in a shallow baking dish and cover with a sauce made by combining soup, mustard, and lemon juice. Bake in a moderate oven (350°F.) about 15 minutes. Serves 4.

PEACH OMELET WITH MINT CHEESE SPREAD

1 tablespoon butter or margarine
6 eggs, slightly beaten
6 tablespoons cream
½ teaspoon salt
2 tablespoons melted butter or margarine
1 cup sliced, cooked peaches
¼ cup sugar
1 tablespoon lemon juice

Melt butter in a skillet. Combine beaten eggs, cream, salt, and butter. Pour egg mixture into a skillet. As mixture cooks on the bottom and sides, prick with a fork so that the uncooked egg mixture will flow to the bottom of the skillet.

Just before it is ready to be folded, place the sliced peaches on half of the omelet. Fold, and sprinkle with sugar and lemon juice.

Place skillet under a preheated broiler (300°F.) for a few minutes. Turn out on a hot platter and serve immediately. Serve with toast spread with Mint Cheese Spread. Serves 6.

Mint Cheese Spread:

1 3-ounce package cream cheese
1 tablespoon chopped mint leaves
1 tablespoon cream

Combine cream cheese, mint, and cream. Makes ½ cup.

SHERRIED SCRAMBLED EGGS WITH MUSHROOMS

2 tablespoons butter or margarine
1 cup sliced mushrooms
8 eggs, beaten
¼ cup light cream
¼ cup sherry
2 teaspoons salt
¼ teaspoon pepper
¼ teaspoon paprika

Melt butter or margarine in saucepan or chafing dish. Add mushrooms and cook slowly 5 minutes.

Add beaten eggs to which cream, sherry, salt, pepper, and paprika have been added.

Cook over hot water (or over very low heat), stirring constantly as mixture begins to thicken. Cook until creamy and to the desired degree of firmness. Serve at once. Serves 4 or more.

Eggs A La King on Corn Rings

EGGS A LA KING ON CORN RINGS

1 tablespoon butter or meat drippings
1 tablespoon minced onion
3 tablespoons flour
2 cups milk
1 teaspoon salt
⅛ teaspoon pepper
½ teaspoon Worcestershire sauce
¼ cup chopped green pepper
6 hard-cooked eggs, sliced
6 slices fried corn meal mush

Melt butter in top of double boiler over direct heat. Add minced onion and cook until tender.

Stir in flour and add milk, seasonings, Worcestershire sauce, and green pepper.

Cook over hot water, stirring until smooth and thickened. Add hard-cooked egg slices.

Serve on rounds of fried corn meal mush. Serves 6.

Corn Meal Mush: Pour cooked cornmeal into a round can or mold that has been rinsed in cold water. Cover, and chill until firm.

Cut into ½-inch slices; dip in flour and sauté in drippings until crisp and brown.

HOLLANDAISE SARDINE-EGG NESTS

2 English muffins
4 eggs
2 3¼-ounce cans sardines
1 cup Hollandaise sauce

Cut muffins in half and toast. Poach eggs.

Place sardines on muffins; add a poached egg to each serving and top with sauce. Serves 4.

Hollandaise Sardine-Egg Nests

STUFFED EGG AND SPINACH CASSEROLE

2 cups cooked spinach
3 tablespoons melted butter or margarine
1 small onion, chopped
1/4 cup flour
1 cup milk
1/2 cup spinach liquid
1 teaspoon salt
Dash of pepper
1/2 teaspoon prepared horseradish
1/2 teaspoon prepared mustard
6 hard-cooked eggs

Drain spinach (reserve liquid) and chop fine. Melt butter in top of double boiler over boiling water. Add onion and cook until tender. Stir in flour until well blended.

Add milk and spinach liquid and cook, stirring constantly, until mixture thickens. Season with salt and pepper. Add horseradish and mustard. Fold in chopped spinach and reheat. Pour into greased casserole.

Top with stuffed eggs made as follows: Cut hard-cooked eggs in halves lengthwise. Remove yolks and mash with 2 tablespoons minced onion, 1/4 teaspoon prepared mustard, 3 tablespoons salad dressing, 1/4 teaspoon salt, and a dash of pepper.

Refill whites with mixture. Place stuffed eggs on top of creamed spinach.

Cover and bake in moderate oven (375°F.) 15 minutes. Serves 6.

OMELET WITH MUSHROOMS IN WINE

1/4 cup butter or margarine
Juice of 1 lemon
Salt and pepper
1/2 cup rhine or sauterne wine
1/2 pound fresh mushrooms, sliced
6 eggs, separated
6 tablespoons milk

Heat 2 tablespoons butter or margarine in a skillet. Add lemon juice, 1/2 teaspoon salt, dash of pepper, and the wine. Simmer mushrooms in this mixture until cooked.

Prepare omelet as follows: Add milk, 1/2 teaspoon salt, and dash of pepper to the egg yolks which have been beaten until light.

Fold into stiffly beaten egg whites.

Melt remaining 2 tablespoons butter or margarine in skillet, and heat well.

Pour omelet mixture into hot skillet, and cook over low heat for 3 to 5 minutes.

Then place omelet in a moderate oven (350°F.), and bake for about 15 minutes. The omelet is done when it springs back when indented with the fingertip.

Crease omelet through the center and place half the mushrooms on one side of the omelet, folding the other half of omelet over mushrooms. Serve on hot platter topped with remaining mushrooms. Serves 6.

STUFFED EGGS ON RICE WITH CURRY SAUCE

1/4 cup margarine
1/4 cup flour
2 cups milk
1/2 teaspoon salt
1/2 teaspoon curry powder
Dash of black pepper
4 cups fluffy cooked rice
2 tablespoons margarine
3 hard-cooked eggs
3 tablespoons minced cooked shrimp
1/4 teaspoon salt
1/4 teaspoon dry mustard
1 tablespoon mayonnaise
1 pound cooked shrimp

Melt 1/4 cup margarine in a saucepan. Blend in flour. Remove from heat and stir in milk. Cook until it is medium thick, stirring constantly.

Add salt, curry powder, and pepper. Spoon 2 tablespoons of the sauce into each casserole.

Mix rice with the 2 tablespoons margarine and place 2/3 cup in each casserole over the sauce.

Stuff egg whites with egg yolks mixed with minced shrimp, salt, mustard, and mayonnaise. Place over the rice.

Place 5 to 6 whole shrimp around each egg. Brush with melted margarine.

Heat in moderate oven (350°F.) 15 to 20 minutes. Serve with hot curry sauce. Serves 6.

CREOLE SCRAMBLED EGGS IN BREAD BASKETS

6 eggs, unbeaten
1/4 cup cream
1/2 teaspoon salt
Dash of pepper
1/2 teaspoon onion juice
1/2 cup chopped, cooked bacon
2 tablespoons finely chopped pimiento or green pepper
2 tablespoons butter or margarine

Break eggs into a mixing bowl; add cream, salt, pepper, onion juice, bacon, and pimiento. Beat slightly.

Melt butter in a skillet over low heat. Pour egg mixture into skillet and cook slowly without stirring until eggs are partially cooked. Then stir with fork, loosening sides and scraping bottom of pan so liquid portion can pour down.

Continue cooking until eggs are done to firmness desired. Spoon egg mixture into bread baskets. Serves 6.

Eggs de Jonghe

EGGS DE JONGHE

8 poached eggs
2 cups soft breadcrumbs
1/4 cup butter or margarine, melted
1/2 teaspoon garlic salt
1/2 teaspoon pepper
6 slices luncheon meat, halved
Paprika

Poach eggs for 2 or 3 minutes only. If necessary, keep eggs hot until all are poached by holding them in a shallow pan of warm water.

Combine crumbs with melted butter or margarine and seasonings. Put a thin layer in the bottom of 4 preheated shallow baking dishes.

Place 2 poached eggs in each dish with 3 half slices of luncheon meat on the side. Top with remaining crumbs.

Place under broiler or in a very hot oven (450°F.) until crumbs are browned, 3 to 8 minutes. (If placed under broiler, watch carefully!) Add a dash of paprika before serving. Serves 4.

Note: A crushed or minced garlic clove and salt may be used instead of garlic salt for seasoning.

EGGS ON TOAST WITH SHERRY CREAM SAUCE

2 tablespoons butter or margarine
2 tablespoons chopped green pepper
2 tablespoons flour
3/4 cup milk
1/4 cup sherry
1/2 teaspoon salt
1/4 teaspoon pepper
1/2 teaspoon Worcestershire sauce
1 teaspoon sugar
1/4 cup chili sauce (optional)
6 slices buttered toast
6 hard-cooked eggs

Melt butter or margarine; add green pepper and cook 3 minutes.

Shake flour and milk in a covered container until the mixture is smooth. Add to butter and green pepper and cook, stirring constantly, until thickened and smooth.

Add sherry, salt, pepper, Worcestershire sauce, and sugar. Add chili sauce if desired.

Slice eggs and arrange 1 sliced egg on each slice of toast. Pour sauce over the eggs on toast. Serve hot. Serves 6.

FACTS ABOUT FOOD AND COOKING

Guides to Better Cooking

SUCCESS WITH RECIPES

1. Read the recipe carefully.
2. Check your supplies to see that you have the necessary ingredients.
3. Assemble the ingredients and equipment needed for measuring, mixing, cooking, or baking—spoons, cups, bowl, pans, etc.
4. Light the oven if a preheated oven is necessary.
5. Use level measurements; measure the ingredients accurately.
6. Follow the procedure given for combining ingredients.
7. Follow directions given for cooking and baking. Use as nearly as possible the size pan indicated. Follow cooking time or baking time and temperatures given; also test for doneness by physical means since oven heat varies. Use thermometers for baking, deep fat frying, and candy making.
8. Handle finished product as indicated. Follow directions for removing from pan, molding, chilling, etc.
9. In making substitutions in a recipe, follow the rules for substitution and equivalents carefully.
10. To reduce a recipe choose a recipe in which the ingredients may be divided easily. Measure smaller quantities carefully. It is not practical to reduce successfully certain recipes as boiled frosting, steamed puddings, etc.
11. To increase a recipe, it is best not to exceed doubling the quantities of ingredients at one time. When the recipe is doubled, the cooking time is not necessarily increased since the larger quantity may be baked in two pans or a larger pan of no greater depth.

CORRECT MEASURING METHODS

Use standard measuring cups and spoons. Measure dry ingredients before measuring liquids to save extra dish.

Part of cup: Use tablespoons or the smaller measuring cups—½, ⅓, ¼—for greater accuracy.

White sugar: If lumpy, sift before measuring. Do not pack down; lift lightly into cup. Level off with spatula or straight knife.

Brown sugar: Pack firmly into cup or spoon, so that when turned out it will hold shape of cup or spoon. If lumpy, roll and sift before measuring.

Syrup and molasses: Rinse spoon or cup in cold water before measuring.

Solid fats: When fat comes in 1-pound rectangular form, 1 cup or fraction can be cut from pound which measures about 2 cups. Or measure cupful by packing firmly into cup and leveling off top with spatula or straight knife.

Water method may be used for part of cup. To measure ½ cup fat, for instance, put ½ cup cold water in 1-cup measure. Add fat, pushing under water until water level stands at 1-cup mark. Pour out water and remove fat.

White flour: Sift once. Lift lightly into cup. Level off top with spatula or straight knife.

Other flours, fine meals, fine crumbs, dried eggs, dry milk: Stir instead of sifting. Measure like flour.

Baking powder, cornstarch, cream of tartar, spices: Stir to loosen. Dip measuring spoon into can, bring up heaping full, level with spatula or knife.

Liquids: Place standard glass measuring cup on a flat surface. Bend down so that you can read the measure at eye level. A safety rim above the full cup mark is provided so that you can get accurate measurements without spilling a drop.

Oil or melted fat: When it's necessary to measure by spoon, pour oil into a cup. Dip measuring spoon into the oil. Lift out carefully; the spoon should be so full it won't hold another drop.

OVEN TEMPERATURES

At least once a year have your oven regulator tested for accuracy by the utility company that serves your area, because even the best range becomes inaccurate occasionally and requires expert attention to re-set it.

Very slow oven	250°–275°F.
Slow oven	300°–325°F.
Moderate oven	350°–375°F.
Hot oven	400°–425°F.
Very hot oven	450°–475°F.
Extremely hot oven	500°–525°F.

CAN SIZES

Of the different sizes of cans used by commercial canners the most common are:

8 ounces	=	1 cup
No. 1 flat	=	1 cup or 9 oz.
No. 1 tall	=	2 cups or 16 oz.
No. 303	=	2 cups or 16 oz.
No. 2 vacuum	=	1¾ cups or 12 oz.
No. 2	=	2½ cups or 20 oz.
No. 2½	=	3½ cups or 28 oz.
No. 3 cylinder	=	5¾ cups or 46 oz.
No. 10	=	13 cups or 6 lbs., 10 oz.

For accurate measuring use standard utensils, not table cups and spoons.

HANDY EQUIVALENTS

	Unit	Measure
Almonds	1 lb.	1 cup, shelled
Apricots, dried	1 lb. (3½ cups)	4½ cups, cooked
Beans, dried	1 cup, dry	2½ cups, cooked
Breadcrumbs, dry	3 to 4 slices bread	1 cup
Breadcrumbs, soft	1 slice bread	¾ cup
Butter or margarine	1 oz.	2 tablespoons
Butter or margarine	¼ lb. or 1 stick	½ cup
Cabbage	1 pound	4 cups, shredded
Cheese, American	1 pound	4 to 5 cups, grated
Cherries, red	1 quart	2 cups, pitted
Chocolate	1 oz.	1 square
Coconut-shredded	1 lb.	6 cups
Corn meal	1 cup	4 cups, cooked
Cottage cheese	1 lb.	2 cups
Crackers, graham	9 crackers, coarsely crumbled	1 cup
Crackers, graham	11 crackers, finely crumbled	1 cup
Crackers, salted, large	7 crackers, coarsely crumbled	1 cup
Crackers, salted, large	9 crackers, finely crumbled	1 cup
Crackers, soda	16 small squares	1 cup coarse crumbs
Crackers, soda	20 to 22 small squares	1 cup fine crumbs
Cranberries	1 lb.	3 to 3½ cups sauce
Cream cheese	3 oz. package	6⅔ tablespoons
Currants	1 lb.	3 cups
Dates, pitted	1 lb.	2½ cups
Eggs, whole	4–6	1 cup
Eggs, whites	8–10	1 cup
Eggs, yolks	12–14	1 cup
Flour:		
All-purpose-enriched	1 lb.	4 cups, unsifted
Cake	1 lb.	4½ cups, unsifted
Whole wheat	1 lb.	4 cups
Lemon juice	1 aver. lemon	3 to 4 tablespoons
Lemon rind	1 aver. lemon	1½ teaspoons grated rind
Macaroni, spaghetti, noodles	½ lb.	4 cups, cooked
Marshmallows	¼ lb.	16 marshmallows
Marshmallows	1 lb.	4 cups (64)
Molasses	1 lb.	1½ cups
Nutmeats	1 lb.	4 cups, shelled
Nutmeats, chopped	¼ lb.	1 cup
Oats, quick-cooking	1 cup	1¾ cups, cooked
Orange juice	1 aver. orange	6 to 8 tablespoons juice
Orange rind	1 aver. orange	1 tablespoon grated rind
Peaches, dried	1 lb. (3 cups)	4 cups, cooked
Prunes, dried	1 lb. (2¾ cups)	4 cups, cooked
Raisins	1 lb.	2 cups, packed
Rice	1 lb.	2 cups, uncooked; about 6 cups cooked
Rice, precooked	1 cup	2 cups, cooked
Sugar:		
Brown	1 lb.	2 cups, firmly packed
Confectioners'	1 lb.	4 cups, sifted
Granulated	1 lb.	2 cups
Vanilla wafers, small	20 wafers, coarsely crumbled	1 cup
Vanilla wafers, small	30 wafers, finely crumbled	1 cup
Walnuts, in shell	1 lb.	2 cups, shelled
Whipping cream	½ pint	2 cups when whipped
Zwieback	7 coarsely crumbled	1 cup
Zwieback	9 finely crumbled	1 cup

WEIGHTS AND MEASURES

Measurements in all recipes are level and based on standard measuring spoons, cups, etc. Table silverware spoons do not correspond accurately with the capacity of measuring spoons.

Dash, pinch	=	Less than ⅛ teaspoon
3 teaspoons	=	1 tablespoon
2 tablespoons	=	1 ounce liquid or fat
2 tablespoons	=	⅛ cup
4 tablespoons	=	¼ cup
5⅓ tablespoons	=	⅓ cup
8 tablespoons	=	½ cup
10⅔ tablespoons	=	⅔ cup
12 tablespoons	=	¾ cup
16 tablespoons	=	1 cup or 8 ounces
½ cup	=	1 gill
4 gills	=	1 pint
1 cup	=	½ pint (8 oz.)
16 ounces	=	1 pound
2 cups	=	1 pint
1 pint	=	1 pound liquid or fat
2 pints or 4 cups	=	1 quart or 32 ounces
4 quarts (liquid)	=	1 gallon
8 quarts, solid	=	1 peck
4 pecks	=	1 bushel
1 pony	=	⅓ ounce
1 jigger	=	1½ ounces
1 shell	=	1½ ounces

1 wine glass = 4 ounces = 8 tablespoons = ½ cup (This is a claret glass and is most commonly used in the average home.)

1 sherry glass = 3 ounces = 6 tablespoons

1 port glass = 2 ounces = 4 tablespoons = ¼ cup

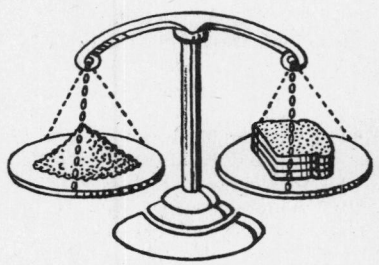

HOW MUCH TO BUY

How much meat to buy for dinner? How many servings will come from a pound of fresh beans, a No. 2½ can, or a frozen package? The food shopper with an eye to thrift and good management learns to buy carefully just what she can use.

The figures below and on the following page can help you decide how much to buy and, when reading market ads, you can use these figures to help decide what are real bargains.

The amount of meat, poultry, and fish per serving varies with the amount of bone and fat. It also varies with the amount of extenders—such as stuffing, potatoes, rice—used with the meat.

Size of serving for each fruit and vegetable is given for whichever way it is most commonly served—cooked or uncooked. Size of serving for dry beans and peas and for cereals and cereal products—except flaked and puffed—is given for the cooked form.

MEAT

	Amount to buy per serving
Much bone or gristle ...	1/2 to 1 pound
Medium amounts of bone	1/3 to 1/2 pound
Little bone	1/4 to 1/3 pound
No bone	1/8 to 1/4 pound

POULTRY
(Dressed weight[1])

Chicken:	
Broiling	1/4 to 1/2 bird
Frying and roasting ..	3/4 to 1 pound
Stewing	1/3 to 3/4 pound
Ducks	1 to 1 1/4 pounds
Geese	3/4 to 1 pound
Turkeys	2/3 to 3/4 pound

POULTRY
(Ready-to-cook weight[1])

Chicken:	
Broiling	1/4 to 1/2 bird
Frying, roasting	2/3 to 3/4 pound
Stewing	1/4 to 2/3 pound
Ducks	3/4 to 1 pound
Geese	2/3 to 3/4 pound
Turkeys	About 1/2 pound

1 Number of servings depends on kind, weight, age, sex, grade and way prepared.

FISH

Whole or round	1 pound
Dressed, large	1/2 pound
Steaks, fillets	1/4 pound

CEREALS AND CEREAL PRODUCTS

	Size of serving	Servings per pound
Flaked corn cereals	1 cup	18–24
Other flaked cereals	3/4 cup	21
Puffed cereals	1 cup	32–38
Corn meal	3/4 cup	16
Wheat cereals:		
Coarse	3/4 cup	12
Fine	3/4 cup	16–22
Oatmeal	3/4 cup	13
Hominy grits	1/2 cup	20
Macaroni and noodles	3/4 cup	12
Rice	1/2 cup	16
Spaghetti	3/4 cup	13

VEGETABLES AND FRUITS

Fresh	Size of serving	Servings per pound[2]
Asparagus:		
Cut	1/2 cup	4
Spears	4–5 stalks	4
Beans, lima	1/2 cup	2[3]
Beans, snap	1/2 cup	6
Beets, diced	1/2 cup	4
Broccoli	2 stalks	3–4
Brussels sprouts	1/2 cup	5–6
Cabbage:		
Raw, shredded	1/2 cup	7–8
Cooked	1/2 cup	4–5
Carrots:		
Raw, shredded	1/2 cup	8
Cooked	1/2 cup	5
Cauliflower	1/2 cup	3
Celery, cooked	1/2 cup	3–4
Collards	1/2 cup	2
Corn, cut	1/2 cup	2[4]
Eggplant	1/2 cup	4
Onions, cooked	1/2 cup	4
Parsnips	1/2 cup	4
Peas	1/2 cup	2[3]
Potatoes	1/2 cup	4–5
Spinach	1/2 cup	3–4
Squash	1/2 cup	2–3
Sweet potatoes	1/2 cup	3–4
Turnips	1/2 cup	4
Apricots	2 medium	5–6
Berries, raw	1/2 cup	4–5
Cherries, pitted, cooked	1/2 cup	2
Plums	2 large	4
Rhubarb, cooked	1/2 cup	4

For apples, bananas, oranges, and pears, count on about 3 to a pound; peaches, 4 to a pound.

Dry		
Dry beans	3/4 cup	9
Dry peas, lentils	3/4 cup	7

Canned		Per can
8-ounce can	1/2 cup	2
No. 2 can	1/2 cup	4–5
No. 2 1/2 can	1/2 cup	6–7
No. 3 cylinder (46 oz.)	1/2 cup	11–12

Frozen		Per package
Family-size packages	1/2 cup	3–4
Juices, concentrated, 6 fluid ounces	1/2 cup	6

2 As purchased. 3 In pod. 4 In husk.

EMERGENCY SUBSTITUTIONS

For these	You may use these
1 whole egg, for thickening or baking	2 egg yolks. Or 2 tablespoons dried whole egg plus 2 1/2 tablespoons water.
1 cup butter or margarine for shortening	7/8 cup lard, or rendered fat, with 1/2 teaspoon salt. Or 1 cup hydrogenated fat (cooking fat sold under brand name) with 1/2 teaspoon salt.
1 square (ounce) chocolate	3 or 4 tablespoons cocoa plus 1/2 tablespoon fat.
1 teaspoon double-acting baking powder	1 1/2 teaspoons phosphate baking powder. Or 2 teaspoons tartrate baking powder.
Sweet milk and baking powder, for baking	Equal amount of sour milk plus 1/2 teaspoon baking soda per cup. (Each half teaspoon soda with 1 cup sour milk takes the place of 2 teaspoons baking powder and 1 cup sweet milk.)
1 cup sour milk, for baking	1 cup sweet milk mixed with one of the following: 1 tablespoon vinegar. Or 1 tablespoon lemon juice. Or 1 3/4 teaspoons cream of tartar.
1 cup whole milk	1/2 cup evaporated milk plus 1/2 cup water. Or 4 tablespoons dry whole milk plus 1 cup water. Or 4 tablespoons nonfat dry milk plus 2 teaspoons table fat and 1 cup water.
1 cup skim milk	4 tablespoons nonfat dry milk plus 1 cup water.
1 tablespoon flour, for thickening	1/2 tablespoon cornstarch, potato starch, rice starch, or arrowroot starch. Or 1 tablespoon granulated tapioca.
1 cup cake flour, for baking	7/8 cup all-purpose (enriched) flour.
1 cup all-purpose (enriched) flour, for baking breads	Up to 1/2 cup bran, whole-wheat flour, or corn meal plus enough all-purpose (enriched) flour to fill cup.

Terms Used in Recipes

Certain terms which might require further explanation recur in recipes; also some words which are occasionally found in recipes are not generally familiar. If any of the cookery methods and terms are new to you, read below and you'll find precise definitions.

AGE

A term often applied to the ripening and tenderizing of game and other meats by allowing them to hang for a time in a cool place, usually a refrigerator. Cheese, wine, and other food products are similarly aged in order to develop their flavor fully.

ASPIC

A jelly made from meat, poultry, or fish stock that has been boiled down sufficiently to become firm when cold. Also fish or vegetable stock or tomato juice that has been thickened with gelatin. It is used to make molded salads or to give a shiny, transparent coat to meats and other foods. In classical cookery the term is applied only to the entire dish, not to the jelly itself.

BAKE

To cook by dry heat, usually in an oven or ovenlike appliance. As modern recipes use it, "bake" simply means to cook in the oven. When applied to certain meats in uncovered containers, it's generally called roasting.

A recipe should tell you the kind and size of pan; whether the dish should be baked with or without a cover; the temperature, and baking time or similar way to determine when the dish is done. See also **Roast.**

BARBECUE

A term of West Indian or South American origin. As an American institution, started in the South, a barbecue is traditionally an open-air gathering (political or social) at which a hog or a steer is broiled or roasted whole over an open fire and food and drink are liberally enjoyed.

To barbecue: to cook with direct heat in a broiler, over coals, or in the oven, basting frequently with a highly seasoned sauce. The word may also mean any food, especially sliced or chopped meat, that is cooked or served in such a sauce.

BARD

To cover lean meat, poultry, or fish with a layer of fat before cooking it, in order to prevent it from drying out. See **Lard.**

BASTE

To moisten foods during cooking with pan drippings, water, or special sauce, to prevent drying, or to add flavor.

BATTER

A flour and liquid mixture usually containing eggs, sugar, and leavening, soft enough to be stirred or mixed with a spoon, as opposed to dough, a similar mixture which is so stiff that it must be mixed with the hands, or rolled on a board or cloth and cut. Usually you speak of cake or pancake batter, cooky or bread dough.

BEAT

To make a mixture smooth, or add air by using a brisk whipping or stirring motion with a spoon, an electric mixer, or a hand rotary beater.

If you use a spoon, mix vigorously with a rapid over-and-over rotary motion. If you are doing your beating with an electric mixer or a hand rotary beater, use medium-to-fast speed.

BIND

To thicken with a binder, i.e., ingredients such as flour, starch, eggs, cream; to mix chopped meat, vegetables, etc., with a sauce.

BIRD

This is a general term applied to poultry and game birds.

It also refers to "meat birds," a dish made in various ways but usually consisting of stuffed thin oblong pieces of beef or veal, rolled, and tied or skewered. They are then coated with flour, browned, and cooked in a small amount of liquid.

BLANCH

To preheat in boiling water or steam. Used to aid in removal of skins from nuts, fruits, and some vegetables. Also used to inactivate enzymes and shrink food in preparation for canning, freezing, and drying. Vegetables are blanched in boiling water or steam; fruits in boiling water, syrup, fruit juice, or steam.

Blanch—Pour hot water over foods to blanch them. Soak for a few minutes.

BLEND

To combine (mix) two or more ingredients together to bring about a change of color, texture, or flavor. It's done by stirring or creaming, or by a combination of the two techniques. When you're adding or blending a thin liquid into a thick mixture in an electric mixer, low is not only the best speed but the least likely to be splashy.

BOIL

To boil means to cook in liquid at boiling temperature (212°F.) at sea level. When this point is reached, adjust heat to maintain it.

The term "boiling" is so frequently misunderstood by cooks that it requires elaboration. For example, many a cook mistakenly thinks that the harder a food boils, the quicker it is done. And the term is often incorrectly applied to such foods as "boiled" beef. Actually most foods are simmered, not boiled, as water below the boiling point is kinder to food proteins. Eggs, meat, poultry, fish, are or should be simmered. Jellies and vegetables are boiled.

Here we explain everyday recipe phrases for boiling.

Bring to the Boiling Point or Bring to a Boil: This signifies the step before cooking. You'll know that water or any liquid is reaching that point when bubbles appear at the bottom, rise to the top, then break. When a vapor appears and all liquid is in motion, it's come to a boil.

Boil Rapidly: This follows boiling. The liquid goes into rapid motion; the surface breaks into small lumpy waves.

A rapid boil won't cook food faster, but for some uses it's better; it starts cereals (keep particles separated), to evaporate soup or jam, to concentrate candy.

Full Rolling Boil: This is the point at which the liquid rises in the pan, then tumbles into great waves that can't be stirred down. It happens only in heavy sugar mixtures like candy or frosting, and in jelly-making when jelly is about done or when liquid pectin is about to be added.

See also: **Simmer: Parboil: Scald: Steam: Blanch: Poach: Steep.**

BONE (In meat cookery)

To bone meat is to remove the bone from it. This is usually done to make carving easier or to allow for stuffing.

BOUILLON

Clear, seasoned stock or broth usually made from browned beef. For many purposes, a quick substitute is 1 meat bouillon cube or ½ teaspoon concentrated meat extract dissolved in 1 cup hot water.

BOUILLON CUBE

A small cube of concentrated chicken meat, or vegetable stock used with boiling water to make a kind of broth.

BRAISE

To cook slowly in a small amount of liquid in a tightly covered utensil on top of range or in the oven. The food may or may not be browned (usually it is browned) in a small amount of fat before braising. It's a highly recommended method for the less tender cuts of meat or poultry.

BREAD

To coat with fine breadcrumbs alone, or to coat with breadcrumbs, then with slightly diluted beaten egg or milk, and again with breadcrumbs.

HINTS FOR COOKING BREADED FOODS

● Breaded foods have a tendency to stick to the pan and to lose their coating when they are fried in shallow fat. The best way to prevent this is to bread the foods ahead of time and let them stand on waxed paper at least 20 minutes, turning them over several times.

● When cooking these foods in shallow fat, turn them carefully with a spatula or pancake turner.

● If breaded meats are to be braised in gravy after frying, keep the temperature just at simmering. Boiling loosens the delicate coating more than simmering.

● In deep-fat frying the breading may have a tendency to break off if the surface of the foods is not completely covered with egg and crumbs or the foods are fried too soon after they are crumbed.

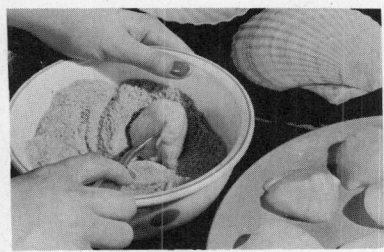

Breading

BREW

To cook or steep in hot liquid until the flavor is extracted, as with tea.

BRINE

A solution of salt to which other preservatives may be added; used for preserving meats, vegetables, etc.

BRITTLE

A test used in sugar cookery; it has the same meaning as crack; also a very hard, brittle candy, as peanut brittle.

BROIL

To cook by exposing to direct heat, usually in a broiler or over coals. The recommended method is to use constant moderate temperatures. See also **Pan-Broil; Barbecue; Toast.**

BROTH

Clear soup, obtained by simmering meat, poultry, game, fish, or shellfish, in water, generally with the addition of vegetables or herbs, then removing fat and straining.

BROWN

To make food brown either by cooking it in a small amount of fat on top of the range or by exposing it to dry heat in the oven.

BRUSH

To spread with butter or margarine, egg, etc., thinly with a brush or small paper or cloth.

BURNT SUGAR

See **Caramel.**

BUTTERSCOTCH

A term applied to various foods flavored with a large proportion of brown sugar and butter.

CANDY

To cook in sugar or syrup when applied to sweet potatoes and carrots. When applied to fruit, fruit peel, or ginger, to cook in heavy syrup until plump and transparent, then drain and dry.

CARAMEL

Burnt sugar, made by slowly melting the sugar and heating it until it is golden brown—a process called caramelizing. The browning of the sugar produces a distinctive flavor. When cooked until all its sweetness has disappeared, caramel is used to color brown sauces. The term caramel also means a chewy candy made from sugar, milk or cream, and corn syrup.

TO CARAMELIZE SUGAR

Rub a heavy skillet lightly with butter. Pour in sugar, not more than $1/2$ cup at a time, and set skillet over moderate heat. Stir constantly until the sugar melts. Add more sugar, $1/2$ cup at a time, and stir as before until you have as much clear brown syrup as desired.

CARAMEL SYRUP

Caramelize 1 cup sugar as above, and add $1/2$ cup boiling water very slowly so that the mixture will not boil over. Simmer 10 minutes.

CARAMEL COLORING FOR GRAVIES

Caramelize sugar and continue cooking it until it is almost black. Then add boiling water very slowly and let simmer until the sugar dissolves. Store in a covered container and use as needed to color gravy. No sweet flavor remains.

CASING

A covering into which sausage meat is packed. Formerly cleaned animal intestine was always used; nowadays various synthetic substitutes are common.

CHILL

To allow to become thoroughly cold but not frozen.

CHOP (The food)

A small cut of meat, usually from the rib or loin; the name is derived from the fact that the piece is chopped off.

CHOP (The cooking term)

To cut food into smaller pieces with a scissors, a knife and cutting board, chopping knife and bowl, or some type of mechanical cutter. When a large knife and cutting board are used, one hand holds knife tip on board; the other moves knife blade up and down through food. For a quick job, cut a whole bunch of celery, onions, or rhubarb at one time.

Chop—A heavy knife and hardwood board do a quick chopping job.

CHOWDER

A thick unstrained soup, especially one made of fish, clams, etc., cooked with vegetables, often in milk.

CLARIFY

To clear a liquid, such as consommé, by adding slightly beaten egg white and egg shells. The beaten egg coagulates in the hot liquid and the particles which cause cloudiness adhere to it. The mixture is then strained.

CLOVE

A segment of a bulb, as of garlic.

COAT

To cover the surface with fine crumbs, batter, or seasoned flour, sugar, etc. To do this, use shaker-top can or sifter to sprinkle with flour, sugar, etc. Or roll in these until coated. Or shake with flour, breadcrumbs, etc., in paper bag until coated.

COATS SPOON

A term used with reference to mixtures, such as custards, that thicken when cooked. It indicates the point at which a thin, even film adheres to a spoon that is dipped into the mixture and then allowed to drip.

CODDLE

To cook gently, as an egg, by heating in water just below the boiling point.

COLANDER

A bowl-shaped, footed sieve or perforated container used for draining off liquids.

COMPOTE

A mixture of stewed fruit, often dried, but whole or halved with special attention given to retaining their shape. Served cold in a syrup.

Compote

CONDIMENT

A seasoning or relish for food, as pepper, mustard, sauces, etc.

CONFECTION

A synonym for candy, but it is often used to include a wide range of sweet foods.

CONNECTIVE TISSUE

A tissue in meats, usually of white elastic fiber that binds together and supports outside tissue.

CONSOMMÉ

A clear, concentrated stock or broth usually made from a combination of two or more kinds of meat, such as beef, veal, and poultry plus some vegetables for seasoning. It is well seasoned, strained, and clarified.

For many purposes, a quick substitute is 1 chicken bouillon cube dissolved in 1 cup hot water.

CORN

To preserve or pickle in brine.

CORNUCOPIAS

Cone-shaped paper containers for nuts, candy, etc.; pastry rolls filled with whipped cream or meringue with nuts; cone-shaped slices of bread, meats, fish, etc., with various fillings served as hors d'oeuvres.

CRACKLINGS

The crisp, crunchy morsels left after rendering pork or poultry fat. In earlier days, when families butchered their own hogs, it was much used in corn bread and for nibbling.

CREAM (The cookery term)

To cream means to rub, stir, or beat with spoon or electric mixer until the mixture is soft, smooth and creamy.

If you use a spoon, a wooden one is preferred, and you cream with the back of the spoon, working or pressing one ingredient or more against the side of the bowl continuously until soft and creamy.

If you use an electric mixer, set the speed at low.

The word "cream" is often used instead of "blend" in instructions for combining a fat with sugar.

CREOLE

(French): Pertaining to the Creoles. The Creoles in the United States are descendants of French or Spanish settlers of Louisiana.

The term is applied to soups, garnishes, sauces, etc., prepared in a manner characteristic of the Creoles. Tomatoes, peppers, okra, onions, filé powder and other seasonings are usually characteristic of these dishes.

CRISP

To make firm or brittle in cold water, as vegetables, or in moderate dry heat, as crackers.

CROQUETTE

A term derived from the French *croquer*, to crunch. It is usually a small, rounded or cone-shaped mass of chopped meat, fish, or vegetables, fried or baked to obtain a crisp coat.

Hints for Making Croquettes

Although croquettes are sometimes made with freshly cooked ingredients (finely chopped or ground chicken, oysters, meat, lobster, etc.) more frequently they are a means of utilizing leftover food. Specific directions are given with various croquette recipes throughout this book.

In general, however, to make croquettes prepare thick white sauce (see index) and combine with cooked chicken, meat, fish, or vegetables. Use ¾ to 1 cup thick white sauce to 2 cups ground or finely chopped solids. The solids should always be very well drained, not watery. Add just enough of the sauce to the solid ingredients so that they are well bound but still of a rather stiff consistency. The amount of sauce used with the solids may vary provided that after chilling the mixture can be handled easily.

Spread the combined mixture in a greased pan and chill thoroughly in the refrigerator. If desired, the top may be brushed lightly with butter to avoid forming a crust. When well chilled, form into desired shapes.

To egg and crumb: Beat an egg just enough to blend evenly, and stir in 2 tablespoons water. Coat the prepared food thoroughly with fine dry bread or cracker crumbs. Then dip in the egg mixture carefully covering the entire surface. Roll again in crumbs. Set on a rack or piece of waxed paper. If convenient, it's better to prepare these an hour before frying so that you have time to chill them. The coating is less likely to slip off during frying.

CROUTONS

Small cubes of toasted or fried bread often used as garnish for soups or salads.

To prepare croutons: Butter bread slices (add a bit of garlic if desired). Toast in a little hot fat in skillet or in slow oven (300°F.). Trim, then cut into small squares.

Or cut bread slices into ½-inch squares; toss in melted butter or margarine. Toast under broiler.

Croutons

CRYSTALLIZED

Candied. See **Candy.**

CUBE

To cube is just what it sounds like—to cut a solid into little cubes anywhere from ½ to 1 inch. Use a very sharp knife and a cutting board. Special cubing gadgets are sold. To dice is exactly the same process but the cubes are made smaller—less than ½ inch.

CURE

To preserve by salting, smoking, pickling, or other means.

CUSTARD

A mixture of milk and eggs, cooked until it thickens. Sweetened and flavored custards, often baked, make up a large class of desserts. Whatever the method, a custard must always be cooked at a low-to-moderate temperature or it will curdle. Those cooked on top of the range must be stirred constantly.

CUT IN

To "cut in" means to mix shortening with dry ingredients by using a pastry blender, two knives, or a fork. This is the method that cuts a solid fat into fine particles and mixes them with dry ingredients. It's the initial step, and an important one, when you're making biscuits or pastry and the recipe calls for one of the solid shortenings.

Cutting In

CUTLET

A small slice of meat from the ribs or leg, for frying or broiling, often served breaded. Also a small, flat croquette of chopped meat, fish, etc.

CUTTING TERMINOLOGY

See Chop; Cube; Dice; Flake; Grate; Grind; Julienne; Mince; Shred; Sliver.

Cut food with scissors when you need small pieces.

DECANT

To pour off a liquid gently without stirring up the sediment.

DEEP-FAT FRY

See **Fry.**

DEGLAZE

A term that describes the incorporation in the cooking liquid of the flavorful cooking juices and tidbits that remain in the roasting pan or skillet after meat or poultry has been roasted or browned. To do this, first the pan is degreased (excess fat is removed), then a small amount of liquid required in the recipe is added to the pan. The mixture is returned to the heat, simmered and stirred while scraping in the coagulated cooking juices. It is then blended with the remaining ingredients. This is an important step in the preparation of meat sauces and gravies because in that way some of the flavor of the meat or poultry is incorporated in the sauce.

DEGREASE

To remove excess fat from the surface of hot liquids such as sauces, soups, stocks; from stews, from a roasting pan, or a pan in which meats or poultry have been browned.

DEVILED

Highly seasoned food. Usually refers to food seasoned to make it hot, as with mustard, red pepper, Tabasco sauce, and the like.

DICE

To cut into very small cubes of less than ½ inch. Use a very sharp knife and cutting board.

DISSOLVE

To cause a dry substance to pass into solution in a liquid.

DOT

To scatter small particles, usually butter, over food.

DOUBLE BOILER, COOK IN

Fill bottom part of double boiler with about 2 inches water; bring to boil. Put double-boiler top, containing food, in place. Then cook over hot or boiling water as directed in recipe.

DOUGH

A mixture of flour, liquid, etc., worked into a soft thick mass too stiff to stir, and must, therefore, be kneaded, cut with a knife, or rolled. Doughs may be either soft or stiff, depending upon the amount of flour used. A soft dough is sticky, while a stiff dough is firm to the touch.

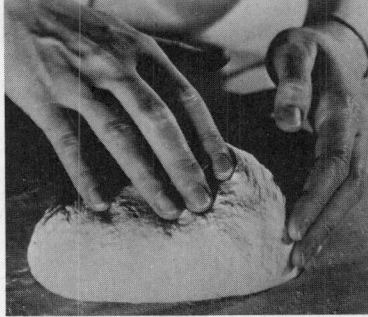

A cook soon learns from experience the "feel" of a pour batter, a soft dough, and a stiff dough.

DRAIN

See in entry for **Strain.**

DREDGE

To sprinkle or coat food with flour, fine crumbs, cereal, or other fine substance. Dredging is very often a preliminary step to frying.

DRESS

To prepare for cooking, as by cleaning or trimming.

DRESSING

A sauce added to salads and other dishes. Also, a stuffing for poultry or meat.

DRIPPINGS

This may refer to the combined fat and juices that drip from meat or poultry while roasting (used for gravy ordinarily), or to just the fats rendered in the process of cooking fat meats such as bacon, salt pork, etc.

DRUG STORE WRAP

This term is often used in directions for sealing aluminum foil packages in cookery or for wrapping packages for freezing. To seal with drug store fold: bring two opposite edges of wrapper together, folding over twice; fold ends in toward center.

DRY

When applied to a beverage, usually wine, this term means low in sugar. Though the opposite of sweet, it never implies sourness.

DRY HEAT

A term applied to roasting, broiling, or panbroiling. As the name implies, it is a method of cooking in which no water is used. Only tender cuts of meat should be cooked in this manner.

DRY INGREDIENTS

When used in recipe instructions, this term refers to flour, baking powder, baking soda, salt, spices, etc.

DUMPLINGS

These may be small pieces of dough, ball-shaped bits of batter or other foods steamed or boiled and served with meat or soup. When served with soups, meat stews, or as the main dish for luncheon, dumplings are usually cooked by steaming on top of the meat and vegetables in a tightly closed kettle. When used as a dessert, dumplings are crusts of dough filled or combined with fruit, and they may be steamed, boiled, or baked.

DUST

To cover lightly with a sprinkling of flour, sugar, or some other powder.

DUTCH OVEN

A deep, heavy cooking utensil with a close-fitting cover. It is sometimes equipped with a trivet or rack, and may be with or without a bail or side handles. It is used for stewing meats or cooking food that requires time and low heat. The capacity of a Dutch oven is stated in quarts.

Dutch Oven

DUXELLES

A French term for a flavoring used in preparing brown sauces and gravies consisting of finely chopped fresh mushrooms sautéed in butter with shallots or onions and seasoned with chopped parsley, salt, and sometimes various herbs. Duxelles may be prepared in advance, stored in the refrigerator, and used not only in brown sauces and gravies but also may be used as a basis for soup or added to stews, stuffings, and vegetables, or wherever a mushroom flavor is wanted. Some cooks like to add a bit of Madeira wine or brandy for additional flavoring. It is named after a famous French gourmet, the Marquis d'Uxelles, and the word is often spelled in this fashion.

How to Prepare Duxelles: Chop ½ pound mushrooms very fine or, if you are using the tops in another way, chop the stems only. Cook ¼ cup chopped onion in 2 tablespoons butter until golden. Add the mushrooms and sauté until the moisture is absorbed. Season delicately to taste with nutmeg and other herbs as desired, and salt and pepper.

ESCALLOP
See **Scallop.**

FELL
A thin paper-like covering over the outside of the lamb carcass. It does not affect the flavor unless the lamb has been aged for some time, and it may be left on or removed from roasts. Normally, it should not be removed from the leg, since this cut keeps its shape better and is juicier if it is left on. Chops, however, are better without it.

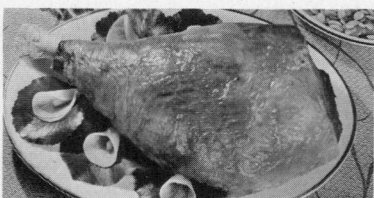

The fell keeps the roast leg of lamb in shape.

FILET
See **Fillet.** Filet mignon: a very small fillet of beef, usually a round cut of beef tenderloin, which is broiled or sautéed.

FILLET
A boneless lean piece of meat or fish. The French spelling filet and the corresponding pronunciation are often used—though never by fish dealers. With animals, the term always refers to the cut from the tenderloin or under-cut from the loin. With poultry and game birds, it is applied to the meat cut from the breast.

FLAKE
To break or pull apart a food like cooked or canned fish or chicken that divides naturally. All you do is follow these divisions, pulling at them gently with one or two forks. Or if you prefer, you can flake with your fingers.

FLORENTINE
In cookery this term usually denotes a dish prepared with spinach, as eggs Florentine, poached eggs served on a bed of spinach and dressed with a cream or cheese sauce.

FLOUR (The recipe term)
To coat food or pans with a thin film of flour. "Dust with flour" refers to this coating of cake pans, and to meats before browning.

FLUTE
To make short rounded grooves, as around the edge of a pie crust.

FOLD IN
To combine ingredients with a large spoon, a whisk, fork, or rubber scraper.
The folding-in motion goes gently down, across, up and over, that is, you cut down through the mixture, the tool slides across the bottom of the bowl, and you bring it up and over the top close to the surface.
The advantage of this easy action is that you prevent the loss of air when you are adding ingredients to a delicate food or mixture, or you are putting light ingredients like whipped cream or egg whites into heavier ones.

FORCEMEAT
Also called stuffing or dressing; a mixture of minced meat and seasonings used as a stuffing.

FORK-TENDER
Softened by cooking until fork pierces easily.

FORM INTO A BALL
This is a step that's important in pastry. Pick up dough with both hands and press (don't pat) firmly together. Turn as you press until you have a ball-shaped mass that holds together with no crumbs.

FOWL
A general term for any of the larger birds used as food, such as chicken, duck, or goose. In modern recipes it is being replaced by the specific name of the bird called for. Nowadays, if it is still used, it means a full-grown older hen used for stewing, as distinguished from a broiler or a fryer.

FRENCH FRYER
An uncovered cooking utensil with a perforated, meshed, or sieve-like insert basket with one handle; also an electric deep fat fryer.
See **Deep-Fat Frying,** in entry for **Fry.**

FRENCHED
A term referring to rib chops or roasts from which some of the fat has been removed to expose the end of the bone.

FRENCHED GREEN BEANS
Green beans cut into narrow length-wise strips.

FRICASSEE
When applied to the dish itself, fricassee usually refers to poultry, veal, or lamb, cut up, stewed, and served in a sauce of its own gravy.
To fricassee is to prepare meat by this method. See **Stew or Fricassee.**

FRIZZLE
To cook in a small amount of fat until the edges are crisp and curled; a term often applied to dried beef.

FRY
Fry means to cook in hot fat or oil in a pan over direct heat; however we must make a distinction among the several methods of frying.

Pan-Fry: (Also called sauté.) This means to brown food lightly in a little hot cooking fat or oil. It is often the first step in braising or stewing. It pro-vides the brown basis you need for most gravies.

Shallow-Fat Frying: This means to cook food in a medium amount of cook-ing fat or oil, about enough to half cover the food. Frying this way in semi-deep fat is sometimes used for foods like fritters, and for chicken when you want it a deep crisp brown but don't care about gravy.

Deep-Fat Frying: This means to cook foods in a lot of hot cooking fat or oil, enough to more than cover them. Deep-fat frying is the method that is often referred to as French frying and is used for such foods as potatoes, doughnuts, and most batter-coated foods.

DEEP FAT FRYING HINTS
The selection of fat and the care given it is important in deep fat frying. Hydrogenated fats, corn oil, and cot-tonseed oil are used for deep-fat frying since they can be heated to a high temperature without smoking or burn-ing.

If particles of flour or crumbs re-main in the fat it will smoke at a lower temperature than normal. The absorp-tion of fat in the fried food increases as the smoking point is lowered. It is therefore important to avoid heating fat to the smoking point, and to clarify fat after it has been used.

To reclaim fat, cook sliced raw po-tatoes in it to absorb flavors and strain through a cheesecloth or fine sieve to remove any particles.

A deep heavy kettle is best to use. A frying basket is convenient to lower the food into the fat and lift it out. A slotted spoon may be used.

A thermometer is an aid although the bread cube test is practical for temperature determinations.

Drop a 1-inch cube of stale bread into the hot fat. If bread browns in 60 to 70 seconds the temperature is satisfactory for uncooked mixtures (360°–370°F.); if it browns in 40 to 50 seconds, it is right for cooked mixtures (375°–385°F.); and if it browns in 20 to 30 seconds, it is hot enough for most cold foods (380°–390°F.).

For automatically controlled heat use an electric fryer.

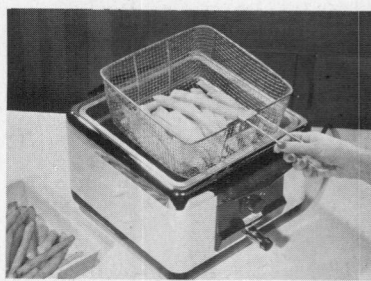

DEEP FAT TIME-TABLE		
FRIED FOODS	TEMPERATURE	MINUTES
Croquettes of cooked food	375°–385°F.	2–4
of uncooked food	370°F.	5–6
Doughnuts	370°–380°F.	2–3
Fritters	365°–375°F.	2–5
French-fried potatoes	370°F.	5–7
then	390°F.	1–1½
Vegetable rings	365°–375°F.	2–5
Oysters	375°F.	1–2
Small fish	375°–385°F.	2–5
Shrimp	375°F.	2–5

DEEP FAT FRYING PROCEDURE

Fill kettle about ⅔ full of melted fat. Heat to desired temperature. Drain food on absorbent paper and lower gently into the hot fat, a few pieces at a time.

Do not fry too much at one time because the temperature of the fat may be lowered too greatly, which would increase the cooking time and also cause the food to absorb more fat.

As soon as food rises to surface of the fat, turn it several times for even browning.

Do not crowd the pieces. When a golden brown, lift food out with wire basket or slotted spoon, allowing fat to drain over the kettle.

Transfer to pan lined with absorbent paper so that excess fat will be absorbed.

The length of time required for frying depends upon the kind of food, size of pieces, and temperature of the fat.

Fat which is reclaimed each time after using may be used over and over again. Keep fat in a cool place away from light. When fat smokes it has been overheated and changed, and is no longer as desirable for deep fat frying.

Hints for Batter-Coated Fried Foods

In deep-fat frying, some batters may have a tendency to peel off. To avoid this, check these hints:
● If batter is too thick, add more liquid.
● If batter is too thin, add more flour.
● If batter is too rich in fat, reduce amount of fat in batter.
● Check temperature of fat; if too low, increase temperature.
● Add less food at a time to deep fat; too much food added at one time reduces temperature too quickly.

GARNISH

To decorate or ornament food, usually with something edible.

GLACÉ

(French): 1. Having a smooth, glossy surface; 2. Covered with icing or sugar, as candied fruits; 3. Frozen or iced. See **Glaze.**

GLAZE

(1) To coat with a thin sugar syrup cooked to crack stage. (2) To give vegetables a brown coating (glazed vegetables) produced by cooking in sugar and fat. (3) To coat meats with a sauce made from brown stock evaporated until thick.

GRATE

To rub on a grater so as to tear off coarse-to-fine particles of food. The degrees of fineness in grating vary from coarse shreds of cheese to powder-fine nutmeg. You can use either one of the hand graters or get a mechanical gadget to do your grating for you.

GRATIN

A French term for the thin crust that forms on the surface of certain foods when they are browned in the oven or under the broiler; hence, any of a number of creamed dishes sprinkled with a topping of crumbs and butter or cheese and browned. Au gratin: having such a crust.

GRAVY

The juice given off by meat in cooking; a sauce made from the fat or stock in which meat has been cooked.

GRAVY BOAT

A dish for serving gravy; so called from its shape.

GREASE

To rub a thin film of cooking fat or oil over surface of frying pan, cake pan, griddle, etc., before it is used.

GRIDDLE

A heavy, flat metal plate or pan for cooking pancakes, etc.

GRILL

This term refers to the act of broiling as well as to the framework of metal wires or bars, commonly used for outdoor broiling. See **Broil.**

GRIND

To reduce to particles by cutting, crushing, or grinding. Usually it means to "grind" by putting food through a food chopper. Food choppers have two or more blades. Use a blade with smaller holes to grind foods fine; one with larger holes for coarser chopping, like meat, for a juicy meat loaf.

GRISTLE

A cartilage; an elastic but very tough tissue, like soft bone.

HARD-COOKED

Used of eggs, this is a better term than hard-boiled, because the proper way to cook them is in water just below the boiling point.

HASH

A chopped mixture of cooked meat and vegetables, usually baked or pan-fried. Also, to chop meat and vegetables into small pieces for cooking.

INFUSION

A method of extracting flavor from a substance by pouring hot liquid over it and allowing it to stand; also, the resulting flavored liquid. Tea and coconut milk are infusions.

JELL

To become or cause to become jelly.

JULIENNE

(French): Match-like strips of meat, vegetables or cheese; also, a clear soup with such vegetables; named for the French chef Jean Julien, who liked to garnish his clear soup with vegetable strips.

KETTLE

A covered or uncovered metal cooking utensil with a bail handle. The capacity is stated in liquid measurement.

KNEAD

Kneading is a process of mixing, in the home usually done by hand. You knead to insure complete mixing, to make some doughs or mixtures smooth and elastic.

To knead yeast dough, shape it first into a ball. Then, using both hands press down with the heels of palms and push dough away from you. Do this twice with quick, even pressure. Give dough a quarter turn and repeat the pushing process. Keep turning and pushing until dough is smooth and satiny.

To knead stiff candy, the mixture is worked into a mass, then pushed and pressed the same way until it's smooth and combined.

LARD

A term not only used to describe the rendered fat of the hog, but also to indicate the process of inserting strips of fat (salt pork, for example) through lean meat with what is known as a larding needle. These strips are called lardoons. It also refers to the placing of fat on top of uncooked lean meat or fish for flavor, or to prevent dryness.

A more correct term for the latter is bard.

LET RISE

This applies to yeast dough. Put dough in a warm place (about 85°F.) so yeast can "grow" and cause dough to expand and get "light." It has risen enough if the dent remains when you press the surface lightly with your fingers.

LIAISON

(French): The process of thickening; a term applied to soups and sauces. The usual agents for producing a liaison are flour, cornstarch, cold butter, egg yolks, and cream, sometimes combined.

MACERATE

To marinate (which see); a term applied to fruits in a syrup or alcoholic liquid.

MARBLING (in meats)

A term used to describe the fat intermingled in the lean of meat. It gives the meat a mottled or streaked appearance. It is not to be confused with the white connective tissue which replaces it when the animal grows past the peak-of-flavor age. Marbling is a definite mark of fine-quality meat.

MARINADE

A liquid in which food is steeped for added flavor and tenderness. It usually includes oil, an acid (wine, vinegar, or lemon juice), and spices and herbs.

MARINATE

To let stand in a marinade (which see). The length of time depends on the food in question.

MARROW

The soft, fatty tissue that fills the cavities of long bones. It is very tasty by itself and is also used in sauces, as a garnish, and in dumplings for soup.

MASK

To cover completely; usually applied to the use of mayonnaise or other thick sauce but may refer to jelly.

MATIGNON

A French term for preparation of seasoned minced vegetables sometimes spread over or under meat or poultry being braised or pot-roasted to flavor them during cooking. It is similar to mirepoix (which see). The term mirepoix is applied when the vegetables are coarsely diced, matignon when the vegetables are minced.

MEAT EXTRACT PASTE

Extract of meat, concentrated to a paste, with seasoning added.

MEAT GLAZE

Stock boiled down to jelly stage. Commercial products are available.

MEAT JUICE

The liquid contained in the meat fibers. It is expressed from slightly heated meat. It is high in flavor and contains some food value.

MEAT TENDERIZERS

These are commercial preparations containing papain, the dried juice of the papaya (a melon-like fruit). This substance, which is harmless to the human digestive system, tenderizes meats by the action of the enzymes it contains.

They should be used in accordance with directions on the labels to improve the tenderness and palatability of less-tender cuts of meat such as chuck steaks or shoulder chops. Such relatively inexpensive cuts of meat are as nutritious as the more expensive cuts and often just as flavorsome. The meat tenderizers are well worth trying on them.

MELTED FAT

Fat heated in small saucepan over low heat until melted. Salad oil may be used in recipes that call for melted fat.

MEUNIÈRE

(French): A method of cooking fish. The fish is sautéed in butter, then this or other browned butter is poured over it, and it is sprinkled with a little lemon juice and with chopped parsley.

MIREPOIX

A French term for a mixture of vegetables (diced carrots, onions, and celery) and herbs which can be made with or without meat (diced bacon, ham, or salt pork) and used as a layer over or under meat, poultry, or shellfish dishes to give flavor to the dishes. It is often used with meat or poultry being braised or pot-roasted. Mirepoix may be used in making soups, stews, and sauces, especially the brown sauces.

To Make Mirepoix: Dice 1 or 2 small carrots, 1 onion, about ½ cup celery heart, 1 tablespoon chopped bacon, ham, or salt pork, and add ½ crushed bay leaf and a sprig of thyme. These may be used raw as a base under the meat. Or heat 1 tablespoon butter in heavy skillet and sauté these ingredients until vegetables are soft, and use on top of meat as a seasoning. If desired, rinse the skillet with a bit of Madeira or sherry and pour over the mirepoix.

MIXED GRILL

A dish of several broiled foods served together; the composition varies.

MOIST HEAT

A method of cooking less tender meat by the application of steam or the addition of liquid.

MULL

To heat, sweeten, and flavor with spices; a term used for beverages such as cider, wine, and beer.

MUSH

A thick porridge made by boiling meal, especially corn meal, in water or milk.

ONION JUICE

Juice scraped with teaspoon from center of halved onion.

PAN-BROIL

To cook uncovered over direct heat on a hot surface, such as a skillet or griddle. Use no fat at all or very little—just enough to keep food from sticking to surface. Fat is poured off as it accumulates.

PAN-FRY

See Fry.

PARBOIL

To cook food in a boiling liquid until partially done. This is usually a preliminary step to further cooking. Beans and ham, for instance, are parboiled, later baked.

PARCH

To cook in dry heat until the outside is dry and sometimes slightly browned.

PARE

To cut or trim away the skin or covering, as potatoes, apples, etc.

PASTE

(1) Dough; specifically a term applied either to certain pastry doughs containing a high proportion of fat or to the shaped and dried doughs usually called pasta or macaroni products. (2) A creamy-textured food made by grinding or pounding, such as almond or meat paste. (3) A jelly-like candy.

PASTEURIZE

To preserve food by heating sufficiently to destroy certain microorganisms and arrest fermentation. Generally applied to liquids, such as milk and fruit juices. The temperature varies with the food but commonly ranges from 140° to 180°F.

PASTRY

Any dough made with shortening and used for the crust of tarts or pies. Also, any food prepared with such a crust; sometimes, by extension, fancy breads or cakes as well.

PASTRY BAG

A cone-shaped bag of firm textile material into which metal tubes of different shapes and sizes may be fitted at the small end.

PASTRY BLENDER

This is a hand-gadget for cutting shortening into flour for pastry. It consists of several wires looped to a handle. It is used with a chopping motion. See **Cutting In.**

PASTRY JAGGER OR WHEEL

A metal wheel used to make a fancy edge on a pie or other form of pastry.

PASTRY SYRINGE

A metal syringe equipped with pastry tubes and used instead of the pastry bag.

PASTRY TUBES

Metal fixtures of assorted sizes and shapes used with pastry bags and syringes.

PATTY

A pastry shell filled with a creamed mixture of food. The term is also used for a small, flat cake of ground meat, fish, etc., usually fried.

Pastry Patty Shell

PEEL

The outer covering of a fruit or vegetable; also, to remove this covering.

PICKLE

To preserve or flavor by steeping in brine or vinegar, often with spices. Also, any food so preserved; usually cucumber, unless some other food is specified.

PIT

To remove pit or seed, as from prunes.

PLANK

A specially made board, usually of kiln-dried oak, on which meat or fish is sometimes broiled and served; also to prepare and serve food on such a board, usually with an elaborate garnish of vegetables, often inside a decorative border of mashed potatoes or other puréed vegetables. The planks often have a tree design cut down their length to drain juices into a shallow depression toward the end.

If all the cooking is done on the plank, it will char rapidly. Steaks are therefore usually broiled on an oven grill fully on one side and partially on the other before being placed on the plank.

New planks should be seasoned by brushing with oil and placing in a very slow oven (225°F.) for at least one hour. To protect it while cooking, oil well any exposed part or cover with a decoration of mashed potatoes.

Planked Whole Fish

POACH

To cook covered by liquid at or below simmering (not boiling) using precautions to retain shape. Eggs cooked in a so-called poacher over hot water are actually steamed, not poached.

POT LIQUOR

The liquid left in the pot after any meat or vegetable is cooked; specifically, in the South, the juice left after greens are boiled with salt pork.

POTPIE

A stew of meat or poultry, usually with potatoes and other vegetables, baked in a casserole with a topping of pastry or biscuit dough. Also, sometimes, a meat stew with dumplings.

Potpies

POT ROAST

Any large cut of beef, or occasionally other meat, that is cooked by braising. Examples are chuck, brisket, and round steak, all of which tend to be tough unless cooked with moist heat. See **Braise.**

POUNDING

A method of making meat more tender or thinner. A meat hammer, the edge of a heavy saucer, or a wooden potato masher may be used to break down the connective tissues.

PRECOOK

To cook partially in a liquid below the boiling point, before preparing in final form.

PREHEAT OVEN

To bring the oven to the desired temperature before putting in the food. Almost all oven-cooked dishes require preheating of the oven.

PULLED BREAD

Fresh unsliced bread, with the crust removed, that is torn or pulled into pieces and toasted in the oven.

PUNGENT

A term implying agreeably sharp or acrid, when applied to taste or smell.

PURÉE

(French): A creamy pulp made by cooking solid food until it is soft and then putting it through a sieve, a colander, or a food mill or crushing it in a mortar or an electric blender; a term also applied to a soup thickened with such a pulp. Also, to make into a purée.

RAMEKIN

Also spelled ramequin; an individual baking dish; also, any food baked in such a dish.

REDUCE

To decrease the quantity of a liquid by continuing cooking, thus concentrating its flavor and sometimes thickening it. A concentrated sauce or stock is made this way, the final product often being a half or a third, etc., of the original quantity. Naturally, reducing applies only to sauces without or before the addition of egg. Those sauces which have a flour base have to be watched carefully and stirred frequently to avoid scorching.

RELISH

A highly flavored food, such as pickles, olives, or chutney, served as a condiment or to stimulate the appetite.

RENDER

To melt fat trimmed from meats and poultry by heating it slowly at a low temperature, in order to obtain only the portion that will liquefy.

RICE

To press potatoes or other food through a container perforated in such a way that the food emerges in rice-like particles.

RIND

A hard or firm outer layer or coating, as the rind of citrus fruits (lemons, oranges, etc.), of cheese, of a side of bacon, and the like.

ROAST

To cook by dry heat in the oven; also, to cook over or in coals. The method is the same as the one called baking, but the two terms are usually applied to different foods. The word roast originally meant to cook by direct exposure to an open fire and is still used for foods that were prepared in that way, such as meats and poultry; the word bake has always meant to cook in the oven and is used for the same old oven-cooked foods, such as bread and pastry. An unsolved mystery, however, is why ham and fish and spareribs are said to be baked while corn and chestnuts are described as being roasted.

ROASTER

A special pan, oven, or apparatus for roasting meat. Pans especially designed for roasting, with or without covers or racks, are made in various sizes designated by the weight of the poultry they will hold. The term is also applied to a young chicken or other animal suitable for roasting, especially whole.

ROLLING BOIL

See **Boil.**

ROLL OUT

Doughs for pastry, biscuits, breads, or cookies are rolled out.

For a pastry circle, flatten out a ball of dough to about 1/2 to 1 inch thick. Then roll with a rolling pin in a press-and-spread motion from center to edge, pressing less near the edge. Continue rolling from center to edge as though following spokes in a wheel, until the dough reaches proper thickness.

ROUX

(French): A mixture of fat and flour to which liquid is added to make gravy or sauce. It is the commonest way to thicken a sauce; butter is the preferred fat. The roux may be blanc (white), blond (golden), or brun (brown). The longer it is cooked, the darker it will be and as a result the darker the sauce in which it is used.

To make a roux, melt the butter and blend in the flour, then cook them together over very low heat, stirring constantly. It may be made in advance and stored in the refrigerator, then reheated in the top of a double boiler.

SALT (The cookery term)

To add salt, or to rub with salt. Also, to cure or season with salt.

SAUTÉ

To pan-fry. See **Fry.**

SCALD

To heat (milk or other liquid) to just below the boiling point; tiny bubbles will appear at the edge of the pan. The term is also used in the same sense as blanch (which see).

SCALLOP

The shell of the scallop or a similarly shaped baking dish. Hence, also, to bake in a style suitable for such a container, usually in a sauce or other liquid and very often with crumbs; actually, a casserole is most commonly used for the purpose. Corn, potatoes, tomatoes, and oysters are frequently scalloped. Also spelled escallop.

SCORE

To cut narrow grooves or gashes part way through the outer surface of food. For example, solid fat like the top of ham is scored to release melting fat and to decorate; tough meats like cubed steaks are scored to make them tender.

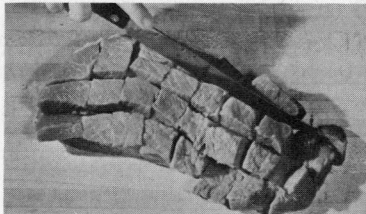

Score

SCRAMBLE

To prepare eggs or mixture containing eggs by stirring while cooking until mixture sets.

SEAR

To cook at a very high temperature for a short time in order to quickly form a brown crust on the outer surface of meat. This method increases shrinkage, but develops flavor, improves appearance.

SHALLOW-FAT FRYING

See **Fry.**

SHRED

To cut or tear into small, long narrow pieces. The fineness varies—recipes will often say that foods should be "finely" or "coarsely" shredded. A knife may be used or a hand or mechanical shredder. Crisp vegetables, like cabbage may be cut to shreds with a sharp knife on a cutting board.

Shred-Make an easy job of shredding with a razor-sharp cutter.

SHUCK

A shuck is the shell of such shellfish as oysters and clams. Recipes will sometimes call for "shucked" oysters or clams, meaning shellfish which have been removed from their shells.

The term shuck is also applied to the outer husk of corn (maize).

SIFT

To put one or more dry ingredients like flour or sugar through a sifter or fine sieve to separate particles; to fluff those that tend to pack; to mix several kinds uniformly.

SIMMER

To cook gently in a liquid just below the boiling point at temperatures of 185° to 210°F. Adjust the heat to maintain this stage.

In simmering, the food cooks so slowly that the surface moves only slightly; no bubbles show because they form slowly and collapse below the surface. See **Boil.**

SINGE (POULTRY)

Hold over flame to burn off all hairs.

SKEWER

To fasten or hold food to keep it in position while it cooks, with metal or wooden pins (skewers).

"Skewer" may also mean assembling, cooking, and serving kabob-style on skewers.

SKILLET

Originally a three-legged, long-handled stewing pot to cook food in a fireplace, sometimes called "spider" because of its resemblance to same.

Nowadays it refers to a fry-pan or frying pan, a shallow, covered or uncovered pan with one handle. The size is stated by the top diameter in inches.

SLIVER

To cut or split into long, thin strips with a knife on a cutting board. For example, the term is applied to almonds and to pimiento pieces used for decoration. See also **Julienne.**

SMOTHER

To cook in a covered dish or in a close mass, as smothered onions; also to cover completely, as with a sauce or gravy.

SNIP

To cut into small pieces, as with a kitchen shears.

SPATULA

A wide, flat, flexible knife-like utensil used for spreading creamy mixtures or for lifting solid foods. Also, a similarly shaped implement of wood or rubber used for folding or stirring.

SPIT

A thin, pointed rod or bar on which food is placed and held to be broiled or roasted over a fire.

SPONGE

A light, fluffy gelatin dessert containing stiffly beaten egg whites or whipped cream. Also the preliminary dough in one method of making yeast bread.

SPRING-FORM PAN

A cake pan with removable sides held in place by a clamp.

STEAM

To cook by steam in a closed container. Dumplings and puddings are examples. Or you can cook by steam under pressure in less time by using a special pressure saucepan.

STEAM-BAKE

To cook in the oven in a pan set over a container of hot water.

STEAM COOKER

A covered saucepan or sauce pot having one or more perforated insert pans equipped with a handle or handles.

STEEP

To let a food stand in hot liquid, below boiling, to extract flavor, color, or both, as in tea.

STERILIZE

To free from living microorganisms by application of intense heat.

STEW OR FRICASSEE

To stew or fricassee means to simmer or cook food slowly in a small amount of liquid in a covered pan. The meat may or may not be browned first. "Stew" usually means meat; "fricassee" most often refers to chicken. Whatever the method is called, it is a fine way to cook tougher cuts of meat.

STIR

When a recipe tells you "to stir" without other specific instructions, it usually means to stir with a spoon, wielding it in a round-and-round motion that follows the outline of the bowl or pan you're using. Keep stirring until you get a smooth, uniform consistency, or according to the directions given in your recipe.

If you're stirring with an electric mixer, set it for slow or medium to get the equivalent speed.

Use a long-handled spoon for hot foods.

STIR-FRYING

A method used in Chinese cooking which results in the tender, crisp, and nicely colored vegetables so typical of Chinese-style dishes. Traditionally, stir-frying is done in a big open conical pan called a *wok* held erect by a ring stand over very high heat. This method of cooking requires only 3 to 4 minutes of cooking time; however preparation time is the slow part since the vegetables must be carefully cut into uniform pieces.

A small amount of cooking oil, usually peanut oil, is added to a preheated pan, then the vegetables are added one at a time. Those that require the longest cooking time go in first. The vegetables are stirred rapidly to make sure they are well coated with hot oil, then stirred constantly over high heat until just tender.

When making combination dishes of meat and vegetables, thin slivers of meat are cooked first, then removed and kept warm. The meat is added to the crisply tender vegetables just before serving.

Chinese Wok

STOCK

The richly flavored liquid in which fish, meat, poultry, or vegetables have been cooked. Used in soups, sauces, and general cooking.

STRAIN

To separate a liquid from solid pieces of food through a coarse sieve or colander. The term "drain" is used when the separation need not be exact.

To strain soup stock, pour it through a piece of cheesecloth fastened over a large bowl.

TART

This term means sharp in taste, sour, acid. In pastry-making, as the term was originally used in Europe, it referred to any open-faced fruit pie. As used nowadays in the United States, the term means a small pastry, usually fruit-filled; actually a tiny pie with no top crust or only part of one.

TENDERIZE

To make meat tender by pounding, marinating, or using a commercial product. See **Meat Tenderizer; Pounding; Marinate.**

THICKEN

See **Thickening Agents,** in Ingredients—How to Use Them.

TIMBALE

A highly flavored custard of meat, chicken, fish, shellfish, or vegetables baked in a small mold.

Timbale

TIMBALE MOLD

Refers to any shape of mold in which delicate creamed mixtures are baked.

TOAST (The cookery term)

To brown by direct heat in a toaster, under a broiler, or by using any other direct heat source.

Sometimes when recipes call for dried-out bread, you may be told to "toast" the bread in a slow oven.

TOSS

To mix ingredients lightly by tumbling them lightly with a lifting motion.

To prevent crushing and to do a thorough job, use two implements: two forks or a fork and a spoon.

The most usual use is mixing greens and other salad ingredients, coating them with dressing. "Tossed" now describes a salad on many menus.

TRIM

To cut away ragged or unsightly parts of food before or after cooking, to improve its appearance for eye appeal.

TRIVET

A short-legged metal plate for holding hot dishes on a table; also a similar type of metal plate used in a skillet, Dutch oven, roasting pan, or saucepan to prevent excessive cooking and scorching of food at the bottom. A trivet is sometimes used when meats are braised or simmered in liquids.

TRUSS

To tie meat or fowl with string or fasten it with metal or wooden pins (skewers) so it keeps its shape during cooking. Chicken, duck, and turkey, for example, are usually trussed before roasting.

TRUSSING NEEDLE

A special needle designed for trussing poultry. It is used to pass string through the bird's body.

TRY OUT

To render fat. An old term not much used any more.

TURK'S HEAD PAN

A round cake pan with spiral-shaped indentations in the walls, and a tube in the center like an angel food pan.

UNMOLD

See **Gelatin,** in Ingredients—How to Use Them.

UNTIL DONE

The phrase "until done" is usually qualified in recipes to indicate precisely what it means in reference to the specific finished product: cake, pie, vegetable, etc. When the unqualified phrase is used, it means, for fish, cook until the flesh is whitely opaque and flakes readily; for meat, until the meat is quite tender and browned; for poultry, until it is so tender that the joints move easily; for vegetables, cook until just tender.

Cakes are done when they begin to shrink slightly from the sides of the pan, when the center surface will spring back when lightly pressed with a finger, and when a wire tester, a straw, or toothpick inserted into the center comes out clean.

UNTIL SET

Until a liquid has become firm, usually applied to a gelatin mixture.

WHIP

To beat rapidly with a rotary beater, an electric mixer set on fast speed, or a wire whisk, to incorporate air and produce expansion.

You'll find the term used most often in instructions about egg whites, whipping cream, gelatin, and other foods like them that expand when whipped and become very light and frothy. Here, in other words, the introduction of air is the main idea; the mixing is only secondary.

WHISK

A device usually made of wire used to beat or stir liquids.

WHITE STOCK

A richly flavored, light-colored liquid in which poultry or light meats have been cooked.

ZESTS

Zests are fine gratings of the colored outermost coatings of oranges, tangerines, limes, or lemons called for in many recipes. Use a small hand grater when grating these and avoid the inclusion of any part of the white part beneath the colored parts because the white is bitter. The outer colored portions of the rinds provide a stronger flavor than the citrus juices because of a heavy concentration of oil in them. Some cooks like to grate colored coatings coarsely and to squeeze them through a piece of cheesecloth onto sugar. They let the sugar stand at least 15 minutes before using it.

Ingredients—How to Use Them

FACTS ABOUT FLOURS AND MEALS

Flour is a product produced by grinding and sifting cleaned grain, especially wheat. Flour should be bought according to the purpose for which it is to be used and should be stored in a dry place.

Enriched Flour: A common name for all-purpose flour (which see). The name arises from the fact that a number of elements having been removed in modern milling some are replaced by an enriching process.

All-Purpose Flour: This flour, often referred to as enriched flour, family flour, general-purpose flour, is the kind customarily used. It is suitable for most home baking. In northern United States, it is made from a blend of hard wheats. In southern states, a blend of soft wheats is used.

Cake Flour: This is made of soft wheats. It has a low protein content and makes a more tender product than all-purpose flour. It is used for fine cakes.

Self-Rising Flour: This is an all-purpose flour to which a leavening agent and salt have been added. Using it for home baking saves time, but recipes have to be changed to omit salt and baking powder called for in them. For best results, follow the manufacturer's directions.

Bleached Flour: Flour that has been whitened to create a more uniform flour, and to improve the quality of baked goods.

Pre-sifted Flour: Flour to be used in batters and doughs should be sifted before measuring. Nowadays some flours have been sifted for you. We suggest you follow the directions on the containers of such flour.

Potato Flour: This is produced from potatoes that have been cooked, dried, and ground. Potato flour makes an especially desirable thickening agent. It cooks quickly and smoothly in a liquid and leaves no raw taste. Use $\frac{1}{3}$ the amount of flour called for in the recipe.

Buckwheat Flour: A meal or flour ground from buckwheat kernels. It is especially tasty in pancakes or waffles.

Rice Flour: A fine white flour ground from rice kernels. It is used in cookies and in some quick breads and cakes but has too little gluten to make satisfactory bread.

Rye Flour: A flour produced generally from the whole grain, from either winter or spring varieties. It is used in baking rye and pumpernickel breads and for rolls. Rye meal is simply coarsely ground whole rye flour.

Whole Wheat Flour: This is made of the entire grain of wheat, including a large part of the bran; it may be finely or coarsely ground. The term is really a misnomer because usually part of the bran has been removed, and sometimes the wheat germ. It is used in bread, rolls, and cookies.

Graham Flour: According to a Federal ruling, the same as whole-wheat and entire-wheat flour; formerly, a wheat flour made by grinding the cleaned whole grain. It was named after Sylvester Graham (1794-1851), an American food reformer who advocated the use of coarsely ground whole-wheat flour. The term is not used much any more.

Seasoned Flour: Flour mixed with seasonings; commonly used proportions are $\frac{1}{4}$ cup flour to $\frac{3}{4}$ teaspoon salt plus $\frac{1}{4}$ teaspoon each of pepper and paprika.

Other Flours: Barley, corn, cottonseed, lima-bean, peanut, and soy flours are available for special purposes. These as well as rye, buckwheat, rice, and potato flours are usually used in combination with wheat flour because, with the exception of rye, they lack gluten-forming proteins. Rye flour produces gluten of low elasticity. Bread and pastry flours are used principally by commercial bakers.

MEAL

Any edible grain, or the edible part of any grain, coarsely ground.

BRAN

The skin or husk of a cereal grain, such as wheat, rye, oats, or corn, which is separated from the flour or meal by sifting or bolting.

CORN MEAL

A meal produced from white or yellow corn (maize), and ground to varying degrees from coarse to fine. It is particularly good for making corn breads, or as a cereal. Water-ground corn meal made of white corn retains much of the rich skin and germ and although nutritionally excellent tends to spoil more quickly than other kinds.

DURUM

A variety of hard wheat; flour made from it is used in macaroni and other pasta products.

FARINA

Strictly, meal made from any grain. In common usage, the term refers to a particular wheat cereal used as a breakfast food and for puddings. It is similar to but finer than semolina and is sometimes used instead of it.

GROATS

Hulled, or hulled and coarsely cracked, grain, especially wheat or oats.

MILLET

Millet is a cereal grass with a small grain used for food in Europe and Asia. In the United States millet is usually available in health-food stores.

OATMEAL

While this name does mean oats crushed into meal or flakes as well as rolled or ground oats, for the sake of clarity the term "oats" is used in recipes when uncooked rolled oats are called for in the recipe. In recipes, oatmeal refers to cooked oats.

SEMOLINA

Coarsely ground wheat, a by-product in the manufacture of fine flour. It is used in making pastas and in puddings and other dishes.

WHEAT GERM

The embryo of a grain of wheat; it is nutritionally rich and has a pleasant nut-like flavor and texture. Wheat germ may be sprinkled over breakfast cereals and other foods, or it may be added to meat loaf and especially to breads, pancakes, waffles, or muffins.

FACTS ABOUT BUTTER, MARGARINE, OILS, SHORTENING, AND OTHER FATS

Butter: Butter is the solidified fat of milk, made by churning cream. It contains not less than 80 per cent by weight of milk fat, an important amount of vitamin A, and 100 calories per tablespoon. Federal standards do not permit any preservatives or additives except approved food coloring and salt which are optional. Butter may be government graded on the basis of taste, aroma, body, and texture. The two top grades are rated as U.S. 93 Score, or U. S. D. A. Grade AA; and U.S. 92 Score, or U. S. D. A. Grade A. Lower rated butter is U. S. D. A. Grade B, or below 92 score.

Buying Butter: There are several types of butter as well as different grades. There is salted butter, unsalted or sweet butter, and whipped butter.

Whipped butter is made from butter with air or inert gas incorporated to improve spreadability and increase volume. *Do not* substitute whipped

butter for butter in recipes.

Unsalted or sweet butter is made from a fine flavored sweet cream with no added salt. Because it lacks this preservative its keeping qualities are less than those of salted butter. Its fine, pleasing aroma and delicate sweet flavor is preferred by many discriminating consumers for table use and required in certain baked goods.

Salt butter is sold in any of the above mentioned several grades; it keeps longer than sweet butter. The top grade (AA) is made from fine flavored sweet cream; grade A is made from cream with only slightly less fresh flavor; grade B, or butter below 92 score, may be made from sweet or sour cream. Although grade B lacks the fine fresh flavor of the two top grades, it is readily acceptable to many consumers.

Look for these grades on butter labels:

To Store Butter

Store butter in the coldest part of the food compartment of your refrigerator in its original package. Any portion which has been partially used should be kept in a covered dish to protect its delicate flavor. If your refrigerator has a special butter compartment, keep butter in it only for immediate use.

Homemade Whipped Butter

This whipped butter mixture is sometimes used by dieters. Soften ¼ cup (4 tablespoons or envelopes) plain gelatin in 2 cups (1 pint) milk and heat over hot water until dissolved.

Cut 1 pound butter in pieces and place in a bowl over hot water. Whip the gelatin mixture gradually into the butter. Season with salt to taste. If milk bubbles appear, continue beating until they disappear. Pour the butter into molds and chill well before using.

SHAPING BUTTER FOR SERVING

Butter Pats: To cut neatly, cover knife blade with a fold of waxed paper or parchment paper in which the butter has been wrapped. Dip a fork in hot water and draw scores across squares of butter diagonally. Garnish with small sprigs of parsley.

Butter Balls: Scald, then chill a pair of wooden butter paddles. Measure butter by teaspoonfuls for uniformity. Roll lightly between paddles to form a ball. To shape rolls, flatten balls into cylinders between paddles. Drop but-

ter balls onto chilled plate, cracked ice, or into ice water.

Butter Curls: Use butter curler. Dip it in hot water each time. Beginning at the far side of a pound print of butter, draw curler lightly and rapidly toward you, making a thin shaving of butter which curls up.

Butter Molds: Scald and chill fancy butter molds. Pack solidly with butter and level off with knife. Press out and chill.

Margarine: Most of today's margarine is made from refined food fats other than butter fat (primarily cotton and soybean oils). Like butter, it is 80 percent fat. Skim milk used in the manufacturing process is largely responsible for its appetizing flavor.

Since margarine is fortified with vitamin A, it is nutritionally comparable to butter and is uniform in food value throughout the year. It makes a fine table spread, and is also used extensively in cooking and baking.

In many recipes it is suggested that margarine may be substituted for butter, weight for weight or measure for measure; however this is usually an economy measure. It should be noted that margarines lack the desirable butter flavor and usually produce textures somewhat different from butter in both cooking and baking. For added butter flavor, some margarines have added dairy fat. To determine this read the label.

To Store Margarine

Margarine should be kept refrigerated in the store in which you buy, and at home should be carefully wrapped or covered and stored in the refrigerator.

Hydrogenated All-Vegetable Shortening: The shortenings, which are sold under various trade names, are made of vegetable oils refined and chemically treated with hydrogen to make them solid fats. They may also be treated in various other ways such as by homogenization or with emulsifying agents.

Although especially adapted for use in quick-method cakes, as most labels indicate, they are used with equal success in other types of cakes, baking, frying, deep fat cookery.

These are packed in cans and require no refrigeration.

Combination Meat Fat and Vegetable Shortening: These shortenings are similar in appearance to all-vegetable types and are used in exactly the same ways.

They are packed in cans and require no refrigeration.

Lard: Lard is the rendered fat of hogs. Most lard is steam rendered.

Leaf lard, of which only a small amount is made, is kettle rendered. It has a characteristic flavor which some people prefer.

Dry rendering is a third method of preparing lard.

Lard may be stabilized by the addition of an anti-oxidant, by hydrogenation or treated by other methods to give it improved flavor and cooking and keeping qualities.

Lard has excellent shortening qualities. It is also used for pan-frying, shallow and deep fat frying, baking breads, etc.

Keep lard, covered, in refrigerator.

Poultry Fat: This is the rendered fat from chicken, duck, goose, or turkey. It is sold in specialty shops in jars or cans but mainly rendered at home. Used in cooking, baking, frying.

Suet: This is the rather stiff white fat stripped from beef. Sold by the pound in meat markets. Used for larding lean meat and also as an ingredient in steamed puddings.

TO RENDER SUET

Place chopped suet in saucepan over medium heat. As it melts, pour into bowl. Don't overheat melted suet or it will turn dark and have a strong flavor.

Store in a cool place until ready to use.

Drippings: These are fats usually rendered in the process of cooking fat meats, such as bacon, salt pork, ham, beef, or lamb. Drippings are sometimes home-rendered from meat scraps.

Oils: Cooking oils are made from cottonseed, corn, peanuts, and soya, or from olives. Some may be a blend of two or more oils.

Cooking oils are purchased for salad dressing bases, for frying (pan-frying, deep, or shallow frying), for preparing dishes calling for melted fat, and are now used frequently (except olive oil) in pastry, cakes and quick breads.

You'll find cooking oils (except olive oil) ideal for deep fat frying because they can be heated to a high temperature without smoking and can be used over and over again.

Olive oil, with its unique flavor, is popular for salad dressings, in Italian-style dishes, etc.; however it is too unstable for deep fat frying.

Fats used for deep frying should be strained when cool and stored in a covered container. Slices of potato may be cooked in the fat to remove strong flavors.

To Store Oils

After pouring what you need from a bottle of salad or olive oil, before screwing cap back on again, be sure to wipe off neck of bottle and inside of cap with a paper towel.

Salad oils should be stored in a cool dark place; most do not require refrigeration. Check the labels.

FACTS ABOUT MILK AND CREAM

Everyone needs milk every day, so never skimp on that daily quota. Children should have three to four glasses a day; adults two to three glasses. Pregnant and nursing mothers need more than other adults. Milk products whose value is equivalent to fresh whole milk can be used for part or all of the requirement.

Insist That Milk Be Pasteurized: Be sure that the milk you buy comes from a reputable dealer, and be certain that it is pasteurized. Pasteurization means the heating of milk in a special way to destroy or make harmless all the organisms in it that cause disease. In some communities, several grades of milk are sold. Ask your health department to explain the difference, then buy the best you can afford.

Whole Milk: Contains not less than 8% milk solids, not less than 3.25% butterfat. When left standing, it shows a collar of cream at top of bottle.

Homogenized Milk: This is pasteurized whole fluid milk treated in such a way that the cream is permanently mixed through and it can't rise to the top.

Skim Milk: This is milk with the cream removed—that is, most of the butterfat removed. Contains half the energy value of whole milk. Used in reducing and low fat diets.

2% Milk: A low fat milk which has had part of the fat removed. Most 2% milk has added nonfat dry milk solids as well as added vitamins A and D.

Top Milk: Top cream layer removed from bottle of whole, nonhomogenized milk.

Certified Milk: This milk is available in some markets. It is milk produced and handled according to rigid sanitary regulations. It may be either raw or pasteurized; may be homogenized and have vitamin D added. It is used mostly on prescription.

Buttermilk: Strictly speaking, this is the liquid remaining after milk or cream has been churned into butter. The usually available beverage is actually cultured buttermilk made from fresh fluid skim milk. A specially prepared culture of bacteria is added to the milk to produce the desirable acidity, body, flavor and aroma so characteristic of buttermilk. Salt is usually added. The yellow flecks in some buttermilk are bits of real butter added for extra flavor. Because it is relatively low in calories it is popular in reducing diets.

Special Fortified, Multiple Vitamin, and/or Mineral Milk: These contain added amounts of one or more of the essential nutrients.

To Make Sour Milk

If you have an old favorite recipe calling for sour milk, substitute the same amount of buttermilk. If you want to make your own sour milk for cooking, pour 1 tablespoon of lemon juice or vinegar into measuring cup and add milk to make 1 cup. Some old-time recipes called for whole or skim milk allowed to sour naturally. Since the milk supply sold in the United States is generally a pasteurized and homogenized product, it will not sour naturally, but merely spoil.

Frozen Milk

It is not recommended that milk be frozen, but if it does freeze it can be used after thawing. You will notice only a slight change in the appearance.

Chocolate Milks: When buying these flavored milks, note that there is a distinction among the types available. *Chocolate milk* is whole milk to which has been added chocolate syrup. If it is made with skim milk or partially skimmed milk, it is called *chocolate milk drink* or *chocolate milk beverage*. When made from whole milk and cocoa, it is called *chocolate-flavored milk*. When made from skim milk and cocoa, it is called *chocolate-flavored drink*.

Malted Milk: This is a soluble powder from whole dried milk and dried malted cereals. It's an easily digested concentrated food because the starch is predigested. To serve, the food value may be increased by preparing it with hot or cold milk.

Dry or Powdered Milk: This is milk with the water removed. Whole dry milk, seldom sold in groceries, has the nutritive content of fresh whole milk.

Dry skim milk, officially called "nonfat dry milk solids," is made by removing virtually all butterfat and water from fresh whole milk. The remaining portion is a nonfat or skim milk powder which contains all of the important nutrients of fresh whole milk except vitamins A and D and, of course, the butterfat.

Instant dry skim milk products differ from non-instant dry skim milk products only in ease of reconstitution into liquid milk.

Dry milks, especially the nonfat types, are finding more and more uses in home cooking. They are thrifty buys. Even if you have a pronounced distaste for the flavor of skim milk, you can still enjoy the economy of the product by using it in cooking. Simply mix in the powder with the other dry ingredients and add water at the point where the recipe calls for milk. Or reconstitute it as directed on the label and use in the recipe in place of fresh milk.

In many recipes you can step up the food value of a dish by adding some nonfat dry milk without adding water; for example, in meat loaves.

Whole fresh milk may be fortified by the addition of 1 tablespoon powdered milk for each glass of liquid milk, and many children prefer the flavor of this enriched milk.

To Whip Instant Nonfat Dry Milk

Equal parts of instant nonfat dry milk and water or juices may be whipped. While it is possible to whip with cold liquids, more volume and stability of foam are produced if all ingredients are at room temperature. Lemon juice (2 tablespoons for each 1/2 cup instant nonfat dry milk) is often added to the whipped topping after soft peaks are formed. This stabilizes the whip and accents the flavor, especially when bland fruit juices are used. Sugar and flavorings to suit the taste may be added after the stiff peaks form.

Evaporated Milk: This is whole milk from which a little more than half of the water has been removed—that is, concentrated to double richness. It is homogenized and pasteurized before it is put in the can, then sterilized after the can is sealed. It is fortified with a large amount of vitamin D. When it is mixed half-and-half with water, it may be used as whole milk and has the same nutritive value. It can be used as it comes from the can in place of cream, or, when it has been thoroughly chilled, it can be whipped.

Keep evaporated milk in the can after opening. Cover the top with a food cover or a piece of aluminum foil pressed close against top edge. Refrigerate when not in use.

Condensed Milk: This is a mixture of whole milk and sugar from which about 60 percent of the water has been removed before the mixture is canned. It is used to sweeten coffee and for special cooking purposes. It is rarely used with sugar.

Note that canned sweetened condensed milk is not the same as evaporated milk.

TO WHIP EVAPORATED MILK

● Pour 1 cup undiluted evaporated milk into a refrigerator tray and put in the ice cube section of the refrigerator to chill.

● When very cold, the milk will have soft crystals through the milk. (That will take about 20 to 30 minutes.)

● Pour the chilled milk into a medium-sized bowl.

● Whip it with an egg beater until it is beginning to get stiff, about 1 minute.

● Add 3 tablespoons lemon juice.

● Whip until very stiff. If you are using the whipped milk for a topping, sweeten to taste. This makes 3 cups whipped topping.

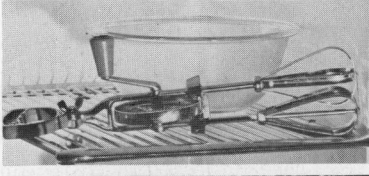

CREAM

Cream is a part of milk containing a high percentage of butter fat.

Light, Coffee, or Table Cream: Cream containing not less than 18 percent butter fat.

Half and Half Cream: A mixture of milk and cream which contains between 10% and 12% milk fat.

Heavy or Whipping Cream: Cream sufficiently heavy to thicken and hold its shape when beaten, containing not less than 30 percent butter fat. It should be very cold at time of beating. It's a good plan to chill the bowl and beater, too. Use a rotary, or electric beater; beat with continuous motion.

Cream in Aerosol Cans: A cream packed under pressure in an aerosol container to cause whipping of the product. It may also contain sugar, flavoring, and a stabilizer. Since there are many whipped toppings in this form, be sure to check the label before purchasing if you want real cream.

How to Whip Cream

Keep it cold! The bowl and beaters as well as the cream should all be chilled in the refrigerator for at least 2 hours before whipping. Use a deep bowl with straight sides. Whip rapidly; stop whipping in time, before churning starts and butter begins to form. If the cream really threatens to turn into butter, whip in 2 or more tablespoons evaporated milk or cream and continue to beat. If you are using an electric beater, use medium high speed until the chilled cream begins to thicken, then lower the speed and watch carefully. It is not advisable to try to whip cream in a blender.

To Store Milk and Cream

Milk and cream should be kept covered in the refrigerator, since both pick up flavors from other food.

Milk from different bottles should not be mixed and unused liquid should not be poured back into the original container if there is other milk in it. This will cause either milk or cream to sour faster. If either does sour, it can be used in cooking.

Nonfat dry, evaporated, or condensed milk can be kept in the cupboard until opened or reconstituted. Then they must be treated like fresh milk.

SOUR CREAM

Cream especially soured for cooking purposes and table use is generally available, often labeled cultured sour cream. It is a light cream of custardlike consistency with a characteristic tangy flavor produced by the addition of a culture or lactic acid starter. It is made from fresh sweet cream (with approximately 18 to 20% milk fat content) which is pasteurized and homogenized. After the culture has been added the cream is allowed to ripen until the desired flavor and consistency have been reached. Modern recipes calling for sour cream mean dairy sour cream—not to be confused with the old-fashioned homemade soured cream. As a safety measure it is always advisable to use only sour cream and milk that have been pasteurized and cultured.

In many markets a Sour Half and Half is available. This is a comparable product with a lower fat content.

Caution: Do not substitute sour half and half in baked foods calling for dairy sour cream.

To Store Dairy Sour Cream

Keep it clean, cold, and covered. Store in original container in the coldest part of the refrigerator. Dairy sour cream should not be frozen. Some prepared dishes made with sour cream may be frozen successfully.

Sour Cream Cookery Hints

When cooking with dairy sour cream, handle it with care. Heat gently, but do not boil. Add to other ingredients just before serving. If it does happen to curdle, only the appearance is affected not the taste. Always fold sour cream into other ingredients carefully, as over-stirring may thin it.

Most dairy sour cream can be whipped. Follow general directions for whipping cream. It will take about 5 minutes. The sour cream will thin out at the beginning of the whipping process, will never become as thick as whipped cream. It will double in volume.

When dairy sour cream is used in dressings or sauces along with vinegar, lemon juice, or comparable acid foods, the sour cream may become thin when stirred to mix. Upon storing the product in the refrigerator it will return to its original consistency.

When dairy sour cream is added to condensed canned soups or if flour is added to the sauce made with sour cream, the cream will not separate or curdle. Sour cream will enhance the flavor of either soup or sauce.

SOUR CREAM SUBSTITUTES

These are lower calorie substitutes for sour cream and are to be used only for garnish or in uncooked dressings.

Blender Cream: Combine 1 cup small curd cottage cheese, 1/3 cup buttermilk, and 1 tablespoon lemon or lime juice. Blend for 2 or 3 seconds.

Evaporated Milk: Use 1 cup evaporated milk at room temperature (70°F.); mix with 1 tablespoon vinegar. Let stand until it clabbers and thickens.

DEVONSHIRE CREAM (CLOTTED CREAM)

This is cream prepared in clotted form used as a topping for berries or other desserts or as a spread for bread. The name comes from Devonshire, England, which together with neighboring Cornwall, is noted for it. It has a characteristic sweet flavor.

To make Devonshire cream, pour 2 gallons rich fresh milk (not homogenized) into a large shallow pan. Let it stand until the cream rises, about 6 hours.

Move it very gently onto the range and heat it very slowly until bubbles begin to appear around the edges. This should take about an hour and the milk must never be allowed to boil or the richness and texture of the cream will spoil.

Remove from heat and let it cool for a full 24 hours, then skim off the cream. It will be thick and clotted.

TO MAKE SOUR CREAM

Place 1 cup of 20 percent pasteurized cream in a quart glass jar. The cream may be heavier, and the heavier the cream, the better the end product.

Add 5 teaspoons buttermilk. The commercial type which has 1 percent acid and has carefully controlled bacteria is easier to use than the less-acid and less-controlled home product.

Cover the jar and shake these ingredients vigorously.

Then stir in an additional 1 cup of 20 percent pasteurized cream.

Cover the jar and allow this mixture to stand at 80°F. for 24 hours. The sour cream may then be used at once although storage in the refrigerator for another 24 hours makes a finer product.

YOGURT

Yogurt (also spelled yoghurt, yohourt) is a thick, custard-like, smooth textured dairy product with a tangy flavor. It is a cultured milk product that has been prepared with a mixed culture of lactic bacteria. It is usually made with fresh, partially skimmed milk that has been enriched by the addition of nonfat dry milk. The milk is pasteurized and homogenized before the culture is added. The nutritive value of yogurt is the same as the milk from which it is made. In addition to the plain yogurt, you may find flavors such as strawberry, coffee, vanilla, orange, lime, prune, or pineapple.

About Serving Yogurt

Yogurt is most popular in dips, toppings, and salad dressings. It can also be served as a dessert, spooned right from the container onto fruit, or "as is" with sugar and preserves.

Since it was originally a Bulgarian fermented milk, a great many Near Eastern recipes call for yogurt. When using yogurt in cooking, stir or fold it into the other ingredients. The custard-like texture or body of the

yogurt will be broken down by any vigorous beating, so treat it gently. When cooked, yogurt thins out even more than sour cream. However, it is stabilized by flour or cornstarch and water.

To Store Yogurt

To retain the fresh flavor and smooth texture of yogurt, store it in the refrigerator but do not freeze.

To Prepare Yogurt: Let 3 tablespoons prepared yogurt stand at room temperature for about 3 hours.

Bring 1 quart milk to boiling point in top part of double boiler. Let it cool to temperature of 120°F. Combine with the 3 tablespoons prepared yogurt and set over hot water.

Keep at a temperature of 100°F. to 105°F. about 3 hours, or until mixture has the consistency of thick custard. Pour into 5 or 6 custard glasses.

Chill thoroughly in the refrigerator. Always reserve 3 tablespoons of this batch to use as a "starter" for the next quart.

SOYBEAN "MILK"

A liquid somewhat similar to milk can be made from soybeans. In the Orient it has been used for hundreds of years as milk for babies. This "vegetable milk" is not equal to cow's milk in food value but it contains most of the food elements in slightly smaller amounts.

It can be used in making custards, soups, breads, cakes, sauces, and drinks such as cocoa, and it can be drunk as a beverage with a little sugar and salt to season it.

The two methods that follow have been used for centuries in the Orient.

Method 1: Wash dry soybeans and soak them overnight. Remove the skins by rubbing them in the water; they will float to the surface and can be discarded.

Grind the beans fine in a food grinder. Put the ground beans in a cheesecloth bag and immerse it in a bowl of lukewarm water, using 3 quarts of water to a pound of dry beans. Work thoroughly with the hands for 5 to 10 minutes, then wring the bag until it is dry.

Boil the creamy white liquid over low heat for 30 minutes, stirring frequently to prevent scorching. Add sugar and salt to taste. Keep in refrigerator.

Method 2: Wash soybeans. Dry them thoroughly, then crack them by crushing coarsely in a food grinder. The skins then can be easily removed. Grind fine in the grinder. To each pound add 3 quarts of water and soak for 2 hours. Boil for 20 minutes, stirring constantly, then strain through cheesecloth. Add sugar and salt to taste. Keep in refrigerator.

FACTS ABOUT LEAVENING AGENTS

To leaven means "to make dough rise." Leavening agents are substances that form bubbles of gas (carbon dioxide) which expand when a batter or dough is heated. They make a batter or dough rise, increase in volume or bulk, and become light and porous during preparation and subsequent baking. Three common sources of carbon dioxide gas are yeast, baking powder, and baking soda plus food acid.

Physical leavenings such as steam and air also make products rise. Steam is formed in any batter or dough as it is heated. It is the principal leavening agent in products such as popovers and cream puffs. Air is beaten or folded into mixtures or introduced into ingredients by beating, creaming, and sifting. Air leavens by expansion during heating.

Bacteria of certain species, under suitable conditions of temperature and moisture, grow rapidly and produce gases from sugar. Salt-rising bread is made from dough leavened in this manner.

Leavening Changes at High Altitudes

For guidance about amounts of leavening to use in your sea level recipes, see **Cooking at High Altitudes.** For specific recipes for various altitudes, see **Cakes at High Altitudes,** in cake section.

BAKING POWDERS

Baking powders are classified according to the acid ingredients they contain. There are three available types: tartrate, phosphate, and SAS-phosphate (usually referred to as double-acting). These terms refer to the chemicals that react with the baking soda in the powder, when liquid is added, to release carbon dioxide gas, the leavening agent. The various brands clearly indicate the type on the labels.

Tartrate Baking Powder: This type reacts rapidly, almost entirely at room temperature when the liquid is added to the dry ingredients. The gas formed then expands when the batter or dough is heated.

Phosphate Baking Powder: This type releases most of its gas at room temperature when combined with liquid, but retains some until the batter or dough is heated.

SAS-Phosphate Baking Powder: This type, often called double-acting or double-action, releases only a small amount of its gas when combined with liquid, then the major portion is given off during baking.

The advantages of a "double-acting" baking powder is that it allows a little more latitude in the mixing and a longer time interval between preparing the batter or dough and putting it into the oven.

Recipes in this book are based on double-acting (SAS-phosphate) baking powder. In general, if you use a single-acting baking powder (tartrate) as a substitute for double-acting baking powder, use 1½ times the amount specified in the recipe.

Because different brands differ in both activity and bulk, the cook who changes from one brand to another, particularly if it is a different type, may find that her usually successful cake recipe doesn't come out just right. A little more baking powder if the cake doesn't rise properly—a little less if it is too porous—will usually take care of the problem. Many cooks prefer to adjust their recipes to a brand and then stick to that brand.

BAKING SODA

Baking soda (also known as sodium bicarbonate or bicarbonate of soda) is used alone or with baking powder to leaven cakes and other products made with buttermilk, sour milk, chocolate, molasses, vinegar, lemon juice and other fruit juices, etc. Acid from these ingredients reacts with baking soda to release a leavening gas. When using baking soda, don't delay mixing or baking.

One-half teaspoon baking soda plus 1 cup sour milk or molasses is equivalent in leavening power to 1 teaspoon double-acting baking powder. You can make sour milk from sweet milk by adding vinegar or lemon juice.

YEAST

Yeast in compressed or dry form is a microscopic living plant that produces a gas (carbon dioxide) from sugar when temperature and moisture are favorable for its growth.

Compressed yeast is a perishable moist mixture of yeast and starch which must be kept in the refrigerator. To use, soften compressed yeast in lukewarm water or milk (85–95°F.) for 5 to 10 minutes.

Dry yeast is similar to compressed yeast except that the yeast-and-filler mixture has been dried and is then packaged in granular form. Before you use dry yeast, soften it in warm water (105–110°F.) for 5 to 10 minutes.

CREAM OF TARTAR

Cream of tartar is an acid substance used extensively before baking powders became common. It seems to be an essential ingredient in angel food cake. Without cream of tartar this cake has a tendency to shrink excessively and is less tender. It also gives very desirable results in sponge cakes and in recipes calling for a large amount of egg whites.

HARTSHORN

A baking ammonia, used in some old-time recipes, and still occasionally used by bakers in cookies and cream puffs. It may be purchased in drug stores in coarse crystals, and should be completely dissolved in a liquid before it is added to a dough or batter. Hartshorn is a powerful leavening agent and should be used cautiously.

FACTS ABOUT THICKENING AGENTS

Flour: Unsifted flour is the most commonly used thickener, especially in sauces. The new easy-blending flour is excellent for sauce making. Flour may be thoroughly blended with fat over very low heat before the liquid is added. Frequent stirring keeps the sauce smooth as it cooks.

Note: The mixture of flour and fat is called a roux. White roux is made without browning. Brown roux for dark sauces is made by browning the fat and flour before adding the liquid.

Or flour may be blended with a cold liquid before combining with the hot mixture. For example, to thicken a hot mixture such as a stew, measure liquid to be thickened. For each cupful, mix 1½ tablespoons flour with 3 tablespoons cold water until smooth. Stir into hot liquid; cook until thickened. Flour requires at least 5 minutes cooking time.

In sweet mixtures, flour may be combined with the sugar before the hot liquid is added.

Cornstarch: This is an especially useful thickener in clear sauces, in some Chinese sauces, and in dessert sauces. Cornstarch should be mixed with a little cold water before being added to the hot liquid. One tablespoon cornstarch will thicken 1½ to 2 cups of liquid. To substitute cornstarch for flour in thickening, use 1½ teaspoons cornstarch for 1 tablespoon flour. Since there are several types of cornstarch on the market, it is best to follow the manufacturer's directions for length of cooking time. In general, it is usually advisable to thicken dessert sauces with cornstarch in the top of a double boiler over (not in) hot water until the raw taste of the cornstarch disappears. Other sauces, particularly the clear Chinese types, are usually thickened over direct heat.

Other Starches: See **Table of Substitutions** for use of other starches in place of flour.

Eggs: Egg yolks not only thicken but enrich a dish. When used for thickening, eggs are slightly beaten and are never added directly to a hot liquid.

To add them to a hot mixture, first stir a small amount of the hot mixture into the eggs, then stir the egg mixture into the remaining hot mixture. If additional cooking is required, use low heat and stir constantly.

TAPIOCA

A starch obtained from cassava root, used to thicken soups and puddings. It is marketed chiefly in pearl and quick-cooking forms. Besides taking longer to cook, pearl tapioca must first be soaked for some time.

SAGO

A starch made from the pith of an East Indian palm tree, used chiefly to thicken puddings and fillings. Sago is used more in England than in the United States.

ARROWROOT

An easily digestible starch made from the roots of a tropical plant. Clear and almost tasteless when cooked, it is used to thicken sauces and puddings and also in baking.

FACTS ABOUT GELATIN

Gelatin is a tasteless, odorless, brittle substance extracted by boiling bones, hoofs, and animal tissues; also, a somewhat similar product made chiefly from seaweeds (vegetable gelatin). Gelatin dissolves in hot water and forms a jelly, also called gelatin, when cool. When the term gelatin is used in a recipe without further description, it means granulated, unsweetened, and unflavored gelatin.

To use, first soften it in a small amount of cold liquid for about 5 minutes, then dissolve it in a hot liquid or over hot water. To hasten setting, part of the added liquid may be cold, once the gelatin has dissolved. One envelope of unflavored gelatin is equivalent to 1 tablespoon and is enough to set 2 cups of liquid firmly. Remember to count the cold liquid used for softening as part of the total.

Packaged gelatin desserts are mixtures of plain gelatin, sugar, fruit acids, flavorings, and colorings. Dissolve them in hot liquid, using 2 cups per package.

Hints About Unmolding Gelatin

Before the mixture is poured in, the mold should be dipped in cold water or (for salads) brushed with salad oil, so that the set gelatin will come out easily.

To unmold, loosen the edge of the mold with a spatula or a small knife dipped in warm water. Then quickly immerse the mold just to the top in lukewarm water (hot water will melt the gelatin). Shake the mold. Place an inverted serving dish on top, turn dish and mold over, and lift the mold off carefully. If the mold is large, moisten the gelatin surface and the plate;

this makes it easy to center the mold. Remove excess moisture with a towel.

Surround large molds with salad greens after turning them out; they may break if unmolded on crisp greens.

Caution About Fresh or Frozen Pineapple

Gelatin will not jell with fresh or frozen pineapple. Always bring fresh or frozen pineapple to a boil, or use canned pineapple. Fresh pineapple contains an enzyme (bromelin) that inhibits jelling. Canned pineapple presents. no problem.

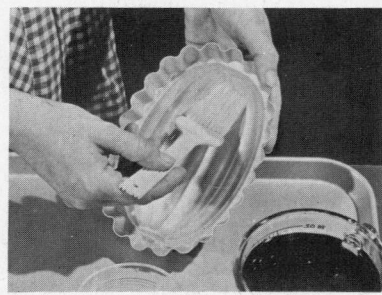

For salads, brush salad oil in mold so the set gelatin will unmold easily.

Shake the set molded salad lightly and turn onto serving plate.

FACTS ABOUT SUGARS, SYRUPS, AND SYNTHETIC SWEETENERS

As used in recipes, the term sugar refers to beet or cane granulated sugar. When another sugar is called for it will be specifically named as: brown sugar or confectioners' sugar.

White sugar can be made from either sugar cane or beet sugar; the two products are identical and either kind can be used interchangeably in all cookery.

Granulated Sugar: This is the standard product made for general use. There are several different granulations variously named by the different manufacturers. Examples are: "granulated," "fine granulated," "extra fine granulated," and "superfine granulated." The last named is a specially screened, uniformly fine-grained sugar, sometimes called "fruit and berry" sugar.

The very fine granulated sugars are desirable where quick dissolving and quick creaming are useful as in mixed

drinks, on cereals and fruits, and in making cakes, cookies, cooked frostings, etc.

Cubes and Tablets: These pressed or cut lumps of sugar are handy for sweetening hot drinks. They are sold in handy 1- and 2-pound cartons.

Confectioners' or Powdered Sugar: These are granulated sugars pulverized and screened to a desired fineness. There is no exact and uniform terminology. Some brands indicate the degree of fineness with X's on the packages. The more X's, the finer the sugar. Some brands may even refer to a superfine granulated sugar as "powdered" sugar.

Very fine confectioners' sugar may be pure sugar or sugar mixed with a very small percentage of cornstarch to keep it from caking.

These sugars are used for frostings, quick candies, and for dusting cakes, cookies, pastries, doughnuts, candies, etc.

Brown Sugar: These sugars have varying amounts of molasses in them which gives them their color. They may be variously named as "yellow," "golden brown," "light brown," and "dark" or "old-fashioned" brown.

The molasses flavor increases with color. The light brown sugars have more delicate flavors and are desirable for general cookery. The darker brown sugars impart more color and flavor, and are desirable for such foods as baked beans, baked hams, and other cookery where more intensity of molasses flavor is preferred.

SEASONED SUGARS

Cinnamon Sugar: Blend 2 tablespoons cinnamon with 1 cup sugar. Use with toast and coffeecake toppings.

Citrus Flavored Sugars: Scrub and rinse thoroughly. the desired citrus fruit (lemon, orange, or tangerine). Grate the colored outermost part of the rind very fine. Combine 1 to 2 teaspoons grated rind to 1 cup sugar. Store covered in a cool place. Use with custards and other desserts.

Vanilla Sugar: Make this by keeping a whole vanilla bean in a closed container of sugar. Or crush the bean with a few tablespoons of sugar before adding it to the stored sugar. Then, strain the sugar and replace it with new sugar until the bean has lost its flavoring power.

TO STORE SUGARS

Store sugars in the original or other covered containers. Confectioner's, and sometimes granulated, sugar have a tendency to cake because they pick up moisture much the same as salt does. These usually can be broken up with a spoon or by putting the sugar through a sieve.

Modern brown sugar packages are designed to retain the sugar's moisture longer and thus to keep it soft and fresh. After each use, fold down the inner paper liner carefully, and tuck in the flap. Storing it in the refrigerator keeps it best because there it obtains the small amount of moisture from the air that it needs to keep it soft.

If brown sugar should lump, place it in a jar with a damp piece of cheesecloth over the top of the jar or put a slice or two of very fresh white bread or apple in the jar. Replace cover and sugar should be soft within a few hours.

SUGAR SUBSTITUTES (SYNTHETIC SWEETENERS)

These are produced under many trade names; however they may be divided into two main types. One is saccharin or saccharin based, the other is based on cyclamate sodium. They have approximately equal sweetening power. The saccharin types should not be used in cooking since they produce a bitter flavor. The cyclamate sodium types can usually be used in cooking and baking since they retain their sweetness when heated. Some types actually increase their sweetening power with some cooked foods. Many recipes that call for sugar to add sweetness, *not bulk,* can be adapted to these sweeteners. Baked goods, however, in which sugar produces volume, as in creaming it with shortening or beating it with eggs, are still off-limits for these sugar substitutes. Hence, the cyclamate sodium substitutes should be used only in baking recipes especially developed for them.

Note: Because of the ban on cyclamates consult your physician before using them.

MOLASSES

Molasses is a by-product of cane sugar, an important source of iron and should be used often.

Light molasses has a mellow flavor and is excellent for general cooking purposes.

Dark molasses is less sweet and has a stronger molasses taste. It is excellent for all cooking in which many spices are present, as in gingerbreads, Indian pudding, etc.

Blackstrap molasses tastes bitter, but contains more iron and calcium than higher grades. It is what's left after the better quality molasses has been drawn off, and is generally regarded as unfit for human consumption except by certain food faddists. It is used for cattle feeding and industrial purposes, and is sold at "health stores" and some groceries.

Old-fashioned molasses is made by a special process. It is unsulfured and has a distinctive flavor.

MAPLE SUGAR AND SYRUP

These are made from the sap of hard maple trees. Maple sugar is sold as maple cream, which has the consistency of peanut butter, as stirred sugar, which is similar to brown sugar, and as soft and hard maple sugar. Maple candies are a fondant made of pure maple frosted with a crystal of pure maple sugar.

Maple syrup is made by concentrating maple sap or by solution of maple sugar. Syrups which are not pure maple are less expensive than the pure syrups. The composition of blended syrups is stated on the label.

CORN SYRUP

A purified syrup made from corn sugar available in light and dark forms. The term corn syrup as specified in recipes usually means the light type. The stronger tasting dark syrup should be specified in recipes, if needed.

HONEY

Honey is a natural sugar manufactured by the honey bee. Its flavor and color depend on the flowers from whose nectar it was made. Dandelion, heather, white clover, and buckwheat are examples.

Comb Honey: Honey sold in the comb. It is sometimes cut into small pieces, packaged, and sold as *cut comb honey.*

Chunk Honey: Consists of pieces of comb placed in glass jars with enough extracted honey added to fill.

Extracted Honey: Liquid honey which has been removed from the comb.

Granulated and solidly crystallized honey are also available.

To Store Honey

It should be stored at room temperature. If it crystallizes, the container can be placed in a bowl of lukewarm water until the crystals are melted.

FACTS ABOUT CHOCOLATE AND COCOA

Chocolate and cocoa are products of the bean of the cacao tree, which is native to tropical America. The word cocoa is a corruption of cacao (the Spanish version of the Aztec word cacahuatl), which is now used in the trade to refer to the raw beans.

Chocolate is the manufactured product when it appears in solidified form such as bars. Cocoa is a powder made from the beans with part of the cocoa butter removed. Breakfast cocoa contains at least 22 percent cocoa butter.

Dutch Process Cocoa: This is made by a chemical treatment that produces a cocoa of a darker color and somewhat different flavor from other prod-

ucts. The method originated in Holland, but also is used domestically.

Instant Cocoas and Ready-to-Serve Cocoas: These require only the addition of hot or cold water or milk to be served as a beverage.

Unsweetened Chocolate: This is made from carefully selected beans, with no cocoa butter removed.

Semisweet Chocolate: This has just enough flavoring sweetening added to give a pleasing, half-sweet flavor. Some cocoa butter is removed.

To Melt Chocolate

Place chocolate in small bowl or custard cup (or aluminum foil or parchment paper); set over hot, not boiling, water until melted. Or melt in original wrapping, on piece of aluminum foil, placed in oven while oven is heating or cooling off. Remove chocolate as soon as it is melted. Never melt chocolate over direct heat. Cool slightly before using.

FACTS ABOUT SALT

Salt is sodium chloride, a white crystalline substance used for seasoning and preserving food and essential to the diet. It is mined from natural beds or obtained by evaporation from sea water.

Table Salt: Finely ground salt, used at table or in cooking.

Iodized Salt: Table salt to which iodine has been added. This is done to prevent goiter.

Coarse or Kosher Salt: Salt in large crystals, used in cooking and as a garnish on such baked goods as rolls and pretzels.

Rock Salt: A non-edible unrefined type of salt used in freezing ice cream and sometimes as a base for baking oysters and potatoes.

Seasoned Salts: Various commercial mixtures of table salt and ground herbs or spices. The commonest are celery, garlic, and onion salts.

Salt substitutes: Various substances resembling table salt in appearance and taste but containing no sodium.

FOOD COLORING

Food colors have to be "U.S. Certified," i.e., certified as safe for use in foods by the Food and Drug Administration. They are available in liquid and paste forms and in a variety of colors. Follow the directions on the containers for using them. In general, however, food color should be added a drop at a time either with an eyedropper or with the tip of a wooden pick. Blend in until desired color is reached.

FACTS ABOUT EXTRACTS

An extract is a preparation containing a food or flavoring in concentrated form, solid or liquid.

Flavoring extracts are essential oils in solution, usually with an alcohol added. When a recipe refers simply to vanilla, it means the extract; with other extracts such as almond, lemon, and orange, the word is always included.

Flavoring extracts should be purchased in small quantities and kept tightly closed because their flavors deteriorate quickly when exposed to air.

Pure vanilla extract is an extract of the vanilla bean, conforming to required standards. The bean is the fruit of a climbing vine of the orchid family native to Mexico and Central America. Vanilla flavoring has been popular since pre-Columbian times, when the Aztecs used it in chocolate.

Imitation vanilla extract is a solution of synthetic flavorings that yield a product simulating pure vanilla extract.

In using vanilla or other flavoring extracts, try to add them to cooled ingredients only. Because they have an alcohol base, much of the flavor evaporates when they are cooked or added to hot substances.

The vanilla bean is far more flavorful than the extract made from it. To use it, steep a small piece in whatever hot liquid you are using—about a ½-inch piece for 2 cups liquid. It may be taken out or finely crushed and left in; if taken out it can be washed, dried, and used to make vanilla sugar. To flavor an uncooked dessert, split the piece of bean, scrape it well, and add the pulp to the other ingredients.

Beef extract is a beef preparation used for flavoring. It lacks food value because the fat and protein are almost entirely removed from the concentrated beef broth from which it is made. It is often used as a quick and easy substitute for beef broth or consommé in sauces and other dishes.

FACTS ABOUT COCONUT

Coconut is the fruit of the coco palm, having a thick, fibrous brown oval husk under which is a thin, hard shell enclosing a layer of edible white meat. When it is fresh, its hollow center is filled with a sweet whitish fluid. Coconut is packed shredded or flaked in several styles.

How to Tint Coconut: Blend 1 teaspoon milk or water with a drop or so of desired food color. Add 1½ cups shredded coconut, also a little almond, peppermint, or vanilla extract if desired. Toss with fork until blended.

To Open and Prepare Fresh Coconut: With a long nail or ice pick, puncture the indentations ("eyes") at the end of the coconut. Drain off the coconut water inside (sometimes called the "milk," but to Hawaiian cooks, coconut "milk" means a liquid extracted from the grated meat).

Then bake the whole coconut in a shallow pan in a moderate oven (350° F.); cool it for half an hour, then tap it with a hammer to crack the shell. Pry out the meat in as large pieces as possible. Remove the brown outer skin with a paring knife or vegetable parer.

Then shred the meat on a vegetable shredder. A medium-sized coconut usually yields about 3 cups shredded coconut

To Make Coconut Milk: To make coconut milk to be used in curry sauce, pudding, or pie filling, pour 1 to 2 cups boiling water or coconut water over 3 cups shredded coconut; let stand 15 minutes, then strain or squeeze through doubled thickness of cheesecloth. After the milk has been extracted, the drained coconut still retains enough flavor to be usable in making candy or macaroons.

For a thick coconut milk, or "cream," to serve over puddings or cereals, use only ½ to ¾ cup boiling water or coconut water.

For coconut cream pie filling, part of the shredded coconut is sometimes scalded with the milk, then strained out before making the filling. Fresh coconut is often sprinkled over the pie before serving.

COMMERCIAL SAUCES IN RECIPES

All of them should be used discreetly; amounts are specified in the recipes.

Worcestershire sauce: A pungent, dark-colored condiment containing soy sauce, vinegar, onion juice, lime juice, chili, and spices. It originated in Worcester, England. The composition may vary.

Soy Sauce: A salty brown condiment made from soybeans that have been fermented and steeped in brine. It is essential to Chinese and Japanese cooking. Since the various brands differ in strength and in monosodium glutamate content, be sure to taste the dish you are cooking before using all the soy sauce called for in a recipe.

Tabasco Sauce: A very pungent proprietary condiment sauce made of cayenne peppers. It's used in small quantities for seasoning many foods.

Bottled Sauce for Gravy: Any of a number of commercial preparations such as Kitchen Bouquet, Gravy Master, etc.. used to give rich brown color and flavor to gravies and sauces.

Bottled Meat Sauce: Any of a number of commercial preparations for, not made of, meat, such as A. 1., Heinz Beefsteak Sauce, etc., of a rather thick consistency.

Shoyu: Japanese name for soy sauce (which see).

FACTS ABOUT NUTS

ALMONDS

The edible nut-like seed of a fruit closely resembling the peach, except that the fruit is fleshless. The "nuts" of sweet almond varieties are eaten raw or roasted and are pressed to obtain almond oil. When called for in recipes in this book, the dry sweet form are the type to be used. Bitter almond varieties also yield oil from which the poisonous prussic acid is removed in the extraction process. The bitter almond is sometimes specified in small quantities in certain recipes for flavoring, for example in Orgeat syrup. Almond oil is used in soaps, and cosmetics and medicinally as a demulcent. It is sometimes used for flavoring, especially in some types of European recipes; however it is dangerous to use in excess and in the United States it is available only on prescription.

ALMOND PASTE

A preparation made from finely ground blanched almonds, used as a base for macaroons, candies, and pastry fillings. It is the main ingredient of marzipan (which see).

BEECHNUTS

Edible three-cornered nuts of a number of related trees with smooth, gray bark, hard wood, and dark-green leaves. Beechnuts have a sweet flavor but are now seldom eaten except in the poorer areas of Europe.

BRAZIL NUTS

The edible, oily, three-sided, hard-shelled seed, or nut, of the Brazilnut tree, a very tall tree of tropical America. The nuts grow clumped together in large, round, woody and extremely hard seed pods. The meat of the seed (the "nut") is very rich in oil.

Brazil nut chips may be used as a trim for cakes and cookies or toasted and salted for delicious nibbling.

BUTTERNUT

The hard-shelled nut of the North American white walnut tree used mostly in the manufacture of candy to which it lends a pleasant, buttery flavor. Butternuts are sweet, oily, and nutritious.

CASHEW

A kidney-shaped nut that grows on the outside of the cashew apple, the fruit of a tropical American tree. In the West Indies, the cashew apple, which is white, yellow, or red, juicy and slightly acid, is eaten or fermented to make wine.

CHESTNUTS

These are the smooth-skinned, sweet, edible nuts of any of a group of trees of the beech family. They contain more starch and less fat than most other nuts. Because the American trees have been largely destroyed by blight, the chestnuts on the market are imported, usually from Italy. Chestnuts are eaten cooked—roasted or boiled. They are particularly delicious with Brussels sprouts. Puréed boiled chestnuts are good accompaniments for game, pork, and turkey and often used in stuffings.

Freshly roasted chestnuts are relished as a dessert. The French word marron, which actually refers to a particular type of chestnut, is used for chestnuts preserved in syrup, candied, or dried. Do not confuse these chestnuts with water chestnuts which are usually available in canned form and often called for in various Chinese-style recipes.

Preparation: Wash chestnuts; cut a gash in the flat side of each chestnut.

Place the nuts in a heavy pan; add 1 teaspoon of cooking oil for each cup of nuts. Shake until coated with oil.

Set pan in moderate oven (350°F.) and heat until shells and skins can be removed easily.

Remove shells and skins with a sharp knife; cover with boiling salted water and cook gently until tender when tested with a toothpick, 15 to 20 minutes.

Drain, mash or rice, and season with salt, pepper, and butter or margarine. Serve with medium white sauce or use in stuffing.

Savory Puréed Chestnuts: Prepare as above but add (for 1 pound chestnuts) to the cooking water 1 tablespoon vinegar, 3 stalks of celery, and 1 small peeled onion.

Season the mashed cooked chestnuts with 2 tablespoons butter or margarine, ¼ teaspoon pepper, 2 or more tablespoons hot cream, and salt to taste.

SAUTÉED CHESTNUTS

Sauté drained cooked chestnuts in butter and serve as garnish for turkey, ham, or as a vegetable.

CREAMED CHESTNUTS

Reheat cooked (sliced or whole) chestnuts in small amount of heavy cream.

ROASTED CHESTNUTS

With a sharp knife, make two crosswise slashes on the flat side of each chestnut.

Melt some butter or oil in a saucepan (about 1 teaspoon for each cup of nuts). Drop in the nuts and keep shaking in the pan over a hot flame until all nuts are coated with fat.

Then bake them in a moderate oven (350°F.) until tender and shells and inner skins can be removed easily, about 30 minutes.

FILBERT

Also known as Hazelnut, these small round nuts from the Pacific Northwest are sweet-meated and increasing in popularity. They are much used in cooking, especially for cookies and candy.

LITCHI

Also spelled lichee; the fruit (nut) of a small Chinese evergreen tree now being cultivated to a limited extent in Hawaii and California. Litchi nuts as usually purchased consist of dried raisin-like pulp enclosed in a fragile shell. They are available in Chinese stores. The litchi is also available canned in syrup.

MACADAMIA NUT

A rich, crunchy nut grown in Hawaii, somewhat similar to a hazelnut when shelled and roasted. It is served as a cocktail tidbit.

PARADISE NUT

A South American hard-shelled nut resembling the Brazil nut.

PEANUT

Peanut is the name of a vine of the pea family with yellow flowers as well as brittle pods ripening underground. The seeds—peanuts—are eaten fresh or roasted and are used in cookery and confectionary. Other names for the peanut are goober, pinder, earthnut, groundnut, and ground pea. Peanuts have a high protein content and make an economical contribution to the diet.

Peanuts may be roasted at home; however the commercial method yields a superior product. To roast at home, keep the oven at a low temperature (300°F.) and roast in the shell for 30 to 45 minutes, or 20 to 30 minutes if shelled. Turn them constantly to avoid scorching. Check for doneness by removing skins. The inner brown skins are nutritious and have a pleasant flavor.

BLENDER PEANUT BUTTER

Use fresh roasted or salted peanuts and a bland oil such as vegetable or safflower oil. Combine in blender, allowing 1½ to 3 tablespoons oil per cup of nutmeats. Blend to desired consistency. If nuts are unsalted, add salt to taste.

PECANS

These are olive-shaped nuts with a thin, smooth shell. The tree it grows on is related to the hickory, and is one of the most important nut trees of the United States. A rich food (containing 70% or more of fat) the pecan is the most popular American nut after the peanut. Cultivated American varieties with unusually thin shells (called papershelled pecans) have been developed but wild pecans are gathered in quantities and sold.

PINE NUT OR INDIAN NUT

The pine nut is a tiny, thin-shelled nut found in the cones of certain pines and removed by roasting. It has a sweet, delicate flavor, and is much used in Italian and Near Eastern cooking and baking. Also known by the Italian name pignolia, the Spanish name piñón, and the French name pignon.

PISTACHIO

The greenish seed of a tree native to Asia Minor and now grown also in the Mediterranean regions and to a limited extent in California. Valued for its delicate flavor and color, it is used especially in confections, ice creams, and pastries. It is served salted in the shell as a dessert nut.

WALNUT

A roundish or oval nut with a two-lobed seed; either the strong, distinctively flavored black walnut, or the pale tan, mild-flavored English (or California) walnut. Recipes calling for walnuts refer to the latter, unless specifying the former.

WATER CHESTNUT

The water chestnut is a crunchy nut-like fruit of any of a number of related water plants with floating leaves and small white flowers. It is widely used in Chinese and other Oriental cooking and can be bought canned.

TO STORE NUTMEATS

Nuts are rich in oil, and shelled nutmeats will become rancid if stored in a warm place for any length of time.

Store them in a tightly covered container in refrigerator, preferably for not more than a few months.

To Recrisp Nuts

Spread on a baking sheet and place in a slow oven (300°F.) for about 10 minutes. Let cool and use as desired.

FACTS ABOUT VINEGARS

Vinegar is a sour liquid containing acetic acid, made by bacterial action from various dilute alcoholic liquids. The sharpness, richness, or mellowness of vinegars make quite a difference in various dishes, hence recipes often specify the type of vinegar or dilution if required.

Cider: A vinegar made from fermented apple juice; it is an all-purpose standby for salads and salad dressings.

Malt: A vinegar made from fermented malt; its rich flavor goes well with many fish and meat sauces, salad dressings, and various seafoods.

Wine: Vinegars made from red or white wines; they are preferred by many people for salad dressings, sauces, and many other dishes.

Distilled or white: Clear, colorless vinegar made from plain alcohol; it is ideal for pickling and preserving.

Any of the above may be flavored with various herbs. Recipes for homemade flavored vinegars have been included in this book; however nowadays you can buy a large variety of delightfully flavored vinegars to use in cooking. Here are a few examples:

Tarragon: A herb fragrance that is often preferred in salads, salad dressings, sauces, and pot roasts.

Garlic Wine: Often used instead of garlic in salads, sauces, stews, and hamburgers.

Basil, Mixed Herb, Mixed Herb and Spice: Any of these should be used lightly with cooked greens, cole slaws, salad dressings, sauces, and other dishes.

GARLIC VINEGAR

Mash 6 garlic cloves through a garlic press into just slightly less than a pint of cider vinegar in a scalded pint jar.

Put uncovered jar in shallow pan of water. Bring water to boil and remove from heat. Let stand 45 minutes.

Remove from water to cool. Cover tightly. Let stand a week, shaking jar occasionally. Strain, bottle, and label.

TARRAGON VINEGAR

Put several sprigs of fresh tarragon or 2 tablespoons dried tarragon in vinegar. Proceed as directed for garlic vinegar.

MIXED HERB VINEGAR

Add a pinch each of basil, chopped chives, dill, oregano, parsley, tarragon, and thyme to 1 pint cider vinegar.

Place uncovered jar in pan of water. Bring to boil. Remove from heat and let stand 45 minutes.

Remove from water to cool. When cool, add 1 small onion which has been pierced many times with a fork. Let stand 1 week, then strain, bottle, and label.

QUICK HERB VINEGAR

1   **cup wine or cider vinegar**
1   **teaspoon dried crushed herbs (basil, tarragon, etc.)**
2   **tablespoons chopped parsley**
1   **tablespoon chopped chives**

Combine vinegar and herbs. You may use this at once with salad oil.

You may add ½ clove of garlic and remove it later. Shortly before you serve it, add parsley and chives.

Food Terms You'll Want to Know

Included here are well-known—and not so well-known—dishes and terms of foreign lands, many unique expressions of American regional cooking, and infrequently used utensils and foods.

ACIDOPHILUS MILK

A form of milk fermented with cultures of Lactobacillus acidophilus. It is tart and buttermilk-like and is sometimes prescribed in cases of intestinal disorder.

ADOBO

A Philippine national dish that takes many forms. It is a type of stew, usually with a base of pork, chicken, or fish or some combination of these. Also spelled adobe.

AGAR-AGAR

Also called agar. A gelatinous substance made from several kinds of seaweed, it is used in some Oriental cooking and in preparing various jellied dishes. Although most agar comes from the Far East, California is also a source of supply. It is marketed in the form of dried flakes.

Agar is often prescribed as a laxative in chronic constipation. It may be taken alone, cut into small pieces and eaten as a cereal with cream and sugar, or combined with a drug such as cascara sagrada to increase the cathartic action.

AGNEAU

(French): Lamb.

AGUACATE

(Spanish): Avocado. The name is probably derived from the Aztec name: ahucatl. See **Avocado.**

AIGUILLETTE

(French): A diminutive of aiguille (needle), referring to a manner of carving; a small, narrow strip or slice of cooked meat from a meat animal, fish, or breast of fowl.

À LA

(French): After, or according to, the style of; in the manner of. This phrase (with its variants à l', au, aux) is used to describe different ways of preparing or serving food. Sometimes the style is said to be that of a country—à l'allemande: German; à la russe: Russian. Sometimes the names are more descriptive of the dish and sometimes fanciful —à la printanière: made with spring vegetables; à l'estragon: served or cooked with tarragon; au vert pré: colored green with vegetables or served with a green garnish; aux champignons: served with or containing mushrooms.

AL, ALLA

The Italian equivalents of the French terms (see preceding entry) are also used in cookery—al burro: cooked with butter; alla cacciatore: sautéed with a sauce of tomatoes, mushrooms, and peppers; al forno: roasted or baked.

ALBACORE

Strictly speaking, albacore is a fish of the tuna family; commonly, any of several related fishes, including the bonito. See **Tuna.**

ALEWIFE

Fish resembling herring and shad, caught on the east coast and also in some lakes and streams.

ALLUMETTE

(French): Match; a term sometimes applied to foods cut in matchlike strips. Pommes allumettes: potato straws; allumettes au fromage: cheese straws.

AMANDINE

(French): Garnished with or containing almonds. Fish such as fillet of sole or trout are sometimes covered with a butter sauce to which slivered almonds have been added. Vegetables may also be served this way.

AMÉRICAINE

(French): American; à la Américaine: "in American style."

ANANAS

(French): Pineapple.

ANCHOVY

The anchovy is a small, slender, salt-water fish of the herring family. In the Mediterranean countries where they are caught, anchovies are often eaten fresh; in the United States they are available only salted, spiced, and canned in oil or made into a paste. They are used as appetizers and to flavor other food, particularly salads and sauces. For recipes see index.

ANDALOUSE

(French): A term indicating that the dish to which it is applied contains tomatoes and sweet pimientos.

ANGLAISE

(French): English; in English style: à la Anglaise.

ANTIPASTO

(Italian): The first, or appetizer, course of a meal. It consists of cold or spicy hors d'oeuvres such as anchovy, salami, hot peppers, olives, celery, and pickled relishes. Prepared jars of antipasto are available in many food stores. They are a convenience to have on hand. Just chill and prepare colorful appetizing arrangements on individual plates.

APÉRITIF

(French): A drink of moderate alcoholic content taken before meals to stimulate the appetite.

APFEL

(German): Apple; apfel kuchen: apple cake or tart; apfel strudel: a delicate pastry made of paper-thin dough covered with an apple filling, then rolled and baked.

APPLE SNOW

A whipped dessert consisting of apple pulp and stiffly beaten egg whites, usually flavored with lemon and vanilla.

ARTICHAUT

(French): Artichoke.

ASH BREAD

A name applied to early types of cornbread made in the South. Ash bread was usually wrapped in cabbage leaves and baked in the ashes of an open fire.

ASPERGES

(French): Asparagus.

AU, AUX

See in À La.

BAIN-MARIE

(French): A utensil for cooking or keeping hot certain delicate foods that should not be exposed to a direct flame. The vessel containing the food is placed in or over another pan, in which water is kept at or below the boiling point. The double boiler is a type of bain-marie.

BALLOTTINE

(French): A piece of meat, poultry, or game; boned, stuffed, and rolled up—usually served hot.

BANNOCK

In Scotland and northern England, a thick, round flattened cake made of oat, rye, or barley meal, usually unleavened and baked on a griddle. Also, a type of Irish soda bread.

BAR-LE-DUC

A preserve of seeded whole red (or sometimes white) currants, named after the French town in which it is said to have originated. Nowadays, the term is also applied to similar preserves made with gooseberries and other berries.

BARLEY

A cereal grass whose seed or grain is used in making liquors and beers and also in soups. Barley as the source of strong alcoholic liquor, especially whiskey, is humorously personified as John Barleycorn—a term also applied to the liquor itself.

BARLEY SUGAR

An English confection made by heating sugar until it begins to melt and caramelize, forming coarse grains. This clear, hard candy was formerly made with a barley extract—hence the name.

BARQUETTE

(French): A small oval or boat-shaped pastry shell. Barquettes may be filled with various mixtures for hot or cold hors d'oeuvres, or with fruit, custards, etc., for desserts.

BAVAROISE

(French): Molded dessert of Bavarian cream; à la Bavaroise: Bavarian style.

BEEF À LA MODE

A well-larded piece of beef slowly cooked in a little water or wine with vegetables; a form of braised beef.

BEIGNET

(French): A fritter.

BEURRE

(French): Butter. Au beurre noir: with black butter. The butter is not really black but browned in a pan. With lemon added, this makes a nice sauce for fish and vegetables. Beurre fondue: melted butter; beurre manié: butter and flour kneaded together and gradually added to a sauce to thicken it.

BIRD'S NEST SOUP

A Chinese soup thickened with the mucilaginous substance used by a certain species of birds (swifts) to hold their nests together.

BISCUIT

In American usage, a quick bread baked in small shapes cut out or dropped from a dough leavened with baking powder or baking soda; in British usage, a cracker or cooky; French usage, sponge cake.

BISMARCK HERRING

The fillets of herring are pickled with their roe in a mixture of white wine and vinegar, seasoned with onions, salt, and whole black peppers. They are served as an appetizer.

BISQUE

A thick, rich cream soup made from shellfish or, formerly, from game; hence, also, various thick vegetable soups. Also, a frozen dessert containing powdered nuts or macaroons.

BITOCHKY SMETANA

(Russian): Russian meatballs in a sour-cream sauce.

BITTERS

An infusion of bark, herbs, roots, and other aromatic materials used to flavor cocktails and other drinks and some foods. There are a number of trademarked brands, whose formulas are usually secret. Abbott's, Angostura, Fernet Branca, and Peychaud's are among the most popular brands. Angostura bitters have been used in a number of the food recipes in this book calling for aromatic bitters.

BLANQUETTE

(French): A stew of white meat (chicken, veal, or lamb) made with white sauce.

BLOATER

A specially selected fat herring or mackerel that has been cured (bloated), i.e., salted and smoked.

BOEUF

(French): Beef; boeuf rôti: roast beef; boeuf à la mode: well larded, sometimes marinated, beef, braised with vegetables; boeuf salé: corned beef; boeuf braisé: braised beef.

BOLOGNA

(Italian): Also called Bologna sausage; a mildly seasoned smoked sausage, usually made of beef, pork, and veal.

BOMBAY DUCK

A strong-flavored dried fish served in India and elsewhere with curries.

BOMBE

(French): A dessert made by freezing two or more ices, ice creams, or sherbets of contrasting colors and flavors in concentric layers in a round or melon-shaped mold.

BONBON

(French): A confection or candy that has a fondant center or is dipped in fondant.

BONNE FEMME, À LA

(French): Literally, in the manner of a good woman; hence, originally, cooked in a plain, home style. The term now refers to a garnish of vegetables cooked with meat or of mushrooms cooked with fish.

BOUCHÉE

(French): Literally "mouthful." A small patty of light pastry usually filled with a savory creamed fish or meat mixture.

BOURGEOISE, À LA

(French): In simple family style; a kind of garnish consisting of vegetables such as onions and carrots.

BOURGUIGNONNE

(French): À la bourguignonne: in the style of Burgundy, a region of France noted for its food and wine. Escargots à la bourguignonne: snails in a garlic-flavored butter sauce; sauce bourguignonne: a red-wine sauce with many variations—depending on whether it is intended to accompany meat, poultry, fish, or eggs—but usually containing shallots or onions, butter, and mushrooms.

BRAID

A fancy bread in which the dough is cut into strips which are braided, either three or four strands being used. The braids are wider at the center than at the ends.

Braid

BRATWURST

(German): Small, highly seasoned pork link sausages, served hot.

BRAUNSCHWEIGER

(German): Soft liver sausage.

BREWER'S YEAST

This is obtained as a by-product in the brewing of beer. It does not have leavening power. Brewer's yeast is a concentrated source of high-quality protein and of many of the B vitamins. Because it is also a good source of the minerals iron and phosphorus, it sometimes is prescribed for patients needing dietary supplements.

BRILLAT-SAVARIN, JEAN ANTHELME

A French gastronome (1755-1826), the author of *The Physiology of Taste*, a classic work on cookery. His name has been given to various dishes.

BROCHETTE

(French): A small skewer. En brochette: Broiled or served on a skewer.

BROWN STEW

Stew in which the meat is browned in fat before liquid is added.

BRULE

(French): Burnt; a term usually applied to caramelized sugar. Crème brulée: a rich custard with a caramelized sugar coating.

BRUNOISE

(French): The cutting of vegetables into shreds or into tiny rounds, cubes, or other uniform shapes. The term also describes a mixture of vegetables slowly cooked in butter or some other fat and used for making soups, sauces, or other dishes.

BUBBLE AND SQUEAK

An old English dish of beef and cabbage, so named because of the sound it makes while cooking.

BUCK RABBIT

Welsh rabbit topped with a poached egg.

BUN

A large round roll, made of yeast dough usually somewhat sweetened and often spiced or enriched with raisins, etc.

BUNDKUCHEN

(German): A circular-shaped cake.

BURRO

(Italian): Butter.

CABINET PUDDING

A cold, molded dessert of layers of gelatin, thickened custard, and cake or fruit.

CAFFEINE

An alkaloid present in coffee, tea (in which it is known as theine), and cola drinks and, in small amounts, in cocoa. When taken in moderation, caffeine is a mild stimulant; taken to excess, it can have a harmful effect on the heart and nervous system.

CALF'S-FOOT JELLY

A jelly made from the gelatin extract from calf's feet by long, gentle cooking; an old-time Jewish dish known in Yiddish as pitcha or sülze.

CANARD

(French): Duck.

CANNELON

(French): When used alone, the word usually refers to a small roll or "stick" of pastry, stuffed with minced meat or sweets, baked or fried. When applied to meat, as "cannelon of beef," it means a stuffed roll of beef, cooked usually by braising.

CANNOLI

(Italian): A Sicilian pastry made of thin dough shaped into a cylinder and fried in deep fat, then filled with ricotta cheese, pudding, whipped cream, or ice cream.

CAPE COD TURKEY

Codfish.

CAPONETTE OR CAPETTE

A hormone treated chicken of either sex, usually marketed at an earlier age than a capon. It is usually lighter in weight but retains all the advantages of a capon.

CARBOHYDRATE

The class of foodstuffs that includes starches and sugars (the two other main food classes are proteins and fats). Carbohydrate foods are used by the body essentially for immediate energy; when eaten in excess of need, they are converted rapidly into stores of fat.

CARNATZLACH

(Yiddish): A highly seasoned ground-meat dish of Rumanian origin. The meat is formed into small sausage-like shapes and broiled.

CAROB

An evergreen tree native to the Mediterranean area with long, fleshy, edible pods which have been used as food for animal and man since prehistoric times. The pods have numerous names including locust pod, St. John's bread, and bokser. The pods are eaten fresh or dried. The carob pod is often found in Italian food shops.

A powder made from the carob pod is sometimes available and is used in baking to add flavor to wheat flour; a lower oven temperature (not over 350°-F.) must be used because carob powder scorches easily. About $\frac{1}{8}$ to $\frac{1}{4}$ cup carob powder may be substituted in each cup wheat flour, and a similar amount of wheat flour must be deducted from the recipe.

CARTE, À LA

(French): Literally, from the bill of fare. This term refers to the practice of listing dishes on a menu item by item, with a separate price for each, as opposed to table d'hôte, in which a price is fixed for the entire meal.

CARTE DU JOUR

(French): Bill of fare or menu for the day.

CASSAVA

Any of a number of related tropical plants with edible starchy roots; also called manioc. Bitter cassava, the kind most commonly used, contains hydrocyanic acid and is deadly poisonous until it is cooked. In South America cassava is cooked like sweet potatoes, ground into a flour used for bread, and fermented to make an intoxicating beverage; elsewhere it is known chiefly as the source of tapioca.

CASSOLETTE

(French): Individual heatproof dish; food cooked and served in such a dish. In the U.S. this is usually called an individual casserole.

Cassolette

CASSOULET

(French): A complex stew made in many versions with a large variety of ingredients; however white beans and pork are basic ingredients in most recipes.

CECI

(Italian): Chick-peas.

CELLULOSE

The substance (chemically, a carbohydrate) that makes up the cell walls or woody parts of plants. Since it is not digested by human beings, vegetables such as cabbage that contain a high proportion of it form a residue (bulk) in the bowel.

CERVELAT

A sausage made of beef and pork.

CHAMPIGNONS

(French): Mushrooms.

CHANTILLY

(French): A term applied to a great many dishes made or served with whipped cream.

CHAPON

(French): A crust or cube of bread usually rubbed with garlic and tossed with salad to give it flavor. Caesar salad is made with chapons. Also the French term for capon.

CHAROSES OR KHAROSES

(Yiddish): A mixture of nuts, apples, and wine served by Jewish people at dinner on the eve of the first two days of their Passover holiday. It symbolizes the mortar used by the Israelites when they were slaves in ancient Egypt.

CHICKEN-FRIED STEAK

Steak dredged in flour and seasonings, pan-fried, and served smothered in gravy.

CHIFFONADE

(French): Literally, "rags." Refers to a garnish of finely shredded vegetables used for soups and salads.

Chiffonade dressing is a salad dressing (usually French dressing) with minced or shredded vegetables in it.

CHOP (The food)

A cut of meat; the name is derived from the fact that the piece is chopped off.

CHOU

(French): Cabbage.

CHOU-FLEUR

(French): Cauliflower.

CHOUX DE BRUXELLES

(French): Brussels sprouts.

CHOWCHOW

Chopped vegetable pickle in a highly seasoned mustard sauce. Also, chopped preserved fruits.

CIVET

(French): A highly seasoned stew of rabbit or other game. The animal's blood is always used in the sauce of a true civet.

CLABBER

Milk that has soured to the stage where a firm custard has been formed but not to the point of separation of the whey.

COBBLER

A deep-dish pie of sweetened fruit topped sometimes with biscuit dough rather than piecrust. Also, a type of alcoholic beverage served over shaved ice.

Cobbler

COCKTAIL

An appetizer—either a short, mixed alcoholic beverage or liquid or solid food (fruit or vegetable juice, chilled mixed fruits, seafood).

COCOTTE

(French): An earthenware or porcelain-covered casserole. Small cocottes are generally used for such dishes as shirred (baked) eggs. Larger sizes are used for chicken and other entrées. Foods so cooked (which are described as being en cocotte) should be served from the dish.

Cocotte

COLCANNON

Irish dish of potatoes, salt pork, cabbage. It is similar in character to the English dish called, "Bubble and Squeak."

COLLOP

A small piece or slice, especially a thin, boneless piece of meat, dipped into eggs and crumbs and sautéed.

CON CARNE

(Spanish): With meat.

CONDÉ

(French): Stewed fruit served with rice. Also a French almond-paste cake.

CONFITURE

(French): Jam.

COQUILLE

(French): Literally, shell; usually that of the scallop. Hence, a similarly shaped cooking vessel or food prepared in one. En coquille: served in a shell.

En Coquille

CORAL

The ovaries of the female lobster. Considered a delicacy.

CORBEILLE

(French): Literally, basket; used on menus to mean a basket of fruit.

CORDON BLEU

(French): Literally, blue ribbon; the name of a famous French cooking school. Often used loosely to denote any exceptionally fine cook.

CÔTELETTE

(French): Cutlet, a small boneless slice of meat.

COUPES

(French): Fruit sundaes, i.e., a combination of ice creams with various flavors usually served in stemmed glasses. Although sundaes are common in the U.S., the idea is of French origin. **Coupe Jacques:** vanilla ice cream served with mixed fruit. **Coupe Melba:** vanilla ice cream topped with a peach half with sweetened puréed raspberries spooned over it, and garnished with whipped cream and slivered almonds.

COUSCOUS

A dish that takes many forms throughout the various North African countries. It commonly refers to a coarse ground grain or meal (wheat semolina, cracked millet, cracked wheat, or buckwheat) steamed in beef, chicken, or mutton stock served separately with the meat or poultry used for the stock. Or couscous may be a complex all-in-one dish of chicken, lamb or mutton, or beef cooked with a variety of vegetables and served with one of the grains mentioned above.

CRÈME

(French): Cream; frequently used in the names of liqueurs. Crème d'ananas: flavored with pineapple; crème de bananes: flavored with bananas; crème de cacao: made from cacao and vanilla beans; crème de café: flavored with coffee; crème de Cassis: mildly alcoholic, made from black currants; crème de menthe: green or colorless, flavored chiefly with peppermint; crème de moka: flavored with coffee; crème de rose: flavored with rose-petal oil and vanilla; crème de thé: flavored with tea; crème de vanilla: flavored with vanilla bean: crème de violette: made from vanilla and cacao, perfumed with oil of violets; crème Yvette: lavender-colored, similar to crème de violette. À la crème: with cream.

CRESSON

(French): Watercress.

CREVETTE

(French): Shrimp.

CROQUEMBOUCHE

(French): A spectacular pyramid-like dessert made from about 100 walnut-size cream puff shells filled with French pastry cream or other filling. After filling, these are dipped in caramelized sugar syrup which serves both as a glaze and adherent to keep the cream puffs in place in row upon row to form the pyramid around some suitably shaped dish.

CROUSTADE

(French): A hollowed-out chunk of fried or toasted bread, or a pastry shell, made to hold creamed or other soft food. Croustades are made in various shapes.

Croustades

CROÛTE

(French): A bread crust, pastry crust, or crust formed on anything. En croûte: baked in a crust, or covered with a crust.

"CUBE" STEAKS

Usually pieces of round steak put through a cube machine. This breaks the fibers and makes the steaks tender.

CUISINE

(French): Kitchen, cookery, or a particular style of cooking.

DAGWOOD

A huge sandwich containing many different fillings, named for the comic strip character addicted to them.

DAMPFNUDELN

(German): Steamed noodles.

DAMSON

A variety of small, purple plum.

DARIOLE

(French): (1) A small cup-shaped mold filled with various savory mixtures and baked or steamed. (2) A small cream-filled tart.

DAUBE

(French): A style of braised meat, poultry, or game; usually beef braised in a wine stock. Also, a Creole-style pot roast.

DÉJEUNER

(French): Lunch, Petit déjeuner: breakfast; the French breakfast usually consists of hot rolls and coffee.

DELMONICO

Delmonico steak: club steak: Potatoes Delmonico: sliced cooked potatoes baked with white sauce, crumbs, and cheese. Both are named for a famous New York restaurant of the 19th century.

Delmonico Steaks

DEMI-TASSE

(French): Literally, half-cup. After-dinner coffee, served in small cups, usually black, although cream and sugar may be added if desired.

DENTE, AL

(Italian): Literally, to the tooth; a term describing pasta products cooked only until they are barely tender. When they are to be served plain or with a sauce, this is how they should be.

DENVER OR "WESTERN" SANDWICH

A sandwich made of scrambled egg with bits of ham and sometimes green pepper and onion in it.

DIABLE, À LA

(French): Deviled, or seasoned with spicy condiments.

DITALINI

(Italian): A tubular-shape macaroni product about 1/4 inch in both diameter and length and usually used in soups.

DIVINITY

A kind of candy; soft, light, and creamy.

DRIED BEEF

A form of preserved beef cured by salting, smoking, and drying.

DUCHESS

Duchess Potatoes: potatoes whipped very light with seasonings and beaten egg yolk, usually piped through a pastry tube as a border for broiled or planked meats; also called Potatoes Duchesse. Duchess apples: an early cooking variety.

DUCK, PRESSED

An epicurean dish of roasted duck that is squeezed in a special press at the diner's table and is served with a sauce prepared in a chafing dish. Called Canard à la Presse in French, this dish is served only in the most elaborate restaurants.

Pressed Duck

DUFF

An old-time English thick flour pudding boiled or steamed in a cloth bag. Also, an English fruit dumpling.

DU JOUR

(French): A term used on menus to indicate feature of the day, as soupe du jour (soup).

DULSE

Any of several edible seaweeds with large, red, wedge-shaped fronds.

DUTCH APPLE CAKE

A form of sweet bread, usually a biscuit or shortcake dough, baked in a flat sheet with tart, wedge-shaped slices of apple arranged in regular rows on the top and spread with sugar and cinnamon.

ÉCREVISSE

(French): The fresh-water crayfish.

ENTRÉE

(French): Correctly used, this term means a small dish served between the main courses at a formal dinner. However, in the United States it is used for the main course of a meal, the one preceded by an appetizer and followed by dessert.

ENTREMETS

(French): Literally, between dishes. In earlier centuries, this term referred to a variety of sweet or vegetable side dishes served between the many courses of the elaborate French meals then in fashion. Nowadays it means dessert.

ESCALOPE

(French): A small thin slice of meat or fish.

ESCARGOTS

(French): Snails.

ESCOFFIER

A French chef (1847-1935), one of the great names in French cookery.

ESPAGNOLE

(French): Spanish. Espagnole sauce: a brown sauce.

FARCE

(French): A forcemeat; a mixture of minced meat and seasonings used as stuffing for meats and poultry.

FARCI

(French): Stuffed with forcemeat or some other filling, as cabbage stuffed with sausage meat.

FARFEL

(Yiddish): Noodle dough chopped into fine grains and boiled, usually in soups.

FECULA

Any form of starch, used for thickening, often produced from potatoes, manioc (cassava), or other food plants rather than from a cereal grain. Potato flour (which see) is a good example.

FISH AND CHIPS

Fish fillets with sliced potatoes, both fried in deep fat; popular in England.

FLAMBÉ

(French): Literally, burned; a term applied to food that has a liquor, usually brandy, poured over it and ignited.

FLAN

(French): An open-faced pie or tart. Also, a baked custard.

FLANNEL CAKE

A thin, tender griddlecake, often one made with yeast.

FLEISHIGS

(Yiddish): Meat or meat derivatives, or dishes made with these. See **Kosher**.

FLOUNDER

Any of several sea flat-fishes with high-quality white meat. Much of the so-called sole found in U.S. markets is actually flounder, since the true sole does not inhabit American waters. See Sole in the index.

FLUFF

A dessert of stiffly beaten egg whites or whipped cream, sugar, and fruit pulp, cooked or uncooked; also called whip, snow, foam, sillabub, and soufflé.

Orange Fluff

FLUMMERY

A dessert made of rice or oatmeal with milk and flavorings; also, a type of custard dessert.

FOIE

(French): Liver. Foie gras: fat goose liver; foie de veau: calf's liver. See also **Pâté**, for pâté de foie gras.

FONDANT

Candy used as centers for bon bons and chocolates, coating for nuts, as base for mints and patties. There are two kinds, one a cooked mixture of sugar and water, the other uncooked confectioners' sugar, butter, and milk or water.

FONDUE

(French): Swiss fondue (which see); also, a baked soufflé made with eggs, cheese, milk, and crumbs. In French, the term is used in addition for various vegetable preparations cooked to a pulp. Fondue à la bourguignonne: chunks of beef cooked individually in a chafing dish by the diners, who then choose a sauce for them from among a variety set out.

FOOL

A dessert of chilled stewed strained fruits and sweet cream. It is an old-time American dish.

FOUR

(French): Oven.

FRAISE

(French): A strawberry; also, a French brandy made from strawberries.

FRAMBOISE

(French): A raspberry; also, a French brandy made from raspberries.

FRANCAISE, À LA

(French): In the French manner: a term applied to various dishes with no specific meaning.

FRAPPÉ

(French): Fruit juice sweetened with sugar, diluted with water, and frozen to a slushy consistency. Also, a beverage poured over shaved ice.

FRENCH DOUGHNUT

A doughnut made of puff paste.

FRENCH PASTRY

Individual pastries, most frequently made of puff paste with various fillings.

FRENCH ROLL

A hard, crisp roll; also called Vienna roll.

FRICANDEAU

(French): Larded meat, usually veal, in a sauce.

FRITTO MISTO

(Italian): A fried or sometimes pan-broiled mixture of delicate meats and vegetables.

FROMAGE

(French): Cheese.

FRUITS DE MER

(French): Seafood.

FUMÉ

(French): Smoked; saumon fumé: smoked salmon.

FUMET

(French): The concentrated stock or broth of meat, fish, or vegetables.

FUNNY CAKE

A Pennsylvania-Dutch favorite. A cake batter and sauce, baked in a pie shell. The sauce forms a layer between cake and pie shell.

GALANTINE

(French): Boned poultry, game, or meat stuffed and roasted, simmered, or braised, then pressed into a symmetrical shape and cut into slices or molded in aspic.

GALUPTZE

(Russian): Ground meat rolled in cabbage leaves.

GÂTEAU

(French): Cake; petits gâteaux: small cakes; gâteaux assortis: assorted cakes.

GAUFRE

(French): A waffle of the French type, made of a very light, sweetened dough or batter.

GELÉE

(French): Jelly or jellied.

GEM

A term variously used; often applied to muffins or cupcakes.

GHEE

A clarified butter used in India, considered choicer as it ages as much as 10 years. It is one of the commonest articles of diet in India, and is used extensively in all forms of cooking.

GHERKIN

A small, knobby variety of cucumber, or the immature fruit of the common cucumber, used for pickling.

GOLDEN BUCK

Welsh Rabbit topped with a poached egg.

GOOBER

A peanut. The term is a corruption of an African (Bantu) word.

GOURMAND

Originally, a glutton; now a person who likes and is a judge of fine foods. In the latter sense it has the same meaning as epicure and gourmet, but the implication is still one of heartiness rather than delicacy.

GOURMET

An epicure; a person who likes and is a judge of fine foods and drinks. In French, the term originally referred to a winetaster.

GROUNDNUT

Any of several plants with edible tubers or tuber-like parts; specifically, a British term for peanut.

GRUEL

A thin porridge.

HACHE

(French): Minced or chopped.

HACHIS

(French): Mincemeat or hash.

HAGGIS

Considered the national dish of Scotland, it is a sort of meat pudding made of liver, lungs, and other parts of mutton mixed with oatmeal, onion, suet, and herbs, and cooked in a sheep's stomach. Since the stomach is tripe, the whole pudding is considered edible.

American Scots have haggis flown in from Scotland for the feast o' the haggis annually on St. Andrew's Day.

HALKE

(Yiddish): A potato or flour dumpling. Also called knaidel.

HALVAH OR HALVA

A confection consisting of a paste made with ground sesame seeds and nuts mixed with honey and other ingredients. It is highly favored in Turkey and other countries of the Near East. A variation of it is popular with American Jews.

HANGTOWN FRY

Usually a combination of scrambled eggs and fried oysters.

HARD TACK

Unsalted, hard, dry biscuit; the name given by sailors in early days to the ship's crackers or bread.

HARICOT

(French): Bean. Haricots verts: green beans. Also a stew, usually of mutton; this term has nothing to do with the word for bean but comes from halicoter, to chop.

HARLEQUIN

See Neapolitan.

HASTY PUDDING

In New England, corn-meal mush; in Great Britain, a flour or oat porridge.

HOTCHPOTCH

Also called hodgepodge; a thick Scottish stew of meat (usually mutton) and various vegetables in a very little brown stock. It needs stirring because it may stick to the bottom of the pot.

HOMARD

(French): Lobster.

HONGROISE, Â LA

(French): Hungarian style. It usually refers to a paprika sauce, pink or red, depending upon the amount of paprika used, with chopped onion and sour cream. Served hot with fish, lamb, veal and poultry.

HOOTSLA

A Pennsylvania-Dutch dish consisting of bread cubes which are first browned in butter, then a mixture of beaten eggs, milk, and seasoning is poured over and fried until brown.

HOT POT

An English meat stew with many variations.

HUILE

(French): Oil.

HUÎTRES

(French): Oysters.

HYSON

A variety of Chinese green tea; the early crop is called young hyson, and the inferior leaves are called hyson skin.

IMBOTTITO

(Italian): Stuffed. The plural forms are imbottiti and imbottite.

INDIENNE, À LA

(French): In the Indian manner; generally, with curry or similar East Indian seasonings.

IRISH MOSS

An edible seaweed (carrageen) dried and bleached for use in medicine and as a thickening agent, particularly in milk desserts. Also, blancmange, which is sometimes made with it.

IRRADIATE

To treat with ultra-violet light in order to increase the vitamin D content. Milk is commonly irradiated.

JAMBON

(French): Ham.

JARDINIÈRE À LA

(French) : Literally, gardener's style; garnished with diced mixed vegetables.

JERKED BEEF

Beef preserved by slicing it into strips and drying these in the sun or over a fire.

JOHNNYCAKE

A type of corn bread. The name comes from the term journey cake—that is, one that would keep well on a journey.

JUGGED HARE

A rabbit stew in a wine sauce.

JULEP

A cold beverage with a distinctive flavor, often of herbs; specifically, a mint julep.

JUMBLES

Name used for several kinds of English cookies.

JUNKET

A sweetened, flavored milk dessert curdled or jellied by rennet (which see).

JUS

(French): Juice or gravy; au jus: served in the natural juice or gravy.

KARTOFFEL

(German): Potato. Kartoffel klösse: potato dumplings.

KÄSE

(German): Cheese.

KEBAB

Also spelled kabob or cabob; highly seasoned meat or other foods cooked on skewers. The word is derived from shish kebab.

KEBI

Also spelled kibbie; a Syrian national dish made primarily of ground lamb and other meats, bulgur (cracked wheat), and pine nuts.

KING, À LA

Usually applies to a method of preparing chicken, served in a rich cream sauce usually containing mushrooms, pimientos, and green peppers; sometimes flavored with sherry.

KLÖSSE

(German): Dumplings.

KOCH KÄSE

(German): Boiled cheese.

KOSHER

(Yiddish): A term designating foods selected and prepared in accordance with Jewish dietary law; derived from a Hebrew word meaning fit, right, proper. Kashruth, as the dietary law is called, makes demands both difficult and subtle. At Passover, for instance, when leavened foods (see Matzo) are prohibited, Orthodox Jews must not use soda pop containing food coloring with an alcoholic base, since this is often made from leavened grain. The Old Testament prohibition against cooking a kid (a young goat) in its mother's milk is extended to keeping separate dishes for meat and dairy products, some pareve (neutral) dishes, and additional sets used only during Passover.

One reason kosher meat is more expensive is that it must be ritually examined before and after slaughter under rabbinical supervision.

Kosher products, often indicated by the letter U, are put out under many national brand names. Kosher cheeses are also made, without animal rennet; they are identified by a label and come in cream, cottage, Gouda, Limburger, and other types.

KRANZKUCHEN

(German): A sweet cake in the form of a braid.

KUCHEN

(German): A cake, often a coffee cake.

KUMISS

Fermented or distilled mare's or camel's milk, drunk by Tatar nomads of Asia. Imitations made of cow's milk are used in certain special diets. Also spelled koumis, koumiss, koumyss.

LACHS

(German): Salmon.

LAIT

(French): Milk. Au lait: made or served with milk.

LANGOUSTE

(French): A sea crayfish or spiny lobster.

LANGUE

(French): Tongue. Langue de veau: veal tongue; langue de chat: cat's tongue, a flat, narrow chocolate candy or a similarly shaped cooky.

LEGUME

The term, legume, refers to any plant of the pea family; also, the edible pod of any of these including beans, peas, peanuts, carob, lentils, and soybeans. In French the word is used to mean any vegetable. Legumes provide valuable and nutritive foods because the food stored for the embryo in the seed (the pea) is rich in protein. In many areas of the world, especially where meat is scarce or expensive, legumes are staples of the diet. See index for recipes for beans, peas, lentils, etc.

LEMON OIL

An oil obtained from the rind of lemons.

LINGUINE

(Italian): A narrow, flat noodle about ⅛ inch wide, meaning literally "little tongues."

LINSEN

(German): Lentils.

LIVER SAUSAGE OR LIVERWURST

A sausage made from pork livers and trimmings, seasoned, and packed in casings of various sizes.

LOX

(Yiddish): Smoked salmon.

LUTFISK

Lutfisk is often called Swedish Christmas Fish for this fish is usually served only during the holiday season. It is a type of dried salt cod which is soaked in lye water or baking soda water for several days to a week, then in fresh water, before it is cooked. It is used almost exclusively by Scandinavians and it can be bought in Scandinavian delicatessen stores in the U.S. ready to cook, especially at Christmastime.

LYONNAISE

Prepared with finely sliced, fried onions; said especially of potatoes sautéed with onions.

MACÉDOINE

(French): A mixture usually of fruits or vegetables, cut into small, uniform pieces.

MADRILÈNE

(French): A clear, tomato-flavored consommé, served hot or jellied.

MAÎTRE D'HÔTEL

(French): The man in charge of hotel catering or restaurant food service. Also, a term implying the use of chopped parsley. Maître d'hôtel butter: creamed, seasoned butter mixed with minced parsley and lemon juice, served on broiled meats, broiled or poached fish, and certain vegetables; maître d'hôtel sauce: béchamel sauce with minced parsley, butter, and lemon juice added.

MANDELTORTE

(German): Almond Torte.

MARGUERITE

(1) An unsweetened cracker spread with boiled frosting, sprinkled with coconut, nuts, or chocolate pieces, and baked until golden. (2) a cracker with a melted marshmallow on it. (3) A spongecake batter baked in small shapes.

MARMITE

(French): A stock pot used for cooking soups or stews. Petite Marmite: A French soup served in small earthenware casseroles.

MASA

(Spanish): Dough; a term sometimes used specifically to mean the dough for tortillas, which is made of corn kernels soaked in lime water and then ground fine.

MATÉ

Also known as Paraguay tea and yerba mate; a kind of tea made from the dried leaves of a South American evergreen tree of the holly family. It is a popular beverage in some parts of South America. In Spanish the word is spelled without the accent, which is used in English so that the second syllable will be pronounced.

MATELOTE

(French): A stew of fish with wine, mushrooms, onions, and garlic, properly made only with fresh-water fish; also, a sauce for fish with similar ingredients.

MATZO

(Hebrew): A Jewish unleavened bread made of flour and water. It is thin and cracker-like, pricked in a pattern that resembles stitching. As a reminder of the Biblical Israelites, who departed so hastily from their slavery in Egypt that they took with them dough that was still unleavened, religious Jews eat no other bread during the week of Passover. The plural of the word is matzoth.

MATZOON

(Armenian): Yogurt.

MEAT BIRDS (PAUPIETTES)

Meat birds, or in French, paupiettes, is a dish made in various ways but usually consisting of thin, oblong pieces of beef or veal that are stuffed, rolled, and tied or skewered. They are then coated with flour, browned, and cooked in a small amount of liquid.

MELBA

The name of a famous Australian operatic star who died in 1931, Dame Nellie Melba, who gave her name to many dishes. The most famous is Peach Melba, originally made in her honor by the great French chef Escoffier. This dish consists of halves of peaches on a layer of ice cream covered with a raspberry sauce. Nowadays almost any fruit is served in the same way.

MERINGUE

(French): Stiffly beaten egg whites sweetened and flavored if desired and baked to a delicate brown. It is used on pastry, puddings, cakes, and other desserts, and as small cakes (kisses). It is also made in the form of shells which are filled with ice cream.

MIGNON

(French): Dainty. Filet mignon: a small choice fillet of beef tenderloin or occasionally some other meat.

MILANAISE, À LA

(French): In the style of Milan. Applied to meats, this term usually indicates a coating of breadcrumbs mixed with Parmesan cheese; with other dishes it most frequently implies the use of macaroni, cheese, chopped cooked meat, and a tomato sauce.

MILLE-FEUILLES

(French): Literally, a thousand leaves; a delicate pastry made of many thin leaves of puff paste, with a cream filling.

MILT

The reproductive glands of male fishes, especially when filled with germ cells, and the milky fluid containing them. It is cooked like fish roe and is considered a delicacy by some people. Also called soft roe. Milter; a male fish in breeding time.

MINESTRA

(Italian): Pottage, soup, broth.

MIROTON

(French): Cooked, sliced leftover meat heated in various ways, usually in a brown gravy to which onions and pickles are often added.

MOCHA

A variety of coffee originally exported from Mocha, a port on the Red Sea, and noted for its quality: hence, a term often applied to foods flavored with coffee or with coffee and chocolate.

MOCK CHICKEN LEG

Meat, usually seasoned ground veal or pork or a combination, formed around a wooden skewer in the shape of a chicken leg. It is usually coated with crumbs before cooking.

MOCK DUCK

A meat prepared in a duck-like shape. Leg of lamb is commonly used.

MOCK TURTLE SOUP

A soup made from calf's head with a variety of seasonings.

MODE, À LA

(French): Literally, fashionable or according to a particular custom; a term applied to a method of braising beef and also, with no specific significance, to various other ways of cooking or serving food.

MOLLET

(French): Soft. Oeufs mollets: soft-cooked eggs.

MONGOLE

(French): Literally, Mongolian style. Purée mongole: a split-pea soup containing tomatoes, garnished with julienne vegetables.

MORTADELLA

(Italian): A large smoked sausage.

MOSTACCIOLI

(Italian): A tubular pasta about $\frac{1}{2}$-inch in diameter, cut obliquely about $2\frac{1}{2}$ inches long.

MOUSSAKA

Also spelled mousaka or mussaca, a Near Eastern casserole dish made in many variations, often of lamb and vegetables, frequently including eggplant.

MOUSSE

(French): Literally, froth. A frozen dessert of sweetened, flavored whipped cream, with or without fruits; also, a chilled dessert of whipped cream or beaten egg whites, variously flavored. The term is also applied to a number of molded dishes of ground fish, meat, or poultry prepared with beaten egg white or with gelatin.

MOUSSELINE

(French): A term applied to a number of preparations made with whipped cream; also, any of several very light cakes. Sauce mousseline: usually Hollandaise sauce with whipped cream, sometimes mayonnaise with whipped cream.

MULLIGAN STEW

A stew made of odds and ends of meat and vegetables; a slang term originating with hoboes.

MUTTON

The meat of a sheep one or more years of age.

NATUREL

(French): Natural; au naturel: in plain or simple style.

NAVARIN

(French): A mutton or lamb stew with turnips, onions, and potatoes and a rich gravy.

NEAPOLITAN

Brick ice cream layered in different flavors; also, sometimes, a gelatin mold arranged in layers of different colors. Also called harlequin.

NOISETTE

(French): Hazelnut. Hence, also, small round pieces of lean meat or browned potato balls.

NORMANDE, À LA

(French): In the style of Normandy, a region of northern France; a term often implying the presence of cream, cider, or apples or a combination of these. Normande sauce: a rich cream sauce containing fish or shellfish stock and mushrooms or mushroom stock, served with seafood.

NOUGAT

(French): Any of several varieties of candy; usually, a paste containing chopped nuts, such as pistachios or almonds.

NOUVEAU

(French): New. Applies to peas, potatoes, etc.

NÜSSE

(German): Nuts; also, small nut-sized or nut-shaped cakes.

OATEN

Of or made of oats or oatmeal.

OB'L PUFFER

A Pennsylvania Dutch type of apple fritter.

O'BRIEN POTATOES

Cooked, diced potatoes pan-fried with chopped onions and green pepper, pimientos, or both.

OEUF

(French): Egg. Oeuf brouillé: scrambled egg; oeuf dur: hard-cooked egg; oeuf en cocotte or oeuf sur le plat: baked or shirred egg; oeuf frit: fried egg; oeuf farci: stuffed egg; oeuf mollet: soft-cooked egg; oeuf poché: poached egg.

OLEOMARGARINE

Margarine. This name, which dates from the time when the product was made with beef fat (oleo), is falling into disuse now that most margarine consists of vegetable oils.

OLLA PODRIDA

(Spanish): A rich stew of sausages, poultry, beans, beef, cabbage, and other ingredients baked slowly in an earthenware pot, from which it takes its name. The term is no longer used much in Spain; such a stew is usually now called a cocido.

OMELETTE

(French): Omelet; omelette au fromage: cheese omelet; omelette au jambon: ham omelet; omelet au rhum: omelet flavored with rum; omelette parmentier: omelet with potatoes; omelette aux fines herbes: omelet with finely chopped herbs.

OOLONG TEA

A type of Chinese and Japanese tea that is only partly fermented before being dried. It therefore differs both in color and in flavor from virtually all the other tea used in the United States, which is black or fully fermented. Oolong makes a lighter-colored beverage with a slightly astringent taste.

ORANGE PEKOE

A black tea grown in Ceylon and India, made from the small leaves at the tips of the stem. The term denotes the size of the leaf, not the quality of the tea.

ORETIKA

(Greek): Hors d'oeuvres or appetizers.

PAIN

(French): Bread. Pain rôti or pain grillé: toast; pain perdu (literally, lost bread): French toast, or, in Creole cookery, a kind of fritter.

PAN BREAD

A quick bread baked in a covered saucepan on top of the range.

PAN FISH

A general term for small fish for cooking whole in a small amount of fat.

PANADA

Originally, any dish containing soaked breadcrumbs (the name comes from the Spanish word for breaded); hence, a simple French soup made of stale crusts of bread gently cooked in water or milk to the consistency of gruel, then enriched with butter and egg and seasoned with salt and pepper. Also, and more commonly, a paste of bread, flour, or cereal cooked with milk or stock to form the foundation for forcemeat or stuffing or to be used in thickening sauces.

PANÉ

(French): Prepared with or coated with breadcrumbs.

PANOCHA

A candy made of brown sugar, milk, butter, and nuts. Also a coarse sugar made in Mexico. Also spelled penuche or penuchi.

PAPILLOTE, EN

(French): Cooked in parchment or in a paper bag. Nowadays, aluminum foil is usually substituted for the paper.

Aluminum foil cookery is a modern version of "en papillote."

PAREVE

(Yiddish): A term applied to food that is neither a dairy (milchig) nor a meat (fleishig) product and can therefore, according to the dietary laws, be eaten with either by Orthodox Jews. Also spelled parve. See **Kosher.**

PARFAIT

A frozen dessert made of whipped cream and flavoring folded into a foundation of beaten egg yolks cooked with hot syrup. Also, a dessert of several layers of ice cream, fruit or syrup, and whipped cream served in a tall glass called a parfait glass.

Parfaits

PARMENTIER

(French): A name applied to dishes containing potatoes; from Antoine-Auguste Parmentier (1737-1817), who popularized the potato in France and invented many ways of cooking it.

PASTRAMI

A type of highly seasoned, peppery, cured smoked beef, usually plate, of Rumanian origin. Available either uncooked or cooked and ready to eat, it is good for sandwiches or for hors d'oeuvres.

PÂTE

(French): Any pastry dough or batter.

PÂTÉ

(French): Any pie with both top and bottom crusts. Also, by extension, any of a number of ground- or chopped-meat mixtures originally prepared in pie form. The most famous of these is pâté de foie gras (literally, fat livers), which is made from the oversized white livers of geese that have been fattened by being confined to pens and stuffed with food; they are cooked with Madeira, seasonings, and usually truffles.

PÂTÉ A CHOUX

(French): Cream-puff paste.

PÂTISSERIE

(French): Pastry; pastry shop; pastry-making.

PAUPIETTE

(French): A meat bird. See **Bird.**

PAYSANNE, À LA

(French): Cooked plainly or peasant-style; specifically, a term applied to braised meats or poultry served with root vegetables and celery.

PÊCHE

(French): Peach.

PEMMICAN

Also spelled pemican, pressed lean venison or buffalo (bison) meat pounded to a paste with fat and berries and pressed into cakes, made by American Indians as a travel food. It keeps a long time; therefore, a similar preparation made of dried beef, raisins or other dried fruits, and suet is used as a concentrated food for explorers and hunters.

PEPPERONI

(Italian): A highly peppered sausage of the salami type.

PÉRIGOURDINE, À LA

(French): In the style of Périgord, a region of western France; a term always implying the presence of truffles and sometimes of pâté de foie gras, two specialties of the region.

PERSILLADE

(French): Prepared with parsley, as potatoes persillade.

PETIT, PETITE

(French): Small.

PETITS POIS

(French): Very small green peas.

PIÈCE DE RÉSISTANCE

(French): The main course or dish of a meal.

PIGS IN BLANKETS

Small sausages wrapped in dough and baked. The term is sometimes applied also to angels on horseback: oysters rolled in bacon and broiled or cooked in a small amount of fat.

PILCHARD

A small fish of the herring family, common along the European coast. Its young is the sardine.

PIQUANT

Agreeably pungent or stimulating to the taste; pleasantly sharp or biting.

PIZZAIOLA

(Italian): In the style of a pizza; a term applied to dishes, usually meat, with a highly seasoned topping of tomatoes and sometimes cheese.

PLOMBIÈRES

(French): A frozen dessert of ice cream and candied fruit, with whipped cream. Also, an almond-flavored ice cream with a custard base.

PLUCK

Term applied by the English to heart, liver, and lungs of animals. We call them variety or specialty meats.

POI

A fermented paste made from ground or pounded taro root. Of Polynesian origin, it is popular in Hawaii.

POIS

(French): Peas. Petits pois: very small peas; pois cassés: split peas.

POIVRADE

(French): Pepper sauce.

POIVRE

(French): Pepper; au poivre: cooked or heavily seasoned with pepper.

POLLO

Chicken in Italian and Spanish.

POLONAISE, À LA

(French): In the Polish style. When applied to meat dishes, this term generally indicates the use of red cabbage, beets, horseradish, or sour cream; applied to vegetables (mainly asparagus, cauliflower, and broccoli), it refers to a sauce of melted butter, breadcrumbs, and chopped egg yolk.

POMME

(French): Apple; pomme bonne femme: baked apple.

POMME DE TERRE

(French): Apple of the earth or potato.

POMODORO

(Italian): Tomato.

PORRIDGE

A soft food made of cereal or meal boiled in water or milk until thick.

PORTERHOUSE

A choice cut of beef from the center of the short loin. Its name is said to come from its having been a specialty of a famous New York porterhouse or tavern. The porterhouses were so called because they served the dark ale known as porter, which in turn got its name from its popularity with porters—that is, load-carriers.

PORTUGAISE SAUCE

(French): A type of tomato sauce.

POTAGE

(French): Soup.

POULET, POULARDE, POULE, POUSSIN

(French): Types of chicken. Poulet: chicken in general, but commonly a bird no larger than about 3½ pounds; poularde: a specially fattened hen or a large roaster; poule: a stewing chicken; poussin: a very young broiler or squab chicken.

PRESSED MEAT

Gelatin-molded meat, often made of chopped, cooked meat mixed with concentrated, well-seasoned stock with a high gelatin content. This is poured into a mold and allowed to stand several hours. In the mold, it may be pressed by use of weights.

Pressed Meat

PRINTANIER

(French): Literally, springlike; a term applied to dishes made or garnished with mixed fresh vegetables. The form à la printanière is also used. Consommé printanier: a chicken consommé containing a variety of vegetables. Printanière sauce: a white sauce colored with green vegetables.

PROVENÇALE, À LA

(French): In the style of Provence, a region of southern France. Dishes in this style always contain garlic (usually a great deal of it) and often tomatoes.

PULLET

A female chicken of 3 to 6 pounds ready-to-cook weight (depending upon the breed), that is in the first six months of egg production. It is usually plump and juicy, and generally fine. Pullets can be fried or roasted, but usually are stewed, fricasseed, or used in chicken pie, creamed chicken, etc.

PUNCH

A sweetened, variously flavored, sometimes spiced beverage often made with a distilled liquor or with wine. The name is derived from the Hindu word for five, which refers to the original number of ingredients.

QUENELLE

(French): A dumpling made of pounded or finely ground meat or fish. Small quenelles are used as a garnish for soups or other dishes; larger ones are served with a sauce as a first course or a luncheon dish.

QUEUE

(French): Tail. Queue de boeuf: oxtail.

QUICHE

(French): A quiche may be an individual tart or a pie served as an appetizer or a main luncheon dish. There are many versions; however the most famous is Quiche Lorraine, a rich custard pie.

Quiche

RACK OF LAMB

The rib section.

RAGOÛT

(French): Stew; as used in English, one that is highly seasoned and thick.

RASHER

A thin slice of bacon; sometimes (in restaurants) three slices of bacon.

RASSOLNIK

(Russian): A soup made of pickled cucumbers, various other vegetables, chicken giblets and other meats (often veal kidneys), and sour cream.

RAVIGOTE SAUCE

(French): Any of several sauces flavored with vinegar: a French dressing with chopped onion, capers, tarragon, sometimes hard-cooked egg, and other seasonings; a hot white sauce with herbs; a highly seasoned mayonnaise containing anchovy paste.

RÉCHAUFFÉ

(French): Reheated or warmed over in sauce. Refers especially to meats.

REINE, À LA

(French): Literally, in queenly style; a term applied to various dishes made with a purée of chicken.

RELEVÉ

French term for meat, fish, or poultry served after hors d'oeuvres, before the roast. Much the same as the French entrées, though there used to be more of a distinction.

RENNET

Rennet is any substance containing the digestive enzyme rennin, which has the property of curdling milk; specifically, an extract prepared from the stomachs of calves. It is used in making cheese and milk puddings. Rennet is available in tablet, powder, and liquid forms under various trade names.

RIBBON CAKE

A cake made from batter that is divided into equal parts, variously colored, and put into a pan in even layers to produce a striped effect. Sometimes the different colors are baked as separate layers and put together with fillings.

RIJSTTAFEL

An Indonesian term which means literally, rice table, and refers to a meal consisting of boiled rice and a wide variety of curried dishes and/or various other hot spicy dishes and the accompanying relishes.

RILLETTES

(French): A highly seasoned pâté of minced or mashed pork, served as an appetizer.

RIS

(French): Sweetbread. Ris d'agneau: sweetbread of lamb; ris de veau: sweetbread of veal.

RISI E BISI

(Italian): A soup of rice and peas.

RISSOLES

(French): Savory ground or chopped mixtures, usually meat, wrapped in rich pastry and fried; meat pies. Also called a pasty as in Cornish pasty. The term is sometimes also applied to fruit-filled turnovers.

Rissoles

RIZ

(French): Rice.

ROCK CANDY

Large, hard, clear crystals of sugar, made by pouring a sugar syrup cooked to a certain density into deep pans that have been laced with heavy thread on which the crystals deposit while being formed.

ROE

Fish eggs, especially when still massed in the ovarian membrane, a film-like skin. Those chiefly used are from the sturgeon, shad, carp, cod, salmon, white-fish, and mullet. Caviar is the salted roe, particularly of sturgeon.

ROGNONS

(French): Kidneys.

ROLLMOP

A small herring fillet rolled around a tiny gherkin, marinated, and usually served as an appetizer.

ROLY POLY

A fruit dessert consisting of a sheet of biscuit dough spread with sugar, spice, and fruit or jam and rolled like a jelly roll. It is then steamed, boiled or baked.

Roly Poly

RÔTI

(French): Roast; roasted.

RÔTIE

(French): Toast. Rôtie au beurre: buttered toast.

ROTISSERIE

An oven, oven-like device, or grill equipped with an automatically rotating spit. Also, a restaurant specializing in grilled and roasted meats or a part of the kitchen reserved for grilling meats.

ROULADE

(French): A rolled, sometimes stuffed piece of meat.

ROYALE

(French): A thick, unsweetened custard cut into various shapes and used as a garnish for soup. À la royale: garnished with custard shapes; also, a term applied to various dishes coated with a thick cream sauce.

RUM TUM TIDDY

Also known as rink tum tiddy, a tomato flavored variation of Welsh

Rabbit, sometimes made with onion and egg.

RUSK

A slice of light bread, cake, or slightly sweetened biscuit dried and toasted in an oven.

RUSSEL

(Yiddish): A soured beet juice, used especially by Jewish people to make borsht (beet soup) during the Passover holiday.

RUSSIAN DRESSING

Mayonnaise plus chili sauce and a variety of other seasonings, if desired. Very similar to Thousand Island dressing, but usually with a smaller variety of added ingredients.

SADDLE

A cut of lamb or mutton from an unsplit carcass, including part of the backbone and the two loins. Long saddle: loin and rump; short saddle: loin only.

ST. GERMAIN

(French): A term applied to many dishes made or garnished with green peas. St. Germain Soup: a green pea soup.

ST. JOHN'S BREAD

See **Carob**.

SALAMI

A highly spiced, salted sausage, originally Italian.

SALMAGUNDI

Any mixture or medley, especially a dish of chopped meat, eggs, etc. flavored with onions, anchovies, pepper, vinegar, and oil.

SALMIS

(French): Also spelled salmi; a type of stew made of game birds. They are first roasted until about two-thirds done, then cut up, trimmed, and stewed in a rich sauce that usually contains wine, truffles, and mushrooms. The final stages, or at least the finishing touches, are often performed at the table in a chafing dish.

SALPICON

(French): Any kind of mixture (fish, meat, poultry, or vegetables) chopped up or cut into very small pieces and bound with a sauce. Salpicons are used as stuffings, made into croquettes, or put into various pastry or bread cases.

SALT FISH

Fish preserved by salting, either with a dry salt or a brine.

SALT PORK

Pork cured in salt, usually in a brine, especially the fatty parts from the back, side, or belly of a hog, and used most frequently as a seasoning in various dishes.

SAMOVAR

(Russian): A metal urn for heating

water to make tea. It is heated by charcoal placed in an internal tube and has a spigot for drawing off the water.

SARATOGA POTATOES

Potato chips.

SARDINE

Any of a variety of young fish preserved in various sauces in tightly packed tins. The true sardine is the pilchard, but sprats and herrings are also commonly used.

SARMA

A Balkan and Near Eastern dish of wilted grape leaves or cabbage leaves stuffed with a well-seasoned mixture of ground meat and often rice, then rolled and cooked in a sauce, most commonly a tomato sauce.

SAUCISSON

(French): Sausage; saucisse: very small sausage.

SAUMON

(French): Salmon.

SAUSAGE

Ground, highly seasoned meat, often combined with other ingredients and usually stuffed into a casing made of animal intestine or other membranous tissue. More than a hundred distinct varieties are known, some of them very ancient. One of the earliest is said to have been made of mixed shellfish. The common U.S. sausage is composed of pork, potato flour, water, and seasonings—a very simple product by sausage standards. Sausages are classified as wet or dry, depending on whether the ingredients are fresh or cooked.

SAVORY

This name is applied not only to the herb, savory (which see) but also by the English to a piquantly flavored food served at the end of dinner. This English custom is unknown in the United States; the British spelling is savoury (plural: savouries).

SCHMALTZ

This Yiddish term derived from German for melted fat refers to rendered chicken or goose fat. It has become a slang expression in English for anything very sentimental and unctuous, as certain music, literature, etc., that is, unctuous sentimentalism.

SCHMIERKÄSE

(German): A type of cottage cheese.

SCHNITZEL

Schnitzel is German for a cutlet of meat, usually veal. Wiener schnitzel (Vienna schnitzel): a thin slice of veal, breaded and fried, then often served with anchovies and capers; schnitzel Holstein: veal cutlet with a fried egg on top, garnished with anchovies.

SCHNITZ UN GNEPP

Also spelled Schnitz und Kneph, a Pennsylvania-Dutch dish of ham and dried apples with dumplings.

SHASHLIK

(Russian): Lamb on skewers.

SHEEPSHEAD

Lean, white meated fish found in both salt and fresh water—along the Atlantic and Gulf coasts, and the Mississippi and other rivers and lakes. It sometimes grows to 50 and 60 pounds but choice eating weight is about 1 to 5 pounds. Has a sheepish look (head and teeth).

SHORTCAKE

A light, rich biscuit; often, specifically, a biscuit of this kind served with fruit (commonly strawberries) and plain or whipped cream. The term is sometimes applied to a similar dessert made with sponge cake.

SHREWSBURY CAKE

A rich rolled English cooky, often cut in star shape.

SILVER CAKE

A delicate, rich, white cake.

SILVER DRAGEES

Tiny ball-shaped, silver-colored candies.

SIMNEL CAKE

Rich fruit cake with an almond paste layer, baked in position, not put in later, traditional in England for the fourth Sunday of Lent, or "Mothering Sunday," a holiday for servant girls by old custom, so that they could visit their mothers. The name "Simnel" is derived from the Latin word simila which means "the finest wheat flour."

Those who prefer a more far-fetched explanation may like to know of a theory that the name of the cake arose out of a squabble, between a husband and wife called Simon and Nellie, as to how a cake should be cooked, whether boiled or baked. In the end, they compromised by boiling it first and then baking it; and in some old recipes Simnel Cake is boiled first and then baked.

SIZZLING STEAK

Steak served on an aluminum platter which has been heated so that the steak and juices sizzle.

SKATE

A flat fish of the ray family, ugly but edible.

SLAW

Cole slaw.

SMÖRGÅSBORD

(Swedish): Literally, bread-and-butter table; a buffet intended for appetizers or for a light lunch or supper. American enthusiasts often make a dinner of it. It may contain as many as 50 different dishes, including several types of bread; many kinds of fish, cheese, and cold cuts; a variety of salads and relishes; and a number of hot foods.

SOLE

Sole is a European sea flatfish highly valued as food. It has white flesh, close-grained but delicate. True sole is not found in American waters but is sometimes imported, chiefly from Britain (where it is called Dover sole) and Denmark. Most of the so-called fillets of sole found in U. S. markets are some species of flounder or fluke. For recipes, see index.

SORBET

(French): Another name for sherbet.

SORGHUM

Any of a number of related tropical cereal grasses. Some are grown chiefly as fodder, others for the sweet juice extracted from their stalks. Also, the syrup made from the juice, which is similar to molasses.

SOUPÇON

(French): Literally, a suspicion; hence, a very small amount, especially of a given seasoning or flavor.

SOUR SALT

A citric acid sometimes used as a substitute for lemon juice as flavoring or to avoid the discoloration of fruits and canned foods.

SOUVLAKIA

(Greek): Lamb on skewers.

SPUMONE

(Italian): A molded frozen dessert often made of 2 or more colors, flavors, and textures of ice cream, often with candied fruits, nuts, and rum flavoring.

SPUN SUGAR

Sugar syrup which has been boiled to the long-thread stage, then drawn out into threads over bars; it is often colored.

STAG

A male chicken, usually under 10 months of age, and 5 to 9 pounds, ready-to-cook weight. Its flesh has begun to darken and toughen slightly, it's skin is coarse, and its breastbone has hardened considerably. This bird is best cooked as a stewing chicken.

STOCKFISH

Fish, usually cod, dried hard in the open air. The best known is a heavily salted Norwegian cod that must be soaked for at least 3 days before it is cooked. It is widely used in northern Europe and — despite a good deal of locally produced dried salt cod — on the Mediterranean coast of France.

STREUSEL

(German): A crumb-like topping for cakes, usually made of butter, flour, sugar, and cinnamon. Fine bread or cake crumbs and chopped nuts, such as almonds, are sometimes included.

STURGEON

Any of several large food fishes with rows of spiny plates along the body and a projecting snout. The largest species is the Russian or beluga of the Caspian and Black Seas and the Sea of Azov; it reaches a length of 13 feet and a weight of up to a ton. Although the meat is coarse, smoked sturgeon is considered a delicacy in many areas. Sturgeon eggs are the source of better grades of caviar. See **Caviar** in index.

SUBGUM

(Chinese): With mixed vegetables.

SUISSE, A LA

(French): Swiss style.

SÜLZE

German for "in aspic"—that is, jellied; also the name of an old-time Jewish dish, a calves foot jelly also known as "pitcha."

SUNDAE

Ice cream topped with a sauce or syrup. Nuts or fruit and whipped cream may be added.

SUNSHINE CAKE

A yellow sponge cake, usually containing more egg whites than yolks.

SUPRÊME

(French): A delicate and tender portion of boneless meat, poultry, or fish; also a term applied to various elaborate desserts. Suprême de volaille: boned chicken breast; suprême sauce: a cream sauce made with reduced chicken stock, served with poultry, eggs, and vegetables.

SYLLABUB

A form of eggnog made of sweetened milk or cream mixed with wine, cider, or brandy and beaten to a froth; sometimes whipped cream is added. When combined with gelatin it becomes a chilled dessert. Also spelled sillabub.

TABLE D'HÔTE

(French): Literally, table of the host; a complete meal of a definite number of courses for which an all-inclusive price is specified on the menu.

TAGLIARINI

(Italian): A ribbon-shaped pasta.

TARTE

(French): Pie; tart. Note that what Americans call a pie is a tarte in France and a tart in England. American tarts are small individual pies, which in France are tartelettes.

TARTELETTE

(French): A little tart.

TASSE
(French): Cup. Demitasse: literally, half a cup; a small cup used for black coffee.

TAVOUK DOLMA
(Armenian): Chicken stuffed with rice.

TERRINE
(French): An earthenware pot resembling a casserole. Also, a cold jellied dish of chopped or diced meat cooked in such a pot.

THURINGER
(German): A mildly seasoned sausage of beef and pork, usually in an edible casing.

TOAD-IN-THE-HOLE
An English meat pie. Also, an egg fried and served in a slice of bread with the center cut out.

TOFFEE
A chewy candy made by cooking a sugar solution with butter until it melts; as it cools it hardens. It may be flavored or coated in various ways.

TOFU
(Chinese and Japanese): Soybean curd. It has a cheese-like consistency and is used in many Oriental dishes. It is available in Chinese and Japanese grocery stores.

TOMALLEY
The liver of the lobster, which turns green when cooked and is considered a delicacy.

TORTCHEN
(German): A small pastry or tart.

TOURTIÈRE
A French-Canadian two-crust pie, usually of ground pork seasoned with nutmeg, mace, garlic, salt, and pepper. It is generally served hot.

TREACLE
The British term for molasses.

TRIFLE
An English dessert, usually of sponge cake sliced and soaked in wine or fruit juice, then spread with jam, and served with custard sauce or whipped cream. In the United States the name is applied to various other desserts.

TUNA OR BONITO
The tuna (also called tunny) is a large game fish of the mackerel family, which inhabits warm waters in the Atlantic, the Pacific, and the Mediterranean. Its weight averages 60 to 200 pounds and has been known to reach 1,500. In Europe and in certain coastal areas of the United States it is eaten fresh, but it is chiefly used canned. The related albacore and bonito taste much the same when canned and are often confused with tuna.
Fresh tuna or bonito may be braised

or roasted in the same way as veal. For canned tuna recipes, see index.

TURBAN
A rolled fillet, usually of fish. Also, a ring or border of food.

TURBOT
Turbot is a large European flatfish, highly regarded as food. It may weigh up to 40 pounds. It is particularly choice when small and is then called chicken turbot in English, turbotin in French. The name is also applied to a number of other similar flatfish.

TURKISH DELIGHT
Also called Turkish paste; a soft jelly-like candy made of a fruit-flavored syrup, cut into cubes or rectangles and dusted with sugar.

TUTTI-FRUTTI
(Italian): Literally, all fruits; a mixture of preserved or candied fruits, usually cut small. Also, as used in English, a confection of mixed fruits with ice cream or pudding.

TZIMMES
(Yiddish): A traditional stew with many variations. It usually contains carrots, potatoes, and sweet potatoes and may or may not include meat. The word has become a Jewish colloquialism meaning fuss.

UOVA
(Italian): Eggs; uova fritte: fried eggs; uova affogate: poached eggs; uova con funghi: eggs with mushrooms; uova con pomodoro: eggs with tomatoes; uova strapazzati: scrambled eggs; uova sodo: hard-cooked eggs.

UVA
(Italian): Grapes.

VANILLIN
The fragrant component of vanilla, a white crystalline substance produced from the vanilla bean or made synthetically.

VEAU
(French): Veal.

VERMICELLI
(Italian): Literally, little worms; very thin spaghetti.

VÉRONIQUE
(French): A garnish of seedless white grapes, used chiefly with chicken. On U.S. menus this dish sometimes appears as Chicken Veronica.

VERT, VERTE
(French): Green. Vert-pré: literally, a green meadow; a term applied either to a garnish of shoestring potatoes and watercress or to chicken or fish coated with a green sauce of mayonnaise mixed with chopped spinach and herbs.

VIANDE
(French): Meat.

VIENNA BREAD
French bread.

VIENNA COFFEE
Coffee served with thin cream and garnished with whipped cream.

VIENNA SAUSAGE
A slender sausage 3 to $3\frac{1}{2}$ inches long, often made of a mildly seasoned mixture of lean beef and pork in a soft, edible casing. Also called wienerwurst.

VIENNESE COFFEE RING
A yeast-raised sweet bread.

VITELLO
(Italian): Veal.

VOLAILLE
(French): Poultry.

VORSPEISEN
(German): Appetizers.

WAFER
A very thin, crisp cooky or cracker; also, a thin, flat, usually round piece of candy.

WASHINGTON PIE
Traditionally, sponge cake layers put together with jelly or jam, sprinkled on top with confectioners' sugar; however, the name is often applied to cake layers put together with custard, chocolate, and the like.

WHEY
The thin, watery part of milk which separates from the thicker part (curds) after coagulation, as in cheesemaking. It has considerable food value as well as a refreshing quality.

WIENER
A hot dog. The name is a shortening of wienerwurst (Vienna sausage); the product now called by this name differs in being smaller.

WIGGLE
A dish of creamed shellfish, especially shrimp, or flaked fish with peas.

WURST
(German): Sausage.

YANKEE POT ROAST
Braised beef served in its own thickened gravy with fresh vegetables and corn fritters.

YERBA MATE
See Maté.

ZAKUSKI
(Russian): Appetizers.

ZWIEBACK
(German): Literally, twice-baked; a type of rusk (which see). Also called Brussels biscuit.

ZWIEBELN
(German): Onions.

FISH AND SHELLFISH

Guides for Buying and Preparing Fish

Fish is frequently less costly than meat and, like meat, it is a primary source of protein and the essential vitamins and minerals. Fish dishes, very often, are time-savers for the busy homemaker, inasmuch as the cooking time for most fish is short. Fish, then, should always be kept in mind as an alternate, not a substitute, for meat in the daily menu. The flavor of fish is delicate. When properly cooked and skillfully combined with other foods it soon becomes a favorite dish several times a week.

Variety is one of the keys to successful meal planning. Very few people realize how many varieties of fish are available on the market. Only about seven species of fish are well known to the average consumer from coast to coast, although there are actually about 160 varieties sold in the United States. Modern refrigeration, quick-freezing, and rapid transportation make it possible for inlanders as well as those living on the shores to enjoy the great variety of fish all the year round.

HOW TO BUY FRESH FISH

Most varieties of fish, like many other types of food products, are particularly abundant fresh during some one season of the year. Local fish dealers will gladly furnish information concerning seasonal offerings, and indicate those varieties that can be used to the best advantage, including the less familiar varieties. If it is desired to save time in preparation and cooking, fish should be purchased as fillets, steaks, or dressed.

In buying fish in the round, the following points should be observed to insure freshness:

Eyes: Bright, clear, full, and bulging.

Gills: Reddish-pink, free from slime or odor.

Scales: Adhering tightly to the skin, bright colored with characteristic sheen.

Flesh: Firm and elastic, springing back when pressed, not separating from the bones.

Odor: Fresh, free from objectionable odors.

Quantity to Buy

Servings of fish are generally based on $1/3$ to $1/2$ pound of the edible flesh per person. When serving steaks, fillets, or sticks, allow $1/3$ pound per person or 2 pounds for 6 people. For dressed fish, allow $1/2$ pound per person or 3 pounds for 6 people. For whole fish, allow about 1 pound per person or 5 pounds for 6 people.

STORING OF FRESH FISH

Fish, like many other food products, will spoil easily if not handled with care. When fish is received from the market, it should be wrapped in moisture-proof paper or placed in a tightly covered dish and stored immediately in the refrigerator. Stored in this manner, the odor of fish will not penetrate other foods. If fish cannot be thoroughly refrigerated, it should be cooked at once and reheated for serving.

HOW TO BUY FROZEN FISH

In recent years a considerable trade has developed in frozen fish, so that now most varieties are available the year round to consumers both in the interior of the country and those living near the source of supply. Frozen fish may be used interchangeably with fresh fish.

Quantity to Buy: In purchasing frozen fish, the allowance for each person is the same as for fresh fish: $1/3$ to $1/2$ pound of the edible flesh per person.

CARE AND STORAGE OF FROZEN FISH

When frozen fish which is wrapped in parchment paper or cellophane is to be used shortly after purchasing, it should be enclosed in another wrapping of paper before being placed in the refrigerator. The additional wrapping prevents the absorption of odors by other foods as the fish thaws. Packaged frozen fish should remain in the unopened package until time to use.

If you wish to keep the fish frozen for several days, place the unopened package in the freezing unit or frozen foods compartment of your refrigerator. Fish will keep as long as it remains solidly frozen, but once it thaws, it should be used immediately. Never refreeze fish after it thaws.

THAWING FROZEN FISH

Fillets, steaks, and dressed fish may be cooked as if they were in the unfrozen form; however, additional cooking must be allowed. When fish are to be breaded or stuffed, it is more convenient to thaw them first to permit easier handling. Thawing is necessary for the cleaning and dressing of whole or drawn fish.

Thawing fish in the refrigerator at a temperature of 37° to 40° has become the accepted practice. The fish should be held at this temperature only long enough to permit ease in preparation. Whole or drawn fish may be thawed more readily by immersing them in cold running water. Thawing at room temperature, although sometimes practiced, is not recommended since a considerable amount of drip usually results.

BASIC FISH COOKERY HINTS

Although the flavor, texture, appearance, and size vary according to the species, the fundamental rules for cooking most fish are few and easy to follow. For this reason, the use of basic recipes, such as frying, broiling, planking, boiling, and steaming are emphasized through this section.

The principal differentiation in types of fish, as related to fish cookery, is the variation in fat content.

As a rule, fat fish, such as salmon or shad, are most desirable for baking, broiling, and planking because their fat content will keep them from becoming dry.

Lean fish, such as cod and haddock, are preferred by some for boiling and steaming as their flesh is firm, and will not easily fall apart while cooking. Both fat and lean fish are suitable for frying.

There are, however, so many exceptions to these rules that actually all fish may be cooked by any of the basic methods with excellent results if allowances are made for the fat content. For example, lean fish, such as halibut, may be broiled or baked if basted frequently with melted fat; otherwise they will have a tendency to become dry.

Most Important Cookery Rule: The most important thing to remember in cooking fish is that it is too often overcooked. Just enough cooking to enable the flesh to be flaked easily from the bones will leave the fish moist and tender and bring out its delicate flavor.

MARKET FORMS OF FRESH AND FROZEN FISH

Fish is marketed in various forms for different uses. Knowing these forms or "cuts" is important in buying fish. The best known forms of fish are given below.

Whole or Round Fish

Whole or round fish are those marketed just as they come from the water. Before cooking, they must be scaled and eviscerated (which means removing the entrails). The head, tail, and fins may be removed if desired, and the fish either split or cut into serving-size portions, except in fish intended for baking. Some small fish, like smelt, are frequently cooked with only the entrails removed.

Drawn Fish

Drawn fish are marketed with only the entrails removed. In preparation for cooking, they generally are scaled. Head, tail, and fins are removed, if desired, and the fish split or cut into serving-size portions. Small drawn fish, or larger sizes intended for baking, may be cooked in the form purchased after being scaled.

Dressed or Pan-Dressed Fish

Dressed fish are scaled and eviscerated, usually with the head, tails, and fins removed. The smaller sizes are ready for cooking as purchased (pan-dressed). The larger sizes of dressed fish may be baked as purchased but frequently are cut into steaks or serving-size portions.

Steaks

Steaks are cross-section slices of the larger sizes of dressed fish. They are ready to cook as purchased, except for dividing the very largest into serving-size portions. A cross-section of the backbone is usually the only bone in the steak.

Fillets

The sides of the fish, cut lengthwise away from the backbone, are called fillets. They are practically boneless and require no preparation for cooking. Sometimes the skin, with the scales removed, is left on the fillets; others are skinned. A fillet cut from one side of a fish is called a single fillet. This is the type of fillet most generally seen in the market.

Butterfly Fillets

Butterfly fillets are the two sides of the fish corresponding to two single fillets held together by uncut flesh and the skin.

Sticks

Sticks are pieces of fish cut lengthwise or crosswise from fillets or steaks into portions of uniform width and length.

CLEANING AND DRESSING FISH

Today the homemaker can obtain almost any variety of fish—fresh or frozen—already cleaned and dressed, filleted or steaked. Therefore, most of the time, there will be no need for cleaning and dressing fish for cooking.

However, freshly caught fish may be available at times, so information on cleaning and preparing fish for cooking is presented here.

Scaling: Lay the fish on the table and with one hand hold the fish firmly by the head. Holding a knife almost vertical, scrape off the scales, working from tail toward head. A scaler may be used instead of a knife. Since scales are more easily removed from a wet fish, it is advisable to soak the fish in cold water for a few minutes before scaling. Take care to remove all the scales near the base of the fins and head.

Cleaning: Remove the entrails after cutting the entire length of the belly from the vent (anal opening) to the head. Cut around the pelvic fins and remove them. Remove the head, including the pectoral fins, by cutting above the collarbone. If the backbone is large, cut down to it on each side of the fish, and then snap the backbone by bending it over the edge of the cutting board or table. Cut any remaining flesh which holds the head attached to the body. Cut off the tail.

Fish Fins: Remove the dorsal or large back fin by cutting the flesh along both sides of the fin. Then, giving a quick pull forward toward the head of the fish, remove the fin with the root bones attached. Remove the other fins in the same manner. Never trim the fins off with shears or a knife since the bones at the base will be left in the fish. Wash the fish in cold running water, removing the blood, any remaining viscera, and membranes. The fish is now dressed or pan dressed, depending on its size, and is ready for cooking. Large fish may be cut crosswise into steaks.

Filleting: With a sharp knife, cut through the flesh along the back from the tail to just behind the head. Then cut down to the backbone just above the collarbone. Turn the knife flat and cut the flesh along the backbone to the tail, allowing the knife to run over the rib bones. Lift off the entire side of the fish in one piece. Turn the fish over and repeat the operation on the other side.

Skinning: If you wish, you may skin the fillets. Lay the fillets flat on the cutting board or table, skin side down. Hold the tail end with your fingers, and with a knife cut through the flesh to the skin about one-half inch from the end of the fillet. Flatten the knife on the skin and cut the flesh away from the skin by pushing the knife forward while holding the free end of the skin firmly between your fingers.

Fish Fins

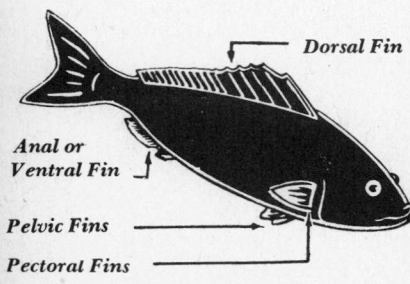

Scaling Fish

Cutting a Steak

Removing Head

Cutting Fillet from Tail to Head

Breaking Backbone

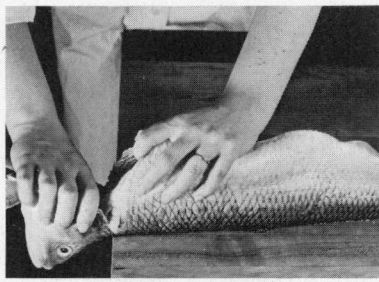

Cutting Along Backbone to Remove Fillets

Cutting to Remove Dorsal Fin

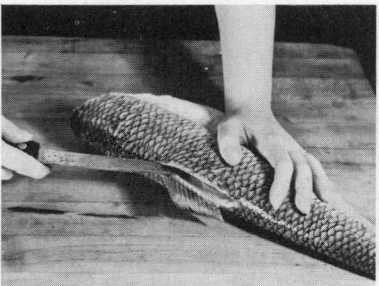

Freeing Fillet at the Tail

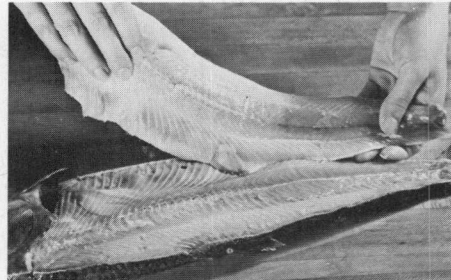

Removing Fin

Removing the Skin from a Fillet

USUAL MARKET FORMS, SIZES, AND PRODUCING AREAS OF FISH

Species	Fat or Lean	Usual market range of round fish	Usual market forms	Main production areas [1]
SALT-WATER FISH				
Bluefish	Lean	1 to 7 pounds	Whole and drawn	Middle and South Atlantic
Butterfish	Fat	¼ to 1 pound	Whole and dressed	North and Middle Atlantic
Cod	Lean	3 to 20 pounds	Drawn, dressed, steaks, and fillets	North Atlantic; North Pacific
Croaker	Lean	½ to 2½ pounds	Whole, dressed, and fillets	Middle and South Atlantic
Eel	Fat	2 to 4 pounds	Alive	Atlantic, Maine to Gulf
Flounder	Lean	¼ to 5 pounds	Whole, dressed, and fillets	All Coastal Areas
Fluke	Lean	1 to 5 pounds	Whole, dressed, and fillets	North Atlantic
Grouper	Lean	5 to 15 pounds	Whole, drawn, dressed, steaks, and fillets	South Atlantic; Gulf
Haddock	Lean	1½ to 7 pounds	Drawn and fillets	North Atlantic
Hake	Lean	2 to 5 pounds	Whole, drawn, dressed, and fillets	North and Middle Atlantic
Halibut	Lean	8 to 75 pounds	Dressed and steaks	Pacific
Herring, sea	Fat	¼ to 1 pound	Whole	North Atlantic; North Pacific
Kingfish	Fat	15 to 30 pounds	Whole, dressed, and steaks	South Atlantic and the Gulf
Lingcod	Lean	5 to 20 pounds	Dressed, steaks, and fillets	Pacific
Mackerel	Fat	¾ to 3 pounds	Whole, drawn, and fillets	North and Middle Atlantic; California
Mullet	Lean	½ to 3 pounds	Whole	South Atlantic; Gulf
Pilchard	Fat	1½ to 2 ounces	Whole, canned	Atlantic and Pacific
Pollock	Lean	3 to 14 pounds	Drawn, dressed, steaks, and fillets	North Atlantic
Pompano	Fat	1½ pounds	Whole, dressed, and fillets	South Atlantic and Gulf
Rockfish	Lean	2 to 5 pounds	Dressed and fillets	Pacific
Rosefish	Lean	½ to 1¼ pounds	Fillets	North Atlantic
Salmon	Fat	3 to 30 pounds	Drawn, dressed, steaks, and fillets	Pacific
Scup (Porgy)	Lean	½ to 2 pounds	Whole and dressed	North and Middle Atlantic
Sea bass	Lean	¼ to 4 pounds	Whole, dressed, and fillets	Middle and South Atlantic; California
Sea trout	Lean	1 to 6 pounds	Whole, drawn, dressed, and fillets	Middle and South Atlantic; Gulf
Shad	Fat	1½ to 7 pounds	Whole, drawn, and fillets	Middle and South Atlantic; Pacific
Snapper, red	Lean	2 to 15 pounds	Drawn, dressed, steaks, and fillets	South Atlantic; Gulf
Sole, Lemon	Lean	2 pounds	Whole, dressed, and fillets	North Atlantic; North and South Pacific
Spanish mackerel	Fat	1 to 4 pounds	Whole, drawn, dressed, and fillets	South Atlantic; Gulf
Spot	Lean	¼ to 1¼ pounds	Whole and dressed	Middle and South Atlantic
Swordfish	Fat	200 to 600 pounds	Steaks	Atlantic and Pacific oceans
Whiting	Lean	½ to 1½ pounds	Whole, drawn, dressed, and fillets	North and Middle Atlantic
FRESH-WATER FISH				
Bass	Lean	¾ to 1 pound	Whole and drawn, also reserved as game fishes	Great Lakes, Lakes, and Rivers
Buffalo fish	Lean	5 to 15 pounds	Whole, drawn, dressed, and steaks	Mississippi Valley
Carp	Lean	2 to 8 pounds	Whole and fillets	Lakes and Rivers
Catfish	Fat	1 to 10 pounds	Whole, dressed, and skinned	Lakes and Rivers
Crappie	Lean	1 to 4 pounds	Reserved as game fishes	Lakes and Rivers, Ponds and Creeks
Lake herring	Lean	½ to 1 pound	Whole, drawn, and fillets	Great Lakes
Lake trout	Fat	1½ to 10 pounds	Drawn, dressed, and fillets	Great Lakes and Lakes
Muskellunge (Musky)	Lean	3 to 10 pounds	Reserved as game fishes	Great Lakes, Lakes, and Rivers
Sheepshead	Lean	½ to 3 pounds	Whole, drawn, dressed, and fillets	Lakes and Rivers
Suckers	Lean	½ to 4 pounds	Whole, drawn, dressed, and fillets	Lakes and Rivers
Smelt	Lean	2 ounces	Whole	Great Lakes and Tributary streams
Trout, Brook	Lean	1 to 2 pounds	Reserved as game fishes	Mountain streams of eastern, northern, western states
Whitefish	Fat	2 to 6 pounds	Whole, drawn, dressed, and fillets	Great Lakes
Yellow perch	Lean	½ to 1 pound	Whole and fillets	Great Lakes, Lakes and Rivers
Yellow pike	Lean	1½ to 10 pounds	Whole, dressed, and fillets	Great Lakes and Lakes

1 North Atlantic area includes the Coastal States from Maine to Connecticut; Middle Atlantic area, New York to Virginia; South Atlantic area, North Carolina to Florida; Gulf area, Alabama to Texas; Pacific area, Washington to California (North Pacific, Washington, Oregon, and Alaska); and Midwest area, Central and Inland States.

Baked Fish

BAKED STUFFED WHOLE FISH

3   or 4 pound fish, dressed
1½ teaspoons salt
Bread stuffing (see Index)
4   tablespoons butter or other fat,
    melted
3   slices of bacon (optional)

Clean, wash, and dry fish. Sprinkle inside and out with salt.

Stuff fish loosely, and sew opening with needle and string, or close with skewers.

Place fish in greased baking pan. Brush with melted fat. Lay slices of bacon over top. Bake in moderate oven (350°F.) 40 to 60 minutes or until fish flakes easily when tested with a fork. If fish seems dry while baking, baste occasionally with drippings or melted fat.

Remove string or skewers and serve immediately on hot platter, plain or with a sauce. Serves 6.

BAKED STUFFED FISH FILLETS OR STEAKS

2   fillets or steaks, about 1 pound each
1   teaspoon salt
⅛ teaspoon pepper
Bread stuffing (½ recipe, below)
4   tablespoons butter or other fat,
    melted
3   slices bacon (optional)

Remove skins from fillets, if skins have not been removed. Sprinkle both sides with salt and pepper.

Place one fillet or steak in well greased baking pan. Place stuffing on fish and cover with remaining fillet or steak. Fasten together with toothpicks or skewers. Brush top with melted fat and lay slices of bacon on top.

Bake in moderate oven (350°F.) 30 to 40 minutes or until fish flakes easily when tested with a fork. Remove carefully to hot platter, take out fasteners, garnish and serve hot with a sauce. Serves 6.

BREAD STUFFING FOR FISH

3   tablespoons chopped onions
¾ cup chopped celery
6   tablespoons butter or other fat,
    melted
1   teaspoon salt
⅛ teaspoon pepper
1   teaspoon thyme, sage, or savory
    seasoning
4   cups day-old breadcrumbs

Cook celery and onions in melted fat for about 10 minutes, or until tender. Add cooked vegetables and seasonings to breadcrumbs; mix thoroughly.

If dressing seems very dry, add 2 tablespoons water, milk, or fish stock to moisten.

PLANKED WHOLE FISH

3   or 4 pound fish, dressed
1½ teaspoons salt
⅛ teaspoon pepper
4   tablespoons butter or other fat
Seasoned mashed potatoes
Seasoned cooked vegetables (peas, carrots, cauliflower, tomatoes, or onions)

If hardwood plank is used, oil well and place in a cold oven and heat thoroughly as oven preheats.

Clean, wash, and dry fish. Sprinkle inside and out with salt and pepper. Brush with melted fat.

Place fish on the hot oiled plank or on a greased oven glass or metal platter. Bake in a hot oven (400°F.) 35 to 45 minutes or until fish flakes easily when tested with a fork.

Remove from oven and quickly arrange a border of hot mashed potatoes around fish. Place in preheated broiler until potatoes are slightly browned, about 5 minutes.

Remove and arrange two or more hot vegetables around fish. Garnish with parsley and lemon or tomato wedges. Serve immediately on the plank. Serves 6.

BAKED FISH FILLETS OR STEAKS

2   pounds fish fillets or steaks
1   teaspoon salt
⅛ teaspoon pepper
2   tablespoons lemon juice
1   teaspoon grated onion
4   tablespoons butter or other fat,
    melted
Paprika

Cut fish into serving-size portions. Sprinkle both sides with salt and pepper. Add lemon juice and onion to melted fat.

Dip each piece of fish into this mixture and place in a greased baking pan. Pour rest of fat over fish.

Bake in moderate oven (350°F.) 25 to 30 minutes or until fish flakes easily when tested with a fork. Sprinkle with paprika. Serve immediately on a hot platter. Serves 6.

A whole fish, stuffed and baked, is one of the most attractive ways to serve fish.

BAKED HALIBUT WITH CHEESE SAUCE

2   1-pound halibut steaks
2   tablespoons butter
Paprika
2   tablespoons lemon juice
4   tablespoons butter
4   tablespoons flour
2   cups milk
1   teaspoon salt
⅛ teaspoon pepper
1   cup shredded sharp Cheddar
    cheese
3   tablespoons grated Parmesan
    cheese
2   hard-cooked eggs, sieved

Place halibut steaks on broiler pan. Dot with 2 tablespoons butter and sprinkle with paprika. Broil about 15 minutes, or until fish flakes when tested with a fork. Place in a shallow buttered baking dish and sprinkle with lemon juice.

While the fish is broiling, melt the 4 tablespoons of butter in a saucepan. Add flour, mixing to a smooth paste. Cook over medium heat about 1 minute. Remove from heat. Add one-half of milk, salt and pepper, stirring until blended.

Return to heat and stir constantly until mixture begins to thicken. Add remaining milk. Heat to simmering point. Cook about 5 minutes. Blend in Cheddar cheese slowly, stirring until melted. Pour sauce over fish and top with Parmesan cheese.

Bake in moderate oven (350°F.) 20 minutes. Sprinkle with sieved hard-cooked eggs and serve at once. Serves 4 to 5.

Baked Halibut with Cheese Sauce

FISH COOKED IN ALUMINUM FOIL

Use small or medium fish such as porgies, trout, sunfish, or yellow perch.

Clean and wash fish; remove heads and tails, if desired. Wipe dry and sprinkle inside and out with salt and pepper.

Cut sheets of foil large enough to wrap each fish separately. Spread center of each sheet with 1 tablespoon butter or margarine. Wrap up fish and fold over foil to seal edges.

To Cook Indoors: Put wrapped fish on baking sheet. Bake in moderate oven (375°F.) about 30 minutes.

To Cook Outdoors: Put wrapped fish directly on hot coals and cover with more coals. Cook 10 to 15 minutes, depending on size of fish.

SHAD

Shad is a delectable fish of the herring family, found along the North Atlantic coast. It is caught chiefly in the spring, when the fish ascend the rivers to spawn. It is notorious for its many bones but nowadays is generally available filleted. The roe is as highly valued as the flesh and is served with it or alone. Both may be baked or broiled; the roe is often parboiled first.

BAKED OR PLANKED SHAD

Clean and split shad. Place skin side down on hot buttered plank or in greased shallow baking dish.

Sprinkle with salt and pepper. Brush with melted butter.

Bake in hot oven (400°F.) 20 to 25 minutes, basting frequently with melted butter. Garnish with parsley. Serve at once.

With Creamed Roe: After baking, spread creamed roe (below) over fish. Sprinkle with 1/2 cup buttered bread-crumbs. Brown under broiler.

Creamed Roe:

1 shad roe, parboiled
2 tablespoons butter or margarine
1 teaspoon grated onion
2 tablespoons flour
1/2 cup light cream
2 slightly beaten egg yolks
1 tablespoon lemon juice

Discard outer membrane of roe. Mash the roe. Melt butter in a saucepan.

Add onion and blend in flour. Slowly stir in cream and cook over low heat until thickened, about 5 minutes. Slowly add to beaten egg yolks, stirring constantly. Add lemon juice and roe. Season to taste with salt and pepper.

POMPANO

This fish is found in the warmer coastal waters of the South Atlantic and Gulf of Mexico.

The Florida pompano is regarded as one of the most delicately flavored fish. Fillets may be broiled, poached, or sauteed.

POMPANO EN PAPILLOTTE

3 medium-sized pompano
3 cups water
1 chopped shallot or 2 tablespoons chopped onion
6 tablespoons butter or margarine
2¼ cups white wine
1 cup crabmeat
1 cup diced cooked shrimp
1/2 clove garlic, minced
1½ cups chopped onions
Pinch of thyme
1 bay leaf
2 cups fish stock
2 tablespoons flour
2 egg yolks
Salt and pepper

Clean pompano and cut into 6 fillets, removing heads and backbones.

Combine heads, bones, and water. Simmer until there are 2 cups stock.

Sauté shallot and fillets in 2 tablespoons butter. Add 2 cups wine; cover and simmer gently until fillets are tender, 5 to 8 minutes.

Sauté crabmeat, shrimp, and 1/4 clove garlic in 1 tablespoon butter. Add onions and remaining 1/4 clove garlic and cook 10 minutes. Add thyme, bay leaf, and 1¾ cups fish stock; simmer 10 minutes.

Blend together 2 tablespoons butter and flour and gradually add remaining 1/4 cup fish stock. Add to crabmeat mixture with stock drained from fillets. Cook, stirring constantly, until thickened.

Beat egg yolks and add hot sauce and 1/4 cup wine. Mix thoroughly. Place in refrigerator to chill until firm.

Cut 6 parchment-shaped hearts 8 inches long and 12 inches wide. Oil well and place spoonfuls of sauce on side of each heart. Lay poached fillet on sauce and fold over. Seal edges.

Lay sealed hearts on an oiled baking sheet. Bake in very hot oven (450°F.) 15 minutes, or until paper hearts are browned. Serve at once in paper hearts. Serves 6.

Variations: Sea trout, striped bass, or fresh salmon may be substituted for pompano.

BAKED BROOK TROUT

Wipe the cleaned trout and wrap each in a strip of bacon. Place in baking pan.

Bake in moderate oven (350°F.) 20 minutes without turning.

Haddock Bake with Sour Cream Topping

HADDOCK BAKE WITH SOUR CREAM TOPPING

1 pound frozen haddock fillets
1/4 cup flour
1 teaspoon salt
1/4 teaspoon ground black pepper
1/2 cup milk
1/2 cup crumbled buttery crackers
2 tablespoons butter or margarine, melted
1/2 cup sour cream

Cut fish in serving size pieces. Coat with mixed flour, salt, and pepper. Arrange in a single layer in baking dish. Pour milk over fish.

Bake in moderate oven (350°F.) 45 minutes. Toast crumbs lightly in melted butter or margarine. Spoon sour cream over fish. Sprinkle with toasted crumbs. Bake 10 minutes longer. Serves 4.

FISH FILLETS BAKED IN WINE-MUSHROOM SAUCE

3 tablespoons butter or margarine
3 tablespoons flour
1 can condensed cream of mushroom soup
1/2 cup sauterne or other white dinner wine
2 tablespoons grated Parmesan cheese
2 tablespoons chopped parsley
1 to 1⅓ pounds fish fillets (sole, halibut, etc.)

Melt butter and stir in flour; add soup and wine and cook, stirring constantly, until mixture boils and thickens; add Parmesan cheese and parsley.

Arrange fillets in a single layer in a greased shallow baking dish, or in 3 or 4 shallow individual casseroles. Pour sauce over fish.

Bake in moderate oven (375°F.) about 25 minutes, or until fish flakes when tested with a fork. Serves 3 or 4.

Fish Fillets Baked in Wine-Mushroom Sauce

Baked Ocean Perch

RED SNAPPER WITH TOMATO SAUCE

1   3-pound red snapper (or other large fish)
Seasoned flour
6   tablespoons butter or margarine
½ cup chopped onion
2   cups chopped celery
¼ cup chopped green pepper
3   cups canned tomatoes
1   tablespoon Worcestershire sauce
1   tablespoon ketchup
1   teaspoon chili powder
½ lemon, finely sliced
2   bay leaves
1   clove garlic, minced
1   teaspoon salt
Few grains red pepper

Sprinkle fish inside and out with seasoned flour. Place in baking pan lined with greased paper.

Melt butter; add onion, celery, and green pepper; simmer 15 minutes.

Add tomatoes, Worcestershire sauce, ketchup, chili powder, lemon, bay leaves, garlic, salt, and red pepper. Simmer until celery is very tender, then put the mixture through a potato ricer or food mill.

Pour the sauce around fish.

Bake in slow oven (325°F.) about 45 minutes.

Baste frequently with sauce. Serves 6.

FISH STEAKS IN WHITE WINE

3   thick fish slices or fillets
1   cup sauterne or rhine wine
3   carrots
1   onion, sliced
3   tablespoons butter or margarine
2   tablespoons flour
1   bouillon cube
Lemon slices

Marinate the fish slices or fillets in wine for several hours in refrigerator.

An hour before dinner, cut carrots in strips, parboil 8 minutes in 1 cup of boiling salted water; pour into shallow baking dish without draining. Add onion. Place fish on top.

For sauce, melt butter or margarine, add flour; stir in bouillon cube and wine in which fish was marinated. Pour over fish. Season with salt and pepper; top with lemon slices.

Bake uncovered in hot oven (450°F.) 25 minutes, or until tender. Heap hot string beans around fish. Serves 6.

Fish Piquant

FILLET OF FISH MARGUERY

3   tablespoons butter or margarine
1   onion, minced
6   cooked or canned shrimp
1   cup hot medium white sauce
2   egg yolks
½ cup cream
1   tablespoon minced parsley
Dash of nutmeg
Juice of ½ lemon
¼ cup sherry
2   pounds fish fillets

Sauté onion and shrimp about 5 minutes in 2 tablespoons melted butter.

Beat egg yolks with cream and slowly pour hot white sauce into egg-cream mixture, stirring constantly. Return to heat and cook 1 minute. Add remaining butter, parsley, nutmeg, and lemon juice; mix well. Remove from heat and add wine.

Place fish fillets in greased casserole. Arrange sautéed onion and seafood on fillets. Cover with sauce.

Bake in moderate oven (350°F.) about 20 minutes. Serves 6.

Note: Oysters and mushrooms may be added to shrimp.

FISH STEAKS FRANCISCO

Marinate 4 fish steaks in 1 cup sauterne or rhine for 3 or 4 hours in refrigerator. Place fish and wine in shallow baking dish. Sprinkle with salt and pepper.

Bake in moderate oven (375°F.) about 25 minutes, or until fish flakes when tested with fork. Drain off liquid.

Before serving, pour melted butter or margarine over it and top with lemon slices. Heap hot string beans and carrots around the fish steaks. Serves 4.

Note: Halibut, swordfish, salmon or any favorite fish may be used in this recipe.

FISH PIQUANT

4   onions, sliced
2   pounds fish fillets--cod, sole, haddock, or perch
½ cup mayonnaise
2   teaspoons Worcestershire sauce
2   tablespoons lemon juice
¼ cup grated Parmesan cheese
2   tablespoons chopped parsley

Cover sliced onions with water and cook until tender but crisp. Spread drained onions in a shallow well greased baking pan.

Cut fish into individual serving pieces. Place fish pieces over onions. Combine remaining ingredients. Blend well. Spread mixture on fish pieces.

Bake in moderate oven (350°F.) 30 to 40 minutes or until fish flakes. Serves 6.

BAKED OCEAN PERCH

Place two 1-pound packages ocean perch in glass baking dish. Season with salt and pepper.

Melt ¼ pound butter (½ cup) and mix in 2¼ cups cracker meal. Cover fillets with butter-crumb mixture. Sprinkle with chopped parsley, if desired.

Bake in moderate oven (350°F.) 30 minutes, or until fish is tender and crumbs browned.

Serve with pickled onions and beets, if desired. Serves 6.

Variations: Haddock or flounder fillets may be substituted for ocean perch.

SPENCER METHOD FOR FISH FILLETS

2   pounds fish fillets
1   cup milk
2   teaspoons salt
¾ cup fine, dry breadcrumbs

Cut fillets in individual portions, and soak 3 minutes in milk to which salt has been added. Drain, and roll in dry breadcrumbs.

Place fish on a greased baking dish and dot with butter.

Bake in very hot oven (500°F.), allowing 10 minutes per inch thickness of fish. Heat may be reduced for larger fish, towards end of cooking time. Serves 6.

BAKED FISH IN SOUR CREAM

3   pounds frozen fish fillets
½ teaspoon salt
⅛ teaspoon pepper
1½ teaspoons Ac'cent
Onion rings
1   cup thick sour cream

Thaw fish; place in buttered or oiled flat baking dish or oven-glass platter. Sprinkle both sides of fillets with salt, pepper, and Ac'cent; let stand 10 minutes.

Cover fish with onion rings (slice onions thin; separate into rings); pour or spoon sour cream over onions.

Bake uncovered in moderate oven (350°F.) until fish flakes easily when tested with a fork, about 30 to 35 minutes.

Baste fish occasionally with the cream and if liquid evaporates too fast, or fish seems dry, add a tablespoon or two hot water.

Serve from baking dish, adding watercress or any other fresh green garnish, at the last moment just before serving. Serves 6.

Baked Stuffed Fresh Salmon

BAKED STUFFED FRESH SALMON

Remove head, tail, and fins from 8 to 10-pound fresh or frozen whole salmon.

Sprinkle Ac'cent lightly inside cavity; fill with stuffing (below), being careful to fill loosely.

Skewer or truss fish to shape. Brush with oil; place on strip of foil (for easy removal later) in shallow roasting pan.

Bake in moderate oven (350°F.), allowing 12 minutes per pound.

Garnish with parsley and lemon slices. Slice and serve with egg sauce accompanied by boiled new potatoes and peas.

Savory Stuffing for Salmon:

¼ cup minced onion
2 tablespoons butter or margarine
¼ teaspoon dried savory, crumbled
¼ teaspoon powdered marjoram
⅛ teaspoon powdered thyme
1 teaspoon finely chopped parsley
1 teaspoon finely grated lemon rind
1 teaspoon salt
⅛ teaspoon pepper
1 teaspoon Ac'cent
2 cups soft breadcrumbs, toasted
1 slightly beaten egg

Brown onion lightly in butter or margarine. Add herbs, lemon rind, salt, pepper, and Ac'cent. Blend well. Lightly stir in breadcrumbs and egg.

Fill cavity of fish; skewer or truss closed.

Makes enough for 8- to 10-pound dressed fish.

BAKED FISH PARMIGIANA

4 servings any fish fillets or steak
Salt and pepper
1 cup tomato sauce
½ cup grated Parmesan cheese
2 tablespoons melted butter or margarine (optional)

Place fish (thawed, if frozen) in shallow baking dish. Season lightly with salt and pepper.

Spread tomato sauce over each fillet; sprinkle with cheese. For a more attractive appearance, sprinkle with melted butter or margarine.

Bake in hot oven (425°F.) until fish flakes easily, 15 to 20 minutes. Serves 4.

FISH CREOLE

1½ pounds fish fillets
2 tablespoons butter or margarine
1 cup chopped onion
½ cup chopped green pepper
1½ teaspoons salt
¼ teaspoon pepper
¼ teaspoon paprika
2 cups canned tomatoes, drained

Haddock, flounder, red snapper, ocean perch, cod, halibut, pollack, blue pike may be used. If desired, 2 pounds whole fish may be used.

Arrange fish in greased shallow baking pan or casserole.

Sauté onion and green pepper in butter. Add seasonings and tomatoes. Pour over fish.

Bake in moderate oven (375°F.) 30 minutes. Serves 4 to 5.

COD OR HADDOCK—ITALIAN STYLE

1 pound cod or haddock
½ teaspoon salt
1 cup tomato sauce
1 tablespoon lemon juice
½ cup grated American or ¼ cup grated Parmesan cheese
2 tablespoons butter or margarine

Cut fish into 3 servings; sprinkle with salt. Place in greased oven-glass pie pan.

Pour tomato sauce (the better its flavor the better the dish) and lemon juice over fish. Sprinkle with cheese and dot with bits of butter.

Bake in hot oven (400°F.) until fish flakes and cheese has browned lightly, about 25 minutes. Serves 3.

RED SNAPPER À LA CREOLE

1 3-pound red snapper
½ teaspoon salt
Dash of pepper
1 large onion, chopped
1 bay leaf, crumbled
3 sprigs parsley, chopped
1 sprig thyme, chopped
1 cup white wine
3 tablespoons butter or margarine
2 tablespoons flour
½ cup chopped mushrooms
6 tomatoes, chopped fine
½ cup cracker crumbs

Clean and wash fish. Season with salt and pepper.

Mix onion, bay leaf, parsley, and thyme. Spread evenly over bottom of baking pan. Put fish in pan. Pour wine over fish.

Bake in moderate oven (350°F.) 20 minutes.

Melt 2 tablespoons butter in a saucepan. Sprinkle in flour, and when browned add mushrooms and tomatoes. Simmer 10 minutes. Pour over fish. Cover with crumbs. Dot with remain-

ing butter. Bake 10 minutes longer. Serves 6.

Variations: Flounder, haddock, pompano, or redfish may be prepared in the same manner.

BAKED HADDOCK AU GRATIN

1 whole or filleted haddock, about 3 pounds
1 No. 2 can tomatoes
1 clove garlic, chopped fine
4 tablespoons American or Parmesan cheese, cut in bits
Salt and pepper, to taste
1 tablespoon chopped thyme

Place fillets in greased baking dish. Add remaining ingredients.

Bake in moderate oven (350°F.) until fish flakes when pierced with fork, about 1 hour. Serves 6.

Note: Flounder, cod, or ocean perch fillets may be substituted for haddock. Cut down baking time to 35 minutes.

BAKED FISH FILLETS IN SWEET-SOUR PINEAPPLE

1 green pepper, cut in strips
1 coarsely chopped, medium onion
2 tablespoons salad oil
1 teaspoon powdered ginger
1 tablespoon brown sugar
1 tablespoon cornstarch
1 tablespoon soy sauce
¼ cup vinegar
1 No. 2 can (2½ cups) pineapple tidbits, not drained
1 to 1½ pounds thawed quick-frozen or fresh fish fillets, or 2 pounds fish steaks, 1-inch thick (cod, haddock, ocean perch, sole, whitefish, halibut)

Sauté green pepper and onion in salad oil in skillet 5 minutes; add ginger and next 5 ingredients. Cook, stirring, until blended and thickened.

Arrange fillets in shallow baking dish; sprinkle with salt and pepper; pour on sauce.

Bake in moderate oven (350°F.) 30 minutes. Serves 4 to 6.

Baked Fillets in
Sweet-Sour Pineapple

Broiled Fish

BROILED FISH FILLETS OR STEAKS

2   pounds fillets or steaks
1   teaspoon salt
1/8 teaspoon pepper
4   tablespoons butter or other fat, melted

Cut fish into serving-size portions. Sprinkle both sides with salt and pepper.

Place fish on a preheated greased broiler pan about 2 inches from the heat, skin side up, if skin has not been removed from fillets.

Brush fish with melted fat. Broil for 5 to 8 minutes or until slightly brown, baste with melted fat, and turn carefully. Brush other side with melted fat and cook 5 to 8 minutes or until fish flakes easily when tested with a fork.

Remove carefully to a hot platter, garnish, and serve immediately plain or with a sauce. Serves 6.

SCROD

Scrod is a young haddock or cod split down the back with most of the backbone removed, ready for cooking. The term, which is native to the Boston area, comes from an old Dutch word for shred and originally referred to shredded fish, particularly cod.

BROILED SCROD

To broil a scrod, brush with melted butter or dip in olive oil, then in fine breadcrumbs. Sprinkle with salt and pepper.

Broil on a preheated greased broiler pan about 2 inches from heat, skin side up, until browned, about 5 minutes or until fish flakes easily when tested by a fork.

Baste with melted butter or olive oil, turn and broil other side.

BROILED BROOK TROUT

(Or Other Small, Fresh-Water Fish)

Line baking sheet with aluminum foil, or grease thoroughly.

Brush whole, cleaned fish, inside and out with melted fat. Sprinkle inside and out with salt, pepper, and Ac'cent. Place on foil.

Broil, with surface or fish 3 inches below source of heat 5 minutes. Turn; broil 4 to 5 minutes longer. Brush with melted butter or margarine several times during broiling. Serve with cucumber sauce.

Low-Calorie Fish Broil

CRUMBLE TOP FISH FILLETS

1   pound frozen fish fillets (cod, haddock, or ocean perch)
1/4 cup butter, melted
1/2 cup soft breadcrumbs
1/3 cup grated Swiss cheese
1   tablespoon grated onion
1/2 teaspoon salt
1/8 teaspoon pepper
Dash of paprika

Let frozen fillets thaw on bottom shelf of refrigerator or at room temperature until they can be pulled apart. Place in broiler pan. Brush with a little melted butter. Broil about 3 inches from source of heat 10 to 15 minutes or until fish flakes easily when tested with a fork.

Meanwhile combine remaining butter with remaining ingredients. Remove fillets from heat; turn with pancake turner. Spread with breadcrumb mixture. Broil 2 to 3 minutes or until crumbs are brown. If desired, garnish with lemon slices and parsley. Serves 3 to 4.

LOW-CALORIE FISH BROIL

Select a lean fish such as flounder (171 calories per pound), haddock, halibut, ocean perch, or red snapper. If in doubt about which fish are lean and which are fat, ask the fish dealer; he will be able to tell you. Have the fish cut thin if it isn't already cut. A serving is a serving, thick or thin; you'll never miss that extra little bit.

The pan in which the fish is broiled need not be greased (calories saved); the moisture from the fish keeps it from sticking. Preheat broiler pan and arrange fish in hot pan. Cover with any of the following low-calorie toppings and broil 2 to 3 inches from the source of heat—4 minutes if fish is thin; 8 minutes, turning once, if fish is thicker than flounder, for example. Fish is done when it flakes easily with a fork.

The toppings given below are created to give flavor and appetite appeal to the fish by adding the fewest calories possible. Ordinarily the browned and colorful appetizing color is achieved with butter and paprika. Not an ounce of butter, margarine, or shortening is used here.

1. Brush with a thin layer of Worcestershire sauce, sprinkle with paprika.
2. Cover during last three minutes of cooking with a mixture of minced cucumber, pimiento, onion, and salt and pepper.
3. Sprinkle during last three minutes of cooking with fish herb mixture (or your own favorite combination) and a little grated fresh carrot for color.
4. Spread with a thin layer of ketchup or chili sauce (fewer calories than butter).

Crumble Top Fish Fillets

BROILED SWORDFISH STEAKS

2   swordfish steaks about 1-inch thick (2 pounds)
1   teaspoon Ac'cent
Salt and pepper
Melted butter or margarine

Sprinkle surface of fish with Ac'cent, following the rule of 1/2 teaspoon per pound. Let stand 5 minutes.

Sprinkle with salt and pepper. Brush with melted butter or margarine. Place on greased broiler rack in broiler, with surface of fish about 3-inches below heat.

Broil about 8 minutes on each side, brushing frequently with melted butter or margarine. Serves 6.

HALIBUT STEAKS WITH PIMIENTO SAUCE

Plan on one half halibut steak for each person. If steaks are frozen, let thaw on refrigerator shelf or at room temperature. Brush with melted butter, sprinkle with salt and pepper. Broil 2 or 3 inches from source of heat, 5 to 8 minutes.

Turn steaks carefully. Season again and brush with melted butter and broil 5 to 8 minutes, or until fish flakes easily when tested with a fork. Serve on heated platter. Pour pimiento sauce (below) over fish and arrange vegetables on a border. Garnish with lemon wedges.

Pimiento Sauce: For 3 halibut steak halves, melt 3 tablespoons butter, add the juice of half a lemon, season with half teaspoon of salt and a dash of pepper. Slice 1 pimiento into thin strips and add to sauce.

Halibut Steaks with Pimiento Sauce

BROILED MACKEREL WITH ONION SLICES

4 1-pound mackerel or other small
    whole fish
3 onions, sliced
2 tablespoons butter

Rub inside of fish with salt. Make several slits on each side of the fish. Slip a slice of onion and a dot of butter in each slit on the top side, pushing the slice of onion well into the slit.

Place fish under broiler. Fish should be about 6 inches from source of heat. Broil for 3 minutes, turn fish and insert onion slices and dots of butter. Broil 6 minutes or until fish flakes easily when tested with a fork. Serves 4 to 6.

Broiled Mackerel with Onion Slices

BROILED SALMON STEAKS WITH MAYONNAISE SAUCE

4 salmon steaks, about ¾ inch thick
¼ cup mayonnaise
2 tablespoons chopped parsley
2 tablespoons chili sauce

Preheat broiler at (550°F.) for 10 minutes.

Arrange salmon steaks on greased baking sheet. Place under broiler and broil about 8 minutes or until lightly browned.

Combine mayonnaise, parsley, and chili sauce; blend well. Spread broiled salmon steaks generously with mixture. Broil 2 to 3 minutes longer, or until sauce is delicately browned.

Serve with romaine or lettuce on a large platter. Garnish with slices of tomato and cucumber. Serves 4.

Broiled Salmon Steaks with Mayonnaise Sauce

BROILED STUFFED FISH FILLETS

1 medium onion, grated
6 flounder fillets (about 2 pounds)
1 teaspoon salt
⅛ teaspoon pepper
2 teaspoons Ac'cent
½ cup finely chopped celery
⅓ cup melted butter or margarine
1 teaspoon savory
4 cups soft breadcrumbs
Creole sauce

Grate onion over surface of fish fillets; sprinkle with salt, pepper, and Ac'cent.

Combine celery, melted butter, savory and breadcrumbs; spread over fillets. Roll up and tie or secure with wooden picks.

Broil with surface of fish 4 inches below source of heat for 15 to 20 minutes. Do not turn. Serve with Creole sauce. Serves 6.

BROILED EEL

Skin and clean eel, remove backbone and cut in individual pieces. Rub with salt and let stand 10 minutes.

Wipe to remove salt, brush with melted butter or oil, and place on oiled broiler 4 inches from heat.

Broil in moderately hot oven (400°F.) 10 minutes, or until golden brown.

The flesh should flake easily with a fork. Sprinkle with salt and pepper and minced parsley. Serve with maître d'hôtel sauce or lemon juice.

TROUT BROILED WITH BACON

Have trout cleaned and ready for the pan. Wrap each trout in bacon strip, fastening bacon with a wooden pick.

Lay them flat in broiler pan and cook with moderate heat until bacon is crisp on side next to heat source. Turn and crisp the other side.

BARBECUED FISH STEAKS

Cut 3 pounds ¾-inch-thick salmon, halibut, or swordfish steaks into serving pieces. Place in shallow dish. Cover with mixture of juice of 1 lemon and ¼ cup salad oil. Chill ½ hour, turning once.

Arrange fish in folding wire broiler; brush well with hot barbecue sauce. Cook close to coals until golden brown, about 3 minutes. (Cook fish quickly to prevent its drying.)

Brush with sauce, turn, cook other side and brush with sauce. Serves 8.

Variations: Place the fish steaks in shallow dish. Cover with Texas barbecue sauce or lemon barbecue sauce (see Sauces) and let stand 1 hour. Cook as above.

Broiled Stuffed Fillets

BROILED SMELTS

Clean as for deep fried smelts. Dip in olive oil, then in breadcrumbs. Dust with paprika.

Broil quickly until golden brown. Put on hot platter. Sprinkle with melted butter.

BROILED FISH CALIFORNIA

2 to 4 small whole fish
¼ cup lemon juice
½ teaspoon Ac'cent
½ teaspoon salt
Few grains pepper
Melted butter or margarine

Remove heads from fish and clean; do not split. Rub inside with lemon juice, Ac'cent, salt, and pepper.

Place on broiler rack; brush with melted butter. Broil, with surface of fish 3 to 4 inches below source of heat 8 minutes; turn; brush with melted butter; broil 5 to 8 minutes longer, depending on size of fish, or until fish flakes easily with fork.

Serve with California sauce (below); garnish with lemon wedges and fresh mint. Serves 4.

California Sauce:

2 tablespoons butter or margarine
2 tablespoons flour
½ teaspoon salt
½ teaspoon Ac'cent
4 tablespoons brown sugar
½ cup lemon juice
½ cup water
½ cup golden seedless raisins

Melt butter or margarine; blend in flour, salt, Ac'cent, and brown sugar.

Combine lemon juice and water; add and stir over low heat until smooth and thickened. Add raisins; simmer 5 minutes. Makes about 2 cups.

Broiled Fish California

Fried Fish

PAN-FRIED FISH

2 pounds fillets, steaks or pan-dressed fish
1 teaspoon salt
1/8 teaspoon pepper
1 egg
1 tablespoon milk or water
1 cup breadcrumbs, cracker crumbs, corn meal, or flour

Cut fish into serving-size portions. Sprinkle both sides with salt and pepper.

Beat egg slightly, and blend in the milk. Dip fish in the egg and roll in crumbs.

Place fish in a heavy frying pan which contains about 1/8 inch melted fat, hot but not smoking. Fry at a moderate heat. When fish is brown on one side, turn carefully and brown the other side. Cooking time about 10 minutes, depending on the thickness of the fish. Drain on absorbent paper.

Serve immediately on a hot platter, plain or with a sauce. Serves 6.

Pan-Fried Fish Fillets: If frozen fish is used for frying, it is better to partially thaw it on refrigerator shelf for even cooking throughout.

OVEN FRIED FISH FILLETS

2 pounds fish fillets
1 teaspoon salt
1 tablespoon paprika
1/4 teaspoon pepper
1 cup milk
1 cup breadcrumbs
4 tablespoons butter or other fat

Cut fillets into serving pieces. Season with salt, pepper, and paprika. (If frozen fillets are used, let them thaw before cutting.)

Dip the fish in milk and roll in crumbs. Place in a well greased baking pan. Pour melted fat over fish.

Place pan on shelf near the top of a very hot oven (500°F.) and bake 10 to 12 minutes, or until fish flakes easily when tested with a fork. Serve immediately on a hot platter, plain or with a sauce. Serves 6.

FRIED FISH IN BATTER

2 pounds fish fillets
1/2 teaspoon salt
Batter:
1 1/2 cups all-purpose flour
3 teaspoons baking powder
1 teaspoon salt
2 eggs
1 cup milk

Season fish and cut in serving-size pieces or smaller pieces if desired. If the pieces of fish are more than half an inch thick but not thick enough to slice conveniently, make three or four slits in the sides. The fish will cook more evenly and quickly.

To make batter, mix and sift dry ingredients. Beat eggs well and stir milk into eggs. Pour liquid into dry ingredients and beat until smooth.

Dip pieces of fish into batter and fry in deep fat (375°F.) until golden brown, turning once. This will take about 7 minutes. Drain on absorbent paper. Serves 6.

Batter No. 2: Beat 1 egg and add 1 cup water. Stir in 1 cup all-purpose flour just until dampened. Batter will be lumpy.

Note: As a general rule, a batter made with water will be crisp while a batter made with milk will be tender.

SAUTÉED BROOK TROUT

Wipe the cleaned trout. Sprinkle with salt. Roll in corn meal or flour. Sauté in butter until delicately brown. Remove trout to hot platter.

To the drippings in pan add additional butter, salt, and lemon juice. Let it brown slightly and pour over fish. Sprinkle with chopped parsley.

For Trout Amandine, sprinkle sautéed brook trout with slivered almonds which have been sautéed with additional butter in the pan drippings.

FISH FILLETS IN WINE, PORTUGUESE STYLE

Crush or chop 3 cloves garlic. Add 1 teaspoon salt, 1/4 teaspoon red pepper, 1 cup wine vinegar, and 1 1/2 cups water.

Pour over 2 pounds fish fillets and leave overnight. Drain from liquid, fry in deep fat, or sauté until delicately browned. Serves 6.

Batter-Dipped Fried Fish: Sprinkle prepared fillets with salt and dip in batter.

Fry batter-dipped fish in hot fat at 375°F. until golden brown. Drain on absorbent paper.

DEEP FRIED SMELTS

Remove small scales with a sharp knife. Slit fish along the underside and remove entrails. Then remove silver lining from stomach by grasping with thumb and index finger. Rinse and dry.

Dip fish in egg beaten with a little milk. Roll in corn meal or fine cracker crumbs. Or use a combination of corn meal and cracker crumbs.

Fry in hot deep fat (370°F.) until golden brown, 3 to 5 minutes. Drain on absorbent paper. Sprinkle with salt, pepper, and lemon juice. Serve with tartar sauce or ketchup and lemon wedges.

Note: Smelt fanciers usually like these fish fried whole and the bones are eaten.

PAN-FRIED OR SAUTÉED SMELTS

Clean as for deep fried smelts. For best results use a half inch of bacon fat in a heavy skillet. Brown until crisp on one side. Turn and brown other side.

Smelts may also be sautéed in butter until brown on both sides.

Smelts Meunière: Sauté smelts in butter. Remove to hot platter. Sprinkle with chopped parsley. Melt additional butter in pan. Pour over smelts. Serve with lemon wedges.

Smelts Amandine: Sauté smelts in olive oil. To serve, sprinkle with slivered almonds sautéed in oil.

Smelts Au Beurre Noir (With Black Butter): Serve sautéed smelts with black butter (See Index) poured over fish.

Frozen breaded fish portions just seem to be made for busy days. Since they were dipped in batter and seasoned breadcrumbs before being packaged and frozen, all you need do is follow directions on the package for deep-fat frying or for pan-frying. Serve them with a well-seasoned sauce.

FISH FILLETS MEUNIÈRE

Season and dredge fish fillets with flour. Fry in butter. When done, remove from pan.

Place a little sweet butter in the same pan and cook it until nut-brown in color. Pour over the fish. Sprinkle with chopped parsley and a little lemon juice.

With Almonds: Sprinkle fish fillets meunière with slivered almonds, sautéed in butter.

BROOK TROUT SUPREME

Sprinkle cleaned and dressed brook trout inside and out with lemon juice, salt, and pepper. Dip in egg beaten with 2 tablespoons milk, then in fine dry breadcrumbs.

Melt enough butter or margarine in skillet to just cover the bottom. Add fish and sauté until golden brown on both sides, about 3 to 4 minutes, or until fish flakes easily when tested with fork.

Remove to hot platter and serve with mushroom-butter sauce (below). Garnish, if desired, with toast cornucopias.

Mushroom-Butter Sauce:
¼ cup (½ stick) butter
1 2-ounce can sliced mushrooms, drained
1 tablespoon lemon juice
½ teaspoon salt

Melt butter. Add mushrooms, lemon juice, and salt. Serve hot with trout. Makes enough for 3 to 4 small trout.

Brook Trout Supreme

DEEP FAT FRIED FISH

Prepare 2 pounds fish as for pan-fried fish.

Use a deep kettle with a frying basket and enough fat to cover the fish, but do not have the kettle more than half full of fat. Heat the fat to 375°F.

Place a layer of fish in the frying basket and cook to an even golden brown, about 3 to 5 minutes. Raise basket, remove fish, and drain on absorbent paper.

Serve immediately on a hot platter, plain or with a sauce. Serves 6.

EELS

Eels should be alive when bought and will be skinned, cut up, and cleaned on request.

To prepare at home, cut off the head and slit the skin lengthwise. Peel off, cut open and remove entrails. Wash in salt water and cut into convenient lengths.

FRIED EEL

Cut eel in 2-inch lengths. Wash and dry thoroughly. Season with salt and pepper.

Dip in crumbs, then in egg, and again in crumbs. Brown quickly in a small amount of fat. Cover, reduce heat, and cook slowly until tender.

Serve with tomato sauce or other desired sauce.

Poached or "Boiled" Fish

LIQUIDS USED FOR BOILING FISH

Boiled fish may be improved in flavor by cooking in one of the following liquids: **Acid Water, Fish Stock,** or **Court Bouillon.**

ACID WATER

To each quart of water add 1½ tablespoons of salt and 3 tablespoons of lemon juice or vinegar.

FISH STOCK

3 pounds fish bones
2 tablespoons butter
4 quarts water
2 stalks celery with leaves
2 large carrots, in pieces
2 onions, in pieces
1 cup chopped leeks
3 bay leaves
2 or 3 cloves garlic
8 peppercorns
2 teaspoons salt
1 teaspoon thyme

Wash fish bones in several changes of water. Melt butter in large kettle; add fish bones and water and cook, stirring about 5 minutes.

Add remaining ingredients and bring to a boil. Reduce heat and simmer ½ hour. Strain and store in refrigerator for a week or longer. Makes about 3 quarts.

Note: This stock may be frozen and defrosted as needed.

COURT BOUILLON

Court bouillon is a well-seasoned liquid in which fish is poached. It is usually made of water, carrots, onion, celery, wine or vinegar, and various herbs and spices.

⅓ cup diced carrots
⅓ cup chopped onion
⅓ cup chopped celery
2 sprigs parsley
2 tablespoons butter or other fat, melted
2 quarts water
6 whole black peppers
2 whole cloves
1 bay leaf
2 tablespoons salt
2 tablespoons vinegar

Cook the vegetables in fat about 5 minutes to brown slightly.

Add water, spices (tied in a bag), and vinegar; simmer 30 minutes. Strain.

Court Bouillon with Wine: Omit vinegar in Court Bouillon recipe, and add 2 cups dry white or red wine.

Fish Stock with Court Bouillon: Cover fish bones and scraps with Court Bouillon. Simmer 30 minutes or longer and strain. Use as liquid in making sauces to serve with fish or in fish soups.

POACHED OR "BOILED" FISH

2 pounds fillets
2 quarts water
3 tablespoons salt

Cut fillets into serving-size portions.

Place fish in a wire basket or on a plate. The plate if used should be tied in a piece of cheesecloth. Lower the fish into the salted, boiling water and simmer (never boil), about 10 minutes or until fish flakes easily when tested with a fork.

Remove fish carefully to a hot platter. Garnish and serve hot with a rich, bright colored sauce. Serves 6.

STEAMED FISH FILLETS

2 pounds fillets
1½ teaspoons salt

Salt fish on both sides. Place fish in a well greased steamer pan, and cook over boiling water for 10 to 12 minutes or until fish flakes easily when tested with a fork.

Remove fish carefully to a hot platter, and serve hot with a rich brightly colored sauce. Serves 6.

GEFILTE FISH
(Traditional Jewish Filled Fish)

Gefilte Fish means literally, stuffed fish in Yiddish. It is an old-time Jewish dish of chopped fish mixed with other ingredients, highly seasoned. It is stuffed into the fish skin or into pieces of it, or shaped into balls, then cooked. Some variation of it was prepared in every country of Central and Eastern Europe. It is sold in jars in the form of balls. Serve it with prepared horseradish.

3   **pounds fish (see below)**
2   **onions**
1   **egg**
2   **tablespoons breadcrumbs or matzo meal**
About 1 teaspoon salt
About 1/8 teaspoon pepper
Few dashes of cinnamon
About 1/2 cup water
1   carrot, sliced
1   potato, sliced (optional)
1   stalk celery, sliced

Use any firm-fleshed fish, preferably pike, carp, whitefish, buffalo, or a combination of these.

Clean and wash fish thoroughly; sprinkle with salt and place in refrigerator until ready to prepare.

Either leave fish whole or cut it into 2-inch slices. If the fish is left whole, do not remove head or tail. In either case, fillet the fish by removing flesh with bones leaving the skin intact.

Remove the flesh from bones; put the filleted parts or flesh and 1 onion through food chopper, then place in wooden chopping bowl.

Add egg, breadcrumbs, or matzo meal, seasoning, and enough water to make a soft light mixture. Chop until thoroughly blended and smooth.

Wet the hands with cold water and fill the skin with this mixture. If the fish has been sliced form the mixture into oval cakes and fit them into bands of skin.

Place the bones, 1 sliced onion, carrot, potato, and celery in a deep kettle. Season with salt, pepper, and cinnamon.

Place fish sections neatly on top; add cold water to cover. Cover kettle and bring to quick boil. Remove cover, turn down heat, and keep fish at a slow boil 1 1/2 to 2 hours.

The liquid should be reduced by half. When cool, remove to a platter carefully to retain shape of each section. Strain liquid over fish or into a separate bowl.

Chill thoroughly before serving, using carrot for garnish.

The jelled sauce may be cut and served separately or as an additional garnish. Serves 4 to 6.

Gefilte Fish Balls: Place bones, head, and skin removed in the process of filleting fish on bottom of deep kettle. Arrange several stalks of celery across.

Form the fish mixture into balls and place on top of celery to make removal easier when cooked.

The bones and skin add flavor to the fish sauce; discard after removing fish and straining sauce.

SQUID AND OCTOPUS

Squid is a long, slender sea creature with ten arms, two of which are much longer than the others. It is a mollusk, but its shell is very small and is on the inside. Small squids are used as food and for fish bait. They have a sweet, rich flavor and appear in many Mediterranean and Oriental dishes. In seaboard areas they are available fresh, and they are occasionally frozen and shipped inland. They are sometimes available canned in specialty stores.

The similarly shaped octopus come in enormous sizes; however the very small ones are often used as food in the same way as squid.

SQUID À LA GRUCCI

1 1/2   **pounds squid**
1   **medium onion, chopped**
3   **tablespoons olive oil**
1   **tablespoon chopped parsley**
1   **clove garlic**
1/2   **teaspoon rosemary**
1/4   **pound mushrooms, sliced**
2   **tablespoons tomato sauce**
1/2   **cup water**

Clean squid and remove skin; cut meat into small pieces.

Brown onion in hot olive oil. Add parsley, garlic, rosemary, and mushrooms; cook 5 minutes.

Add tomato sauce, water, and squid; cover pan and cook gently about 40 minutes, or until squid is tender. Cooking time will depend on size of squid. Serves 4.

WHALE

Although whale is usually classified in the fish section of cook books, this is meat, not fish, since the whale is a mammal. Whale meat is imported frozen and is often available in specialty food stores and in some restaurants. When braised on top of the range or in the oven, it has a flavor resembling that of beef.

For best results, whale meat should be kept frozen right up to the moment of preparation for cooking. If it is allowed to thaw out too long in advance it develops a fishy taste, which starts by being pleasantly suggestive of salmon but may later become overly strong. This flavor may be removed by parboiling the meat with a sliced onion and then draining off any oil that may accumulate.

BLUE TROUT OR TRUITE AU BLEU

This is a method of cooking freshwater fish very quickly by plunging it into boiling court bouillon. It is used especially for trout. With this method it is essential that the fish be not only fresh but actually alive when brought to the kitchen. The fish is stunned, cleaned quickly, plunged into the court bouillon, and removed the instant it is done, usually in 10 to 12 minutes. It is then served with melted butter, plain boiled potatoes, and chopped parsley. The name comes from the vinegar in the court bouillon, which turns the fish slightly blue.

CIOPPINO
(San Francisco Fish Stew)

Cioppino is a fish or fish-and-shellfish stew simmered in highly seasoned tomato sauce, often with wine added. The name is Italian, but the dish as usually prepared originated in San Francisco.

1/4   **cup salad or olive oil**
2   **cloves garlic, minced**
1   **cup chopped onion**
1   **cup chopped green pepper**
1   **can (1 pound, 4 ounces) tomatoes**
1   **8-ounce can tomato sauce**
1   **bay leaf**
1/8   **teaspoon oregano**
Salt and pepper to taste
2   **cups dry white wine**
1   **pound frozen lobster tails**
1   **pound frozen cod or flounder fillets**
1   **10-ounce package frozen shrimp**
1   **10 1/2-ounce can minced clams**

Heat oil in large heavy skillet or Dutch oven over medium heat; add garlic, onion, and green pepper; cook until lightly browned, 8 to 10 minutes.

Add tomatoes, tomato sauce, bay leaf, oregano, salt and pepper.

Cover and cook slowly, stirring frequently, about 1 hour, adding wine during last 10 minutes.

Add lobster and cod or flounder; simmer about 10 minutes. Add shrimp and clams and simmer until tender, about 10 minutes. Serves 6 to 8.

Cioppino

Fish Fillets Duglere

FISH FILLETS DUGLERE

1   pound frozen fish fillets
2   tablespoons butter or margarine
1   medium onion, chopped
1   clove garlic, minced
1   No. 2 can tomatoes
1/4 cup white wine or lemon juice
1   tablespoon minced parsley
1   tablespoon flour
1/4 teaspoon oregano
2   tablespoons heavy cream

Let fillets thaw on the bottom shelf of the refrigerator or at room temperature. Cut fillets in serving-sized pieces.

Melt 1 tablespoon butter or margarine in a skillet; add onion and garlic. Place fish on top; cover with tomatoes, wine or lemon juice, and parsley. Bring to a boil; lower heat; cover skillet and cook 10 to 15 minutes.

Remove fish to chafing dish to keep warm. Cream remaining butter with flour and stir into sauce. Add oregano. Cook, stirring occasionally, for about 5 minutes. Blend in heavy cream. Garnish with additional parsley. Serves 4.

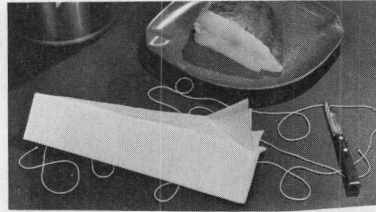

BUTTER BARBECUED FISH FILLETS

1/2 cup (1 stick) butter or margarine
1/2 cup minced onion
2   tablespoons chopped green pepper
1   tablespoon Worcestershire sauce
2   tablespoons ketchup
2   teaspoons vinegar
2   slices lemon
1   teaspoon prepared mustard
2   pounds frozen fish fillets (2 boxes)

Sauté onion and green pepper in butter in a large skillet. Add Worcestershire sauce, ketchup, vinegar, lemon slices, and prepared mustard and simmer for 5 minutes.

Cut each package of fish fillets into 4 equal pieces and place in the skillet. Cover and simmer for 10 minutes. Turn.

Simmer 10 to 15 minutes more or until the fish is done and can be flaked with a fork. Serves 4 to 6.

FISH COOKED IN MILK

2   pounds fish fillets
5   cups water
1   tablespoon salt
3   cups milk

Wipe the fish with a damp cloth, and cut in serving pieces. Soak 5 minutes in 5 cups water to which 1 tablespoon salt has been added. Drain.

Place in hot milk, and simmer until fish flakes easily with a fork, allowing about 15 minutes per inch thickness of fish. Prepare a medium white sauce, using the milk in which the fish was cooked. Serves 6.

FISH COOKED IN WATER
(Flavor-Saving Method)

Portions of whole fish or fillets which are to be used for salads, casseroles, fish cakes, or creamed fish dishes may be cooked in water.

Wipe fish with a damp cloth. Sprinkle fish with salt and place on a sheet of dampened parchment paper or a piece of greased aluminum foil. Measure thickness of fish.

Add 1 tablespoon each of chopped onion and celery. Wrap securely. Draw up corners of parchment paper, pouch fashion, and tie with string. Or fold foil over fish securing open edges with double folds to make package water tight.

Place the package in rapidly boiling water and cover. When water returns to the boil, time the cooking period. Boil 10 minutes per inch thickness for fresh fish and about 20 minutes per inch thickness for frozen fish.

When removing fish from the package, save the juices which can be substituted for liquid in sauces or casseroles.

Fish Fillets with Brazil Nut Sauce

FISH FILLETS WITH BRAZIL NUT SAUCE

Let 1 pound fish fillets thaw until they can be separated. Place in a frying pan. Add 1/4 cup water and 1 tablespoon lemon juice. Cover pan and let simmer 8 to 10 minutes or until fish flakes easily when tested with a fork.

Place on heated platter and pour Brazil Nut Sauce (below) over fish. Serves 3.

Brown Butter Sauce with Brazil Nuts: Put 3 tablespoons butter in a heavy saucepan; melt and cook very slowly until it is hazelnut brown. Serve over fish fillets garnished with toasted Brazil nuts.

To Prepare Brazil Nuts: Cover shelled Brazil nuts with cold water. Bring water slowly to boil and let simmer 3 to 4 minutes. Drain. Slice nuts. Brush slices with butter, place on cooky sheet or in baking dish. Place in moderate oven (350°F.) 10 or 15 minutes until golden brown. Turn occasionally.

"BOILED" HADDOCK OR COD, NEW ENGLAND STYLE

Split a 3 to 4 pound haddock or cod. Clean and rub inside well with salt. Let stand 3 hours.

Rinse fish and wrap in cheesecloth, leaving long ends of the cloth for handles. Simmer in boiling salted water 25 to 35 minutes or until fish flakes easily when tested with fork.

Remove to hot platter. Garnish with crisp bits of salt pork, and surround with boiled potatoes and boiled buttered beets. Serve with parsley sauce or egg sauce. Serves 4 to 6.

"Boiled" Haddock, New England Style

COD PROVENÇAL

4 thick slices cod
Salt and pepper
1 medium onion, finely chopped
1 clove garlic, crushed
2 tablespoons chopped parsley
Pinch of thyme
2 medium tomatoes, peeled and
 chopped
1 cup thinly sliced mushrooms, sautéed in butter or margarine
1 cup white wine
1 tablespoon butter or margarine

Season fish with salt and pepper. Place in well greased shallow baking dish. Sprinkle with onion, garlic, parsley, and thyme. Add tomatoes, sautéed mushrooms, and wine.

Place over low heat and simmer gently until fish is tender and flakes apart 15 to 20 minutes.

Remove fish to heated platter and keep warm while sauce cooks down to about half its original volume. Add butter and pour sauce over fish. Serve at once. Serves 4.

Note: Haddock, ocean perch, or flounder fillets may be substituted for cod.

CURRIED FISH

1½ to 2 pounds fish
2 tablespoons fat
1 tablespoon chopped green pepper
1 small onion, chopped
¼ cup chopped celery
2 tablespoons flour
1 cup liquid from simmered fish
¼ to 1 teaspoon curry powder
Salt, to taste
2 to 3 cups cooked rice
3 tablespoons chopped parsley

Simmer fish about 10 minutes in a small quantity of water in a shallow pan. Drain and save liquid.

Melt fat. Cook green pepper, onion, and celery in fat a few minutes. Stir in flour, then add fish liquid with milk or water to bring the quantity to 1 cup. Cook until thickened, stirring constantly.

Add curry powder and salt, to taste. Remove skin and bones from cooked fish. Arrange on a hot platter with a border of rice. Pour sauce over fish and sprinkle with chopped parsley. Serves 6.

CREOLE BOUILLABAISSE

2 pounds fish fillets
¼ pound mushrooms
1 tablespoon margarine or butter
1 large onion, minced
1 clove garlic, mashed
1 tablespoon flour
2 cups tomato pulp
1 cup water
1½ bay leaves
¾ teaspoon curry powder
¼ cup sherry

Dash of Tabasco sauce
½ teaspoon salt
4 whole cloves

For best results, use 2 kinds of fish such as redfish and red snapper.

Poach fish in boiling water for 15 minutes.

Slice mushrooms very thin and sauté in fat with onion, garlic, and flour. When golden brown, add remaining ingredients and simmer for 30 minutes.

Add this sauce to drained fish and cook about 5 minutes. Place pieces of fish on buttered toast, cover with the sauce and serve. Serves 6 to 8.

POACHED SALMON WITH HERB DRESSING

Select salmon steaks of even thickness, buying 1 steak for 2 servings.

Place piece of aluminum foil in bottom of frying basket. Place 1 steak on foil, top with another piece of foil; continue until all the steaks are added. Place basket in kettle; add 1 or 2 slices of onion, 3 slices of lemon, 3 or 4 whole black peppers, a piece of bay leaf, 1 to 2 teaspoons salt, and ½ teaspoon Ac'cent per pound of fish.

Add enough boiling water to cover fish. Set over low heat; simmer 15 to 20 minutes depending on amount of fish.

Lift out basket. Remove steaks by lifting foil under each. Cool; then chill.

To serve, top with chilled cooked asparagus and herb dressing. Garnish with cucumber slices, watercress, and capers.

Herb Salad Dressing:

1½ tablespoons sugar
1 teaspoon salt
¼ teaspoon Ac'cent
2 teaspoons prepared mustard
¼ teaspoon rosemary
⅛ teaspoon thyme
¼ teaspoon savory
2 tablespoons flour
1 slightly beaten egg
¾ cup milk
¼ cup lemon juice
1 tablespoon butter or margarine

In top of double boiler combine sugar, salt, Ac'cent, mustard, herbs, and flour. Add egg; blend well.

Add milk slowly, blending well. Add lemon juice.

Cook over hot water, stirring constantly, until thickened. Add butter or margarine; stir until melted. Cool, then chill.

Add ¼ to ½ cup light cream if a thinner dressing is desired. Makes about 1 cup dressing.

French Rolled Fish Fillets

FRENCH ROLLED FISH FILLETS

1 tablespoon butter or margarine
2 tablespoons minced onion
1½ pounds fish fillets
1½ teaspoons salt
Speck of pepper
4 peeled, quartered small tomatoes
¼ pound mushrooms, sliced
½ cup dry wine
½ cup cold water

Grease a large frying pan with butter. Strew onion over it.

Roll each fillet like a jelly roll, place in frying pan, seam side down. Sprinkle salt and pepper over fillets.

Arrange tomatoes around and place mushrooms over top. Pour over wine and water. Cover and simmer 10 minutes, or until fish is tender.

Remove fish to hot platter, keeping warm while preparing sauce.

Sauce: To prepare sauce cook liquid left in frying pan until about 1 cupful remains. Cream 3 tablespoons softened butter. Add 3 tablespoons flour. Add to the liquid and simmer until thickened. Sprinkle fish with parsley. Pour sauce over fish. Broil until browned over top.

If desired, small cooked potato balls may be placed around fish before pouring over sauce and broiling. Serves 4.

Poached Salmon with Herb Dressing

Dried, Smoked, and Salt-Cured Fish

CODFISH BALLS
(Master Recipe)

2   cups flaked salt codfish
3½ cups diced, pared raw potatoes
2   slightly beaten eggs
2   tablespoons butter or margarine
¼   cup milk
⅛   teaspoon pepper
Dash of celery salt
Paprika

Shred fish into small flakes; place in saucepan. Cover with cold water. Heat slowly to boiling point. Drain. Repeat, using fresh water if fish is hard and salty.

Combine with potatoes and cook, covered, in about 2 cups boiling water, until potatoes are tender. Drain well and mash thoroughly. Add remaining ingredients. Beat with spoon until light and fluffy. Chill.

Shape into balls or drop by spoonfuls into hot deep fat (375°F.). Fry until browned. Drain on absorbent paper.

Serve with tomato sauce, ketchup, egg sauce, or chili sauce. Serves 6.

Variations of Codfish Balls

Codfish Hash: Spread mixture evenly in a large, hot, well greased skillet. Cook slowly until a brown crust forms on bottom. Fold like an omelet.

Codfish Patties: Shape into patties. Brown on both sides in hot fat.

Curried Codfish Balls: Add 1 teaspoon curry powder to mixture.

CREAMED CODFISH

2   cups shredded codfish
4   tablespoons butter or margarine
4   tablespoons flour
2   cups milk
⅛   teaspoon pepper

Cover codfish with water. Heat slowly to boiling point. Repeat once or twice if fish is hard and very salty. Drain well.

Heat butter. Add codfish and cook over low heat about 2 minutes. Blend in flour. Slowly add milk. Cook until thickened, stirring constantly. Add pepper.

Serve on toast or baked potatoes. Serves 6.

CODFISH CAKES

1   cup (5 ounces) shredded salt codfish
1   cup hot mashed potatoes
20 saltine crackers, finely rolled
1   egg
1   tablespoon minced onion
Few grains pepper

Cracker meal

Place fish in cheesecloth or fine strainer and run cold water through it for 1 minute before using.

Blend together fish, potatoes, cracker crumbs, egg, onion, and pepper.

Shape into 8 patties; roll in cracker meal. Sauté until golden brown. Serve with tomato sauce. Serves 4.

FINNAN HADDIE

Finnan haddie is smoked haddock. The name is a corruption of Findon haddock, Findon being a fishing port on the coast of Scotland famous for its cured haddock.

CREAMED FINNAN HADDIE

2   pounds finnan haddie
2   tablespoons butter or margarine
½   cup cream or top milk

Cover fish with water and simmer 10 minutes. Drain.

Place on a hot platter; dot with butter and add hot milk or cream before serving. Garnish with parsley. Serves 6.

STEAMED FINNAN HADDIE

Steam over boiling water until tender, 15 to 20 minutes. Each piece should be exposed to steam. Do not pile on top of each other. Serve with butter sauce.

FINNAN HADDIE RABBIT

In double boiler, heat ½ pound old English cheese, cut small, with 1 cup heavy cream and 1 cup flaked steamed finnan haddie. When well blended, stir in 1 beaten egg and serve on toast. Serves 6.

FINNAN HADDIE BAKED IN MILK

2   pounds finnan haddie
2   tablespoons butter or margarine
1   cup milk

Cover fish with boiling water; simmer 10 minutes. Drain.

Add milk and butter to fish. Bake in moderate oven (350°F.) 15 minutes. Serves 6.

KIPPERS

To kipper means to preserve fish by splitting, salting, and smoking it. A fish cured by this method, usually a herring, is often referred to simply as a kipper. A bloater is a large, specially selected herring or mackerel that has been cured (bloated) by salting and smoking.

BROILED KIPPERED HERRING

Remove head and tail from herring; wipe with a damp cloth.

Place skin side up, on a broiler 4 inches from heat and broil 3 minutes. Turn fish, dot with butter, broil 3 minutes longer. Serve with lemon.

BAKED KIPPERED HERRING

4   kippered herring
½   green pepper, minced
¼   cup minced onion
1   tablespoon butter or margarine
1½ cups tomato juice
¼   teaspoon pepper

Remove head and tail from herring and wipe with a damp cloth. Place in a greased baking dish.

Sauté minced green pepper and onion in butter; spread over fish. Pour tomato juice over fish; sprinkle with pepper.

Bake in hot oven (425°F.) 15 minutes. Serves 4.

SAUTÉED KIPPERED HERRING

Soak smoked kippers in boiling water to cover 10 minutes. Drain.

Sauté in hot oil or butter in skillet about 5 minutes, turning once. Serve with butter sauce.

CANNED KIPPERED HERRING

Place kippers in a shallow baking dish or ovenproof platter. Brush with melted butter and lemon juice. Sprinkle with pepper. Pour over juice from can.

Heat in oven. Garnish with lemon wedges and chopped parsley.

BOILED SALT MACKEREL

Soak salt mackerel, skin up, well covered with cold water overnight.

Drain and place in a shallow pan. Cover with water and simmer until tender, about 12 minutes. Drain well.

Place on hot platter; pour melted butter over it, to which add chopped chives or parsley and lemon juice or Worcestershire sauce.

BAKED SALT MACKEREL

Soak salt mackerel 8 to 12 hours in cold water. Drain. Dry and dredge with flour.

Place in greased baking dish. Add ½ cup milk per 2 pounds fish. Sprinkle with paprika. Bake in moderate oven (350°F.) about 25 minutes.

BROILED SALT MACKEREL

Soak salt mackerel 8 to 12 hours in cold water. Drain and wipe dry.

Place skin side down on greased broiler rack. Brush with melted butter. Broil 10 to 12 minutes, basting frequently.

Serve with butter and lemon wedges or any fish sauce. Allow about ⅓ pound per serving.

MARINATED (PICKLED) HERRING

12 milter herring
2 lemons, sliced very thin
4 large onions, sliced
12 bay leaves
2 tablespoons mustard seed
2 tablespoons whole black peppers
2 cups vinegar
1 cup water
3 tablespoons sugar

Soak herring in cold water to cover for 3 hours, changing water twice. (Or soak in cold water to cover overnight.)

Drain. Cut off heads and tails. Split the herring. Remove and reserve the milt. If desired, skin and bone the herring. Remove the skin by running a knife from head to tail. Leave fillets whole or cut into 3-inch pieces.

Place herring in a crock in alternating layers with sliced lemon, sliced onions, a few pieces of bay leaf, and a sprinkling of mustard seed and whole black peppers.

Bring the combined vinegar, water, and sugar to a boil; cool. Mash the milt with a fork; add a little of the cooled vinegar mixture to thin it. Put through a sieve, then combine with remaining vinegar mixture. Pour over herring to cover.

Cover crock and put in a cool place. The herring are ready to be served in 4 to 6 days.

Note: If desired, 1 large apple, grated, may be added with the vinegar mixture.

JIFFY HERRING IN WINE WITH SOUR CREAM

1 2-pound jar herring in wine
1 cup sour cream
1 tablespoon grated onion
2 tablespoons chopped chives
1 tablespoon chopped basil

Drain the sauce from the herring and add to it the remaining ingredients. Pour this mixture over the herring. Serve chilled as an appetizer on lettuce. Serves 6.

Pickled herring appetizers are quick and easy to prepare with the ready-made varieties available in most grocery stores. For a drink accompaniment serve herring in a bowl with small slices of pumpernickel and rye breads.

MARINATED HERRING WITH CREAM

6 milter herring
¼ cup vinegar
1 lemon, very thinly sliced
1 onion, thinly sliced
2½ tablespoons mixed pickling spices
1 cup sour cream

Soak, clean, and fillet herring as directed in marinated herring recipe. Cut fillets into 1½-inch pieces.

Mash ½ the milt; combine with vinegar. (Dilute the vinegar with a little water if it is very strong.)

Place remaining milt and herring in a crock in alternating layers with the lemon, onion, and a sprinkling of pickling spices.

Pour vinegar mixture over herring. Add sour cream. Keep in a cool place. Serve it after 48 hours.

FINNAN HADDIE CASSEROLE

¾ pound finnan haddie
3 tablespoons butter or margarine
3 tablespoons flour
1½ cups milk
½ teaspoon salt
⅛ teaspoon pepper
2 cooked potatoes, diced
1 hard-cooked egg, sliced
2 slices bread
2 tablespoons butter

Wash finnan haddie. Soak 30 minutes in half milk and half water to cover. Bring to boil in same liquid and simmer gently 20 minutes. Drain; remove any skin and bones; flake fish.

Melt butter; blend in flour. Slowly add milk, salt, and pepper and cook, stirring constantly, until thickened. Add flaked fish, potatoes, and egg. Pour into individual casseroles.

Remove crusts from bread; cut into small cubes, and brown carefully in 2 tablespoons melted butter. Top casserole with brown cubes.

Bake in moderate oven (350°F.) 30 minutes. Serves 4.

Roe and Milt

Roe are the eggs of fish which are removed intact. They are commonly found in fish in the spring. Roe may be bought by the pound or in cans.

Milt are the spermatic glands of the male fish. It is prepared like roe.

Canned roe may be used in place of parboiled roe. Shad roe is considered a great delicacy and it is the most expensive; however roe is commonly obtained from cod, haddock, herring, flounder, mackerel, and salmon as well as shad. Salt herring and mackerel usually contain roe or milt.

Roe should be parboiled before using in recipes. Follow the method for parboiled shad roe, but cut the time for roe from smaller fish. Five to 10 minutes is usually enough, depending upon size of roe. The roe is sufficiently done when it blanches (whitens).

A pair of roe from 1 shad will serve 2. For other roe or milt, allow about 1 pound to serve 4 to 5, depending upon how it is served.

PARBOILED SHAD ROE

Handle roe carefully in pairs with the membrane intact. Cover with boiling water and for each quart of water add 1 tablespoon vinegar or lemon juice, ½ teaspoon salt, and, if desired, ½ teaspoon pickling spice.

Lower heat and simmer until white and firm, 5 to 20 minutes, depending on size of roe. Drain, cover with cold water, cool, and drain again. Remove membrane or not as desired.

Note: Roe of very small shad do not have to be parboiled or at the most parboil for 2 minutes.

BROILED SHAD ROE

Brush dried parboiled shad roe with melted butter or margarine seasoned with salt and pepper, and a little lemon juice if desired.

Place in shallow greased baking dish or pan. Broil about 2 inches from heat source until golden brown. Turn and broil other side.

Baste several times with melted butter or margarine. It should be firm but not dry or hard. Serve with lemon wedges.

SHAD ROE MEUNIÈRE

Cook parboiled shad roe in butter or oil. Add lemon juice, salt, and pepper to taste. Sprinkle with chopped parsley. Cover with melted browned butter.

Shad Roe Amandine: Follow recipe for Shad Roe Meunière, and garnish with chopped almonds which have been browned in the oven.

BAKED SHAD ROE

Place drained parboiled shad roe in a greased baking dish. Cover with tomato sauce.

Bake in hot oven (400°F.) about 20 minutes, basting 5 times with sauce in pan. Serve with additional tomato sauce.

FRIED OR SAUTÉED SHAD ROE

Season drained, parboiled shad roe with salt and pepper. Sprinkle with lemon juice if desired.

Dip in fine cracker crumbs, then in beaten egg, diluted with 1 tablespoon milk or water, and again in crumbs.

Sauté in butter or margarine until done throughout and lightly browned or fry in hot deep fat (390°F.).

Serve with lemon wedges or tartar sauce.

Dishes with Canned or Cooked Fish

BUYING CANNED FISH

In using canned fish, the more attractive high grades are better for salads or serving plain. For such dishes as casseroles or fish cakes, lower grades will do. They are just as nutritious and flavorful as top quality.

The oil or salty liquid from canned fish adds flavor and food value to seafood dishes. Use the oil, for instance, as fat in the white sauce in making creamed tuna fish. Brine may be part of the liquid in jellied fish salad.

SALMON-MACARONI LOAF WITH TOMATO SAUCE

- 1 cup elbow macaroni
- 2 cups (1-lb. can) salmon, drained and flaked
- 1 cup grated Cheddar cheese
- 1½ cups corn flakes
- 1 cup milk
- 2 eggs, slightly beaten
- ¼ cup chopped pimiento
- 1 tablespoon chopped parsley
- ½ teaspoon finely chopped garlic
- 1 teaspoon salt
- ½ teaspoon pepper
- 2 cups corn flakes or ½ cup packaged corn flake crumbs
- ¼ cup grated Cheddar cheese
- 1 tablespoon butter, melted
- ¼ teaspoon paprika

Cook macaroni in boiling salted water only until tender. Drain, rinse, and drain again. Combine with salmon, 1 cup cheese, 1½ cups corn flakes, milk, eggs, pimiento, parsley, garlic, salt, and pepper. Spread evenly in greased 10 x 6 inch baking dish.

If using corn flakes, crush 2 cups into fine crumbs. Combine with ¼ cup cheese, butter, and paprika. Sprinkle over salmon mixture.

Bake in moderate oven (350°F.) about 40 minutes. Cut into 3 x 2½-inch pieces and serve, accompanied with hot tomato sauce. Serves 8.

Tomato Sauce. Sauté ½ cup each chopped onions and green pepper in 2 tablespoons butter. Then stir in salt, pepper, and chili powder to taste and a can of condensed tomato soup. Serve hot.

Salmon-Macaroni Loaf with Tomato Sauce

CREAMED FISH
(Master Recipe)

Combine 1½ cups flaked fish (cooked or canned) and 1½ cups medium white sauce. Heat in double boiler over hot water.

Season to taste with salt and pepper. Serve on toast, crisp crackers, or corn bread. Serves 4 to 6.

Note: Tomato or Creole sauce may be substituted for white sauce.

Creamed Fish Variations

Creamed Fish with Eggs: In master recipe use 1 cup flaked fish and 2 or 3 hard-cooked eggs, sliced.

Creamed Fish with Vegetables: In master recipe increase white sauce to 2 cups and add 1½ cups diced cooked vegetables.

Fish Au Gratin: Place creamed fish in greased baking dish and cover with ½ cup buttered crumbs mixed with ¼ cup of grated cheese.

Bake in hot oven (400°F.) until sauce is bubbly and the top is well browned, 20 to 30 minutes.

Creamed Fish in Noodle Ring: Prepare noodle ring. Place on hot serving plate. Place creamed fish in center. Garnish.

SCALLOPED FISH
(Master Recipe)

- 2 cups flaked, cooked fish
- 2 teaspoons grated onion
- 1 teaspoon lemon juice
- 1½ cups medium white sauce
- 1 cup buttered crumbs

Arrange fish in a greased casserole or individual ramekins. Sprinkle with onion and lemon juice. Add white sauce. Cover with buttered crumbs.

Bake in moderate oven (375°F.) until crumbs are brown, 20 to 25 minutes. Serves 6.

Scalloped Fish Variations

Scalloped Fish Mushroom Casserole: In master recipe, substitute canned cream of mushroom soup for white sauce. If necessary, dilute soup with a little milk.

Scalloped Fish with Potato Border: In master recipe, substitute mashed potatoes for buttered crumbs.

Scalloped Fish and Eggs: In master recipe, increase medium white sauce to 2 cups. Arrange fish, 3 sliced hard-cooked eggs, and sauce in alternate layers in casserole, sprinkling each layer with onion and lemon juice.

SALMON DIABLE

- ¾ cup sour cream
- ¼ cup sherry
- 1 tablespoon lemon juice
- 1 teaspoon Worcestershire sauce
- ½ teaspoon dry mustard
- 2 eggs, slightly beaten
- 1 1-pound can salmon, drained and flaked
- ⅓ cup fine cracker crumbs
- ¼ cup minced parsley
- 1 tablespoon minced onion
- Salt and pepper
- 6 thin lemon slices
- Paprika

Mix sour cream, wine, lemon juice, Worcestershire sauce, mustard, and eggs. Stir in salmon, cracker crumbs, parsley, and onion. Add salt and pepper.

Spoon mixture into 6 greased baking shells or individual casseroles. Top each with a lemon slice and sprinkle with paprika. Bake in moderate oven (350°-F.) 30 minutes. Serves 6.

Salmon Diable

TUNA IN MUSHROOM SAUCE

- 2 cans (6½ or 7 ounces each) tuna in vegetable oil
- 1 can condensed cream of mushroom soup
- 1 can (4 ounces) sliced mushrooms
- ½ cup sour cream
- 1 tablespoon chopped parsley, optional

Combine tuna, undiluted mushroom soup, and mushrooms with liquid from can in skillet or saucepan. Bring to a boil; simmer gently 5 minutes.

Remove from heat; stir in sour cream. Sprinkle with chopped parsley and serve over hot cooked noodles or rice. Serves 4.

Tuna in Mushroom Sauce

SALMON CROQUETTES

1   1-pound can salmon or 2 cups
    fresh cooked salmon
½ teaspoon salt
Dash of cayenne pepper
1   tablespoon chopped parsley
½ teaspoon grated onion
¼ cup cracker crumbs
1   well beaten egg

Flake fish, removing any skin or
bones. Mix well with remaining ingredients. Shape into croquettes. Roll in
extra bread or cracker crumbs.

Beat 1 additional egg lightly with
1 tablespoon water. Dip croquettes in
egg-water mixture, then again in
crumbs. Let stand in refrigerator at
least 30 minutes.

Fry in deep hot fat (375°F.) until
golden brown. Drain on absorbent
paper. Serve with Tartar Sauce.

KEDGEREE

Kedgeree is a hash of flaked fish with
rice. The name comes from India,
where it is applied to various more or
less similar spiced rice dishes.

1   pound cooked fish (see below)
2   cups hot cooked rice
4   hard-cooked eggs, cut in quarters
    or chopped
⅛ teaspoon pepper
3   tablespoons minced parsley
½ cup light cream
1   tablespoon butter or margarine
1   teaspoon salt

Use cod fillets, pickerel, pike, sole,
flounder, or haddock. Flake fish; place
in top part of double boiler with remaining ingredients. Heat thoroughly
over boiling water. Pinch of curry
powder may be added, if desired.
Serves 4.

BAKED SALMON CUTLETS

2   cups thick white sauce
2   teaspoons Worcestershire sauce
2   teaspoons lemon juice
1   tablespoon minced onion
⅛ teaspoon celery salt
2   cups cooked or canned salmon

Prepare 2 cups thick white sauce.
Add Worcestershire sauce, lemon juice,
minced onion, and celery salt. Mix
well.

Flake salmon, removing skin but
using soft bones and oil, and add fish
to sauce. Chill well.

Form into cutlets and roll in finely sifted dry breadcrumbs. Place on
greased pan. Bake in hot oven (400°F.)
20 minutes.

Serve with lemon sections, chili, or
tartar sauce. Serves 6.

TUNA-CORN CASSEROLE

¼ cup chopped onion
3   tablespoons chopped green pep-
    per
2   tablespoons butter or margarine
1   tablespoon flour
1   teaspoon salt
⅛ teaspoon white pepper
1   teaspoon paprika
1½ cups milk
1   cup cooked or canned corn
1   7-ounce can tuna
About ½ cup breadcrumbs
2   tablespoons melted butter

Sauté onion and green pepper in 2
tablespoons melted butter or margarine
until tender.

Blend in flour, salt, pepper, and paprika. Gradually add milk, and cook, stirring constantly, until mixture is smooth
and thickened. Add corn and flaked
tuna. Mix thoroughly.

Turn into 4 individual greased casseroles or 1 large casserole. Bake in
slow oven (325°F.) 20 minutes.

Toss the breadcrumbs with 2 tablespoons melted butter and sprinkle over
casseroles just a few minutes before
they are served. Serves 4.

SALMON LOAF

1   cup soft breadcrumbs
½ cup evaporated milk diluted with
    ½ cup water
1   No. 1 can salmon, drained and
    flaked
1   teaspoon salt
1   tablespoon butter or margarine
1   tablespoon minced onion
1   teaspoon lemon juice
2   beaten egg yolks
2   egg whites, stiffly beaten
4   hard-cooked eggs

Soak breadcrumbs in diluted milk
for 10 minutes. Add salmon, salt, butter, onion, lemon juice, and egg yolks.
Blend.

Fold in stiffly beaten egg whites.

Fill well greased loaf pan (8½ x-
4½ x 2½ inches) half full; top with a
row of 4 hard-cooked eggs. Pack rest
of mixture firmly around and over eggs.

Bake in moderate oven (350°F.)
about 45 minutes.

Unmold on platter. Serve with Creole
or tomato sauce. Serves 6.

Deviled Tuna

DEVILED TUNA

1   tablespoon chopped onion
1   4-ounce can sliced mushrooms,
    drained
¼ cup butter or margarine
¼ cup flour
½ teaspoon salt
½ teaspoon dry mustard
¼ teaspoon paprika
⅛ teaspoon black pepper
Dash of cayenne pepper
1½ cups milk
½ teaspoon Worcestershire sauce
1   teaspoon lemon juice
2   hard-cooked eggs, sliced
1   7-ounce can tuna, drained and
    flaked

Sauté onion and mushrooms in butter or margarine. Stir in next 6 ingredients. Add milk, Worcestershire
sauce, and lemon juice.

Cook, stirring constantly until sauce
thickens. Add sliced eggs and tuna.
Heat and serve over crackers. Serves
4 to 6.

FISH PATTIES

1½ cups flaked, cooked or canned fish
½ teaspoon salt
1   egg
1½ cups mashed potatoes
1   tablespoon minced onion
⅛ teaspoon pepper
Flour and fat

Combine all ingredients except flour
and fat. Shape mixture into patties and
roll in flour. Brown in fat. Serve with
creamed peas. Serves 4.

Fish Potato Puffs: In fish patties
recipe, add 2 egg yolks instead of a
whole egg to the mixture of fish and
potato. Add seasonings and fold in
stiffly beaten egg whites.

Put mixture into greased custard
cups and bake in a moderate oven
(350°F.) 30 minutes. Serves 4.

Fish Patties with Creamed Peas

Salmon Loaf

Cheese Salmon Ring with Creamed Vegetables

CHEESE SALMON RING WITH CREAMED VEGETABLES

4 tablespoons butter or margarine
½ cup diced onion
½ cup diced green pepper
4 tablespoons flour
1½ teaspoons salt
¼ teaspoon pepper
2½ cups milk
2 eggs, separated
2 tablespoons lemon juice
1 cup grated American cheese
1 cup dry breadcrumbs
1 cup diced cooked celery
1 1-pound can salmon, flaked

Cook onion and green pepper in butter until tender. Add flour and seasonings and blend. Stir in milk and cook until sauce boils and thickens, stirring constantly.

Pour a little hot mixture into slightly beaten egg yolks. Return to sauce. Add remaining ingredients and stir to blend. Fold in stiffly beaten egg whites.

Turn mixture into a buttered 1½-quart ring mold.

Bake in a moderate oven (350°F.) for about 40 to 45 minutes. Unmold on hot serving plate. Fill center with creamed peas. Serves 6.

FISH LOAF

3 tablespoons butter or margarine
4 tablespoons chopped onion
1½ tablespoons flour
1½ cups tomato juice
1 tablespoon lemon juice
¼ teaspoon marjoram
1½ cups cooked fish, flaked (leftover or canned)
1½ cups breadcrumbs
2 lightly beaten eggs
Oil and breadcrumbs for loaf pan

Fish Loaf

Cook onion in melted butter 5 minutes. Blend in flour; add tomato juice gradually. Cook a few minutes, stirring to avoid lumps.

Add lemon juice and marjoram; cook a few minutes longer. Remove from heat.

Add fish and breadcrumbs; mix, then add beaten eggs. Blend well and turn into a 9 x 5-inch loaf pan, well oiled and dusted with breadcrumbs.

Bake in moderate oven (350°F.) 35 to 40 minutes.

Let stand 5 minutes before unmolding. Serves 6.

TUNA-CELERY-NOODLE BAKE

1 6-ounce package egg noodles
1 10½- or 11-ounce can condensed celery soup
½ cup milk
1 6½- or 7-ounce can tuna, flaked
⅓ cup buttered crumbs
½ cup grated American cheese

Cook noodles in boiling, salted water until tender. Drain. Combine soup and milk.

Alternate layers of noodles and tuna in greased 1½-quart casserole. Pour soup mixture over tuna and noodles. Top with buttered crumbs and grated cheese. Bake in moderate oven (350°F.) 20 minutes.

Garnish with stuffed olive slices and parsley. Serves 6.

CREOLE TUNA

2 tablespoons butter or margarine
2 tablespoons chopped green pepper
1 small tomato, peeled and cut in eighths
2 tablespoons flour
1½ cups milk
Salt and pepper
1 7-ounce can tuna, flaked

Melt butter in a saucepan. Add green pepper and tomato; cook 3 minutes. Blend in flour. Gradually add milk and cook, stirring until smooth.

Season with salt and pepper to taste. Add tuna and cook for about 10 minutes. Serve on toast. Serves 6.

TUNA-MUSHROOM LOAF

1 2-ounce can sliced mushroom buttons
1 7-ounce can tuna
1 can condensed cream or mushroom soup
1½ cups soft breadcrumbs
1 tablespoon chopped pimiento
1 tablespoon parsley flakes
¼ teaspoon salt
2 beaten eggs

Arrange 2 rows of mushroom slices on bottom of greased loaf pan. Add re-mainder of mushrooms to rest of ingredients. Mix well.

Put mixture in pan. Bake in moderate oven (375°F.) 45 minutes, until firm. Serves 6.

TUNA CHEESE RABBIT

¼ cup butter or margarine
3 tablespoons enriched flour
1½ cups milk
2 cups grated processed Cheddar cheese (½ pound)
½ teaspoon salt
¼ teaspoon dry mustard
¼ teaspoon paprika
Dash of red pepper
1 tablespoon grated onion
1 teaspoon Worcestershire sauce
½ cup canned tomatoes
1 7-ounce can solid-pack tuna

In a saucepan, melt butter or margarine over low heat; add flour and blend. Add milk and cook until thickened, stirring constantly.

Add cheese, salt, mustard, paprika, pepper, onion, Worcestershire sauce, and tomatoes. Stir until cheese is melted.

Add undrained tuna; mix lightly with fork, breaking tuna into large chunks.

Serve over toasted bread or rolls. Serves 6.

BAKED SEAFOOD NEWBURG

2 cups medium cream sauce
1 tablespoon instant minced onion
½ teaspoon dry mustard
1 teaspoon parsley flakes
1 teaspoon Worcestershire sauce
1 tablespoon lemon juice
3 tablespoons dry sherry
¼ cup pimiento strips
1 can (7 ounces) solid pack tuna
1 can (4½ to 6½ ounces) shrimp
1 can (5 to 6 ounces) crabmeat
⅔ cup corn flake crumbs
3 tablespoons butter or margarine

Combine cream sauce, seasonings, lemon juice, and sherry; mix well. Add pimiento, oil from tuna, tuna broken into chunks, and drained shrimp and crabmeat; mix lightly. Put in baking dish.

Mix corn flake crumbs and melted butter; put in border on top of mixture. Bake in hot oven (425°F.) about 20 minutes, until heated through. Serves 6.

Baked Seafood Newburg

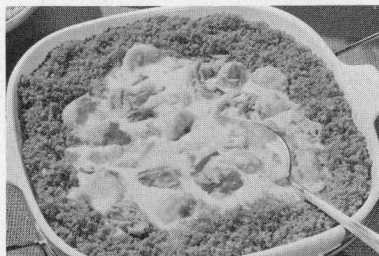

SALMON, RICE, AND TOMATOES

2   cups cooked or canned tomatoes and juice
¼   cup diced onion
¼   cup diced green pepper
2   tablespoons bacon fat or meat drippings
1½ cups boiling water
Salt and pepper
⅓   cup uncooked rice
¼   cup chopped olives, if desired
2   cups flaked canned or cooked salmon

Combine tomatoes, onion, green pepper, fat, water, salt, and pepper in a large saucepan. Bring to boil. (2½ cups raw tomatoes, cut in pieces, may be used instead of 2 cups cooked.)

Add rice and simmer until rice is tender (20 to 25 minutes), adding more water if needed.

Add olives and fish and cook 2 or 3 minutes longer to blend flavors.

Serves 6.

Variations: Other cooked fish may be used in place of salmon.

One cup of cooked rice may be used instead of the uncooked rice. Omit boiling water. Add the rice, olives, and fish as soon as the vegetables are tender and cook 5 to 10 minutes longer.

Celery may be used instead of green pepper.

CREAMED MUSHROOMS AND FLAKED FISH

⅔   cup sliced mushrooms
2   tablespoons butter or margarine
4   tablespoons flour
½   teaspoon salt
Few grains pepper
2   cups milk
2   cups cooked or canned flaked fish
1   tablespoon chopped parsley
Toast slices

Sauté mushrooms in butter or margarine; blend in flour, salt, and pepper. Gradually add milk.

Cook over hot water, stirring constantly, until thick. Add fish and parsley; heat. Serve on toast, or in rice ring. Serves 4.

Creamed Mushrooms and Flaked Fish in Rice Ring

SALMON SHORTCAKE AU GRATIN

3   cups medium white sauce
1   cup freshly grated cheese
1½ cups flaked salmon
1   cup cooked peas
1   tablespoon lemon juice
Baking powder biscuit dough

Make 3 cups medium white sauce. Add cheese, salmon, peas, and lemon juice. Heat thoroughly.

Make baking powder biscuit dough and bake in a round cake pan. Split and serve hot salmon mixture as a filling and topping for biscuit shortcake. Or serve on split hot biscuits, or on toasted bread. Serves 6.

CREAMED SALMON AND CORN

2   tablespoons butter or margarine
4   tablespoons flour
¾   teaspoon salt
Few grains pepper
1   teaspoon sugar
2   cups milk
¾   cup cooked or canned salmon
1½ cups cooked or canned whole kernel corn
1   tablespoon chopped pimiento
Toast slices

Melt butter or margarine; blend in flour, salt, pepper, and sugar. Gradually add milk.

Cook over hot water, stirring constantly, until thick. Add salmon, corn, and pimiento. Serve on toast. Serves 4.

CELERY SALMON LOAF

1   1-pound can (2 cups) salmon with juice, flaked
1½ cups dry breadcrumbs
½   cup minced green pepper
2   slightly beaten eggs
1   can (1¼ cups) condensed cream of celery soup

Combine ingredients as listed and mix. Pack lightly into a greased, small loaf pan.

Bake in a moderate oven (350°F.) about 1 hour or until done. Pour off extra juice and turn out on a warm platter. Serve with celery sauce. Serves 6.

FISH SHORTCAKE

2   to 3 tablespoons chopped onion
4   tablespoons fat
4   tablespoons flour
2   cups milk
⅓   cup grated cheese
1½ cups flaked cooked fish
Salt and pepper to taste
Hot biscuits or corn bread

Cook onion slowly in fat until tender. Blend in flour. Add milk slowly, stirring constantly, and cook until sauce is thickened.

Salmon Shortcake Au Gratin

Add cheese and fish. Season with salt and pepper. Heat mixture through, stirring occasionally. Serve on hot biscuits or corn bread. Serves 4.

Salmon Potpie: Prepare fish mixture as above, using cooked or canned salmon. Turn it into a greased baking dish, top with unbaked biscuits, and bake in hot oven (425°F.).

SALMON VEGETABLE PIE

Cheese Biscuits:
1   cup grated American cheese
2   cups prepared biscuit mix
⅔   cup milk

Combine cheese and biscuit mix; add milk and stir to make a soft dough.

Turn out onto lightly floured board; knead 30 seconds. Roll or pat out to ½- to ¾-inch thickness.

Cut with a floured biscuit cutter and place on top of salmon pie.

Salmon Vegetable Pie:
3   tablespoons butter
¼   cup diced onions
5   tablespoons flour
1½ teaspoons salt
⅛   teaspoon pepper
1   teaspoon Worcestershire sauce
2½ cups milk
2   cups cooked celery, diced
½   pound cooked, sliced mushrooms
1½ cups flaked, boned salmon
2   tablespoons minced parsley

Melt butter, add onions and cook over low heat until tender. Add flour, seasonings, and Worcestershire sauce; blend.

Gradually stir in milk and cook until thick and smooth, stirring constantly.

Add celery, mushrooms, salmon, and parsley, stirring to blend.

Turn into a 1½-quart buttered casserole; top with cheese biscuits and bake in a very hot oven (450°F.), 15 minutes, or until lightly browned. Serves 6.

Salmon Vegetable Pie

Tuna Piquant

TUNA PIQUANT

3 tablespoons butter or margarine
½ cup finely chopped green pepper
3 tablespoons flour
1¼ cups milk
⅓ cup chili sauce
⅓ cup sherry
2 7-ounce cans tuna, flaked
Salt to taste

Melt butter in a saucepan; add green pepper and cook gently for 5 minutes.

Blend in flour; add milk, chili sauce, and sherry; cook, stirring constantly, until mixture is thickened and smooth.

Add tuna and salt; heat gently for 5 minutes or so before serving.

Serve in patty shells, on toast or with rice. Serves 6.

Note: The above sauce may curdle when the liquids are added but will become smooth when mixture boils and thickens.

BAKED FISH TURBOT

Almost any type of fish may be used in this baked dish. Cod or haddock are particularly good.

To 2 cups medium white sauce add 2½ cups of cooked flaked fish.

Pour into a greased casserole. Cover with buttered crumbs.

Bake in moderate oven (375°F.) ½ hour. Grated cheese may be sprinkled over top before baking. Serves 6.

SALMON CASSEROLE

1 1-pound can salmon
½ cup finely chopped onion
½ cup chopped green pepper
½ teaspoon salt
⅛ teaspoon pepper
Dash of chili powder
1 beaten egg
1 cup tomato purée
1 cup breadcrumbs
1 cup condensed mushroom soup
2 tablespoons chopped parsley
2 tablespoons lemon juice
2 tablespoons melted butter

In a saucepan, combine salmon, onion, green pepper, salt, pepper, chili powder, egg, tomato purée, and ½ cup breadcrumbs.

Simmer 5 minutes. Then add mushroom soup, parsley, and lemon juice. Simmer 5 minutes longer.

Turn into buttered 2-quart casserole. Toss remaining breadcrumbs with melted butter; sprinkle on top of casserole. Bake in moderate oven (350°F.) 20 minutes. Serves 6.

TUNA OR SALMON PIE

4 tablespoons butter
½ cup enriched flour
4 cups hot milk and vegetable stock
2 teaspoons salt
⅛ teaspoon pepper
1 tablespoon minced onion
2 cups cooked peas
2 cups cooked carrots
2 7-ounce cans tuna or salmon
Cheese pastry strips (see Index)

Melt butter in top of double boiler. Add flour and blend. Add liquid gradually, stirring until smooth.

Add salt, pepper, and onion and continue cooking, stirring occasionally, until thickened.

Add peas, carrots, and fish and turn into large rectangular or square casserole.

Arrange cheese pastry strips on top of casserole in crisscross or lattice fashion.

Bake in moderate oven (375°F.) 30 minutes, or until crust is baked. Serves 6 to 8.

FISH TURNOVERS

Piecrust made from 2 cups flour or prepared piecrust mix
¾ cup cooked fish, flaked (or use canned tuna or salmon)
½ cup canned condensed mushroom soup or medium white sauce
1 slightly beaten egg
½ tablespoon chopped parsley
1 teaspoon lemon juice
1 hard-cooked egg, chopped
Salt and pepper to taste
1 beaten egg yolk, for brushing turnover tops

Roll out piecrust dough about ⅛ inch thick and cut into 12 equal squares.

Combine fish, mushroom soup or white sauce, beaten egg, parsley, lemon juice, and hard-cooked egg; blend well. Taste for seasoning.

Put a tablespoonful of this mixture on each square. Brush edges with water and fold over. Press edges with a floured fork to seal them.

Brush with beaten egg yolk and prick with fork. Set on greased baking sheet.

Bake in moderate oven (375°F.) 20 minutes. Serve with green salad. Serves 6.

CREAMED FISH CASSEROLE

2 tablespoons butter or margarine
1 cup mashed potatoes
About 3 cups cooked fish in lumps, salmon, tuna, or bonito (leftover or canned), well drained
1 cup sour cream
1 egg
Salt and pepper to taste
About 4 tablespoons grated cheese

1 tablespoon butter or margarine

Butter a baking dish or deep-dish pie plate very well. Line bottom and sides with a thin layer of mashed potatoes. If potatoes are too dry, add milk and beat in. Put fish into potato shell.

Beat sour cream; add egg and seasonings and beat again; add 2 tablespoons grated cheese.

Pour mixture over fish pieces. Dot with 1 tablespoon butter.

Bake in moderate oven (350°F.) 30 minutes, until browned. Sprinkle top with more grated cheese before serving. Serves 6.

TUNA TREAT

1 No. 2½ can cling peach halves
½ cup water
6 whole cloves
½ teaspoon cinnamon
¼ teaspoon nutmeg
¼ cup vinegar
1 3-ounce can sliced broiled mushrooms
1 tablespoon cornstarch
1 5-ounce package precooked rice, cooked according to package directions
2 7-ounce cans solid-pack tuna, drained
½ teaspoon salt
Pepper to taste

Drain peaches and reserve syrup. Combine peach syrup, water, cloves, cinnamon, nutmeg, and vinegar; bring to boiling point over medium heat.

Drain mushrooms and reserve liquid. Combine mushroom liquid and cornstarch; mix well.

Gradually add cornstarch mixture to hot syrup and continue cooking until thickened and clear, stirring occasionally. Add mushrooms and cooked rice.

Break tuna into large pieces with a fork and add to rice mixture.

Arrange alternate layers of tuna mixture and peach halves in a 2-quart casserole.

Cover and bake in moderate oven (350°F.) 30 minutes. Serve piping hot. Serves 6.

Tuna Treat

Shellfish

Shellfish include any aquatic animal with a shell; the most important are abalone, clams, crabs, crayfish, lobsters, mussels, oysters, prawns, scallops, and shrimps. Snails, though land animals, are often classified as shellfish in cookbooks; so are frog legs and turtles, which are zoologically unrelated.

Clams

There are three varieties of clams generally used—the hard-shell or quahog as they are known in New England, the soft-shell, and the razor clam.

The hard-shell is the one that is most usually available. It has a stronger flavor than the soft-shell and is the one used in chowders. The smallest hard-shell clams are known as "little necks." The medium-sized hard-shell clams are the type generally served raw on the half-shell and are called "cherry stones." The large hard-shell, although parts of it are tender, are usually tough and have to be chopped before being eaten. Soft-shell clams have a tender meat somewhat resembling oysters.

Clams bought in the shell must be tightly closed, thereby proving that they are alive. They will usually be opened on request at the market. To prepare them at home, scrub thoroughly, rinse and steam open or force open with a special heavy knife.

For clam chowder, buy whole or chopped clams in bulk by the pint or quart. Whole or chopped canned clams are also available.

CLAMS CASINO

Open clams carefully to retain juice. Remove upper shell, leaving clams in deeper half.

Sprinkle each with few drops of lemon juice, a bit of finely minced green pepper, and chopped onion. Season with salt and pepper. Put 3 bits of bacon on each.

Set in pan and bake in very hot oven (450°F.) or under broiler until bacon crisps.

BROILED CLAMS

Arrange small hard-shell clams on half-shells. Sprinkle with breadcrumbs. Dot with bits of butter. Broil 5 to 7 minutes. Serve very hot.

FRIED CLAMS

Clean and dry soft-shell clams. Roll clams in seasoned flour or roll in fine corn meal and shake off excess corn meal by placing in a strainer.

Fry in hot deep fat (375°F.) until browned. Drain on absorbent paper.

ROASTED CLAMS

Scrub clams well with a brush and wash thoroughly. Place them in a flat layer in a pan over a layer of rock salt, if desired. Bake in hot oven (425°F.) until shells open.

Remove upper shells carefully to avoid spilling liquor. Serve with seasonings, melted butter, and lemon wedges.

STEAMED CLAMS

Allow 10 to 15 per person. Soft-shell clams are best for steaming. Tightly closed shells indicate that the clams are fresh. Scrub thoroughly and wash in running water to remove all sand. Steam in covered kettle with ½ cup water per 4 quarts of clams, over moderate heat until shells partially open, 15 to 20 minutes. Do not overcook.

Remove clams to hot platters. Strain the clam broth left in kettle into small glasses. Serve with clams together with small individual dishes of melted butter seasoned with lemon juice, salt, and pepper.

To eat steamed clams, remove from shells by neck, and dip in clam broth, then in butter. Eat all but the hard black skin of neck.

CLAMBAKE CLAMS

The traditional clambake of New England frequently calls for a deep pit and a variety of seafood. For the most simple type, make a wood fire and preheat a bed of stones. After the fire dies down, cover the hot stones with a very thin layer of sea weed.

Have the clams thoroughly scrubbed with sea water and place them on this. Cover with sea weed and a piece of sail cloth to keep in the steam. Let the clams steam until they open.

CLAM FRITTERS

Drain 1 pint clams. Chop very fine and add to fritter binding batter. Fry in hot deep fat (375°F.) 3 to 5 minutes. Drain on absorbent paper. Serve with tomato or Creole sauce.

Serves 4 to 6.

Deviled Clams

DEVILED CLAMS

2 cups clams
½ cup clam liquor
2 tablespoons minced onion
2 tablespoons each minced green pepper and celery leaves
¼ cup chopped celery
4 tablespoons butter or margarine
⅛ teaspoon pepper
½ teaspoon prepared mustard
¾ cup cracker crumbs or fine bread-crumbs

Chop clams fine and simmer in their own liquor 5 minutes.

Cook onion, green pepper, celery leaves, and celery in melted butter until tender. Mix with remaining ingredients.

Combine with clams and mix well. Fill greased scallop shells or custard cups.

Bake in moderate oven (350°F.) 20 minutes. Serves 4 to 6.

Variation: Lemon juice may be substituted for the onion or green pepper or it may be added to the clam liquor before simmering.

NEW ENGLAND CLAM PIE

1 cup hard-shell clams, finely chopped
¾ cup milk
2 tablespoons clam liquor
½ teaspoon dry mustard
1 beaten egg
1 teaspoon chopped parsley
1 tablespoon butter or margarine
Dash of salt
Pastry made from 2 cups flour or pastry mix

Mix all ingredients except pastry, adding salt to taste.

Roll pastry for bottom crust. Fit into an 8-inch pan. Trim edges. Fill with clam mixture.

Roll pastry for top. Cut gashes to allow escape of steam. Place on pie. Seal well.

Bake in hot oven (425°F.) until crust is brown, about 25 minutes. Serves 4.

Clams Casino: Piping hot stuffed clams may be served as hors d'oeuvres or for an informal luncheon or supper.

Crabs

A crab is a shellfish (crustacean) with a short, broad covering shell and five pairs of legs, the first pair bearing claws or pincers.

Blue Crab: This is the common crab of the Atlantic coast much used as food. The hardshell blue crab is sold on the East coast alive. It is sold as a soft-shell crab if it is caught after it has shed its shell (molted) and before the new shell has hardened. Because the entire soft-shell crab, including the shell, is edible these are usually broiled, sautéed (pan-fried), or deep-fat fried.

Dungeness Crab: This is a Pacific coast crab and is best in the 2½ to 3 pound weight. It is marketed alive, as packaged frozen cooked meat, or canned.

King Crab: This is the largest (up to 15 pounds) of the edible crabs found in the North Pacific. It is marketed canned or frozen.

Rock Crab: A delicate-meated crab from the Atlantic coast, especially New England. It is marketed alive in the East and usually available frozen or canned elsewhere.

HOW TO PREPARE SOFT-SHELL CRABS

Stick a knifepoint into the body between the eyes. Lift the pointed ends of the top shell and scrape off the spongy white substance between the shell and body on each side.

Place the crab on its back and, with a small sharp knife, remove the "apron" or small loose shell which comes to a point at about the middle of the undershell. Wash the crabs and cook at once.

FRIED SOFT-SHELL CRABS

Prepare as above. Dry and sprinkle with salt and pepper. Dip in slightly beaten egg and roll in crumbs. Fry in hot deep fat (365° to 375°F.) until well browned, 3 to 5 minutes. Being very light, the crabs will rise to the top and should be turned 2 or 3 times while frying. Drain on absorbent paper.

Serve at once with tartar sauce and lemon wedges. The entire crab, including shell, is edible.

SAUTÉED SOFT-SHELLED CRABS

Sauté, cleaned prepared crabs in butter or other fat over moderate heat. Transfer to hot platter. Pour the drippings over them.

BROILED SOFT-SHELL CRABS

Sprinkle the cleaned, dried soft-shell crabs with salt, pepper, and lemon juice. Brush with melted butter.

Broil about 2 inches from heat. Cook until brown on both sides, about 5 minutes for each side or a total of 10 minutes in all.

Serve with tartar sauce and lemon wedges.

BOILED HARD-SHELL CRABS

Plunge live crabs head first into boiling salted water, using 1 teaspoon salt per quart water. Boil in covered kettle until shell is red and meat white, 20 to 25 minutes.

Fold back tapering points on each side of back shell and remove spongy material underneath. Remove apron, small pointed piece at lower part of shell.

Serve in shell or remove the meat for other dishes. The edible crabmeat is in the inner top of the back and in the claws. Crack claws with nutcracker.

Allow 1 hard-shell crab or ½ cup meat per serving.

DEVILED FRESH CRABS

8 hard-shell crabs, boiled
4 slices bread, crumbled
¼ cup butter
1 tablespoon Worcestershire sauce
Salt and pepper
Milk
Dash of Tabasco sauce
Buttered crumbs

Remove meat from crab shells and wash shells carefully.

Combine meat, crumbled bread, butter, Worcestershire sauce, salt and pepper to taste. Moisten with a little milk seasoned with Tabasco sauce. The mixture should be soft.

Pack loosely into shells. Top with buttered crumbs. Bake in moderate oven (350°F.) until delicately browned.

CREAMED CRABMEAT

Heat 1 cup crabmeat in 1 cup medium white sauce or cream sauce. Serve on toast or in patty shells. Serves 4.

Variations of Creamed Crabmeat

Crabmeat À La King: To above, add 1 tablespoon finely chopped red and green pepper and ½ cup cooked or canned sliced mushrooms. Season to taste with sherry.

Crabmeat Creamed with Mushrooms: Combine the white sauce with 1 cup crabmeat, ½ cup sliced mushrooms, and 1 diced pimiento.

Cook in top of double boiler over hot water for 10 minutes.

Crabmeat Au Gratin: Pour creamed crabmeat in casserole or ramekins. Top with a mixture of ⅓ cup buttered crumbs and ¼ cup grated cheese.

Bake in moderate oven (350°F.) until crumbs are lightly browned.

Deviled Crabmeat

DEVILED CANNED CRABMEAT

1 can (1¼ cups) condensed cream of celery soup
1 7-ounce can (1 cup) crabmeat
2 tablespoons chopped green pepper
2 teaspoons chopped onion
2 teaspoons lemon juice
½ teaspoon prepared mustard
2 tablespoons breadcrumbs
2 tablespoons melted butter

Combine soup, crabmeat, green pepper, onion, lemon juice, and mustard. Place in 1 large or 6 small buttered casseroles. (Clam shells are nice for this.)

Combine breadcrumbs and butter; sprinkle over crab mixture. Bake in moderate oven (350°F.) about 20 minutes or until lightly browned. Serves 6.

CRABMEAT CREOLE

1 7¾-ounce can King crabmeat
1 (No. 2½) can tomatoes
1 clove garlic, crushed
1½ cups chopped onion
2 teaspoons paprika
½ cup ketchup
¼ cup chopped parsley
1 chopped green pepper
1 cup thinly sliced celery
½ teaspoon filé powder
1 5-ounce package pre-cooked rice

Remove hard membrane from crabmeat, leave in large chunks, set aside.

Put all other ingredients, except rice and filé powder in a heavy skillet. Stir well. Cook over low heat, covered, until vegetables are tender. Season with salt and pepper to taste. Stir in filé powder. Combine with crabmeat and reheat.

Prepare rice according to package directions. Serves 3 to 4.

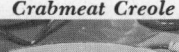

Crabmeat Creole

CRABMEAT SUPREME

2 cups flaked crabmeat
1/2 cup grated cheese
2 well beaten eggs
2 cups milk
Cracker crumbs
2 tablespoons melted butter or margarine
Juice of 1 lemon

Combine crabmeat and cheese. Add beaten eggs and milk. Pour into buttered casserole.

Cover with cracker crumbs mixed with melted butter. Pour lemon juice over all. Cover and set casserole in a pan of warm water.

Bake in moderate oven (350°F.) about 30 minutes. Serves 6 to 8.

Salmon or Lobster Supreme: Use 2 cups canned salmon or 2 cups canned lobster instead of crabmeat.

DEVILED CRAB IN AVOCADO HALVES

1/2 cup slivered blanched almonds
2 tablespoons butter
2 1/2 tablespoons sifted flour
1/2 teaspoon salt
1 cup milk
1 teaspoon prepared mustard
1/2 teaspoon Worcestershire sauce
2 teaspoons lemon juice
2 cups (1 pound) cooked crabmeat
3 to 4 medium-size avocado halves
Fresh lime or lemon juice

Toast almond slivers in slow oven (300° F.) 10 to 15 minutes, until lightly browned.

Melt butter, blend in flour and salt; stir in milk. Cook and stir until mixture boils and thickens. Add mustard, Worcestershire sauce, and lemon juice. Add crab and half of almonds; heat but do not boil.

Cut avocados in halves, lengthwise; remove seed but do not skin. Squeeze a little lime or lemon juice over cut surface of avocados to prevent darkening. Spoon hot crab mixture into avocado halves and sprinkle with remaining almonds. Serve at once. Serves 3 to 4.

Note: Avocados should be at room temperature, not chilled. Recipe may be doubled, if desired.

Deviled Crab in Avocado Halves

CRABMEAT CASSEROLE

6 slices bread, crusts trimmed
1 1/2 cups (2 7-ounce cans) crabmeat
1/2 pound Cheddar cheese, shredded
4 eggs
2 cups milk
About 1 teaspoon salt
Dash of pepper
Dash of cayenne

Arrange slices of bread in bottom of greased casserole. Cover with flaked crabmeat. Sprinkle with cheese.

Beat eggs; add milk and season to taste. Pour over cheese.

Bake in slow oven (325°F.) until set, 45 to 50 minutes. Serves 6 to 8.

CRABMEAT POTATO CHIP CASSEROLE

1/4 cup butter or margarine
1/2 cup flour
Dash of celery salt
2 cups milk
1/2 cup mayonnaise
1 can crabmeat, flaked
3 cups crushed potato chips
1/2 cup shredded Cheddar cheese
1/8 teaspoon paprika

Melt butter in saucepan over low heat. Stir in flour and celery salt.

Add milk gradually; stir until thickened and smooth. Stir in mayonnaise.

Put alternate layers of flaked crabmeat, sauce, and crushed potato chips in greased 1 1/2-quart casserole. Sprinkle cheese and paprika over top.

Bake in moderate oven (350°F.) 20 to 30 minutes. Serves 6.

SPANISH CRABMEAT

2 tablespoons butter or margarine
1 green pepper, finely shredded
2 tablespoons flour
1/2 teaspoon salt
1/4 teaspoon mustard or 1/8 teaspoon paprika
3/4 cup scalded milk
1 beaten egg
1 cup grated cheese
1 can condensed tomato soup
1 can (7 ounces) crabmeat, flaked
Crisp crackers or thin toast

Melt butter or margarine in a saucepan over low heat. Add green pepper and sauté gently without browning.

Combine flour, salt, and mustard or paprika, and stir into the saucepan, cooking and stirring over low heat until the mixture is smooth and well blended. Gradually add scalded milk, stirring constantly until mixture has thickened.

Remove from heat and add a little of hot mixture to beaten egg. Stir well and add egg mixture to first mixture, blending well. Stir in cheese.

Heat the soup in another saucepan and, when just at the boiling point, add to the thickened mixture with the crabmeat.

Place over heat just long enough to heat through. Do not boil.

Serve at once over crackers or toast. Serves 6 to 8.

CURRIED CRABMEAT

3 tablespoons butter or margarine
1 1/2 teaspoons minced onion
4 tablespoons flour
3/4 teaspoon salt
1 tablespoon curry powder
1 1/2 cups chicken stock
1 1/2 cups canned crabmeat
1 tablespoon lemon juice

Heat butter in saucepan. Add onion; cook until clear and limp.

Add flour, salt, and curry powder. Stir until smooth. Blend in chicken stock.

When thickened and smooth, add crabmeat and lemon juice. Heat through and serve with hot rice. Serves 6.

CHAFING DISH KING CRAB NEWBURG

2 7 3/4-ounce cans King crabmeat
1/4 cup butter
1/2 cup sherry
4 egg yolks
About 1 1/2 cups heavy cream
1/2 teaspoon salt
Paprika

Remove cartilage from crabmeat, keeping chunks whole. Place crab, butter, and sherry in chafing dish over direct heat and cook down sherry about one-half.

Place egg yolks in measuring cup and add enough cream to make 2 cups. Beat until smooth and add salt. Stir cream mixture into crab mixture and place over hot water pan. Cook, stirring, until mixture thickens. Sprinkle with paprika. Serve over rice. Serves 6.

Chafing Dish King Crab Newburg

CRABMEAT DELIGHT

In a chafing dish, or in the top of a double boiler melt 1 pound of pasteurized process cheese food. Add ½ cup milk gradually, stirring constantly until the sauce is smooth.

Add one 6¼-ounce can crabmeat, boned and flaked.

Serve on crisp fresh toast triangles. An easy recipe for Sunday night supper.

CRABMEAT ALASKA

1½ cups flaked crabmeat, canned or fresh
½ cup cream
1 egg yolk
1 teaspoon salt
Dash of pepper
¼ teaspoon Worcestershire sauce
6 slices white bread
4 tablespoons butter or margarine
6 large oysters
¼ cup buttered breadcrumbs

Combine the crabmeat, cream, egg yolk, and seasonings.

Remove crusts from bread; fry slices in butter until golden brown. Spread each slice with crab mixture; top with an oyster and sprinkle with buttered breadcrumbs.

Arrange slices on a cooky sheet; place in hot oven (400°F.) for about 10 minutes or until delicately browned. Serve hot. Serves 6.

CRABMEAT OR LOBSTER CUTLETS

2½ tablespoons butter or margarine
⅓ cup flour
1 cup warm milk
1 egg yolk
½ teaspoon salt
¼ teaspoon pepper
1½ tablespoons lemon juice
2 cups cooked or canned crabmeat or lobster

Melt butter. Blend in flour. Gradually add milk, stirring until sauce boils. Add egg yolk, seasonings, lemon juice, and seafood.

Spread on plate to cool. When cold, shape in cones or cutlets. Dip in fine, dry breadcrumbs, then in beaten egg and again in crumbs.

Fry 1 minute in deep, hot fat (375°F.). Serve with green peas. Serves 6.

HOT CRABMEAT SALAD

1 cup crabmeat, flaked
1 cup soft breadcrumbs
1 cup light cream or top milk
1½ cups mayonnaise
6 hard-cooked eggs, diced
1 tablespoon minced parsley
1 teaspoon minced onion
½ teaspoon salt
⅛ teaspoon pepper
Few grains red pepper
½ cup buttered crumbs

Combine all ingredients except buttered crumbs. Place in greased ramekins or shells; sprinkle with buttered crumbs.

Bake in moderate oven (350°F.) until crumbs are golden brown, about 20 minutes. Serves 8.

CRAB DELICIOUS

1 cup light cream
1 cup boiled rice
Salt and paprika, to taste
1 cup flaked crabmeat
2 tablespoons melted butter or margarine
3 tablespoons ketchup
Patty shells or toast

Heat cream and cooked rice together in top of double boiler over hot water. Season to taste, adding celery or parsley salt, if preferred to paprika.

When well heated and blended, stir in crabmeat and butter. Heat through and, just before serving, stir in ketchup.

Serve at once in patty shells or on crisp toast. Serves 4.

CRABMEAT COQUILLES

1 4-ounce can sliced mushrooms
3 tablespoons butter or margarine
3 tablespoons flour
Milk
½ teaspoon salt
Dash of pepper
2 tablespoons chopped green pepper
1 6-ounce can crabmeat
2 tablespoons breadcrumbs

Drain mushrooms and reserve liquid.

Melt butter. Add flour and blend thoroughly.

Add milk to mushroom liquid to make 2 cups and add to butter and flour mixture. Cook until thickened, stirring constantly.

Add mushrooms, salt, pepper, and green pepper.

Remove hard fiber from crabmeat. Flake, and add to cream sauce. Pour into individual shells or medium sized baking dish. Top with breadcrumbs.

Bake in moderate oven (375°F.) 20 minutes. Serves 4 or 5.

ASPARAGUS-TOPPED CRABMEAT IMPERIAL

2 cups lump crabmeat
4 tablespoons butter or margarine
4 tablespoons flour
1¾ cups milk
1 teaspoon salt
½ teaspoon Ac'cent
½ teaspoon dry mustard
2 teaspoons lemon juice
2 teaspoons chopped green pepper
½ teaspoon Worcestershire sauce
1 teaspoon finely chopped onion
Dash of mace
2 beaten eggs
18 asparagus tips, canned or fresh cooked
¼ cup grated Parmesan cheese

Melt butter; stir in flour; cook until smooth. Add milk; cook until thick, stirring constantly.

Add remaining ingredients except eggs. Remove from heat; quickly stir in eggs. Blend carefully so as not to break up crab lumps.

Fill scallop shells or ramekins; top with asparagus tips and cheese.

Bake in hot oven (400°F.) until golden brown. Serves 6 to 8.

Asparagus-Topped Crabmeat Imperial

Lobsters and Rock Lobster Tails

LOBSTER

Any of a group of edible sea crustaceans* distinguished by huge claws or pincers, which constitute the first of five pairs of legs. They are found off the North Atlantic coast. Most of the U. S. supply comes from New England, the largest part of it from Maine. When the true lobster is boiled or broiled as soon as it is taken from the sea, it has a juicy, tender taste that defies description. The meat of the claws is especially succulent.

Lobsters may be bought alive or already cooked. Live lobsters should be active and mottled green in color. Cooked lobster is red. Test it to make sure it was alive when it was cooked: the tail will spring back into position when straightened, and it will be heavy for its size.

Chicken lobsters weigh 3/4 to 1 pound, medium lobsters up to 1 1/4 pounds, and large or select lobsters 1 1/2 to 2 pounds. Cooked lobster meat may also be purchased canned or frozen.

*Note: Crustacean: Any of various types of shellfish with jointed shells. Lobsters, shrimps, and crabs are examples.

LOBSTER TAIL

Lobster tail comes from the sea crayfish, which is not closely related to the true New England lobster, though often confused with it. The tail sections are marketed, usually frozen, under the name rock lobster to distinguish them from the true lobster. Most of those sold in the United States come from South Africa and Australia.

The meat of the rock-lobster tail, although not quite as fine-textured, tastes very much like the true lobster and can be prepared in any of the same ways.

BOILED LOBSTER

Pick up the lobster from behind the head and plunge it into boiling salted water (1 tablespoon of salt to 2 quarts of water).

Boil 7 to 10 minutes, depending upon size of lobster. If lobster weighs less than 2 pounds, 7 minutes is sufficient.

When the lobster is cool, split it from end to end, starting at the head. Remove the stomach and the intestinal vein. Do not remove the tomalley (liver). Crack the claws. Extract the meat.

BROILED BOILED LOBSTER

Boil and clean as above. Flatten halves. Season with salt and pepper. Brush with melted butter.

Broil under moderate heat until lightly browned, about 5 minutes. Serve with hot melted butter.

HOW TO SPLIT A LIVE LOBSTER FOR BROILING

Place the lobster on its back. Cross the large claws and hold firmly with the left hand. Insert the point of a sharp knife into the lobster at the head and cut the shell open from head to tail.

Cut through the back shell. Remove the stomach and the intestinal vein that runs the length of the tail section close to the back.

Do not remove juices, or liver. The liver (called tomalley) is the grayish-looking meat found in the body cavity. It turns green when cooked.

To Broil: Place split lobster in preheated broiling pan. Brush with butter. Broil 15 to 20 minutes, never longer. Have the pan far enough from the heat so the lobster will not scorch. Serve with melted butter and lemon wedges.

BAKED STUFFED LOBSTER

Split the live lobsters as for broiling. Fill the cavity in the head with dressing (below).

Pour melted butter over lobster and bake in very hot oven (450°F.) 20 minutes. Serve with melted butter.

Dressing: Mix together 1 1/2 cups cracker crumbs and 1/2 teaspoon salt. Moisten with 2 tablespoons Worcestershire sauce and 4 tablespoons butter. Makes enough stuffing for 4 lobsters.

TO BOIL LOBSTER TAILS

Place lobster tails, either thawed or frozen, into a large kettle of boiling salted water (1 teaspoon salt for each quart of water). When water reboils, lower heat and boil tails gently 1 minute longer than their individual weight in ounces. (Boil 6-ounce tails, 7 minutes; 8-ounce tails, 9 minutes.) If tails are frozen, add 2 minutes more. Drain off hot water; drench tails with cold water.

To remove meat from shell, use a scissors and cut lengthwise through center of membrane covering meat. Insert fingers under meat at open end and pull meat out. Use meat in recipes calling for cooked lobster meat.

BROILED LOBSTER TAILS

Thaw the lobster tails and preheat the broiler. Using scissors, cut lengthwise down sides of membrane covering flesh, and remove membrane. Grasp tail in both hands and bend backwards toward shell side to crack and prevent curling. Arrange tails, shell side up, in preheated broiler. Turn heat to medium and broil 5 minutes 5 inches from heat. Turn flesh side up, spread

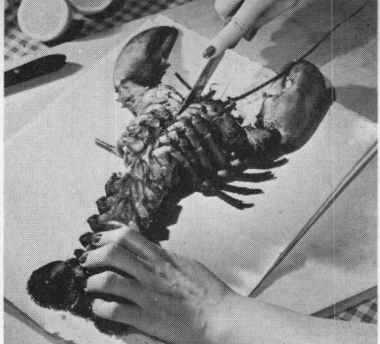

Cut through the back shell

Remove the stomach and intestinal vein

Baked Stuffed Lobster

with butter and broil about 8 or 9 minutes on flesh side, until meat is opaque. Serve with cups of melted butter and lemon wedges.

LOBSTER TAILS WITH DRAWN BUTTER

Cook 6 lobster tails in boiling salted water (as above) or in accordance with package directions.

Drain, cut along each edge, and remove thin top covering. Flatten with hand and insert a skewer into tail to keep tail flat.

Drawn Butter Sauce: Melt 1/2 pound butter over low heat and let stand 15 minutes.

Carefully pour off the liquid fat, leaving the solids. Add lemon juice to taste, 1 teaspoon salt, and 1/4 teaspoon white pepper. Reheat and serve hot. If any sauce remains, it may be refrigerated and used later.

Brush lobster meat with drawn butter; sprinkle lightly with salt and pepper. Broil 3 inches from heat about 5 minutes or until sufficiently brown. Serve remaining sauce with lobster. Serves 6.

LOBSTER NEWBURG
(Master Recipe)

Newburg sauce is a rich cream sauce made with egg yolks and sherry. Although it is usually lobster that is served this way, almost any kind of reheated food may have a Newburg sauce.

Lobster Newburg, a creation of Delmonico's Restaurant in New York, is believed to have been named for Delmonico's friend and customer, Gus Wenburg, a fruit importer. When the two friends had a falling out, Delmonico, the story goes, reversed two letters in the name. Originally light rum, not sherry, was used in the sauce.

1½ cups diced cooked or canned lobster
2 tablespoons butter or margarine
½ tablespoon flour
½ cup light cream
2 tablespoons sherry
2 slightly beaten egg yolks
½ teaspoon salt
Few grains cayenne

Cook lobster (3 pounds of lobster in shell gives 1½ cups of meat) in melted butter over low heat 5 minutes.

Sprinkle in flour. Add cream slowly, stirring constantly, until sauce boils.

Stir in sherry and egg yolks. Cook 1 minute. Remove from heat.

Overcooking will curdle sauce. Season with salt and cayenne. Serve on crisp toast or in patty shells. Serves 4 to 5.

Variations of Lobster Newburg

Clam Newburg: Drain liquid from 1 pint clams.

Chop hard parts fine. Leave soft parts whole. Use in place of lobster. Canned clams may also be used.

Crab Newburg: Use 1½ cups flaked crabmeat instead of lobster.

Scallops Newburg: Cook 1 pint of scallops in their own liquid for 3 minutes. Drain and substitute for lobster.

Shrimp Newburg: Use 1½ cups cooked or canned shrimp instead of lobster.

For elegant serving, save the shells of the cooked lobsters and serve Lobster Newburg in them.

LOBSTER THERMIDOR

Cooked lobster meat cut up and mixed with a cream sauce, then returned to the shell, sprinkled with cheese and sometimes crumbs, and browned in the oven or under the broiler.

2 live lobsters, weighing about 2 pounds each
3 tablespoons butter or margarine
¾ cup sliced mushrooms
1 teaspoon grated onion
3 tablespoons flour
1½ cups light cream (may be part milk)
2 slightly beaten egg yolks
1 teaspoon salt
½ to ¾ teaspoon mustard
Dash of cayenne
⅓ cup grated Parmesan cheese or 1 cup grated American cheese
2 to 3 tablespoons sherry (optional)
1 tablespoon lemon juice

Plunge lobster headfirst into boiling salted water to cover. Boil 8 minutes after water returns to a boil.

Remove lobsters and cool. Split lengthwise from head to tail and remove meat, discarding hard sack (lady) near head and dark intestinal vein. Twist off big claws, crack and remove the meat.

Dice meat from body and claws. Wash shells and reserve.

Heat butter, add mushrooms and onion. Cook slowly until tender but not browned.

Add flour and blend well. Add all but 2 tablespoons of cream. Cook, stirring, until mixture thickens.

Add egg yolks, while stirring briskly, and then cook, stirring, until thickened again.

Add salt, mustard, cayenne, and about ⅔ of cheese. When cheese has melted, add sherry and lemon juice. Add lobster meat.

Fill the reserved lobster shells with the lobster in the thickened sauce.

Spread the surface with remaining 2 tablespoons cream. Sprinkle with remaining cheese.

Slide the stuffed lobsters under the broiler flame. Broil until the surfaces are brown and bubbling. Good accompaniments are cucumbers and rice pilaf. Serves 4.

LOBSTER TAILS THERMIDOR

4 to 6 (6 to 8-ounce) lobster tails
⅓ cup butter or margarine
1 teaspoon minced onion
3 tablespoons flour
½ teaspoon salt
¼ teaspoon white pepper
1 tablespoon lemon juice
⅓ cup dry vermouth
2 cups light cream
3 egg yolks

Lobster Tails Thermidor

Cook and remove meat from lobster tails as directed in Boiled Lobster Tails. Save lobster shells. Dice meat and chill.

Melt butter or margarine in a saucepan. Add onion and cook until onion is soft. Remove pan from heat. Stir in flour, salt, and pepper. Mix lemon juice with vermouth. Gradually add to flour mixture, stirring to blend. Stir in light cream. Return pan to heat and cook over low heat, stirring constantly, until thickened.

Add a little of the hot mixture to beaten egg yolks, then stir egg yolks into sauce. Add lobster meat and continue cooking until lobster is heated. Do not let sauce boil. Spoon into lobster shells. Serve immediately. Serves 4 to 6.

LOBSTER TAILS, CHINESE STYLE

6 (4-ounce) lobster tails
1 clove garlic, minced
2 tablespoons vegetable oil
¼ teaspoon salt
1 cup water
1 tablespoon cornstarch
1 tablespoon soy sauce
2 large green onions (scallions), sliced
1 egg, beaten
3 cups cooked white rice
Sharp mustard sauce

Parboil frozen lobster tails by dropping into kettle of boiling salted water. When water reboils, drain immediately, drench with cold water and cut away thin underside membrane. Remove meat from shells and cut it into bite-size pieces.

In heavy frying pan, lightly sauté garlic in oil. Add lobster meat, salt, and water. Mix cornstarch with soy sauce and add to mixture. Stir gently until sauce thickens. Add sliced green onions.

Just before serving, stir in beaten egg. Serve with bowls of fluffy white rice and a sharp mustard sauce. Serves 6.

Lobster Tails, Chinese Style

LOBSTER À L'AMÉRICAINE

French and American chefs have argued for years about the origin of this truly deluxe dish for special occasions. American chefs claim it was created by an American chef and French chefs claim it as a French creation. Américaine is French for "in the American manner." It sometimes appears incorrectly as "à l'Armoricaine"; the latter meaning "in the manner of Brittany" from the old Roman name for that part of France, Armorica.

2 live lobsters, 1½ to 2 pounds each
¼ cup olive oil
1 tablespoon butter or margarine
1 bay leaf
Pinch of thyme
2 tablespoons chopped shallot or onion
Pinch of cayenne pepper
¼ cup tomato paste or tomato sauce
1 clove garlic, crushed (optional)
About ½ cup dry white wine

Remove and crack claws of lobsters. Remove tail sections from the bodies and cut into 3 or 4 slices. Split lobsters in halves, lengthwise. Discard veins and sacs. Remove and save livers and corals. Season lobsters with salt.

Heat oil and butter in large heavy skillet. Add bay leaf, thyme, and shallot or onion. Add lobster. Sprinkle with cayenne. Add tomato paste. Add garlic, if desired.

Cover and cook very gently until shells are red and lobster tender, 10 to 15 minutes.

Take lobster meat from shells. Strain sauce. Add livers and corals to strained sauce. Cook, stirring constantly, 3 to 4 minutes, or until thickened. Add wine to taste. Add lobster meat and reheat, without cooking. Serves 4.

LOBSTER TAIL AMBASSADOR

4 4- to 6-ounce lobster tails
6 ounces cream cheese
1 cup sour cream
Vinegar to taste
1 cup pimiento-stuffed olives, chopped
Red hot sauce to taste
Salt

Lobster Tail Ambassador

Cook lobster tails as directed on package, or see index. Drench with cold water, cut down both sides of undershell with scissors. Remove from shell in one piece by inserting thumb between meat and shell and gently pulling meat away from shell. Chill. Slice chilled lobster into medallions (thin round slices).

Cream the cheese; beat in sour cream and add 1 tablespoon vinegar. Add additional vinegar to taste, and to thin dressing to desired consistency. Add olives, season with hot sauce and salt to taste. On a flat plate arrange lobster medallions in overlapping circles around generous heap of dressing. Garnish with olive slices.

Serve this dish either as an appetizer with toothpicks so your guests can pick and dip, or as an entree with a crisp green salad and cool drink any warm day.

LOBSTER AND MUSHROOM CASSEROLE

6 tablespoons butter or margarine
½ pound mushrooms, sliced
3 stalks celery, diced
½ small onion, grated
½ green pepper, minced
⅛ teaspoon basil
1 pound lobster meat
2 cups medium white sauce
½ cup cracker crumbs
¼ cup grated Cheddar cheese

Melt 4 tablespoons butter in a large saucepan over moderate heat. Add mushrooms, celery, onion, green pepper, and basil; simmer gently until mushrooms and celery are tender, but not soft, about 10 minutes.

Add lobster to mushroom mixture. Mix well and heat 5 minutes. Add white sauce and mix thoroughly.

Turn into casserole. Cover with layer of cracker crumbs, then with layer of grated cheese. Dot with remaining butter.

Bake in moderate oven (350°F.) until golden brown, about 25 minutes.

Serve very hot from casserole. Serves 4.

Variations: Raw oysters, clams, or scallops may be substituted for lobster. Clams or oysters are heated only 2 minutes and baking time is reduced to 15 to 20 minutes.

HOT LOBSTER MOUSSE

2 cups lobster meat, ground very fine
½ cup medium white sauce
2 beaten eggs
Salt, pepper, and paprika
2 tablespoons sherry

Use cooked or canned lobster. Combine very finely ground lobster with white sauce, eggs, seasonings, and sherry.

Turn into a buttered casserole or individual molds. Set in pan of hot water. Cover with greased paper.

Bake in moderate oven (350°F.) 35 to 40 minutes for casserole, about 20 minutes for small molds.

Unmold and serve with mushroom sauce. Serves 4.

Hot Crab or Shrimp Mousse: Substitute cooked or canned shrimp or crabmeat for lobster in above recipe.

LOBSTER CANTONESE

2 tablespoons fat or salad oil
1½ teaspoons salt
Pepper
½ pound lean pork, ground coarsely
1 tablespoon finely diced carrot
1 tablespoon finely chopped celery
1 tablespoon chopped green onion
2 live baby lobsters or 1 10-ounce can cooked lobster
1 cup chicken bouillon
1 egg, slightly beaten
2 tablespoons cornstarch
2 teaspoons soy sauce
¼ cup water

In a preheated, heavy 10-inch frying pan place fat or salad oil, 1 teaspoon salt, and dash of pepper.

Grind pork and place in mixing bowl with carrot, celery, and green onion. Add ½ teaspoon salt and dash of pepper and mix thoroughly.

Cook lobsters in boiling water 5 minutes. Take out of water, remove and crack claws, cut edible portion of belly in several pieces with heavy knife or cleaver.

Place pork mixture and lobster in frying pan. Add chicken bouillon. Cover pan tightly and cook over moderate heat about 10 minutes.

Add slightly beaten egg. Cook over high heat 2 minutes, stirring constantly.

Blend together and add cornstarch, soy sauce, and water. Cook a few more minutes, stirring constantly, until juice thickens and mixture is very hot. Serve immediately with hot boiled rice. Serves 4.

STEAMED LOBSTER

Place live lobsters in steam cooker and cover tightly. Keep water in steamer boiling rapidly and steam 20 to 40 minutes, depending upon size of lobsters.

BUTTERED LOBSTER

Use cooked or canned lobster meat or the meat from lobster tails. Sauté in hot melted butter until heated through. Season with salt, pepper, and lemon juice.

SCALLOPED LOBSTER

2 tablespoons butter or margarine
3 tablespoons flour
1/2 teaspoon celery seed
1 teaspoon salt
1/2 teaspoon paprika
2 cups milk
1 cup cooked lobster meat
1 cup cooked green peas
2 hard-cooked eggs, sliced
1/2 cup bread cubes
1 tablespoon melted butter or margarine

Melt butter or margarine. Add flour, celery seed, salt, and paprika, stirring until all ingredients are well blended.

Add milk and cook over low heat, stirring constantly, until thickened.

Cut lobster into pieces about 1 inch in size, reserving about 4 fairly large pieces for garnishing. Add lobster to cream sauce.

Pour half of creamed lobster into well greased 1-quart baking dish. Cover with cooked peas and with layer of sliced eggs. Place remaining creamed lobster over ingredients in dish. Top with bread cubes and large pieces of lobster. Pour melted butter over bread cubes and large pieces of lobster.

Bake in moderate oven (350°F.) about 30 minutes. Garnish with parsley. Serves 6.

STUFFED LOBSTER TAILS

4 6-ounce lobster tails
1 tablespoon butter
3/4 cup milk
1 cup soft breadcrumbs
1 egg
1/4 teaspoon salt
1 tablespoon prepared mustard
1 teaspoon aromatic bitters

Cook and remove meat from lobster tails as directed in Boiled Lobster Tails. Flake the meat.

Melt butter in saucepan, add milk and breadcrumbs. Simmer 2 minutes.

Remove from heat. Add egg, salt, mustard, bitters, and flaked lobster meat. Mix well. Pack in shells loosely. Reheat in hot oven (400° F.) 5 minutes. Serves 4.

Stuffed Lobster Tails

LOBSTER FARCI

2 hard-cooked egg yolks
1 cup cooked lobster meat
1 tablespoon minced parsley
1 cup medium white sauce
3 tablespoons sherry
Salt to taste
Few grains white pepper
1/2 cup buttered crumbs

Rub egg yolks through a fine sieve. Combine with lobster, parsley, sauce, sherry, and salt and pepper to taste.

Mix well and use to fill split lobster shells or place in buttered casserole. Top with crumbs.

Bake in moderate oven (375°F.) until brown, about 15 minutes. Serves 2.

Note: Canned lobster meat may be used and the mixture may be baked in scallop shells or individual ramekins.

DEVILED LOBSTER TAILS

4 lobster tails (1/2 pound each)
1/4 cup butter or margarine
1/2 teaspoon dry mustard
1 small onion, minced
1 teaspoon Worcestershire Sauce
2 cups medium white sauce
Salt and pepper
Grated Parmesan cheese
Butter or margarine

Steam or simmer lobster tails 8 to 10 minutes. Cool and split. Remove and dice meat.

Melt 1/4 cup butter; add mustard, onion, and Worcestershire sauce. Simmer 5 minutes.

Add white sauce and lobster meat. Season with salt and pepper.

Fill shells. Sprinkle with Parmesan cheese and dot with butter. Broil until browned. Serves 4.

LOBSTER AND CRABMEAT SOUR CREAM RAMEKINS

1/2 pound lobster meat
1/2 pound crabmeat
1 cup sour cream
1/8 teaspoon salt
Dash of cayenne
4 sprigs tarragon, chopped

Use freshly cooked lobster and crabmeat. Remove bony particles from crabmeat.

Mix the seafood and place in 4 individual ramekins. Mix sour cream with salt, cayenne, and tarragon. Pour over seafood.

Bake in moderate oven (350°F.) until thoroughly heated and bubbly. Serve at once. Serves 4.

Variations: If desired, substitute cooked cleaned shrimp for lobster.

CURRIED LOBSTER TAILS

3 quarts boiling water
3 teaspoons salt
6 frozen rock lobster tails
1 teaspoon Ac'cent
4 tablespoons butter or margarine
4 tablespoons flour
1 teaspoon salt
1/2 teaspoon paprika
1/2 teaspoon Ac'cent
1/8 teaspoon nutmeg
1 1/2 teaspoons curry powder
2 cups milk
2 1/2 tablespoons lemon juice

Bring water to boil in large kettle. Add salt, lobster tails and 1 teaspoon Ac'cent.

When water returns to a boil, lower heat and cook length of time indicated in package directions.

Drain; flush with cold water; remove meat from shells; chill, then dice.

Melt butter or margarine; blend in flour, salt, paprika, 1/2 teaspoon Ac'cent, nutmeg, and curry powder. Add milk; stir over low heat until smooth and thickened.

Add lemon juice and diced lobster meat. Heat thoroughly; refill shells. Serves 6.

LOBSTER TAILS BAKED IN ALUMINUM FOIL

Thaw and cut undershell around edge and remove. Fold each tail securely into a piece of foil cut 4 inches longer than length of tail.

Place on baking pan. Bake in very hot oven (450°F.) 25 minutes for tails weighing 4 to 8 ounces, 30 minutes for tails weighing 9 to 12 ounces, and 35 minutes for tails weighing 13 to 16 ounces.

LOBSTER TAILS IN SAUCE

1/2 pound butter or margarine
1 teaspoon flour
1 teaspoon A-1 sauce
2 teaspoons Worcestershire sauce
1 teaspoon paprika
2 drops Tabasco sauce
3 tablespoons ketchup
1 teaspoon salt
1/2 teaspoon pepper
Juice of 1 lemon
4 lobster tails, cooked and removed from shell

Melt butter in chafing dish, stirring with wooden spoon constantly. Stir in the flour and blend until smooth.

Add A-1 sauce, Worcestershire, paprika, Tabasco, ketchup, salt, pepper, and lemon juice. Stir constantly until thickened and smooth. Simmer for about 10 minutes longer.

Cut cooked lobster into serving pieces. Add pieces to the hot sauce and coat well with mixture. Serve immediately over toast. Serves 4.

Mussels

Mussels include any of various bi-valve mollusks, especially a salt-water variety that tastes somewhat like a clam. If you buy them fresh, make sure the shells are tightly closed. They are also available canned.

HOW TO PREPARE MUSSELS

Mussels must be carefully cleaned; they help to do the job themselves if soaked in a colander in cold running water for a couple of hours. Scrub and rinse them. Steam them open or force the shells with a knife; remove and discard the hairy beard. Mussels are called for in many European recipes and may also be prepared like oysters or clams.

MUSSEL STEW

Clean the mussels and remove the beard. Steam, strain, and reserve the liquid. Follow recipe for Oyster Stew, substituting mussels for oysters.

ROASTED MUSSELS

Scrub and rinse mussels. Spread in flat layer in a pan. Bake in very hot oven (450°F.) until shells open.

Remove upper shells and bearded parts carefully to avoid spilling juice. Serve with seasonings, melted butter and cups of hot broth.

MUSSELS MARINIÈRE

4 to 5 dozen mussels
1 cup dry white wine
1 tablespoon minced shallots or minced onion
1 tablespoon minced parsley
Few grains cayenne
½ bay leaf
2 tablespoons butter or margarine
About 1 tablespoon extra parsley

Scrub mussels thoroughly, scraping shells with a knife and changing the water several times.

Place in a saucepan with the wine, shallots, 1 tablespoon parsley, cayenne, bay leaf, and butter. Cover tightly and cook over low heat until shells open, 5 to 10 minutes, shaking the pan from time to time.

Remove the mussels. Drain and reserve the liquid. Cut off the beards. Loosen from shells and place in half shells on hot serving dishes.

Pour reserved liquid into saucepan, being careful not to mix in any sediment. Boil down to ¾ cup.

Add additional butter and seasonings if necessary. Pour over mussels. Sprinkle with extra parsley. Serve very hot. Serves about 6.

Oysters

Oysters include any of a group of bivalve mollusks that live in the coastal waters of most temperate regions. In many places they are harvested only from September through April; this is done to protect the beds from depletion, not because the oysters are unsafe to eat during the summer.

Oysters may be bought in 3 forms: live in the shell, fresh or frozen shelled, and canned.

Oysters in the shell are generally sold by the dozen and must be alive when purchased. The shells must be tightly closed.

Shelled oysters are sold by the pint or quart. They should be plump and have a natural creamy color, with clear liquid and free from particles.

Canned oysters are sold in a variety of can sizes.

The quantity to buy depends to a large extent on how the oysters are to be served. In general, for 6 servings allow 3 dozen shell oysters, 1 quart shucked oysters, 2 No. 1 cans, or 2 packages frozen oysters.

SHUCKING (OPENING) OYSTERS

Wash and rinse the oysters thoroughly in cold water. Open or shuck an oyster by placing it on a table flat shell up and holding it with the left hand. With the right hand, force an oyster knife between the shells at or near the thin end.

To make it easier to insert the knife, the thin end or "bill" may be broken off with a hammer—a method preferred by some cooks.

Now cut the large adductor muscle close to the flat upper shell in which it is attached and remove the shell.

Cut the lower end of the same muscle, which is attached to the deep half of the shell, and leave the oyster loose in the shell if it is to be served on the half shell, or drop it into a container.

After shucking, examine the oysters for bits of shell, paying particular attention to the muscle to which pieces of shell sometimes adhere.

Oysters on Half Shell

OYSTERS ON THE HALF-SHELL

Open oysters. Loosen oysters from the deeper half shells but let them remain in the shells. Discard the other half shells.

Serve on a bed of crushed ice in shallow bowls or soup plates. Place 6 half-shell oysters on the ice, with a small container of cocktail sauce in the center. Garnish with lemon wedges.

FRIED OYSTERS #1

Drain oysters. Dry carefully between towels. Roll in flour, seasoned with salt and pepper, then in beaten egg diluted with 1 tablespoon water. Roll in dry bread or cracker crumbs.

Fry in deep fat (365°–375°F.) until golden brown. Drain on absorbent paper. Serve with tartar sauce.

Fried Oysters #2: Dip dried oysters in fritter cover batter and fry as above.

Fried Oysters #3: Dip dried oysters in fine dry crumbs, then in mayonnaise, and again in crumbs. Fry as above.

Sautéed Oysters: Prepare as in #1 or #2 and sauté in a single layer in butter.

OVEN-FRIED OYSTERS

Prepare oysters as in Fried Oysters #1. After coating with crumbs, dip in olive oil. Arrange in shallow baking pan.

Bake in hot oven (400°F.) until browned, about 15 minutes.

BROILED OYSTERS

Roll fresh oysters in mixture of half bread and half cracker crumbs. Press flat with hands. Broil 2 minutes on each side.

Salt lightly and brush with melted butter. Serve on buttered hot toast.

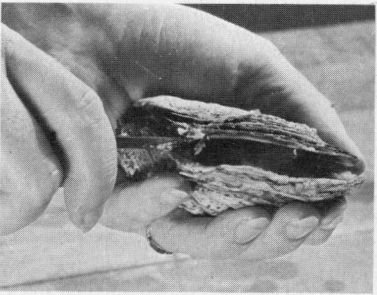

Cutting Muscle

Cutting Oyster from Shell

CREAMED OYSTERS

1   pint oysters
2   tablespoons butter or margarine
2   tablespoons flour
Milk, cream, or stock
About ¾ teaspoon salt
About ⅛ teaspoon pepper
½ teaspoon Worcestershire sauce or
1 teaspoon sherry

Drain oysters, reserving liquid.

Melt butter in saucepan. Slowly blend in flour. Gradually add oyster liquid with enough milk, cream, or stock to make 1 cup.

Cook over low heat, stirring constantly, until smooth. When boiling, add drained oysters. Heat thoroughly but do not boil.

Season with salt, pepper, and Worcestershire sauce or sherry. Serve on toast or in patty shells. Serves 4.

Variation: For a richer dish, blend a little of the creamed mixture with 2 egg yolks, beating constantly. Return to remaining mixture and cook, stirring constantly, for 1 minute to thicken slightly. Season to taste.

QUICK SCALLOPED OYSTERS

1   pint oysters
1   can (10½ ounces) condensed asparagus, celery, or mushroom soup
1   cup dry breadcrumbs
3   tablespoons melted butter or margarine
1   tablespoon finely chopped parsley
About ¼ teaspoon salt

Drain oysters, reserving liquid. Combine soup and oyster liquid and heat to boiling point. Add oysters and cook until edges curl.

Toss crumbs with melted butter, parsley, and salt.

Line bottom of heated casserole with half the crumb mixture. Add oyster-soup mixture and top with remaining crumbs.

Brown under a moderate broiler. Serves 6.

OYSTERS CASINO

1   pint oysters
½ cup finely minced green pepper
½ cup finely minced bacon
1   tablespoon lemon juice
Pepper to taste

Drain oysters and arrange on a greased oven-proof platter. Sprinkle with green pepper, minced bacon, lemon juice, and pepper.

Bake in very hot oven (450°F.) about 10 minutes. Serves 6.

OYSTERS MEUNIÈRE

Dip drained oysters in flour. Brown quickly but gently in butter. Serve on toast, with melted butter and lemon juice poured over each serving.

OYSTERS ROCKEFELLER

This is a famous New Orleans dish of oysters on the half shell topped with a purée of spinach and herbs, and buttered crumbs. The prepared oysters in half shells are then imbedded in pans of rock salt and baked until plump. It's also a good way to use bulk oysters in separately bought shells.

36   oysters in shell
2   cups cooked spinach
4   tablespoons onion
2   bay leaves
1   tablespoon parsley
½ teaspoon celery salt
½ teaspoon salt
6   drops Tabasco sauce
6   tablespoons butter or margarine
½ cup breadcrumbs

Open shells and drain oysters; place on deep half of shells.

Put spinach, onion, bay leaves, and parsley through food chopper. Add seasonings to mixture, and cook in butter for 5 minutes. Add breadcrumbs and mix well. Spread mixture over oysters.

Bake in hot oven (400°F.) about 10 minutes. Garnish with lemon slices. Serves 6.

Note: If shell oysters are not available, 1½ pints select oysters may be used. Drain oysters and arrange on shallow buttered baking dish. Spread with seasonings and cook as above.

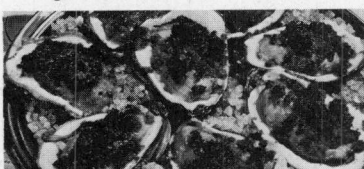

Oysters Rockefeller

DEVILED OYSTERS

1½ pints oysters
2   tablespoons minced onion
2   tablespoons butter or margarine
4   tablespoons flour
1½ cups milk
1   teaspoon salt
¼ teaspoon nutmeg
Few grains cayenne
1   teaspoon prepared mustard
1   tablespoon Worcestershire sauce
1   teaspoon chopped parsley
1   beaten egg
½ cup breadcrumbs
2   tablespoons butter or margarine

Chop oysters. Cook onion in butter until tender. Blend in flour. Add milk and cook until thick, stirring constantly.

Add seasonings, beaten egg, and oysters, and heat.

Turn mixture in buttered ramekins. Cover with crumbs tossed with 2 tablespoons butter.

Bake in hot oven (400°F.) 10 minutes, or until brown. Serves 6.

OYSTER FRITTERS

Prepare fritter binding batter (see Index). Add 1 pint drained and chopped oysters. Fry in hot deep fat (365°-375°F.). Drain on absorbent paper. Serves 4 to 6.

OYSTER LUNCHEON LOAF

1   large loaf unsliced bread
Melted butter or margarine
12   oysters
Evaporated milk
1   8-ounce can tomato sauce
6   tablespoons butter or margarine
1   green pepper, diced
4   tablespoons flour
1   teaspoon salt
Few grains pepper
½ teaspoon Ac'cent
¼ teaspoon rosemary
¼ teaspoon savory
6   hard-cooked eggs

Remove top of loaf of bread in one thin slice; do not remove crusts on sides and ends. With a sharp knife, remove center of loaf in one piece, leaving a shell about ¾-inch thick.

Cut center into cubes and toast golden brown in moderate oven. With a star-cookie cutter, cut 4 stars from top slice. Brush shell and stars with melted butter or margarine and toast in moderate oven.

Measure oyster liquid; add enough evaporated milk to make 2 cups; add tomato sauce.

Melt 6 tablespoons butter or margarine; cook green pepper in this until soft; blend in flour, salt, pepper, and Ac'cent. Add evaporated milk mixture; stir over low heat until smooth and thickened.

Add oysters, rosemary, and savory; cover and cook over hot water 15 minutes. Add toasted bread cubes.

Place toasted bread shell on platter; surround with halves of hard-cooked eggs. Fill case with oyster mixture; cover eggs with remaining oyster mixture. Place stars on top. Serve at once. Serves 6.

Oyster Luncheon Loaf

OYSTER NOODLE CASSEROLE

1   pint oysters
3   tablespoons butter or margarine
3   tablespoons flour
1½   cups milk
1½   cups cooked noodles
2   tablespoons minced green pepper
½   teaspoon salt
⅛   teaspoon pepper
½   cup breadcrumbs
2   tablespoons butter or margarine

Drain oysters. Melt butter in top of double boiler. Blend in flour. Add milk and cook until thickened, stirring constantly.

Place layer of noodles in buttered casserole. Cover with layer of oysters. Sprinkle with green pepper, salt, and pepper. Repeat with alternate layers. Pour sauce over all. Cover with buttered crumbs. Bake in moderate oven (350° F.) 30 minutes or until brown. Serves 6.

OYSTERS LOUISIANA

Coarse rock salt
Large oysters on half shell
Salt, black pepper, paprika
1½   teaspoons minced green pepper
½   teaspoon minced pimiento
Chopped bacon

Fill shallow pans with coarse rock salt and heat to smoking hot in oven. Remove from oven.

Lay on the hot salt large oysters on half shell. Season them with salt, black pepper, paprika, green pepper, and pimiento. Sprinkle with chopped bacon.

Put under broiler flame; cook at high heat 5 to 6 minutes. When bacon is crisp and oysters done, serve at once in shells, placing the pans of hot salt on platters. These are extremely popular in New Orleans.

OYSTER PIE

1   pint oysters
½   cup diced celery
½   cup diced green pepper
4   tablespoons butter or margarine
5   tablespoons flour
2   cups milk
1   teaspoon salt
⅛   teaspoon pepper
2   tablespoons pimiento, chopped
Plain pastry

Cook oysters in their liquid about 5 minutes or until edges begin to curl. Drain.

Cook celery and green pepper in butter until tender. Blend in flour. Add milk and cook until thickened, stirring constantly. Add oysters and seasonings. Heat thoroughly. Pour in casserole. Top with pastry.

Bake in hot oven (425°F.) 15 minutes or until crust is brown. Serves 6.

BROILED OYSTERS ON HALF SHELL

36   oysters in shell
½   teaspoon salt
⅛   teaspoon pepper
½   cup breadcrumbs
2   tablespoons butter or margarine

Open shells and drain oysters. Place on deep half of shells.

Sprinkle with salt, pepper, and buttered breadcrumbs.

Place on preheated broiler pan about 3 inches from heat. Broil until brown, 5 minutes. Serves 6.

OYSTERS À LA CREOLE

1   small onion, minced
2   tablespoons butter or margarine, melted
1½   tablespoons flour
1   cup canned tomato juice
2   dozen raw oysters, drained
2   tablespoons minced parsley
½   teaspoon Tabasco sauce
¾   teaspoon salt
Buttered toast

Sauté onion in butter in saucepan until tender. Blend in flour; then add tomato juice, and cook, stirring, until thickened.

Add oysters, parsley, Tabasco sauce, and salt, and heat until edges of oysters curl. Serve on toast. Serves 4 to 6.

CREAMED OYSTERS AND MUSHROOMS

3   tablespoons fat
5   tablespoons flour
1   teaspoon salt
¼   teaspoon pepper
1½   cups milk
½   cup chopped mushrooms
1   pint oysters

Heat fat in top of double boiler. Add flour, salt, and pepper. Mix until smooth. Add milk gradually, stirring constantly. Cook over hot water 8 minutes.

Fry mushrooms in a little fat until tender.

Drain oysters, clean and pick over. Heat in oyster liquid until edges curl. Add to white sauce with mushrooms.

Serve over hot biscuits or toast or in patty shells. Serves 6.

BAKED OYSTERS ON THE HALF SHELL

36   oysters in shell
½   teaspon salt
⅛   teaspoon pepper
2   tablespoons minced onion
4   tablespoons butter or margarine

Remove shells and drain oysters. Place on deep half of shells.

Sprinkle with salt, pepper, and onion. Dot with butter.

Place oysters in baking pan. Bake in hot oven (400°F.) until edges begin to curl, about 10 minutes. Serves 6.

SCALLOPED OYSTERS

1   pint oysters
2   cups cracker crumbs
½   teaspoon salt
⅛   teaspoon pepper
½   cup butter or margarine, melted
¼   teaspoon Worcestershire sauce
1   cup milk

Drain oysters. Combine cracker crumbs, salt, pepper, and butter; sprinkle ⅓ in a buttered casserole. Cover with a layer of oysters. Repeat layer.

Add Worcestershire sauce to milk, and pour over contents of casserole. Sprinkle remaining crumbs on top.

Bake in moderate oven (350°F.) until brown, 30 minutes. Serves 6.

PANNED OYSTERS

1   pint oysters
4   tablespoons butter or margarine
2   tablespoons lemon juice
Salt and pepper
Lemon slices

Drain oysters. Place in frying pan and cook over low heat until edges curl.

Add butter, lemon juice, and pepper and salt, to taste. Bring to boil. Add a dash of Worcestershire sauce, if desired.

Serve on hot toast and garnish with lemon slices. Serves 4 to 6.

OYSTERS AU GRATIN

6   slices buttered toast
2   beaten eggs
1   teaspoon salt
1   teaspoon prepared mustard
½   teaspoon paprika
½   cup milk
1   pint oysters
1   cup grated cheese

Trim crusts from bread. Cut each slice into quarters.

Combine beaten eggs, seasonings, and milk.

Arrange layer of bread in buttered casserole. Cover with layer of oysters. Sprinkle with grated cheese. Repeat layer.

Pour milk mixture over contents of dish. Cover with grated cheese.

Place casserole in pan of hot water and bake in moderate oven (350°F.) until brown, 30 minutes. Serves 6.

Oysters Au Gratin

Scallops

Scallops include any of a number of bivalve mollusks with deeply grooved shells.

The only part of the scallop that is sold in the stores is the cube-shaped large muscle which opens and closes the scallop shells and it is the only part of the scallop that is used. The rest is discarded.

Two types of scallops are available, the small bay or cape scallops and the considerably larger sea scallops. The bay scallops are slightly more delicate than the larger sea scallops. Scallops should be cream colored, not white, and odorless.

Allow about 1½ to 2 pounds or 1½ to 2 pints for serving 6 to 8, or 2 packages frozen scallops. Buy the smaller quantities if the scallops are to be served in a scalloped dish or in a sauce, the larger quantities if they are to be served sautéed or fried.

BROILED SCALLOPS

Drain and wash scallops. Dip in milk and roll in breadcrumbs. Place in single layer in greased shallow pan. Dot with butter.

Broil, turning frequently, until browned on all sides, about 3 minutes. Serve with melted butter and lemon juice.

SAUTÉED SCALLOPS

Prepared as for broiled scallops. Fry in a well greased frying pan, turning frequently, until brown on all sides, about 3 minutes.

SCALLOPS SAUTÉ PROVENÇAL

1½ pounds sea scallops, fresh or
    frozen
Seasoned flour
6   tablespoons olive or salad oil
1   or 2 garlic cloves, minced
Salt and pepper to taste
½ cup chopped parsley

Defrost scallops, if frozen; dust with seasoned flour.

Heat oil; add scallops and garlic; cook quickly, tossing to brown evenly. Add salt and pepper to taste.

Remove from heat; add parsley; toss to coat scallops evenly. Serves 4.

Scallops Sauté Provençal

COQUILLES SAINT-JACQUES
(Scallops Baked in Shells)

Coquilles Saint-Jacques is French for scallops; however on menus in the U. S. the name is usually applied to a preparation of scallops served in shells such as the recipe given here.

2   pounds scallops
2   cups dry white wine
1   cup water
1   teaspoon salt
Few celery tops
Few sprigs parsley
1   bay leaf
1   small onion
½ pound mushrooms
6   tablespoons butter or margarine
1   teaspoon lemon juice, fresh, frozen
    or canned
¼ cup flour
2   egg yolks
¼ cup heavy cream
4   tablespoons dry breadcrumbs

Cook scallops, wine, water, salt, celery tops, several sprigs parsley, and bay leaf together over a low heat for about 10 minutes or until scallops are tender.

Scoop out the greenery and save liquid to use later on. Chop scallops into little chunks.

Chop onion, mushrooms, and several more parsley sprigs rather fine. Cook in 2 tablespoons melted butter or margarine and lemon juice for about 10 minutes, then mix with cooked scallops.

Make the sauce by melting remaining butter or margarine, stir in flour smoothly and gradually add the liquid in which scallops cooked. Cook, stirring constantly, until sauce thickens. Takes about 5 minutes.

Beat egg yolks slightly, add cream, stir in a little hot sauce slowly, then combine all the sauce with egg yolks (no curdling this way). Cook over a low heat, still stirring for 5 minutes longer or until thick.

Mix vegetable-scallop mixture, spoon into 6 to 8 baking shells. Sprinkle with crumbs. Dot with butter, brown in broiler. Serves 6.

SCALLOPED SCALLOPS

1½ pounds scallops
¼ cup butter or margarine
4   cups soft breadcrumbs
1¼ teaspoons salt
1   teaspoon grated onion
1   teaspoon minced parsley
1   teaspoon minced chives
1   tablespoon lemon juice

If large sea scallops are used, quarter or slice them.

Melt butter and add all the ingredients except scallops; toss together until well mixed.

Coquilles St. Jacques

Place in alternate layers with scallops in a well greased baking dish, with crumb mixture for top layer.

Bake in hot oven (400°F.) until crumbs are brown, about 20 minutes. Serves 6.

SCALLOPS AU GRATIN

3   tablespoons butter or margarine
3   tablespoons flour
1½ cups milk
½ cup grated Cheddar cheese
1   pound sea scallops, sliced
Celery salt to taste
Juice of ½ lemon
Cracker crumbs

Melt butter or margarine. Add flour and mix to a smooth paste. Add milk gradually, stirring over low heat until mixture is smooth and thick.

Add cheese and continue stirring until cheese is melted.

Place a layer of scallop slices in the bottom of greased casserole.

Add celery salt, lemon juice, and a layer of cheese sauce. Repeat until all ingredients are used up. Sprinkle with cracker crumbs.

Bake in moderate oven (375°F.) until crumbs are browned and scallops tender, about 30 minutes. Serves 4 to 6.

FRENCH FRIED SCALLOPS

Method #1: Wipe scallops with damp cloth. Dip in batter and fry in hot deep fat (375°F.) 3 to 4 minutes, or until golden brown. Serve with a tartar sauce.

Method #2: Wipe scallops with damp cloth. Roll in flour, dip in beaten egg, and roll in dry breadcrumbs. Fry in hot deep fat (375°F.) 3 to 4 minutes, or until golden brown. Serve with tartar, chili, or tomato sauce.

Scallops Side-By-Side: Here you see stallops, side-by-side, showing the entire mollusk before the muscle (that marshmallow-shaped part) is removed. The crescent-shaped part that encircles the muscle is the roe, coral colored in the female. The roe is considered a delicacy abroad and is an important part of most European scallop recipes.

SCALLOPS IN GARLIC SAUCE

1 pound scallops
1/4 pound butter or margarine, melted
1 1/2 teaspoons chopped chives
1 1/2 teaspoons parsley flakes
1/4 teaspoon tarragon, if desired
1/4 teaspoon garlic salt
1/2 teaspoon onion salt
Dash of black pepper
Breadcrumbs

Mix butter and seasonings. If large scallops are used, cut into small pieces.

Arrange 18 cherrystone clam shells on baking pan. Place some of butter mixture in bottom of each shell.

Put about 4 pieces of scallop in each shell and top with remaining butter mixture. Sprinkle with breadcrumbs.

Bake in moderate oven (350°F.) for 5 minutes. Serve as an hors d'oeuvre. Serves 6.

Note: If clam shells are not available, scallops may be prepared in shallow baking dish and served on small plates, or individual ramekins.

SCALLOPS IN WINE SAUCE

1/4 cup butter or margarine
1 teaspoon Worcestershire sauce
1/4 cup minced onion
1 pint bay scallops
1/4 cup white wine

Melt butter in small frying pan with Worcestershire sauce. Add onion and cook until golden.

Pick over and rinse scallops. Divide into 4 large scallop shells or individual bakers.

Divide butter-onion mixture evenly over scallops. Add 1 tablespoon wine to each.

Bake in very hot oven (500°F.) 10 minutes. Serve at once. Serves 4.

SCALLOPS ORIENTAL

2 pounds sea scallops, fresh or frozen
1/4 cup honey
1/4 cup prepared mustard
2 teaspoons curry powder
1 teaspoon lemon juice

Line broiler pan with aluminum foil. Arrange scallops in bottom of pan.

Combine remaining ingredients; mix well. Brush scallops generously with curry mixture. Place broiler pan in lowest position under source of heat. Broil slowly 10 minutes.

Turn scallops; brush with curry mixture; broil 10 minutes longer or until nicely browned. Serves 4.

Scallops Oriental

Shrimp

Any of a number of small, slender, long-tailed crustaceans with ten jointed legs. In the marketplace there is no basic difference between a shrimp and a prawn; the latter differs from the true shrimp in having a toothed beak (rostrum) projecting from its head. Both are widely distributed in temperate and tropical fresh and salt waters. They may grow as long as 9 inches, but most are smaller.

The word green, often applied to raw shrimp, is misleading, because some are greenish-grey, some pink, and some brown; the color does not indicate the flavor or the quality. The cellophane-like shell turns pink when cooked. Shrimp in the shell may be bought raw, cooked, or frozen. Peeled shrimp are available cooked, canned, or frozen.

TO SHELL SHRIMP

Raw shrimp (fresh or quick frozen) may be shelled either before or after boiling. Some people think it is easier to remove the small sand vein when the shrimp is raw, while others prefer to cook the shrimp before shelling. The odor of cooking shrimp will not be as strong if they are shelled before cooking.

Wash the shrimp. Let frozen shrimp stand in cold water about 15 minutes.

To clean shrimp, hold tail end in left hand, slip thumb under shell, between feelers, and lift off 2 or 3 segments in one motion. Then still holding firmly to tail, pull out shrimp from remaining shell section and tail.

With a knife, cut along outside curvature and lift out black sand vein, if desired. Vein is harmless, but some people object to the appearance of the black line. Then, rinse with cold water.

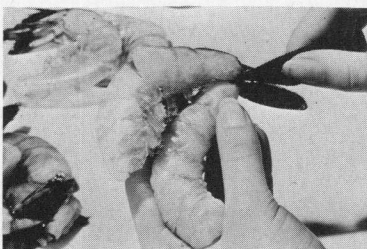

Removing shell from raw shrimp
Removing black sand vein

BOILED SHRIMP

Add 1 tablespoon salt to 1 quart water. Bring to boil.

Add 1 pound shrimp and bring to boil again. Turn heat down so that water just simmers. Cover saucepan and cook 2 to 5 minutes, never longer. Drain shrimp.

SHRIMP COOKED IN COURT BOUILLON

1 quart water
1/2 stalk celery
1 carrot, sliced
1 small white onion, sliced
Juice of 1/2 lemon
1 teaspoon salt
1/2 teaspoon pepper
1 pound raw shrimp, fresh or frozen

Put water in saucepan. Add all ingredients except shrimp. Bring water to boil.

Add shrimp and let water come to boil again. Turn heat down so water just simmers. Cover saucepan and let shrimp cook 2 to 5 minutes, never longer. Drain shrimp.

FRIED FRESH SHRIMP

1 1/2 pounds raw shrimp
1 cup milk
1/8 teaspoon paprika
1/4 teaspoon salt
Corn meal

Shell and remove black vein from shrimp.

Combine milk, paprika, and salt.

Soak shrimp in seasoned milk 30 minutes. Season with additional salt and roll in corn meal.

Fry in deep fat (375°F.) until golden brown. Drain on absorbent paper. Serve with tartar sauce. Serves 4 to 5.

Fried Cooked or Canned Shrimp: Season cleaned shrimp with salt and pepper. Dip in milk and roll in corn meal. Fry as above.

BUTTERFLY SHRIMP

1 1/2 pounds very large shrimp
2 eggs
3 tablespoons flour
1/2 teaspoon salt
Dash of pepper

Remove shells from shrimp but leave tail on. Split along the back and remove black vein but do not cut all the way through. Wash and dry with towel.

Combine eggs, flour, salt, and pepper in bowl; mix to smooth batter.

Drop in shrimp and coat thoroughly. Lift out shrimp one at a time with a fork and drop into deep hot fat (375°F.) and fry until golden brown, 2 to 5 minutes. Serve hot. Serves 4 to 5.

SAUTÉED SHRIMP

Sauté cooked or canned cleaned shrimp in melted butter lightly. Place on hot serving dish. Pour butter over the shrimp. Sprinkle with chopped parsley.

Serve on picks as an hors d'oeuvre. Serve with melted butter flavored with lemon juice and freshly ground pepper.

FRIED SHRIMP—BATTER COATED

1/2 cup sifted enriched flour
1/2 teaspoon baking powder
1/2 teaspoon salt
1/4 teaspoon black pepper
1 egg, slightly beaten
1/3 cup milk
2 or 3 drops Tabasco sauce
2 pounds peeled cleaned shrimp

Sift flour with baking powder, salt, and pepper. Mix egg and milk. Add to dry ingredients and beat smooth. Add Tabasco sauce.

Dip shrimp in batter and fry in hot deep fat (375°F.) until golden.

Serve hot. Provide a dipping sauce.

SCAMPI

(Shrimp in Garlic Butter)

Scampi is the Italian word for prawns. They are a specialty of Venice and are often prepared in Venetian style: broiled or sautéed and served in a garlic sauce. In the United States large shrimp are generally used in scampi recipes.

2 pounds shrimp, fresh or frozen
1/4 pound butter or margarine
1 clove garlic, minced fine
Salt to taste
Pepper to taste

Remove shells from shrimp, except portion which covers tail. Cut down center of back and remove sand vein.

Melt butter and add garlic. Simmer 3 minutes.

Place shrimp on individual flame-proof platters, or large broiling pan. Pour garlic butter over them. Sprinkle with salt and pepper.

Place in preheated broiler 3 inches from heat and broil 5 to 7 minutes or until browned and tender.

Serves 4 to 5.

Scampi

SHRIMP DE JONGHE

1 clove garlic
3/4 cup butter or margarine
1 teaspoon salt
1 cup fine dry breadcrumbs
1/2 cup dry sherry
2 1/2 to 3 pounds cooked shrimp
Chopped parsley

Mash garlic clove until it is almost paste.

Cream together the garlic, butter, and salt until well blended. Add crumbs and sherry. Blend well.

Place alternate layers of cooked cleaned shrimp and crumb mixture in 6 individual casseroles, ending with crumbs. Sprinkle chopped parsley over top of each.

Bake in hot oven (400°F.) 20 to 25 minutes. Serve at once. Serves 6.

SHRIMP ARNAUD—APPETIZER

2 tablespoons tarragon or cider vinegar
1/3 cup olive oil
1 tablespoon paprika
1/4 cup strong prepared mustard (Creole mustard preferred)
About 1 teaspoon salt (more or less to suit taste)
1 cup very finely chopped celery
1/2 cup very finely chopped green onions and tops
1/4 cup very finely chopped parsley
2 pounds shrimp, cooked, peeled, and cleaned

Combine all ingredients except shrimp in a bowl and blend thoroughly.

Pour enough sauce over shrimp to moisten them and mix well. Cover and set in refrigerator 30 minutes to 2 hours before using so the sauce flavor permeates the shrimp.

Pour remaining sauce over shrimp just before serving.

BROILED FRESH SHRIMP

Remove shells, leaving on last segment and tail. Remove black veins. Dip raw shrimp in melted butter or salad oil.

Broil under moderate heat 4 to 6 minutes, depending upon size of shrimp. Season to taste with salt and pepper. Serve with a butter sauce.

CREAMED SHRIMP

Heat cleaned, cooked or canned shrimp in medium white sauce or cream sauce. Season to taste with salt and pepper.

If desired, additional seasonings may be added as given in variations of white sauce (see Index).

For color, add chopped pimiento or chopped parsley. Serve on toast. Sprinkle with paprika.

SWEET AND PUNGENT SHRIMP

1 pound shrimp, fresh or frozen
1 flat can sliced pineapple
1/2 cup brown sugar
1/2 cup vinegar
2 tablespoons soy sauce
1 1/4 cups water
3 tablespoons cornstarch
1 green pepper, cut in strips
1 tomato, cut into wedges

Clean and cook shrimp. Drain syrup from pineapple into a saucepan. Cut pineapple slices in half and reserve. Add brown sugar, vinegar, soy sauce, and 1 cup water to pineapple syrup. Bring to boil.

Combine cornstarch and 1/4 cup water. Add to sugar mixture. Cook stirring constantly until thickened. Add green pepper, pineapple, and tomato wedges. Cook 2 minutes. Add shrimp and cook to heat shrimp through. Serve immediately. Serves 4.

Sweet and Pungent Shrimp

SHRIMP CREOLE

4 tablespoons butter or margarine
1 large onion, chopped
1/2 cup minced green pepper
1 clove garlic, minced
1 teaspoon salt
Dash of pepper
1/8 teaspoon paprika
1/8 teaspoon rosemary (optional)
2 cups canned tomatoes
1 pound cooked shrimp
2 to 3 cups cooked rice

Melt butter in saucepan; add onion, green pepper, and garlic. Sauté 10 minutes or until tender.

Add salt, pepper, paprika, rosemary, and tomatoes. Bring to boiling point; cover, reduce heat. Simmer 15 minutes.

Add shrimp, heat thoroughly. Serve on rice. Serves 4.

Shrimp Creole

SHRIMP TEMPURA

Tempura is a Japanese term for any food dipped in an egg batter and deep-fried in oil. Fish, shellfish, and vegetables are commonly prepared in this way. Tempura is served with a soy sauce dipping mixture and small bowls of grated radish, horseradish, and ginger.

1 pound shrimp
Oil for frying
1 cup sifted flour
½ teaspoon salt
1 beaten egg
¾ cup milk

Shell shrimp, leaving tail shell on. Slash back. Heat oil for deep frying.

Combine flour and salt. Add egg and milk; beat together.

Dip shrimp in batter; add to hot oil (375°F.). Fry 2 to 3 minutes, until golden, turning once. Drain.

Serves 6 to 8 as appetizer or 4 as entrée, with tangy dip.

Sauce: Combine ⅓ cup sherry, 2 tablespoons soy sauce, 1 teaspoon sugar, and pinch of ginger.

SEAFOOD À LA KING

2 tablespoons butter or margarine
1 green pepper, diced
2 tablespoons sliced pimiento
1 cup canned or cooked sliced mushrooms
1 tablespoon flour
½ teaspoon salt
⅛ teaspoon pepper
¼ teaspoon paprika
1 cup light cream
1 cup cooked shrimp
1 cup cooked flaked fish
3 egg yolks
¼ cup sherry

Melt butter or margarine in chafing dish; add green pepper, pimiento, and mushrooms. Cook and stir for 3 minutes, or until pepper is soft.

Stir in flour, salt, pepper, and paprika and gradually add cream, stirring constantly. Add shrimp and flaked fish.

Beat egg yolks lightly; add sherry and stir into à la King mixture. Cook, stirring constantly, until mixture thickens. Serve on toast. Serves 4.

Seafood À La King

SHRIMP SOUFFLÉ CASSEROLE

6 slices buttered bread
Dry mustard
2 8-ounce cans shrimp, cleaned
½ pound American cheese, grated (about 2 cups)
3 eggs
2 cups milk
Salt and pepper

Spread bread lightly with dry mustard. Remove crusts and cut into ½-inch cubes.

Put alternate layers of bread cubes, shrimp, and cheese in a greased casserole.

Beat eggs and combine with milk. Season with salt and pepper. Pour over other ingredients.

Place in pan of hot water and bake in moderate oven (350°F.) 1¼ hours, or until silver knife inserted in center comes out clean. Serves 6 to 8.

QUICK SHRIMP CASSEROLE

3 ounces thin noodles
1 No. 1 can shrimp
1 12-ounce can whole kernel corn
1 4-ounce can mushrooms
2 tablespoons butter or margarine
2½ tablespoons flour
1 cup milk
¼ pound sharp American cheese, shredded
Salt and pepper

Cook noodles until tender in boiling salted water. Drain and place in casserole.

Clean black veins from shrimp. Arrange corn, shrimp, and sliced mushrooms over noodles. (Save liquid from mushrooms and shrimp.)

Melt butter in saucepan. Blend in flour. Add mixture of milk and liquid from shrimp and mushrooms gradually; cook over low heat, stirring constantly, until thickened and smooth.

Add half the cheese, salt and pepper to taste; stir over low heat until cheese is melted. Pour sauce over other ingredients. Mix gently. Sprinkle with remaining cheese.

Bake in hot oven (400°F.) until heated through, about 30 minutes. Serves 6.

Variations: Substitute peas for corn. Substitute clams or oysters for shrimp.

MEXICAN SHRIMP IN SAUCE

1 onion, minced
¼ cup butter or margarine
1 teaspoon chili powder
¼ cup flour
1 cup milk
2 tablespoons minced parsley
¼ cup ketchup
2 cups cooked or canned shrimp

Sauté onion in butter until lightly browned. Stir in chili powder and flour. Slowly add milk.

Cook, stirring over low heat, for 10 minutes.

Add parsley, ketchup, shrimp; bring to a boil. Serve immediately. Serves 4.

CURRIED SHRIMP À LA CEYLON

2 tablespoons butter or margarine
1 cup chopped onion
½ cup chopped green pepper
½ cup chopped celery
2 tablespoons flour
2 teaspoons curry powder (more if desired)
3 teaspoons soy sauce
1 cup water
1 No. 303 can tomatoes
1 cup uncooked white rice
1 teaspoon salt
2 cups water
1 pound frozen thawed shrimp or 2 5-ounce cans shrimp

Melt butter or margarine in skillet or saucepan. Add onion, green pepper, and celery. Cook, stirring occasionally, until the onion is yellow.

Blend in flour. Stir in curry powder and soy sauce. Stir in 1 cup of water and the tomatoes. Cover and simmer 20 minutes.

While the sauce cooks, put rice, salt, and water in a 2-quart saucepan. Bring to vigorous boil. Turn the heat as low as possible. Leave over this low heat 14 minutes.

Remove saucepan from heat but leave lid on until ready to serve rice or at least 10 minutes.

While rice cooks, peel frozen thawed shrimp. Remove sand vein easily by running knife along back of shrimp from head to tail. This pulls out vein.

Wash in water. Place shrimp in boiling salted water. Cover and return to boiling point. Turn heat down and simmer 5 minutes. Drain.

After sauce cooks, stir in cooked frozen thawed or canned shrimp. Heat 5 minutes.

Arrange cooked rice on a hot platter. Pour shrimp and sauce over rice. Serves 6.

Curried Shrimp À La Ceylon

SHRIMP TERIYAKI

½ cup pineapple juice
2 to 4 tablespoons soy sauce
½ cup vegetable or peanut oil
1 pound shelled, cleaned shrimp

Combine pineapple juice, soy sauce, and oil. Pour over shrimp and let soak (marinate) about 15 minutes.

Drain and broil shrimp in broiler or on outdoor grill about 4 inches from heat source for 3 or 4 minutes on each side. Serve with rice. Serves 3.

SHRIMP WITH LOBSTER STYLE SAUCE (Chinese)

½ pound ground fresh pork
1 tablespoon chopped green onion
1 tablespoon chopped carrot
1 tablespoon chopped celery
Salt and pepper
2 tablespoons salad oil
2 pounds raw shrimp
1 cup chicken stock
1 beaten egg
2 tablespoons cornstarch
2 tablespoons cold water
1 tablespoon soy sauce

Combine pork, vegetables, and seasonings in pan with hot oil and cook about 5 minutes.

Add cleaned, washed, and deveined shrimp and stir-fry until they turn pink.

Add stock and cook covered for 10 minutes.

Add egg and stir for 2 minutes and then add remaining ingredients which have been well blended. Stir until thickened. Serve with boiled rice.

Serves 4 to 6.

SHRIMP AU GRATIN

½ pound cooked shrimp, cleaned
2 tablespoons butter
2 tablespoons flour
⅔ cup evaporated milk
⅓ cup water
1 teaspoon paprika
1 cup cubed sharp Cheddar cheese
3 slices white bread, cubed
2 tablespoons butter, melted
Grated Parmesan cheese

Arrange shrimp in 4 individual cas-

Shrimp Au Gratin

seroles or in the bottom of a buttered 1-quart casserole.

Melt butter in a saucepan. Add flour, then blend in evaporated milk and water. Stir until smooth and thickened. Add paprika and cubed cheese and stir until cheese is melted.

Pour over shrimp and top with bread cubes which have been tossed with the last 2 tablespoons of butter.

Sprinkle with grated Parmesan cheese and bake in a hot oven (400°F.) for 20 minutes. Serves 4.

LICHEE GARDENS SHRIMP

2½ pounds or 30 large shrimp
¼ cup finely minced green onions
½ cup finely minced mushrooms
¼ cup finely chopped almonds
2 tablespoons butter or margarine
Salt and pepper
¼ teaspoon Ac'cent

If shrimp are frozen, thaw. Shell and remove veins from shrimp.

Mix green onions, mushrooms, and almonds; sauté in butter until tender; sprinkle with salt, pepper, and Ac'cent.

Make a slit or pocket in shrimp at thickest part. Fill with about 1 teaspoon sautéed mixture. Place on slotted spoon; dip in batter and drain.

Lower into deep hot fat (375°F.) 2 minutes or until golden brown. Serves 5 to 6.

Batter For Lichee Gardens Shrimp:

2 eggs
¾ cup milk
1⅔ cups flour
1½ teaspoons salt
½ teaspoon Ac'cent
1½ tablespoons butter or margarine, softened

Beat eggs until thick and lemon colored; add milk. Sift in flour, salt, and Ac'cent; add butter. Mix until just smooth.

NEAPOLITAN SHRIMP

1 pound shrimp, fresh or frozen
1 clove garlic, finely minced
¼ cup olive or other salad oil
3 anchovy fillets (optional)
1 No. 2 can Italian tomatoes
¼ teaspoon oregano
Pinch crushed red pepper
1 tablespoon chopped parsley

Remove shells from shrimp. Make a slash along back of shrimp, cutting deeply but not all the way through. Wash away sand vein. Drain shrimp on paper toweling.

Heat olive oil in large frying pan. Add garlic and shrimp, placing shrimp in the pan with backs down. Fry shrimp about 5 minutes, turning to sides to finish cooking. Remove shrimp and place on backs in a chafing dish.

Add remaining ingredients to pan.

Lichee Gardens Shrimp

Mix thoroughly, breaking up tomatoes. Cook slowly at least 15 minutes.

Pour sauce around shrimp in chafing dish. Serve with slices of fried French bread. Serves 3 to 4.

SHRIMP WIGGLE WITH TOMATO SAUCE

1 pound shrimp
1 cup water
2 whole black peppers
1 teaspoon salt
1 small bay leaf
½ stalk celery
½ teaspoon Ac'cent
1 cup sliced onions
3 tablespoons butter or margarine
2 8-ounce cans tomato sauce
2 tablespoons cornstarch
2 tablespoons cold water
½ teaspoon Ac'cent
Salt and pepper
Toast points

Wash shrimp under cold running water. Bring water to boil; add whole black peppers, salt, bay leaf, celery, and the ½ teaspoon Ac'cent.

Add shrimp, cover; simmer 5 minutes; drain; shell; remove black sand veins.

Sauté onions in butter or margarine until golden brown. Add tomato sauce. Simmer 5 minutes.

Blend cornstarch and cold water; add; stir until thickened. Add remaining Ac'cent and shrimp; heat thoroughly. Season to taste. Garnish with toast points. Serves 4.

Neapolitan Shrimp

INDIVIDUAL SHRIMP-VEGETABLE CASSEROLES

1½ cups medium white sauce
⅛ teaspoon dry mustard
¼ teaspoon Worcestershire sauce
2 drops Tabasco sauce
1½ cups cooked or canned whole kernel corn, drained
2 cups cooked or canned peas, drained
1 cup cooked or canned shrimp, cleaned
Soft breadcrumbs and butter or margarine or cereal herb topping

Combine sauce and seasonings. Add corn and peas.

Place in individual casseroles or shells. Top with shrimp. Sprinkle with crumbs. Dot with butter.

Bake in hot oven (400°F.) 20 minutes. Serves 4.

SHRIMP WITH RICE IN WINE SAUCE

6 tablespoons butter or margarine
1 large onion, finely chopped
1½ cups rice, washed and drained
½ teaspoon salt
½ teaspoon pepper
2 large mushrooms, sliced
½ cup dry white wine
2½ cups hot stock or water
2 tablespoons chopped parsley
½ teaspoon thyme
2 teaspoons lemon juice
2 pounds uncooked shrimp, shelled and deveined

Melt butter over medium heat in a heavy saucepan or electric skillet and add onion, rice, salt, and pepper. Stir frequently until rice is golden. Add mushrooms and wine. Cook until wine is reduced, about 4 minutes.

Add stock, parsley, thyme, lemon juice, and shrimp. Cover skillet and simmer until rice is tender, about 10 minutes. Remove cover and fluff rice. Serves 4 to 6.

Shrimp with Rice in Wine Sauce

SHRIMP AND LOBSTER IN RICE RING

1½ cups raw rice
3 tablespoons butter or margarine
3 tablespoons flour
1½ cup liquid (juice from canned lobster and shrimp, milk to make up difference)
1 teaspoon salt
½ teaspoon paprika
1 9-ounce can lobster, flaked
1 7-ounce can shrimp

Cook rice in boiling salted water until tender, about 30 minutes. Drain and rinse with hot water. Place over hot water or in oven to dry out.

Pack in buttered ring mold. Keep hot while making lobster and shrimp mixture.

Melt butter in saucepan over low heat. Remove from heat and blend in flour until smooth. Gradually add liquid. Return to heat, cook, stirring constantly until thick.

Add seasonings, flaked lobster, and shrimp. Heat thoroughly.

For serving, turn rice ring onto a hot serving platter and fill center with lobster and shrimp mixture. Serves 6.

SHRIMP AND GREEN PEPPERS (Chinese Style)

1 pound fresh shrimp
1 pound green peppers
1 clove garlic, minced
¼ cup salad oil
About 1¼ teaspoons salt
¼ teaspoon pepper
⅓ teaspoon rosemary
1½ tablespoons cornstarch
¾ cup stock or 1 bouillon cube and water
1 teaspoon gravy coloring

Remove shells and sand veins from shrimp. If shrimp are very large, cut in halves lengthwise.

Cut cleaned peppers into strips about 1 inch wide.

Heat oil in heavy skillet; add green peppers and garlic. Cook until peppers are soft, about 3 to 4 minutes.

Add shrimp. Add salt, pepper, and rosemary. Gently mix and turn peppers and shrimp to cook evenly on all sides. Cover and cook over low heat about 7 minutes.

Dissolve cornstarch in stock and add to green pepper-shrimp mixture. Add gravy coloring. Cover and cook about 5 minutes longer.

Serve with cooked rice or with cooked macaroni or noodles. Serves 4 to 6.

CREAMED SEAFOOD IN SHELLS

2 tablespoons flour
1 cup water
1 cup evaporated milk
½ teaspoon salt

Shrimp and Lobster in Rice Ring

Dash of pepper
1 cup boned lobster or crabmeat, cooked or canned
1 cup shrimp, cooked or canned
About 2 cups mashed potatoes
Cheese, if desired

Stir water slowly into flour to keep smooth. Bring mixture to a boil, stirring constantly to prevent lumping.

Add milk and seasonings and continue cooking over hot water until thickened, about 10 minutes. Add lobster or crabmeat and shrimp, and pour into individual baking dishes.

Garnish with mashed potatoes. Sprinkle with grated cheese, if desired.

Brown in very hot oven (450°F.). Serves 6.

SHRIMP CURRY—HAWAIIAN

4 large onions, chopped
3 large cloves garlic, chopped
4 tablespoons butter or margarine
3 cups water or coconut milk
3 large tomatoes, peeled and chopped
2 large apples, chopped
1 cup chopped celery
1 tablespoon shredded coconut
1 piece fresh ginger root or ¾ teaspoon powdered ginger
1 tablespoon sugar
1½ tablespoons curry powder
1½ tablespoons flour
1½ teaspoons salt
¼ teaspoon pepper
1½ pounds cleaned raw shrimp

Sauté onions and garlic in butter until lightly browned. Add water, bring to a boil.

Add tomatoes, apples, celery, coconut, and fresh ginger root if available.

If powdered ginger is used, blend it with sugar, curry powder, flour, salt, and pepper. Add cold water to moisten to a paste and add, stirring, to boiling mixture. Simmer, stirring occasionally, until vegetables are very tender, or about 40 minutes.

Add shrimp and cook 5 minutes. Serve on rice. Makes about 2 quarts, or 12 or more servings.

SHRIMP LOUISIANE

1/4 cup butter or oil
2 medium onions, chopped fine
2 green peppers, chopped fine
1/2 cup shrimp stock, chicken bouillon, or water
2 cups tomato sauce
2 cups cooked rice
2 pounds cooked shrimp, shelled and deveined
Salt, celery salt, Tabasco sauce
4 egg yolks
2 cups cream

Melt butter in top part of chafing dish over direct heat. Add chopped onions and peppers, and cook until soft but not brown.

Add shrimp stock, chicken bouillon, or water, and simmer until vegetables are tender.

Add tomato sauce, rice, and shrimp. Season with salt, celery salt, and a dash of Tabasco.

Beat egg yolks, add to cream, and stir into hot shrimp mixture a few minutes before serving. This sauce should not boil. Serves 6 to 8.

SHRIMP AND PEPPERS

1 pound green or uncooked shrimp*
6 tablespoons flour
2 tablespoons grated Parmesan cheese
1 teaspoon salt
1 clove garlic
6 medium peppers
1/2 cup olive or salad oil
1/4 cup dry white wine
3/4 teaspoon salt
Dash of pepper

Peel shrimp if necessary. To coat shrimp: mix flour, cheese, and salt in a paper bag, add shrimp and give bag a good shake.

Crush or mince garlic; remove seeds and stems from peppers and cut peppers in inch-wide strips.

Heat oil in a large skillet, toss in shrimp and garlic and cook about 5 minutes or until shrimp are golden.

Now scoop shrimp from pan and set aside for the moment. Put pepper strips in the skillet, cover tightly and cook over a medium heat for 10 to 15 minutes or until tender but still slightly crisp.

Add shrimp, wine, salt, pepper and heat through. Serves 4.

*Note: 2 8-ounce cans shrimp or 2 10-ounce packages frozen shrimp may be substituted.

SHRIMP WITH EGG (CHINESE)

1 cup shredded lean pork
1 clove garlic, minced or crushed
4 water chestnuts, crushed
2 tablespoons salad oil
2 cups peeled raw shrimp, cleaned
1 tablespoon soy sauce
1 tablespoon cornstarch
1/2 cup water
2 tablespoons chopped green onion tops
1 egg
Salt

Sauté pork, garlic, and chestnuts in oil until lightly browned. Add shrimp and cook, stirring often, 3 to 5 minutes. Add soy sauce.

Mix cornstarch with water and add to mixture. Cook, stirring until thickened. Simmer 2 minutes.

Add green onions and egg, stirring constantly, and cook slowly until egg resembles a soft jelly. Add salt to taste. Serve with rice. Serves 2 to 3.

SWEET AND SOUR SHRIMP (CHINESE)

Sauce Ingredients:

3 large green peppers
2 large tomatoes
1 cup vinegar
1 cup water
3/4 teaspoon salt
Dash of pepper
1 No. 2 can (2 1/2 cups) pineapple chunks
1 cup sugar
1 1/2 teaspoons Ac'cent, optional
3 tablespoons cornstarch
3 tablespoons ketchup
2 tablespoons salad oil

Cut each large cleaned green pepper diagonally into 8 pieces. Cut each large tomato into 8 wedges. Set aside.

Batter Ingredients:

2 slightly beaten eggs
3/4 cup enriched flour
1/2 teaspoon salt
2 tablespoons cold water
1 1/2 pounds very large shrimp

Combine eggs, flour, salt, and cold water; mix well.

Remove shells from shrimp. Split down the back but do not cut all the way through. Remove black vein, wash, and drain.

Dip prepared shrimp in batter, coating well. Fry shrimp in deep hot oil (375°F.) until golden brown, 2 to 5 minutes.

Combine all sauce ingredients except tomatoes in a saucepan. Mix well and bring to boil.

Add shrimp and tomatoes. Mix thoroughly and cook 3 minutes. Serves 4.

SHERRIED SHRIMP CREOLE

2 pounds fresh shrimp or 4 cups cooked and cleaned
1/4 cup butter or margarine
2 tablespoons finely chopped onion
1 cup canned tomatoes or 2 large tomatoes, cut in pieces
1 bay leaf
1/2 teaspoon salt
1/2 teaspoon thyme
Dash of cayenne
1 teaspoon sugar
1 can condensed mushroom soup
1/3 cup sherry
2 pimientos, cut in strips

Wash shrimp in cold water. Drop into boiling salted water and cook 6 to 8 minutes. Drain. Cover with cold water. Remove shells, and dark vein along back of each shrimp.

Melt butter or margarine. Cook onion in butter or margarine until it turns yellow. Add tomatoes, bay leaf, salt, thyme, cayenne, and sugar.

Dilute mushroom soup with sherry; add to tomato mixture. Finally add shrimp and pimientos. Cook 5 minutes. Serve with hot boiled rice. Serves 6.

SHRIMP WIGGLE IN TOAST CUPS

1 cup cooked shrimp
4 tablespoons butter
4 tablespoons flour
2 cups milk
1 teaspoon salt
Pepper
1 cup cooked peas

Cook shrimp by boiling 3 or 4 minutes in salted water.

Melt butter in a saucepan. Remove pan from heat. Stir in flour until blended. Gradually add milk, stirring until smooth.

Return pan to heat and cook, stirring constantly until thickened. Add salt and pepper, shrimp, and peas.

Continue cooking until shrimp and peas are heated through. Serve in toast cups. Makes 8 toast cups, enough to serve 4.

To Make Toast Cups: Trim crusts from slices of enriched white bread. (Sandwich sliced bread works best.) Butter both sides of bread slices.

Press each slice into a muffin cup so that corners turn up. Toast in moderate oven (375°F.) until golden brown.

Toast cups can be made ahead and heated just before serving.

Sherried Shrimp Creole

Miscellaneous Shellfish

ABALONE

An abalone is a very large sea mollusk with an oval, somewhat spiral shell perforated along the rim and lined with mother-of-pearl. It is harvested off the California coast but may not be shipped out of the state. The rest of the American market is supplied from Mexico and Japan. The edible part is the central muscle, which resembles a giant scallop. It is sold fresh or canned. The fresh meat is tough if not pounded before cooking.

It is best chopped and served in chowders or fish soups; however, it is often served fried (though this method runs the risk of overcooking it) or creamed or used in canapé or sandwich spreads. Simmer abalone in water until tender. Chop it fine and use it in recipes for chowder or fish soup.

FRIED ABALONE

Pound the raw slices with a wooden mallet. Wipe dry. Roll in seasoned crumbs, then in beaten egg diluted with water, and again in crumbs. Sauté in oil or butter 1 to 1½ minutes on each side. Take care not to overcook because it toughens.

CREAMED ABALONE

Add 1½ cups diced raw abalone to 2 cups medium white sauce. Season to taste and simmer 2 minutes. Stir in 1 slightly beaten egg yolk. Serve on hot toast. Garnish with chopped hard-cooked egg. Serves 4.

FROGS' LEGS

The hind legs of the frog are the only ones used. If bought in the market they will come skinned, cleaned, and ready for use.

If you catch your own, cut them close to the body. The skin is thin and loose and may be turned down so that it pulls off like a glove.

Allow 4 to 6 large legs or ½ pound (8 to 10) small legs per serving.

FROGS' LEGS PROVENÇAL

12   frogs' legs
Flour
6   tablespoons butter or margarine
3   cloves garlic, crushed
1   tablespoon lemon juice
3   tablespoons chopped chives
2   tablespoons chopped tarragon
1½ tablespoons chopped parsley
Salt and pepper
1½ ounces brandy
¼   cup dry white wine

Dry cleaned frogs' legs and roll in flour.

Melt butter in skillet; add garlic and lemon juice. Blend well.

Add frogs' legs and shake skillet gently occasionally to prevent sticking.

Slowly brown well on all sides, 6 to 8 minutes.

Add chives, tarragon, parsley, and salt and pepper to taste. Cook 1 to 2 minutes, then add ignited brandy and the wine. Cook 1 minute longer. Serve at once. Serves 2 or 3.

FRIED FROGS' LEGS

Season legs with salt, pepper, and lemon juice. Dip in sifted breadcrumbs, then in egg diluted with 2 tablespoons water, and again in crumbs. Chill 1 hour.

Fry in hot deep fat (375°F.) 3 minutes, or sauté in butter until brown Serve with tartar sauce.

COCKLE

A marine bivalve mollusk with shells of equal size marked by radial ribs which ray out from the base. In Europe, especially the British Isles, edible varieties are eaten in the same way as oysters or clams. The American varieties are closely related to the European cockles but are seldom eaten as food.

CRAYFISH OR CRAWFISH

These delicate-tasting fresh-water crustaceans look like infant lobsters. To cook, wash live crayfish thoroughly and drop them into boiling salted water or court bouillon for 5 minutes. Let them cool in the water. Scandinavians frequently add fresh dill to the boiling water. To serve, pull out the tail fin and the intestinal vein with it. Crayfish are usually served in their bright-red shells.

The spiny lobster, from which lobster tails are obtained, is sometimes called sea crayfish. See **Lobster Tail.**

CONCH AND WHELK

The conch is a shellfish (a marine mollusk) probably best known for its attractive shell. Some varieties are edible, especially the queen conch of the Atlantic coast. The conch is often confused with the whelk, another species of marine mollusk with similar types of shells found in temperate waters. The latter is commonly used for food in Europe.

The meat of either of these shellfish is tasty but tough and must be tenderized before using in recipes. To use in a chowder, cover the shellfish with cold water, bring to a boil, and simmer about 25 to 30 minutes. Remove from the shell and pound the white body meat until it begins to disintegrate. (After pounding the meat may be marinated in lime juice for extra tenderness.) Then substitute for other fish or shellfish in chowder recipes. Allow a little longer cooking period.

Note: Conch meat may be ground

and made into fritters or sliced very thin and fried.

SNAILS

Any of a large number of mollusks living on land or in water; specifically, a land variety with a short, thick, worm-like body and a protective spiral shell. This is used as food, especially in Europe where it is considered a delicacy. Large quantities of snails are eaten in France, but the consumption is gradually declining. The best type is known as the Burgundy large white. Most snails are gathered in vineyards; some are raised on special farms. They are available in cans.

While snails are becoming increasingly popular in this country, nevertheless the preparation is a laborious and wearisome task.

To serve 5 to 6, use 1 pound fresh snails (2 to 2½ dozen). Soak in heavily salted water 3 to 4 hours, then wash in several waters and simmer 30 minutes.

Remove snails from shells and cook in court bouillon (see Index) about 3 to 4 hours.

Meanwhile wash shells and dry thoroughly. Replace cooked snails in shells and pack with butter mixture (below). (It may be desirable to use 2 cooked snails in each shell.)

Place in shallow baking pan and, if desired, sprinkle with fine breadcrumbs. Bake in hot oven (400°F.) until heated through, about 20 minutes. Serve with a tiny fork or pick.

BUTTER MIXTURE FOR SNAILS

½ cup butter or margarine
¼ cup finely chopped parsley
1   teaspoon chopped onion or shallot
1   clove crushed garlic
About ½ teaspoon salt
Dash of freshly ground pepper

Cream butter until soft and work in remaining ingredients.

Leftover butter mixture may be used as sauce for fish or vegetables.

CANNED SNAILS

Canned snails are sold in special containers, with the prepared snails in one container and the cleaned shells in another.

To serve, place snails in shells, pack with butter mixture and serve as for fresh snails.

If desired, canned snails may be heated in a little white wine seasoned with chopped onion or shallot before placing in shells.

Another favorite stuffing frequently used instead of the butter mixture is a mixture of equal parts butter and ground filberts which have been creamed together in a bowl which was rubbed slightly with a cut clove of garlic.

SNAILS IN WHITE WINE

2 cups dry white wine
1 tablespoon chopped shallot
48 canned snails and shells
   Parsley butter (below)

Boil wine with chopped shallot until the wine is reduced to ¾ cup. Strain through a fine sieve.

Pour 1 scant teaspoon of the reduced wine into each shell. Put snails in shell and seal in with parsley butter. Put prepared snails on a baking sheet or in a shallow pan and place in hot oven (400°F.) until heated through, about 10 minutes. Serves 6.

Parsley Butter: Cream together ½ pound butter, ½ cup finely chopped parsley, and a few drops lemon juice.

PERIWINKLES, BAKED

Periwinkles are various types of salt-water snails of which an edible European species are found on the Atlantic coast of North America. Many people consider them a delicacy.

6 dozen periwinkles
½ cup soft butter
⅓ cup finely chopped parsley
2 cloves garlic, finely chopped
   Salt
24 large snail shells

Cover the periwinkles with warm water and soak long enough to break the membranes that seal them in their shells. Discard any that do not emerge from the shells.

Drain, then cover the periwinkles with salted water; bring to a boil. The periwinkles will recede into their shells because of the heat. Drain.

With a nut pick or the tip of a small paring knife, remove the periwinkles from their shells. Rinse several times in cold water.

Cream together the butter, parsley, garlic, and salt to taste. Grease the inside of 24 large snail shells; insert 3 periwinkles in each, and fill the shells with creamed butter mixture.

Arrange butter side up in baking dish and let stand 2 hours. Then bake in very hot oven (450°F.) 10 minutes. Serves 4.

OYSTER OR PEA CRABS

These little crabs are frequently found in the oyster shell where they live. They are considered a delicious and delicate morsel and are eaten whole, shells and all. They may be bought by the pound.

To prepare them, wash and drain thoroughly. Drop into a paper bag containing flour and shake to thor-oughly coat. Transfer to a sieve and shake to remove excess flour. Fry in basket in hot deep fat (390°F.) or sauté in sweet butter.

TURTLE AND TERRAPIN

A considerable variety of turtles are used for food in various localities. The name terrapin is commonly applied to fresh water turtles and the name tortoise to land species. The marine green turtle is the usual source of turtle soup and canned turtle meat; however the brackish-water diamond back terrapin is the one most favored as a table delicacy in the United States. It is found in marshes along the Atlantic and Gulf coasts. Terrapin should be alive when purchased. The meat from a 6 to 7-inch terrapin should serve 2. Canned terrapin meat is also available.

TO PREPARE AND COOK TERRAPIN

Wash and scrub the terrapin thoroughly. Plunge the live terrapin into freshly boiling unsalted water and boil 5 to 10 minutes.

Remove from kettle and place in cold water until cool enough to handle.

Rub off the skin from the legs and tail with a towel. Pull out the head with a skewer or other sharp pointed instrument and rub off the skin.

Rinse and cover with boiling salted water. Cook until meat is tender. The time will vary but rarely will it be more than 45 minutes for the average terrapin. It is done when the meat of the legs is soft when pinched by the fingers.

If desired, add a stalk of celery, and 2 or 3 slices each of carrot and onion to the boiling water.

When done, remove from the stock, lay the terrapin on its back and let it cool enough to handle. Pull out the nails from the feet. Cut the undershell loose from the upper shell. Carefully remove the meat. Separate the legs from the body, cut in small pieces and set aside.

Empty the upper shell and discard the gall bladder, being careful not to let any particle of the gall bladder remain in the meat or it will give the dish a bitter flavor.

Remove and discard the sandbag, heart, tail, and the thick heavy part of the intestines as well as the white inside muscles.

The small intestines are usually cut small and added to the meat. The liver and eggs are also added to the meat. Cut the meat into small pieces, 1 to 2 inches. Most terrapin experts leave the bones in the meat.

Combine the meat, liver, eggs, and small intestines, if desired, in a kettle. Barely cover with cold salted water. Add a few slices each of carrot and onion, 1 bay leaf, and 2 cloves.

Cover, bring to boiling point, and simmer 30 to 40 minutes. (Some experts prefer to use the seasoned stock from the previous cooking instead of fresh water.)

When done, if the meat isn't going to be used at once, pack into a bowl, cover tightly and keep in refrigerator until wanted.

TERRAPIN BALTIMORE

Combine ¾ cup chicken stock and terrapin meat. Simmer very gently until stock is reduced by half its original volume.

Add the liver, cut into small pieces, 2 tablespoons butter, salt and black pepper to taste, and 2 well beaten egg yolks, stirring constantly while adding. (If desired, omit the egg yolks and increase the butter to ½ cup, adding the butter bit by bit.)

Before serving, season with 1½ to 2 tablespoons sherry.

TERRAPIN WASHINGTON

Melt 1½ tablespoons butter. Blend in 1½ tablespoons flour until smooth. Add 1 cup cream and bring to boiling point, stirring constantly.

Add the cooked terrapin meat with the liver cut into small pieces, chopped small intestines, terrapin eggs, ½ cup sautéed sliced mushrooms, and 1 hard-cooked egg, coarsely chopped. Simmer gently 3 to 5 minutes.

Just before serving, stir in 2 slightly beaten egg yolks. Season to taste with salt and pepper. If desired, add 1½ to 2 tablespoons sherry. Serve very hot.

TURTLE OR TERRAPIN STEW

1 cup sliced fresh or canned mushrooms
2 tablespoons butter or margarine
1 can condensed cream of mushroom soup
1 cup milk
   About ½ teaspoon salt
2 cups chopped, cooked turtle or terrapin meat
¼ cup dry white wine

Pan fry the mushrooms in butter 5 minutes.

Add soup and milk; taste and add more salt if necessary. Then add cooked meat and heat 1 or 2 minutes.

Add wine and heat through, about 1 minute.

Serve hot on buttered toast or corn sticks. Serves 4 to 6.

FRITTERS

The term fritter, which is derived from the Latin frigere meaning to fry, is applied to several kinds of fried food. Some fritters are small batter cakes belonging, like doughnuts and crullers, to the bread family and are always deep-fat fried. Other fritters are combinations of small pieces of fruit, vegetables, meats, fish, etc., and batter which are usually deep-fat fried; however some types are pan-fried (sautéed).

Sometimes the term is also applied to such fried items as timbale cases and rosettes which are intended to hold other foods.

Correct frying procedure is perhaps the most important step in making good fritters. See deep fat frying hints in **Facts About Food and Cooking.**

For a complete list of the frittered foods in this book, consult the index.

BASIC FRITTER BINDING BATTER

1¾ cups sifted enriched flour
3   teaspoons baking powder
1   tablespoon sugar
½   teaspoon salt
2   eggs, slightly beaten
1   cup milk
1   tablespoon melted shortening

Sift dry ingredients. Omit sugar unless batter is to be used for fruit.

Combine eggs, milk, and shortening. Mix liquid and dry ingredients and stir until smooth.

Add 1 to 2 cups chopped vegetables, cooked or canned, or chopped fruit, well drained, or 1 to 2 cups drained corn.

Drop from a tablespoon into deep hot fat (365° to 370°F.). Turn as soon as fritter comes to surface. Remove from fat when well browned on both sides. Drain on absorbent paper. Serves 6.

Banana Fritters

BASIC FRITTER COVER BATTER

1   egg, slightly beaten
1   cup milk or 1 cup water or 1 cup fruit juice
1   tablespoon melted shortening
1   cup sifted enriched flour
½   teaspoon sugar
¼   teaspoon salt

Combine egg, milk, water, or fruit juice and shortening. Add gradually to dry ingredients. Mix until smooth.

Dip fruit into cover batter and fry in deep fat, heated to 365°–370°F. Remove when light brown on both sides. Drain on absorbent paper.

This cover batter may be used for apple, banana, or pineapple slices or for orange sections. Serve fruit fritters sprinkled with confectioners' sugar.

It may also be used for seafoods or meats, but omit sugar from batter. Serves 6.

Variation 1: For a thicker batter decrease milk to ⅔ cup and add 1 teaspoon baking powder to flour with sugar and salt. Use with berries or very juicy fruits.

Variation 2: Vary by adding ¼ teaspoon cinnamon, nutmeg, or grated rind of lemon or orange.

ORANGE FRITTERS

3   oranges
2   cups water
1   cup sugar
4   tablespoons brandy
Fritter cover batter (see index)

Peel oranges, separate the sections, and carefully remove the seeds and pith.

Prepare a sugar syrup by boiling water, sugar, and brandy. Reduce heat to simmer; add orange sections, and simmer gently 10 minutes. Drain

orange sections well and let them cool.

At serving time, pour fritter batter over sections and let fruit and batter stand 10 minutes.

Fry in hot deep fat (375°F.) a few at a time, until they are delicately browned all over, turning them with a wooden spoon. Drain on absorbent paper; dust with confectioners' sugar. Serves 5 to 6.

BANANA FRITTERS

1   cup sifted enriched flour
¼   cup sugar
2   teaspoons baking powder
1¼   teaspoons salt
1   beaten egg
⅓   cup milk
2   teaspoons shortening, melted
3   medium green-tipped bananas, cut diagonally in 3 pieces
2   to 3 tablespoons enriched flour
Fat
Fluffy hard sauce (below)

Sift together flour, sugar, baking powder, and salt.

Combine egg, milk, and melted shortening; add to dry ingredients; mix smooth.

Roll banana pieces in 2 to 3 tablespoons flour; spread with batter, making sure they are well coated. (This batter is stiff—do not thin.)

Fry in deep hot fat (375°F.) until golden brown, about 1 to 2 minutes. (Fritters stay crisp 15 to 20 minutes.)

Serve with fluffy hard sauce. Serves 4.

Fluffy Hard Sauce: Thoroughly cream ¼ cup butter or margarine with 1 cup sifted confectioners' sugar in mixer; add ½ teaspoon vanilla. Chill before serving, if desired.

Variations: Vary flavor with lemon or orange juice and grated rind. Sprinkle with nutmeg, if desired. Makes about ¾ cup.

FRITTER BATTER FOR HORS D'OEUVRES

1/2 cup all-purpose flour
1/4 teaspoon salt
1 whole egg
1 tablespoon melted butter
1/2 cup flat beer
1 stiffly beaten egg white

Sift flour with salt. Beat egg; add butter and combine with flour. Add beer and stir only until the mixture is smooth.

Let batter stand at room temperature until light and foamy, about 1 to 2 hours. Then fold in stiffly beaten egg white.

FRITTERS FOR HORS D'OEUVRES

Prepare fritter batter for hors d'oeuvres (above). To the fritter batter add one of the following. Drop by tablespoons into deep hot fat (375°F.) and fry until golden brown. Drain and serve hot with or without a dipping sauce.

Ham Fritters: Combine 1 cup ground ham, 1 tablespoon chopped parsley, and freshly ground black pepper to taste.

Chicken or Turkey Fritters: Combine 1 cup ground cooked chicken or turkey, 1 tablespoon finely chopped chives or green onion, and salt, pepper, and nutmeg to taste.

Tuna Fritters: Combine 1 cup finely chopped tuna, 2 tablespoons minced celery, and lemon juice and salt and pepper to taste.

ROSETTES

Rosettes are a type of fried cake made from a thin pour batter fried in fancy shapes by means of a special rosette iron. They are usually used as a base for creamed foods such as creamed chicken or for desserts topped with a fruit sauce.

2 eggs
1 tablespoon sugar (see below)
1/4 teaspoon salt
1 cup sifted all-purpose flour
1 cup milk
2 tablespoons melted butter

Beat eggs until blended, then beat in sugar and salt. Stir in flour alternately with combined milk and butter.

To fry, dip iron in deep hot fat (375°F.), then into batter. Do not let batter cover top of iron or it will be difficult to remove rosette. Dip the batter-coated iron into the hot fat for 20 to 35 seconds. Remove rosette with a fork. Repeat process, alternately dipping iron into hot fat and then into batter and frying. Drain on absorbent paper. Makes about 3 dozen.

Variations: If rosettes are not to be used as a dessert omit sugar from above recipe. If served as a dessert, sprinkle the fried rosettes with confectioners' sugar.

HUSH PUPPIES

A hush puppy is a corn-meal fritter served with fried fish and traditionally fried in the same deep fat used for the fish. It is an old-time Southern dish. The name is said to have originated at outdoor fish fries, at which bits of the frying batter would be cooked and thrown to the dogs to quiet them.

2 cups corn meal
1 tablespoon flour
1 teaspoon baking powder
1/2 teaspoon baking soda
1 teaspoon salt
3 tablespoons finely chopped onion
1 egg, well beaten
1 cup buttermilk

Mix and sift dry ingredients. Add onion, well beaten egg, and buttermilk.

Drop by the spoonful into hot fat. Fry until golden brown. Drain on absorbent paper. Serves 6 to 8.

FRENCH FRITTERS (BEIGNETS)

Prepare Cream Puff Paste (see index) but instead of baking, drop by teaspoonful at a time into deep, hot fat (370°F.) and cook until delicately brown. As soon as they are cooked enough on one side, they will turn themselves over. Remove when browned on both sides. Drain and sprinkle lightly with powdered sugar.

Queen Fritters: Cook as above, but cut slit in each and fill with preserves or marmalade, or with chocolate cream filling. Sprinkle with powdered sugar.

BLUEBERRY FRITTERS

1 cup sifted enriched flour
1 teaspoon baking powder
1/2 teaspoon salt
2 tablespoons sugar
2 eggs, separated
2 to 3 tablespoons water
3/4 cup blueberries

Mix and sift dry ingredients. Combine egg yolks with water and stir into dry ingredients, mixing only until smooth.

Fold in stiffly beaten egg whites, then mix in the blueberries.

Drop by spoonfuls into hot deep fat (365°F.) and fry until lightly browned.

Drain on absorbent paper and serve with confectioners' sugar or fruit sauce.

Variations: Other fruits, such as diced peaches, apples, or bananas, or other berries, may be used. If cranberries are used, they must first be cooked in 1/2 cup water and 1/2 cup sugar until the skins burst, then drained and cooled.

APPLE FRITTERS

1 egg, separated
1 teaspoon water
1 tablespoon oil
1/8 teaspoon salt
2/3 cup sifted enriched flour
2 medium apples
Confectioners' sugar

Beat egg yolk with water, oil, and salt. Add flour; beat well until thick and smooth. Allow to "rest or ripen" at room temperature for about 2 hours.

Peel 2 apples; core and cut them into 1/4-inch wedges.

Just before frying, beat egg white until it holds a peak. Blend carefully into first mixture.

Dip slices of apples into batter; fry in deep fat (375°F.) until golden brown. Drain. Before serving, sprinkle with confectioners' sugar. Serves 4 to 6.

SWEDISH TIMBALE CASES
(Patty Shell Cases)

These are pastry shells of fried batter, made with a special iron, in which creamy foods are served. Most people find the fluted irons easier to handle than the plain ones.

1/2 cup milk
2 egg yolks, beaten
3/4 cup sifted enriched flour
1/2 teaspoon salt

Add milk to egg yolks. Gradually stir in flour sifted with salt.

Mix well, cover, and set aside 1 hour.

Heat deep fat to 370°F. and heat timbale iron in it for 2 to 3 minutes.

Drain and dip into batter to within 3/4 inch of top. Immediately return to hot fat and hold there until case is crisp and lightly browned.

If batter slips off, the iron is too cold. If it sticks to iron, it is too hot. Makes 24 timbale cases.

ANDALUSIAN HONEY FRITTERS

1 tablespoon creamed butter or margarine
1/2 cup sugar
4 eggs, well beaten
1 teaspoon grated orange rind
1 tablespoon sherry
1/4 teaspoon salt
1 1/2 cups sifted enriched flour
1 1/2 teaspoons baking powder

Cream together the butter and sugar. Beat in eggs, orange rind, sherry, and salt. Beat to a perfect cream.

Sift together flour and baking powder. Stir this slowly into first mixture until blended.

Let stand 15 minutes, then roll out thin on slightly floured board. Cut into pieces 1 x 4 inches and fry in deep hot fat (360° to 370°F.). Drain; serve hot with honey or maple syrup. Serves 6.

FRESH FRUIT FRITTERS

1 cup sifted enriched flour
1/4 teaspoon salt
2 eggs
2/3 cup milk
1 teaspoon salad oil
Salad oil or shortening for deep frying
Apples, peaches, or bananas

Sift flour with salt into bowl.

Beat eggs, stir in milk and teaspoon of salad oil. Add dry ingredients and beat to a smooth batter. Cover and chill several hours.

To Prepare Fruit: Apples: core, pare and slice in rings 1/2 inch thick. Peaches: pare, and quarter. Bananas: peel, slice once lengthwise, and once crosswise.

Dip into batter and drain off excess batter. Deep-fry in oil or shortening heated to 370°F. until golden brown, 3 to 4 minutes. Drain on absorbent paper.

Serve with meat, or sprinkle with confectioners' sugar and serve with lemon sauce as a dessert. Serves 6 to 8.

CHERRY FRITTERS

3/4 cup well drained pitted sour red cherries
2 tablespoons sugar
1 tablespoon brandy, kirsch, or rum (optional)
1 cup sifted enriched flour
1/4 teaspoon salt
1 teaspoon baking powder
1 beaten egg
About 1/2 cup milk
1 tablespoon melted butter or margarine
Confectioners' sugar

Mix cherries, sugar, and liquor.

Sift together flour, salt, and baking powder.

Mix egg, 1/2 cup milk, and butter. Add milk mixture to dry ingredients and stir only until smooth. Add and fold in cherry mixture. Add additional milk if batter is too thick.

Drop by tablespoonfuls into hot deep fat (365° to 375°F.) and fry until browned, turning as fritters rise to the surface.

Drain on absorbent paper. Sprinkle with confectioners' sugar and, if desired, serve with cherry sauce that has been flavored with the same liquor that was used in batter. Serves 4.

SWISS FRIED CAKES

1 cup light cream
2 beaten eggs
1 teaspoon salt
2 cups sifted enriched flour
1/2 cup butter

Combine cream, eggs, and salt; mix well. Add flour to make a soft dough and turn out onto a floured board.

Dot dough with butter and with the hands work it into the dough. The butter should be firm but not hard.

Chill dough in refrigerator 1 hour then roll out 1/8 inch thick.

Cut in any desired shape, making a 1/2-inch gash through the center of each. Fry in deep hot fat (370°F.).

Drain on absorbent paper and roll in sugar while still hot. Makes about 36.

OB'L PUFFERS
(Pennsylvania-Dutch Apple Fritters)

1 cup sifted enriched flour
2 tablespoons sugar
1 1/2 teaspoons baking powder
1/4 teaspoon salt
1 beaten egg
1/2 cup milk
2 medium apples, pared, cut in 1/8 inch rings or wedges

Sift together dry ingredients.

Add milk to egg and blend with dry ingredients. Add the cut apples to batter.

Dip a long-handled spoon or tongs in the hot fat, then lift a batter-covered piece of apple with it and slide into deep hot fat (375°F.).

Re-dip the spoon about every fourth or fifth "puffer." (This process makes it easier and less messy in handling the food in the batter stage.)

Brown completely on one side and then turn for cooking the other side. Drain on absorbent paper and sprinkle with confectioners' sugar.

Serve piping hot. Makes 12 to 16 "puffers."

HAM AND CORN FRITTERS

1 cup ground cooked ham
1 cup cooked or canned whole kernel corn
1 tablespoon minced onion
2/3 cup enriched flour
1 1/2 teaspoons baking powder
1/4 cup milk or corn liquid

Mix ground ham, corn, and onion.

Sift dry ingredients together. Add to corn mixture. Add liquid and mix well.

Drop by teaspoonfuls into deep fat at 365°F. Fry until golden brown. Drain. Serves 4.

APRICOT FRITTERS WITH RUM SAUCE

1 teaspoon sugar
1 1/4 cups sifted enriched flour
1/3 teaspoon baking powder
Pinch of salt
2 eggs
1/3 cup milk
1/2 tablespoon butter
Apricots

Mix and sift dry ingredients. Beat eggs well; add eggs, milk, and butter to dry ingredients. Mix to a stiff batter.

Remove pits from apricots and cut into quarters. Dust with flour and dip each apricot into batter. Drop into hot deep fat (370°F.). Fry until brown. Serve with Rum Sauce.

Rum Sauce:

1 cup mixed fruit juice
3/4 cup sugar
1/4 teaspoon red food coloring
1/4 cup rum flavoring

Mix all ingredients and cook slowly for one hour. Stir occasionally.

CHEESE FRITTERS

1 1/4 cups sifted enriched flour
1/4 teaspoon salt
2 teaspoons baking powder
2/3 cup milk
1 egg, well beaten
3/4 cup grated American cheese

Mix and sift flour, salt, and baking powder. Mix together the milk and egg. Combine the two mixtures.

Add grated cheese and beat 3 minutes vigorously, or until smooth.

Drop by tablespoons into deep hot fat (360° to 370°F.). Fry until brown. Drain on paper. Serve hot. Serves 6.

Ham and Corn Fritters

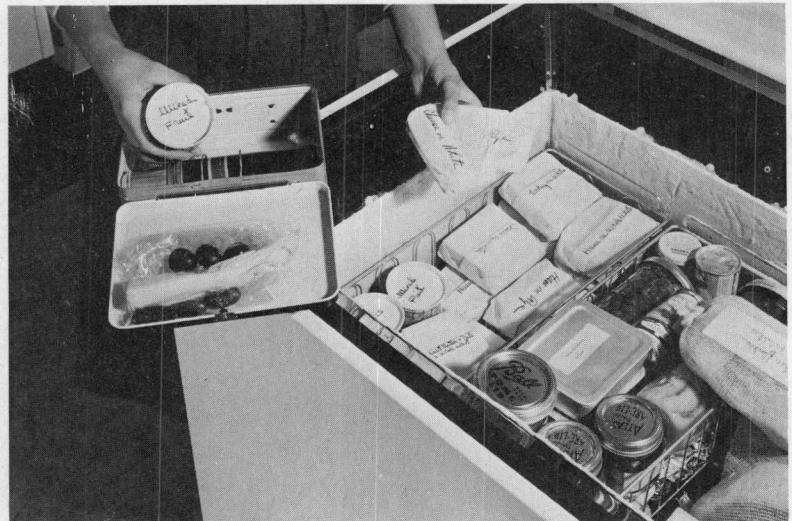

FROZEN FOODS

Having a freezer and making proper use of it can be like having an extra pair of hands in the kitchen or like having an extra day in every week. Begin by thinking of your freezer as more than just a place for food storage. Think of it as part of your daily cooking equipment, plan around it, and rely on it every day to help you.

However to enjoy the advantages of a freezer to the fullest, you'll find it wise in the very beginning to take a little time to learn the facts about freezing—how to prepare, package, freeze, store, and cook frozen foods properly.

BASIC PRINCIPLES OF SUCCESSFUL FREEZING

Frozen foods are attractive, flavorful, and high in nutritive value when carefully prepared with strict attention to basic principles of freezing. There is a great difference, however, between frozen foods of quality and foods that are merely safe to eat because they have been frozen. Carelessness in any of the basic steps may easily produce foods that are entirely safe, yet whose quality is so diminished that you will have little pleasure in eating them.

1. Choose high quality foods. The frozen product will be no better than the food in its original state. Freezing does not improve the flavor or quality of any food.

2. Process foods carefully. Follow instructions about blanching vegetables, cutting and trimming meat and poultry, cooking and chilling prepared foods. Speed in handling is essential at all stages.

3. Package foods properly. Choose only freezer packaging materials which will protect food from air. Wrap tightly and seal with freezer tape. When air reaches food during storage, the result is loss of moisture accompanied by a change in flavor. This is the condition known as "freezer burn."

4. Label all foods accurately. Label each package with date, name of product, weight (if meat) and number of pieces or servings. It is helpful to add an "expiration date" to the label —the maximum storage time. All foods should be used before their expiration date.

5. Freeze at 0°F. or lower. Foods should always be frozen as rapidly as possible. Put unfrozen foods in the fastest freezing area or in direct contact with freezer walls or shelves and away from already frozen foods. Place packages so air can circulate between them.

6. Do not overload freezer with unfrozen foods. Put in only as much food as your freezer will freeze without unduly raising the temperature of foods already stored there. Overloading also keeps the new items from freezing quickly enough for optimum quality. Follow the directions with your freezer to determine how much food may be frozen at one time. If you have more than recommended amounts, have food frozen at a central locker plant, then store at home.

7. Store foods at 0°F. Keep a thermometer in the storage compartment, and make sure the temperature remains at zero or below. Foods stored at temperatures above zero lose flavor and nutritive value rapidly. Ice or snow inside the package usually indicates fluctuation of temperatures above zero.

8. Avoid long storage. No food remains at top quality indefinitely even though frozen. Freezing retards bacterial and enzymatic action greatly but cannot stop it entirely, and it is best to plan on normal seasonal turnover of foods. Foods frozen first should always be used first.

How to Freeze Fruits

Fruits are especially easy to freeze, so allow ample space in your freezer for a complete variety. Most fruits have a high sugar content and, for best results, should be frozen quickly.

Which Fruits to Select

Most fruits, berries and melons can be frozen satisfactorily, but some freeze better than others. In the same manner, certain varieties of each fruit freeze better than others. Directions for freezing specific fruits rate varieties as to suitability for freezing. If in doubt about freezing certain fruits, consult your local nurseryman, county agent or State Agricultural College for further information.

Whole citrus fruits should not be frozen, but serving slices, sections and juices are delicious and easy to freeze. Red raspberries are delicious when frozen.

When to Gather Fruits

The ideal time to freeze most fruits is at the height of maturity. It is best to allow most fruits to reach this stage on the vine, bush, or tree. However, fruits like peaches, plums, and figs are apt to become soft on the plant and are easily bruised in handling. Gather such fruits in the "firm ripe" stage and store overnight . . . insures more even ripening and, with peaches, they are easier to peel.

Gather fruit in the cool of the morning. Sun-heated fruit may bruise excessively from handling and result in an inferior frozen product. Gather no more fruit than can be quickly prepared, packaged, and frozen at one time.

While speed of handling is not so critical with fruits as with vegetables, the shorter the holding time after gathering for most fruits, the better the frozen fruit will be.

Wash Fruit Thoroughly

This is one of the most important steps in preparing fruits for freezing. Low-growing fruits and all wild fruits should be washed twice or more to remove sand and dust.

Wash no more than one quart of small fruit (berries or cherries) at one time. This can be done in a colander, using a spray when possible. Never allow fruit to stand in water more than one minute as water-soaked fruit will not freeze successfully.

After washing, drain fruit thoroughly. Spread fruit carefully on a tray or large utility dish on which several thicknesses of absorbent paper toweling have been placed. If possible, set tray in refrigerator about one hour to cool and firm the fruit.

Stem Fruits Carefully

Never squeeze the stems off berries. The stems of raspberries, dewberries, and gooseberries may be lifted off with the fingers. Use a sharp knife to stem strawberries.

Peel Fruits Rapidly

Apples, apricots, peaches, nectarines, and pears oxidize and discolor rapidly after the skin is removed.

To prevent this, peel and slice fruit directly into a solution of 3 tablespoons lemon juice (or 3 tablespoons salt OR 4½ teaspoons citric acid) to each gallon of cold water.

Don't allow fruit to remain in solution longer than one minute, so do no more than one package at a time.

Rinse in cold water and drain before packaging. Then continue to peel, slice, and package until all fruit has been prepared.

Remove Seeds Carefully

Fruits with seeds (plums, prunes, peaches, apricots, and nectarines) must have the seed removed before freezing. Avoid bruising fruit.

Pulp

Fruit to be pulped (puréed) may be cooked before forcing through a purée strainer or electric food blender. Such fruits as strawberries, grapes, raspberries, peaches, and plums may be forced through purée strainer or food blender without cooking.

Sweeten Fruits Properly

Many fruits retain better flavor if sweetened before freezing. There are two methods of sweetening fruit: dry sugar method and syrup method.

DRY SUGAR METHOD

Method #1: After the fruit has been washed, drained, and cooled, carefully transfer fruit to a bowl. Sprinkle sugar over fruit. Sweeten one quart at a time to avoid bruising.

A clean flour sifter will give more even distribution of sugar.

To mix sugar through fruit, use wooden slotted spoon and gently lift fruit through sugar. Package at once.

Method #2: Wash, cool, and drain fruit. Fill package about ¼ full. Sprinkle in ¼ of sugar, about one or two tablespoons. Continue filling container in this way.

Container may be shaken occasionally to distribute sugar, but avoid pressure on container. Seal at once.

SYRUP METHOD

Syrup is the most satisfactory sweetening agent if fruit is to be used for sauce. Syrup is preferable for apricots, pears, and figs.

The simplest way to add the syrup to the fruit is to first fill the container with fruit and then add syrup to cover. Seal at once.

The syrup must always be cold before using . . . a good idea is to make the syrup a day in advance and store it in a covered container in the refrigerator.

SUGAR SYRUP

Add sugar to boiling water and cook until sugar is thoroughly dissolved.

The sweetness desired in the frozen fruit should govern the syrup to be used. See specific directions for recommended syrup with each particular fruit.

Very Thin: 1 cup sugar to 4 cups boiling water.

Thin: 1 cup sugar to 3 cups boiling water.

Medium: 1 cup sugar to 2 cups boiling water.

Heavy: 1 cup sugar to 1 cup boiling water.

Package Fruits Carefully

Polyethylene bags are excellent, but care should be taken when sealing and handling the bag before the fruit is frozen. Rigid cartons, tin cans (if lacquered inside), and special glass freezing jars may be used.

Containers must also be moisture-vaporproof because air leakage causes destruction of vitamins and minerals and also spoils the appearance of the fruit.

Package According to Use

Decide how the frozen fruit is to be used and then package the fresh fruit accordingly. For instance, fruits to be used for pies or jams need not be sweetened before freezing, with the exception of apricots and peaches which sometimes discolor unless sugar or syrup is added.

As a sauce, a pint carton of fruit will serve 3 or 4. A pint will make a skimpy 8-inch pie but a quart will make four generous individual shortcakes. But if used as a topping over ice cream, a pint of strawberries will serve 5 or 6.

Select package sizes that adequately take care of a meal, with no save-overs. Frozen fruits lose their flavor if left standing several hours after thawing. *Never refreeze fruit.*

Allow for Expansion and Seal Carefully

Package fruit firmly but do not use pressure or crush the fruit. If using a rigid container, there should be sufficient air space to allow for some expansion. Fill container to within ½ inch of top for dry sugar packs and ½ to ¾ inch for syrup packs. Make packages airtight.

Label Clearly and Freeze at Once

After sugar or syrup has been added to fruit in container, package should be sealed, labeled clearly, and placed immediately on quick-freeze shelf with the sealed side up to prevent leakage. If this is not practical, place packages in freezer compartment of refrigerator until ready to load the freezer.

A Hint for Mothers of Small Children

When sorting fruits for freezing, use only those which are firm and ripe. Those which are overripe but still usable can be puréed for the baby and young children. Peaches, apples, apricots, plums, and pineapple are easy to purée and will save both time and money in the preparation of the children's meals.

How It's Done: Peel (or pare) the fruit and then cook thoroughly . . . be careful not to overcook. You may want to add a bit of sugar as the fruit cooks. Then force it through a sieve or food mill or put it through an electric food blender. Cool thoroughly.

After the fruit is cool, pour into refrigerator ice cube tray with the dividers in place. Freeze. When cubes are firmly frozen, remove them from the tray and package one or two cubes, enough for an individual serving, in small polyethylene bags.

To serve: Let cubes stand at room temperature until suitable for serving.

How to Prepare Fruits for Freezing

APPLES FOR SAUCE

Varieties suitable for freezing: good—Baldwin, Greening, Northern Spy, and Yellow Transparent. 1¼ pounds yield approximately 1 pint.

Peel and core the apples. Cut into eighths. Place in saucepan and add only enough water to start the apples cooking. Bring to a quick boil. Reduce heat to simmer and cook about 10 minutes until apples are mushy. Add sugar to taste and stir.

Some apples cook to a fine mush without straining, but if straining is necessary, force the sauce through a purée strainer. Cool thoroughly. Package in polyethylene bags. Freeze.

APPLES FOR PIE

Varieties suitable for freezing: good—any high-acid variety. 1 pound yields about 1 pint.

Freeze enough in one container for a pie . . . a quart container holds apples for a 9-inch pie. *Do not freeze apples which have turned brown on the inside or have started to mold.*

Peel and core the apples. Cut into slices for pie. Apples discolor rapidly after the skin has been removed, so slice apples directly into a solution of 3 tablespoons lemon juice (or 3 tablespoons salt OR 4½ teaspoons citric acid) to 1 gallon cold water. Never allow apples to remain in solution more than one minute. Rinse in cold water before draining.

Place slices on a tray covered with several thicknesses of absorbent paper toweling. Place tray in refrigerator and allow to drain. Thorough draining before packaging makes slices easier to separate for making pies.

Immediately after draining, pack into polyethylene bags and freeze. Add sugar, if desired, in the proportion of 1 part sugar to 4 parts apples.

APRICOTS

Varieties suitable for freezing: good—any tree-ripened variety. ¾ to 1 pound yields approximately 1 pint.

With skins: Select firm, fully ripened fruit of bright apricot color, with no traces of green. Wash thoroughly. Remove stem. Cut in half and remove pit.

Dip pitted halves in a solution of 1 tablespoon lemon juice and 1 quart water. Drain by placing cut side down on a tray covered with several thicknesses of absorbent toweling.

Place in polyethylene bags or rigid containers. Cover with cold, medium syrup. Seal. Freeze at once.

Without skins (Preferred): Place about 20 apricots in a wire basket. Plunge into boiling water to cover for 1 minute. Remove and plunge into cold water to cover for 1 minute . . . or until cool.

Remove skin. Cut in half and remove pit. Dip pitted halves in a solution of 1 tablespoon lemon juice to 1 quart water. Drain by placing cut side down on a tray covered with several thicknesses of absorbent toweling.

Place in polyethylene bags or rigid containers. Cover with cold, medium syrup. Seal. Freeze at once.

BLACKBERRIES

Variety suitable for freezing: fair—Wild Eldorado. 1 quart berries yields about 1 quart frozen fruit.

Select firm, fully matured fruit. Immature blackberries, even though a good black in color, turn reddish black when frozen.

Wash carefully in cold water, never more than 1 quart of berries at a time. Gently move the berries through the water by hand, then lift them to a tray covered with several thicknesses of absorbent paper toweling. Spread them only one layer thick.

Place immediately in refrigerator to cool before packaging. If you wish to add sugar to berries, use the same method as for red raspberries. Package in polyethylene bags, seal and freeze.

For use as a sauce, pack berries in polyethylene bags or rigid containers and cover with a thin or medium syrup. Seal and freeze immediately.

BLUEBERRIES

Variety suitable for freezing: excellent—any small-seeded variety. 1 pint berries yields approximately 1 pint frozen fruit.

Carefully remove leaves, foreign matter and immature berries. Wash thoroughly. Remove stems. Drain on absorbent paper toweling. Place in bowl. Add sugar in proportion of 2 tablespoons sugar to 1 cup berries. Stir gently to avoid bruising the fruit.

Package in polyethylene bags or rigid containers. Seal. Freeze.

CANTALOUPE

Variety suitable for freezing: good—any fully ripened, deep yellow variety. 1 cantaloupe yields approximately 3 pints.

Good for fruit cups or salads during the winter months. Select firm, fully ripened cantaloupe. Cut in half and remove seeds. A French potato ball cutter is ideal for scooping out the cantaloupe. If one is not available, remove rind, cut melon in slices and cube. Drain before packaging.

Package in polyethylene bags. Seal and freeze. Once thawed, cantaloupe must be used immediately.

Before freezing cherries, remove the pits with a salad fork or three-pronged kitchen fork.

CHERRIES, SOUR

Variety suitable for freezing: excellent—Montmorency. 1 quart cherries yields about 1 pint frozen fruit.

Wash thoroughly and quickly. Remove from water at once. Remove stems. Place on tray covered with several thicknesses of absorbent paper toweling.

Set tray in refrigerator until cherries are firm again.

Then remove pits. A salad fork or three-pronged kitchen fork is excellent to do this. With the fork, gently press prong into stem end and lift out the pit. Squeezing the pit out bruises the fruit. Work with only 1 quart at a time because juice accumulates and the cherries may have to be drained again.

Add 2 tablespoons sugar to 1 cup cherries and package in polyethylene bags. Freeze.

Cherries for pies may be frozen without sugar.

CHERRIES, SWEET

Varieties suitable for freezing: fair—Bing and Lambert. 1 quart cherries yields about 1 pint frozen fruit.

Select fully tree-ripened cherries. Proceed as for sour cherries. A medium syrup may be used if the sweet cherries are to be used as a sauce.

Package in polyethylene bags or rigid containers. Seal and freeze at once.

CRANBERRIES

Variety suitable for freezing: excellent—Howes. ½ pound yields approximately 1 pint.

Sort berries carefully. Remove stems and all spongy or poorly formed cranberries. Wash berries carefully. Drain.

Package in polyethylene bags. Freeze. Cranberries do not need sugar for successful freezing.

CURRANTS

Varieties suitable for freezing: good—any large variety. ¾ pound yields about 1 pint.

Wash and drain currants before removing from stem. Then remove stem and place currants in a bowl. Mix with sugar in proportion of 1 part sugar to 4 parts currants.

Place in polyethylene bags. If currants are to be used as a sauce, place in rigid containers and cover with a medium syrup. Seal and freeze.

DEWBERRIES

Variety suitable for freezing: fair—Boysenberries. 1 quart berries yields about 1 quart frozen fruit.

Same procedure as for blackberries.

FIGS

Varieties suitable for freezing: excellent—Magnolia, Brown Turkey, and Celestial.

Gather figs that are completely ripe but not bruised or softened. Figs may be frozen with or without skin.

Peeled Figs: Wash thoroughly. Remove stem. Using a sharp knife, peel very thin. Package according to size of family, allowing 4 or 5 figs per serving. Freeze.

Place figs in polyethylene bags. When bag is ¼ filled, sprinkle sugar over figs Continue alternating figs and sugar. Use 1 part sugar to 4 parts figs. Seal and freeze. Prepared this way, figs are delicious served with cream.

Or fill container. Cover figs with a medium syrup. Seal and freeze.

If figs are to be used as a topping over ice cream, use a heavy syrup.

Unpeeled Figs: Sprinkle 6 quarts of figs with 1 cup baking soda. Pour 6 quarts boiling water over them. Let stand 10 minutes. Rinse in clear, cold water. Drain thoroughly on absorbent paper toweling on a tray. Set tray in refrigerator to chill.

Package in polyethylene bags. Add medium syrup. Seal and freeze.

GOOSEBERRIES

Varieties suitable for freezing: excellent—wild, any large-sized variety. 1 pint fresh berries yields approximately 1 pint frozen fruit.

Frozen gooseberries are excellent for pie. Select fully matured green gooseberries. Wash thoroughly. Remove stem and blossom end. Drain. Place berries in bowl. Add sugar, if desired, in proportion of 2 tablespoons sugar to 1 cup gooseberries. Package. Freeze.

GRAPEFRUIT AND ORANGE SECTIONS

Chill fruit thoroughly. Then, peel and section the fruit, making sure all skin and membrane are removed. Drain on absorbent paper toweling. Prepare only enough for 3 or 4 packages at one time as a protection against vitamin loss.

Package in polyethylene bags with rounds of waxed paper between layers. Seal and freeze. Sugar may be added to grapefruit sections, if desired.

HUCKLEBERRIES

Same procedure as blueberries.

NECTARINES

Practically all varieties suitable for freezing.

Same procedure as for peaches.

PEACHES

Varieties suitable for freezing: Yellow, excellent—Hale Haven, J. H. Hale, and Red Haven. White, excellent—Golden Jubilee and Georgia Belle. 1 to 1½ pounds yield approximately 1 pint.

Select tree-ripened peaches. Peel, rather than scald peaches . . . doing only a few at a time.

Slice peaches directly into the polyethylene bag in which they are to be frozen.

Add sugar alternately with the peaches in proportion of 2 tablespoons sugar to 1 cup peaches. Seal and freeze. This method helps to retard browning or oxidation of peaches.

Or, you may peel and slice about one quart at one time. Place in a bowl and sprinkle 1 tablespoon lemon juice over them to retard discoloring.

Add sugar in proportion of 2 tablespoons sugar to 1 cup peaches. Turn peaches over and over in bowl with wooden spoon.

Handle gently. If you desire, peaches may be packed in medium syrup in polyethylene bags or rigid containers.

Note: Sometimes, due to growing season and the variety of peaches selected for freezing, the peaches may discolor in spite of anything that can be done.

PEARS

(Not especially recommended for freezing.)

Varieties suitable for freezing: fair—Kieffer and Baldwin. 1 to 1¼ pounds yield approximately 1 pint.

Select tree-ripened fruit. Wash, peel and cut into desired sizes. Place peeled and cored fruit in a solution of 1 tablespoon lemon juice (or 1 tablespoon salt OR 1 teaspoon citric acid) to 1 quart of cold water. Drain on tray covered with several thicknesses of absorbent paper toweling. Set tray in refrigerator to chill pears.

Pack in polyethylene bags or rigid containers. Add medium syrup to completely cover pears. Seal and freeze.

PINEAPPLE

Excellent for freezing. 1 pineapple yields approximately 3 pints or 12 to 14 slices.

An easy way to peel pineapple is to lay the fruit, side down, on a good cutting board. Grasp the stem end with one hand. With a sharp knife, cut bottom end off pineapple. Place pineapple upright on cutting board and, while holding by stem, remove peeling by slicing downward. When peeling is removed, return pineapple to its side and cut in ½-inch slices. Discard stem when last piece is sliced. Remove any "eyes" remaining in each slice. Cut out core

These slices may be frozen whole. Place in freezer foil (use drugstore wrap) or in polyethylene bags. Pineapple may be shredded and 2 tablespoons of sugar added to each cup. Or, a thin syrup may be used. Place in polyethylene bags or rigid containers. Seal. Freeze.

> **Note:** If frozen pineapple is to be used in gelatin dessert, it must be brought to the boiling point and cooked a minute or two before using, otherwise gelatin will not congeal.

PLUMS

Varieties suitable for freezing: Plums, very good—Damson and Red June. Prunes, very good—Italian. 1¼ pounds yield approximately 1 pint.

Select fully ripened fruit, not yet brown around the pit. Wash, sort, stem and cut in half, removing the pit. Drain on tray with several thicknesses of paper toweling. Set tray in refrigerator to chill fruit.

Place fruit in bowl. Add sugar in proportion of 1 cup sugar to 5 cups fruit or use medium syrup. Package in polyethylene bags. Freeze.

RED RASPBERRIES

Varieties suitable for freezing: excellent—Cuthbert, Latham, and Viking. 1 pint fresh berries yields approximately 1 pint frozen ones.

Raspberries are exceptionally fragile. Great care should be used in washing them, as they bruise easily.

If possible, wash raspberries in water which has been cooled, with ice, to about 40°F. Wash only a few berries at a time and do not allow them to remain in the water more than 30 seconds.

Use the same procedure as strawberries (see below). Drain thoroughly. Then place berries on tray covered with several thicknesses of absorbent paper toweling.

Set tray in refrigerator to cool and firm the fruit . . . about one hour.

Package raspberries in polyethylene bags or rigid containers. When container is ¼ filled with berries, add ¼ of the sugar (use proportion of 2 tablespoons sugar to 1 cup raspberries). Continue alternately adding berries and sugar until container is filled. Seal. Freeze immediately.

Red Raspberries, Continued

Raspberries make their own syrup when sugar is added. A pint of raspberries makes 4 servings. Purple varieties may also be frozen by this procedure.

RHUBARB

Variety suitable for freezing: excellent—Victoria. 1¼ pounds yield approximately 1 pint.

Freeze rhubarb as early in the spring as possible, before the rhubarb becomes tough and stringy.

Wash under running water. Remove stem and leaf end.

Cut in 1-inch pieces (cuts much easier with scissors). Drain. Package in polyethylene bags. Seal and freeze.

Rhubarb keeps beautifully without sugar or syrup. A quart makes one 9-inch pie.

STRAWBERRIES

Varieties suitable for freezing: excellent—Marshall, Sparkle, Gem, Senator Dunlap, and Fairfax. ⅔ quart yields approximately 1 pint.

Do not remove cap from fruit until after berries are washed. Sort and place in colander. Wash strawberries with fine spray, if possible. If not, dip colander in large container filled with very cold water. Gently lift colander up and down in water two or three times. Drain thoroughly.

To remove cap, use a sharp paring knife. Do not squeeze cap off with fingers. Slip knife directly under the cap, taking care not to cut through into the center of the fruit. Pry cap off.

Place fruit on tray covered with several thicknesses of absorbent paper toweling and put tray in refrigerator to chill the strawberries. Strawberries may be frozen in syrup or by adding sugar.

Add sugar in proportion of 2 tablespoons sugar to 1 cup strawberries. The drained and cooled strawberries may be placed in a bowl and the sugar sprinkled over them, or they may be sweetened in container in which they are to be frozen. When container is ¼ full, add ¼ of the sugar, repeating until container is filled.

Package in polyethylene bags or rigid containers. Seal and freeze at once.

WATERMELON

Variety suitable for freezing: any variety is fair for freezing if thoroughly ripened. Centers of melons are best to use.

Same as for cantaloupe.

Note: The freezer is an ideal place for quickly cooling a watermelon for picnics. Place whole melon in freezer for 3 or 4 hours.

Wash fruit in cold running water or use a gentle spray.

Use a sharp knife and gently remove strawberry cap.

Drain fruit on tray with absorbent paper toweling.

Fruit may be sweetened by mixing with sugar before packaging.

Sugar may be added alternately with fruit as it is packaged.

Seal tightly by twisting polyethylene. Fasten with acetate bands.

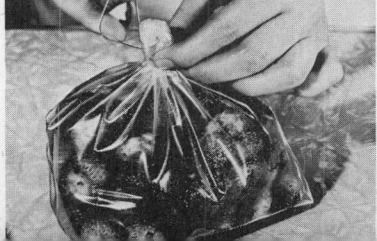

HOW TO PREPARE FROZEN FRUITS FOR SERVING

Always thaw fruit in the container in which it was frozen. This usually requires about 2 to 3 hours at room temperature.

Do not open the container until the fruit is nearly thawed . . . since frozen fruit, once thawed, collapses quickly.

Remove from freezer only the quantity of fruit you plan to use at one time.

Frozen fruit cannot satisfactorily be refrozen once it is thawed.

How to Freeze Fresh Vegetables

When to Gather or Buy Vegetables

Select only those which are in prime condition for freezing. In general, immature vegetables have not fully developed all their sweetness and flavor. Overripe vegetables will neither taste good nor keep satisfactorily. The best time to gather vegetables is in the cool of the morning when the dew is gone. Never pick vegetables at night and keep them in the refrigerator until the next day . . . they lose that garden-fresh flavor.

If you do not raise your own vegetables, buy freshly picked ones from local gardens or nearby farms. The vegetables you buy are satisfactory for freezing only if you *arrange to get them within an hour or two after picking.* Vegetables which have stood longer will not be as tender, nutritive or well-flavored as garden-fresh ones. Freezing captures and preserves the flavor and goodness but it cannot improve them. Frozen foods come from the freezer only as good as when they were frozen.

Speed Is Essential

Gather only as many vegetables as can be completely processed and placed in the freezer within two hours. The *"2 hours from vine to freezer"* rule is an excellent one to remember.

Wash, sort, scald, chill, drain, package, and freeze without wasting any time between steps.

Having all your supplies and materials ready before you begin is a big step toward accomplishing this "2-hour" rule.

Learn these steps, follow them closely and results will be excellent. Have all packaging materials ready before you start freezing. It saves valuable time.

1. Gather vegetables in the cool of morning, selecting the choice grades and only quantities that can be handled speedily.

2. Wash and sort vegetables carefully.

3. Scald according to directions for each vegetable.

4. Cool and drain quickly.

5. Pack in airtight containers.

6. Freeze at once.

7. Enter item in your freezer inventory file.

Which Vegetables to Select

Most vegetables can be frozen satisfactorily. Exceptions: salad greens, celery, radishes, and whole tomatoes. Certain varieties of vegetables freeze better than others. Directions for freezing specific vegetables rate varieties as to suitability for freezing. For success of freezing other varieties, consult your local seed company, county agent or State Agricultural College.

Wash and Sort Vegetables Carefully

Vegetables are prepared for freezing in much the same manner as for cooking. Wash carefully and thoroughly. While washing, sort for size and discard all inferior vegetables. For the best frozen vegetables, freeze only the choice fresh vegetables. Size-sorting of many vegetables (peas, beans, etc.) is important because you can obtain better uniformity.

Scald Vegetables Properly

Scalding is a must . . . never to be omitted! It retards enzymatic action, thus holds back the "growing process." Scalding "locks in" color, preserves flavor and saves vitamins so that, when served, the vegetable is as fresh as it was when taken from the garden.

Scald only one pound of any vegetable at a time. Live steam cannot penetrate evenly through larger amounts. Too many vegetables scalded at once may cause an inferior product.

Live Steam Scalding

This is the preferred method.

Necessary Equipment: Any large utensil with a tight-fitting cover, a trivet or rack, and a fine-mesh wire basket. If a wire basket is not available, a colander with small perforations may be used. It must not interfere with the cover's tight fit. If neither basket nor colander is available, loosely tie the vegetables in cheesecloth.

Procedure: Place rack in utensil. Add sufficient water to keep the utensil from boiling dry during scalding, but not enough to touch the vegetables.

Keep this water boiling vigorously throughout the entire scalding period.

Place vegetables into basket. When water is boiling violently, set basket in utensil and cover at once. Start counting scalding time when the lid is replaced.

Water Bath Scalding

Necessary Equipment: Large utensil with tight-fitting lid, (deep well cooker in electric range is ideal), fine-mesh wire basket or cheesecloth.

Procedure: Boil at least a gallon of water in the cooker or utensil. Have water boiling briskly so that temperature will not drop when vegetables are added.

Place vegetables in wire basket or tie loosely in cheesecloth. Lower basket into rapidly boiling water and cover immediately.

Start counting scalding time from the moment vegetables are placed in the boiling water.

Cool and Drain Quickly

Quick, effective cooling makes better frozen products. Draining is also most important. Moisture clinging to the vegetables when they are packed will form ice crystals and make it difficult to separate frozen vegetables when ready to cook.

Necessary Equipment: Large pan or sink filled with ice water, clean dish towels or absorbent paper toweling.

Procedure: Immediately after scalding, cool vegetables quickly in ice water.

With small vegetables (peas, beans, etc.) leave vegetables in container used during scalding and immerse it in ice water. Move basket back and forth to speed the cooling.

Drain thoroughly by placing several thicknesses of absorbent toweling on a tray. Carefully spread the vegetables on toweling. Shake tray slightly to bring all sides of vegetables in contact with toweling.

Package in Convenient Quantities

Determine the size packages that will best suit your family's needs. For instance, a pint carton of vegetables will usually serve 3 large or 4 small portions. A quart carton will serve from 6 to 8 portions. Containers larger than pints and quarts are not recommended for average-sized families because they waste valuable freezer space. Also food not eaten at one meal may be wasted as it is never advisable to refreeze thawed vegetables.

If freezing for a family of two, freeze in one bag just enough to serve two persons and enclose several of these bags in a larger one. Mark number of smaller bags on outside of larger one.

Never Skimp on Packaging

Buy only packaging materials that are both moistureproof and vaporproof.

Glass freezing jars and outer cardboard cartons may be used over and over again.

Polyethylene bags may be washed and reused providing they are free from pricks and holes.

Plain tin cans, which can be sealed airtight, may also be used except for asparagus and New Zealand spinach, which require enamel or lacquer-lined cans.

Freezing always results in expansion of the food; therefore it is necessary to leave head space to allow for this expansion.

Pint cartons: $1/2$-inch head space.
Quart cartons: $3/4$-inch head space.
Glass jars: 1- to $11/2$-inch head space.
Tin cans: 1-inch head space.

Seal Carefully

Be sure all packages are airtight!

To close polyethylene bags: Put food in polyethylene bag. Then, starting at the bottom, *gently* press all the air out the bag. When the top of the food is reached, twist the top of the bag tightly several times. Loop the top of the bag over and secure tightly with either a piece of string or an acetate band. Rubber bands do not hold at low temperatures.

Freeze at Once

When packages are filled, sealed and labeled, place them immediately in the freezer. If this is not practical, place packages in freezer compartment of refrigerator until you are ready to load the freezer.

Never allow filled packages to stand at room temperature.

A Hint for Mothers of Small Children

When sorting vegetables such as green beans, peas, carrots, or beets, you will find some that are too mature for freezing. Set these aside until after you have frozen the rest. These can be cooked, puréed, frozen, and used later for the baby and young children.

Here's how it's done: Steam the vegetable until it is well cooked . . . not overcooked. Purée in an electric food blender or by forcing through a food mill. Thoroughly cool the puréed vegetable.

After vegetable is cool, pour into refrigerator ice cube tray with the dividers in place. Freeze. When cubes are firmly frozen, remove them from the tray and package one or two cubes, enough for an individual serving, in small polyethylene bags.

To serve: Heat cubes in a covered saucepan. Start with low heat until food is thawed.

How to Prepare Vegetables for Freezing

ASPARAGUS

(Do not use iron utensil ... will discolor asparagus.)

Varieties suitable for freezing: excellent—Mary Washington and Martha Washington. 1½ pounds yield approximately 1 pint.

Scalding time:

Small Spears
By steam, 5 minutes.
By boiling water, 3 minutes.

Large Spears
By steam, 6 minutes.
By boiling water, 4 minutes.

Wash thoroughly. Discard all woody portions. Sort by size of butt end.

Cut stalks correct length to fit polyethylene bag—usually about 5 inches for quart-sized bag.

If you are planning to wrap asparagus in freezer foil, it is not necessary to cut all stalks a specific length.

Remove all scales by slipping sharp knife under scale and snipping off. Sand collects under these scales. Also, sweetness of frozen product is much improved if scales are removed. Do not bruise stem.

When scalding, stand asparagus with tips up. Cool and drain. Pack stalks parallel in polyethylene bags or freezer foil, placing heads in opposite directions. Freeze at once.

BEANS, GREEN SNAP OR YELLOW WAX

(Do not use iron utensil ... will discolor beans.)

Varieties suitable for freezing: Green snap, excellent—Tendergreen, Stringless Green Pod, Kentucky Wonder. Yellow wax, fair—consult your local seed man. ⅔ to 1 pound yields approximately 1 pint.

Scalding time:

By steam, 5 minutes.
By boiling water, 3 minutes.

Wash thoroughly. Sort for size. Remove the stem end. Leave blossom end on, it is particularly rich in vitamins and minerals.

For quick preparation, grasp as many beans as can be easily held in one hand. With small, sharp knife held in other hand, snip off stem end. Cut in 1-inch pieces, or in French style.

Do not scald small and large beans together. Cool, drain, pack and freeze. Package in polyethylene bags.

BEANS, LIMA

Varieties suitable for freezing: excellent—Fordhook (bush) and King of the Garden (pole). 2 to 2½ pounds in pods yield approximately 1 pint.

Scalding time:

Baby Lima Beans
By steam, 5 minutes.
By boiling water, 3 minutes.

Large Fordhook
By steam, 6 minutes.
By boiling water, 4 minutes.

Wash pods, shell beans. Sort for size. Overmatured beans are not recommended for freezing. Scald, cool and drain. Package in polyethylene bags. Freeze.

Lima beans still in their pods may be scalded in boiling water for 1 minute longer than shelled beans. Then cool, shell, drain, sort and package.

BEETS

Variety suitable for freezing: good—Detroit Dark Red. 1¼ pounds, without tops, yield approximately 1 pint.

Scalding time:

Young tender beets, up to 1½ inches in diameter, 3 minutes submerged in boiling water. **All other beets,** cook until tender.

Wash thoroughly before scalding or cooking. Immediately after scalding, cool beets and remove skin.

Small beets may be frozen whole. Large beets may be sliced, diced or quartered.

Cool, drain on absorbent paper toweling, pack in polyethylene bags. Freeze.

BROCCOLI

Variety suitable for freezing: excellent—Italian Green Sprouting. 2 pounds yield approximately 1 pint.

Scalding time:

Medium-Sized Pieces
By steam, 5 minutes.
By boiling water, 3 minutes.

Large Pieces
By steam, 6 minutes.
By boiling water, 5 minutes.

Select compact heads of uniform color. Immerse broccoli for ½ hour in a solution of salt water to remove any insects. Use 1 cup salt to 1 gallon of water. Wash carefully.

Remove woody portions. Separate heads in convenient size for packaging.

Scald, cool and drain. Package in freezer foil or polyethylene bags. Freeze.

Scald not more than one pound of any vegetable at one time.

Cool vegetable quickly by immersing in ice water.

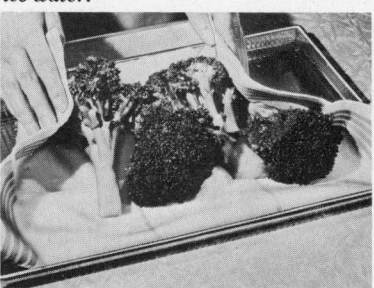
Drain vegetable thoroughly on absorbent toweling.

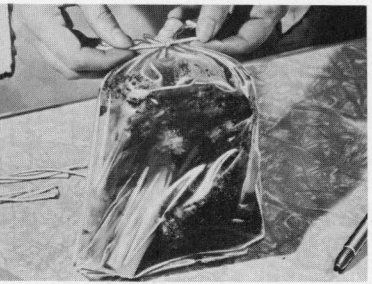
Package and gently force out any air pockets. Seal securely. Freeze immediately.

BRUSSELS SPROUTS

Variety suitable for freezing: excellent—Long Island Improved. 1½ pounds yield approximately 1 pint.

Scalding time:

By steam, 5 minutes.
By boiling water, 4 minutes.

Sprouts should be firm and dark green in color.

Immerse in salt water as for broccoli. Remove stem. If wilted, remove the outer leaves.

Scald, cool, drain, package in polyethylene bags. Freeze. Allow 5 to 6 sprouts to a serving.

CARROTS

Varieties suitable for freezing: excellent—Chantenay, Red Cored, Half Long. 1¼ to 1½ pounds yield approximately 1 pint.

Scalding time:

Sliced

By steam, 4 minutes.
By boiling water, 2 minutes.

Whole

By steam, 5 minutes.
By boiling water, 3 minutes.

Select only young, small carrots. Never attempt to freeze carrots which have grown to full maturity.

Wash and scrape. Sort for size. Scald, cool, drain and package in polyethylene bags.

Alternate top and tip of whole carrots when packaging. Package. Freeze.

CAULIFLOWER

Variety suitable for freezing: good—Snowball. 1 pound yields approximately 1 pint.

Scalding time:

By steam, 4 minutes.
By boiling water, 3 minutes.

Select compact, tender white heads. Trim and cut in pieces about 1 inch thick, or break small flowerets in medium-sized pieces.

Sometimes it is necessary to immerse cauliflower in a salt solution (as for broccoli) to remove insects.

Allow 5 to 6 medium pieces for each serving.

Scald, cool, drain and package in polyethylene bags. Remove as much air as possible from the package. Freeze.

CORN ON THE COB

(Follow directions and corn will be just like fresh-picked.)

Varieties suitable for freezing: excellent—Golden Bantam Hybrids, Golden Cross Bantam, Cherokee, DeKalb Hybrid.

Scalding time:

By boiling water—ears 1½ to 2 inches at base, 8 minutes.

Larger ears require 11 minutes.

Select corn with kernels well formed, while milk is thin and sweet.

Corn on the cob frozen at the peak of summertime perfection is undeniably a treat on a winter menu. The prepared corn may be wrapped individually in freezer wrap, and taped securely.

With sharp knife, cut a section about ½ inch wide from both ends. Husks will come off easier. Husk corn and remove silk.

If necessary, wash corn. Sort for size. Scald for length of time indicated and cool in ice water the same length of time. Drain.

Package in freezer foil or polyethylene bags according to your family's serving needs . . . with not more than 6 ears to a package. Freeze.

CORN, WHOLE KERNEL

Varieties suitable for freezing: Same as corn on the cob. 6 ears yield approximately 1 pint when cut from cob.

Scalding time:

Same as for corn on the cob.

Scald corn. Cool. To remove kernels from cob: Impale base end of cob on large nail driven through a board.

Place in flat dish or on two thicknesses of waxed paper.

Cut corn from cob, holding knife not flat but at a sharp angle.

Examine kernels carefully, removing any bits of silk. Package in polyethylene bags. Freeze.

EGGPLANT

Variety suitable for freezing: good—Black Beauty. 1½ to 2 pounds yield approximately 1 pint.

Scalding time:

By steam, 5 minutes.
By boiling water, 4 minutes.

Select mature eggplant. Peel and cut into about ½-inch slices.

If boiling water method of scalding is used, add 4½ teaspoons pure citric acid to 1 gallon of water.

If steam method is used, add same amount of citric acid, or 3 tablespoons lemon juice, to cooling water.

Put through another cold water rinse. Drain.

Place waxed paper between each slice. Package in polyethylene bags or aluminum foil. Freeze.

GREENS

(Spinach, Kale, Swiss Chard, Mustard Greens, and Turnip Tops)

Varieties suitable for freezing: Spinach, good—King of Denmark. Kale excellent—Dwarf Green Curled. Swiss chard, excellent—Fordhook. Mustard, good—Mammoth. 1 to 1½ pounds yield approximately 1 pint.

Spinach, Kale, Swiss Chard

Scalding time:

By steam, 2½ minutes. Best method: Use wire basket, if possible.
By boiling water, 2 minutes.

Mustard Greens and Turnip Tops

Scalding time:

By steam, 3 to 3½ minutes.
By boiling water, 2 minutes.

Use 2 gallons of water for each pound of greens.

Select young, tender greens. Discard all bruised leaves and cut off stems before washing.

Wash through several waters. *Lift* leaves from one pan of water to the other . . . don't pour off water . . . it may leave sand on the leaves.

Scald only a small amount of greens at one time, and wire basket is preferable. This is particularly true of spinach. Drain.

Complete draining of spinach is impossible, some water will remain in leaves.

If these suggestions are followed, there will be little matting of greens. Do not use pressure when packing. Polyethylene bags are excellent for greens of all kinds. Freeze.

MUSHROOMS

Scalding time:

Button Size—Steam 3 minutes.

Medium Size—Steam 4 minutes.

Sliced—Steam 3 minutes.

Warning: Unless you are completely familiar with wild mushrooms and can accurately identify edible ones, never attempt to freeze them.

Mushrooms must be handled quickly to prevent blackening.

Wash thoroughly. Remove tough portion of stem. Scald, cool quickly and drain.

Package in polyethylene bags. Start freezing immediately to avoid darkening.

OKRA

Varieties suitable for freezing: good—Clemson Spineless, White Lightning. 1½ pounds yield approximately 1 pint.

Scalding time:

Small to Medium Pods—Steam 2 minutes. This is the only method recommended for okra.

Select young, tender pods. Scrub thoroughly. Rinse.

Remove stem end but do not cut into seed section. Care in cutting prevents the sticky juice from oozing out.

Scald, cool and drain. Pack compactly in polyethylene bags . . . alternating top and tip ends. Freeze.

PEAS

Varieties suitable for freezing: Green, excellent—Thomas Laxton and Alderman. Field, very good—Crowder and Black Eye. 1½ to 2 pounds yield approximately 1 pint.

Peas, Continued

Scalding time:

By steam, 3 minutes.
By boiling water, 1 minute.

Select peas that are tender and are not fully matured.

Wash pods before shelling. Discard all immature and wrinkled peas while shelling. If pods are very full and difficult to shell, plunge pods in boiling water for 1 minute, then cool at once in ice water.

Scalding the pods does not take the place of scalding the peas. Scald, cool, drain and package in polyethylene bags. Freeze at once.

PIMIENTOS AND GREEN PEPPERS

Varieties suitable for freezing: Pimientos, excellent—Perfection. Green peppers, very good—California Wonder.

Sliced or Diced: Do not scald! Wash carefully, remove stem end and seeds.

Slice or dice and package in small polyethylene bags in amounts you will use at one time. Several small bags may be packaged in a pint or quart carton. Freeze at once.

Halved for Stuffing: Cut green pepper in half, lengthwise. Remove stem end and seeds.

Scald in boiling water 2 minutes. Cool in ice water, drain well.

When packaging, separate halves with waxed paper, place in polyethylene bags. Freeze immediately.

SQUASH

Variety suitable for freezing: excellent—Yellow Summer. 1 pound yields approximately 1 pint.

Scalding time:

By steam, 3 minutes.

Select squash not fully matured. Outer skin should be easily punctured with fingernail.

Wash thoroughly. Use a vegetable brush to remove dirt lodged in crevices.

Remove stem end. Do not peel. Cut in $\frac{1}{2}$- to 1-inch slices. Do not remove seeds.

Scald. Cool $1\frac{1}{2}$ to 2 minutes. To avoid longer soaking, use quantities of ice in the water.

Drain carefully. Package in polyethylene bags. Freeze.

SUCCOTASH

Prepare corn and lima beans as given under directions for each. Use baby beans only.

Steam corn first, and while it is cooling and being cut from cob, scald and cool the beans.

Mix together in equal portions. Package in polyethylene bags. Freeze.

HOW TO PREPARE FROZEN VEGETABLES FOR SERVING

All vegetables . . . *except* corn on the cob and eggplant . . . are best cooked from the frozen state.

Break frozen vegetables into 3 or 4 chunks before placing in pan. Add about $\frac{1}{4}$ cup of water. Salt to taste.

Cook about $\frac{1}{3}$ to $\frac{1}{2}$ of the time recommended for fresh vegetables. Frozen vegetables are scalded before freezing, so need less cooking time.

Corn on the cob and eggplant should be thawed before cooking. Thaw at room temperature. Thawing requires about 20 minutes for eggplant; 2 hours for corn on the cob.

Cook corn in boiling water 4 to 5 minutes.

Prepare eggplant according to your favorite method.

Caution: Do not overcook vegetables . . . either frozen or fresh. Overcooking causes loss of color and flavor, as well as vitamins.

How to Freeze Meats, Poultry and Game

Freezing meat is quite easy. Only a few simple rules must be followed to assure a delicious product.

When selecting or specifying animals for freezing, choose healthy ones of the size and finish which will produce the weight and quality of cuts preferred by the family.

Excessive finish or fatness is unnecessary, but an ample fat covering increases the desirability of the meat and protects the lean from drying out during the frozen storage. This does not apply to veal which rarely has surplus fat.

The same general rules apply to meats purchased from a meat market or produce house. Ask for quality cuts from prime cattle. If the meat dealer knows you intend to freeze the meat, he may be more careful in his selection and will trim it to your preference.

Proper Wrapping of Meat Is Important

The quality of frozen meat is partly determined by the proper selection of wrapping material and the method of wrapping.

Improper wrapping results in "drying out" of meat and game which affects both the appearance and flavor. This condition is called "freezer burn."

It is unwise to attempt to economize on wrapping materials. Regular butcher paper, ordinary waxed paper, or grocery bags must never be used.

Polyethylene laminated to aluminum foil is best. Aluminum foil with a stockinette outer wrap is also satisfactory.

If a bone protrudes, use a double thickness of waxed paper as "padding" over the bone, then wrap all in aluminum foil. Be sure to work as much air as possible out of the packages before sealing.

Wrapping of meat is simple, yet requires care. Wrappings for meats must be moisture-vaporproof, easy to handle, tough enough to resist tearing and easy to label.

Keep meat cool both during and immediately after wrapping.

When wrapping, the foil must be pulled tightly around the meat to eliminate all posssible air. The finished package should be smooth and firmly packed to conserve storage space.

Place two sheets of waxed paper or polyethylene between chops, steaks, or hamburg patties (if they are to be wrapped together) to facilitate separating them when ready to use. This also makes it easier to broil or pan fry meat from the frozen state.

In general, each package should contain the meat needed for a single meal for the family.

Which Meats to Select

When selecting or specifying meats for freezing, choose healthy ones which will produce the weight and quality of cuts preferred by the family.

Excessive fatness is unnecessary, but an ample fat covering is desirable and protects the lean from drying out during frozen storage. This does not apply to veal since it rarely has surplus fat.

As often as possible, try to select quality meat that is U. S. Government graded. A stamp (a harmless vegetable dye) will appear on all major portions of the carcass. Grading classifies meat according to relative tenderness and quality. Beef and veal grades are: Prime, Choice, Good, Commercial, and Utility. Lamb is graded Prime, Choice, and Good. Pork is of such uniformity that it is not generally graded.

Chill Meat Thoroughly

Meat should be chilled promptly, once the carcass has been prepared. Chilling removes body heat and arrests the destructive growth of bacteria, molds and yeasts which multiply rapidly at temperatures around 70°F., but slowly at temperatures between 30°F. to 40°F. Improper chilling may ruin the flavor of the meat or even render it unfit for use.

Cut Meat to Family Preferences

Again, this is no job for the novice. Most locker plants employ expert meat cutters or can direct you to one. Specify the cuts your family enjoys most and have the meat cut in family-sized portions. This eliminates waste.

Boning meat is recommended because less storage space is required and the danger of bones puncturing the wrapping is eliminated.

Label Clearly

After the meat is packaged, the next important step is proper labeling. Write on the package the type meat enclosed, the approximate number of servings and the date of the packaging. If meat is to be used with a definite recipe, label accordingly.

Start Freezing Immediately

Just as soon as the meat is packaged and labeled, it should be placed in the freezer. If this is not practical, place the packages in the freezer compartment of your refrigerator until ready to load the freezer. Do not allow packaged meat to remain at room temperature any longer than is absolutely necessary.

Do Not Refreeze
Thawed Uncooked Meat

Never refreeze thawed uncooked meat! The meat will still be good but some of the flavor will be lost. Uncooked meat, that you wish to refreeze, must be cooked first.

A Guide to Remember: Meat may be frozen successfully once when raw and once after it has been cooked.

Consult a Skilled Beef Cutter

For meat of high quality, it is imperative that the carcass be properly prepared and chilled. Few persons, except skilled meat cutters, know how to do this correctly.

If weather is not cold enough to do a proper job of chilling, make advance arrangements to have the cleaned and dressed carcass removed immediately to a chilling room. The temperature of slaughtered meat is around 100°F. and body temperature of the carcass must be reduced to between 33°F. and 40°F. within 24 hours after slaughtering.

Beef should be aged, but that is a job for the expert. Aging or ripening tenderizes and improves the flavor of the beef. Prime beef with a one-inch coating of fat all over should be aged a little longer than the poorer qualities of beef.

Cutting the Beef

If the beef carcass is from a reasonably young, well-bred and well-fed animal, the rib and top round can be cut into satisfactory steaks and the first cuts of the rib and arm side of the chuck are usually sufficiently tender to be cooked as oven roasts.

If the animal was old and thin, even the loin steaks may not be sufficiently tender for broiling or frying, but should be cut for braising.

If there is any doubt as to the suitability of the meat for various cuts and methods of cooking, it is advisable to engage an expert cutter who will help you in classifying the meat cuts.

Roasts are usually boned and rolled to save space. Also the bone may be removed from the rump and arm pieces cut from the chuck.

Less-tender cuts such as shank, brisket, plate, neck and flank are most often boned, then ground, or cut into one-inch cubes without gristle or too much fat, and packaged in suitable amounts for stews and casserole dishes.

Ground meat is not salted before freezing. If it is to be broiled or fried, make into patties before wrapping. A pound of meat makes 6 generous-size hamburg patties. If this is done before freezing, it is not necessary to thaw the patties before cooking.

The liver may be sliced before freezing. The heart and tongue may be cleaned and frozen whole.

Packaging and wrapping of beef is same as for all meats. Freeze at once. *Quality meat properly wrapped, frozen, and stored should come out of the freezer juicy, full of flavor, and bright in color.*

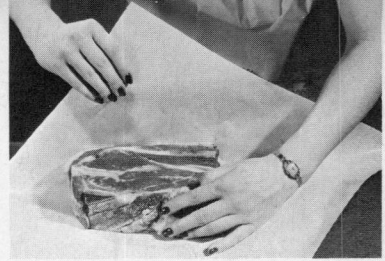

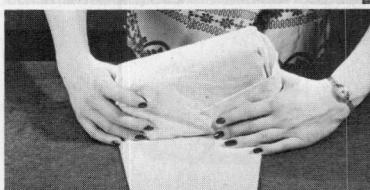

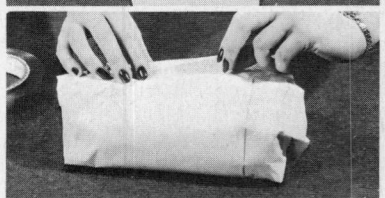

To wrap meats for the freezer, either a "drug store wrap" or a "butcher's wrap" may be used, as you choose, These illustrations show the butcher's wrap. Fasten the loose end securely with freezer tape. Label with date, kind of meat, cut, and number of servings or weight. Freeze quickly, and store at 0°F. or lower.

Approximate Yield of Beef Carcass

Live weight			750 lbs.
Whole carcass			420 lbs.

Trimmed cuts from whole carcass:	Live Weight	Carcass Weight	
Steaks and oven roasts	23%	40%	172 lbs.
Pot roasts	11%	20%	83 lbs.
Stews and ground meat	11%	20%	83 lbs.
	45%	80%	338 lbs.*
Forequarters will yield:			
Steaks and oven roasts		25%	55 lbs.
Pot roasts		32%	70 lbs.
Stews and ground meat		27%	59 lbs.
		84%	184 lbs.
Hindquarters will yield:			
Steaks, oven roasts and pot roasts		58%	117 lbs.
Stews and ground meat		18%	37 lbs.
		76%	154 lbs.

("Freezing Meat," U.S. Dept. of Agriculture Bulletin AW1-75)

* The loss of 82 pounds between the actual yield of finished product and the dressed carcass is due to bones which are removed before packaging, plus normal shrinkage, fat and meat trimming, and the liver, tongue and heart. To conserve freezer space, it is advisable to remove as much bone as possible, as well as unnecessary fat.

LAMB

Lamb may carry a fat covering which is comparable to the various grades of beef. Since it comes from an animal which is less than a year old, any longer than a five-day holding or aging period would result in excessive shrinkage.

The weight of the dressed carcass is usually about half that of the live animal.

As with all other meat, rapid chilling is extremely important. Since the lamb is small, the temperature of the carcass should reach between 33°F. and 40°F. in 24 hours or less. Longer first chilling is apt to destroy the fine flavor of the meat.

Lamb is packaged as other meats. Label and freeze at once.

VEAL

The calf should weigh from 110 to 200 pounds. As with beef, it is desirable to cut veal to suit the immediate needs of the family.

The veal carcass will yield about 80 to 90 pounds of roasts, chops, stew and ground meat.

The hindquarter of the veal is cut into round, rump, loin and flank.

The forequarter is cut into shank, shoulder, rack and breast. Cutlets are made from the round. The loin and rack may be cut into chops.

The rump, shoulder and breast may be boned, rolled and tied for roasting. The flanks and shanks are usually ground.

Veal is slaughtered and cared for in the same manner as beef. However, because veal has little or no fat, it is packaged immediately after the chilling period is finished, and does not go through any aging process.

Veal must be chilled to 33°F. to 40°F. within 24 hours after slaughtering.

Veal should be packaged or wrapped immediately after chilling. Freeze at once.

Store meats in small packages wherever possible. They freeze more quickly and thus retain more of their original quality.

Approximate Yield of Pork Carcass

Live weight			225 lbs.
Whole carcass			176 lbs.

Trimmed cuts:	Live Weight	Carcass Weight	
Fresh hams, shoulders, bacon, jowls	40%	50%	90 lbs.
Loins, ribs, sausage	15%	20%	34 lbs.
	55%	70%	124 lbs.
Lard, rendered	12%	15%	27 lbs.

("Freezing Meat," U.S. Dept. of Agriculture Bulletin, AWI-75)

PORK

Pork is a highly perishable meat, and great care must be exercised in caring for the carcass after the hog is slaughtered.

Pork may sour in 12 hours if hung at warm air temperatures; therefore, *rapid chilling is essential.* The carcass must cool to between 33°F. and 40°F. in a maximum of 24 hours.

Immediately after the chilling, the carcass should be cut, wrapped and frozen.

Pork does not require aging; on the contrary, the speedier pork can be frozen after chilling, the better the quality of the frozen meat.

When to Butcher Pork

On the farm, butchering should be done when the weather is as favorable as possible. Temperatures between 33°F. and 40°F. are best.

Should the weather be extremely cold, hang the carcass in a shed and protect it from freezing by wrapping with a sheet.

If the hog is butchered in warm weather, and chilling facilities are not available at home, arrangements should be made with your local locker plant or meat market to hang the carcass in their chilling rooms immediately after the carcass is cut and cleaned. These arrangements should be made in advance.

Cutting the Pork

As with beef, pork should be cut in family-sized pieces.

Chops should be cut in size desirable for frying.

The hams and bacon are usually cured, but the shoulders may be sliced for frying, or cut into roasts for freezing. Fresh ham may be sliced for frying or cut into roasts.

Spareribs consume considerable room in a storage compartment due to their bony structure. However, frozen spareribs are excellent and keep as satisfactorily as any other portion of the hog.

Speed Chilling of Pork

Split the warm hog and pull the leaf fat as soon as the internal organs have been removed. It also aids chilling to remove the head before hanging.

Unless care is taken, the fat bellies and hams of warm, freshly slaughtered hogs often overlap each other during the cooling process, which closes the body cavity to air circulation. Warm hogs, carelessly hung, will frequently show spoilage the next day, even when held at low temperature.

Whole or half carcasses should be suspended to chill so they do not touch. Never lay hog carcasses on floor to chill. When hams touch each other, chilling is frequently delayed too long and spoilage is the result.

If warm carcasses are held overnight at temperatures slightly above freezing, the internal temperature of the hams will not always be below 40°F. It is suggested that cuts from such meat be spread out during the second night to permit complete chilling.

It is imperative that pork be completely chilled before freezing, even though it delays the wrapping of the meat an additional 12 to 24 hours.

If a ham thermometer is available, test the temperature of the large pieces with it. The need for prompt and thorough chilling of warm carcasses cannot be overemphasized. The heavier and fatter the hog, the greater is the need for careful handling.

Such meats as pork chops and lamb chops will retain their natural flavor and moisture content longer if cut thick for freezing.

Approximate Yield of Lamb Carcass

Live weight			85 lbs.
Whole carcass			41 lbs.

Trimmed cuts:	Live Weight	Carcass Weight	
Legs, chops, shoulders	37%	75%	31 lbs.
Breast and stew	8%	15%	7 lbs.
	45%	90%	38 lbs.

("Lamb and Mutton on the Farm," U.S. Dept. of Agriculture Bulletin 1807)

SAUSAGE, CURED HAMS, BACON

These pork products do not lend well to freezing and should not be kept over 3 weeks. The salt used as a seasoning and preservative activates oxidation which, in turn, results in rancidity.

Sausage

Freezing seasoned sausage is a controversial subject at present. Many authorities state that sausage is the only meat which may be seasoned before freezing. Seasoning includes the addition of salt, black pepper, red pepper, sage, smoking or the addition of cereals. According to Dr. J. G. Woodroof of the Georgia Experiment Station, smoking improves flavor, stabilizes color, partially sterilizes the meat, improves appearance, increases tenderness, prevents rancidity and drives off up to 20% of the water.

Cured Hams and Bacon

Cured hams may be frozen either sliced or whole. Bacon also may be frozen, but does not adapt itself as well to freezing as does ham.

If the bacon is sliced before freezing, dehydration may occur.

If the supply of bacon is greater than can be used within a limited time, it may be desirable to freeze a portion of it.

It is advisable to cut the smoked bacon into 1- or 2-pound slabs, wrap, freeze, take out packages as needed and slice after thawing.

RABBITS AND OTHER SMALL GAME*

Freeze rabbits and other small game in much the same way as poultry.

Immediately after killing, skin, behead and remove entrails. The carcass should then be thoroughly and carefully washed, chilled and cut into pieces for cooking.

Package as for chicken fricassee.

VENISON AND OTHER LARGE GAME*

Prepare, package and freeze in much the same way as beef or veal.

*Note: Some states do not permit game to be kept more than 10 days. Consult your game warden or State Conservation Department before freezing game for longer storage.

How Long May Meat Be Held at 0°?

This also is a controversial subject and depends upon many factors, such as proper slaughtering, chilling, aging, wrapping and the speed with which the meat starts on its way to being frozen, after wrapping. However, the

Government Bulletin, "Freezing Meat and Poultry Products" AWI-75, gives the following times at 0°F:

Product	Storage Period
Ground meat	1 to 3 months
Fresh pork and fish	3 to 6 months
Lamb and veal	6 to 9 months
Beef, poultry and eggs	6 to 12 months

HOW TO COOK FROZEN MEATS

There are two satisfactory methods of cooking frozen meats: (1) remove from frozen storage, unwrap and cook from the frozen state or (2) thaw before cooking the meat.

Cooking meats from the frozen state is preferred as there is a minimum loss of weight and juices, resulting in better flavor and a more tender piece of meat... but it is necessary to add extra minutes to the cooking time.

Roasting: A five-pound roast thaws completely in about 24 hours at room temperature.

If placed in the food compartment of a refrigerator, it requires from 36 to 48 hours to thaw.

If roasts are thawed, and if there is any doubt of the complete thawing of the meat, allow longer roasting time than for fresh meat.

In roasting meat from the frozen state, add an additional 15 to 20 minutes per pound of meat.

The ideal method is to place the meat in the oven immediately after removing from the freezer.

When the meat is completely thawed, place a meat thermometer through the thickest part and cook by temperature. The meat thermometer is the most accurate method of cooking meat whether it is frozen or fresh.

Broiling: Broiling steaks from the frozen state requires an additional 10 to 15 minutes per side, depending upon the degree of broiling desired.

From tests which we have conducted, we have found broiling from the frozen state gives a juicier and better-flavored steak.

Caution About Cooking Pork

Pork must be thoroughly cooked whether it is cooked from the frozen or thawed state.

Allow an additional 15 to 20 minutes per pound of pork.

One may become infected with a serious disease called Trichinosis through the eating of pork which has not been thoroughly cooked. There is some belief that freezing kills trichinae, but until that fact is definitely proved, frozen pork should be given the same thorough cooking as fresh pork.

WRAPPING HAMBURGER PATTIES WITH PLASTIC WRAP

1. The "butcher wrap" method is convenient for ground beef patties. Separate patties with small pieces of plastic wrap, turn stack on its side, and place diagonally on the large outer piece of wrap. Smooth the back corner of wrap forward across the patties as closely as possible.

2. Fold in each side in turn, pressing snugly to the meat to eliminate as much air as possible. Be sure to use enough wrap to allow for a sufficient overlap as each corner is folded into place.

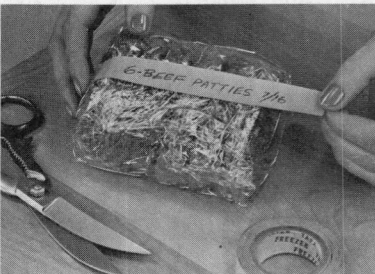

3. After sides are folded in, bring up the remaining corner, pulling it up tightly. Seal with freezer tape and label. Wrapping in this way makes individual patties easy to remove if you do not need them all at one time.

Time-saver hint: When making meat loaf for a family dinner, prepare a double or triple quantity. Freeze the remainder as individual meat loaves in a muffin tin. Package singly or in family size units.

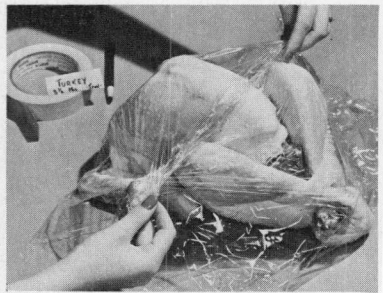

The same basic guides for success in freezing meat also apply to the freezing of poultry. All kinds of poultry may be frozen, but freeze only birds of high quality.

Wrap Poultry Carefully

Poultry must be protected so that it will not lose moisture or flavor during freezing or storage.

Poorly wrapped birds dry out and are tough and dry when cooked. This condition is often referred to as "freezer burn."

Birds may also become rancid or take on foreign flavors if not properly wrapped.

Polyethylene laminated to Aluminum Foil (best)—Can be molded easily to shape of bird. No outer wrap necessary.

Aluminum Foil (recommended)—Can be smoothed to conform to the shape of the bird, thus eliminating air pockets. Use outer wrap for extra protection.

Polyethylene (recommended)—Wrap polyethylene sheets or bags carefully around the bird and force out any air pockets which might form during wrapping. Secure tightly. Use outer wrap of stockinette for extra protection.

Cut-Up Poultry

Cut-up poultry can be packed in aluminum foil, polyethylene bags or wrapped in laminated paper to form a neat, compact package.

To Freeze Giblets

Clean giblets thoroughly and package in polyethylene bags for freezing.

Seal Securely

Inner wrappings should be securely sealed with acetate tape.

Protective sheet wrappings should also be sealed with acetate tape. If stockinette is used, knot ends tightly against bird.

Aluminum foil is sealed securely if edges are tightly folded and pressed firmly against bird. No further sealing is necessary.

Label Informatively

With china marking pencil or water-proof ink, make notation of kind of poultry, how prepared, weight and date of freezing.

If a stockinette outer covering is used, the information can be written on a slip of paper and placed between the stockinette and inner wrapping before ends are secured.

Thaw Poultry Before Stuffing

Frozen poultry must be thawed completely before stuffing.

It may be thawed in one of three ways: (1) at room temperature, (2) in the refrigerator for slow defrosting, or (3) in a 300°F. oven for quickest defrosting.

Do not soak frozen poultry in water to speed thawing.

A whole chicken requires 6 to 8 hours to thaw at room temperature or 3 to 5 hours per pound if thawed in the main food compartment of refrigerator.

An average-sized turkey requires 24 to 36 hours to thaw at room temperature. This same turkey will thaw in about 2 hours in a 300°F. oven.

Caution When Freezing Poultry

The American Institute of Baking states that poultry (chicken, duck, turkey, and other birds) should never be stuffed before it is frozen!

Extensive research done by the American Institute of Baking indicates that three different organisms which are frequently found in poultry can cause extreme illness—even death. While it is true that a sufficiently high oven temperature will destroy most of these organisms, the thawing time of a frozen stuffed bird is so slow that it makes a perfect "breeding ground" for these bacteria.

Therefore, the American Institute of Baking recommends that all poultry be frozen without stuffing . . . and then, after thawing, the bird may be stuffed just before it is placed in the oven for roasting.

The Institute also recommends a dry stuffing in preference to a moist one.

The stuffing may be made the evening before it is to be used, and stored in the refrigerator overnight.

The frozen bird, if kept at room temperature overnight, will be thawed sufficiently by morning to permit easy stuffing. In this way, the bird may be stuffed quickly on the morning it is to be roasted.

Note: Commercially frozen stuffed turkeys are frozen under carefully controlled conditions which cannot be duplicated in the home and hence are safe to use. Follow the cooking directions on the wrapper. *Do not thaw* commercially frozen stuffed poultry before cooking.

HOW TO COOK FROZEN POULTRY

For Frying or Fricassee: Frozen pieces of chicken or young turkey may be rolled in seasoned flour and fried immediately without any preliminary thawing. Or, pieces may be thawed and fried the same as unfrozen chicken.

For Stewing: Remove wrapping and place frozen chicken in kettle. Cover with boiling water and cook as unfrozen chicken.

For Broiling: Broil without any preliminary thawing. Put broiler pan at least 5 inches away from broiling unit.

Allow 20 to 30 additional minutes for each half chicken.

Otherwise, thaw broilers overnight and cook as unfrozen broilers.

WRAPPING POULTRY FOR FREEZING

1. Wrap giblets separately and place in center of wrap. Arrange legs and wings around them.

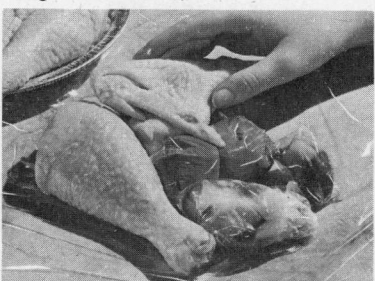

2. Fit thighs, breast, and back pieces compactly together on top. Using the drug store wrap shown, fold wrap down tightly.

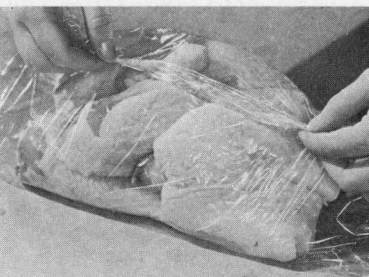

3. Fold in ends of wrap and seal with freezer tape. Label with type of poultry and date.

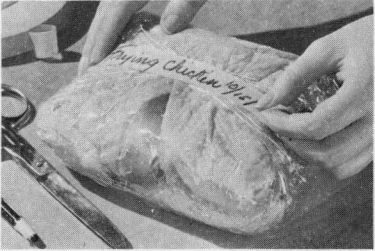

How to Freeze Fish and Shellfish

Fish is an exceptionally perishable food. Contamination by bacteria from the air and water begins within a few hours after they are caught.

Chilling fish with ice or placing in the household refrigerator retards bacterial action but does not prevent it. Organisms which attack fish normally live at lower temperatures than those which attack meats. Speed in preparing and freezing fish is, therefore, essential.

The storage period for frozen fish is relatively short. One to three months usually is considered the maximum.

Selection for Freezing

Fish that contain a high fat content, such as salmon, mackerel, carp, and herring, do not keep as long or as satisfactorily as the non-oily varieties, such as halibut, haddock, and trout.

Preparation for Freezing

Fish to be frozen should be prepared for freezing immediately after catching. Or, in case of delay, it should be promptly packed in quantities of ice.

Prepare as for cooking. Remove fins, tails, entrails, and scales, if any. Fillet large fish. Rinse or dip in salt water, about 1 cup pickling salt to 1 gallon of water.

Individual servings of fish are more convenient to use if first wrapped in polyethylene or aluminum foil.

To prevent any possible exchange of odors with other foods during storage, the individually wrapped packages should be wrapped in a second layer of aluminum foil, polyethylene bag, or laminated papers.

Two pieces of waxed paper between the individual fillets or slices of fish will not only aid the retention of the original quality, but facilitate handling when preparing for cooking.

Place two sheets of waxed paper between fish fillets so they will be easy to separate when frozen.

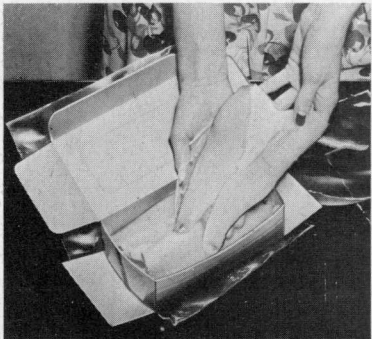

HOW TO FREEZE CRABS AND LOBSTERS

In sections of the country where crabs and lobsters are available, it is often desirable to freeze their meat. Frozen meat is excellent, makes delicious salads.

Lobsters are handled the same as crabs.

1. Use only live crabs.
2. Remove back shell. (Note: Iced or chilled crabs will be less active than those fresh out of the water.)
3. Eviscerate and wash. Be sure to remove the jelly-like substance which is the newly forming shell.
4. Break crabs in half. Pre-cook by placing in a pressure cooker, a steamer or a large kettle containing an inch of vigorously boiling water.

When using a pressure cooker, exhaust steam from petcock 7 to 10 minutes, then tighten the petcock and raise the pressure to 2 pounds. Cook from 12 to 15 minutes.

When using a steamer or large kettle, count time from when steam flutters the lid or escapes rapidly. Steam the crabs 20 to 22 minutes.

5. Remove meat. A small amount of cold water may be used to cool down a few crabs to start with, but it is better if the meat does not come in contact with water at this point. Keep leg and body meat separate to facilitate packing.
6. Pack meat for freezing in rigid containers or polyethylene-lined containers.
7. Cover meat with a salt brine (1 level tablespoon of salt for each quart of water), leaving head space for expansion. Seal.
8. Freeze immediately.

Optional Method for Killing and Cooking

Live crabs may be killed and cooked by dropping into a large amount of vigorously boiling salted water and boiling 20 to 25 minutes.

The method outlined above, however (killing and cleaning before cooking), is preferred, since it produces a more desirable meat.

Note: The information on clams, oysters, and crabs was prepared by Dr. E. W. Harvey of the Seafood Laboratory at Astoria, Oregon; State Circular No. 164, Oregon State College.

HOW TO FREEZE CLAMS

Razor clams are of the best quality if dug between September and April, although they may be taken the year around.

Dead clams should not be used; and care in cleaning clams for freezing should be exercised.

1. Rinse off external sand by hosing or washing under water tap.
2. Place clams in cold water to which salt has been added in the proportion of 3 ounces (about 4 tablespoons) to each gallon of water. Allow to stand for about an hour so that the clams will clean themselves of most of the sand held within the body.
3. Open or shuck as follows in order of preference:
   a. Shuck raw, saving liquid.
   b. Steam open; subject to live steam until majority of shells open.
   c. Immerse in boiling water for 2 to 3 minutes to open shells.
4. Wash clams well under running water, having slit the neck and digger lengthwise to remove any dirt, sand or foreign material and stomach contents. Drain off excess water.
5. If desired, the necks may be cut off, ground and packed separately for use in chowder.
6. Pack body, whole or minced, in glass freezing jars, waxed tubs or polyethylene-lined cartons.

Cover with clam liquid. A salt solution (1 level tablespoon to a quart of water) may be substituted for the clam liquid.

The meats should be thoroughly covered with the liquid or brine to prevent "freezer burn" and off-flavor development during storage. Leave head space for expansion. Seal well.

7. Freeze.

Note: If there is any question about "mussel poisoning" or "clam poisoning" during the late spring or summer months, consult the nearest city or county health officer.

For more detailed information regarding clam freezing, see Oregon Agricultural Experiment Station Circular of Information No. 301, Freezing Razor Clams.

HOW TO FREEZE SHRIMP

The procedure for freezing shrimp varies according to location. For complete information, consult your local State Agricultural College.

HOW TO FREEZE OYSTERS

Oysters are more susceptible to various types of spoilage than are some of the other marine foods. They must be handled with care and *as rapidly as possible.*

Assemble everything needed before starting.

1. Use only live oysters.
2. Hose off or wash under tap to remove external debris from shell.
3. Shuck or open raw in usual manner, saving oyster liquid.
4. Wash thoroughly in salt brine (1 level tablespoon salt to a quart of wa-

ter). Leave oysters in brine for one hour but no longer.

5. Drain off excess water or brine.

6. Package in polyethylene-lined carton, waxed tubs or glass jars.

7. Cover surface with oyster liquid to prevent exposure to air. Leave head space for expansion.

8. Seal and freeze.

HOW TO COOK FROZEN FISH AND SHELLFISH

Fish is best when cooked from the frozen state. Cook just as you would unfrozen fish but allow a little extra time.

For stews, chowders and soups, seafood is cooked from the frozen state.

For use in appetizers and salads, or for frying and scalloping, seafood is thawed in food compartment of the refrigerator. Thaw in sealed freezing container in which seafood was frozen.

How to Freeze Dairy Products

HOW TO FREEZE EGGS

Eggs are among the most satisfactory of all foods to freeze. They keep well for 6 to 8 months and, when used, it is impossible to tell them from fresh eggs.

The volume of the frozen egg white is equal to fresh egg whites and, if frozen properly, they continue to keep their fresh taste.

There is one important fact to remember when freezing eggs. They must be strictly fresh, for the frozen product is only as good as the fresh or original product.

However, we do not recommend freezing quantities of eggs in one container, unless that full amount will be used at once when the eggs are removed from the freezer.

Eggs do not hold up long after they have thawed and there may be considerable waste of the frozen product if more eggs are frozen in one container than will be used at one time.

In the Institute, we have found it advisable to freeze in one envelope only the amount of whole eggs, egg yolks, or egg whites that will be used at one time.

For example, if you make 3-egg cakes frequently, package three eggs to an envelope. Then when you want to make a cake, lift out one envelope.

Freeze egg whites for angel food cake the same way.

For omelets, separate the egg whites and yolks, put them in separate polyethylene bags, then package several of each together. Then when you want to make an omelet, take out one package containing the proper assortment of whites and yolks.

WHOLE EGGS

Beat eggs slightly with fork, just enough to mix yolk and white.

Add ¼ teaspoon salt for each 3 eggs.

Pour into small polyethylene bags, seal package in rigid carton and freeze.

EGG WHITES

Measure out the amount needed in a specific recipe which you prepare often.

Pour into polyethylene bag, seal package in rigid carton and freeze. Egg whites do not need any mixing before freezing.

EGG YOLKS

Egg yolks should be slightly beaten, but not enough to make them fluffy or lemon colored.

To each 3 egg yolks, add ¼ teaspoon salt. The addition of salt prevents coagulation of yolk solids during storage. Package and freeze.

COTTAGE CHEESE

Cottage cheese may be frozen and kept in rigid containers for 2 to 3 months.

It should be of good quality and made from pasteurized milk, the curd washed and salted but not creamed.

In packaging, be sure to leave head space for expansion.

Thawing cottage cheese takes 3½ to 4 hours at room temperature.

How to Thaw Frozen Eggs and Cottage Cheese

Place sealed envelope of eggs in a bowl of cold water. They will defrost in about 30 minutes. Or, they can be left in the sealed envelope at room temperature which requires about 2 hours to thaw.

Cottage cheese should be thawed slowly in the refrigerator. If thawed at room temperature, it will take 3½ to 4 hours. When thawed, add cream and use immediately.

CREAM

Pasteurized cream may be frozen and kept for 2 to 3 months. Unpasteurized cream does not keep satisfactorily for more than 2 to 3 weeks.

When sweet cream is frozen, the water and milk solids separate so, after thawing, do not mix to their original form. For that reason, frozen cream does not ship as satisfactorily as fresh cream.

Cream may be frozen in polyethylene bags or rigid containers. Leave 1-inch head space for expansion.

WHIPPED CREAM

Whip, season and flavor cream as usual.

Spoon out, in serving-size portions, onto cooky sheet that has been cov-

Serve whipped cream while still frozen as it will thaw quickly.

ered with waxed paper.

Set cooky sheet in freezer. When whipped cream is frozen solid, remove cream with a spatula and package in polyethylene bags. Seal and freeze immediately.

BUTTER

Butter may be frozen satisfactorily. Recommended storage period is approximately 3 months.

Butter for freezing should be made from freshly pasteurized cream, well salted and thoroughly worked to remove all traces of buttermilk.

Butter made from unpasteurized cream will turn rancid rapidly and should *never* be frozen.

Wrap butter in double thickness of aluminum foil to prevent transfer of odor.

It is not advisable to freeze more than two pounds of butter in any one package.

Ice cream in the half-gallon or gallon container is often a "specially-priced" item. To keep ice cream at its quality peak, place a piece of plastic wrap directly on the remaining ice cream each time some of it is dipped out to prevent the formation of ice crystals. Overwrap the outer container, and use within a short time.

Freezing Garnishes: Individual ingredients of various dishes or garnishes may sometimes be advantageously frozen. Nutmeats freeze well; so do whipped cream rosettes and hard sauce for dessert toppings. Candied fruits often can be purchased only at certain seasons and must be frozen then if you want to use them later. A little grated cheese in the freezer is a convenience, too.

How to Freeze Ready-Cooked Foods

Freezing ready-cooked foods in advance of their need saves times. Cook more than is needed at one meal, for instance, and freeze what is left to use at some future date. Much of the food for holiday meals or dinner parties can be prepared, cooked, and frozen a week, a month or even more in advance, thus eliminating last-minute confusion and clutter in the kitchen. Frozen food needs only to be reheated or refreshed when wanted.

Practically every cooked food that is commonly used has been tested for freezing. Some frozen cooked foods are far more satisfactory than others. In this book, we are giving directions for freezing only those cooked foods which retain a high quality of flavor, texture, and general appearance after freezing and which represent a substantial saving in time for the homemaker when cooked and frozen in advance.

Three Important Things to Remember

1. The quality of food to be frozen should be top notch. Freezing may slightly improve the flavor of some foods, but it never makes a high-quality product out of inferior food. Don't waste valuable freezer space on ready-cooked foods that do not freeze well or are below standard quality.

2. Ready-cooked foods must be packaged properly. Like all other foods to be frozen, ready-cooked foods must be stored in moisture-vapor-proof containers or wrapping materials. Particular care must be taken so moisture will not evaporate, causing the foods to lose flavor and texture.

3. Follow reheating or refreshing procedures given on chart. This is most important in retaining original flavor and texture of food.

How to Freeze Breads

Breads which are most satisfactory for freezing are:

Yeast Breads—white and whole wheat
Yeast Rolls—clover leaf, Parker House, cinnamon, tea rolls
Baking Powder Nut Bread
Steamed Brown Bread
Swedish Tea Ring

All these are baked before freezing, except brown bread which is steamed. All bread must be cooled to room temperature before freezing.

Swedish tea ring, pancakes, and waffles are particularly nice for Sunday morning breakfast, or any morning for that matter, and will reheat while the rest of the breakfast is being prepared.

If the family is small, yet enjoys homemade bread, a four-loaf recipe may be made and two or three loaves frozen. When reheated, it tastes exactly like freshly baked bread.

Frozen rolls always make a hit with the family or guests because two or three kinds may be frozen in a single bag or carton, which provides a nice variety for the meal. It is impossible to tell them from freshly baked rolls.

Use your favorite recipe for any of these breads. Nut bread is excellent for sandwiches or slicing for any occasion.

The chart will guide you as to packaging, freezing, and reheating.

Homemade breads, yeast rolls, pecan rolls, coffee cakes, and other leavened baked goods should be baked before freezing. Always cool to room temperature before wrapping, then wrap, seal securely, and label.

PACKAGING, STORING AND REHEATING BREADS AND ROLLS

FOOD	SIZE OF PACKAGE	HOW PACKAGED	STORAGE TIME	HOW TO REHEAT
Yeast Bread	One loaf	↑	Not to exceed six months	Thaw at room temperature for 1 hour, then warm in preheated 300°F. oven 10 to 15 minutes. OR, remove from wrappings, reheat unthawed bread in preheated 300°F. oven 25 to 30 minutes.
Steamed Brown Bread	According to size of family		Not to exceed six months	Thaw at room temperature for 1 hour or longer, then reheat in oven in wrappings for 15 to 20 minutes at 300° F.
Baking Powder Biscuits	As desired	Freezer-weight aluminum foil is ideal for packaging all breads and rolls. Can be placed directly in oven for heating without removing wrapping.	Not over six months	In foil for 30 to 40 minutes in 375°F. oven.
Swedish Tea Ring	One, usually. If two are wrapped together, separate with sheet of polyethylene or waxed paper		Not to exceed four months	Unwrap. One half hour on baking sheet in 350°F. oven.
Yeast Rolls	One or two dozen, assorted		Not to exceed six months	In foil for 30 to 40 minutes in 375°F. oven.
Nut Bread	One loaf	↓	Not to exceed four months	Thaw at room temperature for 3 hours.
Pancakes Waffles	According to size of family	Separate by waxed paper	Not over two months	Remove wrapping. Reheat in automatic toaster set on "light" degree. Put through toasting twice to heat thoroughly.

If polyethylene laminated to aluminum foil is used for packaging, transfer bread or rolls to household foil or paper bag for reheating.

How to Freeze Cakes

Cakes may be frozen either frosted or unfrosted, as preferred. Both are satisfactory. While the uncooked batter may be successfully frozen, we prefer to freeze the cake after it has been baked. Saves considerable time when the cake is needed.

Also does not tie up the cake pans, because a piece of cardboard covered with polyethylene or aluminum foil can be used to support the cake.

It is often a good idea to freeze cakes in portions as well as whole. If the family is small, a half cake or even a quarter may be better suited to its needs.

Angel Food Cakes, and any of the other air-leavened cakes such as sunshine and lemon sponge, freeze beautifully. There is little, if any, change in texture of the cakes after freezing.

Butter Cakes also freeze well, though the texture may become a little finer and the cake more firm.

Fruit Cakes definitely improve with freezing. May be made well in advance of need. Fruit cakes which have been frozen do not crumble when sliced after they are thawed.

Frosted Cakes should be frozen before wrapping to prevent damaging the soft icing.

Bake cake, frost it, put in freezing compartment for a couple of hours, then wrap. This is particularly advisable for special birthday cakes with ornamental decorations.

Iced cakes must be unwrapped immediately after removing from freezer to prevent frosting from sticking to wrapping.

Unfrosted Layer Cakes should be separated by a round of polyethylene between each layer before wrapping and freezing. Or, layers may be wrapped separately.

How to Freeze Pies

You may freeze pies before or after baking. The majority of taste testers at the Institute voted for pies frozen *after* baking. When properly thawed, it is almost impossible to tell them from freshly baked pies.

Not all pies freeze to advantage. Mince pies and pies made of fruit or berries are most satisfactory. Double-crust pies freeze best. It is not worth the effort or storage space to attempt to freeze pies with meringue.

In making berry pies, it is essential to add extra thickening, since freezing develops more juice in the fruit. Otherwise, the pies will be too "runny." See recipes for fillings.

Such fruits as apples, peaches, and apricots do not generally require a great deal of thickening. However, especially in the case of apples, it is necessary to judge whether the fruit is juicy or dry and to add thickening accordingly. Even with the juiciest fruits, 4 tablespoons of flour or cornstarch are sufficient.

If frozen fruit is used for pie, add same amount of thickening recommended for fresh fruit pie to be frozen.

How to Wrap: Pies may be wrapped in polyethylene and aluminum foil; in polyethylene and stockinette; or in laminated paper.

Recommended Storage Time: Unbaked fruit or berry pies may be stored for 2 months—unbaked mince pies for

PACKAGING, STORING AND THAWING CAKES AND COOKIES

FOOD	HOW PACKAGED	STORAGE TIME	HOW TO THAW
Plain Layer Cake, Iced	Polyethylene laminated to aluminum foil, aluminum foil, or polyethylene bags are excellent for all packaging of cakes and cookies.	Not to exceed four months	Remove wrappings, let stand at room temperature 2 hours.
Chocolate Cake, Iced		Not to exceed four months	Remove wrappings, let stand at room temperature 2 hours.
Angel Food, Sunshine, Sponge Cake		Six to eight months	Remove wrappings, let stand at room temperature 2 hours.
Fruit Cake		One year	Thaw in wrappings. Requires about 2 hours for 2 pounds of cake.
Baked Cookies		Two months	Remove wrappings, let stand at room temperature for ½ hour.

4 months. Baked fruit or berry pies may be stored for 4 months—baked mince pies for 4 months.

How to Thaw: All *baked* frozen pies are thawed by placing them unwrapped in a preheated 375°F. oven for 45 minutes.

Thaw *unbaked* pies, unwrapped, in preheated 375° F. oven for 1 hour.

To keep top crust from becoming too brown, place a piece of aluminum foil or brown paper over pie the last 20 minutes of baking.

How to Make Pie Fillings from Frozen Fruit: Place frozen fruit in a saucepan. Break gently with a table fork. Start over low heat.

Mix sugar and flour (cornstarch, if used) together. When fruit begins to melt, add sugar mix. Stir with fork to avoid breaking fruit. Cook until thickened.

Be sure to cool fruit before placing filling in pie shell. Bake pie the usual length of time. Serve pie hot or cold.

Do not freeze pie baked with frozen fruit filling . . . the second freezing will cause additional loss of flavor and juice.

Recipes for Fillings Using Fresh or Frozen Fruit

APPLE PIE FILLING

3½ cups apples, sliced
1¼ cups sugar
4   tablespoons flour (maximum)

BLUEBERRY PIE FILLING

3   cups berries
⅔ to ¾ cup sugar
2   tablespoons flour and
    2   tablespoons cornstarch OR
    4   tablespoons flour

CHERRY PIE FILLING

3½ cups pitted fresh cherries
⅔ to ¾ cup sugar
2   tablespoons flour and
    2   tablespoons cornstarch OR
    4   tablespoons flour

Caution: Not even best wraps nor the most careful packaging techniques will prevent dehydration of foods if storage temperature rises above zero frequently.

GOOSEBERRY PIE FILLING

4   cups berries
4   tablespoons cornstarch (or flour)
1½ cups sugar
2   tablespoons water

MINCE PIE FILLING

Follow your regular recipe. No extra thickening is required.

PEACH PIE FILLING

3½ cups peaches
¾   cup sugar
4   tablespoons flour (maximum)

RHUBARB PIE FILLING

3½ cups rhubarb
1½ cups sugar
2   tablespoons flour and
    2   tablespoons cornstarch OR
    4   tablespoons flour

In general, pies may be frozen baked or unbaked. You'll find fruit, berry, mince, and chiffon pies especially good to freeze. Custard or cream-filled pies, however, tend to become grainy, and are not good for freezing. Meringues toughen during freezing and should not be used.

How to Freeze Ready-Cooked Meats and Poultry

Meats which require long, slow cooking, such as stews and meat sauces, can be frozen satisfactorily. However, cool all meat dishes before freezing. Partially cool in the kettle in which it was cooked and finish cooling mixture in the refrigerator.

HINTS ABOUT INGREDIENTS IN MAIN DISHES

● In general, fried foods do not freeze successfully. French-fried potatoes and French-fried onion rings are the exceptions.

● Crumb or cheese toppings should be added when the food is reheated for serving.

● Rice is a good binder in casseroles and freezes well. "Converted" rice is preferable to the quick-cooking variety.

● Add unblanched or thawed uncooked peas to casseroles, stews, and soups to be frozen. The peas will cook during the reheating time.

● Do not include potatoes in stews and other dishes unless the product is to be consumed in a very short time. Potatoes tend to become soft and have a poor flavor when frozen. Add during reheating.

● Sauces containing a large amount of milk frequently separate during freezing and thawing but often may be stirred or beaten smooth again.

● Meat pies and turnovers are best frozen uncooked.

EFFECT OF FREEZING ON SPICES AND SEASONINGS

Pepper, cloves, and synthetic vanilla have a tendency to get strong and bitter. Onion also intensifies tremendously under freezing, and many commercial firms have turned to dried onions successfully to combat this. Celery seasonings also become strong, and curry sometimes develops a musty off-flavor. Salt loses flavor and may tend to increase rancidity of any item containing fat.

Consequently, it is best to season foods very lightly before freezing, and add flavoring as needed during the reheating.

MAIN DISHES WHICH FREEZE WELL

Meat loaves; pot roast of beef with vegetables; beef or veal stew; hash; stuffed peppers; meat balls in sauce; veal fricassee; veal birds; ham loaf; ham or chicken turnovers; chicken loaf with sauce; roast turkey or chicken slices packed in gravy; creamed chicken; chicken or turkey à la king; chicken gumbo; stewed chicken; creamed fish; fish loaves; shrimp à la king; shrimp Creole; lobster newburg; chili con carne; Spanish rice; chop suey; Mexican rice; Hungarian goulash; lasagna.

How to Freeze Ready-Cooked Soups

Soups with a milk base do not freeze satisfactorily. Vegetable, chicken, lentil and other dried legume soups are excellent when frozen. When making any of these soups which require long, slow cooking, make an extra amount and freeze whatever is not used immediately. Be sure to cool soups before starting to freeze them.

Clear broths (chicken, turkey, or beef) freeze satisfactory. Do not add noodles or rice when planning to freeze these broths . . . add when broth is reheating.

How to Package: When cool, soups may be poured into ice cube trays, frozen and cubes removed and packaged in polyethylene bags.

Or, package in glass jars suitable for freezing, polyethylene bags, or rigid cartons.

Storage Time: Not over 4 months.

How to Reheat: Remove from package. Heat in covered saucepan on low heat for 45 minutes to one hour.

Hint: Three of the frozen cubes will make one serving of soup when heated.

Caution: When packaging soups, sauces, or other liquids, leave at least one inch of head space in the container to allow for expansion during freezing.

PARTY FARE FROM YOUR FREEZER

When you are planning a large entertainment and have space available, freezing most or all the foods to be served is worthwhile. You can be as elaborate as you like with your most imaginative canapés and sandwiches when you prepare them at leisure days before the party. Canapés or open-face sandwiches should be frozen first and wrapped as soon as filling or topping is firm. Canapés may be stored in freezer containers in layers with a sheet of freezer wrap between each layer and then overwrapped. Separate the layers when thawing so that fillings will not be damaged as they thaw.

For lunch boxes and impromptu picnics, along with sandwiches also keep in the freezer an assortment of cookies, cupcakes, brownies, and other lunch box foods packaged individually.

WHEN THE POWER FAILS

Keep the freezer tightly closed. If the freezer is full when the power goes off, food will stay frozen at least 48 hours; if half full, about 24 hours. Some manufacturers may tell you in their instruction booklets how long power can be off without food damage. Check with your utility company to see when service will be restored. If the interruption will be more than a reasonable length of time, you have two alternatives: (1) put dry ice into the freezer, or (2) transfer the food to another freezer or commercial locker plant which has standby power.

SHOULD THAWED FOODS BE REFROZEN?

In general, frozen foods which have been thawed should not be refrozen. Frozen meat which has been thawed may be held in the refrigerator for a limited time, or it may be cooked and frozen again. This is not actually refreezing.

If you suspect a food has been thawed too long and are in doubt about your ability to recognize spoilage, do not take a chance on using it.

HINTS ABOUT COMMERCIALLY FROZEN FOODS

Correct handling of commercially frozen foods is equally as important as handling of home-processed frozen foods if quality is to be maintained.

The greatest threat to quality lies in permitting temperature to rise above zero. This is most likely to occur from time foods are selected at the supermarket until placed in the freezer at home. These four precautions will help you prevent excessive temperature changes:

1. Make frozen foods the final items selected at the store.

2. Place them in the insulated bags provided for this purpose before putting them in the shopping cart.

3. Avoid allowing frozen foods to stand for long periods in a heated car or one parked in summer sun.

4. Do not let frozen foods stand on the kitchen counter unnecessarily before being put in the freezer.

The higher the temperature to which a package of frozen food is allowed to rise, the greater the speed with which unfavorable changes in quality take place. Even products stored for a full year at $0°F.$ without fluctuation will be of considerably better quality than those which rise as high as $25°F.$ for only one day due to careless handling.

Squeezing a package of frozen foods is not a reliable way to find out if the food is cold enough. Many packages feel frozen hard at temperatures as high as 15 or $20°F.$ Although foods will not "spoil" at those temperatures, serious losses of quality, including discoloration, losses of nutritive value, and off flavors, already are occurring rapidly.

El Patio Fruit Platter

FRUITS

In this section are suggestions about selecting, storing, and preparing all the well-known—and many not so well-known—fruits. The recipes included here may be varied in innumerable ways by making different combinations of fruits, varying the flavors with wine, brandy, rum, or a bit of lemon juice, or by substituting one sweetening for another such as brown sugar, maple sugar, honey, and flavored syrups instead of white sugar.

Fruit in some form is a good addition to any meal and is an especially desirable dessert to top a heavy meal. Fruits are not only high in essential nutrients but they also have a general appeal, are simple to prepare, and are low in calories compared with cakes, puddings, pies, and most other desserts. To find all the recipes containing fruit that are included in this book, consult the index.

HINTS ABOUT FRUIT

Wash All Fruit: All fruit should be washed carefully before using, because the sprays used on some fruit trees may be harmful. This also applies to wrapped fruit because there is always a possibility of traces of the spray lingering on the fruit even though it is usually washed before packaging.

To Prevent Darkening of Peeled Fruit: Many fruits darken when peeled. This is harmless but detracts from the appearance, and can be avoided if the fruit is dipped immediately into citrus or pineapple juice.

Dried Fruits: The dried fruits (prunes, apricots, dates, raisins, peaches, apples, currants, figs, and pears) are among the magic fruits of the kitchen. They are popular either stewed as a breakfast fruit or in preparing tempting, tasty desserts.

To Stew Dried Fruits: Modern processing methods have removed the necessity of long soaking of most types of dried fruits. Always check the package directions. Or use the directions given below.

Wash fruit quickly in several waters or until the water is clear. Drain, cover with water, bring to a boil, then simmer until tender. Add more water if needed. Unless otherwise specified, add sugar to taste 5 minutes before removing from heat. Specific recipes for various dried fruits are given throughout this book.

STEWED UNPARED FRUIT

1 quart unpared fruit
2 cups boiling water
½ to 1 cup sugar

Add unpared fruit to boiling water. Simmer until nearly tender.

Add sugar; cook until fruit is tender. This method keeps the skin soft.

STEWED PARED FRUIT

2 cups water
½ to 1 cup sugar
⅛ teaspoon salt
1 quart prepared fruit

Boil water, sugar, and salt 3 minutes.

Drop prepared fruit into boiling syrup. Cook gently until tender.

FRUIT WHIP OR SNOW

1 cup fruit, dried or sliced
Sugar to taste
1 teaspoon lemon juice
2 egg whites

Use soft, fresh fruit or any stewed fruit (apples, prunes, bananas, peaches, or apricots). If very juicy fruits are used, the juice should be drained thoroughly before rubbing through a sieve. Sour, raw apples may be grated.

Sweeten fruit pulp to taste and add lemon juice.

Beat egg whites until stiff, then beat in sweetened fruit pulp and continue beating until the mixture is very fluffy.

Pile lightly in individual serving dishes and chill thoroughly. Serve with cream or soft custard. Garnish with jelly. Serves 4 to 6.

EL PATIO FRUIT PLATTER

1 No. 2½ can cling peach halves
1 cup strawberries
Salad greens
1 avocado
Lemon juice
Salt
1 large grapefruit
10 large cooked prunes
1 3-ounce package cream cheese
2 tablespoons peach syrup or prune liquid
1 banana
Mint sprigs

Drain peaches and arrange in ring around strawberries on crisp greens.

Cut avocado into halves and remove seed and skin. Cut crosswise in slices and sprinkle with lemon juice and salt.

Pare and section grapefruit. Drain and pit prunes.

Soften cheese with a fork and blend in peach syrup. Fill pitted prunes with cheese. Cut banana into thick slices.

Alternate grapefruit sections and avocado slices between peaches. Circle with banana slices and stuffed prunes.

Decorate with mint sprigs. Serve with lemon-honey dressing. Serves 5 to 7.

STEWED MIXED DRIED FRUIT

Wash fruit; remove cores from apples and pears. Cover generously with water; boil 35 to 45 minutes. Add ¼ cup sugar for each cup of fruit about 5 minutes before removing from heat.

DRIED FRUIT PURÉES

Cook the fruit slightly longer than when it is to be served whole. Put the cooked fruit through a sieve, colander, or ricer. If a ricer is used, remove the pits from prunes before ricing.

For some recipes such as whips and sauces, the cooked fruit may be beaten to a pulp instead of being puréed. One cup of uncooked fruit yields about 1 cup of purée.

BAKED FRESH FRUIT COMPOTE

Combine several varieties of fresh fruits in a baking dish. Add syrup made of 1 part water to 1 part sugar.

Cover and bake in a moderate oven (350°F.) until tender, 15 to 20 minutes.

FRUIT WITH YOGURT

Sweeten yogurt with sugar and vanilla to taste. Sprinkle the top with cinnamon. Serve well chilled with crushed fresh or frozen strawberries, apricots or peaches, or with stewed cherries.

Fruit with Cottage or Cream Cheese: Prepare and serve either in the same way as yogurt (above).

FRUIT SALAD COMPOTE

Pineapple wedges, fresh, frozen, or canned
Mandarin orange sections, canned
Peach slices, fresh, frozen, or canned
Strawberries, fresh or frozen
Cherries, fresh or canned
1½ cups fruit juice and water
Sugar
2 teaspoons aromatic bitters
2 teaspoons poppy seeds

Prepare fruit and chill. Combine juice from fruit with enough water to make 1½ cups. Place in small saucepan. Add sugar to taste and stir over low heat until sugar is dissolved. Cover and cook 3 minutes. Chill.

Add bitters and poppy seeds. Arrange fruit in a glass bowl and pour syrup over.

Fruit Salad Compote

WINE FRUIT COMPOTES

1. Sprinkle melon balls (watermelon, honeydew, cantaloupe) with powdered sugar; add port, angelica, or sauterne wine to about half-cover the balls, and chill thoroughly, stirring once or twice.

2. Arrange drained canned pear halves and black sweet cherries in a shallow bowl.

Heat enough port wine to almost cover the fruit, add 2 or 3 thin strips each of lemon and orange peel, and a little sugar; heat just to the boiling point.

Cool slightly, pour over fruit, chill thoroughly.

3. Pour port or sauterne wine over lightly sugared strawberries in sherbet glasses. Serve for appetizer or dessert.

SPICY DRIED FRUIT COMPOTE

1 11-ounce package mixed dried fruits
⅔ cup brown sugar
2 tablespoons lemon juice
1 teaspoon whole cloves
1 1-inch stick cinnamon

Combine ingredients in 1½-quart casserole. Add water to cover, about 2 cups.

Cover and bake in moderate oven (350°F.) 1½ hours. Serves 6.

FRUITS BAKED IN WINE

4 pears, apples, or peaches or 12 plums
2 tablespoons lemon juice (optional)
½ cup Marsala, Madeira, or Port
About ¼ cup water
1 tablespoon or more brandy (optional)

Peel pears, apples, or peaches. Cut fruit in half and remove seeds. Arrange in covered baking dish with cut sides up.

Fill cavities with sugar and add lemon juice and wine. Pour water around fruit.

Cover and bake in moderate oven (350°F.) until fruit is tender, basting several times with juice in pan.

Soft fruits will require 20 to 30 minutes, hard pears about 1 hour. Add water as needed. Add brandy to juice in pan and pour over fruit. Serve warm or cold, plain or with cream. Serves 4.

Chocolate Minted Pears: Bake pears as above but omit lemon juice and wine. When tender, place a plain or chocolate mint patty or 2 in each cavity. Reheat uncovered until chocolate melts to form a sauce.

FRUIT WITH SOUR CREAM

Serve chilled canned or almost defrosted frozen fruits, such as apricots, peaches, and blueberries with sour cream and a sprinkling of grated nutmeg.

Fresh Fruit Dessert Cups

FRESH FRUIT DESSERT CUPS

¼ cup brown sugar (packed)
2 tablespoons cornstarch
2 cups orange juice
1 teaspoon grated lemon rind
3 tablespoons lemon juice
Dash of nutmeg
6 whole cloves
1 (3-inch) stick cinnamon
3 cups sliced fresh nectarines
2 cups pitted Bing cherry halves
2 cups cantaloupe balls
½ pint sour cream (optional)

Combine sugar and cornstarch in a small saucepan. Gradually blend in orange juice until smooth. Add lemon rind and juice, nutmeg, cloves, and cinnamon. Cook, stirring constantly, until thickened and clear. Cool.

Pour over nectarines, cherries, and cantaloupe balls. Chill 2 to 3 hours. Serve plain or topped with sour cream. Serves 10 to 12.

HOW TO GLAZE CANNED FRUITS FOR SALADS AND DESSERTS

Soften 1½ tablespoons (1½ envelopes) unflavored gelatin in ⅓ cup cold water 5 minutes. Add 1½ cups boiling water and stir to dissolve gelatin. Tint a delicate yellow with a drop or two of yellow food coloring.

Arrange chilled canned fruit on a cake rack which has been placed over a cooky sheet. When glaze is slightly congealed, pour small amounts over fruit. The excess that falls into cooky sheet may be spooned up, stirred, and used over again.

If glaze becomes too thick while being used, place over lukewarm water, stir until smooth, and chill over ice water to proper consistency.

Glazing may be done a day before fruit is to be served. Remove fruit from cake rack with spatula and store in refrigerator.

To add color to a pale fruit such as pears before glazing, add a few drops of yellow food coloring to the syrup of the canned fruit and let the fruit remain in the syrup until delicately colored.

To add a "blush" to fruits after glazing, brush lightly with red food coloring.

Apples

Historians tell us that the apple was known to ancient cavemen and to the early Greeks and Romans—perhaps not in the succulent form in which expert horticulturists give it to you today, but nevertheless with many of the desirable eating qualities which make it known as the "King of Fruits."

Today, apples are a "stand by" of American cooks . . . for pies, sauces, baking individually or for scores of appetizing new dishes. Too many homemakers, however, buy apples without regard to variety and consequently fail to get the best the market affords. There is no such thing as the typical apple flavor, as each variety has its own distinctive taste—sweet, mellow, or tart, as the case may be. Some apples are better suited for baking, some for eating out of hand, while others make better sauce because of their flavor characteristics. Over 500 different varieties are to be found in the U. S. but you need to know only a few to get the best for your particular purpose.

HINTS ABOUT BUYING APPLES

Here are a few points to bear in mind when buying apples. Those that measure $2\frac{1}{2}$ inches or more in diameter are ideal for general all-around use. The large sizes (3 inches and up) of the baking varieties are best for that purpose. This does not mean that those smaller should be neglected entirely for often they are priced so as to be more economical for cooking than the larger ones.

In selecting apples, try to get those that have good color for their variety and are firm to the touch. This latter point is particularly important when buying the large sizes. Big apples tend to mature more rapidly than the smaller ones and, when soft, usually have a mealy or mushy texture with an overripe flavor too mellow for real taste enjoyment.

Warm temperatures hasten the ripening process and cause apples to lose very rapidly their crispness and tangy flavor. If you keep reserve supplies in the refrigerator or some equally cool spot, they will be at their best when you are ready to use them.

COMMONLY USED APPLE VARIETIES

Arkansas Black: Darkest red, waxy mahogany blackness; a good cooking and baking apple; November to May.
Baldwin: Bright red mottling over yellow skin; a good pie apple, excellent for all purposes: November to April.
Delicious: Recognized by five knob-like points on blossom end; striped red to solid red over yellow skin; excellent for eating out of hand and in salads.

Mildly sweet, crisp, juicy; October to April.
Golden Delicious: Same shape as regular Delicious but light yellow; marvelous eating, one of best salad apples grown. In season from October to April.
Red Delicious: Luscious taste; in all points like the Delicious, but darker red. Same eating qualities and season.
Gravenstein: A yellowish, red-striped apple, good for eating or cooking; July to September.
Grimes Golden: Yellow; fine eating, good cooker; October to January.
Jonathan: Rich red, overlaying a straw-colored background; excellent for all purposes; October to February.
King David: Dark red; not large but juicy, good general all-purpose apple, best from September to December.
McIntosh: Red, an ideal soft-fleshed eating variety and good for cooking; September to January.
Northern Spy: A good all-purpose apple, large in size, bright red color striped over yellow skin; October to March.
Rhode Island Greening: Green or yellowish; the premier cooking apple; in season October to March.
Rome Beauty: The ideal baker; large yellow or green mottled with bright red and striped with carmine; November to May.
Spitzenberg: Strawberry-red in color; slightly elongated shape, excellent for all purposes; rich spicy flavor, crisp, juicy; October to March.
Stayman: Very smooth skin, somewhat thick, nearly covered with dull, mixed red color, indistinctly striped with carmine, often with light gray or russet dots; very juicy, wonderful flavor. An excellent variety for all purposes; November to April.
Wealthy: Red, suitable for all purposes; August to December.
Winesap: A good cooking and eating apple, fine keeper, very juicy, slightly tart, good for all purposes. Roundish in form, bright deep red to purplish red in color; January to May.
Winter Banana: Clear, waxy yellowish skin with pinkish-red blush, white flesh turning yellow when ripened. Good eating, sauce, or pie variety; September to December.
Yellow Newtown: Yellow or yellowish-green, excellent for all uses; unexcelled as a dessert apple or where quality is desired. Medium to large, uniform in color; January to May.
Yellow Transparent: Light green to yellow, good for cooking although sometimes used as a dessert apple, too; June to August.
York Imperial: Red over a yellow background; a good general-purpose apple; October to January.

PREVENTING DISCOLORATION OF APPLES

Place slices as they are peeled in a pan of cold water in which a pinch of salt has been added for each whole apple peeled.

APPLE COMPOTE
(Master Recipe)

$1\frac{1}{2}$ to 2 pounds cooking apples
$1\frac{1}{2}$ cups water
$\frac{3}{4}$ cup sugar
Few grains salt
Slice of lemon (optional)
Candied orange peel (optional)

Wash, pare, and quarter ripe apples. Drop into cold water to prevent discoloration.

Bring to a boil the water, sugar, salt, lemon, and orange peel. Drop apple quarters, a few sections at a time, into syrup.

Cover and simmer gently until fruit is transparent and tender, turning apples when half done.

Serve hot or cold. If fruit is very hard, pre-cook before adding to syrup. Serves 6.

Apple Compote Variations

Apple Raisin Compote: In master recipe, add $\frac{3}{4}$ cup seedless raisins. Cook with apples.

Apple Slices: Follow master recipe. Cut apples crosswise into circles. Add to syrup and simmer until tender.

Cinnamon Apple Rings: Cut apples in rings. Add $\frac{1}{2}$ cup red cinnamon candies to sugar and water in master recipe.

Glazed Apples: Core apples. Cook whole, unpeeled, in colored syrup. Score the skin in small squares before cooking to keep fruit from bursting.

Minted Apples: Color syrup pale green. When apples are done, flavor syrup with oil of peppermint.

SNOW-CAPPED APPLE SLICES

Core red apples; cut crosswise in $\frac{1}{2}$-inch slices. Spread generously with whipped dessert topping. Sprinkle with toasted flaked coconut.
Variation: Spread apple slices with tart red jelly or preserves before adding topping.

Snow-Capped Apple Slices

BAKED APPLES
(Master Recipe)

Wash baking apples. Core 2/3 of the way down from top of apples. Do not break through blossom end of skins. Put in baking dish.

Fill each cavity with sugar, cinnamon, and nutmeg. Allow 1/4 teaspoon cinnamon or nutmeg to 8 apples. If nutmeg is used, add to each apple a few drops of lemon juice and a few gratings of lemon rind.

Cover dish with boiling water 1/4 inch in depth. Cover and bake in moderate oven (375°F.) about 40 minutes, or until apples are soft.

Remove cover, bake 10 minutes longer. If baked uncovered, baste occasionally with syrup in pan.

Remove apples. Boil syrup until thick and pour over apples. Serve hot or cold with cream.

Baked Apple Variations

Honey Baked Apples: In master recipe, substitute honey for sugar.

Maple or Brown Sugar Baked Apples: In master recipe, substitute maple or brown sugar for granulated.

Rosy Cinnamon Apples: In master recipe, add red cinnamon candies to water before baking.

Baked Apple Rings: Cut apples crosswise in rings and place in casserole. Add sugar, water, and lemon juice as for baked apples. Bake until tender.

Praline Apples: Bake apples as in master recipe, adding only the sugar and cinnamon.

Cool them and place in sherbet or dessert dishes.

Place 2/3 cup granulated sugar and 1/2 cup blanched and shredded almonds in a saucepan over medium heat. Heat until sugar is caramelized golden brown. Spoon quickly over apples. Cool. Serve with whipped cream.

Stuffed Baked Apples: Follow master recipe. Before baking, stuff cavities with mincemeat, chopped dates and nuts, sliced bananas, or bananas and cranberries combined, marmalade, jelly, crushed pineapple, etc.

Baked apples become a surprise dish with the many variations in sauces and stuffings given in the master recipe.

Marshmallow Baked Apples: Follow master recipe. Stuff cavities with any suggested stuffings. When baked, top with marshmallow and return to oven to brown, about 5 minutes.

Cranberries in Baked Stuffed Apples: Fill the cavity in the center of each apple with cranberry sauce or jelly. Add sugar to water in pan if filling is not sufficiently sweet. Bake.

BAKED APPLESAUCE
(Master Recipe)

6 to 8 tart apples
Cinnamon to taste, or 2 thin slices lemon
2/3 cup water
About 3/4 cup sugar

Wash apples (do not peel), remove bruised spots, and cut in quarters.

Place in a baking dish. Add cinnamon or lemon and water.

Cover and bake in moderate oven (375°F.) until tender, 20 to 30 minutes.

Put through a strainer. Add sugar and mix. Serve hot or cold.

Serves 6 to 8.

Baked Applesauce Variations

Creamed Applesauce: Substitute 2/3 cup light cream for water. Add 1/2 teaspoon cinnamon and 1/4 teaspoon nutmeg with sugar.

Honey Applesauce: Substitute honey for sugar. Add 1 tablespoon grated lemon rind.

Maple Applesauce: Substitute 1 cup maple syrup for sugar and water.

Orange Applesauce: Add 2 tablespoons grated orange rind while cooking.

APPLESAUCE
(Master Recipe)

Wash, pare, and core 8 cooking apples. Add about 1/2 cup water and 1/8 teaspoon salt. Cook in covered pot until soft.

Add about 1/2 cup sugar while hot. Simmer just long enough to melt sugar. Amount of sugar and water varies with sweetness and juiciness of apples.

For additional flavoring, add with sugar, nutmeg, cinnamon, grated lemon rind or juice, or a combination of spices. Serves 8.

Applesauce Variations

Honey Applesauce: In master recipe, substitute 1/2 cup honey for sugar. Add 1 to 2 teaspoons grated lemon rind.

Minted Applesauce: In master recipe, add 1/4 cup chopped mint with sugar.

Orange Applesauce: In master recipe, add 2 to 3 teaspoons grated orange rind with sugar.

Rosy Cinnamon Applesauce: In master recipe, cook 1/3 cup red cinnamon

candies with apples.

Spiced Applesauce: In master recipe, substitute 1/3 cup firmly packed brown sugar for granulated sugar. Add 1/4 teaspoon cinnamon and 1 teaspoon grated lemon rind.

Strained Applesauce: Do not pare apples. Remove any bruised spots. Cut into quarters and cook until soft. Force through a coarse sieve. Add sugar and flavoring. Simmer to dissolve sugar.

SPICED APPLES TO SERVE WITH MEAT

4   pounds sweet apples (12)
Whole cloves
1   cup cider vinegar
1/4 cup water
1 1/2 cups brown sugar
1   tablespoon ginger root
2   tablespoons mixed pickling spice
1   tablespoon lemon juice
1   teaspoon grated lemon rind

Wash apples; stick each apple with 4 whole cloves.

Make a syrup of vinegar, water, and brown sugar. Add spices, tied in a bag, lemon juice, and rind. Simmer 5 minutes.

Add apples; cook slowly until tender, spooning liquid over them occasionally.

Lift out on a platter and chill. Serve around the meat. Makes 12 apples.

BRANDIED FRIED APPLES

Peel and core small, soft, sweet apples. Cut in thin rounds.

Soak in a mixture of equal parts brandy, lemon juice, and sugar. Drain and dust with flour.

Sauté in butter until light brown, turning carefully.

Sprinkle with powdered sugar and cinnamon mixture. Serve very hot.

FRIED APPLES

Wash, quarter, and core firm apples. Slice in medium thin pieces. Sauté in small amount of hot fat until brown. If tart, sprinkle with a little brown sugar or honey while cooking.

BROILED APPLES

Core and slice firm apples about 1/2 inch thick. Arrange in pan. Sprinkle with brown sugar and butter if tart.

Bake in broiling oven until brown and tender.

CRABAPPLES

Crabapples are mostly used in the making of jellies, jams, and preserves. They are small in size (about 1 1/2 inches in diameter), with a sour taste that makes them unsuitable for eating out of hand. Choose them in the same manner as you would regular varieties of apples.

Apricots

Fresh apricots, which date back to the days of the ancient Persians, have a flavor (between a peach and a plum) entirely different from that of the dried variety.

Selection: Golden-yellow color, plumpness, and firmness are indications of quality in apricots. Since they are an extremely delicate fruit, you should avoid buying those that are soft to the touch or have a wilted or shriveled look about them. Such fruit decays quickly and lacks a good flavor.

Fresh apricots may be used in most dishes that call for peaches; cooked and puréed apricots may be used in any dish that calls for applesauce. In French cookery, the apricot is probably the most popular of all fruits.

To Peel Apricots: Drop raw apricots into boiling water. Remove from heat and let stand 1/2 minute. Remove apricots and plunge into cold water. The skin will pull off easily.

APRICOT SAUCE

Follow method in master recipe for applesauce or any of its variations.

ORANGE APRICOT PORCUPINES

    32 whole firm apricots
    1/4 cup blanched almonds slivered
    2   cups sugar
    1/2 cup white vinegar
    1/2 cup orange juice
    1/2 teaspoon salt
    1/2 teaspoon almond extract

Scald apricots 1 minute in boiling water; plunge into cold water; drain and peel. Press about 3 pieces of almond into each apricot.

Combine sugar, vinegar, orange juice, salt, and almond extract in a 1 1/2-quart saucepan; bring to boil on high heat.

Lower apricots, studded with almonds, carefully into hot syrup; cook on high heat about 3 minutes. Remove from heat.

Lift apricots into hot sterilized, wide-mouthed pint jars, using slotted spoon. Pour on syrup, working out bubbles by running a spatula down sides of the jars. Seal. Makes 4 pints.

Orange Apricot Porcupines

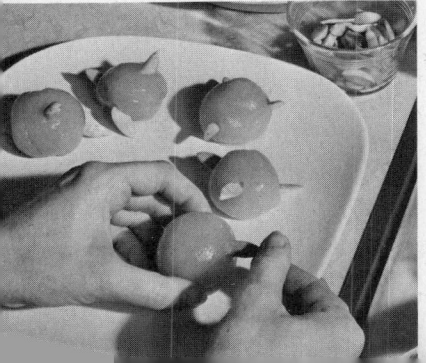

STEWED DRIED APRICOTS

Wash and drain apricots. Cover with water; boil until tender, 30 to 40 minutes. Add 1/4 to 1/2 cup sugar for each cup of fruit for the last 5 minutes of cooking.

PICKLED CANNED APRICOTS

    1   No. 2 1/2 can whole peeled apricots
    1/3 cup vinegar
    2   sticks cinnamon
    2   or 3 pieces ginger root
    2   whole cloves

Drain apricots. Combine juice, vinegar, cinnamon, ginger root, and cloves; simmer 10 minutes.

Add apricots; simmer 10 minutes longer. Chill before serving.

Serves 4 to 6.

APRICOT-APPLESAUCE

    1/4 pound dried apricots
    2   cups water
    5   cooking apples
    2/3 cup sugar

Wash apricots in cold water; cover with water and soak 4 hours.

Drain; add 2 cups water and cook 10 minutes.

Wash, pare, core, and slice apples very thin; add to apricots and cook 10 minutes.

Add sugar, stir to mix thoroughly, and cook 1 or 2 minutes longer. Put through a coarse strainer or serve unstrained. Serves 4 to 6.

ARMENIAN APRICOT DESSERT

    1   pound dried apricots
    1/4 pound prunes
    1/4 pound seedless raisins
        Sugar to taste
        Almonds

Cover apricots and prunes with cold water and soak 4 hours. Put fruits in a saucepan with the same water.

Add raisins and additional water to cover. Let boil gently, adding sugar to taste.

When tender, remove from heat and cool. Serve cold with 6 or 7 blanched, skinned almonds on each portion. Serves 6 to 8.

APRICOTS SUPREME

    1   teaspoon cinnamon
    1/2 teaspoon cloves
    1/4 cup mayonnaise
    16 peeled apricots

Combine cinnamon and cloves. Sprinkle in centers of apricots. Spoon mayonnaise in centers of half the apricots. Top with remaining half.

Place on cooky sheet or broiler pan and broil about 5 minutes or until apricots begin to brown. Serve with baked ham.

Avocados

The avocado (also called alligator pear) is a pear-shaped tropical fruit native to Mexico and northern South America and now grown in other countries. It is yellowish-green to purplish-black and has a single large seed embedded in a firm, buttery yellowish flesh. It varies greatly in size and weight and contains from 10 to 20 per cent fat.

Selection: This rich, mild-flavored fruit is best when fully ripe. (The flesh of a ripe avocado will yield somewhat to pressure, and the seed will move slightly if the fruit is shaken.) It is usually eaten raw with salt, pepper, and lemon juice or with a salad dressing. Allow half a medium-sized avocado per serving for a main-dish luncheon salad. Allow 3 to 4 servings per avocado if it is puréed, seasoned with a French or other dressing, and used as a topping for salads. Because of its mildness, the avocado mixes well with other fruits or with vegetables in salads or first-course cocktails. It is used also in fish, shellfish, and poultry salads and in other dishes.

Note: Avocado flesh rapidly discolors when exposed. To prevent discoloration sprinkle with citrus or pineapple juice. If using only part of an avocado, keep the unused part unpeeled preferably with the seed embedded in it; wrap in foil and store in the refrigerator. When combining with cooked foods, add at the last moment, and away from heat.

AVOCADO AND BACON

Mash the pulp of 1 avocado with a fork. Season with lemon juice, salt, and onion juice. Heap in small mounds on 2 plates.

Garnish with strips of fried bacon, chopped parsley, and paprika. Serves 2.

AVOCADO DESSERT

Pare ripe avocados and put the pulp through a fine sieve. Flavor with lemon juice, powdered sugar, and, if desired, a dash of cloves.

Beat mixture with a rotary beater until fluffy. Chill thoroughly.

Avocado may be cut into interesting shapes to use as attractive edible garnishes.

BAKED AVOCADO

3 ripe avocados (4 cups mashed)
3 tablespoons lemon juice
1/4 teaspoon salt
1 cup confectioners' sugar

Scoop avocado pulp from shells. Mash and put through a sieve. Combine with lemon juice, salt, and sugar in a buttered baking dish.

Bake in moderate oven (350°F.) 30 minutes, or until brown crust forms on top. Serves 6.

AVOCADOS STUFFED WITH CHEESE (NICARAGUAN)

Peel medium-sized avocados. Cut lengthwise and remove pits. Stuff halves with any fresh cream cheese. (Nicaraguans use their own special curd cheese.)

Dip in beaten egg, then in crumbs. Sauté in butter until brown or fry in deep hot fat in basket.

Cover with any desired tomato sauce and heat through in oven. Serve as a vegetable.

FRUIT FILLED AVOCADO

2 medium-sized avocados
Salt
2 cups grapefruit sections
1 1/2 dozen stuffed olives
French dressing

Cut avocados in half and remove pits. Scoop out flesh, leaving a thin layer to hold shells in form. Cut portion removed into cubes and sprinkle with salt.

Cut grapefruit sections into cubes. Cut olives into rounds.

Toss fruit together lightly and refill shells. Add dressing and chill. Serves 4.

AVOCADO-SOUR CREAM DIP FOR SHRIMP

2 ripe avocados
1 cup sour cream
1/2 teaspoon Ac'cent
1/4 teaspoon salt
2 tablespoons prepared horseradish
1 small onion, grated

Mash avocados to smooth pulp with wooden spoon or in electric blender. Whip in remaining ingredients.

Serve with chilled cooked shrimp.

For a buffet luncheon: avocado half-shells with creamed chicken or Creole shrimp for filling.

Bananas

Selection: The color and condition of the peel are good indications of the use that should be made of bananas. When the skin is all yellow, the banana is firm enough to cook and serve as a vegetable and ripe enough to be eaten uncooked. If the peel is yellow but flecked with brown, the banana is fully ripe and ideal for immediate serving with cereals, in fruit cups, salads, and desserts. Fruit with a moldy skin that has turned black is of poor quality, although some bananas with a dark skin are very ripe but still good eating.

Red bananas are merely another variety of this delicious tropical fruit. They are preferred by some people to the common yellow kind, although there actually is not much difference between the taste of the two.

For proper ripening and best flavor, let bananas ripen at comfortable room temperature.

Don't keep bananas in refrigerator—except ones already fully ripe and flecked with brown.

To whip or mash 3 or more bananas: Break in pieces; beat with electric mixer or blender. For 1 or 2 bananas: Slice into bowl and mash with fork, or use mixer or blender.

BAKED BANANAS

6 firm bananas
2 tablespoons melted butter or margarine
Salt

Peel bananas. Place into a well buttered baking pan. Brush well with butter and sprinkle with salt.

Bake in moderate oven (375°F.) 15 to 18 minutes, or until bananas are tender, easily pierced with a fork.

If desired, bake until almost done; then place under broiler heat until tender and browned. Serves 6.

Serve hot as a vegetable or as a dessert with cream or a hot fruit sauce.

Baked Banana Variations

Bananas Baked with Molasses: Just before baking, brush bananas with lemon juice. Pour 3/4 to 1 cup of molasses over bananas. Bake as above.

Serve hot as a sweet entrée with beef or ham, or garnish with chopped toasted almonds and serve as a hot dessert. Maple syrup may be substituted.

Bananas Baked with Brown Sugar: Just before baking, sprinkle bananas lightly with brown sugar. Bake as above.

Serve hot as a sweet entrée with beef, ham, lamb, or chicken.

Bananas Baked with Curry Sauce: Pour 2 cups of your favorite curry sauce over bananas. Bake as above.

Serve hot with rice, pork, lamb, chicken, duck, or shrimp.

Baked Bananas Served with Sour Cream: To serve as a vegetable, top each hot banana with 1/4 cup sour cream. Sprinkle with paprika, if desired.

To serve as a hot dessert, top each banana with 1/4 cup sour cream. Sprinkle with sugar, nutmeg, or cinnamon, if desired.

Bananas Baked with Cranberries: Pour 1 cup hot cranberry sauce over bananas. Bake as above. Serve hot with beef, chicken, or turkey. Tart jams, jellies or marmalades may be used in place of cranberry sauce.

Baked Bananas with Applesauce or Apple Butter: Spread bananas evenly from tip to tip with applesauce or apple butter. Use 1/4 cup for each banana. Bake as above. Serve as a hot dessert.

Honey Baked Bananas: Sprinkle honey over bananas with the butter. Add a sprinkling of lemon juice, if desired.

Baked Bananas with Sherry or Rum: Pour a little sherry or rum over bananas while baking.

FRIED BANANAS

Peel and cut firm bananas in half lengthwise. Fry bananas slowly in butter until tender and golden brown, turning them to brown evenly. Serve hot as a vegetable.

Fried Banana Variations

Glazed for Dessert: Brush well with lemon juice before frying and sprinkle with brown sugar while frying.

Banana Newburg: Sprinkle fried bananas with brown sugar while cooking. Add a little sherry and let them simmer a few minutes.

Fried Bananas with Rum: Pour some rum into the pan when fried bananas are done. Light it. Baste bananas with flaming syrup. Serve immediately.

RUM-FLAMED BANANAS

4 bananas
4 tablespoons butter
2 tablespoons confectioners' sugar
2 tablespoons brown sugar
1/4 cup rum

Peel bananas, cut in half crosswise. Melt butter in chafing dish pan over direct heat.

Place bananas in hot butter; sprinkle with mixed sugars and cook until browned lightly on all sides, about 4 to 6 minutes.

Pour the rum over the bananas; ignite the rum, and serve on dessert plates. Serves 4.

Banana Scallops

BANANA SCALLOPS

1   egg
1½ teaspoons salt
6   firm bananas
¾   cup fine cereal crumbs, bread, or
     cracker crumbs

Beat egg slightly and add salt. Slice peeled bananas crosswise into 1-inch thick pieces. Dip into egg and roll in crumbs.

Fry in hot deep fat (375°F.) 1½ to 2 minutes or until brown and tender. Drain and serve immediately. Serves 6.

Note: Bananas may be prepared for frying several hours in advance.

BANANAS IN BLANKETS

Peel and cut firm ripe bananas into quarters crosswise. Dip in lemon juice and sprinkle very lightly with sugar.

Roll in very thin slices of bacon or boiled ham.

Secure the bacon with toothpicks. Sauté bananas in a skillet or bake in moderate oven (350°F.) until bacon is crisp. When using ham, grease the skillet lightly.

BROILED BANANAS

Peel firm, ripe bananas. Place on broiler rack or into pan containing rack. Brush bananas well with melted butter or margarine and sprinkle lightly with salt.

Broil 3 to 4 inches from heat about 5 minutes on each side or until bananas are browned and tender and easily pierced with fork. Serve hot as vegetable.

Broiled Banana Variations

Broiled Bananas with Curry Sauce: To serve as hot vegetable, top broiled bananas with hot curry sauce.

Broiled Bananas with Applesauce: For a delicious new flavor, cover each banana with about ¼ cup applesauce or apple butter. Top with plain, whipped or sour cream.

Broiled Bananas with Cream: To serve as vegetable, top each banana with about ¼ cup sour cream. Sprinkle with paprika, if desired. To serve as hot dessert, top each banana with plain, whipped or sour cream. Sprinkle with sugar, nutmeg, or cinnamon, if desired.

Berries

Here are two good tips to remember about berries. First, keep in mind that only the popular strawberry is privileged to wear a cap as a sign of maturity. All other berries that are mature should be free of their hull. Second, for best quality and taste, choose those berries that are firm, plump, and full colored for the variety.

TO SERVE FRESH BERRIES

Spread berries on a tray; remove soft or moldy berries. Chill until ready to serve. Then wash in a colander; drain thoroughly. Remove caps of stems.

Sprinkle with sugar if desired and chill a little longer. If fruit is too tart, sprinkle with sugar and let stand 1 to 2 hours. A sprinkling of lemon juice will neutralize excess tartness.

BARBERRIES

Barberry is the name of a family of perennial herbs and shrubs. The bright red berries of several species of the shrubs often used for landscaping are edible but are seldom eaten raw; however they are sometimes used for the making of preserves. They have a tart pleasant flavor.

BOYSENBERRIES

The boysenberry is a dark-red or, when ripe, almost black berry; a hybrid bramble developed in California from several varieties of raspberry and blackberry. It is named after its originator, Rudolph Boysen.

CRANBERRIES

The cranberry is a firm, sour, red berry, the fruit of a trailing evergreen shrub that grows in bogs or marshes. These berries are a good source of vitamin C. The commercially cultivated varieties are native to North America, and are cultivated chiefly in New Jersey, Massachusetts, and Wisconsin. The serving of cranberry sauce with the Thanksgiving turkey is traditional in the United States. Color is no indication of maturity in cranberries, as they vary from a bright red to a dark, blackish red according to variety. They are in season from September to February.

CRANBERRY SAUCE
(Master Recipe)

1   pound (4 cups) cranberries
1½ cups sugar
2   cups water

Wash, pick over, and drain cranberries.

Put berries, sugar, and water in saucepan. Bring slowly to boiling point. Cover and cook slowly about 10 minutes, or until skins burst. Skim and cool. Makes about 4 cups.

Cranberry Sauce Variations

Molded Cranberry Sauce: Increase sugar to 2 cups. Cook until a thin syrup is formed, about 20 minutes. Pour into mold; chill.

Glazed Cranberries: Prepare as in master recipe. Do not drain thoroughly.

Measure and mix equal parts sugar and berries in the top of double boiler.

Cook over hot water until sugar forms thick syrup, about 1 hour, and berries are glazed. Stir carefully a few times at the start.

Minted Cranberry Sauce: In master recipe, stir in teaspoon chopped fresh mint or few drops mint extract.

BAKED CRANBERRY SAUCE

Wash and pick over berries. Place in a baking dish. Add 1¾ cups sugar and 1 cup water for each quart of berries.

Cover and bake in slow oven (325°F.) 30 minutes, or until berries are tender.

CRANBERRY STRAWBERRY COMPOTE

Cook 1 pound cranberries, in water to cover, in covered pot about 5 minutes.

Add 1 cup sugar and 2 cups strawberries. Cook 5 to 8 minutes. Serve cold.

FROSTED CRANBERRIES

1   egg white
½   teaspoon water
1   cup fresh cranberries
1   cup granulated sugar

Lightly beat egg white and water together just until blended. Dip cranberries in mixture until completely coated. Roll in sugar. Let stand until dry at room temperature or in refrigerator.

Frosted Cranberries keep for weeks in the refrigerator. Use them as nibblers or as decorations on ice cream and sherbet.

CURRANTS

Two different fruits are described by the term currant. One is the dried fruit of a small, seedless grape grown in the Mediterranean region, used in cooking; however in the U. S. the name commonly refers to the small, sour, red, white, or black berry of a large group of hardy shrubs. They are used for jellies and jams. Select firm, ripe currants for jelly-making. Over-ripe fruit does not "jell" so well. These berries are in season June to August.

TO SERVE FRESH CURRANTS

Wash, drain, and remove stems from chilled red or white currants. Sprinkle liberally with sugar, since these berries are sharply acid. They are particularly good when combined with other and sweeter berries.

If served with cream, serve the cream separately because the acid may turn the cream.

Ripe black currants are decorative but not as flavorful as the red or white.

ELDERBERRIES

These are the small black berries of the elder bush, principally used in jelly and wine-making.

GOOSEBERRIES

The gooseberry is a small, sour berry resembling a currant but larger. Ripe gooseberries are soft and have a light amber color—the large ones being generally of preferred quality. Gooseberries are usually cooked with sugar for 10 or 15 minutes before they are eaten. Their chief use is in preserves and pies.

GOOSEBERRY FOOL

This old-time American dessert is sometimes made of other chilled stewed fruits.

1 pint green or ripe gooseberries
3/4 cup water
1/2 cup sugar
1 tablespoon butter or margarine
1/8 teaspoon salt
2 eggs, separated
1/4 cup sugar

Stem berries; wash in cold water and drain. Put into saucepan with water.

Cover the pan and boil gently until the berries are soft, 8 to 10 minutes.

Put through colander or food mill, making sure to push through all pulp. Return purée to saucepan; add sugar, butter, and salt; stir to mix.

Beat egg yolks well; stir into purée.

Beat egg whites to stiff foam; gradually add sugar and beat until stiff and shiny.

Place purée over heat; stir constantly until mixture bubbles and thickens. Quickly pour hot berry mixture over whites; cut and fold in until thoroughly blended. Cover; chill in refrigerator.

Serve in chilled dessert cups with a topping of whipped cream, a sliced strawberry, or finely chopped nuts. Serves 4.

HUCKLEBERRIES OR BLUEBERRIES

The huckleberry is an edible dark-blue berry resembling a blueberry, the fruit of any of a number of related shrubs. These are all loosely termed blueberries.

The blueberries commonly sold are really a development through horticultural research of the wild huckleberry. Improved taste, flavor, and size are so noticeable that it might almost be said that blueberries are a separate species. Large size blueberries are preferred to smaller ones, as they have a better flavor.

STEWED BLUEBERRIES

Cook blueberries in very little water. When they are nearly tender, add a few grains salt and sugar to taste. Cook a minute longer.

BLUEBERRY SLUMP

1 quart blueberries
1 cup sugar
4 tablespoons arrowroot or cornstarch
Juice of 1 lemon
4 tablespoons butter or margarine
1/2 cup sugar
1/4 teaspoon salt
1 egg
1/2 cup milk
1 1/2 cups sifted cake flour
2 teaspoons baking powder

Wash berries and drain. Mix sugar and arrowroot; add to berries. Place in greased casserole; sprinkle with lemon juice.

Cream together butter and sugar Add salt. Beat egg and add to creamed mixture. Add milk and mix well. Stir in flour and baking powder briskly and spoon over berries.

Bake in hot oven (425°F.) 20 to 25 minutes. Serve warm with vanilla ice cream. Serves 8.

Note: If fresh blueberries are not available, frozen ones may be used. In that case, use two packages and let defrost slightly.

BLUEBERRY FLUMMERY

1 pint blueberries
2 cups water
1/2 cup sugar
3 1/2 tablespoons cornstarch
1/4 cup cold water
Dash of salt
Juice of 1 lemon

Simmer berries in 2 cups water until very tender. Put through sieve, pressing through as much pulp and skin as possible.

Add sugar to juice and sieved pulp; bring to boil.

Dissolve cornstarch in 1/4 cup cold water, and add with salt to hot mixture. Cook, stirring constantly, until mixture thickens.

Remove from heat; stir in lemon juice. Cool, then pour into serving dish, and chill. Serve with sugar and cream, if desired. Serves 4.

JUNIPER BERRIES

The juniper berry is the fruit of the juniper shrub or tree. It is often used to flavor stuffings and sauces for meat and game, and is the dominant flavoring in gin.

LINGONBERRIES

The lingonberry (also called lingberry) is a red berry, smaller than the cranberry but much like it. It is used as a sauce for Swedish pancakes, in jellies and jams, and as juice.

LOGANBERRIES

The loganberry is a red berry of uncertain origin, cultivated on the Pacific coast. It is either a variety of dewberry or a cross between the dewberry and the red raspberry. These sweet berries are used like raspberries.

MULBERRIES

Mulberries are very sweet and may be eaten raw, usually served with lemon juice or cream. In recipes they are prepared in the same way as raspberries.

STRAWBERRIES

Large strawberries are the choicest for eating, as they usually have the sweetest taste. For canning and preserving, medium size, tart-flavored berries are best. The strawberry season is at its height from mid-April to mid-June.

STRAWBERRY-APPLESAUCE DELIGHT

1/2 pint fresh strawberries or 1 package frozen strawberries
1 3/4 cups applesauce, chilled

Wash fresh strawberries; hull and halve. Combine with applesauce. Sweeten to taste. Place in serving dish. Top with whipped cream, if desired. Serves 4 to 6.

Strawberry-Applesauce Delight

STRAWBERRIES ROMANOFF

2 quarts strawberries
Sugar
1 pint vanilla ice cream
1 cup heavy cream, whipped
Juice of 1 lemon
1/4 cup Cointreau or Curaçao
2 tablespoons gold label rum

Clean and hull strawberries. Sweeten with sugar.

Whip ice cream slightly and fold in whipped cream. Add lemon juice, Cointreau, and rum. Pour over berries. Spoon into chilled sherbet glasses to serve. Serves 8.

Note: To ripen flavors correctly, prepare the topping several hours before serving and store in refrigerator tray with temperature control at normal.

DIPPED STRAWBERRIES

Wash fresh, ripe strawberries. Drain, but do not remove stems and hulls.

Pile whipped sweet or heavy sour cream in center of individual serving dishes.

Arrange fruit around cream, so guests may, using the stems to hold them, dip the berries into the cream.

If desired, a cup of shredded coconut may be folded into a cup of heavy cream, which has been whipped and sweetened with a couple teaspoons of sugar and a dash of vanilla.

STRAWBERRIES WITH KIRSCH CREAM

1 quart ripe strawberries
1/2 cup confectioners' sugar
1 cup heavy cream
3 tablespoons kirsch

Wash berries. Reserve 12 unhulled berries. Remove hulls and cut remaining berries into halves. Sprinkle with confectioners' sugar and let stand for 10 minutes.

Whip cream until stiff; flavor with kirsch.

Fold berries into cream and serve in sherbet glasses garnished with the whole berries. Serves 6.

STEWED RASPBERRIES

1 quart raspberries
1 cup water
1/2 to 1 cup sugar
1 tablespoon lemon juice

Wash, drain, and hull raspberries. Heat water with sugar in a glass saucepan. (Use more sugar for red raspberries than for black.)

When the water-sugar mixture simmers, add berries, cover and simmer 10 minutes.

Add lemon juice and chill. Serves 4 to 6 as a sauce over ice cream, cake, and puddings.

BRAZILIAN STRAWBERRY COMPOTE

1 quart ripe strawberries
Powdered sugar, to taste
Grated rind of 1 orange
About 1/4 to 1/2 cup Cointreau or Triple Sec
1 tablespoon Kirschwasser

Stem and wash strawberries. Dust them with fine powdered sugar.

Grate in the orange rind. Moisten with Cointreau; point up with Kirschwasser. Toss well; chill for at least 4 hours.

Serve each portion with 1 tablespoon well chilled rose-tinted whipped cream on top, sprinkled with slivers of blanched almonds. Serves 4 to 6.

BERRY AND COTTAGE CHEESE PARFAIT

1 cup cottage cheese
1 egg white
2 tablespoons sugar
1/2 teaspoon salt
1 cup heavy cream
1/2 teaspoon almond extract
1 box frozen strawberries, defrosted, or fresh strawberries, crushed and sweetened

Beat cottage cheese until smooth.

Beat egg white until frothy, then beat until stiff, adding sugar and salt. Fold into cottage cheese.

Whip cream, adding almond extract. Fold into mixture. Alternate spoonfuls of cottage cheese mixture and fruit into individual serving dishes. Serves 6.

STRAWBERRIES AND CLABBERED CREAM

1 pint sour cream
1 cup cottage cheese
1 tablespoon sugar
2 cups strawberries, washed, drained dry and hulled

Combine cream, cottage cheese, and sugar. Beat with a spoon until blended.

Just before serving, stir in berries. Serve with toasted crackers or split hot biscuits. Makes 4 cups.

BLACKBERRY WHIP

2 egg whites
Dash of salt
1/4 cup sugar
1 tablespoon lemon juice
Grated rind of 1 lemon
1 pint fresh blackberries

Beat egg whites with salt until stiff, then gradually beat in sugar, 1 tablespoon at a time.

Fold in lemon juice, rind, and washed, well drained blackberries. Chill. Serve plain or with custard sauce. Serves 4.

JIFFY STRAWBERRY FLUFF

1 package strawberry instant pudding
1 package (10-ounce) frozen strawberries, defrosted
3 egg whites
Light cream

Sprinkle dry pudding mix over strawberries. Mix only until combined. Let stand for 5 minutes.

Beat egg whites until stiff but not dry. Fold into strawberries. Serve with light cream or favorite garnish. Serves 4.

Cherries

High quality in cherries is denoted by plumpness with a bright appearance, firmness, and good color. Cherries at their best are on the market from June to September. You'll need a quick handy tool for pitting if you're going to make full use of this delicious fruit for pies, jellies, salads, or fruit cups. The use of a clean pen holder with a strong point inserted in it is suggested or a strong hair pin.

STEWED SOUR CHERRIES

1 quart sour cherries
1 cup water
1 cup sugar

Pick over the cherries, wash and remove pits and stems.

Combine water and sugar; stir over low heat until sugar is dissolved. Bring to a boil and boil for 5 minutes.

Add cherries and boil gently 5 to 10 minutes or until cherries are tender.

MARASCHINO CHERRIES

Originally, these were cherries preserved in maraschino, a very sweet, colorless liqueur. Most of those so called nowadays are in an artificially colored and flavored sugar syrup.

CHERRIES JUBILEE

Cherries Jubilee always involves the use of a liqueur or brandy. If you do not wish to ignite the brandy, it may be added to the cherries well ahead of time so they can absorb the flavor.

1 No. 2 can Bing cherries, pitted
1 teaspoon cornstarch
1/2 cup Cognac or kirsch
1 quart vanilla ice cream

Drain juice from canned cherries. Cook 1 cup juice down to 3/4 cup.

Make paste of cornstarch and 2 tablespoons of remaining cherry juice. Add to hot juice and cook, stirring until thick and clear. Remove from heat.

Add cherries. Pour into metal pan, heat-resistant casserole, or chafing dish.

Carefully pour Cognac on top. Ignite and spoon flaming cherries over individual servings of ice cream. Serve immediately. Serves 8.

Citrus Fruits

GRAPEFRUIT

Grapefruit, occasionally referred to as the "shaddock" or "pomelo," has been a native of North America since its importation by the old Spanish settlers. How this name originated is still a moot question, but it is generally attributed to the fact that the fruit grows in clusters like grapes.

Buying Hints: You may find that two grapefruit of the same size will often vary in taste and juiciness. The one will be heavy, firm, and smoothly textured, with a well-rounded shape—a good indication of fine, juicy grapefruit. The other will be coarse, puffy, and rough—indicative of lack of juice, as well as taste. Since grapefruit is, on the average, over three-quarters liquid, heaviness is a good indication of juice content.

Do not rely solely on color for an index to flavor, as good grapefruit can range from pale yellow to russet or bronze. Brightly colored fruit is naturally more appealing—yet a russeted fruit may often be tastier and juicier. Minor surface blemishes do not affect the eating quality although the presence of a bad bruise may indicate some internal breakdown which is not apparent on the outside. The pink-meated grapefruit is a cross-bred creation, and many people consider the "pink-meats" somewhat sweeter than others.

BROILED OR BAKED GRAPEFRUIT

Wash grapefruit and cut in halves. Remove seeds, core, and loosen segments. Sprinkle each half with 1 tablespoon brown sugar, then pour 1 tablespoon sherry or brandy over each.

Put under the broiler until the sugar melts, or bake in moderate oven. Serve at once as a dessert.

Broiled Honeyed Grapefruit: Prepare grapefruit as above. Spread with honey and sprinkle with cinnamon and mace instead of other ingredients. Brown lightly under moderate broiler heat.

Grapefruit with French Dressing: Use French dressing instead of above ingredients. Spoon 2 tablespoons over each prepared grapefruit half, being careful that all is covered. Bake or broil as directed. Serve hot as a first course.

GRAPEFRUIT COCKTAIL

Cut chilled grapefruit in halves. Loosen the pulp from the peel with a very sharp knife. Remove the seeds and cut out the tough fibrous center with a grapefruit knife or a scissors.

Five minutes before serving sprinkle the grapefruit with confectioners' sugar. Just before serving add 1 tablespoon sherry to each half.

For a party touch, notch the edge of the grapefruit and put a maraschino cherry in the center.

TO PEEL AND SECTION GRAPEFRUIT

Chill whole fruit thoroughly. With a straight-sided sharp knife cut a slice from the top, then cut off peel in strips from top to bottom. Or cut off peel round and round in one long spiraling cut. Always cut deep enough to remove white membrane.

Go over fruit again removing any remaining white membrane.

Cut along membrane of each section from outside to the core. Tip knife outward and roll the whole section out one at a time. Section fruit over a bowl to retain juices.

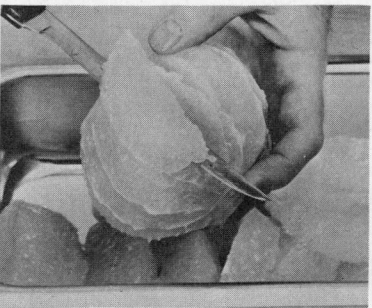

TANGERINES AND SATSUMAS

Tangerines are small, slightly flattened oranges with easily removed skins and loosely adhering sections. They are also called mandarin oranges. This fruit (raised principally in Florida) is best when it is deep orange in color and firm in texture, rather than puffy. It is in season from November to April. Satsumas are similar to tangerines and are generally available during October and November.

TANGERINES IN KIRSCH

Peel the tangerines and separate the segments. Arrange in glass serving dish and sprinkle with powdered sugar.

Sprinkle with kirsch and refrigerate 2 hours before serving.

KUMQUATS

The kumquat is a citrus fruit of Chinese origin. It is about the size of a small plum, orange in color, with an acid pulp partway between that of an orange and a lemon in flavor. It has a thin, sweet, aromatic rind. The entire fruit, rind and all, is edible if it is fully ripe; however, kumquats are used mainly in preserves and jelly or candied. They may be sliced very thin and used in salads; remove the large seeds.

Stuffed Kumquats: Slice in halves. Remove the large seeds. Stuff the fruit with cream cheese or chopped nuts and use to garnish salads.

BOILED KUMQUATS

Wash 1 pound kumquats. Cover with cold water; bring to a boil, then cover and simmer 30 minutes.

Add 2 cups sugar and, if desired, ¼ teaspoon powdered cinnamon, and boil 5 minutes.

The kumquats may be served whole or they may be cut into halves, in which case remove the large seeds. Chill thoroughly and use as a garnish for a meat platter or in salads.

Note: Kumquats may also be cooked in water to cover (without sugar) until the skin is clear and tender, about 20 to 30 minutes.

CITRON

The citron is a yellow, thick-skinned fruit resembling a lime or lemon but larger and less acid. It is cultivated for its thick, spongy rind, which is candied or glacéed for use as a confection or in fruit cakes.

CALAMONDIN

The calamondin is a citrus fruit that looks like a small tangerine but is more like a lime in flavor and acidity.

TANGELO

The tangelo is a citrus fruit produced by crossing the tangerine with the grapefruit or shaddock.

ORANGES

China is placed as the home of this citrus fruit, with Columbus being given credit for introducing seeds to the New World.

Selection: As in any other member of the citrus family, the weight of an orange is indicative of its juice content. Also bear this point in mind: make sure the fruit is firm and has a skin that is not too rough. Color is not a sure guide to quality as much as the Texas and Florida crop has coloring added. Such fruit is dipped in, or sprayed with, a harmless vegetable dye solution at packing time. This process has absolutely no effect on the eating quality of the fruit. It simply gives the outer skin the deep orange color expected by consumers. The law requires that all oranges treated this way must be stamped "Color Added" and must have passed very strict maturity tests.

POACHED ORANGES

    6 seedless oranges
    2 cups sugar
    2 cups water

Cut oranges in half crosswise. Cover with water; bring to boil. Pour off and discard water.

Combine sugar and 2 cups water; bring to boil. Add oranges; cook gently until skins can be easily pierced with wooden pick (20 to 30 minutes). Chill.

GLORIFIED GRAPEFRUIT

    3 medium-size grapefruit
    1 can (1 pound, 1-ounce) fruit
         cocktail
    2 tablespoons maraschino cherry
         syrup
    2 to 3 tablespoons brown sugar

Cut grapefruit in halves. With curved grapefruit knife, remove fruit in one piece, leaving shell intact. Section fruit, removing membranes.

Drain fruit cocktail thoroughly and add to grapefruit, along with maraschino cherry syrup. Mix lightly and spoon into grapefruit shells. Sprinkle with brown sugar.

Place in shallow pan and broil about 4 inches from heat until thoroughly heated and tinged with brown. Serve warm. Serves 6.

LEMONS

Lemons, which come mostly from California, should be fine textured, heavy for their size and moderately firm. These points are indicative of juiciness. Avoid green-tinged fruit, as generally this has not been fully "cured." Of all the members of the citrus family, lemons are the most versatile. Many uses for juice and rind are given in individual recipes throughout this book.

LIMES

The lime is a small, almost round, greenish-yellow citrus fruit. The juice is aromatic, refreshing, sour, and rich in vitamin C. The characteristic flavor of limes makes them especially useful for cold drinks or for squeezing over melon or fruit compote. They are at their best when their skins are bright green. Limes should be kept in the refrigerator.

SHADDOCK

The shaddock is a large, yellow, coarse-grained, pear-shaped fruit closely related to the grapefruit. It is imported from various West Indian islands and may be used like other citrus fruit. It was named for a Captain Shaddock, who introduced it into Barbados from the East Indies in 1696.

POMELO

Pomelo is a name applied to the grapefruit; also, occasionally, the shaddock (which see).

ORANGE BANANA AMBROSIA

Ambrosia is a versatile old favorite dish consisting usually of sliced oranges, bananas, and shredded coconut; however it is often varied by the addition of honeydew and cantaloupe balls and sometimes sprinkled with lime juice.

    2 medium-sized oranges
    2 ripe firm bananas
    2 tablespoons sugar
  1/2 to 3/4 cup shredded coconut

Peel oranges and cut crosswise into thin slices, removing seeds and fibrous portions. Peel bananas and slice about 1/4 inch thick.

Arrange alternate layers of orange and banana slices in large shallow dish, sprinkling each layer with sugar.

Use orange slices for bottom and top layers. Sprinkle top generously with coconut. Chill about 1 hour before serving.

Just before serving, garnish with additional ripe banana and orange slices, if desired. Serves 4 to 6.

◄ *Glorified Grapefruit: The sweet fruits of canned fruit cocktail combine with fresh grapefruit to make a delicious breakfast treat.*

ORANGE COMPOTE

    2 seedless oranges
    1 cup water
  3/4 cup sugar
  1/8 teaspoon salt
    3 additional oranges
    1 tablespoon rum or liqueur (optional)

Cut yellow rind off 2 oranges. Cut rind into thin slices and add water, sugar, and salt. Boil 20 minutes.

Skin and remove membrane from the 2 oranges and from 3 additional oranges. Place the sections in a serving bowl. Pour the hot syrup and rind over them. Chill the compote. If desired, add rum or liqueur before serving. Serves 4.

BAKED GRAPEFRUIT

    2 cups crushed corn flakes
  1/2 cup brown sugar, firmly packed
  1/2 teaspoon cinnamon
  1/4 cup melted butter or margarine
    2 grapefruit, halved and cored

Combine corn flakes, sugar, cinnamon, and butter. Fill and top the halves of grapefruit in which the sections have been loosened.

Bake in hot oven (400°F.) about 10 to 12 minutes. Serve at once. Serves 4.

TANGERINE SURPRISE

    8 medium tangerines
 1 1/2 cups water
  1/2 cup sugar
    5 2-inch cinnamon sticks
    6 whole cloves
    2 tablespoons lemon juice

Wash, peel, and section tangerines, placing rind from 3 tangerines in saucepan. Remove all white fiber from fruit; add fiber to rind, along with water, sugar, spices, and lemon juice. Bring to full, rolling boil; boil, uncovered, 10 minutes.

Remove rind, add tangerine sections and bring to boil again. Boil 1 minute, then cool. Refrigerate. Serve with cream cheese and crackers. Serves 4.

An oversized brandy snifter makes a dramatic serving dish for ambrosia as well as other fruit combinations.

Dates and Figs

DATES

Fresh dates are commercially grown in the U. S. in California and Arizona, as the date palm bears fruit only in extremely dry areas. This fruit is available between September and December and should be selected according to its appearance. Fresh dates, when fully ripe, have a golden brown color and are slightly moist. Their origin may be traced back to ancient Africa where the appearance of date palms usually heralded the location of a water-hole or spring in the midst of a desert.

To serve fresh dates, wash carefully, remove stems, and serve as part of a fruit salad or platter.

SPICED FRESH DATES

3   pounds fresh dates
Shelled walnuts or almonds
4   cups sugar
1½   cups vinegar
½   cup water
½   teaspoon salt
Few drops extract or oil of cinnamon
    and cloves

Pit dates and stuff with large pieces of nuts; the almonds may be blanched or not, as preferred.

Pack into small jars, standing dates on end.

Make a syrup of remaining ingredients, simmer for 5 minutes, and pour over dates in jars. Seal while hot.

GOLD DESSERT COMPOTE

12   dried figs
1   cup flaked coconut
2   oranges, peeled and sliced
6   thin slivers candied ginger
¼   cup honey
⅓   cup orange juice
1   tablespoon grated orange rind

Arrange figs, coconut, oranges, and ginger in glass bowl.

Combine honey, orange juice, and rind; pour over fruits. Chill for an hour before serving. Serves 6.

Gold Dessert Compote

FIGS

The fresh fig is a prime favorite of epicures and is in season June to September. Best known to the Oriental people, this fruit is fairly abundant in hot, tropical areas. Varieties include Mission, large dark purple; Calimyrna, large white; Adriatic, white; Kadota, smaller and white. Figs are highly perishable; ripeness can be ascertained by the degree of softness to the touch, while over-ripeness is detectable by a sour odor which is due to fermentation of the juice.

Serve sliced fresh figs with cream, or with lemon or orange juice. If they are thoroughly ripe they need no sweetening.

Use them in practically any other way that you make use of other fresh fruits—in fruit cups, salads, etc.

STEWED DRIED FIGS

Rinse figs; cover with water and boil 20 to 30 minutes. For each cup of fruit add 1 tablespoon sugar for the last 15 minutes of cooking.

Stewed Figs with Oranges: Cook as above, adding ½ slice orange for each 6 figs for the last 5 minutes of cooking. Serve room warm. Sugar may be added if desired.

SPICED CANNED FIGS

1   No. 2½ jar figs
½   cup sugar
¼   cup cider vinegar
⅛   teaspoon salt
1   stick cinnamon
¼   teaspoon whole allspice
Whole cloves

Drain fruit. Combine syrup, sugar, vinegar, salt, and cinnamon. Add allspice in cheesecloth bag. Bring to full rolling boil and boil 2 minutes.

Stick 2 cloves in each fig and add to hot syrup. Simmer 10 minutes. Do not boil.

Remove spice bag. Cover. Chill 24 hours before serving.

SPICED DRIED FIGS

1   pound dried figs
2   cups cold water
Sliced lemon peel
1   1-inch piece ginger root
½   cup sugar
2   tablespoons lemon juice

Wash figs and remove tough stems. Combine with water, lemon peel, and ginger root in a saucepan. Simmer until figs are tender, about 30 minutes.

Add sugar and simmer 10 minutes. Remove from heat and add lemon juice. Stir and chill. Serves 6 to 8.

Melons

Melons are fruits of the gourd family, one that includes many trailing or climbing plants such as the squash and pumpkin. There are many varieties of melons; the watermelon, cantaloupe or muskmelon, honeydew, and honeyball are perhaps the best known.

Hints on Buying Melons

Melons of all types are at their best when fully matured. Ripeness in almost all kinds of melons is indicated by the softening at the part of the fruit which surrounds the "eye" or stem end and should yield to pressure of the finger. In some melons a change of color to a more or less yellowish tinge is also a sign of ripeness. Usually the fragrant aroma that most melons diffuse becomes stronger and is most perceptible when a melon is fully ripe. No one indication is infallible. Sometimes one, and sometimes a combination of indications must serve as a guide. If melons have soft spots on them, they are overripe and may not taste or look right.

Watermelon is tested for ripeness by thumping with the knuckle; if ripe, it gives a resonant, hollow sound.

Unripe melons should never be chilled, because they do not then fully ripen. In quantity, melons are stored at a temperature of 70°F. until ripe, and then chilled just before serving. An unripe melon will ripen in 1 or 2 days on a sunny window ledge.

A cut melon should always be wrapped in waxed paper or the cut section covered with moistened waxed paper before placing in refrigerator to prevent its odor permeating other foods.

To Serve Melons

Melons should be washed and chilled thoroughly before serving fresh in the shell or cut into various shapes and served in fruit cups, salads, etc. Lemon or lime wedges are usually served with melons in the shell such as cantaloupe, honeydew, honey ball, or casaba because the citrus juice emphasizes the melon's flavor. If desired, melon may be served on ice, but the cavity should never be filled with ice because that injures the fruit and dilutes the flavor.

FRUITED MELON

Top melon wedges with canned fruit cocktail and bit of grated orange rind. Or serve a pitcher of lime, lemon, or orange juice.

SPIKED WATERMELON

To impregnate a watermelon with rum or other liquor, remove a small plug, add the liquor slowly. Replace plug and let stand about 8 hours.

MELON SPIKED WITH WINE

Cut a plug in the upperside of the melon. Dig out the seeds with a long handled spoon. Pour in ¾ to 1 cup port wine. Chill melon in bowl of ice in the refrigerator. Slice and serve with rind removed. Use the marinating wine as a dressing.

STUFFED MELON SLICES

Peel cantaloupe or honeydew melons. Cut off enough of one end so you can remove the seeds. Fill the cavity with a fruit gelatin mixture. Allow it to set. Cut the melon in slices and serve on crisp lettuce leaves. If desired, garnish with sour cream or yoghurt.

MELON SLICES WITH RASPBERRIES OR STRAWBERRIES

Cut chilled cantaloupe or honeydew melon into 1- to 2-inch crosswise slices, allowing one slice for each serving.

Remove the seeds and place slices on individual serving plates. Fill the centers with chilled, sugared raspberries or strawberries. Serve with lemon or lime wedges.

WATERMELON BOWL

Cut a watermelon in half; scoop out meat from both halves with a rounded spoon. Prepare cantaloupe and perhaps honeydew balls in same way.

Mix melon balls with any other desired fruits—pineapple, grapes, sliced peaches, figs. Pour enough wine (sherry, port, or sauterne) over fruit to cover; chill for several hours.

Just before serving, drain fruit thoroughly and heap into one half of the scooped-out watermelon shell. Set filled shell on a platter for serving.

Fruit Pinwheel: Vari-hued melon balls topped with shimmering grapefruit sections either chilled, canned, or frozen make a tempting summer dessert.

Cantaloupe Seafood Appetizer: Cut cantaloupes in halves with a zigzag cut. Trace zigzag line around middle, then make deep thrust with knife into center one way, then the other way, all the way around. Remove seeds. Fill cavity with tomato cocktail sauce and set each half shell in shallow bowl of crushed ice. Arrange shrimp around cantaloupe on ice. Garnish with lime or lemon wedges. Serve with a cocktail fork and a teaspoon.

BAKED CANTALOUPE

2 cantaloupes
3 cups sliced peaches
½ cup sugar
Few grains mace
Mint sprigs

Halve cantaloupes; remove seeds. Combine peaches, sugar, and mace. Fill cantaloupes with peaches, arranging slices in radiating pattern on top.

Bake in hot oven (425°F.) 15 minutes. Garnish with mint. Serve at once. Serves 4.

Peaches and Nectarines

PEACHES

Selection: When purchasing peaches, the best thing to remember is that they must look good to be good. Size and color should play an important part in your choice. Make sure they are plump, smooth skinned, and well filled out. The color on the underside of a peach should be creamy white or yellow, blushed with red. Over-ripeness is generally indicated by the deeper reddish-brown color and a softness of the fruit. Peaches in this stage are suitable for immediate use, but cannot be held for any length of time.

Either the white or yellow-fleshed varieties of peaches are suitable for any number of delicious dishes—the white varieties being just as sweet and tasty as the yellow. But remember to select fruit that is not too deeply green tinged, for such fruit is immature and will not ripen properly at home.

NECTARINES

The nectarine is a smooth-skinned variety of peach, often mistakenly believed to be a cross between a peach and a plum. Peach trees occasionally produce nectarines and nectarine trees may produce peaches. The nectarine can be served in exactly the same way as the peach and substituted for it in recipes.

BROILED PEACHES

Place fresh or canned peach halves, cut side up, in a buttered shallow pan. Place 1 teaspoon butter in each cavity. Sprinkle with brown sugar.

Place under broiler about 3 inches from heat until lightly browned.

Curried: To above, add a dash of curry powder.

With Coconut: Before broiling peaches, sprinkle with brown sugar, then with shredded coconut, and dot with butter. Broil until coconut is delicately browned.

GLACIER PEACHES

1 can (1 pound, 13-ounces) cling peach halves
¼ cup brown sugar (packed)
2 or 3 tablespoons wine vinegar
1 teaspoon instant minced onion
¼ teaspoon seasoned or hickory smoke salt

Glacier Topping:
1 package (8-ounce) cream cheese
2 tablespoons spiced syrup from peaches
2 tablespoons mayonnaise or sour cream
2 or 3 drops Tabasco sauce
¼ teaspoon seasoned salt
2 tablespoons sweet pickle relish, drained (or, 1 tablespoon each chopped green pepper and pimiento)

Drain peaches, saving syrup. Combine 1 cup peach syrup with sugar, vinegar, onion, and salt. Bring to boil; pour over drained peaches and chill thoroughly 4 or 5 hours or overnight.

When ready to serve, drain peaches and fill each one with a snowy cap of Glacier Topping. Serve with sandwich-salad plates or with barbecued or other meats or turkey.

Glacier Topping: Soften cheese; beat in syrup and mayonnaise until smooth. Add all remaining ingredients; chill until ready to use. Serves 5 or 6.

BAKED PEACHES

Peel, cut in halves, and remove pits from firm juicy peaches. Place in baking dish.

Fill each hollow with ½ teaspoon butter, 1 teaspoon sugar, a sprinkling of lemon juice, and a dusting of nutmeg or cinnamon.

Place 2 tablespoons water in the bottom of dish. Bake in moderate oven (350°F.) 20 minutes.

Glacier Peaches

FRUIT BAKED IN WINE

4 peaches, apples, or pears
2/3 cup red wine
2/3 cup sugar
1/2 stick cinnamon
4 whole cloves
1/8 teaspoon salt
1/2 thinly sliced seeded lemon

Pare peaches, apples, or pears; place in a baking dish.

Combine wine, sugar, cinnamon, cloves, salt, and lemon. Heat but do not boil and stir; pour over fruit.

Cover and bake in moderate oven (350°F.) until tender when tested with fork. Baste it every 10 minutes. Turn it so that it will cook evenly. Serves 4.

FLAMING FRESH PEACHES

6 large fresh peach halves, peeled
6 tablespoons brown sugar
2 tablespoons butter or margarine
6 maraschino cherries
1/3 cup brandy
Whipped cream or chilled custard

Place peach halves in baking dish. Sprinkle hollows with brown sugar and dot with butter. Broil until sugar crusts, about 3 minutes.

Place cherry in each peach hollow. Pour brandy over all. Ignite and serve while flaming. Serve with whipped cream or chilled custard. Serves 6.

PEACHES WITH BRANDIED CREAM

1/2 cup heavy cream
1 tablespoon brandy flavoring
Few grains salt
3 tablespoons powdered sugar
Few grains mace
8 fresh peaches

Whip cream slightly. Add flavoring, salt, 1 tablespoon sugar, and mace. Whip until cream is thickened.

Peel and slice peaches. Add remaining sugar and mix well. Arrange in serving dishes and top with cream. Serves 4.

SPICED PEACHES

1 No. 2 1/2 can peach halves
1 tablespoon vinegar
1 to 2 sticks cinnamon
1 teaspoon whole cloves

Combine ingredients in saucepan and heat to boiling. Simmer 5 minutes. Chill.

Drain before serving. Stud peaches with whole cloves.

STEWED DRIED PEACHES

Rinse peaches; cover with water and boil 5 minutes. Drain and remove skins.

Cover with fresh water and boil 35 to 45 minutes. Allow 1/4 cup sugar for each cup of peaches and add for last 5 minutes of cooking.

Pears

There are about 800 known varieties of pears, but only a few of these are grown for commercial marketing today. Behind the cultivation of such a large number of varieties lies a story about the landed gentry who lived in France about 1850. At that time it was the style, just as dog or horse raising is today, to see who could produce the finest species of pears. As a result, scores of new types came into being very quickly, and almost all of them were just as quickly forgotten once the fad was dropped. From this French "horticultural spree" came many of the fall and winter pears found on the market today, such as d'Anjou, Du Comice, Bosc, and Nelis.

Selection: When buying pears, don't be misled by a scar or minor surface blemish, as this in no way affects the fruit's inner delicacy. As a matter of fact, many of the most delectable pears have a highly russeted skin.

Pears are packed and shipped green because it is characteristic that they develop a finer flavor and smoother texture when ripened off the tree. Remember that they should be fully ripe for "fresh" use, such as eating out of hand, salads, or shortcakes. If they are hard and unyielding to the touch at time of purchasing, allow them to stand at ordinary room temperature until the flesh responds readily to a gentle pressure of the hand just as a ripe peach does. They are then in prime condition for eating. However, for baking and cooking purposes, pears are best when they are still firm and slightly underripe.

Bartletts are the summer pears. They're creamy yellow when ripe, with an attractive red blush. The Seckel, a late summer pear, is small, sweet, and luscious, richly russeted and excellent for eating from hand. D'Anjou pears are usually medium to large in size with a smooth, thin, light green or creamy yellow skin when ripe. The Bosc, with its long tapering neck, ripens to a rich golden cinnamon, with brownish mottles running to almost solid russet at the blossom end. Another russet pear, very sweet in flavor, is the Winter Nelis, while probably the most luscious of all is the Du Comice. This latter variety has become widely known through being shipped in special gift boxes under a variety of trade names.

FLAMING PEARS

Allow 1 ripe pear per serving. Cut unchilled pears into halves. Remove core and place on an oven-proof plate.

Prick them with a fork and sprinkle with confectioners' sugar. Pour over each pear half 1 tablespoon brandy. Ignite the brandy at the table.

Toasted Pears with Lemon Cream Sauce

TOASTED PEARS WITH LEMON CREAM SAUCE

6 large fresh pears
3 tablespoons lemon juice
1/4 cup sugar
1/4 cup melted butter or margarine
2 1/2 cups corn flakes

Sauce:

1/3 cup confectioners' sugar
1 cup sour cream
2 tablespoons lemon juice

Peel, halve, and core pears. Dip at once into lemon juice in which sugar has been dissolved.

Dip in melted butter. Roll in crushed corn flakes. Arrange cut side up on a shallow baking pan.

Bake in moderate oven (350°–375°F.) for 20 to 25 minutes or until pears are tender but not soft.

To make lemon cream sauce, beat confectioners' sugar into sour cream and flavor with lemon juice. Serves 6.

PEARS BAKED IN PINEAPPLE JUICE

4 winter pears
1 teaspoon grated orange rind
Juice of 1 lemon
1/2 cup canned pineapple juice
1/4 cup sugar

Cut pears in half, peel, and core. Put in 1 1/2-quart casserole. Mix remaining ingredients and pour over pears.

Cover and bake in hot oven (400°F.) for 45 minutes, or until pears are tender. Baste pears every 15 minutes with some of the syrup in bottom of casserole. Chill. Serves 4.

STEWED FRESH GINGER PEARS

3 winter pears
1/2 cup firmly packed brown sugar
1/4 to 1/2 cup granulated sugar
Grated rind and juice 1/2 lemon
Dash of salt
1 teaspoon ground ginger
1/8 teaspoon ground cinnamon
1/2 cup water

Peel, core, and dice pears.

Combine remaining ingredients in saucepan; bring to boil. Add pears. Simmer, covered, for 20 minutes, or until pears are tender. Serves 4.

For an easy fruit plate, brush halved and cored Bartlett pears with pineapple juice to prevent darkening. Separate grapes into small bunches. Peel bananas and flute by lightly pressing tines of fork down sides. Cut into chunks and dip in pineapple juice. Arrange on fresh garden leaves with pineapple slices.

SOUTHERN BAKED PEARS

6   canned pear halves, drained
6   whole cloves
⅔ cup firmly packed light brown sugar
3   tablespoons pear juice
2   teaspoons lemon juice
3   tablespoons orange juice
¼ teaspoon grated orange rind
1   tablespoon butter or margarine
2   tablespoons chopped nuts

Arrange pear halves, with cored side up, in greased baking dish. Stick a clove in each pear.

Mix light brown sugar, fruit juices, orange rind, and butter in a saucepan. Bring to a boil and boil for 10 minutes, stirring occasionally.

Add nuts. Pour syrup over pears. Bake in moderate oven (350°F.) about 30 minutes. Serve hot with meat course or use as a dessert. Or serve cold with whipped cream. Serves 6.

SPICED PEARS

1   No. 2½ can Bartlett pears
1   stick cinnamon
8   to 12 whole cloves
¼ cup vinegar or lemon juice

Drain syrup from pears. Heat it with stick cinnamon and cloves for 5 minutes.

Remove from heat and add vinegar or lemon juice. Pour back over pears and let stand overnight in refrigerator.

PEARS IN PORT WINE

3   large fresh pears
1   cup water
½ cup brown sugar
2   cups port wine

Stew pears, halved, peeled and cored, in 1 cup water and brown sugar, until tender, taking care not to break them.

Drain; add port wine. Chill in refrigerator after they are cold. Serve cold.

Pineapple

Selection: Fully ripe pineapples are slightly soft to the touch, golden yellow in color, and have a "piney" aroma. Size has little to do with quality but you should avoid fruit that appears too green, as it may not ripen well. In fact, the exquisite flavor is only full appreciated when it is eaten where the fruit is field-ripened because it does not increase in sweetness if picked green. If field-ripened, even the core is tender and can be eaten. Over-maturity on the other hand, is most frequently shown by slight decay at the base or on the sides in dark, soft, watery spots. Fresh pineapples bruise easily, so they should be handled as carefully as possible. Store at 70°F. and away from sunlight. Rounded, plump pineapples have more flesh than the tapering ones. The aroma of ripeness is noticeable at the leafy end when one or two leaves are pulled out. A pineapple weighing 2 pounds yields about 2½ cups cubed or 4 cups grated fruit.

PREPARATION OF FRESH PINEAPPLE

Wash pineapple. Cut off leafy end and a slice from stem end. Stand pineapple upright and cut off skin in strips from top to bottom. Remove eyes with pointed knife or special pineapple knife.

Prepare as below. Sprinkle with sugar and chill. Sugar will dissolve as it stands.

Shredded Pineapple: Cut very thin slices. Shred with a fork.

Pineapple Slices: Cut into thin serving slices. Cut out round core.

Pineapple Spears: Cut prepared pineapple into wedges with core removed. Cut into strips.

Pineapple Wedges or Cubes: Cut slices into wedges or cubes after core is removed.

Pineapple Ambrosia: Cut prepared pineapple into slices or cubes. Add 1 cup each of orange and grapefruit sections and ½ cup shredded coconut. Chill 1 hour or more before serving.

PINEAPPLE TRIFLE

1   cup canned crushed pineapple, drained
10 marshmallows, cut in pieces
1   cup macaroon crumbs
1   cup chopped dates
¾ cup heavy cream, whipped

Combine pineapple, marshmallows, macaroon crumbs, and dates in a bowl. Fold whipped cream into above ingredients. Chill. Serves 6 to 8.

GLAZED PINEAPPLE

Method #1: Drain canned pineapple slices or spears; dip in brown sugar. Brown by cooking in hot bacon fat, pan drippings, or butter.

Method #2: Drain canned pineapple slices. Place in shallow buttered baking pan. Do not let the slices overlap.

Dot with butter or margarine. Bake in slow oven (325°F.) 1 hour. Serve with a maraschino cherry in each slice.

Method #3: Sprinkle drained canned pineapple slices or spears with grated cheese. Season with a few grains red pepper. Broil or bake in moderate oven to melt cheese.

PINEAPPLE IN SPICED WINE

1   cup Port or Madeira
1   cup sugar
18 whole cloves or 1 4-inch stick cinnamon
12 slices fresh or canned pineapple

Simmer wine, sugar, and cloves or cinnamon in a saucepan for 5 minutes.

Add pineapple slices and simmer 5 minutes. Turn the slices several times. Serve as a dessert. Serves 6.

CANDIED PINEAPPLE

1   can (1 pound, 4 ounces) sliced pineapple
1¾ cups granulated sugar
Confectioners' sugar

Drain syrup from pineapple thoroughly. (Allow to drain in a colander several minutes.)

Put part of granulated sugar in the bottom of a large pan; then pineapple, and cover with remaining sugar. Store covered about 24 hours at room temperature.

Empty into large skillet and boil 5 minutes. Reduce heat and gently simmer 15 minutes. Turn occasionally during the cooking, taking care that it does not scorch or turn brown. Remove slices to a wire rack to dry about 24 hours.

Pat sides and edges of slices heavily with sifted confectioners' sugar. A crusty glaze will form after standing on the wire rack overnight.

Note: If surface is not dry after standing, reroll in confectioners' sugar.

SPICED PINEAPPLE CHUNKS

¼ cup vinegar
1½ cups sugar
8   whole cloves
Small piece whole ginger
Grated rind of 1 lemon
½ large, ripe pineapple, cut in small chunks

Combine vinegar, sugar, spices, and lemon rind in saucepan. Bring to boil.

Add pineapple and boil until transparent, about 15 minutes. Serve as accompaniment to meat. Makes about 2 cups.

Plums

Selection: When shopping for fresh plums or prunes you will find the best quality ripe fruit is plump, full colored for the variety, and soft enough to yield to slight pressure.

Plums vary in color, according to variety from a greenish-yellow to the familiar deep bluish-purple. The degree of softness of the flesh, in both plums and prunes, is a fairly reliable guide to maturity—the softer ones being more ripe. Overripe fruit, of course, is very mushy to the touch and, unless used quickly, is a poor buy.

Prunes are actually a variety of plum particularly suitable for drying purposes, as a fresh ripe prune can be separated from the pit like a freestone peach. They are blue-black, oval, firm-fleshed, and represent the late plum crop. The Italian variety is most commonly shipped in the fresh stage.

PLUMCOTS

A cross between the plum and apricot, plumcots have a red flesh and a purple skin. Select them as you would apricots. Plumcots have very little acceptance in the market, as they are not very widely known.

SLOE

A small, acid blue-black plum that grows on the blackthorn tree. It is used chiefly to flavor sloe gin.

STEWED PLUMS

4 cups plums
1½ cups boiling water
½ to 1 cup sugar

Cut into halves and remove pits from plums, or use whole plums.

Drop into boiling water. When they are nearly tender, add sugar. Cook a few minutes longer.

PLUM-FIG AMANDINE

1 can (1 pound, 13 ounces) purple plums, or prunes
1 can (1 pound) Kadota figs
¼ cup orange juice
⅓ cup slivered toasted almonds

Add 1 cup syrup from plums and figs to orange juice. Pour over drained fruits and chill. Add almonds just before serving. Serves 6 to 8.

Plum-Fig Amandine

Prunes and Raisins

CLARET PRUNES

1 jar (about 1 pound) stewed prunes
⅔ cup claret wine
⅓ cup prune liquid
¼ cup brown sugar
¼ teaspoon powdered cinnamon
⅛ teaspoon powdered allspice
6 whole cloves

Remove lid from jar; set lid aside. Drain liquid from prunes; save liquid.

Place wine, prune liquid, sugar, and spices in saucepan. Cook, stirring occasionally, until mixture comes to a boil. Reduce heat and cook gently 5 minutes.

Remove from heat and cool slightly before pouring over prunes. Recap jar tightly. Store in refrigerator until ready to use.

SPICED OR PICKLED PRUNES

1 pound prunes
Whole cloves
3 cups water
1 cup dark brown sugar
1 cup vinegar
4 3-inch sticks cinnamon

Wash prunes. Stick 2 cloves in each prune. Soak in water for 2 hours.

Add sugar, vinegar, and cinnamon. Bring to a boil. Simmer 30 minutes. Chill overnight in syrup. Makes 1 quart.

PRUNE PURÉE

1 pound prunes
2 cups water
⅔ cup sugar

Wash prunes; cover with water and soak 2 to 3 hours. Then cover pan and cook in the same water until tender, about 35 minutes.

Add sugar for the last 5 minutes of cooking. Drain off liquid and put prunes through a sieve. Makes about 2 cups purée.

PRUNE WHIP

1½ cups unsweetened cooked prune pulp
⅓ to ½ cup sugar
Grated rind and juice of ½ lemon
⅛ teaspoon salt
2 egg whites

Drain the cooked prunes before pitting so that the pulp is not too moist.

Place all ingredients in deep bowl and beat until mixture is thick and holds its shape. Electric mixer may be used. Place in serving dishes. Chill. Serve with cream or custard sauce. Serves 4 to 5.

Variation: Fold in ¼ cup chopped nuts or coconut after mixture is beaten until stiff.

STEWED PRUNES
(Master Recipe)

½ pound dried prunes
3 cups hot water
1 to 2 tablespoons sugar
Slice of orange or lemon

Wash prunes and soak in hot water 1 to 2 hours. Simmer in same water until tender, about 30 minutes.

Add sugar and lemon or orange slice last 5 minutes of cooking.

If syrup is very thin, remove prunes and boil down syrup. Serve hot or cold.

Variations:

Stewed Prunes and Apricots: Use ¼ pound each of dried prunes and dried apricots. Double the amount of sugar.

Stewed Prunes and Peaches or Pears: Use ¼ pound each of dried prunes and dried peaches or pears. Increase sugar slightly.

PRUNE PUDDING

To 1½ cups pitted stewed prune pulp and juice add a mixture of ¼ cup cornstarch, ¼ teaspoon cinnamon, and ¼ cup cold water.

Cook until clear and thick, stirring constantly. Chill. Serves 4 to 5.

RAISINS

Seeded raisins sometimes called for in recipes are the large variety from which the seeds have been removed. The sweetness released when they were slit open makes them sticky.

Seedless raisins are the small variety; both light and dark are dried from seedless grapes. Cut or chop them to get the full sweetness and flavor.

PLUMPED RAISINS

Wash raisins, cover with boiling water and let stand about 15 minutes or until cool. Drain, cover again with boiling water and soak 15 minutes. Drain and use in recipes.

STEWED RAISINS

Wash raisins. Add 1 cup water for each cup of raisins. Cover and simmer 10 minutes. Add ½ tablespoon sugar for each cup of raisins and cook 5 minutes longer.

Prune Whip

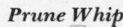

Rhubarb

The rhubarb plant, sometimes referred to as pie plant, is classified as an herb and sometimes as a vegetable; however for cookery it is classed with fruits.

Fresh field or hothouse rhubarb is available. When making your selection, get fresh, large, crisp, and straight stalks of red or cherry color. Condition of the leaves is a reliable guide in judging freshness.

STEWED RHUBARB

Wash 2 pounds rhubarb. Cut off leaves and root ends. Peel only if stalks are tough.

Cut into 1-inch pieces. Add ½ cup hot water. Simmer, covered, 10 minutes.

Add ¾ cup sugar and simmer 5 minutes longer, or until tender.

The amount of sugar necessary may vary with the tartness of the rhubarb. Add dash of cinnamon, if desired. Serves 6 to 8.

Steamed Rhubarb: Prepare as above and cook in top of double boiler until tender, about ½ hour.

STEWED RHUBARB AND PINEAPPLE

Mix equal parts diced washed rhubarb and diced fresh pineapple. Sweeten to taste. Let stand 1 hour or more.

Heat slowly until sugar dissolves. Simmer until rhubarb is tender.

STEWED RHUBARB AND BERRIES

Mix equal amounts of diced washed rhubarb and fresh berries. Add sugar to taste. Let stand 1 hour or more.

Heat slowly until sugar dissolves. Simmer without stirring until rhubarb is tender.

BAKED RHUBARB

Arrange alternate layers of cleaned diced rhubarb and sugar in baking dish. Sprinkle top with sugar.

Bake in slow oven (300°F.) until rhubarb is deep red in color, about 1 hour.

RHUBARB WHIP

Whip 1 pint of heavy cream until stiff. Sweeten. Fold into 1 cup stewed rhubarb.

Place each serving in a sherbet glass which has been lined with lady fingers or pineapple spears. Chill. Serves 6.

RHUBARB BANANA DESSERT

Cook fresh or quick-frozen rhubarb; sweeten to taste. While rhubarb is still warm, add sliced bananas. (3 bananas to 4 cups cooked rhubarb.) Chill. Serve with cream if desired.

Miscellaneous Fruits

ANCHOVY PEAR

The russet-colored fruit of a West Indian tree. Somewhat larger than a chicken egg, it is pickled and eaten like a mango, which it resembles in taste.

BREADFRUIT

The breadfruit is a large, round fruit with a starchy whitish pulp, breadlike when baked. It grows on a tree found in the South Pacific.

CARAMBOLA

This is a fruit of the carambola tree originally cultivated in India and China. The fruit has a thin smooth yellow skin and brown seeds. They vary in size from that of an egg to an orange. The juicy pulp may be pleasantly acid or sweet in flavor. It is eaten raw only. For juice, squeeze the fruit through a sieve. About 15 to 20 fruits will be required to make 2 cups juice. For a beverage resembling lemonade dilute 2 cups juice with 4 cups water and sweeten to taste with sugar.

CHERIMOYAS

Other names for this tropical fruit grown in parts of California are custard apple, sweet sop, and sherbet fruit.

Cherimoyas are tree-ripened, but must stand several days before they become soft and edible.

The perfumy flesh, creamy smooth in texture, has a flavor suggesting a mixture of strawberry and pineapple. To serve, chill the soft fruit thoroughly, then cut in halves if small, quarters or wedges if large, and serve on plates, to be eaten with spoons. The seeds are discarded as one does cherry pits.

The fruit may also be peeled and sieved and used in ice creams and custards. It is especially good combined with bananas.

DURIAN

A large (coconut-sized) fruit which grows in the East Indies and Malay States. It is seldom seen in our markets. It has a spiny outer husk and highly flavored, cream-colored pulp in which are embedded several seeds that resemble chestnuts. These may be roasted.

The unripe fruit often is cooked and served as a vegetable. It has an odor considered offensive to those who come in contact with it for the first time; however, persons who are able to overcome that feature say that it is delicious.

GUAVA

The guava is a tropical pear-like fruit, somewhat like a peach in texture. It is grown in Florida and California and is seldom seen fresh except where grown. The fruit is red to yellow in color. Some guavas are sweet, some sour. The sweeter types are best for eating out of hand, for using fresh in salads and desserts, and for cooking or canning; the sour ones are best for making jellies and jams. To be served fresh, the guava should be washed and served unpeeled. The peel is not eaten.

GROUND CHERRY

Fruit the size of a cherry which grows along the ground in cornfields and elsewhere, wild or cultivated. The berry is covered with a papery husk. Used for preserves, primarily, but good raw.

GRAPES

When you select grapes, choose those bunches that are well formed and good looking. You will find color is a good guide to ripeness. The darker varieties should be free of a green tinge, while white grapes should have a decided amber coloring when completely matured. Fully ripened grapes are fairly soft to the touch and tender to the taste. When ripe for eating, grapes are highly perishable and should be stored in the refrigerator.

California produces most of the early table and juice grapes, while the Eastern states have the later crop.

You will find that the skin of a California grape adheres tightly to the pulp, but that its seeds are easily removed. This, however, is just the opposite of the Eastern grape, for the skin of the latter separates from the pulp easily, while its seeds are difficult to pry away from the meat.

Generally speaking, the Western varieties are the sweeter of the two, although Eastern varieties are eaten out of hand just as much as they are made into jellies, wines, or grape juices.

Listed below are the most important varieties. The first six are from California; the last two are products of the Eastern United States.

Thompson Seedless: White; small, olive-shaped berries, but large bunches, practically seedless; July to October.

Malaga: *White Malaga*, medium-size bunches, round white medium-size berries; August to November. *Red Malaga*, larger, round red berries; August to September.

Flame Tokay: Red; large oval berries and medium to large bunches; September to November.

Cornichon: Blue; long, olive-shaped berries in large bunches, fruit rather soft; September to November.

Emperor: Red, similar in appearance to Tokays, but smaller bunches. Fruit quite hard, even when ripe; November and December.

Ribier: Black, large, round berries, small to large bunches; August to October.

Concord: Blue; the standard Eastern variety, unexcelled for grape juice, jelly, or table use; berries round; August to early November.

Niagara: White, leading Eastern white table variety; September to early November.

Other juice varieties are Alicante (very dark blue), Muscat (white), and Zinfandel (dark blue).

GRAPE LEAVES

The large, tender leaves of Thompson seedless grapes can be used for making dolma (see index). Pickled grape leaves in cans or jars may be bought in Greek, Armenian, or Syrian stores.

CRYSTALLIZED GRAPES

Select perfect red or purple grapes. Wash and drain well. Cut into small clusters.

For each pound of grapes, use 1/2 cup water and 1 cup sugar. Combine water and sugar and boil 5 minutes.

Dip each cluster of grapes separately into hot syrup. Let excess syrup drain off. Sprinkle grapes at once with granulated sugar.

Place on cake rack to harden and place rack in refrigerator.

FROSTED GRAPES

Select perfect red or purple grapes. Wash and dry well. Cut into small clusters.

Beat egg white until slightly frothy. Sprinkle it over the grapes. Dust with granulated sugar. Let dry.

JUJUBE

The jujube is a datelike fruit of any of a number of trees and shrubs of the buckthorn family growing in warm climates. It is gaining favor as a home fruit in the drier sections of the West. The fruit varies considerably in size and is shaped somewhat like a plum, has a pit, and is brownish or reddish brown in color.

It may be eaten fresh or the dried fruits may be chopped and added to breads, cakes, and cooked cereals. The fresh fruit is sometimes made into jujube butter or skinned and pickled.

LOQUAT

The loquat is a delicious plumlike fruit of an ornamental fruiting tree, very popular in parts of California. Fruits of the better varieties grow as large as eggs.

Loquats may be used as table fruits, in preserves, pickled, or in pies. For loquat pie, follow ordinary fruit pie recipes, allowing 2 to 3 cups of pitted loquats for a pie.

MANGO

The mango is a yellowish-red oblong tropical fruit with a thick rind, a somewhat acid and juicy orange pulp, and a hard seed. It tastes like a combination of peach, pineapple, and cantaloupe. The variety commonly sold in the United States is the Hayden mango, larger than a pear, with a smooth rosy skin. It is good raw; stewed like any other fruit; used in puddings, sherbets or ice cream; or made into preserves, jelly or sweet pickles (mango is an important ingredient in chutney). Raw mangoes may be chilled but are delicious at room temperature. Halve them, remove the pit, and eat the soft pulp with a spoon. Or peel and slice the flesh and eat it with a fork, with or without cream and sugar. A sprig of mint and a half lime make a pleasant garnish.

Note: Mango also refers to a pickled pepper, melon, or other fruit or vegetable stuffed with a savory mixture.

OLIVE

The small oval fruit of an evergreen tree with leathery leaves and yellow flowers. Olives are eaten green or ripe as a relish or are pressed to extract olive oil. Olive trees have been grown since prehistoric times in Asia Minor, and their cultivation spread very early to all Mediterranean countries. About 1769 they were introduced by Franciscan missionaries into California, where the entire U. S. crop comes from.

Green olives are picked when full grown but unripe. In the United States they are usually cured and packed in a simple brine. In other countries the brine may be spiced or the olives later pickled in vinegar. Green olives are often pitted and stuffed with pimiento, anchovies, onions, or nuts.

California ripe olives are canned without being pickled. In Europe, black olives are salted or pickled in many styles, often in oil.

PAWPAWS

Pawpaws (also spelled papaw) are often confused with papayas but these two fruits are different botanically. Pawpaws can grow in colder climates than papayas and the fruit is entirely different. Pawpaws are about 6 inches in length, with a width of about 3 inches and an average weight of 3/4 pound. The flesh is yellow, creamy in texture, and has a pungent odor. They often are not enjoyed at first, a taste for them having to be acquired.

There is another variety of the pawpaw tree whose fruit is shaped like a banana but is dark brown in color and flat in appearance. This is sometimes called "johnny-bread." The common name for the species of trees on which the pawpaw grows is custard-apple.

PAPAYA

The papaya is a large, yellowish-orange tropical fruit that resembles a melon. It is common in Hawaii and is now grown in some parts of the continental United States. It has a soft flesh ranging in color from yellow to deep salmon pink.

A papaya is ripe when it is soft enough to yield to slight pressure with the thumb. It is eaten raw. Small papayas may be served at room temperature, with a fruit knife; large ones are chilled and served in any of the ways suitable for melon. They combine well with other fruits in cocktails or salads. They may be made into jam, pickles, or ketchup or into sherbets and other desserts. In Hawaii, green papayas are steamed or baked and served as a vegetable.

PASSION FRUIT (GRANADILLA)

Passion fruit, sometimes called the granadilla, grows extensively in South America and Australia and is also cultivated in California in increasing quantities. The fruit is the size and shape of an egg and has a tough, purple skin. The meat is yellow with many black seeds, and generally is eaten in the fresh stage with a spoon; otherwise it is used in making jelly and as a base for fruit punch.

The passion fruit is said to derive its name from the fact that early Christian missionaries to South America, noticing it for the first time, saw in its flower formation symbols of the Crucifixion—the crown of thorns, nails, etc.

PERSIMMONS

The persimmon is the fruit of any of several trees of the ebony family. A number of varieties are available, including the small, puckery ones native to the eastern part of the United States and the large Japanese persimmons cultivated in the South and on the Pacific coast. The latter, which are the type usually found in markets, are about the size and texture of tomatoes and range in color from rosy orange or salmon pink to yellow. They should be tested for ripeness in the same way as tomatoes; an unripe persimmon is inedibly acid-testing.

Persimmons are most commonly used as a dessert fruit. They should be thoroughly chilled. To serve, set the persimmon stem-end down on a plate and cut off a bit of the top, so that the pulp may be spooned out. Or quarter it from the top, cutting not quite through the stem end, and spread out the sections petal-fashion.

In season October to February, persimmons ripen best in a cool, dark place. This fruit is extremely delicate and should receive no unnecessary handling. It is ready to eat when soft, but when storing it temporarily you should be sure it is kept dry.

PLANTAIN

The plantain is a type of banana, starchier and less sweet than the common species. It is a staple food of the tropics; it is picked green and cooked as a vegetable. It is good sliced thin and fried in deep fat like a potato chip and sprinkled with salt. The slices should be very crisp even when cold. **Note:** The name is also applied to any of a number of related weeds with ribbed leaves. Some are cooked and eaten as greens when young and tender.

POMEGRANATE

The pomegranate is a tropical fruit, the berry of a somewhat thorny shrub or small tree now cultivated in Arizona and California. It is about the size of a large orange, and its leathery skin varies in color from light yellow to deep purplish red. Those with a thin skin of bright color and fresh appearance are considered preferable. The enclosed seeds and crimson juice are used in salads, cocktails, and punches. To serve pomegranates as a dessert, mix the scooped-out seeds with powdered sugar or honey and chill them. The fruit may also be eaten out of hand. Pomegranate juice is the basis of grenadine syrup. In the Near East it is made into wines.

PRICKLY PEARS

Prickly pears (Indian fig, barberry fig, and tuna) are the delicious fruit of a species of cactus and are most abundant during fall and early winter. They range in color from yellow to crimson and have spines which can be easily removed by singeing before the fruit is peeled. Prickly pears have a juicy, acid pulp that may be eaten raw or cooked and is often made into jam.

Choose those that are firm but not hard, with a bright, fresh appearance, when shopping for this unusual fruit.

QUINCE

The quince is an autumn fruit which is generally grown locally for use in jelly-making and preserving. They may also be stewed, baked, or used in pies or tarts. Good-quality quinces are firm, free from blemishes and show a pale yellow color when fully ripe. They bruise very easily and must be handled carefully, although they may be kept for a period of time in a dry, cool place.

Quinces resemble a yellow apple a great deal, although their flesh is more acid-bitter with numerous hard seeds throughout.

BAKED QUINCES

6   medium quinces
1½ cups water
1   cup sugar

Pare, core, and slice the quinces into a casserole. Add water and sugar. Cover and bake very slowly until the fruit is tender and deep red in color.

If the water evaporates, add a little from time to time to insure enough syrup to surround the fruit when it is served.

SAPODILLA

Also called sapodilla plum, sapota, sapote, the sapodilla is the lemon-shaped fruit of a tropical American evergreen tree that also yields chicle. Sapodilla is a rough-skinned fruit with a sweet, yellowish pulp. It has an appealing flavor and may be served in any of the same ways as peaches.

SOURSOP OR GUANABANA

The soursop is a large, pulpy, acid tropical fruit, used for ices and conserves.

TAMARIND

The tamarind is a tropical fruit with a brown pod 3 to 8 inches long, which contains a juicy, acid pulp used in chutneys and preserves, especially in guava jellies. A drink is made by adding sugar and water to the pulp. The tamarind is grown in the East and West Indies and also in Florida.

A marmalade can be made from tamarind as follows: Wash 1 quart tamarinds; drain and combine with 1½ cups water. Bring to a boil, reduce heat and simmer until soft. Put through a sieve to remove fibers and seeds. Heat the pulp and add 1 cup sugar for each cup pulp. Simmer, stirring constantly, until the mixture thickens. Seal and store as for other preserves (see index).

Fruit Soups

Fruit soups are an old world invention especially favored in the Scandinavian countries and in Israel. Colorful, tart, and appetizing, they are particularly delightful for summer meals.

When served cold, they should be thoroughly chilled. Serve hot fruit soups when the remainder of the menu consists of cold food.

CHILLED FRUIT SOUP
(Master Recipe)

2   tablespoons quick-cooking tapioca
1½ cups water
1   tablespoon sugar
Dash of salt
½   cup quick-frozen concentrated orange juice
2½ cups diced fresh fruits (peaches, cherries, apples, bananas, etc.)

Place tapioca and water in saucepan. Bring to boil, stirring constantly. Remove from heat.

Add sugar, salt, and concentrated orange juice; blend. Cool, stirring once after 15 to 20 minutes. Cover and chill.

Before serving, add fruits. If thinner soup is desired, add more juice or less fruit.

Garnish bowl with fruit such as halved strawberries, orange sections, cherries, blueberries, bananas.

Serves 5 to 6.

SWEDISH FRUIT SOUP

½ pound mixed dried fruits (prunes, peaches, apricots)
½ cup dried apples
¼ cup currants
¼ cup seedless raisins
2   quarts cold water
¼ cup red sago (roda sago-gryn)
1   inch stick cinnamon
⅛ teaspoon salt
2   tablespoons sugar
1   tablespoon grated lemon rind
2   cups raspberry juice

Wash dried fruits thoroughly. Cover with cold water; let stand overnight.

In the morning add sago (or tapioca) and cinnamon. Bring to boiling point; cover, reduce heat and simmer 1¼ hours. Add remaining ingredients.

Chill soup. Serve very cold as dessert, sprinkled with finely sliced almonds. Serves 6.

BERRY SOUP

1   pint blueberries, raspberries, or other berries
3½ cups water
2   cups apple juice
¼ teaspoon salt
⅛ teaspoon nutmeg
Sugar to taste
2   tablespoons cornstarch
¼ cup lemon juice

Combine berries and water in saucepan; bring to boil. Cover and cook 20 minutes or until soft; put through sieve.

Add apple juice, salt, nutmeg, and sugar to taste. Add cornstarch dissolved in 2 tablespoons cold water. Cook until clear, stirring constantly. Chill and add lemon juice.

Top each serving with a spoonful of whipped cream if desired. Sprinkle with chopped mint. Serves 6.

Berry Cream Soup: After chilling add 1 cup thick sour cream.

Chilled Fruit Soup

HERBS, SPICES, AND CONDIMENTS

Everyday cooking becomes a culinary triumph with just a little addition of the right herb or spice.

Herbs are spices, but in practice a distinction is made between the two. A spice may be the roots, bark, stems, leaves, seeds, or fruits of a plant, and many of the seasonings that are called spices come from the tropics; herbs are the leaves of soft-stemmed or grassy plants, usually from the temperate zone.

The packaged herbs and spices in stores are dried. Besides the unmixed varieties, many blends are sold—poultry seasoning, chili powder, curry powder, pumpkin-pie spice, and others.

The word condiment can be applied to any herb or spice and also to salt and monosodium glutamate (which are chemicals, not spices) and to bottled seasonings like ketchup or prepared mustard.

HINTS FOR COOKING WITH HERBS

● Since experience is obviously the best teacher, use herbs sparingly until you become acquainted with them.
● The important thing to remember is that herbs never should dominate the foods with which they are used. Herbs are meant to season, to add flavor, to point up natural flavors.
● Use 1/4 teaspoon of dried herbs for a dish serving four unless you are sure you like more. Do not use over 1/2 teaspoon of mixed herbs in a dish serving four.
● Do not use herbs in several dishes at the same meal—use them for variety and accent only.
● Remember that there is a difference in the strength of fresh, dried and powdered herbs.
● Dried herb leaves are four times stronger than the same measure of fresh leaves.
● A powdered herb is two times stronger than the same measure of the crumbled dried leaves of the same herb.

● Since dried herbs tend to lose their fragrance, soaking them in a few drops of water or lemon juice for 15 minutes before using helps to point up the flavor.
● Fresh herbs from the garden can be used just as successfully in cooking as freshly dried herbs, but you always use less of the dried than the fresh.
● Always cut, crush, or mince fresh herbs before using to bring out the volatile oils and true flavors. For some purposes, grind them in a mortar. The more the cut surface is exposed the more completely the aromatic oil can be absorbed.
● Blending or heating herbs with butter or other fats is a good way to draw out and extend the flavor of aromatic oils.
● Remember that the strength of the flavor herbs give food is increased by the length of time they cook, by a cover on the pot, the freshness of the herb.
● Herbs left too long in soups or gravies will impart unpleasantly strong flavors. They are best added a short time before the cooking is finished.
● For soups or gravies, add sprigs of fresh herbs tied in tiny bunches or use ground herbs in cheesecloth bags and remove them after they have served their purpose.
● In uncooked foods, like tomato cocktail, herbs must stand overnight to release their full flavor.

HERBS AND SPICES IN SALT-FREE DIETS

Pure herbs and spices (not blended mixes or sauces) are often allowed in salt-free diets to add interest and zest to bland foods. Many different flavors resulting from a variety of combinations of herbs and spices help cover up the lack of salt in most dishes.

Note that celery and parsley flakes may contain too much sodium for inclusion in these diets.

HOW TO START HERB AND SPICE SHELF

Don't buy everything at once. The beginner would be wise to buy the most used and most versatile herbs and spices first and learn to enjoy them. When you are an expert in the use of these, add others to your seasoning shelf.

It pays to buy only small quantities of quality brands for full natural flavor. Among the herbs basil, marjoram, savory, tarragon, thyme, and rosemary are especially versatile. Less versatile but very popular is sage.

TO FREEZE FRESH GARDEN HERBS

Select young sprays of parsley, mint, or dill or make bundles of herb bouquets. Wash; then blanch in boiling water 10 seconds. Chill in ice water 1 minute and pat dry.

Seal enough herb for a single use in a small freezer bag or foil. Clip or staple all bags of the same herb to a piece of cardboard and label. To use: While still frosty, snip into soup, casserole, butter, etc.

CARE OF HERBS AND SPICES

Since spices are subtle perfume oils trapped within the cell walls of various plants, they must be carefully guarded lest their exotic fragrances evaporate. Observe these simple rules to keep your spices in top condition.

1. Always keep your spice jars tightly covered. If jars are left open, dust and airborne bacteria promote spice spoilage and flavor destruction. Likewise, evaporation causes loss of spice oils and flavor potency.

2. Keep spices in a clean, dry, cool place, preferably in the dark. Do not keep near a stove, radiator, or any other warm place, since heat hastens evaporation and loss of flavor. Do not keep in a humid place. Dampness promotes "caking" and the growth of mold—re-

sulting in a musty odor and flavor.

3. Keep your spices dry. Do not dip a wet spoon into a jar of spices. Any moisture introduced into the spice itself may cause deterioration.

4. If they lose their delicate aroma, replace them with fresh ones.

TO DRY FRESH HERBS

When fresh herbs begin to flower, pick off tops and perfect leaves.

Wash; spread on cheesecloth on a tray. Dry in warm, sunshiny spot, turning occasionally, 2 to 3 days. Then crush leaves (no stems) and store in jars.

THE NAMES, DESCRIPTIONS, HINTS FOR USING THEM

AC'CENT

A trade name for monosodium glutamate (which see).

AJI-NO-MOTO

Originally a trade name, this is now the usual term in Japan for the vegetable protein known in the United States as monosodium glutamate (which see).

ALLSPICE

Pea-sized fruit of a West Indian tree. Sometimes called Jamaica pepper. Flavor resembles a blend of cinnamon, nutmeg, and cloves—hence the name.

Uses: Whole in pickling, gravies, meats, fish dishes; ground in or on cakes, cookies, puddings, relishes, tomato sauce, preserves, pot roast, steak.

ANGELICA

An aromatic plant of the carrot family, native to the Northern Hemisphere and New Zealand. The young leafstalks and stems are candied and used in decorating confections and cakes, and an herb tea is brewed from the leaves.

ANISE

A plant of the carrot family, native to the Mediterranean region but long cultivated elsewhere for its aromatic and medicinal qualities. It has clusters of small white or yellow flowers and a greenish-brown oval seed (aniseed) similar in appearance to caraway.

Uses: The seeds, resembling licorice in flavor, are used in candy, pastry, anisette, and herb tea and in some cheese dishes. Try some on sweet rolls or in cooky batter.

BASIL

Leaf of a plant of the mint family, native to India and Persia.

Uses: Italians use it in tomato paste. French flavor soups, meat pies, stews. Add some to peas, squash, string beans.

Sprinkle over lamb chops before broiling. Wonderful in spaghetti sauces, tomato soup, on fish, cheese and egg dishes, especially omelets.

BAY LEAVES

Aromatic shiny green leaf of evergreen laurel tree, native to Mediterranean area. Used by Greeks to crown heroes.

Uses: For pickling, stews, pot roasts, sauerbraten, sauces for shrimp and fish, gravies, soups, spiced vinegars, tomato mixtures.

BEE BALM

This name is applied to several herbs, especially *Melissa officinalis* and *Monarda didyma*, both perennials of the mint family. The former is sometimes cultivated for its lemon-like odor and flavor. The leaves and the oil distilled from them (known as melissa or balm) are much used for seasonings and beverages. Monarda didyma, also called Oswego tea, was used by the Indians and colonists for tea.

BERGAMOT

(1) A perennial herb of the mint family, used to make a kind of tea. (2) A type of citrus fruit, grown chiefly in Italy, whose thin yellow rind yields an oil used in some perfumes. (3) A variety of pear.

BORAGE

An herb with large, hairy leaves and blue flowers, used in salads and with green vegetables and to flavor soups and stews.

BOUQUET GARNI

Bunches of herbs and sometimes spices tied together or enclosed in a piece of cheesecloth and removed and discarded after cooking.

A usual combination consists of parsley, celery leaves, and onion, and a sprig of thyme. Various combinations are used for soups and stews. For example, parsley, thyme, and clove are often used for lamb stew.

BURNET

An herb of the rose family, with lacy leaves. It is used in salads (especially with cucumbers) and sometimes for herb teas and vinegars.

CAMOMILE OR CHAMOMILE

The name of several herbs of the composite family. One variety *Anthemis nobilis,* has an apple-like aroma and is used for "camomile tea" which is made from the dried flower heads.

CAPER

The flower bud of a southern European shrub, which is pickled and used as a garnish or for seasoning. Excellent with shrimp salad or to season lamb gravy.

CARAWAY

Dried fruit of plant of parsley family, grown in Northern Europe.

Uses: In rye bread and rolls. Add to sauerkraut, cabbage, noodles, asparagus, French fried potatoes, soft cheese spread, cookies. Sprinkle on liver, kidneys before cooking.

CARDAMOM

Tiny brown seeds in small pod—from India, Guatemala.

Uses: To flavor Danish pastry, coffee cake, buns, stewed fruit, grape jelly. Try seeds in demitasse. Sprinkle ground cardamom on iced melon.

In the Orient people chew the seeds to sweeten the breath.

The extract may be used in place of ground form. Seeds may be steeped in hot water or milk, strained out and the flavor carrying liquid used for the recipe.

CASSIA

Dried bark of evergreen tree of laurel family, native to China and Malay States. Ground cassia resembles cinnamon in flavor and in this country is sold as cinnamon. Most persons can't tell the difference between genuine cinnamon and cassia.

CASSIA BUDS

Cassia "buds" are dried unripe or ripe buds of tree from which cassia bark is obtained. Has rich flavor and high oil content.

Uses: In pickling, notably in bread and butter pickles.

CAYENNE PEPPER—RED PEPPER

Most of our cayenne and red pepper comes from Louisiana; some cayenne comes from Africa. Cayenne is a ground spice made of the hottest of hot pepper pods. Red pepper is milder, but brighter in color.

Uses: Cayenne is used in Tabasco sauce, chili powder, curry, and in moderation peps up many a soup, fish dish, barbecue sauce, cheese mixture.

Red pepper goes into commercial ginger ales, and gingersnaps, and is an excellent seasoning for meat and fish dishes.

Cayenne must be used most discreetly, since it is fiery-hot.

These peppers are no relation to black and white pepper. They are vegetables, not fruits. They are cousins to chili peppers.

CELERY SALT

A combination of ground celery seed and salt.

Uses: Add to tomato juice, soups, potato salad, salad dressings, bouillon, oyster stew, clam juice, croquettes. Try it on "boiled" or fried eggs.

CELERY SEED

It is not the seed of the common celery but the tiny seed-like brown fruit of parsley family, with taste akin to celery. Grown in many countries, especially India and France.

Uses: For pickling, salads, salad dressings, sauces. Add it to pastry when baked to be used as a salad accompaniment. Try it with vegetables, stews, and hamburger.

CHERVIL

Leaf of herb grown in many countries in the temperate zone. Resembles parsley in flavor but is sweeter and more aromatic.

Uses: It may be used in any way that parsley is used. Include it in mixed herb preparations for salads. Good in soups, egg and cheese dishes, and with fish.

Try it chopped fine and sprinkled over broiled fish just a couple of minutes before removing from broiler.

CHIVES

A hardy plant of the onion family with small, slender, hollow green leaves which have a delicate onion flavor. To use, snip fine or chop and add to cheese and egg dishes, meat and poultry dishes, stews, salads, soups, and vegetables, etc.

CHILI PEPPERS

Long red pods that are mild or hot. Any number of varieties are used.

Uses: Mexican varieties go into chili powder. Whole chilies are most frequently used in pickling. Mixed pickling spices contain them. Break up one or two for soups and stews.

CHILI POWDER

A mixture of chili pepper and other spices which may be bought either mild or hot. Oregano and cumin seeds and sometimes garlic go into it.

Uses: It is the basic seasoning for Mexican cooking including the popular chili con carne.

Used in cocktail sauces, barbecue sauces, casseroles, bean dishes, in some spaghetti sauces, soups, stews. Try it with hamburger, meat loaf.

CINNAMON

Aromatic bark of cinnamon tree, grown mostly in Ceylon. Most people can't tell the difference between true cinnamon and cassia "cinnamon." The former is lighter in color and milder in flavor than cassia. Stick cinnamon is the dried bark of the tree. Ground cinnamon is made from stick cinnamon.

Uses: It is the most popular spice of all and used in many types of cooking and baking.

Sticks are often used in pickling, for spiced coffee, cider, chocolate, and wine.

Pumpkin pie, puddings, rolls, spice cake, and the popular cinnamon toast are just a few recipients of this ground spice flavor.

CLOVES

Nail-shaped dried brown buds of evergreen clove tree, grown in East and West Indies.

Uses: Whole, for baked ham, pickling, special syrups.

Ground, for chocolate pudding, candy, cake.

Stud a small onion with 3 whole cloves; add to meat stew.

CORIANDER

Dried fruit of small plant of parsley family. Flavor resembles combination of lemon peel and sage. Grown in North Africa and Argentina.

Uses: Whole, in mixed pickles, gingerbread, cookies, cakes, poultry stuffings, mixed green salads.

Rub ground coriander on pork before roasting.

CUMIN OR COMINO

Aromatic seed of a caraway type herb which it resembles in shape. It comes from Mediterranean islands, Mexico, Syria, Iran, India, and other places. It is one of the oldest known spices but isn't used much in the United States.

Uses: It is a favorite in Mexican and South American cooking. Used in Germany to flavor bread, in Holland for cheese, and in Norway for anchovies. It's an ingredient in sausage, pickles, chili, and curry powder.

If you want to try it add a little to stews or boil the seed briefly and pound it. Then use it in cheese, stuffed eggs, pies, soups, and in some canapé spreads.

CURRY POWDER

It is a blend of spices (about 16 ingredients) which include cumin and other seed, several varieties of red peppers, ginger, and turmeric.

Uses: It is basic in the cookery of India where curried dishes include fish, meats, poultry, and rice.

It's good with eggs, in cheese spreads, and in fish chowders. Try it in tomato soup, French dressing, and in scalloped tomatoes.

Because of the yellow turmeric which it contains, curry powder colors as well as flavors the foods in which it is used.

DILL

This is an herb of the parsley family, and though much of the dill seed is imported (grown chiefly in India and Europe), dill for our pickling is homegrown.

Uses: Dill should be used more often to flavor potatoes; it's good with sauerkraut, fish, and in salad dressings and stews.

Try it with green apple pies, cabbage, turnips, and cauliflower.

The dried seed may be purchased in most food stores where herbs are sold.

FAGGOT

A bouquet garni (which see) tied into a bundle.

FENNEL

This small seed-like fruit of a plant of parsley family has a flavor akin to licorice.

Uses: The seed is used in sweet pickles, "boiled" fish, candies, pastry, and liqueurs. Italian bakers use the seed on rolls and breads. Try a dash of the seed in apple pie.

Note: The vegetable fennel as found in the markets resembles celery but smells and tastes more like anise. It may be cooked like celery. The roots are cooked like celery root. Relished particularly by Italians. Also known as finocchio.

FILÉ POWDER

This is an aromatic powder of dried sassafrass leaves. It is used in many Creole dishes, especially the gumbos.

It is sold in New Orleans at markets and grocery stores, elsewhere in stores with large herb assortments.

It is usually added to a dish shortly before serving because the powder becomes gummy on cooking.

FENUGREEK

Hard seed, strong and pleasant aroma. Planted as a cover crop in citrus fruit areas.

Uses: It is not particularly useful to the homemaker. It is used in curry powder, in mango pickle and green mango chutney recipes.

FINES HERBES

A French term for fine herbs. These are combinations of several herbs which are used in stews, soups, fish sauces, fish and meat stuffings, and other recipes.

The herbs are mixed, finely chopped, and added to food just before serving. For example, in pork dishes 1 tablespoon each of sage, basil, and savory are sometimes used this way.

GARLIC

Garlic is the strong-flavored bulb of a plant of the lily family, made up of small sections called cloves. It is an indispensable seasoning in much of the world's cooking—including the French, the Italian, and the Chinese, which are among the most celebrated.

Good quality garlic is thoroughly dry, with firm and well-shaped bulblets or cloves. White and red varieties are obtainable but there is little difference in flavor between the two.

Unless garlic is kept in a closed jar, its strong, pungent odor penetrates all food close to it. Because of this, many grocers sell fresh garlic from which the tops have been removed, handily packaged in small cellophane bags containing 4 to 5 segments.

To Use Garlic: A peeled clove may be added whole or halved to a dish; if a toothpick is inserted in clove it is easy to remove after cooking. Or it may be crushed in a garlic press. Or clove may be sprinkled with a little salt and crushed to a paste with back of spoon. Or rub a cut garlic clove on inside of salad bowl or other bowl used for mixing ingredients.

GARLIC SALT

Ground garlic cloves mixed with salt. Gives famous French and Italian dishes their distinction.

Uses: It's a convenient way to get the tangy garlic flavor and aroma. Use it in addition to or in place of plain salt in many dishes.

Add it to tomato juice, salad dressings, salads, meat, vegetable, spaghetti dishes, and on steaks just before broiling.

GERANIUM

Some varieties of this common garden flower have leaves with aromas which make them popular for culinary use—especially the rose, apple, lemon, nutmeg, and orange scented geranium leaves. Among the dishes in which they are used are baked apples, fruit compote, custards, jellies, and sometimes just as a garnish in fruit drinks.

GINGER

This is the pungent-flavored root of a plant grown in Jamaica, China, Japan.

Uses: Preserved in syrup or candied, ginger is a pepper-upper of many a sauce and pudding.

Gingerbread, ginger cookies, and like baked products make use of the ground dried spice.

Try chopped candied ginger in sauce for ham or chicken, or add it to a meringue or whipped cream topping for pumpkin pie. Add a pinch of powdered ginger to hot cider or wine.

HERB BOUQUET
See **Bouquet Garni**

HOREHOUND OR HOARHOUND

A bitter herb of the mint family, with downy leaves and little white flowers; also a bitter juice extracted from the leaves.

Uses: Its most familiar use is in horehound candy and cough medicines. The tender leaves and flowers may also be used (discreetly, because of the bitter flavor) in seasoning cakes, cookies, or meat stews.

HORSERADISH

The potent-flavored root of a plant of the mustard family. Ground and mixed with vinegar and salt, it is a favorite seasoner for beef, corned beef, ham, or other meats, and an ingredient in many sauces.

HYSSOP

A fragrant, blue-flowered herb of the mint family. The flowers and young leaves are used in fish, meat, and game dishes, sometimes also in fruit cocktails and soups.

LAUREL LEAF
See **Bay Leaves**

LAVENDER

The dried flowers, leaves, and stalks of this plant of the mint family are usually used to fill sachets and to perfume closets. Some people, however, use minute quantities of the flowers and leaves as a seasoner in salads, beverages, jellies, and desserts.

LEMON BALM

An herb related to mint. The fragrant leaves are prized for herb teas and for flavoring other beverages, soups, stuffings, salads, and sauces. See **Bee Balm.**

LEMON VERBENA

An aromatic herb from a shrub of the verbena or vervain family, with a delicate flavor similar to that of lime or lemon. The fresh leaves are used to flavor fruit salads, fruit cups, jellies, and cold drinks. An herb tea may be made from them.

LICORICE

A small plant of the pea family, native to Europe. A juice obtained from the root is used in flavoring candy and drinks and for medicines. Also spelled liquorice.

LOVAGE

A European herb of the carrot family, formerly cultivated for use as a home medicine. The stalks may be eaten like celery. The roots yield an oil used to flavor tobaccos and perfumes. The seeds and leaves are used to season meats and salads. Like lavender, lovage is often used to fill sachets and to perfume closets.

MACE

Fleshy orange-red skin covering nutmeg, the fruit of an evergreen tree. Native to Molucca (Spice) Islands. Has a softer flavor than nutmeg itself.

Uses: Ground, gives pound cake golden color and exotic flavor. Makes cherry pie a gourmet dish. Good in sauces, meat stuffings.

Add a teaspoonful to 1 pint whipped cream to increase delicacy.

The whole mace (called blade mace) is used most often in pickling and

sauces.

Try a chopped blade in stewed cherries or gingerbread batter.

MARIGOLD

Flower petals of the hardy annual plant have been used in cooking for hundreds of years. Fresh petals are used as a garnish for salads. A yellow coloring has been made from it as a substitute for saffron. It is used for coloring butter, cheese, cakes, cookies, as well as for making such unusual specialties as marigold buns. The petals give a rather exotic flavor for shellfish dishes, chowders, stews.

MARJORAM

Dried leaf of grey-green herb of mint family. Imported from France, South America.

Uses: It has a thousand uses—stews, gravies, roasts, fish, omelets, poultry seasonings, in the manufacture of sausage. May be used as a herb salad.

Sprinkle dried marjoram leaves into lamb dishes; use powdered marjoram on lima beans, peas, green beans.

When used discreetly, the mint relationship of marjoram can be capitalized upon for fruit salads.

Most packers use quantities of marjoram for their many loaves, liverwurst, bologna, etc.

MINT

Any of various aromatic plants whose leaves are used for flavoring. Spearmint or peppermint makes the dried product, which is used whole, crushed, or pulverized to flavor soup, stews, meat, fish, sauces, and jelly.

MONOSODIUM GLUTAMATE

A white crystalline substance derived from a vegetable protein, which emphasizes natural food flavors without adding any flavor, color, or aroma of its own. It has long been a standard ingredient in Japanese cooking. It may be used as a basic seasoning, like salt and pepper, in practically all cooked dishes.

Monosodium glutamate is sold under various trade names; however, one brand, Ac'cent, is so widely distributed that the name is now frequently used in recipes. Also called MSG.

MSG
Monosodium glutamate (which see).

MUSTARD

Small seed of annual plant of mustard family. Black, brown, white, or yellow varieties. Best sources are Holland and England, although mustard is now extensively cultivated in the United States.

Uses: This seed of an herb may be purchased whole for pickling, ground for sauces and salad dressings or "prepared" as a sauce for meats.

Deviled eggs and potato salad need mustard as much as a "hot dog."

White sauce flavored with mustard makes an excellent dressing for fish, meat, or vegetables.

NASTURTIUM

A rather common flower, the leaves of which are sometimes used in salads or to flavor jelly or sauces. The seeds are pickled and used as a substitute for capers.

NUTMEG

It is really the seed of the fruit of the nutmeg tree which grows in the East and West Indies. The whole fruit consists of an outer husk, the mace (see **Mace**), an inner shell around which the mace curls, and the nutmeg or kernel. May be purchased whole or ground. The ground spice is more popular. The whole nutmeg is ground as needed.

Uses: The ground spice is used in cakes, pies, many different puddings, and other desserts. Very good with such vegetables as asparagus, cauliflower, and spinach. Excellent with fruit salads.

It's almost a "must" for eggnog and custards and a dash certainly improves lemon sauce for puddings. Rice puddings, applesauce, and sweet potato soufflé are improved with it.

Try it sprinkled on fried bananas or on bananas and berries with cream. It's the best spice for doughnuts.

ONION SALT

Mixture of ground dehydrated onions and salt.

Uses: Use for any dish where onions are used.

ORACH

A garden herb with red or green leaves that are sometimes used as a vegetable. Also spelled orache.

OREGANO

Dried leaf of mint family herb. Grown in Mexico, Italy. Has strong aromatic flavor. It's a cousin to marjoram.

Uses: Flavors pork, beef stew, meat sauces, omelets, "boiled" eggs, chili con carne.

Use it in tomato dishes, especially Italian spaghetti sauce, in mixed green salads with or without tomatoes.

PAPRIKA

Mildest of the peppers, paprika is made by grinding dried large red peppers of mild flavor. Hungarian and Spanish paprika are best.

Uses: The bright color makes it a popular garnish for such white foods as fish, potatoes, cottage cheese, cauliflower.

Used in salad dressings, ketchups, chili sauces, in large amounts in such dishes as Hungarian goulash or chicken paprikash.

PARSLEY-DRIED

Our most common herb; the dried leaves of parsley are also known as "parsley flakes."

Uses: Fresh parsley is a garnish for almost anything up to dessert.

The dried parsley is worth keeping on hand for times when the fresh green is unavailable. Dried parsley is especially nice for soups and stews, in dumplings for flavor and color.

PENNYROYAL

Either of two similar hairy plants of the mint family, used for an herb tea and sometimes for stews and soups.

PEPPER, WHITE OR BLACK

Totally unrelated to the capsicums (cayenne, paprika, red pepper, etc.) these peppers are the small dried berries of a climbing vine. World's most popular spice, they are native to the East Indies.

Black pepper is ground from the whole outer dried berry (peppercorn). White pepper is made from the same peppercorns with the outer hull removed. It is milder, liked especially in light foods where the black specks might be unattractive.

Grind your peppercorns in your own little pepper mill for the most pungent flavor.

PEPPERCORN

The whole dried berry of the pepper plant before grinding. See **Pepper, White or Black.**

PICKLING SPICE

This is generally a mixture of a dozen or more whole spices.

Uses: Used for pickling and preserving relishes, meats, and vegetables. Sometimes used when boiling beets and cabbage.

Try a little bag of spice in a stew but remove it as soon as stew is flavored to your liking.

PIMENTO

Also spelled pimiento; refers to the sweet red pepper, the kind from which paprika is made and which is available canned. Also the allspice tree and berry. See **Paprika; Pepper; Allspice.**

POPPY SEED

Seed of a plant of poppy family, native to Asia; however, Holland is the home of the best of these tiny blue-black seeds used so much by bakers. They have a nut-like flavor, no narcotic properties.

Uses: Whole seed used as topping for rolls, bread, cakes, cookies. Good in salads, with noodles, with cottage cheese.

POTHERB

Any plant whose leaves or stems are used in cooking.

POULTRY SEASONING

Mixture of herbs and spices, often of sage, thyme, marjoram, savory, rosemary. A "must" for seasoning poultry.

Uses: For poultry, veal, pork, fish stuffings. Use in meat loaf.

Add 1/8 teaspoon to batter for French fried onions.

PUMPKIN PIE SPICE

Blend of spices, often of cinnamon, cloves, ginger, ready-mixed for finest flavor.

Uses: For pumpkin pie, cookies, gingerbread.

PURSLANE

The common name for a number of related weeds with pink, fleshy stems and small round leaves some of which are used as herbs in salads or cooked as a vegetable. Purslane is sometimes cultivated.

To serve purslane as a vegetable, use only the tips and leaves. Wash well with cold water, then cover with salted boiling water and simmer for a few minutes. Drain well and reheat in a small amount of melted butter. Season to taste and serve immediately.

ROSEMARY

The herb "for remembrance" is a native of Mediterranean regions. It is a sweet, fresh tasting herb resembling curved pine needle.

Uses: Good with roast beef, lamb, beef and lamb stews.

Try it in green salads, with fish, in soups. Delicious with green beans, potatoes, turnips, cauliflower.

Used commercially in meat packing, and in pickles and perfumes.

Dried rosemary needs to steep in liquid before its flavor is fully aroused. Add it to the dressing for salad instead of directly to the salad, or steep it in the vinegar for a few minutes.

RAMPION

A garden herb, a variety of European bellflower with thick, fleshy white roots that are used as a vegetable or, raw or cooked, in salads.

ROCAMBOLE

A European leek, used like garlic but milder in flavor.

ROSE HIPS

The fleshy red berries of some rose plants, especially wild roses, which have been found to contain considerable vitamin C. They are sometimes used to make a jelly.

ROSELLE

A plant of the mallow family that resembles okra. It is grown for its bright-red calyxes, from which beverages and jellies are made.

RUE

A strong-scented herb with yellow flowers and bitter-tasting leaves that were formerly much used in medicine. It is sometimes used, especially in the South, as a seasoning. The leaves may be blended with cheese or used in salads or to add savor to vegetable cocktails.

SAFFLOWER

A thistle-like herb long cultivated in various parts of the world for food, medicine, and as a substitute for the costly saffron. In the United States, where it is sometimes called American saffron, it is more important as the source of a cooking oil.

SAFFRON

The dried stigma of a plant of the crocus family. It is the world's most expensive spice, because the stigmas of at least 64,000 flowers are needed to make a pound. It is yellow and has a pleasantly bitter flavor. It is imported from Spain and other Mediterranean regions.

Uses: Because of its cost, saffron is often used in such small quantities that its delicate flavor is lost and only its color is apparent; this has made possible the ancient practice of substituting other yellow coloring agents. Saffron is used a great deal in Mediterranean and Latin American cooking, especially in rice dishes. In France it appears in chicken fricassee and is essential to bouillabaisse. The English make saffron breads and cakes. For a golden color and an Oriental flavor, add a dash to water in which rice is to be boiled.

SAGE

Dried leaf of herb of mint family. It's America's most popular herb leaf.

Uses: It's an old-time favorite for stuffings and sausages.

Use with poultry, baked fish, and in salad greens. Goes well with pork.

SARSAPARILLA

Any of a number of related tropical American plants with large, fragrant roots and heart-shaped leaves. An extract of the dried root is used as a tonic and especially as a flavoring for carbonated drinks.

SASSAFRAS

The fragrant dried root bark of the sassafras tree, used in an old-time tea and in root beer. In the South it is sometimes used as a condiment.

SAUSAGE SEASONING

Blend of herbs and spices including white pepper, coriander, and nutmeg.

Uses: Excellent ready-mixed seasoning for the home sausage maker. Used also in meat loaf, veal birds, etc.

SAVORY

Dried leaf of widely grown herb of mint family.

Uses: Good in stuffings, stews, egg dishes, meat sauces, gravies, and casseroles which include meat.

Savory is sometimes called the "bean herb" because it dresses up so many kinds of beans including all fresh and dried beans as well as peas.

SESAME SEED

The small seed of an herb native to Asia and widely grown throughout the tropics. There are black and white varieties; the white, or honey-colored, is the one found in most stores.

Uses: It has a pleasant nut-like flavor and is used in baking and in various candies (it is the basic ingredient of the Near Eastern confection halvah). Try it on cookies, breads, and biscuits. The seed also yields a distinctively flavored oil that is widely used in Near Eastern and Oriental cooking. Also called benne seed.

SHALLOTS

Shallots, which belong to the green onion family, look like small dried onions but are generally red in color with purplish white cloves beneath the outer skin. Shallots have a mild, faintly garlicky flavor. They are called for in many recipes throughout this book. When they are sautéed, they should not be allowed to become brown as they become bitter. Three or four shallots may be substituted for one medium-sized onion.

SWEET CICELY

The name of several plants (European, Asiatic, and American herbs) all closely related and all of the parsley family. They are fragrant perennials with aromatic, licorice-flavored roots, once considered medicinal. The seeds and leaves are sometimes used as a garnish for salads and cold vegetables. Dried seeds are sometimes used in cakes, candies, and liqueurs.

TANSY

Any of a number of plants of the aster family, especially one species with bitter leaves that are used sometimes for seasoning but more frequently as a home medicine.

TARRAGON

Dried leaves and tops of perennial herb. Anise-type flavor.

Uses: Flavoring for tarragon vinegar, sauces, tomato dishes. Sprinkle on broiled chicken.

Try it in tomato juice cocktail, any salad made with tomatoes, with green beans. Sprinkle over steaks or chops.

Tarragon flavored vinegar is available commercially or may be prepared at home by steeping the dried leaves in vinegar. Use tarragon vinegar in sauces

for fish and shellfish, especially lobster. Use it to flavor mayonnaise for any fish salad.

THYME

Leaves and stems of widely grown mint family plant. Strong, distinctive flavor.

Uses: Stews, soups, stuffings are better for that "pinch of thyme." Italians use it in some of their special dishes. Greeks use it in green salads.

Excellent in clam chowder, clam juice, poultry, meat loaf.

Try it in onion soup, chicken fricassee, on baked or broiled fish.

Thyme is particularly nice with lamb in almost any form. Good also with carrots, peas, or creamed onions.

TURMERIC

Aromatic root of ginger family Orange-yellow color.

Uses: For turmeric pickles, chow chow, relishes. Used in curry powder. Often used to replace saffron as coloring agent.

VERBENA

See **Lemon Verbena**

WATERCRESS

A pungent plant of the mustard family that grows in wet soil or water. It has a pleasant peppery taste, and should be selected with an eye to its fresh, deep green color and crispness of its rather long stems. The leaves are used chiefly in salads and soups, or as a garnish, but may also be cooked as a vegetable.

Garden cress and upland cress are varieties similar to watercress, but grown on land rather than in shallow water. All these varieties are well known in Europe, where they have been cultivated for centuries.

To Keep Watercress: Cut off about 1/2 inch of the stem end. If purchased in a bunch, loosen the tie and set in a large jar or other container which does not press it on the sides or top. Fill the container with about 1 inch of cold water, cover, and store in refrigerator.

WINTERGREEN

Also called checkerberry; an evergreen shrub with red berries, white bell-shaped flowers, and egg-shaped leaves. An oil made from the leaves is used in medicine and as a flavoring for candy and chewing gum. The leaves are also used to make a hot drink known as mountain tea.

WOODRUFF OR WALDMEISTER

A sweet European herb used especially to flavor the German punch called May wine. It is sometimes used in other fruit punches; however it should not be left in more than half an hour.

JELLIES, JAMS, AND PRESERVES

Jelly, jam, conserve, marmalade, preserves—any of these fruit products can add zest to meals. Most of them also provide a good way to use fruit not at its best for canning or freezing—the largest or smallest fruits and berries and those that are imperfect or are irregularly shaped.

Basically these products are much alike; all of them are fruit preserved by means of sugar, and usually all are jellied to some extent. Their individual characteristics depend on the kind of fruit used and the way it is prepared, the proportions of different ingredients used in the mixture, and the method of cooking.

The following definitions will help the homemaker to understand recipes for these fruit products preserved by cooking with sugar.

Conserves: Made of 2 or more fruits, one of them usually a citrus fruit, with nutmeats, raisins or both added.

Fruit Butters: Made from strained fruit pulp cooked with sugar and spice to a thick, smooth consistency.

The pulp of some fruits from which the juice has been extracted for jelly is often used if it has enough flavor and pectin.

Jams: Made from crushed fruits cooked with sugar until the mixture is homogeneous and thick.

Jelly: Made by cooking extracted fruit juices with sugar. A transparent, quivery product which hold its shape when unmolded; delicately tender but not syrupy or gummy.

Marmalades: Made from pulpy fruits, usually one or more citrus fruits being used and cut into comparatively large pieces cooked so as to hold their shape in a thick jellied transparent syrup.

Preserves: Contains whole fruits or distinct pieces of fruit preserved in a heavy sugar syrup.

SEALING JELLIES, JAMS, AND PRESERVES

If jelly glasses are used, leave about 1/4-inch head space when filling jars. Cover immediately with about 1/8-inch layer of hot paraffin. Prick any air bubbles that appear. These cause holes to form in paraffin as it hardens and make a poor seal. (A double boiler will prove handy for melting paraffin and keeping it hot.)

Allow jellies and jams to stand, undisturbed, overnight or until cool. Cover glasses or jars with lids.

If canning jars and lids are used, the paraffin may be omitted. Prepare jars according to manufacturer's directions. Fill hot, sterilized jars with boiling hot jelly or jam. Wipe top and threads of jar with clean, damp cloth. Put lid on, rubber sealing compound next to jar. Screw band down evenly and tight.

Invert jar for about 30 seconds so hot jelly can destroy mold or yeast which may have settled on lid. Then stand upright to cool. When jars are cold, test for seal by pressing center of lid. If dome is down, or stays down when pressed, jar is sealed. If the product was not hot enough to produce a vacuum seal, the bands must be left on to keep the jars tightly closed; otherwise bands are not needed after jars are sealed.

Jellies

ESSENTIALS IN MAKING JELLY

In order to "jell," a fruit must contain the right amount of pectin and acid. The amount and quality of pectin in fruits varies according to the stages of ripeness.

A combination of fruits low in pectin and one rich in pectin will often bring about satisfactory results, or a commercial pectin (which can be bought in powder or liquid form) may be added. Carefully follow the manufacturer's directions given with these products.

Fruits Rich in Pectin: Sour apples, crabapples, unripe grapes, blackberries, currants, cranberries, gooseberries, huckleberries, plums, and quinces.

Fruits Low in Pectin: Sweet apples, cherries, peaches, pears, pineapple, rhubarb, strawberries, and some others. With these, added pectin is required or combination with one rich in pectin.

To Test for Pectin: To 1 teaspoon cooked juice, add 1 teaspoon grain alcohol and stir slowly. Wood or denatured alcohol may be used, but do not taste, as these are poison.

A large mass (solid) indicates a large amount of pectin. If moderately rich, there will be a few pieces of gelatin, and, if poor in pectin, only a small flaky sediment.

Jelly Tests: The jelly is done when two drops of the syrup will run together and "sheet off" as one from the side of a spoon.

With a thermometer, cook syrup until it registers between 216° and 220°F.

APPLE OR CRABAPPLE JELLY

Wash 15 pounds tart apples and quarter without peeling.

Place in preserving kettle, just cover with cold water, and simmer gently until soft and tender.

Drain through jelly bag. Shift pulp occasionally to keep juice flowing.

Measure 4 cups juice into 12-quart kettle and boil 5 minutes.

Add 3 cups sugar and boil 5 to 8 minutes longer, or until a drop jells on a cold plate.

Turn into hot sterilized glasses. Cover with melted paraffin and lid.

Continue cooking 4 cups at a time until all juice is used. Use pulp for apple butter.

Mint Apple Jelly: Cook a few sprigs of fresh mint with apples when preparing to extract juice. (1 or 2 drops of mint extract may be used if fresh mint is not available.)

Add a few drops green food coloring and mint extract just before pouring into the glasses. Avoid adding too much flavoring and coloring.

Spiced Apple Jelly: Tie a few whole spices in a piece of muslin. Drop into juice at the beginning of cooking and let remain until jelly is poured into the glasses.

BERRY JELLY

Blackberries, blueberries, and loganberries are but a few of the many which may be used for jelly.

Select firm fruit, using a mixture of ripe and slightly underripe fruit. Pectin is most abundant in slightly underripe fruits. Ripened fruits give the best flavor.

Wash and stem the berries. Drain, then mash to release some of the juice.

To every quart of berries, add 1/4 cup water. If the berries are very juicy, do not add any water.

Boil gently from 10 to 15 minutes, pour into a jelly bag and drain.

Measure juice. Place in large preserving kettle and let boil for 5 minutes.

Add 3/4 cup sugar for each cup juice. Stir until sugar dissolves, then boil rapidly without stirring or skimming until liquid forms a jelly when cool.

Skim and pour into hot, clean glasses. Seal.

CURRANT AND RASPBERRY JELLY

2 quarts currants
3 quarts raspberries
Sugar, as directed

Wash currants, place in kettle, and mash. Add washed, well drained, and mashed raspberries. Stir.

Cover and simmer gently 40 minutes. This must not boil.

Place in jelly bag to drain. Do not squeeze bag.

Measure 4 cups juice into 12-quart kettle. Bring to boiling point, and boil hard 5 minutes.

Add 3 cups sugar and boil with overroll boil 3 minutes.

Pour into hot, sterilized glasses. Cover with melted paraffin and lid.

Continue cooking 4 cups juice with 3 cups sugar until all juice is used.

CURRANT JELLY

Pick over currants. Do not remove stems. Wash and drain. Place in preserving kettle. Mash with potato masher.

Add 1/2 cup water to about 2 quarts fruit. Bring to a boil, simmer until currants appear white.

Strain through jelly bag. Measure juice.

Add 3/4 cup honey and 3/4 cup sugar for every 2 cups juice.

Cook only 4 cupfuls juice at a time. Stir until sugar dissolves.

Cook until a drop jells on a cold plate and jelly sheets from edge of spoon.

Fill hot, sterilized glasses. Cover with paraffin.

GRAPE JELLY

Pick over and wash 4 pounds Concord grapes. Crush and boil together with 1 pint water for 20 minutes.

Press through a jelly bag and allow to drain.

Use 3/4 to 1 cup sugar for each cup of grape juice. Bring grape juice to boil. Add sugar and stir until sugar is dissolved.

Continue boiling until jelly stage is reached and jelly sheets from edge of spoon. Remove from heat and skim.

Pour into hot, sterilized glasses. Cover with hot paraffin at once.

For grape jelly at its best, use canned unsweetened juice. Fresh grape juice contains tartaric acid crystals which form readily in jelly. Canned unsweetened grape juice has much of the acid in crystal form removed.

WINE JELLY

Measure 3 cups sugar into top of double boiler. Add 2 cups wine (sherry, sauterne, burgundy, port, muscatel, or tokay); mix well.

Place over rapidly boiling water and heat 2 minutes, stirring constantly.

Remove from water and at once stir in 1/2 bottle liquid fruit pectin. Pour quickly into glasses. Paraffin at once. Makes about 5 6-ounce glasses.

Jams

STRAWBERRY JAM

1 quart strawberries (4 cups)
4 cups sugar
1/2 cup unstrained lemon juice

Wash, drain, and hull berries. Measure 4 cups. Crush berries in large kettle.

Place in layers in 12-quart preserving kettle, covering each layer with sugar. Let stand 4 hours.

Bring slowly to full rolling boil and boil vigorously 8 minutes.

Add lemon juice and again bring to full rolling boil. Then boil 2 minutes

longer.

Skim, then turn into hot, sterilized jars, filling to 1/2 inch of top, and seal at once. Makes 3 1/2 pints.

GRAPE JAM

Wash and pick over 4 pounds Concord grapes. Separate pulp from skins, putting into separate kettles.

Bring pulp slowly to boiling point, stirring continually until seeds separate from pulp.

Force through sieve to remove seeds. Add skins to pulp, stir thoroughly, and measure.

Add 3/4 cup sugar for each cup fruit. Stir well and cook about 15 minutes, or until thick.

Fill hot sterilized jars to 1/2 inch of top and seal at once. Makes 6 1/2-pint jars.

DAMSON PLUM JAM

4 quarts plums
1 quart water
Sugar

Wash and drain plums. Cut in halves. Add water, bring to boiling point, and simmer 15 minutes.

Cool slightly. Remove pits.

Measure pulp and juice and add 3/4 cup sugar for each cup. Stir until thoroughly mixed.

Bring slowly to boiling point and boil gently until clear and thick, about 20 minutes, stirring constantly to prevent burning.

Pour into hot, sterilized jars, filling to 1/2 inch of top. Seal at once.

BLACK OR RED RASPBERRY JAM

Wash raspberries, crush, and measure. If berries are sour, add equal measurements of sugar. If sweet, use 3/4 as much sugar as berry mixture.

Cook in own juice until thickened, stirring to prevent burning. Boil rapidly because long cooking tends to darken the fruit.

Pack while boiling hot into hot jars and seal immediately.

APRICOT-PINEAPPLE JAM

Pit 5 pounds apricots. Cut into pieces. Combine with 5 cups shredded pineapple and 7 1/2 cups sugar.

Simmer until thick and clear, stirring frequently to prevent scorching.

Pour into clean, hot glasses. Seal when cool.

QUINCE JAM

Wash, pare, and remove core from 4 pounds quinces. Chop into very small pieces.

Add 8 cups sugar, 1/4 pound chopped crystallized ginger and juice, and grated rind of 2 lemons.

Cook until thick and clear. Pour into sterilized jars. Seal.

CHERRY JAM

4 cups chopped cherries
½ cup lemon juice
4 cups sugar

Wash and drain cherries. Remove stems and pits. Put cherries through food chopper, using coarse blade and saving all juice.

Measure 4 cups chopped cherries and juice into 10- or 12-quart kettle. Add sugar. Let stand 4 hours.

Bring slowly to full rolling boil and boil hard for 12 minutes, stirring occasionally.

Add lemon juice and again bring to full rolling boil, then boil 2 minutes longer.

Skim, then turn into hot sterilized jars, filling to ½ inch from top, and seal at once. Makes 1 to 1½ pints.

Note: It takes almost 2 quart boxes of cherries to make 4 cups after they are stemmed, pitted, and put through food chopper.

NEW METHOD UNCOOKED JAMS

This method saves time and effort; however, because the jams are not sterilized by cooking they must be kept in the refrigerator or freezer. They keep well in the refrigerator for several weeks and, of course, much longer in the freezer.

UNCOOKED CHERRY OR STRAWBERRY JAM

2 cups puréed sour cherries or finely mashed or sieved strawberries
4 cups sugar
½ cup liquid pectin (half bottle)

Combine fruit and sugar. Let stand about 20 minutes, stirring occasionally. The cherry purée should be as nearly uniform as possible.

Grind fruit with fine blade of food chopper or use electric blender. Add fruit-sugar mixture to liquid pectin and stir about 2 minutes.

Pour into jelly glasses. Let stand at room temperature 48 hours, or until jelled. Seal with paraffin. Store in refrigerator or freezer. Makes 6 glasses.

Note: Powdered pectin may be substituted for liquid pectin. Use 1 package. Combine with 1 cup water.

Heat to boiling point and boil rapidly for 1 minute, stirring constantly.

Remove from heat and add fruit-sugar mixture, which has stood for 20 minutes. Proceed as above.

Uncooked Red Raspberry Jam: Use 3 cups finely mashed or sieved red raspberries and 6 cups sugar.

Proceed as above but let stand after jam has been poured into glasses, only 24 hours. Makes 9 glasses.

Preserves

STRAWBERRY PRESERVES

● Wash and hull ripe, firm strawberries. Measure a heaping pint after draining the berries thoroughly. Add a pint of sugar and start over low heat. When juice begins to flow from berries, shake the kettle to mix juice, berries, and sugar.

● When sugar is dissolved, increase heat and bring to a good rolling boil as soon as possible. Then start counting cooking time. Boil rapidly for 10 minutes, shaking kettle instead of stirring preserves.

● Remove kettle from heat and allow to cool. Add another heaping pint of berries and another pint of sugar. Bring slowly to a good rolling boil. Shake kettle frequently and boil another 10 minutes.

● Pour the hot preserves into shallow trays or baking dishes and remove foam. Shake pan occasionally while cooling. Let set overnight for berries to plump.

● Pack the cold preserves into sterilized jars—the half-pints are nice for small families—fill jars to within ¼ inch of top.

● Clean inside neck of jar above surface of the preserves. Cover preserves with a thin layer of smoking hot paraffin. Rotate the jar so the paraffin will stick to glass above surface of preserves. Put self-sealing cap on and screw the band tight. This keeps out dust and insects. Store in cool, dry place.

SWEET CHERRY PRESERVES

2 quarts dark sweet cherries
¼ cup strained lemon juice
1 box powdered pectin
6½ cups sugar

Wash, pit, and halve cherries. Place in preserving kettle. Sprinkle with lemon juice and place over medium heat.

Add pectin and blend thoroughly. Bring to a boil. As soon as mixture boils rapidly, gradually add sugar. Blend well.

Bring to a full rolling boil and continue boiling for 2 minutes.

Remove from heat and skim. Pour into hot, sterilized glasses and seal. Makes 8 ½ pints.

PEACH PRESERVES

2 pounds peaches
3 cups sugar

Scald peaches. Dip into cold water and peel. Remove pits. Cut into halves, quarters, or thick slices.

Make a heavy syrup of sugar and water. Cook peaches in syrup until mixture is thick and clear.

Pour into hot, sterilized jars and seal.

EASY RED RASPBERRY PRESERVES

1 12-ounce package frozen raspberries
2 cups sugar

Let berries thaw with sugar, in saucepan.

Place over low heat, bring to boil slowly. (Use larger saucepan than ingredients would indicate as mixture tends to boil over in too small a pan.) Skim off any froth as it forms.

Cook until mixture is thick and translucent.

Test a spoonful of the syrup on a cold saucer; if it "jells" slightly, it is thick enough.

Remove from heat; cover and let stand overnight.

Fill hot, sterilized glasses to within ½ inch of top. Paraffin at once. **Cool.** Makes about 6 6-ounce glasses.

RASPBERRY PRESERVES

Mix thoroughly equal amounts of raspberries and sugar.

Cook slowly and stir until mixture boils. Boil gently for 6 minutes.

Pour into clean, hot jars. Seal at at once.

TOMATO PRESERVES

2 quarts tomatoes
3 lemons
4 cups sugar

Scald red or yellow tomatoes and peel. Cut into small pieces and drain in colander or sieve. (Use juice for soup, sauce, or can for future use.)

Measure 2 quarts pulp. Place in preserving kettle with thinly sliced lemons.

Cook gently uncovered 40 minutes or until lemon skins are tender.

Add sugar, continue cooking 15 minutes, stirring occasionally.

Turn into hot, sterilized jars and seal at once.

Conserves

GRAPE CONSERVE

6 cups grapes, measured after removing stems
2 cups water
6 cups sugar
Juice of 3 oranges
½ pound seedless raisins
¼ pound walnuts, chopped

Remove pulp from grapes. Save skins. Add water to pulp and cook until seeds settle. Strain out seeds.

Combine pulp with skins and remaining ingredients, except walnuts. Cook until a few drops jell on a cold plate.

Add nuts. Pour into hot, clean jars. Seal.

Cranberry or Plum Conserve: Follow above recipe, substituting cranberries or plums for grapes and adding juice of 3 lemons.

PLUM CONSERVE

2 cups plum pulp
1 to 1½ cups sugar
Juice and grated rind of ½ lemon
Juice and grated rind of ½ orange
1 cup seedless raisins
½ cup nutmeats

Wash Damson plums. Remove pits. Put through food chopper and measure.

Mix ingredients, except nutmeats. Cook mixture until thick and clear.

Add nutmeats. Pack in clean, hot jars. Seal.

GOOSEBERRY AND PINEAPPLE CONSERVE

3 quarts gooseberries
1 pound ground or shredded pineapple
8 cups sugar
1 pound raisins, chopped fine
2 cups walnut meats, cut in pieces

Wash gooseberries and boil in small amount of water until they burst.

Add sugar, pineapple, and raisins. Boil mixture slowly until thick. Add walnut meats.

Pack into hot, sterilized jars. Seal.

FIG CONSERVE

2 pounds figs (any kind)
1 cup diced canned pineapple
Sugar
½ cup coarsely chopped almonds or walnuts

Prepare the figs as you ordinarily do for cooking, slicing them if you wish.

Add the pineapple, with its juice, to the figs. Weigh or measure and add an equal amount of sugar.

Place kettle on asbestos mat and boil, stirring occasionally, until thick but still runny.

Add the broken walnut meats just before taking the conserve from the stove. Makes about 2 pints.

PEACH CONSERVE—QUICK METHOD

1. Peel and slice fresh, ripe peaches. Place in cooker with thinly sliced oranges and peel of one orange, thinly sliced peeled lemon including 1 teaspoon grated lemon rind, and water.

4. Add sugar (1½ cups to each pound of fresh peaches) and remaining ingredients (raisins, blanched shredded almonds or walnuts) and cook. Test conserve for jell stage; two drops from spoon indicates conserve has reached correct stage.

2. Place cover on cooker.

5. Fill sterilized jars when cool. Cover with coating of melted paraffin.

3. When steam escapes, put indicator weight on cooker and pressure cook 5 minutes at 15-pounds pressure. Quick cool. Remove cover.

6. Supply of beautiful yellow glossy peach conserve.

STRAWBERRY AND RHUBARB CONSERVE

Cut 1 quart rhubarb into ½-inch pieces, being careful not to peel.

Mix together 1 quart strawberries, the rhubarb, and 6 cups sugar.

Cook mixture slowly until it is thick and clear. Pour into clean, hot jars. Seal.

Miscellaneous Preserves

ORANGE MARMALADE

    8 oranges
    2 lemons
    Water
    Sugar

Wash and dry fruit. Cut unpeeled oranges and lemons into quarters lengthwise. Slice very thin crosswise.

Measure sliced fruit. Add twice as much water as fruit and juice. Let stand overnight.

Next morning, cover kettle, bring to boiling point, and cook 1 hour. Then set aside for 24 hours.

Stir well and measure out 2 cups juice and fruit. Put into a 4- or 6-quart kettle.

Add 2 cups sugar. Bring to full rolling boil and boil 9 minutes only, or to temperature of 220°F.

Pour into hot, sterilized jelly glasses or jars. When cold, cover with melted paraffin and lid.

Continue cooking 2 cups fruit and juice with 2 cups sugar, as given above, until all fruit is cooked. Makes approximately 10 6-ounce glasses.

Amber Marmalade: Follow method for Orange Marmalade, using 1 grapefruit, 1 orange, 1 lemon, sugar, and water.

PEAR MARMALADE

Peel fresh pears. Slice and cover with sugar, using ¾ cup sugar to each cup of fruit. Let stand until it forms a syrup.

Boil slowly until thick.

When fruit is partly cooked, add ½ (No. 2) can shredded pineapple for every 8 cups pears. Pour into sterilized jars. Seal.

PLUM BUTTER

Wash fruit. Place in kettle. Add 2 cups water to 4 pounds of plums.

Cook slowly until pulp separates from pits. Press pulp through sieve. Measure.

If pulp is thin, cook until thick enough to round up on spoon.

Add sugar, allowing ⅔ cup sugar to each cup of pulp.

Cook rapidly, stirring constantly to prevent scorching. Pour into clean, hot jars. Seal.

PEACH BUTTER

    4 pounds peaches
    2 cups water
    Sugar
    2 teaspoons cinnamon
    1 teaspoon cloves

Peel peaches. Remove pits and spots. Place in kettle with water and cook until tender. Rub through sieve and measure.

To each cup of pulp, allow ⅔ cup sugar. Add spices. Cook until thick, stirring frequently.

Pour into sterilized hot jars. Seal.

GUAVA BUTTER

    4 cups strained cooked guava pulp
    3 cups sugar
    1 to 2 tablespoons grated green ginger root
    3 tablespoons lime or lemon juice
    ¼ to ½ teaspoon cinnamon
    ¼ teaspoon allspice

Combine ingredients and cook slowly, stirring almost constantly, until thick. Seal hot, in hot sterilized jars. Makes about 1¼ pints.

Guava Jam: For guava jam, omit the cinnamon and allspice.

PINEAPPLE MARMALADE

    1 pineapple
    3 cups sugar
    3 lemons
    2 cups raisins

Pare pineapple, saving all juice. Cut into small cubes.

Add sugar and grated rind and juice of lemons and pineapple.

Cook 30 minutes or until thick. Add raisins. Cook 5 minutes longer.

Pour into sterilized jars. Seal. Makes about 6 ½-pint jars.

APPLE BUTTER

    10 pounds cooking apples
    3   cups water
    4   cups sweet cider
    8   cups sugar
    1½ teaspoons ground cloves
    3   teaspoons cinnamon
    1½ teaspoons nutmeg
    1½ teaspoons allspice

Wash and core apples. Cook in water until soft and press through sieve.

Boil cider down to 2 cups.

Combine cider, apples, sugar, and spices in preserving kettle and cook slowly until it sheets from spoon. Stir about 3 or 4 times.

Pour into hot, sterilized jars. Seal and adjust lids.

Process 10 minutes in boiling water bath. Makes 6 pints.

PINEAPPLE HONEY

    2 cups water
    4 cups sugar
    2 cups raw pineapple, coarsely grated

Boil sugar and water together for 5 minutes. Add pineapple, and boil until translucent, about 10 minutes.

Pack in sterilized jars, filled to overflowing. Seal.

QUINCE HONEY

    1 pint raw quince, coarsely grated
    1 pint water
    1 quart sugar

Boil sugar and water together 5 minutes. Add quince, and boil until translucent, about 10 minutes.

Pour into sterilized jars, filled to overflowing. Seal.

GRAPE BUTTER

Use 1 pound sugar to 4 pounds grapes.

Wash and stem grapes. Cook in a small amount of water until skins are soft. Press pulp through strainer to remove seeds and skins.

Add sugar and cook until thick and clear.

Pour into hot, clean glasses. Cool and seal.

APPLE AND PLUM BUTTER

    4½ pounds apples
    3   pounds plums
    2   cups water
    6   cups sugar
    1   teaspoon cinnamon

Wash and cut apples and plums, including peels and cores.

Add water and cook until fruit is tender. Press through a sieve.

Add sugar and cinnamon. Cook until thick and clear. Stir occasionally to prevent sticking.

Fill sterilized glasses. Seal. Makes 6 glasses.

CALIFORNIA BAR-LE-DUC

    5 pounds fresh apricots or 3 pounds dried apricots
    2 cups water
    4 cups raisins, chopped
    Juice of 2 lemons
    6 cups sugar

Cut fresh apricots in half and remove pits. Add water. Cook slowly until tender.

Rub through a coarse strainer. Add raisins, lemon juice, and sugar.

Cook slowly until a rich, heavy syrup is formed. Pour into hot jars and seal.

If dried apricots are used wash and soak overnight in water to cover. Cook in same water until soft and press through a coarse strainer.

MEAT AND GAME MEAT

Meat makes the meal—if it's cooked properly! The fame of each cut of meat depends upon the way you cook it. For instance, a prime porterhouse steak would be quite tasteless if it were *braised* and a low-grade round steak would be unchewable if it were *broiled*. The illustrations of each meat cut with the guidance offered for the best way to cook them will help you treat each cut right.

GRADING OF MEAT

The best guides for selecting the meat you want are the U. S. Department of Agriculture grades—which more retail stores will use as consumers request graded meat. The grades you are most likely to find on the market are Choice, Good, and Commercial. The Federal grade name appears in purple on most of the retail cuts of meat.

Another purple stamp which may appear on retail cuts is the round one, indicating that the meat has been inspected and passed on as wholesome food. All graded meat is inspected, but not all inspected meat is graded.

Meat packers, wholesalers, or retailers may use their own brand names, not to be confused with USDA grades. Letters such as AA and A are never used as meat grades by the USDA.

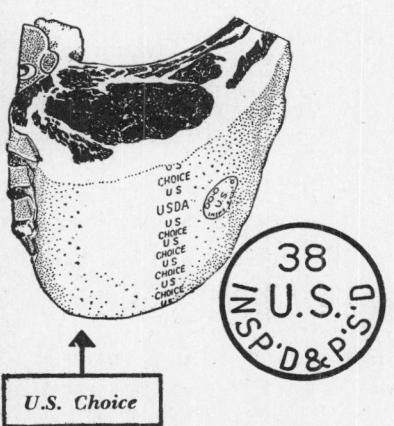

U.S. Choice

The round purple stamp used for marking meat to show it has passed federal inspection. The number appearing on the stamp indicates the establishment.

BUYING MEAT

The amount of bone and fat must be considered in figuring the cost of meat—beef, pork, lamb, or veal. For example, beef short ribs may cost less per pound than hamburger but will yield only 1/3 to 1/2 as many servings.

In buying beef when you plan to have broiled steaks or rare roasts, select Choice or Good grades. But when you want pot roasts, you may do just as well to buy Commercial grade. For hamburger, meat loaf, and stews, Commercial beef may be just as satisfactory as Choice or Good and is often more economical. How much meat to buy per serving is found in **Facts About Food and Cooking.**

HOW TO STORE MEATS

It's important to keep it cold, so store in refrigerator at 36°F. to 40°F. Unsmoked meat such as roasts, chops, and steaks must be allowed some air. Loosen any tight transparent coverings. Cover again loosely and use within a few days.

Ground fresh meat and variety meats, especially liver and brains, spoil more quickly than others. Store loosely wrapped and cook within 2 days for best flavor.

Smoked meats, such as ham, frankfurters, bacon, and sausage (smoked or unsmoked), may be kept tightly wrapped during storage. They keep longer than unsmoked meats, although bacon and sausage are likely to change flavor.

Keep cooked meat as well as broths and gravies covered and in the refrigerator. Use within a few days.

MEAT STORAGE CHARTS

A chart giving time limits meats may be held for maximum flavor and eating pleasure can only be a general guide.

Many factors influence storage limits, including the quality and the age of meat when bought, the method of preparation and handling, and the conditions in the home refrigerator.

	Storage Limit at 36° to 40° F.
Beef:	
Corned Beef	7 days
Pot Roast	5 to 6 days
Rib Roast	5 to 8 days
Steak	3 to 5 days
Stew Meat	2 days
Hamburger	2 days
Lamb:	
Roasts	5 days
Chops	3 days
Shank	2 days
Stew Meat	2 days
Pork:	
Roasts	5 to 6 days
Chops	3 days
Sausage	2 to 3 days
Spareribs	3 days
Bacon	7 days
Whole Ham	2 weeks
Half Ham	7 days
Veal:	
Chops and Steaks	4 days
Roasts	5 to 6 days
Stew Meat	2 days
Variety Meats:	
Liver (sliced)	2 days
Heart	2 days
Others	1 day
Cooked Meats:	
Home-Cooked Meats	4 days
Frankfurters	4 to 5 days
Luncheon Meats (sliced)	3 days
Liver Sausage (sliced)	2 to 3 days
Liver Sausage (uncut)	4 to 6 days
Dry and Semi-Dry Sausage (uncut)	2 to 3 weeks

Beef Cuts and How to Cook Them

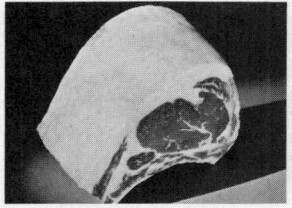

Standing Rib
Roast

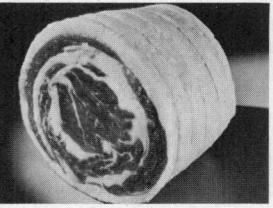

Rolled Rib
Roast

Sirloin Steak
Broil, Panbroil, Panfry

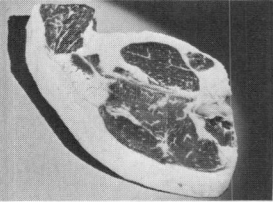

Pinbone Sirloin Steak
Broil, Panbroil, Panfry

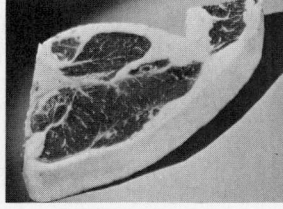

Porterhouse Steak
Broil, Panbroil, Panfry

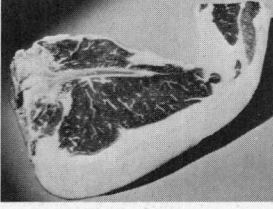

T-Bone Steak
Broil, Panbroil, Panfry

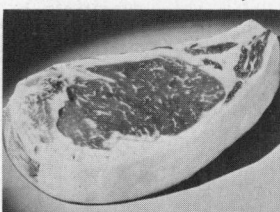

Club Steak
Broil, Panbroil, Panfry

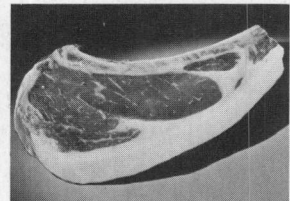

Rib Steak
Broil, Panbroil. Panfry

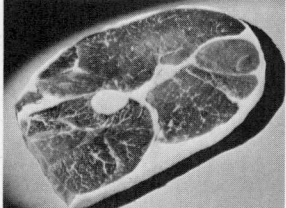

Round Steak (Full Cut)
Braise

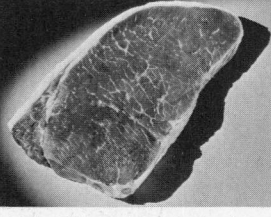

Top Round Steak *Braise*
Broil, Panbroil, Panfry,

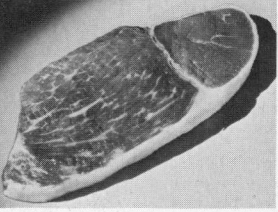

Bottom Round Steak
Braise

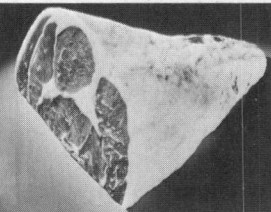

Heel of Round
Braise, Cook in Liquid

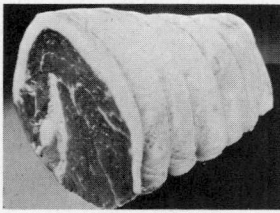

Rolled Rump
Braise, Roast

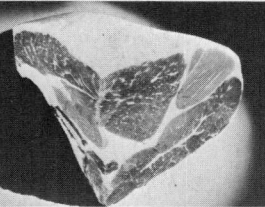

Standing Rump
Braise, Roast

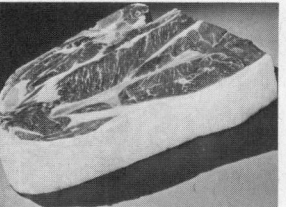

Blade Pot-Roast
(Chuck) *Braise*

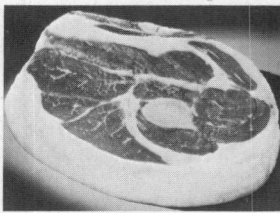

Arm Pot-Roast
(Chuck) *Braise*

Boneless Chuck
Braise

English Cut
(Chuck) *Braise*

Shank Cross Cuts
Braise, Cook in Liquid

Short Ribs
Braise, Cook in Liquid

Flank Steak
Braise

Plate Beef
Braise, Cook in Liquid

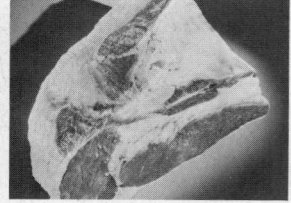

Brisket (Bone In)
Braise, Cook in Liquid

Corned Beef (Brisket)
Cook in Liquid

BEEF CHART

RETAIL CUTS OF BEEF — WHERE THEY COME FROM AND HOW TO COOK THEM

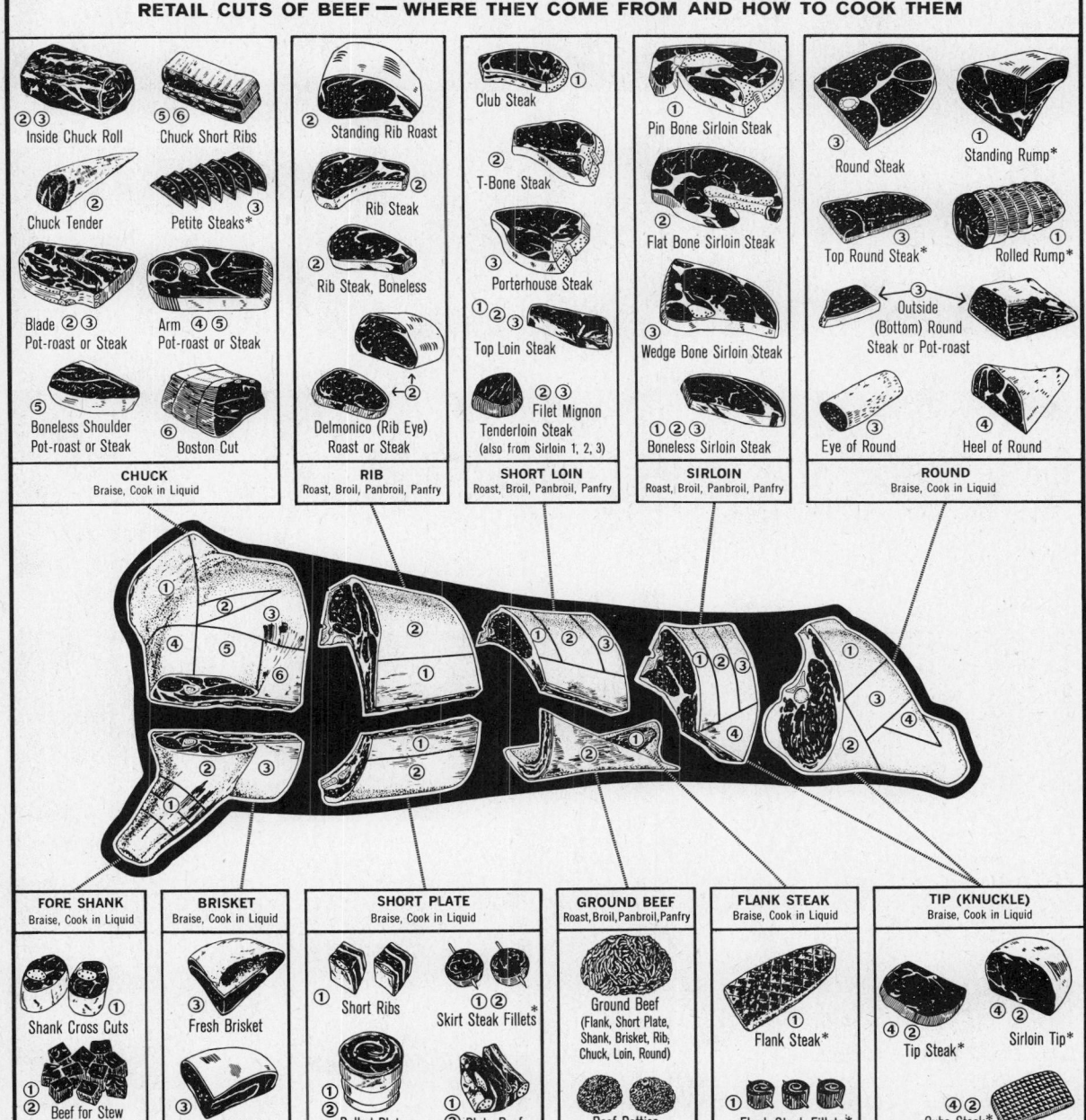

CHUCK
Braise, Cook in Liquid

- ② ③ Inside Chuck Roll
- ⑤ ⑥ Chuck Short Ribs
- ② Chuck Tender
- ③ Petite Steaks*
- Blade ② ③ Pot-roast or Steak
- Arm ④ ⑤ Pot-roast or Steak
- ⑤ Boneless Shoulder Pot-roast or Steak
- ⑥ Boston Cut

RIB
Roast, Broil, Panbroil, Panfry

- ① Standing Rib Roast
- ② Rib Steak
- ② Rib Steak, Boneless
- ② Delmonico (Rib Eye) Roast or Steak

SHORT LOIN
Roast, Broil, Panbroil, Panfry

- ① Club Steak
- ② T-Bone Steak
- ③ Porterhouse Steak
- ① ② ③ Top Loin Steak
- ② ③ Filet Mignon Tenderloin Steak (also from Sirloin 1, 2, 3)

SIRLOIN
Roast, Broil, Panbroil, Panfry

- ① Pin Bone Sirloin Steak
- ② Flat Bone Sirloin Steak
- ③ Wedge Bone Sirloin Steak
- ① ② ③ Boneless Sirloin Steak

ROUND
Braise, Cook in Liquid

- ③ Round Steak
- ① Standing Rump*
- ③ Top Round Steak*
- ① Rolled Rump*
- ③ Outside (Bottom) Round Steak or Pot-roast
- ③ Eye of Round
- ④ Heel of Round

FORE SHANK
Braise, Cook in Liquid

- ① Shank Cross Cuts
- ① ② Beef for Stew (also from other cuts)

BRISKET
Braise, Cook in Liquid

- ③ Fresh Brisket
- ③ Corned Brisket

SHORT PLATE
Braise, Cook in Liquid

- ① Short Ribs
- ① ② Skirt Steak Fillets*
- ① ② Rolled Plate
- ② Plate Beef

GROUND BEEF
Roast, Broil, Panbroil, Panfry

- Ground Beef (Flank, Short Plate, Shank, Brisket, Rib, Chuck, Loin, Round)
- Beef Patties

FLANK STEAK
Braise, Cook in Liquid

- ① Flank Steak*
- ① Flank Steak Fillets*

TIP (KNUCKLE)
Braise, Cook in Liquid

- ④ ② Tip Steak*
- ④ ② Sirloin Tip*
- ④ ② Cube Steak*

*May be Roasted, Broiled, Panbroiled or Panfried from high quality beef.

NLS&MB

Pork Cuts and How to Cook Them

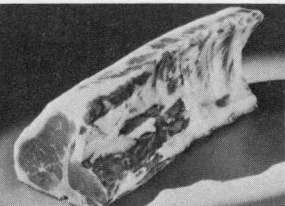

Loin Roast
(Center Cut) Roast

Blade Loin
Roast

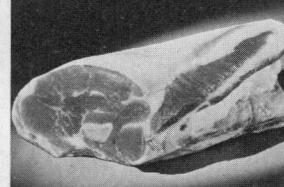

Sirloin Roast
Roast

Boneless Sirloin Roast
Roast

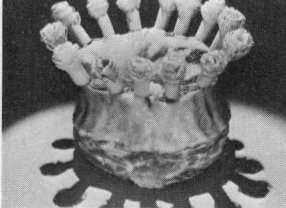

Crown Roast
Roast

Fresh Picnic Shoulder
Roast

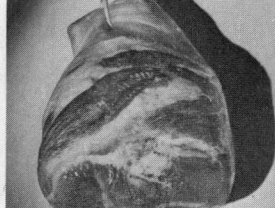

Smoked Picnic Shoulder
Roast (Bake), Cook in Liquid

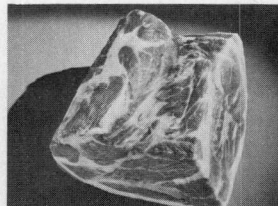

Boston Butt (Shoulder)
Roast

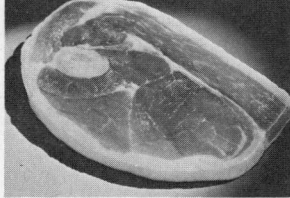

Arm Steak (Shoulder)
Braise, Panfry

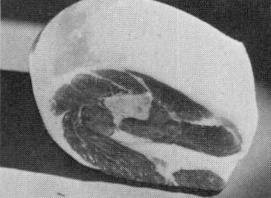

Arm Roast (Shoulder)
Roast

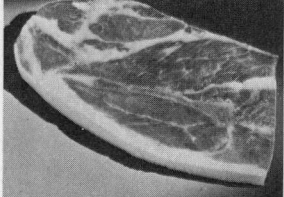

Blade Steak (Shoulder)
Braise, Panfry

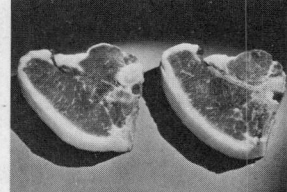

Loin Chops
Braise, Panfry

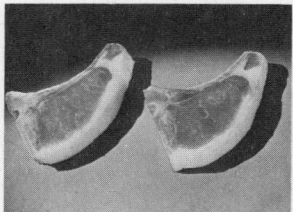

Rib Chops
Braise, Panfry

Spareribs - *Roast (Bake),
Braise, Cook In Liquid*

Tenderloin
Roast, Braise, Panfry

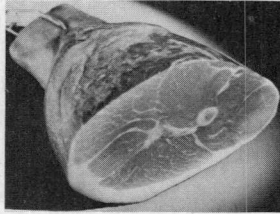

Half Ham (Shank End)
Roast (Bake), Cook in Liquid

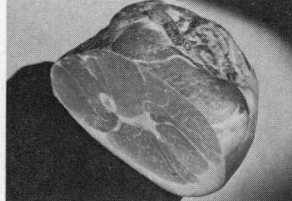

Half Ham (Butt End)
Roast (Bake), Cook in Liquid

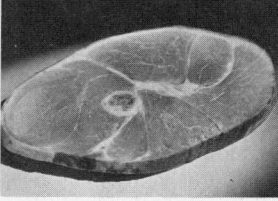

Center Ham Slice
Broil, Panbroil, Panfry

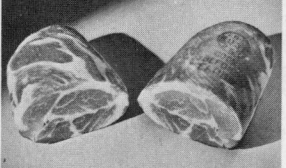

Smoked Shoulder Butt
*Roast, Cook In Liquid,
Broil, Panbroil, Panfry*

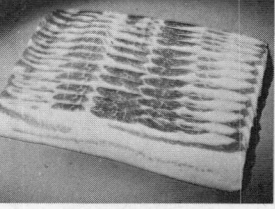

Sliced Bacon
Panbroil, Panfry, Broil

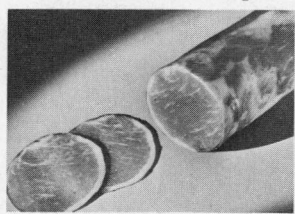

Canadian Style Bacon
Roast, Broil, Panbroil, Panfry

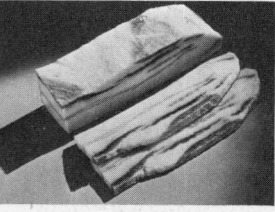

Salt Pork (Side)
*Cook in Liquid,
Panbroil, Panfry*

Jowl Bacon Square
*Cook In Liquid, Broil,
Panbroil, Panfry*

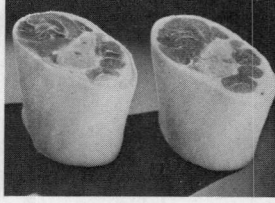

Hocks
Braise, Cook In Liquid

PORK CHART

RETAIL CUTS OF PORK — WHERE THEY COME FROM AND HOW TO COOK THEM

Boston Butt — *Roast*

Rolled Boston Butt — *Roast*

Blade Steak — *Braise, Panfry*

Smoked Shoulder Butt — *Roast (bake), Cook in Liquid, Broil, Panbroil, Panfry*

Sausage * — *Panfry, Braise, Bake*

Porklet — *Braise, Panfry*

Fat Back — *Panfry, Cook in Liquid*

Lard — *Pastry, Cookies, Quick Breads, Cakes, Frying*

Blade Loin Roast — *Roast*

Center Loin Roast

Tenderloin — *Roast, Braise, Panfry*

Rolled Loin Roast

Sirloin Roast

Back Ribs — *Roast (bake), Braise, Cook in Liquid*

Rib Chop

Loin Chop

Sirloin Chop

Butterfly Chop

Blade Chop

Top Loin Chop

Braise, Broil, Panfry

Country Style Backbone

Canadian Style Bacon — *Roast, Broil, Panbroil, Panfry*

Smoked Loin Chop — *Broil, Panfry*

Smoked Ham Shank Portion

Smoked Ham Butt Portion

Roast (bake), Cook in Liquid

Rolled Fresh Ham (leg)

Smoked Ham Boneless Roll

Roast (bake)

Canned Ham — *Roast, (bake)*

Sliced Cooked "Boiled" Ham

Smoked Ham Center Slice

Broil, Panbroil, Panfry

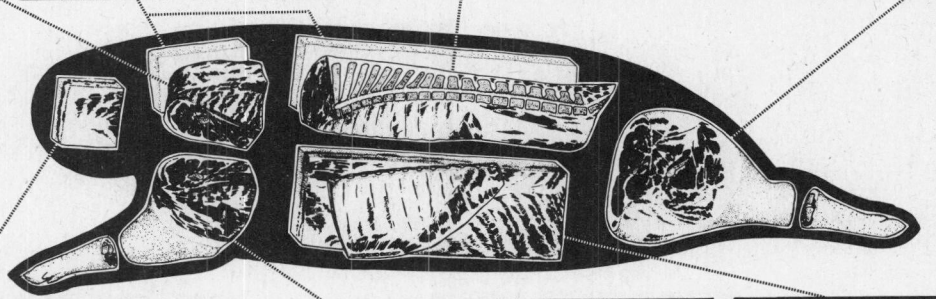

Jowl Bacon — *Cook in Liquid, Broil, Panbroil, Panfry*

Pig's Feet — *Cook in Liquid, Braise*

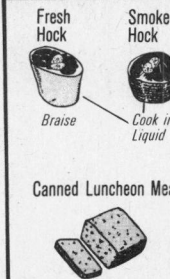

Fresh Hock — *Braise*

Smoked Hock — *Cook in Liquid*

Canned Luncheon Meat * — *Roast (bake), Broil, Panbroil*

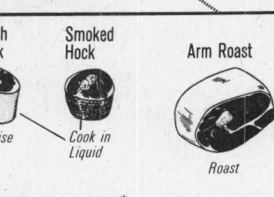

Arm Roast — *Roast*

Arm Steak — *Braise, Panfry*

Fresh Picnic — *Roast*

Rolled Fresh Picnic — *Roast*

Smoked Picnic — *Roast (bake), Cook in Liquid*

Canned Picnic — *Roast, (bake)*

Salt Pork — *Broil, Panbroil, Panfry, Cook in Liquid, Bake*

Spareribs — *Roast (bake), Braise, Cook in Liquid*

Sliced Bacon

Slab Bacon

Broil, Panbroil, Panfry, Bake

*These items may come from several areas of the pork side.

NLS&MB

Veal Cuts and How to Cook Them

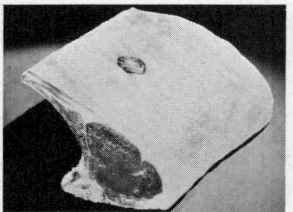

Rib Roast
Roast

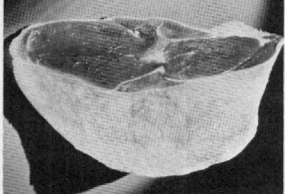

Sirloin Roast
Roast, Braise

Loin Roast
Roast, Braise

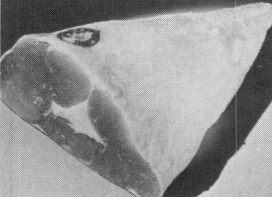

Heel Of Round
Braise, Cook In Liquid

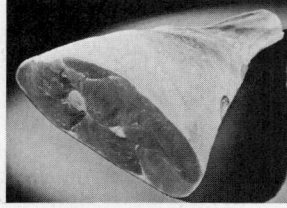

Shank Half Of Leg
Roast, Braise

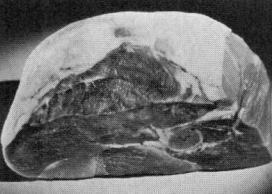

Center Cut Of Leg
Roast, Braise

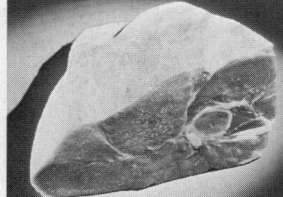

Standing Rump
Roast, Braise

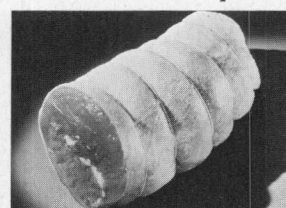

Boneless Rump
Roast, Braise

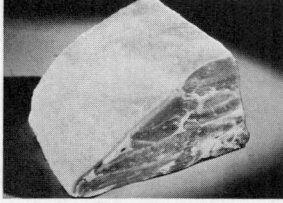

Blade Roast (Shoulder)
Roast, Braise

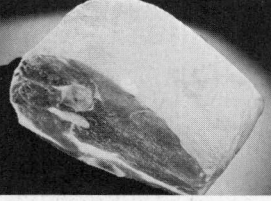

Arm Roast (Shoulder)
Roast, Braise

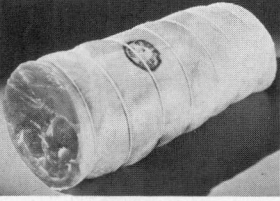

Rolled Shoulder
Roast, Braise

Blade Steak (Shoulder)
Braise, Panfry

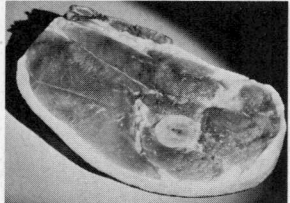

Arm Steak (Shoulder)
Braise, Panfry

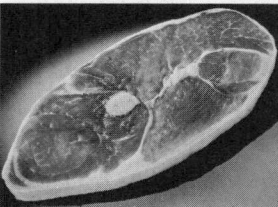

Round Steak (Cutlet)
Braise, Panfry

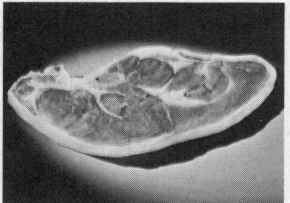

Sirloin Steak
Braise, Panfry

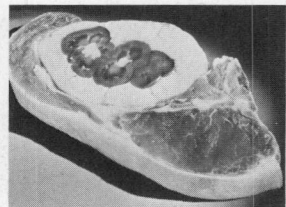

Kidney Chop
Braise, Panfry

Loin Chop
Braise, Panfry

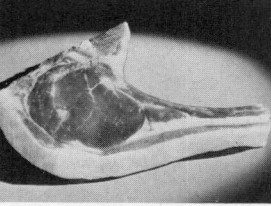

Rib Chop
Braise, Panfry

Breast
Roast, Braise, Cook In Liquid

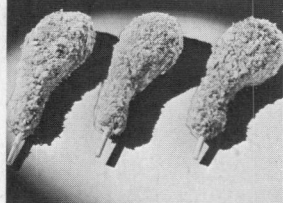

Mock Chicken Legs
Braise, Panfry

Boneless Stew
Braise, Cook In Liquid

Riblets (Breast)
Braise, Cook In Liquid

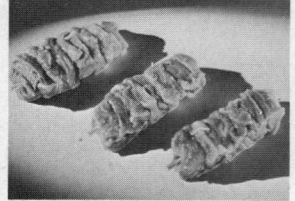

City Chicken
Braise, Panfry

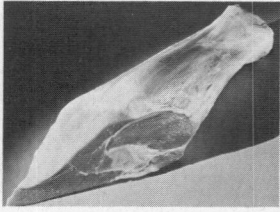

Fore Shank
Braise, Cook In Liquid

VEAL CHART

RETAIL CUTS OF VEAL — WHERE THEY COME FROM AND HOW TO COOK THEM

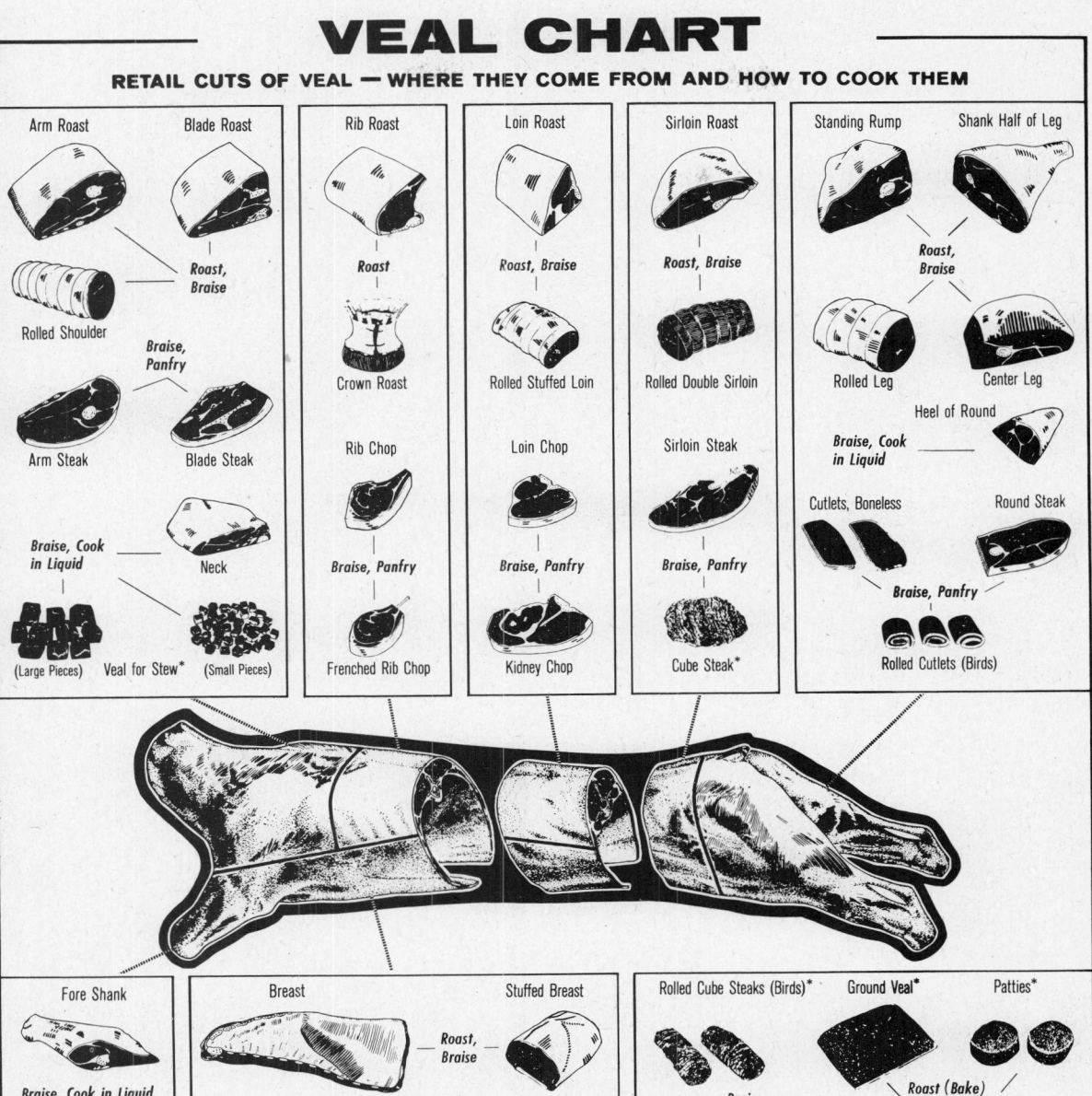

Arm Roast   **Blade Roast**

Roast, Braise

Rolled Shoulder

Braise, Panfry

Arm Steak   **Blade Steak**

Neck

Braise, Cook in Liquid

(Large Pieces)   Veal for Stew*   (Small Pieces)

Rib Roast

Roast

Crown Roast

Rib Chop

Braise, Panfry

Frenched Rib Chop

Loin Roast

Roast, Braise

Rolled Stuffed Loin

Loin Chop

Braise, Panfry

Kidney Chop

Sirloin Roast

Roast, Braise

Rolled Double Sirloin

Sirloin Steak

Braise, Panfry

Cube Steak*

Standing Rump   **Shank Half of Leg**

Roast, Braise

Rolled Leg   **Center Leg**

Heel of Round

Braise, Cook in Liquid

Cutlets, Boneless   **Round Steak**

Braise, Panfry

Rolled Cutlets (Birds)

Fore Shank

Braise, Cook in Liquid

Brisket Rolls

Braise

Breast   **Stuffed Breast**

Roast, Braise

Riblets   **Brisket Pieces**   **Stuffed Chops**

Braise, Cook in Liquid   *Braise, Panfry*

Rolled Cube Steaks (Birds)*   **Ground Veal***   **Patties***

Braise   *Roast (Bake) Braise, Panfry*

Mock Chicken Legs*   **City Chicken***   **Choplets***

Braise, Panfry

*VEAL FOR STEW, GRINDING OR CUBING MAY COME FROM ANY WHOLESALE CUT

Lamb Cuts and How to Cook Them

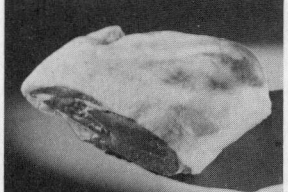

American Leg
Roast

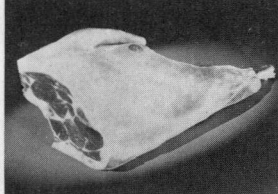

Frenched Leg
Roast

Boneless Sirloin Roast
Roast

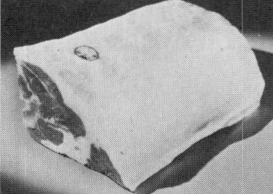

Loin Roast
Roast

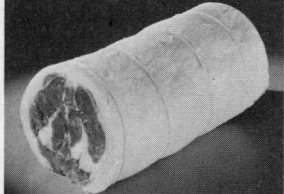

Rolled Loin
Roast

Rib Roast (Rack)
Roast

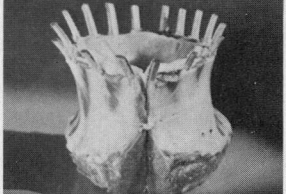

Crown Roast
Roast

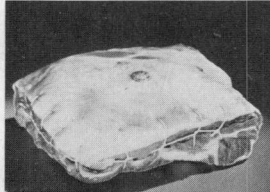

Cushion Shoulder
Roast

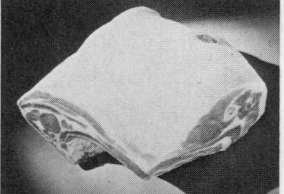

Square Cut Shoulder
Roast

Rolled Shoulder
Roast, Braise

Rolled Breast
Braise, Roast

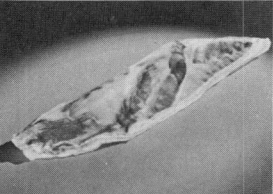

Breast
Braise, Roast

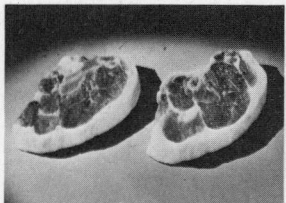

Sirloin Chops
Broil, Panbroil, Panfry

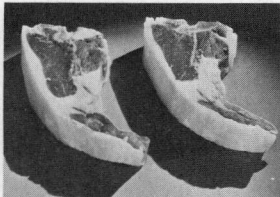

Loin Chops
Broil, Panbroil, Panfry

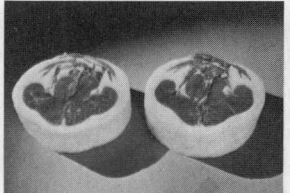

English Chops
Broil, Panbroil, Panfry

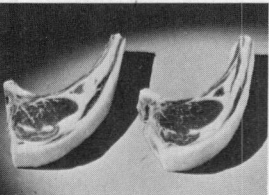

Rib Chops
Broil, Panbroil, Panfry

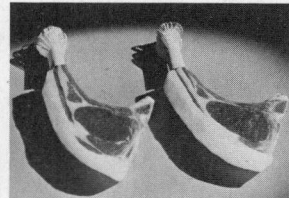

Frenched Chops (Rib)
Broil, Panbroil, Panfry

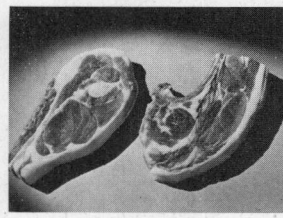

Shoulder Chops
Broil, Panbroil, Panfry, Braise

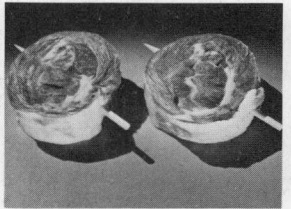

Saratoga Chops (Shoulder)
Broil, Panbroil, Panfry, Braise

Patties
Broil, Panbroil, Panfry

Ground Lamb Loaf
Roast (Bake)

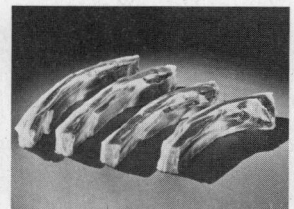

Riblets (Breast)
Braise, Cook In Liquid

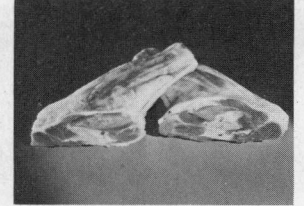

Shanks
Braise, Cook In Liquid

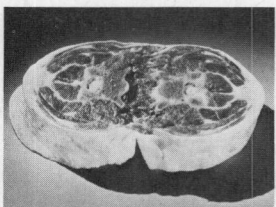

Neck Slices
Braise, Cook In Liquid

LAMB CHART

RETAIL CUTS OF LAMB — WHERE THEY COME FROM AND HOW TO COOK THEM

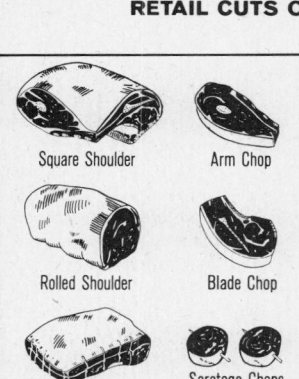

Square Shoulder   Arm Chop

Rolled Shoulder   Blade Chop

Cushion Shoulder   Saratoga Chops

Cubes for Kabobs*

Neck Slices

Rib Roast

Crown Roast

Rib Chops

Frenched Rib Chops

Loin Roast

Rolled Double Loin

English Chop

Loin Chops

Sirloin Half of Leg

Sirloin Roast

Rolled Double Sirloin

Sirloin Chop

Shank Half of Leg

Leg Chop (Steak)

Rolled Leg

Combination Leg

Leg, Sirloin on

Leg, Sirloin off

American Leg

Center Leg

SHOULDER	NECK	RACK	LOIN	SIRLOIN	LEG
Roast, Broil, Panbroil. Panfry	Braise, Cook in Liquid	Roast, Broil, Panbroil, Panfry	Roast, Broil, Panbroil, Panfry	Roast, Broil, Panbroil, Panfry	Roast, Broil, Panbroil, Panfry

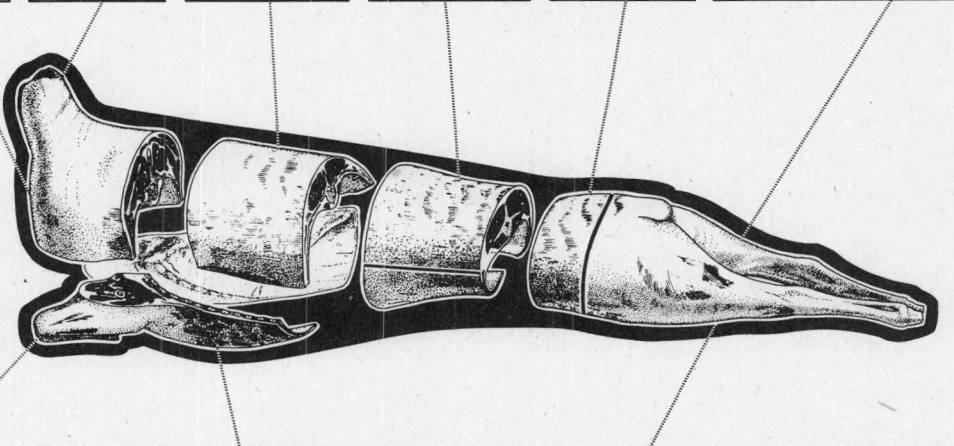

FORE SHANK
Braise, Cook in Liquid

Fore Shank

Riblets

BREAST
Roast. Braise, Broil, Panbroil, Panfry, Cook in Liquid

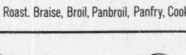

Breast

Ribs (for Barbecue, etc.)

Rolled Breast

Brisket Pieces

Stuffed Breast

Stuffed Chops

HIND SHANK
Braise, Cook in Liquid

Hind Shank

GROUND OR CUBED LAMB
Roast, Broil, Panbroil, Panfry, Braise, Cook in Liquid

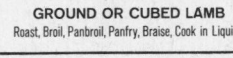

(Large Pieces)   Lamb for Stew*   (Small Pieces)

Cube Steak*

Ground Lamb*

Lamburgers*

*LAMB FOR STEW, GRINDING OR CUBING MAY COME FROM ANY WHOLESALE CUT

How to Carve Meats

STANDING RIB ROAST

When a standing rib roast is purchased, the meat retailer will, on request, remove the short ribs and separate the backbone from the ribs. The backbone can then be removed in the kitchen after roasting. This makes the carving much easier, as only the rib bones remain.

The roast is placed on the platter with the small cut surface up and the rib side to your left.

Either the standard carving set or the roast meat slicer and carver's helper can be used on this roast.

With the guard up, insert the fork firmly between the two top ribs. From the far outside edge slice across the grain toward the ribs. (*first illustration*) Make the slices an eighth to three-eighths of an inch thick.

Release each slice by cutting close along the rib with the knife tip. (*second illustration*)

After each cut, lift the slice on the blade of the knife to the side of the platter. (*third illustration*) If the platter is not large enough, have another hot platter near to receive the slices.

Make sufficient slices to serve all guests before transferring the servings to individual plates.

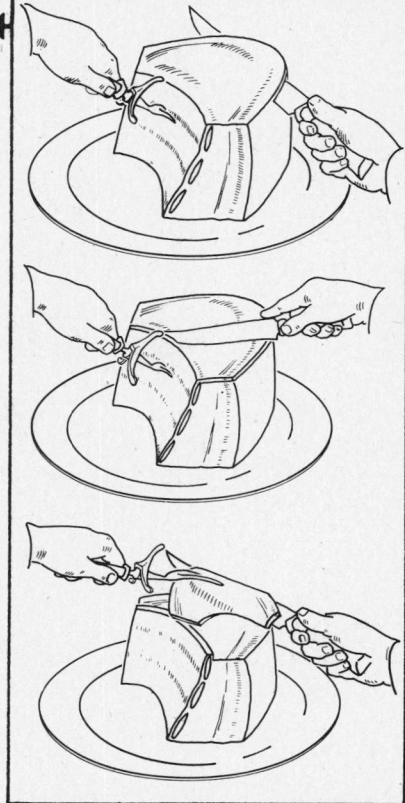

ROLLED RIB ROAST

The roast is placed on the platter with the larger cut surface down.

Use the standard carving set or the slicer and carver's helper.

With the guard up, push the fork firmly into the roast on the left side an inch or two from the top.

Slice across the grain toward the fork from the far right side. (*first illustration*) Uniform slices of an eighth to three-eighths of an inch thick make desirable servings.

As each slice is carved, lift it to the side of the platter or to another hot serving platter. (*second illustration*)

Remove each cord only as it is approached in making slices. Sever it with the tip of the blade, loosen it with the fork and allow it to drop to platter.

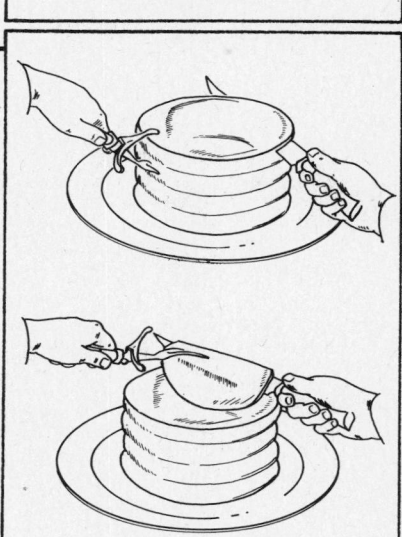

Rolled Roasts

Because of the difficulty of carving shoulder and rump cuts they are often boned and rolled at the market. All are sliced across the face in the same way as the rolled rib, but since many of them make a long roll you will find carving easier with the roast lying horizontally on the platter.

PORTERHOUSE STEAK

Contrary to most carving rules a steak is carved with the grain. A steak need not be cut across the grain because the meat fibers are tender and already relatively short.

Use the steak set, a blade of six or seven inches.

Holding the steak with the fork inserted at the left, cut close around the bone. (*first illustration*) Then lift the bone to the side of the platter where it will not interfere with carving.

With the fork in position, cut across the full width of the steak. (*second illustration*) Make wedge-shaped portions, widest at the far side. Each serving will be a piece of the tenderloin and a piece of the large muscle.

Serve the flank end last if additional servings are needed. (*third illustration*)

In order to protect the cutting edge of the knife, as well as the platter, a board cut to fit the center section of the steak platter is almost a necessity when carving a steak.

BEEF TONGUE

Slice off excess tissue and cartilage from the large end of the tongue. Continue making thin, even and parallel slices. This gives lengthwise slices from the small end of the tongue, as in diagram.

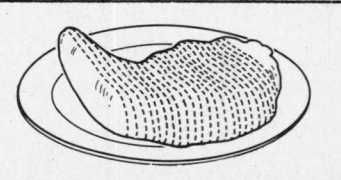

BLADE POT-ROAST

The blade pot-roast contains at least part of one rib and a portion of the blade bone. The long cooking process softens the tissues attached to the bones, therefore the bones can be slippd out easily before the roast is placed on the table.

Either the steak set or the standard carving set may be used for carving the pot-roast.

Hold the pot-roast firmly with the fork inserted at the left and separate a section by running the knife between two muscles, then close to the bone, if the bone has not been removed. (*first illustration*)

Turn the section just separated so that the grain of the meat is parallel with the platter. (*second illustration*) This enables you to cut the slices across the grain of the meat.

Holding the piece with the fork, cut slices of one-fourth to three-eighths of an inch thick. (*third illustration*)

Separate the remaining sections of the roast; note the direction of the meat fibers and carve across the grain.

Two or three slices, depending on size, are served to each person.

ROAST LEG OF LAMB

The leg of lamb should be placed before the carver so that the shank bone is to his right and the thick meaty section, or cushion, is on the far side of the platter. Different roasts will not always have the same surface uppermost because of the difference in right and left legs. However, this does not effect the method of carving. The illustrations show a right leg of lamb resting on the large smooth side.

A standard carving set is a convenient size for this roast.

Insert the fork firmly in the large end of the leg and carve two or three lengthwise slices from the near thin side. (*first illustration*)

Turn the roast so that it rests on the surface just cut. The shank bone now points up from the platter.

Insert the fork in the left of the roast. Starting at the shank end slice down to the leg bone. Parallel slices may be made until the aitch bone is reached. (*second illustration*) One-quarter to three-eighths of an inch is a desirable thickness.

With the fork still in place, run the knife along the leg bone releasing all the slices. (*third illustration*)

LAMB CROWN ROAST

A lamb crown roast is made from the rack or rib section, of the lamb. A pork crown is made from the rib sections of two or more loins of pork. Either cut is carved in a method similar to that of the pork loin roast.

Use a standard carving set.

Move to the side of the platter any garnish in the center which may interfere with carving. Dressing can be cut and served along with the slices.

Steady the roast by placing the fork firmly between the ribs.

Cut down between the ribs, allowing one rib to each slice. (*first illustration*)

Lift the slice on the knife blade, using the fork to steady it. (*second illustration*)

Crown Roasts

For a party or special occasion a crown roast adds a festive touch. Frills may be put on rib ends and attractive garnishes are easy to arrange. If dressing is used to fill the center it should be of a consistency that can be sliced with the chops. If cauliflower is the center garnish ample platter space will be needed so that the carver may place the cauliflower out of his way.

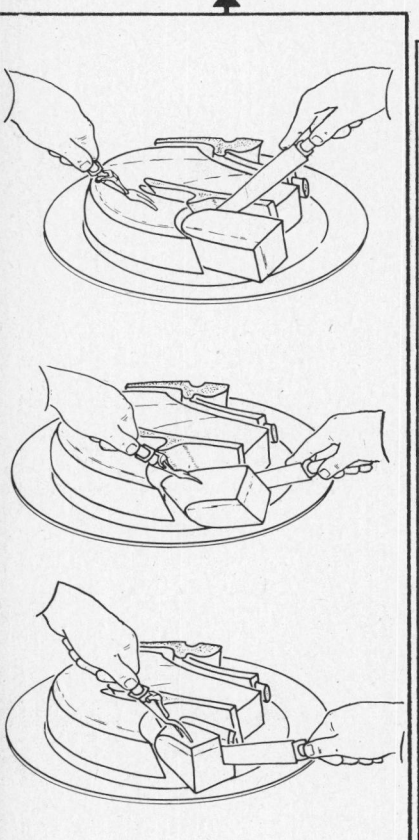

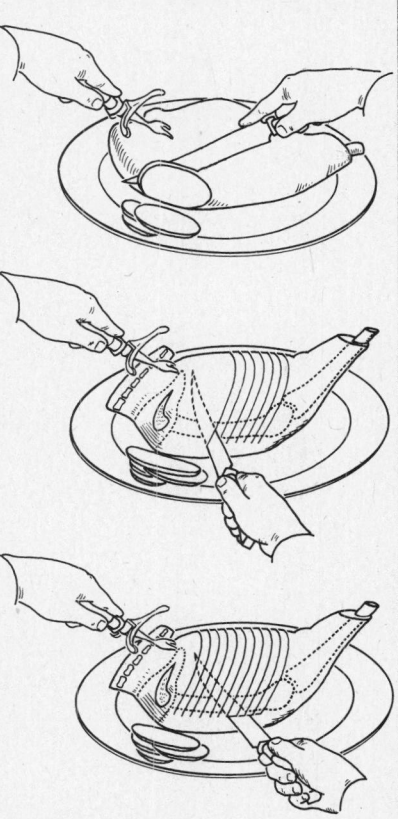

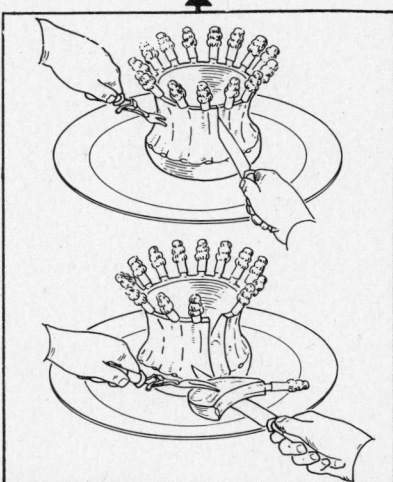

BEEF BRISKET

Place on the platter with the round side away from you. Trim off excess fat. Make slices in rotation from three sides as shown in illustration. Slices should be thin and at a slight angle. Carving in this way makes all cuts across the grain.

PORK LOIN ROAST

It is much easier to carve a pork loin roast if the backbone is separated from the ribs. This is done at the market by sawing across the ribs close to the backbone. The backbone becomes loosened during roasting; note in the first illustration that it has fallen away from the ribs.

The standard carving set is preferred for carving the pork loin, although a smaller size may be used.

Before the roast is brought to the table remove the backbone by cutting between it and the rib ends. (*second illustration*)

The roast is placed on the platter so that the rib side faces you. This makes it easy to follow the rib bones, which are the guides for slicing. Make sure of the slant of the ribs before you carve, as all the ribs are not perpendicular to the platter.

Insert the fork firmly in the top of the roast. Cut close against both sides of each rib. You alternately make one slice with a bone and one without. Roast pork is more tempting when sliced fairly thin. In a small loin each slice may contain a rib; if the loin is large it is possible to cut two boneless slices between ribs.

Two slices for each person is the usual serving.

BAKED WHOLE HAM

The ham is placed on the platter with the fat or decorated side up. The shank end should always be to the carver's right. The thin side of the ham, from which the first slices are made, will be nearest or farthest from the carver, depending on whether the ham is from a right or a left side of pork. The illustrations show a left ham with the first slices cut nearest the carver.

Use a standard carving set or the slicer and carver's helper on the baked ham.

Insert the fork and cut several slices parallel to the length of the ham on the nearest side (*first illustration*)

Turn the ham so that it rests on the surface just cut. Hold the ham firmly with the fork and cut a small wedge from the shank end. (*second illustration*) By removing this wedge the succeeding slices are easier to cut and to release from the bone.

Keep the fork in place to steady the ham and cut thin slices down to the leg bone. (*second illustration*)

Release slices by cutting along bone at right angles to slices. (*third illustration*)

For more servings turn the ham back to its original position and slice at right angles to the bone. (*fourth illustration*)

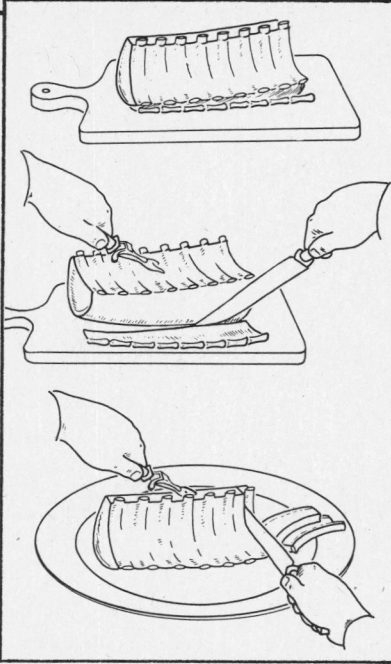

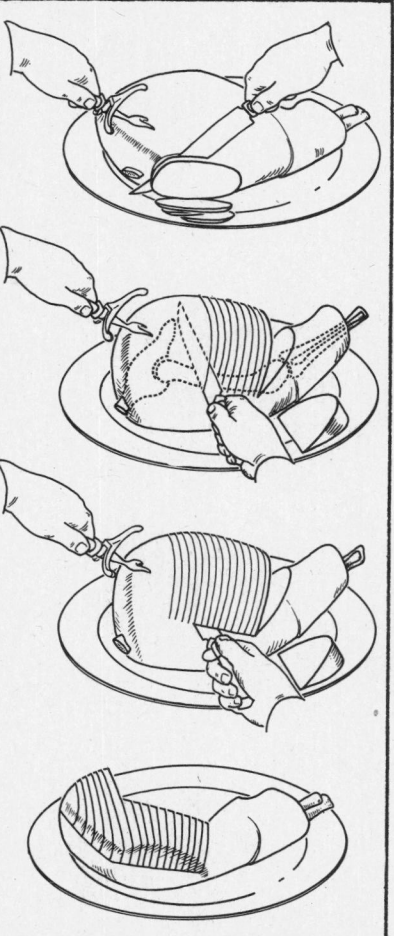

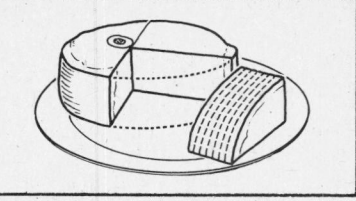

CENTER CUT HAM SLICE

Divide into thirds and turn one of the sections on its side as shown in illustration. Make slices the desired thickness across the grain. Carve·other sections in the same way. The bone must be removed from the end section before slicing.

PICNIC SHOULDER

Procedure is almost identical with that of the baked ham. Take slices from the smaller meaty side; turn the shoulder to stand on this surface. Slice to bone starting at shank end. Release slices by cutting along bone.

CUSHION LAMB SHOULDER

This cut is boneless and easy to carve. Cut slices about three-eighths of an inch thick through the meat and dressing.

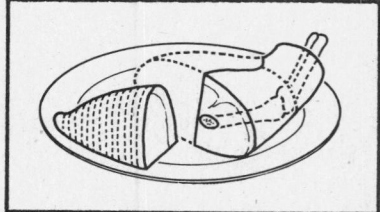

HALF HAM (Shank End)

Remove the cushion section, turn it on the cut side, as shown in the illustration, and make slices beginning at the large end. For further servings from the remaining section, separate it from the shank by cutting through the joint; remove bone, turn and slice.

Meat Cookery — Basic Methods

The most important guide to follow in all meat cookery is to use a *low* cooking temperature. This keeps the juice and flavor in the meat, cuts down shrinkage, keeps the meat more tender and palatable, and prevents burnt fat drippings.

General rules for the basic methods for cooking meats are described below; however more specific instructions are given in each recipe throughout this book. These methods fall into two basic groups: with dry heat or moist heat, depending on whether liquid is used.

Dry Heat Methods	Moist Heat Methods
Roasting	Braising
Broiling	Cooking in Liquid:
Pan-broiling	Soup-Making
Pan-frying	Stewing
Rotisserie cooking	Pressure cooking

Note: For pressure cooking, soup-making, and rotisserie cooking, see separate sections or consult index for specific recipes.

For hints about cooking frozen meats, see **Frozen Food** section.

TIME AND TEMPERATURE CHARTS FOR COOKING MEATS

Specific times are given in each recipe. In addition, you will find time and temperature charts for cooking meats preceding major subdivisions of this section; for example, preceding the beef, pork, veal, and lamb sections. The times given are necessarily only approximate. This is particularly true in roasting meat. The quality of the meat, size, and shape of roast, and its temperature at the start, all affect the time required.

The use of a meat thermometer is recommended. If you use one, insert it so the bulb is at the center of thickest part of meat and does not touch fat or bone. Where a range of times is given, use lower figure for larger roast.

Broiling

HOW TO ROAST

The modern method of roasting meats at low temperature does away with spattered ovens, cuts down shrinkage, and gives more and juicier servings per pound. ("Baking" is the term usually applied to roasting smoked hams and picnics.)

1. Sprinkle meat with salt and pepper.
2. Place fat-side-up on rack in open roaster. (For lean meats, such as veal, ask your meat dealer for a piece of pork or beef fat to lay over the top, or use a few strips of bacon or salt pork.)
3. If you have a meat thermometer, insert through the outside fat into thickest part of muscle so point does not rest on fat or bone.
4. Roast in slow oven (300° to 350°F.). Use this same temperature throughout cooking period. Do not add water. Do not sear meat. Do not cover pan. Do not baste.
5. Remove from oven when meat thermometer registers desired degree of doneness, or follow the time schedule given in time and temperature chart or recipe.

HOW TO PAN-FRY

"Pan-frying" is a term applied to cooking meats in a small amount of fat in a skillet.

Pan-frying rather than pan-broiling is necessary when meat has very little fat or when meat is breaded or floured.

Procedure is the same as for pan-broiling except that fat is added first.

HOW TO BROIL

The length of time to broil a steak or chop depends upon a number of factors—the thickness, your preference for rare, medium, or well done, and the fact that there are so many different makes and models of stoves in use in American kitchens. Here, however, are some general rules to follow:

1. Set regulator at 550°F. or "broil."
2. Put meat on broiler rack and place under broiling unit so that top surface of meat is about 2 inches from heat. Use a greater distance for very thick chops or steaks.
3. Broil with door closed if using a gas oven; leave door slightly ajar if broiling by electricity.
4. Broil until meat is well browned. Season with salt and pepper.
5. Turn and brown other side. Only one turning is necessary.
6. Serve broiled meats immediately on hot platter "to save the sizzle."

Note: Fresh pork and veal chops, steaks and cutlets should not be broiled. See **Braising**.

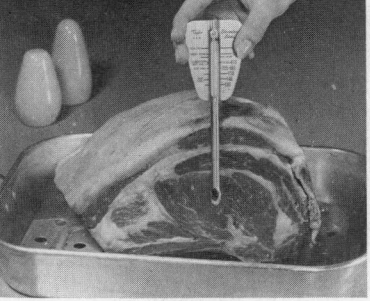

Roasting

HOW TO PAN-BROIL

1. Preheat a heavy cast aluminum or iron skillet, or griddle. Do not add fat except with ground meat patties. If you believe the meat will stick, rub pan with a piece of suet or grease lightly with other fat.
2. When pan is very hot, put in meat, brown quickly on both sides. Do not cover pan.
3. Reduce heat and cook slowly until done. If fat collects in pan, pour it off. Season before serving.

Pan-Broiling

HOW TO MAKE A STEW

"Stewing" is the term applied to the braising method when enough liquid is used to cover the meat.

1. Have beef, veal, or lamb cut into uniform pieces, 1 to 2 inches square. Season with salt and pepper. Flour the meat if you want a deep brown color.
2. Brown on all sides in hot cooking fat. If desired, brown chopped onions along with the meat.
3. Barely cover meat with hot water, stock, or other liquid. (To make a quick meat stock, dissolve a bouillon cube or 1 teaspoon beef extract in a cup of hot water or liquid from cooked vegetables.)
4. Cover kettle closely and cook slowly until meat is tender. Simmer, do not boil. Add extra liquid if necessary.
5. Add vegetables just long enough before meat is tender to be done but not over-cooked.
6. Thicken gravy with a smooth flour and water paste, using a few tablespoons of flour and enough water to moisten.

Braising

HOW TO BRAISE

"Pot roasting" is a popular term applied to braising large cuts.

Braising is a method of moist-heat cookery in which the meat is browned in a little hot fat, then cooked slowly in a covered utensil, usually with a small amount of added liquid. Examples are: pot roast and Swiss steak.

1. Season meat with salt and pepper. For a richer brown, sprinkle with flour.

2. Brown meat slowly on all sides in a little hot fat.

3. Add small amount of liquid. As liquid cooks away, a little more may be added.

4. Cover tightly. Cook over low heat at simmering temperature on top of stove or in moderately slow oven (325°F.) until meat is tender, 2 to 3 hours for a pot roast, 1 to 2 hours for Swiss steak.

5. Vegetables may be added 30 to 45 minutes before meat is done. Continue cooking until meat and vegetables are tender.

HOW TO COOK MEATS IN WATER

"Boiling" is the popular term used for cooking meats in water. Tests prove that these meats are more tender if cooked at a *simmering* rather than a *boiling* temperature.

This is a method often used for cooking cuts such as corned beef, fresh brisket, hocks, ham shank, and smoked tongue.

1. Cover meat with hot water.

2. Season with salt and pepper unless cooking cured or smoked meats such as corned beef, ham, or smoked tongue. Add a peeled onion and herbs and spices, if desired.

3. Cover and cook over low heat at simmering temperature (just below the boiling point) until done. Allow 40 to 50 minutes per pound for fresh or corned beef, 35 to 40 minutes per pound for smoked pork, and 50 minutes per pound for tongue.

4. If vegetables are to be cooked with the meat, add them 30 to 45 minutes before meat is done.

Beef Recipes

HINTS FOR COOKING BEEF

The different cuts of beef vary in tenderness. It is necessary, therefore, to determine the cooking method to be followed and to select the cuts of meat best suited to that method.

For cooking by dry heat—roasting, broiling, and pan-broiling—select tender cuts with small amounts of connective tissue.

For cooking by moist heat—braising, stewing, and soup-making—select the less-tender cuts. The less-tender cuts are more economical and are equal in food value to the tender cuts.

All cuts of meat may be made equally tender and tasty through the selection of the proper cooking method. Other means for making meat tender are grinding, pounding, and marinating. Grinding cuts up the connective tissue and the meat may then be cooked like any other tender meat. Pounding tenderizes by cutting through the connective tissue. Marinating, which is accomplished by letting the meat stand in an oil-acid mixture like French dressing, softens the connective tissue.

Beef Oven Roasts and Pot Roasts

STANDING RIB ROAST OF BEEF

Select a 2- or 3-rib roast (4 to 5 pounds). Have the chine bone removed to make carving easier. Season with salt and pepper.

Use a meat thermometer to assure you of a perfect roast. It registers the internal temperature of meat or its degree of doneness. The bulb should not touch bone or rest on fat.

Place meat fat-side-up on a rack in an open roasting pan. Do not add water. Do not cover.

Roast in a slow oven (300°–325°F.) to desired degree of doneness. Allow 18 to 20 minutes per pound for cooking a rare roast, 22 to 25 minutes per pound for medium, and 27 to 30 minutes per pound for a well done roast.

With meat thermometer, there will be no overcooking and undercooking. Thermometer will read 140° for rare, 160° for medium, and 170° for well done.

Serve on a heated platter, attractively garnished. Allow 2 to 3 servings per pound.

ROLLED RIB ROAST OF BEEF

Select a 3-rib boned and rolled roast. Season with salt and pepper.

Place roast fat-side-up on rack in pan. Insert meat thermometer in thickest part of meat.

If roast hasn't a generous fat cover-ing, place suet over top.

Proceed as for standing rib roast, increasing roasting time 10 to 15 minutes per pound. Allow 3 to 4 servings per pound.

BEEF ROASTING CHART		
Roasted at 325° F. Oven Temperature		
Cut	*Meat Thermometer Reading*	*Minutes Per Lb.*
Standing Ribs (rare)	140°F.	18–20
Standing Ribs (medium)	160°F.	22–25
Standing Ribs (well done)	170°F.	27–30
Rolled Ribs	Same as above	Add 10–15 per lb.
Blade: 3rd to 5th rib (high quality only)	150°–170°F.	25–30
Rump (high quality only)	150°–170°F.	25–30
Tenderloin	140°–170°F.	20–25
Beef Loaf	160°–170°F.	25–30

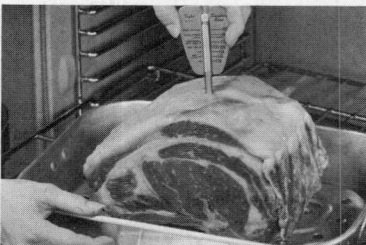

Standing Rib Roast of Beef

Rolled Rib Roast of Beef

YORKSHIRE PUDDING

(Accompaniment to Roast Beef)

This batter pudding of English origin is served with roast beef. Traditionally, Yorkshire pudding was baked in the pan with the roast or under the roast, letting the drippings fall upon it. Since roast beef is now cooked in a slow oven and the pudding requires a moderately hot oven, it is best to bake it in a separate pan or in muffin cups.

1 cup sifted enriched flour
1/2 teaspoon salt
2 eggs
1 cup milk
4 1/2 tablespoons beef drippings or fat

Sift and mix flour and salt. Combine eggs and milk and beat with a rotary beater; add to flour and salt mixture and beat well. Chill batter 1 hour in refrigerator.

Place half a tablespoon drippings or fat in bottom of each muffin pan (1 1/2 inches deep and 3 inches in diameter); heat in oven until fat is hot.

Place 3 tablespoons of chilled batter in each pan (1/2 full).

Bake in moderate oven (375°F.) 30 minutes. Makes 9 individual puddings.

ROAST FILLET OF BEEF

(Beef Tenderloin)

Sprinkle fillet with salt and pepper. Place on rack in open roasting pan. Lay 4 or 5 bacon slices or slices of salt pork over meat.

Roast in slow oven (325°F.) until done, 22 minutes per pound for rare and 25 minutes per pound for medium.

Because of the lack of fat in this meat cut, it is not advisable to roast until well done. Do not cover. Do not add water. Do not baste while roasting.

STUFFED FILLET OF BEEF

(Beef Tenderloin)

1 3- to 3 1/2-pound beef tenderloin
1/4 cup butter or margarine
1 very small onion, chopped
1 can (4 ounces) mushrooms
1 1/2 cups soft breadcrumbs
1/2 cup diced celery
Hot water
Salt and pepper
4 or 5 slices bacon

Have meat dealer split and flatten tenderloin.

Brown onion and mushrooms lightly in butter or margarine. Add breadcrumbs, celery, and hot water to moisten.

Season and spread over half the meat. Bring second half over top and fasten edges together with wooden picks.

Season with salt and pepper. Lay bacon slices over top.

Roast uncovered in moderate oven (350°F.) 1 hour. Serves 6 to 8.

BEEF RUMP ROAST

If a rump roast is of top quality, it may be oven roasted (cooked like a rib roast). If it's from the lower grades, braising (pot roasting) is the better method to use. Allow 3 to 4 servings per pound.

Sprinkle meat with salt and pepper. Place fat-side-up on rack in open roasting pan.

Insert meat thermometer through outside fat into thickest part of muscle so point does not rest on fat or bone.

Do not add water, do not cover, do not baste.

Roast in slow oven (325°F.). For rare, roast 22 to 26 minutes per pound or until meat thermometer registers 140°F.; for medium, roast 26 to 30 minutes per pound or until meat thermometer registers 160°F.; for well done, roast 33 to 35 minutes per pound or until meat thermometer registers 170°F.

BRAISED BEEF RUMP ROAST

Season meat with salt and pepper. Sprinkle with flour for a richer brown.

Brown meat slowly on all sides in a little hot fat.

Add small amount liquid. As liquid cooks away, a little more may be added.

Cover tightly. Simmer over low heat on top of range, or in slow oven (325°F.) until meat is tender, 2 to 3 hours for a pot roast.

Rump Swiss Steak: Follow recipe for Braised Rump Roast. Use canned tomatoes, tomato juice or drained liquid from canned mushrooms as liquid in cooking steaks. Simmer 1 to 2 hours.

BEEF À LA MODE

4 pounds beef round or chuck
1/2 pound salt pork, cut in thin strips
2 teaspoons salt
1/8 teaspoon pepper
1/2 cup flour
1/2 cup fat
1 cup peas
1/2 cup diced carrots
1/2 cup diced celery
1/2 cup diced onions

Lard beef with salt pork, using a larding needle to insert 1/4-inch strips of salt pork into meat.

Season with salt and pepper. Coat with flour and brown in fat.

Add cup of hot water, cover and cook slowly about 2 1/2 to 3 hours or until meat is tender.

Add peas, carrots, celery, and onions 1/2 hour before meat is done, adding more water if necessary to cover the vegetables.

When meat is done, place on hot platter with vegetables arranged around it and serve with brown gravy.

Serves 6 to 8.

Rump Roast

SAUERBRATEN

Sauerbraten is a German term meaning, literally, sour roast; it is a pot roast of beef that has been marinated for several days in spiced vinegar and is then braised in the marinade. The gravy is sometimes thickened with gingersnaps.

4- to 5-pound beef pot roast
2 cups water
2 cups vinegar
1 tablespoon salt
1/2 teaspoon pepper
2 tablespoons white or brown sugar
2 medium onions, sliced
1 clove garlic
6 cloves
2 bay leaves
3 or 4 celery tops
12 gingersnaps

Place meat in large earthenware or glass bowl.

Heat vinegar and water; dissolve salt, pepper, and sugar in it. Top meat with sliced onions; pour vinegar mixture over.

Add remaining ingredients except old-fashion gingersnaps to vinegar around meat. Cover and refrigerate 3 to 4 days, turning meat daily.

Remove meat and drain well. Strain liquid and save.

Dredge meat with flour; brown in hot fat in heavy pan. Add 1/2 cup of the strained liquid, cover and cook over low heat until meat is tender (3 to 4 hours). Add more liquid as needed.

Remove meat and keep hot. To make gravy, add more strained vinegar mixture to juice in the pan to make 3 cups liquid. Bring to boil and stir to dissolve all brown drippings. Add 12 gingersnaps, simmer and stir until gravy is thickened and smooth. Serves 8 to 10.

Sauerbraten

BEEF POT ROAST WITH PRUNES AND OLIVES

1   4-pound pot roast
Salt and pepper
1/8 teaspoon ground ginger
2   cloves garlic
3   onions, sliced
1/2 cup oil
2   cups water
1/2 cup dried mushrooms
1 1/2 cups prunes
1   cup ripe olives

Rub roast with salt, pepper, and ground ginger.

Chop garlic fine, slice onions, and cook in oil. Add meat and brown on all sides; then add 1/2 cup water. Cover tightly and simmer for 1 1/2 hours. Turn frequently.

While the meat is cooking, soak 1/2 cup dried mushrooms and 1 1/2 cups prunes in water.

Add prunes, mushrooms, soaking water, and ripe olives to meat, and continue cooking another hour, or until tender.

Remove meat to platter and surround with olives and prunes. The sauce may be thickened if desired. Serves 6 to 8.

BLADE POT ROAST WITH VEGETABLES

1/4 cup flour
1/2 teaspoon salt
1/8 teaspoon pepper
1/2 teaspoon Ac'cent
1   blade pot roast (bone in) 2-inches thick (about 3 pounds)
2   tablespoons fat
1   cup water
12 small carrots
12 small onions
1/4 cup flour
1/2 teaspoon salt, or to taste
1/8 teaspoon pepper
1/2 teaspoon Ac'cent

Combine first 4 ingredients; coat pot roast with this mixture.

Heat fat in Dutch oven or kettle; brown meat slowly on each side. Pour off excess fat. Add water.

Slip a low rack under meat; cover kettle; simmer 2 1/2 hours, adding more water if necessary, to keep at least 1/2 inch in bottom of kettle.

Blade Pot Roast with Vegetables

Add vegetables; cook 45 minutes longer, or until meat and vegetables are fork-tender.

Arrange meat and vegetables on hot platter; keep warm.

Add 2 cups water to liquid in kettle. Combine last 4 ingredients; blend to smooth paste with 1/2 cup cold water; add to liquid in kettle; stir over low heat until smooth and thickened. Serve with pot roast. Serves 6.

FLEMISH ROAST BEEF RUMP

3 to 4 pounds boneless rump of beef
1/2 pound salt pork
2 teaspoons salt
Dash of pepper
2 tablespoons dry mustard
1/2 cup fat
4 large onions, sliced thin
1 cup (or more) beef stock or canned bouillon
3 medium tomatoes, peeled
2 tablespoons red wine vinegar

Lard beef, using thin strips of salt pork in larding needle. Combine salt, pepper, and mustard, and rub into meat on both sides.

Melt fat in skillet or Dutch oven. Brown meat on both sides; remove from skillet.

Add onions to skillet and cook until golden brown. Then put meat on bed of onions and add beef stock or bouillon.

Cook covered 2 1/2 to 3 hours in slow oven (325°F.). During last half hour of cooking, add tomatoes cut in half and red wine vinegar. Continue cooking until meat is tender.

Serve on platter, surrounded by onions. Garnish with parsley or watercress. Serves 6 to 8.

BAVARIAN POT ROAST

1 4-pound boned beef rump pot roast
2 teaspoons salt
1/4 teaspoon pepper
1/2 pint (1 cup) sour cream
1 tablespoon flour
3/4 cup dry red wine (burgundy, claret, etc.)
1 medium onion, minced
6 carrots, pared, halved

Sprinkle beef with salt and pepper. Brown beef well on all sides in hot fat in Dutch oven about 15 to 20 minutes. Combine sour cream and flour in bowl; pour over beef. Add wine and onion.

Cover Dutch oven; simmer beef slowly about 2 1/2 to 3 hours, or until almost fork-tender, turning occasionally or basting with liquid in Dutch oven.

Then add carrots; cook 30 minutes, or until tender.

On heated platter, arrange roast and carrots, and boiled potatoes or rice if desired. Pass gravy separately. Serves 6.

Creole Pot Roast

BEEF POT ROAST CREOLE

4- to 5-pound chuck pot roast
Salt and pepper
1 bottle stuffed olives
1/4 cup water
1 cup condensed tomato soup
1 medium onion, chopped

Flour the pot roast and brown slowly in a little hot fat. Sprinkle with salt and pepper.

Mix together 1/4 cup liquid from bottled olives, 1/4 cup water, and the condensed tomato soup. Pour half of this over and around meat.

Top roast with 1/4 cup thinly sliced stuffed olives and chopped onion.

Cover the roaster and place in slow oven (325°F.). Cook for 2 1/2 to 3 hours, or until the meat is tender.

Or cook roast in a Dutch oven on top of range at a simmering temperature for the same length of time.

As the liquid cooks away (after about the first hour), add rest of liquid.

Thicken gravy with flour, adding more water to make of the desired consistency. Serve gravy over rice or noodles. Serves 8.

HERB BEEF POT ROAST

4- to 5-pound chuck pot roast
Flour, salt, pepper, and lard
2 celery stalks with leaves
2 medium onions
1/2 teaspoon basil
1/2 teaspoon marjoram
1/2 teaspoon rosemary

Dredge pot roast with flour and brown slowly in a little hot lard in a Dutch oven or other large, heavy utensil. Sprinkle with salt and pepper.

Place meat on a rack and top with sliced celery and onions. Add herbs to 1/2 cup of water or bouillon, add seasonings and pour over and around meat.

Cover and cook over low heat until tender, 2 1/2 to 3 hours, adding more liquid as needed. Make gravy from drippings. Serves 8.

1. For a beef pot roast use the less tender cuts. Season meat with salt and pepper. Sprinkle with flour (optional).

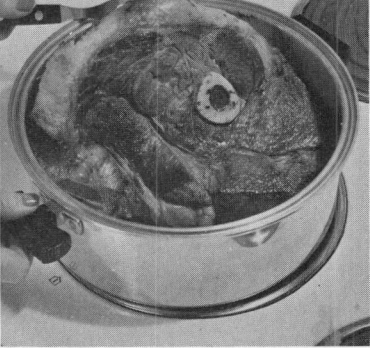

2. Brown meat on all sides in hot fat.

3. Add a small amount of liquid. Cover closely; simmer until tender (2½ to 3 hours). Add whole vegetables just long enough before serving time for them to be cooked tender but not over-cooked.

4. Serve on a heated platter attractively garnished.

BEEF POT ROAST
(Master Recipe)

    2   onions, sliced
    2   tablespoons fat or salad oil
    3   to 5 pounds beef (chuck or rump)
        Flour
        Salt and pepper
    1   cup boiling water or stock
    2   bay leaves (optional)

Brown onions in hot fat. Sprinkle meat with flour; brown on all sides; season with salt and pepper. Add water or stock and bay leaves.

Cover tightly; simmer slowly until meat is tender, 2½ to 3 hours. Add more water or stock if necessary.

Serves 6 to 8.

Beef Pot Roast Variations

Pot Roast with Chili Sauce: Add 2 cups chili sauce when meat has been simmering 1½ hours. Continue cooking another 1½ hours.

Pot Roast with Olives: Before browning, cut slits in meat and insert stuffed olives. Continue as in master recipe.

Pot Roast with Potatoes: Boil peeled potatoes for 15 minutes. Drain and add to pot roast during last 45 minutes of cooking.

Pot Roast with Tomato Juice: Substitute tomato juice or stewed tomatoes for water.

Pot Roast with Vegetables: Add whole carrots, onions, and potatoes during last 45 minutes of cooking time.

Other Pot Roast Variations: Use these miscellaneous seasoning suggestions, chili powder, curry powder, oregano, dill seed or chopped dill pickles, liquid from sweet pickles, caraway seed, horseradish, and vinegar.

Oven Pot Roast: After seasoning meat, lay pieces of suet over the top. Put meat on rack in roasting pan.

Cover closely and cook until tender in moderate oven (375°F.) about 1½ to 2½ hours.

About 45 minutes before meat is done, place six peeled medium potatoes in pan around meat. Turn potatoes in drippings and sprinkle with salt.

Cover and cook until meat and potatoes are tender. Before serving, remove lid to allow potatoes to brown.

BEEF POT ROAST WITH BARBECUE SAUCE

    3   pounds beef pot roast, blade or
            arm cut
    2   teaspoons salt
    ¼   teaspoon pepper
    3   tablespoons fat
    ½   cup water
    1   8-ounce can tomato sauce
    3   medium onions, sliced
    2   cloves garlic, minced
    2   tablespoons brown sugar
    ½   teaspoon dry mustard
    ¼   cup lemon juice
    ¼   cup ketchup
    ¼   cup vinegar
    1   tablespoon Worcestershire sauce

Season meat with salt and pepper. Brown in hot fat. Add water, tomato sauce, onions, and garlic. Cover and cook over low heat 1½ hours.

Combine remaining ingredients and pour over meat. Cover and cook until tender, about 1 hour. Remove meat to hot platter.

Skim most of fat from gravy. Dilute gravy with water to suit taste, then thicken with 2 tablespoons flour mixed to a smooth paste with a little water. Serves 6.

SWEDISH POT ROAST

    3   tablespoons fat
    2   medium onions, sliced
    1   clove garlic, minced
    3   to 3½ pounds pot roast
    1   tablespoon salt
    1   cup thick sour cream
    1   cup water
    4- or 5-ounce package noodles

In a Dutch oven or other heavy utensil, lightly brown onion and garlic in hot fat. Push to one side of pan. Rub meat with salt and brown well.

Combine sour cream with water and pour over meat. Top with browned onions, cover and cook over low heat (or in 325°F. oven) for 2½ hours, or until tender.

Cook noodles in boiling salted water.

Remove roast from pan and make gravy from drippings, adding to it the sour cream and onion mixture from top of roast. Season to taste with salt, pepper, and paprika.

Serve noodles and meat topped with gravy. Serves 6 or more.

CRANBERRY POT ROAST

    3- to 4-pound rolled chuck roast
        Flour
    3   tablespoons fat
        Salt and pepper
    2   cups unsweetened cranberry sauce
    1   cup hot water

Coat meat with flour. Brown in hot fat. Season with salt and pepper. Pour cranberry sauce and water over roast.

Cover and cook in slow oven (325°F.) until tender, about 3 hours, adding water from time to time if necessary.

Remove to hot platter when done and thicken liquid in pan for gravy. Serves 6 to 8.

QUICK SAUERBRATEN WITH RAISINS

3 to 4 pounds chuck pot roast
Salt
2 tablespoons lard
2 medium onions, sliced
1 bay leaf
1/4 cup water
1/4 cup vinegar
1 tablespoon brown sugar
1/8 teaspoon cinnamon
1/4 teaspoon allspice
1/8 teaspoon ground cloves
1/2 cup raisins

Sprinkle roast with salt. Brown in hot lard in a Dutch oven or other large, heavy utensil. Top with sliced onions and bay leaf.

Combine water and vinegar. Add sugar and stir until dissolved. Add remaining seasonings and pour over meat. Cover and cook over low heat until almost tender, about 2 hours, adding more water as needed.

Turn meat and top with raisins. Cover and continue cooking until meat is tender, 1/2 to 1 hour.

Remove roast to serving platter. Spoon off most of fat. Dilute liquid with water, if necessary, and thicken with a flour-and-water paste. Season to taste. Serves 6 to 8.

DUTCH POT ROAST OF CHUCK WITH VEGETABLES

4- to 5-pound beef chuck, boned and rolled
Salt and pepper
Flour
3 tablespoons salt pork or bacon fat
1 cup boiling water
1 cup sliced carrots
1 cup chopped onions
1 cup diced celery
1 cup diced turnips
1/4 clove garlic, minced
2 tablespoons minced parsley
2 cups stock or bouillon cubes and water
1/2 cup red wine or grape juice

Season meat with salt and pepper. Roll in flour until thickly covered. Heat fat in heavy kettle and brown meat all over.

Add boiling water and cover tightly. Simmer 4 hours, turning 3 times during cooking and adding water as necessary to maintain level.

Add remaining ingredients. Cover and simmer until vegetables are tender, about 1/2 hour.

Remove meat to hot platter and mask with vegetables; keep warm.

Strain gravy and return it to kettle. Reduce to 2 cups by rapid boiling and stir in a smooth paste of 1 to 2 tablespoons each of butter and flour, depending on thickness of reduced liquid. Serve gravy in separate dish. Serves 10.

ROAST BEEF IN WINE MARINADE

3 to 4 pounds top sirloin or bottom round of beef
1 pint red wine
1/2 teaspoon garlic salt or onion salt or 1 tablespoon minced onion
1/8 teaspoon thyme
1 bay leaf
3 to 4 thin slices onion
Drippings or margarine
1/2 cup boiling water

Mix wine and remaining ingredients. Pour over the roast and allow to stand in cool place for at least 5 hours. (Note: If chuck or rump cuts are used, then marinate overnight before roasting.)

Remove from marinade. Rub with salt.

Place in roasting pan. Dot top well with drippings or margarine.

Place, uncovered, in moderate oven (350°F.) until meat begins to brown; then add marinating sauce and boiling water.

Cover. Continue to cook 3 to 4 hours, basting occasionally, until meat is tender. Serves 6 to 8.

BEEF POT ROAST WITH HORSERADISH SAUCE

3 pounds beef pot roast
2 tablespoons melted fat
1 teaspoon garlic salt
1 6-ounce bottle horseradish
6 onions, peeled
3 tablespoons enriched flour
2 tablespoons water

Brown meat in fat in deep-well cooker or Dutch oven. Sprinkle with garlic salt. Add enough water to horseradish to make 1 cup; pour over meat.

Cover and cook over low heat for 2 hours. Add onions and cook, covered, for 30 minutes or until onions are tender. Remove meat and onions.

Add enough water to sauce to make 2 cups. Blend flour and 2 tablespoons water until smooth. Add thickening to sauce and cook over low heat, stirring constantly, until thickened. Serves 6.

SPICED BEEF WITH RED WINE

2 cups water
1/2 cup vinegar
1 teaspoon whole black peppers
1/2 teaspoon mace
2 onions, sliced
1/2 cup brown sugar
2 teaspoons mixed pickle spices
1 1/2 cups claret or burgundy
3 to 4 pounds beef pot roast
4 teaspoons salt
Carrots
Flour to thicken gravy

Combine water, vinegar, whole black peppers, mace, sliced onions, brown sugar, and pickle spices. Bring to boiling point. Add wine; pour over the meat. Store in refrigerator overnight.

Rub roast with salt; brown on all sides in a little hot fat.

Pour half the sauce over roast and simmer, covered, for about 2 hours.

Add remaining spice sauce and the carrots; simmer 1 hour longer.

Measure liquid in bottom of pan. Thicken with flour, allowing 2 tablespoons flour for each cup of liquid. Serve with noodles or dumplings. Serves 6 to 8.

CALIFORNIA POT ROAST

3 to 4 pounds beef chuck, bottom round or boneless sirloin
1 cup sour cream
1 teaspoon salt
1/2 teaspoon paprika
1/2 teaspoon pepper
1 clove garlic
1 large carrot
1 large onion
1 cup burgundy or other red wine
3 tablespoons flour
1/2 cup water
1 tablespoon lemon juice or vinegar

Purchase pot roast that is boned, rolled, and larded. Remove sour cream from refrigerator so it's at room temperature.

Mix salt, paprika, and pepper, and rub thoroughly over meat. Brown on all sides in a heavy kettle over high heat, about 10 to 15 minutes.

Meanwhile, chop garlic, pare and slice carrot, peel and cut onion into rings. Add to meat in kettle and cook until onions are golden, about 3 or 4 minutes.

Heat wine and add to meat along with sour cream. Turn down heat, cover tightly and cook over very low heat so mixture barely simmers until meat is tender, about 2 1/2 hours.

Remove meat to hot plate while making gravy. Skim any excess fat.

Blend flour and water to a smooth paste and stir into hot liquid. Cook and stir about 5 minutes.

Add a little more water if gravy is too thick. Add lemon juice and serve at once. Serves 6 to 8.

California Pot Roast

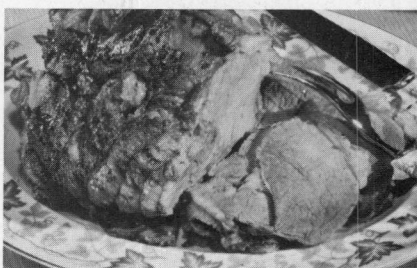

Swiss Steaks

SWISS STEAK

(Master Recipe)

Swiss steak is a thick cut of round steak, or sometimes chuck or rump, that has been coated with flour and then pounded, in order to tenderize it, then braised with or without vegetables.

2 pounds beef, 1 inch thick
Salt and pepper, to taste
1/3 cup flour
2 cups cooked or canned tomatoes

Season meat with salt and pepper. Sprinkle with flour. Pounding helps make meat tender.

Cut meat into serving pieces and brown in fat. Add tomatoes or juice. Cover and simmer gently until tender, 2 to 2 1/2 hours. Serves 6.

Swiss Steak Variations

Swiss Steak with Brown Gravy: Use water instead of tomatoes. When done, remove meat. Add water if needed to make 2 cups total liquid, and, if necessary, thicken with flour blended with cold water.

Swiss Steak with Onion Gravy: Add 2 1/2 cups thinly sliced onions to Swiss Steak with Brown Gravy during last 1/2 hour of cooking.

SPANISH STEAK

Follow master recipe for Swiss Steak, using 1 1/2 pounds of meat.

Brown 3/4 cup chopped onion and 1 1/2 cups chopped green pepper in fat.

Cook 1 1/2 cups macaroni in boiling salted water. Mix macaroni, onions, and pepper with tomato sauce. Serve over meat. Serves 6.

SWISS STEAK SUPREME

2 pounds round steak, 1 inch thick
3/4 cup flour
2 cups sliced onions
2 tablespoons fat
1 teaspoon dry mustard
2 teaspoons salt
1/4 teaspoon pepper
1 clove garlic, finely chopped
1/2 cup water
1/2 cup chili sauce or cooked tomatoes

Pound flour into steak with a meat mallet or edge of heavy saucer.

Pan-fry onions in hot fat in a skillet. Remove from pan.

Brown steak on both sides. Cover with onions. Add mustard, salt, pepper, garlic, water, and chili sauce or cooked tomatoes.

Cover and cook over low heat or bake in moderate oven (350°F.) about 1 1/2 hours. Serves 6.

SWISS STEAK #2

2 pounds round or chuck steak, 1 to 2 inches thick
Flour, salt, pepper, garlic salt, and fat
1 No. 2 can (2 1/2 cups) tomatoes
2 medium onions, sliced
1 stalk celery
1 bay leaf
2 teaspoons Worcestershire sauce

Sprinkle steak well with flour and pound it thoroughly into meat with edge of a heavy saucer or a meat pounder.

Brown steak slowly in hot fat in a Dutch oven or other heavy utensil. Drain off excess fat and sprinkle steak with salt, pepper, and garlic salt.

Pour tomatoes over and around meat; top with sliced onions and celery; add bay leaf and sprinkle with Worcestershire sauce.

Cover and cook over low heat or in slow oven (325°F.) until tender, 1 1/2 to 2 hours, depending on thickness of steak. Serve steak with the tomato gravy spooned over it. Serves 4 to 6.

SWISS STEAK IN SOUR CREAM

3 pounds round steak, 1 inch thick
Salt, pepper, and Ac'cent
1 teaspoon paprika
Flour
1/2 cup chopped onion
1/2 cup sour cream
Boiling water

Wipe steak with damp cloth; rub in seasonings; pound with meat mallet or heavy knife until meat fibers are well broken, adding a little flour at a time and pounding it well into the steak.

Brown meat on both sides in hot fat along with onion, tossing onion around and over top of steak.

Pour off excess fat; add sour cream and enough boiling water to barely cover steak. Cover and simmer until tender, about 2 1/2 hours. Serves 6 to 8.

SWISS STEAK IN RED WINE

1/2 cup flour
1 1/2 teaspoons salt
1/2 teaspoon pepper
2 pounds round steak, cut 3/4 to 1 inch thick
3 tablespoons bacon drippings or other fat
1 cup burgundy, claret, or other red wine
1 can (3 ounces) chopped broiled-in-butter mushrooms
1 onion, thinly sliced
6 medium-sized carrots, cut crosswise in halves and lengthwise in quarters

Mix flour, salt, and pepper. Place meat on a board and pound flour mixture into it with a wooden potato masher or the edge of a heavy plate. Cut meat into serving-size pieces.

Heat bacon drippings in large, heavy skillet; add meat and sauté until well browned on both sides. Place on trivet in pressure saucepan. Add wine and liquid from mushrooms.

If any flour remains on board, sprinkle it over the meat. Close saucepan and bring to 15-pound pressure. Cook for 18 minutes. Reduce pressure according to manufacturer's directions.

Add vegetables and again bring to pressure. Cook for 3 minutes. Reduce pressure.

Before serving, taste and add additional salt and pepper, if necessary. Buttered noodles and a tossed green salad are excellent accompaniments to this dish. Serves 6.

Note: If you do not have a pressure saucepan, flour and brown meat as directed; add all remaining ingredients (including mushroom liquid and any flour remaining on board.) Cover skillet and simmer, stirring occasionally, for 1 1/2 to 2 hours, or until meat is very tender.

Swiss Steak in Red Wine

Beef Steaks

BROILED STEAK

Have a tender porterhouse, T-bone, club, or sirloin steak cut 1 to 2 inches thick. Slash the fatty edge of the steak but do not cut into the meat or you'll lose good meat juice.

Turn the oven regulator to "broil." The broiler may be preheated or not, as desired. With some broilers, thick steaks may be cooked without preheating the broiler.

Place steak on rack of broiler pan, 2 to 3 inches from the heat. Steaks 1½ to 2 inches thick should be at least 3 inches from the heat; those 1 inch or less in thickness, about 2 inches. Broil until top side is brown. The steak should be approximately half done by the time it is browned on top.

Season the top side with salt and pepper. Steaks brown better if browned before salting. Turn and brown the other side. For determining accurately the degree of doneness of a thick steak, a meat thermometer may be used. Season and serve at once. To keep broiled steak hot, the platter should be heated. For 1-inch steak, allow 15 to 20 minutes. For 1½-inch steak, allow 25 to 35 minutes. For 2-inch steaks, allow 30 to 40 minutes.

BROILED STEAK-SEARING METHOD

Preheat broiler until very hot (450° to 500°F.). Place steak under heat so that top of steak is 2 to 3 inches from source of heat. Sear or brown on each side, turning only once, allowing 5 minutes for each. Leave door open.

Reduce heat to slow (300°F.) or place steak 6 to 7 inches from source of heat and finish cooking.

When half done, season top side, turn, and finish cooking. Season other side and serve.

Allow the same time as for even temperature method, including searing in total time. The searing method produces a steak with surface nicely browned while interior may be rare or medium.

PLANKED STEAK

Broil steak, cutting time for top side by 5 minutes. Place less-done side up on a greased broiling plank. Season.

With pastry tube, arrange border of mashed potatoes around edge of plank. Place one or more cooked vegetables between steak and potatoes. Brush all with melted fat.

Place in broiler 3 inches from heat and brown potatoes. Garnish with parsley, watercress, tomato wedges or slices.

GARLIC SEASONED STEAK

Rub broiled steak with cut garlic clove.

STEAK WITH MUSHROOMS

After broiling steak, top with mushroom caps which have been browned in butter.

STEAK WITH ROQUEFORT TOPPING

Blend ¼ cup Roquefort or other blue cheese with 2 tablespoons cream. Season with a few drops Worcestershire sauce and spread over hot broiled steak.

STEAK WITH OYSTERS

Broil beef steak until nearly done. Place it in a pan. Cover with drained oysters. Season oysters lightly with salt and pepper and dot with butter. Bake in moderate oven (375°F.) until oysters are plump. Serve with lemon butter. Garnish with chopped parsley.

PAN-BROILED STEAK

Use tender steak ¾ to 1 inch thick. Trim off excess fat.

Heat heavy skillet moderately and grease very lightly. Place steak in it. Brown quickly on both sides.

Reduce heat. Cook slowly until done, pouring off fat as it accumulates. To test, cut near bone. Season with salt and pepper and serve.

BROILED TENDERLOIN (FILET MIGNON)

Have a fillet cut ¾ to 1½ inches thick. The very thick steaks are called "double fillets."

Shape each cut into a nice round shape and wrap a slice of bacon around the edge. Fasten in place with a toothpick.

Broil or pan-broil until cooked, 10 to 15 minutes. Serve rare but not raw.

CHICKEN-FRIED ROUND STEAK

1½ to 2 pounds round steak, ½ inch thick
2   tablespoons milk
2   beaten eggs
1   cup fine cracker crumbs
¼   cup fat
Salt and pepper

Pound steak thoroughly with meat mallet or edge of heavy saucer.

Mix milk and eggs; dip steak in mixture, then in crumbs. Brown on both sides in hot fat in skillet. Season.

Cover and cook over very low heat 45 to 60 minutes. Serves 6.

LONDON BROIL (FLANK STEAK)

Use a large prime-quality flank steak. Marinate at least 2 hours in French dressing.

Broil on a greased rack about 3 inches from heat, allowing 5 minutes for each side.

To serve, cut in thin slices diagonally across the grain. Season with salt, pepper, and melted butter.

BEEF BROILING CHART		
Cut	**Broiled***	
	Meat Thermometer Reading	**Total Time in Minutes**
Steaks (1-inch) rare: medium:	140°F. 160°F.	15–20 20–30
Steaks (1½-inch) rare: medium:	140°F. 160°F.	25–30 35–50
Steaks (2-inch) rare: medium:	140°F. 160°F.	30–40 50–70
Beef Patties (1-inch) rare: medium:	140°F. 160°F.	12–15 18–20

* Pan-broiling or griddle-broiling requires about half the time for broiling.

TENDERIZED STEAK

Select round, chuck, or rump steak, 1-inch thick. Use instant meat tenderizer according to label directions. Broil to desired doneness. Meat tenderizer cuts cooking time—don't overcook.

CUBE OR MINUTE STEAKS

Minute steaks are small individual steaks, ¼ to ½ inch thick, cut from any tender cut. Sometimes they are scored by a special machine that cuts the connective tissue.

If scored, pan-broil quickly without fat, allowing about a minute for each side in hot frying pan.

If not scored, allow 4 to 5 minutes for entire cooking.

If cooked longer, steaks become dry and tough.

SAUTEED ROUND STEAK

Use round steak about ⅓ inch thick. Cut into serving-size pieces. Dip in flour.

Sauté until brown in hot fat over moderately high heat. Reduce heat to low. Cover and cook until steak is tender.

Planked Steak

Beef Tenderloin with Red Wine Sauce

BEEF TENDERLOIN WITH RED WINE SAUCE

8 to 10 slices beef tenderloin, about 1/2-inch thick
1/4 cup butter
1/2 pound mushrooms
3 tablespoons flour
3/4 cup red table wine
1 cup beef stock, fresh or canned

Sauté beef slices in about 1 tablespoon butter, about 3 minutes per side. Remember the meat is very tender, so do not overcook.

While meat is browning, melt remaining 3 tablespoons butter in another pan, slice mushrooms and sauté until lightly browned. Blend in flour. Add wine and beef stock and cook until the mixture comes to a boil. Simmer 5 minutes.

Just before serving, add beef slices with any pan juice to gravy and cook until heated through. Serves 4 to 5.

PEPPERED STEAK (STEAK AU POIVRE)

A generous amount of fresh coarsely crushed or ground black pepper is the secret to success of this very popular dish.

6 portions 1-inch thick club or filet mignon steaks or strip sirloin steaks
2 tablespoons black pepper, coarsely ground
Salt
2 tablespoons butter
Worcestershire sauce
Tabasco sauce
Lemon juice
2 ounces cognac, optional
Chopped parsley, optional
Chopped chives, optional

Sprinkle both sides of each steak with pepper and work it into the meat with the heel of the hand or with the flat side of a cleaver. Let stand 30 minutes.

Sprinkle a light layer of salt (about 2 teaspoons) over the bottom of a heavy skillet. Place over high heat and when the salt begins to brown, add the steaks. Cook uncovered over high heat until browned on one side.

Lower the heat to moderate, turn the steaks, and cook to desired degree of rareness.

Place a teaspoon of butter on each steak and add Worcestershire, Tabasco,

and lemon juice to taste. Reduce the heat to low; flame the steaks with the cognac and transfer to a heated serving platter. Pour the sauce in the skillet over the steaks and, if desired, sprinkle with parsley and chives. Serves 6.

CHATEAUBRIAND

Chateaubriand is a French term for a steak cut from the thickest part of the fillet of beef (tenderloin), weighing usually 1 to 2 pounds. It is grilled or sautéed rare and served with any of the sauces suggested for steak. Inasmuch as the steak is always thick, care must be taken to avoid charring the outside while the inside remains raw.

STEAK DIANE

1 to 1 1/2 tablespoons butter or margarine
1/4 teaspoon salt
Freshly ground black pepper to taste
1/2 to 1 teaspoon each finely chopped chives and parsley
1 teaspoon Worcestershire sauce
Individual steak of any thickness (1-pound with bone, 8 to 10 ounces without bone and fat)

Mix all ingredients except meat in heavy fry pan and, when very hot, place steak in pan.

Cook at very high heat until done. Serve immediately, pouring residue of sauce over meat. Serves 1.

FLANK FINGER STEAKS

1 flank steak
Flour
1/4 cup drippings
1 teaspoon salt
1/2 teaspoon pepper
1 cup beef bouillon
2 tablespoons minced parsley
2 tablespoons ketchup
1 tablespoon prepared mustard
1 tablespoon vinegar
2 tablespoons minced onion
1 4-ounce can mushrooms

Cut steak into 6 portions. Dredge with flour and brown in drippings.

Remove from skillet. Add and mix remaining ingredients with drippings.

Return steak to skillet. Cover tightly and bring to boil. Reduce heat and simmer 1 1/4 hours. Serves 6.

PAN-BARBECUED STEAK

2 pounds steak (round or flank, 1 1/2 to 2 inches thick)
1/2 teaspoon salt
1/2 teaspoon pepper
3 tablespoons fat
1/3 cup minced onion
1/3 cup minced celery
1/2 clove garlic, minced
1 can (1 1/4 cups) condensed tomato soup
2 tablespoons brown sugar

2 tablespoons Worcestershire sauce
2 tablespoons lemon juice
2 teaspoons prepared mustard
Dash of Tabasco sauce

Sprinkle steak with salt and pepper; pound thoroughly.

Melt fat in heavy saucepan or skillet. Brown steak, onion, celery, and garlic in hot fat.

Add remaining ingredients. Stir well and cover. Cook in moderate oven (350°F.) or on top of range for about 1 1/2 hours or until tender.

Double all the sauce ingredients for additional barbecue sauce to serve over fluffy rice or mashed potatoes. Serves 6.

COUNTRY FRIED ARM STEAK

1. Select an arm steak, 1/2- to 3/4-inch thick. Cut into individual servings. Pound seasoned flour into each side of individual steaks. Melt 2 to 4 tablespoons fat in frying pan.

2. Brown steaks slowly on both sides. Cover and cook at a low temperature 45 minutes to 1 hour.

3. Remove steaks from pan, stir 1/4 cup flour into drippings. Add 2 cups stock stirring constantly until thickened. Serve gravy over or with steaks.

CONTINENTAL STEAK

½ cup fat
2 onions, sliced thin
2 pounds chuck or round steak
1 teaspoon salt
⅛ teaspoon pepper
1 clove garlic, mashed
½ pound fresh mushrooms, sliced
1 green pepper, sliced thin
1 8-ounce can tomato sauce
1 cup water

Melt fat in heavy skillet. Add onions and cook until golden brown; remove onions.

Rub meat with salt, pepper, and mashed garlic; place in hot skillet and sear quickly on both sides. Add browned onions, sliced mushrooms, green pepper, and tomato sauce.

Cook 15 minutes, then add water. Simmer over slow heat about 1½ hours or until meat is tender and sauce has thickened.

Remove to hot platter. Serve hot with parsley buttered potato balls. Serves 5 to 6.

STUFFED FLANK STEAK

1 flank steak
Salt and pepper
2 tablespoons butter or margarine
½ cup finely chopped onion
2 cups soft breadcrumbs
¼ teaspoon caraway seed
½ teaspoon celery salt
1 cup tomato juice

Have meat man score flank steak. Sprinkle with salt and pepper. Melt fat and in it lightly cook onion. Mix with breadcrumbs, caraway seed, celery salt, and salt and pepper to taste.

Spread stuffing on unscored side of steak and roll parallel to its length. Tie in 3 or 4 places with string or fasten with short metal skewers and lace with string.

In a skillet or other heavy utensil, brown steak in a little hot fat. Add tomato juice, cover and cook over low heat or in moderate oven (350°F.) 2 hours, or until tender. Serves 4 to 6.

Savory Flank Steak

BRAISED STEAK AND ONIONS

¾ to 1 pound beef rump or round, cut 1 inch thick
Salt, pepper, flour
Fat
Water
1 or 2 large onions, sliced

Season meat with salt and pepper; sprinkle with flour.

Pound on both sides with meat mallet or the edge of a heavy saucer to help make meat tender.

Cut meat into serving pieces and brown in a little fat in a fry pan.

Add water to ½-inch depth. Cover pan and cook slowly until meat is very tender, about 2 hours, adding onions during last half hour.

To serve, place steak on hot platter and cover with onions. Make gravy with the drippings. Serves 4.

ROUND STEAK BRAISED WITH OLIVES

1½ pounds round steak, ¾-inch thick
2 tablespoons fat
1 medium onion, chopped
1 small green pepper, chopped
1 bottle (3½ ounces) pimiento stuffed olives, sliced
1 can (10½ ounces) cream of tomato soup

Cut steak into serving pieces. Brown with onion and green pepper in hot fat in heavy skillet or flame-resistant casserole. Add olives and olive brine. Add tomato soup. Cover tightly and bake in moderate oven (350°F.) or cook over low heat until tender, about 1½ hours. Serves 4 to 5.

SAVORY FLANK STEAK

1 flank steak, well scored
Salt and pepper
2 tablespoons chopped parsley
1 clove garlic, minced
⅓ cup grated Parmesan cheese
2 tablespoons shortening
2 cans condensed cream of tomato soup, diluted with an equal quantity of water
1 teaspoon cider or salad vinegar
1 teaspoon oregano

Sprinkle one side of flank steak with salt, pepper, parsley, garlic, and cheese.

Roll steak up tightly, jelly-roll fashion, and secure with string. Brown on all sides in shortening in large skillet or Dutch oven.

Combine soup, water, vinegar, and oregano; pour over flank steak. Simmer, covered, 3½ to 4 hours, or until tender.

Serve with noodles or spaghetti. Serves 4 to 6.

Dilly Flank Steak

DILLY FLANK STEAK

¼ cup wine vinegar
¼ cup oil
¾ cup water
1 tablespoon instant minced onion
¼ teaspoon dried dill
⅛ teaspoon garlic powder
½ teaspoon salt
⅛ teaspoon pepper
1 flank steak (1½ to 2 pounds)
1 tablespoon cornstarch
1½ teaspoons sugar

Combine vinegar, oil, ¼ cup water, onion, dill, garlic powder, salt, and pepper. Place flank steak in shallow glass dish. Pour vinegar-oil mixture over steak. Cover and let stand 2 to 3 hours.

Drain steak and remove to broiling pan, reserving marinade. Broil in oven (or over grill) about 5 minutes on first side, 4 minutes on second side for rare. Remove to heated serving platter.

Combine cornstarch, sugar, and remaining ½ cup water with reserved marinade. Add to drippings in broiler pan. Cook, stirring constantly, until mixture boils and is thickened.

To serve, slice steak thin, diagonally to the grain, and top with sauce. Serves 6 to 8.

SKIRT STEAK

Skirt steak is a cut from the diaphragm, so called because it skirts the ribs. When properly trimmed, it is all lean meat. Its long, tough fibers may be tenderized by marinating or light scoring with a knife. It is usually an economical and convenient cut for broiling or sautéing. It is often rolled into pinwheels before being cut into individual portions. Sometimes erroneously called tenderloin, a term properly applied to a long strip on either side of the backbone.

BRAISED FLANK STEAK

Have the meat scored. Dip into flour, season with salt and pepper.

Brown in hot fat. Add ½ cup hot water. Cover and cook over low heat or in moderate oven (350°F.) until tender, about 1½ hours.

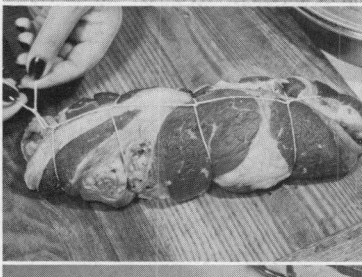

Rolled Stuffed Round Steak

TOURNEDOS

Tournedos is a French term for a small, uniform slice cut from the heart of the fillet of beef (tenderloin), then usually encased in a thin layer of fat and securely tied. They are so cut for quick cooking. These are most often sautéed in butter or olive oil or in a mixture of the two. They may also be grilled but are generally considered better if sautéed and served with a sauce.

COUNTRY FRIED ROUND STEAK

1   pound round steak, cut ½-inch
       thick
1   teaspoon salt
Dash of pepper
¼   cup flour
1   tablespoon fat
2   tablespoons water

Cut steak into serving pieces. Season with salt and pepper. Roll in flour. Brown on both sides in hot fat.

Add water; cover and simmer until steak is tender, 15 to 20 minutes. Serve with hot meat drippings poured over steak. Serves 4.

Variation: If desired, the flour may be seasoned with the salt and pepper and pounded into steak before browning.

With Milk Gravy: Make milk gravy by adding enough milk to drippings to make 2 cups liquid. Combine 3 tablespoons flour with ½ cup of the milk and add slowly to the boiling liquid in pan. Stir and boil 5 minutes. Add more salt if necessary.

ROLLED STUFFED ROUND STEAK

3   cups soft breadcrumbs
¼   cup chopped onion
¼   cup chopped celery
1   tablespoon chopped parsley
½   teaspoon powdered sage
½   teaspoon salt
Pepper
⅓   cup soup stock or hot water
Round steak, cut ½-inch thick
3   tablespoons fat or drippings
¼   cup water

Combine breadcrumbs, onion, celery, parsley, seasonings, and enough stock or water to moisten.

Spread stuffing on steak and roll like a jelly roll. Tie in several places or fasten with skewers.

Brown roll on all sides in fat or drippings. Add water. Cover closely and cook slowly about 1½ hours, or until meat is tender.

Remove to hot platter and make gravy with drippings in the pan. Serves 6 to 8.

MARINATED SIRLOIN STEAK WITH FRIED ONIONS

Sirloin steak, 1½ inches thick
½   cup olive oil
Worcestershire sauce
Salt and pepper
2   tablespoons lemon juice
3   large Spanish onions, sliced
½   cup evaporated milk
Flour

Rub steak with cut clove of garlic, if desired.

Season olive oil to taste with Worcestershire sauce, salt, and pepper. Add lemon juice and pour mixture over steak in a shallow pan. Let stand 2 hours.

Broil steak under moderate heat. About 20 to 30 minutes will be required for medium well-done steak, or 10 to 15 minutes on a side.

Break onion slices into rings and dip in milk, then in flour. Drop into a skillet containing hot fat and cook until delicately browned. Serve over steak. Serves 5 to 6.

STEAK MARINATED IN WINE

4   servings round steak ½- to ¾-inch
       thick
Salt and pepper
¼   cup dry red wine
1   small clove garlic, minced
1   small onion, sliced
Flour, shortening

Combine meat and other ingredients except flour and shortening. Refrigerate at least 1 hour.

Remove meat from marinade. Dry. Coat lightly with flour and brown in shortening. Add marinade. Simmer until tender, about 1½ to 2 hours. Serve with drippings from the pan. Serves 4.

DEVILED FLANK STEAK

1½ pounds flank steak
2   tablespoons flour
2   tablespoons butter or margarine
1   teaspoon chopped onion
1   teaspoon salt
½   teaspoon pepper
1   teaspoon mustard
⅛   teaspoon paprika
1   tablespoon vinegar
2   cups water

Cut steak into small pieces and coat with 1 tablespoon flour.

Brown onion in melted butter in skillet. Remove onion and brown steak in butter. Remove meat from skillet.

Add salt, pepper, mustard, paprika, and remaining flour to butter in skillet, blending well.

Add vinegar and water slowly. Bring to boil, stirring to prevent lumping. Add meat and onion.

Cover tightly and simmer gently until meat is tender, about 2 hours. Serve with the pan gravy. Serves 6.

FLANK STEAK PINWHEELS

Roll flank steak as jelly roll and fasten with wooden skewers at approximately 1-inch intervals.

Brown rolls on both sides in 3 tablespoons hot fat. Season with salt and pepper.

Add ¼ cup water. Cover and cook slowly for 1 hour or until tender. Serves 4.

Flank Steak Pinwheels

BACHELORS' STEAK
(Beef with Beer)

1 thick porterhouse steak
Vinegar and olive oil
Salt and pepper
4 tablespoons butter or margarine
1 pound fresh or canned mushrooms
2 tablespoons flour
2 cups beer

Rub steak with oil and vinegar, season on both sides and let stand in refrigerator.

For a 2-inch steak, broil 6 to 12 minutes on each side in preheated broiler (475°F.).

A few minutes before the steak is done, fry sliced mushrooms in butter, season with salt and pepper, add flour, then steak juice from broiler pan and beer. Stir well while cooking, let come to a boil, pour over steak and serve.

SPANISH ARM STEAK

1½ teaspoons salt
⅛ teaspoon pepper
¼ cup flour
Arm steak, cut 1 inch thick
3 tablespoons fat
1 large onion, sliced
1 green pepper, chopped
1 No. 303 can tomatoes

Mix salt, pepper, and flour. Coat steak with seasoned flour and brown in fat. Add onion, green pepper, and tomatoes.

Cover and cook slowly on top of range or in slow oven (300°F.) 1½ hours or until tender.

Thicken cooking liquid for gravy, if desired. Serves 4 to 6.

STEAK À LA DRAKE

1 10-ounce sirloin steak, well trimmed
1½ tablespoons butter or margarine
1 tablespoon brandy
2 tablespoons sherry
1 tablespoon sweet butter creamed with 1 teaspoon chopped chives

Pound meat very thin with mallet or steak hammer.

Heat butter in a skillet. Fry the steak quickly in the butter, turning it once.

Add brandy. Flame. Add sherry and butter creamed with chives.

Place steak on a warm plate and pour gravy over it. Serves 1.

CHUCK STEAK—SPANISH STYLE

1½ to 2 pounds chuck steak
2 tablespoons melted meat drippings
2 tablespoons vinegar
1½ teaspoons salt
¼ teaspoon pepper
1 onion, chopped
1 tablespoon minced parsley
1 tablespoon minced celery leaves
1 small green pepper, chopped
2 cups tomato sauce

Score steak on both sides. Cover with a marinade dressing made of fat, vinegar, onion, and other seasonings. Soak for 1 hour or longer.

Sear meat, using extra meat drippings of bacon fat if needed. Then place in a shallow baking dish or casserole.

Add what is left of the marinade dressing and the tomato sauce. Bake in slow oven (325°F.) until meat is tender, about 2 hours. Serves 4.

GINGER STEAK STRIPS

2 tablespoons prepared mustard
1 tablespoon salt
1 teaspoon ground black pepper
1 teaspoon chili powder
1 teaspoon sugar
1 tablespoon lemon juice
⅓ cup salad oil
1 clove garlic, sliced
1 onion, sliced
2 cups water
1½ cups cider vinegar
2 pounds bottom round of beef
16 to 18 small white onions, peeled
3 green peppers, cut in strips
1 cup gingersnap crumbs, finely rolled, about 15 cookies
½ cup water

Mix first 11 ingredients in a large bowl. Add beef, cut in strips about ½ x 1 x 2 inches. Marinate 5 to 6 hours.

Boil onions and green peppers together 10 minutes.

Remove meat from marinade. Drain. Place meat in shallow pan and broil in preheated broiler, about 5 inches from heat, 15 minutes, turning frequently. During last 10 minutes of cooking, add onions and green peppers.

To two cups of marinade add gingersnap crumbs and water. Heat to boiling, stirring constantly. Pour over meat and vegetables before serving. Serve over shredded wheat wafers, crumbled or whole. Serves 4 to 6.

Ginger Steak Strips: Marinate a less tender cut of beef for marvelous flavor development — use the marinade to make a zippy sauce.

Chuck Steak—Spanish Style

BEEF ROLLS—BORDELAISE SAUCE

3 pounds round steak, sliced thin
3 hard-cooked eggs, chopped fine
1 large onion, thinly sliced
2 teaspoons salt
Dash of pepper
¼ teaspoon nutmeg
½ cup finely chopped parsley
3 anchovies, chopped
2 tablespoons chopped suet or other fat
¼ cup fat

Cut steak into 12 pieces. Combine remaining ingredients except the ¼ cup fat, and mix well.

Spread over the pieces of meat and roll each carefully and tightly. Fasten with skewers or string. Dust with flour.

Brown well on all sides in ¼ cup fat. Add ½ cup water. Cover and simmer gently until tender, about 2 hours.

Thicken drippings to make gravy. Serve over beef rolls. Serves 6.

ROUND STEAK SPECIAL

1 round steak, ½ inch thick
Salt, pepper, flour, fat
1 cup sliced onions
2 8-ounce cans tomato sauce
2 tablespoons soy sauce
1 tablespoon sugar
1 bay leaf
½ teaspoon herbs (thyme, basil, marjoram, or oregano)

Sprinkle steak with salt, pepper, and flour. Pound on both sides with meat pounder or edge of heavy saucer.

In a large, heavy skillet or Dutch oven, brown steak well in a few tablespoons hot fat. Top with sliced onions.

Combine tomato sauce with rest of ingredients and pour over meat.

Cover and cook over low heat until tender, about 1½ hours. Watch carefully to prevent sticking. Add water as tomato sauce cooks away.

Remove steak to platter. Skim fat from sauce and pour over meat. Serves 4.

Round Steak Special

Beef Brisket and Corned Beef

Brisket is the breast of a meat animal, usually cooked by braising. It is also a popular cut for corned beef.

"BOILED" BEEF WITH HORSERADISH SAUCE

4 pounds fresh brisket of beef
Salted water
3 or 4 whole black peppers
1 bay leaf
1 onion
1 stalk celery
1 tablespoon butter or margarine
1 tablespoon flour
1 cup milk
1 tablespoon lemon juice
Salt and pepper
½ cup prepared horseradish

Place brisket in kettle with salted water to cover. Add whole black peppers, bay leaf, onion, and celery. Cover and simmer until meat is tender, about 3 hours.

If desired, cook potatoes in the stock.

To make sauce, blend flour into melted butter over low heat. Add milk gradually, stirring constantly, until smooth and thickened. Season sauce with salt, pepper, lemon juice and horseradish. Serves 8 or more.

BEEF BRISKET WITH SAUERKRAUT

3 pounds beef brisket
3 tablespoons bacon or other fat
½ cup chopped onions
2 pounds sauerkraut
2 cups boiling water

Tie beef brisket into a compact shape.

Melt fat in a deep kettle; add and brown onions lightly.

Add meat and cover with sauerkraut. Add boiling water and simmer until meat is tender, about 2½ hours.

Season to taste with salt and pepper and, if desired, caraway seed and dry white wine.

Slice meat and serve with boiled potatoes covered with sour cream and sprinkled with chopped parsley. Serves 6.

PICKLING BRINE FOR CORNED BEEF

2 quarts water
1 cup salt
3 tablespoons sugar
1 bay leaf
6 whole black peppers
1 clove garlic, minced
2 teaspoons mixed pickling spices

Combine ingredients in a stoneware crock and stir well.

Add 5 or 6 pounds beef (brisket or rump). Cover with a plate and place a heavy weight on it. (A tightly sealed jar filled with water or a washed rock will serve as the weight to keep the meat well under the solution.)

Leave the meat in the brine for 36 hours.

PICKLING BRINE FOR CORNED BEEF (KOSHER STYLE)

2 cups coarse salt
About 4 quarts water
1 teaspoon saltpeter
¼ cup sugar
1 tablespoon mixed whole spices
1 teaspoon paprika
12 to 15 bay leaves
4 to 5 cloves garlic

Dissolve salt in water. Combine with remaining ingredients except garlic and boil for 5 minutes. Cool.

Place beef in a stoneware crock. Add 4 to 5 cloves of sliced garlic and pour over the brine.

Cover with a large heavy plate and weight it down with a tightly sealed jar filled with water or a heavy rock to keep the meat well under the solution.

Cover with two thicknesses of heavy muslin tied securely around crock.

Store the covered crock in a cool place 2 to 3 weeks, turning meat once a week.

The crock cover may be adjusted; however, see that it is propped up so that air circulates between it and the muslin cover.

This amount will pickle up to 10 pounds of beef or tongue. If the brine is not salty enough, more salt may be added during the pickling process.

NEW ENGLAND "BOILED" DINNER

4 pounds corned beef
6 whole small carrots
6 turnips, diced
6 whole small potatoes, peeled
6 whole small onions
1 head cabbage, cut in wedges

Cover beef with cold water. Bring to boiling. Simmer slowly 40 to 50 minutes per pound, about 3½ hours.

Add carrots, turnips, potatoes, and onions 45 minutes before beef is done.

Add cabbage for last 15 minutes. Serves 6 to 8.

Corned Beef Hash: Combine equal parts chopped cooked corned beef and chopped boiled potatoes. Shape into patties and brown in hot fat.

Thrifty Corned Beef Hash: Chop all leftovers from New England Boiled Dinner. Form into patties and brown in hot fat.

HOW TO "BOIL" CORNED BEEF

Cover corned beef with water. Bring to boil. Reduce heat so that water just simmers. Keep kettle tightly covered.

A 2- to 3-pound piece of corned beef will cook tender in 2½ to 3 hours. A whole brisket (10 to 12 pounds) will take about 6 hours.

No seasonings are needed in the cooking water but you may add a few whole black peppers, an onion, and a stalk of celery or a carrot.

To Cook Kosher-Style Corned Beef: Cook as above, but add 1 clove garlic to the water for each pound corned beef. Let cool in the water.

To serve hot, drain and sprinkle heavily with paprika. Heat in moderate oven (350°F.) ½ hour.

CORNED BEEF AND CABBAGE

Cook corned beef as directed above. No seasoning is needed in water. About 20 minutes before meat is tender, remove enough stock to cook cabbage.

Skim off excess fat. Add cabbage cut in small wedges. Boil, uncovered, until cabbage is just tender, 15 to 20 minutes.

Place meat on hot platter. Drain cabbage and arrange around meat. Sprinkle with salt and paprika.

ROAST BRISKET OF BEEF

Beef brisket is a cut that usually should be braised (pot-roasted) or cooked in water; however the method given here for oven roasting in a pan with a tight-fitting cover is successful and has been a favorite dish with Jewish homemakers for many years.

3 pounds lean beef brisket
1 teaspoon salt
½ teaspoon pepper
¼ teaspoon ground ginger
⅛ teaspoon garlic powder
2 tablespoons fat
3 large onions, peeled

Choose a piece of beef brisket with as little fat as possible. Rub the salt, pepper, ginger, and garlic powder into the meat; let stand about 1 hour.

Melt the fat (or use oil) in a roasting pan with a tight fitting cover. Slice onions and mix with the fat in pan. Place meat over onions; cover pan tightly and cook in moderate oven (350°F.) until the meat is very tender, about 3 hours. Timing will vary with the quality of the meat.

To serve, slice the meat across the grain, arrange on a heated platter and garnish with the onions. Serve the pan gravy separately. Sliced brisket is also delicious served cold. Serves 6.

With Potatoes: Small cooked and peeled potatoes may be placed around the meat during the last half hour of cooking.

*Glazed Corned Beef with
Noodles and Peas*

GLAZED CORNED BEEF BRISKET

Remove the hot "boiled" brisket from cooking liquid.

Score fat covering of brisket into diagonal strips, then score into diamond shapes.

Spread lightly with prepared mustard. Sprinkle lightly with sifted brown sugar. Stud each center of diamonds with a whole clove.

Place meat in shallow pan. Bake in hot oven (400°F.) to melt sugar and glaze surface of brisket, about 20 minutes.

CHOLENT

Like the Puritans who baked beans on Saturday so that they would not have to cook on Sunday, Orthodox Jewish homemakers traditionally prepared cholent for the Sabbath because of a similar religious prohibition. There are many versions of the dish, which is basically a mixture of lima or pea beans, potatoes, beef, and onions. It owes its distinctive savor to very slow overnight cooking; in some places the local baker's brick oven was used by the entire community. Some scholars believe that the Yiddish term, cholent, is a corruption of schul ende, referring to the fact that the dish would be ready when the synagogue service was over on Saturday morning; by others it is believed to be derived from the French chaud (hot).

- 2 large onions, diced
- 2 tablespoons chicken fat or other shortening
- ½ pound dried lima beans, soaked overnight in cold water
- 8 to 10 medium potatoes, pared and cut in quarters
- ½ cup medium barley
- 2 pounds brisket of beef, in one piece
- 2 tablespoons flour

Salt, pepper, and paprika to taste

Sauté onions in fat in large Dutch oven or the deep-well cooker of an electric range.

When onions are light brown, add presoaked beans, potatoes, and barley. Sink the beef in center.

Mix flour with seasonings and sprinkle over top. Add boiling water to cover.

Adjust lid and cook on top of range over very low heat (a low simmer) 5 hours. Or cook in deep-well cooker of electric range at warm (150°F.) overnight, or as long as 18 to 24 hours. Serves 6.

Beef Short Ribs

"BOILED" BEEF SHORT RIBS

Use beef short ribs and follow method for New England "Boiled" Dinner. Simmer until short ribs are tender. Add vegetables, and salt and pepper to taste.

BRAISED SHORT RIBS OF BEEF

- 4 pounds short ribs
- Flour
- 2 teaspoons salt
- Dash of pepper
- 2 tablespoons salad oil or melted fat
- 1 cup boiling water
- 1 cup cooked or canned tomatoes
- 1 clove garlic
- 6 medium potatoes
- 12 small onions
- 6 medium carrots

Roll short ribs in flour seasoned with salt and pepper. Brown on all sides in hot oil or fat.

Place in heavy kettle and add water, tomatoes, and garlic. Cover and simmer over low heat 1½ hours.

Add pared vegetables. Cook until vegetables and meat are tender, ½ to 1 hour.

Arrange meat and vegetables on platter. Thicken gravy with 1½ tablespoons flour and 2 tablespoons water for each cup of liquid. Serve over meat. Serves 6.

SHORT RIBS—SAUERBRATEN STYLE

- 3 pounds beef short ribs, cut into serving pieces
- 1 cup water
- 1 cup ketchup
- 1 tablespoon vinegar
- 1 tablespoon Worcestershire sauce
- 1 tablespoon horseradish
- 1 tablespoon sugar
- 1 tablespoon dry mustard
- ¼ teaspoon pepper
- 1 teaspoon salt
- 2 onions, sliced
- 1 bay leaf
- Flour
- 3 tablespoons fat

Place short ribs in a bowl. Mix remaining ingredients together except flour and fat and pour over ribs. Cover. Place in refrigerator overnight.

Remove ribs; drain and roll in flour. Brown floured ribs in hot fat, then add liquid in which ribs were soaked.

Cover and cook slowly until meat is tender, about 1½ hours. Serves 4 to 5.

BARBECUED SHORT RIBS

- 3 pounds beef short ribs
- 1 medium sized onion, chopped
- 2 tablespoons fat
- ½ cup water
- ¼ cup vinegar
- 1 cup ketchup
- ½ cup sliced celery
- 2 tablespoons sugar
- 2 teaspoons salt
- 3 tablespoons Worcestershire sauce
- 1 teaspoon prepared mustard

Cut short ribs into serving pieces. Brown with onions in hot fat. Add remaining ingredients.

Cover and bake in moderate oven (350°F.) until tender, or cook over very low heat 1½ to 2 hours. Serves 4 to 5.

SWEET-SOUR SHORT RIBS

- 2½ to 3 pounds short ribs
- Salt, pepper, flour, and lard
- 1 cup sliced onions
- 1 clove garlic
- 1½ cups hot water
- 1 small bay leaf
- 3 tablespoons brown sugar
- ⅓ cup ketchup
- ¼ cup vinegar

Cut short ribs into individual servings. Trim off excess fat. Sprinkle with salt and pepper and roll in flour.

Brown well on all sides in large skillet in several tablespoons hot lard. Remove to a Dutch oven or other heavy utensil.

Add onions and sliced garlic to fat in skillet and cook until lightly browned; add to short ribs.

Combine remaining ingredients with ½ teaspoon salt and pour over ribs. Cover and cook over low heat until tender, 2½ to 3 hours. Remove ribs to serving dish and keep in warm place.

Pour off most of fat from gravy, stir in 2 tablespoons flour and enough water to dilute to strength desired. Cook until thickened.

Serve short ribs on hot buttered noodles topped with sauce. Serves 4.

Sweet-Sour Short Ribs

Beef Stews

BROWN BEEF STEW WITH POTATO FRILL

1 to 1½ pounds boneless beef chuck, neck, flank, or shank meat or similar cuts from loin or rib of beef, cut in 1½-inch cubes
2 tablespoons flour
2 tablespoons fat or drippings
1 cup chopped onion
2 teaspoons salt
½ teaspoon pepper
1 bay leaf
4 whole cloves
2 cups boiling water
4 carrots, sliced
3 small potatoes, quartered
1 cup peas, frozen or canned

Roll meat in flour and brown slowly and thoroughly in hot fat 15 to 20 minutes. Brown onion at same time.

To browned meat and onion add salt, pepper, bay leaf, cloves, and boiling water.

Turn the heat very low, then cover pan and simmer gently 2 to 3 hours.

Add sliced carrots, potatoes, and peas. Add another cup of water and 1 more teaspoon salt (for vegetables); cover and cook 45 minutes or until vegetables are tender. Serves 4 to 6.

To Thicken Gravy: Remove meat and vegetables to a casserole.

Mix 1 tablespoon flour with 3 tablespoons cold water, and stir into gravy of the stew to thicken it. Pour over meat and vegetables.

Surround with frill of seasoned mashed potatoes. Heat in oven or under broiling unit until potato peaks are browned.

Variations: Stew may omit frill of mashed potatoes and, instead, small puffy biscuits may be used for topping. Different combinations of vegetables, also dumplings, help make stews interesting.

Beef stew becomes a company dish when served from a chafing dish accompanied by crisply fried corn meal fritters (hush puppies).

BEEF STEW WITH WINE OR BOEUF BOURGUIGNONNE

5 medium-sized onions, sliced or 12 whole small white onions
2 tablespoons bacon drippings or 2 ounces salt pork or suet
2 pounds lean beef (round steak)
2 tablespoons flour
Salt, pepper, marjoram, and thyme
1 cup beef bouillon
1 cup dry red wine
½ to 1 pound sliced fresh mushrooms
12 small new potatoes (optional)

Fry onions in bacon drippings in a heavy deep skillet until brown.

Remove onions and set aside. Add beef cut into 1-inch cubes and brown well, adding a little more fat if necessary.

Sprinkle with flour and seasonings, about a pinch each of salt, pepper, marjoram, and thyme. Add bouillon and wine. Stir slightly.

Cover and simmer as slowly as possible, 3½ hours. Or, place in a casserole in extremely slow oven (250°F.).

Add onions, mushrooms, and, if desired, potatoes and cook until vegetables are tender, about 45 minutes longer. Adjust seasoning to taste. Serves 6.

HUNGARIAN BEEF STEW WITH SAUERKRAUT

2 pounds boneless beef chuck cut into 1-inch cubes
¼ cup flour
¼ cup salad oil or shortening
½ cup chopped onion
1 teaspoon salt
¼ teaspoon pepper
1 teaspoon caraway seed
½ teaspoon paprika
2 cups water
1 can (1 pound 13 ounces) sauerkraut
2 teaspoons sugar
1 cup sour cream

Roll meat in flour to coat evenly or shake in paper bag with flour.

Heat oil or shortening in a heavy skillet or Dutch oven over medium heat; put in meat and brown well on all sides.

Add onion, salt, pepper, caraway seed, paprika, and water. Reduce heat, cover and cook slowly until meat is almost tender, about 1¼ hours.

Add sauerkraut and sugar; cook an additional 30 minutes or until meat is tender.

Just before serving, add sour cream; leave over low heat 2 to 3 minutes. Serves 6 to 8.

Beef Stew with Potato Frill

BEEF GOULASH

Goulash is a dish of Hungarian origin, and its name is a corruption of gulyás. It is a thick stew of beef or veal and vegetables seasoned with paprika. Some variations contain sauerkraut, sour cream, or both.

1 pound beef stew meat
1 clove garlic
2 medium onions
2 teaspoons paprika
1 teaspoon salt
⅛ teaspoon pepper
2 bouillon cubes
2 cups boiling water
2 cups diced potatoes

Cut meat into 1-inch cubes and brown in a little hot fat.

Add minced garlic, sliced onions, seasonings, and bouillon cubes dissolved in hot water. Cover and simmer 2½ hours.

Add 1 cup hot water and potatoes cut in ¾-inch cubes. Cook 20 minutes longer, or until potatoes are tender. Season to taste and thicken, if necessary. Serves 4.

FRENCH CANADIAN BRAISED BEEF

2 pounds stewing beef
¼ cup cornstarch
2 teaspoons salt
Dash of pepper
¼ cup fat
1 medium onion, finely chopped
1½ cups water
1 cup carrots, diced
1 cup green beans (cut in 1-inch lengths)
12 new potatoes
1 cup condensed cream of mushroom soup

Cut meat in serving pieces. With meat mallet or edge of a saucer, pound in as much cornstarch as it will take. Sprinkle with salt and pepper.

Heat fat in heavy frying pan or Dutch oven; add chopped onion; cook until golden brown.

Turn in beef; sear on all sides. Cover with water. Simmer gently until almost tender.

Add carrots, beans, and new potatoes; add mushroom soup. Simmer until vegetables are tender. Serves 6.

HOLLAND STEW

¾ pound beef
½ pound fresh pork
½ pound beef liver
2 quarts boiling water
2 small onions, sliced
1 teaspoon salt
¼ teaspoon pepper
¼ cup flour
¼ cup cold water
1 recipe plain dumplings

Cut meat in small pieces; add water, cover, and simmer 2 hours, adding onions and seasonings the last half hour of cooking.

Thicken with flour and cold water mixed to a smooth paste.

Drop dumplings by spoonfuls into hot stew and cook, covered, 15 minutes. Serve at once. Serves 6.

BEEF POT POI
(Pennsylvania-Dutch)

2 pounds stewing beef
6 cups boiling water
2 teaspoons salt
1 teaspoon minced onion
1 teaspoon minced parsley
1 egg
3 tablespoons milk
2 cups sifted enriched flour
8 medium-sized potatoes, cubed

Simmer meat in salted water until tender. Remove meat from broth.

Add onion and parsley to broth and bring broth to boiling point.

To make pot pie dough, beat egg and add milk. Add flour to make a stiff dough. Roll out thin and cut into 2-inch squares.

With broth at boiling point (this is important), add alternate layers of cubed potatoes and squares of dough. Cover and cook 20 minutes, add more water if needed.

Add meat and stir through pot pie. Serves 8.

HODGEPODGE
(Dutch Vegetable Beef Stew)

1½ pounds chuck
1 quart water
1 tablespoon salt
4 carrots, sliced
4 potatoes, quartered
4 onions, chopped

Put meat in large kettle or saucepan with water and salt. Cover and simmer for 2 hours.

Add vegetables, cook another half hour. More water may be added during cooking period, if necessary, but all the water should be cooked away when dish is ready to serve.

Remove meat from pan, put on platter, keep hot.

Mash together all the vegetables in pan with potato masher. Serve with sliced meat. Serves 4.

BEEF STEW WITH WINE AND HERBS

2 pounds stewing beef, cut into 2-inch cubes
1 cup red wine
1 large bay leaf
1 clove garlic, sliced
1 teaspoon salt
½ teaspoon freshly ground black pepper
2 tablespoons drippings or other fat
1½ cups beef stock
1 stalk celery (diced) with leaves
1 onion, sliced
Few sprigs parsley
¼ teaspoon thyme
8 cloves
1 piece ginger root

Place meat in a deep bowl. Add wine, bay leaf, garlic, salt, and pepper; refrigerate several hours, turning frequently.

Drain meat, reserving marinade, and brown meat thoroughly in drippings.

Simmer together for 10 minutes reserved marinade, stock, and remaining ingredients, tied in a cheesecloth bag.

Add meat, cover, and simmer until tender, about 2½ to 3 hours. Add water if necessary.

If desired, when meat is just tender, vegetables such as peas, carrots and onion may be added. Cook until vegetables are tender.

Discard herb bag and remove meat to a hot platter.

Thicken gravy with cornstarch mixed with a little cold water, using ½ tablespoon cornstarch per cup of broth. Boil, stirring, 2 minutes. Serve sauce over meat with vegetables, if used, arranged attractively around it.

Serves 4 to 5.

BEEF STEW WITH DUMPLINGS

1½ pounds stew beef, cut into 2-inch cubes
Salt
Bacon drippings or fat
1 cup water
6 large carrots, diced
6 potatoes, diced
8 small white onions, diced
2 cups sifted enriched flour
4 teaspoons baking powder
1 teaspoon salt
2 tablespoons shortening
1 cup milk

Season cubed meat with salt; brown well in small amount of bacon drippings or fat in deep kettle.

Add water; cover and cook 1 hour on low heat which allows liquid just to bubble.

Add vegetables to meat. If necessary, add more water. Cover and continue cooking until vegetables are tender, about ½ hour longer.

To Make Dumplings: Sift together flour, baking powder, and salt. Cut in shortening as for pastry.

Stir in milk, blending to form soft dough.

Have at least 1 cup of boiling broth in stew kettle before dropping in dumplings.

Dip a tablespoon into broth, scoop up a spoonful of batter and slip it on top of vegetables in kettle. Work quickly; arrange dumplings so that steam circulates around all sides.

Cover kettle tightly and steam 10 minutes. As soon as dumplings are tender, arrange them with vegetables and meat on large platter. Serve immediately.

Thicken liquid in pan if necessary and serve gravy with stew. Serves 6 to 8.

PRESIDENT EISENHOWER'S OLD-FASHIONED BEEF STEW

4 tablespoons fat
2 pounds round of beef, cut into 1½-inch cubes
Bouquet garni (see below)
3 cans beef bouillon
1 pound small Irish potatoes
1 bunch carrots, cubed
8 to 10 small onions
2 tomatoes, chopped
3 tablespoons flour
3 tablespoons water

Heat fat. Add cubed beef and brown. Add bouquet garni and canned beef bouillon. Cover; simmer 1 hour.

Add potatoes, carrots, onions, and tomatoes. Simmer, uncovered, 40 minutes, or until vegetables are tender.

Remove spices. Combine flour and water with 3 tablespoons stew stock; blend, add to stew, stirring well. Simmer until slightly thickened. Serves 6.

Bouquet Garni: Use 2 whole black peppers, 1 bay leaf, 3 cloves, ½ teaspoon thyme, pinch cayenne, and 1 garlic clove, halved. Tie in a small cheesecloth bag.

Stew with Dumplings

Ragoût with Endive

DANISH BEEF STEW

1½ pounds round steak, cut in cubes
Flour
4 tablespoons butter or margarine
1 small onion, sliced
Salt and pepper
½ teaspoon sugar
Juice of 1 lemon
Hot water
4 cups diced raw potatoes

Roll meat in flour and brown in hot melted butter. Add onion and brown lightly. Season to taste with salt and pepper.

Mix sugar and lemon juice and stir in. Simmer gently 3 or 4 minutes.

Add hot water to just cover meat. Cover tightly and simmer until meat is tender.

Turn into heated casserole. Add potatoes, cover and bake in moderate oven (375°F.) 30 minutes. Serves 6.

BAVARIAN STYLE STEW
WITH RED CABBAGE

2 pounds beef rump, chuck, round, or stew meat
2 medium-sized onions
3 tablespoons fat
3 cups hot water
1 bay leaf
3 teaspoons salt
¼ teaspoon black pepper
1½ teaspoons caraway seed
¼ cup vinegar
1 medium-sized red cabbage
½ cup broken gingersnaps

Cut meat into 2-inch cubes. Brown beef and sliced onions in hot fat in heavy saucepan or Dutch oven.

Add water, bay leaf, salt, pepper, and caraway seed. Cover tightly and cook slowly 1½ hours.

Then add vinegar and place cabbage wedges on top. Cover and cook about 45 minutes to 1 hour more, or until tender.

Meanwhile, soak gingersnaps in ¼ cup warm water.

Lift out cabbage and meat. Add gingersnaps to liquid and bring to boil, stirring to make smooth gravy.

Add meat to gravy. Reheat and serve in cheese noodle ring or on bed of plain boiled noodles. Surround with red cabbage wedges. Serves 6.

RAGOÛT WITH ENDIVE

4 large (or 8 small) heads Belgian or French endive
¼ cup cooking oil
¾ cup thinly sliced onions
1 pound lean boneless beef
½ pound lean boneless pork
1 cup beef bouillon
Salt to taste
1 tablespoon paprika
½ teaspoon marjoram
4 ounces wide noodles, cooked
1 teaspoon caraway seeds
1 tablespoon cornstarch
2 tablespoons cold water
½ cup sour cream

If large heads of endive are used cut in half lengthwise beginning at root end.

Heat oil in large heavy skillet over moderate heat. Add onions and cook until transparent. Add meat cut into 1-inch cubes and brown on all sides, stirring frequently. Add beef bouillon and salt, if needed. Simmer, tightly covered, over low heat until meat is very tender, about 1 hour. Add water if necessary to replace liquid lost by evaporation.

When meat is tender be sure the liquid is ½-inch deep in pan. Stir in paprika and marjoram. Then carefully place the endive on the meat, cut side up, cover tightly and simmer gently until tender and transparent, but not overcooked, 10 to 15 minutes.

Place noodles which have been cooked according to package directions on serving platter. Arrange endive on noodles around edge of platter. Sprinkle with caraway seeds, and keep in warm place.

Into liquid in skillet pour cornstarch and water which have been blended together. Cook, stirring gently, until thickened. Stir in sour cream which has been allowed to stand at room temperature and stirred to soften. Heat gently, but do not allow to boil. Spoon meat mixture over platter, being careful not to cover points of endive. Serve immediately. Serves 4.

BEEF STEW WITH WINE

1 pound chuck beef, cut in cubes
¼ cup flour
1½ teaspoons salt
¼ teaspoon pepper
1 cup cold water
½ cup claret or burgundy
4 onions
4 small potatoes
8 small carrots

Roll beef in mixture of flour, salt, and pepper.

Sauté in hot fat until browned on all sides. Add water and wine; simmer very slowly about 1 hour.

Add onions, potatoes, and carrots; cook for 25 to 30 minutes longer. Serves 4.

TOMATO BEEF STEW

2 tablespoons flour
2 teaspoons salt
¼ teaspoon pepper
2 pounds beef, cubed
2 tablespoons shortening
3 cups water
1 can (1¼ cups) condensed tomato soup
6 small onions
6 small carrots
3 potatoes, quartered

Combine flour, salt, and pepper; roll meat in this mixture.

Brown meat in shortening in a heavy saucepan. Add water; cover and simmer 1½ hours, stirring occasionally.

Add soup, onions, carrots, and potatoes; cook until vegetables are tender, about ½ hour. Serves 6.

RAGOUT OF BEEF

1 pound stewing beef, cut in cubes
Salt, pepper, flour
2 to 3 tablespoons fat
1 small onion, chopped
¼ cup chopped green pepper
¾ cup chopped celery
2 tablespoons chopped parsley
Paprika
Hot water

Sprinkle beef with salt, pepper, and flour. Brown well in fat in heavy pan. While meat is browning, add chopped vegetables.

Sprinkle with paprika and add hot water to cover. Cover pan. Cook slowly 2½ to 3 hours.

If gravy is not thick enough, blend 1 to 2 tablespoons flour with a little cold water and stir into the stew. Cook 3 to 5 minutes.

Season to taste with salt and pepper. If additional seasoning is desired, add ketchup, chili sauce, or grated horseradish. Serves 4.

BELGIAN BEEF STEW

2 tablespoons butter or margarine
3 onions, sliced
1 pound beef, cut in cubes
1 bay leaf
1 cup water
Salt and pepper

Melt butter in saucepan and cook sliced onions until brown.

Add meat, bay leaf, and water. Cover and simmer slowly until meat is tender, adding more water as needed.

One-half hour before serving, season with salt and pepper to taste. Serve with boiled potatoes. Serves 4.

Miscellaneous Beef Recipes

BEEF STROGANOFF

1½ pounds lean beef round or fillet
    of beef
Salt and pepper
3   tablespoons butter or margarine
½   pound fresh mushrooms, sliced
2   medium-sized onions, sliced
2   tablespoons flour
2   cups canned beef bouillon
2   tablespoons tomato paste
1   teaspoon dry mustard
3   tablespoons sherry
¾   cup sour cream

Cut meat into strips about 2 inches long and the width of a pencil. Sprinkle with salt and pepper and let stand in cool place for 2 hours.

Melt 2 tablespoons butter in a heavy skillet. Sauté mushrooms until tender, about 15 minutes. Remove mushrooms and set aside.

Sauté onions until browned. Remove and set aside.

Melt remaining tablespoon butter Brown meat on all sides but leave it rare. Remove meat and set aside.

Blend flour into butter remaining in skillet. Gradually add beef bouillon, stirring constantly, until smooth and slightly thickened. Add tomato paste, dry mustard, and sherry and blend thoroughly.

Combine sauce with meat, mushrooms, and onions and cook slowly in top of double boiler or over a very tiny flame for 20 minutes.

Blend in sour cream about 5 minutes before serving and heat thoroughly.

Serve with riced potatoes, potato balls, or boiled rice. Serves 4 to 5.

CREOLE GRILLADES

2   pounds beef or veal round steak
    cut ¾-inch thick
¼ cup butter or margarine
1 tablespoon salt
1 teaspoon Ac'cent
¼ teaspoon pepper
1 tablespoon butter or margarine
1 tablespoon flour
1 medium-sized onion, chopped
½ cup water or tomato juice
1 clove garlic, finely minced
Boiled rice

Cut meat into serving pieces, removing and discarding bone.

Heat ¼ cup butter or margarine in large, heavy skillet over low heat. Add meat and brown well on one side.

Turn and sprinkle with one-half of a mixture of salt, Ac'cent, and pepper. Brown well on second side and sprinkle with remaining seasoning mixture. Remove meat from skillet.

Heat 1 tablespoon butter or margarine in the skillet over low heat. Blend in flour. Heat until mixture bubbles, stirring constantly.

Stir in onion and cook, stirring constantly, until mixture is lightly browned.

Remove from heat and blend in water or tomato juice. Return skillet to heat.

Add meat and garlic. Cover tightly and cook slowly over low heat about 1 hour, or until meat is tender. Turn meat occasionally. Add more liquid if necessary.

While meat is cooking, prepare boiled rice. Serve meat on hot rice, with sauce spooned over meat. Serves 4 to 6.

MEAT BIRDS (PAUPIETTES)
(Master Recipe)

1½ to 2 pounds beef, cut ¼ to ½
    inch thick
1½ to 2 cups bread stuffing
Salt and pepper
Flour
2   tablespoons fat or salad oil
1   cup tomato juice or meat stock

Cut meat into pieces about 3 x 5 inches. Pound to any desired thinness.

Put mound of stuffing in center of each piece; roll and fasten with wooden picks or tie with cord.

Sprinkle with salt and pepper, roll in flour, and brown on all sides in hot fat.

Add about ½ cup liquid. Cover tightly and simmer until tender, about 1 hour. Add liquid in small quantities as required.

Remove picks or cord before serving. Gravy may be thickened. Serves 6.

Variations: Lamb or veal may be substituted for beef.

Meat Bird Casserole: Prepare birds as above. Brush with 2 tablespoons fat and place in greased casserole.

Bake in slow oven (325°F.), basting occasionally with fat and hot water. Remove cover for last 10 minutes to brown birds.

BEEF KABOBS (BEEF ON SKEWERS)

Use tender steak and cut into 1½-inch cubes. Alternate cubes on skewers with wedges of slightly underripe tomatoes, small mushrooms, slices of raw or par-boiled onion, pieces of bacon, etc.

Brush the filled skewers with melted butter. Broil in preheated broiler about 3 inches from heat source with door partly open.

While broiling, brush with more melted butter. Turn to cook evenly on all sides. Season to taste when done.

Note: If desired, kabobs may be breaded before broiling.

Meat Birds or paupiettes may be varied by using any of your favorite stuffings.

OVEN-BAKED CHUCK STEAK

1¾ pounds chuck steak, at least 1-
    inch thick
4   tablespoons olive oil or butter
1   clove garlic, crushed
1   can (6 ounces) tomato paste
Stock or water
Pinch of rosemary
Salt and pepper
8   to 10 small potatoes, peeled

Sprinkle meat lightly with flour.

Brown garlic in hot oil or butter. Remove garlic; add meat and brown on both sides in hot fat. Transfer to casserole.

Combine tomato paste with enough stock or water to make 2 cups liquid; season to taste. Pour into casserole with meat.

Cover and bake in moderate oven (350°F.) until tender, about 1 hour. About 20 minutes before meat is done, add potatoes. Serves 4 to 6.

BEEF WITH TOMATOES AND GREEN PEPPERS (Pepper Steak)

2   tablespoons fat or salad oil
1   pound round or flank steak, cut
    into ⅛-inch thick slices
1   teaspoon salt
Dash of pepper
2   tablespoons minced onion
1   clove garlic, minced
1   cup beef bouillon
2   green peppers, diced
4   small tomatoes, quartered
2   tablespoons cornstarch
2   teaspoons soy sauce
¼   cup water
Boiled rice

Heat fat in heavy skillet. Add meat, salt, pepper, onion, and garlic. Cook over moderately hot heat, stirring constantly, until meat is brown.

Add bouillon and green peppers. Cover closely and cook over low heat 10 minutes. Add tomatoes and cook 1 minute longer.

Blend together cornstarch, soy sauce, and water. Add to skillet and cook 3 or 4 minutes longer, stirring constantly, until mixture is hot and sauce is thickened.

Serve at once with hot boiled rice. Serves 4.

BEEF WITH PEA PODS (Chinese)

¼ cup peanut oil
½ teaspoon salt
½ pound beef tenderloin, sliced about ¼ inch thick and 2 inches square
¼ pound Chinese pea pods (about 1 cup), cut in 2 pieces diagonally
½ cup (4-ounce can) button mushrooms, cut in halves if large
½ cup water chestnuts, peeled and sliced crosswise in thin slices
1 tablespoon cornstarch
¼ teaspoon Chinese molasses
1 teaspoon soy sauce
1 teaspoon salt
½ teaspoon Ac'cent
¼ teaspoon black pepper
¾ cup chicken stock

Heat oil with ½ teaspoon salt in a heavy saucepan; add beef and cook gently until lightly browned but not dry, about 2 minutes on each side.

Add pea pods, mushrooms, and water chestnuts; cook, turning often, over moderate heat for about 5 minutes.

Blend cornstarch and seasonings with chicken stock; add to vegetable-beef mixture. Cover and cook over low heat until mixture is thick and glazy, about 5 minutes, turning a few times. Serve with fried rice. Serves 2 to 3.

Note: For additional color, add about 2 tablespoons pimiento (cut in 1-inch squares) with the other vegetables.

PEPPER CHUCK STEAK

¼ cup melted fat or salad oil
3 pounds beef chuck, in 2 cuts
6 green peppers, seeded
Salt and pepper
3 large onions, sliced thin
2½ cups canned tomatoes
1 cup tomato sauce
½ cup beef stock or water
2 bay leaves
2 sprigs green celery leaves
1 sprig thyme
8 sprigs fresh parsley

Brown beef well on both sides in hot fat. Place 1 steak in baking pan. Cover steak with 3 green peppers, cut in strips. Season with salt and pepper.

Over this, place other steak and cover with remaining green peppers cut in strips and mixed with onions.

Combine tomatoes and sauce and pour over all. Season with salt and pepper. Pour beef stock or water over this. Add a bouquet garni made up of bay leaves, celery leaves, thyme, and parsley tied with thread. Bring to a boil.

Cover and bake in moderate oven (350°F.) 2 to 2½ hours. Baste several times with gravy. Remove bouquet garni. Serve steak on hot platter. Serves 6.

STEAK AND SPANISH SAUCE

1 pound round or shoulder arm steak
1 tablespoon vinegar
1 teaspoon salt
¼ teaspoon pepper
2 tablespoons chopped onion
1 . tablespoon chopped parsley
2 tablespoons chopped celery leaves
3 tablespoons chopped green pepper
2 cups canned tomatoes or 2 cups peeled, diced fresh tomatoes
2 tablespoons fat

Pound steak on both sides. Cover with mixture of remaining ingredients except fat. Let stand 1 hour, turning once or twice so that meat is thoroughly seasoned.

Brown meat slowly on both sides in hot fat. Place in shallow casserole. Pour over mixture in which meat was soaked.

Cover and bake in slow oven (325°F.) until meat is tender, about 2 hours. Serve at once. Serves 4.

BEEF WITH MUSHROOMS— CHINESE STYLE

2 tablespoons oil or fat
1 teaspoon salt
Dash of pepper
1 pound flank or round steak
2 tablespoons finely chopped onion
1 clove garlic, finely chopped
½ cup beef bouillon
1 pound fresh mushrooms, sliced
2 tablespoons cornstarch
2 teaspoons soy sauce
¼ cup water

Place oil or fat, salt, and pepper in a preheated, heavy 10-inch frying pan.

Cut meat into ⅛-inch-thick slices, and add with onion and garlic.

Cook over moderately hot heat, stirring constantly, until meat is brown.

Add bouillon and mushrooms. Cover pan tightly and cook over low heat for 10 minutes.

Blend together cornstarch, soy sauce, and water and add. Cook a few minutes more, stirring constantly, until the juice thickens and the mixture is very hot.

Serve immediately with hot, boiled rice. Serves 4.

PAPRIKA BEEF

2 pounds round steak, cut ½ inch thick
1 teaspoon salt
⅛ teaspoon paprika
1 clove garlic, peeled
2 tablespoons fat
1 cup water
2 tablespoons Worcestershire sauce
¾ cup sour cream
1 teaspoon paprika
2 tablespoons flour

Rub meat with salt and ⅛ teaspoon paprika. Brown garlic in hot fat. Remove garlic. Add meat and brown it well.

Add water and Worcestershire sauce. Cover and cook slowly about 2 hours.

Add sour cream and 1 teaspoon paprika. Cook slowly 15 minutes longer.

Remove steak to hot platter. Thicken broth with flour mixed with ½ cup cold water. Stir and boil 5 minutes. Serve gravy over meat. Serves 6.

QUEBEC BOILED DINNER

1 pound lean beef
¼ pound lean pork
½ pound lamb flank
1 tablespoon mild drippings
6 cups hot water
2 whole cloves
1 large onion
¼ turnip, cut in 4 or 6 pieces
6 carrots
1 small cabbage
1 pound green beans tied in bunches
6 potatoes quartered
Salt and pepper

Cut the meat in pieces or leave whole. Sear in hot drippings in a heavy pan. Or do not sear the meat and add the boiling water.

Stick the cloves in the onion. Add to the meat and cook gently until the meat is almost tender.

Add the vegetables and continue to cook until done. Season to taste with salt and pepper. (One pound salt pork can be added, if desired.) Serves 6.

STEAK NEW ORLEANS

1½ pounds round steak, 1-inch thick
Seasoned flour
3 tablespoons fat
2 medium-sized onions, thinly sliced
1 No. 303 can (2 cups) tomatoes
1 cup tomato juice
1 tablespoon grated Parmesan cheese
1 green pepper, cut into rings
4 medium-sized Louisiana yams, peeled and sliced ¾-inch thick
Salt and pepper to taste

Dredge meat in flour seasoned with salt and pepper.

Melt fat over low heat; add onion slices and cook until golden brown. Remove.

Brown meat well on both sides. Add tomatoes, tomato juice, cheese, and green pepper rings. Top with onion rings.

Cover; cook over low heat until meat is tender (about 1 hour). Add yam slices.

Cover; continue cooking until yams are tender, about 15 minutes. Season to taste with salt and pepper.

Serves 4 to 6.

TZIMMES

A traditional Jewish dish with many variations, usually a combination of meat, carrots, potatoes, and sweet potatoes; sometimes made of a combination of meat, prunes, and potatoes; frequently it is a meatless dish made of carrots, potatoes, and sweet potatoes, with a large dumpling (knaidle) tucked into its center.

The word Tzimmes has gone into the foodlore and folklore of the Jewish people, and has come to mean "making a fuss over someone or something, or some event," in a favorable and friendly sort of way.

The traditional method of making tzimmes of carrots, potatoes, and sweet potatoes is the slow cooking procedure given below.

6   medium-sized carrots
6   medium-sized whole potatoes
3   medium-sized sweet potatoes
2½ to 3 pounds fresh beef brisket
        (short ribs or "soup meat")
1   teaspoon salt
½   cup sugar or honey
Cold water to cover
1   small onion (optional)
2   tablespoons chicken fat or vege-
        table shortening
2   tablespoons flour

Scrape and slice or dice carrots. Pare and cut potatoes and sweet potatoes into 1-inch rounds.

Sear meat in kettle to be used (a heavy aluminum kettle or Dutch Oven is best).

When meat is browned on all sides, add prepared vegetables, salt, and sugar or honey. Cover with cold water (about 1 inch over all). Bring to boil over moderate heat.

Remove cover and skim. Reduce heat and simmer, uncovered, 2½ to 3 hours or until meat is very tender. Do not stir.

To prevent sticking, shake kettle occasionally. Boiling water may be added if required a little at a time.

If onion is used, it should be peeled and cut into thick wedges to permit flow of juice and added after boiling begins. (The onion should not be permitted to cook apart but lifted out before it disintegrates.)

When the liquid has been reduced by half and meat is tender, brown flour in melted fat in skillet.

Stir in about ½ cup of liquid from kettle to make a smooth paste. Add this paste to tzimmes and shake kettle slightly to distribute evenly.

Turn into casserole and bake in moderate oven (350° F.) 30 minutes or until brown on top. Serves 6 to 8.

Pressure Cooker Method: Sear meat in cooker first, then let cool.

Add prepared vegetables, salt, sugar, and onion (if used). Add 1 to 1½ cups cold water.

Cook according to directions for cooker (at 15 pounds pressure for 20 minutes).

Cool cooker quickly as directed by manufacturer before turning contents into casserole for baking as above.

Thickening may be added just before placing in oven or under broiler heat until lightly browned.

OVEN BEEF STEW #2

1   pound beef stew meat
Salt, pepper, flour
3   tablespoons lard
2   medium onions, chopped
1¾ cups water
1   can condensed tomato soup
1   small bay leaf
2   whole cloves
1   stalk celery, sliced
4   carrots, sliced
3   medium potatoes
1   cup canned peas (8-ounce can)

Cut meat into 1-inch cubes; sprinkle with salt and pepper and dredge with flour. Melt lard in skillet and in it brown meat thoroughly. Transfer meat to a 2-quart casserole.

Lightly brown chopped onion in the hot lard; add to meat. Heat water with tomato soup and pour over meat. Add seasonings and sliced celery.

Cover and bake in a slow oven (325° F.) for 1½ hours, or until meat is nearly tender.

Add sliced carrots, potatoes cut in eighths, and peas; sprinkle with salt and pepper and mix in with beef and gravy. Cover and continue baking for 45 minutes. Serves 4.

SHORT RIBS OF BEEF EN CASSEROLE

2   pounds short ribs of beef
1   teaspoon dry mustard
1   teaspoon salt
¼   teaspoon pepper
½   teaspoon Ac'cent
2   tablespoons vinegar
1   large onion, sliced
2   cups water
2   beef bouillon cubes
6   potatoes, pared and quartered

Have ribs cut into serving-size pieces. Trim off excess fat. Brush meat with mixture of mustard, salt, pepper, Ac'cent, and vinegar. Place meat in 3-quart casserole.

Add onion, water, and bouillon cubes.

Cover and bake in moderate oven (350°F.) 1¾ hours.

Place potatoes around meat and bake until potatoes and meat are tender, about 35 minutes longer. Uncover to brown. Serves 4.

SWISS STEAK WITH HERBS

¼   cup flour
2   teaspoons salt
1   teaspoon pepper
1   clove garlic, mashed
1   teaspoon dill seed
¼   teaspoon dried marjoram
¼   teaspoon dried tarragon
2   pounds beef round steak, cut 1-inch
        thick
½   cup fat
½   cup sliced onion
2   cups hot water
½   cup white wine (optional)

Combine flour, salt, pepper, garlic, dill, marjoram, and tarragon. Spread half over steak; pound with a meat hammer or edge of a heavy saucer until seasoned flour is worked into the meat.

Turn; spread remaining flour mixture over steak, and pound into meat.

Brown steak on both sides in hot fat. Sprinkle any remaining flour mixture over meat. Add onion; pour in water.

Cover and simmer or bake in moderate oven (350° F.) until tender, 1½ to 2 hours. Add more water if necessary to keep the meat moist.

Before serving, pour wine over meat and heat through, about 2 minutes. Serves 6.

Variation: Omit dill. Add ¼ cup ketchup, 1 teaspoon oregano, and 1 tablespoon paprika to the water.

GERMAN BEEF ROLLS

4   very thin slices of top round steak
Salt and pepper
4   strips bacon
1   large onion, chopped
2   tablespoons chopped sweet pickle
½   cup water
1   8-ounce can tomato sauce
1   teaspoon meat glaze

Flatten slices of steak and season with salt and pepper.

Broil bacon and save fat. Brown onion in fat.

Crumble crisp bacon and mix it with browned, drained onions and pickle. Place spoonful of mixture in center of each slice of beef. Roll beef and tie ends.

Brown rolls in bacon fat. Add tomato sauce and meat glaze. Simmer gently until tender. Season to taste.

Serve hot. Serves 4.

BEEF SHORT RIB CROWN

Sew ends of two sections of short ribs together or tie with cord to form crown. Season with salt and pepper. Place in roasting pan. Fill center with bread stuffing.

Roast, uncovered, in moderate oven 1 hour.

Add 1½ cups hot water. Cover tightly and cook 2 hours longer. Serves 6 to 8.

POLISH ROUND STEAK ROASTED IN SOUR CREAM

3½ pounds round steak
Flour
2   tablespoons bacon fat
1½ cups sour cream
Water
1   large onion, sliced
1   small bay leaf
¾   teaspoon salt
⅛   teaspoon black pepper
1   sweet pepper, minced

Pound flour into meat, as much as it will take, using meat mallet.

Melt bacon fat in heavy deep pan. Add meat; brown all over.

Then add sour cream, enough water to come up to level of meat, onion, bay leaf, salt, black pepper, and sweet pepper.

Set pan in another containing hot water. Let cook, covered, until tender.

Remove steak to hot platter. Pour over gravy; serve hot. Serves 6.

STUFFED FLANK STEAK #2

2- to 3-pound flank steak
1   teaspoon meat tenderizer
6   large mushrooms, thinly sliced
1   small onion, thinly sliced
1   tablespoon butter or margarine
½   teaspoon rosemary
½   teaspoon salt
Dash of pepper
½   cup red wine

Have the meat man cut a sizable pocket in meat. Treat it with meat tenderizer according to directions on label of container.

Cook mushrooms and onion in melted butter or margarine for several minutes. Season with rosemary, salt (if you use seasoned tenderizer, omit salt), pepper, and wine.

Cook a few more minutes or until onions are tender.

Drain vegetables (save liquid to use later on) and stuff into pocket of flank.

Sprinkle meat with additional salt and broil 8 to 10 minutes on each side. Baste occasionally with liquid from vegetables. Carve in thin bias slices. Serves 6.

DUTCH BRISKET OF BEEF WITH SAUERKRAUT

2   tablespoons flour
1   tablespoon brown sugar
1   tart apple, grated
1   small onion, minced
1   quart sauerkraut
2½ to 3 pounds beef brisket
Salt and pepper

Add flour, sugar, apple, and onion to kraut and place half of kraut in heavy pot with snug-fitting lid.

Season meat with salt and pepper and lay on kraut. Top with remaining sauerkraut. Cover with water.

Cover tightly and simmer very slowly 3 hours. Serves 8.

BEEF SCALOPPINE

¼   cup flour
1   teaspoon salt
⅛   teaspoon pepper
1   teaspoon paprika
2   pounds beef, cut for scaloppine*
4   tablespoons salad oil or shortening
1   clove garlic
1   bay leaf
1   cup claret wine
1   cup ripe olives, cut in quarters
1   beef bouillon cube

Combine flour, salt, pepper, and paprika on a piece of waxed paper; dip pieces of beef into it to coat lightly

In heavy skillet, heat oil or shortening; add beef, cook over medium heat until browned on both sides.

Add garlic (stick it on a toothpick so it will be easy to remove), bay leaf, wine, olives, and bouillon cube.

Cover, bring to a boil; reduce heat and simmer for 30 minutes, stirring occasionally.

Remove garlic and bay leaf before serving. Serves 6 to 8.

*Note: Buy round steak sliced about ¼ inch thick; cut in strips about 2 x 5 inches; flatten by pounding with meat mallet or rolling pin.

BEEF STROGANOFF #2

1½ pounds beef tenderloin, cut in shoestring strips
Salt and pepper
1   tablespoon flour
2   tablespoons butter or margarine
2   cups stock (canned beef bouillon may be used)
1   tablespoon tomato paste
½   pound mushrooms, cut not too fine
1   tablespoon chopped onion
2   tablespoons sour cream

Season meat well with salt and pepper; let stand 2 hours.

Brown flour in melted butter; work to a smooth paste, then gradually stir in stock. Bring to a boil.

Stir in tomato paste. Add mushrooms.

Sear meat in butter with chopped onion. When the meat is brown, add meat and onions to sauce and simmer 5 minutes.

Add sour cream, heat through and serve at once. Serves 6.

BEEF WELLINGTON
(Whole Tenderloin of Beef Baked in Pastry)

Pastry:

4   cups enriched flour
1   teaspoon salt
½   cup butter
½   cup shortening
1   egg, lightly beaten
About ½ cup ice water

Combine flour, salt, butter, and shortening in a large bowl; blend with pastry blender or tips of fingers until a sandy mass has been obtained. Add egg and just enough water to make a dough. Form into a ball; wrap in waxed paper and chill thoroughly.

Filling:

1   whole beef tenderloin (filet), about 3 pounds
2   tablespoons brandy
Salt and pepper
6   slices bacon
5 to 8 ounces canned pâté de foie gras or pâté of chicken livers (see Index)
3 or 4 truffles, optional
1   egg for brushing pastry

Have outside membrane and excess fat removed from meat. Rub beef all over with brandy and season with salt and freshly-ground pepper.

Place bacon over top and fasten with string if necessary. Place on rack in roasting pan; roast, uncovered, in preheated very hot oven (450°F.) 15 minutes for rare, 20 to 25 minutes for medium.

Remove from oven and remove bacon; cool to room temperature before continuing. Spread pâté all over top and sides of cooled meat.

Roll out the well chilled pastry into a rectangular shape about 18 x 12 inches and ¼ inch thick, large enough to envelop the meat.

Cut truffles into halves and arrange in a row in center of pastry so that the pieces will be covered by the meat. Place meat in center with that side down which you want eventually to be up.

Fold pastry over meat, trimming ends if necessary, and seal seams and ends with water or beaten egg.

Place seam side down, on buttered cooky sheet and brush top and sides with one egg well beaten and mixed with a little water or cream. Prick pastry thoroughly with fork in crisscross design, to allow escape of steam.

If desired, decorative shapes may be cut from pastry trimmings and the pieces arranged down the center of the pastry. Brush the shapes with remaining egg mixture.

Bake in preheated hot oven (425°F.) 30 minutes, until pastry is cooked.

Serve hot with Madeira Sauce (see Index). Serves 4 to 8.

Note: Puff pastry may be used but be sure to roll it very thin.

Recipes with Leftover Beef

RED FLANNEL HASH

A New England dish of corned-beef hash with chopped beets in it.

1 cup chopped leftover corned beef
2 cups chopped cooked potatoes
½ raw onion, minced
1 cup cooked leftover vegetables, chopped (carrots or other)
1 cup chopped cooked beets
Salt and pepper
Stock from corned beef

Combine ingredients with enough stock to moisten.

Spread in hot, greased skillet, cover, reduce heat, and cook until well browned on bottom. Then fold over like an omelet and serve. Serves 6.

ROAST BEEF HASH

3 cups cooked beef
3 medium carrots
3 medium potatoes, pared
1 cup celery
2 small onions
1 cup milk
1 cup tomato soup
¾ teaspoon salt
½ teaspoon pepper
Buttered breadcrumbs

Grind meat and vegetables with coarse blade of meat chopper. Add remaining ingredients except breadcrumbs.

Place in well greased casserole; cover top with buttered crumbs. Bake in moderate oven (350°F.) 1 hour. Serves 6.

MEAT CROQUETTES – FRIED

2 cups ground cooked meat (beef, veal, lamb, pork, or ham)
1 cup thick white sauce
2 teaspoons grated onion
1½ teaspoons Worcestershire sauce
½ teaspoon dry mustard
1 egg
Fine dry breadcrumbs

Combine sauce with rest of ingredients, except egg and crumbs. Add salt and pepper to suit taste. Chill several hours or overnight.

Divide chilled mixture into 8 portions and shape into cylinders, cones, or balls. Chill again ½ hour.

Dip in beaten egg mixed with 1 tablespoon water, then roll in breadcrumbs.

Fry croquettes, a few at a time, in deep fat, which has been heated to a temperature of 365°F. Turn occasionally to brown evenly; fry 2 to 5 minutes, or until golden brown. Makes 8.

Note: To make thick white sauce, use 4 tablespoons each of fat and flour, 1 cup milk, and ½ teaspoon salt.

BEEF MIROTON

2 onions, finely chopped
3 tablespoons fat
1 tablespoon flour
1½ to 2 cups stock
1 tablespoon vinegar
¾ pound cooked beef
Salt and pepper to taste
Pinch of thyme
1½ cups sliced, cooked potatoes
2 gherkins, sliced
1 teaspoon minced parsley
⅓ cup breadcrumbs

Cook onions in hot fat until golden brown. Stir in flour and add liquid slowly. When well combined, add vinegar. Boil 8 to 10 minutes.

Pour some of the sauce in bottom of greased casserole. Add slices of beef. Season with salt, pepper, and thyme.

Put potatoes in border around beef. Pour in remaining sauce. Arrange sliced gherkins and minced parsley over top. Sprinkle with crumbs. Dot with fat.

Brown in moderate oven (375°F.) 20 to 25 minutes. Serves 6.

OVEN MEAT CROQUETTES

2 cups ground cooked beef, veal, lamb, or pork
1 cup grated raw carrots
1 cup soft breadcrumbs
¼ cup grated onion
1 beaten egg
1 teaspoon salt
⅛ teaspoon pepper
Bacon drippings, butter, or margarine
Dry breadcrumbs

Combine ground meat, carrots, breadcrumbs, onion, egg, and seasonings. Mix well.

Divide mixture into 6 parts and shape into croquettes.

Roll in melted bacon drippings, butter, or margarine; then in dry breadcrumbs.

Place on cooky sheet and bake in moderate oven (350°F.) 40 minutes. Serve with mustard or mushroom sauce. Serves 4 to 6.

JELLIED MEAT LOAF

1 tablespoon (1 envelope) unflavored gelatin
¼ cup cold water
¾ cup boiling water
¼ cup vinegar
½ teaspoon salt
¼ cup diced celery
1 chopped pimiento
½ chopped green pepper
2 tablespoons finely minced onion
½ cup mayonnaise or boiled dressing
2 cups finely diced cooked meat
2 hard-cooked eggs, sliced

Soak gelatin in cold water, then dissolve in boiling water. Add vinegar and salt. Cool.

When mixture begins to thicken, mix in all other ingredients except eggs.

Rinse mold in cold water and arrange egg slices on bottom and sides. Pour in meat mixture.

Chill until very firm. Serve on a bed of shredded lettuce. Serves 6.

LEFTOVER BEEFSTEAK WITH ONIONS

Slice onions thin. Place in skillet with a little fat and season with salt and pepper. Cover and brown slightly and put onions to one side.

Place leftover steak in skillet; smother with onions, cover tightly, and cook over low heat until steak is heated through. When ready to serve, spread onions on top.

MEAT CAKES

Combine 1 cup ground cooked meat with 1 slice of bread (crumbled), 1 tablespoon milk, and ½ teaspoon prepared mustard.

Beat 1 egg slightly. Combine half of egg with meat mixture and form into 2 ½-inch patties.

Dip patties into remaining egg mixed with a tablespoon of water or milk. Roll patties in flour, brown on both sides in a little fat in a skillet.

Serve with ketchup, chili sauce, or mustard. Makes 2 large cakes.

Oven Meat Croquettes

Meat Pie with Biscuit Topping

MEAT PIE WITH BISCUIT TOPPING

2   tablespoons shortening, fat, or salad oil
2   cup cooked meat, cut in ¾-inch cubes
2   tablespoons enriched flour
½   teaspoon salt
2   cups thin leftover gravy
½   teaspoon dried rosemary
1   cup cooked carrots, cut in 1-inch strips
1   cup cooked peas
8   very small cooked onions
1   cup sifted enriched flour
1½ teaspoons baking powder
½   teaspoon salt
2   tablespoons shortening
¼   cup grated sharp processed cheese
1   tablespoon finely chopped pimiento
6   tablespoons milk

Heat fat in large skillet on high heat. Switch to medium heat; add meat and brown slightly. Add 2 tablespoons flour and ½ teaspoon salt and blend.

Add gravy and rosemary to skillet, and stir constantly until mixture begins to thicken.

Switch to low heat. Add carrots, peas, and onions to first mixture. Cover and heat thoroughly while making biscuit topping.

Sift flour, baking powder, and ½ teaspoon salt together into a small mixing bowl. Cut in shortening with pastry blender or 2 knives until mixture resembles fine meal.

Add cheese and pimiento and mix. Add milk to flour mixture and mix with a fork to make a soft dough.

Turn onto a lightly floured pastry cloth or board and knead dough about 20 strokes. Roll dough into rectangle 9 x 7 inches and ¼ inch thick. Using a 2-inch round biscuit cutter, cut 12 biscuits.

Pour hot meat mixture into a 10 x 6 x 2-inch baking dish, and arrange biscuits on top. Bake in very hot oven (450°F.) for 10 to 15 minutes. Serves 4 to 6.

HOTEL CLARIDGE CORNED BEEF HASH

1   cup chopped onion
2   green peppers, chopped fine
2   celery stalks, chopped fine
1   clove garlic, minced
3   tablespoons butter or margarine
2   pounds cooked corned beef coarsely ground
5   medium potatoes, cooked and diced
1   tablespoon minced parsley
1   tablespoon Worcestershire sauce
½   cup beef stock

Sauté onion, peppers, celery, and garlic in butter until onions are golden. Add beef, potatoes, and parsley; sprinkle with Worcestershire.

Heat mixture over medium heat, adding beef stock a little at a time. Stir constantly as mixture cooks until well blended.

Transfer hash to buttered skillet and brown on both sides, turning once.

May be served with poached eggs. Serves 6.

BUBBLE AND SQUEAK (ENGLAND)

1 to 1½ pounds cabbage, finely chopped
1   onion, sliced
4   tablespoons butter or margarine
½   teaspoon salt
Pepper
4   servings thinly sliced cooked beef (roast, pot roast, or boiled)

Boil cabbage in salted water until barely tender. Drain.

Sauté it and the onion in 3 tablespoons of the fat until onion is tender. Season with salt and pepper to taste.

In another frying pan, sauté beef gently in the remaining fat until very hot. Place on platter and top with cabbage. Serves 4.

BEEF PARMIGIANA

4   servings sliced cooked beef (about 1 pound)
1   beaten egg
2   tablespoons milk
1   teaspoon salt
¼   teaspoon pepper
1   teaspoon dry mustard
½   cup fine breadcrumbs
½   cup grated Parmesan cheese
½   cup shortening
1   8-ounce can tomato sauce

Combine egg, milk, salt, pepper, and mustard. Melt shortening in heavy skillet.

Dip pieces of beef into egg mixture, then into breadcrumbs and last into cheese.

Pan-fry in hot shortening until browned on both sides. Serve with hot tomato sauce. Serves 4.

BRUNSWICK STEW

2   cups cold roast meat, beef or lamb cut into 2-inch cubes
3½ cups water
1½ teaspoons salt
¼   teaspoon pepper
2   teaspoons Worcestershire sauce
1   cup diced green string beans
1   cup diced wax beans
8   small new potatoes
8   small white onions, peeled
1   cup green peas
1½ cups young carrots, peeled and sliced

Place meat, water, salt, pepper, and Worcestershire sauce in 3-quart casserole.

Cover and bake in moderate oven (350°F.) about 1 hour.

Remove cover. Add vegetables and bake about 45 minutes longer, or until vegetables are tender and gravy is somewhat thickened. Serves 8.

YORKSHIRE BEEF PUFF

Using leftover roast or pot roast, cut 2 cups of meat into small thin pieces and arrange over the bottom of a 9 x 9-inch glass baking dish that contains about ⅛-inch meat drippings.

Beat 2 minutes 1 cup each flour and milk, 2 eggs, and ¼ teaspoon salt. Pour over meat in pan.

Bake in very hot oven (450°F.) about 30 minutes. Serve with leftover gravy or mushroom sauce. Serves 4.

CREOLE BEEF WITH RICE OR MACARONI

1   cup ground or chopped cooked beef
2   tablespoons fat
1   tablespoon chopped onion
¼   cup chopped celery
1   tablespoon flour
1   cup cooked tomatoes
¼   teaspoon chili powder
½   teaspoon salt
1   teaspoon Worcestershire sauce
½   cup water
2   cups cooked rice, spaghetti, or macaroni

Stir and brown meat in fat in heavy skillet. Add onion and celery and brown lightly.

Sprinkle flour over meat and vegetables, then add tomatoes, seasonings, and water. Stir and simmer about 10 minutes to blend flavors. Taste and season more if necessary.

Serve over hot cooked rice, spaghetti, or macaroni. Serves 2 to 3.

Note: If leftover rice is used, pour it into kettle of boiling water and boil 5 minutes. Then drain in a strainer and shake to dry rice.

Hamburger and Other Ground Meats

HOW TO BUY GROUND BEEF

Ground beef (hamburger) varies in quality of beef and the proportion of fat and lean meat. The ready-ground beef sold by a reliable meat dealer is good fresh beef and is supposed to be sold in two styles: (1) regular ground beef with not more than 25 per cent fat and (2) lean ground beef with not more than 12 per cent fat. Both types are ground twice.

When beef is ground to order as round steak, shoulder (chuck), flank, etc., check the leanness of the meat and if it is very lean have 2 ounces suet ground with each pound of meat. This is particularly necessary with ground round steak.

Have the meat ground twice for most uses. Twice-ground meat is more compact. For extra juicy, tender patties have the meat ground only once. Freshly ground beef is bright red in color.

HANDLING GROUND BEEF

The less handling ground beef gets, the more juicy and tender it will be. When mixing meat loaves, toss together lightly.

Pat patties loosely into shape. When you cook, don't pack them down with the spatula.

HOW TO STORE GROUND BEEF

Wrap the mound of beef loosely in waxed paper with ends slightly open. Or, if desired, shape at once into patties and place between squares of waxed paper and cover. Store at once in refrigerator. Use within two days.

Frozen ground beef should be kept frozen until ready to use, or thawed in refrigerator just before cooking. Frozen ground beef should be used within 2 to 3 months.

Meat Balls

TO SHAPE MEAT BALLS

For easier handling rinse hands with cold water before shaping meat balls.

SWEDISH MEAT BALLS —FAMILY STYLE

3 tablespoons chopped onion
2 tablespoons fat
½ pound finely ground beef
¼ pound finely ground veal
¼ pound finely ground pork
3 slices fresh white bread, crusts removed
½ cup milk or water
1 egg
1 teaspoon salt
⅛ teaspoon freshly ground black pepper

Brown the onion in 1 tablespoon fat. Mix together the browned onion, meats, bread, milk, egg, salt, and pepper. Mix with the hands until thoroughly blended. Form into 12 balls.

Brown the meat balls in the same pan, using the remaining fat. Shake pan to keep balls round. When cooked, remove balls to a hot platter and keep hot.

For gravy, add to 2 tablespoons of fat in the pan 2 tablespoons of flour. Brown the flour, stirring, over low heat. Add a cup of milk, stirring, and cook, stirring, until mixture boils. Season to taste and, if desired, add ¼ cup sour cream. Serves 4.

Note: For appetizers, to be served on picks with cocktails, make the meat balls marble size, cook as indicated above, but omit gravy. The same size balls may be served in clear or vegetable soup.

TOMATO MEAT BALLS
("Porcupines")

1 pound ground beef
1 egg
1 medium onion, minced
2 tablespoons minced parsley
1 teaspoon salt
¼ teaspoon basil, if desired
⅛ teaspoon pepper
Dash of cayenne
¼ cup raw rice
2½ cups canned tomato juice
1 cup thinly sliced celery
½ teaspoon chili powder
¼ teaspoon salt
¼ cup water

Place ground beef, egg, onion, parsley, salt, basil, pepper, and cayenne in medium-size bowl; toss together lightly with two-tined fork.

Shape into 12 small balls; pat rice on balls.

Combine tomato juice, celery, chili powder, salt, and water in large frying pan; bring to boiling; add meat balls. Simmer, covered, 35 to 40 minutes, or until rice is cooked. Serves 4.

KOENIGSBERGER KLOPS
(German Meat Balls)

½ pound ground beef
¼ pound ground veal
¼ pound ground pork
1 tablespoon minced onion
¼ cup breadcrumbs
1 teaspoon salt
1 egg, slightly beaten
Flour
1 can (10½-ounces) beef bouillon
1 cup water
½ lemon, sliced

Combine meat, onion, crumbs, salt, and egg. Shape into 1-inch balls. Roll balls in flour.

Heat bouillon and 1 cup water in saucepan. Add floured balls. Simmer 15 to 20 minutes.

Mix 2 tablespoons flour with ¼ cup cold water. Add to beef bouillon and cook, stirring constantly, until thickened. Serve with lemon slices. Serves 4.

MEAT BALLS STROGANOFF

1 pound ground beef
¾ pound ground pork
1 cup cracker crumbs
2 teaspoons salt
Dash of pepper
Dash of thyme
Dash of oregano
½ cup milk
2 eggs
2 tablespoons fat
2 cups sour cream
1 6-ounce can sliced broiled mushrooms, drained

Combine meats, crumbs, seasonings, milk, and eggs. Mix well and form into 1½-inch balls. Brown in hot fat.

Drain off excess fat. Add 1½ cups sour cream. Cover and simmer 1 hour.

Remove meat balls to warm serving dish. Stir ½ cup sour cream into mixture in skillet. Add mushrooms. Heat to boiling point. Pour over meat balls. Serves 6 to 8.

GROUND BEEF KABOBS

⅔ cup (small can) undiluted evaporated milk
1½ pounds ground beef
½ cup fine cracker meal
1 egg
½ cup chopped onion
1 teaspoon garlic salt
½ teaspoon salt
1 tablespoon prepared mustard
Small tomatoes
Thick onion slices

Combine evaporated milk, beef, cracker meal, egg, onion, garlic salt, salt, and mustard in large mixing bowl. Mix thoroughly. Shape meat mixture into 12 balls.

Alternate meat balls with small tomatoes and thick onion slices on 6 skewers. Place on broiling pan. Broil 5 to 7 inches from heat about 5 minutes on each side, or to taste. Serves 6.

Ground Beef Kabobs

*Meat Balls with Celery
Sauce and Noodles*

MEAT BALLS WITH CELERY SAUCE AND NOODLES

½ pound ground beef
½ pound ground pork
1 cup fine dry breadcrumbs
1 tablespoon minced onion
¼ teaspoon nutmeg
1 teaspoon salt
¼ teaspoon pepper
1 cup evaporated milk
1 slightly beaten egg
2 tablespoons shortening
1 can condensed cream of celery soup
1⅔ cups (1 tall can) evaporated milk
¼ cup finely chopped parsley
8 ounces broad noodles

Mix meat with crumbs, onion, nutmeg, salt, and pepper. Stir in the 1 cup milk and egg, and blend well.

Shape mixture into balls, using about 1 tablespoon of the mixture for each.

Melt shortening in large fry pan. Add meat balls and cook over low heat, cooking and turning until balls are browned on all sides. Remove meat balls and discard any drippings in pan.

Empty contents of can of celery soup into pan. Gradually stir in the 1⅔ cups milk, keeping mixture smooth. Add parsley and meat balls.

Cover and let simmer gently, stirring occasionally, until heated through, about 15 minutes.

While meat balls are simmering in sauce, drop noodles into 3 quarts boiling water to which 1 tablespoon salt has been added. Cook until tender.

Drain well, then toss in bowl with about 1 tablespoon butter. Shape into border on heated chop plate. Fill center with meat balls and sauce.

Serves 4 to 6.

BARBECUED MEAT BALLS AND BAKED BEANS

1 pound ground beef
1 teaspoon salt
¼ teaspoon pepper
⅓ cup fine, dry breadcrumbs
¼ cup ketchup
2 tablespoons brown sugar
2 tablespoons vinegar
2 teaspoons Worcestershire sauce
1 teaspoon prepared mustard
2 16-ounce cans beans with pork

Mix beef, salt, pepper, breadcrumbs,

and ¾ cup water. Form in small balls about 1½ inches in diameter; brown over medium heat. Pour off fat.

Add remaining ingredients, except beans; simmer 5 minutes. Add beans; put in 1½-quart casserole.

Bake in moderate oven (350°F.) 25 minutes, or until hot and bubbly. Serves 4.

MEAT BALLS WITH RICH WINE SAUCE

1 pound chuck or round ground beef
1 large apple, peeled and shredded
1 slightly beaten egg
1¼ teaspoons salt
⅛ teaspoon pepper
¼ cup flour
2 tablespoons shortening or salad oil
¼ cup chopped onion
¾ cup burgundy
¼ cup water
2 8-ounce cans tomato sauce
½ teaspoon basil
¼ teaspoon rosemary
¼ teaspoon sugar

Combine ground beef, apple, egg, salt, and pepper; shape into balls about 1 inch in diameter; roll in flour.

Heat shortening or salad oil in large skillet; add meat balls and onion; cook over medium heat about 10 minutes, until lightly browned on all sides.

Combine wine, water, tomato sauce, basil, rosemary, and sugar. Pour over meat balls; cover and simmer 15 minutes. Serve over hot cooked spaghetti. Serves 4 to 6.

MEXICAN MEAT BALLS

1 pound ground beef
¼ cup white corn meal
1 egg
1 clove garlic, minced
1 small onion, minced
1¼ teaspoons coriander seed, pounded (optional)
1¼ teaspoons salt
½ teaspoon pepper
Chili tomato sauce (below)

Mix beef, corn meal, egg, garlic, onion, and seasonings. Shape in tiny balls about ½ inch in diameter.

Drop into boiling chili tomato sauce; cover, and simmer 5 minutes. Serves 4.

Chili Tomato Sauce:

1 tablespoon fat
1 small onion, chopped
1 clove garlic, minced
2 to 3 tablespoons chili powder
3 cups tomato juice
Salt

Melt fat in large saucepan. Add onion and garlic, and cook slowly until

lightly browned. Add chili powder, tomato juice, and salt to taste; cook 10 minutes.

ZESTY HAMBURGER BALLS ON NOODLES

1 pound hamburger
1 teaspoon salt
6 ounces noodles, cooked
¼ cup chili sauce
1 cup tomato juice
1 teaspoon Worcestershire sauce
1 teaspoon prepared mustard

Combine meat and salt. Form into 6 balls. Spread noodles in a lightly buttered baking dish. Top with meat balls.

Combine chili sauce, tomato juice, Worcestershire sauce, and mustard. Pour over noodles. Bake in moderate oven (350°F.) 25 minutes. Serves 6.

SWEET AND SOUR MEAT BALLS

1 pound ground round steak
1 egg, slightly beaten
2 tablespoons flour
Salt and pepper
½ cup peanut oil
1 cup chicken bouillon or broth
2 large green peppers, cut in small pieces
4 slices canned pineapple, cut in small pieces
3 tablespoons cornstarch
1 tablespoon soy sauce
½ teaspoon Ac'cent
½ cup vinegar
½ cup pineapple juice
½ cup sugar

Form meat into 16 small balls.

Combine egg, flour, salt and pepper to taste to form a smooth batter.

Heat oil in heavy skillet. Dip meat balls in batter. Fry in hot oil until brown on all sides. Remove meat balls and keep warm.

Pour all but 1 tablespoon fat from skillet. Add ½ cup bouillon or broth, green pepper, and pineapple. Cover and cook over medium heat 10 minutes.

Blend remaining ingredients and add to skillet. Cook, stirring constantly, until mixture comes to boil and is thickened.

Return meat balls to sauce and heat through. Serve with hot, fluffy boiled rice. Serves 4.

Sweet and Sour Meat Balls

SWEDISH MEAT BALLS —PARTY STYLE

1   pound ground beef
1/2 pound lean pork
1   pound veal
4   slices bread
3/4 cup milk
1   onion, finely chopped
2   teaspoons salt
1/8 teaspoon nutmeg
1/8 teaspoon allspice
1   clove garlic, mashed fine
1/4 teaspoon pepper
2   lightly beaten eggs
Shortening for frying
2   cups beef bouillon

Have the beef, pork, and veal ground together 2 or 3 times.

Crumble bread and add milk. Stir to blend until it is of paste-like consistency. Combine with meat in a mixing bowl. Add seasonings and eggs. Beat and stir with wooden spoon until the mixture is stiff.

Dip out rounded teaspoonfuls and roll between hands into 1-inch balls. Place on waxed paper about half an hour to dry a bit.

Heat enough shortening in heavy skillet to make it 1/2 inch deep. Brown meat balls in this hot fat.

Put meat balls in a single layer in a large shallow baking pan. Add hot bouillon.

Bake in moderate oven (350°F.) about 30 minutes, or until the broth is absorbed. Serve the balls without gravy or sauce. Makes 80 1-inch meat balls.

Variation: Remove browned balls from skillet. Pour off all but 3 tablespoons of shortening. Stir in 4 tablespoons flour. Add enough water to make desired consistency of gravy. Boil 3 minutes. Put in top of double boiler. Add meat balls. Keep warm until served.

MEAT BALLS WITH BURGUNDY

3/4 pound ground beef
3/4 cup fine dry breadcrumbs
1/4 cup minced onion
3/4 teaspoon cornstarch
1/8 teaspoon allspice
1   egg, slightly beaten
3/4 cup milk
1/2 teaspoon pepper
3/4 teaspoon salt
1/4 cup fat
3   tablespoons flour
2   cups water
1   cup Burgundy wine
2   bouillon cubes
1/4 teaspoon salt

Combine beef, breadcrumbs, onion, cornstarch, allspice, egg, milk, salt, and pepper.

Shape into about 30 small balls and brown balls in melted fat. Remove balls from pan and add flour and blend.

Stir in water, Burgundy, bouillon cubes, and 1/4 teaspoon salt. Cook, stirring constantly, until smooth.

Place balls in sauce; cover, and simmer 30 minutes. Transfer to chafing dish and keep hot on buffet table. Serve with rice or noodles. Serves 6.

SWEET AND PUNGENT MEAT BALLS

3   large green peppers
1   pound ground beef
1   beaten egg
2   tablespoons flour
1 1/2 teaspoons salt
Few grains pepper
1/4 cup salad oil
1   cup chicken bouillon
4   slices canned pineapple, diced
12 maraschino cherries
3   tablespoons cornstarch
2   teaspoons soy sauce
1/2 cup vinegar
1/2 cup light corn syrup

Cut green peppers in sixths. Form seasoned beef into 16 small balls.

Combine egg, flour, 1/2 teaspoon salt, and pepper; dip meat balls in this batter.

Heat salad oil; add remaining salt. Fry meat balls in hot oil, turning to brown on all sides.

Remove meat balls; drain off all but 1 tablespoon of oil. Add 1/3 cup bouillon, diced pineapple, cherries, and green peppers; simmer 10 minutes.

Blend cornstarch, soy sauce, vinegar, corn syrup, and remaining bouillon. Add to pineapple mixture. Cook slowly, stirring until thickened. Pour over meat. Serve with fluffy boiled rice. Serves 4.

CHINESE MEAT BALLS

3   tablespoons fat
1   teaspoon salt
1/2 pound ground beef
1/4 cup diced onion
1   cup diced celery
1   cup sliced carrots
2   cups cooked lima beans
1   cup beef broth
2   tablespoons cornstarch
1   tablespoon soy sauce
1/4 cup water

Melt fat. Add salt to meat and shape into small balls. Cook in fat with onion until tender.

Add celery, carrots, lima beans, and broth. Cover and cook 15 minutes.

Blend cornstarch, soy sauce, and water. Add to hot mixture and cook, stirring until thick. Serve with fluffy rice. Serves 6.

MEAT BALLS IN SOUR CREAM SAUCE

1   slightly beaten egg
1   cup milk
1   teaspoon salt
1/4 teaspoon pepper
1   cup fine dry breadcrumbs
1   teaspoon grated onion
1 1/2 pounds ground lean beef
2   tablespoons bacon drippings
1   medium onion, chopped
2   tablespoons flour
2   8-ounce cans tomato sauce
1   cup sour cream
1   cup coarsely chopped ripe olives

Prepare the meat balls ahead of time. Beat egg with milk, salt, pepper, crumbs, and grated onion. Allow to stand for a few minutes.

Add ground beef; mix lightly with a fork and shape into 2-inch balls.

Cover with waxed paper or foil; keep in refrigerator until ready to use.

Heat drippings in chafing dish over direct heat. Sauté meat balls until uniformly browned. This may have to be done in two or three batches, depending on the size of your pan.

Remove from pan. Sauté onion in pan juices for 5 minutes.

Blend in flour; then add tomato sauce and meat balls.

Place over hot water. Cover and simmer 30 minutes.

Add sour cream and mix gently with a wooden spoon until meat balls are coated with cream. Scatter olives over all. Heat through and serve.

Serves 8 to 10.

LILLIPUT MEAT BALLS

1   pound ground beef
1/2 cup grated soft breadcrumbs
1/4 cup milk
1   tablespoon finely chopped onion
2   tablespoons butter or margarine
1/2 cup sherry
1/2 cup ketchup
1/4 teaspoon oregano (optional)

Mix beef, breadcrumbs, milk, onion, and 1 teaspoon salt. Shape mixture into little balls, using 1 teaspoon per ball.

Melt butter in a large, heavy skillet; brown balls nicely on all sides. Pour off most of fat from pan.

Mix wine, ketchup, and oregano; pour over balls; add salt to taste. Cover and simmer gently about 20 minutes, shaking pan gently from time to time to cook balls evenly.

Serve in a chafing dish or in a pottery casserole set over a candle warmer, and provide toothpicks for spearing the balls. Makes about 60 tiny balls.

Hamburger Sandwiches and Patties

HINTS ABOUT PREPARING HAMBURGERS

1. It is not necessary to use round steak for hamburgers, as the less expensive ground chuck is just as satisfactory. In fact, many people prefer chuck to round because it contains more fat and makes a juicier hamburger. High quality, ready-ground hamburger also may be used.

2. Use 1 teaspoon salt and 1/8 teaspoon pepper for each pound of ground beef.

3. For extra-juicy hamburgers, add 1/4 cup water or evaporated milk per pound of meat.

4. Add some finely chopped onion, if desired, also one or several of the following seasonings: Worcestershire sauce, mustard, ketchup, thyme, poultry seasoning, caraway seed, horseradish. Or add 1/4 cup finely chopped nuts or parsley to each pound of meat.

5. A good variation in preparing hamburgers is to put two thin hamburger patties together with well seasoned bread dressing. Pinch edges together before cooking.

6. Frying is the easiest method for cooking hamburgers. However, they may be broiled if the patties are not too thin.

7. A good seasoning tip when broiling hamburgers: After patties have been turned, spread with ketchup or chili sauce or with butter that has been blended with crumbled blue or American cheese. Continue broiling until done.

BROILED DEVILED HAMBURGERS #1

1 pound ground beef
4 tablespoons ketchup
1½ teaspoons Worcestershire sauce
1 teaspoon salt
Dash of pepper
6 hamburger buns, split

Combine all ingredients except buns. Toast uncut surfaces of buns under broiler and spread with meat mixture.

Broil about 6 minutes, with meat surface about 3 inches from the unit. Serves 3.

Frankburgers with Bacon

STANDARD AMERICAN HAMBURGER

1 pound ground beef
1 teaspoon salt
2 tablespoons chopped onion, optional
1 teaspoon fat

Combine hamburger, salt, and onion thoroughly.

Shape into 4 thick or 8 thin patties. Pan-brown in fat in skillet. Do not press the patties. Do not overcook. Turn to brown other side.

Serve hot as dinner meat or sandwich filling. Serves 4.

With Sauce: When patties are done, remove from pan.

Add to pan 2 tablespoons flour, 1 tablespoon Worcestershire sauce or ketchup. Stir and pour over hamburgers.

BROILED DE LUXE HAMBURGERS

Shape Standard American Hamburgers into 2 thick patties. Place on a pie pan.

Broil 3 inches from heat source 5 to 10 minutes, turning once.

To serve, spread with a mixture of one of the following:

1. Two tablespoons butter mixed with 2 tablespoons Worcestershire sauce.

2. Two tablespoons butter mixed with 1 tablespoon prepared mustard.

3. Two tablespoons butter mixed with 2 tablespoons ketchup, 1 teaspoon prepared mustard or chili powder.

4. Two tablespoons butter mixed with 2 tablespoons chopped chives.

5. Two tablespoons butter mixed with 2 tablespoons blue cheese.

BROILED DELUXE CHEESEBURGERS

Prepare Broiled Deluxe Hamburgers. Before removing from broiler, top each with a slice of cheese. Broil until cheese melts, about 2 minutes.

FRANKBURGERS WITH BACON

2 cups corn flakes
½ cup milk
1 teaspoon salt
1/8 teaspoon pepper
2 tablespoons finely chopped onions
1 pound lean ground beef
8 slices bacon
8 frankfurter rolls

Crush corn flakes slightly; combine with milk. Let stand a few minutes until soft. Add salt, pepper, onions, and ground beef; mix well. Shape meat mixture into 8 frankfurter shaped portions. Wrap each spirally with a bacon slice, fastening with toothpick.

Broil until meat is brown and bacon is crisp, about 6 minutes per side. Serve in warm frankfurter rolls. Makes 8.

Big Boy Cheeseburgers

BIG BOY CHEESEBURGERS

2 cups corn flakes or ½ cup corn flake crumbs
1 pound lean ground beef
1 teaspoon salt
1/4 teaspoon pepper
1 tablespoon Worcestershire sauce
1/4 cup ketchup or chili sauce
1/4 cup finely chopped onions
1/3 cup evaporated milk
2 9- or 11-inch loaves brown 'n serve French bread
3/4 cup grated natural sharp Cheddar cheese

If using corn flakes, crush into fine crumbs. Combine beef, salt, pepper, Worcestershire sauce, ketchup, onions, corn flake crumbs, and evaporated milk in 2-quart bowl; mix lightly but thoroughly.

Cut unbaked loaves in half lengthwise. On cut side of each half-loaf bread spread one-fourth of meat mixture, covering to edges. Place on baking sheets crust side down.

Bake in hot oven (400°F.) about 25 minutes or until beef is done. Top with grated cheese or cheese strips during last 5 minutes of baking. Remove from oven; serve immediately. Makes 4 servings, ½ loaf each or 8 servings, 1/4 loaf each.

BARBECUED HAMBURGERS

1 pound hamburger
1/4 cup finely chopped onion
1 teaspoon salt
1/4 teaspoon pepper
1 tablespoon fat
1 cup ketchup
1 onion, sliced
1/4 cup vinegar
1 tablespoon sugar
½ teaspoon dry mustard

Mix together hamburger, onion, salt, and pepper. Shape into 4 large patties.

Pan-fry in hot fat to brown on both sides. Combine remaining ingredients. Pour over hamburgers. Cover and simmer 20 minutes more. Serve with hot, fluffy rice. Serves 4.

Note: Store leftover barbecue sauce in refrigerator. Use for barbecued franks or for combining with cooked rice or macaroni for a quick casserole.

SALISBURY STEAKS
(Master Recipe)

Salisbury steak is another name for hamburger (ground raw meat); however as used on menus it usually means a fancy form, often with cream added, and sometimes coated with fresh bread-crumbs. It is formed in a fairly thick patty, broiled or pan-fried, and served with a sauce. Popular versions are given below.

Patty:

1 pound hamburger
1/4 teaspoon pepper
1 teaspoon salt
2 tablespoons fat

Combine hamburger, pepper, and salt. Shape into patties about 2 inches in diameter.

Pan-fry in hot fat in a heavy skillet. Serves 4.

Bacon Salisbury Steaks: Chop 4 slices cooked bacon and add to above recipe. Form into 6 patties.

Pan-fry in hot fat in a heavy skillet.

Salisbury Steaks with Curry Sauce:

1 recipe master Salisbury steaks
1/4 cup sliced mushrooms (optional)
2 tablespoons flour
1 cup water
1 beef bouillon cube
1/2 teaspoon curry powder

Remove patties to a warm plate. Pan-fry mushrooms. Add flour to drippings in pan. Stir. Add water, bouillon cube, and curry powder.

Cook until mixture boils, cube is dissolved, and sauce is thickened. Pour over patties.

Salisbury Steaks with Sour Cream Sauce:

1 recipe master Salisbury steaks
2 tablespoons flour
1/2 cup water
1/2 cup sour cream
1 teaspoon horseradish
1/4 teaspoon thyme

Remove patties to a warm plate. Stir in flour to drippings in pan. Add remaining ingredients. Bring to boiling point. Pour over patties.

Open-Face Cheeseburgers

CHEESE HAMBURGER

1 pound hamburger
1 cup shredded Cheddar type cheese (1/4 pound)
1 teaspoon salt
1/8 teaspoon pepper
1/4 cup water
1 tablespoon fat

Thoroughly combine hamburger, cheese, salt, pepper, and water. Form into 5 large, flat patties.

Slowly brown patties on each side in hot fat in a heavy skillet. Cook slowly until meat is cooked as desired. Serves 5.

WINE HAMBURGERS

3/4 cup claret, burgundy, cabernet or or any red wine
1 cup whole bran or 1 1/2 cups dry breadcrumbs
1 medium onion, minced
1 beaten egg
1 pound ground beef
1 1/2 teaspoons salt
1/4 teaspoon pepper

Pour wine over bran or breadcrumbs. Add minced onion. When bread is soft, add beaten egg, ground beef, salt and pepper. Mix well. Form into 8 patties.

Brown in hot fat in skillet. Serve on buns, if desired. Serves 4 to 6.

OPEN-FACE CHEESEBURGERS

Place on cooky sheet the lower halves of large round buns which have been spread liberally with butter, mixed with prepared mustard if desired.

Toast under broiler until golden brown. Keep hot in oven until needed.

In the meantime, quickly cook seasoned hamburger patties on griddle or under broiler.

Arrange on each bun half a crisp lettuce leaf, onion rings or thin slices, thinly sliced tomato, a spoonful of hot baked beans—any one or all as fancy and taste dictate.

Top each with a hot hamburger patty.

Place on each:

(1) A slice of American Cheddar cheese, or—

(2) A mixture of blue cheese, 1/2 cup, mixed with 1/4 cup butter, 2 teaspoons Worcestershire sauce, or—

(3) 1/2 cup sharp Cheddar cheese spread mixed with 2 teaspoons Worcestershire sauce.

Place low under broiler until the cheese is bubbly, browned, and melted. Serve at once.

Have the hot butter-toasted bun tops handy to clap on the sandwich, if you like, but this creation is more easily eaten with a fork than as a portable meal!

Barbecued Hamburger Stacks

BARBECUED HAMBURGER STACKS

2 cups (1 pound) ground beef
1/2 teaspoon salt
1/8 teaspoon pepper
5 bread stuffing patties (see below)

Combine ground beef, salt, and pepper. Shape into 10 meat balls.

Place 3 inches apart on sheet of waxed paper. Cover with another sheet of waxed paper.

Flatten meat balls into patties about 3 inches in diameter.

Bread Stuffing Patties:

4 cups soft 1/2-inch bread cubes
1/4 cup hot milk
1 beaten egg
1/4 cup melted fat or meat drippings
1/4 teaspoon salt
1/8 teaspoon pepper
2 tablespoons chopped onion

Combine soft bread cubes, hot milk, beaten egg, fat, salt, pepper, and onion.

Shape into 5 bread patties about 3 inches in diameter.

Barbecue Sauce:

1/4 cup shortening or meat drippings
2 tablespoons chopped onion
1/4 cup finely chopped celery
1/4 cup vinegar
1/4 cup tomato purée or tomato paste
1 tablespoon Worcestershire sauce
1/2 teaspoon garlic salt
2 tablespoons sugar
1/2 cup water
1/4 teaspoon pepper
1/2 teaspoon salt

Melt shortening in skillet. Add onion and celery and sauté until tender.

Add vinegar, tomato purée, Worcestershire sauce, garlic salt, sugar, water, pepper, and salt. Simmer 10 minutes.

To Make Hamburger Stacks: Place 5 meat patties in shallow baking dish or pan. Top each with bread patty.

Finish by placing a meat patty on top of each bread patty. Pour barbecue sauce over hamburger stacks.

Bake in moderate oven (375°F.) 30 minutes, occasionally basting stacks with barbecue sauce. Serves 5.

*Hamburger Tuck-Ins
Cheese-Cross Burgers*

SPECIAL HAMBURGER DINNER PATTIES

2 pounds ground beef or round steak
2 teaspoons salt
2 tablespoons chopped onion
1/2 cup chopped mushrooms (optional)
1 tablespoon fat
2 tablespoons butter or margarine
1 tablespoon lemon juice

Spread beef on pan; sprinkle with salt. (Add 1/4 teaspoon pepper, if desired.) Brown onion and mushrooms lightly in fat and add to beef.

Use hand to combine ingredients thoroughly. Shape into 4 giant patties 1 1/2 inches thick.

Place patties on pan or aluminum foil and broil about 3 inches below source of heat, about 10 minutes on each side or until crispy brown on both sides and rare inside.

Mix together butter and lemon juice (may add 1 tablespoon chopped parsley). Spread over hamburgers. Serves 4.

Variations: (1) Spread top of broiled beef patties with crumbled blue cheese or blue cheese spread.
(2) Brush top of beef patties with French dressing or thin barbecue sauce before and after broiling each side.
(3) Add chopped green onions to butter topping for patties.
(4) Make 8 1-inch patties of the beef mixture. Melt a tablespoon of fat in heavy frying pan and pan broil. Turn 2 or 3 times to cook and brown evenly, about 15 minutes.

HAMBURGER MUSHROOM STEAK ON TOAST

1/4 pound mushrooms, sliced
Butter or margarine
1 pound ground beef
1 teaspoon onion juice
1 teaspoon salt
1/4 teaspoon pepper
4 slices bread, toasted on one side

Cook mushrooms in 1 tablespoon butter until lightly browned. Mix with beef, onion juice, and seasonings.

Butter untoasted side of bread; spread with meat mixture, and dot with butter. Put under broiler until browned. Serves 4.

HAMBURGER TUCK-INS

1 pound ground beef
1 teaspoon salt
1/8 teaspoon pepper
2 teaspoons Worcestershire sauce
4 tablespoons finely chopped onion

Mix ground beef with salt and pepper. Shape into 8 thin patties.

Combine Worcestershire sauce and onion. On each of 4 patties, place 1 tablespoon chopped onion.

Top with a second patty and pinch edges together well.

Pan-fry or broil about 15 minutes, turning once. Serves 4.

CHEESE-CROSS 'BURGERS

Combine 1 pound ground beef with 1/4 cup water, 1 teaspoon salt, and 1/8 teaspoon pepper.

Shape into 4 or 5 patties and pan-fry or broil until well browned. The last few minutes of the cooking time, top each patty with 2 strips of processed cheese, arranged criss-cross.

Continue cooking until cheese begins to melt. Garnish each with a slice of stuffed olive. Serves 4 or 5.

HAMBURGER PARMIGIANA

1 pound ground beef
3/4 teaspoon salt
1 beaten egg
2 tablespoons milk
1 teaspoon dry mustard
1/4 teaspoon pepper
1/3 cup fine dry breadcrumbs
1/4 cup grated Parmesan cheese
2 tablespoons butter or margarine
1 8-ounce can tomato sauce

Mix beef and salt; shape in 8 rectangular patties about 1/2 inch thick.

Mix egg, milk, and seasonings. Dip patties in mixture, then in crumbs, then in cheese.

Fry in butter over medium heat until browned on both sides. Serve with heated tomato sauce. Serves 4.

SCOTCH-POCKET HAMBURGERS

1 pound ground beef
1 teaspoon salt
1/8 teaspoon pepper
2 teaspoons Worcestershire sauce
4 tablespoons finely chopped onion
4 thin slices tomato (medium size)

Mix ground beef with salt and pepper. Flatten beef into a large square. Divide into 8 equal parts and make a thin patty of each.

Mix together the Worcestershire sauce and onion. On half the patties place a slice of tomato and a tablespoon of chopped onions. Top with a second patty and pinch edges together.

Place in a shallow pan and broil about 15 minutes, turning once. Serves 4.

BEEF À LA LINDSTROM
(Swedish Meat Cakes)

3 small potatoes, cooked
2 medium beets, cooked
2 small onions
1/2 cup water
1/2 teaspoon salt
1 pound finely ground round steak
4 egg yolks
1/3 cup light cream
1 tablespoon minced capers
1 teaspoon salt
1/4 teaspoon white pepper
4 tablespoons butter or margarine
1 cup consommé

Chop cooked potatoes and beets into tiny cubes.

Mince onions; add water and 1/2 teaspoon salt. Cook, uncovered, until water has evaporated, about 3 minutes.

Pound meat with potato masher. Mix egg yolks and cream and add gradually to meat, mashing thoroughly. Add potatoes, beets, onions, capers, and seasonings.

Shape into flat cakes 1/2 inch thick. Fry quickly in butter, 1 1/2 minutes on each side. Remove to warm platter.

Add consommé to pan. Bring to boil and pour over meat. Makes 12 cakes.

SLOPPY JOES

1 pound ground beef
1 cup finely chopped onion
1 cup finely chopped green pepper
1 tablespoon sugar
2 tablespoons prepared mustard
1 tablespoon vinegar
1 teaspoon salt
1 cup ketchup
1/2 teaspoon ground olives
4 to 6 hamburger buns

Brown meat slowly until crumbly but not hard. Combine remaining ingredients and add to meat.

Cover and simmer about 30 minutes. Serve on split buns. Serves 4 to 6.

TEXASBURGERS

1 pound ground beef
1 small onion, chopped
1 teaspoon salt
1/4 teaspoon pepper
2 tablespoons fine, dry breadcrumbs
1/3 cup milk
6 sandwich rolls, split and toasted
2 large tomatoes, sliced
1 1/2 cups coleslaw
Pickle relish

Mix beef, onion, salt, pepper, breadcrumbs, and milk; form in 6 patties. Broil until browned on both sides.

Put patties on bottom halves of rolls. Top with slice tomato, spoonful coleslaw, and a little pickle relish.

Cover with top halves of rolls. Serve at once. Serves 6.

HAMBURGER SANDWICH BAKE

2 tablespoons butter or margarine
8 slices bread
½ pound ground beef
A little chopped onion
1 stalk celery, chopped
1 teaspoon prepared mustard
1 cup shredded process American cheese
3 eggs, beaten
2 cups milk
¾ teaspoon salt
⅛ teaspoon pepper

Butter 4 slices bread, and put, butter side up, in baking pan; brown lightly in moderate oven (350°F.).

Meanwhile, brown beef with onion and celery, stirring with fork. Add mustard.

Spread meat mixture on toasted bread; sprinkle cheese on top; cover with remaining bread slices.

Combine eggs, milk, salt, and pepper; pour over sandwiches. Bake in moderate oven (350°F.) about 45 minutes. Serves 4.

HAWAIIAN HAMBURGERS

1 pound ground beef
1 medium onion, minced
1 clove garlic, minced
½ cup soy sauce
¼ teaspoon ground ginger

Mix beef and onion. Shape in 8 patties. Put in shallow dish.

Combine remaining ingredients, and pour over patties. Let stand 30 minutes, turning once.

Drain, and broil or pan-fry. Serve with spiced pineapple. Serves 4.

HAMBURGER SHORTCAKES

1 pound hamburger
2 teaspoons prepared mustard
1 teaspoon salt
¼ teaspoon savory
2 cups biscuit mix
About ½ cup milk
Ketchup or tomato sauce

Combine hamburger, mustard, salt, and savory. Shape into 6 patties.

Combine biscuit mix and milk. Turn out onto sheet of waxed paper. Knead 6 times. Roll out ¼ inch thick on a lightly floured pastry cloth or board. Cut 12 circles the size of the patties (a No. 2 can is about right).

Place 2 biscuit circles together shortcake fashion. Place patties and biscuits on a baking sheet or jelly roll pan.

Bake in a hot oven (400°F.) for 15 minutes. Serve patties between biscuit shortcakes with ketchup or tomato sauce. Serves 6.

WIENERBURGERS ON ROLLS

2 pounds ground beef
1 tablespoon chopped onion
2 tablespoons cream
1 teaspoon Worcestershire sauce
1 teaspoon salt
¼ teaspoon pepper
3 dill pickles
12 frankfurter rolls, split and toasted

Mix beef, onion, cream, Worcestershire, salt, and pepper.

Cut dill pickles in quarters, lengthwise.

Shape meat mixture around pieces of pickle to form wiener shape.

Bake in hot oven (425°F.) about 15 minutes. Serve on frankfurter rolls. Makes 12.

"ORIENTAL" HAMBURGER SANDWICH

1 tablespoon finely chopped fresh ginger root (or 2 teaspoons powdered ginger)
2 cloves garlic, chopped fine
½ cup chopped onion
2 tablespoons sugar
½ cup soy sauce
¼ cup water
1 pound hamburger

Make sauce from ginger root, garlic, onion, sugar, soy sauce, and water. Pour over meat. Let stand 1 to 2 hours in refrigerator.

Spread mixture on 6 hamburger buns. Broil about 3 inches from heat source, 3 to 5 minutes. Serves 6.

HAMBURGER WESTERN SANDWICHES

¼ pound ground beef
1 small onion, chopped
½ medium green pepper, chopped
Salt and pepper
4 eggs, slightly beaten
Butter or margarine
8 slices bread or toast

Cook beef, onion, and green pepper, stirring with fork, until meat loses its red color. Sprinkle with salt and pepper.

Pour eggs over mixture. Reduce heat to medium, and cook until eggs are set; do not stir.

Cut in quarters; turn, and brown on other side. Serve hot between buttered bread or toast. Serves 4.

CREOLE HAMBURGER ON ROLLS

1 pound ground beef
2 medium onions, chopped
1 medium green pepper, chopped
1 teaspoon salt
¼ teaspoon pepper
1 8-ounce can tomato sauce
½ cup corn flakes
6 frankfurter or sandwich rolls, split and toasted

Cook beef, stirring with fork, until it loses its red color. Add onions, green pepper, salt, and pepper.

Blend ½ cup water with tomato sauce. Add sauce and corn flakes to first mixture; bring to boil, and simmer 15 minutes. Serve on rolls. Serves 6.

BROILED DEVILED HAMBURGERS #2

1 pound ground beef
4 tablespoons ketchup
1½ teaspoons prepared mustard
2 teaspoons horseradish
2 teaspoons minced onion
1½ teaspoons Worcestershire sauce
1 teaspoon salt
Dash of pepper

Combine all ingredients. Split 6 hamburger buns and toast uncut surfaces under the broiler. Spread cut sides with the meat mixture.

Return to the broiler and broil about 6 minutes, having meat surface about 3 inches from the unit. (Buns may be used untoasted, but toasting makes buns crisper.) Serves 4.

HURRY-UP BURGERS

1 pound hamburger
1 cup diced celery
1 teaspoon salt
1 tablespoon fat
1 tablespoon Worcestershire sauce
4 hamburger buns, split and buttered

Brown and cook hamburger, celery, and salt in fat in a heavy skillet.

Add Worcestershire sauce. Heap meat mixture on halves of large round buns. Serves 6.

Cheese Hurry-Ups: Follow the above recipe. After heaping each bun with meat mixture, top with a slice of cheese food. Broil until cheese melts. Serve hot.

HERB HAMBURGERS

1 pound ground beef
¼ cup chopped onions
1 tablespoon fat
¼ teaspoon celery flakes
¼ teaspoon garlic salt
1 teaspoon dried parsley
⅛ teaspoon marjoram
⅛ teaspoon thyme
½ teaspoon salt

Thoroughly combine all ingredients. Shape into patties ¾ inch thick.

Broil or pan-broil about 5 minutes on each side.

Spread each while piping hot with a little butter or margarine. Serves 4.

With Lemon Butter: Combine 1 tablespoon lemon juice with ¼ cup softened butter or margarine; spread on the broiled hamburgers.

With Cheese: Sprinkle shredded aged cheese over the hot hamburgers.

OLIVE CHEESEBURGERS

1½ cups breadcrumbs
3 tablespoons olive brine
3 tablespoons water
¾ teaspoon Ac'cent
⅛ teaspoon pepper
1½ pounds ground lean beef
Prepared mustard
12 large stuffed olives
8 slices (½-pound package) process Swiss cheese

Combine crumbs, olive brine, water, Ac'cent, and pepper; mix well; add to ground beef.

Form into 8 large patties; broil on 1 side about 7 minutes, with meat about 3 inches below source of heat.

Turn; spread with mustard; cover with sliced olives; top each with slice of cheese.

Broil 5 minutes longer, or until cheese melts and is delicately browned. Serves 8.

TOASTED DEVILED HAMBURGERS

1 pound ground beef
2 tablespoons chili sauce
1½ teaspoons prepared mustard
1½ teaspoons prepared horseradish
1 teaspoon minced onion
1½ teaspoons Worcestershire sauce
1 teaspoon salt
¼ teaspoon pepper
8 buns or bread slices

Combine ingredients and spread on buns. Broil for about 8 minutes at moderate heat and serve immediately. Serves 8.

TABASCO HAMBURGERS

3 pounds round steak, ground
1 cup chopped onion
¾ cup chopped green pepper
½ cup special hot barbecue sauce (see sauces)

Combine ingredients; shape into 12 patties.

Broil 5 to 8 minutes. Baste and serve with additional special hot barbecue sauce. Makes 12 servings.

BOHEMIAN BEEF PATTIES

1 pound hamburger
3 tablespoons finely chopped onion
3 tablespoons chopped dill pickle
½ cup chopped pickled beets
1 cup cooked diced potatoes
¼ cup milk
½ teaspoon salt
2 tablespoons fat

Mix all ingredients except fat. Shape into 8 patties 1 inch thick.

Pan-fry in hot fat in heavy skillet about 15 minutes or until well done and browned on both sides. Makes 8 patties.

PEPPERBURGERS

1½ pounds ground beef
1 teaspoon salt
¼ teaspoon pepper
4 green peppers, halved
8 sandwich rolls

Mix ground beef with salt and pepper. Shape into 8 patties. Broil or cook in hot, greased skillet to degree of doneness desired.

Fry or boil green peppers until tender. Place on top of patties. Serve between split, heated rolls. Makes 8.

BLUE CHEESE BURGERS

2 pounds hamburger
3 tomatoes
Onion salt
Salt and pepper
⅓ cup blue cheese
2 tablespoons chopped green pepper

Shape hamburger into 6 oblong steaks 1 inch thick. Broil to about half desired doneness. Turn, and make a shallow, lengthwise slit down centers.

Sprinkle tomato halves with onion salt, and broil with meat until meat is almost of desired doneness. Sprinkle with salt and pepper.

Press a spoonful of cheese into slit in each hamburger. Top tomatoes with green pepper. Return to broiler until cheese is melted. Serves 6.

MINT MEAT PATTIES

1 pound hamburger
¼ cup chopped fresh mint
1 teaspoon salt
Pinch of pepper and nutmeg
2 slices white bread, crusts removed
½ cup sour cream
¼ cup bacon fat

Combine meat, mint, salt, pepper, and nutmeg. Soften bread in sour cream 10 minutes. Blend with meat mixture. Shape into small patties and brown in bacon fat. Makes about 12 patties.

POTATO 'BURGERS

½ pound ground beef chuck
1 cup grated raw potatoes
2 tablespoons minced onion
⅛ teaspoon pepper
1 teaspoon salt
3 tablespoons fat or salad oil
½ teaspoon dry mustard
1 tablespoon chopped parsley

Mix together beef, potato, onion, pepper, and salt. Shape into 8 patties.

In hot fat in skillet, sauté until crisp, and brown; then remove from skillet; keep warm.

Add mustard and parsley to drippings in skillet; heat; pour over patties. Serves 4.

HAMBURGER ROLLS

3 pounds ground beef
2 10½-ounce cans tomato soup
1 cup pickle relish
1 tablespoon salt
½ teaspoon pepper
24 frankfurter or sandwich rolls, split and heated

Cook beef until browned, stirring with fork.

Add soup, relish, salt, and pepper; simmer about 15 minutes. Serve on rolls. Makes 24.

BEEF AND MUSHROOMS ON TOAST

1 pound ground beef
1 medium onion, minced
½ cup diced celery
½ medium green pepper, minced
1 cup sliced mushrooms
1½ teaspoons salt
⅛ teaspoon pepper
Dash of cayenne
2 tablespoons quick-cooking tapioca
8 slices toast

Brown beef, stirring with fork. Add onion, celery, green pepper, mushrooms, seasonings, and 2 cups water.

Cover, and simmer 25 minutes. Add tapioca, and cook until gravy thickens slightly and tapioca is clear. Serve on toast. Serves 4.

BARBECUED SPOONBURGERS

3 tablespoons fat
1 onion, chopped
1 green pepper, chopped
1 pound hamburger
1 cup ketchup
1 teaspoon salt
¼ teaspoon pepper
8 hamburger buns

Melt fat in heavy skillet. Add onion and green pepper and fry about 5 minutes. Add hamburger and continue cooking and stirring until pink color of meat has disappeared.

Add ketchup, salt, and pepper and cook slowly until flavors are blended, about 15 minutes. (Add some red pepper if a "hotter" mixture is desired.) Serve in hot split buttered buns. Serves 8.

Note: Make this barbecue mixture in advance; then heat for serving.

STUFFED HAMBURGER PATTIES

Press seasoned ground beef into thin patties between waxed paper.

Put 2 patties together with a filling made of chopped raw onion mixed with a little bottled steak sauce, crimping the edges of the patties firmly together.

Broil and serve in hot buttered buns.

With Cheese: Substitute cheese slices for onion in above.

Ground Meat Loaves

MASTER MEAT LOAF

1   pound ground beef
1/2 pound ground pork
2   slightly beaten eggs
2/3 cup soft breadcrumbs
1   cup milk
1/4 cup minced onion
2   teaspoons salt
1/8 teaspoon pepper
1/2 teaspoon sage

Combine all ingredients and pack lightly into meat loaf pan.

Bake in moderate oven (350°F.) 1 hour. Serve with tomato sauce, mushroom sauce, or white sauce with vegetables added. Serves 4 to 6.

Master Meat Loaf Variations

1. Meats: In place of pork, use bulk pork sausage or 1/2 pound bologna, ground; or use 1/4 pound pork and 1/4 pound veal.

2. Liquids: In place of milk, use meat stock or bouillon, tomato juice, diluted canned soups, or half ketchup or chili sauce and half water.

3. Seasonings: Worcestershire sauce, mustard, horseradish, garlic salt, celery salt, poultry seasoning, thyme, parsley, chili powder, savory.

4. Picnic Meat Loaf: Place a row of hard-cooked eggs in center of loaf before baking.

5. Glazed Loaf: Invert baked loaf on a baking sheet and brush with a mixture of mustard and ketchup. Return to hot oven 10 minutes.

6. Meat Ring: Pack meat loaf mixture into a ring mold and bake 45 minutes. Let stand in a warm place for a few minutes before serving.

Then invert on a round or square platter and fill center with a buttered vegetable.

7. Midget Loaves: Bake meat loaf mixture in muffin pans. Bake 30 minutes.

8. White-Capped Loaf: Thirty minutes before loaf is done, cover top with a row of overlapping onion slices. Continue baking.

Picnic Meat Loaf

9. Blue Cheese Meat Loaf: Shape half the mixture in loaf pan or on a shallow pan.

Spread with filling made by crumbling 1/4 pound blue cheese and combining with 1/4 cup soft margarine, 2 teaspoons Worcestershire sauce, and 1/2 teaspoon dry mustard. Shape rest of meat mixture on top; bake.

PORCUPINE MEAT LOAF

1 1/2 pounds hamburger
1/2   cup uncooked rice
1   large onion, minced
1 1/2 teaspoons salt
1/4   teaspoon pepper
1 1/2 teaspoons poultry seasoning
1   teaspoon Worcestershire sauce
2   bouillon cubes
1/4   cup flour

Mix meat, rice, onion, 1/2 cup water, salt, pepper, poultry seasoning, and Worcestershire sauce. Shape into a round loaf and put in 2-quart casserole.

Dissolve bouillon cubes in 2 cups hot water and pour around loaf.

Cover; bake in moderate oven (350°F.) for 2 hours. Remove loaf to hot platter.

Thicken liquid remaining in casserole with a paste of the flour and 1/3 cup cold water. Season to taste. Serve hot with the gravy and glazed apple rings, if desired. Serves 6.

PENNY-PINCHER'S PLANKED STEAK

1   pound ground beef
1   teaspoon garlic salt
1   tablespoon Worcestershire sauce
1   egg
4   tomatoes
2   tablespoons chopped green pepper
1/2 cup grated process Cheddar cheese

Combine beef, garlic salt, Worcestershire sauce, and egg; shape into patty.

Broil 3 inches from broiling unit 7 to 8 minutes.

Remove stem ends of tomatoes. Combine green pepper and cheese. Top tomatoes with cheese mixture.

Turn meat. Arrange tomatoes on broiler rack. Broil 6 to 8 minutes. Serve with butter pats topped with chopped chives, if desired.

Arrange steak and tomatoes on a plank or heat-proof platter. Whip up fluffy mashed potatoes from the packaged quick-cooking variety and make a border around edge of plank. Serves 4.

Variation: This deviled steak is a delicious change: Add 1/2 cup chopped onions, 1/2 cup chopped green pepper to basic meat mixture; when patty is turned, spread the top with 1/4 cup chili sauce.

Frosted Meat Loaf

FROSTED MEAT LOAF

4   cups corn flakes
2   slightly beaten eggs
1   cup milk
2   teaspoons salt
1/8   teaspoon pepper
1   teaspoon Worcestershire sauce
1/4   cup chopped parsley
1   tablespoon chopped onion
1 1/4 pounds ground beef
1/4   pound ground pork

Crush corn flakes slightly; combine with remaining ingredients and mix thoroughly. Spread in greased 9 1/2 x 5 1/2-inch loaf pan.

Bake in moderate oven (350°F.) about 1 hour. Unmold loaf and place on greased baking sheet or ovenproof platter.

Frosting:

4   cups seasoned mashed potatoes
1   cup corn flakes
1   tablespoon melted butter or margarine

Frost loaf with mashed potatoes. Crush corn flakes into fine crumbs; mix with melted butter. Sprinkle over mashed potatoes.

Bake in moderate oven (350°F.) about 20 minutes longer. Serves 8.

KETCHUP MEAT LOAF

1 1/2 pounds ground beef
1   cup soft breadcrumbs
1   slightly beaten egg
1/3   cup tomato ketchup
1 1/2 teaspoons salt
1/4   teaspoon pepper
1/2   cup chopped onions

Combine all ingredients. Mix lightly but well. Shape into a loaf in shallow baking pan.

Bake in moderate oven (350°F.) 1 hour. Serves 6 to 8.

Penny-Pincher's Planked Steak

Upside-Down Meat Loaf

UPSIDE-DOWN MEAT LOAF

¾ cup packaged bread stuffing
½ cup milk
⅓ cup ketchup
1 medium onion, chopped
1½ pounds ground beef
¾ teaspoon salt
Few grains pepper
¾ teaspoon Ac'cent
Few drops Tabasco sauce
½ teaspoon Worcestershire sauce
3 to 4 canned cling peach halves

Empty measured stuffing into large bowl. Combine milk and ketchup; pour over stuffing; let stand 15 minutes or until stuffing is soft.

Add remaining ingredients, except peaches; mix thoroughly until all ingredients are well blended.

Arrange peach halves, cut side down, in greased loaf pan; cover with meat mixture.

Bake in moderate oven (350°F.) 1 hour. Unmold on serving platter. Fill centers of peach halves with currant jelly. Serves 6.

PICKLE BEEF PINWHEELS

1 pound ground beef chuck
1 unbeaten egg
¼ cup sweet pickle relish
1 tablespoon grated onion
1½ teaspoons salt
⅛ teaspoon pepper
1 cup seasoned mashed potatoes

Combine beef, egg, sweet pickle relish, onion, salt, and pepper. Mix thoroughly.

Place on waxed paper and pat out to a rectangle, about 8 x 10 inches.

Spread mashed potatoes over meat. Carefully roll up like jelly roll.

Cut into slices and broil about 3 inches from source of heat, 10 to 15 minutes, or until done. Serves 4 to 6.

Pickle Beef Pinwheels

TOMATO MEAT LOAF

2 cans (2½ cups) condensed tomato soup (save 2 cups for the sauce)
1 pound ground beef
½ pound ground pork
1½ cups soft bread cubes
¼ cup chopped parsley
1 slightly beaten egg
1 tablespoon Worcestershire sauce
1 teaspoon salt
¼ teaspoon pepper
1 small onion, chopped

For Sauce:

2 cups soup (saved from meat loaf)
Dash of allspice
⅓ cup drippings

Combine ½ cup soup with other loaf ingredients (save rest of soup for sauce).

Shape meat mixture into a loaf or pack lightly into a greased loaf pan.

Bake in moderate oven (350°F.) about 1 hour or until cooked through.

Remove loaf from pan and combine ingredients for sauce. Heat for 5 minutes. Serve hot sauce with loaf. Serves 6.

Tomato Meat Loaf Variations

Mushroom Meat Loaf: Follow recipe for tomato meat loaf but use condensed cream of mushroom soup instead of condensed tomato soup.

For sauce: Leave out allspice; instead, add ⅓ cup chopped pimiento.

Celery Meat Loaf: Follow recipe for tomato meat loaf but use condensed cream of celery soup instead of condensed tomato soup.

For sauce: Leave out allspice; instead, add 2 tablespoons chopped parsley.

HAMBURGER-BISCUIT PINWHEELS

Baking Powder Biscuit Dough:

About ⅔ cup milk
2 cups biscuit mix

Filling:

1 small onion, chopped
2 tablespoons fat
1 pound hamburger
½ teaspoon salt
¼ teaspoon pepper
3 tablespoons ketchup

Fry onion in fat until golden brown. Add hamburger and brown. Season with salt, pepper, and ketchup. Cool.

Spread over biscuit dough made by adding milk gradually to biscuit mix. Blend with fork until a soft dough is formed. Turn onto a floured board and knead 6 times. Roll or pat into a rectangle ⅓ inch thick.

Spread with filling. Roll as for jelly roll.

Cut into 1-inch thick slices. Place on ungreased baking sheet. Bake in

very hot oven (450°F.) about 15 minutes. Serve hot with mushroom sauce. Serves 6.

15-MINUTE MEAT LOAF WITH TOMATO SAUCE

1½ pounds ground beef
1½ teaspoons salt
⅛ teaspoon pepper
2 tablespoons chopped green pepper (optional)
2 tablespoons chopped onion
2 8-ounce cans tomato sauce
2 tablespoons sugar
¼ tablespoon Worcestershire sauce

Combine beef, salt, pepper, onion, green pepper, and ½ can tomato sauce. Press into greased 9 x 12 x 2-inch baking dish.

Bake on lowest shelf in very hot oven (450°F.) for 10 minutes. Broil 5 minutes longer.

While meat is cooking, combine remaining tomato sauce, sugar, and Worcestershire sauce. Bring to a boil. Boil about 3 minutes. Add meat drippings if desired.

Cut meat in half crosswise. Arrange sandwich fashion on platter, pouring tomato sauce between and on top of meat. Serves 6.

TAMALE LOAF

1 onion, chopped
1 small clove garlic, chopped
⅓ cup olive oil
¾ pound ground beef
2 teaspoons salt
3 cups tomatoes, skinned and mashed
2 teaspoons chili powder
Dash of cayenne or Tabasco sauce
¾ cup corn meal
¾ cup milk
¾ can (No. 2) cream-style corn
¾ cup pitted ripe olives

Cook onion and garlic in olive oil for 5 minutes. Put in the ground meat and, stirring often, cook until meat begins to brown. Add salt, tomatoes, chili powder, and cayenne. Cook 15 minutes.

Mix corn meal with milk, and add mixture to meat. Stir and cook another 15 minutes. Then add corn and olives, and when all is well mixed pour into a greased 8 x 12-inch pan. Spread olive oil lightly over top and bake in moderate oven (350°F.) for 1 hour. Serves 8.

Hamburger-Biscuit Pinwheels

MEAT LOAF—MEXICAN STYLE

1   pound ground beef
1   pound ground pork
1   egg
1/2 cup corn meal
1/2 cup chopped onion
1/4 cup chopped green pepper
1 1/4 cups canned tomatoes
2   teaspoons salt
1/4 teaspoon pepper
1/2 teaspoon sage
1/4 teaspoon chili powder

Mix all ingredients thoroughly. Put into 9 1/2 x 5 1/2 x 3-inch loaf pan.

Bake in moderate oven (350°F.) 1 1/2 hours. Garnish with ketchup and serve with hot, buttered whole kernel corn. Serves 8 to 10.

SAVORY MEAT LOAF

2   pounds ground beef
1/2 pound ground pork
1/2 cup fine dry breadcrumbs
2   tablespoons milk
1   tablespoon lemon juice
2   tablespoons chopped onion
2   teaspoons salt
1/4 teaspoon pepper
4   hard-cooked eggs

Combine all ingredients except hard-cooked eggs. Pack half the meat mixture into a 5 x 9-inch loaf pan.

Arrange shelled hard-cooked eggs in a lengthwise row through center of loaf. Pack remaining meat mixture over eggs.

Bake in moderate oven (350°F.) until done, about 1 1/2 hours. Serve hot or cold. Serves 8.

SWEET AND SOUR MEAT LOAF

1   8-ounce can tomato sauce
1/4 cup brown sugar
1/4 cup vinegar
1   teaspoon prepared mustard
1   egg
1   small onion, minced
1/4 cup crushed crackers
2   pounds ground beef
1 1/2 teaspoons salt
1/4 teaspoon pepper

Mix tomato sauce with sugar, vinegar, and mustard until sugar is dissolved.

Beat egg slightly; add onion, crackers, beef, salt, pepper, and 1/2 cup tomato sauce mixture; combine lightly but thoroughly.

Shape meat into oval loaf in a bowl; turn into shallow baking dish, keeping loaf shapely. Pour on rest of tomato sauce mixture.

Bake in hot oven (400°F.) 45 minutes, basting occasionally. With 2 broad spatulas, lift onto platter. Pass juices, after spooning off as much fat as possible. Serves 8.

GOLDEN MEAT LOAF

4   cups corn flakes
1 1/4 pounds ground beef
1/4 pound ground pork
2   slightly beaten eggs
1   cup milk
2   teaspoons salt
1/8 teaspoon pepper
1   teaspoon Worcestershire sauce
1/4 cup chopped onions
1   cup grated raw carrots
1/4 cup chopped parsley

Crush corn flakes slightly. Combine with remaining ingredients and mix well.

Spread in greased 9 1/2 x 5 1/4-inch loaf pan. Bake in moderate oven (350°F.) about 1 1/4 hours. Serves 8.

MEAT LOAF WITH MUSHROOM SAUCE

1   10 1/2-ounce can cream of mushroom soup
1 1/2 pounds ground beef
1 1/2 cups soft breadcrumbs
1   medium onion, chopped
1/4 cup chopped parsley
1   egg
1   tablespoon Worcestershire sauce
1 1/4 teaspoons salt
1/4 teaspoon pepper
1/4 cup milk
1   pimiento, chopped

Combine 1/2 cup soup with remaining ingredients, except milk and pimiento. Pack into 9 x 5 x 3-inch loaf pan.

Bake in moderate oven (350°F.) 1 1/4 hours. Pour off liquid; turn loaf out on hot platter.

Heat remaining soup with milk. Add pimiento and pour over loaf. Serves 6.

WESTERN RANCH MEAT LOAF

1/2 cup chopped onion
3/4 cup diced celery
1/4 cup fat
1/3 cup diced green pepper (optional)
1   tablespoon salt
2   eggs
3   cups soft breadcrumbs
1/2 cup water
2   pounds hamburger
1/2 cup tomato juice
2   tablespoons butter or margarine, melted

Brown onion and celery in the fat. Combine with green pepper, salt, eggs, breadcrumbs, and water to make a stuffing.

Add half of the stuffing (1 1/2 cups) to the meat, mixing well. Pat out half the meat mixture in a 2-quart loaf pan. Cover with remaining stuffing, then top with remaining meat mixture.

Bake in a moderate oven (350°F.) 1 1/4 hours. Baste twice with tomato juice and melted butter to keep loaf moist. Serves 10 to 12.

Golden Meat Loaf

JIFFY HAMBURGER LOAVES

1   pound ground chuck
1/2 minced small onion
1   teaspoon salt
1/2 teaspoon Ac'cent
1/2 cup fresh breadcrumbs
1   can condensed vegetable soup, undiluted

With fork, mix meat lightly but thoroughly with rest of ingredients.

Spoon into 12 2-inch cupcake cups. Bake in very hot oven (450°F.) 15 minutes. Serves 6.

BACON-LATTICED MEAT LOAF

1 1/2 pounds ground lean beef
1   cup chopped parsley
1   cup chopped onion
1 1/2 teaspoons salt
1/4 teaspoon pepper
3/4 teaspoon Ac'cent
1 1/2 teaspoons Worcestershire sauce
1/2 cup fine dry breadcrumbs
1   cup water
6   slices bacon, partially cooked

Combine all ingredients except bacon; blend well. Pack into 8 x 4 x 3-inch loaf pan. Bake in slow oven (325°F.) 45 to 50 minutes.

Arrange half-cooked bacon lattice fashion over top of meat loaf. Continue baking 10 to 15 minutes longer or place under broiler heat until bacon is crisp.

If desired, garnish loaf on its platter with scoops of sweet potato (seasoned with salt, pepper, and Ac'cent) arranged on fried pineapple slices and topped with sprinkling of coconut. Serves 6.

Bacon-Latticed Meat Loaf

GROUND BEEF STEAK SUPREME

1   pound ground beef
1/4 cup fine dry breadcrumbs
1   beaten egg
1   teaspoon salt
1/8 teaspoon pepper
3   tablespoons minced onion
1/4 cup finely chopped celery
1   can condensed mushroom soup
1/2 cup water

Mix all ingredients except mushroom soup and water. Shape into an oval about 1-inch thick.

Brown in a skillet in hot fat; carefully turn and brown other side.

Pour over the meat the mushroom soup which has been diluted with the 1/2 cup water. Cook slowly in covered skillet 25 minutes.

Serve mushroom gravy over boiled or mashed potatoes. Serves 5 to 6.

ORANGE-GLAZED HAMBURGER LOAVES

6   tablespoons brown sugar
1/2 teaspoon dry mustard
6   slices small orange, unpeeled
1 1/2 pounds ground beef
2   cups soft breadcrumbs
1   egg
1   medium onion, minced
1   medium green pepper, minced
1/4 teaspoon pepper
1   teaspoon salt
1/2 cup orange juice
Juice of 1 lemon

Put brown sugar in 6 greased, small baking dishes. Sprinkle with mustard, and top each with orange slice.

Combine remaining ingredients; mix well. Press into baking dishes.

Bake in moderate oven (350°F.) 1 hour. Let stand a few minutes before turning upside down on platter. Serves 6.

PLANKED GROUND STEAK

1   small chopped onion
2   tablespoons margarine
2   eggs
1 1/2 pounds ground beef
1/2 pound ground pork
1   cup milk
2   teaspoons salt
1/8 teaspoon pepper
1   teaspoon Worcestershire sauce
1/4 cup chopped parsley
1 2/3 cups oats, uncooked
3   cups mashed potatoes
6   parboiled onion cups filled with cooked, seasoned peas

Sauté onion in margarine for a few minutes.

Beat eggs and add to meat with milk, onion, seasonings, and oats. Mix thoroughly.

Form into a flat loaf on a greased plank, shallow baking dish, or ovenproof platter; score in diamond shapes across top.

Bake in hot oven (425°F.) 40 minutes. Arrange mashed potatoes along the two long sides of loaf and filled onion cups at ends. Brown in hot oven. Serves 6.

HERBAL MEAT LOAF

1   pound ground beef
1/2 pound ground pork
1/3 cup toast crumbs
2   medium onions, chopped
1   garlic clove, minced
1   tablespoon olive oil
1/4 teaspoon marjoram
1/4 teaspoon savory
1/2 teaspoon salt
1/8 teaspoon pepper

Basting Sauce:

1   tablespoon bacon fat
1   tablespoon olive oil
1   teaspoon dry red wine
1   tablespoon ketchup
Salt and pepper

Herbal Meat Loaf: Combine all ingredients; mix well. Pack in greased loaf pan.

Bake in moderate oven (375°F.) 1 hour. Baste every 15 minutes with hot basting sauce.

Basting Sauce: Combine all ingredients; heat. Serves 6.

BROILED BEEF PINWHEELS

1   pound hamburger
1 1/2 teaspoons salt
1/8 teaspoon pepper
1   egg
2   tablespoons melted fat
6   tablespoons breadcrumbs
2   tablespoons tomato juice or milk
1 1/2 cups mashed potatoes, seasoned
1 1/2 cups mashed peas, seasoned
Butter or margarine, melted

Mix together all but the last 3 ingredients. Pat out on waxed paper to form rectangular sheet 1/2 inch thick.

Spread mashed potatoes on crosswise half of meat. Spread other half with mashed peas. Roll meat firmly, jelly-roll fashion, starting with the end covered with peas.

Wrap in waxed paper and chill several hours. When ready to cook, cut with sharp knife into six 1-inch slices.

Place on preheated broiler, 3 to 4 inches below source of heat. Brush with melted butter and broil slowly about 5 minutes. Turn and brush again with melted butter and finish broiling. Serves 6.

Baked Pinwheels: Place 2-inch slices on a greased baking pan. Brush surface with melted butter. Bake in a hot oven (400°F.) 30 minutes.

POT ROASTED MEAT LOAVES

1 1/4 pounds ground beef
1   egg
1 3/4 teaspoons salt
1/8 teaspoon pepper
1/2 cup soft breadcrumbs
1/3 cup milk
Flour
2   tablespoons fat

Mix beef, egg, 1 1/4 teaspoons salt, pepper, crumbs, and milk. Shape in 4 individual meat loaves. Dredge with flour.

Brown on all sides in fat in skillet. Drain off fat. Add 1/2 cup water and remaining 1/2 teaspoon salt. Cover, and simmer 30 minutes, or until done. Serve with potato pancakes. Serves 4.

BURGUNDY MEAT LOAF

3/4 pound ground beef, lamb, or veal
3/4 cup rolled oats
1/2 cup burgundy or claret wine
3   tablespoons chopped onion
1 1/4 teaspoons salt
1/4 teaspoon pepper
1/8 teaspoon poultry seasoning
1   beaten egg
2   tablespoons melted meat drippings

Combine ingredients in order given. Pack into greased small loaf pan. Bake in moderate oven (350°F.) 1 hour or until done. Serves 4 or 5.

VELVET-SMOOTH MEAT LOAF

1   pound fresh ground beef
1   egg
1 1/2 teaspoons salt
1/2 cup finely chopped onion
1   tall can evaporated milk, undiluted
2   cups soft breadcrumbs

Combine all ingredients, mixing thoroughly.

Pack into a greased loaf pan and bake in moderate oven (350°–375°F.) about 1 hour. Slice and serve hot or cold. Serves 6.

CHEESE MEAT CUPS

1 1/2 pounds ground beef
1/2 cup cheese-cracker crumbs
1/4 cup finely chopped onion
2   tablespoons finely chopped green pepper
1/4 cup chili sauce
2   to 3 drops Tabasco sauce
2/3 cup milk
2   eggs
3/4 teaspoon salt
Dash of pepper

Mix ingredients thoroughly. Fill greased muffin pans.

Bake in moderate oven (350°F.) 45 minutes. Makes about 10 "cups." Or bake in 8 1/2 x 4 1/2 x 2 1/2-inch loaf pan about 1 hour. Serves 6 to 8.

JUICY MEAT LOAF

1 pound ground beef
1/2 cup oats (quick or old fashioned, uncooked)
1 beaten egg
1/4 cup chopped onion
1 1/2 teaspoons salt
1/4 teaspoon pepper
2/3 cup tomato juice

Combine all ingredients thoroughly; pack firmly into a loaf pan.

Bake in moderate oven (350°F.) 45 to 50 minutes. Let stand 5 minutes before slicing. Serves 6.

Variations:

Dinner Hamburgers: Use meat loaf recipe above, omitting beaten egg. Combine ingredients thoroughly. Shape into 6 dinner hamburgers; chill.

Pan-fry in hot fat and serve sizzling hot.

Meat Balls: Use meat loaf recipe above, omitting beaten egg. Shape combined ingredients into 12 meat balls; roll in flour; then brown in hot fat.

Add tomato sauce; simmer 20 to 25 minutes.

Mock Drumsticks: Use meat loaf recipe above, omitting beaten egg. Shape combined ingredients into 6 drumsticks. Insert a wooden skewer into each drumstick; chill.

Roll in breadcrumbs. Brown on all sides in hot fat; cover and cook slowly 10 minutes longer.

SOY MEAT LOAF

3/4 pound ground meat
1 1/2 cups vegetable liquid, tomato juice, or milk
2 ounces salt pork, diced (about 1/3 cup)
2 tablespoons chopped onion
1/2 cup chopped celery
3/4 cup soy grits
2 tablespoons chopped parsley
2 teaspoons salt
3/4 cup breadcrumbs
1/8 teaspoon pepper

Select one kind of meat or a mixture of two or more kinds.

Blend vegetable liquid, tomato juice, or milk with the meat.

Fry salt pork until crisp and remove from fat. Cook onion and celery in the fat for a few minutes.

Add all the ingredients to the meat and mix well. Pack mixture into a loaf pan or mold it into a loaf and place in an uncovered baking pan.

Bake loaf in a moderate oven (350°F.) until well done and brown, about 1 hour. Serves 6 to 8.

Variation: To vary the flavor, serve the loaf with brown gravy or tomato sauce.

LOUISIANA YAM BEEF ROLL

1 1/2 pounds ground beef chuck
1 slightly beaten egg
3/4 cup soft breadcrumbs
2 tablespoons finely chopped onions
1 1/2 teaspoons salt
1/4 teaspoon pepper
1 tablespoon horseradish
1/4 teaspoon dry mustard
1 1/4 cups mashed yams or 1 No. 2 can yams, drained and mashed
2 tablespoons chopped parsley
2 tablespoons chopped onion
Salt
3 slices lean bacon

Combine beef, egg, crumbs, onion, salt, pepper, horseradish and mustard. Mix well.

Spread meat mixture on a piece of heavy waxed paper to make a rectangle about 8 x 10 inches.

Combine yams, parsley, onion, and salt to taste. Mix well, and spread evenly over beef. Roll like a jelly roll.

Place in shallow baking pan and top with bacon slices. Bake in moderate oven (350°F.) 45 minutes to 1 hour. Serve with tomato sauce. Serves 6.

INDIVIDUAL BEEF FILLED RICE LOAVES

1 cup uncooked rice
1/4 cup margarine
1 pound ground beef
2 tablespoons chopped onion
1/2 teaspoon salt
1/4 teaspoon pepper
6 tablespoons ketchup

Cook rice in boiling salted water until tender and fluffy.

Melt 2 tablespoons margarine in skillet. Add ground beef and cook over medium heat until red color disappears, stirring constantly with fork. Add onion, salt, and pepper. Mix well.

Into well greased custard cups or individual baking dishes put 1/2 the hot rice, pressing down firmly.

On top of rice arrange layer of beef. Over meat spread 1 tablespoon ketchup in each dish.

Cover meat with remaining rice, pressing down firmly. Dot with remaining 2 tablespoons margarine.

Set baking dishes in shallow pan or on baking sheet. Bake in moderate oven (350°F.) 25 to 30 minutes.

Unmold on hot plates or platter. Serve hot with creamed peas or creamed asparagus. Serves 6.

Note: May also be baked in well greased 8 x 8 x 2-inch pan.

Put layer of rice into pan, then layer of meat. Spread with ketchup and cover with rice.

Dot with margarine and bake as directed. Cut in squares to serve.

STANDARD AMERICAN MEAT LOAF
(Master Recipe)

1 beaten egg
1 cup rolled oats, uncooked
1 1/2 pounds ground beef
1/4 cup chopped onion
2 teaspoons salt
1/4 teaspoon pepper
1 tablespoon Worcestershire sauce
1 cup water or milk

Mix all ingredients together thoroughly. Pack into 9 x 5 x 3-inch greased loaf pan.

Bake in moderate oven (350°–375°F.) 1 hour. Serves 8.

Variations:

Company Meat Loaf: Add 1/2 teaspoon rubbed sage to master recipe.

Combine 3 tablespoons brown sugar, 1/4 cup ketchup, 1/4 teaspoon nutmeg, and 1 teaspoon dry mustard and spread over loaf before baking.

Filled Cheeseburgers: Shape meat mixture into 20 very thin patties.

Combine 2 1/2 ounces Roquefort cheese, 2 tablespoons mayonnaise, and 1 teaspoon prepared mustard.

Spoon this mixture on 10 patties. Top with remaining patties, and press edges together.

Broil 6 inches from heat 12 minutes on first side, and 8 minutes on other side.

SPICY MEAT LOAF

1 1/2 pounds ground beef
1/2 pound sausage meat
1 medium onion, grated
1 egg
1 cup soft breadcrumbs
1/2 cup milk
1 teaspoon salt
1/4 teaspoon pepper
1/2 teaspoon nutmeg
1/2 teaspoon allspice
1/8 teaspoon ginger

Combine all ingredients, mixing lightly but thoroughly. Shape in a loaf.

Bake in moderate oven (350°F.) about 1 1/4 hours. Serves 8.

MOCK PORTERHOUSE

1 1/2 pounds hamburger
1 1/2 teaspoons salt
1/2 cup quick-cooking rolled oats
1/4 cup finely chopped onion
1/2 cup top milk
Butter or margarine

Mix together the hamburger, salt, rolled oats, onion, and milk. Pat this mixture into a mound about 2 inches thick.

Broil 4 inches from heat source about 20 minutes. Dot surface with butter and serve on a hot platter. Serves 6.

Top-of-Range Main Dishes with Ground Beef

CREAMED GROUND BEEF
(Master Recipe)

1 pound ground beef
1/2 cup chopped onion
1 tablespoon fat
1 cup shredded carrots (optional)
2 teaspoons salt
1/4 cup flour
2 cups water

Brown meat and onion in hot fat in heavy skillet. Add carrots and salt. Cook and stir 15 minutes.

Sprinkle flour over meat and stir until blended. Add water. Cook until thickened.

Add seasonings to taste, such as Worcestershire sauce, dry mustard, or pepper. Serve hot over toast, baked or mashed potatoes, or rice. Serves 8.

Creamed Hamburger and Almonds: Add 1/2 cup sliced almonds to master recipe.

Creamed Hamburger and Corn: Add 1 cup whole kernel corn to master recipe.

EASY BURGER SKILLET

1 pound hamburger
1 teaspoon Worcestershire sauce
1/2 10 1/2-ounce can condensed cream of celery soup
1/3 cup shredded cheese

Brown hamburger lightly in a skillet. Stir in Worcestershire sauce. Spread soup over all.

Top with shredded cheese. Cover. Cook slowly for 10 minutes. Serves 4.

STUFFED CABBAGE—SWEET AND SOUR

10 to 12 large cabbage leaves
1 pound ground beef
1/2 cup cooked rice
1 egg
1 teaspoon salt
1/8 teaspoon pepper
1/2 cup raisins
1 onion, sliced thin
Juice of 1 lemon
About 1/4 cup brown sugar
2 cups canned tomatoes
1 cup water

Use large, whole, outside leaves of cabbage. Place in boiling water for 5 minutes to soften.

Combine meat, rice, egg, salt, pepper, and half the raisins. Put a generous amount on each leaf. Fold in sides. Roll up and fasten with wooden picks.

Shred the heart of cabbage. Line bottom of kettle with shredded cabbage. Put stuffed cabbage on top, close together.

Add remaining shredded cabbage, onion, raisins, lemon juice, sugar, tomatoes, and water. Simmer gently 2 1/2 to 3 hours. Serves 6.

SQUAW RICE

1 pound ground beef
2 cups cooked rice
2 teaspoons salt
1/8 teaspoon pepper
1 cup whole kernel corn, drained
1 medium onion, sliced
1 cup canned tomatoes, drained
1 cup tomato juice

Lightly brown beef, rice, salt, and pepper.

Add remaining ingredients; cover and simmer about 30 minutes. Serves 8.

GROUND BEEF CHOP SUEY

1/2 pound hamburger
1 large onion, sliced
1 cup celery strips
2 tablespoons salad oil
1 No. 2 can bean sprouts, drained
1 1/2 cups consommé or bouillon
1/2 cup sliced mushrooms
1 tablespoon cornstarch
1 tablespoon salt
1/4 cup soy sauce
Hot cooked rice

Pan-fry hamburger, onion, and celery in oil in a heavy kettle. Add bean sprouts, consommé, and mushrooms.

Mix cornstarch with 1/4 cup water and add. Cook and stir 10 minutes. Season to taste with salt and soy sauce. Serve on hot cooked rice with additional soy sauce. Serves 6.

Ground Beef Chow Mein: Prepare ground beef chop suey and serve on chow mein noodles with additional soy sauce.

STUFFED WHOLE CABBAGE

1 1/2 pounds ground beef
2 teaspoons salt
1/4 teaspoon pepper
1/2 cup fine dry breadcrumbs
1 medium onion, chopped
1 medium head cabbage
2 beef bouillon cubes

Combine all ingredients, except cabbage and bouillon, with 1 cup water.

Remove core from cabbage; cook cabbage in boiling salted water about 5 minutes; drain. Separate leaves.

Line colander with large piece of several thicknesses of cheesecloth. Form cabbage head again by lining cheesecloth with cabbage leaves, then a layer of beef mixture, continuing until all meat and cabbage are used, making 4 or 5 layers of each. Pull cloth tightly around cabbage head; tie top firmly with string.

Put in large kettle, and almost cover with boiling water. Add bouillon cubes; cover, and simmer about 1 1/2 hours.

Remove from liquid; drain, and untie. Put on plate; remove cheesecloth; cut in large wedges. Serve with ketchup or horseradish. Serves 6.

CHILI CON CARNE

Chili or Chile Con Carne is Spanish for peppers with meat. It is a dish of Mexican origin now popular in the United States in various versions. Its chief ingredients are beef, tomato sauce, beans, and chili peppers. Chili powder is usually substituted for the crushed chili peppers.

1 1/2 to 2 cups pinto beans (red beans)
Salt and pepper
1 pound ground beef
2 tablespoons shortening
2 large onions, cut fine
2 cloves garlic, cut fine
2 cans tomato paste
1 to 4 tablespoons chili powder

Wash and soak beans overnight. Simmer until tender (about 2 hours). Season with salt and pepper.

Brown ground beef in large, heavy skillet, turning frequently to keep from sticking.

Melt shortening in small skillet and brown onion and garlic.

Combine onion, garlic, tomato paste, and chili powder with browned meat, in large skillet. Simmer about 20 minutes.

Add chili mixture to cooked, seasoned beans and simmer over low heat about 1 hour, stirring often to prevent sticking. Serves 6.

QUICK CHILI CON CARNE

1 pound hamburger
2 medium onions, chopped
2 tablespoons fat
1 teaspoon salt
1 teaspoon chili powder
1/4 teaspoon pepper
2 cups cooked tomatoes, or tomato soup
2 cups cooked kidney beans

Brown hamburger and onions in hot fat. Season meat well. Add tomatoes and kidney beans. Cook over low heat 20 to 30 minutes. Serves 6 to 8.

Steaming bowls of chili and a crisp green salad are all that's needed for a simple but satisfying supper.

LIMA BEAN CHILI

1 medium onion, chopped
1 pound ground beef
2 or 3 teaspoons chili powder
1¼ teaspoons salt
1 package frozen lima beans
1 19-ounce can (2½ cups) tomatoes

Cook onion and beef in large saucepan, stirring with fork, until meat loses its red color.

Add remaining ingredients; bring to boil; cover, and simmer about 30 minutes, stirring occasionally. Serves 4.

TROPICAL HAMBURGER

1 cup shredded coconut
½ pound hamburger
¼ teaspoon nutmeg
1 teaspoon salt
1 cup pineapple juice
2 tablespoons lemon juice
½ cup water
2 tablespoons cornstarch
Fried noodles

Brown coconut in skillet until crispy. Stir in hamburger and cook until lightly browned. Add nutmeg and salt.

Combine pineapple juice, lemon juice, and water with cornstarch. Stir into meat mixture. Stir and heat 5 to 10 minutes.

Serve on fried noodles, garnished with salted, slivered almonds. Serves 4.

RICE AND HAMBURGER SKILLET

1 pound ground beef
2 cups cooked rice
1 teaspoon salt
⅛ teaspoon pepper
1 cup whole kernel corn, drained
1 cup sliced onions
1 teaspoon salt
1 cup tomatoes, drained
1 cup tomato juice

In a skillet or large saucepan, mix together ground beef, rice, salt, and pepper. Fry, stirring frequently, until ground beef is browned.

Stir in corn, onions, salt, tomatoes, and tomato juice. Cover and cook over low heat 30 minutes. Serves 10.

BARBECUED BEEFBURGERS WITH RICE

1 pound ground beef
1 egg
⅛ teaspoon pepper
1 teaspoon salt
3 tablespoons fat
1 cup chopped onion
2 tablespoons Worcestershire sauce
1 tablespoon vinegar
2 tablespoons sugar
2 8-ounce cans tomato sauce
4½ cups hot cooked rice

Mix together the beef, egg, salt, and pepper. Shape into 6 flat cakes, using about ⅓ cup of mixture for each cake.

Melt 1 tablespoon fat in a skillet and brown cakes, first on one side, then on other.

While cakes are browning, melt remaining 2 tablespoons fat in saucepan. Add onions and cook in fat until tender.

Add Worcestershire sauce, vinegar, sugar, and tomato sauce and mix well. Pour this sauce over cakes.

Cover skillet and simmer 15 minutes. To serve, arrange hot rice on a platter. Place beef cakes over rice and pour sauce over beef cakes and rice. Serves 6.

Barbecued Beefburgers with Rice

Master Freezer Sauce for Delicious Dishes

From one frozen "starter" recipe in the freezer you can quickly prepare a variety of dishes. The master Italian meat sauce "starter" is excellent on rice, potatoes, or frankfurters as well as in preparing the dishes given here.

ITALIAN MEAT SAUCE
"Starter"

1 cup oil or cooking fat
3 cloves garlic, crushed
3 green peppers, chopped
3 large onions, sliced fine
3 pounds ground beef
3 6-ounce cans tomato paste
3 8-ounce cans tomato sauce
3 cups boiling water
1 tablespoon salt
1 tablespoon paprika
1 teaspoon celery salt
1 teaspoon garlic salt
1 teaspoon chili powder
2 tablespoons Worcestershire sauce
3 tablespoons A-1 sauce
3 tablespoons chili sauce

Heat oil in large heavy kettle. Add crushed garlic, green pepper, and onions. Cook over low heat 5 minutes.

Add meat; mix well and cook on high heat until lightly browned.

Add tomato paste, tomato sauce, and water. Cook over low heat for 2 hours. Add seasonings.

Cool quickly. Package and freeze in pint containers. Makes 10 pints.

To Thaw: Put container under hot water and let hot water run long enough so that contents can be slipped out.

Or remove from freezer and let stand at room temperature several hours before using.

Or remove from freezer the night before using and keep in refrigerator.

MEAT SAUCE AND SPAGHETTI

2 pints Meat Sauce Starter
½ cup tomato juice
1 8-ounce package spaghetti
1 tablespoon salt
Grated Parmesan cheese

Thaw meat sauce with tomato juice. Cook spaghetti in boiling salted water until tender. Drain. Serve with meat sauce and cheese.

TAMALE PIE

2 pints Meat Sauce Starter, thawed
½ package corn muffin mix

Pour meat sauce into a 2-quart casserole.

Prepare corn muffin mix according to directions on package. Pour muffin mix over sauce. Bake in hot oven (425°F.) for 30 minutes.

MEAT SAUCE WITH RED KIDNEY BEANS

1 pint Meat Sauce Starter
2 cans red kidney beans, drained
⅓ cup red wine

Combine all ingredients in a 1½-quart casserole. Bake in moderate oven (350°F.) for 1 hour.

EGGPLANT WITH MEAT SAUCE

1 eggplant
1 pint Meat Sauce Starter, thawed
2 tablespoons grated Parmesan cheese

Peel and slice eggplant in ½-inch slices.

Alternate slices of eggplant with meat sauce and cheese in a 1½-quart casserole. Bake in moderate oven (350°F.) for 1 hour.

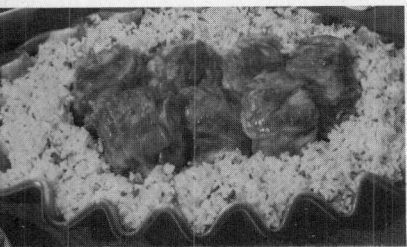

Skillet Cabbage Rolls

SKILLET CABBAGE ROLLS

8 large cabbage leaves
1/2 pound hamburger
1/2 cup cooked rice
1 egg
1 teaspoon salt
1/4 teaspoon pepper
2 tablespoons chopped onion
2 tablespoons fat
1/2 cup cooked tomatoes or ketchup
1/4 cup chopped onion
1 bay leaf (optional)
4 whole cloves (optional)

Cook cabbage leaves in salted water for 5 minutes.

Combine hamburger, rice, egg, salt, pepper, and onion. Brown lightly in hot fat.

Place a spoonful of meat mixture in each leaf and roll up. Secure with a pick. Place in skillet.

Add tomatoes, onion, bay leaf, and cloves. Cover and simmer 45 minutes. Serve with parsleyed rice. Serves 4.

BEEF AND GREEN BEANS
(Chinese)

1 large onion, slivered
1 small clove garlic, minced
1 tablespoon fat
3/4 pound ground beef
3 cups water
3 tablespoons soy sauce
1 pound green beans, diced
2 1/2 tablespoons cornstarch
Hot cooked rice

Brown onion and garlic lightly in fat in heavy saucepan. Add meat and cook 3 minutes, stirring to break up meat.

Add water and soy sauce and heat to boiling. Add beans and cook 10 minutes.

Blend cornstarch with a little cold water. Add to mixture and cook until thickened, stirring constantly. Serve with hot rice. Serves 4.

HAMBURGER PILAF

2/3 cup rice
1 pound ground beef
1 large onion, chopped
1 6-ounce can tomato paste
2 teaspoons salt
1/4 teaspoon pepper

Cook rice, beef, and onion, stirring with fork, until lightly browned.

Add remaining ingredients and 2

cups water; stir and bring to boil.

Cover and simmer 35 to 40 minutes, or until rice is tender. Stir gently with a fork once during cooking.

Serves 4 to 6.

HAMBURGER-SPAGHETTI SUPPER

1 16-ounce can tomatoes
1/2 clove garlic
1 bay leaf
1 pound ground beef
1 medium onion, chopped
1/2 medium green pepper, chopped
2 tablespoons flour
1 teaspoon sugar
1 teaspoon salt
1/8 teaspoon pepper
Hot cooked spaghetti or noodles

Put tomatoes, garlic, and bay leaf in saucepan; bring to boil, and simmer, uncovered, 10 minutes. Force through sieve.

Cook beef, onion, and green pepper in skillet, stirring with fork, until beef is browned.

Blend in flour, sugar, and seasonings. Add sieved tomato mixture, and cook until thickened, stirring constantly. Serve on spaghetti or noodles. Serves 4.

BEEF AND LIMA SKILLET

1 pound ground beef
1 small onion, minced
1 clove garlic, minced
2 stalks celery, sliced
2 cups cooked dried lima beans
3/4 cup bean liquid
1 teaspoon Worcestershire sauce
1/2 teaspoon chili powder
Salt and pepper to taste
3/4 cup shredded sharp Cheddar cheese

Cook beef, onion, garlic, and celery, stirring with fork, until meat loses its red color.

Add remaining ingredients, except cheese. Bring to boil; cover, and simmer 10 minutes, stirring occasionally. Add cheese. Serves 4.

CREAMED HAMBURG-
CABBAGE SKILLET

3/4 pound hamburger
1/2 cup diced onion
3 tablespoons fat
4 cups coarsely chopped cabbage
1/4 cup flour
1 1/2 teaspoons salt
1/4 teaspoon paprika
1/2 teaspoon celery seed
2 cups milk

Brown hamburger and onion in hot fat. Add cabbage. Fry lightly with onion and hamburger. Add flour and seasonings. Blend into mixture.

Pour milk over all. Cover. Simmer 15 to 20 minutes, or until cabbage is tender. Serves 6.

BEEF WITH SPANISH RICE

2 tablespoons fat
3/4 cup rice
2 tablespoons chopped onion
3 tablespoons chopped celery
1 pound hamburger
1 tablespoon salt
2 1/2 cups tomatoes (No. 2 can)
1 cup bouillon
1 teaspoon soy sauce
1 teaspoon sugar

Brown rice slowly in hot fat in heavy skillet, stirring constantly.

Add onion, celery, and hamburger, and continue browning.

Add remaining ingredients. Cover and simmer 45 minutes or until rice is tender. Serves 4.

BEEF DINNER-IN-A-SKILLET

1/2 pound ground beef
1 slightly beaten egg
1/4 cup milk
1/4 cup fine dry breadcrumbs
1 1/2 tablespoons finely chopped onion
1/2 teaspoon salt
1/4 teaspoon dry mustard
Few grains pepper
2 tablespoons flour
1/4 cup salad oil
1 10 1/2-ounce can condensed soup (tomato or cream of mushroom)
3/4 cup milk
1 1/2 cups cooked assorted vegetables
1/2 teaspoon salt

Combine first 8 ingredients. Shape into 12 small meat balls, using about 1 tablespoon meat mixture for each. Roll in flour.

Heat salad oil in skillet over medium heat about 3 minutes. Add meat balls and fry about 10 minutes. When brown, arrange meat balls around the side.

Gradually pour condensed soup and milk which have been mixed together in center of skillet.

Place vegetables over soup; add salt. Cover and simmer about 10 minutes. Serves 4.

Note: One 12-ounce package frozen mixed vegetables may be substituted for the cooked vegetables. Allow an additional 15 minutes for cooking.

Beef Dinner-in-a-Skillet

Miscellaneous Ground Beef Recipes

CORNISH PASTIES

A pasty is a small pie or turnover of meat wrapped in pastry. Some are baked; others are fried. The most famous is the Cornish pasty, named after Cornwall, England; its filling is beef, potatoes, onions, and sometimes carrots.

Pastry:

- 3 cups sifted enriched flour
- 1 teaspoon salt
- 1 cup shortening
- About ½ cup water

Filling:

- 1 pound ground beef
- 1 tablespoon fat
- 1 cup cubed potatoes
- 1 cup cubed carrots
- ½ cup chopped onion
- 1½ teaspoons salt

Prepare pastry from flour, salt, shortening, and water. Roll out into 6-inch circles.

Brown meat in hot fat in heavy skillet. Add potatoes, carrots, onion, and salt. Cook 5 minutes.

Place equal portions of filling on half of each pastry circle. Moisten edges with water. Fold over half of circle and seal with a fork. Place on baking sheet.

Bake in very hot oven (450°F.) 15 minutes. Reduce heat to moderate (350°F.) and bake 30 minutes longer.

Serve hot with ketchup, hot gravy, or mushroom sauce. Makes 6 pasties.

STUFFED HAMBURGER PIE

- 1 pound hamburger
- 1 teaspoon salt
- ¼ cup milk
- 2 cups soft bread cubes
- ½ cup grated raw carrot
- ¼ cup finely chopped celery
- 1 tablespoon finely chopped onion
- 1 teaspoon salt
- ½ teaspoon poultry seasoning

Mix hamburger, salt, and milk. Make a stuffing of remaining ingredients.

Place half of meat mixture in an 8-inch pie plate. Place stuffing on top of meat. Top with remaining meat, pack-

Twin Beef Turnovers

ing firmly.

Bake in a hot oven (400°F.) for 25 minutes. Serves 4.

Note: Vegetables will be crisp. If a softer texture is desired, precook carrots and celery 5 minutes before adding to stuffing.

GROUND BEEF COMPANY CASSEROLE

- 1 pound ground beef
- 1 tablespoon butter or margarine
- 2 8-ounce cans tomato sauce
- 8 ounces noodles
- 1 cup cottage cheese
- 8 ounces cream cheese
- ¼ cup thick sour cream
- ⅓ cup chopped green onions
- 1 tablespoon chopped green pepper
- 2 tablespoons melted butter or margarine

Brown meat in 1 tablespoon butter in heavy skillet. Stir in tomato sauce. Remove from heat.

Cook noodles in boiling salted water 10 minutes. Drain.

Combine cottage cheese, cream cheese, sour cream, onions, and green pepper.

Spread half the noodles in a buttered 2-quart casserole. Cover with cheese mixture; then cover with remaining noodles. Pour the melted butter over noodles. Pat the beef-tomato sauce mixture over top. Bake in moderate oven (350°F.) 20 to 30 minutes. Serves 6.

TWIN BEEF TURNOVERS

- 4 tablespoons butter or margarine
- ¼ cup chopped onion
- ¼ cup chopped green pepper
- 1 pound ground beef
- 2 cups canned peas, drained
- ½ cup shredded carrot
- 1 teaspoon salt
- ¼ teaspoon pepper
- 3 tablespoons flour

Pastry made with 2½ cups flour

Melt butter or margarine in skillet; add onion, green pepper, and beef; brown lightly.

Add peas and carrots and sprinkle with salt, pepper, and flour. Stir well.

Prepare pastry dough and divide in half. Roll each into a 12-inch circle on floured pastry cloth. Remove to cooky sheet.

Pile filling on half of each circle. Moisten edges of dough with water. Fold pastry over filling like a giant turnover and press edges together to seal. Cut open design for escape of steam.

Bake in very hot oven (450°F.) 15 minutes. Reduce heat to moderate (375°F.) and continue baking for 20 minutes. Serves 6.

HAMBURGER - VEGETABLE PIE

- 1 pound hamburger
- 1 teaspoon onion salt
- Salt and pepper
- 2 teaspoons prepared mustard
- 2 teaspoons Worcestershire sauce
- 2 tablespoons fat
- 1 can beef gravy
- 1 8-ounce can tomato sauce
- 1 No. 2 can green peas, drained, or use 3 to 4 cups leftover vegetables
- 1 No. 2 can onions, drained

Combine hamburger, onion salt, salt, pepper, mustard, and Worcestershire sauce; form into 8 patties; brown in fat.

Remove patties; add gravy and tomato sauce to pan; heat.

Arrange patties, peas, and onions in casserole. Add gravy.

Make biscuits, using 1½ cups biscuit mix, according to package directions; place on casserole.

Bake in very hot oven (450°F.) 20 minutes. Serves 4.

GROUND BEEF AND MACARONI (Italian Style)

- ¾ pound macaroni or spaghetti
- 1 can (6 ounces) tomato paste
- 1½ cups water
- ¼ teaspoon baking soda
- ½ pound bacon, cut in small pieces
- 1 pound ground beef
- ½ pound sliced fresh mushrooms
- ½ cup finely sliced green pepper
- ½ cup chopped onions
- 1½ teaspoons salt
- ⅛ teaspoon oregano
- 1 medium clove garlic, chopped fine
- ¼ cup chopped parsley
- ¾ cup grated Parmesan cheese

Cook macaroni in boiling salted water until tender; rinse with cold water.

Combine tomato paste, water, and baking soda.

Fry bacon in a saucepan until medium done, then add ground beef, stirring constantly, about 5 minutes.

In another saucepan, fry mushrooms and green pepper in 2 tablespoons butter about 5 minutes. Add all vegetables, seasonings, and half of tomato mixture to meat. Cover pan and cook about 7 minutes.

Place half of the cooked macaroni in well greased casserole (8 x 12 x 1½ inches). Sprinkle with half the Parmesan cheese. Cover with all of the meat and vegetable mixture. Then cover with remaining macaroni mixture. Sprinkle with remaining Parmesan cheese. Finally, top with remaining half of tomato mixture. Cover casserole tightly. Bake in moderate oven (375°F.) 30 minutes. Serves 8.

HAMBURGER PIE WITH GREEN BEANS

1 pound hamburger
1 cup chopped onion
1 tablespoon fat
1 10½-ounce can condensed cream of tomato soup
1½ teaspoons salt
1 cup cooked green beans
1 egg
2 tablespoons butter or margarine
3 cups mashed potatoes

Cook hamburger and onion in melted fat in heavy skillet. Stir and cook until they are browned.

Mix in soup, 1 teaspoon salt, and green beans. Place in a 1½-quart casserole.

Mix egg, butter, and ½ teaspoon salt with mashed potatoes. Place potatoes on top of meat-and-bean mixture in casserole. Bake in moderate oven (350°F.) 30 minutes. Serves 4 to 6.

HAMBURGER SWEET POTATO PIE

1 cup corn flakes
½ cup soft breadcrumbs
2 tablespoons butter or margarine
¾ pound ground beef
1 egg
1 teaspoon salt
⅛ teaspoon pepper
⅛ teaspoon thyme
⅛ teaspoon sage
1 bay leaf, crumbled
1 small onion, minced
3 cups hot, seasoned mashed sweet potato
Paprika

Crumble corn flakes with crumbs, and spread on bottom and sides of greased, deep 8-inch pie pan. Dot with butter, and put in oven until butter melts.

Mix beef, egg, seasonings, and onion; spread in crumbed pan, and bake in moderate oven (350°F.) 10 minutes.

Whip potatoes until light. Arrange around edge of pie pan; sprinkle with paprika. Return to oven 10 minutes, or until lightly browned. Serves 4.

PEDERNALES RIVER CHILI
(Mrs. Lyndon B. Johnson's Recipe)

4 pounds chili meat**
1 large onion, chopped
2 cloves garlic
1 teaspoon ground oregano
1 teaspoon comino seed
6 teaspoons chili powder, (more if needed)
1½ cups canned whole tomatoes
2 to 6 generous dashes liquid hot pepper sauce
Salt to taste
2 cups hot water

Place meat, onion, and garlic in large heavy frying pan or Dutch oven. Cook until light-colored.

Add oregano, comino seed, chili powder, tomatoes, hot pepper sauce, salt, and hot water. Bring to boil, lower heat, and simmer about 1 hour. Skim off fat during cooking. Serves 8 to 10.

**Chili meat is coarsely ground round steak or well-trimmed chuck meat. If specially ground, ask meat man to use ¾-inch plate for coarse grind.

GROUND BEEF PARTY CASSEROLE

1 pound ground beef
1 cup chopped onions
2 cups canned or cooked tomatoes
1 teaspoon chili powder or curry powder, or 1 tablespoon Worcestershire sauce
2 teaspoons salt
2 potatoes, sliced thin
⅓ cup flour
2 cups drained whole kernel corn
2 cups drained, cooked lima beans
½ cup sliced green pepper
1½ cups shredded cheese or buttered crumbs

Combine beef, onions, tomatoes, chili powder, and salt. Pat into 1-inch layer in 3-quart casserole.

Over this place layers of potatoes, flour, corn, lima beans, and green pepper. Top with cheese or crumbs.

Bake in moderate oven (350°F.) 1 hour. Serves 8 to 10.

SCALLOPED BEEF AND EGGPLANT

1½ pounds ground chuck
1 teaspoon onion salt
¼ teaspoon pepper
2 tablespoons salad oil
1 medium eggplant
⅓ cup flour
½ teaspoon salt
⅛ teaspoon pepper
¼ cup salad oil
2 8-ounce cans tomato sauce
1 cup grated sharp American cheese
¼ teaspoon oregano

Mix ground beef, onion salt, and ¼ teaspoon pepper; lightly form into 8 patties. Sauté patties in 2 tablespoons hot salad oil until brown on both sides but rare inside. Remove from skillet.

Cut washed eggplant into 8 ½-inch thick slices. Sprinkle with mixture of flour, salt, and ⅛ teaspoon pepper. Sauté in ¼ cup hot salad oil until golden on both sides.

Arrange half of eggplant slices with half of patties in greased casserole (12 x 8 x 2-inches). Spread with 1 can tomato sauce. Sprinkle with half of cheese and oregano. Repeat layers.

Bake uncovered in moderate oven (350°F.) until cheese is bubbly, about 30 minutes. Serves 4.

GROUND BEEF À LA GRUCCI

1 green pepper, chopped fine
1 pound ground beef
2 tablespoons olive oil
½ pound sharp cheese, grated
1 small onion, grated
1 clove garlic, crushed
½ cup sliced stuffed olives
½ cup sliced ripe olives
¼ cup olive liquid
¼ pound noodles, cooked
1 can whole kernel corn
1 No. 2 can tomatoes
½ teaspoon salt
¼ teaspoon pepper

Blend green pepper with meat and brown in olive oil. Add remaining ingredients and blend thoroughly. Pour into greased casserole. Bake in moderate oven (350°F.) 45 to 60 minutes. Serves 8.

CREOLE MEAT SHORTCAKES
Meat Sauce:

½ pound hamburger
2 tablespoons chopped onion
½ cup finely chopped celery
2 tablespoons fat
2 tablespoons flour
1 cup boiling water
½ teaspoon chili powder
1 teaspoon salt
½ teaspoon Worcestershire sauce
2 cups cooked tomatoes
1 tablespoon chopped green pepper

Biscuit:

2½ cups biscuit mix
About 1 cup milk

Brown the hamburger, onion, and celery in fat. Stir in flour. Add water to make a sauce. Add seasonings, tomatoes, and green pepper. Cook slowly 1 hour.

Put biscuit mix into mixing bowl. Pour milk quickly into dry ingredients. Stir until well blended. Turn onto lightly floured board. Knead 6 times. Roll or pat to ½-inch thickness. Cut 6 biscuits with 3-inch cutter.

Place on baking sheet and bake in a very hot oven (450°F.) 15 minutes.

Serve hot with ⅔ cup meat sauce, between and over top of each split biscuit. Serves 6.

CREAMED HAMBURGER AND EGGS

½ pound hamburger
1 10½-ounce can condensed cream of celery soup
1 cup milk
4 hard-cooked eggs, sliced
4 slices hot buttered toast

Stir and cook hamburger until red color disappears. Stir in celery soup and milk. Heat.

Stir in sliced eggs carefully. Serve hot on hot toast or in patty shells. Serves 4.

Miscellaneous Ground Meats— Pork, Ham, Lamb, and Veal

BROILED LAMB PATTIES

Use ground lamb shoulder or breast, allowing 1/4 pound per person.

Season with salt and pepper; shape into patties 1 inch thick and 3 inches in diameter.

If desired, wrap bacon strip around each patty; fasten with pick.

Place on broiler rack, with top of food 2 inches below unit or tip of flame. Broil, turning when 1/2 total cooking time is completed.

For medium patties, allow 18 minutes; for well done, allow 20 to 24 minutes.

Pan-Broiled Lamb Patties: Prepare patties as above. Rub heavy skillet with small amount of fat or salad oil. Brown patties on both sides.

Cook slowly, turning frequently, about 10 to 12 minutes, or until done, pouring off any fat which accumulates.

SAVOY CABBAGE, STUFFED WHOLE

1 Savoy cabbage
1 pound ground veal
3/4 pound ground cooked ham
1 medium onion, chopped
1 garlic clove, minced
1 1/2 teaspoons salt
Few grains pepper
1 teaspoon Ac'cent
2 chicken bouillon cubes
1 cup boiling water
1 bay leaf, crumbled
1/4 teaspoon thyme

Hold cabbage under running hot water and gently separate leaves without removing them, being careful not to tear them. Drain thoroughly.

Combine ground meats, onion, garlic, salt, pepper, and Ac'cent. Stuff meat mixture between cabbage leaves. Tie firmly with string.

Place cabbage in deep saucepan slightly larger than the cabbage in diameter.

Dissolve bouillon cubes in the boiling water. Pour over cabbage; add bay leaf and thyme.

Cover saucepan tightly. Simmer 1 1/2 hours or until tender. Remove strings. Serves 6.

Savoy Cabbage, Stuffed Whole

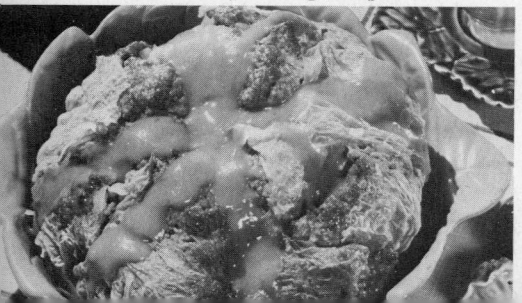

Lamb Patties

TOURTIERE (CANADIAN PORK PIE)

1 teaspoon salt
1/4 teaspoon pepper
1/4 teaspoon nutmeg
1 clove garlic
1/8 teaspoon mace
Few grains cayenne pepper (optional)
1/2 tablespoon cornstarch
1 cup water
1 pound ground lean pork (shoulder or leg)
Pastry for 2-crust, 8-inch pie

Add seasonings, cornstarch, and water to pork, and simmer covered in a kettle or saucepan 30 minutes.

Uncover and cook 10 minutes more. Remove garlic.

Pour mixture into pastry-lined 8-inch pie pan. Cover with top pastry which has been pricked in several places to allow escape of steam during baking. Fold upper crust over bottom crust at edge and press together firmly.

Bake in hot oven (425°F.) about 10 minutes. Then reduce heat to moderate (350°F.) and continue baking 30 minutes more. Serve hot. Makes 1 8-inch pie or 6 servings.

Here are two famous Mexican dishes, so easy to prepare. Empanadas: light pastry surrounding a chili, pork, and tomato filling which is also served as a sauce. For dessert, try a Mexican Flan: banana flavored caramel custard garnished with mandarin orange sections, rich but so good.

PORK EMPANADAS

Empanadas are turnovers made with a pie crust (often spicy) and with a vast variety of fillings, either sweet or spicy, popular in Mexico and in most other South and Central American countries. Mincemeat makes a very desirable filling. They may be baked or fried, served hot or cold, and served as an appetizer, main dish, or dessert. If served as an hors d'oeuvre, they should be made very small. The version given below should be served hot as a main dish.

2 cups sifted all-purpose flour
1 teaspoon salt
3/4 cup shortening
4 to 5 tablespoons ice water
2 medium onions, chopped
2 tablespoons butter or margarine
1 1/2 pounds ground pork
1 6-ounce can tomato paste
1/2 cup chopped pimiento
1/3 cup chopped pitted olives
2 hard-cooked eggs, chopped
1/2 cup tomato ketchup
3 tablespoons chili powder
1 teaspoon salt
1/8 teaspoon ground black pepper
1/4 teaspoon ground cumin
1 to 1 1/2 cups chicken broth

Sift flour and salt. Cut in shortening until mixture resembles breadcrumbs. Add water. Toss lightly until dough forms a ball. Chill until ready to use.

In a skillet sauté onion in butter or margarine, add pork and sauté until cooked. Drain off excess fat. Add tomato paste, pimiento, olives, hard-cooked eggs, ketchup, chili powder, salt, pepper, and cumin. Mix well.

Roll dough out on a floured board to 1/10-inch thickness. Cut into circles about 5 inches in diameter. Makes 12.

Place 1 tablespoon of pork mixture on one half of the dough. Brush edges with water. Fold over and seal edges firmly.

Place on an ungreased baking sheet. Bake in hot oven (425°F.) 15 to 20 minutes or until golden brown. Add chicken broth to remaining meat mixture to make a sauce consistency. Pour over empanadas. Makes 12 empanadas.

Veal and Ham Loaf

VEAL AND HAM LOAF

2 pounds veal shoulder, ground
½ pound ham, ground
3 tablespoons minced parsley
2 tablespoons grated onion
1½ cups soft breadcrumbs
½ cup evaporated milk
1 unbeaten egg
1 teaspoon salt
⅛ teaspoon pepper
1½ teaspoons Ac'cent
¼ teaspoon Tabasco sauce
Canned pineapple slices
¼ cup brown sugar

Combine veal, ham, parsley, onion, crumbs, evaporated milk, egg, and seasonings; mix well.

Arrange pineapple slices in a design in bottom of greased loaf pan (9 x 5 x 3 inches). Sprinkle with brown sugar.

Pack meat mixture in loaf pan. Cover with aluminum foil.

Bake in moderate oven (350°F.) ½ hour; remove foil. Continue baking 1 hour longer. Serves 8.

STUFFED CABBAGE ROLLS

¾ pound ground beef
½ pound ground pork
1½ teaspoons salt
½ teaspoon pepper
½ cup grated raw onion
½ cup raw rice
1 head cabbage

Combine all ingredients except cabbage. Remove core from cabbage and place in boiling water for a few minutes to wilt leaves.

Shape meat and rice mixture into loose rolls and wrap each meat roll in a cabbage leaf. Fasten with a wooden pick. Place in baking dish.

Cover with water. Cover and cook in moderate oven (350°F.) for 1½ hours, or until rice is done. Serves 6.

Stuffed Cabbage Rolls

HAM-PINEAPPLE LOAF

1 pound ground ham
½ pound ground pork
¾ cup milk
½ cup breadcrumbs
Pepper
1 No. 2 can (2½ cups) pineapple pie filling
½ cup seedless raisins
2 tablespoons prepared mustard
½ teaspoon horseradish

Combine ham, pork, milk, breadcrumbs, and pepper. Pat out to a 15 x 10-inch rectangle on waxed paper.

Combine pie filling, raisins, mustard, and horseradish; spoon one-half of mixture down center of meat rectangle. Spread to cover meat but do not bring to the edges. Lifting waxed paper, roll jelly roll fashion starting at the short end. Pat ends to seal.

Wrap loaf in waxed paper and refrigerate about 2 hours. Place in a 7 x 11 x 2-inch baking dish. Bake in moderate oven (350°F.) 1 hour; spoon remaining pineapple sauce over loaf and bake 15 to 20 minutes longer. Serves 6 to 8.

Ham-Pineapple Loaf

INDIVIDUAL HAM LOAVES

¾ pound smoked ham, ground fine
¾ pound lean pork, ground fine
½ teaspoon salt
Dash of pepper
3 tablespoons finely chopped onion
½ cup fine breadcrumbs
1 egg, beaten
¾ cup milk

Combine ingredients and mix well. Pack lightly in large muffin pans.

Bake in moderate oven (350°F.) 45 minutes. Serve with horseradish sauce or mustard sauce.

The mixture may be baked in a loaf pan, 9½ x 5¼ x 2¾ inches, if desired. Serves 6 to 8.

ORANGE UPSIDE-DOWN HAM LOAVES

6 tablespoons brown sugar
½ teaspoon dry mustard
6 thin unpeeled orange slices
2 cups ground, cooked ham
1 pound pork-sausage meat
1 small onion, minced

½ cup fresh breadcrumbs
1 egg
½ cup orange juice
½ teaspoon paprika
½ teaspoon Worcestershire sauce
½ teaspoon dry mustard
Pinch of ground cloves

In each of 6 custard cups or individual casseroles (about 3½ inches in diameter) place 1 tablespoon brown sugar; sprinkle on a little of mustard; top with orange slice.

Combine ham and remaining ingredients; pack lightly into cups.

Bake in moderate oven (350°F.) 45 minutes; let stand 5 minutes. Drain; then invert onto serving platter. Serves 6.

Note: This may also be baked in 9 x 5 x 3-inch loaf pan, 1¼ hours, using 3 or 4 orange slices.

BEEF AND PORK COMPANY LOAF

1½ pounds ground beef
½ pound ground pork
¼ cup finely chopped onion
2 teaspoons salt
¼ teaspoon pepper
¼ teaspoon sage
¼ teaspoon poultry seasoning
1 tablespoon Worcestershire sauce
2 eggs
1 cup tomato juice
4 slices bread

Combine meat with onions and seasonings.

Beat eggs and add to tomato juice. Cube bread and soak in liquid mixture. Beat well. Add to meat and mix lightly.

Pack into a 5 x 9-inch meat loaf pan and bake in moderate oven (350°F.) 1¼ hours.

Let loaf stand 10 minutes, then drain off liquid and turn out of pan. Spread with ketchup or hot tomato sauce. Serves 6 to 8.

Variation: If desired, the loaf may be spread with ⅓ cup ketchup before baking. This adds moisture and interesting flavor.

Beef and Pork Company Loaf

PINEAPPLE UPSIDE DOWN HAM LOAF

Topping:

1 tablespoon butter or margarine
2 tablespoons molasses
1 tablespoon sugar
3 slices pineapple
3 maraschino cherries

Ham Loaf:

2½ cups (1 pound) cooked, ground ham
2 cups (1 pound) uncooked, ground pork
1 cup crushed corn flakes
½ teaspoon salt
¼ teaspoon pepper
1 teaspoon dry mustard
2 beaten eggs
¼ cup milk

Melt butter or margarine in 4 x 9 x 3-inch loaf pan, measured across bottom. Stir in molasses and sugar; spread uniformly over bottom of pan.

Arrange pineapple and cherries over molasses-butter mixture.

Mix all ingredients for ham loaf in order given.

Spread mixture in pan over pineapple; press down. Bake in moderate oven (350°F.) 1 hour.

Turn out on hot platter with pineapple and cherries on top. Yield: 16 slices, ½-inch thick.

KEBI (Syrian National Dish)

1 pound ground lamb
1 pound fine bourlgour (cracked wheat)
3 onions, chopped
1 pound cooked meat, chopped
1 cup pine nuts (pignolia)

Mix together the lamb and bourlgour and knead thoroughly, adding a small amount of water.

Sear onions in a little hot fat; combine with cooked meat and pine nuts. Season with salt and pepper.

Place a layer of half the lamb mixture in a baking dish. Add a layer of the second mixture (cooked meat). Cover with a layer of the first mixture (lamb).

Cut into diamond-shaped pieces and lightly cover with butter or olive oil. Bake in moderate oven (350°F.) 1 hour. Serves 8.

Note: Bourlgour (cracked wheat) can be bought in Armenian, Syrian, and Greek stores.

LEMON PORK LOAF

2 pounds ground pork
4 cups breadcrumbs
1 beaten egg
2 teaspoons salt
Grated rind of 3 lemons
6 slices bacon
1 cup sour cream or chopped tomatoes
Paprika

Combine ground pork, breadcrumbs, egg, seasonings, and grated lemon rind; shape into loaf.

Place in baking dish and add water to cover bottom of dish. Cover with bacon slices.

Bake covered in moderate oven (350°F.) 1 hour. Remove cover and pour over sour cream or tomatoes. Sprinkle with paprika. Bake 30 minutes longer. Serves 8 to 10.

LAMB AND BACON WHIRLS

½ pound sliced bacon
1½ pounds ground lamb shoulder
1 teaspoon salt
⅛ teaspoon pepper
¼ teaspoon marjoram
1 tablespoon Worcestershire sauce
1 cup crushed corn flakes
3 tablespoons water

Place bacon on waxed paper on a cutting board so that the lean edge overlaps the preceding strip about 1 inch.

Combine remaining ingredients and mix well. Spread out in an even layer over the bacon.

Roll up like a jelly roll and fasten with toothpicks or skewers.

Slice in serving-size rounds, and broil or pan-broil, allowing about 8 to 10 minutes on each side. Serves 8.

STUFFED CABBAGE CASSEROLE

1 small cabbage
1 medium onion, minced
2 tablespoons butter or margarine
1 pound lamb shoulder, ground (about 2 cups)
2 cups cooked rice
1 teaspoon salt
Few grains pepper
1 teaspoon Ac'cent
½ teaspoon paprika
½ cup ketchup
1 tablespoon lemon juice
1 teaspoon sugar
1 teaspoon dried mint leaves

Cook cabbage in boiling salted water to cover 15 minutes. Cool. Strip off leaves.

Cook onion in butter or margarine until soft but not brown; combine with remaining ingredients.

Line shallow baking dish with large cabbage leaves.

Make 6 "cups" of smaller cabbage leaves; fill cups with meat mixture. Cover with remaining large leaves.

Bake in moderate oven (350°F.) 1 hour. Serve with a tomato sauce. Serves 6.

Lamb and Bacon Whirls

CURRIED LAMB PATTIES

1½ pounds ground lean lamb
1 large onion, finely chopped
2 tablespoons quick-cooking tapioca
1½ cups milk
2 teaspoons salt
¼ teaspoon pepper
1 teaspoon Ac'cent
1 teaspoon curry powder

Place all ingredients in bowl; blend lightly but thoroughly.

Form into small patties. Roll in flour and brown well in hot oil or fat.

Pour off excess fat; add enough hot water to cover meat. Cover and cook over low heat until meat is tender, about 30 minutes.

As gravy cooks down, add a few spoons hot water. Thicken gravy. Turn meat and gravy out on hot platter; surround with a border of hot buttered rice or noodles. Serves 6.

Stuffed Cabbage Casserole

CHOPPED LAMB PILAF
(Armenian)

1 pound chopped or ground lamb shoulder
1 onion, chopped
1 No. 2 can tomatoes
2 teaspoons allspice
1/2 teaspoon cinnamon
1 teaspoon marjoram
Salt to taste
1/2 cup sherry
2 cups precooked rice
2 tablespoons butter or olive oil

Sauté lamb in a large skillet until lightly browned, pouring off excess fat.

Add onion and cook slowly for 5 minutes. Then stir in chopped tomatoes and juice and cook for about 15 minutes. Add seasonings and wine.

Cook raw rice in butter or olive oil until rice turns light golden color.

Form a hollow in center of lamb mixture; fill with rice. Liquid should cover both meat and rice, so add water, if necessary, to supplement tomatoes. Bring to a boil, cover, and cook slowly for about 15 minutes.

Turn heat off and, with cover still on pan, let rice steam fluffy for about 10 minutes longer.

To serve, fill warm casserole dish and garnish with chopped fresh parsley, green onions, and tomatoes. Serves 4.

LAMB LOAF

2 pounds ground lamb
2 teaspoons salt
1/4 teaspoon black pepper
1/2 clove garlic, minced (optional)
2 tablespoons minced onion
1 green pepper, finely chopped
2 tablespoons chopped parsley
1 beaten egg
1 cup milk
1 cup crumbled cracker crumbs

Mix ingredients thoroughly. Pack into greased loaf pan or ring mold.

Bake in slow oven (325°F.) 1 hour and 20 minutes. If desired, serve with an olive sauce. Serves 8.

Olive Sauce: Blend 1/4 cup butter or drippings and 1/4 cup flour. Add 2 cups milk gradually and stir over moderate heat until thickened.

Add 1/3 cup sliced or chopped stuffed olives and salt and pepper to taste.

SWEDISH HAM BALLS IN SWEET-SOUR SAUCE

1 1/2 pounds fresh boneless pork, ground
1 pound ground cooked ham
2 cups cracker or breadcrumbs
2 well beaten eggs
1 cup milk
Salt and Ac'cent

Combine pork, ham, crumbs, beaten eggs, milk, and seasonings; mix well. Form into small round balls about the size of a walnut. Place in shallow 9-inch baking dish.

Bake in moderate oven (350°F.), basting frequently with sweet-sour sauce (below) until meat is tender, about 50 minutes.

Sweet-Sour Sauce:

1 cup brown sugar, firmly packed
1 teaspoon dry mustard
1/2 cup vinegar
1/2 cup hot water
1/4 cup small raisins

Combine ingredients, stirring to dissolve sugar. Pour over ham balls after they have begun to cook, about 10 minutes after placing in oven.

VEAL LOAF

2 pounds ground veal
1/2 pound ground pork
1/4 pound ground suet
1/2 pound sliced mushrooms
2 tablespoons butter
2 teaspoons salt
1/2 teaspoon pepper
1 teaspoon marjoram
1 teaspoon chopped parsley
2 beaten eggs
1 10 1/2-ounce can tomato soup, undiluted

Grind meat together. Cook mushrooms in butter for 5 minutes. Add to meat along with seasonings, parsley, eggs, and soup. Shape into loaf.

Bake in moderate oven (350°F.) for 1 hour. Bacon may be placed on top of loaf before baking. Serves 10.

BITOCHKY SMETANA
(Russian Meat Balls)

1 1/2 pounds ground veal
4 medium-sized potatoes, cooked and chopped
1 1/2 small onions, grated
1 1/2 teaspoons salt
1/8 teaspoon pepper
1 egg, beaten
1/4 cup butter or margarine
1 1/4 cups heavy sour cream

Mix together veal, potatoes, onions, seasonings, and egg. Shape in round balls and fry in butter until well browned.

Add 3/4 cup sour cream and simmer, covered, 15 minutes.

Just before serving, add remaining 1/2 cup cream and bring to a boil. Makes 12 balls (6 servings).

LAMB PATTIES WITH BURGUNDY

1 onion, minced
1 1/2 cups dry breadcrumbs
3/4 cup burgundy
1 well beaten egg
1 pound ground lamb
1 1/2 teaspoons salt

1/4 teaspoon pepper

Mix onion and breadcrumbs together; add wine and egg. Mix well. Combine with meat and seasonings.

Shape into 8 small patties or loaves. Pan-fry slowly in hot fat. Serves 4.

BAKED PORK LOAF WITH MUSHROOM GRAVY

2 pounds fresh, lean pork shoulder
1/2 pound smoked picnic ham
3 cups corn flakes, crushed
2 eggs, beaten
1 (11-ounce) can condensed tomato soup
1 teaspoon salt
Few grains pepper
1 teaspoon Ac'cent
1 (11-ounce) can condensed mushroom soup
1/2 cup water

Have the fresh pork and ham ground together. Place meat in bowl; add corn flakes, eggs, tomato soup, salt, pepper, and Ac'cent. Mix lightly but thoroughly.

Pack into loaf pan. Bake in moderate oven (375°F.) about 1 1/2 hours. Pour off fat after loaf is baked.

Heat mushroom soup and water together to make gravy. Serves 6.

ORIENTAL LAMBURGERS

2 pounds ground lamb shoulder
1 clove garlic, chopped fine
1 1/2 teaspoons salt
1 teaspoon pepper
3 tablespoons shelled pine nuts
1/4 cup chopped parsley
1 egg
8 slices bacon

Mix the lamb with garlic, salt, pepper, pine nuts, and parsley. Add egg, slightly beaten, and mix well. Form into round patties.

Wrap each patty with a slice of bacon and secure with a small skewer or wooden pick.

Broil slowly and turn so that lamb is browned on both sides and cooked through but with a tinge of pink in the middle.

Serve lamburgers with English mustard or with your favorite barbecue sauce. Makes 8 patties.

SAVORY HAM AND PORK BALLS

1 pound ground ham
3/4 pound ground pork
1 beaten egg
1/4 cup milk
1/8 teaspoon pepper

Mix all ingredients and shape into 2 1/2-inch balls. Brown slowly in a shallow pan with a small amount of fat.

Add enough water to just cover the bottom of the pan. Cover tightly and simmer gently for 45 minutes. Serve with chili sauce. Makes 8 balls.

Pork Recipes

HINTS FOR COOKING PORK

Some cuts of pork are in demand as fresh pork, while others are in greatest demand as cured pork. Many pork cuts are sold both fresh and cured.

All cuts of pork are tender, therefore all large or chunky cuts, both fresh and cured, may be cooked by roasting. Roasting of cured (smoked) cuts is usually referred to as "baking." Roasting and baking, however, so far as meat is concerned, are synonymous.

Fresh pork is usually roasted at 350°F., and cured pork at 300°F. or 325°F. Slow cooking helps retain much of the flavor of pork. The use of a meat thermometer is desirable. Specific times are given in each recipe or consult the time charts.

Pork chops, cutlets, sliced fresh ham or shoulder, and sliced pork liver are best if cooked by braising, rather than by broiling, pan-broiling, or griddle-broiling. Braising cooks them well done without drying them out. They may also be cooked by frying.

Sliced cured ham and bacon may be pan-fried, deep-fat fried, or oven-cooked on a rack in an open roasting pan at 325°F.

Pork should always be cooked well done. The cooked lean of fresh pork should be grayish white without even a tinge of pink.

FRESH PORK ROASTING CHART
Roasted at 350°F.
Oven Temperature

Cut	Meat Thermometer Reading	Minutes Per Lb.
Loin:		
Center	185°F.	35–40
Whole	185°F.	15–20
Ends	185°F.	45–50
Shoulder:		
Rolled	185°F.	45–50
Cushion	185°F.	35–40
Boston Butt	185°F.	45–50
Leg or Ham	185°F.	30–35
Spareribs		30–35
Pork and Ham Loaf		30–35

PORK ROAST
(Master Recipe)

If rib of loin is selected, have the meat man separate backbone from ribs to make carving easy.

Season with salt and pepper. If desired, rub with cut clove of garlic and dredge with flour.

Place in shallow pan, fat side up. Roast in preheated moderate oven (350°F.).

For center loin cut weighing 4 to 5 pounds, allow 35 to 40 minutes per pound.

For end cuts weighing 4 to 5 pounds, allow 45 to 50 minutes per pound.

Do not cover. Do not add water.

If meat thermometer is used, insert so that bulb is in center of the largest part.

Roast until well done or thermometer registers 185°F.

Rib roast may be boned, stuffed, rolled, and cooked in same manner. With boned and rolled pork roasts, add 10 to 15 minutes per pound to cooking time.

CROWN ROAST OF PORK

Have meat man prepare crown of 10 or 12 ribs. Season with salt and pepper. Tie strips of salt pork or bacon around end of each rib to keep bones from charring.

Put in roasting pan bone-ends-up. Fill center with favorite stuffing.

Roast in moderate oven (350°F.), allowing 30 to 35 minutes per pound.

To serve, place paper frills over bone ends. If stuffing isn't used, do not cover bones and cook roast upside down.

Fill center with vegetables when serving. Serves 10 to 12.

ROLLED SHOULDER OF PORK

Have the shoulder boned and rolled. Prepare meat as suggested under Pork Roast. Place on rack in shallow pan. Put the removed bones in the pan.

Roast in moderate oven (350°F.), allowing 45 minutes per pound. Turn every 30 minutes. Prepare gravy from drippings.

BAKED STUFFED TENDERLOIN ROLL

Have 2 tenderloins split and flattened. Season with salt and pepper.

Spread bread, mushroom, or potato stuffing over one. Lay the other on top. Roll and tie securely.

Sprinkle outside with salt and pepper. Put 4 or 5 slices bacon over top.

Place on rack in open roasting pan. Roast in slow-to-moderate oven (325° or 350°F.) until tender, 1 to 1½ hours.

ROAST FRESH HAM

A fresh ham (leg of pork) is prepared like pork loin roast.

Roast it on rack in uncovered pan in slow oven (325°F.) 35 to 40 minutes per pound for whole ham, 45 to 50 minutes per pound for half leg of pork. "Skin" roast, if necessary, 30 minutes before end of cooking time.

Crown Roast of Pork

FRESH HAM WITH MEXICAN CORN STUFFING

Order an 8- to 12-pound fresh ham, boned and scored. Sprinkle inside cavity of ham generously with Ac'cent; let stand 30 minutes.

Fill cavity with Mexican Corn Stuffing (below). Truss ham to hold shape during roasting.

Place in open roasting pan. Bake in moderate oven (350°F.), allowing 35 to 40 minutes per pound or until ham reaches an internal temperature of 185°F.

Mexican Corn Stuffing:

6	slices bacon, chopped
3	tablespoons bacon fat
¾	cup chopped celery
1	cup chopped onions
1	cup soft breadcrumbs
4	cups canned Mexican corn, drained
½	teaspoon powdered sage
1	teaspoon salt
½	teaspoon pepper
1½	teaspoons Ac'cent

Fry bacon until crisp; drain on absorbent paper.

Measure fat into skillet. Cook celery and onions in hot fat until tender. Add breadcrumbs; toss lightly over high heat until golden.

Add remaining ingredients; mix well; remove from heat.

Fill boned ham cavity; bake as directed above. Garnish with poached oranges (see Index). Serves 10 to 12 generously.

Fresh Ham with Mexican Corn Stuffing

Roast Fresh Shoulder of Pork with Almond-Rice Stuffing

ROAST FRESH SHOULDER OF PORK WITH ALMOND-RICE STUFFING

1 medium onion, chopped fine
1/3 cup butter or margarine
1 teaspoon salt
Few grains pepper
1/2 teaspoon Ac'cent
1 teaspoon poultry seasoning
3 cups cooked rice
1/3 cup chopped roasted almonds
1 boned fresh pork shoulder (about 5 pounds)

Cook onion in butter until soft. Add seasonings, rice, almonds.

Fill cavity in boned fresh pork shoulder. Skewer.

Place on rack in open roaster. Bake in moderate oven (350°F.), calculating 40 minutes per pound of weight before stuffing. Serves 6 to 8.

Gravy: Pour off all but 4 tablespoons of fat from roaster, leaving brown drippings.

Set roaster over low heat; stir in 1/4 cup flour, 1/4 teaspoon Ac'cent, 1 teaspoon salt, few grains pepper.

Slowly add 2 1/2 cups water, blending after each addition. Cook and stir until gravy is smooth and thickened. Add more salt and pepper if necessary. Makes about 2 1/2 cups gravy.

STUFFED ROAST SUCKLING PIG

1 suckling pig, about 10 pounds
1 clove garlic
3 tablespoons butter or margarine
1/2 cup chopped celery
1/4 cup chopped onion
3 cups soft breadcrumbs
1/2 cup apple cider
Dash of ground cloves
Dash of nutmeg
1/4 teaspoon thyme
1/2 teaspoon salt

Wash pig in several waters and dry. Rub inside with cut clove of garlic.

Heat butter and sauté celery and onion until tender but not brown. Mix in remaining ingredients, using enough cider to moisten this stuffing slightly. Stuff pig.

Truss fore and hind legs forward separately under the body. With ice pick or sharp knife, make little gashes in top of pig to allow fat to drain while roasting.

Place a small block of wood in pig's mouth. Cover ears with aluminum foil to prevent burning.

Roast in slow oven (325°F.) 4 hours. Baste frequently with fat from pan.

Remove block from mouth and insert raw apple. Place on large board or platter and garnish as desired. Serves 8 to 10.

BOILED PIGS' FEET

Wash, scrape, and rinse pigs' feet. Put in a large pot with 1/2 sliced onion, 1 bay leaf, and 1/2 teaspoon salt. Cover with cold water. Bring to boiling point and simmer 4 to 6 hours. Store in stock until used.

Serve cold or hot with vinegar. Use one per serving. Serve with sauerkraut and mashed potatoes.

Broiled Pigs' Feet: Boil as above and drain. Sprinkle with salt and pepper.

Place on greased broiler and broil 5 minutes on each side. Serve with vinegar, lemon juice, or Maître d'Hôtel butter.

Fried Pigs' Feet: Boil as above and drain. Dip in a batter of flour, salt, and water. Fry in deep fat (385°F.) until brown. Serve with Maître d'Hôtel butter.

Pickled Pigs' Feet: Boil as above and drain. Pour hot vinegar over the pigs' feet and leave in the liquid for several days. Serve cold.

STEWED PORK NECK BONES

Cover neck bones with seasoned boiling water. Cover and simmer until tender.

Vegetables may be added for the last half hour of cooking.

STEWED PORK HOCKS

Cover pork hocks with seasoned boiling water. Cover and simmer until tender, 1 1/2 to 3 hours.

To cook vegetables with the hocks, add potatoes for the last 1/2 hour of cooking or cabbage or greens for the last 15 minutes of cooking.

JELLIED PIGS' FEET

6 pigs' feet, split into halves
1 cut clove of garlic
1 large onion, sliced
1 lemon, sliced
2 bay leaves
6 whole cloves
4 whole black peppers
White vinegar or dry wine
Salt, if necessary

Cover the washed pigs' feet with water. Bring to boiling point, cover kettle, reduce heat and simmer for 3 hours.

Add remaining ingredients except salt and vinegar or wine. Add boiling water if necessary.

Cover and simmer pigs' feet 1 hour longer.

Strain the stock through a sieve. Remove skin and bones from pigs' feet. Return the meat to the stock and season with salt if necessary and a little vinegar or dry wine.

Pour into mold and chill until firm. If desired, 1 chopped pimiento may be added to the mold before chilling. Serves 6.

FRUITED PORK STEAKS

4 pork shoulder steaks
Flour, salt, paprika
2 cooking apples (Jonathan, Winesap, or Rome Beauty)
Raisins, brown sugar

Trim fat from edge of pork steaks and fry out in large skillet or Dutch oven. Remove pieces.

Flour pork steaks and brown on both sides in hot fat. Sprinkle each side with salt and paprika. Pour off excess fat.

Core apples, but do not pare; cut into thick slices. Top each steak with 1 or 2 apple slices and fill centers with raisins. Sprinkle apples with brown sugar.

Pour 1/4 cup water around steaks. Cover and cook over low heat 45 minutes or until steaks are tender. Baste once or twice during cooking with liquid in pan. Add more water, if needed.

(If desired, pork steaks may be baked with the fruit in a large covered baking dish in moderate oven (350°F.) 45 minutes.) Serves 4.

Fruited Pork Steaks

PORK BIRDS

2 pounds pork shoulder steak, cut very thin
2 teaspoons lemon juice
½ teaspoon salt
¼ teaspoon pepper
¼ teaspoon Ac'cent (optional)
2 cups dry breadcrumbs
½ cup seedless raisins, cut into halves
¾ cup cream or evaporated milk
2 tablespoons flour
2 tablespoons fat
1 cup boiling stock or water

Pound the shoulder steaks to a thickness of ¼ inch. Cut into 6 oblong pieces. Season by rubbing with a mixture of lemon juice, ½ teaspoon salt, pepper, and Ac'cent.

Combine breadcrumbs, raisins, cream or milk, and 1 teaspoon salt. Spread the meat with breadcrumb mixture. Roll up and fasten with wooden picks or tie with string.

Sprinkle the rolls with flour and brown in hot fat. Add boiling water or stock.

Cover pan and simmer about 20 minutes. Serve with the juices in pan. Serves 6.

FRESH PORK BUTT
COOKED WITH VEGETABLES

1 fresh pork butt
4 large carrots, cut lengthwise
4 large parsnips, cut lengthwise
1 small cabbage, quartered
½ teaspoon salt
⅓ teaspoon pepper

Simmer pork butt in water to cover 1½ hours.

One hour before serving, add vegetables and seasonings. Cook until tender.

Cut pork in slices. Arrange in center of platter, with vegetables around meat. Serves 6 to 8.

BRAISED PORK
TENDERLOIN PATTIES

Flour and brown patties in a little fat in skillet; then add seasonings and a small amount of liquid. Cover skillet tightly, and cook slowly until tender, 35 to 45 minutes.

Herbs, spices, or seasonings, such as Worcestershire and Tabasco sauce, added to the liquid during braising, give pork tenderloin patties an interesting flavor.

Braised Pork Tenderloin Patties

SWEET AND SOUR PORK

1 pound lean pork shoulder
Fat, salt, pepper
1 cup bouillon
2 medium green peppers
3 tablespoons chopped onion
4 slices canned pineapple
3 tablespoons cornstarch
¼ cup sugar
¼ cup vinegar
2 teaspoons soy sauce
½ cup pineapple syrup
4 cups boiled rice

Cut pork into ½-inch cubes and brown well in a little hot fat in skillet. Sprinkle well with salt and pepper.

Add bouillon and cook, covered, over low heat 20 minutes. Cut green peppers into 1-inch strips and add. Add onion and pineapple slices cut into eighths. Cook another 10 minutes.

Blend cornstarch with sugar, vinegar, soy sauce, and pineapple syrup and add to mixture. Stir constantly until thickened. Cook 5 minutes longer.

Add more salt and pepper if necessary. Serve in individual rice rings or nests of boiled rice. Serves 4.

BRAISED PORK STEAK

Have lean pork sliced 1½ inches thick. Place in baking dish. Sprinkle with salt, pepper, and flour.

Add ½ cup consommé or bouillon, and arrange half slices of pineapple or thick slices of tomato over pork.

Cover and bake in moderate oven (350°F.) until tender, about 1½ hours. Allow 1¼ pounds pork to serve 4.

ROAST PORK SHOULDER BUTT

Rub roast with salt, pepper, and a little sage, if desired. Place on rack in shallow roasting pan and roast in slow oven (325°F.) 50 minutes per pound.

Place roast on a platter and surround with a ring of fried apple wedges. To prepare apple wedges, heat a little butter or margarine in a skillet, add apples, sprinkle with brown sugar, cover and cook until tender.

PORK TENDERLOIN,
BAKED IN SOUR CREAM

1½ pounds pork tenderloin
½ teaspoon salt
⅛ teaspoon pepper
½ teaspoon Ac'cent
Flour, fat
1 cup sour cream

Wipe meat with damp cloth. Sprinkle with salt, pepper, and Ac'cent; cut into 1¼-inch slices.

Roll slices in flour; brown quickly in hot fat.

Place in 9-inch pie plate; cover with sour cream. Bake in moderate oven (350°F.) about 30 minutes.

When tender, pour off liquid and thicken for pan gravy. Strain gravy over meat; return to oven until sauce is hot and bubbly. Serves 6.

Sweet and Sour Pork

KENTUCKY BURGOO

Kentucky Burgoo is a famous stew, dating back to the early part of the 19th century. Traditionally it was made in vast quantities, calling for such ingredients as 600 or 800 pounds lean meat, 200 or more pounds of fat hens, etc. The following recipe is trimmed down to serve 20 to 25.

2 pounds pork shank
2 pounds veal shank
2 pounds beef shank
2 pounds breast of lamb
1 4-pound hen
8 quarts water
1½ pounds Irish potatoes, peeled and diced
1½ pounds onions, peeled and diced
3 large carrots, scraped and diced
2 green peppers, seeds removed, then diced
2 cups chopped cabbage
1 quart cooked tomatoes
2 cups fresh or canned corn kernels
2 pods red pepper
1 cup diced celery
2 cups diced okra
2 cups fresh or canned lima beans (optional)
1 bunch parsley, chopped
Salt and cayenne to taste
About 4 teaspoons Worcestershire sauce

Cover the meat with cold water; bring slowly to a boil. Simmer until meat is tender enough to fall from the bones.

Remove the meat from the stock. Cool, dice the meat, removing the bones.

Return meat to stock; add prepared vegetables except parsley. Let simmer until thick. (Burgoo should be thick but still soupy.)

Season gradually while cooking, but not too much until stew is almost done. As stew simmers down, the seasoning will become more pronounced.

Stir frequently with a long-handled wooden spoon during the first part of cooking and almost constantly after it thickens. Add the chopped parsley near the end of cooking time.

The total cooking time is about 8 to 10 hours; however, the time may be cut in half by cooking the meat one day and completing the cooking on a second day.

Roast Pork Loin with Stuffing

ROAST PORK LOIN WITH STUFFING

Spread a 4- to 5-pound pork loin with 1/4 cup prepared mustard. Place on rack in open roasting pan with fat side up and roast in slow oven (325°F.).

During the last hour of roasting, place stuffing (below) under meat and peeled potatoes around roast. Brush with drippings. Continue baking until potatoes are cooked and nicely browned. Serves 6 to 8.

Stuffing:

1 cup diced celery
1 tablespoon crushed onion flakes
1/2 cup water
1/3 cup butter or margarine
1 teaspoon salt
1/4 teaspoon pepper
1/2 teaspoon sage
4 cups stale breadcrumbs

Simmer celery and onion flakes in water for 5 minutes. Mix in remaining ingredients. Arrange in mound on foil or dish.

Place roast over stuffing during last hour of cooking.

TENDERLOIN PATTIES WITH VEGETABLES

1 pork tenderloin, about 1¼ pounds
1 tablespoon drippings
1 teaspoon salt
1 medium onion, chopped
1/2 cup chopped celery
1 cup finely cut carrots
1/2 cup cooked peas
1 cup bouillon or meat stock
2 tablespoons flour
1/4 cup water

Cut meat crosswise in 2-inch pieces. Flatten slightly with meat mallet and brown in drippings. Season with salt.

Add vegetables to skillet. Add bouillon. Cover and cook slowly about 45 minutes, either in moderate oven (350°F.) or on top of range.

Remove meat from skillet. Blend flour with water and add to vegetables. Cook until thickened. Serve vegetables with meat. Serves 5.

ROAST PORK CANTONESE STYLE

1/2 teaspoon salt
1/3 cup soy sauce
3 tablespoons lemon juice
1/4 cup sugar
1/8 teaspoon red food coloring
1 pound lean pork
1 small onion, sliced
4 green onions, cut in 1-inch lengths
3 pieces fresh ginger, crushed, or 1/4 teaspoon ground ginger
6 cloves garlic, crushed
1/2 cup chicken stock or canned consommé

Combine salt, soy sauce, lemon juice, sugar, and red coloring. Rub onto pork. Add onion, green onions, ginger, and garlic. Allow to stand 1/2 hour.

Place in roasting pan. Add 1/2 cup chicken stock. Cook in slow oven (325°F.) 1 hour. Slice in 1/4-inch slices. Serve hot with rice. Serves 3 to 4.

SWEET AND PUNGENT PORK (Chinese)

1 pound lean pork shoulder, cut into 1-inch cubes
2 tablespoons sherry or 1 teaspoon soy sauce or rice wine
1 egg, slightly beaten
1/2 cup flour
1/2 teaspoon salt
1/4 cup water
Oil for frying
1 cup fresh pineapple cubes
1 cup water
1 green pepper, cut into 1-inch strips
1/4 cup vinegar
1/4 to 1/3 cup brown sugar
1 tablespoon molasses
1 tomato, cut into wedges
2 tablespoons cornstarch

Toss meat in sherry, soy sauce, or rice wine, and let stand 20 minutes, turning once or twice.

Mix egg, flour, salt, and water until smooth. Add pork and turn to coat each cube with batter.

Fry pork in deep hot oil (350°F.) until brown. Place on absorbent paper and keep warm.

To prepare sauce, cook pineapple in water, covered, until just tender. Add pepper strips, vinegar, brown sugar, molasses, and tomatoes. Boil 2 minutes.

Mix cornstarch with enough water to give a thin mixture. Add to boiling sauce, stirring, and cook, stirring, until thickened.

Add pork and serve at once with rice. Serves 4

PORK STEAK WITH GARLIC SAUCE

1 small onion, coarsely chopped
1 small carrot, coarsely chopped
1½ tablespoons butter or margarine
2 tablespoons flour
1 cup tomatoes

3/4 cup beef bouillon
2 cloves garlic, minced
1/2 teaspoon salt
1/2 teaspoon sugar
Freshly ground black pepper
Bouquet garni (see below)
2 pork steaks, 1-inch thick

Sauté onion and carrot in butter until soft but not brown.

Add flour, stirring until smooth. Add tomatoes, bouillon, garlic, salt, sugar, pepper, and bouquet garni tied in cheesecloth. Cook and stir until mixture thickens. Cover and simmer 1 hour.

Strain. While sauce is cooking, season pork steaks with salt and pepper. Brown both sides of steak and sauté over low heat until tender, about 40 minutes. Serve garlic sauce hot over steak. Serves 6.

Bouquet Garni: Use 1 small bay leaf, pinch of thyme, 4 sprigs of parsley, 1 sprig of celery leaves, and 1 whole clove. Tie in piece of cheesecloth.

PORK AND GREEN NOODLE CASSEROLE

1 cup water
1 can (6 ounces) tomato paste
1½ pounds pork shoulder, cut in 1/2-inch pieces
About 1/2 cup butter or margarine
1/2 cup chopped onions
1 cup celery, sliced in 1/4-inch strips
3 teaspoons salt
1/4 teaspoon pepper
1/2 teaspoon thyme
1/2 teaspoon Ac'cent
1/2 pound green noodles
1/2 can (5½ ounces) mushroom soup, undiluted
1 package frozen peas, cooked
1/2 cup grated American or Parmesan cheese

Combine water and tomato paste.

In a saucepan, fry pork in hot fat, then add onions and fry until light brown, about 3 minutes.

Add celery, 2 teaspoons salt, pepper, thyme, Ac'cent, and tomato paste-water mixture.

Cover pan and simmer over low heat until meat is tender, about 45 minutes. Every 10 minutes, stir all ingredients well.

Cook noodles in 2 quarts boiling salted water until tender, about 8 minutes. Drain noodles and add 1/4 cup butter and 1 teaspoon salt, blending well.

Combine noodles with cooked meat mixture. Add mushroom soup and cooked peas. Blend all ingredients and turn into a greased 2-quart casserole. Sprinkle top with cheese.

Bake in moderate oven (375°F.) 30 minutes. Serves 6 to 8.

PORK PIE WITH SAGE BISCUITS

1½ to 2 pounds boneless pork shoulder, cut in 1½-inch cubes
¼ cup flour
1½ to 2 teaspoons salt
¼ teaspoon pepper
2 tablespoons lard
1 cup chopped celery
½ cup chopped onion
2 chicken bouillon cubes
2 cups hot water
2 cups cooked peas

Dredge meat in flour combined with seasonings and brown on all sides in hot lard. Add celery, onion, and bouillon cubes dissolved in hot water. Cover and simmer for 1½ hours.

Thicken with a paste made of a little flour and cold water. Add peas, reserving about ¼ cup for a garnish, and season to taste. Place mixture in casserole. Top with sage biscuit rings. (Add ½ teaspoon powdered sage to 2 cups flour in standard biscuit recipe.)

Bake in hot oven (425° F.) 15 to 20 minutes. Fill centers of rings with remaining hot buttered peas. Serves 6 to 8.

PORK WITH ALMONDS AND VEGETABLES—CANTONESE

½ cup chopped blanched almonds
¼ cup oil
1 pound lean pork, cut in ½-inch cubes
½ cup chicken stock or canned consommé
1 teaspoon salt
1 cup diced cooked carrots
2 cups cooked peas
1½ cups diced celery
2 tablespoons cornstarch
2 teaspoons soy sauce
⅓ cup cold water

Brown almonds in 1 tablespoon of the oil.

Put remainder of oil in a heavy skillet; add pork and cook until golden brown.

Add chicken stock and salt and cook about 30 minutes or until pork is tender.

Add carrots, peas, and celery; cook 10 to 15 minutes longer.

Blend cornstarch, soy sauce, and water. Add to meat mixture and cook until juice thickens. Turn into serving dish. Garnish with almonds.

Serve immediately with hot boiled rice. Add additional soy sauce, if desired. Serves 6 to 8.

CUSHION STYLE PICNIC SHOULDER

Have picnic shoulder boned and sewed on 2 sides. This leaves 1 side open for inserting stuffing. Season inside and out with salt and pepper.

Fill cavity with bread stuffing (see Index). Sew or skewer edges together. Place fat-side-up on rack in open pan.

Roast in moderate oven (350° F.) until done. Allow 40 to 45 minutes per pound.

PORK AND NOODLES— HAWAIIAN

1½ pounds lean pork shoulder, cut in 1-inch cubes
2 tablespoons fat
4 medium onions, coarsely chopped
3 carrots, sliced
3 cups water
1 tablespoon salt
1 9-ounce can pineapple chunks
2 tablespoons lemon juice
1 tablespoon soy sauce
4 tablespoons cornstarch
4 tablespoons brown sugar
4 ounces medium noodles, cooked and drained
2 green peppers, cut into pieces

Brown pork on all sides in hot fat in heavy skillet. Add vegetables and brown very lightly. Add water and salt. Simmer very gently until meat is almost tender, about 40 minutes.

Make a smooth paste of pineapple juice from canned pineapple, lemon juice, soy sauce, cornstarch, and brown sugar. Pour over pork and cook, stirring occasionally, until sauce thickens.

Carefully mix in noodles, green peppers, and pineapple. Pour into casserole.

Bake in moderate oven (350° F.) 15 to 20 minutes. Serves 6.

VEAL AND PORK PARTY CASSEROLE

1 pound diced veal
1 pound diced pork
1 cup sliced fresh mushrooms
3 tablespoons fat
½ pound noodles
1 small can pimiento, chopped
2 tablespoons grated onion
½ pound American cheese, grated
1 No. 2 can cream-style corn
1 can condensed chicken soup
2 teaspoons salt
½ teaspoon pepper
½ cup buttered crumbs

Brown meat and mushrooms in hot fat.

Cook noodles in boiling salted water. Drain and rinse.

Combine meat, mushrooms, noodles, chopped pimiento, grated onion, grated cheese, corn, soup, salt, and pepper. Pour into casserole.

Bake in moderate oven (350° F.) 45 minutes.

Remove cover, sprinkle with crumbs and cook uncovered 15 minutes longer. Serves 10 to 12.

CHINESE ROAST PORK

4 teaspoons sugar
1 teaspoon salt
4 teaspoons honey
3 teaspoons soy sauce
3 tablespoons chicken bouillon
2 pounds fresh pork butt or shoulder of pork

Place all ingredients except meat in bowl. Mix well.

Cut meat lengthwise in 3 pieces and add. Soak pork for ¾ of an hour, turning occasionally.

Remove from bowl and place on rack in a roasting pan, adding a few tablespoons of water to prevent smoking.

Roast in moderate oven (350° F.) for about 1 hour and 15 minutes, turning occasionally. Slice pork and serve immediately with English mustard. Serves 6.

PINEAPPLE PORK (CHINESE)

Part #1:

1 cup lean pork, sliced in ½-inch pieces
1 small egg, well beaten
¼ teaspoon salt
½ teaspoon Ac'cent
½ cup flour
Fat, for deep frying

Coat pork pieces by dipping in egg; transfer to paper bag containing combined salt, Ac'cent, and flour. Shake until meat is well and evenly coated. Remove pork; dust off excess flour.

Deep-fry pork in hot fat or oil (360° F.) 6 to 8 minutes or until tender.

Remove pork to absorbent paper to drain. Keep warm.

Part #2:

1 tablespoon cooking oil
⅓ cup clear chicken stock (free from fat)
½ cup canned pineapple chunks
1 medium green pepper, cut in ½-inch pieces
¼ cup (½-inch) onion pieces
1 teaspoon cornstarch
1 teaspoon soy sauce
2 tablespoons sugar, brown or white
⅓ cup pineapple juice
1 teaspoon ketchup

Lightly toss together in hot oil in hot fry-pan or skillet, the stock, pineapple, green pepper, and onion. When mixed, cover and cook 2 minutes.

Add fried pork pieces; cook uncovered 2 minutes longer.

Combine remaining ingredients; blend smooth. Add to pork mixture; toss lightly and continuously until juice has thickened.

Turn out and mound up on hot serving dish. Serves 2.

Leftover Pork

CHINESE PORK AND RICE

2   tablespoons butter or margarine
2/3 cup uncooked long grain rice
1   teaspoon salt
1   large onion, cut in thin slices
1½ cups boiling water
1   bouillon cube
1   green pepper, cut in thin strips
2   stalks celery, cut in thin strips
1   cup cooked, cubed pork
2   teaspoons soy sauce

Melt butter in heavy skillet. Add uncooked rice. Season with salt and cook until rice grains turn golden, stirring occasionally.

Add onion to rice and cook several minutes, then pour in boiling water in which bouillon cube has been dissolved. Cover tightly and cook until rice is tender, about 20 minutes.

Add pepper, celery, and pork. Cover tightly and place over very low heat about 10 minutes more or until vegetables are tender but still slightly crisp.

Just before serving, stir in soy sauce. Serves 4.

CREOLE PORK SKILLET

1   large onion, sliced
2   cups diced cooked pork
2   tablespoons oil
2½ cups canned tomatoes
¼   cup diced green pepper
⅓   cup diced celery
½   teaspoon chili powder
1   teaspoon sugar
1½ teaspoons salt
Freshly ground black pepper
1   tablespoon flour

Sauté onion and pork in oil until onion is golden brown.

Add tomatoes, green pepper, celery, chili powder, sugar, salt, and pepper. Cover and simmer 45 minutes.

Combine flour and 2 tablespoons water and stir into tomato mixture. Cook and stir 5 minutes. Serves 6.

PORK SUPPER

1   tablespoon chopped onion
1   tablespoon fat
¼   cup vinegar
¾   cup water
1   tablespoon cornstarch
2   tablespoons brown or granulated sugar
1   teaspoon salt
1   cup ground cooked pork
2   cups cooked green beans
2   cups cooked, diced carrots

Brown onion in fat in heavy skillet. Combine vinegar, water, cornstarch, sugar, and salt. Stir into onions. Heat.

Add pork and cook 10 minutes. Add drained beans and carrots. Heat slowly 25 to 30 minutes. Serve hot. Serves 4.

FRUITED PORK LOAF

4   ounces dry noodles
1½ cups sweetened applesauce
1   tablespoon lemon juice
½   cup orange juice
1   tablespoon grated orange rind
¼   teaspoon salt
⅛   teaspoon dry mustard
⅛   teaspoon cloves
1   tablespoon brown sugar
1   cup cubed cooked pork

Cook noodles in boiling salted water until tender, about 6 minutes. Drain and rinse.

Combine with remaining ingredients and mix well. Turn into greased loaf pan.

Cover and bake in moderate oven (350°F.) 25 minutes. Serves 6.

SCALLOPED PORK AND POTATO CASSEROLE

2   cups chopped cooked pork
3   cups thinly sliced potatoes
2   tablespoons finely chopped green pepper
2   tablespoons finely chopped onion
1   10½-ounce can condensed cream of celery soup
½   cup milk
1   teaspoon salt
⅛   teaspoon pepper
⅛   teaspoon savory
½   cup shredded cheese (optional)

Combine all ingredients except cheese in a 1-quart casserole.

Bake in moderate oven (350°F.) 30 minutes. Remove from oven. Sprinkle cheese on top.

Return to oven and continue baking for 30 minutes or until potatoes are done. Serves 4 to 5.

SAVORY PORK IN SWEET POTATO NESTS

2   cups mashed sweet potatoes
Milk
1   tablespoon melted butter or margarine
1½ cups finely chopped cooked pork
1   cup peas
½   cup gravy
½   teaspoon salt
⅛   teaspoon thyme

To the mashed sweet potatoes add enough milk to make mixture smooth and easy to shape. Divide in 4 mounds on a baking sheet. Make a well in the center of each mound with the back of a spoon. Brush with melted butter.

Combine pork, peas, gravy, and seasonings in a saucepan or baking dish. Place pork mixture and sweet potato mounds in moderate oven (350°F.) 15 to 20 minutes. Spoon pork into sweet potato nests. Serve hot. Serves 4.

Fruited Pork Loaf

BARBECUED PORK BUNS

¼   cup drippings
1   medium onion, minced
½   cup finely minced celery
1   or 2 cloves garlic, crushed
½   cup water
¼   cup vinegar
⅓   cup Worcestershire sauce
⅓   cup chili sauce
1   teaspoon salt
¼   teaspoon pepper
¾   teaspoon Ac'cent
¾   teaspoon chili powder
2   tablespoons brown sugar
Thinly sliced roast pork (for 6)
Toasted bun halves

Heat drippings in saucepan; add onion, celery, garlic; simmer 2 to 3 minutes.

Add all remaining ingredients except pork slices and buns. Cover; simmer 5 minutes.

Add sliced, leftover pork (trim off surplus fat); cover and simmer 5 to 10 minutes longer.

Arrange hot pork slices on toasted bun halves; pour sauce on top. Garnish as desired. Serves 6.

PORK AND MUSHROOM RING

1   tablespoon finely minced onion
5   tablespoons melted butter or margarine
4   tablespoons flour
½   teaspoon salt
2   cups scalded milk
2   egg yolks, beaten
1   cup sliced mushrooms
1½ cups diced cooked pork
1   package corn bread mix

Sauté onion in 4 tablespoons butter until golden brown.

Add flour, salt and blend. Add hot milk gradually, stirring constantly. Simmer 10 minutes, stirring occasionally.

Strain and add gradually to egg yolks, stirring constantly. Heat but do not boil.

Sauté mushrooms in 1 tablespoon butter. Add mushrooms and pork to sauce; heat thoroughly.

Pour in center of hot corn bread ring made with 1 package corn bread mix. Serve immediately. Serves 6.

Pork Chops

PAN-BROILED PORK CHOPS

Rub pork chops with garlic or rosemary, or other desired seasoning.

Brown on both sides in a heavy skillet in just enough fat to keep them from sticking. Reduce heat. Season with salt and pepper. Cover pan closely.

Cook on top of stove or bake in slow oven (325°F.) until chops are tender, 45 minutes to 1 hour, depending upon thickness of chops.

Pour off excess fat as they cook. Use drippings to prepare gravy.

BRAISED PORK CHOPS

Use 1-inch-thick rib or loin chops. Trim off a little fat and heat in heavy skillet.

Brown chops slowly on both sides, about 10 minutes. Add 2 to 4 tablespoons water, depending upon size of skillet. Cover and cook slowly over low heat or in moderate oven (350°F.) until well done and tender, about 40 minutes.

Season chops after cooking. If desired, dredge chops with flour before browning. Make gravy from the drippings.

Thin chops do not need the added water, but use cover and very low heat to keep chops moist.

Variations: Instead of water, use barbecue sauce, tomato juice, canned tomatoes, consommé or bouillon, orange juice, pineapple juice, or diluted lemon juice.

Chops may be rubbed with a cut clove of garlic before braising or with a little dry mustard, sage, or soy sauce.

BAKED PORK CHOPS

4 pork chops (1½ pounds)
Fat
2 8-ounce cans tomato sauce
½ cup water
⅓ cup finely diced celery
2 tablespoons brown sugar
Juice of ½ lemon
½ teaspoon salt
½ teaspoon dry mustard
⅛ teaspoon pepper

Brown chops in fat. Place in shallow greased baking dish.

Combine tomato sauce, water, celery, brown sugar, lemon juice, and seasonings. Pour over chops.

Cover and bake in moderate oven (350°F.) 1¼ hours or until chops are tender. Serves 4.

TO BROWN EDGES ON PORK CHOPS

Place chops side by side, bone edge up, in small amount of hot fat. Hold in position with spatula and fork. Rock chops back and forth to brown evenly.

CHICKEN-FRIED PORK CHOPS

6 pork chops, ¾-inch thick
2 beaten eggs
2 tablespoons milk
1 cup fine cracker crumbs
¼ cup fat
½ teaspoon salt
Dash of pepper
¼ cup water

Pound chops thoroughly with meat mallet to ½-inch thick. Mix eggs and milk. Dip meat into mixture, then into crumbs.

Brown on both sides in hot fat. Season with salt and pepper. Add water. Cover and cook over low heat 45 to 60 minutes. Lift chops occasionally to prevent sticking.

For crisp coating, remove cover the last 15 minutes. Garnish with spiced crabapples on bed of greens. Serves 6.

PORK CHOPS IN SOUR CREAM

4 thick pork chops
Salt and pepper
4 slices each lemon and onion
4 green pepper rings
¼ cup brown sugar, honey, or molasses
¾ cup sour cream
¼ cup chili sauce

Brown pork chops on both sides in a skillet. Season with salt and pepper.

Put a slice each of lemon and onion, and a green pepper ring on each chop. Top each with 1 tablespoon brown sugar, honey, or molasses.

Mix sour cream and chili sauce and pour over all. Cover tightly. Cook gently until chops are tender, about 45 to 60 minutes, depending upon thickness of chops. Serves 4.

PORK CHOPS WITH HOPPING JOHN

4 pork chops
¼ cup chopped onions
½ cup converted rice
1 can (15 to 16 ounces) blackeyed peas, drained
¾ teaspoon salt
Pepper, cayenne, and garlic seasoning, to suit taste
2 cups water

Brown pork chops in skillet; if thick simmer slowly, covered, to partially cook. Lift out chops and drain skillet.

Add remaining ingredients and place chops on top. Bring to a boil. Stir, cover, and lower heat. Cook 20 to 25 minutes or until rice is tender, most of liquid is absorbed, and chops are done. Serves 4.

Pork Chops with Red Beans and Rice: Substitute a 15 to 16 ounce can red or kidney beans, drained, for the blackeyed peas in above recipe.

Stuffed Pork Chops: Pockets may be cut in double thick chops to hold the stuffing.

STUFFED PORK CHOPS – BAKED

2 tablespoons melted butter or margarine
3 cups soft breadcrumbs
¼ cup diced celery
2 tablespoons chopped onion
2 tablespoons chopped parsley
Salt and pepper
8 pork chops, cut thin
¼ cup tomato juice

Mix butter, crumbs, celery, onion, parsley, and salt and pepper to taste.

Wipe chops with damp cloth. Season with salt and pepper. Place chops together with stuffing between (sandwich style). Put in greased baking dish. Add tomato juice.

Bake in moderate oven (350°F.) until tender, about 1 hour. Serves 4.

Variations: Pockets may be cut in double-thick chops and filled with dressing. Sliced tart apples or half slices of pineapple may be used instead of bread stuffing.

BREADED PORK CHOPS OR STEAKS

Wipe meat with a damp cloth. Roll in seasoned breadcrumbs. Dip in slightly beaten egg diluted with 2 tablespoons water and roll again in crumbs.

Brown slowly in minimum of hot fat. Pour off excess fat and cook until done.

Serve with a highly seasoned sauce made by thickening the drippings with flour.

Or, after browning chops, remove from pan. Add minced green pepper, minced onion, and canned tomato to drippings. Place chops in sauce. Cover and simmer 1 hour.

Pork Chops with Hopping John

Pork Chops with Tomato Sauce

PORK CHOPS WITH TOMATO SAUCE

6 pork chops
1 tablespoon shortening
Dash of black pepper
6 slices onion
6 green pepper rings
1 can (1¼ cups) condensed tomato soup

Brown chops in shortening in heavy skillet; sprinkle with pepper.

Place an onion slice and a pepper ring on each chop; pour soup over all. Cover and simmer about 1 hour. Serves 6.

PORK CHOP—PINEAPPLE BAKE

Sear 6 chops in hot bacon fat in skillet. Place in casserole. Brown 6 slices pineapple lightly in fat and put on chops. Add ¾ cup pineapple juice.

Cover and bake in moderate oven (350°F.) until done, about 35 minutes. Baste often. Thicken juice with flour. Serves 6.

PORK CHOP-SWEET POTATO SKILLET

2 tablespoons salad oil
6 shoulder pork chops
6 medium sweet potatoes, pared and thinly sliced
1 large onion, thinly sliced
1 medium green pepper, cut into rings
Salt and pepper
¼ teaspoon crushed thyme
¼ teaspoon crushed marjoram
1 can (1 pound, 4 ounces) tomatoes

Heat oil in skillet; add pork chops and brown on both sides.

Arrange sweet potato slices, onion slices, and green pepper rings over pork chops. Sprinkle with salt and pepper, thyme, and marjoram. Pour tomatoes over all. Cover and cook over low heat 1 hour, or until pork chops and sweet potatoes are tender. Serves 6.

Pork Chop-Sweet Potato Skillet

FRUITED PORK CHOPS

1 small onion, chopped
¼ cup chopped celery
3 tablespoons butter or margarine
2 cups corn flavored cracker crumbs
½ cup dried apricots, chopped
1 teaspoon salt
⅛ teaspoon pepper
8 loin pork chops

Sauté onion and celery in butter or margarine until golden. Combine with crumbled corn crackers, dried apricots, salt and pepper; toss lightly.

Divide stuffing onto 4 pork chops. Top each with another chop; fasten together with cocktail picks or skewers.

Bake in moderate oven (350°F.) 1¼ hours or until chops are tender and browned. Serves 4.

Fruited Pork Chops

DEVILED PORK CHOPS

4 pork chops, cut 1-inch thick
¼ cup chili sauce
1 tablespoon lemon juice
1 small onion, minced
¼ teaspoon dry mustard
½ teaspoon salt
Dash of pepper
1 teaspoon Worcestershire sauce
½ cup water

Marinate chops in a mixture made by combining all the ingredients (except meat of course). Let soak an hour or longer.

Drain, reserving marinade, and dry chops with paper towels.

Sauté in bacon or other fat until browned. Add reserved liquid and cook, covered, until tender or about 40 minutes.

Remove chops to platter and cover with sauce in pan. Serves 4.

PORK CHOPS Ā LA CREOLE

4 loin pork chops
3 tablespoons flour
1 teaspoon salt
¼ teaspoon pepper
¼ teaspoon garlic salt
¼ teaspoon thyme
4 onion slices
½ cup uncooked rice
1 No. 2 can (2½ cups) tomatoes

Dip chops in flour seasoned with half the salt, pepper, garlic salt, and thyme. Brown chops in a little fat. Place chops in bottom of casserole.

Top with onion slices and rice. Season with remaining salt, pepper, garlic salt, and thyme. Pour tomatoes over rice and chops.

Cover and bake in moderate oven (350°F.) 30 minutes. Remove cover and bake 30 minutes longer, basting occasionally. Serves 4.

CRANBERRY PORK CHOPS

6 pork chops
½ teaspoon salt
4 cups cranberries, ground
¾ cup honey
½ teaspoon cloves

Brown chops quickly on both sides in hot skillet. Sprinkle with salt. Place 3 chops in greased casserole or baking dish.

Combine cranberries, honey, and cloves. Spread half over chops in casserole. Place remaining chops on top. Cover with remaining cranberry mixture.

Cover. Bake in moderate oven (350°F.) about 1 hour. Serves 6.

PORK CHOP—VEGETABLE SKILLET

4 pork chops
4 cups pared sliced potatoes
⅔ cup coarsely diced green pepper
1 cup diced celery
1 cup sliced onion
2 teaspoons salt
⅛ teaspoon pepper
1 can condensed tomato soup
½ cup water
¼ teaspoon Tabasco sauce

Brown pork chops in skillet; remove from pan.

Starting with potatoes, put vegetables in layers in a deep 2-quart skillet. (Reserve about ⅓ of green pepper, celery, and onion.) Sprinkle each layer with part of the salt and pepper.

Place browned pork chops on top of vegetables. Top with remaining green pepper, celery, and onion. Sprinkle with remaining salt and pepper.

Mix together tomato soup, water, and Tabasco; pour over meat.

Cover and cook on top of range over low heat 1 to 1½ hours. Serves 4.

Pork Chop-Vegetable Skillet

Pork Chop, Corn and Apple Skillet

PORK CHOP, CORN AND APPLE SKILLET

- 4 loin pork chops
- ½ teaspoon Ac'cent
- Salt and pepper
- ¼ cup water
- 2 cans (12-ounces each) Mexican-style kernel corn
- ½ teaspoon Ac'cent
- 4 thick, unpeeled apple rings
- Cinnamon-sugar

Sprinkle chops with ½ teaspoon Ac'cent, salt, and pepper. Brown slowly in their own fat in skillet, turning to brown both sides. Add ¼ cup water to pan; cover; simmer 30 minutes. Remove from skillet.

Pour corn into skillet without draining. Season to taste with salt, pepper, and remaining ½ teaspoon Ac'cent.

Place chops on corn. Top each chop with apple ring dusted with cinnamon-sugar. Cover; cook 10 minutes or until apple rings are tender. Serves 4.

SPANISH PORK CHOPS

- 1 large onion
- 1 tablespoon shortening
- 4 pork chops
- Salt and pepper
- 1½ cups canned tomatoes
- 1 small green pepper, chopped
- ½ teaspoon chili powder

Cut onion into ½-inch-thick slices. Brown in shortening in heavy frying pan. Remove onion and reserve.

Season pork chops with salt and pepper and brown in same pan. Top the chops with onion, tomatoes, green pepper, and chili powder.

Cover and cook slowly about 1 hour or until chops are fork-tender. Serves 4.

Pork Chop-Rice Skillet

PORK CHOP—VEGETABLE SKILLET #2

- 4 end or shoulder pork chops (about 1½ pounds)
- 1 tablespoon fat
- ½ cup water
- 4 large potatoes, quartered
- 8 small onions, halved
- 8 small carrots
- 1 cup fresh lima beans
- 1½ teaspoons salt
- ⅛ teaspoon pepper

Brown chops in fat in large skillet with tight-fitting cover. Add water; cover, and simmer 30 minutes.

Add vegetables and seasonings. Cover, and simmer 30 minutes, or until vegetables are tender. Serves 4.

Variations: Shoulder lamb chops may be substituted for pork.

PORK CHOPS WITH MACARONI AND CORN

- 1 cup elbow macaroni
- 4 loin pork chops, ½-inch thick
- 2 teaspoons salt
- ¼ teaspoon pepper
- 2 tablespoons finely chopped onion
- ¼ cup finely chopped green pepper
- 2 tablespoons flour
- ½ cup water
- ½ cup chili sauce
- 1 tablespoon brown sugar
- 1 tablespoon vinegar
- 1 No. 2 can cream-style corn

Cook macaroni until tender in boiling salted water; drain.

Season chops with 2 teaspoons salt and the pepper. Brown chops on both sides in skillet. Remove chops and brown onion and pepper lightly.

Blend in flour, then add water, chili sauce, sugar, and vinegar. Cook, stirring constantly, until thickened.

Mix in macaroni and corn. Turn into 2-quart casserole. Arrange chops on top.

Cover and bake in moderate oven (350°F.) until chops are tender, about 1 hour. Serves 4.

PORK CHOP-RICE SKILLET

- 6 pork chops
- ⅔ cup uncooked rice
- 1 cup water
- 2 teaspoons salt
- ½ cup chopped onion
- 1 can (1 pound) tomatoes, broken up
- 1 cup whole kernel yellow corn
- ¼ teaspoon black pepper

Trim some fat from pork chops. Fry out in a large skillet. Add chops and brown very slowly on both sides. Lift out. Pour off excess fat.

Spread rice over bottom of skillet. Add water. Sprinkle with 1 teaspoon salt. Arrange chops over rice. Sprinkle with the other 1 teaspoon salt. Add onion and tomatoes. Spoon on the corn. Sprinkle with black pepper. Bring to a boil.

Turn heat down low. Cover and simmer 25 to 35 minutes or until the rice is tender. Add a small amount of water, should mixture cook dry. Serve at the table from one of the colorful, oven-proof skillets. Serves 6.

PORK CHOPS ON SPAGHETTI WITH APPLE GRAVY

- 4 loin pork chops
- Salt and pepper
- 2 tablespoons fat
- ¼ cup water
- 6 tablespoons butter or margarine
- 6 tablespoons enriched flour
- 2 cups apple juice
- Salt and pepper to taste
- Dash celery salt
- 8 ounces spaghetti, cooked

Season pork chops with salt and pepper. Melt fat over low heat in skillet; add chops and brown well on both sides.

Add water and cover. Cook over low heat until tender, 30 to 45 minutes.

Meanwhile, melt butter or margarine over low heat; add flour and blend. Cook over low heat until flour mixture is golden brown, stirring constantly.

Gradually stir in apple juice and continue cooking until thickened, stirring constantly. Add salt, pepper, and celery salt.

Serve pork chops and apple gravy with cooked spaghetti. Serves 4.

PORK CHOPS NEAPOLITAN

- 2 tablespoons olive oil
- 1 clove garlic, minced
- 6 rib or loin pork chops, cut about ¾- to 1-inch thick
- 1 teaspoon salt
- ½ teaspoon Ac'cent
- ¼ teaspoon pepper
- 1 pound mushrooms, sliced
- 2 green peppers, chopped
- ½ cup canned tomatoes, sieved
- 3 tablespoons dry white wine

Heat olive oil in large, heavy skillet having a tight-fitting cover. Add garlic and cook until lightly browned.

Meanwhile, wipe pork chops with a clean, damp cloth. Season with a mixture of salt, Ac'cent, and pepper. Place into skillet, and slowly brown chops on both sides.

When chops are browned, add mushrooms and peppers. Stir in slowly a mixture of tomatoes and wine.

Cover skillet and cook over low heat 1 to 1½ hours, depending on thickness of chops. Add small amounts of water as needed.

Test for doneness by cutting meat near bone; no part of meat should be pink in color. Serves 6.

Spareribs

"BOILED" SPARERIBS

Combine spareribs with boiling water to cover, seasoned with salt and pepper. Add chopped onion, carrot, celery, and parsley.

Cover and simmer until meat is tender, 1½ to 2 hours.

Drain and serve with sauerkraut and mashed or boiled potatoes.

BAKED STUFFED SPARERIBS

Select a whole sparerib piece or part of two, so that one part can be laid over the other. Have the breast bone cracked so that you can cut between the ribs when cooked.

Rub with 1 teaspoon salt and ¼ teaspoon pepper to each pound. Spread prune or apple stuffing (see Index) over larger piece. Cover with other part. Fasten with small skewers.

Bake in moderate oven (350°F.) 1½ hours. Allow ¾ to 1 pound ribs per person.

If necessary, to prevent burning, pour ¼ cup water in pan.

Baked Without Stuffing: Allow about 1 hour for a sheet of ribs. If desired, sprinkle ribs with flour after seasoning.

BAKED SPARERIBS WITH SAUERKRAUT

    2   sides spareribs
    Salt, pepper, paprika
    1   large can sauerkraut
    1   small onion, chopped
    1   apple, chopped
    3   cloves
    ½   teaspoon caraway seed
    3   tablespoons brown sugar

Have spareribs cut into serving-size pieces. Put a layer of ribs in bottom of a large roasting pan. Sprinkle with salt and pepper.

Combine kraut with chopped onion, chopped apple, cloves, caraway seed, and brown sugar.

Cover ribs with kraut mixture, then top with rest of ribs. Sprinkle with salt, pepper, and paprika. Add a little water if sauerkraut seems dry.

Cover pan and bake in slow oven (325°F.) 1 hour. Uncover and cook another half hour. Serves 4.

Baked Spareribs with Sauerkraut

SWEET AND SOUR SPARERIBS

    2   sides well-fleshed spareribs
    1   tablespoon fat or salad oil
    ½   teaspoon salt
    1   small garlic clove
    1   No. 303 can sliced pineapple
    2   medium green peppers
    2   tablespoons cornstarch
    1   teaspoon soy sauce
    1   teaspoon Ac'cent
    ½   cup wine vinegar
    ¼   cup sugar
    1   cup water
    Maraschino cherries

Have spareribs cut in serving-size pieces. Place on rack in open roaster. Roast in slow oven (325°F.) 1½ hours.

Meanwhile heat fat or salad oil; add salt and garlic; cook over low heat 10 minutes; remove garlic.

Add syrup from pineapple. Cut green peppers in 1-inch pieces; add; cook over low heat 10 minutes.

Blend remaining ingredients, except cherries; add. Cook, stirring constantly until thickened and clear. Add pineapple slices and cherries; heat. Pour sauce over spareribs. Serves 6.

OVEN-BARBECUED SPARERIBS

    3   to 4 pounds spareribs, cut in pieces
    1   lemon, sliced with peel
    1   large onion, thinly sliced
    1   cup ketchup
    2   cups water
    ⅓   cup Worcestershire sauce
    1   teaspoon chili powder
    2   or 3 dashes of Tabasco sauce
    1   teaspoon salt

Place spareribs, fat sides up, in a shallow roasting pan. Put a thin slice each of lemon and onion on each piece of sparerib.

Roast in very hot oven (450°F.) ½ hour.

Combine remaining ingredients in a saucepan. Bring to a boil and pour over ribs.

Reduce heat to moderate (350°F.) and roast until tender, about 45 to 60 minutes. Baste ribs every 15 minutes with the sauce in pan, adding a little more water if needed. Serves 4.

CHINESE BARBECUED SPARERIBS

    2   tablespoons sugar
    3   tablespoons honey
    1   cup chicken stock
    ½   teaspoon salt
    Dash of pepper
    2   tablespoons soy sauce
    3   pounds spareribs

Mix sauce ingredients together and soak ribs in mixture for 1 hour, turning frequently.

Remove ribs to rack of roasting pan. Place small amount of water in pan.

Roast in moderate oven for 1 to 1½ hours, turning from time to time. Serves 4.

Sweet and Sour Spareribs

GLAZED SPARERIBS

Three pounds of spareribs will serve 3 or 4 persons.

Place ribs on rack in an open roasting pan.

Bake in slow oven (325°F.) 1½ hours, basting frequently with this mixture: 1 cup stock or bouillon, ⅓ cup honey or molasses, 1 teaspoon salt, and 2 tablespoons vinegar.

WINE-BAKED SPARERIBS

    3   pounds spareribs, fresh or cured
    1½ cups cabernet, claret, burgundy or
        any red wine
    Salt, pepper and mustard
    1   cup brown sugar

Have the sheets of spareribs cracked through center. Parboil smoked, cured ribs about 20 minutes to remove, excess cure. Wipe fresh ribs with damp cloth.

Arrange parboiled, smoked ribs or fresh ribs on baking sheet. Sprinkle surface with salt and pepper. Rub with dry mustard.

Bake in moderately slow oven (325°F. to 350° F.) about 1 hour, basting at intervals with red wine.

After 1 hour of baking, remove from oven and rub brown sugar over surface of spareribs. Return to oven and bake ½ hour longer basting occasionally with wine and drippings from bottom of pan. Serves 4 to 5.

HAWAIIAN SPARERIBS

    2   sides spareribs
    3   tablespoons brown sugar
    2   tablespoons cornstarch
    ½   teaspoon salt
    ¼   cup vinegar
    ½   cup ketchup
    1   9-ounce can crushed pineapple
    1   tablespoon soy sauce

Have ribs cut into serving pieces.

Combine sugar, cornstarch, and salt; stir in vinegar, ketchup, pineapple and juice, and soy sauce. Cook until slightly thickened, about 5 minutes, stirring constantly.

Arrange a layer of spareribs in roasting pan. Cover with part of pineapple mixture. Add another layer of ribs and top with remaining sauce.

Cover tightly. Bake in moderate oven (350°F.) 1½ to 2 hours. Serves 4.

Pork Sausage

ABOUT HOMEMADE SAUSAGE

The recipes for homemade sausage are old-time favorites that have been in use for many years and have wide appeal. Tastes for various seasonings, however, differ and the strength of spices is variable. Adjustment of seasonings to personal taste is recommended but uncooked pork cannot be tasted. We suggest, therefore, that you mix a small sample of any desired recipe and cook it in the form of patties for taste-testing before you season the entire recipe.

OLD-TIME COUNTRY SAUSAGE MEAT

9 pounds fresh lean pork
2 tablespoons thyme or sage
1 teaspoon red pepper
2 tablespoons black pepper
1/4 cup salt

Cut pork in small pieces and put through meat grinder, using medium blade. Mix thoroughly with the seasonings.

Pack tightly into cotton bags 3 inches wide and 12 inches long. Tie the bags at one end.

When ready to use, turn back the end of a bag, and cut meat into 1/2 inch slices. To cook, start slices in a cold ungreased frying pan over moderate heat and cook until medium brown on both sides and done throughout. This sausage will keep for several weeks in the refrigerator. Makes 9 pounds.

CREOLE PORK SAUSAGE

This Creole sausage is often called chaurice, a name that was probably derived from the Spanish chorizo, a Spanish and Mexican sausage which is sometimes similarly seasoned.

4 pounds lean pork
2 pounds pork fat
2 large onions, finely chopped
1 clove garlic, mashed to a pulp
3 teaspoons salt
2 teaspoons black pepper
1 teaspoon chili pepper
1 teaspoon paprika
1/2 teaspoon cayenne
2 tablespoons finely chopped parsley
1/4 teaspoon thyme
1/2 teaspoon allspice
2 bay leaves, finely minced
5 yards sausage casing

Put pork and pork fat through the meat grinder, using medium blade. Place the ground meat in a large bowl; add remaining ingredients and mix until thoroughly blended.

Remove the cutting blade from the grinder and attach the sausage stuffer. Using a yard of casing at a time, work all but a few inches of casing onto the sausage stuffer. Tie a knot at the end of the casing. Refeed the meat through the grinder and into the casing. Twist into links. Keep the sausages in the refrigerator. Makes about 6 pounds.

ITALIAN HOT SAUSAGE

4 1/2 pounds fresh lean pork
1 1/2 pounds fresh fat pork (use pork siding)
1 medium onion, chopped
1 large clove garlic, finely minced
3 tablespoons salt
1 1/2 tablespoons black pepper, freshly ground
1 1/2 teaspoons paprika
2 tablespoons crushed dried red peppers
2 teaspoons fennel seeds
1/2 teaspoon crushed bay leaf
1/4 teaspoon thyme
Pinch of coriander
2/3 cup red wine or water
2 1/2 yards sausage casing

Cut the meats into small pieces and put through the meat grinder with the onion and garlic, using the fine blade. Sprinkle the seasonings and wine over the ground mixture and mix thoroughly.

Remove the cutting blade from the grinder and attach sausage stuffer. Work about half the sausage casing onto the stuffer, leaving a few inches off and tie a knot at the end of the casing.

Put the seasoned ground meat through the grinder and into the casing twisting into desired links. Store the filled sausage in the refrigerator; it is perishable. Makes about 6 pounds.

SPICED PORK SAUSAGES

9 pounds fresh lean pork
3 tablespoons salt
3/4 teaspoon red pepper
1 1/2 tablespoons black pepper, freshly ground
1 1/2 tablespoons crushed sage
6 yards sausage casing

Cut the pork into small pieces and put through the meat grinder, using the fine blade. Sprinkle the seasonings over the ground meat and mix thoroughly.

Remove the cutting blade from the grinder and attach the sausage stuffer. Use a yard of sausage casing at a time, and work all but a few inches of the casing onto the stuffer. Tie a knot at the end of the casing.

Put the ground meat through the grinder and into the case twisting into desired links. Store the filled sausage in the refrigerator; it is perishable. Makes about 9 pounds.

SPANISH AND MEXICAN HOT SAUSAGE (CHORIZO)

2 pounds lean pork
1/2 teaspoon crushed hot pepper or 2 small hot red peppers, finely chopped
2 teaspoons salt
3 cloves garlic, finely minced
2 tablespoons chili powder
1 teaspoon black pepper, freshly ground
1 teaspoon oregano
1/4 teaspoon ground cumin
1/4 cup vinegar
1 yard sausage casing

Cut the pork into small pieces and put through the meat grinder, using the coarse blade. Add remaining ingredients and mix well.

Remove cutting blade from grinder and attach the sausage stuffer. Work all but a few inches of casing onto stuffer; tie a knot at the end of casing. Put meat mixture through the grinder and into casing twisting into desired links. If desired, hang the sausage in cool place to dry. The dried sausage may be kept for a few weeks. Cook as for fresh sausage. Makes about 2 pounds.

CAPE COD SAUSAGE CAKES

1/2 teaspoon Ac'cent
1 pound pork sausage meat
1 cup sugar
1 cup water
2 cups fresh cranberries

Add Ac'cent to sausage meat; mix well. Form into 6 cakes. Fry until well browned; drain on absorbent paper.

Combine sugar and water in saucepan; cook, stirring, until sugar dissolves; simmer 5 minutes.

Pour cranberries into shallow baking pan; add hot syrup. Arrange sausage cakes in pan.

Bake in hot oven (400°F.) 30 minutes or until cranberries have popped open. Serves 6.

Cape Cod Sausage Cakes

PORK SAUSAGE LINKS

Method #1: Place sausage links in a cold skillet. Cook over low heat 12 to 15 minutes, pouring off fat as it accumulates.

Method #2: Put links in a skillet with 2 tablespoons water. Cover and steam 5 minutes.

Drain off water and cook links over low heat, turning frequently, until sausage is well browned.

Do not puncture skins during cooking.

FRIED PORK SAUSAGE PATTIES

Shape bulk sausage into thin patties. Place in cold skillet.

Cook slowly, turning occasionally, until center has lost pink color. Drain off fat as it accumulates.

SAUSAGE WITH GLAZED APPLES

2 firm tart apples
1/2 cup sugar
1/2 cup water
1 teaspoon butter or margarine
4 sausage patties (1/2 pound) or sausage links
1 tablespoon flour
1/4 teaspoon sugar

Core and cut apples into 1/2-inch slices. Combine sugar and water and boil 5 minutes. Add butter.

Drop apple rings into syrup and cook slowly until nearly tender, about 5 minutes. Drain.

If sausage meat is used, form into patties, roll in mixture of flour and 1/4 teaspoon sugar. Broil under moderate heat about 8 minutes. If links are used, cook as directed in preceding recipe. Serves 4.

PORK SAUSAGE-SWEET POTATO-APPLE CASSEROLE

3 medium sweet potatoes
3 medium tart apples
1/2 cup brown sugar
1/2 teaspoon salt
1/8 teaspoon allspice
1 pound pork sausage links
2 tablespoons drippings
1/4 cup boiling water

Boil sweet potatoes until tender; pare and cut in thick slices. Lay half the slices in greased casserole.

Core unpeeled apples and cut across into 1/8-inch slices. Put half the slices on top of potato slices.

Sprinkle with brown sugar mixed with allspice and salt. Add remaining potatoes and apples.

Fry sausage links 10 minutes and place in casserole.

Mix drippings and water; pour over all. Bake in moderate oven (375°F.) 40 minutes. Serves 4.

SAUSAGE SURPRISES

2 cups packaged ready-mix for pancakes or biscuits
1/4 cup shortening
2/3 to 3/4 cup milk
10 small pork sausage links, cooked

To make dough, cut shortening into ready-mix until mixture resembles coarse crumbs. Add milk, stirring lightly only until mixture is dampened. Turn out on lightly floured board and knead gently a few seconds.

Roll out to a scant 1/4-inch thickness. Cut twenty circles of dough, using a floured biscuit cutter (about 3-inch size).

Place a cooked sausage link on ten of the circles. Place a second circle on top of each, sealing edges with the tines of a fork. Cut a slit about an inch long in the center of each.

Place on an ungreased baking sheet. Bake in hot oven (425°F.) 12 to 15 minutes. Serve plain as an appetizer or with warm applesauce or sausage gravy for a main dish. Makes 10 surprises.

BAKED PORK SAUSAGE PATTIES

Break 1 slice of bread into small pieces. Combine with 1 pound pork sausage, 1 egg, 1/2 cup grated apple, and 1 teaspoon salt.

Mix well. Shape into 6 uniform patties 3/4 inch thick.

Place on rack in open roasting pan. Bake in moderate oven (350°F.) 1 hour. Serves 6.

BAKED SAUSAGES

Place sausages on a rack over a pan. Cook in moderate oven (350°F.) until done.

SAUSAGES IN WHITE WINE

1 tablespoon butter or margarine
1 onion, finely chopped
12 large pork sausages
1 cup rich consommé
1 cup white wine
2 tablespoons tomato purée
Buttered toast
Manie butter (1 1/2 tablespoons flour kneaded with 2 tablespoons butter)

Melt butter in a large skillet; add onion and pork sausages, pricked with a fork. Cook until the onions and sausages are lightly browned.

Add consommé, white wine, and tomato purée. Simmer, covered, for 10 to 15 minutes.

Place sausages over slices of buttered toast on a heated platter and keep them warm.

Continue to cook the sauce until it is reduced to 1 cup and thicken it with bits of manie butter. Stir well until the sauce is smooth and thick. Taste for seasoning and pour the sauce over the sausages. Serves 6.

Sausage Surprises

SOUTHERN SAUSAGE LOAF

1 pound sausage meat
1 pound lean ground beef
1/2 cup fine breadcrumbs
1/4 teaspoon pepper
1 teaspoon sage
1 teaspoon salt
2 well beaten eggs
1/4 cup light cream

Mix all ingredients thoroughly. Form into loaf and bake in moderate oven (350°F.) 1 hour, or until done.

This is delicious served with a cream sauce. Serves 6.

HUNGARIAN PORK SAUSAGE LOAF

Combine 2 pounds bulk pork sausage with 4 cups breadcrumbs, 1 slightly beaten egg, and 1 cup sour cream. Season with paprika.

Pack firmly into loaf pan. Bake in moderate oven (350°F.) about 1 1/2 hours. Serves 5 to 6.

RICE AND SAUSAGE CASSEROLE

1/2 pound bulk pork sausage
1 can condensed vegetable soup (without meat)
1 1/2 cups cooked rice
1/4 cup water

Fry bulk sausage (loose, not formed into patties) until brown. Drain off fat to save or discard.

Combine sausage, soup, rice, and water in skillet. Mix well.

Bake in greased casserole or in individual casseroles in moderate oven (350°F.) 20 minutes.

For a decorative touch, fry some sausage in small balls and use these with some of peas and carrots out of soup as a top garnish. Add this garnish during final minutes of cooking period. Serves 6.

Rice and Sausage Casserole

Ham and Other Cured Pork

How to Tell Whether a Ham Must Be Cooked Before Eating

Most hams on the market have complete identification and cookery copy on the wrapper telling you whether the ham must be cooked before eating. Half hams, pieces, and slices are more difficult to identify because the lettering on the edge of the meat may be difficult to read.

"Fully Cooked" means that the ham or picnic is completely cooked, ready to use without further cooking, or it may be reheated if desired hot.

"Ready to Eat" means the ham is probably safe to eat without cooking but the texture and flavor are improved by cooking just like uncooked ham.

"Cook Before Eating" means that the ham must be cooked before it is eaten.

"Tenderized," "Tendered" and similar terms are advertising slogans without reference to government terminology to explain the degree of heat to which the ham has been subjected by the meat packer. The terms are not a guide to buying the type of ham you want.

Canned hams are ready to use as taken from the can or may be reheated. If the ham is sliced before heating, the oven period will be shortened.

HOW AND WHERE TO STORE HAMS

The type of ham influences the storage period. Modern mild-cured hams are very different from the old-style or country-type hams that were cured in a strong salt-sugar brine which helped preserve or keep the hams.

Today most hams on the market are given a mild salt-and-sugar cure; then smoked to a definite internal temperature. Specialty hams like Smithfield and Tennessee have old-style cures, so these may be kept in a cool place for several months.

However, the modern mild-cured hams, whether uncooked or cooked, should be kept in the refrigerator and used within a week or so to prevent loss of flavor and deterioration.

Full-sized canned hams and picnics must be kept in the refrigerator, too, as directed on the label.

Cured meats (as ham, picnics, and bacon) do not keep well in the freezer because salt increases the development or rancidity in the fat. However, canned hams and picnics frozen in the unopened can keep very well.

BAKED HAM

Place whole or half ham fat-side-up on rack in open roasting pan. Do not add water. Do not cover.

If you have a meat thermometer, insert it through outside fat into center of thickest muscle so that bulb does not rest on bone or fat. Bake in a slow oven (300°–325°F.) according to timetable.

Times given in the chart are for ham at room temperature when started. Since heat penetrates a thick piece of meat like a ham very slowly, additional time should be allowed when meat has been taken from refrigerator a short time before roasting.

Note: Many hams on the market carry cooking directions which should be used for that particular kind.

Half an hour before ham is done, take from oven and remove rind. Score fat in diamond shapes; stick a whole clove in each diamond and rub surface with dry mustard and brown sugar moistened with ham drippings. Or follow directions for glazes (below).

Or ham may be basted during cooking period with honey, syrup from canned fruit, or cider.

BAKED PICNIC SHOULDER

Picnics may be baked and glazed like ham of the same type.

Decorated Baked Ham: Cut stems for flowers from green pepper. Make blossoms by cutting canned pineapple into small rings, cutting kumquats and maraschino cherries in half. Arrange on ham to form gay bouquet, holding in place with toothpicks. Brush with a little additional glaze and return to oven until fruit and ham are glazed to perfection. Remove toothpicks before serving.

SMOKED SHOULDER BUTT

Use a 2- to 2½-pound smoked Boston-style butt. Place in deep kettle and cover with cold water. Bring just to boiling; reduce heat and simmer (*do not boil*) 45 to 60 minutes per pound, or until tender. Remove from water.

Place in shallow pan. Spread butt with prepared mustard. Stud with whole cloves. Sprinkle with brown sugar. Bake in moderate oven (350°F.) until glazed, about 30 minutes. Serves 8.

GLAZES FOR BAKED HAM AND PICNICS

General Directions: Thirty minutes before end of baking time, remove the ham from oven, score fat (cut shallow crisscross gashes), stick with cloves, spread with a glaze and return to oven.

Brown Sugar-Orange Glaze: Mix together 1 cup brown sugar, 1 teaspoon dry mustard, and enough orange juice to moisten.

Brown Sugar-Pineapple Glaze: Mix ¾ cup brown sugar with ¾ cup crushed pineapple.

Molasses Glaze: Mix dark molasses with a very little vinegar from sweet pickles. Spread sparingly on ham. Sprinkle with fine breadcrumbs.

Maple-Cider Glaze: Mix ½ cup maple syrup, ½ cup cider, and 2 tablespoons dry mustard.

Spiced Honey Glaze: Mix 1 cup honey with 2 tablespoons mustard. Spread over ham. Sprinkle with fine dry breadcrumbs.

Jelly Glaze: Mix 1 cup red jelly with 4 tablespoons horseradish.

Cranberry Glaze: Mix 1 can whole or jellied cranberry sauce, mashed with a fork, with ½ cup light corn syrup. Or, use cranberry sauce alone.

BAKED HAM TIMETABLE
(Oven Temperature 300°F.–325°F.)

	Thermometer Reading	Minutes Per Lb.
Ham, whole: Uncooked, 10-12 lbs.	160°F.	18–20
Ready-to-eat type, 10-12 lbs.	130°F.	10
Ham, half: Uncooked, 6-8 lbs.	160°F.	22–25
Ready-to-eat type, 6-8 lbs.	130°F.	10
Picnic (Shoulder)	170°F.	30–35
Boneless Butt (Cottage Roll)	170°F.	40–45

ROTISSERIE-ROASTED HAM

Buy a boneless and *fully cooked* ham. Center ham lengthwise on spit and tie with cord if necessary. Place on rotisserie. Roast about 10 minutes per pound or until meat thermometer reads 130°F. During the last 30 minutes glaze by occasionally spooning orange marmalade over the turning ham.

COUNTRY HAMS: TENNESSEE, VIRGINIA, SMITHFIELD, KENTUCKY, ETC.

The majority of country-cured hams require soaking and boiling before baking because they are hung for a considerable time and they develop an exterior mold.

The distinctive flavors of these hams are due to a special diet of peanuts and acorns and to long aging after curing and smoking.

To prepare them, scrub well with a stiff brush and warm water. Rinse well in several waters. Cut off any discolored spots. Cover with cold water and soak 12 to 24 hours.

Drain and place skin-side-up in a large pot. Cover with cold water. Bring to boiling point. Cover closely. Reduce heat and simmer until tender. Allow 25 to 30 minutes per pound.

Glazed Virginia Ham: Prepare as above, then remove skin. Sprinkle with brown sugar. Stud with cloves.

Bake in slow oven (325°F.) about 30 minutes, until glazed. Slice very thin.

SPICED COTTAGE ROLL (BONELESS BUTT)

Place cottage roll in a deep kettle. Cover with water. Add 6 whole cloves, 1/2 bay leaf, 1 stick cinnamon, 1/2 teaspoon celery seed, 1 sliced onion, and 1/2 cup vinegar.

Cover tightly. Let simmer until done. Allow 40 to 45 minutes per pound.

HOLIDAY CANNED BAKED HAM

Place one 8-pound canned ham on rack in roasting pan. Spread a 1-pound jar candied fruits and peels over top of ham.

Bake in moderate oven (350°F.) 45 minutes, basting occasionally. Sprinkle one 8-ounce jar red candied whole

◄ *Decorate and flavor a holiday baked ham with candied whole cherries and candied fruits and peels for a festive main dish.*

cherries over fruit. Bake, basting frequently, for 30 minutes. Makes 16 to 20 servings.

"BOILED" HAM

Place smoked ham in kettle with water to cover. Bring to boiling point. Reduce heat until water just simmers but does not bubble. Cover closely and simmer until tender.

For a very large ham (12 to 16 pounds), allow 25 minutes per pound; for a 10- to 12-pound ham, allow 30 minutes per pound; for a half ham, allow 35 minutes per pound.

If ham is not to be served hot, let it cool in the water in which it was cooked.

If ham is to be baked, remove from liquid, remove rind, score and glaze ham as in baked ham.

Bake in moderate oven (350°F.) about 30 minutes.

PROSCIUTTO

This Italian-style ham is becoming increasingly popular and generally available everywhere. It is a pepper-covered and air-dried ready-to-eat ham which may be served hot or cold. It is most commonly used on an hors d'oeuvres tray.

It should be sliced very thin. It goes very well with potato salad and makes an excellent wrap-around for tiny pickles.

A classic hors d'oeuvre is prosciutto wrapped around fresh figs or chunks of melon.

CAPOCOLLO

Capocollo is an Italian term for cooked, boneless pork butt that has been rolled in spices and pepper. It is served in thin slices as an appetizer.

GLAZED SMOKED PORK BUTT WITH CHERRIES

- 1 2½-pound smoked pork butt
- 6 whole cloves
- 1 bay leaf
- 2 tablespoons brown sugar
- 1 teaspoon dry mustard
- ½ No. 2 can sour cherries, drained

Cover pork butt with water. Add cloves and bay leaf and simmer until tender, about 2 hours. Remove and place in shallow roasting pan. (Save broth for cooking vegetables such as beans or cabbage.)

Mix sugar and mustard and sprinkle over pork. Pour cherry juice into pan.

Bake in moderate oven (350°F.), basting often with juice in pan, about 25 minutes or until well glazed.

Heat cherries in roasting pan and serve with pork. Serves 6 to 8.

Ham En Croûte

HAM EN CROÛTE

- 1 cup onion-flavored cracker crumbs
- 1 cup all-purpose flour
- 1/2 cup shortening
- 1/4 cup cold water
- 1 (1½ to 2 pounds) canned ham

Mix cracker crumbs and flour. Cut in shortening. Stir in cold water to form a very stiff dough. Turn out on heavily floured board and roll into a rectangle about 8 x 12 inches.

Remove gelatin and fat from ham. Place ham in center of pastry and fold pastry over ham. Invert on shallow baking pan.

Flute edges of crust if desired and prick with a fork along top and sides. Bake in hot oven (400°F.) 50 minutes or until brown. Serve hot or cold. Serves 4.

SLICED BUFFET HAM

Have the meatman slice canned ham, preferably on a food-slicing machine, and then tie with a heavy cord. Bake in slow oven (325°F.). See timetable for baking time. During the last 30 minutes, spoon over orange marmalade. Bake until glazed. Place on platter and remove cord.

BAKED ORANGE PICNIC

Place smoked picnic in slow oven (325°F.). Bake uncooked picnics 30 minutes per pound. Heat ready-to-eat cooked picnics 15 minutes per pound.

Half an hour before end of baking period, remove picnic from oven. With sharp knife, cut fat into crisscross gashes.

Mix 3/4 cup brown sugar with grated rind and juice of 1 small orange; spread over fat.

Using whole cloves, stick a few half orange slices and maraschino cherries onto fat.

Return to oven to brown. The last 10 minutes, increase oven heat to 400°F.

Baked Orange Picnic

Jiffy Ways with Cooked Ham

CREAMED HAM
(Master Recipe)

2   cups medium white sauce
1½ cups diced cooked ham
¼   teaspoon dry mustard

Combine all ingredients in top of double boiler. Heat thoroughly.

Adjust seasoning to taste with additional mustard or a few drops Tabasco sauce.

Serve on toast, baking powder biscuits, split squares of buttered corn bread, in patty shells, croustades, with mashed potatoes, or with croquettes. Serves 6.

Ham À La King: Add 1 canned pimiento, minced, 3 tablespoons minced green pepper, and, if desired, ½ pound sliced and sautéed mushrooms.

Other Variations of Creamed Ham: Add any of the following to creamed ham: ½ cup cooked corn, canned whole kernels, or cut from the cob, ½ cup cooked or canned green peas, 1 tablespoon chopped ripe olives, or 3 tablespoons chili sauce.

Ham with Cheese Sauce: Substitute cheese sauce for medium white sauce in master recipe.

CREAMED HAM, CELERY, AND WALNUTS

2   cups sliced celery
1   cup water
Milk, as needed
⅓   cup butter or margarine
⅓   cup flour
Few grains pepper
½   teaspoon Ac'cent
1   tablespoon cut chives
2   cups diced, leftover ham
½   cup coarsely broken walnut meats
Salt to taste

Cook sliced celery in water until tender. Drain; measure water; add enough milk to make 3 cups.

Melt butter or margarine; blend in flour, pepper, and Ac'cent. Add milk mixture; cook over low heat until smooth and thickened.

Add chives, ham, walnuts, and cooked celery. Salt to taste. Serve with hot toasted garlic bread. Serves 6.

Creamed Ham, Celery, and Walnuts

HAM WITH PINEAPPLE AND SWEET POTATOES

3   tablespoons chopped onion
¼   cup butter or margarine
2   tablespoons flour
½   cup pineapple juice
½   cup pineapple bits
⅓   cup brown sugar, firmly packed
3   cups chopped cooked ham
3   cups sliced cooked sweet potatoes

Pan-fry onion in butter in chafing dish. Blend in flour.

Add pineapple juice and cook until thickened.

Stir in pineapple bits, brown sugar, and ham.

Arrange sweet potatoes on top. Cover and simmer for 10 minutes. Serve hot. Serves 4 to 6.

HAM AND MUSHROOM CASSEROLE

1½ cups uncooked noodles
2   cups medium white sauce
½   cup grated American cheese
½   teaspoon onion powder or 1 tablespoon grated onion
2   stalks celery
1   4-ounce can mushrooms
2   cups diced leftover ham
Salt and pepper
Buttered crumbs

Cook noodles in boiling, slightly salted water.

Make white sauce and melt cheese in hot sauce. Add onion, sliced celery, and mushrooms, which have been browned in a little hot fat.

Add noodles, ham, and salt and pepper to taste.

Turn into greased baking dish; cover with fine buttered crumbs and bake in moderate oven (375°F.) 30 minutes, or until crumbs are brown. Serves 4.

SHERRIED HAM-CHEESE PUFF

6   slices bread, buttered and cubed
1½ cups grated American cheese
1   cup slivered or finely diced baked or boiled ham
2   slightly beaten eggs
1   cup milk
⅓   cup sherry
½   teaspoon Worcestershire sauce
Salt and pepper to taste

Arrange alternate layers of bread cubes, cheese, and ham in a greased baking dish, ending with a layer of bread cubes on top.

Mix remaining ingredients; pour over contents of baking dish. Bake in a slow oven (325°F.) for 1 hour. Serves 4.

Ham with Pineapple and Sweet Potatoes

HAM AND CORN CUSTARD

2   tablespoons minced onions
2   tablespoons ham drippings
3   beaten eggs
1   cup milk
1   cup whole kernel corn
1   cup diced, baked ham
1   tablespoon minced parsley
Salt and pepper

Sauté onions in drippings until tender. Beat eggs; add milk, corn, ham, parsley, and salt and pepper to taste. Stir in onions.

Pour into oiled casserole and bake in moderate oven (350°F.) 30 to 40 minutes or until custard is firm.

This makes a good luncheon or supper dish and may be served with a tomato or mushroom sauce. Serves 4 to 6.

SOUTHERN CREAMED HAM

1   can (1¼ cups) condensed cream of mushroom soup
¼   cup milk
1   cup cubed cooked ham
2   tablespoons diced pimiento
Corn bread

Blend soup, milk, ham, and pimiento in saucepan; heat thoroughly.

Pour over corn bread or waffles. Serves 4.

HAM AND SWEET POTATO PATTIES

2   cups cooked ham, cut fine
2   cups mashed sweet potatoes (use 4 medium sized potatoes)
½   teaspoon salt
¼   cup milk
1   tablespoon butter or margarine
1   egg
⅛   teaspoon nutmeg
⅛   teaspoon cinnamon
½   cup pineapple, cut fine
2   cups crushed corn flakes
2   to 4 tablespoons fat

Combine all ingredients except corn flakes and drippings. Shape into 8 patties. Dip in corn flakes.

Melt 2 tablespoons fat in skillet. Brown patties slowly, adding more fat as necessary. Fry on both sides until crisp and well browned. Serves 4.

Ham Ring with Creamed Peas

HAM LOAF OR RING

4 slices slightly stale bread
1 cup milk
1 egg
2 cups ground canned ham
½ pound ground beef
1 small onion, chopped
Salt and pepper

Tear bread into fine crumbs and soak in milk about 5 minutes. Beat egg slightly and add with meats and onion to crumbs. Season to taste with salt and pepper.

Put in greased loaf pan or ring mold. Bake in moderate oven (375°F.) 1 hour. To serve, fill center with creamed peas. Serves 6.

Variation: Use ¾ cup milk and ¼ cup ketchup in place of 1 cup milk.

UPSIDE-DOWN HAM LOAF

2 tablespoons butter
¼ cup brown sugar
8 to 12 canned pineapple wedges
Whole cloves
4 cups ground cooked ham
2 tablespoons grated onion
½ teaspoon dry mustard
1 cup breadcrumbs
½ cup pineapple juice
2 slightly beaten eggs
Dash of cayenne

Melt butter in bottom of greased loaf pan or casserole; sprinkle with brown sugar. Stud pineapple wedges with whole cloves and arrange on top of sugar.

Combine ham and remaining ingredients; pack into pan or casserole on top of pineapple wedges.

Bake covered in moderate oven (375°F.) about 30 minutes.

Turn out upside-down on hot platter. Serves 6 to 8

Golden Ham Casserole

HAM AND CORN AU GRATIN

2 cups diced cooked ham
2½ cups canned or cooked whole kernel corn
2 tablespoons grated onion
¼ cup finely chopped green pepper
1½ cups medium white sauce
½ teaspoon dry mustard
½ cup grated cheese
½ cup buttered crumbs

Arrange ham, corn, onion, and green pepper in layers in greased casserole.

Mix mustard with white sauce; pour into casserole. Top with grated cheese and buttered crumbs, mixed. Sprinkle with paprika.

Bake in moderate oven (375°F.) about 25 minutes or until browned. Serves 6.

HAM AND RICE ROUNDUP

1 5-ounce package precooked rice
1 can (1¼ cups) condensed cream of mushroom soup
⅔ cup milk
2 tablespoons grated onion
1 cup cubed cooked ham
2 tablespoons chopped parsley
2 tablespoons chopped pimiento
¼ cup corn flakes

Cook rice according to directions on package.

Combine soup, milk, and grated onion in 1½-quart casserole; mix well.

Add cooked rice, ham, parsley, and pimiento; sprinkle corn flakes over top.

Bake in moderate oven (375°F.) about 25 minutes, or until hot. Serves 6.

GOLDEN HAM CASSEROLE

1 tablespoon vinegar or lemon juice
1 cup milk
1½ to 2 cups diced cooked ham
2 eggs, slightly beaten
Salt and pepper
1 cup grated cheese
2½ cups uncooked noodles
1 tablespoon grated onion
Choice of ½ cup sliced, stuffed olives, sliced celery, fried mushrooms, or cooked peas

Stir vinegar or lemon juice into milk and let stand a few minutes.

Combine ham, milk, eggs, ½ teaspoon salt, ⅛ teaspoon pepper, cheese, and noodles which have been cooked in boiling salted water until barely tender, then rinsed in warm water.

Add onion, olives, celery, mushrooms, or cooked peas (or use more than one of these if desired.) Pour mixture into greased casserole.

Top with buttered breadcrumbs or crushed cereal flakes. Bake in moderate oven (375° F.) 35 minutes.

Serves 5 to 6.

HAM TREAT

2 tablespoons butter or margarine
2 tablespoons flour
1½ cups milk
1½ cups leftover chopped ham (or any leftover meat)
3 eggs, separated
2 tablespoons grated onion
1 teaspoon salt
¼ teaspoon pepper
1 teaspoon Worcestershire sauce
1½ cups finely crumbled soda crackers

In a double boiler, melt 2 tablespoons butter, blend in flour and gradually stir in milk. When sauce thickens, add chopped ham, slightly beaten egg yolks, grated onion, seasonings and Worcestershire sauce. Cool.

Mix in crumbled crackers and then fold in egg whites, which have been beaten stiff.

Pour into greased casserole; bake in moderate oven (350°F.) 1 hour.

Serves 4 to 6.

HAM LOAF

3 cups cooked ground ham
1 tablespoon brown sugar
1 tablespoon vinegar
2½ cups soft breadcrumbs
¼ cup finely chopped onion
2 tablespoons minced parsley
¼ teaspoon pepper
1¼ cups milk
2 beaten eggs

Combine ingredients and fill greased loaf pan.

Place in another pan of hot water. Bake in moderate oven (350°F.) 1 hour. Serves 6.

HAM AND PINEAPPLE FRITTERS

⅔ cup sifted flour
1 teaspoon baking powder
⅓ cup milk
2 eggs
1 tablespoon Angostura bitters
2 cups ground, cooked ham
½ cup crushed, drained pineapple
Fat for deep frying

In mixing bowl, sift flour with baking powder. Add milk, eggs, and bitters; mix until smooth. Fold in ham and well-drained pineapple.

Drop by teaspoonfuls into deep hot fat (350°F.) and fry until golden brown. Drain on paper towels. Makes 20 to 30 small fritters.

Ham and Pineapple Fritters

HAM, GREEN BEAN, AND MUSHROOM CASSEROLE

1 pound green beans, cut in 2-inch pieces
1 pound fresh mushrooms
1/4 cup butter
1/3 cup sifted enriched flour
2 cups milk
1 cup cream
1 teaspoon salt
Dash of white pepper
3 cups cooked ham, cut in strips
1/3 cup pimiento, cut in strips
Grated cheese for top

Cook beans until tender. Cut mushrooms lengthwise and in quarters and sauté in butter 5 minutes.

Sauté a few mushrooms whole for top garnish and set them aside. Blend in sifted flour gradually to butter and mushrooms; add milk, cream, salt, and pepper and cook until thickened.

Add cut ham, beans and pimiento to above sauce; mix and place in a 2-quart casserole. Top with whole mushrooms. Sprinkle with grated cheese.

Bake in moderate oven (350°F.) for 20 minutes. Serves 6 to 8.

HAM WITH ORANGE CURRIED RICE

2 tablespoons butter or margarine
2 tablespoons chopped green pepper
1 tablespoon chopped onion
2 tablespoons brown sugar, firmly packed
2 cups small cooked ham pieces
1 teaspoon salt
1/8 teaspoon curry powder
1/2 cup orange juice
1 tablespoon slivered orange peel
2 cups cooked rice

Pan-fry green pepper and onion in butter for 5 minutes. Add brown sugar and ham. Stir and continue cooking for 5 minutes.

Add remaining ingredients. Mix well. Cover and cook for 10 minutes. Serves 4.

HAM AND SWEET POTATO CASSEROLE

1 1/2 cups diced cooked ham
1 tablespoon butter or ham fat
6 cups hot mashed sweet potatoes (about 1 1/2 pounds potatoes)
2 beaten eggs
1/2 cup milk
1 1/2 tablespoons lemon juice
About 1/2 teaspoon salt

Brown ham slightly in hot fat.

Whip potatoes until smooth and mix with beaten eggs, milk, lemon juice, and salt to taste. Whip again.

Mix with browned ham and drippings. Turn into greased 2-quart casserole.

Bake, uncovered, in moderate oven (350° F.) 45 minutes. Serves 4 to 5.

BACON AND HAM STACKS

Mix 2 cups of ground leftover ham with a beaten egg. Make into 5 patties.

Cross two slices of bacon; lay on them one slice of pineapple, one patty of mashed seasoned sweet potato, and one patty of ground ham.

Fold over ends of bacon and fasten with a toothpick. Place in baking dish and bake in moderate oven (350°F.) for 1 hour. Serves 5.

BAKED HAM TIMBALES

4 eggs
2 cups ground cooked ham or picnic
1 1/2 cups milk
1/2 teaspoon salt
1/2 teaspoon paprika
1/4 teaspoon celery salt
1 teaspoon chopped onion
1 tablespoon chopped parsley

Beat eggs and add to other ingredients. Mix well. Pour into buttered custard cups.

Place cups in pan of water. Place in slow oven (325°F.) 1 hour. Remove from custard cups to serve. Serves 6.

HAM BALLS IN SOUR CREAM GRAVY

1/4 cup chopped onion
4 tablespoons fat
1 pound ground cooked ham
1/4 teaspoon pepper
1 egg
2 tablespoons flour
1/2 cup water
1 cup sour cream

Pan-fry onion in fat in skillet. Remove and combine with ham, pepper, and egg.

Shape mixture into 2-inch balls and brown in hot fat. When evenly browned remove from pan onto platter.

Combine flour with remaining fat in skillet. Add water and sour cream and cook until thickened. Pour over ham balls and serve. Serves 4 to 5.

GLAZED HAM PATTIES

1 pound cooked or baked ham, ground (4 cups lightly packed)
1/3 cracker crumbs
1 beaten egg
2/3 cup evaporated milk
1/16 teaspoon pepper
1/8 teaspoon thyme
1/4 cup finely chopped onion
1/2 cup brown sugar
1 1/2 tablespoons vinegar
1/2 teaspoon dry mustard

Use medium blade of food chopper in grinding ham. Mix ham thoroughly with cracker crumbs, egg, milk, pepper, thyme, and chopped onion.

For baking patties, use a muffin pan

Bacon and Ham Stacks

for 12 large muffins. Grease pans lightly and pack ham mixture lightly into pans, filling about 2/3 full. Bake in moderate oven (350°F.) 10 minutes.

Meanwhile, blend brown sugar, vinegar, and dry mustard in saucepan. Boil syrup 1 minute, stirring occasionally.

After 10 minutes of baking, remove patties from oven and spoon syrup over each. Return to oven and bake 10 minutes longer to glaze patties. Makes 12 patties (6 servings).

HAM CONES, HAWAIIAN

3 cups (1 pound) ground cooked ham
1 tablespoon grated onion
1 tablespoon chopped parsley
1 tablespoon prepared mustard
2 tablespoons pineapple syrup
1 slightly beaten egg
1/2 cup crushed corn flakes (about 2 cups whole flakes, crushed)
10 drained pineapple slices (No. 2 can)

Mix first 6 ingredients together thoroughly. Shape into 10 cone-shaped patties.

Roll cones carefully in crushed corn flakes and place on drained pineapple slices in shallow baking dish.

Bake in moderate oven (375°F.) about 25 minutes. Serve with creamy sauce (below). Makes 10 cones.

Creamy Sauce: Melt 1 tablespoon butter. Blend in 1 tablespoon flour.

Add 1/4 teaspoon salt, dash of black pepper, dash of Ac'cent, and 3/4 cup milk, stirring constantly to keep mixture smooth while cooking until slightly thickened, about 5 minutes.

Glazed Ham Patties

HAM AND SWEET POTATOES—HAWAIIAN

6 medium sweet potatoes
3 tablespoons butter or margarine
1/2 teaspoon salt
1/8 teaspoon pepper
Pinch of nutmeg
Milk
2 cups diced cooked ham
1 No. 2 can pineapple chunks, drained
1/2 cup green pepper strips
2 tablespoons brown sugar
1 tablespoon cornstarch
3/4 cup juice, drained from pineapple
2 tablespoons vinegar

Cook and mash sweet potatoes, then add 1 tablespoon butter, salt, pepper, nutmeg, and enough milk to whip potatoes.

Pan-fry ham in butter until golden. Add pineapple and green pepper; cook 3 minutes. Combine and stir in sugar and cornstarch. Then blend in pineapple juice and vinegar.

Cook, stirring constantly, until clear and thickened. Pour mixture into a shallow casserole. Drop spoonfuls of whipped sweet potato on top.

Bake in hot oven (400°F.) until thoroughly heated, about 20 minutes.
Serves 4 to 5.

PLANKED HAM PUFF

1 cup chopped cooked ham
1 cup mashed potatoes
1/4 teaspoon salt
1 egg, separated
1/2 cup grated American cheese
Buttered julienne carrots

Mix ham, potatoes, and salt. Add egg yolk and fold in beaten egg white.

Pile mixture in center of a buttered pan or shallow glass baking dish and sprinkle with cheese.

Bake in moderate oven (350°F.) 30 minutes. Serve with a border of hot buttered julienne carrots. Serves 4.

HAM WITH SWEET POTATOES AND PEAS

2 cups diced, cooked ham
2 cups cooked peas or 1 No. 2 can peas, drained
1 can condensed cream of mushroom soup
4 hot cooked medium sweet potatoes
2 tablespoons butter or margarine
1/4 teaspoon salt
1/2 teaspoon cinnamon

Combine ham, peas, and soup in greased 1 1/2-quart casserole.

Mash sweet potatoes; add butter, salt, and cinnamon. Place in 6 mounds on top of mixture in casserole.

Bake in moderate oven (350°F.) 30 minutes. Serves 6.

BARBECUED PORKIES IN A SKILLET

1/2 cup minced onion
2 tablespoons butter or margarine
1/4 cup light brown sugar, firmly packed
1 teaspoon salt
1/2 cup chili sauce
1 cup tomato juice
2 tablespoons Worcestershire sauce
6 tablespoons cider or salad vinegar
2 pounds cooked boneless smoked pork shoulder butt

Sauté onion in butter in skillet until lightly browned.

Add remaining ingredients except meat; simmer, uncovered, 20 minutes, stirring occasionally.

Slice meat 1/8 to 1/4 inch thick; place in barbecue sauce. Simmer, covered, 20 minutes.

Skim off any excess fat. Serve in heated sandwich buns. Makes 10 to 12 sandwiches.

HAM WITH MACARONI AND SPINACH

8 ounces elbow macaroni
2 cups milk
1/2 pound process cheese, cubed
2 teaspoons prepared mustard
1 cup cubed cooked ham
2 cups chopped cooked spinach
1 tomato, cut in wedges

Cook macaroni in boiling salted water until tender; drain.

Combine milk, cheese, mustard, and ham. Add to drained macaroni and mix lightly.

Place spinach in bottom of greased shallow casserole. Pour macaroni mixture over spinach.

Arrange tomato wedges in a ring on top of macaroni mixture, pressing gently into macaroni. Dot with butter, if desired.

Bake in moderate oven (375° F.) 20 to 30 minutes. Serve at once. Serves 4 to 6.

HAM BURGERS

2 cups canned or cooked sweet potatoes, mashed
1 1/2 cups ground cooked ham
3/4 cup brown sugar
1 teaspoon dry mustard
3 tablespoons milk
1 teaspoon salt
1/4 teaspoon pepper
Crushed cereal flakes

Mix all ingredients, except cereal flakes, thoroughly.

Form into flat patties. Coat with cereal flakes.

Brown slowly on both sides in small amount of drippings. Serves 6.

HAM AND POTATOES IN SOUR CREAM SAUCE

2 cups sour cream
1 tablespoon melted butter
1 tablespoon flour
1 lightly beaten egg
Pinch of salt
Pinch of nutmeg
Breadcrumbs
1/2 pound ham, thinly sliced
2 cups cooked potatoes, sliced
Shredded Swiss cheese
1 tablespoon butter

Blend together sour cream, 1 tablespoon melted butter, and flour. Gradually stir in egg, keeping mixture smooth. Add salt and nutmeg. Cook over medium heat, stirring constantly, until smooth and thickened. Remove from heat at once and let cool.

Sprinkle a well buttered 1-quart casserole liberally with breadcrumbs.

Arrange ham in casserole. Put layer of potatoes on ham. Cover with layer of sour cream mixture. Repeat until all ingredients are used up.

Sprinkle top with Swiss cheese. Dot with butter. Bake in slow oven (300°F.) 1 hour. Serves 3 to 4.

SCALLOPED HAM, APPLESAUCE, AND EGGPLANT

1 medium eggplant, pared and sliced
1 large onion, chopped
1/4 cup butter or margarine
1 cup canned applesauce
1 pound (2 cups) diced cooked ham
1/2 teaspoon sage
1/4 teaspoon salt
1 cup soft buttered breadcrumbs

Cook eggplant until tender in boiling salted water; drain and chop.

Pan fry onion in butter and add to eggplant with applesauce, ham, and seasonings. Turn into 1 1/2-quart casserole. Top with crumbs.

Bake in moderate oven (375°F.) 25 minutes. Serves 4 to 6.

CRANBERRY HAM ROLLS

2 cups ground cooked ham
2/3 cup fine breadcrumbs
1 slightly beaten egg
2 tablespoons milk
1/4 teaspoon allspice
1/8 teaspoon pepper
1/4 teaspoon cloves
2 tablespoons butter or margarine
1 can jellied cranberry sauce
1 teaspoon vinegar

Combine all ingredients except butter, cranberry sauce, and vinegar. Form into 6 balls. Brown on all sides in butter in a skillet.

Heat cranberry sauce and vinegar in a small saucepan until melted. Pour over balls. Cover pan and cook slowly for 20 minutes. Serves 6.

Jiffy Ways with Ham Slices

BARBECUED HAM STEAK

1   ham steak, cut 1-inch thick
2   tablespoons dry mustard
2   tablespoons brown sugar
3   drops Tabasco sauce
1/3 cup vinegar
Few grains cayenne
1/2 teaspoon paprika
2   tablespoons hot water
3   tablespoons currant jelly

Parboil ham steak for 5 minutes in water to just cover. Drain. Sear on both sides under broiler heat.

Place in greased casserole which, if desired, may be first rubbed with cut clove of garlic.

Combine remaining ingredients and spread over ham. Add 2 tablespoons water or stock.

Cover closely. Bake in moderate oven (350°F.) 35 to 40 minutes. Serves 4.

FRIED HAM SLICE

Trim rind from smoked ham slice. Heat skillet and rub with ham fat. Brown slice on both sides.

Cover and cook over low heat slowly until tender, turning several times.

Allow about 10 minutes for 1/4-inch-thick slice and about 15 minutes for 1/2-inch-thick slice.

HAM SLICE HAWAIIAN WITH WHOLE BEETS

1   No. 2 can crushed pineapple
1   1-inch thick ham slice
1/2 cup brown sugar

Drain pineapple; reserve syrup. Place ham on rack in shallow baking pan. Pour pineapple syrup over ham. Bake in slow oven (325°F.) 1 hour.

Combine pineapple with brown sugar. Spread over top of ham. Bake in hot oven (400°F.) an additional 15 minutes.

Garnish with canned whole beets which have been hollowed out a bit and filled with Horseradish sauce (below). Serves 4 to 6.

Horseradish Sauce: Combine 1/2 cup whipping cream, whipped stiff, with 3 tablespoons drained, prepared horseradish and 1/4 teaspoon salt.

Ham Slice Hawaiian with Whole Beets

BROILED HAM SLICE

Preheat the broiler and grease broiler rack with a piece of ham fat.

Gash fat edge on the ham slice in several places to prevent curling during cooking.

Place meat on rack, and adjust rack 2 inches under the broiling unit for a 1-inch-thick slice of ham.

If you are broiling a slice of cooked ready-to-eat ham, allow 5 minutes for each side. For the cook-before-eating type of ham, allow 15 minutes per side.

Ham Broiler Meal: The cooked dinner vegetables may be heated at the same time as the ham slice is being broiled, by placing them in the lower part of the broiler pan to catch the rich ham drippings and take on added flavor.

Ham Slice with Peaches: When the ham slice is turned, arrange well drained cling peach halves on the broiler rack.

Brush the peaches with melted margarine or butter and broil until heated through and slightly browned.

HAM SLICE WITH SWEET POTATOES

3/4 to 1 pound slice of ham
2   medium-sized sweet potatoes, pared
2   tablespoons brown sugar
1   cup hot water

Cut ham in serving pieces and brown lightly in skillet. Place ham in baking dish.

Slice sweet potatoes over it and sprinkle with sugar. Add water to drippings and pour over sweet potatoes.

Bake in moderate oven (350°F.) about 45 minutes, basting occasionally with the liquid. Remove cover for last 15 minutes. Serves 4.

BAKED HAM STEAK— COUNTRY STYLE

1   ham steak, cut 1-inch thick
Pepper to taste
Pinch of thyme
1 1/2 cups canned tomatoes
4   sprigs parsley, chopped
1/4 pound grated American cheese, (about 1 cup)
1/4 cup minced onions
1   bay leaf

Put ham in greased casserole or baking dish with a tight-fitting cover.

Sprinkle with pepper and thyme. Cover with remaining ingredients which have been well mixed.

Cover tightly and bake in moderate oven (350°F.) about 45 minutes, turning once during the cooking. Serves 4.

Baked Stuffed Ham Slices

BAKED STUFFED HAM SLICES

4   cups soft breadcrumbs
1/2 cup raisins
1/4 cup brown sugar
1   teaspoon dry mustard
1/4 cup melted butter
2   slices (2 pounds) smoked ham, 1/2 inch thick
9   slices pineapple
30 whole cloves
Parsley

Mix breadcrumbs, raisins, sugar, and mustard together. Pour butter evenly over mixture.

Place 1 slice of ham in 3-quart shallow baking dish. Spread dressing lightly over slice. Top with second slice of ham. Stick cloves in fat around edge.

Cut 1 pineapple slice into wedges to make flower petals for top of ham. Place 2 pineapple slices, 1 on top of the other, in each corner of the dish.

Bake in slow oven (325°F.) 1 hour. Garnish with parsley and serve. Serves 6 to 8.

SAVORY HAM SLICE IN CREAM GRAVY

2   tablespoons dry mustard
2   tablespoons water
1   slice ham, about 1 1/2 inches thick (weight about 2 pounds)
1   cup milk

Make a paste of the mustard and water. Spread on both sides of ham slice.

Place ham in a shallow baking dish. Add milk and bake in slow oven (325°F.) until ham is tender and nicely browned. Serves 6.

SPICY BAKED HAM SLICE

1/2 teaspoon each of caraway seeds, chervil, garlic salt, nutmeg, and oregano
1   teaspoon each of minced parsley and tarragon
1   cup water
1   cup wine vinegar
1   2-inch thick ham slice

Combine herbs and spices with water and vinegar; heat through and pour over ham slice.

Bake in moderate oven (350°F.) 2 hours. Spoon sauce over the ham once or twice while baking. Serves 6.

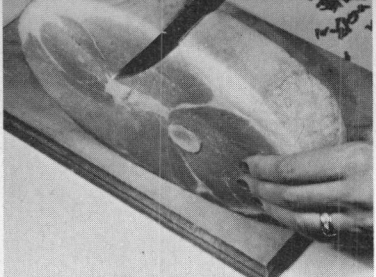

Slash edges of fat about 2 inches apart.

Add brown sugar and bake.

Holiday Baked Ham Slice

BROILED HAM WITH ASPARAGUS

Sliced ham (to serve 4)
Cooked asparagus spears
4   thick slices jellied cranberry sauce
4   thick slices Cheddar cheese, halved

Broil ham to desired degree of doneness. Place ham slices in flat casserole dish. Place 2 or 3 spears of cooked asparagus on top of each serving. Then place a slice of cranberry sauce and slices of cheese (in opposite directions so that the cranberry sauce shows).

Place under broiler until cheese melts. Serve immediately. Serves 4.

Broiled Ham with Asparagus

HOLIDAY BAKED HAM SLICE

A baked ham slice is a fine meat for the holiday small dinner. The slice can be from 1 to 2 inches thick and can be cut from either the "cook-before-eating" or the fully-cooked type of ham.

A center-cut slice is best for a party meal, but any slice from a quality ham is fine eating. Horseshoe slices make handsome individual roasts which require no at-the-table carving.

First, slash the edges of the fat about 2 inches apart. These slashes will keep the slice from curling as the ham heats. Stud the fat with whole cloves and place the slice in a shallow baking pan.

Pour 1½ cups of fruit juice over and around the slice. Use pineapple juice or the syrup from canned pears or spiced peaches. If pear syrup is used, add a piece of stick cinnamon or a few pieces of chopped ginger root or candied ginger.

Now, cover the surface of the ham slice with brown sugar. This is done most evenly by forcing the sugar through a sieve.

Bake in slow oven (325°F.). A cook-before-eating type ham slice will require 1½ hours for a 2-inch slice. Allow about 45 minutes for heating a fully-cooked ham slice of the same thickness.

Spoon the syrup over the slice once or twice during baking.

Garnish festively: Pineapple slices form the base for the edible "holly" (three maraschino cherries with leaves cut out of green pepper).

CRANBERRY GLAZED HAM SLICE

2   slices ham, cut 1 inch thick
1   can (17-ounces) cranberry sauce
½   cup light corn syrup
2   tablespoons whole cloves

Gash fat several places around edge of ham slices. Place 1 slice in greased baking dish.

Cover with mixture of cranberry sauce and corn syrup. Cover with a second slice of ham.

Cover with remaining cranberry sauce-syrup mixture.

Stick whole cloves in fat around edge.

Bake, uncovered, in slow oven (325°F.) 1½ hours, basting occasionally. Serves 6.

BAKED HAM SLICE WITH ORANGE GLAZE

2   tablespoons fat
1   slice smoked ham, 1½-inches thick
2   oranges, thinly sliced
2   tablespoons brown sugar
½   teaspoon cinnamon

Heat fat in a heavy frying pan; sear ham well on both sides.

Remove from heat; cover ham slice

with thinly sliced oranges. Sprinkle with a mixture of sugar and cinnamon. Cover closely.

Bake in moderate oven (350°F.) until ham is tender, about 1 hour. Uncover for last 10 minutes of baking. Serves 5.

BAKED HAM SLICES WITH RICE AND CHEESE

1   slice smoked ham, cut 1-inch thick
¼   cup molasses
¼   cup water
1   cup cooked rice
¼   cup grated Cheddar cheese

Slash fat edge of ham slice in several places. Place in baking dish.

Add molasses and let stand 15 minutes.

Add ¼ cup water. Cover and bake in moderate oven (350°F.) until tender, 40 minutes.

Cover with rice. Sprinkle with cheese. Broil until cheese melts and browns. Serves 6.

HAM STEAK FRANCOIS

1   1-inch center cut slice uncooked ham
1   cup apricot jam
1   cup sauterne or other white wine

Trim rind from ham. Slice and slash fat on edge in several places to prevent curling.

Place ham in shallow baking pan. Combine jam and wine. Pour over ham.

Bake in moderate oven (350°F.) 1 hour. Baste frequently. Serves 4 to 6.

HAM STEAK WITH APRICOT GLAZE

2   1-inch thick ham steaks
1   12-ounce can apricot nectar
2   teaspoons Worcestershire sauce
2   tablespoons brown sugar

Score fat edges of ham steaks to prevent curling. Place ham steaks side by side in a lightly greased shallow baking pan. Combine remaining ingredients and blend well. Spoon ½ of the mixture evenly over the ham steaks.

Place in moderate oven (350°F.) and bake uncovered 45 minutes. During cooking period baste ham steaks every few minutes with some of the remaining sauce. Cut into serving pieces and serve with some of the pan drippings. Serves 6.

Ham Steak with Apricot Glaze

Bacon and Salt Pork

Bacon is the salted and smoked meat from the back or sides of a hog. Canadian-style bacon is a cured, smoked boneless strip of pork loin.

HOW TO COOK BACON

Pan-Broiled Bacon: Place slices in a cold skillet over moderate heat.

Turn frequently for 8 to 10 minutes, until all parts of bacon are evenly crisp but not brittle.

Do not let the fat smoke or bacon will have a burnt flavor.

Pour off fat as it accumulates during cooking.

Broiled Bacon: Place slices on preheated broiler rack, 3 to 3½ inches from heat source.

Broil at moderate temperature 2½ to 3 minutes per side, turning only once.

This bacon needs no draining. If only a small quantity is prepared, a shallow pan with wire rack may be used.

Oven-Cooked Bacon: Lay slices on a wire rack in a shallow pan.

Bake in hot oven (400°F.) about 10 minutes, or until the desired crispness.

This bacon needs no draining and browns evenly from end to end without curling. This method is recommended when cooking large quantities because bacon requires less watching and needs no turning at all.

BACON AND BANANAS

Cut bananas in half. Roll with bacon slices. Fasten with toothpicks.

Broil or bake in moderate oven (350°F.) until bananas are tender and bacon is crisp. Turn frequently.

FRIED SALT PORK AND MILK GRAVY

Cut salt pork into thin slices, about ⅛ inch thick. Gash each rind in 3 or 4 places.

Fry in heavy frying pan over moderate heat until crisp and brown, turning often and removing fat as it accumulates.

Drain on absorbent paper and keep hot. Serve with medium white sauce made with milk and pork drippings instead of other fat.

Variations: If desired, dip pork slices in flour and corn meal before frying. Add cubed boiled potatoes to the white sauce. Serve on hot plates with sauce and potatoes in center surrounded by pork slices. Garnish with minced parsley.

Allow 1 pound salt pork, 1 cup sauce, and 1½ cups cubed boiled potatoes to serve 4.

PAN-BROILED BACON

Place bacon slices in cold frying pan.

Turn bacon frequently while cooking over low heat. Pour off drippings as they collect.

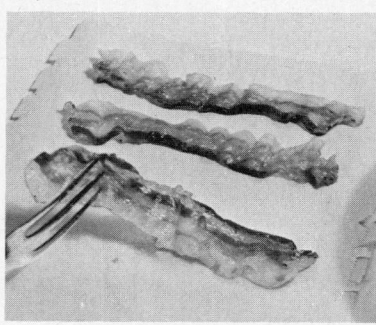

Drain bacon on absorbent paper before serving.

BACON AND PINEAPPLE RINGS

Pan-broil bacon. Drain.

Dip canned pineapple slices in seasoned flour and sauté in bacon fat until brown. Serve with crisp bacon.

CANADIAN BACON AND LIMA BEAN SKILLET

¾ pound Canadian bacon, sliced thin
1 pound can green lima beans

Fry bacon quickly on both sides in skillet. Remove from skillet, and keep hot.

Add undrained beans to fat in skillet and heat thoroughly. Pour into serving dish and top with bacon. Serves 4.

CANADIAN BACON—BROILED

Place ¼-inch slices Canadian bacon on broiler rack. Broil 3 inches from heat source about 5 minutes on each side.

CANADIAN BACON SAUTÉED

This is a lean meat usually cut in thin slices.

Place slices in a heavy skillet and cook over low heat about 5 minutes. Turn slices frequently.

When done, the lean part is a red brown and the fat is a light golden brown. It rarely requires draining.

GLAZED CANADIAN BACON

Slip off casing from 3½ to 4 pound piece of Canadian bacon. Place fat side up in shallow pan. Bake in slow oven (325°F.) about 1½ hours.

Score top of bacon; stud with cloves if desired. Spread with ⅓ cup honey mixed with 2 tablespoons sherry. Continue baking until glazed, about 20 minutes longer.

Serve hot with Golden West Raisin Pineapple Sauce (below), spooning a little of the sauce over the roll to add further glaze. Serve remainder separately.

Golden West Raisin Pineapple Sauce

¼ cup butter or margarine
1 teaspoon dry mustard
½ teaspoon ginger
½ cup pineapple-apricot jam
1 tablespoon vinegar
1 can (13½ ounces) pineapple tidbits
1 tablespoon cornstarch
2 tablespoons water
½ cup dark or golden raisins
¼ cup brandy

Heat butter, mustard, and ginger until bubbly. Stir in jam. Add vinegar and ¾ cup syrup drained from pineapple. Stir in cornstarch blended with water. Cook, stirring until thickened, 3 or 4 minutes. Add drained pineapple tidbits and raisins.

Heat brandy, pour into sauce and flame. Serve hot over baked ham or Canadian bacon. Makes 2½ cups sauce (enough for 10 to 12 servings).

Glazed Canadian Bacon with Golden West Raisin Pineapple Sauce

Veal Recipes

Veal is the flesh of a calf usually weighing from 110 to 200 pounds. The carcass yields 80 to 90 pounds of veal. The lighter the color the better the meat; the most desirable is that from a milk-fed calf, which is almost white and not usually available in most markets. Older and darker veal may be improved by soaking overnight in milk in the refrigerator or by blanching briefly, starting in cold water.

HINTS FOR COOKING VEAL

Because veal comes from immature animals it lacks fat and, although it is tender, it has considerable connective tissue which means that it requires long, slow cooking.

Veal is delicate in color and becomes lighter when cooked. It also has a fine delicate flavor. Cooking methods which intensify color and make the flavor more pronounced should be used.

The best methods of cooking veal are roasting, frying, and braising. Veal is also cooked in liquid for stews. Veal chops, steaks, and cutlets are best if fried or braised.

Rich colorful sauces and gravies are delicious with veal because it combines so well with many flavors. Veal frequently appears in many interesting Italian and French dishes.

For broiling or pan-broiling, only loin and rib chops from high-quality heavy or more-mature veal should be used, and a lower temperature than that for beef and lamb is advisable. Always cook veal to the well-done stage.

VEAL ROASTING CHART Roasted at 300°F. Oven Temperature		
Cut	Meat Thermometer Reading	Minutes Per Lb.
Leg	170°F.	25
Loin	170°F.	30–35
Rack	170°F.	30–35
Shoulder: Whole	170°F.	25
Rolled	170°F.	40–45
Cushion	170°F.	30–35
Breast: Stuffed	170°F.	40–45
Rolled	170°F.	40–45
Loaf	170°F.	25–30

VEAL ROAST

Select roast from leg, loin, rib, or shoulder. Bacon or salt pork strips or suet placed over roast improve the flavor. More seasoning is required for veal than for other meats. An onion added while roasting helps.

Dredge meat with flour before placing in pan. Add sliced onion. Season with salt and pepper.

Place fat-side-up on rack in open roasting pan. Roast in slow oven (300°F), allowing 25 minutes per pound for leg, 30 to 35 minutes per pound for loin. If roast is rolled, allow additional 10 to 15 minutes per pound.

Serve with brown gravy made from fat in pan.

If meat thermometer is used, it will register 170° when veal is well done. For more detailed roasting times, see Veal Roasting Chart.

SPICED POT ROAST OF VEAL

```
5   pound piece veal rump
1   tablespoon dry mustard
2   tablespoons flour
1   tablespoon brown sugar
1   tablespoon salt
1   teaspoon poultry seasoning
1/8 teaspoon black pepper
3   tablespoons fat or salad oil
2   tablespoons vinegar
1   large onion, chopped
1   tablespoon parsley
1   teaspoon celery seed
12  small carrots
```

Roll meat in mixture of mustard, flour, sugar, salt, and seasonings.

Brown well on all sides in a little fat or salad oil in a Dutch oven-type utensil or one with a tight lid.

Add vinegar, onion, parsley, and celery seed. Cover and simmer for 2 to 2¼ hours or until tender.

During last half hour of cooking, small whole carrots may be added. Make gravy from juice. Serves 8.

ROLLED STUFFED SHOULDER OF VEAL

```
Veal shoulder
3   tablespoons bacon fat
1/4 cup chopped onion
1/4 cup chopped green pepper
1/4 cup chopped celery
2   quarts day-old bread cubes
1   teaspoon salt
1/4 teaspoon pepper
1/4 teaspoon marjoram
1/3 cup milk
```

Have bones removed from veal shoulder.

Melt bacon fat; add onion, green pepper, and celery and cook until soft, but not brown.

Add mixture to bread cubes. Add seasonings and milk and mix well.

Spread veal open, spread with stuffing and roll like a jelly roll. Tie roast firmly with string (about 7 strings around the roast will hold it firm).

Place roast on rack in shallow pan and bake uncovered in slow oven (300°–325°F.) until meat thermometer registers 170°F., or about 35 to 40 minutes per pound.

Serve with gravy made from drippings in pan. Serves 12 to 14 or leftover roast to slice cold next day.

CITY CHICKEN OR VEAL ON SKEWERS

```
1½  pounds veal steak (3/4-inch thick,
       cut in 1-inch cubes)
1/2 cup fine crumbs
1   teaspoon salt
1   egg
2   tablespoons water
Fat
```

Thread pieces of veal on wooden or metal skewers.

Dip meat in salted crumbs, then in egg beaten with water, and again in crumbs.

Pan fry in hot fat. When well browned reduce heat, cover and cook until tender, about 35 minutes. Serves 6.

BRAISED VEAL SHOULDER

Brown rolled shoulder in hot fat. Season with salt and pepper.

Place on rack in roasting pan. Add small amount of water. Cook in slow oven (300°F.) until tender, about 35 to 40 minutes per pound.

Add vegetables for last 45 minutes of cooking. Make gravy with drippings.

VEAL SWISS STEAK

Substitute veal for beef in master recipe for Swiss Steak.

BRAISED VEAL WITH WINE

Use a shoulder of veal. Coat with flour, seasoned with salt and pepper.

Brown in hot fat. Add 2 onions, sliced and 1 cup water or stock. Cover closely and simmer until tender, about 3 hours.

Add ½ cup dry white wine and finish cooking. Remove meat and thicken liquid for gravy.

Rolled Stuffed Shoulder of Veal

Breast of Veal with Cracker Stuffing

BREAST OF VEAL WITH CRACKER STUFFING

1 medium onion, minced
4 large stalks of celery, minced
½ cup butter or margarine
About 4 cups crumbled saltine cracker crumbs
2 tablespoons chopped parsley
½ teaspoon sage
¼ teaspoon pepper
2 cups bouillon
3 to 4 pounds breast of veal

Sauté onion and celery in butter or margarine until onions are golden. Combine with cracker crumbs, parsley, sage, pepper, and 1 cup bouillon.

Cut breast of veal in half widthwise. Spread stuffing evenly over one section; cover with remaining section. Skewer evenly on all sides with cocktail picks or poultry pins; lace with cotton thread.

Place on low rack in baking pan. Spread top with thin layer of shortening. Pour in remaining cup of bouillon, cover.

Bake in moderate oven (350°F.) 2 hours. Uncover and bake 30 minutes longer. Serve with gravy (below). Serves 6 to 8.

Note: For mushroom and sour cream gravy, dissolve 1 tablespoon flour in a little water. Add to pan drippings along with 1 tablespoon grated onion and the contents of a small can of mushroom slices. Cook until mixture boils and thickens.

Spoon in 1 cup sour cream. Season to taste with salt, pepper and a dash of nutmeg. Bring to boiling and serve.

VEAL BRAISING CHART

Cut	Total Time in Hours
Breast: Stuffed	1½–2
Rolled	1½–2
Birds	¾–1
Chops	¾–1
Steaks	¾–1

Veal Chops, Cutlets, Steaks

VEAL SCALOPPINE ALLA MARSALA

Scaloppine is the Italian term for small, thin slices of meat, generally veal. They are prepared in a number of styles. The basic method is usually to sauté them until brown, then cook them in wine or a sauce until they are tender. The word is commonly misspelled in various ways.

1½ pounds boned veal, cut into very thin, even slices
Flour
Salt and pepper
¼ cup butter
⅓ cup Marsala wine
3 tablespoons canned concentrated bouillon

Pound the veal lightly until very thin. Dip in flour seasoned with salt and pepper.

Heat butter in a heavy skillet; add the veal and brown on both sides. Add wine and cook 1 minute longer over moderately high heat.

Remove meat to warm serving dish. Add bouillon to pan drippings. Scrape all brown particles loose and bring to a boil. Pour over meat. Serves 4.

Veal Scaloppine with Mushrooms: Pan-fry ½ pound sliced fresh mushrooms in 2 tablespoons butter. Transfer mushrooms to warm serving dish. Proceed as for Veal Scaloppine Alla Marsala. Serve veal and sauce on the same serving dish with the mushrooms.

VEAL CHOPS FLAMENCO

6 loin veal chops
Salt and pepper
Flour
¼ cup olive oil
1 can (10 ounces) condensed beef consommé
2 teaspoons grated lemon rind
1 tablespoon Worcestershire sauce
½ cup chopped green pepper
½ cup chopped onion
½ cup whole pitted black olives
¼ cup chopped pimiento
2 tablespoons capers
1 tablespoon cornstarch
¼ cup cold water

Sprinkle veal chops with salt and pepper. Roll chops in flour. Brown veal chops on all sides in hot olive oil.

Add consommé, lemon rind, Worcestershire sauce, green pepper, olives, onion, pimiento, and capers. Cover skillet tightly. Cook over low heat, turning chops occasionally until meat is tender, about 40 to 45 minutes. Add water occasionally to keep up the level of the liquid.

Thicken the sauce with a mixture of 1 tablespoon cornstarch mixed with ¼ cup cold water. Serve with buttered noodles. Serves 6.

VEAL PARMIGIANA

Parmigiana, or alla parmigiana, is an Italian term applied to a number of dishes containing Parmesan cheese, often in combination with tomato sauce.

4 veal cutlets
1 teaspoon salt
¼ teaspoon pepper
2 eggs
1 cup fine breadcrumbs
3 tablespoons grated Parmesan cheese
6 tablespoons olive oil
1 can (8 ounces) tomato sauce
½ pound Mozzarella cheese, sliced

Pound the cutlets with the edge of a avy saucer or with a mallet.

Add salt and pepper to eggs and beat well.

Mix crumbs with Parmesan cheese. Dip cutlets in egg, then in crumbs.

Heat oil in a flame-proof casserole. Add cutlets and sauté until golden brown, about 5 minutes on each side. Pour tomato sauce over cutlets. Top with slices of Mozzarella cheese.

Bake in slow oven (325° F.) until cheese is melted and delicately browned, about 15 minutes. Serves 4.

VEAL MARENGO CASSEROLE

1½ pounds veal cutlets, cut into serving pieces
1 clove garlic, minced
2 tablespoons olive or salad oil
2 tablespoons flour
1½ cups stock or canned bouillon
Salt and pepper
4 medium tomatoes, peeled and cut in thin slices
1 cup sliced fresh mushrooms

Dredge meat with flour and brown with garlic in hot oil. Remove to greased casserole.

Add flour to pan; stir until browned then add stock, salt, and pepper. Cook, stirring constantly, until slightly thickened and smooth. Lay tomatoes on meat. Pour in sauce.

Cover and bake in moderate oven (350°F.) at least 1½ hours. Add mushrooms during last hour of cooking. Serves 6.

Veal Chops Flamenco

VEAL SCALOPPINE

1½ pounds veal steak, cut ½-inch thick
1 teaspoon salt
1 teaspoon paprika
½ cup salad oil
¼ cup lemon juice
1 clove garlic
1 teaspoon prepared mustard
¼ teaspoon nutmeg
½ teaspoon sugar
¼ cup flour
¼ cup shortening
1 medium onion, sliced thin
1 green pepper, cut in strips
1 10½-ounce can chicken bouillon
¼ pound mushrooms
1 tablespoon butter or margarine
6 pimiento olives, sliced

Cut veal into serving pieces.

Make sauce by combining salt, paprika, oil, lemon juice, garlic, mustard, nutmeg, and sugar. Beat well, or shake in bottle to combine thoroughly.

Lay veal flat in baking pan. Pour sauce over veal. Turn pieces of veal to coat with sauce. Let stand 15 minutes.

Remove garlic. Lift veal from sauce. Dip into flour. Brown well in heated shortening in skillet.

Add onion and green pepper. Combine chicken bouillon with remaining sauce and pour over veal. Cover and cook slowly until veal is tender, about 40 minutes.

Clean and slice mushrooms. Brown lightly in butter. Add mushrooms and olives to veal. Stir and dip sauce over veal. Cook about 5 minutes more. Serve veal with sauce poured over it. Serves 6.

BREADED VEAL CHOPS

About ½ cup flour
1 teaspoon salt
Pepper
4 veal chops, cut ¾-inch thick
1 slightly beaten egg
2 tablespoons water
½ cup sifted dry crumbs
½ cup fat
2 cups water
2 tablespoons chopped parsley
1 teaspoon Worcestershire sauce

Mix flour, salt, and pepper to taste and coat chops with mixture.

Mix egg with water and dip chops first in egg and then in crumbs.

Sauté chops in fat until well browned and remove to a platter.

If necessary, add more fat to that in pan to make 4 tablespoons. Add 4 tablespoons flour (use any left over from flour mixture, adding enough to make 4 tablespoons). Brown well.

Add water and cook, stirring until thickened. Return chops to gravy and season with parsley, Worcestershire sauce, and additional salt and pepper.

Simmer, covered, until tender, about 40 minutes. Serves 4.

VEAL STEAKS—MEXICAN STYLE

1 clove garlic, minced fine
1 medium onion, finely chopped
¼ cup shortening
4 veal steaks (about 6 ounces each) cut ½ inch thick
¼ cup flour
1 teaspoon salt
¼ teaspoon pepper
1 No. 2 can tomatoes
¼ cup tomato paste
½ teaspoon salt
1 teaspoon brown sugar
1 teaspoon curry powder
½ teaspoon thyme
1 teaspoon soy sauce
¼ cup chopped pimiento

Cook garlic and onion in hot shortening until golden brown. Remove from pan.

Dredge veal in flour sifted with 1 teaspoon salt and ¼ teaspoon pepper. Brown in shortening. Add remaining ingredients. Cover tightly. Simmer slowly until tender, about 45 minutes. Serves 4.

CALIFORNIA VEAL CHOPS

4 ¾-inch veal loin or rib chops
Salt and pepper
4 slices pineapple
4 dried prunes
8 medium carrots
½ cup hot water

Brown chops in hot fat. Season with salt and pepper.

Place pineapple on each chop with prune in center. Add carrots. Add water. Cover and cook slowly 1½ hours. Serves 4.

ITALIAN-STYLE VEAL WITH TOMATO SAUCE AND CHEESE

¾-pound veal cutlet, thinly sliced
Salt and pepper
Cracker crumbs
1 beaten egg
3 tablespoons hot melted shortening or salad oil
1 8-ounce can tomato sauce, heated
¼ pound Mozzarella cheese, thinly sliced

Have veal cut into servings and pounded thin. Season with salt and pepper. Dip in crumbs, then in beaten egg, and again in crumbs.

Brown meat quickly on both sides in hot fat.

Place browned cutlets in flameproof dish and pour hot tomato sauce over them. Top with cheese.

Broil until cheese melts, bubbles, and browns. Serves 2.

Note: If Mozzarella cheese is not available, other cheeses may be substituted.

VEAL BIRDS—FRENCH STYLE

6 veal cutlets, cut 3 per pound
½ cup fine breadcrumbs
¼ cup milk
¼ pound bulk pork sausage
¼ cup chopped onion
½ clove garlic, minced
2 slices bacon, cooked and diced
1 tablespoon minced parsley
1 egg yolk
2 tablespoons fat
2 cups veal stock or canned consommé
1 tablespoon flour

Pound veal until it is ¼ inch thick.

Combine crumbs with milk, then mix with sausage, onion, garlic, bacon, parsley, and egg yolk.

Put 1 tablespoon of filling across center of each piece of meat. Roll up and fasten with a wooden pick.

Cook over low heat in hot fat in a heavy skillet until brown on all sides.

Add hot stock and simmer until done, 45 minutes to 1 hour.

Thicken the sauce with a paste made of the 1 tablespoon flour and a little cold water.

To serve, place birds on a heated platter and pour sauce over them. Garnish with parsley and slices of lemon. Serves 6.

VEAL CHOP AND POTATO BAKE

4 veal loin or rib chops, cut ¾-inch thick
2 tablespoons lard or drippings
4 potatoes, pared and sliced
Salt and pepper
¼ cup flour
2 cups milk
¼ cup grated cheese

Brown chops on both sides in lard or drippings. Season.

Place half the sliced potatoes in greased casserole. Season with salt and pepper. Sprinkle with flour. Add remaining potatoes and flour. Pour milk over all.

Place browned chops on top of potatoes. Sprinkle with grated cheese.

Cover and cook in slow oven (300°F.) until tender, about 1½ hours. Serves 4.

Italian-Style Veal

PAPRIKA VEAL STEAK

Chop 1 bunch green onions, including part of tops (or use ½ cup chopped white onions) and brown lightly in hot fat. Skim out onions.

Coat veal steak with flour and brown in hot fat. When browned, sprinkle each side well with salt, pepper, and enough paprika to make meat quite red. Scatter onions over steak.

Dilute ½ cup sour cream with 2 tablespoons milk. Pour over veal steak.

Cover skillet, and cook slowly 35 to 40 minutes or until very tender.

During cooking, turn veal steak and spoon sour cream over top.

Remove meat from skillet, and make gravy from sour cream and drippings in pan, adding a little flour blended with cold water.

WIENER SCHNITZEL
(Breaded Veal Cutlet)

This is one of the classic, traditional Sunday dishes in Vienna—served with cucumber salad and boiled potatoes, or with mixed fruit compote and rice.

1½ pounds veal round
Flour
2 well beaten eggs
1 tablespoon milk
Salt and pepper to taste
Finely sifted breadcrumbs (dry)
Lemon slices
Parsley sprigs
Fat for deep frying

Have the meat cut into very thin slices (like fillets) and pounded flat. Meat must be paper-thin.

Wash and dry meat. Slash corners if necessary, and pound again if necessary. Dredge meat with flour.

Blend eggs, milk, and seasonings with wire whisk. Dip meat into egg mixture, letting excess drip off.

Cover with breadcrumbs. Shake off excess crumbs.

Fry schnitzel in deep hot fat (375°F.) 5 to 6 minutes or until golden brown.

Drain on absorbent paper. Garnish with lemon slices and parsley sprigs.

The lemon slices are part of the dish; sprinkle schnitzel with a few drops of lemon juice before serving. Serves 5 to 6.

Wiener Schnitzel

STUFFED VEAL ROLLS

1¼ pounds veal steak, ½-inch thick, (4 pieces)
1 small onion, chopped
¼ cup butter or margarine
1 cup coarsely chopped dill pickles
About 1 cup saltine cracker crumbs
½ cup liquid from dill pickles
¼ teaspoon pepper
2 eggs, beaten

Have meatman flatten veal ¼-inch thick. Sauté onion in butter or margarine. Stir in remaining ingredients. Place large spoonful of stuffing on each piece of veal. Roll and secure with toothpicks, if necessary.

Place in covered baking dish and bake in moderate oven (350°F.) 1½ hours. Serve with your favorite cheese sauce. Serves 4.

VEAL CUTLETS IN WINE SAUCE

2 pounds veal cutlet
Salt and pepper
2 tablespoons olive oil or salad oil
¼ cup chopped onion
¾ cup sliced mushrooms
1 tablespoon minced parsley
2 tablespoons flour
1½ cups stock or water
¼ cup white wine
2 tablespoons lemon juice

Sprinkle cutlets with salt and pepper; fry in fat until browned on both sides. Place meat in a casserole.

To fat in frying pan, add onions, mushrooms, and parsley and cook for a few minutes.

Stir in and brown the flour. Add remaining ingredients.

Cook until smooth and thick, stirring constantly. Pour over cutlets. Bake in slow oven (325°F.) 1 hour. Serves 6.

BAKED VEAL CHOPS

4 shoulder veal chops (2 pounds)
Salt and pepper
1 egg, beaten
Breadcrumbs
1 medium onion, sliced
1 can (10½ ounces) condensed tomato soup
½ soup can water
1½ tablespoons Angostura bitters
1 teaspoon oregano
Salt and pepper to taste

Sprinkle chops with salt and pepper. Dip each chop first in egg and then in breadcrumbs. Brown slowly on both sides in skillet.

Put chops in baking dish and place onion slices on top of chops. Mix tomato soup with water and heat until blended. Add bitters, oregano, and salt and pepper to taste. Pour sauce over chops. Bake in moderate oven (350°F.) 30 minutes. Serves 4.

Stuffed Veal Rolls

VEAL CHOPS GENOVESE

1 clove garlic
6 loin veal chops, ¾ inch thick
Flour
1 teaspoon salt
¼ teaspoon pepper
3 tablespoons fat
2½ cups cooked tomatoes
2 medium onions, sliced thin
½ cup sherry
½ pound mushrooms, sliced
3 tablespoons butter or margarine
8 ripe olives, sliced

Cut gashes in peeled garlic clove; rub over skillet; discard. Coat veal chops with flour and seasonings.

Brown in hot fat. Add tomatoes, onion, and sherry. Simmer 1 hour and 15 minutes. Sauté mushrooms in butter; add with ripe olives. Simmer 15 minutes longer. Serves 6.

VEAL VEGETABLE BUNDLES

2 pounds veal steak, cut ¼-inch thick
6 small carrots
1 onion, sliced
Salt and pepper
1 egg plus 2 tablespoons water
Sifted crumbs
¼ cup fat
1 cup water or chicken broth

Cut steak into servings about 2 by 3 inches.

Wrap a clean whole carrot and a slice of onion in each piece of veal. Season and fasten with wooden picks.

Dip in diluted egg, then in crumbs. Brown in hot fat, turning to brown all sides.

Add water or broth. Cover and cook slowly until carrots and veal are done, about 1 hour.

For sauce thicken liquid in pan with a blend of flour and cold water (2 tablespoons flour for each cup of gravy). Serves 6.

Baked Veal Chops

FRENCH VEAL CASSEROLE

1½ pounds veal round, ½ inch thick
Flour, salt, and pepper
½ cup fat
1 small onion, chopped
1 clove garlic, minced
4 tablespoons flour
1½ cups beef stock or canned bouillon
4 medium tomatoes or 2 cups canned tomatoes
½ pound fresh mushrooms or 1 cup canned mushrooms

Cut the veal into 6 pieces. Dip in flour seasoned with salt and pepper. Heat fat in skillet; add onion and garlic and cook until golden brown; remove from fat.

Brown meat in flavored fat; remove from skillet.

Add 4 tablespoons flour to fat and stir until browned. Add stock to make brown sauce, cooking until smooth. Season well and add onion and garlic.

Peel and slice tomatoes (if fresh ones are used) and arrange in greased 1½-quart casserole. Lay meat on layer of tomatoes and pour brown sauce over meat.

Cover and bake in moderate oven (350°F.) 45 to 50 minutes. During the last 15 minutes of cooking add mushrooms, and finish cooking with cover off. Serves 6.

HUNGARIAN VEAL BIRDS

2 pounds veal steak
Salt, pepper, paprika, and thyme
2 cups soft breadcrumbs
1 tablespoon each minced parsley, onion, and mushrooms
¼ cup fat
1 tablespoon minced sweet-sour gherkins
1 tablespoon minced olives
Flour
Melted shortening
Clove of garlic
¾ cup boiling water or stock

Cut veal into 6 servings ¼ inch thick. Season with salt, pepper, paprika, and thyme.

Combine breadcrumbs with parsley, onion, and mushrooms. Brown this mixture lightly in hot fat for 2 to 3 minutes, stirring constantly.

Remove from heat. Stir in gherkins and olives. Season with salt and pepper.

Divide this mixture evenly among the 6 portions of veal. Roll up and tie with string.

Brush with melted shortening. Roll in flour and brown in 2 or 3 tablespoons shortening. Rub a casserole with garlic clove and grease it. Place meat birds in casserole. Add boiling water or stock.

Bake, covered, in moderate oven (375°F.) 45 minutes. Turn birds once during baking process. Serves 6.

STUFFED VEAL CHOPS CHABLIS

4 veal chops, about 1¼ inches thick
1½ cups soft breadcrumbs
½ cup ground or minced, cooked ham
1 tablespoon minced onion
3 tablespoons melted butter or margarine
Salt and pepper to taste
Flour
3 tablespoons bacon drippings or other fat
1 cup chablis, sauterne, or other white wine
1 can condensed cream of mushroom soup

Have each chop slit from fat side to bone to form pocket.

Mix breadcrumbs, ham, onion, and butter; season with salt and pepper. Stuff chops with mixture. Fasten openings securely with skewers or wooden picks.

Coat chops with flour seasoned with salt and pepper. Heat bacon drippings in large, heavy skillet and brown chops nicely on both sides.

Add wine; cover and simmer gently about 45 minutes, or until chops are very tender. Place chops on heated platter.

Measure 1 cup of skillet liquid, adding water if necessary to make that amount. Combine with mushroom soup and heat to boiling. Season to taste with salt and pepper. Pour gravy over chops or serve separately. Serves 4.

VEAL AND NOODLES BAKED IN WINE SAUCE

1 pound veal steak, cut in ¾-inch cubes
1 medium onion, sliced
3 tablespoons fat
¾ cup sauterne, Rhine, or other white wine
¾ cup canned consommé or 1 bouillon cube dissolved in water
1 can condensed mushroom soup
1 can (4 ounces) sliced mushrooms and liquid
1 teaspoon Worcestershire sauce
Salt and pepper
½ pound fine noodles
Grated Parmesan cheese

Sauté veal and onion in fat until meat loses its red color.

Add wine, consommé, mushroom soup, mushrooms and liquid, Worcestershire sauce, and salt and pepper to taste.

Mix well and bring to boil, then add noodles. Cook and stir until noodles are limp and well mixed with other ingredients, about 5 minutes. Turn into greased casserole.

Cover and bake in moderate oven (350°F.) 1 hour. Serve with grated Parmesan cheese. Serves 4 to 5.

VEAL SKILLET WITH SAUSAGES, TOMATOES, AND RICE

4 link pork sausages
1 slice veal cutlet (about ¾ pound), pounded very thin
3 tablespoons flour
1 teaspoon salt
¼ teaspoon pepper
1 medium onion, sliced
¾ cup raw rice
½ cup thinly sliced celery
1 No. 2½ can (3½ cups) tomatoes
1 teaspoon salt
⅛ teaspoon pepper
1 tablespoon Worcestershire sauce

Brown sausages in a large skillet; reserve the fat.

Cut veal in 4 pieces; wrap each around 1 sausage and secure with a wooden pick.

Coat the rolls with flour seasoned with 1 teaspoon salt and ¼ teaspoon pepper.

Brown the veal-sausage rolls in sausage fat in skillet; remove rolls.

Add onion and rice to fat in skillet and cook, stirring, 5 minutes. Add veal rolls, celery, tomatoes, 1 teaspoon salt, ⅛ teaspoon pepper, and Worcestershire sauce.

Cover and simmer, stirring occasionally, until veal rolls and rice are tender and the liquid has been absorbed, about 40 minutes. Serve sprinkled with chopped parsley. Serves 4 to 5.

VEAL CUTLETS FRENCH STYLE

6 or 8 veal cutlets
3 tablespoons butter or margarine
1 cup stock
2 teaspoons chopped parsley
1 teaspoon chopped onion
Salt and pepper to taste
2 tablespoons white wine

The veal cutlets should be cut about a half-inch thick. Have the meat man pound them thin or do so at home by wrapping the meat in waxed paper and flattening it with a heavy plate.

Heat butter in a frying pan until it is very hot. Cook cutlets 3 minutes on each side.

Add remaining ingredients except wine. Cover. Simmer 20 minutes.

Remove veal to hot platter and keep hot.

Add wine to drippings in pan. Heat, simmer briefly and pour over meat.

Serve with rice, noodles, or riced potatoes. Serve 4.

Note: If desired, serve tomato sauce in place of sauce indicated.

Miscellaneous Veal Dishes

SAVORY VEAL STEW

2 pounds veal (shoulder or round)
cut in 1-inch cubes
⅓ cup flour
2 teaspoons salt
½ cup chopped onion
⅓ cup shortening
2 cups water
1 cup 2-inch celery slices
6 to 8 small whole carrots
1 tablespoon Worcestershire sauce

Dip veal cubes in seasoned flour. Brown veal and onion in shortening in heavy skillet or Dutch oven.

When well browned, add water, cover, and cook over low heat until veal is tender, about 40 minutes.

Add celery, carrots, and Worcestershire sauce, and continue cooking until vegetables are tender, about 20 minutes. Serve in rice ring if desired.

Serves 4 to 6.

VEAL AND PEPPERS—
ITALIAN STYLE

1½ pounds boneless lean veal
3 tablespoons salad oil
2 medium green peppers, cut in eighths
1 3-ounce can sliced mushrooms, undrained
Pinch of crushed red pepper
2 8-ounce cans tomato sauce
Salt and pepper

Cut meat in bite-size pieces. Brown meat on all sides in hot oil in skillet.

Add peppers. Cover and reduce heat. Cook 10 minutes, stirring occasionally.

Add mushrooms and liquid, red pepper, and sauce. Cover and simmer until tender, 30 minutes longer.

Season to taste. Serve on hot cooked rice, macaroni, or spaghetti. Serves 4.

HUNGARIAN VEAL PAPRIKA

1 pound boneless veal, cut into 1-inch cubes
2 tablespoons bacon fat or shortening
1 large Spanish onion, sliced thin
1 can beef bouillon
1 teaspoon salt
1 tablespoon paprika
1 cup sour cream
1 tablespoon flour
8 ounces noodles, cooked

Brown meat well in bacon fat in heavy skillet.

Add onion and stir and cook until onion is lightly browned.

Add beef bouillon diluted with 1 can water, salt, and paprika.

Cover. Cook slowly on surface heat or in moderate oven (350° F.) about 1 hour or until veal is tender.

Combine sour cream and flour and stir into broth around veal. Cook to thicken. Serve on hot noodles. Serves 4.

VEAL AND SAUERKRAUT
GOULASH

2½ pounds lean veal
3 tablespoons fat
½ cup diced onion
2 tablespoons diced green pepper
1 teaspoon salt
1 teaspoon paprika
¼ teaspoon pepper
½ teaspoon marjoram
1 teaspoon caraway seeds
1 cup canned tomatoes
1 cup diced carrots
2 cups sauerkraut

Cut meat into 1-inch cubes. Heat fat in skillet; add meat and brown.

Add onion and green pepper; sauté 5 minutes.

Add seasonings, caraway, and tomatoes. Cover, simmer 40 to 45 minutes or until meat is tender.

Add carrots and sauerkraut. Cook 20 minutes longer. Add a little water if necessary. Serves 6.

VEAL WITH MUSHROOMS
IN SOUR CREAM

3 pounds veal for stew
1 teaspoon sugar
2 tablespoons butter or margarine
2 tablespoons finely chopped onion
2 tablespoons flour
1½ teaspoons salt
⅛ teaspoon pepper
¼ teaspoon Ac'cent
Grated rind of ¼ lemon
4 cups boiling water
¼ pound fresh mushrooms, sliced
½ cup sour cream

Remove bones and cut meat into bite-size pieces.

Melt sugar in skillet; add butter or margarine and onion. Stir until onion is coated.

Add veal and stir until it slightly changes color. Add flour, salt, pepper, Ac'cent, and lemon rind.

Pour in boiling water, then transfer to casserole. Cover and bake in moderate oven (350°F.) 1 hour.

Stir in mushrooms, cover, and bake an additional hour. Stir in sour cream, heat through, and serve garnished with parsley. Serves 4.

VEAL SCALLOPS Â LA
PROVENCALE

1½ to 2 pounds veal scallops (thinly sliced round or loin of veal)
Flour
4 tablespoons olive oil
½ pound fresh mushrooms, sliced
2 cloves garlic, minced
½ cup dry white wine
4 medium tomatoes, peeled and chopped
Salt and pepper
Chopped parsley

Dip veal in flour; brown in olive oil in chafing dish over direct heat.

Push veal to side of pan; add mushrooms and cook, stirring often, 2 or 3 minutes.

Arrange mushrooms on veal; add garlic, wine, tomatoes, and salt and pepper to taste. Simmer about 10 minutes. Serve sprinkled with parsley. Serves 6 to 8.

SUPREME OF VEAL WITH
RHINE WINE

4 tablespoons butter or margarine
½ pound mushrooms, sliced or 1 3-ounce can sliced, broiled-in-butter mushrooms
¼ cup diced green pepper
¼ cup flour
½ cup light cream or evaporated milk
1 cup veal stock or chicken bouillon*
Salt and pepper to taste
2 cups diced, cooked veal
2 tablespoons minced pimiento
¼ teaspoon oregano or marjoram
½ cup Rhine wine

Melt butter in a chafing dish or electric frying pan. Add fresh mushrooms or drained, canned mushrooms and green pepper; cook about 5 minutes, or until mushrooms are golden brown and tender.

Sprinkle with flour, stir and mix. Add cream or milk and stock or bouillon. Stir until thickened. Add salt and pepper if needed. Add veal, pimiento, oregano or marjoram, and Rhine wine. Cook 5 minutes longer.

Serve on parslied, freshly cooked macaroni. Serves 6.

*Two instant chicken bouillon cubes dissolved in 1 cup hot water

Supreme of Veal with Rhine Wine

Minced Veal À La Suisse

MINCED VEAL À LA SUISSE (SWISS VEAL)

1½ pounds leg of veal (tender part), cut in thin strips about one-half inch wide
1 medium onion, chopped
2 large mushrooms, sliced
6 tablespoons butter or margarine
1 cup light cream
1 tablespoon sifted flour
1 cup dry white wine
1 tablespoon chopped parsley
Salt and pepper, to taste

In Electric Skillet: Preheat uncovered electric skillet on high (7) for 3 minutes. Meantime, mix veal with onion and mushrooms. Turn heat to 5½ setting and melt butter. Add meat mixture and stir until slightly browned (8 to 10 minutes).

Blend cream with flour. Add to meat and stir until food comes to boil (about ½ minute). Turn to 4 setting; cover electric skillet and allow to cook for 5 or 6 minutes or until veal is tender.

Mix wine with parsley. Add to meat and let come to boil once, stirring constantly. Turn heat to 1½ setting; cover skillet and simmer for 2 minutes. Serve immediately. Serves 6.

In a Regular Frying Pan: Heat a heavy frying pan over high heat; add butter and reduce heat to moderately high. Mix veal, onion, and mushrooms, sauté in butter, stirring often, until slightly browned, 8 to 10 minutes.

Blend cream with flour; add to meat and cook, stirring, until mixture boils. Turn heat to low; cover and simmer until veal is tender, 5 to 6 minutes.

Mix wine and parsley; add to meat and let mixture boil up once, stirring constantly. Turn heat to very low, cover and let simmer 2 minutes.

JELLIED VEAL LOAF

2 pounds veal shoulder
2 knuckles of veal
2 whole black peppers
1 bay leaf
2 tablespoons vinegar
2 teaspoons salt
1 green pepper, chopped
2 stalks celery, chopped
2 hard-cooked eggs, diced
1 cup cooked peas
1 tablespoon (1 envelope) unflavored gelatin
¼ cup cold water

Cover veal and knuckles with warm water. Add seasonings and simmer until meat is tender.

Strain stock; there should be 1 quart.

Dice meat; add green pepper, celery, eggs, and peas. Place in oiled ring or other mold.

Soften gelatin in cold water; dissolve in hot meat stock. Pour into mold. Chill until firm.

To serve, unmold and serve with cucumber sauce (see Index). Serves 8.

VEAL SUPREME WITH RICE

1 pound boneless veal
2 teaspoons salt
1 onion
Few celery leaves
6 whole black peppers
½ cup flour
⅛ teaspoon mace
Dash of cayenne
Salt to taste
3 hard-cooked eggs
2 tablespoons sherry (optional)

Cover veal with 1¾ cups water. Add salt, onion, celery leaves, and whole peppers. Simmer covered until meat is tender.

Remove celery leaves and whole peppers. Cut meat into short strips.

Thicken broth with flour and stir in meat. Add mace, cayenne, and salt to taste.

Press egg yolks through fine sieve, cut egg whites lengthwise and add to meat.

Cook until thickened; add sherry, if desired. Serve on steamed rice. Serves 5.

VEAL AND POTATO CASSEROLE

1 pound boneless veal, cut in 1½-inch cubes
4 to 5 tablespoons butter or margarine
3 to 4 medium potatoes, pared (2 cups 1-inch cubes)
3 to 4 medium onions, peeled (1½ to 2 cups 1-inch cubes)
1 small clove garlic, minced
2 teaspoons salt
½ teaspoon pepper
½ teaspoon oregano
2 tablespoons minced parsley
1 No. 2 can (2½ cups) tomatoes
2 tablespoons cornstarch

Brown meat well on all sides in hot fat. Add potatoes, onions, and garlic and cook until vegetables are lightly browned. Add seasonings, parsley, and tomatoes.

Blend cornstarch with 2 tablespoons cold water or tomato juice; add and simmer about 5 minutes. Turn mixture into casserole.

Cover and bake in slow oven (325°F.) until meat and vegetables are tender, about 40 to 45 minutes. Serves 4 to 6.

VEAL RAGOUT (Ragoût De Veau)

2 slices bacon
1 large onion, sliced
3 green onions, chopped
3 tablespoons butter or margarine
2 pounds boneless veal, cut in 1½ inch cubes
2 tablespoons flour
1½ teaspoons salt
¼ teaspoon pepper
⅛ teaspoon oregano
½ cup water
1 cup sour cream
Chopped parsley or chives

Cut bacon into 1-inch pieces. Stir and cook in heavy skillet until lightly cooked but not brown.

Add onions and butter. Stir and cook until onions are partially cooked but not brown.

Roll veal in flour seasoned with salt, pepper, and oregano. Add to skillet and brown. Stir and mix to brown veal.

Add ½ cup water. Cover and simmer about 1 hour. Do not scorch.

When veal is tender, push to one side of pan. Stir sour cream into drippings. Stir all together.

Cover and heat about 15 minutes over very low heat to blend flavors. Serve garnished with chopped parsley or chives. Serves 6.

GREEN BEAN AND VEAL STEW (GERMAN)

1 pound boned veal shoulder
3 cups cold water
2 teaspoons Ac'cent
2 pounds green beans
3 tablespoons butter or margarine
3 tablespoons flour
1 tablespoon sugar
1 teaspoon salt
2 tablespoons vinegar
¼ teaspoon summer savory
1 tablespoon chopped parsley
⅛ teaspoon pepper

Cut veal in ½-inch pieces. Add cold water and 1 teaspoon of the Ac'cent. Bring slowly to boil; lower heat; simmer 1 hour.

Wash beans; break off tips; remove strings, if any. Break into 1-inch pieces; add to veal; cover; cook 25 minutes, or until tender.

Melt butter or margarine; blend in flour, sugar, salt and remaining Ac'cent.

Measure liquid from green beans mixture; add enough water to make 4 cups; add to flour mixture with vinegar. Cook, stirring, until smooth and thickened; return to green bean mixture.

Add savory, parsley, and pepper. Cook, uncovered, over low heat 15 minutes. Top each serving with generous mound of mashed potatoes. Serves 6.

Leftover Veal

VEAL CROQUETTES

2 tablespoons butter or margarine
4 tablespoons flour
1 cup milk
2 cups ground cooked veal
1 teaspoon salt
2 tablespoons chopped onion
Fine cracker crumbs

Make a white sauce of butter, flour, and milk. Add veal, salt, and onion. Cool.

Shape into 6 croquettes. Roll in cracker crumbs.

Fry croquettes in deep hot fat until well browned. Drain on absorbent paper.

Serve with hot spicy beets or other tart relish. Serves 6.

Note: One can creamed chicken soup may be substituted for white sauce.

Variations: Add one of these to veal mixture: 1/4 cup shredded cheese, 1/2 mashed clove garlic, 1 tablespoon ketchup, or 1 tablespoon chopped parsley.

VEAL Â LA KING

1 cup diced cooked veal
1 10 1/2-ounce can cream of chicken soup
1/2 cup top milk
1/4 cup sliced ripe olives or canned mushrooms
1 tablespoon butter or margarine
1/8 teaspoon nutmeg
1 tablespoon pickle relish or chopped green pepper
4 slices toast, buttered

Heat soup and milk in saucepan. Add remaining ingredients except toast. Stir and heat slowly.

Taste and season. Serve hot on hot toast. Serves 4.

CURRIED VEAL OR LAMB PIE

2 tablespoons butter or margarine
1/2 cup hot milk
Salt and pepper to taste
3 cups mashed potatoes
1 well beaten egg
3 cups ground cooked veal or lamb
1 medium onion, chopped
2 cups curry white sauce (see Index)

Melt butter in hot milk; add salt and pepper. Beat into mashed potatoes. Add well beaten egg and beat until light.

Fill a greased 1 1/2-quart casserole with part of potato mixture.

Combine meat, onion, and curry sauce; turn into casserole and top with remaining potato mixture.

Bake in hot oven (425°F.) about 30 minutes or until heated through and lightly browned. Serves 6.

VEAL TERRAPIN

1 cup thin white sauce
3 cups chopped cooked veal
3 hard-cooked eggs, chopped
1 teaspoon lemon juice
1 tablespoon Worcestershire sauce
3 cups cooked rice

Prepare white sauce with thin cream or evaporated milk; add veal and egg and heat thoroughly.

Just before serving, add lemon juice and Worcestershire sauce; serve with a border of rice. Serves 6.

PINEAPPLE-VEAL PATTIES

2 cups ground leftover roast veal
1/4 cup fine, dry breadcrumbs
1/4 cup ketchup
1/4 cup minced onion
1/2 teaspoon salt
1/8 teaspoon pepper
1/8 teaspoon thyme
1 slightly beaten egg
4 or 5 slices canned pineapple
3 tablespoons butter or margarine
1/3 cup brown sugar
1/2 cup pineapple syrup

Combine meat, crumbs, ketchup, onion, seasonings, and egg; mix well.

Shape into 4 or 5 large patties. Place on pineapple slices in greased shallow casserole. Combine remaining ingredients and spoon over patties. Cover.

Bake in moderate oven (350°F.) 30 minutes. Uncover and bake 10 minutes; baste occasionally. Serves 4 to 5.

VEAL TIMBALES

2 tablespoons fat
2 tablespoons flour
1 cup meat broth or thin gravy
2 well beaten eggs
Salt and pepper to taste
Lemon juice to taste
2 cups ground cooked veal
1 tablespoon chopped parsley

Make a sauce of fat, flour, and liquid.

Add eggs, seasoning, and meat. Mix thoroughly.

Pour into greased timbale molds or custard cups. Place cups in pan of water.

Bake in moderate oven (350°F.) about 1/2 hour, until set in center.

Turn timbales out and serve hot sprinkled with parsley. Serves 6.

Variations: Chicken, lamb, or other leftover meat may be used instead of veal.

VEAL IN SOUR CREAM

Place cooked, sliced veal in a shallow oven-proof dish. Cover lightly with sour cream and sprinkle with a bit of nutmeg.

Bake in moderate oven (350°F.) until well heated.

Creamed Veal and Vegetables in Parsley Noodle Ring

CREAMED VEAL AND VEGETABLES IN PARSLEY NOODLE RING

4 tablespoons butter or margarine
1/4 cup flour
2 cups milk
1 teaspoon salt
Few grains of pepper
2 cups diced cooked veal
1 cup diced cooked celery
1 cup cooked peas
2 tablespoons butter or margarine
1/8 teaspoon thyme (optional)
1/4 cup minced parsley
4 cups cooked noodles

Melt 4 tablespoons butter in a saucepan; blend in flour; gradually add milk. Cook over low heat, stirring constantly, until thick.

Add salt and pepper. Cook 5 minutes, stirring occasionally. Add veal, celery and peas. Season more if necessary.

Combine 2 tablespoons butter, thyme and parsley; add to hot noodles; mix well. Press into oiled ring mold.

Unmold on hot serving plate; fill center with veal mixture. Garnish with parsley. Serves 8.

VEAL AND OKRA CASSEROLE

1/4 cup milk
1 cup condensed mushroom soup
1 teaspoon grated onion
1 cup chopped cooked veal
1 cup canned or cooked sliced okra

Mix all ingredients. Pour into greased casserole.

Bake in moderate oven (350°F.) 20 minutes. Top with potato chips and bake 5 more minutes. Serves 4.

CELERY VEAL RING

2 cups diced cooked veal (pork or lamb also may be used)
1 3/4 cups chopped celery
3 cups soft white bread cubes (3 slices)
1 teaspoon salt
3 beaten eggs
Dash of curry powder
2 tablespoons minced onion
1 tablespoon melted shortening or margarine
1 3/4 cups hot gravy or milk

Combine veal, celery, bread cubes, salt, eggs, curry powder, onion, and shortening. Add gravy and mix well.

Bake in greased 9-inch ring mold or loaf pan in moderate oven (350°F.) 1 hour. Serve with tomato sauce. Serves 6.

Lamb and Mutton Recipes

COOKING HINTS FOR LAMB AND MUTTON

The thin paper-like covering over the outside of the lamb carcass is known as the "fell." It does not affect the flavor unless the lamb has been aged for some time, and it may be left on or removed from roasts. Under normal conditions, the fell should not be removed from the leg, since this cut keeps in shape better and is juicier if the fell is left on. Chops, however, will be more desirable if the fell is removed before cooking.

Most cuts of high-quality lamb are tender, therefore roasting, broiling, and pan-broiling or griddle-broiling are the cooking methods most used.

Lamb and mutton contain a very small amount of fat and very little moisture. If cooked too long or at too high a temperature the meat will dry and harden.

The neck, shanks, and breasts may be prepared for braising or cut into small pieces for stew, which is cooked in liquid. The meat from these cuts also may be ground for patties or loaf, then cooked by dry heat. Most cuts of the lower-quality Utility lamb are best if cooked by moist heat.

While mutton (mature sheep) is very popular in Great Britain and some other countries, only a small amount of it is sold in this country. Mutton requires slightly longer cooking periods.

Lamb is cooked medium or well done. If cooked so that it is still slightly pink on the inside, there will be less shrinkage and the meat will be juicy and delicious.

Always serve lamb very hot or cold. It should never be served lukewarm.

Roast Leg of Lamb is one of the easiest meats to prepare for Sunday dinner or any festive occasion. Lamb calls mint to mind. But lamb is companionable with lemon, orange, and pineapple flavors, too. A subdued tomato barbecue sauce is favored on lamb by some, but use it sparingly to avoid overpowering the delicate flavor of the meat.

LAMB ROASTING CHART

Roasted at 300° F. Oven Temperature		
Cut	Meat Thermometer Reading	Minutes Per Lb.
Leg	175°–180°F.	30–35
Shoulder: Whole	175°–180°F.	30–35
Rolled	175°–180°F.	40–45
Cushion	175°–180°F.	30–35
Breast: Stuffed	175°–180°F.	30–35
Rolled	175°–180°F.	30–35
Lamb Loaf	175°–180°F.	30–35

ROAST LEG OF LAMB

Do not remove fell or thick skin. If desired, gash meat and tuck in slivers of garlic. Rub surface with salt and pepper.

Place skin-side-down with cut surface up on rack in an open shallow roasting pan.

If fat covering is thin, lay bacon strips over cut side.

If a meat thermometer is used, insert it in the center of the meatiest part so it does not touch the bone.

Roast in slow oven (300°F.) 30 to 35 minutes per pound or until meat thermometer registers 175°F. for medium, 180°F. for well done.

Serve with gravy, mint sauce, or jelly.

Roasted Lamb with Minted Pineapple: Rub a 5- to 6-pound leg of lamb with about 2½ to 3 teaspoons Ac'cent (pure monosodium glutamate) and roast as above.

Half hour before roast is done, heat 5 or 6 slices canned pineapple in ½ cup minted jelly. Place on roast; return to oven and finish roasting. Baste lamb occasionally with remaining jelly. To serve, drain off fat and make gravy from drippings. Serves 6 to 8.

CUSHION LAMB SHOULDER ROAST—STUFFED

Use 3- to 4-pound square-cut lamb shoulder. Have bones removed from side to form pocket.

Fill cavity with favorite stuffing. Fasten edges together by sewing or with skewers.

Place fat-side-up on rack in roasting pan. Roast uncovered, without basting and without adding water, in slow oven (300°F.) until done. Allow 35 to 40 minutes per pound, or until meat thermometer registers 180°F.

Crown Roast of Lamb filled with your favorite stuffing, garnished with hot chutney-filled pear halves. Cooked small white onions cover the rib ends.

CROWN ROAST OF LAMB

Have crown of 10 to 16 ribs prepared at market. Season with salt and pepper. Wrap rib ends with salt pork or bacon or aluminum foil to prevent charring. Fill center with favorite stuffing.

Place roast on rack in open roasting pan. Roast in slow oven (300°F.), allowing 30 to 35 minutes per pound or until meat thermometer inserted in thickest part of roast registers 175°F. to 180°F.

Remove salt pork, bacon, or aluminum foil and replace with paper frills. Serve with pan gravy.

If dressing isn't used, place roast upside down in roasting pan so fat from roast will baste rib ends. Fill center with cooked peas, tiny carrots, or cooked cauliflower at serving time.

SQUARE SHOULDER LAMB ROAST WITH PINEAPPLE GLAZE

1   4- to 5-pound square-cut shoulder of lamb
2   teaspoons salt
½   teaspoon pepper
1   tablespoon curry powder
1   can (1 pound, 4 ounces) crushed pineapple

Place lamb on rack in roasting pan. Sprinkle with salt and pepper. Bake in slow oven (300°F.) 2½ hours.

Combine curry powder and pineapple and add to lamb. Cook 15 minutes, turning occasionally. Garnish with pineapple and cherries. Serves 4 to 6.

Square Shoulder Lamb Roast with Pineapple Glaze

Lamb Shoulder Roll

LAMB SHOULDER ROLL

Season 5- to 6-pound lamb shoulder with salt and pepper. Place on rack in open roasting pan. Insert meat thermometer so that bulb reaches center of thickest part. Do not add water. Do not cover.

Roast in slow oven (300°F.), basting every half hour with French dressing (use total of 1 cup). For medium-done lamb, meat thermometer should register 175°F., and 180°F. for well-done lamb. Allow 30 to 35 minutes to pound. Serves 10 to 12.

MINTED BRAISED LAMB BREAST WITH BREAD STUFFING

Lamb breast
Salt and pepper
3 tablespoons chopped celery
1½ tablespoons chopped onion
2 tablespoons fat
2 cups fine breadcrumbs
½ cup mint leaves
¾ teaspoon salt
¼ teaspoon pepper
6 tablespoons salad oil

Have pocket cut into lamb breast from the large end. Sprinkle inside and out with salt and pepper.

To make the stuffing, brown the celery and onion in hot fat. Add breadcrumbs, mint leaves, and seasoning. Mix well.

Stuff pocket of roast. Fasten edges together with skewers.

Brown breast on all sides in hot fat. Add ½ cup hot water and cover tightly. Cook slowly until done, about 1½ to 2 hours. Serves 4 to 6.

Braised Stuffed Lamb Breast

BRAISED SHOULDER OF LAMB

Rub meat with cut clove of garlic, then with salt. Brown well on all sides in a little fat in a heavy kettle.

Add ¼ cup water, ¼ cup chopped celery, ½ cup chopped onions, 1 cup canned tomatoes, and a bay leaf.

Cover and cook over very low heat or in moderate oven until tender. A 4-pound shoulder will take about 2½ hours.

LAMB PINWHEEL ROLL-BRAISED

Have breast of lamb boned. Spread with sausage or favorite stuffing, then roll jelly-roll fashion. Hold together with skewers or tie with string.

Brown in small amount of hot fat. Add ¼ cup water to pan. Cover and simmer gently until meat is tender, about 2 hours. Add water as necessary. Remove skewers or string before serving.

Variations: Use a can of condensed tomato juice instead of water. Or, use cream of mushroom soup diluted with half as much water, and, if desired, add a little sour cream.

JELLY GLAZED ROAST LEG OR SHOULDER OF LAMB

Select a leg or a boned and rolled shoulder of lamb. Rub with chopped mint leaves. Season with salt and pepper.

Roast as directed for Roast Leg of Lamb. During last 30 minutes, baste often with ½ cup grape jelly diluted with ½ cup hot water.

Make gravy from drippings in pan thickened with a little flour-water paste.

BREAST OF LAMB WITH RICE AND NUT STUFFING

1 lamb breast
1 clove garlic, cut
¾ cup rice, brown or white
¼ cup chopped nuts (pecans, peanuts, or any mixed nuts)
1 teaspoon salt
2 tablespoons chopped parsley
¼ cup flour or sifted fine breadcrumbs
¼ cup shortening or salad oil
2 cups boiling soup stock or water

Have a deep pocket cut into lamb breast for the stuffing.

Precook rice in boiling salted water for 14 minutes; drain.

Rub the lamb breast inside and out with cut clove of garlic. Trim off bits of fat and chop or cut fine; combine with drained rice, nuts, salt, and parsley.

Stuff the breast and fasten opening with skewers. Coat all over with flour or sifted fine breadcrumbs.

Heat shortening or oil in roasting pan; place stuffed breast in it and

spoon some of the oil over meat.

Add stock or water and cook 1½ to 2 hours in slow oven (300°F.) or 30 to 35 minutes per pound of meat. Baste occasionally with drippings in pan. Serves 4 to 6.

BARBECUED LEG OF LAMB

1 5-pound leg of lamb
Salt and pepper
Flour
2 tablespoons Worcestershire sauce
2 tablespoons sugar
½ teaspoon dry mustard
¼ cup vinegar
1 cup water
½ cup ketchup
2 medium onions, chopped

Sprinkle meat with salt and pepper and rub with flour. Place in roasting pan.

Combine remaining ingredients; mix well and pour over meat.

Cover pan and roast in slow oven (325°F.) until tender, 30 to 35 minutes per pound. Baste occasionally with sauce in pan.

Remove cover 30 minutes before meat is done to let it brown. Serve with the sauce. Serves 6 to 8.

BARBECUED BREAST OF LAMB

2 pounds lamb breast, cut into 4 pieces
2 teaspoons salt
2 tablespoons fat
1 medium onion, sliced
½ cup chili sauce
¼ teaspoon cayenne pepper
1 tablespoon vinegar
1 cup water

Season lamb with salt. Brown in hot fat in skillet.

Add onion, chili sauce, cayenne, vinegar, and water.

Cover and simmer or bake in moderate oven (350°F.) about 1½ hours.

Uncover and cook until the sauce is almost absorbed, about 20 minutes. Serves 4.

	LAMB BRAISING CHART	
Cut		Total Time in Hours
Breast: Stuffed		1½–2
Rolled		1½–2
Neck Slices		1
Shanks		1½
Stew (Cooked in Liquid)		1½–2

Leftover Lamb

RED NOODLES AND LAMB

2 cups diced, roast lamb
2 tablespoons lamb fat
2 cloves garlic, minced
1 6-ounce can tomato paste
3½ cups water
1½ teaspoons salt
⅛ teaspoon pepper
2 teaspoons paprika
1 8-ounce package broad noodles
Grated Parmesan cheese

Brown lamb lightly in fat. Add garlic, tomato paste, water, and seasonings. Bring to boil; cover; and simmer 1 hour.

Add noodles, and continue cooking until noodles are tender, stirring occasionally to prevent sticking. Add more water, if necessary.

Sprinkle with cheese just before serving. Serves 4.

LAMB CASSEROLE

3 cups cooked lamb, cut in pieces
1 tablespoon fat
1 cup cooked carrots, cut in cubes
1 cup cooked potato balls
8 cooked small onions
1 to 1½ cups leftover gravy

Brown lamb in fat. Place in baking dish.

Add carrots, potato balls, and onions. Add gravy and enough hot water to moisten. Season with salt and pepper if necessary.

Cover and bake in moderate oven (350°F.) 20 to 25 minutes or until thoroughly heated. Serves 6.

LAMB WITH EGGPLANT, BALKAN STYLE

4 tablespoons oil
1 small onion, cut into thin slices
1 small eggplant, cut into 1½-inch chunks
1 No. 2 can tomatoes
1 tablespoon chopped dill or parsley
1 teaspoon salt
¼ teaspoon pepper
1 slightly beaten egg
1 tablespoon water
1 tablespoon lemon juice
2 pounds cooked lamb, cut into 1½-inch chunks

Heat oil in chafing dish over direct heat. Brown onion and eggplant, then push to one side.

Add tomatoes, dill or parsley, salt and pepper to chafing dish. Cover and cook until eggplant is tender.

Place pan over hot water. Combine egg, water, and lemon juice, then stir in 2 tablespoons of hot sauce from chafing dish. Spoon back into chafing dish. Add lamb. Heat but do not boil, stirring occasionally. Serves 6 to 8.

JIFFY LAMB CURRY

1 cup sliced mushrooms
1 cup diced apple
⅓ cup finely chopped onion
3 tablespoons butter or margarine
2 cans (2½ cups) condensed cream of celery soup
2 teaspoons curry powder
3 cups cubed cooked lamb
3 cups hot cooked rice (1 cup uncooked)
Shredded coconut

Cook mushrooms, apple, and onion until soft in butter. Add soup, curry powder, and lamb; simmer about 20 minutes.

Heap curried lamb on hot rice; top with coconut. Serves 6.

LEFTOVER LAMB KEBABS

Lamb kebabs are usually made with uncooked lamb, but the leftover roast may be used in this way, too.

The trick is to cut the lamb into fairly uniform 1½- to 2-inch cubes. To assure even browning, dip lamb cubes into French dressing, garlic, or lemon-flavored melted butter, or a tart barbecue sauce before broiling. Then brush with sauce during broiling.

Pineapple chunks, mushrooms, sliced bacon, tomato sections, and small boiled onions may be threaded alternately on the skewers to make interesting combinations.

Since the lamb is cooked, broil about 2 inches from heat source to brown quickly and turn to brown evenly.

LAMB PUFFS

2 cups chopped, cooked lamb
1 well beaten egg
2 cups hot mashed potatoes
Salt and pepper to taste
⅛ teaspoon paprika
Flour

Add enough leftover gravy to seasoned lamb to make it spreadable.

Blend egg, seasoned potatoes, and enough flour to make a mixture stiff enough to roll out on floured board. Roll ¼ inch thick and cut with a large biscuit cutter.

Drop a spoonful of lamb mixture into center of each round. Bring up edges to form a three-cornered puff. Press edges together and brush with melted butter or margarine.

Place puffs on greased baking sheet and bake in hot oven (400°F.) 10 to 15 minutes, or until hot and browned. Serve with lamb gravy or tomato sauce. Serves 6.

Variation: One recipe for pastry can be used in place of potato shells, if desired.

Jiffy Lamb Curry

LAMB STEW

2 cups cubed cooked lamb
2 tablespoons fat or salad oil
3½ cups water
2 teaspoons salt
1 teaspoon Worcestershire sauce
8 small white onions
1 cup sliced carrots
1 cup cooked or canned peas
Flour
Hot canned chow mein noodles
Hot cooked rice

Brown lamb in fat or salad oil. Add water, salt, and Worcestershire sauce; simmer 5 minutes.

Add onions and carrots; cook 20 minutes. Add peas; heat. Drain off liquid in pan.

Blend a little flour to smooth paste with water; add to liquid. Cook slowly, stirring constantly, until thickened. Add to lamb and vegetable mixture.

Arrange lamb mixture on platter with noodles and rice. Serves 4.

SPANISH LAMB AND RICE

1 cup uncooked rice
4 tablespoons bacon fat or butter
1 medium onion, chopped
1 cup diced celery
1 No. 2 can tomatoes
1 cup water or lamb broth
1 teaspoon salt
¼ teaspoon pepper
2 cups cubed or slivered cooked lamb

Brown rice lightly in bacon fat or butter, stirring often. Add onion and celery and brown a few minutes longer.

Add tomatoes, lamb broth or water, salt, and pepper. Cook, covered, over low heat, stirring occasionally, until rice is tender, about 25 minutes.

Add lamb, reheat and adjust seasonings. Serves 4.

LEFTOVER LAMB AND EGGPLANT

Sauté 1 large onion and 1 clove garlic, both chopped, in 2 tablespoons olive oil until yellow.

Add 1 cup chopped tomatoes, 1 medium eggplant, peeled and cubed, 1 bay leaf, and ½ teaspoon salt. Cook until eggplant is just tender, stirring often.

Add 2 cups diced or ground cooked lamb and heat to simmering. Adjust seasonings.

Serve on rice. Serves 4 to 5.

Lamb or Mutton Chops and Steaks

PAN-BROILED LAMB OR MUTTON CHOPS

Rib, shoulder, or loin chops may be used. Place chops in heavy frying pan and brown on both sides.

Reduce heat and cook to desired degree of doneness. Add no fat or water. Do not cover pan.

Pour off excess fat as it collects in pan. Turn the chops frequently to cook uniformly. Sprinkle with salt. Serve at once on hot platter.

BRAISED LAMB SHOULDER CHOPS

4 lamb shoulder chops, cut ½-inch thick
1 teaspoon salt
¼ teaspoon black pepper
Garlic or garlic salt
1 teaspoon paprika
1 tablespoon lemon juice
2 tablespoons water

Brown chops thoroughly on both sides in heavy skillet.

Combine seasonings, lemon juice, and water and pour over chops. (If garlic clove is used, rub cut clove over chops.)

Cover and simmer 25 to 30 minutes, turning once during cooking. Serves 4.

LAMB SHOULDER CHOPS, HUNTER STYLE

2 tablespoons butter or margarine
4 shoulder lamb chops, about 1½ inches thick
½ cup sliced onion
2 cloves garlic, sliced
1 can (1 pound, 4 ounces) tomatoes
½ pound mushrooms, sliced
½ teaspoon oregano
Salt and pepper to taste
½ cup dry red wine
1 pound spaghetti

Melt butter or margarine; add lamb chops and cook until lightly browned on both sides.

Add onion, garlic, tomatoes, mushrooms, oregano, salt, and pepper. Cook covered over low heat about 45 minutes or until lamb is tender. Add wine. Cook 15 minutes.

Meanwhile, cook spaghetti in boiling salted water. Drain in colander. Serve with chops. Serves 4.

Lamb Shoulder Chops, Hunter Style

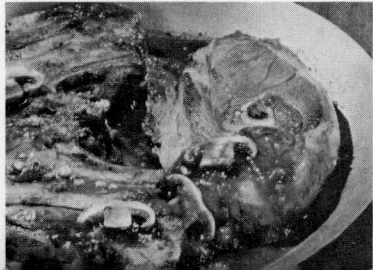

BAKED LAMB SHOULDER CHOPS

6 shoulder lamb chops
1 clove garlic
Salt and pepper
2 tablespoons fat
2 medium onions, chopped
2 cups cooked carrots, diced
4 tablespoons flour
4 tablespoons chili sauce
½ cup sauterne or rhine wine

Rub chops with cut clove of garlic; sprinkle with salt and pepper. Brown on both sides in hot fat in frying pan. Remove to baking dish.

Sauté onions and carrots in pan until onions are soft. Add flour, chili sauce, and wine; cook until thickened.

Place a mound of carrot mixture on top of each chop. Bake in moderate oven (350°F.) for 45 minutes. Serves 6.

STUFFED LAMB CHOPS

8 thick lamb chops with pockets cut at market
Flour seasoned with salt
6 large mushrooms, finely chopped
1 clove garlic, minced
1 teaspoon finely chopped parsley
2 tablespoons breadcrumbs
1 tablespoon cream
Salt and pepper to taste
1 egg yolk
2 tablespoons melted butter or margarine
½ cup boiling water

Roll chops in seasoned flour. Mix remaining ingredients except butter and water. Stuff chops.

Brown in butter. Place in roasting pan. Add butter in which chops were browned. Add water. Cover and cook in slow oven (325° F.) 1¼ to 1½ hours. Serves 8.

LAMB BROILING CHART		
Cut	Meat Thermometer Reading	Time in Minutes
Chops (1-inch)	170°F.	12
Chops (1½-inch)	170°F.	18
Chops (2-inch)	170°F.	22
Lamb Patties (1-inch)		15–18

Note: Pan-broiling or griddle-broiling requires about half the time for broiling.

Broiled Lamb Sirloin Steaks with Mint Glaze

BROILED LAMB SIRLOIN STEAKS WITH MINT GLAZE

4 lamb sirloin steaks, about 1 to 1½ inches thick
½ cup mint jelly
Salt and pepper
¼ cup chopped parsley

Broil lamb steaks 3 to 4 inches from source of heat 7 to 8 minutes, or until lightly browned. Turn. Spread with jelly; sprinkle with remaining ingredients. Broil 8 minutes or to desired degree of doneness.

Serve with escalloped potatoes, seasoned peas, and fresh vegetable salad. Serves 4.

BROILED LAMB OR MUTTON CHOPS

Have loin, rib, or shoulder chops cut ¾ to 1 inch thick. Place in broiler 2 inches below heat.

When brown, season; turn and brown other side. Allow total time of 12 to 15 minutes for chops 1 inch thick. Allow 2 to 3 minutes longer for mutton chops. Serve on a heated platter attractively garnished with vegetables.

ENGLISH LAMB HOT-POT

6 loin mutton or lamb chops
1 lamb kidney
6 large or 12 small oysters
4 mushrooms, chopped
½ teaspoon salt
¼ teaspoon pepper
2 teaspoons Worcestershire sauce
Oyster liquid or stock
Potatoes, sliced
Parsnips, sliced
2 tablespoons melted butter or margarine

Place in a large baking dish in overlapping layers the trimmed mutton or lamb chops. Cut the lamb kidney in 12 slices and place 2 slices on each chop.

Place 1 large or 2 small oysters on each chop. Sprinkle the chopped mushrooms, salt, pepper, and Worcestershire sauce over all. Barely cover all this with oyster liquid, stock or both.

Fill dish with equal parts of sliced potatoes and parsnips. Pour in melted butter.

Cover tightly and bake in slow oven (300°F.) 2 hours. Serve with cranberry jelly. Serves 6.

PLANKED LAMB STEAK DINNER

2 lamb steaks
3 tomatoes, halved
Canned asparagus tips
2 tablespoons butter or margarine
3 egg yolks
Salt and pepper
2 cups hot riced potatoes

Have slices from leg of lamb cut 1 to 2 inches thick.

Brown on one side in hot pan. Season and transfer, with brown side down, to heated plank or fireproof platter.

Place tomato halves around steaks. Arrange asparagus tips tied in bundles on platter; dot with butter.

Add 2 tablespoons butter, egg yolks, and seasonings to potatoes and beat. Make border around other foods with potatoes.

Place in hot oven (400°F.) or under broiler, to brown and finish cooking lamb and to heat vegetables. Serves 6.

LAMB CHOPS VIENNESE

Have rib or loin chops cut 1 inch thick. With a sharp knife, cut a pocket in each chop, to the bone.

Insert a thin slice of fried ham in each pocket. Fasten cut edges with toothpicks. Broil chops about 8 minutes to the side. Season with salt and pepper and serve.

Paper frills may be slipped over the rib ends. Rib chops are small, so allow two to a person. One loin chop should satisfy a normal appetite.

ENGLISH MUTTON CHOPS, COUNTRY STYLE

6 mutton chops, 2 inches thick
Olive oil
Salt and pepper
3 beaten egg yolks
3 tablespoons cream
Salt
Freshly ground black pepper
Dry breadcrumbs
Grated cheese
Melted butter or margarine

Trim chops and flatten slightly with broad side of cleaver. Brush chops with olive oil and broil on 1 side 4 minutes. Remove from broiler.

Season lightly with salt and pepper and spread over broiled side a mixture of egg yolks, cream, salt and pepper to taste. Coat with equal parts breadcrumbs and grated cheese.

Place chops in greased shallow pan. Brush with melted butter. Bake in hot oven (400°F.) 15 minutes. Serves 6.

MUTTON CHOPS, MAÎTRE D'HÔTEL

6 mutton chops, 2 inches thick
Salt and pepper
¼ cup creamed butter or margarine
½ teaspoon lemon juice
1 tablespoon minced parsley
Crisp bacon
Parsley

Trim excess fat from chops and flatten slightly wtih flat side of cleaver or meat mallet.

Broil about 6 to 8 minutes on each side. Season with salt and pepper.

Just before serving, place 1 teaspoon maître d'hôtel butter on each.

Garnish with crisp bacon and parsley.

Prepare butter by adding lemon juice, minced parsley, a sprinkle of salt and pepper to creamed butter. Serves 6.

BAKED LAMB CHOPS

½ cup bacon drippings
½ cup cracker crumbs
2 teaspoons minced onion
1 teaspoon salt
¼ teaspoon pepper
1 teaspoon Worcestershire sauce
2 hard-cooked eggs (optional)
4 lamb chops, cut thick

Put drippings in skillet and brown crumbs, onion, and seasonings in it. Add Worcestershire sauce.

Chop whites of eggs, force yolks through a sieve and add to crumb mixture.

Wipe chops with damp cloth and bread with crumb mixture. Place in baking pan. Bake, covered, in slow oven (325° F.) 1¼ hours. Serves 4.

LAMB CHOPS WITH MUSHROOMS

6 lamb chops
½ pound large mushrooms
1 egg, slightly beaten
Fine cracker crumbs
3 tablespoons butter or margarine
Buttered hot toast
Parsley

Broil or pan-broil chops, allowing 12 to 20 minutes.

While chops are broiling, wash mushrooms, dry and cut in halves lengthwise through caps and stems.

Dip each half in egg, roll in crumbs, and fry slowly in butter in heavy frying pan about 10 minutes, or until golden brown, turning frequently; remove and keep hot.

Serve broiled chops on buttered toast, placing mushrooms over each chop so as to completely cover it. Garnish with parsley. Serves 6.

QUICK AND EASY BROILER MEAL

Remove the fell from lamb shoulder chops and arrange chops on broiler rack. Place cooked green beans and sliced carrots in broiler pan. Season vegetables with salt and pepper.

Place broiler rack over vegetables and set pan and rack in broiler so the surface of the meat is about 3 inches from heat. Broil on one side until chops are browned, about 6 to 8 minutes.
Season, turn and broil on the second side until brown. Season only when turning is necessary. The vegetables will heat while meat is cooking.
Serve chops on a heated platter accompanied with green beans and carrots tastily seasoned with meat drippings.

Miscellaneous Lamb Dishes

OVEN SHISH KEBABS

- 3. pounds boneless lamb shoulder, cut in 1½-inch cubes
- 1 large onion, thinly sliced
- 1 clove garlic, cut in half
- 2 green peppers, cut in 1-inch squares
- 1 teaspoon salt
- ½ teaspoon coarse black pepper
- ¾ teaspoon oregano
- ¼ cup salad oil
- ¾ cup sherry

Put meat, onion, garlic, and green peppers in a bowl; add seasonings, oil, and wine; mix well. Let stand in refrigerator several hours or overnight, stirring occasionally.

An hour or so before serving time, remove from refrigerator and string meat cubes on metal skewers alternately with pieces of green pepper

Lay filled skewers on a rack in a shallow baking pan, or suspend them between the sides of a loaf pan.

Bake in very hot oven (450°F.) for 35 to 40 minutes. Serve on the skewers. Serves 6.

BAKED LAMB (OR VEAL) STEW

- 2 pounds lamb or veal shoulder
- 2 tablespoons fat
- 1 sliced onion
- Salt to taste
- 1½ cups sliced raw carrots
- 1 cup diced celery
- 1 cup raw peas
- ¼ cup chopped parsley

Brown 1-inch cubes of meat in hot fat. Add onion and brown slightly.

Add salt and vegetables, except parsley. Barely cover with water and bring to boiling point.

Thicken with 2 tablespoons flour stirred to smooth paste with water. Pour into casserole.

Cover and bake in slow oven (325°F.) until meat is tender, 1½ to 2 hours. Garnish with chopped parsley. Serves 4.

Sweet and Sour Lamb Riblets

LAMB (OR VEAL) CURRY

- 1½ pounds lamb or veal stew meat
- ½ cup chopped onions
- 1 tart apple
- 1½ teaspoons salt
- ⅛ teaspoon pepper
- 1 teaspoon curry powder
- ½ teaspoon ginger
- 1 teaspoon sugar
- 2 cups bouillon or water
- ¼ cup raisins (optional)
- Hot boiled rice

Brown meat cubes in a little hot fat or oil.

Add onions, apple, seasonings, and liquid. Cover and cook gently 1 hour.

Thicken, if desired, with a flour-water paste. Add raisins and cook 15 minutes longer.

Serve over hot boiled rice. If desired, sprinkle with chopped nuts or coconut. Serves 4 or 5.

SWEET AND SOUR LAMB RIBLETS

- 2 pounds lamb riblets, cut in halves
- 1 teaspoon salt
- 4 cups boiling water
- 1 tablespoon peanut or vegetable oil
- ¼ cup onion, diced
- 1 cup carrots, thinly sliced
- 1 cup pineapple tidbits or chunks
- 1 green pepper, cut in 1-inch squares
- 6 small sweet pickles, sliced

Sweet and Sour Sauce:
- 1 clove garlic mashed with ½ teaspoon salt
- 1 teaspoon monosodium glutamate
- 2 tablespoons cornstarch
- 2 tablespoons brown sugar
- 2 tablespoons soy sauce
- ¼ cup vinegar
- ½ cup cold water
- 1 cup pineapple juice
- 1 bouillon cube (chicken or beef) dissolved in ¼ cup boiling water

Have your meatman chop riblets in halves. Add salt and lamb to boiling water in kettle. Cover kettle. Simmer 1 hour or until tender. Drain, saving liquid for soup or sauces. Brown the lamb pieces slowly in the oil.

Mix together all of the sauce ingredients. Add to the browned lamb, and cook, stirring constantly, until sauce is transparent. Add onion, carrots, pineapple, green pepper, and sweet pickles. Simmer mixture, covered, until vegetables are tender, but still a little crisp. Serve with steamed rice and/or fried noodles. Serve with dishes of mustard, pickle relish, a tart jelly, and a raw vegetable salad. Serves 4.

Lamb Curry is a perfect buffet dish. Serve on plain rice, rice pilaff, or rice into which raisins (white or dark) and slivered almonds have been stirred. Include a variety of accompaniments such as chutney, fine coconut, chopped hard-cooked egg white and bacon, pineapple cubes, etc.

IRISH STEW

- 2 pounds lamb or mutton
- About 4 cups boiling water
- 3 medium-sized carrots, cut into ½-inch slices
- ½ cup diced raw turnip
- 1 medium-sized onion, sliced
- 3 tablespoons chopped parsley
- 2 teaspoons salt
- ¼ teaspoon pepper
- 1 bay leaf

Select meat from shank, neck, shoulder, breast or flank. Cut into 2-inch pieces. Place in kettle and cover with water. Cover and simmer 2 hours.

Add vegetables and seasonings and cook about ½ hour longer.

Thicken liquid with 2 tablespoons flour mixed smooth with ¼ cup cold water. Serves 6.

With Dumplings: Mix and sift 1 cup enriched flour, 1½ teaspoons baking powder, and ½ teaspoon salt. Add ½ cup milk and 2 tablespoons melted shortening or salad oil to make a soft dough.

Bring the stew to a boil, then drop in dumplings from a spoon. Cover tightly and steam, without lifting cover, 12 to 15 minutes.

Irish stew may be made of lamb or mutton. The meat is not browned before it is stewed.

Serve hot braised lamb shanks on a bed of rice and sautéed mushrooms. Pass the gravy separately.

BRAISED LAMB SHANKS

4 large lamb shanks
Salt and pepper
2 tablespoons fat
2 cups hot water
1 cup diced raw potatoes
1 cup diced raw carrots
½ cup diced celery
1 medium-sized onion, chopped

Season shanks with salt and pepper. Brown on all sides in hot fat.

Add water. Cover and bake in moderate oven (350°F.) 1½ hours.

If necessary, add more water to prevent shanks from burning.

Add potatoes, carrots, celery, and onion. Cook until vegetables are tender, about 30 minutes longer. Serves 4.

Note: If desired, the shanks may be cooked on top of range over very low heat.

BARBECUED LAMB SHANKS

4 lamb shanks, about 1½ pounds each
2 tablespoons fat
2 onions, sliced
1 cup ketchup
1 cup water
2 teaspoons salt
2 tablespoons Worcestershire sauce
½ cup vinegar
¼ cup brown sugar
2 teaspoons dry mustard

Brown shanks in hot fat in heavy skillet or Dutch oven. Combine remaining ingredients and pour over shanks.

Cover and simmer on top of range or bake in moderate oven (350°F.) until meat is tender, about 2 hours. Spoon sauce over shanks 2 or 3 times during cooking period.

Uncover and cook 15 minutes longer. Serves 4.

LAMB STEW WITH SOUR CREAM

2 pounds lamb shoulder or breast
2 tablespoons flour
2 tablespoons fat
2 small onions, sliced
2 cups tomatoes or 1 can tomato soup
2 tablespoons chopped parsley
Salt, pepper, paprika
Dill seed, if desired
1 cup thick sour cream

Have meat boned and cut into cubes. Roll in flour and brown in fat. Brown onions with meat. Add tomatoes, parsley, and seasonings. Cook slowly about 2 hours. Add sour cream just before serving and blend it well with the tomato sauce. Serves 4.

EAST INDIAN CURRY

1½ pounds lean lamb, cut in 1-inch square pieces
2 tablespoons butter or margarine
3 small onions, chopped fine
1 clove garlic, minced
1 tablespoon curry powder (more or less)
1 apple, peeled, cored and cut in pieces
3 tomatoes, peeled and cut in pieces
2 cups water or stock
1 teaspoon salt
⅛ teaspoon pepper
3 tablespoons flour

Brown lamb lightly in butter with onions and garlic. Add curry, apple and tomatoes.

Add water, salt, and pepper. Stir well; simmer, covered, until lamb is tender, about 1 to 1½ hours. Remove lamb.

Strain sauce and thicken with flour mixed to smooth paste with little cold water. Return meat to sauce, and heat through.

Serve with plain boiled rice or rice pilaff. Serves 4.

BARBECUED LAMB RIBLETS IN A SKILLET

10 to 12 lamb riblets
Salt and pepper
Smoked salt, if desired
2 onions, sliced
½ cup ketchup
½ cup water
2 tablespoons vinegar
1 tablespoon sugar
2 teaspoons Worcestershire sauce
Dash of Tabasco sauce
1 teaspoon dry mustard
Clove of garlic, mashed or minced

Brown the riblets slowly and thoroughly in a skillet. Drain off the fat. Sprinkle the meat with salt, pepper, and smoked salt, if desired.

Add sliced onions. Combine remaining ingredients and pour over the meat and onions.

Cover and cook slowly until fork-tender, about 1 hour. Stir occasionally while cooking. Serves 4.

Lamb Stew with Mashed Potato Topping

LAMB STEW WITH MASHED POTATO TOPPING

2 pounds lamb breast, shank, or neck
Flour
3 tablespoons lard
Salt and pepper
Rosemary or thyme, to taste
1 cup water
6 carrots
6 small onions
Hot mashed potatoes

Cut meat into 1½-inch cubes. Dredge in a few tablespoons flour and brown well on all sides in hot lard.

Season with salt and pepper, rosemary or thyme; add 1 cup water and simmer about 1½ hours.

Cut up carrots and add with onions. Season. Cover and continue cooking until vegetables are tender, about ½ hour.

Pour into casserole and top with hot mashed potatoes.

Bake in very hot oven (450°F.) until potatoes are brown. Serves 4 to 6.

BAKED VEGETABLES WITH LAMB (BULGARIAN)

3 onions, sliced
1 pound lamb, cut into cubes
2 green peppers, cut into small pieces
Salt and paprika
2 potatoes, pared and quartered
1 cup canned or fresh string beans
1 cup canned or fresh peas
1 cup canned or fresh tomatoes

Brown onions in a little fat in a flameproof casserole. Add lamb and peppers. Season with salt and paprika.

Bake in moderate oven (350°F.) until meat is tender, about 45 minutes. Add potatoes, string beans, peas, and tomatoes. Bake about 20 minutes longer. If fresh vegetables are used, bake about ½ hour longer. Serves 4 to 5.

Barbecued Lamb Riblets

LAMB PILAFF

1 pound lamb shoulder, cut into
   small pieces
3/4 cup butter or margarine
Juice of 1/2 lemon
Salt
Water
1 cup rice
1/2 No. 2 can tomatoes or yogurt

Sauté lamb slowly in 1/4 cup butter
until brown.

Add lemon juice, salt to taste, and a
few drops of water.

Simmer until lamb is tender, adding
water a little at a time as needed to
prevent sticking.

While lamb is cooking, prepare rice.
Place remaining 1/2 cup butter in a
heavy saucepan. Add rice and cook,
stirring often, until golden brown.

Add 1/2 teaspoon salt and 2 cups water. Cover and cook without stirring
over very low heat until rice is tender
and grains are separate.

If desired, rice may be flavored with
tomatoes or it may be left plain and
the final dish served with yogurt.

If tomatoes are used, reduce water
1/4 cup and add them when rice is half
tender.

Add hot lamb to hot rice. Serves 4.

SKILLET LAMB RIBLETS
AND VEGETABLES

2 pounds lamb riblets
2 tablespoons lard, melted
Salt and pepper
1/2 cup water
2 carrots, diced
2 potatoes, diced
1 large onion, diced
1 green pepper, diced

Brown lamb riblets well on all sides
in melted lard. Spoon off drippings.

Season with salt and pepper. Add
water. Cover and simmer 1 hour.

Add carrots, potatoes, onion, and
green pepper. Cover and simmer 1/2
hour longer.

Thicken gravy and serve with meat
and vegetables. Serves 4.

Skillet Lamb Riblets and Vegetables

ITALIAN STYLE LAMB

1 large onion, sliced thin
1 clove garlic, minced fine
1/4 cup olive oil
1/2 cup flour
1 1/2 teaspoons salt
1/2 teaspoon pepper
1 teaspoon paprika
2 pounds cubed, lean stewing lamb
1 can (6 ounces) tomato paste
2 cups warm water
Cooked rice

Cook onion and garlic slowly in hot
oil until light yellow. Remove from oil.

Roll lamb cubes in flour seasoned
with salt, pepper, and paprika. Brown
meat on all sides in hot oil.

Return onion and garlic to pan. Pour
tomato paste and water over all.

Cover tightly and cook slowly until
tender, 1 hour. Serve over cooked rice.
Serves 6.

LAMB-APPLE CASSEROLE

1 pound lamb shoulder, diced
Salt and pepper
1 tablespoon fat
2 cups sliced tart apples
1 teaspoon grated lemon rind
3 whole cloves
2 tablespoons water
1/3 cup dry breadcrumbs
1/4 cup brown sugar

Season meat with salt and pepper.
Brown on all sides in hot fat. Transfer
meat to shallow casserole.

Add apples, lemon rind, cloves, and
water. Sprinkle with crumbs, then with
brown sugar.

Cover and bake in moderate oven
(350°F.) 1/2 hour. Uncover and bake
until nicely browned on top, about 15
minutes longer. Serves 4.

PERSIAN PILAFF

1 pound shoulder of lamb
2/3 cup chopped onion
1/2 cup chopped fresh or canned tomatoes
2 cups uncooked rice
2 tablespoons butter or margarine
1 cup broth or water
Salt and pepper

Cut lamb in 1-inch cubes and brown
well.

Add chopped onions and brown
lightly. Add tomatoes and cook 15 minutes.

Meanwhile soak rice in heavily salted
water. Wash well in cold water and put
over the top of meat.

Top with butter; add broth or water
around the edges of meat. Season to
taste.

Bake in moderate oven (350°F.) 1
hour. Turn out on platter and serve
immediately. Serves 4.

South-Of- The-Border Chili

SOUTH-OF-THE-BORDER CHILI

1/4 cup oil or drippings
2 pounds lean lamb, beef, or pork,
   cubed
2 tablespoons flour
2 tablespoons chili powder
1 medium onion, chopped
2 cloves garlic, minced
2 cups stock or water
2 teaspoons salt
1 teaspoon Ac'cent

Heat oil in heavy skillet; add meat;
brown lightly over moderate heat. Push
meat to one side.

Mix flour with chili powder; add to
skillet with onion and garlic. Continue cooking until onions are lightly
browned.

Add stock or water, salt, and Ac'cent.
Cover tightly; simmer over low heat until meat is very tender, about 2 hours.

Serve over hot cooked rice accompanied by boiled pinto beans. Serves 6.

Variations: In place of chili powder,
use 6 to 8 chilies (seeds removed), 1 teaspoon oregano, 1/4 teaspoon comino
seed, and 2 tiny hot red peppers. Remove stems and seeds from the chili
pods; cut in very thin strips with scissors. Add after adding stock or water;
continue as directed.

LAMB WITH VEGETABLES

2 1/2 pounds lamb shoulder or neck
2 tablespoons flour
3 tablespoons butter or margarine
4 carrots, scraped and diced
1 cup diced celery
1 cup diced, peeled summer squash
1 No. 1 can (2 cups) tomatoes
1 1/2 teaspoons salt
1 teaspoon Ac'cent
1/4 teaspoon powdered mint
4 small mild onions, cut in halves

Remove excess fat from meat. Cut in
small cubes and roll in flour. Brown in
butter; transfer to casserole.

Cover with carrots, celery, squash,
and tomatoes mixed with seasonings.
Put onions on top, Cover and bake in
moderate oven (350°F.) until lamb is
tender about 1 1/2 hours. To serve,
sprinkle with chopped parsley. Serves 4.

SPANISH LAMB STEW

2 pounds breast of lamb
2 tablespoons fat
2 quarts hot water
1 large onion, chopped
1 green pepper, chopped
1/2 cup rice
1 teaspoon salt
1/4 teaspoon pepper
1 1/2 cups canned tomatoes
1 cup canned peas
1 beaten egg
1 teaspoon olive oil
1/2 teaspoon vinegar

Cut lamb in small pieces. Brown lightly in fat; add hot water and simmer, covered, 1 1/2 hours.

Add onion, green pepper, rice, and seasonings and simmer 1/2 hour longer, or until vegetables and rice are done, adding tomatoes and peas the last 10 minutes of cooking.

Combine egg, olive oil and vinegar; add to stew, stirring until thickened; serve at once. Serves 6.

BLANQUETTE OF LAMB

4 pound boneless breast or shoulder lamb
2 tablespoons shortening
1 teaspoon salt
Dash of pepper
1 pound small white onions
5 tablespoons butter or margarine
1/2 pound mushrooms, sliced
2 tablespoons flour
1 cup milk
1/4 cup sherry or white wine
1/2 cup heavy cream

Cut lamb into small chunks, brown in melted shortening for about 20 minutes.

Season with salt and pepper; cook slowly for 15 minutes longer.

Peel onions and cook whole in 3 tablespoons melted butter until barely tender. Add mushrooms; cook 5 minutes more.

To make sauce: Melt remaining butter (2 tablespoons) in a separate saucepan; stir in flour smoothly, add milk gradually and cook slowly, stirring constantly, until sauce bubbles.

Add lamb to onion-mushroom mixture.

Rinse lamb pan with wine and add to meat mixture. Stir in sauce and heavy cream, cover and cook slowly for 35 minutes. Serves 6.

ENGLISH COLYS

2 tablespoons fat
2 onions, chopped
1 clove garlic, minced
1/2 teaspoon salt
1/2 teaspoon freshly ground pepper
1 teaspoon marjoram
2 tomatoes, cut in quarters

1 tablespoon chopped parsley
2 pounds lamb or veal (neck or shoulder)
1 cup water
2 cups diced potato or potato balls

Melt fat and sauté onion and garlic. Add seasonings, tomatoes, and parsley. Turn into casserole. Add meat cut in large cubes.

Cover closely and simmer or bake 30 minutes.

Add water and potatoes. Cover and cook 1 1/2 hours longer. Serves 6.

LAMB SHANKS WITH POTATOES AND CARROTS

4 lamb shanks
1 or 2 cloves garlic, cut in slivers
1/4 cup flour
1/4 teaspoon salt
2 tablespoons fat
1 1/4 cups tomato juice
1 small onion, sliced
1/2 teaspoon salt
Dash of pepper
1/8 teaspoon oregano
1/2 cup sherry
4 to 6 medium potatoes, pared
4 to 8 medium carrots, scraped

Have meat dealer crack shank bones. Slit skin of each shank in several places and insert garlic slivers. Coat shanks with flour seasoned with 1/4 teaspoon salt. Brown shanks on all sides in hot fat in heavy skillet. Transfer to large casserole.

Combine tomato juice, onion, salt, pepper, oregano, and sherry in a saucepan. Heat to boiling point and pour over shanks.

Cover and cook in moderate oven (350°F.) until fat begins to pull away from bone, about 1 1/2 to 2 hours. Skim off excess fat. Add potatoes and carrots. Cook until tender, about 30 minutes longer. Serves 4.

LAMB AND EGGPLANT SUPREME

2 large eggplants
1 pound lamb breast or shoulder, cut in 1-inch squares
1 small onion, chopped
1 teaspoon salt
Dash of pepper
2 tablespoons tomato purée
1 cup water or meat stock
1 cup medium white sauce
1/4 cup grated sharp American or Parmesan cheese

Bake whole eggplants in moderate oven (350°F.) while preparing meat.

Sauté lamb and onion in small amount of butter or oil until browned. Add salt, pepper, tomato purée, and stock. Cover and cook very gently 1 hour.

When eggplants have baked soft, remove skins and mash pulp. Place in top

of double boiler. Add well seasoned white sauce and grated cheese. Beat until very fluffy.

Serve hot, with lamb and its sauce topping the portions of eggplant. Serves 6.

LAMB STEW WITH DUMPLINGS

2 pounds lamb, cubed
1 tablespoon fat
2 teaspoons salt
1/2 teaspoon pepper
4 cups water
6 medium carrots
6 small whole onions
1 1/2 cups green beans
1 tablespoon melted butter or margarine
1 1/2 tablespoons flour

Brown meat in hot fat, then simmer in covered pan with salt, pepper, and water for 1 1/2 hours.

Add carrots, onions, and beans and cook 1/2 hour more.

Mix melted butter and flour into a paste and stir into stew. Cook until slightly thickened.

Dumplings: Sift together 1 1/2 cups sifted enriched flour, 2 teaspoons baking powder, and 1 teaspoon salt.

Beat 1 egg and mix with 3/4 cup milk. Add to dry ingredients, stirring only enough to moisten flour.

Drop by tablespoonsful into hot stew. Cook covered for 5 minutes.

Remove lid and cook 15 minutes more. Serves 8.

LAMB STEW Â LA MASI

Butter or margarine
12 green onions, cooked
6 medium turnips, halved and cooked
12 young carrots, cooked
1 pound green beans, cooked
12 small new potatoes, cooked
1 package frozen lima beans, cooked
1 can consommé
1/4 cup dry wine
1 teaspoon sugar
Salt and pepper
2 pounds shoulder of lamb, diced

Prepare vegetables first. Cook young onions in butter, other vegetables in water, separately, except the potatoes. Cook these in canned consommé. Combine vegetables, adding the consommé from the potatoes and the wine and sugar. Season to taste with salt and pepper.

Now cook the lamb in butter for 5 minutes, or until done. Season.

Add vegetables and liquid and rock the skillet over moderate heat until meat and vegetables have become permeated with the sauce. Serve in small casserole. Serves 6.

Variety Meats

The culinary reputations of many noted chefs have been made with the cooking of variety meats such as liver, tongue, sweetbreads, and other "meat specialties" including hearts, brains, kidneys, oxtails, and tripe.

This delicate art is worth perpetuating, for such meats are well flavored, highly nutritious, and usually quite inexpensive.

When including any of these variety meats in your menus, take our tips on buying, storing, and serving. They'll prove a handy guide to the skillful preparation of some delicious main dishes.

BRAINS

Brains of calf, lamb, beef, and pork may be used. Although there is very little difference in the tenderness or flavor, calf brains are the most popular and highest priced.

Brains may be used in most recipes calling for sweetbreads or may be combined with sweetbreads. Brains combine well with other food and need only a little pep in flavor (Worcestershire sauce, sherry, etc.) to make them very good.

Allow 1 pound to make 4 servings. Beef brains weigh about 3/4 pound each, calf brains about 1/2 pound, lamb and pork brains about 1/4 pound each.

Brains are a very delicate and perishable food and should be cooked within 24 hours after purchase. Keep covered in refrigerator.

HOW TO COOK BRAINS

Soak brains in cold salted water (1 tablespoon salt per quart water) for 15 minutes.

Drop into 1 quart boiling water; add 1 tablespoon vinegar or lemon juice.

Cover, reduce heat and simmer (do not boil) 15 minutes. Drain, cover with cold water, then drain well.

Use at once or cover and store in refrigerator. If brains are to be kept in the refrigerator, leave the membrane on until ready to use, then remove it with the tip of a paring knife.

Brains

From Left To Right, Beef, Veal, Pork, Lamb—Broil, Braise, Cook In Liquid

Note: Brains are sometimes used without precooking, particularly when scrambled with eggs. They may also be steamed before using in recipes, instead of being precooked as above.

FRIED BRAINS

Cut precooked brains into pieces. Season with salt and pepper. Roll in dry crumbs; dip in beaten egg diluted with 1 tablespoon water, then roll again in crumbs.

Fry in shallow fat or salad oil or in deep hot fat (370°F.) until brown. Drain on absorbent paper. Serve with mushroom sauce.

BROILED BRAINS

Brush cooked brains with oil or melted butter. Sprinkle with paprika.

Broil under moderate heat until done, turning to brown both sides, 10 to 12 minutes. Baste occasionally with melted butter. Serve garnished with chopped parsley and lemon wedges.

BRAINS AND BACON

Cut each precooked brain into several pieces. Wrap each piece with a strip of bacon. Fasten with a wooden pick.

Place in an oiled pan. Sprinkle with paprika. Dot with butter.

Bake in moderate oven (350°F.) until brains and bacon are done, about 20 minutes.

BRAINS Ā LA KING

1 pound cooked brains
2 chopped green peppers
2 teaspoons grated onion
1/2 cup diced celery
2 tablespoons fat
2 cups medium white sauce
2 tablespoons chopped pimiento
1/2 teaspoon salt
1/8 teaspoon pepper
6 slices toast

Separate cooked brains into small cubes.

Sauté green peppers, onion, and celery in fat. Add white sauce with pimiento, salt, and pepper.

Add brains and heat thoroughly. Serve on toast. Serves 6 to 8.

STEAMED BRAINS

Wash 1 pair of brains under cold running water; remove membrane with the tip of a paring knife.

Place in a saucepan and add 3 tablespoons water and 1 tablespoon vinegar. Cover tightly and simmer 15 minutes. Chill thoroughly.

SCRAMBLED BRAINS WITH EGGS

1/2 pound cooked brains
4 eggs
2 tablespoons ketchup

Broiled Brains

1/4 teaspoon salt
Dash of Worcestershire sauce
4 tablespoons fat
4 slices toast
2 tablespoons minced parsley

Cut cooked brains in 1/2-inch pieces. Beat eggs slightly and add seasonings and brains.

Heat fat in frying pan. Pour in brain-egg mixture. Cook slowly, stirring enough to scramble. Serve on hot toast, garnished with parsley. Serves 6.

FRITTO MISTO
(Italian Mixed Fry)

Cover Batter:

2 cups sifted enriched flour
1 teaspoon salt
1/4 teaspoon pepper
1 1/2 cups milk
3 well beaten eggs
2 tablespoons melted shortening

Mixed Meats And Vegetables:

1/2 pound liver, sliced 1/4 to 1/2 inch thick, cut into small pieces, and seasoned with salt, pepper, and Ac'cent
1/2 pound brains, precooked and cut into small pieces
6 artichoke hearts (canned in water), drained
2 zucchini squash, cut crosswise into 1-inch slices
3 stalks celery, cut into 3-inch pieces

Note: This is an excellent way to use leftover vegetables such as cauliflower, string beans, strips of onion, carrots, and squash as well as cold cooked chicken or veal.

To prepare cover batter, mix and sift flour, salt, and pepper.

Combine milk, eggs, and shortening; gradually add sifted flour mixture beating until smooth.

Drop each vegetable and piece of meat into batter. Lift the batter-coated pieces with a teaspoon and drop into deep hot fat (365°–375° F.)

Cook until golden brown, 4 to 5 minutes. Turn the pieces occasionally during frying.

Do not fry too many pieces at one time. Fry only as many pieces as will float uncrowded one layer deep in the fat. Drain on absorbent paper and serve on warm platter. Serves 6.

HOW TO COOK HEART

Use beef, calf, lamb, veal, or pork heart. Veal heart is the most tender and delicate in flavor. All hearts require moist cooking over low heat.

Remove large arteries and veins at top and inside of heart. Wash in cold water.

Cover heart with water. Add ½ teaspoon salt per pound heart. Cover and simmer until tender.

Beef and pork heart take about 2 hours. Lamb and veal heart 1 to 1½ hours.

When done, slice crosswise, grind or chop and use in meat pies or casserole dishes calling for cooked meat, or serve sliced heart with gravy made from stock, or serve chopped heart on buttered toast.

A beef heart weighing 3 to 3½ pounds will serve 8 to 10, pork hearts weigh about ½ pound and will serve 2, lamb hearts weigh about ¼ pound and will serve one, veal hearts weigh about ¾ pound and will serve 2 to 3.

HEART IN SWEET AND SOUR SAUCE

1   beef heart or 2 veal hearts
Fat or salad oil
1½ cups canned tomatoes
¼   cup water
½   cup vinegar
¼   cup brown sugar
2   tablespoons flour
1   teaspoon salt
⅛   teaspoon paprika

Trim heart and cut into small cubes.
Heat 3 to 4 tablespoons fat or oil in heavy saucepan. Add heart and sauté over moderate heat 10 minutes.

Add tomatoes, water, vinegar, and sugar. Cover and simmer until heart is tender, 35 to 40 minutes.

Add flour to 2 tablespoons fat melted in a skillet. Stir in ¼ cup sauce from hearts. Cook, stirring constantly, until smooth. Combine with hearts.

Add more salt, if necessary, and paprika. Cook 5 minutes longer.
Serves 6 to 8.

Hearts

From Left To Right, Beef, Veal, Pork, Lamb—Braise, Cook In Liquid

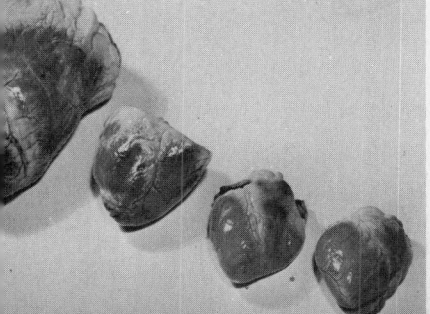

Glazed Stuffed Beef Heart

GLAZED STUFFED BEEF HEART

1   beef heart (about 5 pounds)
Parsley dressing (below)
1   cup sliced onions
3   tablespoons fat
6   cups boiling water
2   teaspoons salt
¼   teaspoon pepper
1   teaspoon Ac'cent
1   teaspoon celery salt
1   teaspoon leaf marjoram
½   cup red currant jelly
1   tablespoon water
2   teaspoons lemon juice
6   tablespoons flour
½   cup cold water

Remove fat, veins, and arteries from beef heart. Stuff with parsley dressing.

Cook onions in fat in deep kettle or Dutch oven until lightly browned; push to one side; brown beef heart on all sides.

Add boiling water, salt, pepper, Ac'cent, and celery salt. Simmer, covered, 2½ to 3 hours, or until meat is tender.

Add marjoram about 15 minutes before end of cooking time.

Remove beef heart from liquid.
Break up currant jelly with fork, add 1 tablespoon water; melt over low heat; brush over beef heart to glaze.

Strain liquid; measure 3 cups back into kettle. Add lemon juice. Thicken with flour mixed to smooth paste with ½ cup cold water. Serve gravy separately.

Parsley Dressing:

4   cups soft breadcrumbs
½   teaspoon salt
Few grains pepper
¼   teaspoon Ac'cent
1   teaspoon poultry seasoning
1   tablespoon minced parsley
¼   cup butter or margarine
¼   cup minced onion

Combine crumbs, salt, pepper, Ac'cent, poultry seasoning, and parsley.

Melt butter or margarine; add onion; simmer until onion is soft but not brown. Stir in crumb mixture; blend well.

Makes enough stuffing for 5-pound beef heart.

KIDNEYS

Kidneys cooked alone or attached to veal and lamb chops and sold as kidney chops are prized highly by many people. Like all variety meats, they are highly nutritious.

Beef, pork, lamb, and veal kidneys can all be used to good advantage.

Veal and lamb kidneys require very little cooking. Beef kidney is most often well cooked and served in beef and kidney pie.

Pork kidney is seldom available in most markets.

All kidneys should be used within 24 hours. Keep loosely wrapped in the refrigerator.

HOW TO COOK KIDNEYS

To cook beef and pork kidneys, remove outer membrane. Split in half. Trim off all fat and white veins. Rinse well in cold water.

Simmer in water about 30 minutes, or brown in fat and then cook slowly in a little water.

To cook lamb or veal kidneys, remove outer membrane. Trim white veins and fat. Broil or pan fry.

BAKED VEAL KIDNEY

Place kidneys in a pan, fat side up. Bake uncovered in slow oven (300°F.) until tender, about 1¼ hours.

One veal kidney weighing 8 to 12 ounces makes a nice small roast for 1 person.

BROILED KIDNEYS

Use lamb or veal kidneys. Have meat man leave about ¼ inch of fat on kidneys.

Split and place on broiler rack with fat side up.

Broil with kidneys about 3 inches from source of heat until fat is brown and crisp.

Season with salt and pepper and turn. Continue broiling until done. Total broiling time about 20 minutes.

Broil butter-brushed mushroom caps or 1-inch thick slices of tomato and slices of bacon with the kidneys, if desired. Serve as a mixed grill.

Kidneys

From Left To Right, Veal, Beef, Lamb, Pork
Beef And Pork—Braise, Cook In Liquid
Veal And Lamb—Broil, Panbroil, Braise, Cook In Liquid

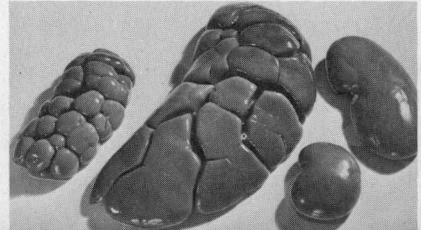

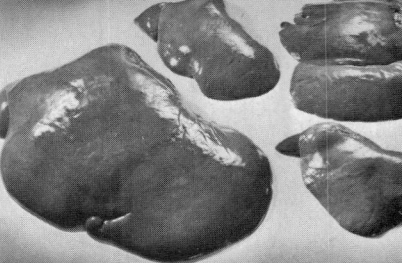

BEEFSTEAK AND KIDNEY PIE (ENGLISH)

¾ pound boneless stew beef
¾ pound beef kidney, trimmed
⅓ cup flour
1½ tablespoons fat
⅓ cup chopped onion
3⅓ cups hot water
1½ teaspoons salt
⅛ teaspoon pepper
3 whole cloves
½ teaspoon mixed pickling spice
Biscuit dough or pastry

Cut beef and kidney in 1-inch cubes and dredge with flour.

Melt fat, add onion and sauté until lightly brown. Remove onion, add meat and brown well. Remove meat.

Add water to the pan, stirring until smooth. Return onion and meat to pan, add salt and pepper, cloves, and pickling spice tied in cheesecloth. If necessary, add more water to cover meat.

Cover tightly and simmer 1½ to 2 hours or until meat is tender. Remove spices.

Place meat in greased 6-cup casserole. Cover with biscuit dough or pastry and bake in hot oven (400°F.) 25 to 30 minutes, until crust is cooked. Serves 6.

If Using Pressure Cooker: Reduce water to 1½ cups and cook 20 minutes at 15 pounds pressure. Cool cooker slowly. Then place meat in casserole and finish as above.

KIDNEY SPOON CAKES

1 pound kidney
1 teaspoon salt
⅛ teaspoon pepper
2 eggs
Sausage or bacon drippings

Use beef, pork, lamb, or veal kidneys. Wash kidney and put through food chopper. Add seasonings and eggs and beat until well mixed.

Drop into hot drippings by tablespoonfuls. Brown second side until crisp. Serve hot with creamed onions. Serves 6.

Kidneys and mushrooms on toast are nice for a Sunday buffet-brunch.

BAKED KIDNEYS WITH BACON

4 lamb kidneys
1 slightly beaten egg
3 teaspoons Worcestershire sauce
½ teaspoon salt
Fine cracker crumbs
4 slices bacon

Cut kidneys in half. Wash and remove tubes.

Mix egg, Worcestershire sauce, and salt. Dip kidneys in sauce, then in crumbs.

Wrap each with a bacon slice. Secure with toothpicks. Place in shallow baking pan.

Bake in hot oven (400°F.) until bacon is crisp and kidneys are browned, about 20 minutes. Serves 4.

SAVORY SAUTÉED KIDNEYS

1 pound veal or lamb kidney
Garlic
¼ cup butter or margarine
½ cup sliced onions
Salt and paprika
1 tablespoon lemon juice or ¼ cup sherry or dry red wine

Remove some of the fat from the kidneys. Cut them crosswise into slices. Cut away all the white tissue.

Rub a skillet with a cut clove of garlic. Melt the butter and pan fry the onions until very lightly browned.

Add the kidneys and pan fry until tender, about 5 minutes.

Season with salt, paprika, and the lemon juice or wine. Serves 4.

KIDNEYS AND MUSHROOMS ON TOAST

8 lamb kidneys
2 tablespoons flour
1 medium onion, minced
4 tablespoons butter or margarine
1 beef bouillon cube
¾ cup water
1 3-ounce can sliced mushrooms with liquid
½ teaspoon salt
⅛ teaspoon pepper
2 tablespoons sherry
Hot toast

Wash kidneys, cut in quarters, and remove tubes and fat. Sprinkle kidneys with flour.

Cook onion in 2 tablespoons butter or margarine. Remove onion and set aside.

Put remaining 2 tablespoons butter or margarine in skillet and brown kidneys on all sides, stirring frequently.

Add onion and remaining ingredients except sherry and toast. Bring to boil, cover, and simmer 25 minutes. Add sherry and serve on toast.

Serves 4.

Liver

Beef: Lower Left—Roast, Braise, Fry
Veal: Upper Left—Broil, Panbroil, Fry
Pork: Upper Right—Roast, Braise, Fry
Lamb: Lower Right—Broil, Panbroil, Fry

LIVER

Beef livers are plump and easy to distinguish because of the one large and one small lobe, or section. Pork, veal, and lamb livers are smaller in size. Veal and lamb livers are particularly mild in flavor. Ordinarily, dealers carry the one or two types for which demand is greatest in their neighborhoods.

Allow 1 pound for 4 servings.

Preparation and Refrigeration: Do not soak or scald liver. Precook liver only when it is to be ground. Refrigerate and use soon after purchase.

FRIED (SAUTÉED) LIVER

Remove outer membrane (skin) from ¼- to ½-inch slices of liver. Veins are easily removed with a kitchen shears.

Dip slices in well seasoned flour. Brown quickly in very little hot bacon drippings or melted butter over moderate heat, a matter of 2 or 3 minutes. The liver will be done when the second side is brown. Don't overcook—liver toughens easily.

Variations: If desired, rub the pan with a cut clove of garlic before frying the liver, or flavor the liver when cooked with grated lemon rind and juice.

Liver with Wine Sauce: After frying liver as above, rinse the skillet with a few tablespoons dry red wine and use for sauce.

Liver with Sautéed Onions: Slice onions crosswise; sauté them in a small amount of bacon fat or shortening. Brown evenly, season, and keep them hot while frying liver.

Cook liver on one side as directed above, turn it, pile the onions on the cooked side and continue to cook the liver until done.

Liver and Bacon: Cook the bacon first; keep it hot while preparing the liver as above. Liver, bacon, and onions are a good combination.

FRENCH-FRIED LIVER

Cut pork liver in ½-inch strips. Let stand in French dressing ½ hour; drain. Dip in beaten egg; roll in cracker crumbs. Fry in deep, hot fat (360°F.) until browned. Drain on paper towels.

BROILED SLICED LIVER

Use calf, lamb, or beef liver sliced ⅓ to ½ inch thick.

Place on broiling rack about 3 inches from moderate heat. Leave the door of broiling oven open and broil 1 minute on each side for the thinner slices, 1½ minutes per side for thicker slices. Then, season to taste.

Method #2: Brush the slices with melted butter or oil and increase broiling time ½ minute for each side.

Serve with bacon and sliced sweet onions, previously broiled. Garnish with lemon wedges and parsley.

BRAISED LIVER

Dip slices of beef or pork liver in flour. Season with salt and pepper. Brown quickly on both sides in a little hot fat. Reduce heat. Add 1 bouillon cube dissolved in ½ cup hot water, and thinly sliced onions. Cook until tender, about 20 minutes.

HOW TO "BOIL" LIVER

Wash liver thoroughly. Place in water to cover. Cover pan and simmer gently until tender, adding ½ teaspoon salt per pound when half done.

Very thin slices will take 5 to 15 minutes. Solid pieces weighing 2 pounds or more will take 1 to 1½ hours.

Drain, grind, and use in salads, sandwich fillings, creamed dishes, etc.

BRAISED LIVER IN WHITE WINE

1½ pounds beef or pork liver, sliced thin
1 cup Sauterne, Rhine, Chablis or other white wine
Flour, salt, pepper
¼ cup bacon drippings or other fat
Pinch of thyme
½ cup water

Wash liver. Let stand in wine for an hour.

Pour off wine, reserving wine for later use. Coat liver with seasoned flour. Brown on both sides in hot fat in chafing dish over direct heat.

Add wine and thyme. Cover and simmer 10 minutes.

Add water and continue simmering for 20 minutes, or until tender. Serves 6.

Liver and Bacon Patties

LIVER LOAF

3 stalks celery
1 medium-sized onion, chopped
1 cup water
1 pound sliced liver (beef, pork, or lamb)
2 slices bacon
1 or 2 beaten eggs
¾ teaspoon salt
⅛ teaspoon pepper
1 cup cracker or dry breadcrumbs
½ teaspoon thyme or marjoram
1 cup liquid (liver stock, tomato juice, milk, or bouillon)
½ cup ketchup

Boil the water with celery and onion for 5 minutes; add liver and simmer 3 minutes. Drain, reserving liquid.

Put liver, vegetables, and bacon through food chopper. Add remaining ingredients except the ketchup; blend well.

Pour the ketchup in a greased loaf pan. Pack the liver mixture into the pan. Bake in moderate oven (350°F.) about 40 minutes. Serves 6 to 8.

LIVER CREOLE

2 slices bacon
½ pound liver (¼ inch thick)
2 tablespoons flour
1 can (1¼ cups) condensed tomato soup
¼ cup chopped green pepper
¼ teaspoon chili powder

Cut bacon into small pieces; fry until crisp in a skillet, then remove from pan.

Dust liver with flour; brown in bacon drippings. Add bacon bits and remaining ingredients. Cover; simmer 45 minutes. Serves 4.

LIVER AND BACON PATTIES

1 pound pork liver
2 tablespoons ketchup
¼ teaspoon salt
1 large onion
4 slices bacon

Simmer liver in water until firm. Then grind or chop liver.

Combine with ketchup and salt. Shape into 4 large patties.

Cut onion in ½-inch slices. Place a patty on an onion slice. Wrap bacon around patty and onion. Fasten with a wooden pick.

Bake in hot oven (400°F.) until bacon is crisply brown, about 30 minutes. Serves 4.

FRIED LIVER CUBES

1 pound liver, cut in 1-inch cubes
½ cup French dressing
¼ cup enriched flour
12 broiled bacon slices

Marinate liver cubes in French dressing 1 hour, drain.

Dredge cubes in flour and fry in hot deep fat (375°F.) 2 minutes or until well browned. Serve with bacon slices. Serves 4.

CALF LIVER-BURGUNDY CASSEROLE

4 slices bacon
1 pound calf liver, cut in 4 slices
Flour
2 cups cooked rice
½ eggplant, peeled and cut in 1-inch cubes
4 raw tomatoes, cut in quarters
½ cup sliced onions
Salt, pepper, paprika
½ cup Burgundy wine
1 tablespoon butter

Cook bacon until crisp and brown. Remove from pan.

Dust liver with flour and brown lightly on both sides.

Line a greased casserole with 1 cup cooked rice. Add half the eggplant, 2 tomatoes, onions, and seasonings to taste, calf liver, and bacon, crumbled into pieces.

Cover with rest of rice, eggplant, and tomatoes. Add wine to moisten. Dot top with bits of butter.

Cover and cook in moderate oven (350°F.) 30 minutes. Remove cover and cook 10 minutes. Serves 4.

MEXICAN BRAISED LIVER

1½ pounds liver, sliced
8 tablespoons bacon drippings
6 carrots, diced
2 green peppers, diced
6 small onions, diced
Salt and pepper to taste
½ cup water
Cooked brown rice

Dredge liver with flour. Brown in bacon drippings.

Prepare and dice the carrots, green peppers, and the onions. Arrange in mounds on pieces of liver. Season with salt and pepper and add water; cover.

Simmer gently for about 45 minutes or until vegetables are tender, adding more water if necessary.

Serve on a bed of fluffy brown rice. Serves 6.

Mexican Braised Liver

SWEETBREADS

These are the thymus gland; they have a tender, delicate flavor. Veal, beef, and lamb sweetbreads are available; pork sweetbreads are not used. Veal sweetbreads are often sold as "pair stock" (neck and heart without separation of connective tissue). However, they are also sold as individual pieces. In the case of beef, usually only the neck sweetbreads are sold.

Allow 1 pound for 4 to 6 servings.

Preparation And Refrigeration: Do not soak. Wash and precook in simmering water to cover (beef 25 minutes, veal and lamb 15 to 20 minutes). If sweetbreads are frozen, increase cooking time 10 minutes. Many cooks prefer to add 1 tablespoon vinegar or lemon juice and 1 teaspoon salt per quart of cooking water.

Drain, cover with cold water, and let stand until cool enough to handle. Remove membrane and tubes. Refrigerate or broil, sauté, or prepare as desired.

BROILED SWEETBREADS

Method #1: Cut precooked sweetbreads in half crosswise. Sprinkle with salt and pepper. Brush with melted butter or margarine.

Place on broiler rack with top of food 3 inches below unit or tip of flame. Broil about 10 minutes, turning once.

Method #2: Break precooked sweetbreads into large pieces. Dry well and roll in seasoned flour.

Wrap in bacon strips and secure with wooden picks. Dot well with butter and broil, basting frequently with the juices that drip from them and if they are rather dry baste with additional butter.

Season the drippings with lemon juice or sherry and serve with the sweetbreads.

DEEP FAT-FRIED SWEETBREADS

Prepare as for pan-fried sweetbreads. Fry in deep hot fat (360°F.) until golden brown, 7 to 10 minutes.

Sweetbreads

From Left To Right, Beef, Veal, Lamb, —Broil, Fry, Braise, Cook In Liquid

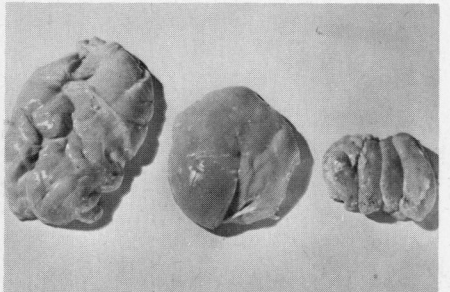

PAN-FRIED SWEETBREADS

Cut precooked sweetbreads in half. Dry thoroughly. Dip them in seasoned very fine breadcrumbs. Then dip in 1 slightly beaten egg diluted with 2 tablespoons water. Dip again in crumbs.

Pan-fry them in hot butter until they are a rich brown. Serve with a well seasoned white or tomato sauce or a creamed vegetable.

BRAISED SWEETBREADS

Use calf or lamb sweetbreads, allowing 1/2 to 1 pair per serving.

Cover with cold water; let stand 30 minutes. Drain and remove membrane. Dip sweetbreads in seasoned flour and pan fry in a small amount butter or salad oil, turning to brown on all sides.

Cover and cook slowly 20 minutes.

Blend together a little flour and water; add to drippings in pan. Cook, stirring constantly, until thickened. Serve on sweetbreads.

If desired the drippings may be seasoned with a little sherry.

CREAMED SWEETBREADS
(Master Recipe)

1   **pound cooked sweetbreads, cubed**
2   **cups medium white sauce**
1   **cup cooked or canned peas**
Seasoning to taste

Add cubed sweetbreads to white sauce. Heat thoroughly, stirring gently. Add peas. Season to taste.

Serve hot on toast, in timbale cases, or in patty shells. If desired, stir in 1 slightly beaten egg yolk before serving. Serves 4 to 6.

Creamed Sweetbread Variations
Creamed Sweetbreads and Mushrooms: Substitute 1 cup cooked or canned mushrooms for peas.

With Almonds: Add 1/4 cup slivered toasted almonds to Creamed Sweetbreads with Mushrooms.

With Asparagus Tips: Substitute cooked or canned asparagus tips for peas.

With Oysters: Substitute oysters for peas. Heat oysters in their own liquor until edges curl before adding.

With Other Meats: Substitute diced cooked chicken, ham, or veal for peas.

Quick Creamed Sweetbreads: Substitute 1 can (10 1/2 ounces) condensed cream of mushroom soup diluted with 1/2 can milk for medium white sauce.

SWEETBREADS WITH PINEAPPLE

Slice 3 pairs precooked calf or lamb sweetbreads and brown in hot fat. Brown 6 pineapple slices in the fat.

Add 1/4 cup water to 1 can condensed cream of mushroom soup; heat and pour over sweetbreads and pineapple. Serves 6.

Sweetbreads Melba

SWEETBREADS MELBA

3   **pairs sweetbreads**
Juice of 2 lemons
1   **teaspoon salt**
1/2   **teaspoon Ac'cent**
2   **cups beef stock or bouillon**
2   **celery stalks and leaves, chopped**
Several sprigs parsley
1/4   **teaspoon thyme**
1/4   **teaspoon mace**
1/8   **teaspoon allspice**
6   **tablespoons butter or margarine**
2   **tablespoons prepared mustard**
Few grains pepper
1   **teaspoon Ac'cent**
1   **tablespoon lemon juice**
Melba toast

Cover sweetbreads with cold water; soak 1 hour, changing water several times.

Cover with fresh cold water, add juice of 2 lemons, salt, and the 1/2 teaspoon Ac'cent. Bring slowly to boil; simmer 15 minutes.

Plunge into cold water. Carefully remove tubes and membranes; place in saucepan with stock, celery, parsley, thyme, and spices; bring to boil; simmer 1/2 hour. Drain, saving broth.

Melt butter or margarine; blend in mustard, pepper, 1 teaspoon Ac'cent, and 1 tablespoon lemon juice. Add 1 cup strained broth.

Slice sweetbreads; add to sauce; reheat. Serve on Melba toast. Serves 6.

TONGUE

Available fresh, smoked, corned, pickled. Pork and lamb tongues being small are mostly canned whole. The larger size of beef and veal tongues makes them better for home use.

Preparation and Refrigeration: Wipe with a damp cloth. Refrigerate or use at once.

To Cook Fresh Tongue: Cover with cold water; add 1 1/2 teaspoons salt to each quart of water; bring to a boil. Fresh tongues are better when spice and seasonings are added to cooking water. Simmer slowly until tender.

Allow 2 1/2 to 4 hours for beef tongue, 1 to 1 1/2 hours for calf or pork tongue. Remove the outer skin and the roots.

To Cook Pickled Tongue: Cover with cold water, bring to boil. Reduce heat and simmer 2 1/2 to 4 hours, or

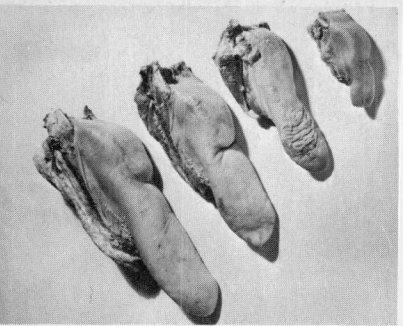

Tongues

From Left To Right, Beef, Veal, Pork, Lamb—Cook In Liquid

Tongue, Continued

until tender. Remove the outer skin and roots.

To Cook Smoked Tongue: Cover with water and simmer 50 minutes per pound or until tender. Remove the outer skin and roots.

"BOILED" SEASONED BEEF TONGUE

1 beef tongue
6 whole black peppers
4 whole cloves
1 tablespoon vinegar

Fresh, corned, or smoked tongues may be used. A 4-pound tongue serves 8 to 10.

Corned or smoked tongues are improved by soaking in cold water for several hours before cooking.

Scrub tongue under running water. Place in deep kettle. Add seasonings and boiling water to cover. Boil 10 minutes, then lower heat and simmer until a fork will penetrate easily to the center, 2½ to 4 hours.

Let tongue remain in water until cool enough to handle. Peel off outer skin. Cut out membranous portions of roots.

Press into shape for serving. Serve hot with horseradish or raisin sauce, use in other recipes, or slice and serve cold.

Variations of "Boiled" Seasoned Beef Tongue

Tongue with Cranberries: Place sliced cooked tongue in a pan.

Combine ½ cup water or tongue liquid, ½ cup stewed cranberries, ¼ cup brown sugar, 2 tablespoons melted fat, and 3 slices lemon.

Add to tongue. Simmer until heated through. Serve hot.

Baked Fresh Tongue: After peeling fresh cooked tongue, place in a shallow roasting pan. Rub with hot fat.

Bake in moderate oven (350°F.) about 50 to 60 minutes.

Beef Tongue Piquant: After peeling cooked fresh tongue, dust with flour seasoned with salt and pepper. Brown in hot fat.

Combine ¾ cup tart grape jelly and

1 cup hot water. Mix thoroughly. Pour over tongue. Simmer about 40 minutes.

Jellied Tongue: Peel and trim cooked fresh tongue. Place in a mold.

Strain tongue liquid. Measure enough to fill mold.

Soften 2 tablespoons (2 envelopes) unflavored gelatin in ½ cup cold tongue liquid and add to measured liquid.

Bring to boiling point and pour over tongue. Chill until firm.

TONGUE—SWEET AND SOUR

1 cooked beef tongue
1 large onion, chopped
1 tablespoon fat
1 tablespoon flour
2 cups hot tongue liquid
½ teaspoon salt
1 tablespoon finely chopped almonds
1 stick cinnamon
4 cloves
¼ cup raisins
¼ cup brown sugar
1 tablespoon molasses
Juice of 1 lemon

Peel and slice cooked tongue.

Brown onion slightly in hot fat. Remove onion and set aside.

Stir flour into hot fat and cook 3 minutes. Gradually add hot tongue liquid and salt and simmer gently until smooth and thickened, about 5 minutes.

Add browned onions, almonds, cinnamon, cloves, and raisins. Mix well.

Blend together the brown sugar, molasses, and lemon juice and stir into the mixture. Simmer about 10 minutes, stirring constantly.

If desired, add more salt, sugar, and lemon juice to taste. Add sliced tongue and simmer until heated through. Serve hot with sauce.

SUGAR-GLAZED TONGUE

1 fresh smoked beef tongue, about 4 pounds
⅓ cup cider vinegar
1½ teaspoons salt
8 whole cloves
3 tablespoons brown sugar
1 tablespoon lemon juice

Cover tongue with cold water; bring to boiling point and drain.

Again cover with water; add vinegar and salt; simmer until tender. Let cool in the liquid.

Remove skin, small bones, and cartilage. Stud with cloves and place in a shallow baking dish.

Mix together the brown sugar and lemon juice; brush over the tongue.

Bake in moderate oven (350°F.) ½ hour, basting frequently. Slice and serve hot. Serves 6.

OXTAILS

Oxtails are usually sold disjointed or the meat man will disjoint them when

purchased. The meat is fine flavored and oxtails make excellent soup. The proportion of bone is large so allow 1 pound for 2 servings.

HOW TO COOK OXTAILS

Wash throughly in cold water. Cover with water. Add salt.

Simmer until meat is tender, about 2 hours. Serve in a hot tomato sauce or other desired spicy sauce.

BRAISED OXTAILS WITH VEGETABLES

4 tablespoons butter or beef drippings
1 large onion, chopped
2 oxtails, disjointed
Flour
2 teaspoons salt
¼ teaspoon pepper
1 tablespoon vinegar
2½ cups water
4 carrots, sliced
1 cup diced celery
1 large green pepper, chopped
4 medium-sized potatoes, cut in half

Heat fat in a skillet; add onion. Roll oxtails in flour and brown in the hot fat with onion.

Add salt, pepper, vinegar, and water. Cover tightly and simmer 3 hours. Add more water as necessary to prevent burning.

Add carrots, celery, green pepper, and potatoes. Cover; increase heat to start vegetables cooking, then reduce heat and simmer 45 minutes.

Remove vegetables to a hot platter. Thicken the broth for gravy with a little flour-water paste. Serves 5 to 6.

TRIPE

Tripe is the inner lining of the stomach of meat animals. It is a most important ingredient in the preparation of Philadelphia pepper pot and it can be prepared in many other delicious ways. In England and in some continental countries it is a favorite breakfast food.

Two forms of tripe are commonly sold, one plain, one honeycomb. Plain is the lining of the first stomach of beef; honeycomb (the more delicate of the two) is the lining of the second stomach. Either may be purchased fresh, pickled, or canned.

Fresh tripe is usually partially cooked before selling. Further cooking in water is preliminary to all ways of serving, at least two hours' cooking at a simmering temperature being required to make it tender.

Pickled tripe is usually thoroughly cooked but requires soaking before using. Canned tripe is ready to heat and serve.

HOW TO COOK "FRESH" TRIPE

Wash tripe well in several waters. Cover with water. Cover, heat to boiling, then reduce heat and simmer until fork tender, 2 hours or more. Add ½ teaspoon salt per pound when half done.

Use for various dishes. Allow ¼ to ⅓ pound per serving.

Note: If fresh tripe has not been partially cooked (as it usually is before being sold) whole tripe calls for 4 hours or more simmering; if it is cut into strips you may allow 2 hours or more.

FRIED TRIPE

Dip boiled tripe in egg diluted with 2 tablespoons cold water. Roll in fine breadcrumbs.

Repeat and fry in a little hot fat until brown on both sides.

TRIPE À LA MODE DE CAEN

A classic French dish from Normandy.
3 pounds fresh honeycomb tripe
2 calf's feet, split
2 pounds onions, sliced
¼ pound beef suet, cut in small cubes
1 onion, stuck with 3 cloves
1 bay leaf
Bouquet Garni (see below)
¼ cup calvados or other apple brandy
Cider or water
Thick paste made of flour and water
Salt and freshly ground pepper

Wash the tripe carefully in several changes of water. Drain and slice the tripe into pieces two inches square. In two separate kettles, cover the tripe with cold water and the calf's feet with cold water. Bring each to a boil. Immediately add two cups cold water to each kettle to stop the cooking, then drain well.

Line the bottom of a large earthenware casserole with a layer of onions, then a layer of tripe and a sprinkling of beef suet. Build successive layers, topping with the split calf's feet, the onion stuck with whole cloves, bay leaf, and bouquet garni.

Add the calvados or other apple brandy and enough cider or water to cover all ingredients. Bring to boiling point on top of range. Remove from

Tripe À La Creole

heat. Cover the casserole with a lid and seal the cover with a thick paste made of flour and water.

Bake in very slow oven (250°F.) at least 12 hours.

At serving time, break and discard the pastry seal. Remove the bouquet garni, the whole onion, and bay leaf. Skim the fat from the liquid and season to taste with salt and pepper.

Pick the meat from the calf's feet and discard the bones. Return the meat to the casserole. Heat through and serve in individual heated casseroles with hot boiled potatoes on the side. Serves 8.
Note: For bouquet garni use 1 bay leaf, 1 clove, 2 sprigs parsley, 1 clove garlic, 1 teaspoon thyme, and 10 peppercorns, all tied securely in a cheesecloth bag.

TRIPE Á LA CREOLE

1 pound tripe
Water
3 tablespoons butter or drippings
3 tablespoons chopped green pepper
3 tablespoons chopped onion
3 tablespoons flour
1½ cups tomatoes
1 teaspoon salt
¼ teaspoon pepper

Cover tripe with water and simmer 2 hours, or until the cut surface has a clear, jelly-like appearance. Drain and cut into 2-inch pieces.

Melt fat and cook green pepper and onion in it until tender. Add flour; stir until smooth, then add tomatoes, stirring constantly until thickened. Season and add tripe. Simmer 10 minutes. Serves 6.

HEADCHEESE

This is a jellied loaf made from the head of a hog or calf, with the trimmings and sometimes the feet included. It is highly seasoned and is molded in its natural aspic.

1 hog's or calf's head with ears, tongue, and brain
Water
1 large onion
4 whole cloves
Salt
10 whole black peppers
Bouquet garni of mixed herbs
Nutmeg, sage, cayenne pepper

Have the meat dealer scrape and clean the head, split it, remove the eyes, brain, and tongue. Scrub the tongue well. Rinse all thoroughly.

Place head and tongue in deep kettle. Cover with cold water. (Half water and half white wine may be used.)

Add the onion stuck with whole

cloves, salt, whole black peppers, and bouquet garni. Bring to boiling and skim carefully.

Let simmer until meat is very tender, 3 to 4 hours. Let cool in stock.

If tongue is done early remove it. Carefully cut any rind from head. Cut ears into small slices. Cut tongue and other meat into various 1-inch shapes.

Parboil the brains in a little of the cooking liquid.

Combine all meat and season to taste with nutmeg, sage, and cayenne. If wine was not used, add ½ cup vinegar. If vinegar is used, add ½ cup of the cooking liquid. Toss to mix thoroughly.

Press the mixture firmly into a bread pan or other mold. Cover and press down with a heavy weight.

Chill 2 to 3 days, in the refrigerator. Serve cold in thin slices with salads.

To serve hot, dip slices in slightly beaten egg, roll in fine crumbs, and fry in a little fat.

CHITTERLINGS

Chitterlings are the intestines (usually the small ones) of pigs prepared in various ways, especially in the South. Usually they are boiled, well seasoned, then dipped in batter of flour or corn meal, and fried in deep fat. A common pronunciation is "chittlin's" without an "e," "r," and "g."

5 pounds chitterlings
2 garlic cloves
1 lemon, quartered
2 medium onions, sliced
¼ cup vinegar
2 bay leaves
Several sprigs of parsley
1 teaspoon salt
1 teaspoon pepper
1 tablespoon thyme
1 teaspoon whole cloves
1 teaspoon mace
1 teaspoon allspice
1 tablespoon marjoram
½ cup ketchup or 1 cup tomato sauce
Soak chitterlings overnight. Wash through 4 or 5 waters. Turn inside out, remove excess fat but leave a small amount for seasoning.

Put chitterlings in heavy kettle. Add remaining ingredients except ketchup or tomato sauce.

Cover with water; bring to boiling point, lower heat and simmer until tender. Cut into small pieces.

During last 30 minutes of cooking, add the ½ cup ketchup or 1 cup tomato sauce and hot pepper to taste.

FRIED CHITTERLINGS

Prepare chitterlings as in above recipe. Omit vinegar and ketchup or tomato sauce. When tender, drain well.

Cut into 2-inch squares. Dip in fritter batter and fry in deep hot fat. Drain on absorbent paper.

Game Meats

The history of America is the story of gradual depletion of the country's natural resources, including the wild game that the first settlers found so plentiful.

As many of the native animals and birds became almost extinct, the government began a program of conservation that has resulted in such vast game preserves as the national forests. Here, the deer and the elk are flourishing again to the point where they can be hunted. Private growers, too, have added to the supply of game.

Much game is now specifically raised for sale, but that doesn't make it different from that shot in the wilds—the same growers stock forests for future hunting. In this way, certain government-protected birds can be sold commercially.

Whether you hunt your own quarry or find it at the market, the best of preparation is suggested for these rare meats.

CARE OF LARGE GAME
(Deer, Elk, Moose, Bear, Etc.)

Bleed, draw, clean, and cool immediately. Spread cavity with a stick and hang by hind legs or antlers with or without hide (controversial points) until cooled. Transport, being careful not to heat animal. Hang or age in a cooler or in open air where temperature ranges between 36 to 40 degrees. Allow a week to firm the meat of young animals, 2 to 3 weeks for older animals. Some authorities recommend hanging as long as 4 weeks. Remove hide (if still on) and carve into cuts similar to beef cuts. Cook immediately or wrap in freezer paper and store at 0°F.

Note: Unless you are an expert and have the proper tools, have a meatman cut your venison like beef into roasts, steaks, chops, and stew meat. Have the fat trimmed completely. It is strong flavored and should be replaced with fat salt pork.

VENISON

Venison actually means the flesh of any antlered game animal such as deer, caribou, elk, moose, and reindeer; however, in popular usage it generally refers to the deer, when used as a food.

Venison is cooked in much the same manner as domestic meats, particularly lamb or mutton. Because the meat is considered somewhat of a "treat," an attempt is usually made to give it extra attention in preparation by the addition of wine, cream, mushrooms, etc.

The texture is very similar to beef. Tender cuts of young animals are cooked by dry heat: broiling or roasting. Tough cuts such as the shoulder are cooked by moist heat: braising or stewing.

Venison tends to be lean, therefore bacon, butter, or other fat has to be added generously to keep moist and juicy.

Large herds of Alaskan reindeer are making considerable quantities of frozen reindeer meat available for tender steaks, roasts, stews, etc. Allow it to thaw slowly at room temperature before cooking. While the flavor is somewhat "gamy" it is not strong. It has an excellent texture and is usually tender.

VENISON STEAKS, CHOPS, LOIN CUTLETS

Use tender cuts from loin or leg, about ½ to 1½ inches thick. Sprinkle with salt and pepper. Brush with butter or oil.

Place on greased broiler rack in moderate broiler. Cook 5 to 10 minutes on each side or until well browned, turning once during cooking.

To pan-broil: Place in hot frying pan which has been brushed lightly with fat. Cook over moderate heat.

If desired, rub both sides with cut clove of garlic before broiling. If desired, steaks may be marinated in French dressing for 1 hour before cooking.

Serve with fresh mushrooms which have been sautéed in butter or with melted butter seasoned with lemon juice, or with a mixture of half butter and half currant jelly.

BRAISED VENISON

Use a 4- to 6-pound cut from shoulder or leg. Lard lean side with strips of fat pork, drawing them through with a larding needle. Rub with softened butter. Coat well with seasoned flour.

Brown on all sides in ½ cup hot fat, turning often. Add ¼ cup hot water. Cook, covered, over low heat until tender, about 2 to 2½ hours. Add small amounts of water if necessary and turn frequently.

If desired, add 2 medium-sized sliced carrots, ½ cup chopped celery, 1 medium-sized onion, sliced, and 1 tablespoon lemon juice during the last half hour of cooking.

STEWED VENISON

Do not lard. Cut the meat into 1½- to 2-inch cubes. Otherwise prepare in the same manner as braised venison.

A full cup of water may be added instead of the half cup after the meat is browned.

ROAST VENISON

Use thick loin or upper leg cuts from young venison. Rub with butter. Sprinkle with salt and pepper.

Place in roasting pan. Cover with strips of fat salt pork. If desired, stick a few cloves of garlic deep into flesh.

Roast in moderate oven (350°F.) until done, allowing about 25 minutes per pound. Baste frequently throughout roasting period with melted butter.

Make brown gravy from the drippings. Serve with a tart jelly.

ROAST RACCOON

Skin and dress, being careful to remove scent glands under each front leg and on either side of spine in small of back. Wash in cold water.

Parboil in freshly boiling water ½ hour, repeating if animal is not young. Drain and dry carefully.

Stuff with bread stuffing to which a quartered tart apple has been added. Place in baking pan.

Roast in moderate oven (350°F.) until tender and delicately browned.

ROAST OPOSSUM ('POSSUM)

The flavor of 'possum is improved if the animal is caught alive and fed for a week or longer on persimmons, apples, berries, etc. Some 'possum fanciers insist that mashed persimmons and warm water is the best diet. The 'possum is then killed and dressed in much the same way as a suckling pig.

The animal is at its best when it is fat; however as much fat as possible should be removed. The head and tail may be left on or removed.

Rub the cleaned cavity with onion or sage. Sprinkle with salt and pepper. Fill with apple or onion stuffing.

In many parts of the South a herb-seasoned mixture of persimmons, sweet potatoes, and breadcrumbs, moistened with beef stock, is a favorite stuffing.

Truss and place on rack in shallow pan underside down. Add 2 tablespoons water and roast in slow oven (300°–325°F.) until well done, 2 to 2½ hours, basting occasionally with drippings from pan. Skim fat from gravy and serve with sweet potatoes and stewed persimmons.

If desired, small parboiled sweet potatoes may be placed around the 'possum when it's nearly done and basted with drippings from time to time.

MOUNTAIN GOAT

Mountain goat is tough, dark, and usually dry meat. It should be marinated and the use of a pressure cooker is advisable.

MUSKRAT

The fur-bearing muskrat lives on water plants, and this diet produces succulent meat that can be prepared in any of the ways suggested for hare and rabbit.

The meat is usually cut up and soaked overnight in salted water before cooking.

BUFFALO

Herds of buffalo are raised on Western ranges like beef cattle, and an increasing supply of buffalo meat is available in some markets. Buffalo steaks and roasts have a pleasant gamy flavor. The meat is lean and should be cooked with added fat by larding or otherwise, then prepared like beef. Many people consider buffalo liver a greater delicacy than calf's liver which it resembles.

BEAR

Bear meat is very dark, and usually dry and tough. The meat should be marinated before cooking and, like pork, it must be very thoroughly cooked before eating.

The use of a pressure cooker is advisable. Cub bear meat is tender when very young.

MOUNTAIN SHEEP

This highly prized meat should be roasted in the same way as lamb. The fell from the legs is not removed but it should be removed from chops.

Roast in open pan, basting frequently with a little water in pan. If the meat is dry, use a little butter in the pan with the water. Serve with a mint jelly or sauce.

PORCUPINE

Skin in the same manner as a rabbit. Dress and wipe with damp cloth.

Roast, whole or cut up depending on size, in an open roasting pan. Add no water. Bake in moderate oven (350°F.) until tender and richly browned.

WOODCHUCK

This is another name for the weather-prophesying ground hog, a rather common burrowing and hibernating marmot with coarse red-brown fur.

To use as a game food, they are at their best shot in the autumn when they are well fattened in preparation for the winter hibernation.

They may be cooked like rabbit, except that under the front legs and in the small of the back of the woodchuck there are seven to nine white musclelike sacs, or kernels. These must be cut out, or the meat will be too strong.

Woodchuck meat is preferably soaked overnight in salted water before cooking.

RABBIT OR HARE

As used in the United States, the term hare refers to any wild rabbit eaten as game; some are true hares, that is, born with fur and with eyes open, and some are not. The European hare is larger. Young, tender rabbits have light meat and can be cooked in most of the ways suitable for young,

tender chicken. Larger, dark-meated hare should be braised, stewed, or marinated, just as older chicken is cooked. Note: An important fact to remember is never to handle wild rabbit (or any wild meat) without using gloves because of the danger of tularemia infection.

Domestic rabbit is fine-grained, mild-flavored meat that is becoming increasingly available in retail markets. Like other lean meats, poultry, and lean fish, it is a good source of high-quality protein.

HOW TO SKIN A RABBIT, HARE, OR SQUIRREL

Hang up by hind legs in cool place for several days. To skin it, leave it hanging. Carefully cut up the front from tail to throat with a sharp knife. Take out entrails. Cut out bile sack from liver, saving liver and heart. Discard other parts.

Cut fur around each of the 4 ankles, pulling legs through. Cut off ears.

Strip the fur skin, separated from the inner skin, from the hind legs down and over the head.

Cut off the head, throat, and paws and discard these parts together with the skin from the belly. Remove small waxy kernels directly between body and forelegs.

Wipe thoroughly inside and out with a cloth dipped in a mixture of 1 cup water and 1 tablespoon vinegar. Serving portion: ¾ to 1 pound.

BUYING RABBIT

Rabbits are sold live or ready-to-cook. Like poultry, ready-to-cook rabbits may be government inspected for wholesomeness.

Most commercially produced rabbits are marketed when they are 8 to 12 weeks old. These young rabbits are known as "fryers" and weigh not less than 1½ pounds and rarely over 3½ pounds, ready-to-cook. Rabbits known as "roasters" usually weigh over 4 pounds, ready-to-cook, and are ordinarily 8 months or older.

A large volume of the ready-to-cook rabbit is marketed in frozen form—usually pieces of one rabbit are packaged and frozen together. The giblets—heart, kidneys, and liver—are often included.

THAWING FROZEN RABBIT

A 2½-pound frozen rabbit packaged in pieces needs about 3 hours to thaw under cold running water, about 6 hours at room temperature (75°F.), or 8 to 10 hours, or overnight, in the refrigerator.

Large rabbits—over 3 pounds—should not be thawed at room temperature

unless they are to be cooked immediately.

POINTERS ON COOKING RABBIT

Small young rabbits (fryers, 1½ to 2 pounds ready-to-cook) may be fried satisfactorily in much the same way that chicken is fried. Or they may be stewed and the meat used in various recipes.

Large fryers and roasters need long, slow cooking in a covered pan to make them tender. Best methods of cooking them are stewing—that is, simmering in a small amount of water—and braising—first browning in a little fat and then cooking slowly, with or without added liquid, on top of the range or in the oven. Liquid used in braising may be a sauce that adds flavor to the dish.

For most recipes, the rabbit is cut in serving pieces before it is cooked. Dealers usually cut large rabbits into 9 or 11 pieces—the 2 forelegs, 4 pieces from the 2 hind legs, and 3 or 5 sections of back.

The kidneys are usually attached inside the lower back and are cooked and served with this piece. The liver and heart may be cooked with the rest of the rabbit in any recipe you are using, or stewed separately and used in gravy.

Yield of Stewed Rabbit Meat

From a small rabbit 1½ to 3½ pounds, ready-to-cook, you may expect 2 to 4½ cups of cooked meat. From larger rabbits you may count on about 1½ cups of cooked meat per pound of ready-to-cook weight.

FRIED RABBIT

Small young rabbit (1½ to 2 pounds ready-to-cook) cut in serving pieces
Flour, salt, pepper
Cooking fat or oil

Roll rabbit in mixture of flour, salt, and pepper. Heat fat or oil about ¼ inch deep in a heavy fry pan large enough to hold the pieces without crowding.

Use moderate heat for frying. Put in the large meaty pieces of rabbit first and cook about 10 minutes before adding the smaller pieces and giblets. Turn the pieces often for even cooking, and cook until well browned and tender (30 to 35 minutes total time).

Serves 3 to 4.

BROILED RABBIT OR SQUIRREL

Squirrel meat is similar to rabbit but more delicate in flavor. Clean and wipe young animals with damp cloth. Rub inside and out with melted butter.

Lay on side and cover with strips of bacon. Broil under moderate heat until well browned on all sides.

FRIED SQUIRREL

Use only young, fresh squirrels that are free of any strong, unpleasant odors. Follow method for frying rabbit. If animal is old, add a little water, cover and cook until tender.

ROAST RABBIT OR SQUIRREL

Rub inside of cleaned, dressed rabbit or squirrel with salt.

Fill with desired stuffing. Sew up and truss. Brush with melted fat or bacon drippings. Sprinkle with salt and pepper. Place on side in roaster.

Roast, uncovered, in slow oven (325°F.) until tender, about 1½ hours. Turn at least once while cooking. Baste frequently with melted fat.

RABBIT STEW

2 cups dried lima beans
1 small rabbit, dressed and cut in serving-size pieces
Boiling water
2 teaspoons salt
⅛ teaspoon pepper
1 teaspoon Ac'cent
1 bay leaf
1 medium-sized onion, sliced
1 bunch carrots, sliced
2 large green peppers
2 tablespoons butter or margarine

Soak beans overnight in 1½ quarts cold water; drain.

Wash rabbit; place in large kettle with drained beans; cover with boiling water; add salt, pepper, Ac'cent, bay leaf, and onion; simmer ½ hour.

Add carrots; cook 1 hour longer or until rabbit is tender. Add more boiling water as needed.

Cut seeded green peppers in rings; add during last 15 minutes, with butter or margarine. Thicken gravy if desired. Serves 6.

HASENPFEFFER

A German dish of rabbit marinated, seasoned, and braised.

½ cup vinegar
2 cups water
2 teaspoons salt
¼ teaspoon pepper
½ teaspoon whole cloves
2 teaspoons sugar
4 bay leaves
1 medium onion, sliced
Small rabbit (about 2½ pounds ready-to-cook) cut in serving pieces
Flour
3 tablespoons fat
2 teaspoons Worcestershire sauce
3 tablespoons flour

Make pickling mixture by combining the vinegar, water, salt, pepper, cloves, sugar, bay leaves, and onion in a glass or enameled-ware bowl.

Add pieces of rabbit and sliced giblets and cover the bowl. Let stand in refrigerator 8 to 12 hours, turning the pieces occasionally so that they will absorb the flavor evenly.

Remove the rabbit pieces. Save liquid and onions but discard bay leaves and cloves.

Roll the rabbit in flour. Heat fat or oil in a heavy pan and brown the rabbit in it, turning to brown all sides.

Pour the pickling mixture over the rabbit. Cover pan and cook over low heat about 1 hour, or until rabbit is tender.

Take rabbit from pan and keep it hot. Add Worcestershire sauce to the liquid. Mix the 3 tablespoons flour with a little cold water, add a few tablespoons of hot liquid to it, and pour the mixture back into the pan. Stir and cook until the sauce is thick and smooth, then cook a little longer.

Pour sauce over rabbit. Serves 4.

To use a large rabbit (about 4 to 5 pounds ready-to-cook), double the amounts of ingredients for the pickling

mixture. It is important to have enough to flavor all of the meat.

Use ⅓ cup fat to brown the rabbit and ⅓ cup flour to thicken the sauce. It may be necessary to skim off part of the fat before thickening the sauce. Serves 8 to 10.

RABBIT OR HARE FRICASSEE WITH VEGETABLES

Rabbit (about 3 pounds ready-to-cook) cut in serving pieces
Flour, salt, pepper
⅓ cup cooking fat or oil
2 cups hot water
4 cups raw vegetables (peas and coarsely chopped carrots, onions, and celery)
1 teaspoon salt
¼ cup sifted flour

Roll rabbit in mixture of flour, salt, and pepper.

Heat fat or oil and brown the rabbit slowly, turning often. Add water and cover pan.

Cook slowly on top of range about 1 hour, or until rabbit is almost tender. Add water if needed during cooking. Add vegetables and salt and cook about 20 minutes longer, or until vegetables are done.

Or, after browning, bake the rabbit in slow oven (325°F.) about 1½ hours, add vegetables, and bake about 30 minutes longer.

Mix the ¼ cup flour with a little cold water, add a few tablespoons of hot liquid from the pan, and stir the mixture into the liquid in pan. Cook 15 minutes longer, or until sauce is smooth and thick. Serves 8.

To fricassee a smaller rabbit (about 2 pounds ready-to-cook), use ¼ cup fat or oil for browning, and half the quantity of the other ingredients in the recipe above. Cooking time on top of range before adding vegetables is about 30 minutes; in oven, about 45 minutes. Serves 4.

RABBIT IN CASSEROLE

1 rabbit, cut up
3 tablespoons flour
1 teaspoon salt
½ teaspoon pepper
2 tablespoons butter or margarine
2 tablespoons cooking oil
1 cup claret or burgundy
½ cup canned or diced fresh tomato
½ cup diced celery
3 tablespoons sugar

Shake rabbit pieces in paper bag with flour, salt, and pepper. Brown in butter and oil in skillet. Remove to casserole.

Pour wine into skillet; stir well, then pour over rabbit.

Add remaining ingredients; cover and bake in slow oven (325°F.) 1 hour. Serves 6.

Rabbit Stew

NUTRITION AND WEIGHT CONTROL

In building the human body, the best foods in the right proportions are needed.

The ABC's of Nutrition

Nutrition is the science that deals with food at work—food on the job for you.

Modern knowledge of food at work brings a new kind of mastery over life. When you—and your family—eat the right food, it does far more than just keep you alive and going.

The right food helps you to be at your best in health and vitality. It can even help you to stay young longer, postponing old age. An individual well fed from babyhood has a more likely chance to enjoy a long prime of life. But, at any age, you are better off when you are better fed.

Food's Three Big Jobs

1. Food provides materials for the body's building and repair. Protein and minerals (and water) are what tissue and bone are chiefly made of. Children must have these food materials to grow on; and all life long the body continues to require supplies for upkeep.

2. Food provides regulators that enable the body to use other materials and to run smoothly. Vitamins do important work in this line, and minerals and protein too.

3. Food provides fuel for the body's energy and warmth. There is some fuel in every food.

Body's Needs, A to Z

From vitamin A to the mineral zinc, a list of nutrients—chemical substances that the body is known to require from food—would total more than 40. And there may be some not yet detected.

You can put nutrition knowledge to use without being introduced to all of the body's A-to-Z needs. When daily meals provide sufficiently for the following key nutrients, you can be reasonably sure of getting the rest.

PROTEIN

Protein was named from a Greek word meaning "first." Nearly a hundred years ago, it was recognized as the main substance in all of the body's muscles and organs, skin, hair, and other tissues. No simple substance could build and renew such different tissues, and protein has proved to be complex and varied.

Protein in different foods is made up of varying combinations of 22 simpler materials called amino acids. If need be, the body can make its own supply of more than half of these amino acids. But the remaining amino acids must come ready-made from food. And to get the best use from these special ones, the body needs them all together, either in one food or in some combination of foods.

The best quality proteins have all of these especially important amino acids, and worthwhile amounts of each.

You get top-rating proteins in foods from animal sources, as in meat, poultry, fish, eggs, milk, cheese. Some of these protein foods are needed each day; and it is an advantage to include some in each meal.

Next best for proteins are soybeans and nuts and dry beans and peas. When these are featured in main dishes, try to combine them with a little top-rating protein food, if you can.

The rest of the protein required will then come from cereals, bread, vegetables, and fruits. Many American-style dishes, such as meat and vegetable stew, egg sandwiches, macaroni and cheese, cereal and milk, are highly nourishing combinations. For in the body's remarkable chemistry, the high-grade proteins team with the less complete proteins in many companion foods and make the latter more useful than if eaten alone.

CALCIUM

Calcium is one of the chief mineral materials in bones and teeth. About 99 percent of all the calcium in the body is used for framework. Small but important, the other 1 percent remains in body fluids, such as the blood. Without this calcium, muscles can't contract and relax and nerves can't carry their messages.

For calcium to be used properly, other substances are needed too in right quantities, vitamin D and phosphorus, for example.

Many people go through life with bones that are calcium-poor. If a child gets too little calcium in his food or if his bones fail to deposit the calcium properly, then the bones will be smaller than they should be, or malformed as when legs are bent in rickets. Older people who are calcium-poor may have brittle bones that break easily and mend slowly. Whether you are young or old, it's a good thing for the diet to be calcium-rich.

The outstanding food for calcium is milk. You can hardly get enough calcium without using a good deal of milk in some form. Next-best foods for calcium are some of the leafy green vegetables—notably turnip tops, mustard greens, and kale.

These build, repair and regulate.

IRON

One of the essential materials for red blood cells is iron. Without its iron supply, the blood could not carry oxygen from the lungs to each body cell.

When meals are varied, you get some iron from many different foods. Liver is outstanding for iron. And one good reason for eating leafy green vegetables is their iron content.

Some of the other foods that add iron are egg yolks, meat in general, peas and beans of all kinds, dried fruits, molasses, bread and other cereal foods made from the whole grain or enriched.

IODINE

Your body must have small but steady amounts of iodine to help the thyroid gland to work properly. The most familiar bad effect of getting too little iodine is a swelling of the gland, called goiter.

Along the sea coast, and in some other parts of the United States, iodine is contained in the drinking water and vegetables and fruits grown in local soil. But too little iodine in water and soil is the cause of a wide "goiter belt" across the country, particularly around the Great Lakes and in northwestern States.

It is well to plan for iodine, particularly if you live inland. Eating salt-water fish or other food from the sea at least once a week will help. But the best line of defense is to use iodized table salt regularly. In this kind of table salt, the iodine lost from natural salt in refining is restored.

One point of warning must be added. Using iodized salt regularly can prevent simple goiter, but it may be harmful to a goiter far-advanced. If in doubt about its use, see a competent physician.

VITAMINS

Nearly 20 vitamins that are known or believed to be important to human well-being have thus far been discovered. A few more vitamins are known to be important to such creatures as fish, chickens, or insects, but not to people.

When you eat a variety of food you are pretty sure of getting a well-rounded assortment of the vitamins you need—except perhaps vitamin D. And you may also be getting other vitamins still undetected in food, but serving you just the same.

Separate doses of one or more selected vitamins are best taken under doctors' orders. For research is showing more and more instances in which a vitamin or other nutrient seeks a different nutrient in a meal as a special partner to assist in its work. When a vitamin pill brings in a mass army, the right partners may not be ready to use so much specialized help.

The following vitamins are of practical importance in planning family meals.

The B-Vitamin Family

There was once supposed to be just one vitamin B. Then, vitamin B was found to be complex and it has in time been separated into about a dozen vitamins, each with particular duties and importance. Most of them are now called by names that tell something about their chemical nature.

Thiamine, riboflavin, and niacin are the most generally known and best understood B's. Getting enough of these in food helps with steady nerves, normal appetite, good digestion, good morale, healthy skin. When these B's are seriously wanting in diet, malnutrition ills such as beri-beri and pellagra follow. But far more common in this country are borderline cases. The chronic grouch, the lazy-bones, the nervous man, the housewife with vague complaints, may be showing effects of food providing too little of these important B's.

Recently identified B's are folic acid and vitamin B[12], both important for healthy state of the blood. Folic acid and B[12] are being used medically with success in treating two hard-to-cure diseases—pernicious anemia and sprue.

Few foods contain real wealth of B vitamins, but in a varied diet many foods contribute some and so build an adequate supply.

One way to make sure of raising your B level is to use regularly bread and flour that have been made from whole grain or that have been enriched so as to restore important B vitamins.

Getting ample milk in diet is important for B's, too, and for riboflavin in particular.

B vitamins play a part in converting fuel in foods into energy. It follows that any one who eats large quantities of starches and sugars also requires more food containing B vitamins.

Vitamin A

Vitamin A is important to the young for growth. And at all ages it is important for normal vision, especially in dim light.

In one way or another, many vitamins help protect the body against infection, and vitamin A's guard duty is to help keep the skin and the linings of nose, mouth, and inner organs in good condition. If these surfaces are weakened, bacteria can invade more easily.

You can get vitamin A from some animal foods. Good sources are liver, egg yolks, butter, whole milk and cream, and cheese made from whole milk or cream. Fish-liver oils which children take for vitamin D are rich in vitamin A besides.

From many vegetable foods you can get carotenes, which are yellow-orange substances that the body converts into vitamin A. Green, yellow, and some red vegetables are good sources of carotene. One good reason for including a vegetable from the "leafy, green, and yellow group" every day is to keep stocked with this vitamin. Margarine, a vegetable fat, is nearly always fortified with vitamin A or carotene.

Some vitamin A can be stored in the body. So it is to your advantage to eat heartily of foods that provide for it, such as the green and yellow vegetables. A savings account of vitamin A in your system may be drawn upon, if in any emergency this vitamin is wanting in the diet.

Vitamin C

The first vitamin separated out from food was vitamin C, now also called ascorbic acid. Tissues throughout the body can't keep in good condition without vitamin C.

When diet is very low in this vitamin, gums are tender and bleed easily,

Concentrated sources of energy.

joints swell and hurt, and muscles weaken. In advanced stages, the disease called scurvy results. This misery used to attack sailors on long voyages when they got no fresh food. In time, they found they could fight scurvy with lemon, lime, or orange juice added to rations. Much later, vitamin C, the scurvy-fighter itself, was discovered.

Scurvy is rare now in this country. But many people get too little vitamin C for their best state of health.

You need some food rich in vitamin C daily, because the body can't store much of this vitamin.

All of the familiar citrus fruits are bountiful sources of vitamin C. Half a glass (4 ounces) of orange or grapefruit juice, fresh or canned, goes far toward meeting a day's needs. The same is true of half a grapefruit, a whole orange, or a couple of tangerines.

Other good sources of vitamin C include tomatoes and tomato juice, canned or fresh; fresh strawberries and cantaloup; also raw green food, such as cabbage, green pepper, and green lettuce. The potato's many values include some vitamin C.

Vitamin D

Vitamin D is especially important to the young, because it works with minerals to form straight, strong bones, and sound teeth. Babies with bowlegs may have too little vitamin D. An individual should get some of this vitamin regularly, at least through the growing stage. It is also important for pregnant and nursing mothers.

"Sunshine vitamin" is vitamin D's nickname, because the sun's rays striking the skin have power to change certain substances in the skin into vitamin D.

From baby days on, children can make good use of sunshine. But they should be protected well against sunburn or sunstroke.

Children can't get much vitamin D from the sun when they must wear thick warm clothes for cold weather, or when sunlight is cut off by clouds, smoke, fog, dust, or ordinary window glass.

A few foods, such as egg yolk, butter,

Vegetables and fruits are regulators and defenders of the body.

salmon, tuna, and sardines, help out with vitamin D; and some milk, both fresh and evaporated, has vitamin D added. But to supplement sunshine and food, babies and young children usually need to take a special vitamin D preparation or one of the fish-liver oils regularly. These oils from halibut, shark, and cod are the richest natural sources of this vitamin known.

FUEL

For the body's energy in work and play, fuel must come from food. The value of foods for this purpose is figured in calories. Main sources are starches and sugars, and fats, but all foods furnish calories—some many, some few, in a given-size portion.

Your needs for food as fuel depend mainly on two things—the size of your body and how active you are. An average-size man who is a desk worker with no strenuous sport or hobby needs about 2,400 calories from daily food. A fast-growing, lively teen-ager, boy or girl, may need more calories than this grown man.

If body weight stays about right for your health and build it's a sign that fuel intake from food matches your needs. The calories are taking care of themselves.

But suppose you are overweight... what then?

When the body gets more energy food than it can use, it stores up the excess as fat. Accumulation of too much fat is sometimes termed the most frequent malnutrition problem among adults in this country. To put it more plainly, many adults eat too much.

Up to 35 years of age, if you can't be just right in weight, it is better to be plump than skinny. Beyond 35, excess fat becomes a greater health liability than thinness. Ills such as high blood pressure and heart and kidney ailments are more common among overweights. Underweights tend to tire readily and may be an easy prey to infections.

FINDING OUT WHAT'S IN FOODS

Taking foods apart chemically, scientists are learning more exactly, nutrient by nutrient, what each familiar food can provide for the body's needs.

The table on a following page gives a rough idea of how well different kinds of foods in this country's diet can provide for the body's various needs. You can judge from this table that no one food has a wealth of all nutrients— not even milk, "the most nearly perfect food." Most foods contain more than one nutrient, and so help in more ways than one.

SERVING BY SERVING
Foods Provide for Daily Needs

Stars in the chart that follows give a rough idea of how servings from groups of familiar foods contribute toward dietary needs.

A serving that rates 5 stars provides more than 50 percent of the day's need for a nutrient. A 4-star serving provides about 40 percent; 3-star serving, 30 percent; 2-star serving, 20 percent; 1-star serving, 10 percent. Smaller amounts of nutrients are not shown.

These ratings are based on daily allowances of nutrients for a moderately active man as recommended by the National Research Council.

Some foods within a group have more of a nutrient, some less; but in a varied diet, which is common in this country, a group is likely to average as shown.

It's Up to You

● To get all the nutrients needed, it's wise to choose a variety of foods. It is also important to get enough of the different nutrients from food. A food plan worked out by nutritionists, such as the one that follows, is a handy guide.

● You will be off to a good start nutritionally if you plan meals by some orderly plan, so that daily food includes needed quantities of protein, minerals, and other nutrients.

● You are following through effectively when you cook by up-to-date methods that keep delicate vitamins and minerals from being wasted.

● And, rounding out a family nutrition program, you can make mealtime interesting and food associations pleasant. For, after all, food must be eaten to count for good nutrition. You can, for example...

● Select nutritious recipes that the whole family enjoys, and use them reasonably often.

● When re-using one of these favorites, vary the meal with different food combinations.

● If an inexpensive dish seems dull, vary flavor with seasonings, or combine with others foods different ways.

● Use contrast in food colors, flavors, textures. Some bright-colored food, something crisp, for example, can heighten the eye appeal and appetite appeal of a meal.

● Give children small servings, remembering that big amounts may be discouraging. It's better for a child to form the habit of cleaning his plate and asking for a second helping, if wanted.

● Introduce a new food to a young child in sample tastes, and at the start of a meal when he is hungry... and if he doesn't like it at first, try another day.

Kind of food	Size of Serving	Protein	Calcium	Iron	Vitamin A value	B-vitamins			Vitamin C (ascorbic acid)	Food energy (in calories)
						Thiamine	Riboflavin	Niacin		
Leafy, green, yellow vegetables.	½ cup			★	★★★★				★★	30
Tomatoes, tomato products.	½ cup			★	★★★			★	★★★	35
Potatoes ...	1 medium			★		★		★	★	105
Sweetpotatoes	1 medium			★	★★★★★	★		★	★★★	165
Other vegetables	½ cup								★	40
Citrus fruits	½ cup								★★★★★	55
Other fruits	½ cup				★				★	70
Milk, cheese, ice cream.	1 cup milk	★	★★★		★	★	★★			170
Meat, poultry, fish	4 ounces	★★		★★	★	★★	★	★★★		225
Eggs	1 egg	★		★	★		★			80
Dry beans and peas, nuts.	¾ cup beans cooked	★★	★	★★★		★★	★	★★		215
Baked goods, flour, cereals.	2 slices bread	★		★		★	★	★		130
Butter, fortified margarine.	1 pat				★					50
Other fats (includes bacon, salt pork).	2 tablespoons									230
Sugar, all kinds	2 teaspoons									35
Molasses, sirups, preserves.	2 tablespoons			★						115

★★★★★ More than 50 percent of daily need.
★★★★ About 40 percent of daily need.
★★★ About 30 percent of daily need.
★★ About 20 percent of daily need.
★ About 10 percent of daily need.

Have a Food Plan

To see that your family is well fed, it's wise to use a plan. This way you can be sure to provide each important kind of food—and enough of it.

A food fact worth knowing is: When families in this country are poorly fed, the foods they neglect are most often milk and milk products, and vegetables and fruits—especially the leafy, green, and yellow vegetables and citrus fruits. Watch for these in planning.

A Ready-Made Food Plan

A helpful guide for weekly shopping and meal planning is a food plan worked out by nutritionists. Such a plan is given on a following page. Other plans could be made that would measure up—as this plan does—to the National Research Council's yardstick of good nutrition. Any plan that does measure up must bring into the kitchen the makings of meals that offer recommended amounts of protein, minerals and vitamins, and food energy.

In the plan given, foods are in groups according to their major contributions of nutrients, as well as their place in the meal. Amounts to provide for adequate diets are shown in pounds and quarts of food for a week.

More information about planning by food groups, and the way they work out in servings, is also given on the following pages and in ABC's for Cooks. You can see that there is ample choice within groups to allow for varied meals from day to day wherever you live. The groups allow, too, for stressing family favorites among the foods.

In the pages on food groups, the "plan to use" headings are intended as a guide, if you follow a food plan of your own, not exactly like the one given.

Ways to Use This Plan

You can make use of the food plan for good nutrition in several ways. It can serve as a shopping guide, as it stands, to show the approximate amount of food needed for each member of the family. Or you can compare it to kinds and quantities of food you regularly use, just to make sure that you are not short in any important kind.

If you have a garden or put up food for the winter, the food plan can help as a general guide to amounts of foods that the family will use.

To Figure Your Family's Needs

To use the food plan, figure weekly amounts of the food groups that will fit your family.

The rows of figures in the plan are arranged to show food quantities according to age, sex, and how active the individual is. Where a range is given: For children, the first quantity is for the youngest age. For adults, the first quantity is for the less active. The most active adults do really heavy work or take strenuous exercise.

For pregnant and nursing women, the first quantity is for pregnant and the second for nursing women.

No figures are given for children under 1 year because they are often breast-fed or have formulas or other food prepared especially for them.

Guided by these ranges, you can estimate the quantity needed for each person in the family. Use judgment in doing this. If a child is having a spurt of growing, he may need the amount of food usually suggested for children a year or two older.

As you add up the amount of each kind of food your family members need in a week, write the figure in the column provided at right of the food plan sheet. This is your shopping guide, to use as it stands or to compare with amounts you've been buying.

YOUR FOOD AND YOUR MONEY

Quantities in the food plan can be bought for about the same money that the average family in this country spends for food. This assumes that you will choose moderate-price foods, or mix some cheaper foods with more expensive ones.

If you have more money to spend, you can choose now and again the more expensive items, such as luxury foods and those out of season. On the other hand, if you want to cut down food costs, reduce somewhat—perhaps by about one-third—the quantities of meat, poultry, and fish in the plan, and also the group described as "other vegetables and fruits." To take their place, increase potatoes and cereals by about one-fourth.

In either case, try not to change very much the quantities given in the plan for milk and milk products, leafy, green, and yellow vegetables, and tomatoes and citrus fruits.

A FOOD PLAN FOR GOOD NUTRITION (Quantities for One Week)

Kinds of food	For children 1 to 6 years	For children 7 to 12 years	For girls 13 to 20 years	For boys 13 to 20 years	For women		For men, all activities	Total suggested for your family
					All activities	Pregnant and nursing		
Leafy, green, and yellow vegetables	2–2½ lbs.	2½–3 lbs.	3½ lbs.	3½–4 lbs.	3½–4 lbs.	4 lbs.	3½–4 lbs.	
Citrus fruits, tomatoes	2–2½ lbs.	2½–3 lbs.	3 lbs.	3–3½ lbs.	2½–3 lbs.	3½–4½ lbs.	2½–3½ lbs.	
Potatoes, sweet potatoes	½–1 lb.	1½–2 lbs.	2½ lbs.	3½–4½ lbs.	2–3 lbs.	2–3 lbs.	3–5 lbs.	
Other vegetables and fruits	2 lbs.	2½ lbs.	3½ lbs.	3½ lbs.	3–4 lbs.	3–3½ lbs.	3–4 lbs.	
Milk, cheese, ice cream[1]	6 qts.	7 qts.	6–7 qts.[2]	7 qts.	5 qts.	7½–10½ qts.	5 qts.	
Meat, poultry, fish[3] Eggs Dry beans and peas, nuts	1–1¼ lbs. 6–7 eggs 1 oz.	2 lbs. 7 eggs 2 ozs.	2½–3 lbs. 7 eggs 2 ozs.	3 lbs. 7 eggs 4–6 ozs.	2½–3 lbs. 7 eggs 2–4 ozs.	3 lbs. 6–7 eggs 2–4 ozs.	3–3½ lbs. 6–7 eggs 4 ozs.	
Baked goods, flour, cereals[1] Whole-grain, enriched, or restored	1–1½ lbs.	2–3 lbs.	2½–3 lbs.[2]	4–5 lbs.	2–4 lbs.	2–2½ lbs.	3–7 lbs.	
Fats, oils	¼ lb.	½–1 lb.	¾ lb.	1–1½ lbs.	¾–1 lb.	¾ lb.	1–2 lbs.	
Sugar, syrups, preserves	¼–½ lb.	¾ lb.	1 lb.	1–1½ lbs.	¾–1 lb.	¾ lb.	1–1½ lbs.	

[1] For explanation of milk-equivalent and flour-equivalent foods see What's In Each Food Group.

[2] Larger quantities are for the younger girls.

[3] To meet the iron allowance needed by children 1 to 6 years, girls 13 to 20, and pregnant and nursing women, include weekly 1 large or 2 small servings of liver or other organ meats.

What's in Each Food Group

Here are common foods grouped as in The Food Plan for Good Nutrition. Foods in each group can be used similarly in meals, so within the group there is room for variety. Foods in each group provide about the same nutrients but some are better providers than others.

Leafy, Green, and Yellow Vegetables

Leafy, green, and yellow vegetables are rich in vitamin A value, especially the dark green leafy kinds, and carrots. They also provide worth-while amounts of riboflavin, iron, and some calcium; and cabbage, broccoli, Brussels sprouts, and greens offer vitamin C.

Plan to use: 1 or more servings daily. The food plan provides: 10 to 12 servings per week.

All kinds of greens—collards. kale. turnip greens, spinach, and many others, cultivated and wild; carrots, peas, snap beans, okra, green asparagus, broccoli, Brussels sprouts, green lima beans, pumpkin, yellow squash, green cabbage.

Citrus Fruits, Tomatoes

Citrus fruits and tomatoes are mainstay sources of vitamin C.

Plan to use: 1 or more servings daily. The food plan provides: 7 to 10 servings a week.

Oranges, grapefruit, tangerines, other citrus fruit, tomatoes.

The following foods are also good sources of vitamin C and may be used as alternates:

If eaten raw—cabbage, salad greens, green peppers, turnips, strawberries, pineapple, cantaloup. If cooked briefly, in very little water—cabbage, broccoli, Brussels sprouts, greens.

Potatoes, Sweet Potatoes

Potatoes and sweet potatoes contain a number of nutrients. Because of the quantities in which they are eaten, white potatoes can become quite important as a source of vitamin C. Sweet potatoes are valuable for vitamin A in addition to vitamin C.

Plan to use: 1 or more servings daily. The food plan provides: 7 to 9 servings a week.

Other Vegetables and Fruits

These vegetables and fruits help toward a good diet with vitamins and minerals.

Plan to use: 1 or more servings daily. The food plan provides: 10 to 12 servings a week.

Beets, cauliflower, corn, cucumbers, onions, sauerkraut, turnips, white cabbage, apples, peaches, bananas, berries, rhubarb, dried fruit—all vegetables and fruits not included in other groups.

Milk, Cheese, Ice Cream

Milk—whole, skim, evaporated, condensed, dry, buttermilk—is our leading source of calcium. Milk also provides high-quality protein, riboflavin, vitamin A, and many other vitamins and minerals.

Plan to use, as the food plan provides, the following amounts of milk daily.

Include milk used for drinking as well as cooking:

Children through teen age: 3½ to 4 cups.

Adults: 2½ to 3 cups.

Pregnant women: A little more than 1 quart.

Nursing mothers: 1½ quarts.

On the basis of calcium they contain, the following may be used as alternates for 1 cup of milk: Cheddar cheese, 1½ ounces; cream cheese, 15 ounces; cottage cheese, 11 ounces; ice cream, 2 to 3 large dips.

Meat, Poultry, Fish

Meat, poultry, and fish are important primarily for high-quality protein. Foods in this group also provide iron, thiamine, riboflavin, niacin, vitamin A.

Plan to use: 1 serving daily, if possible.

The food plan provides: 7 to 8 servings a week.

All kinds, including liver, heart, and other variety meats.

Count bacon and salt pork in with fats.

Eggs

Eggs are a source of high-quality protein, iron, vitamin A, riboflavin, vitamin D, and provide some calcium and thiamine.

Plan to use: 4 or more a week.

The food plan provides: 6 or 7 a week.

Dry Beans and Peas, Nuts

Dry beans and peas and nuts contain good protein, also some calcium, iron, thiamine, riboflavin, and niacin.

Plan to use: 1 or more servings a week.

The food plan provides: 1 to 2 servings a week.

Dry beans of all kinds, dry peas, lentils; soybeans, soya products; peanuts, other nuts; peanut butter.

Baked Goods, Flour, Cereals

Whole-grain cereals, or those with added vitamins and minerals or restored to whole-grain value, provide significant amounts of iron, thiamine, riboflavin, niacin. Foods in this group also help out with protein and calories.

Plan to use as the food plan provides: Some every day.

Flour or meal made from wheat, corn, oats, buckwheat, rye; cooked and ready-to-eat cereals; rice, barley, hominy, noodles, macaroni; breads, other baked goods.

Quantities suggested in the food plan are in terms of pounds of flour and cereal. Bread and other baked goods average two-thirds flour by weight. Therefore, count 1½ pounds of bread and other baked goods as 1 pound of flour.

Fat, Oils

Butter and fortified margarine are rich in vitamin-A value. Like all fats, they furnish many calories.

Plan to use as the food plan provides: Some butter or margarine daily; other fats as needed in cooking.

Butter, margarine, salad oil, shortening, bacon, salt pork, lard, suet, drippings.

Sugar, Syrups, Preserves

Sugar, syrups, preserves are useful mainly for the calories they provide for bodily energy.

The food plan includes for the average person about a pound a week.

Any kind of sugar—granulated (beet or cane), confectioners', brown, and maple; molasses or any kind of syrup or honey; jams and jellies; candy.

CONTROLLING WEIGHT

If you are under 20 years of age, don't try to reduce except under a physician's guidance. This is also advisable if you are a young mother or have anything wrong with heart or other organs. If you are not in these groups, and need to reduce, take it slowly. A pound or two off a week is plenty.

To reduce calories without starving your body of its other needs:

Eat three meals a day, but don't be tempted by between-meal snacks.

Avoid high-calorie foods like the fat on meat, cooking fat, salad oil, fried foods, gravies and rich sauces, nuts, pastries, cakes, cookies, rich desserts, candies, jellies, and jams. Eat small-size servings of bread or cereal.

Don't skimp on fruits and vegetables. Eat a variety—yes, potatoes, too. A medium-sized potato has no more calories than a big orange or a big apple. But take fruits and vegetables straight—vegetables without cream sauce, or fat, fruit without sugar and cream. Don't skimp on protein-rich foods, for you need plenty of lean meat, milk and eggs.

If you are underweight you need to turn the tables to put some fat on your bones. You need three balanced meals, as overweights do. To these meals, you can freely add the extras shunned by the weight reducers—such as rich gravies and desserts, salad dressings, and jams. And you can well take some extra food as between-meal snacks.

Calorie Counter's Guide

A calorie is a unit of heat, or energy, generated in the body by food, used to measure the amount of heat, or energy, required by the body at different ages and under various conditions.

If you eat more in total calories for the day than the body needs, it's stored as fat. By counting calories, dieters can and should eat well balanced meals—and still lose or gain weight.

Calorie values can seldom be exact, especially for "made" foods. For example, two dishes of ice cream, even of the same flavor, can vary considerably in calorie value because the ingredients vary. One may have more sugar than another, or be made with richer cream. One might have more chocolate or fruit in its composition. But even approximate calorie values can be very helpful to one who is dieting for one reason or another.

The data given here are in quantities that can be readily adjusted to servings of different sizes.

Values for prepared foods and food mixtures have been calculated from typical recipes.

Values for cooked vegetables are without added fat.

HOW TO ESTIMATE YOUR CALORIE NEEDS

Dieters should know the number of calories the body needs just to keep in top physical condition.

1. Estimate your "ideal" weight for height and build. Weight charts are usually for the average person. Large-boned people may top this average by 10 to 20 percent; slender-boned people fall under it.

2. Multiply your "ideal" weight by 15. Your body needs 15 to 20 calories per pound per day.

3. In order to lose weight, reduce the answer above by one-third. In order to gain, in most cases add one-third. The result is your calorie quota for one day.

4. Divide your total for your three meals.

BREADS, ROLLS; OTHER GRAIN PRODUCTS

	Measure	Calories
Barley (pearled, light, dry)	1 cup	710
Biscuits (baking powder, enriched flour)	1 biscuit (2½" diam.)	130
Bran flakes	1 cup	115
Breads:		
Boston Brown (unenriched)	1 slice	105
Corn bread	2" cube	200
Cracked wheat bread	1 slice	55
French toast	1 slice	230
Gluten bread	1 slice	65
Melba toast	1 slice	25
Pumpernickel	1 slice	70
Rye	1 slice	55
Rye Crisp	1 piece	20
White bread, raisin	1 slice	100
White, unenriched, 4% nonfat milk solids	1 slice	65
White, enriched, 4% nonfat milk solids	1 slice	65
White, enriched, 6% nonfat milk solids	1 slice	65
Whole wheat	1 slice	55
raisin	1 slice	100
Cereal foods, dry, precooked (infant food)	1 ounce	105

BREADS, ROLLS; OTHER GRAIN PRODUCTS

	Measure	Calories
Corn flakes	1 cup	95
Corn grits, degermed, cooked, unenriched	1 cup	120
Corn grits, degermed, cooked, enriched	1 cup	120
Crackers:		
Graham	4 small or 2 med.	55
Matzo wafer	1 small	80
Oyster	10	40
Rye wafer	1 small	22
Soda (plain)	2 crackers (2½" diam.)	45
Wheat wafer	1 small	24
Farina, enriched, cooked	1 cup	105
Flours and Meals:		
All-purpose or family flour, enriched or unenriched	1 cup, sifted	400
Buckwheat flour	1 cup	564
Cornmeal, yellow or white	1 cup	456
Gluten flour	1 cup	463
Graham flour	1 cup	360
Rice flour	1 cup	356
Rye flour	1 cup	361
Soybean flour	1 cup	353
Whole wheat flour	1 cup, stirred	400
Grape nuts	½ cup	205
Grape nut flakes	1 cup	130
Hominy grits, cooked	½ cup	100
Macaroni, cooked, unenriched	1 cup	210
Macaroni, cooked, enriched	1 cup	210
Muffins, made with enriched flour	1 muffin (2¾" diam.)	135
Muffins, corn, made with degermed corn meal	1 muffin (2¾" diam.)	105
Muffins, bran	1 muffin (2¾" diam.)	100
Noodles, containing egg, unenriched, cooked	1 cup	105
Oatmeal or rolled oats, cooked	1 cup	150
Oatmeal, precooked, (infant food), dry	1 ounce	105
Pancakes, baked, wheat, with enriched flour	1 cake (4" diam.)	60
Popovers	1 medium	105
Popcorn, popped	1 cup	40
Pretzels	5 small sticks	20
Rice, cooked, converted	1 cup	205
Rice, cooked, white or milled	1 cup	200
Rice, puffed	1 cup	55
Rolls, plain, enriched	1 roll (12 per lb.)	120
Rolls, Parkerhouse	1 small	100
Rolls, sweet, with frosting	1 med. size	300
Rolls, Vienna	1 aver.	140
Spaghetti, unenriched, cooked	1 cup	220
Waffles, baked with enriched flour	1 waffle (4½x5⅝")	215
Wheat germ	1 cup, stirred	245
Wheat, puffed	1 cup	65
Wheat, shredded	1 large biscuit (1 ounce)	100
Zwieback	1 piece	35

EGGS

	Measure	Calories
Whole egg, raw, medium	1 egg	75
Egg yolk, raw, medium	1 yolk	60
Egg white, raw, medium	1 egg white	15
Eggs, dried, whole	1 cup	640
Egg, fried	1	110
Egg, poached	1	75
Egg, scrambled	1	145
Egg, soft or hard-cooked	1	75

FISH AND SEAFOOD

	Measure	Calories
Anchovy paste	1 tbsp.	20
Anchovies	3	18
Caviar, pressed	1 tbsp.	72
Clams, raw, meat only	4 ounces	90
Clams, raw, with juice	6 aver. size	100
Cod, dried	1 ounce	105
Crabmeat, canned or cooked	3 ounces	90
Finnan Haddie	¾ cup	95
Fish, fried (most fish)	aver. serving	215
Fish, broiled or steamed, lean (bass, cod, haddock, halibut)	aver. serving	110
Fish, broiled or steamed fat (mackeral, tuna, etc.)	aver. serving	190
Flounder, raw	4 ounces	80
Frog legs	4 medium	45
Herring, fresh	1 7" fish	165
Herring, smoked	3" piece	115
Lobster	½ small or ½ cup canned	65
Mackerel, canned solids and liquid	3 ounces	155
Oysters, meat only, raw	1 cup (13–19 med. size, selects)	200
Oysters, raw, with juice	4 to 6 med. size	80
Oyster stew	1 cup with 6–8 oysters	245
Perch	1 4½" fish	55
Salmon, canned, pink	3 ounces	120
Salmon, fresh	2½" piece	195
Sardines, canned in oil, drained solids	3 ounces	180
Scallops, raw	4 ounces	90
Shad, raw	4 ounces	190
Shrimp, canned, meat only	3 ounces	110
Shrimp	1 medium	10
Tuna fish, drained solids	3 ounces	170
Trout	6" piece	80
Whitefish	1 piece (3x3 in.)	165

MEATS, POULTRY, GAME

	Measure	Calories
Beef, canned:		
Corned beef, medium fat	3 ounces	180
Corned beef hash	3 ounces	120
Strained (infant food)	1 ounce	30
Beef, dried	2 ounces	115
Beef, without bone, cooked:		
Brisket	1 slice (4x2½x1")	400
Chuck	3 ounces	265
Corned, boiled	1 slice (4x1½x1)	100
Hamburger	3 oz. patty	315
Round, lean	3 ounces	150
Sirloin, lean	3 ounces	150
Swiss steak, cooked	3x2½x1½"	320
Rib roast, medium fat	3 ounces	320
Beef and vegetable stew	1 cup	390
Chile con carne, canned without beans	⅓ cup	170
Pork:		
Bacon, medium fat, broiled or fried	2 slices	95
Canadian bacon	1 slice	70
Ham, smoked, boiled, fat trimmed	1 slice (4½x4x½")	260
Spareribs	4 ribs	330
Luncheon meat, canned, spiced	2 ounces	165
Loin or chops, cooked	3 oz. without bone	285
Veal:		
Cutlet, cooked	3 oz. without bone	185
Roast	1 slice (3x3¾x½")	120
Chop	1⅝" thick	210
Lamb:		
Leg roast, cooked	3 ounces	230
Canned, strained (infant food)	1 ounce	30
Rib chop, lean only	1	100
Stew meat, breast	2 pieces (2x1¼")	225
Sausage:		
Bologna	1 slice (2x½" thick)	100
Frankfurter, cooked	1	125

MEATS, POULTRY, GAME

Pork sausage, canned	4 ounces	340
Pork sausage, links	1 3″ long	60
Pork sausage	1 patty	270
Liver sausage	1 slice	100
	(3¼x1½″ thick)	

Variety Meats:

Beef heart, raw	3 ounces	90
Brains	2	150
Kidneys, beef, raw	3 ounces	120
Liver, beef, fried	2 ounces	120
Liver, canned, strained (infant food)	1 ounce	30
Sweetbreads	1 piece	400
	(4x3″)	
Tongue, beef, raw	4 ounces	235
Tongue, cooked	2 slices	50
	(3x2x⅛″)	

Chicken:

Canned, boned	3 ounces	170
Creamed	½ cup	160
Fried	1 thigh and 1 leg	330
Liver	3 aver.	90
Roast	1 thigh and 1 leg	335
Duck, roast	¼ breast and 1 thigh	170
Goose, roast	3x3″ piece	155
Rabbit, fried	1 thigh and 1 leg	410
Turkey, roast	aver. serving	170

FRUITS AND FRUIT JUICES

	Measure	Calories
Apples, baked, sweet	1 medium	170
Apples, raw	1 medium	75
	(2½″ diam.)	
Apple juice, fresh or canned	1 cup	125
Applesauce, canned, sweetened	1 cup	185
Apricots, raw	3 apricots	55
Apricots, canned in syrup	4 med. halves and 2 tbsps. syrup	95
Apricots, canned, strained (infant food)	1 ounce	15
Apricots, dried, cooked unsweetened, fruit and liquid	1 cup	240
Avocadoes, raw	½ peeled fruit	280
	(3½x3″)	
Bananas, raw	1 medium	90
	(6x1½″)	
Blackberries, raw	1 cup	80
Blueberries, raw	1 cup	85
Cantaloupes, raw	½ melon	35
	(5″ diam.)	
Cherries, raw, pitted	1 cup	65
Cherries, canned, red sour	1 cup	120
Cider, sweet	1 cup	115
Cranberry juice, sweet	1 cup	245
Cranberry sauce, sweetened	1 cup	550
Dates "fresh" and dried, pitted and cut	1 cup	505

Figs, raw	3 small	90
	(1½″ diam.)	
Figs, dried	1 large (2x1″)	55
Fruit cocktail, canned, solids and liquid	1 cup	180
Grapefruit, raw	1 cup sections	75
Grapefruit, raw	½ medium	45
Grapefruit juice, canned, unsweetened	1 cup	90
Grapefruit juice, frozen concentrate	6 ounce can	295
Grapes, American type (slip skin)	1 cup	85
Grapes, European type (adherent skin)	1 cup	100
Grape juice, bottled	1 cup	170
Honeydew melon, diced	1 cup	80
Lemon juice, fresh	1 cup	60
Lime juice, fresh	1 cup	60
Oranges	1 medium	70
	(3″ diam.)	
Orange juice, canned, unsweetened	1 cup	110
Orange juice, fresh	1 cup	110
Orange juice, frozen concentrate	6 ounce can	300
Papayas, raw, cubed	1 cup	70
Peaches, raw	1 medium	45
	(2½x2″ diam.)	
Peaches, canned in syrup, solids and liquid	1 cup	175
Peaches, canned, strained, (infant food)	1 ounce	15
Peaches, dried, cooked, unsweetened	1 cup	225
	(10-12 halves and 6 tbsps. liquid)	
Pears, raw	1 pear	95
	(3x2½″ diam.)	
Pears, canned in syrup	2 medium halves and 2 tbsps. syrup	80
Pears, strained (infant food)	1 ounce	15
Persimmons, Japanese, raw, seedless kind	1 persimmon	95
	(2¼″ diam.)	
Pineapple, raw, diced	1 cup	75
Pineapple, canned in syrup	2 small or 1 large slice and 2 tbsps. juice	95
Pineapple juice, canned	1 cup	120
Plums, raw	1 plum	30
	(2″ diam.)	
Prunes, cooked unsweetened	1 cup (16–18 prunes and ⅓ cup liquid)	310
Prune juice, canned	1 cup	170
Raisins, dried	1 cup	430
Raspberries, red, raw	1 cup	70
Rhubarb, cooked with sugar	1 cup	385
Strawberries, raw	1 cup	55
Strawberries, frozen	3 ounces	90

Tangerines	1 med.	35
	(2½″ diam.)	
Tangerine juice, canned	1 cup	95
Watermelons	½ slice (¾x10″)	45

VEGETABLES AND VEGETABLE JUICES

	Measure	Calories
Asparagus, cooked	1 cup cut spears	35
Asparagus, canned green	6 med. size spears	20
Asparagus, canned bleached	6 med. size spears	20
Beans, lima, immature, cooked	1 cup	150
Beans, snap, green cooked	1 cup	25
Beets, cooked, diced	1 cup	70
Beet greens, cooked	1 cup	70
Broccoli, cooked, flower stalks	1 cup	45
Brussels sprouts, cooked	1 cup	60
Cabbage, raw, shredded	1 cup	25
Cabbage, cooked	1 cup	40
Carrots, raw, grated	1 cup	45
Carrots, cooked, diced	1 cup	45
Carrots, strained (infant food)	1 ounce	10
Cauliflower, cooked, flower buds	1 cup	30
Celery, raw, diced	1 cup	20
Celery, cooked, diced	1 cup	25
Collards, cooked	1 cup	75
Corn, sweet, cooked	1 ear (5″ long)	85
Corn, sweet, canned, solids and liquid	1 cup	170
Cowpeas, immature seed, cooked	1 cup	150
Cucumbers, raw	6 slices (⅛″ thick, center section)	5
Dandelion greens, cooked	1 cup	80
Endive, raw	1 pound	90
Kale, cooked	1 cup	45
Lettuce, headed, raw	2 large or 4 small leaves	5
Mushrooms, canned, solids and liquid	1 cup	30
Mushrooms, fresh	1 large	2
Mustard greens, cooked	1 cup	30
Okra, cooked	8 pods (3″ long, ⅝″ diam.)	30
Onions, raw, mature	1 onion (2½″ diam.)	50
Onions, young green	6 small onions without tops	25
Parsnips, cooked	1 cup	95
Peas, green, cooked	1 cup	110
Peas, canned, strained (infant food)	1 ounce	15
Peppers, green, raw	1 medium	15
Potatoes, baked	1 medium (2½″ diam.)	95

VEGETABLES AND VEGETABLE JUICES

Potatoes, boiled in skin	1 medium (2½" diam.)	120
Potatoes, boiled after peeling	1 medium (2½" diam.)	105
Potatoes, creamed	½ cup	100
Potatoes, French-fried	8 pieces (2x½x½")	155
Potatoes, hash-brown	½ cup	175
Potatoes, scalloped	½ cup	100
Potato chips	10 medium (2" diam.)	110
Pumpkin, canned	1 cup	75
Radishes, raw	4 small	5
Rutabagas, cooked, cubed or sliced	1 cup	50
Sauerkraut, canned, drained solids	1 cup	30
Soybean sprouts, raw	1 cup	50
Spinach, cooked	1 cup	45
Spinach, canned, strained (infant food)	1 ounce	5
Squash, summer, cooked, diced	1 cup	35
Squash, winter, baked, mashed	1 cup	95
Squash, winter, canned, strained (infant food)	1 ounce	10
Sweet Potatoes, peeled, baked	1 sweet potato (5x2")	185
Sweet Potatoes, peeled, boiled	1 sweet potato (5x2½")	250
Tomatoes, raw	1 medium (2x2½")	30
Tomatoes, canned or cooked	1 cup	45
Tomato juice, canned	1 cup	50
Turnips, cooked, diced	1 cup	40
Turnip greens, cooked	1 cup	45
Vegetables, mixed, canned, strained (infant food)	1 ounce	10

MATURE BEANS AND PEAS; NUTS

	Measure	Calories
Almonds, shelled, unblanched	1 cup	850
Almonds, salted	10 to 12	100
Beans, canned or cooked:		
Red Kidney	1 cup	230
Navy or other varieties with:		
Pork and tomato sauce	1 cup	295
Pork and molasses	1 cup	325
Beans, lima, dry	1 cup	610
Brazil nuts	1 average	45
Brazil nuts, shelled	1 cup	905
Cashews	1	20
Coconut, dried, shredded (sweetened)	1 cup	345
Cowpeas, dry	1 cup	685
Filberts	6	50

Peanuts	10 kernels	55
Peanuts, roasted, shelled	1 cup	805
Peanut butter	1 tablespoon	90
Peas, split, dry	1 cup	690
Pecan	1 half	10
Pecans	1 cup halves	750
Soybeans, dry	1 cup	695
Walnut	1 half	10
Walnuts, English	1 cup halves	655

MILK AND MILK PRODUCTS

	Measure	Calories
Buttermilk, from skim milk	1 cup	85
Milk, cow:		
Fluid, whole	1 cup	165
Fluid, nonfat (skim)	1 cup	85
Evaporated (undiluted)	1 cup	345
Condensed, undiluted)	1 cup	980
Dry, whole	1 tbsp.	40
Dry, nonfat solids	1 tbsp.	30
Milk, goat, fluid	1 cup	165
Whey	1 cup	55
Yogurt, plain	1 cup	160
Cheese:		
Camembert	1 ounce	85
Cheddar	1 ounce cube (1")	115
Cheddar, grated	3 tbsps.	110
Cheddar, processed	1 ounce	105
Cheese foods, Cheddar	1 ounce	90
Cottage, from skim milk	1 ounce	25
Cream	1 ounce	105
Limburger	1 ounce	100
Roquefort or blue	1 ounce	100
Swiss	1 ounce	105
Cream:		
Light	1 tbsp.	30
Heavy	1 tbsp.	50
Milk Beverages:		
Chocolate (all milk)	1 cup	240
Cocoa (all milk)	1 cup	235
Chocolate flavored milk	1 cup	185
Eggnog	1 cup	215
Malted milk	1 cup	215
	Fountain size	460

BEVERAGES

	Measure	Calories
Cola type	6 oz. bottle	80
Root beer	1 cup	65
Ginger ale	1 cup	75
Coffee	1 cup	0
Tea	1 cup	0
Postum	1 cup	16

BEVERAGES—ALCOHOLIC

	Measure	Calories
Ale	8 ounces	135

Beer	8 ounces	120
Brandy	1 ounce	85
Cordials	1 ounce	90
Gin	1 ounce	80
Rum	1 ounce	150
Whiskey-Bourbon, Rye, Irish	1 ounce	100
Whiskey-Scotch	1 ounce	95
Cocktails:		
Bacardi	½ cup	244
Daiquiri	½ cup	199
Manhattan	½ cup	236
Martini	½ cup	102
Old-Fashioned	⅓ cup	177
Mixed Drinks:		
Tom & Jerry	1 cup	266
Tom Collins	1 cup	235
Whiskey Sour	⅓ cup	98
Wines:		
Dry	4 ounces	90
Sweet	4 ounces	95
Champagne	4 ounces	120
Port	1 ounce	55
Sherry	1 ounce	40

SOUPS, CANNED, READY TO SERVE

	Measure	Calories
Beef	1 cup	100
Chicken	1 cup	75
Chicken, strained (infant food)	1 ounce	15
Clam chowder	1 cup	85
Bouillon or consommé	1 cup	35
Asparagus, cream of	1 cup	120
Bean	1 cup	235
Celery, cream of	1 cup	160
Corn, cream of	1 cup	155
Mushroom, cream of	1 cup	125
Pea, cream of	1 cup	165
Pea, split	1 cup	165
Potato	1 cup	200
Tomato, cream of	1 cup	155
Vegetable	1 cup	90

SALADS

	Measure	Calories
Aspic	½ cup	30
Cole slaw, with mayonnaise	½ cup	55
Cole slaw, with vinegar	½ cup	15
Molded fruit	½ cup	145
Perfection, clear gelatin	½ cup	35
Potato salad	½ cup	200
Tossed green salad, no dressing	¾ cup	25
Waldorf salad	½ cup	240
Chicken, fish, or meat	½ cup	200

SANDWICHES

	Measure	Calories
Bacon, tomato, with mayonnaise	1	290
Cheese, American	1	330
Cheese, toasted	1	390
Cream cheese—jelly	1	350
Cream cheese—olive—nut	1	385
Chicken, plain	1	315

SANDWICHES

Club (chicken, bacon, tomato, lettuce, mayonnaise	1	350
Egg salad	1	300
Frankfurter on bun, with mustard	1	235
Ham, boiled	1	325
Hamburger on bun, with mustard	1	300
Lettuce-tomato, with mayonnaise	1	250
Peanut butter	1	365
Tuna salad	1	400

SAUCES

	Measure	Calories
Butterscotch sauce	¼ cup	292
Chocolate sauce	¼ cup	144
Creole sauce	¼ cup	100
Drawn butter	1 tbsp.	110
Gravy	¼ cup	85
Hard sauce	1 tbsp.	100
Hollandaise sauce	1 tbsp.	70
Tartare sauce	1 tbsp.	100
Tomato sauce	¼ cup	85
White sauce	¼ cup	100

DESSERTS—FROZEN

	Measure	Calories
Ice—lemon or orange	½ cup	150
Ice, berry	½ cup	190
Ice cream, plain	⅐ of qt. brick	165
Ice cream, chocolate	½ cup	250
Ice cream, vanilla	½ cup	200
Ice cream soda, most flavors	1 fountain size	350
Sherbet, milk	½ cup	170
Sundae, chocolate ice cream, chocolate sauce, nut-sprinkled	1 average fountain size	425
Sundae, fruit ice cream, fruit sauce	1 average fountain size	260

DESSERTS—MISCELLANEOUS

	Measure	Calories
Apple dumpling	1 average	215
Cakes:		
Angel food cake	2" sector (1/12 of cake, 8" diam.)	110
Cheese cake, moderately rich	3" wedge	300
Chocolate cake (2 layers)	2½" wedge	450
Foundation cake	1 square (3x2x1¾")	230
Foundation cake, plain icing	2" sector (1/16 of cake, 10" diam.)	410
Fruit cake, dark	1 piece (2x2x1½")	105
Gingerbread	1 piece (2x2x2")	180
Plain cake and cupcakes	1 cupcake (2¾" diam.)	130

Sponge cake	2" sector (1/12 of cake, 8" diam.)	115
Cookies, plain and assorted	1 3" cookie	110
Pies:		
Apple	4" sector (9" pie)	330
Custard	4" sector (9" pie)	265
Lemon meringue	4" sector (9" pie)	300
Mince	4" sector (9" pie)	340
Pumpkin	4" sector (9" pie)	265
Strawberry shortcake (old-fashioned biscuit with whipped cream)	1 aver. size	300

DESSERTS—PUDDINGS

	Measure	Calories
Apple betty	½ cup	175
Bavarian cream	½ cup	148
Bread pudding	½ cup	200
Brown betty	½ cup	427
Caramel	½ cup	179
Chocolate	½ cup	231
Cornstarch, plain	½ cup	186
Custard, baked	1 cup	285
Custard pudding, canned, strained (infant food)	1 ounce	30
Cottage pudding (cake with sauce)	3x3x2 in.	188
Fruit-flavored gelatin, plain	½ cup	85
Fruit snow	¾ cup	90
Plum pudding	4" piece	119
Rice with raisins	½ cup	272
Spanish cream	½ cup	74
Soufflé, fruit	⅔ cup	313
Tapioca cream	½ cup	135
Prune whip	⅔ cup	127
Junket	⅔ cup	100

SUGARS, SWEETS

	Measure	Calories
Candied Fruit:		
Apricots	1	105
Cherries	1	18
Figs	1	93
Ginger, crystallized	1½" strip	18
Lemon and orange peel	1 piece	35
Pineapple	1 slice	124
Caramels	1 ounce	120
Chocolate candy bar	1 average	450
Chocolate-coated raisins	10	50
Chocolate-covered peanuts	1 cluster	85
Chocolate cream	1 1-inch	60
Chocolate, unsweetened	1 ounce	140
Divinity	1½" square	105
Fondant	1½" square	70

Fudge, plain	1 ounce	115
Gum	1 stick	7
Gum drops	5 small	25
Hard candy	1 ounce	110
Honey, strained or extracted	1 tbsp.	40
Jams, marmalades, preserves	1 tbsp.	55
Jelly beans	5	90
Marshmallow	1	20
Milk chocolate bar	1 average	240
Mint	1" diam.	35
Molasses, cane, light	1 tbsp.	50
Molasses, cane, blackstrap	1 tbsp.	45
Peanut brittle	2" piece	100
Pecan pralines	2x3" piece	415
Penuche	1" piece	100
Sorghum	1 tbsp.	55
Suckers	1 average	80
Sugar, brown	1 tbsp.	45
Sugar, confectioners'	1 tbsp.	45
Sugar, granulated	1 tbsp.	60
Sugar, loaf	1 cube	30
Sugar, maple	1 tbsp.	50
Syrup, table blends	1 tbsp.	55
Taffy	1" cube	42
Turkish delight	1½" cube	102

FATS, OILS RELATED PRODUCTS

	Measure	Calories
Bacon fat	1 tbsp.	90
Beef fat	1 tbsp.	80
Butter	1 tbsp.	100
Chicken fat	1 tbsp.	115
Fats, cooking (vegetable fats)	1 cup	1770
	1 tbsp.	110
Lard	1 tbsp.	125
Margarine	1 tbsp.	100
Oils, salad or cooking	1 tbsp.	125
Salad Dressings:		
Blue cheese dressing	1 tbsp.	80
French dressing	1 tbsp.	60
Home-cooked dressing	1 tbsp.	30
Mayonnaise	1 tbsp.	90
Russian dressing	1 tbsp.	145

MISCELLANEOUS

	Measure	Calories
Bouillon cube	1	2
Ketchup	1 tbsp.	20
Chili sauce	1 tbsp.	25
Olives, pickled "mammoth" size:		
Green	10 olives	70
Ripe, mission variety	10 olives	105
Pickles:		
Dill, cucumber	1 4" long	15
Sweet, cucumber, or mixed	1 2¾" long	20
Vinegar	1 tbsp.	2
Yeast:		
Compressed, baker's	1 ounce	25
Dried brewer's	1 tbsp.	20
Mustard	1 tbsp.	17
Bread stuffing	½ cup	170

OVEN MEALS

Oven meals can be our best time and labor savers on busy days. Usually the main dish, vegetables, bread and/or dessert can be baked at one time. If your range has an automatic clock, the food can even be placed in the oven as much as two hours before cooking begins. Set the clock for the time you want your oven heat to turn on and the time the heat should go off—and the food cooks quietly out of sight while you go about your other business. At dinnertime, make the salad and coffee—and everything's ready.

Oven meals can also save a lot of pot washing too, if the food is baked right in the casserole in which it will be served. Then you can sit down to dinner with a clean orderly kitchen. This helps to make cooking a pleasure.

Here's How to Plan an Oven Meal

The magic key to time saving oven meals is to plan first and plan wisely.

The Main Dish: Plan this first. It might be a meat loaf, one-dish casserole, oven brown stew, baked pork chops, Swiss steak, or pot roast. What oven temperature does this dish take? Most meat, cheese, milk, and egg dishes require slow to moderate oven (325° to 350° F.).

This temperature should be used for the rest of the meal and will determine what other foods to combine with the main dish. Then choose vegetables and dessert that can be baked at the same temperature for about the same time.

You can still make the most of oven heat even if you select vegetables and dessert that require less time than the main dish. Put in the main dish, then with the aid of a minute timer, you slide each dish into the oven at its correct time.

Remember—if you have a roast or bread or other dishes which need to be browned, do not plan foods that make steam—unless of course, you can brown the dessert or casserole dish at the end when the "steamy" foods are out of the oven.

Vegetables: Many vegetables can be cooked in the oven in a tightly covered pan. Place just enough water on the vegetables to form steam, usually not more than 2 to 4 tablespoons. Add seasonings and cover tightly.

If the oven meal is to cook an hour cut the vegetables into strips, thin slices, or small cubes. If the meal takes longer to cook, leave the vegetables in larger pieces or even whole.

Vegetables which may be cooked by this method are potatoes, carrots, squash, parsnips, corn, turnips, onions, sauerkraut, beets, dried beans, and tomatoes. Peas, green beans, and asparagus may be cooked by this method. Frozen asparagus requires about 30 minutes and peas require 14 minutes at 350° F.

It's usually better to omit the green vegetables since they keep their color and vitamins best if they're cooked on top of the range.

If your meal is to cook a short time, give your potatoes a head start by placing them in boiling water for 15 minutes before putting them in to bake.

Desserts: Fruit puddings, fruit cobblers, custards, stewed dried fruits, whole baked apples or pears, gingerbread, and upside-down cakes bake well with oven meals. Cakes and pies usually do not brown well if there are a lot of "steaming" foods in the oven—unless they can be removed during the last 15 minutes of baking.

Breads: When the oven is in use, the wise homemaker usually likes to give her family a special treat with a hot bread. Yeast rolls and quick breads such as corn bread, muffins, coffee cakes, rolls, and nut breads can be baked with oven meals. They may need to be baked alone the last 15 minutes in order to brown. These can be made from your own recipe or from a packaged mix.

If you want to cut preparation time still more, heat bakery rolls or French bread. Garlic bread or herb French bread and similar jiffy tricks are good with oven meals.

Make the Most of Oven Heat with These Oven Meal Suggestions

FOR HOT OVEN (400°F.) TIME: 25 TO 30 MINUTES

Main Dishes:

Meat or Chicken Pie (Leftover Meat —biscuit top)
Meat Biscuit Roll-ups
Baked Canned Luncheon Meat
Baked Canned Salmon or Tuna

Vegetables:

Scalloped Corn
Scalloped Onions
Scalloped Tomatoes

Breads:

Corn Bread
Muffins
Coffee Cake—quick or yeast
Plain Yeast Rolls

Desserts:

Baked Apples (precooked in syrup 5 minutes)
Apple Dumplings
Fruit Cobblers
Fruit Roll-ups
Shortcake

FOR MODERATE OVEN (350°F.) TIME: 45 TO 60 MINUTES

Main Dishes:

Casseroles
Individual Meat Loaves
Mock Chicken Legs
Shepherd's Pie
Spanish Rice
Stuffed Peppers
Baked Fish

Vegetables:

Baked Potatoes (medium)
Baked Sweet Potatoes (medium)
Steamed Carrots (strips)
Stuffed Onions
Quick Baked Beans

Breads:

Sweet Rolls
Yeast Coffee Cakes

Desserts:

Baked Apples or Pears
Apple Dumplings
Brown Betty
Apple Crisp
Upside-Down Cake
Cottage Pudding
Gingerbread

FOR MODERATE OVEN (350°F.) TIME: 1 TO 1½ HOURS

Main Dishes:

Meat Loaf
Pork Chops
Sausage Patties
Spareribs
Scalloped Potatoes and Ham
Ham Shanks
Meat Balls in Sauce
Ham Slice
Oven-Fried Chicken
Scalloped Chicken
Scalloped Oysters
Salmon or Cheese Soufflés
Macaroni and Cheese
Braised Lamb

Vegetables:

Baked Potatoes (large)
Baked Sweet Potatoes (large)
Scalloped Potatoes
Apple and Sweet Potato Scallop
Baked Squash
Steamed Carrots (quarters, halves)

Breads:

Nut and Fruit Breads
Spoon Breads

Desserts:

Bread Pudding
Date Pudding
Dried Fruits (presoaked-covered with water)
Baked Apples (large)

45-MINUTE OVEN DINNER FOR 6

Meat Loaf with Tomato Sauce
Baked Frozen Green Peas
Baked Acorn Squash
Graham Brown Betty

Hints: Entire meal goes into moderate oven (375°F.) at the same time, and cooked for 45 minutes.

Frozen green peas are cooked in covered baking dish with 2 tablespoons butter or margarine, no water.

Scrub the skin of small squash, cut in halves, scrape out seeds and strings from center. Sprinkle with salt and brush well with butter. Place in a shallow pan with a little water in the bottom. Bake until tender. If baked uncovered, baste occasionally. Season to taste and served filled with the baked green peas.

MEAT LOAF WITH TOMATO SAUCE

3 slices bread, cubed
2 pounds ground beef
2 teaspoons salt
¼ teaspoon pepper
1 medium onion, grated
2 eggs, slightly beaten
½ cup milk
1 8-ounce can tomato sauce

½ teaspoon Worcestershire sauce
3 drops Tabasco sauce
1 teaspoon salt
1 teaspoon sugar

Blend bread into ground beef mixed with 2 teaspoons salt and ¼ teaspoon pepper.

Reserve 2 tablespoons grated onion; add remainder to meat mixture with the eggs and milk.

Shape meat into loaf pan or on center of lightly greased shallow baking pan.

Prepare sauce by mixing together tomato sauce, remaining grated onion, Worcestershire sauce, Tabasco sauce, salt and sugar.

Pour sauce over meat loaf and bake, uncovered, in moderate oven (375° F.) about 45 minutes. Serves 6 to 8.

GRAHAM BROWN BETTY

24 graham crackers, finely rolled (2 cups crumbs)
3 tablespoons softened butter or margarine
½ cup brown sugar
3 to 4 medium apples, pared, cored, and sliced
1 tablespoon lemon juice
½ teaspoon grated lemon rind
⅓ cup hot water

Thoroughly blend together graham cracker crumbs, softened butter or margarine, and sugar.

Place ⅓ crumb mixture in greased 1½-quart baking dish. Arrange half of apple slices over crumbs; sprinkle with half of lemon juice and rind. Add second layer of crumbs and remaining apple slices, lemon juice, and rind.

Cover with remaining crumbs. Pour water over. Bake in moderate oven (375°F.) 45 minutes. Serves 6.

45-Minute Oven Dinner for 6

1-HOUR OVEN DINNER #1 FOR 6

Savory Stuffed Pork Chops
Candied Tomato Sauce
Corn and Lima Beans
Apple Dumplings

Hints: Set oven for moderate (350°F.) Put all foods in the oven and cook for 1 hour.

SAVORY STUFFED PORK CHOPS

    3 cups soft breadcrumbs
    1 cup finely chopped, cooked ham
    1/4 teaspoon salt
    1/8 teaspoon pepper
    1/4 teaspoon nutmeg
    1 beef bouillon cube
    1/4 cup boiling water
    6 1-inch thick rib pork chops, cut
         with pockets
    1/4 cup enriched flour
    3/4 teaspoon salt
         Pepper to taste
    1/8 teaspoon ground sage
    1/8 teaspoon thyme
    1/2 cup water

To make stuffing, combine crumbs, ham, salt, pepper, and nutmeg. Dissolve bouillon cube in boiling water; pour over mixture and toss lightly.

Stuff pork chops and fasten with wooden toothpicks. Coat chops with mixture of flour, salt, pepper, sage, and thyme.

Brown chops in hot fat in skillet on top of range. Arrange in baking dish, add water; cover with aluminum foil. Cook on lower oven rack of moderate oven (350°F.) 1 hour. Serves 6.

CANDIED TOMATO SAUCE

    1 10½-ounce can tomato purée
    1 cup sugar
    2 tablespoons lemon juice

Combine tomato purée, sugar, and lemon juice in saucepan and cook for 5 minutes. Pour into a 1-pint greased casserole.

Cover and cook on lower oven rack in moderate oven (350°F.) 1 hour. Serve over pork chops. Serves 6.

CORN AND LIMA BEANS

Partially break up 1 10-ounce package of frozen corn and 1 12-ounce package of frozen lima beans. Place in buttered 1½-quart casserole; add 2 tablespoons butter or margarine, salt and pepper to taste, and 2 tablespoons light cream.

Cover and cook on top oven rack in moderate oven (350°F.) 1 hour. Serves 6.

APPLE DUMPLINGS

    2 cups sugar
    1 cup water
    3 tablespoons cinnamon candies
    1/4 cup butter or margarine
    6 apples
    1 tablespoon lemon juice
    1/4 teaspoon nutmeg
    1/4 teaspoon cinnamon
    2 cups enriched flour
    1 teaspoon salt
    1 tablespoon baking powder
    3/4 cup shortening
    1/2 cup milk

Make syrup of 1 cup sugar, water, and cinnamon candies; cook until dissolved. Add butter or margarine; set aside.

Pare, core, and slice apples. Sprinkle with lemon juice, 1 cup sugar, nutmeg, and cinnamon.

Sift flour, measure, add salt and baking powder, sift into bowl; cut in shortening. Add milk; stir until moistened. Roll out in sheet about 18 by 12 inches. Cut into 6 6-inch squares.

Put mound of apples on each square of pastry. Moisten edges of squares with water; bring four corners up over apples; pinch sides together.

Place in individual greased baking dishes; pour syrup around dumplings. Bake on upper rack in moderate oven (350°F.) 1 hour. Serves 6.

1-HOUR OVEN DINNER #2 FOR 6

Spicy Round Steak
Oven-Browned Potatoes
Green Bean Casserole
Lemon-Coconut Pudding

Hints: Put all foods in the oven and cook for 1 hour at moderate heat (350°F.).

SPICY ROUND STEAK

    1/4 cup enriched flour
    1 teaspoon salt
    1/4 teaspoon pepper
    2 pounds round steak, ½-inch thick
    3 tablespoons shortening
    1 cup ketchup
    1/2 cup water
    1 medium onion, thinly sliced
    1 lemon, thinly sliced
    1 green pepper, sliced
    5 whole cloves

Combine flour, salt, and pepper; pound into steak.

Melt shortening in a skillet and brown steak. Place in baking dish.

Blend ketchup and water; pour around steak. Add onion, lemon, green pepper, and cloves.

Cover with aluminum foil; place on lower oven rack. Cook in moderate oven (350°F.) 1 hour. Serves 6.

OVEN-BROWNED POTATOES

Peel 12 small potatoes and dip in melted fat. Bake uncovered in shallow baking dish on top rack in moderate oven (350°F.). Serves 6.

GREEN BEAN CASSEROLE

Partially thaw 2 10-ounce packages of frozen French-style green beans. Arrange in alternate layers with condensed mushroom soup (1 10½-ounce can) in buttered 1½-quart baking dish.

Sprinkle top with 2 tablespoons grated Parmesan or American cheese and 2 tablespoons toasted breadcrumbs.

Cover; place on lower oven rack in moderate oven (350°F.). Serves 6.

LEMON COCONUT PUDDING

    2 tablespoons butter or margarine
    1 cup sugar
    4 eggs, separated
    1/3 cup lemon juice
    1 tablespoon grated lemon rind
    1/4 teaspoon salt
    1¼ cups shredded coconut
    2 tablespoons enriched flour
    1 cup milk
    2 tablespoons currant jelly

Cream butter or margarine, adding sugar gradually. Add egg yolks to butter-sugar mixture and beat well.

Add lemon juice, grated lemon rind, and salt; blend thoroughly.

Fold in 3/4 cup of the coconut and the flour. Stir in milk.

Beat egg whites until stiff but not dry. Fold into lemon mixture.

Pour into 1½-quart baking dish. Set in pan containing ½-inch hot water. Bake on upper oven rack in moderate oven (350°F.) 1 hour.

Before serving, toast rest of coconut in oven; use as garnish with jelly. Serves 6.

1¼-HOUR OVEN DINNER FOR 4

Savory Pork Chops
Crusty Baked Potatoes
Creamy Carrots and Onions
Baked Apples Connecticut

Hints: Set oven for moderate (350°F.). Put all the foods in the oven and bake for 1¼ hours. Scrub the potatoes before baking on oven rack.

SAVORY PORK CHOPS

4 pork chops, ¾-inch thick
1 teaspoon salt
¼ teaspoon pepper
¼ teaspoon sage

Arrange chops in single layer in open roasting pan.
Sprinkle with salt, pepper, and sage.
Bake in moderate oven (350°F.) 1¼ hours. Serves 4.

CREAMY CARROTS AND ONIONS

2 cups sliced carrots
1 bunch chopped green onions
½ teaspoon salt
½ teaspoon sugar
¼ cup water
1 cup light cream

Place all ingredients except cream in baking dish. Cover. Bake in moderate oven (350°F.) 1¼ hours.
To serve, heat cream and pour over baked carrots and onions. Serves 4.

BAKED APPLES CONNECTICUT

4 baking apples, cored
Lemon juice
¾ cup sugar
¼ teaspoon nutmeg
2 tablespoons butter or margarine
¼ cup water

Dip cut ends of apples in lemon juice, place in baking dish.
Combine sugar and nutmeg, fill centers of apples with sugar mixture. Dot apple tops with butter.
Pour water into bottom of baking dish. Cover. Bake in moderate oven (350°F.) 1¼ hours. Serves 4.

1-HOUR OVEN DINNER #1 FOR 4

Honeyed-Orange Ham Slice
Frenched Beans Amandine
Cherry Crumb Dessert

Hints: Put all foods in the oven and cook for 1 hour at slow heat (325°F.).

1-Hour Oven Dinner # 1 for 4

HONEYED-ORANGE HAM SLICE

1 pound ham slice, 1-inch thick
½ cup honey
1 tablespoon grated orange rind

Place ham in shallow baking pan. Combine honey and orange rind; spread over ham.
Bake in slow oven (325° F.) 1 hour. Serves 4.

FRENCHED BEANS AMANDINE

Place 1 package frozen green beans, French style, ¼ cup boiling water, 2 tablespoons butter or margarine, and ¼ cup slivered blanched almonds in greased baking dish. Cover.
Bake in slow oven (325°F.) 1 hour. Serves 4.

CHERRY CRUMB DESSERT

1 20-ounce can frozen cherries, thawed
¼ teaspoon almond extract
½ cup sifted enriched flour
½ cup firmly packed brown sugar
½ teaspoon allspice
¼ teaspoon nutmeg
¼ cup butter or margarine

Combine cherries and almond extract. Turn into 8x8-inch baking pan.
Blend flour, sugar, spices, and butter; sprinkle over cherries.
Bake in slow oven (325°F.) 1 hour. Serves 4.

1-HOUR OVEN DINNER #2 FOR 4

Veal Chops Hungarian
Continental Green Beans
Sweet Potato and Apple Bake
Fruit and Bread Scallop

Hints: Put veal and green beans on lower rack and sweet potatoes and fruit scallop on upper rack of oven. Set oven control at moderate (375°F.) and bake for 1 hour.

VEAL CHOPS HUNGARIAN #2

¼ cup enriched flour
⅓ teaspoon salt
⅛ teaspoon pepper
4 veal chops
2 tablespoons shortening
1¼ cups sour cream

Mix flour, salt, and pepper; coat chops with seasoned flour.
Brown chops on all sides in hot shortening, then arrange in greased 2½-quart casserole.
Pour over sour cream. Cover tightly and bake in moderate oven (375°F.) for 1 hour. Serves 4.

CONTINENTAL GREEN BEANS

½ cup chopped onion
⅔ cup diced bacon
2 tablespoons enriched flour
2 cups cooked or canned tomatoes
2 cups cooked or canned green beans
½ teaspoon salt
¼ teaspoon pepper
¼ teaspoon paprika
1 bay leaf
1 cup coarse cracker crumbs
2 tablespoons melted butter or margarine

Brown onion with bacon in a large saucepan, then blend in flour.
Add tomatoes, green beans, salt, pepper, paprika, and bay leaf. Mix together, then turn into greased 1-quart baking dish.
Combine cracker crumbs with melted butter. Sprinkle over top.
Bake in moderate oven (375°F.) 1 hour. Serves 4 to 6.

SWEET POTATO—APPLE BAKE

1 No. 2½ can (3½ cups) sweet potatoes
2 tablespoons butter or margarine
2 tablespoons cream
1 teaspoon salt
⅛ teaspoon pepper
2 firm baking apples
8 marshmallows

Heat sweet potatoes and mash, blending in butter, cream, salt, and pepper.
Spread mashed sweet potatoes in 8-inch square baking dish.
Wash and core apples; cut in halves but do not pare.
Arrange apples on sweet potato layer. Decorate top with marshmallows.
Bake in moderate oven (375° F.) 1 hour. Serves 4.

FRUIT AND BREAD SCALLOP

¼ cup butter or margarine
3 cups soft breadcrumbs
1 cup brown sugar
½ teaspoon cinnamon
¼ teaspoon nutmeg
2 cups rhubarb, cut in 1-inch pieces
1 cup thick applesauce
2 firm bananas, sliced
1 tablespoon lemon juice
3 tablespoons light corn syrup

Melt butter and brown the crumbs in it. Mix the sugar, cinnamon, and nutmeg.
Use a large greased loaf pan; arrange alternate layers of breadcrumbs, sugar mixture, rhubarb, apple sauce, and bananas, starting and ending with breadcrumbs.
Sprinkle the top with a mixture of lemon juice and corn syrup.
Bake in moderate oven (375°F.) for 1 hour. Serves 4 to 6.

1-HOUR OVEN DINNER #3 FOR 6

Ham Loaf and Gravy
Baked Frozen Corn
Baked Potatoes
Cherry Crumb Pie

Hints: Set oven control for hot oven (400°F.) and preheat oven. Toward the back of lower rack place the ham loaf and frozen corn, and in front of these 6 medium-sized potatoes.

The two pies go on the front section of the upper rack. They may be put in at the start of the oven meal baking period or after 20 minutes, since they require 20 minutes less baking time.

When the meal is done, turn the oven off. Invert the ham loaf on a heat-resistant platter and return to the warm oven.

Cut a cross on the top side of the potatoes and gently press the potatoes to soften and to push some of the potato up through the opening. After putting one tablespoon of butter or margarine on top of each potato, place them in a 12¼x8x2-inch baking dish and place them back in the oven.

Make gravy and serve the meal hot from the oven.

HAM LOAF AND GRAVY

½ cup firmly packed brown sugar
1   No. 1 flat can sliced pineapple
6   whole maraschino cherries, drained
1   pound ham, ground
½   pound fresh pork, ground
1   cup fine soft breadcrumbs
1   egg, unbeaten
1   cup milk
¼   cup minced onion
¼   cup minced celery
½   teaspoon salt
¼   teaspoon pepper
Juice from pineapple, meat liquid, and water to make 1 cup
⅛   teaspoon bottled brown seasoning sauce
1   cup water
3   tablespoons enriched flour

Spread brown sugar in bottom of greased 9½x5¼x2¾-inch aluminum pan.

Remove and drain 2 slices of pineapple, reserving remainder of can for making gravy. Cut each pineapple slice in 3 pieces. Arrange pineapple and cherries on brown sugar so some of each can be served with each serving of meat.

Mix ham, pork, breadcrumbs, egg, milk, onion, celery, salt, and pepper. Pack meat mixture firmly in loaf pan over pineapple and cherries.

Bake in hot oven (400°F.) for 1 hour. Remove from oven; pour juice from pan and reserve for gravy.

Invert meat loaf onto heat resistant serving platter and keep warm in oven while making gravy.

Put juice, meat liquid, seasoning sauce, water, and remainder of pineapple, diced, in 1-quart saucepan.

Shake water and flour vigorously in covered jar until thoroughly blended. Add to liquid in saucepan.

Bring to boil on a high heat, stirring constantly. Switch to a low heat and boil 1 minute. Serves 6.

BAKED FROZEN CORN

2   10-ounce packages frozen cut corn
¼   cup water
½   teaspoon salt
2   tablespoons butter or margarine

Place corn, water, salt, butter in 2-quart casserole. Cover.

Bake in hot oven (400°F.) for 1 hour. Serves 6.

CHERRY CRUMB PIES

1   recipe pastry for two-crust pie
4   cups cherries, drained (use two 1-pound, 3-ounce cans)
2   cups cherry juice and water
2   cups sugar
4   tablespoons quick-cooking tapioca
1½ teaspoons salt
½   teaspoon almond extract
1   tablespoon butter or margarine, melted
4   drops red food coloring
1½ cups sifted enriched flour
½   cup butter or margarine

Line two 9-inch pie plates with pastry making high fluted edges.

Combine cherries, juice and water, 1½ cups sugar, tapioca, ½ teaspoon salt, almond extract, butter or margarine, and food coloring. Divide evenly into the two pie shells.

←

Make the Most of Oven Heat

Ready to serve hot from the oven is this meal of ham loaf, baked potatoes, and baked frozen corn with two cherry crumb pies baked at the same time—the extra pie to freeze for future use.

Combine flour, 1 teaspoon salt, and ½ cup sugar in small mixing bowl. Cut in butter or margarine with pastry blender until mixture resembles fine meal. Sprinkle one-half of crumb mixture evenly over each pie.

Bake in hot oven (400°F.) for 40 to 50 minutes. Makes 6 to 8 servings for each pie.

1½-HOUR OVEN DINNER FOR 6

Chicken Casserole
Tomato Rice
Cherry Scallop

Hints: Preheat moderate oven (350°F.). Place chicken casserole and tomato rice on lower rack, cherry scallop on upper rack. Cook for 1½ hours. Serve with a bowl of pre-crisped salad greens.

BAKED CHICKEN

4   pounds cut-up chicken
Milk, flour, salt, and pepper
½   cup fat
½   pound fresh mushrooms
1   tablespoon finely chopped onion
2   cups top milk, heated

Dip pieces of chicken in milk, then in seasoned flour. Fry in fat until nicely browned. Place in casserole.

Fry mushrooms and onion in pan about 2 or 3 minutes. Sprinkle over chicken. Pour hot milk over all.

Cook on the lower rack of moderate oven (350°F.) for 1½ hours. Serves 6.

TOMATO RICE

4   cups strained tomatoes
1   cup water
1½ teaspoons salt
1   tablespoon sugar
2   tablespoons butter or margarine
1½ cups uncooked rice, washed

Combine first five ingredients and boil for five minutes.

Place washed rice in buttered casserole. Pour tomato mixture over rice. Cover.

Cook on lower rack of moderate oven (350°F.) for 1½ hours. Serves 6.

CHERRY SCALLOP

6   slices bread, toasted slightly
1   can cherries
1   cup sugar
½   teaspoon nutmeg
¼   cup butter or margarine

Toast bread lightly and cut in cubes.

Place alternate layers of bread, cherries, sugar and nutmeg in buttered casserole.

Pour cherry juice over top layer. Dot with butter. Cover.

Bake on upper rack of moderate oven (350°F.) 1½ hours. Serves 6.

1-Hour Oven Dinner # 3 for 4

1-HOUR OVEN DINNER #3 FOR 4

Ham Slice with Crushed Pineapple
Baked Sweet Potatoes
French Style Green Beans
Date-Nut Pudding with
Whipped Cream

Hints: On the lower rack, place sweet potatoes and ham slice. On upper rack, put saucepan with string beans, place custard cups in baking pan and pour warm water around them to a depth of one inch. Set your oven at moderate (350°F.) for 1 hour.

Either whip the cream while waiting for coffee, or do it early, and place in the refrigerator until you need it for dessert.

HAM SLICE WITH CRUSHED PINEAPPLE

2 pound, 1-inch thick ham slice
8 whole cloves
2 tablespoons brown sugar
1 cup crushed pineapple with juice
1 tablespoon cherry juice
1/4 cup frozen, canned, or maraschino cherries

Place ham slice in greased 5x8-inch baking pan; press cloves into fat which you have slit to prevent curling.

Cover ham with brown sugar and crushed pineapple, the fruit juices, and use the cherries for decoration.

Cook on lower rack of moderate oven (350°F.) for 1 hour. Serves 4.

FRENCH STYLE GREEN BEANS

1 package frozen French cut green beans

2 tablespoons butter or margarine
1/2 cup water

Place in saucepan, cover tightly. Cook on upper rack of moderate oven (350°F.) for 1 hour. Serves 4.

DATE-NUT PUDDING

3 eggs
1 cup sugar
1/2 teaspoon vanilla
1/4 cup enriched flour
1/4 teaspoon salt
1 teaspoon baking powder
1/2 teaspoon nutmeg
1 cup chopped dates
1 cup chopped nuts
1/2 pint heavy cream, whipped

Beat the eggs, gradually add sugar and vanilla.

Sift dry ingredients together and stir into egg mixture.

Fold in dates and nuts. Blend well and pour batter into 4 large greased custard cups.

Place the cups in a baking pan, and pour warm water around them to a depth of 1 inch. Cook on upper rack of moderate oven (350°F.) 1 hour.

When baked, unmold, cover with whipped cream. Serves 4.

35-MINUTE OVEN DINNER FOR 4

Salmon Casserole
Buttered Broccoli
Potatoes Au Gratin
Apricot Cobbler

Hints: Preheat moderate oven (375°F.). Put broccoli and potatoes on lower shelf. Place salmon casserole and apricot cobbler on upper shelf. Bake for 35 minutes.

SALMON CASSEROLE

2 teaspoons finely chopped onion
1/4 cup butter or margarine
1 1/2 cups soft breadcrumbs
1 1-pound can salmon
Milk
1 beaten egg
1 tablespoon chopped parsley
1/4 teaspoon grated lemon rind
1 teaspoon lemon juice
1/2 teaspoon salt
1/8 teaspoon pepper

Lightly brown onion in melted butter. Add crumbs and toss to mix the butter with crumbs. Then brown the crumbs slightly.

Drain liquid from salmon and add milk to make 1 cup liquid. Remove bones and skin, then flake salmon.

Combine all ingredients; mix well

and turn into greased 1 1/2-quart casserole.

Bake in moderate oven (375°F.) 35 minutes. Serves 4.

BUTTERED FROZEN BROCCOLI

1 package frozen broccoli
1/2 cup water
1/4 teaspoon salt
2 tablespoons melted butter or margarine

Place broccoli, water, and salt in oven dish. Cover tightly. Cook in oven with dinner. To serve, drain, and season with melted butter. Serves 4.

POTATOES AU GRATIN

1/4 cup butter or margarine
1/4 cup enriched flour
1/2 teaspoon salt
1/8 teaspoon pepper
1/4 teaspoon dry mustard
2 cups milk
1 1/2 tablespoons prepared horseradish
3 cups diced cooked potatoes
1/2 cup grated Cheddar cheese

Melt butter in a saucepan; blend in flour, salt, pepper, and mustard until smooth.

Gradually add milk, stirring constantly. Cook until thickened, then add horseradish.

Mix sauce with diced cooked potatoes.

Turn into greased 1 1/2-quart baking dish.

Sprinkle cheese over the top.

Bake in moderate oven (375°F.) for 35 minutes. Serves 4.

APRICOT COBBLER

1 1/2 cups cooked dried apricots
3/4 cup hot apricot juice
1/4 cup melted butter or margarine
1 teaspoon grated orange rind
5 tablespoons granulated sugar
1/2 cup brown sugar
2 cups biscuit mix
2 tablespoons shortening
2/3 cup milk
1 well beaten egg

Place drained apricots, skin side down, in greased 9-inch square baking dish.

Combine the hot apricot juice with butter, orange rind, 3 tablespoons granulated sugar, and 1/2 cup brown sugar; carefully pour over apricots.

With a pastry blender cut shortening into biscuit mix.

Blend in 2 tablespoons granulated sugar, milk, and well beaten egg.

Drop dough with a tablespoon onto hot apricot mixture.

Bake in moderate oven (375°F.) 35 minutes. Serves 4.

PANCAKES AND WAFFLES

A pancake is a griddlecake or any of various similar thin, fried cakes. Pancake is the term usually used when the batter is of a distinctive kind, as in potato, blueberry, or Swedish pancakes.

Whether they are called pancakes, griddlecakes, hotcakes, flapjacks, wheatcakes, flannel cakes they are among the most popular of our foods—and in one form or another are included in the cookery of all nations.

GRIDDLECAKES (PANCAKES)
(Master Recipe)

1   or 2 eggs, well beaten
1½   cups milk, scant
2   tablespoons melted shortening
2   cups sifted enriched flour
3   teaspoons baking powder
½   teaspoon salt
1   tablespoon sugar

Combine egg, milk, shortening. Add to sifted dry ingredients. Beat only until smooth. Pour by spoonfuls onto hot, lightly greased or ungreased griddle.

Bake until bubbles on top burst. Turn and bake on other side. Makes about 15 medium sized cakes.

Variations of Griddlecakes

Apple Griddlecakes: Add 1 cup finely chopped tart apple to batter.

Banana Griddlecakes: Add 1 thinly sliced banana to batter.

Blueberry Griddlecakes: Add 1 cup fresh, or drained canned blueberries to batter.

Buckwheat Griddlecakes: Substitute 1 cup buckwheat for 1 cup white flour.

Cherry or Peach Griddlecakes. Add to batter 1 cup drained, chopped cherries or peaches, fresh or canned. Serve hot with butter and a syrup of sugar and cherry juice or sugar and peach juice.

Chocolate Griddlecakes: Increase sugar to ⅓ cup. Add 1 square melted, unsweetened chocolate to liquid ingredi-

Although traditionally served at breakfast, pancakes and waffles appear at other times as well—around the clock. With crisp bacon or tasty sausages, pancakes and waffles are hearty enough for lunch. Waffles are a welcome dessert after a simple main course.

ents. Serve as dessert with sweetened, flavored whipped cream.

Corn Meal Griddlecakes: Substitute ¾ cup corn meal for ¾ cup white flour and 1 tablespoon dark molasses for 1 tablespoon sugar.

Crumb Griddlecakes: Substitute 1 cup breadcrumbs for ½ cup flour.

Meat Griddlecakes: Add ¾ cup any chopped cooked meat to batter.

Nut Griddlecakes: Add ¼ cup chopped pecans to dry ingredients.

Griddlecake Sandwich: Place a thin slice of cooked ham or sausage over first cake, cover with batter, brown and turn.

Pineapple Griddlecakes: Add 1 cup drained, crushed pineapple to batter. Bake slowly on greased hot griddle.

Rice Griddlecakes: Substitute 1 cup cooked rice for 1 cup flour. Reduce milk to 1 cup. Add rice to egg-milk mixture.

Sour Milk Griddlecakes: Substitute scant 2 cups sour milk or scant 2 cups buttermilk for sweet milk. Use only 2 teaspoons baking powder and add 1 teaspoon baking soda.

Soy Griddlecakes: Substitute ⅓ cup soy flour for ⅓ cup white flour.

Whole Wheat Griddlecakes: Substitute 1 cup whole wheat flour for 1 cup white flour.

GRIDDLECAKE (PANCAKE) MAKING HINTS

Prepare griddlecake batter by one of the following recipes. Stir the batter only until blended. Do not overmix. The stiffer the batter, the less mixing is required. The batter becomes thicker as baking powder is increased, but with more baking powder the finished product is more porous and tender and has greater volume.

Heat a heavy griddle and grease it with a bit of bacon. If 2 or more tablespoons fat are used for each cup liquid, griddle need not be greased.

Test griddle by letting a few drops of cold water fall upon it. If the water bounces and sputters ("dances on surface") the griddle is ready for cakes.

Pour the batter from spoon onto the hot griddle. To get a round cake pour it from the tip of the spoon. Bake until bubbles appear on the surface and begin to burst, then lift the cakes with a spatula to see if the under surface is well browned before turning. Usually 2 to 3 minutes is sufficient baking before turning. Turn only once. Griddle or pancake batter may be thinned or thickened as desired. After making a small test cake, thin with a tablespoon milk or thicken with a tablespoon flour.

Griddlecakes should be served as soon as possible. If they cannot be served at once, keep them on a cooky sheet in a very slow oven separated by and covered with a tea towel to keep them from getting soggy. Prepared flours requiring only the addition of liquid are timesaving and many of the variations of the master recipe may be used.

Egg Roll

EGG ROLL

Egg roll is a Chinese dish; a very thin pancake (called egg roll skins) made of a batter of flour, cornstarch, eggs, water, and salt and filled with various mixtures; among the possible ingredients are finely chopped or shredded raw carrot, celery, green onion, water chestnut, cooked pork, and cooked shrimp. The completed egg rolls are fried in deep fat and are usually served with an apricot sauce and a mustard sauce.

Filling:

- 2 cups finely chopped cooked pork
- 1 cup finely chopped cooked shrimp or lobster
- 2 cups finely chopped celery
- 1 cup finely chopped green onions
- 1 cup finely chopped water chestnuts
- 1 tablespoon Ac'cent
- 1 tablespoon soy sauce
- 2 teaspoons sugar
- 1 teaspoon salt
- 1 small egg
- ¼ cup melted shortening

Egg Roll Skins:

- 1⅓ cups sifted enriched flour
- ⅔ cup cornstarch
- ½ teaspoon salt
- 2 unbeaten eggs
- 1½ cups water

For filling, combine first 5 ingredients in a large bowl. Blend in next 6 ingredients and mix thoroughly; refrigerate.

Next make egg-roll skins. Sift together flour, cornstarch, and salt.

Blend together with a fork the eggs and ½ cup water. Add gradually to dry ingredients, blending thoroughly with spoon or rotary beater. Gradually add remaining 1 cup water, beat until smooth.

Reserve about ⅓ cup batter for sealing edges of egg rolls.

Brush heavy skillet lightly with shortening; place over medium heat.

Holding it at a slight angle, pour about 2 tablespoons batter all at once into skillet. Tip quickly in all directions to make a thin 7-inch pancake.

Cook until mixture looks dry and begins to curl around edges. Remove from heat.

Repeat with remaining batter, stacking egg rolls until all are baked.

Place a scant ¼ cup filling in center of each egg roll, then fold 2 sides over filling.

Brush edges with reserved batter. Beginning at one open end, roll up egg roll, pressing edges *gently* to seal.

Fry immediately or store in refrigerator several hours before frying.

Fry in deep, hot fat (360°F.) until crisp and golden brown, about 5 to 8 minutes; turn only once. Serve hot with apricot sauce, hot mustard sauce or both. Makes 24 egg rolls.

For Apricot Sauce: Combine 2 cups apricot jam, ¼ cup finely chopped pimiento, and 2 tablespoons vinegar in saucepan. Bring to boil and simmer for 2 minutes, stirring occasionally. Cool.

For Hot Mustard Sauce: Blend together dry mustard and water to form a paste.

JIFFY ORANGE PANCAKES

- 1 beaten egg
- 1 cup light cream
- 1 6-ounce can frozen orange juice concentrate
- 1 cup packaged pancake mix
  Orange Syrup (below)

Combine egg, cream, and ¼ cup of the orange juice concentrate (reserve remainder). Add pancake mix, stirring to remove most of lumps.

Bake on hot greased griddle, turning once. Serve with warm orange syrup. Makes about 18 pancakes.

Orange Syrup: Combine ½ cup butter or margarine, 1 cup sugar, and reserved orange juice concentrate. Heat just to boiling, stirring occasionally. Makes about 1½ cups.

SWEDISH PANCAKES

- 2 cups sifted enriched flour
- ½ teaspoon salt
- 1 tablespoon sugar
- 3 eggs
- 4 cups milk

Mix and sift flour, salt, and sugar. Beat eggs well and combine with milk. Gradually add flour mixture, beating until smooth.

Use a special Swedish griddle containing several small molds or bake quickly in a greased, heavy, hot frying pan, making one large pancake at a time.

Spread with jam. Roll large cakes and dust with powdered sugar. Stack small cakes. Reheat and serve. Makes 14 to 16 large cakes or 24 to 30 small cakes.

LATKES OR GRATED POTATO PANCAKES

Latke is a Yiddish term for pancakes, especially those made of grated raw potatoes as in the following recipe. The Yiddish term kugel is applied to a potato pie made of similar ingredients. They are old-time Jewish dishes.

- 6 medium raw potatoes
- 1 small onion
- 2 slightly beaten eggs
- 3 tablespoons flour
  Dash of pepper
- 1 teaspoon salt
- ½ teaspoon baking powder (optional)

Pare and grate raw potatoes and onion. Let stand 10 minutes so that liquid will rise to top.

Remove liquid. Stir in eggs. Add other ingredients and blend together.

Drop by spoonfuls into a hot well greased skillet. Brown on both sides over moderate heat. Drain on absorbent paper.

Serve hot with applesauce, sugar, or sour cream. Serves 6.

Potato Pancake Variations

Potato Cakes with Meat: Add ½ cup diced, cooked meat or cracklings. Substitute fine bread or cracker crumbs for flour. Fry same as above.

Potato Cupcakes: Bake potato pancake mixture in well greased custard cups in moderate oven (350°F.) until brown, about 40 minutes. Serve hot.

Potato Pie (Kugel): Prepare potato pancake mixture and bake in a shallow greased casserole in a moderate oven (350°F.) until brown, about 40 minutes. Serve hot.

SWISS-APPLE CINNAMON PANCAKE

- 1 cup sifted enriched flour
- ½ teaspoon baking powder
  Pinch of salt
- 2 beaten eggs
- ½ cup milk
- 1 teaspoon melted butter
- 3 large apples
  Sugar and cinnamon

Mix and sift flour, baking powder, and salt. Mix with eggs, milk, and melted butter. Beat until batter is smooth.

Peel and slice apples. Sauté in a little butter in 9 or 10 inch frying pan until apples are turning soft. Sprinkle lightly with cinnamon and sugar.

Pour batter over apples, smoothing it to edges of pan. Bake in hot oven (400°F.) until golden brown. Serve very hot, sprinkled liberally with sugar and cinnamon. Serves 4.

BLINTZES

Blintzes is a Yiddish term for a Jewish dish of very thin pancakes filled with a cottage-cheese mixture or sometimes with berries or other fruit, rolled up, then browned in butter or baked. Blintzes are usually served with sour cream.

Batter:

1 cup sifted enriched flour
1 teaspoon salt
4 eggs, well beaten
1 cup milk or 1 cup water

Cheese Filling:

1½ pounds dry cottage cheese
1 or 2 egg yolks, beaten
1 tablespoon melted butter
Salt, sugar, and cinnamon to taste

Pancakes: Sift flour and salt. Mix eggs with liquid. Stir in flour. Mix until smooth to form thin batter.

Pour onto a hot lightly greased 6-inch skillet enough batter to form very thin cake, tilting the pan from side to side so that batter spreads evenly.

Cook over a low heat on one side only until the top of cake is dry and blistered. Turn out on clean cloth, cooked side up. Allow to cool. Repeat until all batter is used.

Filling: Mix cheese with egg yolks and butter and with salt, sugar, and cinnamon to taste. Place a tablespoon of mixture in center of each cake. Fold edges over to form envelope.

Blintzes may be prepared and filled in advance and kept in refrigerator until ready to fry. Just before serving, fry in butter until brown on both sides, or bake in a moderate oven.

Serve hot with sour cream, or with sugar and cinnamon mixture. Makes about 10 blintzes.

Variations of Blintzes:

Apple Blintzes: Mix 2 cups peeled and cored chopped apples, 1½ tablespoons ground almonds, 1 egg white, powdered sugar, and cinnamon to taste. Proceed as for cheese blintzes. Serve with sugar and cinnamon mixture.

Blintzes may be made very small, filled with a fruit filling such as blueberries, and served as a dessert with a light main course.

Cherry Blintzes: Mix 1 cup drained, pitted canned cherries, dash of cinnamon, 1 tablespoon flour, and sugar to taste. Proceed as for cheese blintzes. Serve with sour cream or with cinnamon and sugar.

Blueberry Blintzes: Substitute blueberries for cherries and proceed as directed above.

CREPES SUZETTE

Crêpes Suzette is a French term for very thin pancakes (crêpes) rolled up and served with a flaming brandy sauce.

Batter:

¾ cup sifted enriched flour
2 teaspoons sugar
½ teaspoon salt
¾ cup milk
3 eggs, slightly beaten

Sauce:

½ cup sweet butter
½ cup powdered sugar
1 orange, juice and grated rind
¼ cup curaçao or brandy

Mix flour, sugar, and salt. Add milk alternately with eggs. Beat until smooth.

Grease bottom of heavy frying pan when very hot. Cover bottom of pan with thin layer of batter and quickly tilt pan so that the pancake is evenly paper-thin. Brown on both sides.

Successful making of crêpes depends upon the thinness of the batter. If made ahead of time, pancakes may be reheated in oven. Roll each and serve with following sauce.

Crêpe Suzette Sauce: Cream butter (do not melt). Add powdered sugar, grated rind and juice of orange, and brandy.

Arrange pancakes in row on hot platter. Pour over some of the sauce, sprinkle with brandy, and light just before serving. Makes 10 to 12 5-inch pancakes.

FRENCH PANCAKES WITH PINEAPPLE

Prepare crêpe batter. Drain canned pineapple rings; slice each piece into 3 parts to make 3 very thin rings, and dry the rings on a towel.

Heat and butter a very small frying pan, the bottom of which is only slightly larger than the pineapple rings.

Pour in a little batter to cover the bottom and when it is set and brown on the underside, place a ring of pineapple on it.

Pour another very thin layer of batter over it, turn and brown the pancake on the other side.

Place the pancakes on a hot serving platter and sprinkle with confectioners' sugar.

Crêpes Suzette: Special pans are often used by restaurants specializing in these famous pancakes; however you can make them at the table in a chafing dish or electric skillet. Otherwise, make them ahead in the kitchen, put them on a warmed serving dish and pour sauce over them. At serving time, sprinkle with warmed brandy and light with a match.

FRENCH PANCAKES WITH KIRSCH

Prepare crêpe batter and make small pancakes about 5 to 6 inches in diameter.

Spread them with a little butter that has been creamed with sugar and flavored with a little kirsch.

Roll the pancakes and place them in a shallow baking pan. Sprinkle with fine granulated sugar and glaze them very quickly under the broiler.

NORWEGIAN PANCAKES

Use same batter and fry as for Crêpes Suzette, but do not roll. Pile several flat pancakes on serving plate.

Spread jelly or butter and maple sugar between them and over the top. Serve hot in pie-shaped wedges.

OATMEAL GRIDDLECAKES

2 cups milk
2 cups quick-cooking oats, uncooked
⅓ cup sifted enriched flour
2½ teaspoons baking powder
1 teaspoon salt
2 eggs, separated
⅓ cup melted fat

Heat milk and pour over oats. Allow to cool. Sift together flour, baking powder, and salt. Beat egg yolks and add to oat mixture. Add melted fat and stir in dry ingredients. Fold in stiffly beaten egg whites.

Drop batter by spoonfuls onto hot greased griddle. When surface is covered with bubbles, turn and brown on other side. Oatmeal griddlecakes take longer to brown than plain griddlecakes.

Apple Oatmeal Griddlecakes: Add ¼ teaspoon cinnamon, 2 tablespoons brown sugar, and 1 cup finely chopped, pared apples to batter before adding egg whites.

SWEDISH DESSERT PANCAKES
(Plättar)

3 eggs
1/2 teaspoon salt
1/4 cup sugar
1 cup sifted enriched flour
2 cups milk
1 teaspoon vanilla
3 tablespoons melted butter or margarine

Beat eggs well with hand beater; gradually add salt, sugar, flour, milk, and vanilla, beating well after each addition. Stir in butter.

Heat pancake griddle; grease lightly. Make little thin pancakes. Spread each pancake with whipped cream, lingonberries, preserves, applesauce, cottage cheese, or sour cream.

Stack in groups of six; or roll up each cake. Or, as each pancake comes from griddle, roll it up; sprinkle lightly with sugar; pass bowl of whipped cream, lingonberries, etc. Serves 4 to 6.

BUTTERMILK GRIDDLECAKES

3 well beaten egg yolks
1 2/3 cups buttermilk or sour milk
1/4 cup melted butter
1 1/2 cups sifted enriched flour
1/2 teaspoon salt
1 teaspoon baking powder
1 teaspoon baking soda
1 teaspoon sugar
3 egg whites, stiffly beaten

Mix egg yolks, buttermilk, and melted butter. Stir in sifted dry ingredients and beat until smooth. Fold in egg whites. Pour batter onto hot, lightly greased griddle.

Bake on 1 side until bubbles appear on surface, then turn and bake on other side until lightly browned. Makes about 24 small griddlecakes.

COTTAGE CHEESE PANCAKES

2 eggs
1/2 cup sieved cottage cheese
3/4 cup thin sour cream
3/4 cup sifted enriched flour
1/2 teaspoon baking soda
1 teaspoon salt

Beat eggs, and blend with cottage cheese; stir in sour cream.

Sift flour with baking soda and salt. Add to egg mixture and beat thoroughly.

Let batter stand a few minutes before baking. Cook on hot, lightly greased griddle until browned, turning once.

Serve hot with butter and applesauce. Makes 10 to 12 pancakes 3 1/2 to 4 inches in diameter.

RHODE ISLAND JOHNNY CAKES

1 cup water-ground corn meal
1 tablespoon flour
1 teaspoon sugar
1/2 teaspoon salt
1 cup boiling water
1/2 cup milk

Combine and stir the dry ingredients. Pour the boiling water over them and stir in. Add the milk.

Cook on a griddle generously greased with bacon fat. Makes 10 to 12 pancakes.

BUTTERMILK BUCKWHEAT PANCAKES

1/2 cup sifted enriched flour
1/2 teaspoon baking powder
1/2 teaspoon salt
2 teaspoons sugar
1 teaspoon baking soda
1 1/2 cups buckwheat flour
3 1/4 cups buttermilk or sour milk
2 tablespoons melted butter

Mix and sift flour, baking powder, salt, sugar, and soda.

Add buckwheat flour and mix well. Stir in milk and melted shortening and beat only until batter is blended. Bake on a hot greased griddle.

MASHED POTATO PANCAKES

1 cup mashed potatoes
2 cups sifted enriched flour
1 teaspoon salt
3 teaspoons baking powder
2 eggs, beaten
1 cup milk
4 tablespoons light corn syrup
1 teaspoon nutmeg

Combine potatoes, sifted flour, salt, and baking powder.

Mix together the eggs and milk and stir lightly into the potato-flour mixture. Add corn syrup and nutmeg and beat well.

Bake on a greased griddle until cakes are brown on both sides. Makes 12.

QUICK RUSSIAN PANCAKES
(BLINI)

3/4 cup sifted enriched flour
1/3 teaspoon baking powder
1/4 teaspoon salt
1/2 cup milk
1 egg, slightly beaten
2 tablespoons sour cream

Sift flour, baking powder, and salt together. Add remaining ingredients. Stir well.

Bake on greased griddle, making each pancake very small (about 1 1/2 inches across) and very thin. Brown on both sides, turning only once.

Serve with caviar, melted butter, or sour cream. Makes about 30 pancakes.

MATZO MEAL PANCAKES

1/2 cup matzo meal
1 teaspoon salt
1 tablespoon sugar
2 eggs, separated
1 cup milk or water

Mix matzo meal, salt, and sugar. Beat egg yolks; add milk and combine with dry ingredients. Let stand 1/2 hour, then fold in stiffly beaten egg whites.

Bake on hot greased griddle until bubbly on top and brown on underside, then turn and brown the other side. Serve with syrup or sprinkled with sugar.

PINEAPPLE CRÊPES

1/2 teaspoon salt
1 tablespoon powdered sugar
1/2 cup sifted flour
2 eggs, beaten
1 tablespoon melted butter
2/3 cup milk
1/2 teaspoon grated orange rind
Tidbit Sauce (below)

Add salt and sugar to flour. Mix remaining ingredients; add to flour, beating until smooth.

Heat 5-inch frying pan, butter lightly. Fry each crêpe separately, dropping 1 tablespoon batter into pan and tilting pan so batter covers bottom. Fry about one minute on each side.

Spoon 1 tablespoon tidbits (from sauce) on each crêpe. Roll. Place crêpes in shallow pan or chafing dish, pour over remaining sauce. Heat in chafing dish or in moderate oven (350°F.) about 10 minutes. Makes 16 crêpes.

Tidbit Sauce:
1/2 cup pineapple syrup (drained from tidbits)
1 orange, grated rind and juice
1/4 cup granulated sugar
3 tablespoons butter
2 cups (1 No. 2 can) drained pineapple tidbits

Mix together all ingredients except tidbits; simmer 10 minutes. Add tidbits and heat.

Pineapple Crêpes

LACY GRAHAM CRACKER PANCAKES

- ½ cup sifted enriched flour
- ¾ cup sugar
- 1 teaspoon baking soda
- 1½ teaspoons baking powder
- 1 teaspoon salt
- 1 cup coarsely crushed graham crackers
- 4 eggs, beaten
- 1 cup sour cream
- About 3 tablespoons water

Mix and sift flour, sugar, baking soda, baking powder, and salt.

Add graham cracker crumbs and fold in the eggs, which have been beaten until they are thick and lemon-colored. Then stir in the sour cream and the water.

The batter should be just thin enough so that the cakes will run a little at the edges, when dropped on a hot griddle.

The griddle should be completely covered with a thin layer of fat. Try using half butter and half bacon fat. The cakes should be dark brown in color, with a crisp, lacy surface texture and uneven edges.

If they are almost impossible to turn, the batter is the right consistency. Serve hot with butter and syrup, or with powdered sugar and jam.

DOWN EAST PANCAKES

- 2 cups sifted enriched flour
- 1 teaspoon baking soda
- 3 tablespoons sugar
- ¾ teaspoon salt
- 2 well beaten eggs
- ¼ cup vinegar
- 1¾ cups sweet milk
- ¼ cup shortening

Mix and sift flour, soda, sugar, and salt. Combine eggs, vinegar, milk, and shortening and mix well. Add to dry ingredients and stir only until smooth.

Pour batter from tip of large spoon or from pitcher onto large frying pan or griddle. When underside is browned and before bubbles burst on top, turn and brown second side. Makes about 20 medium pancakes.

Variations: For apple pancakes add 1 cup grated raw apples. For blueberry pancakes add ½ cup well-drained blueberries.

CRÊPES WITH KIRSCH

- 3 eggs, separated
- 2 tablespoons sugar
- ¼ teaspoon salt
- ½ cup melted butter
- 1 cup milk
- ½ cup sifted enriched flour
- ½ cup confectioners' sugar
- ½ cup Kirsch

Beat egg yolks well; add 2 tablespoons sugar, salt, and 2 tablespoons melted butter. Add milk and flour; beat until smooth.

Beat egg whites until stiff and fold into first mixture until well blended.

Spoon small portions of the batter into a greased 6-inch skillet. When slightly browned on underside, turn and brown other side.

Roll and place over heat in chafing dish. When 4 or 5 crêpes are made, sprinkle generously with confectioners' sugar, melted butter, and Kirsch. Ignite liqueur and burn until it goes out.

Add other crêpes as they are cooked and repeat additions of sugar, butter, and Kirsch, serving as needed. Serves about 6.

BUTTER PANCAKES

- 3 cups sifted enriched flour
- 3 teaspoons baking powder
- 1 teaspoon salt
- 2 tablespoons sugar
- 3 eggs, separated
- 3 cups milk
- ½ cup butter, melted

Sift flour twice with baking powder, salt, and sugar.

Beat egg yolks, add milk and melted butter. Add flour all at once; beat until batter is smooth.

Beat egg whites until stiff and fold into batter thoroughly.

Bake on a moderately hot, buttered griddle, using a scant ¼ cup for each cake. Bake until golden brown on under side; then turn and bake until browned on second side. Turn only once.

Serve hot with butter and sprinkle with a mixture of brown sugar and chopped pecans. Makes 3 dozen 4-inch pancakes.

GERMAN APPLE PANCAKE

- 1 cup sifted enriched flour
- ½ teaspoon baking powder
- Pinch of salt
- 1 cup milk
- 5 eggs
- 2 tablespoons melted butter
- Thinly sliced apples sautéed in butter, or hot applesauce

Mix and sift dry ingredients. Stir in milk. Add unbeaten eggs one at a time, beating each separately into batter. Add melted butter.

Pour into hot greased skillet. Put on direct heat for 1 minute, then bake in hot oven (425°F.) until browned, puffed, and curled up at edges, 20 to 25 minutes.

Sprinkle with powdered sugar and lemon juice if desired. Serve at once with hot thin slices of apple which have been sautéed in butter or with hot applesauce. Serves 4 to 6.

RUMANIAN PANCAKES

- 1 cup sifted enriched flour
- 1 cup milk
- 1 egg, beaten
- ¼ teaspoon salt
- 1 tablespoon sugar
- Dash of cinnamon, optional
- Canned cherries
- Powdered sugar

Add flour to milk and beat until well blended. Add egg, salt, sugar, and cinnamon. Mix thoroughly.

Bake on a greased griddle until brown on one side. Turn and brown on other side.

Spread cherries over pancakes while hot. Roll up and sprinkle with powdered sugar.

Serve hot as dessert. Serves 4.

ICELANDIC PANCAKES

- 1 cup sifted enriched flour
- 2 eggs
- About ½ cup milk
- 2 to 3 tablespoons melted butter or margarine
- 2 teaspoons vanilla

Sift flour into a bowl. Beat eggs and add half the milk.

Stir egg-milk mixture, melted butter, and vanilla into flour.

Add enough more milk to make a batter of the thickness of whipping cream.

Use a small (5- to 6-inch) skillet. Cover bottom of lightly buttered hot skillet with a thin layer of batter by tilting the skillet slightly.

Brown lightly on both sides. When cooked, spread 1 teaspoon of jam and a tablespoon of whipped cream over pancake. Fold twice and place on warm serving plate. Serves 6.

A tasty way to make leftovers into a hearty luncheon is to serve pancakes with such dishes as creamed chicken, mushrooms, tuna, or ham. If desired, put the pancakes together, sandwich fashion, using the creamed mixtures as fillings. Serve immediately or keep the pancakes warm in a very slow oven.

GOLDEN EGG PANCAKE

2 eggs
1/2 teaspoon salt
1 tablespoon sugar
1/3 cup sifted enriched flour
1/2 cup milk
1 teaspoon fat

Beat eggs, salt, and sugar together. Add flour and milk to eggs. Beat until smooth.

Heat fat in deep skillet (10- to 12-inch) until drop of water in skillet sizzles. Pour in all of batter. Cook 2 minutes.

Place in very hot oven (450°F.) and bake 15 minutes or until surface is brown. Let stand in pan until ready to serve.

Dot with butter and sweetened fruit or marmalade, syrup, or honey. Roll or fold from opposite sides to center, making 3 layers. Turn out on warm platter. Sprinkle with confectioners' sugar. Serves 1 to 2.

Variations of Egg Pancake

Place one of the following over the batter just before placing it in the oven.

Apple: 1 layer of thinly sliced apples.

Bacon: 3 to 4 slices crisply cooked bacon, diced. Reduce salt to 1/4 teaspoon.

Ham: 1/4 cup finely diced cooked ham. Reduce salt to 1/4 teaspoon.

BLINI

Blini is a Russian term for very small yeast-raised pancakes, often made with buckwheat flour. They are served as a rule with caviar, sour cream, cheese, or melted butter. The name is sometimes also applied to small pancakes made with baking powder.

3 cups warm milk
1 cake compressed yeast
2 cups fine buckwheat flour
4 eggs, separated
1/2 teaspoon salt
1 tablespoon sugar
2 teaspoons melted butter

Pour 1 1/2 cups warm milk over crumbled yeast. Stir to dissolve and add enough flour to make a thick sponge. Cover with a warm cloth. Set in a warm place (80 to 85°F.) for about 2 1/2 hours.

Beat egg yolks with salt and sugar and stir in remaining warm milk. Add butter and stir into the raised sponge. Mix in remaining flour and stiffly beaten egg whites. Cover again and let rise at least 20 minutes.

Bake small pancakes (about 3 inches across and not more than 1/4 inch thick) on a hot, greased griddle. Brown lightly on both sides, turning only once. Serve with caviar or with melted butter and sour cream. Makes about 30 pancakes.

GOLDEN EGG PANCAKE HINTS

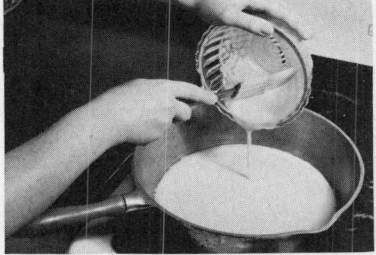

1. Pour batter into a 10- or 12-inch hot greased skillet.

2. Cook on top of range over moderate heat 2 minutes, then bake in very hot oven (450°F.) until surface is browned, about 15 minutes.

3. Roll or fold from opposite sides to center making three layers.

4. Turn out on a warm platter and garnish with sweetened fruit or marmalade, syrup, or honey. Sprinkle with confectioners' sugar.

GERMAN SKILLET PANCAKES

6 eggs, separated
1/2 cup sifted enriched flour
1 teaspoon baking powder
Pinch of salt
1/2 cup milk

Beat the egg yolks until thick and lemon-colored.

Mix and sift flour, baking powder, and salt; add to the egg yolks alternately with the milk.

When all ingredients are combined, fold in egg whites, which have been stiffly beaten.

Melt a little butter in a skillet and pour in a tablespoon of the batter. Tip pan so that batter will cover bottom of skillet in a thin layer. When brown on one side, turn and brown the other.

Serve very hot with sugar and wedges of lemon.

HUNGARIAN PANCAKES (Palascinta)

1 egg
3/4 cup enriched flour
2 cups milk
1/8 teaspoon salt
1 teaspoon sugar

Mix all ingredients together well with rotary beater or electric mixer. Let batter stand about 30 minutes.

Put enough butter in small frying pan to coat bottom of pan lightly. Heat until pan is hot.

Pour in just enough batter to make a very thin layer on the bottom of pan, tipping pan when batter is added so entire bottom of pan is covered.

Pan-fry over low heat until browned on one side. Transfer to heated platter.

Spread a thin layer of jelly on half the pancake, then roll up.

Sprinkle powdered sugar over top. Serve at once. Makes about 10 pancakes.

RAISED BUCKWHEAT CAKES

2 1/4 cups boiling water
1/2 cake compressed yeast
2 tablespoons lukewarm water
1 1/2 cups buckwheat flour
1 teaspoon salt
4 teaspoons sugar
1/2 cup sifted enriched flour
1/4 teaspoon baking soda

Boil 2 cups water, cool to lukewarm. While it is cooling, dissolve yeast in 2 tablespoons lukewarm water.

Reserve baking soda and 3 teaspoons sugar to add next morning, then add remaining ingredients and dissolved yeast to the 2 cups lukewarm water. Cover and let stand in a fairly warm place 12 hours (overnight).

The next morning add the other 1/4 cup water, cooled to lukewarm, with soda and 3 teaspoons sugar dissolved in it. Mix well and bake on griddle.

One-half cup of batter may be reserved as "seed." Use "seed" in place of yeast after first day. "Seed" should be stored in cool place. Makes about 12 pancakes.

Waffles

A waffle is a soft but crisp cake cooked in a utensil called a waffle iron —two metal plates studded on the inside, which are hinged together and shut upon each other. Waffle batter is similar to that used for pancakes, but richer. Waffles are usually served with butter and syrup but may also be accompanied by fresh or stewed fruit, preserves, ice cream, or creamed chicken.

WAFFLE BAKING HINTS

Waffles should be evenly browned and uniform in shape, well filled out to the edges. They should be crisp, light, and tender.

Correct baking temperature is important. If the baker is too hot, the outside will brown before the inside is cooked. If too cold, the waffles will stick or appear spotted.

If the baker is not thermostatically controlled the iron may be tested by throwing drops of water upon it. The baker is ready to use when the drops form into balls and "skid" across.

Pour the batter from a pitcher around the center of the grid, filling the iron only two-thirds full to prevent overflow. Cook until steaming stops. It takes 3 to 5 minutes to bake the average waffle, a little longer for a thin batter. Lift waffle off griddle with a fork.

Store leftover batter in the refrigerator; it will keep for about 3 days in a covered container.

BAKING WAFFLES AT HIGH ALTITUDES

For general information about baking at high altitudes, see **Cooking at High Altitudes.** Some reduction in leavening (usually about 1/4 less of baking powder or baking soda) will be required at high altitudes when using sea level recipes.

CARE OF WAFFLE BAKERS

Modern waffle irons usually require no greasing and some do not require tempering. The manufacturer's directions should be followed regarding tempering of the grids, use of heat control and indicator, and cleaning after use.

If manufacturer's directions are not available, the following general cleaning hints may usually be followed. Wash off the outside with a damp cloth wrung out of hot soapy water, then polish the baker with a dry cloth. Remove excess batter from the grids with slightly dampened steel wool. Then brush the grids with an even film of melted unsalted fat. Close the baker, turn on the current, and heat for 2 minutes. Wipe off excess fat with paper towels.

WAFFLES (Master Recipe)

2   cups sifted enriched flour
3   teaspoons baking powder
2   tablespoons sugar (optional)
1   teaspoon salt
3   eggs, separated
1¼ cups milk
4   tablespoons melted shortening

Sift dry ingredients. Beat egg yolks. Add milk and melted shortening. Beat thoroughly. Add to dry ingredients. Combine quickly.

Gently fold in egg whites, beaten stiff but not dry. Bake 3 or 4 minutes in a hot waffle iron. Makes 5 to 6 waffles.

Variations of Waffles:

Apple Waffles: Follow master recipe. Just before baking, add 1 cup of 1/2-inch cubes of raw apples to batter. Serve with cinnamon-sugar mixture, and butter.

Bacon Waffles: Follow master recipe. Sprinkle cooked, diced bacon over batter in waffle iron before baking.

Blueberry Waffles: Follow master recipe. Mix 1 cup blueberries with 2 tablespoons sugar, and add to batter just before baking. Serve with powdered sugar.

Cheese Waffles: In master recipe add 1 cup grated American cheese to batter before folding in beaten egg whites.

Coconut Waffles: Follow master recipe. Before closing grids, sprinkle coconut over each waffle or add 1 cup shredded coconut to batter.

Corn Meal Waffles: In master recipe substitute 1/2 cup corn meal for 1/2 cup white flour.

Date or Fig Waffles: Follow master recipe; add 1 cup chopped dates or dried figs to batter just before baking. Serve with powdered sugar.

Ginger Waffles: In master recipe add 4 tablespoons molasses and 1½ teaspoons ginger. Omit 4 tablespoons milk.

Ham Waffles: Prepare master recipe. Sprinkle 2 tablespoons finely diced, cooked ham over batter of each waffle before closing grids.

Orange Waffles: Follow master recipe. Add 2 teaspoons grated orange rind to the egg yolk and milk mixture. If desired, substitute 1/2 cup orange juice for 1/2 cup milk.

Pecan Waffles: In master recipe add 1 cup chopped pecans to batter or sprinkle over batter of each waffle before closing iron.

Sour Cream Waffles: In master recipe use only 1 teaspoon baking powder. Add 1/2 teaspoon baking soda. Substitute 1¼ cups thick sour cream for milk and shortening.

Sour Milk or Buttermilk Waffles: In master recipe substitute 1½ cups sour milk or 1½ cups buttermilk for sweet milk. Add 3/4 teaspoon baking soda and use only 2¼ teaspoons baking powder.

Whole Wheat Waffles: In master recipe substitute 1/2 cup whole wheat flour for 1/2 cup white flour.

SPONGE CAKE WAFFLES

1   cup sifted cake flour
1   teaspoon baking powder
1/4 teaspoon salt
3   eggs, well beaten
1   cup sugar
3   tablespoons melted butter
1/4 cup cold water
1   teaspoon vanilla

Sift together the flour, baking powder, and salt.

Combine well beaten eggs and sugar. Add sifted dry ingredients, melted butter, water, and vanilla, beating until smooth.

Bake in a hot waffle iron until delicately browned, about 2 minutes.

May be served as a shortcake. Sprinkle with powdered sugar, and serve with berries and whipped cream or ice cream. Makes 6 waffles.

SWEET POTATO WAFFLES

4   tablespoons shortening
1   tablespoon sugar
1   egg, separated
1   cup milk
Salt, cayenne, and nutmeg
3/4 cup sifted enriched flour
1   cup mashed sweet potatoes
2   teaspoons baking powder

Cream shortening and sugar until smooth. Add well beaten egg yolk, milk, and seasoning, continuing to beat until smooth.

Beat in the flour, sweet potatoes, and baking powder. Fold in the stiffly beaten egg white.

Bake in a heated waffle iron until golden brown. Serve sprinkled with sugar and cinnamon. Serves 5 to 6.

Waffle ice cream sandwiches are always popular with the youngsters.

FRENCH TOAST WAFFLES

1   beaten egg
1/4 cup milk
2   tablespoons melted butter
1/8 teaspoon salt
Sliced bread

Combine egg, milk, butter and salt. Cut sliced bread into pieces to fit a waffle iron, then coat bread well in the batter. Toast in a hot waffle iron.

CREAM DESSERT WAFFLES

1   cup sifted cake flour
2   teaspoons baking powder
1/2 teaspoon salt
2   eggs, separated
1   cup heavy cream

Mix and sift the dry ingredients; mix to a smooth batter with beaten egg yolks and cream.

Fold in stiffly beaten egg whites. Bake in a hot waffle iron. Makes 4 waffles.

Variations:

Chocolate Waffles: Stir into the batter 2 squares melted unsweetened chocolate and 6 tablespoons sugar.

Spiced Chocolate Waffles: Add to chocolate waffle batter 1/4 teaspoon ground cinnamon, 1/4 teaspoon ground nutmeg, and 1 teaspoon vanilla.

BUTTERMILK WAFFLES

1 3/4 cups sifted enriched flour
2   teaspoons baking powder
1   teaspoon baking soda
1/2 teaspoon salt
3   eggs, separated
1 1/2 cups buttermilk or sour milk
1/2 cup melted butter or shortening

Mix and sift dry ingredients. Mix to a light batter with the egg yolks, which have been well beaten, and the milk.

Stir in melted butter. Fold in egg whites which have been stiffly beaten. Bake in hot waffle iron. Makes 8 waffles.

Variations:

Yogurt Waffles: Use 2 cups yogurt in place of buttermilk in above recipe.

Sour Cream Waffles: Use 2 cups sour cream in place of buttermilk and stir in only 2 tablespoons melted butter.

SOUR CREAM WAFFLES #2

2   eggs, separated
2   cups sour cream
2   cups sifted enriched flour
1   tablespoon corn meal
1   teaspoon baking soda
1/2 teaspoon salt

Beat whites and yolks of eggs separately.

Mix with the beaten yolks, the sour cream, flour, corn meal, baking soda, and salt.

Finally fold in the egg whites. Bake at once on a hot iron. Makes 6 waffles.

WHOLE WHEAT WAFFLES
(Yeast-Raised)

1 1/2 cups milk
1/2 cup honey
1 1/2 teaspoons salt
2   tablespoons shortening
1/2 cup warm (not hot) water
1   package or cake yeast, active dry or compressed
2   eggs, beaten
3   cups whole wheat flour

Scald milk. Stir in honey, salt, and shortening. Cool to lukewarm.

Measure 1/2 cup warm water into bowl (cool to lukewarm for compressed yeast). Sprinkle or crumble in yeast. Stir until dissolved. Stir in lukewarm milk mixture.

Add beaten eggs and flour. Beat until smooth. Cover. Let rise in warm place, free from draft, until doubled in bulk, about 40 minutes.

Stir batter down.

Bake in waffle iron at medium heat until golden brown, about 8 minutes.

Serve with margarine or butter and hot syrup. Makes 5 large waffles.

BROWNIE WAFFLES

1 1/2 cups sifted enriched flour
1/2 teaspoon salt
3/4 cup shortening
2/3 cup sugar
2   egg yolks
3/4 cup milk
2   squares unsweetened chocolate, melted
1/2 cup chopped nuts
2   egg whites, stiffly beaten

Sift together flour and salt. Cream shortening and add sugar gradually. Beat until light and fluffy. Add egg yolks and mix well.

Add milk to creamed mixture alternately with flour. Fold in remaining ingredients.

Bake in moderately hot waffle iron about 5 minutes. Serve with a scoop of vanilla ice cream or whipped cream topped with chocolate sauce.

GINGERBREAD WAFFLES

2   eggs
1/4 cup sugar
1/2 cup molasses
1   cup sour milk
1 1/2 cups sifted enriched flour
1   teaspoon ginger
1/4 teaspoon salt
1   teaspoon baking soda
1   teaspoon baking powder
1/3 cup melted shortening

Beat eggs until light. Add sugar, molasses, sour milk, and remaining dry in-

gredients sifted together. Beat until smooth and add shortening. Cinnamon and clove may be added if desired.

Bake in a hot waffle iron. Serve with whipped cream, ice cream, or cold applesauce. Makes about 5 waffles.

OLD-FASHIONED WAFFLES

2   cups sifted enriched flour
1   teaspoon baking soda
1   tablespoon sugar
1/2 teaspoon salt
2   eggs, separated
1/4 cup vinegar
1 3/4 cups sweet milk
1/3 cup melted shortening

Mix and sift flour, soda, sugar, and salt. Beat egg yolks, vinegar, and milk together. Add dry ingredients and melted shortening. Stir until batter is smooth.

Beat egg whites until stiff but not dry and fold into batter.

Pour batter on heated waffle iron to about 1-inch of edge. Bake 3 to 4 minutes or until waffles stop steaming.

Serve with butter and syrup. Or, use under creamed meat, poultry, or fish for luncheon or supper dish. Makes 6 to 7 waffles.

Pecan Waffles: Add 3/4 cup chopped pecans.

CHOCOLATE WAFFLES #2

2   cups sifted enriched flour
4   teaspoons baking powder
1/2 teaspoon salt
1/4 cup sugar
1/2 cup cocoa
2   eggs, separated
1 3/4 cups milk
1/2 cup melted butter or margarine

Mix and sift flour, baking powder, salt, sugar, and cocoa.

Combine egg yolks, milk, and melted butter or margarine and add to dry ingredients. Beat slightly.

Beat egg whites until stiff but not dry and fold into batter. Bake in hot waffle baker. Serve with chocolate sauce. Makes 8 waffles.

For a heartier dish, serve waffles with creamed eggs, chicken, or mushrooms, or with sausages, bacon, or fried chicken.

PICKLES AND RELISHES

Although food markets today offer a wide variety of pickles and relishes, many homemakers like to make their own pickle products when garden vegetables and fresh fruits are in abundant supply. This section gives specific directions for a wide variety of old-time favorites as well as some new jiffy-type recipes.

PICKLING HINTS

Use only fresh, good quality fruits and vegetables. Cucumbers and green tomatoes are best pickled within 24 hours of picking. Fruits may be slightly underripe.

Use a good, clear standard vinegar—free from sediment—one with 4 to 5 percent of acetic acid. Use white vinegar (barley malt, corn, rye) if the pickles are light in color; cider (apple) vinegar for all others.

Use pure granulated salt. A medium coarse salt is preferable to table salt because the carbonates, or bicarbonates of sodium, calcium, or magnesium added to table salt to prevent lumping may not give you as good results.

Use soft water for best results.

Use fresh, whole spices for longer lasting flavor.

Store pickles in jars with glass tops or in well-sealed crocks to avoid corrosion.

For a Bright-Colored Pickle: Use glass or pottery for soaking pickles. Enamel is preferred for heating acid pickling liquids; however brightly scoured aluminum, or stainless steel kettle may be used.

Iron utensils darken pickles, copper ones impart an undesirable greenish hue.

A stronger vinegar than recommended may give a darker color than desired.

To give pickles a fresh, green color, spinach or grape leaves may be added.

Hollow or Limp Pickles: These result from overripe or imperfect vegetables or when vegetables have been standing too long before pickling.

Cloudy Pickles: These are caused by a weak brine and a weak vinegar solution.

Soft Pickles: These may result from too weak a brine solution or from neglecting to cover pickles completely in the brine.

Tough or Shriveled Pickles: May be caused by excessive salt, or sugar, or excessively strong vinegar.

If very sour or very sweet pickles are desired it is best to put them in a weak solution at first and increase the strength later. Hurrying the processes of cooking or brining may cause shriveling.

CUCUMBER OIL PICKLES

4 quarts small, sliced cucumbers
1/2 cup salt
2 quarts water
1 1/2 cups cider vinegar
1/2 cup sugar
1/3 cup mustard seed
1 teaspoon celery seed
1 teaspoon whole black peppers
1/2 cup olive oil or salad oil

Place cucumbers in a bowl. Dissolve salt in water and pour over cucumbers. Add more water if needed to cover cucumbers. Let stand overnight.

Drain cucumbers, cover with fresh water, heat to boiling and drain again. Pack into hot sterilized jars.

Heat vinegar, sugar, spice, and oil to boiling point, stirring until sugar is dissolved. Pour over pickles, filling jars almost to rim. Seal immediately. Makes about 6 pints.

SWEET GHERKINS

Use cucumbers no larger than 2 inches in length. Leave 1/4 inch or more of the stem on each. Wash and place in stone jars. Salt, using 1 cup of salt to a gallon of the cucumbers.

Pour boiling water over them and let stand 24 to 36 hours.

Remove pickles from the brine and drop them into a solution of equal parts vinegar and water. Heat to the boiling point and remove pickles to clean jars.

Add a teaspoonful of mixed pickling spices to each quart, and also a fairly long strip of horseradish root, if it is available.

Pour over the pickles the hot vinegar and water to which a cup of sugar per quart has been added. Seal.

EASY KOSHER DILL PICKLES

1 quart cucumbers
1/2 cup lemon juice
2 tablespoons salt
Spray of dill
Water
Clove of garlic

Sterilize jars and pack with firm, clean cucumbers.

Add lemon juice and salt. Fill to the neck of the jar with clear, cold water.

Put the spray of dill and clove of garlic on top and seal loosely.

This pickle is not ready for use for six weeks. Complete seal at that time. Makes 1 quart.

ICICLE PICKLES

Cut large cucumbers into 4 to 8 pieces lengthwise. Let stand in ice water 8 hours or overnight.

Pack into hot sterilized jars. Fill center of each jar with 2 pieces of celery and 6 pickling onions.

Combine 1 quart cider vinegar, 1/3 cup medium-coarse salt, and 1 cup sugar; heat to a boil. Fill jars and seal.

In these recipes "hot sterile jars" mean containers and lids that have been scrubbed in hot sudsy water, rinsed and then boiled 15 to 20 minutes just before use.

MIXED MUSTARD PICKLES

4 cups sliced cucumbers
2 cups quartered, small, green tomatoes
2 cups cauliflower flowerets
2 cups string beans, cut in 1-inch pieces
2 cups small whole onions or large onions, sliced
1½ cups sliced young tender carrots
3 sweet red peppers, cut in small pieces
3 sweet green peppers, cut in small pieces
Salt

Cover vegetables with a brine made with ½ cup salt to 1 quart water. Let stand overnight.

Drain, rinse in fresh water; drain again and cover mixture with equal parts of strong white vinegar and water (about 3 cups each, water and vinegar). Let stand 1 hour.

Heat to a rapid boil. Drain, add mustard dressing. Simmer 5 minutes.

Pack into hot, sterilized jars and seal airtight. Makes about 5 pints.

To Make Mustard Dressing:

9 tablespoons flour
5 tablespoons dry mustard
2½ teaspoons turmeric
1½ teaspoons celery seed
1 quart strong white vinegar
1¼ cups molasses or sugar

Mix flour with spices. Slowly add vinegar. Mix thoroughly and stir in molasses or sugar.

Cook until thick, stirring constantly.

EASY DILL PICKLES

Cucumbers of even size
1 head dill for each jar
3 quarts water
1 quart cider vinegar
1 cup salt

Scrub small, firm cucumbers thoroughly and rinse. Pack closely into quart jars. Place a head of dill in the top of each jar.

Mix water, vinegar, and salt; bring to a boil, and pour at once over cucumbers.

Seal jars and store in a cool, dark place for at least six weeks before opening. During this period the cure is completed. Pickles canned this way are best eaten within a period of 6 or 8 months.

COLD VINEGAR PICKLES

Wash and dry small cucumbers. Pack closely into sterilized jars.

To each quart, add 1 tablespoon crushed rock salt, 2 tablespoon sugar, 1 tablespoon mixed pickling spices. Fill jar with cold vinegar, seal, and store in a cool place.

A few slices of onion may be added to each jar, if desired.

SWEET SPICED CUCUMBERS

3 quarts sliced cucumbers
½ cup salt
1 quart vinegar
1½ to 2 cups white granulated sugar or tightly packed brown sugar
1 teaspoon whole allspice
2 sticks whole cinnamon, broken
1 teaspoon whole cloves
1 tablespoon white mustard seed

Arrange cucumbers and salt in a bowl or stone crock and let stand 3 hours.

As soon as cucumbers have been prepared, boil, covered, for 10 minutes the vinegar, sugar, and spices (spices should first be put in a square of cheese cloth and tied together in a bag). Let mixture stand, covered.

After 3 hours drain cucumbers and press to remove excess moisture. Remove spice bag from vinegar mixture and add cucumbers to it. Bring to a simmering point. Do not boil.

Pack in hot, clean jars, seal or partially seal, according to type of closure. Process in a boiling water bath 10 minutes. Makes about 5 pints.

BREAD AND BUTTER PICKLES

25 medium cucumbers, sliced
12 onions, sliced
½ cup salt
2 cups sugar
2 teaspoons turmeric
2 teaspoons cassia buds (optional)
1 quart vinegar
2 teaspoons mustard seed
2 teaspoons celery seed

Soak cucumbers and onions in ice water with salt for 3 hours.

Combine remaining ingredients and heat to boiling.

Add cucumbers and onion and heat for 2 minutes. Do not allow to boil. Fill clean jars. Seal at once.

MILD DILL PICKLES

4½ pounds cucumbers
6 tablespoons salt
1½ tablespoons yellow mustard seed
3 cups distilled white vinegar
3 cups water
¾ cup dill seed
6 bay leaves
6 peeled cloves garlic

Wash cucumbers and halve crosswise. Quarter each half lengthwise.

Pack in clean pint jars that have been rinsed in hot water.

Combine salt, mustard seed, vinegar, and water. Heat to boiling.

Pour liquid over cucumbers in jars, covering them. Add to each pint 2 tablespoons dill seed, a bay leaf, and a clove of garlic. Be sure jars are filled to not more than a half-inch from top.

Seal jars according to type of closure used and process immediately in a boiling water bath for 10 minutes. Makes 6 pints.

Note: Garlic may be omitted.

DILL PICKLES IN A CROCK

¼ bushel (about 12 pounds) cucumbers
4 tablespoons whole mixed pickling spice
Grape or cherry leaves
Dill
2 gallons soft water
2 cups cooking salt
2 cups vinegar

Wash and scald 4 or 5 gallon crock and cover the bottom with a layer of well washed grape or cherry leaves.

Add a layer of dill. Sprinkle a third of the spice over dill.

Wash the cucumbers well and pack half of them into the crock.

Add another layer of grape or cherry leaves, dill, and a sprinkling of spices.

Pack in remaining cucumbers and top with a third layer of leaves, dill, and spices.

Boil water, salt, vinegar together for 5 minutes and cool. Pour over cucumbers and place a cover or plate with a weight on it, over them so the cucumbers will be kept below the brine during fermentation.

Place a clean cloth over the top of the crock and leave crock in a fairly warm place, between 80–85 degrees to ferment. Active fermentation will begin in a few days and will be completed after 2 or 3 weeks, possibly a little longer.

Remove scum from top of pickles two or three times a week, for if scum remains it will cause spoilage. If brine evaporates, add more made in the same proportion. When fermentation ceases, no more scum will form.

Draw off the brine, pack pickles into clean jars with a sprig of dill in each jar.

Bring brine to the boiling point, pour over pickles and seal. Store in a cool place. Pickles will be ready for use after 4 to 6 weeks.

Kosher Dill Pickles: Make these in the same way as above, but add when canning, 1 clove garlic, 2 bay leaves, 1 teaspoon mustard seed, ¼ cup sugar, a strip of hot red pepper, and 1 cup vinegar for every 3 cups brine. Boil 2 minutes, pour over packed pickles and seal at once.

SAUERKRAUT
(Glass-Jar Method)

20   to 25 pounds cabbage
½ pound salt

Remove the outer leaves and wash cabbage; drain. Cut in halves or quarters; remove the core. Shred about 5 pounds of cabbage at a time and, using the hands, mix thoroughly with 3½ tablespoons salt. Measure accurately—oversalting prevents proper fermentation.

Pack into clean glass jars, pressing down firmly and evenly. Fill with cabbage to shoulder of jar (1½ to 2 inches from top) and be sure juice completely covers cabbage. A quart jar takes about 2 pounds of cabbage.

Wipe off top of jar. Cover cabbage with two or three layers of thin, clean white cloth, and tuck edges down against inside of jar. Crisscross two dry, clean wood strips (ice cream spoons or wooden garden labels cut to right size are suitable) over cloth to keep cabbage pressed under brine. Put lid on jar; don't seal tightly.

Set jars on a tray or pan to catch juice that leaks out. Keep at room temperature, about 70°F. is best. Every few days, remove scum if it forms. Add a little weak brine to keep cabbage covered (1½ tablespoons salt to 1 quart water). Let ferment about 10 days, or until liquid settles and bubbles no longer rise to surface.

If you are planning to use the kraut in a few weeks, it isn't necessary to process in a boiling-water bath. Seal the jars tightly and keep in a cool place.

To Store: Remove lids and set jars in a kettle, with cold water to shoulders of jars. Cover kettle. Bring water to boiling and boil 10 minutes.

Remove jars. Add boiling-hot brine if needed to fill jars to ½ inch of top (1½ tablespoons salt to 1 quart water). Wipe off jar rims and adjust lids. Boil jars in boiling-water bath—25 minutes for pints, 30 minutes for quarts—making sure that water covers jars. Remove jars; complete seals. Makes 8 to 10 quarts.

KOSHER STYLE GREEN TOMATO DILLS

Choose small, firm, green tomatoes. Wash thoroughly, and pack into clean jars.

To each quart jar add a garlic clove, a stalk of celery, and a quarter of a green pepper.

Make a solution in the following proportions: 2 quarts water, 1 quart vinegar, and 1 cup salt. Add 1 head of dill for each jar and boil solution 5 minutes.

Pour over green tomatoes in jars, placing dill in each. Seal and store 6 weeks. Pickles will not be thoroughly cured before that time.

GREEN TOMATO PICKLE

4   pounds green tomatoes
6   medium onions, sliced
½ cup salt
1   to 2 green peppers, chopped
2   cups sugar
2   cups vinegar
2   tablespoons each celery and mustard seed
1   tablespoon whole cloves
1   teaspoon whole black peppers
2   3-inch sticks cinnamon

Slice tomatoes ¼ inch thick. Place layers of tomatoes and onions in a large bowl, sprinkling each with salt; let stand overnight.

Drain and rinse in cold water.

Place in kettle and add green peppers, sugar, vinegar, celery, and mustard seed. Tie cloves, whole black peppers, and cinnamon in cheesecloth and add to mixture.

Bring to a rapid boil, stirring, and cook, stirring often, until thickened, about 20 minutes. Remove spice bag, pour into hot sterile jars and seal. Makes about 3½ pints.

PICKLED ONIONS

4   quarts small pickling onions (silver-skins)
Boiling water
Cold water
1   cup salt
¼ cup mixed pickle spice
2   quarts vinegar
2   cups sugar

Cover onions with boiling water; let stand 5 minutes. Drain; cover with cold water. Peel onions; place in bowl or enamel pan. Add salt; cover with fresh cold water; let stand overnight.

Next day, drain onions; rinse with cold water; drain again.

Tie spices in muslin or cheesecloth bag; boil with vinegar and sugar 5 minutes.

Remove spice bag. Add onions to boiling liquid; boil 2 to 3 minutes.

Pour into clean hot jars; fill to overflowing with liquid. Seal at once. Store at least 1 week before serving. Makes 6 or 7 pints.

BEET PICKLES

2½ quarts cooked beets
2   teaspoons each mustard seed and celery seed
4   teaspoons salt
1   teaspoon whole cloves
2   sticks cinnamon
1   quart strong vinegar
1   cup sugar
5   small onions, sliced (optional)

Peel beets. If small, leave whole. If large, slice or quarter them.

Tie spices in cheesecloth bag. Put spices and remaining ingredients, except the onions and beets, in a large kettle and bring to a boil.

Add beets and onions, and reheat to boiling. Remove spice bag.

Pack in hot, sterilized jars. Pour the hot liquid over beets and seal air-tight. Makes 6 pints.

PICKLED PEPPERS

6   red peppers
6   green peppers
2   cups vinegar
2   cups water
½ cup sugar
2   teaspoons salt
1   teaspoon mustard seed
1   teaspoon whole allspice

Remove tops and seeds from peppers. Cut in quarters lengthwise.

Combine vinegar, water, and sugar; heat to boiling. Add peppers; heat through slowly.

Pack in hot, sterilized jars. To each pint add ½ teaspoon salt, ¼ teaspoon mustard seed, and ¼ teaspoon whole allspice. Cover with hot vinegar liquid. Seal. Makes 4 pints.

PICKLED CAULIFLOWER

3   medium heads cauliflower
1   quart small white onions
1   cup salt
1   tablespoon mustard seed
1   tablespoon celery seed
1   teaspoon whole cloves
2   sticks cinnamon, broken
2   quarts white vinegar
2½ cups sugar

Separate cauliflower into flowerets. Peel onions. Place in large bowl or crock and cover with water in which salt has been dissolved. Let stand overnight.

Drain vegetables, rinse in cold water and drain.

Tie spices in square of cheesecloth. Boil with vinegar and sugar 5 minutes.

Add vegetables and boil 3 minutes. Remove spice bag.

Pack vegetables in hot sterile jars. Cover with boiling syrup. Seal tightly. Makes about 8 pints.

PICKLED GREEN BEANS

2   to 3 quarts fresh green beans
Salt
1½ cups sugar
2   cups vinegar
2   cups water
¼ cup lemon juice

Cook whole beans in salted water until tender.

Drain and pack in hot, sterilized jars.

Combine remaining ingredients; heat to boiling, simmer 5 minutes. Pour over beans. Seal.

Spiced and Pickled Fruits

SPICED FRUIT
(Master Recipe)

1/2 peck fruit
Whole cloves
3 cups vinegar
3 pounds brown sugar
1 ounce stick cinnamon

Use peaches, pears, crabapples, or apples. Select fine, firm fruit.

Remove skin from peaches or pears, leaving the fruit whole.

With crabapples, the skin and stem should be left on but the fruit carefully washed and cleaned.

Remove skin from apples. Cut into quarters or eighths, depending on size of apples.

If using more than one variety of fruit do not combine. Pickle each kind separately.

Place 3 or 4 cloves in each piece of fruit. To help retain shape of fruit, cook until tender a few pieces at a time in vinegar, sugar, and cinnamon syrup.

Place in sterilized jars. Fill with syrup. Seal.

WATERMELON PICKLES

4 pounds prepared watermelon rind
Limewater
2 tablespoons whole allspice
2 tablespoons whole cloves
10 2-inch pieces stick cinnamon
1 1/2 quarts white vinegar
1 lemon, sliced thin
1 quart water
4 1/2 pounds sugar

To prepare melon, pare skin and pink flesh. Cut into 1 1/2 to 2-inch squares.

Soak for 2 1/2 hours in limewater made with 2 quarts cold water and 2 tablespoons lime of calcium oxide, purchased from the drug store.

Drain, cover with fresh water, and cook until tender, about 1 1/2 hours, adding more water as needed. Let stand several hours or overnight. Drain.

Put spices in cheesecloth bag, tying loosely. Bring to boil spices, vinegar, lemon, water, and sugar.

Add rind and boil slowly for 2 hours, or until syrup is fairly thick.

Remove spice bag. Pack pickles in clean, hot jars; fill with boiling syrup, and seal.

WHOLE PICKLED GRAPES

Select bunches of grapes of the same size and ripeness. Any type of grape may be used, but they should not be overripe.

Leave grapes on stems and, after washing and drying, pack the bunches closely into clean glass jars. To avoid bruising, do not pack tightly.

Prepare syrup of 1 1/2 cups sugar to each cup white vinegar. Boil 5 minutes. Pour over grapes to fill jars. Seal.

PICKLED PEACHES

8 pounds small or medium-sized peaches
2 tablespoons whole cloves
8 two-inch pieces stick cinnamon
2 pounds sugar
1 quart vinegar

Wash and pare peaches; stick 2 cloves in each peach. Or put cloves and cinnamon loosely in a clean, thin white cloth and tie top tightly. Cook together spices, sugar, and vinegar for 10 minutes. Add peaches; cook slowly until tender, but not broken. Let stand overnight.

In the morning, remove spices if they have been cooked in a bag. Drain syrup from peaches; boil syrup rapidly until thickened.

Pack peaches in clean, hot, sterile jars. Pour hot syrup over peaches, filling jars to top. Seal tightly.

Keep in a cool place several weeks before serving to blend flavor. Makes about 6 pints.

BRANDIED CHERRIES

Select ripe, large white or red cherries. Wash and drain. Cut stems short. Pack into wide-mouthed quart bottles.

To each quart container, allow 1/4 cup granulated sugar, alternating layers of cherries and sugar until the jars are 3/4 full.

Fill to brim with brandy, using about 1 cup for each quart. Seal securely.

Turn jars upside down, and turn them end for end again every hour for 4 consecutive hours, so as to mix sugar and brandy.

Then store in a cool, dry, dark place at least 3 months before using.

PICKLED SWEET CHERRIES

Fill clean fruit jars with large sweet cherries, leaving the stems on. Pack the fruit as closely as possible.

Mix together 1 tablespoon salt and 1 cup vinegar for each quart of cherries and pour over fruit.

Fill each jar with cold water and seal. Allow the cherries to stand in this brine for at least 2 weeks before opening any of the jars.

Pickled cherries are an excellent garnish and accompaniment for meats.

SPICED CRANBERRIES

2 cups sugar
1/2 cup vinegar
3/4 teaspoon whole cloves
3 inches stick cinnamon
4 cups cranberries

Combine sugar, vinegar, and spices. Bring to boiling point.

Add cranberries and cook slowly, without stirring, until skins pop open. Pack in clean, hot jars. Fill with syrup. Seal.

PICKLED CRABAPPLES OR SECKEL PEARS

7 pounds crabapples or seckel pears
1 quart white vinegar
8 cups sugar
1/4 cup whole cloves
1 stick cinnamon
1 1/2 teaspoons whole ginger

Wash and remove blossom ends from fruit. Prick each piece several times.

Heat vinegar and sugar to boiling. Add spices tied loosely in a cheesecloth bag. Add fruit and boil gently until tender but not broken. Remove spice bag.

Quickly pack one hot sterilized jar at a time. Fill to 1/8 inch from top. Be sure vinegar solution covers the fruit. Seal each jar at once. Makes 6 pints.

Relishes

CORN RELISH

1/2 cup flour
1 tablespoon turmeric
1/4 cup dry mustard
6 cups corn, cut from cob
2 red peppers, chopped
1 cup chopped cabbage
4 onions, chopped
1 quart vinegar
2 tablespoons salt
2 cups sugar
1 1/2 tablespoons celery seed

Blend flour, turmeric, and mustard to a paste with a little of the vinegar.

Mix all ingredients and simmer for 45 minutes, stirring frequently to prevent scorching. Seal in clean, hot jars.

INDIA RELISH

12 large green tomatoes
1 red pepper
1 green pepper
4 large onions
1 tablespoon salt
1 cup dark corn syrup
1 cup vinegar
1 tablespoon mustard seed
1 tablespoon celery seed

Put the tomatoes, peppers, and onions through food chopper, using coarse knife.

Drain well, reserving juice for soup or beverage.

Add remaining ingredients and mix well. Cook gently until vegetables are tender and mixture is thick, about 15 minutes.

Turn into hot, sterilized jars, filling to 1/2 inch from top. Seal at once. Makes 3 pints.

CHUTNEY

Chutney is a highly seasoned relish made in many different ways. It originated in India and is served with curries. It is often based on mangoes, but homemade chutneys include tomatoes, peppers, apples, pears, peaches, and other fruits. The following is a popular version.

12 green tomatoes, peeled
6 sweet red peppers, chopped
1 hot red pepper, chopped (optional)
1 cup chopped onion
½ cup chopped celery
2 tablespoons salt
1 pint vinegar
2 cups white or brown sugar
3 tablespoons whole mixed pickling spice
1 tablespoon ginger root
6 sour apples, peeled and chopped
½ pound seedless raisins (optional)

Mix vegetables with salt and let stand overnight.

Add remaining ingredients and cook, stirring often, until mixture is thick and clear.

Pour into sterile, hot, jars and seal. Makes about 3 pints.

CHILI SAUCE

7 pounds ripe tomatoes, cored and peeled
½ pound sweet green peppers
½ pound sweet red peppers
1 cup chopped onion
1 tablespoon salt
1 bay leaf
1 tablespoon celery seed
½ teaspoon whole cloves
½ teaspoon whole allspice
1 teaspoon mustard seed
½ cup sugar
1½ cups vinegar

Chop all vegetables. Add salt and spices that have been tied in a piece of cheesecloth.

Simmer until mixture begins to thicken, stirring occasionally.

Add sugar and vinegar and cook, stirring often, until mixture is a thick sauce. Remove spice bag.

Pack into hot, sterile jars and seal. Makes about 3 pints.

PEPPER-ONION RELISH

1 quart finely chopped onion
2 cups finely chopped sweet red pepper
2 cups finely chopped green pepper
1 cup sugar
1 quart vinegar
4 teaspoons salt

Combine all ingredients and bring slowly to boil. Cook until slightly thickened.

Pour into clean, hot, sterile jars. Fill jars to top; seal tightly.

TOMATO KETCHUP

6 quarts sliced red tomatoes (about 9 pounds)
4 red peppers
5 large onions
1 stalk celery
1 cup cider vinegar
1½ cups sugar
2 tablespoons salt
¼ cup whole mixed pickling spices

Simmer sliced tomatoes until soft, about ½ hour. Place in sieve or colander. Drain off juice.

Put peppers, onions, and celery through food chopper. Add to tomato pulp.

Simmer 1 hour and press through fine sieve.

Add vinegar, sugar, salt and spices tied in a cheesecloth bag. Simmer 1½ to 2 hours, or until thick.

Turn into hot, sterilized jars. Seal at once. Makes about 2 pints.

Note: Use drained juice for beverage or bottle for future use.

PEACH CHUTNEY

2 quarts sliced peaches
2 cups vinegar
1 cup brown sugar
1 cup white raisins
1 medium onion, chopped
1 green pepper, chopped
1 clove garlic, minced (optional)
¼ cup chopped candied ginger
2 teaspoons salt
⅛ teaspoon cayenne pepper

Combine ingredients. Simmer until thick, stirring frequently.

Seal in sterilized jars. Makes 2 pints.

PICCALILLI

Originally from India, hence piccalilli is often called Indian pickle.

1 quart chopped green tomatoes
2 medium-sized sweet red peppers, chopped
2 medium-sized sweet green peppers, chopped
2 large mild onions, chopped
1 small head cabbage, chopped
½ cup salt
3 cups vinegar
1 pound (2 cups firmly packed) brown sugar
1 teaspoon mustard, or 2 tablespoons mixed pickle spices, tied in cheesecloth bag

Combine the vegetables, cover with salt and let stand overnight.

Drain and press in a clean, thin white cloth to remove all the liquid possible.

Add the vinegar, sugar, and spices and simmer until clear.

Discard spice bag and pack into clean, hot, sterile jars. Fill jars to top, seal tightly. Makes about 3 pints.

SWEET CHUTNEY

2 pounds cooking apples
1 pound sugar
1 pound seedless raisins
1 ounce red chilies
1 ounce garlic, ground
1 ounce ginger, minced
½ tablespoon salt
½ pint vinegar

Peel and core apples and chop coarsely.

Combine all ingredients in a pan, simmer gently and stir occasionally until the chutney thickens. Put into jars and, when cold, cover tightly.

CRANBERRY GRAPE RELISH

With fork, break up contents of 1-pound can whole cranberry sauce, chilled. Add 1 teaspoon grated orange rind and ½ cup seedless grapes, cut in half.

CRANBERRY ORANGE RELISH

4 cups (1 pound) fresh cranberries
2 oranges, quartered and seeded
2 cups sugar

Put cranberries and oranges (including the rind) through the food grinder (coarse blade). Stir in the sugar and chill. Makes 2 cups. Keeps well for weeks stored in the refrigerator.

Note: 4 tablespoons sucaryl solution may be substituted for sugar if desired. **Variations:** (1) To 1 cup basic relish add ¼ cup shredded coconut; (2) To 1 cup basic relish add 1 teaspoon lemon juice and ½ cup thinly sliced celery; (3) To 1 cup basic relish add 2 tablespoons raisins and ¼ cup chopped walnuts; (4) To 1 cup basic relish add ¼ teaspoon ginger and 1 tablespoon slivered lemon or orange rind.

Flair for Family Meals from the Freezer: Simple garnishes and relishes add a "dress-up" touch to family meals. Cranberry relishes, for example, can be frozen in cubes for a quick garnish any time.

PIES
AND
PASTRY

Whether you serve a fruit pie warm from the oven for a family dinner or a party pie from the refrigerator or freezer, you'll find either the quick and convenient or the lavish and lovely types are all popular desserts.

PIE-PASTRY HINTS

Enriched (all-purpose) flour is generally used, although some cooks prefer a special pastry flour.

Use chilled water and be very sparing with it.

Don't overmix. Handle dough as little as possible and as lightly as possible.

Chill after mixing.

Plain pastry, made by the standard method, is tender and flaky. Hot water pastry is tender but has a tendency to crumble. It is somewhat difficult to handle, although some cooks consider it easier to make.

ABOUT EQUIPMENT

A board, rolling pin, a wire pastry blender or blending fork, a measuring cup, knife, and spoon are all that are necessary.

If a pastry blender is not available, use two knives.

A pastry cloth (medium-weight cotton canvas or duck) for the board and stockinette for the rolling pin reduces flour needed to roll dough and makes handling of pastry easier, especially in hot weather.

ABOUT PIE PANS

A standard pie pan with a slanting rim is best.

Pastry will brown more readily on the bottom in a glass baking dish or enamel pan, or in a tin that has grown dark from use than in a new tin or aluminum pan. Glass has the advantage that you can inspect the bottom to see if the crust is thoroughly baked, and it does make a more attractive serving dish.

PIE MAKING AT HIGH ALTITUDES

For general information about high altitude cooking, see **Cooking at High Altitudes.** Pie crust is usually not affected by altitude except for the faster rate of evaporation. Therefore, you may get better results if you add a little more liquid.

PIE FAULTS—
HOW TO OVERCOME THEM

Although you think you have followed directions very carefully for making your pie, it may not turn out as expected. This is not a matter of chance but is caused by something you did or failed to do during the preparation or baking. Study the following chart, note the sections that name any faults of your pie, and try to determine where you have slipped.

Pastry has shrunk:

a. Pastry should be allowed to rest about 10 minutes before trimming and baking.

b. Not letting upper crust extend over rim of pan so that it can be molded into rim with lower crust.

c. Pastry should not be stretched to fit into pan. Fit it loosely and press gently into shape of pan.

Pastry crumbles:

a. Flour and fat over-mixed.

Pastry is tough:

a. Too much water added to flour-fat mixture.

b. Too little fat in proportion to flour.

c. Too much handling and rolling.

d. Too much flour on board. It works into pastry.

e. Pastry over-mixed.

Bumps and bubbles on baked pie shells:

a. Air trapped under pastry when fitted into or over pan.

b. Bottom and sides of crust not pricked with tines of fork before baking.

Pies do not brown:

a. With fruit or custard pies use a glass pie pan or an enamel pan. Try baking such pies at a constant temperature of 400°F. to 425°F.

Bottom crust of filled pie is soggy:

a. Too low a temperature was used.

b. Pastry too damp to begin with.

Fruit pie filling has bubbled over:

a. Not enough thickening with watery fruit.

b. Use a pie vent to form funnel so juice can bubble up but not over, or bind edge of juicy fruit pies with pie tape, strip of gauze, or cloth dipped in cold water. Remove after pie is baked.

c. Make lower crust large enough to fold over edge of fruit.

d. Oven was too hot.

Cream pie filling is runny although the same recipe was used which gave good results at another time:

a. Eggs not as fresh or smaller than usual.

b. Filling may not have been cooked long enough after eggs were added.

c. Occasionally when starch is used for thickening, it is affected by very acid ingredients. This may particularly occur with brown sugar, chocolate, or lemon fillings.

Meringue is tough, shrinks, or "weeps":

a. Oven too slow.

b. Meringue was not spread well out on the edge of outer crust all around.

c. Too much sugar was used or sugar is too coarse.

d. Egg whites may have been under-beaten.

e. Sugar may not have been thoroughly blended into egg whites.

Why butter and margarine are generally not recommended for pastry:

a. Butter and margarine scorch at lower temperature.

b. They contain water and milk solids which do not give as tender crusts as pure fats.

Pastries for Pies

PASTRY FOR DOUBLE-CRUST PIE

For 8-inch 2-crust pie:

- 1½ cups sifted enriched flour
- ¾ teaspoon salt
- ½ cup shortening
- 3 to 4 tablespoons ice water

For 9-inch 2-crust pie:

- 2 cups sifted enriched flour
- 1 teaspoon salt
- ⅔ cup shortening
- 4 to 6 tablespoons ice water

Step 1: Sift together the flour and salt. Cut in the shortening with a pastry blender or blending fork (or two knives used scissors fashion) until pieces are size of small peas.

To make pastry extra tender and flaky, divide shortening in half. Cut in first half until mixture looks like corn meal. Then cut in remaining half until pieces are the size of peas.

Step 2: Sprinkle water, a tablespoon at a time, over part of mixture. Gently mix with a fork and push to one side of bowl. Sprinkle next tablespoon water over dry part; mix lightly and push to moistened part at side. Repeat until all is moistened. Be sparing with water because too much makes pastry tough.

Step 3: Use just enough water to make it possible to gather dough together with the fingers so it cleans the bowl. Chill about ½ hour, if time permits.

Step 4: Divide dough about in half. Use a little more than half for under crust. Use fingers rather than the palm of hand to shape the portion that is to be rolled into a ball. Press lightly and evenly all over to make a smooth circle of dough, round and somewhat flat in shape.

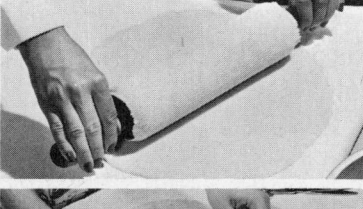

Step 5: Roll dough for bottom crust on lightly floured board or pastry cloth, using a stockinet-covered rolling pin. Roll lightly, but evenly, from center to edges. If edges split, pinch together. Keep it in a circle ⅛ inch thick and large enough to extend ½ inch over edge of pie pan. (Estimate by holding pan over the dough.)

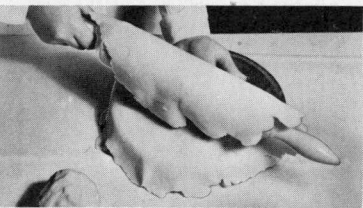

Step 6: Transfer to pie pan folding dough in half for easy transfer to pie pan, or roll it on rolling pin unrolling it into pie pan. Do not stretch pastry but pat and fit it loosely down into pan. It should cover rim of pan well.

Step 7: Trim off overhanging edges with scissors.

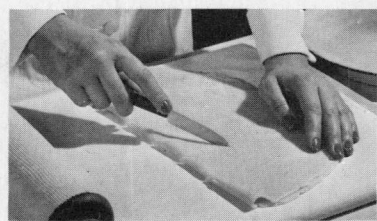

Step 8: Roll second ball of dough as described above. Make several gashes in a design to allow escape of steam. Place filling in pie according to pie recipe used.

Step 9: Place top crust over filling. by rolling it over the rolling pin, transferring to pie pan, and unrolling into place. Crust will not break if this method is used.

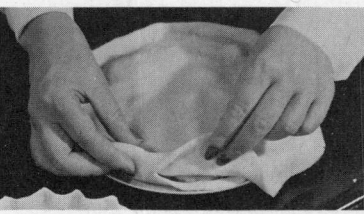

Step 10: Moisten the edge of the lower crust. With scissors, trim the upper crust half an inch beyond edge and tuck it under the edge of the lower crust. Then crimp edges together with fork, spoon, or fingers. Bake according to directions given in recipe for pie.

TO CUT A PIE BEFORE BAKING

1. Outline wedges of pie before baking. For a 2-crust pie, cut slits into top crust using toothpicks and a string as a guide.

2. For a single-crust pie, cut ½-inch strips of pastry. Outline wedges with the pastry instead of making regular lattice top.

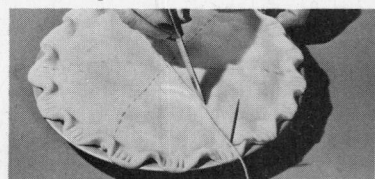

TO MAKE THREE EASY EDGES ON A DOUBLE-CRUST PIE

1. To put a high fluted edge on a pie crust, cut dough off ½ inch beyond rim of pan. Fold under. Then crimp dough between knuckle of left forefinger and thumb and forefinger of right hand.

2. Press edges together with the tines of a fork.

3. For a pretty scalloped edge, press edges together with the tip of a teaspoon.

FLAKY HOT WATER PASTRY

¼ cup boiling water
½ cup lard or vegetable shortening
1½ cups sifted enriched flour
½ teaspoon baking powder
¼ teaspoon salt
1 teaspoon sugar

Pour boiling water over shortening in mixing bowl; stir until smooth and well blended; cool.

Combine remaining dry ingredients in sifter; sift over cooled shortening; stir only enough to mix well. Chill before rolling. Makes 1 8-inch two-crust pie.

EGG PASTRY

2 cups sifted all-purpose flour
1 teaspoon salt
⅔ cup shortening
1 slightly beaten egg
2 tablespoons water
2 teaspoons lemon juice

Mix and sift flour with salt into mixing bowl. Cut in shortening with a pastry blender or 2 knives until particles are the size of small peas.

Combine egg, water, and lemon juice; sprinkle over flour mixture while tossing and stirring lightly with fork until dough is just moist enough to hold together. If necessary add a few more drops water.

Divide in half and form into balls. Roll out one ball on floured surface to a circle 1½ inches larger than inverted 8- or 9-inch pie pan. Fit loosely into pan. Fill with desired filling.

Roll out remaining dough. Cut slits for escape of steam. Place top crust over filling. Bake according to recipe for filling. Makes 2-crust 8- or 9-inch pie.

QUICK OIL PIE CRUST

2 cups sifted enriched flour
½ teaspoon salt
¼ teaspoon baking powder
½ cup vegetable oil
¼ cup water

Sift dry ingredients together.

Combine oil and water and stir lightly.

Toss dry ingredients with a fork while adding liquid ingredients in a small steady stream; work rapidly.

Press dough together; divide into 2 balls and place ball of dough on lightly floured board. Cover with waxed paper to prevent dough from sticking to rolling pin and roll immediately.

Pie Shell: Bake 15 minutes in a hot oven (425°F.).

Two-crust Fruit Pie: Bake 10 minutes in very hot oven (450°F.), then reduce heat to moderate (350°F.) and bake until fruit is tender, usually 25 to 35 minutes.

Makes 2 9-inch pie shells or pastry for 1 9-inch 2-crust pie.

CHEESE PASTRY

To recipe for plain pastry (9-inch double-crust) add 1 tablespoon more shortening.

Combine flour, salt, and shortening with pastry blender, then stir in ⅓ cup grated sharp cheese.

Then add ice water and continue as directed in plain pastry.

This is excellent for apple pies, and it is sometimes used for cherry pies.

SPICED PASTRY

Sift ½ teaspoon cinnamon, ¼ teaspoon ginger, and ¼ teaspoon cloves with the flour and salt in recipe for 2-crust 9-inch plain pastry. Good for apple pie.

BUTTER-CRUST PASTRY

½ cup butter
2 tablespoons sugar
1 cup sifted all-purpose flour

Combine butter, sugar, and flour in small mixing bowl. Using low speed of mixer, mix just until dough forms.

Place ¼ to ⅓ cup of mixture in small pan. With well-floured fingers press remaining mixture evenly over bottom and sides of 9-inch pie pan.

Bake in moderate oven (375°F.) until golden brown, 12 to 15 minutes. Bake the crumbs 10 to 12 minutes.

Cool, then fill with desired filling. Sprinkle top with crumb mixture. Makes a 9-inch pie crust.

Variations: Stir in ¼ cup chopped nuts or packaged flaked coconut before pressing into pie pan.

TO MAKE A LATTICE TOP FOR A FRUIT PIE

Using recipe for 2-crust pie, fit lower crust into pan, cut off pastry to allow ½-inch overhang. With knife or pastry-wheel, cut strips ½ inch wide. Cover pie with half of the strips. Starting at center, fold back every other strip and weave additional strips diagonally across pie, under and over until top is covered. Press ends of strips to rim, fold the overhanging crust up and over and crimp edge. Pastry strips may be woven into lattice on wax paper. Whole lattice may be flipped over onto filling and wax paper peeled off.

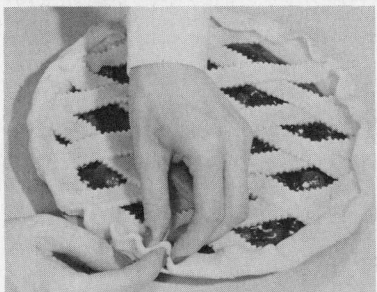

PASTRY FOR SINGLE-CRUST PIE
(Makes 8- or 9-inch shell)

1 cup sifted enriched flour
½ teaspoon salt
⅓ cup shortening
2 to 3 tablespoons ice water

Step 1: Mix and sift flour and salt.

Step 2: Cut in shortening with a pastry blender.

Step 3: Sprinkle with cold water. Gather dough together and press firmly into a ball.

Step 4: Roll out into a circle 1 inch larger than pan, all around.

Step 5: Fit loosely into pan. Avoid stretching to prevent shrinkage.

(**Note:** For precise instructions regarding above steps, see plain pastry for 2-crust pie.)

Step 6: Let pastry rest a few minutes, then fold extra pastry back and under, and build up a high fluted edge even with pan rim.

Step 7: Prick bottom of unfilled shell with fork to keep pastry from puffing up and warping during baking. Bake in very hot oven (450°F.) until delicately browned, 12 to 15 minutes. (After 5 minutes of baking look at pastry shell and quickly collapse any bubbles by pricking.)

Step 8: Cool pastry shell in the pan on a cake rack out of draft before adding filling.

Step 9: Or, if filling and pastry are baked together do not prick the crust. Bake according to recipe directions for the pie.

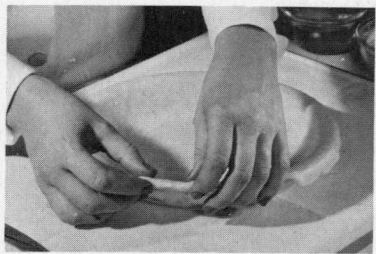

After letting pastry in pan rest a few minutes, fold extra pastry back and under.

Build up a high fluted edge to hold a generous amount of filling.

TO KEEP CRUST FROM SHRINKING WHEN MAKING A PIE SHELL

1. Fit pastry loosely into pan and shape without stretching. Build up fluted edge, then prick all over to prevent puffing up and warping during baking. Let cool, then fill.

2. Pie shells hold to shape and shrink less when baked on the back of the pie pan. Let dough fall loosely over pan and shape without stretching. Crimp edges and prick all over to prevent blistering.

3. Pie shells may be baked between 2 pans of equal size. Fit dough into pan without stretching, trim and press down edges with tines of fork and prick all over. Place second pan on top of dough. After 8 minutes of baking time, remove top pan to allow shell to brown.

HINT FOR CRISPER UNDERCRUSTS

For crisper undercrusts in pumpkin or custard pies freeze unbaked pie shells before you fill them. Brush pastry with a little beaten egg, then place shell in freezing compartment or in food freezer. Before baking, fill frozen shells and place in oven without defrosting.

NUT PASTRY SHELL

Follow recipe for plain pastry for 1-crust pie, adding ¼ cup ground nuts to the flour. This is most frequently used for cream pies.

ORANGE PASTRY SHELL

Follow recipe for plain pastry for 1-crust pie, substituting orange juice for the water, and adding ½ teaspoon grated orange rind. This is used with orange and lemon pies, and sometimes for other pies.

CHOCOLATE PASTRY

1½ cups sifted enriched flour
2½ tablespoons cocoa
2 teaspoons sugar
½ teaspoon salt
½ cup hard lard or vegetable shortening
About 6 tablespoons cold water

Mix and sift flour, cocoa, sugar, and salt.

Cut in lard until mixture is of a coarse consistency.

Add only enough water to hold ingredients together.

Pat pastry into a ball. Chill 1 hour, if time allows.

Roll out and fit into pie pan. Prick with tines of fork to prevent bubbles.

Bake in hot oven (400°F.) about 12 minutes. Makes 1 9-inch pie shell.

MUERBETEIG
(Rich Egg Pastry)

1 cup enriched flour
1 egg yolk
1 tablespoon sugar
½ cup butter or margarine
Grated rind of 1 lemon
Pinch of salt

Sift flour onto a pastry board or into a bowl.

Make a "well" in the center of the flour and put into it the egg yolk, sugar, butter, lemon rind, and salt.

Mix these center ingredients into a smooth paste and then quickly work in the flour, adding a very little ice water to moisten the dough, if necessary.

Press the dough, with the fingers, into a 9-inch pie plate, or chill it for 1 hour in the refrigerator and roll it out ¼ inch thick to fit a spring form pan.

This paste or dough is used for many types of kuchens, fruit pies, and desserts.

Chill the lined pie plate or spring form pan for 30 minutes before covering it with fruit, sugar, and spices. Bake as directed in recipe.

HOW TO USE LEFTOVER PASTRY

Roll out trimmings from pie crusts. Sprinkle with grated cheese, or sugar and cinnamon. Cut in fancy shapes, and bake. Serve with hors d'oeuvres, salads.

Crumb Pie Crusts

GRAHAM CRACKER PIE CRUST (Master Recipe)

1⅓ cups graham cracker crumbs (16 or 18 crackers)
⅓ cup soft butter or margarine
3 tablespoons sugar

Use only crisp crackers. Roll into fine crumbs on waxed paper or in plastic bag. Or crush crumbs in food mill or blender.

Combine and mix dry ingredients, then add butter softened at room temperature. (Don't melt; the softened fat mixes more easily and evenly.)

Blend all ingredients well with pastry blender, blending fork, or your hands.

Turn mixture into a 9-inch pie pan. Using a flat bottomed glass or custard cup, press firmly, making the bottom slightly thicker than the sides. Use the back of a tablespoon to pack crumbs firmly into angles of pan and firmly against sides of pan. Use hands to finish molding crust firmly around rim; make it slightly rounded and at least ¼ inch thick for easier cutting and serving of pie.

Chill thoroughly before using. This crust may be baked in preheated moderate oven (350°F.) for 8 to 10 minutes, which gives a firmer crust and is desirable if a cooked filling rather than an instant pudding or a gelatin filling is used. Chill the baked crust before filling.

Or for a pie to be covered with meringue, pour cold filling into the freshly shaped crust, spread on meringue in usual way, then bake in moderate oven (350°F.) 12 to 15 minutes to brown meringue.

Chocolate Graham Cracker Crust: Follow method for graham cracker crust, using half chocolate wafer crumbs and half graham cracker crumbs.

CRUMB CRUSTS—QUICK WAY

Empty crumb mixture into a 9-inch pie pan and spread evenly across the bottom.

Place an 8-inch pie pan, which has been greased on the outside, on the crumb mixture, and press mixture firmly into an even layer against the bottom and sides.

Remove greased pie pan and chill or bake, as desired.

Use only crisp crackers. Roll into fine crumbs.

To the mixed dry ingredients, add butter softened at room temperature.

Pack crumbs firmly into angles of pan and firmly against sides of pan.

OTHER CRUMB CRUSTS

Chocolate Cooky Crust: Use 1½ cups chocolate cooky crumbs and ⅓ cup soft butter or margarine. Follow method for graham cracker crust.

Corn Flake Crust: Use 1½ cups finely crushed corn flakes (or other ready-to-eat cereal), ⅓ cup sugar, and ⅓ cup soft butter or margarine. Follow method for graham cracker crust.

Gingersnap Crust: Use 1⅓ cups gingersnap crumbs, ⅓ cup soft butter or margarine, and a dash of salt. Follow method for graham cracker crust.

Vanilla Wafer Crust: Use 1⅓ cups vanilla wafer crumbs and ¼ cup soft butter or margarine. Follow method for graham cracker crust.

Zwieback Crust: Use 1¼ cups crumbs, ⅓ cup soft butter or margarine, and 2 tablespoons sugar. Follow method for graham cracker crust.

Other Variations: Almost any crisp cookies may be used in the same way. Some people prefer to use melted butter; in that case grease the pie pan well before spreading the crumb mixture.

If desired, spread only the bottom of the pie pan with cooky crumbs and line sides of pan with whole wafers, cut in halves.

Meringues

MERINGUE TOPPING

This meringue may be used for other desserts as well as pies.

For 9-inch Pie:

3 egg whites
¼ teaspoon salt
6 tablespoons sugar
½ teaspoon flavoring (optional)

For 8-inch Pie:

2 egg whites
¼ teaspoon salt
4 tablespoons sugar
¼ teaspoon flavoring (optional)

Beat egg whites with salt until frothy. (Whites will whip fluffier if they are at room temperature.)

Then beat in sugar, 1 tablespoon at a time. Beat until meringue is stiff and glossy. The meringue is ready for the pie when the sugar has dissolved and the meringue is stiff enough to hold a point, yet still looks moist.

Add ½ teaspoon flavoring, if desired. Beat only enough to blend.

Swirl meringue lightly on pie, sealing to edge of crust to prevent shrinking.

Bake in moderate oven (350°F.) 12 to 15 minutes, until delicately browned.

Always pile meringue thick and high.

Swirl meringue lightly on pie, sealing to edge of crust to prevent shrinkage.

Meringue may be spooned onto filling to make a wreath. Leave in peaks.

MERINGUE SHELLS

    4   egg whites
    1   teaspoon cream of tartar
    1/2 teaspoon salt
    1/2 teaspoon vanilla
    1   cup sifted granulated sugar

(*Note:* Egg whites should be at room temperature to whip up extra fluffy, but eggs should be separated while cold.)

To Mix: Add cream of tartar, salt and vanilla to egg whites in large bowl. Using rotary egg beater or electric mixer, beat egg whites until stiff (mixture holds a peak) but not dry. The stiff peaks are still glossy.

Add sugar gradually, 1 tablespoon at a time. Beat after each addition until well blended and sugar is dissolved. If you taste a little, there should be no sugar crystals.

To Shape and Bake: Line cooky sheet with unglazed brown paper, cut to fit. Trace a heart on it, or other desired shape, using a cardboard pattern or heart-shaped cake pan.

Using a full recipe of meringue, smooth out to edge of pattern with back of tablespoon and build up rim.

Bake meringue heart in very slow oven (250°F.) for 1¼ hours. The heart will be tinged with golden brown. The outside will be crisp, the inside tender and a little moist.

To Serve: Just before serving, fill cooled meringue with ice cream, lemon pie filling, or other desired filling.

Individual Meringues: These may be heart-shaped or round. Drop by spoonfuls on small heart pattern drawn on liner paper or heap in a circle. Hollow out with back of spoon.

Bake individual meringues in slow oven (275°F.) for 50 minutes.

To Freeze Meringues: Place in freezer or freezing compartment of refrigerator. When frozen, wrap in freezer paper and seal.

To serve, remove from freezer and allow to stand at room temperature 30 to 45 minutes.

Heart-Shaped Meringue

Fruit Pies
APPLE PIE (Master Recipe)

Pastry for 9-inch 2-crust pie
    7 to 8 medium-sized tart, juicy apples (2¼ pounds)
    1   tablespoon flour
Dash of salt
    ⅔ to ¾ cup sugar (larger amount for very tart apples)
    1   tablespoon butter or margarine
    1   tablespoon lemon juice (optional)
    ¼   teaspoon cinnamon or nutmeg

Prepare pastry. Roll out bottom crust; line pan and trim off even with pan rim.

Roll out top crust; cut design in center for escape of steam. Cover pastry with waxed paper while preparing filling.

Wash apples, pare, quarter, remove cores, and cut quarters lengthwise into 3 or 4 slices. There should be a full quart (4 cups) of sliced apples, firmly packed.

Blend flour, salt, and sugar; sprinkle ¼ of mixture over bottom of pastry lined pan.

Stir the remaining mixture lightly through apples; turn into pie pan, placing them close together and piling them higher than the rim of the pie pan. Fruit should be slightly rounded in center.

Dot with butter. Sprinkle with lemon juice, then with cinnamon.

Moisten the edge of lower pastry with a little cold water. Then carefully place the pastry for top crust evenly on top of the filling, allowing it to fall loosely in place. Press down gently around edge to seal.

Trim off any extra edges wth a scissors, but leave ½ inch overhanging edge of pan.

Fold the extra edge of top pastry under edge of lower pastry so fold is even with pan rim.

Again press down gently all around edge and flute with the fingers or crimp with the tines of a fork.

Bake in very hot oven (450°F.) 15 minutes, then reduce heat to slow (325°F.) and bake until apples are tender and juice boils out of vents, about 35 minutes. Remove to cake rack to cool.

To Make 8-Inch Pie: Use pastry for 2-crust 8-inch pie, 1½ pounds medium-sized tart juicy apples, 2 teaspoons flour, pinch of salt, 7 tablespoons to ½ cup sugar, 1 teaspoon butter or margarine, 2 teaspoons lemon juice, and a scant ¼ teaspoon cinnamon.

Deep-Dish Apple Pie: Bake ingredients for apple pie above in pastry lined 6½ x 10½-inch oblong baking dish.

Cheese Crumble Apple Pie

CHEESE CRUMBLE APPLE PIE

    1   package pie crust mix
    ½   cup sugar
    ½   cup finely packed brown sugar
    ¾   teaspoon cinnamon
    3   tablespoons butter
    2   cups shredded Cheddar cheese
    3   pounds cooking apples, peeled and sliced
    1   tablespoon flour

For crumble topping: Measure 1 cup of pie crust mix and combine with sugars and cinnamon. Cut in butter thoroughly. Set aside.

Mix 1 cup Cheddar cheese into remaining pie crust mix. Blend with 2 to 2½ tablespoons water. Roll dough and line pie plate.

Place apples in pastry-lined 9-inch pie plate, sprinkling flour evenly through them. Sprinkle with nutmeg and cover with half of crumble mixture.

Sprinkle remaining 1 cup Cheddar cheese over all. Top with remaining crumble mixture. Bake in moderate oven (375°F.) about 40 minutes or until apples are tender.

TO KEEP JUICE FROM BOILING OVER WHEN MAKING FRUIT PIES

1. Cut off lower crust at edge of pan. With scissors, cut off top crust ½ inch beyond edge. Tuck this under the lower crust before crimping. This seals in the juices of the pie.

2. Place 1½-inch pieces of uncooked macaroni or straws in top. The juice boils up into these little "chimneys" instead of boiling over the sides. May be used with a lattice or 2-crust pie.

3. Cut a circular piece of pastry the size of the inside top of the pie pan. When this is placed over the filling, it leaves a narrow opening around the edge and permits the steam to escape—thus the juice does not bubble over the top.

CANNED APPLE PIE

1½ tablespoons quick-cooking tapi-
    oca
¾ cup sugar
⅛ teaspoon salt
¾ teaspoon cinnamon
¼ teaspoon nutmeg
2½ cups (1 can) sliced apples
Pastry for 8-inch double crust pie
2 tablespoons butter or margarine

Mix tapioca, sugar, salt, cinnamon, nutmeg, and apples.

Line pie pan with pastry rolled ⅛ inch thick.

Fill with apple mixture; dot with butter. Moisten edge of pastry.

Cut slits in top crust to permit escape of steam and adjust, opening slits with knife. Bake in hot oven (425°F.) 55 minutes or until syrup boils with heavy bubbles that do not burst.

CANNED PINEAPPLE PIE

1 No. 2½ can pineapple slices or
    3 cups pineapple tidbits
½ cup pineapple juice
3 tablespoons cornstarch
¾ cup sugar
Grated rind and juice of 1 lemon
3 tablespoons butter
Pastry for 2-crust 9-inch pie

Drain pineapple and cut into pieces. Heat juice. Blend cornstarch with sugar and add to hot juice. Cook over low heat until mixture is clear and thickened, stirring constantly. Add lemon juice and rind, butter, and pineapple. Let cool while making pie crust.

Fit lower crust into 9-inch pie pan and fill. Fit on top crust, trim and crimp edges. Cut gashes to allow steam to escape. Bake in hot oven (425°F.) 25 to 30 minutes or until crust is browned.

FRESH PINEAPPLE PIE

2 eggs
1½ cups sugar
1 tablespoon lemon juice
3 cups shredded fresh pineapple
Pastry for 9-inch double crust

Beat eggs slightly and combine with sugar, lemon juice, and pineapple.

Line 9-inch pie pan with pastry; pour in filling. Cover with pastry.

Bake in very hot oven (450°F.) 10 minutes. Reduce heat to moderate (350°F.) and bake 30 minutes, or until crust is nicely browned and pineapple is tender.

Pineapple and Strawberry Pie: Use 1½ cups shredded fresh pineapple and 1½ cups sliced strawberries.

GUAVA PIE

Pastry for 9-inch double crust
2½ pounds ripe guavas
Scant 1 cup sugar
1 tablespoon butter or margarine
Dash of nutmeg

Pare guavas thinly and scoop out seedy part in center. Rub through food mill and discard seeds.

Cut the fleshy guava shells into thin slices and combine with purée. (There should be 3 cups purée and slices.)

Stir sugar into fruit and turn into pastry lined pan. Spread evenly and dot with butter. Sprinkle with nutmeg.

Fit top pastry over filling, sealing well. Bake in very hot oven (450°F.) 15 minutes. Reduce heat to slow oven (325°F.) and bake 30 minutes, or until pastry is lightly browned and fruit is tender. Let cool on rack before cutting.

CONCORD GRAPE PIE

2 pounds (4 cups) Concord grapes
⅔ to ¾ cup sugar
¼ cup flour or 1 tablespoon quick-
    cooking tapioca
⅛ teaspoon salt
Grated rind and juice of ½ lemon
Pastry for 9-inch 2-crust pie

Slip pulp out of grape skins. Reserve skins. Cook pulp until seeds loosen and press through colander or food mill.

Mix sugar, flour or tapioca, salt, lemon rind, and juice. Add grape juice and skins.

If tapioca has been used, let mixture stand 15 minutes.

Turn into pastry lined 9-inch pan and cover with pastry.

Bake on lower rack of very hot oven (450°F.) 15 minutes. Lower heat to moderate (350°F.) and bake about 20 minutes longer.

GALETTE FRUIT PIE

Use 3 cups fruit such as apples, apricots, peaches, and plums. Fresh fruit or cooked or canned fruit may be used.

Line pan with Galette Pastry (below). Fill with fruit. Sprinkle with sugar to taste.

Bake in hot oven (425°F.) about 25 minutes.

GALETTE PASTRY

This sweet, rich pastry, very similar to Muerbeteig, is generally used in France and other European countries for open fruit pies.

1 cup sifted enriched flour
½ teaspoon salt
1 tablespoon sugar
6 tablespoons butter or margarine
1 egg yolk
1 tablespoon water
1½ tablespoons lemon juice or 1½
    tablespoons rum

Mix and sift flour, salt, and sugar. Cut in butter with pastry blender or 2 knives.

Beat egg yolk with water and lemon juice and work into dough with the fingers. Chill thoroughly.

Roll or pat ¼-inch thick to fit 9-inch pie pan or roll ⅛-inch thick to fit 9 x 12-inch pan.

Fill and bake as directed in Galette Fruit Pie.

There are many versions of this classic pastry. Yeast coffee cake dough is often used. After the last rising, pat it out very thin, and make a rim by pinching the edges of the dough all the way around. Fill with the fruit and cover with a streusel topping (see index). Bake as directed for the coffee cake dough.

FRENCH FRUIT TART

About 1⅔ cups vanilla wafer crumbs,
    finely rolled
¼ cup butter or margarine, melted
1 tablespoon instant coffee
5 egg yolks
¾ cup sugar
3 tablespoons flour
2 cups milk
1 teaspoon vanilla
Fresh peaches, pared and sliced
Fresh strawberries, hulled and washed
Fresh blueberries
½ cup red currant jelly

Combine vanilla wafer crumbs and melted butter into which the instant coffee has been stirred. Pour crumb mixture into a 9-inch pie plate pressing crumbs firmly against bottom and sides using an 8-inch pie plate. Bake in moderate oven (375°F.) 8 minutes. Cool.

Beat egg yolks and sugar until thick and lemon-colored. Slowly beat in flour until well blended.

Scald milk with vanilla and stir into egg mixture. Return custard to saucepan and cook over medium heat, stirring constantly until custard thickens and boils. Boil for 1 minute.

Cool in a bowl, covering the surface of the custard with wax paper to prevent a skin forming. Spoon into pie shell. Top custard with the fresh fruit in any pattern you wish.

Melt red currant jelly in a saucepan and brush over the fruit to glaze. Refrigerate until ready to serve. Makes 8 servings.

French Fruit Tart

FRESH BERRY PIE
(Master Recipe)

Pastry for 2-crust 9-inch pie
4 cups (1 quart) fresh berries
7/8 to 1 cup sugar
4 tablespoons flour
2 teaspoons quick-cooking tapioca
1/2 teaspoon cinnamon
1 tablespoon butter or margarine

Use fresh ripe berries (strawberries, raspberries, blueberries, blackberries, or loganberries, etc.). Wash them, pick over, and remove stems and hulls.

Drain and increase or decrease sugar in accordance with sweetness of fruit (up to 1 1/2 cups sugar for 1 quart berries).

Fill pastry lined 9-inch pan with berries, sprinkling them with the sugar-flour mixture. Sprinkle tapioca over when half the berries are in the pan and again toward top.

Sprinkle with cinnamon and dot with butter. If fruit is dry, sprinkle with 1 to 2 tablespoons water. Cover with top crust.

Bake in very hot oven (450°F.) 10 minutes, then in moderate oven (350°F.) about 30 minutes, until crust is nicely browned and berries are cooked through. Serve slightly warm, not hot.

CANNED BERRY PIE
(Master Recipe)

Pastry for 9-inch double crust
2 2/3 cups canned berries
1/2 to 3/4 cup sugar
4 tablespoons flour
1/2 teaspoon cinnamon (optional)
1 tablespoon butter or margarine
1/2 cup juice from berries

Drain berries well. Taste juice and use minimum amount of sugar.

Mix sugar and flour; sprinkle 1/2 of it over chilled pastry in 9-inch pan.

Add berries, sprinkling remaining flour and sugar through them. Sprinkle with cinnamon. Dot with butter. Add juice. Quickly cover with top crust.

Bake in very hot oven (450°F.) 15 minutes, then about 20 minutes in moderate oven (350°F.) until nicely browned. Serve slightly warm, not hot.

Deep Dish Strawberry Pie

FROZEN BERRY PIE
(Master Recipe)

Pastry for 9-inch double crust
1 quart sugar packed berries, thawed
4 tablespoons flour
2 tablespoons butter or margarine

Line a 9-inch pie pan with pastry. Berries should be thawed enough to separate fruit easily.

Sprinkle 1 tablespoon flour over bottom of pastry shell.

Blend remaining flour with some of the berry juice, making a smooth paste. Stir into remaining berries and juice.

Fill pastry lined pan. Dot with butter. Cover with top crust.

Bake in very hot oven (450°F.) 15 minutes. Reduce heat to moderate (375°F.) and bake 20 minutes longer.

Note: If unsweetened berries are used, add 1/2 to 1 cup sugar to them as in master recipe.

If syrup-packed berries are used, pour off syrup after thawing, measure 1/3 cup syrup and add to 1 quart drained berries. Add no sugar.

STRAWBERRY GLAZE PIE

1 9-inch baked pie shell
3 1/2 cups (1 quart) fresh hulled strawberries
3/4 cup sugar
2 tablespoons cornstarch
1/4 teaspoon salt
1 cup water

Line baked shell with strawberries.

Combine sugar, cornstarch, salt, and water. Cook over low heat slowly until thickened and clear, about 10 to 15 minutes.

Pour glaze over strawberries. Chill. Just before serving, garnish with whipped cream and whole berries.

Peach or Raspberry Glaze Pie: Fresh sliced peaches or whole raspberries may be substituted for strawberries, if desired.

DEEP DISH STRAWBERRY PIE

1/2 to 1 cup sugar (depending on sweetness of berries)
1/4 cup flour
1/8 teaspoon salt
4 cups washed and hulled strawberries
2 tablespoons butter
Pastry for 2-crust 9-inch pie

Mix sugar with flour and salt. Toss lightly with the berries. Fill a 1-quart baking dish with the fruit mixture and dot with butter.

Top with the pastry which has been rolled out on pastry cloth to size 1 inch larger all around than top of baking dish. Fold edges of pastry under and press firmly to rim of dish.

Flute edges and cut gashes in pastry to allow steam to escape.

Bake in hot oven (425°F.) 25 minutes or until crust is browned. Serve slightly warm with plain or whipped cream.

FRESH CHERRY PIE

Pastry for double crust 9-inch pie
1 quart cherries, pitted
1 cup sugar (1 1/4 cups for very sour cherries)
1/4 teaspoon salt
2 tablespoons cornstarch or 2 1/2 tablespoons tapioca
2 tablespoons butter or margarine

Combine sugar, salt, and cornstarch. Add to the pitted cherries. Place fruit in pastry lined pie plate. Dot with butter.

Cover with top crust, slashed toward the center to allow for escape of steam. Press the edges of the two crusts together tightly, so that the juices will not run out.

If a glaze is wanted, brush the top pastry with milk or cream.

Bake in very hot oven (450°F.) 15 minutes, then reduce heat to 350°F. and bake about 30 minutes longer.

CANNED CHERRY PIE

Pastry for 9-inch double crust
2 No. 2 cans or 3 cups unsweetened cherries
4 tablespoons cornstarch
1/2 cup cherry juice
1 cup sugar
1 tablespoon butter or margarine
1/4 teaspoon salt
1/2 teaspoon almond flavoring

Prepare pastry as directed for 2 crusts.

Drain cherries. Combine cornstarch and cherry juice and bring to boil. Cook, stirring constantly, until thick and clear. Add sugar.

Remove from heat and add butter or margarine, salt, cherries, and almond flavoring, stirring carefully to prevent crushing cherries. Cool.

Fill pie shell. Place top crust over filling. Trim pastry and seal as directed for double-crust pie. Bake in hot oven (425°F.) 35 minutes.

The Liberty Bell topping this fruit pie was made from leftover bits of pastry baked on a cooky sheet.

FROZEN CHERRY PIE

1 quart frozen cherries
Plain pastry for 9-inch double crust
3 tablespoons flour
4 teaspoons cornstarch
1/8 teaspoon salt
2/3 cup sugar
3/4 cup cherry juice, drained from cherries
1 tablespoon butter or margarine
Few drops red food coloring (optional)

Thaw cherries and drain; there should be 1 1/4 to 1 1/3 cups juice and 3 cups drained cherries.

Make pastry; roll out 1/2 of it and line 9-inch pie pan.

Blend flour, cornstarch, salt, and sugar in 3-quart saucepan. Stir in cherry juice gradually until smooth. (Thicken leftover juice and serve over pie.) Cook and stir until thickened.

Remove from heat; stir in butter, coloring, and cherries. Cool thoroughly, then turn into pastry lined pan, spreading level. Cover with top crust.

Bake in very hot oven (450°F.) 15 minutes, then reduce heat to moderate (350°F.) and bake 25 minutes longer, or until nicely browned. Remove to cake rack to cool.

LATTICE CANNED CHERRY PIE

Plain pastry using 2 cups flour
4 cups canned red cherries, drained
1/2 cup juice
4 tablespoons cornstarch
1 cup sugar
1/4 teaspoon salt
1 tablespoon butter or margarine

Mix cherries, juice, cornstarch, sugar, salt, and dots of butter. Pour into lined 9-inch pie plate.

Roll out remainder of dough and cut into strips. Make a lattice work across top of pie.

Bake in hot oven (425°F.) 10 minutes; continue baking 40 to 45 minutes at 350°F. Cool and serve. Serves 6 to 8.

FRESH APRICOT PIE

3 cups fresh apricots, halved
3 tablespoons flour
3/4 to 1 cup sugar
1/2 teaspoon nutmeg
1 tablespoon lemon juice
1 tablespoon butter or margarine
Pastry for 9-inch double crust

Line a pie plate with pastry. Arrange fresh ripe apricots close together.

Combine flour, sugar, and nutmeg. Sprinkle over fruit. Add sprinklings of lemon juice. Dot with butter.

Cover with top crust, perforated to allow steam to escape.

Bake in hot oven (400°F.) 50 to 60 minutes. May be sprinkled with cinnamon if desired.

DRIED APRICOT PIE

1/2 pound dried apricots
2 cups cold water
1 cup sugar
Water or canned peach syrup
1 1/2 tablespoons cornstarch
1/8 teaspoon salt
1 tablespoon butter or margarine
Pastry using 1 1/2 cups flour

Wash apricots quickly but thoroughly with cold water.

Place in saucepan with water. Cover and let soak at least 2 hours.

Then add 1/2 cup sugar; place over heat, cover and simmer gently about 20 minutes, or until fruit is about tender. Drain off and measure juice; add enough water or peach syrup to make 1 cup.

Blend 1/2 cup sugar with cornstarch and salt; sprinkle 2 tablespoons of mixture over bottom of pastry lined 9-inch pan.

Stir remainder gently into apricots and turn into lined pan. Dot with butter. Cover with lattice top.

Bake in hot oven (425°F.) about 30 minutes, or until crust is nicely browned and juice bubbles up through lattice. Remove to cake rack to cool. Makes 1 9-inch pie.

FRESH PEACH PIE

Pastry for 9-inch double crust
4 cups sliced fresh peaches
1 cup granulated sugar or 1/2 cup brown sugar and 1/2 cup granulated sugar
1/4 teaspoon salt
1 tablespoon flour
2 tablespoons butter or margarine

Fill pastry lined 9-inch pie pan with sliced peaches and cover with mixture of sugar, salt, and flour. Dot with butter. Top with gashed upper crust or lattice strips.

Bake in very hot oven (450°F.) 10 minutes. Reduce heat to moderate (350°F.) and bake about 30 minutes longer.

CANNED PEACH PIE

2 No. 2 1/2 cans peaches, well drained
2/3 cup granulated sugar
1/4 teaspoon salt
1/8 teaspoon nutmeg
1/4 teaspoon cinnamon
1 tablespoon flour
1 tablespoon melted butter or margarine
1 tablespoon lemon juice
Pastry for 9-inch double crust

Thoroughly drain peaches in colander, then slice them. Mix sugar, salt, spices, and flour. Lightly combine with peaches.

Fill pastry lined 9-inch pie pan; drizzle melted butter and lemon juice over top.

Roll remaining pastry thin and cut about 7 2-inch circles. Arrange them on top fruit.

Bake in very hot oven (450°F.) 10 minutes; reduce heat to 350°F. and bake about 30 minutes longer, or until crust is nicely browned. Cool before slicing. (If you wish, bake pastry circles on a cooky sheet in hot oven 5 to 10 minutes, then set them on top the baked pie to avoid overbrowning.)

PERSIMMON PIE

1 8-inch baked pie shell
2 cups persimmon pulp
1/2 cup sugar
1/2 teaspoon mace
1 teaspoon grated lemon rind
2 teaspoons butter or margarine
2 beaten egg yolks
2 stiffly beaten egg whites
4 tablespoons sugar

Press enough sweet, ripe persimmons through a colander to make 2 cups pulp free from seed and skin.

Add sugar mixed with mace and lemon rind and place over low heat. Add butter and beaten egg yolks.

Cook and stir until mixture is slightly thickened. Pour into baked pie shell. Cool.

Cover with meringue made from egg whites and 4 tablespoons sugar. Brown lightly in moderate oven (350°F.).

CONCORD RAISIN PIE

2 cups dark seedless raisins
2 cups bottled grape juice
3 tablespoons vinegar
1/2 cup sugar
3 tablespoons cornstarch
1/4 teaspoon salt
1/3 cup water
2 tablespoons butter or margarine
Pastry for single (9-inch) crust

Combine raisins, grape juice, and vinegar. Heat to boiling, lower heat and simmer 5 minutes. Stir in sugar blended with cornstarch, salt, and water. Add butter. Cook, stirring, until mixture boils and becomes clear and thickened.

Cool slightly. Pour into pastry lined pie pan. Bake in very hot oven (450°F.) 25 to 30 minutes until crust is golden brown.

Serve warm or cold, either plain or with whipped cream. Makes 1 9-inch pie.

Note: Single crust pie may be decorated with a few baked pastry cut-outs, if desired. To make a double crust pie, cover filling with top crust, flute rim and cut a few slits in top.

PRUNE PIE

    2   cups cooked dried prunes
    1   orange
    ½   cup brown sugar
    ¼   teaspoon salt
    2   tablespoons cornstarch
    1   cup liquid from prunes
    2   tablespoons butter or margarine
    1   9-inch baked pastry shell
    2   egg whites
    ¼   cup granulated sugar

Pit prunes and cut in halves. Peel orange and remove inner white peel. Dice the orange.

Combine sugar, salt, and cornstarch. Add prune liquid. Bring to boil and cook, stirring constantly, until thickened.

Add prunes, orange, and butter and cook 10 minutes longer, stirring frequently.

Cool slightly and pour into baked pie shell.

Cover with meringue made by whipping egg whites until stiff and gradually folding in the sugar. Brown in moderate oven (350°F.) about 12 to 15 minutes.

SOUR CREAM PRUNE PIE

    2   whole eggs
    1   egg yolk
    ½   cup brown sugar, firmly packed
    ¼   cup granulated sugar
    1   cup sour cream
    1   cup plumped, chopped prunes
    ⅓   cup prune juice (water in which
        prunes were plumped)
    1   9-inch baked pastry shell

Beat eggs and yolk lightly; stir in sugars and sour cream. Combine with prunes and prune juice in saucepan. Place over medium heat and cook until thickened, about 10 minutes, stirring constantly.

Remove from heat, cool slightly. Pour into baked pastry shell. Cool and top with wreath of meringue.

Meringue: Beat 1 egg white until slightly stiff; gradually add 2 tablespoons brown sugar, beating until stiff. Spoon in wreath around edge of pie. Brown lightly in hot oven (400°F.) 6 minutes.

Sour Cream Prune Pie

CRANBERRY ORANGE PIE

    2   cups sugar
    ¾   cup water
    4   cups fresh cranberries (1 pound)
    ¼   cup cornstarch
    ⅛   teaspoon salt
    2   tablespoons butter
    1   cup orange sections or slices
    Recipe for 9-inch 2-crust pie

Combine sugar and water; bring to boil. Add cranberries and cook over low heat until cranberries begin to pop.

Mix cornstarch to a smooth paste with a little cold water. Add to cranberries and cook over low heat until thickened, stirring constantly. Add salt and butter and allow to cool. Fold in orange.

Fit lower crust in 9-inch pie pan and fill. Cut circle from center of top crust and cover filling. Trim and crimp edges. Bake in hot oven (425°F.) 25 to 30 minutes or until crust is browned.

From leftover pastry, cut leaves and bake on cooky sheet until lightly browned. Just before serving, place leaves on top crust with whole berries for garnish.

CRANBERRY PIE

    2½ cups sugar
    ¾   cup water
    4   cups cranberries
    ¼   cup quick-cooking tapioca
    ¼   teaspoon salt
    2   tablespoons butter or margarine
    1   9-inch unbaked pie shell
    Pastry strips for top

Boil sugar and water 5 minutes; add cranberries and boil until all berries have popped. Cool.

Add tapioca, salt, and butter; let stand 15 minutes.

Fill pastry lined pan with cranberry mixture. Adjust lattice strips on top.

Bake in very hot oven (450°F.) 15 minutes. Reduce heat to moderate (350°F.) and bake 25 minutes longer.

CRANBERRY APPLE PIE

    1   pound can cranberry sauce (whole
        berries)
    2   cups chopped apple
    ½   cup sugar
    ¼   teaspoon salt
    1   teaspoon tapioca
    Pastry for 9-inch double crust

Mix ingredients together in a bowl, then put mixture in a chilled pastry lined pie plate.

Dot with butter, sprinkle with 2 teaspoons grated orange rind and cover with top crust.

Bake in hot oven (400°F.) 30 to 40 minutes, or until done.

Cranberry Orange Pie

RHUBARB PIE

    Pastry for 9-inch shell and strips for
        top
    2   well beaten eggs
    1¾ cups sugar (about)
    ¼   cup enriched flour
    ¼   teaspoon salt
    4   cups sliced rhubarb
    Butter or margarine

Combine eggs, sugar, flour, and salt. Add rhubarb and mix well.

Arrange in pie shell. Dot with butter or margarine.

Top with pastry strips to form a star design.

Bake in very hot oven (450°F.) 15 minutes. Reduce heat to moderate oven (350°F.) and bake 30 minutes longer.

RHUBARB-STRAWBERRY PIE

    Pastry for 9-inch shell and top strips
    3   cups pink rhubarb, cut in ½-inch
        pieces
    1   cup large whole fresh strawber-
        ries
    3   tablespoons butter or margarine
    2   well beaten eggs
    2¼ cups sugar
    4   tablespoons cornstarch

Wash rhubarb; do not peel. Wash and drain strawberries; remove hulls.

Cream butter until soft; add beaten eggs; stir until smooth.

Combine sugar and cornstarch; add to butter-egg mixture; mix well.

Put fruits together in pastry-lined pan; pour egg mixture over.

Adjust crisscross pastry strips for top. Moisten rim with cold water.

Bake at once in very hot oven (450° F.) 10 minutes; reduce heat to 325°F. and bake until filling has thickened and top is nicely browned, about 25 to 30 minutes.

Cool completely before serving. Serve soon after making. This is not a pie to stand and wait for several hours.

Rhubarb-Strawberry Pie

AVOCADO PIE

Graham cracker crust for 9- or 10-inch pie
2 large avocados, sieved
¾ cup lemon juice
1 cup sweetened condensed milk

Prepare crust and chill while mixing filling.

Choose fully ripe avocados, cut in halves, remove seeds, and peel.

Mash to fine pulp or put through sieve. Mix with lemon juice and the sweetened condensed milk.

Fill graham cracker shell and bake in moderate oven (350°F.) 20 minutes. Chill before serving.

CANNED GOOSEBERRY PIE

Pastry for 8-inch double crust
1 tablespoon enriched flour
⅓ to ½ cup sugar
1 No. 303 can (2 cups) gooseberries in heavy syrup
1 tablespoon butter or margarine

Blend flour and sugar in a bowl; turn berries into bowl and stir gently to mix well.

Turn berries into pastry lined 8-inch pan. Dot with butter. Cover with top crust.

Bake in very hot oven (450°F.) 15 minutes; reduce heat to moderate (350°F.) and bake 25 to 30 minutes longer or until nicely browned. Remove to cake rack to cool to lukewarm before serving.

RED CURRANT PIE

Pastry for 9-inch double crust
1 quart red currants
1 cup sugar
2 tablespoons cornstarch
1 tablespoon butter or margarine (optional)

Wash currants carefully through 2 or 3 cold waters. Drain in colander, then strip fruit from stems. There should be about 3½ cups stemmed fruit. Chill thoroughly in refrigerator.

Blend sugar and cornstarch; sprinkle 3 tablespoons of mixture over bottom of pastry lined 9-inch pan.

Turn in chilled currants, leveling surface. Sprinkle rest of sugar mixture over top. Dot with butter. Cover with top crust.

Bake in very hot oven (450°F.) 12 minutes; reduce heat to moderate (350°F.) and bake 25 to 30 minutes longer or until nicely browned and juice bubbles up through vents.

CINNAMON CANDY APPLE PIE

6 medium-sized apples
¾ cup sugar
½ cup water
1 4-ounce package red cinnamon candies
1 tablespoon flour
1 teaspoon lemon juice
1 tablespoon butter or margarine
Pastry for 8-inch 2-crust pie

Pare and slice apples. Combine sugar, water, and cinnamon candies; cook until candies dissolve. Add apples and simmer until apples are red; drain, reserving syrup.

Blend flour with ½ cup cooled syrup; add lemon juice. Pour over apples in pastry lined pie pan. Dot with butter. Cover with top crust.

Bake in very hot oven (450°F.) 10 minutes. Reduce heat to moderate oven (350°F.) and bake 15 minutes longer.

DUTCH APPLE PIE

7 or 8 juicy tart cooking apples
3 tablespoons butter or margarine
¾ cup sugar
½ teaspoon cinnamon, if desired
Unbaked 8-inch pie shell

Streusel Topping:

¾ cup enriched flour
½ teaspoon cinnamon
⅓ cup light brown sugar, firmly packed
⅓ cup butter or margarine

Peel apples; quarter and remove core. Cut each quarter into 4 slices lengthwise.

Melt butter in saucepan; add apples and toss about until each slice is well coated.

Add sugar which may be mixed with cinnamon, and again toss about to distribute through apples.

Arrange apples compactly in pastry lined pan. They should be slightly heaped in center.

Make streusel by mixing flour thoroughly with cinnamon. Stir in brown sugar.

Cream butter until soft and smooth and work in the flour-cinnamon-sugar mixture until well blended. Sprinkle this crumbly mixture over top of pie.

Bake in very hot oven (450°F.) about 20 minutes, or until crust is well browned. Reduce heat to slow oven (325°F.) and continue baking about 30 minutes more, or until apples are translucent and tender. Cool.

VERMONT APPLE PIE

Pastry for 2-crust 9-inch pie
4 cups peeled, sliced apples
½ cup maple syrup
¼ cup sugar
¼ teaspoon salt
3 tablespoons flour
1 tablespoon butter or margarine

Combine all ingredients except butter and let stand while preparing pastry.

Fill unbaked pie shell with fruit mixture. Dot with butter. Slightly moisten edge of bottom crust with cold water.

Roll out top crust, cut slits to let out steam and place it over filling, folding top crust over, then under edge of bottom crust.

Press the two crusts into fluting to make a "crinkle edge." Press lightly so as not to tear pastry.

Bake in moderate oven (375°F.) about 60 minutes, until crust is a light brown. Cool.

NEW ENGLAND BLUEBERRY PIE

1 cup blueberries
1 cup sugar
¾ cup water
2 tablespoons flour
¼ cup water
3 cups blueberries
1 baked 9-inch pastry shell
½ pint heavy cream, whipped, or 1 pint vanilla ice cream

Cook 1 cup blueberries with sugar and ¾ cup water until berries are soft. Put through sieve.

Mix flour and ¼ cup water to a paste and add to sieved blueberry mixture. Cook slowly until thickened. Cool.

Then add to 3 cups uncooked blueberries.

Pour into pastry shell and chill several hours. Serve topped with whipped cream or ice cream.

FROSTED BERRY PIE

1 8-inch crumb crust
1 egg white
1 cup sugar
¼ cup water
Pinch of salt
½ teaspoon cream of tartar
1 teaspoon vanilla
2 cups drained, sliced strawberries

Place unbeaten egg white, sugar, water, salt, and cream of tartar in double boiler.

Cook over boiling water, beating constantly, until mixture thickens and forms peaks, about 7 minutes.

Remove from heat, add vanilla, and continue beating until cool.

Arrange sliced strawberries in crumb crust. Pour filling over fruit. Garnish with whole berries. Chill 1 hour before serving. Serves 6.

Frosted Berry Pie

Miscellaneous Pies

PUMPKIN PIE

For 8-Inch Pie:

½ cup brown sugar
2 teaspoons flour
¼ teaspoon salt
1½ teaspoons pumpkin pie spice
1 cup cooked or canned pumpkin
1 cup evaporated milk
1 slightly beaten egg
4 teaspoons dark molasses

For 9-Inch Pie:

¾ cup brown sugar
1 tablespoon flour
½ teaspoon salt
2¼ teaspoons pumpkin pie spice
1½ cups cooked or canned pumpkin
1½ cups evaporated milk
1 slightly beaten egg
2 tablespoons dark molasses

Mix in a bowl the sugar, flour, salt, and spice. Add pumpkin, evaporated milk, egg, and molasses; stir until smooth.

Pour into pie pan lined with unbaked pastry made with pie crust mix or from pastry recipe.

Bake on center rack in moderate oven (375°F.) about 40 to 45 minutes, until firm.

For a More Mildly Spiced Pumpkin Pie: Omit molasses and pumpkin pie spice. For 8-inch pie, use ¾ teaspoon cinnamon, ¼ teaspoon each of nutmeg and ginger and add 2 teaspoons lemon juice.

For 9-inch pie, use 1 teaspoon cinnamon, ½ teaspoon each of nutmeg and ginger, and add 1 tablespoon lemon juice. Bake as directed above.

Squash Pie: Substitute well drained, mashed, cooked winter squash for pumpkin.

Sweet Potato Pie: Omit molasses and substitute sieved, cooked or canned sweet potatoes for pumpkin.

Reduce sugar for 8-inch pie to ⅓ cup and add 2 teaspoons melted shortening; use ½ cup sugar and 2 tablespoons melted shortening for 9-inch pie.

PECAN PIE

1 9-inch unbaked pie shell
1½ cups dark corn syrup
1 cup brown sugar
¼ cup butter or margarine
¼ teaspoon salt
2 eggs
1 cup pecans

Cook corn syrup and brown sugar together until mixture begins to boil.

Remove from heat; stir in butter or margarine. Add ¼ teaspoon salt. Cool.

Beat eggs and add to syrup mixture.

Pour filling into 9-inch unbaked pastry shell. Sprinkle pecans on top of filling.

Bake in moderate oven (350°F.) about 50 minutes or until done.

MINCEMEAT PIE

2½ to 3 cups mincemeat (homemade or commercial)
½ cup chopped apple, if desired
1 to 2 tablespoons orange juice or brandy
Pastry for 9-inch double crust

Mix mincemeat, apple, and orange juice or brandy. Fill pastry-lined pie pan. Cover with top crust.

Bake in very hot oven (450°F.) about 30 minutes.

MINCEMEAT

1 pound stewing beef
2 cups boiling water
1 teaspoon salt
4 cups chopped apples
½ package seeded raisins
1 package seedless raisins
1 cup ground orange peel
1 cup chopped citron
½ pound chopped suet
1 cup each molasses and sugar
2 cups strong fresh coffee
1 cup cider or fruit juice
1 teaspoon each cinnamon and nutmeg
½ teaspoon each cloves and allspice

Simmer beef with boiling water and salt until very tender. Drain, reserve stock and chop meat.

Combine in large kettle meat with remaining ingredients and a cup of the meat stock. Stir over heat until thoroughly mixed.

Continue cooking over low heat about 2 hours, or until most of the liquid is absorbed. Stir occasionally during cooking and often as mixture thickens.

Pour into hot sterilized jars and seal completely. Makes about 5½ pints.

GREEN TOMATO MINCEMEAT

½ peck (about 5½ pounds) firm green tomatoes
1 pound chopped tart apples
½ cup ground citron
½ cup orange juice
½ cup vinegar
½ cup finely ground veal kidney suet
2½ cups brown sugar
1 teaspoon salt
1 teaspoon whole allspice
1 teaspoon whole cloves
1 teaspoon cracked cinnamon
1 pound dark seedless raisins

Wash tomatoes; remove stems; cut in pieces; put through food chopper.

Put all ingredients except raisins in kettle, tying spices in muslin or cheesecloth bag.

Cook over low heat, stirring frequently, 1 hour.

Add raisins; continue cooking until mixture is thick.

Remove spice bag and discard. Fill hot sterilized jars. Seal at once. Makes about 5½ pints.

WALNUT PIE

½ cup soft butter or margarine
½ cup firmly packed brown sugar
¾ cup granulated sugar
4 well beaten eggs
¼ teaspoon salt
¼ cup light corn syrup
½ cup heavy cream
1½ cups chopped walnuts
1 teaspoon vanilla
1 9-inch unbaked pie shell, chilled

Combine butter or margarine with both sugars in top of large double boiler. Cream until fluffy.

Stir in eggs, salt, corn syrup, and cream. Place over boiling water and cook 5 minutes, stirring constantly. Add walnuts and vanilla.

Pour into pastry lined pie pan. Bake in moderate oven (350°F.) 1 hour.

Cool. Top with ring of whipped cream studded with walnut halves.

LEMON SPONGE PIE

¼ cup melted butter or margarine
1 cup sugar
3 tablespoons flour
3 slightly beaten egg yolks
Juice and grated rind of 1 lemon
1½ cups milk
3 stiffly beaten egg whites
Plain pastry for 9-inch pie shell

Blend butter with sugar and flour; add egg yolks, lemon juice and rind, and milk.

Fold in egg whites and pour into 9-inch pastry lined pie pan.

Bake in very hot oven (450°F.) 8 minutes. Reduce heat to slow oven (325°F.) and bake 25 minutes.

To make the stars in this mincemeat pie, cut through the top crust with a star cooky cutter after placing the crust in place, but do not remove the stars. This will allow steam to escape.

Lemon Angel Pie

LEMON ANGEL PIE

4 egg yolks
¾ cup sugar
¼ cup fresh lemon juice
1 tablespoon butter or margarine
2 egg whites, stiffly beaten
1 8-inch baked pie shell

Cream egg yolks and sugar together thoroughly. Add lemon juice and cook in double boiler until thickened (about 10 minutes), stirring often. Add butter.

Remove from heat and fold in beaten egg whites. Pour into an 8-inch baked pie shell.

Top with lemon-flavored meringue made with 2 remaining egg whites. Brown in slow oven (325°F.) for 15 minutes.

Lemon Meringue: Add 4 tablespoons sugar gradually to 2 egg whites which have been beaten until frothy, and continue beating until egg holds its shape in peaks. Fold in 1 teaspoon lemon juice.

LEMON MERINGUE PIE #2

6 tablespoons cornstarch
¼ teaspoon salt
1 cup sugar
2 cups water
3 egg yolks
2 tablespoons butter or margarine
1½ teaspoons grated lemon rind
5 tablespoons lemon juice
3 egg whites
¼ teaspoon cream of tartar
6 tablespoons sugar
1 baked 9-inch pie shell

Combine cornstarch, salt, and ½ cup sugar in top of double boiler; gradually add water.

Place over boiling water and cook, stirring constantly, until mixture thickens. Cover and cook 10 minutes, stirring occasionally.

Stir small amount of hot mixture into egg yolks which have been mixed with remaining ½ cup sugar. Immediately pour back into remaining hot mixture over boiling water. Blend thoroughly and cook 2 minutes longer, stirring constantly.

Remove from heat; add butter, lemon juice, and rind. Cool to room temperature without stirring. Pour into pie shell.

Add cream of tartar to egg whites and beat until frothy. Gradually beat in sugar and continue beating until mixture is stiff and glossy.

Spread meringue lightly on filling, sealing edges to crust. Bake in hot oven (400°F.) until delicately browned, 8 to 10 minutes.

KEY LIME PIE

4 eggs, separated
1 can (15-ounce) sweetened condensed milk
⅓ cup lime juice
1 teaspoon grated lime rind
1 baked 9-inch pie shell

Beat 4 egg yolks and 1 egg white together until light colored and thick.

Add milk and beat thoroughly. Add lime juice and rind and stir until mixture thickens.

Fold in remaining egg whites which have been beaten stiff. Turn into baked pie shell.

Bake in slow oven (325°F.) about 15 to 20 minutes or until set.

Decorate edge of pie with chocolate kisses, if desired.

ICE CREAM PARFAIT PIES (Master Recipe)

1¼ cups hot fruit juice or water
1 package fruit-flavored gelatin
1 pint ice cream
1 to 1½ cups drained fruit or berries (optional)
1 baked 8- or 9-inch pie shell

Prepare 8- or 9-inch pie shell with pie crust mix or plain pastry. Bake and cool.

Heat liquid to boiling in 2-quart saucepan. Remove from heat. Add gelatin; stir until dissolved.

Add ice cream, cut into pieces, to hot liquid; immediately stir until melted. Chill until mixture is thickened but not set, 10 to 35 minutes.

Fold in drained fruit, if desired. Turn into cooled, baked pie shell. Chill until set, 10 to 30 minutes.

STRAWBERRY PARFAIT PIE

Follow master recipe. Prepare 1½ cups sliced fresh strawberries; sweeten if desired. Drain well; reserve juice. (One package frozen strawberries, thawed and drained, may be substituted.)

Fold the fruit into parfait made with 1¼ cups liquid (reserved strawberry juice plus water), 1 package lemon-flavored gelatin, and 1 pint vanilla ice cream.

PEACH PARFAIT PIE

Follow master recipe, using an 8-inch baked pie shell, 1 package strawberry gelatin, 1¼ cups hot water, 1 pint vanilla ice cream, and 1 cup thoroughly drained, sweetened sliced peaches, fresh or frozen. Garnish pie with whipped cream and additional peaches, if desired.

SHOO-FLY PIE

A Pennsylvania Dutch single-crust pie with a cake-like filling, topped with crumbs made of flour, sugar, and shortening.

¼ cup sifted enriched flour
½ cup sugar
⅛ teaspoon salt
3 tablespoons shortening
1 egg
⅓ cup molasses
2 tablespoons boiling water
½ teaspoon baking soda
1 unbaked 9-inch pie shell

Mix flour, sugar, salt, and shortening together until crumbs are formed.

Beat egg until light and fluffy. Add egg to molasses, boiling water, and soda, and beat until soda is dissolved.

Add all but ¼ cup crumb mixture to molasses mixture and stir until well blended. Pour into pastry lined pan. Sprinkle top with reserved crumbs.

Bake in moderate oven (375°F.) 35 minutes.

LIME ANGEL PIE

3 eggs, separated
¼ teaspoon cream of tartar
1½ cups sugar
⅛ teaspoon salt
½ cup lime juice
1 teaspoon grated lime rind
1 cup heavy cream

Beat egg whites until frothy; add cream of tartar and 1 cup sugar gradually, beating constantly. Continue beating until stiff.

Spread egg white mixture evenly over bottom and sides of greased 9 inch pie pan. Bake in very slow oven (275°F.) for 1 hour. Cool thoroughly.

Beat egg yolks slightly; add ½ cup sugar, salt, lime juice, and lime rind. Cook over medium heat, stirring constantly, until thickened. Cool thoroughly.

Beat cream until stiff. Fold into lime mixture. Cool thoroughly. Pour into meringue shell and chill until firm.

Strawberry Parfait Pie

GREEN TOMATO PIE

Pastry for 9-inch lower crust and narrow strips for top
1 quart sliced green tomatoes
Boiling water
1¼ cups sugar
¼ teaspoon salt
3 tablespoons flour
¼ teaspoon ground nutmeg
Small pinch ground cloves
Grated rind and juice of 1 medium lemon
2 tablespoons water
2 tablespoons butter or margarine

Line deep pie pan with pastry. Cut strips for lattice top.

Wash tomatoes; do not peel. Slice ⅛ inch thick into bowl. Pour on boiling water to cover; let stand 5 minutes. Drain.

Stir sugar, salt, flour, and spices until well mixed. Combine lemon rind, lemon juice, and water.

Fill pastry lined pan with layers of tomato slices, sprinkling each layer with sugar mixture and dotting each layer with butter.

When pan is filled, pour lemon mixture over top. Arrange pastry strips to make a lattice top over filling. Moisten rim of pastry with cold water.

Bake in very hot oven (450°F.) 8 to 10 minutes to set crust; reduce heat to moderate (375°F.) and bake until tomatoes are tender, about 40 minutes. Or, bake at 425°F. about 50 minutes. Cool pie completely before serving.

PINEAPPLE SPONGE PIE

3 eggs, separated
1 teaspoon grated lemon rind
3 tablespoons lemon juice
1 cup sugar
3 tablespoons flour
½ teaspoon salt
1 cup pineapple chunks
1 cup hot milk
⅛ teaspoon salt
18 pineapple chunks
6 maraschino cherries
Plain pastry for 10-inch pie shell

Add grated lemon rind and lemon juice to egg yolks and beat until light.

Sift sugar, 3 tablespoons flour, and ½ teaspoon salt together and stir into egg mixture.

Cut pineapple chunks into smaller pieces and add to egg mixture. Stir in hot milk.

Add ⅛ teaspoon salt to egg whites and beat until stiff. Carefully fold egg whites into rest of mixture. Pour into 10-inch unbaked crust.

Bake in hot oven (425°F.) 10 minutes. Lower temperature to 350°F. and continue baking about 35 minutes longer.

Cool pie before serving and garnish with pineapple chunks and maraschino cherries.

CHOCOLATE BROWNIE PIE

Pastry for 1 9-inch pie crust
2 squares (2 ounces) unsweetened chocolate
2 tablespoons butter or margarine
3 large eggs
½ cup sugar
¾ cup dark corn syrup
¾ cup pecan halves

Melt together over hot water the unsweetened chocolate and butter.

Beat eggs, sugar, chocolate mixture, and corn syrup thoroughly with rotary beater.

Mix in pecan halves. Pour into pastry lined pan.

Bake in moderate oven (375°F.) 45 to 50 minutes, just until set.

Serve slightly warm or cold garnished with ice cream or whipped cream.

Note: To use cocoa, omit chocolate and sift ½ cup cocoa with sugar. Then add ¼ cup melted butter to egg and sugar mixture.

MAGIC LEMON PIE

1 crumb or baked pastry 8-inch pie shell
1⅓ cups (15-ounce can) sweetened condensed milk
½ cup lemon juice
1 teaspoon grated lemon rind or ¼ teaspoon lemon extract
2 eggs, separated
¼ teaspoon cream of tartar, if desired
4 tablespoons sugar

Put condensed milk, lemon juice, lemon rind or extract, and egg yolks into mixing bowl; stir until mixture thickens. Pour into chilled crumb crust or cooled pastry shell.

Add cream of tartar to egg whites; beat until almost stiff enough to hold a peak. Add sugar gradually, beating until stiff and glossy but not dry. Pile lightly on pie filling.

Bake in slow oven (325°F.) until lightly browned, about 15 minutes. Cool.

GRAPEFRUIT PIE

1⅓ cups (15-ounce can) sweetened condensed milk
¼ cup lemon juice
1 teaspoon grated grapefruit rind
1 cup grapefruit segments
1 8-inch baked pastry shell
2 egg whites, beaten stiff with ¼ cup sugar
½ cup coconut, if desired

Stir together condensed milk, lemon juice, and grapefruit rind. Filling will thicken as though cooked. Add grapefruit.

Pour into the baked pastry shell. Cover with meringue made from the egg whites and sugar. Sprinkle with co-

conut, if desired. Brown in oven. Chill and serve.

MOLASSES PIE

Plain pastry for 8-inch pie shell
½ cup broken pecans
3 eggs
1 tablespoon flour
1 cup sugar
1 cup molasses
2 tablespoons melted butter or margarine
Pinch of salt

Sprinkle nuts on the bottom of pastry lined 8-inch pan.

Beat eggs, flour, and sugar together until well combined. Add molasses, melted butter, and salt; mix thoroughly. Pour over nuts in pan.

Bake in very hot oven (450°F.) 10 minutes. Reduce heat to slow oven (300°F.) and bake 30 minutes.

Cool and top with whipped cream, if desired.

ALOHA PIE

1 9-inch baked pastry shell
1 No. 2 can pineapple chunks
⅔ cup sugar
2 tablespoons cornstarch
¼ teaspoon salt
2 eggs
1 cup milk
2 tablespoons butter or margarine
½ teaspoon vanilla
3 drops green food coloring

Drain pineapple chunks, reserving syrup.

Combine in saucepan the sugar, cornstarch, salt, and eggs; stir in milk and ⅓ cup of pineapple syrup. Cook over medium heat 5 minutes, stirring constantly, until mixture thickens.

Remove from heat and add butter or margarine, vanilla, and food coloring. Beat with electric or rotary beater to smooth. Cool completely.

Pour into baked pastry shell. Spoon glazed pineapple chunks (below) around edge. Wreath with whipped cream. Chill about 2 hours.

Glazed Pineapple Chunks: Combine in saucepan ⅓ cup sugar, 3 tablespoons cornstarch, and ¾ cup pineapple syrup.

Cook on medium heat for 5 minutes, or until thickened and clear.

Remove from heat, stir in 2 drops yellow food color. Fold in 1⅔ cups pineapple chunks. Cool.

Aloha Pie

SWEET POTATO PIE #2

2 cups mashed, hot sweet potatoes
3 tablespoons melted butter or margarine
1 teaspoon cinnamon
1/2 teaspoon nutmeg
1/2 teaspoon ginger
1¼ teaspoons salt
1/2 cup molasses
1/4 cup orange juice
1 tablespoon grated orange rind
3 well beaten eggs
1 cup milk
Plain pastry for 9-inch pie shell

Mix together ingredients in order given. Turn into unbaked pie shell.

Bake in very hot oven (450°F.) 10 minutes, then reduce heat to moderate (350°F.). Bake until set, about 40 minutes.

Cool. Serve with whipped cream flavored with a dash of cinnamon.

PUMPKIN PIE #2

2/3 cup brown sugar, firmly packed
1 slightly rounded cup cooked or canned pumpkin
1/2 teaspoon salt
2 unbeaten eggs
1 tall can (1⅔ cups) evaporated milk
2 teaspoons cinnamon
1/2 teaspoon ginger
1/4 teaspoon mace
1/4 teaspoon nutmeg
1/3 cup boiling water
1 9-inch unbaked pie shell

Combine brown sugar, pumpkin, salt, and eggs. Mix well. Gradually add evaporated milk.

Mix spices together and add boiling water. Stir this into pumpkin mixture and blend well.

Pour into a 9-inch unbaked pie shell.

Bake in hot oven (400°F.) 35 to 40 minutes. If a glass pie plate is used, bake at 375°F. approximately 55 minutes.

OLD SOUTH SUGAR PIE

1 unbaked 9-inch pie shell
3 eggs
3 cups moist light brown sugar
1/2 cup milk
1/8 teaspoon salt
1 teaspoon vanilla
1/2 cup melted butter

Beat eggs; then beat in brown sugar. Add milk, salt, vanilla, and melted butter.

Pour into pastry lined pan. Bake in very hot oven (450°F.) 10 minutes. Reduce heat to slow oven (325°F.) and bake 25 minutes.

With Pecans: Add 1/2 cup halved pecans before baking.

PECAN PUMPKIN PIE

Plain pastry for 1-crust 9-inch pie
3 slightly beaten eggs
1/2 cup granulated sugar
1/2 cup firmly packed brown sugar
2 tablespoons flour
1/2 teaspoon salt
1 teaspoon cinnamon
1/2 teaspoon nutmeg
1/2 teaspoon allspice
1½ cups pumpkin, cooked or canned
1½ cups light cream, heated
1 tablespoon butter or margarine
2 tablespoons brown sugar
3/4 cup pecan halves

Combine eggs, granulated sugar, brown sugar, flour, salt, cinnamon, nutmeg, and allspice. Add pumpkin; mix well.

Gradually add heated light cream; mix well. Turn into pastry lined pan.

Bake in very hot oven (450°F.) 10 minutes, then at 350°F. 20 minutes.

Melt butter and 2 tablespoons brown sugar together. Add pecan halves and stir until nuts are thoroughly coated.

Remove pie from oven and immediately cover with pecan mixture.

Bake in moderate oven (350°F.) 20 to 30 minutes, until a knife inserted about half way between center and edge of filling comes out clean.

TEXAS PECAN PIE

1 unbaked 9-inch pie shell
1/4 cup butter or margarine
1/2 cup granulated sugar
3 eggs, unbeaten
3/4 cup molasses
Juice of 1 lemon
3/4 cup broken pecans
1/4 cup pecan halves

Line a 9-inch pie pan with pastry. Cream butter and sugar; add eggs, molasses, and lemon juice. Beat with rotary beater.

Add broken pecans and pour into pastry lined pie pan. Place halves around the edges of the crust.

Bake in very hot oven (450°F.) 10 minutes. Then decrease heat to moderate (350°F.) and bake 30 minutes longer.

OATMEAL CRUST FRUIT PIE

1/2 cup sifted enriched flour
1½ cups uncooked oats
2/3 cup brown sugar
1 teaspoon salt
1 teaspoon cinnamon
1/2 cup melted shortening
2½ cups sweetened fruit (sliced peaches, apples, or apricots either fresh or cooked)

Combine dry ingredients; add melted shortening, mixing thoroughly.

Pack all but 1 cup of this mixture firmly in bottom and on sides of a pie plate.

Arrange sliced fruit on top; cover with remaining crumb mixture.

Bake in moderate oven (375°F.) 30 minutes, or until brown. Serve hot or cold, plain or with cream. Serves 6.

PEAR-MINCEMEAT PIE

2 Bosc or Anjou pears
2 cups homemade or commercially canned mincemeat
Pastry for 9-inch double crust

To mincemeat, add pears which have been washed, cored, and diced. Pour into pie shell and cover with lattice crust.

Bake in hot oven (425°F.) for 35 to 45 minutes. Serve warm or cold.

QUANTITY PASTRY MIX

6 cups sifted enriched flour
1 tablespoon salt
2 cups shortening

Sift flour with salt. With a pastry blender, or 2 knives cut in shortening until the mixture is the consistency of small peas.

Store in covered container in a cool place.

For a 9-inch single-crust pie, use 1⅓ cups pastry mix with 1 to 3 tablespoons water.

For a double-crust pie use 2½ cups with 4 to 6 tablespoons water.

Follow directions for handling pastry given in the recipe for plain pastry.

TO KEEP BOTTOM CRUST FROM SOAKING

1. When making custard or pumpkin pie, take a little of the beaten egg and spread over the unbaked crust with pastry brush or back of spoon. Place in refrigerator to let egg dry while making filling.

2. When making fruit pies, combine flour with sugar, salt, and spices. Sprinkle some of this mixture over bottom crust before filling pie. Combine rest of mixture with fruit and toss lightly, so that all fruit is coated.

Cream and Custard Pies

CUSTARD PIE
(Master Recipe)

Plain pastry for one 9-inch pie shell
4   eggs (or 2 eggs and 4 yolks),
      slightly beaten
½   cup sugar
¼   teaspoon salt
½   teaspoon vanilla
½   teaspoon almond extract
2½ cups scalded milk
Nutmeg (optional)

Line 9-inch pie pan with pastry. Be sure there are no bubbles under pastry and no holes in pastry. For best results have pastry slightly thicker than usual. Place in refrigerator while preparing filling.

Blend eggs with sugar, salt, and flavorings.

Slowly pour scalded milk into egg mixture, stirring constantly.

Pour custard mixture into pastry lined 9-inch pie pan. To avoid custard spilling over edges while transferring pie to oven pour in last cup of filling after pie is in position for baking.

Bake in hot oven (400°F.) until knife inserted halfway between outside and center of custard comes out clean, 25 to 30 minutes.

Remove promptly to cooling rack. Do not cut pie until just before serving. If desired, sprinkle surface with nutmeg.

Avoid spills by pouring the last cup of custard pie filling after pie is in position for baking. This is a good trick with cup custards, too.

Test custard pie by inserting knife halfway between outside and center of custard. When done, knife comes out clean.

Custard Pie Variations

Almond Custard Pie: Brown 1 cup chopped blanched almonds in 2 tablespoons of butter in the oven. Sprinkle over bottom of pastry.

Butter Custard Pie: Add 2 tablespoons butter to milk before scalding. Makes a nicely browned top on finished pie.

Coconut Custard Pie: Sprinkle 1 cup finely cut shredded coconut in unbaked pastry shell. Pour custard over coconut. Bake the same as plain custard pie.

Graham Cracker Pastry: Roll out regular pastry. Sprinkle with ⅓ cup fine graham cracker crumbs. Roll crumbs lightly into crust. Place pastry in pie plate—crumb side down. Bake as directed above.

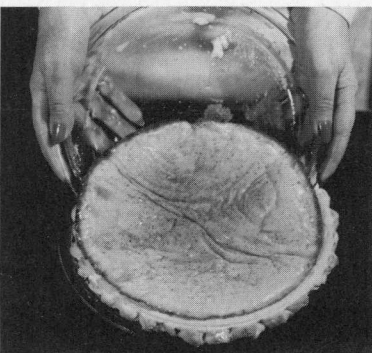

Slip-Slide Custard Pie: A sure way to keep the crust crisp under a delicate custard pie is to bake the custard in a separate pie pan the same size as the baked pie shell.

SLIP-SLIDE CUSTARD PIE

1   baked 9-inch pie shell
4   eggs
½   cup sugar
¼   teaspoon salt
3   cups milk
⅛   teaspoon grated nutmeg

Cool the pie shell in pan in which it was baked. Butter a second pan of the same size.

Beat eggs slightly; add sugar and salt. Add milk. Strain mixture into the buttered pan. Grate nutmeg over top.

Set pie pan in a larger dish in which you have about ½ inch of water.

Bake in very hot oven (450°F.) 10 minutes. Then reduce heat to slow oven (325°F.) and bake until a knife blade inserted in center comes out clean, about 25 to 30 minutes.

Remove from oven. Let custard cool, having loosened the edges after taking from the oven.

Slide the baked custard into the baked pie shell. It works if you have courage, a deft hand, and a firm custard.

Broiled Pineapple Custard Pie

BROILED PINEAPPLE CUSTARD PIE

4   eggs
½   cup sugar
¼   teaspoon salt
¼   teaspoon nutmeg
1   teaspoon vanilla
2   cups light cream
½   cup syrup drained from pineapple
1   unbaked 9-inch pastry shell, fluted
      rim

Topping:
½   cup flaked coconut
3   tablespoons brown sugar
1   tablespoon melted butter
5   pineapple slices

Beat eggs lightly, then beat in sugar, salt, nutmeg, and vanilla. Add cream and pineapple syrup.

Turn mixture into pastry-lined pie pan. Bake on lower shelf in hot oven (425°F.) until filling is barely set in center, about 30 minutes.

Remove pie from oven and let stand 5 to 10 minutes. (Heat contained in pie will continue cooking so center will set.)

Topping: Combine coconut, brown sugar, and butter. Arrange drained pineapple slices on top of pie; sprinkle with topping.

Cover edge of crust with foil to prevent excessive browning. Place pie under broiler a minute or two until topping is bubbly. Remove from oven and cool.

JEFFERSON DAVIS PIE

½   cup butter or margarine
2   cups light brown sugar
4   egg yolks
2   tablespoons sifted enriched flour
1   teaspoon cinnamon
1   teaspoon freshly grated nutmeg
½   teaspoon allspice
1   cup cream
½   cup chopped dates
½   cup raisins
½   cup broken pecan meats
1   9-inch baked pie shell
Meringue

Cream butter and sugar together. Beat in egg yolks.

Mix and sift flour, cinnamon, nutmeg, and allspice. Add to first mixture.

Add cream, dates, raisins, and pecans.

Turn into baked pie shell and bake in moderate oven (375°F.) 35 to 40 minutes, until set.

When cool, cover with meringue and bake as directed in recipe for meringue.

Chocolate-Topped Cream Pie: Fill baked pie shell with vanilla cream filling. Melt one 6-ounce package semi-sweet chocolate bits over hot water and blend in 3 tablespoons light cream or top milk. Spread over cream filling. Top with unsweetened whipped cream at serving time.

MASTER CREAM PIE
(Vanilla Cream Pie)

1 cup sugar
½ cup flour
½ teaspoon salt
2 cups scalded milk
3 eggs, separated
2 tablespoons butter or margarine
1 teaspoon vanilla
1 9-inch baked pastry shell

Mix ⅔ cup sugar, flour, and salt. Gradually stir in milk and set over hot water. Stir until thoroughly thickened.

Cover, and cook 10 minutes, stirring a few times to keep smooth.

Blend a small amount of hot mixture into slightly beaten egg yolks. Combine with mixture in double boiler.

Cook about 2 minutes, stirring constantly. Add butter and vanilla.

Cool slightly. Pour into cooled, baked pastry shell.

Cover with meringue made by gradually beating ⅓ cup sugar into stiffly beaten egg whites.

Bake in moderate oven (350°F.) until lightly browned, about 15 minutes. Chill.

Note: Meringue may be omitted and pie served with whipped cream. If pie is made with only 2 eggs, reduce sugar to ¾ cup.

Variations of Master Cream Pie

Almond Cream Pie: In master cream pie, substitute ⅓ teaspoon almond extract for vanilla.

Add toasted slivered almonds to cooled filling just before pouring into pastry shell.

Top with whipped cream. Garnish with toasted slivered almonds.

Banana Cream Pie: Prepare master cream pie filling. Alternate layers of sliced bananas and cream filling or add 1 cup mashed bananas to cooked filling.

Butterscotch Cream Pie: In master cream pie, substitute ½ cup firmly packed brown sugar for granulated sugar.

Increase butter to 3 tablespoons.

Chocolate Cream Pie: Add 2 ounces (2 squares) chocolate to milk in recipe for master cream pie. When melted, beat until smooth.

Reduce flour to 6 tablespoons. Proceed as for master cream pie.

Chocolate Sponge Pie: Prepare Chocolate Cream Pie Filling.

Fold meringue into filling. Bake as for master cream pie. Chill. Serve with whipped cream.

Coconut Cream Pie: Stir ½ cup shredded coconut into master cream pie filling.

Cover with meringue and sprinkle with coconut before or after browning.

Fruit Cream Pie: Lightly stir 1 cup fresh berries, ½ cup well drained crushed pineapple, 1 cup chopped dates, or 1 cup raisins into cooked master cream pie filling just before turning into baked shell.

Cover with meringue and brown.

VINEGAR PIE

1 9-inch baked pie shell
¼ cup sifted enriched flour
½ cup sugar
1 cup water
Additional ½ cup sugar
3 beaten egg yolks
⅛ teaspoon salt
1 tablespoon butter or margarine
¼ teaspoon lemon extract
3 tablespoons vinegar

Line a 9-inch pie pan with rich pie pastry and bake as usual.

Mix together the flour and ½ cup sugar in top of double boiler. Add water gradually and cook over hot water 15 minutes or until thickened, stirring constantly.

In a bowl combine additional ½ cup sugar with beaten egg yolks and salt. Beat until sugar is dissolved.

Pour first (hot) mixture into this gradually, beating vigorously until blended well.

Return to double boiler; cook over hot water 3 minutes longer or until thick and smooth. Add butter, lemon extract, vinegar. Blend well and cool.

Pour into baked shell; top with meringue; bake in slow oven (325°F.) 15 minutes, or until delicately brown. Serve hot.

STRAWBERRY CREAM PIE

1 cup sugar
6 tablespoons cornstarch
½ teaspoon salt
2½ cups milk, scalded
2 slightly beaten eggs
3 tablespoons butter or margarine
½ teaspoon vanilla
1 9-inch baked pastry shell
1 pint strawberries, sliced
1 cup heavy cream, whipped

Mix sugar, cornstarch, and salt; gradually add milk and cook in double boiler until thick.

Add small amount of hot mixture to eggs; stir into remaining hot mixture. Cook until thick, stirring constantly.

Remove from heat; add butter and vanilla. Chill.

Pour into cooled baked shell. Cover with strawberries. Chill.

Spread with sweetened whipped cream just before serving. Garnish with halved berries.

ORANGE MERINGUE CREAM PIE

1 baked 9-inch pie shell or crumb crust
1 cup sugar
5 tablespoons cornstarch
¼ teaspoon salt
2 cups strained orange juice
4 egg yolks
2 tablespoons butter or margarine
⅓ cup lemon juice
1 tablespoon grated orange rind
4 egg whites

In top of double boiler, stir together ¾ cup sugar, the cornstarch, and salt until well mixed.

Stir in orange juice, keeping mixture smooth.

Place over hot water. Cook, stirring constantly, until mixture thickens and is clear.

Beat egg yolks; add little of hot mixture and stir together. Return to cooked mixture in double boiler; stir and cook until egg yolks thicken, 3 to 5 minutes.

Remove from heat. Stir in butter. Gradually stir in lemon juice and grated orange rind. Cool.

Beat egg whites until stiff but not dry; gradually beat in remaining sugar to make stiff meringue. Fold lightly and carefully into cooled orange filling.

Pour into pie shell; chill until firm.

Whipped cream, lightly sweetened, may be served over top of pie; or, a thin spread of orange marmalade. If marmalade is very thick, thin it down with a little water or fruit juice. Drained fresh orange sections are also a pretty garnish.

Garnish Strawberry Cream Pie with whole or halved berries.

Garnish Banana Chocolate Cream Pie with additional banana slices just before serving.

BANANA CHOCOLATE CREAM PIE

1½ squares (1½ ounces) unsweetened chocolate)
2 cups milk
¾ cup sugar
5 tablespoons flour
½ teaspoon salt
2 egg yolks, slightly beaten
1 tablespoon butter or margarine
½ teaspoon vanilla
1 baked 9-inch pie shell or 6 3½-inch tart shells
3 ripe bananas

Melt chocolate in milk in top of double boiler over rapidly boiling water, beating until blended.

Mix sugar, flour, and salt. Stir into chocolate mixture. Keep stirring and cook until well thickened.

Cook 10 minutes longer, stirring occasionally.

Stir hot mixture into egg yolks. Cook 1 minute. Add butter or margarine and vanilla.

Cool thoroughly. Cover bottom of pie shell with small amount of filling.

Peel bananas and slice into pie shell. Cover with remaining filling.

Top with meringue or sweetened whipped cream, if desired. Makes 1 pie or 6 tarts.

With Pudding Mixes: Packaged commercial pudding mixes of any flavor may be used as filling for this pie. Prepare according to directions on package. Then cool thoroughly and follow the above recipe directions for placing filling and bananas into pie shell.

French Silk Chocolate Pie

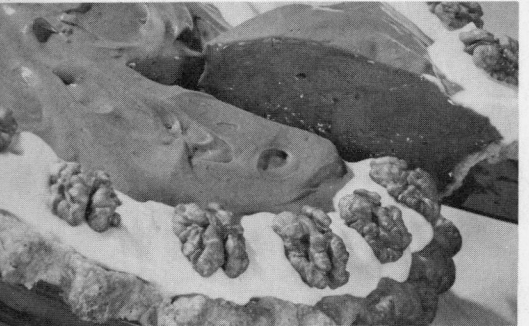

CHOCOLATE CAKE PIE

Plain pastry for 1 9-inch pie shell
1 cup sugar
2 tablespoons enriched flour
Pinch of salt
3 eggs, separated
2 ounces (2 squares) unsweetened chocolate, melted
1 cup rich milk

Sift together sugar, flour, and salt.

Beat egg yolks until light and fluffy; stir in sifted dry ingredients. Stir in melted chocolate and milk.

Beat egg whites until stiff; fold into chocolate-egg yolk mixture.

Pour into pastry lined 9-inch pan. Bake in very hot oven (450°F.) 15 minutes. Reduce heat to moderate oven (350°F.) and bake 30 minutes.

Variations:

Pineapple Cake Pie: Omit chocolate and add 1 teaspoon grated lemon rind, 2 tablespoons lemon juice, and ½ cup drained crushed pineapple.

Strawberry Cake Pie: Omit chocolate and add 1 tablespoon lemon juice and ½ cup strawberry purée.

EGGNOG PIE

3 beaten egg yolks
½ cup sugar
2 cups light cream
⅛ teaspoon salt
⅛ teaspoon nutmeg
½ teaspoon vanilla
3 stiffly beaten egg whites
Plain pastry for 9-inch pie shell

Beat egg yolks, sugar, and cream. Add salt, nutmeg, and vanilla. Fold in egg whites.

Pour into 9-inch pastry lined pie pan.

Bake in very hot oven (450°F.) 10 minutes. Reduce heat to slow oven (325°F.) and bake until firm, about 25 minutes.

Variations: Sherry or rum to taste may be substituted for vanilla.

FRENCH SILK CHOCOLATE PIE

1 8-inch baked pie shell
½ cup butter
¾ cup sugar
2 squares (2 ounces) unsweetened chocolate, melted
1 teaspoon vanilla
2 eggs

Cream butter; gradually add sugar, creaming well.

Blend in melted and thoroughly cooled chocolate and vanilla.

Add eggs, one at a time, beating 5 minutes after each addition. (With electric mixer use medium speed.)

Turn into cooled, baked pie shell. Chill at least 2 hours.

Before serving top with whipped cream and walnuts, if desired.

PUMPKIN CREAM PIE

Pastry for 9-inch pie shell
2 cups strained, cooked pumpkin, fresh, frozen, or canned
2 teaspoons cinnamon
⅔ cup brown sugar
½ teaspoon ginger
½ teaspoon salt
1½ cups milk
2 well beaten eggs
½ cup heavy cream

Combine pumpkin, cinnamon, sugar, ginger, and salt.

Slowly add milk and beat with rotary beater until thoroughly blended. (If you have a blender, use it instead of the rotary beater to blend the mixure.) Stir in eggs and cream.

Pour pumpkin mixture in pastry lined 9-inch pan. Sprinkle top with cinnamon.

Bake in slow oven (325°F.) 50 minutes. Serve warm with whipped cream, if desired.

ONTARIO MAPLE SYRUP PIE

2 tablespoons cornstarch
Pinch of salt
1 cup milk
2 cups maple syrup
2 egg yolks
1 9-inch baked pie shell
2 egg whites
2 tablespoons granulated sugar

Blend cornstarch and salt with a little of the milk.

Heat rest of milk with maple syrup to boiling point. Add cornstarch mixture and cook 5 minutes in double boiler, stirring constantly.

Pour some of the mixture over beaten egg yolks, return to double boiler and cook 5 minutes longer, stirring continually.

Pour into baked pie shell. Top with meringue made from well beaten egg whites and sugar.

PEACHES AND CREAM PIE

1 unbaked 9-inch pastry shell
About 8 large ripe peaches
Few grains salt
3 tablespoons flour
½ cup sugar
1 cup light cream
2 drops almond flavoring

Peel peaches; cut each in half; remove stone. Arrange peach halves, hollow side up, in pastry lined pan, without crowding. Fill in between peach halves with few peach slices.

Stir salt, flour, and sugar together until well mixed; stir in cream and flavoring. Pour over peaches.

Bake in moderate oven (350°F.) on low rack, until peaches are tender (test with a fork). Cool pie on wire rack. Serve soon after cooling.

Gelatin Pies

FRESH FRUIT CHIFFON PIE
(Master Recipe)

1 pint any fresh fruit
1¼ cups sugar
2 tablespoons arrowroot or corn-starch
Water
2 teaspoons (⅔ envelope) unfla-vored gelatin
4 egg whites
1 baked 9-inch pastry shell
½ cup heavy cream, whipped
Dash of liqueur or ½ teaspoon va-nilla

Peel, pit, or prepare fruit accord-ing to variety chosen. Crush and add ½ cup sugar. Cook until tender and purée if desired.

Heat to boiling; add arrowroot or cornstarch, which has been blended with small amount of cold water. Cook, stirring, until thickened. Boil, stirring, 2 minutes.

Soften gelatin in 2 tablespoons cold water; add to hot fruit mixture and stir until dissolved.

Beat egg whites until almost stiff; add remaining ¾ cup sugar gradually and beat until stiff. Fold into fruit mixture.

Pour into baked pie shell and chill until set. Flavor whipped cream with liqueur or vanilla and spread over pie.

ORANGE CHIFFON PIE

¼ cup cold water
1 envelope (1 tablespoon) unfla-vored gelatin
4 eggs, separated
1 cup sugar
½ teaspoon salt
½ cup orange juice
1 teaspoon lemon juice
1 teaspoon finely grated orange rind
1 9-inch pie shell, baked and cooled
½ cup heavy cream (optional)

Sprinkle gelatin over cold water, stir slightly, and set aside.

Place egg yolks in small mixing bowl and beat until light and lemon colored. Add ½ cup sugar and the salt and blend thoroughly. Add juices gradually and blend.

Pour mixture into 1-quart saucepan

Orange Chiffon Pie

and cook on medium heat, stirring con-stantly, until mixture just begins to thicken (about 2 minutes).

Switch to low heat, and continue cooking, stirring constantly, until mix-ture resembles consistency of a soft custard (about 4 minutes). Remove from heat.

Add orange rind and gelatin mixture to hot egg yolk mixture and stir until gelatin is dissolved.

Chill in refrigerator until mixture is very thick, but not stiff.

Place egg whites in large-sized mix-ing bowl. With clean beater, beat until stiff but not dry. Add remaining ½ cup sugar, 1 tablespoon at a time, while beating until very stiff.

Add egg yolk mixture and fold in until completely blended.

Pour mixture into baked pie shell and spread evenly. Chill in refrigera-tor until firm (about 1 hour).

Just before serving, spread whipped cream over filling.

NESSELRODE PIE

Originally, the name Nesselrode was applied to a frozen pudding made with chestnuts, fruit, and cream, invented by the chef of an early-19th-century Russian statesman of German descent, Count Karl Robert Nesselrode. The name is also applied nowadays to vari-ous other desserts and dessert sauces, and especially to a pie flavored with rum, containing preserved fruits, and often topped with shaved chocolate.

2 teaspoons light rum
¼ cup chopped candied fruit
2 tablespoons (envelopes) plain gel-atin
¼ cup sugar
½ teaspoon salt
2 cups cold milk
3 eggs, separated
Additional ⅓ cup sugar
1 cup heavy cream, whipped
Baked 9-inch pie shell
Shaved chocolate or candied fruit, op-tional

Sprinkle rum over candied fruit and set aside. Combine gelatin, ¼ cup su-gar, and salt in top part of double boiler. Gradually stir in milk and cook over hot water, stirring until gelatin has dissolved.

Beat egg yolks in a bowl, then gradu-ally stir milk mixture into egg yolks. Return to double boiler and cook, stir-ring constantly, until mixture is slightly thickened and coats a spoon. Let cool, then add candied fruit.

Beat egg whites until stiff, then grad-ually beat in ⅓ cup sugar. Gently fold into gelatin mixture. Fold in whipped cream. Turn into the baked pie shell; chill until firm. If desired, garnish with shaved chocolate or can-died fruit.

PEPPERMINT CHIFFON PIE

1 tablespoon (1 envelope) unfla-vored gelatin
¼ cup cold water
3 egg whites
⅓ cup sugar
1 cup heavy cream, whipped
Few drops oil of peppermint
½ cup crushed peppermint stick candy
1 9-inch chocolate wafer crumb crust

Soften gelatin in cold water and dis-solve over boiling water. Cool.

Beat egg whites until stiff and beat in sugar gradually.

Add dissolved gelatin to egg whites and fold in whipped cream, flavor-ing, and crushed candy.

Turn into crumb crust and chill.

CHOCOLATE CHIFFON PIE

1 tablespoon (1 envelope) unfla-vored gelatin
¼ cup water
2 ounces (2 squares) unsweetened chocolate
½ cup water
3 eggs, separated
¼ teaspoon salt
1 teaspoon vanilla
¼ teaspoon cream of tartar
½ cup sugar
1 9-inch graham cracker pie shell

Soften gelatin in ¼ cup water.

Meanwhile melt chocolate in re-maining ½ cup water in top of double boiler. Stir into egg yolks.

Return to double boiler; cook and stir until creamy. Stir in gelatin until dissolved. Blend in salt and vanilla; cool.

Beat egg whites and cream of tartar until almost stiff. Gradually beat in sugar until very stiff and glossy. Fold in slightly thickened chocolate mixture.

Spoon into crumb crust. Garnish with lattice of whipped cream for that extra special touch.

Chocolate Chiffon Pie

LEMON CHIFFON PIE

1 9-inch graham cracker crumb crust
1 tablespoon (1 envelope) unfla-
    vored gelatin
1/4 cup cold water
3 eggs, separated
3/4 cup sugar
1/2 teaspoon salt
1/2 cup lemon juice
1 teaspoon grated lemon rind
Chopped nuts for garnish

Soften gelatin in cold water at least 5 minutes.

Beat egg yolks; add 1/2 cup sugar, salt, and lemon juice. Cook over boiling water, stirring constantly, until of custard consistency.

Add lemon rind and gelatin, stir until gelatin dissolves. Cool until slightly thickened.

Beat egg whites until they form soft peaks. Gradually add remaining sugar; beat until stiff. Fold into custard mixture. Pour into graham cracker crumb crust.

Chill to set. Before serving, garnish with chopped nuts.

Note: For a quick and easy method, substitute 1/2 cup bottled lemon juice for 1/2 cup fresh lemon juice and lemon rind.

RASPBERRY CHIFFON PIE

1 package raspberry-flavored gela-
    tin
1 cup boiling water and juice from
    berries
1/3 cup sugar
Dash of salt
2 tablespoons lemon juice
1/2 cup cold water and juice from ber-
    ries
1/3 cup ice water
1/3 cup nonfat dry milk solids
1 package frozen raspberries,
    thawed and drained or 1 1/2
    cups fresh raspberries plus 3
    tablespoons sugar
1 baked 9-inch pie shell

Thaw raspberries in strainer over bowl and reserve juice.

Dissolve raspberry gelatin in boiling water. When thoroughly dissolved, add sugar and salt. Stir until dissolved.

Add cold juice and lemon juice and

Raspberry Chiffon Pie

allow to chill until of jelly-like consistency.

When ready, place ice water into the small bowl of mixer, add nonfat dry milk and beat until stiff. Remove to smaller bowl.

Beat partially set gelatin until thick and fluffy. Fold in drained berries and whipped milk.

Turn into baked pie shell and chill until firm. Decorate with whipped cream and fresh berries.

PINEAPPLE CHIFFON PIE

1 9-inch graham cracker crumb crust
1 tablespoon (1 envelope) unfla-
    vored gelatin
1/4 cup cold water
1 cup (8-ounce can) undrained
    crushed pineapple
1/4 cup sugar
3 eggs, separated
1 tablespoon butter or margarine
1/4 teaspoon salt
1/2 cup sugar
1/2 cup heavy cream (optional)

Soften gelatin in cold water.

Combine pineapple, 1/4 cup sugar, and egg yolks. Cook over low heat until mixture coats a metal spoon, stirring frequently.

Blend in margarine. Stir in softened gelatin. Chill until mixture begins to thicken.

Add salt to egg whites and beat until they stand in soft peaks.

Gradually beat in 1/2 cup sugar, one tablespoon at a time. Fold into pineapple mixture.

Pour into cold graham cracker pie crust.

Chill until ready to serve. If desired, top with whipped cream.

COFFEE CHIFFON PIE

1 tablespoon (1 envelope) unfla-
    vored gelatin
1/4 cup cold water
2 tablespoons instant coffee
3/4 cup hot water
1/4 teaspoon salt
1/2 cup sugar, divided
3 eggs, separated
1 9-inch chocolate cooky crumb
    crust

Soften gelatin in cold water.

Dissolve coffee in hot water in top of double boiler. Add salt and 1/4 cup sugar. Cook over direct heat until sugar is dissolved.

Beat egg yolks slightly. Slowly add hot liquid, stirring constantly. Return to top of double boiler and cook over hot water, stirring constantly, until mixture is slightly thickened.

Remove from heat and add softened gelatin, and stir until dissolved.

Chill until consistency of unbeaten egg whites.

Beat egg whites until stiff, gradually beat in remaining 1/4 cup sugar. Fold in chilled coffee mixture.

Turn into 9-inch chocolate cooky crumb crust and chill until firm. If desired, garnish with whipped cream and shaved chocolate.

Coffee Chiffon Pie

EGGNOG CHIFFON PIE

2 tablespoons (2 envelopes) unfla-
    vored gelatin
4 cups bottled eggnog
1/4 cup sugar
1/4 teaspoon nutmeg (optional)
4 teaspoons rum flavoring (op-
    tional)
1 cup heavy cream, whipped
1 10-inch baked pie shell

Sprinkle gelatin in 1 cup of cold eggnog in top of double boiler to soften.

Place over boiling water. Add sugar and stir until gelatin and sugar are dissolved. Add remaining eggnog.

If additional flavoring is desired, add nutmeg and flavoring. Chill until consistency of unbeaten egg white.

Whip gelatin mixture until light and fluffy; fold into whipped cream. Turn into pie shell; chill until firm.

Garnish with additional whipped cream, shaved chocolate, chopped maraschino cherries, orange peel, and citron.

Variation: To make Nesselrode Pie, fold in 1/2 cup chopped maraschino cherries and 1/2 cup chopped nuts just before turning into pie shell.

Eggnog Chiffon Pie

Pumpkin Chiffon Pie

PUMPKIN CHIFFON PIE

1   9-inch crumb crust
3   egg yolks
3/4 cup brown sugar
1½ cups cooked or canned pumpkin
½   cup milk
½   teaspoon salt
½   teaspoon ginger
1   teaspoon cinnamon
½   teaspoon nutmeg
1   tablespoon (1 envelope) unfla-
     vored gelatin
¼   cup cold water
3   egg whites
6   tablespoons granulated sugar

Beat egg yolks and brown sugar until thick; add pumpkin, milk, salt, and spices; cook in double boiler until thick.

Add gelatin softened in cold water; stir until gelatin dissolves. Cool mixture until it begins to set.

Beat egg whites until fluffy. Gradually add granulated sugar, beating well after each addition, until stiff. Fold egg whites into pumpkin mixture. Pour into baked shell and chill.

If desired, top with whipped cream and sprinkle with cereal crumbs.

APRICOT CLOUD PIE

1   tablespoon (1 envelope) unfla-
     vored gelatin
¼   cup cold water
2   eggs, separated
½   cup sugar
¼   teaspoon salt
1   cup apricot pulp and juice
2   tablespoons lemon juice
⅓   cup ice water
⅓   cup nonfat dry milk solids
¼   cup sugar
3   tablespoons apricot brandy
1   9-inch baked pie shell

Soften gelatin in cold water.

Beat egg yolks in top of double boiler. Add ½ cup sugar, salt, apricot pulp and juice, and lemon juice. Cook over hot water until mixture coats spoon.

Add gelatin. Stir until dissolved. Cool until slightly jelled.

Place egg whites and ice water in small bowl of electric mixer. Add nonfat dry milk solids. Beat at low speed until smooth.

Beat at high speed until it forms stiff peaks. Add ¼ cup sugar gradually.

Fold this and brandy into gelatin mixture. Turn into crust. Chill until firm.

Variations of Apricot Cloud Pie

Lemon Cloud Pie: Omit apricot pulp, juice and brandy. Increase lemon juice to ½ cup. Add 1½ teaspoons grated lemon rind.

Or, use 1 6-ounce can frozen lemonade concentrate and omit sugar, lemon juice and rind.

Orange Cloud Pie: Reduce lemon juice to 1 tablespoon. Add ⅓ cup undiluted frozen orange concentrate.

Cranberry Cloud Pie: Omit lemon juice and rind. Use 1 cup strained cranberry pulp, ¼ cup frozen orange concentrate and 1 teaspoon grated orange rind.

BRAZIL NUT BLACK BOTTOM PIE

1   tablespoon (1 envelope) unfla-
     vored gelatin
¼   cup cold water
⅔   cup sugar
1   tablespoon cornstarch
4   eggs, separated
2   cups milk, scalded
1   package semi-sweet chocolate
     pieces
1   teaspoon vanilla
¼   teaspoon salt
1   10-inch Brazil nut pie crust

Soften gelatin in cold water.

Combine ⅓ cup sugar and cornstarch.

Beat egg yolks slightly; slowly add scalded milk. Stir in sugar mixture. Cook in double boiler, stirring constantly, until mixture is slightly thickened.

To 1 cup custard, add semi-sweet chocolate pieces. Stir until chocolate is melted; set aside.

To remaining custard, add softened gelatin. Stir until gelatin is dissolved; add vanilla. Chill until consistency of unbeaten egg white.

Beat egg whites until stiff; gradually beat in salt and remaining ⅓ cup sugar. Fold in custard-gelatin mixture.

Stir chocolate mixture; turn into pie shell. Spoon gelatin mixture over chocolate layer and chill until firm.

Garnish with whipped cream, maraschino cherries, and Brazil nut slices.

BRAZIL NUT PIE CRUST

1½ cups ground Brazil nuts (¾
     pound unshelled nuts)
3   tablespoons sugar

Mix Brazil nuts with sugar in a 10-inch pie plate. Press this mixture with back of tablespoon against bottom and sides, up to rim of pie plate.

If a toasted flavor is desired, bake in hot oven (400°F.) 8 minutes, or until lightly browned. Cool. Makes 1 10-inch crust.

PEACH CHIFFON PIE

1   9-inch crumb or baked pastry
     shell
2   teaspoons (⅔ envelope) unfla-
     vored gelatin
¼   cup cold water
3   eggs, separated
½   teaspoon salt
2   teaspoons lemon juice
⅔   cup sugar
1½ cups fresh peaches, crushed or
     sieved

Soften gelatin in cold water.

Beat egg yolks slightly and add salt, lemon juice, and about ¼ cup sugar. Cook over hot, not boiling, water until thickened, stirring constantly.

Stir softened gelatin into hot mixture until dissolved.

Remove from hot water. Add peaches and chill until mixture begins to thicken.

Beat egg whites until stiff but not dry; gradually beat in remaining sugar. Fold into peach mixture.

Pile lightly into crumb shell and chill until firm. Top with whipped cream and garnish with sliced peaches.

SHERRY CHIFFON PIE

1   baked 9-inch pie shell
1   tablespoon (1 envelope) unflavored
     gelatin
⅓   cup cold water
4   eggs, separated
1   cup sugar, divided
⅔   cup sherry
⅓   teaspoon salt
½   cup whipping cream (optional)

Soften gelatin in cold water 5 minutes.

Beat egg yolks light; add gradually ½ cup sugar while continuing to beat. Add sherry.

Cook over hot water, stirring constantly, until mixture is the consistency of soft custard. Add gelatin; stir until dissolved and let cool.

Beat egg whites stiff; beat in remaining ½ cup sugar and salt. Combine with the custard. Spoon into pastry shell. Chill until firm, about 3 hours.

When ready to serve, garnish with whipped cream and a dash of nutmeg, if desired.

Sherry Chiffon Pie

BUTTERSCOTCH CHIFFON PIE

- 1 tablespoon (1 envelope) unflavored gelatin
- ¼ cup cold water
- 3 well beaten egg yolks
- 1 cup firmly packed brown sugar
- ¼ teaspoon salt
- 1 cup scalded milk
- 1 teaspoon vanilla
- 3 egg whites, beaten stiff
- 1 cup heavy cream, whipped
- 1 9-inch baked pie shell or crumb crust

Soften gelatin in cold water.

Mix egg yolks, sugar, salt, and milk. Cook over boiling water, stirring constantly, until mixture is slightly thickened.

Add gelatin and stir until dissolved. Chill until mixture is thick. Fold in vanilla, egg whites, and cream.

Turn into pie shell and chill several hours or overnight.

Half of the whipped cream could be reserved and used as topping for pie.

STRAWBERRY-ORANGE CHIFFON PIE

- 2 egg yolks
- ¼ cup sugar
- ¼ teaspoon salt
- 2 tablespoons cornstarch
- ⅛ teaspoon nutmeg
- 1 cup orange juice
- 1¼ cups milk
- 1 tablespoon (1 envelope) unflavored gelatin
- ¼ cup cold water
- ½ teaspoon vanilla
- 1 cup strawberries, sliced
- 2 egg whites
- ¼ cup sugar
- 1 cup heavy cream, whipped
- 1 9-inch corn flake crust

Combine egg yolks, ¼ cup sugar, salt, cornstarch, and nutmeg. Add orange juice and milk gradually. Cook over low heat, stirring constantly, until thickened.

Soften gelatin in cold water. Add gelatin to custard, stirring until gelatin is dissolved.

Cool custard until thickened. Add vanilla. Add strawberries.

Beat egg whites until peaks begin to form. Gradually add sugar and continue beating until a soft meringue is formed.

Fold meringue into custard mixture. Turn into crust and chill 2 hours or more before serving.

Serve with cream which has been whipped, and sweetened if desired.

Raspberry or Peach-Orange Chiffon Pie: Substitute raspberries or very ripe fresh peaches for strawberries.

BITTERSWEET MINT PIE

- 1 9-inch baked graham cracker crumb crust
- 1 tablespoon (1 envelope) unflavored gelatin
- ½ cup cold milk
- 1 cup milk, scalded
- ¾ cup sugar
- 3 eggs, separated
- 2 ounces (2 squares) unsweetened chocolate, melted
- ½ cup heavy cream
- ¼ cup creme de menthe

Soften gelatin in cold milk.

Pour a little scalded milk into sugar and slightly beaten egg yolks; combine with remaining milk. Cook over hot water, stirring constantly, until mixture coats spoon.

Stir in gelatin; divide in half.

To one half, add melted chocolate. Chill both mixtures until partially set.

Whip cream stiff; fold into chocolate mixture. Pour into graham cracker crumb crust; chill.

Beat egg whites stiff; fold into remaining custard with creme de menthe. Pour over chocolate mixture. Chill until firm.

RHUBARB AND STRAWBERRY BAVARIAN PIE

- 1 baked 9-inch pie shell
- 1 cup sugar
- 1 pound rhubarb, cut in 1-inch pieces
- 2 tablespoons (2 envelopes) unflavored gelatin
- ¼ cup cold water
- 1 cup mashed strawberries
- 1 cup cream, whipped
- 2 egg whites, stiffly beaten

Sprinkle ¾ cup sugar over rhubarb and let stand to extract juice while making pie shell.

Soften gelatin in cold water.

Heat rhubarb to boiling; lower heat and simmer until just tender, 5 minutes or longer. Stir gently or shake pan to prevent sticking.

Add softened gelatin and stir gently until dissolved. If desired, remove the most-perfect pieces of rhubarb for garnishing, and put a spoonful of syrup over them. Set them aside, but do not chill.

Add strawberries to rhubarb mixture and more sugar if desired. Cool and then chill until beginning to set.

Fold in half the whipped cream and the meringue made by beating remaining sugar into beaten egg whites. Turn into pie shell and chill until set.

At serving time, garnish with reserved whipped cream, reserved pieces of rhubarb, and additional whole strawberries.

SWEET POTATO CHIFFON PIE

Crumb Crust:

- 20 graham crackers finely rolled (1⅔ cups crumbs)
- ¼ cup softened butter or margarine
- ¼ cup sugar
- ¼ teaspoon cinnamon

Thoroughly blend together crumbs, softened butter or margarine, sugar, and cinnamon.

Pour mixture into 9-inch pie plate; firmly press against bottom and sides of plate.

Bake in moderate oven (375°F.) 8 minutes. Cool.

Filling:

- 1 tablespoon (1 envelope unflavored gelatin
- 1¼ cups milk
- 3 eggs, separated
- ⅔ cup sugar
- ½ teaspoon cinnamon
- 1 cup mashed, cooked sweet potato

Soften gelatin in ¼ cup milk. In top of double boiler, beat egg yolks; stir in remaining 1 cup milk, ⅓ cup sugar, cinnamon, and sweet potato. Cook over hot water, stirring constantly, until thickened.

Stir in gelatin until dissolved; chill until slightly thickened.

Beat egg whites until fairly stiff; gradually beat in remaining ⅓ cup sugar until stiff peaks form. Fold in custard mixture. Heap into crumb crust. Chill.

Before serving, garnish with a wreath of whipped cream and sprinkling of golden raisins.

RHUBARB CHIFFON PIE

- 2 cups finely chopped fresh rhubarb
- ¾ cup sugar
- ¼ cup hot water
- 1 tablespoon (1 envelope) unflavored gelatin
- ¼ cup cold water
- 2 egg whites
- ½ cup heavy cream, whipped
- 1 tablespoon grated orange rind
- 1 baked 9-inch pie shell

Cook rhubarb with ½ cup sugar and hot water until tender. Force through coarse sieve.

Soften gelatin in cold water and add to hot rhubarb mixture. Chill until almost firm.

Beat egg whites until frothy and add remaining sugar gradually, beating until stiff. Fold into cold rhubarb mixture which has been beaten until fluffy.

Fold grated orange rind into whipped cream and fold into mixture. Turn into pie shell. Chill until firm.

Turnovers and Tarts or Miniature Pies

TURNOVERS

This is an excellent way to use left-over pastry trimmings. Roll pastry 1/8 inch thick. Cut into 3- to 4-inch circles or squares.

Place a teaspoon of fruit filling or preserves on half of each pastry. Moisten the edge of half of each pastry. Fold over to form half a circle or a triangle, and seal the edges by pressing together with the tines of a fork.

Prick the tops to form small steam vents. Bake in hot oven (425°F.) about 15 minutes.

PEACH TURNOVERS
(Master Recipe)

2   cups sifted enriched flour
3   teaspoons baking powder
1/2 teaspoon salt
1/4 cup shortening
2/3 to 3/4 cup milk
1   cup sliced peaches
2   tablespoons butter or margarine
2   tablespoons brown sugar

Sift together flour, baking powder, and salt. Cut or rub in shortening until mixture is crumbly. Add milk to make a soft dough.

Turn out on lightly floured board or pastry cloth and knead gently 30 seconds.

Roll out into rectangular sheet about 1/4 inch thick. Cut into 8 rectangles 6 x 3 inches.

Place peach slices on half of each rectangle. Dot with butter or margarine and sugar. Fold over and seal.

Bake in hot oven (425°F.) 15 to 18 minutes. Makes 8 turnovers.

Variations: Other fruits may be substituted for peaches.

BANBURY TARTS

These small triangular turnovers are named for an English town noted for its pastry.

Pastry for 9-inch double crust pie
1/2 cup sugar
1   tablespoon flour
1   egg
1   cup seedless raisins
1/4 cup chopped nuts
1   tablespoon lemon juice
2   teaspoons grated lemon rind

Roll pastry 1/8 inch thick; cut 4-inch squares.

Combine sugar and flour and stir into slightly beaten egg. Combine with remaining ingredients.

Place filling on half of each square; fold pastry to form triangle. Seal edges and flute with fingers or a fork. Cut or prick small steam vents.

Bake in hot oven (425°F.) about 15 minutes. Makes 12.

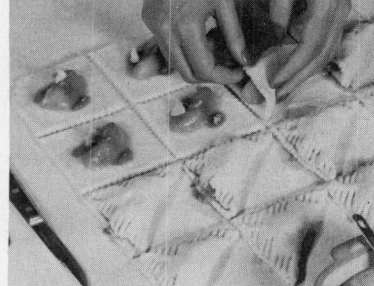

Place filling on half of each square; fold pastry to form triangle. Seal.

CHEESE APRICOT TURNOVERS

3   3-ounce packages cream cheese
1/3 cup butter or margarine
2   cups sifted enriched flour
1   teaspoon salt
1/2 pound dried apricots, cooked and puréed
1/2 cup sugar

Blend together cream cheese and butter. Gradually cut in mixed and sifted dry ingredients; chill.

Roll out very thin on a lightly floured board. Cut into 4-inch squares.

Combine apricots and sugar. Place 1 tablespoon of apricot mixture on each square of pastry. Fold squares into triangles and seal edges with a fork. Prick tops with a fork.

Place on cooky sheet. Bake in moderate oven (375°F.) 20 to 25 minutes. Makes 18 to 20 turnovers.

OLD-FASHIONED FRIED PIES

2   cups sifted enriched flour
1   teaspoon salt
1/3 cup shortening
Ice water
Filling (below)
Shortening for frying

Sift flour and salt together. Cut in shortening until crumbs are the size of small peas. Gradually add water (about 1/3 cup) to make a soft dough.

Roll out to 1/8-inch thickness on lightly floured pastry cloth. Cut in 5-inch rounds (use a sharp-pointed knife and a cardboard cut-out or the top of a coffee can).

Put 1 1/2 tablespoons filling on half of each circle, keeping it 1/2 inch from the edge.

Moisten edge of pastry with water and fold the empty half over the filling to make a half circle. Seal the edges by pressing together with tines of a fork. Prick the tops 2 or 3 times with a fork.

With a pancake turner, slide 3 or 4 at a time into deep hot fat (360°F.) and fry until golden brown on the underside, 2 to 3 minutes. Turn and brown other side.

Lift out and drain on absorbent paper. Serve warm or cold. Sprinkle with confectioners' sugar, if desired. Makes 10 to 12 pies.

Dried Apricot Filling:

2   cups stewed dried apricots, drained
1/4 cup sugar
2   tablespoons melted butter or margarine

Cook the apricots; stir in sugar and butter.

Dried Apple Filling:

2   cups stewed dried apples, drained
1/4 cup sugar
2   tablespoons melted butter or margarine
1/4 teaspoon nutmeg or cloves

Cook apples; stir in sugar, butter, and spice.

Applesauce Filling:

1   cup applesauce
1/4 cup firmly packed brown sugar
1/4 cup seedless raisins
1/4 teaspoon allspice
1 1/2 teaspoons lemon juice
1   tablespoon melted butter or margarine

Mix ingredients thoroughly.

Old-Fashioned Fried Pies

CHESS TARTS

1   cup seedless raisins
1/2 cup butter or margarine
3/4 cup firmly packed brown sugar
3   unbeaten eggs
1   cup broken walnuts
1   tablespoon brandy extract
6   4-inch pastry lined tart shells

Rinse and drain raisins. With electric mixer at medium speed, or "cream" (or with spoon), thoroughly mix butter with sugar.

Add eggs, 1 at a time, beating well after each addition. Stir in nuts, brandy, and raisins. Spoon into shells.

Bake in hot oven (425°F.) 10 minutes. Reduce heat to moderate (350°F.) and bake 25 minutes longer. Cool. Serve with whipped cream.

Assorted Fruit Tarts: Make muffin pan tart shells. Just before serving, fill baked shells with fresh fruit in season. Picture shows blueberries, sliced peaches, and strawberries. Serve with sweetened whipped cream.

TART SHELLS

Roll out pastry 1/8 inch thick as directed in recipe for plain pastry. (The 9-inch double-crust recipe will make 8 medium-sized tart shells.)

Cut into circles, using a sharp-pointed knife to cut around cardboard pattern or a can.

Line tart pans with pastry circles and press into the flutings on sides of pans with back of a knife.

Press pastry overhang against sharp pan edges to cut off neatly.

Prick pastry with tines of fork or not, according to recipe directions for filling.

Bake filled tart shells according to directions given in recipe for tarts.

To prevent puffing, prick unfilled tart shells thoroughly all over with tines of fork and bake in very hot oven (450°F.) until delicately browned, 10 to 15 minutes. Cool thoroughly before filling.

DOUBLE CRUST TARTS

Line tart pans, being careful not to stretch the dough. Trim off pastry with scissors 1/4 inch beyond pan rim.

Cut design in center of circles for top crusts to make steam vents.

After filling tarts, moisten edge of trimmed lower crust, cover with top crust and press gently around edge to seal.

Trim with scissors 1/4 inch beyond rim of pan. Turn overhang under lower crust so fold is even with edge of pan.

Flute or crimp as for full-sized double-crust pie.

Note: Fruit tarts may also be covered with lattice top if desired.

MUFFIN PAN TART SHELLS

Use muffin pans with cups 3 to 3½ inches in diameter. Cut 5-inch pastry circles, using a sharp-pointed knife and a cardboard pattern or the top of a coffee can.

Fit the circles over the backs of muffin cups. Pinch edges together 6 or 7 times to fit dough to cup. Prick liberally with tines of fork over "tops" of cups and "down" sides.

Bake in very hot oven (450°F.) until lightly browned, about 10 minutes.

Cool before removing tart shells from muffin cups.

PETAL TART SHELLS

Roll out plain pastry. Cut 5 circles the same size as the bottom of the muffin cup.

Lay one circle in bottom of muffin cup; press 4 circles to sides and bottom of cup so that they overlap.

Prick well and bake in very hot oven (450°F.) 10 to 15 minutes, or until golden brown.

Cool and lift out carefully. Fill with favorite filling and top with whipped cream if desired.

COOKY TART SHELLS

1/3   cup butter or margarine
1/2   cup sugar
1   egg
1   tablespoon orange juice
1½   cups sifted enriched flour
1   teaspoon baking powder
1/4   teaspoon salt

Cream butter or margarine; add sugar gradually and mix well. Add egg and orange juice; mix well.

Sift flour, baking powder, and salt together. Add to creamed mixture and blend well. Chill dough.

Roll dough on a lightly floured board to 1/8-inch thickness; cut into rounds.

Invert muffin pans and grease outside of cups. Place rounds over cups, press down and pinch edges of dough at intervals to fit cups. Prick with a fork.

Bake in moderate oven (375°F.) 6 to 8 minutes.

Cool 1 minute before removing shells. Fill with berries, pudding, or ice cream for serving. Makes 10 or 12 tart shells.

PATTY SHELLS

Roll out plain pastry 1/4 inch thick. Cut with round, floured cutter. Remove centers from 1/2 these circles with a small cutter.

Wet edges of the whole circles. Place the rings on them.

Brush tops carefully with an egg slightly beaten with 1 tablespoon water. Take care not to moisten sides. Chill until stiff.

Bake in very hot oven (450°F.) 10 to 20 minutes. Bake small centers 10 minutes and use as tops after shells are filled.

GLAZED STRAWBERRY CREAM CHEESE TARTS

1   3-ounce package cream cheese
2   tablespoons cream
6   baked tart shells
1½   pints strawberries
Glaze No. 1 or No. 2 (see following recipes)
1/2   cup cream, whipped

Blend cheese and cream. Spread in bottom of tart shells.

Fill shells with strawberries that have been washed, hulled, and drained.

Cover fruit with glaze and chill. Garnish with whipped cream, sweetened if desired.

GLAZE FOR TARTS #1

1   pint strawberries
1/2   cup water
1   cup sugar
2½   tablespoons cornstarch
1   tablespoon butter or margarine
Red food coloring

Crush berries. Add water, sugar, and cornstarch. Cook, stirring, until thickened and clear.

Add butter and enough coloring to give a bright red. Strain. Makes enough for 6 tarts.

GLAZE FOR TARTS #2

Melt any good fruit jelly (currant, quince, apple, crabapple, etc.) in top of double boiler. Pour over fruit. One cup of jelly is enough for 6 tarts.

MINCEMEAT PIE FACES

Make up recipe for a 2-crust pie. Cut 8 circles from rolled out dough. With sharp knife, cut "faces" in four of the circles.

Place 1/4 cup of mincemeat in center of the 4 remaining circles. Moisten edge of dough with water. Top with "faces" and press crusts together with tines of fork. Bake on cooky sheet in hot oven (400°F.) about 15 minutes.

Mincemeat Pie Faces

VIENNESE CREAM CHEESE TARTS

1/2 cup butter or margarine
1 3-ounce package cream cheese
1 cup sifted enriched flour
1/4 cup red currant, raspberry, strawberry, or grape jelly
1 egg yolk
2 tablespoons milk
1/2 cup finely chopped nuts
Confectioners' sugar

Work butter or margarine and cream cheese together until soft, then stir in flour thoroughly. Chill in refrigerator for about an hour or until manageable.

Roll dough about 1/8 inch thick on a lightly floured board and cut into 2-inch squares.

Spoon a bit of jelly (1/4 teaspoonful or better) near center of square.

Fold a corner of dough over jelly to form a triangle and pinch edges to seal.

Pull 2 corners of the triangle around to shape a crescent and dip into a mixture of egg yolk and milk.

Roll crescents in chopped nuts.

Place on an ungreased cooky sheet and bake in hot oven (400°F.) 8 to 10 minutes. Sprinkle with confectioners' sugar and cool. Makes 2 dozen.

GLAZED GRAPE TARTS

4 cups Concord grapes
2/3 cup sugar
1 tablespoon cornstarch
1 to 2 tablespoons lemon juice
5 to 6 unbaked tart shells
3/4 cup currant or apple jelly

Slip pulp out of skins. Reserve skins. Cook pulp until seeds loosen; put through sieve to remove seeds.

Mix sugar and cornstarch. Add to pulp. Add skins and lemon juice; pour into tart shells.

Bake in very hot oven (450°F.) 10 minutes. Lower heat to moderate (350°F.) and bake 20 minutes longer.

Heat jelly with 1 to 2 teaspoons water, stirring until thin and smooth. Pour over grapes to glaze. Cool. Serve with whipped cream.

Cherry Cream Tarts

PINEAPPLE LIME TARTS

1 No. 2 1/2 can sliced pineapple
1 package lime-flavored gelatin
3/4 cup whipping cream
6 baked and cooled pastry shells

Drain pineapple; cover and refrigerate.

Add enough water to syrup to make 1 3/4 cups liquid. Heat and dissolve gelatin in it. Chill until slightly thickened.

Whip cream until stiff and fold into gelatin. Fill tart shells. Chill.

Just before serving, top with a pineapple slice and garnish with a maraschino cherry.

Pineapple Lime Tarts

WALNUT TARTS

1 cup walnuts, coarsely chopped
1/3 cup hot milk
6 tablespoons sugar
2 teaspoons rum
4 unbaked 3-inch tart shells

Mix all ingredients well. Pour into tart shells.

Bake in hot oven (425°F.) 15 to 20 minutes.

CHERRY CREAM TARTS

6 baked tart shells
1 3-ounce package cream cheese
2 tablespoons sugar
1/4 teaspoon lemon juice
1/2 teaspoon grated lemon rind
1/3 cup heavy cream, whipped
1 No. 2 can (2 1/2 cups) sour, red, pitted cherries, well drained
3 tablespoons sugar
1 tablespoon cornstarch
3/4 cup cherry juice

Soften cream cheese at room temperature; cream until smooth. Gradually add sugar while stirring; beat with spoon until fluffy.

Add lemon juice and lemon rind. Fold in whipped cream.

Put 2 1/2 tablespoons cream cheese mixture into each baked tart shell. Chill in refrigerator 1 hour.

Combine 3 tablespoons sugar and cornstarch in saucepan. Gradually stir in cherry juice. Cook over medium heat until thick and clear. Cool slightly.

Spoon cherries over cream cheese mixture. Cover with cherry-cornstarch mixture. Makes 6 3 3/4-inch tarts.

Cooky Tarts

COOKY TARTS

Cut out rounds of pie dough with scalloped cooky cutter. Cut centers from half of these rounds. Bake on cooky sheet in hot oven (425°F.) 10 minutes. Spread whole rounds with preserves and top with circles.

RASPBERRY TARTS

2 tablespoons sugar
1 tablespoon cornstarch
1/8 teaspoon salt
3/4 cup fruit juice
1 teaspoon lemon juice
4 to 6 baked tart shells
1 pint fresh raspberries

Blend together the sugar, cornstarch, and salt in a saucepan.

Stir in fruit juice and cook over low heat until thick and clear. Cool. Add lemon juice.

Fill tart shells with raspberries. Pour fruit sauce over berries. Chill. Top with whipped cream, if desired.

PUMPKIN CHIFFON TARTS

3 slightly beaten egg yolks
1/2 cup sugar
1 1/2 cups canned pumpkin
1/2 cup milk
1/2 teaspoon salt
1 teaspoon ginger
1/2 teaspoon nutmeg
1/2 teaspoon cinnamon
1 tablespoon (1 envelope) unflavored gelatin
1/4 cup cold water
1/2 cup sugar
3 stiffly-beaten egg whites
8 baked pastry tart shells

Combine egg yolks, 1/2 cup sugar, pumpkin, milk, salt, and spices; cook in double boiler until thick. Add gelatin which has been softened in cold water. Mix thoroughly and cool.

Add remaining 1/2 cup sugar to egg whites; fold into pumpkin mixture. Pour into baked tart shells and chill. Garnish with whipped cream.

COTTAGE CHEESE AND CHERRY TARTS

Heat canned red cherries; add sugar to taste, and thicken to desired consistency with cornstarch. Cool.

Fill cooled, baked tart shells with creamed cottage cheese and top each with the cooked and sweetened cherries.

Any pie may be made in the form of individual tarts for festive desserts and they make group service simple when the party is large.

CALIFORNIA CHESS TARTS

1/2 cup butter or margarine
1   cup sugar
1/4 teaspoon salt
1/4 teaspoon cinnamon
1/4 teaspoon nutmeg
1/4 teaspoon cloves
4   egg yolks, unbeaten
1   cup seedless raisins
1   cup chopped walnuts or pecans
1/2 cup sherry
8   unbaked tart shells

Cream 1/2 cup butter or margarine and 1 cup sugar together until light and fluffy.

Add salt, cinnamon, nutmeg, and cloves.

Add unbeaten egg yolks, one at a time, beating well after each addition.

Add raisins (rinsed with boiling water and drained well), walnuts or pecans, and sherry; blend thoroughly.

Spoon mixture into unbaked tart shells. Bake in moderate oven (350°F.) about 40 minutes, or until firm.

Serve warm or cold, topped with either whipped cream or vanilla ice cream. Serves 8.

CRANBERRY TARTS

4   cups chopped cranberries
1   teaspoon grated orange rind
2   oranges, peeled and chopped
2   cups sugar
3   tablespoons quick-cooking tapioca
1   tablespoon butter or margarine, melted
1/2 teaspoon salt
1   orange, sectioned
6   unbaked tart shells

Combine cranberries, orange rind, oranges, sugar, tapioca, butter, and salt.

Pour into tart shells. Arrange orange sections on top of filling.

Bake in very hot oven (450°F.) 10 minutes; reduce temperature to moderate (350°F.) and bake 25 to 30 minutes.

QUICK LEMON MERINGUE TARTS

1   package lemon pudding or pie mix
1/2 cup sugar
2 1/2 cups water
2   eggs, separated
6   large or 12 small baked tart shells
1/4 cup sugar

Combine lemon pudding, sugar, and water in a saucepan.

Beat yolks slightly and add to mixture. Cook over medium heat, stirring constantly, until mixture thickens and comes to a boil.

Cool slightly. Pour into baked tart shells.

Beat egg whites until stiff but not dry; gradually beat in sugar until mixture stands in peaks. Pile lightly on tarts.

Bake in hot oven (425°F.) about 5 minutes, until lightly browned. Makes 6 large or 12 small tarts.

BRUNSWICK MINCEMEAT TARTS

Prepare pastry, using 1 1/2 (9-ounce) packages piecrust mix and following directions on carton.

Roll out thin and cut in rounds with a 4-inch cutter. Line the inside of tiny (2-inch) muffin cups with these rounds. Prick pastry.

Bake shells in a very hot oven (450°F.) 12 minutes. Cool. (Leave shells right in the muffin cups.)

Fill shells with mincemeat filling (below). Bake in a moderate oven (350°F.) for 45 minutes.

Remove from cups while still warm. Serve warm or cold, plain or topped with a bit of sherry-flavored hard sauce. Makes 24 miniature tarts.

Mincemeat Filling:

1/2 cup softened butter or margarine
1   cup firmly packed brown sugar
1 1/2 tablespoons flour
4   egg yolks
1 1/2 cups mincemeat
1/2 cup chopped walnuts
1/3 cup sherry
1/4 teaspoon each cinnamon and nutmeg
1/4 teaspoon salt

Cream butter, sugar, and flour together until thoroughly blended. Beat in egg yolks, one at a time.

Add remaining ingredients; mix well. Spoon into tart shells as directed above.

GLAZED WALNUT MINCE TARTS

Spoon canned moist mincemeat into baked tart shells; top with coarsely broken walnut meats.

Drizzle a little honey over the nuts; place under broiler heat a few minutes to glaze.

MAPLE SYRUP BUTTER TARTS

2   eggs
1   cup brown sugar
1/4 teaspoon salt
2   teaspoons vinegar
1/2 cup maple syrup
6   tablespoons melted butter
2/3 cup chopped nuts
Pastry

Beat eggs only until yolks and whites are well blended.

Beat in sugar and salt and add vinegar and maple syrup. Mix well and add melted butter and nuts.

Line patty cups with pastry, and fill 1/2 to 2/3 full.

Bake in very hot oven (450°F.) 10 minutes, then reduce heat to moderate (350°F.) and bake 20 to 25 minutes more, or until filling is firm.

DEEP DISH APPLE PIE, TOKAY

Pastry for 6 individual pies with lattice strips (basis 1 1/2 cups flour)
3   cups sliced apples
3/4 cup sugar
1/2 teaspoon salt
1/2 teaspoon cinnamon
1/8 teaspoon nutmeg
2   tablespoons flour
2   tablespoons butter or margarine
2   tablespoons lemon juice
3/4 cup port, tokay, angelica, muscatel or any dessert wine

Arrange a layer of sliced apples in each individual deep dish pie shell.

Mix sugar, salt, spices, and flour. Sprinkle half the dry ingredients over layers of apples.

Add remaining apples and remaining dry ingredients in succeeding layers.

Dot with butter or margarine. Sprinkle with lemon juice. Add two tablespoons wine to each pie. Top with lattice pastry.

Bake in very hot oven (450°F.) 10 minutes, then reduce heat to moderate (350°F.) and bake 30 to 35 minutes longer until apples are done and crust is browned.

Deep Dish Apple Pie, Tokay

Cream Puff Paste (Pâte à Choux)

Far from being an item reserved for special desserts, cream puff paste can become something to be served at almost any point in the meal. For example, thimble-sized puffs can be made for hors d'oeuvre and stuffed with those thirst-provoking mixtures that fit them for cocktail companions. Larger shells may be fried in deep fat, producing a crisp surface that is a good accent for creamed fish or poultry.

Or after forcing the batter through a pastry tube, éclairs are created which with a rich homemade filling put ordinary bake shop éclairs into complete eclipse.

CREAM PUFF PASTE
(Master Recipe)

- 1 cup water
- 1/2 cup butter or 1/4 cup butter, 1/4 cup vegetable shortening
- 1/4 teaspoon salt
- 1 cup sifted enriched flour
- 4 eggs

Heat water, fat, and salt to boiling. Simmer until fat has melted.

Reduce heat as much as possible without eliminating it altogether. Add flour all at once. Stir briskly until mixture forms a ball that leaves the sides of the saucepan, but no longer.

Remove from heat. Add eggs one at a time, beating after each addition until mixture is stiff and glossy.

The batter having been prepared, the next step is to shape it. The size and form chosen depend on the method of presentation—very small for hors d'oeuvre shells, larger for main course and dessert purposes.

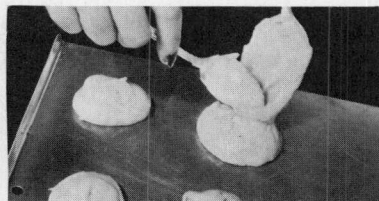

To make cream puff shells, scrape a tablespoonful of batter per puff onto a lightly greased cooky sheet. Bake in a hot oven until puffy, light, delicately brown.

For éclair shells, the puff paste may be forced from a pastry tube or dropped from a spoon. Make éclairs an inch wide, four inches long.

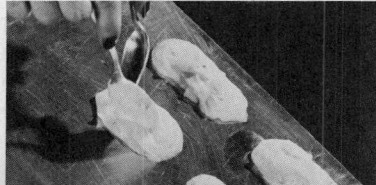

When cream puff paste is baked or deep-fat fried, it expands to many times its original size and a mass of air occurs in the center.

SHAPING CREAM PUFF PASTE

Cocktail Puff Shells: Use about 3/4 teaspoon of paste. Scrape off end of spoon onto lightly greased surface, arranging shells about 2 inches apart.

Bake only until brown and dry, or about 30 minutes in a hot oven (425° F.). The master recipe yields 4 dozen cocktail shells.

Fried Puff Shells (for main dish salads, creamed mixtures): Scrape mixture from spoon into deep, hot fat (370°F.). Use one rounded tablespoon per puff. Turn often. Fry about 12 minutes. Drain on unglazed paper. Yield of master recipe: 12 large puffs.

Cream Puff Shells (for dessert): Scrape rounded tablespoonfuls of paste onto lightly greased baking sheet about 2 inches apart. Bake in hot oven (425° F.) about 50 minutes or until brown and no bubbles show on surface. Yield of master recipe: 12 large puffs.

Éclair Shells (for dessert): Force puff paste through pastry bag, using largest plain tube or no tube at all if set includes only the small type. Make éclairs about an inch wide and four inches long. Bake as for cream puffs. The master recipe yields 12 to 18 shells.

CREAM PUFF SWANS

To make the swan neck and head, pipe cream puff pastry through a large pastry tube, using a large star tip, onto a buttered baking sheet into the shape of an "S."

For the tail, pipe a comma-shaped piece separately.

After filling cream puffs, insert a "head" and a "tail" in each to make a swan, cutting holes if necessary.

The cream puff tops that have been cut off to admit the filling may be cut in two and replaced to simulate lifted wings.

HINTS FOR FILLING AND FINISHING PUFF PASTE SHELLS

Fill puff paste shells as near serving time as possible.

Cut a hole in the side and use a pastry bag and tube to insert the stuffing.

Or cut off a portion of the top and fill with a spoon.

Cream puffs and éclairs are best finished off with a sifting of confectioners' sugar. For devotees of very sweet desserts, an icing is perhaps indicated, or whipped cream, or any dessert sauce that would harmonize with the filling.

Cream puff shells may be prepared in advance of serving and stored in foil or covered container. After filling, cream puffs should be refrigerated unless served promptly.

CREAM FILLING FOR CREAM PUFFS AND ÉCLAIRS

- 3 cups milk
- 1/2 cup enriched flour
- 1/2 teaspoon salt
- 3/4 cup sugar
- 3 eggs or 6 yolks, slightly beaten
- 1 1/2 teaspoons vanilla
- 3 tablespoons butter or margarine or 1/2 to 1 cup heavy cream, whipped

Scald milk in top of a double boiler.

Mix flour, salt, and sugar. Add milk while stirring.

Return to top of double boiler and cook, stirring, until thickened. Leave in double boiler, cover and cook 5 minutes.

While stirring, add mixture gradually to beaten eggs. Return to double boiler and cook, stirring until thickened, or about 2 minutes.

Add vanilla and butter. Chill. Whipped cream gives a richer, lighter textured filling. If used, add it just before filling shells. Makes enough for 12 large cream puffs.

Variations of Cream Filling

Butterscotch: Substitute 1 cup dark brown sugar for granulated and cook butter in the mixture.

Chocolate: Increase sugar to 1 cup. Add 3 to 4 ounces (squares) chocolate, shredded or grated, to mixture before cooking.

Coffee: Substitute 3/4 cup very strong coffee for that same amount of milk.

Fruit: Fold into mixture just before filling shells 1 cup sliced or chopped fruit, well drained. Strawberries, bananas, and pineapple are recommended.

Ginger: Add 1/4 cup finely chopped preserved ginger to vanilla or butterscotch filling.

Maple: Substitute maple sugar for granulated.

Nut or Coconut: Add 3/4 cup chopped nuts or coconut to vanilla, chocolate, coffee, or maple filling.

Rum or Sherry: Omit vanilla and add 2 tablespoons or more rum or sherry to the cream filling.

Profiteroles is a French term for walnut-size puff shells, which may be filled with custard or cream to make a dessert or with meat or other savory fillings to be served as an appetizer or with soup.

PROFITEROLES

Bake small cream puffs. Cool and fill with Crème Patissière à la Vanille (below), whipped cream, or ice cream.

Serve with hot chocolate or other dessert sauce.

Crème Patissière à la Vanille:

½ cup sugar
¼ cup flour
2 tablespoons cornstarch
¼ teaspoon salt
1 egg yolk
½ cup milk
2 cups hot milk
1 tablespoon butter
2 teaspoons vanilla

Combine sugar, flour, cornstarch, and salt in top of double boiler.

Beat egg yolk slightly. Add cold milk. Blend in dry ingredients and stir until smooth.

Blend in hot milk. Cook over boiling water, stirring constantly, until thick. Cover and cook for 5 minutes.

Remove from heat. Add butter and vanilla. Cover and cool.

Miscellaneous Pastries

STRUDEL

Strudel is a German term for a Central European pastry of stretched paper-thin dough rolled up with a filling of fruit, nuts, poppy seeds, cottage cheese, vegetables, or even meat and baked. It is superlatively fragile and delicious. Americans tend to be afraid of trying to make the stretched dough, but once they have done so many agree that it is no more difficult than making a good pie crust.

STRUDEL DOUGH

3 cups sifted enriched flour
½ teaspoon salt
1 tablespoon vegetable oil
1 beaten egg
1 cup lukewarm water

To Mix and Knead Dough: Sift flour and salt into a large bowl. Make a "well" in the center of the flour; place oil and egg in the depression.

Work flour gently into oil and egg and gradually add water to make a soft dough. (The dough will be sticky.)

Turn dough out onto a lightly floured pastry board. Hold dough high above board and crash it down against the board. Repeat this about 100 to 125 times or until the dough is smooth and elastic and leaves the board clean. (After 15 or 20 times it will no longer stick.)

Knead slightly and pat it into a round. Lightly brush surface of dough with oil (not olive oil).

Cover dough with an inverted warmed bowl and allow to rest from 30 minutes to 1 hour.

To Stretch Dough: Spread a large table (about 3 x 5 feet) with a clean cloth, allowing cloth to hang down.

Sprinkle cloth lightly but thoroughly with about ½ cup flour.

Place dough in center of cloth and roll it into a large oblong, turning it several times to prevent its sticking to the cloth, and rolling the outer edges as thinly as possible.

With a soft brush, lightly brush the dough with cooking oil (not olive oil); the oil aids in preventing the formation of holes during stretching.

Now reach under the dough and start stretching (do not pull) gently from the center to the outer edge.

Some people work with the backs of the hands. They turn the palms downward and stretch with slightly raised knuckles only. Others prefer to keep the palms up with the fingers straight out, working with a circular motion under the dough. You will soon learn which method is most convenient for you.

Work around the table until the evenly stretched dough is as thin as paper and drapes over the edges of the table on all sides.

As you stretch, keep the dough close to the table. The dough should not have any torn spots. If some should appear, do not try to patch them.

With kitchen scissors, trim off the thick outer edges that overhang the table.

Allow the stretched dough to dry a little, about 10 minutes. It should lose its stickiness but avoid drying too long because it becomes brittle.

To Fill and Roll: Brush the entire surface with cooled melted butter. Sprinkle with breadcrumbs as directed in recipe for filling. Cover from a half to two-thirds of the surface with remaining ingredients for the filling.

Fold over the overhanging flaps on three sides over the filling. Butter the turned-up edges, and then with the aid of the table cloth start to roll the dough over, pulling the cloth and dough toward you with both hands. Roll fairly loosely to give room for expansion.

With the last roll slide the strudel on a well buttered baking sheet, bending it into a horseshoe shape.

Or cut the strudel in halves, and lifting each half on cloth, gently roll onto the baking sheet.

To Bake: Brush the surface with melted butter and bake in moderate oven (350°F.) until golden brown, 35 to 45 minutes. Baste and brush with melted butter several times during baking.

When strudel makes a crackly sound on touching it is done. (Strudel should not be smooth.)

To Serve: Remove to cooling rack; cool slightly. Sift confectioners' sugar generously over it. Remove to a cutting board and cut into 2-inch slices. Serve warm with unsweetened whipped cream. Makes 12 to 15 servings.

Note: The trimmings of dough may be kneaded with a little flour, rolled out, and when dry, cut into broad noodles.

APPLE STRUDEL

1 recipe strudel dough
½ cup (¼ pound) butter, melted and cooled
½ cup fine breadcrumbs
1½ pounds tart apples, peeled, cored, and finely sliced (4 to 6 apples)
½ to ¾ cup sugar (depending on tartness of apples)
1 teaspoon cinnamon
1 cup raisins
1 cup chopped walnuts or almonds, if desired

Make and stretch strudel dough. Brush dough with some of the melted butter. Sprinkle two-thirds of the surface with breadcrumbs and apples.

Sprinkle over this the sugar, cinnamon, raisins, and nuts. Roll, place on buttered baking sheet. Brush with butter.

Bake in moderate oven (350°F.) 35 to 45 minutes, basting frequently with melted butter.

Variations:

Sour Cherry Strudel: Use 2 pounds sour cherries, pitted, in place of apples. Omit raisins.

Sweet Cherry Strudel: Use 2 pounds sweet black cherries, pitted, in place of apples. Use only ½ cup sugar. Omit cinnamon and raisins.

Fresh Peach Strudel: Use sliced peaches in place of apples.

Plum Strudel: Use sliced pitted plums in place of apples.

CABBAGE STRUDEL

1 recipe strudel dough
1 head (about 3 pounds) cabbage
(about 3 quarts, shredded)
2 tablespoons salt
1/4 cup butter
3/4 to 1 teaspoon pepper
1/4 cup thick sour cream
1/4 cup fine, dry breadcrumbs

Remove and discard wilted outer leaves of cabbage. Rinse; cut into quarters (discarding core) and finely shred.

Place cabbage in a large bowl and mix with salt. Let stand 1/2 hour, mixing occasionally.

Melt butter in a 3-quart saucepan. Squeeze cabbage, a small amount at a time, discarding juice; put cabbage into saucepan. Cook, uncovered, over medium heat, stirring frequently, 10 to 15 minutes, or until just tender.

Remove cabbage from heat and mix in pepper. Set cabbage aside.

After strudel dough is stretched and slightly dried, spoon sour cream over entire surface in small mounds. Carefully spread mounds of cream with spatula.

Sprinkle breadcrumbs over the sour cream. Spoon cabbage in small mounds over breadcrumbs. With spatula spread mounds carefully.

Roll, bake and slice as directed in strudel dough recipe. Do not sprinkle with confectioner's sugar. Serve warm. Makes 12 slices.

POPPY SEED STRUDEL

1 recipe strudel dough
1/2 pound (about 2 1/2 cups) freshly
ground poppy seeds
1 cup sugar
1/2 cup raisins
2 teaspoons grated lemon rind
1/2 cup butter, melted and cooled

Mix poppy seeds, sugar, raisins, and lemon rind together. Set aside.

After strudel dough is stretched and slightly dried, sprinkle cooled, melted butter over it. Spoon poppy seed mixture over the butter.

Roll and bake as directed in recipe for strudel dough.

Viennese Tarts

CANNOLI .

A Sicilian fried pastry usually filled with a ricotta cheese filling, as given below; however pudding, whipped cream, and ice cream fillings are often used.

4 cups sifted enriched flour
1/4 teaspoon cinnamon
1 tablespoon powdered instant
coffee
Grated rind of 1/2 lemon
1/4 cup sugar
1 egg, slightly beaten
1 egg yolk, slightly beaten
2 tablespoons cooking oil
About 1 cup sauterne or other
semi-sweet white wine
Additional 2 egg yolks, slightly beaten

Mix and sift flour, cinnamon, and coffee into a bowl. Stir in lemon rind, sugar, egg and egg yolk, and oil.

Mix with your hands, adding just enough wine to hold ingredients together to form a dough. Turn out on a floured board and knead until smooth and elastic, about 10 minutes. Chill dough several hours.

Cut off pieces of dough about the size of a walnut, and roll out very thin on a well-floured board. Using a 5-inch cutter or a saucer cut into 5-inch rounds. Wrap each around a cannoli tube (a metal tube about 1-inch in diameter) or use pieces of clean broomstick handle about 5 inches long. Seal dough by brushing with remaining egg yolks.

Fry 2 or 3 at a time by dropping wrapped tubes into deep hot fat (375°F.) until lightly browned, about 1 minute. Drain on absorbent paper; let cool slightly then push molds out one end.

Just before serving fill cannoli, garnish ends with chopped nuts and sprinkle cannoli with confectioners' sugar. Makes about 30.

Ricotta Cheese Filling: Combine 2 pounds ricotta cheese, 1 1/2 cups sugar, 1/2 cup semi-sweet chocolate pieces, 1/4 cup finely chopped citron, and 1 teaspoon vanilla.

VIENNESE TARTS

1 cup sifted enriched flour
1/4 teaspoon salt
1/3 cup shortening
1/2 cup cottage cheese
Marmalade or jam

Sift together flour and salt. Cut or rub in shortening. Add cottage cheese and mix well.

Form into smooth ball. Chill 30 minutes or longer.

Roll out on lightly floured board or pastry cloth. Cut into 3-inch squares.

Put a teaspoon of tart marmalade or jam in center of each square. Pinch all edges together to hold filling. Place on ungreased baking sheet.

Bake in hot oven (425°F.) about 10 minutes or until browned. Makes about 2 dozen 1 1/2-inch tarts.

BAKLAVA

A sweet, rich Near Eastern dessert made of many paper-thin layers of pastry dough that are filled with a mixture of butter and nuts and covered with syrup. Stores featuring Greek and Syrian specialties often sell it canned.

Pastry:

2 cups sifted flour
1/2 cup shortening
1 teaspoon salt
1 egg and water to make 1/2 cup

Cut shortening into flour and salt until mixture looks like corn meal.

With a fork, blend the egg and water. Add to dry ingredients, mixing until all dry ingredients are thoroughly dampened.

Turn onto waxed paper. Knead 8 times. Roll into ball and let rest 1/2 hour.

Filling:

2 cups slivered almonds
1/2 cup brown sugar, firmly packed
1 cup melted butter or margarine
1 teaspoon cinnamon
1/2 teaspoon nutmeg

Mix together all ingredients for filling.

Divide pastry into 4 portions. Roll out 1 portion very thin on a lightly floured pastry cloth into a rectangle 8 x 16 inches.

Cut rectangle in half to form 2 8-inch squares.

Place 1 square in bottom of 8 x 8 x 2-inch baking pan. Spread 2 tablespoons of the filling over this pastry.

Place second layer of pastry on top of filling.

Roll out another portion of pastry as above. Continue making layers of pastry and filling.

Spread no filling on the top layer of pastry.

Syrup:

1 cup water
1 cup sugar
Grated rind of 1 orange
Grated rind of 1 lemon

Mix ingredients for syrup in saucepan. Boil 5 minutes.

Cut baklava into 8 servings. Pour 3 tablespoons of syrup over baklava.

Bake in moderate oven (350°F.) 35 to 40 minutes.

Serve remaining sauce (cooled) over the hot baklava. Serves 8.

PUFF PASTRY
(Master Recipe)

Puff pastry is a flaky, air-filled butter-rich product with infinite uses.

2 cups (1 pound) sweet butter
4 cups (1 pound) enriched flour
1 teaspoon salt
1 to 1⅓ cups ice water

Wash the butter by putting it in a bowl of ice water and kneading and squeezing it with the hands until it is smooth, waxy, and as pliable as putty.

Remove it from the water. Place it in a clean cloth and press out any water that may have been trapped in it.

Set aside 2 tablespoons butter. Shape the remaining butter into a flat, square cake about ½ inch thick. Wrap in waxed paper and chill in coldest part of the refrigerator.

Sift flour with salt into a large mixing bowl or in a mound on a board.

Add the 2 tablespoons washed butter to the flour and, with the fingertips, work it into flour.

Add ice water gradually and, again using the fingertips, mix quickly and lightly to make a dough with about the consistency of the washed butter. The dough should be firm but not hard.

Place the dough on a lightly floured board and roll it out in a rectangle ½ inch thick.

Place the ½-inch-thick square cake of butter in the center of the dough.

Fold the upper flap of dough down to cover the butter. Fold the lower flap of dough up over the upper flap, making 3 layers and completely covering the butter.

Press the side edges of the dough firmly together to enclose as much air as possible. Chill the paste in the refrigerator for 20 minutes.

Place the chilled dough on a board with either side facing you.

Gently roll the paste away from you to make a long rectangle about ½ inch thick and about 20 inches long. The dough should be rolled without letting the butter break through the surface of the dough. This is one of the secrets of making puff pastry. If you let the butter break through, it means enclosed air is being lost, and it is this enclosed air that will make the pastry puff.

Fold the rectangle of dough into thirds as you did the first time and turn it so one of the edges faces you. This rolling, folding, and turning is called a "turn."

Make another turn and again chill the dough in the refrigerator for 20 minutes.

Then make 2 more turns and chill again in the refrigerator for 20 minutes.

Then make 2 more turns (this makes six turns in all) and chill for 15 min-utes before rolling and cutting the dough for baking.

If the paste is not used at once, wrap it in waxed paper and store in the refrigerator; it may be kept several days before using.

When ready to use, roll ¼ to ⅓ inch thick, cut as desired and place on baking sheet rinsed with cold water and drained thoroughly. Prick shapes and chill it again before baking. The paste should be ice cold when placed in the oven.

Bake in very hot oven (450°F.) about 8 minutes, or until paste has risen its full height; then reduce heat to moderate (350°F.) and bake 10 to 20 minutes, or until delicately browned. This amount of dough will make 2½ to 4 dozen fancy pastries.

CREAM HORNS

Use a small amount of puff pastry at a time, leaving remaining pastry in refrigerator until needed.

Roll puff pastry on a pastry cloth ⅛ inch thick, keeping shape rectangular.

With a sharp knife, cut it into long strips ½ to ¾ inch wide.

Roll these strips around metal cream horn forms, overlapping edges slightly. Or use cornucopias made out of stiff brown paper, one for each strip of pastry. Place on cold dampened baking sheet and bake in very hot oven (450°F.) until well puffed and lightly browned, about 20 minutes. Quickly remove from oven; quickly brush with egg white wash (1 slightly beaten egg white combined with 1 teaspoon water) and return to oven to finish baking, about 5 minutes.

Remove from metal horns or paper cornucopias and cool on cake rack. When cool, fill with vanilla-flavored whipped cream or cream filling.

NAPOLEONS

Roll puff pastry on pastry cloth that has practically no flour on it, into a rectangle about ⅛ inch thick.

Cut into strips 2½ inches wide. Prick all over with a fork. Place on a baking sheet that has had cold water run over it and excess shaken off. Chill until dough is very stiff.

Bake in very hot oven (450°F.) about 8 minutes, or until paste has risen its full height. Then reduce heat to moderate (350°F.) and bake until dry and delicately browned, 10 to 20 minutes.

Cool thoroughly and cut into 3-inch bars. Sandwich two bars together with whipped cream or a rich cream filling.

BOUCHÉES

Roll puff pastry about ⅛ inch thick. Shape in the same way as puff pastry patty shells, making them much smaller (1½ to 2 inches in diameter).

VOL-AU-VENT

This is a large puff pastry shell, usually 6 to 8 inches in diameter, to be filled with meat, poultry, or game mixtures. A vol-au-vent may be shaped on the back of a deep pan or may be fashioned in the same manner as individual patty shells.

Roll puff pastry about ⅓ inch thick. Cut 2 large ovals or rounds, using floured mold or sharp-pointed knife (cutting around a cardboard pattern).

Brush outer edge of one with cold water. Cut off a ¾-inch-wide band around edge of remaining oval and place this ring on plain oval, pressing lightly.

Then press in very lightly the inside edge of ring to prevent uneven rising. Prick several places with a fork and chill thoroughly.

Roll the remaining cut-out piece ¼ inch thick and cut shape for cover.

Bake in very hot oven (450°F.) about 8 minutes. Then reduce heat to moderate (350°F.) and bake 20 to 30 minutes, until delicately browned. Cover with paper if pastry browns too quickly.

PUFF PASTRY PATTY SHELLS

Use a small amount of the pastry at a time, leaving the rest in the refrigerator until needed.

Roll the pastry out on a pastry cloth that has practically no flour on it to a thickness of ¼ inch.

Cut into 3-inch rounds with a lightly floured cutter. Cut out centers from half the rounds with a small cutter.

Moisten underside of each ring with cold water and place on remaining plain rounds, pressing down lightly. Then press in lightly the inside edge of ring to prevent uneven rising.

Brush the surface with beaten egg or with milk mixed with beaten egg. Chill thoroughly.

Bake in very hot oven (450°F.) 8 minutes, or until paste has risen its full height; then reduce heat to moderate (350°F.) and bake 10 to 20 minutes, or until delicately browned.

The small rounds cut out from the circles may be baked separately for caps.

Baked patty shells are sold ready-to-serve in many bakeries; frozen patty shells are available in groceries. Just split the baked shells and fill them with whipped cream or any desired pudding. Garnish with fruits and berries.

PIZZA

Pizza is the Italian word for pie; specifically a pie of Neapolitan origin with a crust of bread dough that is spread with tomatoes or tomato sauce, cheese (usually mozzarella), oregano, and sometimes various other toppings. It is eaten hot, generally with the fingers.

PIZZA

(For two 12-inch round pies)

Dough:

1 cup warm (not hot) water
1 package active dry or 1 cake compressed yeast
1 teaspoon sugar
1 teaspoon salt
2 tablespoons olive or salad oil
2 cups sifted enriched flour
Additional 1½ cups sifted enriched flour (about)

Topping:

1 6-ounce can (⅔ cup) tomato paste
½ cup water
1 teaspoon salt
1 teaspoon crushed oregano
Dash of pepper
½ pound Mozzarella cheese, sliced about ⅛ inch thick
4 tablespoons olive or salad oil
4 tablespoons grated Parmesan cheese

Sprinkle or crumble yeast into the 1 cup water and stir until dissolved. Stir in 1 teaspoon sugar, 1 teaspoon salt, and 2 tablespoons oil.

Add 2 cups flour and beat until smooth, then gradually stir in the additional 1½ cups flour. Dough should be as soft as biscuit dough. Turn out on lightly floured board and knead until smooth and elastic.

Place in greased bowl; brush top with soft shortening. Cover and let rise in warm place (85°F.), free from draft, until doubled in bulk, about 45 minutes.

Mix together the tomato paste, ½ cup water, 1 teaspoon salt, 1 teaspoon oregano, and dash of pepper.

When dough is doubled in bulk, punch down and divide in half. Form each half into a ball and place on greased baking sheet. Press out with palms of hands into circles about 12 inches in diameter, making edges slightly thick.

On each circle of dough arrange half of the Mozzarella cheese. Spread evenly half of the tomato mixture; sprinkle evenly 2 tablespoons oil and 2 tablespoons grated Parmesan cheese.

Bake in hot oven (400°F.) about 25 minutes. Serve hot. Makes 2 12-inch pies.

PIZZA #2

(For an 11 x 15-inch pan)

1 package active dry or 1 cake compressed yeast
⅞ cup warm (not hot) water
1½ tablespoons olive or salad oil
¼ teaspoon salt
2⅔ cups sifted enriched flour
¼ pound fresh Italian sausage
1½ cups solid part Italian plum tomatoes
2 tablespoons olive oil
1 teaspoon crushed oregano
½ to 1 teaspoon crushed basil
Freshly ground pepper
¾ pound Mozzarella cheese, sliced about ⅛ inch thick
4 ounces anchovies in oil

Add yeast to water and stir until dissolved. Add the oil, salt, and flour and mix well. Dough should be as soft as biscuit dough. Add a bit more flour if necessary.

Turn onto a floured board and knead until very smooth and elastic. Place in a greased bowl; grease surface and let stand in a warm place (85°F.), free from draft, until doubled in bulk. On cool days bowl of dough may be put in pan of warm water.

While dough is rising prick skin of sausages and cook, covered, in a little water 5 minutes. Uncover and brown lightly. Cool and slice.

Turn dough out of bowl and shape into a smooth ball. Place in a greased shallow pan, about 11 x 15 inches, and press until the dough fits pan.

Cover with pieces of tomato and sprinkle with oil. Sprinkle with oregano, basil, and pepper.

Cover two-thirds of dough with Mozzarella, leaving uncovered the third adjacent to a lengthwise rim.

Arrange anchovies on outer half of cheese-covered dough. Put sausage on dough that has no cheese on it. This leaves center part with only cheese on it.

Bake in very hot oven (450°F) 15 to 20 minutes or until brown. Cut into strips or squares and serve piping hot. Makes 30 to 36 strips.

Early Preparation Methods for Pizza

(1) Prepare the yeast dough several hours before serving time and chill it in the refrigerator.

About 2 hours before time to bake the pizza, spread the dough in the pan, apply the topping and cover with waxed paper or aluminum foil. Return to the refrigerator.

Remove to a warm place for 20 minutes or while heating the oven and bake as directed, using the lower shelf of the oven.

(2) Bake the pizza until half done or until the dough is set. Cool the pizza, cover well and let stand at room temperature. Complete the baking just before serving.

The first method gives a fresher topping, but requires more judgment, for it is difficult to estimate the rate of rising in the refrigerator. Partial baking gives a very acceptable product.

PIZZA WITH HOT ROLL MIX BASE

1 package hot roll mix
1/2 cup minced onion
1 tablespoon olive oil
1 can (8 ounces) tomato sauce
1 can (6 ounces) tomato paste
1 teaspoon salt
1/4 teaspoon oregano
1/8 teaspoon garlic salt
1/8 teaspoon pepper
Olive oil or salad oil
1/2 pound Italian or other white cheese
1/4 cup finely-cut parsley
2 to 3 tablespoons grated Parmesan cheese, if desired

Prepare dough and let rise as directed in basic recipe on hot roll mix package.

Sauté 1/2 cup minced onion in 1 tablespoon olive oil until golden brown.

Combine and add tomato sauce, tomato paste, salt, oregano, garlic salt and pepper.

Divide dough into 4 parts. Flatten each piece and pat into bottoms of 4 9 or 10-inch piepans. (If desired, dough may be divided in half, rolled to 2 12 x 8 x 2-inch rectangles and placed on ungreased baking sheets.)

Brush with olive oil or salad oil.

Slice thin or grate 1/2 pound Italian or other white cheese. Arrange half of cheese on dough. Cover with the tomato sauce. Top with remaining cheese and additional topping as desired. See suggestions below.

Sprinkle with 1/4 cup finely-cut parsley and 2 to 3 tablespoons grated Parmesan cheese, if desired.

Bake immediately in very hot oven (450°F.) 15 to 20 minutes. Serve hot.

Pizza Variations:

Mushroom Pizza: Place 1 cup mushrooms, chopped or sliced, over dough.

Anchovy Pizza: Place 12 to 14 anchovies (whole or pieces) over dough.

Italian Sausage Pizza: Arrange 1 cup pepperoni or other Italian sausage, diced or sliced thin, over dough.

Salami Pizza: Arrange 1 cup salami, cut into thin strips, over dough.

Pork Sausage Pizza: Place 1 cup cooked pork sausage over dough.

QUICK PIZZA CRACKER SNACKS

1 can (1 1/4 cups) condensed tomato soup
1 small clove garlic, minced
1/4 teaspoon oregano
3/4 pound sharp Cheddar cheese, sliced
50 saltines

Combine soup, garlic, and oregano. Let stand for at least 20 minutes. Top each saltine with a bit of tomato sauce and a slice of cheese.

Sprinkle with additional oregano if desired.

Bake on cooky sheet in hot oven (400°F.) until cheese melts, about 3 to 5 minutes. Makes about 50.

PIZZA WITH BISCUIT BASE

1 No. 2 can (2 1/2 cups) cooked tomatoes
1/2 cup chopped green pepper
1 clove garlic, minced
1 teaspoon salt
1/2 teaspoon oregano, optional
Dash of pepper
2 cups sifted enriched flour
3 teaspoons baking powder
1 teaspoon salt
1/4 cup shortening
2/3 to 3/4 cup milk
Melted butter or margarine
2 cups shredded Italian or sharp Cheddar cheese (1/2 pound)

Combine tomatoes, green pepper, garlic, salt, oregano, and pepper. Mix well and let stand while preparing biscuit dough.

Sift together flour, baking powder, and salt. Cut or rub in shortening until mixture is crumbly. Add milk to make a soft dough. Mix well.

Divide dough in 4 equal portions. Pat each portion out on greased baking sheet to circle about 7 inches in diameter, making a slight ridge around the edge. Brush lightly with butter or margarine.

Sprinkle 1/4 cup cheese over each biscuit round. Spoon tomato mixture over cheese. Top with remaining cheese.

Bake in hot oven (425°F.) 15 minutes. Reduce heat and bake in moderate oven (350°F.) 15 minutes longer.

Cut into pie-shaped pieces and serve hot. Makes 4 individual pizza-style pies.

PIZZA-STYLE SNACKS WITH ENGLISH MUFFINS

6 English muffins
3 ripe tomatoes or 1 1/4 cups drained stewed tomatoes
24 anchovy fillets or dash of rosemary
12 thin slices of cheese
Olive oil
Salt and pepper

Break muffins apart; toast until slightly crispy.

Thinly slice tomatoes and place 1 slice or 2 tablespoons stewed tomatoes on each muffin half.

Add either 2 anchovy fillets or dash of rosemary. Add another layer of fresh tomato or stewed tomato and top with slice of cheese.

Sprinkle with olive oil, salt, and pepper. Place under broiler and broil until cheese melts. Serves 6.

PIZZA-STYLE SNACKS

2 cups sifted enriched flour
3 teaspoons baking powder
1 teaspoon salt
1/3 cup salad oil
2/3 cup milk
Salad oil
Tomato Topping (below)
1/2 pound pasteurized process cheese food

Sift flour, baking powder, and salt into bowl. Pour 1/3 cup oil into measuring cup; add milk and pour all at once into dry ingredients. Stir with fork until mixture rounds up into a ball. Knead about 10 times without flour.

Roll dough between waxed paper to 1/4 inch thickness. Cut into 6 3 1/2-inch rounds. Place on ungreased cooky sheet. Brush top of each round with oil. Spread with Tomato Topping.

Bake in hot oven (400°F.) 15 minutes or until edges are lightly browned.

Remove from oven and arrange strips of cheese in spoke fashion on top. Bake 5 minutes more, or until cheese is melted. Makes 6 individual snacks.

Tomato Topping:

1 cup canned drained tomatoes
1/2 cup chopped stuffed olives
2 tablespoons finely chopped green onions
1/4 teaspoon oregano
1/2 teaspoon salt
1/8 teaspoon pepper

Break up tomatoes and combine with olives, onions, and seasonings. Drain well just before placing on rounds of dough.

PIZZA-STYLE SNACKS WITH ENGLISH MUFFINS #2

Split 6 large English muffins in half. Remove centers, reserving crumbs for casserole dishes.

Brush each half with butter and add filling as given above. Broil until filling is bubbly and hot and cheese melts. Serves 6.

Pizza-Style Snacks

POULTRY AND GAME BIRDS

MODERN POULTRY

The biggest differences between modern poultry and the chickens, turkeys, and ducks our mothers were able to buy are in tenderness, amount of available meat per pound, and constancy of supply. Modern poultry raising is such a streamlined process that a steady flow of tender meaty poultry comes to our markets the year round, maintaining a fairly constant quality and price.

All modern poultry is fed a carefully balanced diet, designed to produce a high percentage of meat, compared to total weight, at a very early age. As a result chickens and turkeys have more breast meat and larger drumsticks; ducklings have a minimum amount of excess fat. The younger marketing ages mean lower prices for the consumer, too.

The inspection mark of the U. S. Department of Agriculture in the form of a circle denotes wholesomeness. It is required on all poultry sold across state lines. The grade mark may be used only on poultry that has been inspected and has met rigid sanitary requirements set up by the Federal Government. Usually the inspection circle and the grade shield appear on the wrapper, wing tag, giblet wrap, package insert, or label.

CHICKEN SELECTION HINTS

Chicken is available in different classes; size, age, and sex of the chicken determine the class. Age influences tenderness which, in turn, determines the cooking method.

The common classes are: Broiler or Fryer, Roaster and Hen—the latter also called Stewing Chicken or Fowl. The latter term is gradually being discontinued. Capon is another class found in some markets.

Age and sex cannot be determined readily. However, it is unnecessary for the consumer to judge them because there are easy guides for selection:

(1) Quality (in reference to the general appearance, the meatiness and the finish—that is, the amount and distribution of fat) or grade labeling; (2) characteristics which identify each class and quality of chicken.

Guides for quality selection are based on brand names, government grades, or both. These may be found on a wing band, a stamp on the bird, a tag, the wrap or package.

When this labeling information is not present, there are identifying characteristics which are helpful in selecting chicken: The size; the texture and thickness of the skin; the firmness of the flesh; the amount and distribution of fat; and the breastbone flexibility. These characteristics are described in the following definition of each class:

Broiler or Fryer: A young chicken (either sex, usually 10 to 16 weeks of age) with smooth, thin, soft skin; tender-meated, soft flesh; small amount of fat underneath skin along backbone, over drumsticks and thighs and along the sides of breast; and flexible-tipped (cartilaginous) breastbone.

Roaster: A young chicken (either sex, usually under 8 months of age) having the same characteristics as a broiler or

fryer. There is usually slightly more fat, the chicken is larger and the breastbone is slightly less flexible.

Capon: A young chicken (unsexed male, usually under 10 months of age) having the same characteristics as the roaster, but with exceptionally good finish, flavor, and tenderness brought about by caponizing. It has a large proportion of white meat.

Stewing Chicken: A mature chicken (female, usually more than 10 months of age). It has less-tender, firm flesh; thick, firm skin; well developed connective tissue; a layer of fat underneath the skin, giving the chicken a full, well rounded appearance; and a non-flexible breastbone.

PREPARATION OF POULTRY FOR COOKING

Fresh Poultry: Ready-to-cook birds should need no preparation before cooking. But you may have to remove a few pinfeathers. Wash and dry bird.

If poultry is purchased "dressed" style, it should be drawn promptly, and refrigerated at 36–40°F. loosely wrapped. If whole, use it within 2 to 3 days; if cut-up, within 1 or 2 days. Wash the bird in cold water and pat dry just before cooking.

How to Clean Poultry: Dry-picked poultry is preferred or it may be dipped into hot, not boiling, water until water penetrates to skin.

Grasp feathers close to skin and pull in direction they grow, not against it. ("Dressed" birds have been bled and picked but the head and feet and internal organs have not been removed.)

Singe off hairs by holding dry bird over direct flame, turning to expose all parts of the body. Remove pinfeathers with dull edge of knife or tweezers. Cut off head and feet and wing tip, if desired.

Cut out the oil sac on top of tail. Cut circle around vent below tail, leaving it free to be removed with internal organs. Make a crosswise slit, large enough for drawing, between the two cuts.

Insert hand and carefully loosen entrails from back and sides; draw out internal organs, making sure lungs are removed. Save heart, liver, and gizzard.

Slit skin lengthwise at back of neck, leaving skin on bird. Slip skin down and remove crop and windpipe. Cut neck off short and save.

How to Clean Giblets: Giblets include the gizzard, heart, and liver. The giblets and neck are usually included when a whole bird is purchased.

To clean giblets from a "dressed" bird, cut blood vessels from heart and carefully cut away green gall sac from liver. Be careful not to break the gall sac. Gall is bitter and will spoil the flavor of any meat it touches.

Cut through one side of gizzard to inner lining, remove lining and discard.

When the giblets are included with the ready-to-cook poultry they should also be cleaned promptly.

Any blood vessels at the heart and any gall stain on the liver should be cut away. Be sure the gizzard has been split open and the inner sac removed. Scrape the lining of the gizzard with a knife.

Giblets may be kept 1 or 2 days wrapped and placed close to the freezing compartment. If quick-frozen, cook promptly after defrosting.

DEFROSTING FROZEN POULTRY

Follow package directions or defrost poultry by one or a combination of these methods.

1. Leave bird in its original body wrap. Place on shelf in refrigerator. A chicken will defrost in the refrigerator overnight; a turkey may take from 2 to 4 days.

2. Place bird, still in its original body wrap, under running cold water, 2 to 4 hours for chicken and up to 6 hours for turkey.

Prompt cooking after defrosting is preferable. Do not refreeze. A defrosted, ready-to-cook or a fresh-drawn bird can be kept for two or three days in a refrigerator at 38°F. or less. Wrap bird loosely in aluminum foil or moisture-proof paper.

In whole birds, be sure to remove the giblets and neck, which are wrapped separately and placed in either the body cavity or wishbone area.

Rinse the bird, giblets, and neck in cold water and pat dry before cooking.

Poultry may be put on to cook when partly defrosted; that is, when whole birds are pliable enough to remove giblets, and cut-up poultry pliable enough

to separate the parts. Allow additional cooking time.

CARE OF COOKED POULTRY

Refrigerate cooked poultry immediately after the meal. If poultry has been cooked several hours, or a day or two in advance of service, cool it rapidly and refrigerate promptly. Cover or wrap it well to prevent drying out or loss of flavor.

If roast poultry has been stuffed, remove any stuffing from the cavities and store it separately, well covered.

Do not allow the poultry, the stuffing, or the gravy to stand in the kitchen after the meal.

Use leftover stuffing within a day or two and heat very thoroughly for service.

For the best flavor, use poultry meat within 2 or 3 days after cooking and broth within 1 or 2 days unless properly wrapped and frozen.

GIBLET COOKERY

The neck is usually included with the giblets when whole birds are purchased, fresh or quick-frozen.

Moist heat is required to soften the gizzard, heart, and neck. When they are added to gravy, sauces, or stuffing or served with broiled and fried chicken, the giblets and neck must be precooked by simmering in seasoned water until the gizzard is fork-tender.

When poultry is braised or stewed, the giblets and the neck may be cooked with the bird.

Liver is very tender and requires only 10 to 15 minutes' cooking at low temperature. It is so tender that it may be broiled or fried without the preliminary cooking required for gizzard, heart, and neck.

HOW TO RENDER CHICKEN OR GOOSE FAT

If a chicken is to be used for soup, or if goose has excess fat, it is advisable to remove the excess fat and render it. The rendered fat and the cracklings are used in a number of recipes given in this and other sections of the book.

Cut the excess fat from the bird and, if cracklings are desired, also remove the fatty parts of skin. Cut into small (1-inch-square) pieces.

Place in a heavy skillet. Add cold water to cover. Cover and bring to a boil. Cook about 20 minutes.

Uncover and cook over low heat until all water has evaporated and only the melted fat and cracklings remain.

Add 1 diced onion and continue cooking until the skin is crisp and well browned and the onion brown but not burned.

Strain off the fat. Chill and use in cooking. Serve the cracklings with rye bread and crackers.

Recipes with Chicken Breasts

HOW TO BONE CHICKEN BREASTS

Boneless chicken breasts are the basis of many elegant dishes and are called for in a number of recipes in this book. Breast of chicken when it is removed raw from one side of the bird in a skinless, boneless piece is called a suprême. Some meatmen will bone the breasts for you, but it is not difficult to do yourself, and with a little practice you can easily master the technique.

Cut the chicken breasts in halves. Place the breasts on a flat surface and, using your fingers, pull off the skin. Then with a sharp paring knife, cut against the ridge of the breastbone to loosen the flesh. Continue cutting along the rib cage, pulling flesh from bone as you cut until meat from one side of the breast separates from the bone in one piece. Be careful not to tear the meat. Cut and pull out the white tendon that runs about two-thirds down the under side of the meat. Flatten the suprêmes lightly with the side of a heavy knife.

LEMON CHICKEN ROLLS

½ pound fresh mushrooms, sliced
2 tablespoons butter
½ teaspoon dill seed
½ teaspoon salt
⅛ teaspoon ground black pepper
2 tablespoons chopped chives
2 teaspoons grated lemon rind
About 1⅔ cups buttery cracker crumbs, finely rolled
4 chicken breasts, boned and split
2 tablespoons butter, melted

Sauté mushroom in butter with dill seed. Stir in salt, pepper, chives, lemon rind, and cracker crumbs. Mix lightly but well.

Place chicken breasts between 2 sheets of waxed paper. Flatten to about ⅛-inch thick with a rolling pin. Place ⅛ of the stuffing on each chicken breast. Roll up and secure with toothpicks.

Place on an ungreased baking sheet. Brush with melted butter. Sprinkle with paprika, if desired. Bake in moderate oven (350°F.) 25 to 30 minutes. Serves 8.

Lemon Chicken Rolls

Bacony Chicken Breasts

BACONY CHICKEN BREASTS

2   whole chicken breasts, split
4   strips bacon
⅓   cup butter
2   tablespoons Worcestershire sauce
2   tablespoons chopped chives

Split chicken breasts. Cut 2 slashes across each half of chicken breast. Place ½ strip of raw bacon into each slash.

Cream butter. Beat in Worcestershire sauce and chopped chives. Spread mixture over chicken breasts.

Bake in moderate oven (375°F.) 40 minutes, or until breasts are tender and brown. Brush chicken breasts with pan drippings 4 to 5 times during cooking. Serve with pan drippings, noodles Romanoff (use a mix), and Frenched green beans. Serves 2.

CHICKEN À LA KIEV

A classic recipe created during the Czarist days in Russia. It is rolled, boneless breast of chicken stuffed with butter, often seasoned with chives. The butter should spurt forth when a knife slices into it.

3   whole breasts of chicken or
      6 fresh or frozen halves
½   cup chilled sweet firm butter
Salt and pepper
2   tablespoons chopped chives
Flour for dusting
2   eggs, lightly beaten
1   cup very fine dry breadcrumbs
Fat for deep frying

Cut the breasts in half. Remove the bone from the breasts of chicken. Place them between pieces of waxed paper and pound flat and very thin with a mallet. Do not split the flesh. Remove the waxed paper.

Cut the butter into six finger-shaped pieces. Place a piece in the middle of each breast and sprinkle with salt, pepper, and chives. Roll the chicken around it and fold the flaps in envelope fashion, completely enclosing the butter. Secure with a toothpick, if necessary. Dust lightly with flour. Brush with beaten egg. Roll in dry breadcrumbs. Refrigerate one hour or more so the crumbs will adhere.

Fill a fryer or kettle with enough fat to completely cover the breasts. Heat the fat until hot (360°F.). Add chicken gradually and fry until golden brown on all sides. Drain on absorbent paper. One half breast makes a portion. Serves 6.

CHICKEN BREASTS EN PAPILLOTE

En papillote is a French term meaning cooked in parchment or in a paper bag. Nowadays, aluminum foil is usually substituted for the paper.

3   chicken breasts, cut in halves
Chicken broth or lightly salted water
¼   cup butter
2   tablespoons flour
¼   cup milk
½   cup dry white wine
1   lightly beaten egg yolk
Salt and pepper
Pinch of cayenne pepper
Pinch of nutmeg or mace
Pinch of ground cloves
¼   cup finely chopped mushrooms
1   teaspoon chopped onions or chives

Place chicken breasts in small pot and barely cover with broth. Bring to a boil, reduce heat, cover and simmer gently until tender, 20 to 40 minutes, depending upon the size of the breasts.

Remove chicken from broth and let cool. Then carefully remove skin and bones from the meat.

Cut 6 pieces of aluminum foil large enough to make an envelope for each breast half. Spread the foil with half the butter.

Melt remaining butter in a saucepan; add the flour and stir until blended. In another pan, bring milk, wine, and ½ cup of the chicken broth to a boil; add all at once to the butter-flour mixture, stirring vigorously until sauce is smooth and thickened.

Pour a little of the hot sauce into the beaten egg yolk, then combine with remaining sauce, and stir gently until thickened. Do not let boil. Add seasonings; stir in mushrooms and onions or chives.

Place a half chicken breast in center of each square of foil; spoon some sauce over top. Fold the foil to make a secure package, crimping the edges to seal tightly. Arrange on baking sheet and bake in hot oven (400°F) 10 minutes. Serve wrapped in the foil. Serves 6.

CHICKEN AND GRAPES

1   cup cracker crumbs, finely rolled
½   teaspoon salt
¼   teaspoon ground black pepper
¼   teaspoon basil leaves
¼   teaspoon tarragon leaves
3   chicken breasts, split
¼   cup butter
¼   cup minced onion
¼   cup water
¾   cup white wine
1   chicken bouillon cube
½   pound fresh mushrooms, sliced
3   tablespoons butter
2   cups Thompson seedless grapes or
      Muscat grapes, seeded

Mix crumbs, salt, pepper, basil, and tarragon. Remove skin from chicken

breasts. Coat chicken in cracker crumbs. Heat ¼ cup butter in large skillet and brown chicken on all sides.

Place chicken in single layer in large baking pan. Add minced onion to butter in skillet and cook until soft. Pour in water and wine. Add chicken bouillon cube. Bring liquid to a boil, stirring to dissolve bouillon cube and pour around chicken. Bake, uncovered, in moderate oven (375°F.) 40 minutes.

Meanwhile, sauté mushrooms in 3 tablespoons butter. At end of 40 minutes baking time add mushrooms and grapes to chicken. Continue to cook 8 to 10 minutes. Serves 6.

Note: Another part of the chicken may be used, if desired.

Chicken and Grapes

CHICKEN SUPREME, FOIL-BAKED

6   chicken breasts
1½   teaspoons salt
Dash of pepper
1   tablespoon minced green onion
2   tablespoons minced parsley
1   clove garlic, minced
½   teaspoon crushed tarragon
Dash of thyme
1   can condensed cream of mushroom soup

Sprinkle chicken with salt and pepper. Combine remaining ingredients; spread on surface and in cavity of chicken breasts.

Place each piece of chicken on square of aluminum foil; bring edges together and seal with drugstore wrap, folding corners under.

Place on cooky sheet. Bake in very hot oven (450°F.) 20 to 25 minutes; turn packages over; bake 20 minutes. Serve in foil. Serves 6.

Chicken Supreme, Foil Baked

How to Carve Poultry

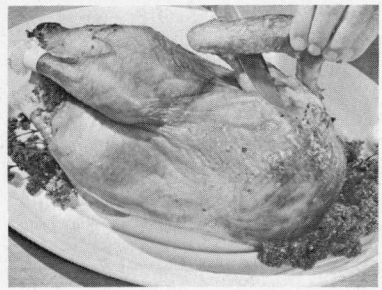

1. Cut off tip and first joint. This may be done in advance of placing bird on platter in the kitchen. (The one next to the platter must be cut off in advance.)

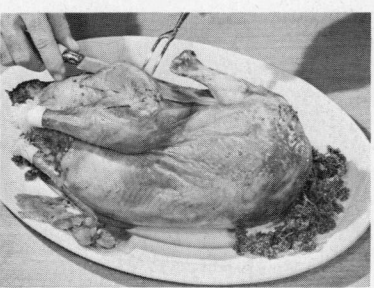

2. Insert fork, just below the thigh, to steady the bird while slicing. Cut thin slices of leg meat, away from carver, parallel to the bone until thigh bone and joints are exposed. Arrange slices of meat in neat overlapping style around platter's edge.

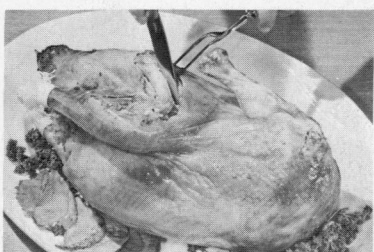

3. With point of knife cut around the thigh bone, loosening meat and skin adjacent to the bone.

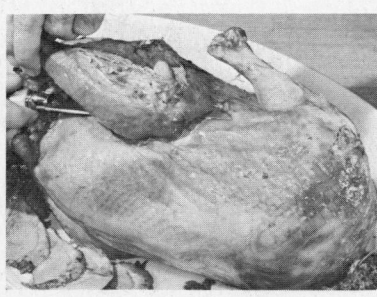

4. Cut skin underneath the leg to free it from the body.

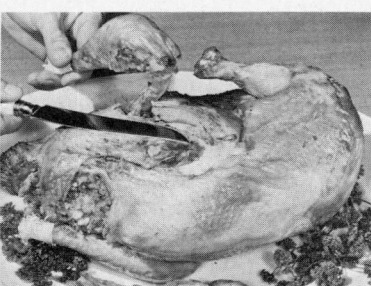

5. Lift drumstick up taking thigh bone with it—in one piece. If the bird is properly cooked, the joint holding the leg to the body should give easily. Place this piece behind the bird at the back of the platter. If drumstick meat is to be served, cut joint separating leg into drumstick and thigh bone. Transfer drumstick to side plate or platter.

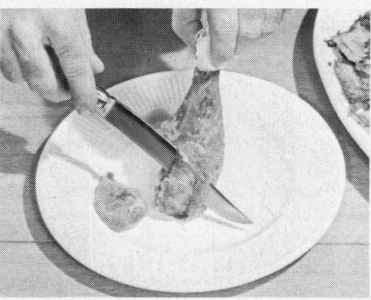

6. Hold drumstick upright, or at a convenient angle to the plate. Slice meat turning drumstick to obtain uniform slices. Avoid cutting into tendons that may be present.

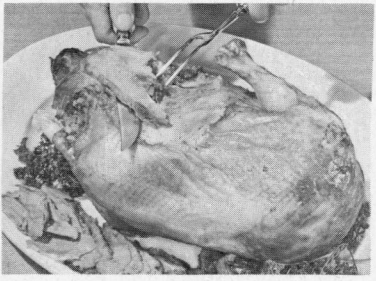

7. Slice remaining thigh meat down to the body. If possible, include some of the "oyster" meat with each slice.

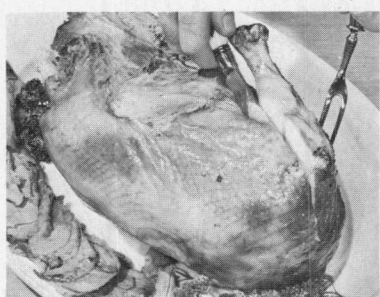

8. Insert fork into the body, just below the wing joint. Make a cut in front of and parallel to the wing joint, cutting into the breast meat down to the bone.

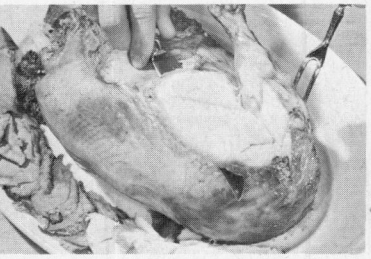

9. Keeping fork in the same position and holding knife parallel to the platter, cut slices of white meat until enough slices are obtained or until keel bone is exposed. Arrange slices as they are carved, around the edge of the platter.

10. Unless stuffing is exposed, cut an opening, large enough to insert a serving spoon, in the tissue. Remove stuffing with spoon and place serving portions on dinner plates.

11. For each serving, lay slices of dark and white meat over the hot stuffing.

Roast Chicken — Oven-Baked Chicken

ROAST CHICKEN
(Master Recipe)

All sizes of tender chicken may be roasted. Plumpness is a desirable quality.

Stuffing: Rub cavity of prepared bird with ½ to 1 teaspoon salt. If desired, stuff. *Do not stuff bird ahead of time, but just before roasting.* Stuffing prepared in advance must be refrigerated. Stuff body and wishbone cavities lightly.

Trussing (or Shaping): This assures compactness to permit even cooking and browning. The chicken is more attractive and easier to carve.

To truss: Fasten neck skin to the back with skewers. Shape wings "akimbo" style and bring wing tips onto the back.

Close abdominal opening with skewers and cord.

Tie drumsticks to tail. A skewer above the tail on the back helps to hold this cord in place.

If there is a bridge of skin at abdominal opening, push drumsticks underneath this bridge. It will hold them down without skewers and cord.

Roasting: Brush skin thoroughly with fat.

Place trussed bird breast up or down, as desired, on a rack at least ½ inch high in shallow open pan.

Cover top of chicken with fat-moistened thin cloth. Do not wrap bird in the cloth.

The cloth helps in uniform browning and makes basting unnecessary.

Roast at a constant low temperature. See timetable below.

Do not sear. Do not add water. Do not cover.

If cloth dries during cooking, moisten cloth with fat from drippings in the pan.

If bird was started breast down, turn breast up when about ¾ done.

To test, press the thickest part of the drumstick between the fingers—meat should be very soft. Protect the fingers with paper or cloth.

Another test is to move the drumsticks up and down; leg joints should move readily or break.

A low roasting temperature assures excellent drippings, rich in color and flavor for the gravy, not burned or dried in the pan.

Remove skewers and any cord. Place on warm platter while preparing gravy with the drippings in the roasting pan.

Do not partly roast stuffed poultry on one day and complete roasting the following day.

STUFFING AND TRUSSING POULTRY FOR ROASTING

Here's how to get a chicken or turkey ready to go into the oven.

Fill neck cavity with stuffing.

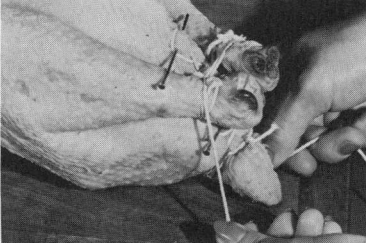
Tie drumsticks to tail, or push them under bridge of skin if it is present.

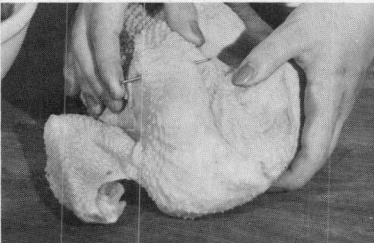
Skewer neck skin to back.

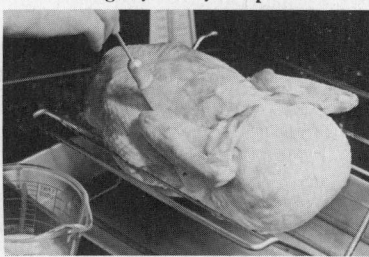
Brush skin with fat.

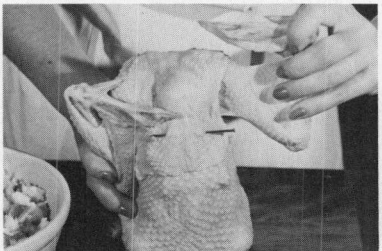
Lift wing up and out forcing the tip back until it rests flat against neck skin.

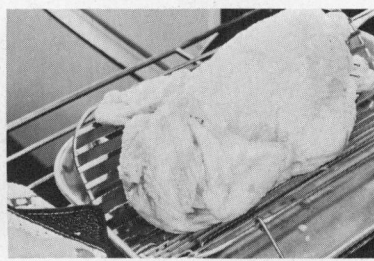
Roast at a low temperature.

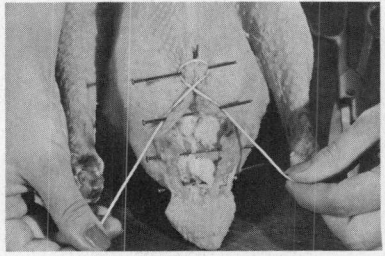
Lace abdominal opening to hold stuffing.

Test for doneness.

TIMETABLE FOR ROASTING CHICKEN

Dressed Weight	Ready-to-Cook Weight	Oven Temperature	Approximate Roasting Time
2 to 3½ lbs.	1⅓ to 2½ lbs.	350°F.	1¼ to 2 hrs.
3½ to 4½ lbs.	2½ to 3½ lbs.	350°F.	2 to 3 hrs.
4½ to 6 lbs.	3½ to 4¾ lbs.	325°F.	3 to 3½ hrs.
6 lbs. and up	4¾ lbs. and up	325°F.	3½ to 3¾ hrs.

JELLY GLAZED ROAST CHICKEN

Whip ½ cup currant jelly. Spread over roast chicken last 30 minutes of cooking. Complete roasting uncovered. Baste frequently with jelly and drippings.

CHICKEN ROASTED IN PARCHMENT PAPER

Prepare chicken as directed in Roast Chicken. Omit fat-moistened cheesecloth.

Wrap in parchment paper (or waxed paper), doubling the paper over breast. Secure with pins.

Roast in slow oven (325°F.), allowing 30 to 40 minutes per pound, depending upon size. Unwrap for last half hour to let bird brown.

CHICKEN COOKED IN ALUMINUM FOIL

Have the chicken at room temperature. Prepare for roasting and wrap completely in aluminum foil.

Roast in hot oven (400°F.) for 20 minutes. Reduce heat to moderate (350°F.) and roast from then on at 25 minutes per pound.

Open the foil about 30 minutes before roasting time is up to let chicken brown. Baste frequently during this period with pan drippings.

SAVORY CHICKEN LEGS

¾ cup corn flake crumbs
½ teaspoon onion salt
½ teaspoon garlic salt
¼ teaspoon pepper
¼ teaspoon crushed savory
¼ teaspoon curry powder
¼ teaspoon monosodium glutamate
8 to 10 chicken legs with thigh removed (about 2 pounds)
½ cup evaporated milk
1 cup mayonnaise

Combine corn flake crumbs and seasonings. Dip chicken legs in evaporated milk, then coat generously with seasoned corn flake crumbs. Place in foil-lined shallow baking pan. Do not crowd. Bake in hot oven (400°F.) about 15 minutes to set corn flake crumbs.

Spoon mayonnaise generously on top of chicken legs. Reduce heat to slow oven (300°F.) and bake about 1 hour until tender but not dry. Hot buttered biscuits and honey complement this entree. Serves 4 to 6.

Savory Chicken Legs

COUNTRY-STYLE ROAST CHICKEN

Place chicken in an uncovered pan in very hot oven (450°F.) and sear for 20 minutes, or until chicken is brown on all sides.

Reduce heat to slow oven (275° to 300°F.). Pour ¼ cup boiling water into pan. Cover pan and roast until bird is tender, allowing 25 to 30 minutes per pound.

Do not baste. For a crisp crust, uncover during last 30 minutes. Prepare gravy from drippings.

ROAST CHICKEN WITH POTATO-BREAD STUFFING

1 4-pound roasting chicken
3 cups stale bread cubes (firmly packed)
½ cup instant potato powder
2 teaspoons rubbed sage
1 teaspoon salt
⅛ teaspoon pepper
½ teaspoon celery salt
1 medium onion, minced
1½ cups milk
¼ cup butter or margarine

Prepare dressing, combining bread cubes, instant potato powder, sage, salt, pepper, celery salt, and onion. Heat milk and butter over low flame until butter is melted; add to bread mixture; mix thoroughly.

Clean chicken. Sprinkle cavity with 1 teaspoon salt and a pinch of pepper. Stuff and truss chicken.

Place on rack in open roaster. Rub with 2 tablespoons butter or margarine; sprinkle with a mixture of 1 teaspoon salt, pinch of pepper, and ½ teaspoon paprika.

Roast in moderate oven (350°F.), calculating 25 minutes per pound weight before stuffing. Serves 5 to 6.

ROAST CHICKEN WITH SAUSAGE-BREAD STUFFING

1 4- to 5-pound roasting chicken
¼ pound sausage meat
1 chicken liver, chopped fine
½ cup mushrooms, chopped fine
½ cup onions, chopped fine
2 cups small dry bread cubes
1 teaspoon salt
½ teaspoon poultry seasoning
Pinch of powdered thyme
½ teaspoon Ac'cent

Rinse chicken and pat dry. Mix remaining ingredients for stuffing, blending lightly but thoroughly. Fill cavity of chicken with stuffing; truss.

Bake in slow oven (325° F.) until tender, allowing 35 minutes per pound stuffed weight of chicken.

Baste with following mixture:

½ cup white wine
¾ teaspoon Ac'cent
¼ cup butter or margarine

Heat ingredients together in saucepan and keep warm. Baste chicken frequently while roasting. Use up all the mixture. Serve chicken with unthickened pan juices. Serves 6.

OVEN CRUSTY CHICKEN

This easy oven method that requires no attention while baking to golden goodness has become one of America's favorite ways of preparing chicken. Quantities can be increased readily for a crowd-pleasing party dish.

1 2½ to 3-pound frying chicken, cut up
½ to ⅔ cup butter or margarine, melted
1 teaspoon salt
½ teaspoon pepper
1 cup corn flake crumbs

Wash chicken pieces and dry thoroughly. Combine melted butter or margarine with salt and pepper. Dip chicken pieces in seasoned butter, then roll in corn flake crumbs until well-coated. Place skin side up in shallow baking pan lined with aluminum foil; do not crowd pieces.

Bake in moderate oven (350°F.) about 1 hour or until tender. Do not cover pan or turn chicken while cooking. Serves 4 to 5.

Note: For **Corn-Crisped Chicken,** add salt and pepper to corn flake crumbs; substitute evaporated milk for butter.

Variations of Oven Crusty Chicken:
Barbecued Crusty Chicken: Use ⅔ cup barbecue sauce in place of seasoned butter.

California Crusty Chicken: Mix 2 to 3 tablespoons lemon juice with the seasoned butter.

Gourmet Crusty Chicken: Omit pepper. Combine ¼ teaspoon thyme, ¼ teaspoon paprika, and ¼ teaspoon curry powder with corn flake crumbs.

Italian Crusty Chicken: Combine ¼ teaspoon crushed oregano, ¼ teaspoon garlic salt, and ½ teaspoon paprika with corn flake crumbs.

Parmesan Crusty Chicken: Combine ½ cup grated Parmesan cheese with corn flake crumbs.

Sesame Crusty Chicken: 2 tablespoons sesame seeds may be added to corn flake crumbs with salt and pepper.

Oven Crusty Chicken

TO ROAST FROZEN COMMERCIALLY STUFFED POULTRY

To roast this type of poultry, follow directions on the package or either of the methods given here. Frozen commercially stuffed poultry is ready for the oven and *must not be thawed before cooking.*

Remove wrapping from poultry; leave the foil-wrapped giblets in place and roast with poultry. Place poultry breast side up on a rack in a shallow roasting pan. Brush with melted fat.

Roast uncovered at 325°F. (slow oven) or in a covered pan at 400°F. (hot oven). Do not add water in either method. If uncovered poultry browns too fast, cover breast and legs lightly with a tent of aluminum foil.

Approximate roasting time for frozen commercially stuffed poultry of various weights are given in the chart. A meat thermometer is the best guide to doneness. When the bird has thawed sufficiently—about half or two-thirds through the roasting time—insert thermometer into the center of the inner thigh muscle. Make certain that the thermometer is not touching bone. The poultry is done when the thermometer reaches 185°F.

To check the stuffing temperature, remove thermometer from the thigh as soon as poultry comes out of the oven, and insert it in the stuffing in the body cavity for about 5 minutes. Stuffing temperature should be at least 165°F. If the temperature is not this high, return the poultry to oven and continue to roast until the stuffing temperature reaches 165°F.

BAKED CHICKEN QUARTERS WITH RAISIN-NUT STUFFING

2 broilers, quartered
Ac'cent, salt, and pepper
4 cups day-old breadcrumbs
2/3 cup melted butter or margarine
1 cup light seedless raisins
1 cup broken walnut meats
2 teaspoons salt
1/2 teaspoon Ac'cent
1/4 teaspoon pepper
1/2 teaspoon oregano
1/2 teaspoon poultry seasoning

Have broilers quartered at market,

Baked Chicken Quarters with Raisin-Nut Stuffing

RECOMMENDED COOKING TIMES FOR FROZEN COMMERCIALLY STUFFED POULTRY *(Do not thaw before cooking)*

Kind and Class	Weight as purchased	Approximate time, uncovered, at 325°F.	Approximate time, covered, at 400°F.
	Pounds	*Hours*	*Hours*
Turkeys	5 to 7	4½ to 6	2½ to 3½.
	7 to 9	6 to 6¾	3½ to 4.
	9 to 11	6¾ to 7¼	4 to 4½.
	11 to 13	7¼ to 8	4½ to 5.
	13 to 15	8 to 8½	5 to 5½.
	15 to 17	8½ to 10	5½ to 6.
Chickens:			
Cornish game hens	2 to 2½	2½ to 3½	
Roasters	4 to 5		2¾ to 3.
	5 to 6		3 to 3¼.
	6 and over		3¼ to 3½.

with necks and backbones removed. (Save them for soup or stock.)

Sprinkle chicken pieces inside and out with Ac'cent, salt, and pepper; let stand while preparing stuffing.

Combine remaining ingredients; toss lightly with fork to mix. Place in open roasting pan.

Arrange chicken quarters over stuffing. Brush with additional melted butter or margarine.

Bake in moderate oven (350°F.) 1½ hours, or until chicken is golden brown and tender. Brush occasionally with melted butter or margarine during baking. Serves 8.

ROAST CHICKEN STUFFED WITH PARSLEY (DANISH STYLE)

1 ready-to-cook young chicken, 2 to 3 pounds
Salt
1 bunch parsley
1 cup melted butter
1/2 cup cream
Broth or water

Rub chicken inside thoroughly with salt. Stuff with parsley mixed with butter.

Grease skin thoroughly and place on rack in shallow pan. Roast in moderate oven (350°F.) until tender, 1½ to 2 hours.

If desired, baste occasionally during roasting with melted butter and juices from bottom of pan.

About ½ hour before done, pour ½ cup cream over chicken. Place chicken on warm serving platter while preparing gravy. Serves 4.

Gravy: For 2 cups of gravy, use the pan drippings, 3 tablespoons flour, and 2 cups of chicken broth previously prepared by cooking giblets and neck in seasoned water.

CHICKEN AND BISCUIT OVEN DINNER

1 2½ to 3-pound frying chicken, cut up
1/2 cup flour
1/2 cup wheat germ
1½ teaspoons paprika
2 teaspoons salt
1/2 cup butter or margarine (1 stick)

Dip chicken pieces in mixture of flour, wheat germ, paprika, and salt. Coat well.

Melt butter or margarine in shallow baking dish (9 x 13 x 2 inches) in hot oven (425°F.). Remove baking dish from oven and place chicken skin side down in a single layer. Bake in hot oven (425°F.) 45 minutes. Turn chicken.

Now prepare your favorite packaged biscuit mix according to directions on package. Enrich by adding 1/3 cup wheat germ to dry mix. Add milk called for in directions plus 1 extra tablespoon. Roll dough; cut biscuits. Place in one end of baking pan, pushing chicken to other end. Be sure both chicken and biscuits remain in single layer.

Bake another 15 minutes or until biscuits are lightly browned. Serves 4.

Chicken and Biscuit Oven Dinner

BAKED BROILERS

Cut small broilers in halves. Rub liberally with sweet butter. Season to taste. Place in pan.

Bake in hot oven (400°F.) ½ hour, turning once and basting several times with drippings. Serve on hot buttered toast, with drippings poured over.

ROAST CHICKEN—SOUTHERN STYLE

1 4½-pound ready-to-cook roasting chicken
Salt
5 cups southern dressing (below)
½ lemon
1 tablespoon melted butter or margarine
1 tablespoon minced celery leaves
¼ teaspoon tarragon
1 tablespoon chopped chives
2 tablespoons cream
3 oranges

Rinse chicken and wipe dry; rub cavity with salt and stuff with dressing (do not pack). Skewer or sew opening.

Truss chicken and rub with lemon and butter. Sprinkle with celery leaves, tarragon, and chives. Wrap loosely in aluminum foil.

Roast on rack in an open, shallow pan in hot oven (400°F.) for 1½ hours.

Open foil; brush with cream and continue roasting at 350°F. until brown and tender, about 45 minutes.

Meanwhile, cook whole oranges in boiling water for 15 minutes; drain, cut in half and roast cut-side-up for the last 20 minutes. Arrange around chicken on platter before serving. Serves 6.

Southern Dressing:

½ cup sausage meat
1 small onion, chopped
½ teaspoon paprika
½ teaspoon salt
¼ cup diced carrots
¼ cup chopped celery
3 cups soft breadcrumbs
2 tablespoons parsley
2 tablespoons milk

Cook sausage meat and onion, stirring frequently until lightly browned.

Combine with remaining ingredients and mix well. Makes 3½ cups dressing.

Roast Chicken—Southern Style

BAKED MARYLAND CHICKEN

Use 2 frying chickens weighing about 2½ pounds each; disjoint, cut in pieces for serving, and wash and dry.

Roll in seasoned flour; dip in egg, beaten slightly with 2 tablespoons water, and roll in coarse breadcrumbs. Place close together in well greased pan or casserole.

Bake, uncovered, in moderate oven (375°F.) 45 to 60 minutes, or until tender. Baste frequently with hot mixture of ⅓ cup butter, 2 tablespoons water, and 1 teaspoon lemon juice.

Serve with gravy made from giblet stock and cream. The crusty crumb covering serves as a dressing. Serves 6.

SAVORY FLORIDA BAKED CHICKEN

2 broiling chickens, cut in halves
Seasoned flour
¼ cup fat or salad oil
1 cup water
2 whole cloves
1 bay leaf
Pinch of thyme
Pinch of marjoram
Few grains of mace
¾ cup orange juice
Orange slices

Shake chicken in paper bag containing flour seasoned with salt and pepper. Brown on both sides in hot fat or salad oil in frying pan.

Remove to large roasting pan. Pour water into frying pan in which chicken was browned. Add herbs and mace. Simmer 10 minutes and strain over chicken in roaster.

Cover and bake in moderate oven (350°F.) 1 hour.

Add orange juice. Bake ½ hour longer, or until chicken is tender. Thicken gravy if desired. Garnish with orange slices. Serves 4.

CANADIAN BAKED CHICKEN

1 roasting chicken (5 to 5½ pounds)
10 strips bacon
Whole cloves
¼ cup brown sugar
1 teaspoon salt
Dash of pepper
1 tablespoon cornstarch
2 tablespoons fat
½ cup hot water

Have the chicken cut in serving pieces.

Roll each piece in a slice of bacon and fasten with wooden picks.

Stick 3 whole cloves in each section; place in roasting pan. Sprinkle with a mixture of sugar, salt, pepper, and cornstarch; add fat and hot water.

Cover tightly and bake in hot oven (400°F.) 1 hour, or until tender. Serve with creamy mashed potatoes. Serves 6.

Chicken International

CHICKEN INTERNATIONAL

2 ready-to-cook young chickens, 2½ pounds

Stuffing:

2 cups cooked rice
2 tablespoons melted butter or margarine
1½ cups drained, canned tomatoes
½ cup chopped onions
½ cup chopped green peppers
½ cup chopped celery
2 chicken livers, chopped
1¼ teaspoons salt
½ teaspoon curry powder
¼ teaspoon pepper
1 teaspoon Ac'cent
1 egg

Sauce:

2 tablespoons cornstarch
1 cup chicken broth
½ cup vinegar
¾ cup sugar
1 teaspoon salt
½ teaspoon Ac'cent
2 tablespoons soy sauce
1 clove garlic, whole or minced
½ cup chopped green pepper
2 cups pineapple chunks
3 tablespoons grated orange rind
2 pimientos, sliced

Stuffing: Put rice into mixing bowl; add butter or margarine; blend. Add remaining stuffing ingredients; mix well.

Stuff body and wishbone cavities of chickens lightly. Truss.

Place birds breast-side-down on rack in shallow open pan. Roast in moderate oven (350°F.) 1½ to 2 hours, until tender. Turn breast-up when about ¾ done.

Sauce: Blend cornstarch with ¼ cup of the broth. Combine with remaining sauce ingredients except pimientos in saucepan.

Cook, stirring constantly, until thickened and clear.

Pour sauce over chickens 20 minutes before they are done. Baste several times.

Add pimientos to sauce about 5 minutes before serving. (For added color and crispness, garnish with slices of red apples.) Serves 8.

ROAST CHICKEN HAWAIIAN

2 3-pound plump chickens
Salt
6 cups rice and orange dressing (below)
3 tablespoons melted butter or margarine
1 tablespoon cornstarch
1 cup broth
1/2 cup vinegar
3/4 cup sugar
1/2 teaspoon Ac'cent
2 tablespoons soy sauce
1 clove garlic, minced
1/2 cup chopped green pepper
2 cups pineapple chunks
3 tablespoons grated orange rind

Rub birds inside and out with salt; stuff bodies and wishbone cavities lightly with dressing, and truss. Brush with melted butter.

Place birds breast-side-down on rack in shallow open pan. Roast in slow oven (325°F.) about 2 to 2½ hours, or until tender. Turn breast up, when about 2/3 done.

Meanwhile, blend cornstarch with 1/4 cup broth. Combine with remaining ingredients and cook over low heat, stirring constantly until thickened and clear. Pour over chickens 20 minutes before they are done. Baste every 8 minutes. Serves 8.

Rice and Orange Dressing:

1 cup raw rice
1 small onion, minced
2 tablespoons shortening or chicken fat
1 large orange
2 tablespoons seedless raisins
1/2 teaspoon salt
1/8 teaspoon pepper
1/2 teaspoon celery salt

Cook rice in boiling lightly salted water until barely tender. Drain thoroughly.

Sauté onion in shortening until golden. Grate rind of orange; peel and remove membrane and seeds; chop orange meat coarsely. Place rind, chopped orange, rice, onion, and raisins in a bowl. Add combined seasonings and mix well.

Makes about 4 cups of dressing, enough for a 5- to 6-pound bird. Use for duck, turkey, chicken, or goose.

BAKED FRYERS

Cut cleaned chicken into quarters. Brown on all sides in melted butter or margarine in frying pan.

Place in baking dish. Pour over 1/2 cup hot chicken stock or milk. Season to taste with salt and pepper.

Cover and bake in slow oven (325°F.) about 1 hour.

To serve, remove chicken from dish

and thicken gravy with flour-water paste. Season to taste. Additional stock, cream, or milk may be used to increase amount of gravy.

ROAST CHICKEN KUCERA

1 3-pound ready-to-cook broiler-fryer
1/2 lemon
1/4 cup pork sausage meat
1/4 cup butter or margarine
3 tablespoons chopped onion
1/2 teaspoon paprika
3/4 teaspoon salt
1/4 cup chopped celery
1/4 cup chopped parsley
4 cups soft breadcrumbs
Milk
1 tablespoon chicken or sausage fat
2 tablespoons chopped celery leaves
1/2 teaspoon rosemary
1/2 cup cream

Rub skin of chicken with cut lemon and set aside.

Cook sausage over low heat until golden brown, breaking it into small pieces as it cooks. Add butter and 2 tablespoons chopped onion. Continue cooking until the onion has softened but not browned.

Remove from heat and add paprika, salt, celery, parsley, and breadcrumbs. Add enough milk to give desired moisture.

Stuff body and neck cavities lightly; then truss. Rub skin with chicken fat, and sprinkle with celery leaves, rosemary, and remaining 1 tablespoon onion.

Wrap loosely in aluminum foil. Place on rack in open shallow pan. Roast in slow oven (325°F.) 1 hour.

Open foil and pull it back to expose chicken so it will brown. Brush with cream and continue to cook until nicely browned and tender, about 45 minutes. Serves 4.

ROAST STUFFED CHICKEN
(IRANIAN STYLE)

1/4 cup cracked wheat cereal
1/2 teaspoon salt
1 tablespoon butter
1 cup water
1 cup canned garbanzos (chick peas)
1 cup chopped, toasted almonds
1 ready-to-cook young chicken, 3 to 3½ pounds
Salt and pepper
Butter or margarine
1/2 cup broth or water
1/3 cup butter or margarine

Cook cracked wheat, salt, 1 tablespoon butter, and water over simmering water until wheat is tender, 1½ to 2 hours. Water should be absorbed by this time.

For stuffing, combine cereal with garbanzos and almonds.

Add black pepper and additional salt to taste.

Meanwhile rub salt, pepper, and softened butter on inside of chicken. Stuff and truss bird as usual. Grease outside skin.

Place on rack in shallow open pan and roast in moderate oven (350°F.) until tender and nicely browned, 2½ to 3 hours. Baste during roasting, with broth and butter mixed together.

Serves 5 to 6.

ROAST CAPON WITH
CHESTNUT STUFFING

1 6-pound ready-to-cook capon
Salt
6 cups chestnut stuffing (below)
3 slices bacon
1/2 cup hot chicken broth
3 tablespoons butter or margarine

Rinse capon, pat dry and rub inside and out with salt.

Stuff with chestnut stuffing (do not pack). Close opening with skewers and truss.

Place on rack in baking pan breast up. Lay bacon over breast. Bake uncovered in moderate oven (375°F.) 30 minutes.

Reduce heat to slow oven (325°F.) and roast for 1¾ hours or until the capon's second joints move easily. Baste often during roasting with hot broth mixed with butter.

Transfer bird to a warm platter. Prepare gravy from drippings.

Serves 6 to 8.

Chestnut Stuffing:

1/2 pound chestnuts
2 cups lightly packed breadcrumbs
3 tablespoons melted butter or margarine
1 teaspoon salt
1 teaspoon dried sage
1/8 teaspoon pepper
1 well beaten egg
1/4 cup cream or top milk

Wash chestnuts and make a gash in each shell. Bake in extremely hot oven (500°F.) 15 minutes.

Cool and remove shells and skins. Cook in boiling salted water for 20 minutes. Drain and chop fine.

Add remaining ingredients and mix well. Makes about 4 cups stuffing.

The meat thermometer tells when it's done. For greater accuracy, insert it between thigh and lowest rib to center of stuffing.

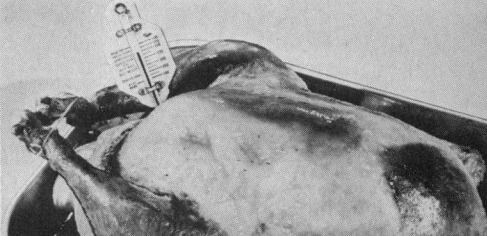

Turkeys

TURKEY SELECTION

Turkeys are sold fresh or frozen, dressed (formerly called New York or market dressed), or ready-to-cook.

Top quality frozen ready-to-cook turkeys have the tendons removed from the drumsticks to make carving easier. If a dressed turkey is bought, have the dealer pull out the tendons and clean the bird so it is ready to cook.

The smallest turkeys may be as little as 2 pounds ready-to-cook weight (broiler-fryers) to more than 25 pounds ready-to-cook weight for the largest turkeys.

Buy a hen turkey if you want an 8- to 15-pound bird. Hen turkeys mature faster and are usually better finished than toms of the same weight. Buy a tom if you want a 16- to 25-pound bird.

WHAT SIZE BIRD TO BUY

When buying medium or heavy birds, 12 pounds or over, allow $\frac{1}{2}$ to $\frac{3}{4}$ pound (ready-to-cook weight) per serving. When buying turkeys under 12 pounds, allow $\frac{3}{4}$ to 1 pound per serving. The table below suggests the number of servings.

Ready-to-Cook Turkey (pounds)	Number of Servings
6 to 8	6 to 10
8 to 12	10 to 20
12 to 16	20 to 32
16 to 20	32 to 40
20 to 24	40 to 50

The actual number of servings depends on the quality of the turkey, correct cooking and carving skill.

ROAST TURKEY

Stuffing: A turkey may or may not be stuffed for roasting. The stuffing may be cooked separately in a casserole or suitable baking pan—loaf or muffin size.

When birds are stuffed, these directions should be followed: *Combine ingredients just before stuffing bird.*

Dry ingredients may be measured and prepared ahead of time. Liquid or moist ingredients may be measured but must be kept in the refrigerator until they are to be combined with the dry ingredients. Meats, if one of the ingredients, such as ground beef, giblets, liver, oysters, or sausage must be thoroughly cooked before combining them with other ingredients.

Stuff the turkey just before it is placed in the oven.

Allow $\frac{3}{4}$ cup stuffing per pound of turkey, ready-to-cook weight.

TIMETABLE FOR ROASTING WHOLE TURKEY

Ready-to-Cook Weight*	Oven Temperature	Total Approximate Roasting Time (Stuffed Bird)
4 to 8 lbs.	325°F.	$3\frac{3}{4}$ to $4\frac{1}{2}$ hrs.
8 to 12 lbs.	325°F.	4 to 5 hrs.
12 to 16 lbs.	325°F.	5 to 6 hrs.
16 to 20 lbs.	325°F.	6 to $7\frac{1}{2}$ hrs.
20 to 24 lbs.	325°F.	$7\frac{1}{2}$ to 9 hrs.

* If you buy a Dressed turkey, subtract 15 to 20% of the dressed weight to obtain the approximate Ready-To-Cook weight.

To Stuff Turkey: Rub $\frac{1}{2}$ to $1\frac{1}{2}$ teaspoons salt, depending upon turkey size, into the cavity. Stuff body and wishbone cavities lightly to avoid a soggy, compact stuffing.

To Cook Stuffing Separately: Prepare stuffing in customary manner. Pile lightly into roasting pan from which drippings have been removed, greased casserole, loaf pan, or muffin cups.

Cover, if a moist stuffing is desired. Bake in moderate oven (350°F.) 30 to 50 minutes, depending upon shape and depth of stuffing.

If covered, remove cover the last 10 minutes to brown top.

To Truss Turkey: Fasten the neck skin to the back with 1 or 2 skewers.

Shape wings "akimbo" style and bring wing tips onto the back.

Close abdominal opening with skewers and cord.

Tie drumsticks to tail. A skewer above or through the tail helps to hold this cord in place.

If there is a bridge of skin at abdominal opening, push drumsticks underneath this bridge. It will hold them down without skewers and cord.

To Roast Turkey: Brush skin of bird thoroughly with cooking fat.

Place bird, breast up, on a rack at least $\frac{1}{2}$ inch high in shallow open pan. If a meat thermometer is used, insert it so that the bulb rests in the center of the inside thigh muscle adjoining the body cavity. If a V-rack is used, place turkey breast-down.

Take a piece of aluminum foil 4 to 5 inches longer than the turkey. Lay it over bird. Pinch the foil at the drumstick and breast ends, pressing it lightly at those ends to anchor it. Leave the cap loose over the top and at the sides.

Or, the turkey may be covered with fat-moistened cheesecloth, large enough to cover the top and drape down on all sides. Do not wrap bird in the cloth. Aluminum foil or cloth helps in uniform browning. Basting is unnecessary.

Place in preheated slow oven (325°F.). Do not sear. Do not add water. Do not cover. If cheesecloth dries during cooking, moisten with drippings in the bottom of the pan.

When the turkey is about $\frac{2}{3}$ done, according to the timetable, cut the cord or the band of skin, holding the drumstick ends to the tail, to release the legs. This permits the heat to reach the inside thigh to assure thorough cooking.

About 20 minutes before the turkey is done according to the approximate total time prescribed in the timetable, or if a meat thermometer is used it should register 190°F., apply these physical tests for doneness:

(a) Press the fleshy part of the drumstick between the fingers, protected with paper or cloth. Meat should feel very soft.

(b) Move the drumstick up and down; the drumstick should move readily or twist out of the joint.

When turkey is done, remove from oven. Keep hot while preparing gravy with drippings in roasting pan.

HOW TO COOK SMOKED TURKEY

Wash bird thoroughly. Soak overnight in enough cold water to cover. Wipe dry throughout.

Stuff bird if desired, but omit salt in stuffing.

Truss bird and place on V-shaped rack breast-side up in a slow oven (250°F.).

Turn the bird for even cooking. Do not baste with pan dripping as it is likely to be too strong. Use a mixture of brown sugar and vinegar, flavored with a dash of cloves and mustard.

At this temperature, a young 10-pound turkey will require about $4\frac{1}{2}$ hours. If the bird is an older smoked turkey, wash thoroughly and simmer in water (do not boil), whole or in pieces.

A sliced onion and several stalks of celery may be added to the broth.

Cooking time will range from 4 to 5 hours. Cool bird in broth. Serve baked or boiled smoked turkey in thin slices, hot or cold.

TURKEY COOKED IN ALUMINUM FOIL

The procedure given here is based on unstuffed turkeys weighing 8 to 24 pounds, ready-to-cook weight. Two distinct advantages are the shortened cooking time and the fact that spattering of the oven is prevented—important factors for the homemaker.

The skin of turkeys cooked in foil may be less brown (the color may be spotty), have a light color, and be very soft. The 15- to 20-minute cooking with the foil folded back gives it the desired golden-brown appearance.

Although cooking results in tests were the same irrespective of the foil weight, medium weight of aluminum foil ("heavy duty") is preferred. Thin foil tears easily during wrapping and heavy foil tends to be too stiff. An 18-inch foil is a good width.

To Wrap the Turkey in Aluminum Foil: Tie drumsticks to tail. Press wings to body, with wings tips flat against sides of breast.

Place the bird in the center of the aluminum foil. The foil should be wide enough to have 5 to 6 inches extending beyond the leg and breast ends of the bird. If it is not wide enough, join two pieces tightly together with a drugstore or lock fold to prevent leakage of the drippings.

Bring one side of the foil strip snugly up and over the breast. Then bring the opposite side up and over, using a simple lap fold. These ends should overlap 2 to 3 inches.

Fold the foil down snugly at each end of the bird, breast and legs. Then bring ends up. The top of these ends should be high enough to prevent the drippings from escaping from the top and into the pan. If the drippings escape into the pan, they brown quickly and cause sharp odors and smoke.

To Cook the Turkey: Place the aluminum foil-wrapped turkey, breast up, in the bottom—not on a rack—of shallow pan.

Place pan with turkey in a preheated very hot oven (450° F.) and cook to within 15 or 20 minutes of the total cooking time given in the timetable.

Remove from oven. Quickly fold foil back away from the bird to the edges of the pan. If a meat thermometer is used to judge doneness, insert it at this time. Insert it so the bulb reaches the center of the inside thigh muscle—the side next to the body cavity.

Return to the very hot oven (450° F.) and continue cooking according to the timetable. Apply the physical tests (given in recipe for whole Roast Turkey) and meat thermometer reading to

TIMETABLE FOR COOKING TURKEY IN ALUMINUM FOIL			
Ready-to-Cook Weight (Pounds—Unstuffed)	Oven Temperature (A Very Hot Oven)	Total Cooking Time (Hours—Approximate)	Interior Temperature
8–10	450° F.	2¼ to 2½	185–190° F.
10–12	450° F.	2¾ to 3	185–190° F.
14–16	450° F.	3 to 3¼	185–190° F.
18–20	450° F.	3¼ to 3½	185–190° F.
22–24	450° F.	3¼ to 3¾	185–190° F.

judge doneness.

Lift turkey from the foil to a warm serving platter. Keep hot.

Pour the drippings into a saucepan. If desired, concentrate drippings by boiling to reduce the volume and to intensify the color.

Prepare gravy with these drippings as directed for gravy (see Index). If desired, add additional color.

ROAST HALF OR QUARTER TURKEY

Rub cavity (cut side) with salt. Skewer skin to meat along cut edges to prevent shrinking from meat during roasting.

Tie leg to tail. Lay wing flat over white meat and tie cord around breast end to hold wing down.

Place turkey skin-side-down on a rack in a shallow pan. Grease with cooking fat and cover with aluminum foil or a fat-moistened cheesecloth.

Place in preheated slow oven (325° F.). Do not sear. Do not add water. Do not cover. (When the turkey is about ⅔ done, according to the timetable, cut the cord holding the drumstick end to the tail, to release the leg. This permits the heat to reach the inside thigh to assure thorough cooking.)

If cheesecloth dries during cooking, moisten with drippings in the bottom of the pan. Turn skin-side-up when about ¾ done.

Test as for whole turkey, above. If the breast quarter is roasted, the meat in the thickest area should be soft.

Stuffing the Half or Quarter Turkey: Prepare stuffing, allowing about ⅔ cup per serving. Press lightly into greased pan or casserole or place in aluminum foil. Cover or not as desired. Bake with turkey the last 1 to 1½

hours of turkey roasting time.

Or, when half or quarter turkey is ¾ done, remove from pan. Arrange stuffing on a piece of foil or parchment paper to fit area of turkey cavity. Replace turkey skin-side-up atop stuffing. Continue roasting until turkey is done.

TURKEY-BY-THE-PIECE WITH WHOLE WHEAT WALNUT STUFFING

Place turkey pieces or quarters around mound of stuffing. Lay fat-moistened cheesecloth over all.

Roast in moderate oven (350° F.) 1½ to 2 hours for cut-up pieces or 50 minutes per pound for quarters.

Whole Wheat Walnut Stuffing:

2 medium onions
½ cup butter or margarine
8 cups soft whole wheat bread-crumbs
1 cup broken walnut meats
½ cup golden seedless raisins
1 cup diced celery
1½ teaspoons salt
Few grains pepper
1½ teaspoons Ac'cent
1 tablespoon poultry seasoning
Hot water

Grate onions with coarse grater; cook in butter or margarine until soft but not brown; add to crumbs.

Add remaining ingredients with enough hot water to make fairly moist.

Makes enough stuffing for 8- to 10-pound turkey.

BONELESS TURKEY ROAST (ROLLS)

Place on a rack in an open pan. Roast in a slow oven (325° F) until a meat thermometer inserted in the center registers 170° to 175° F. Or, follow cooking directions printed on the package.

TIMETABLE FOR ROASTING HALF OR QUARTER TURKEY		
Ready-to-Cook Weight	Oven Temperature	Approximate Roasting Time
3½ to 5 lbs.	325° F.	3 to 3½ hrs.
5 to 8 lbs.	325° F.	3½ to 4 hrs.
8 to 12 lbs.	325° F.	4 to 5 hrs.

OVEN-BARBECUED SMALL TURKEY

1 5- to 6-pound turkey, cut into serving pieces

Herb Barbecue Sauce:

1 cup tomato juice
1 can (1¼ cups) consommé
1 cup water
½ cup salad oil
¼ cup wine vinegar
½ teaspoon salt
⅛ teaspoon cayenne
¼ teaspoon crumbled tarragon
¼ teaspoon powdered thyme
¼ teaspoon freshly ground black pepper
4 whole cloves
2 cloves garlic, mashed
2 tablespoons brown sugar
¼ cup finely chopped onion
¼ cup finely chopped green pepper
1 tablespoon dried parsley
½ cup sherry wine

Combine all sauce ingredients except sherry; simmer 30 minutes.

Spread turkey pieces flat in a baking pan. Pour barbecue sauce over turkey.

Bake in slow oven (300°F.) for 3 hours. Dip the sauce over turkey 2 or 3 times during baking. Add water to the sauce if necessary to keep turkey moist.

Before serving, pour the sherry over the turkey and heat through about 15 minutes. Serve the sauce with turkey. Serves 6.

Variations: Add to the sauce before serving 1 cup lightly browned sliced mushrooms, 1 cup sliced ripe olives, and ½ cup slivered toasted almonds.

WESTERN BARBECUED TURKEY

1 turkey (4 to 6 pounds, ready-to-cook weight), cut in pieces for serving
1 cup ketchup
1¼ cups water
½ cup Burgundy wine or other red wine
1 tablespoon wine vinegar
½ cup butter, margarine, or oil
½ cup minced onion
Grated garlic or garlic powder to taste
2 teaspoons Worcestershire sauce
1 tablespoon sugar
2 teaspoons paprika
½ teaspoon salt (or to taste)

Place turkey skin-side-down in a roasting pan.

Combine remaining ingredients; heat to boiling; pour over turkey. Cover and bake in a moderate oven (375°F.) 1 hour, basting occasionally.

Remove cover and turn turkey skin-side-up. Continue baking, uncovered, about ¾ to 1¼ hours, or until turkey is tender, basting and turning turkey occasionally. (Thin sauce with more wine if necessary.) Serves 4 to 6.

TURKEY QUARTER WITH APPLE CIDER

1 4- to 5-pound turkey breast or hind quarter
2 teaspoons salt
½ teaspoon pepper
1 teaspoon allspice
¼ cup butter or margarine
2 medium onions, thinly sliced
2 carrots, finely diced
1 cup apple cider

Sprinkle turkey quarter with salt, pepper, and allspice. Brown in a heavy skillet in moderately hot butter, turning frequently for about 30 minutes. Remove from pan.

Arrange a bed of onions and carrots in the skillet with turkey on top. Pour apple cider over.

Cover and cook over low heat for about 2½ hours or until fork-tender in the thickest parts.

Baste occasionally and add more cider if necessary.

Remove turkey to a warm serving dish.

Strain pan juices, mashing the vegetables through a sieve to make a rich gravy. Season to taste.

Garnish platter with garlic croutons and halves of canned fruit filled with seedless raisins. Serves 6.

TOM TURKEY WITH CRANBERRY STUFFING

1 16-pound ready-to-cook turkey
2 teaspoons Ac'cent
1 pound fresh cranberries
1 cup sugar
4 quarts small bread cubes
1 cup melted butter or margarine
2 cups raisins
1 tablespoon salt
1 teaspoon cinnamon
2 teaspoons lemon rind
1 cup turkey broth*

Prepare turkey for roasting and dust cavity with Ac'cent.

Chop cranberries and place in a saucepan with sugar. Bring to a boil and remove from heat.

Moisten bread cubes with melted butter and combine with cranberries, raisins, seasonings, lemon rind, and broth; mix well.

Stuff and truss turkey. Roast according to chart. Serves 18.

* Note: Prepare the turkey broth by cooking the turkey giblets.

Roast Chicken or Turkey with Wine
Prepare chicken or turkey for roasting in the usual way (see Index). Mix ¾ cup of warm table wine with ¼ cup melted butter or margarine and spoon it over the bird while it roasts. For chicken, use a white table wine like sauterne, chablis, or rhine wine. For turkey, use a red table wine like burgundy, zinfandel, or claret.

ROAST SMALL TURKEY

1 Beltsville turkey, 6 to 8 pounds
Ac'cent, salt, pepper
1 cup diced celery
½ cup finely chopped onion
2 tablespoons butter or margarine
3 cups crumbled corn bread
2 to 3 cups soft breadcrumbs
2 teaspoons poultry seasoning
1 teaspoon Ac'cent
½ cup seedless raisins
⅓ cup melted butter or margarine
2 beaten eggs
Salt and pepper to taste

Sprinkle body and neck cavities of turkey with Ac'cent, salt, and pepper. Let stand while preparing stuffing.

Cook celery and onion in 2 tablespoons butter or margarine until onion is soft but not brown; combine with corn bread and breadcrumbs. Add poultry seasoning, Ac'cent, raisins, and ⅓ cup melted butter or margarine. Toss to mix well. Stir in eggs.

Stuff turkey lightly with this mixture; do not pack. (Any extra stuffing may be dotted with butter and baked in separate pan.) Truss turkey.

Sprinkle lightly with Ac'cent; place breast-side-down on rack in open, shallow roasting pan. Lay fat-moistened cheesecloth over turkey.

Roast in slow oven (325°F.) 3½ to 4 hours. Turn turkey breast-up when about ¾ done. If cloth dries out, moisten with drippings in pan. Serve hot or cold. Makes about 8 servings.

Note: For turkeys weighing 4 to 6 pounds, the approximate cooking time in a slow oven (325°F.) is 3 to 3½ hours. Roasting time will vary with individual birds.

Broiled and Barbecued Poultry

POULTRY TO BROIL

Because younger marketing ages have resulted from the scientific mass production of all poultry, you can broil chicken, ducklings, and even small turkeys, or half turkeys, with every assurance that the cooked meat will be tender and delicious. The recipes for broiling poultry include the basic timing and technique for cooking modern poultry in this modern way.

BROILED CHICKEN
(Master Recipe)

All sizes of tender, small chicken may be broiled, but the preference is usually a 1½- to 2½-pound bird, ready-to-cook weight. This gives a meaty, flavorful chicken and the broiling time is relatively short.

The chicken is split in half, lengthwise, with the backbone, neck and keel bone removed. Larger sizes may be cut crosswise after broiling to give quarters.

Steps in Broiling

Place chicken halves in bottom of broiling pan—not on the rack—so that chicken is kept moist in the juices. Bring wing tip onto back under the shoulder joint.

Season with ¼ to ½ teaspoon salt and ⅛ teaspoon pepper for each half. Brush well with butter, margarine, or any desired fat. Flatten halves skin side down in pan.

Place pan in broiler so that surface of chicken is 7 to 9 inches from the heat. Broil slowly, regulating heat or pan position so that browning begins after 10 to 15 minutes of cooking.

Turn every 15 minutes, brushing with additional fat each time.

Broil until tender, nicely browned and crisp on the outside. Chicken is done when the drumstick and wing joints yield easily to fork pressure. The broiling time for a 2- to 2½-pound chicken is 50 to 60 minutes.

The liver (uncooked) and the precooked gizzard, heart, and neck (see Giblet Cookery) may be brushed with fat and placed in broiler pan the last 15 minutes, or long enough to heat and brown.

Serve on warm platter skin side up. Pour the pan drippings over the chicken.

Variations: Herbs may be rubbed into the chicken before broiling or the chicken may be marinated in French dressing 1 to 3 hours.

Lemon juice may be drizzled over the chicken during the broiling.

BROILING FROZEN CHICKEN

See package directions or hints given under Defrosting Frozen Chicken.

Sprinkle with seasoning.

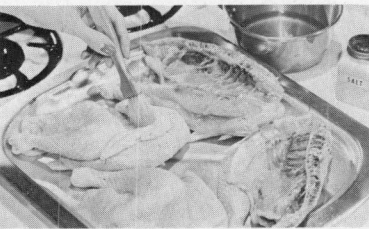
Brush broiler halves with fat.

Test for "doneness" when golden.

Serve attractively garnished.

BROILED-PARBOILED CHICKEN

Large chickens may be parboiled about 10 to 15 minutes before broiling.

BROILED-STEAMED CHICKEN

Place bird on rack in shallow pan. Add enough water to reach just below bird.

Cover and steam in moderate oven (350°F.) 30 minutes.

Brush bird with melted fat. Sprinkle with salt. Broil in hot oven.

BARBECUED CHICKEN

Broil chicken and baste with barbecue sauce during the broiling. Thick sauces should be diluted with water.

Chicken may also be marinated in barbecue sauce before broiling.

Still another method is to serve barbecue sauce with broiled chicken for individual use at the table.

BAKED-BROILED CHICKEN

Bake bird in an open pan in moderate oven (350°F.) 15 minutes. Sprinkle with salt. Brush with melted fat. Broil until evenly browned.

BROILED SMALL TURKEY

Choose a young turkey about 3 to 4 pounds. Have turkey split in half lengthwise for broiling. Snap drumstick, hip and wing joints to keep bird flat during broiling.

Flatten halves and skewer leg to body. Fold wing tip back under wing. Skewer wing flat against cut edge of backbone.

Season each half turkey with about ¼ teaspoon salt and a sprinkling of pepper.

Place turkey in broiler pan (not on rack). Brush with melted fat and then place skin-side-down.

Broil Slowly: Place in broiler 7 to 10 inches under heat source. Regulate heat or pan position so that turkey just begins to brown lightly in 15 minutes. Cook slowly.

Turn and brush with fat. Baste frequently during broiling to brown and cook evenly. Total cooking time, about 60 minutes for 4-pound ready-to-cook turkey.

Test for Doneness: The turkey is done when meat on the thickest part of the drumstick cuts easily and there is no pink color visible.

Serve on warm platter, with pan drippings poured over turkey.

If giblets are served with broiled turkey, coat the liver and precooked heart and gizzard with fat, season and broil just long enough to brown.

SKILLET CHICKEN BARBECUE

1   3-pound ready-to-cook chicken, cut up for frying
¼ cup shortening
⅓ cup thinly sliced onion
⅓ cup chopped green pepper
1   small clove garlic, minced
1   can condensed tomato soup
2   tablespoons brown sugar
2   tablespoons Worcestershire sauce
2   tablespoons lemon juice or vinegar
2   teaspoons prepared mustard
Dash of Tabasco sauce

Brown chicken on all sides in hot shortening in a heavy skillet.

Remove chicken and gently fry onion, green pepper, and garlic for 5 minutes.

Mix in remaining ingredients and simmer until thoroughly blended.

Return chicken to skillet, and spoon sauce over. Cover and simmer about 30 minutes, or until chicken is done, turning occasionally. Serves 4.

OVEN BARBECUED CHICKEN OR TURKEY

You may want to use plump broiler-fryer chickens, cut in halves, or young fryer-roaster turkeys (4 to 7 pounds, ready-to-cook) halved or quartered. Or, cut-up poultry fresh or quick-frozen.

Place halves or quarters, skin side up, in roasting or broiling pans and pour all-purpose barbecue sauce over them ½ to 1 inch deep.

Bake uncovered in slow oven (325°F.). Turn occasionally and baste each time, leaving sauce in the rib cages when the halves are turned up.

As the birds cook, the sauce will thicken into rich gravy. If the sauce becomes too thick, add a little hot water.

Chickens will be done in from 1½ to 2¼ hours, depending on size. Young turkeys will require ½ hour or more extra time. Test legs for doneness as in grill barbecuing.

For rich crustiness, place cooked birds skin side up, baste and turn up heat to 500°F. or place under broiler heat. Watch carefully! Two or three minutes may be plenty.

Serve the birds, with thick sauce poured over them, on warm plates or platter. Or, serve sauce separately.

LEMON BARBECUED SMALL TURKEY

Have a young turkey about 3 to 4 pounds prepared for broiling. Place turkey halves in broiling pan.

Barbecue Mixture: Rub both sides of turkey with cut lemon, squeezing lemon to obtain plenty of juice. Brush with melted fat.

Sprinkle with a mixture of 1 teaspoon each of salt and sugar, ¼ teaspoon paprika, and ⅛ teaspoon black pepper for each half. Place skin-side-down in broiler (not on rack).

To Broil: Follow directions for broiling.

FIESTA BROILED CHICKEN

2 2½- to 3-pound ready-to-cook chickens, split
2 teaspoons salt
¼ cup apple jelly
¼ pound butter or margarine
¼ cup white wine

Wipe chicken, sprinkle with salt and place in broiler pan skin-side-down.

Combine apple jelly, butter, and wine; bring to a boil and brush mixture over chicken with pastry brush.

Place under broiler unit for 20 minutes. Turn chicken to brown evenly, baste again and continue to cook for 30 minutes. Serve with hot biscuits and jelly. Serves 6.

Fried Poultry

FRIED CHICKEN (Master Recipe)

Select young chicken. Disjoint and cut up for cooking.

Mix ¼ teaspoon pepper, 1½ teaspoons salt, and 1½ tablespoons paprika with 1 cup flour for every 3 pounds of meat. Rub flour into pieces. Save leftover flour for gravy.

Melt fat in a heavy skillet to depth of ½ to ¾ inch. Brown meaty pieces first in the hot fat, slipping less-meaty pieces in between as chicken browns. Avoid crowding, use two skillets if necessary.

As soon as chicken begins to brown, about 10 minutes, reduce heat, and cook slowly until tender, 30 to 60 minutes, depending upon size of pieces. Cover tightly as soon as it is a light, uniform tan.

Add 1 to 2 tablespoons water before covering if pan cannot be covered tightly or if bird is heavier than 3 pounds.

Uncover last 15 minutes to brown. Turn several times to brown evenly.

To Test: Cut thickest part of any piece to the bone. If done, the meat should cut easily and no pink color be visible.

To Fry Giblets: Simmer gizzard until tender. Drain well and rub seasoned flour into giblets. Fry until browned, about 10 minutes.

MARYLAND FRIED CHICKEN

1 young chicken (3 pounds)
Salt and pepper
1 cup flour
2 eggs, slightly beaten
4 tablespoons water
1 cup dry breadcrumbs
¼ cup butter or margarine
¼ cup lard

Cut chicken in pieces for serving, wash and dry. Season with salt and pepper, roll in flour, dip in slightly beaten eggs, diluted with water, and roll in crumbs.

Sauté in butter and pork fat in heavy frying pan until browned on all sides; cover and place in slow oven (300°F.) ½ to ¾ hour, or until tender.

If chicken weighs more than 3 pounds, add ½ cup hot water to pan in oven.

Serve with cream gravy made from drippings in pan. Serves 6.

Chicken Cream Gravy: To 4 tablespoons of drippings add 4 tablespoons of flour. Stir until blended.

Slowly add 2 to 3 cups of milk or half milk and half cream. Heat slowly over low heat, stirring constantly until thick and smooth. Season to taste.

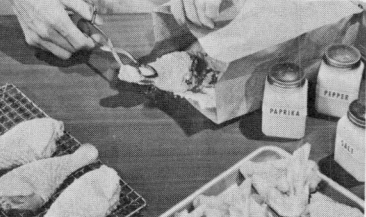

Use young chicken, cut-up, for frying. Coat chicken with seasoned flour.

Brown in shallow fat. Start the larger pieces first.

Add a little water; cover and cook slowly.

Test for doneness.

FRENCH-FRIED CHICKEN

2 1¾-pound ready-to-cook fryers, split in halves
1 tablespoon salt
¾ teaspoon pepper
1 cup flour
Fat for frying

Coat each chicken half with seasoned flour.

Heat deep fat to 370°F. on frying thermometer, or until a 1-inch bread cube browns in 1 minute.

Put chicken in fryer basket, 1 or 2 pieces at a time; lower carefully into hot fat. Fry chicken 12 to 15 minutes, or until golden brown and tender.

Drain on absorbent paper. Keep hot in heated oven until all pieces are fried. Serves 6.

Variations: If desired, use 1 large fryer—2¾ pounds ready-to-cook—quartered. To vary flavor, add 1 teaspoon ground ginger to the flour.

CHICKEN SAUTÉ SEC

1 frying chicken (about 3½ pounds), cut in pieces for serving
Flour, salt, and pepper
4 tablespoons butter or margarine
2 shallots or green onions, finely chopped
2 tablespoons chopped parsley
Sprinkling of thyme and basil
½ cup sauterne wine
1 4-ounce can sliced mushrooms

Dust pieces of chicken with flour seasoned with salt and pepper. Melt butter in a large, heavy skillet; add chicken and sauté until golden brown, turning the pieces frequently and adding more butter, if necessary.

Add shallots, parsley, thyme, basil, and wine; cover tightly and simmer gently for 30 minutes.

Drain mushrooms and add; continue cooking for 15 minutes, or until chicken is tender and no liquid remains in the pan. Serves 3 or 4.

CANTONESE FRIED CHICKEN

1 2½ to 3½-pound fryer, cut up
3 tablespoons Chinese brown gravy sauce
1 teaspoon salt
¼ teaspoon pepper
1 teaspoon sugar
¼ teaspoon monosodium glutamate (optional)
3 tablespoons butter
3 tablespoons shortening
6 canned water chestnuts, sliced
1½ cups sliced fresh mushrooms
1 cup chicken broth
1 tablespoon soy sauce
½ teaspoon salt
½ teaspoon sugar
1 tablespoon cornstarch
1 tablespoon water
Green onions

Place chicken in enough boiling water to cover. Add brown gravy sauce, salt, pepper, sugar, and monosodium glutamate. Cook slowly for 15 minutes. Drain and pat dry.

Brown chicken in mixture of hot butter and shortening until a golden brown. Cover and cook slowly for 20 minutes.

Remove and place on a platter. Pour off all but 3 tablespoons fat; add water

Cantonese Fried Chicken

chestnuts, mushrooms, broth, soy sauce, salt, and sugar. Cover and simmer about 5 minutes.

Combine cornstarch and water; pour into vegetable mixture. Cook until thickened. Pour sauce over chicken and serve garnished with green onions. Serves 4 to 6.

OVEN-FRIED CHICKEN

Prepare chicken as in master recipe for fried chicken. When pieces are uniformly and delicately browned, transfer to covered roasting pan or casserole. Add a little water if desired. Bake in slow oven (325°F.) until tender, 1 to 1½ hours. To crisp, remove cover the last 5 to 10 minutes of cooking.

MANDARIN CHICKEN

1 young chicken, 2 to 2½ pounds ready-to-cook weight, cut up
½ cup flour
2 teaspoons salt
1 teaspoon paprika
¼ teaspoon ground pepper
½ cup fat for frying
¼ teaspoon ground cloves
¼ teaspoon ground nutmeg
1 tablespoon water
¼ cup flour
½ cup water
1 cup pineapple juice
1 cup orange juice (2 to 3 medium oranges or frozen juice)
About ⅔ cup pineapple cubes
2 small oranges or tangerines, sectioned
½ cup (about 2 ounces) salted almonds, slivered
3 cups fluffy hot rice

Blend ½ cup flour, salt, paprika, and pepper in plastic or sturdy paper bag.

Drop chicken, 2 or 3 pieces at a time, into bag and shake to coat evenly.

Heat fat in heavy skillet until drop of water just sizzles.

Start browning meaty pieces first, slipping less-meaty pieces in between as chicken browns. Turn as necessary to brown evenly, 15 to 20 minutes. Sprinkle with cloves and nutmeg.

Add 1 tablespoon water. Cover tightly and cook over low heat until thickest pieces are fork-tender, 25 to 30 minutes. Turn pieces as necessary to cook evenly.

Meanwhile, blend ¼ cup flour and ½ cup water until free of lumps. Blend with pineapple and orange juice. Cook in saucepan until thickened throughout, stirring constantly.

Add pineapple cubes, orange sections, and almonds. (Some of almonds may be reserved for garnishing rice.)

Pour over chicken and cook over low heat, uncovered, about 10 minutes to blend flavors. Serve with rice. Serves 4 to 5.

CHICKEN SAUTÉ CHASSEURS

Chasseur is a French term meaning hunter; it often appears on menus as "à la chasseur," meaning hunter's style and it is applied to various ways of cooking chicken, meat, and game. Usually popular versions of this dish as given below contain tomatoes.

3 tablespoons butter or margarine
¼ cup flour
2 teaspoons salt
¼ teaspoon pepper
¼ teaspoon thyme
2- to 2½-pound frying chicken (cut pieces)*
4 green onions, chopped
¼ pound mushrooms, cut into quarters
2 tablespoons lemon juice
1 teaspoon sugar
1 teaspoon salt
⅓ cup apple juice
2 medium tomatoes, diced (or 2 whole canned tomatoes, drained and diced)
2 tablespoons chopped parsley and chives

Heat butter in heavy skillet.

Mix flour, salt, pepper, and thyme in a paper bag. Shake pieces of chicken in seasoned flour mixture and brown thoroughly in butter in skillet.

Add onions and mushrooms. Cover and simmer 3 minutes.

Mix lemon juice, sugar, salt, and apple juice and pour over chicken. Cover and simmer 5 minutes. Add tomatoes.

Cook slowly over low heat about 1 hour or until chicken is fork tender. Sprinkle with parsley and chives. Serve hot. Serves 4 to 5.

*Note: If an older chicken is used, cook slowly for 2 hours.

WINE-FRIED CHICKEN

Disjoint a good-sized fryer; season but do not flour.

In skillet, heat 2 tablespoons butter and 1 tablespoon oil. Add chicken and brown thoroughly on all sides. Then add ¾ cup sauterne wine; cover tightly and simmer 20 minutes or until tender.

Add ½ cup cream (sweet or sour), heat again and serve on a platter with the wine-and-cream gravy poured over the chicken. Serves 4.

Mandarin Chicken

PAN-FRIED SMALL TURKEY

A young turkey weighing 4 to 5 pounds (ready-to-cook weight) is suitable for frying. It is usually disjointed and cut up.

Coating: For each pound of turkey, blend 1/4 cup flour, 1 teaspoon paprika, 3/4 teaspoon salt, and 1/8 teaspoon pepper (1/8 teaspoon poultry seasoning optional) in a paper bag.

Shake turkey, 2 or 3 pieces at a time, in bag to coat evenly. Save any leftover flour for gravy.

Preliminary Browning: Heat 1/2 inch of vegetable oil or shortening in a skillet until a drop of water just sizzles. Start browning meaty pieces first, slipping less-meaty pieces in between as turkey browns.

To brown evenly, turn as necessary with kitchen tongs or two spoons. This browning takes 15 to 20 minutes.

Slow Cooking: Reduce heat, cover tightly and cook slowly until tender, 45 minutes for 4-pound ready-to-cook weight, 50 to 60 minutes for 5-pound ready-to-cook weight.

If pan cannot be covered tightly, add 1 to 2 tablespoons water and cover.

The liver and precooked heart, gizzard, and neck may be floured and browned with turkey the last 15 minutes.

Uncover last 10 minutes to recrisp skin.

Test for Doneness: The turkey is done when meat on the thickest part of the drumstick cuts easily and there is no pink color visible.

Lift turkey to a warm platter. If desired, prepare gravy with pan drippings.

SAVORY PAN-FRIED TURKEY

Use butter or margarine in place of oil or shortening. Add one or more additional seasonings to coating flour such as Ac'cent, garlic powder, or thyme.

OVEN-FRIED SMALL TURKEY

This method is excellent when two or more turkeys are being fried.

Coating and Browning: Coat the cut-up turkey with seasoned flour. See Pan-Fried Small Turkey.

Brown in at least 1/2-inch layer of fat in a heavy skillet. If a large quantity of turkey is prepared, it may be deep-fat browned. Place golden-browned turkey, one layer deep, in a shallow baking pan.

Slow Oven Cooking: For each 2 pounds of turkey, spoon a mixture of 2 tablespoons of melted butter and 2 tablespoons of broth or milk over the turkey.

Continue the cooking in a moderate oven (350°F.) until turkey is tender, 50

to 60 minutes. Turn once to crisp evenly. During the cooking, broth or milk may be drizzled over turkey if it appears dry.

Test the doneness the same as for pan-fried turkey.

SPANISH FRIED CHICKEN

1 chopped onion
4 tablespoons fat
1 frying chicken, cut up
Seasoned flour
1 chopped green pepper
1 cup chopped tomatoes
1/2 tablespoon chili powder
1/2 cup uncooked rice
1 cup milk or 1/2 cup evaporated milk diluted with 1/2 cup water

Cook onion in hot fat for a few minutes.

Roll chicken in flour and brown on both sides. Arrange in casserole. Add other ingredients and enough water to cook rice. Cook slowly, covered, in moderate oven (350°F.) until chicken is tender.

If necessary add more milk, but only enough to cook rice, as it must be quite dry when served. Serves 4 to 6.

SMOTHERED-FRIED CHICKEN

1 2 1/4-pound ready-to-cook fryer
1 1/2 teaspoons salt
3/4 teaspoon pepper
1/2 cup flour
1/2 cup fat
2 cups water

Cut chicken in frying pieces and coat with seasoned flour.

Brown quickly on all sides in hot fat in large skillet.

Pour off fat. Add water. Cover and simmer until chicken is tender, about 30 minutes. Add more seasoning if necessary. Serves 4.

Variations: Substitute 1 cup white wine for 1 cup water or, if desired, milk or half milk and half water may be substituted for all the water.

Vary seasoning by adding 1 to 2 teaspoons poultry seasoning, ground marjoram, or sage to the flour.

NORTHWEST FRIED CHICKEN

Prepare young fryers, 1 1/2 to 2 1/2 pounds, for frying. Cut into halves, quarters or pieces, whichever way is preferred.

Heat in iron or heavy aluminum skillet enough fat, oil, or half butter and half fat, to cover half the depth of the chicken.

Dip chicken in 3/4 cup cream or evaporated milk. Dredge in a mixture of well-blended 1/2 cup flour, 1/2 teaspoon salt, 1/2 teaspoon pepper, and 1/4 teaspoon paprika.

Fry slowly until golden brown; turn and brown other side until same color and until done, 25 to 30 minutes.

Place on platter with sprigs of parsley and serve hot.

GARLIC CHICKEN

1/2 cup butter or margarine
1 young chicken, about 3 1/2 pounds, cut up
1 teaspoon salt
8 cloves garlic
1/2 cup chopped parsley

Melt half of butter in heavy skillet or Dutch oven. Place chicken in skillet and brown on all sides over low to medium heat. Sprinkle with salt.

Mash garlic with fork or put through garlic press. Combine with remaining butter, chopped parsley, and cream all ingredients well. Add to chicken.

Cover and cook over low heat until tender, about 30 to 40 minutes. During cooking turn chicken occasionally and spoon sauce over it. Serve sauce with chicken. Serves 4.

CHICKEN SUBLIME

1 tablespoon aromatic bitters
1 tablespoon lemon juice
1/4 cup water
1 2 to 2 1/2-pound broiler or fryer, cut in serving pieces
1 tablespoon salt
2 teaspoons monosodium glutamate
1 teaspoon garlic salt
2 eggs, well beaten
6 cups corn flakes or 1 1/2 cups corn flake crumbs
1/2 cup flour
1 cup vegetable oil

Combine bitters, lemon juice, and water in small saucepan. Heat to boiling.

Season chicken pieces with combined salt, monosodium glutamate, and garlic salt. Place chicken pieces in shallow pan. Pour hot sauce over chicken. Let stand at room temperature 1 hour, turning pieces frequently. Drain, saving leftover sauce; combine with eggs.

If using corn flakes, crush into fine crumbs. Coat chicken pieces first with flour, then dip in egg mixture and then in corn flake crumbs. Fry in 1 inch of oil until golden brown on both sides, about 15 minutes per side. Serves 4.

Chicken Sublime

Oven-Fried Chicken with
Tropical Fruit Sauce

OVEN-FRIED CHICKEN WITH TROPICAL FRUIT SAUCE

1/2 cup wheat germ
1/2 cup fine cereal crumbs or dry breadcrumbs
1/2 teaspoon salt
1/2 teaspoon onion salt
1/4 teaspoon garlic salt
1/2 teaspoon summer savory
1/2 teaspoon curry powder
1/8 teaspoon pepper
1   3-pound frying chicken, cleaned and cut into serving pieces
1/4 cup melted butter or margarine

Combine wheat germ, breadcrumbs, salt, onion salt, garlic salt, summer savory, curry powder, and pepper. Brush chicken pieces with melted butter or margarine then dip in crumb mixture to coat outer surface.

Place skin side up in shallow baking dish. Drizzle with any remaining butter or margarine. Bake in hot oven (400°F.) until tender, 50 to 60 minutes. For a lightly browned chicken, cover dish with aluminum foil during last 15 minutes of cooking.

Serve with Tropical Fruit Sauce. If preferred, sauce may be poured over chicken during last 5 to 10 minutes cooking time. Serves 4.

Tropical Fruit Sauce:

1   can (13 1/2 ounces) pineapple chunks
1/2 green pepper, optional
1/2 cup orange juice
2   tablespoons lemon juice
1   tablespoon cornstarch
1/4 cup sugar
1   tablespoon chopped preserved ginger, optional
1   teaspoon grated orange rind

Drain pineapple chunks; save syrup. Remove stem and seeds of green pepper; wash and cut into strips or 1-inch cubes.

Combine pineapple syrup, orange and lemon juice, cornstarch, and sugar; stir until blended. Cook, stirring constantly, until clear and thickened.

Stir in ginger, orange rind, pineapple chunks, and peppers; heat thoroughly. Serve over or with Oven-Fried Chicken. Makes about 2 cups sauce.

CHICKEN SAUTÉED CREOLE STYLE

2   frying chickens
2   tablespoons butter or margarine
2   large onions, sliced
2   tablespoons flour
6   tomatoes, sliced
3   green peppers or pimientos, chopped
1   clove garlic, chopped fine
1   sprig thyme
1   sprig parsley, chopped
1   bay leaf
2   cups chicken consommé or stock
Salt and pepper
Cooked rice

Cut up the chickens into frying pieces. Season well with salt and pepper.

Melt butter in a large saucepan; add chicken and brown on all sides.

Add onions and brown lightly, then sprinkle with flour and mix well.

Add tomatoes, peppers or pimientos, garlic, and herbs. Simmer for 20 minutes, then add the hot consommé which has been highly seasoned with salt and pepper. Simmer for 45 minutes.

To serve, put pieces of chicken on a hot platter and cover with sauce. Serve with boiled rice. Serves 6.

CHICKEN MARSALA

2 1/2- to 3-pound ready-to-cook broiler-fryer (cut for frying)
Flour
4   tablespoons butter or margarine
1   medium onion, chopped
1   green pepper, chopped
1   canned pimiento, sliced
1   3-ounce can button mushrooms
1   to 2 tablespoons minced parsley
1   clove garlic, mashed or cut fine
1   teaspoon salt
1/4 teaspoon pepper
1   cup soup stock or water
1/2 cup water
1/3 cup (dry) marsala wine
1/2 cup light cream and 1/2 cup water if sauce is desired

Have the chicken cut either in 4 pieces; or in 2 drumsticks, 2 thighs, 2 wings and center breast.

Melt butter and heat in a heavy skillet or electric skillet. Brown meaty pieces of chicken first, slip less meaty ones in between. Brown chicken evenly on all sides about 10 minutes.

Meanwhile blend all vegetables with seasonings and soup stock; add to chicken. Cover and cook over moderate heat for 10 minutes.

Turn chicken pieces with spatula; add water and wine. Cover skillet and cook until chicken is tender, about 30 minutes if chicken is cut into 4 pieces, and 20 to 25 minutes if chicken is cut into smaller pieces as indicated above. Turn chicken once or twice during cooking.

If gravy is desired, remove chicken to heated platter, add cream and water to gravy in skillet. Cook over moderate heat for 3 to 5 minutes until gravy is smooth and well blended. stirring constantly.

Add chicken and serve directly from skillet. Serves 4 to 6.

Note: Serve with fluffy rice, cranberry sauce, and salad bowl, if desired.

PUNGENT-FRIED CHICKEN

1   young chicken, 2 to 2 1/2 pounds, ready-to-cook weight, cut up
Grated rind and juice of 2 medium oranges
1   tablespoon grated onion
1/2 teaspoon salt
1/2 teaspoon dry mustard
1/8 teaspoon pepper
Dash of Tabasco sauce
3/4 cup enriched flour
1 1/2 teaspoons salt
1   teaspoon paprika
1/8 teaspoon pepper
About 1/2 cup fat
About 1 tablespoon water

Place chicken one layer deep in shallow dish. Combine orange rind, orange juice, onion, salt, dry mustard, pepper, and Tabasco. Pour mixture over chicken. Marinate 1 to 3 hours.

Drain, reserving marinade for gravy.

Combine flour, salt, paprika, and pepper and coat chicken thoroughly with this mixture. Save any leftover flour mixture for gravy.

Brown chicken in heavy skillet containing 1/2 inch hot fat. Turn occasionally to brown evenly.

When chicken is lightly browned, 15 to 20 minutes, add the water and cover skillet tightly. Cook slowly until thickest pieces are fork-tender, 20 to 30 minutes. Turn chicken as necessary to brown and cook evenly.

Uncover and continue cooking slowly to recrisp coating, about 5 minutes. Remove chicken to warm platter and prepare gravy, using marinade mixture as part of liquid. Serves 4 to 5.

Chicken Marsala

OVEN-FRIED HERB CHICKEN

1 young chicken, 3 to 3½ pounds ready-to-cook weight, disjointed
½ teaspoon thyme
½ teaspoon marjoram
Flour
Fat
½ teaspoon rosemary
2 tablespoons fresh minced parsley
1 teaspoon salt
¼ teaspoon pepper
½ cup hot water

Sprinkle the chicken with thyme and marjoram; let stand ½ to 1 hour.

Roll in flour and fry in ¼-inch hot fat just long enough to brown on both sides.

Remove each piece as it browns, and place in shallow baking pan. Sprinkle with rosemary, parsley, salt, and pepper.

Pour the hot water into skillet; stir thoroughly. Pour the hot liquid over chicken.

Bake uncovered in moderate oven (375° F.) about 45 minutes. Serves 6.

SAUTÉED CHICKEN BREASTS

Remove breasts from 2 cleaned, dressed chickens. Wash and dry them and cut each in 2 pieces. Sprinkle each with salt and pepper.

Dip in light cream or evaporated milk; roll in flour and sauté in butter or margarine until golden brown.

Arrange sautéed chicken breasts in a baking pan. Dot with 2 tablespoons butter or margarine. Cover with parchment paper and bake in moderate oven (375°F.) 20 minutes. Serves 4.

CHICKEN SAXONY

1 2½- to 3-pound frying chicken, cut in serving pieces
1 teaspoon salt
¼ teaspoon pepper
1 small garlic clove
¼ cup salad oil
½ cup lemon juice
2 tablespoons grated onion
½ teaspoon thyme
Salt and pepper
½ cup butter or margarine

Season chicken with salt and pepper. Keep in covered dish in the refrigerator until thoroughly chilled.

Mix the garlic, oil, lemon juice, onion and thyme together, season with a little salt and pepper. Let stand 30 minutes or longer, then remove garlic.

Melt butter or margarine in chafing dish pan over direct heat. Brown chicken on all sides. Turn the pieces skin-side up and pour the garlic mixture over.

Cover pan; cook gently until chicken is tender, about 40 minutes. Serves 4.

WESTERN FRIED CHICKEN

½ teaspoon onion salt
1 teaspoon paprika
Dash of garlic salt
½ teaspoon pepper
1 cup enriched flour
1 tablespoon salt
2 3-pound broiler-fryers, cut in pieces
2 cups vegetable shortening
½ cup butter or margarine
Parsley and vegetables for garnish

Combine dry ingredients in a paper bag. Place chicken pieces, a few at a time, in bag and shake well.

Place pieces in hot shortening and butter in a heavy skillet. Cover and cook for 20 minutes.

Turn chicken and continue to cook for 20 minutes or until golden brown.

Sprinkle with ¼ cup water. Cover again and cook for 5 minutes. Remove from pan and drain on paper. Garnish with parsley and fresh vegetables. Serves 6 to 8.

CALIFORNIA CHICKEN DINNER

2 frying chickens, cut in serving pieces
1 teaspoon salt
¼ teaspoon pepper
½ cup olive or peanut oil
1 garlic clove, minced
6 green onions, whole
2 cups canned tomato sauce (2 8-ounce cans)
1 cup chicken bouillon or broth
½ cup mushroom liquid
1 cup button mushrooms

Season chicken well with salt and pepper. Heat oil in chafing dish over direct heat and sauté chicken until well browned, all sides.

Add garlic and onions. Pour tomato sauce and bouillon over chicken. Add mushroom liquid.

Cover pan and cook about 30 minutes, or until chicken is tender and the sauce is cooked down around it.

Add mushrooms about 10 minutes before serving. Serves 4 to 6.

SOUTHERN FRIED CHICKEN

2 broilers; or 1 large fryer, or 1 young roasting chicken
½ cup sifted flour
½ teaspoon salt
⅛ teaspoon pepper
1 egg, slightly beaten
⅓ cup milk
1 pound salt pork

Rinse the cleaned and dressed chickens, wipe dry and cut in serving pieces.

Sift the flour with the salt and pepper; combine beaten egg and milk and stir into the dry ingredients; mix thor-

oughly. Dip the pieces of chicken into this batter.

Cut the salt pork in small cubes and heat in a heavy frying pan to make fat 1-inch deep. Remove bits of pork.

When fat is hot, lay the pieces of chicken in, brown quickly, then cover the pan and cook slowly until tender, 35 to 60 minutes. Serve with cream gravy. Serves 4 to 6.

CHICKEN SAUTÉ BURGUNDY WITH MUSHROOM SAUCE

1 frying chicken (about 3½ pounds), cut in pieces for serving
Flour
Salt and pepper to taste
2 tablespoons butter or margarine
2 tablespoons salad oil
¼ cup burgundy or other red wine

Dust chicken with flour seasoned with salt and pepper.

Heat butter and oil in large, heavy skillet with a tight-fitting lid. Add chicken and sauté until nicely browned on all sides.

Add ¼ cup wine. Cover and cook over low heat 45 minutes, or until chicken is tender.

Meantime, prepare sauce as follows:

½ cup diced celery
¼ cup diced onion
4 tablespoons butter or margarine
3 tablespoons flour
1¼ cups chicken stock (canned or bouillon-cube broth may be used)
½ cup burgundy or other red wine
1 4-ounce can mushroom stems and pieces
Dash of thyme
Dash of marjoram
Dash of paprika
Salt and pepper to taste
2 tablespoons chopped parsley

Sauté celery and onion gently in butter 5 minutes. Blend in flour; add stock; cook, stirring constantly, until mixture boils and thickens.

Add wine, mushrooms (undrained), and seasonings; bring to a boil, then simmer 5 minutes, stirring frequently.

Just before serving, add parsley. Pour sauce over chicken, or serve separately. Serves 3 to 4.

Southern Fried Chicken with Cream Gravy

Rock Cornish Hens

The Rock Cornish hen (also called Cornish game hen) is a small-boned, all-white-meat bird of fine flavor developed by cross-breeding the Cornish hen with other breeds of chicken. It is generally marketed at 5 to 8 weeks, and the ready-to-cook weight is seldom more than a pound. Although it is usually cooked whole—in the oven, on a spit, or on coals—it may also be cut into halves and broiled or fried.

ROAST ROCK CORNISH HEN

Place defrosted hens on baking sheet or shallow pan breast-side-up. Brush entire bird with melted butter, margarine, or shortening. Season to taste.

Roast in hot oven (425°F.) 20 minutes. Reduce heat to moderate oven (350°F.) and roast 25 minutes more, then turn bird breast down and continue to roast until golden brown, about 15 minutes.

Baste during cooking, adding hot water or consommé to drippings to make a gravy.

FLAMING ROCK CORNISH HENS

Pour ¼ cup heated brandy over roasted game hens and sauce. Ignite with a match and allow flames to burn out. This French touch adds to the flavor and appearance.

BROILED ROCK CORNISH HENS

Split defrosted birds; sprinkle with salt and pepper and rub with melted butter, margarine, or shortening and a few drops seasoning sauce.

Place flesh-side-down 3 to 5 inches from moderate flame for 15 to 20 minutes.

Turn; add a cup of white wine to broiling pan and baste frequently until done, 15 to 20 minutes.

Candlelight dinner for two features roast Rock Cornish game hens with a moist stuffing of crumbs, prunes, and walnuts.

ROCK CORNISH HENS WITH CHINESE GLAZE

4   Rock Cornish hens, about 14 ounces each
1   teaspoon salt
¼   teaspoon pepper
1   large onion, cut in large pieces
2   stalks celery, cut in 1-inch pieces
4   medium carrots, cut in ½-inch pieces
2   tablespoons melted butter or margarine

Rub hens inside and out with salt and pepper. Stuff with vegetables.

Place breast-side-up on rack in shallow pan; brush with butter or margarine. Roast, uncovered, in moderate oven (350°F.) for 30 minutes.

Remove from oven; brush with glaze. Return to oven; roast another 30 minutes, or until tender; baste occasionally. Serves 4.

Chinese Glaze: Use a prepared Chinese duck sauce or make your own as follows: Cook ½ cup dried apricots as directed on package; drain.

Press through wire strainer or food mill. Add 1½ teaspoons grated orange rind, ¼ cup orange juice, 1 tablespoon light corn syrup, 1 tablespoon vinegar, 1½ teaspoons soy sauce, and dash of ground ginger. Bring slowly to boil, stirring often.

STUFFED CORNISH GAME HENS

1   cup shredded wheat wafer crumbs
2   tablespoons butter or margarine
½   cup chopped walnuts
1   tablespoon grated lemon rind
½   cup chopped prunes
½   teaspoon salt
1   teaspoon ground allspice
1   teaspoon ground marjoram
¼   cup cranberry juice cocktail
1   teaspoon ground ginger
2   frozen Rock Cornish game hens, thawed

Mix crumbs with next 9 ingredients. Stuff hens. Truss.

Place on rack in a shallow baking pan and roast in moderate oven (350°F.) about 1 hour. Brush with melted butter or margarine and baste occasionally while cooking. Serves 2.

ROCK CORNISH HENS GRUCCI

4   whole Cornish hens, defrosted
Salt and pepper
¾   cup cooked wild rice
⅓   cup diced ham or Canadian bacon
⅓   cup chopped mushrooms
2   shallots, minced
½   cup sherry
¼   cup brandy
¼   cup butter
¼   cup broth or consommé

Season hens inside and out with salt and pepper.

Combine rice, bacon, mushrooms, and shallots; moisten with ¼ cup sherry and ¼ cup brandy. Stuff loosely into cavities. Skewer openings and truss birds.

Place breast-side-up in baking dish. Dot with butter. Roast in moderate oven (350°F.) until nicely browned and done through, about 45 minutes.

Remove hens to a warm platter. Add ¼ cup sherry and broth to juices in pan. Stir up brown bits and thicken sauce with 1 teaspoon flour, if desired. Pour over hens. Serves 4.

CORNISH HEN APPLE CASSOULET

2   teaspoons instant minced onion
2   tablespoons water
2   tablespoons salad oil
½   pound sweet Italian sausages
2   Rock Cornish hens, split into halves
½   teaspoon salt
3   tart apples, peeled and sliced
1   green pepper, cut in rings
1   can (1 pound, 4 ounces) white kidney beans (Cannellini)
¼   teaspoon Tabasco sauce
1   teaspoon Worcestershire sauce

Combine onion and water; let stand until water is absorbed.

Heat salad oil in large skillet. Cut sausages in chunks; brown in oil; remove. Rub hens with salt; brown in same skillet; remove.

Add apples and green pepper rings to skillet; cook 5 minutes. Add beans, Tabasco, Worcestershire sauce, and onions; mix well. Spoon bean mixture into 4 individual casseroles; place hens on top; cover.

Bake in moderate oven (350°F.) 45 to 60 minutes, or until hens are done. Serves 4.

Cornish Hen Apple Cassoulet

Stewing and Braising Poultry— Top of Range Recipes

CHICKEN STEW WITH HERB DUMPLINGS

2   medium-sized onions, minced
1   green pepper, minced
1   garlic clove, minced
2   tablespoons fat
1   3- to 3½-pound chicken, disjointed
1   8-ounce can tomato sauce
½   cup water
1½   teaspoons salt
⅛   teaspoon pepper
1   teaspoon Ac'cent
1   teaspoon poultry seasoning
About 4 cups boiling water
2   cups cooked or canned green peas

In deep kettle cook onions, green pepper, and garlic in hot fat until soft but not brown. Add chicken.

Combine tomato sauce, ½ cup water, and seasonings; pour over chicken.

Add enough boiling water to cover; simmer 1½ hours, adding more water if necessary.

Add peas; drop in dumpling batter; cover; boil 12 minutes longer. Serves 6.

Herb Dumplings: Use favorite recipe, or follow directions on package of prepared biscuit mix, adding 1 teaspoon oregano or marjoram to dry ingredients.

SMOTHERED CHICKEN WITH CREAM GRAVY

1   4½-pound dressed roasting chicken, cut for frying
½   cup flour
2   teaspoons paprika
2   teaspoons salt
¼   teaspoon pepper
⅓   cup chicken fat or shortening
2   cans condensed cream of mushroom soup

Shake chicken in a sack with flour, paprika, salt, and pepper.

Brown on all sides in fat in a heavy skillet.

Pour soup over chicken. Cover and simmer over low heat about 1 hour, or until tender. Spoon sauce over chicken occasionally. Serves 6.

Mediterranean Chicken

Chicken Stew with Herb Dumplings

MEDITERRANEAN CHICKEN

1   frying chicken (3 pounds)
¼   cup butter or margarine
2   pounds (about 16) small new potatoes
2   teaspoons tomato paste
Salt and pepper
1   can (9 ounces) pitted ripe olives
1   can (1 pound) artichoke hearts
½   cup sherry

Have chicken cut into quarters. Wash with cold water and dry with absorbent paper. Brown slowly in 2 tablespoons butter in Dutch oven, or other deep pan, uncovered.

Wash potatoes, scraping if desired, and brown lightly in remaining butter.

After chicken has cooked 30 minutes, stir tomato paste into juices in bottom of pan; then add potatoes. Season with salt and pepper. Cook, covered, over low heat until potatoes and chicken are tender, about 20 minutes.

Add drained olives and artichoke hearts; cook 5 minutes longer. Remove to serving dish and rinse out pan with sherry, scraping well. Spoon over chicken and serve. Serves 4.

Note: Chicken isn't salted at beginning because it makes butter too brown.

COQ AU VIN

Coq au Vin is French for chicken with wine of which there are many versions; however the name is usually applied to cut-up chicken browned in butter, transferred to a casserole, and braised in red wine as in the following recipe. Any good red wine may be used in preparing it.

2   broilers, about 2½ pounds each, cut in halves
2   onions, diced
2   carrots, diced
3   bay leaves
2   stalks celery, cut in 1-inch pieces
Salt and pepper
Burgundy or other dry red wine to cover
Flour
¼   cup butter

Combine the chicken, onions, carrots, bay leaves, and celery in a bowl; add a sprinkling of salt and a dash of pepper and cover with wine. Let stand 2 to 4 days in the refrigerator.

At cooking time, remove the chicken from the marinade and dry thoroughly with a towel. Sprinkle all over with flour.

Heat butter in a heavy skillet; add chicken and brown on all sides. Transfer chicken to a flame-proof casserole with a cover or to a Dutch oven.

Add the marinade with the vegetables and cook over very low heat until the chicken is tender and the marinade has been reduced to a rich brown sauce. The cover should be lifted slightly off-center to allow the escape of steam. Transfer the chicken to a hot platter; strain the sauce and pour over it. Serves 4.

BRAISED CHICKEN MONTE CARLO

3   tablespoons butter or margarine
3   tablespoons olive or salad oil
2   2½-pound ready-to-cook broilers, quartered
1   teaspoon salt
¼   teaspoon white pepper
1   teaspoon Ac'cent
⅔   cup thinly sliced onions
½   cup sauterne wine
1   cup light cream
1   4-ounce can button mushrooms
6   radishes, sliced

Heat butter and oil in a large skillet. Brown chicken pieces on all sides. Sprinkle with salt, pepper, and Ac'cent.

Add onions and cook until onions are soft.

Pour wine over. Cover and simmer gently for 20 minutes.

Stir in cream and drained mushrooms. Heat through and serve at once garnished with radish slices. Serves 8.

STEWED CHICKEN PICTURE HINTS

Cut up into serving pieces or leave chicken whole. Add water and seasonings.

Simmer, covered, until tender. Test for doneness.

For variety, brown chicken before stewing.

Prepare gravy from the broth.

Stewed Chicken with Dumplings

STEWED CHICKEN
(Master Recipe)

Select a 3½- to 5-pound chicken. Place the chicken, whole or cut up, in kettle. Choose one with a tight-fitting cover.

Add ½ cup water and ½ teaspoon salt for each pound of chicken ready-to-cook including giblets and neck. If the chicken is to be served with gravy and dumplings, biscuit or mashed potatoes increase water to 1 cup and the salt to a scant ¾ teaspoon per pound of chicken, ready-to-cook weight.

For additional flavor, 1 small carrot, 1 small onion, 2 or 3 ribs of celery, a clove, and 2 or 3 whole black peppers may be added.

Bring water to a rapid boil. Skim any froth from surface, reduce heat to simmering. Cook gently until thickest pieces are fork-tender, 2½ to 4 hours.

Remove chicken, strain broth, and cool meat and broth promptly. Cover and refrigerate unless it is served immediately.

Steps in Preparing Gravy for Stewed Chicken

Remove chicken from broth.

Skim fat from the surface of the broth. Set this fat aside. Some will be used for the gravy.

If necessary, strain the broth and then measure it. For gravy allow about ½ cup broth per serving. Add milk or water to broth if necessary to make up the needed amount.

For each cup of gravy, mix 1½ tablespoons each of flour and chicken fat and ¼ cup water until smooth.

Pour slowly into the simmering broth, stirring constantly until smooth and thickened throughout. Cover and simmer 5 to 10 minutes depending upon the amount of gravy.

Replace chicken in gravy. Season gravy well to taste. Serve very hot.

Variations: Sometimes stewed chicken with gravy is referred to as a White Stew or a Brown Stew.

To prepare White Stew follow directions for cooking the chicken. Add 1 cup milk to the broth before preparing the gravy.

Brown Stew is prepared by browning the flour-coated pieces as in braising before the water and salt are added.

BRAISED CHICKEN
(Master Recipe)

Any size of mature, less-tender chicken may be cooked by braising.

Coat the cut-up chicken, giblets, and neck with seasoning and flour. For each 1 pound of chicken use 2 tablespoons flour, ½ teaspoon salt, ¼ teaspoon paprika, and ⅛ teaspoon pepper.

Use a heavy kettle with a well-fitting lid. Brown slowly in a thin layer of moderately hot fat, turning with tongs or 2 spoons. About ½ hour is required to brown 4 pounds of chicken.

Remove pan from heat while adding ½ to ⅓ cup water. Cover tightly.

Replace over very *low* heat or place in slow oven (325°F.) and cook slowly until the thickest pieces are fork-tender, 2½ to 3½ hours. Should the liquid be used up before chicken is tender, add more water in ¼- to ½-cup amounts.

Lift chicken to warm serving dish.

Prepare gravy with the pan drippings.

Variations: Milk, sweet or sour cream, fruit or vegetable juices, cider, or wine may be used instead of water. When chicken is oven-braised, ketchup, chili or barbecue sauce, tomatoes or creamed soups give flavor and variety. Seasonings in addition to salt and pepper may be selected from allspice, bay leaf, cloves, ginger, nutmeg, onion, or garlic.

BRAISED CHICKEN PICTURE HINTS

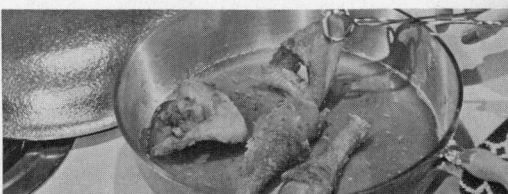

To braise stewing chicken, first flour and brown.

Add liquid, cover tightly and cook on range or in oven.

Serve braised chicken with rice or vegetables.

CHICKEN FRICASSEE

Cut up chicken and cook as for Stewed Chicken.

Roll cooked pieces in well seasoned flour and sauté in chicken fat in a heavy skillet until browned.

Thicken 1½ cups of the stock with 2 tablespoons flour blended into 2 tablespoons chicken or other fat.

Or, mash the vegetables and use to thicken stock. Serve with rice, spaghetti, or noodles.

CHICKEN CACCIATORE

Cacciatore, or as it often appears on menus, "alla cacciatore," is an Italian term meaning hunter's style. It is a method of cooking chicken and sometimes veal in a well-seasoned sauce of tomatoes and wine. Mushrooms and peppers are often included in various versions of chicken cacciatore.

1 ready-to-cook chicken, 2½ to 3 pounds, disjointed
½ cup olive oil, scant
1 teaspoon paprika
1 finely sliced onion
3½ cups canned tomatoes or 8 medium tomatoes
1 clove garlic
1 teaspoon salt
¼ teaspoon pepper
½ cup white wine (optional)

Dry chicken. Cook gently in hot olive oil until well browned. Sprinkle with paprika to aid browning. Turn occasionally to brown evenly.

Spoon off 2 or 3 tablespoons oil. Add onions, tomatoes, garlic, salt, and pepper. Cover tightly and simmer until chicken is tender, about ¾ hour.

If sauce is watery, remove chicken and simmer sauce for several minutes to thicken it.

Return chicken to sauce. Add wine and heat. Remove garlic before serving. Serves 5.

Note: Flour, brown, and cook giblets and neck with chicken. If desired, before serving, cut neck in 3 sections and slice gizzard, heart, and liver meat into thin slices and serve all in sauce.

EASY CHICKEN PAPRIKA

1 3-pound chicken, cut into pieces
Flour
¼ cup shortening
¼ cup finely chopped onion
1 cup sliced mushrooms
1 can (1¼ cups) condensed tomato soup
1 cup sour cream
1 bay leaf
½ teaspoon salt
¼ teaspoon pepper
2 teaspoons paprika

Dust chicken with flour; brown on both sides in hot melted shortening in a heavy skillet.

Add onion and mushrooms and cook until lightly browned.

Blend in remaining ingredients; cover and simmer slowly, stirring occasionally, for 45 minutes, or until tender.

Remove bay leaf before serving. Serves 6.

CHICKEN BRUNSWICK STEW

Brunswick stew is a name for a popular Southern dish which may be made of chicken, rabbit, squirrel, or pork and may include such vegetables as corn, green lima beans, okra, and tomatoes. A popular version is given below.

1 5-pound ready-to-cook stewing chicken
2 quarts water
1 tablespoon salt
1 cup diced onion
2 cups cooked tomatoes
2 cups cooked lima beans
1 cup cream-style corn
1 cup okra, cleaned
1 teaspoon salt
½ teaspoon black pepper
⅛ teaspoon thyme
1 bay leaf

Wash the chicken inside and out. Cut into pieces or leave whole. Put into a deep kettle. Add water, salt, and onion. Cover and simmer about 3 hours or until the chicken is tender.

Remove chicken from the broth and strip the meat from the bones. Cut the

Easy Chicken Paprika

meat into bite-sized pieces.

Use a big spoon to skim off most of the fat from the broth. Return the chicken meat to the broth. Add all the vegetables and remaining seasoning. Simmer 1 hour.

Taste and season if necessary. Remove bay leaf before serving.

Serves 6 to 8.

Note: This is a one-dish meal. It should be fairly thick and served in soup bowls to be eaten with a soup spoon. Serve with crusty rolls or French bread.

CHICKEN CREOLE

1 frying chicken, 3½ pounds
1 teaspoon salt
Few grains black pepper
¼ cup olive oil
2 tablespoons butter or margarine
1 tablespoon flour
½ cup minced onion or 6 chopped shallots
5 tablespoons chopped green pepper
1 No. 2 can tomatoes
Few grains cayenne
1 sprig thyme or ¼ teaspoon powdered thyme
1 tablespoon minced parsley
1 bay leaf
2 cloves garlic, minced
½ cup white wine
Cooked rice

Cut chicken into frying pieces. Sprinkle with salt and pepper. Brown on all sides in olive oil.

In another pan, melt the butter, blend in flour, and cook until brown. Add onion or shallots and green pepper and brown slightly.

Add tomatoes, cayenne, thyme, parsley, bay leaf, and garlic. Cook over low heat until sauce is thickened, about 15 minutes.

Add chicken, cover and simmer over low heat until chicken is perfectly tender, about 45 minutes.

Add wine 15 minutes before cooking time is up. Serve over cooked rice. Garnish with parsley and avocado slices, if desired. Serves 4 to 6.

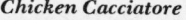

Chicken Cacciatore

Olive Chicketti

OLIVE CHICKETTI

1   5-pound stewing chicken
1/4 cup oil or shortening
6   cups hot water
1   tablespoon salt
1/3 cup chopped onion
1/3 cup diced green sweet pepper
2   cups sliced celery
1/2 cup diced pimiento
1   pound spaghetti
1 1/2 cups ripe olives
2   cups grated Cheddar cheese

Disjoint chicken and brown in hot oil. Add hot water and salt, cover and cook slowly until tender. Cool sufficiently to handle.

Skim off excess fat. Remove skin and bones from chicken, leaving meat in large pieces.

Cook onion, pepper, and celery in a little of the chicken fat until wilted and clear. Stir into chicken and broth, add pimiento and heat to boiling.

Add broken spaghetti. Boil until spaghetti is tender, adding more water if needed.

Cut some of olives into large pieces and leave some whole.

Just before serving, stir olives and cheese into chicken mixture and heat slowly until cheese is melted.

Serves 8 to 10.

ARROZ CON POLLO
(Latin American Chicken with Rice)

Arroz is the Spanish term for rice; arroz con pollo: chicken with rice.

1   young 3 1/2-pound chicken
1/2 cup olive oil
1/2 cup diced onion
1 1/2 teaspoons salt
Pepper to taste
3   cups canned tomatoes
1   clove garlic
1   bay leaf
1   cup raw rice

Cut up and fry chicken in oil gently until evenly browned. Remove chicken.

Cook onions lightly. Replace chicken. Add salt and pepper.

Add tomatoes heated to boiling. Drop garlic clove and bay leaf on top. Add rice.

Cook gently over low heat (or in moderate oven, 350°F.) until rice is tender and fluffy, about 1 hour.

Lift and stir once after first 15 minutes.

Remove garlic and bay leaf. Serve on warm platter, garnished with slivers of olives and green pepper rings.

Serves 5 to 6.

Arroz De Franzo: In Portugal, white wine is added.

Spanish Arroz Con Pollo: In Spain, saffron and cummin seed are added.

CHICKEN ROMANO

1   2 1/2-pound ready-to-cook chicken, cut in pieces
1/4 cup flour
1   teaspoon salt
1/4 teaspoon pepper
1/4 cup olive or salad oil
1   No. 1 can small white onions
1   medium-sized green pepper, cut in strips
1   4-ounce can mushrooms, drained
1   small clove garlic, minced
1   10 1/2-ounce can condensed tomato soup
1/2 cup water
2   tablespoons vinegar or lemon juice
1   tablespoon Worcestershire sauce
1/2 teaspoon oregano

Wash chicken pieces and pat dry. Roll in flour seasoned with salt and pepper. Brown chicken in olive oil in a large skillet; remove chicken.

Sauté onions, green pepper, mushrooms, and garlic in same skillet; blend in remaining ingredients.

Add chicken; cover and simmer about 30 minutes, or until chicken is done. Stir occasionally. Serve over cooked spaghetti. Serves 4.

CHICKEN IN RED WINE

4   tablespoons fat
1   stewing chicken (4 to 5 pounds), cut in pieces for serving
1   cup chicken broth (canned or bouillon-cube broth may be used)
1   8-ounce can tomato sauce
1/2 cup Burgundy or other red wine
1   medium onion, thinly sliced
2   stalks celery, chopped
2   tablespoons chopped parsley
Salt and pepper to taste
6   medium carrots, scraped and sliced
1   cup fresh or frozen peas, cooked
1/3 cup flour
2   tablespoons sherry wine

Heat fat in a Dutch oven or other heavy kettle; add chicken and fry gently until nicely browned on all sides.

Add chicken broth, tomato sauce, wine, onion, celery, parsley, and salt and pepper. Bring to a boil, then cover and simmer gently for 2 to 2 1/2 hours (or longer, if necessary), until chicken is almost tender.

Add carrots; continue cooking for 1/2 hour, or until chicken and carrots are tender.

Remove chicken and vegetables from liquid. Pour liquid into a measuring pitcher or bowl; skim off excess fat and add water to make 3 cups. Return to Dutch oven and heat to boiling.

Mix flour with 2/3 cup water to a smooth paste. Add slowly to the boiling liquid, stirring constantly. Simmer about 5 minutes. Season to taste with salt and pepper. Add sherry.

Return chicken and vegetables to gravy. Add peas. Heat thoroughly before serving. Serves 5 or 6.

CHICKEN ALMOND CURRY

1   chicken (3 1/2 to 4 pounds), disjointed
2   teaspoons salt
Few grains pepper
1 1/2 teaspoons Ac'cent
1   medium onion, sliced
Boiling water
1   tart apple, diced
6   tablespoons butter or margarine
6   tablespoons flour
1   tablespoon curry powder, or to taste
Salt and pepper
1/2 cup chopped, toasted almonds

Place chicken in deep kettle. Add salt, pepper, 1 teaspoon Ac'cent, and onion. Cover with boiling water. Simmer 1 1/2 hours, or until chicken is tender. Add apple during last half hour.

Strain broth; measure 3 cups.

Bone chicken, leaving meat in as large pieces as possible.

Melt butter or margarine; blend in flour, remaining Ac'cent, and curry powder. Add broth; stir over low heat until thickened; add chicken; heat thoroughly.

Season to taste with additional salt and pepper. Pour into serving dish; top with almonds.

Serve with whole, sautéed bananas and curry accompaniments, such as chutney, coconut, and golden raisins. Serves 6.

Chicken Almond Curry

Miscellaneous Dishes with Fresh or Frozen Chicken

CHICKEN MOLÉ

Molé is a highly seasoned Mexican sauce for poultry containing a small amount of chocolate. In Mexico the word is spelled without the accent, which is added in English so that the second syllable will be pronounced.

1 ready-to-cook stewing chicken, 3 pounds
3 dried sweet red peppers, broken into small pieces
2 dried hot red peppers, broken into small pieces
1 teaspoon salt
½ cup water
1 slice white bread, cubed
2 tablespoons sesame seed
½ cup olive oil
2 tablespoons flour
2 cups chicken broth
1 teaspoon salt
2 whole cloves
½ ounce unsweetened chocolate

Disjoint and cut up chicken. Simmer in seasoned water to cover with giblets and neck until tender, 2½ to 3 hours.

Prepare sauce: Remove stems and seeds from peppers; break into cold salted water and soak 20 minutes.

Drain. Brown drained peppers, bread cubes, and sesame seed in olive oil. Add remaining ingredients and chocolate. Cook slowly until chocolate is melted, about 10 minutes.

Force through fine sieve. Serve sauce over hot chicken. Serves 5 to 6.

CHICKEN BARCELONA

1 broiler-fryer chicken (3 pounds), quartered
2 teaspoons salt
1 teaspoon paprika
¼ cup olive or salad oil
1 teaspoon rosemary
½ teaspoon thyme
1 clove garlic, sliced
2½ cups water
¼ teaspoon saffron
1 cup raw regular rice
2 bay leaves
1 package (10 ounces) frozen green peas
½ cup sliced pimiento-stuffed olives

Chicken Barcelona

Sprinkle chicken with 1 teaspoon salt and paprika. Brown on all sides in hot oil in skillet.

Meanwhile, mix together remaining 1 teaspoon salt, rosemary, thyme, garlic, and water in saucepan; bring to a boil; add chicken neck and giblets. Simmer 25 minutes; strain and reserve 2 cups stock.

Remove chicken from skillet; drain off all but 3 tablespoons drippings. Stir saffron and rice into skillet. Toast 15 minutes or until rice is golden, stirring occasionally. Add bay leaves, peas, reserved stock, and olives; mix well.

Add chicken; cover and cook over low heat 30 minutes or until chicken and rice are tender; stir occasionally. Serves 4.

CHICKEN TETRAZZINI

Tetrazzini is a term applied to a casserole of chicken baked with mushrooms and spaghetti in a rich wine-flavored sauce. The original dish was named for the Italian opera soprano Luisa Tetrazzini (1874-1940). Turkey, lobster, and veal are often prepared in much the same manner. Although Luisa Tetrazzini was distinctly Italian, the dishes named for her are usually distinctly American.

1 4-pound chicken
1 teaspoon salt
½ pound fresh mushrooms, sliced
6 tablespoons butter or margarine
½ pound spaghetti
3 tablespoons flour
2 cups chicken broth
1 cup heavy cream
2 tablespoons sherry
Grated Parmesan cheese

Cover cleaned chicken with hot water. Add salt and simmer until tender. Cool in broth, then shred chicken and put skin and bones back in broth. Cook broth down to little more than 2 cupfuls, so that when strained there will be 2 cupfuls.

Sauté mushrooms in 3 tablespoons butter 2 to 3 minutes.

Cook spaghetti in boiling salted water.

Make sauce: Melt 3 tablespoons butter, blend in flour, and add broth, stirring and cooking over low heat until smooth and thickened. Add cream and sherry.

Divide sauce and add chicken to one part and spaghetti and mushrooms to other part. Put spaghetti in baking dish, making a well in center for chicken mixture.

Sprinkle grated cheese over all. Bake in moderate oven (350°F.) until lightly browned. Serve at once. Serves 8.

CHICKEN MILANO

1 frying chicken (2½ to 3 pounds)
2 tablespoons olive or cooking oil
2 tablespoons butter or margarine
Salt and pepper
1 clove garlic, sliced
1 onion, minced
½ cup canned or diced fresh peeled tomato
½ cup water
Juice of 1 lemon
1 tablespoon chopped parsley

Cut chicken as for fricassee. Wipe pieces dry, then sauté slowly until brown in oil and butter. Sprinkle with salt and pepper while cooking.

When well browned, add garlic and onion. Cook slowly until onion is soft, then add tomato, water, and lemon. Cover and cook slowly for 30 minutes longer.

Sprinkle with parsley before serving. Any juice left in the pan should be served over the chicken. Serves 4.

CHICKEN MARENGO

According to legend Chicken Marengo is supposed to have been invented for Napoleon at Marengo, Italy, after one of his most important victories. Traditionally the dish contained mushrooms, tomatoes, wine, garlic, and was garnished with crawfish and fried eggs. Nowadays there are many versions of this dish and the name is also applied to veal dishes.

1 3- to 4-pound chicken, disjointed
Cooking fat or oil
Salt, pepper, thyme
6 green onions, chopped
1¼ cups chicken broth
¾ cup sauterne or rhine wine
2 tablespoons tomato paste
1 tablespoon flour

Heat 1 inch melted cooking fat in skillet or frying pan. Dry chicken pieces, and fry to golden brown on both sides. Season with salt, pepper, and thyme. Transfer to baking dish.

Sprinkle with chopped onions. Add ½ cup chicken broth, and bake, uncovered, in moderate oven (325°F.) 30 minutes.

Add ½ cup wine and tomato paste. Cover, and bake 20 minutes longer.

Uncover, and bake 10 minutes. Remove chicken to hot platter.

Add remaining broth and wine to drippings in pan. Shake flour with ¼ cup cold water and add to gravy. Cook until slightly thickened. Serve sauce over chicken. Serves 4.

Chicken Mexicana

CHICKEN STEAMED IN LEMON BUTTER

1/2 cup butter or margarine
2 tablespoons lemon juice
1 teaspoon salt
1 clove garlic, peeled
1/8 teaspoon pepper
1/2 teaspoon paprika
1 frying chicken, cut up

Put all ingredients except chicken in skillet and bring to boil.

Arrange chicken in skillet; bring again to boil. Cover and simmer for 30 minutes, or until chicken is tender, turning several times. Serves 4.

REGAL CHICKEN

1 10-ounce package corn frozen in butter sauce, in cooking pouch
2 cups dry breadcrumbs
1/2 teaspoon salt
1/4 teaspoon poultry seasoning
4 whole chicken breasts
1/2 cup butter or margarine, melted
1 cup sour cream

Drop frozen pouch of corn in butter sauce into boiling water to cover. Bring to a second boil. Heat several minutes or until butter sauce is melted. Do not cover pan. Remove pouch by grasping top flap. Open and pour into medium-sized bowl. Add breadcrumbs, salt, and poultry seasoning; toss lightly.

Fill cavity of each chicken breast with stuffing. Skewer with toothpicks. Place in shallow baking dish in melted butter or margarine; turn once to coat both sides. Bake in slow oven (325°F.) 45 minutes.

Turn and bake an additional 45 minutes or until tender. Remove to warm platter or serving plates.

Stir sour cream into cooled pan drippings. Heat over low heat several minutes. Do not boil. Spoon over chicken. Serves 4 to 6.

Regal Chicken

CHICKEN MEXICANA

1 4-pound chicken, disjointed
2 cups boiling water
2 tablespoons chili powder
1/4 teaspoon pepper
1/4 teaspoon cinnamon
2 tablespoons grated onion
1 teaspoon Ac'cent
1 teaspoon salt
1/4 cup fat or drippings
2 cups pineapple juice
2 cups pineapple chunks
1 teaspoon sugar
2 bananas, sliced
1 ripe avocado
1/2 pound white grapes

Place chicken in deep kettle; add boiling water, chili powder, pepper, cinnamon, grated onion, Ac'cent, and salt. Cover; simmer 1 hour.

Drain chicken; brown pieces on all sides in hot fat or drippings; arrange in baking pan.

Add pineapple juice to broth in which chicken was cooked; heat and pour over chicken.

Arrange pineapple chunks over chicken; sprinkle with sugar.

Bake in moderate oven (375°F.) 30 minutes.

Remove chicken and fruit to serving dish; garnish with lengthwise slices of banana, avocado slices, and grapes. Serve gravy separately. Serves 6.

CHICKEN-RICE DINNER

1 5-pound chicken
1 onion, chopped
Fat for browning
1 cup uncooked rice
1 teaspoon salt
1/8 teaspoon white pepper
1 can mushrooms or 2 carrots
2 cups stock or tomatoes

Cut chicken in serving pieces. Brown with onion in small amount of fat.

Add boiling water to partially cover. Add uncooked rice, salt, pepper, mushrooms or chopped carrots, and stock or tomatoes.

Simmer on top of range or in moderate oven (350°F.) until chicken is almost, but not quite, falling off bones. The time depends on tenderness of the chicken, but do allow about 1 1/2 hours for the chicken.

Serve generous amount of rice with pieces of chicken. Serves 4 to 6.

CHICKEN GUMBO WITH RICE

1 large stewing chicken
2 tablespoons fat
1 slice ham, diced
2 teaspoons salt
1/4 teaspoon pepper
1/2 cup chopped onion
1 cup chopped green pepper
1/4 teaspoon thyme

1 No. 2 can tomatoes
1 quart water
3 cups sliced okra
6 cups hot cooked rice

Cut chicken into serving pieces. Wash thoroughly in cold water. Pat dry.

Heat fat in a soup kettle. Add chicken and ham. Cover and cook 15 minutes.

Add salt, pepper, onion, green pepper, thyme, and tomatoes. Add water. Cover and allow to simmer 2 hours, or until chicken is tender.

Add okra. Cover and cook 20 minutes, or until okra is tender. If desired, remove chicken meat from bones.

Serve the gumbo in soup tureen, if desired. Place rice in soup bowls and pour gumbo over rice. Be certain to have gumbo steaming hot when it is served. Serves 8.

CREAMY SMOTHERED CHICKEN AND MUSHROOMS

3 1/2- to 4-pound chicken
1/2 cup flour
1/4 cup fat
3/4 cup hot water
1/2 pound mushrooms
Cooked rice or noodles

Wash chicken, dry and disjoint.

Mix 1/4 cup flour, 1 teaspoon salt, and few grains pepper; use to dredge chicken.

Brown chicken in fat. Add hot water, cover and simmer until chicken is tender, about 40 minutes. There should be about 1/4 cup stock in pan. Add milk to make 2 cups.

Blend remaining flour to smooth paste with cold water; add to stock and milk in pan and cook slowly, stirring constantly until thick.

Sauté mushrooms in butter. Arrange hot cooked rice or noodles, chicken, and mushrooms on serving dish. Pour a little milk gravy over chicken. Pass remaining gravy. If desired, serve chutney in green pepper rings. Serves 6.

Chicken Gumbo with Rice

CHICKEN PAPRIKASH (HUNGARIAN)

    1   ready-to-cook chicken about 2½
          pounds
    ¼   cup flour
    ¾   teaspoon salt
    ⅛   teaspoon pepper
    ½   cup fat for frying
    ½   cup finely chopped onion
    2   to 3 tablespoons water
    1   tablespoon paprika or more
    3   tablespoons flour
    1   cup sour cream
    1   cup water
        Grated rind of 1 lemon
    1   tablespoon lemon juice or more

Disjoint chicken and coat with blended flour, salt, and pepper.

Brown chicken in hot fat. Add onion and water. Sprinkle chicken generously with paprika.

Cover tightly and cook gently over low heat or in moderate oven (350°F.) until chicken is fork-tender, 40 to 50 minutes. If necessary, add more water in tablespoon amounts to prevent sticking.

Remove chicken to serving dish and keep hot.

Prepare gravy: Add flour to juices in pan and blend thoroughly. Cook over low heat until bubbly. Add sour cream and water and cook, stirring constantly, until thickened throughout.

Cover and simmer about 5 minutes. Add lemon rind and juice. Season well to taste. Serve gravy around chicken or separately. Serves 4 to 5.

Note: Unless some other use is planned, flour, brown, and cook giblets and neck with chicken. For service, cut neck into 3 pieces and gizzard, heart, and liver into slices. Add all to gravy.

DEVILED CHICKEN

    2   2½- to 3-pound ready-to-cook
          broilers, split
    6   tablespoons butter or margarine
    1   teaspoon salt
    1   tablespoon vinegar
    1   tablespoon Worcestershire sauce
    1   cup dry breadcrumbs

Place broiler halves skin-side-down in shallow pan and broil 6 inches from heat about 5 minutes on each side. Turn broilers.

Mix 4 tablespoons butter with rest of ingredients, except crumbs, and spread over the chicken. Melt rest of butter, stir in crumbs, and spread over chicken.

Bake uncovered in a moderate oven (350°F.) until chicken is tender and crumbs are browned (about 50 to 60 minutes). Potatoes may be pan-roasted with chicken if desired. Serves 4.

BAKED CHICKEN WITH MUSHROOMS

    1   roasting chicken, 3½ to 4 pounds
        Milk, flour, salt, and pepper
    ½   cup fat
    ½   pound fresh mushrooms
    1   small onion, sliced thin
    2   cups hot cream or top milk

Cut chicken into serving pieces; dip in milk, then in seasoned flour.

Fry in hot fat until nicely browned. Put in 1½-quart casserole.

Clean mushrooms and cut caps and stems into pieces. Fry mushrooms in fat about 2 or 3 minutes. Add mushrooms and onion slices to chicken, and add hot cream or top milk.

Bake in moderate oven (350°F.) 1½ to 2 hours, or until chicken is tender and cream is a thick sauce. Serve on a hot platter. Serves 6.

Note: If cream is used, it may curdle slightly. A little water can be added to it and stirred until sauce is smooth.

SKILLET LEMON BARBECUED CHICKEN

    1   frying chicken
        Salt and pepper
    6   tablespoons butter or margarine
    ¾   cup lemon sauce (below)

Have chicken drawn and cut into serving pieces, or, if quick-frozen, thaw according to directions on the box. Rinse in cold water and dry. Season with salt and pepper.

Melt butter in a heavy aluminum or stainless steel skillet and brown chicken, skin side down. Turn and brown.

Pour lemon sauce over chicken pieces. Cover and cook slowly until tender, about 30 to 40 minutes.

Arrange chicken on platter and pour sauce over pieces. Serves 4.

Lemon Sauce:

    1   small clove garlic
    ½   teaspoon salt
    ¼   cup salad oil
    ½   cup lemon juice
    2   tablespoons grated onion
    ½   teaspoon celery salt
    ½   teaspoon black pepper
    ½   teaspoon dried thyme

Mash garlic clove with salt in a bowl. Add remaining ingredients and mix together.

If possible, allow sauce to stand overnight to blend flavors before using. Makes ¾ cup.

IMPERIAL CHICKEN

    1   2½ to 3-pound frying chicken,
          cut up
    3   to 4 cups oven-toasted rice cereal
    ¾   cup grated Parmesan or Romano
          cheese

    2   teaspoons salt
    ⅛   teaspoon pepper
    1   clove garlic, crushed
    ¼   cup chopped parsley
    ½   to ⅔ cup butter or margarine,
          melted

Wash chicken pieces and dry thoroughly. Crush oven-toasted rice cereal into medium-fine crumbs; combine with grated cheese, salt, pepper, garlic, and parsley. Dip chicken pieces in melted butter, then roll in cereal crumbs until well coated.

Place skin side up in shallow baking pan lined with aluminum foil; do not crowd pieces. Bake in moderate oven (350°F.) about 1 hour or until tender. Do not cover pan or turn chicken while cooking. Serves 4 to 5.

GUMBO FILE (CREOLE)

    1   3-pound chicken
    1½ teaspoons salt
    ¼   teaspoon black pepper
    2   tablespoons fat
    2   tablespoons flour
    1   small onion, chopped fine
    1   tomato, sliced
    2   quarts hot water
    ½   teaspoon thyme
        Dash of cayenne
    ½   cup minced celery
    2   dozen oysters
    2   tablespoons minced parsley
    2   tablespoons filé powder
        Boiled rice

Remove chicken from bones. Cut meat in small pieces and combine with salt and pepper and brown lightly in fat in frying pan.

Remove chicken and add flour, stirring constantly until brown and smooth. Add onion and cook until yellow; add tomato and cook a few minutes.

Put in chicken, hot water, thyme, cayenne, and celery. Simmer until meat is tender, 1½ to 2 hours.

Add oysters and parsley and cook until edges of oysters curl.

Remove from heat and stir in filé powder. Do *not* cook after adding filé powder. Serve with a spoonful of rice in each soup plate. Serves 8.

Imperial Chicken

CHICKEN PIE (ENGLISH STYLE)

1   stewing chicken, 3 to 6 pounds,
        cut up, giblets and neck
4   tablespoons chicken fat
1/2 cup flour
3   cups chicken broth
1   cup top milk or thin cream
1/2 teaspoon ginger
3/4 teaspoon pepper
2   to 4 hard-cooked eggs, sliced
Biscuit dough

Cook chicken several hours or a day in advance, simmering chicken, giblets, and neck until tender in seasoned water to cover, 2 1/2 to 3 hours. Refrigerate until pie is prepared.

Melt fat over low heat. Add flour and blend thoroughly. Add broth and milk all at once. Cook, stirring constantly, until thickened throughout. Add seasonings.

Meanwhile, trim giblets and cut into thin slices. Remove meat from neck or cut neck into 2 or 3 sections. Add all to gravy.

Arrange chicken in 2-quart shallow casserole, dividing larger pieces. If bones are left in, alternate meaty and less-meaty pieces. Add eggs and hot gravy.

Cover with biscuit dough rolled 1/4 inch thick. Brush top with milk. Bake in hot oven (425°F.) until top is nicely browned and sauce is bubbly, 20 to 25 minutes. Serves 6 from 3-pound chicken.

If the larger-sized chicken is cooked, gravy and biscuit dough may be increased. For biscuit topping, use favorite biscuit recipe made with 2 cups flour or 2 cups biscuit mix.

SAUCY MUSHROOM CHICKEN WITH BROCCOLI

1   2 1/2-pound package frozen frying
        chicken, cut up, thawed
2   tablespoons butter or margarine
1/4 cup chopped onion
1   can condensed cream of mush-
        room soup
1   cup chicken stock
1   teaspoon salt
1   head broccoli, cut into florets

Brown chicken in butter. Add onion, soup, stock, and salt. Cover and cook over low heat 40 minutes.

Arrange broccoli over chicken. Cover and cook 10 minutes.

If desired, serve with lemon slices. Serves 4.

Herb Chicken Skillet: For a gourmet trick, substitute 1/2 cup sauterne wine for soup. Reduce chicken stock to 1/2 cup. Make a garni of 1 bay leaf, 3 whole black peppers, 3 sprigs parsley, and 1 clove garlic. Add garni with onion, wine, stock, and salt.

CHICKEN PUFF CASSEROLE

1   3-pound frying chicken
3   tablespoons flour
1   teaspoon salt
1/4 teaspoon pepper
4   tablespoons fat
1   cup corn meal
2   cups boiling water
1   tablespoon butter or margarine
1 1/2 teaspoons salt
1/2 cup sifted enriched flour
1   tablespoon sugar
3   teaspoons baking powder
4   eggs, separated
1/2 cup milk

Cut chicken into serving size pieces. Coat with flour seasoned wth 1 teaspoon salt and 1/4 teaspoon pepper. Melt fat in skillet and fry chicken until well browned on all sides. Remove chicken to large casserole. Save drippings to make gravy.

Slowly stir corn meal into boiling water. Add butter and 1 1/2 teaspoons salt. Cook over low heat, stirring frequently, until mixture thickens, about 5 minutes. Pour into large bowl.

Mix and sift flour, sugar, and baking powder. Beat egg yolks until light and thick; stir into corn meal mixture with milk. Stir in sifted dry ingredients.

Beat egg whites until stiff and gently fold into mixture. Pour over chicken.

Bake in moderate oven (350°F.) until set and lightly browned, about 1 hour.

Make milk gravy from chicken drippings. Serve at once with milk gravy. Serves 4.

CHICKEN PILAF CREOLE

2   frying chickens, disjointed
1/2 cup butter or margarine
1   small onion, chopped
1   No. 2 can tomatoes
1/2 cup chopped celery
4   chicken bouillon cubes
4   cups boiling water
1 1/2 cups uncooked rice
1   teaspoon salt
1/8 teaspoon pepper
1/4 teaspoon nutmeg

Roll each piece of chicken in flour seasoned with salt and pepper.

Melt butter or margarine in deep frying pan over low heat. Put in pieces of chicken. Add onion. Turn chicken frequently until each piece is well browned.

Add tomatoes and celery and continue cooking 5 minutes.

Dissolve bouillon cubes in boiling water. In a large kettle, cook rice in bouillon 10 minutes.

Lay chicken pieces on top of rice and pour tomato mixture over. Season with salt, pepper, and nutmeg.

Cover closely and continue cooking slowly over low heat until rice and chicken are done, about 30 minutes. If necessary, add more water with bouillon cube dissolved in it.

When done, arrange rice and tomatoes in center of platter and flank with chicken. Serves 6.

CHICKEN BREASTS AND OYSTERS BIARRITZ

4   chicken breasts, boned
1/2 cup butter or margarine
1/2 pound fresh mushrooms, sliced
1   pint oysters and liquid
2   cups chicken broth
3   tablespoons flour
2   tablespoons cream
1/2 teaspoon salt
Dash of cayenne
1/2 teaspoon fresh dill (optional)
1   cup toasted bread cubes

Gently fry chicken breasts in 1/4 cup butter until lightly browned on both sides; remove from pan.

Cook mushrooms in the same pan for 3 or 4 minutes.

Arrange in 3-quart casserole a layer each of chicken, mushrooms, and drained oysters.

Combine chicken broth with oyster liquid; thicken with flour mixed to a paste with a little cold water. Add cream and seasonings. Pour over chicken.

Top with bread cubes and drizzle remaining 1/4 cup melted butter over.

Bake, uncovered, in moderate oven (375°F.) 30 minutes. Serves 4.

PUERTO RICAN ARROZ CON POLLO

1   4-pound chicken
Salt and pepper
Lard for browning
1   dozen olives
1   tablespoon capers
1   onion, sliced
1/2 large red sweet pepper
2   medium-sized tomatoes, cut in
        pieces
2   cups rice
3   cups boiling water
1   can peas
Pimientos

Cut chicken in serving-size pieces; rub with salt and pepper and brown in a skillet with melted lard.

Add olives, capers, onion, red pepper, and tomatoes.

Cover and cook slowly, stirring occasionally, until tender. If the chicken is old, add a small amount of water.

When tender, add rice and boiling water. Cover and cook until rice is done, stirring occasionally.

Heat peas separately.

To serve, surround a mound of rice with chicken pieces. Cover with peas and garnish with pimiento. Serves 6.

UNITED NATIONS CHICKEN

1 ready-to-cook young chicken, 2½ pounds
¼ cup flour
¾ teaspoon salt
¼ teaspoon ginger
⅛ teaspoon pepper
1 garlic clove
½ cup fat for frying
3 cups steamed rice
1½ teaspoons salt
¼ teaspoon oregano
¼ teaspoon curry
12 tiny white onions, cooked
6 small carrots, cooked
Paprika
3 to 4 tablespoons finely chopped chives
2 cups chicken gravy (below)

Coat disjointed chicken with blended flour, salt, ginger, and pepper. Include giblets and neck. Add garlic clove to fat and fry chicken until nicely browned and fork-tender, about 40 minutes.

Meanwhile steam rice, adding salt, oregano, and curry for seasoning.

Mound rice in shallow 3-quart casserole. Arrange chicken, onions, and carrots, whole or cut in uniform pieces, in rows with chicken at edge of casserole. Sprinkle chicken generously with paprika.

Reheat to serving temperature in moderate oven (350°F.) 15 to 20 minutes. Then sprinkle rice with chives. Serve with chicken gravy. Serves 5 to 6.

Prepare gravy: Use 2 tablespoons fat from frying and 3 tablespoons flour. Blend and add 2 cups broth all at once stirring constantly until thickened throughout. Season to taste.

Variations: Stewing chicken may also be used. Cook chicken in seasoned water 2½ to 3 hours until fork-tender. Drain, cut into serving pieces. Coat with blended flour and seasoning given in recipe. Brown and proceed as above.

BAKED CHICKEN AND CORN

1 3½-pound ready-to-cook chicken
2 tablespoons butter or margarine
2 cups (No. 303 can) whole kernel corn
Milk
½ cup fine dry breadcrumbs
2 slightly beaten eggs
½ teaspoon salt

Season cut-up chicken with salt and pepper. Brown on all sides in melted butter in large skillet over medium heat.

Drain corn. Measure liquid and add enough milk to make 1½ cups.

Combine corn, crumbs, eggs, and salt. Slowly stir in milk mixture. Spread evenly in 2-quart greased shallow casserole. Arrange chicken on top. Pour

drippings from skillet over all.

Bake uncovered in moderate oven (350°F.) until chicken is tender, about 1 hour. Serves 4.

COUNTRY-STYLE BAKED CHICKEN

2 eggs
2 teaspoons Worcestershire sauce
1 teaspoon onion juice
2 3-pound ready-to-cook broiler-fryers, cut in pieces
2 cups fine breadcrumbs
1 teaspoon sage
½ teaspoon paprika
Dash of garlic salt
½ teaspoon salt
⅛ teaspoon pepper
¼ cup vegetable oil
4 slices bacon
⅓ cup milk

Beat eggs, Worcestershire sauce, and onion juice until thoroughly mixed.

Dip chicken pieces in this mixture, then roll in a combination of breadcrumbs and seasonings.

Pour oil in a flat baking dish. Arrange chicken in dish, with bacon slices spread over it.

Bake in moderate oven (350°F.) 1 hour. Add milk. Cover with a lid or foil and continue to bake for 15 to 20 minutes. Serves 6.

BAKED CHICKEN WITH OYSTERS

1 frying chicken, cut up (2½ to 3½ pounds)
1½ cups cracker crumbs
½ teaspoon salt
Pinch of pepper (optional)
1 cup butter or margarine
½ pint oysters
1 cup top milk or thin cream

Roll chicken in crumbs seasoned with salt and pepper. Brown in half the butter and place in casserole.

Roll oysters in crumbs and fit into spaces between chicken.

Heat milk and melt remaining butter in it. Pour over all. Cover with remaining crumbs.

Cover and bake in moderate oven (350°F.) until chicken is tender, about 1 hour.

Uncover during last 15 minutes to let top brown. Add more milk during baking if mixture gets dry.
Serves 4 to 6.

CHICKEN RAMEKINS—NORMANDY

1 frying chicken (3½ pounds)
Salt and pepper
½ cup flour
6 tablespoons butter
¾ cup cider
¾ cup bouillon
½ cup canned mushrooms
6 medium potatoes

¼ cup hot milk
2 eggs

Cut chicken in frying pieces. Dredge in well seasoned flour. Fry in 4 tablespoons butter until lightly browned and almost tender. Remove from heat. When cool enough to handle, remove meat from bones and cut into pieces.

Place chicken in 6 ramekins. Sprinkle with flour, then add 2 tablespoons cider and 2 tablespoons bouillon to each ramekin.

Bake in moderate oven (350°F.) 15 minutes. Then add mushrooms and additional liquid if chicken is cooking dry and bake 10 minutes more, or until chicken is tender.

Meanwhile boil the potatoes, drain and mash. Add 2 tablespoons butter to them, 1 teaspoon salt, dash of pepper, and hot milk. Then beat in the eggs.

The potatoes will be soft and yellow. Cover each ramekin with potato-egg mixture, allowing room at the edges for expansion. Brown under broiler. Serves 6.

CHICKEN FRICASSEE CASSEROLE

1 4-pound chicken
⅔ cup flour
1 teaspoon salt
Dash of pepper
3 tablespoons fat
½ cup chopped celery
¼ cup chopped onion
2 pimientos, chopped
1 can condensed mushroom soup
¾ cup water
Steamed rice

Cut chicken into serving pieces. Rub with seasoned flour. Brown in hot fat. Remove chicken to casserole.

Cook celery and onion in fat until golden. Drain off excess fat and add to chicken.

Add pimientos, soup, and water. Stir lightly to blend.

Cover and bake in slow oven (325°F.) until tender, 1½ to 2 hours. Serve from the casserole or around a mound of hot steamed rice on a platter. Serves 6.

Chicken Fricassee Casserole

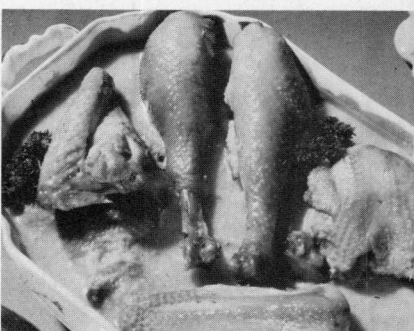

FRICASSEED CHICKEN (GERMAN STYLE)

1 ready-to-cook stewing chicken, about 3 pounds, cut-up
1 medium onion
4 whole black peppers
2 cloves
Tip of bay leaf
1 tablespoon salt
3 tablespoons chicken fat
7 tablespoons flour
3 cups chicken broth
1/2 teaspoon grated lemon rind
1/4 teaspoon black pepper
2 to 3 tablespoons white wine
1 egg yolk
1/4 cup cream

Place chicken in kettle and just cover with boiling water. Add onion, whole black peppers, cloves, bay leaf, and salt. Cook gently until meat is tender, 2 1/2 to 3 hours.

Lift out chicken and strain broth.

Prepare fricassee gravy: Mix chicken fat and flour in saucepan. Add 3 cups broth and place over heat. Cook, stirring constantly, until uniformly thickened.

Add lemon rind and pepper. Add wine. Taste for additional seasoning. Simmer about 5 minutes.

Place chicken in gravy to heat.

Blend egg yolk and cream in sauce dish or cup. To it add, while stirring, some of the hot gravy. Then pour back into chicken and gravy mixture and cook 2 or 3 minutes stirring constantly. Serve promptly. Serves 5 to 6.

BROILED CHICKEN (PAKISTAN STYLE)

1 ready-to-cook broiler, not over 2 1/2 pounds
2 tablespoons melted fat
1/2 cup onions, minced
1/2 garlic clove, minced
2 green chilies (canned style), minced
1/4 teaspoon each ginger, black pepper, cloves, cardamom, and cumin
1/2 teaspoon salt
Juice from chilies

Split chicken in half lengthwise. Break drumstick, hip, and wing joints to keep bird flat during broiling. Skewer wing and leg to body to make a compact flat piece of chicken.

Brush with melted fat and then rub with paste made of seasonings and chili juice.

Place skin-side-down on broiler pan (not rack). Place broiler pan at least 7 inches under heat source. Chicken should be broiled slowly. When rib cage is browned, 10 to 15 minutes, turn chicken over. Broil 15 minutes. Brush with melted fat as needed. Total broiling time about 45 minutes. Serves 2.

CHICKEN WITH RICE (GREEK)

1 ready-to-cook young chicken, 2 1/2 to 3 pounds, disjointed
1/2 cup butter or margarine
1 medium onion, chopped
1 teaspoon salt
1/4 teaspoon black pepper
1 6-ounce can tomato paste
1/2 teaspoon sugar
3 cups boiling water
1 cup rice
1/4 cup butter or margarine

Brown chicken in 1/2 cup butter, turning to brown evenly.

Add onion, salt, pepper, tomato paste, sugar, and 2 or 3 tablespoons water. Cover and cook gently until chicken is barely tender.

Add boiling water. Sprinkle rice over top. Cover and steam until rice is tender, about 40 minutes.

Arrange on serving dish. Melt 1/4 cup butter in cooking pan and pour over rice and chicken. Serves 4 to 5.

CHICKEN BELVEDERE

1 clove garlic, halved
1/4 cup salad oil
1 young chicken, 2 1/2 pounds ready-to-cook weight, disjointed
1 1/2 teaspoons salt
1/2 teaspoon pepper
1/2 teaspoon oregano
1 clove garlic, minced
1 4-ounce can (1 cup) mushrooms
1/2 cup sliced celery
1 6-ounce can (2/3 cup) tomato paste

Brown halved garlic clove in hot oil; remove garlic.

Season chicken with salt, pepper, oregano, and minced garlic.

Fry chicken in hot oil 10 to 12 minutes, or until golden brown.

Drain mushrooms, reserving liquid. Combine mushroom liquid plus water to make 3/4 cup, celery, and tomato paste; add to chicken.

Cover; simmer 30 minutes; add mushrooms; simmer 15 minutes.

Serves 4.

FRICASSEE OF CHICKEN POPUCH

1 3-pound broiling chicken
1 1/2 tablespoons flour
1/2 cup butter or margarine
6 fresh mushrooms
1 tablespoon salt
1/4 teaspoon pepper
2 cups heavy cream
1/4 cup Cognac

Disjoint chicken and roll in flour. Heat butter in frying pan; add chicken and slowly cook, covered, until golden brown, about 20 minutes.

Peel mushrooms, quarter, and add to chicken. Cook, covered, 5 minutes longer. Add salt, pepper, and cream and cook, covered, slowly 20 minutes. Add Cognac just before serving. Serves 3.

KOREAN CHICKEN AND PORK

1 frying chicken, 2 1/2 to 3 pounds
1/2 pound pork, cut in 1-inch cubes
1/2 cup vinegar
2 cloves garlic, crushed
3 bay leaves
3 tablespoons soy sauce
1 1/2 teaspoons salt
1/8 teaspoon pepper
1/4 cup fat or oil

Disjoint chicken and cut into serving pieces. Put chicken and pork into 3-quart saucepan.

Add vinegar, garlic, bay leaves, soy sauce, and seasonings; let stand 1 hour. Then add enough boiling water to just cover the meat.

Simmer over low heat until meat is tender. Remove garlic, bay leaves, and any excess liquid. Add fat; fry pork and chicken, one piece at a time, so that each piece is nicely browned.

After the meat has been removed from the pan, add 1/2 cup of the meat stock and stir to remove any bits of chicken or pork from bottom of pan. Simmer for about 5 minutes and pour over chicken and pork. Serve hot with dry, flaky rice. Serves 4.

QUICK CURRIED CHICKEN HAWAIIAN

1 frying chicken, 3 to 4 pounds
3 tablespoons salad oil
1 clove garlic, mashed
6 to 8 green onions, tops and all, cut in 1 inch lengths
Salt and pepper
1/2 cup hot water
1 1/2 cups top milk
3 tablespoons flour
1 to 2 tablespoons curry powder

Have poultry man chop the legs, thighs, wing, breast, wishbone, and back of chicken crosswise, right through bone and meat, into pieces about an inch long. At home, cut the thickest pieces of meat into smaller chunks. (There will be about 50 chunks of chicken altogether.)

Add mashed garlic to oil in a large skillet and heat slowly 5 minutes. Remove garlic.

Put in chicken and cook over medium heat about 15 minutes, turning occasionally, until lightly browned.

Sprinkle with salt and pepper, add chopped onions and hot water, cover snugly and simmer about 20 minutes, until chicken is tender.

Into a pint jar measure top milk, flour, and curry powder. Cover jar, shake until smooth, then add all at once to chicken and cook, stirring gently, until smoothly thickened.

Serve on mounds of hot cooked rice, or on hot biscuits. Serves 6 to 8.

CHICKEN BREASTS EPICUREAN

2 whole chicken breasts
1 slightly beaten egg
1 cup fine breadcrumbs
1 teaspoon salt
1/4 teaspoon thyme
1/4 teaspoon marjoram
1/4 teaspoon paprika
Fat for frying
1 cup pineapple juice
2 tablespoons lemon juice
1 tablespoon cornstarch
1/4 teaspoon curry powder
1 tablespoon sugar
2 tablespoons sherry wine
4 slices hot toast
Slivered almonds

Split breasts in half. Remove bones but keep meat in one piece.

Dip chicken in beaten egg. Roll in crumbs mixed with salt, thyme, marjoram, and paprika.

Fry chicken in 1/4-inch of hot fat in skillet until brown on both sides.

Drain fat from pan. Combine juices, cornstarch, curry, and sugar. Pour over chicken.

Cover and cook slowly 25 minutes. Then stir in sherry. Serve on hot toast. Top with slivered almonds. Serves 4.

CHICKEN IN WINE-CHERRY SAUCE

2 1/2 to 3 1/2 pounds chicken, cut up for frying
1 can (20 ounces) dark sweet cherries
1 cup Port or Burgundy wine
3 tablespoons lemon juice
2 cloves garlic, chopped
1/4 teaspoon ginger
1/2 teaspoon oregano
1/2 cup flour
2 teaspoons salt
Dash of pepper
1/4 cup shortening or salad oil
1 chicken bouillon cube

Wash chicken; dry. Drain cherries; make marinade by combining 1 cup of the cherry syrup with wine, lemon juice, garlic, ginger, and oregano. Pour over chicken and let stand several hours or overnight. Then remove chicken; wipe dry, saving the marinade.

Combine flour, salt, and pepper; coat each piece of chicken with flour mixture.

Heat shortening or salad oil in large skillet; add chicken and cook over medium heat until brown on all sides.

Strain garlic from marinade; pour over chicken. Bring to boil; add bouillon cube and stir to dissolve.

Reduce heat and simmer about 30 minutes. Add cherries; cook about 15 minutes longer. Serves 4 to 6.

EASY CHICKEN BREASTS SUPREME

1 can condensed cream of mushroom soup, undiluted
1 teaspoon poultry seasoning
1/4 teaspoon salt
1/2 cup milk
2 12-ounce packages frozen chicken breasts
1/4 cup grated process American cheese

In large skillet or flameproof casserole with cover, combine soup, poultry seasoning, salt, and milk. Mix well; bring to boil over low heat.

Add frozen chicken breasts. Cover and cook over low heat 15 minutes.

Uncover; with help of forks, carefully separate chicken pieces.

Place breasts, with meaty sides down, in sauce. Cook, covered, 20 to 25 minutes longer, or until tender.

Sprinkle with cheese; put under broiler long enough to melt and lightly brown cheese. Serves 4 to 6.

TARRAGON CHICKEN

1 3 1/2-pound dressed fryer, cut in pieces
Salt
1/2 lemon
1/2 teaspoon celery salt
1 teaspoon Ac'cent
1/4 teaspoon pepper
1/4 pound butter or margarine
1 teaspoon dried or 3 teaspoons fresh tarragon

Soak chicken in heavily salted cold water for 30 minutes. Drain and pat dry.

Rub thoroughly with lemon. Sprinkle with mixture of 1/2 teaspoon salt, celery salt, Ac'cent, and pepper.

Place in a shallow pan skin-side-down. Dot with 2 tablespoons of butter. Preheat broiler and brown chicken pieces lightly on both sides.

Meanwhile, melt remaining butter with tarragon and cook over low heat for 10 minutes.

Pour butter evenly over chicken and continue to broil 5 minutes on each side under medium heat.

Then bake in moderate oven (350°F.) 25 minutes, basting twice with sauce. Serve with cranberry relish. Serves 4.

SWEDISH CHICKEN

1 frying chicken, cut up
3/4 cup flour
2 teaspoons salt
2 cups evaporated milk or 2 cups thin cream

Coat chicken with flour and place in heavy skillet.

Mix salt with milk or cream and pour over chicken. Cover tightly and simmer over low heat 45 minutes.

As chicken cooks, the milk will thicken and the chicken will brown lightly. Serves 4 to 5.

HAWAIIAN CHICKEN LUAU

1 2 1/2-pound chicken, cut-up for frying
Flour
1/2 cup butter or margarine
1 teaspoon salt
1 cup water
1 cup milk, heated
1 package (4-ounce) shredded coconut
2 pounds fresh spinach
2 tablespoons finely chopped onion
1/2 teaspoon salt
1/4 cup water

Dip pieces of chicken in flour.

Melt butter in heavy skillet. Add chicken and fry until lightly brown. Add salt and water. Cover and simmer until chicken is tender (about 30 minutes).

Pour hot milk over shredded coconut. Let stand 15 minutes and simmer 10 minutes.

Wash spinach, remove stems. Lay bunches on cutting board and cut into 2-inch strips. Boil with onion in salted water about 5 minutes. Drain.

Add spinach and coconut with milk to chicken. Simmer 3 minutes. Serve hot. Serves 6.

BUFFET CHICKEN CURRY

5-pound stewing chicken, cut in pieces
1/3 cup butter or margarine (part chicken fat may be used)
1/4 cup minced onion
1 to 2 tablespoons curry powder
Scant 1/2 cup flour
1 1/2 cups milk
2 cups chicken broth
1/4 teaspoon sugar
Salt
2 tablespoons sherry

Steam chicken in kettle or pressure cooker until tender.

Melt butter and sauté onion until limp and golden. Blend in curry powder and flour.

Gradually add milk and strained chicken broth; cook, stirring constantly, until mixture is thickened and smooth.

Transfer to a double boiler. Add sugar and salt to taste.

Remove cooked chicken meat from bones, cut in fairly good-sized pieces and add to sauce. Cover and cook over gently boiling water for 30 minutes. Just before serving add sherry. Serve with rice and a selection of curry accompaniments. Serves 6 to 8.

Curried Lamb: Substitute cooked lamb for chicken in above.

Duck or Duckling

Duck producers aim to have young ducks ready for market at 7 or 8 weeks of age. About 90 per cent of the ducks on the retail market are frozen, and ready to cook. Most ducks are marketed as ducklings or young ducks and usually weigh 4 to 6 pounds.

Ducks usually marketed as "roaster ducklings," have tender, flavorful meat that makes a delicious roast. Small ducks can be cut up and fried or broiled. Larger whole ducks can be put on a spit and cooked over coals on a rotisserie.

When buying, allow at least 1 pound ready-to-cook weight per person.

Thawing time in the refrigerator for frozen ducks weighing 3 to 5 pounds is 1 to 1½ days.

ROAST DUCKLING

The modern-type ducklings are prepared for roasting just like chicken. Place duckling breast-side-up on a rack in a shallow open pan in slow oven (325°F.).

If roasted for 1½ to 2 hours, or until meat thermometer inserted in stuffing records an interior temperature of 165°F., the duckling will be moderately well done but juicy and delicious. Allow 18 minutes per pound for dressed weight (5 to 7 pounds).

For very well done duckling, the interior temperature should read about 185°F. Allow 22 to 25 minutes per pound.

For ducklings with drawn (ready-to-cook) weight of 3½ to 5 pounds, allow 25 minutes per pound for medium well done, 30 to 35 minutes per pound for very well done.

When well done, the thick flesh on the drumstick feels soft when pressed, and leg joint moves easily.

Roast Fat Duckling: If a duck has excess fat, prick the skin over back and around tail to let fat drain off in cooking. Roast as above, but pour off fat as it accumulates in the pan to keep drippings light-colored and delicately flavored. Allow at least 30 minutes per pound, then test for doneness. No basting is needed.

Stuffing Hints for Duckling: Tart, well seasoned stuffings (especially fruits) combine well with rich duck meat. Some cooks just put a whole orange or a whole, cored apple inside; others fill small birds with chopped onion and celery, or chopped onion and quartered apple. A stuffing of rice and apricot or other dried fruit is another favorite.

Glazed Roast Duckling: Roast as directed in Roast Duckling. Remove from oven just before duck is done. Raise oven temperature to very hot (450°F.).

Combine and mix well: 1 cup apricot preserves, ½ cup clover honey, 1 tablespoon Cointreau or other orange-flavored liqueur, and 1 tablespoon brandy. Coat the duck with this thick glaze and return to oven until the glaze caramelizes, 10 to 15 minutes.

ROAST DUCK BIGARADE

Bigarade is the French term for the bitter or Seville orange, which should be used in preparing this dish.

Prepare duck for roasting. Do not stuff. Season with salt and pepper. If desired, fill cavity with orange slices.

Roast, uncovered, on rack in slow oven (325°F.), allowing 20 to 25 minutes per pound.

Do not baste. Prick skin several times and turn to brown all sides.

Skim fat from drippings and prepare gravy, using ½ cup orange juice and ½ cup water.

Boil whole peel of 1 orange in water to cover for 5 minutes. Drain, scrape out white pulp and discard. Cut peel into thin julienne strips and add to gravy. Season to taste.

If desired, a little lemon juice, white wine, or curaçao may be added.

BROILED DUCKLING

Have the meat dealer prepare the duckling for broiling by removing the backbone and keel from breastbone.

Place duck skin-side-down on ungreased pan in preheated moderate broiler 4 to 5 inches from heat source.

Broil for a total of 20 to 25 minutes on each side, turning pieces when golden brown. Baste if desired. (For more detailed directions, see Broiled Chicken.)

With Honey Glaze: Just before serving, brush duckling with a mixture of 2 tablespoons honey and 1 teaspoon Kitchen Bouquet. Return to broiling compartment for 2 minutes. Serve immediately.

DUCK EN CASSEROLE

1   duck, 4 to 5 pounds
⅓   cup flour
1½   teaspoons salt
¼   teaspoon pepper

½   teaspoon Ac'cent
⅓   cup butter or margarine
1   small onion, finely chopped
1   teaspoon powdered mint
3   cups boiling water
3   chicken bouillon cubes
1   No. 2 can (2½ cups) green peas, drained

Clean duck well, removing pin feathers. Dry and cut in sections as for fricassee. Dip duck pieces in mixture of flour, salt, pepper, and Ac'cent. Pan-fry in hot fat until lightly browned on all sides.

Transfer to 2-quart casserole. Add onion and mint. Pour in water in which the bouillon cubes have been dissolved.

Cover and bake in moderate oven (350°F.) until tender, about 1¾ hours. Add drained peas about 10 minutes before duck is done. Serves 4.

DUCKLING AU VIN

2   tablespoons corn oil
2   3-pound ducklings, quartered
2   teaspoons salt
1   tablespoon Worcestershire sauce
1   cup sliced celery
1   large onion, sliced
2   cups white wine
Chicken broth
2   tablespoons butter
2   tablespoons flour
2   4-ounce cans button mushrooms, drained
2   16-ounce cans white onions, drained

Heat oil in a skillet. Brown ducklings well on all sides. Drain off excess fat.

Sprinkle duckling with salt and Worcestershire sauce. Add celery, onion, and white wine. Cover tightly. Cook over a medium heat, turning occasionally, for 1 hour or until duckling is tender. Add chicken broth if necessary during cooking to maintain level of liquid.

When duckling is tender, transfer pieces to a casserole, keep warm.

Cream butter. Stir in flour to form a paste. Skim excess fat from the stock in the skillet. Add paste to the hot stock. Cook over a low heat stirring constantly until smooth and thickened. Add mushrooms and onions. Reheat and pour hot sauce over duckling. Serve with wild rice and peas cooked with green grapes. Serves 6 to 8.

Duckling Au Vin

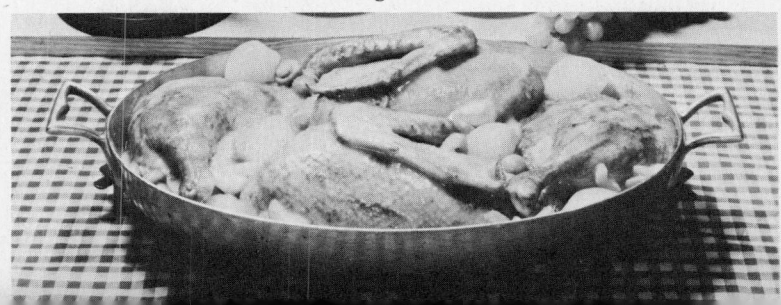

FRIED DUCKLING

1 duckling, 3½ to 4 pounds
1 cup flour
2 teaspoons salt
¼ teaspoon pepper
2 teaspoons paprika
¼ cup butter or margarine
¼ cup fat
¼ cup water

Cut duckling into serving pieces, or, if quick-frozen, thaw according to directions on wrapper. Rinse in cold water, and drain.

Mix flour, salt, pepper, and paprika in a paper sack. Shake 2 or 3 pieces of duckling at a time in sack in order to coat thoroughly with flour.

Heat butter and enough of the fat in a heavy skillet to make a layer of fat ¼ inch deep. With kitchen tongs, place duckling in hot fat skin-side-down. Brown and turn.

Add water and cover tightly. Reduce heat and cook slowly about 1½ hours, or until duckling is tender. To crisp the crust, remove the cover during last 10 minutes. Serves 4 to 5.

Oven-Fried Duckling: Prepare as above; after adding water, bake in moderate oven (350°F.) about 1 hour. Uncover and bake about 30 minutes longer.

DUCKLING QUARTERS, BAKED IN FOIL

1 4½-pound ready-to-cook duckling, quartered
1 clove garlic
½ teaspoon salt
¼ teaspoon pepper
1 teaspoon Ac'cent
Heavy foil
8 small white onions
1 large juicy grapefruit, peeled and cut in sections
½ cup giblet broth
2 teaspoons cornstarch
½ cup white wine

Rub the cleaned duckling with garlic. Sprinkle with a mixture of salt, pepper, and Ac'cent.

Arrange skin-side-down in a roasting pan lined with heavy foil. Brown in hot oven (425°F.), turning several times so both sides are browned. Pour off fat.

Arrange onions and grapefruit sections over and around duckling. Crimp another piece of foil over pan to fit snugly.

Bake in moderate oven (350°F.) for 1 hour, or until tender.

Discard grapefruit sections. Remove duck and onions to a warm platter.

Skim excess fat from pan juices. Add broth. Bring to a boil and thicken with cornstarch mixed with wine. Season to taste and serve in a separate dish. Serves 4.

DEVILED DUCKLING

1 4-pound ready-to-cook duckling
1½ tablespoons soy sauce
2 small onions
2 celery tops
1 teaspoon dry mustard
½ teaspoon powdered ginger
¼ teaspoon pepper

Clean and rinse duckling; pat dry. Brush inside and out with soy sauce.

Insert onions and celery tops into cavity. Pin neck skin to back with skewers.

Stir mustard, ginger, and pepper until well mixed; sprinkle a good coating over the soy-dampened duck.

Place on a rack in an open roasting pan. Roast in a preheated hot oven (400°F.) ½ hour. By now a nice crust should be formed.

Reduce heat to slow oven (325°F.) and continue to roast for 1 hour, or until duckling is tender. The crisp skin is so spicy and delicious that the duckling is equally good served hot or cold. Serves 4.

ROAST DUCK WITH ORANGE-WINE SAUCE (FRENCH)

1 duck
1 cup orange juice
½ cup port wine
1 teaspoon salt
1 whole orange, preferably seedless

Rinse the duck inside and outside with clear water. Dry well with a towel. Truss and place on a rack in an open pan breast-side-up.

Roast in slow oven (325°F.) for 35 minutes per pound. Baste every 10 minutes with a mixture of the orange juice, port wine, and salt.

Cut the whole orange (with skin) in thin slices. Arrange slices around the duck and on rack in the roasting pan (not in the sauce) about 10 minutes before the end of the cooking time. Garnish the duck with the orange slices for serving.

Allow 1 pound dressed weight per person when estimating number of servings.

HOW TO SKIN DUCKLING

With sharp-pointed knife, cut the skin from the neck to the vent, first along breast of duck, then along backbone.

Loosen the skin by running knife underneath, close to flesh of duck. Peel skin back as it is loosened, cutting the skin where necessary but keeping the flesh intact.

It is really easy and simple to remove the skin since there is a solid layer of fat between skin and flesh, but, if you prefer, ask your meat dealer to skin the duck for you.

BRAISED DUCKLING
(Master Recipe)

Cut the cleaned duckling into quarters. Place skin-side-up on rack in shallow roasting pan. Roast in slow oven (325°F.) for 1 hour.

Meanwhile, cook giblets and prepare desired sauce, using duck broth (from cooking giblets) or fruit juice.

Transfer duck to covered pan. Pour sauce over duck and cover tightly. Continue baking in sauce until duck is tender, about 30 minutes longer.

For a brown finish, brush duck with 1 teaspoon Kitchen Bouquet and 2 tablespoons of honey before cooking in sauce.

ROAST DUCK WITH WINE SAUCE

1 4- to 5-pound duck
2 cups claret or other wine
⅓ cup brandy
⅓ cup chopped onions
2 tablespoons minced parsley
¾ teaspoon salt
¼ teaspoon pepper
½ pound sliced mushrooms
2 tablespoons flour
¼ cup cold water

Cut duck in quarters. Arrange pieces on rack in shallow roasting pan. Brown in hot oven (400°F.) for 30 minutes. Pour off all except ¼ cup of drippings. Remove rack from pan and place duck in bottom.

Add wine and brandy to chopped onion, parsley, salt, pepper, and mushrooms. Pour over duck. Return to oven; reduce heat to 375°F. Bake 1½ hours, or until duck is tender; baste frequently with sauce. Remove from pan and keep hot while preparing gravy.

Blend flour in cold water until smooth. Add to liquid in pan. Cook, stirring constantly, until thickened. Add salt and pepper to taste.

Place duck on hot platter and serve sauce in a bowl; or place duck on platter, cover with thickened wine sauce. Serves 4.

ROAST DUCK—CHINESE STYLE

4 teaspoons sugar
1 teaspoon salt
4 teaspoons honey
3 teaspoons soy sauce
3 tablespoons chicken bouillon
•1 4-pound duckling

Place all ingredients except duckling in a large mixing bowl. Mix well.

Clean and add duckling. Soak duck for 40 minutes, turning occasionally.

Remove from bowl and place on rack in a roasting pan, adding a few tablespoons of water to prevent smoking.

Roast in slow oven (325°F.) until tender, turning occasionally, about 1¾ hours. Serve immediately. Serves 4.

Duckling Italienne

DUCKLING ITALIENNE

1   duckling, 4 to 5 pounds,
      ready-to-cook weight
2   tablespoons fat
½   cup finely diced onion
¼   cup finely diced celery
1   cup tomato sauce
1   teaspoon Kitchen Bouquet
1½ teaspoons sugar
1½ teaspoons salt
⅛   teaspoon oregano
12 ounces spaghetti, cooked

Wash duckling in cold water and dry carefully. Cut off wing tips. Cut duckling in serving size pieces. Melt fat in deep frying pan or Dutch oven. Add pieces of duckling and brown on all sides over moderate heat. Add onion and celery and let cook about 5 minutes longer.

Combine tomato sauce, Kitchen Bouquet, sugar, salt, and oregano, Pour over duckling. Cover tightly and bring to boil. Let cook until duckling is tender, about 45 minutes.

Meanwhile, cook giblets and neck in boiling salted water until tender. Cook spaghetti.

When ready to serve, remove pieces of duckling from sauce. Pour off fat. Chop giblets and add to tomato sauce if desired. Drain spaghetti, then pour sauce over spaghetti and mix well. Arrange spaghetti on serving platter. Top with pieces of duckling and serve immediately with a tossed green salad. Serves 6.

PINEAPPLE DUCK

1   4-pound duckling, quartered
6   cups cold water
2   teaspoons salt
2   tablespoons salad oil or fat
1½ cups duck broth
1   No. 2 can (2 cups) pineapple
      chunks, drained
¼   teaspoon ground ginger
1   medium green pepper, cut in
      small pieces
2   tablespoons cornstarch
1   tablespoon soy sauce
⅛   teaspoon pepper
6   tablespoons pineapple juice

Place quartered duckling in saucepan. Add cold water and salt. Bring to boil over high heat. Reduce heat, cover, and simmer gently 45 minutes.

Remove duckling and drain thoroughly. Reserve broth.

Heat oil or fat in large skillet. Add drained duckling and cook gently, turning frequently, until golden brown, about 15 minutes.

Add 1½ cups duck broth, pineapple chunks, ginger, and green pepper. Cover and cook over moderate heat 15 minutes. Remove duck and keep warm.

Combine and blend cornstarch, soy sauce, pepper, and pineapple juice; stir into broth and pineapple mixture in skillet. Stir until thickened.

Return duck to sauce. Cover and heat thoroughly, about 10 minutes. Serve with hot boiled rice. Serves 4 to 5.

BRAISED DUCK IN BLACK CHERRY SAUCE

1   5- to 6-pound duckling
¼   cup fat
1   tablespoon duck fat
1   tablespoon minced onion
1½ cups duck broth
½   teaspoon salt
1   bay leaf
⅛   teaspoon marjoram
1   No. 2 can black cherries
2   tablespoons cornstarch

Have duck cut in quarters. Brown duck in fat in heavy saucepan; roast uncovered in slow oven (325°F.).

Meanwhile, cook giblets. Drain off liquid. Allow fat to rise to top and pour it off.

Place 1 tablespoon fat in saucepan. Add onion. Cook over low heat about 3 minutes. Add duck broth, salt, bay leaf and marjoram.

Drain cherries. Combine ½ cup cherry juice and cornstarch. Stir into hot broth. Cook, stirring constantly, until sauce thickens and boils. Remove bay leaf.

Add cherries and heat thoroughly. Serve hot over braised duck quarters.

If desired, substitute ½ cup red wine for ½ cup broth. Serves 4.

CANTONESE DUCK

5- to 6-pound duckling, dressed
      weight
¼   cup sherry
¼   cup honey
Salt and pepper

With sharp pointed knife, cut through duck skin along center of breast from neck to vent. Loosen skin by pulling away from flesh and at the same time running knife underneath.

Cut skin where necessary, but keep flesh intact. Discard skin.

Cut skinned duck in serving-size pieces and place in bowl.

Combine remaining ingredients and pour over duck meat. Cover and let marinate in cool place 3 hours, turning occasionally.

Place duck and marinade in large covered frying pan and cook over low heat until tender, about 45 minutes to 1 hour.

Serve immediately or, if crisp brown crust is desired, place pieces of duck in uncovered baking dish and heat in moderate oven (350°F.) at least 15 minutes. Serve hot or cold. Serves 4.

BRAISED DUCKLING, BURGUNDY

1   Long Island duckling, 5 to 6
      pounds
½   garlic clove, minced
2   tablespoons flour
2   cups burgundy wine
1   6-ounce can broiled mushrooms
1   small bay leaf
¼   teaspoon rosemary
1   teaspoon salt
1   teaspoon Ac'cent

Cut duckling in serving pieces with poultry shears, or have this done at the market. Remove skins and fat from pieces.

Cook skin and fat with giblets and neck; drain off liquid. Chill until fat rises to top; pour off.

Measure 2 tablespoons of this fat into heavy skillet. Heat; brown duckling in hot fat; remove to casserole with cooked giblets.

Add garlic to fat; cook 1 minute. Stir in flour. Add wine, mushrooms, bay leaf, rosemary, salt, and Ac'cent. Cook over low heat, stirring, until sauce thickens; pour into casserole; cover.

Bake in moderate oven (350°F.) 1½ hours, or until duckling is well done and tender. Serves 4.

Braised Duckling, Burgundy

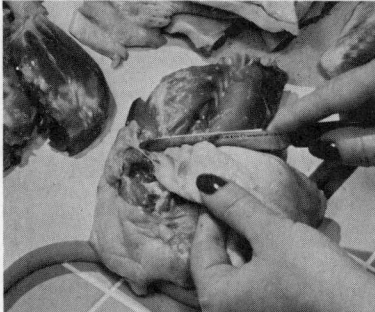

Squab

A squab is a young pigeon. Squabs are best at the age of 4 to 5 weeks and at a weight of 12 to 14 ounces. The flesh is very tender. Very young chickens are sometimes called squab chickens.

BROILED SQUABS ON TOAST

Split the cleaned, dressed squabs down the back and spread open. Rub the meat with lemon juice, brush with melted butter, margarine, or bacon fat and sprinkle with salt and pepper.

Place on greased rack in broiler and broil under moderate broiler heat 2 to 3 inches below the heat, 15 to 20 minutes. Turn the squabs to brown both sides.

Serve on hot buttered toast and spread with squab giblet paste. Allow 1 whole small squab, or 1/2 of a large squab to a serving.

Squab Giblet Paste: Simmer giblets of 3 squabs in water to cover for 15 minutes, or until tender. Mash, season to taste with salt and paprika and add 1 tablespoon Worcestershire sauce and 2 tablespoons of any tart jelly.

ROAST SQUABS

Rub the inside of cleaned squabs with salt. Stuff lightly with wild rice or mushroom stuffing.

Place on rack in roasting pan. Spread with melted butter, margarine, or bacon fat. Sprinkle with salt and dust with flour.

Roast, uncovered, in slow oven (325°F.) 45 minutes, or until tender. Baste frequently with a mixture of 1/3 cup butter or margarine, 2/3 cup boiling water, and 1/2 cup currant jelly stirred in. Remove the roasted birds to a hot serving platter.

Thicken the pan drippings with 1 tablespoon flour mixed with a little water to make a smooth paste; bring to boiling point, cook 2 minutes and serve with the birds. Allow 1 small or 1/2 large squab to a serving.

SQUABS EN CASSEROLE

4   squabs
Salt and pepper
1 1/2   cups uncooked rice
1/2   pound whole mushrooms, washed
1   package frozen peas, thawed just enough to separate
8   small peeled white onions
2   small sweet pickles, chopped
Chopped squab livers
1   cup chicken broth
1   cup dry white wine

Have the poultry dealer clean the squabs but do not split them. Keep the livers and add to casserole. Season squabs well inside and out.

Brown rice in a dry skillet over low heat. Place in layer in a deep casserole. Place squabs on rice. Put mushrooms, peas, onions, pickles, and livers around squabs.

Heat broth and wine but do not boil; add to casserole.

Cover and cook in moderate oven (350°F.) until squabs are tender, about 1 hour. Serves 4.

SQUABS IN WINE SAUCE WITH WHITE GRAPES

4   squabs, cleaned
1/4   cup softened butter or margarine
1   teaspoon salt
1/3   cup chicken consommé
1/3   cup white wine
1 1/2   cups seedless white grapes

Rub squabs with butter. Sprinkle cavities with salt. Place in a buttered casserole; cover and bake in moderate oven (375°F.) for 10 minutes.

Add consommé and wine. Cover again and continue to bake in slow oven (325°F.) 45 minutes, or until tender. Five minutes before squabs are done, add grapes. Serves 4.

Geese

Geese generally are marketed young because weight gained after the first 11 weeks is mostly in the form of fat.

Chilled or frozen ready-to-cook young geese (goslings) usually weigh from 6 to 12 pounds. Young geese have tender, flavorful meat that makes a delicious roast. Small geese braise well cut up. Thawing time in the refrigerator for frozen geese weighing 4 to 14 pounds is 1 to 2 days.

ROAST GOOSE

When buying goose, allow 1 to 1 1/4 pounds per person. Goose is cleaned, stuffed, trussed, and roasted like chicken. If very fat, prick the skin lightly in several places with a sharp-pointed fork after the goose has baked for an hour. This permits some of the fat to drain out.

Roast on a rack in slow oven (325°F.), allowing 25 to 30 minutes per pound for total roasting. A 10- to 12-pound goose will require 3 1/2 to 4 1/2 hours. Tests for doneness are the same as for chicken.

Make gravy for goose, using 4 tablespoons each of drippings and flour and 2 cups stock prepared by cooking the giblets in seasoned water.

BOHEMIAN ROAST GOOSE-POTATO STUFFING

5   large potatoes
1/4   cup grated onion
1   tablespoon minced parsley
1   teaspoon caraway seed
1   egg

1   tablespoons melted poultry fat
1   roasting goose
Salt and pepper to taste

Wash potatoes. Boil with skins on. When done, peel, mash and add onion, parsley, caraway seed, egg, and fat. Mix well and season to taste.

Wash and dry goose. Remove excess fat. Stuff and truss.

Melt down excess fat in pan on top of range. Rub melted fat into goose. Sprinkle with flour, salt and pepper.

Place on rack in roasting pan. Do not add water. Prick skin several times to let fat run out.

Roast, uncovered, in slow oven (325°F.) 20 to 25 minutes per pound. Baste every 15 minutes. Serves 6 to 8.

Gravy: Remove all but 2 tablespoons fat from roasting pan. Sift into pan 3 tablespoons flour. Blend smoothly with fat. Add 3 cups water.

Place pan over low heat and stir constantly until gravy thickens, blending in brown juice from bottom of pan. Season with salt and pepper.

FRICASSEED GOOSE (GAENSEKLEIN) (Pennsylvania-Dutch)

Back, wings, neck, gizzard, and heart of goose
Salt, pepper, ginger
1   clove garlic, minced
1/2   onion, sliced
2   stalks celery, diced
2   tablespoons fat
2   tablespoons flour
1   cup goose broth
1   teaspoon chopped parsley

Season meat well with salt, pepper, ginger, and garlic. Let stand about 12 hours or overnight.

Cover with boiling water; add onion and celery. Simmer gently until meat is tender, about 2 hours.

When done, remove meat from broth. Heat fat; blend in flour, then gradually add the hot goose broth. Cook until thickened, stirring constantly. Add parsley; simmer for several minutes and serve the sauce over the cooked meat. Serve with dumplings. Serves 4.

Roast Goose

Game Birds

In general, before being cooked it is necessary to hang many freshly killed wild birds to tenderize and improve the flavor. The actual length of time to allow game birds to hang is best determined by preference and experience. For example, the English like their birds "high" and let them hang for 10 days or longer in a cool place. This is not practical in our climate and, as a matter of fact, the flavor which is thus developed is not well liked in this country. Two days is usually sufficient ripening time for most birds. Ducks must never be allowed to hang "until high."

The most commonly used wild birds are grouse, pheasant, quail, and wild duck. When purchased in the market, they are dressed, drawn, and if desired, cut up ready for use. Like other game, birds are lean and require generous use of extra fat during cooking to prevent drying out. The light-meated birds such as partridge and quail should always be cooked until well done. Dark-meated birds may be served rare.

Any of the stuffings used for domestic poultry may be used for game; however, wild rice stuffing is the favorite for game birds. The addition of tart apple or orange to bread stuffing is an improvement in strong-flavored birds.

Drippings are made into gravy with a little wine frequently added, or a wine sauce may be made from the pan drippings. A tart jelly is a good accompaniment for roasted or broiled birds. The latter are generally served on toast.

HOW TO DRESS BIRDS

Ducks, geese, grouse, and turkeys are usually dry picked. To do this, hang the bird up by one leg. Pluck the pinion and tail feathers first, then the small feathers from shanks and inside of thighs. Then pluck the remaining body feathers.

To pluck and avoid tearing the skin, grasp only a few feathers at a time and pull downward in the direction the feathers grow.

Game birds are drawn (entrails removed) in the same way as with domestic fowl.

FISH EATING GAME BIRDS

The flavor of birds depends upon the type of food they eat. Birds that eat fish have a "fishy" flavor which some people find objectionable. This flavor may be eliminated by parboiling the birds for 10 to 20 minutes, depending upon size of birds.

Add to enough water to cover 2 birds 1 teaspoon baking soda and 1 teaspoon black pepper, then parboil.

Drain well and rub with salt and pepper. Tie a piece of bacon over breast. Brown the birds in melted butter in heavy kettle. Cover tightly and cook over low heat until tender, about 1½ hours. Add giblet stock during last part of cooking. Serve with gravy.

ROAST WILD DUCK OR WILD GOOSE

Cut off tail, removing oil sack. Draw and wipe with damp cloth. Rub inside with salt and pepper.

Fill with savory stuffing or wild rice stuffing or omit stuffing and put a small stalk of celery, or a whole apple or a whole onion in the cavity. If desired, add 1 tablespoon wine and 1 tablespoon melted butter. Close openings with small skewers. Truss wings to body.

Cover breast side with strips of fat salt pork or bacon, or rub skin with butter or oil. Sprinkle with salt and pepper.

Bake, uncovered, breast side up in slow oven (300°F.) until done. Allow 15 to 20 minutes per pound or ½ to 1 hour, depending upon size of bird. Duck should be served rare; therefore take care to avoid overcooking. Baste frequently with drippings from pan. Serve with gravy made from drippings and giblet stock.

BROILED WILD DUCK

Use young mallards and canvas backs. Cut off tail, removing oil sack. Split down the back. Draw and wipe well with a damp cloth. Do not wash.

Rub with salt and pepper and then with melted butter or oil, or spread with slices of bacon.

Spread open and lay skin side down on broiler rack. Broil under moderate heat until tender, 15 to 20 minutes, turning at least once. Take care to avoid overcooking.

Serve with melted butter seasoned with a little lemon juice and chopped parsley. A tart jelly is a natural accompaniment.

ROAST WILD TURKEY

The wild turkey is the largest of American upland game birds; it is a highly prized and delicious meat. Young hens average 8 pounds; young toms, 12 pounds, undressed.

Follow method used for preparing, stuffing, trussing, and roasting domestic turkey (see Index).

SAGE HENS

Use young hens. Dress immediately after killing to prevent too strong a sage taste. Fry or roast as ordinary chicken.

Pheasant Muscatel with Nutted Rice in Fluted Orange Cups

PHEASANT MUSCATEL

3 1½-pound broiler pheasants, dressed, split in half
½ lemon
Salt and pepper
⅓ cup butter or margarine
Juice of 3 oranges (save shells)
1 cup white raisins
1 teaspoon grated lemon rind
⅓ cup muscatel wine
1 cup chicken broth or stock

Rinse pheasants inside and outside with warm water. Drain well.

Rub pheasants inside with lemon. Season with salt and pepper. Place in a baking dish, breast side up. Spread with butter. Add orange juice, raisins, lemon rind, wine, and chicken stock to the baking dish.

Bake in moderate oven (350°F.) 45 minutes, basting about every 10 minutes. Serve with Nutted Rice in Fluted Orange Cups (below). Serves 6.

Nutted Rice in Fluted Orange Cups: In a saucepan, combine 2 cups chicken stock and 1 cup uncooked rice. Bring to a boil, stir, cover and cook over low heat 14 minutes. Remove from heat. Stir in 2 tablespoons butter or margarine, ⅔ cup chopped pecans, and 2 tablespoons minced parsley. Season to taste with salt. Flute orange cups and spoon the rice into shells.

ROAST PHEASANT

Use young hens weighing about 3 pounds each when dressed. Draw and truss as for chicken.

Rub inside with butter or oil. Sprinkle with salt. Fill lightly with a bread or wild rice stuffing. Cover with strips of bacon or fat salt pork or rub skin with butter or oil.

Bake, uncovered, in slow oven (325°F.) until tender, about 1 hour. Baste often with butter or drippings. Serve with gravy made from drippings.

PHEASANT BAKED IN SOUR CREAM

Cut bird into serving pieces. Roll in flour and sprinkle with salt and pepper. Brown in melted butter in heavy skillet. Add 1 cup light cream.

Cover and bake in moderate oven (350°F.) 30 minutes. Turn occasionally. Serve with gravy made from **cream** in pan.

WOODCOCK AND SNIPE

Woodcock and snipe are small, highly esteemed game birds. Dark-fleshed and strong-flavored, they are cooked whole and are often eaten entrails and all; indeed, this is considered the most delicate part. The entrails (called the trail) shrivel in cooking and are easily removed at the table. The squeamish may remove the lower end before cooking the birds. Woodcock may be wrapped in thin slices of bacon or salt pork, roasted in 10 to 15 minutes, and served on toast with a gravy of the pan juices; snipe roasts in even less time. Allowing for the difference in size, either of these birds may be substituted in recipes for quail, grouse, or partridge. Unlike quail and grouse, however, they must first be hung for 3 to 4 days.

PARTRIDGE

The game birds of this name that are shot in the United States are not partridge at all but ruffed grouse or some species of quail. True partridges of several varieties are imported from England and continental Europe and are sometimes available in markets; they are also bred commercially in the United States. Partridge, grouse, and quail can be treated alike in cookery. Fanciers like it to hang for at least four days so that its delicate, fragile flavor can develop.

ROAST PARTRIDGE

Wipe cleaned birds with a damp cloth. Rub with melted butter or oil. Sprinkle inside and out with salt and pepper.

Bake in roasting pan in slow oven (325°F.) until tender, 30 to 40 minutes.

ROAST GROUSE OR PRAIRIE CHICKEN

Wipe inside and out with damp cloth. Rub inside and out with salt.

Fill with bread or wild rice stuffing, or if preferred, put a strip of bacon or salt pork inside. Do not fasten opening.

Cover breast with strips of bacon or salt pork. Bake in slow oven (325°F.) until tender, about 30 minutes.

BROILED WOODCOCK

Woodcock is not drawn. The entrails shrivel up when cooked and are easily removed at the table. If one is finicky about this, the lower end of the trail (intestines) may be removed.

Clean birds and wipe with damp cloth. Rub with butter. Wrap completely in bacon slices or thin strips of fat salt pork. Broil under very moderate heat about 15 minutes, turning frequently.

BROILED PARTRIDGE, PHEASANT, QUAIL, OR GROUSE

Clean birds and split them down back. Sprinkle with salt and pepper. Dust with flour to keep juices in.

Broil on wire rack, laying the inside first toward the fire. Length of broiling time will depend upon size of bird and how well done you like the meat. Allow 10 to 15 minutes for quail, 15 to 20 minutes for grouse, and 20 to 30 minutes for young partridge and pheasant.

When done, place on warm platter and butter or oil well on both sides. If the breasts are quite thick, use very moderate heat.

ROAST QUAIL

Wipe the cleaned bird with a damp cloth. Brush inside and out with butter. Rub with salt. Place a large mushroom inside the bird.

Place in pan. Cover with buttered parchment paper. Roast, uncovered, in slow oven (325°F.) 25 to 30 minutes. Remove paper after first 20 minutes.

COOT OR MUDHEN

Skin the birds. Cut off legs and breast. Discard remainder of carcass. Split breast in half.

Wash all parts thoroughly in cold water. Roll in seasoned flour.

Fry in hot bacon fat until well browned on all sides. Cover and let steam until tender. Make milk gravy in the skillet.

SPIT ROASTED WILD DUCKS

2 wild ducks
1 apple or orange
1 teaspoon salt
1/4 teaspoon pepper
3 tablespoons oil
4 tablespoons melted butter or margarine
4 tablespoons orange juice
1 tablespoon chopped parsley

Stuff ducks with pieces of apple or orange. Sprinkle with salt and pepper; rub with oil. Truss well.

Place on the spit. Turn frequently and baste with oil. Cook about 20 minutes, or until blood will not run when meat is pricked. Wild duck should not be overcooked. It has a much finer flavor if served rare.

Remove fruit. Pour melted butter mixed with orange juice and parsley over ducks. Serves 4.

PTARMIGAN

A game bird of the grouse family. Most species live in arctic or sub-arctic regions. They have feathered legs and feet, and their plumage changes color with the season. To cook, follow recipes for grouse or quail.

WILD DUCKS À LA PABLO MASI

2 wild ducks, cleaned and drawn
Salt and pepper
1/4 cup butter or margarine
4 slices bacon
3 cups sauerkraut, drained
2 apples, pared and chopped
1/2 cup rhine wine
1 teaspoon cornstarch

Season ducks lightly with salt and pepper. Brown on all sides in hot butter. Bind with bacon slices and place in a casserole.

Arrange sauerkraut and apple around birds; pour wine over.

Cover and bake in moderate oven (350°F.) 1 1/2 hours or until birds are tender. Transfer them to a warm serving dish.

Stir cornstarch, mixed to a thin paste with 1/4 cup cool water, into the 'kraut. Cook until slightly thickened. Serve separately. Serves 4.

ROAST GUINEA HEN

A guinea hen or fowl is a small domestic bird with a slightly gamey flavor. It has a rounded body and dark feathers spotted with white. It is so called because it was originally imported from Guinea.

Squab guinea are young birds, weighing 3/4 to 1 1/4 pounds; guinea chickens weigh 1 1/2 to 2 1/4 pounds, guinea hens weigh 2 1/2 to 3 pounds. Allow 3/4 to 1 pound per serving.

Clean guinea, following directions for poultry.

Rub inside with butter. Season cavity with salt and pepper. Put 1 medium-sized quartered onion in cavity or stuff with well seasoned stuffing.

Place breast-side-down on rack in roasting pan. Arrange thin strips of salt pork over back.

Roast, uncovered, in slow oven (325°F.) 30 minutes.

Turn breast-side-up. Season with salt and pepper. Transfer salt pork to breast. Roast about 30 minutes longer. Allow 35 to 45 minutes per pound for total roasting. If onion was used, remove from cavity before serving.

Serve with giblet gravy made from drippings in pan and giblet stock with ground or chopped giblets and 1/4 cup currant jelly added to gravy. Allow about 1 pound per portion.

FRIED GUINEA BREASTS

Use breasts from young guinea chickens. Sprinkle with salt and pepper and fry very slowly in butter or bacon drippings in heavy frying pan about 20 minutes, or until browned and tender.

Place on hot platter and serve with buttered mushroom caps and sauce made from drippings in pan and cream. Allow 1 breast per portion.

Recipes for Using Cooked or Canned Poultry

CREAMED CHICKEN OR TURKEY (Master Recipe)

Chicken, turkey, or veal may be used interchangeably in the master recipe or any of its variations. You should feel free to follow any creative urge in creating your own variations in proportions, seasonings, etc., provided that good combinations are used.

3   tablespoons butter or margarine
4   tablespoons flour
1   cup chicken or turkey broth
1   cup milk
1/2 teaspoon salt
1/2 teaspoon paprika
1/8 teaspoon pepper
1   teaspoon finely grated onion
1 1/2 cups diced cooked turkey
2   tablespoons sherry (optional)

Melt butter, add flour and stir over low heat until blended. Add cold broth and milk all at once. Cook, stirring constantly, until uniformly thickened.

Then set over hot water. Add seasonings and turkey and heat thoroughly.

Add more seasoning if desired. Blend in sherry just before serving.

Serve over biscuits, toast, plain or fried noodles or rice. Serves 6.

Note: If creamed mixture is thicker than desired, thin with hot milk or water. All recipes below serve 6.

Variations of Creamed Chicken or Turkey

Turkey À La King: Cook 1/4 cup finely chopped green pepper in the butter for a few minutes before adding flour. Proceed as for Creamed Turkey.

Add 1 chopped pimiento and a small can (4-ounce) well drained mushrooms with seasonings.

Turkey Terrapin: Prepare Creamed Turkey, reducing the turkey meat to 1 cup.

Just before serving, add 4 chopped hard-cooked eggs and 1/4 cup chopped ripe olives.

Turkey Curry: Prepare Creamed Turkey. To above seasonings add 1/2 to 1 1/2 teaspoons curry powder and 1/2 cup grated fresh coconut.

If canned shredded coconut is used, it should be chopped finer. Serve over rice.

Turkey Curry, Hawaiian Style: Prepare Turkey Curry. Serve in coconut shells which have been sawed in half crosswise to make 6 serving shells. Remove some of coconut meat and use in preparation of curry.

Prepare 6 cups of cooked rice. Grease inside of shells. Line shells with 1/2-inch layer of rice, reserving enough to cover top. Pour in turkey curry. Top with rice.

Bake in a hot oven (400°F.) about 20 minutes.

Creamed Turkey and Pineapple: Prepare Creamed Turkey. Just before serving, add 1/2 cup well drained canned shredded pineapple or 1/2 cup finely diced fresh pineapple and 1/4 cup slivered almonds.

This may be served in hollowed-out fresh pineapple shells cut lengthwise and with stem still on.

Top with Parmesan cheese and place in broiler as far as possible from heat. Broil until top is lightly browned.

Turkey, Rarebit Style: Prepare Creamed Turkey, reducing turkey meat to 1 cup. Add a well drained 4-ounce can of mushrooms.

Just before serving, stir in 1/2 cup grated Cheddar cheese and 1 chopped canned pimiento.

Serve over toast or rusks. For variation, top each serving with a slice of pineapple heated in its own juice or sautéed in small amount of butter.

Creamed Turkey and Ham: Prepare Creamed Turkey, substituting 3/4 cup diced cooked ham for half of turkey (3/4 cup).

Creamed Turkey and Shrimp: Prepare Creamed Turkey, substituting 3/4 cup cooked or canned shrimp for half of turkey (3/4 cup).

Creamed Turkey with Vegetables: Prepare Creamed Turkey, substituting 1/2 cup cooked vegetables (peas, corn or mixed vegetables) for 1/2 cup of turkey.

JIFFY CREAMED CHICKEN AND MUSHROOMS

2   tablespoons butter or margarine
1 1/2 cups diced cooked chicken
3   tablespoons flour
1   can cream of mushroom soup
4   hard-cooked eggs
Salt and pepper

Melt butter and brown chicken in it slightly. Add flour and blend well.

Add soup and cook until thick, stirring constantly. Add sliced egg whites and allow them to heat through. Season to taste.

Serve on toast cubes and sprinkle with sieved egg yolks. Garnish with watercress. Serves 4.

Creamed Chicken in Toast Cups

EASY CHICKEN À LA KING

1/4 cup chopped green pepper
2   tablespoons diced celery
2   tablespoons butter or margarine
1   tablespoon enriched flour
1   can condensed cream of chicken soup
2   3-ounce cans (1 1/2 cups) broiled sliced mushrooms
1   5 1/2-ounce can (3/4 cup) chicken, diced
1/4 cup chopped pimiento
1/4 teaspoon Ac'cent
Salt and pepper

Cook green pepper and celery in butter until tender. Blend in flour. Gradually add soup. Add mushrooms and liquid. Cook until thick, stirring constantly.

Add chicken, pimiento, and seasonings; heat thoroughly. Serve over toast triangles. Serves 4 to 6.

CHICKEN SQUARES

3   cups diced or sliced cooked chicken
1   cup cooked rice
1 1/2 tablespoons chopped parsley
1 1/2 tablespoons chopped pimiento
1   teaspoon salt
1/8 teaspoon pepper
3   eggs, slightly beaten
1 1/2 cups hot seasoned chicken stock
1   cup oven-toasted rice cereal
1   tablespoon melted butter or margarine

Combine chicken, rice, parsley, pimiento, salt, pepper, and eggs; mix carefully. Stir in hot chicken stock. Pour into greased 8 x 8-inch pan.

Combine rice cereal and melted butter; sprinkle over chicken mixture. Set in pan of hot water. Bake in moderate oven (350°F.) about 40 minutes, or until set. Makes 9 2 1/2-inch squares.

Chicken Squares

PARTY CHICKEN LOAF

Filling:

- **3** to 4 cups diced, cooked chicken (1 large stewing chicken)
- **½** cup chopped celery
- **1** egg, unbeaten
- **2** tablespoons chopped pimiento
- **1** to 1½ teaspoons salt
- **½** teaspoon Worcestershire sauce
- **⅛** teaspoon pepper
- **¼** cup chicken fat or butter
- **¼** cup enriched flour
- **⅔** cup chicken stock

Combine cooked chicken, celery, egg, pimiento, salt, Worcestershire sauce, and pepper.

Melt chicken fat or butter in saucepan; blend in flour. Mix until smooth. Gradually add chicken stock; cook over medium heat, stirring constantly until very thick. Blend thoroughly with chicken mixture. Refrigerate while preparing pastry.

Pastry:

- **2** cups sifted enriched flour
- **1** teaspoon salt
- **⅔** cup shortening
- **6** to 7 tablespoons cold water

Sift together flour and salt into mixing bowl. Cut in shortening until particles are the size of small peas.

Sprinkle cold water gradually over mixture while tossing and stirring lightly with fork. Add water to driest particles, pushing lumps to side, until dough is just moist enough to hold together.

Divide into two portions, one twice as large as the other. Form into balls. Flatten to about ½-inch thickness; smooth dough at edges.

Roll out larger portion on floured pastry cloth or board to 15 x 10-inch rectangle. Fit loosely into small loaf pan, approximately 9 x 5 x 3 inches. Fill with chicken mixture.

Roll out remaining dough to 10 x 6-inch rectangle. Cut several slits for escape of steam. Moisten rim of bottom crust. Place top crust over filling; fold edge over bottom crust. Flute edge against inside of pan. Brush top with milk.

Bake in hot oven (425° F) 30 to 40 minutes until golden brown. Cool in

Party Chicken Loaf

pan 5 minutes. Gently turn out on wire rack; then place right side up on serving plate. Cut into 2½-inch slices; serve hot with mushroom sauce (below).

For Individual Tarts: Divide dough into two portions, one slightly larger. Form into balls as above. Roll out larger portion to ⅛-inch thickness. Cut out six 6-inch circles; fit loosely into six 4-inch tart pans. Fill each with about ½ cup chicken filling.

Roll out remaining dough to ⅛-inch thickness; cut six 5-inch circles (dough will need to be re-rolled). Cut two or three slits in the center of each for escape of steam. Moisten rims of bottom crusts. Place a top crust over filling of each tart; fold edge under bottom crust. Press to seal; flute edge. Bake at 425° F. for 20 to 25 minutes.

Mushroom Sauce: Melt 3 tablespoons chicken fat or butter in saucepan over medium heat. Blend in 3 tablespoons flour. Gradually add 1½ cups chicken stock, stirring constantly. Continue cooking and stirring until thickened. Add ¾ cup (4-ounce can) mushrooms and ¼ to ½ teaspoon salt.

Turkey Loaf-Gourmet

TURKEY LOAF-GOURMET

- **2** cups cooked turkey
- **2** cups soft breadcrumbs
- **¼** cup celery, chopped very fine
- **3** egg yolks
- **⅓** cup sherry wine
- **2** tablespoons cream
- **1** teaspoon salt
- **1** teaspoon minced onion

Cut turkey into very small pieces. Add breadcrumbs and chopped celery.

Beat egg yolks. Add wine and cream to egg yolks. Add salt and minced onion. Mix all together lightly.

Pack into greased loaf pan (8 x 4 x 3 inches). Bake in moderate oven (350°F.) about 40 minutes.

Serve with giblet gravy, mushroom, or cheese sauce. Serves 4 to 5.

CHICKEN-IN-A-RING

- **1½** cups uncooked rice
- **1** medium green pepper, diced
- **¼** cup butter, margarine, or chicken fat
- **¼** cup flour

- **2** cups chicken stock
- **½** teaspoon salt

Dash of pepper

- **2** teaspoons lemon juice
- **3** cups diced cooked chicken
- **1** 4-ounce can mushrooms and juice
- **¼** cup chopped pimiento
- **1** egg, slightly beaten

Cook rice, keep hot. Cook green pepper in butter until soft; mix in flour. Add chicken stock, stirring until thickened. Add remaining ingredients except rice.

Heat thoroughly, stirring constantly. Pile hot rice in ring around serving plate or mold in ring. Place chicken in center. Serves 6 to 7.

CHICKEN SPIRAL LOAF

Chicken Filling:

- **1** cup diced cooked chicken
- **1** cup chopped celery
- **¼** cup chopped green pepper (optional)
- **1** tablespoon chopped onion
- **3** sliced hard-cooked eggs
- **½** teaspoon salt

Pastry:

- **1½** cups sifted enriched flour
- **½** cup enriched corn meal
- **1** teaspoon baking powder
- **1** teaspoon salt
- **½** cup shortening
- **½** cup milk

For chicken filling, combine all ingredients, mixing well.

For pastry, sift together dry ingredients. Cut in shortening until mixture resembles coarse crumbs. Add milk, tossing lightly with a fork until mixture will just hold together.

Knead gently a few seconds on a lightly floured board. Roll dough out to form a 10 x 12-inch rectangle. Transfer dough to baking sheet.

Spoon chicken filling onto dough, spreading mixture evenly over the dough. Roll up, beginning on the long side, as for a jelly roll.

Place seam on underneath side. Seal ends by pressing dough together.

Bake in hot oven (425°F.) 20 to 25 minutes. Slice and serve with a cheese sauce. Serves 6.

Chicken Spiral Loaf

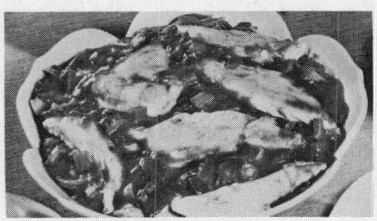

Pimiento Chicken

PIMIENTO CHICKEN

4   onions, thinly sliced
¼   cup butter or margarine
¼   cup flour
1   tablespoon curry powder (or to taste)
2   cups chicken broth
4   cups cut-up cooked chicken
1   teaspoon salt
¼   teaspoon pepper
1   7-ounce jar pimientos, whole pod, chopped

Sauté onions in butter or margarine. Stir in flour and curry powder. Add chicken broth and chicken. Simmer 30 minutes.

Add salt, pepper, and pimientos. Keep hot and serve over shredded wheat biscuits. Serves 4.

CRUNCHY CHICKEN WITH RICE

1⅓ cups packaged precooked rice
2   tablespoons butter or margarine
1   medium onion, sliced
1   medium green pepper, cut into strips
3   cups sliced celery
1¼ cups chicken broth
1   tablespoon soy sauce
2   cups cooked or canned chicken
1   3-ounce can mushrooms, drained
2   tablespoons cornstarch
3   tablespoons mushroom liquid
½   cup walnuts or slivered almonds

Cook rice as directed on package; keep hot.

Cook onion in butter until tender. Stir in green pepper, celery, chicken broth, and soy sauce; simmer 10 minutes. Add chicken and mushrooms.

Blend cornstarch with mushroom liquid to a smooth paste; stir into chicken mixture. Bring to a boil; add nuts and serve over hot rice. Serves 6.

Crunchy Chicken with Rice

CHICKEN OR TURKEY HASH

4   tablespoons butter or margarine
2   tablespoons chopped onion
½   cup fresh or canned mushrooms, sliced
2   cups diced, boiled potatoes
2   cups diced, cooked chicken
⅔   to 1 cup rich milk or cream
Salt, pepper, and paprika to taste

Cook onions and mushrooms in fat until onions are lightly browned.

Add potatoes, chicken, and enough milk or cream to moisten well. Cook slowly over low heat until thickened.

Add salt, pepper, and paprika to taste. Serves 4.

Baked Chicken or Turkey Hash: Turn into a casserole. Top with buttered crumbs. Bake in moderate oven (375° F.) about 30 minutes, until hot and top is browned.

CHICKEN CROQUETTES

2   cups chopped cooked or canned chicken
1   cup thick white sauce
2   teaspoons chopped parsley
Salt and pepper
2   eggs
2   tablespoons water
Dry crumbs

Combine chicken, sauce, and parsley; season with salt and pepper.

Pack into greased pan 8 x 8 x 2 inches; chill thoroughly. Form into croquettes.

Beat eggs; add water. Roll croquettes in crumbs; dip in egg; roll in crumbs.

Fry in shallow fat or deep hot fat (375° F.) 5 minutes, or until brown. Drain on absorbent paper. Serves 4.

Chicken Croquettes

CHICKEN WITH PINEAPPLE

2   tablespoons peanut oil
½   cup sliced water chestnuts
½   cup bamboo shoots
½   cup finely diced celery
½   cup finely chopped spinach
1   teaspoon sugar
1   teaspoon Ac'cent
1   tablespoon soy sauce
1   cup chicken broth
1½ tablespoons cornstarch
3   tablespoons water

1   cooked breast of chicken, thinly sliced
½   cup pineapple tidbits, drained
3   to 4 cups cooked rice

Cook vegetables in oil 3 to 5 minutes. Add seasonings and broth and bring to boil.

Blend cornstarch and water until free of lumps. Add slowly to simmering broth, stirring constantly until thickened throughout.

Add chicken and pineapple and heat to serving temperature. Serve hot with fluffy rice. Serves 4.

CHICKEN AND VEGETABLE LOAF

2   cups diced cooked chicken
2   cups cooked or canned peas or peas and carrots
1   cup soft breadcrumbs
¼   cup chopped celery
½   cup chicken stock or milk
2   slightly beaten eggs
1½ teaspoons salt
1   tablespoon minced onion
1   tablespoon minced pimiento

Combine ingredients and pack lightly into greased pan.

Bake in moderate oven (350° F.) about 40 minutes.

Turn out on serving platter. Serve with chicken gravy or mushroom sauce. Condensed cream of mushroom soup may be thinned slightly with milk for a sauce. Serves 6.

ALMOND-PINEAPPLE CHICKEN

2   tablespoons butter or margarine
½   cup crushed pineapple
½   cup pineapple juice
1½ tablespoons cornstarch
2   cups chicken stock
2   cups cubed cooked chicken
½   cup slivered toasted almonds
½   cup sliced celery
1½ teaspoons salt
Chow mein noodles

Let pineapple sauté in butter 5 minutes. Add pineapple juice mixed with cornstarch.

Add chicken stock and stir over low heat until thickened. Add cubed chicken, almonds, celery, and salt. Let heat through.

Serve with chow mein noodles. Serves 6 to 8.

Almond-Pineapple Chicken

CHICKEN ALMOND WITH RICE

½ cup blanched almonds
3 tablespoons salad oil
1 teaspoon salt
1 clove garlic, mashed
1 cup diced cooked chicken
1 cup cubed bamboo shoots
½ cup sliced canned or fresh mushrooms
2 tablespoons liquid (use 1 tablespoon each from bamboo shoots and water chestnuts cans)
½ cup thinly sliced water chestnuts
½ cup thinly sliced celery
2 teaspoons cornstarch
½ teaspoon sugar
¼ cup water
4 teaspoons soy sauce
½ cup sliced green onions
Hot boiled rice

Brown almonds in 1 tablespoon oil. Set aside.

Combine salt, mashed garlic clove, and 1 tablespoon oil in skillet which has a tight-fitting lid. Heat and add the chicken and brown lightly.

Add 1 tablespoon oil, bamboo shoots, and mushrooms. Brown lightly.

Add 2 tablespoons liquid. Cover and cook over low heat 5 minutes.

Add water chestnuts, celery, and half of almonds. Heat through. Celery and chestnuts should stay crisp.

Blend cornstarch, sugar, water, and soy sauce; stir into rice mixture. Cook until thickened and smooth.

Serve over hot cooked rice, sprinkling remaining almonds and green onions over top. Serves 4.

HOT TURKEY AND HAM MOUSSE

3 tablespoons butter or margarine
3 tablespoons flour
1 cup milk
Salt and pepper
1½ cups minced leftover turkey
½ cup minced cooked or canned ham
½ cup soft breadcrumbs
2 eggs

Melt butter or margarine; blend in flour. Gradually add milk; cook over hot water, stirring constantly, until thick. Season with salt and pepper.

Cool slightly; add turkey, ham, and crumbs. Beat eggs; add.

Pour into individual greased molds. Place in pan of warm water.

Bake in moderate oven (350°F.) 45 minutes, or until inserted knife comes out clean. Serves 4.

CHICKEN FINALE

2 tablespoons finely chopped green pepper
1 tablespoon butter or margarine

Chicken Almond with Rice

1 can (1¼ cups) condensed cream of chicken soup
2 cups cooked noodles
½ to 1 cup diced cooked chicken

Cook green pepper until tender in butter in saucepan.

Add soup, noodles, and chicken. Mix well. Cook over low heat about 10 minutes.

Serve on warm platter. Garnish with green pepper rings and additional slivers of chicken if desired. Serves 4.

CHICKEN CUSTARD LOAF

2½ cups coarsely ground cooked chicken
1½ cups soft breadcrumbs
¾ cup chicken broth
½ cup minced celery
1 tablespoon minced parsley
1 teaspoon grated onion
1 teaspoon salt
⅛ teaspoon pepper
¾ teaspoon Ac'cent
2 teaspoons lemon juice
2 beaten eggs
½ cup evaporated milk

Combine ingredients in order given, mixing lightly and thoroughly. Fill well greased 8 x 5 x 3-inch loaf pan; set in pan of hot water.

Bake in moderate oven (350°F.) until loaf is firm and top delicately browned, about 1 hour.

Remove from hot water; let stand 5 to 10 minutes before unmolding. Slice and serve with thin gravy, either chicken-mushroom or plain chicken gravy. Serves 6.

Note: If the chicken was cooked originally with Ac'cent, or if it was used in the broth, then only ½ teaspoon Ac'cent is needed in the recipe.

CHICKEN À LA BORDELAISE

2 tablespoons butter
2 tablespoons flour
1 cup chicken stock
1 teaspoon Worcestershire sauce
1 clove garlic, mashed
Salt and pepper to taste
12 large mushroom caps
¼ cup sherry or Madeira
2 cups cold cooked chicken, diced
¼ cup heavy cream

Heat butter in the top pan of the chafing dish placed directly over a low flame and when melted, stir in flour and chicken stock. Continue to stir until it is thick and smooth.

Add Worcestershire sauce, garlic, salt and pepper to taste.

Add mushrooms and sherry or Madeira and simmer for 5 minutes.

Add diced chicken, heat, and stir in heavy cream. Serves 6.

CHICKEN-SPAGHETTI LOAF WITH MUSHROOM SAUCE

1 cup broken spaghetti
1 cup diced cooked chicken
1 cup dry breadcrumbs
1 cup grated American cheese
1½ cups warm milk
¼ cup melted butter or margarine
¼ cup chopped green pepper
2 tablespoons chopped pimiento
1 teaspoon salt
3 slightly beaten eggs

Cook spaghetti in boiling, salted water. Drain; add remaining ingredients.

Bake in greased 10 x 6 x 1½-inch baking dish in moderate oven (350°F.) 1 hour. Serve with mushroom sauce. Serves 6.

Mushroom Sauce: Stir ¼ cup milk into 1 can condensed cream of mushroom soup. Heat.

With a freezer, leftovers are banished. Leftover turkey can be packaged for various uses as turkey sandwich slices, turkey bits, or turkey pieces as required for your recipes.

HAWAIIAN CURRY

2   cups hot milk
1   package (4-ounce) shredded coco-
      nut
2   cloves garlic, chopped
2   teaspoons ground ginger
3   green onions, chopped
1   to 2 tablespoons curry powder
2   tablespoons soft butter or mar-
      garine
1/3 cup flour
6   tablespoons butter or margarine
1/2 teaspoon salt
1/2 cup cream
3   cups cooked, boned chicken meat

Pour hot milk over coconut and let
stand 30 minutes. Add garlic, ginger
and onion to coconut (in milk).

Combine curry powder and 2 tablespoons of butter in top of double
boiler. Stir in coconut milk mixture
and cook over hot water about 2 hours,
stirring frequently. Strain through double thickness of cheesecloth.

Blend flour and remaining butter in
top of double boiler. Add strained coconut milk. Stir and cook over hot water until the sauce is thick and smooth.
Stir in salt and cream. Add chicken
and cook slowly to prevent curdling,
about 20 minutes. Serve hot on hot
cooked rice. Serves 6.

Accompany with an assortment of six
of the following condiments:

Chopped crisp bacon
Chutney
Chopped green onions
Chopped hard-cooked egg yolks
Finely chopped parsley
Chopped peanuts
Shredded coconut
Chopped hard-cooked egg whites

CREAMED CHICKEN
(CHINESE STYLE)

3   tablespoons cornstarch
2   cups milk
1   can condensed cream of mushroom
      soup, undiluted
2   cups diced, cooked, or canned
      chicken
1   3-ounce can chopped mushrooms,
      undrained
1   8-ounce can water chestnuts,
      drained, sliced
1/8 teaspoon each salt, pepper, dried
      marjoram, and Ac'cent
1/2 teaspoon paprika
1   tablespoon sherry
Chow mein noodles

Blend cornstarch in a saucepan with
some of the milk to form a smooth
paste, then mix in remaining milk and
soup.

Add remaining ingredients except
noodles. Cook over low heat until bubbling hot.

Arrange noodles on large heated
platter; cover with chicken mixture.
Serves 6.

CHICKEN Â LA REINE

6   tablespoons butter or margarine
6   tablespoons flour
3   cups chicken stock
Salt and pepper
3/4 teaspoon Ac'cent
1/8 teaspoon ground nutmeg
2   beaten egg yolks
2   to 3 tablespoons dry sherry
      (optional)
2   to 3 cups diced cooked or canned
      chicken
3   cups hot well seasoned mashed
      potatoes

Melt butter or margarine; blend in
flour until smooth. Add chicken stock;
cook over low heat, stirring until
smooth and thickened. Season with salt
and pepper to taste. Add Ac'cent and
nutmeg.

Add slowly to beaten egg yolks; stir
and cook 2 minutes over low heat.

Remove from heat; add sherry and
chicken. Turn into 6 individual ramekins.

Make a border of mashed potato
around each ramekin. Brown under
broiler heat. Serves 6.

TURKEY CHEESE TURNOVERS

Cheese pastry (see below)
4   tablespoons butter
2   tablespoons minced onion
1/2 cup finely diced celery
3   tablespoons flour
1   teaspoon salt
1/8 teaspoon pepper
1   cup milk
2   cups diced, cooked turkey
2   tablespoons minced parsley

Make your favorite pastry with 2 1/4
cups flour, reducing shortening in
recipe to 2/3 cup; blend in 1 cup grated
cheese when cutting in shortening.

Roll out to 1/8-inch thickness on a
floured board and cut in 6-inch squares
or 4-inch circles.

To make filling: Melt butter; add
onion and celery; cook over low heat
until tender.

Blend in flour and seasonings; gradually stir in milk and cook until mixture
boils and thickens, stirring constantly.
Add turkey and parsley; remove from
heat.

Pile turkey filling on each piece of
pastry; fold pastry to make triangle or
half-circle. Press edges together with
fork. Prick tops to let steam escape.

Bake in very hot oven (450°F.) for 10
minutes; reduce heat to 400°F., and
bake 15 minutes longer, until lightly
browned. Serve hot with mushroom
sauce. Serves 6.

ORIENTAL CHICKEN PILAF

1/2 cup butter or margarine
2   cups cooked chicken, cut into
      strips about 1 1/2 inches long
1/4 cup diced onion
2   teaspoons salt
1/8 teaspoon pepper
1/2 teaspoon oregano or thyme
1   cup uncooked white rice
2 1/2 cups chicken stock or 2 1/2 cups
      water and 3 chicken bouillon
      cubes
1/2 cup chopped fresh or canned to-
      matoes, drained
1/2 cup chopped walnuts

Melt butter or margarine in a large
saucepan. Add chicken and onion and
cook until chicken browns. Add salt,
pepper, and oregano or thyme.

Add rice and cook, stirring occasionally, for 5 minutes.

Slowly add chicken stock or water
and bouillon cubes. Add tomatoes and
walnuts. Bring to a boil.

Cover and simmer 20 minutes or until rice is tender. Do not stir. Serve hot.
Serves 8.

HOT CHICKEN MOUSSE

6   tablespoons butter or margarine
3/4 cup dry breadcrumbs
2   cups thin cream or evaporated
      milk
1/8 teaspoon salt
1/4 teaspoon nutmeg
3   cups chopped cooked chicken
6   slightly beaten eggs
1/3 cup sherry wine
3   large avocados
1 1/2 cups mayonnaise

Melt butter in top of double boiler.
Add crumbs, cream, salt, and nutmeg;
cook 10 minutes, stirring frequently.

Mix together chicken, eggs, and
sherry; add hot cream sauce.

Pour into well greased mold. Place
mold in pan of water and cover with
sheet of waxed paper.

Bake in moderate oven (350°F.) 45
to 60 minutes, or until firm. A ring
mold will take about 30 to 35 minutes.

Cube avocados; mix with mayonnaise
and pour around mousse or fill the
center of a ring mold. Serves 6.

Turkey Cheese Turnovers

CHICKEN ROYALE

3½ cups cooked chicken (1 4½-pound fowl)
2 cups soft breadcrumbs
1 cup cooked rice
1 teaspoon salt
½ teaspoon paprika
¾ cup nonfat dry milk solids
¼ cup chopped pimiento
4 well beaten eggs
3 cups chicken broth
¼ cup butter or chicken fat

Disjoint fowl, cook in water to cover until tender; cool, remove meat from bones and dice.

Combine ingredients in order given and mix well. Turn into buttered 10-inch ring mold or 13½ x 8½-inch baking dish and place in pan of hot water.

Bake in moderate oven (350°F.) 1 hour.

Allow to stand 10 minutes before unmolding on hot chop plate. Fill center with mushroom sauce and garnish with parsley. Serves 8.

Mushroom Sauce:
½ cup butter
1 pound fresh mushrooms, sliced
½ cup flour
1 cup nonfat dry milk solids
1 quart rich chicken broth
2 well beaten egg yolks
½ cup cream
½ teaspoon salt
Paprika
1 tablespoon chopped parsley
1 tablespoon lemon juice

Melt butter in heavy skillet; add sliced mushrooms and cook gently 5 minutes.

Remove mushrooms from butter and keep hot.

Transfer butter from skillet to a double boiler; add flour and dry milk solids and mix well; gradually stir in chicken broth, place over hot water and cook until thick, stirring until smooth.

Stir in egg yolks mixed with cream; add seasoning, lemon juice, and mushrooms. Serve hot in chicken ring.

TURKEY SUPPER RING

4 tablespoons butter or margarine
4 tablespoons flour
2 cups milk
3 chicken bouillon cubes
2 well beaten eggs
1 cup mayonnaise
1 to 2 cups diced cooked turkey
½ cup slivered blanched almonds
1 can Chinese fried noodles

Melt butter; blend in flour; add milk and chicken cubes; stir over low heat until smooth and thickened. Cool slightly.

Add to eggs. Stir in mayonnaise. Fold in turkey, almonds, and noodles.

Bake in well greased ring mold in moderate oven (350°F.) 50 to 60 minutes or until set.

Let stand 5 minutes. Unmold. Fill center with mushroom sauce.

Serves 4 to 6.

Mushroom Sauce: Slice ½ pound mushrooms; cook in 3 tablespoons butter until golden brown.

Blend in 3 tablespoons flour and ½ teaspoon salt. Combine 1 can cream of celery soup and ⅓ cup cream; add; stir smooth over low heat.

CHICKEN AND MUSHROOM DELIGHT

4 tablespoons butter or margarine
1 tablespoon cornstarch
2 tablespoons flour
1½ cups chicken stock
1 cup light cream
½ cup heavy cream
Salt and pepper
2 cups cold, boiled chicken, cut in generous blocks or diced
1 cup broiled, fresh mushrooms
½ cup sliced pimiento
1 truffle (optional)
¼ cup thinly sliced celery, cooked 10 minutes
2 slightly beaten egg yolks

Melt butter in saucepan. Mix cornstarch and flour; add to butter; stir until blended.

Add chicken stock and cream. Add seasonings, and heat to boiling point, stirring constantly.

Add chicken, mushrooms, pimiento, shredded truffle, if possible, and celery. Heat to boiling.

Remove from heat; add yolks, stirring constantly. Serves 4 to 6.

CHICKEN TERRAPIN #2

3 tablespoons butter or margarine
3 hard-cooked eggs
5 tablespoons flour
¾ teaspoon dry mustard
1 teaspoon salt
¼ teaspoon white pepper
2 cups milk or milk and stock
1½ cups diced, cooked chicken
1 pimiento, chopped
1 tablespoon chopped green pepper
4 ripe olives, coarsely chopped
1 tablespoon lemon juice

Melt butter or margarine. Blend in mashed egg yolks, flour, and seasonings. Add liquid and cook until thickened.

Add chopped egg whites and remaining ingredients except lemon juice. Heat thoroughly.

Taste and add more seasoning if needed. Add lemon juice last. Serve on toast. Serves 4 to 6.

BUFFET CHICKEN PIE

5 tablespoons flour
1 teaspoon salt
⅛ teaspoon pepper
1 cup cold water
2 cups hot chicken stock
9 small onions
1 cup chopped celery
2 cups cooked peas
2 cups cooked carrot slices
3 cups cooked chicken

Crust:

1½ cups sifted enriched flour
¼ teaspoon baking powder
½ teaspoon salt
½ cup shortening
5 to 6 tablespoons ice water

Mix together 5 tablespoons flour, 1 teaspoon salt, pepper, and 1 cup cold water. Add to hot chicken stock and cook until thick and no starchy taste remains; stir constantly.

Parboil onions about 10 minutes. To thickened chicken stock add onions, celery, cooked peas, cooked carrots, and chicken. Pour into 2½-quart baking dish.

Crust: Sift together 1½ cups flour, baking powder, and ½ teaspoon salt. Cut in shortening until it is the size of peas.

Add ice water a little at a time, mixing only enough to hold ingredients together.

Place dough on lightly floured board and roll to about ⅛-inch thickness. Cut dough into strips and arrange in lattice work effect across top of pie.

Bake in hot oven (400°F.) about 25 minutes or until crust is browned. Serve with tomato-cucumber salad in individual ramekins. Serves 9.

CHICKEN À LA KING #2

6 tablespoons butter
6 tablespoons flour
½ teaspoon salt
2 cups milk
1½ cups cooked chicken in 1½-inch or larger pieces
½ cup diced cooked celery
3 tablespoons diced cooked green peppers
2 tablespoons chopped pimiento
2 beaten egg yolks
1 tablespoon Worcestershire sauce

Melt butter, blend in flour and salt, add milk and cook, stirring constantly over low heat or in chafing dish until sauce is thick and bubbly.

Add chicken, celery, green peppers, and pimiento and heat through.

Beat eggs with Worcestershire, add a small amount of creamed mixture, stir well, and add to rest of creamed mix.

Stir in well, away from heat, and serve at once over slices of toast or noodle squares. Serves 8.

Party Creamed Chicken

PARTY CREAMED CHICKEN

1/4 cup butter or margarine
1/4 cup chicken fat
3/4 teaspoon salt
1/2 teaspoon garlic salt
7 tablespoons enriched flour
3 cups milk or 1 1/2 cups each milk and chicken stock
3 to 4 cups cooked seasoned large chicken pieces
1 1/2 cups cooked seasoned frozen peas

Melt butter and chicken fat. Combine seasonings and flour. Add to fat and stir until free of lumps. Remove from heat.

Add milk and stir until thoroughly mixed.

Return to low heat. Cook, stirring constantly, until sauce has thickened. Add chicken and peas.

Pour into heated casserole. Garnish with hot buttered bite-size shredded whole wheat (below). Serves 6.

Hot Buttered Bite-Size Shredded Whole Wheat:

1/3 cup melted butter or margarine
2 cups bite-size shredded whole wheat
3/4 teaspoon salt

Pour melted butter over bite-size shredded whole wheat. Sprinkle with salt. Mix carefully. Turn into a flat baking pan.

Heat in moderate oven (375°F.) 20 minutes, stirring gently after 10 minutes. Serves 6.

CURRIED CREAMED CHICKEN WITH NOODLES

6 tablespoons butter or margarine
1/4 cup chopped onion
1/3 cup chopped celery
6 tablespoons flour
1 tablespoon curry powder
3 cups chicken stock or bouillon
Salt
2 cups diced, cooked chicken or turkey
1 8-ounce package noodles
1/3 cup chopped peanuts

Melt butter in top of double boiler; add onion and celery and cook until tender.

Place over boiling water; add flour and curry powder and stir until well blended.

Gradually add chicken stock and cook, stirring constantly, until mixture thickens. Season to taste with salt. Add chicken and reheat.

Cook noodles in boiling, salted water until tender. Drain, rinse with boiling water and place in casserole.

Pour curried chicken into center of noodles. Sprinkle with chopped peanuts and serve. Serves 6.

SPAGHETTI AND TURKEY CASSEROLE

1/2 pound spaghetti, broken in 2-inch pieces
2 cups coarsely diced cooked turkey
4 tablespoons butter or margarine
1/2 pound mushrooms, sliced
3 tablespoons flour
1/2 teaspoon salt
1/8 teaspoon white pepper
2 cups chicken bouillon or stock
1 cup evaporated milk
1/2 cup breadcrumbs
2 tablespoons melted butter or margarine

Cook spaghetti in boiling salted water until tender. Drain and combine with diced turkey.

Melt 4 tablespoons butter in saucepan and pan-fry mushrooms 5 minutes. Push to one side and blend flour and seasonings in drippings. Add bouillon slowly and cook over low heat until thickened, stirring constantly. Stir in evaporated milk.

In a greased baking dish, arrange alternate layers of turkey mixture and sauce. Combine fine breadcrumbs with melted butter and sprinkle over spaghetti and turkey. Bake in very hot oven (450°F.) until brown and bubbling, 20 to 25 minutes. Serves 6.

TURKEY (OR CHICKEN) BUDGET PIE

1 1/2 cups cooked, chopped turkey
1 1/2 cups cooked, diced potatoes
1/2 cup diced carrots or celery
2 tablespoons finely minced onion
1/2 cup grated cheese
1 1/2 cups medium white sauce or canned creamed soup
Salt and pepper
Plain pastry

Combine turkey, potatoes, carrots, and onion. Add cheese and sauce.

Season to taste with salt and pepper. Place in shallow baking dish.

Roll out pastry and cut it slightly larger than baking dish.

Cover dish with pastry, pressing firmly just below edge of dish.

Cut "turkeys" from scraps of dough and arrange on top of pastry. Cut slits in the pastry for steam vents.

Bake in hot oven (400°F.) until pastry is nicely browned and filling begins to bubble. Serve very hot. Serves 4 to 5.

CHICKEN AND MUSHROOM CROQUETTES

4 tablespoons shortening
5 tablespoons flour
1 teaspoon salt
1/4 teaspoon pepper
1 cup liquid (milk, canned chicken soup, or mushroom liquid)
2 cups cooked chicken, chopped or cut very fine
1 can mushrooms (4 ounces), drained and chopped
Fine breadcrumbs
1 egg, slightly beaten with 1 tablespoon water

Melt shortening in saucepan. Add flour, salt, and pepper and blend. Add liquid and cook until smooth and thick, stirring constantly. Add chicken and mushrooms and blend well.

Spread mixture in shallow pan, 7 x 11 inches, and chill until stiff.

Cut into rounds with biscuit cutter. Coat with crumbs, then dip in egg, and again in crumbs.

Fry in deep hot fat (375°F.) about 1 1/2 inches deep until brown. Drain on absorbent paper. Serve with mushroom sauce. Serves 6.

Chicken King Cutlets: Omit mushrooms; add 2 tablespoons chopped pimiento and 2 teaspoons chopped parsley.

CREAMED CHICKEN IN RICE RING

Creamed Chicken:

1 1/2 tablespoons butter or margarine
2 tablespoons flour
1 cup chicken broth
1 cup evaporated milk, undiluted
1/2 teaspoon salt
2 cups diced cooked chicken

Make a sauce of butter, flour, broth, evaporated milk, and salt. Add diced chicken and heat in double boiler.

Pour creamed chicken into center of rice ring. Garnish with parsley. Serves 8.

Rice Ring:

1 egg
1/2 teaspoon salt
1 teaspoon grated onion
1 cup evaporated milk, undiluted
1/2 cup chicken broth
3 cups cooked rice

Beat egg. Add remaining ingredients. Pour into well buttered ring mold. Set in pan of hot water.

Bake in moderate oven (350°–375°F.) until set, about 45 minutes. Serves 6 to 8.

CHICKEN OR TURKEY TETRAZZINI AU SAUTERNE

1/2   pound spaghetti
1/2   cup sliced mushrooms
3   tablespoons butter or margarine
3   tablespoons flour
3/4   cup consommé
3/4   cup sauterne or rhine wine
1/2   cup evaporated milk
1 1/2 cups leftover turkey or chicken,
       cubed
       Buttered crumbs
       Grated Parmesan cheese

Cook spaghetti in salted water until tender; drain and rinse with hot water.

Cook mushrooms in butter or margarine for 5 minutes. Sprinkle with flour, stir, add consommé and wine; cook, stirring until smooth. Add evaporated milk; season to taste.

In a greased baking dish, put a layer of spaghetti, then a layer of turkey, and a layer of mushroom sauce. Repeat, ending with a top layer of spaghetti.

Sprinkle top generously with buttered breadcrumbs mixed with grated Parmesan-type cheese.

Bake in hot oven (450°F.) until lightly browned and bubbling.

Serves 5 to 6.

TURKEY RICE CASSEROLE

1   cup uncooked rice
1/3   cup chopped onion
1/3   cup chopped celery
5   cups turkey broth or water and 4
       chicken bouillon cubes
1/4   cup chopped green pepper
1/4   cup chopped pimiento
3/4   teaspoon Worcestershire sauce
1 1/2 teaspoons salt
3   cups cubed cooked turkey or
       chicken
1/4   cup breadcrumbs mixed with 1
       tablespoon melted butter

Cook rice, onion, and celery in broth until all but about 1 cup broth is absorbed by rice.

Then add green pepper, pimiento, Worcestershire sauce, salt, and cubed turkey.

Place in casserole and top with buttered breadcrumbs. Bake in moderate oven (350°F.) 1 hour. Serves 5 to 6.

DEVILED MOCK DRUMSTICKS

2   eggs
1   cup thick white sauce
1   teaspoon Worcestershire sauce
2   tablespoons chopped parsley
2   tablespoons minced onion
1/2   teaspoon salt
       Few drops Tabasco sauce
1 1/2 cups ground leftover turkey
2   tablespoons water
       Dry crumbs

Beat 1 egg; add to sauce. Add Worcestershire sauce, parsley, onion,

salt, Tabasco, and turkey; mix well. Chill. Shape like drumsticks.

Beat remaining egg; add water. Roll drumsticks in crumbs; dip in egg; roll in crumbs.

Fry in deep fat or salad oil heated to 375°F. 5 to 7 minutes, or until brown. Drain on absorbent paper. Insert wooden skewers; place paper frills on skewers. Serves 4.

CHICKEN-RICE TIMBALES

1 1/2 cups cooked rice
1 1/2 cups diced cooked chicken
1   tablespoon finely diced onion
2   beaten eggs
1   cup milk
1/3   cup chicken broth or milk
1/2   teaspoon salt
       Pepper

Mix all ingredients together. Divide mixture among custard cups or individual baking dishes.

Place cups in pan of very hot water and bake in moderate oven (350°F.) about 30 minutes, or until a knife inserted in center of timbale comes out clean. Serves 5 to 6.

Variations: Cooked ham, pork, turkey, fish, or rabbit may be used in place of chicken.

If you have less than the 1 1/2 cups of chicken (or other meat) the recipe calls for, stretch meat with sliced hard-cooked eggs and cooked peas. For a company meal, add mushrooms, fresh or canned.

Creamed mushroom sauce may be served on timbales. Cooked macaroni, spaghetti, or noodles may be substituted for cooked rice.

TURKEY-MACARONI LOAF

1 1/2 cups hot milk
1/4   cup fat
4   well beaten eggs
1   cup soft breadcrumbs
1   cup grated cheese (1/4 pound)
2   cups diced cooked turkey
2   cups cooked macaroni or noodles
2   tablespoons chopped parsley
1   small onion, finely chopped
1   tablespoon chopped pimiento
1   teaspoon salt
1/8   teaspoon pepper
1/2   teaspoon Ac'cent (optional)

Melt fat in hot milk. Combine remaining ingredients. Pour milk and fat over mixture, stirring constantly.

Pour into a 2 1/2 x 8 x 3 1/2-inch loaf pan. Set in a pan of hot water. Bake in moderate oven (350°F.) until a knife inserted half-way between center and outside edge comes out clean, 50 to 60 minutes.

Let stand in pan about 5 minutes before inverting on platter. Slice or cut in squares. Serve plain or with mushroom sauce. Serves 8 to 10.

CHICKEN VALENCIA

1   medium onion, chopped
3   cloves garlic, crushed
3   tablespoons fat
1   No. 2 can tomatoes
1   No. 1/2 can Vienna sausage
1 1/2 cups diced cooked chicken
1/2   pound ham, diced
3   cups chicken broth
2   cups rice
1   teaspoon salt
1   cup cooked peas
1/2   cup diced pimientos
3   hard-cooked eggs, cut into
       quarters

Sauté the onion and garlic in hot fat until lightly browned. Add tomatoes, sausage, chicken, and ham. Cook for 10 minutes and then add chicken broth, rice, and salt.

Cook until rice is done. Add peas and pimientos.

Turn onto platter and garnish with hard-cooked eggs. Serves 8 to 10.

CHICKEN DINNER-IN-A-DISH

1   cup celery, cut in 1-inch lengths,
       plus a few minced leaves
1   small onion, chopped
2   cups cooked chicken, cut in 1-inch
       cubes
2 1/2 cups chicken stock
1   cup uncooked brown rice
1 1/2 teaspoons salt
1   bay leaf
       Dash of Tabasco sauce
2   tablespoons butter or chicken fat
3   medium carrots, cut in 1/2-inch
       rounds
1   medium green pepper, cut in inch
       strips

In a greased 2-quart casserole arrange celery, onion, and chicken evenly. Add chicken stock, rice, salt, bay leaf (tuck to one side for easy removal), Tabasco, and butter.

Cover and bake in moderate oven (350°F.) for 45 minutes.

With a fork, lightly mix in carrots and green pepper; cover and bake 45 minutes longer. Serves 6.

Or cook all ingredients, covered, except carrots and green pepper in a heavy kettle or Dutch oven over low heat on top of stove for 35 minutes. Add carrots and green pepper; cook 40 minutes longer.

Chicken Dinner-In-A-Dish

QUICK AND EASY COOKING

This section is for working wives and mothers, career girls and bachelors, many of whom keep apartments and cook for themselves, and any other busy people who love to entertain and serve good food but find time scarce for preparing elaborate spreads. It is possible to wine and dine guests lavishly without stirring, simmering, watching, and garnishing for hours. Many gastronomic concoctions can be made quickly and the quality of the food need not be sacrificed. In every section of this book you'll find many good quick and easy recipes. Here, however, we have assembled recipes and tips designed to put you on an easy route to good simple cookery—even gourmet cookery—and guaranteed to save you many hours in the kitchen. Your helpers in many of these quick and easy recipes are packaged, canned, or frozen foods.

Quick and Easy Meat Recipes

BARBECUED CANNED PORK LOAF

1 tablespoon butter or margarine
½ cup chopped onion
1 teaspoon paprika
¼ teaspoon pepper
3 tablespoons lemon juice or vinegar
1½ tablespoons sugar
1 teaspoon dry mustard
1 tablespoon Worcestershire sauce
¼ cup ketchup
1 12-ounce can pork loaf

Cook onion in melted butter until tender.

Add remaining ingredients except meat.

Cut meat into 8 slices. Bake in the sauce in moderate oven (350°F.) 30 minutes. Serve between toasted buns. Serves 4.

GOLDEN ROUND-UP

1 cup rice, uncooked
2¼ cups chicken broth
1 teaspoon salt
½ teaspoon Ac'cent
½ cup chopped onion
1 No. 2½ can whole tomatoes
1 12-ounce can luncheon meat, cut in finger-lengths (½ inch by 2 inches)
1 cup grated sharp Cheddar cheese

Place rice, broth, salt, Ac'cent, and onion in 2-quart casserole. Stir well.

Cover and bake in moderate oven (350°F.) 45 minutes or until rice is barely done.

Remove casserole from oven. Drain tomatoes and place down in rice. Place meat on top of rice; sprinkle cheese over meat.

Cover; return casserole to oven. Bake 20 to 30 minutes longer or until cheese is melted. Serves 6.

QUICK HASH WITH BROWN PEAR CRUST

1 12-ounce can luncheon meat, grated
1½ cups cooked diced potatoes
1 cup chopped onion
½ cup diced celery
¼ cup diced green pepper
1 teaspoon Ac'cent
1 cup broth
1 No. 2 can pear halves, drained
Butter, softened
Brown sugar

Lightly toss together all ingredients except pears, brown sugar, and butter.

Blend well; turn into buttered 1½-quart shallow casserole. Bake in hot oven (400°F.) 30 minutes.

Remove from oven; arrange pears on top. Lightly butter pears; sprinkle with brown sugar.

Return to oven; bake 15 minutes longer. Lightly brown under broiler, if desired. Serves 4 to 6.

BROILED PINEAPPLE TOP HATS

1 12-ounce can luncheon meat, ground
½ cup oats, quick or old fashioned, uncooked
¼ cup pineapple juice
2 tablespoons ketchup
1 teaspoon prepared mustard
6 slices pineapple, drained

Combine luncheon meat, rolled oats, pineapple juice, ketchup, and mustard. Shape into 6 patties. (Chill if desired.)

Arrange pineapple slices on broiler rack; place a patty on each. Broil about 4 inches from heat until meat is lightly browned, 7 or 8 minutes. Serves 6.

LUNCHEON MEAT BROILER MEAL

Arrange slices of canned luncheon meat, parboiled potato slices, and thick tomato slices on broiler rack. Brush with melted fat or salad oil.

Cook in preheated broiler, on one side only, until hot and lightly browned.

Variations: Another good combination for the broiler: canned luncheon meat slices, par-boiled sweet potatoes cut in thick slices, and sliced pineapple or apple dotted with brown sugar and butter.

Quick Hash with Brown Pear Crust

BAKED CANNED CORNED BEEF

Remove corned beef whole from can. Stud it with whole cloves.

Make a paste by stirring a little water into 1/4 cup brown sugar and 1 teaspoon chili powder.

Add 2 tablespoons chopped pickles to it and spread over the beef.

Bake in moderate oven (350°F.) 10 minutes.

CANNED CORNED BEEF HASH PATTIES

3 tablespoons chopped onion
2 tablespoons butter or margarine
2 tablespoons prepared horseradish
1/2 teaspoon thyme
1 1-pound can corned beef hash

Brown onion lightly in melted butter. Add remaining ingredients and mix well. Form into patties.

Brown patties lightly on both sides in hot melted butter or drippings.

Serve with slices of firm tomato which have been pan-fried in drippings, and then seasoned with brown sugar and salt and pepper. Serves 4.

LUNCHEON MEAT RICE BAKE

1 18-ounce can tomato juice
1/4 cup ketchup
1 package (1 1/8 cups) precooked rice
1 medium-sized onion, chopped
1/2 cup chopped celery
1/2 green pepper, chopped
1/2 teaspoon sugar
1/2 teaspoon salt
1/8 teaspoon pepper
1/8 teaspoon marjoram or oregano
Small piece of bay leaf
1 12-ounce can luncheon meat
1/2 lemon, thinly sliced

Combine tomato juice, ketchup, rice, onion, celery, green pepper. and seasonings (sugar, salt, pepper, marjoram or oregano, and bay leaf) in 2-quart baking dish.

Cut luncheon meat in eight slices. Place the meat on top of rice mixture, overlapping slices slightly.

Insert lemon slices between meat slices.

Bake, covered, in moderate oven (375°F.) 30 to 35 minutes, or until rice is tender. Serves 4.

Luncheon Meat Rice Bake

SPICY HAM LOAF-BAKED

Score top of 12-ounce ham loaf. Stick in 10 cloves. Bake in moderate oven (350°F.) 10 minutes.

Combine 1/3 cup brown sugar, 1/2 teaspoon cinnamon, 1 teaspoon prepared mustard, 1/4 teaspoon vinegar, and 1 teaspoon water; spread over top. Bake additional 15 minutes. Serves 3.

CANNED CORNED BEEF HASH SUGGESTIONS

Fried with Eggs: Slide hash out of can in one piece without breaking it. Slice and brown in a little fat.

Serve topped with fried eggs, sunny-side-up.

With Macaroni Casserole: Slice whole corned beef hash. Brown one side in skillet.

Place browned side up on casserole of cooked macaroni. Pour cheese sauce over all.

Bake in moderate oven (375°F.) until heated through.

With Scrambled Eggs: Brown corned beef hash cubes in butter. Then scramble eggs with the cubes.

With Cabbage: Heat 2 tablespoons fat in large pan. Add 6 cups shredded cabbage. Cover and cook 8 to 10 minutes, stirring frequently.

Add flaked corned beef hash and heat thoroughly. Season to taste.

Patties with Sauce: Add 2 well beaten egg yolks to 2 cups flaked corned beef hash. Fold in 2 stiffly beaten egg whites.

Drop by spoonfuls on buttered baking sheet.

Brown under broiler. Serve with well seasoned tomato sauce.

RING-AROUND-ROSY BEEF

1 can (1 1/4 cups) condensed tomato soup
1/2 cup water
1 teaspoon chopped parsley
1 12-ounce can corned beef, broken into chunks
3 cups cooked rice, (1 cup uncooked)

Combine soup, water, parsley; heat. Add corned beef chunks; stir gently. Serve in a ring of hot cooked rice. Serves 6.

EGGS IN CANNED CORNED BEEF HASH

Divide the contents of a 1-pound can of corned beef hash into 4 parts.

Press each portion into a buttered oven-proof ramekin. Make a depression in each and put 1 egg in the center.

Sprinkle tops with grated American cheese and paprika.

Bake in moderate oven (375°F.) until the eggs are set. Garnish with chopped parsley. Serves 4.

Easy Chop Suey

EASY CHOP SUEY

1 pound pork, cut in 1-inch cubes
1 tablespoon shortening
1 large onion, chopped
1 can (1 1/4 cups) condensed cream of celery soup
1 4-ounce can (1/3 cup) mushrooms (save juice)
1/2 cup water
2 teaspoons Worcestershire sauce
3 cups hot, cooked rice (1 cup uncooked)

Brown pork cubes in shortening in heavy saucepan. Add onion and cook until soft.

Blend in soup, mushrooms and juice, water, and Worcestershire sauce.

Cover; simmer 30 minutes. Remove cover; cook 15 minutes longer or until pork is tender. Serve over hot rice. Serves 6.

HAM PLATTER DINNER

1 24-ounce can baked ham
1 No. 2 can whole sweet potatoes, cut in half
4 spiced peach halves
2 cups fresh or frozen peas

Slice ham in fourths; arrange in center of ovenproof plate.

Arrange sweet potatoes and spiced peach halves around ham. Spread with mixture of 1/2 cup brown sugar, 1/2 teaspoon dry mustard, and 1/2 cup peach pickle juice.

Broil about 7 minutes. Brush with 2 tablespoons melted butter; turn and broil 7 minutes.

Cook peas until tender; drain. Arrange food on large or individual platters. Serve at once. Serves 4.

Corned Beef Hash Topped with Eggs

Creamed Dried Beef

CREAMED DRIED BEEF
(Master Recipe)

- 2 tablespoons butter or margarine
- 2 tablespoons flour
- 2 cups milk or light cream
- ½ pound dried beef, shredded and scalded
- ¼ teaspoon pepper

Melt butter. Stir in flour until smooth. Gradually add milk, stirring constantly until mixture boils and thickens.

Add beef, pepper, and salt if required. Serve on toast. Serves 6.

Creamed Dried Beef Variations

Frizzled Dried Beef: Sauté beef in butter until it curls. Proceed as above, adding flour and cream to butter in pan.

Creole Dried Beef: Prepare Frizzled Dried Beef. At the last, add 4 tablespoons chili sauce.

Dried Beef Curry on Rice: Prepare Frizzled Dried Beef. Season sauce with ¼ teaspoon curry powder. Serve on freshly boiled rice.

DRIED BEEF IN CANNED SOUP

- 2 tablespoons butter or margarine
- 1 small onion, chopped
- 4 ounces dried beef, cut in strips
- 1 can (1¼ cups) condensed cream of celery soup
- ½ cup milk
- 1 pound asparagus, cooked (fresh, canned or frozen)

Melt butter in saucepan; add onion and cook until golden.

Add dried beef, soup, and milk; heat thoroughly. Serve over hot asparagus. Serves 4.

Sweet-Sour Pork Orientale

HAM STEAKS WITH FRUIT

- 2 1-inch tenderized ham steaks
- ½ cup brown sugar
- ½ teaspoon dry mustard
- 1 No. 2 can fruit cocktail

Place one ham steak in a shallow baking pan. Mix brown sugar and mustard together and sprinkle half over ham. Pour over ½ can of the fruit cocktail.

Cover with remaining ham steak and top with remaining mixture and fruit cocktail.

Bake in moderate oven (350°F.) 25 to 35 minutes or until done, basting with juice in pan. Serve with candied sweet potatoes.

If tenderized ham is not available, cover slices of regular ham with cold water, bring to a simmer and cook, covered, 20 minutes. Then drain and proceed as above. Serves 4 to 6.

MUSHROOM-SMOTHERED VEAL

- 4 veal cutlets
- 1 egg
- 2 tablespoons water
- ½ cup fine dry breadcrumbs
- 3 tablespoons shortening
- 2 cans (2½ cups) condensed cream of mushroom soup

Wipe cutlets dry. Combine egg and water; beat lightly. Dip pieces of meat first in egg mixture, then in breadcrumbs.

Brown cutlets on both sides in shortening in a heavy skillet. Pour soup over cutlets; cover and cook slowly for about 30 minutes or until done. Serve on a warm platter. Serves 4.

SWEET-SOUR PORK ORIENTALE

- 2 tablespoons butter or margarine
- ½ green pepper, cut in thin strips
- 1 12-ounce can luncheon meat, diced
- 1 1-pound, 4-ounce can pineapple chunks or tidbits
- 1 1-pound can bean sprouts, well drained
- ½ cup vinegar
- ⅓ cup firmly packed brown sugar
- 1½ tablespoons soy sauce
- 2½ tablespoons cornstarch
- 2 cups hot cooked rice

Melt butter or margarine in large frying pan; add green pepper and luncheon meat; cook 5 minutes, stirring occasionally.

Add pineapple and pineapple juice, bean sprouts, vinegar, brown sugar, and soy sauce; heat thoroughly.

Blend cornstarch to smooth paste with 3 tablespoons water; stir into hot mixture. Bring to boiling, stirring constantly; cook until slightly thick.

Serve with hot, fluffy rice; pass extra soy sauce. Serves 4.

QUICK SHEPHERD'S PIE

Heat 2 1-pound cans lamb stew; turn into 1-quart baking dish. Cover with crust made from 1 package pie crust mix following package directions. (Save remaining crust for a deep-dish pie.)

Bake in hot oven (425°F.) about 20 minutes, or until crust is baked and browned. Serves 4.

Beef and Kidney Pie: Follow recipe for Shepherd's Pie, substituting 2 10-ounce cans beef and kidneys in gravy for lamb stew.

BEEF STEW WITH BISCUIT TOPPING

Pour a can of beef stew in a shallow casserole. Cover with a thin layer of biscuit dough to which grated onion has been added.

Bake in hot oven (425°F.) until biscuits are done and stew is heated through.

FRONTIER BEEF STEW

- 1 large onion, coarsely chopped
- ½ cup uncooked regular rice
- 1 teaspoon salt
- ¼ teaspoon black pepper
- 1½ cups liquid from peas and carrots, plus water
- 1 1-pound can tomatoes and juice
- 2 teaspoons Worcestershire sauce
- 1 1-pound can meatballs and gravy (use 2 cans for more meat)
- 1 1-pound can peas and carrots, drained

Put the onion, rice, salt, pepper, and 1½ cups liquid from peas and carrots (including added water) in a 2-quart saucepan. Bring to a vigorous boil. Turn heat down. Cover and simmer 14 minutes.

Stir in tomatoes. Break into small pieces. Add Worcestershire sauce, meatballs in gravy, and peas and carrots.

Cover and simmer about 15 minutes. Add water if a thinner mixture is desired. Add salt and pepper to taste. Serves 5 to 6.

Frontier Beef Stew

BAKED BEANS WITH HAM

Pour canned baked beans into a shallow casserole. Cover with small slices cooked ham or other ready-to-eat pork-type meat. Spread with chili sauce or drizzle honey over top. Bake in moderate oven (375° F.) 20 to 30 minutes.

LUNCHEON HAM ROLLS

4 tablespoons butter or margarine
4 tablespoons finely chopped onion
4 tablespoons chopped celery
2 cups cooked rice
Salt and pepper
8 slices (1/8-inch slices) boned boiled ham
Cranberry glaze (below)

Melt butter in small saucepan. Add onion and celery. Cook until soft.

Remove from heat. Add rice and seasoning. Spread on each ham slice. Roll up. Fasten with toothpick. Place in greased shallow pan.

Make cranberry glaze. Spoon over ham rolls. Bake in moderate oven (350°F.) 15 to 20 minutes. Makes 8.

Cranberry Glaze: Crush contents of a 1-pound can jellied cranberry sauce and 1/2 cup brown sugar. Spoon over ham rolls before baking.

FRITOQUE

This is an easily prepared and very flavorful dish from the Southwest. Alternate in a casserole layers of canned chili con carne (either plain or with beans), cheese, onions, and corn chips.

Heat in a moderate oven until cheese is thoroughly melted.

TAMALE-CHILI DINNER

1/4 cup chopped onion
1 tablespoon fat
1 10½-ounce can tamales
1 No. 2 can (2½ cups) chili
1/2 cup grated sharp cheese

Cook onion in hot fat until golden. Remove shucks from tamales. Add tamales and chili to onion. Cover. Heat thoroughly.

Arrange in serving dish. Top with additional hot tamales if desired. Sprinkle with grated cheese. Serves 4 to 6.

Tamale-Chili Dinner

CHILI BEAN BAKE

1 small can chili con carne without beans
1 cup canned red kidney beans
1 small can Vienna sausage, drained and sliced
1/2 cup coarsely crushed corn chips or potato chips

Combine chili con carne, kidney beans, and Vienna sausage.

Turn into 1-quart baking dish; top with corn chips or potato chips. Bake in moderate oven (375°F.) until bubbling hot, about 25 minutes. Serves 2.

Note: Stir in additional chili powder, if you like extra hot chili.

JIFFY VEAL BIRDS

2 thin large slices veal cutlets
Salt and pepper
Dash of Worcestershire sauce
2 hard-cooked eggs, shelled
2 tablespoons butter
1 can (10 ounces) condensed cream of chicken soup
1 teaspoon Worcestershire sauce
2 tablespoons pimiento
2 tablespoons chopped parsley

Pound veal until very thin. Sprinkle with salt, pepper, and dash of Worcestershire sauce. Place 1 hard-cooked egg on each piece of veal. Wrap veal around egg. Fasten with a toothpick.

Melt butter. Brown veal birds on all sides. Add soup mixed with 1 teaspoon Worcestershire sauce. Add pimiento and parsley. Cover and cook about 20 to 25 minutes, or until veal is tender. Serves 2.

Jiffy Veal Birds

EASY LUNCHEON HAM DISH

4 1/4-inch slices cooked ham
4 slices canned pineapple
2 cups mashed sweet potatoes
1/2 cup orange or apricot marmalade

Place slices of ham in baking pan. Top each slice with slice of pineapple. Shape 1/2 cup sweet potatoes in a mound on each slice of pineapple. Spread mounds with marmalade.

Bake in hot oven (400°F.) about 20 minutes to heat and brown. Serve hot. Serves 4.

Chili Bean Bake

HAM PIE WITH CHEESE BISCUIT TOP

3 tablespoons minced onion
4 tablespoons chopped green pepper
4 tablespoons butter or margarine
6 tablespoons flour
1 10½-ounce can condensed chicken soup
1⅓ cups milk
1⅓ cups diced ham
1 tablespoon lemon juice

Cook onion and green pepper in butter or margarine until soft but not browned. Add flour and stir until frothy.

Add soup and milk and cook until thick and smooth. Add ham and lemon juice; pour into buttered casserole.

Cheese Biscuit Top:

1½ cups prepared biscuit mix
1/2 cup grated cheese
6 tablespoons milk

Mix biscuit mix and cheese together and stir in milk to make a medium soft dough.

Roll out on a floured board and cut with a biscuit or doughnut cutter.

Arrange biscuits on top of ham pie and bake in very hot oven (450°F.) 20 minutes, or until biscuits are golden brown. Serves 4 to 6.

EASY BEEF PIE WITH CHEESE

1 16-ounce can beef stew
1 teaspoon Worcestershire sauce
Buttered white bread triangles
4 tablespoons grated Cheddar cheese

Add Worcestershire to beef stew and heat. Place in a shallow baking dish.

Arrange bread triangles around edge and sprinkle top with cheese. Brown under broiler. Serves 3.

Easy Beef Pie with Cheese

Ham Loaf with Pickle Stuffing

HAM LOAF WITH PICKLE STUFFING

1   12-ounce can luncheon meat
1   cup fine dry breadcrumbs
⅛ teaspoon black pepper
⅛ teaspoon thyme
¼ cup finely chopped onion
1   egg
1   cup evaporated milk

Stuffing:

1   teaspoon prepared mustard
¼ cup evaporated milk
½ cup fine dry breadcrumbs
½ to ¾ cup pickle relish

Empty can of luncheon meat into large mixing bowl. Shred meat into bits by running tines of fork over the meat.

Add the 1 cup crumbs, seasonings and onion, and mix thoroughly. Beat in egg and the 1 cup milk.

Divide meat mixture in half. Pack one half in bottom of a well greased loaf pan, about 2¼ x 8½ x 4¾ inches.

Stir mustard into the ¼ cup evaporated milk. Add the ½ cup crumbs and pickle relish, and blend thoroughly. Spread pickle stuffing evenly and firmly on top of meat.

Pack remaining half of meat mixture over pickle layer.

Bake in moderate oven (375°F.) 45 minutes. Makes 6 generous servings.

Note: 4 cups lightly packed ground leftover cooked or baked ham can be used in place of luncheon meat. Ham should be put through medium blade of food chopper.

If ham is used, reduce amount of fine dry breadcrumbs used in meat mixture to ½ cup.

CANNED PORK LOAF O'BRIEN

1   12-ounce can pork loaf
¼ cup bacon drippings
1   cup diced cooked potatoes
1   cup chopped onions
½ cup chopped green pepper
1   teaspoon salt

Cut 5 thin slices from loaf. Dice the rest.

Brown potatoes and onion in hot fat. Add diced meat, green pepper, and salt when potatoes are beginning to brown.

Brown slices of meat and serve with potato mixture. Serves 5.

DEVILED HAM CASSEROLE

1   small can deviled ham or ½ cup ground cooked ham
1   teaspoon finely chopped onion
2   tablespoons chili sauce
1   teaspoon horseradish
1   teaspoon prepared mustard
1   teaspoon Worcestershire sauce
4   slices slightly stale bread
¼ cup grated sharp process Cheddar cheese
2   teaspoons butter or margarine
3   beaten eggs
2   cups milk
½ teaspoon salt

Combine ham, onion, chili sauce, horseradish, mustard, and Worcestershire sauce. Spread bread slices with mixture and cut slices into ½-inch cubes.

In 1½-quart buttered casserole, alternate layers of cubes and cheese, ending with bread cubes. Dot with butter. Combine eggs, milk, and salt; pour over all.

Place casserole in pan of hot water and bake in moderate oven (350°F.) 1¼ hours. Serves 6.

SPANISH KIDNEY BEANS

4   slices bacon
1   onion, chopped
½ green pepper, minced
1   pound ground beef
1   can tomato purée
¼ teaspoon each salt and pepper
1   can red kidney beans
Buttered crumbs

Fry bacon in heavy skillet. When lightly browned, add onion and green pepper and sauté 3 to 5 minutes. Add meat and cook until meat loses its red color. Add tomato purée, salt, and pepper. Add kidney beans and their liquid.

Place in casserole. Top with crumbs. Heat and brown top in 350°F. oven. Serves 4.

CHILI STUFFED PEPPERS

6   green peppers
1   cup boiling water
½ pound ground meat
1   can chili con carne (plain or with beans) drained, save liquid
1   medium onion, chopped
1½ teaspoons salt
1   raw or canned tomato, chopped

Remove stems and seeds from peppers. Parboil in boiling water for 5 minutes.

Combine meat, chili con carne, onion, salt, and tomato.

Stuff peppers and arrange in shallow baking pan or casserole. Pour liquid from chili con carne plus ½ cup water over peppers. Bake in moderate oven (350°F.) for 45 minutes. Serves 6.

LAMB CHOP BROILER MEAL

4   medium zucchini squash
8   rib or loin chops or 4 shoulder chops, cut ¾ inch thick
Salt and pepper
2   large tomatoes, cut in half
4   large mushrooms
¼ cup butter or margarine, melted

Wash squash, slice, and simmer until tender.

Place chops on broiler rack. Insert broiler pan and rack so top of chops is 2 inches from heat. When one side is browned, season and turn.

Place tomatoes cut side up on broiler rack and top with a mushroom button. Arrange squash slices on rack.

Brush tomatoes, mushrooms, and squash with melted butter.

Continue broiling until chops are done and vegetables lightly browned. Serves 4.

JIFFY CORNED BEEF AND CABBAGE

1   small head of cabbage
1   12-ounce can corned beef, sliced
Butter or margarine
1   tablespoon lemon juice
Salt and pepper

Cut cabbage into thick wedges and place in large kettle with small amount of boiling, salted water.

Place corned beef in a strainer, suspended over top of cooking kettle but not in contact with the water. Cook 8 to 10 minutes. The steam from the cabbage will heat the corned beef.

Season cabbage with melted fat, lemon juice, salt, and pepper. Serve on warm platter with corned beef slices. Serves 4.

ORANGE HAM LOAF WITH RAISIN SAUCE

1   12-ounce can pork-ham luncheon meat
2   large oranges

Slice meat crosswise in ¼-inch slices to within 1 inch of bottom. Place loaf in shallow baking pan.

Peel and section oranges. Place orange sections between meat slices to form fan-shaped loaf.

Pour raisin sauce over loaf.

Bake in moderate oven (375°F.) 20 minutes. Baste occasionally during baking. Serves 4.

Raisin Sauce: Combine ½ cup brown sugar, 1 tablespoon flour, 1 teaspoon dry mustard, 1 teaspoon grated lemon rind, 1½ tablespoons lemon juice, 1½ tablespoons vinegar, and ⅓ cup seedless raisins in saucepan. Heat to boiling point and cook over low heat 1 minute, stirring constantly.

Frankfurters

BARBECUED GRILLED OR ROASTED FRANKFURTERS

Grill or put franks on a rack in roasting pan. During cooking baste them constantly with barbecue sauce.

SAUTÉED FRANKFURTERS

Cover frankfurters with boiling water. Let stand 7 to 8 minutes.

Split lengthwise and sauté in a little cooking fat or salad oil. Turn to brown both sides.

"BOILED" FRANKFURTERS

Cover frankfurters with boiling water. Simmer gently 7 to 8 minutes.

BROILED FRANKFURTERS

Cover frankfurters with boiling water. Let stand 7 to 8 minutes.

Split lengthwise and brush with cooking fat or salad oil.

Place skin-side-down on broiler rack about 2 inches from heat. Broil until brown.

FRANKFURTER KEBOBS

- 1 cup chili sauce
- 1 to 2 tablespoons brown sugar
- 3 tablespoons vinegar
- 3 drops Tabasco sauce
- 3 slices onion
- 12 frankfurters
- 8 slices bacon

Combine chili sauce, brown sugar, vinegar, Tabasco, and onion in saucepan. Simmer 5 minutes.

Cut each frankfurter into quarters and each slice of bacon into 6 pieces. Arrange alternately on skewers.

Place on baking sheet and spread with half the sauce. Broil 5 minutes under moderate heat. Turn, spread with remaining sauce, and broil 5 minutes longer. Serves 6.

FRANK FRITTERS

Split frankfurters lengthwise and spread inside with prepared mustard. Press together.

Dip into fritter cover batter (see Index) and fry in deep hot fat (365°F.) until browned. Serve two per portion.

Frankly delicious! Top pork and beans, lima beans, or kidney beans (the three are great together) with broiled or pan-broiled frankfurters. Pour on ketchup or chili sauce.

BAKED OR BROILED STUFFED FRANKFURTERS

- 2½ cups breadcrumbs
- ¼ teaspoon salt
- ⅛ teaspoon pepper
- 1 teaspoon each sage and thyme
- 1 small onion, minced
- ⅓ cup melted butter or margarine
- 10 frankfurters
- 10 bacon slices

Combine crumbs, seasonings, onion, and butter or margarine. Blend well.

Split frankfurters lengthwise and fill with stuffing. Wrap each with a slice of bacon. Fasten with toothpicks.

Broil 10 minutes or bake in moderate oven (350°F.) 30 minutes. Serves 5 or more.

Variations:

Apple-Stuffed Frankfurters: Use chopped apple instead of stuffing.

Cheese-Stuffed Frankfurters: Use slice of cheese instead of stuffing. Broil or bake until cheese melts and bacon is browned.

Relish-Stuffed Frankfurters: Combine 1 cup sweet pickle relish and 2 tablespoons prepared mustard. Use instead of stuffing.

FRANKFURTERS STUFFED WITH SAUERKRAUT

Gash frankfurters lengthwise; spread the outside with mustard and fill the gash with sauerkraut.

Wrap each stuffed frankfurter with a slice of bacon; fasten with a wooden pick.

Broil or bake in hot oven (400°F.) until bacon is crisp and the franks are well cooked.

Variation: Substitute pickles for sauerkraut.

BARBECUED FRANKFURTERS

- 1½ cups canned tomatoes
- ½ cup red wine or water
- 2 cloves garlic, minced
- 1 onion, finely chopped
- 1 carrot, minced
- 2 tablespoons chili powder
- 1 teaspoon curry powder
- ½ teaspoon ground mustard
- 1½ teaspoons Worcestershire sauce

Salt to taste
- 2 tablespoons bacon fat
- 1 dozen frankfurters

Simmer together for 30 minutes the tomatoes, wine, garlic, onion, carrot, chili powder, curry powder, mustard, Worcestershire, and salt.

When sauce has almost finished cooking, melt the bacon fat in a skillet, add frankfurters and sauté. Then pour the finished sauce over frankfurters, cover and cook over low heat about 10 minutes. Serves 6.

Franks with Sweet and Pungent Sauce

FRANKS WITH SWEET AND PUNGENT SAUCE

- ¼ cup butter or margarine
- 1 clove garlic, crushed
- ¼ cup chopped green pepper
- 2 tablespoons brown sugar
- ¼ teaspoon ground ginger
- 1 pound frankfurters, sliced crosswise
- ½ cup raisins
- 1 8¾-ounce can pineapple tidbits, drained
- 1 cup apple juice
- ½ cup cider vinegar
- ½ teaspoon salt
- 1 tablespoon cornstarch
- ¼ cup cold water

Melt butter or margarine and sauté garlic and green pepper. Stir in brown sugar and ginger.

Add frankfurters and cook until tender, about 10 minutes. Add raisins, pineapple, apple juice, vinegar, and salt. Mix well.

Stir cornstarch into cold water. Add to frankfurter mixture. Simmer, stirring occasionally, 15 minutes or until raisins are soft. Serve on crackers.

CREOLE FRANKFURTERS

- 4 frankfurters
- 1½ tablespoons finely chopped onion
- 1 tablespoon finely chopped green pepper
- 1½ teaspoons shortening
- ¼ cup ketchup
- ¼ cup water
- ¼ teaspoon salad or cider vinegar
- 1 cup cooked rice
- 2 tablespoons chopped parsley

Lightly brown frankfurters, onion, and green pepper in shortening in skillet. Stir in ketchup and remaining ingredients; cook over low heat 5 minutes. Serves 2.

Creole Frankfurters

*Onion Frankfurters
with Spiced Sauerkraut*

ONION FRANKFURTERS WITH SPICED SAUERKRAUT

1 No. 2½ can sauerkraut
1 teaspoon celery seed
Dash celery salt
½ teaspoon dry mustard
6 frankfurters
3 small onions
¼ cup butter or margarine, melted

In a bowl, combine sauerkraut, celery seed, celery salt, and mustard; toss lightly but thoroughly.

Slash each frankfurter diagonally in four places. Peel onions and cut each into 8 thin slices. Insert an onion slice into each slit in frankfurters.

Arrange half of sauerkraut mixture in bottom of 1½-quart casserole. Place 3 frankfurters on top of sauerkraut mixture in casserole. Top with remaining sauerkraut mixture.

Place remaining 3 frankfurters side by side on top of casserole. Pour melted butter or margarine over all.

Bake in moderate oven (350°F.) 25 minutes. Serves 4 to 6.

GRILLED CHEESE AND FRANKFURTER SPECIAL

8 frankfurters
¾ pound American cheese
8 bread slices

Parboil 8 frankfurters and split lengthwise. Cut cheese in thin slices; place on 8 bread slices, reserving several strips for garnish.

Broil until cheese is melted and slightly browned.

Top each slice with split frankfurter and remaining cheese. Broil until cheese strips are slightly melted.

Arrange on serving tray. Garnish with olives, pickles, and celery leaves. Serve with mustard. Serves 4 to 8.

Grilled Cheese And Frankfurter Special

FRANKFURTER PUFFS

Pour boiling water over 6 frankfurters; cover; let stand 8 minutes. Slit each frank lengthwise. Spread with mustard.

Combine 2 cups well seasoned mashed potatoes, ¼ cup minced onion, 1 to 2 tablespoons chopped pimiento, and ¼ cup chopped parsley.

Spread over split franks. Brown in broiler or oven. Serves 6.

FRANKFURTERS IN BLANKET

Lay a frankfurter on a piece of bread. Spread frankfurter with mustard or chili sauce.

Wrap bread around frankfurter and secure with small metal skewers.

Brush bread with melted butter. Place on baking sheet or pie pan. Bake in hot oven (425°F.) about 15 minutes.

CHEESE AND FRANKFURTERS

1 pound frankfurters
1 cup grated sharp natural Cheddar cheese
½ cup chopped peanuts
2 tablespoons salad dressing
Frankfurter buns

Cut a long slit in each frankfurter. Combine cheese, peanuts, and salad dressing. Fill each frankfurter with cheese mixture.

Place frankfurters on cooky sheet. Bake in slow oven (325°F.) 10 minutes or until cheese is melted and frankfurters are heated through. Serve in warmed buns.

SWISS PUPPIES

Slash 4 frankfurters diagonally and stuff with slices of process Swiss cheese.

Broil 3 inches from broiling unit until cheese melts. Serve on frankfurter rolls.

STUFFED FRANKFURTER CASSEROLE

1 cup uncooked macaroni
1 cup milk
2 tablespoons diced pimiento
1½ teaspoons salt
1½ teaspoons Worcestershire sauce
1 cup grated cheese
¼ cup pickle relish
¼ cup minced onion
8 frankfurters

Cook macaroni in boiling salted water until tender. Drain.

Combine macaroni, milk, pimiento, salt, Worcestershire sauce, and ¾ cup cheese. Pour into greased, shallow casserole.

Combine pickle relish and chopped onion. Slit frankfurters lengthwise but do not cut all the way through. Fill frankfurters with relish mixture, top with remaining cheese and place on macaroni.

Bake in moderate oven (350°F.) 25 minutes. Serves 6 to 8.

FRANKFURTER, APPLE AND CHEESE BAKE

8 frankfurters
3 tart apples, peeled and thinly sliced
¼ cup granulated or brown sugar
½ cup grated American cheese

Put the frankfurters in a layer in baking dish. Spread lightly with mustard.

Cover with apple slices. Sprinkle with sugar and bake in moderate oven (350°F.) about 20 minutes.

Sprinkle with cheese and bake or broil until cheese melts. Serves 4.

SKILLET FRANKS

1 pound frankfurters
2 tablespoons butter or margarine
¼ cup ketchup
1 tablespoon prepared mustard
9 to 10 frankfurt buns

Fry franks in butter in heavy skillet until browned.

Combine ketchup and mustard and pour over franks. Turn franks to coat well with sauce. Heat 2 or 3 minutes. Serve frank in a split bun. Serves 6 to 8.

FRANKFURTERS IN TOMATO YEAST ROLLS

1 package roll mix
Tomato juice
½ cup grated Parmesan cheese
1 tablespoon chopped parsley
12 frankfurters
2 tablespoons melted butter or margarine

Prepare roll mix according to directions on package, substituting tomato juice for liquid required.

Roll into 12-inch circle and sprinkle with grated cheese and chopped parsley.

Cut into 12 pie-shaped pieces and roll a frankfurter in each piece, rolling from wide edge of dough.

Brush with melted butter or margarine and bake in hot oven (400°F.) for 15 to 20 minutes. Serves 12.

Frankfurters In Tomato Yeast Rolls

Quick and Easy Poultry Recipes

CHICKEN CASSEROLE

1 package frozen chicken à la king
½ cup light cream
¼ pound sliced mushrooms
2 tablespoons butter or margarine
3 tablespoons sherry
¼ pound process Cheddar cheese, sliced

In saucepan over low heat, heat frozen chicken à la king with cream 20 minutes, stirring often to prevent sticking.

In skillet, sauté mushrooms in butter 5 minutes, or until tender. Add, with sherry, to chicken.

Pour into 10 x 6 x 2-inch baking dish; top with cheese; broil a few seconds in a preheated broiler. Serve on toast points. Serves 4.

BAKED CHICKEN PUFF

1 can (1¼ cups) condensed cream of mushroom soup
⅓ cup milk
1 cup cubed cooked chicken
2 cups cooked green beans, drained
4 eggs, separated
¼ cup shredded American cheese

Combine soup and milk in 1½-quart casserole; add chicken and beans. Bake in moderate oven (375°F.) 10 minutes.

Meanwhile, beat egg yolks well; add cheese. Beat egg whites until stiff and fold into egg-cheese mixture.

Pile fluffy egg topping on hot chicken; continue baking 30 minutes. Serves 6.

Baked Beef Puff: Follow recipe for Baked Chicken Puff, except use 1 can of condensed cream of celery soup instead of mushroom, cooked beef instead of chicken, and cooked, diced carrots instead of green beans.

Baked Tuna Puff: Follow recipe for Baked Chicken Puff, except use 1 7-ounce can (1 cup) flaked tuna instead of chicken, and cooked green peas instead of beans.

For whole meal sandwiches in casseroles: place ½ inch thick, oblong slices of whole wheat bread on a baking sheet in moderate oven (350° F.) and bake until crisp and toasted. Then place a slice of toast in a shallow casserole, cover with slice of cooked turkey, then a crisp, cooked bacon slice. Cover all with about ⅓ cup thick, well seasoned cheese sauce. Bake in moderate oven (350° F.) until cheese is bubbly, 15 to 20 minutes. Serve at once.

CHICKEN-IN-CREAM POTATO PIE

1 tablespoon butter or margarine
3 cups thick seasoned mashed potato
1½ cups creamed chicken, or 1 can chicken à la king
Salt, pepper, and Ac'cent to taste

Spread butter over inside of 8-inch pie plate or pan. Spread 2 cups of mashed potato over bottom and sides of pan. Build up edge slightly.

Season creamed chicken mixture with salt, pepper, and Ac'cent to taste.

Pour into potato-lined pan. Put remaining potato through pastry bag to make a fluted edge and to decorate top.

Place in moderate oven (375°F.) 25 to 30 minutes until heated through and bubbly hot. Serves 4 to 6.

CHICKEN TETRAZZINI

2 cups narrow noodles (¼ pound)
¼ pound sliced mushrooms
3 tablespoons butter or margarine
1 14- or 16-ounce can chicken fricassee
1 tablespoon sherry
3 tablespoons grated Parmesan cheese

Cook noodles in boiling salted water until tender; drain.

Meanwhile, sauté mushrooms in butter until tender. Add fricassee; heat quickly; don't simmer or stir. Stir in sherry.

Placed drained noodles in 10 x 6 x 2-inch baking dish. Pour fricassee into center. Sprinkle with Parmesan cheese; broil until golden in preheated broiler. Serves 2 to 3.

CHICKEN ALMONDINE

1 14- or 16-ounce can chicken fricassee
¼ cup slivered almonds
⅛ teaspoon salt

Heat fricassee quickly; don't simmer or stir. Stir in almonds and salt with a fork. Serves 2 or 3.

Chicken-in-Cream Potato Pie

CHICKEN PAPRIKA

1 sliced onion
2 tablespoons butter or margarine
1 14- or 16-ounce can chicken fricassee
½ cup sour cream
½ teaspoon paprika

Sauté onion in butter until tender. Add fricassee. Heat quickly; don't simmer or stir.

With fork, stir in sour cream and paprika. Heat. Serves 2 or 3.

SPAGHETTI-POULTRY CASSEROLE

Top a casserole of plain cooked spaghetti with a jar of sliced turkey or chicken.

Cover with a can of cream of mushroom soup and bake in a moderate oven (350°F.) 25 minutes.

BAKED CHICKEN SALAD

2 5-ounce cans boned chicken, coarsely cut up (1½ cups)
1½ cups sliced celery
½ cup chopped walnuts
½ teaspoon salt
Dash of pepper
2 teaspoons minced onion
2 tablespoons lemon juice
¾ cup mayonnaise
1 cup crushed potato chips

Combine all ingredients except potato chips; toss lightly.

Heap into 4 individual baking dishes or 9-inch deep pie plate. Crush potato chips; sprinkle over all.

Bake in very hot oven (450°F.) 15 minutes, or until lightly browned. Serves 4.

CHICKEN CURRY

1 cup diced onion
¼ cup diced green pepper
2 tablespoons lemon juice
½ cup tomato sauce
1 clove garlic, crushed
1 can boneless chicken fricassee
¼ teaspoon curry powder

Dice onion and green pepper. Add lemon juice, tomato sauce, and crushed garlic clove. Simmer together until sauce has cooked down almost dry.

Cut chicken into bite-size pieces. Add chicken and gravy to sauce. Season with curry and heat thoroughly. Serves 4.

*Chicken Fricassee
in Green Bean and Rice Ring*

CHICKEN FRICASSEE IN GREEN BEAN AND RICE RING

1   cup uncooked rice
2¼ cups water
1   teaspoon salt
¼   teaspoon Ac'cent
1   No. 2 can (1 pound) cut green beans
¼   teaspoon Ac'cent
1   No. 2 can chicken fricassee
¼   teaspoon Ac'cent
Salt to taste

Cook rice with water, salt, and ¼ teaspoon Ac'cent until tender and all water is absorbed. Spoon a layer of rice into bottom of well oiled 8-inch ring mold.

Heat beans in their liquid with Ac'cent. Use remaining rice and hot green beans alternately to fill mold level full.

Place in moderate oven (350°F.) to heat through.

Heat chicken in saucepan. Turn mold out upside-down on hot platter. Fill center with hot chicken mixture. Serves 4 to 5.

CHICKEN CURRY FREDONA

1   can (1¼ cups) condensed cream of chicken soup
1   6-ounce can evaporated milk
½   cup chicken broth
1   teaspoon curry powder
3   6-ounce cans boned chicken or turkey, cut into large pieces
½   teaspoon chopped ginger
1   6-ounce can mushrooms
½   cup shredded coconut
2   cans chow mein noodles

Combine soup, milk, broth, and curry powder.

Heat combined liquids in chafing dish pan over low heat, stirring until blended.

Add chicken, ginger, mushrooms and coconut. Heat through.

Serve over heated noodles with condiment tray of chopped peanuts, pickled peaches and shredded coconut.

Serves 6.

CHICKEN À LA SHERMAN

1   8-ounce can or 14-ounce package quick-frozen chicken à la king
½   cup cooked ham
Lightly cooked asparagus tips
Butter or margarine
Breadcrumbs

To an 8-ounce can or a 14-ounce package of quick-frozen chicken à la king, add ham cut into small squares. Heat.

Place in a shallow oven-proof casserole or heat-proof glass pie dish. Top with lightly cooked asparagus tips. Dot with butter. Sprinkle with breadcrumbs and set under the broiler just long enough to brown crumbs.

Serve bubbling hot from the casserole. This same combination may also be placed on buttered toast. Serves 4.

CRUNCHY CHICKEN CASSEROLE

1   can condensed cream of chicken soup
½   cup milk
1   cup cubed cooked chicken
1¼ cups corn flakes
1   cup unsalted cooked lima beans, drained

Empty soup into a small casserole. Add milk and mix thoroughly.

Add chicken, 1 cup corn flakes, and beans. Stir well.

Sprinkle top with remaining corn flakes.

Bake in moderate oven (375°F.) 25 minutes. Serves 4.

CHICKEN CASSEROLE

Turn 1 can of chicken à la king into greased casserole. Top with 1 package frozen spinach or broccoli, cooked and seasoned, and grated Parmesan cheese.

Bake in moderate oven (375°F.) 15 to 20 minutes. Serves 2 to 3.

QUICK CHICKEN CHOW MEIN

2   cans (1 pound each) chicken chop suey
1   tablespoon brown sugar
1   tablespoon vinegar
1   can (4-, 5-, or 6-ounce) boned chicken, cut in strips
2   3-ounce cans chow mein noodles
Soy sauce

Carefully combine chop suey, brown sugar, vinegar, and chicken in medium-sized saucepan, reserving a few strips of chicken for garnish. Heat, stirring gently.

Place chow mein noodles in shallow baking pan; heat in moderate oven (375°F.) 5 minutes.

Serve piping hot over heated chow mein noodles; pass soy sauce. Serves 4 to 5 generously.

CHICKEN RABBIT

1   package frozen broccoli
1   12-ounce jar Welsh rabbit
1½ cups hot chicken bouillon
1   12-ounce can chicken or turkey
1   cup cooked, diced celery

Cook broccoli according to the directions on the package. Drain and reserve liquid for soup.

Arrange broccoli in a greased baking dish. Place the Welsh rabbit in the top of a double boiler over boiling water. Add the chicken bouillon and stir until the mixture is well blended.

Cut chicken into 1-inch pieces and add with the celery to the rabbit. Pour over the broccoli and bake in a moderate oven (350°F.) about 15 minutes or until thoroughly heated. Serves 4.

CHICKEN À LA KING ON CORN WAFFLES

1   package waffle mix (see note below)
1   12-ounce can whole kernel corn, chopped
2   11-ounce packages frozen chicken à la king or 2½ cups canned
1   cup canned peas

Mix waffles according to the directions on the package. Add corn to the batter and bake as directed.

Heat chicken à la king in the top of a double boiler; add peas and serve over the hot waffles. Serves 6.

Note: Biscuit or pancake mix may be used. Follow directions for waffles given on package.

CORN AND CHICKEN BAKE

2   cups diced cooked or canned chicken
1   cup crushed potato chips
1   (No. 2) can cream-style corn
1½ cups milk
Few grains pepper
¾   teaspoon Ac'cent
2   beaten eggs

Combine all ingredients; pour into casserole; top with additional crushed potato chips if desired.

Set casserole in pan of warm water. Bake in slow oven (325°F.) until knife inserted comes out clean, about 1 hour. Serves 6.

Quick Chicken Chow Mein

Chicken Livers and Giblets

CREAMED CHICKEN LIVERS

Drop chicken livers into boiling chicken stock to cover; reduce heat and simmer until tender, about 6 to 8 minutes.

Drain and add them to medium white sauce made with part rich milk or cream and part chicken stock. Use about half as much sauce as there are livers.

Season with about 1 tablespoon sherry and salt and pepper to taste. Serve with scrambled eggs, rice, or on toast.

GIBLETS AND NOODLES

1 pound chicken giblets
1 teaspoon salt
4 cups water
1 package chicken-noodle soup mix
2 cups uncooked egg noodles

Simmer giblets in salted water until tender. Cool; remove meat, and slice.

Measure stock to 4 cups, adding water, if necessary. Add soup mix and noodles; cook for 10 minutes. Add giblets; simmer few minutes. Serves 4 to 6.

CHICKEN LIVER SAUTÉ

1 pound fresh or thawed frozen chicken livers
¼ cup butter or margarine
1 minced small onion (optional)
¼ cup flour
2 cups water
1 teaspoon salt
Sherry to taste, or 2 teaspoons bottled thick meat sauce

Cut livers in half. In butter in skillet, sauté livers and onion over low heat, turning often, about 5 minutes. Remove livers.

Stir flour into fat; gradually stir in water; cook, stirring, until thickened. Add salt, sherry, and livers. Serve on toast or toasted English muffins. Serves 4.

Liver-Mushroom Sauté: Sauté few sliced mushrooms with livers.

Curried Liver Sauté: Substitute curry to taste for sherry.

Chicken Liver Sauté with Rice

FRICASSEED GIBLETS

Chicken giblets including livers
¼ cup chopped green pepper
¼ cup chopped celery
2 tablespoons butter or margarine
2 tablespoons flour
1 cup stock
Salt and pepper

Simmer the giblets in slightly salted water to cover until tender. Add the chicken livers, green pepper, and celery for the last 15 minutes.

When cooked, drain and reserve the stock.

Melt butter or margarine and stir in flour, mixing until smooth. Gradually pour in the stock; stir until mixture boils and thickens, then cook about 3 minutes longer, stirring occasionally. Season to taste.

Add the giblets and reheat. Serve on toast. Makes about 1½ cups.

CHICKEN LIVERS SUPREME

1 cup uncooked rice
2 tablespoons butter or margarine
1 pound chicken livers, fresh or frozen
1 3-ounce can mushroom slices
1 10½-ounce can mushroom soup
⅓ cup milk
Dash of pepper
Few sprigs parsley
2 tablespoons white wine
¼ cup chopped toasted almonds

Cook rice until tender according to package directions. Drain off any excess liquid.

Melt butter or margarine in a skillet; toss in chicken livers and brown quickly.

Add mushrooms and mushroom liquid, mushroom soup, milk, pepper, chopped parsley, and wine. Cook until hot and smooth, then mix with rice.

Pour into 2-quart casserole; top with almonds and bake in moderate oven (350°F.) 30 minutes. Serves 4 to 6.

CHICKEN LIVERS WITH OLIVES IN WINE SAUCE

1 pound chicken livers
¼ cup butter or margarine
3 tablespoons flour
1 cup chicken broth or bouillon
⅓ cup sherry
½ teaspoon salt
⅛ teaspoon pepper
⅓ cup sliced stuffed olives

Rinse chicken livers; remove gall spots, drain and dry.

Sauté livers in hot butter in chafing dish over direct heat until nicely browned, turning frequently; remove from pan.

Blend in flour. Gradually add broth, sherry, and seasonings. Cook and stir until thickened and smooth.

Add livers and olives to sauce. Heat to piping hot. Serve at once on hot cooked noodles or rice. Serves 4.

CHICKEN LIVERS WITH PINEAPPLE AND PEPPERS

4 slices canned or fresh pineapple
2 medium green peppers, slivered
2 tablespoons oil or drippings
1 pound chicken livers
½ teaspoon salt
Dash of pepper
1 cup chicken broth or bouillon
2 tablespoons cornstarch
2 teaspoons soy sauce
½ cup wine vinegar
½ cup sugar

Sauté pineapple (cut each slice in 6 pieces) and peppers in oil until peppers are slightly soft. Don't allow them to brown.

Remove from pan and add livers with salt and pepper. When livers are lightly browned and tender, remove to hot platter.

Mix cornstarch to paste with a little of broth; add remaining broth, soy sauce, vinegar, and sugar.

Add to skillet in which livers were browned. Cook and stir until sauce thickens and is clear.

Add peppers and pineapple. Heat thoroughly and pour over livers. Serve with rice. Serves 4.

CHICKEN LIVERS EN CASSEROLE

1 pound chicken livers
¼ cup butter or margarine
¼ teaspoon ground black pepper
1 large bay leaf, crumbled
1 tablespoon instant minced onion
1 4-ounce can mushroom crowns, drained
1 can (1 pound) stewed tomatoes, slightly drained
1 10-ounce package frozen mixed vegetables
1½ cups chicken-flavored cracker crumbs, finely rolled

Sauté chicken livers in butter or margarine. Add remaining ingredients, reserving 2 tablespoons cracker crumbs for topping. Mix well.

Cook over medium heat 5 minutes, stirring constantly. Pour into a 1½-quart casserole. Bake in moderate oven (350°F.) 1 hour. Serves 4.

Chicken Livers En Casserole

Curried Chicken Livers

CURRIED CHICKEN LIVERS

1 pound fresh or thawed frozen
    chicken livers
4 tablespoons butter or margarine
1/4 cup minced onion
1 teaspoon salt
1/4 teaspoon pepper
1 tablespoon curry powder
2/3 cup beer or ale
Hot cooked rice

Cut chicken livers in halves. Melt butter in skillet or chafing dish. Add livers and onion and sauté 5 to 8 minutes, turning often, until livers are cooked.

Add salt, pepper, curry powder, and beer and bring to a simmer; continue cooking over low heat 3 minutes longer. Serve over rice. Serves 4.

SAVORY CHICKEN LIVERS WITH RICE

3 tablespoons butter or margarine
1 pound chicken livers
Salt and pepper to taste
1/8 teaspoon rosemary
1/2 cup white wine
Fluffy cooked rice

Melt butter; when bubbling, add chicken livers and season with salt, pepper, and rosemary. Cook until well browned, stirring occasionally.

Add wine and simmer 10 minutes. Serve over rice. Serves 4.

CHICKEN LIVERS WITH FINE HERBS (Appetizer)

1 pound chicken livers
1 tablespoon minced onion
1 tablespoon chopped parsley
1/2 teaspoon salt
Dash of pepper
1/2 teaspoon Ac'cent
1/2 teaspoon crushed oregano
2 tablespoons olive oil
Flour as needed
Shortening, oil, or butter as needed
Few crystals Ac'cent
Minced parsley as needed

Remove gall spots completely; wash livers; drain well.

Combine all ingredients; pour over livers. Let stand 1/2 hour to marinate.

Drain livers; roll in flour. Sauté lightly in fat 5 minutes. Place each liver on cocktail pick; arrange on plate; sprinkle with Ac'cent and parsley just before serving. Yield: 1 pound (16 individual portions).

CHICKEN LIVERS AND MUSHROOMS IN WINE SAUCE

1 pound chicken livers, cut in
    halves
16 to 20 mushroom caps, depend-
    ing on size
Melted butter
2 more tablespoons butter
3 tablespoons flour
1 1/2 cups strong chicken broth
1/2 cup dry white wine
Salt and paprika

Brush chicken livers and mushroom caps with melted butter and put under a broiler briefly. The chicken livers will take 5 to 8 minutes, including both sides, and the mushroom caps 3 to 5 minutes.

Arrange 4 or 5 mushroom caps in each of 4 individual au gratin dishes, preferably something pretty like copper. Put 1 piece of chicken liver on each mushroom cap.

Cover with sauce made this way: Melt 2 tablespoons butter; blend in flour and add chicken broth slowly, stirring until thick and smooth. Add the white wine, salt, and paprika and cook until smooth.

Pour over mushrooms and chicken livers and place in moderate oven (350°F.) 10 to 15 minutes, or until hot and bubbly. Serves 4.

CHICKEN LIVERS IN MADEIRA SAUCE

1 pound chicken livers, cut in large
    pieces
3 tablespoons olive oil
1 tablespoon tarragon vinegar
Salt and pepper
1 clove garlic
1/2 cup madeira wine
Pinch of sugar
2 tablespoons butter or margarine
1 1/2 tablespoons flour
3/4 cup chicken stock or broth
Finely shredded or grated rind of 1
    orange

Cover livers with a mixture of olive oil, vinegar, salt, pepper, garlic, 1/4 cup madeira, and sugar. Set in refrigerator overnight.

Drain livers on paper towels. Sauté in butter; transfer livers to a warm plate.

Thicken juices in pan by adding flour mixed with enough water to make a thin paste. Then add chicken stock and 1/4 cup madeira, stirring constantly until smooth and thickened.

Finally, add shredded orange rind. The shredding may be done rather simply by peeling a whole orange with a potato peeler and then chopping it very fine, or it may be grated the usual way.

Serve on freshly buttered toast. Serves 4.

CHICKEN LIVERS FLORENTINE

6 ounces long spaghetti
1/4 cup butter or margarine
1/4 cup chopped green onions (scal-
    lions)
1 small clove garlic, chopped
1/2 pound chicken livers, diced
3 tablespoons flour
1/2 teaspoon salt
Dash freshly ground pepper
1/8 teaspoon oregano
Pinch sweet basil
3/4 cup beef broth or consommé
1/2 cup dry red wine

Cook spaghetti in boiling salted water until tender (about 15 minutes). Drain and rinse.

While spaghetti is cooking, melt butter or margarine in skillet. Add green onions, chopped with some of the green stems, and garlic; brown lightly.

Add chicken livers which have been diced and brown well.

Stir in flour and seasonings. Add broth or consommé and wine and cook until thickened, stirring constantly.

Arrange spaghetti on hot platter and top with chicken liver sauce. Sprinkle lightly with chopped parsley.

Serves 4 to 5.

CRUSTY CHICKEN LIVERS AND MUSHROOMS ON TOAST

12 chicken livers
1 egg, well beaten
2 teaspoons Worcestershire sauce
1 cup biscuit mix
1/4 cup butter or margarine
1 can (10 1/2 ounces) mushrooms in
    brown gravy
2 tablespoons sherry
6 slices toast

Cut chicken livers in half. Beat egg with 1 teaspoon Worcestershire sauce. Dip chicken livers into egg mixture. Roll livers in biscuit mix, coating generously.

Melt butter or margarine in a skillet. Fry livers until golden brown and crisp.

Heat mushroom gravy to the boiling point. Add 1 teaspoon Worcestershire sauce and sherry. Place chicken livers on toast. Spoon gravy over all. Serve with crisp bacon strips and hot applesauce. Serves 6.

Crusty Chicken Livers and
Mushrooms on Toast

Quick and Easy Fish and Shellfish Recipes

QUICK SHRIMP NEWBURG

Blend 1½ tablespoons flour with ⅓ cup cream of shrimp soup (from 1 13-ounce can). Add remaining soup and 2 egg yolks, beaten; cook until thickened, stirring often.

Add 1 5-ounce can shrimp, drained and deveined; heat thoroughly.

Just before serving, add 2 tablespoons sherry; serve in pastry shells, on toast or over hot, seasoned rice.

Serves 3 or 4.

Lobster or Crab Newburg: Use 1 6-ounce can lobster or 1 6½-ounce can crabmeat in place of shrimp.

SALMON-RICE CASSEROLE

1   5-ounce package (1⅓ cups) pre-cooked rice
½ cup milk
½ pound process American cheese, shredded
¾ teaspoon salt
Dash of pepper
1   cup canned salmon, flaked
¼ cup chopped stuffed green olives

Cook rice as directed on package.

Combine milk, cheese, salt, and pepper in top part of double boiler. Heat and stir occasionally until well blended and smooth.

Place in 1½-quart casserole alternate layers of rice, salmon, olives, and cheese sauce, having a top layer of cheese sauce. Bake in moderate oven (350°F.) 30 minutes. Serves 6.

Tuna-Rice Casserole: Substitute 1 cup solid-pack tuna, flaked, for salmon.

SHRIMP CHOP SUEY

2   1-pound cans meatless chop suey
1   5- or 7-ounce can shrimp, drained and deveined
1   3- or 4-ounce can sliced mushrooms
1   tablespoon soy sauce

Carefully combine all ingredients in medium-sized saucepan. Heat, stirring gently.

Serve with hot rice; pass extra soy sauce. Serves 4.

Creamed Seafood with Wine

SALMON AND POTATO BAKE

4   tablespoons butter or margarine
2   tablespoons cornstarch
2½ cups milk
1   medium onion, chopped fine
1   teaspoon salt
¼ teaspoon pepper
1   tablespoon minced green pepper
4   cups thinly sliced raw potatoes
1   can (1 pound) salmon, flaked
1   cup crushed potato chips

Melt butter and blend in cornstarch. Add milk, onion, salt, pepper, and green pepper. Cook, stirring constantly, until thickened.

Place alternate layers of potatoes, salmon with liquid from can, and sauce in greased casserole.

Cover, and bake in moderate oven (350°F.) about 20 minutes. Remove cover and sprinkle with potato chips. Bake until potatoes are tender, about 25 minutes. Serves 6.

JIFFY LOBSTER THERMIDOR

1   can condensed cream of mushroom soup
¼ can white wine or ¼ can water
1   tablespoon lemon juice
4   tablespoons grated Parmesan or Romano cheese
Pinch of dry mustard or ½ teaspoon prepared mustard
2   to 3 cups cooked or canned lobster meat

To a can of condensed cream of mushroom soup, add white wine or water, lemon juice, grated cheese, and mustard.

Heat in top of double boiler and add lobster meat, cut into good-sized cubes.

Place in shallow buttered casserole or in lobster shells. Sprinkle with cheese and bake in very hot oven (450°F.) 15 minutes or set under the broiler about 5 minutes until cheese melts and slightly browns.

Serve bubbling hot and serve from shells or baking dish. Serves 4 to 6.

CREAMED SEAFOOD WITH WINE

¼ cup cream
1   medium-sized can of tuna, salmon, shrimp, or crab
1   can (10½ ounces) condensed cream of mushroom soup
2   tablespoons sherry

Add cream and coarsely flaked seafood to soup and heat gently over direct heat or over hot water.

Add wine, reheat and serve on hot buttered toast. Serves 4.

JIFFY SHRIMP JAMBALAYA

2   tablespoons butter, margarine, or shortening
⅔ cup chopped celery
½ cup minced onion
½ cup chopped green pepper
2   tablespoons enriched flour
4   tablespoons tomato paste
1¾ cups water
1   teaspoon salt
Dash of pepper
2   7-ounce cans shrimp
2   cups cooked rice

Melt butter in a skillet; add celery, onion, and green pepper and cook until tender.

Stir in flour and gradually pour in tomato paste and water mixed together. Add seasoning and cook 5 minutes longer, stirring constantly.

Add shrimp and heat thoroughly. Serve over rice. Serves 6.

SHRIMP AND CRABMEAT CASSEROLE

1   medium green pepper, chopped
1   medium onion, chopped
1   cup chopped celery
1   6½-ounce can crabmeat, flaked
1   7-ounce can shrimp, cleaned
½ teaspoon salt
⅛ teaspoon pepper
1   teaspoon Worcestershire sauce
1   cup mayonnaise
1   cup buttered crumbs

Combine all ingredients except crumbs. Turn into buttered casserole or individual ramekins.

Sprinkle with crumbs. Bake in moderate oven (350°F.) 30 minutes. Serves 6 to 8.

NOODLE SHRIMP CURRY

8   ounces medium egg noodles
1   cup condensed cream of celery soup
3   tablespoons ketchup
½ teaspoon paprika
1   teaspoon curry powder
⅛ teaspoon ginger
1   pound fresh or quick-frozen shrimp (cooked and cleaned)

Cook noodles in 3 quarts boiling salted water (1 tablespoon salt). Drain in colander.

Combine soup, ketchup, paprika, curry powder, and ginger; mix thoroughly. Cook over low heat 5 minutes, stirring occasionally. Add shrimp; heat thoroughly.

Turn cooked noodles into heated serving bowl; top with shrimp curry.

Serve with accompaniments such as pickled onions, chutney, sieved or chopped hard-cooked eggs, chopped or whole peanuts, grated fresh coconut, or crumbled crisp bacon. Serves 4.

Quick and Easy Rice and Pasta Recipes

EASY MACARONI AND CHEESE

1. Melt ½ pound of natural Cheddar cheese in top of double boiler.

2. When cheese is melted, slowly add a large can (13 liquid ounces) of evaporated milk, stirring constantly.

Add 1 teaspoon salt and ⅛ teaspoon pepper to cheese sauce.

3. Place 1 8-ounce package elbow macaroni (which has been cooked until tender in boiling salted water, and drained) in 1½-quart casserole.

Pour cheese sauce over macaroni and mix lightly.

Mix 1½ cups coarse soft breadcrumbs, lightly packed with 1 tablespoon melted margarine or butter, and sprinkle over top of macaroni.

4. Bake in moderate oven (350°F.) 25 minutes. Serve at once. Serves 6.

NOODLE-SAUSAGE SKILLET MEAL

½ 8-ounce package (about 2 cups) noodles
1 pound tiny link sausages
1 cup cooked peas, canned or frozen
1½ cups canned tomato juice
1 teaspoon salt
¼ teaspoon pepper

Cook noodles in boiling, salted water until tender. Drain.

Brown sausages over low heat; pour off any excess fat.

Add noodles, peas, tomato juice, and seasonings. Simmer, uncovered, 15 minutes, stirring occasionally. Serves 6.

TOMATO CHEESE MACARONI

1 can (1¼ cups) condensed tomato soup
½ cup milk
2 cups shredded sharp American cheese
¼ cup finely chopped parsley
4 cups cooked macaroni (2 cups uncooked)
2 tablespoons buttered breadcrumbs, if desired

Heat soup, milk, and 1½ cups cheese over low heat; when cheese melts, add parsley. Blend with macaroni; pour into a buttered 2-quart casserole.

Top with remaining cheese and buttered breadcrumbs. Bake in hot oven (400°F.) 20 minutes. Serves 6.

CHILI RICE MEXICALI

2 tablespoons butter or margarine
1 teaspoon chili powder
1 package pre-cooked rice
1½ cups cold water
2 tablespoons shortening
1 medium onion, sliced
1 green pepper, diced
1 No. 2 can kidney beans
2 tomatoes, diced
1 12-ounce can whole kernel corn
2 tablespoons chili powder
Salt and pepper to taste
1 teaspoon Ac'cent
½ pound sharp Cheddar cheese, grated

Melt butter or margarine; blend in 1 teaspoon chili powder. Add rice and cold water. Bring to a full boil, fluffing rice occasionally with fork. Boil 2 minutes. Remove from heat; cover, let stand 10 minutes.

Meanwhile melt shortening; cook onion and green pepper in shortening until soft but not brown.

Add beans, tomatoes, corn, and seasonings; mix well. Add cheese; stir over low heat until cheese melts.

Pack hot rice into ring mold; invert on serving plate. Fill center with bean mixture. Garnish with fried banana quarters. Serves 6.

MACARONI AND CHILI DE LUXE

1 tablespoon salt
3 quarts boiling water
2 cups elbow macaroni (8 ounces)
3 tablespoons butter or margarine
½ cup diced green pepper
2 medium-sized onions, thinly sliced
1 15½-ounce can chili con carne with beans
¾ cup tomato juice

Add 1 tablespoon salt to rapidly boiling water. Gradually add macaroni so that water continues to boil. Cook uncovered, stirring occasionally, until tender. Drain in colander.

Melt butter or margarine over medium heat; add green pepper and onions and sauté until tender.

Add macaroni, chili, and tomato juice; mix well. Cook over low heat until thoroughly heated, stirring occasionally. Serves 4 to 6.

SPAGHETTI CASSEROLE DE LUXE

4 tablespoons butter or margarine
3 tablespoons flour
1 teaspoon salt
⅛ teaspoon pepper
1 cup milk
1 cup chicken broth or vegetable stock
4 cups cooked spaghetti
½ pound fresh mushrooms, sliced
1 cup diced, cooked chicken
½ cup grated Parmesan cheese

Melt butter in saucepan. Stir in flour and seasonings. Add milk and stock gradually, stirring constantly to prevent lumping. Let come to boil and cook 3 minutes.

Place spaghetti in buttered casserole. Scatter mushrooms and chicken over it. Pour sauce over all. Sprinkle cheese on top.

Bake in slow oven (325°F.) until mushrooms are tender (about 30 minutes). Serves 6.

Variations: Veal or tuna fish may be substituted for chicken.

If canned mushrooms are used, bake just until cheese is melted and mixture heated through.

If stock is not available, use 1 bouillon cube with 1 cup hot water.

Chili Rice Mexicali

Quick and Easy Cheese Recipes

EASY SWISS FONDUE

1 pound Swiss cheese
¾ cup white wine
Hot toast or bread sticks

Cut the cheese in small pieces. Place in top of double boiler or in a chafing dish over hot water.

Add wine; heat and stir until cheese melts and the mixture is smooth.

Serve with hot toast, long bread sticks, or chunks of French bread. Serves 4.

Variation: Omit wine. Use ¼ cup butter or margarine; season with ½ teaspoon salt and ⅛ teaspoon white pepper.

MONTEREY JACK

4 slices bacon, diced
1 medium onion, sliced
1 green pepper, diced
2 No. 2 cans red kidney beans
3 tomatoes, diced
2 tablespoons chili powder
½ teaspoon salt
Few grains pepper
1 teaspoon Ac'cent
½ pound sharp Cheddar cheese, grated

Fry bacon crisp; drain on absorbent paper.

Cook onion and green pepper in 2 tablespoons of the bacon fat until soft but not brown.

Add kidney beans, tomatoes, bacon, seasonings, and cheese. Stir over low heat until cheese melts. Serves 8.

Note: One pound dried kidney beans soaked overnight and cooked until tender may be used instead of canned beans.

BROILED TOMATOES AND CHEESE TOAST

4 large tomatoes
½ teaspoon salt
1 teaspoon sugar
1 tablespoon butter or margarine
4 slices bread
¼ to ½ pound American cheese, sliced thin
12 dill pickle slices

Cut tomatoes in half and sprinkle with salt and sugar; dot with butter or margarine.

Remove broiler pan and preheat broiler for 5 minutes. Place tomatoes on rack of broiling pan. Broil slowly for 6 minutes; place slices of bread on rack and toast on one side.

Turn bread over and top with cheese slices. Continue broiling tomatoes and cheese toast for for 3 to 5 minutes until tomatoes are tender and cheese melts.

Remove from broiler; cut cheese toast diagonally into quarters. Serve all on platter, with 4 of the tomato halves placed on the cheese toast and topped with pickle slices. Serves 4.

CHEESE FONDUE

1½ cups scalded milk
1½ cups bread cubes, tightly packed
¼ pound American cheese, diced
1 tablespoon butter or margarine
½ teaspoon salt
¼ teaspoon mustard
2 eggs, separated

Mix scalded milk with bread cubes, cheese, butter, salt, and mustard.

Beat egg yolks until lemon colored; blend cheese mixture into egg yolks.

Beat egg whites until stiff and fold into first mixture.

Pour into an oiled baking dish, 9 inches in diameter. Bake in moderate oven (350°F.) 20 to 30 minutes, or until set. Serve immediately. Serves 4 to 5.

SPIEDANO ROMANO

1 loaf unsliced white bread
½ cup margarine or butter
¼ cup finely minced or grated onion
¼ cup prepared mustard
1 tablespoon poppy seeds
½ pound sliced process Swiss cheese
½ teaspoon Ac'cent
2 or 3 slices bacon, cut in half

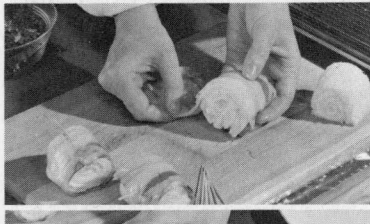

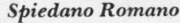

Spiedano Romano

Remove all crusts from bread. Make regular diagonal cuts about 1½ inches apart, but do not cut completely through loaf.

Soften margarine or butter; blend in onion, mustard, and poppy seeds. Spread all but 2 tablespoons of mixture between cuts.

Fill cuts with cheese, sprinkling each cheese slice with Ac'cent. Press loaf together. Spread outside and over top with reserved mixture. Arrange bacon on top.

Place in greased shallow baking dish. Bake in moderate oven (350°F.) until cheese is melted and loaf is browned, about 15 minutes. Serve at once.

Serves 4 to 6.

Note: If the loaf of bread is sliced, discard the heels; trim off crusts and spread some of the butter mixture on each slice. Top with cheese; sprinkle with Ac'cent.

As you go along, press slices together in buttered loaf pan to make a bread-loaf shape. Put bacon or anchovy butter on top, as you prefer; bake as directed.

BACON PINWHEELS

Trim the crusts from a fresh loaf of white bread and cut ¼-inch lengthwise slices. Spread each slice with cream cheese which has softened at room temperature.

Roll up each slice like a jelly roll. Cut each roll in half crosswise, and wrap a slice of bacon around each pinwheel, fastening it with a toothpick.

Place the pinwheels on a broiler rack, and toast them under moderate broiler heat, turning often until the bacon is cooked.

Arrange the pinwheels on a chop plate and serve with stuffed olives.

Bacon Pinwheels

Pressure Cooked Recipes

SPAGHETTI MEAT SAUCE

2 tablespoons salad oil
1 pound ground beef
4 or 5 medium onions, sliced
3 or 4 cloves garlic, chopped
1 8-ounce can tomato sauce
2 6-ounce cans tomato paste
1/2 teaspoon red pepper
1 tablespoon chili powder
1 teaspoon salt
Dash of pepper
2 cups water

Combine all ingredients in pressure pan. Adjust cover. Exhaust air from cooker. Cook at 15-pound pressure 20 minutes.

Reduce pressure quickly. Serve over cooked spaghetti (one 8-ounce package long spaghetti). Top with grated Parmesan cheese. Serves 6.

CHICKEN FRICASSEE

1 2- to 3-pound ready-to-cook chicken, cut in pieces, or 2 1-pound packages frozen chicken pieces
1/4 cup fat
1 cup water
2 small onions, sliced
2 bay leaves
1/4 cup chopped celery leaves
2 teaspoons salt
Dash of pepper
Milk
1/3 cup enriched flour
1/2 teaspoon salt
1/4 teaspoon Kitchen Bouquet

Roll chicken in seasoned flour (2 teaspoons salt and 2 teaspoons paprika to 1/2 cup flour). Brown in hot fat in pressure cooker.

Add water, onions, bay leaves, celery leaves, 2 teaspoons salt, and pepper. Cook at 15-pound pressure 35 minutes.

Allow pressure to go down normally. Remove chicken. Strain broth; add milk to make 3 cups.

Mix 1 cup of the liquid with flour until blended. Add remaining liquid. Return to pressure pan. Cook, stirring constantly, until gravy is thick.

Add 1/2 teaspoon salt and Kitchen Bouquet. Pour over chicken.

Serves 4 to 6.

Chicken Fricassee

QUICK SAUERBRATEN

3 pounds rolled rump or chuck pot roast
1/3 cup grape jelly
2 large onions, cut in 1/4-inch slices
6 whole black peppers
2 bay leaves, crushed
2 teaspoons salt
1/2 teaspoon allspice
1/2 teaspoon ginger
1/4 teaspoon pepper
1/3 cup vinegar
1/4 cup water
1 teaspoon Kitchen Bouquet

Trim excess fat from meat and fry the fat lightly in pressure pan.

Brown meat slowly on all sides in the hot fat. Allow 10 to 20 minutes for browning.

Spread with grape jelly; top with onion slices and sprinkle with seasonings.

Combine vinegar, water, and Kitchen Bouquet; pour over meat.

Cook at 15-pound pressure 40 to 45 minutes. Allow pressure to go down normally. Serves 6 to 8.

PORCUPINE MEAT BALLS

1 1/2 pounds ground beef
1/2 cup rice
1 teaspoon salt
1/2 teaspoon pepper
1 tablespoon chopped onion
1 10 1/2- or 11-ounce can condensed tomato soup
1/2 cup water

Combine meat, rice, salt, pepper, and onion. Form in small balls.

Blend soup and water; heat in pressure cooker until mixture begins to simmer.

Add meat balls. Cook at 15-pound pressure 10 minutes.

Allow the pressure to go down normally. Serves 4 to 6.

TEXAS CHILI CON CARNE

1 pound ground beef
1 No. 2 can (2 1/2 cups) tomatoes
1 1-pound can (2 cups) chili beans
1 cup sliced onion
1/4 cup chopped green pepper
1 clove garlic, minced
2 bay leaves
1 tablespoon flour
1 tablespoon chili powder
1 tablespoon brown sugar
1 teaspoon salt
1 teaspoon ground oregano
1/2 teaspoon basil
Dash of cayenne

Combine all ingredients. Cook at 15-pound pressure 15 minutes. Let pressure go down normally. Serves 6 to 8.

Lamb Shanks in Wine Sauce

LAMB SHANKS IN WINE SAUCE

4 lamb shanks
Flour
Salt and pepper
3 tablespoons salad oil
1 clove garlic, cut in half
1 carrot quartered
1 onion, chopped
1 stalk celery and leaves, chopped
3 tablespoons chopped parsley
1 bay leaf
1 cup red wine
3/4 cup water

Flour the lamb shanks lightly; season with salt and pepper. Brown on all sides in hot oil.

Add remaining ingredients plus 3/4 cup of water.

Cover and cook at 15-pound pressure for 30 minutes. Reduce pressure immediately.

Thicken gravy with 1 tablespoon flour blended with 2 tablespoons cold water. Serves 4.

CHICKEN VESUVIO (Italian)

2 tablespoons butter or margarine
2 medium onions, minced
1 green pepper, chopped
1 clove garlic, minced
1 tablespoon minced parsley
1/2 cup tomato paste
1 cup dry wine
1 teaspoon salt
3- to 4-pound chicken
1/4 cup seedless raisins

Brown vegetables in butter in pressure cooker. Add tomato paste, wine, and salt.

Cut chicken into serving pieces; place in sauce and cook 40 minutes at 15-pound pressure.

Reduce pressure at once and remove chicken bones, leaving the meat in the sauce.

Add raisins and cook 5 minutes more at 15-pound pressure. Serve with cooked spaghetti or rice. Serves 6.

Texas Chili Con Carne

NEW ENGLAND BOILED DINNER

1½ pounds ham shank
1 cup water
4 small potatoes, halved
4 small onions
1 small rutabaga or turnip, sliced
4 medium carrots
1 small cabbage, quartered
⅛ teaspoon pepper

Place ham and water in cooker. Adjust cover and exhaust all air from cooker according to directions for cooker. Cook 20 minutes at 15-pound pressure. Reduce pressure rapidly.

Open cooker, add vegetables and pepper. Do not fill cooker over ⅔ full.

Return cooker to stove. Adjust cover and exhaust all air from cooker. Cook at 15-pound pressure 5 to 8 minutes, depending on size of vegetables. Cool cooker at once. Serves 4.

TENDERLOINS IN SOUR CREAM

2 pork tenderloins
2 tablespoons butter or margarine
1 small onion, minced
1 pint sour cream

Cut tenderloins in 4 pieces each; flatten by pounding.

Brown in butter in pressure cooker, frying onion slightly toward end of browning period.

Pour in sour cream. Cover and cook 25 minutes at 15-pound pressure.

Serves 4 to 6.

LAMB OR VEAL CURRY

1½ pounds veal or lamb
4 tablespoons flour, seasoned
4 tablespoons fat or cooking oil
1 large onion, sliced
1½ teaspoons curry powder
2 tablespoons lemon juice
2 cups tomato juice
1 tablespoon cornstarch
¼ cup water

Cut veal into serving pieces and roll in seasoned flour.

Heat cooker and add fat. Brown meat. Add onions and cook until limp. Add curry powder, lemon juice, and tomato juice. Mix well.

Adjust cover and exhaust all air from

Lamb or Veal Curry

cooker. Cook 15 minutes at 15-pound pressure. Cool cooker gradually.

Thicken with a paste made from cornstarch and water. Serve on a bed of rice. Serves 4 to 6.

HAWAIIAN CHICKEN

4 tablespoons salad oil
1 onion, minced
½ cup thinly sliced celery
½ cup sliced fresh or canned mushrooms
1 cup diced cooked chicken
½ cup canned water chestnuts (optional)
1 cup drained bean sprouts
½ cup strong chicken broth
4 tablespoons soy sauce
¼ teaspoon sugar
2 teaspoons cornstarch
½ cup blanched almonds

Heat cooker and add 3 tablespoons oil. Lightly brown onion, celery, mushrooms, chicken, and water chestnuts.

Add bean sprouts, chicken broth, soy sauce, and sugar. Cook at 15-pound pressure 1 minute.

Reduce pressure. Remove cover and thicken with a paste made of cornstarch and 2 tablespoons water.

Add blanched almonds which have been browned in remaining tablespoon salad oil. Serve with steamed rice or fried noodles. Serves 4 to 5.

CHICKEN CURRY

1 chicken (about 3½ pounds), cut up
1½ cups water
1 large sweet onion, minced
1 large tart apple, minced
3 stalks celery, cut
¼ cup olive oil
2 tablespoons flour
1 teaspoon salt
2 tablespoons curry powder
½ teaspoon ginger
4 drops Tabasco sauce
2 teaspoons Worcestershire sauce
2 egg yolks, beaten
1 cup light cream
3 cups cooked rice or noodles

Place chicken on rack in pressure cooker; add water and cook 35 minutes at 15-pound pressure.

Cool quickly; remove chicken pieces; pour off and reserve the liquid.

Remove meat from bones and cut into small pieces, using shears.

Brown onion, apple and celery in hot oil in pressure cooker. Stir in flour; add seasonings and chicken stock, adding enough water to make 2 cups.

Return chicken meat to mixture. Bring to a boil uncovered, then set aside to cool.

If time permits, cool 3 hours for seasoning thoroughly to permeate the meat. Just before serving reheat and stir in mixed egg and cream. Serve on boiled rice or noodles. Serves 6.

SPANISH POT ROAST

5 pounds rump roast
2 tablespoons olive oil
10 bacon slices, cut in halves
10 cloves garlic, cut in halves
Allspice
4 cups tomato juice
6 carrots, diced
1 bunch celery, cut
6 onions, chopped
½ cup vinegar
1 bay leaf, crushed
2 teaspoons salt
¼ teaspoon pepper

Brush meat with olive oil.

Sprinkle each bacon piece with allspice, and make rolls of bacon half slices around the half cloves of garlic.

With a sharp-pointed knife, make deep gashes in roast. Push bacon and garlic rolls into the gashes at uniform distances over entire surface.

Brown roast on all sides in cooker. Lift and put rack in place.

Add tomato juice and sprinkle remaining ingredients over roast. Adjust cover and cook 1 hour at 15-pound pressure, opening to add potatoes the last of cooking period, if desired.

Serve, using the tomato and vegetable mixture as a sauce. Serves 6 to 8.

SCOTCH LAMB STEW

½ cup barley
1½ cups warm water
2 pounds lamb, cut in pieces ½-inch thick
1 tablespoon fat
½ cup water
3 or 4 potatoes
6 small onions
3 carrots, cut in half
3 or 4 stalks celery, cut in 3-inch pieces
2 teaspoons flour
2 teaspoons salt
½ teaspoon pepper
2 tablespoons boiling water

Soak barley in 1½ cups warm water overnight.

Flour the meat; brown in hot fat, then drain. Add ½ cup water, potatoes, onions, carrots, and celery to browned meat. Sprinkle with 2 teaspoons flour, salt, and pepper.

Drain barley; turn into 12-inch square of aluminum foil shaped to form a pouch; add 2 tablespoons boiling water to the pouch. Pinch corners of foil together; don't tie. Add to pressure cooker.

Cook at 15-pound pressure 8 minutes. Let pressure return to normal. Serves 4.

Spareribs with Barbecue Sauce

SPARERIBS WITH BARBECUE SAUCE

2 sides spareribs (about 4 pounds)
Salt, pepper, paprika
2 tablespoons lard or shortening
1 large onion
¼ cup ketchup
2 tablespoons water
2 tablespoons vinegar
1 teaspoon sugar
1 teaspoon Worcestershire sauce
¼ teaspoon chili powder
¼ teaspoon celery seed

Have spareribs cut into serving pieces; sprinkle with salt, pepper and paprika.

Melt lard in pressure cooker, and in it brown spareribs a few at a time until all are well browned.

Slice onion; mix ketchup with rest of ingredients.

Put half the spareribs in the pressure cooker; cover with half the sliced onions and half the barbecue sauce. Add rest of spareribs, onions and sauce.

Place cover on pressure cooker and cook for 15 minutes at 15-pound pressure. Reduce pressure slowly. Serves 4.

SPARERIBS AND SAUERKRAUT

2 pounds spareribs
1 tablespoon fat
Salt and pepper
1 quart sauerkraut
1 tablespoon brown sugar

Cut ribs into serving pieces. Heat pressure cooker and add fat. Brown ribs on both sides.

Season with salt and pepper. Place sauerkraut over ribs and sprinkle with brown sugar. Do not fill cooker over ⅔ full.

Cook 15 minutes at 15-pound pressure. Cool cooker at once. Serves 4 to 6.

HUNGARIAN VEAL GOULASH WITH NOODLES

¼ cup shortening
1½ pounds onions, sliced
1½ pounds veal shoulder, cut in 1½-inch pieces
2 tablespoons paprika
½ bay leaf
1 clove garlic, chopped fine
1 quart consommé or white stock
1 medium tomato, peeled and chopped fine
Salt and pepper to taste

Heat cooker and add shortening. Add onions and cook until yellow. Add veal and brown.

Mix in paprika, bay leaf, garlic, consommé or white stock, tomato, and salt and pepper to taste.

Pressure cook 35 minutes at 15-pound pressure. Remove bay leaf and serve with hot buttered noodles,—a green salad on the side. Serves 4 to 5.

POT ROAST WITH VEGETABLES

1 tablespoon fat
3 to 4 pounds beef chuck or rump pot roast
Salt and pepper
½ cup water
4 to 6 small potatoes
4 to 6 medium onions
4 to 6 medium carrots

Heat pressure pan; add fat. Brown roast on all sides.

Season. Add water. Adjust the cover; exhaust air from cooker.

Cook roast at 15-pound pressure 30 to 35 minutes.

Let pressure return to normal. Open cooker. Place potatoes, onions, and carrots on top. Season.

Adjust cover; exhaust air from cooker. Cook at 15-pound pressure 10 minutes.

Reduce pressure rapidly; serve vegetables on platter with meat.

Serves 4 to 6.

FRESH TONGUE

3 pounds tongue
2 cups water in cooker with rack
1 tablespoon salt
2 bay leaves
6 whole black peppers
6 cloves
1 onion, quartered

Wash tongue. Place on rack with water and other ingredients in cooker. Adjust cover and exhaust all air from cooker.

Cook 45 minutes at 15-pound pressure. Then cool cooker.

Remove skin; strain liquid. Keep tongue in liquid until ready to serve.

Tongue may be served with cucumber or raisin sauce. (See Index.)

Serves 6 to 8.

BEEF BRISKET WITH SAUERKRAUT

2 tablespoons fat
3 pounds beef brisket
2 tablespoons flour
2 teaspoons salt
⅛ teaspoon pepper
1 quart sauerkraut
1 tablespoon sugar
1 cup grated raw potato
1 teaspoon caraway seed
¼ cup grated onion

Heat fat in cooker. Rub flour and seasonings over the brisket and brown on all sides.

Lift meat from cooker; put rack in place and place sauerkraut on rack.

Return meat to cooker and sprinkle with remaining ingredients. Cook 1 hour at 15-pound pressure.

Serve with boiled potatoes which may be put in cooker, around meat, for last 15 minutes of cooking period.

Serves 6 to 8.

BRAISED SHORT RIBS

4 pounds short ribs of beef
1 tablespoon salt
¼ teaspoon pepper
1 onion, chopped
1 clove garlic, minced
1 bay leaf
½ cup water

Have meatman cut meat into individual servings. Season meat with salt and pepper. Place fat-side-down in pressure cooker or skillet and brown well, turning to brown all sides.

Place in pressure cooker on a rack with bone side down. Add onion, garlic, bay leaf, and water.

Cook in pressure cooker at 15-pound pressure for 25 minutes.

Remove meat to hot platter and make gravy from liquid in pan.

Serves 6 to 8.

BEEF STEW

1 to 1½ pounds beef, chuck or brisket, cut in 1-inch cubes
2 tablespoons fat
Salt and pepper
1 cup water
3 cups potatoes, cut in 1-inch cubes
2 cups carrots, cut in 1-inch pieces
4 to 5 small onions, halved
½ cup fresh or frozen peas
½ cup frozen lima beans

Heat pressure cooker, add fat and brown meat well.

Season with salt and pepper. Add water. Cook 12 minutes at 15-pound pressure. Cool cooker at once.

Add potatoes, carrots, onions, peas, and lima beans. Mix well. Cook 5 minutes at 15-pound pressure. Cool cooker at once. Serves 4 to 5.

BURGUNDY DUCK

1 duck (about 5½ pounds), cut up
1 onion, cut in quarters
1 leek, washed and quartered
3 stalks celery, cut in pieces
1 lemon, cut into wedges
1 cup Burgundy wine
Salt and pepper
12 small white whole onions, peeled, or 1 can or jar onions
4 apples, cored and quartered
1 can cranberry jelly

Flour duck lightly and fry gently in a little olive or salad oil until golden brown.

Put duck in pressure cooker with onion, leek, celery, lemon, Burgundy, and salt and pepper. Cook at 15-pound pressure for 30 minutes.

Reduce pressure gradually.

Meanwhile, boil onions, unless you are using canned onions. Add onions, apples, and cranberry jelly, broken up a bit with a fork, and cook without pressure on top of range until the jelly is melted. Serve in a deep platter with juices from duck and the jelly mixture. Serves 4.

SAVORY DUCKLING WITH SOUR CREAM

1 duckling (about 4 pounds), cut up
2 cloves garlic, halved
1 medium onion, quartered
⅓ cup finely chopped parsley
1 teaspoon rosemary
½ teaspoon marjoram
1 can frozen orange juice concentrate, diluted with 1 can water
1 lemon, sliced thin
Salt and pepper
1 pint sour cream

Flour the duck lightly and fry gently with garlic until golden brown.

Drain off excess fat; remove garlic, and put duck in the pressure cooker with onion, seasonings, diluted orange juice, lemon, salt, and pepper.

Cover and cook at 15-pound pressure for 30 minutes. Reduce pressure grad-

Almond Chicken Gizzards in Burgundy Wine

ually.

Skim off fat and add sour cream, stirring it well into the juices. Serves 4.

LOUISIANA CHICKEN SUPPER

1 3½-pound frying chicken, cut in serving pieces
⅓ cup corn meal
⅓ cup flour
2 teaspoons salt
½ teaspoon celery salt
¼ teaspoon pepper
3 tablespoons shortening
4 medium-sized sweet potatoes, pared
4 slices pineapple
⅛ teaspoon allspice
½ teaspoon cinnamon
¼ cup brown sugar
2 tablespoons melted butter or margarine
1 tablespoon lemon juice
Parsley

Shake chicken pieces in paper bag containing mixture of corn meal, flour, 1 teaspoon salt, celery salt, and pepper.

Heat shortening in pressure cooker over medium heat and fry chicken to an even golden brown.

Place sweet potatoes on an 18-inch square of aluminum foil. Arrange pineapple slices over them. Sprinkle with spices, sugar, and remaining teaspoon salt; drizzle with melted butter.

Pull edges of aluminum foil up and twist together making a tightly sealed package.

Put rack under chicken; sprinkle with lemon juice and add ½ cup water and foil package. Cover and cook at 15-pound pressure for 15 minutes. Let pressure reduce gradually. Serves 4.

ALMOND CHICKEN GIZZARDS IN BURGUNDY WINE

2 cups chicken broth or 2 chicken bouillon cubes, dissolved in 2 cups hot water
1 pound chicken gizzards (about 10 or 12)
2 tablespoons finely chopped parsley
Cornstarch
½ teaspoon salt
¼ teaspoon pepper
¼ cup burgundy wine
Slivered toasted almonds

Place chicken broth, parsley, and gizzards in the cooker. Place cover on cooker. Release all air from cooker. Cook 30 minutes at 15-pound pressure. Quick cool.

Remove gizzards from broth and slice thin.

Thicken broth with cornstarch. Add seasonings, sliced gizzards, and wine. Reheat. Serve on toast points with slivered almonds sprinkled over.

Serves 4 to 6.

CHICKEN AND BEEF BRUNSWICK STEW

1 4-pound stewing chicken, cut up
2 cups water
1 pound beef brisket, cut in cubes
2 teaspoons salt
1 teaspoon paprika
4 slices bacon, cut in small pieces
1 medium onion, minced
2 cups lima beans
2 cups whole kernel corn
2 cups cooked tomatoes
3 large potatoes, diced

Cook chicken with 2 cups water in cooker 35 minutes at 15-pound pressure.

While chicken cooks, sprinkle brisket with salt and paprika and let stand until ready to use.

Remove chicken from liquid; pour off remaining liquid and reserve.

Fry bacon in pressure cooker until crisp; add onion and fry to light brown.

Add beef and brown, while removing chicken meat from bones. Cut chicken to desired size, add, and brown slightly.

Now add liquid in which chicken was cooked, adding enough to nearly cover the meat. Cover and cook 30 minutes at 15-pound pressure.

Reduce pressure at once; add vegetables and cook 10 minutes at 15-pound pressure. Serves 8.

STEWED CHICKEN WITH DUMPLINGS

1 3½-pound chicken, cut in pieces
⅓ cup sliced onion
1 quart hot water
1 bay leaf
Salt and pepper

Dumplings:

1 cup sifted enriched flour
2 teaspoons baking powder
1 teaspoon salt
3 tablespoons shortening
½ cup milk

Cook the chicken, onion, and seasonings in 1 quart hot water for 22 minutes at 15-pound pressure.

Reduce pressure immediately and transfer chicken to a hot deep platter, leaving the juices in the pan. Keep chicken hot.

While chicken is cooking, make dumplings. Sift dry ingredients into a bowl. Cut in shortening with a pastry blender until the dough has the consistency of corn meal. Add milk.

Drop dumplings into juice in the cooker from a tablespoon which has been dipped in the hot juice. Cover and steam without pressure for 8 minutes. Add dumplings to chicken and serve. Serves 4 to 6.

Quick and Easy Salads

JIFFY TOMATO ASPIC

Heat 1 cup tomato juice or vegetable juice cocktail; add to 1 package lemon-flavored gelatin and stir until thoroughly blended. Add 1 more cup of juice.

Pour into lightly oiled mold or molds and chill. Serves 4.

TOMATO TOP HATTERS

Wash 3 tomatoes and slice in half. Season cottage cheese with salt, pepper, finely chopped green onion, carrot, and cucumber. Pile spoonfuls of cheese on tomato halves.

CORN TOSSUP

1   No. 2 can whole kernel corn
1   No. 2 can cut green beans
1   cup sliced radishes
1/2 cup mayonnaise
2   tablespoons chili sauce

Drain corn and beans, then mix together. Add radishes.

Blend mayonnaise with chili sauce. Add to vegetables and toss lightly. Serve on salad greens. Serves 6.

TOSSED SALAD, GOURMET

Cut or break up leaves of lettuce or other greens into bowl. Add sections of pink or white grapefruit and slices of avocado.

Sprinkle a few capers over top and toss with French dressing.

AVOCADO-CRANBERRY SALAD

Arrange avocado halves or quarters on lettuce. Heap with cubed canned cranberry sauce, mixed with diced celery. Serve with French dressing.

AVOCADO WITH CHIVED COTTAGE CHEESE

Peel avocados; cut each in half lengthwise and remove the pits.

For each serving place half an avocado on curly endive. Fill the center with creamed chive cottage cheese. Serve with French dressing.

The richness of avocado is set off by the filling of chived cottage cheese.

FLOWER GARDEN SALADS

Flower garden salads make an attractive luncheon dish—or, in a smaller size, a dinner salad.

First, arrange a bed of lettuce or greens. Next, place cottage cheese on top of this. Then arrange sliced cling peaches or peach halves in flower formation on or around cottage cheese.

A slice of green pepper can be the stem, and bits of cut green pepper the leaves. Maraschino cherry adds a colorful center.

PINEAPPLE FRUIT COCKTAIL

Arrange drained canned pineapple slices on salad greens. Fill centers with drained canned fruit cocktail.

PEAR SALAD

Use canned or fresh pears, placing one half, hollow side up, on a bed of greens. Fill with chopped nuts and maraschino cherries.

APRICOT 'N' CREAM CHEESE

Place drained halves of canned apricots cut-side-up on salad greens. Top with softened cream cheese and chopped dates.

Apricot 'n' Cream Cheese

PINEAPPLE CUCUMBER SALAD

Arrange drained canned pineapple slices on salad greens.

Score a cucumber with a fork, leaving peeling on. Cut in thin slices.

Overlap 3 cucumber slices on each pineapple slice. Place a mound of pimiento cream cheese in center.

APPLE AND ORANGE TOSS

Dice a tart apple into a bowl.

Grate the yellow rind of an orange over apple, then peel the orange and dice it into bowl with the apple.

Add a sprinkling of broken walnuts. Toss with salad dressing, and serve on lettuce. Serves 2 to 3.

MELON RING SALAD

Place ring of honeydew on lettuce leaf. Center with scoop of raspberry sherbet.

Arrange fresh peach and pear slices, dipped in lemon juice, around sides.

Serve with honey-lime dressing made by combining 2 parts honey and 1 part lime juice.

Flower Garden Salads

MINTED PEACH SALAD

Place peach halves on bed of greens. Sprinkle with lemon juice and chopped mint. Serve with whipped cream dressing.

PEACH CREAM CHEESE SALAD

Arrange drained canned peach halves, cut side up, on salad greens.

Fill centers with cream cheese which has been softened with a small amount of peach syrup. Top with chopped nuts.

CORONATION SALAD

Drain canned pear halves well. Put two halves together with cream cheese which has been softened with a small amount of the pear syrup. Sprinkle paprika on one side to form a blush.

Place a small strip of green pepper or a pretzel stick on top of pear for a stem. Arrange upright on salad greens.

AVOCADO AND ORANGE SALAD

Alternate sections of oranges with slices of peeled avocado.

Serve with lemon wedges and French dressing.

GRATED CARROT SALAD

Wash young, tender carrots. Grate on fine grater. Using a fork, gently combine with French dressing.

Place on lettuce leaves. Serve at once. A bit of cheese may be grated with carrots.

Easy Fruit Salad Platter: Line serving plate with crisp romaine or other greens. Arrange drained chilled canned fruits on greens. Garnish with watercress and sprinkle with chopped nuts. Serve with fruit salad dressing. Fruit combinations to use: pear halves and light sweet cherries; apricot halves and purple plums; fruits for salad and dark sweet cherries; citrus sections and pineapple chunks.

Quick and Easy Breads and Rolls

BUTTERSCOTCH DINNER ROLLS

Combine 1/4 cup soft butter, 1/2 cup firmly packed brown sugar, and 1/4 teaspoon nutmeg.

Spread butter mixture over brown-and-serve rolls. Bake.

JIFFY BISMARCKS

Remove refrigerated biscuits from tube and flatten to 1/4 inch. Place 1 teaspoon jam or jelly on half the biscuits; cover with remaining biscuits; seal edges well.

Fry in deep hot fat (375°F.) 3 minutes on each side. Drain on paper towels. Dust with confectioners' sugar, if you like. Serve these warm with hot coffee for dessert.

COCONUT COFFEE CAKES

1/4 cup butter or margarine
1/4 cup brown sugar
1/3 cup dark corn syrup
1/2 cup shredded coconut
8 brown-and-serve cloverleaf rolls
Melted butter or margarine

Cook 1/4 cup butter, sugar, and syrup together until butter melts and mixture is syrupy.

Pour into 8 muffin cups. Sprinkle part of coconut in each, then add rolls. Brush rolls with melted butter.

Bake in moderate oven (375°F.) until lightly browned, about 15 minutes.

CRANBERRY GLAZED ROLLS

1/4 cup chopped nuts
1/2 cup jellied cranberry sauce
1/4 cup brown sugar
6 to 8 brown 'n serve rolls

Grease muffin pans or custard cups. Sprinkle a few chopped nuts into each.

Combine cranberry sauce that has been crushed with a fork and brown sugar. Put a tablespoon of the mixture in each muffin cup.

Turn brown 'n serve rolls upside down and press into each muffin cup. Bake in hot oven (400°F.) for 12 to 15 minutes. Let cool for 4 to 5 minutes. Invert pans and gently remove rolls.

Cranberry Glazed Rolls

ALMOND CINNAMON RING

Separate rolls from 2 cans refrigerator quick raisin cinnamon rolls. Overlap rolls to form a 9-inch ring on cooky sheet.

Bake in moderate oven (375°F.) for 15 to 20 minutes until golden brown. Spread with icing. Sprinkle with slivered almonds. If desired, garnish with maraschino cherries. Serve warm. Makes 1 large coffee cake.

CARAMEL PECAN ROLLS

1/4 cup butter or margarine
1/4 cup brown sugar
1/3 cup dark corn syrup
Pecans
8 brown-and-serve cloverleaf rolls

Melt butter; blend in brown sugar and syrup. Boil 1 minute.

Pour into 8 muffin cups. Add a few pecan halves to each, then add rolls.

Bake in moderate oven (375°F.) until lightly browned, about 15 minutes.

HONEY NUT PAN ROLLS

2 tablespoons honey
2 tablespoons sugar
2 tablespoons soft butter or margarine
2 tablespoons flour
8 brown-and-serve pan rolls
1/4 cup broken walnuts

Combine honey, sugar, butter, and flour. Spread on top of rolls. Sprinkle with walnuts.

Place on greased baking sheet; bake in moderate oven (375°F.) until lightly browned, about 15 minutes.

ORANGE-NUT COFFEE CAKE

2 cups biscuit mix
1/4 cup sugar
2/3 cup milk
2 well beaten eggs
1/2 cup chopped walnuts

Combine biscuit mix and sugar. Add alternately with milk to well beaten eggs. Stir in nuts.

Spread batter in greased 8 x 11½-inch round pan. Bake in hot oven (400°F.) about 25 minutes.

Orange Topping: Melt 1/3 cup butter or margarine; mix with 2/3 cup brown sugar. Spread over warm cake; sprinkle with 1/2 cup grated orange rind and 1/2 cup broken walnuts.

Pour 1/2 cup orange juice over mixture and place cake under broiler until bubbly. Serve warm.

ORANGE BLOSSOM BUNS

Place 1 teaspoon melted butter and 1 tablespoon orange marmalade in bottom of each muffin cup.

Arrange a brown-and-serve roll topside down in each cup and bake.

Almond Cinnamon Ring

BACON CORN BREAD

Prepare 1 package corn muffin or corn bread mix according to directions on package.

Sprinkle with 6 or 7 slices bacon, broiled and crumbled. Bake as directed.

HERB-BUTTERED ROLLS

Combine 1/3 cup softened butter, 1 tablespoon lemon juice, 1/4 teaspoon garlic salt, 2 tablespoons finely chopped parsley, and 1/2 teaspoon thyme.

Top brown-and-serve rolls with butter mixture and bake.

ROUND-THE-CLOCK COFFEE LOAF

3/4 cup sugar
3/4 teaspoon cinnamon
1/3 cup walnuts, chopped
2 packages refrigerated unbaked biscuits
1/4 cup butter or margarine, melted
1 ounce (1/3 of 3-ounce package) cream cheese
3/4 cup sifted confectioners' sugar
1 teaspoon milk
1/4 teaspoon vanilla

Combine sugar, cinnamon, and nuts. Dip biscuits in butter, then in sugar mixture.

Place 13 biscuits in bottom of 12 x 8 x 2-inch pan, then top with second layer of 7 biscuits, overlapping slightly.

Bake in hot oven (425°F.) until golden brown, 20 to 25 minutes.

Combine cream cheese, confectioners' sugar, milk, and vanilla; cream well. Frost warm loaf. Sprinkle remaining sugar-nut mixture over top. Serves 8.

Round-the-Clock Coffee Loaf

Quick and Easy Desserts

APPLE PAN DOWDY

2 cups canned apple slices, drained
1/4 cup molasses or brown sugar
1/4 teaspoon nutmeg
1/4 teaspoon cinnamon
1/4 teaspoon salt
1 package white cake mix

In the bottom of a buttered baking dish, arrange apple slices. Sprinkle with molasses or brown sugar, nutmeg, cinnamon, and salt.

Make up white cake mix according to directions. Pour batter over apples.

Bake in moderate oven (350°F.) 20 to 25 minutes or until cake is done.

At serving time, bring to the table in its own baking dish. Cut into squares and serve with sweetened whipped cream or ready-whipped cream. Serves 6.

QUICK CHOCOLATE MOUSSE

1/2 6-ounce package chocolate pieces
3 eggs, separated
1 teaspoon vanilla

Melt chocolate pieces over hot water. Remove from heat and beat in egg yolks one at a time. Add vanilla.

Beat egg whites until stiff, but not dry; gently fold into chocolate mixture.

Spoon into sherbet glasses, and chill. Serve garnished with cream or soft vanilla ice cream. Serves 4.

BLUEBERRY DELIGHT

1/2 cup sugar
3 tablespoons cornstarch
1/4 teaspoon salt
3 cups blueberries, slightly crushed
Juice and grated rind of 1 lemon
18 shortbread cookies, coarsely crumbled

Mix together sugar, cornstarch, and salt in saucepan.

Combine blueberries, lemon juice, and rind; stir into sugar mixture, blending well. Cook over low heat, stirring constantly, until thick and clear; cool.

Alternate layers of blueberry mixture and shortbread crumbs in 6 parfait glasses. Top with whipped cream. Serves 6.

Peach Crisp Pudding

BRAZILIAN CREAM

1 tablespoon instant coffee
1 package vanilla pudding
2 cups milk
1/2 cup cream, whipped

Combine coffee and pudding powder in a saucepan. Add milk gradually, blending well. Cook and stir over medium heat until mixture comes to a boil and is thickened. Turn into bowl, cover, and chill well.

Then beat slowly with rotary egg beater and fold in whipped cream. Turn into sherbet glasses. Garnish with ladyfinger strips, coconut, and maraschino cherries with stems. Serves 5.

GEORGIA CRUNCH

1 No. 2 1/2 can sliced peaches
1/2 cup butter or margarine
3/4 cup wheat cereal flakes
1/2 cup firmly packed brown sugar
1/2 teaspoon cinnamon
1/2 teaspoon nutmeg
1 cup chopped walnuts

Drain peaches well. Arrange in the bottom of a shallow baking pan.

Cut cereal flakes and brown sugar into butter. Add cinnamon and nutmeg. Sprinkle evenly over peach slices. Top with chopped walnuts.

Bake in moderate oven (375°F.) 10 minutes. Serves 6.

FRENCH CHOCOLATE CREAM PUDDING

1 package chocolate pudding
1 cup cold milk
2 squares (2 ounces) unsweetened chocolate
1/2 teaspoon vanilla
1 cup heavy cream

Empty contents of chocolate pudding mix into a heavy saucepan. Stir in milk gradually and keep stirring until mixture is absolutely smooth.

Add chocolate and cook very slowly, stirring constantly, until chocolate has melted and the pudding is as thick as mayonnaise.

Remove from range and allow pudding to cool. Add vanilla to cream and beat until thick.

Mix or fold the whipped cream into cooled chocolate pudding. Pour into custard cups. Serves 6.

PEACH CRISP PUDDING

Cream 1/4 cup butter and 1/2 cup sugar together. Combine with 1 quart soft 1/2-inch bread cubes and 2 cups sliced peaches.

Bake in greased 1 1/2-quart casserole in moderate oven (375°F.) for 30 minutes. Serve with whipped cream. Serves 8.

A variety of party parfaits can be quickly prepared with packaged pudding mixes. Alternate the chilled prepared puddings with sweetened, flavored whipped cream in parfait glasses.

JIFFY LEMON CHIFFON PUDDING

2 eggs, separated
3 1/4- to 4 1/4-ounce package lemon pie filling
Dash of salt
4 tablespoons sugar

With egg yolks, cook lemon pie filling as directed on package; cool about 10 minutes.

Add salt to egg whites; beat until foamy and just stiff enough to hold a peak; gradually beat in sugar until smooth and glossy. Fold into lemon mixture. Spoon into dessert dishes and chill. Serves 4 to 6.

JIFFY CHOCOLATE PUFF

1/2 6-ounce package chocolate pieces
1 cup milk
3 tablespoons sugar
Dash of salt
1 teaspoon vanilla
3 eggs

Melt chocolate pieces and milk over hot water; beat with egg beater until smooth. Add sugar, salt, vanilla, and eggs.

Beat with egg beater one minute. Cover and cook over boiling water for 20 minutes without lifting the cover. Remove from heat and serve immediately with cream. Serves 6.

FIG BROWNIE PUDDING

24 fig cookies (about)
1 cup sweetened condensed milk
1/2 cup water
1 1/2 teaspoons baking powder
1 square (1 ounce) baking chocolate, melted
1 package chocolate bits
1 teaspoon vanilla
1/2 cup chopped walnut meats

Crumble the fig cookies into the milk, add the remaining ingredients and stir together.

Place in a generously buttered baking dish. Bake in moderate oven (350°F.) for about 25 minutes or until a little puffy. Serve in dessert dishes while warm, with whipped cream or the type of cream you desire.

Serves 5 to 6.

"DIFFERENT" PASTRY SHELLS

Prepare 1 package pastry mix according to label directions:

Coffee Pecan Crust (perfect for a chocolate chiffon pie): Substitute coffee for liquid in recipe. Add ½ cup ground pecans.

Spiced Crust (for ice cream pie): Add 1½ teaspoons cinnamon, ½ teaspoon nutmeg, ¼ teaspoon allspice, and ¼ cup sugar.

Cheddar Crust (for apple pie): Add ½ cup grated Cheddar cheese.

"DIFFERENT" PIE FILLINGS

Prepare 1 package vanilla pudding mix according to directions on label.

Rich Coffee Pecan: Substitute 1 cup strong coffee for 1 cup liquid.

Fold in ½ cup heavy cream, whipped, and ½ cup finely chopped pecans just before turning into shell.

Brazil Nut: Fold ½ cup slivered toasted Brazil nuts through filling before turning into shell.

Fudge-Coated Orange: Combine pudding mix, 2 teaspoons grated orange rind, and 1½ cups milk. Cook according to label directions.

Remove from heat and add ½ cup orange juice.

Melt ½ package semi-sweet chocolate pieces over low heat.

Spread melted chocolate over bottom of pastry shell. Pour cooled filling over chocolate. Chill.

Banana: Arrange sliced bananas in shell before adding filling.

Top with whipped cream and shaved chocolate before serving.

BLUEBERRY CREAM CHEESE TARTS

Start with a package of pie crust mix. Makes 6 shells. If time is really at a premium, store-purchased sponge cake shells can be used.

Beat a package of cream cheese until smooth. Add luscious plump blueberries, a bit of sour cream, and sugar.

At serving time, fill the cooled pastry or sponge cake shells with chilled cheese mixture.

Jiffy Strawberry Cream Pie

PEACHES AND COCONUT CREAM PIE

Make your favorite cream pie filling, or prepare a package of vanilla pudding according to the directions on the box.

Cool slightly, then fold in 1 cup toasted coconut. Pour into a baked and cooled pastry shell. Chill.

Just before serving, top with well drained and chilled canned peach halves. Garnish centers with more toasted coconut. Nice, too, made in individual tart shells. Serve with sweetened whipped cream, if desired.

To toast coconut: Spread in a shallow pan and bake in moderate oven (350°F.) about 10 minutes.

Peaches and Coconut Cream Pie

JIFFY PECAN PUMPKIN PIE

Combine 1½ tablespoons melted butter and ⅓ cup firmly packed brown sugar. Add ½ cup chopped pecans.

Spread mixture over top of bought pumpkin pie.

Bake under a preheated broiler (350°F.) for 10 minutes. Serve while hot.

CHOCOLATE BANANA TARTS

Line 5 cooled tart shells with sliced bananas. Add chocolate pudding, made from a prepared mix. Chill.

Top with additional banana slices and whipped cream just before serving.

JIFFY STRAWBERRY CREAM PIE

Filling: Prepare vanilla-flavor instant pudding according to directions on package.

Pour into well chilled cereal crumb crust (see index). Cover with fresh strawberry halves.

Melt 1 cup currant jelly over low heat, beating until smooth. When cool but still syrupy, pour over strawberry topping. Chill again before serving. Other fruits of the season may be used.

Note: If using prepared pudding mix that requires cooking or a standard recipe for cream pie filling, it is better to bake the cereal crumb crust in moderate oven (350°F.) 7 to 10 minutes.

Chill thoroughly before adding filling. Crust will harden while it cools.

Lazy Girlie Fig Pie

LAZY GIRLIE FIG PIE

Bake a 10-inch pie shell and cool.

Meanwhile, crumble about 14 fig cookies into 2 cups milk. Add 1 package vanilla-flavored packaged pudding. Stir over heat until pudding bubbles.

Remove from heat and stir in ½ cup light molasses, 1 teaspoon cinnamon, and ½ teaspoon allspice. Add 1 teaspoon vanilla and ½ teaspoon salt. Cool.

Then place in a cooled pie shell. Top with sweetened, vanilla-flavored whipped cream. Serves 6 to 8.

MAGIC APPLE PIE

1 package refrigerator biscuits
1 15-ounce can sweetened condensed milk
⅓ cup lemon juice
1 No. 2 can processed sliced apples or 2½ cups cooked, sliced apples
1 teaspoon cinnamon

Remove biscuits from package. Flatten each biscuit to ¼-inch thickness.

Press biscuits in greased baking pan (8 x 12½ x 2-inch) to cover bottom; arrange remaining biscuits around sides of pan, so edges resemble a scalloped edge.

Brush biscuits with about 4 to 5 tablespoons sweetened condensed milk, covering bottom and sides completely.

Bake in hot oven (400°F.) about 20 minutes or until browned.

Add lemon juice to remaining sweetened condensed milk, stirring until mixture thickens. Fold in apples and cinnamon. Pour mixture into baked biscuit shell. Chill. Garnish with whipped cream. Serves 6.

CHOCOLATE-MINT BROWNIES

Prepare fudge brownies as directed on package of brownie mix. When done, remove from oven and place 16 mint-chocolate wafers on top.

Return to oven 5 minutes or until chocolate wafers soften.

Using spatula, spread chocolate evenly over top of brownies. Cool, then cut into 16 squares.

BERRY CAKES

Split 2 sponge cake layers to form 4 layers. Fill with sweetened berries.

Cut into wedges; top with ice cream, whipped cream, or custard sauce.

Ten Minute Boston Cream Pie

TIPSY PARSON

2 bought sponge cake layers (sold for shortcake)
Currant, grape, or apple jelly
Shredded almonds

Place between the sponge cake layers, currant, grape, or apple jelly. Sprinkle jelly liberally with canned shredded almonds. Place top layer over jelly.

Spread top of cake with a thin layer of jelly and sprinkle with almonds.

Tipsy Sauce: Prepare the sauce from a package of vanilla-flavored pudding mix by using 1½ as much liquid as required for a regular pudding. Cook according to package directions. Add ½ cup sherry or Madeira wine. Stir and chill.

At serving time, cut cake into regular servings and pass chilled sauce in a separate bowl. Serves 6 to 8.

RIBBON ICE CREAM CAKE

1 6-inch round angel food cake
½ pint chocolate ice cream
½ pint peppermint ice cream
1 cup heavy cream, whipped and sweetened
½ cup shredded coconut, lightly toasted

Split cake crosswise into 3 layers. Slightly soften ice creams and spread chocolate ice cream on bottom layer. Put middle layer of cake into place and spread this with peppermint ice cream. Replace top of cake.

Cover entire cake with whipped, sweetened cream and sprinkle with toasted coconut. Place in freezer for 20 minutes or longer. Serves 6 to 8.

Variations: Any two flavors of ice cream that taste well together may be used.

Quick Cranberry Refrigerator Cake

TEN MINUTE BOSTON CREAM PIE

1 package semi-sweet chocolate morsels
¾ cup evaporated milk
2 8-inch bought sponge layers
Confectioners' sugar

Put semi-sweet chocolate morsels and evaporated milk in saucepan; place over low heat. Cook, stirring occasionally, until mixture is blended.

Bring to a boil and cook, stirring constantly, until mixture thickens, about 3 to 5 minutes. Cool.

Spread frosting between layers, reserving about 2 tablespoons to thinly spread over top layer.

Sprinkle with confectioners' sugar or, if attractive design is desired, place paper doily on top of cake and sprinkle with confectioners' sugar. Remove doily. Makes 8 servings.

PINEAPPLE-CREAM CAKE

1 8-inch bought angel food ring
⅔ cup pineapple jam
1½ cups heavy cream, whipped

Slice cake and put on individual serving plates. Fold jam into cream and use to top cake slices.

ORANGE SPONGE CAKE

Sprinkle 2 sponge cake layers with ¼ cup orange juice. Fill with whipped cream. Top with grated orange rind and chopped walnuts.

COCONUT BARS

Butter slices of bought pound cake; cut into bars and sprinkle with coconut, then broil.

CHOCOLATE CREAM CUPCAKES

Gash chocolate cupcakes part way. Fill with whipped cream; sprinkle with walnuts.

PEACH SPONGE LAYER CAKE

Fill 2 sponge cake layers with slightly thawed frozen peaches; top with whipped cream.

QUICK CRANBERRY REFRIGERATOR CAKE

1 egg white, stiffly beaten
2 cups whole cranberry sauce
1 bought 8-ounce angel food cake
¾ cup heavy cream, whipped

Fold stiffly beaten egg white into cranberry sauce.

Slice angel food cake into 3 horizontal sections. Alternate layers of sliced angel food cake and sauce in a shallow pan, with cake as both top and bottom layer.

Cover the top and sides of cake with whipped cream. Refrigerate until ready to serve. Serves 8.

COCONUT HONEY BARS

Slice pound cake ½ inch thick. Cut each slice in 4 strips.

Spread 3 sides with butter and honey; roll in coconut and place on greased cooky sheet. Toast a delicate brown in moderate oven (375°F.) 5 to 10 minutes.

BUTTERSCOTCH POUND CAKE DESSERT

1 (4½ ounce) package butterscotch pudding
1 (14 ounce) loaf pound cake

Prepare butterscotch pudding according to directions on package.

Cut pound cake in half lengthwise. With a 2-inch cooky cutter, cut each lengthwise strip into 3 circles.

Arrange cake circles in dessert dishes. Pour butterscotch pudding over each cake circle. Serves 6.

JIFFY SHORTCAKE

Make shortcake from biscuit mix according to directions on the package, or use bought dessert shells.

Fill and top with fresh, or thawed frozen strawberries, raspberries, or sliced peaches and whipped cream.

TEA CAKES

1 8-ounce bought loaf cake
1 cup butter frosting
½ ounce unsweetened chocolate, melted
1 teaspoon hot water
1 tablespoon grated orange rind
½ teaspoon orange extract

Slice cake horizontally into 3 equal-size layers. Even off cake top if it is rounded.

Spread ⅓ cup butter frosting on bottom layer and cover with middle layer.

Add melted chocolate and hot water to ⅓ cup butter frosting and spread over middle layer.

Place top layer over chocolate frosting. Add orange rind and juice to remaining butter frosting.

Spread orange butter frosting over top of cake, leaving sides unfrosted. After frosting has set, cut cake into 8 small squares.

Tea Cakes

BERRIES JUBILEE WITH ICE CREAM

Peel from 1 lemon
2 tablespoons quick-frozen orange juice, undiluted
1 pint fresh or quick-frozen whole strawberries
1/4 cup brandy

Cut the peel from 1 lemon and leave it curled cork-screw style. Place in a shallow pan—a chafing dish if convenient. Add orange juice. Heat gently about 3 minutes, pressing the peel to get all the flavor.

Add strawberries and toss berries around in the hot juice. Pour on brandy. Warm and light with a match.

At serving time, do all this at the table if you can and serve the flaming berries over vanilla ice cream, lemon or orange sherbet.

Raspberries Jubilee: Raspberries can be done in the same fashion.

PEACH DELIGHT

1 No. 2 1/2 can peach halves, drained
1/2 cup vanilla wafer crumbs
1 cup heavy cream, whipped
Walnut halves

Roll peach halves in vanilla wafer crumbs until well coated. Place halves, cut side down, in sherbet glasses.

Top each with spoonful of whipped cream and a walnut half. Serves 6.

SPICED FRUIT COMPOTE

3 1/2 cups (1 No. 2 1/2 can) fruits for salad or canned fruits of your choice
1 tablespoon vinegar
6 inches stick cinnamon
1 teaspoon whole cloves

Combine fruits (with their syrup), vinegar, cinnamon, and cloves in saucepan; heat to boiling. Simmer 5 minutes.

Garnish with a few spiced crabapples if desired. Keep hot in chafing dish. Serves 6 to 8.

BANANAS JUBILEE

Cut bananas into thin slices. Arrange in layer, on top of angel-cake wedges. Serve with warm spiced cherry sauce.

Drain syrup from 1 can (about 1 pound) dark sweet cherries; add water, if needed, to make 1 cup.

Place 1 tablespoon cornstarch and a dash each of salt and ground cloves in small saucepan; stir in syrup. Cook and stir until sauce thickens and boils 1 minute; add cherries; heat through.

ORANGE FLUFF CAKES

Whip 1 cup heavy cream; mix with 1 cup coconut, 2 tablespoons orange juice, 1 teaspoon grated orange rind; use to top sponge cake wedges.

CHOCOLATE BAKED ALASKA CAKE

4 egg whites
6 tablespoons sugar
1/2 teaspoon vanilla
1 8-inch bakers' layer cake
1 quart firm chocolate ice cream

Beat egg whites until stiff, but not dry. Blend in sugar and vanilla. Continue beating until meringue stands in peaks and is well blended.

Place cake on a sheet of brown paper on a cooky sheet. Pile ice cream on cake, leaving about 1/2 inch around edge of cake uncovered.

Cover ice cream and cake with meringue, making sure that ice cream is well covered by the meringue.

Brown quickly in very hot oven (450°F.) for about 5 minutes. Serve immediately. Serves 6 to 8.

BLUE CHEESE PEARS WITH WINE SAUCE

1/2 cup crumbled blue cheese (about 3 ounces)
1 tablespoon milk
8 canned pear halves
3/4 cup pear juice
2 tablespoons sherry

Combine cheese and milk; mix until well blended. Fill pear halves with cheese mixture.

Place in shallow baking pan and bake in hot oven (400°F.) about 10 minutes, or until cheese is melted and pears are heated through.

Meanwhile, combine pear juice and sherry; heat to boiling point.

Place 2 pear halves in each serving dish and cover with wine sauce. Serve hot. Serves 4.

JIFFY CHEESE CAKE

1 8-ounce bought pound cake
1 tablespoon lemon juice
1/2 pound cottage cheese
1/4 teaspoon cinnamon
3 tablespoons granulated sugar
2 cups sour cream
1 No. 2 can sliced peaches
3 tablespoons brown sugar
1/2 teaspoon vanilla

Cut pound cake into thin slices. Line a 9 x 9-inch baking pan with cake slices and sprinkle the lemon juice over cake.

Combine cottage cheese, cinnamon, granulated sugar, and 1/2 cup sour cream.

Drain peaches and finely chop 1 cup. Mix chopped peaches with cheese mixture and pour over cake slices.

Combine remaining 1 1/2 cups sour cream with brown sugar and vanilla; spread over cheese mixture.

Arrange remaining peach slices on top. Bake in hot oven (400°F.) 15 minutes. Serves 6 to 8.

APRICOT CREAM TORTE

Crush 1 1/2 cups drained canned apricots. Stir in 2 tablespoons sugar. Spoon onto 1 sponge cake layer. Circle with whipped cream.

PINEAPPLE FLUFF

1 fresh pineapple
1/4 cup sugar
1/2 pound marshmallows, cut in small pieces
1 cup heavy cream, whipped
Sliced maraschino cherries

Pare and cut pineapple into fine pieces. Place in bowl in layers, sprinkling each layer with sugar and marshmallow pieces. Cover and let stand several hours.

To serve, fold in whipped cream and spoon into serving dishes. Garnish with maraschino cherries. Serves 8.

STEWED FIGS À LA GLACE

Canned figs, thoroughly chilled
Vanilla ice cream
Rum or brandy (optional)

Place a scoop of vanilla ice cream into individual dessert dishes, sherbet glasses, or champagne glasses of the saucer type. On top of the ice cream, carefully place 2 or 3 figs together with a little of the syrup.

Add a teaspoonful of rum or brandy to each portion.

QUICK CHOCOLATE TORTE

1 large bought angel food cake
1 cup sweet butter or margarine
2 cups confectioners' sugar
1 teaspoon vanilla
2 1-ounce squares chocolate, melted
1/2 cup confectioners' sugar
6 tablespoons cocoa
1/8 teaspoon salt
2 cups whipping cream
1/2 cup chopped salted pistachio nuts

Slice cake into 3 layers, using long, thin, sharp-bladed knife.

Cream butter well. Beat the 2 cups confectioners' sugar into butter; cream well. Add vanilla and melted chocolate. Mix well, then spread between layers of cake.

Sift together 1/2 cup confectioners' sugar, cocoa, and salt. Add to unwhipped cream. Chill 2 hours or more.

Add vanilla to cream and whip until stiff. Spread on tops and sides of cake. Sprinkle chopped nuts around sides of cake. Chill several hours before serving. Makes 16 servings.

BANANAS ON HALF SHELL

Halve each banana crosswise. Remove half of peel lengthwise, without removing fruit; cut fruit crosswise (not through peel) into 1/2-inch slices. Top with whipped cream and sprinkle with nutmeg.

Quick and Easy Timed Menus with Recipes

50-MINUTE SUNDAY SPECIAL MENU

Serves 4

Chilled Vichyssoise with Chives
Glazed Baked Ham
Hot Spiced Cherries
Browned Potatoes—
Parsley-Butter Carrots
Garden Salad Bowl
Pineapple-Peppermint Delight
Coffee   Milk

Bake the ham first—

GLAZED BAKED HAM

Remove one 3- to 4-pound ham from can. Place ham, fat side up, on rack in shallow baking pan. Stud top with cloves; drizzle with ½ cup honey.

Bake in slow oven (325°F.) 45 minutes, basting often with additional honey. (Use remaining ham for another meal.)

Chill the soup next—

VICHYSSOISE WITH CHIVES

Place 2 cans ready-to-serve vichyssoise in ice cube compartment; chill, but do not freeze.

Just before serving, beat with rotary beater; sprinkle with chopped chives.

Now for the creamy-rich dessert—

PINEAPPLE-PEPPERMINT DELIGHT

Drain well 1 can (9-ounce) crushed pineapple. (Pineapple juice may be added to cherry sauce.)

Whip ½ pint (1 cup) heavy cream, beating in 2 tablespoons sugar. Fold in pineapple and ½ cup coarsely crushed peppermint stick candy; spoon into sherbet glasses; chill.

Then the cherries—

HOT SPICED CHERRIES

Combine 1½ tablespoons cornstarch, ¼ cup sugar, ¼ teaspoon each allspice and ground cloves in small saucepan.

Gradually stir in juice drained from 1 No. 2 can (1 pound, 4 ounces) red sour pitted cherries and juice drained from crushed pineapple, if desired.

Cook until thick and clear, stirring constantly: blend in few drops red food coloring and cherries. Serve hot with baked ham.

Hints: There's time to skillet-brown 1 No. 2 can (1 pound, 4 ounces) whole white potatoes in 2 tablespoons butter or margarine, and to heat and season 1 No. 303 can (1 pound) carrots.

Prepare the salad and coffee, and set the table. Dinner will be ready in about 50 minutes.

20-MINUTE TAKE-IT-EASY DINNER

Serves 4

Chicken à la King
Chow Mein Noodles
French-Style Green Beans
Whole-Kernel Corn
Tomato Aspic Salad
Hot Spiced Applesauce Sundaes
Coffee   Milk

First the—

CHICKEN À LA KING

Combine 1 10½-ounce can chicken à la king, 1 can condensed cream of mushroom soup, 1 6-ounce can boned chicken, and ¼ cup milk in saucepan; heat thoroughly.

Serve hot over 1 3¾-ounce can chow mein noodles heated according to label directions.

Then the dessert—

HOT SPICED APPLESAUCE SUNDAES

Combine 1 No. 303 can (1 pound) applesauce, 2 tablespoons sugar, ¼ teaspoon cinnamon, and dash each of allspice and cloves in small saucepan.

To serve, heat well and spoon over individual dishes of vanilla ice cream.

Hints: For the vegetables, heat separately 1 No. 303 can (1 pound) whole-kernel corn and 1 No. 303 can (1 pound) French-style green beans. Drain and season each with butter or margarine, salt and pepper.

Slice 1 can tomato aspic; serve on watercress with French dressing.

Have applesauce ready to heat while you're clearing the main course. After you've made coffee and set the table, this quick meal is ready in about 20 minutes.

45-MINUTE MENU WHEN COMPANY COMES

Serves 4

Grapefruit-Cranberry Cocktail
Chicken 'n' Dumplings
Pimiento Asparagus   Pickled Peaches
Lettuce Wedges
with Blue Cheese Dressing
Broiled Pineapple-Topped Spicecake
Coffee   Milk

Dessert comes first—

BROILED PINEAPPLE-TOPPED SPICECAKE

Prepare 1 package spicecake mix according to package directions, using 9 x 9 x 2-inch or 11 x 7 x 1½-inch baking pan.

When cake is baked, remove from oven and arrange 1 No. 2 can (1 pound, 4 ounces) sliced pineapple, well drained, over top of cake, reserving juice for first course.

Sprinkle cake with ½ cup brown sugar and ¼ teaspoon ground ginger; dot with 2 tablespoons butter or margarine.

Broil 1 to 2 minutes, or until topping browns. Cool on wire cake rack; cut in squares.

Note: Have topping ingredients ready to put on as soon as cake is baked. Sliced peaches, drained, may be substituted.

Next, the meal-starter—

GRAPEFRUIT-CRANBERRY COCKTAIL

Divide 1 No. 2 can (1 pound, 4 ounces) grapefruit sections among 4 sherbet glasses; add reserved pineapple juice.

Top each with several small cubes of jellied cranberry sauce. Chill until serving time.

Then the salad dressing—

BLUE CHEESE DRESSING

Blend ½ cup mayonnaise or salad dressing with 2 tablespoons crumbled blue cheese.

Sharpen with canned lemon juice or red wine vinegar, if desired. Spoon over crisp lettuce wedges.

Now for the main course—

CHICKEN 'N' DUMPLINGS

Heat 2 cans (about 1 pound each) chicken fricassee in large saucepan with tight-fitting cover.

When hot and bubbling, open 1 container refrigerator biscuits. Place biscuits on top of fricassee. Simmer, tightly covered, 15 minutes.

Hints: While chicken simmers, you've time to heat and season 1 No. 2 can (1 pound, 4 ounces) asparagus; garnish with 1 pimiento, diced.

Spoon 1 No. 2 can (1 pound, 4 ounces) pickled peaches into serving dish, make coffee and set the table. You're ready to serve in 45 minutes.

Chicken 'N' Dumplings

30-MINUTE SUPPER FROM THE SHELF

Serves 4

Chilled Pineapple Juice
Tuna 'n' Noodle Bake
Buttered Peas and Whole Onions
Tomato-Cucumber-Chive Salad
Plum Good Shortcake
Coffee   Milk

First the casserole—

TUNA 'N' NOODLE BAKE

Combine 2 15-ounce cans tuna and noodle dinner, 1 can condensed cream of mushroom soup, 1/2 cup milk and 1/2 cup ripe olives sliced from pits (about 12 olives).

Turn into 1-quart baking dish; sprinkle with crushed potato chips (about 1/2 cup).

Bake in very hot oven (450°F.) 20 minutes, or until bubbling hot.

Note: Or substitute 2 cans egg noodles and beef for tuna and noodle dinner.

Next, dessert—

PLUM GOOD SHORTCAKE

Combine 1/4 cup sugar, 1 1/2 tablespoons cornstarch, and dash of salt in medium-sized saucepan.

Gradually stir in juice drained from 1 No. 2 1/2 can (1 pound, 15 ounces) halved, pitted purple prune plums; cook until thick and clear, stirring constantly.

Add 1/4 teaspoon almond extract and plums.

Serve warm over refrigerator biscuits baked according to label directions, reserving extra biscuits and sauce for another meal.

Garnish with whipped cream, if desired—the quick-pressurized kind.

Hints: Heat together 1 No. 303 can (1 pound) peas and 1 No. 2 can (1 pound, 4 ounces) whole onions, drained; season with butter or margarine, salt and pepper.

For salad, arrange tomato and cucumber slices on crisp greens; serve with salad dressing and a sprinkling of chopped chives.

Pour pineapple juice over ice. After

Old-Fashioned Beef Stew

coffee is made and the table set, you'll have a hearty meal ready to serve in less than 30 minutes—short-order cooking!

25-MINUTE HOT AND HEARTY SUPPER

Serves 4

Tomato and Sauerkraut Blend
Old-Fashioned Beef Stew
Hot Biscuits   Cherry Jam
Apple Betty
Coffee   Milk

First the dessert—

APPLE BETTY

Combine 1 No. 2 can (1 pound, 4 ounces) unsweetened sliced apples, 1/4 cup brown sugar, 1/2 teaspoon cinnamon, and 1/8 teaspoon salt in 1-quart baking dish. Top with 3 slices bread, cut in cubes; drizzle with 1/4 cup honey.

Bake in hot oven (400°F.) 20 minutes, or until bubbling. Serve warm with cream or whipped cream from pressurized cream container.

Then first course—

TOMATO AND SAUER-KRAUT BLEND

Blend 1 No. 2 can (1 pint, 2 ounces; 2 1/2 cups) tomato juice, chilled, with 1/2 cup canned sauerkraut juice; season with juice of 1/2 lemon and few drops Tabasco sauce; chill until serving time.

Next the stew—

OLD-FASHIONED BEEF STEW

Combine in large saucepan 1 1-pound can beef and gravy, 1 can condensed cream of celery soup, 1 8-ounce can whole onions (drained), 1 8-ounce can peas and carrots, and 1/2 cup chili sauce or ketchup. Heat thoroughly; serve in soup bowls.

OR to vary the main dish, serve—

QUICK BRUNSWICK STEW

Combine in large saucepan 1 can (about 1 1/2 pounds) beef stew, 1 can (about 1 pound) chicken stew, 1 No. 303 can (1 pound) lima beans, 1 6-ounce can tomato paste, 1/2 teaspoon Worcestershire sauce, and 2 dashes of Tabasco sauce; heat thoroughly.

Serve in soup bowls. (Chilled pineapple juice makes a good first course with this stew.)

Hints: Open 1 container refrigerator biscuits and pop in oven with dessert to bake about 10 minutes, or until brown.

With coffee made and table set, dinner's ready in about 25 minutes.

35-MINUTE SUNDAY DINNER

Serves 4

Hot Madrilene with Lemon Wheels
Turkey and Mushroom Casserole
Potatoes with Cheese
Peas and Carrots
Pineapple-Cranberry-Cress Salad
Steamed Fig Pudding
        with Orange Sauce
Coffee   Milk

First the casserole—

TURKEY AND MUSHROOM CASSEROLE

Combine 1 can condensed cream of chicken soup, 1 4- or 6-ounce can sliced mushrooms, and 1/4 teaspoon Worcestershire sauce in 1-quart baking dish.

Add 1 6-ounce can boned turkey or chicken, diced. Sprinkle with 1/2 cup packaged bread stuffing for poultry.

Bake in moderate oven (375°F.) 25 minutes, or until bubbling hot. (Or bake in 4 individual baking dishes 20 minutes.)

Next—

POTATOES WITH CHEESE

Place 1 No. 2 can (1 pound, 4 ounces) whole white potatoes, drained, in 8-inch pie pan. Sprinkle with 1/2 cup shredded Cheddar cheese and 3 tablespoons milk.

Place in oven with turkey casserole to heat thoroughly. (Bake at 375°F. 20 minutes.)

Then dessert—

STEAMED FIG PUDDING WITH ORANGE SAUCE

To heat pudding, open 1 12-ounce can fig pudding; place in top of double boiler over boiling water; heat, covered, about 20 minutes.

To make sauce, gradually stir syrup drained from 1 No. 2 can (1 pound, 4 ounces) orange sections into 1 tablespoon cornstarch in small saucepan. Cook, stirring constantly, until thick and clear.

Add orange sections; serve hot over pudding. (Add 2 tablespoons of rum or brandy to sauce, if desired.)

Hints: There's still time to combine, season and heat 1 No. 303 can (1 pound) peas with 1 8-ounce can julienne carrots—a bit of fresh mint does wonders here.

Make coffee and arrange 4 slices drained canned pineapple (9-ounce can) with spoonful of whole or jellied cranberry sauce on crisp watercress; serve with French dressing.

Heat 2 cans madrilene and serve with thin slices of lemon. When you have the table set, dinner is ready in about 35 minutes.

45-MINUTE FESTIVE FARE

Serves 4
Orange-Grapefruit Cocktail
Ham Parisienne
Aspic and Artichoke Salad
Peach Cream Cake
Coffee   Milk

Begin with dessert—

PEACH CREAM CAKE

Whip 1 cup heavy cream; sweeten with 2 tablespoons sugar. Spread thin layer of cream over top of one bought 8-inch sponge layer.

Drain well 1 No. 2½ can (1 pound, 13 ounces) sliced peaches; arrange half of peaches over cake layer; top with second cake layer.

Spread remaining cream over top and sides of cake. Arrange remaining peaches over top of cake. Put chopped toasted almonds (½ of 5-ounce can) on sides of cake; refrigerate until dessert-time.

Note: Almonds come in cans already chopped and toasted. Refrigerate left-over cake for another meal.

Now for the main dish—

HAM PARISIENNE

Prepare 1 package corn muffin mix according to package directions, using 8 x 8 x 2-inch baking pan.

While corn bread bakes, cut 8 slices canned ham (½ of 3-pound canned ham; use remaining ham for another meal). Heat ham in covered frying pan with 2 tablespoons gelatin from ham can or water; keep hot until serving time.

Heat 1 No. 2 can (1 pound, 4 ounces) asparagus spears; drain well; keep warm.

Combine 1 can condensed cream of mushroom soup, 1 4- or 6-ounce can sliced mushrooms including liquid and 1 pimiento, diced; heat thoroughly; add 1 tablespoon sherry, if desired.

To serve, cut corn bread into 4 squares. Split and place squares on large platter. Arrange ham, then asparagus on corn bread; spoon hot mushroom sauce over top.

Hints: To make salad, arrange 1 can tomato aspic, chilled and sliced, and 1 8-ounce can artichoke hearts, chilled and drained, on lettuce; serve with tart French dressing.

For first course, blend 1 6-ounce can frozen concentrated orange and grapefruit juice with water according to label directions; serve over ice.

Make coffee, set the table, and you're ready to serve in about 45 minutes.

30-MINUTE SATURDAY NIGHT FAVORITE

Serves 4
Skillet Corned Beef and Cabbage
Mustard Sauce
Buttered Potatoes
Tomatoes with Pickles
Celery
Broiled Ginger Pear Halves
Vanilla Wafers
Coffee   Milk

Start with—

SKILLET CORNED BEEF AND CABBAGE

Brown in large frying pan 1 12-ounce can corned beef in 2 tablespoons butter or margarine, breaking up meat with fork.

Wash, core and coarsely chop 1 medium-sized head cabbage (about 1½ pounds). Add cabbage to corned beef with 1 teaspoon salt and dash of pepper; toss lightly.

Simmer, tightly covered, 10 minutes, or until cabbage is just fork-tender, stirring often.

Then the—

MUSTARD SAUCE

Heat 1 8-ounce can white sauce according to label direction, blending in 2½ tablespoons prepared mustard. (Or combine 1 can condensed cream of celery soup with 1 to 2 tablespoons prepared mustard; heat thoroughly.)

Serve hot as a sauce with the corned beef and cabbage.

Next the—

TOMATOES WITH PICKLES

Combine 1 No. 2 can (1 pound, 4 ounces) tomatoes, ½ cup drained bread and butter pickles (coarsely chopped), 2 teaspoons sugar, ½ teaspoon salt, and dash of pepper; heat thoroughly.

Dessert last—

BROILED GINGER PEAR HALVES

Arrange 1 No. 2½ can (1 pound, 13 ounces) pear halves with syrup in shallow baking dish.

Fill each pear center with honey; sprinkle lightly with ground ginger or thinly sliced candied ginger.

Place under broiler until bubbling hot; serve at once.

Hints: Heat 1 No. 2 can (1 pound, 4 ounces) whole white potatoes; drain and season with butter or margarine, salt, and pepper.

Have pears ready to pop into hot

broiler while you're clearing the table. You've still time to fix celery, make coffee, set the table. You'll be serving dinner in about 30 minutes.

25-MINUTE MENU FOR CRISP FALL DAYS

Serves 4
Franks 'n' Sauerkraut
Stewed Tomatoes
Green-Gold Salad
Hot Doughnuts à la Mode
Coffee   Milk

Main dish first—

FRANKS 'N' SAUERKRAUT

Combine in large saucepan 1 No. 2½ can (1 pound, 13 ounces) sauerkraut, 1 No. 2 can (1 pound, 4 ounces) unsweetened sliced apples, 1 12-ounce can frankfurters, 1 tablespoon sugar, and 1 teaspoon caraway seeds.

Toss lightly with fork; simmer, covered, 15 minutes, or until thoroughly heated.

Next—

STEWED TOMATOES

Combine in medium-sized saucepan 1 No. 2 can (1 pound, 4 ounces) tomatoes, 2 slices bread (cut in cubes), 1 tablespoon sugar, 2 tablespoons butter or margarine, ½ teaspoon each salt and onion salt and dash of pepper. Heat thoroughly.

Then the salad—

GREEN-GOLD SALAD

Drain 1 No. 303 can (1 pound) peas, reserving liquid for soup or gravy.

Toss peas lightly with ½ cup each sliced celery and cubed processed American cheese, ½ teaspoon salt, and 2 tablespoons mayonnaise or salad dressing blended with a bit of canned lemon juice or red wine vinegar. Spoon into lettuce cups.

For dessert—

HOT DOUGHNUTS À LA MODE

Put 4 doughnuts in top of double boiler over boiling water to heat while you sit down to dinner.

At dessert-time, heat about ½ cup canned chocolate syrup in small saucepan.

Arrange doughnuts in individual serving dishes; top each with scoop of vanilla ice cream, hot chocolate syrup and a sprinkling of canned chopped nuts.

Note: Spongecake or leftover cake may be substituted for doughnuts.

Hints: With coffee made and table set, you're serving in 25 minutes.

30-MINUTE DOWN-EAST DINNER

Serves 4
Quick Baked Beans
Codfish Cakes   Tomato Sauce
Coleslaw   Brown Bread
Indian Pudding
Coffee   Milk

Begin with the beans—

QUICK BAKED BEANS

Combine in medium-sized saucepan 2 1-pound cans baked beans in tomato sauce with ¼ cup ketchup or chili sauce, 1 tablespoon prepared mustard, and ½ teaspoon Worcestershire sauce. Heat thoroughly.

Then—

CODFISH CAKES

Shape four codfish cakes, using 2 10-ounce cans codfish cakes. Dust lightly with flour; brown on both sides in 2 tablespoons butter or margarine in frying pan.

Heat 1 8-ounce can tomato sauce; serve with hot codfish cakes.

Hints: Because it takes time to heat, open 1 11-ounce can brown bread; slice and heat in top of double boiler over boiling water after preparing the baked beans. Serve brown bread hot.

Use top of same double boiler to heat 1 1-pound can Indian Pudding while you serve the main course.

At dessert-time, top hot pudding with cream, bought hard sauce or vanilla ice cream. (For a light fruit dessert, substitute canned purple plums.)

Make your favorite coleslaw, adding 1 9-ounce can crushed pineapple, well drained, if desired. Then set the table and make coffee. Your dinner—New England style—is ready in about 30 minutes.

15-MINUTE MENU

Serves 4
Jiffy Spaghetti and Meat Balls
Swiss Spinach
Celery and Ripe Olives
Crusty Bread   Butter
Fruited Poundcake
Coffee   Milk

First—

JIFFY SPAGHETTI AND MEAT BALLS

Combine 2 1-pound cans spaghetti in tomato sauce and 1 15-ounce can meat balls with gravy. Simmer, covered, 10 minutes, or until thoroughly heated, stirring carefully.

Serve with sprinkling of Parmesan cheese; pass extra cheese.

Note: Or use 1 15-ounce can hamburgers.

Then—

SWISS SPINACH

Heat 1 No. 2 can (1 pound, 4 ounces) chopped spinach in medium-sized saucepan; drain thoroughly.

Return to saucepan; toss lightly with ¼ cup top milk, cream, or evaporated milk, ½ teaspoon onion salt and ¼ teaspoon nutmeg. Heat well, but do not boil.

Dessert next—

FRUITED POUNDCAKE

Have ingredients ready to put together after you've cleared the main course.

Place 4 slices poundcake on baking sheet ready to toast on both sides in broiler. Open 1 1-pound can fruits for salad.

At dessert-time, put 1 slice toasted poundcake on each serving plate; spoon fruit over cake and top with whipped cream, if desired. (A little green crème de menthe sprinkled over the fruit adds interest, color and flavor.)

Hints: While the spaghetti and spinach heat, fix relishes, make coffee and set the table. A good meal in about 15 minutes.

30-MINUTE HOT-OFF-THE-GRIDDLE SUPPER

Serves 4
Corn Cakes and Sausages
Hot Syrup
Celery Sticks
Grapefruit Surprise
Coffee   Milk

Dessert first—

GRAPEFRUIT SURPRISE

Spoon 1 No. 2 can (1 pound, 4 ounces) grapefruit sections into 4 individual sauce dishes.

Top with 1 10½-ounce can frozen strawberries, partially thawed. Chill until dessert-time.

Pancakes last—

CORN CAKES AND SAUSAGES

Combine and sift together 1 cup sifted enriched flour, 1½ teaspoons baking powder and ½ teaspoon salt.

Combine 1 well beaten egg, 1 cup (8-ounce can) cream-style corn, and 1 cup milk; stir into dry ingredients with 2 tablespoons melted butter or margarine.

Bake on lightly greased griddle or in frying pan until golden brown, turning once. Put pancakes in warm oven to keep hot until all cakes are baked.

Serve hot with heated, canned maple syrup and 1 8-ounce can breakfast sausages heated according to label directions.

Note: Or you may use sliced bacon in place of sausages for a quick variation.

Hints: Corn cakes are best when they're hot off the griddle, so have the table set, celery sticks cut and coffee made before you start baking the cakes. This short-order supper or lunch is ready in less than 30 minutes.

40-MINUTE MENU FOR WINTRY DAYS

Serves 4
Chili-Topped Corned Beef Hash 'n' Eggs
Buttered Green Beans
French-Fried Onion Rings
Cabbage and Tomato Slaw
Hot Biscuits
Cherry Dumplings
Coffee   Milk

Baked dish first—

CHILI-TOPPED CORNED BEEF HASH 'N' EGGS

Spread 1 1-pound can corned beef hash in 9-inch pie pan. Top hash with 1 No. 303 can (1 pound) whole-kernel corn, well drained; make 4 depressions in corn and break 1 egg into each; top with ½ cup chili sauce.

Bake in hot oven (400°F.) 20 minutes, or until thoroughly heated and eggs are set.

Then dessert—

CHERRY DUMPLINGS

Combine ⅓ cup sugar and 1½ tablespoons cornstarch in medium-sized frying pan with tight-fitted cover.

Gradually add juice drained from 1 No. 2 can (1 pound, 4 ounces) red sour pitted cherries and few drops red food coloring.

Cook until thick and clear, stirring constantly. Add cherries; heat to bubbling hot.

Open 1 can refrigerator biscuits; put 4 biscuits on top of cherries; simmer, tightly covered, 15 minutes. (Put remaining biscuits on baking sheet; pop in oven to bake and serve with hash.)

Keep dumplings warm until dessert-time; serve with cream or, for a special treat, top with vanilla ice cream.

Hints: While you're waiting for hash to bake and dumplings to cook, heat 1 3½-ounce can French-fried onions according to label directions.

Heat 1 No. 303 can (1 pound) French-style green beans; season with butter or margarine, salt and pepper.

Then make coffee and coleslaw, and set the table. Here's a 40-minute meal—one sure to please.

Quick Eggs Benedict

30-MINUTE SAVE-A-PENNY SUPPER

Serves 4
Tomato Cocktail
Quick Eggs Benedict
Chick Peas and Bean Sprouts Marinade
Cherry-Graham Cracker Pudding
Coffee   Milk

Salad first—

CHICK PEAS AND BEAN SPROUTS MARINADE

Drain and combine 1 No. 2 can (1 pound, 4 ounces) chick peas and 1 No. 2 can (1 pound, 4 ounces) bean sprouts, reserving liquid for first course.

Toss lightly with 2 tablespoons French dressing, 1 tablespoon soy sauce, and 1/2 teaspoon salt; chill.

When ready to serve, spoon into lettuce cups; top with sliced ripe olives.

First course next—

TOMATO COCKTAIL

Combine liquid reserved from chick peas and bean sprouts and 2 1/2 cups tomato juice (1 No. 2 can).

Season with 1 teaspoon canned lemon juice and a few drops Tabasco sauce. Chill until serving time, or serve over ice.

Then dessert—

CHERRY-GRAHAM CRACKER PUDDING

Prepare 1 package vanilla pudding mix according to package directions.

Fold in 1 8-ounce can dark sweet cherries, well drained, and 10 graham crackers broken into bite-sized pieces. Chill until serving time.

Note: Canned crushed pineapple, applesauce, fruit cocktail, or strained fruits for babies may be used in place of cherries.

Now for—

QUICK EGGS BENEDICT

Heat 1 8 1/2- or 9-ounce can cheese rabbit in top of double boiler over boiling water.

Split and toast 4 English muffins; spread with 2 cans (2 1/4-ounces each) deviled ham.

Just before serving, top each muffin half with 1 hot poached egg; spoon hot rabbit over eggs. Serve at once, two halves per person.

Note: Or use 1 cup of favorite cheese sauce in place of rabbit.

Hints: Make coffee and set table for a 30-Minute Meal.

30-MINUTE MENU FOR MAN SIZED APPETITES

Serves 4
Hamburgers and Gravy on Rice
Buttered Green Beans
4-Fruit Salad
French Bread
Chocolate Crunch Pudding
Coffee   Milk

First the—

HAMBURGERS AND GRAVY ON RICE

Combine 1 10-ounce can beef gravy and 1 15-ounce can hamburgers and gravy in saucepan; simmer, covered, 10 minutes, or until hamburgers are thoroughly heated.

Serve over 2 12-ounce cans cooked rice, heated according to label directions; or use 1 package (5 ounces) precooked rice prepared according to package directions.

Note: Canned Salisbury steaks or canned beefsteaks with gravy may be substituted for hamburgers and gravy.

Then dessert—

CHOCOLATE CRUNCH PUDDING

Prepare 1 package instant chocolate pudding mix according to package directions.

Fold in 1/3 cup coarsely crushed canned peanut brittle or chopped canned peanuts.

Chill until serving time. If you have any leftover cake, fold in 1 or 2 slices cut in bite-sized pieces.

Now the salad—

4-FRUIT SALAD

Drain syrup from 1 8-ounce can each of sliced peaches, Bing cherries, pear halves, and pineapple tidbits. (Reserve syrup for fruit drinks.)

Arrange fruit on crisp salad greens; top each salad with spoonful of sweet

or sour cream and a generous sprinkling of nutmeg.

Hints: There's time to heat and season 1 No. 303 can (1 pound) green beans, adding 2 tablespoons each tartar sauce and chili sauce.

Make coffee and set the table for another 30-minute meal.

40-MINUTE MENU FOR EASY ENTERTAINING

Serves 4
Onion Soup
Chicken and Shrimp Curry on Parsley Rice
Raisins — Pineapple—
Chutney — Coconut
Buttered Peas   Julienne Beets
Garden Greens   French Dressing
Choco-Mint Cake
Coffee   Milk

It's dessert first—

CHOCO-MINT CAKE

Prepare and bake 1 package white cake mix according to package directions, using 13 x 9 x 2-inch baking pan.

When cake is baked, remove from oven; arrange 1 package (8 1/2 ounces) chocolate mint-flavored candy wafers over top of cake. Return cake to oven for 3 minutes, or until chocolate is melted.

Score top lightly with fork; sprinkle with 1/2 cup coarsely chopped canned peanuts; cool on wire cake rack. Cut in squares.

While cake bakes—

CHICKEN AND SHRIMP CURRY ON PARSLEY RICE

Blend 1 can condensed cream of chicken soup with 1/4 cup milk. Add 1 to 2 teaspoons curry powder (real curry fans will like the larger amount); 1 6-ounce can boned chicken and 1 5-ounce can shrimp, drained and deveined. Heat thoroughly.

Serve over 2 12-ounce cans cooked white or wild rice, heated according to label directions and tossed with 2 tablespoons chopped parsley, 1 tablespoon butter or margarine, and 1/4 teaspoon salt. (Or use 1 package (5 ounces) precooked rice prepared according to label directions.)

Hints: Next heat and season vegetables, using 1 No. 303 can (1 pound) sugar peas and 1 No. 303 can (1 pound) julienne beets.

Fill small condiment dishes with raisins, pineapple chunks (1 No. 1 tall can: 1 pound), chutney and canned coconut.

Then heat 2 cans ready-to-serve onion soup, arrange salad greens, make coffee and set table—all done in about 40 minutes.

Chili and Tamales

25-MINUTE DOWN MEXICO WAY MENU
Serves 4
Chili and Tamales
Crisp Crackers   French Bread
Tossed Salad
Hot Spiced Apricots
Coffee   Milk

First—

CHILI AND TAMALES

Combine 2 15-ounce cans chili con carne with beans and 1 15-ounce can red kidney beans, drained, in medium-sized saucepan; heat.

Place 1 15-ounce can tamales over chili; heat thoroughly.

Dessert next—

HOT SPICED APRICOTS

Drain into saucepan syrup from 1 No. 2½ can (1 pound, 13 ounces) apricot halves or whole apricots.

Add 3 lemon slices, 8 whole cloves, and ⅛ teaspoon allspice; simmer 5 minutes. Add apricots; heat thoroughly and serve hot.

Note: Peaches, pears, pineapple, or sweet cherries may be substituted for apricots.

Hints: Make your favorite tossed salad, adding a little crumbled Roquefort cheese. Fix coffee; set the table.

Heat the French bread and crackers. You're ready to serve this hearty meal in less than 25 minutes.

35-MINUTE FRIDAY DINNER
Serves 4
Vegetable Juice Cocktail
Salmon Scallop
Herb Peas
Lettuce Wedges   French Dressing
Bread Sticks
Prune-Peach Whip
Coffee   .Milk

The casserole first—

SALMON SCALLOP

Drain and flake 1 7¾-ounce can salmon.

Combine 2 cups coarsely crushed salted cracker crumbs, ⅓ cup melted butter or margarine, 1 tablespoon minced parsley, 1 teaspoon grated on-

ion and dash of pepper.

Spread 1 cup crumb mixture in 8-inch pie pan. Cover with salmon; sprinkle with remaining crumb mixture Pour 1 cup milk or undiluted evaporated milk over crumbs.

Bake in hot oven (400°F.) 20 minutes, or until crumbs brown and casserole is thoroughly heated.

Note: Or use 1 6-ounce can lobster or 1 6½-ounce can crabmeat in place of salmon.

Dessert next—

PRUNE-PEACH WHIP

Whip 1 cup heavy cream, beating in 2 teaspoons sugar. Carefully fold in 1 can (4¾ ounces) strained prunes and 1 can (4¾ ounces) strained peaches—baby-food pack.

Arrange lady fingers around sides of dessert dishes; pile prune-peach mixture in center. Chill until serving time.

For the vegetable—

HERB PEAS

Drain liquid from 1 No. 303 can (1 pound) peas into saucepan; boil quickly to reduce to about ⅓ cup.

Add peas, 1 tablespoon butter or margarine, ½ teaspoon salt, and ⅛ teaspoon mixed herbs; toss lightly; heat well.

Hints: While scallop bakes, fix the salad, make coffee, set the table and pour the chilled juice or serve over ice (12-ounce can vegetable juice cocktail to serve 4). Dinner's ready in 35 to 40 minutes.

25-MINUTE SOUP TUREEN SUPPER
Serves 4
Quick Lobster Chowder
Tossed Salad   Parmesan Dressing
Potato Chips   Refrigerator Biscuits
Orange Nut Roll   Whipped Cream
Coffee   Milk

Soup first—

QUICK LOBSTER CHOWDER

Blend 1 can condensed cream of mushroom soup, 1 can condensed cream of tomato soup, 1 soup can milk and 1 cup light cream; heat, but do not boil.

Drain 1 6-ounce can lobster; pick over meat, discarding any hard fiber; flake meat. Add to soup; heat well.

Note: As a substitute for the lobster, any one of the following may be used: 1 6½-ounce can crabmeat, 1 5-ounce can shrimp, 1 7-ounce can solid-pack tuna, 1 7¾-ounce can salmon, or 1 7- or 10½-ounce can minced clams.

Hints: Next, open 1 can Orange Nut Roll (about 8 ounces) and place in top of double boiler; heat, covered, over

boiling water about 20 minutes. (For party flavor, add 2 to 3 tablespoons of rum while heating.)

At dessert-time, slice roll and top with whipped cream from pressurized cream container.

Toss salad lightly with French dressing and 1 tablespoon grated Parmesan cheese.

Bake 1 container refrigerator biscuits according to label directions. Now there's time to make coffee and set the table.

For extra crisp potato chips, pop them in oven with biscuits just to heat. In about 25 minutes the meal's ready—wonderful enough for easy party food, filling enough for hearty family fare.

30-MINUTE SUPPER
Serves 4
Macaroni and Cheese Stuffed Peppers
Stewed Tomatoes   Curried Carrots
Celery Sticks
Strawberry and Pineapple Compote
Cookies
Coffee   Milk

First—

MACARONI AND CHEESE STUFFED PEPPERS

Cut 2 large, or 4 small, green peppers in half lengthwise; remove all seeds and veins; wash. Steam, covered, in simmering water 10 minutes, or until just tender; drain well.

Meanwhile, heat 2 cans (about 1 pound each) macaroni with cheese sauce.

Place hot drained peppers in shallow baking pan; fill with hot macaroni and cheese. Top with shredded Cheddar cheese (about 1 tablespoon for each pepper) and sprinkle with paprika.

Just before serving, put under broiler until cheese topping melts.

Note: You may use 2 cans (about 15 ounces each) Spanish rice in place of macaroni and cheese.

Then—

CURRIED CARROTS

Heat 1 No. 303 can (1 pound) diced carrots; drain and season with butter or margarine, salt, pepper, and ½ to ¾ teaspoon curry powder; toss lightly.

Hints: Heat 1 No. 303 can (1 pound) stewed tomatoes; cut celery sticks; make coffee and set the table.

Open 1 10½-ounce can frozen pineapple chunks and 1 10½-ounce can frozen strawberries; let thaw while you're serving main course.

At dessert-time, spoon fruits into dessert dishes; sprinkle a teaspoon of Cointreau over each, if desired.

SALADS

The salad-wise homemaker will choose salads to fit the meal. If they accompany the main course of the dinner, she will choose a light salad. If served as a first course, the salad will be made up of tart fruits or seafood. A frozen salad or a fruit salad will be chosen for the dessert course.

If a salad is chosen as the main course of the meal, it should have some protein-rich food such as meat, poultry, fish, eggs, or cheese as the main ingredient.

Garnishes for Salads

Suitable garnishings for meat and vegetable salads are: sliced cucumbers, quartered and sliced tomatoes, canned beets cut into cubes, sticks, or slices, sliced or quartered hard-cooked eggs, green and red pepper, pimiento, stuffed olives, carrot sticks, sliced or diced pickles, cheese strips, cubes, or slices, and other suggested garnishes.

Fruit salads may be garnished with maraschino cherries, melon balls, mint leaves, herbs, strawberries, dark fruits, ripe olives, nuts, coconut, shredded dates, figs, and pitted prunes.

ASPARAGUS TIPS

Marinate small canned asparagus tips in French dressing. Sprinkle ends with paprika.

TO MAKE CARROT FLOWERS

Scrape tender carrots. Make lengthwise cuts 1/8 inch deep into carrots. Cut crosswise into paperthin slices. Keep slices in ice water an hour or so to curl petals.

CARROT STRIPS

Wash and scrape young, tender carrots. Cut into thin strips lengthwise. Chill in ice water.

CARROT CURLS

Slice carrot paper-thin lengthwise. Roll up each slice and fasten with wooden pick. Crisp in ice water. Remove pick.

CARROT STICK BUNDLES

Slice carrot lengthwise into small strips.

Cut pits from large olives. Push 3 or 4 strips through openings in olives.

CUCUMBER BALLS

With a French vegetable cutter, cut large cucumbers into balls.

Marinate in dressing. Sprinkle with paprika.

FLUTED CUCUMBERS

Cucumbers may be left unpeeled or peeled. Run a fork down the length of cucumber, repeating completely around the cucumber. Slice.

CUCUMBER RADISH FANS

Cut ends of 2 unpeeled cucumbers. Quarter lengthwise. Slash each quarter in 1/8-inch slices. Do not cut all the way through.

Cut 8 large radishes crosswise into thin slices. Insert radishes between cucumber slices.

RADISH ROSES

Cut down thin strips of red peel of radishes almost through to stems to form petals.

Place radishes in ice water. As they chill the peel will curl back like petals.

CALLA LILIES

Pare a white turnip. Cut into thin lengthwise slices. Chill in ice water until they curl and resemble calla lilies. Form stems from carrot strips.

STUFFED PICKLES

Core large pickles. Fill with cream cheese. Chill thoroughly and slice.

CUCUMBER BOATS

Remove seeds and pulp from a cucumber. Fill with cream cheese.

Chill well and slice again, if desired.

Beets and carrots may be cooked until just done and then filled with cottage cheese.

LETTUCE CUPS

For lettuce cups to lie flat on the plate, cut each leaf up from the stem end about 2 or 3 inches.

Fit 2 leaves together on each plate, interlocking the slits.

GREEN OR RED PEPPER RINGS

Cut off tops. Remove seeds and centers. Cut crosswise into thin slices.

Crisp in ice water. Dry before using.

GREEN ONIONS (Scallions)

Trim washed green stalks, leaving about 3 inches. Trim onion if skin is loose or shriveled. Chill in ice water.

ONION RINGS

Cut large Bermuda or Spanish onion into thin slices. Crisp in ice water, then loosen rings and drain well.

RADISH FANS

Select firm and rather long radishes. With a thin, very sharp knife, cut thin slices crosswise almost through radish.

Chill in ice water. The slices spread fan-shaped as they chill.

TO MAKE CELERY CURLS

Cut small stalks or short pieces of celery lengthwise into thin shreds, cutting to within 1/2 inch of the leaves or end of piece. Place in ice water to curl.

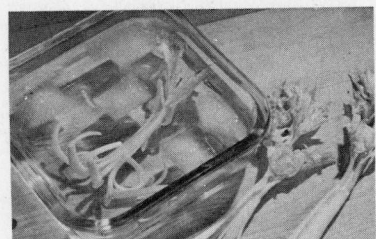

SALAD-MAKING HINTS

- Buy the freshest salad greens possible, wash them, dry thoroughly, and store in refrigerator in the vegetable compartment or bag or in a damp towel until ready to serve. Fresh, clean, crisp, tender greens are the basis of a good green salad.
- All ingredients should be well drained before they are combined with the dressing, to avoid giving the dressing a watery consistency. Dry greens thoroughly by patting with a towel.
- Use a variety of greens. Try shredded cabbage, endive, watercress, and romaine as a change from head or leaf lettuce. Tear lettuce into bite-size pieces instead of cutting. Outer leaves of lettuce should be discarded only when they are bruised.
- When mixing salads, toss ingredients gently until mixed. Don't stir vigorously.
- Add the dressing to salads at serving time to avoid wilting the greens, or, better still, serve the dressing from a separate bowl. People differ in the amount of dressing they prefer.
- Use leftover vegetables in salad bowls.
- The flavor of some salads, especially those containing cooked vegetables or meats, is improved by marinating the ingredients in French dressing. To do this, let foods stand in the dressing in a cool place until they are well seasoned. Drain before serving.
- Wooden salad bowls should not be washed. Wipe clean with a cold damp cloth. Before using, season with warm salad oil, followed by rubbing the bowl with a cut clove of garlic.
- Use a variety of dressings. It is not necessary to make a dressing for each salad. Most dressings keep well in the refrigerator.
- Avoid too much garnish. Depend upon the natural color and flavor of foods for an attractive appetizing salad. Arrange salads lightly and attractively.

Grapefruit Appetizer

First Course Appetizer Salads

Appetizer salads are usually miniature salads served as a first course for luncheon or dinner. Almost any favorite salad could be used for this purpose if arranged attractively on a small bed of salad greens placed on an individual plate, and accompanied with a tart dressing. Naturally the type of salad depends somewhat on the courses that are to follow but the variety is endless. Because salads have become so popular and can be made so tasty and attractive it's the wise homemaker who turns to them as a curtain raiser.

ITALIAN APPETIZER SALAD (Antipasto)

Lettuce
Thick tomato slices
Thin Italian salami slices
Cole slaw
Anchovies
Olives

Arrange lettuce leaves on individual salad plates. Cover with tomato and salami slices.

Pile well-seasoned cole slaw into a cone on top of this. Cross the top with 2 anchovies. Garnish with black and stuffed olives.

Serve olive oil and wine vinegar in cruets to accompany the salad.

ITALIAN APPETIZER SALAD #2

On each serving dish arrange thin, unpeeled apple slices, strips of green pepper, a mound of cole slaw, a pimiento, one or two sardines, stuffed pickled onions, black olives and stuffed olives.

Serve olive oil and wine vinegar in cruets to accompany the salad.

BARBECUED EGGPLANT SALAD

Broil 2 medium eggplants until rather burned and very soft.

Peel eggplants carefully.

Then chop and add ½ cup each minced onions and parsley, ¼ cup each vinegar and salad or olive oil, and 1½ teaspoons salt and ¼ teaspoon pepper. Chill well. Serves 8 to 10.

TOMATO-CHEESE APPETIZER

For each serving arrange 2 slices of tomato, a ball of cream cheese and chives, and 2 radish roses on a lettuce leaf. Serve with mayonnaise.

GRAPEFRUIT APPETIZER

For each serving arrange grapefruit sections alternately with strips of green pepper on a lettuce leaf.

Serve with Thousand Island dressing made by blending 1 cup mayonnaise with ⅓ cup chili sauce.

HONEYDEW WITH PROSCIUTTO

1 large honeydew melon
½ pound prosciutto ham

Have the ham sliced paper thin. Cut the melon into 8 wedges and arrange a wedge of melon with 2 or 3 slices of ham on an individual plate for each person. Serve with a small knife and fork.

TOMATO AND EGG APPETIZERS

Lettuce
Slices of large tomatoes
Slices of hard-cooked eggs
Stuffed olive slices
1 3-ounce package cream cheese
1½ tablespoons French dressing

Arrange tomato slices on lettuce leaves on individual dishes. On each slice of tomato arrange 3 slices of hard-cooked egg topped with olive slices.

Moisten cheese with French dressing. Press mixture through pastry tube around edge of tomatoes.

Variations: Omit cream cheese and French dressing. Spread tomatoes with prepared mustard before topping with egg slices. Sprinkle egg slices with cayenne or paprika.

PACIFIC COAST APPETIZER

Hollow out chilled, fresh tomatoes, reserving the pulp and juice for Close-To-The-Border Sauce (below).

Fill tomato cups with your favorite seafood cocktail, and serve on chilled, crisp iceberg lettuce.

Close-To-The-Border Sauce: A flavorful, uncooked sauce to serve with meat, fish, and other first course foods.

Combine 2 cups fresh tomato pulp and juice with 2 tablespoons each minced green pepper, celery, and cucumber. Add 1 tablespoon of wine vinegar and salt and pepper to taste.

A bit of chili powder will add "heat" for those who want it. This sauce is especially good on enchiladas, tamales, and other Mexican foods.

Pacific Coast Appetizer

DICED CUCUMBER COCKTAIL

2 large cucumbers
1/4 cup ketchup
1/4 cup chili sauce
1 teaspoon Worcestershire sauce
Juice of 1/2 lemon
1 teaspoon prepared horseradish
Dash of Tabasco or cayenne
4 lettuce leaves

Chill cucumbers. Combine remaining ingredients except lettuce to make sauce and chill.

Just before serving, peel cucumbers; make lengthwise parallel grooves with tines of fork. Dice in 1/4 inch pieces. Place on lettuce leaves in cocktail glasses. Top with sauce. Serves 4.

AVOCADO-TOMATO COCKTAIL

1 avocado
2 tomatoes
Small lettuce leaves
1/2 cup chili sauce
1 tablespoon horseradish
Juice 1/2 lemon
1/2 teaspoon salt
1/8 teaspoon pepper

Peel and dice chilled avocado and tomatoes. Put on lettuce in cocktail glasses.

Mix remaining ingredients, and serve as sauce. Serves 4.

CAULIFLOWER COCKTAIL

1 head of cauliflower
1/2 cup mayonnaise
3 tablespoons chopped sweet pickle
1 tablespoon capers
1/2 teaspoon prepared mustard
1 tablespoon lemon juice
Few grains of salt

Cook the cauliflower until just tender. Chill thoroughly and separate into flowerets.

Serve in cocktail cups on lettuce topped with a dressing made of the remaining ingredients.

AVOCADO-OLIVE APPETIZER

1 large, ripe avocado
1 cup highly seasoned French dressing
1/3 cup chopped stuffed olives

Peel avocado. Cut in two and remove seed. Cut in 1/4 inch lengthwise slices. Cover with French dressing and let stand in refrigerator 30 minutes.

Drain and reserve dressing for future salads. Sprinkle with olives. Serves 4.

FROZEN TOMATO AND CUCUMBER COCKTAIL

4 large tomatoes, diced
2 large cucumbers, diced
1/2 cup chili sauce
2 teaspoons horseradish
1 teaspoon Worcestershire sauce
1 tablespoon lemon juice

Put tomatoes in refrigerator tray and partially freeze. Spoon into cocktail glasses, filling each about half full. Fill with cucumber.

Mix remaining ingredients and use for topping cocktail. Serves 6 to 8.

TOMATO-CAVIAR-SHRIMP APPETIZERS

Lettuce leaves
Caviar
Chopped hard-cooked egg yolks
Few drops of lemon juice
Thin slices of tomato
Chopped hard-cooked egg whites
Marinated cooked or canned shrimp

Arrange lettuce leaves on individual plates. Combine caviar and chopped egg yolks; season with lemon juice. Spread this mixture on tomato slices. Garnish with chopped egg whites.

Place in center of lettuce leaves. Garnish the centers with shrimp.

ENDIVE APPETIZER

6 endive leaves
2 tablespoons caviar
2 lemon wedges
1 3-ounce package cream cheese
Seasonings
Mayonnaise

Fill endive with caviar and arrange 3 leaves on each plate, meeting at the center on a lemon wedge.

Season cheese highly and moisten with mayonnaise; shape in balls and arrange 3 on each plate between endive leaves. Serves 2.

EGG-SARDINE APPETIZER

Cut hard-cooked eggs in halves, lengthwise. Season with salt, pepper, and paprika.

Place a small well-drained sardine or rolled fillet of anchovy over each egg half.

Arrange on a crisp lettuce leaf. Garnish with a bit of lemon.

HAM AND TOMATO APPETIZERS

8 tablespoons deviled ham
3 tablespoons mayonnaise
1/2 teaspoon minced onion
4 large tomatoes
Parsley

Combine ham, mayonnaise, and onion. Wash, dry, core, and cut each tomato in to 4 1/4-inch crosswise slices.

Spread deviled ham mixture on half the tomato slices and top each with a second tomato slice to make sandwiches.

Arrange on lettuce on individual dishes. Garnish with mayonnaise and a sprig of parsley. Serves 8.

EGG AND TOMATO APPETIZER

4 eggs
1/4 teaspoon salt
1/4 teaspoon paprika
3 large, firm tomatoes

Hard-cook eggs and chop 3 of them while still warm. Add salt, paprika, and a few drops of onion juice. Pack tightly into small buttered molds; chill 4 to 5 hours.

Remove from mold and cut into 1/2-inch slices. Place thick slices of tomato on lettuce; add egg slices. Cover with desired dressing.

SARDINE APPETIZER

2 large cans boneless, skinless sardines
1/4 pound butter, creamed
Lemon juice
Paprika
1 cup pimiento olives, sliced

Mash sardines with fork; add creamed butter. Mix and season with lemon juice and paprika. Chill until firm.

Mold as desired. Cover with sliced olives. Chill. Serve with sliced lemon.

AVOCADO AND SHRIMP APPETIZER SALAD

2 avocados
1/2 pound cooked, cleaned shrimp

Sauce:

1/2 cup mayonnaise
1/4 cup chili sauce
1/4 teaspoon grated onion
1 tablespoon finely chopped green pepper
1 1/2 teaspoons Worcestershire sauce
1 tablespoon lemon juice
1/4 teaspoon salt
Dash of Tabasco sauce

Prepare sauce by combining all sauce ingredients. Chill until ready to serve.

Cut avocados into halves, lengthwise, and peel if desired. Place each avocado half on lettuce leaf. Place shrimp over cut side of fruit. Serve with sauce. Serves 4.

TOMATO-GRAPEFRUIT SALAD

4 tomatoes, peeled
1/2 bunch watercress
2 grapefruit, peeled and sectioned
Pimiento strips
Mayonnaise, salad dressing, or French dressing

For each serving place a tomato, whole, quartered or sliced, on watercress on a salad plate. Surround the tomato with grapefruit sections. Garnish with pimiento strips.

Serve with mayonnaise, salad dressing, or French dressing. Serves 4.

Tossed Salads and Vegetable Salad Bowls

BASIC TOSSED SALAD

This is the simplest of all bowl salads. Any number of fresh or cooked vegetables may be used. Choose one or several kinds of following greens: lettuce, chicory, romaine, endive, escarole, watercress, green dandelions, or raw spinach.

Add any of following: sliced or chopped radishes, onions, celery, green pepper, cucumber, tomato, carrot, bits of leftover snap beans, beets, carrots, peas, sliced cauliflower, etc.

Be sure greens are crisp, clean, and dry. Wash them thoroughly in cold water, then dry by shaking in a towel. No salad should ever be watery.

Break greens into desired pieces. Add chopped or sliced vegetables. Mix in salad dressing, using two forks, being sure not to break the vegetables. Serve on lettuce leaves or in individual salad bowls.

For a suggestion of garlic or onion, rub bowl, before adding ingredients, with a freshly cut surface of either.

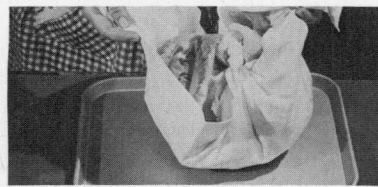

Tie washed "greens" in a dry towel and shake well before storing.

Store cleaned salad vegetables in refrigerator to chill them.

For tossed salads, tear salad greens to bite-size pieces.

Add dressing to salad greens just before serving.

ITALIAN SALAD BOWL

1 clove garlic
1 2-ounce can rolled anchovy fillets
¼ cup olive or other salad oil
1 tablespoon tarragon vinegar
1 tablespoon fresh lemon juice
1 teaspoon dry mustard
½ teaspoon salt
Freshly ground pepper
1 tablespoon capers
2 large potatoes
1 (No. 2) can green beans
Lettuce
1 or 2 tomatoes
Ripe olives

Peel garlic and mash with 2 anchovies. Add oil, vinegar, lemon juice, seasonings, and capers. Let stand 1 hour.

Cook potatoes in jackets until tender; peel and dice. Drain beans, add potatoes and pour dressing over them; toss to coat well and chill in refrigerator at least 1 hour.

Just before serving, toss again. Garnish with a ruffle of lettuce, tomatoes cut into wedges, ripe olives, and remaining anchovies. Serves 4 to 6.

TOSSED GREENS SALAD BOWL WITH DRESSING

1 small clove garlic, if desired
½ cup salad oil
3 tablespoons vinegar
¾ teaspoon salt
⅛ teaspoon pepper
½ teaspoon sugar
½ teaspoon dry mustard
½ teaspoon paprika
1 medium head lettuce, broken into 1½-inch chunks
4 large romaine leaves, cut into 1½-inch lengths
¼ bunch watercress, stems removed

Have all salad ingredients except seasonings chilled. Rub inside of salad bowl with cut surface of garlic clove and then discard garlic.

Add next 7 ingredients and beat with fork until well blended. Break lettuce and romaine into salad bowl in alternate layers. Add watercress.

Toss ingredients lightly until each piece of salad green is coated with dressing. Serve immediately. Serves 6.

STRING BEAN AND RADISH SALAD

Use 2 cups cooked slivered string beans, 1 teaspoon chopped chives, and ½ cup thinly sliced crisp radishes tossed with a few greens and French dressing. If desired, add a few tablespoons crumbled Roquefort cheese.

Italian Salad Bowl

GREEK SALAD

Cut 1 head lettuce and the following vegetables very fine: 3 peeled tomatoes, 4 spring onions, 1 large cucumber, 2 green peppers, 1 bunch roka (Greek watercress) or substitute our watercress.

Toss mixture with 3 tablespoons vinegar, 1 teaspoon salt, and 12 black ripe olives.

Pour ⅓ cup olive oil over all; let stand ¼ hour to ripen and serve. Serves 6.

CAESAR SALAD

1 clove garlic
½ cup salad oil
½ head lettuce
½ bunch curly endive
1 cup croutons
1 2-ounce can anchovy fillets
3 or 4 tomatoes, diced
1 beaten egg
1 tablespoon Worcestershire sauce
¼ cup lemon juice
½ teaspoon pepper
½ teaspoon salt
½ cup grated Parmesan cheese

Mash garlic and add to salad oil. Break lettuce into large wooden salad bowl. Tear endive.

Add croutons, anchovies, and tomatoes. Strain oil to remove garlic and pour over vegetables.

Combine remaining ingredients and beat well. Pour over salad and toss lightly. Serves 4 to 6.

Croutons: Work 1 teaspoon thick bottled meat sauce or Worcestershire sauce into ½ cup butter and spread on slices of stale bread.

Cut into cubes and brown in the oven or in a frying pan. Sprinkle lightly with salt and use as a garnish for Caesar salad.

Caesar Salad

Grapefruit Spinach Salad Oriental

GRAPEFRUIT SPINACH SALAD ORIENTAL

10 ounces raw spinach, washed and drained
1 can (4 ounces) sliced mushrooms, drained
1 can (5 ounces) water chestnuts, diced
2 grapefruit, sectioned and diced
1/4 cup salad oil
2 tablespoons vinegar
2 tablespoons grapefruit juice
1 tablespoon soy sauce
1/4 teaspoon Tabasco sauce
1/4 teaspoon salt
1/4 teaspoon dry mustard

Coarsely tear spinach into large salad bowl. Add mushrooms, water chestnuts, and grapefruit.

Mix oil, vinegar, grapefruit juice, soy sauce, Tabasco, salt, and dry mustard. Toss with spinach mixture. Serves 6 to 8.

HEARTY GARDEN SALAD BOWL

1/3 cup garlic French dressing
3 tablespoons mayonnaise
1 can (1 pound) mixed vegetables
1 small onion, thinly sliced
1/2 cup chopped celery
1/4 cup pimiento strips
2 hard-cooked eggs, diced
1 cup slivered canned tongue
Salt and pepper

Combine French dressing and mayonnaise. Add drained mixed vegetables, onion, and celery. Chill about 1 hour to blend flavors.

Add pimiento, eggs, and tongue. Mix gently. Add salt and pepper to taste. Chill. Serve on crisp salad greens. Serves 4 to 6.

Hearty Garden Salad Bowl

SHREDDED RAW VEGETABLE SALAD

1/3 cup shredded cucumbers
1/4 cup shredded raw beets
2 teaspoons wine vinegar
1/4 teaspoon sugar
1/3 cup shredded raw carrots
1/3 cup shredded or chopped celery or apple
1/2 cup sour cream or yogurt
1/4 teaspoon salt
Pepper
1/4 teaspoon dry mustard or curry powder
1 tablespoon lemon juice

Sprinkle cucumbers and beets with vinegar and sugar. Let stand while preparing other ingredients.

Add carrots and celery or apple and chill.

Mix sour cream, salt, pepper, mustard or curry powder, and lemon juice. Blend with vegetables just before serving. Serve on any salad greens. Serves 4 to 5 as a dinner salad.

Luncheon Salad: Serve Shredded Raw Vegetable Salad with cottage cheese as a luncheon main dish, in which case portions would be reduced to 3.

Appetizer Salad: Prepare Shredded Raw Vegetable Salad and garnish servings with anchovies to use as appetizer salad. Serves 8.

TOSSED SALAD, WINE DRESSING

1 head of lettuce, cut up
2 tomatoes, cut in eighths
1 stalk celery, cut in strips
3 carrots, cut in strips
2 green onions, sliced
1/2 unpeeled cucumber, sliced thin
Watercress
1/2 cup salad oil
2 tablespoons lemon juice
1 tablespoon sugar
1/2 teaspoon salt
1/8 teaspoon pepper
1/2 cup burgundy or claret

Combine lettuce, tomatoes, celery, carrots, onions, cucumber, and watercress in a bowl.

Mix salad oil through salad before bringing to the table.

Blend lemon juice, salt, pepper, and wine in small bowl at table. Pour over salad; toss lightly. Serves 6.

COMBINATION SALAD

1 cup cooked snap beans
1/2 cup shredded raw carrots
1/2 cup celery strips
2 cups shredded lettuce
1 hard-cooked egg
French dressing

Combine snap beans, raw carrots, celery strips, and lettuce. Mix lightly.

Arrange sliced egg on vegetables. Serve with French dressing. Serves 5.

Vegetable and Egg Combination Salad: Increase eggs to 3 and add 1/2 cup chopped green peppers to Combination Salad recipe.

BEAN SPROUTS SALAD BOWL

Use 1 cup bean sprouts, 1/2 cup chopped celery, 1 sliced cucumber, 1/4 cup sliced radishes, and 4 or 5 rings of green pepper. Toss with French dressing seasoned with a little soy sauce.

RAW BEET SALAD

Use 2 cups ground raw beets and 1/2 cup piccalilli. Toss with French dressing or thin mayonnaise and a few salad greens.

CUCUMBER AND CARROT SALAD

Use 1 cucumber (unpeeled and sliced), 1 green pepper (cut in strips), 3 grated carrots, 1/2 cup chopped celery, and 1/2 small head of lettuce or other greens. Toss with thinned mayonnaise.

LUNCHEON SALAD BOWL WITH CHEESE AND HAM

Chopped lettuce
10 dried figs, cooked and sliced
4 slices Swiss cheese, cut into strips
5 slices ham, cut into strips
2 oranges, peeled and sectioned
French dressing

Make a bed of chopped lettuce in bottom of salad bowl. Toss figs with cheese, ham, oranges, and additional lettuce.

Garnish with whole figs, orange sections, and ham strips rolled up. Serve with thick French dressing. Serves 5.

Luncheon Salad Bowl with
Cheese and Ham

Miscellaneous Vegetable Salads

ARTICHOKE SALAD

8 canned artichoke hearts, drained
1 cup French dressing
Bibb lettuce
8 anchovy fillets
4 thin strips of pimiento
Freshly ground pepper
Salad dressing

Cut the artichoke hearts in half lengthwise and marinate in French dressing for several hours. Drain.

Arrange on crisp lettuce and top each serving with two anchovy fillets and a strip of pimiento. Season with pepper. Serve with salad dressing. Serves 4.

MARINATED CUCUMBERS

Wash and slice 2 large chilled, unpeeled cucumbers in very thin slices. Sprinkle with 2 teaspoons salt and 6 tablespoons sugar.

Add 2/3 cup vinegar. Then press slices with the back of spoon until salad is quite juicy.

SIMPLE ASPARAGUS SALAD

Drain and chill cooked or canned asparagus tips. Marinate 1/2 to 1 hour in French or other desired dressing.

Arrange 4 to 6 tips on tomato slices over crisp salad greens on individual plates. Serve with French dressing.

STRIPED TOMATO SALAD

Remove stems from unpeeled tomatoes and make 4 or 5 parallel cuts through each almost to the bottom.

Put a generous spoonful of well seasoned cottage cheese between the slices. Serve on thick slices of iceberg lettuce. If desired, cottage cheese may be seasoned with chives, green onions, or garlic.

Striped Tomato Salad

VEGETABLE SALAD PARISIENNE

2 cups cooked peas
2 cups cooked green beans
2 cups cooked sliced carrots
1/2 cup minced green onion tops
1/2 cup minced parsley
1/3 cup vinegar
2 teaspoons seasoned salt
1/2 teaspoon sugar
2/3 cup salad oil
6 to 8 lettuce cups
1 cup sour cream

Combine drained peas, beans, and carrots in a bowl with green onions and parsley.

In a screw-top, pint-size jar combine vinegar, seasoned salt, and sugar. Add oil and shake thoroughly. Pour over vegetables and toss until well coated. Marinate 1 hour or longer.

When ready to serve, drain vegetables, saving the marinade. Fill lettuce cups, topping with sour cream which has been seasoned to taste with part of the marinade. Garnish with a top sprinkling of seasoned salt. Serves 6 to 8.

WILTED LETTUCE SALAD

2 bunches leaf lettuce
1 teaspoon sugar
1/2 teaspoon salt
1/8 teaspoon pepper
6 slices bacon
1/4 cup vinegar
2 tablespoons sweet or sour cream (optional)
2 hard-cooked eggs, sliced

Wash, drain, and shred lettuce into warm serving bowl. Sprinkle with sugar, salt, and pepper. Mix with fork and let stand about 10 minutes to wilt slightly.

Cut bacon in small pieces and fry until crisp. Add vinegar and cream and bring to boil. Pour over lettuce, mixing lightly with fork.

Serve immediately, garnished with sliced hard-cooked eggs. Serves 6.

MARINATED TOMATOES

4 to 6 tomatoes
1 clove garlic
1 tablespoon chopped chives
1/4 cup highly seasoned French dressing
2 sprigs parsley, chopped
1 teaspoon mixed dried herbs (mint, tarragon, and basil)

Wash tomatoes and cut in large chunks. Drain if necessary. Put in bowl.

Add remaining ingredients and toss lightly. Cover and marinate in refrigerator several hours. Remove garlic before serving. Serves 4.

Vegetable Salad Parisienne

WATERCRESS SALAD

Wash 2 bunches watercress thoroughly. Remove yellow leaves. Mix with 1/2 cup French dressing and serve at once.

Onion rings may be mixed with the watercress. Serves 4.

LUNCHEON SALAD WITH WINE-CHEESE DRESSING

Lettuce or other salad greens
1/2 peeled tomato
2 or 3 stalks cooked broccoli
2 anchovy fillets
2 deviled egg halves
1 canned artichoke heart, halved

To assemble salad, line a salad plate with crisp salad greens. Place tomato half cut-side-up in center of plate; top tomato with broccoli stalks; lay anchovy fillets crisscross over broccoli.

Arrange deviled egg halves and artichoke hearts around tomato. Serve with wine-cheese dressing (below). Serves 1.

Wine-Cheese Dressing:

1 cup salad oil
1/2 cup sauterne or other white wine
1/4 cup wine vinegar
1/2 cup grated Parmesan cheese
2 raw eggs
1 teaspoon salt
1/2 teaspoon each: onion salt, garlic salt, coarsely ground black pepper, and paprika
1/4 teaspoon Worcestershire sauce

Combine all ingredients in mixing bowl. Beat with rotary beater until well blended.

If dressing is not to be used at once, store it in covered jar in refrigerator and beat well just before serving. Makes about 2 cups dressing.

Luncheon Salad with Wine-Cheese Dressing

FRENCH ENDIVE SALAD

Wash about ½ pound or 4 heads French endive thoroughly. Cut into quarters. Drain and place 4 quarters on individual salad plates.

Garnish plates with sprigs of watercress. Serve salad with Lorenzo dressing. Serves 4.

CUCUMBERS WITH SOUR CREAM

Pare and slice 3 cucumbers. Add 1½ teaspoons salt, ⅛ teaspoon pepper, 3 tablespoons minced chives or green onions, 1 cup sour cream, and 2 tablespoons lemon juice. Chill about 10 minutes. Serves 4 to 6.

CARROT AND RAISIN SALAD

Combine 3 cups shredded carrots, ¼ teaspoon salt, and 1 cup seedless raisins.

Add ½ cup mayonnaise and mix lightly. Serve on crisp lettuce. Serves 6.

CARROT AND APPLE SALAD

Coarsely dice 3 unpeeled apples. Combine with 2 cups grated carrots and 1 tablespoon finely minced onion.

Add ½ cup sweet or freshly soured cream blended with 2 tablespoons lemon juice, ¾ teaspoon salt, and ⅛ teaspoon pepper. Mix well. Serve on lettuce. Serves 6.

CELERY VICTOR

4 hearts of celery (1½ pounds)
1 cup chicken broth
¼ teaspoon Ac'cent
½ cup French dressing
Anchovies
Tomato wedges
Lettuce or watercress

Wash celery thoroughly without separating stalks. Cut lengthwise into 2 or 4 pieces, depending on size. Cut off most of leafy tops.

Place celery in pressure saucepan with broth and Ac'cent. Cook at 15-pound pressure for 6 to 8 minutes. Remove and drain.

Place celery in shallow dish; pour French dressing over and marinate 1 hour or more as it cools. Turn occasionally. Chill thoroughly.

Arrange celery with two strips of anchovies over each heart, with tomato wedges, on watercress or lettuce.

Serves 6 to 8.

Celery Victor

ASPARAGUS AND DEVILED EGG SALAD

Cut 6 hard-cooked eggs in half lengthwise. Remove the yolks.

Mash or sieve the egg yolks. Blend in 3 tablespoons of mayonnaise, and season with salt and pepper.

Fill a pastry tube with the egg yolk mixture.

Arrange lettuce on individual salad plates and on each plate place, alternately, 3 groups of cooked asparagus tips and 3 hard-cooked egg white halves, radiating the asparagus tips from the center. Fill the egg whites with the egg yolk mixture by forcing it through the pastry tube.

Place a spoonful of mayonnase on the center of each salad. Serve as a main dish for luncheon or supper.

TURKISH EGGPLANT SALAD

3 medium eggplants
6 tablespoons olive oil
Salt
Juice of 1 lemon
1 tablespoon vinegar
2 medium tomatoes, sliced
2 green peppers, sliced and seeded
1 medium onion, chopped
10 black olives

Put eggplants on spit or hold with tongs and cook, preferably over charcoal fire, but gas flame will do. Skin must be allowed to burn black as this gives a delicious smoked flavor to salad.

Skin eggplants while still hot (the skin will come off like that of a scalded tomato).

Place eggplants in bowl containing olive oil and sprinkle with salt and lemon juice. Mash with potato masher.

Add vinegar and beat smooth. Shape into a form and place on platter. Decorate with tomatoes, peppers, onion, and black olives. Serves about 6.

Variation: Mayonnaise can be used in place of olive oil, vinegar, and lemon juice.

GREEN BEANS PARMESAN

Cook 1 box French-style green beans as package label directs. Drain and cool.

Mix 1 small, minced onion, ¼ cup olive oil, 3 tablespoons wine vinegar, 1 tablespoon chopped parsley, and ¼ cup grated Parmesan cheese. Pour over beans. Chill.

Serve on salad greens. Serves 4.

Variations: Cut green or wax beans, broccoli, or asparagus are also good in this salad.

MARINATED BROCCOLI SALAD

Cook 1 package frozen broccoli as label directs. Drain and cool.

Rub a small bowl with cut clove of garlic. Put 2 tablespoons oil in bowl. Add juice of 1 lemon and small pinch each of tarragon and oregano. Season and pour over broccoli.

Chill. Serve on salad greens. Serves 3.

Variations: Also try marinated asparagus, cauliflower, green or wax beans, peas, or peas and carrots.

CORN AND TOMATO SALAD

Use 2 tomatoes (cut in chunks), ½ cup whole kernel corn, 2 tablespoons chopped green pepper, and about 1 cup salad greens. Toss with French dressing.

FRESH TOMATO RELISH

Chop 2 pounds tomatoes, 2 medium green peppers, 2 peeled medium onions; drain slightly.

Add 2 teaspoons salt, 1 teaspoon each dry mustard and celery seeds, ¼ cup each vinegar and salad oil; mix; chill. Makes 1 quart.

STUFFED TOMATO SALADS

Select medium-sized smooth tomatoes. Scald and peel tomatoes. Cut a slice from top and remove some of the pulp.

Sprinkle inside with salt, invert, and let stand in refrigerator 30 minutes to chill. Fill with stuffing. Serve on salad greens.

Avocado Stuffing: Mix diced avocado with chopped celery hearts. Moisten with French dressing.

Cabbage Stuffing: Mix 1½ cups shredded cabbage, ¼ teaspoon celery seed, ¼ teaspoon salt, and 2 tablespoons French dressing.

Chicken Stuffing: Mix diced cooked chicken, diced cucumber, and chopped tomato pulp. Moisten with mayonnaise.

Cottage Cheese and Chives: Mix cottage cheese and chopped chives. Stuff tomatoes.

Top with a spoonful of desired dressing and stuffed olives.

Pineapple-Cheese Stuffing: Combine finely chopped fresh or canned pineapple, tomato pulp, cream cheese, and minced watercress. Moisten with mayonnaise.

Crabmeat Stuffing: Mix flaked crabmeat, diced celery, shredded carrot, tomato and cucumber pulp. Moisten with mayonnaise.

Other Suggested Stuffings: Waldorf salad, egg salad, tuna fish, or any meat salad.

Red tomatoes filled with a variety of stuffings appeal to both eyes and appetite.

DUTCH ASPARAGUS SALAD

2 pounds fresh asparagus
½ pound bacon, cut into tiny squares
3 to 4 tablespoons wine vinegar
1 teaspoon sugar
Salt
Pepper, freshly ground
2 hard-cooked eggs, sliced
2 green onions
Iceberg head lettuce

Prepare and cook whole asparagus spears until tender. Chill.

Fry tiny bacon squares until crisp and brown. Remove browned bacon and stir vinegar, sugar, and seasonings into hot bacon fat.

Arrange chilled asparagus on lettuce-lined chop plate. Cover with sliced eggs. Sprinkle with bacon and finely cut green onions. Pour hot dressing over salad. Serve immediately. Serves 6.

CUCUMBER "BOATS"

3 medium-sized cucumbers
1 cup cooked elbow macaroni
1 12-ounce can luncheon meat, cubed
½ cup grated carrots
¼ cup chopped green pepper
½ cup mayonnaise
2 tablespoons vinegar
2 tablespoons horseradish
Salt and pepper

Cut cucumbers in half lengthwise. Scoop out pulp from each half, leaving a shell ¼ inch thick.

Chop pulp and combine with macaroni, luncheon meat, carrot, and green pepper.

Blend together mayonnaise, vinegar, and horseradish. Add to meat mixture and toss lightly. Season to taste with salt and pepper. Pile salad into cucumber shells. Serves 6.

CAULIFLOWER SALAD BOWL

1 medium head cauliflower
¾ cup French dressing
Lettuce
1 green onion, chopped
2 teaspoons lemon juice
1 tablespoon milk
½ cup mayonnaise
Slices of cucumber
Tomato wedges

Remove leaves and all of woody base and wash head of cauliflower. Cook whole in small amount of salted water in covered kettle about 15 minutes or until just tender.

Chill. Marinate in French dressing ½ hour.

Place head of cauliflower in salad bowl lined with lettuce. Combine green onion, lemon juice, milk, and mayonnaise and pour over cauliflower.

Garnish with cucumber slices and tomato wedges. Serves 6.

Dutch Asparagus Salad

KIDNEY BEAN MEDLEY SALAD

2 cups drained cooked or canned kidney beans
⅓ cup tart French dressing
1 small onion, sliced in rings
⅓ cup chopped celery
¼ cup chopped sweet pickles
Salt and pepper to taste

Mix beans and dressing; chill an hour or more. Turn beans in the dressing occasionally so they absorb the flavor.

Just before serving, add rest of ingredients. Mix lightly. Season to taste. Serve in lettuce cups, garnished with slices of hard-cooked egg. Serves 4 to 6.

CALIFORNIA VEGETABLE SALAD

Slice ½ cup ripe olives from pits and combine with 2 cups finely shredded cabbage or coarsely grated carrot, 2 tablespoons diced green sweet pepper, and ¼ cup thinly sliced green onion.

Toss together lightly with ¼ cup mayonnaise seasoned with 1 teaspoon Worcestershire sauce, ½ teaspoon salt, ¼ teaspoon dill seed, and pepper to taste. Serves 4.

CARROT, EGG, AND CELERY SALAD

Use 1½ cups cooked diced carrots, ¾ cup diced celery, 1 chopped hard-cooked egg, greens, and ½ teaspoon minced onion. Toss with thinned cooked dressing.

BEANS AND PEAS SALAD BOWL

Use 1 cup cooked string beans, ½ cup cooked peas, ½ cup sliced celery, ½ cup chopped apple, and about 1 cup salad greens. Toss with French dressing.

Cauliflower Salad Bowl

September Salad Bowl: Wedges of rosy tomatoes and crisp green leaves of iceberg lettuce heaped in a big bowl is almost everybody's favorite salad. Mayonnaise is the favorite dressing for this tomato and lettuce combination but many other popular dressings are good here, too.

EGGPLANT AND PEPPER SALAD

1 medium eggplant (about 1½ pounds)
3 sweet red peppers
1 small onion, chopped
¼ cup garlic French dressing
Salt and pepper

Wash eggplant and peppers. Bake in hot oven (400°F.) until tender when pierced with a fork, about 30 minutes for eggplant and 20 minutes for peppers. Cool.

Cut eggplant in halves. Scoop out pulp and break up with spoon. Remove seeds from peppers and cut into ¼-inch slices.

Add remaining ingredients and mix well. Chill and serve on lettuce. Serves 4.

CARROT AND GREEN PEPPER SALAD

Combine 3 cups shredded carrots with 1 cup chopped green pepper, and 3 mint leaves, chopped.

Moisten with mayonnaise. Serve in lettuce cups. Serves 6.

NAVY BEAN AND RADISH SALAD

Use 1½ cups well seasoned boiled navy beans, ½ cup sliced radishes, about 1 cup of shredded lettuce or other greens, and a few pitted olives. Toss with French dressing seasoned with onion juice.

Luncheon Salad Bowl

KIDNEY BEAN SALAD

3 cups cooked red kidney beans
1 cup diced celery
4 hard-cooked eggs, diced
4 green onions, with tops, sliced thin
¼ cup piccalilli or chopped sweet pickle
1 cup diced cooked cold potato
2 teaspoons minced parsley
Salt and pepper
Cooked dressing or mayonnaise

Combine ingredients with salt and pepper to taste and chill for several hours before serving. The dressing for this salad should be on the sharp side, so if mayonnaise is used, add a little vinegar and some prepared horseradish.

Sliced radishes and diced cucumbers may also be added, but, if used, should be combined with the other ingredients shortly before serving. Serves 8.

BROCCOLI AND EGG SALAD

Use 1½ cups cooked broccoli (chilled), 4 chopped hard-cooked eggs, 4 tablespoons crumbled Roquefort cheese, and thinned salad dressing.

CORN SALAD BOWL

Use 2 cups drained whole kernel corn, 2 tablespoons chopped green pepper, 1 tablespoon minced onion, ½ chopped pimiento, and 1 chopped hard-cooked egg. Toss with thinned cooked dressing and lettuce.

CHINESE CELERY CABBAGE SALAD

Place 2 cups shredded Chinese celery cabbage on crisp outer leaves.

Serve with Thousand Island dressing or nippy mayonnaise. Serves 4.

LUNCHEON SALAD BOWL

2 pounds fresh asparagus
2 hard-cooked eggs
1 cucumber
3 green onions
2 tomatoes
1 small head lettuce
½ cup sliced ripe olives
Wine vinegar French dressing

Wash asparagus, break off tough ends and cook in small amount of boiling salted water until tender. Drain and cool.

Slice eggs. Peel and slice cucumber. Slice onions very thin. Cut tomatoes into wedges. Break lettuce into bite-sized pieces in salad bowl.

Arrange asparagus stalks, tomato, and cucumber in groups over lettuce as shown in picture. Sprinkle onions over all. Center with egg slices and sliced olives. Serve with wine vinegar French dressing. Serves 5.

HOW TO PREPARE A PICNIC TOSSED SALAD

Here is what you do if you'd like to serve a crisp, cold tossed vegetable salad in all its glory far from home:

1. Wash and separate leaves from a head of lettuce. Dry lettuce in a dish towel and leave wrapped.

2. Assemble and wash 2 large tomatoes, 1 cucumber, ½ dozen or so radishes, 1 whole uncut avocado. Pack these vegetables in plastic cartons.

3. Hard-cook two or three eggs and chill.

4. Carry these ingredients to the picnic with large wooden bowl, fork and spoon, individual serving dishes of wood or paper, and bottle of dressing.

5. When ready to serve picnic meal, break lettuce leaves into salad bowl, slice vegetables and eggs into bowl, and season with salt and pepper.

6. Drizzle on a commercial French dressing or your homemade variety which you've prepared ahead and stored in a tightly closed bottle.

GRAPEFRUIT ASPARAGUS SALAD

On bed of endive, chicory, or lettuce, center 5 cooked or canned asparagus stalks. Arrange 5 grapefruit segments on each side of asparagus and garnish with strips of pimiento.

Serve with mayonnaise made with lemon juice. Serves 1.

A buffet style salad is an ideal accompaniment for a barbecue or patio supper. Combine greens (romaine, iceberg, Boston lettuce), torn into bite-size pieces, in a large salad bowl. Surround with a selection of condiments (chopped pimiento, onion rings, anchovies, ripe olives, sliced cucumber, and cottage cheese), and a choice of dressings.

Cole Slaws

COLE SLAW—MASTER RECIPE

Sometimes erroneously called cold slaw, the name of this popular salad is derived from the Dutch words for cabbage and salad.

Use fresh, tender cabbage. Red cabbage may be used or equal amounts of red and white cabbage. Remove and discard the wilted outer leaves and the hard core from a small firm head of cabbage. Shred the cabbage extra-fine, using a chef's knife or grater, cutting only as much as is needed for immediate use. To avoid last minute rush, toss cabbage with ice cubes; hold in refrigerator 1 hour. Remove ice; drain well and dry between towels.

If desired, to 3 cups shredded cabbage add 1/4 cup chopped green pepper or minced onion, or 1 cup grated raw carrots and 1/2 cup raisins.

Immediately before serving, moisten by tossing with one of the following dressings:
- Cooked dressing or salad dressing; French dressing; sour cream dressing.
- Mix 2 to 3 tablespoons sugar, 3 tablespoons vinegar, 2 tablespoons salad oil, and 1 teaspoon salt. Stir until sugar dissolves.
- Mix 1/3 cup mayonnaise or salad dressing, 1 tablespoon vinegar, 2 teaspoons sugar, 1/2 teaspoon salt, and 1/2 teaspoon celery seed. Stir until sugar dissolves.
- Mix 1/2 cup salad dressing, 2 tablespoons vinegar, and 1 teaspoon prepared mustard.

For an outdoor meal, serve cole slaw in a hollowed-out cabbage surrounded by hard-cooked "penguin" eggs. Pieces of black olive form the wings and trim. They can be attached with toothpicks or unflavored gelatin which has been softened in a small amount of cold water and melted over low heat. A skewered whole olive is used for each head.

DUTCH SLAW

- 1 cup chopped bacon
- 1/4 cup lemon juice
- 1 teaspoon salt
- 1/2 cup mayonnaise
- 1 quart finely shredded cabbage
- 1/2 cup chopped green pepper
- 1/4 cup chopped parsley
- 1/4 cup chopped celery
- 2 tablespoons minced onion

Fry bacon until crisp. Remove from pan.

Mix 1/4 cup bacon drippings, lemon juice, and salt. Add to mayonnaise and blend.

Pour over combined vegetables and bacon and toss lightly. Chill before serving. Serves 6.

APPLE COLE SLAW WITH SOUR CREAM DRESSING

- 1 cup thick sour cream
- 1 tablespoon vinegar
- 2 teaspoons prepared mustard
- 1/2 teaspoon onion powder
- 1/4 teaspoon salt
- Dash of cayenne
- 4 cups shredded cabbage
- 1 cup diced red apple
- 1 teaspoon celery seed

Combine cream, vinegar and seasonings. Mix thoroughly.

Pour over cabbage, apple, and celery seed. Toss lightly. Garnish with paprika. Serves 8.

PINEAPPLE SLAW

- 3 cups shredded cabbage
- 2 tablespoons chopped green pepper
- 1/2 cup diced unpeeled apple
- 4 slices pineapple
- 1 teaspoon salt
- 1 tablespoon sugar
- 1/2 cup vinegar
- Salad greens
- 1 cup shredded carrots

Combine cabbage, green pepper, apple, and 2 slices pineapple, cut into sections.

Mix salt, sugar, and vinegar, and add. Place in bowl lined with salad greens.

Top with shredded carrots and remaining drained pineapple slices cut into halves. Serves 4.

HONEY COLE SLAW

Beat 1 cup cold sour cream until thick. Add 1/4 cup honey, 1 teaspoon salt, and 2 teaspoons celery salt. Pour over 4 cups finely shredded cabbage.

RIO GRANDE SLAW

Add salt and celery seeds to shredded cabbage. Pour heated barbecue sauce over the mixture, toss and serve while hot.

For color and flavor contrasts, make several types of cole slaw for a party cole slaw platter.

PENNSYLVANIA PEPPER CABBAGE

- 2 cups shredded cabbage
- 1 green pepper, cut fine
- 1 teaspoon salt

Mix shredded cabbage, pepper, and salt and let stand about 1 hour.

Drain off all liquid. Pour hot salad dressing (below) over the cabbage and mix well. Serve at once. Serves 4 to 5.

Hot Salad Dressing:

- 3 slices bacon
- 1 tablespoon flour
- 1/2 cup vinegar
- 1 tablespoon sugar
- 1/2 teaspoon dry mustard
- 1/2 teaspoon salt
- 1/8 teaspoon pepper
- 1 egg yolk, beaten

Cut bacon in small cubes and fry crisp. Remove cubes of bacon from grease and put aside.

Blend flour into grease and brown. Add vinegar and stir until it thickens.

Mix together sugar, mustard, salt, and pepper and add to the mixture. Pour over the beaten egg yolk and mix well.

Put on heat again and cook 1 minute longer. Add bacon cubes when ready to use.

CABBAGE AND CARROT SLAW
(Master Recipe)

- 1 1/2 cups shredded carrots
- 3 cups shredded cabbage
- 1/2 teaspoon salt
- 2 teaspoons sugar
- 1 tablespoon vinegar
- 3 tablespoons mayonnaise

Combine carrots, cabbage, salt, sugar, and vinegar. Moisten with mayonnaise. Mix lightly.

Arrange on crisp lettuce. Sprinkle with minced parsley or paprika. May be garnished with orange slices. Serves 6.

Cabbage and Apple Salad: In master recipe, substitute 1 1/2 cups thinly sliced unpeeled tart red apples for carrots.

Cabbage, Carrot and Celery Salad: In master recipe, decrease shredded cabbage to 2 cups. Add 1 cup thinly sliced celery.

Bull's Eye Salad

BULL'S EYE SALAD

2 large tomatoes
1/4 head cabbage
3 large carrots
2 tablespoons chopped chives
1 cucumber
1 head escarole, curly endive, or romaine
Mayonnaise

Double an 18-inch strip of waxed paper lengthwise and then double again. Lap ends to form circle about 5 inches in diameter and fasten with wooden pick.

Cut slice from stem end of tomatoes so they will set flat. Cut in eighths and stand up inside paper. Fill center with mayonnaise and garnish with chopped chives.

Radiate greens from tomatoes to edge of plate. Place ring of crisp shredded cabbage around tomatoes, half slices of unpeeled cucumber, and shredded carrots.

Garnish with cucumber twists, made by cutting from center through each. Turn one cut edge to right, the other to left and fasten with pick. Let stand in ice water 1/2 hour and remove pick. Remove waxed paper. Serves 6.

CABBAGE SALAD IN PIMIENTO CUPS

1 1/2 cups finely chopped cabbage
1/2 tablespoon chopped onion
1 tablespoon chopped green pepper
2 tablespoons vinegar
Salt and pepper
1/2 teaspoon celery salt
3/4 cup chopped, drained tomato
1/4 cup salad dressing
8 pimientos (3 4-ounce cans)

Combine cabbage, onion, and green pepper; add vinegar and seasonings. Let stand 1 hour; drain.

Add tomato and salad dressing; toss lightly. Fill pimiento cups. Serves 8.

CABBAGE AND ONION SALAD

Shred cabbage. Cut onions into very thin rings. Season with salt, celery salt, pepper, and paprika.

Mix with mayonnaise or French dressing. Serve on cabbage leaf.

HOT SLAW

Combine in saucepan 2 slightly beaten egg yolks, 1/4 cup cold water, 1/4 cup vinegar, 1 tablespoon butter or margarine, 1 tablespoon sugar, and 1/2 teaspoon salt.

Cook on low heat, stirring constantly until mixture thickens.

Add 3 cups shredded cabbage and reheat. Serves 5.

HERB COLE SLAW

4 cups finely shredded cabbage
1/2 teaspoon salt
3/4 teaspoon dried thyme
2 tablespoons chopped parsley
1/2 cup French dressing

Toss cabbage with salt, thyme, and parsley. Then toss well with French dressing. Serve at once. Serves 4.

MEXICAN SLAW

Crisp a small head of cabbage by removing a few of the outer leaves, then cutting in half, and let stand in ice water 1/2 hour. Shake out water well, and shred.

Dice cold cooked ham or tongue, celery, green pepper, and pimiento. Sprinkle with salt.

Mix salad with mayonnaise which has been thinned with sweet or sour cream.

Line a serving dish with outside leaves of cabbage and fill center with slaw. Squeeze 1/2 lemon over all.

SOUR CREAM SLAW

1/2 cup mayonnaise
1/4 cup sour cream
1/2 teaspoon salt
1/2 teaspoon sugar
1 teaspoon tarragon vinegar
4 cups shredded cabbage

Combine mayonnaise, sour cream, salt, sugar, and vinegar.

Toss with shredded cabbage until well coated. Serve after chilling thoroughly. Serves 6.

RED CABBAGE SLAW

2 cups red cabbage, shredded
3 tart red apples, diced
1 cup grated carrot
1/4 cup brown sugar
3 tablespoons vinegar
2 tablespoons French dressing

Combine cabbage, apple, and carrot. Mix sugar, vinegar, and dressing and pour over salad.

Toss lightly until dressing coats salad. Serves 6.

VEGETABLE AND APPLE SALAD

1 cup grated raw carrots
1 cup shredded cabbage
1 cup diced celery
1 cup thin apple strips
Dash of salt
Salad dressing
Lettuce

Toss vegetables, apples, and a dash of salt with salad dressing to moisten. Chill. Serve in crisp lettuce cups. Serves 6.

ITALIAN PEPPER SLAW

1 clove garlic
2 cups finely shredded cabbage
1/4 cup chopped green pepper
1/4 cup chopped pimiento
1/2 teaspoon salt
1/2 teaspoon celery seed
Dash of red pepper
Dash of paprika
1 tablespoon soft breadcrumbs
2 tablespoons tomato paste
2 1/2 teaspoons water
1/4 teaspoon salt
1/8 teaspoon sugar
2 1/2 teaspoons salad oil
2 teaspoons cider vinegar

Rub salad bowl with cut garlic clove. Put vegetables, 1/2 teaspoon salt, celery seed, red pepper, and dash paprika in bowl.

Mix remaining ingredients thoroughly. Pour over contents of salad bowl. Toss. Serves 6.

HOT CABBAGE SALAD—WINE DRESSING

4 frankfurters
1/4 cup butter or margarine
1 large or 2 small onions
3/4 cup chablis, hock, sauterne, riesling, or any white wine
2 tablespoons sugar
1 tablespoon flour
1/2 teaspoon salt
1/4 teaspoon pepper
2 cups shredded cabbage

Split frankfurters and sauté in butter or margarine until lightly browned. Remove to hot platter.

Sauté onion until yellow. Combine wine, sugar, flour, salt, and pepper in small covered jar and shake vigorously until well blended. Add to onions in skillet and cook, stirring constantly, until smooth and slightly thickened.

Add cabbage and cook, mixing constantly with wine dressing for about 6 minutes.

Serve topped with sautéed frankfurters and garnish with green onions. Serves 4.

Hot Cabbage Salad with Wine Dressing

Potato, Macaroni, Rice Salads

MASTER POTATO SALAD

    3   cups diced cooked potatoes, cooked
          in jackets
    1   tablespoon grated onion
    3   tablespoons French dressing
    1   tablespoon minced parsley
    1   teaspoon salt
    1/4 teaspoon paprika
        Mayonnaise

Combine ingredients, except mayonnaise, tossing lightly with a fork. Chill 3 to 4 hours.

Just before serving add mayonnaise, mixing carefully. Serve on lettuce or watercress. Serves 6.

Potato Salad Variations

Potato Salad with Celery: To master potato salad, add 1 cup diced celery.

Potato-Egg Salad: To master potato salad, add 1 cup diced celery and 3 chopped hard-cooked eggs.

Gourmet Potato Salad: To master potato salad, add 1/2 cup tartar sauce and 1/3 cup chow-chow and stuffed olives, minced.

Potato Salad with Carrots: To master potato salad, add 1 cup diced celery and 1 cup grated raw carrot.

Potato Salad with Cabbage: To master potato salad, add 1 cup finely cut cabbage.

Potato Salad with Nuts: To master potato salad, add 1 cup diced celery and 3/4 cup salted peanuts, chopped Brazil nuts, or toasted filberts.

Potato Salad with Cucumber: To master potato salad, add 1 cup diced celery and 1 diced cucumber.

Cornucopia Potato Salads: Roll thin slices of bologna to form cornucopias Fill with potato salad.

Molded Potato Salad Ring: Pack potato salad into medium-sized ring mold. Chill.

Unmold on bed of greens. Garnish with assorted sliced cold meats, radish roses, and quartered tomatoes.

HOT POTATO SALAD

    1   cup finely chopped onions
    6   cups thinly sliced cooked pota-
          toes
    2   tablespoons minced parsley
    2/3 cup cider vinegar
    1/3 cup hot water
    1   teaspoon sugar
    1   slightly beaten egg
    1/3 cup salad oil
    1 1/2 teaspoons salt
        Few grains pepper
    1 1/2 teaspoons Ac'cent

Combine onions, potatoes, and parsley.

Combine vinegar and water; heat to boiling; add sugar; stir until dissolved.

Add hot mixture slowly to egg. Add salad oil, salt, pepper, and Ac'cent.

Beat vigorously with rotary egg beater until well blended.

Pour over potato mixture; stir with fork until thoroughly mixed. Heat gently or let stand in warm place 10 to 15 minutes. Serves 6 to 8.

MASTER MACARONI SALAD

    3   cups cooked elbow macaroni,
          chilled
    1/2 green pepper, minced
    1 1/2 tablespoons minced onion
    1/2 cup chopped celery
    1/3 cup French dressing
        Lettuce
        Mayonnaise or cooked dressing

Combine macaroni, green pepper, onion, celery, and French dressing. Chill.

Arrange on lettuce and garnish with mayonnaise or cooked dressing. Serves 6.

Macaroni Salad Variations

Macaroni Salad with Hard-Cooked Eggs: Slice and add 3 hard-cooked eggs to master macaroni salad.

Macaroni Salad with Tuna Fish: In master macaroni salad, use a little less macaroni. Add a 7-ounce can flaked tuna fish. Use additional mayonnaise.

Macaroni Salad with Vegetables: To master macaroni salad, add 1 cup mixed cooked or canned carrots, peas, and diced string beans. If desired, marinate vegetables first.

Baked Bean Salad: Follow master macaroni salad recipe and substitute cold baked beans for macaroni.

Brown Bean Salad: Follow master macaroni salad recipe and substitute cold baked brown beans for macaroni.

Hot potato salad, attractively garnished, is equally tempting in summer or winter.

HOT DUTCH POTATO SALAD

    4   slices bacon
    1/2 cup chopped onion
    1/2 cup chopped green pepper
    1/4 cup vinegar
    1   teaspoon salt
    1/8 teaspoon pepper
    1   teaspoon sugar
    1   slightly beaten egg
    1   quart hot, cooked, cubed potatoes
    1/4 cup chopped pimiento
    3   hard-cooked eggs, diced

Cut bacon into strips and pan-fry. Add onion and green pepper. Cook 3 minutes.

Add vinegar, salt, pepper, sugar, and beaten egg. Cook slightly.

Add cubed potatoes, pimiento, and hard-cooked eggs. Blend lightly. Serve hot. Serves 8.

Note: If desired, dilute vinegar with 3 tablespoons water.

WESTERN RICE SALAD BOWL

    1   garlic clove, peeled
    1   No. 2 can bean sprouts, drained
          and rinsed
    1   cup thinly sliced unpeeled radishes
    1   cup diced unpeeled cucumber
    1   cup thinly sliced celery
    1   cup chopped watercress
    2   small sweet onions, chopped
    1/4 cup chopped green pepper
    1   to 1 1/2 cups cold cooked rice
    1   to 1 1/2 teaspoons Ac'cent
    1   cup mayonnaise
        Soy sauce (optional)

Rub salad bowl with garlic. Have all vegetables and rice well chilled; layer them into bowl in order given.

Blend Ac'cent into mayonnaise; pour over top layer of salad (which should be rice). Lift and toss carefully to blend but not crush.

Taste and if salt is needed try adding soy sauce. Serves 6 to 8.

Cold Cuts with Macaroni Salad

HAWAIIAN POTATO SALAD

    4 hard-cooked eggs
    1 cup hot cooked rice
    1 large potato, hot mashed
    ¼ cup French dressing
    ½ teaspoon salt
    2 tablespoons chopped pimiento
    1 tablespoon chopped green pepper
    1 tablespoon finely chopped onion
    1 tablespoon chopped parsley

Press 2 of the hard-cooked eggs through a sieve and combine with rice and potatoes. Blend in French dressing. Chill.

Just before serving, add remaining ingredients. If desired, add more seasoning. Garnish with remaining eggs, sliced or sieved, and parsley. Serves 4.

SOUR CREAM POTATO SALAD

    5 cups sliced cooked potato
    ½ cup minced celery
    1 onion, chopped
    4 radishes, sliced
    ¼ cup French dressing
    1 cup sour cream
    Salt, pepper, and cayenne
    Chopped fresh dill

Combine potato, celery, onion, and radishes. Pour French dressing over mixture, and let stand in refrigerator for several hours.

Just before serving, fold in sour cream. Season to taste. Sprinkle with chopped dill. Serves 4.

MACARONI AND CHICKEN SALAD

    ½ cup diced cooked chicken
    2 cups cooked elbow macaroni
    1 tablespoon grated onion
    ¾ cup cooked mushrooms
    1 teaspoon salt
    ¼ teaspoon pepper
    ¾ cup cooked salad dressing or mayonnaise
    Curly endive
    2 tomatoes, quartered

Combine all ingredients except endive and tomatoes. Place in refrigerator about 2 hours to chill.

Wash endive thoroughly and arrange it in 9-inch crinkle-edge glass pie plate.

Place salad mixture on endive and garnish with quartered tomatoes. Serves 6 to 8.

Macaroni and Chicken Salad

EL PATIO POTATO SALAD

    3 to 4 medium potatoes
    ¼ cup sauterne wine
    3 green onions
    ⅓ cup whole or pitted ripe olives
    ¾ cup chopped celery
    2 tablespoons chopped parsley
    Salt and pepper
    ⅓ cup mayonnaise
    1 teaspoon vinegar

Boil potatoes in salted water until tender. Drain and cool sufficiently to handle. Peel and dice. Pour wine over potatoes and allow to stand until cold.

Slice onions thin. Cut olives into large pieces. (Remove pits from whole olives.)

Add onions, olives, celery, and parsley to potatoes. Season with salt and pepper.

Blend mayonnaise and vinegar; pour over salad mixture and mix lightly. Serves 4.

BOLOGNA CUPS WITH POTATO SALAD

Sauté bologna slices with skins on in a small amount of butter or margarine until they form well-shaped cups.

Remove skins. Pile potato salad into bologna cups and arrange on a large platter. Garnish with sliced tomatoes on lettuce leaves.

Bologna Cups With Potato Salad

RAINBOW MACARONI SALAD

    1 8-ounce package elbow macaroni
    ¼ cup French dressing
    ¼ cup sliced green onion
    ¼ cup diced pimiento
    ½ cup finely chopped sweet pickles
    ½ cup thinly sliced carrots
    2 tablespoons prepared mustard
    Mayonnaise, salt, and pepper

Cook macaroni in boiling, salted water until tender. Drain and rinse with cold water. Add French dressing and chill for several hours, if possible.

Add remaining ingredients, using about 1 cup mayonnaise and salt and pepper to taste; mix thoroughly but lightly. Chill several hours.

Serve in lettuce lined bowl; sprinkle with chopped fresh parsley and top with hard-cooked egg slices, if desired. Serves 8.

Chinese Salad Bowl

CHINESE SALAD BOWL

    1 package (1⅓ cups) precooked rice
    2 cups cooked green peas
    1 can water chestnuts
    1 can bean sprouts
    1 head Chinese cabbage or escarole
    ½ cup mayonnaise
    ½ cup sour cream
    1 teaspoon celery seed
    ½ teaspoon Ac'cent
    1 cup roast pork, cut in thin strips

Cook rice according to directions on package. Chill; place in salad bowl. Add peas.

Drain water chestnuts: slice: add. Drain bean sprouts; add. Tear cabbage or escarole leaves into small pieces; add.

Combine mayonnaise, sour cream, celery seed, and Ac'cent; beat well; pour into salad bowl.

Toss until all ingredients are well-mixed. Scatter strips of pork on top. Serves 6 to 8.

LUNCHEON RICE SALAD

    3 cups cooked rice, chilled
    ½ cup French dressing
    ½ cup minced onion (young green onions preferred)
    1 head lettuce
    Grated sharp cheese (optional)
    1 pint pickled beets
    Watercress or other greens to garnish
    4 whole tomatoes, peeled and quartered
    1 pimiento, cut in long thin strips
    Egg slices and radish roses to garnish

Pour French dressing over rice and toss lightly with fork. Let stand 1 hour, then drain thoroughly.

Add minced onion and mold in timbales (glass custard cups make a nice size mold).

Unmold timbales of rice in center of lettuce cups. Sprinkle with grated cheese if desired; garnish with pickled beets, watercress, peeled and quartered tomatoes, and top the rice with thin strips of pimiento. Egg slices and radish roses may be added. Mayonnaise may accompany this salad if desired. Serves 6.

Luncheon Rice Salad

Fish and Shellfish Salads

MASTER FISH SALAD

Use cooked or canned fish. Cut into ¼- to ½-inch cubes or flake. Toss lightly with mayonnaise or cooked salad dressing. Add salt, if necessary.

Chill and serve in salad bowl or individual plates. Garnish with dressing, crisp greens, cooked or raw vegetables.

Apple and Fish Salad: Use 2 cups flaked fish and 2 cups diced tart apple.

Cucumber and Fish Salad: Use 2 cups flaked fish, ½ cup each of diced cucumber and celery, ½ shredded head lettuce, 1 finely chopped small onion, and a few diced radishes.

Seafood Salad: Use 1 cup cooked or canned shrimp, 1 cup flaked canned crabmeat, and 1½ cup diced tart apple. Marinate in French dressing.

Lobster Salad: Use 2 cups cooked or canned lobster meat and 1 cup chopped celery. Marinate in French dressing for 20 minutes. Mix with mayonnaise.

SHRIMP SALAD

½ cup sharp mayonnaise
1 tablespoon lemon juice
2 cups canned or cooked shrimp
2½ cups canned peas
3 sliced hard-cooked eggs
⅔ cup thinly sliced celery
Salad greens
3 stuffed olives
Lemon wedges

Thin mayonnaise with lemon juice and 2 tablespoons liquid from shrimp. Add drained shrimp, peas, eggs, and celery. Mix gently.

Place on salad greens. Garnish with sliced stuffed olives and lemon wedges. Serves 6.

Variations: Crabmeat, lobster, salmon, tuna, or flaked fish may be used instead of shrimp.

SHRIMP SALAD—GUEST STYLE

1 pound shrimp
½ cup diced celery
¼ cup sliced black olives
1 hard-cooked egg, coarsely cut
½ cup sour cream
¼ cup mayonnaise
1 tablespoon lemon juice

Salt and pepper to taste
Dash of cayenne

Shell, cook, and chill shrimp. Combine chilled shrimp with remaining ingredients.

Serve on mixed greens, preferably with thin-sliced pumpernickel or salty rye. Serves 5 to 6.

CRAB LOUIS

Whole lettuce leaves
Shredded lettuce leaves
2 cups cooked or canned crabmeat
2 hard-cooked eggs, sliced
Chopped chives
½ cup French dressing
½ cup chili sauce
2 tablespoons mayonnaise
½ teaspoon Worcestershire sauce (optional)
Salt and pepper to taste

Arrange lettuce leaves around the inside of a salad bowl. Place some shredded lettuce leaves on bottom.

Heap crabmeat on top of shredded lettuce. Garnish with slices of hard-cooked egg. Sprinkle with chopped chives.

Mix remaining ingredients in another bowl and pour over salad. Serves 4.

BUFFET TUNA SALAD

1 small head lettuce
2 cans (6½ or 7 ounces each) tuna in vegetable oil
3 hard-cooked eggs, halved
3 whole pimientos
6 green pepper rings
6 green onions (scallions)
12 radishes
12 carrot sticks
12 ripe olives
12 cucumber slices

Cover large platter with lettuce. Place tuna in center. Surround with remaining ingredients. Serve with Tangy Salad Dressing (below). Serves 6.

Tangy Salad Dressing: Blend together ½ cup mayonnaise, ½ teaspoon salt, 1 teaspoon lemon juice, and 2 teaspoons Worcestershire sauce.

Buffet Tuna Salad

Lobster and Macaroni Salad

LOBSTER AND MACARONI SALAD

6 (3 to 5 ounces) lobster tails
1 package (8 ounces) macaroni shells
½ cup green pepper, finely diced
½ cup celery, finely diced
1 teaspoon onion juice
½ cup stuffed olives, sliced
½ cup mayonnaise
¼ cup ketchup
½ teaspoon aromatic bitters
Salt and pepper to taste

Cook lobster tails according to package directions. Remove shells and dice meat.

Cook macaroni shells according to package directions. Drain in colander and rinse with cold water. Chill.

Mix together macaroni, lobster, green pepper, celery, onion juice, and olives. Combine mayonnaise, ketchup, and bitters and add to salad. Toss all together lightly but thoroughly. Add salt and pepper to taste. Chill well.

At serving time, decorate bowl with empty lobster shell. Serves 6.

OYSTER SALAD

1 pint oysters
¼ teaspoon celery salt
1 tablespoon butter or margarine
¼ cup chopped lettuce
2 hard-cooked eggs, diced
½ cup diced celery
1 pimiento, chopped
1 teaspoon grated onion
1 teaspoon lemon juice
½ cup mayonnaise or salad dressing
½ teaspoon salt
⅛ teaspoon pepper
Lettuce

Drain oysters. Add celery salt and cook in butter until edges begin to curl. Chill and dice oysters.

Combine all ingredients and serve on lettuce cups. Garnish with paprika. Serves 6.

SALMON COTTAGE CHEESE SALAD

1 cup minced salmon
1 cup cottage cheese
½ cup chopped celery
¼ cup chopped sweet pickle
Salad dressing

Combine all ingredients. Chill. Serve on lettuce. Serves 6.

West Coast Salad with Mushroom Dressing

WEST COAST SALAD WITH MUSHROOM DRESSING

1 head iceberg lettuce
¼ cup wine vinegar
½ cup olive or salad oil
1½ teaspoons salt
1 teaspoon paprika
Freshly ground black pepper
1 small clove garlic, crushed
½ pound fresh mushrooms, sliced
½ pound cooked, cleaned shrimp
1 cup cooked or canned lobster or crabmeat
1 cup sliced celery
1 package (10 ounces) frozen asparagus, cooked
1 package (10 ounces) frozen fresh peas, cooked
2 hard-cooked eggs, sliced
2 tomatoes, cut in wedges

Core lettuce; wash in cold water and drain well. Place in plastic bag or transparent plastic wrap; refrigerate.

Combine vinegar, oil, salt, paprika, pepper, and garlic in bowl; mix well. Add mushrooms, chill 1 hour.

Half an hour before serving, separate lettuce leaves and line salad bowl; shred remaining lettuce into bottom of bowl. Arrange shrimp, lobster, celery, drained asparagus, and peas in rows over lettuce. Spoon mushrooms onto salad.

Stir the dressing and pour over salad. Garnish with egg slices and tomato wedges. Chill. Toss lightly before serving. Serves 6 to 8.

Salmon Hollandaise Mold

SALMON AND CUCUMBER SALAD

2 cups diced cucumber
1 cup sliced celery
1 teaspoon Ac'cent
1 1-pound can salmon
1 tablespoon capers (optional)
½ cup mayonnaise
Melon balls
Celery seed dressing (below)

Combine cucumber and celery; sprinkle with Ac'cent; toss well to mix. Let stand while preparing remaining ingredients and dressing.

Flake salmon, removing skin and bones; add capers. Combine with cucumber mixture and mayonnaise.

Serve on salad greens; garnish with melon balls. Serve dressing separately. Serves 4 to 6.

Celery Seed Dressing:

½ cup mayonnaise
½ cup sour cream
1 teaspoon celery seed
¼ teaspoon Ac'cent
2 tablespoons ketchup

Combine all ingredients; mix well

Salmon and Cucumber Salad

SALMON HOLLANDAISE MOLD

Hollandaise Sauce:

2 egg yolks
Dash of cayenne pepper
½ cup butter or margarine, melted
3 tablespoons lemon juice

Beat egg yolks until thick and lemon colored; stir in pepper. Blend in 3 tablespoons butter, a little at a time, beating constantly.

Slowly beat in remaining butter with lemon juice.

Mold:

34 saltine crackers, finely crushed
1 1-pound can salmon, well drained
2 cups chopped celery
½ medium onion, chopped
¼ teaspoon pepper
Hollandaise sauce (above)

Combine all ingredients; blend well. Pack into 1-quart mold; chill.

When ready to serve, unmold on bed of chicory and garnish with olives and lemon wedges. Serves 6 to 8.

SWEDISH HERRING SALAD

2 No. 2 cans ocean herring or 3 salt herrings, cooked
4 cups diced cooked beets
3 medium apples, diced small
½ cup chopped onion
½ cup minced dill pickle
3 hard-cooked eggs, minced
French dressing
Hard-cooked egg, sliced
Watercress

Drain canned herring. (Soak salt herring in cold water 1 hour; drain; cook until tender in boiling water.)

Remove skin and bones; cut into small pieces.

Combine all ingredients, mixing lightly with French dressing.

Decorate with slices of hard-cooked egg and sprigs of watercress. Serves 12.

GRAPEFRUIT SALMON SALAD

2 grapefruit
1 1-pound can salmon
½ cup mayonnaise
¼ cup chili sauce
½ teaspoon Ac'cent

Halve grapefruit, making scalloped edge if desired. Spoon out pulp; remove all membrane with scissors.

Drain salmon; flake, removing skin. Combine salmon and grapefruit pulp.

Combine mayonnaise, chili sauce, and Ac'cent; add to salmon mixture; toss to mix. Fill grapefruit shells.

Serve on watercress or other salad greens. Serves 4.

SHRIMP ARTICHOKE SALAD

2 pounds medium-size shrimp, cooked, shelled, and cleaned
2 10-ounce packages artichoke hearts, cooked and drained
2 8-ounce cans mandarin oranges, drained
1 head iceberg lettuce, cubed

Combine all ingredients. Place in a salad bowl. Chill well. Just before serving toss with French dressing. Serves 6.

Shrimp Artichoke Salad

LOBSTER SALAD

2 cups (16 ounces) diced, boiled rock lobster tail meat
1/4 cup French dressing
2 tablespoons minced, sweet onion
1 1/2 cups diced celery
1/2 cup mayonnaise
1/2 teaspoon salt
1/8 teaspoon paprika
Lettuce leaves
Pimiento strips
Green olives
Lemon wedges

Stir together lobster meat and French dressing. Chill thoroughly.

Add onion and celery. Stir in mayonnaise until all ingredients are well mixed, with salt and paprika. Correct seasoning if necessary.

Line salad bowl with crisp lettuce leaves. Pile salad in center.

Garnish with pimiento strips, green olives, and additional mayonnaise if desired. Serve with lemon wedges. Serves 4.

CURRIED TUNA-RICE SALAD

2/3 cup packaged pre-cooked rice
1 cup water
1/4 teaspoon salt
1 cup mayonnaise
2 teaspoons curry powder
2 tablespoons diced pimiento
1 teaspoon salt
1/2 teaspoon Ac'cent
1 cup cooked peas
1 6 1/2-ounce can chunk style tuna

Combine rice, water, and the 1/4 teaspoon salt in saucepan. Mix just until all rice is moistened. Bring quickly to boil over high heat, fluffing rice gently once or twice with fork (do not stir). Cover; remove from heat; let cool to room temperature.

Blend mayonnaise and curry powder; add pimiento, the 1 teaspoon salt, and Ac'cent; add remaining ingredients and rice; toss well to mix. Chill.

Serve on salad greens with additional mayonnaise. Serves 6.

Note: If the brand of tuna fish already contains monosodium glutamate, slightly less Ac'cent will be needed.

Curried Tuna-Rice Salad

SALMON SALAD TROPICAL

1 cup sliced or diced, ripe firm bananas
1/2 cup drained, diced, canned pineapple
1 to 1 1/2 cups cooked, flaked salmon (1 7-ounce or 1 16-ounce can)
1/2 to 1 cup diced celery
2 tablespoons chopped, sweet pickle
1 teaspoon salt
1 tablespoon mayonnaise or salad dressing
1 tablespoon prepared mustard
Lettuce
Salad greens for garnish

Combine bananas and pineapple. Add salmon, celery, pickle, and salt.

Mix together mayonnaise or salad dressing and mustard and add to salad mixture. Mix lightly.

Combine 2 or 3 crisp lettuce leaves to form a cup and arrange on each salad plate. Fill each lettuce cup with salad mixture.

Garnish salad with crisp salad greens. Serves 4 to 6.

Variations of Salmon Salad Tropical

Tuna and Banana Salad: In place of salmon, use 1 to 1 1/2 cups (1 7-ounce or 1 12-ounce can) flaked tuna.

Chicken Salad Tropical: In place of salmon, use 1 to 1 1/2 cups diced cooked chicken.

Note: When canned salmon or tuna is used, drain and mix liquid with mayonnaise or salad dressing. One tablespoon lemon juice may be added to mayonnaise or salad dressing, if desired.

For additional color and texture contrast, cold cooked peas, crisp carrot strips or radishes may be arranged on each salad.

SHRIMP BOUQUET SALAD

1 pound fresh or frozen shrimp
4 medium-sized tomatoes
3 radishes, sliced
Lettuce
Coral Dressing (below)

Cook and clean shrimp. Chill. Arrange tomatoes, shrimp, and radishes on beds of shredded lettuce to form red and pink bouquet. Serve with Coral Dressing. Serves 3.

Coral Dressing:

1/2 cup mayonnaise
2 tablespoons ketchup
1/2 teaspoon Worcestershire sauce
1 teaspoon horseradish
Dash of Tabasco sauce
1/4 teaspoon salt
1/8 teaspoon black pepper
1 tablespoon lemon juice

Blend ingredients. Chill.

Egg and Cheese Salads

TOMATO ROSE SALAD

Peel one firm tomato for each tomato rose salad.

Slightly soften a 3-ounce package of cream cheese with milk.

Form a row of petals on the upper side of each tomato by pressing level teaspoons of the softened cheese against the side of the tomato, then drawing the teaspoon down with a curving motion.

Make a second row of petals on the lower side of the tomato, placing each of these petals between the two petals above it on the top row.

Place each tomato on watercress on a salad plate. Press hard-cooked egg yolk through a sieve onto the center of the tomato. Serve with French dressing.

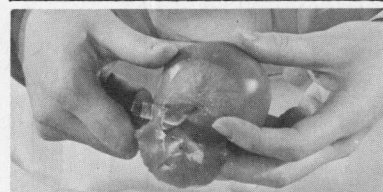

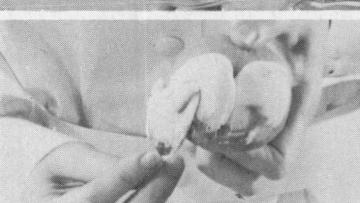

Cottage Cheese and Vegetable Salad

COTTAGE CHEESE AND VEGETABLE SALAD

1 garlic clove (optional)
2 cups cottage cheese
1 teaspoon salt
Paprika
2 tablespoons chopped chives or green onion
2 tablespoons chopped pimiento
1/4 cup chopped celery
2 cucumbers
1 medium-sized onion
2 large tomatoes
2 carrots
French dressing
Salad greens

Rub mixing bowl with cut clove of garlic. Add cottage cheese, salt, and paprika. Fold in chopped chives, pimiento, and chopped celery. Turn into bowl that has been rinsed in cold water; chill in refrigerator.

Unmold on center of large salad plate; surround with watercress, thin cucumber slices, onion rings, carrot flowers, and tomato wedges. Serve with French dressing. Serves 6.

Variation: The cottage cheese mixture can be served in whole tomatoes in lettuce cups, topped with toasted almonds or peanuts. French dressing is served with it.

CHEESE AND ANCHOVY APPETIZER SALAD

1/2 pound Roquefort or blue cheese
1 3-ounce package cream cheese
1/2 teaspoon minced onion
11/2 teaspoons prepared mustard
Dash of Tabasco sauce
4 thick slices tomato
4 leaves lettuce
8 rolled anchovies

Blend the 2 cheeses with onion, mustard, and Tabasco. When smooth, pack into pastry tube.

Place slice of tomato on lettuce leaf on small salad plate. Pipe cheese spread into mound on tomato slice. Top each with 2 rolled anchovies.

Serve with crisp crackers or Melba toast. Serves 4.

SIMPLE COTTAGE CHEESE SALADS

Season 2 cups cottage cheese with salt and pepper to taste. Add light cream to form desired consistency.

Serve on lettuce leaves topped with French dressing or vary as suggested below. Serves 6.

Cottage Cheese with Chives: Season and cream as above. Add 1/4 cup chopped chives. Serves 6.

Cottage Cheese with Olives: Add whole or sliced stuffed olives to seasoned, creamed cottage cheese.

Cottage Cheese with Orange Wedges: Combine 1 cup orange wedges with 11/2 cups seasoned, creamed cottage cheese. Flavor with a little chopped fresh mint. Serves 6.

Cottage Cheese with Raisins and Green Pepper: To 11/2 cups seasoned, creamed cottage cheese add 1/2 cup seedless raisins and 1/4 cup chopped green pepper.

If desired, use mayonnaise instead of cream with the cottage cheese. Serves 6.

Cottage Cheese with Fresh Strawberries: Fold 1 cup fresh strawberries into 11/2 cups seasoned, creamed cottage cheese. Flavor with a little chopped fresh mint. Serves 6.

EGG-OLIVE TIMBALES WITH SEAFOOD DRESSING

1 cup pitted ripe olives
12 hard-cooked eggs
2 pimientos
2 green onions
2 tablespoons sour cream
2 tablespoons mayonnaise
1/2 teaspoon salt
1/2 teaspoon seasoned salt
Endive or other salad greens
Seafood Dressing (below)
Whole pitted ripe olives for garnish
Seafood Dressing:
1/3 cup mayonnaise
1/3 cup sour cream
1/3 cup chili sauce
Juice of 1 lemon
11/2 cups cooked cleaned shrimp, crabmeat, or lobster

Slice 1 cup olives into rings. Arrange 3 overlapping slices in bottom of each of 6 lightly oiled custard cups.

Peel eggs and grate on medium fine grater. Chop pimientos and green onions. Combine with eggs, sour cream, mayonnaise, salt, seasoned salt, and remaining sliced olives and toss lightly. Spoon into custard cups and pack down lightly. Chill several hours.

Unmold unto plate garnished with endive. Garnish with Seafood Dressing and whole ripe olives.

Seafood Dressing: Blend together

mayonnaise, sour cream, chili sauce, and lemon juice. Fold in shrimp or other seafood. Chill thoroughly before serving. Serves 6.

ANCHOVY CHEESE SALAD

1 2-ounce can anchovies, drained
1 teaspoon finely cut chives
1 pint creamed cottage cheese
Crisp lettuce leaves
6 small tomatoes, peeled and sliced

Chop 2/3 of the anchovies into small pieces. Cut 1/3 into long strips for garnish.

Add chives and anchovy pieces to cottage cheese, and mix lightly.

Cover and place in refrigerator for at least 1/2 hour to blend flavors.

Arrange lettuce cups on large chop plate.

Put mound of cottage cheese in center and overlap tomato slices on lettuce around edge.

Place strips of anchovies on top of cheese as a garnish.

Serve mayonnaise or French dressing on the side. Serves 6.

MOLDED EGG SALAD

8 hard-cooked eggs
1 cup finely diced celery
1/4 cup salad dressing
1 teaspoon Worcestershire sauce
1 tablespoon lemon juice
1 teaspoon scraped onion
Salt and pepper
6 thick slices of tomato
Salad greens
Paprika
Celery curls

Chop eggs coarsely. Add celery, dressing, and seasoning. Season to taste with salt and pepper. Press into molds and chill.

Unmold on tomato slices placed in a bed of salad greens. Sprinkle with paprika. Garnish with celery curls and additional dressing if desired. Serves 6.

Egg-Olive Timbales with Seafood Dressing

Meat and Poultry Salads

CHICKEN, TURKEY, OR DUCK SALAD

2 cups diced cooked or canned chicken, turkey, or duck
2 cups diced celery
1 cup mayonnaise or salad dressing
Salt and pepper
Lemon juice
Lettuce or other greens

Combine chicken, celery, and salad dressing. Season to taste with salt, pepper, and lemon juice.

Chill and serve on lettuce or other greens.

If desired, pimiento strips, sliced olives, or sliced cucumbers, toasted almonds, or marinated asparagus tips may be used for a garnish. Serves 4.

With French Dressing: Marinate chicken in French dressing. Chill. Drain and combine with other ingredients. Blend with mayonnaise, if desired. Season to taste.

Chicken Salad Variations

Chicken-Nut Salad: Add ¼ to ½ cup slivered toasted almonds just before serving.

Avocado-Chicken Salad: Add ½ cup diced avocado. If desired, serve in halved avocados.

Cranberry-Chicken Salad: Garnish or serve salad with cranberry sauce.

Egg-Vegetable-Chicken Salad: Add 2 chopped hard-cooked eggs, 2 tablespoons chopped green pepper, and 1 teaspoon finely grated onion.

Grape-Chicken Salad: Add 1 cup fresh seedless white grapes.

Pineapple-Chicken Salad: Add 1 cup diced fresh or canned pineapple.

Ham and Chicken: Substitute half diced cooked ham for half the chicken.

Note: A 4-pound drawn bird yields about 4 cups cooked chicken; a 10-pound drawn turkey yields 7 to 8 cups cooked turkey.

Ham and Orange Salad Bowl

CHICKEN AND MUSHROOM SALAD

Use 2 cups diced cooked chicken, ½ cup sautéed button or sliced mushrooms, and ½ cup diced celery. Moisten with desired dressing.

CHICKEN WITH NUTS AND OLIVES SALAD

Use 2 cups diced cooked chicken, ½ cup diced celery, ½ cup sliced ripe olives, and ½ cup sliced toasted almonds. Moisten with mayonnaise.

CHICKEN AND SWEETBREADS SALAD

Use 2 cups diced cooked chicken, 1 cup diced cooked sweetbreads, and ½ cup chopped cucumber. Moisten with mayonnaise.

CHICKEN-FRUIT-NUT SALAD

Use 2 cups diced cooked chicken, ½ cup chopped celery, ½ cup diced pineapple (or whole grapes or cherries), and ½ cup sliced toasted almonds. Moisten with mayonnaise.

CHICKEN-TOMATO SALAD

Use 1 cup diced cooked chicken, ½ cup diced crisp cracklings, and 1 cup diced tomato. Moisten with desired dressing.

CHICKEN-TONGUE SALAD

Use 1 cup diced cooked chicken, 1 cup diced cooked tongue, ½ cup chopped celery, and ½ cup chopped stuffed olives. Moisten with desired dressing.

MEAT SALAD

In master recipe for Chicken Salad, substitute any kind of diced cooked meat for chicken. For large groups, veal may be economically combined with chicken. For 25 servings, use 3 quarts meat and/or chicken or turkey and 2 quarts diced celery.

HAM AND ORANGE SALAD BOWL

1   clove garlic (optional)
2   cups cubed ham
1½ cups orange sections
1   cup chopped celery
½   cup chopped walnuts
⅓   cup minced onion (optional)
⅓   to ½ cup mayonnaise
2   tablespoons cream
1   tablespoon vinegar
Dash of pepper

Rub salad bowl with garlic. Mix ham, orange sections, celery, walnuts, and onion in bowl.

Combine other ingredients; then add to ham mixture and toss. Serves 6 to 8.

Chilled Chicken Salad Pie

CHILLED CHICKEN SALAD PIE

1   baked and chilled, 9-inch pie shell, made with pie crust mix or 1 cup flour, ½ teaspoon salt, ⅓ cup shortening, and 3 to 4 tablespoons cold water

Chicken Salad Filling:

2   cups cooked chicken, cut into pieces
¾   cup grated American cheese
½   cup diced celery
½   cup (9-ounce can) drained crushed pineapple
⅓   cup blanched slivered almonds or chopped walnuts
½   teaspoon paprika
½   teaspoon salt
½   cup mayonnaise
½   cup whipping cream
¼   cup mayonnaise
Grated carrot

Combine cooked chicken, American cheese, celery, crushed pineapple, almonds or walnuts, paprika, salt, and mayonnaise. Toss lightly. Turn into cooled baked pie shell.

Whip whipping cream until thick and stiff. Carefully fold in mayonnaise. Spread over salad in pie shell, leaving 1 inch of salad around edge uncovered.

Garnish with grated carrot. Chill until serving time, at least 30 minutes. Serves 6.

CHEF'S SALAD BOWL

Line a salad bowl with romaine; fill in center with bite-sized pieces of chicory or any combination of greens.

Arrange strips of ham, turkey, and Cheddar cheese in groups on top of chicory, with tomato wedges and thin sliced unpeeled cucumber between. Top with wedges of hard-cooked eggs.

Carry to the table for all to see, then toss with your stoutest French dressing and serve.

Dutch Salad

DUTCH SALAD

2   medium red apples
2   cups diced, cooked beef
1   large dill pickle, minced
4   cups diced, cooked potatoes
1   medium onion, minced
2   tablespoons vegetable oil
3   tablespoons vinegar
¼   cup mayonnaise
Halved hard-cooked eggs
Pickled beets

Wash and core apples; do not peel; dice. Combine with beef, pickle, potatoes, and onion.

Combine oil, vinegar, and mayonnaise; pour over apple mixture; toss to mix well. Serve on salad greens, garnished with halved hard-cooked eggs and pickled beets. Serves 8.

CHICKEN LIVER AND EGG SALAD

3   onions, minced
3   tablespoons chicken fat or salad oil
½   pound chicken livers
4   hard-cooked eggs
2   ribs of celery, minced
Salt and pepper

Sauté onions in melted fat until lightly browned. Remove onions. Sauté livers until tender.

Chop livers with eggs and celery. Mix with browned onions. Season with salt and pepper.

Moisten with fat in which onions were fried. Serve on salad greens. Serves 6.

HAM SALAD

3   cups cubed, cooked ham (about 1 pound cut into ½-inch cubes)
15   radishes, sliced thin
8   sweet pickles, sliced thin
2   hard-cooked eggs, chopped
½   cup cooked salad dressing
½   cup mayonnaise
1   teaspoon prepared mustard
½   teaspoon salt
⅛   teaspoon pepper
Hard-cooked egg slices

Combine ham, radishes, pickles, and chopped hard-cooked eggs.

Blend salad dressing and mayonnaise; season with mustard, salt, and pepper. Stir salad ingredients into dressing.

Pile salad into lettuce cups placed in individual bowls or on large serving platter.

Garnish each serving with hard-cooked egg slices. Serves 6.

MEAT SALAD BOWL
(Master Recipe)

¼   cup sliced onions
1   small head lettuce
2   tomatoes, cut in wedges
2   cups cooked or canned peas
¼   cup sliced, stuffed olives
1   cup cooked meat, cut in strips
1   teaspoon salt
1   cup French dressing

Separate onion rings. Break lettuce in bite-sized pieces. Arrange vegetables and meat on lettuce. Sprinkle with salt. Add dressing. Toss lightly. Serves 6.

Variations: Tongue, beef, veal, lamb, duck, turkey, liver, or chicken may be used for the meat. Cabbage may be used in place of celery.

Tuna or Salmon Salad Bowl: Use tuna or salmon in place of the meat. Omit onion. Add 1 cup chopped celery.

RICE AND CHICKEN SALAD WITH ORANGES

2   tablespoons butter or margarine
⅔   cup uncooked rice
1¾   cups warm water or chicken broth
½   teaspoon salt
2   cups diced, cooked chicken
1   cup diced celery
2   cups orange sections
½   cup French dressing
½   teaspoon salt
1   head lettuce

In a 2-quart saucepan, melt butter or margarine. Add rice and cook until grains are a brownish color. Stir occasionally.

Add water slowly, add salt and bring to vigorous boil. Turn heat as low as possible. Cover and leave over low heat 20 minutes. Chill rice.

Add chicken, celery, orange sections (save some for garnish), French dressing, and salt to chilled rice. Toss together.

Place in lettuce cups or line bowl or platter with lettuce and place rice and chicken salad on lettuce. Garnish with remaining orange sections. Serves 8 to 10.

HORNS OF PLENTY

1   tablespoon instant minced onion
2   tablespoons table wine or broth
1   tablespoon chopped pimiento
⅛   teaspoon garlic powder, or 1 crushed garlic clove
2   tablespoons sweet pickle relish
2   tablespoons wine vinegar
3   tablespoons salad oil
¼   teaspoon salt
¼   teaspoon sugar
1   or 2 (1 pound each) cans green beans
Sliced baked ham or turkey
Spiced peaches

Measure instant minced onion into wine. Combine all ingredients except green beans, ham, and spiced peaches. Drain beans; combine with marinade and let stand several hours.

When ready to serve, roll ham or turkey into cornucopias; hold together with toothpicks, if necessary. Fill each cornucopia with beans. Serve as salad or entree with hot or cold spiced peaches. Serves 6 entrees or 12 salads.

Note: Marinade is sufficient for 1 or 2 cans green beans. To serve Horns of Plenty hot; heat marinade gently with drained beans. Spoon into hot ham or turkey cornucopias.

Horns of Plenty may be served as a salad or entree; will be enjoyed hot or cold. They are especially good accompanied by hot or cold spiced peaches.

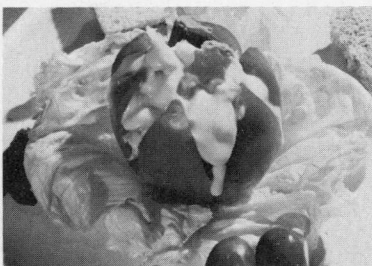

For a summer luncheon serve chicken salad in a tomato.

Florida Chicken Salad

WHOLE-MEAL SALAD BOWL

1   clove garlic, if desired
½ cup salad oil
2   tablespoons vinegar
¾ teaspoon salt
⅛ teaspoon pepper
½ teaspoon dry mustard
¼ teaspoon paprika
½ head lettuce, broken into 1½-inch
      chunks
2   tablespoons chopped green pepper
½ cup sliced celery
½ cup thinly sliced raw cauliflowerets
1   cup cooked asparagus tips
1   hard-cooked egg, cut in eighths
½ pound baked ham or salami, cut
      julienne style

Have all salad ingredients chilled. Rub inside of salad bowl with cut surface of garlic clove and then discard garlic.

Stir in salad oil and vinegar. Add seasonings and beat with fork until well mixed.

Combine remaining ingredients in order given. Toss lightly until each piece of salad is coated with dressing. Serve immediately. Serves 6 to 8.

CHICKEN SALAD—CALIFORNIA STYLE

3   avocados, cut in half
¼ cup orange juice
2   cups cooked diced chicken
1   cup diced celery
2   oranges, sectioned and diced
½ cup mayonnaise
3   tablespoons chili sauce
⅛ teaspoon paprika
1   teaspoon salt
2   tablespoons chopped pimiento
Salad greens

Brush halved avocados with orange juice. Combine chicken and celery with diced oranges; mix well.

Blend mayonnaise, chili sauce, and seasonings; fold into chicken mixture, mixing until thoroughly blended.

Fill cavity of avocados with chicken salad. Top with chopped pimiento. Serve on bed of salad greens. Garnish with additional orange sections. Serves 6.

PORK SALAD

2   cups cubed cooked pork
1   cup diced pared apples
1½ cups chopped celery
1   teaspoon minced onion
¼ cup minced parsley
¼ cup chopped green pepper
1   teaspoon salt
¼ cup cooked salad dressing
¼ cup mayonnaise
¼ cup sour cream
1   tablespoon lemon juice
1   can jellied cranberry sauce
Crisp salad greens

Combine pork, apples, celery, onion, parsley, and green pepper.

Blend together salt, salad dressing, mayonnaise, sour cream, and lemon juice. Mix dressing lightly with meat and vegetables.

Serve salad on crisp salad greens. Garnish with slices of jellied cranberry sauce. Serves 4.

TONGUE AND VEGETABLE SALAD

1   cup cooked tongue
2½ cups canned or cooked vegetables
1   cup thinly sliced celery
1   tablespoon chopped onion
2   tablespoons chopped sweet pickle
½ cup sharp mayonnaise
1   head lettuce
1   hard-cooked egg, sliced

Cut tongue in strips. Drain chilled vegetables.

Combine tongue, vegetables, onion, and pickles with mayonnaise. Chill 1 hour to blend flavors.

Serve in lettuce cups. Garnish each serving with a slice of egg. Serves 6.

Variations: Use cooked or canned chicken, canned tuna, salmon, or other cooked meats or fish instead of tongue.

Snappy Sauerkraut Salad: Add 1 cup sauerkraut to tongue and vegetable salad with the mixed vegetables.

*Chicken Salad—
California Style*

FLORIDA CHICKEN SALAD

1   No. 2 can orange and grapefruit
      sections
2   cups diced cooked chicken
1   cup diced celery
2   tablespoons lime juice
¼ cup mayonnaise
¼ teaspoon salt
⅛ teaspoon pepper
Salad greens

Drain citrus sections thoroughly. Add drained sections to chicken and celery in mixing bowl.

Mix together lime juice, mayonnaise, and seasonings. Add to salad and toss lightly.

Serve with salad greens and garnish with additional fruit sections.

Serves 5 to 6.

CHICKEN SALAD—GUEST STYLE

2   cups diced, cooked or canned
      chicken
1   cup chopped celery
1   cup seedless green grapes, or
      seeded Tokay grape halves
½ cup toasted almonds
½ cup mayonnaise
Crisp lettuce

Combine chicken, celery, grapes, and nuts. Chill.

Add mayonnaise and toss lightly. Serve in lettuce cups. Serves 4 to 6.

Fruit Salads

WALDORF SALAD

Combine 2 cups cubed apples, 1/4 cup chopped nuts, and 1 cup cubed celery.

Moisten with 1/2 cup mayonniase. Mix lightly with 2 forks. Serve on lettuce. Serves 5.

WALDORF SALAD SPECIAL

6 apples
2 tablespoons lemon juice
1 1/2 cups chopped celery
1/2 cup chopped walnuts or pecans
3/4 cup mayonnaise or cooked salad dressing
1/2 cup heavy cream, whipped
Apple slices and whole nuts for garnish

Wash, core, and dice apples coarsely without peeling. Sprinkle apples with lemon juice and toss quickly to prevent discoloration.

Add chopped celery and nuts and blend well. Fold mayonnaise or cooked salad dressing into whipped cream. Gently mix dressing with fruit.

Place in large bowl. Garnish with apple slices and nuts. Serves 8.

APPLE AND GRAPE SALAD

3 unpeeled red apples, diced
1 cup halved seeded Tokay grapes
Mayonnaise or salad dressing
Lettuce
1/2 cup shredded Cheddar cheese

Combine the apples and grapes and toss with sufficient mayonnaise or salad dressing to moisten and season well.

For each serving place a mound of the salad on lettuce on a salad plate; sprinkle generously with shredded cheese.

Serve with additional mayonnaise or salad dressing. Serves 4.

APPLE-CARROT-RAISIN SALAD

Combine bite-sized pieces of unpeeled red apple with shredded carrot and seeded raisins. Serve with mayonnaise.

Avocado-Fruit Cocktail Salad: Fill avocado halves with chilled drained fruit cocktail. Sprinkle fruit with a few drops of lemon juice. Serve on crisp salad greens.

APPLE-CUCUMBER SALAD

1 1/2 cups diced unpeeled red apples
1 1/2 cups diced peeled cucumbers
1/2 teaspoon salt
Dash of pepper
1/4 cup pineapple or lemon juice
1/3 cup mayonnaise or salad dressing
1/4 cup pecan pieces
Lettuce

Season the apples and cucumbers with salt and pepper; sprinkle with the pineapple or lemon juice.

Add the mayonnaise or salad dressing and pecans.

Serve in crisp lettuce cups. Serves 4.

APPLE AND PINEAPPLE SALAD

1 1/2 cups diced unpeeled red apples
French dressing
6 slices pineapple
Lettuce

Toss apples with enough French dressing to moisten. For each serving, place a slice of pineapple on lettuce, with a mound of the apple salad in the center. Serves 6.

TOMATO SLICES FILLED WITH AVOCADO

Peel, then mash avocado and season with lemon juice, grated onion, salt, and paprika. Spread the mixture between slices of tomato.

Garnish with a bit of mayonnaise and arrange individual servings on lettuce.

STUFFED AVOCADO SLICES

2 avocados
2 tablespoons lemon juice
Salt
1/4 cup cream
1 8-ounce package cream cheese
1/4 cup finely chopped sweet pickles
2 tablespoons minced green onion
1 tablespoon minced parsley
1/2 teaspoon salt
6 slices pineapple
Lettuce
French dressing

Cut each avocado into halves lengthwise; remove the pit, and peel. Sprinkle inside and out with lemon juice and salt.

Gradually add the cream to the cream cheese, blending until smooth. Add the pickles, onion, parsley, and salt.

Fill the cavity of each avocado half with the cheese filling, spreading it well to the sides. Put the halves together and wrap in waxed paper; chill.

Slice crosswise into rings. For each serving place a slice of pineapple on lettuce on a salad plate; top with a stuffed avocado slice. Serve with French dressing. Serves 6.

Colorful, piquant Ambassador Salad makes an impressive main dish for luncheon tables.

AMBASSADOR SALAD WITH ONION DRESSING

2 large or 3 small avocados
Crisp lettuce leaves
1 1/2 dozen cooked large shrimp
6 hard-cooked eggs
12 cooked asparagus spears
Tiny tomatoes
Ripe olives
Onion Dressing (below)

Cut avocados in halves lengthwise, remove seeds and skin. Cut avocados crosswise into thick half circles (you will need 18).

Arrange crisp lettuce on salad plates. Alternate 3 avocado pieces and 3 shrimps in center of plate. Arrange 2 hard-cooked egg halves and 2 asparagus spears on salad; garnish with tiny whole tomatoes and ripe olives. Serve with Onion Dressing. Serves 6.

Onion Dressing:
1/4 cup wine vinegar
2 teaspoons instant minced onion
1/4 teaspoon paprika
1/2 cup salad oil
1 teaspoon soy sauce
2 drops Tabasco sauce
1/2 teaspoon dry mustard
1/8 teaspoon dried dill (optional)
1/2 teaspoon salt

Combine all ingredients in a covered jar. Shake to blend. Let stand at least 1 hour before using.

AVOCADO-ORANGE SALAD

3 oranges, peeled and sliced
1 large sweet onion, thinly sliced
French dressing
2 large avocados
2 tablespoons lemon juice
Lettuce

Marinate the orange and onion slices in the French dressing, in the refrigerator, for several hours. Drain.

Cut the avocados in half lengthwise; remove the pits, peel and slice. Sprinkle with lemon juice to prevent darkening.

For each serving place alternate slices of orange, onion, and avocado on lettuce.

Serve with the French dressing drained from the oranges and onion. Serves 6 to 8.

AVOCADO-CREAM CHEESE SALAD

2   medium-sized avocados
3   3-ounce packages cream cheese
1   teaspoon minced onion
½ teaspoon celery salt

Peel avocados halved lengthwise and hollow out stem ends slightly. Sprinkle inside and out with lemon or lime juice and salt.

Combine cheese, onion, and celery salt, and blend thoroughly. Fill halves with cheese mixture and press two filled halves together. Wrap in waxed paper and chill thoroughly. Cut into thick lengthwise slices and lay on lettuce garnished salad plates.

Allow one filled oval to each serving. Top with mayonnaise if desired. Serves 8.

Variations: Filling may be varied in flavor with minced capers; chopped celery; green pepper or sweet pickles; chopped green or ripe olives; chopped chives; chopped salted nuts; minced pimiento; finely shredded pineapple.

SPRING FRUIT SALAD

On a large tray, arrange mounds of grapefruit sections, halved seeded grapes, blueberries, banana fans, and small scoops of cottage cheese.

Let each person make his own selection of fruit, crisp salad greens and lots of crackers. Serve with lemon allspice dressing (below).

Note: Cut grapefruit in half and then section. Shells may then be used as novel serving dishes.

Lemon Allspice Dressing:

½ cup mayonnaise
¼ cup powdered sugar
3   tablespoons lemon juice
⅛ teaspoon salt
½ teaspoon allspice
½ cup heavy cream whipped

Blend mayonnaise with sugar, lemon juice, salt, and allspice. Fold in whipped cream. Makes 1½ cups.

Egg and Grapefruit Salad

AVOCADO-CANTALOUPE RINGS

2   avocados
Lemon juice
1   cantaloupe, peeled
Bibb lettuce
1   cup pitted Bing cherries
French dressing, sweetened

Cut the avocados in half lengthwise; remove the pits and peel. Cut in thin slices and dip in lemon juice.

For each serving cut thin slices of the cantaloupe and alternate with the avocado slices on lettuce on a salad plate.

Fill the center with cherries. Serve with sweetened French dressing. Serves 4.

GUACAMOLE (AVOCADO) SALAD

2   small avocados
½ to 1 tablespoon onion juice
¼ to ⅓ cup chopped pimiento
Juice of 1 lemon
½ teaspoon salt
⅛ teaspoon pepper
Lettuce
2   tomatoes, quartered
Paprika

Pare and mash avocados. Add onion juice, pimiento, lemon juice, and salt and pepper to taste. Blend well.

Arrange lettuce in nests on 4 salad plates. Mound avocado mixture in each lettuce nest.

Garnish with tomatoes. Sprinkle paprika on top of each salad. Serves 4.

EGG AND GRAPEFRUIT SALAD

2   tablespoons lemon juice
1½ cups diced celery
2   large firm grapefruit
6   hard-cooked eggs
½ teaspoon salt
¼ cup mayonnaise
Paprika
2   olives (optional)

Pour lemon juice over celery placed in chilled bowl. Refrigerate while preparing other ingredients.

Peel and separate grapefruit sections, keeping as whole as possible and free from membrane.

Slice 1 hard-cooked egg, and set aside for garnish.

Add the 5 eggs coarsely cut, salt, half the mayonnaise, and the grapefruit to celery. Mix gently with 2 forks. Add more seasoning if desired. Heap into prepared grapefruit shells or lettuce cups.

Garnish top with egg slices. Finish with a dash of paprika. Place on chilled plates and serve promptly. Serve salad dressing on side if desired. Serves 4.

Note: Green celery makes an especially colorful salad. If used, add chopped olives to salad mixture. Pink grapefruit is especially nice.

APPLE CUPS

Use red-skinned unpeeled apples. Wash apples. Cut off a thin slice from stem end. Core without cutting through bottom of apple. With spoon, scoop out apple to form cup.

Fill with any of the following. Serve on crisp greens.

1. Combine equal amounts of chopped celery, peas, and chopped nuts. Moisten with mayonnaise.

2. Mix fruit salad with French dressing.

3. Add chopped celery and nutmeats to any fruit-flavored packaged gelatin. Fill apple cups; chill until set. Serve topped with a sour cream dressing.

4. Combine minced chicken with halved red grapes, chopped celery, and pecans; moisten with mayonnaise. Top with dressing.

FIG AND PEACH SALAD

Arrange a peach half in a crisp cup-shaped lettuce leaf on each plate, using shredded lettuce underneath to hold cup in place.

Cut a fig in half and place, bowtie-fashion, beside the peach.

Cut remaining figs coarsely with scissors, and mix with about ½ cup mayonnaise, ¼ cup sliced celery, and 1 tablespoon lemon juice. Heap a spoonful of this in each peach half and put a dot of it on figs. Decorate with walnut pieces, and serve.

Variation: For a luncheon salad, put a big spoonful of cottage cheese under peach, serve with cinnamon toast or hot muffins, and you have a complete meal.

FRUIT AND VEGETABLE CHEESE SALAD

2   red apples, cut in wedges
1   cup cubed pineapple or orange slices
1   small bunch red grapes, cut in halves, or berries in season
2   or 3 tomatoes, cut in slices
2   medium-sized cucumbers, cut in strips
1   small bunch green onions or sliced sweet onion
Salad greens (chicory, watercress, or lettuce)
3   cups shredded American cheese

Arrange wedges of apple in a semi-circle on one side of large chop plate or tray. In center of the half-circle, pile pineapple cubes. At each, place grapes.

On opposite side, arrange vegetables on bed of salad greens. Fill center of plate with shredded American cheese.

Garnish with salad greens. Serve with sour cream salad dressing. Serves 6.

GRAPE CLUSTER SALAD

Blend cream cheese with a small amount of milk. For each salad place a pear half, round side up, on lettuce on a salad plate. Spread it with the cream cheese.

Cut grapes in half lengthwise, and arrange them, cut side down, on each cream cheese covered pear, to resemble a bunch of grapes. Put a bit of grape stem in the large end of each pear.

Serve the Grape Cluster Salads with French dressing.

STUFFED PEACH SALAD

¼ cup milk
1 3-ounce package cream cheese
½ cup chopped walnuts
½ cup chopped white seedless raisins
8 peach halves
8 large cooked prunes, pitted
Leaf lettuce
French dressing

Gradually add milk to cream cheese, blending until smooth. Add nuts and raisins and mix well.

Fill centers of peaches with mixture.

For each salad, arrange 2 stuffed peach halves and 2 pitted prunes on lettuce. Serve with French dressing. Serves 4.

Cottage Cheese Coronation Salad

ROSE PETAL SALAD

4 pineapple slices
Lettuce
1 3-ounce package cream cheese
Milk
4 radishes, thinly sliced
French dressing

For each serving, place a slice of pineapple in a lettuce cup.

Soften the cream cheese slightly with a small amount of milk and place a rounded scoop in the center of each pineapple slice.

Press thin radish slices into the cheese to resemble rose petals. Serve with French dressing. Serves 4.

LANAI SALAD

1 3-ounce package soft cream cheese
¼ cup mayonnaise
2 tablespoons pineapple syrup
1 banana, sliced
4 maraschino cherries, cut in fourths
¼ cup chopped nuts
4 pineapple slices, drained

Mix cream cheese, mayonnaise, and pineapple syrup together until smooth. Fold in banana slices, cherries, and nuts.

Arrange drained pineapple slices on a bed of crisp greens. Pile cheese-fruit mixture on top. Serves 4.

COTTAGE CHEESE CORONA-TION SALAD

This easy-to-make salad combines a serving of cottage cheese with a delicious canned cling peach half, cut as a crown, with red and green maraschino cherries as crown jewels.

Nest the salad in endive or leaf lettuce to make a very attractive setting and add a sprig of watercress.

PARTY FRUIT SALAD

1 3-ounce package cream cheese
1 tablespoon mayonnaise
1 No. 2½ can sliced pineapple
½ cup finely chopped parsley
2 cups watermelon wedges
2 cups cantaloupe wedges
2 bananas
Leaf lettuce or escarole
½ pound Tokay grapes

Mix cheese and mayonnaise; spread on edges of chilled pineapple slices. Roll edges in parsley.

Combine chilled watermelon and cantaloupe wedges.

Cut peeled bananas in half and into strips.

Outline platter with lettuce, and group fruit attractively. Garnish with French dressing. Serves 8.

Note: When melons are not available, use such fruits as apples, pears, or plums.

PEAR-CHEESE SALAD

Arrange pear halves on lettuce leaves. Top with mayonnaise, then a sprinkle of grated American cheese.

COTTAGE CHEESE WITH FRESH FRUIT

2 cups cottage cheese
1 teaspoon salt
1 teaspoon lemon juice
¼ cup chopped pecans
Salad greens
1 melon, cut in round slices
2 oranges
2 bananas
1 pint fresh sweet cherries, or 1 pint strawberries
3 pineapple slices

Add salt and lemon juice to cottage cheese. Fold in part of chopped pecans. Turn into bowl that has been rinsed in cold water and place in refrigerator to chill.

Just before serving, unmold on large salad plate; surround with crisp salad greens or lettuce cups filled with fresh fruits—melon rounds, orange sections, banana slices (soaked in lemon or pineapple juice), pineapple sections, and red cherries or strawberries. Serves 6.

Cottage Cheese with Fresh Fruit

GEORGIA FRUIT SALAD

1 cup drained canned fruit cocktail
    (or coarsely diced peaches)
1 banana, diced
¼ cup finely diced celery
½ cup salad dressing
Lettuce

Combine the fruit, celery, and salad dressing; toss until well blended. Serve on lettuce. Serves 4.

JIFFY ORANGE SALAD

12 peeled orange slices
  Leaf lettuce
  Mayonnaise or salad dressing
4 maraschino cherries

For each portion arrange 3 orange slices on lettuce. Garnish with mayonnaise or salad dressing and a cherry.

Serve as an appetizer salad. Serves 4.

PINEAPPLE SALADS

Pineapple-Apricot: Arrange pineapple slices on salad greens. Top each slice with an apricot half.

Pineapple-Apple: Alternate half slices of pineapple with lengthwise slices of unpeeled red apples on salad greens.

Pineapple-Cream Cheese: Arrange pineapple slices on salad greens. Garnish with watercress and cream cheese that has been formed into balls and rolled in chopped nuts.

Pineapple-Cottage Cheese: Arrange mounds of cottage cheese on salad greens. Surround each mound with pineapple slices, cut in quarters.

Pineapple-Banana: Arrange pineapple chunks and thick slices of banana (dip in pineapple syrup and roll in finely chopped nuts) on salad greens. Garnish with maraschino cherries.

Pineapple Chunks 'n' Cherries: Arrange drained canned pineapple chunks and dark sweet cherries on salad greens.

Pineapple - Banana - Nut: Arrange drained canned pineapple slices on salad greens. Place banana slices (which have been dipped in pineapple syrup) atop the pineapple and sprinkle with salted peanuts.

Pineapple Salads

PEACH-PINEAPPLE DAISIES

Arrange leaf lettuce in 5 separate nests on a round chop plate.

Place a slice of canned pineapple in each lettuce nest.

On each slice of pineapple place 4 slices of canned peaches, petal fashion.

Place a spoonful of salad dressing in the center of each daisy.

Garnish each daisy with a maraschino cherry.

HONEYDEW RING FRUIT SALAD

6 slices honeydew melon, peeled
Lettuce
2 cups cantaloupe balls
2 cups fresh raspberries
2 cups seedless grapes
Fresh mint
¼ cup salad oil
¼ cup lime juice

Place melon slices on lettuce, and fill centers with other fruits, combined.

Garnish with mint; serve with mixed oil and juice. Serves 6.

CANTALOUPE FRUIT RINGS

Lettuce
4 peeled cantaloupe rings
1 cup red raspberries
1 cup seedless grapes
1 cup red plums, diced
1 cup watermelon balls
Cream cheese dressing

Cover large individual dishes with crisp lettuce. Arrange the cantaloupe rings on the lettuce.

Toss the raspberries, grapes, plums, and watermelon balls lightly together. Heap in the cantaloupe rings.

Serve with cream cheese dressing. Serves 4.

WINE FRUIT SALAD

Prepare sliced bananas, pineapple, and orange sections. Cover with dressing made by blending ½ cup sugar, ⅓ cup sherry, and 2 tablespoons madeira.

Allow to stand in a cold place for an hour before serving. May be served as dessert.

Old-Fashioned Fruit Salad

OLD-FASHIONED FRUIT SALAD

1 large orange
2 cups halved, seeded Tokay grapes
1 cup diced fresh or canned pineapple
1 cup diced tart apple
½ cup whipping cream
1½ tablespoons fresh lemon juice·
1 tablespoon sugar
Few grains salt
Salad greens
Clusters of Tokay grapes for garnish

Pare and section orange. Combine with grapes, pineapple, and apple.

Whip cream until stiff. Add lemon juice, sugar, and salt, and blend gently. Fold into fruit mixture. Garnish with crisp salad greens and tiny clusters of Tokay grapes. Serves 4 to 6.

EASY FRUIT WALDORF

1 No. 2½ can fruit cocktail
½ cup sliced celery
½ cup chopped walnuts
Salad greens
Mayonnaise or cream dressing

Drain fruit cocktail well and mix lightly with celery and walnuts.

Serve on salad greens and top with mayonnaise. Serves 6.

Variation: Instead of mayonnaise, serve lemon-honey dressing in a separate bowl, to be spooned over the fruit at the table. Make the dressing by combining equal parts lemon juice and honey.

SPICED PEACH SALAD

½ cup vinegar
1 teaspoon cloves
1 stick cinnamon
½ cup sugar
6 canned peach halves
1 package (3 ounces) cream cheese
1 teaspoon lemon juice
¼ cup chopped pecans

Put vinegar in saucepan; add spices and sugar and cook 3 minutes. Pour over drained peaches. Chill 3 hours.

Drain and fill peach cavities with cream cheese seasoned with lemon juice and mixed with chopped pecans.

Arrange on lettuce and garnish with mayonnaise. Serves 6.

FRESH GRAPEFRUIT WINTER SALADS

Arrange on lettuce-covered salad plate.

Poinsettia: On 5 or 6 grapefruit segments arranged flower-petal fashion, place thin strips of pimiento. Center with 4 or 5 small pimiento cheese balls, sprinkle with paprika. Pass mayonnaise. Serves 1.

Grapefruit-Banana: Alternate 6 grapefruit segments with 6 banana fingers, rolled in chopped nuts, coconut, or vanilla wafer crumbs. Serve with any desired dressing. Serves 1.

Grapefruit-Apple: Alternate 6 grapefruit segments with 6 wedges of unpeeled, red-skinned apple. Serve with grapefruit French dressing. Serves 1.

Holiday: Fill center of an individual ring mold of cranberry jelly with 4 or 5 avocado or banana balls. Around base arrange 6 or 7 grapefruit segments. Garnish with chicory. Pass grapefruit French dressing.

If canned cranberry jelly is used, cut in inch-thick slices and cut out center with cooky cutter to simulate ring molds. Serves 1.

FRESH GRAPEFRUIT SUMMER SALADS

Arrange on lettuce-covered salad plate.

Fruit-Cheese Luncheon Plate: Fill a peach or pear half with cream or cottage cheese, moistened with fruit mayonnaise. Circle with 5 or 6 grapefruit segments. Garnish with cube of red jelly. Pass fruit mayonnaise. Serves 1.

Grapefruit, Pear and Grape: Combine ¼ cup each of grapefruit pieces, diced pear, and seeded grapes. Serve with fruit mayonnaise. Serves 1.

Grapefruit-Egg: Cut a deviled egg in 6 lengthwise slices. Alternate these with grapefruit segments. Garnish with sliced stuffed olives. Serve with mayonnaise. Serves 1.

Grapefruit-Melon: Arrange 6 grapefruit segments in flower-petal pattern, alternately with long fingers of cantaloupe or honeydew melon. Marinate melon slices first in sweetened grapefruit juice. Serve with sweet grapefruit French dressing. Serves 1.

MELON BALL SALAD

1 cantaloupe
Lettuce
2 cups watermelon balls
1½ cups honeydew melon balls
Sprigs of mint
Mayonnaise, sweetened

Slice the cantaloupe into rings about an inch thick. Peel each ring and place on lettuce on a salad plate.

Fill each ring with watermelon and honeydew balls. Garnish with sprigs of mint.

Serve with sweetened mayonnaise. Serves 4.

GRAPEFRUIT-MELON BALL SALAD

2 grapefruit, peeled and sectioned
Lettuce
1½ cups watermelon or cantaloupe balls

For each serving arrange grapefruit sections, petal fashion, on crisp lettuce on a salad plate.

Fill the center with melon balls and serve with a sweetened dressing. Serves 4 to 6.

FLOWER PETAL SALAD

2 oranges, peeled and sectioned
2 grapefruit, peeled and sectioned
Lettuce
Mayonnaise or salad dressing
4 pecan halves

For each salad arrange alternate orange and grapefruit sections, petal fashion, on lettuce on a salad plate.

Place a spoonful of mayonnaise or salad dressing in the center. Garnish with a pecan half. Serves 4.

Grapefruit sections encircled by orange slices and sweet onion rings make an eye-catching and delicious salad served with a fruit dressing.

WATERMELON BOWL CENTERPIECE

½ watermelon
2 cups cantaloupe balls
1 cup pineapple chunks
1 cup blueberries
Green galax leaves
French dressing

With a ball cutter, remove the center from half of a short thick watermelon.

Toss together the watermelon and cantaloupe balls, pineapple chunks, and blueberries.

Place the watermelon bowl on galax leaves on a round platter, and fill it with the mixed fruit. Serve the salad with French dressing. Serves 4 to 6.

CARLTON FRUIT SALAD

1 cup grapefruit sections
1½ cups orange sections
½ cup Tokay grapes, cut in half and seeded
Lettuce
Honey French dressing

Combine the grapefruit and orange sections and the grapes. Place in a mound on lettuce. Serve with honey French dressing. Serves 4.

FRUIT SALAD DELIGHT

8 peach halves
1 cup blueberries
Leaf lettuce
1 cup watermelon balls
1 cup honeydew melon balls
12 peeled cantaloupe slices
Mayonnaise or salad dressing

For each serving, place 2 peach halves filled with blueberries opposite each other on lettuce arranged on a salad plate.

Between the peaches on one side of the plate place a mound of melon balls, and opposite it place 3 cantaloupe slices, petal fashion.

Garnish the center of the plate with mayonnaise or salad dressing. Serves 4.

For an appetizing luncheon plate: Combine cottage cheese and chopped dried figs (4 figs to 1 pint cheese). Place a mound of cottage cheese-fig mixture on each lettuce-lined plate. Garnish each plate with 2 whole dried figs, pineapple spears, orange slices, and strawberries or cherries.

PACIFIC SALAD COOLER

For each serving, peel two seedless oranges and cut them into thin cartwheel-like slices.

Arrange two melon slices on a bed of lettuce that has been placed on a large salad or luncheon plate.

Take the cartwheel slices of oranges and form two semi-circles with them, overlapping each slice, at one end of plate.

For a bright touch of color, add several large strawberries, sliced, and tucked in around the edge of the orange slices and several at one side of plate.

Drop a large scoop of lemon sherbet in center and serve immediately.

Serve hot rolls or cinnamon toast plus tall glasses of fresh lemonade and you'll have a complete summer lunch.

Pacific Salad Cooler

PEACH 'N' COTTAGE CHEESE

Place drained halves of canned peaches cut-side-up on salad greens. Top with cottage cheese to which chives have been added.

WINTER PEAR WALDORF SALAD

2 cups diced, pared pear, or 1 cup each diced pear and unpared red apple
2 tablespoons lemon juice
1 teaspoon sugar
½ cup mayonnaise
1 cup thinly sliced celery
½ cup coarsely chopped walnuts

Toss fruit with lemon juice, sugar, and 1 tablespoon mayonnaise.

Just before serving, add celery, walnuts, and remaining mayonnaise. Toss and serve on crisp lettuce. Sprinkle with French dressing. Serves 6.

Variations: Substitute, for pears, cubes of fresh or canned pineapple or banana or 1 cup orange sections and 1 cup grapes, or 2 cups apple, plus ½ cup raisins or fresh dates.

Coconut Waldorf: Substitute shredded coconut for nuts.

A citrus salad of orange slices and grapefruit sections served with cottage cheese and a garnish of strawberries make an attractive low calorie luncheon.

GOLDEN SALAD

4 pineapple slices
Leaf lettuce
2 oranges, peeled and sectioned
1 grapefruit, peeled and sectioned
6 maraschino cherries, sliced
Watercress
Mayonnaise or salad dressing

For each serving, place a slice of pineapple on lettuce on a salad plate.

Arrange alternate orange and grapefruit sections on the pineapple, with thin slices of maraschino cherry between the sections.

Garnish each salad with watercress. Serve with mayonnaise or salad dressing. Serves 4.

COTTON BLOSSOM SALAD

4 red apples
4 large oranges
1 pound cottage cheese
1 teaspoon grated orange rind
½ cup chopped maraschino cherries
½ cup sour cream
½ teaspoon salt
Watercress
Mayonnaise or salad dressing

Wash apples, quarter, core, and slice thin. Peel oranges and remove sections.

Combine cottage cheese, orange rind, cherries, sour cream, and salt; mix well.

Place ring of crisp watercress around edge of large round plate. Plate alternate slices of apple and orange sections in a ring on watercress. Mound cottage cheese mixture in center.

Serve with mayonnaise or salad dressing. Serves 6.

Cotton Blossom Salad

FESTIVE SALAD

3   well beaten egg yolks
1/2 cup cream
1/4 cup lemon juice
1/8 teaspoon salt
1   No. 2½ can Royal Anne cherries, pitted
1   No. 2 can pineapple, cut in small pieces
1½ cups almonds, blanched and slivered
1/2 pound marshmallows, cut in pieces
1   cup heavy cream, whipped

Combine egg yolks, 1/2 cup cream, lemon juice, and salt. Place in top of double boiler and cook over boiling water, stirring constantly until thick.

Cool mixture. Fold fruit, nuts, and marshmallows into cooled sauce. Then fold in whipped cream.

Pour into large shallow pan or bowl and chill for several hours or overnight.

Serve on lettuce with cherry garnish. This salad may be served for dessert, if desired. Serves 12.

CLUB FRUIT PLATE

6   oranges, peeled and sliced
3   bananas, cut in sixths
3   cups melon or avocado balls
1   pound (2 cups) cottage cheese
1   3-ounce package cream cheese
Walnuts
Salad greens

Arrange fruits, cottage cheese, and walnut bonbons (below) on salad greens for individual servings. Serve with lemon French dressing. Serves 6.

Walnut Bonbons: Place balls of cream cheese between walnut halves.

BLUSHING PEAR

Drain canned pear halves and put 2 halves together with softened cream cheese. If desired, sprinkle paprika on one side to make a blush.

Top with cream cheese and a short strip of green pepper or a leaf of watercress for a stem. Stand upright on salad greens.

Blushing Pear

SALAD BUFFET PLATTER

Here are eight lovely fruit salads made from a variety of canned fruits. Back row: ready-to-serve fruits for salad; fruit cocktail molded in lemon gelatin with pecans; orange and grapefruit sections with cheese topped with a walnut; apricot halves put together with cream cheese.

Front row: a pear half filled with grated cheese; pineapple slices topped with coconut and maraschino cherries; a peach half filled with cream cheese and raisins; cottage cheese topped with pineapple chunks. These are all ideal dinner salads.

CRANBERRY-PEACH SALAD

Place a slice of canned jellied cranberry sauce on curly endive. Around it make a ring of overlapping canned peach slices.

Top cranberry sauce with a spoonful of cottage cheese. Pass mayonnaise.

PEACH BOWL SALAD

Mix drained canned sliced peaches, sliced celery, sliced stuffed olives, and shredded lettuce—to the cook's taste. Toss with French dressing or mayonnaise.

Cottage Cheese Showcap with Fruit Salad Cups

BANANA GRAPEFRUIT SALAD

3   grapefruit sections, fresh or canned
1   fully ripe banana
Salad greens
Berries or cherries

Arrange overlapping grapefruit sections along center section of salad plate. Peel banana and slice crosswise into pieces about 1/4-inch thick. Arrange 2 rows of overlapping banana slices around sides of plate.

Garnish the center with crisp green salad greens and berries or cherries, if desired. Serve with a sweet or tart dressing. Serves 1.

Note: Pink and white grapefruit sections combined, make an especially pretty salad arrangement.

If desired, orange sections may be used in place of, or combined with, the grapefruit sections.

COTTAGE CHEESE SNOWCAP WITH FRUIT SALAD CUPS

1   pound cream-style cottage cheese
1/2 teaspoon salt
1   teaspoon grated lemon rind
2   tablespoons lemon juice
1/2 cup slivered, candied ginger

Combine ingredients, reserving a little ginger to garnish top of cottage cheese, and blend. Turn into a chilled bowl.

Serve with chilled fruit salad cups: Wash and drain 9 individual lettuce cups. On 3 cups place peach halves with centers filled with blueberries; alternate grapefruit and orange sections on 3 other cups. Fill 3 remaining cups with pineapple cubes and halved strawberries.

Arrange cups on a large platter around a snowcap of cottage cheese. Serves 9.

FRUIT SALAD BOATS

2 pineapples
2 cups grape halves
2 large bananas, sliced
8 ounces cottage cheese
Watercress

Cut pineapples in half and scoop out center. Remove core and cut in bite-sized pieces.

Mix pineapple with grape halves and banana. Pile back into pineapple shell.

Divide cottage cheese in four balls; place one on each salad. Garnish with watercress. Serve with crisp crackers. Serves 4.

PEAR DESSERT SALAD

2 large fresh pears
1 tablespoon lemon juice
1 pound cottage cheese
2 to 4 tablespoons sour cream
2 to 4 tablespoons chopped preserved ginger
1/8 teaspoon salt
Lettuce or other salad green
Mayonnaise

Cut pears into quarters, core, and slice. Brush cut surfaces with lemon juice.

Mix cheese, sour cream (enough to soften), ginger, and salt.

Place salad green on individual plates and top with a mound of cheese. Insert pear slices.

Serve with mayonnaise and a garnish of any other fresh fruits, if desired. Serves 4.

CURRIED APPLE-ONION-PEPPER SALAD

Combine strips of apple with thin onion rings and crisp slivers of red and green peppers. Serve with mayonnaise seasoned with curry powder.

SUMMER CLUSTERS

For each serving place a slice of pineapple on curly endive. Cover it with a slice of peeled orange. Place 3 slices of fluted banana on orange.

Quarter fresh strawberries and place 1/4 between banana slices around edge of orange.

Garnish center with a whole strawberry. Serve with salad dressing.

Summer Clusters

FRESH FRUIT SALAD

1 large honeydew melon
Lettuce
1/4 cup lemon juice
4 medium peaches, peeled and halved
4 bananas, sliced diagonally
1/2 pound fresh Bing cherries, pitted
Mayonnaise

Have all ingredients chilled. Cut honeydew melon into halves lengthwise. Remove seeds and cut halves into 4 lengthwise boat-shaped pieces. Peel and place on lettuce cups.

Drizzle lemon juice over peach halves and banana slices. Place a peach half in each slice of melon. Add several banana slices. Top with a few Bing cherries. Serve with mayonnaise. Serves 8.

PINEAPPLE-CUCUMBER SALAD

1 unpeeled cucumber, scored, thinly sliced
4 pineapple slices
Lettuce
French dressing

For each serving place overlapping slices of cucumber on a slice of pineapple and place on crisp lettuce. Serve with French dressing. Serves 4.

CALIFORNIA FRUIT PLATE

3 ripe Bartlett pears
1 melon, cut in 6 slices
1/2 cup blueberries
1 lime, cut in sixths
Lettuce

Halve and core ripe, chilled Bartlett pears. Cut melon in 6 slices; remove skin and seeds. Scallop edge with paring knife or score with fork.

Place a melon slice on each dish; put a pear half in the center of each melon slice. In core cavity of pear put a few ripe blueberries.

Add a wedge of lime for dessert plate or line plate with crisp lettuce for salad. Serves 6.

PINEAPPLE AND CHEESE SALAD

4 pineapple slices
Lettuce
1/2 cup shredded Cheddar cheese
French dressing

For each serving, place a slice of pineapple on lettuce on a salad plate, with a mound of shredded cheese in the center of the pineapple. Serve with French dressing. Serves 4.

FRUIT IN COTTAGE CHEESE RING

Drain a chilled can of mixed fruits. Add sliced celery for crunchiness.

Spoon cottage cheese in a ring on lettuce-covered plates. Put fruits in center.

Sunshine Cottage Cheese Salad

SUNSHINE COTTAGE CHEESE SALAD

2 cups creamed cottage cheese
1/2 teaspoon salt
1 teaspoon grated lemon rind
2 tablespoons lemon juice
3 tablespoons shredded orange rind
3 large oranges, peeled, sliced
1 head lettuce or other salad greens
Fresh strawberries

Add salt, lemon rind, lemon juice, and 2 tablespoons orange rind to cottage cheese; stir lightly to blend. Turn into oiled bowl and chill.

Wash and drain crisp lettuce and arrange on plate. Turn out cottage cheese in center of plate, sprinkling remaining orange rind on top.

Surround cottage cheese mound with overlapping sliced oranges and whole fresh strawberries. Serves 6.

AVOCADO RING

Cut avocado in half and peel thinly. Remove pit and fill cavity with pineapple or pimiento cheese. Press halves together; wrap in waxed paper. Chill.

Cut into slices 1/4 inch thick. Arrange 2 or 3 slices in lettuce cup. Serve with French dressing.

CRANBERRY COTTAGE CHEESE

Combine 1 1/2 cups cottage cheese with 3/4 cup well drained cranberry jelly and 1/4 cup broken pecan meats. Serve with mayonnaise.

Rainbow Fruit Salad: For entertaining the girls at a warm weather luncheon, serve a fruit salad, buffet style. This one allows you time to enjoy your own party. Combine 2 pints cottage cheese, 1 cup pitted chopped dates, 1/2 cup coarsely chopped nutmeats, and 1 tablespoon sugar. Place in center of lettuce-lined platter. Surround with assorted fruits in season. Serve with muffins.

Frozen Grapefruit Salad

Frozen Salads

Frozen salads are especially suitable when the thermometer soars in summer or for entertaining menus when so much of the food preparation must be done well in advance. When the salad is frozen, you simply cut it in squares or slice, place a serving on a bed of salad greens and garnish with a little dressing.

TO FREEZE SALADS

(1) Turn the mixture into refrigerator trays or other molds and place in freezing compartment of refrigerator or in the freezer. Set refrigerator at coldest point. Freeze until firm.

(2) Pack mixture into oiled mold. Seal tightly with paraffin or adhesive tape. Cans with lids such as baking powder cans make good molds. Pack mold in 5 parts ice to 1 part salt and let stand about 4 hours or until firm.

Note: Do not freeze salad long enough for fruits to become frozen or icy.

FROZEN FRUIT-CHEESE SALAD

1 can (No. 2½) fruit cocktail
1 teaspoon unflavored gelatin
2 tablespoons lemon juice
1 3-ounce package cream cheese
¼ cup mayonnaise
Dash of salt
⅔ cup whipping cream, chilled
½ cup sugar
½ cup chopped nuts

Drain fruit cocktail. Soften gelatin in lemon juice, then dissolve over hot water. Blend cream cheese with mayonnaise and salt. Stir in gelatin.

Whip cream until stiff, adding sugar gradually during last stages of beating. Fold in cheese mixture, nuts, and fruit cocktail. Pour into refrigerator tray that has been lined with waxed paper.

Freeze until firm with refrigerator set at coldest setting (approximately 4 hours).

Turn out on platter, remove paper, cut into thick slices. Garnish with watercress. Serves 8.

Note: Let the salad stand at room temperature for a few minutes just before serving. The flavor and texture are ever so much better.

Frozen Fruit-Cheese Salad

FROZEN BANANA SALAD

4 ripe bananas
2 tablespoons lemon juice
1 cup heavy cream, whipped
½ cup mayonnaise
½ pound marshmallows, cut in pieces
3 pimientos, puréed, and juice
¾ teaspoon salt

Slice bananas and mix with lemon juice. Fold in whipped cream, mayonnaise, marshmallows, and pimientos. Add salt.

Mix well and turn into refrigerator trays. Freeze until stiff, about 3 hours.

To serve, cut into squares. Serve on lettuce or watercress with French dressing. Serves 6.

FROZEN ROQUEFORT CHEESE SALAD

¼ pound Roquefort cheese
2 tablespoons cream cheese
1 teaspoon lemon juice
1 cup celery, chopped fine
Chopped onion or chives
Paprika
1 cup heavy cream, whipped

Blend Roquefort and cream cheese with lemon juice, using a silver fork. Add remaining ingredients, folding in whipped cream. Freeze. Serves 6.

FROZEN CREAM CHEESE AND FRUIT SALAD

1 3-ounce package cream cheese
½ cup mayonnaise
½ cup heavy cream, whipped
½ cup canned or fresh seedless grapes
¼ cup red maraschino cherries
1 cup (9-ounce can) canned crushed pineapple, drained
1½ cups diced marshmallows (about 14)

Blend cheese and mayonnaise until smooth. Fold in whipped cream, fruits, and marshmallows.

Turn into refrigerator tray. Freeze until firm. Serve on lettuce. Serves 6.

EASY FROZEN FRUIT SALAD

Freeze overnight 1 17-ounce can fruit cocktail or other canned fruit.

Immerse can in hot water a few seconds. Open both ends. Push frozen fruit through and slice.

Or pour fruit into refrigerator tray and freeze. Turn out and cut into slices. Serve at once on lettuce with mayonnaise. Serves 6.

FROZEN GRAPEFRUIT SALAD

1 package (8 ounces) cream cheese
1 cup sour cream
¼ teaspoon salt
½ cup sugar
1 grapefruit, sectioned
1 avocado, diced
1 cup seedless white grapes, halved
½ cup pecan pieces

Soften cream cheese; blend in sour cream. Add salt and sugar and stir until well blended. Add grapefruit sections, avocado, grapes, and pecans.

Pour into 9 x 5-inch loaf pan and freeze until firm. Slice and serve on salad greens with French dressing. Serves 6 to 8.

FROZEN DELIGHT SALAD

1 cup heavy cream, whipped
¼ cup mayonnaise
1 teaspoon (⅓ envelope) unflavored gelatin
3 tablespoons syrup from pineapple
1 cup crushed canned pineapple
½ cup chopped ripe olives
½ cup chopped celery
½ teaspoon prepared horseradish
Salt
Salad greens

Fold mayonnaise into whipped cream. Soften gelatin in cold syrup and heat over hot water until dissolved. Cool slightly and fold into cream mixture.

Fold in pineapple, olives, celery, horseradish, and salt to taste.

Pour into refrigerator tray and freeze. Stir occasionally during freezing. When firm, cut into squares and serve on salad greens. Serves 8.

CALIFORNIA FROZEN SALAD

1 3-ounce package cream cheese
3 tablespoons mayonnaise
⅛ teaspoon salt
1 cup heavy cream, whipped
¼ cup chopped kumquats
¼ cup chopped dates
¼ cup chopped maraschino cherries
¼ cup crushed pineapple
1 tablespoon finely chopped preserved ginger
½ cup chopped blanched almonds

Blend cheese smoothly with mayonnaise; add salt. Fold in whipped cream and fruit and ginger mixture.

Pour into refrigerator tray; sprinkle almonds over top. Freeze. Serve on crisp lettuce. Serves 8.

Frozen Cranberry Loaf

FROZEN CRANBERRY LOAF

- ¾ cup finely ground toast crumbs
- ½ cup brown sugar
- 1 teaspoon cinnamon
- ½ teaspoon nutmeg
- ¼ teaspoon allspice
- ¼ teaspoon cloves
- ¼ teaspoon ginger
- 3 tablespoons melted butter or margarine
- 1 1-pound can jellied cranberry sauce
- ½ cup heavy cream
- 1 3-ounce package cream cheese
- Green food coloring

Mix first 7 ingredients together. Work in melted butter. Press mixture evenly against sides and bottom of an ice cube tray. Chill in freezing compartment for at least 1 hour.

Crush jellied cranberry sauce with a fork and spread over crumb crust.

Whip cream. Soften cream cheese and whip with cream. Tint green with green food coloring. Spread whipped cream-cheese mixture over cranberry sauce.

Place in freezing compartment and freeze until firm. Slice to serve. Serves 8.

FROSTED STRAWBERRY SALAD

- 1 pint strawberries
- 1 10-ounce package marshmallows, cut small
- 2 3-ounce packages cream cheese
- ⅔ cup mayonnaise
- 1 cup heavy cream, whipped
- Chicory

Wash and hull berries; reserve some for garnish and slice remaining ones.

Combine sliced berries with marshmallows and let stand while preparing other ingredients.

Mash cream cheese with fork and blend in mayonnaise. Fold in whipped cream. Fold in berry mixture and pour into freezing tray or loaf pan and freeze until firm.

Unmold on serving tray; garnish with chicory and whole strawberries. Slice and serve with additional mayonnaise, if desired. Serves 6 to 8.

FROZEN CHICKEN SALAD

- 1 teaspoon (⅓ envelope) unflavored gelatin
- 2 tablespoons cold water
- ⅔ cup mayonnaise
- 1½ cups cold minced cooked chicken
- ¼ cup chopped blanched almonds
- ½ cup halved Malaga grapes
- ⅛ teaspoon salt
- ⅔ cup heavy cream, whipped

Soften gelatin in cold water 5 minutes, then dissolve over boiling water.

Cool and combine well with mayonnaise. Add other ingredients, folding in whipped cream last.

Turn into refrigerator tray and freeze. Slice and serve on crisp greens. Serves 6.

FROZEN PEACH SALAD

- 1 No. 2½ can peach halves
- 1 tablespoon butter or margarine
- 1½ tablespoons flour
- 1 tablespoon sugar
- ¼ teaspoon salt
- ½ cup syrup from peach halves
- ¼ cup orange juice
- 1 stiffly beaten egg white
- ½ cup evaporated milk, whipped

Place 8 drained peach halves cut-side-down in refrigerator tray.

Melt butter; add flour and blend. Add sugar, salt, peach syrup, and orange juice. Cook, stirring constantly, until thick and smooth.

Fold in stiffly beaten egg white. Cool. Dice remaining peaches and add to mixture. Fold in whipped evaporated milk. Pour over peaches. Freeze until firm.

Cut in squares and place in lettuce cups, peach half up. Place a maraschino cherry in center of each peach. Serves 8.

FROZEN TOMATO MOUSSE

- 1¾ cups canned tomatoes
- 2 teaspoons vinegar
- ½ teaspoon minced onion
- ½ teaspoon salt
- ½ teaspoon celery seed
- ½ teaspoon allspice
- 1 tablespoon (1 envelope) unflavored gelatin
- 1½ cups heavy cream, whipped stiff

Simmer tomatoes, vinegar, and seasoning 15 minutes and strain carefully.

Add gelatin, which has been softened 5 minutes in ¼ cup cold water, and

stir until dissolved.

Cool and, when partially congealed, fold in cream. Turn into refrigerator tray and freeze. Serve on bed of watercress. Garnish with latticed cucumber slices. Serves 6.

FROZEN FRUIT SALAD

Finely cut fruit from 1 No. 1 can mixed fruits.

Combine with ½ cup fruit salad dressing or honey dressing and ½ cup heavy cream, whipped. Freeze. Serves 6.

FROSTY FRUIT CREAM

- 1 3-ounce package cream cheese
- 1 tablespoon lemon juice
- ⅛ teaspoon salt
- ¼ cup sugar
- 1 cup diced canned peaches, well drained
- 1 cup fresh blueberries, washed and well drained
- 2 cups (1 pint) sour cream
- Chicory
- Blueberry cream dressing

Set refrigerator control at coldest point.

Let cream cheese soften at room temperature. Gradually stir in lemon juice, salt, and sugar. Add peaches and blueberries, stirring until well blended. Fold in sour cream.

Pour into freezing tray lined with waxed paper or aluminum foil. Fold ends of waxed paper or aluminum foil over top of fruit salad. Freeze until firm, about 1½ to 2 hours.

Unmold on chilled platter on bed of chicory. If desired, garnish with additional peaches and blueberries and serve with blueberry cream dressing. Serves 6.

Blueberry Cream Dressing:

- 1 tablespoon lemon juice
- 1 to 2 tablespoon sugar
- ⅛ teaspoon salt
- ¼ cup crushed blueberries
- 1 cup sour cream

Add lemon juice, sugar, and salt to blueberries, mixing well. Fold in sour cream. Chill. Makes 1¼ cups.

Frosty Fruit Cream

Molded Salads, Aspics, Mousses

GELATIN SALAD HINTS

Please read about gelatin in **Ingredients—How to Use Them.**

Gelatin molded salads are especially suitable when you entertain a crowd and so much of the food preparation has to be done well in advance. They are not tricky to prepare, but a few "do's" and "don'ts" may be helpful.

● Use syrup from canned fruits as part of liquid in gelatin salads for added flavor.
● For large molds, cut liquid to 1¾ cups for 1 package fruit-flavored gelatin, or 1 tablespoon (1 envelope) unflavored gelatin.
● Chill gelatin until slightly thickened (unbeaten egg white consistency) before adding solid ingredients. Carefully fold well drained fruits and vegetables into thickened gelatin, distributing them evenly.
● A gelatin salad may be molded in several ways—in large ring or fancy mold, in individual molds, or in shallow pan.
● To mold fruits or vegetables in definite pattern, arrange in thin layer of slightly thickened gelatin. Chill until firm, then add balance of gelatin.
● To make molded layered salads, be sure each layer is firm before adding next layer.
● Prepare large gelatin molds a day ahead of serving, so they will be thoroughly set before unmolding.
● Fill molds as full as possible for easy unmolding.

Gelatin Molds with Vegetables

CARDINAL SALAD

1   package lemon-flavored gelatin
1   cup hot water
¾   cup beet juice
3   tablespoons vinegar
½   teaspoon salt
1   tablespoon prepared horseradish
2   teaspoons grated onion
¾   cup diced celery
1   cup cooked diced beets
Mayonnaise

Dissolve gelatin in hot water. Add beet juice, vinegar, salt, horseradish, and onion. Chill until partly set.

Fold in celery and beets. Pour into mold rinsed in cold water and chill.

Serve on watercress garnished with mayonnaise. Serves 6.

FRUITED SLAW SALAD MOLD

1   can (1 pound, 1 ounce) fruit cocktail
1   package lemon-flavored gelatin
1¾ cups boiling water
3   tablespoons lemon juice
¼   teaspoon salt
1   cup finely shredded raw cabbage
Mustard Dressing (below)

Drain fruit cocktail thoroughly.

Dissolve lemon gelatin in boiling water. Add lemon juice and salt; chill until mixture begins to thicken.

Stir in 1¼ cups well-drained fruit cocktail (saving remainder for garnish) and the cabbage. Turn into a lightly oiled mold or individual molds and chill until firm.

Unmold, garnish with fruit cocktail, and serve with Mustard Dressing. Serves 6 to 8.

Mustard Dressing: Blend ¼ cup mayonnaise, ½ cup sour cream, ¼ teaspoon salt, ½ teaspoon prepared mustard, and 1½ teaspoons lemon juice together until smooth.

EASY ASPIC (Master Recipe)

1   tablespoon (1 envelope) unflavored gelatin
½   cup cold canned mixed vegetable juices
1¼ cups hot canned mixed vegetable juices

Soften gelatin in the cold vegetable juices. Add hot vegetable juice and stir until dissolved. Pour into individual molds and chill until firm.

Unmold on salad greens and serve with mayonnaise or French dressing. Serves 4.

Variations:

Ring Mold: For ring mold double the recipe, and pour into 1-quart ring mold. Unmold and fill center with chicken, turkey, or tuna fish salad. Serves 8.

Seafood Aspic: Make Easy Aspic. Chill until the mixture is the consistency of unbeaten egg white.

Fold in 1 cup diced or shredded shrimp, crabmeat, lobster, and ½ cup diced celery. Serves 6.

Olive Cucumber Aspic: Make Easy Aspic. Chill until the mixture is the consistency of unbeaten egg white.

Fold in ¼ cup sliced stuffed olives and 1 cup diced cucumber. Serves 6.

Perfection Aspic: Make Easy Aspic. Chill until the mixture is the consistency of unbeaten egg white.

Fold in 1 cup finely shredded cabbage, 1½ cups diced celery, and 2 tablespoons chopped green pepper. Serves 6.

Fruited Slaw Salad Mold

TOMATO ASPIC (Master Recipe)

2   tablespoons (2 envelopes) unflavored gelatin
½   cup cold water
2½ cups canned tomatoes
1   tablespoon minced onion
1   tablespoon sugar
1   teaspoon salt
4   whole black peppers
½   bay leaf
4   cloves
2   tablespoons lemon juice

Soften gelatin in cold water 5 minutes.

Cook tomatoes and seasonings (except lemon juice) 5 to 10 minutes. Strain.

Pour 2 cups hot tomato mixture over softened gelatin.

Add lemon juice and pour into molds rinsed with cold water. Chill.

Unmold on lettuce. Serve with mayonnaise or cooked dressing. Serves 6.

Tomato Aspic Ring: Prepare master tomato aspic. Pour into large ring mold or individual small molds. Chill until firm.

Unmold and fill center with chicken, tuna, or salmon salad.

Tomato Aspic with Celery and Peas: Prepare master tomato aspic; add 1 cup canned peas and 1 cup diced celery to thickened aspic.

Tomato Aspic with Cottage Cheese: Prepare master tomato aspic; fill molds only ⅔ full of tomato aspic.

When firm, complete filling molds with seasoned cottage cheese. Unmold with cottage cheese on the bottom.

Tomato Aspic with Cucumber: Prepare master tomato aspic and add 2 cups diced cucumber to thickened aspic.

To Chill Individual Salad Molds: Place individual salad molds in muffin pans and partially fill. Place in refrigerator and add remaining liquid.

HORSERADISH MOLD WITH COLESLAW

1 tablespoon (1 envelope) unflavored gelatin
1/4 cup cold water
1/2 cup boiling water
1/2 cup mayonnaise or salad dressing
1/3 cup prepared horseradish
1/4 teaspoon salt
1/4 teaspoon paprika
1/2 cup heavy cream, whipped
1 small head red cabbage, shredded
1/4 cup diced green pepper
2 tablespoons diced pimiento
Mayonnaise or salad dressing
Salt and pepper

Soften gelatin in cold water. Add boiling water and stir until dissolved.

Combine with the 1/2 cup of mayonnaise or salad dressing, horseradish, 1/4 teaspoon salt, and paprika.

Fold in the whipped cream. Pour into a 1-quart mold; chill until firm.

Toss cabbage with green pepper, pimiento, and just enough mayonnaise or salad dressing to moisten. Season to taste with salt and pepper.

Unmold the gelatin on a platter; surround with coleslaw. Serve with mayonnaise or salad dressing. Serves 4 to 6.

CUCUMBER AND OLIVE MOLD

2 packages lime-flavored gelatin
3 cups hot water
1/2 teaspoon salt
1/2 cup sliced stuffed olives
1 cup cubed cucumber, drained
1 cup crushed, canned pineapple, drained

Dissolve gelatin in hot water. Add salt. Place slices of stuffed olives on the bottom of a 1 1/2-quart ring mold. Add enough gelatin to cover. Chill until firm.

Chill remaining gelatin until slightly thickened. Add cucumber and pineapple and pour into the mold. Chill until firm.

Unmold and surround with crisp lettuce. Serve with salad dressing. Serves 8 to 10.

BROCCOLI SALAD MOLD

1 tablespoon (1 envelope) unflavored gelatin
1/4 cup cold water
1 cup hot consommé or bouillon
3/4 cup mayonnaise
1/4 teaspoon salt
1/8 teaspoon pepper
2 cups chopped cooked broccoli
2 hard-cooked eggs, chopped
2 hard-cooked eggs, sliced
Greens

Soften gelatin in cold water 5 minutes. Dissolve in very hot consommé. Chill until slightly thickened.

Fold in mayonnaise and seasonings,

mixing until well blended. Fold in broccoli and chopped eggs. Turn into 1-quart mold. Chill until firm.

Unmold on large platter. Garnish with crisp greens and sliced hard-cooked eggs. Serves 6.

TOMATO ASPIC IN GREEN PEPPER SLICES

5 large green peppers
1 1/2 tablespoons (1 1/2 envelopes) unflavored gelatin
1/2 cup cold water
2 1/2 cups tomato juice
1/2 cup tomato purée
2 teaspoons salt
1/4 teaspoon pepper
1 cup chopped celery
Lettuce
1 cup thin strips Cheddar cheese
Salad dressing

Cut a slice from the top of each pepper. Remove the seeds and membrane and place in ice water until crisp. Drain well.

Soften gelatin in cold water and dissolve it over hot water. Add tomato juice and purée, and the seasonings. Chill until slightly thickened.

Fold in the celery. Fill the pepper shells and chill until the aspic is firm. Cut each pepper into 1/2-inch slices.

For each serving place 3 slices on lettuce. Garnish with strips of cheese and serve with salad dressing. Serves 8 to 10.

TOMATO SALAD MOLD

2 tablespoons (2 envelopes) unflavored gelatin
1/2 cup cold water
1 cup condensed tomato soup, undiluted, heated
1 8-ounce package cream cheese
1 cup mayonnaise or salad dressing
1 cup chopped celery
1/4 cup chopped green pepper
1 tablespoon chopped onion
Salt and pepper

Soften gelatin in cold water and dissolve in hot soup. Gradually add to cream cheese, blending until smooth. Chill until slightly thickened.

Fold in mayonnaise or salad dressing and chopped vegetables. Season to taste.

Pour into a 1 1/4-quart mold and chill until firm.

Unmold and garnish with crisp lettuce. Serve with mayonnaise or salad dressing. Serves 6 to 8.

MOLDED BEET SALAD

1 package lemon-flavored gelatin
2 cups hot water
1/4 cup vinegar
2 cups diced cooked beets, drained
1/4 cup chopped celery

1 tablespoon prepared horseradish
1/2 teaspoon salt

Dissolve gelatin in hot water. Add vinegar, and chill until slightly thickened. Add beets, celery, horseradish, and salt. Pour into 4 or 6 individual molds and chill until firm. Unmold and garnish with endive. Serve with mayonnaise or salad dressing. Serves 4 to 6.

LAYERED TOMATO ASPIC SALAD

First Layer—Tomato Aspic:
1 bay leaf
Dash of Tabasco sauce
1/3 cup finely chopped onion
1/2 teaspoon salt
3 3/4 cups tomato juice
3 tablespoons (3 envelopes) unflavored gelatin
2/3 cup water
2 tablespoons vinegar

Place bay leaf, Tabasco sauce, onion, salt, and tomato juice in 2-quart saucepan. Bring to boil on high heat; lower heat, and cook 10 minutes.

Soften gelatin in water 5 minutes; dissolve in juice mixture, add vinegar, and strain. Cool slightly.

Pour 2 cups of aspic mixture in lightly oiled 9 1/2 x 5 1/4 x 2 3/4-inch baking pan. Chill in refrigerator until firm, about 60 to 70 minutes.

Cool remaining aspic mixture for later use, but do not allow to congeal.

Second Layer—Cottage Cheese:
1 3-ounce package cream cheese
1 1/2 cups drained cottage cheese
1 1/2 teaspoons salt
2 tablespoons finely chopped parsley
1 tablespoon finely chopped onion
2 tablespoons aspic mixture

Mix cream cheese, cottage cheese, salt, parsley, onion, and aspic mixture. Spread over firm layer of aspic in baking pan.

Third Layer—Tomato Aspic:
Pour remaining aspic mixture over cottage cheese layer and chill in refrigerator about 1 hour or until firm.

Fourth Layer—Chopped Ham Salad:
1 cup very finely chopped ham or luncheon meat
1/2 cup mayonnaise
1/4 cup finely chopped celery
1/4 cup finely chopped green pepper
1 teaspoon prepared mustard
1 tablespoon (1 envelope) unflavored gelatin
1/4 cup cold water

Combine meat, mayonnaise, celery, green pepper, and mustard.

Soften gelatin in water 5 minutes. Heat on low heat until gelatin is dissolved, add slowly to meat mixture; mix.

Spread over firm aspic in pan. Chill until firm. Serves 8 to 10.

The bright color of the molded salad ring filled in the center with a salad of contrasting color makes a real picture.

MASTER VEGETABLE SALAD MOLD

1   tablespoon (1 envelope) unfla-vored gelatin
¼   cup cold water
1   cup hot water
¼   cup mild vinegar
1   tablespoon lemon juice
½   teaspoon salt
2   tablespoons sugar
⅛   teaspoon pepper
1½   cups diced or shredded vegetables (below)
1   tablespoon minced onion

Use raw or cooked vegetables. Add more sugar if desired.

Soften gelatin in cold water 5 minutes. Dissolve in hot water. Add vinegar, lemon juice, salt, sugar, and pepper. Cool until syrupy.

Fold in vegetables. Turn into mold which has been rinsed in cold water. Chill until firm.

Unmold on lettuce. Serve with desired dressing. Serves 6.

Vegetable Salad Mold Variations

1. ½ cup diced celery, ½ cup diced cucumber, ¼ cup sliced radishes, and 2 tablespoons chopped green pepper.

2. ½ cup shredded raw cabbage, ½ cup grated raw carrots, ¼ cup diced apples, and ¼ cup chopped nuts.

3. 1 cup shredded raw cabbage, ½ cup chopped celery, and 2 tablespoons chopped green pepper or pimiento.

4. ½ cup each chopped celery, shredded raw carrots, and cooked peas.

5. 1 cup shredded raw cabbage and ½ cup sliced green olives.

6. ¾ cup each shredded raw cabbage and shredded raw carrots.

Vary the fruit (or vegetable) filling with the season so your family will enjoy ring molds the year 'round.

7. ½ cup each canned asparagus tips, canned green peas, shredded raw carrots, and 2 tablespoons chopped pimiento.

8. ¾ cup each cubed pickled beets and chopped celery.

9. ½ cup each chopped celery, diced cooked beets, and shredded raw cabbage.

10. ¾ cup each cooked peas and chopped roasted peanuts.

11. ½ cup each diced celery, canned lima beans, and diced or shredded carrots, raw or cooked.

12. ½ cup each canned red kidney beans and peas, ½ cup chopped celery, ¼ cup chopped green pepper, and 1 tablespoon grated onion.

Molded Kraut Cooler

MOLDED KRAUT COOLER

2   3-ounce packages lemon-flavored gelatin
1   cup boiling water
2   cups cold water
½   cup sour cream
1   No. 2 can sauerkraut, drained and cut into short lengths
1   large red apple, cored and diced
1   cup diced cucumber
¼   cup minced onion

Dissolve gelatin in boiling water; add cold water and sour cream. Beat until well blended. Chill in refrigerator until slightly thickened.

Fold in sauerkraut and remaining ingredients; mix well and turn into 2-quart mold. If desired a layer of clear gelatin may be poured in bottom of mold. Chill in refrigerator until firm.

Unmold and garnish with cucumber slices and apple wedges. Serves 4 to 6.

EASY TOMATO ASPIC

1   package lemon-flavored gelatin
1   cup (8-ounce can) tomato sauce
1   cup hot water
½   teaspoon salt
1   tablespoon lemon juice

Dissolve gelatin in hot water. Stir until dissolved.

Add tomato sauce, salt, and lemon juice. Mix thoroughly. Chill until syrupy. Pour into molds and chill until firm. Unmold on crisp lettuce leaves.

Serves 4.

SUNSET SALAD

1   tablespoon (1 envelope) unfla-vored gelatin
¼   cup cold water
1   egg yolk
½   teaspoon salt
1   cup pineapple juice
2   tablespoons lemon juice
½   cup chilled evaporated milk
2   cups shredded cabbage
1   cup canned pineapple, either shredded or cut very fine
½   cup shredded carrot

Soak gelatin in cold water for at least 5 minutes.

Beat egg yolk, add salt, pineapple juice, and lemon juice. Bring to a boil, stirring constantly. Remove from heat, add gelatin and stir until gelatin is dissolved. Cool until mixture begins to thicken.

Whip the evaporated milk and fold the gelatin, cabbage, pineapple, and carrot into the milk. Pour into molds which have been rinsed with cold water.

Serve on salad greens. Serves 8.

LEMON VEGETABLE MOLD

Dissolve 1 package lemon-flavored gelatin in 1 cup hot water. Add 1 cup cold water and 1 tablespoon lemon juice. Cool.

Add 1 cup shredded raw cabbage, ½ cup cooked peas, ½ cup cooked diced carrots, and ¼ teaspoon salt.

Mix well. Pour into molds and chill. Serves 4 to 6.

ALMOND TOMATO MOLD SALAD

1¾   cups tomato juice
1   tablespoon pickling spices
¼   teaspoon salt
1   package lemon-flavored gelatin
2   tablespoons lemon juice
1   teaspoon grated onion
1   teaspoon Worcestershire sauce
¼   teaspoon oregano
½   cup diced cucumber
½   cup diced celery
¼   cup blanched almonds, chopped

Heat tomato juice, spices, and salt to boiling point; strain. Add gelatin and stir until dissolved. Chill until slightly thickened.

Add remaining ingredients. Pour into 1-quart mold and chill until firm.

Tomato Mold Salad

Christmas Tree Salads

CHRISTMAS TREE SALADS

1   tablespoon (1 envelope) unfla-
    vored gelatin
1/4 cup cold water
1   1-pound can jellied cranberry
    sauce, crushed with a fork
1   cup finely shredded cabbage
1/4 cup diced celery
1/2 cup chopped walnuts
Soft cream cheese, tinted green

Place gelatin in custard cup. Add cold water. Let stand 2 minutes.

Place cup with gelatin in pan of boiling water and heat until gelatin is dissolved. Mix with crushed cranberry sauce, cabbage, celery, and nuts.

Spoon into cone-shaped paper cups supported in small glasses. Chill until firm. Place on lettuce and peel off paper cups. Trim with softened cream cheese. Makes 4 to 6 salads.

JELLIED COLESLAW

1   package lemon-flavored gelatin
1   cup hot water
1   small onion, minced
1   cup crushed pineapple, with juice
1   chopped pimiento
3   tablespoons wine vinegar
1/2 green pepper, minced
1/2 teaspoon salt
1/8 teaspoon black pepper
2   cups shredded cabbage

Place gelatin in bowl and add hot water. Stir until gelatin dissolves. Mix in remaining ingredients.

Pour mixture into 10 x 6 x 2-in baking dish, then chill until set.

Cut into squares; arrange on lettuce. Serve salad dressing separately. Serves 6.

TOMATO RELISH SLICES

4   large firm tomatoes, peeled
1   tablespoon (1 envelope) unfla-
    vored gelatin
1/4 cup cold water
1   8-ounce package cream cheese
1   tablespoon chopped celery
1   tablespoon chopped green pepper
1   tablespoon chopped pickle
1   tablespoon chili sauce
1/4 teaspoon salt
1/4 teaspoon paprika

Cut a thin slice from the stem end of each tomato. Scoop pulp out carefully and drain upside down.

Soften gelatin in cold water; dissolve over hot water.

Gradually add to the cream cheese, blending until smooth. Add celery, green pepper, pickle, chili sauce, salt, and paprika.

Pour into the tomato shells and chill until firm.

Slice with a sharp knife and arrange on crisp lettuce. Serve with mayonnaise. Serves 6.

CUCUMBER SALAD MOLD

1   package lime-flavored gelatin
2   cups hot water
1   tablespoon lemon juice or vinegar
1   teaspoon scraped onion
1/2 teaspoon salt
Dash of pepper
1   cup finely chopped cucumber

Dissolve gelatin in 2 cups hot water. Add lemon juice or vinegar and seasoning. Chill.

When slightly thickened, fold in cucumber. Turn into square pan and chill until firm.

Cut into squares and serve on lettuce. Serves 4 to 6.

Pineapple and Carrot: Use orange-flavored gelatin with shredded carrot and pineapple instead of cucumber.

Pineapple and Cucumber: Substitute 1/2 cup crushed canned pineapple for 1/2 cup cucumber.

JELLIED GREEN PEPPER RINGS

4   large green peppers
1   package lemon-flavored gelatin
2   cups boiling water
1   cup chopped celery
1   cup chopped raw carrots
1   cup shredded cabbage
1   cup drained chopped cucumbers

Cut the stem ends from green peppers; remove seeds.

Dissolve gelatin in boiling water. When gelatin is cool and somewhat thickened, add remaining ingredients.

Spoon gelatin-vegetable mixture into pepper shells and chill until firm.

Cut each pepper into 6 crosswise slices. For each portion of salad, place 2 slices on crisp lettuce.

Garnish with a radish rose and serve with mayonnaise. Serves 6.

TEXAS BUFFET MOLD

2   tablespoons (2 envelopes) unfla-
    vored gelatin
1/2 cup cold water
2   cups boiling water
1/3 cup mild vinegar
2   tablespoons lemon juice
1/2 cup sugar
1   teaspoon salt
2   cups chopped celery
3/4 cup diced raw carrots
1   cup finely chopped cabbage
2   pimientos, finely chopped
1   red apple, unpeeled, diced

Soften gelatin in cold water and dissolve it in boiling water. Add vinegar, lemon juice, sugar, and salt. Chill until slightly thickened.

Fold in celery, carrots, cabbage, pimientos, and apple. Pour into 2-quart mold and chill until firm.

Unmold and surround with crisp lettuce. Serve with mayonnaise or salad dressing. Serves 10 to 12.

ASPARAGUS AND TOMATO MOLD

Simmer 2 cups tomato juice, bit of bay leaf, 1 clove, 1/2 teaspoon salt, and 1/2 onion (sliced) 15 minutes.

Add 1 tablespoon (1 envelope) unflavored gelatin soaked in 4 tablespoons cold water. Dissolve. Strain and cool mixture.

When slightly thickened, add 1 1/2 cups tender cooked or canned asparagus cut into 1/2-inch pieces. Turn into molds and chill. Serves 4 to 6.

Pineapple Cucumber Mold

PINEAPPLE CUCUMBER MOLD

Pineapple Layer:

1 cup crushed canned pineapple (not drained)
1 package lemon-flavored gelatin
1/2 teaspoon salt
1/2 cup finely grated carrots

Cucumber Layer:

1 tablespoon (1 envelope) unflavored gelatin
1/4 cup cold water
1 cup mayonnaise
1/2 cup light cream
1/2 teaspoon salt
1 tablespoon grated onion
1/2 cup finely chopped celery
1/2 cup grated cucumber, drained

Pineapple Layer: Drain pineapple. Add enough water to syrup to make 1¾ cups liquid. Heat to boiling; dissolve gelatin in it.

Chill until the consistency of unbeaten egg whites. Add salt, carrots, and crushed pineapple.

Turn into a 1½-quart ring or fancy mold. Chill until firm.

Cucumber Layer: Soften gelatin in cold water; dissolve over hot water.

Combine remaining ingredients. Add gelatin and blend. If desired, tint pale green. Pour over pineapple layer.

Chill until firm. Unmold and garnish with salad greens. Serves 8 to 10.

CUCUMBER AND SOUR CREAM SALAD MOLD

1 tablespoon (1 envelope) unflavored gelatin
1/4 cup cold water
1/2 cup hot water
1/4 cup sugar
1 cup grated cucumber, well drained
1 cup thick sour cream
2 tablespoons lemon juice
1 tablespoon grated onion and juice
1/2 teaspoon salt
Cucumber slices, ripe olives, and watercress

Soften gelatin in cold water. Combine hot water and sugar and heat to boiling point. Add softened gelatin, stirring until dissolved. Chill until slightly thickened.

Fold in cucumber, sour cream, lemon juice, onion juice, and salt. Pour into mold and chill until firm.

Unmold and garnish with thin slices of cucumber, ripe olives, and parsley or watercress. Serves 4.

PERFECTION SALAD

1 tablespoon (1 envelope) unflavored gelatin
1/4 cup cold water
1 cup hot water
1/4 cup sugar
1/2 teaspoon salt
1 tablespoon lemon juice
1/4 cup vinegar
1/2 cup finely shredded cabbage
1 cup finely diced celery
1 pimiento, finely chopped or 2 tablespoons chopped sweet red or green pepper

Soften gelatin in cold water in top of double boiler. Add hot water, sugar, and salt. Stir over boiling water until dissolved.

Add lemon juice and vinegar. Chill until mixture is consistency of unbeaten egg whites.

Stir in vegetables. Pour into mold. Chill until firm.

Unmold on salad greens. Garnish with mayonnaise. Or, cut salad in cubes and serve in green pepper cases. Serves 6.

JELLIED CABBAGE AND PINEAPPLE SALAD

2 tablespoons (2 envelopes) unflavored gelatin
1/2 cup cold water
1¼ cups boiling water
1/2 cup sugar
1 teaspoon salt
1/2 cup syrup drained from pineapple slices
1/2 cup vinegar
1/4 cup lemon juice
2 pineapple slices
Pimiento
3 cups finely shredded cabbage
1 cup diced celery
1/4 cup diced green pepper
1/4 cup diced pimiento
1 or 2 slices pineapple, diced
Mayonnaise

Add gelatin to 1/2 cup cold water; let stand 5 minutes, then add 1¼ cups boiling water, sugar, and salt; stir until dissolved. Add syrup drained from pineapple slices, vinegar, and lemon juice.

Pour a thin layer of this into an 8 x 4 x 4-inch loaf pan, chill until almost firm; arrange 2 slices of pineapple over the gelatin, center with pimiento, chill until firm.

Mix shredded cabbage, celery, green pepper, pimiento, and diced pineapple;

add, then fold in remaining gelatin. Pour over pineapple in pan; chill. Unmold and serve with mayonnaise. Serves 6 to 8.

Note: If you prefer to mold this in a ring, use pineapple chunks in place of slices, arranging them attractively in the mold, or mixing them with the cabbage.

RING MOLDS WITH SALAD

1 tablespoon (1 envelope) unflavored gelatin
1/4 cup cold water
1 cup boiling water
1 tablespoon vinegar
1 tablespoon minced onion
2 tablespoons chopped parsley
6 hard-cooked eggs, chopped
2 tablespoons salad dressing
1 teaspoon salt
Dash of freshly ground pepper
Dash of paprika
Chicken, shrimp, or vegetable salad

Soften gelatin in cold water and dissolve it in boiling water. Add the vinegar and chill until slightly thickened.

Combine onion, parsley, eggs, salad dressing, and seasonings. Add the gelatin. Pour into 4 individual ring molds and chill until firm.

Unmold and fill the centers with chicken, shrimp, or vegetable salad. Garnish with curly endive or watercress. Serves 4.

HOME GARDEN BARBECUE SALAD

1 package lemon-flavored gelatin
1¼ cups hot water
1 8-ounce can tomato sauce
1½ tablespoons vinegar
1/2 teaspoon salt
Few grains pepper
1 cup diced cucumber
1 cup sliced radishes
1/2 cup sliced green onions
1 teaspoon Ac'cent

Dissolve gelatin in hot water. Add tomato sauce, vinegar, salt, and pepper. Chill until consistency of mayonnaise. Meanwhile combine vegetables; sprinkle with Ac'cent; toss well to mix.

Fold into gelatin mixture; fill into oiled ring mold. Chill until firm.

Unmold; fill center with salad greens. Serve with mayonnaise. Serves 4 to 6.

Home Garden Barbecue Salad

Gelatin Molds with Meat and Poultry

MEAT LOAF MOLD
(With Leftover Meats)

1 tablespoon (1 envelope) unflavored gelatin
¾ cup cold water
1 10½-ounce can condensed consommé
2 tablespoons lemon juice
¼ teaspoon salt
1 cup finely diced leftover meat (lamb, veal, beef, pork, chicken, etc.)
½ cup chopped celery
2 tablespoons chopped green pepper (optional)

Soften gelatin in ¼ cup cold water. Combine soup with remaining ½ cup water and bring to boil.

Add softened gelatin and stir until dissolved. Add lemon juice and salt. Cool.

When mixture begins to thicken, fold in meat and celery and green pepper if used.

Turn into 4-cup mold, loaf pan, or individual molds that have been rinsed in cold water. Chill.

Unmold on salad greens. Serve with mayonnaise. Serves 6.

Variations: 1½ cups boiling water and 2 bouillon cubes may be used instead of canned consommé. Homemade soup stock may also be used, in which case you would soften gelatin in ¼ cup cold water and dissolve it in 1½ cups hot soup.

Any desired combination of leftover vegetables such as corn, string beans, cabbage, carrots, peas, etc., may be used instead of celery.

JELLIED HAM MOLD

2 tablespoons (2 envelopes) unflavored gelatin
2 tablespoons cold water
3 cups consommé
1 tablespoon prepared horseradish
2 teaspoons prepared mustard
1 tablespoon minced onion
Dash of pepper
3½ cups ground cooked ham (or ground luncheon meat)

Soak gelatin in cold water. Heat con-

Jellied Ham Mold

sommé and add gelatin, stirring until dissolved. Cool.

Add horseradish, mustard, onion, and pepper. Place in refrigerator.

When mixture begins to thicken, stir in ham. Pour into ring mold, loaf pan, or decorative mold, which has been well rubbed with salad oil or rinsed with cold water. Serves 6 to 8.

MOLDED CHICKEN SALAD

1 tablespoon (1 envelope) unflavored gelatin
2 tablespoons lemon juice
2 chicken bouillon cubes
½ teaspoon salt
1¾ cups hot water
⅓ cup mayonnaise
1 diced, peeled avocado
1 cup diced, cooked chicken
¾ cup diced apples
Salad greens

Soften gelatin in lemon juice.

Dissolve bouillon cubes and salt in hot water; add gelatin. Cool until consistency of unbeaten egg white.

Fold in mayonnaise, avocado, chicken, and apples. Pour into 6 small molds; refrigerate until firm. Unmold on crisp salad greens. Serves 4.

Molded Chicken Salad

HAM MOUSSE

1 tablespoon (1 envelope) unflavored gelatin
2 tablespoons cold water
½ cup boiling water
1 teaspoon dry mustard
½ teaspoon salt
1 tablespoon prepared horseradish
½ teaspoon brown sugar
Speck of cayenne
2 cups ground cooked ham
1 cup heavy cream, whipped

Soften gelatin in cold water. Dissolve in boiling water. Chill until partially thickened.

Mix remaining ingredients except cream together. Add gelatin and mix lightly. Fold in cream.

Turn into mold. Chill until firm. Unmold and garnish with crisp salad greens, pickles, and radishes. Serves 6.

Lemon Chicken Mold: A tasty versatile mold to serve as an appetizer spread or salad with crisp snack crackers.

LEMON CHICKEN MOLD

1 chicken bouillon cube
1 cup boiling water
1 tablespoon (1 envelope) unflavored gelatin
2 cups chopped, cooked chicken
1½ teaspoons salt
⅛ teaspoon pepper
1 tablespoon lemon juice
¼ cup finely chopped celery
¼ cup finely chopped onion
2 tablespoons finely chopped sweet pickle
2 tablespoons chopped parsley
2 tablespoons chopped pimiento

Dissolve bouillon cube in boiling water. Remove and cool ¼ cup bouillon.

Soften gelatin in cooled bouillon. Add to remaining bouillon and stir until dissolved. Cool until mixture starts to thicken.

Add remaining ingredients. Pour into 1½-quart mixing bowl. Cool. Unmold.

Glaze: Dissolve 1 3-ounce package lemon-flavored gelatin in 1 cup hot water. Cool. Pour into mixing bowl used as mold.

Put chicken mold back into bowl pushing down gently to force gelatin up sides of mold. Chill.

Unmold. Garnish with rosettes of softened cream cheese and serve with assorted crackers.

HAM AND CABBAGE MOLDS

1 tablespoon (1 envelope) unflavored gelatin
¼ cup cold water
1¼ cups hot water
1 tablespoon vinegar
½ teaspoon salt
¾ cup mayonnaise or salad dressing
1 teaspoon prepared mustard
1½ cups cubed cooked ham
1 cup shredded cabbage
2 tablespoons minced onion

Soften gelatin in cold water. Add hot water and stir to dissolve. Add vinegar and salt. Cool to room temperature.

Stir in mayonnaise and mustard. Chill until partially set.

Fold in ham, cabbage, and onion. Pour into custard cups. Chill until firm. Serves 5.

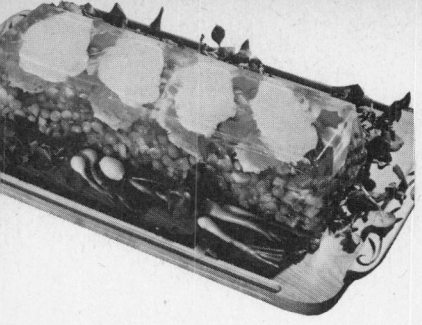

Jellied Chicken Loaf

JELLIED CHICKEN LOAF

9   slices cooked white meat of chicken
2   tablespoons (2 envelopes) unflavored gelatin
¼   cup cold water
4   cups chicken stock
2½ cups diced cooked chicken
¼   cup diced pimiento
2   cups diced celery
2   cups cooked peas
¼   cup lemon juice
2   tablespoons Worcestershire sauce
Salt

Arrange white meat in well-oiled loaf pan (8½ x 4½ x 2½ inches).

Soften gelatin in cold water; dissolve in hot chicken stock. Cool; pour ½ cup over white meat; chill until set.

Add diced chicken and rest of ingredients to remainder of gelatin mixture. Fill pan. Chill until firm, invert to unmold. Garnish as desired. Serves 8 to 10.

TOMATO-HAM SALAD MOLD

1½ tablespoons (1½ envelopes) unflavored gelatin
⅔   cup water
1   chicken bouillon cube
1⅓ cups condensed tomato soup
1   tablespoon finely chopped onion
2   cups ground cooked ham or luncheon meat
½   cup chopped celery
¼   cup chopped pimiento
½   cup chilled evaporated milk, whipped
2   tomatoes, thinly sliced
2   hard-cooked eggs
½   cup mayonnaise
1   teaspoon mustard-with-horseradish
Salad greens

Tomato-Ham Salad Mold

Soften gelatin in ⅓ cup cold water. Mix bouillon cube with rest of water and dissolve in hot soup.

Add onion and ground meat and cool until slightly thickened.

Fold in celery, pimiento, and stiffly whipped evaporated milk. Turn into heart-shaped mold (1¼ quarts) rinsed in cold water and chill until firm.

Unmold and surround with salad greens. Form heart outline with sliced egg white on top of mold. Fill with mayonnaise mixed with mustard-with-horseradish and arrange thinly sliced tomatoes around edge. Serves 6.

BUFFET PARTY LOAF

1   No. 2½ can fruit cocktail, well-drained
2   tablespoons (2 envelopes) unflavored gelatin
2   tablespoons vinegar
½   teaspoon cinnamon
⅛   teaspoon ground cloves
Syrup from fruit cocktail
2   12-ounce cans ham-type luncheon meat, chopped very fine
½   cup very finely chopped celery
¼   cup finely chopped green pepper or olives
½   cup mayonnaise-type salad dressing
1   tablespoon prepared mustard
½   teaspoon salt

Arrange drained fruit cocktail in 9 x 5 x 3-inch loaf pan. Add gelatin, vinegar, cinnamon, cloves to cold syrup; dissolve over hot water. Carefully pour ¼ cup dissolved gelatin over fruit.

Mix ham, celery, green pepper, or olives. Mix salad dressing with mustard, salt, rest of dissolved gelatin. Add to ham mixture; mix well.

Spread on fruit; chill until firm (at least 4 hours). Serves 8 to 10.

CHICKEN IN ASPIC (NORWEGIAN)

1   ready-to-cook chicken, 3 to 3½ pounds, cut up
1   cup diced carrot, celery, and onion
1   tip bay leaf
4   whole black peppers
2   cloves
1   tablespoon salt
4   tablespoons (4 envelopes) unflavored gelatin
½   cup cold water
3½ cups chicken broth
About 1 teaspoon salt
¼   teaspoon ginger
¼   teaspoon white pepper
1   tablespoon brandy or 2 tablespoons sherry
2   cups cooked peas, drained

Cook chicken several hours in advance of preparing this dish as follows: Place in kettle with vegetables and spices tied in cheesecloth "bag," the salt and 3 cups boiling water. Sim-

mer, covered, until meat is tender, 2½ to 3 hours.

Remove meat and strain broth. Chop meat, discarding skin and bones.

Meanwhile soften gelatin in ½ cup cold water about 5 minutes. Add to boiling chicken broth and stir until gelatin is dissolved. Season rather highly. Add more seasoning if necessary. Add brandy. Chill until syrupy.

Pour layer of broth in 7-cup mold. When almost firm, add chicken, broth, and peas, chilling each layer before adding next. Fill mold with remaining broth. Chill several hours or overnight.

Unmold. Serve with mayonnaise, garnishing as desired. Serves 12 to 14.

TWO-TONE JELLIED CHICKEN DINNER

Chicken Salad Layer:

1   tablespoon (1 envelope) unflavored gelatin
¾   cup cold chicken broth
¼   teaspoon salt
¼   teaspoon Ac'cent
1   tablespoon lemon juice
¾   cup mayonnaise
1   cup diced steamed chicken
3   tablespoons finely diced green pepper
¾   cup thinly sliced celery

Pour gelatin into top of double boiler; add cold chicken broth; dissolve over hot water. Cool.

Add salt, Ac'cent, and lemon juice; add slowly to mayonnaise, blending well. Stir in chicken, green pepper, and celery.

Turn into 6-cup mold; chill until almost firm.

Vegetable Aspic Layer:

1   tablespoon (1 envelope) unflavored gelatin
1¾ cups cold canned mixed vegetable juice
¼   teaspoon Ac'cent

Pour gelatin into top of double boiler. Add vegetable juice and Ac'cent; dissolve over hot water. Chill until consistency of unbeaten egg white.

Spoon on top of first layer; chill until firm. Garnish with salad greens, cucumber slices, and radish roses. Serves 8.

Two-Tone Jellied Chicken Dinner

MOLDED CHICKEN AND TONGUE SLICES

1 tablespoon (1 envelope) unflavored gelatin
3 tablespoons cold water
1¾ cups chicken stock
2 teaspoons grated onion
1½ teaspoons salt
⅛ teaspoon pepper
½ teaspoon Ac'cent
¼ teaspoon powdered poultry seasoning
½ to ¾ pound cooked smoked tongue, sliced
2 cups diced cooked chicken
¾ cup chopped celery
½ cup mayonnaise

Soften gelatin in cold water. Heat chicken stock with onion and seasonings to boiling; dissolve softened gelatin in hot mixture. Strain a little hot gelatin liquid over bottom of loaf pan; chill until firm.

Arrange overlapping slices of tongue on top of firm gelatin. Cover tongue slices with additional gelatin. Chill.

Layer chicken and celery alternately on top of tongue.

Stir mayonnaise into remaining gelatin; mix well and pour over chicken and celery. Chill until firm.

Unmold on bed of crisp watercress. Garnish with thinly sliced cucumber, radish roses, and olives. Serves 6 to 8.

DEVILED HAM MOUSSE

1 tablespoon (1 envelope) unflavored gelatin
¼ cup cold water
¾ cup mayonnaise
2 3-ounce cans deviled ham
1½ teaspoons grated onion
½ cup chopped celery
¼ cup chopped green pepper
¼ cup chopped sweet pickles

Soften gelatin in cold water; dissolve over hot water.

Blend mayonnaise with deviled ham, onion, celery, green pepper, and pickles. Stir in dissolved gelatin. Pour mixture into a pint mold; chill until firm.

Unmold and garnish with salad greens. Surround with chilled Vienna sausages and slices of corned beef. Serves 6 to 8.

Deviled Ham Mousse

CHICKEN ALMOND MOUSSE

1½ tablespoons (1½ envelopes) unflavored gelatin
3 cups chicken stock or broth
1 teaspoon salt
¼ teaspoon pepper
1 teaspoon minced onion
⅛ teaspoon paprika
3 egg yolks
½ cup finely chopped almonds
2 cups diced cooked chicken
1 cup heavy cream, whipped

Soften gelatin in ½ cup cold chicken stock. Add salt, pepper, onion, and paprika to remaining stock and heat.

Stir a little of hot stock into egg yolks. Mix well and return to double boiler. Cook over hot water until smooth and thick. Strain if necessary.

Stir in and blend softened gelatin. Cool until partially thickened.

Fold in nuts, chicken, and whipped cream. Turn into ring mold. Chill until firm.

Unmold on serving platter. Fill center with crisp greens. Garnish with tomato wedges. Serves 6.

Variations: Vary seasonings by adding a little horseradish and dry mustard. *

CHICKEN MOUSSE

1 tablespoon (1 envelope) unflavored gelatin
¼ cup cold water
½ cup milk, scalded
1 can condensed cream of chicken soup
2 cups ground cooked chicken
¼ cup mayonnaise
1 tablespoon grated onion
½ teaspoon salt
¼ teaspoon pepper
1 cup heavy cream

Soak gelatin in cold water 5 minutes; dissolve in hot milk. Combine with undiluted soup, chicken, mayonnaise, onion, salt and pepper; blend well. Chill until almost set.

Whip cream stiff; fold into chicken mixture. Pour into 5- or 6-cup mold rinsed with cold water. Chill about 4 hours or until set.

Unmold just before serving and garnish with mayonnaise. Accompany with marinated asparagus, cranberry sauce, and crackers. Serves 8.

PRESSED CHICKEN LOAF

1 3½- to 4-pound chicken
1 carrot
1 slice onion
1 whole clove
2 whole black peppers
2 teaspoons salt
1 tablespoon (1 envelope) unflavored gelatin

¼ cup cold water
½ cup chopped parsley
6 hard-cooked eggs, sliced

Cut chicken in pieces. Cover with hot water; add carrot, onion, and seasonings. Cook slowly until tender. Remove chicken and cook stock down to 2 cups.

Soften gelatin in cold water. Chop carrot cooked with chicken and combine with parsley. Arrange egg slices on bottom of well greased loaf pan. Alternate layers of chicken, egg, and parsley-carrot mixture.

Dissolve softened gelatin in hot stock. Pour over arrangement in loaf pan. Cover with waxed paper. Place weight on top to hold chicken mixture in stock. Chill overnight.

Unmold. Garnish with crisp greens. Slice for serving. Serves 6 to 8.

CHICKEN SAUTERNE SOUFFLÉ SALAD

1 package lemon-flavored gelatin
1 cup hot water
½ cup sauterne or other white wine
1 tablespoon lemon juice
½ cup mayonnaise
½ teaspoon salt
4 to 5 drops Tabasco sauce
1 cup diced, cooked chicken
½ cup diced celery
⅓ cup toasted, slivered, blanched almonds

Dissolve gelatin in hot water. Add wine, lemon juice, mayonnaise, salt, and Tabasco. Blend well with rotary beater.

Pour into refrigerator freezing tray. Quick-chill in freezing unit (without changing control) 20 to 25 minutes, or until firm about 1 inch from edge but soft in center.

Turn mixture into bowl and whip with rotary beater until fluffy. Fold in chicken, celery, and almonds. Pour into individual molds.

Chill until firm in refrigerator (not freezing unit) 30 to 60 minutes.

Unmold and garnish with salad greens. Serve with additional mayonnaise, if desired. Serves 4.

Chicken Mousse

Gelatin Molds with Fish and Shellfish

Double Decker Salmon Loaf

SHRIMP MOLDS

1 package lime-flavored gelatin
1 cup hot water
1 teaspoon salt
1 teaspoon dry mustard
1 tablespoon prepared horseradish
1 tablespoon lemon juice
1 cup thick sour cream
1 tablespoon minced chives
2 cups cooked or canned shrimp
1 cup drained shredded cucumber
1/4 cup minced parsley

Dissolve gelatin in hot water. Cool. Add salt, mustard, horseradish, lemon juice, and sour cream. Chill until slightly thickened.

Add chives, shrimp, cucumber, and parsley. Pour into 6 or 8 individual molds. Chill until firm.

Unmold on crisp lettuce. Garnish with watercress. Serves 6 to 8.

TUNA-COTTAGE CHEESE MOLD SAUTERNE

2 tablespoons (2 envelopes) unflavored gelatin
1/4 cup cold water
1 cup sauterne, rhine, or other white wine
1 cup undiluted evaporated milk
1 cup mayonnaise
1 pint cottage cheese with chives
1 6 1/2-ounce can grated-style tuna
1 cup finely diced celery
2 tablespoons minced parsley
Salt and pepper to taste

Soften gelatin in mixture of cold water and 1/4 cup wine for 5 minutes; dissolve over boiling water.

Add remaining wine, milk, and mayonnaise; beat until well blended. Chill until slightly thickened.

Add remaining ingredients and mix well. Pour into an oiled fish mold or loaf pan; chill until firm.

Unmold and surround with crisp salad greens and serve with French dressing or mayonnaise. Serves 8.

Tuna-Cottage Cheese Mold Sauterne

SEA GARDEN SALAD

1 pound fillet of halibut or other white fish
1/2 teaspoon Ac'cent
2 packages lime-flavored gelatin
3 cups hot water
1 cup pineapple juice
2 tablespoons lime juice
1 cup diced canned pineapple
1/2 cup seedless white grapes (optional)
1 cup diced melon

"Poach" fish in water to cover to which Ac'cent has been added, about 10 minutes or until done. Drain; cool; break into small chunks.

Dissolve gelatin in hot water; add pineapple juice and lime juice. Chill until consistency of unbeaten egg white.

Fold in fruits and fish. Turn into lightly oiled mold. Chill until firm.

Unmold on salad greens. Serve with mayonnaise. Serves 6 to 8.

Sea Garden Salad

TUNA MOUSSE

2 tablespoons (2 envelopes) unflavored gelatin
1/2 cup cold water
1 cup mayonnaise
2 6 1/2- or 7-ounce cans tuna
1/2 cup chopped cucumber
3 tablespoons chopped stuffed olives
1/4 cup lemon juice
1 1/2 teaspoons prepared horseradish
2 teaspoons onion juice
1/4 teaspoon salt
1/4 teaspoon paprika
1 cup heavy cream, whipped

Soften gelatin in cold water. Dissolve over boiling water and stir into mayonnaise.

Flake tuna and add with remaining ingredients except cream. Mix well.

Fold in whipped cream. Pour into 1 1/2-quart mold. Chill until firm. Unmold on crisp lettuce. Serves 8.

Shrimp Mousse: Substitute cooked or canned flaked shrimp for tuna.

DOUBLE DECKER SALMON LOAF
Salmon Layer:
1 tablespoon (1 envelope) unflavored gelatin
1 1/4 cups cold water
1 cup chopped celery
1 can (7 3/4 ounces) salmon
1 tablespoon grated onion
1/2 cup sharp mayonnaise
1 tablespoon prepared mustard
Consommé Layer:
1 tablespoon (1 envelope) unflavored gelatin
1/2 cup cold water
1 can condensed consommé
2 tablespoons lemon juice
Few dashes Tabasco sauce

Salmon Layer: Soften gelatin in 1/4 cup cold water 5 minutes. Heat remaining water to boiling and pour over gelatin; stir until dissolved.

Add celery, flaked salmon, onion, mayonnaise, and mustard. Season with salt if needed. Mix well and pour into a loaf pan and chill. When almost firm, begin consommé layer.

Consommé Layer: Soften gelatin in cold water for 5 minutes. Add hot consommé and stir until dissolved. Add lemon juice and Tabasco sauce. Cool. Pour over salmon mixture.

Chill until firm. Unmold on platter. Serves 6 to 8.

Variation: Tuna may be used instead of salmon.

LOBSTER IN ASPIC

2 1/2 tablespoons (2 1/2 envelopes) unflavored gelatin
1/2 cup cold water
2 cups boiling water
1 1/2 teaspoons salt
4 tablespoons sugar
1/4 cup lemon juice
1/2 cup lobster liquid or cold water
2 cups shredded, cooked lobster
1 cup blanched almonds

Soak gelatin in cold water 5 minutes. Add boiling water, salt, sugar, and lemon juice. Cool.

Add lobster liquid, shredded lobster and blanched almonds. Pour into a mold which has been dipped in cold water. Chill until firm. Unmold and serve on lettuce. Serves 6.

SALMON AND CUCUMBER MOUSSE

1   tablespoon (1 envelope) unflavored gelatin
1/4   cup cold water
1   bouillon cube
1/2   cup boiling water
1/2   cup mayonnaise
1   teaspoon Worcestershire sauce
1   tablespoon onion, scraped
1   tablespoon vinegar
1   teaspoon salt
1/4   teaspoon pepper
2   cups flaked cooked or canned salmon
1 1/2   cups diced cucumber
1/2   cup heavy cream, whipped

Soften gelatin in cold water. Dissolve bouillon cube in boiling water and add to gelatin. Stir until gelatin dissolves.

Let cool. Add mayonnaise, Worcestershire, onion, vinegar, salt, and pepper. Blend well and chill until thick.

Beat with rotary egg beater until light and foamy. Fold in salmon, cucumber, and whipped cream.

Turn into 1-quart fish-shaped mold. Chill until firm. Serve on greens with slices of cucumber. Serve with mayonnaise. Serves 4.

LEMON-TUNA MOUSSE

1   package lemon-flavored gelatin
1 3/4   cups boiling water
2   tablespoons vinegar
1   tablespoon grated onion
1   can (7-ounces) tuna, drained and flaked
1/4   cup chopped green pepper
1   pimiento, chopped
1/2   teaspoon salt
2   teaspoons prepared horseradish
1   cup heavy cream, whipped

Dissolve gelatin in boiling water; add vinegar and onion; chill until partially firm.

Combine remaining ingredients, except cream; fold into gelatin mixture. Fold in whipped cream.

Pour into oiled 1-quart mold; chill until firm. Unmold on salad greens. Serves 4 to 6.

JELLIED FISH SALAD

1   tablespoon (1 envelope) unflavored gelatin
1/4   cup cold water
1/2   teaspoon salt
1/2   teaspoon celery seed
1/4   cup vinegar
1/4   cup water
2   eggs, beaten
2   cups flaked cooked or canned fish

Soften gelatin in cold water. Add seasonings, vinegar, and water to eggs. Cook over boiling water until thick-

ened, stirring constantly.

Add gelatin and stir until it is dissolved.

Add fish and mix thoroughly. Pour into individual molds or large ring mold and chill. Serves 6.

MOLDED TUNA LOAF

1   tablespoon (1 envelope) unflavored gelatin
1/4   cup cold water
1   cup hot water
3/4   cup mayonnaise or salad dressing
1   tablespoon lemon juice
1   tablespoon prepared mustard
2   6 1/2- or 7-ounce cans (2 cups) tuna, flaked
1   cup thinly sliced celery
1/3   cup diced cucumber
1   tablespoon thinly sliced green onion

Soften gelatin in cold water. Add hot water and stir to dissolve gelatin. Cool to room temperature.

Blend in mayonnaise, lemon juice, and mustard. Chill until partially set.

Fold in tuna, celery, cucumber, and onion. Pour into 8 1/2 x 4 1/2 x 2 1/2-inch loaf pan. Chill until firm.

Garnish with tomato slices and lemon wedges, if desired. Serves 4 to 6.

SHRIMP SALAD MOLD

2   tablespoons (2 envelopes) unflavored gelatin
2 1/2   cups cold water
1   cup boiling water
1/2   cup lemon juice
1/2   teaspoon salt
1   teaspoon Worcestershire sauce
1   or 2 drops Tabasco sauce
1   teaspoon grated onion
1   pound shrimp, cooked and cleaned
1   cup diced celery
1/2   cup diced green pepper
1/2   cup sliced pimiento stuffed olives
Deviled eggs
Sliced olives

Soften gelatin in 1 cup cold water. Add 1 cup boiling water and stir until gelatin is dissolved.

Add remaining water and lemon juice. Stir in salt, Worcestershire, Tabasco, and onion.

Pour thin layer of gelatin mixture into 1-quart mold and arrange shrimp in it. Chill until set.

Chill remaining gelatin mixture until slightly thickened, then fold in celery, pepper, and olives. Carefully pour over shrimp. Chill until firm.

Unmold and garnish with additional sliced olives, deviled eggs, and salad greens. Serve with mayonnaise or sour cream dressing. Serves 6.

Tuna Soufflé Salad

MOLDED SEAFOOD OR VEGETABLE SALAD TO FREEZE

1   tablespoon (1 envelope) unflavored gelatin
1/3   cup cold water
1   6-ounce can frozen lemonade concentrate
4   tablespoons ketchup or chili sauce
1   cup sour cream

Soak gelatin in cold water, then heat in top of double boiler until dissolved. Remove from double boiler.

Add concentrate for lemonade, ketchup or chili sauce, and sour cream.

Freeze plain in mold or containers; or add 1 cup of any cooked seafood, poultry, meat, or cooked vegetables, and freeze.

TUNA SOUFFLÉ SALAD

1   package lemon-flavored gelatin
1   cup hot water
1/2   cup cold water
1/2   cup mayonnaise
1   tablespoon lemon juice
1/4   teaspoon salt
Dash of pepper
1/2   cup flaked tuna
1/2   medium cucumber, diced
1   hard-cooked egg, diced
1   tablespoon chopped onion

Dissolve gelatin in hot water. Mix in cold water, mayonnaise, lemon juice, salt, and pepper.

Pour into refrigerator tray. Quick-chill in freezing unit 15 to 20 minutes, or until firm about 1 inch from edge but soft in center.

Turn into bowl and whip with rotary egg beater. Fold in remaining ingredients; pour into 1-quart mold. Chill in refrigerator until firm (about 60 minutes). Unmold onto a bed of chicory; garnish with cucumber slices.

Serves 4 to 6.

Shrimp Salad Mold

Molded Shrimp And Egg Buffet Style

MOLDED SHRIMP AND EGG BUFFET STYLE

Shrimp Salad:

1 tablespoon (1 envelope) unflavored gelatin
½ cup cold water
2 tablespoons lemon juice
½ teaspoon salt
¼ teaspoon Worcestershire sauce
⅛ teaspoon Tabasco sauce
¾ cup salad dressing
1½ teaspoons grated onion
½ cup finely diced celery
¼ cup finely diced green pepper
¼ cup chopped pimiento
2 cups fresh, frozen or canned shrimp, cut in small pieces

Sprinkle gelatin on cold water to soften. Place over boiling water and stir until gelatin is dissolved.

Add lemon juice, salt, Worcestershire sauce, and Tabasco sauce. Cool.

Add salad dressing; mix in remaining ingredients. Turn into large or individual molds and chill until firm. Serves 6.

Egg Salad: Follow recipe for shrimp salad increasing salt to 1 teaspoon and 4 hard-cooked eggs (chopped) are substituted for the shrimp. Serves 6.

Note: To serve 12 from either mold as illustrated in picture, double all ingredients and turn into 1½ quart mold.

TUNA LUNCHEON MOLD

1 tablespoon (1 envelope) unflavored gelatin
½ cup cold water
1 cup mayonnaise
⅓ cup lemon juice
¾ cup diced celery
⅓ cup diced green pepper
Salt and pepper
2 6½-ounce cans grated or flaked tuna

Soften gelatin in cold water and dis-

solve it over hot water. Combine mayonnaise and lemon juice and add to celery, green pepper, seasonings, and tuna which have been tossed together.

Add gelatin to mixture, and mix lightly. Pour into ring mold and chill until firm.

Unmold ring on curly endive arranged on chop plate. Fill center with radish roses. Serves 6 to 8.

MASTER SOUFFLÉ SALAD

Ingredients:

1 package lemon-flavored gelatin
1 cup hot water
½ cup cold water
3 tablespoons vinegar or canned lemon juice
½ cup mayonnaise
¼ teaspoon salt
Dash of pepper
1 cup minced celery
4 tablespoons minced parsley
1½ tablespoons minced onion

Choose One:

1 1-pound can salmon, drained and flaked
2 7-ounce cans tuna, drained and flaked
1 12-ounce can luncheon meat, chopped
1 No. 303 can (1 pound) peas, peas and carrots, or mixed vegetables, drained (Use 1 cup hot tomato juice in place of hot water.)
1 12-ounce can boned chicken, diced
2 6-ounce cans boned turkey, diced
1 12-ounce can tongue or tongue loaf

Dissolve gelatin in hot water. Add cold water, vinegar or lemon juice, mayonnaise, salt, and pepper; blend well with rotary beater; pour into refrigerator tray.

Chill in freezing unit 15 to 20 minutes, or until firm around edges but soft in center.

Turn into bowl; whip with rotary

beater until fluffy; fold in remaining ingredients. Pour into 1-quart mold or 6 individual molds.

Chill (not in freezing unit) 30 to 60 minutes, or until firm. Unmold; garnish with salad greens. Serves 6.

Note: For Fruit-Soufflé Salad, omit pepper, parsley, and onion; reduce salt to ⅛ teaspoon and vinegar to 1 tablespoon. Choose 1 No. 303 or No. 2 can fruit cocktail, peaches, apricots, grapefruit sections, or pears. Use syrup drained from fruit as part of liquid. Follow same directions.

CANADIAN SALMON MOLD

2 tablespoons (2 envelopes) unflavored gelatin
½ cup cold water
1 cup hot chicken broth or bouillon
1 cup salad dressing or mayonnaise
3 tablespoons chili sauce
2 tablespoons lemon juice
1 tablespoon grated onion
½ teaspoon Worcestershire sauce
Dash of cayenne
½ teaspoon Ac'cent
Salt to taste
1 8-ounce can salmon, or 1 cup cooked salmon
1 cup finely diced celery
½ cup sliced stuffed olives

Soften gelatin in cold water; dissolve in hot chicken broth.

Cool slightly. Add slowly to mayonnaise, blending well after each addition.

Add chili sauce, lemon juice, onion, Worcestershire sauce, cayenne, Ac'cent, and salt. Chill until consistency of unbeaten egg whites.

Flake salmon; fold in with celery and olives. Turn into an oiled 5-cup mold; chill until firm.

Unmold on crisp salad greens. Serve with any desired dressing. Serves 8.

Variations: Use 1 package lemon- or lime-flavored gelatin instead of unflavored gelatin. Substitute water for chicken broth.

Canadian Salmon Mold

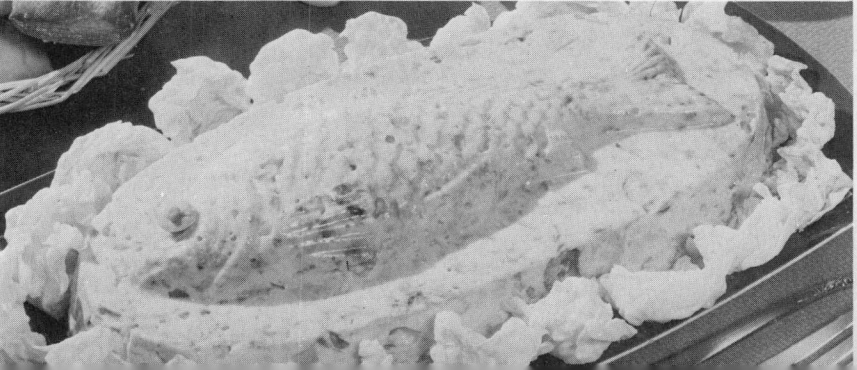

AVOCADO AND TUNA LOAF

Tuna Layer:

1   tablespoon (1 envelope) unflavored
    gelatin
½ cup cold water
¾ cup boiling water
3   tablespoons lemon juice
1   teaspoon salt
1   7-ounce can tuna, flaked
1   cup diced celery
⅓ cup diced pimiento

Sprinkle gelatin on cold water to soften. Add boiling water and stir until gelatin is dissolved.

Add lemon juice and salt. Chill until mixture is consistency of unbeaten egg white. Fold in flaked tuna, celery, and pimiento.

Turn into a 9 x 5 x 3-inch loaf pan; chill until almost firm.

Avocado Layer:

1   tablespoon (1 envelope) unflavored
    gelatin
¾ cup cold water
1   teaspoon sugar
2   tablespoons lemon juice
1   cup mashed avocado (1 large)
½ cup sour cream
½ cup mayonnaise
1   teaspoon salt
⅛ teaspoon Tabasco sauce

Sprinkle gelatin on cold water to soften. Place over boiling water and stir until gelatin is dissolved.

Add sugar and 1 tablespoon lemon juice.

Chill until mixture is consistency of unbeaten egg white.

Immediately after mashing avocado, add remaining tablespoon lemon juice, sour cream, mayonnaise, salt, and Tabasco. Fold in gelatin mixture.

Turn on top of almost firm first layer; chill until firm.

Unmold; if desired, garnish with additional avocado slices, ripe and stuffed olives. Serves 8.

Avocado and Tuna Loaf

SHRIMP PARTY RING SALAD

2   tablespoons (2 envelopes) unflavored gelatin
¾ cup cold water
1½ cups hot water
¼ cup honey
¾ teaspoon salt
6   tablespoons lemon juice
1   cup mayonnaise
1   cup cooked shrimp pieces
1   cup chopped celery
1   tablespoon minced onion
2   tablespoons chopped parsley
2   tablespoons chopped pimiento
Chicory
Spinach leaves
Cooked whole shrimp
Pimiento strips
1   cup mayonnaise
½ teaspoon grated lemon rind
2   teaspoons lemon juice
Thin lemon slices

Soften gelatin in cold water. Add hot water, honey, salt, and lemon juice. Chill.

Stir mixture into 1 cup mayonnaise. Pour ½ cup of mixture in an 8½-inch ring mold. Chill until firm.

To remaining mixture add shrimp pieces, celery, onion, parsley, and pimiento. Chill until beginning to thicken. Pour into ring mold and chill until firm.

Unmold on serving platter. Place chicory and spinach leaves in center of mold. Garnish with whole shrimp and additional chicory and spinach leaves. Place pimiento strips on top of mold in a pattern.

Combine 1 cup mayonnaise with lemon rind and juice thoroughly. Serve salad garnished with thin slices of lemon. Serves 6.

SALMON MOUSSE

1   tablespoon (1 envelope) unflavored gelatin
¼ cup cold water
1   cup mayonnaise
½ cup light cream or top milk
2   tablespoons lemon juice
1   teaspoon salt
1   cup finely chopped celery
¼ cup finely chopped sweet pickles
1   tablespoon grated onion
2   teaspoons prepared horseradish
1   1-pound can salmon, drained and flaked

Soften gelatin in cold water; dissolve over hot water.

Combine remaining ingredients. Add gelatin and blend. Pour into a 1-quart mold. Chill until firm.

Unmold and garnish with salad greens, deviled eggs, and slices of lemon. Serves 6 to 8.

Shrimp Party Ring Salad

MOLDED KING CRAB SALAD

2   6-ounce packages frozen king crabmeat
1   cup chopped celery
¼ cup French dressing
1   package lemon-flavored gelatin
1½ cups hot water
½ cup lemon juice
½ teaspoon salt
Salad greens
½ cup mayonnaise or salad dressing

Thaw crabmeat and remove any cartilage. Marinate crabmeat and celery in French dressing.

Dissolve gelatin in hot water. Add lemon juice and salt. Place about ⅓ of the gelatin in a ring mold; chill until almost congealed.

Arrange crabmeat and celery attractively over the gelatin base and cover with remaining gelatin. Chill until firm.

Unmold on round platter and garnish with salad greens. Fill center with mayonnaise. Serves 6.

SHRIMP-AVOCADO ASPIC

1   tablespoon (1 envelope) unflavored gelatin
2   tablespoons cold water
1   cup boiling water
1   cup sieved avocado
1½ tablespoons lemon juice
¾ teaspoon salt
½ teaspoon Worcestershire sauce
Dash of Tabasco sauce
1   pimiento, minced
1½ cups cooked or canned shrimp, cleaned

Soften gelatin in cold water. Dissolve in boiling water. Add avocado, seasonings, and pimiento. Chill until mixture begins to thicken.

Add shrimp and turn into mold rinsed in cold water. Chill until firm. Unmold on lettuce. Serves 6.

Salmon Mousse

Gelatin Molds with Cheese

Pineapple Cheese Mold

CHRISTMAS SALAD MOLD

1st Layer:

1 tablespoon (1 envelope) unflavored gelatin
½ cup cold water
¾ cup hot water
½ teaspoon salt
1 tablespoon lemon juice
1 8-ounce package cream cheese, softened
Green pepper; cut in shape of holly leaves, about 8
Pimiento; cut in shape of holly berries, about 12

Soften gelatin in cold water; add hot water and salt. Stir until gelatin dissolves. Add lemon juice and cream cheese; mix until smooth.

Pour 3 tablespoons in bottom of 9-inch ring mold. Press green pepper holly leaves and pimiento berries alternately in design on bottom of mold.

Chill until firm, then add remaining gelatin mixture and chill.

2nd Layer:

4 cups tomato juice
1 tablespoon chopped onion
1 teaspoon salt
Dash of cayenne pepper
2 tablespoons (2 envelopes) unflavored gelatin
½ cup cold water
1 teaspoon Worcestershire sauce
1 teaspoon lemon juice
½ cup chopped celery

Combine tomato juice, onion, salt, and cayenne. Simmer 15 minutes.

Soften gelatin in cold water. Add Worcestershire sauce, lemon juice, softened gelatin, and celery to tomato juice mixture. Cool and pour over cream cheese layer.

Chill. Unmold. Fill center with leaves of iceberg lettuce. Serves 8 to 10.

Christmas Salad Mold

PINEAPPLE CHEESE MOLD

1 tablespoon (1 envelope) unflavored gelatin
¼ cup cold water
1 can crushed pineapple
1 tablespoon lemon juice
½ teaspoon salt
1 cup shredded mild Cheddar cheese
1 cup cream, whipped
Strawberries
Curly endive

Soften gelatin in cold water. Heat ½ cup juice from crushed pineapple and, when hot, add to gelatin.

Cool until partially thickened, then fold in 1 cup well-drained crushed pineapple, the lemon juice, salt, cheese, and the whipped cream.

Pour into a round oiled ring mold and return to refrigerator until firm. Unmold onto large chop plate. Garnish with strawberries and curly endive. Serve with salad dressing. Serves 6.

BUFFET PARTY MOLD

1 No. 2 can (2½ cups) crushed pineapple
1 3-ounce package lime-flavored gelatin
2 3-ounce packages cream cheese
⅓ cup chopped pimiento
1 cup heavy cream, whipped
1 cup diced celery
1 cup chopped walnuts

Heat pineapple to boiling point; add gelatin and stir until dissolved. Chill until partially set.

Soften cream cheese; stir in pimiento; add to gelatin mixture and blend. Fold in whipped cream, celery, and nuts.

Pour into 1½-quart fluted mold. Chill until firm. Serves 6 to 8.

ROQUEFORT-CREAM CHEESE MOLD

½ pound Roquefort or blue cheese
2 3-ounce packages cream cheese
1 tablespoon (1 envelope) unflavored gelatin
½ cup heavy cream, whipped

Mash cheeses to a smooth paste.

Soften gelatin in ½ cup cold water and stir over hot water until dissolved.

Add cheese paste to whipped cream and stir in gelatin. Turn into mold rinsed in cold water. Chill until firm. Serve with mayonnaise or French dressing. Serves 6 to 8.

BLUE CHEESE-COTTAGE CHEESE MOLDS

1 package lemon-flavored gelatin
1 cup boiling water
½ cup cold water
¼ cup mayonnaise
1½ cups cottage cheese
⅓ cup crumbled blue cheese

Dissolve gelatin in hot water. Add cold water. Chill until of a jelly-like consistency.

Beat with a rotary beater until frothy. Add mayonnaise, cottage cheese, and blue cheese and mix well.

Pour into individual molds which have been oiled or dipped in cold water. Makes 8 individual molds.

SPRING BEAUTY SALAD

1½ tablespoons (1½ envelopes) unflavored gelatin
3 tablespoons cold water
1 cup cottage cheese, sieved
1 cup American cheese, grated
1 teaspoon salt
⅛ teaspoon white pepper
2 tablespoons chopped pimiento
2 tablespoons chopped green pepper
½ cup diced American cheese
1 pint heavy cream, whipped

Soften gelatin in cold water 5 minutes and dissolve over hot water.

Soften cottage cheese with a little plain cream and press through sieve. Add grated American cheese, gelatin, seasonings, pimiento, pepper, and diced American cheese. (Some of diced cheese may be sprinkled in bottom of mold.)

Fold in stiffly beaten cream. Turn mixture into wet mold and chill.

Serve on large chop plate with center filled with fresh fruit or vegetable salad. Garnish with crisp lettuce, endive, or watercress. Serves 6.

Spring Beauty Salad

APPLE AND CHEESE LAYERED MOLD

1   package lemon-flavored gelatin
2   cups boiling water
2   tablespoons lemon juice
1/2 teaspoon salt
1   diced red apple
1   teaspoon sugar
1   3-ounce package cream cheese
1/2 cup broken nutmeats

Dissolve gelatin in boiling water. Add 1 tablespoon lemon juice and salt. Chill.

Combine apple, sugar, and remaining lemon juice. When gelatin mixture is slightly thickened, fold apples into half the mixture. Turn into mold and chill until firm.

Place remaining gelatin mixture in a bowl of cracked ice and beat with a rotary beater until thick and fluffy like whipped cream. Fold in mashed cheese and nuts. Pour over gelatin-apple layer and chill until firm.

To serve, cut in slices and arrange on lettuce leaves. Top with mayonnaise or any desired dressing. Serves 6.

CRANBERRY COTTAGE SALADS

1   tablespoon (1 envelope) unflavored gelatin
1/4 cup cold water
1   1-pound can cranberry sauce (jellied or whole)
2   teaspoons prepared horseradish
3/4 teaspoon dry mustard
1/4 cup lemon juice
1   teaspoon grated lemon rind
1/4 teaspoon salt
Pinch of cayenne
1/4 cup cottage cheese

Place gelatin in custard cup. Add cold water. Let stand 2 minutes. Place custard cup in pan of boiling water until gelatin dissolves.

Combine cranberry sauce and gelatin. Stir in other ingredients, beating slightly to blend.

Spoon into molds which have been rinsed in cold water. Chill until firm.

Unmold and serve in lettuce cups. Serves 4 to 6. An excellent accompaniment for fish.

Cranberry Cottage Salads

LAYERED CHEESE AND FRUIT SALAD

First Layer—Fruit Gelatin:

2   cups hot water
2   packages lime-flavored gelatin
2   cups pear juice drained from 1 No. 303 can of pears (add water to make 2 full cups)
2   medium bananas
16 to 20 halves of maraschino cherries

Heat water in 2-quart saucepan until it steams. Remove from heat and add gelatin dessert. Stir until dissolved, add pear juice and water mixture; cool.

Pour 1/2 cup of gelatin mixture into lightly oiled 9 1/2 x 5 1/4 x 2 3/4-inch loaf pan, and chill in refrigerator until firm. Chill remaining mixture in refrigerator, but do not allow to congeal.

Arrange banana slices on firm gelatin in two outside rows lengthwise of the pan, and cherries, cut side up, in two center rows. Pour 1 1/2 cups cooled gelatin mixture slowly down the side of pan, being careful not to disturb fruit arrangement. Place in refrigerator, and chill until firm.

Second Layer—Cream Cheese:

3   3-ounce packages cream cheese
1/2 cup mayonnaise
2   tablespoons fruit gelatin mixture
1/2 cup finely chopped salted peanuts
1/3 cup chopped cherries

Beat cream cheese at a medium speed on electric mixer until light and fluffy. Add mayonnaise and gelatin mixture; fold in nuts and cherries.

Spread in an even layer over firm fruit gelatin in loaf pan.

Third Layer—Fruit Gelatin:

1   cup diced canned pears

Add diced pears to remaining gelatin mixture, and pour over cheese layer.

Chill layered salad in refrigerator until firm. Serves 8 to 10.

TOMATO CHEESE MOLD

1   tablespoon (1 envelope) unflavored gelatin
1/4 cup cold water
2   cups canned tomato sauce
2   teaspoons finely minced onion
Salt and pepper
1/2 pound Cheddar cheese, shredded

Soften gelatin in cold water and dissolve over hot water.

Add to tomato sauce and onion. Season to taste. Chill until slightly thickened.

Fold in shredded cheese. Pour into 4 or 6 individual molds. Chill until firm; unmold on lettuce and serve with mayonnaise or salad dressing. Serves 4 to 6.

Molded Plum and Cottage Cheese Salad

MOLDED PLUM AND COTTAGE CHEESE SALAD

1   No. 303 can blue plums
1   package orange-flavored gelatin
Plum syrup plus water to make 1 cup
1   cup creamed cottage cheese
1/2 cup chopped celery
1/2 cup chopped pecans
2   tablespoons lemon juice
1/2 cup evaporated milk, chilled icy cold

Drain plums and save syrup. Cut plums in halves, remove and discard pits. Place plum halves fairly close together in the bottom of an 8-inch ring mold or in 8 individual molds. If any plum halves remain, save for use for some other purpose.

Empty gelatin into a medium-sized mixing bowl. Heat syrup and water to boiling. Add to gelatin and stir until gelatin is dissolved.

Chill gelatin until it begins to thicken, then add cottage cheese, celery, pecans, and lemon juice.

Whip milk until it will hold a stiff peak. Fold into chilled gelatin mixture. Spoon carefully over plums. Chill until firm, about 2 to 3 hours.

Unmold on chilled platter. Garnish with orange or grapefruit segments, if desired. Serves 6 to 8.

SUPERB SALAD MOLDS

1/4 cup milk
1   8-ounce package cream cheese
1   cup shredded Cheddar cheese
1/2 teaspoon salt
1/4 teaspoon paprika
1   tablespoon (1 envelope) unflavored gelatin
1/4 cup cold water
1   cup heavy cream, whipped
6   pineapple slices

Gradually add the milk to the cream cheese, blending until smooth. Add the shredded cheese, salt, and paprika.

Add the gelatin which has been softened in the cold water and dissolved over hot water. Chill until slightly thickened.

Fold in the whipped cream. Pour into 6 individual molds. Chill until firm. For each serving, place a slice of pineapple on crisp watercress. Unmold a gelatin salad in the center of the pineapple. Serves 6.

Emerald Mold

EMERALD MOLD

1   3-ounce package lime-flavored gelatin
1½ cups hot water
1   can (1 pound, 4½ ounces) crushed pineapple, well drained
1   teaspoon peppermint extract
1   tablespoon (1 envelope) unflavored gelatin
¼   cup cold water
2   8-ounce packages cream cheese, softened
½   cup sugar
2   eggs
½   teaspoon vanilla

Dissolve lime-flavored gelatin in hot water. Chill until syrupy. Fold in crushed pineapple and peppermint extract. Pour half of mixture into a lightly oiled 1-quart mold. Chill until set.

Soften unflavored gelatin in cold water. Dissolve over hot water. Add to softened cream cheese. Stir in sugar, eggs, and vanilla. Beat until smooth. Pour half of cheese mixture over gelatin layer in mold. Chill until firm.

Repeat layers chilling after each addition. Serves 8 to 10.

CREAMY CHEESE SALAD MOLD

1   tablespoon (1 envelope) unflavored gelatin
¼   cup cold water
3   eggs
2   cups milk
¼   teaspoon salt
1½ cups diced American cheese
¾   teaspoon onion juice
½   cup sliced stuffed olives
¼   cup chopped sweet pickles
½   cup finely diced celery
1   tablespoon vinegar or pickle juice
Lettuce, chicory, or watercress
Paprika

Creamy Cheese Salad Mold

Soften gelatin in cold water.

Beat eggs, add milk and salt, and cook over boiling water, stirring constantly, until mixture thickens slightly.

Remove from heat and stir in softened gelatin until dissolved. Add remaining ingredients (except greens and paprika) until well mixed, not until cheese melts.

Decorate large or individual molds with additional olive and pickle slices. Pour in a little of gelatin mixture (not enough to float garnish) and chill until firm.

Then add remainder of mixture and chill until whole mold is firm.

Unmold on crisp salad greens, on one large or individual plates. Garnish with paprika. Serves 6 to 8.

RED AND WHITE SALAD

1   tablespoon (1 envelope) unflavored gelatin
½   cup water
1   can (1¼ cups) condensed tomato soup
1   teaspoon grated onion
1   cup creamy cottage cheese

Soften gelatin in cold water. Heat soup; mix in softened gelatin and grated onion.

Pour into 1 large or 4 individual molds that have been rinsed with cold water. Chill until firm.

Unmold on lettuce. Serve with top knot of cottage cheese. Serves 4.

Red and White Salad

OLIVE SALAD LOAF

2   tablespoons (2 envelopes) unflavored gelatin
¼   cup cold water
1   cup tomato sauce
2   tablespoons vinegar
½   teaspoon salt
2   cups cottage cheese
1   cup ripe olives
½   cup mayonnaise
1   cup finely chopped celery
⅓   cup finely chopped green sweet pepper
¼   cup diced pimiento

Soften gelatin in cold water. Heat tomato sauce to boiling. Add gelatin and stir until it is dissolved.

Blend in vinegar and salt. Cool to room temperature.

Force cottage cheese through sieve. Cut olives into large pieces.

Blend cheese, olives, mayonnaise, celery, green pepper, and pimiento into gelatin mixture. Turn into loaf pan (about 8½ x 4½ x 2½ inches), and chill until firm.

Unmold on salad greens to serve. Serves 8 to 10.

PINEAPPLE-COTTAGE CHEESE MOLD

2   teaspoons (⅔ envelope) unflavored gelatin
3   tablespoons cold water
1   cup pineapple juice or pineapple juice plus water
2   tablespoons lemon juice
2   tablespoons sugar
Pinch of salt
½   cup drained crushed pineapple (9-ounce can)
⅓   cup finely chopped celery
⅓   cup cottage cheese

Sprinkle gelatin on cold water and soak a few minutes.

Heat fruit juices; add sugar, salt, and gelatin. Stir until gelatin is dissolved.

Chill until thick enough to hold solid food in place. Stir in pineapple, celery, and cottage cheese. Chill until firm. Serves 4.

LEMON-PECAN-COTTAGE CHEESE MOLDS

1   package lemon-flavored gelatin
1   cup boiling water
½   cup cold water
1½ cups cottage cheese
¼   cup mayonnaise
¼   cup chopped pecans
1   tablespoon lemon juice

Dissolve gelatin in boiling water. Add cold water. Chill until of a jelly-like consistency.

Beat with rotary beater until frothy. Add mayonnaise, cottage cheese, pecans, and lemon juice. Mix ingredients well.

Pour into individual molds which have been oiled or dipped in cold water. Makes 8 individual molds.

Olive Salad Loaf

Gelatin Molds with Fruit

WALDORF SALAD MOLD

1   package lemon-flavored gelatin
2   cups hot water
1   tablespoon vinegar
½   teaspoon salt
1½ cups tart apples, diced
½   cup coarsely chopped walnuts
¾   cup diced celery
Bibb lettuce

Dissolve gelatin in hot water. Add vinegar and salt.

Cover bottom of 1-quart mold with a thin layer of gelatin. Chill until firm.

Chill remaining gelatin until slightly thickened. Add apples, nuts, and celery. Pour into mold. Chill until firm.

Unmold on a platter. Surround with lettuce. Serve with a cream cheese dressing. Serves 4 to 6.

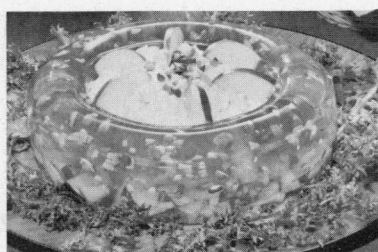

Prepare a Waldorf Salad Mold in a ring and fill the center with cottage cheese garnished with apple slices dipped in lemon juice to prevent fruit from darkening. Garnish with nuts.

GINGER ALE-LEMON MOLD

Dissolve 1 package lemon-flavored gelatin in ½ cup boiling water. When cool, add 1½ cups ginger ale.

Chill until slightly thickened and fold in 1 cup diced mixed fruits (fresh or canned and drained), ¼ cup chopped celery, and ¼ cup chopped nuts. Pour into molds and chill. Serves 6.

APPLE-LIME MOLD

Dissolve 1 package lime-flavored gelatin in 1 cup hot water. Add 1½ cups sweetened, unflavored applesauce. Pour into molds and chill. Serves 4 to 6.

Two-Tone Rainbow Salad

INDIVIDUAL PEACH AND BLUEBERRY RINGS

1   package lemon-flavored gelatin
1   cup boiling water
¾   cup liquid from canned Cling peaches
1   No. 303 (1 lb. 1 oz.) can sliced Cling peaches
1   cup sweetened fresh, frozen, or canned blueberries

Dissolve gelatin in boiling water. Add peach liquid and mix. Pour a small amount into the bottoms of 8 well oiled individual ring molds. Let stand until partially set.

Press three Cling peach slices into the bottom of each mold.

Chill remaining gelatin until partially set.

Add the blueberries and any remaining peaches, chopped.

Pour on top of the peach slices in the molds. Chill until set.

Unmold on mounds of cottage cheese which have been arranged on greens. Fill the centers with additional cottage cheese. Serves 8.

Individual Peach And Blueberry Rings

TWO-TONE RAINBOW SALAD

1   No. 2½ can fruit cocktail
1   package fruit-flavored gelatin
1   tablespoon lemon juice
1   package (3 ounces) cream cheese or 1 cup cottage cheese
Mayonnaise

Drain fruit cocktail and measure syrup; add water to make 2 cups liquid. Heat to boiling and dissolve gelatin in hot liquid. Add lemon juice.

Arrange drained fruit cocktail in a 1-quart ring mold. Pour in 1 cup of gelatin mixture; chill until firm.

Meanwhile, mix together until smooth the remaining gelatin and cream cheese (or cottage cheese). Pour over firm gelatin and fruit mixture in the mold and chill. Turn out upside-down on plate and serve with mayonnaise. Serves 6 to 8.

Lemonade Layered Salad With Melon Balls

LEMONADE LAYERED SALAD WITH MELON BALLS

First Layer:

1   tablespoon (1 envelope) unflavored gelatin
¼   cup cold water
½   cup hot water
1   6-ounce can frozen concentrate for lemonade
½   cup salad dressing

Soak gelatin in cold water 5 minutes. Add hot water and stir until gelatin is completely dissolved. Add undiluted concentrate for lemonade. Mix well.

Then add salad dressing and stir, or whip with rotary beater, until dressing and gelatin mixture are thoroughly blended.

Pour into 5 x 9-inch loaf pan which has been rinsed with cold water or oiled. Chill in refrigerator until firm before adding second layer.

Second Layer:

1   tablespoon (1 envelope) unflavored gelatin
¼   cup cold water
½   cup hot water
4   tablespoons frozen concentrate for lemonade
2   tablespoons maraschino cherry juice
1   cup ginger ale (let settle for accurate measurement)
¼   cup sliced maraschino cherries
16   melon balls (fresh or frozen)
Additional melon balls and sprigs of mint for garnish

Soak gelatin in cold water 5 minutes. Add hot water and stir until gelatin is completely dissolved.

Add concentrate for lemonade, cherry juice, and ginger ale, stirring well. Chill until mixture begins to thicken, then add sliced cherries and melon balls and mix well.

Pour mixture on top of chilled first layer of salad. Chill until firm.

Unmold on platter and, before serving, garnish salad loaf.

MOLDED CRUSHED PINEAPPLE

Dissolve 1 package lemon-flavored gelatin in 2 cups hot water. Chill until slightly thickened.

Fold in ½ cup drained crushed canned pineapple, 1 cup diced unpeeled red apple, and ¼ cup chopped pecans.

Turn into individual molds. Chill until firm; unmold. Serves 4 to 6.

Hidden Apricot Salad

MASTER FRUIT SALAD MOLD

1   tablespoon (1 envelope) unfla-
      vored gelatin
1/4   cup cold water
1   cup hot fruit juice or water
1/4   cup lemon juice
1/4   cup sugar
1/4   teaspoon salt
1 1/2 cups canned or fresh fruit (below)

Soften gelatin in cold water 5 minutes. Add hot fruit juice or water and stir until dissolved.

Add lemon juice, sugar and salt. Chill until syrupy.

Fold in diced fruits. Rinse mold in cold water. Line bottom with thinly sliced fruits. Pour in thickened mixture. Chill until firm.

Unmold on lettuce. Serve with desired dressing. Serves 6.

Master Fruit Salad
Mold Variations

1. 1/2 cup diced apples, 1/2 cup cut up orange segments, 1/4 cup chopped dates, and 1/4 cup chopped nuts.

2. 1/2 cup each diced grapefruit, orange sections, and diced canned pineapple.

3. 1/2 cup each diced orange sections, diced pears, and peaches, fresh or canned.

4. 3/4 cup diced apple, 1/2 cup chopped celery, and 1/4 cup chopped nuts.

5. 1/2 cup each diced canned pineapple, diced apple, and sliced strawberries.

6. 1/2 cup each diced canned pineapple, shredded raw carrot, and shredded new cabbage.

7. 3/4 cup each diced pears, fresh or canned, and diced cucumber.

8. 3/4 cup each diced canned pineapple and diced raw cucumber.

9. 1/2 cup each sliced bananas, diced orange sections, and white grapes.

10. 1/2 cup each sliced red cherries, diced melon, and diced orange sections.

11. 1 1/2 cups of cantaloupe and honeydew melon balls.

Harvest Fruits In Wine Jelly

HIDDEN APRICOT SALAD

1   can (1 pound, 14 ounces) apricot
      halves, drained
1   package orange gelatin
1   cup boiling apricot syrup
1/2   cup water
1   package (3 ounces) cream cheese,
      softened
1   tablespoon salad dressing (see
      note below)
1   cup evaporated milk

Drain and save syrup from apricot halves. Measure 1 cup apricot syrup and heat to boiling. Dissolve gelatin in hot syrup. Stir in water and allow to cool slightly.

Meanwhile, fill drained apricot halves with a mixture of creamed cheese and salad dressing. Put the halves together and place whole apricots in bottom of a 1-quart ring mold.

Stir evaporated milk into cooled gelatin mixture. (Mixture may be a little curdled but becomes smooth when chilled.) Pour gelatin mixture over stuffed apricots. Refrigerate until firm. To serve, unmold and garnish with lettuce.

Note: Use salad dressing that comes in a jar, not a bottle.

HARVEST FRUITS IN WINE JELLY

1   package lime-flavored gelatin
1   package lemon-flavored gelatin
2   cups hot water
Juice of 2 fresh limes
1   cup sauterne, rhine, chablis, or any
      white wine
3/4   cup boiled salad dressing
1/2   cup diced unpeeled apples
1/2   cup diced fresh pears
1/2   cup seeded grapes
1/2   cup walnuts or pecans
Lettuce
Fruits for garnish

Dissolve gelatin in hot water. Cool. Add lime juice and wine. Chill slightly.

Divide in 2 portions. Add salad dressing to first half of gelatin mixture and allow to congeal slightly.

Rinse a ring mold in cold water and pour enough of second half of gelatin mixture in mold to just cover bottom. Set in refrigerator to congeal slightly.

Arrange a design of fruits and nuts on the layer of gelatin. Add remaining fruits to rest of gelatin and pour over design layer. Chill.

Whip gelatin-salad dressing mixture with rotary beater until smooth. Pour into ring mold. Chill until firm.

Unmold on large salad plate. Fill center of ring with crisp lettuce. Garnish platter with pears and grapes. Serves 8.

MOLDED PINEAPPLE-CUCUMBER
SALAD CHABLIS

2   tablespoons (2 envelopes) unfla-
      vored gelatin
1/2   cup cold water
1   9-ounce can crushed pineapple
1 1/2 cups chablis wine
2   tablespoons lemon juice
1/2   cup sugar
1   teaspoon salt
1   green pepper, minced
1   cup finely diced cucumber

Soften gelatin in cold water 5 minutes.

Drain pineapple and to the juice add wine, lemon juice, and enough water to make 2 cups liquid. Bring this to boil; add soaked gelatin, sugar, and salt; stir until gelatin and sugar are dissolved; chill until slightly thickened.

Fold in drained pineapple, green pepper, and cucumber; pour into ring mold or individual molds; chill until firm.

Unmold and surround with crisp salad greens and serve with mayonnaise. Serves 6.

DELLA ROBBIA WREATH

2   tablespoons (2 envelopes) plain
      gelatin
1/2   cup cold water
1   can (1 pound, 14 ounces) fruit
      cocktail
1/3   cup lemon juice
1   cup canned cranberry sauce
Curly endive

Soften gelatin in cold water. Drain syrup from fruit cocktail and add water, if necessary, to make 2 1/2 cups. Heat. Add gelatin to syrup mixture and stir until dissolved. Add lemon juice.

Pour a little of the gelatin mixture into 9-inch ring mold; chill until partially set; arrange a wreath of fruit cocktail in it. Chill until firm.

Divide remaining gelatin mixture into two equal parts. To one part, add cranberry sauce; to the other fruit cocktail.

Spoon cranberry portion into ring mold, chill until firm. Spoon fruit cocktail into ring mold; chill until firm. Unmold on bed of curly endive. Makes one 9-inch ring mold.

Della Robbia Wreath

CRANBERRY SALAD MOLD

1 cup sugar
1 cup water
2 cups fresh cranberries
1 tablespoon (1 envelope) unflavored gelatin
½ cup cold water
½ teaspoon salt
½ cup diced celery
½ cup chopped nuts

Make cranberry sauce by combining sugar and 1 cup water. Boil 5 minutes. Add cranberries. Cook without stirring until all skins pop open, about 5 minutes.

Soften gelatin in cold water. Add to hot cranberries with salt. Stir until gelatin is dissolved. Strain.

Chill until mixture is consistency of unbeaten egg whites.

Stir in celery and chopped nuts. Pour into individual molds. Chill until firm.

Unmold on salad greens. Garnish with whole nutmeats. Serve with mayonnaise. Serves 6.

Variation: Canned cranberry jelly, (1½ cups) may be used in place of fresh cranberry sauce. Either may also be used without straining.

SPICY FRUIT RING

1 No. 2½ can (3½ cups) fruit cocktail
1 3-inch stick cinnamon
1 teaspoon whole cloves
1 teaspoon whole allspice
2 envelopes (2 tablespoons) unflavored gelatin
⅓ cup lemon juice

Drain fruit cocktail. Simmer syrup with spices 10 minutes. Strain out spices, measure syrup and add water to make 3½ cups liquid. Heat.

Soften gelatin in lemon juice and dissolve in hot liquid. Cool until slightly thickened.

Fold in fruit cocktail. Turn into 8½-inch ring mold and chill until firm.

Unmold and garnish with watercress. Fill ring with chicken salad. Garnish with avocado balls and slivered almonds. Serves 8.

Spicy Fruit Ring

AVOCADO SALAD RING MOLD

1½ tablespoons (1½ envelopes) unflavored gelatin
¼ cup cold water
2½ cup tomato juice or purée
2 bay leaves
5 whole cloves
¼ cup chopped onion
½ teaspoon salt
Pepper
Few drops of Tabasco sauce
2 avocados
½ cup diced celery
Lettuce hearts

Soften gelatin in cold water. Combine tomato juice or purée, bay leaves, cloves, onion, salt, pepper, and Tabasco sauce. Boil 5 minutes and strain. Add softened gelatin and stir until dissolved. Cool.

When gelatin begins to set, stir in 1 cubed avocado and celery. Mold in ring mold.

To serve, fill center of ring with lettuce hearts and remaining avocado sliced. Serve with desired dressing. Serves 6 to 8.

Variations:

Substitute any flavored gelatin mold, and vary form of avocado pieces as desired.

Emerald Mold: Lime gelatin, sliced stuffed olives and cocktail onions, and diced cucumbers.

Waldorf Mold: Lemon gelatin, diced apple, finely cut celery, and a few walnuts or almonds.

Seafood Mold: Lime or lemon gelatin flavored with lemon juice and condiments, and seafood.

Nectar Mold: Apricot, plum, nectarine, or berry gelatin base, bananas, and pineapple.

SELF-LAYERING SALAD

2 packages orange-flavored gelatin
2 cups hot water
2 cups cold water
¼ teaspoon almond extract
2 cups sliced canned Cling peaches, drained (No. 2½ can)
3 medium bananas, sliced

Empty gelatin dessert into 2-quart bowl. Add hot water and stir until gelatin dessert has dissolved.

Add cold water and almond extract to gelatin mixture. Cool and pour into a lightly oiled 9½ x 5¼ x 2¾-inch loaf pan.

Add peaches and banana slices to gelatin mixture. Be sure bananas are coated with gelatin mixture. Stir to distribute fruit evenly. Chill in refrigerator until firm.

Peaches will sink to bottom of loaf pan and bananas will float, making a self-layered salad. Serves 6 to 8.

Party Fruit Ring Mold

PARTY FRUIT RING MOLD

2 packages lemon-flavored gelatin
1½ cups hot water
2 cups fruit syrup (drained from peaches and pineapple)
Peach halves, drained
Pineapple slices, canned, drained
Dark sweet cherries, drained
Salad greens

Dissolve gelatin in hot water. Add fruit syrup and chill mixture until slightly thickened.

Pour ½ cup gelatin into the bottom of an 8-inch ring mold (1½ quarts) and chill until almost firm.

Set pineapple slices in gelatin with a dark sweet cherry in the center and pour in gelatin just to cover. Chill until firm.

Stand peach halves upright against sides of mold and place cherries above pineapple slices.

Pour in gelatin to cover peaches about one-half and chill until firm.

Add remaining gelatin and chill thoroughly. Unmold and garnish with salad greens. Serve with a whipped cream dressing. Serves 6 to 8.

SPICED PEACH SOUFFLÉ SALAD

1½ cups peach juice
4 whole cloves
¼ teaspoon cinnamon
2 tablespoons vinegar
2 tablespoons sugar
1 package orange-flavored gelatin
Mayonnaise
2½ cups chopped canned peaches

Combine peach juice, cloves, cinnamon, vinegar, and sugar. Heat just to boiling.

Empty gelatin into small bowl. Pour hot liquid through fine strainer and over gelatin; stir until gelatin is dissolved.

Add mayonnaise and blend at a medium to high speed on mixer or with rotary beater.

Pour into ice tray. Chill in freezer compartment of refrigerator about ½ hour or until set but not icy.

Empty mixture into small mixer bowl and beat at a high speed until smooth and fluffy. Fold in chopped peaches.

Pour into 1-quart lightly oiled mold. Chill in fresh foods compartment of refrigerator until firm, about 1 hour. Serves 6 to 8.

Tawny Salad Molds

TAWNY SALAD MOLDS

1 No. 2½ can fruit cocktail
1½ tablespoons (1½ envelopes) unflavored gelatin
3 tablespoons lemon juice
1 6-ounce can frozen orange juice
Salad greens

Drain syrup from fruit cocktail, measure, and add water to make 1½ cups
liquid. Heat.

Soften gelatin in ⅓ cup cold water
and dissolve in hot syrup. Stir in lemon
juice and undiluted orange juice. Cool
until slightly thickened.

Fold in fruit cocktail. Turn into
molds and chill until firm.

Unmold on salad greens and garnish
with additional fruit cocktail as desired.
Makes 8 6-ounce molds.

BANANA GELATIN SALAD

1 package fruit-flavored gelatin or 1
tablespoon (1 envelope) unflavored gelatin
2 ripe bananas
Salad greens
Salad dressing

Mix gelatin according to package
directions. Chill only until slightly
thickened.

Partly fill 1 pint-sized mold with gelatin. Peel bananas, slice and arrange on
top of gelatin. Fill mold with remaining
gelatin. Chill until firm.

Unmold. Garnish with additional
slices of ripe banana or other fruit if
desired. Garnish with crisp salad greens.
Serve with sour cream, mayonnaise, or
a tart French-style salad dressing.

Serves 4 to 6.

Note: Four to six individual molds may
be used in place of 1 large mold.

Banana Gelatin Salad

APPLE SALAD MOLD

1 package cherry-flavored gelatin
1 cup hot water
¼ cup red cinnamon candies
¾ cup boiling water
½ cup chopped peeled apples
½ cup chopped celery
½ cup chopped walnuts

Dissolve gelatin in hot water. Add
cinnamon candies to boiling water; stir
until dissolved. Add to gelatin. Chill
until slightly thickened.

Add apples, celery, and walnuts.
Pour into 6 or 8 individual molds; chill
until firm.

Unmold and surround with crisp lettuce. Serve with a sweet dressing. Serves
6 to 8.

AVOCADO-GRAPEFRUIT SALAD

1 package lemon-flavored gelatin
2 cups hot water
1 avocado, peeled and sliced
1 grapefruit, peeled and sectioned
Lettuce
Thin cantaloupe slices
French dressing

Dissolve the gelatin in the hot water.
Cool. Arrange avocado slices and grapefruit sections in the bottom of a 1-quart
mold. Add enough gelatin to cover and
chill until firm.

Chill the remaining gelatin until
slightly thickened and fold in the remaining avocado slices and grapefruit
sections. Pour over the firm gelatin in
the mold. Chill until firm.

Unmold and surround with lettuce.
Garnish with cantaloupe slices. Serve
with French dressing. Serves 4.

WHITE BEAUTY MOLD

4 slightly beaten egg yolks
1 cup milk
1 teaspoon unflavored gelatin
2 tablespoons lemon juice
2 cups heavy cream, whipped
1 No. 2 can (2½ cups) pineapple tidbits, drained
1 No. 303 can (2 cups) white cherries,
pitted and halved
¾ pound (about 48) marshmallows,
cut in fourths
2 cups chopped blanched almonds

Mix egg yolks with milk in double
boiler; cook, stirring constantly, until
thick.

Soften gelatin in lemon juice; dissolve in hot mixture. Cool slightly. Fold
in whipped cream and remaining ingredients.

Turn into 11 x 7 x 1½-inch pan and
chill until firm. Cut in squares. Cut
each square in half diagonally.

Serve 2 of the triangles on each plate
on a bed of endive. Serves 6 to 8.

RASPBERRY FRUIT RING

1 package raspberry-flavored gelatin
2 cups hot water
1 cup pitted white cherries
1 cup diced canned pineapple
1 cup orange sections

Dissolve gelatin in hot water. Chill
until slightly thickened.

Add well drained fruit. Pour into a
1¼-quart ring mold and chill until
firm.

Unmold and garnish with curly endive. Fill center with mayonnaise or
salad dressing. Serves 6 to 8.

GREENGAGE-LIME MOLD

Dissolve 1 package lime-flavored gelatin in 1 cup hot water. Add 1 cup plum
juice and water, and 2 cups canned
greengage plums. Chill. Serves 4 to 6.

GINGER ALE-GRAPE MOLD

Dissolve 1 package lemon-flavored
gelatin in 1 cup hot grape juice. Cool.
Add 1 cup ginger ale. Turn into molds
and chill. Serves 4 to 5.

STRAWBERRY BAVARIAN SLIMMER

1 package strawberry-flavored gelatin
¼ cup sugar
1 package frozen strawberries,
thawed and drained
⅓ cup ice water
1 tablespoon lemon juice
⅓ cup non-fat dry milk

Combine gelatin and sugar. Make
gelatin according to label directions,
using 1 cup hot water. Add ½ cup berry
syrup. Cool.

Add berries and chill until slightly
thickened.

Combine ice water and lemon juice,
sprinkle non-fat dry milk over top. Beat
until stiff, 8 to 10 minutes.

Fold into thickened gelatin mixture.
Turn into 1-quart mold and chill until
firm. Serves 8.

Strawberry Bavarian Slimmer

TOP-AND-BOTTOM FRUIT LOAF

2   packages fruit-flavored gelatin
1¾ cups boiling apricot juice and water
2   tablespoons lemon juice
2   cups cold water
1½ cups drained apricots, cut small
1   cup seeded Tokay grape halves
1½ cups sliced apples
2   firm bananas, sliced

Dissolve gelatin in hot apricot juice (measure juice drained from apricots and add water to measure 1¾ cups; heat to boiling). Add lemon juice and cold water. Cool completely but do not chill.

Lightly oil loaf pan (8 x 3½ x 2½-inches); place apricots and grapes in layer over bottom. Pour in cooled gelatin.

Place sliced apples and bananas in layer on top; pressing fruit just below surface of gelatin. Chill until firm. Fruits will stay in place with layer of clear gelatin between.

Cut in slices and serve on watercress with a fruit salad dressing. Serves 8.

EASTER BONNET SALAD

2   packages lime-flavored gelatin
4   cups boiling water
Salad greens
1   cup mayonnaise
3   tablespoons orange juice
Maraschino cherries

Dissolve gelatin in 4 cups boiling water. Pour 3 cups into a 7-inch round mold which has been rinsed in cold water. Place in refrigerator to set.

Allow remaining cup of liquid to chill until thick and syrupy. Whip with a rotary beater until light and fluffy. Pile into a 5-inch round mold and allow to set until firm.

Unmold plain gelatin on a bed of lettuce. Unmold whipped gelatin on top of larger one.

With a pastry tube, decorate "bonnet" with ¼ cup mayonnaise. Garnish with maraschino cherries.

Serve with ¾ cup mayonnaise combined with orange juice. Fresh fruit makes a delicious accompaniment. Serves 6 to 8.

Easter Bonnet Salad

GRAPEFRUIT-SAUTERNE MOLD

2   tablespoons (2 envelopes) unflavored gelatin
Water
2   large or 3 medium grapefruit
½ cup honey
Dash of salt
¾ cup sauterne wine
⅓ cup lemon juice

Soften gelatin in ½ cup cold water 5 minutes.

Peel grapefruit, and cut in segments, reserving all juice. Add enough water to juice to make 2 cups; heat to boiling.

Add gelatin, and stir until dissolved. Add honey, salt, sauterne, and lemon juice; blend well. Cool until mixture begins to thicken.

Fold in grapefruit segments.

Pour into oiled, 2-quart ring mold; chill until firm.

Unmold onto salad greens. Serve with French dressing. Serves 6.

GOLDEN SALAD MOLD

1   tablespoon (1 envelope) unflavored gelatin
¼ cup cold water
¼ cup sugar
¼ teaspoon salt
1   cup hot pineapple syrup or juice
¼ cup cold orange juice
¼ cup vinegar
¾ cup coarsely grated raw carrots
¾ cup orange sections, cut into small pieces
1½ cups drained canned pineapple, cut into small pieces

Soften gelatin in cold water. Add sugar, salt, and hot pineapple syrup. If necessary add water to pineapple syrup to complete measurement. Stir until dissolved.

Add orange juice and vinegar. Chill until consistency of unbeaten egg whites. Stir in carrots, oranges, and pineapple.

Pour into mold. Or, if individual molds are used, place 1 teaspoon clear jelly in bottom of each. When nearly firm, place on it 1 tablespoon mayonnaise. When this is firm fill molds with salad mixture. Chill until firm.

Unmold on salad greens. Decorate with pineapple. Serve with mayonnaise or salad dressing, if desired. Serves 6.

CHERRY-OLIVE MOLD

Dissolve 1 package cherry-flavored gelatin in 1 cup hot water. Add 1 cup cherry juice and cold water.

When slightly thickened, add 1½ cups pitted sour red cherries (slightly sweetened), ¼ cup chopped pickle, and ¼ cup sliced stuffed olives. Chill. Serves 6.

Cranberry-Orange Salad

CRANBERRY-ORANGE SALAD

1   tablespoon (1 envelope) unflavored gelatin
2   tablespoons cold water
1   cup orange juice, heated to boiling
⅔ cup evaporated milk, chilled icy cold
1   teaspoon lemon juice
1   12-ounce package frozen cranberry orange relish, thawed

Soak gelatin in cold water and dissolve in hot orange juice. Chill until mixture is of a jelly-like consistency.

Meanwhile, chill a bowl and beater and chill evaporated milk in refrigerator tray until ice crystals form around edge.

Beat evaporated milk in chilled bowl until it forms peaks; add lemon juice, and beat until stiff. Fold whipped evaporated milk and cranberry-orange relish into gelatin.

Pour into an oiled star-shaped mold and chill until set.

Unmold on greens and garnish with orange slices and cranberry sauce. Serves 6.

GUACAMOLE RING MOLD

2   tablespoons (2 envelopes) unflavored gelatin
½ cup cold water
1¼ cups hot water
6   tablespoons lemon juice
2   tablespoons sugar
½ teaspoon salt
3   avocados, sieved
¾ cup mayonnaise

Soften gelatin in cold water and dissolve in hot water. Add lemon juice, sugar, and salt. Cool.

Add avocado and mayonnaise and stir only until blended. Turn into 5-cup ring mold and chill until firm.

Unmold and garnish with avocado slices and parsley. Fill center with marinated fruits. Serves 10.

Ginger Guacamole Ring Mold: Fold ⅓ cup minced preserved ginger or chutney in with mayonnaise. Fill center with poultry or fruit salad.

Zesty Guacamole Ring Mold: Omit sugar from recipe and add 1 teaspoon chili powder, juice of 1 clove garlic, 1 teaspoon minced onion, and 1 green or red pepper, minced. Serve with fish, meat, poultry, or vegetable salad.

FRUIT SALAD MOLD WITH CURRY MAYONNAISE

1   package orange-flavored gelatin
1   cup boiling water
1/2 cup orange juice
1/4 cup grapefruit juice
1   tablespoon lemon juice
1/2 cup orange sections
1/2 cup grapefruit sections
1   cup mayonnaise
1   to 2 teaspoons curry powder

Dissolve gelatin in boiling water. Cool.

Add fruit juices, and let stand until partially thickened.

Add orange and grapefruit sections. Pour into mold rinsed in cold water, and chill until firm.

Unmold, and serve with mayonnaise combined with curry powder. Serves 4.

GRAPEFRUIT-CUCUMBER SALAD

1   package lemon-flavored gelatin
1 1/2 cups hot water
1/2 teaspoon salt
1   tablespoon lemon juice
1   grapefruit, peeled and diced
1   cup peeled, diced cucumber, drained
1/2 cup chopped celery
1   tablespoon chopped pimiento

Dissolve gelatin in hot water. Add salt and lemon juice. Chill until slightly thickened.

Add grapefruit, cucumber, celery, and pimiento. Pour into a 1-quart mold and chill until firm.

Unmold and surround with crisp lettuce. Serve with sour cream dressing. Serves 4 to 6.

GRAPEFRUIT MOLDS WITH AVOCADO

1   package lime-flavored gelatin
2   cups hot water
1   grapefruit, peeled and sectioned
1   avocado
Lettuce
Mayonnaise or salad dressing

Dissolve the gelatin in the hot water. Pour into 4 individual molds in each of which place 2 sections of grapefruit. Chill until firm.

Cut the avocado in half crosswise; remove the pit; peel and slice.

Unmold each serving on lettuce on a salad plate and surround with slices of avocado.

Garnish the slices with mayonnaise or salad dressing forced through a pastry tube. Serves 4.

PINEAPPLE-COTTAGE CHEESE SALAD

Dissolve 1 package lemon- or lime-flavored gelatin in 1 cup hot water. Add 1 cup cold water. Cool.

Add 1 cup seasoned cottage cheese and 1/2 cup drained crushed canned pineapple. Pour into mold rinsed in cold water and chill until firm.

Unmold on crisp lettuce and garnish with mayonnaise. Serves 6.

STUFFED CHERRY SALAD MOLD

1   3-ounce package cream cheese
1/2 cup chopped nuts
1   cup drained pitted Bing cherries
1   package lemon-flavored gelatin
1   cup hot cherry juice
1   cup grapefruit juice
1   grapefruit, peeled and sectioned
Bibb lettuce

Combine cream cheese and nuts. Stuff cherries with this mixture.

Dissolve gelatin in hot cherry juice. Add grapefruit juice.

Arrange cherries and grapefruit sections in bottom of 1-quart mold; add enough gelatin to cover and chill until firm.

Chill remaining gelatin until slightly thickened. Pour into mold. Chill until firm.

Unmold and garnish with lettuce. Serve with sweetened mayonnaise. Serves 4 to 6.

GRAPEFRUIT-CHEESE MOLD

1 1/2 tablespoons (1 1/2 envelopes) unflavored gelatin
1 1/2 cups unsweetened grapefruit juice
1/2 cup lime juice
1/2 cup sugar
1/2 cup finely diced celery
1   3-ounce package cream cheese

Soften gelatin in 1/2 cup of grapefruit juice. Dissolve over hot water. Add to the remaining grapefruit juice. Add the lime juice and sugar. Chill until slightly thickened.

Add the celery to half of this gelatin mixture and pour into a 1-quart ring mold. Chill until firm.

Gradually add the remaining gelatin mixture to the cream cheese, blending until smooth. Chill until slightly thickened. Pour over the firm gelatin in the mold. Chill until firm.

Unmold on a platter and garnish with watercress. Serve with mayonnaise or salad dressing. Serves 4 to 6.

COTTAGE CHEESE AND CANTALOUPE SOUFFLÉ SALAD

1   package lime-flavored gelatin
1   cup hot water
1/2 cup cold water
1   tablespoon lemon juice
1/2 cup mayonnaise
1   cup cottage cheese
1 1/2 cups diced cantaloupe

Empty gelatin into small bowl; pour hot water over it and stir until dissolved.

Add cold water, lemon juice, and mayonnaise. Blend ingredients at a medium to high speed on mixer or with rotary beater.

Pour into ice tray. Chill in freezer compartment of refrigerator about 1/2 hour or until set but not icy. Empty mixture into small bowl and beat at high speed until smooth and fluffy.

Fold in cottage cheese and cantaloupe. Pour into 1-quart lightly oiled mold. Chill in fresh food compartment of refrigerator until firm, about 1 hour. Serves 6 to 8.

CRANBERRY-LEMON MOLD

Dissolve 1 package lemon-flavored gelatin in 1 cup boiling water.

Put 1 cup raw cranberries through food chopper and add 1 cup orange juice and 1/2 cup sugar. Add to cooled gelatin.

Pour into mold and chill. Serves 6.

PEACH AND GRAPE EMERALD SALAD

2   packages lime-flavored gelatin
1   cup boiling water
1   cup liquid from canned cling peach slices
2   cups cold water
1   No. 303 (1 pound, 1 ounce) can sliced cling peaches
1   cup red or green grapes, seeded and halved
1   red maraschino cherry

Dissolve gelatin in boiling water. Add peach liquid and cold water and mix well. Pour a small amount of this mixture into bottom of a well-oiled 6-cup mold. Let chill until partially set.

When set, press peaches into gelatin in bottom of mold and place a cherry in center. Chill remaining gelatin until partially set also.

Dice any peach pieces that are not used in decoration. Then add sliced grapes and diced peach slices. Pour into the mold and chill until set.

Unmold on a serving plate and surround with lettuce leaves filled with cottage cheese. Serves 8 to 10.

Peach and Grape Emerald Salad

Miscellaneous Gelatin Molds

MACARONI AND CHEESE MOLD

1 tablespoon (1 envelope) unflavored gelatin
½ cup cold water
¾ cup hot water
1 cup grated American cheese
1 tablespoon lemon juice
2 teaspoons grated onion
1 teaspoon salt
2 tablespoons chopped parsley
1 tablespoon chopped pimiento
½ cup diced celery
1½ cups cooked, broken macaroni
½ cup mayonnaise or salad dressing

Soften gelatin in cold water. Add hot water. Stir constantly until gelatin is dissolved.

Add grated cheese. Stir until cheese has softened.

Stir in lemon juice, grated onion, and salt. Chill until mixture is consistency of unbeaten egg whites.

Stir in remaining ingredients. Pour into 1 large or 6 individual molds. Chill until firm. Unmold on salad greens. Serves 6.

ASPARAGUS-EGG MOLD

1 tablespoon (1 envelope) unflavored gelatin
¼ cup cold water
1 cup hot asparagus liquid
½ teaspoon salt
⅛ teaspoon pepper
1 tablespoon minced onion
2 tablespoons lemon juice
2 cups diced cooked or canned asparagus
4 hard-cooked eggs
1 cup chopped celery
1 cup sour cream

Soften gelatin in cold water and dissolve in hot asparagus liquid. Add salt, pepper, onion, and lemon juice. Cool.

When mixture begins to thicken, fold in asparagus, 3 chopped eggs, celery, and sour cream.

Slice remaining hard-cooked egg and place around side of rinsed mold. Pour asparagus mixture into mold. Chill until firm.

Unmold and garnish with sliced tomatoes. Serve with French dressing. Serves 4 to 6.

Asparagus-Egg Mold

CREAMY RAISIN MUSTARD RING

⅔ cup sugar
1 tablespoon (1 envelope) unflavored gelatin
2 tablespoons dry mustard
1 teaspoon salt
4 eggs
½ cup cider vinegar
1 cup water
1 teaspoon prepared horseradish
1 tablespoon lemon juice
1 cup dark seedless raisins, coarsely chopped
2 tablespoons finely chopped green onion
2 tablespoons finely chopped pimiento
½ cup finely chopped celery
1 cup whipping cream

Combine sugar, gelatin, mustard, and salt. Blend in beaten eggs, vinegar, and water. Cook over simmering water until mixture thickens, about 15 minutes; stir frequently to keep smooth. Add horseradish, lemon juice, and raisins.

Cool. When mixture begins to jell, fold in vegetables and stiffly beaten cream. Spoon into 6-cup ring mold. Chill until firm. Unmold on serving plate. Serves 8.

EGG SALAD MOLD

2 tablespoons (2 envelopes) unflavored gelatin
1 cup cold water
1½ cups mayonnaise or salad dressing
Juice of 1 lemon
½ teaspoon salt
2 drops Tabasco sauce
1 teaspoon grated onion
12 hard-cooked eggs
¼ cup chopped parsley
½ cup finely chopped green pepper or celery

Soften gelatin in cold water. Dissolve over boiling water. Cool slightly.

Add mayonnaise, lemon juice, salt, Tabasco sauce, and grated onion.

Place center slices of hard-cooked egg around inside of oiled 1- to 1½-quart ring mold.

Separate remaining yolks and whites of eggs. Sieve yolks. Chop whites.

Combine yolks and ½ the gelatin mixture; place as a layer in ring mold. Then add parsley and green pepper as a layer. Cover with egg whites mixed with remaining ½ of gelatin mixture. Chill until set.

Unmold on large platter. Fill center of ring with chicken or vegetable salad. Garnish with salad greens. Serve with French dressing. Serves 6 to 8.

Creamy Raisin Mustard Ring

HAM AND MACARONI MOLD

4 ounces macaroni
1 tablespoon (1 envelope) unflavored gelatin
¼ cup cold water
2 tablespoons butter or margarine
2 tablespoons flour
2 cups milk
½ teaspoon salt
¼ cup pickle juice
½ teaspoon Worcestershire sauce
½ cup chopped or sliced stuffed olives
½ cup chopped sweet pickles
1¼ cups diced celery
3 cups ground cooked ham
3 hard-cooked eggs, sliced

Cook macaroni in salted boiling water until tender (about 20 minutes). Drain and rinse thoroughly with cold water; drain.

Soak gelatin in cold water.

Melt butter, blend in flour, add milk, and cook over direct heat, stirring constantly, until sauce boils and thickens; add salt. Remove from heat and stir in softened gelatin until dissolved.

Add pickle juice and Worcestershire sauce, and cool.

Combine cold macaroni with olives, pickles, celery, ham, and eggs, reserving a few center slices of egg and a few olive slices for garnishing. Add cold sauce and mix lightly with other ingredients.

Rinse a 6-cup mold with cold water and arrange reserved egg and olive slices in the bottom in any desired pattern. Pack the salad mixture into mold and chill until firm.

When ready to serve, unmold onto chilled serving plate and garnish with pickle fans and lettuce. Serves 6.

Ham and Macaroni Mold

SALAD DRESSINGS

HINTS ABOUT SALAD DRESSINGS

We have suggested suitable dressings for individual salads in most cases. We advise, however, experimentation with variations of the master recipes to suit the ingredients and your individual taste. The dressing as well as garnishes should enhance the salad with contrasts in color, flavor, and texture.

What type of dressing to choose—sweet or tart, thick or thin—may be determined by your family's taste. Main-dish salads made with meat, fish, poultry, eggs, beans, cheese or potatoes usually call for a mayonnaise-type or cooked salad dressing. But some of these more substantial salads are good with tart French dressing—salad oil combined with lemon juice or vinegar plus seasonings.

Tart French dressing is the most likely choice for vegetable salads and vegetable-fruit combinations. But some vegetable salads may well take a mayonnaise or cooked dressing.

Reserve the sweet, clear French dressings for fruit salads. Mayonnaise made milder with whipped cream or thinned and sweetened with fruit juice is good for fruit salads too.

MAYONNAISE (Master Recipe)

1 whole egg or 2 egg yolks
1 teaspoon dry mustard
1 teaspoon salt
1 teaspoon syrup
Pepper
Cayenne pepper
Dash of paprika
1½ cups cold salad oil
2 tablespoons vinegar or lemon juice

Combine the first 7 ingredients and beat thoroughly. Add oil 1 tablespoon at a time, beating thoroughly after each addition, until half the oil has been added.

Then add remaining oil in larger quantities, and lastly add vinegar or lemon juice. Makes 2 cups.

Note: If the mayonnaise should curdle, wash the beater, beat 1 egg yolk in another bowl, and very slowly add the curdled mayonnaise to the egg yolk, beating constantly to form a new emulsion.

MAYONNAISE VARIATIONS

Use these variations with homemade or purchased mayonnaise.

Caper Mayonnaise: To 1 cup mayonnaise, add a scant ½ cup finely chopped well-washed capers.

Caviar Mayonnaise: To 1 cup mayonnaise add 1 tablespoon caviar.

Horseradish Caviar Mayonnaise: To 1 cup mayonnaise add 1 tablespoon each of drained horseradish and caviar.

Anchovy Caviar Mayonnaise: To 1 cup mayonnaise, add 4 washed, dried, and finely chopped anchovy fillets and 1 tablespoon caviar.

Chili Mayonnaise: To 1 cup mayonnaise add ¼ cup chili sauce, 1½ tablespoons vinegar, ¾ tablespoon Worcestershire sauce, and ¼ teaspoon chopped chives. Serve with fish salads.

Chutney Mayonnaise: To 1 cup mayonnaise add 1½ tablespoons chopped chutney.

Cranberry Mayonnaise: To 1 cup mayonnaise add 2 tablespoons well-beaten cranberry jelly and 1 teaspoon grated orange rind.

Curry Mayonnaise: To 1 cup mayonnaise, add and blend well ½ to 1 teaspoon curry powder, 1 mashed garlic clove, ¼ teaspoon ginger, 1 tablespoon lime juice, and 1 teaspoon honey. Serve with fish or fruit.

Green Mayonnaise: Color mayonnaise with green food coloring or spinach juice.

Honey Cream Dressing: Blend ¼ teaspoon dry mustard with 1 tablespoon honey and ½ teaspoon lemon juice. Add to mayonnaise. Serve with fruit salads.

Horseradish Mayonnaise: To 1 cup mayonnaise add 3 tablespoons prepared horseradish. Serve with cold beef.

Ideal Salad Dressing: To 1 cup mayonnaise add 2 tablespoons condensed tomato soup, ½ tablespoon lemon juice, 1 teaspoon Worcestershire sauce, and 1½ teaspoons powdered sugar.

Nippy Mayonnaise: To 1 cup mayonnaise add 3 teaspoons prepared horseradish, 3 teaspoons prepared mustard and 1 small chopped sweet pickle. Serve with tomato salads, head lettuce, or salad bowl.

Piquante Mayonnaise: To 1 cup mayonnaise add 2 tablespoons each finely chopped olives and pickles and 1 teaspoon each chopped onion and chives.

Ravigotte Mayonnaise: Mix and chop ½ cup watercress, ½ cup parsley, 2 teaspoons chives, 1 tablespoon capers, and 4 anchovies.

Force mixture through fine sieve and add to 1 cup mayonnaise. Serve with fish and vegetable salads.

Red Beet Mayonnaise: To 1 cup mayonnaise add 1 tablespoon strained beet juice and 2 tablespoons finely chopped cooked beets.

Red Mayonnaise: Tint mayonnaise with red food coloring.

Roquefort Mayonnaise: To 1 cup mayonnaise add 2 tablespoons crumbled Roquefort cheese, a few drops Worcestershire sauce, 1 tablespoon French dressing, and 1 tablespoon minced chives.

Rum Cream Mayonnaise: To 1 cup mayonnaise add 1 teaspoon rum, mixed with ½ cup whipped cream, and add ¼ cup chopped toasted almonds. Serve with fruit salads.

Russian Dressing: To 1 cup mayonnaise add 1 chopped hard-cooked egg, ¼ cup chili sauce, and 2 tablespoons chopped green pepper.

MAYONNAISE VARIATIONS

Spicy Mayonnaise: To 1 cup mayonnaise add ¼ teaspoon each Worcestershire sauce, paprika, and dry mustard. Serve with fish, meat, or vegetable salads.

Thousand Island Dressing: To 1 cup mayonnaise add 2 tablespoons chili sauce, 2 tablespoons chopped green pepper, 2 tablespoons pimiento, and 2 tablespoons chopped sweet pickle. Serve with vegetable salads.

Whipped Cream Mayonnaise: Fold 1 cup mayonnaise into ⅓ cup heavy cream, whipped. Serve with fruit salads.

Whipped Cream Fruit Mayonnaise: Fold into 1 cup mayonnaise, ½ cup heavy cream, whipped, and ¼ cup each chopped almonds and currant jelly.

GREEN MAYONNAISE #2
(Sauce Verte)

Use 2 cups mayonnaise; blend in 2 tablespoons parsley, 1 tablespoon chives, 2 tablespoon tarragon, 1 teaspoon dill, and 1 teaspoon chervil, all finely chopped. Let stand in a cool place for 2 hours to blend flavors. Serve with cold fish or shellfish or vegetables. Makes about 2 cups.

FRUIT MAYONNAISE

⅓ cup grapefruit juice
½ cup mayonnaise
1½ teaspoons sugar

Blend thoroughly. Serves 8.

COOKED DRESSING
(Master Recipe)

¼ tablespoon salt
2 tablespoons sugar
1 tablespoon flour
¾ teaspoon dry mustard
Few grains cayenne
2 slightly beaten eggs
2 tablespoons butter or margarine
¾ cup milk
¼ cup vinegar or lemon juice

Sift dry ingredients; add eggs, butter, milk, and vinegar very slowly.

Stir and cook over boiling water until mixture begins to thicken. Strain and cool. Makes about 1 cup.

Note: For a thinner dressing use one egg yolk. Store covered until ready to use.

Cooked Dressing Variations

Almond and Cucumber Dressing: To cooled dressing add ½ cup diced cucumber and ¼ cup blanched and shredded almonds. Serve with fruit salad.

Banana Nut Dressing: To ¼ cup cooked dressing add 3 tablespoons peanut butter and 1 mashed banana. Thin with a little cream, if necessary. Serve with fruit salads.

Chutney Dressing: To ¾ cup cooked dressing add 2 tablespoons chopped chutney and ¼ cup whipped cream. Serve with fruit or vegetable salads.

Cream Dressing: In master recipe omit butter; use 1 cup light cream instead of milk.

Fruit Dressing: In master recipe increase flour to 2 tablespoons. Substitute 1 cup orange juice for milk.

Ham Salad Dressing: To 1 cup cooked dressing add ½ cup minced ham and 1 tablespoon minced green pepper. Serve with any vegetable or green salad.

Honey Dressing: In master recipe, substitute 2 to 4 tablespoons honey for sugar.

Peanut Butter Dressing: Prepare master recipe. Blend ¼ cup peanut butter with hot dressing after removing from heat.

Sardine Cooked Dressing: Skin, bone, and mash 6 sardines. Mix with 1 tablespoon lemon juice. Add to 1 cup cooked dressing. Serve with fish or vegetable salad.

Sour Cream Dressing: Prepare master recipe. Fold in 1 cup whipped sour cream when cool.

Toasted Nut Dressing: Prepare master recipe. Add ⅓ cup toasted chopped nuts when cool. Serve with potato, tomato, or plain fruit salads.

Whipped Cream Dressing: Prepare master recipe. Fold in ½ cup heavy cream, whipped, when cool.

SOUR CREAM DRESSING FOR VEGETABLE OR FRUIT SALADS

1 cup thick sour cream
1 tablespoon lemon juice
1 tablespoon prepared horseradish
2 tablespoons sugar
½ teaspoon salt
⅛ teaspoon dry mustard

Whip sour cream; fold in remaining ingredients. Serve at once. Makes about 2 cups.

SOUR CREAM-CURRY DRESSING FOR FRUIT SALAD

¼ to ½ teaspoon curry powder
1 teaspoon sugar
1 tablespoon lemon juice
2 tablespoons mild vinegar
1 cup sour cream

Blend curry, sugar, lemon juice, and vinegar, then stir into sour cream. Makes about 1 cup.

LOW CALORIE SALAD DRESSING

16 non-caloric sweetening tablets, crushed
2 beaten eggs
2 tablespoons cornstarch
½ teaspoon dry mustard
1 teaspoon celery seed
Salt and pepper
¼ cup lemon juice
2 cups water

Add crushed non-caloric sweetening tablets to eggs and mix well. Add cornstarch, dry mustard, celery seed, salt, and pepper. Add lemon juice and mix well.

Add water. Cook over medium heat, stirring constantly, until mixture begins to thicken. Cool. Makes 40 tablespoons dressing, each containing 5 calories.

Tomato Salad Dressing: To 1 cup of low calorie salad dressing, add 1 cup tomato juice, 1 teaspoon grated onion, 8 non-caloric sweetening tablets, crushed, and 1 teaspoon cornstarch.

Mix well and cook over medium heat, stirring constantly, until mixture thickens. Cool. Makes 32 tablespoons dressing, each containing 5 calories.

Thousand Island Dressing: To 1 cup low calorie salad dressing, add ½ cup each chopped pimiento, chopped olives, chopped dill pickle, and chili sauce or ketchup.

Chop 1 hard-cooked egg fine and add to mixture. Makes 32 tablespoons, each containing 10 calories.

LOW CALORIE SALAD DRESSING #2

1 cup tomato juice
2 tablespoons salad oil
1 tablespoon Worcestershire sauce
¼ teaspoon salt
2 tablespoons vinegar
¼ cup grated onion
2 tablespoons chopped parsley
¼ teaspoon pepper

Combine all ingredients. Chill. Shake thoroughly for serving.

BLUE CHEESE (OR ROQUEFORT) DRESSING

1 cup salad oil
½ cup cider vinegar
1½ teaspoons salt
Few grains cayenne
¼ teaspoon paprika
1½ teaspoons sugar
½ cup crumbled or chopped blue cheese (2 ounces)

Combine all ingredients but the cheese and beat with rotary beater.

Add cheese. Store in covered jar in refrigerator. Stir or shake well before using. Makes 1½ cups.

MASTER ITALIAN DRESSING

1 clove garlic
1/2 teaspoon dry mustard
1/2 teaspoon salt
4 tablespoons wine vinegar
1/2 cup olive oil

Cut garlic clove in half. Mix mustard, salt, garlic, and vinegar thoroughly. Add oil and stir until all ingredients are blended.

Store in covered jar in cold place. Shake well just before using. Makes 3/4 cup.

Variations of Italian Dressing

Roquefort Cheese Italian Dressing: Crumble 2 ounces cheese. Add to dressing just before using.

Gorgonzola Cheese Dressing: Crumble 2 ounces cheese. Add to dressing just before using.

Other Variations: Most of the variations of French or cooked dressing may be used.

LEMON-SHERRY DRESSING FOR FRUIT SALAD

1/4 cup lemon juice
1/8 teaspoon salt
1/4 cup sugar
2 tablespoons dry sherry

Blend lemon juice, salt, and sugar until sugar has dissolved. Add sherry. Makes about 1/2 cup.

YOGHURT SALAD DRESSING

1 8-ounce carton yoghurt
1 teaspoon unsweetened lemon juice
2 to 3 teaspoons prepared mustard
1/4 teaspoon onion salt
1/2 teaspoon liquid artificial sweetener

Combine ingredients in jar. Mix well. Cover and store in refrigerator. Serve with tossed greens or potato salad. Makes 1 cup.

Celery Seed Dressing: Add 1 teaspoon celery seed.

Chive Bacon Dressing: Add 2 tablespoons chopped chives. If desired, add 2 slices crisp, crumbled bacon. Serve with or on vegetables, baked potatoes, salads. Makes about 1 cup.

FRUIT SALAD DRESSING WITH CREAM CHEESE

1 3-ounce package cream cheese
3/4 cup cream
2 tablespoons currant jelly
1 tablespoon lemon juice

Soften the cream cheese with a fork and beat until smooth. Slowly blend in remaining ingredients. Chill 1 hour before serving. Makes about 1 1/4 cups.

WHIPPED CREAM DRESSING
(Master Recipe)

1/2 cup heavy cream
1/4 teaspoon salt
2 tablespoons lemon juice or vinegar
Few grains of pepper

Beat cream until stiff. Fold in other ingredients very slowly. Chill and add to salad just before serving.

Whipped cream dressing may be used as a sweet or savory dressing by the addition of flavorings and seasonings. It may be delicately tinted with a very small amount of liquid or paste food coloring.

Whipped Cream Dressing Variations

Anchovy Cream Dressing: Add 3 anchovy fillets, washed, dried, and minced fine, with 1 teaspoon grated lemon rind to 1 cup whipped cream dressing just before serving.

Caviar Cream Dressing: Add 1 tablespoon red or black caviar and a few drops onion juice to 1 cup whipped cream dressing just before serving.

Ginger Cream Dressing: Add 1 teaspoon chopped, candied ginger and 1 teaspoon grated lemon rind to 1 cup whipped cream dressing just before serving.

Savory Cream Dressing: Add 1/4 teaspoon anchovy paste and a little minced parsley and chives to 1 cup whipped cream dressing just before serving.

Horseradish Cream Dressing: Fold 2 tablespoons grated fresh horseradish into 1 cup whipped cream dressing just before serving. Omit vinegar in master recipe if bottled horseradish is used.

Jelly Cream Dressing: Add 1/2 cup tart red jelly, such as currant, cranberry, or raspberry, to 1 cup whipped cream dressing just before serving.

Mustard Cream Dressing: In master recipe, beat in 1 tablespoon prepared mustard as cream begins to thicken. Add salt to taste.

Nut Cream Dressing: Add 3 tablespoons chopped nuts to 1 cup whipped cream dressing just before serving.

California Cream Dressing: Add 1 tablespoon each chopped dates, figs, and raisins to 1 cup whipped cream dressing just before serving.

Pepper Cream Dressing: Add 1/3 cup finely chopped green pepper and 2 tablespoons finely chopped pimiento to 1 cup whipped cream dressing just before serving.

GREEN GODDESS DRESSING

1 cup mayonnaise
1 clove garlic, minced or grated
3 anchovies, chopped
1/4 cup finely cut chives or green onions with tops
1/4 cup chopped parsley
1 tablespoon tarragon vinegar
1 tablespoon fresh lemon juice
1/2 teaspoon salt
Pepper, coarsely ground
1/2 cup sour cream, whipped

Combine ingredients, folding in the whipped sour cream after the other ingredients have been blended.

Tear iceberg lettuce into bite-sized pieces and toss with a generous amount of dressing. Makes 2 cups.

GARLIC DRESSING

1 1/3 cups salad oil
1/2 cup vinegar
4 cloves garlic, peeled and halved
1 1/2 teaspoons salt
1 teaspoon sugar
1/2 teaspoon dry mustard

Combine ingredients in a jar or bottle. Cover, shake well, and store in refrigerator for several hours to blend flavors.

Shake well before serving. Makes 2 cups.

TOMATO SALAD DRESSING

1 clove garlic, peeled
1 slice soft bread
1 can (1 pound) tomatoes
1/3 cup salad oil
2 tablespoons vinegar
1/2 teaspoon salt
1/4 teaspoon pepper
1 teaspoon sugar
2 teaspoons Angostura aromatic bitters

Cut garlic in 3 or 4 pieces and insert in bread. Let stand half an hour and remove garlic.

Mix tomatoes, oil, vinegar, and seasonings. Add bread and beat until thoroughly mixed. Serve as a dressing for a mixed green salad.

Tomato Salad Dressing

MASTER FRENCH DRESSING

¼ teaspoon dry mustard
⅛ teaspoon freshly ground pepper
¾ teaspoon salt
¼ cup vinegar
¼ to ½ teaspoon paprika
1 teaspoon sugar
¾ cup salad oil

Measure all ingredients into a mixing bowl or glass jar. Beat with a fork or rotary beater or cover jar tightly and shake to mix thoroughly.

French dressing may be made in larger quantities and stored in the refrigerator. Always beat again or shake well just before serving. Makes 1 cup.

Variations of French Dressing

Brandy French Dressing: To master recipe add 2 tablespoons brandy, 2 tablespoons tarragon vinegar, 6 tablespoons olive oil, and salt and pepper to taste.

Chiffonade Dressing: To master recipe add following finely chopped: 2 tablespoons parsley, 2 hard-cooked eggs, 2 tablespoons chopped red pepper, 1 tablespoon each chopped olives and cucumber pickle, and ¼ teaspoon paprika.

Chutney French Dressing: In master recipe, use half lemon juice and half vinegar. Add ¼ cup finely chopped chutney.

Cottage Cheese French Dressing: To master recipe add ¼ to ½ cup cottage cheese and shake.

Cream French Dressing: To master recipe add 2 tablespoons sweet or sour cream.

Cream Cheese French Dressing: Mash 1 3-ounce package cream cheese. Stir in French dressing to form a smooth paste. Add to remainder of French dressing and shake well.

Cucumber French Dressing: To master recipe add 1 cup well drained, grated cucumber. Serve very cold with fish salads.

Curry French Dressing: To master recipe add ¾ teaspoon curry powder before beating.

Egg-Cheese French Dressing: To master recipe add 1 hard-cooked egg (chopped fine), 4 tablespoons grated American cheese, 1 tablespoon each chopped parsley and chives, and 1 tablespoon each chopped green pepper and pimiento.

Foamy French Dressing: Prepare cream French dressing and fold in 1 egg white, beaten until dry but not stiff.

Fruit French Dressing: In master recipe, substitute ¼ cup orange juice for ¼ cup vinegar. Add 1 tablespoon lemon juice. May be sweetened with additional sugar or corn syrup or honey.

Garlic French Dressing: Before preparing master recipe, pare and rub clove of garlic over bottom of bowl. If desired, clove of garlic may be left in dressing about 1 hour.

Ginger French Dressing: To master recipe add 1½ tablespoons finely chopped preserved ginger. Use on fruit salads.

Grapefruit French Dressing: Use grapefruit juice instead of vinegar in master recipe.

Honey French Dressing: In master recipe, omit mustard and pepper. Add ½ cup strained honey and beat until frothy. Use on fruit salads.

Horseradish French Dressing: To master recipe add 2 tablespoons horseradish before serving.

Lemon French Dressing: In master recipe, substitute lemon juice for vinegar.

Lime French Dressing: In master recipe, use equal parts lime and lemon juice, or 3 tablespoons lime and 1 tablespoon lemon juice instead of vinegar.

Mint French Dressing: To master recipe add 1 tablespoon chopped mint.

Olive French Dressing: To master recipe add ¼ cup chopped olives before serving.

Roquefort French Dressing: Crumble ½ cup Roquefort cheese and add to French dressing before serving.

Spanish Dressing: To master recipe add ½ teaspoon chili powder.

Spicy French Dressing: To master recipe add 2 tablespoons prepared mustard and 2 teaspoons Worcestershire sauce.

Swiss Dressing: To master recipe add ¼ cup grated Swiss cheese and ¼ teaspoon Worcestershire sauce.

Tarragon French Dressing: In master recipe, use tarragon vinegar.

Tomato French Dressing: To master recipe add 2 teaspoons tomato juice and a few drops onion juice.

Vinaigrette French Dressing: Follow master recipe. Before beating, add 1 tablespoon chopped pickles, 1 tablespoon minced capers, 1 tablespoon chopped green olives, 1 tablespoon chopped pimiento, 1 teaspoon minced onion, and 1 teaspoon dry mustard.

"TRADITIONAL" FRENCH DRESSING

Many food experts insist this is the only "genuine" French dressing. To ½ cup vinegar (wine, cider, or malt vinegar) add ¾ teaspoon salt and ¼ teaspoon ground white pepper. Stir well with a fork and add 1½ cups olive oil. Beat the mixture with fork until it thickens.

For a garlic flavor, hang a garlic clove by a thread into the bottle containing the vinegar for at least 3 or 4 days before making the dressing.

SPECIAL FRENCH DRESSING

1 clove garlic, grated fine
½ cup sugar
⅓ cup mild vinegar
1 teaspoon Worcestershire sauce
1 small onion, grated
⅔ cup tomato ketchup
1 teaspoon salt
2 cups salad oil

Mix in order given and beat thoroughly. Pour into quart jar. Store in cool place.

LOUIS DRESSING

½ cup chili sauce
½ cup mayonnaise or salad dressing
½ cup creamy French dressing
1 teaspoon Worcestershire sauce

Slowly stir chili sauce into mayonnaise. Add French dressing and Worcestershire sauce. Mix well.

Serve with lettuce and tomato salads. Makes 1½ cups.

LORENZO DRESSING

½ cup French dressing
2 tablespoons chopped watercress
2 tablespoons chili sauce
1 teaspoon minced pimiento
1 teaspoon minced chives or onion

Blend ingredients thoroughly and serve over salad greens. Makes ¾ cup.

BLENDER MAYONNAISE

1 egg
¼ teaspoon dry mustard
½ teaspoon salt
2 teaspoons lemon juice or wine vinegar
⅔ cup vegetable oil or equal amounts of vegetable and olive oil

Combine egg, mustard, and salt in container of electric blender. Cover and blend at high speed for 30 seconds.

Pour in lemon juice or vinegar and, still blending at high speed, pour in oil as slowly as possible. If the mayonnaise thickens too much at any point, add a few more drops of lemon juice or vinegar.

Makes about 1 cup.

SANDWICHES

Sandwich Hints

Bread for Sandwiches

There probably are 10 to 15 different kinds of sandwich bread available from bakeries, besides the long, hard-crusted loaves of Italian and French white bread, and the odd-shaped and unusually flavored loaves to be found in many small bakeries. Rolls, hamburger and frankfurter buns, biscuits, muffins, and fruit breads are excellent for sandwiches.

- For more interesting sandwiches, use different kinds of bread—even in the same sandwich.
- To facilitate slicing and spreading of ordinary sandwiches, use day-old bread of firm texture.
- For rolled sandwiches, use very fresh bread.
- For very thin, dainty sandwiches, buy unsliced bread and cut with a razor-sharp knife into slices not more than 1/4 inch thick. If many sandwiches are to be made, sharpen knife frequently.
- When a lot of sandwiches are to be made without crust, cut the crust from the loaf before slicing. Incidentally, sandwiches will stay moist longer if the crust is left on and there'll be no waste.
- For fancy sandwiches to be cut with cooky cutter, slice the bread lengthwise.

Butter for Sandwiches

- Cream butter or margarine until softened before spreading. Never melt butter. To facilitate creaming, keep butter at room temperature for about an hour.
- Butter prevents the sandwich from becoming soggy when a moist filling is used.
- For savory sandwiches, soften butter with mayonnaise; for sweet sandwiches, with a little cream or whipped cream.

Sandwich Fillings

- Sandwich fillings are often a blend of the cook's ingenuity and whatever there is on hand. The recipes and hints that follow should serve as suggestions—starting points for your imagination. An infinite variety of fillings will be developed from them.
- For additional fillings, refer to the spreads in the appetizer and salad sections. The canapé spreads should be used for dainty, attractive tea sandwiches.
- Use a variety of fillings for contrast in color, flavor, shape, and texture.
- Vegetables, such as cucumber, sliced tomato, and lettuce, should be prepared and added just before serving.
- Sliced fillings such as meat and cheese should be cut very thin and arranged to fit the sandwich.
- For color in fillings, add chopped pimiento, pepper, parsley, olives, or pickle.

To Keep Sandwiches

- If possible, avoid making sandwiches with moist fillings in advance, since the bread tends to become soggy.
- If sandwiches must be made in advance, wrap in waxed paper or slightly dampened cloth.
- To keep sandwiches for an hour or longer, wrap first in waxed paper, then in a damp cloth, and place in refrigerator.
- To prevent an interchange of flavors from various fillings, wrap each variety of sandwich separately in waxed paper.
- Ribbon, checkerboard, loaf, and other sandwiches, which have to be chilled or even frozen in the refrigerator, should always be well wrapped to preserve the flavor and prevent drying out.

Keep Frozen Sandwiches on Hand

- Sandwich fillings that freeze are those made of sliced cooked meat, meat loaf, chicken, or cheese.

- Sandwich spreads also lend themselves to freezing—especially those made of chopped or ground meat, chicken, canned fish (tuna, salmon, etc.), cheese, peanut butter.
- All sandwich fillings should be thoroughly chilled before being used.
- Butter both slices of bread before adding the filling. This will prevent the filling soaking into the bread.
- Work quickly and wrap each sandwich separately in moisture-vapor-proof freezer paper, excluding as much air as possible. Seal or tape and freeze.
- Sandwiches may be stored 2 to 3 months.
- When making sandwiches for the freezer, include a variety of breads such as white, cracked wheat, rye, raisin, or other family preferences.
- Pack sandwiches, right from freezer, in lunchbox.

Vary not only the bread and fillings but also the way you cut the sandwiches.

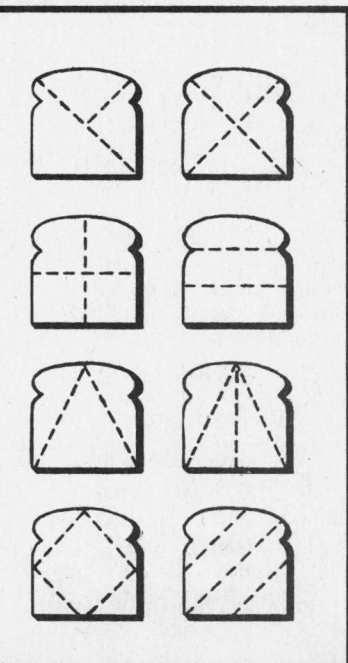

Hot Sandwiches

PICNIC ITALIANOS

1 loaf French bread
2 4½-ounce cans deviled ham
3 tomatoes, sliced
½ teaspoon oregano
4 slices American or Mozzarella cheese

Split bread in two lengthwise. Spread cut slices generously with deviled ham. Top with tomato slices, sprinkle with oregano, then add cheese slices.

Bake in moderate oven (375°F.) until cheese is melted and sandwiches thoroughly heated. Serves 8 to 10.

Suggestions: These may be cooked over an open fire when wrapped in aluminum foil. Especially popular with men and teen-agers. For spicier flavor add chili sauce on top of the cheese.

BARBECUED SANDWICHES

(1) Heat sliced roast beef, pork, ham, turkey, or meat loaf in barbecue sauce. Serve in toasted buns. (2) Cover toasted buns with cold or hot sliced meat and pour hot barbecue sauce over buns.

HOT DOG LOAF

¼ cup chopped onion
2 tablespoons vegetable oil
1 can (8 ounces) tomato sauce
1 tablespoon prepared mustard
2 teaspoons brown sugar
2 teaspoons vinegar
1 teaspoon Worcestershire sauce
1 loaf French bread
½ cup shredded mild natural Cheddar cheese
15 frankfurters, cut in half crosswise

Cook onion in oil until golden. Add tomato sauce and seasonings. Simmer about 10 minutes.

Cut ends off French bread. Cut loaf in ¾-inch slices. Every other cut should be all the way through the crust so that the loaf will separate into sandwiches.

Between the attached slices, spread the sauce and sprinkle in half of the cheese. Insert 3 frank halves, letting uncut ends protrude. Sprinkle with remaining cheese. Wrap loaf in aluminum foil, place on cooky sheet and bake in hot oven (425°F.) 25 minutes. Serve hot. Makes 10 sandwiches.

Hot Dog Loaf

Picnic Italianos

OPEN-FACE SANDWICHES
(Italian Style)

½ pound ground beef
½ pound sausage meat
8 thin slices Mozzarella or Muenster cheese
8 slices brown-and-serve French bread
Oregano

Mix beef and sausage and shape in 8 thin patties. Broil under medium heat until well browned on both sides.

Put a slice of cheese on each slice of bread. Sprinkle with oregano. Broil until cheese is slightly melted.

While still hot, press a meat patty on each slice.

Makes 8 small sandwiches.

CHICKEN SANDWICH ROYAL

8 slices buttered toast
Slices of cooked chicken
Slices of tomato
Salt
1 cup grated Cheddar cheese
2 teaspoons Worcestershire sauce

Lay slices of buttered toast in shallow baking pan. Place sliced chicken on toast. Place slices of tomato on the chicken. Sprinkle with salt.

Spread thickly with grated cheese mixed with Worcestershire sauce.

Broil quickly until cheese is melted and browned. Serve at once. Makes 8.

CHEESE AND CHIPPED BEEF SANDWICHES

¼ pound chipped beef, ground or chopped
1 clove garlic, finely minced
1 8-ounce can tomato sauce
¼ pound cheese, grated
1 slightly beaten egg
Dash of cayenne pepper

Combine all ingredients in top of double boiler and cook until cheese melts, stirring constantly. Serve on toasted bread. Serves 6.

HOT ROAST BEEF SANDWICHES

Make sandwiches with toasted bread and slices of roast beef.

Serve on hot plates, with hot gravy poured over the sandwiches. Garnish with a sprig of parsley and a pickle.

CURRY FRIED PORK
SANDWICHES

¼ cup vinegar
4 to 6 slices cooked pork
3 tablespoons flour
2 teaspoons curry powder
½ teaspoon salt
1 tablespoon shortening
4 slices bread
Butter or margarine

Pour vinegar over pork. Let stand 15 to 30 minutes.

Combine flour, curry powder, and salt. Drain pork slices and dip in flour mixture. Fry in melted shortening until crisp.

Place between slices of buttered bread. Serve hot. Serves 2.

SAUTÉED MEAT SANDWICHES

Moisten ground leftover meat with thick white sauce or gravy. Put between slices of bread. Brown on each side in hot fat.

BAKED BEANS AND SALAMI

¼ pound salami
1½ cups canned baked beans with tomato sauce
2 tablespoons chili sauce
2 tablespoons prepared mustard
½ teaspoon minced onion

Cut salami into small bits and combine with remaining ingredients. Mash with a fork.

Spread between slices of bread. Broil the sandwiches, turning to brown both sides.

For Chicken Rabbit Sandwiches, arrange toast in a shallow baking dish; top with thick slices of chicken. Cover with cheese sauce; sprinkle lightly with paprika. Heat under broiler only until cheese sauce begins to brown lightly.

Cheese Strata

CHEESE STRATA

Arrange 6 slices of bread (crusts trimmed) in bottom of rectangular dish.

Place a slice of pasteurized process American cheese on each slice of bread. Cover with 6 slices of bread (crusts trimmed).

Beat 4 eggs. Add 2½ cups milk and salt and pepper.

Pour egg and milk mixture over bread and cheese sandwiches. Let stand an hour.

Bake in slow oven (325°F.) about 40 minutes. Serve plain or with your favorite jelly.

SOUFFLÉED CHEESE SANDWICH

4 to 6 slices of bread
½ teaspoon salt
3 eggs, separated
Dash of pepper
Dash of paprika
½ cup grated sharp cheese

Toast bread (crust removed, if desired) on one side.

Add salt to egg whites and beat until stiff, but not dry.

Add pepper and paprika to yolks. Beat until light. Add cheese and fold into beaten egg whites.

Heap on untoasted side of bread. Place on greased baking sheet. Bake in moderate oven (350°F.) for 15 minutes or until puffy and delicately browned. Serve at once.

Makes 4 to 6 sandwiches, depending upon size of slice and thickness of egg mixture desired.

SAUTÉED TOMATO AND CHEESE

Spread slices of bread with nippy mayonnaise.

Put a slice of tomato and a slice of American cheese between each 2 slices.

Dip in an egg-milk mixture; fry as for French toast.

DENVER OR WESTERN SANDWICH

For each sandwich, fry 1 tablespoon minced onion in butter until slightly browned.

Add 1 tablespoon minced cooked ham and stir in 1 slightly beaten egg.

Cook slowly until firm and season with salt and pepper. Serve hot.

OLIVE-CHEESE SANDWICHES

1 cup ripe olives
1½ cups grated American cheese
⅓ cup mayonnaise
½ teaspoon grated onion
½ teaspoon Worcestershire sauce
6 round French rolls
Butter or margarine
Tomatoes

Cut olives in small pieces. Blend with cheese, mayonnaise, onion, and Worcestershire sauce.

Make 2 cuts part way through each roll from top to bottom, and spread cut edges lightly with butter, then quickly with cheese-olive mixture.

Cut tomatoes in halves and then into thin slices. Put a half slice in each cut.

Place rolls on baking sheet. Bake in moderate oven (375°F.) about 15 minutes. Serve at once. Makes 6 rolls.

Olive-Cheese Sandwiches

CHEESE BARBECUE

Grind together 1 pound Cheddar cheese, ½ green pepper, 1 medium onion, 2 hard-cooked eggs, and 1 cup stuffed olives.

Add ½ can condensed tomato soup and 2 tablespoons melted butter. Mix well.

Spread on bun halves or rye bread and broil.

BROILED COTTAGE CHEESE SANDWICHES

Season cottage cheese with salt and paprika.

Spread on buttered toast. Top with bacon strips and broil slowly until bacon is crisp.

BACON, CHEESE AND TOMATO DOUBLE DECKERS

12 slices white bread
⅓ cup butter or margarine
12 slices American cheese
6 tomato slices
Salt
12 bacon slices

Trim crusts from white bread slices and toast on one side. Spread untoasted side generously with butter.

Cover 6 slices each with a slice of cheese and remaining 6 slices of bread, double-decker fashion.

Put slices of peeled tomato on top of bread, salt, and then top with a slice of cheese.

Place in moderate oven until cheese begins to soften.

Place 2 slices of partially broiled bacon on top. Place under low broiler heat until cheese is thoroughly melted and bacon is crisp.

Makes 6 double-decker sandwiches.

BAKED TURKEY SANDWICH PUFF

8 slices buttered bread
Thin slices cooked turkey
Thin slices American cheese
3 eggs, slightly beaten
1½ cups milk
½ cup sherry
Salt, celery salt, and pepper

Prepare 4 turkey-cheese sandwiches, using bread, turkey, and cheese. Arrange sandwiches in a greased shallow baking pan.

Mix together eggs, milk, sherry, and seasonings. Pour mixture over sandwiches and let stand for hour or so. Bake in slow oven (325°F.) 1 hour.

To serve, separate sandwiches with a sharp knife and lift onto plates with a broad spatula. Serves 4.

Variations: Slices of cooked chicken or ham may be substituted for the turkey in this recipe.

WAFFLE-GRILLED CHEESE SANDWICHES

For each sandwich, place 1 slice of process American cheese between 2 slices of bread.

Brush top and bottom of sandwich with melted buter or margarine.

Put sandwiches in waffle iron until bread is golden brown, and cheese is melted.

Waffle-Grilled Cheese Sandwiches

BARBECUED TUNA BURGERS

1 clove garlic, minced
1 tablespoon butter or margarine
1 can (8 ounces) tomato sauce
2 tablespoons vinegar
1 tablespoon brown sugar
½ teaspoon salt
½ teaspoon dry mustard
½ teaspoon chili powder
1 can (7 ounces) tuna, drained and flaked
4 hamburger buns, split

Cook garlic in butter or margarine 1 minute; add remaining ingredients, except tuna and buns; simmer 5 minutes. Add tuna; heat thoroughly.

Toast buns; spoon barbecued tuna over buns. Makes 4 sandwiches.

HOT FISH SANDWICHES

1 tablespoon fat
1½ tablespoons minced green pepper
1 tablespoon minced onion
2 slightly beaten eggs
¼ cup milk
½ teaspoon salt
¾ cup flaked canned or cooked fish
Toasted rolls

Heat fat and cook green pepper and onion in it until they are tender.

Combine remaining ingredients and add to vegetables. Cook over low heat or boiling water, stirring constantly, until thick and creamy. Serve hot on toasted rolls. Makes 4.

SOUFFLÉED SHRIMP SANDWICH

8 slices enriched bread
2 eggs, separated
4 ounces Cheddar cheese, grated
Dash of pepper
Dash of paprika
1 pound shrimp, cleaned

Trim crusts from bread; toast lightly and cut in half. Beat egg yolks.

Melt cheese in top of double boiler. Gradually add to the beaten egg yolks. Add seasonings and fold this mixture into stiffly beaten egg whites.

Arrange toast points in 4 individual or 1 large greased baking dish. Top with cleaned shrimp, then the sauce.

Bake in slow oven (325°F.) until brown and puffy. Serves 4.

Souffléed Shrimp Sandwich

SALMON SANDWICH FONDUE

1 8-ounce can salmon
1 cup minced celery
¼ cup mayonnaise
1 tablespoon prepared mustard
¼ teaspoon salt
12 thin slices whole wheat bread
6 slices American Cheddar cheese
3 beaten eggs
2½ cups milk
2 teaspoons Worcestershire sauce
½ teaspoon Ac'cent

Drain salmon; flake, removing bones; add celery.

Blend mayonnaise, mustard, and salt; add to salmon mixture; mix well.

Spread between bread slices to make 6 sandwiches. Arrange sandwiches in shallow baking dish; top each with slice of cheese.

Combine eggs, milk, Worcestershire sauce, and Ac'cent. Pour over sandwiches.

Bake in slow oven (325°F.) 45 minutes. Makes 6 sandwiches.

FRENCH-TOASTED TUNA CHEESE SANDWICHES

1 7-ounce can tuna flakes
1 teaspoon lemon juice
½ cup diced celery
3 tablespoons mayonnaise
4 tablespoons butter or margarine
12 slices bread
6 slices American cheese
2 eggs, beaten
½ teaspoon salt
1 cup milk
2 tablespoons butter or margarine

Combine tuna flakes, lemon juice, celery, and mayonnaise.

Butter slices of bread on one side; spread 6 buttered slices with tuna mixture.

Top each with a slice of cheese and place remaining slices on top; chill.

Combine eggs, salt, and milk; stir to blend. Dip each sandwich in mixture to coat both sides.

Melt butter in frying pan or on griddle over medium heat and lightly brown sandwiches on both sides, turning only once. Serve immediately. Serves 6.

Fish-Stick Buns: Prepare frozen fish sticks according to package directions. Split frankfurter buns and toast. On each bun half, place a lettuce leaf and two fish sticks. Put a heaping tablespoon of tartar sauce on the sticks. Cover with remaining bun halves. Serve while fish sticks are warm.

OYSTER CLUB SANDWICHES

12 slices bacon
1 pint oysters
½ cup flour
½ teaspoon salt
⅛ teaspoon pepper
12 lettuce leaves
12 slices tomato
½ cup mayonnaise
18 slices buttered toast

Fry bacon and drain on absorbent paper.

Drain oysters, roll in flour seasoned with salt and pepper. Fry in bacon fat. When brown on one side, turn and brown on other side. Cooking time is about 5 minutes. Drain on absorbent paper.

Arrange lettuce, oysters, bacon, tomatoes, and mayonnaise between 3 slices of toast. Fasten with wooden picks. Serves 6.

FISH BUN BROIL

12 long frankfurter buns
6 large sardines or 6 pickled herring fillets
1 egg white, beaten stiff
¾ cup mayonnaise
2 tablespoons chopped onion
Melted butter or margarine

Pull buns apart lengthwise. Fit sardines or divide herring fillets and place on lower half of bun.

Beat egg white stiff and fold into mayonnaise. Place line of mixture on top of fish. Sprinkle finely chopped onion over mayonnaise.

Brush top halves of bun with melted butter or margarine. Arrange both kinds of halves on cooky sheet.

Place under broiler or in very hot oven (450°F.) until lightly browned and both fish and buns are piping hot. Garnish with radishes and green onions. Serves 6.

Cheese-Ham Rolls

CHEESE-HAM ROLLS

1 tablespoon finely chopped onion
2 tablespoons chili sauce
2 tablespoons chopped green pepper
2 tablespoons sweet piccalilli
¼ cup deviled ham
1½ cups grated process cheese, firmly packed
8 frankfurter buns

Combine onion, chili sauce, green pepper, piccalilli, ham, and cheese. Cut buns in half and place 3 tablespoons cheese-ham mixture between matched bun halves.

Wrap and seal each filled bun in aluminum foil. Heat in moderate oven (350°F.) for 8 to 10 minutes, or until cheese melts. Makes 8 cheese-ham rolls.

CHEESE CLUB SANDWICH

Melt ½ pound (2 cups) sharp Cheddar cheese in chafing dish or top of double boiler. Add ⅓ cup milk gradually, stirring until sauce is smooth.

Add ½ teaspoon salt, ¼ teaspoon pepper, 1 teaspoon Worcestershire sauce, and ⅛ teaspoon dry mustard.

Trim crusts from 12 slices white bread and toast slices on both sides.

For each sandwich, spread toast slice with mayonnaise, cover with peeled sliced tomatoes, and second toast slice spread with mayonnaise on both sides; add 2 slices broiled bacon and a lettuce leaf. Cover with third toast slice spread with mayonnaise.

Cut diagonally and serve each sandwich with generous amount of hot cheese sauce. Garnish with pickle fan. Makes 4.

BROILED HAM, CHICKEN AND PICKLE SANDWICHES

4 slices bread, toasted on 1 side
Butter or margarine
4 slices cooked or canned chicken
4 slices cooked or canned ham
Thin sliced dill pickles
4 slices process cheese

Spread untoasted side of bread with butter or margarine.

Place slice of chicken, then slice of ham on each.

Cover with a layer of pickle, then slice of cheese. Broil until cheese melts. Serve hot. Makes 4.

EGG 'N' BACON SQUARE

Combine 4 chopped hard-cooked eggs, ¼ cup chopped green pepper, ½ teaspoon salt, and enough Thousand Island salad dressing to moisten.

Spread egg mixture over 4 slices whole wheat bread. Top with ⅓ cup crumbled cooked bacon.

Broil 3 inches from broiling unit 3 minutes.

TURKEY SANDWICH GRILL

1 cup chopped cooked turkey
1 cup finely diced celery
1 tablespoon sweet pickle relish
⅓ cup mayonnaise or salad dressing
Salt and pepper
6 slices buttered toast
1 cup (¼ pound) grated cheese

Combine turkey, celery, pickle relish, and mayonnaise. Season to taste with salt and pepper.

Spread turkey mixture atop toast. Sprinkle cheese over each.

Place in hot oven (425°F.) or under broiler to melt cheese, 2 to 5 minutes.

Serve with a dot of chili sauce and a sprig of parsley atop each sandwich.

If desired, serve with triangles of additional toast, grilled tomatoes and crisp bacon. Makes 6 sandwiches.

CRANBERRY MEAT SANDWICH

Toast bread. Place a slice of broiled or roast meat on each slice of bread. Pour over gravy, if desired. Top with generous spoonful of hot cranberry sauce.

CHEESE SAUCE OVER MEAT SANDWICHES

Melt 1 cup grated American cheese in 1 cup medium white sauce. Pour over any meat sandwich.

SWISS LOAF

1 1-pound loaf unsliced bread
¼ cup butter or margarine
½ cup finely chopped onion
¼ cup chili sauce
1 tablespoon celery seeds
8 slices (½ pound) Swiss cheese

With a sharp knife, make 9 equal diagonal slices, almost through to the bottom crust.

Melt butter in a skillet; add onion and sauté about 5 minutes. Add chili sauce and celery seeds and heat 5 minutes. Remove from heat.

Spread onion mixture and 1 slice of cheese between each slice of bread. Place loaf on cookie sheet. Pour remaining onion mixture over top.

Bake in a moderate oven (350°F.) for 20 minutes. Serves 8.

TURKEY RED DEVILS

Buttered toast
Sliced sharp cheese
Sliced tomatoes
Sliced cooked turkey
1 can condensed cream of mushroom soup
½ can of broth, milk, or water
Cayenne and mustard (optional)
Paprika

Arrange on a shallow baking pan for individual servings—toast topped with the cheese, tomato seasoned with salt and pepper, and the turkey.

Blend soup with broth and season with cayenne and mustard if desired. Top each sandwich with 3 or 4 spoonfuls of the soup. Sprinkle with paprika.

Place in hot oven (425°F.) until cheese begins to melt and top is browned, about 15 minutes. The diluted mushroom soup is enough for 4 or 5 sandwiches.

BACON, CHEESE AND TOMATO SANDWICHES

Trim the crusts from slices of bread and toast them on one side. Spread the untoasted sides with mayonnaise.

Place a slice of peeled tomato on each slice of toast.

Place a slice of pasteurized process American cheese on each slice of tomato.

Arrange two slices of partially broiled bacon on each slice of cheese. Place under moderate broiler heat until the cheese melts.

Serve piping hot, and see why it's called America's favorite sandwich.

Dainty Party Sandwiches

HUMPTY-DUMPTY

From a slice of whole wheat bread, cut an egg-shaped piece attached at bottom end to a small rectangle of bread. Spread egg-shaped section with filling and cover with egg-shaped piece cut from enriched bread.

Decorate Humpty-Dumpty egg face with diamond shaped cucumber peel for eyes, a strip of raisin for the nose, pimiento cut in half-moon shape for mouth, and a strip of pimiento for belt.

To simulate a wall on which egg is sitting, pipe cream cheese across the rectangular section of bread, representing the cement between the bricks of a wall. Pipe cream cheese on the wall for Humpty-Dumpty's legs.

SAILBOATS

Cut a slice of whole wheat bread into the shape of a sailboat, butter and spread with filling.

Cut two sails for each boat from enriched bread and place them on the whole wheat bread, leaving a narrow strip of whole wheat showing between sails for the boat's mast.

Cut the hull of the boat from whole wheat bread and place it over filling. Cut a flag of pimiento and place it at the top of the mast.

To simulate portholes and waves, pipe cream cheese on the lower part of the hull.

For added interest and color, coconut that has been tinted green with food coloring may be placed on the cream cheese waves.

FACES

With a cooky cutter, cut slices of whole wheat and enriched bread into circles, about 2½ inches in diameter. Butter the bread circles and spread a filling between each two.

To make the face, pipe cream cheese around the top of circle, and sprinkle grated carrot over the cream cheese to simulate hair.

Use strips of raisins for eyebrows and nose, diamond-shaped cucumber peel or green pepper for eyes, and pimiento cut in half-moon shape for mouth.

Young Folk's Sandwich Tray

COTTAGES

Remove crusts from slices of whole wheat bread and cut off top corners to form a pointed roof. Each sandwich requires two slices of whole wheat bread cut in the above shape. Butter the first slice and spread with sandwich filling.

It is suggested that red jelly or meat be used as filling to make colorful windows and door.

From second slice, cut door and windows, and place it over first slice.

Decorate house by piping cream cheese shutters at sides of windows and along edge of roof.

CLOWNS

From a slice of whole wheat bread, cut a round clown's head with a cone-shaped hat on one side. Butter and spread with filling.

Place a circle of enriched bread over the filling for the face, and a triangle of whole wheat for the hat.

Trim the hat and hair sections of the clown face with cream cheese. Sprinkle the "cheese hair" with coconut that has been tinted green with food coloring.

Cut round eyes from black olives, a halfmoon-shaped mouth from pimiento, and tiny triangles of pimiento for cheeks.

Lily Sandwiches

LILY SANDWICHES

Cut thinly sliced fresh bread into 2¾-inch rounds. Roll each round with a rolling pin to remove the "spring" of the bread.

Spread each round with cheese, softened at room temperature, and place a carrot strip in the center to represent the stamen. Fold over at one edge to form a lily and pinch together to hold in place.

Put a parsley stem in the end of each lily, to represent the stem.

MOSAICS

From the center of a slice of buttered whole wheat and enriched breads, cut out a small chicken design with a cooky cutter.

Reverse chicken cut-outs, placing the enriched bread cut-out into the whole wheat slice and the whole wheat bread cut-out into the enriched bread slice.

Place each slice, buttered side down, on alternate slices of enriched or whole wheat bread spread with a sandwich filling. Trim crusts from sandwiches. Use raisins for chicken's eyes.

Other cut-outs such as stars, rabbits, or hearts may be used for variety.

TEA SANDWICHES

Cut an equal number of slices of white and whole wheat bread. Cut into desired shapes with fancy sandwich cutters.

Cut fancy designs in half of the slices of white and whole wheat bread.

Spread whole slices of bread with desired sandwich filling. Top spread slices with cut-out slices.

The shapes cut out of the white bread in forming fancy designs may be fitted into the cuts made in the dark bread, and vice versa.

RIBBON SANDWICHES

Start with 2 slices white bread and 2 slices whole wheat.

Stack these alternately (light-dark-light-dark) with a filling of softened butter or margarine, cream cheese, meat or fish spread, jam or jelly between each slice.

Press stack firmly together and slice crusts from all sides.

Wrap tightly in waxed paper and chill in refrigerator for several hours.

Just before serving cut stack down into ¼ inch thick ribbon slices.

Ribbon Sandwiches

Little Layers

Checkerboard Sandwiches

Roll-ups

Valentine Sandwiches

Pinwheels

PINWHEELS

Using an unsliced loaf of bread, cut crusts off all sides.

Cut into lengthwise slices about ¼ inch thick.

Run rolling pin lightly over the slices to make the bread easy to handle and less likely to crack.

Spread with softened butter or margarine, then if desired with a spread.

Arrange stuffed olives, pickles, or Vienna sausage across short end of bread.

Roll up tightly as you do a jelly roll. Wrap rolls individually in waxed paper or aluminum foil, twisting ends securely. Chill several hours or overnight.

To serve, cut each chilled roll down into ¼ to ½ inch slices.

LITTLE LAYERS

Cut crusts from slices of sandwich bread. Spread with softened butter or margarine.

Cut into circles with a 2½-inch biscuit cutter.

Use three rounds for each sandwich. Cover bottom round with pimiento cheese spread. Top with another circle of bread and spread with egg salad. Now place a buttered circle, plain side up, on top.

Frost sandwiches all over with cream cheese, moistened with a little cream.

CHECKERBOARD SANDWICHES

Prepare 2 stacks as directed for ribbon sandwiches.

Cut each stack into ½ inch slices. Then put 3 alternating slices together, with softened butter or a spread between, so that light and dark breads alternate to form a checkerboard design.

Wrap each block in waxed paper and chill for several hours.

To serve, remove from refrigerator and with a sharp knife, immediately cut each block crosswise into checkerboard slices, ½ inch thick.

ROLL-UPS

Cut crusts from thin-sliced white or whole wheat bread. Lightly flatten out with rolling pin.

Spread with softened butter or margarine to keep bread from getting soggy.

Place asparagus tip, celery heart, or watercress sprig across one end of slice.

Roll up each slice jelly-roll fashion into a tight roll.

Cover with a damp cloth until serving time. Serve roll-ups whole or cut in half.

VALENTINE SANDWICHES

Trim crusts from slices of bread, then with a heart-shaped cooky cutter, cut out a heart design from the center of each slice.

Spread half of the "hearts" with sandwich filling and top with a matching heart.

Let the remaining portion of the bread, from which the heart was taken, serve as top or a second sandwich to eliminate waste of bread. Just trim the edges of the two slices to be sure they are the same size.

CARD PARTY SANDWICHES

Slice bread thin. Spread with any desired sandwich filling and place a second slice on top of the first. Press lightly together, then cut out with cooky cutters in the form of hearts, diamonds, clubs, and spades.

Garnish top with tiny pieces of pimiento cut in heart or diamond shapes with garnish cutters, or pieces of ripe olives cut to form spades or clubs.

For a children's party, serve tiny sandwiches cut in animal shapes.

Garnish heart-shaped sandwiches with tiny hearts cut from cranberry sauce or red jelly.

Party glamor is added to the snack tray by a patterned arrangement of the sandwiches.

Many of these tiny finger sandwiches can be prepared beforehand, chilled in the refrigerator and brought to the serving table freshly sliced and tempting.

Sandwich Loaves

SHERRY-CHEESE FROSTED SANDWICH LOAF

Remove all crusts from a day-old 12-inch loaf of sandwich bread. (If only a longer loaf is available, slice off the extra bread and reserve for other purposes.) Cut the loaf lengthwise into 4 slices of equal thickness; keep slices in order.

Place bottom slice on a serving platter or tray; spread with softened butter or margarine, then with Filling 1 (below). Butter both sides of the next slice; press in place over bottom slice; spread with Filling 2 (below). Butter both sides of the third slice; press in place; spread with Filling 3 (below). Butter bottom of the top slice; press in position.

Spread Sherry-Cheese Frosting (below) over top and sides of loaf.

If desired, decorate top of loaf with slices of stuffed olive, strips of pimiento, green pepper, etc.

Chill in the refrigerator for several hours. Before serving, garnish platter with bunches of parsley or watercress or crisp lettuce leaves. Slice crosswise with a sharp knife and serve accompanied by forks.

Filling 1: Mix 2 small cans deviled ham, ½ cup finely chopped celery and enough mayonnaise to moisten.

Filling 2: Peel 2 medium-sized tomatoes; slice crosswise in very thin slices. Arrange slices on the bread; spread with mayonnaise; sprinkle with salt and pepper.

Filling 3: Grate or chop 4 hard-cooked eggs. Mix eggs with ¼ cup cottage cheese, enough mayonnaise to moisten, and seasonings to taste.

Sherry-Cheese Frosting: Blend ½ pound cream cheese with 1 5-ounce jar process American cheese spread. Gradually beat in about ½ cup sherry (enough to make a fluffy mixture that will spread easily). Season with ¼ teaspoon each Worcestershire sauce and prepared mustard, and salt to taste.

Sherry-Cheese Frosted Sandwich Loaf

TULIP SANDWICH LOAF

½ pound cold boiled ham
½ pound American cheese
6 sweet pickles
Mayonnaise
1 loaf unsliced sandwich bread
3 3-ounce packages cream cheese
Cream
1 small can pimiento
1 green pepper

Grind ham and grate cheese. Combine ham, cheese, and chopped pickles and add enough mayonnaise to moisten.

Remove crusts from loaf of bread. Cut a ½- to ¾-inch slice of bread the length of the loaf. Remove center of remaining loaf, so there is a box made of bread having ½ to ¾" thick sides and bottom.

Spread inside of loaf of bread and one side of slice generously with softened butter. Put sandwich filling inside loaf and put top slice on with butter side down.

Soften the cream cheese with a small amount of cream until you have a spreading consistency. Cover loaf with cream cheese.

Cut small tulips and leaves from the pimiento and green pepper and decorate the sides of the loaf.

Chill for at least one hour and when ready to serve cut in one-inch slices. Serves 12 to 15.

FROSTED SALMON SANDWICH LOAF

1 large loaf bread
Butter or margarine
1 small can salmon
3 tablespoons chopped pickle
Mayonnaise
2 large tomatoes
Salt and pepper to taste
½ green pepper, chopped
1 cup grated raw carrots
½ cup chopped celery
¾ pound cream cheese
1½ cups cream

Remove crusts from bread. Cut into four slices lengthwise. Spread each slice with softened butter.

Drain and flake salmon. Combine with chopped pickle, moisten with mayonnaise, and spread on first slice.

Cover second slice of bread with sliced tomatoes. Season.

Combine green pepper with mayonnaise. Spread over sliced tomatoes.

Combine grated carrots and chopped celery. Season with salt and pepper, moisten with mayonnaise, and spread on third slice of bread.

Put the four slices together, press into loaf shape, wrap tightly in waxed pa-

Tulip Sandwich Loaf

per. Chill.

Spread top and sides with cream cheese softened with cream. Keep in refrigerator until ready to serve.

Garnish with radish roses, parsley, carrot strips, stuffed olives, pimiento, etc. Cut into 1-inch-thick slices.

BAKED TUNA OR SALMON SANDWICH LOAF

1 medium loaf white or whole wheat bread
1 6-ounce can tuna or salmon
3 hard-cooked eggs, chopped
1 can condensed mushroom soup
½ teaspoon celery salt
¼ teaspoon onion salt
Dash of pepper
¼ cup melted shortening or salad oil
⅓ cup milk

Remove crusts from the loaf of bread and slice lengthwise in thirds.

Combine tuna and eggs and moisten with ⅓ cup of the mushroom soup. Season with celery and onion salt and pepper. Spread filling between bread slices.

Brush top and sides of loaf with melted shortening or oil. Bake in moderate oven (375°F.) 20 minutes or until lightly browned.

Add milk to remaining soup; heat and serve as a sauce. Serves 6.

MEAT STUFFED RYE LOAF

1 large onion, sliced
2 tablespoons fat
½ pound ground beef
¼ cup chopped parsley
1 carrot, grated
2 teaspoons salt
1 tablespoon chili sauce
¼ teaspoon pepper
¼ teaspoon paprika
1 loaf rye bread, unsliced
1 medium onion, grated

Cook sliced onion in fat until lightly browned. Add beef, and cook until browned. Add parsley, carrot, and seasonings; cook 5 minutes.

Cut a slice from one end of bread, and put aside; take out soft center of bread, and mix with meat mixture. Add grated onion, ½ cup water; mix well; stuff into loaf. Put back cut slice, and fasten with toothpicks.

Bake in moderate oven (350°F.) 25 minutes. Slice to serve. Serves 4.

SALMON SALAD SURPRISE LOAF

1 (20-ounce) loaf day-old enriched bread, unsliced
4 hard-cooked eggs, chopped
1 No. 1 can red salmon, flaked and boned
1 tablespoon grated lemon rind
1 tablespoon lemon juice
¾ cup finely chopped celery
1½ teaspoons salt
⅔ cup mayonnaise or salad dressing
1 tablespoon chopped green pepper
2 tablespoons sliced green olives

With a sharp knife, remove the crusts from a loaf of bread to make an even, box-shaped loaf. Cut a lengthwise slice from the top (see right).

Hollow out the center of the loaf, leaving side walls and bottom at least ½ inch thick. Place on a cooky sheet. (Save center of loaf for breadcrumbs or stuffing.)

Combine chopped eggs, flaked salmon, lemon rind, lemon juice, celery, salt, mayonnaise, pepper, and olives.

Loaf Topping:

1 tablespoon (1 envelope) unflavored gelatin
1 tablespoon dilute vinegar
1 cup mayonnaise or salad dressing
¼ teaspoon cayenne pepper
½ teaspoon Worcestershire sauce
1 hard-cooked egg, sliced
3 sliced olives

Mix gelatin with vinegar and dissolve over hot water. Slowly combine mayonnaise and dissolved gelatin. Add pepper and Worcestershire sauce.

To Complete Salmon Salad Surprise Loaf: Fill center of the loaf of bread with salmon salad. Cover with top slice of bread. Spread top and sides of loaf with topping mixture. Garnish with sliced egg and olives.

Cover finished loaf with heavy waxed paper to prevent discoloration of mayonnaise from moisture.

Place in refrigerator for 12 hours. To serve: Slice in 1-inch cuts. Serves 8.

1. Remove crusts from loaf of bread. Cut a lengthwise slice from top.

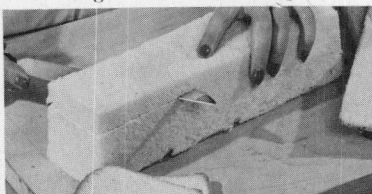

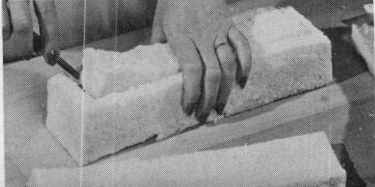

2. Hollow out center of the loaf, leaving side walls and bottom at least half an inch thick. Fill center of loaf.

HAM 'N' EGG SALAD SANDWICH LOAF

Remove crusts from small loaf of unsliced bread, leaving top rounded. Cut in 3 lengthwise slices.

Spread bottom slice with egg filling (below); cover with middle slice. Spread with ham filling (below). Cover with rounded top slice.

Wrap in waxed paper. Chill. Frost thinly with mayonnaise.

Garnish with "flowers" made of pimiento strips and capers and sprays of chicory. Cut in slices to serve. Serves 8.

Egg Filling:

4 hard-cooked eggs, chopped
2 tablespoons minced green pepper
Few grains pepper
¼ teaspoon Ac'cent
2 tablespoons mayonnaise

Combine all ingredients; mix well.

Ham Filling:

¼ pound cooked ham, ground
3 tablespoons minced celery
Few grains pepper
¼ teaspoon Ac'cent
1½ tablespoons mayonnaise

Combine all ingredients; mix well.

POOR BOY, SUBMARINE, HERO, OR GRINDER

These are various names used in different parts of the country for giant sandwiches usually made with long loaves of French bread and a vast variety of fillings. The Poor Boy of New Orleans is a popular example.

POOR BOY SANDWICH

This hearty snack, native to New Orleans, is made in dozens of different ways, depending on the tastes of the maker and what is available.

A medium-long, thin loaf of French bread is slit in half lengthwise and generously buttered. Then the loaf is sliced in thirds or fourths, not quite through the bottom crust. A different

3. Spread top and sides with topping mixture. Garnish and cover with waxed paper. Chill in refrigerator 12 hours.

Salmon Salad Surprise Loaf

Ham 'n' Egg Salad Sandwich Loaf

kind of filling goes in each section.

Fried oysters almost invariably go in one part. The other sections can be filled with slices of well seasoned tomato with a slice of broiled bacon, another with sausage, chicken salad, fried egg with hot chili sauce, or chopped green pepper and onion, and so on, using any appetizing tidbit desired.

HOT CHICKEN SALAD LOAF

1 (1 pound) loaf day-old white bread, unsliced
1 tablespoon soft butter or margarine
1½ cups chopped, cooked chicken
¾ cup finely chopped celery
2 teaspoons chopped onion
1½ teaspoons chopped parsley
½ cup mayonnaise or salad dressing
¼ teaspoon salt
Dash of pepper

With a sharp knife, remove crusts from loaf of bread to make an even, box-shaped loaf. Cut a lengthwise slice from the top.

Hollow out the center of loaf, leaving sides and bottom at least ½ inch thick. Spread butter on inside walls of the cavity. (Save center of loaf for breadcrumbs or stuffing.)

Combine chicken, celery, onion, parsley, mayonnaise, salt, and pepper. Fill center of the loaf with chicken salad.

Cover with top slice of bread. Wrap loaf with heavy waxed paper. Chill in refrigerator for 6 hours.

Loaf Topping: Beat 2 egg whites until stiff. Fold in ¼ cup mayonnaise and a dash of salt.

To Complete Loaf: Unwrap and spread top and sides of loaf with topping mixture. Place on cooky sheet and brown in very hot oven (450°F.) 10 minutes. Serve hot and cut crosswise into 6 sections. Serve with whole cranberry sauce. Serves 6.

GOURMET SANDWICH LOAF

- 4 hard-cooked eggs
- 1 cup finely chopped cooked turkey
- 1/4 cup chopped sweet pickles or pickle relish
- 1 can cream of mushroom soup
- Salt and pepper
- 12 slices bread
- 2 tablespoons softened butter or margarine
- 1/4 cup milk

Chop 2 of the eggs. Combine with turkey, pickles, and half of the soup. Season to taste with salt and pepper.

Trim crusts from bread and cut slices in half to make 24 pieces. Place 6 pieces of bread close together on baking sheet or heat-proof serving platter. Spread with turkey mixture. Top with layer of bread.

Repeat until there are 3 layers of turkey and 4 layers of bread. Brush top with softened butter.

Bake in moderate oven (375°F.) until lightly browned, 15 minutes.

Blend milk with remaining soup. Heat to boiling. Add remaining chopped eggs. Serve over 6 sandwiches.

TEA SANDWICH LOAF

Prepare the following sandwich fillings: salmon salad, olive and nut, and egg salad.

Remove crusts from an unsliced loaf of enriched bread and cut lengthwise into five slices.

Spread each bread slice with softened butter. Spread salmon salad between first and second slices of bread; olive and nut between second and third slices; egg salad between third and fourth slices; sharp process cheese spread topped with a layer of tomatoes between fourth and fifth slices.

Press loaf firmly together. Wrap in waxed paper and chill for an hour.

Frost top and sides of loaf with cream cheese softened with cream. Arrange chopped parsley, sliced cucumber, and a fish-shaped slice of pimiento on top of loaf. Garnish platter with lemon wedges, tomato slices, and parsley. Cut into thick slices when serving.

Turkey 'n' Cranberry Rounds

MINCEMEAT PARTY LOAVES

- 6 3-ounce packages cream cheese
- 1 9-ounce package mincemeat
- 1/2 cup water
- 32 slices white bread, cut 3 inches square
- 1 5-ounce jar pineapple cheese spread
- 1 cup whole cranberry sauce, drained
- 1/2 cup light cream

Let cream cheese soften at room temperature. Break mincemeat into small pieces and put in small saucepan. Add water. Place over low heat and stir until lumps are thoroughly broken. Increase heat and boil briskly for 3 to 5 minutes or until mixture is dry, stirring frequently. Chill.

To make each loaf, spread about 2 tablespoons of mincemeat on a slice of bread, about 1 1/2 tablespoons of cheese spread on second slice of bread and about 2 tablespoons of cranberry sauce on third slice of bread. Pile spread bread slices one on top of the other. Top with fourth slice of plain bread.

Wrap in waxed paper and chill in refrigerator. Repeat procedure for each loaf. Meanwhile beat cream cheese until light and fluffy. Gradually add cream, blending until smooth and fluffy. Frost each loaf on all sides and top. Garnish with candied fruit.

Return to refrigerator and chill. To serve, slice diagonally. Makes 8 3-inch square loaves.

TURKEY 'N' CRANBERRY ROUNDS

- 18 slices bread
- 4 tablespoons softened butter or margarine
- 1 1-pound can jellied cranberry sauce
- 3/4 cup diced turkey
- 3 tablespoons sliced olives
- 3 tablespoons chopped pickle
- 1/4 cup diced celery
- 1 tablespoon minced onion
- 3 tablespoons mayonnaise
- 1/2 teaspoon salt
- 1 teaspoon poultry seasoning, optional
- 3 3-ounce packages cream cheese, softened

Cut bread slices into rounds the size of cranberry slices. Spread with softened butter or margarine.

Cut cranberry sauce into 6 plump slices. Place a slice on 6 rounds of bread.

Top each with 2nd round of bread. Spread 2nd round with turkey filling made by combining turkey, olives, pickles, celery, onion, mayonnaise, salt, and poultry seasoning.

Top with 3rd bread round. Frost with cheese. Serves 6.

YULE LOG SANDWICH

Prepare the following fillings: Deviled ham-peanut butter; egg-bacon; avocado-pineapple; cheese-shrimp; cranberry-cheese.

Remove crusts from an unsliced loaf of enriched bread and cut lengthwise into 5 slices.

Butter slices and spread each with one of the first four fillings as named. Stack and top with 5th bread slice.

Press loaf firmly together. Wrap in waxed paper and chill for 1 hour.

Frost top and sides of loaf with cranberry-cheese mixture, making lengthwise ridges with a spatula.

Garnish platter with cinnamon pear halves set on lettuce leaves, with their cherry bell clappers. Cut into thick slices to serve.

Sandwich Fillings for Yule Log

Deviled Ham-Peanut Butter: Combine 1/3 cup peanut butter, a 3-ounce can deviled ham, 1/4 cup mayonnaise, 3 tablespoons chopped dill pickle.

Egg-Bacon: Combine 2 chopped hard-cooked eggs, 1/3 cup chopped cooked bacon, 3 tablespoons mayonnaise.

Avocado-Pineapple: Combine 1/3 cup mashed avocado, 2 tablespoons drained crushed pineapple, 1 teaspoon lemon juice, 1 tablespoon mayonnaise, and a dash of salt.

Cheese-Shrimp: Combine 1/2 cup pimiento cream cheese, 1/2 teaspoon chili sauce, 1/3 cup finely chopped cooked shrimp, and 1/2 teaspoon lemon juice.

Cranberry-Cheese: Combine two 3-ounce packages cream cheese with 2/3 cup strained cranberry sauce, mixing with a rotary beater until smooth.

A delicious sandwich loaf makes a good party food that is easy to make. For a Christmas party, the pimiento tree arranged on the cream cheese frosting adds the festive note.

Fish and Shellfish Sandwiches

SARDINE-PICKLE FILLING

1 4-ounce can sardines, packed in oil, drained, flaked
1 dill pickle, chopped or 2 tablespoons plus 1 teaspoon sweet pickle relish
1 tablespoon softened butter or margarine
1 teaspoon prepared mustard
1 tablespoon salad dressing or mayonnaise

Combine ingredients and spread on toast. Makes spread for 4 sandwiches.

TUNA-SLAW SUBMARINES

2 tablespoons mayonnaise or salad dressing
2 tablespoons chili sauce
1 tablespoon lemon juice
Dash of salt
1 can (7 ounces) tuna, drained and flaked
2 small loaves or 1 large loaf French bread
1 cup cole slaw, well drained

Blend mayonnaise or salad dressing, chili sauce, lemon juice, and salt; add tuna; toss lightly.

Split French bread lengthwise almost through; spread with additional mayonnaise or salad dressing; line with lettuce, if desired.

Fill first with tuna mixture, then with slaw. Cut in serving-sized slices. Serves 4.

SARDINE-EGG FILLING

Combine 1 can drained, mashed sardines and 2 chopped hard-cooked eggs. Moisten with lemon juice to taste.

Danish Open Sandwiches: A colorful open sandwich buffet could be luncheon for the next meeting of your club. Your imagination is the only limit when it comes to the filling—all delicious on rolls made from a mix. Pictured here are toppings of roast beef with horseradish, egg and asparagus, and shrimp with fresh dill. Each roll half was spread with mayonnaise glaze before the toppings were added.

To make mayonnaise glaze: Soften 1 envelope of unflavored gelatin in 1/4 cup cold water. Stir in 1 cup mayonnaise and heat, stirring constantly, until gelatin is dissolved.

EGG-CRABMEAT-ALMOND SANDWICH BARS

1 3-ounce package cream cheese
2 tablespoons milk
2 tablespoons chopped, toasted almonds
1 hard-cooked egg, chopped
1/4 cup flaked crabmeat
1/4 teaspoon celery salt
2 tablespoons mayonnaise or salad dressing
1 teaspoon lemon juice
3 lengthwise slices whole wheat bread (cut from unsliced sandwich loaf)
1/4 cup soft butter or margarine

Combine cream cheese, milk, and almonds. Combine chopped egg, crabmeat, celery salt, mayonnaise, and lemon juice.

Spread each slice of bread with butter. Spread cheese-almond mixture on 1 slice of bread; top with second slice, buttered side up.

Spread egg-crabmeat mixture on second slice of bread; top with third slice, buttered side down.

Press loaf together gently. Wrap in waxed paper, twisting ends of paper; chill.

To serve: unwrap and cut sandwich loaf in half lengthwise. Cut each lengthwise strip into 16 sections. Makes 32.

SALMON SALAD FILLING

1 1/2 cups flaked salmon
1/4 cup chopped celery
1 tablespoon chopped green pepper
2 tablespoons salad dressing

Combine salmon, celery, and green pepper. Add salad dressing and mix thoroughly. Makes 1 1/2 cups filling, enough for 6 sandwiches.

SALMON BOATS

1 can (7 3/4 or 8 ounces) salmon, drained and flaked
1 cup diced celery
1/4 cup salad dressing
2 hard-cooked eggs, chopped
1/2 teaspoon onion salt
1/8 teaspoon pepper
6 frankfurter rolls
Lettuce

Combine salmon, celery, salad dressing, eggs, and seasonings.

Split 6 frankfurter rolls; line with lettuce; spoon salmon salad into rolls. Makes 6 salad rolls.

TUNA AND EGG FILLING

Combine 1 cup flaked tuna, 2 chopped hard-cooked eggs, and 1/4 cup chopped stuffed olives. Moisten with mayonnaise.

Lobster Tail Party Sandwiches: Flaked cooked lobster tail meat was combined with minced celery and minced onion, then moistened with mayonnaise to make the topping for the half slices of whole wheat bread.

ANCHOVY FILLING

1/2 cup mashed anchovies or anchovy paste
1/4 cup chopped olives
1/4 cup butter or margarine

Mix ingredients together to form a smooth paste. Store in refrigerator. Makes 1 cup.

FLAKED FISH FILLING

1 cup canned fish flakes
1 tablespoon chopped celery
1 tablespoon chopped pickle (sweet or sour)
3 tablespoons mayonnaise
1/2 tablespoon horseradish
1/4 teaspoon salt
1/8 teaspoon pepper

Combine all ingredients and mix well.

SHRIMP SPECIAL FILLING

1 cup chopped, cooked or canned shrimp
3 tablespoons chopped celery
1/4 teaspoon salt
1 teaspoon lemon juice
Mayonnaise

Combine all ingredients well and moisten with mayonnaise.

SARDINE FILLING

Mix sardines with chopped hard-cooked eggs, grated cheese, butter, and lemon juice. Season with curry powder.

SALAD FILLED ROLLS

2/3 cup ripe olives
2 hard-cooked eggs
1 7-ounce can tuna
3/4 cup chopped celery
1/2 cup mayonnaise
6 finger rolls
Butter or margarine
Lettuce

Cut olives into large pieces. Dice eggs. Drain oil from tuna and flake coarsely. Combine olives, eggs, tuna, and celery and blend lightly with mayonnaise.

Cut rolls in half leaving one side attached, and hollow slightly. Butter insides, and heap with filling. Tuck a crisp lettuce leaf inside each roll. Serves 6.

Cheese and Egg Sandwiches

EGGS AND LIVER FILLING

4 chopped, hard-cooked eggs
1/2 cup minced cooked liver
Salt and pepper
Prepared horseradish
Mayonnaise

Combine hard-cooked eggs with minced cooked liver. Season with salt and pepper and prepared horseradish. Moisten with mayonnaise.

DEVILED EGG FILLING

3 hard-cooked eggs
3 teaspoons chopped parsley
3 teaspoons vinegar
1/8 teaspoon dry mustard
1/4 teaspoon salt
1/8 teaspoon pepper

Chop hard-cooked eggs fine. Combine with parsley, vinegar, dry mustard, salt, and pepper. Blend well.

EGG-CELERY FILLING

3 hard-cooked eggs
Salt and pepper
1/2 cup finely chopped celery
Mayonnaise or prepared sandwich
spread

Chop hard-cooked eggs well. Season with salt and pepper. Mix with celery and mayonnaise or prepared sandwich spread. Makes 4 sandwiches.

EGG SALAD FILLING

3 hard-cooked eggs
1/4 cup chopped ripe olives
1/4 cup mayonnaise
1/4 teaspoon prepared mustard
1/4 teaspoon salt
Black pepper to taste

onion
pickles
celery or
celery
seed

Chop eggs and blend with remaining ingredients. Makes about 1 cup.

EGG-HAM FILLING

Combine 4 chopped hard-cooked eggs and 1/4 to 1/2 cup chopped boiled ham. Moisten with mayonnaise.

EGG-BACON FILLING

4 chopped hard-cooked eggs
6 slices chopped crisp bacon
3 tablespoons chopped olives
1/4 teaspoon salt
Mayonnaise

Combine hard-cooked eggs, bacon, olives, and salt. Moisten with mayonnaise.

EGG AND WATERCRESS FILLING

Mix chopped hard-cooked egg, watercress, and mayonnaise.

EGGS AND SPINACH FILLING

Mix ground hard-cooked eggs with half the amount of spinach.

CREAMY CHEESE FILLING

1/4 cup mayonnaise
3 3-ounce packages cream cheese
1/4 cup chopped green pepper
1 1/2 teaspoons minced onion

Blend all ingredients to spreading consistency. Makes 1 1/3 cups.

CREAMY CHEESE-OLIVE FILLING

1 3-ounce package cream cheese
1 to 2 tablespoons milk or cream
1/3 cup chopped ripe olives
Dash of Tabasco sauce
Salt to taste

Soften cheese and gradually blend in milk to make spreading consistency. Blend in olives and seasonings to taste. Makes about 1 cup.

COTTAGE CHEESE-CUCUMBER FILLING

1 large cucumber
1 tablespoon grated onion
1/2 teaspoon salt
1 pint cottage cheese
Dash of pepper

Peel cucumber and remove seeds. Grate or grind and mix with onion and salt. Put in a strainer and let set over a bowl until just ready to make sandwiches.

Mix well with cottage cheese and dash of pepper. Additional salt to taste may be added. Makes 8 to 10 sandwiches.

ROQUEFORT-OLIVE SWIRL SANDWICHES

3 tablespoons cream cheese
2 tablespoons grated Roquefort cheese
1/2 tablespoon milk
4 slices enriched bread
2 or 3 ripe olives

Combine cream cheese, Roquefort cheese, and milk. Cut each slice of bread into 4 1 1/2-inch circles with a cooky cutter. Spread 1 teaspoon cheese mixture on each circle.

Garnish top of each sandwich with slivers of ripe olives arranged in a swirl pattern. Makes 16.

COTTAGE CHEESE-GREEN PEPPER FILLING

1/2 pound dry cottage cheese
1/3 cup evaporated milk
1 teaspoon salt
1/8 teaspoon pepper
3 tablespoons chopped green pepper
1 tablespoon minced onion

Cream cottage cheese with evaporated milk until smooth. Add salt, pepper, green pepper, and minced onion. Mix well. Makes 5 sandwiches.

Flower Sandwiches

FLOWER SANDWICHES

White bread
Pimiento cheese spread
Olive-pimiento cheese spread
Cream cheese
Milk
Old English cheese spread
Sliced stuffed olives
Small squares of green pepper
Slivers of green pepper

Cut thinly sliced bread with flower cutters. Spread half of the flowers with pimiento cheese spread and the other half with olive-pimiento cheese spread.

Spread the stems of the pimiento cheese flowers with cream cheese softened with milk, and spread the stems of the olive-pimiento cheese flowers with Old English.

Top the centers of the flowers with olive slices or small squares of green pepper. Decorate the leaves and stems with slivers of green pepper.

CHERRY-CHEESE ROLLS

1 3-ounce package cream cheese
2 tablespoons chopped maraschino cherries
2 tablespoons soft butter or margarine
20 maraschino cherries
2 lengthwise thin slices enriched bread (cut from unsliced sandwich loaf)

Combine cream cheese and chopped cherries. Spread each slice of bread with butter, then with cheese-cherry mixture.

Cut each slice in equal halves crosswise. Place a row of five cherries across width of each half slice of bread, pressing cherries firmly together end to end.

Roll each half slice of bread as for jelly roll, starting at cherry end, being careful to keep first turn firm and cherries in place.

Wrap each roll in waxed paper, twisting ends of paper. Place on a flat surface so that roll rests on last turn of bread; chill.

To serve: unwrap and cut each roll into 6 slices. Makes 24.

Meat and Poultry Sandwiches

HAM-OLIVE PINWHEELS

6 tablespoons ground boiled ham
2 tablespoons mayonnaise
1 teaspoon prepared horseradish
1 loaf sandwich bread, unsliced
4 tablespoons butter
6 stuffed olives

Combine ham, mayonnaise, and horseradish. Remove all crusts from bread.

Cut bread lengthwise into slices 1/4-inch thick. Spread with softened butter and with ham mixture.

Place olives in a line crosswise at 1 end of the bread; roll bread starting at the end of slice.

Wrap roll in a damp cloth or waxed paper and place in refrigerator for several hours.

When ready to serve cut crosswise into slices any thickness desired. This makes sufficient filling for 1 full-length slice of bread which will cut into 8 thin pinwheels.

Other Meat or Fish Fillings: Use ground cooked or canned chicken or turkey or canned or cooked fish instead of ham.

Peanut Butter Filling: Omit horseradish and substitute peanut butter for the ham.

Cream Cheese Filling: Spread with a mixture of cream cheese and just enough chili sauce to give the cheese a spreading consistency.

ROLLED CHICKEN SANDWICHES
(For a Crowd)

3 3-ounce packages soft cream cheese
2 cups firmly packed, very finely ground cooked chicken
1/2 cup firmly packed, finely ground celery
1/4 cup chopped parsley
1/2 cup sauterne or other dry white wine
2 teaspoons grated onion
1 teaspoon Worcestershire sauce
Salt to taste
Softened butter or margarine
36 to 40 thin slices very fresh white bread, crusts trimmed

Blend cheese, chicken, celery, and parsley. Gradually beat in wine. Add onion and seasonings.

Spread bread with butter after rolling lightly with rolling pin, and spread with filling. Roll up like jelly roll.

Place seam-side-down on platter or shallow pan. Cover with waxed paper, then wrap in damp towel and chill 1/2 hour or longer before serving. Makes 36 to 40.

TURKEY OR CHICKEN CLUB SANDWICHES

Spread a slice of toast with butter and mayonnaise. Add layer of thin sliced cooked chicken or turkey. Top with another buttered slice of toast.

Then add strips of crisp bacon, slices of tomato and a leaf of lettuce. Cover with third slice of toast. Skewer together with wooden picks and cut into quarters.

GROUND BEEF FILLINGS

1. Cook ground beef with chopped celery and onion. Mix with a little horseradish and salad dressing.
2. Cook ground beef with a little chopped onion. Mix with chili sauce and mayonnaise.
3. Cooked ground beef mixed with pickle relish and mayonnaise.
4. Slice each of meat loaf, tomato, and cheese, spread with prepared mustard.
5. Slice meat loaf, pickle relish, sliced hard-cooked egg, and salad dressing.

GROUND HAM FILLING

1/2 cup vinegar
1 teaspoon prepared mustard
1/2 teaspoon salt
1/4 cup light brown sugar
1 egg, well beaten
1/2 pound ground, cooked ham

Combine all ingredients except ham, and cook, stirring constantly, until boiling. Boil 5 minutes.

Cool, then add ham and mix well. Spread between buttered slices of enriched white or whole wheat bread. Serve with pickle.

ZESTY CHICKEN LIVER FILLING

3 slices bacon
1/2 pound chicken livers
1/4 pound chopped mushrooms
1 tablespoon minced onion
3/4 teaspoon salt
Dash of pepper
8 slices rye bread

Fry bacon until crisp. Remove from skillet.

In bacon drippings, sauté chicken livers with mushrooms until tender.

Turn into chopping bowl with bacon; chop fine. Add onion, salt, and pepper. Blend well. Makes 4 sandwiches.

HAM-CABBAGE FILLING

Combine chopped cooked or canned ham and chopped or finely shredded cabbage. Moisten with mayonnaise or salad dressing. Season with prepared mustard.

Sandwich Trees: Sandwich trees are a delightfully different way to serve a group—large or small. Cut bread into rounds of 4 sizes from 1 3/4 to 3 3/4 inches in diameter. Spread one of the larger rounds with your favorite sandwich spread (deviled ham spreads were used in this photo). Top with round of the same size. Repeat the rounds. Build trees with sandwiches of graduated rounds. Top with parsley or tiny bread star. Each tree makes 4 servings.

HAM SALAD FILLING

1/2 pound (1 1/2 cups) baked ham or minced ham (luncheon meat)
1 cup sweet pickles or pickle relish
4 hard-cooked eggs
1 teaspoon lemon juice
About 1/2 cup mayonnaise

Grind meat and sweet pickles; chop hard-cooked eggs (chop whites very fine). Add lemon juice. Mix with mayonnaise. Makes 6 to 8 sandwiches.

CHICKEN-RIPE OLIVE FILLING

Combine 1 cup chopped cooked chicken with 1/2 cup chopped celery and 1/4 cup chopped olives. Moisten with mayonnaise.

CREAM CHEESE-DEVILED HAM RIBBON SANDWICHES

1 3-ounce can deviled ham
1 3-ounce package cream cheese
2 lengthwise slices enriched bread (cut from unsliced 1 1/2 pound loaf)
1 lengthwise slice whole wheat bread (cut from unsliced 1 1/2 pound loaf)
3 tablespoons soft butter or margarine

Combine deviled ham and cream cheese. Spread each slice of bread with butter. Spread half of the cheese-ham mixture on 1 slice of enriched bread; top with whole wheat slice, butter side down.

Spread the remaining mixture on whole wheat bread. Top with second slice of enriched bread, buttered side down.

Wrap in waxed paper, twisting ends of paper; chill. To serve: unwrap and cut sandwich loaf crosswise into 16 sections. Makes 16.

Whole-Meal Sandwich

WHOLE-MEAL SANDWICH

For each serving, butter a large round slice of rye bread. Place butter-side-up on dinner plate.

First put on several leaves of head lettuce, then a layer of thin slices of Swiss cheese.

Then add large lettuce cup, reverse side up. Cover it with slices of white meat of chicken. Now pour Thousand Island dressing over all.

Top with a tomato slice, then a hard-cooked egg slice. Garnish sandwich with crisp, hot bacon slices, ripe olives, and topper of parsley.

BOLOGNA-EGG FILLING

1/2 pound bologna
1/4 cup chopped pickles
1/2 cup mayonnaise
1/2 teaspoon minced onion
Dash of Tabasco sauce
2 tablespoons pickle juice
3 chopped hard-cooked eggs
1/2 teaspoon salt

Grind bologna and mix well with remaining ingredients.
Makes 7 sandwiches.

SALAMI-BEAN FILLING

1/2 pound salami, finely chopped
3/4 cup canned baked beans with to-
    mato sauce, drained
2 teaspoons minced onion
2 tablespoons chili sauce
2 teaspoons prepared mustard
1 teaspoon prepared horseradish

Place salami, baked beans, onion, chili sauce, mustard, and horseradish in mixing bowl. Mash well with fork. Makes 2½ cups.

TONGUE-OLIVE FILLING

Combine 1 cup chopped cooked or canned tongue with 1/2 cup chopped stuffed olives. Moisten with mayonnaise or salad dressing.

BACON-PICKLE FILLING

Fry 6 slices of bacon crisp. Crumble and combine with 1/2 cup chopped dill pickle, and 1/4 cup mayonnaise. Makes 4 sandwiches.

HAM-CHUTNEY FILLING

Combine ground cooked or canned ham and chutney. Moisten with mayonnaise or salad dressing.

HAM-CHEESE FILLING

2 cups process American cheese
1/2 teaspoon Ac'cent
About 1/2 cup ketchup
2 or 3 slices boiled ham

Coarsely grate cheese. Add Ac'cent and enough ketchup for spreading consistency. Cut ham into 1/4-inch strips and use for tops. Makes filling for 4 to 6 sandwiches.

CORNED BEEF FILLING

4 tablespoons sharp American cheese
2 tablespoons mayonnaise
1/4 pound cooked corned beef
6 tablespoons minced sweet pickle
2 teaspoons finely minced onion
1 teaspoon prepared mustard
1/4 teaspoon salt
1/8 teaspoon pepper

Cut cheese into small pieces and blend thoroughly with mayonnaise until smooth and soft. Add shredded corned beef and other ingredients.

Spread on half slices of buttered whole wheat and white bread. A slice of tomato and crisp lettuce may be added to each sandwich. Makes 12 sandwiches.

LIVERWURST FILLING

1/4 cup sweet pickle relish
1/4 cup liverwurst
1/4 cup cream cheese

Blend ingredients well. Makes spread for 3 to 4 sandwiches.

GROUND LIVER FILLING

1 cup ground, cooked liver
1 teaspoon chopped pickle
1 tablespoon pickle juice
4 tablespoons mayonnaise
Dash of Tabasco (optional)
Salt and pepper to taste

Combine all ingredients and mix thoroughly. Makes 5 sandwiches.

SALAMI-EGG FILLING

Combine chopped salami and hard-cooked egg. Top with sliced onion or tomato.

DRIED BEEF FILLING

1 2½-ounce jar dried beef
1 3-ounce package cream cheese
1 teaspoon horseradish
1 tablespoon minced onion
Pepper, if desired

Cut dried beef into thin strips with scissors. Combine with remaining ingredients. Makes 4 sandwiches.

HAM-CUCUMBER FILLING

Combine 1 cup ground, cooked ham, 1/4 cup diced cucumber, 3 tablespoons mayonnaise, and salt to taste. Mix well.

CHICKEN SALAD FILLING

3 cups minced cooked chicken or tur-
    key
1 cup minced celery
1 pimiento, minced
6 large stuffed olives, minced
Salad dressing to moisten

Mix all ingredients and season to taste.

Spread liberally between slices of light or dark bread. A leaf of lettuce may be added. Spreads 12 whole sandwiches.

Note: The same mixture may be used for salad if meat and celery is cubed rather than minced.

MOCK PÂTÉ FILLING

Blend liverwurst with cream cheese. Season with grated onion.

PORK-EGG-PICKLE RELISH FILLING

Combine chopped canned spiced pork, chopped hard-cooked egg, and pickle relish. Moisten with mayonnaise or salad dressing.

LIVER-EGG FILLING

2/3 pound steamed pork liver
2 hard-cooked eggs
1 small chopped onion
1 tablespoon shortening
1/2 cup cream or top milk
Salt and pepper
Few drops Tabasco sauce

Steam liver 25 minutes in deep-well cooker or large kettle.

Cool, put through food grinder. Chop eggs coarsely. Brown onion in the shortening. Mix all ingredients well. Keep in a cool place.

Sandwiches in the lunch box can be made more fun for children and adults alike if cut sometimes into triangles, on the diagonal, or into strips.

These sandwich filling ingredients freeze well: cooked egg yolk; peanut butter; cooked or canned meat, poultry, or fish; dried beef; Roquefort or Bleu cheese; nut pastes; olives; pickles. Not recommended: mayonnaise; jelly; whites of hard-cooked egg; lettuce, tomatoes; cucumber; celery; watercress.

SAUCES, GRAVIES, MARINADES, AND SEASONED BUTTERS

Many elegant dishes owe their special appeal to a fine subtly seasoned sauce and many simply cooked foods become superb company fare when served with a classic sauce or one of its interesting variations. The art of making sauces was developed in France, hence many sauces have French names. In French cooking, the word sauce means any liquid or semi-liquid adjunct that complements a dish. This includes, of course, the gravy in a stew and the white or cream sauce on a vegetable. It also encompasses the salad dressings, the melted butter dressings, the savory butters for canapés, marinades for meats and other foods, and other appetite-provoking additions which Americans do not ordinarily consider to be sauces.

In this section are the most versatile, the most commonly used, and the most famous sauces for meats, poultry, fish, game, and vegetables. Salad dressings, dessert sauces, and canapé butters are given in separate sections.

Many sauces are prepared with the dishes they are intended to complete—dishes that create their own sauce in the cooking; therefore many sauces are given with specific recipes throughout this book. For a complete list of the sauces contained in this book, consult the index.

Commercial sauces are often used to flavor or "pep up" homemade varieties. They have a very definite place on the pantry shelf and are often used as a convenience accessory in cooking and for the most part they have developed from sauces once laboriously made in the home kitchen.

As long as there are good cooks, new sauces will continue to be invented, and new variations will be given to old ones; therefore do not hesitate to apply your imagination and creative abilities in the creation of your own variations of the standard classics.

Seasoned Butters

CLARIFIED BUTTER

This is merely melted butter with the sediment removed. To make clarified butter, place butter in a heatproof cup and stand the cup in hot water. When completely melted, remove from heat, let stand for a few minutes to allow the milk solids to settle to the bottom. Pour off the butter fat and discard the milky sediment in the cup. Use as indicated in recipes.

KNEADED BUTTER OR BEURRE MANIÉ

This is butter and flour kneaded together and used as a thickening agent for sauces rather than a real sauce or butter. Knead or cream together butter and flour in proportions varying from 1 tablespoon butter to 1 to 2 teaspoons flour. Add to the hot gravy, sauce, or other liquid to be thickened. Simmer, but do not boil sauce after adding kneaded butter, just long enough to thicken sauce and dispel the floury taste.

BROWN BUTTER (BEURRE NOISETTE)

This is melted butter cooked slowly until light brown. A better flavor and appearance will be obtained if clarified butter is used. Use with vegetables such as asparagus and broccoli, and with fish.

BROWN BUTTER SAUCE

Brown slowly but do not burn, 1/4 cup butter or margarine, stirring constantly. Add 2 teaspoons lemon juice and 1/4 teaspoon salt.

ALMOND BUTTER

Blanch 1/4 cup almonds in boiling water; remove skins. Pound almonds to a smooth paste, adding 1 teaspoon water if necessary. Cream 1/4 cup butter and blend in almonds. If desired, rub through a fine sieve. Use in cream sauces.

BLACK BUTTER (BEURRE NOIR)

This is melted butter cooked until it is very dark brown. A better flavor will be obtained if clarified butter is used. If desired, flavor to taste with lemon juice or vinegar. Use with vegetables and brains.

BLACK BUTTER SAUCE

4 tablespoons butter or margarine
4 sprigs parsley, stripped of stems
2 tablespoons lemon juice

Melt butter and when very hot add parsley. Fry until crisp and brown.

When butter is brown but not burnt, pour into serving dish.

Heat lemon juice very hot and add to butter before serving.

GREEN BUTTER

2 shallots, chopped fine
1 teaspoon chopped chervil
1 teaspoon chopped tarragon
6 to 8 spinach leaves, chopped
1 tablespoon chopped parsley
1/4 cup butter, creamed

Combine all ingredients except butter; cover with boiling water and cook 5 minutes. Drain and dry well in a towel.

Rub them through a fine sieve or pound in a mortar or bowl. Blend with creamed butter. Use for fish or to give sauces a green color.

MAÎTRE D'HÔTEL BUTTER

Cream 1/2 cup butter. Add 1 tablespoon chopped parsley and gradually blend in 3 tablespoons lemon juice, 1/2 teaspoon salt, and 1/8 teaspoon pepper. Serve with broiled fish. Makes 2/3 cup sauce.

COLBERT BUTTER

To 1/2 cup maître d'hôtel butter add 1/2 teaspoon melted beef extract or meat glaze, and 1/4 teaspoon chopped tarragon.

LOBSTER OR SHRIMP BUTTER

Dry the shells from 1 pound shrimp or from 1 large cooked lobster in a slow oven for a short time. Pound the shells in a mortar until they are pulverized or put them through a food chopper so they are broken up as fine as possible.

Melt 1/4 pound (1/2 cup) butter in the top of a double boiler over (not in) hot water. Add the shells with 2 tablespoons water. (If you are using lobster shell, add also the coral if available.) Simmer 10 to 12 minutes. Do not let the butter boil.

Strain the butter through a fine cheesecloth into a bowl of ice water. Set bowl in refrigerator until butter hardens. Skim off the butter and store in covered jar in refrigerator to use in recipes for fish or shellfish sauces, or serve with shellfish.

DRAWN BUTTER

Drawn butter is melted butter, used as a sauce. It is sometimes thickened.

DRAWN BUTTER SAUCE

1/3 cup butter or margarine
3   tablespoons flour
1 1/2 cups vegetable or fish stock
1/2 teaspoon salt
1/8 teaspoon pepper
1   teaspoon lemon juice

Melt half the butter. Add flour and blend until smooth. Gradually add stock.

Bring to boiling point, stirring constantly. Cook 3 minutes. Add seasonings and remaining butter.

Drawn Butter with Anchovy: Season Drawn Butter Sauce to taste with anchovy paste.

Drawn Butter with Capers: Add 1 tablespoon drained capers to Drawn Butter Sauce.

Drawn Butter with Egg: Add 2 sliced hard-cooked eggs to Drawn Butter Sauce.

Drawn Butter with Seafood: Add 1/2 cup cooked or canned shrimp or other seafood to Drawn Butter Sauce.

PAPRIKA BUTTER

Melt 2 tablespoons butter (clarified butter is preferred) in a saucepan. Cook 2 tablespoons finely chopped onion in it until light brown. Blend in 1 teaspoon paprika and cool.

Cream 4 tablespoons butter and blend into the paprika mixture. Strain through a fine sieve. Serve with fish or poultry or for finishing a paprika sauce.

MUSTARD BUTTER FOR FISH

Melt 1/4 cup butter and add to it a little at a time 1 1/2 teaspoons prepared mustard.

CHILI SAUCE BUTTER

Heat 1/4 cup butter or margarine. Add 2 tablespoons chili sauce and 1 tablespoon lemon juice.

BERÇY BUTTER

2   teaspoons finely chopped shallots
3/4 cup dry white wine
1/4 cup butter
2   teaspoons chopped parsley
Salt and pepper

Simmer shallots and wine in a saucepan until reduced to about 1/4 original quantity. Cool.

Cream butter with parsley and blend into wine-shallot mixture. Season to taste with salt and pepper. Serve on broiled meats.

MARCHAND DE VIN BUTTER

Prepare Berçy Butter using dry red wine instead of white wine. Use only 1 teaspoon chopped parsley. Use on broiled meats.

LEMON BUTTER

Combine 2 to 3 tablespoons lemon juice with 1/2 cup melted butter or margarine. Add 1 tablespoon chopped parsley and a dash of paprika.

Quick Sauces with Canned Soups

Condensed soups when heated may be the right consistency for the sauce you want. Use such soups as asparagus, celery, mushroom, tomato, etc.

Vary the seasonings by using about 2 tablespoons sherry wine, a little salt, pepper, chili powder, cayenne or Tabasco sauce, Worcestershire sauce, curry powder, dry mustard, etc.

If the sauce is too thick, dilute with a little milk or stock.

Ready-to-serve soups may be thickened with a roux made of flour blended into melted butter, but be sure to cook several minutes after blending in the roux. Specific examples of such sauces are given in this section.

QUICK CREOLE SAUCE

1/4 cup finely chopped onion
1/4 cup finely chopped green pepper
2   tablespoons melted shortening or oil
1/2 cup water
1   can (1 1/4 cups) condensed tomato soup
1   teaspoon vinegar
Black or cayenne pepper to taste
Dash of Tabasco sauce

Cook onion and green pepper until tender in shortening in heavy skillet.

Add remaining ingredients and cook over low heat about 10 minutes.

Use on rice, seafood, roast meats, or as a hot "dunking" sauce. Makes about 2 cups.

QUICK TOMATO SAUCE

1   can (1 1/4 cups) condensed tomato soup
1/4 bay leaf
4   whole cloves
1   sprig parsley

Combine and heat thoroughly. Strain before serving.

QUICK À LA KING SAUCE

1   finely chopped green pepper
1   tablespoon butter or margarine
1   can (1 1/4 cups) condensed cream of mushroom soup
1   pimiento, chopped

Sauté green pepper in melted butter. Add to heated mushroom soup with pimiento.

QUICK SPANISH SAUCE

2   tablespoons finely chopped onion
1   tablespoon finely chopped green pepper
2   tablespoons shortening or bacon drippings
1   can (1 1/4 cups) condensed tomato soup
1/2 cup cooked mushrooms, if desired

Cook onion and green pepper until tender in shortening.

Stir in soup and mushrooms; continue cooking over low heat about 5 minutes.

This sauce is especially good on omelets, meat, or cooked rice. Makes about 2 cups.

QUICK MUSHROOM SAUCE

Combine 1 can (1 1/4 cups) condensed cream of mushroom soup with 1/2 cup hot milk. Heat thoroughly. Serve at once.

QUICK ONION SAUCE

Heat 1 can ready-to-serve onion soup. Blend in a little flour to thicken it and cook a few minutes.

If desired, add a little grated cheese just before serving.

QUICK HOT MUSTARD SAUCE

Blend 1 can (1 1/4 cups) condensed cream of celery soup, 1/2 cup milk, and 2 tablespoons prepared mustard; heat well.

Serve over broccoli, asparagus, cauliflower, carrots, or with tongue, ham, corned beef. Makes 2 cups.

SAUCES WITH DRIED SOUPS

Interesting time-saving sauces may be made from the packaged dried soups although they take a little longer than the canned soups. For a well-flavored base, use about half the liquid called for normally. These packaged mixes are particularly suitable in making casserole dishes; however go easy on seasonings until the dish has cooked for at least 20 minutes and you have tasted it.

Cold Sauces

AIOLA SAUCE

A famous French sauce of the mayonnaise type, with a strong garlic flavor, sometimes called Garlic Mayonnaise.

2 or 3 garlic cloves
2 egg yolks
7 or 8 tablespoons olive oil
1 teaspoon strained lemon juice, scant
Few drops cold water
Salt and freshly-ground pepper

Skin and mash the garlic cloves very thoroughly; combine with egg yolks. Beat in the olive oil, drop by drop at first, increasing to a thin stream as the sauce begins to thicken.

Blend well, stirring constantly, and when half the oil has been beaten in, alternate with the remaining oil the lemon juice and a few drops of cold water.

Adjust seasonings to taste with salt and freshly-ground pepper. Serve very cold with poached fish and boiled beef. Makes about 1/2 cup.

Note: If the sauce should curdle, place another egg yolk into a bowl and beat the curdled sauce into it very very slowly.

GRIBICHE SAUCE (HARD-COOKED EGG MAYONNAISE)

3 hard-cooked eggs
1/2 teaspoon salt
1 teaspoon prepared mustard
Dash of pepper
1 1/2 cups olive oil or salad oil
1/2 cup vinegar
1/2 cup chopped sour pickles
1 tablespoon mixed chopped parsley, chervil, tarragon, and chives

Separate the eggs and crush the yolks in a bowl until smooth. Blend in salt, mustard, and pepper.

Add oil a few drops at a time, beating constantly, until about 2 tablespoons of the oil have been added. Then add the oil in a thin stream while beating constantly, and adding the vinegar a little at a time whenever the mixture starts to get too thick.

Chop the egg whites finely. Press out all of the moisture from the sour pickles. Blend these into the sauce along with the mixed herbs. Serve with fish and cold meat. Makes about 3 cups.

ASPIC GLAZE FOR MEATS

1 tablespoon (1 envelope) unflavored gelatin
1/2 cup cold meat or vegetable stock
2 cups hot meat or vegetable stock
Seasoning to taste

Soften gelatin in cold stock. Dissolve it over hot water and add to hot stock. Season to taste.

Chill until somewhat thickened, then use as a glaze for cold meats, fish, and hors d'oeuvres.

RAVIGOTE SAUCE

Ravigote sauce may be any of several sauces flavored with vinegar: a French dressing with chopped onion, capers, tarragon, sometimes hard-cooked egg, and other seasonings; a hot white sauce with herbs; a highly seasoned mayonnaise containing anchovy paste.

A popular version of a cold sauce is given below.

RAVIGOTE OR VINAIGRETTE SAUCE

1 cup salad oil
1/3 cup tarragon vinegar
1 tablespoon capers
1 tablespoon minced onion
2 tablespoons minced parsley
Salt and pepper
1 hard-cooked egg, sieved or chopped fine

Combine ingredients and mix thoroughly.

Serve with cold meats, vegetables, vegetable salads, and fish. Makes about 1 1/2 cups.

GELATIN MAYONNAISE OR MAYONNAISE CHAUD-FROID

2 tablespoons (2 envelopes) unflavored gelatin
1/2 cup cold water
2 cups mayonnaise

Soften gelatin in cold water for 5 minutes and stir over hot water until the gelatin is dissolved.

Add mayonnaise and blend well. This sauce is used to bind salad mixtures which are to be molded.

It is used to coat cold fish, lobster, poultry, and meats, and fix decorations on them.

CHAUD-FROID SAUCE

Chaud-froid is a French term meaning, literally, hot-cold. It is thick cooked white sauce cooled and jellied as a coating for meats and fish.

3 tablespoons butter
1/4 cup flour
4 cups clear chicken or turkey broth
2 tablespoons (2 envelopes) plain gelatin
1/2 cup cold water
2 egg yolks
1/2 cup cream

Melt butter in a saucepan and stir in the flour. In another pan bring broth to a boil; add all at once to butter-flour mixture, stirring vigorously. When mixture is thickened and smooth, cook 5 minutes over low heat.

Soften gelatin in cold water, then add to sauce. Stir until gelatin is dissolved. Remove from heat.

Beat egg yolks with cream and slowly stir into hot sauce. Heat but do not boil. Cool but do not chill. Makes about 5 cups.

RÉMOULADE SAUCE

Rémoulade sauce is mayonnaise seasoned with various ingredients such as mustard, chopped pickle, chopped herbs, and capers. It is served with fried fish or with cold fish and shellfish.

1/2 cup finely chopped sour pickles
2 tablespoons finely chopped capers
1 tablespoon prepared mustard
1 tablespoon mixed finely chopped parsley, tarragon, chervil, and chives
2 cups mayonnaise

Press all moisture out of pickles and capers. Add with remaining ingredients to mayonnaise.

TARTARE SAUCE

Tartare (or tartar) sauce may be a cold sauce made of mayonnaise with lemon juice and various other ingredients as given below; or it may be a hot version made of white sauce with similar additions. Both are served with fried or broiled fish or shellfish.

1 cup mayonnaise or cooked dressing
1/4 cup chopped pickles
1 teaspoon minced onion
1 tablespoon capers (optional)
1 tablespoon chopped ripe olives
1 tablespoon minced parsley
1 hard-cooked egg, chopped
1 tablespoon chopped green pepper
Lemon juice

Blend ingredients and add lemon juice to thin slightly and point up flavors. Makes about 1 1/2 cups.

CHINESE MUSTARD

Stir 6 tablespoons boiling water into 2 tablespoons dry mustard. Add 1/2 teaspoon salt and 2 teaspoons salad oil. For additional yellow coloring, add some turmeric.

Chaud-froid glaze is often used to decorate a cold baked ham.

Marinades and Barbecue Sauces

A marinade is a liquid in which food is soaked (marinated) for added flavor and tenderness. Marinades usually include oil, an acid (wine, vinegar, or lemon juice), and spices and herbs. The length of time depends upon the food in question. The marinade is also used to baste meats and fish during cooking.

A commonly used marinade is the master recipe for French Dressing or one of the variations given in the salad dressing section. For a variety of marinades as well as additional barbecue sauces, see barbecue cooking section. For a complete listing of all in this book, see index.

COOKED MARINADE FOR MEATS

4   cups water
1½ cups vinegar
2   onions, chopped
1   carrot, chopped
1   clove garlic
3 or 4 sprigs parsley
12   peppercorns, bruised
1   tablespoon salt

Combine all ingredients in a saucepan. Bring to a boil; reduce heat and simmer gently for 1 hour.

Let cool, then pour over meat to be marinated. Store the cold marinade and meat in a cool place or in the refrigerator. Turn the meat occasionally. After removing the meat from the marinade, wipe it carefully with a dry cloth before cooking.

WINE MARINADE

1   cup dry wine (see note below)
1   cup olive oil
2 or 3 cloves garlic, split
2   teaspoons dried herbs such as marjoram, rosemary, or thyme
¼   cup chopped parsley
¼   teaspoon freshly ground pepper

Mix ingredients and use for meat and poultry.
Note: Use white wine with poultry and veal, red for other meats. If desired, add ½ cup orange or pineapple juice when using with chicken or duck.

FRENCH DRESSING MARINADE

1   cup French dressing
1   clove garlic, crushed
1   teaspoon chopped parsley
Dash each of dried tarragon and thyme

Mix ingredients and use for fish, lamb, veal, chicken, or vegetables. The French dressing should preferably be made with wine vinegar.

UNCOOKED MARINADE FOR MEATS

1   large onion, thinly sliced
2   large carrots, thinly sliced
2 to 4 shallots, chopped
3   sprigs parsley
1   teaspoon salt
8   peppercorns, bruised
2   stalks celery, cut up
1   clove garlic
2   bay leaves
2   cloves
Pinch of thyme
2   cups red or white wine
½   cup salad oil

Mix all ingredients together and pour over the meat to be marinated. Store in a cool place or in the refrigerator, turning the meat occasionally. When ready to cook, wipe the meat with a cloth and reserve the marinade which is often used in cooking the meat.

SOY SAUCE MARINADE FOR STEAK

1   cup soy sauce
¼   cup brown sugar
1   tablespoon ground ginger root

Combine ingredients; pour over steak and marinate, covered, in refrigerator 2 to 3 hours.

BARBECUE SAUCE

1   medium onion, chopped
2   tablespoons fat
2   tablespoons lemon juice
1   cup water
½   cup chopped celery
½   teaspoon dry mustard
2   tablespoons vinegar
2   tablespoons brown sugar
1   cup ketchup
2   tablespoons Worcestershire sauce
⅛   teaspoon pepper
1   teaspoon salt

Brown onion in hot fat. Add remaining ingredients and simmer gently 20 to 30 minutes. Pour over meat before cooking or baste meat during roasting.

Use over baked or broiled chicken, frankfurters, braised beef, steaks, hamburgers, etc. Makes about 2 cups sauce.

LEMON BARBECUE SAUCE

1   clove garlic
½   teaspoon salt
¼   cup salad or olive oil
½   cup lemon juice
2   tablespoons grated onion
½   teaspoon black pepper
1   teaspoon Worcestershire sauce

Mash garlic with salt in bowl; stir in remaining ingredients.
Chill 24 hours. Especially nice for chicken. Makes ¾ cup.

For a barbecued touch, spoon barbecue sauce over chicken toward end of broiling.

QUICK BARBECUE SAUCE

1   can (1¼ cups) condensed cream of tomato soup, undiluted
½   cup India relish
¼   cup finely chopped onion
1   tablespoon Worcestershire sauce
1   tablespoon flour

Combine soup, relish, onion, and Worcestershire. Blend in flour, stirring constantly, over low heat.
Bring to boiling point and simmer 3 minutes.
Use for barbecued meat, poultry, or fish, or serve hot with meat or fish loaf, on frankfurters, etc.

QUICK BARBECUE SAUCE #2

⅓   cup finely chopped onion
⅓   cup finely chopped celery
½   clove garlic, minced
3   tablespoons melted shortening or oil
1   can (1¼ cups) condensed tomato soup
2   tablespoons brown sugar
2   tablespoons Worcestershire sauce
2   tablespoons lemon juice or vinegar
2   teaspoons prepared mustard
4   drops Tabasco sauce, if desired

Cook onion, celery, and garlic until soft in shortening in heavy skillet.
Add remaining ingredients; stir well and simmer 10 minutes.
Excellent on broiled steaks, chops, chicken, baked spareribs, meat loaf or with hot dogs or hamburgers. Makes about 2½ cups.

KETCHUP BARBECUE SAUCE

2   medium onions, chopped
4   tablespoons fat
½   clove garlic, grated
½   cup ketchup
1   bouillon cube dissolved in 1 cup water
2   tablespoons Worcestershire sauce
Salt and pepper to taste

Cook onion in fat until golden; add rest of ingredients. Simmer for 30 minutes.
Use as a baste for turkey broilers, chickens, short ribs, and hamburgers. Makes about 1 pint.

Master Sauces

WHITE SAUCE (Master Recipe)

Every cook should learn to make a perfect white sauce, often called cream sauce, although it is usually made with milk. It is used for creaming foods like fish, poultry, and vegetables. It is the basis of many dishes such as cream soups, soufflés, and scalloped dishes, and also is the basis for many other sauces.

Thin White Sauce:

1 tablespoon butter or fat
1 tablespoon flour
1/4 teaspoon salt
1 cup milk, cream, or stock

Medium White Sauce:

2 tablespoons butter or fat
2 tablespoons flour
1/4 teaspoon salt
1 cup milk, cream, or stock

Thick White Sauce:

3 tablespoons butter or fat
3 to 4 tablespoons flour
1/4 teaspoon or more salt
1 cup milk, cream, or stock

Use methods 1, 2, or 3 (below). Makes about 1 cup sauce.

Method 1: Melt fat, stir in flour and salt. Cook until mixture bubbles.

Remove from heat; add liquid, and stir until smooth.

Cook in double boiler or over low heat until mixture thickens, stirring constantly or not at all.

Method 2: Melt fat and remove from heat. Add flour and salt. Stir until smooth.

Add liquid gradually, stirring constantly over low heat until mixture thickens.

Method 3: Stir enough liquid into flour and salt to form a thin smooth paste.

Scald remainder of liquid in double boiler. Add flour paste to hot liquid, stirring constantly until mixture thickens.

Cover and cook 20 minutes longer. Stir in fat just before serving.

To keep hot and prevent crust from forming over sauce, place over hot water and cover tightly.

WHITE SAUCE USES

Thin Sauce: Use as base for cream soups and other sauces.

Medium Sauce: Use for creamed and scalloped dishes, and gravies.

Thick Sauce: Use for croquettes and soufflés.

WHITE SAUCE VARIATIONS

Anchovy Egg Sauce: To 1 cup thin white sauce add 1/4 teaspoon anchovy paste. Boil the mixture, stirring it constantly, for 3 minutes. Remove the saucepan from the heat and add 2 hard-cooked eggs, finely chopped.

Asparagus Sauce: Add 1/2 cup cooked or canned asparagus, cut into small pieces, to hot medium white sauce. Serve with omelets or soufflés.

Caper Sauce: Add 3 to 4 tablespoons chopped capers and 1 teaspoon lemon juice to white sauce. Serve with fish.

Cheese Sauce: Add 1/2 to 1 cup chopped or grated American cheese and a dash of Worcestershire sauce or paprika (optional) to white sauce.

Stir over hot, not boiling, water until cheese is melted. Serve with fish, eggs, macaroni, or rice.

Cheese Olive Sauce: Prepare thin white sauce and omit salt. Add 1/2 to 1 cup chopped or grated American cheese and 1/2 cup sliced stuffed olives to white sauce.

Stir over hot, not boiling, water until cheese is melted. Serve with macaroni, rice, or vegetables.

Cheese Tomato Sauce: Use 1/2 cup tomato juice or strained tomatoes and 1/2 cup milk in preparing medium sauce.

Add 1/4 cup grated or finely cut American cheese to hot sauce. Stir until melted. Serve over cauliflower.

Cold Chiffon Sauce: Stir 1 egg yolk into 1 cup medium white sauce. Add salt and pepper to taste. Let sauce stand for 10 minutes and add 2 tablespoons tarragon vinegar. Cool and fold in 1 stiffly beaten egg white. Serve well chilled with cold fish.

Rich Cheese Sauce: To 1 cup thick white sauce, add 2 well beaten egg yolks, and 1/4 cup grated cheese. Heat in double boiler over hot water without boiling until the cheese melts.

Chivry Sauce: Combine 1/2 cup dry white wine, 1 teaspoon each chopped chives, chervil, and tarragon, and 1 tablespoon chopped watercress in a saucepan; cook until it is reduced to a third of original quantity.

Add 2 cups medium white sauce and rub through a fine sieve.

Cook 1 tablespoon chopped spinach with a teaspoon of chopped tarragon and chervil in a little water for a few minutes. Rub through a fine sieve: add to the sauce to color it. Use for eggs and poultry.

Chestnut Sauce: Roast or broil a dozen chestnuts until they are tender, then put them through a food chopper using the finest blade or rub them through a sieve. Season with salt, pepper, cayenne, and grated nutmeg to taste. Combine with 2 cups thin white sauce mixed with 1/2 cup scalded cream. Serve with poultry.

Crabmeat Sauce: Remove bony particles from crabmeat and add 1/2 to 1 cup flaked canned crabmeat to seasoned medium white sauce.

Flavor with 1 tablespoon dry white wine if desired.

Cream Onion or Celery Sauce: Sauté 1/4 cup finely chopped onion or celery in 1 tablespoon butter or margarine. Add to 1 cup medium white sauce.

Creole Sauce: Use tomato juice or strained tomatoes for the liquid.

Sauté minced onion, chopped green pepper, and minced celery in the butter before flour is added.

Curry Sauce: Add 1/4 to 1/2 teaspoon curry powder with dry ingredients. Serve with chicken, lamb, rice or fish.

Dill Sauce: Add 3 tablespoons minced fresh dill to 1 cup hot, seasoned medium white sauce.

Egg Sauce: Add 2 chopped hard-cooked eggs to white sauce, additional salt, and a dash of paprika. Serve with fish.

Goldenrod Sauce: Add 2 chopped hard-cooked egg whites to 1 cup seasoned medium white sauce. Pour over fish and sprinkle with chopped hard-cooked egg yolks.

Green Pea Sauce: Add 1/2 cup hot cooked or canned peas and 1 tablespoon chopped pimiento to hot medium white sauce. Serve with omelets or salmon or tuna loaf.

Horseradish Sauce: Add 2 to 4 tablespoons prepared drained horseradish, and 1/4 to 1/2 teaspoon prepared mustard to white sauce. Serve with boiled beef or corned beef.

A perfect white sauce is smooth, glossy, satiny.

WHITE SAUCE VARIATIONS

Lobster or Shrimp Sauce: Add ½ to 1 cup canned or cooked lobster meat or shrimp, cut into small pieces to seasoned medium white sauce.

For added flavor, add a tablespoon dry white wine. Serve with omelets, baked, broiled, or poached fish.

Milanese Sauce: Use ½ cup veal stock and ½ cup milk in preparing medium white sauce.

Add 2 tablespoons grated Parmesan cheese to the thickened sauce. Serve with veal.

Mock Hollandaise Sauce: To ½ cup well seasoned white sauce, add equal amount of mayonnaise and enough lemon juice to sharpen. Serve on asparagus and other green vegetables.

Mushroom Sauce: Add ½ to 1 cup sliced cooked or canned mushrooms to white sauce. Serve with chicken or vegetables.

Mustard Sauce: Add 1 tablespoon prepared mustard to white sauce. Serve with fish or tongue.

Oyster Sauce: Gently cook ½ cup small oysters in their own liquid until they plump and the edges begin to curl, about 3 minutes.

Add to hot medium white sauce. Serve with omelets, fish patties, and timbales.

Paprika Sauce: Add ½ to 1 teaspoon paprika with dry ingredients. Season with ¼ teaspoon onion juice, if desired. Serve with noodles, macaroni, or chicken.

Pimiento Sauce: Add ¼ cup chopped pimiento to white sauce; ¼ cup chopped green pepper may be added, if desired. Serve with fish or vegetables.

Hot Ravigote Sauce: Combine ⅓ cup dry white wine, ⅓ cup vinegar, and 6 finely chopped shallots in a saucepan; cook until reduced to a third of original quantity.

Add 2 cups medium white sauce and simmer gently for 4 to 6 minutes. Remove from heat; add 2 tablespoons butter and 1 teaspoon mixed chopped chives, chervil, and tarragon. Serve with fish or poultry.

Wine Egg Sauce: To 1½ cups medium white sauce, add 1 teaspoon Worcestershire sauce, 4 chopped hard-cooked eggs, and 2 tablespoons sherry or other white wine. Blend thoroughly and serve hot on fish.

Yellow Sauce: Add a little cold water to a slightly beaten egg yolk, and stir slowly into the white sauce.

Cook for a minute over hot water, stirring constantly. Serve over vegetables, meat or poultry.

WHITE SAUCE MIX WITH DRY MILK
(Master Recipe)

  2 cups nonfat dry milk solids
  1 cup enriched flour
  1 cup butter or margarine

Combine all ingredients with pastry blender until mixture is consistency of coarse corn meal.

Store in covered jars in refrigerator. Makes about 2 quarts medium sauce.

This master mix can be used for thin, medium, or thick white sauces. Just measure the required amount into a saucepan; add water and cook until thickened, adding the desired seasonings.

Thin White Sauce: Use ¼ cup mix with 1 cup water.

Medium White Sauce: Use ½ cup mix with 1 cup water.

Thick White Sauce: Use ¾ cup mix with 1 cup water.

HOLLANDAISE SAUCE
(Master Recipe)

This queen of sauces makes a superb dish out of the plainest and most simply cooked vegetables. It is a favorite with fish, broiled or roasted meats and poultry, and in such special dishes as Eggs Benedict.

The name is derived from the French term, *hollandaise,* the feminine of *hollandais,* meaning of Holland, a country famous for its butter which is used so liberally in this calorie-loaded sauce.

Béarnaise Sauce, which may be considered a special variation of Hollandaise Sauce, was named in honor of the gourmet king, Henry IV of France.

  ½ cup butter or margarine
  4 egg yolks
  2 tablespoons lemon juice
  ¼ teaspoon salt
Dash of cayenne
  ¼ cup boiling water

Divide butter into 3 portions. Beat egg yolks and lemon juice together. Add 1 piece of butter and cook in double boiler, stirring constantly until mixture begins to thicken.

Remove from range, add second piece of butter, and stir rapidly.

Then add remaining butter and continue to stir until mixture is completely blended. Add salt, cayenne, and boiling water.

Return to double boiler; cook until thickened, stirring constantly. Serve at once.

Note: Sauce may separate if cooked too long, or at too high a temperature, or if permitted to stand too long before serving. To smooth, beat in 1 tablespoon boiling water and a little lemon juice drop by drop, with a rotary beater.

Hollandaise Sauce Variations

Béarnaise Sauce: Reduce lemon juice to 1½ tablespoons. Add 1 teaspoon each chopped tarragon and chopped parsley, 1 tablespoon tarragon vinegar, and 1 teaspoon onion juice or ½ teaspoon onion salt. Serve with baked or broiled fish.

Chive Hollandaise Sauce: Add 1½ tablespoons finely chopped chives to sauce. Serve with vegetables.

Cucumber Hollandaise Sauce: Add 1 cup drained, chopped cucumber to sauce. Serve with fish.

Dill Hollandaise Sauce: Add 1 tablespoon chopped dill to sauce.

Mint Hollandaise Sauce: Add 1 tablespoon finely chopped mint to sauce.

BLENDER HOLLANDAISE SAUCE

  ½ cup butter
  3 egg yolks (at room temperature)
  2 tablespoons lemon juice
  ¼ teaspoon salt
Pinch of cayenne

Heat butter to bubbling but do not brown. Combine in the blender the egg yolks, lemon juice, salt, and cayenne. Blend these ingredients at low speed for a few seconds.

Add hot butter gradually and blend a few seconds longer until the sauce is smooth and thickened. Makes about 1 cup.

MALTAISE SAUCE

Prepare 1 cup Hollandaise sauce. Just before serving add 2 or 3 tablespoons orange juice and 1 teaspoon grated orange rind. This sauce should be pink; hence, if desired, add 1 or 2 drops pink vegetable coloring. Use with asparagus.

MOUSSELINE SAUCE

Prepare Hollandaise sauce. Just before serving over fish or vegetables, fold in an equal quantity of whipped cream. Serve hot or cold.

Hollandaise sauce makes a superb dish out of the plainest and simplest cooked vegetables and it is a favorite with meats, poultry, and fish.

FIGARO SAUCE

Prepare 1 cup Hollandaise Sauce. Beat in very slowly ¼ cup warm tomato purée. Fold in 1 tablespoon finely chopped parsley. Correct seasoning with salt to taste and a few grains cayenne.

VELOUTÉ SAUCE
(Master Recipe)

Velouté is French for velvety. Velouté sauce is a basic French sauce from which many other famous sauces are derived such as the variations given here. Fish, chicken, or veal stock is used in its preparation depending on how it is to be used. For example, in Normandy (or Normande) sauce, fish or shellfish stock is used because it is to be served with seafood. Allemande sauce is a smooth yellow sauce served on eggs, fish, meats, and vegetables, and also on chicken and fish loaves and croquettes. Soubise sauce contains onions and is served with meats, especially lamb and veal.

2 tablespoons butter or margarine
2 tablespoons flour
1 cup fish, chicken, or veal stock
Salt to taste
Dash of white pepper
⅛ teaspoon nutmeg (optional)

Melt butter over low heat. Blend in flour. Remove from heat and gradually stir in stock.

Return to heat and cook, stirring constantly, until smooth and thick. Blend in seasonings.

If desired, strain through a very fine sieve. Serve hot over croquettes, baked fish, etc. Makes about 1 cup.

Velouté Sauce Variations

Allemande Sauce: Stir into strained velouté sauce 1 well beaten egg, 1 teaspoon lemon juice, and 2 tablespoons cream or finely grated Parmesan cheese.

Anchovy Velouté Sauce: Omit salt and use fish stock in master recipe.

Blend 1½ teaspoons anchovy paste into flour and butter mixture.

Add 1 tablespoon finely minced parsley just before serving.

Caper Velouté Sauce: Prepare master recipe. Add 1 teaspoon capers to strained sauce. Serve with lamb or vegetables.

If serving with fish, substitute fish stock for chicken or veal stock.

Fish Velouté Sauce: Use fish stock in master recipe.

Normandy Sauce: Use fish stock in master recipe. Beat a little hot sauce into 2 slightly beaten egg yolks and beat into remaining sauce. Blend in 1 tablespoon lemon juice, salt, pepper, and cayenne to taste.

Parsley Sauce: Add 2 tablespoons finely chopped parsley to strained Allemande Sauce.

Soubise Sauce (Onion Sauce): Cover 3 medium-sized onions with boiling water and cook until soft. Drain and rub onion pulp through a sieve into Velouté Sauce.

Add ½ cup cream and stir until boiling point is reached.

Remove from heat and stir in 1 tablespoon butter. Season with salt to taste.

Sauce Poulette: Add ½ cup sliced cooked mushrooms to strained Allemande Sauce.

SUPREME SAUCE

2 cups rich chicken stock
3 or 4 mushrooms or stems and peelings of mushrooms
1 cup Velouté sauce
1 cup sweet cream
Salt and pepper

Cook chicken stock with mushrooms until it is reduced to ⅓ the original quantity.

Combine with Velouté sauce; bring to a boil and reduce to about 1 cup.

Gradually add cream, stirring constantly. Season to taste with salt and pepper. Serve with eggs, fish, and poultry. Makes about 1½ cups.

BASIC BROWN SAUCE

The basic brown sauce is also known as Spanish Sauce or Sauce Espagnole. It is used as the basis of many other sauces and as an ingredient in various dishes. A good quality clear brown beef stock should be used. Throughout the preparation very slow simmering is required for gradual reduction, and retention of flavor.

½ cup fat (beef, veal, or pork drippings)
1 carrot, coarsely chopped
2 onions, coarsely chopped
½ cup flour
8 cups (2 quarts) brown beef stock
1 clove garlic
2 stalks celery
3 sprigs parsley
1 bay leaf
Pinch of thyme
½ cup tomato purée or tomato juice, or ¼ cup tomato sauce

Melt fat in a large heavy saucepan. Add carrot and onions and cook until they just start to turn golden, shaking the pan for even cooking.

Add flour and cook, stirring frequently, until the flour takes on a good brown color (hazelnut-brown) and the carrot and onions are also brown.

Add 3 cups of the boiling stock, the garlic, celery, parsley, bay leaf, and thyme. Cook, stirring constantly, until the mixture thickens, then add 3 more cups of stock.

Simmer very slowly over low heat, stirring occasionally, until the mixture is reduced to about 3 cups. This should take 1 to 1½ hours. As it cooks, skim off the excess fat rising to the surface. Add tomato purée and cook a few minutes longer, then strain through a fine sieve.

Add remaining 2 cups stock and continue cooking slowly until the sauce is reduced to about 4 cups, skimming the surface from time to time as needed. Cool, stirring occasionally.

Store in a covered jar in the refrigerator. If not used within a week, recook it, put in another jar, and return to refrigerator. A little good melted fat over the top will seal it and help keep it a little longer.

Variations: For a richer sauce, cook ½ cup diced fat salt pork along with the carrot and onions. When adding the final 2 cups of beef stock also add ½ cup beef gravy or juice from roast beef.

LYONNAISE SAUCE OR BROWN ONION SAUCE

2 tablespoons butter
2 onions, finely chopped
⅓ cup dry white wine
1 cup basic brown sauce
1 teaspoon finely chopped parsley

Melt butter in a saucepan; add onions and cook until golden brown. Add wine and simmer until reduced to half.

Add brown sauce and simmer 15 minutes. Just before serving stir in parsley. Use with meat, especially leftovers, and vegetables. Makes 1¼ cups.

DIABLE SAUCE
(Brown Devil Sauce)

3 shallots or green onions, finely chopped
7 or 8 peppercorns, finely crushed
⅓ cup dry white wine or vinegar
1 cup basic brown sauce
1 teaspoon Worcestershire sauce
1 teaspoon chopped parsley

Combine shallots, peppercorns, and wine; cook until reduced to one-third.

Add brown sauce, Worcestershire sauce, and parsley. Serve with broiled foods. Makes about 1⅓ cups.

MADEIRA SAUCE #1

Prepare 2 cups basic brown sauce and simmer gently until reduced to about 1¼ cups. Add ⅓ cup Madeira and bring again just to boiling point but do not allow to boil, or the flavor of the wine will be impaired. Serve with game, beef, veal, ham, or poultry.

MASTER BROWN SAUCE
(Quick Method)

4 tablespoons butter or fat
4 tablespoons flour
2 cups meat, vegetable, or fish stock
1 teaspoon salt
1/8 teaspoon pepper

Melt butter, blend in flour and cook until browned, stirring constantly.

Gradually add stock, stirring constantly, until mixture boils and thickens.

Add salt and pepper; cook 3 minutes longer, stirring constantly.

Serve with meat, poultry, fish or vegetables. Makes 2 cups.

Brown Sauce Variations

Creole Brown Sauce: Sauté 1/4 cup chopped onion and 1/2 cup chopped green pepper in fat before adding flour.

Dill Brown Sauce: Add to brown sauce 2 tablespoons wine or cider vinegar and chopped dill to taste. Serve with veal or lamb.

Giblet Gravy #2: Substitute pan drippings for other fat. Add chopped cooked chicken or turkey giblets to gravy.

Mushroom Brown Sauce: Sauté 1 cup sliced mushrooms and 1 teaspoon chopped onion in fat before adding flour.

Olive Brown Sauce: Add about 12 sliced pitted green or ripe olives to brown sauce.

Pan Gravy: In Master Brown Sauce substitute pan drippings for other fat. Use water or stock.

Piquant Brown Sauce: Simmer together for a few minutes 2 tablespoons each tarragon vinegar and finely chopped green pepper, 1 teaspoon each chopped onion and chopped capers. Add to brown sauce with 2 tablespoons chopped pickle.

Serve with fish, beef, veal, or tongue. If used with fish, use fish stock when preparing master brown sauce.

Port Wine Brown Sauce: To 1 cup of brown sauce add 2 tablespoons port wine. Simmer about 5 minutes.

Savory Horseradish Brown Sauce: Add 3 to 4 tablespoons prepared horseradish and 1 tablespoon prepared mustard to brown sauce.

Spanish Brown Sauce: Sauté 1/4 cup chopped onion, 1/2 cup chopped green pepper, 1/2 cup sliced mushrooms in fat before adding flour.

Substitute 1 cut tomato juice or stewed tomatoes for 1 cup stock. Serve with rice, spaghetti, or meat balls.

BECHAMEL SAUCE
(Master Recipe)

This name is often applied to plain white sauce or to any sauce based on it. However, the original or true Béchamel is made of chicken or veal stock, cream or milk, flour, and butter and is usually seasoned with onions. Use it with any of the variations suggested for white sauce. It is said to have originated with the Marquis de Béchamel, maître d'hôtel of Louis XIV.

A famous variation is Mornay Sauce, believed to be named for Philippe de Mornay, premier of France under Henry IV.

1½ cups chicken or veal stock
1 sprig parsley
6 celery leaves
1/2 small onion
1/4 bay leaf
6 whole black peppers
3 tablespoons butter or margarine
3 tablespoons flour
Few grains cayenne
1/4 teaspoon salt
Few grains nutmeg
1 cup scalded milk

Simmer stock with parsley, celery leaves, onion, bay leaf, and whole black peppers for 20 minutes.

Strain and measure. If necessary, add water to make 1 cup.

Melt butter over low heat and blend in flour and seasonings. Gradually add hot stock and scalded milk.

Bring to boiling point and let boil 2 minutes or until thick and smooth.

Strain through fine sieve. Serve on chicken croquettes, chicken mousse, or fried chicken. Makes about 2 cups.

Bechamel Sauce Variations

Fish Bechamel Sauce: Substitute fish stock for chicken or veal stock.

Stir a little hot stock into 1 slightly beaten egg and beat into remaining sauce. Blend in 1 tablespoon lemon juice.

Mornay Sauce: Add 2 to 4 tablespoons grated Parmesan cheese to sauce. Serve with vegetables or fish.

Yellow Bechamel Sauce: Stir 1 slightly beaten egg yolk into sauce.

Mushroom Bechamel Sauce: Sauté 1 cup sliced mushrooms in butter 5 minutes before blending in flour.

PAPRIKA SAUCE OR HUNGARIAN SAUCE

1 cup Béchamel sauce
1 tablespoon finely chopped onion
2 tablespoons butter
2 teaspoons Hungarian paprika

Prepare Béchamel sauce. Sauté onion in 1 tablespoon butter, drain well and add to sauce. Add paprika, then put through a fine sieve. Add 1 tablespoon butter. Serve with fish, poultry, lamb, and veal.

AURORE SAUCE

Prepare 2 cups Béchamel sauce and add to it 3 tablespoons very red tomato purée. Boil slightly before putting through a fine sieve. Then add 1 tablespoon butter. Serve with fish or poultry.

TOMATO SAUCE
(Master Recipe)

2 cups canned tomatoes
2 slices onion
1 teaspoon sugar
1 bay leaf
2 whole allspice
2 whole cloves
Butter or other fat
Flour
Salt and pepper

Simmer tomato, onion, sugar, and spices 10 minutes. Strain through fine sieve and measure the liquid.

For each cup liquid blend 2 tablespoons flour and 2 tablespoons melted fat. Add to tomato juice with salt and pepper to season, and stir until thickened.

Continue to cook over hot water 5 to 10 minutes. Serve hot over croquettes, meat loaf, or spaghetti.

Tomato Sauce Variations

Tomato Cheese Sauce: Add 1/2 cup grated cheese to tomato sauce. Cook until cheese is melted.

Tomato Lobster Sauce: Add 1 cup chopped cooked or canned lobster meat to tomato sauce. Use shrimp or lobster sauces over cooked spaghetti or macaroni.

Tomato Meat Sauce: Brown tiny meat balls in fat before blending in flour. Serve with spaghetti or noodles in casserole.

Tomato Shrimp Sauce: Add 1 cup canned or cooked cleaned shrimp to tomato sauce.

Tomato Wine Sauce: Add 1/4 cup sherry to tomato sauce.

CHINESE SWEET-SOUR SAUCE

1/2 cup pineapple juice
1/4 cup mild vinegar
3 tablespoons peanut or salad oil
2 tablespoons brown sugar
1 teaspoon soy sauce
1/2 teaspoon pepper

Combine ingredients and heat. Serve with fish, shellfish, and meats. For other Chinese sweet-sour sauces, see recipes in index.

MASTER BÉARNAISE SAUCE

1 cup dry white wine
1 tablespoon tarragon vinegar
1 tablespoon finely chopped shallots
    or green onion
1 sprig parsley
2 sprigs tarragon, chopped
1 sprig chervil, chopped
2 peppercorns, bruised
3 egg yolks
1 cup melted butter (½ pound)

Combine in top of double boiler the wine, vinegar, shallots or onions, parsley, tarragon, chervil, and peppercorns. Cook over direct heat until reduced to ⅔ of original volume.

Allow to cool, then place over, not in, hot water and add a little egg yolk and then a little melted butter, combining well before next addition. Continue alternating additions until all butter and eggs are added. When finished the sauce should have the consistency of heavy cream. Note: All of the egg and butter may not be needed to arrive at this consistency.

Drain through a fine sieve before serving, and correct the seasoning with salt to taste and a dash of cayenne. If desired, 1 teaspoon each of chopped chervil and tarragon leaves may be added. Serve with any broiled steak, especially beef tenderloin. It is also a luxurious choice for eggs and fish. Makes about 1½ cups.

VALOIS SAUCE

To 1 cup Béarnaise sauce, add 1 teaspoon melted beef extract to give a light brown color. Serve with eggs or broiled chicken.

CHORON SAUCE

To 1 cup Béarnaise sauce, add ¼ cup tomato purée. Use with fish, chicken, or meat.

CREOLE SAUCE #2

2 tablespoons chopped onion
2 tablespoons butter or margarine
1 tablespoon flour
2 cups canned tomatoes
½ cup chopped celery
1 green pepper, chopped
4 tablespoons chopped cooked ham
    or bacon
Chopped parsley
Salt and pepper to taste

Cook onion in butter for a few minutes. Sprinkle flour over onion and quickly stir in tomatoes, celery, and green pepper. Simmer about 20 minutes.

Add ham or bacon, parsley, and salt and pepper. Serve with omelets, spaghetti and fish. Makes about 2½ cups sauce.

TOMATO SAUCE
(Italian Style)

2 cups chopped onion
3 cloves garlic, chopped
3 tablespoons olive oil
1 No. 2½ can (3½ cups) Italian
    style plum tomatoes
2 6-ounce cans tomato paste
About 2 cups water or meat broth
1 bay leaf
½ teaspoon salt
½ teaspoon oregano or ¼ teaspoon
    each oregano and basil

Sauté onion and garlic in olive oil until brown, stirring often.

Add tomatoes, tomato paste, water or broth, bay leaf, salt, and pepper. Simmer, uncovered, stirring occasionally, about 2 hours. Add additional water as needed.

Add oregano and basil and continue cooking about 15 minutes. The sauce should be thick. Makes about 1½ quarts.

HUNTER'S SAUCE OR
CHASSEUR SAUCE

2 to 4 tablespoons butter
1 cup sliced mushrooms
½ teaspoon salt
Few grains pepper
2 shallots or green onions, finely
    chopped
½ cup red wine
1 cup basic brown sauce
2 tablespoons tomato sauce or purée
1 teaspoon chopped parsley or ½
    teaspoon each of chopped
    parsley and chopped tarragon

Melt butter in a saucepan; add mushrooms, salt, and pepper; sauté until mushrooms are lightly browned. Add shallots or green onions and wine; simmer until reduced to about half.

Add brown sauce, tomato sauce, and parsley. Simmer about 5 minutes. Correct the seasoning. Serve with poultry, game, and red meat. Makes about 2 cups.

HOT RAVIGOTE SAUCE #2

⅓ cup dry white wine
⅓ cup vinegar
5 or 6 shallots, finely chopped
2 cups rich white sauce
2 tablespoons butter
1 teaspoon mixed herbs (chopped
    chives, chervil, and tarragon)

Combine wine, vinegar, and shallots in a saucepan; cook until reduced to ⅓ original quantity.

Add white sauce; boil gently 5 or 6 minutes. Remove from heat and add butter and herbs. Serve with fish, light meats, and poultry. Makes about 2½ cups.

CHEESE SAUCE #2

2 tablespoons butter or margarine
2 tablespoons flour
1 cup milk
1 egg yolk, well beaten
½ teaspoon dry mustard
⅛ teaspoon pepper
¾ teaspoon salt
Few grains cayenne or paprika
2 tablespoons grated Parmesan
    cheese

Melt butter and blend in flour. Add milk slowly, stirring constantly. Cook over hot water until smooth and thick.

Pour over egg yolk, stirring constantly.

Season to taste. Add cheese. Serve with vegetables, fish, macaroni, or rice.

SOUR CREAM SAUCE
(SMITANE SAUCE)

1½ tablespoons butter
2 small onions, finely chopped
½ cup dry white wine
1 cup heavy sour cream, scalded
Salt and pepper
About 1 teaspoon lemon juice (op-
    tional)

Melt butter in a saucepan; add onions and pan-fry until soft but not brown. Add wine and cook until the mixture is reduced to about half, stirring occasionally.

Pour in scalded sour cream, stirring constantly, and stir until thoroughly blended. Simmer very gently 5 minutes but do not let mixture boil after adding sour cream or it will curdle.

Strain sauce through fine sieve and season with salt and pepper to taste. For a sourer effect add lemon juice to taste. Serve with fish, chicken, or light meats. Makes about 1½ cups.

BORDELAISE SAUCE

A famous brown sauce usually served with steak.

2 tablespoons butter or margarine
2 tablespoons flour
2 cups brown stock or consommé
2 cloves garlic, chopped fine
2 tablespoons chopped onion
Bit of bay leaf
2 tablespoons chopped ham
2 slices carrot
2 tablespoons chopped parsley
8 whole black peppers
1 tablespoon Worcestershire sauce
1 tablespoon ketchup
2 tablespoons sherry

Melt butter. Stir in flour until lightly browned. Add remaining ingredients except sherry and simmer 8 minutes.

Strain sauce and season with sherry, salt and pepper to taste. Makes about 2 cups.

Sauces for Meats and Poultry

POIVRADE SAUCE (PEPPER SAUCE)

A dark-brown sauce with black pepper served with meat and game, especially venison.

1/4 cup cooking oil
1 carrot, chopped
1 onion, chopped
3 sprigs parsley
1 bay leaf
Pinch of thyme
1/4 cup vinegar
1/2 cup liquid from marinade used for the meat or game (see note below)
3 cups basic brown sauce
10 peppercorns
1/2 cup dry red wine
Salt and pepper

Heat oil in saucepan; pan-fry in it the carrot and onion until golden brown. Add parsley, bay leaf, thyme, vinegar, and 1/4 cup marinade liquid. Simmer gently until reduced to 1/3 original quantity.

Add brown sauce; bring to a boil, reduce heat and simmer for 1 hour.

Add peppercorns and simmer 5 minutes more. Strain sauce into another saucepan and add remaining 1/4 cup marinade liquid. Cook slowly for 30 minutes, then add wine. Correct seasoning with salt and freshly-ground pepper to make a hot sauce. Serve with meat and game. Makes about 3 cups.
Note: If the meat or game was not marinated, see index for basic uncooked marinade for meat or game.

GRAND VENEUR SAUCE

Add 1 tablespoon truffles, diced or cut into julienne strips, to Poivrade Sauce. The sauce may be thickened with the blood of a hare or rabbit. Add the blood slowly, rotating the pan to swirl it into the sauce. Do not boil the sauce after adding the blood.

JIFFY BROWN SAUCE OR GRAVY

1/2 clove garlic
2 tablespoons butter
2 tablespoons flour
1 cup canned bouillon or 2 bouillon cubes dissolved in 1 cup boiling water
Salt and pepper
Other seasoning as desired, such as Worcestershire sauce, dry sherry, ketchup or chili sauce, lemon juice, and dried herbs

Rub a saucepan with garlic. Melt butter, blend in flour. Stir in bouillon. Bring to boiling point, stirring constantly. Season to taste with salt and pepper, and other seasonings as desired. Makes 1 cup.

ROBERT SAUCE

There is also a commercial Sauce Robert on the market, used for flavoring many dishes, but the sauce found on many menus is often made this way.

2 tablespoons finely chopped onion
1 tablespoon butter
1/3 cup dry white wine
1 tablespoon vinegar
1 cup basic brown sauce
2 tablespoons tomato sauce or tomato purée
1 tablespoon finely chopped sour pickle
1 teaspoon prepared mustard
1 teaspoon chopped parsley

Cook onion in melted butter in a saucepan until onion is golden brown. Add wine and vinegar and cook until reduced to about 3/4 of original quantity.

Add brown sauce and tomato sauce; simmer gently 10 to 15 minutes. Just before serving, stir in pickles, mustard, and parsley. Serve with meats. Makes about 1 1/4 cups.

ENGLISH BREAD SAUCE

1 onion
6 whole cloves
2 cups milk
Few grains cayenne
1 teaspoon salt
1 cup fresh fine breadcrumbs

Stud onion with cloves. Place onion and milk in a saucepan. Add cayenne and salt. Bring to boiling point. Cook 5 minutes.

Strain and add breadcrumbs. Taste and add more salt if necessary.

Serve with roast poultry or game. If a richer sauce is desired, add a little butter or cream at the end.

MARCHAND DE VIN SAUCE (Wine Merchant's Sauce)

6 tablespoons butter
6 green onions (scallions), minced, or 1/2 cup minced onion
3/4 cup dry red wine
1 1/2 cups basic brown sauce or canned beef gravy
2 tablespoons lemon juice

Melt 4 tablespoons butter. Slowly stir in onions and cook until wilted, about 5 minutes. Add wine and simmer uncovered until the liquid is reduced to about 1/4 cup, about 20 minutes.

Add brown sauce and lemon juice; heat and stir in remaining butter bit by bit. Serve with broiled steak or roast beef. Makes about 2 cups.

Mushroom Steak Sauce is a jiffy topping for steaks, chops, and hamburgers.

MUSHROOM STEAK SAUCE

1 6-ounce can sliced broiled mushrooms
1/4 cup water
Few drops Tabasco sauce
1/4 teaspoon Kitchen Bouquet
1 1/2 teaspoons cornstarch

Place all ingredients in small saucepan. Mix well. Bring to boil, stirring constantly. Salt to taste. Serve over steaks, chops, or broiled hamburgers. Makes about 1 cup sauce.

ROSEMARY SAUCE

Heat 1/4 cup dry red wine to boiling point. Remove from heat and add 1/4 teaspoon dried rosemary. Cover and let stand 5 to 10 minutes. (Note: if desired, a mixture of rosemary and other dried herbs may be used such as thyme, basil, bay leaf, sage, and marjoram.)

Strain the herb-flavored wine into 1 cup basic brown sauce. Serve with game. Makes about 1 cup.

CRANBERRY GAME SAUCE

1 teaspoon cinnamon
1/4 teaspoon ground cloves
Dash of nutmeg
3 tablespoons sugar
Grated rind of 1 lemon
1/2 cup port wine
1 can (1 pound) whole cranberry sauce

Simmer above ingredients together for 5 minutes. Stir 1 tablespoon cornstarch into spice wine mixture. Heat thoroughly, stirring until mixture thickens slightly.

To keep hot until serving time, place pan over boiling water in the bottom of the double boiler. Serving suggestions: on rock Cornish hens, pork chops, or baked ham.

CURRANT JELLY SAUCE

1 8-ounce glass currant jelly
2 tablespoons vinegar
1 teaspoon dry mustard
1/4 teaspoon ground cloves
1/4 teaspoon cinnamon

Heat jelly until melted. Add other ingredients and simmer 10 minutes. Serve hot with ham or baked canned meats. Makes about 1 cup.

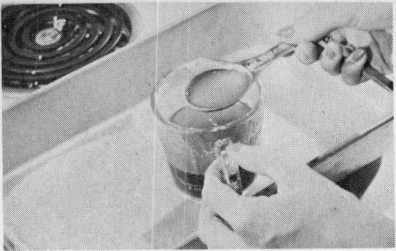

TO PREPARE GRAVY WITH PAN DRIPPINGS

1. Measure the fat and drippings to be used.

2. Measure and add flour, stirring until well blended.

3. Gradually add broth or other liquid called for in recipe.

4. Cook over low heat, stirring until thick and smooth.

HOW TO BROWN FLOUR FOR GRAVY

Spread flour on pan and place in slow oven (300°F.). Stir frequently to prevent burning; 20 to 25 minutes are required to brown 3 cups.

Flour may be browned in a skillet on top of range. Watch carefully to avoid burning flour.

Store browned flour in a tightly covered receptacle.

FLOUR PASTE FOR THICKENING SAUCES AND GRAVIES

A thin paste will give better results. The usual proportions are about 1 part

water to 2 parts flour.

Blend flour and cold water together, then stir as much as required into boiling stock or drippings. Cook until sauce thickens.

ROAST BEEF GRAVY

Skim fat from the roast drippings, leaving about 4 tablespoons in pan. Add 6 to 8 tablespoons flour and stir over moderate heat until flour is thoroughly browned. Do not add water until the flour is thoroughly browned.

Gradually add 2 cups water or stock. Cook, stirring until gravy is smooth and thickened. Season to taste with salt and pepper.

POT ROAST GRAVY

Measure amount of pot roast liquid left in the cooking pan. Add to this enough water, soup, stock, or water in which vegetables have been cooked to make the desired amount of gravy.

For each cup of liquid, measure 2 tablespoons flour and make a smooth paste by adding enough cold water to blend. The water must be cold to prevent lumping. Use a spoon or egg beater to thin flour paste.

Add paste gradually to pot roast liquid, stirring constantly over moderate heat. Bring to a boil and simmer 2 or 3 minutes.

GIBLET GRAVY

Chop cooked giblets fine and save broth in which they were cooked.

Skim off excess fat in roasting pan, leaving about 1/2 cup for quart of gravy.

Add 1/2 cup flour and stir until smooth over low heat.

Gradually add 4 cups broth, using water if there isn't enough broth. Stir constantly to keep gravy smooth as it thickens.

Add chopped giblets, and salt and pepper, to season. For thinner gravy, add more liquid. Makes 1 quart.

COUNTRY GRAVY

2 cups milk
1/4 cup flour
1/4 cup drippings
Salt and pepper

This is milk gravy made after frying chicken, salt pork, or sausage.

Make a smooth thin paste with a little of the milk and flour.

Add paste to hot drippings, stirring constantly.

Add remaining milk, stir and cook until gravy is smooth and thickened. Season to taste.

SOUR CREAM GRAVY

Prepare gravy according to any of given recipes. Add 1/2 cup sour cream for each cup of gravy, just before removing from heat.

Cook just long enough to heat sour cream. Do not boil as sour cream will curdle.

WINE GRAVY

Make gravy according to any of given recipes. Add 2 tablespoons wine for each cup of gravy and cook only long enough to heat through.

Use red wine for beef gravy and white wine for veal.

MADEIRA SAUCE #2

1 cup basic brown sauce
1/4 cup Madeira or dry sherry
1 teaspoon beef extract
1 or 2 tablespoons butter
Additional 2 tablespoons Madeira

Prepare brown sauce, then simmer gently until reduced to about 3/4 cup. Add 1/4 cup Madeira or dry sherry and beef extract. Simmer gently 5 to 10 minutes.

Add butter bit by bit, swirling it in by moving the pan in a circular motion. Keep hot, but do not let sauce boil after adding butter.

Finally add 2 additional tablespoons Madeira, swirling it in the same way. Serve with sautéed fillet of beef. Makes about 1 cup.

Note: This sauce may be made in the same pan in which you have sautéed the meat. Pour off the fat from pan, then proceed as above.

PÉRIGUEUX SAUCE

Make Madeira sauce and add 1 tablespoon chopped truffles and a little liquid from truffles to it. Add 1 tablespoon butter, swirling it in by moving the pan in a circular motion. Keep hot but do not let sauce boil after adding butter. Use with croquettes, shirred eggs, and chicken.

PÉRIGOURDINE SAUCE

This sauce is usually very similar to Sauce Périgueux; however the truffles are diced small instead of chopped.

PIQUANT SAUCE

1 tablespoon butter
2 tablespoons finely chopped onion
2 tablespoons dry white wine or vinegar
1 cup basic brown sauce
1 tablespoon tomato sauce or purée
2 tablespoons finely chopped sour pickle
1 tablespoon chopped parsley

Melt butter in a saucepan; add onion and cook until lightly browned. Add wine and simmer until liquid is almost evaporated. Add brown sauce and tomato sauce and simmer 10 minutes.

Just before serving, add pickle and parsley. Adjust the seasoning with salt. This is good for reheating leftover meats. Makes about 1 1/4 cups.

SOUTHERN CREAM GRAVY FOR FRIED CHICKEN

Pour off all but 2 tablespoons fat from the pan in which chicken has been fried. Stir in 1 tablespoon flour and when the mixture is well blended, pour in slowly, stirring constantly and scraping in the brown bits, 1 cup light cream. When the sauce boils, taste for seasoning and add salt and pepper if required. Pour over fried chicken.

ORANGE SAUCE FOR ROAST DUCK OR GOOSE

⅔ cup sugar
¼ teaspoon salt
2 teaspoons cornstarch
1 cup boiling water
1 teaspoon butter or margarine
Juice and grated rind of 2 oranges

Mix sugar, salt, and cornstarch. Pour hot water over mixture, stirring constantly. Cook until thick and clear.

Add butter, orange juice, and grated rind just before removing from heat. Stir well and serve with duck. Makes about 2 cups.

GINGERSNAP SAUCE

5 crushed gingersnaps
½ cup brown sugar
¼ cup vinegar
1 teaspoon onion juice
1 cup hot water
1 lemon, sliced
¼ cup raisins

Mix ingredients in saucepan and heat, stirring constantly, until smooth and fairly thick. Serve with boiled tongue. Makes 1½ cups.

HORSERADISH SAUCE

1 tablespoon butter or margarine
1 tablespoon flour
1 cup milk
½ cup prepared horseradish
1 tablespoon lemon juice
Salt and pepper
1 tablespoon minced pimiento

Melt butter and blend in flour. Slowly add milk, stirring constantly until the mixture boils.

Add drained horseradish to lemon

Raisin sauce is a traditional accompaniment for smoked tongue.

juice, seasonings, and pimiento. Add to cream sauce and serve hot. Serve with "boiled" meats and poultry. Makes 1½ cups.

CURRY SAUCE

2 tablespoons butter or margarine
1 medium onion, chopped
2 tablespoons flour
½ teaspoon curry powder
1 cup beef broth, bouillon, or consommé

Melt butter; add onion and let cook until tender.

Stir in flour; let it brown slightly, then add curry and liquid. Cook and stir until sauce is thickened and smooth.

A hint of garlic may be added to this sauce by cooking a clove with onion for 1 minute. Serve with veal, lamb, or poultry. Makes 1 cup.

CUMBERLAND SAUCE

This sauce is named for an English duke.

1 tablespoon Port wine
Grated rind of 1 lemon
Juice of 1 lemon
Grated rind of 1 orange
1 tablespoon confectioners' sugar
1 teaspoon prepared mustard
½ cup melted red currant jelly

Combine ingredients and blend well. If the jelly is very stiff, dilute with 1 or 2 tablespoons hot water. Serve with any cold meat or game. Makes about ¾ cup.

MINT SAUCE FOR LAMB

2 to 3 tablespoons sugar
¼ cup hot water
½ cup mild vinegar
½ cup chopped fresh mint leaves
3 tablespoons lemon juice
½ teaspoon salt

Dissolve sugar in water. Add vinegar. Bring to boil.

Pour over fresh mint leaves. Add lemon juice and salt.

Let stand ½ to 1 hour before straining and serving with lamb. Makes about 1 cup sauce.

RAISIN SAUCE FOR TONGUE AND HAM

½ cup brown sugar
1½ teaspoons dry mustard
1 tablespoon cornstarch
1½ cups water
¼ cup vinegar
⅓ cup raisins
1 tablespoon butter or margarine

Combine dry ingredients; slowly add water and vinegar.

Add raisins and cook over low heat, stirring constantly, until thickened.

Cook 10 minutes longer to plump raisins, then add butter or margarine.

SAVORY ONION GRAVY FOR STEAKS

4 cups sliced onions
2 tablespoons fat
2 tablespoons flour
2 cups meat stock
1 tablespoon Worcestershire sauce
Salt and pepper to taste

Cook onions in hot fat until golden; stir in flour.

Add meat stock, Worcestershire, salt and pepper, and cook, stirring constantly, over low heat until thick.

Cover and simmer 10 minutes. Makes 6 to 8 servings.

Note: 2 bouillon cubes dissolved in 2 cups hot water may be used instead of meat stock.

CHINESE BROWN GRAVY

6 tablespoons drippings from roast beef, ham, or chicken
6 tablespoons flour
2 tablespoons soy sauce
1 teaspoon Chinese brown gravy sauce*
1 teaspoon salt
Dash of pepper
½ cup cold water
1½ cups hot water

Mix flour and drippings in bottom of pan. Add sauces, salt, pepper, and cold water. Crush lumps and mix thoroughly.

Add hot water. Stir well and cook to smooth paste.

Pour in hot gravy boat and serve with egg foo yong, cooked or fried rice, biscuits, potatoes, dumplings, egg noodles, chops, roast beef, pork, or veal. Makes 2 cups.

Variations: One beef or chicken bouillon cube may be added, and mushroom juice may be used instead of hot water, if available. Add more flour if thicker gravy is desired. Add more water if thinner gravy is desired.

*Note: Chinese brown gravy sauce may be purchased in most large grocery stores.

WINE SAUCE FOR ROAST CHICKEN

¼ cup sweet white wine
Juice of 1 orange
2 tablespoons butter or margarine, melted
1 stalk celery, chopped
1 small onion, sliced

Combine all ingredients, and pour over breast of dressed and stuffed chicken in roaster.

Roast at 325°F. until tender, basting with wine sauce at 20 minute intervals. Strain drippings in pan for gravy. Makes enough for one 4-pound chicken.

Sauces for Fish and Shellfish

NEWBURG SAUCE
1 tablespoon butter
1 teaspoon Worcestershire sauce
1 tablespoon flour
2 cups cream
2 egg yolks, well beaten
1/4 cup sherry

Melt butter. Stir in Worcestershire sauce and flour. Gradually stir in cream. Cook over low heat, stirring constantly until smooth and thickened.

At this point add cooked and cleaned lobster, shrimp, crabmeat, flaked fish, or tuna fish.

When ready to serve, gradually beat in egg yolks and sherry. Reheat slightly and adjust seasoning. Serve over patty shells, toast points, or biscuits. Makes about 2 cups sauce, enough for 4 cups seafood.

Variation: For chicken à la king, to this amount of sauce add 1 cup cooked peas, 1 4-ounce can mushrooms, 2 tablespoons chopped pimiento, and 3 cups diced cooked chicken.

BERÇY SAUCE
3 tablespoons butter
1 teaspoon finely chopped shallot
1/2 cup white wine
1 teaspoon flour
1/4 teaspoon salt
Few grains pepper
1 teaspoon chopped parsley

Cook shallot in 1 tablespoon melted butter until soft and brown. Add wine and cook until reduced to 1/4 cup.

Meanwhile cream remaining 2 tablespoons butter with flour and cook over low heat, stirring until well blended.

Add to wine sauce and mix together until well blended. Add salt, pepper, and parsley.

This sauce is used with fish. Place the fish in a baking dish. Cover with sauce and bake in oven. Serve from the dish.

HOT MAYONNAISE SAUCE
3/4 cup mayonnaise
1/3 cup milk
1/4 teaspoon salt
Dash of white pepper
Few grains cayenne
1 tablespoon chopped parsley or chives or 1/3 teaspoon dried basil or tarragon

Combine mayonnaise and milk in top of double boiler. Heat over, not in, boiling water, stirring until smooth, about 5 minutes.

Stir in salt, pepper, and cayenne, then remove from heat. Stir in parsley or chives. Serve with hot fish or vegetables. Makes about 1 cup.

BURGUNDY SAUCE OR SAUCE BOURGUIGNONNE
1 small carrot
1 small onion
1 small celery root
3 tablespoons sweet butter
Pinch of thyme
Bit of bay leaf
1 cup red Burgundy wine
1 1/2 cups fish stock
1 clove garlic
Salt and pepper

Cut vegetables into very small pieces. Brown them in 2 tablespoons melted butter in a heavy saucepan. Add thyme, bay leaf, wine, 1/2 cup fish stock, and garlic. Cook over moderate heat until the sauce is reduced to half its original quantity. Then add remaining 1 cup fish stock and simmer gently 15 to 20 minutes.

Strain the liquid through a fine sieve, pressing gently to force some of the pulp through. Season to taste with salt and pepper. Just before serving, stir in 1 tablespoon sweet butter. Strain again and serve with fish. Makes about 1 1/2 cups.

SAUCE MEUNIÈRE
Heat 4 to 5 tablespoons butter or margarine until it is brown.

Stir in 1 teaspoon lemon juice and pour over food already sprinkled with chopped parsley.

SHRIMP SAUCE FOR FISH
2 cups medium white sauce
1/2 cup cooked or canned shrimp, cleaned
1/2 cup canned or sautéed fresh mushrooms
1/4 cup finely chopped celery
1/4 cup chopped olives
2 tablespoons chopped parsley
1 teaspoon Worcestershire sauce

Prepare white sauce and season well to taste; add remaining ingredients and heat just to boiling point.

Serve in sauce dish with baked or poached fish; or place fish on a platter and pour sauce over it. Makes about 3 cups.

Variations: A well-seasoned, thickened tomato sauce may be substituted for the medium white sauce. Other ingredients may be varied as desired.

WATERCRESS SAUCE (MAYONNAISE)
To 3/4 cup mayonnaise, add 1/4 cup finely chopped watercress, 1 tablespoon lemon juice, and salt and pepper to taste. Use with cold fish and shellfish. Makes about 1 cup.

NANTUA SAUCE
1/4 cup heavy cream, scalded
1 cup medium white sauce
Salt and pepper
2 tablespoons lobster or shrimp butter
Finely chopped cooked shrimp

Add scalded cream to white sauce; blend well and put through a fine sieve into a saucepan.

Heat without boiling; add salt and pepper to taste, then stir in lobster or shrimp butter. Garnish the sauce with finely chopped cooked shrimp or lobster. Serve with fish.

Note: Instead of shrimp or lobster butter, you may use 1 tablespoon finely ground shellfish and 1 tablespoon butter made into a smooth paste.

ANCHOVY SAUCE FOR FISH
Prepare 1 cup thin white sauce; add to it 3 anchovy fillets, washed and pounded to a paste. Blend well with the sauce.

ANCHOVY BUTTER SAUCE
Add 1 tablespoon anchovy paste to Maître D'Hôtel Butter with the lemon juice.

GARLIC OR ONION BUTTER SAUCE
Heat 1/4 cup butter or margarine and 1 clove garlic or 1 very small minced onion. Strain.

ALMOND BUTTER SAUCE
Sauté 1/4 cup shredded blanched almonds in 1/4 cup butter or margarine until lightly browned, stirring constantly. Serve with fish. Makes about 1/3 cup.

SOUR CREAM-CUCUMBER SAUCE
1/2 cup thick sour cream
1 cup diced, unpeeled cucumber
1/2 teaspoon salt
4 drops onion juice

Whip sour cream until smooth; add cucumber, salt, and onion juice. Serve with fish. Makes 1 1/4 cups.

HORSERADISH BUTTER SAUCE
Combine 2 to 4 tablespoons horseradish with 1/2 cup melted butter or margarine.

PARSLEY BUTTER SAUCE
Combine 2 to 3 teaspoons finely chopped parsley with 1/2 cup melted butter or margarine.

Add 1 teaspoon lemon juice, 1/2 teaspoon salt, and 1/8 teaspoon pepper.

CHIVES OR CHERVIL BUTTER SAUCE
Heat 1/4 cup butter or margarine and add 2 tablespoons minced chervil or 1 tablespoon minced chives.

Sauces for Vegetables

BUTTER SAUCE FOR CANNED OR BOILED VEGETABLES

Drain vegetables and boil the vegetable liquid until it is reduced by half. Add to it melted butter and seasonings to taste.

SOUR CREAM SAUCE FOR BAKED POTATOES

1 cup sour cream
1 teaspoon Worcestershire sauce
1/2 teaspoon Ac'cent (monosodium glutamate)
Dash of Tabasco sauce
1/2 teaspoon salt
Freshly-ground black pepper to taste
Chopped chives

Blend all ingredients except chives. Garnish with latter. Makes 1 cup.

POLONAISE SAUCE

1/3 cup butter
1/4 cup fine breadcrumbs
Few drops lemon juice
1 teaspoon chopped parsley

Heat butter gently until it begins to brown slightly. Add breadcrumbs and cook until the crumbs are brown and the butter has stopped bubbling. Add lemon juice and parsley and serve immediately as a garnish for vegetables. If desired, sprinkle the vegetable with finely chopped egg.

Variation: If desired, 1 tablespoon finely chopped onion may be cooked in the butter until onion is transparent, before adding breadcrumbs.

SOUR CREAM SAUCE
(Mock Hollandaise)

2 egg yolks
3/4 cup sour cream
1 tablespoon lemon juice
1/2 teaspoon minced parsley
1/8 teaspoon salt
1/4 teaspoon paprika

Beat egg yolks and cream together in top part of double boiler.

Place over simmering water and cook, stirring constantly, until mixture is of custard consistency.

Remove from heat and add remaining ingredients. Serve at once with vegetables or fish.

French Butter Pecan Sauce is quick, tasty, and simple.

VINAIGRETTE SAUCE

The traditional French vinaigrette is classic French salad dressing (oil, vinegar, salt, and pepper) but American vinaigrette usually refers to any of several variations for vegetables, and sometimes for meats and fish. In the recipe given here change the proportions or add other herbs, as desired. This American version may be served cold or hot. This recipe is excellent served cold over a green salad. Cooked vegetables served with this sauce are also excellent cold.

1 teaspoon salt
1/2 teaspoon paprika
1/8 teaspoon pepper
1/2 tablespoon dry mustard
1/2 teaspoon sugar
1 tablespoon tarragon vinegar
2 tablespoons cider vinegar
1/3 cup olive oil or salad oil
1 tablespoon chopped pickles
1 tablespoon chopped stuffed olives
1 teaspoon minced onion

Mix all ingredients together and beat well.

Heat to boiling point and serve with vegetables such as spinach, broccoli, artichokes, and asparagus.

ALMOND BUTTER FOR VEGETABLES

To 1/4 cup melted butter or margarine, add 2 tablespoons chopped salted almonds and 1 tablespoon lemon juice.

Serve over green beans, Brussels sprouts, or broccoli.

SNAPPY MOCK HOLLANDAISE SAUCE

Heat 1/2 cup mayonnaise over very low heat; stir in 1 teaspoon lemon juice and 1/8 teaspoon Tabasco.

Adds glamour to asparagus, broccoli, green beans, and other vegetables. Serves 4.

MINT BUTTER FOR VEGETABLES

To 1/4 cup butter or margarine, add 1 tablespoon chopped fresh mint leaves. Serve on peas, carrots, or a combination of the two.

FRENCH BUTTER PECAN SAUCE

1/2 cup butter, melted
2 tablespoons chopped chives
1/2 teaspoon salt
1/4 teaspoon pepper
1/4 teaspoon marjoram
2 to 4 tablespoons lemon juice
1/2 cup chopped pecans

Combine all ingredients; heat to blend flavors. Serve over cooked vegetables. Makes 1 cup or enough to sauce 4 10-ounce packages frozen vegetables.

Any one of a number of simple sauces made with butter can be used to add flavor and eating enjoyment to fresh or frozen vegetables. One of the most popular is Lemon Butter: butter melted until bubbling, then flavored with lemon juice and grated lemon rind.

ORANGE BUTTER FOR BEETS

To 1/4 cup butter or margarine, add 3 tablespoons orange juice and 1 tablespoon grated orange rind.

Simmer for a few minutes over low heat and serve over beets.

MOCK HOLLANDAISE SAUCE

1. Place an 8-ounce package of cream cheese (which has been standing at room temperature until soft) in the top of double boiler. Cream it with a spoon.

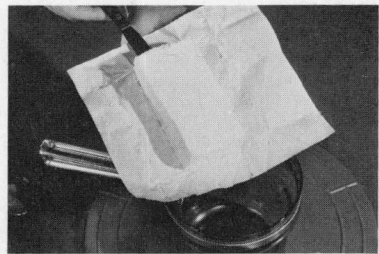

2. Add 2 egg yolks, one at a time, blending thoroughly after each addition.

Slowly add 2 tablespoons lemon juice and a dash of salt.

3. Place over hot water just until the sauce is heated through. Pour over hot cooked asparagus spears placed on toast points.

4. Serve hot. A delicious sauce, too, for broccoli and cauliflower.

SOUFFLÉS

Long considered the final test of an accomplished cook, the soufflé is often held in awe by many people who entertain an exaggerated idea of the difficulties of its composition. The classic French soufflé is actually easy to prepare and has a simple, even thrifty base: butter, flour, and milk for cream sauce, a cup of cheese or almost any leftover, and eggs.

Today, we Americans often simplify this dish even more: a can of condensed soup, cheese, and eggs make a main dish soufflé; a package of prepared pudding mix, some milk, and eggs make the most delectable—and impressive—of desserts.

HINTS ABOUT MAKING SOUFFLÉS

● The secret of a soufflé is primarily the proper beating of the eggs and the incorporation of these beaten eggs into the basic mixture.

● Use eggs at room temperature; however yolks aren't as likely to break if you separate them from the whites while still cold from the refrigerator.

● If you let egg whites warm up to room temperature before beating, they'll fluff up better.

● French chefs always beat an extra egg white into a soufflé for lightness, that is, 4 whites to every 3 yolks.

● Many good cooks add $\frac{1}{4}$ teaspoon cream of tartar to whites while beating—as insurance for a well risen soufflé.

● Egg yolks are beaten until thick and lemon-colored.

● Egg whites are beaten until stiff but still glossy—never until dry.

● Underbeaten eggs make a small, unstable soufflé; overbeaten eggs will cause a tough product.

● The ready and waiting hot sauce is slowly stirred into the beaten egg yolks. This way the yolks are smoothly blended with the sauce.

The size, shape, and preparation of the dish will influence the quality of the soufflé. A straight-sided dish gives maximum volume.

● The *cooled* sauce mixture is *folded* very gently into the beaten egg whites. A blending fork or metal spoon is just the thing for this. Take your time, and gently lift up-and-over in high strokes.

● Soufflés may be prepared in advance, with the exception of the beating of the egg whites, which must be done immediately before the soufflé is put into the oven.

● For a 3- or 4-egg soufflé, use a $1\frac{1}{2}$-quart dish; for a large soufflé with more than 4 eggs, use a 2-quart dish.

● For highest rise, butter or oil the bottom only, but not the sides of a baking dish. The mixture will cling to the dry sides and make a taller and more uniform product.

● For extra height, tie a folded strip of waxed paper around the outside of soufflé dish like a collar to support the rise. Pour soufflé mixture in almost to the top of dish.

● To bake a soufflé with a "top hat," pour the soufflé mixture into the baking dish, then run a teaspoon all around, 1 inch from the edge and about 1 inch deep. This crease will cause the crust to break at this point and form a taller center.

● For a sweet crust dessert soufflé, butter the baking dish and sprinkle with sugar before filling.

● When making a soufflé in a ring mold with the intention of inverting the contents when done, butter the ring pan well. Then fill with soufflé mixture and set in larger pan with 1 inch of hot, not boiling, water. This will facilitate turning out the soufflé from the mold and will give it a uniform consistency. For serving, fill the center of the turned out, inverted mold.

● Once done, serve soufflés promptly, because they start falling as soon as they start cooling. It is better to let your family or guests wait for the soufflé than to let the soufflé do the waiting. If your meal is delayed, turn the oven temperature to very low (250°F.) and leave the soufflé in the oven—but not more than an extra 10 or 15 minutes.

● Soufflés may be cooked in a double boiler over, not in, simmering water. Grease well both the pot and the lid. Pour in the soufflé mixture. Cover it and cook about 45 minutes to 1 hour. Turn out onto a hot platter.

Testing for doneness: the knife inserted in center should come out clean.

With the constant oven temperatures of today's modern ranges it is easier to succeed than to fail in making a perfect soufflé. Check the temperature of your oven with an oven thermometer. Periodic adjustments should be made by your utility serviceman.

Main-Course Soufflés

FISH SOUFFLÉ

2½ cups leftover cooked fish, flaked
    (or use drained canned sal-
    mon, tuna, or bonito)
1   tablespoon lemon juice
Salt and pepper to taste
½ teaspoon paprika
Pinch of nutmeg
¾ cup breadcrumbs
¾ cup milk
4   eggs, separated

Sprinkle flaked fish with lemon juice and mix in seasonings.

Combine breadcrumbs and milk; heat to just boiling point, and add to fish.

Beat egg yolks until light yellow in color; combine with fish and bread-crumb mixture.

Finally, add egg whites which have been beaten until stiff but not dry.

Pour into buttered baking dish. Set into a pan with hot water and bake in moderate oven (350°F.) until set, about 40 to 45 minutes.

Serve immediately in baking dish with an egg sauce, tomato sauce, or lobster sauce. Serves 6.

EASY ASPARAGUS-CHEESE SOUFFLÉ

(Short-Cut Main Dish Soufflé)

1   can (1¼ cups) condensed cream
    of asparagus soup
1   cup shredded American cheese
6   eggs, separated

Heat soup slowly; add cheese and cook, stirring constantly until cheese is melted. Add slightly beaten egg yolks; cool. Fold stiffly beaten egg whites into soup mixture.

Pour into an ungreased 2-quart casse-role. Bake in a slow oven (300°F.) for 1 to 1¼ hours or until soufflé is golden brown. Serve immediately. Serves 6.

Easy Chicken Soufflé: Follow recipe for Easy Asparagus Cheese Soufflé except use cream of chicken soup instead of asparagus; omit cheese and use instead 1 cup finely diced cooked chicken.

Easy Celery Salmon Soufflé: Follow recipe for Easy Asparagus Cheese Soufflé except use cream of celery soup instead of asparagus; omit cheese and use instead, 1 cup finely flaked salmon, drained.

Easy Mushroom Cheese Soufflé: Follow recipe for Easy Asparagus Cheese Soufflé except use cream of mushroom soup instead of cream of asparagus.

"TOP HAT" CHEESE SOUFFLÉ

4   tablespoons butter or margarine
4   tablespoons flour
1   teaspoon salt
Dash of cayenne
1½ cups milk
½ pound process American cheese,
    or "Old English" cheese,
    sliced
6   eggs, separated

Melt the butter or margarine in the top of a double boiler placed over boiling water. Remove from the boiling water, and blend in the flour, salt, and cayenne.

Gradually add the milk, blending well. Return to the boiling water and cook, stirring constantly, until the sauce is thick and smooth.

Add the sliced cheese and continue cooking, stirring frequently, until the cheese has melted.

Remove from the heat and slowly add the beaten egg yolks, blending them in well.

Slightly cool the mixture, then pour onto the stiffly beaten whites of the eggs, cutting and folding the mixture thoroughly together. Pour into an *ungreased* 2-quart casserole.

Run the tip of a teaspoon around in the mixture one inch from the edge of the casserole, making a slight "track" or depression. This forms the "top hat" on the soufflé as it bakes and puffs up.

Bake in a slow oven (300°F.) 1¼ hours. Serve immediately. Serves 6.

RICE AND CHEESE SOUFFLÉ

2   cups cooked rice
⅛ to ¼ pound finely diced or grated
    Cheddar cheese
1   tablespoon melted butter or mar-
    garine
2   beaten egg yolks
1   cup milk
½ teaspoon salt
⅛ teaspoon paprika
Few grains cayenne
1   tablespoon grated onion (optional)
1   teaspoon Worcestershire sauce
    (optional)
3   tablespoons chopped parsley
    (optional)
2   egg whites
⅛ teaspoon salt

Combine rice, cheese, butter, egg yolks, milk, salt, paprika, cayenne, onion, Worcestershire sauce, and parsley.

Beat egg whites and salt until stiff. Fold them into the rice mixture. Bake the soufflé in a moderate oven (350°F.) for about 25 minutes. Serves 4.

1. Make a cream sauce, using the butter, flour, milk, salt, and cayenne.

2. When the sauce is thickened and smooth, add the sliced cheese; stir until cheese melts.

3. Remove from the heat and add the beaten egg yolks while stirring constantly. Cool the mixture slightly.

4. Fold the cheese sauce into the egg whites beaten until stiff but not dry, cutting and folding the mixture thoroughly together.

5. Pour into ungreased 2-quart casserole. With a teaspoon draw a line around the casserole one inch in from the edge to form a "top hat."

6. Bake 1¼ hours in a slow oven (300° F.) and serve immediately.

BLENDER CHEESE AND VEGETABLE SOUFFLÉ

This recipe may be used for any vegetable soufflé. Use 1½ cups of a raw vegetable such as carrots or 2 cups of a leafy vegetable such as spinach.

¾ cup milk
¼ cup soft butter
4 egg yolks
½ cup cubed cheese
1½ cups diced raw carrot
¼ cup flour
1 slice onion
1 teaspoon salt
⅛ teaspoon pepper
4 egg whites, stiffly beaten

Combine all ingredients except egg whites in blender; blend until vegetable is finely cut. Turn into saucepan and cook over moderate heat, stirring until thickened.

Cool slightly, then fold in stiffly beaten egg whites. Turn into greased baking dish; sprinkle with paprika. Bake in slow oven (325°F.) 50 minutes to 1 hour. Serve immediately by itself or with a mushroom or tomato sauce. Serves 5.

SWEET POTATO SOUFFLÉ

2 cups cooked, mashed sweet potatoes
¾ cup hot milk
⅓ cup butter or margarine
1 teaspoon grated lemon rind
¾ teaspoon salt
Few grains pepper
3 stiffly beaten egg whites

To mashed sweet potatoes add hot milk and butter; beat until fluffy. Add lemon rind, salt and pepper.

Fold in egg whites beaten stiff but not dry.

Pile lightly into a greased casserole. Bake in a hot oven (400°F.) 30 to 35 minutes, or until puffy and browned. Serves 6.

OYSTER SOUFFLÉ

1 pint oysters
3 tablespoons butter or margarine
3 tablespoons flour
1 cup milk
1 teaspoon salt
⅛ teaspoon pepper
Dash of nutmeg
3 eggs, separated

Drain and chop oysters. Melt butter and blend in flour. Add milk and bring to boiling point, stirring constantly. Cook 3 minutes.

Add oysters, seasonings, and beaten egg yolks.

Beat egg whites until stiff but not dry. Fold into oyster mixture. Pour into buttered casserole.

Set in pan of hot water and bake in moderate oven (350°F.) until brown, about 30 minutes. Serves 6.

MASTER CHEESE SOUFFLÉ

4 tablespoons butter or margarine
4 tablespoons flour
1 cup milk
¼ pound sharp cheese, chopped
¼ teaspoon dry mustard
⅛ teaspoon pepper
¾ teaspoon salt
4 eggs, separated

Melt butter, add flour, blend well and cook over low heat until bubbly.

Add cold milk all at once and cook, stirring constantly, until thickened throughout. Add cheese to white sauce and stir until melted and well blended.

Add mustard, pepper, and sauce to egg yolks beating constantly.

Add salt to egg whites and beat until shiny and whites leave peaks that fold over when beater is withdrawn.

Pour yolk-cheese mixture gradually over egg whites folding at the same time. Pour into an *ungreased* 1½-quart casserole.

Circle mixture with a spoon about 1-inch from side of casserole and about 1-inch deep.

Set in a pan of hot water and bake in slow oven (325°F.) until puffy, delicately browned, and knife inserted in center comes out clean, 60 to 75 minutes. Serve promptly. Serves 4.

Variations of Cheese Soufflé

Chicken, Turkey, Salmon, or Tuna Soufflé: Omit cheese. Stir 1 cup finely chopped cooked meat and 1 tablespoon minced onion into yolks before combining with hot sauce.

Increase seasonings as needed with salt and add grated rind of 1 lemon and 1 tablespoon lemon juice. Serve plain or with gravy, or mushroom sauce.

Chive Cheese Soufflé: Add ½ teaspoon finely chopped chives and 1 teaspoon finely chopped parsley with the stiffly beaten egg whites.

Mushroom Cheese Soufflé: Sauté ½ cup finely chopped mushrooms in butter for a few minutes. Add with stiffly beaten egg whites.

Spinach or Carrot Soufflé: Omit cheese. Stir 1 cup finely chopped raw spinach or grated raw carrot and 1 tablespoon chopped onion into yolks before combining with hot sauce. Increase salt to 1¼ teaspoons. Cheese, parsley, or tomato sauce is a good accompaniment.

It is always advisable to serve a soufflé the moment it is baked. A soufflé sturdy enough to stand without falling is not delicate enough to be perfect.

"TOP HAT" SPINACH SOUFFLÉ

1 cup packed, chopped fresh spinach, uncooked (½ cup chopped frozen spinach, thawed but uncooked, may also be used)
¼ cup butter or margarine
¼ cup enriched flour
1 cup milk
⅓ cup shredded sharp cheese
3 beaten egg yolks
½ teaspoon salt
1/16 teaspoon pepper
3 egg whites
¼ teaspoon salt

Prepare spinach, wash and drain thoroughly.

Melt butter or margarine in top of double boiler. Blend in flour. Add milk. Cook over hot water, stirring constantly, until thick. Stir in cheese. Remove from heat.

Blend in egg yolks to which a little of the hot mixture has been added. Fold in ½ teaspoon salt, pepper, and drained spinach. Place over hot water.

Beat egg whites with ¼ teaspoon salt until stiff but not dry. Fold in hot spinach mixture gently but thoroughly.

Pour into ungreased 1½-quart casserole. Place casserole inside pan of hot water; water should be level with top of soufflé mixture. With spatula or knife, mark a circle around top of soufflé about 1 inch in from edge and ½ inch deep.

Bake in moderate oven (375°F.) 35 to 40 minutes or until firm to the touch. Serve immediately or, if it must wait a few minutes, leave in oven with heat turned off. Serves 4 to 6.

"Top Hat" Spinach Soufflé: The baking of a soufflé has much to do with its quality. Do not place the dish in hot water unless the recipe calls for it as in this case. The water will keep the soufflé moist and soft, and in other cases it is preferable to have it crisp and crusty.

LOBSTER SOUFFLÉ

5 tablespoons butter or margarine
5 tablespoons flour
1/2 teaspoon salt
1/2 teaspoon paprika
1 1/2 cups milk
5 eggs, separated
1 1/2 cups finely flaked, cooked lobster meat
1 tablespoon ketchup
1 teaspoon Worcestershire sauce

Melt butter. Blend in flour, salt, and paprika. Add milk gradually and cook, stirring constantly, until smooth and thickened.

Remove from heat and beat in egg yolks, one at a time.

Stir in lobster meat, ketchup, and Worcestershire sauce. Fold in stiffly beaten egg whites.

Turn into greased 1 1/2-quart casserole. Bake in hot oven (425°F.) about 25 minutes. Serve at once. Serves 4 to 6.

CHESTNUT SOUFFLÉ

2 tablespoons flour
1/2 teaspoon salt
1/8 teaspoon pepper
1 cup mashed or riced cooked chestnuts
1/2 cup milk
3 egg whites

Mix the flour, salt, and pepper and add to the chestnuts. Mix well. Add the milk, stirring until smooth.

Beat the egg whites stiff and fold lightly into the chestnut mixture.

Pour the mixture into a 1-quart ungreased casserole. Bake in slow oven (325°F.) about 30 minutes, or until firm. Serves 4.

CHICKEN-RICE SOUFFLÉ DELUXE

3 tablespoons butter or margarine
3 tablespoons flour
1 cup heavy cream
Salt and pepper
3 eggs, separated
1 cup cooked rice
1 cup diced cooked or canned chicken
1/3 cup finely chopped ham
1 small onion, finely chopped
1/2 cup grated Swiss or Parmesan cheese

Melt the butter; blend in flour and add cream slowly, cooking until smooth and thickened.

Remove from the heat and stir in the egg yolks and then the rice, chicken, ham, onion, and cheese. Season.

Whip the egg whites until stiff and fold in gently.

Turn into a greased baking dish, preferably one with straight sides, and bake in a moderate oven (350°F.) until the top is lightly browned and springs

back when gently touched with the finger. Serves 4 to 6.

INDIVIDUAL CHEESE CRUMB SOUFFLÉS

1 cup milk, scalded
1 1/4 cups fine, soft breadcrumbs
1 1/2 cups grated sharp American cheese
1/2 teaspoon salt
1/4 teaspoon paprika (optional)
1/2 teaspoon baking powder
4 eggs, separated

Pour scalded milk over crumbs and cheese. Add seasoning and baking powder.

Pour part of mixture into beaten egg yolks. Add egg mixture to remainder of sauce.

Fold in stiffly beaten egg whites. Turn into individual baking dishes.

Bake in moderate oven (350°F.) until delicately browned and firm to touch, about 30 minutes. Serve at once. Serves 6.

Variations of Cheese Crumb Soufflé

Chicken or Veal Soufflé: Substitute finely chopped cooked chicken or veal for cheese and add 1/4 cup finely chopped celery, if desired.

Ham Soufflé: Substitute finely chopped ham for cheese and add 1/4 teaspoon mustard, if desired.

Salmon Soufflé: Substitute 1 1/2 cups finely flaked canned salmon for cheese. Add 1/4 cup minced green pepper, 2 teaspoons lemon juice, and 1/2 teaspoon onion juice.

TOMATO SOUFFLÉ

2 slices bread
1/2 cup milk
5 fresh tomatoes
2 tablespoons butter or margarine
1 teaspoon onion juice
Salt and pepper
4 egg yolks, slightly beaten
5 egg whites, stiffly beaten
2 tablespoons grated cheese

Trim crusts from bread and soak in the milk. Mix bread and milk to a paste.

Peel, seed, and finely chop the tomatoes.

Melt the butter in a saucepan. Add tomatoes, onion juice, bread, and salt and pepper to taste. Cook, stirring until ingredients are thoroughly incorporated.

Remove from heat, stir in beaten egg yolks, and cool.

Fold in egg whites and pour into a well buttered soufflé dish.

Sprinkle grated cheese on top. Bake in moderate oven (350°F.) for 35 to 40 minutes. Sprinkle with paprika.

Serves 4.

BACON SOUFFLÉ

1 cup diced fried bacon (1/2 to 3/4 pound)
6 slices bread
5 beaten eggs
3/4 teaspoon salt or more*
1/4 teaspoon dry mustard
Paprika
2 cups milk

Dice bacon and cook until light brown. Drain, if very fat.

Grease casserole with bacon fat. Arrange bread in layers in casserole, sprinkling the cooked bacon and some bacon fat over each layer. Reserve some bacon for the top.

Add seasonings and milk to eggs and pour over bread. Sprinkle reserved bacon over top.

Bake in moderate oven (350°F.) until puffy and knife inserted in center comes out clean, about 1 hour. Serve from casserole. Serves 6 to 8.

*Note: Saltiness will depend upon saltiness of bacon.

OLIVE RICE SOUFFLÉ

1 cup ripe olives
3 eggs, separated
1/2 cup milk
1 teaspoon salt
1 teaspoon Worcestershire sauce
1 teaspoon grated onion
1 cup chopped raw spinach
1 cup grated American cheese
3 cups cooked rice
1/4 cup melted butter or margarine

Cut olives into large pieces. Separate eggs and beat yolks slightly. Combine with olives and all remaining ingredients except egg whites.

Fold in stiffly beaten egg whites.

Turn into 1 1/2-quart baking dish. Bake in moderate oven (350°F.) about 35 minutes. Serves 5 to 6.

CRABMEAT SOUFFLÉ

1 cup (6 1/2-ounce can) crabmeat
1 cup thick white sauce
1 tablespoon lemon juice
4 eggs, separated
1 1/2 teaspoons grated onion
1 tablespoon finely chopped parsley
1/2 teaspoon paprika
1/4 teaspoon cream of tartar

Pick over crabmeat to remove cartilage and shred fine.

To white sauce add crabmeat, lemon juice, egg yolks beaten until thick and lemon-colored, onion, parsley, and paprika. Cool.

Beat egg whites until frothy; add cream of tartar and continue beating until stiff but not dry. Fold into crabmeat mixture.

Turn into a 1 1/2-quart greased casserole. Bake in slow oven (325°F.) about 1 hour. Serves 4 to 6.

INDIVIDUAL CHEESE SOUFFLÉS

2   tablespoons butter or margarine
2   tablespoons flour
1/3 teaspoon baking soda
1   teaspoon salt
2   teaspoons Worcestershire sauce
1/4 teaspoon paprika
1/2 cup milk
1   cup grated cheese
4   eggs, separated

Melt butter; add flour, soda, salt, Worcestershire sauce, and paprika and stir until well blended.

Add milk gradually, stirring constantly over boiling water until sauce thickens.

Remove from heat and stir in grated cheese and egg yolks, beaten until thick and lemon colored. Then fold in stiffly beaten egg whites.

Bake in individual paper cases or in well buttered custard cups which can be sent to the table. Bake in moderate oven (350°–375°F.) about 12 minutes.

Serve immediately. Makes 8 to 10 soufflés of custard-cup size.

HAM SOUFFLÉ

2   tablespoons melted butter or margarine
2   tablespoons flour
2   cups milk
3   eggs, separated
1   cup dry breadcrumbs
2   cups ground cooked ham
1   tablespoon chopped parsley
Salt and pepper to taste

Prepare a sauce of butter, flour, and milk.

Beat yolks and mix with crumbs, ham, and sauce. Add parsley, salt, and pepper.

Fold in stiffly beaten egg whites. Turn into greased baking dish.

Bake in slow oven (300°F.) until set in center, about 1 hour. Serves 6.

MUSHROOM AND HAM SOUFFLÉ

2   cups thick white sauce
1/3 cup grated American cheese
3/4 cup minced celery
1½ tablespoons minced pimiento
1   cup mushrooms, cooked
3/4 cup chopped boiled ham
4   eggs, separated
3/4 teaspoon curry powder
1½ teaspoons grated onion

To white sauce add cheese, celery, pimiento, mushrooms, ham, well beaten egg yolks, curry powder, and onion. Mix well, then fold in egg whites beaten stiffly but not dry.

Turn into a greased casserole and place in a pan of hot water.

Bake in moderate oven (350°F.) about 30 to 45 minutes, or until nicely browned. Serves 6.

BUDGET CHICKEN SOUFFLÉ

2   tablespoons butter or margarine
2   tablespoons flour
1   10¾-ounce can cream of chicken soup, undiluted
3   eggs, separated

Melt butter in saucepan; stir in flour. Add soup; heat slowly, stirring until mixture bubbles and is thickened. Cool slightly.

Beat egg whites until stiff but not dry.

Add soup mixture gradually to slightly beaten egg yolks. Fold in egg whites.

Spoon into 1-quart casserole. Place casserole in pan of warm water.

Bake in slow oven (325°F.) for 1 hour or until knife, when inserted, comes out clean. Serves 4 to 5.

Note: For 4 to 5 individual casseroles: Bake as above for 30 to 45 minutes.

POTATO SOUFFLÉ WITH CHEESE

3   cups hot mashed potatoes
2   egg yolks
2   tablespoons butter or margarine
1/2 cup hot cream
1   teaspoon salt
1/8 teaspoon paprika
2   egg whites
1/8 teaspoon salt
1/3 cup dry grated cheese, preferably Parmesan

Combine mashed potatoes, egg yolks, butter, cream, 1 teaspoon salt, and paprika; beat well.

Shape these ingredients into a mound on an oven-proof dish.

Whip egg whites and 1/8 teaspoon salt until stiff. Fold in grated cheese. Spread this mixture lightly over the mound.

Bake in slow oven (325°F.) about 15 minutes. Serves 6.

VEGETABLE SOUFFLÉ

1/2 tablespoon finely chopped onion
1/2 tablespoon finely chopped green pepper
1   tablespoon finely chopped celery
2   tablespoons melted fat
2   tablespoons flour
1/2 cup milk
1/2 teaspoon salt
Pepper to taste
3/4 cup diced cooked vegetables
2   eggs, separated

Brown onion, green pepper, and celery lightly in fat.

Blend in flour and add milk. Cook over low heat, stirring constantly, until thickened. Season with salt and pepper.

Stir vegetables into sauce; add hot mixture to beaten egg yolks.

Beat egg whites stiff but not dry. Fold in vegetable mixture. Pour into greased baking dish.

Bake in slow oven (325°F.) 40 to 50 minutes or until set. Serves 4.

CHICKEN LIVER SOUFFLÉ

1/2 pound chicken livers
1   tablespoon finely chopped onion
5   tablespoons butter or margarine
3   slices crumbled cooked bacon
3   tablespoons flour
1   cup milk or chicken broth
3   eggs, separated
Salt and pepper

Sauté chicken livers with onion in 2 tablespoons butter. Mash slightly with a fork and add bacon.

Melt the other 3 tablespoons butter in another pan; stir in flour and blend well. Add the milk or chicken broth and stir constantly until thickened and smooth.

Remove from the heat. Add chicken-livers-and-bacon mixture and beaten egg yolks.

Fold in stiffly beaten egg whites and turn into a greased baking dish with straight sides.

Bake in a moderate oven (350°F.) 45 to 50 minutes or until the top is delicately brown and springs back when gently touched. Serves 4.

CORN MEAL SOUFFLÉ

2   cups milk
1/3 cup white or yellow corn meal
1   tablespoon butter or margarine
3   tablespoons or more grated cheese
1   teaspoon salt
1/4 teaspoon paprika
Few grains cayenne
3   eggs, separated

Heat milk to boiling point and stir in corn meal and butter. Reduce heat and stir in cheese. Cook these ingredients to consistency of mush.

Season them with salt, paprika, and cayenne. Add beaten egg yolks. Cook and stir for 1 minute longer to permit the yolks to thicken. Cool these ingredients.

Whip egg whites until stiff, then fold in.

Bake in an ungreased 7-inch baking dish in moderate oven (350°F.) until it is slightly crusty, about 45 minutes. In Italy bits of ham and seafood are added to the batter which is baked until it is very crisp. Serves 3.

Vegetable Soufflé

Dessert Soufflés

GRAND MARNIER SOUFFLÉ

3   tablespoons butter
3   tablespoons flour
¾ cup milk
3   tablespoons orange marmalade
4   egg yolks, lightly beaten
¼ cup Grand Marnier
6   egg whites

Butter a 1½-quart soufflé dish or casserole and sprinkle bottom and sides with sugar.

Melt butter in a saucepan; stir in flour. Add milk gradually, stirring with a wire whisk, and cook over low heat until mixture thickens. Stir in marmalade and egg yolks. Add Grand Marnier.

Beat egg whites until stiff and gently fold into soufflé mixture. Pour soufflé mixture into prepared dish. Bake in moderate oven (375°F.) until puffed and golden brown, 30 to 45 minutes. Serves 4 to 5.

VANILLA SOUFFLÉ
(Master Recipe)

⅓ cup enriched flour
½ cup sugar
⅛ teaspoon salt
1   cup milk
4   eggs, separated
¼ teaspoon cream of tartar
1   teaspoon vanilla

Combine flour, sugar, and salt in a saucepan. Stir in milk a little at a time. Cook over low heat, stirring constantly, until mixture is smooth and thick.

Beat egg yolks until thick and yellow; slowly fold in the milk mixture.

Beat egg whites until foamy; sprinkle the cream of tartar over them and continue beating until stiff but not dry. Fold into the first mixture with vanilla.

Pour into an ungreased 1½-quart casserole. Bake in slow oven (325°F.) 50 to 60 minutes, or in a hot oven (425°F.) about 25 minutes or until well browned, using a lower shelf in the oven.

The long slow baking makes a soufflé of even moistness throughout; quick baking gives a thicker crust and a soft moist interior. Serve immediately from the baking dish. Serves 6.

Vanilla Soufflé Variations

Butterscotch Pecan Soufflé: In Vanilla Soufflé, substitute ⅔ cup firmly packed brown sugar for granulated sugar; add 2 tablespoons butter or margarine.

Fold in 1 cup finely chopped pecans with the thickened milk mixture.

Chocolate Soufflé: In Vanilla Soufflé, stir 2 squares (2 ounces) melted unsweetened chocolate into thickened milk mixture before stirring into egg yolks.

Pineapple Soufflé: In Vanilla Soufflé, substitute 1 cup pineapple juice for milk. Omit vanilla; add 1 tablespoon lemon juice and ½ teaspoon lemon rind. Fold in ⅔ cup well drained crushed pineapple with the thickened milk mixture.

Orange Soufflé: In Vanilla Soufflé, substitute 1 cup orange juice for milk. Omit vanilla; add 1 tablespoon lemon juice and 1 tablespoon grated orange rind.

Lemon Soufflé: In Vanilla Soufflé, reduce milk to ⅔ cup. Add ⅓ cup lemon juice when thickened. Omit vanilla; add 1 teaspoon grated lemon rind.

STRAWBERRY SOUFFLÉ

1   pint strawberries
½ cup sugar
2   tablespoons kirsch or brandy
¼ cup butter or margarine
3   eggs, separated
1   cup soft breadcrumbs

Slice strawberries; add ¼ cup sugar and liquor and let stand until needed. Drain berries, reserving 1 cup for soufflé and remainder of berries and juice for sauce.

Cream butter with remaining ¼ cup sugar until fluffy. Add well beaten egg yolks, then crumbs and cup of strained berries.

Beat egg whites until stiff and fold into mixture.

Turn into 1½-quart casserole which has been greased only on the bottom or which has been buttered all over and sprinkled with sugar.

Set in pan of hot water and bake in moderate oven (350°F.) until firm, about 45 minutes. Serve with reserved berry and juice mixture. Serves 4 to 5.

FRESH PEACH SOUFFLÉ

1   cup peach pulp
1½ tablespoons lemon juice
¼ cup sugar
4   beaten egg yolks
⅛ teaspooon salt
1   tablespoon grated orange rind
4   stiffly beaten egg whites
Cream

Peel and mash ripe peaches to make 1 cup peach pulp. (Or use an equal amount of canned puréed baby food peaches or other raw or canned fruit pulp.)

Add lemon juice, sugar, egg yolks, salt, and orange rind to peach pulp. Fold in egg whites.

Place the mixture in a 7-inch baking dish. Bake in slow oven (325°F.) for about 45 minutes. Serve hot with cream. Serves 5.

PRUNE SOUFFLÉ
(Master Recipe)

4   tablespoons sugar
1   cup prune pulp
2   teaspoons lemon juice
5   egg whites

Combine sugar and prune pulp and heat until sugar has dissolved. Add lemon juice.

Beat egg whites until frothy. Fold in.

Turn into a baking dish and bake in moderate oven (350°F.) about 40 minutes.

When done, sprinkle with powdered sugar. Serve at once from baking dish with cream. Serves 4.

Variations of Prune Soufflé

Apple Soufflé: Substitute 1 cup thick applesauce for prune pulp.

Apricot Soufflé: Substitute 1 cup apricot pulp for prune pulp. Add ¼ teaspoon almond extract with lemon juice.

Cherry Soufflé: Substitute sweet cherry pulp for prunes and cherry brandy for lemon juice.

Peach Soufflé: Substitute 1 cup peach pulp for prune pulp. Add ¼ teaspoon almond extract with lemon juice.

HAZELNUT SOUFFLÉ

3   eggs, separated
3   tablespoons sugar
3   tablespoons flour
⅛ teaspoon salt
¾ cup hazelnuts
1   cup milk
3   tablespoons butter or margarine
½ teaspoon vanilla or 1 tablespoon rum
1   cup heavy cream, whipped
Caramel or coffee flavoring

Beat egg yolks until light. Gradually beat in sugar, flour, and salt.

Put hazelnuts through a nut grinder. Pour milk over them and heat to just below the boiling point.

Stir in egg mixture. Stir and cook these ingredients over low heat to permit the yolks to thicken slightly. Stir in butter.

Cool, then beat in vanilla or rum.

Beat egg whites until stiff; fold into first mixture.

Bake in a buttered dish in slow oven (325°F.) for about 30 minutes. Serve hot or cold with whipped cream flavored with caramel or coffee. Serves 4 to 5.

ORANGE SOUFFLÉ #2

1/4 cup butter or margarine
6 tablespoons enriched flour
Dash of salt
1 cup milk
1 6-ounce can frozen orange juice
    concentrate
1/2 cup water
1 1/2 teaspoons grated lemon rind
6 eggs, separated
1/4 cup sugar
1 recipe orange sauce (below)

Melt butter; blend in flour and salt. Gradually stir in milk; cook over low heat, stirring constantly, until thick.

Combine 1/4 cup of the orange juice concentrate (reserve remainder for orange sauce), water, and lemon rind. Stir into hot mixture.

Beat egg yolks until thick and lemon colored; gradually add hot mixture; mix well.

Beat egg whites until soft peaks form; gradually add sugar, beating until stiff peaks form.

Fold yolk mixture into egg whites. Pour into ungreased straight-sided 1 1/2-quart casserole around which has been tied a 6-inch collar of greased waxed paper.

Set baking dish in shallow pan, filling pan to 1 inch with hot water.

Bake in slow oven (325°F.) about 1 1/2 hours, or until mixture doesn't adhere to knife. Serve at once with orange sauce. Serves 8.

Orange Sauce: Combine 1/2 cup sugar, 1 1/2 tablespoons cornstarch, and dash of salt.

Stir in reserved orange juice concentrate (1/2 cup) and 1 cup water. Cook, stirring constantly, until thick.

Remove from heat; stir in 1 tablespoon butter or margarine. Serve warm in pitcher or bowl. Makes about 1 1/2 cups.

SHORT-CUT DESSERT SOUFFLÉ

1 package pudding or pie filling
    (vanilla, butterscotch, or chocolate flavor)
1 cup milk
3 eggs, separated
Pinch of salt

Combine in saucepan the pudding or pie filling and milk. Cook and stir over medium heat until mixture thickens and boils. Remove from heat.

Beat egg yolks and add pudding gradually, stirring constantly.

Beat egg whites with a pinch of salt until stiff enough to stand in soft peaks. Carefully fold in egg yolk mixture.

Pour into greased and sugar-sprinkled 1 1/2-quart baking dish. Bake in moderate oven (350°F.) for 45 minutes, or until firm. Serves 6 to 8.

LEMON SOUFFLÉ #2

4 eggs, separated
1/4 cup hot water
1 cup sugar
1/2 teaspoon salt
2 teaspoons grated lemon rind
1/4 cup lemon juice

Beat yolks until thick; add water gradually and continue beating. Add sugar gradually, beating thoroughly after each addition.

Add salt and lemon rind and juice; fold in stiffly beaten egg whites.

Turn into 1 1/2-quart dish, buttered on the bottom.

Place in pan of hot water and bake in moderate oven (350°F.) 30 to 45 minutes, or until firm. Serve at once with lemon sauce. Serves 6.

TOP-OF-RANGE CHOCOLATE SOUFFLÉ

2/3 cup milk
1/3 cup granulated sugar
1 ounce (1 square) unsweetened
    chocolate
1/8 teaspoon salt
1/2 teaspoon vanilla
2 eggs, unbeaten

In double boiler, heat milk with sugar, chocolate, salt, and vanilla until chocolate melts. With egg beater, beat until smooth.

Break eggs into cup; add to chocolate mixture, beating 1 minute.

Cook, covered, over boiling water 35 minutes without removing cover. Serve hot or cold, as is or with light cream. Serves 4.

ALMOND AND STRAWBERRY SOUFFLÉ

3/4 cup almonds
1 tablespoon sugar
1 cup crushed strawberries
1/3 cup sugar
3/4 cup hot milk
2 tablespoons flour
1/4 cup cold milk
1 tablespoon sweet butter or margarine
4 egg yolks, well beaten
6 egg whites, stiffly beaten

Blanch almonds by steeping in boiling water for 5 minutes, then cut lengthwise into slivers.

Add 1 tablespoon sugar to crushed strawberries. Dissolve 1/3 cup sugar in hot milk.

Blend flour in cold milk and add gradually to the hot milk, stirring over the heat for about 2 minutes, or until thick and creamy.

Remove from heat and stir in butter and well beaten egg yolks. Cool.

Fold in strawberries and three quarters of the almonds, then fold in egg whites. Pour into greased baking dish;

sprinkle top with remaining almonds. Bake in moderate oven (350°F.) for 30 minutes. Sprinkle top with powdered sugar. Serves 6.

PINEAPPLE MACAROON SOUFFLÉ

3 tablespoons butter or margarine
3 tablespoons flour
1 cup crushed pineapple
2/3 cup dry crushed macaroons
3 eggs, separated
1/8 teaspoon salt
2 tablespoons sugar
1/2 teaspoon vanilla

Melt butter over low heat. Stir in flour. When blended, stir in pineapple.

Then when thick and smooth, stir in macaroons and egg yolks. Permit the yolks to thicken slightly. Cool the mixture.

Beat egg whites with salt until stiff. Gradually beat in sugar and vanilla. Fold this into the soufflé mixture.

Bake it in a 7-inch baking dish in a slow oven (325°F.) for about 30 minutes. Serves 4.

MOCHA SOUFFLÉ

3 tablespoons butter or margarine
1/4 cup enriched flour
5 tablespoons sugar
2 teaspoons cocoa
2/3 cup milk
1/3 cup strong fresh coffee
4 eggs, separated
1/4 teaspoon salt
1/4 teaspoon vanilla

Melt butter in saucepan; gradually stir in flour combined with sugar and cocoa. Cook, stirring constantly, until mixture bubbles.

Then slowly stir in milk mixed with coffee. Cook, stirring constantly, until thick and smooth. Let cool.

Then stir in well beaten egg yolks, salt, and vanilla. Gently fold in stiffly beaten egg whites.

Turn into 1 1/2-quart casserole, greased on bottom only. Put casserole in pan of hot water.

Bake in slow oven (325°F.) until done, 50 to 60 minutes. Serve at once. Serves 6.

Mocha Soufflé

SOUPS

Soups should be an important part of any low-cost menus, not only because they are highly nutritious, but because to delicious soups may be added food ingredients which the average homemaker may normally discard.

The water in which meats, fish, and vegetables are simmered, as well as the liquids from canned vegetables, contain much of the precious vitamins and minerals and should be used as a liquid in the preparation of soups. They can be saved and stored in the refrigerator for future use.

Scraps of raw or cooked vegetables, fish, meats, and bones should be used in soups together with the addition of the lower-priced cuts of meats. Inexpensive meat cuts have essentially the same nutritive values as the higher-priced cuts. To obtain the full flavor from such soups, always simmer or boil these soups in closely covered kettles. A helpful hint to keep in mind is that soups made from these leftover ingredients may very often be improved with the addition of a can of prepared soup.

SOUP-MAKING HINTS

There are innumerable ways to vary soups and there are many inticing names but, basically, soups are divided into just a few groups.

Soups made from white stock have veal or poultry as a base.

Soups made from brown stock have dark meats as a base.

Bouillon is a clear soup made from beef stock.

Consommé is made from beef, chicken, veal, and vegetables.

Chowders are thick soups made from fish, meat, and vegetables.

Broth is the liquid resulting from meat which has been simmered slowly in water.

The cream soups (purées and bisques) contain both milk and butter, as well as the vegetables after which they are named.

COOKING SOUPS AT HIGH ALTITUDES

Since liquids boil at lower temperatures at high altitudes, soups will require longer cooking periods above 2,500 feet.

HOW TO REMOVE EXCESS FAT FROM SOUP

The easiest method, of course, is to chill the soup for then the fat congeals on the surface and can be scraped off.

If the soup is still simmering use a long-handled spoon and draw it over the surface, dipping up a thin layer of fat. The remaining fat can be removed when the cooking is done. If the soup is still hot, let it settle for 5 minutes so the fat will rise to the surface. Then tip the kettle so that the heavier fat deposit will collect at one side and can be more easily spooned off. When you have taken off as much as you can, roll up a paper towel and use one end to skim off fat. When the end is coated with fat, cut it off and continue the process until the last floating fat globules have been blotted off.

SOUP GARNISHING HINTS

The finishing touch—a bit of colorful garnish—is liked by everyone and should not be forgotten when serving soups. Here are some suggestions.

For Chowders and Meat Soups: Chopped parsley, thin slices of lemon for fish chowder; thin slices of frankfurters in bean and pea soups. See other suggestions with specific recipes.

For Clear Soups: Finely minced parsley, chives, thin slices of lemon, balls or slices of avocado, thin cooked celery rings or celery leaves, sautéed mushroom slices, thinly sliced olive rings, julienned carrots, string beans, rice, macaroni in small shapes.

For Cream Soups: Salted whipped cream alone or with minced parsley or chopped nuts, toast croutons, chopped pimiento, chopped chives, puffed cereals, raw grated carrots, thick sour cream, crumbled crisp bacon, grated cheese.

FRITTER GARNISH FOR SOUP

1   egg
¾ teaspoon salt
½ cup flour
2   tablespoons milk or water

Beat egg until light. Add salt, flour, and milk.

Put through colander into deep hot fat (365°F.). Fry until brown. Drain on paper. Serve in hot soup.

CUSTARD FOR SOUP

1   egg
½ cup milk or stock
⅛ teaspoon salt
⅛ teaspoon nutmeg (optional)
⅛ teaspoon paprika

Beat egg slightly. Add milk or stock and seasonings. Pour into small buttered cup.

Set in pan of hot water and bake in slow oven (325°F.) until it is set.

Remove from bowl and cut into diamonds or fancy shapes. Drop into soup just before serving it.

Royal Custard: Add 3 egg yolks and proceed as above.

CHICKEN FORCEMEAT FOR SOUP (Quenelles)

½ cup fine stale breadcrumbs
½ cup milk
2   tablespoons butter or margarine
1   stiffly beaten egg white
Salt
Few grains cayenne
Slight grating of nutmeg
⅔ cup raw breast of chicken

Cook breadcrumbs and milk to paste. Add butter, egg white, and seasonings.

Add chicken which has been pounded and forced through a purée strainer or food chopper. Form into small balls and cook in soup.

CHEESE PUFF BALLS

½ cup grated Parmesan cheese
1 tablespoon flour
¼ teaspoon salt
Dash of cayenne or paprika
2 egg whites, stiffly beaten
3 tablespoons cracker crumbs

Mix cheese, flour, salt, and pepper; fold into egg whites. If too crumbly to mold, add a few drops of milk.

Shape in small balls; roll in crumbs and fry in hot deep fat (375°F.) about 1 minute, or until golden brown. Drain on absorbent paper. Makes 1½ dozen balls.

FARINA PUFFS FOR SOUP

2 tablespoons butter or margarine
3 tablespoons uncooked farina
½ teaspoon baking powder
1 well beaten egg yolk
⅛ teaspoon salt
⅛ teaspoon nutmeg
Boiling water or soup

Cream the butter or margarine. Mix farina with baking powder and work into the creamed butter. Add egg yolk, salt, and nutmeg.

Drop by ¼ teaspoonfuls into simmering water or soup. Cook about 10 minutes.

Remove with a slotted spoon if cooked in water. The puffs will double or triple in size. Makes 20 small puffs.

WHIPPED CREAM GARNISH

½ cup cream
2 tablespoons horseradish
⅛ teaspoon paprika

Whip cream. Fold in horseradish and paprika.

Place a spoonful on top of an individual serving of soup.

Variations: Omit horseradish and paprika; place a spoonful of whipped cream on top of each serving and garnish with paprika and chopped parsley.

Or add ⅛ teaspoon cayenne or curry to the whipped cream instead of horseradish and paprika.

With Eggs: Fold equal amount of whipped cream into stiffly beaten egg whites to make a fluffy and less rich garnish for soups.

With Color: Add 1 tablespoon tomato paste or puréed pimiento to give whipped cream garnish an attractive pink color. Use with white or green soups.

TOASTED BREAD ANIMALS

Cut animal shapes out of bread with cooky cutters. Butter and toast a golden brown under the broiler. Serve to children with their soup.

EGG DROP FOR SOUP

1 beaten egg
Dash of salt
3 tablespoons flour
¼ cup cold water

Stir all ingredients together until smooth. Drop slowly from end of spoon into boiling soup.

Cover. Cook 5 minutes and serve hot.

Variation: Pour well beaten egg gradually into boiling soup just before serving.

Jiffy Hot Soups

Many new soups are made possible by combining two prepared soups of different yet harmonizing flavors. The addition of herbs, cream, or perhaps wine (madeira or sherry), finely chopped onions, chives, parsley, etc., will improve the flavors as well as seasoning such as curry, Worcestershire, or Tabasco sauce.

Delightful, appetizing combinations result from personal experimentation in "mixing and matching" these soups. Condensed soups are also used as cooking sauces and in preparing main dishes such as casseroles and meat loaves, to enhance the flavor of homemade soups and in recipes calling for soup stock.

The "can" measure in preparing "Quick Change" combinations is your soup can.

BLACK BEAN SOUP

Combine 1 can each bouillon or consommé and black bean soup; heat.

Add a dash of sherry if desired. Garnish each bowl with a thin slice each of lemon and hard-cooked egg.

QUICK MINESTRONE

1 can vegetable soup
2 cans hot water
1 can baked beans in tomato sauce
2 tablespoons elbow macaroni
1 clove garlic, finely sliced
Grated Parmesan cheese

Combine all ingredients. Cook until macaroni is tender, about 12 minutes.

Serve with grated Parmesan cheese sprinkled over each bowl.

CHICKEN CORN CHOWDER

Prepare 1 can condensed cream of chicken soup according to label directions. Add 1 package frozen cut corn.

Cover and cook until corn is tender. Add ¼ cup pimiento strips and 4 slices diced, cooked bacon.

TOMATO SOUP WITH SHERRY

To 1 can condensed tomato soup add 1 can water; heat to boiling; add ⅓ cup sherry, heat and serve with lemon slices. Serves 4.

Onion Soup Italienne

ONION SOUP ITALIENNE

1 can (10½-ounces) condensed onion soup
1½ teaspoons Worcestershire sauce
1 tablespoon butter or margarine
1 egg, well beaten
3 tablespoons flour
¼ teapsoon salt
1 tablespoon grated Parmesan cheese

Prepare onion soup according to directions on the can. Heat and add Worcestershire sauce.

Cream butter. Blend in egg, flour, salt, and Parmesan cheese. Drop batter by tiny teaspoonfuls into simmering soup. Simmer 5 minutes. Serves 2.

QUICK SHRIMP BISQUE

Sauté 1 green pepper cut into rings in 2 tablespoons melted butter. Add 1 package frozen shrimp and cook until lightly browned.

Add 1 can condensed tomato soup and ½ cup light cream. Heat to serving temperature.

HO-HO SOUP

2 10½-ounce cans beef broth
1½ soup cans water
1½ cups (12-ounce can) vegetable juice cocktail
2 tablespoons soy sauce
3 tablespoons vinegar
¼ teaspoon pepper
⅓ cup thinly sliced carrots
¼ cup chopped green beans
½ cup chopped cooked chicken
3 eggs, beaten

Combine all ingredients except eggs. Bring to a boil. Simmer about 10 minutes. Stir in beaten eggs. Serve at once with saltine crackers. Serves 6 to 8.

Ho-Ho Soup: A whimsical version of an Oriental chicken-vegetable soup. It's nutritious and fun to serve in Chinese rice bowls.

CURRY-AVOCADO SOUP

1 tablespoon butter or margarine
1 to 1½ teaspoons curry powder
1 can condensed chicken consommé
1 cup milk or light cream
1 slightly beaten egg yolk
1 medium avocado

In saucepan, melt butter or margarine; stir in curry powder; add consommé. Bring to boil; cover and simmer 10 minutes.

Combine milk or cream with egg yolk and stir into soup.

Mash half the avocado and coarsely chop the other half; add both to soup. Heat, stirring constantly; serve hot or chill thoroughly before serving. Serves 4.

QUICK TUNA SOUP

1 can condensed cream of mushroom soup
1 can condensed cream of asparagus soup
2 cups milk or 1 cup milk and 1 cup light cream
1 7-ounce can tuna, drained and flaked
Chopped parsley or chives

Blend soups and milk or milk and cream; add tuna. Heat slowly, but do not boil. Sprinkle with parsley or chives. Serves 4.

SALMON CHOWDER

1 can cream of tomato soup
1 can cream of mushroom soup
1½ cups milk
2 tablespoons grated onion
1 1-pound can white potatoes, drained and quartered
1 8-ounce can (1 cup) peas, drained
1 1-pound can salmon, drained and flaked
1 cup (½ pint) light cream

Blend tomato soup, mushroom soup, milk, and onion; heat. Add potatoes, peas, and salmon; heat thoroughly, stirring carefully.

Just before serving, add cream; heat but do not boil. Serves 6.

ASPARAGUS AND MUSHROOM SOUP

Combine 1 can each asparagus and mushroom soups. Dilute condensed soups with milk. Heat and garnish with chopped pimiento.

BEEF-CELERY SOUP

Mix 1 can cream of celery soup and 1 can beef soup. Stir well.

Blend in 2 cans of water. Simmer about 5 minutes.

CREOLE TOMATO SOUP

Combine 1 can tomato soup, 1 can chicken gumbo soup, and 2 cans water. Simmer about 5 minutes.

PUMPKIN-TOMATO SOUP

In a saucepan, combine can of condensed tomato soup with an equal amount of milk.

Add ½ cup canned pumpkin, ¼ teaspoon salt, ¼ teaspoon allspice, and a dash each of pepper and thyme; blend well. Heat and serve.

EASY HERBED TOMATO SOUP

½ teaspoon dried basil
1 teaspoon celery seeds
4 whole cloves
1 tablespoon minced onion
½ teaspoon salt
⅛ teaspoon pepper
1½ cups water
1 can condensed tomato soup, undiluted

Combine all ingredients except soup. Simmer, uncovered, about 10 minutes.

Then add soup; heat and serve with crisp crackers. Serves 4.

QUICK HEARTY MAIN-DISH CHOWDER

Combine 1 1-pound can corned beef hash, 1 can condensed tomato soup, 1 soup can milk, and 1 8-ounce can peas.

Heat, stirring often; dilute with additional milk, if desired.

Serve in big bowls with chowder crackers. Serves 4 to 5.

BACON-CLAM CHOWDER

Combine 1 can each clam chowder and cream of celery soup.

Add 1 can milk, ½ teaspoon grated onion, 1 tablespoon chopped parsley, and pinch of thyme. Heat to boiling and simmer a few minutes.

Garnish with generous spoonful of crumbled cooked bacon.

VEGETABLE SOUP, PEASANT STYLE

Combine 1 can vegetable soup, 1 can bean with bacon soup, and 2 cans water. Simmer about 5 minutes.

CREAM OF TOMATO AND BEAN SOUP WITH FRANKFURTERS

Combine 1 can each tomato and bean soup.

Add 2 cans milk and ¼ pound frankfurters, sliced. Heat.

OLD-FASHIONED VELVET

Stir 1 can cream of mushroom soup; add 2 cans water slowly, stirring constantly.

Blend in 1 can chicken noodle soup. Heat, don't boil.

FISH MONGOLE SOUP

Combine 1 can each tomato and pea soup. Add 2 cans milk or water and 1 cup flaked cooked fish.

Bring to boil and add 2 tablespoons sherry, if desired.

Jiffy Bean Soup

JIFFY BEAN SOUP

1 envelope onion soup mix
6 peppercorns
1 bay leaf
1 12-ounce can beef gravy
1 1-pound can beans in tomato sauce
2 tablespoons tomato paste or ketchup

Prepare onion soup mix as directed on package, adding the peppercorns and bay leaf. Add remaining ingredients to onion soup and bring to a boil; simmer for 5 minutes. Serves 5 to 6.

TOMATO CHICKEN-NOODLE SOUP

Combine 1 can each tomato and chicken noodle soup. Add 1 can water and dash of garlic salt.

Heat to boiling and simmer a few minutes.

GREEN PEA AND MUSHROOM SOUP

Mix 1 can green pea soup and 1 can cream of mushroom soup. Stir well.

Slowly add 1 can water, then 1 can milk. Heat thoroughly, but don't boil.

QUICK FRENCH ONION SOUP

4 tablespoons butter or margarine
4 large onions, thinly sliced
6 beef bouillon cubes
6 cups boiling water
1 teaspoon Worcestershire sauce
2 teaspoons salt
½ teaspoon paprika
⅛ teaspoon pepper
2 hard rolls
Grated Parmesan cheese

Melt butter or margarine in large skillet and cook onions until golden.

Pour dissolved bouillon cubes over cooked onions. Add Worcestershire sauce, salt, paprika, and pepper. Bring to boiling point but, for fuller flavor, do not boil.

Pour soup into medium-sized earthenware casserole. For that final French touch, cut rolls into thin slices and sprinkle each slice with cheese. Float these on top of soup.

Slide casserole into broiler, about 4 inches from unit, and broil until cheese turns rich brown color. Remove from broiler and serve at once. Serves 6.

Cottage Cheese Soup: A savory blend that just dares you to be different.

COTTAGE CHEESE SOUP

1 10½-ounce can condensed cream of celery soup
1 soup can milk
2 tablespoons chopped onion
1 tablespoon butter or margarine
½ teaspoon paprika
⅛ teaspoon cayenne pepper
⅛ teaspoon nutmeg
1 cup cottage cheese
2 tablespoons chopped pimiento

Combine soup and milk. Heat. Sauté onion in butter 5 minutes. Add to soup. Add remaining ingredients and heat but do not boil. Serves 4.

VEGETABLE AND BEEF SOUP

½ pound ground beef
1 small onion, minced
½ cup soft breadcrumbs
¼ cup milk
1 egg
½ teaspoon salt
Dash of pepper
1 package vegetable soup mix with noodles

Combine all ingredients, except soup mix. Shape in 1-inch balls; brown.

Prepare soup mix according to package directions. Add beef balls; simmer 5 minutes. Serves 4.

FOUR-SEASON HEARTY SOUP

Prepare 1 can condensed cream of asparagus soup according to label directions.

Drain 1 12-ounce package frozen oysters, and cook oysters in 3 tablespoons melted butter until edges curl.

Add oysters and oyster liquor to asparagus soup. Heat to serving temperature. Top with Parmesan toast strips.

VEGETABLE AND BEEF NOODLE

Combine 1 can vegetable soup, 1 can beef noodle soup and 1½ cans water. Simmer about 5 minutes.

CHICKEN WATERCRESS SOUP

Combine 1 can cream of chicken soup with 1 can milk; heat almost to boiling.

Add ½ cup chopped watercress; simmer a few minutes.

CLAM CHOWDER CREOLE

Combine equal parts clam chowder and chicken gumbo creole.

Chilled Soups

To most people at one time, a cold creamed soup meant Vichyssoise in the most elegant, high-priced restaurants or made with lots of trouble at home. It is not only possible but easy to make good cold soups at home with little effort and at slight expense—in infinite varieties. Many of the recipes given below require only a few minutes preparation.

There are a few points to remember. Canned soups, served cold, are much lighter in flavor than when heated. In some cases they can take double the usual amount of seasoning to make them delicious.

Chill the ingredients thoroughly and use a rotary beater, electric blender, or electric mixer for combining.

Use the soup can for measuring.

To keep the soup cold on the table, put it in a bowl and set in a larger bowl filled with ice. Bowls or serving dishes of copper are ideal because they hold cold well.

VICHYSSOISE
(Cream of Potato and Leek Soup)

Although many Americans think of Vichyssoise as a classic French dish, the original rich cream soup of potatoes and leeks, served chilled and sprinkled with minced chives, was created in 1941 by Louis Diat, then chef of the Ritz-Carlton Hotel, in New York.

4 large potatoes
3 leeks
2 cups chicken stock
1 tablespoon butter or margarine
2 teaspoons salt
¼ teaspoon white pepper
2 cups milk
1 cup cream
4 tablespoons chopped chives
½ teaspoon paprika

Peel and dice potatoes; cook with diced leeks (using green tops also) in stock until very soft (about 20 minutes). Put through a fine strainer.

To this purée add butter, seasonings, milk, and cream and reheat.

Serve cold or hot with minced chives on top and a garnish of paprika. If served cold, more milk or cream may need to be added on serving. Two medium white onions may be used instead of leeks. Serves 6.

CHILLED CREAM OF ASPARAGUS SOUP

Combine 2 cans condensed cream of asparagus soup and 2 cans light cream or rich milk.

Season with ¼ teaspoon each of paprika, garlic salt, and marjoram, and freshly ground pepper to taste. Garnish with minced chives. Serves 6.

CHILLED CREAM OF CHICKEN SOUP

Combine 2 cans condensed cream of chicken soup and 2 cans light cream or rich milk.

Season with salt and freshly ground pepper to taste. Garnish with minced chives. Serves 6.

CHILLED TOMATO SOUP

Stir 2 cans condensed tomato soup; add 1 can light cream and 1 can milk gradually, stirring constantly.

Chill 4 hours. Garnish with parsley. Serves 4.

BORSHT (Chilled Beet Soup)

Borsht may be any of a variety of soups originating in Russia, but popularly it refers to a beet soup made with or without meat and served either hot or cold. Citric acid or lemon juice is sometimes added. Beet borsht is usually served with sour cream. Cabbage and spinach borsht are other versions. Also spelled borsch, borscht, bortsch, and borshch, the last of these being the closest to the Russian pronunciation.

2 bunches young beets
2 quarts water
Salt and pepper to taste
Juice of 1 lemon
Sugar to taste
2 eggs

Use dark red beets. Wash, peel, and grate. Add to water with salt and pepper, to taste. Cook until tender.

Add lemon juice and about 1 tablespoon sugar. Cool. Soup should have distinctly sweet-sour taste. Since beets vary in sugar content, amount of seasonings is added accordingly. Beat eggs slightly and blend slowly with cooled borsht. May be served hot or ice cold topped with a tablespoon of sour cream.

Sliced hard-cooked eggs and chopped cucumber are also used as a garnish. A small sprig of fresh dill added to beets while cooking enhances flavor. If desired, serve with hot boiled potatoes. Serves 8.

BLENDER BORSHT

1 cup stock or bouillon
1 cup beet liquid
2 tablespoons sour cream
2 teaspoons lemon juice
1 cup cooked or canned sliced beets
½ teaspoon salt
Dash of pepper
About 1 tablespoon thin lemon peel
½ cup thick sour cream

Put all ingredients except ½ cup sour cream in container. Blend until smooth, about 2 minutes.

Chill thoroughly. Serve topped with sour cream. Serves 3.

SCHAV BORSHT (SORREL SOUP)

Schav is the Yiddish term for this highly favored Jewish dish.

1½ pounds sorrel (sour grass or schav)
1   quart water
⅓   cup sugar
1   tablespoon vinegar
2   tablespoons lemon juice
1   teaspoon salt
2   lightly beaten eggs
½   cup heavy sour cream

Wash sorrel thoroughly in cold water; remove stems and chop fine. Combine sorrel, water, and sugar in kettle; bring to boiling point. Lower heat and simmer 10 minutes. Add vinegar, lemon juice, and salt. Let cool.

Mix eggs and sour cream until blended. Add to schav and mix thoroughly. Chill and serve very cold with a hot boiled potato per serving, or sliced hard-cooked eggs. Makes about 1½ quarts.

Spinach Borsht: Substitute spinach for sorrel.

COLD YOGURT SOUP
(TURKISH STYLE)

3   medium cucumbers
¼   teaspoon salt
1   clove garlic (optional)
1   tablespoon vinegar
1   teaspoon dill (optional)
1   pint yogurt
2   tablespoons olive oil
1   tablespoon chopped mint leaves or
    ½ teaspoon dried mint leaves

Peel cucumbers, quarter lengthwise, and slice about ⅛ inch thick. Place in bowl and sprinkle with salt.

Rub another bowl with garlic and swish vinegar around in it to collect flavor, then add dill and yogurt.

Stir until mixture is consistency of thick soup, if necessary, adding 3 tablespoons cold water.

Pour over cucumbers and stir. Pour into individual serving dishes, sprinkle with olive oil, and garnish with chopped mint. Serves 6.

CHILLED SPINACH SOUP

Melt 2 tablespoons butter, blend in 2 tablespoons enriched flour, ½ teaspoon onion salt, and ½ teaspoon salt.

Add 2 cups light cream gradually and cook, stirring constantly, until thickened.

Add 1 package frozen chopped spinach. Cover and cook until spinach is tender. Chill thoroughly.

CHILLED BLACK BEAN SOUP

Stir 1 can condensed black bean soup well and add 1 can condensed consommé. Stir in 1 can water and 1½ teaspoons sherry.

Chill 4 hours. Garnish each serving with a lemon slice. Serves 4.

Jellied Soups

Some canned bouillons and consommés will jell when thoroughly chilled in the refrigerator. Others require the addition of gelatin. If a canned bouillon or consommé, ready-to-serve or condensed will jell upon chilling, it is usually so stated on the label.

The cans should be stored in the refrigerator for several hours or preferably overnight. Most rich, concentrated homemade bouillons or consommés will jell when thoroughly chilled.

JELLIED CONSOMMÉ OR BOUILLON

When using a consommé or bouillon which requires the addition of gelatin, allow 1 teaspoon (⅓ envelope) unflavored gelatin for each measuring cup of bouillon or consommé.

Soften the gelatin in a little cold water (1 tablespoon to a teaspoon gelatin). Then add hot bouillon or consommé and stir until gelatin is dissolved. Season to taste.

Pour into a pan; chill until firm. Just before serving, cut into cubes or break up lightly with a fork. Pile lightly in chilled serving cups. Serve with lemon slices.

CANNED MADRILÈNE

Chill in the can. Turn out into a chilled bowl, whip with a fork and serve at once in chilled cups.

Top each serving with 1½ to 2 tablespoons sour cream, or a little chopped parsley, chives or fresh dill, basil or chervil.

ORANGE JELLIED SOUP

½   tablespoon (½ envelope) unflavored gelatin
2   tablespoons cold water
⅓   cup boiling water
¼   cup sugar
1   cup orange juice (about 2 oranges)
⅛   teaspoon salt
2   teaspoons lemon juice
2   whole oranges

Soften gelatin in cold water for 5 minutes and dissolve in boiling water.

Add sugar, orange juice, salt, and lemon juice.

Section oranges and add to gelatin mixture. Fill bouillon cups about half full and place in refrigerator to chill. Serves 6 to 8.

JELLIED MADRILÈNE

2   tablespoons (2 envelopes) unflavored gelatin
¼   cup cold water
5   chicken bouillon cubes
4   cups boiling water
2   teaspoons aromatic bitters
½   cup minced chives

Soak gelatin 5 minutes in cold water.

Jellied Madrilène

Dissolve bouillon cubes in boiling water. Add gelatin and stir until dissolved. Add bitters and chill until mixture begins to set. Stir in ½ cup minced chives and chill until set.

Beat slightly with fork and pile in bouillon cups. Top with sour cream, if desired. Serves 4 to 6.

GAZPACHO

There are many versions of this Spanish dish that is a cross between a soup and a salad. The jellied version given here will be a colorful, refreshing addition to any menu. Spoon it into lettuce-lined bowls and serve it with assorted cold cuts and hot rolls for a simple bit of luxury eating. For a more formal occasion, present it as a first course. Served in bouillon cups or small bowls bedded in crushed ice, it's a peppy appetite teaser.

JELLIED GAZPACHO

1   tablespoon (1 envelope) unflavored gelatin
1   18-ounce can tomato juice
2   tablespoons wine vinegar
2   tablespoons olive oil
½   teaspoon salt
Few drops Tabasco sauce
Dash of cracked black pepper
1   16-ounce can diagonal-cut green beans, drained
1   medium cucumber, peeled and chopped
¼   cup diced green pepper
¼   cup minced onion
1   2½-ounce jar sliced mushrooms, drained

Add gelatin to tomato juice in small saucepan. Heat several minutes over low heat, stirring frequently until gelatin is dissolved. Stir in vinegar, oil, and seasonings. Cool slightly.

While tomato mixture is cooling, combine remaining ingredients in large bowl. Stir in tomato mixture. Chill 4 to 5 hours or until mixture will mound up on a spoon. Serve cold in soup cups or lettuce-lined salad bowls. Garnish with dollops of sour cream and chopped chives, if desired. Makes about 1 quart.

Gazpacho

Creamed Soups

CREAM OF VEGETABLE SOUP
(Master Recipe)

3 tablespoons butter or margarine
2 or 3 medium-sized onion slices
3 tablespoons flour
1½ teaspoons salt
Few grains pepper
3 cups milk
About 2 cups vegetables and cooking
    liquid (see below)
⅓ cup cream (optional)

Melt butter in saucepan; add onion and cook gently until soft but not browned, about 5 minutes.

Stir in flour and seasonings. Remove from heat and slowly add milk, stirring until well blended.

Place over low heat and cook until smooth and thick, stirring constantly.

Add vegetable and cooking liquid prepared as directed below.

Heat thoroughly and add cream if desired. Sprinkle each portion with chopped parsley, watercress, or chives or a dash of paprika. Serves 6.

Cream of Vegetable Soup Variations

With Leftover Vegetables: Reheat vegetables singly or in combination in vegetable cooking liquid or in milk until soft enough to put through electric blender.

Measure purée or finely chopped vegetables and add cooking liquid or milk to make 2 cups.

Cream of Asparagus Soup: Follow master recipe, increasing butter and flour to 4 tablespoons each.

Use 2 pounds of asparagus cut in 1-inch lengths. Cook covered in ¾ cup boiling salted water until very tender.

Save tips for garnish and put remainder through a sieve. Add cooking liquid to make 2 cups purée.

Cream of Carrot Soup: Follow master recipe. Use 3 cups finely shredded carrots which have been cooked covered in 1 cup boiling salted water for 5 to 10 minutes.

Cream of Celery Soup: Follow master recipe. Use 2 cups finely chopped or diced celery. Cook covered in 1 cup milk in top of double boiler or over low heat until very tender. Add cooking liquid to measure 2 cups.

Cream of Corn Soup: Follow master recipe. Use 1 No. 2 can cream-style corn, or cook 2½ cups chopped fresh corn in 1 cup of milk until tender. Press canned or cooked corn through sieve.

Cream of Spinach Soup: Use 1 pound raw spinach. Cook until tender covered in water which clings to leaves after washing.

Put through sieve. Follow master recipe, increasing butter and flour to 4 tablespoons each.

Cream of Watercress Soup: Use 2 bunches of watercress. Wash and chop coarsely. Cook covered in 1 cup boiling salted water until tender.

Put through sieve and add cooking liquid to make 2 cups. Follow master recipe, increasing butter and flour to 4 tablespoons each.

Cream of Mushroom Soup: Use ¼ pound fresh mushrooms. Wash and chop fine; cook gently in ¼ cup butter with 1 teaspoon grated onion until tender, about 10 minutes.

Follow master recipe, adding 1 to 2 teaspoons lemon juice, if desired.

Cream of Lima Bean Soup: Use 1½ to 2 cups cooked or canned lima beans and liquid. Put through sieve and follow master recipe.

Cream of Onion Soup: Use 2½ cups very finely sliced or chopped onions. Cook gently in ¼ cup butter until tender, about 15 minutes, but do not brown. If desired put through sieve. Follow master recipe.

Cream of Pea Soup: Use 2 cups fresh or frozen peas or 1 No. 2 can peas. Cook fresh peas in 1 cup boiling salted water, frozen peas according to package directions until very tender.

Heat canned peas in their own liquid about 10 minutes. Put peas through a sieve. Follow master recipe.

Cream of Potato Soup: Use 2 cups diced, cooked potatoes and 1 tablespoon chopped pimiento. Do not put through sieve. Follow master recipe.

CHESTNUT SOUP—FRENCH STYLE

1 pound chestnuts
Bouquet garni (see below)
¼ teaspoon thyme
Salt and pepper
2 cups chicken stock
½ cup heavy cream, scalded
⅓ cup sherry

Prepare chestnuts: cut gash on flat sides; place in extremely hot oven (500°F.) for about 6 minutes, or until shells may be easily removed, taking care not to burn them. Remove shells and skins with a sharp knife.

Put chestnuts in kettle with bouquet garni, ¼ teaspoon thyme, and just enough water to cover nuts. Season with salt and pepper to taste. Cover and boil gently until nuts are soft, 20 to 25 minutes.

Discard bouquet garni and put chestnuts and liquid through a fine sieve into another kettle. Add chicken stock; bring to boiling point and stir in scalded cream. Adjust seasoning to taste and if the soup is too thick add more chicken stock. Let soup boil up once, then stir in sherry.

If desired, serve garnished with whipped cream sprinkled with crumbled roast chestnuts. Makes about 4 cups.

Bouquet Garni: Wrap in a piece of cheesecloth and tie securely: 8 sprigs parsley, 3 sprigs green celery tops, 2 whole cloves, and 1 bay leaf.

PUMPKIN SOUP

2 pounds cooked fresh pumpkin or
    3 cups canned pumpkin
3 cups milk, scalded
1 tablespoon butter
1 tablespoon sugar or 2 tablespoons
    brown sugar
⅛ teaspoon saffron
½ cup ham, cut in match-stick strips
Salt and pepper to taste
Nutmeg and cinnamon to taste, if desired

Combine pumpkin with scalded milk; add remaining ingredients. Heat to serving temperature but do not boil. Serve immediately. Makes about 4 cups.

ALMOND SOUP

2 cups blanched whole almonds
2 tablespoons instant minced onion
3 cups water
3 tablespoons chicken stock base*
¼ teaspoon salt
½ teaspoon coriander seed
1½ cups milk
Grated orange rind

Finely grind almonds in meat grinder or whiz in blender. In a kettle, combine ground almonds, onion, water, chicken stock base, salt, and coriander. Simmer 30 minutes.

Remove from heat; strain and gradually stir in milk. Heat gently until thoroughly heated through. Serve hot or cold garnished with grated orange rind. Makes 4 large servings or 8 small servings.

*Note: 3 cups chicken broth and 5 chicken bouillon cubes may be substituted.

Almond soup is served hot or cold.

CREAM OF TOMATO SOUP

1   No. 2 can (2½ cups) tomatoes
2   slices onion
1   bay leaf
1   teaspoon salt
¼   teaspoon pepper
¼   teaspoon cinnamon
⅛   teaspoon cloves
2   tablespoons butter or margarine
2   tablespoons flour
2   cups milk

Combine tomatoes, onion, and seasonings. Simmer 10 minutes, then strain.

Make white sauce: melt butter; blend in flour. Gradually add milk and cook over low heat until slightly thick, stirring constantly.

Just before serving, slowly add hot, strained tomatoes to white sauce, stirring constantly. Do not reheat. Serves 6.

MUSHROOM BISQUE

1   pound mushrooms
3   cups water
1   slice onion
½   teaspoon salt
3   tablespoons butter or margarine
¼   cup flour
2   cups milk
Salt and pepper
Paprika
1   egg yolk
⅓   cup heavy cream, whipped

Clean and chop mushrooms. Add water, onion, and ½ teaspoon salt. Simmer ½ hour. Press through a medium sieve.

Melt butter and blend in flour. Gradually add milk and cook over hot water, stirring occasionally until thick.

Add the sieved mushrooms, season with salt, pepper, and paprika to taste.

Beat egg yolk and gradually add to mushroom mixture. Serve with garnish of whipped cream. Serves 4 to 6.

POTATO CARROT CHOWDER

1   white onion, minced
¼   cup butter or margarine
2   cups diced raw potatoes
3   cups boiling water
1   teaspoon salt
¼   teaspoon paprika
1   tablespoon flour
2   cups milk, scalded
2   carrots, diced and cooked

Sauté onion in 2 tablespoons butter in large saucepan until lightly browned.

Add potatoes, boiling water, salt, and paprika. Boil about 15 minutes or until potatoes are soft.

Blend flour with remaining butter and gradually add milk stirring constantly, until smooth and thickened.

Add to potato mixture. Add carrots. Cook 5 minutes, stirring until smooth. Serves 6.

CORN AND POTATO CHOWDER
(Master Recipe)

1   medium onion, chopped fine
3   tablespoons fat
3   cups boiling water
3   medium-sized potatoes, cubed
Dash of pepper
1½   teaspoons salt
1½   cups canned corn
3   cups scalded milk

Sauté onions in fat until lightly browned. Add boiling water, potatoes, and seasonings. Cook until potatoes are tender, about 15 minutes.

Add corn and milk. Heat to boiling point, but do not boil. Serves 6.

Variations of Corn and Potato Chowder

Bean Chowder: Substitute 1½ cups canned lima beans for corn and diced carrots for potatoes.

Fish Chowder: Substitute 1½ pounds fish (haddock or cod) for corn. Add fish with potatoes and cook until both are tender. Then add milk, heat, and serve.

Additional fish bones or heads may be used, if desired.

Potato Soup: Omit corn. Cook 2 tablespoons chopped celery leaves with potatoes.

Garnish each serving with a little butter and dash of paprika.

BLENDER BISQUES
(Master Recipe)

2   cups milk
1   tablespoon flour
2   tablespoons butter or margarine
1   teaspoon salt
Dash of pepper
¼   cup diced celery or 3 sprigs parsley
1   thin slice raw onion, optional
Cooked or canned fish, seafood, or
     meat

Combine all ingredients in container. Blend until smooth.

Heat over low heat, stirring occasionally, until mixture reaches boiling point. Serves 3 to 4.

Variations of Blender Bisques

Crab Bisque: Use ⅔ cup cooked or canned crabmeat.

Fish Bisque: Use ⅔ cup cooked or canned fish flakes.

Lobster Bisque: Use ½ cup cooked or canned lobster meat.

Oyster Bisque: Use 3 or 4 raw oysters.

Salmon Bisque: Use ½ cup cooked or canned salmon.

Shrimp Bisque: Use ⅔ cup cooked or canned shrimp.

Meat Bisque: Use ½ cup diced cooked leftover chicken, beef, lamb, veal, or ham. Substitute 1 cup stock for 1 cup milk.

BLENDER CREAM SOUP
(Master Recipe)

2   cups milk
2   tablespoons flour
2   tablespoons butter or margarine
1   teaspoon salt
Dash of pepper
1   thin slice onion
Few sprigs of parsley or ¼ cup diced
     raw celery
Raw, canned, or cooked vegetables,
     cut up into small pieces

Put all ingredients in container. Blend until smooth. Heat over low heat, stirring occasionally, until mixture boils.

If cooked leftover food is used, season after blending. Frozen vegetables do not have to be defrosted before blending. Serves 3 to 4.

Variations of Blender Cream Soup

Asparagus Cream Soup: Use ⅔ cup asparagus tips.

Carrot Cream Soup: Use 1 cup diced raw or canned carrots.

Corn Cream Soup: Use 1 cup raw or canned corn.

Cucumber Cream Soup: Use 2 cups raw, sliced, unpeeled cucumber.

Mushroom Cream Soup: Use 6 whole sautéed mushrooms.

Pea Cream Soup: Reduce flour to 1 tablespoon. Use 1 cup raw or canned peas.

Spinach Cream Soup: Use 2 cups tightly packed raw spinach or ⅓ cup cooked or canned spinach.

CREAM OF CHICKEN SOUP

2   tablespoons butter or margarine
2   tablespoons flour
2   cups heated chicken stock
1   cup scalded milk or cream
Salt and pepper

Melt butter and blend in flour. Add stock and milk or cream. Cook 5 minutes, stirring constantly.

Season to taste and remove from heat to avoid curdling. Serves 4.

With Egg Yolk: Use only 1 tablespoon flour. Beat an egg yolk slightly. Slowly pour hot soup over it. Strain and serve at once.

HAM AND CORN CHOWDER

½   cup onion slices
½   cup melted butter or margarine
1   No. 2 can cream-style corn
½   cup light cream
1   cup chopped cooked ham
¼   teaspoon salt
⅛   teaspoon pepper

Sauté onion slices in melted butter until tender. Add corn, light cream, cooked ham, salt, and pepper. Heat to serving temperature. Serve with celery croutons. Serves 4 to 5.

Fish and Shellfish Soups

LOBSTER BISQUE (Master Recipe)

3 tablespoons butter or margarine
4 tablespoons flour
1 teaspoon salt
1/8 teaspoon pepper
3 cups milk
1 cup bouillon
1 6-ounce can lobster meat
1 medium-sized onion, sliced
1 sprig parsley
1/2 cup light cream

Melt butter in saucepan. Stir in flour, salt, and pepper. Add milk and bouillon gradually, stirring constantly, and simmer over low heat until mixture thickens.

Add lobster, onion, and parsley. Cover and simmer 10 minutes. Remove from heat.

Strain, pressing as much of the meat as possible through a sieve. Add cream and reheat. Serves 6.

Lobster Bisque Variations

Crab Bisque: Substitute canned crabmeat for lobster.

Shrimp Bisque: Remove black line and wash 1 cup canned or cooked shrimp. Substitute in Lobster Bisque.

Clam Bisque: Substitute canned minced clams for lobster.

SEAFOOD SOUP

1/4 cup butter or margarine
1 cup chopped onion
1 cup chopped green pepper
2 4-ounce cans sliced mushrooms
1 clove garlic, crushed
1 1-pint, 2-ounce can tomato juice
1 cup water
2 chicken bouillon cubes
1/2 teaspoon oregano
1 5-ounce can lobster
2 5-ounce packages frozen, cooked shrimp (2 cups)
1 6 1/2-ounce can crabmeat

Melt butter or margarine. Sauté next 4 ingredients 5 minutes. Stir in tomato juice, water, bouillon cubes, and oregano. Cook over low heat 15 minutes.

Add lobster, shrimp, and crabmeat. Heat. Serve with saltine crackers. Serves 6 to 8.

CLAM CHOWDER, NEW ENGLAND AND MANHATTAN

Clam chowder fanciers are divided into two uncompromising schools. New Englanders are firm in their insistence on milk or cream in chowder; those who prefer Manhattan chowder claim that any chowder worth its salt must contain tomatoes. How New England chowder got its name is obvious. How Manhattan chowder got its name is more mysterious. For chowder with tomatoes is eaten with gusto not only in Manhattan, but the country over.

1 quart shucked clams
6 tablespoons chopped bacon
1 cup sliced onions
3 cups diced potatoes
1/2 teaspoon salt
1/4 teaspoon pepper
2 cups hot water
1 quart milk
8 soda crackers

Drain clams, saving juice. Chop clams.

Cook bacon in large saucepan until crisp. Add onions and brown slightly.

Add potatoes, salt, pepper, and water; cook 10 minutes.

Add clams, milk, and clam juice; cook until potatoes are tender, about 10 minutes.

Pour chowder over plain or crumbled crackers in serving bowls. Serves 6.

Manhattan Clam Chowder: Follow recipe for New England Clam Chowder, substituting 1 cup diced celery for potatoes, and 4 cups canned tomatoes or tomato juice for milk. Add 1 teaspoon thyme.

GULF STATES OYSTER GUMBO

4 tablespoons butter or margarine
1 1/2 tablespoons minced onion
1 pint oysters
4 cups fish stock or canned clam broth
1 cup cooked or canned okra
2 cups cooked or canned tomatoes
Salt and pepper
2 tablespoons flour

Cook onion in 2 tablespoons melted butter until lightly browned.

Add oysters and their liquid, stock, okra, tomatoes, and salt and pepper to taste. Bring slowly to boiling point.

Add a smooth paste made of 2 tablespoons butter and 2 tablespoons flour. Stir until smooth. Serves 4 to 6.

Seafood Soup: From the sea comes a bounty of succulent foods. Three of them combine to make one of the heartiest and best of soups. It's a meal in itself—served with saltine crackers.

CLAM BROTH

Wash and scrub clams in shell with a brush. Place in deep saucepan. Add 1/2 cup water for each quart clams. Cover tightly and cook until clams open wide, 20 to 30 minutes.

Let stand 10 to 15 minutes so any sediment will settle. Strain through cheesecloth. Season to taste.

Serve hot or cold. Chop clams and use for canapé spread or other recipes.

Clam Broth Variations

Clam and Tomato Broth: Combine equal quantities of clam broth and tomato juice or tomato bouillon. Season with celery salt.

Clam and Chicken Frappé: Combine 1 1/2 cups clam broth and 2 1/2 cups highly seasoned chicken stock. Freeze to mush. Serve in chilled cups.

Clam and Chicken Broth: Combine equal quantities of clam broth and chicken stock. Either or both may be fresh or canned. Season to taste with salt and pepper. Garnish with chopped chives or parsley.

TURTLE SOUP

It is a timesaver to buy canned or frozen turtle meat; however if you want to prepare your own, see index.

1 1/2 cups diced fresh turtle meat
2 quarts beef stock
1 bay leaf
1 1/2 tablespoons lemon juice
1 clove mace
Few drops Tabasco sauce
Salt and pepper
Sherry wine
2 hard-cooked egg whites, chopped

Combine turtle meat, stock, bay leaf, mace, lemon juice, and Tabasco sauce. Bring to boiling point. Simmer until turtle meat is tender.

Remove bay leaf and mace. Season with salt and pepper.

Add 1 tablespoon sherry to each serving and garnish with chopped egg white. Serves 8.

LOBSTER STEW

1 2-pound lobster, boiled
1/4 cup butter or margarine
1 quart milk
1 slice onion
1 teaspoon salt
Paprika

Cut lobster meat into small pieces. Sauté lightly without browning in melted butter.

Scald milk with onion slice. Discard onion; add lobster meat and seasonings. Heat thoroughly.

If desired, lobster coral or liver may be rubbed through a sieve and added at the last. Serves 4.

BOUILLABAISSE

Bouillabaisse is an elaborate seafood chowder or stew made of many kinds of fish and shellfish (generally five or six), olive oil, tomatoes, garlic, and usually saffron; it is sometimes seasoned with wine. True bouillabaisse can be made only on the Mediterranean coast of France, since it depends on local varieties of fish. Similar dishes to which the same name is applied are also popular elsewhere, including New Orleans. The American version given below includes ingredients available everywhere.

2/3 cup salad oil
1   carrot, minced
3   onions, minced
3   pounds fish fillets
1   bay leaf
1   cup tomato pulp
3   cups fish stock or water
1   dozen oysters or clams
1   cup cooked shrimp or lobster meat
2   pimientos, minced
2   teaspoons salt
1/3 teaspoon paprika
2   tablespoons lemon juice
Toast
2   tablespoons minced parsley

Use a combination of several kinds of fish such as flounder, haddock, perch, sole, whiting, or whitefish.

Heat oil in large heavy saucepan and cook carrot and onions 5 minutes. Add fish, cut into small pieces, and bay leaf. Cook 5 minutes then add tomato pulp and fish stock.

Cover and simmer, without actually boiling, about 20 minutes or until fish is tender.

Add oysters or clams, shrimp or lobster meat, pimientos, seasonings, and lemon juice. Heat thoroughly.

Serve in soup plates, ladling the Bouillabaisse over toast in plates and sprinkling parsley over the surface. Serves 6.

FISH BISQUE
(Master Recipe)

1 1/2 cups thin white sauce
1   slice onion
1/2 to 3/4 cup canned or cooked fish
Lemon juice
Whipped cream (optional)

Add onion to white sauce. Add flaked or chopped fish and heat thoroughly.

Press through a sieve. Heat carefully. Season to taste.

Just before serving, add a few drops lemon juice. If desired, garnish with whipped cream to which a few grains of salt has been added, and, if desired, a bit of paprika. Serves 3.

Variations: Vary by adding a dash of Tabasco sauce or 1/2 teaspoon Worcestershire sauce. If desired, 1/2 cup cooked celery may be added before pressing through sieve.

QUICK SHRIMP GUMBO

1   medium-sized onion, chopped
1/2 green pepper, chopped
3   tablespoons butter or margarine
4   cups chicken stock or consommé
1 1/2 cups cooked or canned okra, cut in small pieces
1   No. 2 can tomatoes
1   cup cooked or canned shrimp
1/2 teaspoon filé powder

Cook onion and green pepper in melted butter until soft, about 5 minutes. Add stock, okra, and tomatoes and simmer gently 20 minutes.

Add shrimp and filé powder. Heat thoroughly. *Do not boil* after adding filé powder.

Season to taste with salt and pepper. Garnish with minced parsley. Serves 6.

Quick Crab Gumbo: Substitute canned crabmeat for shrimp.

OYSTER STEW

4   tablespoons butter or margarine
1   pint shelled oysters with liquid
1   quart (4 cups) milk
1   teaspoon salt
1/8 teaspoon pepper
1 1/2 tablespoons flour

Heat 2 tablespoons butter with oysters and oyster liquid in top part of a double boiler.

Combine 3 1/2 cups milk, 2 tablespoons butter, salt, and pepper in a saucepan; heat to scald milk.

Stir flour into remaining 1/2 cup milk and blend well. Add to the scalded milk mixture; cook over low heat, stirring constantly, until it thickens.

Pour over the hot oysters and place stew over, not in, hot water for 15 minutes before serving. Serves 4 to 6.

PLANTATION CHOWDER

3   medium onions, sliced
2   green peppers, cut into small pieces
3   large carrots, cubed
1/2 cup olive oil
3   frozen lobster tails, cut into 1-inch pieces (shell on)
2   packages deveined frozen shrimp
1   pound package frozen fish fillets
Water to cover (about 5 cups)
1   cup cooked tomatoes
1 1/2 teaspoons salt
1/4 teaspoon pepper
3   cups cooked rice
Saffron (optional)

Sauté vegetables in oil in a large kettle. Add lobster tails, shrimp, then fish fillets. Add water, tomatoes, and seasonings. Cover and cook to boiling.

Reduce heat and simmer 20 minutes.

Meanwhile, following directions on the package, cook enough rice to make 3 cups. Add saffron for color and flavor, if desired. In individual bowls, serve fish and soup, topped with scoops of freshly cooked rice.

NEW ENGLAND FISH CHOWDER

1 1/2 pounds fresh cod, haddock, or any other large fish
2   cups diced potatoes
1   cup diced carrots
1   quart water
1/4 pound salt pork, diced
1   onion, chopped
2   tablespoons flour
2   cups milk
1/2 teaspoon Ac'cent
Salt and pepper
6   soda crackers
2   tablespoons butter or margarine

Cut fish into small pieces; remove bones and skin. Cook fish, potatoes, and carrots in water 15 minutes.

Fry salt pork until crisp; remove and drain.

Sauté onion in drippings; add flour and stir until well blended. Gradually add milk. Add to fish mixture. Add Ac'cent and salt and pepper to taste. Stir frequently and simmer 10 minutes longer.

Add more seasoning if necessary. Add crackers and butter. Serve at once. Serves 6.

SCALLOP STEW

1   quart milk
1/2 pint light cream
1/3 cup butter or margarine
1   tablespoon sugar
1/2 teaspoon Worcestershire sauce
1   pound scallops

Heat milk and cream in double boiler.

Melt butter in skillet, and add sugar and Worcestershire sauce.

Crush scallops, cut off the hard pieces and dice. Add to mixture in skillet. Simmer until tender.

Pour heated milk and cream over cooked scallops. Season to taste with salt and pepper. Serves 6.

Plantation Chowder

OYSTER STEW, WHITE WINE

2 tablespoons butter or margarine
1 pint oysters
1 pint milk (scalded)
1 cup Chablis, Hock, Sauterne, Riesling or any white wine
1 cup cream

Melt butter or margarine. Add oysters and cook until edges begin to curl. Season with salt and pepper.

Scald milk and oyster liquid. Add to oysters. Heat to boiling point.

Remove from heat; add wine gradually. Finally add the cream. Reheat and serve very hot. Serves 4.

SOUTHERN CRAWFISH BISQUE

2 dozen crawfish
1 quart water
2 onions
2 carrots
2 ribs celery
4 sprigs parsley
1/4 teaspoon thyme
6 tablespoons cracker crumbs
Milk
3 tablespoons butter or margarine
2 tablespoons flour
Salt and pepper
1 beaten egg

Prepare crawfish for soup by soaking in cold salted water (1 tablespoon salt to 4 cups water) for 30 minutes. Wash and scrub under running water to remove all the dirt.

When cleaned, place in a soup kettle with the water, 1 onion, the carrots, celery, half the quantity of parsley, and the thyme. Allow to come to a boil and simmer for 25 minutes.

Drain off the water from the crawfish and set aside for later use.

Remove all the meat from the heads and bodies of the crawfish; set aside the heads which are to be stuffed.

Moisten cracker crumbs with milk. Chop crawfish meat and add to the moistened crumbs.

Mince the remaining onion; melt the butter, add the onion and 1 tablespoon of flour. Add 1 tablespoon of the broth and the remainder of the parsley. Season with salt and pepper to taste.

Simmer slowly for a few minutes; add the crawfish and cracker crumb mixture and cook 2 minutes longer.

Remove from range and let cool slightly. Stir in the beaten egg. Fill the heads with this mixture.

Roll the heads in flour and fry in butter until nicely browned. Drain on paper and keep warm while preparing the stock.

Melt the balance of the butter; add the remainder of the flour and stir until smooth.

Strain reserved stock in order to remove celery and carrots. Add the broth to the butter and flour. Cook slowly for 12 minutes; season with more salt and pepper if desired. Before serving, add the stuffed crawfish heads.

Serves 4 to 5.

CREOLE SHRIMP GUMBO

1 slice (1/2 pound) raw ham, cut in small pieces
2 pounds okra, cut in 3/4-inch pieces
1 1/2 cups chopped onion
2 stalks celery with leaves, chopped
1/2 chopped green pepper, seeds and membrane removed
2 cloves garlic, minced
1 sprig fresh thyme or 1/3 teaspoon dried thyme
1 bay leaf
1 1/2 cups skinned fresh tomatoes or 1 No. 1 can tomatoes
6 cups water
2 pounds fresh shrimp
2 tablespoons chopped parsley
Boiled rice

Sauté ham lightly in a skillet. Sauté okra slowly in ham drippings for 10 minutes. (If you use canned okra, omit the sautéing.) Add onion and sauté for the last 2 minutes.

Add celery, green pepper, garlic, thyme, bay leaf, tomatoes, and water. If a thick gumbo is desired use less water.

Shell and remove black sand veins from shrimp. Let the soup boil then reduce heat and add ham, shrimp, and parsley. Simmer 30 minutes.

Serve with boiled rice. Serves 8 to 10 as a main dish or 10 to 12 as a soup.

VELOUTINE DE CRUSTACES

6 medium blue point oysters with liquid (or small to medium oysters)
1 cup diced scallops
10 cherrystone clams (or canned little neck clams)
5 or 6 celery leaves
2 cups chicken broth
2 tablespoons quick-cooking tapioca
2 egg yolks
1/2 cup light cream
Salt to taste
1/2 teaspoon Ac'cent
Dash of pepper
1 tablespoon butter or margarine

Cook oysters, scallops, clams (if fresh), and celery leaves in oyster liquid for 5 minutes; strain.

Skim liquid; add chicken broth; heat to boiling. Add tapioca; cook until thickened (about 10 minutes).

Beat egg yolks with cream; add to chicken broth while stirring. Add remaining ingredients with oysters, scallops, and clams; heat to boiling but do not boil.

Serve hot in soup bowls; keep hot if for sauce; spoon hot into pastry shells if for entrée.

Garnish with finely chopped chives or sprinkle of paprika. Makes 3 1/2 cups, or 4 to 6 servings.

CLAM CHOWDER À LA CAPE COD

(President John F. Kennedy's Favorite)

4 dozen medium hard-shelled clams
6 cups cold water
1 2-inch cube salt pork, diced
1 large onion, chopped very fine
4 medium-sized potatoes, diced
Salt and pepper
2 cups milk
1 cup light cream

Wash and scrub clams thoroughly. Place in deep saucepan with cold water. (Water should almost cover clams.) Let boil gently until shells open, about 10 minutes.

Strain broth through cheesecloth and save. Remove clams from shells, clean and chop fine.

Fry out salt pork in deep saucepan. Add onion and let cook slowly until it begins to turn golden brown.

Add clams and broth. Skim well, if necessary. Add potatoes and season to taste with salt and pepper. Cook until potatoes are tender.

Remove from heat and slowly add milk and cream which have been heated. Serve at once. Serves 8 to 10.

MARTHA WASHINGTON'S CRAB SOUP

2 hard-cooked eggs
2 tablespoons butter or margarine
2 tablespoons flour
Grated rind of 1/2 lemon
1 1/2 quarts milk, scalded
3/4 pound crabmeat, cooked or canned
1/2 cup cream
2 teaspoons Worcestershire sauce
1 cup sherry of madeira wine
Salt and pepper

Mash yolks of cooked eggs to paste with butter, flour, and grated lemon rind.

Add chopped egg whites. Pour hot milk over mixture. Place over low heat and simmer 5 minutes, stirring constantly.

Add crabmeat and cream; bring to boiling point.

Add Worcestershire sauce and wine. Season to taste with salt and pepper. Heat through but do not boil after wine has been added. Serves 6 to 8.

Note: This is a modern adaptation of the original early American recipe.

Stocks and Soups Made with Meat

BEEF OR BROWN SOUP STOCK
(Master Recipe)

A good stock is the basis of countless thousands of dishes. The preparation is relatively easy; it can be made in large quantities and frozen for later use.

5   pounds beef knuckle
3   quarts cold water
1   medium onion, sliced
2   carrots, sliced
1   medium turnip, diced
4   pieces celery (with leaves), cut into
      ½-inch pieces
½ teaspoon whole black peppers
5   whole cloves
1   small bay leaf
3   sprigs parsley
1   tablespoon salt

Have beef knuckle cut in several pieces. Cut meat from bone and cut in cubes. Brown meat cubes.

Put meat and bone into soup kettle; add water and let stand 1 hour to draw out juices.

Bring to boil; skim and reduce heat to simmering. Cook slowly 4 to 5 hours.

Add vegetables and seasonings during last hour of cooking.

Strain stock. Chill. Remove layer of fat when stock is chilled. Makes about 2 quarts.

CONSOMMÉ

Follow recipe for Brown Soup Stock. Substitute 2 pounds lean beef (cut in 1-inch cubes), 1 pound marrowbone (cracked), and 2 pounds veal knuckle (cut in pieces), for beef knuckle.

Sauté vegetables in 1 tablespoon butter until lightly browned before adding to stock.

Chicken stock or chicken bones may be added to soup kettle. Makes about 2 quarts consommé.

CONSOMMÉ PRINCESS

Serve consommé with shredded chicken and new green peas.

CONSOMMÉ ROYALE

Garnish each serving of consommé with royal custard (see Index) diced or cut in fancy shapes.

HOW TO CLARIFY STOCK

For 1 quart of stock, combine 2 tablespoons water with 1 egg white and shell. Add to cold stock. Heat stock and stir constantly until it boils. Boil 5 to 10 minutes without stirring.

Let stand 15 to 20 minutes at back of range for stock to settle. Strain through two thicknesses of cheesecloth.

VEAL OR WHITE STOCK

Follow recipe for Beef or Brown Soup Stock and substitute 4 to 5 pounds of knuckle of veal or poultry or a combination of both for beef.

Do not brown meat. Cover with cold water and proceed as directed.

LAMB OR MUTTON STOCK

Follow recipe for Beef or Brown Soup Stock and substitute 4 to 5 pounds of lamb or mutton for beef.

Do not brown meat. Remove any excess fat from meat before cooking.

BOUILLON

Prepare brown stock. Cool and clarify as directed.

CONSOMMÉ JARDINIERE

Cut vegetables into fancy shapes with vegetable cutters.

Cook and serve in the consommé, allowing about 1 cup vegetables to 1 quart stock.

CONSOMMÉ MACEDOINE

Add cubed cooked vegetables in various colors to stock and reheat.

TOMATO BOUILLON

Combine 2 cups bouillon and 2 cups tomato juice; stir well and heat to boiling point. Pour into cups. Top with slightly salted whipped cream. Sprinkle with chopped parsley.

BEEF JUICE OR TEA
FOR INVALIDS AND CHILDREN

Cut 1 pound lean round steak into small cubes. Put in a quart glass jar. Add 1 cup cold water and a pinch of salt.

Cover jar tightly and place in a pan of cold water, using as much water a possible without upsetting the jar.

Slowly bring the water in pan to a boil and boil gently for 1 hour.

Remove jar and place on a rack to cool as quickly as possible.

Strain the juice and store in refrigerator until ready to heat and serve.

MADRILÈNE

1½ cups chicken stock or bouillon
1½ cups beef stock or bouillon or use
      cube or canned bouillon
1½ cups tomato juice
1   cup chopped celery
½   cup chopped carrot
1   cup chopped leeks
Salt and pepper

Mix bouillons and tomato juice; bring to a boil.

Add vegetables and simmer 30 minutes. Taste, and add more salt and pepper if needed. Strain. Reheat. Serve hot or chilled. Serves 5 to 6.

Minestrone

MINESTRONE
(Italian Vegetable Soup)

This Italian thick vegetable soup appears in countless versions; however all of them include a pasta and usually dried beans or peas. It is usually served with grated Parmesan cheese.

¼ pound bacon or bacon ends,
      chopped
2   medium onions, sliced
1   clove garlic, minced
½   cup chopped celery and leaves
1   carrot, sliced
¼   cup chopped parsley
1   cup chopped escarole
1   cup chopped cabbage
1½ cups cooked dried beans
1   No. 2 can tomatoes
½   cup canned chickpeas
½   teaspoon dried basil
¼   teaspoon oregano
Salt
½   teaspoon Ac'cent (optional)
½   cup elbow macaroni
Cayenne
1   pound hot Italian sausage, sliced
      and cooked
Grated Parmesan cheese

Brown bacon and onions in large kettle. Add remaining raw vegetables; cook 10 minutes, stirring occasionally.

Add 6 cups water, beans, tomatoes, chickpeas, herbs, ½ teaspoon Ac'cent, and 2 teaspoons salt. Bring to boil; cover and simmer 30 minutes.

Add macaroni, and cook 10 minutes, or until tender. Add salt and cayenne to taste. Serve topped with sausage and cheese. Makes 3 quarts.

MUSHROOM CONSOMMÉ

¾ pound mushrooms
6 cups brown stock or 2 cans con-
      densed consommé diluted with
      3 cups water

Wash mushrooms. Remove stems and chop fine; slice caps.

Place chopped stems and stock in a saucepan; cover and simmer about 30 minutes. Strain, chill and remove excess fat.

Simmer sliced mushroom caps in 1 cup of the stock until tender, about 10 minutes. Combine with remaining stock and reheat. Serves 6 to 8.

JIFFY STOCK, BOUILLON, OR CONSOMMÉ

For quick stock, bouillon, or consommé, use one of the following: canned light soup directly from the can; canned condensed soup diluted with an equal amount of water; 1 or 2 bouillon cubes dissolved in 1 cup boiling water, or 1 to 2 teaspoons beef extract or meat concentrate dissolved in 1 cup boiling water.

PEPPER POT

- 1 pound fresh honeycomb tripe
- 3 tablespoons butter or drippings
- 3 quarts cold water
- 1 pound stewing lamb or mutton, trimmed of fat
- 1/4 pound lean salt pork
- 1 small bay leaf
- 1 clove
- 1 sprig each parsley, thyme, and marjoram
- 2 cups mixed vegetables
- 1 cup diced potatoes

Use a variety of vegetables in season, making up the 2 cups of equal parts of beans, carrots, and celery; peas, onions, and beans; tomato, eggplant, and onion, etc.

Wash tripe, drain well, and cut into cubes. Brown in soup kettle in butter or drippings.

Add water, meat (cut into small pieces), salt pork, and seasonings tied together in a piece of cheesecloth. Cover tightly, bring to boiling point and simmer 2 hours.

Add vegetables and potatoes and cook until tender.

Cool, skim off fat and season to taste with salt and pepper. Thicken with a paste made of 3 to 5 tablespoons flour blended with 3 to 5 tablespoons butter. Bring to boiling point.

If a rich effect is desired, pour boiling soup over 2 egg yolks, while stirring constantly. Serves 6 to 8.

Pepper Pot: The birthplace of many of our American traditions—Philadelphia—is also the home of this flavorful and hearty soup, hence it's often called Philadelphia Pepper Pot. There are many versions but one ingredient—tripe—is in every one of them or it's not a true pepper pot.

CHICKEN SOUP STOCK

- 1 4- to 4½-pound chicken, cut up
- 6 cups cold water
- 2 small onions, sliced
- 2 pieces celery, diced
- 1 carrot, sliced
- 3 sprigs parsley
- 1 teaspoon salt
- Dash of pepper
- 4 whole black peppers

Put chicken in soup kettle and cover with cold water. Bring to boiling point and skim.

Add vegetables and seasonings, and simmer until meat is tender.

Remove chicken and strain stock. Cool. Place in refrigerator until needed.

Before using chicken stock, remove fat film from top. The chicken stock may be used for sauces or as a soup base.

Use the chicken meat in chicken salad, chicken loaf, or soufflé. Makes about 1 quart.

CHICKEN NOODLE SOUP

Heat 4 cups chicken stock in top of double boiler.

Add 1½ cups noodles and cook until noodles are tender, about 25 to 30 minutes. Serves 6.

CHICKEN RICE SOUP

Heat 4 cups chicken stock in top of double boiler. Add 1 cup rice; cook until rice is fluffy, about 40 minutes. Serves 6.

MULLIGATAWNY SOUP

This is an East Indian curry-flavored soup with apples and vegetables. Some versions of this dish are made with mutton instead of chicken.

- 1/4 cup butter or other fat
- 1 cup raw diced chicken
- 1 apple, thinly sliced
- 1 small onion, diced
- 1/3 cup diced celery
- 1/3 cup diced carrot
- 1 green pepper, chopped fine
- 1/4 cup flour
- 1 teaspoon curry powder
- 1 blade mace
- 3 cloves
- 1 cup canned tomatoes
- 2 tablespoons minced parsley
- 1 teaspoon salt
- 1/2 teaspoon pepper
- 1½ quarts chicken stock
- 1 cup cooked rice

Cook chicken, apple, and vegetables (except tomatoes and parsley) in butter until brown.

Add remaining ingredients (except rice) in order given. Simmer gently 1 hour.

Strain and pick out pieces of chicken. Press vegetables through a sieve.

Return chicken and vegetables to soup. Adjust seasoning. Serve very hot over cooked rice. Serves 6 to 8.

COCK-A-LEEKIE (From Scotland)

This famous Scotch soup sometimes appears on menus as cockie-leekie.

- 2 bunches leeks
- 1 3½- to 4-pound chicken
- 1½ teaspoons salt
- 1/2 teaspoon pepper
- 1/2 teaspoon nutmeg
- 2 quarts veal stock or water
- 1 dozen prunes

Wash leeks and cut off green tops. Slice white parts in 1/2-inch pieces. Place half the sliced leeks in a large kettle with closely fitting cover.

Cut chicken into serving pieces and place on top of leeks. Add remaining leeks and seasonings. Cover with stock. Bring to rolling boil and skim the top.

Cover well and simmer until chicken is tender, about 1½ hours.

Add prunes 30 minutes before end of cooking time.

Remove meat from bones and place in soup bowls. Pour soup over chicken. Serves 6 to 8.

SPLIT PEA SOUP

- 2 cups dried split peas
- 3 quarts water
- 1 large onion, chopped
- 2 stalks celery
- Sprig of parsley (optional)
- Ham bones or small shank end of ham
- Salt and pepper

Soak peas overnight in cold water to cover.

Combine peas, onion, celery, parsley, ham bones or shank, and additional water to make 3 quarts. Cover and simmer until peas are tender, 3 to 4 hours.

Rub vegetables through a sieve or leave some of the peas whole. Skim off excess fat. Season to taste with salt and pepper.

If desired, thicken soup with a paste made of 3 tablespoon flour and 3 tablespoons butter. If desired, dilute with additional water or milk.

Serve with croutons or slices of frankfurters or Vienna sausage if desired. Garnish with julienne strips of cooked carrot. Serves 6 to 8.

Variations of Split Pea Soup

Purée Mongole: Use yellow split peas and at end dilute with strained cooked tomatoes instead of water or milk.

Black Bean Soup: Use dried black beans instead of peas. Garnish each portion with a slice of lemon and a slice of hard-cooked egg.

Soup St. Germain: Add 3 or 4 lettuce leaves with the peas. Serve with croutons.

CHICKEN BROTH

Use a 3- to 4-pound ready-to-cook stewing chicken. Clean, remove skin and fat and cut in pieces.

Cover with 2 quarts cold water; heat slowly to a boil. Skim, then cover and simmer until tender, about 3 hours. Add 1 teaspoon salt after 2 hours of cooking.

Remove fat and strain as for clear soup. Season to taste and serve hot. Makes about 1 quart broth.

Note: If desired, 2 tablespoons tapioca, sago, rice, or barley soaked overnight, may be cooked with the broth.

Meat cut from bones may be used in salads, creamed, or in other dishes calling for cooked chicken meat.

PETITE MARMITE PARISIENNE

This is a French meat-and-vegetable soup traditionally served in small individual casseroles (marmites). Beef marrow is often added just before serving and the soup may be garnished with toast or bread crusts and grated cheese. There are innumerable versions of this soup. Either the recipe below or the one for Pot-Au-Feu are suitable for this kind of service. If individual casseroles are used, place them under the broiler flame for a few moments to brown after sprinkling with grated cheese.

    2 quarts meat stock
    6 to 8 chicken wings or pieces of
       chicken
    6 cubes of beef (3/4 inch)
    1 small onion, split and toasted with
       a clove in each half
    2 carrots
    2 sticks celery
    1 white turnip
    1 bunch leeks, cut 1-inch long and
       thick as a pencil
    1/8 head cabbage
    Salt and pepper to taste
    1 tablespoon Ac'cent
    6 marrow bone rings (have meatman
       saw 1/4-inch thick)
    French bread crusts, toasted
    Grated Parmesan cheese
    Sprinkle of chopped chervil

Put meat stock in stew pot and bring slowly to boil. Add chicken, beef, and onion; simmer about 30 minutes.

Add carrots, celery, turnip, and leeks, and continue to simmer.

Parboil cabbage in salted water; drain and wash in cold water. When rest of vegetables are nearly cooked, add cabbage, correct seasoning and add Ac'cent.

Remove from heat and place in earthen pot designed for petite marmite.

You can float marrow bone rings in pot or bring slowly to boil in more shallow dish with stock, to be lifted later

to individual serving.

Serve with bread crust and cheese. Sprinkle with chervil. Serves 6 to 8.

POT-AU-FEU
(French Boiled Dinner)

Pot-au-feu means literally, pot on the fire or stock pot. This meat-and-vegetable soup is considered a French national dish. The meat, although cooked with the soup, may be served as a separate course.

    4 pounds lean beef with bone (bris-
       ket, rump, shin, plate, chuck,
       or round)
    3 quarts cold water
    1 tablespoon salt
    Bouquet Garni (see below)
    2 cups chopped mixed vegetables
    3 large carrots, quartered
    6 cabbage wedges
    6 leeks, white part only
    6 potatoes, whole or quartered

For the bouquet garni, tie in a cheesecloth bag 1 bay leaf, 1/4 teaspoon thyme, 1/2 teaspoon whole black peppers, 3 cloves, 4 sprigs parsley, and a few celery leaves.

For the 2 cups mixed vegetables, use onion, carrots, white turnips, and parsnips.

Place meat, water, salt, and bouquet garni in a large soup kettle. Bring to boiling point, skimming often. Lower heat and simmer until meat is almost tender, 4 hours or longer.

Add chopped vegetables and those cut into larger pieces. Simmer until larger pieces are tender, about 45 minutes.

To serve, remove meat to hot serving platter and surround with large pieces of vegetables. Keep warm.

Serve the broth with chopped vegetables as a first course. Refrigerate the balance. Chill and remove fat. Use for stock. Serves 6 or more.

Note: If a fatty piece of meat is used, it is better to make it a day earlier. Chill and remove fat before serving.

QUEBEC PEA SOUP

    1 pound dried whole peas (2½ cups)
    5 quarts cold water
    1/2 pound fat back salt pork or 1 ham
       bone
    1/3 cup chopped onion
    Salt and pepper

Wash peas and soak overnight in cold water.

Add salt pork and chopped onion. Bring soup gradually to boiling point. Then simmer slowly about 3 hours or until peas are tender and mealy, which gives a thick, velvety soup.

Remove pork. Before serving, add salt, if needed, pepper, and parsley or

savory to taste. Makes 12 servings (about 1 cup each).

Note: If pea soup is made in pressure cooker, use the recipe given above, reducing water to 8 cups and cooking 1 hour at 10-pound pressure. Remove from heat and allow pressure to drop gradually until it is completely down.

OXTAIL SOUP

    2 oxtails
    Flour
    3 tablespoons fat
    1 teaspoon salt
    1/2 teaspoon whole black peppers
    Dash of cayenne
    1 bay leaf
    1/2 cup chopped celery
    1 medium onion or leek, chopped
    1 carrot, diced
    1/2 cup tomato purée
    1 teaspoon Worcestershire sauce
    Chopped parsley
    Salt and pepper

Have oxtails cut in pieces and roll in 1/2 cup flour. Brown in 2 tablespoons fat in large kettle.

Add 2 quarts water, salt, pepper, cayenne, and bay leaf. Bring to boil and skim. Cover and simmer 3 hours, or until meat is tender.

Strain broth. Cool and remove fat. Separate meat from bones.

To broth and meat, add celery, onion, and carrot. Bring to boil. Reduce heat and simmer 30 minutes.

Add tomato purée and simmer 10 minutes.

In skillet, brown 2 tablespoons flour; blend in remaining 1 tablespoon fat. Add to soup and bring to boil.

Add Worcestershire and parsley. Season to taste. Makes about 2 quarts.

SCOTCH BROTH

    1/2 cup barley
    3 pounds lamb or mutton
    2 tablespoons butter or margarine
    1/4 cup each celery, carrots, turnips,
       onions, or leeks, diced
    Salt and pepper
    Minced parsley

Soak barley for 2 hours or overnight in cold water.

Combine meat and cold water to cover in kettle. Bring to boiling point and add barley. Simmer until meat is tender, about 1½ to 2 hours.

Sauté vegetables in butter and add to soup for last half hour. Add salt and pepper to taste. Add more boiling water if soup is too thick. Add parsley just before serving. Serves 6 to 8.

Note: For the meat, use the inexpensive cuts such as breast, neck, or flank. Soaked split peas may be added with the barley. Rice may be substituted for barley. Add with the vegetables.

French Onion Soup

WON TON SOUP

Won ton is a Chinese name for small cases of noodle dough stuffed with various mixtures. Although here they are cooked, then served in a chicken soup, the same won tons are often fried in deep oil until golden brown.

Dough:

2 cups sifted enriched flour
1 teaspoon salt
1 large egg
⅓ cup water

Mix and sift flour and salt into mixing bowl. Beat egg slightly and stir into flour.

Add water, a little at a time, mixing until dough is smooth and right for rolling.

Turn out on lightly floured board and knead until smooth, turning and folding over a few times. Cover and let stand 15 to 20 minutes.

Roll out paper-thin and cut into 3-inch squares.

Filling:

1 pound finely ground cooked pork
1 beaten egg
1 tablespoon soy sauce
½ teaspoon salt
¼ teaspoon pepper

Mix pork and remaining ingredients smoothly together. Place 1 teaspoon of mixture in center of each square. Fold squares in half diagonally to form triangles and press edges together with a fork.

Drop filled won tons a few at a time into 1 quart boiling salted water and cook until they float to the surface, about 15 minutes. Remove with slotted spoon and drain.

Soup:

6 cups chicken stock
2 tablespoons chopped green onions
2 tablespoons soy sauce

Heat stock. Place filled cooked won tons in bowls. Sprinkle with green onions. Season each bowl with a little soy sauce. Pour on hot stock. Serves 4.

Variations: Cooked ground beef or shrimp may be substituted for pork in won ton filling. Finely chopped celery (½ cup and 1 cup tightly packed spinach may be added to chicken stock, in which case cook 1 minute when heating the stock before serving.

FRENCH ONION SOUP

2 tablespoons butter or margarine
1¼ to 2½ cups thinly sliced onions (depending upon desired thickness)
5 cups meat stock, canned bouillon, or diluted bouillon cubes
Salt and pepper to taste
1 cup finely grated aged Cheddar or Parmesan cheese
Croutons or French bread

Melt butter in a saucepan; add onions and sauté until lightly browned, about 5 minutes.

Add stock and simmer, covered, about 20 minutes or until onions are just tender.

Season with salt and pepper. Pour into soup bowls; sprinkle with grated cheese and place croutons on top. If using French bread place slices around edge of soup. Makes about 6 8-ounce cups of soup.

CHICKEN OKRA GUMBO
(Creole)

2 tablespoons butter or margarine
1 3- to 3½-pound chicken
1½ to 2 pounds ham slices
1 onion, chopped
½ pod hot red pepper, seeded
1 sprig thyme or parsley, chopped
6 large tomatoes, peeled and chopped
1 quart (1 pound) okra
3 quarts boiling water
1 bay leaf
Salt and cayenne
2½ cups rice, boiled

Heat butter. Add the chicken and ham, both of which have been cut up into pieces. Cook, covered, about 10 minutes.

Add onion, red pepper, thyme, and solid part of tomatoes, reserving juice. Simmer a few minutes; stir often.

Wash okra well, remove stems and cut into ½-inch slices. Add to onion mixture and simmer, stirring constantly until brown.

Add the reserved tomato juice, boiling water, and bay leaf. Add salt and cayenne to taste. Simmer about 1 hour. Serve with boiled rice. Serves 8 to 10.

Note: Okra quickly burns, and should be watched and often stirred during browning. The traditional New Orleans gumbo is highly seasoned, so add cayenne generously.

The Creoles of the Crescent City make many different gumbos, thickening them wtih powdered filé (sassafras) or with okra. Chicken gumbo, like the above, is done with either. Okra often is preferred to the filé in crab and shrimp gumbos.

Of the thick soup that is the gumbo, it has been said:

"It is an original conception, a something *sui generis* in cooking, peculiar to New Orleans alone, and to the manner born."

BLENDER ONION SOUP

2 cups sliced onions
¼ cup butter or margarine
2 cups beef or chicken stock
2 small sprays celery leaves
2 sprays parsley

Sauté onions in hot fat in covered skillet over low heat until golden brown, about 25 minutes. Uncover and sauté 5 minutes longer. Cool and put in container with other ingredients. Blend about 30 seconds.

Reheat and serve with toast rounds and grated Parmesan cheese. Serves 3.

BLENDER WATERCRESS SOUP

1 bunch watercress
3 cups chicken stock
2 tablespons flour
2 teaspoons butter or margarine
½ teaspoon salt

Put watercress, 1 cup stock, flour, fat, and salt in container. Blend thoroughly, about ½ minute.

Heat remaining stock. Add blended mixture. Bring to boiling point. Strain, if desired. Serves 4.

AVOCADO SOUP

4 cups beef or chicken stock, (canned or cubes and water may be used)
1 large avocado, peeled
3 tablespoons finely minced parsley
Salt
4 tablespoons sherry

Heat stock to boiling point in top part of double boiler over direct heat. Keep hot over hot water.

Put avocado pulp through ricer or sieve.

Stir avocado pulp, minced parsley, salt to taste, and sherry into hot stock just before serving. Serves 4.

Note: Do not heat soup with avocado pulp over direct heat. Flavor of avocado is hurt by too much heat.

CLARET BOUILLON

Heat 2½ cups beef bouillon to boiling point. Remove from heat and add ¾ cup claret wine. Serve at once in bouillon cups and garnish with chopped parsley.

WHAT TO DO IF SOUP IS TOO SALTY

Add a few slices raw potato to the soup. Let the soup boil until potatoes are done. They will absorb excess salt.

RUSSIAN CABBAGE SOUP

1½ pounds flank steak
2½ quarts water
1 tablespoon salt
Pepper to taste
1 No. 2 can tomatoes or 2½ cups
    chopped fresh tomatoes
1 large onion
1 bay leaf (optional)
½ clove garlic, cut fine (optional)
1 medium head cabbage
2 tablespoons sugar
1 tablespoon vinegar or lemon
    juice

Place meat and water in 5-quart soup kettle. Add salt, pepper, tomatoes, onion, bay leaf, and garlic. Bring to boiling point; reduce heat and simmer 1½ hours.

Shred cabbage coarsely and add. Add sugar, vinegar, and a little more salt to taste. Simmer gently for another 1½ hours. Serve hot. Serves 4 to 6.

Note: If desired, top each portion with a heaping tablespoon of sour cream.

CLEAR TOMATO SOUP WITH CHEESE

1½ cups sliced onions
3 tablespoons butter or margarine
1 No. 2 can (2½ cups) tomatoes
½ teaspoon salt
¼ teaspoon pepper
½ teaspoon oregano
3 cups beef bouillon or beef stock
1 cup shredded sharp Cheddar
    cheese

Sauté onion in butter until clear. Add tomatoes and cook 5 minutes longer.

Add seasonings and bouillon or stock. Simmer for 10 minutes.

Strain. Serve with shredded Cheddar cheese. Serve 4.

Note: If 3 cups of meat stock are not available, prepare bouillon using 3 cups of boiling water and 3 beef bouillon cubes.

QUICK CHICKEN GUMBO

3 tablespoons butter or margarine
1 onion, chopped fine
½ green pepper, chopped fine
4 cups chicken stock or consommé
1½ cups cooked or canned okra
1 No. 2 can tomatoes
About 1½ teaspoons salt
About ¼ teaspoon pepper
1 cup finely diced cooked or canned
    chicken

Cook onion and green pepper in melted butter until tender, about 5 minutes.

Add stock and remaining ingredients. Simmer gently about 20 minutes. Serves 6.

CHINESE WATERCRESS SOUP

1 loin pork chop
4 cups water
¼ pound pork liver
1 tablespoon soy sauce
½ tablespoon oil
1 bunch watercress, coarsely chopped
1 slightly beaten egg
Salt

Shred meaty portion of chop and simmer in water with bone until meat is tender.

While meat is cooking, cut liver into shreds. Add soy sauce and oil to it and let marinate.

Add watercress to pork chop and cook about 5 minutes. Add liver in its marinade and bring to boil. Add egg.

Reduce heat and cook until egg is poached. Add salt to taste. Serves 4.

CANADIAN CHEESE BISQUE

4 cups clear chicken or veal stock
1 tablespoon minced carrot
1 tablespoon minced celery
2 tablespoons flour
2 tablespoons butter or margarine
½ pound strong Cheddar cheese, 2
    years old, grated
⅛ teaspoon pepper
½ teaspoon salt
½ teaspoon Worcestershire sauce
1 tablespoon minced green pepper
1 cup strong ale, heated

To the stock add the minced carrot and celery.

Make a roux by blending the flour, butter, and cheese. Stir into the stock and whip until smooth and blended.

Season with pepper, salt, and Worcestershire sauce.

Lastly add the green pepper, then set on top of stove until ready to serve, whereupon add the strong ale, heated. Blend together and serve. Serves 6.

EGG AND LEMON SOUP
(Greece)

8 cups soup stock (below)
½ to 1 cup uncooked rice
3 egg yolks
1 tablespoon cornstarch
1 cup milk
Juice of ½ lemon
1 tablespoon butter or margarine,
    melted
1 teaspoon chopped parsley
Salt and pepper to taste

(To make stock: Cut 1½ to 2 pounds of lean lamb in pieces, add 2 quarts water, 3 teaspoons salt, 4 carrots, 1 onion, 2 potatoes, and 1 celery root (celeriac) if available. The vegetables should be sliced or cut in pieces before adding. Simmer until meat is tender, then strain off the stock and chill.)

Remove fat from stock, measure, and add water to make 8 cups. Heat to boiling. Wash rice and add to hot stock. Cook until rice is tender (about 30 minutes). Mix egg yolks with cornstarch and milk and stir into soup. When the mixture has thickened slightly, remove from heat and stir in lemon juice slowly to avoid curdling. Add butter, chopped parsley, salt, and pepper to soup and serve immediately. Serves 8 to 12.

VEGETABLE SOUP, FAMILY STYLE

Bones and scraps from rib roast or leg
    of lamb
2½ quarts cold water
1 medium onion, sliced
2 stalks celery (with leaves), sliced

Place above ingredients in large kettle. Simmer 1¼ hours.

½ cup barley
2 medium white turnips, diced
2 medium potatoes, diced
4 medium carrots, diced
1½ cups sliced celery
½ cup minced parsley
2 teaspoons salt
¼ teaspoon pepper
1 to 1½ teaspoons Ac'cent
⅛ teaspoon powdered cloves
    (optional)
⅛ teaspoon thyme

At end of 1¼-hour first simmering add barley. Continue cooking, at a gentle boil, until barley is swollen and tender, about 1 to 1¼ hours.

Remove bones from stock. If soup is not to be finished for immediate serving, chill stock to congeal fat on top, then remove it. Otherwise skim off fat from stock; bring to boil and add all remaining ingredients.

Simmer gently until vegetables are tender, about 15 minutes.

Meanwhile remove all meat from bones; chop or dice.

Soup meat
2 cans condensed tomato soup
1 teaspoon sugar
Ac'cent, as needed

Add soup meat, tomato soup, and sugar. Heat soup thoroughly. Correct seasoning with Ac'cent. Makes 2 to 2½ quarts.

Vegetable Soup, Family Style

UKRAINIAN BORSHT

2½ pounds soup meat
Soup bones
1   bunch beets, cleaned and quartered
1   large onion
1   can tomato paste
3   cloves garlic, crushed
2   tablespoons lemon juice
¼   cup sugar
2   to 3 tablespoons salt
½   teaspoon paprika
⅛   teaspoon pepper
2   quarts water
3   pounds cabbage, quartered

Combine all ingredients, except cabbage, in large pot. Cover and simmer slowly for 2 hours or until meat is tender.

Put cabbage wedges on top and simmer about another hour until cabbage is done.

Serve with sour cream and plenty of crisp crackers. Makes about 10 servings but most people will want more than one. If there's any left, it's just as delicious reheated for another meal.

MUSHROOM AND BARLEY SOUP
(With Dried Mushrooms)

¼   pound barley
1   quart bouillon
1   ounce dried mushrooms
1   onion, diced
1   carrot, diced
Few sprigs of parsley
Few sprigs of dill
2   bay leaves
½   cup diced cooked soup meat

Cook the barley in water until tender. Combine bouillon, cooked barley, and dried mushrooms which have been washed and cut into pieces, onion, and carrot.

Wrap the parsley and dill around the bay leaves and tie into a bouquet; add to soup kettle.

Simmer gently until vegetables are tender, then remove bouquet. Add the soup meat and serve hot. Serves 4 to 6.

YETCAMEIN

Boil 5 ounces of fine noodles or vermicelli in a quart of rich chicken, beef, or other broth for 4 minutes.

Divide noodles and broth into serving bowls.

Garnish with halves of hard-cooked eggs, sliced cold roast pork or chicken, and sprinkle with chopped parsley or green onions. Flavor individual portions to taste with soy sauce. Serves 3.

TOMATO-RICE SOUP

Cook ½ cup rice and ¼ cup diced celery in 4 cups chicken broth until tender.

Add 1 can condensed tomato soup, 1 red pepper pod, and salt to taste. Heat and remove pepper pod before serving. Serves 6.

BEEF BROTH

Use 3 to 4 pounds beef (shin, chuck, or neck); cut in pieces and crack bone.

Combine with 1 quart cold water; bring slowly to a boil, skim, then cover and simmer about 4 hours. Add ½ teaspoon salt after 2 hours of cooking.

Remove fat and strain. Reheat and serve in hot cups, or chill and serve as a jelly. Makes about 2 cups broth.

TURKEY BONE SOUP

Bones of 1 turkey
2   quarts cold water
1   carrot, sliced
1   stalk celery, chopped
1   teaspoon chopped onion
1   sprig parsley
¼   bay leaf
3   whole black peppers
½   teaspoon salt

Place all ingredients in large kettle. Bring to a boil and simmer, covered, 2 hours; strain. Makes about 1½ quarts soup.

Miscellaneous Meatless Soups

FRENCH VEGETABLE SOUP
(Potage Julienne)

2   potatoes
2   turnips
2   carrots
2   celery sticks
3   cabbage leaves
2   green onions
½   pound string beans
1   cup sweet green peas
1½ quarts (6 cups) water
1½ teaspoons salt
2   tablespoons butter or margarine

Cut the vegetables in thin, matchlike strips; cook all vegetables for 1 hour in boiling water to which you have added salt and butter. Liquid should be reduced to half its volume.

For a *crème julienne*, press the cooked vegetables through a sieve and add ½ to 1 cup of thin cream or rich milk just before serving. Serves 6 to 8.

MUSHROOM STOCK

This is a good way to use up mushroom skins and ends. Combine with chopped onion, celery pieces and leaves, sliced carrots, and chopped parsley.

Cover with cold water; simmer for 30 minutes.

Strain the stock and when ready to use season with salt, pepper, and sherry.

MEATLESS MINESTRONE
(Italian Vegetable Soup)

1   cup navy beans or garbanzos
5   cups cold water
¼   teaspoon salt
¼   cup oil or butter
1   clove garlic, chopped fine
1   tablespoon onion, chopped fine
2   tablespoons parsley, chopped fine
¾   cup or more celery, chopped fine
¼   teaspoon salt
⅓   teaspoon pepper
1   cup fresh or canned tomato pulp
1   cup coarsely chopped cabbage
1   cup cooked macaroni
Salt and paprika
¼   cup or more grated Parmesan cheese

Soak navy beans or garbanzos. Drain and add cold water. Simmer the beans until tender.

Add boiling water, if needed, and ¼ teaspoon salt.

Heat oil or butter in a saucepan. Sauté the garlic, onion, parsley, and celery in the oil until golden brown. Add ¼ teaspoon salt, pepper, tomato pulp, and cabbage. Bring to boiling point and combine with the cooked beans.

Add cooked macaroni. Simmer 15 minutes longer. Add salt and paprika, if needed. Serve in bowls and sprinkle with Parmesan cheese. Makes about 6 cups soup.

MEATLESS LENTIL SOUP

2   cups lentils
1   onion, diced
2   tablespoons fat
1   carrot, diced
3   stalks celery, diced
1   teaspoon salt
¼   teaspoon pepper
2   quarts hot water
Minced parsley

Soak lentils overnight in cold water to cover.

Drain and add diced onion browned in fat. Stir over heat 5 minutes.

Add carrot, celery, salt, and pepper and 2 quarts hot water. Simmer slowly until lentils are tender, about 45 minutes.

Rub through a sieve. Bring to boil and serve hot garnished with parsley. Serves 6 to 8.

Lentil Soup Variatons

Lentil and Barley Soup: Add ½ cup barley with the lentils.

Lentil Soup With Frankfurters: Slice frankfurters into pieces about ½-inch thick. Cook in a few cups of soup stock. Serve soup with sliced frankfurters.

Lentil Soup With Meat: Add soup bone and 1½ to 2 pounds soup meat. Simmer until meat is tender.

SPAGHETTI, MACARONI, NOODLES, AND OTHER PASTAS

PASTA

Pasta is a general term covering all the Italian thin-dough products, such as macaroni, spaghetti, and noodles. Some are usually made fresh, such as cappelletti and ravioli; most are dried, and it is estimated that more than 150 shapes are made commercially. They taste different because they look different, but the dough is the same for all. Many stories tell of the origins of pasta; these include tales of ancient Romans eating pasta with cheese and, on the other hand, of Marco Polo's bringing them home from China. Actually, the Mongols are believed to have introduced them into Europe when they invaded Germany in the 13th century; similar products have been used in Asia for thousands of years.

Pasta dough is made by adding water with or without salt to semolina, farina, flour, or a mixture of these. The quality depends almost entirely on the wheat used. Pastas made from durum wheat break with a clean, sharp edge and keep their shape when cooked. Egg pastas, which include noodles and egg vermicelli, are made of a similar dough with the addition of a government-specified amount of whole eggs or egg yolks.

Baked or boiled, served with all sorts of sauces or with plain butter, pasta is an integral part of the Italian diet. It cooks quickly and easily, its bland flavor blends well with other foods, and it needs only a green salad to make a well-rounded meal.

Sauces for Pasta

BUTTER SAUCE FOR SPAGHETTI OR OTHER PASTA

Finely chop a generous handful of fresh parsley picked from the stems. Add the parsley and 1/4 pound butter to 1 pound of any cooked and well drained pasta, which has been kept steaming hot.

Toss quickly until the butter is completely melted. Sprinkle with grated Parmesan cheese and toss until the cheese is well blended with the pasta. Serve very hot. Serves 5 to 6.

MARINARA SAUCE FOR SPAGHETTI

2 onions, sliced
1 clove garlic
4 tablespoons olive oil
2 1/2 cups cooked or canned tomatoes seasoned with basil
2 anchovy filets, cut into small pieces
1/4 teaspoon sugar
Salt and pepper to taste
1/4 teaspoon oregano

Sauté onions and garlic in olive oil for about 5 minutes. Discard garlic and stir the tomatoes into the seasoned oil.

Cook over high heat for 5 minutes; lower the heat and simmer for 1 hour.

Add anchovy filets, sugar, and salt and pepper to taste. Simmer for 10 minutes longer. Add oregano.

Pour the sauce over 1 pound cooked spaghetti on a hot platter and sprinkle with grated Romano cheese. Serves 6.

ITALIAN TOMATO-MEAT SAUCE

1 clove garlic, chopped fine or 1 onion
1/4 cup olive or salad oil
1 No. 2 can tomatoes
1 can (6 ounces) tomato paste
2 cups water
1 teaspoon salt
1/8 teaspoon cayenne pepper or 4 small dried red peppers
1/2 pound ground beef
1/2 pound ground veal
2 tablespoons chopped parsley
1/4 cup chopped celery tops

Cook garlic or onion in 2 tablespoons oil 5 minutes. Add tomatoes, tomato paste, water, and seasonings, and simmer while meat is cooking.

Cook meat in remaining oil in a heavy frying pan. Stir and cook until redness is gone.

Combine meat and sauce and simmer 2 hours. Add parsley and celery tops and simmer 1 hour more.

Serve sauce on cooked spaghetti and sprinkle with grated Parmesan cheese. Serves 6

WHITE CLAM SAUCE FOR SPAGHETTI

1 medium onion, chopped
1 clove garlic, chopped fine
1 tablespoon chopped parsley
2 tablespoons olive oil
1 can (10 1/2 ounces) minced clams
1/2 teaspoon salt
1/8 teaspoon pepper

Cook onion, garlic, and parsley in hot oil 5 minutes.

Add clams with liquid and seasonings. Simmer 5 minutes. Serves 4.

RED CLAM SAUCE FOR PASTA

2 tablespoons olive oil
2 cloves garlic, finely chopped
1 onion, chopped
2 stalks celery, chopped
2 cups canned tomatoes
1 6-ounce can tomato paste
1½ cups water
¼ teaspoon thyme
¼ teaspoon basil
½ teaspoon oregano
Salt and pepper
2 cups fresh or bottled clam juice
2 cups finely chopped clams, fresh
    or canned
¼ cup butter
½ cup chopped parsley

Heat oil in heavy kettle; add garlic, onion, and celery; sauté until onion is golden brown.

Add tomatoes, tomato paste, water, thyme, basil, oregano, and salt and pepper to taste. Bring to boiling point; reduce heat and simmer gently uncovered 1 hour. Add clam juice after half an hour.

About 5 minutes before serving add clams and cook gently. Stir in butter and parsley. Correct seasoning to taste with salt and pepper. Heat until the butter melts. Serve with freshly cooked pasta. Makes about 6 cups.

GREEN SAUCE FOR SPAGHETTI

⅓ cup butter or margarine
1 clove garlic, chopped fine
¾ cup finely chopped parsley
Grated Parmesan cheese

Melt butter in saucepan over low heat. Add garlic and cook until lightly browned. Pour over hot cooked spaghetti.

Add parsley and about ½ cup grated cheese. Toss well and serve with additional cheese. Serves 4.

CHICKEN LIVER SAUCE
FOR SPAGHETTI

1 medium onion, chopped fine
2 cloves garlic, chopped fine
4 tablespoons olive or salad oil
1 No. 2 can (2½ cups) tomatoes
1 can (6 ounces) tomato paste
1¾ cups water
2 teaspoons salt
¼ teaspoon pepper
¼ teaspoon poultry seasoning
1 bay leaf
½ pound chicken livers
¼ cup canned sliced mushrooms

Cook onion and garlic in 2 tablespoons hot oil until yellow. Add tomatoes, tomato paste, water, and seasonings.

Cut livers into small pieces and cook in remaining oil until browned. Add with mushrooms and liquid to tomato mixture.

Simmer uncovered over low heat, 2 hours, stirring occasionally. Serves 6.

SHRIMP SAUCE FOR PASTA

2 medium onions, chopped
2 tablespoons olive oil
2 garlic cloves, chopped fine
4 cups canned Italian-style toma-
    toes
1½ pounds raw shrimp, shelled and
    cut in small pieces
Pinch of oregano
Salt and pepper

Sauté onion in hot oil in heavy kettle until it is just golden brown. Add garlic and cook over very low heat about 3 minutes.

Add tomatoes and cook uncovered over moderately high heat about 12 minutes. Add shrimp and oregano. Lower heat and simmer about 5 minutes. Add salt and pepper to taste. Serve with freshly cooked spaghetti or other pasta. Makes about 4 servings.

Other Seafood: Substitute for the shrimp, 2 cups of any of the following: crabmeat, lobster meat in small pieces; raw oysters in small pieces (whole if very small), raw clams in small pieces and without juice, young squid cut in very thin slices, octopus cut in bite-size pieces. With squid and octopus, it will be necessary to cook about 15 minutes longer.

QUICK TOMATO SOUP SAUCE
FOR SPAGHETTI

1 medium onion, minced
1 clove garlic, minced
2 tablespoons salad oil
1 can condensed tomato soup
½ cup water
½ teaspoon salt
Dash of pepper
Dash of Worcestershire sauce

Cook onion and garlic in hot oil until yellowed.

Add remaining ingredients and bring to boiling point.

Lower heat and simmer 5 minutes. Serves 4.

ITALIAN SAUSAGE SAUCE
FOR SPAGHETTI

1 pound hot or sweet Italian sausage
Water
1 medium onion, chopped
1 tablespoon chopped parsley
1 No. 2 can (2½ cups) tomatoes
2 8-ounce cans tomato sauce
1 bay leaf
Salt and pepper

Cut sausage into 1-inch pieces. Cook in large pan in ¼ cup water until water evaporates and sausage begins to brown, about 10 minutes.

Add onion and parsley, and cook until onion is yellow. Add ¼ cup water and remaining ingredients.

Bring to boiling point and simmer, uncovered, 1¼ hours, stirring occasionally. Serves 6.

ITALIAN SPAGHETTI AND
MEAT BALLS

2 medium onions, chopped
2 cloves garlic, minced
2 tablespoons salad oil
1 No. 2½ can (3½ cups) tomatoes
¼ cup chopped parsley
Pinch of dried basil
½ teaspoon thyme
2½ teaspoons salt
¼ teaspoon pepper
¼ teaspoon crushed red pepper
1 6-ounce can tomato paste
Meat balls (below)
1 pound spaghetti, cooked
Grated Parmesan cheese

Cook onion and garlic in oil 5 minutes.

Add tomatoes, and simmer, uncovered, 20 minutes, or until oil comes to surface of sauce.

Add 1 cup water, parsley, seasonings, and tomato paste; bring to boil.

Add meat balls; cover, and simmer at least 2 hours. Add more seasonings, if desired.

Serve over hot, drained spaghetti; sprinkle with cheese. Serves 6.

Meat Balls:

½ pound ground beef
½ pound ground pork
2 medium onions, minced
1 clove garlic, minced
¼ cup chopped parsley
½ cup grated Parmesan cheese
½ cup fine, dry breadcrumbs
1 egg
2 teaspoons salt
½ teaspoon pepper
2 tablespoons salad oil

Combine all ingredients except oil; mix thoroughly. Add a little water if mixture seems dry.

Shape in 24 balls, and brown slowly in hot oil.

CHILI HAMBURGER SAUCE

3 small onions, chopped
1 pound hamburger
1 No. 2 can tomatoes
2 teaspoons chili powder
2 teaspoons salt

Brown onions and hamburger in a skillet for a few minutes, stirring with a fork to break meat into bits.

Add remaining ingredients and simmer gently for 45 minutes. Serves 6.

Note: This hamburger sauce is excellent on spaghetti, rice, potatoes or frankfurters.

MUSHROOM-TOMATO SAUCE FOR SPAGHETTI

1   pound mushrooms, sliced
1   medium onion, chopped
1   clove garlic, finely minced
1/4 cup olive oil
1   No. 2 can tomatoes
1/4 teaspoon dried basil
1/8 teaspoon crushed red pepper
1   teaspoon salt

Cook mushrooms, onion, and garlic in hot oil in a large saucepan about 10 minutes, or until mushrooms are browned. Stir frequently.

Add remaining ingredients. Bring to boiling point. Lower heat and simmer, uncovered, 1 hour, stirring occasionally. Serves 6.

MEAT SAUCE WITH RIPE OLIVES

1   pound ground lean beef
1/4 cup olive oil
1   large onion, chopped
1   clove garlic, minced (optional)
1/3 cup chopped green sweet pepper
1   No. 2 1/2 can (3 1/2 cups) tomatoes
1/2 bay leaf
2   teaspoons salt
1   teaspoon chili powder
1/2 teaspoon basil
1/4 teaspoon black pepper
1   cup whole or pitted ripe olives

Brown meat in olive oil. Add onion, garlic, and green pepper to meat and cook until lightly browned.

Stir in tomatoes and seasonings and simmer 1 hour or longer.

If sauce becomes too thick, add water as needed.

Quarter half of olives and add with remaining olives to sauce a few minutes before serving, heating thoroughly. Serves 6.

EASY SPAGHETTI AND MEAT BALLS

3/4 cup chopped onion
1   clove garlic, minced
4   tablespoons fat
1   teaspoon salt
1   pound ground beef
1   8-ounce can tomato sauce
1   cup water
1/4 teaspoon pepper
2   teaspoons Worcestershire sauce
1   8-ounce package spaghetti, cooked
Grated cheese

Lightly brown onion and garlic in hot oil or drippings.

Add salt to meat, mix lightly, form into 8 meat balls. Brown in drippings in pan.

Add tomato sauce, water, and seasoning. Cover and simmer 40 minutes.

Pour sauce over hot spaghetti. Sprinkle with cheese. Serves 4.

SPAGHETTI SAUCE A LA MASI

4   tablespoons butter or margarine
1   medium-sized onion, chopped
1   large clove garlic, minced
1 1/2 pounds ground round steak
1   small bunch celery hearts and leaves, chopped fine
2   medium-sized carrots, chopped fine
2   6-ounce cans tomato paste
1 1/2 cups water
1   No. 2 1/2 can (3 1/2 cups) plum tomatoes
1   tablespoon chopped parsley
1   tablespoon rosemary
1 1/2 tablespoons sweet basil
1 1/2 tablespoons salt
1   teaspoon pepper

Cook onion and garlic in melted butter in a heavy saucepan until onion is golden.

Add ground beef and cook until browned.

Add remaining ingredients in order listed and simmer slowly until sauce has thickened, about 4 hours. Serves 10.

Note: The "secret ingredient" in this as well as other old-time Italian spaghetti sauce recipes is the long, slow simmering.

ITALIAN HERBED TOMATO SAUCE FOR SPAGHETTI

3   medium onions, minced
3   cloves garlic, minced
1/4 cup olive oil
1   No. 2 1/2 can (3 1/2 cups) solid pack tomatoes
1   6-ounce can tomato paste
1   cup dry red wine
1   teaspoon salt
Pepper
1   bay leaf
1/4 teaspoon basil
1/4 teaspoon thyme or oregano
Bouillon or water

Sauté onions and garlic in olive oil until lightly browned, stirring often.

Add remaining ingredients and, to develop a complete blending of flavor, simmer 2 to 3 hours, adding bouillon or water as needed. The sauce should be thick. Strain if desired. Adjust seasonings.

Serve over cooked spaghetti or use as an ingredient in such dishes as eggplant parmigiana, meat loaf, soups, and stews. Makes about 1 quart.

Herbed Meat Tomato Sauce: Brown 1/2 pound chopped beef in the fat before adding onions and garlic.

SPAGHETTI WITH GARLIC SAUCE

Sauté 3 minced garlic cloves in 1/3 cup olive oil, salad oil, or butter or margarine for 3 minutes, stirring constantly so the bits do not brown. Pour over hot drained cooked spaghetti (8-ounce package). Lift with fork to distribute the oil and garlic throughout.

TOMATO MEAT SAUCE WITH WINE FOR SPAGHETTI

1/4 cup olive oil or salad oil
2   onions, minced
1   clove garlic
1   pound hamburger
2   cups canned tomatoes or 4 fresh tomatoes, cut in pieces
1   6-ounce can tomato paste
Salt and pepper
2   cups red wine
1   small can mushrooms

Sauté onion and garlic in oil until lightly browned.

Remove garlic. Add hamburger and cook, stirring frequently until well browned. Add tomatoes and tomato paste, salt and pepper to season. Add 1/4 cup red wine (chianti, cabernet, claret, burgundy, or any other red wine).

Allow mixture to simmer in covered skillet until thick.

Add second 1/4 cup wine and continue cooking and adding wine as sauce thickens. Simmer at least 1 hour.

Add mushrooms about 10 minutes before the end of the cooking period. Serves 6.

SPAGHETTI WITH SEAFOOD SAUCE

1/4 cup butter or margarine
1   medium-sized onion, chopped
1   medium-sized green pepper, chopped
1   cup chopped celery
2   8-ounce cans tomato sauce
1   cup water
1/2 teaspoon marjoram
1/2 pound shrimp, shelled and deveined
2   cups lobster meat
Salt and pepper to taste
1   tablespoon salt
3   quarts boiling water
8   ounces spaghetti

Melt butter; add onion, green pepper, and celery. Sauté until tender, stirring occasionally.

Add tomato sauce, water, and marjoram, and heat to boiling point, stirring occasionally. Simmer, uncovered for 20 minutes.

Add shrimp and lobster. Cook, covered, 10 minutes, or until tender. Season with salt and pepper.

Meanwhile, add 1 tablespoon salt to rapidly boiling water. Gradually add spaghetti so that water continues to boil. Cook, uncovered, stirring occasionally, until tender. Drain in colander. Serve seafood sauce over spaghetti. Serves 4 to 6.

Miscellaneous Pasta Recipes

HOW TO BOIL MACARONI, SPAGHETTI, AND NOODLES

Directions on package give definite method and time for the product.

If directions are not available, allow about 2 quarts rapidly boiling water and 4 teaspoons salt for 2 to 3 cups uncooked macaroni, spaghetti, or noodles.

Break long sticks of macaroni or spaghetti into short pieces or use elbow macaroni, shells, or other small shapes.

Drop into rapidly boiling salted water. Bring back to a boil as quickly as possible and keep at an active boil.

For most products, boil 9 to 12 minutes or to desired degree of tenderness. Do not overcook.

Drain in a strainer, rinse, and drain again.

If long spaghetti sticks are to be served whole or unbroken, boil by placing one end in the boiling water and gradually coiling in the remainder as the sticks soften.

In most recipes spaghetti, macaroni, and noodles may be used interchangeably. Macaroni and spaghetti double in bulk on cooking.

Serve hot at once or use boiled macaroni, noodles, and spaghetti in other recipes.

A variety of sauces for spaghetti is included in this section. Many of the sauces for fish, meats, and poultry, and vegetables may also be used.

SPINACH NOODLES (GREEN NOODLES)

¼ cup spinach, cooked, drained, and puréed
1 beaten egg
¼ teaspoon salt
2 cups sifted enriched flour

Combine spinach, egg, and salt. Stir flour in gradually. Knead until smooth. Place dough in a covered dish for ½ hour.

Roll into paper-thin sheets. Spread out on cloths to dry.

Before they are too dry to handle, fold over into a roll and cut into very thin shreds. Toss apart and permit them to dry thoroughly.

Store in a glass jar until ready to use.

BUTTERED NOODLE RING

Boil ½ pound noodles. Rinse with hot water and drain.

Add ¼ cup butter and stir well. Pack in a ring mold.

Unmold on platter. Fill center and garnish as above. Serves 6.

HOMEMADE NOODLE DOUGH

About 2 cups sifted enriched flour
½ teaspoon salt
2 eggs
2 or 3 teaspoons cold water

Sift flour with salt into mixing bowl or onto a board. Make a "well" in the center.

Drop in eggs and combine with a fork, adding spoonfuls of water as necessary to form a ball of dough that is compact but not hard.

Knead dough until as smooth and elastic as possible, about 5 minutes.

Roll out on a lightly floured board. Use the rolling pin from the outer edges toward the center, turning the board as necessary for easier rolling.

When the dough is rolled evenly thin, let stand 20 minutes in order to dry so that it will not stick together when rolled up.

Roll up lightly and use a very sharp knife to slice ⅛ inch thick, or ¼ inch thick for broad noodles.

Toss the noodles lightly to separate them and spread on lightly floured surface. Let dry thoroughly at room temperature, about 2 hours, then store in covered jars.

Note: Do not try to make noodle dough in damp weather, especially if you are a novice at it.

To Cook Homemade Noodles: Drop by handfuls into boiling soup or boiling, salted water and cook 10 minutes.

Noodle Puffs: Prepare noodle dough and roll out as for noodles; let stand until almost dry.

Fold dough in two and cut through both thicknesses with a small floured cutter (thimble size), pressing well so edges stick together.

Fry in deep hot fat until brown. They should puff up like small balls. Serve in hot soup.

Noodle Squares: Roll noodle dough out thin as for noodles.

When dry, cut into 3-inch strips.

Place on top of each other and cut in ½ inch strips crosswise.

Pile up again and cut to form ½-inch squares. Dry and store as for noodles.

Cook in boiling soup for 15 minutes.

BUTTERED NOODLES

Boil 1 8-ounce package noodles in 3 quarts boiling salted water until tender. Drain in a colander and rinse with hot water.

Add 3 tablespoons butter, salt and pepper, to taste. Stir gently. Serve as soon as butter melts. Serves 4 to 6.

Noodle Cheese Custard Ring with Vegetables

NOODLE CHEESE CUSTARD RING WITH VEGETABLES

1 8-ounce package fine noodles
1 cup milk, scalded
3 beaten eggs
1½ cups grated sharp Cheddar cheese
1 teaspoon salt
Few grains pepper
½ teaspoon Ac'cent
1 bunch carrots, sliced and cooked
2 cups cooked lima beans
⅓ cup melted butter or margarine
½ cup chopped peanuts

Cook noodles in boiling salted water until tender; drain; rinse with cold water.

Pour scalded milk over eggs; add to noodles with cheese and seasonings.

Pour into greased 9-inch ring mold; set in pan of hot water. Bake in slow oven (325°F.) 45 minutes.

Unmold on serving plate. Fill center with hot vegetables.

Melt butter or margarine; add peanuts; cook until butter begins to brown; pour over vegetables and top of noodle ring. Serves 6.

Note: When cooking vegetables, add ¼ teaspoon Ac'cent to cooking water.

BAKED NOODLE RING

1 8-ounce package noodles
⅓ cup dry breadcrumbs
1 cup grated American cheese
2½ cups milk
4 slightly beaten eggs
1 teaspoon salt
1 teaspoon Worcestershire sauce

Cook noodles in boiling salted water.

Drain in colander, rinse, and drain again.

Put alternate layers of noodles, crumbs, and cheese in greased 2-quart ring mold.

Combine milk, eggs, salt, and Worcestershire sauce; pour over noodles.

Set in pan of hot water.

Bake in moderate oven (350° F.) about 45 minutes. Serves 6.

Note: Cheese may be omitted and 3 tablespoons butter added.

LUKSHEN KUGEL
(Old-World Broad Noodle Pudding)

Lukshen Kugel is Yiddish for noodle pudding; this is old-time broad noodle pudding which has been a favorite dish in many versions among European Jews and continues to be popular in the United States.

    8 ounces broad noodles
    3 tablespoons fat
    3 eggs, separated
    1 teaspoon cinnamon
    ¼ teaspoon nutmeg
    ¾ cup chopped seedless raisins
    ½ cup sugar
    ⅛ teaspoon salt

Boil, drain, and rinse noodles. Add fat, well beaten egg yolks, and remaining ingredients, lastly folding in stiffly beaten egg whites.

Mix well and pour into a greased casserole.

Bake in moderate oven (350°F.) about 45 minutes, or until browned. Serves 4 to 6.

Lukshen Kugel Variations

With Almonds: Reduce raisins to ½ cup. Add ¼ cup chopped almonds.

With Apples and Nuts: Use only ¼ cup raisins. Add ⅔ cup sliced, peeled apple and ¼ cup chopped nuts.

With Breadcrumbs: Sprinkle with 3 tablespoons buttered or dry breadcrumbs before baking.

With Cracklings: Omit nutmeg. Use only ¼ teaspoon cinnamon.

Substitute ¾ cup chopped cracklings for raisins. Use chicken fat for the fat.

With Prunes or Apricots: Substitute chopped dried prunes or apricots for raisins.

Add 1 tablespoon lemon juice and ¼ teaspoon grated lemon rind.

FRIED NOODLES

    1 pound fine egg noodles (vermicelli)
       Peanut oil for deep frying

Add noodles to boiling salted water and boil 3 to 5 minutes. Drain and dry.

Drop noodles, one quarter of amount at a time, into hot deep fat (375°F.), separating them so they will brown on all sides. Drain on absorbent paper.

FRIED NOODLE RINGS

    2 cups fine dry noodles
    1 teaspoon salt
       Fat for deep frying

Cook noodles in boiling salted water until tender. Drain but do not wash the noodles.

Place in individual ring molds. Chill until firm. Remove from ring molds.

Fry in deep fat heated to 365°F. (or when an inch cube of bread browns in 60 seconds) 2 to 3 minutes. Drain on absorbent paper.

Place in oven to reheat just before serving. Serve with creamed seafood, creamed chicken, or chow mein. Serves 6.

NOODLE SQUARES

Cook noodles in boiling salted water until tender. Drain and place in a greased baking dish to about 1 inch thickness.

Pour a mixture of 1 beaten egg and a cup of milk over noodles. Season with salt and bake in a slow oven (325°F.) until firm. Allow to stand a while before cutting into squares.

BAKED SOUR CREAM NOODLE RING

    4 ounces broad noodles
    1 cup sour cream
    1 slightly beaten egg
    1 cup cottage cheese
    ½ teaspoon salt
       Dash of pepper
    ¼ cup melted butter or margarine

Cook, drain, and rinse noodles. Combine with remaining ingredients and turn into buttered ring mold.

Bake in slow oven (300°F.) about 1½ hours.

Unmold and fill center with creamed mushrooms, or fish, as desired. Serves 4.

POPPY SEED NOODLES

    8 ounces broad noodles
    3 tablespoons poppy seeds
    ½ cup blanched toasted almonds, chopped
    1 tablespoon melted butter or margarine
    1 teaspoon lemon juice
    ½ teaspoon salt
    ⅛ teaspoon white pepper
       Sprig parsley, minced

Boil, drain, and rinse noodles.

Blend poppy seeds and almonds with butter. Add remaining ingredients. Mix lightly with hot noodles. Serves 6.

NOODLE BASKETS

Noodle baskets are used to serve creamed foods and are available in some food specialty stores. To make them at home 2 small strainers are needed, one about 3 inches in diameter and another about ⅜'s of an inch smaller to fit into the larger one and allowing space for the swelling of the noodles.

Prepare noodle dough (see index) and when it is dry cut into ¼-inch strips.

Dip the strainers in hot fat to keep from sticking, then line with noodle strips in criss-cross fashion. Cut off any ragged edges and place the smaller strainer over the noodle basket. Fry in deep hot fat (375°F.) until lightly browned. Remove basket from strainer and continue with others. Use immediately or let cool and reheat them briefly without the strainers in hot fat before using.

SPEEDY GREEN NOODLES DE LUXE

    ½ pound green noodles
    1 12-ounce jar spaghetti meat sauce
    1 teaspoon Worcestershire sauce
    1 clove garlic
    2 tablespoons red wine
       Grated Parmesan or Romano cheese

Cook noodles in 2 quarts boiling salted water (½ tablespoon salt) until tender, about 10 to 12 minutes. Drain.

Heat spaghetti sauce with Worcestershire, garlic, and red wine.

Pile noodles on garlic-rubbed plates. Pour sauce in center. Sprinkle liberally with cheese. Serves 4.

MACARONI WITH CHEESE AND OLIVE SAUCE

    2 cups (½ pound) uncooked macaroni
    4 tablespoons butter or margarine
    3 tablespoons flour
    2½ cups milk
    2 cups grated American cheese
    1 teaspoon salt
    ⅛ teaspoon pepper
    ½ to 1 cup sliced, stuffed green olives

Cook macaroni in boiling salted water until tender. Drain and run hot water through macaroni.

Melt butter; add flour and blend until smooth. Add milk and cook in top of double boiler until sauce thickens, stirring constantly.

Reserve a little cheese to garnish top and add remaining cheese with seasonings to white sauce. Stir until cheese is melted. Add sliced olives.

Arrange macaroni on warm serving plate. Pour sauce over it. Garnish top with grated cheese.

Serve with broiled tomatoes on buttered toast rounds. Serves 6.

Macaroni with Cheese and Olive Sauce

KREPLACH

Kreplach is a Yiddish term for noodle dough cut into small squares; filled with meat or cheese, and other fillings; folded into a triangular turnover; cooked, and served in soups or sometimes fried. It is an old-time Jewish dish.

1 recipe homemade noodle dough
2 cups filling (below)

Roll out noodle dough very thin on a lightly floured board. Cut into 3-inch squares.

Place a heaping teaspoon of the filling on each square. Moisten edges lightly with water, and fold over diagonally to form triangles. Press edges firmly together with a fork. These may be wrapped and frozen.

At serving time, drop the kreplach one at a time into a large saucepan of rapidly boiling water to which ½ teaspoon salt has been added. Cover pan and cook 20 minutes. Skim out.

Serve in clear soup or serve meat or kashe kreplach with meat gravy, cheese kreplach with sour cream. Makes 12 to 18 3-inch kreplach.

Note: If bite-size 1½-inch kreplach are made, cook only 10 to 15 minutes.

Chicken Filling for Kreplach:

1½ cups finely cut cooked chicken
1 slightly beaten egg
1 tablespoon minced parsley
1 teaspoon onion juice
Salt and pepper to taste

Mix together and use as filling for kreplach.

Variations: Other cooked leftover meat may be substituted for chicken. Cracklings (greben) may be combined with leftover chicken, seasoned to taste, and used as filling.

Cheese Filling for Kreplach:

1 pound dry cottage cheese
1 slightly beaten egg
1 tablespoon sugar
¼ teaspoon cinnamon
¼ teaspoon salt
¼ cup seedless raisins (optional)

Blend ingredients together. Makes 2 cups.

Chicken Liver and Egg Filling for Kreplach:

Broil chicken livers under moderate heat until tender. Combine with as many shelled hard-cooked eggs as desired and chop together in wooden chopping bowl or put through medium blade of food chopper.

Season with salt and pepper, poultry seasoning, and finely chopped parsley. Blend into a smooth mixture before using.

CAPPELLETTI

Moist stuffed pasta that takes its name from a fancied resemblance to little hats. Cappelletti are served with sauce or in soups.

Stuffing:

1 chicken breast, raw
2 tablespoons butter or margarine
1 pound Ricotta cheese
1 whole egg, unbeaten
1 egg yolk, unbeaten
Pinch of nutmeg
Salt and pepper to taste
3 tablespoons grated Parmesan cheese

Pasta (Dough):

1 pound enriched flour (4 cups sifted)
3 slightly beaten eggs
1 tablespoon butter or margarine
Lukewarm water

To prepare stuffing, brown chicken breast in 2 tablespoons butter.

Chop meat very fine and to it add a mixture of the Ricotta cheese, 1 unbeaten egg, 1 unbeaten egg yolk, nutmeg, salt, and pepper to taste. Add Parmesan cheese and mix well.

To make dough, sift flour onto center of a board. Stir into its center the 3 slightly beaten eggs. Add 1 tablespoon butter and enough lukewarm water (less than 1 cup) to form a firm dough. Knead well until smooth and manageable.

Cut dough in half and roll into thin sheets on a lightly floured board. Cut into rounds with a biscuit cutter.

To prepare the cappelletti, place 1 teaspoon stuffing in center of each round. Fold one side over to form a little hat. Press edges gently but firmly to prevent filling from falling out.

When all the ingredients are used, drop the cappelletti into 6 quarts of rapidly boiling salted water. Cook about 5 minutes or until dough is tender.

Drain and put on hot platter. Serve with any plain Italian-type tomato sauce and grated Parmesan cheese.

These cappelletti may also be boiled in chicken broth and served in the soup.

MACARONI-CAMP STYLE

1 8-ounce package macaroni
2 cups grated Cheddar cheese (½ pound)
¼ cup chili sauce
3 tablespoons Worcestershire sauce
Salt and pepper to taste
¾ cup hot melted butter or margarine

Cook macaroni in boiling salted water until tender. Drain and spread out on a hot large platter.

Sprinkle with cheese, chili sauce, and Worcestershire. Add salt and pepper to taste.

Pour over the hot melted butter and toss with 2 forks until sauce is creamy. Serve at once. Serves 6.

RAVIOLI

Ravioli is an Italian specialty. Small pillows of thinly rolled noodle dough are filled with chopped spinach, meat, cheese, or other forcemeat and cooked in stock or boiling salted water. They are served with butter and cheese or with a sauce and may also be baked with cheese and tomato sauce.

1½ cups sifted enriched flour
1 egg yolk
Water to make a stiff dough
¼ cup fine cracker crumbs
1 egg
¼ cup chopped cooked spinach
Chicken stock
Salt and pepper
½ cup grated Parmesan cheese
4 tablespoons tomato paste
1¼ cups water
2 tablespoons flour

Sift flour onto board. Make a depression in the center and drop in the egg yolk. Moisten with enough warm water to make a stiff dough.

Knead until the mixture is smooth, cover, and let stand 10 minutes.

Roll paper-thin and cut with a pastry jagger into strips three inches wide and as long as the pastry.

Mix crumbs, egg, and spinach. Moisten with stock and season with salt and pepper.

Place spoonfuls of the spinach mixture on the lower half of each strip about 2 inches apart. Fold the upper half of the strip over the lower part. Press pastry together along the edges and between mounds of filling. Cut apart with pastry jagger.

Drop into boiling stock and cook 10 minutes.

Remove to serving dish, placing ravioli in layers with the cheese and covering with tomato sauce made by cooking the tomato paste, water, and flour together until smooth and thickened, or serve any desired tomato spaghetti sauce. Serves 4 to 6.

Macaroni-Camp Style

CHEESE NOODLE RING

1 8-ounce package fine noodles
1 cup milk, scalded
3 eggs, beaten
1½ cups grated Cheddar cheese
1 teaspoon salt
Few grains pepper
½ teaspoon Ac'cent
1 bunch carrots, sliced and cooked
2 cups lima beans, cooked
⅓ cup butter or margarine
½ cup chopped unsalted peanuts

Cook noodles in boiling salted water until tender; drain; rinse with cold water. Pour scalded milk over eggs; add to noodles with cheese and seasonings. Pour into greased 9-inch ring mold; set in pan of hot water. Bake in slow oven (325°F.) until firm, 45 minutes.

Unmold on serving plate. Fill center with hot carrots and lima beans.

Melt butter; add peanuts; cook until butter begins to brown; pour over vegetables and top of noodle ring. Serves 6.

ARGENTINE TAGLIARINI AND BEEF

¼ cup olive oil
1 large onion, chopped
1½ pounds top round steak, cut into 2-inch strips
½ green pepper, cut in small strips
4 tablespoons fresh mushrooms, chopped
1 cup claret or other dry red wine
½ pound hot boiled tagliarini (see below)
Grated cheese (optional)

Heat oil in a skillet. Add onion and cook until clear only. Add steak and green pepper and cook until steak is brown all over.

Add mushrooms and wine. Let simmer, covered, until beef is tender.

Strain this sauce over tagliarini; mix well, adding grated cheese if desired. Spread on a hot platter; put beef on top; serve. Serves 6.

Note: Tagliarini are a very fine strip-type Italian paste, a third the width of ordinary noodle strips. They may be bought in well stocked markets or in stores in Italian neighborhoods.

CHILI SPAGHETTI OR MACARONI

2 tablespoons butter or margarine
3 tablespoons chopped onion
¼ cup diced green pepper
½ pound lean ground beef
1 No. 2 can (2½ cups) tomatoes
1 6-ounce can tomato paste
1 teaspoon salt
2 teaspoons chili powder
1 No. 303 can kidney beans, drained
½ pound spaghetti or macaroni, cooked

Cook onion and green pepper until tender in melted butter in skillet.

Add beef and cook until lightly browned.

Add tomatoes, tomato paste, salt, and chili powder. Simmer over low heat, stirring occasionally, for 20 minutes.

Add kidney beans to chili mixture; heat thoroughly and serve over cooked, drained spaghetti or macaroni. Serves 6.

CREAMY MACARONI PATTIES

4 tablespoons shortening
5 tablespoons flour
1 cup milk
1 teaspoon salt
½ pound grated cheese
1½ cups cooked macaroni
1 tablespoon chopped parsley
1 teaspoon scraped onion
Fine dry breadcrumbs
1 egg
1 tablespoon water
4 tablespoons fat

Melt shortening. Blend in flour. Add milk and salt. Stir until smooth and thickened.

Remove from heat. Add grated cheese and stir until cheese is melted.

Add macaroni, cut into small pieces, parsley, and onion.

Turn into well greased pan. Chill until firm.

Cut into patties. Dip in fine crumbs, then in beaten egg which has been diluted with water, then again in crumbs.

Fry in hot fat until brown. Serve with tomato sauce. Serves 5.

Macaroni Croquettes: Prepare above recipe. Shape into croquettes when chilled.

Fry in deep fat (375°F.) until browned. Drain on absorbent paper. Serve with cheese sauce.

SPAGHETTI GABRIELE

½ cup olive oil
¼ cup butter or margarine
3 cloves garlic, minced
1 cup sliced onions
½ cup chopped celery
1 cup chopped parsley
2 4-ounce cans mushrooms, drained
½ pound coarsely ground beef
½ pound coarsely ground pork
½ pound coarsely ground veal
1 No. 2½ can tomatoes
1 6-ounce can tomato paste
½ teaspoon ground allspice
½ teaspoon black pepper
1 tablespoon salt
1 teaspoon thyme
1½ pounds spaghetti, cooked
¼ cup butter or margarine
2 teaspoons grated Italian cheese
1 tablespoon chopped parsley

Heat olive oil and melt ¼ cup butter or margarine in large heavy skillet. Add garlic, onions, celery, 1 cup parsley, mushrooms, and meat. Sauté until meat is lightly browned.

Add tomatoes and tomato paste; cook over low heat, stirring occasionally, 1 hour.

Add allspice, pepper, 1 tablespoon salt, and thyme; mix thoroughly.

Place hot cooked spaghetti in saucepan; add ¼ cup butter or margarine, cheese, and 1 tablespoon parsley. Cover; let stand 2 to 3 minutes.

Add small amount of sauce to spaghetti mixture; blend well. Serve spaghetti with remaining sauce.

Serves 8 to 10.

TURKEY SPAGHETTI SUPREME

¼ cup butter or margarine
¼ cup chopped green pepper
¼ cup enriched flour
2 cups turkey broth or chicken bouillon
1 cup milk
1 teaspoon salt
⅛ teaspoon pepper
¼ cup chopped canned pimiento
8 ounces spaghetti, cooked
2 cups diced boned cooked turkey or chicken
1 3-ounce can mushrooms, drained
Grated Parmesan cheese

Melt butter or margarine over low heat. Add green pepper and cook until tender.

Blend in flour. Add turkey or chicken broth and milk. Cook, stirring constantly, until mixture thickens. Season with 1 teaspoon salt and pepper. Add pimiento.

Add half the sauce to drained spaghetti and mix well. Turn onto large serving dish.

Add turkey or chicken and mushrooms to remaining sauce and heat thoroughly.

Pour turkey or chicken mixture into center of spaghetti on serving dish; sprinkle with Parmesan cheese.

Serves 4 to 6.

Spaghetti Gabriele

Oven Main Dishes

MANICOTTI

Manicotti is an Italian word which means literally "little muffs." These may be thin rectangles or rounds of noodle dough stuffed with meat or cheese filling, rolled up, and baked in a sauce, but more commonly manicotti refers to a pipelike macaroni about 1 inch across similarly filled and baked. Tufoli, a similarly shaped macaroni product, may be used instead of manicotti.

Sauce:

1 pound ground beef
1/4 cup olive or salad oil
1/2 cup chopped onion
1 large clove garlic, minced
2 6-ounce cans tomato paste
2 cups water
1 1/2 teaspoons salt
Dash of pepper
2 tablespoons chopped parsley
4 teaspoons basil
1 teaspoon aniseed (optional)

Filling:

3/4 pound fresh ricotta cheese or 1 1/2 cups cream-style cottage cheese
1/3 cup grated Parmesan or Romano cheese
1 beaten egg
2 tablespoons chopped parsley
1/4 teaspoon salt
Dash of pepper
1/2 pound manicotti shells
Additional grated Parmesan or Romano cheese

Sauce: Sauté meat in hot oil until lightly browned. Add remaining sauce ingredients (next 9 ingredients). Simmer uncovered, stirring occasionally, about 45 minutes.

Filling: Combine next 6 ingredients. Mix lightly but thoroughly.

Cook manicotti in a large quantity of boiling salted water until half done, about 10 minutes. Drain and rinse in cold water. Return to pot and toss with small amount of melted butter to prevent sticking.

Using a teaspoon or pastry tube, stuff manicotti with filling.

Pour half the tomato-meat sauce into an 11 x 7 x 1 1/2-inch baking dish. Arrange manicotti in a layer, overlapping slightly. Cover with remaining sauce. Sprinkle with grated cheese.

Bake in moderate oven (350°F.) 25 to 30 minutes. Serves 6 to 8.

MACARONI-BEEF CASSEROLE

1 pound lean ground beef
1/2 cup chopped onion
2 tablespoons cooking oil
1/4 cup dry white wine
1 8-ounce can tomato sauce
1 teaspoon salt
1/4 teaspoon cinnamon
1 1/2 tablespoons margarine or butter
1 1/2 tablespoons flour
1 1/2 cups milk
1 egg, well beaten
1 tablespoon breadcrumbs
1/2 pound macaroni, cooked just tender, drained
2/3 cup grated Parmesan cheese

Cook beef and onions in oil until meat is lightly browned. Add wine, tomato sauce, salt, and cinnamon. Simmer 10 minutes.

Melt butter in saucepan; add flour and stir until blended. Slowly add milk and cook, stirring until smooth and thickened.

Add egg and breadcrumbs to meat mixture.

Put half of macaroni into a 2 1/2- or 3-quart greased baking dish. Sprinkle macaroni with 1/3 of the grated Parmesan cheese and spread with meat mixture. Add remaining macaroni and sprinkle with another 1/3 grated Parmesan. Pour white sauce over all and sprinkle with remaining cheese. Bake in hot oven (400°F.) 30 minutes. Serves 6 to 8.

MACARONI PARMIGIANA

2 cloves garlic, minced
2 tablespoons olive oil
1 8-ounce can tomato sauce
1 No. 2 can tomatoes
1 small onion, minced
1 1/2 teaspoons salt
1/4 teaspoon pepper
1 1/2 teaspoons oregano
1 8-ounce package elbow macaroni
1 pound cottage cheese
1/2 pound Mozzarella or Swiss cheese, sliced thin
1/2 cup grated Parmesan cheese

Brown garlic in oil. Stir in tomato sauce, tomatoes, onion, salt, pepper, and oregano.

Cover and simmer until thickened, about 15 to 20 minutes.

Cook macaroni until tender. Drain. Fill a 3-quart casserole with alternate layers of macaroni, cottage cheese, Mozzarella or Swiss cheese, tomato mixture, and Parmesan cheese.

Bake in moderate oven (375°F.) 20 to 25 minutes. Serves 6 to 8.

Macaroni-Beef Casserole

LASAGNE WITH BEEF AND SAUSAGE

Lasagne are a type of very broad noodle. They are prepared like macaroni. The dish that is popularly called lasagne in the United States should be more specifically called lasagne imbottite: stuffed noodles, made by layering cooked noodles in a baking dish with tomato sauce, meat, and cheese and cooking it in the oven. The recipe that follows is a popular version of this dish. It is sometimes called lasagna, which is the singular form of the word.

1/2 pound ground beef
1/2 pound sausage
1 clove garlic, mashed
1/2 cup chopped onion
1/2 cup chopped celery
2 6-ounce cans tomato paste
3 cups hot water
2 teaspoons sugar
2 teaspoons salt
1/2 teaspoon sage
1 pound lasagne noodles, cooked
1/2 pound ricotta cheese
1/2 pound Mozzarella cheese, sliced thin

Cook meat until crumbly. Add garlic, onion, and celery; cook until tender.

Stir in tomato paste, water, and seasonings. Blend well. Cover and simmer 50 minutes. Drain off extra fat.

Arrange alternate layers of cooked noodles, sauce, and cheese in greased 13 x 9 x 2-inch baking dish, ending with Mozzarella.

Bake in moderate oven (375°F.) 25 to 30 minutes, or until cheese melts.

Let stand out of oven 5 minutes. Cut into squares. Serves 6 to 8.

Manicotti

Lasagne with Beef and Sausage

MACARONI-VEGETABLE-MEAT CASSEROLE
(Master Recipe)

2 cups broken macaroni
6 cups boiling water
2½ teaspoons salt
1 tablespoon butter or margarine
1 tablespoon flour
¼ teaspoon pepper
¾ cup vegetable liquid
¾ cup evaporated milk
1 cup grated American cheese
1¼ cups ground cooked meat (see below)
1 cup drained vegetable, freshly cooked or canned (see below)
½ cup breadcrumbs or corn flakes
2 tablespoons melted butter or margarine

Cook macaroni until tender in boiling salted water, using 1½ teaspoons salt. Drain and rinse with hot water.

Melt butter; blend in flour, 1 teaspoon salt, and pepper. Stir in vegetable liquid slowly. Stir and boil 2 minutes. Stir in milk and heat well. Remove from heat.

Add drained macaroni, grated cheese, meat, and vegetable; pour into 2-quart greased casserole.

Sprinkle top with mixture of breadcrumbs or corn flakes and melted butter.

Bake in moderate oven (375°F.) until crumbs are brown (10 minutes). Serves 6.

Variations: Substitute ½ pound noodles or spaghetti for macaroni.

Use ham, corned beef, bologna, frankfurters, or tongue.

Use carrots, green beans, peas, or celery.

LASAGNE AL FORNO
(Italian Baked Cheese and Noodles)

½ pound lasagne (very broad noodles)
3 tablespoons finely chopped green pepper
1 large onion, chopped
¼ cup olive oil
1 8-ounce can tomato sauce
½ teaspoon sugar
Salt and pepper
¾ pound Mozzarella cheese
½ cup grated Parmesan cheese

Cook noodles in boiling salted water and drain.

Brown green pepper and onion in hot oil and add tomato sauce and seasonings.

Place alternate layers of drained noodles and thin slices of Mozzarella cheese in a casserole, sprinkling each layer with Parmesan cheese and sauce.

Sprinkle top with Parmesan cheese.

Bake in moderate oven (350°F.) until cheese is well browned, about 15 minutes. Serves 4 to 6.

NOODLE CASSEROLE SUPREME

1 8-ounce package wide noodles
3 tablespoons butter or margarine
1 cup chopped onion
1 can (17 ounces) whole tomatoes
1 tablespoon Worcestershire sauce
2 tablespoons sugar
1 cup cottage cheese
1 cup sour cream
2 tablespoons finely cut chives
¼ cup grated Parmesan cheese

Cook noodles as directed on package; put in greased 2-quart casserole.

In saucepan melt butter, add onion and cook over medium heat until tender.

Stir in tomatoes, Worcestershire sauce, and sugar; bring to boil.

Remove from heat and stir in cottage cheese, sour cream, and chives. Pour over noodles in casserole; sprinkle with Parmesan cheese.

Bake in moderate oven (350°F.) for 25 to 30 minutes. Serves 8.

SPAGHETTI AND TOMATO CASSEROLE

8 ounces thin spaghetti
1 green pepper, chopped
1 small onion, minced
¼ cup butter or margarine
1 No. 2 can tomatoes
1 can (6-ounces) tomato paste
¾ cup water
1 teaspoon salt
⅛ teaspoon pepper
½ pound sharp process cheese, grated
½ cup sliced ripe olives

Cook spaghetti in boiling salted water until tender. Drain thoroughly.

Sauté green pepper and onion in butter 5 minutes. Add tomatoes, tomato paste, water, seasonings, and half of cheese. Blend thoroughly.

Place in greased casserole. Sprinkle with remaining cheese. Bake in moderate oven (350°F.) 30 minutes. Garnish with olives. Serves 6.

CHESTERFIELD PIE
(Old-Time Southern Hunt Specialty)

1 cup elbow macaroni, cooked
1 cup grated American cheese
½ cup fresh breadcrumbs
3 tablespoons finely chopped green pepper
3 tablespoons finely chopped onion
¼ cup butter or margarine
1 cup milk
1 teaspoon salt
3 eggs, separated
3 cups creamed chicken
1 tablespoon finely chopped parsley

Cook macaroni the previous day or the morning you plan to serve the dish. Drain; and while hot, add cheese, crumbs, pepper, onion, butter, milk, and salt.

Cool. Place covered in refrigerator until ready to bake.

Then add beaten egg yolks. Fold in stiffly beaten egg whites. Pour into well greased 8-inch ring mold.

Place mold in shallow pan of water in slow oven (300°F.) about 20 minutes.

Remove from water and continue baking 10 to 15 minutes longer or until cake tester inserted in center comes out clean.

Unmold on serving dish and fill center of ring with creamed chicken. Garnish with parsley. Serves 6 to 8.

SALAMI-SPAGHETTI DINNER

6 ounces spaghetti
¼ cup margarine
¼ cup flour
1¼ teaspoons salt
⅛ teaspoon pepper
½ teaspoon dry mustard
1 teaspoon Worcestershire sauce
2 cups milk
1 tablespoon minced onion
¾ cup grated American cheese
1½ cups diced salami
½ cup slivered sweet pickle

Cook spaghetti in boiling salted water until tender. Drain and rinse.

Melt margarine in saucepan. Stir in flour, salt, pepper, mustard, and Worcestershire sauce. Mix smooth.

Gradually add milk, stirring constantly until thickened and sauce comes to a boil.

Fold in onion, cheese, salami, and pickle. Fold into spaghetti.

Pour into well greased 2-quart baking dish or into 6 individual bakers. Bake in moderate oven (350°F.) 25 minutes.

If desired, garnish with shredded cheese and a cluster of salami "flowers." Make the "flowers" by folding thin slices of salami. Fasten with wooden picks and insert strips of cheese and pickle into the center. Serves 6.

Salami-Spaghetti Dinner

Baked Macaroni and Cheese

BAKED MACARONI AND CHEESE
(Master Recipe)

2 teaspoons grated onion
1/2 pound grated cheese
2 cups medium white sauce
1 8-ounce package macaroni
1/2 cup buttered crumbs
Paprika

Add onion and half the grated cheese to white sauce. Blend well.

Cook macaroni, drain, and rinse. Place in alternate layers with sauce in buttered casserole.

Sprinkle with crumbs, remaining cheese, and paprika.

Bake uncovered in moderate oven (375°F.) about 25 minutes, or until crumbs are browned. Serves 6 to 8.

BAKED MACARONI VARIATIONS

Baked Macaroni with Ham or Corned Beef: Follow master recipe for baked macaroni and cheese.

Before baking, add 1 cup chopped cooked ham or corned beef. If cheese is omitted, dot meat with butter.

Baked Macaroni with Sausage: Follow master recipe for baked macaroni and cheese.

Substitute 1 1/2 to 2 cups chopped cooked sausage for the cheese.

Baked Macaroni and Hard-Cooked Eggs: Alternate layers of cooked macaroni and slices of hard-cooked egg.

Cover with medium white sauce and bake.

Baked Macaroni with Tomato Sauce: Omit onion and paprika in master recipe.

Substitute tomato sauce for white sauce.

Baked Italian Macaroni: Add sautéed minced onion and garlic to tomato sauce.

Pour on cooked macaroni and sprinkle Parmesan cheese on top. Bake.

Baked Spanish Macaroni: Add 1/4 cup chopped green pepper which has been fried until soft in 1 tablespoon oil, and 1 tablespoon each of minced onion, celery, and pimiento to 2 cups tomato sauce.

Pour on cooked macaroni and bake.

Baked Spaghetti: Substitute spaghetti for macaroni in master recipe or macaroni variations.

NOODLES ROMANOFF

1 cup cottage cheese
1 cup sour cream
2 cups hot boiled noodles (6 ounces uncooked)
1 teaspoon minced onion
1 small clove garlic, minced
1 teaspoon Worcestershire sauce
1/2 teaspoon salt
1/4 cup grated cheese

Mix together gently the cottage cheese, sour cream, and cooked noodles. Add onion, garlic, and seasonings.

Place in greased 2-quart casserole. Sprinkle with cheese.

Bake in moderate oven (350°F.) 40 minutes. Serve hot. Serves 6.

MACARONI BAKED WITH SOUR CREAM

6 ounces macaroni
3 tablespoons melted butter or margarine
1 cup sour cream
1/2 cup grated cheese

Cook macaroni in boiling salted water. Drain and toss with melted butter.

Turn into greased baking dish. Make a well in center. Pour in sour cream. Sprinkle grated cheese over all.

Bake in hot oven (400°F.) until top is brown. Serves 4.

CANELLONI ALLA GRUCCI

Canelloni is an Italian term for pasta stuffed with meat and baked with tomato or cheese sauce.

1 1/3 cups flour
1 egg plus 1 egg yolk
Pinch of salt

Blend flour, egg and egg yolk, and salt to make a smooth paste. Roll the dough out very thinly and cut into 3 1/2-inch squares. Drop the squares into boiling salted water and cook for 8 minutes, or until tender but somewhat firm. Drain and place them on a cloth.

Filling:

6 chicken livers
1 onion, finely chopped
1 clove garlic, finely chopped
3 tablespoons butter
1 1/2 cups cubed cooked chicken or veal
1/4 teaspoon thyme
Salt and pepper
2 eggs, slightly beaten

Topping:

1 1/2 cups tomato sauce, slightly heated
Grated Parmesan cheese

Pan-fry chicken livers with onion and garlic in butter about 5 minutes, or until delicately colored. Put this mixture and the cooked meat through food chopper using the fine blade; season with thyme and salt and pepper to taste. Blend with the eggs.

Put a little of this filling on each noodle square and roll each one to make a tube.

Arrange the canelloni, side by side, in a large shallow baking dish. Cover with heated tomato sauce; sprinkle generously with grated cheese. Brown under broiler. Serves 5 to 6.

MACARONI-TOMATO-GREEN PEPPER CASSEROLE

1 8-ounce package macaroni
3 tablespoons chopped onion
2 tablespoons butter or margarine
1 No. 2 can (2 1/2 cups) tomatoes
1 teaspoon salt
3 medium green peppers
1/2 cup grated sharp Cheddar cheese

Cook macaroni in boiling salted water until tender. Drain thoroughly.

Cook onion in butter until soft and yellow. Add tomatoes and simmer about 5 minutes.

Add drained macaroni and salt. Mix well and simmer 10 minutes longer.

Cut peppers into quarters. Wash, remove white membranes and boil about 5 minutes in salted water (1 teaspoon salt to 1 quart water).

Drain peppers and arrange in bottom of greased casserole. Fill casserole with macaroni-tomato mixture. Sprinkle top with grated cheese.

Bake in hot oven (400°F.) until cheese is nicely browned, about 15 minutes. Serves 5 to 6.

ITALIAN SPAGHETTI CASSEROLE

1/4 cup chopped onion
1 clove garlic, minced
1/2 cup chopped green pepper
1/4 cup salad oil
1/4 pound ground beef
1/4 pound ground pork
1 No. 2 can (2 1/2 cups) tomatoes
1 6-ounce can tomato paste
1/2 cup sliced mushrooms
1 teaspoon sugar
About 1 teaspoon salt
Dash of pepper
1/2 teaspoon chili powder
1/2 cup red wine (claret or burgundy)
3 cups cooked spaghetti
1 cup grated Parmesan cheese

Lightly brown onion, garlic, and green pepper in hot oil. Add beef and pork; brown lightly.

Add tomatoes, tomato paste, mushrooms, and seasonings. Cover and simmer 30 minutes.

Add wine, spaghetti and cheese. Turn into casserole. Bake in slow oven (325°F.) 30 minutes. Serves 6.

Cheese Macaroni with Chopped Eggs

MACARONI-FRANKFURTER LOAF

2 cups uncooked elbow macaroni
3 tablespoons shortening
3 tablespoons soya flour or 2 tablespoons enriched flour
2 teaspoons salt
1 cup milk
2 well beaten eggs
1 cup grated American cheese
2 teaspoons prepared mustard or 1 teaspoon dry mustard
6 to 8 frankfurters

Cook macaroni in boiling salted water until tender; drain.

Melt shortening; blend in flour and salt, then gradually add milk, stirring until thickened.

Pour a little of the hot sauce into beaten eggs, mix and then combine with remaining sauce. Add cheese and mustard and stir until cheese is melted. Mix the sauce with cooked, drained macaroni.

Pour a layer in the bottom of a well greased loaf pan (9 x 5 x 3 inches).

Lay 3 or 4 frankfurters on top, lengthwise of pan. Add another layer of macaroni, then the remaining frankfurters, and top with another layer of macaroni.

Bake in hot oven (400°F.) 45 minutes. Keep top covered most of cooking time with waxed paper to prevent drying.

Turn out on platter and garnish with tomato wedges. When cut, there will be 4 to 5 circles of frankfurters in each slice. Serves 5 to 8.

Coronado Shell Casserole

CHEESE MACARONI WITH CHOPPED EGGS

1/4 cup butter or margarine
1 tablespoon chopped onion
1/4 cup flour
2 cups milk
Salt and pepper to taste
2 tablespoons chopped parsley
2 tablespoons chopped canned pimiento
1/2 teaspoon Worcestershire sauce
2 cups grated processed American cheese (about 1/2 pound cheese)
5 hard-cooked eggs, chopped
2 cups elbow macaroni (8 ounces), cooked

Melt butter or margarine over low heat; add onion and sauté until tender. Add flour and blend.

Gradually add milk and cook, stirring constantly, until sauce thickens.

Add salt, pepper, parsley, pimiento, Worcestershire sauce, and cheese. Stir until cheese is melted.

Combine chopped eggs with cooked macaroni and cheese sauce. Turn into 6 individual casseroles or a 1½-quart casserole.

Bake in moderate oven (350°F.) 20 minutes, or until sauce begins to bubble. If desired, garnish with strips of pimiento. Serves 4 to 6.

CORONADO SHELL CASSEROLE

3 cups macaroni shells (8 ounces)
1/4 cup butter or margarine
1/4 cup enriched flour
3½ cups tomato juice
1¼ teaspoons salt
Dash of cayenne
1 pound shrimp, cooked, shelled and deveined
1 cup cooked peas
1/2 cup grated processed American cheese

Add 1 tablespoon salt to 3 quarts rapidly boiling water.

Gradually add macaroni shells so that water continues to boil.

Cook, uncovered, stirring occasionally, until tender.

Drain in colander.

Melt butter or margarine over low heat; add flour and blend.

Gradually add tomato juice and cook until thickened, stirring constantly.

Add 1¼ teaspoons salt, cayenne, shrimp, and peas; mix well.

Fold in macaroni shells. Turn into greased 2-quart casserole.

Top with grated cheese.

Bake in moderate oven (375°F.) 25 minutes, or until cheese is melted and golden brown. Serves 6.

ITALIAN MACARONI CASSEROLE

2 cups elbow macaroni (8-ounces), cooked
1 cup thin onion slices
1/2 pound Mozzarella or brick cheese, sliced
2 teaspoons salt
Freshly ground pepper
1/2 cup mayonnaise
1 cup light cream
3 hard-cooked eggs
1 slice crisp, cooked bacon, crumbled
1 tablespoon chopped canned pimientos
Mayonnaise to moisten

In a shallow 2-quart baking dish, arrange alternate layers of cooked macaroni, onion slices, and cheese slices. Season with salt and pepper.

Blend 1/2 cup mayonnaise and cream until smooth; pour over macaroni mixture.

Cover and bake in moderate oven (350°F.) 35 minutes.

Uncover and arrange stuffed eggs on top. Bake 10 minutes longer. Serve piping hot. Serves 6.

To Make Stuffed Eggs: Halve hard-cooked eggs lengthwise; remove yolks.

Combine egg yolks, bacon, pimiento, and mayonnaise to moisten; mix lightly but thoroughly. Refill egg whites with mixture.

NOODLES AMANDINE

8 ounces egg noodles
2 tablespoons butter or margarine
3/4 cup blanched almonds, slivered
1/4 cup butter or margarine
2 tablespoons flour
1 cup light cream
1 cup milk
1½ teaspoons salt
White pepper, freshly ground
1/3 cup grated American cheese

Cook noodles in 3 quarts boiling salted water (1 tablespoon salt) until tender. Drain in colander.

Meanwhile, melt 2 tablespoons butter or margarine over low heat. Add slivered almonds and sauté until golden brown.

Melt 1/4 cup butter or margarine over low heat. Add flour, blending well. Slowly stir in cream and milk. Cook, stirring constantly, until sauce is thickened. Add 1½ teaspoons salt and pepper.

Combine cooked noodles, sauce, and half the almonds; mix lightly but thoroughly. Turn into greased 2-quart casserole.

Mix together remaining almonds and grated cheese; sprinkle across top of casserole in diagonal lines.

Bake in moderate oven (350°F.) 20 minutes. Serves 4 to 6.

STUFFINGS FOR FISH, MEATS, AND POULTRY

Don't reserve stuffings for heavy holiday meals; make them part of your daily fare.

HINTS FOR MAKING STUFFINGS

The type of stuffing or dressing to use depends upon the kind of fish, meat, or poultry.

As a general rule, the more rich and oily the meat, the more simple and fruity the stuffing. That's why oysters, sausage, or other rich mixtures are generally used for dry-meated chicken or turkey, and stuffings including chopped apples, prunes, cranberries, pineapple, etc. are used for duck, goose, pork, and similar meats.

Stuffings may be dry or crumbly, or moist and compact, depending upon the amount of liquid used. When a stuffing is used inside poultry, the meat juice will increase the moisture.

All stuffings expand during cooking, therefore stuff lightly and bake any excess stuffing in a separate baking dish. Cover with bacon, salt pork, or poultry fat or pour a little meat stock over the stuffing. Bake slowly with the meat for at least an hour.

The seasonings given in the following recipes may be varied in accordance with personal taste; however, it is wise to remember to use only spices and herbs with full strength and fragrance.

Always taste the stuffing before using and add required seasoning.

Many stuffing recipes call for "day-old" bread, yet, today, bakery bread has "first day" freshness even after several days in the home bread box. If bread is soft when a dry stuffing is desired, toast the bread slices or cubes in the oven until lightly browned. Soft bread and crackers are likely to make a compact stuffing.

For hints on preparing crumbs for stuffings, see breadcrumbs in Index.

DO'S AND DON'TS FOR STUFFING POULTRY

● If stuffing is made before using, do not stuff the bird until just before it goes into the oven.

● Refrigerate the cleaned bird and the stuffing separately in a covered container.

● If you want to freeze the bird, do it with an unstuffed cavity.

● Stuffing may be frozen in a separate container.

● The bird takes a long time to defrost. Stuffing which is in the separate container requires much less time and should be used as soon as it is thawed.

● If there is stuffing left after the bird has been carved and served, take out the stuffing and refrigerate it separately.

● Do not let stuffing stay in the bird while it stays in the refrigerator.

● Cooked stuffing should be used within 3 days. Reheat only enough for 1 meal.

● Fresh pork sausage used in a stuffing always should be browned in a frying pan or otherwise thoroughly cooked before being added to the stuffing mixture.

● Some recipes call for cubes of ham. For these recipes, select either the fully cooked style of ham, or make certain that uncooked ham is cooked before being used in stuffing.

● Cook giblets in water before using in stuffing.

● If meat broth is used in stuffing, make certain the broth is well refrigerated during the period between the making of the broth and the use in the stuffing. Do not make the broth more than 24 hours before stuffing the bird.

AMOUNT OF STUFFING TO MAKE

Allow about 1 to 1¼ cups stuffing for each pound ready-to-cook weight of poultry. Allow ½ to ¾ cup stuffing per serving of meat.

MINT STUFFING FOR LAMB

1½ tablespoons chopped onion
3 tablespoons chopped celery and leaves
4 tablespoons fat
½ cup fresh mint leaves
3 cups soft breadcrumbs
Salt and pepper to taste

Cook onion and celery for a few minutes in fat. Then stir in mint leaves and breadcrumbs. Season with salt and pepper.

Mix all ingredients together until hot. Makes stuffing for 3- to 4-pound cushion-style shoulder of lamb. For a rolled shoulder, use half the recipe.

WILD RICE AND MUSHROOM STUFFING

2 cups wild rice
3 teaspoons chopped onion
¾ cup sliced mushrooms
¼ cup fat or salad oil
1 teaspoon salt
Dash of pepper

Wash rice and cover with salted water. Bring to boil and cook until tender, about 20 minutes. Drain.

Brown onion and mushrooms in hot fat. Mix with rice, salt, and pepper. Makes enough for 4- to 5-pound bird.

Wild Rice and Chestnut Stuffing: In above recipe omit mushrooms. Boil, peel, and chop ½ pound chestnuts. Mix with other ingredients.

Wild Rice and Mushroom Stuffing is the favorite with Cornish hens.

BREAD STUFFING
(Master Recipe)

    4 cups stale bread cubes
    ¼ teaspoon pepper
    1 teaspoon salt
    ¼ teaspoon thyme or marjoram
    ½ to 1 teaspoon poultry seasoning
    ¼ cup finely chopped onion
    ¼ cup melted fat

Combine bread, seasonings, and onion. Slowly add fat, tossing lightly with a fork until blended.

For a more moist stuffing slowly add up to ⅓ cup hot water or stock. Makes about 4 cups stuffing. Allow 1 cup for each pound of poultry.

Bread Stuffing Variations

Celery Stuffing: To master recipe add 1 cup finely chopped celery.

Chestnut Stuffing: To master recipe add ½ cup finely chopped celery and 1 pound of boiled, chopped chestnuts.

Corn Bread Stuffing: In master recipe, substitute corn bread crumbs for bread cubes.

Giblet Stuffing: To master recipe add chopped, cooked giblets. Use giblet stock for moistening.

Mushroom Stuffing: Sauté ½ cup sliced mushrooms in the fat and add to master recipe.

Oyster Stuffing: To master recipe add 1 cup chopped, drained oysters.

Parsley Stuffing: To master recipe add 2 to 3 tablespoons minced parsley.

Prune Stuffing: Omit thyme or marjoram and prepare half of master recipe for bread stuffing.

Remove pits from 1 cup cooked prunes and add with 1 cup diced apple.

Raisin Stuffing: To master recipe add ½ cup seedless raisins.

Sage Stuffing: In master recipe, omit thyme or marjoram. Add 1 tablespoon crumbled sage leaves.

Sausage Stuffing: To master recipe add ½ cup fried sausage meat, well drained.

PINEAPPLE STUFFING FOR LAMB

    3 cups soft white breadcrumbs
    3 cups rye breadcrumbs
    ¾ teaspoon cinnamon
    ½ teaspoon salt
    ½ cup drained, crushed pineapple
    ¼ cup melted butter or margarine

Combine crumbs, cinnamon, pineapple, and salt. Add butter or margarine and mix well.

Use with 14 to 16 rib crown roast of lamb.

MASTER SAVORY STUFFING

    1 cup chopped celery
    ¼ cup chopped parsley
    ¼ cup chopped onion
    ⅓ cup fat
    6 cups breadcrumbs
    ½ to 1 teaspoon salt
    ⅛ teaspoon pepper
    1 teaspoon savory seasoning

Cook celery, parsley, and onion in hot fat for a few minutes. Add breadcrumbs and seasonings. Mix well. Makes stuffing for 5- to 6-pound bird.

Savory Stuffing Variations

Savory Bacon Stuffing: Dice ½ pound bacon and pan-broil until crisp. Drain on paper. Add with the dry ingredients in master recipe. Use for poultry, fish, or fresh pork.

Savory Chestnut Stuffing: To master recipe add 1 pound of cooked, chopped chestnuts. To prepare chestnuts, boil in water 15 minutes, peel off shells and brown skin while still hot.

Savory Corn Bread Stuffing: In master recipe, use crumbled stale corn bread instead of breadcrumbs. Use for poultry, veal, or other meats.

Savory Hazelnut, Filbert, Pecan, or Almond Stuffing: Add 1 cup of any these chopped nuts to master recipe.

RICE STUFFING

    2 tablespoons chopped onion
    1 tablespoon chopped parsley
    1 cup chopped celery and leaves
    2 tablespoons fat
    2 cups cooked rice (brown, white, or wild)
    ½ teaspoon savory seasoning
    Salt and pepper to taste

Cook onion, parsley, and celery in fat a few minutes. Add rice and seasoning. Stir until well mixed and hot.

Use as stuffing in chicken, duck or other poultry or in boned cuts of meat.

ONION STUFFING

    6 medium-sized onions, minced
    ½ cup melted butter or margarine
    3 cups soft breadcrumbs
    1½ teaspoons sage
    ¾ teaspoon salt
    ¼ teaspoon pepper
    3 tablespoons minced parsley
    2 tablespoons water
    2 well beaten eggs

Sauté onions lightly in melted butter. Add crumbs, sage, salt, pepper, parsley, and water and cook until lightly browned.

Remove from heat and stir in eggs. Makes 4 to 5 cups of stuffing for 1 4- to 5-pound bird.

All stuffings expand during cooking, so do not pack too firmly and leave space for the mixture to swell and stay light.

MASHED POTATO OR SWEET POTATO STUFFING

    2 cups hot mashed potatoes
    1 cup soft breadcrumbs
    3 tablespoons melted fat or salad oil
    1 lightly beaten egg
    3 tablespoons chopped onion
    1 teaspoon chopped parsley

Use white or sweet potatoes. Season well while mashing.

Combine all ingredients. Moisten with stock if mixture is dry. Makes 3 cups stuffing for veal or lamb breast or shoulder.

GRATED RAW POTATO STUFFING

    6 medium raw potatoes
    1 onion, grated
    2 eggs
    ½ cup enriched flour
    Dash of pepper
    1 teaspoon salt
    Minced parsley
    ½ cup hot melted shortening or salad oil

Peel and grate raw potatoes. Squeeze out excess water.

Mix all ingredients, adding hot melted shortening last. Let mixture stand a few minutes before stuffing. Makes stuffing for 4- to 5-pound breast of veal.

CHESTNUT STUFFING

    3 cups boiled chestnuts
    ¼ cup cream
    ½ cup melted butter or margarine
    1 cup dry breadcrumbs or cracker crumbs
    About 1 teaspoon salt
    About ⅛ teaspoon pepper
    ¼ cup chopped celery (optional)
    2 tablespoons chopped parsley (optional)

Shell and skin chestnuts. Cook in boiling water until soft.

Put chestnuts through ricer or food mill. Combine with other ingredients. Makes about 4 cups or enough for 3½ to 4 pound chicken.

Chestnut-Oyster Stuffing: Use part oysters and part chestnuts in above recipe.

MASTER STUFFING FOR FISH

1/4 to 1/2 cup melted butter or margarine
1   tablespoon grated onion
2   cups breadcrumbs or cubes
1/2 teaspoon salt
1/8 teaspoon pepper
1   tablespoon lemon juice
1   tablespoon chopped parsley
1   teaspoon capers (optional)

Amount of butter depends upon type of fish. Use smaller amount with lean fish, larger amount with fat fish.

Add onion and crumbs to melted butter. Stir over low heat until crumbs brown slightly.

Add and mix remaining ingredients. If desired, 1/4 teaspoon sage or thyme may be substituted for capers. Makes stuffing for 3- to 4-pound fish.

Variations of Fish Stuffing

Bacon Stuffing: In master stuffing substitute for the butter 3 to 6 slices bacon, diced and browned but not crisp.

Cucumber Stuffing: In master stuffing reduce breadcrumbs or cubes to 1 1/2 cups. Add 1 cup drained chopped cucumbers.

Pickle Stuffing: To master stuffing add 1/4 to 1/3 cup chopped drained sweet or dill pickles.

SHRIMP STUFFING FOR FISH

2   tablespoons butter or margarine
1/2 tablespoon water
1   teaspoon anchovy paste
1   cup soft breadcrumbs
1/2 cup finely cut cooked shrimp
1/4 teaspoon grated onion
1   tablespoon lemon juice
2   teaspoons chopped stuffed olives

Heat butter, water, and anchovy paste together until butter is melted.

Add to crumbs and mix in remaining ingredients. This is especially good with stuffed trout.

CELERY-ONION STUFFING FOR FISH

3   tablespoons shortening or margarine
1/4 cup chopped onion
1/2 cup chopped celery
2 1/2 cups toasted 1/2-inch bread cubes
2   tablespoons minced parsley
1   tablespoon lemon juice
1/2 teaspoon salt
1/4 teaspoon sage
3   tablespoons milk or water

Melt shortening in a skillet; add onion and celery and sauté until tender.

Pour over toasted bread cubes, adding parsley, lemon juice, salt, and sage. Add milk and mix well. Makes stuffing for 1 4- to 5-pound fish.

CRACKER STUFFING

1/3 cup chopped onion
1/2 cup butter or margarine
4   cups unsalted soda cracker crumbs
3/4 teaspoon salt
Few grains of pepper
2   tablespoons chopped parsley
1/2 cup water

Cook onion in butter or margarine until lightly browned. Mix with crumbs, salt, pepper, and parsley. Add water and mix well.

Makes stuffing for 4 to 5 pounds chicken or fish.

APPLE STUFFING

1/2 cup chopped celery and leaves
1/2 cup chopped onion
1/4 cup chopped parsley
2   to 3 tablespoons melted fat
5   tart apples, diced
1/2 cup sugar
Salt and pepper to taste
1   cup soft breadcrumbs

Cook celery, onion, and parsley a few minutes in half of fat. Remove from pan.

Put remaining fat in pan and add apples. Sprinkle apples with sugar. Cover and cook until tender.

Remove cover and cook until apples are candied.

Combine with vegetables, breadcrumbs, and seasonings. Use with goose, duck, lamb, beef, or other meats.

CORN BREAD STUFFING

1/2 cup diced bacon
1/4 cup butter or margarine
1/2 cup minced onion
1   cup diced celery
1   teaspoon salt
1/4 teaspoon pepper
1   teaspoon Ac'cent
1   teaspoon poultry seasoning
2   cups corn bread, cubed or crumbled
1   cup white bread cubes, thoroughly dried

Heat bacon and butter in heavy skillet over low heat until butter melts. Add onion and celery; fry gently until bacon is lightly browned.

Add seasonings. Combine with corn bread and white bread cubes in bowl; mix thoroughly.

Makes enough stuffing for 5- to 6-pound capon or roasting chicken.

Corn Bread Stuffing Variations

1. Reduce onion to 1/3 cup and celery to 1/2 cup; add 3/4 cup finely chopped pecans or blanched almonds.

2. Omit celery and add 1 cup peeled and chopped boiled chestnuts.

3. Omit celery and add 3/4 cup raisins and 1/2 cup finely chopped walnuts.

PRUNE STUFFING FOR CROWN ROAST OF PORK

1   cup prunes
2   cups breadcrumbs
1   cup diced celery
1   medium onion, finely chopped
1/4 cup finely chopped green pepper
Salt and pepper
1   cup meat stock

Cook prunes until tender. Drain and cut in small pieces, removing pits.

Add crumbs, celery, onion, and green pepper. Season to taste with salt and pepper. Moisten with stock. Makes stuffing for 10- to 12-rib crown.

PRUNE STUFFING BALLS

1 1/3 cups cooked prunes
1/4 cup finely chopped onion
1   cup thinly sliced celery
1/2 cup butter or margarine
2   quarts soft stale breadcrumbs
1/2 teaspoon salt
1/4 teaspoon sage or poultry seasoning
Generous dash of black pepper
2   eggs
Hot water

Cut prunes from pits into pieces. Cook onion and celery very slowly in butter 10 minutes. Pour over bread, tossing to blend. Sprinkle with salt, sage, and pepper.

Beat eggs well; mix with bread. Blend in prunes lightly.

Sprinkle with 1 to 4 tablespoons hot water, depending on moisture of bread. Mixture should not be wet, just moist enough to hold together.

Shape lightly into 12 balls and place on greased baking sheet.

Bake in moderate oven (350°F.) 25 to 30 minutes, or until crisp and lightly browned. Serve hot with roast pork or lamb. Serves 6.

Give your next roast pork or lamb a lift by serving these "Prune Stuffing Balls." Just add the chopped, pitted prunes to a barely moistened bread stuffing, shape into balls and bake. Good with turkey, too.

ORANGE STUFFING FOR DUCKS OR GOOSE

- 3/4 cup butter or margarine
- 1/2 cup chopped onion
- 1 1/2 cups chopped celery
- 1 cup boiling water
- 2 teaspoons salt
- 2 teaspoons poultry seasoning
- 1/2 teaspoon pepper
- 2 tablespoons grated orange rind
- 2 tablespoons minced parsley
- 2 quarts toasted bread cubes
- 2 cups diced oranges

Sauté onion in butter. Cook celery in water until tender. Add seasonings, orange rind, and parsley.

Add to cooked onions with bread cubes and oranges. Mix well and stuff goose or ducks. Makes stuffing for 2 ducks or 10- to 12-pound goose.

QUICK SAVORY RICE STUFFING

- 1/4 cup butter or margarine
- 1 1/3 cups packaged pre-cooked rice
- 1 cup diced celery
- 1/4 cup chopped celery leaves
- 1/4 cup chopped onion
- 2 tablespoons chopped parsley
- 1 teaspoon salt
- 1/2 teaspoon sage
- 1/8 teaspoon pepper
- 1 1/2 cups chicken stock or bouillon

Melt butter in saucepan. Add rice and sauté until lightly browned, stirring constantly.

Add celery, celery leaves, onion, parsley, and seasonings. Sauté 2 or 3 minutes longer.

Then add chicken stock. Bring quickly to boil over high heat, uncovered, fluffing rice gently with a fork. (Do not stir.) Cover and remove from heat. Let stand 10 minutes.

Makes 3 cups dressing or enough for chicken, duck, or half turkey.

POTATO STUFFING FOR GOOSE OR DUCKLINGS

- 1/2 cup bacon or salt pork drippings
- 1 cup chopped onions
- 1/2 cup chopped celery
- 10 medium potatoes, cooked and riced
- 4 slices bread, crumbled
- 2 beaten eggs
- 1 tablespoon poultry seasoning
- 1 teaspoon salt
- 1/4 teaspoon pepper
- 1 1/2 teaspoons Ac'cent

Melt fat in frying pan; add onions and celery; cook until soft but not brown.

Combine remaining ingredients; add contents of frying pan; mix well.

Makes enough stuffing for one 10- to 12-pound goose or two 5- to 6-pound ducklings.

BROWN RICE-SAUSAGE STUFFING

- 1/2 pound bulk pork sausage
- 1 medium-sized onion, chopped
- 1 tart apple, peeled and diced
- 1 cup chopped celery, including a few leaves
- 1 teaspoon salt
- Dash of pepper
- 1/2 teaspoon sage or poultry seasoning
- 1 cup raw brown rice
- 2 cups water

In a heavy skillet or kettle, cook sausage until lightly browned, stirring occasionally to keep loose. Drain off all except 3 tablespoons fat.

Mix in onion, apple, and celery; simmer about 5 minutes longer.

Add seasonings, rice, and water. Stir to mix and loosen browned bits. Cover tightly and cook over low heat until almost done, about 30 minutes. Do not stir. Makes stuffing for 4- to 5-pound bird.

PENNSYLVANIA DUTCH STUFFING

- 2 cups hot mashed potatoes
- 1 well beaten egg
- 4 cups dry bread cubes
- 3 tablespoons butter or other fat
- 1/4 cup chopped parsley
- 1/2 cup chopped onion
- 1 teaspoon salt
- 1/2 teaspoon poultry seasoning
- Pepper to taste

Combine potatoes and egg. Sauté bread cubes in butter. Combine potato mixture with bread.

Stir in remaining ingredients. Mix well. Makes 6 1/2 cups of stuffing for 6-pound turkey.

HAMBURGER STUFFING FOR POULTRY OR CABBAGE LEAVES

- 1/2 pound ground beef
- 2 tablespoons fat
- 1 teaspoon salt
- 1/4 teaspoon pepper
- 1/2 cup finely chopped onion
- 1 cup finely chopped celery
- 1/4 teaspoon poultry seasoning
- 2 slightly beaten eggs
- 1/4 cup water
- 6 cups bread cubes

Fry meat in hot fat in heavy skillet. Add salt, pepper, onion, celery, and poultry seasoning. Continue cooking until onion is transparent.

Beat eggs and water. Add egg mixture to bread cubes. Stir in meat mixture. Makes stuffing for 6-pound roasting chicken.

Variations: Use as stuffing for cabbage leaves or pack in 9 x 9 x 2-inch pan. Top with strips of salt pork or bacon and bake in moderate oven (375°F.) 30 minutes.

FRUITED BRAZIL NUT STUFFING

- 4 1/2 cups bread cubes
- 6 tablespoons melted butter or margarine
- 1 1/2 cups chopped tart apples
- 3/4 cup chopped cooked prunes
- 1 1/3 cups chopped Brazil nuts
- 2 1/2 teaspoons salt
- 1/4 teaspoon pepper
- 1 teaspoon poultry seasoning
- 1/3 cup bouillon or broth

Combine ingredients and mix lightly. Use to stuff half a turkey or a goose, duck, or chicken. Makes about 6 cups.

CORN STUFFING FOR POULTRY

- 2 cups canned corn
- 2 1/2 cups breadcrumbs
- 2 eggs
- 1 tablespoon finely minced green pepper
- 1/2 cup chopped mushrooms
- 2/3 teaspoon salt
- 1/4 teaspoon pepper
- 2 tablespoons fat

Mix all ingredients thoroughly. If too dry, add a little stock. If too moist, add a little more breadcrumbs. Makes stuffing for 4- to 5-pound bird.

HAM STUFFING RING

- 1/2 cup finely chopped onion
- 1/2 cup butter or margarine
- 1/2 pound mushrooms, diced
- About 6 cups cracker crumbs (finely rolled)
- 2 cups ground ham
- 1/2 cup snipped parsley
- 2 teaspoons poultry seasoning
- 1/4 teaspoon pepper
- 1 egg
- 1 cup milk

Sauté onion in butter or margarine until transparent; add mushrooms and cook 5 minutes longer.

Combine with cracker crumbs, ham, parsley, poultry seasoning, and pepper.

Beat egg; blend in milk. Lightly stir into crumb mixture.

Pile into well oiled 9-inch ring mold. Bake in slow oven (325°F.) about 50 minutes.

Unmold by running knife around sides. Fill center of ham ring with broccoli and serve to accompany roast capons or small turkeys stuffed with small white onions. Makes about 10 servings.

Ham Stuffing Ring

Spicy Cheese-Olive Loaf

TOASTS AND TRICKS WITH BREAD

FRENCH TOAST
(Master Recipe)

2 eggs
Dash of salt
1 tablespoon sugar
2/3 cup milk
6 slices white bread

Beat eggs slightly. Add salt, sugar, and milk. Dip bread into milk mixture.

Cook on hot, well-greased griddle or skillet. Brown on one side. Turn and brown on other side, or fry in deep hot fat 1 to 2 minutes, or until browned.

Serve with syrup, preserves, or cinnamon and sugar mixture.

Variations:

French Toast Fingers: Cut slices of bread into fingers about 1 inch wide. Prepare as French toast. Serve with confectioners' sugar or tart jelly.

Hawaiian French Toast: In master recipe substitute 2/3 cup pineapple juice for milk. Serve toast on half slices of heated pineapple.

Honey French Toast: In master recipe add 1/4 cup honey to milk mixture of French toast.

Orange French Toast: In master recipe substitute 2/3 cup orange juice and 1 teaspoon orange rind for milk. Serve with honey.

TOAST CORNUCOPIAS

Remove crusts from thin-sliced bread. Spread each slice on both sides with softened butter, sprinkle with garlic salt. Roll to form cornucopias and fasten each with toothpick. Stuff centers with crusts so that cornucopias will retain rounded shape. Toast in moderate oven (350°F.) 20 to 25 minutes or until golden. Remove crusts in cornucopias and fill centers with parsley sprigs.

SPICY CHEESE-OLIVE LOAF

1 (1-pound) loaf unsliced whole wheat bread
1 cup shredded American cheese
1/4 cup finely chopped olives
2 tablespoons minced onion
1/2 cup soft butter or margarine
2 teaspoons prepared mustard

Cut the unsliced loaf lengthwise. Cut each half loaf almost through the bottom crust, into 6 slices.

Combine cheese with remaining ingredients; spread mixture between slices of bread. Wrap loaf in aluminum foil. Heat in a not-too-hot part of the grill until piping hot and crusty. Or just place unwrapped on a cooky sheet and heat in a hot oven (400°F.) about 12 minutes.

GARLIC BREAD

1 loaf French bread
1 clove garlic
1/4 pound butter or margarine

Cut the loaf in 1 1/2 inch slices, cutting diagonally almost through the bread.

Crush garlic and heat in butter or margarine. Let mixture stand a few minutes so garlic permeates butter, then remove garlic and spread the butter over cut surfaces of bread.

Wrap loaf in aluminum foil and place in hot oven (400°F.) 12 to 15 minutes, or until heated through.

HOW TO REHEAT BREAD OR ROLLS

Put the bread or rolls in a paper bag. Close the bag and place in a hot oven (425°F.) for 5 minutes.

Or put the bread or rolls in a hot covered double boiler over boiling water for about the same amount of time. If the bread is old, it may be sprinkled with water.

TEA TOASTS

Cut bread very thin. If desired, remove crusts, cut slices into halves or strips. Spread hot toast with butter, then with desired mixture. Place under broiler long enough to melt sugar, about 2 minutes.

Cinnamon Toast: Use 1 1/2 teaspoons cinnamon and 2 tablespoons brown sugar.

Honey Cinnamon Toast: Use mixture of honey and cinnamon to taste.

Honey Toast: Use strained honey.

Maple Toast: Use maple sugar.

Orange Toast: Use mixture of 1/2 tablespoon grated orange rind, 2 tablespoons orange juice, and 1/4 cup sugar.

TOMATO FRENCH TOAST

2 eggs
1/2 cup condensed tomato soup
1/2 teaspoon salt
1/2 teaspoon paprika
6 slices bread

Beat eggs until blended; then beat in tomato soup, salt, and paprika. Dip bread in this mixture; pan-fry in melted butter until browned. Serve alone or with a cheese sauce.

ROLL BASKETS

Hollow out small rolls. Spread the hollows with melted butter. Toast in slow oven (300°F.) until crisp.

VANILLA BAKED TOAST

Cut slices of bread into thirds. Combine 1/2 cup milk, 1 tablespoon sugar, and 1/2 teaspoon vanilla.

Brush surface of bread. Toast in slow oven (300°F.) until crisp, dry, and golden.

BREAD BASKETS (CROUSTADES)

Trim crusts from 1 large loaf unsliced white bread. Cut bread into blocks 2 x 3 x 2 inches.

With sharp knife, cut centers from blocks of bread to fashion baskets.

Brush baskets with melted butter or margarine. Place on a cooky sheet and toast under a preheated broiler to a light golden brown. Serve with creamed foods.

Note: Use the leftover bread trimmings for breadcrumbs.

SAVORY CROUTONS

Cut bread in small cubes. Fry in small amount of butter, margarine, or fat drippings until brown, stirring constantly.

Sprinkle with curry powder, marjoram, chili seasoning, onion salt, or garlic salt.

MILK TOAST

Place hot buttered toast in cereal bowl. Serve with scalded milk seasoned with salt and pepper. Allow about 1/2 cup per slice.

MELBA TOAST

Cut stale bread into 1/4-inch slices. Bake in slow oven (300°F.) until brown and dry, 15 to 20 minutes.

SEEDED FRENCH BREAD

Slice French bread and spread generously with softened butter or margarine.

Sprinkle slices with caraway, poppy, or sesame seed.

Bake in hot oven (400°F.) until lightly browned, about 10 minutes.

TOASTED CHEESE ROLLS

Split, butter, and toast long rolls; sprinkle with grated nippy cheese and return to moderate oven (350°F.) until cheese melts. Serve warm.

TOAST CUPS

Trim crusts from 1/4-inch thick slices of fresh bread. Brush with melted butter.

Press each slice into custard cup so that bread forms a cup. Bake in moderate oven until crisp and brown, 15 to 20 minutes.

Shrimp Wiggle In Toast Cups

BREAD CUBES OR CRUMBS

Soft Breadcrumbs: Tear a fresh slice of bread into small pieces with the fingers.

Soft Bread Cubes: Stack two or three slices of bread on a bread board and with a sharp knife, using a sawing motion, cut sliced bread into strips of desired width. Cut again in opposite direction to form cubes of even size.

Toasted Bread Cubes: Arrange soft bread cubes on a cooky sheet. Place cooky sheet under a preheated broiler (400°F.) or in a slow oven (300°F.) and toast until bread cubes are golden brown on all sides, turning occasionally.

Dry Breadcrumbs: Grind dry breads through a food chopper, using fine blade. Tie a paper bag on the blade end of the grinder so that crumbs will drop into bag as they are ground. If fine breadcrumbs are desired, sift the crumbs through a sieve and store the coarse dry and fine dry crumbs in covered separate containers.

Buttered Breadcrumbs: Melt 1/3 cup butter in a skillet. When hot, add 1 cup dry breadcrumbs. Stir constantly until crumbs are golden brown.

SLIM JIM BREAD STICKS

Quarter frankfurter rolls lengthwise. Spread cut sides, or all sides, with soft butter or margarine.

Roll in one of these: minced parsley, chives, or nuts, poppy seeds, or grated Parmesan cheese. Bake in hot oven (425°F.) 5 to 10 minutes.

GARLIC BREAD SQUARES

Cut unsliced loaf of bread into 2-inch squares.

Mix thoroughly 1/4 clove garlic, mashed, and 1/4 cup butter or margarine. Spread mixture on outside of squares.

Bake on cooky sheet in very hot oven (450°F.) 10 minutes.

PAIN PERDUE (LOST BREAD)

6 slices bread (not too thick)
1/2 cup milk
2 tablespoons sugar
1/8 teaspoon salt
1 teaspoon vanilla
3 egg yolks, beaten
Butter
Powdered sugar

Remove crusts and dampen bread slightly in milk to which sugar, salt, and vanilla are added. Bread must not break.

Dip in beaten yolks, coating evenly. Fry to a golden brown in hot butter. Drain.

Serve on napkin generously sprinkled with powdered sugar.

Making Soft Breadcrumbs

Making Soft Bread Cubes

Toasted Bread Cubes

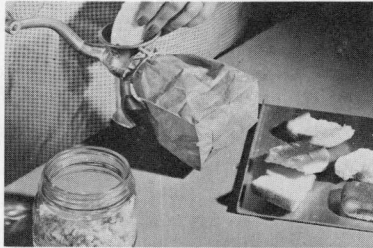

Making Dry Breadcrumbs

SALT STICKS

Cut sliced white bread in 1/2-inch strips. Brush with melted butter or margarine.

Toast in hot oven (400°F.) until lightly browned, 8 to 10 minutes. Sprinkle with coarse salt.

CHEESE FOLD-UPS

Remove crusts from bread slices and spread with butter or margarine. Sprinkle lightly with grated cheese.

Fasten opposite corners together with wooden picks. Bake the fold-ups in very hot oven (450°F.) 10 minutes.

NIPPY CHEESE FINGERS

Mix a sharp spreading cheese with butter or margarine. Remove crusts from bread slices; spread and cut in strips. Bake in moderate oven (350°F.) 10 minutes.

FRENCH TOAST AND PEACHES

Fresh or frozen peaches, an all-year-round delight, can extend to make a good all-around meal.

Here is a meal-on-a-plate for lunch, supper or even breakfast. It's simply hot French toast layered with cottage cheese and lightly sweetened peaches.

French Toast and Peaches

SHERRIED FRENCH TOAST

2 slightly beaten eggs
1/4 teaspoon salt
1/2 cup sherry
5 or 6 slices bread (stale bread is best)

Mix eggs, salt, and sherry in a shallow dish.

Dip bread slices quickly into mixture, coating both sides.

Brown slowly in hot fat in a heavy skillet. Serve hot, sprinkled with sugar. Serves 2 to 3.

BREAD CONFECTIONS

1 15-ounce can sweetened condensed milk
1 teaspoon vanilla
1 1/2 cups dry, shredded coconut
Orange food coloring
1 loaf day-old bread, thinly sliced
Orange marmalade

Combine sweetened condensed milk and vanilla in a small bowl. Put coconut into a jar, add a drop or two of orange food coloring, being careful not to add too much; cover jar and shake until coconut is evenly colored; put into small bowl and break coconut fine.

Cut two 2-inch rounds from each slice of bread. Spread half the rounds with sweetened condensed milk mixture; then spread with marmalade. Top each spread round with a plain bread round. Dip one flat surface and sides of each sandwich in sweetened condensed milk mixture; drain; dip in colored coconut. Put on ungreased cooky sheet, plain surface down. Continue until all circles are coated.

Bake in slow oven (325°F.) 12 to 15 minutes; do not let coconut brown. Remove at once from cooky sheet. Cool. Makes 21.

ROLLS IN LOAF

Trim side and top crusts from a loaf of unsliced enriched white bread.

Cut through the center of the loaf, just to the lower crust, but not through it. Then make crosswise cuts, spacing them so that the "rolls" will be even in size.

Brush with melted margarine or butter and toast in a moderate oven (375°F.) until the edges of the loaf are golden brown. Serve hot.

PEANUT BUTTER BREAD FINGERS

1/2 cup peanut butter
1 cup milk
1/2 teaspoon salt
1/4 teaspoon pepper
1 egg, slightly beaten
12 slices bread

Cream together peanut butter and milk. Add salt and pepper, then add slightly beaten egg.

Remove crusts from bread slices and cut into narrow strips. Dip in the mixture and sauté in butter.

TOASTED CHEESE RINGS

Cut rings from bread slices with doughnut cutter; brush with melted butter or salad oil, then dip into grated cheese. Place in moderate oven (350°F.) until light brown.

ONION-CARAWAY RYE LOAF

With a sharp knife, cut a loaf of caraway rye bread in diamonds without cutting through bottom crust.

Season softened butter or margarine with salt and grated onion; spread generously around diamonds of bread. Bake in hot oven (400°F.) for 10 minutes, or until loaf is hot.

TOAST STRIPS

Cut slices 1/3-inch thick. Remove crusts. Spread butter on both sides. Cut slices in 1/2-inch strips. Lightly brown under broiler.

TOAST POINTS

Remove crusts from 1/2-inch thick slices of bread. Toast. While hot, cut into 4 triangles. Use as a garnish.

GARLIC BREAD STRIPS

Brush slices of party rye bread with melted butter to which garlic salt has been added. Cut in thin strips. Toast in hot oven (400°F.) until lightly browned, about 5 minutes.

SAVORY STUFFED ROLLS

Cut circle, 3/4 inch from edge of sandwich rolls. Remove center with fork, leaving about 1/4 inch on bottom.

Fry until brown a small amount of chopped onion in a generous amount of margarine or fat drippings. Add a few leaves of marjoram and thyme, the bread crumbs, and some chopped parsley. Stuff rolls with mixture.

Heat in moderate oven (375°F.) for 8 to 10 minutes, or until hot.

HOT PUMPERNICKEL SLICES

With a sharp knife, slice day-old round loaf of pumpernickel or rye bread 1/8 to 1/4 thick. Tie together with string. Spread softened butter or margarine over top.

Heat in hot oven (400°F.) for 10 minutes, or until heated through and crust is crisp. Put in serving basket, and remove string.

FRENCH TOASTED MATZOS

6 eggs
1/2 teaspoon salt
2 tablespoons butter, chicken fat, or salad oil
4 matzos
Sugar and cinnamon
Grated lemon rind, optional

Beat eggs very light; add salt. Heat butter in skillet. Break matzos into large equal-sized pieces. Dip each piece in the beaten egg. Fry until lightly browned on both sides. Serve hot, sprinkled with sugar and cinnamon and, if desired, with grated lemon rind.

Bread Confections

HONEY-FRUIT ENGLISH MUFFINS

Split and toast English muffins. Spread with softened butter. Put a slice of pineapple or slices of banana and a little honey on each.

Broil until topping is lightly browned.

CELERY BREAD STICKS

Trim crusts off 5/8-inch thick slices of bread. Brush both sides of bread slices with butter.

Cut each slice into 6 equal size strips. Roll strips in celery seed.

Place on a cooky sheet. Toast in moderate oven (350°F.) 15 minutes.

GARLIC BREAD STICKS

Add 2 cloves cut garlic to 1/2 cup melted butter or margarine and let stand 15 minutes. Remove garlic.

Brush 12 or more Italian bread sticks or sticks cut from stale bread with flavored butter or margarine.

Place in moderate oven (375°F.) until hot, crisp, and delicately browned.

For stronger flavor touch sticks with cut side of garlic and proceed as above.

CRUSTY CHEESE LOAF

Cut crusts from top and side of unsliced sandwich loaf. Slice to, but not through, bottom crust.

Spread top and sides of slices with mixture of 1/2 cup butter or margarine and two 5-ounce jars sharp spreading cheese.

Tie loaf together with string; place in baking pan. Bake in hot oven (400°F.) 20 minutes.

CHEESE-CARAWAY FAN ROLLS

Separate fan rolls almost to bottom. Put slices of sharp Cheddar cheese in slits, and sprinkle with caraway seeds.

Bake in hot oven (400°F.) for 5 minutes, or until cheese is slightly melted and rolls are hot.

FRENCH OVEN TOAST

2 eggs, beaten
1/2 teaspoon salt
2 tablespoons sugar
1 cup milk
1/2 teaspoon almond extract
12 slices enriched bread

Combine beaten eggs, salt, sugar, milk, and almond extract. Dip sliced bread into mixture.

Place slices on well greased cooky sheet and brown in extremely hot oven (500°F.). Turn toast over after 10 minutes and brown on the other side. Serve with honey butter or maple syrup. Makes 6 servings—2 slices per serving.

Note: This toast may be reheated satisfactorily.

CHEESE FRENCH TOAST

3 eggs
2 1/2 cups milk
1/2 teaspoon salt
12 slices day-old bread
6 tablespoons butter
1 1/4 cups grated American cheese

Beat eggs slightly; add milk and salt and blend thoroughly. Dip bread slices in mixture.

Melt butter in a skillet; add soaked bread slices and cook until a delicate brown on one side.

Turn, sprinkle grated cheese over top of each slice and cook until underside is a delicate brown and cheese is melted.

Serve hot with crisp bacon or sausage for luncheon or supper. Serves 6.

Breads for the Barbecue

BARBECUE BREAD HINTS

Bread and rolls are easy to reheat; for convenience, butter the bread indoors, then warm on the grill outside. Simply slice bread and wrap in foil, either the whole loaf or a couple of pieces to a package. Heat on or near the fire.

French or rye bread can be split lengthwise or cut in diagonal slices almost to bottom crust, spread with your choice of spreads, wrapped in foil and put in a not-too-hot part of the grill.

Rolls may be split and spread with a filling before wrapping in foil and heating.

SAVORY SPREADS FOR BREAD AND ROLLS

Garlic Butter: Mash 1 to 2 cloves garlic or use garlic press; cream into 1/2 cup (1/4 pound) butter or margarine.

Cheese-Parsley Butter: Combine 1/4 pound butter or margarine with 1/4 cup each of grated Cheddar or Swiss cheese and minced parsley.

Onion Butter: Chop a small bunch of green onions (scallions), including some tops, and mix with 1/4 pound butter or margarine.

Sesame–Onion Butter: Toast 1/4 cup sesame seeds; mix with onion butter.

Herb Butter: Cream 1/4 pound butter or margarine with 2 tablespoons of fresh rosemary, tarragon, or basil. If desired, add a little chopped onion.

HOT ROLLS AND MUFFINS

Put muffins or rolls in large coffee can. Place can on side on grill or hot coals. Roll occasionally until rolls are heated through.

TOASTED ROLLS AND MUFFINS

Split and spread with butter or margarine or one of the savory spreads. Toast on grill in hinged wire broiler or on skewers.

Or toast by placing buttered side down in skillet on grill. (English muffins are good this way.)

CHEESE BREAD CHUNKS

Spread thick slices of French bread with butter or margarine mixed with grated Parmesan cheese. Toast on skewers over coals.

HERBED FRENCH OR ITALIAN BREAD

Cut a long loaf of French or Italian bread in half the long way.

Mix 1/2 cup softened butter or margarine with 1 cup chopped parsley, 1/4 cup chopped green onions, and 2 finely chopped garlic cloves. Spread on the two bread halves.

Sandwich the two halves together and wrap in foil. Heat on the grill.

POPPY SEED BREAD

Buy a homestyle loaf unsliced and cut in thick slices down to, but not through, the bottom crust. Stand on a large sheet of foil.

Mix softened butter with poppy seeds, or sugar and cinnamon, if preferred. Spread the cut slices.

Bring the foil up over the bread and wrap, but leave opening at top for steam to escape.

Heat for about 20 minutes on the grill over medium heat. Tip over on both sides for part of time for even heating. Serve from foil.

GRILLED SWEET ROLLS

Split sweet rolls crosswise (pecan rolls are especially good). Spread with soft butter or margarine. Toast in heavy skillet or on griddle.

French Bread with Savory Spread: Heat the prepared bread in a snug foil wrapper in a not-too-hot part of the grill. The tender, crunchy crust of French or Vienna bread contrasts delightfully with savory spread drizzling out between the slices.

VEGETABLES

A variety of perfectly cooked vegetables attractively served and beautifully garnished are a real masterpiece.

PREPARATION TRICKS WITH VEGETABLES

● The tightly grown or curled vegetables (cabbage, cauliflower, Brussels sprouts, leeks, artichokes) should be soaked briefly in salted cold water before cooking.

● Some vegetables need a stiff brush to get them clean (potatoes, beets, rutabaga, salsify or oyster plant); others require a soft brush or "hand rubbing" (asparagus, mushrooms, celery). Still others need several washings in clear, cool water (all the leafy vegetables and salad plants).

● If they are to be cooked whole, do not pare beets. Leave at least 2 inches of top on each beet to prevent "bleeding." When tender, drain and rinse quickly with cold water, then slip off skins.

● Wash and pick over the garden herbs and vegetables used for garnishes (chives, parsley, mint, celery leaves, etc.) as carefully as you do the vegetables they are to garnish. Have them crisp if they are used as sprigs, sprays, bunches, or tufts. If they are to be cut fine to sprinkle over a vegetable, snip them with scissors.

● Husk and remove silk from green corn just before cooking; in fact, have the water at a galloping boil before exposing corn to the air. Cook quickly and do not overcook.

● Trim stems to 1/2-inch length and remove coarse, discolored outer leaves from artichokes; cut off about 1/2 inch of tops to expose inner leaves. Clean carefully. Cook *head-down* in slightly acidulated boiling water (lemon juice or vinegar) until stem tests tender. Drain upside down.

QUICK SEASONING TRICKS

● Slivered, chopped, or sliced nuts (almonds, filberts, Brazil nuts, peanuts, walnuts, macadamias, etc.) as a garnish.

● A sliver or two of garlic heated in the butter for vegetables, then removed.

● Chopped or riced hard-cooked egg for garnish or to mix with buttered crumbs.

● Snipped parsley or chives stirred into the butter or margarine, or the cream sauce.

● Sour cream, lemon juice, or herb vinegars, for pleasing tartness.

● Condensed canned soups to use for easy-do sauces.

● Caraway, celery, or dry-toasted sesame seeds to sprinkle on.

● A *little* crushed thyme, oregano, or marjoram for tomatoes and greens. Fresh snipped chervil or tarragon for peas, beans, greens.

HOW TO SHORTEN COOKING TIME

● By removing all inedible or "woody" portions: such as root ends of asparagus, tough midribs of kale, coarse outer leaves of cabbage, Brussels sprouts, etc.

● By paring and slitting thick stems such as broccoli (or cook and serve stems as a separate vegetable).

● By shredding (cabbage, carrots, turnips, etc.) or grating coarsely (beets, carrots, rutabaga, etc.).

● By cubing (potatoes, turnips, etc.); slicing (onions, carrots, celery, etc.); cutting into match-size strips called Julienne (the root vegetables especially; also celery, snap beans, potatoes, etc.).

● By separating cauliflower into flowerets.

● By dividing or cutting large vegetables into individual servings; cabbage into wedges, small vegetables or stem-types tied in portions, etc.

HINTS ABOUT COOKING VEGETABLES

● Clean and keep them cool until cooking time . . . do not *soak* in water unless directed.

● Avoid scraping or paring if possible . . . if removing the skin is necessary, pare *thinly*.

● Use freshly *boiling* water and as little of it as possible—none at all for delicate greens . . . enough water clings to leaves or the vegetable itself is "watery" enough to cook without additional water.

● Boil vegetables gently and cook them only until crisply tender. Vegetables should never be limp or soggy, faded or unattractive looking. The testing fork should meet a little resistance when put into the vegetables.

● Cover most vegetables to speed up cooking. Too slow cooking keeps the vegetables in contact with water or steam unnecessarily long.

● Do **not** use baking soda to "set" the color. Properly cooked vegetables will retain their color.

● Heavy-bottom saucepans with covers, and with bases that fit firmly and completely over the cooking heat, permit cooking in a minimum amount of water and in a minimum time.

● Cook frozen vegetables according to directions on the package. Measure the water—don't guess. Avoid over-cooking and reduce pressure immediately. Never let the vegetable "cool down with the cooker."

● Canned vegetables are already cooked—do *not* cook them further. Heat, but do not boil. Add seasonings; serve immediately. Or, drain liquid from vegetable into saucepan; boil down to about 1/3 or 1/2 cup. Add vegetable and seasonings; heat and serve.

● Do not throw away the water or juice from cooked vegetables . . . if it is not served with the vegetable, save it for soups, sauces, made dishes—or drink it.

Master Recipes for Vegetables

VEGETABLE CROQUETTES
(Master Recipe)

    1   cup thick white sauce
    2   cups cooked or canned minced
        vegetables, well drained
    1   tablespoon chopped onion
    2   tablespoons chopped parsley
    1   or 2 eggs
Salt, pepper, paprika, or other desired
        seasoning
    2   cups sifted seasoned breadcrumbs
    1   egg
    2   tablespoons milk or water

Prepare the sauce and, when it is smooth and boiling, stir in vegetables.

Heat to boiling point, remove from the heat and beat in 1 or 2 eggs.

Cook and stir over low heat to permit the eggs to thicken slightly. Season to taste.

Other seasonings may be used such as a choice of ½ teaspoon curry powder, ½ teaspoon dried herbs, 1 teaspoon Worcestershire sauce, ½ teaspoon Tabasco sauce, etc.

Spread the mixture in a dish. Let cool, then shape it as desired. Roll croquettes in seasoned breadcrumbs, then in 1 egg beaten slightly with milk or water, and again in breadcrumbs.

Be sure to cover the entire croquette with the egg mixture to prevent the fat from penetrating. Let the croquettes dry for about 2 hours.

Fry a few at a time in deep hot fat (390°F.) until delicately browned, 3 to 5 minutes. Drain on absorbent paper. To reheat, place in a hot oven (400°F.).

Serve with tomato, mushroom, or other desired sauce. Serves 6.

VEGETABLE COVER BATTER

    1   cup sifted enriched flour
    ¼   teaspoon salt
    1   slightly beaten egg
    1   cup milk
    1   tablespoon melted fat or salad oil

Sift flour with salt. Mix egg, milk, and fat; gradually add to flour, beating with rotary beater until smooth.

Use for dipping cauliflower, eggplant, and other vegetables.

Dip pieces of vegetable into the batter. Fry in deep hot fat (365°–375°F.) 2 to 5 minutes. Makes 1¼ cups batter.

Vegetable Soufflé

SCALLOPED VEGETABLES
(Master Recipe)

    2   to 3 cups cooked or canned vege-
        tables
    1½ cups medium white sauce
    ½   cup buttered crumbs
Paprika

Arrange prepared vegetables in alternate layers with white sauce. Sprinkle top with buttered crumbs, topped with a dash of paprika.

Bake in moderate oven (375°F.) until browned, about 25 minutes.

Serves 4 to 6.

Note: Almost any vegetables may be used singly or in combination. A good combination is carrots, cauliflower, and green beans. Or, asparagus tips or broccoli with small white onions or new potatoes.

Vegetables Au Gratin (Scalloped Vegetables with Cheese): In master recipe, alternate layers of grated American cheese with vegetables or mix ½ cup grated cheese with buttered crumbs and sprinkle top before baking.

Curried Scalloped Vegetables: In master recipe, season the white sauce with curry powder to taste.

CREAMED VEGETABLES
(Master Recipe)

    2   cups cooked or heated canned veg-
        tables, drained
    1   cup hot medium white sauce

Add hot vegetables to sauce or heat in sauce or place hot vegetables in serving dish and pour white sauce over vegetables.

If desired, add a little grated onion to sauce. Garnish with a little chopped parsley. Serves 4 to 6.

VEGETABLE SOUFFLÉ
(Master Recipe)

    3   eggs, separated
    ½   to 1 cup thick white sauce, sea-
        soned
    ¼   to ½ teaspoon minced onion
    1   cup drained cooked vegetables
        (minced, mashed, puréed)

Beat yolks until thick and lemon colored; stir into white sauce and add vegetables.

Fold in stiffly beaten egg whites. Turn into ungreased casserole.

Bake in slow oven (325°–350°F.) 30 to 45 minutes.

Serve at once with cream sauce or cheese sauce, if desired. Serves 4 to 6.

Note: Vegetable may be increased to 2 cups, if desired.

Vegetable-Cheese Casserole

VEGETABLE-CHEESE CASSEROLE

    2   large Bermuda onions, sliced
        (about 1½ cups)
    3   cups sliced carrots
    1   1-pound jar pasteurized process
        cheese spread
About 1⅔ cups cracker crumbs (but-
        tery crackers, finely rolled)
    ¼   teaspoon pepper
    ½   teaspoon whole thyme
    1   4-ounce jar pimientos, chopped

Cook onions and carrots until tender. Drain. Heat cheese spread over boiling water. Combine crumbs with pepper and thyme.

Layer vegetables, melted cheese, and crumb mixture in a greased shallow 2-quart baking dish. Sprinkle with chopped pimientos.

Bake, covered, 15 minutes in moderate oven (350°F.), then 15 minutes uncovered. Serves 6 to 8.

VEGETABLE LOAF

    2   tablespoons melted fat (shortening,
        butter, or margarine)
    1   cup chopped onion
    1   cup finely chopped celery
    1   cup grated raw carrots
    1   cup finely ground English walnuts
        or mixed nuts
    1   cup dry whole wheat or rye bread-
        crumbs
    1   teaspoon salt
    1   teaspoon poultry seasoning
    2   beaten eggs
    1   cup evaporated milk or cream

Fry onions over low heat in melted fat until light brown.

Add celery, carrots, nuts, crumbs, and seasonings; cook and stir over low heat about 5 minutes.

Beat eggs; stir in cream or evaporated milk. Combine the two mixtures.

Turn into a well greased loaf pan. Bake in moderate oven (350°F.) until nicely browned, about 40 to 45 minutes.

Turn out on a heated platter. Surround with cooked green peas; garnish with sliced hard-cooked eggs. Serve with mushroom or tomato sauce. Condensed cream of mushroom soup, heated just before serving, makes a good sauce. Serves 4 to 6.

Vegetable-Cheese Fondue

VEGETABLE-CHEESE FONDUE

1 cup milk
1 cup soft breadcrumbs
1 tablespoon butter or margarine
1/2 teaspoon salt
Few grains paprika
Few grains pepper
1/2 teaspoon Ac'cent
1/4 pound Cheddar cheese
3 eggs, separated
1 cup green peas

Scald milk; combine with crumbs, butter or margarine, salt, paprika, pepper, and Ac'cent. Grate cheese; add.

Add unbeaten egg yolks; mix well. Add peas. Beat egg whites stiff; fold in.

Bake in greased casserole in moderate oven (350°F.) 45 minutes. Serve at once.

Serves 6.

Note: Any cooked vegetable may be used instead of peas.

VEGETABLE CASSEROLE

(Master Recipe)

3/4 cup cooked or canned peas, drained
3/4 cup cooked or canned sliced carrots, drained
3/4 cup cooked or canned green or wax beans, drained
3/4 cup cooked or canned diced celery, drained
2 tablespoons grated onion
1 1/2 cups medium white sauce
1/2 cup buttered crumbs or 1/2 cup grated cheese
Paprika

Put peas, carrots, beans, and celery in layers in greased casserole, sprinkling each layer with grated onion. Pour sauce over vegetables.

Top with buttered crumbs and a dash of paprika or with grated cheese.

Bake in moderate oven (375°F.) about 25 minutes. Serves 6 to 8.

Vegetable Casserole Variations

Vegetable Casserole with Canned Soup: Follow master recipe, substituting for white sauce 1 can condensed cream of asparagus or mushroom soup diluted with 1/3 cup milk.

Or, omit white sauce and diced celery, and use 1 can condensed cream of celery soup diluted with 1/3 cup milk.

Vegetable Pie: Follow recipe for vegetable casserole. Omit crumbs or cheese topping. Cover casserole with plain pastry, biscuit dough, or 1 tube ready-to-bake biscuits, or toasted bread cubes.

Vegetable Casserole with Mushrooms: Follow recipe for vegetable casserole, adding broiled or pan-fried whole button or sliced mushrooms to top of casserole before sprinkling with breadcrumbs.

TO BRAISE OR "PAN" VEGETABLES

Use a covered pan or skillet. Put in 2 to 4 tablespoons butter, margarine, bacon fat, or salt pork fat. Add a small amount of water or broth, and the vegetable. Cover tightly; cook slowly on direct heat or in moderate oven. Depending upon type and flavor of fat used, add salt to taste when vegetable is done.

You can *braise:* cabbage, chard, collards, mustard, turnip, and other greens (omit water); celery, leeks, green onions (scallions); corn (cut from cob); snap beans, peas, eggplant, thin-skinned squash, and okra.

TO STEAM VEGETABLES

Use a rack or perforated steamer insert over rapidly boiling water. Season after cooking.

Note: Portions of prepared vegetables may be seasoned and buttered first, then then wrapped securely in foil or tied in parchment paper, then steamed or boiled. This method is excellent for retaining all the natural juices.

For easier serving, certain vegetables may be tied in individual servings with thick clean cotton string before cooking: asparagus, celery, leeks, scallions (green onions), whole snap beans, etc.

TO FRENCH FRY VEGETABLES

Cut large vegetables in pieces to facilitate cooking. Season both the vegetable and the breading mix with Ac'cent. Pre-heat fat to correct temperature (see recipe directions) and bring fat to correct temperature again before putting in another batch of vegetables. Serve immediately after cooking. Cooked vegetables are usually seasoned first; others, like French fried potatoes, are sprinkled with salt after cooking.

You can *French fry:* potatoes, parsnips, onions (rings), asparagus, eggplant, green tomatoes, summer squash, carrots, okra, and cauliflower.

TO BROIL VEGETABLES

Choose firm vegetables that will slice well and hold their shape, such as eggplant, tomatoes (green or red), knob celery or celeriac, and parsnips, previously parboiled and drained. Season with salt, pepper, and Ac'cent. Brush or dot with fat. Broil at least 3 inches below heat.

TO BOIL VEGETABLES

Start with boiling water. Add salt. Use high heat until steam appears around edge of cover, then lower heat to a gentle boil until vegetables are just done. Count time from moment water comes to boil again after vegetable is put in.

TO BAKE VEGETABLES

Allow 2 to 3 times longer cooking than for boiling. Some vegetables will require more liquid, or must be covered for part of the baking time. Pierce potatoes when done to let steam escape.

You can *bake:* large onions, tomatoes, potatoes, eggplant, acorn squash, winter squash (Hubbard), corn on the cob, and zucchini.

FROZEN VEGETABLES WITH HERBS

Cook 1 package frozen mixed vegetables as label directs.

Meanwhile, melt 2 tablespoons butter or margarine; add a pinch of marjoram, thyme, or savory. Pour over drained vegetables and season to taste. Serves 3 to 4.

Variations: These herbs also add flavor to peas, peas and carrots, succotash, or green beans.

ANISE

Anise, also called sweet fennel or finocchio, is similar in appearance to celery but has a spicy licorice flavor. It should be tender and have a well-developed bulb when bought in the fresh state. This edible type of anise should not be confused with the variety that is grown only for the oil that is secreted by its leaves.

Selection: Buy 1 medium-sized bulb per serving.

Preparation: Scrape the bulb. Cut bulb and stalk into 1-inch slices.

Cooking Time: 15 to 20 minutes.

Cooking: Cook, covered, in a small amount of boiling salted water 15 to 20 minutes, or until just tender.

Serving: Serve hot seasoned with salt, pepper, melted butter or margarine, and fresh lemon juice.

To Serve Raw: Serve like celery. Cut heads in quarters or eighths, or scrape the bulb, slice thin and use in salads.

ANISE JARDINIERE

3 heads anise
1 clove garlic, minced
1 onion, sliced
1 carrot, sliced or ½ cup green peas
½ cup consommé, chicken broth, or water
Salt
1 tablespoon melted butter or olive oil

Cut tops off anise and remove any outer discolored stalks. Wash well. Cut each head into quarters or sixths, leaving stalks attached at root end.

Combine anise, garlic, onion, carrot or peas, consommé, broth or water, and salt. Cook, covered, until tender, about 15 minutes.

Drain or serve in broth with butter or olive oil. Serves 4.

ARTICHOKES (French or Globe)

Really an unopened flower bud that grows on a thistle-like plant, the French or globe artichoke is native to the Mediterranean region and was popular in Italy as early as 1466. Nowadays almost all the artichokes available in American markets are grown in California.

Artichokes have a delicate nut-like flavor. Though they may be stuffed and are sometimes pickled, they are usually boiled and served hot or cold as indicated below.

Selection: Allow 1 per serving. Size not important to quality and flavor. Choose compact, heavy globular buds which yield slightly to pressure. A good artichoke has large, tightly closed leaf scales. Freshness indicated by green color.

Preparation: Prepare just before cooking. If unusually large, split each in half lengthwise to make 2 servings. Cut off 1 inch of the top, cutting straight across with a sharp knife. Cut off stem about 1 inch from base, leaving a stub. Pull off any loose leaves around the bottom. With scissors, clip off tip of each leaf.

Cooking Time: 20 to 45 minutes.

Cooking—Western Style: Drop into boiling salted water. Season by adding a small clove of garlic, 1 thick slice of lemon, 1 tablespoon olive or other salad oil for *each* artichoke. Add a small piece of bay leaf if desired.

Cover and boil until leaf can be pulled easily from stalk, or stem can be easily pierced with a fork—20 to 45 minutes. Remove carefully from water. Drain. Cut off stub.

Serving as a Hot Vegetable: Place upright on plate. Serve with hot melted butter or margarine, mayonnaise, or Hollandaise sauce. Put sauce in crisp lettuce cups, small crinkled paper cups or tiny custard cups.

Serving as a Salad: Drain and chill cooked artichoke. Place upright on salad plate. Serve with mayonnaise blended with fresh lemon juice and prepared mustard. Westerners often serve artichokes as an appetizer.

How to Eat: Pull off the leaves (petals) one by one and dip the base (the light-colored end) into the sauce. Eat only the tender part of the leaf by drawing it between the teeth. Discard the remaining less-tender tip.

Continue with leaf after leaf until you come to the fuzzy center or "choke."

Remove the small "choke" with a knife and fork and discard it. Cut the heart into bite-sized pieces with a fork, dip in sauce and eat.

ARTICHOKES—ITALIAN STYLE

4 large or 8 small artichokes
3 tablespoons olive oil
2 onions, chopped
2 cloves garlic, chopped
2 tablespoons minced parsley
1 cup minced celery
8 anchovies, chopped
4 tablespoons grated Parmesan cheese
1 cup fine soft breadcrumbs
3 tablespoons capers
¼ teaspoon pepper
Salt to taste

Wash artichokes well. Cut off about ¼ of tops and stems. Remove bottom leaves. Stand in 1½ inches of boiling salted water. Add stems. Cover and cook 30 minutes. Drain. Peel and chop stems and reserve.

Sauté onion and garlic in 1 tablespoon oil until yellow. Add chopped stems, parsley, celery, anchovies, cheese, crumbs, capers, and pepper. Add salt to taste.

Spread the leaves of the cooked artichokes apart and remove choke. Fill center with stuffing and put a little stuffing at base of large leaves.

Place in baking dish. Cover bottom of dish with ¼ inch of water. Pour remaining 2 tablespoons oil over artichokes.

Cover and bake in moderate oven (350°F.) until base of leaves is very tender. Baste occasionally with drippings in pan or more oil. Serves 4.

ARTICHOKE HEARTS

French or Globe artichokes stripped of leaves and chokes. These bottoms of artichokes are delicately flavored and may be cooked fresh or purchased canned. They are delicious in salads or served with mayonnaise or Hollandaise sauce.

Artichokes—French or Globe

FRIED ARTICHOKE BOTTOMS OR HEARTS

Drain cooked artichoke hearts; dip in 1 well beaten egg mixed with 1 tablespoon milk, then dip in fine, dried breadcrumbs.

Fry in deep hot fat (365°F.) 5 minutes. Drain. Serve with tartar sauce; 2 or 3 hearts make 1 serving.

Or cut each heart in half and sauté lightly in sweet butter or margarine.

Sprinkle with a few drops of lemon juice. Serve hot.

ARTICHOKE FRITTERS

3 eggs, well beaten
½ teaspoon salt
½ teaspoon pepper
1 cup evaporated milk
1 small onion, chopped fine
½ clove garlic, minced fine
½ cup grated Parmesan cheese
½ cup flour
1 teaspoon baking powder
6 white crackers, ground fine
2 packages frozen artichoke hearts, coarsely chopped

Combine all ingredients and let stand approximately 10 minutes. Drop by teaspoons into hot deep fat (375°F.) and cook until brown and crisp. Serves 6.

ARTICHOKES—JERUSALEM

The Jerusalem artichoke is a root or tuber vegetable of the sunflower family, native to North America. It has no connection with Jerusalem or with true artichokes; the first part of its name is a corruption of the Italian word for sunflower, and the second part arose from a fancied resemblance in taste. It looks like a small, gnarled white potato but is sweeter and more watery, having a taste somewhat similar to that of a cooked water chestnut. The boiled tubers may be eaten hot, with various sauces, or diced and served cold in a salad.

Selection: Allow 1 pound for 6.

Preparation: Wash, pare, leave whole or slice. Cook until tender in boiling salted water, 15 to 25 minutes, or in pressure saucepan 2 minutes. Overcooking toughens this vegetable. Drain; add ¼ cup butter or margarine, 2 tablespoons lemon juice, 2 tablespoons finely chopped parsley, ¼ teaspoon cayenne, and a few grains pepper. Cook 3 minutes.

Mayonnaise and sliced olives heated in top of double boiler, then poured over cooked asparagus on toast makes a delightful side dish.

ASPARAGUS

Of its two types, white and green asparagus, the latter is generally considered more desirable. The green type is an early spring crop and is usually cut just as soon as the tips of the stalks come above ground about eight inches. The white asparagus is the same variety, but it is clipped while most of the stalk is still below ground.

Selection: Buy 2 pounds for 4 servings. The stalk should be green and tender for almost its entire length. It should be fresh and firm with close, compact tips.

Preparation: Cut off tough ends and remove large scales along the stalk that hold grit. If stalks are peeled, they are as tender as the tips and will cook in the same length of time.

Peeled stalks may be placed horizontally in the saucepan in which they cook, but unpeeled stalks should be tied together and placed upright.

Wash the vegetable thoroughly but gently until no sand remains. A soft brush helps.

Cooking Time: 10 to 20 minutes.

Boiled Whole Stalks: Stand unpeeled stalks upright in the bottom of a double boiler. Add boiling salted water to 1-inch depth. Cover tightly with upper part of double boiler and boil until just tender, 10 to 20 minutes.

Drop peeled stalks into a saucepan which holds boiling salted water to a depth of 1 inch. Cover pan tightly and boil until just tender, 10 to 15 minutes.

Boiled 1-Inch Lengths: Cook, covered, in 1-inch boiling salted water for 10 to 15 minutes, or until tender.

Steamed: Cook in steamer 7 to 15 minutes, or until tender.

Pressure Cooked: Stand in pressure pan; add water to just cover bottom and cook to 15-pound pressure or ½ minute. Lower pressure immediately.

Serving: Remove from water carefully to avoid breaking tips. Serve at once with melted butter or margarine, white sauce, or Hollandaise sauce.

ASPARAGUS AU GRATIN

Follow master recipe for scalloped vegetables with cheese.

FRENCH FRIED ASPARAGUS

Use fresh cooked or canned asparagus tips. Drain and dip in egg and fine crumbs or flour. Chill.

Fry a few at a time in deep hot fat (380°F.) until delicately brown, about 3 minutes. Drain on paper.

With Cheese: Mix grated Parmesan or Romano cheese with the crumbs used for dipping, using half cheese and half crumbs.

SCALLOPED ASPARAGUS

Follow master recipe for scalloped vegetables, using 2-inch lengths of cooked or canned asparagus. Add diced hard-cooked eggs and 1 or 2 tablespoons chopped pimiento.

ASPARAGUS SOUFFLÉ

Follow master recipe for vegetable soufflé.

ASPARAGUS WITH PARMESAN CHEESE

Cook 1 bunch asparagus by a method given above and drain well.

Lay in a shallow heat-resistant baking dish.

Sprinkle with freshly ground pepper, 3 tablespoons butter, and ¼ cup grated Parmesan cheese. Brown lightly under broiler heat. Serves 4.

ASPARAGUS Ā LA GOLDENROD

Cook 1 pound asparagus. Add 3 hard-cooked eggs, sliced in 1½ cups cheese sauce.

Serve hot on buttered toast. If desired, add ¼ cup chopped ripe olives. Serves 6.

CREAMED ASPARAGUS

Cut cooked asparagus into 1-inch pieces. Heat in medium white sauce. Serve on toast.

Diced hard-cooked eggs may be added to sauce. Garnish with minced parsley and pimiento strip.

Canned asparagus with cream sauce and garnish of sliced hard-cooked eggs.

BAMBOO SHOOTS

Grown mostly in the southern states, edible bamboo shoots are the tender young stalks of a species of bamboo plant. They resemble asparagus spears in appearance. Freshness, crispness, and a good green color are general indications of quality. They are commonly available canned, ready to use.

Cooking: Boil fresh bamboo shoots in water to cover about 10 to 15 minutes. Drain and discard the water. The shoots are then ready to use.

BEAN SPROUTS

Young edible soybean sprouts are commonly used in so-called "Chinese" dishes. To cook fresh sprouts, add 4 cups bean sprouts to ¾ cup boiling water. Cover and simmer until almost soft, just long enough to remove the raw bean flavor. Season with salt or soy sauce.

BEANS—GREEN SNAP OR WAX

Green beans were formerly called string beans because they had to have the strings removed before using; however nowadays varieties are usually available that only have to have the ends snipped off. Some varieties are green—others waxy yellow (wax beans). Some are flat and some are round but all are equally good. Selection depends upon personal taste. The fresh beans are found on the market all year and are in reality the immature pods of kidney beans, picked while the seeds are tiny.

Selection: Buy 1½ pounds for 4 servings. They should be clean, firm, crisp, tender and free from blemishes.

Preparation: Young, tender beans need only to be washed and have the ends nipped off. Cut crosswise into inch lengths, or sliver them lengthwise for French style beans.

Cooking Time: 10 to 20 minutes.

Cooking: Cook, covered, in ½ inch of boiling salted water. Allow 15 to 20 minutes for cut beans; 10 minutes for French style beans.

Serving: Season with salt and pepper and butter or margarine. For variety, bacon or ham drippings or crumbled crisp-cooked bacon will add a good flavor.

To Serve Raw: Reserve a few young beans to cut into mixed green salads.

GREEN BEANS WITH ALMONDS

Arrange cooked and seasoned green beans in a buttered casserole. Add a thin white sauce. Cover with slivered almonds.

Bake in hot oven (400°F.) until almonds are browned.

OLD-FASHIONED SNAP BEANS AND BACON

1/4 pound bacon, diced
1/4 cup chopped onion
1 1/2 pounds fresh snap beans
2 medium-sized potatoes, diced
3/4 cup water
1 1/2 teaspoons salt
1/8 teaspoon pepper

Brown the bacon. Add onion and let brown slightly.

Add to other ingredients and bring to boil. Lower heat and cook until beans are tender, 25 to 30 minutes. Serves 5.

Note: If canned beans are used simmer only 20 minutes.

SWEET AND SOUR GREEN BEANS

1 No. 2 can (2 1/2 cups) green beans
3 slices bacon, diced
3 tablespoons sweet pickle juice

Drain beans; cook bean liquid until 1/3 cup remains. Fry bacon until crisp.

Add beans, bacon, and pickle juice to hot liquid. Simmer to blend flavors, about 15 minutes. Serves 4 to 5.

SAUTÉED SNAP OR WAX BEANS

Cook and season 1 1/2 pounds beans cut in strips.

Drain and cook in 1/4 cup butter or margarine about 5 minutes, stirring frequently. Serve hot.

ITALIAN GREEN BEAN CASSEROLE

1 can (2 cups) green beans
1 tablespoon instant minced onion
1/16 teaspoon garlic powder, or 1/2 clove garlic, finely chopped
3 eggs, eaten
1 cup soft stale breadcrumbs
1/4 teaspoon oregano
1/8 teaspoon pepper
1/2 teaspoon salt
1/3 cup grated Parmesan cheese

Drain beans, reserving 1/2 cup liquid. Combine liquid with all remaining ingredients, mixing well. Add beans and mix lightly.

Turn into 1 quart baking dish. Bake in moderate oven (350°F.) about 35 minutes, until set in center. Serve at once, from baking dish. Serves 4 to 5.

Italian Green Bean Casserole

SNAP OR WAX BEANS— ITALIAN STYLE

Cook 1 pound beans until tender. Then simmer 10 minutes longer with 1 cup tomato soup, 1 clove garlic (to be removed at end of cooking period), 2 tablespoons butter or margarine, and salt and pepper to taste.

SCALLOPED SNAP BEANS

Follow master recipe for Scalloped Vegetables.

GREEN BEANS À LA FRANCAISE

Cook covered in 3 tablespoons butter until tender: 1 medium onion, sliced; 1 strip celery, diced; 1 small carrot, chopped.

Add 2 cups green beans and 1 bouillon cube dissolved in 2 tablespoons hot water. Simmer until vegetables are tender but not mushy. Be sure vegetables retain their crispness when you serve them.

GREEN BEANS AND MUSHROOMS

Wash and slice 1/4 pound fresh mushrooms. Mince 1/2 small onion and cook with mushrooms in 1 tablespoon butter or margarine 5 minutes.

Add 1 package frozen green beans, 1/3 cup boiling water, and 1/2 teaspoon salt. Bring to boil; cover, and cook 8 to 12 minutes, or until beans are just tender.

Add 1/4 cup heavy cream to undrained vegetables and season to taste. Heat well. Serves 4.

Variations: Peas or cut asparagus are also good cooked with mushrooms.

MUSTARD BUTTERED GREEN BEANS

Cook 2 cups green beans in boiling, salted water until tender; drain.

Melt 1/4 cup butter or margarine and season to taste with prepared mustard. Pour over green beans. Serves 6.

BEANS—FAVAS

Fava beans are a long, round, velvety-podded variety held in high esteem by epicures. They resemble the lima bean except that they are rounder, with thick, somewhat larger pods.

Selection and Preparation: Same as for green lima beans.

Cooking Time: 20 to 25 minutes.

Cooking: Follow directions for cooking green lima beans. Add a clove of garlic while cooking or season with onion.

Serving: Same as for green lima beans.

DRIED BEANS—BOILED

There are many varieties of dried beans; the best known in the average American grocery are lima, navy, kidney, soy, yellow eye, and black.

Preparation: In general to prepare them, pick over and discard any discolored beans.

Cover with 4 cups water to each cup of beans. Soak overnight. Bring to boiling in same water. Skim. Simmer until tender but not mushy. Add salt when beans are about half done.

Cooking time: The time will vary depending on size and type of beans. Dried limas cook in about 45 minutes, soy beans 2 to 3 hours, some types of soy beans as much as 4 to 6 hours, other beans 1 to 3 hours. Add water from time to time as it cooks away.

Some types of packaged beans are available treated to eliminate the soaking. Follow directions on package for these.

Pressure Cooked Beans: Cook limas 20 minutes, kidney beans 15 minutes, navy beans 30 minutes, soybeans 40 minutes.

Note: Dried beans swell to double or more in bulk as they cook.

Serving: To serve as boiled beans, season with salt and pepper to taste. Dress with butter, margarine, or a little olive oil. Or, add a small amount of fat meat —salt pork, bacon, or ham bone with some meat left on for the last hour of cooking. Minced fresh parsley is a good addition to a serving of boiled beans.

Boiled beans are good hot or cold; they are useful in salad mixtures, as sandwich filler, and in other recipes. One serving of hot boiled beans is usually about 1/2 cup.

PINTO BEAN

A speckled, pink bean related to the kidney bean and common in Mexico and the U. S. Southwest. It is used dried. Also called Mexican beans.

PURÉE OF DRIED BEANS OR LENTILS

Wash well. Soak overnight in cold water to cover. (Specially treated beans should be prepared in accordance with directions on package.)

If the beans are strong in flavor, drain and add fresh water. Otherwise cook in the water in which they were soaked to conserve minerals and vitamins.

Season with salt (about 1 teaspoon to 2 cups beans). Simmer covered until tender, about 1 1/2 to 2 hours. Add water as needed in small amounts.

Drain and put through purée strainer. Season to taste with salt, pepper, and melted butter or margarine.

FRIJOLES

Frijoles is a Spanish term which means literally, beans; specifically, Mexican-style beans, cooked with chili and sometimes with tomatoes. Frijoles refritos: refried (that is, twice-fried) beans, which after cooking are lightly fried, then mashed and fried again.

FRIJOLES, SOUTHWESTERN STYLE

Pick over and wash 1 pound (about 2 cups) pink Mexican beans; soak overnight in water to cover.

Remove seeds and ribs from 6 to 8 dry Mexican chili peppers (the long hot kind that you see hung to dry in brilliant strings on the walls of adobe houses in the Southwest).

Wash peppers; add to beans; simmer, covered, 2 to 3 hours, or until tender enough to mash easily, adding 2 teaspoons salt while cooking. Also add more water if necessary during cooking.

Drain while hot, saving the liquid.

Heat ½ cup bacon drippings in a heavy skillet. Add some of the beans and mash thoroughly with a potato masher. Blend in some bean liquid, then add more beans and mash them. Continue until all beans and liquid are used; cook, stirring constantly, until thick and creamy.

Serve with tortillas which have been reheated quickly on a dry griddle or skillet. Serves 4 to 6.

Mexican Frijoles: Use small red beans, and omit the red chili peppers from above recipe.

Frijoles Refritos (Refried Beans): Simply heat the already mashed and fried beans in additional bacon drippings or lard, stirring constantly, until they are thoroughly hot and completely dry.

Variations: Many people like to add chopped onion, green pepper, and garlic to pink or red beans after they have cooked for an hour or so. Some like to use canned tomatoes in place of part of the water ordinarily used. Some like to add 1 to 2 tablespoons chili powder for each pound of beans. Some add browned hamburger balls, or bits of ham or other meat.

MEXICAN STEWED BEANS

2 cups washed pinto (or kidney) beans
2 teaspoons salt
Cold water
1 tablespoon bacon fat
1 onion, minced
2 cloves garlic, minced
3 seeded green peppers, minced

Combine in saucepan pinto or kidney beans, salt, and cold water to cover. Bring to boil.

Meanwhile, heat bacon fat in another pan. Add onion, garlic, and green peppers. Cook until lightly browned.

Turn the cooking beans into this pan with enough of their water to cover. Cook gently until soft, or about 1½ hours, adding water as necessary.

At moment of serving there should be only enough liquid to make a moist dressing and not enough for a watery sauce.

Note: This is one of the commonest daily dishes of Mexico. The recipe is varied by substituting for the green peppers, *Chile Ancho Pulp*, or pulp from any of the many kinds of chile peppers grown in the country.

SOYBEANS

The soybean (or soya bean) is the seed of any of several hundred plants that have been cultivated in the Orient for probably 5,000 years. It is the most nutritious of legumes, with a high content of good-quality protein. Soybeans are not eaten much in the United States but are grown for flour, oil, feed, and other commercial products. In the Far East they are a basic food. They are ground into meal, pressed into cakes, fermented into cheeses, and boiled and crushed to make a sort of milk.

GREEN SOYBEANS

Fresh green soybeans are very similar to fresh green peas in appearance and flavor. Use young vegetable soybeans (not the field type) while pods are still green.

To shell, drop the pods in boiling water. Cover and let stand 5 minutes. Drain and cool slightly. Press the beans out of pods by squeezing with thumb and forefinger.

Cook beans in lightly salted boiling water until tender, 10 to 25 minutes. (Use 1 cup water to 1 pint beans). Some varieties cook more quickly than others.

If desired, they may be cooked in the pod 25 to 30 minutes, cooled and shelled. The shelled beans may be cooked 5 to 10 minutes more before being served. Or, they may be steamed instead of boiled.

To serve, follow recipes for fresh or canned lima beans, or season simply with salt and pepper to taste and melted butter, or serve with crisply fried bacon or salt pork.

DRIED SOYBEANS

Dry soybeans (either the vegetable or field type) should be prepared and served in practically the same way as other dry beans, except that most of the varieties require a longer period of cooking. They should always be soaked overnight.

After soaking overnight, drain, add fresh water, and simmer. One cup of dry beans will make about 2 cups of cooked soybeans. Some varieties will cook tender in about 2 hours. The field varieties require additional cooking time.

With a pressure cooker at 15 pounds pressure the cooking time required is from 15 to 30 minutes. Three cups of water to 1 cup of beans may be used. The vegetable type softens more quickly than the field type of soybean.

To bake soybeans, first simmer them about 2 hours. After adding such seasonings as salt pork, tomato sauce, mustard, brown sugar, or molasses, and a couple of tablespoons of flour, bake for 3 to 4 hours in a slow oven.

Dried soybeans may be substituted for other dried beans, navy, pea, lima, etc. in other recipes (see index).

CHEESE LIMA BAKE

4 tablespoons butter
3 tablespoons flour
1 teaspoon salt
2 cups milk
1 cup grated American cheese
¼ cup diced pimiento
1 teaspoon grated onion
¼ cup ripe olives (6)
3 cups cooked dry lima beans
(¾ cup uncooked)

Make cream sauce by melting butter, blending in flour and salt. Add milk slowly and cook and stir over low heat until mixture thickens. Add cheese and stir until melted. Stir in pimiento, onion, and ripe olives cut from pits in large pieces.

Pour over drained beans in buttered 1½-quart casserole. Bake in moderate oven (350°F.), until browned and bubbly on top, about 30 to 35 minutes. Serves 6.

Note: Addition of ½ cup chopped ham makes a good variation. If desired, prepare and serve in individual casseroles.

Cheese Lima Bake

BEANS—GREEN LIMAS

Lima beans are flat and kidney shaped, the smaller sizes being known as butter beans and the larger beans as potato limas.

Selection: Buy 3 pounds (purchased in the pod) for 4 servings. Pods should be well-filled, crisp, fresh and dark green in color. The shelled bean should be plump and have a tender skin which is green or greenish-white in color.

Preparation: Wash pods and then shell beans just before cooking. For ease of shelling cut off thin outer edge of pod with a sharp knife or scissors—then slip out the beans.

Cooking Time: 20 to 25 minutes.

Cooking: Cook, covered, in about 1 inch boiling, salted water 20 to 25 minutes.

Serving: Season with salt, pepper, and butter or margarine or cream.

SCALLOPED FRESH LIMA BEANS

Follow master recipe for scalloped vegetables.

BAKED BARBECUED LIMAS

1 pound California large dry limas
1/3 pound diced salt pork
1 chopped large onion
1 minced clove garlic
2 tablespoons cooking oil
1 tablespoon chili powder
1 can condensed tomato soup
1 teaspoon Worcestershire sauce
1 teaspoon soy sauce
2 teaspoons prepared mustard
1/4 cup brown sugar (packed)
1/4 cup lemon juice
3/4 teaspoon salt

Soak limas several hours or overnight in 1 1/2 quarts water. Bring to boil. Add salt pork and boil gently until nearly tender, about 30 to 45 minutes.

Fry onion and garlic in hot oil about 5 minutes. Sprinkle with chili powder; mix well.

Stir in tomato soup, 1 1/2 cups cooking liquid from limas, Worcestershire sauce, soy sauce, mustard, brown sugar, lemon juice, and salt. Heat to boiling.

Pour over beans in earthenware casserole. Top with some salt pork. Bake in moderate oven (350°F.) 1 to 1 1/2 hours. Serves 6.

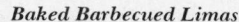

Baked Barbecued Limas

CHILI LIMA BEANS

Cook 1 package frozen lima beans as label directs.

Cook 1 small, minced onion in 3 tablespoons bacon fat, butter, or margarine until yellowed. Add 1/3 cup chili sauce and a dash of cayenne.

Drain beans, add sauce and heat well. Serves 3.

Variations: Green beans, cauliflower, succotash, or cut corn can be substitued for lima beans.

LIMA BEANS AND GREEN ONIONS

Cook 1 box frozen lima beans as label directs.

Meanwhile, slice 6 green onions with tops. Cook in 2 tablespoons butter or margarine 2 minutes. Add 1/4 teaspoon paprika.

Drain beans; add green onions and season. Serves 3.

Variations: Peas, peas and carrots, spinach, green or wax beans, or kale are good with green onions, too.

LIMAS IN MUSHROOM SAUCE

Cook 1 package frozen lima beans as label directs. Drain, reserving 1/4 cup liquid.

Add to lima beans 1 tablespoon minced onion, 1 teaspoon Worcestershire sauce, 1 can condensed cream of mushroom soup, bean liquid, and salt and pepper to taste. Heat well.

Serves 4 to 5.

Variations: Succotash, asparagus, or green beans can also be prepared this way.

DRIED LIMA BEANS IN TOMATO SAUCE

1 cup dried lima beans
3 cups water
3/4 teaspoon salt
1/2 cup chopped onion
1 cup cooked or canned tomatoes
4 slices bacon

Wash beans. Add water, boil 2 minutes, then remove from heat and let soak 1 hour. Or, add water and let soak overnight in a cool place.

Add 1/2 teaspoon salt to beans and boil gently in the same water 45 minutes. Drain.

To bake, put onion and beans in a greased baking dish. Add tomatoes and rest of salt. Arrange bacon strips on top.

Bake in moderate oven (350°F.) until beans are tender and most of the liquid has been absorbed, 45 minutes to 1 hour. Serves 4.

Top-of-Stove Method: Soak, boil, and drain beans as above. Chop bacon and brown it with the onion in a skillet.

Add beans, tomatoes, and salt. Boil gently until beans are tender, stirring occasionally to keep from sticking, about 30 minutes. Add a little water or tomato if the mixture gets too dry.

BEETS

Selection: Beets are marketed with or without tops; the Fall crop, which is sometimes stored, being the one usually sold with only the root part remaining.

Fresh, prime quality beets should have a good globular shape, with a smooth, firm flesh. Those of medium size are less likely to be tough. In the early crop, a poor appearance of the leaves is no certain indication of inferiority, for beet tops deteriorate rapidly without affecting the root quality.

Beet tops are frequently taken from young plants, bunched, and sold as salad greens. Here the color and appearance of the tops are important as their edibility depends upon their being young and tender. Select those that are thin-ribbed, fresh green, and not wilted or slimy.

Preparation: Cut off all but about 2 inches of the tops. *Save* the tops. Wash beets well.

Cooking Time: 30 to 45 minutes.

Cooking: Cook whole beets, covered, in boiling salted water to cover until tender—30 to 45 minutes. Very old, woody beets will never cook tender.

Serving: Drain. Pour cold water over beets and rub off skins. Serve small beets whole; slice or dice large ones. Reheat with butter or margarine, salt, pepper, and a little fresh lemon juice or vinegar.

To Serve Raw Beets: Shred fine and add to salad.

CITRUS HARVARD BEETS

2 tablespoons sugar
1 tablespoon cornstarch
1/4 teaspoon salt
1 can (1 pound) grapefruit sections
1/4 cup vinegar
1 can (1 pound) tiny whole or sliced beets, drained

Combine sugar, cornstarch, and salt in saucepan. Drain grapefruit sections; stir syrup into cornstarch mixture with vinegar.

Place over medium heat and cook, stirring constantly, until mixture comes to a boil. Boil 1/2 minute.

Add drained beets; heat to serving temperature. Remove from heat. Add grapefruit sections. Serves 6.

Citrus Harvard Beets

EASY PICKLED BEETS

Slice cooked beets and cover with mild cider vinegar or 1 cup vinegar boiled 5 minutes with ½ cup sugar. Serve lukewarm or cold.

BEET TOPS

Beet tops contain valuable food elements and are highly palatable. Cut them off, wash and cook them as you do spinach.

HARVARD OR SWEET-SOUR BEETS

½ cup sugar
2 tablespoons flour
¼ cup water
½ cup vinegar
½ teaspoon salt
2 tablespoons butter or margarine
3 cups cooked, diced beets

Mix sugar and flour; add water and vinegar. Cook on medium heat until thick, about 10 minutes.

Add salt, butter and then beets. Cover and continue cooking about 10 minutes. Serves 4 to 5.

BEETS IN ORANGE BUTTER

Wash 6 medium-sized beets. Cook whole beets until tender, remove peel, and shred or chop fine.

Place in casserole. Add 3 tablespoons butter or margarine ¼ cup orange juice, 1 teaspoon grated orange rind, and ½ teaspoon salt.

Cover and bake in moderate oven (350°F.) until well heated. Serves 6.

BRAISED SHREDDED BEETS

Peel and shred 1 pound young beets. Combine with 3 tablespoons butter or margarine in heavy saucepan.

Cover tightly. Simmer 3 to 5 minutes, stirring several times. Season with salt and pepper. Serves 4.

DEVILED BEETS

Heat 3 tablespoons butter or margarine, 2 tablespoons vinegar, ⅓ teaspoon salt, ¼ teaspoon each paprika and dry mustard, 1 tablespoon sugar, and 1 teaspoon Worcestershire sauce.

Pour over 3 cups cooked, diced beets, heat and serve. Serves 6.

Fresh vegetables go gourmet when cooked with a mellow sauce and topped with crisp onion rings as in this Broccoli Casserole with Mushroom-Cheese Sauce.

BROCCOLI

Italian broccoli, which was cultivated as far back as the 16th century, is a first cousin of cauliflower and is served in practically the same way.

Selection: Buy 1½ pounds for 4 servings. Broccoli should be fresh and clean with stalks that are firm and tender. It should have tightly closed green flower buds in compact clusters or heads; there should be no yellow color evident in the buds.

Preparation: Wash well and trim off a bit of the end of the stem, but do not remove the stems. The whole stalk is edible. If any of the stems are more than 1 inch in diameter, it is well to make lengthwise gashes through them (about 4 or 6) almost to the flowerets. The stalks will then cook as quickly as the flower buds.

Cooking Time: 10 to 15 minutes.

Cooking: Drop the prepared broccoli into a small amount of boiling salted water. Cover and cook quickly until just tender—10 to 15 minutes.

Serving: Remove broccoli carefully from water to avoid breaking flower buds. Serve at once seasoned with salt, pepper, and melted butter or margarine or with lemon or almond butter, or with Hollandaise or cheese sauce.

To Serve Raw Broccoli: Use the flowerets in lettuce and tomato salad or serve on the relish tray.

BROCCOLI CASSEROLE WITH MUSHROOM-CHEESE SAUCE

1½ pounds fresh broccoli spears
1 cup grated process American cheese
⅔ cup evaporated milk
1 can condensed cream of mushroom soup
1 3½-ounce can French fried onion rings

Turn on oven and set at very hot (425°F.). Place broccoli spears in shallow 2-quart baking dish. Cover (no water necessary) and bake near center of oven for 25 to 30 minutes or until tender when pierced with fork.

Remove from oven and lower oven temperature to moderate (350°F.). Sprinkle grated cheese over broccoli spears. Mix evaporated milk and mushroom soup until smooth and pour over broccoli. Top with onion rings. Return to oven and bake 15 minutes more uncovered.

Variations: Follow recipe for Broccoli Casserole, except in place of broccoli, use 1 medium head cauliflower, broken apart; 2 pounds fresh asparagus spears; or 1½ pounds fresh green beans.

BROCCOLI WITH PARMESAN CHEESE

Cook broccoli. Season with melted butter or margarine. Serve Parmesan cheese separately to be sprinkled over broccoli.

CREAMED BROCCOLI

Add 2 cups cooked broccoli to 1 cup medium white sauce. Heat thoroughly.

SCALLOPED BROCCOLI

Follow master recipe for Scalloped Vegetables.

BROCCOLI SOUFFLÉ

Follow master recipe for Vegetable Soufflé.

Broccoli dressed up with Mock Hollandaise sauce and garnished with slivered almonds.

BROCCOLI WITH SLIVERED ALMONDS

Cook broccoli. Sauté slivered almonds in butter or margarine until browned. Add drained broccoli and heat thoroughly. Season and serve.

BRUSSELS SPROUTS

Brussels sprouts receive their name from the Belgian city of Brussels, where they were first grown in the 13th century.

Selection: Buy 1 pound for 3 servings. Brussels sprouts should resemble firm, miniature heads of cabbage. They should be compact and bright green in color.

Preparation: Remove any loose or discolored leaves. Cut off a bit of the stem end. Wash thoroughly in cold water.

Cooking Time: 8 to 10 minutes.

Cooking: Cook, covered, in 1 inch of boiling salted water only until tender, about 8 to 10 minutes.

Serving: Serve at once seasoned with pepper and a generous amount of melted butter or margarine or serve with Hollandaise sauce.

BRUSSELS SPROUTS WITH CHESTNUTS

Add 1 cup chopped, boiled, peeled and skinned chestnuts to 4 cups cooked sprouts.

Melted butter or margarine, or cream sauce may be added. Serves 6.

BRUSSELS SPROUTS WITH CHEESE

Heat 4 cups cooked drained sprouts in the top part of a double boiler with ¾ cup grated cheese. Mix. Serves 6.

CREAMED BRUSSELS SPROUTS

Add 1 cup medium white sauce to 2 cups cooked sprouts. Heat thoroughly. If desired, add ½ cup diced crisp bacon.

BRUSSELS SPROUTS WITH MUSHROOMS

Add 1 cup chopped, sautéed mushrooms to 4 cups cooked sprouts. Mix well. Serves 6.

FRENCH FRIED BRUSSELS SPROUTS

Cook sprouts until barely tender. Drain well and dip in egg and crumbs.

Fry in deep hot fat (375°F.) until delicately browned, about 3 minutes. Drain on absorbent paper.

BRUSSELS SPROUTS IN CASSEROLE

Season cooked sprouts with melted butter or margarine. Put in casserole.

Sprinkle with buttered crumbs. Bake in moderate oven (350°F.) until crumbs are brown.

DEVILED BRUSSELS SPROUTS

Cook 1 package frozen sprouts as label directs.

Meanwhile, melt 3 tablespoons butter or margarine; add ¾ teaspoon prepared mustard, ¼ teaspoon salt, ½ teaspoon Worcestershire, and dash of cayenne. Pour over drained sprouts. Serves 3.

Variations: Prepare deviled cauliflower or green beans in the same way.

Brussels sprouts: This picture shows how "sprouts" grow on their stalk. Usually they are marketed in small pint-size containers and sold as a unit for a set price, rather than by the pound.

CABBAGE

Selection: There are numerous common varieties of cabbage but the quality characteristics are generally the same for all types. Well-trimmed, reasonably solid heads that are heavy for their size and show no discolored veins are your best buy. Early or new cabbage is not so firm as some of the Fall and Winter strains which are suitable for storing. One of the most unusual-appearing varieties is called Savoy cabbage. Its yellowish, crimped leaves form a head usually not much harder than that of Iceberg lettuce. Another novel type is celery cabbage also called Chinese cabbage, which has some of the characteristics of both romaine and cabbage. This variety is used principally for salads and its long, oval shaped head should be firm, fresh, and well blanched.

All fresh raw cabbage is very rich in vitamin C and has a fair content of vitamin B_1. Like so many other vegetables, it is also a good source of several important minerals.

Cooking Hint: The typical cabbage odor can be appreciably decreased by dropping a whole walnut into the water in which the vegetable is cooked.

CABBAGE—GREEN

Preparation: Wash well. Cut into wedges and remove the core, or shred for cooking.

Cooking Time: 5 to 15 minutes.

To Cook Wedges: Cook, covered, 10 to 15 minutes, or until just barely tender, in 1 inch of boiling salted water or the water in which a ham or corned beef was cooked.

To Cook Shreds: Cook rapidly, uncovered, in a small amount (not more than ½ inch) of boiling salted water for about 5 minutes, or until just crisply-tender.

Serving: Serve at once while hot. Season with pepper and butter or margarine.

To Serve Cabbage Raw: See Salads.

CABBAGE—RED

Selection And Preparation: Same as for Green Cabbage.

Cooking Time: 8 to 12 minutes.

Cooking: Follow directions for cooking Green Cabbage but add 2 tablespoons fresh lemon juice or vinegar to the cooking water to retain the cherry red color of the cabbage.

Serving: Serve at once while hot. Season with salt, pepper and melted butter or margarine.

To Serve Raw: Same as for Green Cabbage. See Salads.

Properly cooked, well-seasoned vegetables attractively served with sauces soon convert vegetable-haters to vegetable-lovers.

This triple vegetable platter features cabbage with cheese sauce, tomato halves stuffed with seasoned cottage cheese, and buttered green beans.

CREAMED CABBAGE

Heat cooked cabbage in cream or white sauce. Season with grated cheese or curry powder, if desired.

SCALLOPED CABBAGE

Put creamed cabbage in buttered baking dish. Cover with buttered crumbs.

Bake in moderate oven (350°F.) until brown. If desired, add grated cheese to crumbs.

FRIED CABBAGE

Brown drained cooked cabbage lightly in drippings.

SWEDISH STYLE CABBAGE

Heat, but do not boil ½ cup sour cream and ½ teaspoon caraway seeds together. Mix with 2½ cups cooked, drained cabbage. Serves 4.

BUTTERED CABBAGE

Add 1½ to 2 tablespoons melted butter or margarine to each cup of drained, cooked cabbage.

SWEET AND SOUR CABBAGE

1 medium cabbage, red or white
Salt and pepper
3 small sour apples, sliced
2 tablespoons fat
Boiling water
2 tablespoons flour
3 tablespoons lemon juice
4 tablespoons brown sugar

Shred cabbage very fine. Season with salt and pepper.

Add cabbage and apples to melted fat in pan. Pour over boiling water to cover and simmer until tender.

Sprinkle with flour; add lemon juice and sugar. Simmer 10 minutes longer. Serves 6.

Note: Vinegar may be substituted for lemon juice. If red cabbage is used, pour boiling water over several times before cooking. More sugar and lemon juice or vinegar may be added according to taste.

BRAISED CABBAGE

Melt 2 tablespoons butter; add 1 quart shredded green or white cabbage, salt and freshly ground pepper to taste.

Cover tightly and cook, stirring a few times, until just tender. Add water only if necessary. Serves 4.

BAVARIAN CABBAGE

Sauté 1 tablespoon chopped onion in 2 tablespoons bacon drippings 5 minutes.

Add 2 tablespoons vinegar and 1 tablespoon brown sugar. Mix with 2½ cups drained, boiled cabbage. Serves 4.

DUTCH STYLE CABBAGE

Heat together over boiling water, 1 well beaten egg, 1 tablespoon butter or margarine, ½ teaspoon salt, and ¼ cup heavy cream or evaporated milk.

Mix with 2½ cups drained, boiled cabbage. Serves 4.

CHEESED CABBAGE

Melt ½ cup grated Cheddar cheese in ½ cup thin white sauce, then mix with 2½ cups boiled, drained cabbage. Serves 4.

SOUTHERN WILTED CABBAGE

Use 1 medium head raw cabbage, shredded. Cook 4 slices chopped bacon in skillet until crisp.

Add 2 tablespoons sugar, 1 teaspoon salt, few grains pepper, and ¼ cup vinegar.

When hot pour over shredded cabbage. Add ¼ cup minced parsley and serve immediately. Cabbage will be crisp, though warm.

DEVILED CABBAGE

1 large head green cabbage (6 cups), shredded
1 teaspoon prepared mustard
½ teaspoon salt
1 teaspoon sugar
3 tablespoons butter or margarine
1 tablespoon lemon juice

Cook cabbage in covered pan in rapidly boiling salted water about 5 to 7 minutes, until just tender; drain.

Meanwhile, mix remaining ingredients in saucepan. Heat slowly, stirring to blend. Pour over hot cabbage, mixing lightly. Serves 6.

Don't shy away from the more unusual vegetables; try them once and you may want to have them often.

CELERY OR CHINESE CABBAGE

One pound celery cabbage makes 4 servings.

To Boil: Wash and cook whole celery cabbage in water to cover for 15 to 20 minutes; or shred and cook in 1 cup water to 4 cups cabbage with ½ teaspoon salt. Cover the saucepan in each case.

To Serve: Drain cooked cabbage; serve with 2 tablespoons butter or margarine per cup of cooked cabbage, or 1 tablespoon butter or margarine per serving if cooked whole.

Or dress the cooked cabbage with a cream sauce or with Hollandaise sauce, using 2 tablespoons of either per serving.

To Serve Raw: Celery cabbage is popular in salads. Wash and chill it as for any other green.

CARDOON

Cardoon is a vegetable related to the artichoke. It is a tall, thistle-like plant, greenish olive in color. Outwardly it resembles coarse prickly celery, although the taste is not similar. The stalks of this plant have at times attained a height of eight feet or more, although this is unusual. Cardoon is popular in France. Some is grown in the United States; more is imported. The roots and leafstalks are usually cooked and eaten in soups; it may be served as a vegetable or used in stews. It is best when boiled and served in a salad.

Wash and scrape. Cut into short lengths (2 to 3 inches). Cook, covered, until tender in boiling salted water, 15 to 20 minutes, or pressure cook 2 to 3 minutes. Drain and serve with melted butter or margarine.

Cardoon—Italian Style: Cook 10 to 15 minutes. Drain and roll in fine crumbs. Sauté in hot olive oil. Serve with well seasoned tomato sauce.

CARROTS

The carrot owes its chief claim of nutritional fame to the extraordinary amount of vitamin A, also termed "carotene," found in its roots. About ¾ cup of raw carrots can supply over twice the amount needed daily by the average person.

Selection: Brightly colored carrots that have a well-shaped firm flesh are best eating. Usually these are smooth, clean, and free from straggling rootlets. The condition of the green tops in most instances will help you to judge edibility in the early crops. This is no sure guide however, as tops may be damaged in handling without hurting the quality of the roots. Storage carrots are sold with their tops off, but green-topped carrots can usually be found in the stores the year round.

Buy 1 bunch (about 1¼ pounds) or package for 3 servings.

Preparation: Remove tops. Scrape or pare carrots thinly with a knife—or scrub well with a stiff brush. Leave whole, dice, cut into slices or strips, or shred.

Cooking Time: 5 to 20 minutes.

Cooking: Cook, covered, in 1 inch of boiling salted water. Boil gently about 5 minutes for shreds, 10 to 20 minutes for cut pieces, and 15 to 20 minutes for whole carrots.

For Variety: Add finely cut green onion or grated dry onion to carrots while they are cooking.

Serving: Serve hot with a sprinkling of parsley and season with salt, pepper, and butter or margarine or serve with lemon butter or with white sauce. Carrots may be mashed and served hot seasoned with pepper and melted butter or margarine.

CANDIED CARROTS

Cut cooked carrots in halves or quarters, if large. Melt ½ cup butter in heavy pan; add ½ cup brown sugar. Stir until melted; add carrots and cook until well glazed.

CARROT PUFF

⅓ cup seedless raisins
3 tablespoons butter or margarine
4 tablespoons flour
1 cup milk
1 teaspoon salt
1 teaspoon prepared horseradish
2 cups grated raw carrots
1 cup grated American cheese
2 eggs, separated

Rinse and drain raisins. Melt butter and blend in flour. Add milk and cook and stir until mixture boils and is thick.

Add salt, horseradish, carrots, cheese, and raisins, and stir over low heat until cheese is melted. Remove from heat.

Beat egg whites until stiff. Beat yolks lightly. Stir yolks into cooked mixture. Fold in whites.

Turn into greased 1-quart baking dish. Bake in slow oven (325°F.) 1 hour. Serves 5 or 6.

Carrot Puff

Cauliflower and Asparagus au Gratin

OVEN GLAZED CARROTS

Scrape 6 medium-sized carrots and cut in long strips lengthwise. Cook until barely tender.

Place carrots in baking dish. Combine 1 cup brown sugar, 3 tablespoons butter or margarine, and ½ cup water in a saucepan. Cook until sugar is dissolved and pour over carrots.

Bake in moderate oven (350°F.) until glazed, basting occasionally, about 20 minutes. Serves 6.

OVEN GLAZED MINT CARROTS

Add 2 tablespoons fresh, chopped mint to melted butter or margarine and follow recipe for Oven Glazed Carrots.

CARROT RING OR MOLD

2½ cups mashed cooked carrots
2   teaspoons minced onion or onion juice
2   tablespoons melted butter or margarine
2   well beaten eggs
1   tablespoon flour
1   cup rich milk or light cream
Salt, pepper, paprika

Mix ingredients, adding seasonings to taste.

Pack into buttered ring mold. Place in shallow pan of hot water and bake in moderate oven (350°F.) 40 to 50 minutes.

Serve ring filled with green beans, peas, or Brussels sprouts, or as a main dish with creamed chicken. Serves 6.

Carrot Ring with Cheese: Use 2 cups carrots; add 1½ cups grated Parmesan cheese and 1 cup breadcrumbs.

SCALLOPED CARROTS

Follow master recipe for Scalloped Vegetables. Small cooked white onions may be added.

CARROT SOUFFLÉ

Follow master recipe for Vegetable Soufflé.

CARROTS BAKED WITH ROAST

Scrape whole carrots and place around meat roast 1 hour before roast is done. Baste with drippings.

RICED (MASHED) CARROTS

Put cooked carrots through potato ricer. Season with butter, salt, and pepper. Sprinkle with chopped parsley.

CREAMED CARROTS AND CELERY

Cube cooked carrots; add finely cut cooked celery. Heat in medium white sauce.

SAUTÉED CARROTS

Use cooked carrots cut into long thin strips. Dip in slightly beaten egg and cracker crumbs.

Sauté in small amount of butter or margarine in hot skillet until well browned. Serve at once.

CARROT TIMBALES

3   tablespoons butter or margarine
2   teaspoons minced onion
2   tablespoons flour
1   cup light cream or evaporated milk
2   cups mashed, cooked carrots
2   well beaten eggs
½   teaspoon salt
⅛   teaspoon ground mace

Melt butter or margarine; sauté onion in it 3 minutes.

Add flour and blend well; add cream or milk slowly, stir and simmer 5 minutes. Let cool.

Add carrots; mix well and add eggs, salt, and mace.

Pour into 6 greased custard cups; place in a shallow baking pan half full of hot water.

Bake in moderate oven (350°F.) 25 minutes. Serves 6.

MINTED CARROTS

Top drained cooked carrots with melted butter or margarine to which chopped fresh mint has been added.

CAULIFLOWER

Selection: Cauliflower should wear a jacket of bright green, denoting freshness. If it passes this test, make sure the head is white or creamy white, clean and solidly formed. Size of the head does not affect quality nor do the leaves you occasionally find growing through the curds. However, the small flowers in the head must not have started to grow or the cauliflower will be of inferior eating quality. Yellowed, withered leaves are indicative of age, particularly if the head is of "ricy" appearance.

Preparation: Before cooking soak it for 10 minutes or up to an hour, if desired, with the head down in cold water to which has been added a teaspoonful each of vinegar and salt. This will freshen the head and draw out any hidden worms if left in this water for about an hour. This same treatment can be given to cabbage, sprouts, and other vegetables. To cook, remove the green stalks. Leave the head whole or separate into flowerets.

Cooking Time: 8 to 30 minutes.

Cooking: Cook, covered in 1 inch of boiling salted water only until tender when tested with a fork. Flowerets will require no more than 8 to 15 minutes; a whole head of cauliflower will require 20 to 30 minutes.

Serving: Serve hot with butter or margarine or serve with cheese sauce, almond butter, or Hollandaise sauce.

To Serve Raw Cauliflower: Break into flowerets and serve on relish plates. Use as an appetizer with a "dunking" sauce. Add to vegetable salads.

CAULIFLOWER AND ASPARAGUS AU GRATIN

1   medium-sized cauliflower
1½ cups grated American cheese
2   cups medium white sauce
1   No. 1 can asparagus tips, or 1 bunch fresh cooked asparagus
¼   cup breadcrumbs

Break cauliflower into flowerets and cook in boiling salted water; drain well.

Add grated cheese to hot white sauce and blend thoroughly.

Place cooked cauliflower in buttered casserole. Surround with cooked asparagus and cover with sauce. Sprinkle top with buttered crumbs or dot with butter.

Bake in slow oven (325°F.) 20 to 30 minutes, until heated through and crumbs are brown. Serves 6.

CAULIFLOWER WITH MUSHROOMS

Sauté ¼ pound diced mushrooms in butter. Add to cooked flowerets of 1 medium head. Serve on toast with cheese sauce. Serves 6.

CAULIFLOWER WITH CHEESE CRUMB TOPPING

Use large head of hot, cooked cauliflower. Sprinkle top with buttered crumbs, then a generous amount of grated American cheese.

Place in oven or under moderate broiler to brown crumbs and melt cheese. Serves 6.

CREAMED CAULIFLOWER

Combine 1 cup medium white sauce with about 2 cups cooked flowerets. Heat thoroughly and sprinkle with paprika.

SCALLOPED CAULIFLOWER

Follow master recipe for Scalloped Vegetables.

CAULIFLOWER À LA CREOLE

Add 1 teaspoon salt and dash of pepper to 2½ cups canned tomatoes. Cook until most of liquid has evaporated.

Place 4 cups cauliflower flowerets in buttered casserole. Pour over canned tomatoes.

Sprinkle with 1 cup grated American cheese and ¼ cup soft breadcrumbs. Dot with butter.

Bake in slow oven (325°F.) 12 to 20 minutes. Serves 5.

CELERIAC (CELERY ROOT)

Celeriac, also known as celery root, is a type of celery with a root somewhat like a turnip. The root is the only edible portion, and is used for salads and sometimes for cooking as a vegetable. The quality characteristics of celeriac are the same as those of other root vegetables. Buy 1½ pounds for 4 servings.

Preparation: Cut away leaves and root fibers. Scrub well but do not peel before cooking.

Cooking Time: 40 to 60 minutes.

Cooking: Cook, covered, in boiling salted water until tender, from 40 to 60 minutes.

Serving: Peel the cooked root. Slice and serve hot with melted butter or margarine and pepper or with white sauce or Hollandaise sauce.

To serve Raw Celery Root: Pare. then slice very thin and season with salt, pepper, and vinegar to serve as a relish.

CREAMED CELERY ROOT

Combine with medium white sauce (2 cups boiled celery root to 1 cup sauce). Serve hot. Garnish with parsley.

FRIED CELERY ROOT

Cook, drain and chill thoroughly. Dip into beaten egg and breadcrumbs.

Fry in small amount of fat until browned on all sides. Season with salt and pepper.

CELERY

Celery is a vegetable which grew wild for centuries before most people were aware of its food value. Authorities generally agree that to Italians is due the credit for "domesticating" celery and beginning its cultivation for table use. Celery is probably native to England, as old textbooks mentioned it as "smallage." Celery still grows in a wild state there in ditches and country lanes.

Selection: Buy 1 medium stalk for 4 servings. Stalks should be crisp and topped with fresh leaves. There are two types—Pascal (green) and Golden (bleached). Pascal is a "meaty," full-hearted celery with a mild, nutty flavor.

Preparation: Remove leaves and trim roots. Wash thoroughly, using a brush to remove sand. Dice outer branches. Reserve inner branches to serve raw.

Cooking Time: 15 to 20 minutes; in pressure saucepan, cook 2 to 3 minutes.

Cooking: Cook diced celery, covered, in 1 inch of boiling salted water for 15 to 20 minutes.

Serving: Season with salt, pepper, and melted butter or margarine and serve hot, or serve with white sauce.

CREAMED CELERY

Combine with medium white sauce (2 cups cooked celery to 1 cup sauce). Serve hot. If desired, sprinkle with chopped toasted almonds. Serves 4.

For variety, add 1 or 2 green peppers, seeded, precooked, and cut in small pieces.

BRAISED CELERY

Clean, cut off leaves, and cut 1 bunch celery into 3-inch pieces.

Heat 2 tablespoons salad oil in skillet. Brown celery lightly.

Add 1 cup meat stock or consommé. Cook slowly until stock is reduced about ½ cup. Season with salt and pepper.

CELERY AU GRATIN

Follow master recipe for Scalloped Vegetables with Cheese.

CELERY VINAIGRETTE

1 bunch pascal celery
½ cup olive or salad oil
⅓ cup wine or tarragon vinegar
1 tablespoon chopped parsley
1 tablespoon chopped chives or 1 tea-
     spoon grated onion
2 tablespoons finely chopped green
     pepper
½ teaspoon salt
Dash of pepper

Wash celery and cut into pieces about 6 inches long. Cook in boiling salted water until tender but not soft; drain and cool.

Combine oil with vinegar, parsley, chives or onion, green pepper, salt and pepper; pour over celery. Let stand in refrigerator 2 to 3 hours.

To serve, lift out celery; save oil mixture to use again. Serves 4 to 5.

Green Beans Vinaigrette: In above recipe use 1 pound cooked whole green beans instead of celery.

CELTUCE

As the name indicates, celtuce is partly like celery and partly like lettuce. It is now grown in the United States although it is believed to have originated in China.

To Cook: Wash, slice, and cook in any of the ways celery is prepared.

To Serve Celtuce Raw: Wash and remove the skin of the large stalk down to the crisp tender part. Serve the stalk with salt, like celery. Or slice crosswise in ½-inch slices; serve with French dressing or in mixed vegetable or fruit salads.

CHERVIL

Salad chervil is a leafy vegetable generally used like parsley. Turnip-rooted chervil, sometimes called parsnip chervil, is cultivated for its edible root which is cooked and served like parsnips. See also **Chervil**, in **Herbs.**

CHAYOTE

One pound serves 4. This pear-shaped squash is about the size of acorn squash. The meat is pale green much like honeydew melon. It may be halved and baked like acorn squash, seasoned with just salt and pepper or stuffed.

Boiled: Peel very thinly before or after cooking. Cut into halves, quarters, or slice. Leave the seeds in. They are edible and will cook tender. Cook in small amount boiling salted water (½ cup to 1 pound) until tender, 15 to 20 minutes. Serve with melted butter or margarine or cream sauce.

Mashed: Mash boiled chayote. Season with salt and pepper.

Fried: Slice ½ to ¾ inch thick. Cover with fritter cover batter or seasoned corn meal. Fry in deep fat (370°F.) until delicately browned, 3 to 5 minutes. Drain on paper. Serve with cream sauce. Or, dip in beaten egg and crumbs and sauté until nicely browned.

Baked: Arrange sliced cooked chayote in greased casserole. Cover with medium white sauce. Sprinkle with equal amounts of mixed fresh breadcrumbs and grated American cheese. Bake in hot oven (400°F.) 8 to 10 minutes.

CHICK-PEAS (GARBANZOS)

The chick-pea is the dried seed of a bushy plant of the pea family with short, hairy pods. The seeds are round, wrinkled, and somewhat larger than peas. There are white, black, and red varieties; the white is considered the best. Called garbanzos in Spanish, chick-peas are popular in Mexico and in the southwest. They are used in soups, baked like beans, or coated with sugar and eaten as a confection. Chick-peas are available canned.

To prepare dried chick-peas, soak and cook in 3 times their volume of water until tender, seasoning as you do any dried beans; they will require about 2 hours. One pound will serve 5 to 6.

CHICORY

Chicory is a plant with blue flowers, a thick root, and leaves used for salad; also called curly endive and succory. The root is dried, roasted, and ground for use as a coffee substitute; in some places (notably New Orleans) it is mixed with coffee for added flavor, body, and aroma. See **Endive.**

COLLARDS

Collards are sometimes used as a substitute for cabbage. This vegetable resembles kale, and has large, curly leaves that do not form into a solid head. Choose much the same way as cabbage, taking care to avoid wilted-looking, yellow leaves. See **Greens.**

CORN

At one time, in biblical days, all grain was called "corn." In England the British refer to our common corn as "maize" or Indian corn to make the distinction apparent. Corn was cultivated in the New World long before Columbus found this land. Many Indian legends were woven about this "all inclusive food" which in the days of the early settler, had a mixture of red, white, yellow, and black kernels on each ear. Careful breeding since then has produced the present day scientifically developed hybrids that now represent almost all commercially grown corn types.

Selection: Sweet corn may be either white or yellow. In best quality, the husk is a fresh green color while the kernels are tender, milky, and sufficiently large to leave no space between the rows. They should be just firm enough to puncture rather easily when slight pressure is applied. Ears generally should be filled to the tip, with no rows of missing kernels. If you see cobs with kernels that are very soft and very small, you can be quite sure that the corn is immature. When young corn is cooked just after picking it is naturally sweet and tops in flavor. Even a few hours off the stalk brings about changes that lessen this choice eating flavor.

MEXICAN CORN CUSTARD

1/4 cup minced onion
1/4 cup diced green pepper
3 tablespoons butter or bacon fat
3 tablespoons chopped pimiento
2 cups whole kernel corn
2 eggs, slightly beaten
1 teaspoon sugar
2 cups hot milk
1 3/4 teaspoons salt
1/8 teaspoon pepper

Cook minced onion and green pepper in melted butter for 3 minutes; add with pimiento to whole-kernel corn.

Beat eggs slightly, add sugar and hot milk; add seasonings and corn mixture.

Pour into a well greased 1 1/2 quart casserole. Place in a pan of hot water and bake in slow oven (325°F) 1 hour and 15 minutes, or until a clean knife inserted in the center comes out clean. Serves 6.

CORN-ON-THE-COB

Selection: Allow 1 or 2 ears per person. Cobs should be well filled with plump, milky kernels. The husks should be fresh and green.
Preparation: Just before serving, remove husks and silk.
Cooking Time: 3 to 5 minutes.
Cooking: Line the bottom of a pan with some of the corn husks. Put in ears of corn. Cook, covered, in unsalted boiling water from 3 to 5 minutes.
Serving: Lift corn from water and serve at once with salt, pepper, and plenty of butter or margarine.

CORN PUDDING

2 tablespoons butter or margarine
2 tablespoons flour
1 1/2 teaspoons salt
1/2 teaspoon sugar
1/8 teaspoon pepper
3 cups milk
1 teaspoon grated onion
4 slightly beaten eggs
2 packages frozen sweet corn
2 tablespoons chopped pimiento

Melt butter. Add flour, salt, sugar, and pepper, mixing well to blend. Add milk gradually, stirring until smooth. Cook and stir over medium heat until thickened.

Remove from heat. Add onion, eggs, and corn and mix well. Carefully stir in pimiento. Spoon into 1 1/2-quart baking dish.

Place in pan of hot water and bake, uncovered, in moderate oven (350°F.) until firm, about 1 hour. Serves 6 to 8

CORN FRITTERS

1 cup enriched flour
1 teaspoon salt
1 teaspoon baking powder
2 eggs
1/4 cup milk
1 tablespoon melted shortening
1 1/2 cups cooked whole kernel corn
Fat for deep frying

Sift flour, salt, and baking powder into bowl. Beat eggs with milk; add melted fat and whole kernel corn and combine two mixtures lightly.

Drop from teaspoon into deep fat heated to 365°F. (or when an inch cube of bread browns in 60 seconds).

Fry until brown and cooked in center, about 4 to 5 minutes. Drain on absorbent paper.

Makes 8 medium fritters.

ROAST CORN

Place ears of corn with husk in hot oven (400°F.). Bake until corn is tender, about 15 minutes.

Mexican corn custard may be baked either in one large casserole or in individual custard cups or casseroles.

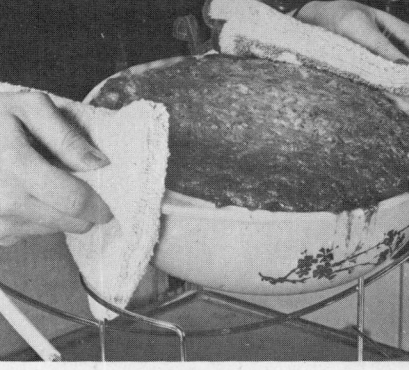

Corn Fondue: Baked fondue must be served immediately—like a soufflé—so plan to have the rest of the meal on the table when your fondue comes out of the oven.

CORN FONDUE

1 cup milk
2 cups cheese cracker crumbs, finely rolled, (about 54 round crackers)
2 cups shredded sharp Cheddar cheese
2 12-ounce cans whole kernel corn, drained
1/4 cup chopped green pepper
1 4-ounce jar pimientos, chopped
2 tablespoons chopped celery
1 tablespoon minced onion
1 teaspoon salt
1/2 teaspoon dry mustard
4 eggs, separated

Scald milk, add cracker crumbs, and next 8 ingredients.

Beat egg yolks; stir into crumb mixture. Beat egg whites. Fold into crumb mixture.

Pour into a buttered 1 1/2-quart baking dish. Bake in moderate oven (350°F.) 1 1/4 to 1 1/2 hours or until brown. Serve immediately. Serves 8.

CORN PATTIES (MOCK OYSTERS)

2 cups grated fresh corn
2 beaten eggs
1/2 cup cracker crumbs
1/2 cup sifted enriched flour
1/2 teaspoon baking powder
1 teaspoon salt
1/4 teaspoon pepper

Grate corn on coarse grater or cut tips from kernels with sharp knife and scrape cobs with dull edge of knife.

Add eggs, cracker crumbs, and flour sifted with baking powder. Add salt and pepper.

Drop from tablespoon into 1 inch of salad oil, hot enough to brown bread cube in 40 seconds. Turn once.

Makes 18 small patties.

STEWED FRESH CORN

Combine corn cut from cob with small amount milk or water. Cover and simmer until corn is just tender, 5 to 6 minutes. Season to taste with salt, pepper, and butter or margarine.

Chuck Wagon Corn Cakes

SCALLOPED CORN
(Master Recipe)

    4 tablespoons butter or margarine
    2 tablespoons flour
    1 cup liquid (use liquid drained
         from corn plus light cream or
         evaporated milk)
    1 teaspoon salt
    1/8 teaspoon pepper
    2 beaten eggs
    1 12-ounce can whole kernel corn,
         drained
    1 tablespoon chopped pimiento
    1/2 cup dry breadcrumbs
    Paprika

Melt 2 tablespoons butter. Blend in flour. Gradually add liquid and cook until thickened, stirring constantly. Season with salt and pepper.

Remove from heat and slowly add beaten eggs, stirring constantly. Mix in corn and pimiento. Turn into greased casserole.

Combine crumbs with 2 tablespoons melted butter and sprinkle over top. Add a sprinkling of paprika.

Set in shallow pan of water. Bake in moderate oven (350°F.) 45 to 50 minutes. Serves 4 to 5.

Scalloped Corn Variations

Scalloped Corn with Pork Sausage or Bacon: Omit butter in preparing sauce. Cook 1/2 pound pork sausage or 4 slices bacon in saucepan until browned and crisp. Blend in flour and continue as directed in master recipe.

Scalloped Corn with Clams: Add 1/2 cup drained, minced canned or fresh clams just before adding eggs in master recipe.

Scalloped Corn with Chipped Beef: Frizzle 1 cup dried beef (about 1 3- to 4-ounce jar) in the butter before blending in flour in master recipe. Decrease salt to 1/2 teaspoon.

Scalloped Corn with Ham: Add 1 small can deviled ham or 1/2 to 3/4 cup chopped cooked ground ham just before adding eggs in master recipe.

Scalloped Corn with Mushrooms: Lightly brown 1 cup chopped or sliced mushrooms in the butter before blending in flour in master recipe.

CHUCK WAGON CORN CAKES

    1/2 cup all-purpose flour, sifted
    2   teaspoons baking powder
    1/2 teaspoon salt
    1   cup cooked rice
    1   cup canned whole kernel corn,
          drained
    1   egg, beaten
    About 3 tablespoons milk

Sift together flour, baking powder, and salt. Stir in rice, corn, and egg. Mix thoroughly. Add enough milk to make a thin batter. Mix thoroughly.

Cook on hot griddle or in skillet in a liberal amount of cooking fat. Cook on both sides until golden brown. Makes 10 cakes.

CREOLE CORN

    1   onion, chopped
    2   tablespoons butter or margarine
    2 1/2 cups peeled, chopped tomatoes
    1   teaspoon sugar
    1   teaspoon salt
    1/4 teaspoon pepper
    2   cups corn cut from cob (about 6
          to 8 ears)
    1/2 medium green pepper, chopped

Fry onion in butter until tender and lightly browned. Add tomatoes, sugar, and seasonings; simmer 10 minutes.

Add corn and green pepper; simmer 5 minutes longer. Serves 6.

STEAMED CORN IN THE HUSK

Remove outer husks from corn; turn back inner husks and remove silk. Replace inner husks over cob and tie. Let stand in cold water in large, heavy kettle about 15 to 20 minutes.

Drain; cover and cook over medium heat until cover gets hot. Turn heat very low and continue cooking until corn is tender, about 15 minutes. Serve with butter or margarine and salt.

GRILLED CORN

Drain boiled corn-on-the-cob. Spread generously with butter or margarine. Place on rack in preheated broiler oven. Use high flame, turning ears to brown. Sprinkle with salt.

SQUAW CORN

    3 slices bacon, diced
    1 No. 2 can corn
    1/2 teaspoon salt
    Dash of pepper
    3 slightly beaten eggs
    6 buttered toast rounds

Pan-broil bacon until crisp, add corn and heat thoroughly.

Add seasonings to eggs and pour over corn. Cook slowly, stirring occasionally until eggs are cooked. Serve on toast. Serves 6.

CUCUMBERS

Selection: A good guide in buying cucumbers is to remember that those which are firm, fresh, and bright green are best. The shade of color is important, as the older ones tend to be of a rather deep black-green or sometimes yellow. Poor quality is also indicated by an outside rind that has a decided "give" to it when slight pressure is applied.

Note: Some of the cucumbers now on the market have a shiny, waxy finish applied to them before shipment. Never use skin that has been waxed. If not waxed the cucumber skin is edible.

Preparation: Pare thinly and cut into thick slices.

Cooking Time: 10 to 15 minutes.

Cooking: Cook, covered, in a small amount of boiling salted water until tender, from 10 to 15 minutes.

Serving: Season with melted butter or margarine and pepper. Serve hot.

To Serve Raw: Do not pare if skins are tender. Slice, cover with vinegar and season with salt, pepper, and finely sliced onion or see recipes and serving suggestions in appetizers and salads.

FRIED (SAUTÉED) CUCUMBERS

Pare and cut in slices at least 1/4 inch thick. Dry on paper towels. Sprinkle with salt, pepper, and flour.

Brown in butter or margarine, or dip in crumbs, then in slightly beaten egg, and again in crumbs and fry in deep hot fat (385°F.). Drain on paper towels.

BAKED STUFFED CUCUMBERS

    4 large cucumbers
    2 tablespoons chopped onion
    2 tablespoons chopped parsley
    4 tablespoons butter or margarine
    1 cup breadcrumbs
    1 cup tomato pulp
    1 teaspoon salt
    Pepper

Wash and pare cucumbers if the skin is tough. Cut in half lengthwise. Scoop out as much of seed portion as possible without breaking the fleshy part.

Parboil cucumber shells in lightly salted water 10 minutes. Drain.

Meanwhile cook onion and parsley in fat. Add other ingredients and cucumber pulp. Cook this mixture 5 minutes.

Fill cucumber shells with hot stuffing. Place in shallow baking dish. Add a little water to keep them from sticking.

Bake in moderate oven (350°F.) 15 minutes. or until stuffing has browned on top Serve in baking dish.

Serves 4 to 6.

DANDELION

When used as a food, dandelions usually are served as a salad green. However, cooked dandelion greens are an excellent source of vitamin A, a half cup supplying more than enough of this element to meet the normal daily requirements.

Good quality is characterized by a fresh green appearance and comparatively large, tender leaves. See **Greens**.

DASHEENS

The dasheen or, if you prefer to call it by its true name, taro, is raised and used mostly in the southern states. This tuber vegetable is somewhat similar to the potato in food properties, appearance, and culinary uses except that it cannot be mashed.

The flesh of cooked dasheens ranges from purple or violet to a cream shade. The deep violet-colored "corms" as the tubers are called, are regarded as having a better flavor than the light or cream-colored ones.

Preparation: Do not pare before cooking. Scrub well with a brush. Cover with boiling salted water and cook until tender, 20 to 40 minutes.

The dasheen is somewhat drier than potatoes, therefore lots of butter should be used or more liquid than with potatoes if dasheens are substituted in potato recipes.

They may be baked; however, they should be parboiled for 15 minutes before baking and the skin should be rubbed with oil or melted butter.

EGGPLANT

Native to the tropics, but widely grown in the United States and Europe, the eggplant has a white or purple color, depending on the variety. The white is more prevalent in Europe, while the purple is more common in this country and is usually obtainable throughout the year.

Selection: Purple eggplant should be of a clear, dark glossy color that covers the entire surface. Heaviness and firmness of flesh are also important. Watch the size of eggplants you buy. A good rule to follow is to choose pear-shaped eggplants from 3 to 6 inches in diameter. Buy one medium eggplant (about 1½ pounds) for 4 servings.

Preparation: It is not necessary to peel eggplant unless the skin is tough. Do not soak in salt or in salt water before cooking. Wash well.

BROILED EGGPLANT

Cut eggplant into ½- to ¾-inch slices. Brush with melted butter or margarine or bacon drippings.

Place about 2½ inches from tip of flame or electric element. Broil about 5 minutes, or until brown. Turn and brown other side.

Season and serve hot. Serve with broiled meats.

SCALLOPED EGGPLANT

1   medium eggplant
4   tablespoons butter or margarine
2   tablespoons chopped green pepper
2   tablespoons chopped onion
2   cups cooked or canned tomatoes
1   teaspoon salt
Pepper to taste
¾ cup bread cubes

Pare eggplant if necessary and cut into small even pieces.

Brown green pepper and onion in 2 tablespoons butter in fry pan.

Add tomatoes, salt, pepper, and eggplant; simmer 10 minutes. Pour into greased baking dish.

Melt rest of butter and mix with bread cubes. Spread over top of eggplant mixture.

Bake in moderate oven (350°F.) 20 minutes, or until eggplant is tender and bread cubes are brown. Serves 4.

EGGPLANT AU GRATIN

1   large eggplant
2   eggs, slightly beaten
About 1⅔ cups cracker crumbs, (finely rolled)
½ cup olive oil or salad oil
2   8-ounce cans tomato sauce
1   clove garlic, chopped
1   tablespoon minced parsley
¼ teaspoon basil
1   teaspoon oregano
1   6-ounce package Mozzarella cheese

Pare eggplant, cut crosswise, making ¼-inch slices. Dip slices in egg, then into crumbs (about 1 cup). Sauté in oil until golden brown. Drain well.

Combine tomato sauce, remaining crumbs, and next 4 ingredients. Simmer gently 20 minutes, stirring frequently.

Alternate slices of eggplant, sauce, and slices of cheese in a 1-quart baking dish. Bake in moderate oven (350°F) 30 minutes. Serves 4 to 6.

STUFFED EGGPLANT

2   small eggplants, cut in half
¼ cup diced green pepper
¼ cup diced onion
¼ cup diced celery
1   tablespoon salad oil
1   can condensed tomato soup
1   cup cooked rice
½ teaspoon salt
Dash of pepper
Dash of thyme
18   cheese crackers, finely rolled
       (about 1½ cups crumbs)
Butter or margarine

Simmer eggplants in salted boiling water until almost tender, about 10 minutes.

Sauté green pepper, onion, and celery in oil until golden brown. Combine with tomato soup, rice, salt, pepper, and thyme.

Scoop out center of eggplant; leave ½-inch layer of pulp around edges. (Save pulp scooped out of eggplant and add to spaghetti sauce another day.)

Sprinkle 2 tablespoons cheese cracker crumbs over bottom of each shell. Fill with rice mixture. Spread remaining crumbs over top; dot with butter or margarine.

Bake in moderate oven (375°F.) 30 minutes. Serves 4.

PAN-FRIED (SAUTÉED) EGGPLANT

Cut eggplant ino ½- or 1-inch slices. Peel if necessary.

Dip in flour, or dip in fine dry breadcrumbs, then in an egg beaten with 2 tablespoons of milk, then dip in flour or crumbs again.

Season and fry slowly in a small amount of hot fat until browned on one side and rather transparent looking. Turn and brown on other side. Serve hot.

BAKED EGGPLANT

Marinate sliced eggplant in French dressing for 15 minutes. Drain or spread with softened butter.

Bake in hot oven (400°F.) until tender, about 15 minutes, turning once. Sprinkle with lemon juice.

Eggplant au Gratin

FRENCH FRIED EGGPLANT

Pare eggplant if necessary and cut in ¼-inch slices crosswise.

Sprinkle with salt and pepper and dip in flour. Dip in egg which has been beaten with 2 tablespoons of milk. Roll in fine, dry breadcrumbs until completely covered.

Fry in hot deep fat from 2 to 4 minutes, or until golden brown.

Drain. Season with salt and pepper. Serve hot.

EGGPLANT CASSEROLE
(Italian Style)

1 eggplant
1 well beaten egg
⅓ cup milk
½ teaspoon salt
½ pound Mozzarella cheese, sliced
3 tomatoes, sliced
Oregano, salt, pepper
1 tablespoon olive oil

Wash eggplant thoroughly, then slice ¼ inch thick without paring.

Dip slices into batter made by blending egg, milk, and salt. Brown in skillet in which 2 tablespoons drippings or fat have been heated.

Place several slices of fried eggplant in bottom of casserole.

Place thin slices of cheese and tomato on top of eggplant. Sprinkle with oregano, using about ½ teaspoon per layer. Season with salt and pepper.

Repeat procedure until eggplant is used. Pour olive oil on top of last layer of cheese.

Cover and bake in moderate oven (350°F.) about 30 minutes, removing cover for last 10 minutes of cooking.

If desired, a garlic flavoring can be given by adding minced clove of garlic to the melted drippings in which eggplant slices are browned. Serves 6.

ENDIVE, ESCAROLE, CHICORY

Considerable confusion in using three terms has resulted throughout the country because of local misinterpretations of the exact vegetable to which they apply. For instance, endive is called escarole or chicory in some localities; chicory is misnamed endive, and so on. However, the descriptions given here should facilitate your identification of each of these leafy greens.

Curly endive grows in a bunchy head, with narrow, ragged-edge leaves which curl at the ends. The center of the head is a yellowish white and has a milder taste than the darker green outer leaves which tend to be slightly bitter. If this center is not so white as desired when the endive is purchased, it can be further bleached by covering overnight with a damp cloth.

There is another variety of endive with broad leaves (Batavian endive) that do not curl at the tips. It is the type which is almost universally marketed as escarole.

Witloof chicory is a rather tightly folded plant that grows upright in a thin, elongated stalk with creamy-white, smooth tapering leaves 1 to 2 inches wide, rather than flat or bushy like endive or escarole. This vegetable is usually bleached a decided white while growing and is known far more commonly as French or Belgian endive than by its true botanical name. Although it is imported from Europe in fairly large quantities, much of the supply used in the United States is grown here.

It should be noted the same confusion about names prevails abroad; the French, the Belgians, and the British each have their own ideas.

BRAISED FRENCH ENDIVE

1 pound endive
¼ to ½ teaspoon salt
1 tablespoon lemon juice
2 tablespoons butter or margarine
⅓ cup water

Wash heads of endive and drain. Arrange in single layer in a saucepan or skillet with tight-fitting cover.

Sprinkle with salt, lemon juice, and bits of butter. Add water.

Cover and boil until tender, 30 minutes or longer, adding water if necessary to prevent sticking. Remove to hot platter.

Boil juice in pan, uncovered, until reduced to about 3 tablespoons. Add ½ to 1 tablespoon additional butter and pour over endive. Serves 4 to 6.

Endive Mornay: Braise endive as above and place on a heat-proof platter. Cover with easy Mornay sauce (below). Sprinkle with crumbs and broil until bubbly and lightly browned.

Mornay Sauce: Season 1 cup white sauce to taste with onion, chopped parsley, and nutmeg. Add 1 egg yolk, ¼ cup grated Parmesan or Gruyere cheese, and 1 tablespoon butter or margarine.

Cook, stirring, until thickened. Fold in 1 tablespoon whipped cream, if desired.

BELGIAN OR FRENCH ENDIVE WITH LEMON-EGG SAUCE

4 large (or 8 small) heads Belgian or French Endive
1 cup chicken bouillon
2 eggs, separated
¼ cup lemon juice

When large heads of endive are used, cut in half lengthwise, beginning at the root end. Arrange endive carefully in a large heavy skillet, cut side up. Add bouillon; cover, bring to a boil and simmer gently until tender and transparent, but not overcooked, 10 to 15 minutes.

Meanwhile with a rotary beater, beat egg whites until frothy but not stiff; add egg yolks and continue beating until blended. Then add lemon juice gradually, and beat until thick and smooth.

When endive is done remove it to a deep preheated vegetable dish.

Measure hot bouillon and add enough boiling water to make ¾ of a cup. Pour hot liquid gradually into the egg mixture, then return to pan and cook over very low heat, stirring gently until thickened (or heat in double boiler). Pour sauce over endive and serve garnished with sprigs of parsley or watercress. Serves 4.

FENNEL OR FINOCCHIO
See **Anise.**

FIDDLEHEADS

The fiddlehead is a fern that grows wild in northern Maine, where it has been used as food for many years.

Selection: Fiddleheads are so named because the tops are curled like the head of a violin. They are picked before they begin to uncurl and are eaten or preserved as soon as possible after picking, usually within 2 days. Canned fiddleheads are available in fine grocery stores. The flavor of young fiddleheads resembles a cross between asparagus and mushrooms. Allow 1 pound to serve 3.

Preparation: Wash thoroughly and drain. Cook, covered, in small amount lightly salted boiling water until tender, 15 to 20 minutes. Drain and season with salt, pepper, and melted butter or margarine.

Serving: Serve on toast. To serve in a salad, chill the drained cooked greens, combine with sliced onion, and season with a liberal amount of olive oil lemon juice, and salt.

Endive with Lemon-Egg Sauce

GREENS

Use young tender beet tops; carrot tops—add to other greens; collards; kale; mustard greens; outer leaves of chicory and escarole; outer leaves of lettuce; radish tops—add to other greens; Swiss chard; turnip tops, and dandelion greens.

Selection: Buy 2 pounds of greens for 4 servings. Select greens which are fresh, crisp, tender and have a good bright fresh color.

Preparation: Same as for Spinach (which see).

Cooking Time: 5 to 25 minutes, depending on variety.

Cooking: Follow directions for cooking spinach. Allow 5 to 15 minutes for beet tops; 15 to 20 minutes for chicory, escarole, lettuce, Swiss chard, or mustard greens; 10 to 15 minutes for collards, and 15 to 25 minutes for turnip tops and kale.

Serving: Season with salt, pepper, and butter or margarine. Small pieces of bacon may be crisped and served mixed with greens.

GREENS WITH BACON DRESSING

1½ to 2 pounds greens (dandelion, young beet, mustard, Swiss chard, spinach, escarole, or a mixture of these)
¼ cup green onions, minced
4 slices bacon
2 tablespoons vinegar
½ teaspoon dry mustard
1½ teaspoons sugar
Salt and pepper
2 hard-cooked eggs, sliced

Pick over greens, removing any tough stems. Wash thoroughly, lifting them from one water to another until no sand remains.

Cook in small amount salted water until tender and drain well.

Chop if leaves are large. Add green onions.

Cook bacon until crisp. Remove and set aside. To fat in pan, add vinegar, mustard, sugar, and salt and pepper to taste.

Add to hot vegetables. Turn into serving dish. Garnish with egg slices and reserved bacon, crumbled. Serves 4.

KALE

Kale (or Borecole) is a large, hardy, curly leafed green of the cabbage family, inexpensive and usually abundant throughout the winter. Dark green kale is best but a few leaves with slightly browned edges are not objectionable, as they can readily be trimmed.

Cut off the root and wash thoroughly. Remove heavy stems from leaves. For 1 pound kale, add 1 cup water and ½ teaspoon salt. Cover and cook 15 to 20 minutes.

Drain, chop, and add 2 tablespoons butter or margarine.

Or add lemon juice and butter or margarine to the hot cooked kale. Mix. Sprinkle the top with chopped hard-cooked egg.

CREAMED KALE

Cook 1 pound kale. Add ¾ cup medium white sauce to drained, chopped kale instead of butter or margarine.

KALE—COUNTRY STYLE

Cook 1 package frozen kale as label directs. Drain and chop. Put back in saucepan.

Add 3 tablespoons bacon fat and 1 tablespoon pickle relish. Heat well and season to taste. Serves 3.

Variations: Other greens or green beans may be prepared in the same way.

KOHLRABI

Kohlrabi is a vegetable of the cabbage family with a turnip-like thickened bulb or root. It should be young, small, and tender, as the large overgrown specimens are tough and woody. The young tender leaves are eaten as greens.

Selection: Allow 1 medium-sized kohlrabi per person. Look for small or medium-sized kohlrabi with fresh tops.

Preparation: Remove leaves. Pare and cut into cubes or slices.

Cooking Time: 25 minutes.

Cooking: Cook, covered, in a small amount of boiling salted water until tender, about 25 minutes.

Serving: Serve hot seasoned with pepper and melted butter or margarine or with white sauce.

Kohlrabi may be diced, cooked, and served with boiled chestnuts or with broiled mushrooms. A topping of grated nuts offers a unique and delicious touch to a dish of kohlrabi.

MASHED KOHLRABI

Mash the cooked bulbs; season with salt, pepper, and butter or margarine.

KOHLRABI PATTIES

Mash the cooked bulbs; season with salt and pepper. Form into small patties; dip in seasoned flour and fry in butter or margarine.

SCALLOPED KOHLRABI

Follow master recipe for Scalloped Vegetables.

LEEKS

This member of the onion family has a mild onion flavor and, although highly acceptable when cooked alone, it is most often combined with other vegetables. Part of the green top, as well as the lower white section, is used.

Selection: Buy 2 bunches for 4 servings.

Preparation: Cut off green tops to within 2 inches of the white part. Wash.

Cooking Time: 15 minutes; in pressure saucepan, cook 2 or 3 minutes.

Cooking: Cook, covered, in boiling salted water until just tender, about 15 minutes.

Serving: Drain and serve hot, seasoned with pepper and melted butter or margarine.

CREAMED LEEKS

Follow master recipe for Creamed Vegetables.

LEEKS AU GRATIN

Arrange cooked stalks in baking dish. Season with salt and pepper. Sprinkle with grated cheese. Place under broiler to melt cheese.

LENTILS

The lentil is the dried seed of a plant of the pea family, round and flattish in shape and purplish green to red in color. Lentils have been used since biblical times. They are prepared and cooked like dried beans or peas and may be substituted for them in many dishes. One pound of lentils serves 6 to 8.

Cooking: Wash, drain, cover with water and soak overnight. Then drain, cover with water and simmer until tender, 20 to 30 minutes.

Serve with butter or margarine and lemon juice, or use in combination with other foods.

Savory Lentils: Add 1 or 2 slices of fat salt pork to the cooking lentils; lower the heat and simmer lentils slowly.

Remove pork before serving. Garnish the cooked lentils with chopped parsley.

Just a bit of effort makes the simplest vegetable plate an artistic thing of beauty.

LETTUCE

While there are several types of lettuce which are commercially important, the variety known as *Iceberg* is by far the most popular and widely known. Available the year round, Iceberg is tightly headed lettuce, medium green on the outside with a very pale green heart. When making your selection at the grocery, look for heads that are heavy for their size with leaves clean and free from burned or rusty-looking tips. Along with freshness of appearance, weight and solidity are the best indications of all-round good quality in lettuce.

Big Boston, sometimes called *"Butterhead,"* is another rather well-known variety of lettuce particularly in the east and south. This type forms heads somewhat softer and lighter than Iceberg and is not so crisp in texture. Boston lettuce is medium in size with light green outer leaves and light yellow leaves inside.

Romaine, or *cos*, has a green, elongated head of moderate firmness with a coarser leaf and stronger flavor than Iceberg lettuce. The long stiff leaves are usually medium dark to dark green on the outside and become greenish white near the center.

Leaf lettuce, as its name implies, grows with leaves loosely branching from its stalk and has a crisp texture preferred by many people. Hanson and New York are other types of head lettuce not so well known. Both these varieties are larger and a deeper green than Iceberg.

Bibb, also called *limestone*, is considered a special delicacy. The tiny Bibb has dark green leaves loosely held together; it is tender and delicious.

Corn salad, a lettuce-like vegetable, is also known as lamb's lettuce or fetticus. Its leaves are generally used in the fresh state but are also sometimes cooked as greens.

Although lettuce is usually regarded as a salad green or garnish—one of the most popular—it may be cooked in simple ways. The French often cook lettuce, mainly by braising.

BRAISED LETTUCE

- **3 small lettuce hearts or 1 large heart, quartered**
- **2 tablespoons butter or margarine**
- **Salt and pepper**
- **Pinch of nutmeg**
- **1 tablespoon lemon juice**

Soak lettuce in cold water 1 hour. Drain. Tie firmly with string. Cook in boiling salted water 10 minutes. Drain and cut off string.

Melt butter in heavy skillet; add lettuce, season and cook slowly 35 minutes. Pour lemon juice over lettuce. Serves 2 to 3.

MOREL

Morel is a member of the truffle family; this edible fungus is usually classed with the mushrooms since it grows above ground, whereas truffles grow underground.

MUSHROOMS

Many edible varieties of mushrooms are known, but the cultivated mushrooms on the market belong, almost entirely, to a single species. There is no need to worry about mushrooms packaged by reputable firms; however it's dangerous to collect wild mushrooms. There is no simple way to identify the edible types and some poisonous mushrooms so closely resemble edible types that they even fool the experts.

Selection: Buy 1 pound for 4 to 6 servings. Buy clean, firm, moist, white to creamy-white mushrooms which are free of spots.

Preparation: Clean by brushing well. Do not wash unless loam clings to them. If it's necessary to wash mushrooms, wash quickly; do not soak. Do not peel unless skin is tough and brown. If you have to peel, save the skin to make mushroom soup. Leave whole, or remove stems and chop fine, leaving caps whole.

Cooking Time: 8 to 10 minutes.

Cooking (Sautéed): Cook in a covered skillet in 1/4 cup butter or margarine for 8 to 10 minutes. Season with salt and pepper.

Serving: Serve as a hot vegetable, or combine with other freshly cooked hot vegetables—peas, snap beans, or green limas, etc.

CREAMED MUSHROOMS

Proceed as for sautéed mushrooms, blending in 2 teaspoons flour for each 1/2 pound mushrooms. Add 1 cup light cream when half done.

CREAMED CANNED MUSHROOMS

Use 2 cups canned mushrooms to 1 cup medium white sauce. Heat thoroughly. Serve very hot on toast.

BROILED MUSHROOMS

Clean mushrooms, removing stems. Chop stems and season with salt and pepper.

Place caps gill-side-down under moderate broiler 2 to 3 minutes. Turn and season with salt and pepper.

Fill hollows with chopped seasoned stems and dot with butter. Broil a few minutes longer.

Lift carefully from broiler so that juices are not lost. Serve on buttered toast.

DRIED MUSHROOMS— CHINESE STYLE

- **1/2 pound dried mushrooms**
- **3 cups cold water**
- **3 teaspoons soy sauce**
- **1 teaspoon salt**
- **2 teaspoons sugar (optional)**

Wash the mushrooms several times in cold water, then cover with boiling water and soak 15 minutes.

Drain; add cold water, soy sauce, salt, and sugar; bring to a boil and cook over high heat 10 minutes. Reduce heat and simmer 50 minutes. Refrigerate in covered jar for use in Chinese-style recipes.

MUSHROOM CROQUETTES

- **1/2 cup thick white sauce**
- **1/2 teaspoon Worcestershire sauce**
- **1/8 teaspoon curry powder**
- **1 slightly beaten egg**
- **2 tablespoons cracker crumbs**
- **1 cup chopped mushrooms**
- **1/2 teaspoon salt**
- **1/4 teaspoon paprika**

Prepare the thick white sauce. Remove from heat and add remaining ingredients.

Shape into croquettes and chill thoroughly.

Fry in deep hot fat (360°F.) until brown. Makes about 6.

MUSHROOMS AND ONIONS IN WINE SAUCE

- **1/2 pound fresh mushrooms, sliced**
- **1/2 pound small pearl onions, peeled**
- **1/4 cup butter or margarine**
- **2 tablespoons minced parsley**
- **1/4 teaspoon grated nutmeg**
- **2 tablespoons flour**
- **1 cup chicken broth or cube or canned bouillon**
- **1/4 cup Madeira or sherry**

Sauté mushrooms and onions in butter 5 minutes. Add parsley and nutmeg; cover and simmer 5 minutes.

Blend in flour until well mixed. Add broth and simmer, stirring 5 minutes.

Add wine. Heat and serve with steamed rice or on buttered toast. Serves 4.

Mushrooms and Onions in Wine Sauce

MUSHROOMS—DRIED

To give dried mushrooms the texture and flavor of fresh mushrooms, they should be soaked 2 to 12 hours. They can then be used just like fresh or canned mushrooms.

They may also be crushed and used dried as a flavoring; 1 tablespoon crushed dried mushrooms equals 1/3 cup fresh mushrooms in flavor. Add them to cooked dishes about 15 minutes before removing from the heat.

MUSHROOMS BAKED IN CREAM

Cut stems from cleaned large mushrooms. Place in shallow buttered baking dish, smooth side down.

Sprinkle with salt and pepper. Dot with butter. Pour a little cream or top milk around them.

Bake in very hot oven (450°F.) 10 minutes. Serve on dry toast, with cream remaining in pan poured over.

MUSHROOMS STUFFED WITH HAM

1 pound fresh mushrooms
1 cup ground ham
1/2 cup thick cream sauce
Breadcrumbs

Remove stems from washed mushrooms and put both cups and stems in a buttered baking pan in a hot oven for 5 minutes.

Chop the cooked stems with the ham; add the cream sauce and fill the mushroom cups.

Sprinkle the tops with breadcrumbs and return to the oven for 7 or 8 minutes.

MUSHROOMS STUFFED WITH CRABMEAT

Use 8 large mushrooms and 1/2 cup crabmeat. Combine crabmeat, 2 tablespoons cream, and seasonings.

Remove stems of mushrooms, wash and peel. Broil rounded-side up 5 minutes. Turn, fill each with crabmeat mixture.

Cover with cheese and crumbs. Broil again 5 minutes.

CHEESE-STUFFED MUSHROOMS

Fill cavities of fresh mushroom caps with small pieces of sharp Cheddar cheese. Dot with butter.

Broil slowly until cheese melts and mushrooms are cooked through. Spear each with a pick. Serve hot.

STUFFED MUSHROOM CAPS

1 can medium-sized mushroom caps
1/2 cup cooked pork sausage meat
2 tablespoons burgundy wine
Dash of red pepper

Scoop out center of mushrooms; fill with a mixture of sausage meat, wine, and pepper.

Place under broiler until tender. Spear with picks to serve hot.

NETTLES

Nettles is the common name for a family of plants and shrubs. Some of them provide edible greens which in Europe are cooked like spinach and considered nourishing and tasty. A soup is sometimes prepared from young nettle greens.

OKRA

Okra are the sticky green pods of a tall, originally African plant. Okra is used chiefly in soups and stews. Known in the United States as a southern favorite, it is also widely eaten in the Near East. It is indispensable to a gumbo (see index) and is often called by this name. It may also be cooked as a vegetable.

Selection: Buy 1 pound for 4 servings. Buy young, tender, clean pods which snap easily. Choose small- to medium-sized pods, from 2 to 4 inches in length.

Preparation: Wash well and cut off stems. Leave small pods whole and cut large pods into 1/2-inch slices.

Cooking Time: 10 minutes.

Cooking: Cook, covered, in a small amount of boiling salted water until just tender, about 10 minutes.

Serving: Season with pepper, a dash of vinegar, and melted butter or margarine. Serve hot.

FRIED (SAUTÉED) OKRA

Wash and dry okra thoroughly before cutting into 1/2-inch pieces.

Heat 3 or 4 tablespoons fat in heavy skillet. Add okra, cover and cook 10 minutes, stirring frequently to prevent burning.

Remove cover and cook until tender and lightly browned. Serve at once.

STEWED OKRA AND TOMATOES

2 tablespoons bacon drippings or other fat
1 small onion, chopped
2 cups sliced okra
2 cups cooked or canned tomatoes
1/2 teaspoon salt
Pepper

Melt fat in fry pan. Brown onion and okra slightly, stirring as it cooks.

Add tomatoes and salt. Cook over moderate heat until vegetables are tender and mixture is thick, about 20 minutes. Stir occasionally to prevent sticking.

Season with pepper and more salt if needed. Serves 4.

Variation: Add 3 tablespoons rice with the tomatoes. Cook until rice is tender, 20 to 30 minutes. Add a little water if needed.

ONIONS—DRY

There are several different varieties of dry onion of which the domestic is probably the most common in the United States. This variety is medium size, globular in shape and may be either red, yellow, or white. The Bermuda is a flat type onion, yellow or white in color, and milder in flavor than the domestic variety. Sweet Spanish onions or "Valencias," as they are sometimes called, are another mild variety, globe shaped and considerably larger than either the domestic or Bermuda. They may be either white or yellowish brown.

Onions of any of the above varieties are often called "boilers" when they range from 1 to 1 1/2 inches in diameter. Any which are still smaller than that are termed "picklers."

Selection: When selecting dry onions, look for those that are well shaped and dry enough to crackle. Thin necks and bright hard bulbs are two other indications of quality. Avoid those with a wet, soggy feeling at the neck, as this is usually, although not invariably, a sign that decay is starting, if not already present.

Selection: Buy 1 1/2 pounds for 4 servings. Buy bright, clean, hard, well shaped onions with dry skins.

Preparation: Peel. To avoid weeping when peeling onions, pour boiling water over them, rinse in cold water, and then slip off skins. Leave whole for boiling.

Cooking Time: 15 to 35 minutes.

Cooking: Drop peeled onions into several inches of boiling salted water. Boil small onions 15 to 20 minutes and large ones 30 to 35 minutes, or add to other vegetables while they are cooking.

Serving: Drain. Serve hot seasoned with salt, pepper, and butter or margarine, or with medium white sauce.

Creamed onions will have a new appeal to the family when you add a few sautéed mushrooms and a different seasoning to the medium white sauce before combining with the boiled onions.

Onion Cheese Squares

ONION CHEESE SQUARES

4   tablespoons butter
3   cups thinly sliced onion
4   eggs, slightly beaten
3   cups scalded milk
1   teaspoon salt
1/2   teaspoon celery salt
1/4   teaspoon paprika
1 1/2   cups grated American cheese
1/2   cup slivered pimiento
1 1/2   cups dry breadcrumbs
1/4   cup minced parsley

Melt butter, add onion and cook over low heat until tender.

Beat eggs slightly and gradually add hot milk, while stirring. Add onions and remaining ingredients and blend.

Turn mixture into a buttered utility pan, 6 x 10 x 2 inches and bake in a slow oven (325°F.), over hot water 50 to 60 minutes. Cut into squares. Serves 6 to 8.

STUFFED ONIONS

6   large onions
1/2   green pepper, chopped
1/2   pound mushrooms or 1 cup cooked
          meat, poultry, fish or shellfish
4   tablespoons butter or margarine
1   cup cooked rice, soft breadcrumbs,
          or mashed potatoes
Salt, pepper, and any other seasoning
          desired (soy sauce, curry pow-
          der)
1/4   cup sifted breadcrumbs or grated
          Parmesan cheese

Peel onions without cutting off root end (in order to keep them whole) and boil in salted water until almost tender. Drain, cut a slice from top of each and remove centers, leaving a rim of 3 or 4 layers of onion. Chop slices and centers.

While onions are boiling, lightly sauté the pepper and mushrooms (or a substitute) in 2 tablespoons butter.

Add rice (or alternative), seasonings, and chopped onion. Fill onion shells.

Sprinkle tops with sifted crumbs or cheese and dot with bits of remaining butter.

Place in a pan that has a film of water over the bottom and bake in a moderate oven (375°F.) until tops are brown, about 15 minutes. Serves 6.

SAUTÉED OR SMOTHERED ONIONS

1 1/2   pounds large sweet onions or
          small boilers
3   tablespoons butter or margarine
Salt
Freshly ground pepper

Peel large onions and cut into wedges or thick slices. The small boilers are easy and almost odorless to peel if they are first boiled about 1 minute and then drained and rinsed with cold water. Leave the onions whole if they are even in size.

Melt fat in a saucepan with a tight-fitting cover or in a pressure saucepan. Add onions and salt and pepper to taste.

Cover and cook until onions are tender, about 20 minutes, adding a bit of water and stirring onions once if closure is loose and steam escapes.

In the pressure saucepan, cook at 15-pound pressure about 3 minutes. Reduce pressure quickly.

If desired, serve sprinkled with minced parsley or paprika.

Serves 3 to 4.

Smothered Mixed Vegetables: Substitute green beans, celery, carrots, or other vegetables for part of the onions in above recipe.

OLIVE-ONION PIE

1   cup ripe olives
2 1/2   cups thinly sliced onions
2   tablespoons butter or margarine
2   eggs
1   cup thick sour cream
1   teaspoon salt
1/8   teaspoon black pepper
Pastry for single crust 9-inch pie
Paprika

Cut olives from pits into large pieces. Cook onions slowly in butter in covered pan 5 to 10 minutes, until transparent.

Beat eggs, add sour cream, salt, and pepper, and beat again. Stir in onions and olives, and turn into pastry-lined pie pan. Sprinkle with paprika.

Bake in hot oven (425°F.) 10 minutes. Reduce heat to moderate (350°F.) about 25 to 30 minutes longer, or until set in center. Serve hot. Serves 6 to 8.

FRENCH FRIED ONION RINGS

2   pounds large Bermuda onions
2/3   cup milk
1/2   cup flour
Shortening for deep frying

Cut cleaned onions into 1/4-inch slices and separate into rings. Dip onion rings in milk and then in seasoned flour.

Fry in deep hot fat (365°F.), or when an inch cube of bread browns in 60 seconds. Fry onion rings, a few at a time, until well browned (about 3 minutes). Drain on absorbent paper.

Serves 4 to 5.

SCALLOPED ONIONS

Put 2 cups cooked onions (quartered) in buttered baking dish. Cover with 1 cup medium white sauce.

Sprinkle with buttered cracker crumbs. Bake in hot oven (400°F.) until crumbs are brown.

If desired, sprinkle with grated cheese before adding white sauce.

ONIONS BAKED IN CREAM

Cut large sweet onions in thin slices. Arrange in baking dish. Sprinkle with salt and pepper. Pour over cream to cover.

Bake in slow oven (325°F.) until tender.

BROILED ONIONS

Slice large mild onions 1/2 inch thick. Put in shallow buttered pan. Season with salt and pepper. Dot with butter.

Broil until tender (about 15 minutes), turning once with spatula.

GREEN ONIONS (SCALLIONS)

A young green onion that has not developed a bulb.

Selection: Buy 2 bunches for 4 servings (cooked). Green onions are marketed in bunches. Buy onions with crisp, green tops and with medium-sized, well-formed necks well blanched 2 or 3 inches from the root.

Preparation: Wash well and remove any loose layers of skin.

Cooking Time: 8 to 10 minutes.

Cooking: Cook in a small amount of boiling salted water until barely tender, 8 to 10 minutes, or chop and cook with other vegetables.

Serving: Carefully remove from water and serve hot seasoned with freshly ground pepper and melted butter or margarine.

To Serve Raw: Trim tops, remove any loose skin and wash well. Serve whole and crisp on relish plate. Use chopped or cut fine in salads.

French Fried Onion Rings

HEART OF PALM

Heart of palm is a very delicate vegetable from the tender center head of the cabbage palmetto tree. It is available in cans and is used chiefly in salads.

PARSNIPS

Parsnips are one of the hardiest vegetables on the market and hold up well under either warm or quite cold temperatures. However, many authorities state that the parsnip's flavor is not really brought out until it has been stored for some time at a temperature close to 32°F.

Selection: Buy 1½ pounds for 4 servings (2 per person). Buy smooth, firm, well-shaped parsnips, small to medium in size.

Preparation: Scrape or peel. Leave whole or cut into halves, quarters, or slices.

Cooking Time: 30 minutes.

Cooking: Cook, covered, in a small amount of boiling salted water until tender, about 30 minutes.

Serving: Season with salt, pepper, and melted butter or margarine and serve hot with a sprinkling of minced parsley.

MASHED PARSNIPS

Mash boiled parsnips or press through ricer. For 3 or 4 cups parsnips add ½ cup hot milk, 3 to 4 tablespoons butter or margarine, salt and pepper to taste. Beat until fluffy.

PARSNIP PATTIES

Mash cooked parsnips. Season with butter or margarine, salt, and pepper.

Shape in small, flat, rounded cakes. Roll in flour. Sauté in butter.

FRENCH FRIED PARSNIPS

Cut raw parsnips into very thin slices. Fry in deep hot fat (380°F.) until delicately brown. 7 to 8 minutes.

PARSNIP SOUFFLÉ

Follow master recipe for Vegetable Soufflé.

Carrot and Parsnip duo: Colorful carrots are intermingled with parsnips, generously coated with butter, sprinkled with parsley and chives and flavor-treated with seasoned salt.

SAUTEED (FRIED) PARSNIPS

Use young boiled parsnips, cut in sixths, lengthwise. Brown lightly in butter or margarine. Season with salt and pepper.

To Candy: Sprinkle with brown sugar, then sauté.

PARSNIP CARAMEL

Scrape parsnips. Cook 20 minutes and drain.

Arrange in shallow baking dish. Sprinkle with brown sugar. Bake in hot oven (400°F.) 20 minutes.

PARSNIP FRITTERS

Cut cooked parsnips in 3-inch pieces. Dip in fritter cover batter.

Fry in deep hot fat (385°F.) until browned.

GLAZED PARSNIPS

Cook 12 medium-sized parsnips until nearly tender. Heat 2 tablespoons butter or margarine, ⅓ cup sugar, and 1 tablespoon water in skillet. Add parsnips and cook until glazed and golden brown. Serves 6.

PARSNIPS BAKED WITH BACON

Cook 12 parsnips. Place in buttered casserole. Sprinkle with salt, pepper, and 1 tablespoon sugar. Cover with 6 strips bacon.

Bake in moderate oven (375°F.) until bacon is crisp and parsnips are heated through. Garnish with parsley. Serves 6.

GREEN PEAS

Selection: Buy 3 pounds for 4 servings. Look for bright green, fresh-looking pods somewhat velvety to the touch.

Preparation: Prepare and serve peas as soon as possible after marketing. Shell and wash just before cooking. Reserve a few pods to cook with the peas.

Cooking Time: 8 to 12 minutes.

Cooking: Cook peas, covered, in 1 inch boiling salted water for 8 to 12 minutes. Drop in a few of the pods for flavor.

Serving: Remove the pods. Season with pepper and with butter or margarine. Try adding a sprinkling of chopped fresh mint leaves for variety. Serve at once while the color is bright and the flavor is fresh and sweet.

MINTED PEAS

Add sprigs of mint to boiling water with peas. When cooked, remove mint. Drain and season with salt and butter.

PURÉE OF GREEN PEAS

Put cooked or canned peas through strainer or vegetable mill.

Beat until light and smooth with hot milk or cream. Season to taste. Keep hot in double boiler. Dust with paprika before serving.

Curried peas and eggs: Canned or frozen green peas and quartered hard-cooked eggs in a rich cream sauce makes a pretty but simple luncheon or supper treat. Add a bit of curry powder to the sauce. Serve with a basket of toasted buns.

MUSHROOM BUTTERED PEAS AND ONIONS

Cook 12 small pearl onions and 1½ cups peas separately in boiling salted water. Drain.

Melt ¼ cup butter over low heat. Add ⅓ cup cooked, diced mushrooms and 1 teaspoon grated onion. Cook slowly until mushrooms are lightly browned.

Combine peas and onions in bowl and pour sauce over. Serves 6.

SAVORY PEAS AND CARROTS

Cook 1 package frozen peas and carrots as label directs.

Cook 1 small minced onion in 3 tablespoons butter or margarine until yellowed. Add ½ cup chopped stuffed olives.

Drain vegetables and add onion mixture. Season with salt and pepper to taste. Serves 3 to 4.

PEAS AND NOODLES SUPREME

1 8-ounce package noodles
2 cups seasoned medium white sauce
1 No. 2 can (2½ cups) peas

Cook noodles in boiling salted water until tender. Drain and blanch with boiling water.

Combine cooked noodles and white sauce. Heat. Place in individual baking shells or casseroles. Top with heated, seasoned peas. Serves 5 to 6.

Variations: ½ cup grated cheese and/or ½ cup sautéed mushrooms may be added to the sauce.

Peas and Noodles Supreme

CREAMED PEAS

Follow master recipe for Creamed Vegetables.

FROZEN PEAS—FRENCH STYLE

Put ¼ cup boiling water, ½ teaspoon each of salt and sugar, and 1 package frozen peas in saucepan. Add 1 small peeled onion, 1 sprig parsley, and 1 or 2 lettuce leaves.

Bring to boil, breaking up peas with fork. Cook slowly about 8 minutes, or until peas are tender.

Remove onion, parsley, and lettuce before serving. Serves 3.

SNOW PEAS

Snow peas, also called podded peas, sugar peas, and Chinese peas, are often used as an ingredient in various Chinese style recipes. They can usually be found only in Chinese shops. To prepare them, wash, cut off the ends and string, and cook in the same way as green beans just until crisply tender.

BOILED DRIED PEAS

Soak dried peas 6 hours or longer in cold water.

Drain and simmer in salted water until tender, about ½ hour.

Dried peas may be substituted in practically all recipes calling for dried beans, although molasses is omitted in baked dried peas. Dried peas need salt to bring out their flavor.

PURÉE OF SPLIT PEAS

1½ cups dried peas
Water to cover
Ham bone or ½ pound salt pork
1 large onion, quartered
1 stalk celery, quartered
2 tablespoons butter or margarine

Wash peas; soak overnight in water to cover.

Drain and add to ham bone or pork in a large kettle. Add water to cover. Add onion and celery. Simmer until peas are tender.

Force through a strainer. Serve purée with melted butter or margarine whipped into it. Serves 4.

HOPPING JOHN
(Carolina Peas and Rice)

Hopping john is a southern dish of dried cowpeas (sometimes dried black-eyed peas or crowder peas), salt pork, rice, and bacon drippings; believed to be native to South Carolina.

2 cups cowpeas, soaked overnight
¼ pound salt pork or other seasoning meat
1 cup uncooked rice
3 tablespoons bacon drippings

Boil the peas with salt pork until tender, 1½ to 2 hours, or 30 minutes in a pressure cooker.

Add the peas and 3 cups of the water in which they were cooked to rice and drippings. Cook over slow heat for 1 hour. Serves 6.
Note: Dried black-eyed peas or crowder peas may be used in above.

BOILED BLACK-EYED PEAS

1 pound dried black-eyed peas
½ pound salt pork, cut into cubes
4 cups boiling water
1 teaspoon salt

Cover peas with cold water and soak overnight.

Drain peas; add salt pork, boiling water, and salt. Simmer for 2 hours, or until peas are done.

Serve with some of the "pot likker" in which the peas were cooked. Serves 6.

PEPPERS

Peppers, which are believed to have originated in South America, are available on the market the year round. The Big Bell or Sweet Pepper is the most popular variety and may be bought either green or red, according to the stage of maturity desired. Best quality peppers are well shaped, thick walled, and firm, with a uniform glossy color. Pale color and soft seeds are signs of immaturity, while sunken, blister-like spots on the surface indicate that decay may set in rather quickly.

Chili, Pimiento, and Cayenne are varieties of hot peppers which are often dried and sold in strings.

FRIED GREEN PEPPERS

Remove seeds from 6 large green peppers, and cut in eighths. Cover with boiling water. Cover and cook 3 minutes; drain.

Fry peppers slowly in ¼ cup hot drippings until lightly browned. Season to taste with salt and pepper. Serves 4.

TO PREPARE PEPPERS FOR STUFFING

Cut off stem ends of peppers. If very large, cut into half lengthwise. Remove seeds and inner white ribs.

Parboil by dropping into boiling water. Remove from heat and let stand in the water about 5 minutes.

Drain well, stuff with desired filling, and bake as directed.

MEAT AND RICE STUFFED PEPPERS

1 cup cooked rice
2 cups chopped cooked meat
1 tablespoon minced onion
1 beaten egg
Salt and pepper
6 green peppers
Crumbs

Combine and mix rice, meat, onion, and egg. Season to taste.

Stuff prepared peppers. Cover with crumbs and dot with fat.

Place upright in baking dish. Surround peppers with water or stock about ¼ inch in depth.

Bake until peppers are tender and tops browned, 30 to 40 minutes.

Serves 6.

Variation: Substitute 1 cup canned or cooked corn for 1 cup meat.

SALMON STUFFED PEPPERS

6 green peppers
1 1-pound can salmon
1 onion, grated
¾ cup soft breadcrumbs
¾ cup milk
1 teaspoon salt
1 beaten egg
2 teaspoons lemon juice
Buttered crumbs

Combine all ingredients. Mix well. Stuff prepared peppers. Top with buttered breadcrumbs.

Bake in moderate oven (375°F.) until just tender, 15 to 20 minutes. Do not allow peppers to brown. Serves 6.

CORNED BEEF HASH STUFFED PEPPERS

4 large or 6 small green peppers
1 1-pound can corned beef hash
¼ cup chopped onion
3 tablespoons sweet pickle relish
2 tablespoons vinegar
½ cup chili sauce
1 tablespoon brown sugar
1 teaspoon prepared mustard
⅛ teaspoon Tabasco sauce

Fill prepared peppers with corned beef hash.

Combine remaining ingredients and bring to a boil. Reduce heat and simmer 5 minutes.

Place filled peppers in casserole. Pour over sauce.

Cover. Bake in hot oven (400°F.) 30 minutes.

Serves 4 to 6.

For added flavor, top cooked beef and rice stuffed peppers with grated cheese or buttered crumbs and brown under broiler just before serving.

CORN AND BACON STUFFED PEPPERS

6   large green peppers
4   slices bacon
1   tablespoon butter or margarine
2   tablespoons finely diced onion
2   tablespoons flour
1   teaspoon sugar (optional)
1½ teaspoons salt
¼   teaspoon pepper
1½ cups milk, scalded
2   cups cooked corn
½   cup soft breadcrumbs
1   slightly beaten egg

Wash peppers. Cut a slice from side of each and remove seeds and fibrous parts. Cover with boiling water and simmer 5 minutes.

Meanwhile, cook bacon, drain and dice. Melt butter in saucepan; add onion and cook until tender. Add flour, sugar, and seasonings and blend. Add milk gradually and cook over low heat until thickened, stirring constantly.

Add corn, crumbs, and bacon, and stir into beaten egg. Fill green pepper shells.

Bake in pan of hot water, in slow oven (325°F.) 45 minutes or until filling is set. Serve with cheese sauce. Serves 6.

STUFFED GREEN PEPPERS—TOP OF STOVE METHOD

4   large green peppers
1½ cups ground, cooked meat (ham, tongue, lamb, pork, beef, or veal)
¼   cup rice
¼   cup minced onion
1½ teaspoons salt
¼   teaspoon pepper
1   8-ounce can tomato sauce
1   cup water or vegetable cooking water
Dash of cayenne
2   basil leaves, or pinch of dry basil, if desired

Cut off tops and remove seeds from peppers.

Mix meat, rice, onion, salt, and pepper. Stuff peppers about ¾ full.

Stand upright in small, heavy saucepan with tight-fitting lid. Pour combined sauce, water, and seasonings over peppers.

Cover and cook very slowly until rice is tender, about 40 minutes. If necessary, add a little more water. Serves 4.

FRENCH FRIED PEPPER RINGS

Slice peppers in thin rings. Cover with boiling water and cook 5 minutes. Drain.

Dip in egg slightly beaten with 1 tablespoon water, then in fine crumbs. Fry, a few at a time, in deep hot fat (370°F.). Drain on paper towels.

CHEESE STUFFED GREEN PEPPERS

6   green peppers
2   cups cooked rice
½   cup milk
2   tablespoons chopped pimiento
1   tablespoon finely minced parsley
1   tablespoon grated onion
1   teaspoon salt
⅛   teaspoon pepper
2   tablespoons melted butter or margarine
1   cup diced American cheese

Prepare peppers for stuffing by cutting off tops. Remove fibers and seeds. Drop into boiling, salted water and simmer gently 5 minutes. Drain.

Combine cooked rice, milk, pimiento, parsley, grated onion, salt, pepper, melted butter, and diced cheese.

Fill peppers with cheese stuffing. Place upright in baking pan; add ½ cup hot water.

Bake in moderate oven (350°F.) 30 minutes, or until peppers are tender. Serves 6.

HUNGARIAN STUFFED PEPPERS

6   green peppers (plump, uniform)
1   pound ground beef
½   cup chopped onion
1   egg
1   cup uncooked rice
1   teaspoon salt
Pepper
1   10½-ounce can tomato soup
1   tablespoon flour
1   cup thick sour cream

Cut tops off green peppers. Use scissors to remove center and all seeds.

Combine ground beef, onion, egg, rice, salt, and pepper. Mix well and stuff loosely into green peppers (allow for rice to swell).

Place upright in a casserole. Pour tomato soup mixed with 2 cans of water into casserole.

Bake in moderate oven (350°F.) at least 1 hour or until rice is tender. (If rice is boiled 10 minutes before combining with meat, 1 hour baking is adequate.)

Remove peppers to hot platter. Combine flour and sour cream and stir into tomato sauce in casserole. Stir and boil to thicken. Pour over peppers. Serves 6.

OTHER STUFFINGS FOR PEPPERS

A vast variety of stuffings can be used besides those already given. In fact, you can make them up yourself. Here are a few suggestions:

1. Tomatoes combined with leftover meats, properly herbed and seasoned.

2. Mashed potatoes seasoned with diced onion or chopped chives and blended with cream or a beaten egg.

3. Leftover spaghetti, tomatoes, and cheese make another combination.

Cheese Stuffed Peppers

POTATOES

A great many people are misinformed about white or Irish potatoes on two counts. First, they are not native to Ireland but to South America, and were not introduced to the Irish until 1585. Second, white potatoes, contrary to popular belief, are not an exceptionally fattening food. As a matter of fact, one medium-size potato contains no more calories than a large apple or single baking powder biscuit of average size.

Furthermore, the potato is a fair source of vitamins B_1, C, and G and, in addition, has an abundant content of iron, phosphorous, and other health-giving minerals. With such a wealth of food values it is therefore obvious that potatoes more than deserve their position as the backbone of our national vegetable diet.

Selection: New potatoes, always characterized by a thin, feathery skin which may be either red or white, are ideally suited for boiling or creaming. The Russet Burbank is a fairly large, well-shaped potato, easily recognized by the peculiar netting marks on its skin. Idaho is the largest producer of this variety, which is a good all-purpose potato but is best known for its baking qualities. Other varieties such as the Red Bliss potato and the Irish Cobbler potato are all commonly found in retail stores and are satisfactory for general use.

Good quality white potatoes are generally clean, firm, and free from cuts, growth cracks, and other unsightly knobs or surface defects. If you choose those that are well shaped and have shallow eyes, your waste in preparation will be kept to a minimum. "Sunburnt" potatoes, characterized by a green color on part of their surface, should be avoided, as they are usually bitter-tasting. Also watch out for frost-damaged potatoes which generally have a watery appearance or show a black ring near the surface when cut across.

The best way to get the most food value from potatoes is to cook them in their jackets. So, if possible, start with potatoes boiled in their jackets, whether you have them mashed, creamed, parslied, or hashed brown. Boiling in the skins conserves even more vitamins than baking potatoes.

Monday—Scalloped potatoes
Tuesday—Potatoes cooked in milk
Wednesday—Franconia potatoes
Thursday—Creamy mashed potatoes
Friday—Buttered parsley potatoes
Saturday—Creamed potatoes with chives

BOILED POTATOES

Wash and scrub with brush if potatoes are to be boiled in their skins.

Cook in boiling salted water in covered pan until tender, 20 to 40 minutes.

Drain and shake in pan over low heat until potatoes are dry and mealy.

Boiled Potato Variations

Boiled New Potatoes: Scrub with brush or scrape, but do not pare. Cook as above for 25 to 30 minutes.

Cheese Potatoes: Cover hot boiled potatoes with cheese sauce or sprinkle grated cheese over potatoes. Add cream and heat.

Parsley Potatoes: For each 5 or 6 potatoes, sprinkle 3 tablespoons chopped parsley and 2 tablespons melted butter or margarine over cooked, pared potatoes.

Potatoes and Carrots: Cook an equal amount of sliced carrots and potatoes together until done. Season and add cream and butter.

Potatoes and Onions: Cook an equal amount of sliced or whole onions and potatoes together until done. Season with cream and butter or margarine.

Potatoes and Peas: Cook whole new potatoes with new peas. Serve creamed.

Quick Browned Potatoes: Sprinkle hot boiled potatoes with flour. Brown in hot fat.

Savory Potatoes: Season hot boiled potatoes with cream and paprika.

Creamed Potatoes: Use cooked sliced or diced potatoes. Prepare thin white sauce.

If potatoes are cold, reheat in sauce. Add chopped pimiento and sprinkle with chopped parsley.

POTATOES COOKED IN MILK

3 cups finely diced raw potato
2/3 cup milk
1 teaspoon salt
Dash of pepper

Mix all ingredients in top part of double boiler.

Cover and cook over boiling water about 45 minutes. Serves 4.

MASHED POTATOES

Boil potatoes. Force through a ricer or mash well. Season to taste with salt and pepper.

Add 1/3 cup hot milk or potato liquid and 3 tablespoons butter, margarine, sour cream, or sour milk for every 5 potatoes. Beat well until light and fluffy.

To keep hot, set over pan of hot water or pile lightly in casserole and place in slow oven (325°F.).

Mashed Potato Variations

Baked Potato Puff: Add 1 egg yolk to 2 cups riced potatoes. Beat well.

Fold in 1 stiffly beaten egg white.

Place in greased baking pan and bake in moderate oven (350°F.) until browned.

Mashed Cheese Potatoes: Add 1/2 cup grated cheese to 2 cups mashed potatoes.

Sprinkle grated cheese and paprika on top. Brown in moderate oven (350°F.).

Duchess Potatoes: Add 2 tablespoons butter or margarine, 1/2 teaspoon salt, and 2 slightly beaten egg yolks to 2 to 3 cups hot riced or mashed potatoes.

Mix thoroughly. Shape into patties or croquettes.

Place in greased shallow baking dish. Brown in very hot oven (450°F.). Serves 4 to 6.

Mashed Potato Cakes: Combine 2 cups seasoned, mashed potatoes with one egg.

Shape into four patties. Dip in flour.

Fry until well browned in hot shortening about 1/4 inch deep in heavy skillet. Serves 4.

Mashed Potatoes with Fried Onions: Prepare mashed potatoes. Before serving, cover with sliced fried onions.

Mayonnaise Potatoes: Prepare mashed potatoes, substituting a little mayonnaise for butter or margarine called for in recipe.

Beat until light and fluffy. Season to taste.

Parsley Mashed Potatoes: Beat finely chopped parsley into mashed potatoes.

Pimiento Potatoes: Add diced pimiento to hot mashed potatoes.

Potato Cakes with Meat: Add 1/2 cup ground leftover meat to 2 cups cold mashed potatoes. Form into cakes. Fry until browned.

Potato Nests: Make a cavity in center of mashed potato mound. Fill with creamed carrots or peas.

Yellow Mashed Potatoes: Rice or mash together boiled potatoes and boiled carrots.

For a well-baked potato, wrap a well-scrubbed, dried and greased baking potato in foil. Bake at from 350° to 425°F. for 40 to 50 minutes, while baking other foods. Keep inside foil until ready to serve—it will keep hot and moist.

BAKED POTATOES

Scrub potatoes, dry, rub skins with soft butter or margarine.

Bake in preheated very hot oven (450°F.) until tender, 45 to 60 minutes.

Remove from oven, cut 2 crossed slits on one side, and pinch potato until it opens at slit.

Put a lump of butter or margarine in opening; sprinkle with paprika.

Baked Stuffed Potatoes: Bake as above, then cut in half lengthwise.

Carefully scoop out potato without breaking skin.

Mash potato with butter or margarine, salt, pepper, and enough milk or potato water to give a fluffy texture.

Pile mixture into shell, sprinkle with grated cheese and paprika. Return to oven to brown.

Baked Stuffed Potatoes with Eggs: Prepare as above and, for every potato, add 1 chopped, hard-cooked egg to the mixture.

Baked Stuffed Potatoes with Meat, Fish, or Vegetables: Omit milk in baked stuffed potatoes. Combine potato with any leftover creamed fish or vegetables, or cooked poultry or meat moistened with fat.

Baked Stuffed Potatoes with Mushrooms: For every potato add 1 tablespoon chopped or sliced sautéed mushrooms to the mixture.

Stuffed Baked Potatoes

POTATOES ANNA

6 medium-sized potatoes (about 2 pounds), pared and thinly sliced
6 tablespoons butter
1½ teaspoons salt
¼ teaspoon pepper
Grated onion
Grated Parmesan cheese

Lightly grease a 10-inch skillet with a heat-resistant handle or a shallow casserole, with tight fitting cover. Arrange the potatoes in slightly overlapping spirals until the bottom of the pan is filled.

Dot with bits of butter. Add a sprinkling of salt, pepper, grated onion, and grated Parmesan cheese. Repeat with 2 additional layers.

Cover pan and bake in hot oven (425°F.) 30 minutes. Remove cover and bake 5 minutes longer. To serve, invert on platter. Serves 6.

SCALLOPED POTATOES

(Master Recipe)

6 medium potatoes
3 tablespoons butter or margarine
2 tablespoons flour
3 cups milk
1 teaspoon salt
¼ teaspoon pepper
2 tablespoons chopped onion

Pare potatoes and slice thin.

Melt butter in saucepan; blend in flour. Slowly add milk; cook over medium heat until thickened, stirring constantly.

Put half the potatoes in greased 2-quart casserole. Cover with half the sauce, seasonings, and onion. Add remaining potatoes, seasoning, and onion. Top with remaining sauce.

Cover and bake in moderate oven (350°F.) about 1 hour. Uncover and bake until top is browned. Serves 4 to 6.

Scalloped Potato Variations

Scalloped Potatoes with Cheese (Au Gratin): Prepare as in master recipe. Sprinkle each layer with cheese. Or, cheese may be melted in white sauce.

Scalloped Potatoes with Seafood: Prepare as in master recipe. Add cooked or canned fish such as finnan haddie, salmon, shrimp, lobster, herring, lox (smoked salmon), crabmeat, etc. in layers with potatoes. Season to taste.

Scalloped Potatoes with Meat: Prepare as in master recipe. Add cooked diced or sliced leftover meat, dried beef, corned beef, franks, bacon, or ham.

If desired, bake a slice of ham or ground meat patties with the potatoes, placing it on the bottom of casserole, on the top, or between layers.

FRANCONIA POTATOES
(Pan-Roasted Potatoes)

Pare potatoes. Cut in half or quarter large potatoes. Place in baking pan with meat which is being roasted about 1¼ hours before meat is through cooking.

Turn and baste occasionally during cooking so that they brown evenly on all sides.

To shorten cooking time, cook potatoes in boiling salted water 10 to 15 minutes before placing in roasting pan; allow 45 minutes to 1 hour for baking.

Variations: Potatoes may be dipped into melted fat, then rolled in dry breadcrumbs and baked in separate pan.

BAKED POTATOES WITH SOUR CREAM

⅔ cup chopped onions
3 tablespoons butter or margarine, melted
1½ cups sour cream
2 eggs, slightly beaten
4 cups sliced, cooked potatoes
½ teaspoon salt
⅛ teaspoon pepper
2 cups corn flakes or ½ cup corn flake crumbs
¼ cup grated Cheddar cheese

Cook onions in 2 tablespoons butter until golden brown. Combine sour cream and eggs.

Place half the potatoes in greased individual casseroles or 1½-quart baking dish. Spread half the onions over potatoes; pour on half the sour cream mixture. Repeat layering, using remaining potatoes, onions, and sour cream mixture. Sprinkle with salt and pepper.

If using corn flakes, crush into fine crumbs. Combine corn flake crumbs, cheese, and remaining butter. Sprinkle corn flake crumb mixture over potatoes. Bake in moderate oven (350°F.) about 25 minutes. Serves 6 to 8.

HASHED-BROWN POTATOES

Chop enough cold boiled or baked potatoes to make 3 cups. Add 3 tablespoons flour and ¼ cup milk; mix well. Season with salt and pepper to taste.

Heat 2 tablespoons bacon fat in heavy 9-inch skillet. Add potatoes and pack with spatula in a large cake. Cook over medium heat until potato is brown and crusty, shaking pan to keep potato from sticking. Turn out onto flat plate.

Wipe pan free of crumbs. Add 1 tablespoon fat. Slide potato back into hot pan.

Cook until brown, packing edges with spatula and shaking pan. Serves 4.

Variations: Add a little minced onion or chopped parsley with the salt and pepper.

POTATOES O'BRIEN

Combine 2 cups cooked, chopped potatoes, ¼ cup each of minced green pepper and onion, and 1 tablespoon diced pimiento.

Fry until golden brown in hot fat about ¼ inch deep in heavy skillet. Serves 4.

FRENCH FRIED POTATOES

Wash, pare, and cut potatoes into lengthwise strips, about ½ inch thick.

Soak in cold water 1 hour. Drain, dry thoroughly between towels.

Heat kettle of deep fat, hot enough to brown a small piece of bread in 60 seconds (375°F.).

Fry about a cupful of sliced potatoes at one time until lightly browned. Drain on absorbent paper.

Just before serving, return to hot fat (385°F.) and fry until crisp and brown.

Drain on absorbent paper and sprinkle with salt. Serve at once.

Variations:

Lattice Potatoes: Cut potatoes with a lattice vegetable cutter. Fry as above.

Potato Balls: Cut potatoes into tiny balls with ball cutter. Fry as above.

Potato Chips: Cut potatoes into thin slices. Fry as above.

Saratoga Chips: Cut potatoes into very thin slices. Soak in cold water, drain, and plunge into boiling water.

Drain, dry, and fry as above.

SKILLET FRIED POTATOES

Cut pared potatoes in ⅛-inch slices. Fry over low heat in heavy skillet in bacon drippings or other fat. Season with salt and pepper.

After potatoes are browned, turn and fry slowly on the other side. Do not cover.

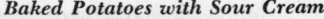

Baked Potatoes with Sour Cream

French Fried Potato Balls

FRENCH FRIED POTATO BALLS

    8   cups corn flakes or 2 cups corn
          flake crumbs
    1   cup cottage cheese, drained
    1/4 cup finely chopped onion
    1   egg, well-beaten
    3   cups mashed potatoes
    1   teaspoon salt
    1/8 teaspoon pepper
    1/8 teaspoon paprika
    1/4 teaspoon dry mustard
    2   teaspoons grated horseradish
    2   eggs
    2   tablespoons milk

If using corn flakes, crush into fine crumbs.

Combine cottage cheese, onion, beaten egg, potatoes, seasonings, and horseradish; mix well. Shape into small balls, 1½ inches in diameter.

Beat eggs and milk together. Roll balls in corn flake crumbs, then in egg-milk mixture; roll again in corn flake crumbs.

Fry in deep hot fat (375°F.) about 2 minutes, or until crisp and well-browned. Serve with horseradish flavored sour cream, if desired. Makes about 2 dozen balls, 1½ inches in diameter.

FRENCH FRIED POTATO BALLS #2

    2   cups hot mashed potatoes
    2   slightly beaten eggs
    1   teaspoon baking powder
    1/4 teaspoon salt
    1/8 teaspoon paprika
    1   tablespoon chopped parsley

Combine all ingredients and beat well.

Drop by teaspoonfuls into deep hot fat (390°F.). Cook until golden brown. Drain on absorbent paper. Serve hot.

SOUFFLÉED POTATO SLICES

Select medium-sized Idaho potatoes of uniform size. Pare and cut on slant in slices about 1/8 inch thick. Dry between towels.

Fry, a few at a time, in medium hot, deep fat (275°–300°F.) 5 minutes, keeping potatoes in motion.

Then lift basket and plunge quickly into very hot, deep fat (400°–425°F.) 1 to 2 minutes, or until puffed and browned, keeping potatoes moving. They should puff at once when dropped into kettle of very hot fat.

Hold basket over kettle for fat to drip, then turn out on absorbent paper to drain. Sprinkle with salt. Serve at once.

The type of potato and the quick changes from a medium hot to a very hot fat are important in making these slices.

POTATO BASKETS

Cut 2 pared potatoes in very fine strips. Soak in cold water, drain, and dry well.

Fry in deep fat heated to 365°F. (or when an inch cube of bread browns in 60 seconds) 2 minutes. Sprinkle with salt and press into muffin pans.

Brown in hot oven (400°F.) 7 to 8 minutes. Makes 4 baskets.

BAKED POTATO WAFERS

    4 to 6 large potatoes
    1/2 cup (1 stick) butter or margarine
    Salt and pepper

Select large potatoes and rub them with butter after scrubbing them well. Cut, without peeling, into slices 1/8 inch thick.

Place in large skillet in which butter has been melted. Sprinkle with salt and pepper and brown slightly on both sides at a low temperature.

Cover and continue cooking over low heat 20 minutes, or until slices are tender. Serves 6.

OVEN-FRIED (TOASTED) POTATOES

Cut potatoes as for French-fried potatoes. Rinse in cold water. Drain and dry on absorbent paper.

Arrange on shallow baking pan. Brush generously with melted butter or margarine.

Bake in very hot oven (450°F.) until golden brown and tender, turning occasionally, 35 to 40 minutes. Sprinkle with salt.

COTTAGE FRIED POTATOES

Cook potatoes in jackets. Remove skins and slice or dice.

Fry in hot fat, turning frequently, until brown and crisp. Season with salt and pepper.

Lyonnaise Potatoes: Proceed as above, frying thinly sliced onions with the potatoes.

BUTTER BROWNED POTATO BALLS

    6 large potatoes
    1/2 cup butter or margarine (1 stick)
          melted
    Salt and pepper

Pare potatoes and cut with a round ball cutter. Cook them in melted butter in large frying pan until golden brown and cooked through. A medium temperature is best for butter cooking.

Sprinkle with salt and pepper and serve at once. Serves 4 to 6.

POTATOES WITH SOUR CREAM

    6 medium potatoes
    2 cups sour cream
    3 tablespoons finely chopped onion
    Salt and pepper

Boil potatoes in jackets until tender. Peel, cool enough to handle, and cut into pieces.

Warm cream and onion, being careful not to heat cream to point where it curdles.

Add potatoes. Season to taste with salt and pepper and serve, if desired, with a garnish of parsley. Serves 6.

CHEESED POTATOES

    8 medium new potatoes
    1/4 cup butter or margarine
    1/3 cup minced chives
    1 teaspoon salt
    1/8 teaspoon paprika
    1/2 cup grated American cheese

Cook potatoes in jackets; drain and return to low heat, 2 to 3 minutes, shaking gently until they are hot and mealy. Turn into hot serving dish.

Meanwhile, melt butter, add minced chives, seasonings, and cheese. Pour hot cheese mixture over potatoes. Sprinkle with extra chives and a dash of paprika. Serves 6.

BAKED POTATOES WITH MUSHROOM SAUCE

    1 can (1¼ cups) condensed cream
          of mushroom soup
    1/3 cup milk
    4 medium potatoes, baked
    2 tablespoons butter or margarine
    Black pepper

Pour soup into saucepan and stir well; blend in milk. Simmer about 2 minutes.

Split hot potatoes and dot each with 1/2 tablespoon butter. Sprinkle with pepper. Pour sauce in and over each potato. Serves 4.

Baked Potato Wafers
Butter Browned Potato Balls
Potatoes with Butter Sauce

GERMAN POTATO PIE

6   to 8 large raw potatoes
1/4 small onion, grated
3   eggs, well beaten
1   cup hot milk
6   tablespoons butter or margarine,
        melted
2 1/2 teaspoons salt

Pare and grate potatoes. Combine with remaining ingredients, blending well. Pour into well greased shallow casserole, about 7 x 12 inches.

Bake in moderate oven (350°F.) until set, about 1 hour and 15 minutes. Serves 6.

POTATO SPINACH PUFF

1   pound (2 large) potatoes
Salt
1   package frozen chopped spinach
2   tablespoons cream
2   tablespoons butter or margarine
1   egg
Pepper and nutmeg

Pare potatoes and cut in quarters. Cook in boiling salted water until tender. Drain and put through ricer.

Meanwhile, cook spinach as directed on package. Drain and add to potatoes.

Add cream, butter, and egg; beat until light and fluffy. Season to taste with salt, pepper, and nutmeg.

Pile into 1-quart casserole. Bake in hot oven (400°F.) 15 minutes. Serves 4.

SURPRISE POTATOES

Foil-bake potatoes. Divide potatoes lengthwise, allowing about 2/3 for the lower half.

Scoop out centers and whip up to feathery lightness with hot milk, butter, and seasonings.

Heap the filling nicely in the larger potato skin shell, discarding the smaller one. Sprinkle with paprika and melted butter.

Wrap these stuffed potatoes in foil and store in freezer. When ready to serve, place direct from freezer in moderate oven (375°F.) and heat 30 minutes. Serve right in the foil, turning it back at the table. These potatoes may also be stored in the refrigerator for short periods and heated in 25 minutes when not frozen.

Surprise Potatoes

POTATO CHEESE CROQUETTES

2   cups cold mashed potatoes
1   beaten egg
1   cup grated Cheddar cheese
Salt to taste
3/4 teaspoon Ac'cent
1/2 cup fine dry breadcrumbs
1/2 cup milk

Break up potatoes. Beat egg in blender until frothy. Add potato pieces gradually, beating at medium speed until blended.

Stir in cheese, salt, and Ac'cent. Shape as desired. Dip into crumbs, then into milk, and again into crumbs.

Fry in shallow hot fat until golden brown on all sides. Serves 4 to 6.

BEEF-STUFFED BAKED POTATOES

4   baking potatoes
1/2 pound hamburger
2   tablespoons chopped onion (or
        sliced green onion or chives)
2   tablespoons butter or margarine
1   teaspoon salt
1/2 cup shredded cheese

Scrub potatoes and bake in very hot oven (450°F.) for 45 to 55 minutes, or until tender when pierced with a fork.

Pan-fry hamburger and onion in butter in a skillet.

Cut a slice from top of each potato and scoop out inside. Mash thoroughly. Add the meat, butter, and onion mixture to the potatoes and whip until light and fluffy.

Pile lightly into potato shells and top each with shredded cheese. Return to very hot oven to reheat and melt cheese. Serves 4.

CASSEROLE-BAKED POTATOES

12   small potatoes
1/2 to 1 teaspoon salt
2/3 cup butter or margarine, melted

Wash potatoes, peel and wash again. Pat dry with absorbent paper or towel.

Place in oven-glass casserole. Salt well and add butter. Cover.

Bake in moderate oven (350°F.) until browned and tender, about 1 hour. Turn potatoes several times, or shake the casserole so they turn themselves, to make sure they brown evenly. Serves 6.

BAKED MASHED POTATOES

1 1/2 cups mashed potatoes
2   tablespoons butter or margarine
1   egg
1/2 cup hot milk or cream
Salt and pepper to taste

Combine ingredients, beat well, and place in greased baking dish.

Sprinkle with a little paprika and bake in moderate oven (375°F.) until top is lightly browned. Serves 4 to 6.

Potato Cheese Croquettes

POTATO CHEESE PUFFS

3   cups hot mashed potatoes
1/2 cup heavy cream, whipped
1/3 cup grated American cheese

Mash potatoes with salt and butter or margarine to taste, and enough milk to give a light fluffy consistency. Place in buttered custard cups.

Whip cream, add cheese, and mix well. Spread over potatoes.

Bake in moderate oven (350°F.) about 15 minutes, or until browned. Serves 6.

POTATOES FRIED WITH BACON

Fry 4 slices bacon in heavy skillet; remove and crumble.

Pare 4 large potatoes; slice very thin. Place in bacon drippings; add 1 teaspoon salt and 1/4 teaspoon pepper.

Fry until almost tender and quite brown. Then cover and move to edge of grill. Add bacon bits and fry until tender. Serves 4 to 6.

CRISPY-TOPPED CHEESE POTATOES

3   tablespoons melted butter or margarine
4   medium-sized boiled potatoes
1   cup corn flakes, finely crushed
1   cup finely shredded cheese
1/2 teaspoon paprika
1   teaspoon salt

Pour 2 tablespoons butter or margarine into shallow baking pan.

Cut potatoes into 1/2-inch slices and place close together in pan. Brush tops with remaining butter or margarine.

Roll corn flakes into fine crumbs; combine with cheese, paprika, and salt; sprinkle over potatoes.

Bake in hot oven (425°F.) about 15 minutes. Serves 6.

Crispy-Topped Cheese Potatoes

Panned Potatoes

PANNED POTATOES

    4 tablespoons butter or margarine
    10 to 12 small potatoes
    4 tablespoons flour
    2 to 3 teaspoons salt
    1 large onion, sliced
    Paprika

Melt butter or margarine in skillet with tight-fitting cover.

Peel and slice potatoes thin. Arrange ½-inch-thick layer in skillet and sprinkle with flour, salt, and bits of onion.

Continue layers until skillet is nearly full. Arrange onion slices on top. Sprinkle with paprika.

Cover and cook slowly until potatoes are tender but not mushy.

If desired, loosen around edge with knife, cover skillet with large plate and invert. Potatoes will come out in one piece, or cut and serve in wedges. Serves 6.

BROILED POTATOES AU GRATIN

    3 cups diced cold cooked potatoes
    6 tablespoons butter or margarine
    3 tablespoons flour
    1½ cups milk
    ¼ pound sharp Cheddar cheese, grated
    Salt and pepper
    ¾ cup soft breadcrumbs

Put potatoes in shallow baking dish.

Melt 3 tablespoons butter in a saucepan; blend in flour. Add milk gradually and cook, stirring constantly, until smooth and thickened. Add cheese and stir until melted. Season to taste with salt and pepper.

Pour over potatoes and mix lightly with fork.

Melt remaining 3 tablespoons butter and mix with crumbs. Sprinkle over contents of baking dish.

Put in broiler under medium heat and broil until golden brown. Serves 4.

POTATOES—SPANISH STYLE

Measure 4 cups thinly sliced pared raw potatoes into 1-quart casserole.

Blend 2 cups tomato sauce, 1 medium onion, chopped, 1 finely chopped garlic clove, 1½ teaspoons salt, dash of pepper, and 1 teaspoon paprika.

Pour sauce over potatoes, stirring lightly. Cover with tight-fitting lid.

Bake in moderate oven (375°F.) until potatoes are tender, 1 hour. Serves 6.

QUICK SCALLOPED POTATOES WITH HAM

    6 large potatoes
    1 large onion, sliced
    1 cup diced cooked ham
    1 teaspoon salt
    ¼ teaspoon pepper
    1 tall can evaporated milk, diluted with ½ cup hot water
    ½ cup crisp breadcrumbs
    2 tablespoons melted butter or margarine

Boil potatoes with skins on for just 5 minutes. Peel and slice potatoes.

Place half the potatoes in 1½-quart buttered baking dish. Arrange sliced onion and ham on top of potatoes. Add remaining potatoes.

Add seasonings to milk diluted with hot water and pour over potatoes.

Mix crumbs and melted butter and sprinkle on top. Bake in moderate oven (350°F.) 30 minutes. Serves 4 to 6.

Variations: Substitute ½ pound chipped beef or other cooked meat for ham. Potatoes may be used without boiling, but increase baking time to 45 minutes.

SCALLOPED POTATOES WITH SAUSAGE AND TOMATOES

    3 cups raw sliced potatoes
    6 diced sausages
    4 tablespoons flour
    1 teaspoon salt
    ⅛ teaspoon pepper
    3 tablespoons minced onion
    1½ cups milk
    3 slices tomato
    Parsley, if desired

Arrange about half the potato slices and diced sausages in well greased 1½-quart casserole. Sprinkle with half the flour, salt, pepper, and onion.

Repeat. Pour milk over ingredients. Top with tomato slices. Cover.

Bake in moderate oven (350°F.) ¾ hour. Remove cover and bake another ½ hour, or until done.

If desired, garnish with sprigs of parsley for serving. Serves 3 to 4.

IRISH POTATO PUFF

    ¼ cup butter or margarine
    1 cup breadcrumbs
    1 teaspoon salt
    1 tablespoon grated lemon rind
    1 teaspoon lemon juice
    3 egg yolks
    1 cup milk
    3 egg whites, beaten stiff
    3 cups mashed potatoes
    ¼ cup grated cheese

Combine butter and crumbs. Mix until well blended. Press on bottom and sides of round baking dish.

Combine salt, lemon rind, lemon juice, and egg yolks. Blend well and stir in milk.

Fold in egg whites and gently fold mixture into mashed potatoes. Fill baking dish and stir in half of grated cheese. Sprinkle remaining cheese on top.

Bake in moderate oven (350°F.) ½ hour, or until firm and delicate brown on top. Serve hot. Serves 6.

BAKED CREAMED POTATO RING

    6 cups diced, cooked potatoes
    1 medium onion, minced
    2 cups thick white sauce
    2 beaten eggs
    ¾ teaspoon Ac'cent
    1 cup grated sharp Cheddar cheese

Combine potatoes and onion.

Pour hot white sauce on beaten eggs; add Ac'cent. Add cheese; stir over low heat until cheese melts.

Combine cheese mixture and potato mixture; mix well. Pack into heavily greased 10-inch ring mold.

Set in pan of hot water. Bake in moderate oven (350°F.) 45 minutes.

To unmold, run knife around edges, invert on large plate, then invert again on serving plate so that browned top will be uppermost.

Fill center with buttered Brussels sprouts. Serves 6.

POTATO KUGEL #2

    6 medium potatoes
    1 small onion
    3 eggs
    ½ teaspoon salt
    Dash of pepper
    About ¾ cup flour
    4 tablespoons shortening

Pare and grate raw potatoes; squeeze out excess liquid. Grate onion into the potatoes.

Add eggs, salt, pepper, and just enough flour to make a batter that will drop from a spoon.

Heat shortening in baking pan; mix into batter. Turn batter into greased baking pan.

Bake in moderate oven (375°F.) until nicely browned and crisp at edges, 30 to 40 minutes. Serves 6.

Potato Kugel

PUMPKIN

Pumpkin, a member of the same family as muskmelons and squash, is usually classified as a vegetable. It is used chiefly for pies and has a golden yellow color when ripe. Size and shape have little to do with a pumpkin's flavor, although the smaller ones have less waste and usually a more tender flesh. They are a good source of vitamin A.

In general, pumpkin is prepared for mashing or other use by boiling like winter squash. Cut pumpkin into small pieces and peel. If pumpkin has been used as a jack-o-lantern, remove portions that are charred or on which candle wax has fallen.

Pressure Cooked: Place on rack in pressure cooker with 1/2 cup water. Cook at 15-pound pressure 10 to 12 minutes. Estimate time by how hard it was to cut pumpkin into pieces. Cool cooker at once under running water. Drain pumpkin. This yields a dryer product than boiling.

Boiled: Cover cut-up pumpkin with water. Cover and cook until tender, 30 minutes or longer. Drain well.

Baked: Cut pumpkin in half. Remove seeds and fibrous matter. Place it cut-side down in a pan with a small amount of water. Bake in slow oven (325°F.) until tender, 1 hour or longer. This yields a dry product.

RADISHES

Good quality in fresh radishes is not indicated by the condition or color of the leaves but by the root, which should be smooth, crisp, and firm, never soft or spongy. The long, white, mild-flavored ones are called "Icicles" but the small, red "button" variety is more popular. Round radishes vary in size from about an inch in diameter up to four inches; the long ones from three inches up to ten inches in length.

RADISHES—RED

Selection: Buy 2 bunches for 4 servings. Buy well-formed, smooth, firm, crisp radishes with fresh, bright green tops.

Preparation: Wash and remove roots. If radishes are large remove leaves. Remove only damaged leaves of small radishes.

Cooking Time: 5 to 10 minutes.

Cooking: Cook whole in a small amount of boiling salted water in a tightly covered saucepan. The small ones and their tops will be done in about 5 minutes. The larger ones will take about 10 minutes.

Serving: Serve piping hot drenched with melted butter or margarine.

To Serve Raw: Serve crisp and cold on the relish tray. Add thin slivers to vegetable or green salads.

RUTABAGA

The rutabaga, also called Swedish turnip and swede, is a large, yellow fleshed, strong-flavored turnip with a good content of vitamin B_1. In Europe, it is usually regarded as cattle feed, but it makes an excellent vegetable if not overcooked. The tops, which are not eaten, show first signs of deterioration and, consequently, are usually trimmed off before they are placed on sale. The roots of good quality rutabagas should be smooth skinned, firm, and heavy for their size.

Storage turnips are generally treated with an edible wax to make them keep better. This comes off when the root is peeled, of course. For cooking methods, see **Turnips.**

SALSIFY (OYSTER PLANT)

Salsify (oyster plant or vegetable oyster) is similar in appearance and quality characteristics to parsnips except that the tops look like heavy grass. It also resembles the parsnip in that its flavor is improved after exposure to cold temperatures. It is also known as oyster plant or vegetable oyster because when cooked it tastes somewhat like an oyster.

Preparation: Wash, scrape and cut into small pieces. Place in cold water, adding 1 teaspoon vinegar or lemon pieces to 1 quart of water to prevent discoloration. Drain.

Cooking: Cover with boiling water. (Do not salt before cooking.) Cover and cook until tender, 20 to 40 minutes (10 minutes in pressure saucepan).

Drain and add melted butter, and season with salt and pepper to taste.

SAUTÉED SALSIFY

Boil salsify and drain. Roll in seasoned flour or breadcrumbs. Sauté in fat until brown on all sides, 7 to 10 minutes.

CREAMED SALSIFY

Reheat boiled salsify in medium white sauce. Sprinkle with chopped parsley.

SALSIFY PATTIES OR FRITTERS

Mash cooked salsify. Season with butter, salt, and pepper.

Shape in small flat cakes. Roll in flour. Brown in butter.

SORREL

Sorrel, which is usually cooked as a green, is a member of the buckwheat family, identifiable by its arrow-shaped leaves. Buy and handle sorrel as you would spinach, with which it is usually cooked to add flavor. Sorrel is also sometimes known as sour grass.

SAUERKRAUT

Sauerkraut is German for sour cabbage; shredded cabbage fermented in a brine of its own juice.

Boiled: One pound serves 4. Drain sauerkraut. Cover with boiling water or stock. Cook slowly, uncovered, 30 to 35 minutes.

Drain and season to taste with salt, butter, and, if needed, pepper. If desired, season with 1 teaspoon caraway or celery seed and 1 to 2 tablespoons brown sugar.

Note: If sauerkraut is very salty, it should be drained, rinsed in cold running water and drained again before cooking.

SAUERKRAUT WITH WINE

Drain sauerkraut. Add 1 1/2 cups white or red wine per pound. Cook slowly until tender.

SAUERKRAUT WITH ONIONS

Dice 1 onion and sauté in 2 tablespoons fat until soft.

Add drained sauerkraut, stir well, cover, and cook slowly at least 30 minutes on top of range or in oven. Season to taste.

SAUERKRAUT AND FRANKFURTERS

2 tablespoons bacon drippings or margarine
1 medium-sized onion, chopped
1 medium-sized green pepper, chopped
1 No. 2 can (2 1/2 cups) sauerkraut
1 cup canned tomatoes
1 teaspoon brown sugar
1 cup canned okra
1 pound frankfurters

In a large heavy skillet, melt drippings or margarine over low heat. Add onion and green pepper; sauté 5 minutes.

Stir in sauerkraut, tomatoes, and sugar; mix thoroughly. Add okra and mix lightly.

Arrange frankfurters on top. Cover and cook over low heat 20 minutes. Serve piping hot. Serves 4 to 6.

Sauerkraut and Frankfurters

Baked Spinach Casserole

SPINACH

Modern boys and girls aren't the only ones who have had to eat spinach, as historical records show that it was cultivated by the Greeks and Romans even before the Christian era. Today spinach, because of its wealth of natural food values, is one of our most commonly used vegetables. Both the crinkly-leaf and flat-leaf types are good for cooking. Incidentally, you won't have to wash spinach so much as usual if a little salt is dissolved in the first water you use.

Selection: Buy 2 to 2½ pounds for 4 servings. Look for well-developed plants with fresh, crisp, clean leaves of good green color. If you buy spinach in cellophane bags, washed and ready to cook, be sure it is young and fresh. Frozen or canned spinach is not as crisp as fresh spinach.

Preparation: Cut off root ends and any damaged leaves. Wash at least 3 times to remove sand unless it is packaged, washed spinach.

Cooking Time: 3 to 10 minutes.

Cooking: Cook, covered, using only the water that clings to the leaves after washing. Boil 3 to 10 minutes. Chop or leave in sprays or cut through several times.

Serving: Serve at once seasoned with salt, pepper, butter or margarine, and a little vinegar or fresh lemon juice.

To Serve Raw: Use crisp and chilled in mixed green salads.

SPINACH WITH ALMONDS

Cook 1 package frozen chopped spinach as label directs.

Cook 2 tablespoons chopped and blanched almonds in 2 tablespoons butter or margarine until lightly browned. Add 2 teaspoons lemon juice. Pour over drained spinach. Season with salt and pepper to taste. Serves 3.

Spinach Ring

BAKED SPINACH CASSEROLE

2   10-ounce packages frozen chopped spinach
2   tablespoons minced onion
3   tablespoons butter or margarine
3   tablespoons flour
2   cups milk
3   hard-cooked eggs, finely chopped
2   teaspoons salt
¼   teaspoon pepper
⅛   teaspoon nutmeg
2   cups corn flakes or ½ cup corn flake crumbs
½   cup grated Cheddar cheese
2   tablespoons butter or margarine, melted
Paprika

Cook spinach according to directions on package; drain thoroughly.

Cook onion in butter until transparent. Stir in flour. Add milk gradually, stirring constantly. Cook until thickened, stirring occasionally. Fold in spinach and eggs; season with salt, pepper, and nutmeg.

Spread in greased shallow baking dish. If using corn flakes, crush into fine crumbs. Combine corn flake crumbs with cheese and butter; sprinkle over spinach. Sprinkle with paprika.

Bake in moderate oven (375°F.) about 20 minutes, or until lightly top of each timbale. Serves 6.

CREAMED SPINACH

Cook 1 package of frozen chopped spinach as label directs.

Melt 2 tablespoons butter or margarine; blend in 1½ tablespoons flour and dash of nutmeg. Stir in ½ cup milk. Add 1 chicken bouillon cube and 1 teaspoon grated onion. Cook, stirring constantly, until thickened.

Add to hot, drained spinach. Season to taste. Serves 3.

Variations: Cream other frozen greens in the same way.

SPINACH RING

3   packages frozen chopped spinach
3   tablespoons butter
3   tablespoons flour
¾   cup milk
1½ teaspoons salt
2   teaspoons aromatic bitters

Thaw spinach and put in colander. Drain off all water by pressing with spoon.

Make cream sauce of butter, flour, and milk. Add salt and bitters. This will make a thick sauce. Add drained spinach and cook over low heat for 5 minutes.

Grease ring mold with butter or cooking oil and press spinach mixture into it evenly. Put ring in hot water to keep warm. Turn spinach ring out on a round platter. Fill ring with creamed chicken. Serves 6 to 8.

Spinach Timbales

SPINACH TIMBALES

3½ cups chopped cooked spinach
3   slightly beaten eggs
¼   cup cream
2   tablespoons melted butter
¾   cup soft, fine breadcrumbs
½   teaspoon salt

Combine ingredients and mix well. Fill buttered custard cups ⅔ full. Place in shallow baking pan of hot water. Bake in moderate oven (350°F.) about 40 minutes, or until firm.

Unmold. Serve with white sauce. Place a slice of hard-cooked egg on top of each timbale. Serves 6.

SQUASH

The term squash refers to any of a number of edible gourds closely related to the pumpkin. The name is of American Indian origin. Squashes fall into 2 categories—summer and winter. Summer squash are used when they are young, before the rind hardens. The skin of summer squashes should be tender enough not to need paring. They may be boiled, steamed, baked, or fried.

Winter squash have hard shells and will keep all winter in a warm, dry room. They are often halved and baked; they may then be mashed or eaten from the shell. If cooked in any other way they must be pared, and they need more cooking time than the summer squashes. All squashes are good stuffed.

WINTER SQUASH

Varieties: Banana, Hubbard, Acorn, Des Moines, Table Queen, or Danish.
Selection: Buy 3 pounds for 4 servings. All winter squash should be very heavy for its size. The rind should be very hard, and the flesh thick and bright orange in color.
Preparation: Wash, cut into individual servings, and remove seeds.
Cooking Time: 30 to 60 minutes.
Cooking—Baked: Season with salt, pepper, butter or margarine, bacon or ham drippings, and bake, covered, in a hot oven (400°F.) until tender. Allow 30 minutes for banana squash, 45 to 60 minutes for Hubbard squash, and 30 to 40 minutes for acorn squash.
Serving: Remove from rind, mash, add additional seasonings, if necessary, or serve the individual pieces on the "half shell."

WINTER SQUASH—BAKED IN SQUARES

Cut in pieces about 3 inches square. Remove seeds and stringy portion.

Place in a greased shallow pan. Sprinkle with salt and pepper. Pour melted butter or margarine over top.

Cover and bake in moderate oven (350°F.) 1 hour, or until squash is tender. Serve hot.

MASHED WINTER SQUASH

Cut in pieces, remove seeds and stringy portions. Pare and cut into small serving pieces.

Cook rapidly in small amount boiling salted water, covered, until tender, 20 to 30 minutes.

Drain, mash, and season to taste with salt, pepper, and butter.

STEAMED WINTER SQUASH

Prepare as above. Steam over boiling water until tender, 30 to 40 minutes. Press through sieve or potato ricer. Beat well. Season with salt, pepper, and butter.

STUFFED ACORN SQUASH

Fill baked or boiled squash with tomatoes Creole, creamed ham, or creamed chicken. Sprinkle with buttered crumbs, if desired. Brown in oven.

Or, fill hot baked or boiled squash with creamed or buttered spinach or other vegetables and serve very hot.

HAM-STUFFED ACORN SQUASH

1¾ cups saltine cracker crumbs
½ cup water
2 cups chopped, cooked ham
1 tablespoon prepared mustard
¼ teaspoon pepper
2 eggs, beaten
3 acorn squash

Combine all ingredients except squash; mix well.

Cut 3 acorn squash in half lengthwise. Remove seeds and fill cavity with stuffing. Bake in covered dish in moderate oven (350°F.) 1 hour, or until squash are tender. Serves 6.

Stuffed Acorn Squash: One of fall's most plentiful vegetables is a perfect teammate with a made-to-order stuffing of saltine crackers and ham. Serve with a crisp tossed salad.

SUMMER SQUASH

Varieties: 1. White—Cymling, patty-pan or scalloped. 2. Yellow—Straight neck or crookneck. 3. Light Green—Chayote. 4. Dark Green—Zucchini or Italian squash.

Selection: Buy 2 pounds for 4 servings. Summer squash must be extremely immature, fresh and heavy for its size. The skin may be smooth or warty (depending on variety) but must be very tender.

Preparation: Wash but do not pare. Remove stem and blossom ends. Cut into ½-inch slices or cubes. The Chayote is cut straight through, seed and all.

Cooking Time: 10 to 15 minutes.

Cooking: Cook, covered, in a very small amount of boiling salted water until tender, 10 to 15 minutes.

Serving: Serve hot seasoned with salt, pepper, and butter or margarine. For variety, add ketchup or tomato sauce or a dash of French dressing, or mash and season with butter, salt and pepper.

BROWNED SUMMER SQUASH SLICES

Wash squash. Do not pare unless skin is quite tough; cut into slices about ½ inch thick. Sprinkle with salt and pepper; dip in flour to coat lightly.

Brown slices in small amount of butter or margarine (about 10 minutes); serve sizzling hot.

FRENCH FRIED SUMMER SQUASH

Cut in ½-inch pieces. Season with salt and pepper. Dip in fine crumbs, then in egg slightly beaten with 1 tablespoon water, and again in crumbs.

Fry in deep hot fat (375°F.) and drain.

CREAMED SUMMER SQUASH

Cut in cubes; cook until nearly done but still firm. Drain and reheat in cream. Season to taste.

GLAZED ACORN SQUASH

Sprinkle baked or boiled squash with brown or maple sugar. Place in oven until sugar melts.

BAKED ZUCCHINI

Cut zucchini in halves, lengthwise. Place cut-side-up in buttered baking dish. Dot with butter or bits of bacon. Season with salt and pepper.

Bake in moderate oven (375°F.) until tender, about 30 minutes. Allow 1 small zucchini per serving. Serve with Hollandaise or tomato sauce.

Zucchini Baked with Tomato: Scoop out some of center. Fill with tomato, cut in pieces. Season and bake as above.

Stuffed Zucchini

STUFFED ZUCCHINI

6 medium-size zucchini
1 can (12-ounce) whole kernel corn, drained
2 teaspoons seasoned salt
2 eggs, beaten
¼ cup frozen chopped chives
½ cup grated sharp Cheddar cheese

Scrub zucchini well. Cut off ends; do not pare. Cook whole in boiling water about 5 to 7 minutes.

Cut squash in half lengthwise. With tip of spoon carefully remove squash from shells. Chop into small pieces; then combine with corn, seasoned salt, eggs, and chives.

Pile mixture lightly into zucchini shells. Place in 2-quart oblong baking dish. Sprinkle with grated cheese. Bake, uncovered, in moderate oven (350°F.) 30 minutes or until brown on top. Serves 6.

ZUCCHINI—ITALIAN STYLE

Cook 1 sliced onion in butter or margarine until yellow. Add 1 pound zucchini, sliced; cook and stir 5 minutes.

Add 1 cup fresh or canned tomatoes; season with salt and pepper. Cover and cook 5 minutes. Lower heat and cook until tender, about 25 minutes.

Variation: Or place in casserole; sprinkle with grated cheese and bake in moderate oven (375°F.) until brown. Serves 4.

SHERRIED SQUASH

3 cups winter squash, fresh or frozen, cooked and mashed
¾ teaspoon salt
¼ teaspoon celery salt
Dash of pepper
1½ tablespoons sherry
1 tablespoon butter or margarine, melted
⅛ teaspoon nutmeg

Combine squash, salt, celery salt, pepper, and wine; pile in greased shallow 1-quart baking dish. Brush with melted butter; sprinkle with nutmeg.

Place in preheated broiler 5 to 7 minutes or in moderate oven (375°F.) 15 to 20 minutes until heated. Serves 6.

Sherried Sweet Potatoes: In place of squash, use 3 cups sweet potatoes cooked and mashed.

SUCCOTASH

A mixture of corn and lima beans. Both the dish and the name are of American Indian origin.

Combine equal parts cooked lima beans and cooked corn kernels. Season with butter and salt. Reheat. Frozen limas and corn are excellent for succotash.

SUCCOTASH #2

2 cups cooked or canned, drained whole kernel corn
2 cups fresh or frozen green limas, cooked and drained
3 tablespoons butter or margarine
Salt and pepper
½ cup light cream or top milk

Combine vegetables in double boiler. Add butter, seasonings, and cream; heat thoroughly. Serves 6.

SWEET POTATOES

Cultivated from ancient times by the Aztecs, sweet potatoes were introduced into Europe in the 16th century and spread from there to Asia.

There are two types of sweet potatoes—one is light-colored, dry, and mealy (Jersey); the other moist, soft, and sugary (Nancy Hall or Porto Rico). In Louisiana and other southern states, the latter type is commonly called a yam. The true yam, however, belongs to another plant family (see index).

Disregard color in sweet potato buying, but remember that thick, chunky, medium-sized sweets which taper toward the ends are preferable. Avoid those with any sign of decay, as such deterioration spreads rapidly, affecting the taste of the entire potato, even in portions not immediately adjacent to the decayed area. Buy bright, clean sweets that are free from blemishes.

SWEET POTATOES—BOILED IN JACKETS

Wash and scrub sweet potatoes. Cook whole in boiling salted water, covered, about 30 minutes, or until tender. Drain.

Peel, and season with butter or meat drippings, salt and pepper to taste.

Baked Sweet Potatoes with Prune Filling

MASHED SWEET POTATOES

Peel hot cooked sweet potatoes (6 medium-sized makes 6 servings). Mash thoroughly and quickly. Add seasoning and butter or margarine.

Beat in hot milk a little at a time until sweet potatoes are fluffy and smooth.

Variations:

1. Shape seasoned mashed potatoes into mounds with small well in center. Brown in hot oven (425°F.).

Fill well with cranberry sauce or jelly, and serve hot.

2. Use orange juice in place of milk, add a little grated orange rind, butter or margarine, and a few raisins.

If desired, place in baking dish, top with meringue, and brown lightly in moderate oven (350°F.). Serve hot.

PAN-FRIED SWEET POTATOES

Boil sweet potatoes in jackets, peel, and slice. Add salt and pepper to taste.

Fry in hot fat in large skillet, turning occasionally until nicely browned.

BAKED SWEET POTATOES

Select medium-sized or large sweet potatoes. Scrub thoroughly, removing any imperfections, and rub skins all over with a little fat of any kind.

Bake in hot oven (400°F.) until potatoes are soft, from 40 to 60 minutes, according to size.

Remove from oven and cut lengthwise, then crosswise to allow steam to escape. Pinch the potatoes, pressing up the pulp so that it will show.

To save time in baking sweet potatoes, they may be parboiled for 15 minutes.

Serve plain, or with a dusting of paprika and a small pat of butter or margarine on each potato.

BAKED SWEET POTATOES WITH PRUNE FILLING

6 medium-sized sweet potatoes (about 3 pounds)
1 cup plumped chopped prunes
¼ teaspoon salt
½ teaspoon nutmeg
¼ cup butter
6 whole plump pitted prunes

Cut off both ends of sweet potatoes and bake in hot oven (400°F.) 40 to 45 minutes.

Remove and cool slightly. Cut off tops, scoop out with teaspoon, leaving shells. Mash sweet potatoes, add chopped prunes, salt, nutmeg, and butter; blend well. Refill shells.

Reheat for serving in moderate oven (350°F.) 15 minutes. Make a small indentation in top center of each sweet potato and place a warm pitted prune on each. Serves 6.

CANDIED SWEET POTATOES

4 medium sweet potatoes (1½ pounds)
2 tablespoons salad oil or shortening
½ cup brown sugar
¼ cup orange juice
¼ teaspoon grated orange rind

Wash sweet potatoes. Cover with water and partially cook until just tender enough to be pierced with a fork. Do not overcook. Drain well and set aside.

Combine remaining ingredients in saucepan; heat to boiling and cook 2 minutes.

Peel sweet potatoes and cut in halves lengthwise. Place in shallow 8-inch square baking pan and pour syrup over them.

Bake in slow oven (300°F.) 55 minutes, or until well glazed. After the first 15 minutes, turn potatoes and baste with syrup every 10 minutes. Serves 8.

BAKED STUFFED SWEET POTATOES

4 medium sweet potatoes
3 tablespoons butter or margarine
½ teaspoon salt
About ¼ cup milk or light cream

Wash potatoes, dry and bake in hot oven (400°F.) about 40 minutes, or until soft when tested with a vegetable knife.

Cut a slice from the top of each potato. Scoop out pulp and run it through a potato ricer or food mill. Reserve shells.

Whip pulp until fluffy with 2 tablespoons butter, salt, and milk or cream, using enough liquid to make mixture about as soft as mashed white potatoes.

Fill shells, and brush with remaining tablespoon of butter, melted. Return to oven and bake until lightly browned. Serves 4.

Variations of Baked Stuffed Sweet Potatoes

Sweet Potato Puffs: Fold 1 stiffly beaten egg white into mashed potato before filling shells.

Sweet Potato Boats: Add 1 of the following to the mashed sweet potato mixture before filling shells: 4 slices of crisp bacon, crumbled; ½ cup chopped cooked chicken or ham, ¼ cup chopped nuts, raisins, or well drained shredded pineapple.

SWEET POTATO PATTIES

Shape cold mashed sweet potatoes into small patties.

Roll in breadcrumbs or crushed dry breakfast cereal. Brown on both sides in a little fat.

Variations: Add to the mashed sweet potatoes, chopped cooked leftover meat or finely chopped apple.

SCALLOPED SWEET POTATOES AND APPLES

(Master Recipe)

Place alternate layers of sliced cooked sweet potatoes and sliced raw apples in a greased baking dish.

Sprinkle apple layers with sugar and a little salt. Dot with fat.

Add just enough hot water to cover bottom of dish. Apples and sweet potatoes do not take up liquid.

Bake covered in moderate oven (375°F.) 30 to 40 minutes, or until apples are tender.

If desired, uncover the dish for last 15 to 20 minutes of cooking and top with crushed dry breakfast cereal or breadcrumbs mixed with a little fat.

Sliced raw sweet potatoes may be used but require longer baking.

Variations: Substitute peeled orange slices, cranberry sauce (not jelly), or sliced fresh pears for apples. With pears, use brown sugar instead of granulated for added flavor. Top with breadcrumbs and bake 20 to 30 minutes.

SCALLOPED SWEET POTATOES WITH ORANGE JUICE

Omit apples and water in master recipe. Pour over sweet potatoes 1/3 to 1/2 cup orange juice containing a little grated orange rind. Top with breadcrumbs, and bake about 20 minutes.

SCALLOPED SWEET POTATOES WITH HAM

Follow recipe for scalloped potatoes and apples. For a main dish, use chopped cooked ham in place of apples. Omit sugar and breadcrumbs. Bake until heated through, 20 to 30 minutes.

SCALLOPED SWEET POTATOES WITH PEANUTS

Substitute chopped roasted peanuts for apples in master recipe. Omit fat and crumbs, and, if nuts are salted, omit salt. Bake 20 to 30 minutes.

Cranberry Candied Sweet Potatoes

OLD-FASHIONED SWEET POTATO PONE

  6 medium sweet potatoes
  2 cups sugar
  1/4 cup butter or margarine
  3 beaten eggs
  1 teaspoon cinnamon
  1 teaspoon allspice
  1 teaspoon ground cloves
  1 teaspoon nutmeg
  1 12-ounce package white raisins

Cook potatoes until tender. Peel and place in single layer in casserole.

Blend sugar and butter; mix in remaining ingredients. Pour over potatoes.

Bake in moderate oven (350°F.) until very hot, about 45 minutes. Serves 6.

SWEET POTATOES WITH MARSHMALLOWS

Boil 4 to 6 medium sweet potatoes until tender, but not soft.

Drain, peel, and put through ricer or mash with fork. Add milk, butter, 4 tablespoons chopped walnut meats, brown sugar, and salt to taste.

Turn mixture into buttered baking dish, allowing enough room between layer of potatoes and top of dish for a layer of marshmallows, which swell and spread during cooking.

Bake in slow oven (325°F.) until marshmallows are puffed and browned. Serve in baking dish. Serves 6.

LOUISIANA CASSEROLED SWEET POTATOES

Arrange 6 whole cooked Louisiana sweet potatoes in a buttered baking dish. Cover with 1 cup honey. Dot with 1/2 cup butter or margarine. Sprinkle with a few drops lemon juice.

Bake in moderate oven (350°F.) 15 to 20 minutes, basting potatoes occasionally with syrup. Serves 6.

CRANBERRY CANDIED SWEET POTATOES

  4 medium sweet potatoes, cooked and peeled, fresh or canned
  1/2 cup canned whole cranberry sauce
  3 tablespoons lemon juice
  1/2 cup light corn syrup
  1 tablespoon melted butter or margarine

Cut sweet potatoes in half lengthwise. Place in greased shallow baking pan. Combine cranberry sauce and lemon juice; mix well. Spread cranberry mixture over sweet potatoes.

Combine corn syrup and butter or margarine. Pour over sweet potato mixture.

Bake in moderate oven (350°F.) 25 minutes, basting occasionally with syrup mixture. Serves 4.

TOMATOES

It may surprise you to learn that tomatoes, once known as "love apples," are actually a fruit, not a vegetable, and that only a generation ago, many people thought they were poisonous. However, it is hardly conceivable that anyone labors under such a misapprehension today, as, whether she pronounces it "Tomayto" or "Tomahto," the American homemaker knows this delicious red-ripe fruit as one of the richest sources of healthful food values.

Selection: Buy 2 pounds for 4 servings. Tomatoes should be firm, well-formed and not overripe.

Preparation: Wash well. The skin is edible, but if necessary, peel. Keep tomatoes covered and refrigerated after peeling.

To Peel: Dip in boiling water for about 1/2 minute, then into cold water to chill; skins can be removed easily; or hold tomato on a fork over flame until skins blister and split. Peel.

Cooking Time: 10 minutes.

Cooking: Cut peeled tomatoes into quarters. Simmer gently, covered, for about 10 minutes. Use no water.

Serving: Season with minced onion, salt, pepper, and butter or margarine.

CHERRY TOMATO

A miniature red or yellow tomato about the size of a small plum, often no more than 1 inch in diameter.

PLUM TOMATO

The small Italian tomatoes shaped like plums; they can be used in any recipes calling for tomatoes.

BAKED OR BROILED TOMATOES

  3 medium tomatoes, cut in halves
  1 teaspoon salt
  1/8 teaspoon pepper
  1/2 cup buttered breadcrumbs
  1/2 cup grated American cheese

Season each tomato half with salt and pepper. Blend crumbs and cheese, and sprinkle on each tomato half.

Arrange in baking pan and bake in moderate oven (375°F.) 15 minutes, or broil 8 to 10 minutes, under low heat. Serves 6.

FRIED RIPE OR GREEN TOMATOES

Slice 6 medium-sized ripe or green tomatoes about 1/2-inch thick. Dip in mixture of 1/2 cup fine, dry breadcrumbs or flour, 1/2 teaspoon salt, and a little pepper.

Cook in small amount fat until brown on both sides.

If desired, dip tomatoes in beaten egg, then in flour or breadcrumbs before cooking. Serves 6.

Tomatoes Provincial

TOMATOES PROVINCIAL

1   cup ripe olives
8   large firm tomatoes
3   tablespoons olive or salad oil
½   cup minced onion
2   minced cloves garlic
1   pound bulk pork sausage
½   teaspoon salt
Dash of pepper
2   tablespoons chopped parsley

Cut up olives, leaving 8 whole. Wash tomatoes; take slice off bottom and with toothpick, put whole olive in top of each.

Scoop out tomatoes; turn upside down to drain on absorbent paper.

Heat oil in skillet; add onion and garlic; cook until soft and yellow. Add sausage and brown slowly about 15 minutes.

Drain off fat. Stir in seasonings, parsley, and cut olives; fill tomatoes.

Place in baking dish. Bake in moderate oven (375°F.) 15 to 20 minutes. Top with tomato slices last 5 minutes of baking time. Serves 6 to 8.

SCALLOPED RIPE OR GREEN TOMATOES

3½ cups sliced fresh or 1 No. 2½ can
        tomatoes
¼   cup minced onion
2   tablespoons minced green pepper,
        if desired
1   teaspoon salt
Pepper
Sugar, if desired—½ teaspoon for ripe
        or canned tomatoes, 1 table-
        spoon for green tomatoes
2   cups soft breadcrumbs
2   tablespoons fat

Combine tomatoes (ripe or green), onion, green pepper, salt, pepper, and sugar if used.

Place in baking dish alternate layers of tomato mixture and breadcrumbs, ending with breadcrumbs. (For a thinner mixture, omit 1 cup of the crumbs.) Dot with fat.

Bake in moderate oven (375°F.) 20 to 30 minutes for ripe tomatoes, about 45 for green.

If desired, sprinkle ½ cup grated cheese over the top for the last 10 to 15 minutes of baking. Serves 6.

Variations: For variety, combine ripe tomatoes with other vegetables. Reduce tomatoes in above recipe to 2½ cups and add 2½ cups cooked whole-kernel corn; or 3 cups shredded cabbage; or 1 medium-sized eggplant, pared and cut in ½-inch pieces; or 4 cups sliced crookneck squash; or 4 medium-sized onions, sliced or quartered, in place of the minced onion. Combine as for scalloped tomatoes.

Cover and bake until vegetables are tender—with corn, 20 to 30 minutes; with onions, about 1 hour; with cabbage, eggplant, or squash, the scallop will need to bake 45 to 50 minutes.

RIPE OR GREEN STEWED TOMATOES

Remove stem ends and quarter 6 medium ripe or green tomatoes (peel ripe tomatoes, if preferred). Add 1 tablespoon minced onion for flavor, if desired. Cover and cook until tender, 10 to 20 minutes for ripe tomatoes, 20 to 35 for green. Add a little water to green tomatoes, if needed.

Season with 1 teaspoon salt; a little pepper; sugar, if desired—½ teaspoon for ripe tomatoes, 1 tablespoon for green; and 1 tablespoon fat.

For variety, add ½ cup soft breadcrumbs before serving or top with toasted bread cubes. Serves 6.

Stewed Canned Tomatoes: Season canned tomatoes in the same way as fresh ripe, and heat (if onion is added cook until onion is tender).

Stewed Tomatoes With Onions or Celery: Cook together half as much sliced onion or chopped celery as ripe tomatoes. Season as above.

Cook covered until onion or celery is tender, about 20 minutes. This is an excellent way to use the outer stalks of celery that are less desirable for eating raw.

BAKED STUFFED TOMATOES
(Master Recipe)

Select smooth, medium-sized tomatoes. Cut thin slice from stem ends; remove seeds and pulp; discard seeds, if desired.

Drain off most of the juice. Sprinkle tomatoes with salt, invert and, if possible, let stand 30 minutes or longer.

Add an equal quantity of breadcrumbs to pulp. Season with salt and pepper, and a few drops onion juice. If desired, finely chopped onion and green pepper may be added. Stuff tomatoes, with mixture.

Place in buttered pan; sprinkle with additional buttered crumbs. Bake in hot oven (400°F.) 20 minutes.

STUFFING VARIATIONS FOR BAKED TOMATOES

This is an excellent way to use up small amounts of leftover seafood, meat, poultry, and vegetables.

Sauté a little chopped onion in butter or margarine; add chopped or ground meat, some of the tomato pulp, and crumbs. Season to taste.

For a firmer stuffing, stir in 1 slightly beaten egg.

Other suggested stuffings follow:

Shrimp Stuffing: Cut canned, or freshly cooked, cleaned shrimp in 2 or 3 pieces; add a little cream, cheese, or curry sauce. Fill tomatoes.

Top with buttered crumbs. Bake in moderate oven (350°F.) until top is brown.

Curried Leftover Meat Stuffing: Use any leftover cooked meat or cold cuts. Put through food chopper.

Bind with a little meat stock; season to taste with curry powder and a little grated onion. Fill tomatoes.

Top with buttered crumbs. Bake in moderate oven (350°F.) until top is brown.

Mixed Vegetable Stuffing: Chop leftover cooked vegetables (cucumber, onion, green pepper, peas, cauliflower, etc.). Mix with a little cream sauce or cheese sauce. Fill tomatoes.

Top with buttered crumbs. Bake in moderate oven (350°F.) until top is brown.

Creole Rice Stuffing: Sauté minced onion in butter or margarine. Add cooked rice, tomato pulp, and seasoning to taste. Fill tomatoes.

Top with buttered crumbs. Bake until top is brown.

Corn Stuffing: Fry gently 1 tablespoon chopped onion and 1 tablespoon green pepper in 2 tablespoons butter or margarine. Add 2 cups drained whole kernel corn, ½ cup fine breadcrumbs, 2 well beaten eggs, and ½ teaspoon salt.

Fill tomatoes. Bake until top is brown.

Corn and Green Pepper Stuffing: Use corn cut from cob. Mix with cooked, chopped green pepper, season with salt, pepper, and onion. Fill tomatoes.

Top with buttered crumbs. Bake until top is brown.

Broccoli Stuffing: Dip cooked broccoli tips in melted butter or margarine. Fill tomatoes.

Top with buttered crumbs. Bake in moderate oven until top is brown.

Green Pea Stuffing: Fry gently 1 tablespoon grated onion and ¼ cup finely cut celery in 2 tablespoons butter or margarine.

Add 2 cups cooked peas and the pulp which has been scooped out of the tomatoes. Mix well. Fill tomatoes. Bake.

Creole Stuffed Tomatoes

CREOLE STUFFED TOMATOES

3 slices bacon
1/4 cup chopped green pepper
1/4 cup chopped onion
6 medium tomatoes
1 cup whole kernel corn
1 teaspoon seasoned salt

Fry bacon in skillet until crisp. Drain and set aside. Remove drippings, leaving about 1 tablespoon. Sauté green pepper and onion slightly.

Meanwhile prepare tomatoes by removing top slice and center core from each. Scoop out pulp.

Add pulp, corn, and seasoned salt to vegetables in skillet. Heat thoroughly. Crumble bacon and add to vegetable mixture saving some of the bacon for garnish.

Fill tomato cups and top with remaining bacon. Bake in shallow dish in moderate oven (350°F.) 15 to 20 minutes. Serves 6.

TOMATOES CREOLE

1 green pepper, shredded
1 large onion, chopped
2 tablespoons minced celery
2 tablespoons butter or margarine
4 to 6 large tomatoes, skinned and sliced

Cook pepper, onion, and celery in melted butter until tender.

Add tomatoes and cook slowly until tender. Season to taste with salt and pepper. Serves 4 to 5.

SWISS CHARD

Swiss chard is a form of beet that is grown for the tops only. Like all salad greens, it is important that the leaves be fresh, crisp, and of a good green color. It is an excellent source of vitamin A and has a fair content of C and G. See **Greens.**

Selection and Preparation: One pound serves 3 to 4. Use young chard; wash thoroughly in 4 or 5 waters to remove sand and dirt.

Cooking: It usually needs no more water than that which clings to the leaves. Cover pan and cook over low heat 10 to 15 minutes. The liquid should be entirely absorbed.

If the green is old or has heavy white stalks, cut these off and cook them separately from the green leaves. Cut the stalks in 2-inch lengths; cover with boiling salted water and simmer until tender, about 25 minutes.

Serving: Chop the cooked vegetable; add 1 tablespoon melted butter or mar-

garine and 1/4 teaspoon salt for each cup of cooked drained chard.

Serve with melted butter or margarine, Hollandaise sauce, or hot mayonnaise as a dressing. Garnish with hard-cooked egg.

TARO

Any of several tropical plants cultivated for their starchy roots. The dasheen is a variety of taro. Taro roots are a staple food on many Pacific islands and in parts of the Far East. The Hawaiian dish poi is made from it. See **Dasheen.**

TOPEPO

This vegetable derives its name from the fact that it is a cross between the tomato and pepper. Topepos are generally used in salads and should be selected the same way as you would tomatoes.

TURNIPS

Turnips originated in Southern Europe where, during the earliest times, they were cultivated for medicinal purposes as well as for food. In fact, it was then popularly believed that broth made from turnips was good for the gout and that the turnip could be made into an excellent scouring soap for beautifying the face and hands. Modern research, however, indicates that turnips are a good source of several vitamins, the fresh green tops being particularly rich in A and C.

Turnips are generally sold with tops removed, although those from early crops are sometimes sold in bunches with tops on. The tops should be young, fresh, and green. Good winter turnips of the purple-top variety should have all the characteristics of quality root vegetables—smooth skin, firmness, and a good weight for their size. The eating quality of turnip greens depends largely on their freshness when purchased.

Turnips can be made sweeter and their flavor greatly improved by adding a teaspoonful of sugar to the cooking water.

Preparation: Turnips and rutabagas are cooked the same way. Scrub, peel as thinly as possible before cooking. Leave whole, cut into large pieces or dice. Save the green tops to serve as another vegetable.

Cooking Time: 15 to 30 minutes.

Cooking: Cook, covered, in a small amount of boiling, salted water. Allow 20 to 30 minutes for the whole turnips and 15 to 20 minutes for sliced or diced turnips.

Serving: Season with salt, pepper, and butter or margarine. Or mash, add a little hot milk and season as above.
Raw: Thin strips of turnip are a good addition to the relish plate.

CREAMED TURNIPS OR RUTABAGAS

Reheat diced, cooked turnips or rutabagas in a little heavy cream.

TURNIP SOUFFLÉ

Follow master recipe for Vegetable Soufflé.

GLAZED TURNIPS

Cook 8 small or 2½ cups diced turnips until tender. Drain.

Place in skillet with 3 tablespoons butter or margarine, 3 tablespoons corn syrup, and 1 blade of mace. Cook slowly until lightly browned, turning often. Serves 6.

TURNIPS EN CASSEROLE

Put cubed raw turnip in casserole. Dot with butter or margarine. Season with salt and pepper.

Add water or consommé to cover bottom of dish. Bake in moderate oven (350°F.) until soft, about 40 minutes.

TRUFFLES

A truffle is a small, fleshy fungus that grows underground, usually in woodlands close to the roots of trees. They are found in several parts of Europe but are valued most highly in France. The several varieties vary in color from gray or brown to nearly black; those of Périgord are especially esteemed. Their piquant, aromatic flavor makes them a prized garnish and sauce ingredient. Because they have not been successfully cultivated and must usually be hunted by hogs or dogs trained to scent them, they are expensive. Truffles in cans or jars are available, imported from France.

UDO

Udo is the Japanese name for the spikenard, a perennial herb of the valerian family. Its blanched shoots resemble celery and are used like asparagus. It is now grown in California.

YAMS

A yam is the starchy tuberous root of any of several tropical or subtropical climbing herbs or shrubs. The sweet potato, though commonly so called in the South, is not a yam. True yams, which often grow to 30 pounds or more, are grown in the West Indies, some Central and South American countries, and other parts of the world and to a limited extent in Florida and Louisiana. They are baked, boiled, or ground into flour and are also fed to livestock.

SPECIAL HELPS

Pressure Cooking

The large variety of pressure pans developed in recent years attest to the popularity of this versatile utensil. A pressure cooker is a saucepan in which food is cooked at temperatures above the normal temperature of boiling water. In ordinary top-of-the-stove cooking the boiling point of water (212°F.) is the highest temperature that can be reached. In a pressure cooker, the temperature is raised above the boiling point by the pressure of live steam and the heat is driven through the food at a much faster rate and in that way cutting the cooking time. For example, at 5 pounds pressure the temperature in the cooker is 228°F., at 10 pounds pressure the temperature inside the cooker is 240°F., and at 15 pounds pressure the temperature is 250°F.

Pressure cookers have regulators with which the pressure and temperature can be kept at the desired level. And they have safety valves intended to release steam (if the regulator clogs) before a dangerous pressure is reached. The pressure pan as we know it today is different in size and weight from the big pressure canners. It is, therefore, used for different purposes and handled differently. For canning, a large cooker of 16-quart capacity is more practical than the pressure pans which range in size from 1½ to 7 quarts, even though some of the manufacturers of large pans recommend them for this purpose.

The pressure cooker is not only a timesaver but it also conserves the vitamin content of food because air and light are excluded during the cooking period. Minerals, too, are conserved because those minerals which are soluble in water are contained in the small amount of water used in pressure cooking, and the cooking water that is left may be used in gravies, sauces, or soups.

GENERAL RULES FOR USING A PRESSURE COOKER

1. Before you use a pressure cooker for the first time, study the instruction booklet thoroughly and follow the manufacturer's directions with great care. They have been worked out in the maker's laboratories to insure safety in operation and the best possible results. Your cooker is a mechanically designed precision tool and cannot be operated by guess work.

2. Be sure the vent opening is properly cleaned and clear of any particles of food.

3. Put in the rack or omit as directed. Use the exact amount of water or other liquid specified in the recipe.

4. Fill the cooker no more than ⅔ or ¾ full of solid food, using ⅔ for a flexible or spring top cooker, ¾ for the solid dome types. Under no circumstances should the food touch the top of the cooker as this might clog the ventpipe or block the safety plug. Note, however, that some manufacturers stipulate that their cookers should never be filled more than ⅔ full of any kind of food.

5. Fill the cooker **no more than half full** of soup, liquids, or cooking cereal.

6. Unless a boiled or stewed effect is desired, use just enough water or liquid to come to the top of the rack, not over it.

7. Be sure that a steady stream of cold air with steam is coming out of the vent before pressure is built up. This takes from 2 to 4 minutes according to the size of the cooker, and the temperature of the liquid and food when put in.

8. Don't start cooking in a pressure cooker unless the lid is tight and well adjusted.

9. Remember, that unless the heat is reduced after pressure is reached, a continuous escape of steam causes so much loss of moisture that foods cook dry and burn.

10. Count pressure time given in a recipe from the time when the indicator, weight, or gauge shows 15 pounds pressure.

11. It may be desirable to use a timer to keep close track of minutes—partiularly to avoid overcooking frozen foods or fresh fruits.

12. Regulate the heat under the cooker so the pressure will keep even. If it tends to go up, even when the heat is lowered, place an asbestos pad under the cooker. The cause is probably that the vent tube is clogged or the heat is too high. If pressure starts to drop during the cooking period, it usually means that all moisture has been exhausted from the cooker. This is usually due to excess heat.

13. If you're called out of the kitchen while using the pressure cooker, turn off the heat or push cooker off the burner. Return it to the heat when you return.

14. When pressuring is finished turn off the heat. Reduce pressure according to the manufacturer's directions. Foods tend to overcook if allowed to stand in the cooker after pressuring. There are some foods, however, such as dried vegetables, puddings, fine cereals, and some casseroles which have a better texture if the pressure is reduced gradually. You will best determine this by experience and personal preference.

15. Always tilt the lid of a pressure cooker toward you when removing it so that any steam left is directed away from the face.

16. **Never attempt to force a cover off.** If you feel any resistance, that means the cooker has not been completely cooled. Scalding may result if the lid is prematurely removed while steam pressure remains in pot. That's why some cookers are so constructed

as to make it impossible to remove the lid until all pressure has been exhausted. If you feel any resistance, follow the manufacturer's directions in immersing the pan in cold water or allowing cold water to run over it for a while before opening it. Food in a cooker cooled to just the point where it can be opened, is usually the right temperature for serving.

HOW TO ADAPT YOUR OWN RECIPES TO PRESSURE COOKER

You don't have to acquire a whole set of new recipes for your pressure cooker. Most manufacturers put out a book of instructions and recipes giving cooking time, amount of water to be added, recipes, etc., but you are not limited. You can easily adapt your favorite recipes.

In general remember to cook things only ⅓ as long, and for most foods such as meats, vegetables, stews, etc., add only the amount of liquid you want in the finished food. Do not count on evaporation. As a general rule, ¼ cup is sufficient for foods requiring less than 10 minutes to cook and ½ cup for foods which take up to 20 minutes.

WHAT PRESSURE TO USE

The recipes and charts in this book are designed as a general guide. If they differ from the instructions in the booklet provided by the manufacturer of your cooker it is wise to follow those instructions because the maker knows best how his cooker performs.

Some of the pans have a pressure guage whereby 5, 10, or 15 pounds pressure may be used. Others are keyed to 15 pounds usage. If you have a pressure pan with various weights, that is, if a choice is possible from 5 to 15 pounds you may want to use the following table which is recommended by some manufacturers: 5 pounds for fruits and vegetables, 10 pounds for meats and dried vegetables, and 15 pounds for fresh vegetables, soups, and one dish meals. Other manufacturers recommend a standard 15 pound pressure, claiming that similar results are obtained at this higher pressure.

Most recipes and all charts in this book use a consistent 15 pound pressure. If you follow this plan you will not find it necessary to learn a variety of timings.

CARE OF PRESSURE COOKERS

1. When the pressure cooker is new, rinse in hot soapy water. To make cleaning easier, pour warm water into cooker as soon as you remove the food. After each use wash thoroughly in fairly hot, soapy water. Scald and dry thoroughly. Store uncovered to prevent accumulation of stale odors.

2. To remove food stains, add 2 teaspoons cream of tartar to 1 quart water and bring to pressure.

3. The steam control valves and weights do not require cleaning and should **never be immersed in water.** Handle indicator control or weight carefully. Dropping it may put it out of commission.

4. When the vent tube needs cleaning use a very tiny brush or a pipe cleaner, or force water through the vent tube to rinse it.

5. Keep the smooth edge of the cooker free of nicks. Avoid hitting the edge of the cooker with utensils such as knives or spoons. A marred uneven edge will allow escape of steam and with it precious vitamins and minerals.

6. Keep the cover away from direct heat such as burner, electric unit, or oven. Direct heat affects the gasket in such a way that it may not create a perfect seal and pressure will not be built up in the cooker.

7. Keep the cover clean and store right side up and not on the pressure pan.

8. Never pour cold water inside a dry overheated cooker or the sudden temperature change may crack or warp the metal.

9. If your cooker has a gauge, have it checked periodically for accuracy.

HINTS FOR PRESSURE COOKING MEATS, POULTRY, GAME

The primary advantage of pressure cooking meats is the fact that you can use the cheaper grades and cuts of meat or older stewing poultry and they can be stewed or pot roasted into a tender, juicy dish in a relatively short time. It is questionable, however, whether you would want to prepare steaks, chops, or high-quality roasts by this manner. We certainly would not recommend it. The pressure cooker, for example, cannot give you the fine broiled flavor of meats done by direct heat as in broiling.

Most meats are usually browned in the pressure cooker or in a skillet before being pressure cooked. It adds to the flavor and helps to seal in the juices; however to avoid unnecessary shrinkage browning should be done slowly. In browning meat before pressuring we suggest that you use as little fat as possible. If more than 2 tablespoons is used, pour off any excess fat after the meat is browned. With some finished dishes it is often desirable to brown and crisp the meat under a moderate broiler or in the oven after pressuring.

It is very difficult to give the exact time for pressure cooking meats. The cut and grade of meat, the size and shape, the amount and distribution of fat, bones, etc., all must be taken into consideration as well as the degree of doneness preferred by your family. In general, a thick, chunky piece of meat will require more time than a thin one, and the larger the amount of fat and the smaller the amount of bone the more minutes per pound will be required for pressuring.

FROZEN MEATS AND POULTRY

It is advisable to thaw any large cuts of meat before pressure cooking or it may cook unevenly. In general, meat does not have to be defrosted before cooking; however it will require a much longer cooking period. Allow ½ to ¾ as much time as given in the recipes and add about double the amount of water or other liquid.

Whole poultry should be entirely defrosted. Cut up poultry may be thawed only to the point where it can be separated into pieces.

CONDENSED RECIPE HINTS

It is very important to watch timing very carefully. An additional minute or two may represent many minutes of ordinary cooking.

If you want to use a lower pressure than the standard pressure of 15 pounds which is followed in these recipes, then

PRESSURE COOKERY AT HIGH ALTITUDES		
As the altitude increases the boiling point of water decreases. At sea level the boiling point of water is 212°F. If your pressure cooker has an adjustable gauge, you may use the following table.	Increase the pressure according to the altitude but the time will remain the same. No adjustment is needed for altitudes below 2000 feet.	

Elevation Above Sea Level	Boiling Point of Water	Increase Pressure
Below 2,000 feet	212°F.	0 pounds
Above 2,000 feet	208°F.	1 pound
Above 3,000 feet	206°F.	2 pounds
Above 4,000 feet	204°F.	2 pounds
Above 5,000 feet	202°F.	3 pounds
Above 6,000 feet	201°F.	3 pounds
Above 7,000 feet	199°F.	4 pounds

consult the directions supplied by the manufacturer of your cooker.

The directions that follow are intended as a guide so that you can, if you desire, make your own combination dishes. You merely take into consideration the difference in cooking time of the combined foods.

For example, if a meat takes 1 hour, the potatoes 15 minutes, and another vegetable only 5 minutes, you reduce pressure after 45 minutes of cooking and add the potatoes. Cook at 15 pounds pressure an additional 10 minutes. Reduce pressure again and add the second vegetable. Cook at 15 pounds pressure 5 minutes or a total time of 1 hour.

Season pressure cooked foods lightly inasmuch as very little liquid is used. You can always season to taste later. If desired you may make substitutions of tomato juice or stock for water and, of course, you may add other seasonings as desired but use seasonings lightly until you have gained experience. For suggestions about seasonings see the Index for other recipes.

Cooking time in the following condensed recipes begins when pressure reaches 15 pounds.

Unless you want a stewed effect, always use a rack in the cooker.

CONDENSED RECIPES
Cook at 15-Pound Pressure
CORNED BEEF

Use 3 to 4 pounds. Soak in cold water before cooking to remove excess salt. Drain. Place on rack in cooker. Add 2 cups water. Cook 20 to 25 minutes per pound. For additional flavoring, add a bay leaf, several whole black peppers, and 1 small sliced onion.

Near the end of cooking time, pour off all but 1 cup water and add potatoes and cabbage wedges.

FLANK STEAK

Use 1½ pounds. Cut into serving pieces. Season meat lightly. Spread with stuffing. Roll and tie. Brown on all sides in fat. Place on rack. Add ½ cup boiling water or tomato juice.

Near the end of cooking period, add potatoes, carrots, and onions, if desired. Total cooking time 35 to 45 minutes.

SHORT RIBS, BRAISED

Season lightly. Brown well in hot fat. Add 1 cup tomato juice. Cook 20 to 25 minutes.

BEEF STEW

Cut 2 pounds beef into 1-inch cubes. Season lightly. Brown in hot fat. Add 2 cups hot water. Cook 25 minutes. Near end of cooking period add mixed vegetables.

POT ROAST

Use 3 to 4 pounds round or rump. Season lightly. Pound flour into surface. Brown on all sides in hot fat. Add ½ cup hot water, 1 medium-sized onion (minced), 1 bay leaf, salt and pepper. Place on rack. Cook 10 minutes per pound.

Add other vegetables near end of cooking period.

SWISS STEAK

Use 2 pounds round steak, cut ¾ inch thick. Season lightly. Pound with flour. Brown slowly on both sides in hot fat. Add ½ cup tomato juice. Cook 25 minutes. Add vegetables near end of cooking period.

PORK SHOULDER

Brown slowly on all sides in hot fat. Pour off excess fat. Season lightly. Add ½ cup hot water. Cook 15 to 18 minutes per pound. When done, crisp in oven.

SPARERIBS

Use 2 pounds spareribs. Brown slowly in hot fat. Season lightly. Add 2 tablespoons hot water. Cook 15 minutes. To brown, brush with barbecue sauce and brown under very moderate broiler.

HAM HOCKS, FRESH

Brown slightly in hot fat. Season lightly. Add ½ cup hot water. Cook 20 minutes. Near end of cooking period add cabbage wedges or sauerkraut.

PICNIC HAM

Use a half or whole regular-type picnic ham. Cover with cold water. Soak 2 hours or more. Discard water. Place on rack in cooker. Add 2 cups hot water or cider. Cook 12 minutes per pound.

To bake, pare off rind and excess fat. Cover with desired glaze and brown in hot oven.

HAM SHANK

Place a 1- to 3-pound ham shank on rack in cooker. Add 1 cup hot water. Cook 35 minutes. Reduce pressure and remove shank. Cook cabbage and rutabagas in shank broth.

VEAL SHANKS

Split shanks. Brown slowly in hot fat. Add ¼ cup hot water. Cook 20 minutes.

VEAL STEW

Brown floured veal cubes in hot fat. Season lightly. Add 1 cup hot water. Cook 15 to 20 minutes. Add vegetables near end of cooking period.

VEAL BIRDS

Use ½-inch-thick slices. Stuff, season, and roll up. Tie and roll in flour. Brown in hot fat. Add ¼ cup hot water. Cook 15 minutes.

LAMB SHANKS

Split shanks. Brown in hot fat. Season lightly. Add ½ cup hot water and 1 small chopped onion, if desired. Cook 20 to 25 minutes. Add vegetables, if desired, near end of cooking period.

LAMB STEW

Cut meat into 1-inch cubes. Season lightly. Roll in flour. Brown on all sides in hot fat. Add 1 cup hot water for 2 pounds meat. Cook 20 minutes. Add vegetables near end of cooking period.

LAMB, NECK PIECES

Brown in hot fat. Season lightly. Add 1 cup hot water or tomato juice. Cook 20 minutes.

BEEF TONGUE, SMOKED

Add 2 cups hot water. Cook 25 minutes per pound.

Note: If tongue is to be served cold, skin and return to liquid and let cool in seasoned liquid. If tongue is to be served hot, remove and skin while cooking vegetables in part of tongue liquid.

BEEF TONGUE, CORNED

Add 2 cups hot water. Cook 20 minutes per pound.

BEEF TONGUE, FRESH

Add 2 cups hot water. Cook 15 minutes per pound.

OXTAILS

Cut into 1½-inch pieces. Brown in hot fat. Season lightly. Add 2 cups water. Cook 45 minutes.

BEEF HEART

Remove veins. Stuff if desired. Brown on all sides in 2 tablespoons hot fat. Season lightly. Add 1 cup hot water or tomato juice. Cook 25 minutes per pound.

CHICKEN FRICASSEE

Dredge serving-size pieces with seasoned flour. Brown on all sides in hot fat. Add ½ cup hot water. Cook 30 to 40 minutes.

CHICKEN, STEWED

Use a large stewing hen. Disjoint. Add 2 cups hot water. Cook 30 to 40 minutes. Use meat for creamed chicken, salads, molds, etc. Use the liquid in sauces.

VENISON STEAK

Season and pound in flour. Brown in hot fat. Add ¼ to ½ cup hot water. Cook 15 to 30 minutes. If young, cook the shortest time, using only ¼ cup hot water.

RABBIT

Clean and cut into serving-size pieces. Season and flour. Brown in hot fat. Add 1 cup hot water. Cook 15 minutes.

Soups—Pressure Cooked

RULES FOR PRESSURE-COOKED SOUPS

A much smaller amount of liquid is used in cooking soups in the pressure cooker than in the usual methods because soup is pressured without evaporation.

Soup is cooked at 15-pound pressure and, in that way, the full flavor and the essential nutrients are quickly extracted from the bones, meats, and other ingredients.

Your pressure cooker should not be filled more than half full of liquid ingredients or two-thirds full of liquids and solids unless the manufacturer's directions state otherwise. If your recipe calls for more liquids than your pressure cooker can hold under that rule or, if the result is too highly concentrated, it can always be diluted at serving time with boiling water, vegetable juices, or milk.

Less seasoning is needed in pressure-cooked soup, so season lightly. That, too, can be adjusted later.

Soup bones should be cracked open so that all the flavor may be extracted in the pressuring.

A minimum amount of fat should be used because fat tends to clog the vent pipe. All excess fat should be trimmed from meat or poultry used in pressure-cooked soups.

To make a clear soup in which vegetables are to be cooked, determine the cooking time of the vegetables in the chart and add them when the soup has been partially cooked. Reduce the pressure, strain the soup, and add the vegetables, then pressure cook until the vegetables are tender.

Your favorite recipes may be adapted to the pressure cooker. Read the instructions above about quantities of liquids and solids and cut the usual time of each step in your recipes about one-sixth. Note, too, that vegetables should be added toward the end of the cooking time; otherwise, they may overcook and be mushlike in consistency.

CHICKEN SOUP

3   pounds chicken
1   teaspoon salt
1   stalk celery, chopped
1   medium-sized carrot, diced
1   small onion, diced
1½ quarts boiling water

Cut chicken into serving pieces. (Wings, necks, and backs make excellent soup.) Put chicken in cooker. Add remaining ingredients. Cover and cook at 15-pound pressure for 15 minutes.

Reduce pressure. Strain soup. Remove skin and bones from chicken. Cut meat into tiny pieces and serve in soup. Serves 6 to 8.

BROWN SOUP STOCK

1½ pounds lean beef, cut into 1-inch cubes
2   tablespoons melted fat
½   cup diced onion
¼   cup carrot
1   small bay leaf
1½ teaspoons salt
⅛   teaspoon pepper
¼   cup chopped celery with leaves
1   teaspoon chopped parsley
1½ quarts boiling water

Brown meat in pressure cooker in the melted fat. Add onion, carrot, bay leaf, salt, pepper, celery, parsley, and water.

Adjust cover. Cook at 15-pound pressure 15 minutes.

Reduce pressure. Uncover and strain. Adjust seasoning. Serve as clear soup, bouillon, or store in refrigerator for soup stock. After soup is made, diced or julienned vegetables, cereals, diced meat, etc., may be served in soup. Serves 6.

ECONOMY SOUP STOCK

1½ pounds small soup bone, cracked
1   teaspoon salt
6   cups water

Place soup bone, salt, and water in cooker. Cook at 15-pound pressure for 20 minutes. Reduce pressure. Strain soup. Serves 6.

CREOLE GUMBO

3   tablespoons ham drippings or other fat
2½ cups cut okra
1   large onion, chopped
2   cloves garlic, chopped
1   medium-sized green pepper, chopped
1   can (8 ounces) tomato sauce
½   cup crabmeat
1   teaspoon thyme
2   tablespoons flour
½   pint oysters with liquid
4   cups water
3   tablespoons diced ham
2   bay leaves
1   teaspoon chopped parsley
1   teaspoon salt
½   teaspoon cayenne pepper

Heat cooker. Brown okra lightly in ham drippings in cooker. Combine remaining ingredients in cooker and mix well.

Cover and cook at 15-pound pressure for 15 minutes. Reduce pressure. Serves 6 to 8.

NAVY BEAN SOUP

1   cup navy beans
1   ham bone
1   onion, chopped
2   carrots, sliced
2   stalks celery, chopped
⅛   cup minced green pepper
½   cup tomato purée
⅛   teaspoon mustard
1   clove
2   peppercorns
4   cups water

Wash beans. Cover with water and soak overnight.

Drain. Put all ingredients in cooker. Season with salt and pepper to taste. Cook at 15-pound pressure for 30 minutes. Serves 6.

VEGETABLE SOUP

1   pound lean soup meat
1   small soup bone
4   cups water
2   teaspoons salt
¼   cup washed rice or barley
2   cups tomatoes
¼   cup diced potatoes
¼   cup diced carrots
¼   cup cut green beans
¼   cup diced celery
1   tablespoon minced parsley

Combine all ingredients except parsley in cooker. Cook 20 minutes at 15-pound pressure. Reduce pressure. Garnish soup with parsley. Serves 4 to 6.

FRENCH ONION SOUP

2   tablespoons butter or margarine
4   large onions, thinly sliced
4   cups brown soup stock
4   slices crisp, buttered toast
½   cup grated Parmesan cheese

Brown onions in melted butter in cooker. Add stock. Cover and cook at 15-pound pressure for 4 minutes.

Place toast in heated bowls. Pour soup over toast and sprinkle with Parmesan cheese. Serves 4.

Creole Gumbo

Packed Lunches

TIPS FOR AN EASIER PACKED LUNCH

1. Plan your lunch menus at the same time that you are planning your other family meals so you get better balanced meals in both. This will save you time, work, and help you to have a better packed lunch.

2. Plan to prepare some foods the day before while you are getting other meals (such as sandwich fillings, custards, puddings, cookies, stewed fruit) to save your time in the mornings (store in the refrigerator or freezer to keep until needed).

3. Have a lunch-packing center on a convenient table, or a cabinet with frequently used utensils, spices, waxed paper, string, etc. assembled together.

4. Wash and air lunch box daily to prevent food odors and flavors from developing.

5. Cream butter well before spreading. Spread on both slices of bread to prevent soaking from the filling.

6. Spread fillings to edge of bread, but do not allow to run over edge.

7. Cut sandwiches in different simple shapes for variety.

8. Wrap foods separately with waxed paper. Self-sealing waxed paper is economical because less paper is needed.

9. Pack heavy foods in bottom of container, with lighter ones on top, to prevent mashing.

10. Small salt and pepper shakers are a convenience. Cover top with paper and rubber band to prevent spilling. Plastic containers give good protection to moist foods.

11. Include napkins with the lunch.

12. Remember: Foods with variety in flavor, color, and texture add more interest and variety to the meal. It helps to prevent tiresome lunches.

SANDWICHES

Sandwiches are usually the foundation of the lunch. Use whole wheat or enriched bread rather than plain white bread. Whenever you use white bread, be sure it is "enriched" as it helps to supply some of the same minerals and vitamins found in the whole grain. Sweet rolls or sweet buns, common rolls, etc., are not required by some state laws to be enriched but may be by choice of the baker.

Make your sandwich fillings tasty and interesting. Most fillings are more tasty if chopped, or ground and combined with salad dressing or some other binder to make a good consistency to spread. Slices of cold meat and cheese are often dry and unappetizing.

Use a variety of breads such as whole wheat, cracked wheat, rye, raisin, nut, corn, and oatmeal bread. Crackers—plain, graham, soy, and rye crisp—make good sandwiches. Spread the bread with butter to prevent filling from soaking into the bread.

Filling Preparations

You will like to vary the flavor of sandwiches with different seasonings such as—mustard, ketchup, chili sauce, horseradish, paprika, olives, pickles, onions, pimiento or pepper, parsley, celery or celery seed. Salad dressing needs to be combined with most fillings to hold the mixture together. Suggested combinations are:

1. Ground meat (ham, beef, heart, liver)—horseradish, pickles.
2. Ground meat—egg, pickle, ketchup.
3. Sliced cold meat, pickle relish.
4. Salmon, pickle, ketchup.
5. Chopped egg, celery, green pepper, lemon juice.
6. Chopped egg, pickle, olives.
7. Chopped egg, cheese, crisp bacon.
8. Cream or cottage cheese, nuts, ground raisins.
9. Cream or cottage cheese, pimiento, onion juice, green pepper.
10. Cream cheese and jam.
11. Cream or cottage cheese, grated pineapple or dried fruit paste.
12. Peanut butter and ground raisins mixed with fruit juice.
13. Peanut butter, grated raw carrots.
14. Peanut butter, applesauce or fruit butters or jelly.
15. Peanut butter, honey.
16. Baked beans (mashed), ketchup, pickle.
17. Apple, celery, carrot, raisins.
18. Apple, celery, nuts.
19. Ground cabbage, carrots, peanuts, lemon juice.
20. Ground prunes, raisins, nuts.

VEGETABLES AND FRUITS

Raw vegetables and fruits add interest and health-protecting values to the lunch menu.

Wrap freshly washed vegetables in waxed paper, aluminum foil, or plastic bags to keep them crisp. Good vegetables to serve raw are: carrots, cabbage leaves, celery, lettuce, raw spinach, onions, radishes, raw cauliflower, tomatoes, and cucumbers.

Wrap lettuce for sandwiches to be placed in bread at the time of eating to prevent wilting.

SOUPS

Soups provide something hot and make the meal more satisfying.

If a thermos bottle is carried, hot soups are good. These may be clear broth, plain vegetable, or any creamed soups. Heat the bottle well with hot water before adding the soups to help retain heat.

DESSERTS TOP OFF THE MEAL

Raw fruits are always good. Simple desserts are more nutritious than rich ones. Heavy desserts such as pie, rich cakes, and puddings tend to make the child feel sluggish after lunch. However, they may be served occasionally to the active working person. Stewed fruit, custards, simple puddings, and plain cake or cookies are always desirable.

Occasional surprises such as a few small pieces of candy, candied fruit, and dried fruit relieve the monotony of carrying a packed lunch. Avoid too much candy or sweets for the child or overweight person.

Always include an orange, an apple, or some other fresh fruit.

Dried fruits washed and wrapped in waxed paper.

Cooked fruits in covered glass container.

Cookies and cake, wholesome ones, made with whole-grain cereals, fruits, and nuts.

Custards and other milk puddings in covered glass container.

BEVERAGES

You will always want to include milk in some form in your lunch. Milk is the most desirable beverage for the lunch. It is a necessary food for both children and adults to protect their health. There is no substitute for milk in the healthful diet. Include it as a beverage or you may make it into cream soups, custards, or puddings.

Fruit juices and tomato juice also offer good variety.

A thermos bottle is necessary to keep beverages hot or cold as desired. Rinse with hot or cold water first to help maintain temperature of the food.

A WORD OF WARNING— AVOID FOOD POISONING

Some foods, such as meats, salads, and egg dishes, spoil very quickly if not kept cool enough. Be especially careful with these in hot weather—or plan sandwich fillings of safe foods such as peanut butter, jelly, ground vegetables or fruits.

Do not pack deviled eggs, potato salads, and deviled ham. Bacteria develops very rapidly in these dishes in warm temperatures and cause poisoning.

SALT IN SUMMER IS IMPORTANT

For the man who does hard active work, put in a little extra salt in hot weather. Losing very much salt in perspiration may cause heat cramps.

Cooking at High Altitudes

The homemaker who moves into a high-altitude region soon finds that she must make changes in her everyday recipes. The lower air pressure at high elevations means that water boils at a lower temperature. Foods boiled or steamed fail to reach as high a cooking temperature as they do at lower levels, and they take longer to cook to the desired stage. Changes in atmospheric pressure make necessary many modifications in cooking procedures. Among these are an increase in the cooking times for most vegetables, a lowering in the end-point temperatures in cooking candies and cake frostings, and modifications of rich dough mixtures.

Fortunately, much experimentation and research has been done to eliminate the mysteries of high-altitude cookery by such organizations as the Colorado Agricultural Experiment Station, Colorado A. & M. College, Fort Collins, Colorado, the Colorado State College, the University of Wyoming Agricultural Experiment Station, Laramie, Wyoming, as well as by homemakers in high-altitude areas working under the direction of various experiment stations and commercial food companies. A homemaker can readily obtain the results of these experiments in booklet form. The information offered in this section, as well as in the Pressure Cookery section, will give a brief résumé of this information and in that way prepare the homemaker for the problems she will encounter and how to overcome them. More detailed information may be obtained from experiment stations maintained by the state colleges in the mountainous areas of the West.

CAKES AT HIGH ALTITUDES

The most perplexing problem that confronts a homemaker at high altitudes is that of baked products, especially cake. Since the air pressure is less, the leavening gas expands more and causes a coarse, crumbly or sometimes fallen product.

As the pressure decreases (with the increase in elevation) a correspondingly smaller weight of carbon dioxide or other leavening gas is required to perform the same amount of leavening. This applies to all flour mixtures, whether they are leavened with carbon dioxide, as in the case of butter cakes, baking powder biscuits, quick breads and yeast breads; or with air, as in angel food and sponge cakes; or with steam, as in popovers and cream puffs.

The structure of cake is very delicate, and increased pressure resulting from expanded carbon dioxide within the cells causes them to expand too much. This makes the texture too coarse, or, if the cells are expanded still more, they will rupture and a fallen cake will result. To produce a satisfactory cake at a high altitude, less baking powder must be used. For cakes made with sour milk and soda, less soda should be used.

The liquid at high altitudes evaporates to a greater extent, causing the sugar solution in the batter to become more concentrated. Excessive sugar in the cell walls weakens the structure and makes them more apt to collapse. Thus, reducing the sugar in a cake recipe gives stronger cell walls and makes the cake less susceptible to falling.

In general, for 5,000 feet, the Colorado Experiment Station recommends a reduction of ½ teaspoon double-acting baking powder, 2½ teaspoons sugar and an increase of ½ to 1 tablespoon liquid for a cake containing 2 cups flour. Contrary to popular opinion, there are no set rules for modification of cake recipes for high altitude. The changes that are necessary depend on the type of cake and the relationship of the ingredients to each other.

In angel food cakes, the leavening is air, and care must be taken not to beat too much air into the egg whites. They should be beaten until they form peaks which just fall over. The sugar should be reduced about 1 tablespoon for each 1,000 feet of altitude. A higher baking temperature for a shorter time is more satisfactory. Less sugar and more liquid should be used for sponge cake. The eggs or egg yolks should not be overbeaten and if baking powder is called for, the amount should be reduced.

QUICK BREADS

With biscuits, muffins, and other quick breads the baking powder may be decreased slightly but the structure of the product is such that it will withstand the increased pressure quite well.

For popovers, the amount of egg in the batter should be increased and the shortening reduced. This makes a stronger batter which will be able to retain the steam long enough for a crust to form. Popovers made by sea-level recipes lose the steam too fast, both by expansion and evaporation, and turn out more like muffins. Cream puff batter, being heavier, holds the steam well and does not require any correction for altitude.

YEAST BREADS

Yeast bread dough rises more rapidly at high altitudes, and it may become over-puffed if it is not watched carefully and allowed to rise only until it is doubled in bulk. Less yeast may be used, but most bakers prefer to let the dough rise for a shorter time. Flour dries out faster at higher altitudes; therefore it may be necessary to use more liquid to compensate for this loss and to make the dough the proper consistency.

COOKIES

Cookies usually do not need adjustment for altitude. A slight reduction in baking powder and sugar may improve them.

PIECRUST

Piecrust is not affected by altitude except for the faster rate of evaporation. Therefore, slightly more liquid may be required.

DOUGHNUTS

Doughnuts made from sea-level recipes are frequently found to be cracked, too high in fat absorption, and too hard and brown. To remedy this difficulty, the sugar also should be reduced.

DOUGHNUTS — HIGH ALTITUDE

2	tablespoons shortening
1	cup sugar
2	eggs
1	cup sour milk or buttermilk
1	teaspoon baking soda
4	to 4½ cups sifted enriched flour
1½	teaspoons baking powder
1	teaspoon salt
1	teaspoon nutmeg

Cream shortening and sugar. Add eggs and beat well. Add sour milk.

Sift dry ingredients and add to first mixture. Mix well, chill.

Roll out and fry in hot deep fat (350°F.). Makes about 3½ dozen.

Smoke Cooking

This is a method of cooking which uses hot smoke in place of direct heat giving to meats, poultry, and fish that wonderful flavor that is characteristic of some Chinese barbecued foods and a variety of expensive foods often seen in specialty shops.

Smoke cooking is an ancient art regaining popularity now that portable smoke ovens are being offered in the stores.

Cooking times and methods vary with the type of oven used, the heat of the fire, and the distance of the smoking rack or hooks from the firebox. The manufacturer's directions accompanying your oven should be followed.

In general, the ovens consist of a firebox and a chimney.

After the fire is started and the oven warmed, food is suspended in the chimney and cooked by the hot air and smoke which escapes past it.

The temperature is controlled by a lid with an adjustable damper.

The fire should be made with hardwoods (chips, sawdust, pressed) such as hickory, oak, hard maple, or fruit woods (apple, cherry, lemon, etc.) to give the foods their characteristic smoke flavor.

To smoke-cook foods in a barbecue with a hood, start with a charcoal fire, then when it burns down to even glowing embers, add slightly dampened hickory or fruit tree chips or sawdust.

Place the food on the grill or spit, close the hood tightly and let it cook. Remember that this is a slow process and can't be hurried.

In all smoke cooking care has to be observed to avoid overcooking as there is a tendency for the food to dry out. For this reason fatty foods are most suitable. And it's usually best to soak the food in a marinade for several hours or overnight to add flavor and to temper the smoky taste.

Chafing Dishes

Chafing dish cookery is fun and almost anything that can be made in a skillet or double boiler can also be made in many chafing dishes. It's that simple!

TYPES OF CHAFING DISHES

You'll find chafing dishes in many handsome styles from tiny ones for individual servings to jumbo size for more than 20.

They come with different kinds of heating devices. For actual cooking at the table, most people vote for heat you can adjust, as the alcohol burner, canned heat, and the electric unit with heat control.

Some chafing dishes are actually a double boiler (bain-marie) with water pan and a cooking pan (blazer). The cooking pan can be used directly over the flame for browning or for foods that don't require the gentle heat of the bain-marie. Other chafing dishes are the deep-skillet type with just one pan.

Then there are food warmers, often pottery casseroles, heated by candles or alcohol burners. These keep cooked foods at serving temperature on the buffet. You may also use a double-boiler chafing dish for the same purpose.

CHAFING DISH COOKERY HINTS

● Plan on a first course such as a large salad to keep your guests busy while you play chef.
● So you won't keep hungry folks waiting too long while you cook, choose a quick-to-make recipe.
● Memorize the recipe thoroughly. If necessary, rehearse it in advance.
● Get most of the fixing out of the way before the doorbell rings. Measure all ingredients carefully in the kitchen.
● Arrange all ingredients and utensils you'll need on a tray or lazy susan near the chafing dish. Have the chafing dish on another tray.
● And remember, part of the fun is collecting pretty tiny dishes and pans to hold these ingredients. Choose conversation pieces that will help make a stunning picture.
● Cook noiselessly. Use long wooden spoons for stirring.
● It's wise to fill the alcohol burner beneath the chafing dish well ahead of lighting. And if you must refuel while cooking, you'll be smart to carry the whole to the kitchen sink.

Cooking for Two

Cooking for two, despite its romantic implications, often poses a problem because most recipes make 4, 6, or 8 servings. For a smaller number of servings, the amount of each ingredient in such recipes as casseroles, salads, and vegetables may be cut in half or thirds. Pies can be prepared as individual tarts. It's best, however, to bake whole recipes for breads and cakes, then freeze half or more. Leftover cake, however, can be turned into a variety of enticing cake desserts. Many such desserts are included in this book.

In many sections of this book you'll find certain types of popular recipes specifically marked "for two." In general, you'll be money and time ahead if you plan several meals at once when you cook for two. You can then make use of small roasts as well as such items as a half ham or a small turkey. Leftovers of these present the minimum problem since they make easily prepared casseroles, meat pies, and sandwiches.

BUYING and COOKING GUIDE for SMALL ROASTS (Roasted at 325°F. Oven Temperature)			
Meat Cut to Buy	**Weight**	**Time: Minutes Per Lb.**	**Meat Thermometer Reading**
Beef: Standing Rib (short cut)	2½–3 lbs. (1 rib roast)	20 / 25 / 30	140°F. (rare) / 160°F. (medium) / 170°F. (well done)
Beef: Rolled Rib	2½–3 lbs. (3–4 inches thick)	30–35 / 35–40 / 40–45	140°F. (rare) / 160°F. (medium) / 170°F. (well done)
Veal: Shoulder, boned and rolled	3½–4 lbs.	55–60	170°F.
Veal: Breast, with pocket	1 breast (about 4 lbs.)	45	170°F.
Veal: Rolled Rump	3–4 lbs.	55–60	170°F.
Lamb: Shoulder, boned and rolled or cushion style	3–3½ lbs.	40	175°F. (medium) / 180°F. (well done)
Fresh Pork: Loin, center cut	2–2½ lbs.	40	185°F.
Fresh Pork: Spareribs	2–2½ lbs.	1½–2 hours (total time)	
Fresh Pork: Tenderloin	2 thick tenderloin pieces	1½ hours (total time)	185°F.
Smoked Ham: Slice	1–2 inches thick	1–2 hours (total time depending on thickness)	
Canadian Bacon	1½ lbs.	1 hour (total time)	170°F.

For any cook, cub or expert, a meat thermometer is a wise investment. It tells at a glance whether meat is rare, medium, or well done.

Ways to Use Leftovers

SOME OF THE DISHES IN WHICH LEFTOVERS MAY BE USED

Egg whites, in

Custard
Fruit whip
Meringue
Soufflés

Hard-cooked egg or yolk, in

Casserole dishes
Garnish
Salads
Sandwiches

Sour cream, in

Cakes, cookies
Dessert sauce
Meat stews
Pie filling
Salad dressing
Sauce for vegetables

Cooked meats, poultry, fish, in

Casserole dishes
Hash
Meat patties
Meat pies
Salads
Sandwiches
Stuffed vegetables

Cooked rice, noodles, macaroni, spaghetti, in

Casseroles
Meat or cheese loaf
Timbales

Egg yolks, in

Cakes
Cornstarch pudding
Custard or sauce
Pie filling
Salad dressing
Scrambled eggs

Cooked snap beans, lima beans, corn, peas, carrots, in

Meat and vegetable pie
Soup
Salad
Stew
Stuffed peppers
Stuffed tomatoes
Vegetables in cheese sauce

Cooked potatoes, in

Croquettes
Fried or creamed potatoes
Meat-pie crust
Potatoes in cheese sauce
Stew or chowder

Cooked leafy vegetables chopped, in

Creamed vegetables
Soup
Meat loaf
Meat patties
Omelet
Soufflé

Cooked or canned fruits, in

Fruit cup
Fruit sauces
Jellied fruit
Quick breads
Shortcake
Upside-down cake
Yeast breads

Cooked wheat, oat, or corn cereals, in

Fried cereal
Meat loaf or patties
Sweet puddings

Cake or cookies, in

Brown betty
Ice-box cake
Toasted, with sweet topping for dessert

Bread

Slices, for
    French toast
Dry crumbs, in
    Brown betty
    Croquettes
    Fried chops
Soft crumbs, in
    Meat loaf
    Stuffings

Sour milk, in

Cakes, cookies
Quick breads

HINTS FOR USING LEFTOVER MEATS

With leftover meats the possibilities are almost limitless. With the price of meat as high as it is, it is wise to see that none is wasted. Some families like a roast and feel that although the initial cost is high, it goes farther than steaks, chops, or even hamburgers or stew meat.

Hash need not be "low man on the totem pole" of menu planning. With proper handling it can become a far more sophisticated dish than cartoonists or comedians would have us believe. It can be just well-seasoned, dry minced meat, or it can be moistened with leftover gravy, milk, cream (even sour cream), cream sauce or soup—with or without onions, peppers, potatoes, or chopped vegetables.

A piece of soup meat or leftover stew can emerge as a good-to-look-at and good-to-eat dish if it is ground, seasoned, moistened with gravy or soup, and used to fill the center of a straight-sided baking dish or casserole which has been buttered and lined with cooked rice or fine noodles. Bake in a moderate oven until well heated. Turn out on a platter and sprinkle with chopped parsley or chives. Serve with leftover gravy, tomato or mushroom sauce poured around the mound of meat and rice (or noodles).

Another variation is to make the ground meat—and it need not be just one meat; it can be a combination of meats, or meats and vegetables—into pastry rolls or pinwheels. Use either pastry dough or a biscuit dough.

For the rolls: Roll the dough into a rectangle. Shape the chopped meat mixture into a roll about one and one-half inches in diameter. Place it along the edge of the rectangle of dough and roll dough until the meat is covered by the crust. Cut into desired lengths. Place on a greased pan and bake until the crust is browned.

The pinwheels are made and cut like a jelly roll. Spread the dough with the meat mixture, roll up, cut in slices about one inch thick, place on greased cooky sheet or pan, and bake. Serve with stewed tomatoes, ketchup, gravy or mushroom sauce.

Pieces of meat from the bone of a roast can be added to a spaghetti sauce or ground and made into a sandwich filling.

Bits of minced ham, chicken or veal are delicious added to an omelet, scrambled eggs, or cut in small strips and added to a tossed salad.

Meat pies from stews, with pastry, biscuit or mashed potato topping, are always popular. Try a well seasoned meat turnover in a lunch box in place of the usual sandwich.

HINTS FOR USING LEFTOVER VEGETABLES AND FRUITS

Vegetables reheated are apt to be unattractive, lacking in flavor, and will lose vitamins in the process. Try a casserole by adding freshly boiled, diced celery and onion to the leftover vegetables and top with an undiluted can of cream soup—chicken, tomato or mushroom—or grated cheese and breadcrumbs.

Leftover broccoli, Brussels sprouts or cauliflower can be placed in a shallow dish, topped with a cheese spread and browned under the broiler. Placed on a slice of boiled ham or cold chicken, this combination will be a main course easily prepared and a welcome change from the usual fare.

Cold vegetables well marinated with a French dressing and served with lettuce or added to a mixed salad will take the place of separate servings of vegetables and salad. Freshly diced tomato added to this dish increases its taste- and eye-appeal.

Almost any combination of cooked or cooked and raw vegetables can be blended and used in soups or sauces. Finely chopped, they may be added to salad dressing, meat loaf, croquettes or hamburgers. Again they might be reseasoned—onion, celery seed, chives, parsley, Worcestershire, a bit of herb, such as tarragon—and a little stiff cream sauce added. Shape as croquettes, dip in egg and crumbs, and bake or sauté ...thus giving the leftover a new personality.

For stuffing peppers, tomatoes, squash, eggplant or cabbage leaves, the combinations of vegetables, crumbs, rice and meat are limited only by the cook's imagination. As in all leftovers, if it tastes good before it is cooked, it will taste better afterwards. Tasting is important all along the line.

Leftover Salad

Salads pose a problem only when prepared as a large salad. A small amount of tossed or chef's salad is often left over. This is good chopped and added to mayonnaise when serving a sliced tomato, cucumber or potato salad. The portion of tossed salad also can be mixed with a sandwich spread, or even added to a soup (French dressing included).

A tomato aspic is just as delicious served hot as a soup. If necessary, stretch with a beef or chicken consommé or bouillon cube. It also can be added to a vegetable soup.

Leftover Fruits

If some mixed fruit salad is left over and cannot be used attractively in a fruit cup, it can be stewed with added sugar and used as a tutti-frutti sauce— or cooked until thick and used as a jam for toast or as filling for a cake. Grated lemon or orange rind will improve the flavor of any fruit combination.

Cooked cut-up fruit may be added to mincemeat or a cranberry-raisin-apple combination for harvest pie.

Fruit juices, fresh or canned, should be saved and used in gelatin salads, desserts, and beverages.

HINTS FOR USING LEFTOVER DESSERTS

A loaf cake which has become too dry can appear as a party dessert.

Slice and toast or crumb the cake. Place in a dish, add a custard sauce, chill and top with jam, whipped cream or coconut. Fruit may be combined with the crumbs.

A crumb crust for a pie is delicious when made from cake or cooky crumbs, either white, spiced or chocolate. It is easier to crumb cake or cookies when they are not too dry. Place on paper napkins in a shallow pan and dry thoroughly in a slightly warm oven. Sift or roll well for an even crumb and store in the refrigerator or a cool, dry place.

A more elaborate dessert is easily made using angel food or sponge cake. If there is only a piece or two left, use it in individual molds.

Make a pattern of fruit in the bottom of the mold, using sliced peaches, canned pineapple, cherries, grapes, orange sections or just well drained fruit cocktail. Cover the fruit with broken pieces of cake. Pour over this a warm ready-mix or a gelatin mix made from fruit juices. Place in the refrigerator to chill. Unmold and serve with cream, custard sauce or cut-up fruit.

Fruit Bettys made with crumbled cake instead of bread will cut down on the sugar and butter needed.

Cake crumbs with a little brown sugar and cinnamon added are good for topping on an open-faced fruit pie.

Fine, sifted white cake crumbs with white sugar and grated lemon rind, sprinkled lightly on a lemon chiffon pie, is a change from whipped cream and is kinder to the figure and the purse. When used as a topping, chocolate crumbs, nuts, and a bit of cinnamon give a pleasing texture combination to cornstarch puddings and pies.

Frequently, when making pies, there will be a little leftover filling. If it is of a pudding or custard type, it can be baked without a crust so that a member of the family who cannot eat pastry can still enjoy the dessert.

If there is a little leftover pastry dough, cut it in rounds with a large cooky cutter, bake and store to use another day to top either a stew, stewed fruit or applesauce.

A little extra pie filling, such as lemon meringue or any of the pudding-type fillings, may be thinned with either fruit juice, milk or cream and put into sherbet glasses for another meal or used undiluted as a cake filling. It is good to remember desserts eaten with a spoon should be less stiff than those eaten with a fork. A little leftover fruit from pie-making can be used in a turnover or a tart, or sometimes saved for for use in filled cookies.

Too many times a little fresh fruit is allowed to spoil when it might be used. Cook it for a sauce or a jam, use it in fruit whips, in a gelatin dessert, or add it to griddlecakes, waffles or muffins.

Leftover griddlecakes spread with jelly or jam, rolled up, reheated in the oven and served with powdered sugar or a lemon sauce will be enjoyed for dessert.

HINTS FOR USING LEFTOVER BREAD

Leftover bread is perhaps the most wasted item of food in many homes— yet it has innumerable uses. If bread puddings are not popular with members of the family, the bread can be used for any number of fruit Bettys.

Fine crumbs (made by drying the bread in a warm oven, then putting it through the food chopper) are handy for breading chops. Crumbs, salt, pepper and a generous amount of paprika is a good combination to use for breading meats.

Fish, sliced liver, sliced eggplant brushed with melted fat and then dusted with this crumb mix may be baked quickly in a very hot oven (500°F.) for 12 to 15 minutes. This combination emerges looking and tasting better than when done in a frying pan; furthermore, it is much less greasy.

Bread cut into tiny squares, or crum-

bled, dried and mixed with herbs and stored, saves time when stuffing the holiday bird. Again, cut the crusts from not too dry, thinly sliced bread and make waffle toast in the waffle iron. Complete drying in the oven and store for use with soups and salads, using it as Melba toast.

Wine Cookery Hints

The American homemaker is catching up with her French counterpart, who has known this little kitchen secret all along: To make a mundane dish sensational, just add a little wine. Even old American standbys like franks-and-beans and cherry pie become subtle mellow dishes with a touch of wine. For wine is a seasoning, like salt and pepper, that complements the natural goodness of foods. And wine blends with foods to create something new and richer in the way of flavor.

There is no trick to cooking with wine. At first you may feel more assurance if you follow a recipe. But in many cases you don't need a recipe. When you add your other seasonings, pour in a little wine as well; taste, and continue adding wine a little at a time until it tastes "just right." (The alcohol passes off as heat is applied just as it does from vanilla.)

While almost any wine can be used with almost any food, there are natural "taste harmonies" between certain wines and foods. Take sherry, for instance. Its flavor harmonizes with a variety of foods, with soups and with fish. It's grand, too, in many chicken dishes and in sauces for ham and other meats. And it's a "natural" in sauces for puddings and fruits.

The white table wines, such as sauterne and rhine wine, are delicate in flavor—the perfect complement to the delicate flavors of fish, chicken, lamb, and veal.

The red table wines, such as burgundy and claret, being more robust in flavor, go well with red meats. They're excellent, too, in spaghetti and cheese dishes. And you can improve the flavor and texture of inexpensive cuts of meat by marinating them in red wine for several hours before cooking.

The dessert wines, such as port, muscatel, and tokay, give extra goodness to desserts and fruits.

You'll find wines are versatile, too. You can substitute one wine for another in a recipe as long as you use the same type of wine. For instance, in a recipe calling for sauterne, you may use chablis or any other white table wine. The same thing applies to red wines—zinfandal or any claret-type wine may be substituted for burgundy.

Cooking for a Crowd

HINTS ON PLANNING FOR AND SERVING A CROWD

● The first step to consider in planning a meal for a large group is to select a thoroughly dependable chairman with whom people like to work. She will have to delegate the work to her assistants and see that they carry it out.

● The various jobs will include the marketing and the accounts, the preparation of the food in the kitchen, arrangements for the dining room—setting and decorating the tables, serving the incidentals such as butter and water, waiting on the tables, and the final cleaning up.

● Planning the menu is the next step. Be sure the food you select fits the group you are serving. Choose dishes that are most generally liked by the greatest number of people, keeping in mind the fact that an all man's group likes one thing, an all woman's group something else, and that a community supper would require food quite different than would be included in a menu for teen-agers.

● Decide upon the type of meal, keeping in mind the cost of each item and any extras.

● Simplify the work by choosing food which can be prepared in advance and which will require a minimum amount of last-minute effort.

● Choose foods that are in season and readily available.

● Consider the cooking facilities as well as the refrigeration. Avoid dishes which can't be made on the available equipment.

● If the equipment is inadequate perhaps some dishes can be prepared at the homes of the committee members and brought in ready to be served. Select foods that can be easily prepared.

● Consider contrasts in color, flavor, shape, and texture. For example, don't serve pea soup if peas are to be included, or tomatoes if tomato soup is included.

● Be prepared for extra guests. Have a supply of canned foods on hand which can be returned.

● And finally, use the simplest form of service whether it's buffet, table service, or family service, doing everything that can be done in advance, leaving time for the things that must be done at the last minute such as placing bread, butter, and water on the tables, tossing the salad, etc.

APPROXIMATE AMOUNTS OF FOODS NEEDED TO SERVE FIFTY PERSONS

Food	Size of Serving	Approximate Amount to Buy for 50
BEVERAGES		
Coffee	1 cup	1 to 1¼ pounds
Cocoa	1 cup	½ pound
Cocoa mix	1 cup	3 pounds
Fruit punch	2 to 3 punch glasses	3½ gallons
Tea, hot	1 cup	⅓ pound
Tea, iced	1 teaspoon leaves per glass	1¼ cups tea leaves
Fruit juices	½ cup	6½ quarts or 2 No. 10 cans
DAIRY PRODUCTS AND EGGS		
Butter or margarine (36 squares to pound)	1 to 1½ pats	1½ pounds
Cheese, American	1 to 2 ounces	4¾ pounds
Cheese, cottage (1 pound-2 cups)	3 to 5 ounces for plain salad	10 to 16 quarts
	3 ounces if part of main course	
Cheese, cream	½ ounce per sandwich	10 3-ounce packages or 25 ounces bulk
Cheese, Swiss (12 to 20 slices per pound)	1 slice per sandwich	4 pounds
Cream, for dessert for coffee	2 to 4 tablespoons 1 tablespoon	1½ to 3 quarts 1 quart
Cream, whipping for garnish	1 tablespoon	1 quart
Ice cream, bulk	No. 12 dipper (½ cup)	2 gallons
Ice cream, brick	⅙ of brick	9 bricks
Eggs, for scrambling	1½ to 2 eggs	6¼ to 8⅓ dozen
Milk	6 ounce glass	2½ gallons
FRUIT		
Canned	½ cup	2 No. 10 cans or 8 No. 2½ cans
Apples for pie	6 to 7 cuts per pie	15 pounds
Berries for shortcake	½ cup	6 to 8 quarts
Frozen fruit for pie	6 to 7 cuts per pie	10 pounds
Frozen fruit for topping for ice cream	1½ ounces	5 pounds
Cranberries for sauce	¼ cup	3 pounds
Cranberry sauce, jellied	½-inch slice	6 1-pound cans
FISH AND SHELLFISH		
Fish, with tail, head bone and skin	½ pound	25 pounds
Fish, without tail or head	¼ pound	14 pounds
Fish fillets	¼ pound	14 pounds
Lobster, fresh or canned	⅓ cup for salad	18 to 20 pounds live or 3 pounds, canned
Oysters, for cocktail	6 to 8 raw	5 to 6 quarts
Oysters, for stew	1 to 1½ cups stew	6 quarts oysters
Oysters, scalloped	½ cup scalloped	6 quarts oysters
Shrimp, fresh or canned	8 to 10 shrimps for cocktail	8 pounds fresh, shelled or canned
Tuna, canned	⅓ cup meat, about 4 servings per can	12 to 13 (7-ounce) cans
POULTRY (Dressed Weight)		
Chicken, roast or baked	4 to 5 ounces	30 to 35 pounds
Chicken, fried	¼ or ½ chicken	13 to 25 fryers (2½ to 3½ pounds)
Chicken for dishes using cut-up meat	5 to 6 ounces	20 to 25 pounds
Turkey, roast	2½ ounces	35 to 40 pounds
Turkey for dishes using cut-up meat	5 to 6 ounces	16 pounds

APPROXIMATE AMOUNTS OF FOODS NEEDED TO SERVE FIFTY PERSONS

Food	Size of Serving	Approximate Amount to Buy for 50
MEATS (Uncooked Weight)		
Beef:		
Country fried steak (round), ½-inch thick	3 ounces	20 pounds
Ground meat patties	3½ ounces	14 pounds
Liver	3 ounces	13 pounds
Pot roast, chuck	3 ounces	20 pounds
Rib roast	2 ounces	20 to 25 pounds
Steaks to broil (sirloin)	4 to 4½ ounces	18 to 20 pounds
(T-bone)	8 ounces	25 pounds
Stew with vegetables	5½ ounces	12 pounds
Swiss steak (round) ¾-inch thick	3½ ounces	16 pounds
Veal:		
Breaded veal, round	3 ounces	12½ pounds
Birds, round, thin	3½ ounces	12½ pounds
Cutlets and chops	3 ounces	12½ to 15 pounds
Lamb:		
Chops	2 each	25 pounds
Roast leg	2½ ounces	25 pounds (4 legs)
Patties	1 5-ounce patty	16 pounds
Pork:		
Ham, cured, baked with bone	3 ounces	25 pounds
Ham, cured, boneless	3 ounces	15 pounds
Pork cutlets, chops	1 each	10 to 15 pounds
Roast loin with bone	4 ounces	20 to 25 pounds
Roast, fresh ham	3 ounces	20 pounds
Sausage, link	2 each	12½ pounds
Sausage, for patties	4 to 5 ounce patty	12½ pounds
VEGETABLES		
Canned vegetables	½ cup	2 No. 10 cans or 14 No. 2 cans
Dried vegetables:		
Kidney beans	4 ounces	5½ pounds
Lima beans	5 ounces	6 pounds
Navy beans	6 ounces	6 pounds
Split peas	4 ounces	5 pounds
Fresh vegetables:		
Beets	3 ounces	13 to 14 pounds
Cabbage, to cook	2½ to 3 ounces	12 pounds
Cabbage, raw	1 to 2 ounces	8 pounds
Carrots	3 ounces	12½ pounds
Cauliflower	3 ounces	28 to 32 pounds
Celery curls	1 piece	2 medium stalks
Lettuce, head	1½ to 2 ounces	8 to 10 heads
Lettuce, head, garnish	2 or 3 leaves	4 to 5 heads
Potatoes, baked	6 ounces	20 pounds
Potatoes, mashed	5 ounces	15 pounds
Potatoes, scalloped	5 ounces	12½ pounds
Potatoes, sweet	4½ to 5 ounces	18 to 20 pounds
Radishes	2 each	10 bunches
Squash	3 ounces	10 to 12 pounds
Tomatoes, sliced	3 slices	10 to 12½ pounds
Frozen vegetables	2¼ to 2½ ounces	8 to 10 pounds or 13 to 17 packages of 10 to 12 ounces of each

APPROXIMATE QUANTITIES OF READY-TO-EAT FOODS FOR FIFTY PERSONS

Food	Quantity for 50
Baked beans	2½ to 3 gallons
Beverages	2½ to 3 gallons
Cakes, layer, angel	3 (10 inch) cakes
sheet	3 (10 inch) cakes / 1 sheet 12 x 20 inches
Chili	6½ quarts
Cooked vegetables	1 to 2 gallons
Cooked potatoes	1 to 2 gallons
Cranberry sauce	2 quarts
Fruit cup	4¼ quarts
Gravy and sauce accompaniments	2 quarts
Pies	8 pies (6 to 7 cuts per pie)
Potato chips	3⅛ pounds or 4 gallons
Salads	1 to 2 gallons
Scalloped dishes	2½ to 3 gallons

1 gallon will yield: 16 cups; 20 ¾-cup portions; 24 ⅔-cup portions; 32 ½-cup portions

APPROXIMATE AMOUNTS OF FOODS NEEDED TO SERVE FIFTY PERSONS

Food	Size of Serving	Approximate Amount to Buy for 50
MISCELLANEOUS		
Bread:		
1 pound, 1 ounce loaf	1½ slices	5 loaves
Pullman loaf	1 to 2 slices	2 to 4 loaves
Hard rolls	1 to 1½ each	4½ to 6½ dozen
Pan rolls	1½ to 2 each	6 to 8½ dozen
Crackers	2 each	1 pound
Jams, jellies	2 tablespoons	3 pounds
Macaroni	6 ounces	6 pounds
Noodles	6 ounces	4 pounds
Salad dressing	1½ to 2 tablespoons	1 to 1½ quarts
Spaghetti	6 ounces	6 pounds
Syrup	¼ cup	3¼ quarts
Sugar, loaf	1 to 2 cubes	1½ pounds
Sugar, granulated	1½ teaspoons	¾ pound

TABLE SETTING AND SERVICE

The Family Meals

Did you ever stop to think that your family, as well as your friends, are your guests when they sit down at your table? For the graciousness with which you have planned and prepared the meal can mean much to them. A pretty table and a pleasing meal make everyone happy.

Mealtime is about the only time in the day that the entire family is together. There are many ways to make it a sociable and friendly hour of relaxation amid the busy day's activities.

You'll find it easier to train the children in good eating habits and table manners, too, if you make each meal a pleasant occasion. Good manners and social poise come through everyday practice.

So put a bowl of flowers on your lunch table, a gay tablecloth on your dinner table, or occasionally use your best china—just for the family's enjoyment. These little things count much at mealtime.

And, when special occasions—holidays, company dinners or parties—come along, every member of your family will be at ease. They will be able to make your guests feel they are really part of a friendly family circle.

FAMILY OR COUNTRY STYLE SERVICE

Our most familiar and popular way of table service is none other than the "country" or "family style" meal. This is the one you probably are using in your home right now. It's informal, and it's easy to place the food in serving dishes and to pass it at the table. Even for company meals, family style service may be the one you prefer to use.

But there's much we can do to make our table, and this way of meal service,

as colorful and inviting and appropriate as the lovely pictures we often see in magazines. It's all in knowing how. There's a customary way to set this kind of table, a correct and convenient way to serve your family and guests, and a dozen and one ideas for using your dishes, glassware and silverware to set a pretty table with an interesting centerpiece.

Perhaps you've become so used to using the dishes nearest at hand, or the regular tablecloths, that you've forgotten about some of the little extras that will brighten up your table. Have you? Now is the time to bring them out.

SELECTING THE TABLE COVERING

Tablecloths—linen, rayon, or cotton damask, or plain or novelty weave cloths—how we enjoy them! And what a variety of colors they come in, from traditional white to lovely pastels or deep rich tones. Each one has its place.

Plastics, oilcloth, paper tablecloths or place mats are real time-savers, and of course you rely on them. But choose them just as carefully as you would a more expensive cloth. You can do wonders with a pretty background even if it's for your everyday breakfast table.

Sometimes it is a problem to get things to go together, isn't it? All of us acquire dishes or silverware, tablecloths or glassware at different times. Here's a simple rule—if your dishes have a design or pattern on them, use plain cloths as much as possible. If your dishes are on the plain side, you can use more pattern in your tablecloth if you choose. This gives the tablecloth a chance to perform its real duty—to be a pretty background for your dishes and glassware.

Use a silence cloth or pad of felt or cotton under your tablecloth. It protects the table top and improves the ap-

pearance and feel of the cloth.

Another thing—your tablecloth will look best if it hangs 10 to 12 inches over the edge of the table.

For those special occasions, bring out your lace cloth, or your sheer linen or embroidered one. Lay it directly on the table with no silence cloth underneath. Use pads under hot dishes. Lace cloths may have more overhang than damask.

PLACE MATS

About place mats—perhaps you haven't used them very often. But they're a good idea for family meals as well as company occasions. They are decorative, they save laundry, and they may even be less expensive than an overall cloth. They come in a wide variety of colors, textures and designs.

Here's a point to remember about place mats. Choose them large enough to hold the entire service of plate, salad plate, cup and saucer, silver and water glass. Lay the place mat close to and parallel to the edge of your table.

SEATING ARRANGEMENT

Before you set your table, you'll want to know the correct places for your family and guests to sit. Perhaps you have a regular place for everyone now. But, once in a while, change helps. Then, too, you'll want to know the most convenient place to have everyone sit when you have company.

Usually the father and mother (host and hostess) sit at the two ends of the table, mother next to the kitchen for convenience. A woman guest of honor will sit at the right of the host; the man guest of honor sits at the right of the hostess. If a child is to help with the serving, she sits at mother's left.

Or try other seating arrangements. When there are four or six at the table omit the two end places and seat your family or guests along the two sides.

Place the decorations at the ends. Or try a horseshoe arrangement with one end or side left open. You'll find it different to put an interesting decoration at that end or side of the table.

Be sure to give each person plenty of room at the table, both for appearance and comfort. Twenty-four to thirty inches between the center of each place setting is comfortable.

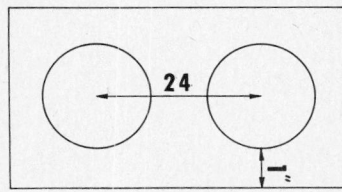

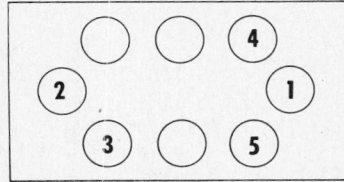

1. Hostess 2. Host 3. Female guest of honor 4. Male guest of honor 5. Child who helps with serving.

HOW TO SET THE TABLE

Now you are going to be an artist. With your everyday or with your company dishes, you are going to set a pretty table. Remember, first, the tablecloth—one that fits the occasion.

The space for each person, together with the necessary silver, glassware, napkins and china is called a "cover." Mark each cover with a plate. Space the plates evenly and directly opposite each other, one inch from the edge of the table.

Now place the silver beside the plate in order of its use, beginning from the outside.

Place forks at the left, with tines up. If you have cocktail forks and want to use them, place them at the right of the spoons, or on the plate.

Place knives at the right with sharp edges toward the plate.

Put spoons at the right of the knife

The space for each person, together with the necessary silver, glassware, napkin and china is called a "cover."

with bowls up. Line the pieces of silver parallel to each other, with their handle ends even and one inch from the edge of the table.

Lay only those pieces of silver required by the menu.

If you have bread and butter plates and plan to use them, place the butter knife on the rim of the plate horizontal to the edge of the table.

If no knife is needed, place the fork on the right in the knife's place.

Place the glass at the tip of the knife, or if no knife is used, at the tip of the fork. If that crowds the setting or forces the glass off the place mat, set the glass slightly to the right of the tip of the knife. Place a second beverage, if used, at the right of the water glass on a line slightly forward. Put the cup and saucer for a hot beverage to the right of the spoons.

Now put the bread and butter plate, if you wish to use it, at the tip of the fork. Other extra dishes, as salad plate, when not served as a separate course, are set at the left of the forks and napkin, or placed just above the dinner plate.

Lay the napkin at the left of the fork one inch from the edge of the table. Fold it simply in a square or rectangle. Fashion now permits us to turn either the folded or the hemmed loose edges toward the plate. If you put the napkin on the service or dinner plate, place it with the loose-edged corner to the right.

Put salt and pepper shakers at the top of the plate, or between every two covers in line with the glasses.

CREATE A BALANCED PICTURE

Now that you've set your table, stand back and look at it. Of course, you haven't added a centerpiece yet, nor are there dishes of food on the table. But

The simple pattern is set off beautifully by the textured place mat in a contrasting color.

just for a moment look at your table as if you were the guest.

Why does it look nice? Because a convenient table is also a beautiful table! All table arrangements have certain good features in common. They are our guide posts.

When you plan your china, glassware, silver and decorations so they "go together," they form a pleasing picture. And when you arrange your table to give that all-over look of balance, from centerpiece to serving dish, serving actually becomes easier.

GIVE THE TABLE BALANCE

Ever notice how crowding all the serving dishes toward the center of the table, or even at one end, makes the table look top-heavy or lopsided? It's out of balance. Let's move a few of the dishes outward, or down the table. We fill up the bare spots and achieve that feeling of balance we want.

Offset the bulk or weight of a large dish at one end of the table by a similar one at the other end. Or use two smaller dishes for the same purpose. You'll feel the restful harmony of your "picture table" when you place one cover opposite another and arrange the serving dishes to balance each other.

Key your table color scheme to that of your dining room.

CREATING COLOR HARMONY

Of course, you'll want to use color. Color schemes are easier to develop when you start with what you have. Of course, the colors in your dining room itself are something to think about. But suppose you have a mixed collection of linen, china and glass. You wonder what you can do with them?

Suppose you have:

White dinner cloth. Blue (or other plain colored) luncheon cloth. Pale green linen or cotton place mats. Clear fine glass tumblers. Blue glass tumblers. Set of pink and white semi-porcelain. Or a set of gold band china or semi-porcelain. Red and white peasant pottery. Or plain but bright colored pottery.

You may not have any or all of these, of course. But for the moment, let's suppose you have. These are the makings of several beautiful table settings.

The green linen, pink china and clear tumblers were made for each other. The blue cloth, with red and white pottery and blue tumblers are just right for breakfast and lunch.

For company meals—the white cloth, white china, thin tumblers or even goblets with your shining silver will be just right. Then you can plan for interesting color in the flowers, food and accessories. Or try the green place mats with your white china and crystal.

Perhaps you would like more color as a background for your white china—then choose a colored cloth of linen or rayon. Even dye a white tablecloth the color you want. Make it do wonders for your dishes and your table.

Almost any combination, as you can see, will give a pleasing effect if you remember a few simple rules. Let one color predominate, use a medium amount of a second color and just an accent of a third. Opposite colors are pretty together if you feature neutral colors such as cream, gray or beige with smaller amounts of the brighter, contrasting colors.

GIVE THE TABLE HARMONY

It's just the little things we do that give harmony to our table. Did you notice that you've chosen dishes and glassware and silver that go best together? They are in keeping or in harmony with each other.

And note that you've placed the table appointments parallel to, or at right angles to, the lines of your table. This gives the harmony of line you want. Even a round doily will fit into the picture if you place it so the threads are parallel to the edge of the table. Avoid diagonal lines by turning the handles of pitchers, bowls and cups parallel to the edges of your table, also.

MAKE EVERY TABLE SETTING DIFFERENT

Any reason why our tables should look alike day after day? Of course not. It's the difference that makes mealtime more interesting. Do use gay colored pottery and linen for your breakfast table, lunch in the garden or supper on the porch. It's the appropriateness that counts. Try a centerpiece of vegetables, fruits or hardy flowers such as zinnias, calendulas or hollyhocks.

For company meals and special occasions bring out your best lace or fine linen or damask tablecloth. Set your table with your nicest china and glassware and silver. Then select flowers in keeping with this feeling of festivity. Try roses from your garden, or lilacs, cosmos, lilies of the valley or sweet peas, just to mention a few. Perhaps you will wish to use crystal or silver candlesticks or china figurines.

Here is your chance to make a table which will be remembered by your family and friends.

CHOOSING A CENTERPIECE— THAT ADDED TOUCH

Isn't it fun to plan a pretty table? And you really don't need to be an artist. Try a single flower, floating in a low container, for your centerpiece. Or perhaps use a china figurine surrounded by a few springs of greenery.

For those special company dinners, fix a low arrangement of flowers in the center with your candles on each end. Or try a cluster of candles for the centerpiece. Maybe you'll want to use a few glass balls with greenery.

All too often we tend to overdecorate. It's really too much work, and the decoration overshadows the rest of the table arrangement and the food served.

Keep the central arrangement low so your family and guests can see each other. About 10 inches is the highest it can be without becoming a nuisance. Perhaps you will want to sit down to see if the centerpiece obstructs the view.

If you use candles, make them stand above eye level so their light is not annoying. Fourteen to sixteen inches above the table is comfortable. Use enough candles to give good light, or don't use them. A minimum of four is really necessary for enough light. Use candles only in late afternoon or when light is needed to add cheer and coziness to your meal.

CENTERPIECE HINTS

The glare of candles burning at eye level or below eye level is annoying.

Flame should be 14 to 16 inches above the table. Use at least four candles or none at all.

Tall arrangements of flowers interfere with vision across the table.

Keep flowers low so everyone can see and speak freely across the table.

FINAL CHECK UP HINTS

Now that you've worked out your lovely table, you will want to check on all those last-minute jobs that need attention just before you invite your family or guests to the table.

● Check the table setting with your menu to be sure all the necessary appointments are on the table.

● Have extra silver which will be needed ready to use on the buffet or service table.

● Make the dining room comfortable by adjusting lights and ventilation.

● Place chairs around the table with front edges even with the edge of the table.

● Fill the glasses seven-eighths full of cool fresh water. Pour milk or other beverages just before the meal is announced, immediately afterwards, or when you serve the dessert.

● Fill a water pitcher with ice water and place on service table.

● Place butter and relishes on the table.

● Salad may also be put on the table before the meal is announced.

● Bread and rolls go on the table just before the meal is served, or, if hot, they are brought in immediately afterward.

● You may have the first course on the table when the family is seated, or you may serve it immediately afterwards; or if you plan to start your meal with an appetizer, you may serve it in the living room. You'll want to choose the method of serving that keeps the food at its best.

● Place serving silver beside the dish of food, not in it.

How to Serve Family or Country Style

Many things, such as family traditions and customs, will influence your choice as to how you serve the family meals.

Probably you use the country style which has been mentioned. Let's see how we serve country style, shall we? Everything is ready and the family is seated at the table.

You, as the hostess, may serve yourself first, beginning with the main dish, or you may prefer to offer it to the person on your right. Other foods follow in the order of their importance.

The meat or main dish, potatoes and vegetables are followed by gravy, bread and relishes.

Pass the food to the left or to the right, whichever seems most agreeable. However, once it is decided, all food should go in the same direction. Suppose you decide to pass to the right.

In this type of service the person nearest a dish of food puts the serving silver in the dish and offers it to the one on his right. That person helps himself and passes the dish to the next one on his right. Each dish goes around the table and is returned to its original place.

The success of this type of service depends on the cooperation of all members of the family in passing food and in foreseeing the needs and wishes of other members of the family.

A side table or tea wagon near the hostess is a great help in holding the water pitcher, the hot or iced beverage, and extra bread or rolls, under a suitable cover. While you may wish to leave the dessert in the kitchen until you are ready to serve it, you may also place it on the serving table or tea wagon. With thoughtful planning no member of the family will need to leave the table to serve the meal.

Following the main course, the serving dishes and individual plates may be passed to the mother who stacks them on the service table or tea wagon, or they may be removed by a family member.

The dessert may be served on individual plates and passed to the guests. Or, the plates may be passed and then the dessert, so the guests may serve themselves.

Country style or "family" service, though simple and informal, may be beautifully done.

English Style Service — Another Way to Serve

You want your children to have good training in serving and being served by other accepted methods. So, you would like to know about other ways of serving your family meals.

Another family style (also called English style) is nice for family or company meals. This is the service which was often used by our grandparents, or no doubt you remember when father served the plates.

This is how we do it:

All food is served at the table by the host or hostess. The host usually serves the meat, potatoes and vegetables, and the hostess serves the soup, salad and dessert. However, the host may serve the dessert while the hostess serves the beverage.

If necessary, rearrange the cover of the host to make room for the meat platter and other foods he serves. Place the platter directly in front of the host's cover, and the dishes containing vegetables and sauces at his right or left so they're easily reached. Stack the plates in front of the host.

Who shall be served first? The answer to this debated question is a matter of opinion and preference. Some authorities say the mother (hostess), while others contend the guest of honor (if there is one) receives the first plate.

Preference is given to serving the hostess first. The host passes the first plate to his left to the hostess. He then passes the next plate to his left to the one on her right, and so on in regular order down that side of the table. Those on the other side are served likewise. The host serves himself last.

An elderly guest may be served first if she is accustomed to that method,

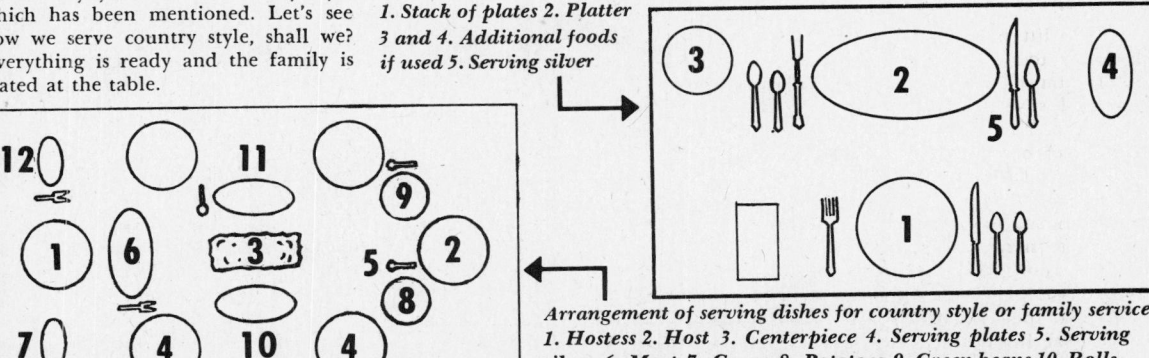

1. Stack of plates 2. Platter 3 and 4. Additional foods if used 5. Serving silver

Arrangement of serving dishes for country style or family service. 1. Hostess 2. Host 3. Centerpiece 4. Serving plates 5. Serving silver 6. Meat 7. Gravy 8. Potatoes 9. Green beans 10. Rolls 11. Relish 12. Pickles

but it avoids confusion if each is served in turn regardless of age, sex or fame.

The hostess serves the salad. So the salad bowl, or platter containing molded or individual salads, is placed before her. Salad plates and a large fork and spoon for serving the salad should be provided. The hostess may serve the salad while the host is serving meat and vegetables. The order in which she serves the guests is similar to the order in which the host serves from his end of the table.

Bread or hot rolls and the gravy are put on the table. These are passed around the table, always in the same direction.

The hostess indicates when all are ready to eat by picking up the appropriate piece of silver.

At the end of the course the food is removed, beginning with the platter of meat, or main dish, the other serving dishes, then the individual plates and silver, and finally everything including salt and pepper. Leave only water glasses and silver to be used for the last course. If coffee or tea has been served with the main course, allow the cup and saucer to remain for another serving.

SERVING THE DESSERT

The hostess usually serves the dessert. It may be placed before her, or she may transfer it from a side table. If the beverage is not served with the main course, it is brought in with or after the dessert and placed together with cups and saucers, cream and sugar in front of the server.

ADAPTED RUSSIAN STYLE SERVICE

You may like to arrange the food on the plates and place them on the table

before the family is seated, or they can be brought in by a family member and placed before each person.

You probably make use of this method often, when serving soup, salad and the dessert when it is served in individual portions to each member of the family.

COMPROMISE SERVICE

There are times when you may want to use a combination of these types of meal services we have mentioned. We call it "compromise service."

The main course, that is, meat and vegetables, are served at the table by the host and hostess. This gives the father an opportunity to carve the chicken, turkey, a roast or a steak at the table. The family, too, will enjoy seeing the meat or main dish before it is cut for serving.

You may prefer to serve up the soup in the kitchen and place the individual bowls before each family member. Likewise, the salad can be arranged on individual plates and placed at each cover.

The compromise service helps make the dessert rather special. After the main course is finished, the leftover food and used dishes are removed, and the dessert is brought on, arranged in individual portions.

The hostess may pour a hot beverage at the table. This style combines the convenience of having much of the serving of the food done in the kitchen, and the hospitality of serving the main course at the table.

Tips on Serving

Just a little practice will make it easy for you and your family helpers to serve everyday or company meals quickly and correctly.

Here are some guides to remember:

● Place and remove dishes from the left with the left hand.
● Offer food, as rolls or relishes, to the left with the left hand.
● Serve or pour beverages from the right with the right hand.
● Refill glasses during the meal without moving the glass. Use a napkin to catch the drip.
● Handle dishes and plates by the outer edge. Do not place the thumb over the rim.
● When a meal is served in courses, remove everything relating to one course before serving the next one.
● Remove food first, then soiled dishes from individual covers, then clean dishes and unused silver.
● Remove one cover at a time.
● Do not stack dishes in front of guests or family members.
● Remove dishes of hostess (mother) first, then in regular order around the table beginning at her right.
● If the hostess removes the dishes, she begins at her right and removes her own service last.
● Crumb the table with a folded napkin and a plate.

Table Etiquette

The basis of all good manners is a kindly thoughtfulness for others whether you are eating at home or in public. Attention to these guides of courtesy will help the family to be more considerate of others, and to be at ease in any gathering:

● Be prompt at meals.
● Give attention to personal grooming before meals. Hands and face should be clean and hair combed.
● Boys and men should remain standing until women and girls are seated. They should seat the ladies.
● Sit down from left side of chair.
● If a blessing is asked, the head is bowed and the hands kept in the lap.
● Serve the hostess, mother at family dinner, first.
● The hostess unfolds her napkin first, takes up her silver to be used and indicates that it is time for all to begin eating.
● Sit up straight and do not lounge at the table.
● Keep elbows at the side, not resting on the table while eating. Don't let elbows interfere with neighbor's eating. Between courses it is permissible to lean on your elbows while talking.
● If you wish something, ask to have it passed. Do not reach in front of anyone.

ORDER OF SERVICE WHEN DAD SERVES

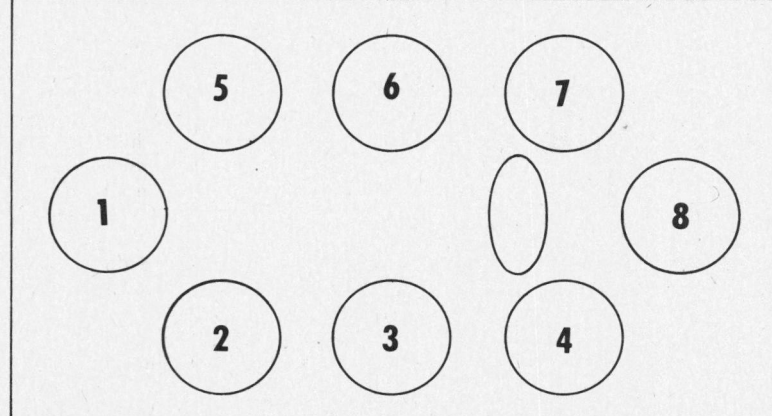

Order of service
1. Hostess receives first plate of food. 2. Person who receives second plate of food. 3, 4, 5, 6, and 7. Receive plates of food in that order. 8. Host serves himself last.

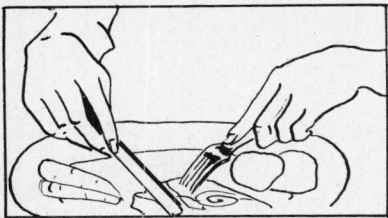

- In cutting food hold the knife in the right hand, the fork in the left, tines down. Grasp the handles firmly and naturally. The ends of the handles rest in the palms of your hands and are not seen. Extend the index fingers along the handles to steady and guide the knife and fork.
- Cut only enough meat or other food for one or two bites at a time.

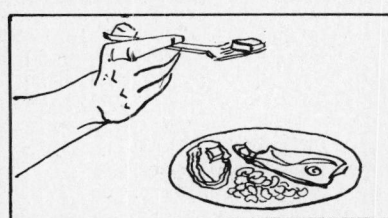

- Carry food to the mouth with the fork in the right hand, tines up. However, in other countries such as Canada, etc., the custom is to carry food to the mouth with the fork in the left hand, tines turned down. The fork is used as a pick. Don't put food on the back of the fork.
- Use fork rather than spoon whenever possible.
- When eating soup, dip toward back of dish and sip from side of spoon. When eating other food with a spoon, dip toward you and take food from end of spoon.
- Use a spoon to stir and test the temperature of a hot drink. Do not leave the spoon standing in the cup. Lay it on the saucer. Never drink from a cup with a spoon standing in it.
- When silver is once used, rest it across the back of the plate, never on the tablecloth nor propped up on the edge of the plate.
- If food or drink is too hot, let it stand until cooler. Never blow on it.
- Do not take a drink while you have food in your mouth.
- Keep mouth closed while chewing. Do not smack lips. Never talk with food in your mouth.
- Eat slowly and quietly. Never appear greedy.
- Never hold food on the fork while talking. Having once picked it up, eat it promptly.
- In passing plate for a second serving, leave knife and fork on plate side by side so that there is no danger of

their slipping off.
- If asked to express a choice of food, do so at once. If not, take what is served without comment.
- To butter bread, break off small piece, hold it on the plate and spread the butter. Do not butter a whole slice at a time. Do not bite from a whole slice of bread. Break it into small pieces as it is to be eaten.

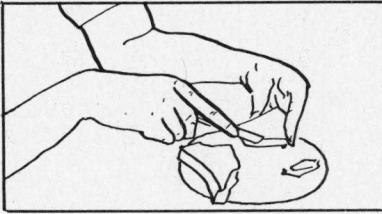

- Never place any food on the tablecloth. This applies to bread, salt, radishes and celery. If the dinner plate is small, use the bread and butter plate or salad plate for these things. Relishes, jams and jellies may be put on the bread and butter plate.
- Do not pick up and hold a dish while eating. Do not tip a dish for the last bit of food.
- Do not eat while passing food or serving others.
- Take only the portion of food into the mouth that can be eaten at once.
- A bit of bread, but nothing else, may be used to help food upon the fork.
- Foods eaten with the fingers include: bread, olives, pickles, radishes, nuts, celery, strips of carrots, French fried potatoes and potato chips, cookies, cake (that isn't sticky), corn on the cob and confections.
- Fish bones, as other bones taken into the mouth, are removed by taking between the finger and thumb and removing between compressed lips.
- The pits of stewed prunes or cherries that are eaten with a spoon are made as clean and dry as possible in the mouth, then dropped into the spoon with which you are eating and put on the edge of the plate. Seeds and skin may be removed with the finger and thumb with lips closed, or you may drop pits or seeds into the cupped hand, held close to the lips.
- The hostess continues eating until all have finished.
- If finger bowls are used, dip only the tips of the fingers of one hand in at a time. Wipe on the napkin.
- Leave dishes in place when you have finished eating.
- Leave the napkin on the lap until the hostess places hers on the table just prior to rising. Leave it at the left of the plate.

- Rise from the left side of the chair. If necessary, push chair close to table so others may pass.
- Do not use toothpicks in the presence of others.
- Do not criticize the manners of elderly people. Customs change. It was once proper to eat with the knife!
- If one must cough or sneeze at the table, cover the mouth and nose with the handkerchief, not the napkin.
- If one must leave the table in the midst of the meal, ask permission of the hostess. Go quietly.

How to Make
the Most
of the Meal Hour

"Take time to live a little every day" might be a good slogan for every family. "Breaking bread" together can bring your family into closer fellowship and help each member to understand and appreciate the others more.

It is important that at least one meal a day, perhaps the evening meal, be observed as a daily family social hour. Serve the meal as leisurely as your family's activities will allow. Make a spirit of happy companionship prevail. Keep the conversation pleasant. Petty troubles and unpleasant topics can spoil any meal. They may have to be talked out at some later time, but never allow unpleasant issues to spoil the pleasure of your family at meal time. Correcting the children at the table should be kept to the minimum.

Encourage everyone to participate in the conversation. The opinions expressed by family members during the gay as well as the more serious moments of the meal hour will have a direct influence on molding the attitudes and thinking of your children. Good manners, honesty, kindness, courage and good citizenship can all be taught around the family table.

Remember special days—birthdays and anniversaries. They are opportunities for family pleasures to cherish a lifetime.

Share responsibility as well as fun. Let the children begin early to help serve meals. Avoid assigning only routine tasks as peeling potatoes and washing dishes. Give children responsibilities that challenge their best abilities, and they will be glad to help.

BUFFET SERVICE

You will like to serve buffet meals. They create a friendly, informal atmosphere. Your guests will enjoy moving around to visit with each other, and serving themselves at your attractive table. Best of all, your meal will be easier to prepare and to serve than the usual type of "company" dinner.

While this seems to suggest that buffet service is just for informal occasions, you can make it more elaborate if you wish, for weddings, anniversaries, and receptions.

Plan a buffet breakfast or brunch— or a one o'clock luncheon. Or even carry over this idea for your bridge or club meetings in the late afternoon, and for early or late evening suppers.

It's the logical service, too, for the covered dish or potluck luncheons and Sunday night suppers we all like. Even church suppers, when the number of people to be served is indefinite, run smoothly when served buffet style.

FIT THE OCCASION

Choose a theme which fits the occasion. It may be a Halloween party with ghosts and goblins; a New Year's supper honoring Father Time; a "feed" after the homecoming football game with appropriate gridiron decorations; a family reunion, or perhaps a family or community supper for new neighbors.

Make your table attractive with tablecloth, dishes, and centerpiece appropriate to each other and to the food you are serving. Peasant linens, bright colored pottery, and wooden bowls go together for informal affairs. Or you may prefer to use a bare table. Your decoration might be fruits, vegetables, nuts, or flowers of the coarser type such as zinnias, hollyhocks, and calendulas. If you wish to use candlesticks, choose those of pottery, wood, pewter, brass, or copper in keeping with the other decorations.

For more dress-up occasions use your best linen and your nicest dishes, glassware, and silver. You may wish to use a cloth which covers the table, but doilies and runners also make interesting backgrounds. Bring in roses, sweet peas, snapdragons, cosmos, chrysanthemums, or other dainty flowers from your garden for your floral centerpiece. And use your silver or crystal candlesticks if you wish.

PLAN A PRETTY TABLE

Whatever the setting, your table is the center of interest. Originally the term "buffet" was applied to service from the buffet or sideboard. Now we use the table but the idea is the same, and often the sideboard is used in addition to the table arrangement.

Place your table to give the best use of space or the effect you desire. It may be in the center of the room, at one end, or at the side. Or you may choose to push the table against the wall. This limits the amount of table edge space, but you can create interesting and unusual decorations at the back of the table against the wall.

CREATE A PICTURE

Now that you are ready to set your table, what are some artistic rules to remember? There is balance. Just make sure that no area of your table is cluttered or overloaded while the rest of the table appears bare. Place the dishes, food, silver, napkins, and decorations so the table has a restful orderly appearance.

Use colors which go together and which set off the food you serve. They may be soft and pastel or the bright, rich hues. The decorations need not always be flowers and candles. You might use figurines, vegetables, fruits, nuts, gourds, grasses, weeds, or pine cones.

Your menu and the way you plan to serve it will determine the way you arrange the food, china, and silver. There are many ways to serve a buffet meal. We shall discuss these as we go along.

For the meal itself, limit your menu to two courses—a main course and a dessert course and beverage. You may serve the beverage from the table with the main course, or from another smaller table, or you may pass it on trays.

MAKE IT CONVENIENT

For the main course, place the principal dish at one end of the table. Set a stack of six or eight plates near it. Bring in other plates as you need them. The serving silver belongs beside the dish of food. If only a spoon is needed, place it at the right. If both spoon and fork are required, place the spoon at the right and the fork at the left of the dish of food.

Here is a suggested buffet menu. Note the arrangement and where the serving silver is placed.

Chicken Loaf   Curry Gravy
Buttered Peas   Fluffy Baked Potatoes
Relish Plate
Clover Leaf Rolls
Lemon Meringue Pudding
with Graham Cracker Topping
Beverage

Place other foods, such as salad, vegetable, buttered rolls, sandwiches and relishes, along the side of the table. Set them near the edge within easy reach of your guests.

You may arrange the food in individual portions, such as sliced meat loaf or individual pies.

In this way, the serving dishes or platters will still look attractive even after several people have served themselves. The meat dish and salad are adaptable to individual servings or portions.

If you serve the beverage with the main course, place it at the end of the table opposite the main dish.

Arrange the cups in an orderly and convenient manner. No more than two should be stacked together. Place the accompaniments for the beverage, such as cream and sugar, on the table next to the beverage so your guests may help themselves.

Arrange silver and napkins on the other side of the table so they may be picked up last.

If your table looks crowded, plan to serve the beverage at a small table near by. You may also use this service table for trays, napkins, and silver.

Have your guests pass around the table either to the left or the right as you wish.

This will depend upon the arrangement of the table and the rooms. Passing to the left is more logical.

This allows the right hand to be toward the table—a convenience in helping oneself to food.

THREE WAYS TO SERVE

Buffet service may be any one of three forms—the informal, the semi-formal, and formal. There is no distinct line between them. Your choice will depend upon the occasion, the number of guests you have, whether they are young or older, the facilities in your home, and the amount of help you have.

Of course, the type of service you choose will depend on the seating arrangement you've planned. At women's parties, it's simpler to let your guests hold the filled plates on their laps. Trays are desirable. They do make lap service somewhat easier.

If there are men guests present, plan to provide small tables. Most men are

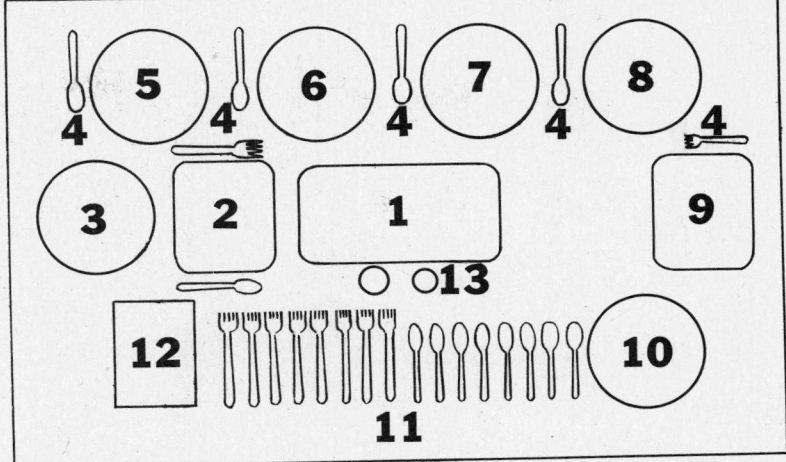

Arrangement when beverage is served from a side table

1. Centerpiece
2. Main dish
3. Stack of plates
4. Serving silver
5–6. Vegetable dishes
7–8. Salads
9. Relish plate
10. Rolls and sandwiches
11. Silver
12. Napkins
13. Salt and pepper shakers

not skilled in holding plates or trays on their laps nor do they enjoy it. Small tables for holding the beverage are helpful, but card tables for the complete meal are preferable.

Cover the tables with luncheon cloths or place mats in keeping with the appointments you have chosen for the buffet. Or use bare tables with mats for hot or very cold dishes. Arrange the silver, napkins, water glasses, and beverage cups and saucers on the small tables. Pour the beverage at the tables. Provide cream and sugar at each table or pass it as you wish.

While there are no set rules for serving a buffet meal, there are certain features of the different types of service for us to keep in mind.

FOR A SMALL GROUP

When you entertain a relatively small group, have an informal buffet. It works best when your guests know each other and all feel free to help themselves. Keep the menu simple, and the service as easy and informal as possible.

You (the hostess) announce the meal and invite your guests to serve themselves. Have the guests come to the table a few at a time. Avoid a long line.

Each guest takes a plate and passes around the table in the direction indicated, choosing the foods he wants. The beverage, silver, and napkin are taken last. Then the guests seat themselves in the living room.

Second servings are always in order. Part of the charm of the buffet is in the freedom your guests have to choose foods each especially enjoys.

If you prefer, pass the serving dishes to your guests for second servings. Also pass the rolls and relishes again, or invite your guests to go back to the table for them.

After the main course has been eaten and second servings have been offered, clear the table of first course foods and arrange the dessert course. Ask your guests to place their first course plates upon the service table. Then invite them to serve dessert to themselves. They may also serve themselves a second cup of coffee.

When your guests have finished, they place their used plates on the service table. The service table must be kept orderly and cleared. This is easier if your guests stack their plates.

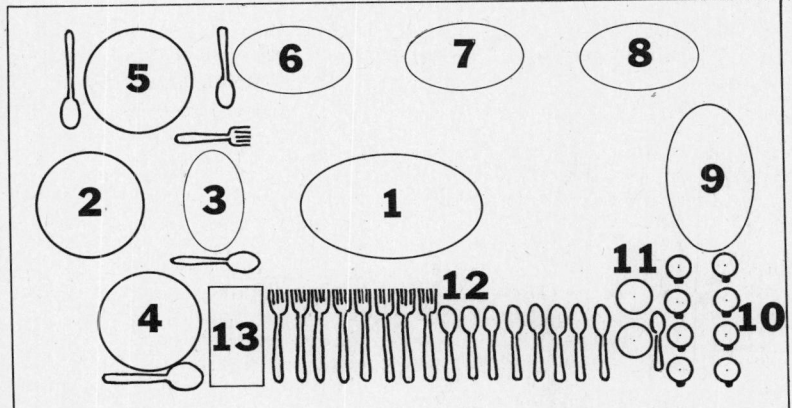

Table arrangement for the main course

1. Centerpiece
2. Plates
3. Main Dish
4. Vegetable
5. Gravy
6. Vegetable
7. Rolls
8. Relish plate
13. Napkins
9. Coffee service
10. Cups
11. Cream and sugar, and spoon
12. Silver

Table arrangement for the dessert course

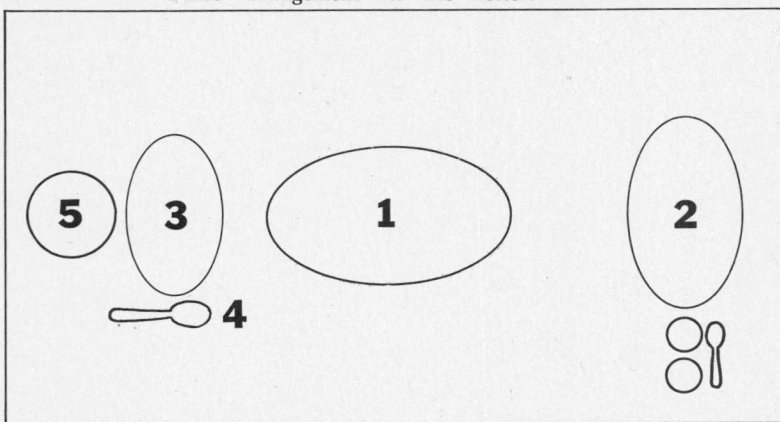

1. Centerpiece   2. Coffee service   3. Dessert   4. Serving silver
5. Dessert plates

There are several ways to serve the dessert course:

(1) Place it on the table as in the case of the informal service. Your guests will serve themselves.

(2) Have it served at the table. A friend of the hostess will do the serving.

(3) Have it carried from the kitchen to your guests.

If this is done, waitresses or young friends of the hostess remove two main course plates from the guests, taking the plates to the kitchen and returning with two desserts. It speeds up the service if each waitress carries two plates at a time as she removes the empty plates and returns with the desserts.

The assisting friends leave the table after they have finished serving the food to the guests. They serve themselves and join the other guests.

FOR MORE SPECIAL EVENTS

There are many occasions when you will wish to entertain with a semi-formal buffet—a luncheon or supper for a group of friends, a meal to celebrate an anniversary, or perhaps a wedding breakfast for a member of your family or a friend.

The semi-formal service differs from the informal in that you may have one or two friends assist at the buffet table. One may sit at one end of the table and serve the main dish, and perhaps a second food or salad. Another friend may be seated at the opposite end of the table to pour the beverage.

Your guests will help themselves to other foods and to silver and napkins. This service is convenient, for it's sometimes difficult to serve oneself while holding a plate.

FOR VERY SPECIAL OCCASIONS

Perhaps you are planning a wedding reception or an anniversary party, or a party in honor of some person of distinction. This is the perfect occasion for a formal buffet. It's a little less formal than a formal dinner. Use it when you plan to have a large number of guests. You may need more room than your home will offer. Then entertain at a hotel or club. The management will help you with your buffet.

When you entertain at home, use your loveliest linen, china, and silver, and set your table with great care. Choose the flowers, candles, and other appointments with equal attention to beauty and their suitability to the occasion.

Seat your guests in the dining room and rooms adjoining. They do not go to the table to serve themselves. Place the plates, napkins, and silver on the buffet or service table to avoid overcrowding the table. Arrange duplicate services of food at each end of the table.

Two friends of the hostess, seated at opposite ends of the table, serve the plates. The filled plates are then taken by waitresses or other friends of the hostess to the seated guests. This is the procedure for the formal service:

The waitress takes two empty plates from the service table and places one (left hand, left side) before the person serving. The waitress takes the filled plate (left hand, left side) and places the empty one (right hand, left side) in its place. She then goes to the service table and places a fork on the plate, a napkin under it, and carries it to the guest. She hands it to the guest with the handle of the fork to the guest's right. She then takes another empty plate from the service table and continues to exchange empty plates for filled ones which she passes to the guests until all are served.

Rolls and relishes are passed twice.

Trays are used to pass small glasses of water. Coffee may be served either with the main course or dessert, or both. It's usually easier to serve the coffee cups from a tray. Another waitress follows with a tray containing cream, sugar, and coffee spoons.

The buffet table is cleared and arranged for dessert.

Then when the guests have finished, the waitresses remove two main course plates at a time, leaving the napkin.

The dessert is served in the same manner as the main course, or it may be served from the kitchen.

The waitress passes nuts and candy. These are repassed once.

When all the guests have been served, the waitresses remove all dishes from the buffet table, leaving the cloth and decorations.

When dessert is finished, the waitresses take plates and napkins from the guests and carry them to the kitchen.

Main course for semi-formal buffet

THE POTLUCK MEAL

All of us like "potluck" meals. They are a convenient way to share the responsibility for feeding a large group. Potluck has become a popular meal for an all-day club meeting, an extension leader training meeting, church social, or a community or family get-together.

The potluck will turn out better if you do some planning beforehand as to what type of food each person or family shall bring. Menus usually include main dishes, vegetable dishes, salads, sandwiches or rolls, and dessert. The hostess usually provides the beverage.

Arrange for a table large enough to hold the food without crowding. The hostess provides a suitable tablecloth, a simple centerpiece or decoration, and necessary serving dishes and serving silver.

You can avoid much confusion and delay by organizing your group before going to the kitchen to prepare the meal. Committees are a good idea. Ask:

● Two women to assist the hostess to make and serve the coffee.

● Two women to arrange the dining table and supervise placing of food for first course.

● Two women to arrange the dessert course.

● Two women to supervise the clearing away after the meal, and see that the hostess' kitchen is left in order.

SERVING THE LUNCH

Many times the potluck table has a helter-skelter look. It is easy to achieve logical order if each woman is told where to place her dish of food. (See diagram.) Place the serving silver on the table beside the dishes.

Very often you are confronted with many foods of the same kind. Plan to place only enough food on the table at one time to give variety to your meal. For example, serve one or two protein dishes, two or three vegetable dishes, two or three salads, and sandwiches and relishes at the beginning of the meal. As the food is taken, replenish with fresh bowls of food.

When the meal is ready, the hostess or chairman invites the guests to serve themselves. Some groups may be accustomed to saying grace before their meal. In that case, the hostess or chairman can call on someone to ask the blessing or lead the guests in singing a grace.

If there are one or more special guests present, they are among the first to be served. The guests, in small groups, start at the end of the table where the main dishes are placed. Each person passes around the table to the left choosing the foods desired.

Beverage may be poured at one end of the table or it may be served from a small table or a buffet. Or it may be put on a tray and passed after the guests are seated. Cream and sugar may be taken with the coffee or passed later.

Guests should feel free to return to the buffet table for second servings, or the hostess may pass extra foods.

SERVING THE DESSERT

When the main course has been finished, the dessert committee clears the table and arranges the dishes of desserts. Then the guests are invited to go back to the table and serve themselves. They may also serve themselves to coffee, or it may be poured at their tables. After the meal is finished each woman assembles her own dishes to take home.

The clearing away committee clears the table, and prepares the hostess' dishes for washing. The kitchen should be left in good order.

Arrangement of potluck table

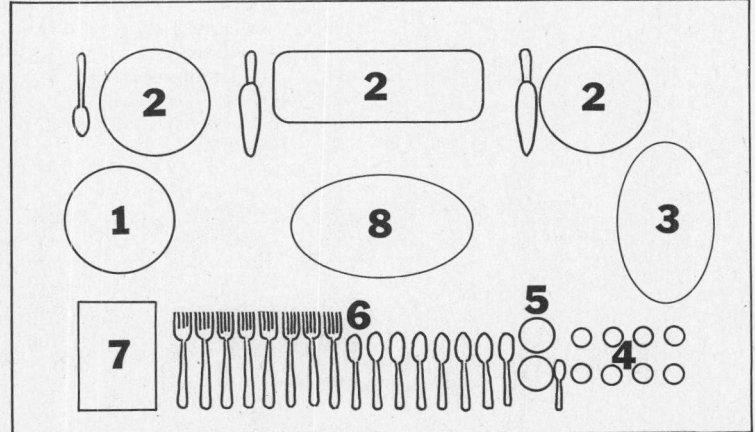

1. Dinner plates
2. Main dishes
3. Vegetables
4. Salads
5. Assorted relishes
6. Sandwiches or rolls
7. Silver
8. Napkins
9. Centerpiece

Make the dessert course special

1. Dessert plates
2. Choice of desserts
3. Beverage service
4. Cups
5. Cream and sugar
6. Silver
7. Napkins
8. Centerpiece

MENUS

Balanced Menus for Each Season

The following daily menus for each season of the year outline appetizing, nutritious meals which are for the most part modestly priced but varied and nourishing. The basic menus have alternate choices so, if you want to make a change, look for a letter to the left of the item on the menu. Substitute a dish marked with the same letter under "Alternates."

BALANCED MENUS—SUMMER 1

Breakfast
Melon Balls
Puffed Wheat   Milk
Cinnamon-Raisin Bread   Butter
Coffee   Milk

Lunch
(A) Creamed Carrot and Potato Soup;
Crisp Crackers
(B) Salmon Salad on
Thick Tomato Slices;
Bread and Butter, Lemonade

Dinner
(C) Baked Stuffed Green Peppers—
Rice and Meat Stuffing;
Tomato Sauce
(D) Corn-on-the-Cob
(E) Vegetable Salad Bowl;
Whole Wheat Bread, Butter
(F) Fresh Fruit, Cookies, Milk

Alternates:
(A) Vegetable Chowder or
Creamed Lima Bean Soup
(B) Sliced Tomatoes and Lettuce
Salad; Waldorf Salad
(C) Carrot Meat Loaf with
Tomato Sauce; Stuffed Cabbage
Rolls; Baked Ham Slice
with Raisin Sauce
(D) Baked Sweet Potatoes
(E) Beet and Leaf Lettuce Salad
(F) Deep-Dish Cherry or Rhubarb Pie

BALANCED MENUS—SUMMER 2

Breakfast
Tomato Juice,
Cantaloupe or Fresh Pineapple
Crisp Rice Cereal with Milk
Whole Wheat Toast   Butter
Coffee   Milk

Lunch
(A) Tomato-Cheese Fondue;
Bread and Butter
(B) Individual Vegetable Salads;
Cookies, Milk or Iced Cocoa

Dinner
(C) Fried Liver and Onions
(D) Baked Potatoes
(E) Summer Squash
(F) Celery Curls, Carrot Sticks,
Green Pepper Strips;
Bread and Butter,
Ice Cream, Cold Fruit Beverage

Alternates:
(A) Fluffy Omelet with Cheese Sauce;
Welsh Rabbit;
Creamed Eggs on Toast;
Spiced Ham and Cheese Sandwich
(B) Health Salad;
Cabbage and Apple Salad
(C) Braised Liver with Vegetables;
Stuffed Eggplant;
Liver Patties with Egg Sauce;
Braised Spareribs;
Baked Pork Chops
(D) French Fried; Creamed Potatoes
(E) Buttered Greens; Broccoli
(F) Tossed Vegetable Salad;
Tossed Spinach Salad;
Tomato and Cucumber Salad

BALANCED MENUS—SUMMER 3

Breakfast
Fresh Fruit or Fruit Juice
Nut or Corn Meal Griddle Cakes
with Syrup
Bacon
Coffee   Milk

Lunch
(A) Cold Plate (Sliced Eggs,
American Cheese, Bologna)
(B) Potato Salad;
Whole Wheat Bread, Butter
(C) Chilled Melon;
Milk or Iced Cocoa

Dinner
(D) Minute Steaks;
Sliced Bermuda Onions
(E) Hashed Browned Potatoes
(F) Buttered Carrots or Spinach;
Sliced Tomatoes or Cole Slaw,
Hot Toasted Buns, Butter
(G) Strawberry Shortcake;
Iced Beverage

Alternates:
(A) Stuffed Tomato Salad—
Canned Fish Stuffing
(B) Tossed Vegetable Salad;
Apple and Celery Salad;
Kidney Bean Salad;
Macaroni Salad
(C) Stewed Fresh Fruit
(D) Grilled Frankfurters;
Broiled Lamb or Beef Patties;
Pan-Broiled Lamb Chops;
Salmon Patties
(E) Steamed New Potatoes
(F) Buttered Beet Greens;
Asparagus with
Mock Hollandaise Sauce
(G) Fresh Fruit in Season;
Apple Brown Betty; Orange
Sherbet; Fresh Peach Cobbler

Basic Summer Breakfast #1

BALANCED MENUS—SUMMER 4

Breakfast

Fresh Fruit Cup
Apple or Blueberry Muffins
Bacon   Butter
Coffee   Milk

Lunch

(A) Grilled Cheese Sandwiches
with Tomato Slices
(B) Waldorf Salad;
Cookies, Milk or Iced Cocoa

Dinner

(C) Fried Chicken with Cream Gravy
(D) Fluffy Mashed Potatoes
(E) Escalloped Carrots and
Green Beans
(F) Relish Plate (Celery, Green
Pepper, Tomato, Pickles);
Cracked Wheat Bread, Butter
(G) Peach Shortcake;
Coffee or Iced Beverage

Alternates:

(A) Broiled Cottage Cheese
Sandwiches
(B) Grapefruit or Orange Salad
(C) Chicken Fricassee;
Stewed Chicken with Noodles;
Chicken Curry with Steamed Rice
(D) Parsley Potatoes;
Creamed New Potatoes
(E) Buttered Greens or Broccoli;
Spinach Molds; Carrots and
Snap Beans au Gratin
(F) Tomato Stuffed with Cole Slaw
(G) Fresh Berry Pie;
Rhubarb Strawberry Roll;
Ginger Ale Sherbet

BALANCED MENUS—FALL 1

Breakfast

Assorted Fall Fruit Basket
Hot Whole Wheat Cereal
with Raisins, Milk
Corn Sticks   Butter   Jam
Coffee   Hot Cocoa

Lunch

(A) Meat Salad Bowl;
Buttered Toast with Jam,
Fruits in Season,
Milk or Hot Cocoa

Dinner

(B) Country-Style Roast Chicken;
Cream Gravy
(C) Buttered Rutabagas or Carrots;
Baked Sweet Potatoes
(D) Tossed Vegetable Salad;
Bread and Butter
(E) Chocolate Cake;
Coffee, Tea or Milk

Alternates:

(A) Tuna or Salmon Salad Bowl;
Egg and Vegetable Salad Bowl
(B) Roast Duck with Apple Stuffing;
Stewed Chicken with Dumplings;
Oven-Braised Chuck Steak
with Browned Potatoes
(C) Fluffy Yellow Squash; Succotash;
Buttered Carrots and Peas
(D) Molded Vegetable Salad;
Cranberry Mold;
Combination Salad
(E) Rhubarb Betty; Ice Cream;
Custard Pie; Pumpkin Pie

BALANCED MENUS—FALL 2

Breakfast

Canned Grapefruit Sections
or Citrus Fruit Cup
Crisp Rice Cereal with Milk
Scrambled or Fried Eggs
Buttered Toast
Coffee   Milk   Hot Cocoa

Lunch

(A) Cream of Tomato Soup
Crisp Crackers
(B) Pineapple and Cheese Salad
Bread and Butter
Milk

Dinner

(C) Spaghetti with Meat Balls—
Grated Parmesan Cheese
(D) Tossed Vegetable Salad with
Italian Dressing;
Hot Italian Bread with
Garlic Butter
(E) Ice Cream;
Coffee, Tea or Milk

Alternates:

(A) Cream of Celery Soup or
Cream of Lima Bean Soup
(B) Cabbage and Carrot Salad;
Apple and Carrot Salad
(C) Lamb, Beef, or Veal Stew with
Dumplings; Meat Loaf with
Tomato Sauce; Lamb Shanks
with Vegetable Gravy;
Potato Pancakes with
Creamed Cooked Meat
(D) Lettuce with Thousand Island
Dressing; Tossed Tomato Salad;
Grapefruit Salad; Tomato Aspic
with Cottage Cheese Salad
(E) Peach Shortcake with Top Milk;
Gelatin with Vanilla Sauce;
Lemon Snow Pudding;
Butterscotch Pudding

BALANCED MENUS—FALL 3

Breakfast

Orange, Grapefruit, or Tomato Juice
Oatmeal
with Milk and Brown Sugar
Buttered Raisin Toast
Preserves
Coffee   Milk   Hot Cocoa

Lunch

(A) Black-Eyed Bean Soup
with Croutons
(B) Relish Plate (Assorted Vegetables
and Sliced Egg);
Whole Wheat Bread, Butter;
Baked Pears or Fruit Cup,
Cookies, Milk

Dinner

(C) Broiled Hamburger Steak—
Onion Rings
(D) French-Fried Potatoes
(E) Buttered Greens
(F) Cole Slaw
(G) Frosted Cup Cakes;
Coffee, Tea or Milk

Alternates:

(A) Vegetable Soup;
Corn and Lima Bean Chowder
(B) Egg and Celery Salad on Lettuce;
Tomato Aspic Salad with
Sliced Egg
(C) Ham Shortcake; Meat Loaf with
Mashed Potatoes;
Ground Beef and Vegetable
Casserole
(D) Fluffy Mashed Potatoes
(E) Buttered Broccoli;
Brussels Sprouts
(F) Watercress Salad; Romaine Salad
(G) One Bowl Cake; Brownies;
Chocolate Bread Pudding;
Upside-Down Cake;
Peach Cobbler

BALANCED MENUS—FALL 4

Breakfast

Fresh Plums,
Tangerine Juice; Orange Wedges
Bacon and Eggs
Hot Biscuits or Whole Wheat Muffins
Butter
Coffee   Milk   Hot Cocoa

Lunch

(A) Vegetable Soup;
Crisp Crackers
(B) Cottage Cheese and Cucumber
Sandwiches on
Whole Wheat Bread
(C) Fresh Fruit in Season;
Raisin Cookies, Milk

Dinner

(D) Veal Birds and Steamed Potatoes
(E) Scalloped Tomatoes
(F) Orange and Coconut Salad;
Parkerhouse Rolls or
Corn Muffins
(G) Fruit Custard Pudding;
Coffee, Tea or Milk

Alternates:

(A) Bean and Barley Soup;
Cream of Split Pea Soup
with Croutons

(B) Cottage Cheese and Green Pepper
or Egg and Celery Sandwiches
(C) Canned Fruit; Stewed Fruit
(D) Barbecued Breast of Lamb with
Browned Potatoes; Beef Chow
Mein with Steamed Rice; Ham
Loaf with Baked Sweet Potatoes;
Pork Chops or Pork Steaks
with Creamed Potatoes;
Spareribs with Browned Potatoes
(E) Buttered Spinach;
Broccoli with Brown Butter Sauce
(F) French Salad Bowl;
Orange and Vegetable Salad Bowl
(G) Butterscotch Pudding;
Plain Cornstarch Pudding

BALANCED MENUS—WINTER 1

Breakfast
Cherry Juice or Tomato Juice
Oatmeal
Topped with Cinnamon Raisins
Orange Honey Muffins
or Coffee Cake
Butter
Milk   Coffee

Lunch
(A) Puffy Cheese Omelet;
Buttered Parsnips,
Whole Wheat Bread, Butter;
Canned Fruit, Milk

Dinner
(B) Breaded Veal Cutlet with
Tomato Sauce;
Mashed Potatoes
(C) Buttered Carrots
(D) Head Lettuce—French Dressing;
Baking Powder Biscuits or
Cloverleaf Rolls
(E) Fruit Cobbler;
Coffee, Tea or Milk
Alternates:
(A) Toasted Cheese Sandwiches;
Baked Eggs au Gratin
(B) Roast Chicken with Celery
Stuffing; Chicken Fricassee;
Scalloped Chicken and Spaghetti;
Stuffed Veal Steak and Browned
Potatoes; Fried Whole Flounder
with Paprika Potatoes
(C) Okra and Tomatoes;
Steamed Winter Squash;
Scalloped Tomatoes
(D) Pear and Celery Salad;
Citrus Salad Bowl; Cabbage Salad
(E) Baked Apples with Cream;
Apple Roly Poly;
Orange Custard Pudding

BALANCED MENUS—WINTER 2

Breakfast
Baked Apple,
Grapefruit, or Orange Juice
Poached or Scrambled Eggs
Buttered Toast
Coffee   Cocoa   Milk

Lunch
(A) Split Pea Soup with Croutons
(B) Broiled Tomato and Cheese
Sandwiches
(C) Applesauce;
Cookies, Milk

Dinner
(D) Escalloped Fish
(E) Baked Potatoes
(F) Buttered Broccoli
(G) Tossed Vegetable Salad;
Hot Biscuits
(H) Peach Brown Betty;
Coffee, Tea or Milk
Alternates:
(A) Navy Bean Soup;
Cream of Lima Bean Soup
(B) Toasted Peanut Butter
Sandwiches;
Dried Fruit and Nut Sandwiches
(C) Stewed Dried Fruit; Bananas
and Cream
(D) Baked Fish Fillets; Salmon or
Tuna Loaf; Fried Fish or
Oysters with Scalloped Potatoes
(E) Dutchess Potatoes; Potato Puffs
(F) Buttered Brussels Sprouts;
Stewed Tomatoes; Harvard Beets
(G) Lettuce-Spinach Salad;
Carrot and Green Pepper Salad
(H) Baked Cereal Custard;
Tapioca Cream Pudding;
Butterscotch Bread Pudding

BALANCED MENUS—WINTER 3

Breakfast
Stewed Fruit or Fruit Juice
Oatmeal
with Milk and Brown Sugar
Graham Muffins or Cinnamon Toast
Butter   Preserves
Coffee   Cocoa   Milk

Lunch
(A) French Toast with Bacon—Syrup
(B) Fruit Gelatin Salad;
Cocoa or Milk

Dinner
(C) Roast Leg of Lamb—Gravy;
Browned Potatoes
(D) Minted Carrots or Buttered Peas
(E) Beet Salad;
Whole Wheat Biscuits or
Butterflake Rolls
(F) Apple Pie;
Coffee, Cocoa or Milk
Alternates:
(A) Waffles with Bacon;
Tomato Rabbit on Toast;
Toasted Cheese Sandwiches
with Bacon
(B) Mixed Fruit Salad;
Peach-Cottage Cheese Salad
(C) Beef Pot Roast with Mashed
Potatoes; Veal Roast with

Baked Potatoes; Pork Shoulder
Roast with Corn Stuffing and
Scalloped Potatoes;
Flank Steak with Celery Stuffing
and Baked Potatoes
(D) Brussels Sprouts;
Baked Winter Squash;
Glazed Carrots
(E) Lettuce with Roquefort Dressing;
Chef's Salad
(F) Lemon Pie;
Fruit Upside-Down Cake

BALANCED MENUS—WINTER 4

Breakfast
Grapefruit Sections or Fruit Juice
Oatmeal or Corn Meal Griddle Cakes
with Syrup
Coffee   Cocoa   Milk

Lunch
(A) Cheese Omelet;
Bread and Butter,
Leaf Lettuce Salad—Mayonnaise
(B) Bananas and Cream;
Cookies, Milk

Dinner
(C) Liver Loaf
(D) Escalloped Potatoes
(E) Buttered Beets or Parsnips
(F) Cabbage and Pepper Slaw;
French Bread and Butter
(G) Tapioca Cream Pudding;
Coffee, Tea or Milk
Alternates:
(A) Shirred Eggs in Toast Cups;
Creamed Eggs on Toast;
Baked Cheesed Eggs
(B) Canned Berries with Cream
(C) Baked Pork Chops with
Creamed Potatoes; Braised Liver
and Vegetables; Braised Oxtails
with Baked Potatoes;
Short Ribs of Beef
with Fluffy Mashed Potatoes
(D) Creamed Potatoes or
Fluffy Mashed Potatoes
(E) Baked Squash
(F) Waldorf Salad; Lettuce Wedges
with French Dressing
(G) Lemon Chiffon Pudding;
One-Egg Cake;
Baked Custard and Cookies

Basic Winter Breakfast #1

Basic Spring Breakfast #1

BALANCED MENUS—SPRING 1

Breakfast

Grapefruit Cup
Filled with
Fresh Grapefruit Sections
and Tokay Grape Halves
Shredded Wheat   Milk
Nut Bread   Butter
Coffee

Lunch

(A) Buttered Asparagus on Toast;
Radishes, Young Onions
(B) Pear and Cottage Cheese Salad;
Whole Wheat Bread, Butter,
Milk

Dinner

(C) Baked Ham;
Candied Sweet Potatoes
(D) Buttered Green Peas
(E) Cabbage and Pineapple Salad;
Hot Biscuits
(F) Gingerbread with Lemon Sauce

Alternates:

(A) Scalloped or Dutch Snap Beans;
Snap Beans au Gratin
(B) Chocolate Pudding;
Orange Custard Pudding
(C) Pork Loin Roast with Browned
Potatoes; Swiss Steak with
Au Gratin Potatoes; Stuffed Breast
of Veal with Browned Potatoes;
Lamb Shoulder Roast with
Baked Potatoes
(D) Buttered Carrots; Asparagus
(E) Combination Salad;
Carrot and Pineapple Toss Salad
(F) Boston Cream Pie;
Deep-Dish Rhubarb Pie

BALANCED MENUS—SPRING 2

Breakfast

Blended Orange and Grapefruit Juice
Griddle Cakes,
Waffles or French Toast
with Syrup
Coffee   Milk   Cocoa

Lunch

(A) Poached Eggs in Cream Sauce;
Carrot Strips, Sliced Tomatoes
(B) Rice Pudding; Cookies, Milk

Dinner

(C) Meat Pie
(D) Fruit Salad Plate;
Whole Wheat Bread, Butter
(E) Hot Gingerbread;
coffee; milk

Alternates:

(A) Creamed Eggs on Toast;
Baked Eggs au Gratin;
Macaroni and Cheese
(B) Cornstarch Pudding; Baked
Cereal Custard; Rennet Custard
(C) Shepherd's Pie; Beef and Kidney
Pie; Macaroni or Spaghetti
and Meat Casserole;
Chicken en Casserole
(D) Cabbage-Pepper Slaw;
Cabbage and Carrot Salad
(E) One Bowl Spice Cake; Fresh
Fruit Shortcake; Spice Cupcakes

BALANCED MENUS—SPRING 3

Breakfast

Fresh Strawberries and Cream
Puffed Corn or Rice Cereal
Popovers or Raisin Muffins
Milk   Coffee

Lunch

(A) Cream of Tomato Soup
(B) Egg Salad Sandwiches
(C) Canned Fruit;
Cookies, Milk

Dinner

(D) Lamb or Beef Patties;
Spanish Rice, Buttered Peas
(E) Carrot and Pineapple Toss Salad;
French Bread
Gingerbread Upside-Down Cake

Alternates:

(A) Sour Cream Cabbage;
Creamed Dry Lima Beans
(B) Melted Cheese and Bacon
Sandwich; Bologna and Hard-
Cooked Egg Sandwich
(C) Stewed Prunes; Prune Whip
(D) Braised Pork Chops with
Parsleyed Potatoes; Barbecued
Frankfurters with Escalloped
Potatoes; Pan-Fried Liver and
Onions with Mashed Potatoes;
Fried Perch with Mashed Potatoes
(E) Leaf Lettuce—Sour Cream
Dressing; Romaine Salad—
French Dressing

BALANCED MENUS—SPRING 4

Breakfast

Orange Slices or Stewed Fruit
Crisp Whole Wheat Cereal with Milk
Fluffy Omelet
Cinnamon Toast
Coffee   Milk

Lunch

(A) Cream of Mushroom Soup
(B) Peanut Butter and Bacon
Sandwich;
Carrot Strips, Spring Onions,
Fresh or Stewed Fruit Cup

Dinner

(C) Fish Loaf with Cheese Sauce;
Mashed, Creamed, or Scalloped
Potatoes; Buttered Broccoli,
Asparagus, or Peas
(D) Cole Slaw;
Whole Wheat Bread, Butter
(E) Jelly Roll

Alternates:

(A) Any Cream of Vegetable Soup
(B) Peanut Butter and Carrot
Sandwich
(C) Baked Fish with Egg Sauce;
Broiled Fish Steak;
Chili Con Carne;
Pan-Broiled Minute Steaks;
Fried Round Steak with
Country Gravy
(D) Grapefruit and Carrot
Molded Salad;
Molded Vegetable Salad
(E) Washington Pie; Pineapple
Chiffon Pie; Lemon Sherbet

SPECIAL OCCASION MENUS

New Year's Eve Buffet Supper

Celery   Olives
Baked Ham   Pineapple Rings
Sweet Potato Puffs
Asparagus Tips
with Hollandaise Sauce
Lobster Salad   Molded Fruit Salad
Tiny Hot Buttered Parkerhouse Rolls
Tutti Frutti Ice Cream
Brandy Sauce
Salted Nuts   Candied Fruit Peel
Coffee

New Year's Day Dinner

Minted Fruit Cup
Celery   Olives
Roast Goose
with Apple-Prune Stuffing
Mashed Potatoes
Fresh or Frozen Green Peas in
Onion Cups
Lettuce Hearts with Russian Dressing
Hot Mincemeat Pie   American Cheese
Coffee

Ringing In the New Year

Cheese Tray   Assorted Crackers
Relish Tray:
Stuffed Celery, Olives, Radishes,
Carrot Curls
Stuffed Dates   Salted Nuts
Candies
Fruitcake   Cookies   Fruit
Punch Bowl   Coffee

Thanksgiving Dinner

Tomato Juice, Hot or Iced
Crackers
Stuffed Celery   Stuffed Pickle Slices
Roast Turkey
with
Oyster Dressing   Giblet Gravy
Fluffy Mashed Potatoes
Buttered Green Beans
Cranberry Ring
Filled with
Spiced Peaches or Pears
Hot Rolls   Butter
Pumpkin or Hot Mincemeat Pie
Cheese   Nuts   Raisins   Coffee

Christmas Dinner

Melon Ball Cocktail
Roast Duckling
with Apple-Celery Stuffing
Baked Acorn Squash
Scalloped Onions
Buttered Peas
Avocado and Tangerine Salad
Plum Pudding   Hard Sauce   Coffee

Easter Dinner

Melon Balls in Ginger Ale
Roast Leg of Lamb
Mint Jelly
Creamed New Potatoes and Peas
Lettuce with Roquefort Dressing
Hot Biscuits
Ice Cream   Cupcakes
Nuts   Coffee

Bridge Luncheon 1

Macaroni, Ham, and Tomato Casserole
Buttered Broccoli
Hard Rolls
Peach Cobbler   Coffee

Bridge Luncheon 2

Tomato Juice Cocktail
Spaghetti
with
Meat Sauce and Parmesan Cheese
Bread Sticks
Tossed Salad with Italian Dressing
Biscuit Tortoni   Coffee

Bridge Luncheon 3

Shrimp and Macaroni Salad
in Tomato Aspic Ring
Buttered Green Beans
Hard Poppyseed Rolls
Lemon Meringue Tarts   Coffee

Following Afternoon Bridge

Fresh Fruit Salad
with Fruit Sherbet Topping
Hot Tiny Butterscotch Pecan Rolls
Nuts   Bon Bons
Coffee

Afternoon Tea

Assorted Tea Sandwiches
Angel Food Cake   Chocolate Cake
Candies   Nuts
Tea or Chocolate

French Dinner

French Onion Soup
with Toast and Grated Cheese
or
Clear Bouillon with Sherry
Beef À la Mode
or
Chicken Sauté Chasseur
Braised Celery   Potato Croquettes
Rolls or French Bread
Sugared Fresh Strawberries
or Fresh Pineapple Sticks
or
Napoleons or Other French Pastries
Red or White Wine   Coffee

Italian Dinner

Antipasto
(shredded salad greens, tomato slices,
fennel sections, pimiento slices, Italian
salami slices, pickled mushrooms, black
olives, anchovy fillets)
Oil and Vinegar
Minestrone
with Grated Parmesan cheese
Italian Bread
Veal Scallopine or Chicken Cacciatore
Biscuit Tortoni or Zabaglione
or Pears in Red Wine
Red Wine   Coffee Espresso

Chinese Dinner

Clear Chicken Soup
or Meat Broth with Egg Drops
or Chicken Subgum Soup
Egg Rolls (Frozen) with Mustard Sauce
Shrimp and Green Peppers
or Beef with
Tomatoes and Green Peppers
Sweet and Pungent Pork
Steamed Rice
Preserved Kumquats
or Almond Cookies
Tea   Rice Wine

Latin-American Dinner

Kidney Bean Soup
or
Chilled Mixed Vegetable Soup
Arroz Con Pollo (Chicken with Rice)
Tamales (canned or homemade)
Mexican Chocolate-Coffee

(made of half hot coffee and half
hot cocoa, flavored with cinnamon)
or
Iced Mexican Coffee

For Buffet Supper

Tomato Juice Cocktail
Baked Ham
Minted Pineapple Sticks
Candied Sweet Potatoes
Tossed Green Salad   Buttered Rolls
Fruit Tart   Coffee
or
Sliced Cold Baked Ham
and Sliced Cold Tongue
Sliced Tomatoes   Sliced Cucumbers
Scalloped Potatoes
Buttered Rolls
Molded Vegetable Salad   Mayonnaise
Cupcakes   Coffee

Meatless Dinners or Suppers

1.
Clam Chowder   Crackers   Butter
Cottage Cheese   Green Pepper Relish
Tossed Vegetable Salad
Baked Apples with Custard Sauce
Milk   Coffee
2.
Baked Fish with Lemon Butter
Scalloped Potatoes   Buttered Broccoli
Head Lettuce
with Cottage Cheese Dressing
Bread   Butter
Chocolate Pudding
Milk   Coffee
3.
Macaroni and Cheese
Green Beans with Butter Crumb Sauce
Watermelon Pickles
Corn Muffins   Butter
Cabbage Slaw
Fruit Cobbler À la Mode
Milk   Coffee
4.
Creamed Fish-Filled Buns
Harvard Beets
Buttered Green Beans
Head Lettuce Salad
Dark Rye Bread   Butter
Lemon Custard Pudding
Milk   Coffee

INDEX

Acknowledgments

For much technical information and the informative photographs which illustrate many of the recipes in this cookbook, we gratefully acknowledge the generous cooperation of: A-1 Sauce — Abbott Laboratories — Ac'cent, International — Aluminum Company of America —American Airlines — American Bakeries Company — American Can Company — American Dairy Association — American Institute of Baking — American Lamb Council — American Meat Institute — American Molasses Company — Angostura-Wupperman Corp. — Armour & Company — Artichoke Industries, Inc. — Ball Brothers — Belgian Endive Association — Bernardin Bottle Cap Co., Inc. — Best Foods, Division Corn Products Company — The Borden Company — Bordo Products Co. — Brer Rabbit Molasses — California Almond Growers Exchange — California Avocado Advisory Board — California Foods Research Institute — California Prune Advisory Board — California Raisin Advisory Board — Calumet Baking Powder — Campbell Soup Company — Canned Salmon Institute — Carnation Company — Cereal Institute — Chun King Division of Corn Products Company — Church & Dwight Co., Inc. — Clabber Girl Baking Powder Co. — Cling Peach Advisory Board — Coldwater Seafood Corp. — Colorado Agricultural Experiment Station, Colorado A & M College — Colorado State College — Cornell University Dept. of Extension Teaching & Information — Corning Glass Works — Cultivated Blueberries of Michigan — Diamond Walnut Growers, Inc. — Dole Corporation — The Dow Chemical Company — Ekco Housewares Co. — Fish and Wildlife Service, United States Dept. of the Interior — The R. T. French Company — Fruit Dispatch Company — General Electric Company — General Foods Corporation — General Mills, Inc. — Gerber Baby Foods — Giroux Co., Inc. — Grandma's West Indies Molasses — Green Giant Co. — Grocery Store Products Co. — Peter F. Heering — H. J. Heinz Company — Hershey Chocolate Co. — Heublein, Inc. — George A. Hormel & Co. — Hunt-Wesson Foods, Inc. — Iowa State College of Agriculture & Mechanic Arts — Kellogg Company — Kerr Glass Mfg. Co. — Kikkoman International, Inc. — Knox Gelatine, Inc. — Kraft Foods Division of National Dairy Products Corporation — Kretschmer Wheat Germ Corp. — La Choy Food Products — Land O'Lakes Creameries, Inc. — Lawry's Foods, Inc. — Lea & Perrins, Inc. — Libby, McNeill & Libby — Louisiana Sweet Potato Advertising & Development Commission — Oscar Mayer & Co. — Metropolitan Life Insurance Co. — Michigan Bean Shippers Assn. — Milnot Co. — John Morrell & Co. — National Biscuit Company — National Broiler Council — National Canners Association — National Dairy Council — National Duckling Council — National Fisheries Institute — National Kraut Packers Assn. — National Live Stock & Meat Board — National Macaroni Institute — National Pickle Packers Assn. — National Presto Industries, Inc. — National Red Cherry Institute — New Bedford Seafood Council — Norbest Turkey Growers Assn. — Northland Foods, Inc. — Ocean Spray Cranberries, Inc. — Olive Advisory Board — John Oster Manufacturing Company — Pel-Freeze Rabbit Meat, Inc. — Pepperidge Farms, Inc. — Pet Milk Company — Pie Filling Institute — Pillsbury Mills, Inc. — Pineapple Growers Association — Pompeian Olive Oil Corp. — Poultry & Egg National Board — Pream Test Kitchens — Processed Apples Institute, Inc. — The Procter & Gamble Company — The Quaker Oats Company — Ralston Purina Company — The Rath Packing Company — Seven-Up Company — Shenandoah Valley Produce Co. — South African Rock Lobster Service Corp. — Spanish Green Olive Commission — Standard Brands Inc., Makers of Planters Peanut Oil — Sunkist Growers — Sun-Maid Raisin Growers of California — Swift & Company — Tabasco — The Taylor Wine Company — Tuna Research Foundation — Tupperware — The Underwood Kitchen — United Air Lines — United Fruit Company — University of Wyoming Agricultural Experiment Station — Fred Usinger, Inc. — Vienna Sausage Mfg. Co. — Vita Food Products, Inc. — Western Growers Association — Westinghouse Electric Corporation — Wheat Flour Institute — Widmer's Wine Cellars, Inc. — Wilson & Co., Inc. — Wine Institute